2008–2009

Accredited Institutions of Postsecondary Education

Includes Candidates for Accreditation and Accredited Programs at Other Facilities

Edited by Kenneth A. Von Alt

Additional copies of this directory are available from:
American Council on Education
Fulfillment Service
Department 191, Item #311695
Washington, DC 20055-0191
(301) 632-6757
Fax: (301) 843-0159
www.acenet.edu/bookstore

American Council on Education

American Council on Education
One Dupont Circle NW
Washington, DC 20036

Printed in the United States of America

printing number
1 2 3 4 5 6 7 8 9 10

Library of Congress Cataloging in Publication Data

The Library of Congress has cataloged this serial as follows:

Accredited institutions of postsecondary education
published by the American Council on Education, Washington, DC

v.; 24 cm.

Annual
Began with issue for 1976–77.
A directory of accredited institutions, professionally accredited programs, and candidates for accreditation.
Description based on: 1980–81.
Spine title: Accredited Institutions of Postsecondary Education.

ISBN-10 0-826-0015-7 / ISBN-13 978-0-8268-0015-2
ISSN 0270-1715 = Accredited institutions of postsecondary education, programs, candidates.

I. Education, Higher—United States—Directories I. American Council on Education.
II. Title: Accredited Institutions of Postsecondary Education.
[DNLM: L901 A172]

L901.A48 378.73 81-641495
AACR2 MARC-S

Table of Contents

Abbreviations and Terms Used in This Directory

Accred. .... institutional accreditor; national or regional
CHEA .... Council for Higher Education Accreditation
Enroll .... student enrollment or headcount
FTE Enroll .... full-time equivalent (enrollment calculation)
Prelim. .... preliminary
Prof. Accred. .... specialized or professional accreditor of programs within an institution
URL .... unique Internet address (Uniform Resource Locator)
USDE .... United States Department of Education

Degree Abbreviations

C .... certificate/diploma
A .... associate degree or equivalent
B .... baccalaureate (bachelor's) degree or equivalent
M................................. master's degree or equivalent
P.................................. first-professional degree; a degree program requiring a minimum of two years of postsecondary education for entrance and a total of six years of postsecondary education for completion
D .... doctoral degree or equivalent

Calendar Terms

3-3 .... academic year of three equal terms
4-1-4............................ academic year of two 4-month terms with a 1-month intersession
4-4-x .... academic year of two 4-month terms with one term of flexible length
Quarter .... quarter (academic year of four equal terms)
Semester .... semester (academic year of two equal terms)
Trimester .... trimester (academic year of three 15-week terms, with students typically attending two of the three terms)

About This Directory

Accredited Institutions of Postsecondary Education (AIPE)—published annually since 1964 by the American Council on Education (ACE)—is the oldest, comprehensive directory of accredited colleges, universities, and other postsecondary institutions in the United States.

Accreditation is a peer-based, external review performed by a variety of nonprofit regional, faith-based, private career, professional, and specialized accrediting organizations. The accrediting organizations, in turn, are recognized by the nongovernmental, nonprofit Council for Higher Education Accreditation (CHEA) and/or the U.S. Department of Education (USDE). "Recognition" simply means that the accrediting organization is certified as legitimate and competent. Appendix A contains a more thorough explanation of the accreditation process.

The list of accredited institutions and programs in this directory is compiled from data collected from each of the recognized accrediting organizations. The data have been reformatted for this directory, but have not otherwise been edited or changed.

Accreditation decisions are made throughout the year; therefore, this annual directory may not contain the most up-to-date information. Users should check with the accreditor for the most current accreditation status. (Addresses, names, and telephone numbers of persons to contact begin on page 839.)

Institutional accreditation granted by a regional, faith-based, or private career accreditor applies to the institution as a whole. An individual program or department within a larger, accredited institution may be separately accredited by a professional or specialized organization and is included in the display for the larger institution. A separate section lists individually accredited programs at nonaccredited, noneducational facilities such as hospitals and clinics (see page 683).

Many disciplines have no established, recognized professional accreditation organization. Therefore, no listings for such departments appear in this directory. The user should note that the institutional accreditation listings include only separately accredited programs, and not a complete list of programs available at the institution.

The dynamic arena of higher education is marked by major changes in organizational structure. To help users locate information for institutions that have modified their identifying information, this directory includes a section listing closures, mergers, and name changes, by state (see page 775). Each instance appears in three consecutive editions before it is removed. Name changes are cross-referenced in the index.

A final section of this directory lists institutions designated as "candidates for accreditation." These institutions are described as progressing toward accreditation with a recognized accrediting organization, but are not ensured of achieving accredited status.

Please take time to review the section How to Use This Directory for guidelines on interpreting the listings (see page vii). For further clarification regarding entries in the directory, contact Kenneth A. Von Alt, database editor, American Council on Education, One Dupont Circle NW, Washington, DC 20036; (202) 939-9382; e-mail: ken_von_alt@ace.nche.edu. For clarification about accreditation or the recognition process, contact the Council for Higher Education Accreditation, One Dupont Circle NW, Suite 510, Washington, DC 20036-1110; (202) 955-6126; e-mail: chea@chea.org.

Key to Major Accrediting Organizations

Regional Institutional Accrediting Organizations

MSA .... Middle States Association of Colleges and Schools, Commission on Higher Education
NWCCU .... Northwest Commission on Colleges and Universities
NCA-HLC.................. North Central Association of Colleges and Schools, Higher Learning Commission
NCA-CASI................. North Central Association of Colleges and Schools, Commission on Accreditation and School Improvement, Board of Trustees
NEASC-CIHE............. New England Association of Schools and Colleges, Inc., Commission on Institutions of Higher Education
NEASC-CTCI............. New England Association of Schools and Colleges, Inc., Commission on Technical and Career Institutions
SACS........................ Southern Association of Colleges and Schools, Commission on Colleges
WASC-ACCJC........... Western Association of Schools and Colleges, Accrediting Commission for Community and Junior Colleges
WASC-ACSCU........... Western Association of Schools and Colleges, Accrediting Commission for Senior Colleges and Universities

National Career-related Accrediting Organizations

ABHES...................... Accrediting Bureau of Health Education Schools
ACCET...................... Accrediting Council for Continuing Education and Training
ACCSCT.................... Accrediting Commission for Career Schools and Colleges of Technology
ACICS....................... Accrediting Council for Independent Colleges and Schools
COE.......................... Council on Occupational Education
DETC........................ Distance Education and Training Council Accrediting Commission
NACCAS .... National Accrediting Commission for Cosmetology Arts and Sciences

National Faith-related Accrediting Organizations

ABHE........................ Association for Biblical Higher Education
AARTS...................... Association of Advanced Rabbinical and Talmudic Schools
ATS .... Commission on Accrediting of the Association of Theological Schools
TRACS...................... Transnational Association of Christian Colleges and Schools

State-based Accrediting Organizations

NYBOR .... New York Board of Regents

How to Use This Directory

Because this directory is divided into several sections, the user is advised to begin his or her search using the index located in the back of this directory. Arranged alphabetically by institution name, the index contains numerous cross-references that make it easier to locate institutions that may use shorter or alternate names, have undergone a name change, merged with another institution, or closed altogether.

The data in every institutional entry are consistently arranged, although not every type of information is available for every institution. The following example demonstrates how a typical entry is arranged.

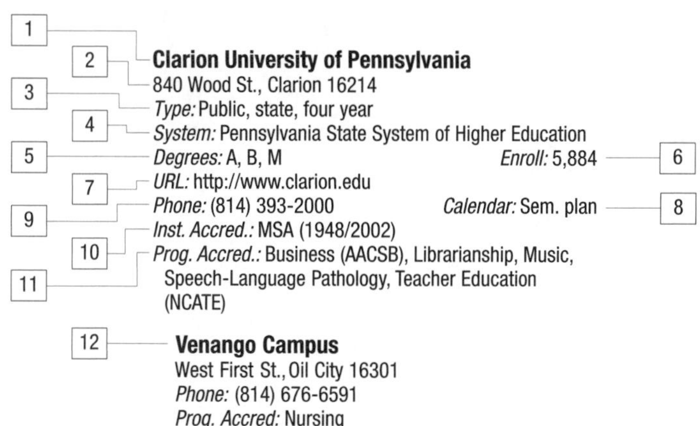

1. Institution name.
2. Address.
3. Type of institution (e.g., public), type of controlling entity (e.g., state), and specific organizational characteristics (e.g., four year).
4. Name of controlling system or entity, public or private (e.g., Ohio Board of Regents).
5. Degrees offered.
6. Enrollment figure, based on most recent enrollment data from the U.S. Department of Education.
7. Web address of institution (Uniform Resource Locator).
8. Type of academic calendar.
9. Main institutional telephone number.
10. Institutional accreditator acronym, date of first accreditation or candidacy/date of most recent renewal or reaffirmation, and, when applicable, accreditation status (e.g., probation, warning). (Consult the specific accrediting body for dates of interruption in or limitations on accreditation status.)
11. Specialized accreditation by any of 65 professional accrediting agencies, including one umbrella organization representing 17 joint review committees.
12. Branch campus(es).

Accredited Degree-Granting Institutions

ALABAMA

Air University
55 LeMay Plaza South, Maxwell AFB 36112-6335
Type: Public, federal, four-year
Degrees: A, M
URL: http://www.au.af.mil/au/index.asp
Phone: (334) 953-5159
Inst. Accred.: SACS (2004)

Community College of the Air Force
130 West Maxwell Blvd., Simler Hall, Ste. 104, Maxwell AFB 36112-6613
Phone: (334) 953-7848
Prog. Accred: Physical Therapy Assisting, Radiography

School of Advanced Air and Space Studies
600 Chennault Circle, Maxwell AFB 36112
Phone: (304) 953-5886

Alabama Agricultural and Mechanical University
4900 Meridian St., Normal 35762
Type: Public, state, four-year
System: Alabama Commission on Higher Education
Degrees: A, B, M, P, D *Enroll:* 5,497
URL: http://www.aamu.edu
Phone: (256) 372-5000 *Calendar:* Sem. plan
Inst. Accred.: SACS (1963/2004, Probation)
Prog. Accred.: Allied Health (speech-language pathology), Computer Science (ABET-CAC), Dietetics (didactic), Dietetics (internship), Engineering (civil, electrical, mechanical), Engineering Technology (electrical, mechanical), Family & Consumer Science, Forestry, Graduate Social Work, Planning, Rehabilitation Counseling, Social Work, Teacher Education (NCATE)

Alabama Southern Community College
PO Box 2000, Monroeville 36461
Type: Public, state, two-year
System: Alabama College System
Degrees: A *Enroll:* 1,004
URL: http://www.ascc.edu
Phone: (251) 575-3156 *Calendar:* Sem. plan
Inst. Accred.: SACS (1992/2006)
Prog. Accred.: Nursing

Thomasville Campus
Highway 43, South, Thomasville 36784
Phone: (205) 636-9642

Alabama State University
915 South Jackson St., Montgomery 36101-0271
Type: Public, state, four-year
System: Alabama Commission on Higher Education
Degrees: A, B, M, P, D *Enroll:* 4,689
URL: http://www.alasu.edu
Phone: (334) 229-4100 *Calendar:* Sem. plan
Inst. Accred.: SACS (1966/2001)
Prog. Accred.: Allied Health (occupational therapy), Business (ACBSP), Music, Physical Therapy, Social Work, Teacher Education (NCATE)

American Sentinel University
2101 Magnolia Ave., Ste. 200, Birmingham 35205-2827
Type: Private, proprietary, four-year
Degrees: A, B, M *FTE Enroll:* 100
URL: http://www.americansentinel.edu
Phone: (205) 323-6191 *Calendar:* Sem. plan
Inst. Accred.: DETC (2000/2005)

Amridge University
1200 Taylor Rd., Montgomery 36117-3553
Type: Private, Church of Christ, four-year
Degrees: A, B, M, D *Enroll:* 569
URL: http://www.amridgeuniversity.edu
Phone: (334) 387-3877 *Calendar:* Sem. plan
Inst. Accred.: SACS (1989/2005)

Andrew Jackson University
2919 John Hawkins Pkwy., Birmingham 35244
Type: Private, independent, four-year
Degrees: A, B, M *FTE Enroll:* 144
URL: http://www.aju.edu
Phone: (205) 871-9288
Inst. Accred.: DETC (1998/2008)

Athens State University
300 North Beaty St., Athens 35611
Type: Public, state, four-year
System: Alabama College System
Degrees: B *Enroll:* 1,727
URL: http://www.athens.edu
Phone: (256) 233-8100 *Calendar:* Sem. plan
Inst. Accred.: SACS (1955/2000)
Prog. Accred.: Business (ACBSP), Teacher Education (NCATE)

Auburn University
Auburn University 36849-5206
Type: Public, state, four-year
System: Auburn University System
Degrees: B, M, P, D *Enroll:* 21,318
URL: http://www.auburn.edu
Phone: (334) 844-4000 *Calendar:* Sem. plan
Inst. Accred.: SACS (1922/2004)
Prog. Accred.: Accounting, Allied Health (audiology, speech-language pathology), Art, Aviation, Business (AACSB), Clinical Psychology, Computer Science (ABET-CAC), Construction Education, Counseling, Counseling Psychology, Dietetics (didactic), Engineering (aerospace, agricultural, chemical, civil, computer, electrical, industrial, materials, mechanical, software, textile), Family & Consumer Science, Forestry, Interior Design, Journalism, Landscape Architecture, Marriage and Family Therapy, Music, Nursing Education, Pharmacy, Planning, Public Administration, Rehabilitation Counseling, Social Work, Teacher Education (NCATE), Theatre, Veterinary Medicine

Auburn University at Montgomery
PO Box 244023, Montgomery 36124-4023
Type: Public, state, four-year
System: Auburn University System
Degrees: B, M, P *Enroll:* 3,782
URL: http://www.aum.edu
Phone: (334) 244-3000 *Calendar:* Sem. plan
Inst. Accred.: SACS (1968/1998)
Prog. Accred.: Allied Health (cytotechnology), Business (AACSB), Clinical Lab Scientist, Nursing Education, Public Administration, Teacher Education (NCATE)

Bevill State Community College
PO Box 800, Sumiton 35148
Type: Public, state, two-year
System: Alabama College System
Degrees: A *Enroll:* 2,774
URL: http://www.bscc.edu
Phone: (205) 648-3271 *Calendar:* Sem. plan
Inst. Accred.: SACS (1994/1999)
Prog. Accred.: Allied Health (EMT-paramedic, surgical technology), Clinical Lab Technology, Nursing, Practical Nursing

Brewer Campus
2631 Temple Ave. North, Fayette 35555
Phone: (205) 932-3221

Walker College
1411 Indiana Ave., Jasper 35501
Phone: (205) 387-0511

Birmingham-Southern College
900 Arkadelphia Rd., Birmingham 35254
Type: Private, United Methodist Church, four-year
System: Alabama Association of Independent Colleges and Universities
Degrees: B, M *Enroll:* 1,361
URL: http://www.bsc.edu
Phone: (205) 226-4700 *Calendar:* 4-1-4 plan
Inst. Accred.: SACS (1922/2004)
Prog. Accred.: Business (AACSB), Music, Teacher Education (NCATE)

Bishop State Community College
351 North Broad St., Mobile 36603-5898
Type: Public, state, two-year
System: Alabama College System
Degrees: A *Enroll:* 3,221
URL: http://www.bishop.edu
Phone: (251) 405-7000 *Calendar:* Sem. plan
Inst. Accred.: SACS (1992/2005, Probation)
Prog. Accred.: Allied Health (EMT-paramedic), Business (ACBSP), Culinary Education, Funeral Service Education (Mortuary Science), Nursing, Physical Therapy Assisting, Practical Nursing

Baker Gains Central Campus
1365 Martin Luther King Ave., Mobile 36603-5362
Phone: (334) 405-4400

Carver Campus
414 Stanton St., Mobile 36617
Phone: (334) 473-8692

Southwest Campus
925 Dauphin Island Pkwy., Mobile 36605-3299
Phone: (334) 479-7476

Calhoun Community College
PO Box 2216, Decatur 35609-2216
Type: Public, state, two-year
System: Alabama College System
Degrees: A *Enroll:* 5,273
URL: http://www.calhoun.edu
Phone: (256) 306-2500 *Calendar:* Sem. plan
Inst. Accred.: SACS (1968/2002)
Prog. Accred.: Allied Health (EMT-paramedic, surgical technology), Business (ACBSP), Dentistry (dental assisting), Nursing, Practical Nursing

Central Alabama Community College
PO Box 699, Alexander City 35011
Type: Public, state, two-year
System: Alabama College System
Degrees: A *Enroll:* 1,510
URL: http://www.cacc.edu
Phone: (256) 234-6346 *Calendar:* Sem. plan
Inst. Accred.: SACS (1969/2005)
Prog. Accred.: Nursing

Chattahoochee Valley Community College
PO Box 1000, 2602 College Dr., Phenix City 36869
Type: Public, state, two-year
System: Alabama College System
Degrees: A *Enroll:* 1,329
URL: http://www.cv.edu
Phone: (334) 291-4900 *Calendar:* Sem. plan
Inst. Accred.: SACS (1976/2002)
Prog. Accred.: Nursing

Columbia Southern University
25326 Canal Rd., Orange Beach 36561
Type: Private, proprietary, four-year
Degrees: A, B, M, D *FTE Enroll:* 313
URL: http://www.columbiasouthern.edu
Phone: (251) 981-3771
Inst. Accred.: DETC (2001/2006)

Concordia College Selma
PO Box 2470, Selma 36702-2470
Type: Private, Lutheran Church-Missouri Synod, four-year
System: Concordia University System
Degrees: A, B *Enroll:* 759
URL: http://www.concordiaselma.edu
Phone: (334) 874-5700 *Calendar:* Sem. plan
Inst. Accred.: SACS (1983/1999)

Enterprise-Ozark Community College
PO Box 1300, Enterprise 36331-1300
Type: Public, state, two-year
System: Alabama College System
Degrees: A *Enroll:* 1,284
URL: http://www.eocc.edu
Phone: (334) 347-2623 *Calendar:* Sem. plan
Inst. Accred.: SACS (1969/2005)

Aviation Campus
3405 South US 231, Ozark 36360
Phone: (334) 774-5113

Faulkner University
5345 Atlanta Hwy., Montgomery 36109-3378
Type: Private, Church of Christ, four-year
System: Alabama Association of Independent Colleges and Universities
Degrees: A, B, M, D *Enroll:* 2,064
URL: http://www.faulkner.edu
Phone: (334) 272-5820 *Calendar:* Sem. plan
Inst. Accred.: SACS (1971/1999)
Prog. Accred.: Law (ABA only), Teacher Education (NCATE)

Gadsden State Community College
PO Box 227, Gadsden 35902-0227
Type: Public, state, two-year
System: Alabama College System
Degrees: A *Enroll:* 3,789
URL: http://www.gadsdenstate.edu
Phone: (256) 549-8200 *Calendar:* Sem. plan
Inst. Accred.: SACS (1968/2003)
Prog. Accred.: Allied Health (EMT-paramedic), Business (ACBSP), Clinical Lab Technology, Nursing, Radiography

Ayers Campus
1801 Coleman Rd., PO Box 1647, Anniston 36202
Phone: (256) 835-5400

George C. Wallace State Community College—Dothan
1141 Wallace Dr., Dothan 36303-9234
Type: Public, state, two-year
System: Alabama College System
Degrees: A *Enroll:* 2,475
URL: http://www.wallace.edu
Phone: (334) 983-3521 *Calendar:* Sem. plan
Inst. Accred.: SACS (2000/2002)
Prog. Accred.: Allied Health (EMT-paramedic, medical assisting (AMA), respiratory therapy), Nursing, Physical Therapy Assisting, Practical Nursing, Radiography

Sparks Campus
3235 South Eufaula Ave., PO Drawer 580, Eufaula 36072-0580
Phone: (334) 687-3543

George Corley Wallace State Community College—Selma
PO Box 2530, Selma 36702-2530
Type: Public, state, two-year
System: Alabama College System
Degrees: A *Enroll:* 1,478
URL: http://www.wccs.edu
Phone: (334) 876-9227 *Calendar:* Sem. plan
Inst. Accred.: SACS (1974/1999)
Prog. Accred.: Nursing, Practical Nursing

H. Councill Trenholm State Technical College
1225 Air Base Blvd., Montgomery 36108
Type: Public, state, two-year
System: Alabama College System
Degrees: A *Enroll:* 958
URL: http://www.trenholmtech.cc.al.us
Phone: (334) 420-4200 *Calendar:* Sem. plan
Inst. Accred.: COE (1972/2005)
Prog. Accred.: Allied Health (EMT-paramedic, medical assisting (AMA)), Culinary Education, Dentistry (dental assisting, dental laboratory technology), Practical Nursing

Patterson Campus
3920 Troy Hwy., Montgomery 36116
Phone: (334) 288-1080
Prog. Accred: Dentistry (dental assisting, dental laboratory technology)

Heritage Christian University
PO Box HCU, Florence 35630-0050
Type: Private, Churches of Christ, four-year
Degrees: A, B, M *Enroll:* 78
URL: http://www.hcu.edu
Phone: (256) 766-6610 *Calendar:* Sem. plan
Inst. Accred.: ABHE (1988/1999)

Herzing College—Birmingham Campus
280 West Valley Ave., Birmingham 35209
Type: Private, proprietary, four-year
System: Herzing College Corporate Offices
Degrees: A, B, M *Enroll:* 288
URL: http://www.herzing.edu
Phone: (205) 916-2800 *Calendar:* Sem. plan
Inst. Accred.: NCA-HLC (2004, *Indirect accreditation through Herzing College Corporate Offices, Milwaukee, WI*)

Huntingdon College
1500 East Fairview Ave., Montgomery 36106-2148
Type: Private, United Methodist Church, four-year
System: Alabama Association of Independent Colleges and Universities
Degrees: A, B *Enroll:* 755
URL: http://www.huntingdon.edu
Phone: (334) 833-4222 *Calendar:* Sem. plan
Inst. Accred.: SACS (1928/2000)
Prog. Accred.: Music

Huntsville Bible College
904 Oakwood Ave. NW, Huntsville 35811-1632
Type: Private, independent, four-year
Degrees: A, B
URL: http://www.huntsvillebiblecollege.com
Phone: (256) 539-0834 *Calendar:* Sem. plan
Inst. Accred.: ABHE (2007)

J.F. Drake State Technical College
3421 Meridian St., North, Huntsville 35811
Type: Public, state, two-year
System: Alabama College System
Degrees: A *Enroll:* 552
URL: http://www.drakestate.edu
Phone: (256) 539-8161 *Calendar:* Qtr. plan
Inst. Accred.: COE (1971/2001)

J.F. Ingram State Technical College
PO Box 220350, Deatsville 36022
Type: Public, state, two-year
System: Alabama College System
Degrees: A *Enroll:* 544
URL: http://www.ingram.cc.al.us
Phone: (334) 285-7870 *Calendar:* Qtr. plan
Inst. Accred.: COE (1977/2004)

Jacksonville State University
700 Pelham Rd., North, Jacksonville 36265-1602
Type: Public, state, four-year
System: Alabama Commission on Higher Education
Degrees: B, M, P *Enroll:* 7,338
URL: http://www.jsu.edu
Phone: (256) 782-5781 *Calendar:* Sem. plan
Inst. Accred.: SACS (1935/2003)
Prog. Accred.: Art, Business (AACSB), Computer Science (ABET-CAC), Dietetics (didactic), Electronic Technology, Health Technology, Industrial Technology, Music, Nursing Education, Social Work, Teacher Education (NCATE), Theatre

James H. Faulkner State Community College
1900 Hwy. 31 South, Bay Minette 36507
Type: Public, state, two-year
System: Alabama College System
Degrees: A *Enroll:* 2,477
URL: http://www.faulkner.cc.al.us
Phone: (251) 580-2100 *Calendar:* Sem. plan
Inst. Accred.: SACS (1970/2006)
Prog. Accred.: Allied Health (surgical technology), Culinary Education, Dentistry (dental assisting), Nursing, Practical Nursing

Jefferson Davis Community College
PO Box 958, Brewton 36427-0958
Type: Public, state, two-year
System: Alabama College System
Degrees: A *Enroll:* 819
URL: http://www.jdcc.edu
Phone: (251) 867-4832 *Calendar:* Sem. plan
Inst. Accred.: SACS (1994/1999)
Prog. Accred.: Nursing

Jefferson State Community College
2601 Carson Rd., Birmingham 35215-3098
Type: Public, state, two-year
System: Alabama College System
Degrees: A *Enroll:* 4,487
URL: http://www.jeffersonstate.edu
Phone: (205) 853-1200 *Calendar:* Sem. plan
Inst. Accred.: SACS (1968/2003)
Prog. Accred.: Business (ACBSP), Clinical Lab Technology, Construction Education, Culinary Education, Funeral Service Education (Mortuary Science), Nursing, Physical Therapy Assisting, Radiography, Veterinary Technology

Judson College
PO Box 120, 302 Bibb St., Marion 36756
Type: Private, Alabama Baptist Convention, four-year
System: Alabama Association of Independent Colleges and Universities
Degrees: B *Enroll:* 286
URL: http://www.judson.edu
Phone: (334) 683-5100 *Calendar:* Sem. plan
Inst. Accred.: SACS (1925/2005)
Prog. Accred.: Music

Lurleen B. Wallace Community College
PO Box 1418, Andalusia 36420
Type: Public, state, two-year
System: Alabama College System
Degrees: A *Enroll:* 1,086
URL: http://www.lbwcc.edu
Phone: (334) 222-6591 *Calendar:* Sem. plan
Inst. Accred.: SACS (2003)
Prog. Accred.: Allied Health (EMT-paramedic)

MacArthur Campus
1708 North Main St., PO Drawer 910, Opp 36467
Phone: (334) 493-3573
Prog. Accred: Allied Health (surgical technology)

Marion Military Institute
1101 Washington St., Marion 36756
Type: Public, state, two-year
System: Alabama College System
Degrees: A *Enroll:* 256
URL: http://www.marionmilitary.edu
Phone: (334) 683-2306 *Calendar:* Sem. plan
Inst. Accred.: SACS (1926/2006)

Miles College
PO Box 3800, Birmingham 35208
Type: Private, Christian Methodist Episcopal Church, four-year
System: Alabama Association of Independent Colleges and Universities
Degrees: A, B *Enroll:* 1,676
URL: http://www.miles.edu
Phone: (205) 929-1000 *Calendar:* Sem. plan
Inst. Accred.: SACS (1969/2003)
Prog. Accred.: Social Work

Northeast Alabama Community College
PO Box 159, Rainsville 35986
Type: Public, state, two-year
System: Alabama College System
Degrees: A *Enroll:* 1,441
URL: http://www.nacc.edu
Phone: (256) 228-6001 *Calendar:* Sem. plan
Inst. Accred.: SACS (1969/2005)
Prog. Accred.: Allied Health (EMT-paramedic), Nursing

Northwest-Shoals Community College
PO Box 2545, Muscle Shoals 35662
Type: Public, state, two-year
System: Alabama College System
Degrees: A *Enroll:* 2,641
URL: http://nwscc.edu
Phone: (256) 331-5200 *Calendar:* Sem. plan
Inst. Accred.: SACS (1994/1999)
Prog. Accred.: Allied Health (EMT-paramedic), Nursing

Oakwood University
7000 Adventist Blvd., NW, Huntsville 35896
Type: Private, Seventh-Day Adventist Church, four-year
System: Alabama Association of Independent Colleges and Universities
Degrees: A, B, M *Enroll:* 1,634
URL: http://www.oakwood.edu
Phone: (256) 726-7000 *Calendar:* Sem. plan
Inst. Accred.: SACS (1958/2001)
Prog. Accred.: Business (ACBSP), Dietetics (didactic), Dietetics (internship), Nursing, Social Work, Teacher Education (NCATE)

Prince Institute of Professional Studies
7735 Atlanta Hwy., Montgomery 36117-4231
Type: Private, proprietary, two-year
System: Stenograph, LLC
Degrees: A *Enroll:* 27
URL: http://www.princeinstitute.edu
Phone: (334) 271-1670 *Calendar:* Qtr. plan
Inst. Accred.: ACICS (1984/2008)

Reid State Technical College
PO Box 588, Evergreen 36401-0588
Type: Public, state, two-year
System: Alabama College System
Degrees: A *Enroll:* 448
URL: http://www.rstc.cc.al.us
Phone: (251) 578-1313 *Calendar:* Sem. plan
Inst. Accred.: COE (1972/2005)
Prog. Accred.: Business (ACBSP)

Remington College—Mobile
828 Downtowner Loop West, Mobile 36609-5404
Type: Private, proprietary, four-year
System: Education America, Inc.
Degrees: A, B *Enroll:* 351
URL: http://www.remingtoncollege.edu
Phone: (251) 343-8200 *Calendar:* Qtr. plan
Inst. Accred.: ACCSCT (1986/2008)

Little Rock Campus
19 Remington Rd., Little Rock, AR 72204
Phone: (501) 312-0007

Memphis Campus
2710 Nonconnah Blvd., Memphis, TN 38132
Phone: (901) 345-1000

Nashville Campus
441 Donelson Pike, Ste. 150, Nashville, TN 37214
Phone: (615) 889-5520
Prog. Accred: Dentistry (dental hygiene)

Samford University
800 Lakeshore Dr., Birmingham 35229
Type: Private, Southern Baptist Church, four-year
System: Alabama Association of Independent Colleges and Universities
Degrees: A, B, M, P, D *Enroll:* 4,232
URL: http://www.samford.edu
Phone: (205) 726-2011 *Calendar:* Sem. plan
Inst. Accred.: ATS (1996/2001), SACS (1920/2007)
Prog. Accred.: Business (AACSB), Dietetics (didactic), Exercise Science, Interior Design, Law, Liberal Education, Music, Nurse Anesthesia Education, Nursing Education, Pharmacy, Teacher Education (NCATE)

Shelton State Community College
9500 Old Greensboro Rd., Tuscaloosa 35405-8522
Type: Public, state, two-year
System: Alabama College System
Degrees: A *Enroll:* 4,166
URL: http://www.sheltonstate.edu
Phone: (205) 391-2211 *Calendar:* Sem. plan
Inst. Accred.: SACS (1994/1999)
Prog. Accred.: Allied Health (EMT-paramedic, respiratory therapy), Nursing

Snead State Community College
PO Box 734, Boaz 35957-0734
Type: Public, state, two-year
System: Alabama College System
Degrees: A *Enroll:* 1,452
URL: http://www.snead.edu
Phone: (256) 593-5120 *Calendar:* Sem. plan
Inst. Accred.: SACS (1941/2003)

Southeastern Bible College
2545 Valleydale Rd., Birmingham 35244-2083
Type: Private, nondenominational, four-year
System: Alabama Association of Independent Colleges and Universities
Degrees: A, B *Enroll:* 212
URL: http://www.sebc.edu
Phone: (205) 970-9200 *Calendar:* Sem. plan
Inst. Accred.: ABHE (1962/2004)

Southern Union State Community College
PO Box 1000, Wadley 36276
Type: Public, state, two-year
System: Alabama College System
Degrees: A *Enroll:* 3,459
URL: http://www.suscc.edu
Phone: (256) 395-2211 *Calendar:* Sem. plan
Inst. Accred.: SACS (1994/2006)
Prog. Accred.: Allied Health (EMT-paramedic, surgical technology), Nursing, Radiography

Opelika Campus
1701 LaFayette Pkwy., Opelika 36803-2268
Phone: (334) 745-6437
Prog. Accred: Nursing

Spring Hill College
4000 Dauphin St., Mobile 36608-1791
Type: Private, Roman Catholic Church, four-year
System: Alabama Association of Independent Colleges and Universities
Degrees: A, B, M *Enroll:* 1,311
URL: http://www.shc.edu
Phone: (251) 380-3030 *Calendar:* Sem. plan
Inst. Accred.: SACS (1922/2006, Warning)
Prog. Accred.: Business (ACBSP), Nursing Education

Stillman College
PO Box 1430, Tuscaloosa 35403
Type: Private, Presbyterian Church (USA), four-year
System: Alabama Association of Independent Colleges and Universities
Degrees: B *Enroll:* 785
URL: http://www.stillman.edu
Phone: (205) 349-4240 *Calendar:* Sem. plan
Inst. Accred.: SACS (1953/2000)
Prog. Accred.: Teacher Education (NCATE)

T.A. Lawson State Community College
3060 Wilson Rd., SW, Birmingham 35221
Type: Public, state, two-year
System: Alabama College System
Degrees: A *Enroll:* 2,288
URL: http://www.lawsonstate.edu
Phone: (205) 925-2515 *Calendar:* Sem. plan
Inst. Accred.: SACS (2005)
Prog. Accred.: Business (ACBSP), Nursing

Bessemer Campus
PO Box 308, 1100 Ninth Ave., SW, Bessemer 35022
Phone: (205) 426-7374
Prog. Accred: Dentistry (dental assisting), Practical Nursing

Talladega College
627 West Battle St., Talladega 35160
Type: Private, Church of Christ, four-year
System: Alabama Association of Independent Colleges and Universities
Degrees: B *Enroll:* 350
URL: http://www.talladega.edu
Phone: (256) 362-0206 *Calendar:* Sem. plan
Inst. Accred.: SACS (1931/1999)
Prog. Accred.: Social Work

Troy University
University Ave., Troy 36082
Type: Public, state, four-year
System: Alabama Commission on Higher Education
Degrees: A, B, M, P, D *Enroll:* 17,510
URL: http://www.troy.edu
Phone: (334) 670-3000 *Calendar:* Sem. plan
Inst. Accred.: SACS (2004)
Prog. Accred.: Business (ACBSP), Counseling, Music, Nursing, Rehabilitation Counseling, Social Work, Teacher Education (NCATE)

Atlantic Region Campus
5425 Robin Hood Rd., Ste. B-1, Norfolk, VA 23513
Phone: (757) 451-8202

Dothan Campus
500 University Dr., Dothan 36303
Phone: (334) 983-6556
Prog. Accred: Business (ACBSP)

Florida Region Campus
81 Beal Pkwy. SE, Fort Walton Beach, FL 32548-5327
Phone: (850) 244-7414

Montgomery Campus
231 Montgomery St., Montgomery 36103-4419
Phone: (334) 834-1400
Prog. Accred: Business (ACBSP), Counseling

Pacific Region Campus
Okinawa, 47, Japan
Phone: 011 81 611-734-3930

Phenix City Campus
One University Place, Phenix City 36869
Phone: (334) 448-5106
Prog. Accred: Counseling

Southeast Region Campus
PO Box 4790, Columbus, GA 31914
Phone: (866) 288-2105

Western Region Campus
5825 Delmonico Dr., Ste. 120, Colorado Springs, CO 80919
Phone: (719) 265-8769

Tuskegee University
308 Kresge Center, Tuskegee 36088
Type: Private, independent, four-year
System: Alabama Association of Independent Colleges and Universities
Degrees: B, M, D *Enroll:* 2,796
URL: http://www.tuskegee.edu
Phone: (334) 727-8011 *Calendar:* Sem. plan
Inst. Accred.: SACS (1933/2008)
Prog. Accred.: Allied Health (occupational therapy), Business (AACSB), Clinical Lab Scientist, Dietetics (didactic), Engineering (aerospace, chemical, electrical, mechanical), Nursing, Social Work, Teacher Education (NCATE), Veterinary Medicine

United States Sports Academy
One Academy Dr., Daphne 36526
Type: Private, independent, four-year
System: Alabama Association of Independent Colleges and Universities
Degrees: B, M, D *Enroll:* 260
URL: http://www.ussa.edu
Phone: (251) 626-3303 *Calendar:* Sem. plan
Inst. Accred.: SACS (1983/2008)

The University of Alabama
PO Box 870100, Tuscaloosa 35487-0100
Type: Public, state, four-year
System: University of Alabama System
Degrees: B, M, P, D *Enroll:* 19,790
URL: http://www.ua.edu
Phone: (205) 348-6010 *Calendar:* Sem. plan
Inst. Accred.: SACS (1897/2005)
Prog. Accred.: Accounting, Allied Health (audiology, speech-language pathology), Art, Business (AACSB), Clinical Psychology, Computer Science (ABET-CAC), Counseling, Dance, Dietetics (coordinated), Dietetics (didactic), Engineering (aerospace, chemical, civil, computer, electrical, industrial, mechanical, metallurgical), English Language Education, Family & Consumer Science, Graduate Social Work, Interior Design, Journalism, Law, Librarianship, Music, Nursing Education, Rehabilitation Counseling, Social Work, Teacher Education (NCATE), Theatre

The University of Alabama at Birmingham
1530 3rd Ave. South, Birmingham 35294-0150
Type: Public, state, four-year
System: University of Alabama System
Degrees: B, M, D *Enroll:* 13,366
URL: http://www.uab.edu
Phone: (205) 934-4011 *Calendar:* Sem. plan
Inst. Accred.: SACS (1970/2005)
Prog. Accred.: Accounting, Allied Health (EMT-paramedic, cytotechnology, health services administration, medicine, occupational therapy, optometric residency, optometry, respiratory therapy), Art, Business (AACSB), Clinical Lab Scientist, Clinical Psychology, Dentistry (advanced education in general dentistry, combined prosthodontics, dental assisting, dental hygiene, dental laboratory technology, dental public health, dentistry, endodontics, general dentistry, general practice residency, maxillofacial prosthetics, oral and maxillofacial pathology, oral and maxillofacial surgery, orthodontic and dentofacial orthopedics, pediatric dentistry, periodontics, prosthodontics), Dietetics (internship), Engineering (civil, electrical, materials, mechanical), Music, Nuclear Medicine Technology, Nurse Anesthesia Education, Nursing Education, Physical Therapy, Physician Assistant, Psychology Internship, Public Administration, Public Health, Radiation Therapy, Radiography, Rehabilitation Counseling, Social Work, Teacher Education (NCATE)

The University Hospital in Birmingham
618 18th St. South, 125 West Pavilion, Birmingham 35249
Phone: (205) 934-5748
Prog. Accred: Clinical Pastoral Education (ACPEI)

The University of Alabama in Huntsville
301 Sparkman Dr., Huntsville 35899
Type: Public, state, four-year
System: University of Alabama System
Degrees: B, M, D *Enroll:* 5,555
URL: http://www.uah.edu
Phone: (256) 824-1000 *Calendar:* Sem. plan
Inst. Accred.: SACS (1970/2006)
Prog. Accred.: Art, Business (AACSB), Computer Science (ABET-CAC), Engineering (aerospace, chemical, civil, computer, electrical, industrial, mechanical, optical/optics), Music, Nursing Education, Teacher Education (NCATE)

University of Atlanta
801 Executive Park Dr., Ste. 204, Mobile 36606
Type: Private, proprietary, four-year
Degrees: B, M
URL: http://www.uofa.edu
Phone: (251) 471-9977
Inst. Accred.: DETC (2008)

University of Mobile
PO Box 13220, Mobile 36663-0220
Type: Private, Southern Baptist Church, four-year
System: Alabama Association of Independent Colleges and Universities
Degrees: A, B, M *Enroll:* 1,488
URL: http://www.umobile.edu
Phone: (251) 675-5990 *Calendar:* Sem. plan
Inst. Accred.: SACS (1968/2003)
Prog. Accred.: Business (ACBSP), Music, Nursing, Nursing Education

University of Montevallo
Station 6001, Montevallo 35115-6001
Type: Public, state, four-year
System: Alabama Commission on Higher Education
Degrees: B, M, P *Enroll:* 2,716
URL: http://www.montevallo.edu
Phone: (205) 665-6000 *Calendar:* Sem. plan
Inst. Accred.: SACS (1925/2000)
Prog. Accred.: Allied Health (audiology, speech-language pathology), Art, Business (AACSB), Counseling, Family & Consumer Science, Music, Social Work, Teacher Education (NCATE)

The University of North Alabama
Florence 35632
Type: Public, state, four-year
System: Alabama Commission on Higher Education
Degrees: B, M, P *Enroll:* 5,329
URL: http://www.una.edu
Phone: (256) 765-4100 *Calendar:* Sem. plan
Inst. Accred.: SACS (1934/2002)
Prog. Accred.: Applied Science (industrial hygiene), Art, Business (ACBSP), English Language Education, Music, Nursing Education, Social Work, Teacher Education (NCATE)

University of South Alabama
307 North University Blvd., Mobile 36608-3053
Type: Public, state, four-year
System: Alabama Commission on Higher Education
Degrees: B, M, P, D *Enroll:* 11,007
URL: http://www.usouthal.edu
Phone: (334) 460-6101 *Calendar:* Sem. plan
Inst. Accred.: SACS (1968/2003)
Prog. Accred.: Allied Health (EMT-paramedic, audiology, medicine, occupational therapy, respiratory therapy, speech-language pathology), Business (AACSB), Clinical Lab Scientist, Computer Science (ABET-CAC), Engineering (chemical, civil, computer, electrical, information systems, mechanical), Music, Nursing Education, Physical Therapy, Physician Assistant, Radiography, Social Work, Teacher Education (NCATE)

The University of West Alabama
205 North Washington St., Station 1, Livingston 35470
Type: Public, state, four-year
System: Alabama Commission on Higher Education
Degrees: A, B, M, P *Enroll:* 2,464
URL: http://www.uwa.edu
Phone: (205) 652-3400 *Calendar:* Sem. plan
Inst. Accred.: SACS (1938/2002)
Prog. Accred.: Business (ACBSP), Nursing, Teacher Education (NCATE)

Virginia College
65 Bagby Dr., Birmingham 35209-3703
Type: Private, proprietary, four-year
System: Education Corporation of America
Degrees: A, B, M *Enroll:* 2,119
URL: http://www.vc.edu
Phone: (205) 802-1200 *Calendar:* Qtr. plan
Inst. Accred.: ACICS (1990/2007)
Prog. Accred.: Allied Health (surgical technology), Interior Design

Austin Campus
6301 East Hwy. 290, Austin, TX 78723
Phone: (512) 371-3500
Prog. Accred: Allied Health (surgical technology)

Culinard at Virginia College
195 Vulcan Rd., Birmingham 35209
Phone: (205) 802-1200
Prog. Accred: Culinary Education

The Golf Academy of America Orlando
1200 East Altamonte Dr., Unit 1010, Altamonte Springs, FL 32701
Phone: (407) 699-1990

The Golf Academy of America Phoenix
670 North Arizona Ave., Ste. #13, Chandler, AZ 85225
Phone: (480) 875-1574

The Golf Academy of America San Diego
1950 Camino Vida Roble, Ste. 125, Carlsbad, CA 92008
Phone: (760) 734-1208

The Golf Academy of the Carolinas
3268 Waccamaw Blvd., Myrtle Beach, SC 29579
Phone: (843) 236-0481

Gulf Coast Biloxi Campus
920 Cedar Lake Rd., Biloxi, MS 39532
Phone: (228) 392-2994

Huntsville Campus
2800-A Bob Wallace Ave., Huntsville 35805
Phone: (256) 533-7387

Jackson Campus
5360 I-55 North, Jackson, MS 39211
Phone: (601) 977-0960

Mobile Campus
2970 Cottage Hill Rd., Ste. 140, Mobile 36606
Phone: (251) 471-6722
Prog. Accred: Allied Health (surgical technology)

Montgomery Campus
6200 Atlanta Hwy., Montgomery 36117
Phone: (334) 277-3390

Pensacola Campus
19 West Garden St., Pensacola, FL 32501
Phone: (850) 436-8444
Prog. Accred: Allied Health (surgical technology)

Virginia College Online
500 Century Park South, Ste. 200, Birmingham 35226
Phone: (205) 397-6600

Virginia College School of Business and Health at Chattanooga
721 Eastgate Loop Rd., Chattanooga, TN 37411
Phone: (888) 232-7887

Wallace State Community College
PO Box 2000, 801 Main St., Hanceville 35077-2000
Type: Public, state, two-year
System: Alabama College System
Degrees: A *Enroll:* 3,738
URL: http://www.wallacestate.edu
Phone: (256) 352-8000 *Calendar:* Sem. plan
Inst. Accred.: SACS (1978/2005)
Prog. Accred.: Allied Health (EMT-paramedic, diagnostic medical sonography, medical assisting (AMA), occupational therapy assisting, respiratory therapy), Business (ACBSP), Clinical Lab Technology, Dentistry (dental assisting, dental hygiene), Nursing, Physical Therapy Assisting, Radiography

ALASKA

Alaska Bible College
PO Box 289, Glenallen 99588-0289
Type: Private, nondenominational, four-year
Degrees: A, B *FTE Enroll:* 35
URL: http://www.akbible.edu
Phone: (907) 822-3201 *Calendar:* Sem. plan
Inst. Accred.: ABHE (1982/2003)

Alaska Pacific University
4101 University Dr., Anchorage 99508-4672
Type: Private, independent, four-year
Degrees: A, B, M *Enroll:* 565
URL: http://www.alaskapacific.edu
Phone: (907) 561-1266 *Calendar:* Sem. plan
Inst. Accred.: NWCCU (1981/2006)
Prog. Accred.: Teacher Education (NCATE)

Charter College
2221 East Northern Lights Blvd., Ste. 120, Anchorage 99508
Type: Private, proprietary, four-year
System: Prospect Colleges, LLC
Degrees: A, B *Enroll:* 258
URL: http://www.chartercollege.edu
Phone: (907) 227-1000 *Calendar:* Qtr. plan
Inst. Accred.: ACICS (1988/2003)

Mat-Su Campus
1451 East Parks Hwy., Ste. B, Wasilla 99654
Phone: (907) 952-1000

Ilisagvik College
PO Box 749, NARL Facilities, Barrow 99723
Type: Public, tribal, two-year
System: American Indian Higher Education Consortium
Degrees: A *Enroll:* 136
URL: http://www.ilisagvik.cc
Phone: (907) 852-3333 *Calendar:* Sem. plan
Inst. Accred.: NWCCU (2002/2007)

Prince William Sound Community College
PO Box 97, Valdez 99686
Type: Public, state, two-year
System: University of Alaska Anchorage
Degrees: A *Enroll:* 328
URL: http://www.pwscc.edu
Phone: (907) 834-1660 *Calendar:* Sem. plan
Inst. Accred.: NWCCU (1989/2008)

University of Alaska Anchorage
3211 Providence Dr., Anchorage 99508
Type: Public, state, four-year
System: University of Alaska System
Degrees: A, B, M *Enroll:* 10,864
URL: http://www.uaa.alaska.edu
Phone: (907) 786-1800 *Calendar:* Sem. plan
Inst. Accred.: NWCCU (1974/2006)
Prog. Accred.: Allied Health (medical assisting (AMA)), Applied Science (surveying/geomatics), Art, Business (AACSB), Clinical Lab Technology, Dentistry (dental assisting, dental hygiene), Dietetics (internship), Engineering (civil), Journalism, Music, Nursing, Social Work, Teacher Education (NCATE)

Kenai Peninsula College
34820 College Dr., Soldotna 99669
Phone: (907) 262-0330

Kodiak College
117 Benny Benson Dr., Kodiak 99615
Phone: (907) 486-4161

Matanuska-Susitna College
Box 2889, Palmer 99645
Phone: (907) 745-9774

University of Alaska Fairbanks
PO Box 757500, 320 Signers' Hall, Fairbanks 99775-6725
Type: Public, state, four-year
System: University of Alaska System
Degrees: A, B, M, D *Enroll:* 5,776
URL: http://www.uaf.edu
Phone: (907) 474-7581 *Calendar:* Sem. plan
Inst. Accred.: NWCCU (1934/2007)
Prog. Accred.: Accounting, Allied Health (medical assisting (AMA)), Business (AACSB), Computer Science (ABET-CAC), Dentistry (dental hygiene), Engineering (civil, electrical, geological/geophysical, mechanical, mining, petroleum), Forestry, Journalism, Music, Social Work, Teacher Education (NCATE)

Bristol Bay Campus
PO Box 1070, Dillingham 99576
Phone: (800) 478-5109

Chukchi Campus
PO Box 297, Kotzebue 99752
Phone: (907) 442-3400

Kuskokwim Campus
UAF-College of Rural Alaska, PO Box 368, Bethel 99559
Phone: (907) 543-4502

Northwest Campus
Pouch 400, Nome 99762
Phone: (907) 443-2201

University of Alaska Southeast
11120 Glacier Hwy., Juneau 99801
Type: Public, state, four-year
System: University of Alaska System
Degrees: A, B, M *Enroll:* 1,805
URL: http://www.uas.alaska.edu
Phone: (907) 465-6457 *Calendar:* Sem. plan
Inst. Accred.: NWCCU (1983/1998)
Prog. Accred.: Teacher Education (NCATE)

Ketchikan Campus
2600 Seventh Ave., Ketchikan 99901
Phone: (907) 225-6177

Sitka Campus
1332 Seward Ave., Sitka 99835
Phone: (907) 747-7701

AMERICAN SAMOA

American Samoa Community College
PO Box 2609, Pago Pago 96799
Type: Public, state, two-year
Degrees: A *Enroll:* 1,038
URL: http://www.ascc.as
Phone: (684) 699-9155 *Calendar:* Sem. plan
Inst. Accred.: WASC-JR. (1976/2003)

ARIZONA

American Indian College of the Assemblies of God
10020 North 15th Ave., Phoenix 85021
Type: Private, General Council of the Assemblies of God, four-year
Degrees: A, B *Enroll:* 60
URL: http://www.aicag.edu
Phone: (602) 944-3335 *Calendar:* Sem. plan
Inst. Accred.: NCA-HLC (1988/2003)

Anthem College—Phoenix
1515 East Indian School Rd., Phoenix 85014-4901
Type: Private, proprietary, four-year
System: High-Tech Institute
Degrees: A, B *Enroll:* 2,853
URL: http://www.anthem.edu
Phone: (602) 279-9700
Inst. Accred.: ACCSCT (1984/2004)
Prog. Accred.: Veterinary Technology

Anthem College Online
2222 West Peoria Ave., Ste. C, Phoenix 85029
Phone: (866) 837-1010

High-Tech Institute—Atlanta
2450 Pledmont Rd. NE, Atlanta, GA 30324
Phone: (678) 279-7000

High-Tech Institute—Kansas City
9001 State Line Rd., Kansas City, MO 64114
Phone: (816) 444-4300

High-Tech Institute—Minneapolis
5100 Gamble Dr., Ste. 200, St. Louis Park, MN 55416
Phone: (952) 417-2200
Prog. Accred: Medical Assisting (ABHES)

High-Tech Institute—Nashville
560 Royal Pkwy., Nashville, TN 37214
Phone: (615) 232-3700
Prog. Accred: Surgical Technology

High-Tech Institute—Sacramento
9738 Lincoln Village Dr., Ste. 100, Sacramento, CA 95827
Phone: (916) 929-9700
Prog. Accred: Medical Assisting (ABHES)

Apollo College—Phoenix Campus
8503 North 27th Ave., Phoenix 85051
Type: Private, proprietary, two-year
System: U.S. Education Corporation
Degrees: A *Enroll:* 2,598
URL: http://www.apollocollege.com
Phone: (602) 864-1571
Inst. Accred.: ABHES (1991/2002), ACICS (2008)

Albuquerque Campus
100 Menaul Blvd. NE, Albuquerque, NM 87107
Phone: (505) 254-7777
Prog. Accred: Medical Assisting (ABHES), Medical Laboratory Technology

Tri-City Campus
630 West Southern Ave., Mesa 85210-5004
Phone: (480) 831-6585
Prog. Accred: Allied Health (respiratory therapy), Medical Assisting (ABHES)

Tucson Campus
3550 North Oracle Rd., Tucson 85705
Phone: (520) 888-5885
Prog. Accred: Medical Assisting (ABHES)

Westside Campus
2701 West Bethany Home Rd., Phoenix 85017
Phone: (602) 433-1333
Prog. Accred: Radiography

Argosy University Phoenix
2233 West Dunlap Ave., Phoenix 85021
Type: Private, proprietary, four-year
System: Argosy University
Degrees: B, M, D
URL: http://www.argosyu.edu/phoenix
Phone: (602) 216-2600 *Calendar:* Tri. plan
Inst. Accred.: NCA-HLC (1981/2008, *Indirect accreditation through Argosy University, Chicago, IL*)
Prog. Accred.: Clinical Psychology

Arizona Automotive Institute
6829 North 46th Ave., Glendale 85301-3597
Type: Private, proprietary, two-year
Degrees: A *Enroll:* 737
URL: http://www.aai.edu
Phone: (623) 934-7273 *Calendar:* Qtr. plan
Inst. Accred.: ACCSCT (1972/2005)

Arizona School of Acupunture and Oriental Medicine
4646 East Fort Lowell Rd., Ste. 104, Tucson 85712
Type: Private, proprietary, four-year
Degrees: M
URL: http://www.asaom.edu
Phone: (520) 795-0787 *Calendar:* Qtr. plan
Inst. Accred.: ACAOM (2003/2007)

Arizona State University
PO Box 872803, Tempe 85287-2803
Type: Public, state, four-year
System: Arizona Board of Regents
Degrees: B, M, D *Enroll:* 44,279
URL: http://www.asu.edu
Phone: (480) 965-9011 *Calendar:* Sem. plan
Inst. Accred.: NCA-HLC (1931/2003)
Prog. Accred.: Accounting, Allied Health (audiology, health services administration, speech-language pathology), Art, Business (AACSB), Clinical Lab Scientist, Clinical Psychology, Computer Science (ABET-CAC), Construction Education, Counseling, Counseling Psychology, Engineering (aerospace, bioengineering, chemical, civil, computer, electrical, industrial, materials, mechanical), Graduate Social Work, Interior Design, Journalism, Landscape Architecture, Law, Music, Planning, Psychology Internship, Public Administration, Recreation and Leisure Services, School Psychology, Social Work

East Campus
7001 East Williams Field Rd., Mesa 85212
Phone: (480) 727-3278
Prog. Accred: Aviation, Dietetics (didactic), Dietetics (internship), Engineering Technology (electrical, manufacturing, mechanical), Industrial Technology

West Campus
PO Box 37100, Phoenix 85069-7100
Phone: (602) 543-5500
Prog. Accred: Accounting, Business (AACSB), Graduate Social Work, Nursing Education, Recreation and Leisure Services, Social Work

Arizona Western College
PO Box 929, Yuma 85366
Type: Public, state/local, two-year
System: Arizona Commission for Postsecondary Education
Degrees: A *Enroll:* 3,503
URL: http://www.azwestern.edu
Phone: (520) 317-6000 *Calendar:* Sem. plan
Inst. Accred.: NCA-HLC (1968/1999)
Prog. Accred.: Nursing

The Art Center Design College
2525 North Country Club Rd., Tucson 85716-2505
Type: Private, proprietary, four-year
Degrees: A, B *Enroll:* 273
URL: http://www.theartcenter.edu
Phone: (520) 325-0123 *Calendar:* Qtr. plan
Inst. Accred.: ACCSCT (1992/2002), NCA-HLC (2006)
Prog. Accred.: Interior Design

Albuquerque Campus
5000 Marble Ave. NE, Albuquerque, NM 87110-6344
Phone: (505) 254-7575

The Art Institute of Phoenix
2233 West Dunlop Ave., Phoenix 85021-2859
Type: Private, proprietary, four-year
System: Education Management Corporation
Degrees: A, B
URL: http://www.aipx.edu
Phone: (602) 331-7500 *Calendar:* Qtr. plan
Inst. Accred.: ACICS (2003)
Prog. Accred.: Culinary Education, Interior Design

The Art Institutes International—Kansas City
8208 Melrose Dr., Lenexa, KS 66214
Phone: (913) 217-4600

The Art Institute of Tucson
5099 East Grant Rd., Ste. 100, Tucson 85712
Type: Private, proprietary, four-year
System: Education Management Corporation
Degrees: A, B
URL: http://www.artinstitutes.edu/tucson
Phone: (520) 881-2900 *Calendar:* Qtr. plan
Inst. Accred.: ACICS (2003)

Asian Institute of Medical Studies
3131 North Country Club, Ste. 100, Tucson 85716
Type: Private, proprietary, four-year
Degrees: M
URL: http://www.asianinstitute.edu
Phone: (520) 322-6330 *Calendar:* Qtr. plan
Inst. Accred.: ACAOM (2006)

Brown Mackie College—Tucson
4585 East Speedway Blvd., Ste. 204, Tucson 85712
Type: Private, proprietary, four-year
System: Education Management Corporation
Degrees: A, B *Enroll:* 385
URL: http://www.brownmackie.edu/Tucson
Phone: (520) 327-6866 *Calendar:* Qtr. plan
Inst. Accred.: ACICS (1969/2006)

North Canton Campus
4300 Munson St. NW, Canton, OH 44718-3674
Phone: (330) 494-1214
Prog. Accred: Surgical Technology

The Bryman School of Arizona
2250 West Peoria Ave., Building A, Ste. 100, Phoenix 85029
Type: Private, proprietary, two-year
System: High-Tech Institute
Degrees: A *Enroll:* 1,429
URL: http://www.brymanschool.edu
Phone: (602) 274-4300
Inst. Accred.: ACCSCT (1989/2005)
Prog. Accred.: Allied Health (medical assisting (AMA)), Medical Assisting (ABHES)

High-Tech Institute—Dallas Campus
4250 North Beltline Rd., Irving, TX 75038-4201
Phone: (972) 871-2824

High-Tech Institute—Las Vegas Campus
2320 South Rancho Dr., Las Vegas, NV 89102
Phone: (702) 385-6700

High-Tech Institute—Memphis Campus
5866 Shelby Oaks Circle, Ste. 100, Memphis, TN 38134
Phone: (901) 432-3800
Prog. Accred: Surgical Technology

High-Tech Institute—Orlando Campus
3710 Maguire Blvd., Orlando, FL 32803
Phone: (407) 893-7400

Tempe Campus
8945 South Harl Dr., Ste. 102, Tempe 85284
Phone: (480) 776-1100

Central Arizona College
8470 North Overfield Rd., Coolidge 85228
Type: Public, local, two-year
System: Arizona Commission for Postsecondary Education
Degrees: A *Enroll:* 3,425
URL: http://www.centralaz.edu
Phone: (520) 494-5444 *Calendar:* Sem. plan
Inst. Accred.: NCA-HLC (1973/2008)
Prog. Accred.: Dietetic Technician, Nursing

Aravaina Campus
Star Route 887, Winkleman 85292
Phone: (529) 357-2000

Superstition Mountain Campus
273 Old West Hwy., Apache Juction 85219
Phone: (480) 288-4005

Chandler-Gilbert Community College
2626 East Pecos Rd., Chandler 85225-2499
Type: Public, state/local, two-year
System: Maricopa County Community College District
Degrees: A *Enroll:* 4,617
URL: http://www.cgc.maricopa.edu
Phone: (480) 732-7000 *Calendar:* Sem. plan
Inst. Accred.: NCA-HLC (1992/2007)
Prog. Accred.: Dietetic Technician, Nursing

Williams Campus
7360 East Tahoe Ave., Mesa 85212
Phone: (480) 988-8000

Cochise College
4190 West Hwy. 80, Douglas 85607
Type: Public, state/local, two-year
System: Arizona Commission for Postsecondary Education
Degrees: A *Enroll:* 2,504
URL: http://www.cochise.edu
Phone: (520) 364-7943 *Calendar:* Sem. plan
Inst. Accred.: NCA-HLC (1969/2006)
Prog. Accred.: Nursing

Coconino Community College
2800 South Lonetree Rd., Flagstaff 86001-2701
Type: Public, state/local, two-year
System: Arizona Commission for Postsecondary Education
Degrees: A *Enroll:* 1,821
URL: http://www.coconino.edu
Phone: (928) 527-1222 *Calendar:* Sem. plan
Inst. Accred.: NCA-HLC (1996/2002)

College of the Humanities and Sciences Harrison Middleton University
1105 East Broadway, Tempe 85282
Type: Private, independent, four-year
Degrees: A, B, M, D
URL: http://www.chumsci.edu
Phone: (480) 317-5955
Inst. Accred.: DETC (2003/2008)

CollegeAmerica
1800 South Military Rd., Flagstaff 86001
Type: Private, proprietary, two-year
Degrees: A
URL: http://www.collegeamerica.edu
Phone: (928) 526-0763
Inst. Accred.: ABHES (1982/2005)

Phoenix Campus
6533 North Black Canyon Hwy., Phoenix 85015
Phone: (802) 246-3041

Collins College
1140 South Priest Dr., Tempe 85281-5206
Type: Private, proprietary, four-year
System: Career Education Corporation
Degrees: A, B *Enroll:* 979
URL: http://www.collinscollege.edu
Phone: (480) 966-3000
Inst. Accred.: ACCSCT (1981/2005)

DeVry University Northeast Phoenix
Scottsdale Corporate Center I, 18500 North Allied Way, Ste. 150, Phoenix 85054
Type: Private, proprietary, four-year
System: DeVry University
Degrees: M
URL: http://www.devry.edu
Phone: (480) 657-3223 *Calendar:* Sem. plan
Inst. Accred.: NCA-HLC (2002, *Indirect accreditation through DeVry University, Oakbrook Terrace, IL*)

Phoenix Metro Campus
2149 West Dunlap Ave., Phoenix 85021
Phone: (602) 870-9222

DeVry University Phoenix
2149 West Dunlap Ave., Phoenix 85021-2995
Type: Private, proprietary
System: DeVry University
Degrees: A, B, M *Enroll:* 1,232
URL: http://www.devry.edu/phoenix
Phone: (602) 870-9222 *Calendar:* Sem. plan
Inst. Accred.: NCA-HLC (2002, *Indirect accreditation through DeVry University, Oakbrook Terrace, IL*)
Prog. Accred.: Engineering Technology (computer, electrical)

DeVry University—Mesa Center
1201 South Alma School Rd., Ste. 5450, Mesa 85210
Type: Private, proprietary, four-year
System: DeVry University Oak Brook
Degrees: M
URL: http://www.devry.edu/keller
Phone: (480) 827-1511 *Calendar:* Sem. plan
Inst. Accred.: NCA-HLC (2002, *Indirect accreditation through DeVry University, Oakbrook Terrace, IL*)

Diné College
1 Circle Dr., Route 12, Tsaile 86556
Type: Public, tribal, four-year
System: American Indian Higher Education Consortium
Degrees: A, B *Enroll:* 1,173
URL: http://www.dinecollege.edu
Phone: (928) 724-6600 *Calendar:* Sem. plan
Inst. Accred.: NCA-HLC (1976/2008)

Shiprock Campus
PO Box 580, Shiprock, NM 87420-0580
Phone: (505) 368-3500

Dunlap-Stone University
11225 North 28th Dr., Ste. B201, Phoenix 85029
Type: Private, independent, four-year
Degrees: B *FTE Enroll:* 297
URL: http://www.expandglobal.com
Phone: (602) 648-5750 *Calendar:* Sem. plan
Inst. Accred.: DETC (2003/2008)

Eastern Arizona College
615 North Stadium Ave., Thatcher 85552
Type: Public, state/local, two-year
System: Arizona Commission for Postsecondary Education
Degrees: A *Enroll:* 2,698
URL: http://www.eac.edu
Phone: (520) 428-8233 *Calendar:* Sem. plan
Inst. Accred.: NCA-HLC (1966/1996)

Estrella Mountain Community College
3000 North Dysart Rd., Avondale 85323-1000
Type: Public, state/local, two-year
System: Maricopa County Community College District
Degrees: A *Enroll:* 2,849
URL: http://www.estrellamountain.edu
Phone: (623) 935-8000 *Calendar:* Sem. plan
Inst. Accred.: NCA-HLC (1997/2002)
Prog. Accred.: Nursing

Everest College—Phoenix
10400 North 25th Ave., Ste. 190, Phoenix 85021
Type: Private, proprietary, four-year
System: Corinthian Colleges, Inc
Degrees: A, B *Enroll:* 545
URL: http://www.everest.edu
Phone: (602) 942-4141
Inst. Accred.: NCA-HLC (1997/2001)

Mesa Campus
5416 East Baseline Rd., Ste. 200, Mesa 85206
Phone: (480) 830-5151

Frank Lloyd Wright School of Architecture
12621 North Frank Lloyd Wright Blvd., Scottsdale 85261-4430
Type: Private, independent, four-year
Degrees: B, M *FTE Enroll:* 21
URL: http://www.taliesin.edu
Phone: (480) 860-2700 *Calendar:* 12-mos. pr
Inst. Accred.: NCA-HLC (1987/2005)

Gateway Community College
108 North 40th St., Phoenix 85034
Type: Public, state/local, two-year
System: Maricopa County Community College District
Degrees: A *Enroll:* 3,358
URL: http://www.gatewaycc.edu
Phone: (602) 392-5000 *Calendar:* Sem. plan
Inst. Accred.: NCA-HLC (1971/2000)
Prog. Accred.: Allied Health (diagnostic medical sonography, respiratory therapy, surgical technology), Nursing, Physical Therapy Assisting, Radiography

Glendale Community College
6000 West Olive Ave., Glendale 85302
Type: Public, state/local, two-year
System: Maricopa County Community College District
Degrees: A *Enroll:* 10,796
URL: http://www.gc.maricopa.edu
Phone: (623) 845-3000 *Calendar:* Sem. plan
Inst. Accred.: NCA-HLC (1967/2002)
Prog. Accred.: Nursing

Grand Canyon University
3300 West Camelback Rd., PO Box 11097, Phoenix 85061-1097
Type: Private, proprietary, four-year
System: Grand Canyon Education, Inc.
Degrees: B, M *Enroll:* 3,994
URL: http://www.grand-canyon.edu
Phone: (602) 589-2500 *Calendar:* Sem. plan
Inst. Accred.: NCA-HLC (1968/2007)
Prog. Accred.: Business (ACBSP), Nursing Education

IIA College
4240 West Bethany Home Rd., Phoenix 85019
Type: Private, proprietary, four-year
System: IIA College
Degrees: A, B *Enroll:* 378
URL: http://iia-online.com
Phone: (602) 242-6265 *Calendar:* Sem. plan
Inst. Accred.: ACICS (1982/2006)

Albuquerque Campus
4201 Central Ave. NW, Ste. J, Albuquerque, NM 87105-1649
Phone: (505) 880-2877

Mesa Campus
925 South Gilbert Rd., Ste. 201, Mesa 85204-4448
Phone: (480) 545-8755

Tucson Campus
5441 East 22d St., Ste. 125, Tucson 85711-5444
Phone: (520) 748-9799

International Baptist College
2150 East Southern Ave., Tempe 85282-7504
Type: Private, independent Baptist, four-year
Degrees: A, B, M, D *Enroll:* 62
URL: http://www.tri-citybaptist.org
Phone: (480) 838-7070 *Calendar:* Sem. plan
Inst. Accred.: TRACS (2000/2005)

ITT Technical Institute
5005 South Wendler Dr., Tempe 85282
Type: Private, proprietary, four-year
System: ITT Educational Services, Inc.
Degrees: A, B *Enroll:* 625
URL: http://www.itt-tech.edu
Phone: (602) 231-0871 *Calendar:* Qtr. plan
Inst. Accred.: ACICS (1999/2004)

ITT Technical Institute
1455 West River Rd., Tucson 85704
Type: Private, proprietary, four-year
System: ITT Educational Services, Inc.
Degrees: A, B *Enroll:* 389
URL: http://www.itt-tech.edu
Phone: (520) 408-7488 *Calendar:* Qtr. plan
Inst. Accred.: ACICS (1999/2003)

Albuquerque Campus
5100 Masthead St., NE, Albuquerque, NM 87109-4366
Phone: (505) 828-1114

Baton Rouge Campus
14141 Airline Hwy., Bldg. 3, Ste. K, Baton Rouge, LA 70817
Phone: (225) 754-5800

Oklahoma City Campus
50 Penn Place Office Tower, 1900 Northwest Expressway, Ste. 305R, Oklahoma City, OK 73118
Phone: (405) 810-4100

Saint Rose Campus
140 James Dr. East, Saint Rose, LA 70087
Phone: (504) 463-0338

Tulsa Campus
4943 South 78th East Ave., Tulsa, OK 74145
Phone: (918) 619-8700

Kaplan College, Phoenix
13610 North Black Canyon Hwy., Ste. 104, Phoenix 85029
Type: Private, proprietary, two-year
System: Kaplan Higher Education Corporation
Degrees: A *Enroll:* 388
URL: http://getinfo.kaplancollege.com
Phone: (602) 548-1955 *Calendar:* Qtr. plan
Inst. Accred.: ACCSCT (1981/2005)
Prog. Accred.: Allied Health (medical assisting (AMA), respiratory therapy), Veterinary Technology

Lamson College
875 West Elliot Rd., Ste. 206, Tempe 85284
Type: Private, proprietary, two-year
System: Delta Education Corporation
Degrees: A *Enroll:* 250
URL: http://www.lamsoncollege.com
Phone: (480) 898-7000 *Calendar:* Qtr. plan
Inst. Accred.: ACICS (1981/2006)
Prog. Accred.: Allied Health (surgical technology)

Mesa Community College
1833 West Southern Ave., Mesa 85202
Type: Public, state/local, two-year
System: Maricopa County Community College District
Degrees: A *Enroll:* 14,337
URL: http://www.mc.maricopa.edu
Phone: (480) 461-7000 *Calendar:* Sem. plan
Inst. Accred.: NCA-HLC (1967/2005)
Prog. Accred.: Funeral Service Education (Mortuary Science), Interior Design, Nursing, Veterinary Technology

Red Mountain Campus
2305 North Power Rd., Mesa 85215
Phone: (480) 654-7200

Mohave Community College
1971 Jagerson Ave., Kingman 86401
Type: Public, state/local, two-year
System: Arizona Commission for Postsecondary Education
Degrees: A *Enroll:* 2,677
URL: http://www.mohave.edu
Phone: (928) 757-4331 *Calendar:* Sem. plan
Inst. Accred.: NCA-HLC (1981/2003)
Prog. Accred.: Allied Health (surgical technology)

Lake Havasu Campus
1977 West Acoma Blvd., Lake Havasu City 86403
Phone: (520) 855-7812
Prog. Accred: Nursing

Mohave Valley Campus
3400 Hwy. 95, Bullhead City 86442
Phone: (520) 758-3926

North Mohave Campus
480 South Central, PO Box 980, Colorado City 86021
Phone: (520) 875-2799

National Paralegal College
6516 North 7th St., Ste. 103, Phoenix 85014
Type: Private, proprietary, two-year
Degrees: A
URL: http://nationalparalegal.edu
Phone: (845) 371-9101
Inst. Accred.: DETC (2006)

Northcentral University
10000 East University Dr., Prescott Valley 86314
Type: Private, proprietary, four-year
Degrees: B, M, D *Enroll:* 1,500
URL: http://www.ncu.edu
Phone: (928) 541-7777 *Calendar:* Sem. plan
Inst. Accred.: NCA-HLC (2003/2008)
Prog. Accred.: Business (ACBSP)

Northern Arizona University
Box 4092, Flagstaff 86011-4092
Type: Public, state, four-year
System: Arizona Board of Regents
Degrees: B, M, D *Enroll:* 15,275
URL: http://www.nau.edu
Phone: (928) 523-9011 *Calendar:* Sem. plan
Inst. Accred.: NCA-HLC (1930/2008)
Prog. Accred.: Allied Health (speech-language pathology), Business (AACSB), Business (ACBSP), Computer Science (ABET-CAC), Construction Education, Counseling, Dentistry (dental hygiene), Engineering (civil, computer, electrical, environmental/sanitary, mechanical), Forestry, Music, Nursing Education, Physical Therapy, Recreation and Leisure Services, Social Work

Northland Pioneer College
PO Box 610, Holbrook 86025-0610
Type: Public, state/local, two-year
System: Arizona Commission for Postsecondary Education
Degrees: A *Enroll:* 1,982
URL: http://www.npc.edu
Phone: (928) 524-7600 *Calendar:* Sem. plan
Inst. Accred.: NCA-HLC (1980/2000)

Little Colorado Campus
1400 East 3rd St., Winslow 86047-4404
Phone: (520) 289-6511

Painted Desert Campus
993 East Hermosa Dr., Holbrook 86025
Phone: (520) 524-7311

Silver Creek Campus
1610 South Main St., Snowflake 85937-5614
Phone: (520) 536-6211

White Mountain Campus
1001 West Deuce of Clubs, Show Low 85901-6211
Phone: (520) 532-6111

Paradise Valley Community College
18401 North 32nd St., Phoenix 85032
Type: Public, state/local, two-year
System: Maricopa County Community College District
Degrees: A *Enroll:* 4,465
URL: http://www.pvc.maricopa.edu
Phone: (602) 787-6500 *Calendar:* Sem. plan
Inst. Accred.: NCA-HLC (1990/2005)
Prog. Accred.: Dietetic Technician, Nursing

The Paralegal Institute, Inc.
18275 North 59th Ave., Ste. 186, Bldg. N, Glendale 85308
Type: Private, proprietary, two-year
Degrees: A *FTE Enroll:* 360
URL: http://www.theparalegalinstitute.edu
Phone: (602) 212-0501
Inst. Accred.: DETC (1979/2003)

Penn Foster College
14300 North Northsight Blvd., Ste. 111, Scottsdale 85260
Type: Private, proprietary, two-year
Degrees: A *FTE Enroll:* 1,705
URL: http://www.pennfostercollege.edu
Phone: (480) 315-4950 *Calendar:* Sem. plan
Inst. Accred.: DETC (1974/2004)
Prog. Accred.: Veterinary Technology

Phoenix College
1202 West Thomas Rd., Phoenix 85013
Type: Public, state/local, two-year
System: Maricopa County Community College District
Degrees: A *Enroll:* 6,189
URL: http://www.pc.maricopa.edu
Phone: (602) 285-7500 *Calendar:* Sem. plan
Inst. Accred.: NCA-HLC (1928/2006)
Prog. Accred.: Dentistry (dental assisting, dental hygiene), Nursing

Phoenix Institute of Herbal Medicine and Acupuncture
301 East Bethany Home Rd., Ste. A-100, Phoenix 85012
Type: Private, proprietary, four-year
Degrees: M
URL: http://pihma.edu
Phone: (602) 274-1885
Inst. Accred.: ACAOM (2003/2007)

Pima County Community College District
401 North Bonita Ave., Tucson 85709-5001
Type: Public, state/local, two-year
System: Arizona Commission for Postsecondary Education
Degrees: A *Enroll:* 16,471
URL: http://www.pima.edu
Phone: (520) 206-4500 *Calendar:* Sem. plan
Inst. Accred.: NCA-HLC (1975/2001)
Prog. Accred.: Allied Health (respiratory therapy, surgical technology), Dentistry (dental assisting, dental hygiene, dental laboratory technology), Nursing, Radiography

Community Campus
401 N. Bonita Ave., Tucson 85709-5000
Phone: (520) 206-3933

Desert Vista Campus
5901 South Calle Santa Cruz, Tucson 85709-6001
Phone: (520) 206-5030

Downtown Campus
1255 North Stone Ave., Tucson 85709-3002
Phone: (520) 206-6135

East Campus
8181 East Irvington Rd., Tucson 85709-4000
Phone: (520) 206-7000
Prog. Accred: Veterinary Technology

Northwest Campus
7600 North Shannon Rd., Tucson 85709-7500
Phone: (520) 206-2090

West Campus
2202 West Anklam Rd., Tucson 85709-0001
Phone: (520) 206-6600
Prog. Accred: Dentistry (dental assisting, dental hygiene, dental laboratory technology)

Pima Medical Institute
3350 East Grant Rd., Ste. 200, Tucson 85716
Type: Private, proprietary, two-year
Degrees: A *Enroll:* 690
URL: http://www.pmi.edu
Phone: (520) 326-1600
Inst. Accred.: ABHES (1982/2003)
Prog. Accred.: Allied Health (respiratory therapy), Medical Assisting (ABHES), Physical Therapy Assisting, Radiography

Albuquerque Campus
2201 San Pedro Dr., NE, Building 3, Ste. 100, Albuquerque, NM 87110
Phone: (505) 881-1234
Prog. Accred: Medical Assisting (ABHES), Radiography

Chula Vista Campus
780 Bay Blvd., Ste. 101, Chula Vista, CA 91910
Phone: (619) 425-3200
Prog. Accred: Medical Assisting (ABHES), Radiography

Colorado Springs Campus
370 Printers Pkwy., Colorado Springs, CO 80910
Phone: (719) 482-7462
Prog. Accred: Medical Assisting (ABHES)

Denver Campus
7475 Dakin St., Denver, CO 80221
Phone: (303) 426-1800
Prog. Accred: Medical Assisting (ABHES), Physical Therapy Assisting, Radiography

Las Vegas Campus
3333 East Flamingo Rd., Las Vegas, NV 89121-4329
Phone: (702) 458-9650
Prog. Accred: Medical Assisting (ABHES), Veterinary Technology

Mesa Campus
957 South Dobson Rd., Mesa 85202
Phone: (480) 644-0267
Prog. Accred: Medical Assisting (ABHES)

Renton Campus
555 South Renton Village Place, Renton, WA 98055
Phone: (425) 228-9600
Prog. Accred: Medical Assisting (ABHES)

Seattle Campus
9709 Third Ave. NE, Ste. 400, Seattle, WA 98102
Phone: (206) 322-6100
Prog. Accred: Medical Assisting (ABHES), Radiography, Veterinary Technology

Prescott College
220 Grove Ave., Prescott 86301
Type: Private, independent, four-year
Degrees: B, M, D *Enroll:* 948
URL: http://www.prescott.edu
Phone: (520) 778-2090 *Calendar:* Qtr. plan
Inst. Accred.: NCA-HLC (1984/2000)

The Refrigeration School
4210 East Washington St., Phoenix 85034-1816
Type: Private, proprietary, two-year
Degrees: A *Enroll:* 208
URL: http://www.refrigerationschool.com
Phone: (602) 275-7133
Inst. Accred.: ACCSCT (1973/2005)

Rio Salado Community College
2323 W. 14th St., Tempe 85281-6950
Type: Public, state/local, two-year
System: Maricopa County Community College District
Degrees: A *Enroll:* 6,924
URL: http://www.riosalado.edu
Phone: (480) 517-8000 *Calendar:* Sem. plan
Inst. Accred.: NCA-HLC (1981/2002)
Prog. Accred.: Dentistry (dental hygiene), Nursing

Scottsdale Community College
9000 East Chaparral Rd., Scottsdale 85250-2699
Type: Public, state/local, two-year
System: Maricopa County Community College District
Degrees: A *Enroll:* 6,001
URL: http://www.sc.maricopa.edu
Phone: (480) 423-6000 *Calendar:* Sem. plan
Inst. Accred.: NCA-HLC (1975/2007)
Prog. Accred.: Culinary Education, Interior Design, Nursing

Scottsdale Culinary Institute
8100 East Camelback Rd., Ste. 1001, Scottsdale 85251-3940
Type: Private, proprietary, four-year
System: Career Education Corporation
Degrees: A, B *Enroll:* 1,328
URL: http://www.chefs.edu
Phone: (480) 990-3773
Inst. Accred.: ACCSCT (1989/2005)
Prog. Accred.: Culinary Education

South Mountain Community College
7050 South 24th St., Phoenix 85040
Type: Public, state/local, two-year
System: Maricopa County Community College District
Degrees: A *Enroll:* 2,170
URL: http://www.southmountaincc.edu
Phone: (602) 243-8000 *Calendar:* Sem. plan
Inst. Accred.: NCA-HLC (1984/1999)

Southwest College of Naturopathic Medicine and Health Sciences
2140 East Broadway Rd., Tempe 85282
Type: Private, proprietary, four-year
Degrees: D *Enroll:* 338
URL: http://www.scnm.edu
Phone: (480) 858-9100
Inst. Accred.: NCA-HLC (2004)
Prog. Accred.: Naturopathic Medicine

Southwestern College
2625 East Cactus Rd., Phoenix 85032-7042
Type: Private, Conservative Baptist Association of America, four-year
Degrees: A, B *Enroll:* 265
URL: http://www.southwesterncollege.edu
Phone: (602) 489-5300 *Calendar:* Sem. plan
Inst. Accred.: ABHE (1977/1998), NCA-HLC (1992/2002)

Thunderbird School of Global Management
15249 North 59th Ave., Glendale 85306
Type: Private, independent, four-year
Degrees: M *Enroll:* 797
URL: http://www.t-bird.edu
Phone: (602) 978-7250 *Calendar:* Tri. plan
Inst. Accred.: NCA-HLC (1969/2006)
Prog. Accred.: Business (AACSB)

Tohono O'odham Community College
PO Box 3129, Sells 85634
Type: Public, tribal, two-year
System: American Indian Higher Education Consortium
Degrees: A
URL: http://www.tocc.cc.az.us
Phone: (520) 383-8401 *Calendar:* Sem. plan
Inst. Accred.: NCA-HLC (2003/2005)

Universal Technical Institute
10695 West Pierce St., Avondale 85323
Type: Private, proprietary, two-year
Degrees: A *Enroll:* 3,516
URL: http://www.uticorp.com
Phone: (623) 245-4600
Inst. Accred.: ACCSCT (1968/2004)

Glendale Heights Campus
601 Regency Dr., Glendale Heights, IL 60139-2208
Phone: (630) 529-2662

NASCAR Technical Institute
220 Byers Creek Rd., Mooresville, NC 28117
Phone: (704) 658-1950

Norwood Campus
One Upland Rd., Building 200, Norwood, MA 02062
Phone: (781) 948-2000

Phoenix Campus
2844 West Deer Valley Rd., Phoenix 85027-2303
Phone: (623) 869-9644

Rancho Cucamonga Campus
9494 Haven Ave., Rancho Cucamonga, CA 91730
Phone: (909) 484-1929

Sacramento Campus
4100 Duckhorn Dr., Sacramento, CA 95834
Phone: (916) 263-9100

University of Advancing Technology
2625 West Baseline Rd., Tempe 85283-1056
Type: Private, independent, four-year
Degrees: A, B, M *Enroll:* 1,202
URL: http://www.uat.edu
Phone: (602) 383-8228
Inst. Accred.: ACICS (1992/2007)

University of Arizona
712 Administration Bldg., PO Box 210066, Tucson 85721-0066
Type: Public, state, four-year
System: Arizona Board of Regents
Degrees: B, M, P, D *Enroll:* 33,198
URL: http://www.arizona.edu
Phone: (520) 621-2211 *Calendar:* Sem. plan
Inst. Accred.: NCA-HLC (1917/2000)
Prog. Accred.: Accounting, Allied Health (audiology, medicine, perfusion, speech-language pathology), Art, Business (AACSB), Clinical Lab Scientist, Clinical Psychology, Dance, Dietetics (didactic), Engineering (aerospace, bioengineering, chemical, civil, computer, electrical, engineering management, geological/geophysical, industrial, materials, mechanical, mining, optical/optics, systems), English Language Education, Journalism, Landscape Architecture, Law, Librarianship, Music, Nursing Education, Pharmacy, Planning, Psychology Internship, Public Administration, Public Health, Rehabilitation Counseling, School Psychology, Theatre

The Arizona International College
1615 East Helen St., Bldg. 410E, Tucson 85719-4511
Phone: (520) 626-0600

Sierra Vista Campus
1140 N. Colombo, Sierra Vista 85635
Phone: (602) 629-0335

University of Phoenix
4615 East Elwood St., Phoenix 85040
Type: Private, proprietary, four-year
System: Apollo Group, Inc.
Degrees: A, B, M, D *Enroll:* 9,413
URL: http://www.phoenix.edu
Phone: (480) 966-9577
Inst. Accred.: NCA-HLC (1978/2003)
Prog. Accred.: Business (ACBSP), Nursing Education

Albuquerque Campus
7471 Pan American Freeway, NE, Albuquerque, NM 87109
Phone: (505) 821-4800

Atlanta Campus
8200 Roberts Dr., Ste. 300, Dunwoody, GA 30350
Phone: (678) 731-0555

Axia College of the University of Phoenix
Phoenix 85040
Phone: (800) 471-9955

Boise Campus
3080 Gentry Way, Ste. 150, Meridian, ID 83642
Phone: (208) 888-1505

Boston Campus
100 Grossman Dr., Ste. 201, Braintree, MA 02184
Phone: (781) 843-0844

Central Massachusetts Campus
One Research Dr., Westborough, MA 01581
Phone: (508) 614-4100

Charlotte Campus
3800 Arco Corporate Dr., Charlotte, NC 28273
Phone: (704) 504-5409

Chicago Campus
1500 McConner Pkwy., Ste. 700, Schaumburg, IL 60173
Phone: (847) 413-1922

Cincinnati Campus
110 Boggs Ln., Ste. 149, Cincinnati, OH 45246
Phone: (513) 772-9600

Cleveland Campus
5005 Rockside Rd., Ste. 325, Independence, OH 44131
Phone: (216) 447-8807

Colorado Campus
10004 Park Meadows Dr., Lone Tree, CO 80124
Phone: (303) 694-9093

Columbus, Georgia Campus
18 9th St., Columbus, GA 31901
Phone: (800) 697-8223

Columbus, Ohio Campus
8405 Pulsar Place, Ste. 120, Columbus, OH 43240
Phone: (800) 697-8223

Dallas Campus
12400 Colt Rd., Churchill Towers, Ste. 200, Dallas, TX 75251
Phone: (972) 385-1055

Ft. Lauderdale Campus
600 North Pine Island Rd., Ste. 500, Plantation, FL 33324
Phone: (954) 382-5303

Hawaii Campus
827 Fort St., Honolulu, HI 96813
Phone: (808) 536-2686

University of Phoenix *(continued)*

Houston Campus
11451 Katy Freeway, Ste. 100, Houston, TX 77079
Phone: (713) 465-9966

Indianapolis Campus
7999 Knue Rd., Ste. 150, Indianapolis, IN 46250
Phone: (317) 585-8610

Jacksonville Campus
4500 Salisbury Rd., Ste. 150, Jacksonville, FL 32216
Phone: (904) 636-6645

Kansas City Campus
901 East 104th St., Ste. 301, Kansas City, MO 64131
Phone: (816) 943-9600

Las Vegas Campus
333 North Rancho Dr., #300, Las Vegas, NV 89106
Phone: (702) 638-7279

Louisiana Campus
One Galleria Blvd., Ste. 725, Metairie, LA 70001
Phone: (504) 461-8852

Maryland Campus
8830 Stanford Blvd., Ste. 100, Columbia, MD 21045
Phone: (410) 872-9001

Metro Detroit Campus
5480 Corporate Dr., Ste. 240, Troy, MI 48098
Phone: (248) 925-4100

Milwaukee Campus
13890 Bishops Dr., Ste. 110, Brookfield, WI 53005
Phone: (262) 785-0608

Nashville Campus
616 Marriott Dr., Ste. 150, Nashville, TN 37214
Phone: (615) 872-0188

Netherlands Campus
Rivium le Straat 1, 2909 LE Capelle a/d Ijssel, Rotterdam
Phone: 011 31 10 288-6344

Northern Virginia Campus
11710 Plaza America Dr., Ste. 2000, Reston, VA 20190
Phone: (703) 435-4402

Oklahoma City Campus
6501 North Broadway Extension, Ste. 100, Oklahoma City, OK 73116
Phone: (405) 842-8007

Online Campus
3201 East Elwood St., Phoenix 85034
Phone: (602) 387-7000

Oregon Campus
13221 Southwest 68th Pkwy., #500, Tigard, OR 97223
Phone: (503) 403-2900

Orlando Campus
2290 Lucien Way, Ste. 400, Maitland, FL 32751
Phone: (407) 667-0555

Philadelphia Campus
170 South Warner Rd., Wayne, PA 19087-9971
Phone: (610) 989-0880

Phoenix Hohokam Campus
4605 East Elmwood St., Phoenix 85072-2076
Phone: (480) 804-7400
Prog. Accred: Counseling

Pittsburgh Campus
Penn Center West Six, Ste. 100, Pittsburgh, PA 15276
Phone: (412) 747-9000

Puerto Rico Campus
PO Box 3870, RD 177 KM 2.0 (Los Filtros), Guaynabo, PR 00970-3870
Phone: (787) 731-5400

Reno Campus
5370 Kietzke Ln., Ste. 102, Reno, NV 89511
Phone: (775) 828-7999

Sacramento Campus
1760 Creekside Oaks Dr., #100, Sacramento, CA 95833
Phone: (916) 923-2107

St. Louis Campus
13801 Riverport Dr., Ste. 100, Riverport Executive Center II, St. Louis, MO 63043
Phone: (314) 298-9755

Salt Lake Campus
5251 Green St., Salt Lake City, UT 84123
Phone: (801) 263-1444
Prog. Accred: Counseling

San Diego Campus
11682 El Camino Real, 2nd Flr., San Diego, CA 92130
Phone: (858) 509-4300

San Jose Campus
3590 North First St., San Jose, CA 95134
Phone: (408) 435-8500

Southern Arizona Campus
5099 East Grant Rd., #120, Tucson 85712
Phone: (520) 881-6512

Southern Colorado Campus
5475 Tech Center Dr., #130, Colorado Springs, CO 80919
Phone: (719) 599-5282

Spokane Campus
1330 North Washington St., Spokane, WA 99201-2446
Phone: (800) 697-8223

Tampa Campus
100 Tampa Oaks Blvd., Ste. 200, Temple Terrace, FL 33637
Phone: (813) 626-7911

Tulsa Campus
10810 East 45th St., Ste. 103, Tulsa, OK 74146
Phone: (918) 622-4877

Vancouver Campus
885 West Georgia St., Vancouver, BC, Canada V6C 3E8
Phone: (604) 408-6606

Washington Campus
7100 Fort Dent Way, #100, Seattle, WA 98188
Phone: (206) 268-5800

West Michigan Campus
318 River Ridge Dr. NW, Walker, MI 49544
Phone: (616) 956-5100

Wichita Campus
3020 North Cypress Dr., Wichita, KS 67226
Phone: (316) 630-8121

Western International University
9215 North Black Canyon Hwy., Phoenix 85021
Type: Private, proprietary, four-year
System: Apollo Group, Inc.
Degrees: A, B, M *Enroll:* 50,544
URL: http://www.wintu.edu
Phone: (602) 943-2311 *Calendar:* Sem. plan
Inst. Accred.: NCA-HLC (1984/2005)

Modi Apollo International Institute
24A, Lajpat Nagar IV, Ring Rd., New Delhi, India 110024
Phone: 011 91-11-264-41203

Shuanglong Campus
120 Shuanglong Nanli, Chaoyang, Beijing, China 100021
Phone: 011 86-10-8731-3311

Yavapai College
1100 East Sheldon St., Prescott 86301
Type: Public, state/local, two-year
System: Arizona Commission for Postsecondary Education
Degrees: A *Enroll:* 3,370
URL: http://www2.yc.edu
Phone: (520) 445-7300 *Calendar:* Sem. plan
Inst. Accred.: NCA-HLC (1975/2003)
Prog. Accred.: Nursing

ARKANSAS

Arkansas Baptist College
1600 Bishop St., Little Rock 72202
Type: Private, Southern Baptist Church, four-year
Degrees: A, B *Enroll:* 270
URL: http://www.arkansasbaptist.edu
Phone: (501) 370-4000 *Calendar:* Sem. plan
Inst. Accred.: NCA-HLC (1987/2006)

Arkansas Northeastern College
PO Drawer 1109, Blytheville 72316
Type: Public, state/local, two-year
System: Arkansas Department of Higher Education
Degrees: A *Enroll:* 1,253
URL: http://www.anc.edu
Phone: (870) 762-1020 *Calendar:* Sem. plan
Inst. Accred.: NCA-HLC (1980/2002)
Prog. Accred.: Allied Health (EMT-paramedic), Nursing

Burdette Center
Box 36, I-55 and Hwy. 148, Burdette 72321
Phone: (870) 763-1486
Prog. Accred: Dentistry (dental assisting)

Paragould Campus
4601 Linwood Dr., Paragould 72450
Phone: (870) 239-3200

Arkansas State University
PO Box 10, State University 72467
Type: Public, state, four-year
System: Arkansas State University System Office
Degrees: A, B, M, P, D *Enroll:* 8,674
URL: http://www.astate.edu
Phone: (870) 972-2100 *Calendar:* Sem. plan
Inst. Accred.: NCA-HLC (1928/2003)
Prog. Accred.: Allied Health (speech-language pathology), Art, Business (AACSB), Clinical Lab Scientist, Clinical Lab Technology, Counseling, Engineering (general), Journalism, Music, Nurse Anesthesia Education, Nursing, Physical Therapy, Physical Therapy Assisting, Public Administration, Radiation Therapy, Radiography, Rehabilitation Counseling, Social Work, Teacher Education (NCATE)

Arkansas State University Mountain Home
1600 South College St., Mountain Home 72653
Type: Public, state, two-year
System: Arkansas State University System Office
Degrees: A
URL: http://www.asumh.edu
Phone: (870) 508-6100 *Calendar:* Sem. plan
Inst. Accred.: NCA-HLC (2003/2008)
Prog. Accred.: Funeral Service Education (Mortuary Science)

Arkansas State University—Beebe
PO Box 1000, Beebe 72012
Type: Public, state, two-year
System: Arkansas State University System Office
Degrees: A *Enroll:* 2,746
URL: http://www.asub.edu
Phone: (501) 882-8356 *Calendar:* Sem. plan
Inst. Accred.: NCA-HLC (1971/2002)
Prog. Accred.: Clinical Lab Technology

Arkansas State University—Newport
7648 Victory Blvd., Newport 72112
Type: Public, state, two-year
System: Arkansas State University System Office
Degrees: A
URL: http://www.asun.edu
Phone: (870) 512-7800 *Calendar:* Sem. plan
Inst. Accred.: NCA-HLC (2002/2007)

Arkansas Tech University
Russellville 72801-2222
Type: Public, state, four-year
System: Arkansas Department of Higher Education
Degrees: A, B, M, P *Enroll:* 6,030
URL: http://www.atu.edu
Phone: (479) 968-0389 *Calendar:* Sem. plan
Inst. Accred.: NCA-HLC (1930/2004)
Prog. Accred.: Allied Health (medical assisting (AMA)), Business (AACSB), Engineering (electrical, mechanical), Music, Nursing, Recreation and Leisure Services, Teacher Education (NCATE)

Ozark Campus
1700 Helberg Ln., Ozark 72949-2013
Phone: (479) 667-2117
Prog. Accred: Allied Health (EMT-paramedic)

Black River Technical College
Highway 304 East, PO Box 468, Pocahontas 72455
Type: Public, state, two-year
System: Arkansas Department of Higher Education
Degrees: A *Enroll:* 1,255
URL: http://www.blackrivertech.org
Phone: (870) 248-4000 *Calendar:* Sem. plan
Inst. Accred.: NCA-HLC (1997/2002)
Prog. Accred.: Allied Health (EMT-paramedic, respiratory therapy), Dietetic Technician

Central Baptist College
1501 College Ave., Conway 72032
Type: Private, Missionary Baptist Association, four-year
Degrees: A, B *Enroll:* 354
URL: http://www.cbc.edu
Phone: (501) 329-6872 *Calendar:* Sem. plan
Inst. Accred.: NCA-HLC (1993/2005)

Cossatot Community College of the University of Arkansas
PO Box 960, 183 Hwy. 399, DeQueen 71832
Type: Public, state, two-year
System: University of Arkansas System Administration
Degrees: A *Enroll:* 543
URL: http://www.cccua.edu
Phone: (870) 584-4471 *Calendar:* Sem. plan
Inst. Accred.: NCA-HLC (1998/2003)
Prog. Accred.: Business (ACBSP)

Crowley's Ridge College
100 College Dr., Paragould 72450-9731
Type: Private, Churches of Christ, four-year
Degrees: A, B *Enroll:* 131
URL: http://www.crowleysridgecollege.edu
Phone: (870) 236-6901 *Calendar:* Sem. plan
Inst. Accred.: NCA-HLC (2000/2005)

East Arkansas Community College
1700 Newcastle Rd., Forrest City 72335-9598
Type: Public, state/local, two-year
System: Arkansas Department of Higher Education
Degrees: A *Enroll:* 991
URL: http://www.eacc.edu
Phone: (870) 633-4480 *Calendar:* Sem. plan
Inst. Accred.: NCA-HLC (1979/1999)
Prog. Accred.: Allied Health (EMT-paramedic), Nursing

Ecclesia College
9653 Nations Dr., Springdale 72762-8159
Type: Private, independent, four-year
Degrees: B
URL: http://www.ecclesiacollege.org
Phone: (479) 248-7236 *Calendar:* Sem. plan
Inst. Accred.: ABHE (2005)

Harding University
Box 10773, 900 East Center Ave., Searcy 72149-0001
Type: Private, Churches of Christ, four-year
Degrees: B, M, D, P *Enroll:* 4,795
URL: http://www.harding.edu
Phone: (501) 279-4274 *Calendar:* Sem. plan
Inst. Accred.: NCA-HLC (1954/2005)
Prog. Accred.: Business (ACBSP), Dietetics (didactic), Music, Nursing, Pharmacy, Social Work, Teacher Education (NCATE)

Henderson State University
1100 Henderson St., Arkadelphia 71999-0001
Type: Public, state, four-year
System: Arkansas Department of Higher Education
Degrees: A, B, M *Enroll:* 3,164
URL: http://www.hsu.edu
Phone: (870) 230-5091 *Calendar:* Sem. plan
Inst. Accred.: NCA-HLC (1934/2002)
Prog. Accred.: Business (AACSB), Dietetics (didactic), Music, Nursing Education, Teacher Education (NCATE)

Hendrix College
1600 Washington Ave., Conway 72032-3080
Type: Private, United Methodist Church, four-year
Degrees: B, M *Enroll:* 1,018
URL: http://www.hendrix.edu
Phone: (501) 450-1273 *Calendar:* Tri. plan
Inst. Accred.: NCA-HLC (1924/1999)
Prog. Accred.: Music, Teacher Education (NCATE)

John Brown University
2000 West University Sreet, Siloam Springs 72761
Type: Private, independent, four-year
Degrees: A, B, M *Enroll:* 1,731
URL: http://www.jbu.edu
Phone: (479) 524-9500 *Calendar:* Sem. plan
Inst. Accred.: NCA-HLC (1962/2002)
Prog. Accred.: Construction Education, Engineering (general), Teacher Education (NCATE)

Lyon College
PO Box 2317, Batesville 72503
Type: Private, Presbyterian Church, four-year
Degrees: B *Enroll:* 470
URL: http://www.lyon.edu
Phone: (870) 793-4201 *Calendar:* Sem. plan
Inst. Accred.: NCA-HLC (1959/2002)
Prog. Accred.: Teacher Education (NCATE)

Mid-South Community College
2000 West Broadway St., West Memphis 72301-3829
Type: Public, state, two-year
System: Arkansas Department of Higher Education
Degrees: A *Enroll:* 796
URL: http://www.midsouthcc.edu
Phone: (870) 733-6722 *Calendar:* Sem. plan
Inst. Accred.: NCA-HLC (1999/2004)

National Park Community College at Hot Springs
101 College Dr., Hot Springs National Park 71913
Type: Public, state/local, two-year
System: Arkansas Department of Higher Education
Degrees: A *Enroll:* 1,857
URL: http://www.npcc.edu
Phone: (501) 760-4222 *Calendar:* Sem. plan
Inst. Accred.: COE (2003), NCA-HLC (1981/2002)
Prog. Accred.: Allied Health (EMT-paramedic), Business (ACBSP), Clinical Lab Technology, Nursing, Radiography

North Arkansas College
1515 Pioneer Ridge, Harrison 72601
Type: Public, state/local, two-year
System: Arkansas Department of Higher Education
Degrees: A *Enroll:* 1,490
URL: http://www.northark.edu
Phone: (870) 391-3000 *Calendar:* Sem. plan
Inst. Accred.: NCA-HLC (1979/2001)
Prog. Accred.: Allied Health (EMT-paramedic, surgical technology), Business (ACBSP), Clinical Lab Technology, Nursing, Radiography

NorthWest Arkansas Community College
One College Dr., Bentonville 72712-5091
Type: Public, state/local, two-year
System: Arkansas Department of Higher Education
Degrees: A *Enroll:* 3,101
URL: http://www.nwacc.edu
Phone: (501) 636-9222 *Calendar:* Sem. plan
Inst. Accred.: NCA-HLC (1995/2000)
Prog. Accred.: Allied Health (EMT-paramedic, respiratory therapy), Physical Therapy Assisting

Ouachita Baptist University
410 Ouachita St., Arkadelphia 71998
Type: Private, Southern Baptist Church, four-year
Degrees: A, B *Enroll:* 1,440
URL: http://www.obu.edu
Phone: (870) 245-5000 *Calendar:* Sem. plan
Inst. Accred.: NCA-HLC (1927/2001)
Prog. Accred.: Business (AACSB), Dietetics (didactic), Music, Teacher Education (NCATE)

Ouachita Technical College
One College Circle, PO Box 816, Malvern 72104
Type: Public, state, two-year
System: Arkansas Department of Higher Education
Degrees: A *Enroll:* 903
URL: http://www.otcweb.edu
Phone: (501) 332-3658 *Calendar:* Sem. plan
Inst. Accred.: NCA-HLC (1996/2001)

Ozarka College
PO Box 10, Melbourne 72556
Type: Public, state, two-year
System: Arkansas Department of Higher Education
Degrees: A *Enroll:* 773
URL: http://www.ozarka.edu
Phone: (870) 368-7371 *Calendar:* Sem. plan
Inst. Accred.: NCA-HLC (1996/2001)

Philander Smith College
One Trudie Kibbe Reed Dive, Little Rock 72202
Type: Private, United Methodist Church, four-year
Degrees: B *Enroll:* 715
URL: http://www.philander.edu
Phone: (501) 370-5275 *Calendar:* Sem. plan
Inst. Accred.: NCA-HLC (1949/2007)
Prog. Accred.: Business (ACBSP), Social Work, Teacher Education (NCATE)

Phillips Community College of the University of Arkansas
1000 Campus Dr., Box 785, Helena 72342-0785
Type: Public, state/local, two-year
System: University of Arkansas System Administration
Degrees: A *Enroll:* 1,430
URL: http://www.pccua.edu
Phone: (870) 338-6474 *Calendar:* Sem. plan
Inst. Accred.: NCA-HLC (1972/2005)
Prog. Accred.: Business (ACBSP), Clinical Lab Technology, Nursing, Phlebotomy

DeWitt Campus
1210 Ricebelt Ave. Hwy. 165, DeWitt 72042
Phone: (870) 946-3506

Stuttgart Campus
2807 Hwy. 165 South, Stuttgart 72160
Phone: (870) 673-4201

Pulaski Technical College
3000 West Scenic Rd., North Little Rock 72118-3399
Type: Public, state/local, two-year
System: Arkansas Department of Higher Education
Degrees: A *Enroll:* 5,206
URL: http://www.pulaskitech.edu
Phone: (501) 821-2216 *Calendar:* Sem. plan
Inst. Accred.: NCA-HLC (1997/2002)
Prog. Accred.: Allied Health (occupational therapy assisting, respiratory therapy), Dentistry (dental assisting)

Rich Mountain Community College
1100 College Dr., Mena 71953
Type: Public, state/local, two-year
System: Arkansas Department of Higher Education
Degrees: A *Enroll:* 539
URL: http://www.rmcc.edu
Phone: (479) 394-7622 *Calendar:* Sem. plan
Inst. Accred.: NCA-HLC (1990/2005)

South Arkansas Community College
PO Box 7010, El Dorado 71731-7010
Type: Public, state/local, two-year
System: Arkansas Department of Higher Education
Degrees: A *Enroll:* 857
URL: http://www.southark.edu
Phone: (870) 864-7107 *Calendar:* Sem. plan
Inst. Accred.: NCA-HLC (1983/2007)
Prog. Accred.: Allied Health (EMT-paramedic, occupational therapy assisting), Clinical Lab Technology, Physical Therapy Assisting, Radiography

Southeast Arkansas College
1900 Hazel St., Pine Bluff 71603
Type: Public, state/local, two-year
System: Arkansas Department of Higher Education
Degrees: A *Enroll:* 1,395
URL: http://www.seark.edu
Phone: (870) 543-5900 *Calendar:* Sem. plan
Inst. Accred.: NCA-HLC (1996/2001)
Prog. Accred.: Allied Health (EMT-paramedic, respiratory therapy, surgical technology), Nursing, Radiography

Southern Arkansas University
PO Box 9392, Magnolia 71754-9392
Type: Public, state, four-year
System: Arkansas Department of Higher Education
Degrees: A, B, M *Enroll:* 2,718
URL: http://www.saumag.edu
Phone: (870) 235-4001 *Calendar:* Sem. plan
Inst. Accred.: NCA-HLC (1929/2003)
Prog. Accred.: Business (AACSB), Music, Nursing, Social Work, Teacher Education (NCATE)

Southern Arkansas University—Tech
SAU Tech Station, PO Box 3499, East Camden 71711-1599
Type: Public, state, two-year
System: Arkansas Department of Higher Education
Degrees: A *Enroll:* 962
URL: http://www.sautech.edu
Phone: (870) 574-4500 *Calendar:* Sem. plan
Inst. Accred.: NCA-HLC (1980/2000)

University of Arkansas at Fayetteville
Administration Bldg. 425, Fayetteville 72701
Type: Public, state, four-year
System: University of Arkansas System Administration
Degrees: B, M, P, D *Enroll:* 15,088
URL: http://www.uark.edu
Phone: (479) 575-2000 *Calendar:* Sem. plan
Inst. Accred.: NCA-HLC (1924/2007)
Prog. Accred.: Accounting, Allied Health (speech-language pathology), Business (AACSB), Clinical Psychology, Counseling, Dietetics (didactic), Engineering (agricultural, chemical, civil, computer, electrical, environmental/sanitary, industrial, mechanical, transportation), Family & Consumer Science, Graduate Social Work, Interior Design, Journalism, Landscape Architecture, Law, Music, Nursing Education, Radiography, Rehabilitation Counseling, Social Work, Teacher Education (NCATE)

University of Arkansas at Fort Smith
5210 Grand Ave., PO Box 3649, Fort Smith 72913-3649
Type: Public, state, four-year
System: Arkansas Department of Higher Education
Degrees: A, B *Enroll:* 5,028
URL: http://www.uafortsmith.edu
Phone: (501) 788-7000 *Calendar:* Sem. plan
Inst. Accred.: NCA-HLC (1973/2005)
Prog. Accred.: Allied Health (surgical technology), Dentistry (dental hygiene), Nursing, Radiography, Teacher Education (NCATE)

University of Arkansas at Little Rock
2801 South University Ave., Little Rock 72204
Type: Public, state, four-year
System: University of Arkansas System Administration
Degrees: A, B, M, P, D *Enroll:* 8,837
URL: http://www.ualr.edu
Phone: (501) 569-3000 *Calendar:* Sem. plan
Inst. Accred.: NCA-HLC (1929/2000)
Prog. Accred.: Allied Health (audiology, health services administration, speech-language pathology), Art, Business (AACSB), Computer Science (ABET-CAC), Construction Education, Engineering (systems), Engineering Technology (computer, mechanical), Graduate Social Work, Law, Music, Nursing, Public Administration, Rehabilitation Counseling, Social Work, Teacher Education (NCATE), Theatre

University of Arkansas at Monticello
PO Box 3596, Monticello 71655-3596
Type: Public, state, four-year
System: University of Arkansas System Administration
Degrees: A, B, M *Enroll:* 2,547
URL: http://www.uamont.edu
Phone: (870) 367-6811 *Calendar:* Sem. plan
Inst. Accred.: NCA-HLC (1928/2005)
Prog. Accred.: Allied Health (EMT-paramedic), Business (ACBSP), Forestry, Music, Nursing, Social Work, Teacher Education (NCATE)

University of Arkansas at Monticello College of Technology-Crossett
1326 Hwy. 52 West, Crosett 71635
Type: Public, local, two-year
Degrees: A
URL: http://www.uamont.edu/UAMCTC
Phone: (870) 364-6414 *Calendar:* Sem. plan
Inst. Accred.: NCA-HLC (1928/2005, *Indirect accreditation through University of Arkansas at Monticello, Monticello, AR*), COE (2005)

University of Arkansas at Pine Bluff
1200 North University Dr., Pine Bluff 71611
Type: Public, state, four-year
System: University of Arkansas System Administration
Degrees: A, B, M *Enroll:* 3,013
URL: http://www.uapb.edu
Phone: (870) 543-8000 *Calendar:* Sem. plan
Inst. Accred.: NCA-HLC (1950/2007)
Prog. Accred.: Art, Dietetics (didactic), Family & Consumer Science, Industrial Technology, Music, Nursing, Social Work, Teacher Education (NCATE)

University of Arkansas Community College at Batesville
PO Box 3350, Batesville 72503
Type: Public, state, two-year
System: University of Arkansas System Administration
Degrees: A *Enroll:* 977
URL: http://www.uaccb.edu
Phone: (870) 793-7581 *Calendar:* Sem. plan
Inst. Accred.: NCA-HLC (1998/2003)
Prog. Accred.: Allied Health (EMT-paramedic, surgical technology), Nursing

University of Arkansas Community College at Hope
2500 South Main, PO Box 140, Hope 71802-0140
Type: Public, state, two-year
System: University of Arkansas System Administration
Degrees: A *Enroll:* 803
URL: http://www.uacch.edu
Phone: (870) 777-5722 *Calendar:* Sem. plan
Inst. Accred.: NCA-HLC (1997/2001)
Prog. Accred.: Allied Health (respiratory therapy), Funeral Service Education (Mortuary Science)

University of Arkansas Community College at Morrilton
One Bruce St., Morrilton 72110
Type: Public, state, two-year
System: Arkansas Department of Higher Education
Degrees: A *Enroll:* 1,408
URL: http://www.uaccm.edu
Phone: (501) 354-2465 *Calendar:* Sem. plan
Inst. Accred.: NCA-HLC (1997/2002)

University of Arkansas for Medical Sciences
4301 West Markham St., Little Rock 72205
Type: Public, state, four-year
System: University of Arkansas System Administration
Degrees: A, B, M, P, D *Enroll:* 1,990
URL: http://www.uams.edu
Phone: (501) 686-5000 *Calendar:* Sem. plan
Inst. Accred.: NCA-HLC (1987/2007)
Prog. Accred.: Allied Health (EMT-paramedic, cytotechnology, diagnostic medical sonography, medicine, respiratory therapy, surgical technology), Clinical Lab Scientist, Dentistry (dental hygiene), Dietetics (internship), Nuclear Medicine Technology, Nursing Education, Pharmacy, Psychology Internship, Public Health, Radiography

Area Health Education Center Northwest
2907 East Joyce St., Fayetteville 72703-5011
Phone: (479) 521-8269
Prog. Accred: Radiography

Area Health Education Center Southwest
300 East 6th St., Texarkana 71854
Phone: (870) 779-6000
Prog. Accred: Allied Health (respiratory therapy), Radiography

University of Central Arkansas
201 Donaghey Ave., Conway 72035
Type: Public, state, four-year
System: Arkansas Department of Higher Education
Degrees: A, B, M, P, D *Enroll:* 10,349
URL: http://www.uca.edu
Phone: (501) 450-5000 *Calendar:* Sem. plan
Inst. Accred.: NCA-HLC (1931/2000)
Prog. Accred.: Allied Health (occupational therapy, speech-language pathology), Art, Business (AACSB), Dietetics (didactic), Dietetics (internship), Interior Design, Music, Nursing, Nursing Education, Physical Therapy, Teacher Education (NCATE), Theatre

University of the Ozarks
415 North College Ave., Clarksville 72830
Type: Private, Presbyterian Church (USA), four-year
Degrees: A, B *Enroll:* 604
URL: http://www.ozarks.edu
Phone: (501) 979-1000 *Calendar:* Sem. plan
Inst. Accred.: NCA-HLC (1931/2003)
Prog. Accred.: Teacher Education (NCATE)

Williams Baptist College
201 Fulbright Ave., Walnut Ridge 72476
Type: Private, Southern Baptist Church, four-year
Degrees: A, B *Enroll:* 540
URL: http://www.wbcoll.edu
Phone: (870) 886-6741 *Calendar:* Sem. plan
Inst. Accred.: NCA-HLC (1963/2002)
Prog. Accred.: Teacher Education (NCATE)

CALIFORNIA

Academy of Art University
79 New Montgomery St., 6th Flr., San Francisco 94105
Type: Private, independent, four-year
Degrees: B, M *Enroll:* 6,597
URL: http://www.academyart.edu
Phone: (415) 274-2200 *Calendar:* Sem. plan
Inst. Accred.: WASC-SR. (2007)
Prog. Accred.: Art, Interior Architecture, Interior Design

Academy of Chinese Culture and Health Sciences
1601 Clay St., Oakland 94612
Type: Private, proprietary, four-year
Degrees: M *Enroll:* 122
URL: http://www.acchs.edu
Phone: (510) 763-7787 *Calendar:* Tri. plan
Inst. Accred.: ACAOM (1992/2004)

Acupuncture and Integrative Medicine College, Berkeley
2550 Shattuck Ave., Berkeley 94704
Type: Private, proprietary, four-year
Degrees: M
URL: http://www.aic-berkeley.edu
Phone: (510) 666-8248 *Calendar:* Qtr. plan
Inst. Accred.: ACAOM (2000/2007)

Advanced College
13180 Paramount Blvd., South Gate 90280
Type: Private, proprietary, two-year
Degrees: A
URL: http://www.advancedcollege.edu
Phone: (562) 408-6969
Inst. Accred.: COE (2003)

Advanced Training Associates, Inc.
1810 Gillespie Way, Ste. 104, El Cajon 92020
Type: Public, proprietary, two-year
Degrees: A
URL: http://www.advancedtraining.net
Phone: (619) 596-2766
Inst. Accred.: COE (2000/2006)

Allan Hancock College
800 South College Dr., Santa Maria 93454-6368
Type: Public, state/local, two-year
System: Allan Hancock Joint Community College District
Degrees: A *Enroll:* 6,098
URL: http://www.hancockcollege.edu
Phone: (805) 922-6966 *Calendar:* Sem. plan
Inst. Accred.: WASC-JR. (1952/2004)

Alliant International University—Fresno
5130 East Clinton Way, Fresno 93727-2014
Type: Private, independent, four-year
System: Alliant International University
Degrees: A, B, M, D *Enroll:* 290
URL: http://www.alliant.edu/fresno
Phone: (559) 456-2777 *Calendar:* Sem. plan
Inst. Accred.: WASC-SR. (1977/2006, *Indirect accreditation through Alliant International University, San Francisco, CA*)
Prog. Accred.: Clinical Psychology

Sacramento Campus
425 University Ave., Ste. 201, Sacramento 95825
Phone: (916) 565-2955
Prog. Accred: Marriage and Family Therapy

Alliant International University—Irvine
2500 Michelson Dr., Bldg. 400, Irvine 92612-1548
Type: Private, independent, four-year
System: Alliant International University
Degrees: A, B, M, D
URL: http://www.alliant.edu
Phone: (949) 833-2651 *Calendar:* Sem. plan
Inst. Accred.: WASC-SR. (1977/2006, *Indirect accreditation through Alliant International University, San Francisco, CA*)
Prog. Accred.: Marriage and Family Therapy

Alliant International University—Los Angeles
1000 South Fremont Ave., Unit 5, Alhambra 91803-1360
Type: Private, independent, four-year
System: Alliant International University
Degrees: A, B, M, D *Enroll:* 577
URL: http://www.alliant.edu/la
Phone: (626) 284-2777 *Calendar:* Sem. plan
Inst. Accred.: WASC-SR. (1977/2006, *Indirect accreditation through Alliant International University, San Francisco, CA*)
Prog. Accred.: Clinical Psychology

Alliant International University—San Diego Cornerstone Court
6161 Cornerstone Ct. East, San Diego 92121-3710
Type: Private, independent, four-year
System: Alliant International University
Degrees: A, B, M, D *Enroll:* 1,229
URL: http://www.alliant.edu/sandiego
Phone: (858) 623-2777 *Calendar:* Sem. plan
Inst. Accred.: WASC-SR. (1977/2006, *Indirect accreditation through Alliant International University, San Francisco, CA*)
Prog. Accred.: Clinical Psychology

**Alliant International University—
San Diego Scripps Ranch**
10455 Pomerado Rd., San Diego 92131-1799
Type: Private, independent, four-year
System: Alliant International University
Degrees: A, B, M, D *Enroll:* 1,085
URL: http://www.alliant.edu/sandiego.htm
Phone: (858) 271-4300 *Calendar:* Sem. plan
Inst. Accred.: WASC-SR. (1977/2006, *Indirect accreditation through Alliant International University, San Francisco, CA*)
Prog. Accred.: Marriage and Family Therapy

**Alliant International University—
San Francisco Bay**
1005 Atlantic Ave., Alameda 94501
Type: Private, independent, four-year
System: Alliant International University
Degrees: A, B, M, D *Enroll:* 642
URL: http://www.alliant.edu/sfbay
Phone: (510) 523-2300 *Calendar:* Sem. plan
Inst. Accred.: WASC-SR. (1977/2006, *Indirect accreditation through Alliant International University, San Francisco, CA*)
Prog. Accred.: Clinical Psychology

Allied American University
22952 Alcalde Dr., Laguna Hills 92653
Type: Private, proprietary, four-year
Degrees: A, B
URL: http://www.allied.edu
Phone: (888) 384-0849 *Calendar:* Sem. plan
Inst. Accred.: DETC (2008)

American Baptist Seminary of the West
2606 Dwight Way, Berkeley 94704-3029
Type: Private, American Baptist Churches (USA), four-year
System: Graduate Theological Union
Degrees: M *Enroll:* 62
URL: http://www.absw.edu
Phone: (510) 841-1905 *Calendar:* Sem. plan
Inst. Accred.: ATS (1938/2004)

American College of Traditional Chinese Medicine
455 Arkansas St., San Francisco 94107-2813
Type: Private, proprietary, four-year
Degrees: M *Enroll:* 247
URL: http://www.actcm.org
Phone: (415) 282-7600 *Calendar:* Qtr. plan
Inst. Accred.: ACAOM (1991/2007)

American Conservatory Theater
30 Grant Ave., 6th Flr., San Francisco 94108-5800
Type: Private, independent, four-year
Degrees: M *Enroll:* 50
URL: http://www.act-sfbay.org
Phone: (415) 439-2350 *Calendar:* Sem. plan
Inst. Accred.: WASC-SR. (1984/2008)

The American Film Institute
2021 North Western Ave., Los Angeles 90027
Type: Private, independent, four-year
Degrees: M *Enroll:* 318
URL: http://www.afionline.org
Phone: (323) 856-7600 *Calendar:* 24-mos. pr
Inst. Accred.: WASC-SR. (2002)
Prog. Accred.: Art

American Graduate University
733 North Dodsworth Ave., Covina 91724
Type: Private, proprietary, four-year
Degrees: M
URL: http://www.agu.edu
Phone: (626) 966-4576
Inst. Accred.: DETC (1998/2008)

American Jewish University
15600 Mulholland Dr., Bel Air 90077
Type: Private, independent, four-year
Degrees: B, M *Enroll:* 265
URL: http://www.ajula.edu
Phone: (310) 476-9777 *Calendar:* Sem. plan
Inst. Accred.: WASC-SR. (1961/2006)

Brandeis-Bardin Campus
1101 Peppertree Ln., Brandeis 93064
Phone: (805) 582-4450

American River College
4700 College Oak Dr., Sacramento 95841-4286
Type: Public, state/local, two-year
System: Los Rios Community College District
Degrees: A *Enroll:* 15,821
URL: http://www.arc.losrios.edu
Phone: (916) 484-8011 *Calendar:* Sem. plan
Inst. Accred.: WASC-JR. (1959/2004)
Prog. Accred.: Allied Health (EMT-paramedic, respiratory therapy), Funeral Service Education (Mortuary Science)

American University of Armenia
300 Lakeside Dr., Fourth Flr., Oakland 94612
Type: Private, independent, four-year
Degrees: M
URL: http://www.aua.am
Phone: (510) 987-9452 *Calendar:* Qtr. plan
Inst. Accred.: WASC-SR. (2006)

American University of Health Sciences
3501 Atlantic Ave., Long Beach 90807
Type: Private, independent, four-year
Degrees: B, M
URL: http://www.auhs.edu
Phone: (562) 988-2278
Inst. Accred.: ACICS (2004/2006)

Antelope Valley College
3041 West Ave. K, Lancaster 93536-5426
Type: Public, state/local, two-year
System: Antelope Valley Community College District
Degrees: A *Enroll:* 6,234
URL: http://www.avc.edu
Phone: (661) 722-6300 *Calendar:* Sem. plan
Inst. Accred.: WASC-JR. (1952/2005)

Antioch University—Los Angeles
400 Corporate Pointe, Culver City 90230
Type: Private, independent, four-year
Degrees: B, M *FTE Enroll:* 2,323
URL: http://www.antiochla.edu
Phone: (310) 578-1080 *Calendar:* Qtr. plan
Inst. Accred.: WASC-SR. (2007)

Antioch University—Santa Barbara
801 Garden St., Santa Barbara 93101
Type: Private, independent, four-year
Degrees: B, M, D
URL: http://www.antiochsb.edu
Phone: (805) 962-8179 *Calendar:* Qtr. plan
Inst. Accred.: WASC-SR. (2007)
Prog. Accred.: Business (ACBSP)

Applied Professional Training, Inc.
PO Box 131717, Carlsbad 92013
Type: Private, proprietary, two-year
Degrees: A
URL: http://www.aptc.com
Phone: (800) 431-8488
Inst. Accred.: DETC (2003/2007)

Argosy University Orange County
3501 West Sunflower Ave., Ste. 110, Santa Ana 92704-9888
Type: Private, proprietary, four-year
System: Argosy University
Degrees: A, B, M, D
URL: http://www.argosy.edu/orangecounty
Phone: (714) 338-6200 *Calendar:* Tri. plan
Inst. Accred.: NCA-HLC (1981/2008, *Indirect accreditation through Argosy University, Chicago, IL*)

Inland Empire Campus
636 East Brier Dr., Ste. 235, San Bernardino 92408
Phone: (909) 915-3800

San Diego Campus
7650 Mission Valley Rd., San Diego 92108
Phone: (858) 598-1900

Santa Monica Campus
2950 31st St., Santa Monica 90405
Phone: (310) 866-4000

Argosy University San Francisco Bay Area
1005 Atlantic Ave., Alameda 94501
Type: Private, proprietary, four-year
System: Argosy University
Degrees: B, M, D
URL: http://www.argosy.edu/sanfrancisco
Phone: (510) 217-4700 *Calendar:* Tri. plan
Inst. Accred.: NCA-HLC (1981/2008, *Indirect accreditation through Argosy University, Chicago, IL*)
Prog. Accred.: Clinical Psychology

Art Center College of Design
1700 Lida St., Pasadena 91103
Type: Private, independent, four-year
Degrees: B, M *Enroll:* 1,501
URL: http://www.artcenter.edu
Phone: (626) 396-2200 *Calendar:* Tri. plan
Inst. Accred.: WASC-SR. (1955/2007)
Prog. Accred.: Art

The Art Institute of California—Hollywood
3440 Wilshire Blvd., 7th Flr., Los Angeles 90010
Type: Private, proprietary, four-year
System: Education Management Corporation
Degrees: A, B
URL: http://www.artinstitutes.edu/hollywood
Phone: (213) 251-3636 *Calendar:* Qtr. plan
Inst. Accred.: ACICS (1995/2004)

Art Institute of California—Inland Empire
630 East Brier Dr., San Bernardino 92408
Type: Private, proprietary, four-year
Degrees: A, B
URL: http://www.artinstitutes.edu/inlandempire
Phone: (909) 915-2100 *Calendar:* Qtr. plan
Inst. Accred.: ACCSCT (2005)

The Art Institute of California—Los Angeles
2900 31st St., Santa Monica 90405-3035
Type: Private, proprietary, four-year
System: Education Management Corporation
Degrees: A, B
URL: http://www.aicala.artinstitutes.edu
Phone: (310) 752-4700 *Calendar:* Qtr. plan
Inst. Accred.: ACICS (2003)

The Art Institute of California—Orange County
3601 Sunflower Ave., Santa Ana 92704
Phone: (714) 830-0200

The Art Institute of California—San Francisco
1170 Market St., San Francisco 94102-4908
Phone: (415) 865-0198

Sacramento Campus
1331 Garden Hwy., Ste. 300, Sacramento 95833-9773
Phone: (916) 830-6320

The Art Institute of California—San Diego
7650 Mission Valley Rd., San Diego 92108-3277
Type: Private, proprietary, four-year
System: Education Management Corporation
Degrees: A, B *Enroll:* 1,723
URL: http://www.artinstitutes.edu/sandiego
Phone: (858) 598-1200 *Calendar:* Qtr. plan
Inst. Accred.: ACCSCT (1986/2006)
Prog. Accred.: Culinary Education

Aviation and Electronic School of America
PO Box 1810, Colfax 95713-1810
Type: Private, proprietary, two-year
Degrees: A
URL: http://www.aesa.com
Phone: (530) 346-6792
Inst. Accred.: COE (1999/2007)

San Diego Campus
7905 Silverton Aveenue, Ste. 101, San Diego 92126
Phone: (858) 566-2184

Azusa Pacific University
901 East Alosta Ave., PO Box 7000, Azusa 91702-7000
Type: Private, Wesleyan Church, four-year
Degrees: A, B, M, P, D *Enroll:* 6,060
URL: http://www.apu.edu
Phone: (626) 812-3434 *Calendar:* 4-1-4 plan
Inst. Accred.: ATS (1990/2006), WASC-SR. (1964/2001)
Prog. Accred.: Clinical Psychology, Nursing Education, Physical Therapy, Social Work, Teacher Education (NCATE)

Bakersfield College
1801 Panorama Dr., Bakersfield 93305-1299
Type: Public, state/local, two-year
System: Kern Community College District
Degrees: A *Enroll:* 8,566
URL: http://www.bakersfieldcollege.edu
Phone: (661) 395-4011 *Calendar:* Sem. plan
Inst. Accred.: WASC-JR. (1952/2007)
Prog. Accred.: Allied Health (EMT-paramedic), Radiography

Barstow College
2700 Barstow Rd., Barstow 92311-6699
Type: Public, state/local, two-year
System: Barstow Community College District
Degrees: A *Enroll:* 1,578
URL: http://www.barstow.edu
Phone: (760) 252-2411 *Calendar:* Sem. plan
Inst. Accred.: WASC-JR. (1962/2006)

Berkeley City College
2020 Milvia St., Berkeley 94704-1183
Type: Public, state/local, two-year
System: Peralta Community College District
Degrees: A *Enroll:* 1,710
URL: http://berkeley.peralta.edu
Phone: (510) 981-2800 *Calendar:* Sem. plan
Inst. Accred.: WASC-JR. (1981/2003)

Bethany University
800 Bethany Dr., Scotts Valley 95066
Type: Private, Assemblies of God, four-year
Degrees: A, B, M *Enroll:* 492
URL: http://www.bethany.edu
Phone: (831) 438-3800 *Calendar:* 4-1-4 plan
Inst. Accred.: WASC-SR. (1966/2001, Warning)

Bethesda Christian University
730 North Euclid St., Anaheim 92801
Type: Private, Full Gospel World Mission, four-year
Degrees: B, M
URL: http://www.bcu.edu
Phone: (714) 517-1945 *Calendar:* Sem. plan
Inst. Accred.: ABHE (1997/2006), TRACS (2006)

Biola University
13800 Biola Ave., La Mirada 90639-0001
Type: Private, interdenominational, four-year
Degrees: B, M, P, D *Enroll:* 4,684
URL: http://www.biola.edu
Phone: (562) 903-6000 *Calendar:* 4-1-4 plan
Inst. Accred.: ATS (1978/2006), WASC-SR. (1961/2005)
Prog. Accred.: Art, Business (ACBSP), Clinical Psychology, Music

Brooks College
4825 East Pacific Coast Hwy., Long Beach 90804
Type: Private, proprietary, two-year
System: Career Education Corporation
Degrees: A *Enroll:* 784
URL: http://www.brookscollege.edu
Phone: (562) 597-6611 *Calendar:* Qtr. plan
Inst. Accred.: WASC-JR. (1977/2004)
Prog. Accred.: Interior Design

Brooks Institute of Photography
801 Alston Rd., Santa Barbara 93108
Type: Private, proprietary, four-year
System: Career Education Corporation
Degrees: A, B, M *Enroll:* 2,563
URL: http://www.brooks.edu
Phone: (805) 690-7667 *Calendar:* Tri. plan
Inst. Accred.: ACICS (1984/2005)

Ventura Campus
5301 North Ventura Ave., Ventura 93001
Phone: (805) 585-8000

Bryan College
3580 Wilshire Blvd., Ste. 400, Los Angeles 90010
Type: Private, proprietary, two-year
Degrees: A
URL: http://www.bryancollege.edu
Phone: (213) 484-8850
Inst. Accred.: ACICS (1975/2005)

Bryan College—Sacramento
2317 Gold Meadow Way, Gold River 95670
Type: Private, proprietary, two-year
Degrees: A *Enroll:* 1,365
URL: http://ws1.bryancollege.edu
Phone: (916) 649-2400
Inst. Accred.: ACCSCT (1999/2007)

Butte College
3536 Butte Campus Dr., Oroville 95965-8399
Type: Public, state/local, two-year
System: Butte-Glenn Community College District
Degrees: A *Enroll:* 8,897
URL: http://www.butte.edu
Phone: (530) 895-2511 *Calendar:* Sem. plan
Inst. Accred.: WASC-JR. (1972/2003)
Prog. Accred.: Allied Health (EMT-paramedic, respiratory therapy)

Cabrillo College
6500 Soquel Dr., Aptos 95003-3119
Type: Public, state/local, two-year
System: Cabrillo Community College District
Degrees: A *Enroll:* 7,800
URL: http://www.cabrillo.edu
Phone: (831) 479-6100 *Calendar:* Sem. plan
Inst. Accred.: WASC-JR. (1961/2008)
Prog. Accred.: Allied Health (medical assisting (AMA)), Dentistry (dental hygiene), Radiography

California Baptist University
8432 Magnolia Ave., Riverside 92504
Type: Private, Southern Baptist Church, four-year
Degrees: B, M *Enroll:* 2,552
URL: http://www.calbaptist.edu
Phone: (951) 689-5771 *Calendar:* Sem. plan
Inst. Accred.: WASC-SR. (1961/2000)
Prog. Accred.: Business (ACBSP), Music, Nursing Education

California Christian College
4881 East University Ave., Fresno 93703-3599
Type: Private, Free Will Baptist Church, four-year
Degrees: A, B
URL: http://www.calchristiancollege.org
Phone: (559) 251-4215 *Calendar:* Sem. plan
Inst. Accred.: TRACS (1993/2003)

California Coast University
700 North Main St., Santa Ana 92701
Type: Private, proprietary, four-year
Degrees: A, B, M *FTE Enroll:* 312
URL: http://www.calcoast.edu
Phone: (714) 547-9625 *Calendar:* Sem. plan
Inst. Accred.: DETC (2005)

California College of the Arts
1111 Eigth St., San Francisco 94107-2247
Type: Private, independent, four-year
Degrees: B, M *Enroll:* 1,560
URL: http://www.ccac-art.edu
Phone: (415) 703-9500 *Calendar:* Tri. plan
Inst. Accred.: WASC-SR. (1954/2008)
Prog. Accred.: Art, Interior Design

Oakland Campus
5212 Broadway, Oakland 94618
Phone: (510) 594-3600

California College San Diego
2820 Camino Del Rio South, Ste. 300, San Diego 92108-3821
Type: Private, proprietary, four-year
Degrees: A, B
URL: http://www.cc-sd.edu
Phone: (619) 295-5785
Inst. Accred.: ACCSCT (1992/2004)
Prog. Accred.: Allied Health (respiratory therapy)

California Culinary Academy
625 Polk St., San Francisco 94102-3368
Type: Private, proprietary, two-year
System: Career Education Corporation
Degrees: A *Enroll:* 3,607
URL: http://www.baychef.com
Phone: (415) 771-3500
Inst. Accred.: ACCSCT (1982/2005)
Prog. Accred.: Culinary Education

California Institute of Integral Studies
1453 Mission St., 4th Flr., San Francisco 94103
Type: Private, independent, four-year
Degrees: B, M, D *Enroll:* 846
URL: http://www.ciis.edu
Phone: (415) 575-6100 *Calendar:* Qtr. plan
Inst. Accred.: WASC-SR. (1981/2008)
Prog. Accred.: Clinical Psychology

California Institute of Technology
1200 East California Blvd., Pasadena 91125-0001
Type: Private, independent, four-year
Degrees: B, M, D *Enroll:* 2,169
URL: http://www.caltech.edu
Phone: (626) 395-6811 *Calendar:* Qtr. plan
Inst. Accred.: WASC-SR. (1949/1998)
Prog. Accred.: Engineering (chemical, electrical, engineering physics/science, mechanical)

California Institute of the Arts
24700 McBean Pkwy., Valencia 91355
Type: Private, independent, four-year
Degrees: B, M *Enroll:* 1,324
URL: http://www.calarts.edu
Phone: (661) 255-1050 *Calendar:* Sem. plan
Inst. Accred.: WASC-SR. (1955/2000)
Prog. Accred.: Art, Dance, Music, Theatre

California International Business University
303 A St., 3rd Flr., San Diego 92101
Type: Private, proprietary, four-year
Degrees: B, M, D
URL: http://cibu.edu
Phone: (619) 702-9400 *Calendar:* Qtr. plan
Inst. Accred.: ACICS (2007)

California Lutheran University
60 West Olsen Rd., Thousand Oaks 91360
Type: Private, Evangelical Lutheran Church in America, four-year
Degrees: B, M *Enroll:* 2,808
URL: http://www.callutheran.edu
Phone: (805) 492-2411 *Calendar:* 4-1-4 plan
Inst. Accred.: WASC-SR. (1962/2007)
Prog. Accred.: Teacher Education (NCATE)

California Maritime Academy
200 Maritime Academy Dr., PO Box 1392, Vallejo 94590-8181
Type: Public, state, four-year
System: California State University System
Degrees: B *Enroll:* 765
URL: http://www.csum.edu
Phone: (707) 654-1000 *Calendar:* Tri. plan
Inst. Accred.: WASC-SR. (1977/2002)
Prog. Accred.: Engineering (mechanical), Engineering Technology (facilities, naval architecture/marine)

California National University for Advanced Studies
8550 Balboa Blvd., Ste. 210, Northridge 91325
Type: Private, proprietary, four-year
Degrees: B, M *FTE Enroll:* 500
URL: http://www.cnuas.edu
Phone: (818) 830-2411 *Calendar:* Tri. plan
Inst. Accred.: DETC (1998/2008)

California Polytechnic State University—San Luis Obispo
San Luis Obispo 93407
Type: Public, state, four-year
System: California State University System
Degrees: B, M *Enroll:* 17,715
URL: http://www.calpoly.edu
Phone: (805) 756-1111 *Calendar:* Qtr. plan
Inst. Accred.: WASC-SR. (1951/2000)
Prog. Accred.: Art, Business (AACSB), Computer Science (ABET-CAC), Construction Education, Dietetics (didactic), Dietetics (internship), Engineering (aerospace, agricultural, architectural, civil, computer, electrical, environmental/sanitary, industrial, manufacturing, materials, mechanical), Forestry, Industrial Technology, Landscape Architecture, Music, Planning, Recreation and Leisure Services

California School of Culinary Arts
521 East Green St., Pasadena 91101
Type: Private, proprietary, two-year
System: Career Education Corporation
Degrees: A
URL: http://www.csca.edu
Phone: (626) 229-1300 *Calendar:* Sem. plan
Inst. Accred.: ACICS (1997/2006)

Hollywood Campus
6360 West Sunset Blvd., Hollywood 90028-7323
Phone: (626) 403-0984

California State Polytechnic University—Pomona
3801 West Temple Ave., Pomona 91768
Type: Public, state, four-year
System: California State University System
Degrees: B, M *Enroll:* 17,257
URL: http://www.csupomona.edu
Phone: (909) 869-7659 *Calendar:* Qtr. plan
Inst. Accred.: WASC-SR. (1970/2001)
Prog. Accred.: Art, Business (AACSB), Computer Science (ABET-CAC), Dietetics (didactic), Dietetics (internship), Engineering (aerospace, chemical, civil, computer, electrical, industrial, manufacturing, mechanical), Engineering Technology (civil/construction, electrical, general), Landscape Architecture, Planning, Public Administration, Veterinary Technology

California State University, Bakersfield
9001 Stockdale Hwy., Bakersfield 93311-1099
Type: Public, state, four-year
System: California State University System
Degrees: B, M, D *Enroll:* 6,441
URL: http://www.csubak.edu
Phone: (661) 664-2011 *Calendar:* Qtr. plan
Inst. Accred.: WASC-SR. (1970/2000)
Prog. Accred.: Business (AACSB), Graduate Social Work, Nursing Education, Public Administration, Teacher Education (NCATE)

California State University, Channel Islands
One University Dr., Camarillo 93012
Type: Public, state, four-year
System: California State University System
Degrees: B, M *Enroll:* 2,190
URL: http://www.csuci.edu
Phone: (805) 383-8400 *Calendar:* Sem. plan
Inst. Accred.: WASC-SR. (2007)

California State University, Chico
400 West First St., Chico 95929
Type: Public, state, four-year
System: California State University System
Degrees: B, M *Enroll:* 14,762
URL: http://www.csuchico.edu
Phone: (530) 898-4636 *Calendar:* Sem. plan
Inst. Accred.: WASC-SR. (1949/2007)
Prog. Accred.: Allied Health (speech-language pathology), Art, Business (AACSB), Computer Science (ABET-CAC), Construction Education, Dietetics (didactic), Dietetics (internship), Engineering (civil, computer, electrical, mechanical), Graduate Social Work, Journalism, Manufacturing Technology, Music, Nursing Education, Public Administration, Recreation and Leisure Services, Social Work, Teacher Education (NCATE)

California State University, Dominguez Hills
1000 East Victoria St., Carson 90747
Type: Public, state, four-year
System: California State University System
Degrees: B, M *Enroll:* 8,909
URL: http://www.csudh.edu
Phone: (310) 243-3300 *Calendar:* Sem. plan
Inst. Accred.: WASC-SR. (1965/2008)
Prog. Accred.: Allied Health (occupational therapy, orthotist/prothetist), Business (ACBSP), Clinical Lab Scientist, Computer Science (ABET-CAC), Graduate Social Work, Music, Nursing Education, Public Administration, Teacher Education (NCATE), Theatre

California State University, East Bay
25800 Carlos Bee Blvd., Hayward 94542-3011
Type: Public, state, four-year
System: California State University System
Degrees: B, M *Enroll:* 10,314
URL: http://www.csueastbay.edu
Phone: (510) 885-3000 *Calendar:* Qtr. plan
Inst. Accred.: WASC-SR. (1961/2008)
Prog. Accred.: Allied Health (speech-language pathology), Art, Business (AACSB), Engineering (industrial), Graduate Social Work, Music, Nursing, Teacher Education (NCATE)

California State University, Fresno
5241 North Maple Ave., Mailstop 48, Fresno 93740-8027
Type: Public, state, four-year
System: California State University System
Degrees: B, M, D *Enroll:* 17,980
URL: http://www.csufresno.edu
Phone: (559) 278-4240 *Calendar:* Sem. plan
Inst. Accred.: WASC-SR. (1949/2005)
Prog. Accred.: Allied Health (speech-language pathology), Business (AACSB), Construction Education, Counseling, Dietetics (didactic), Dietetics (internship), Engineering (civil, computer, electrical, industrial, mechanical, surveying), Graduate Social Work, Interior Design, Music, Nursing Education, Physical Therapy, Public Administration, Public Health, Recreation and Leisure Services, Rehabilitation Counseling, Social Work, Teacher Education (NCATE), Theatre

California State University, Fullerton
PO Box 34080, Fullerton 92834
Type: Public, state, four-year
System: California State University System
Degrees: B, M *Enroll:* 28,019
URL: http://www.fullerton.edu
Phone: (714) 278-2011 *Calendar:* Sem. plan
Inst. Accred.: WASC-SR. (1961/2000)
Prog. Accred.: Accounting, Allied Health (speech-language pathology), Art, Business (AACSB), Computer Science (ABET-CAC), Counseling, Dance, Engineering (civil, electrical, mechanical), Journalism, Music, Nurse Anesthesia Education, Nursing Education, Public Administration, Teacher Education (NCATE), Theatre

California State University, Long Beach
1250 Bellflower Blvd., Long Beach 90840
Type: Public, state, four-year
System: California State University System
Degrees: B, M, D *Enroll:* 28,846
URL: http://www.csulb.edu
Phone: (562) 985-4111 *Calendar:* Sem. plan
Inst. Accred.: WASC-SR. (1957/2002)
Prog. Accred.: Allied Health (audiology, health services administration, kinesiotherapy, speech-language pathology), Art, Business (AACSB), Computer Science (ABET-CAC), Dance, Dietetics (didactic), Dietetics (internship), Engineering (aerospace, chemical, civil, computer, electrical, mechanical), Engineering Technology (computer, electrical, manufacturing), English Language Education, Family & Consumer Science, Graduate Social Work, Music, Nursing Education, Phlebotomy, Physical Therapy, Psychology Internship, Public Administration, Public Health, Radiation Therapy, Recreation and Leisure Services, Social Work, Teacher Education (NCATE), Theatre

California State University, Los Angeles
5151 State University Dr., Los Angeles 90032-4226
Type: Public, state, four-year
System: California State University System
Degrees: B, M, D *Enroll:* 15,731
URL: http://www.calstatela.edu
Phone: (323) 343-3000 *Calendar:* Qtr. plan
Inst. Accred.: WASC-SR. (1954/1999)
Prog. Accred.: Allied Health (audiology, speech-language pathology), Art, Business (AACSB), Counseling, Dietetics (coordinated), Dietetics (didactic), Engineering (civil, electrical, mechanical), Graduate Social Work, Music, Public Administration, Rehabilitation Counseling, Social Work, Teacher Education (NCATE)

California State University, Monterey Bay
100 Campus Center, Building 1, Seaside 93955-8001
Type: Public, state, four-year
System: California State University System
Degrees: B, M, D *Enroll:* 3,413
URL: http://csumb.edu
Phone: (831) 582-3538 *Calendar:* Sem. plan
Inst. Accred.: WASC-SR. (2003)
Prog. Accred.: Teacher Education (NCATE)

California State University, Northridge
18111 Nordhoff St., Northridge 91330
Type: Public, state, four-year
System: California State University System
Degrees: B, M *Enroll:* 26,884
URL: http://www.csun.edu
Phone: (818) 677-2121 *Calendar:* Sem. plan
Inst. Accred.: WASC-SR. (1958/2000)
Prog. Accred.: Allied Health (audiology, speech-language pathology), Applied Science (occupational health & safety), Art, Business (AACSB), Computer Science (ABET-CAC), Counseling, Dietetics (didactic), Dietetics (internship), Engineering (civil, electrical, environmental/sanitary, manufacturing, mechanical), Environmental Health, Environmental Health (graduate), Family & Consumer Science, Graduate Social Work, Interior Design, Journalism, Music, Nursing Education, Physical Therapy, Planning, Public Health, Radiography, Teacher Education (NCATE), Theatre

California State University, Sacramento
6000 J St., Sacramento 95819-6016
Type: Public, state, four-year
System: California State University System
Degrees: B, M, D *Enroll:* 23,370
URL: http://www.csus.edu
Phone: (916) 278-6011 *Calendar:* Sem. plan
Inst. Accred.: WASC-SR. (1951/1997)
Prog. Accred.: Allied Health (audiology, speech-language pathology), Art, Business (AACSB), Computer Science (ABET-CAC), Construction Education, Counseling, Dietetics (didactic), Dietetics (internship), Engineering (civil, computer, electrical, mechanical), Engineering Technology (mechanical), Graduate Social Work, Interior Design, Music, Nursing Education, Physical Therapy, Recreation and Leisure Services, Rehabilitation Counseling, Social Work, Theatre

California State University, San Bernardino
5500 University Pkwy., San Bernardino 92407-2397
Type: Public, state, four-year
System: California State University System
Degrees: B, M *Enroll:* 13,658
URL: http://www.csusb.edu
Phone: (909) 880-5000 *Calendar:* Qtr. plan
Inst. Accred.: WASC-SR. (1965/2004)
Prog. Accred.: Art, Business (AACSB), Computer Science (ABET-CAC), Dietetics (didactic), Graduate Social Work, Music, Nursing Education, Public Administration, Rehabilitation Counseling, Social Work, Teacher Education (NCATE), Theatre

California State University, San Marcos
333 South Twin Oaks Valley Rd., San Marcos 92096-0001
Type: Public, state, four-year
System: California State University System
Degrees: B, M, D *Enroll:* 6,114
URL: http://www.csusm.edu
Phone: (760) 750-4000 *Calendar:* Sem. plan
Inst. Accred.: WASC-SR. (1993/2000)
Prog. Accred.: Teacher Education (NCATE)

California State University, Stanislaus
801 West Monte Vista Ave., Turlock 95382
Type: Public, state, four-year
System: California State University System
Degrees: B, M *Enroll:* 6,364
URL: http://lead.csustan.edu
Phone: (209) 667-3082 *Calendar:* 4-1-4 plan
Inst. Accred.: WASC-SR. (1963/1998)
Prog. Accred.: Art, Business (AACSB), Graduate Social Work, Music, Nursing Education, Public Administration, Teacher Education (NCATE), Theatre

Stockton Campus
612 East Magnolia St., Stockton 95202-1846
Phone: (209) 467-5300

California University of Management and Sciences
721 North Euclid St., Anaheim 92801
Type: Private, independent, four-year
Degrees: A, B, M
URL: http://www.calums.edu
Phone: (714) 533-3946 *Calendar:* Qtr. plan
Inst. Accred.: ACICS (2006)

California Western School of Law
350 Cedar St., San Diego 92101
Type: Private, independent, four-year
Degrees: P *Enroll:* 825
URL: http://www.cwsl.edu
Phone: (619) 239-0391 *Calendar:* Tri. plan
Inst. Accred.: ABA (1962/2000)
Prog. Accred.: Law

Cambridge Junior College
990-A Klamath Ln., Yuba City 95993
Type: Private, proprietary, two-year
Degrees: A
URL: http://www.cambridge.edu
Phone: (530) 674-9199
Inst. Accred.: ACICS (2003/2005)

Cañada College
4200 Farm Hill Blvd., Redwood City 94061-1099
Type: Public, state/local, two-year
System: San Mateo County Community College District
Degrees: A *Enroll:* 2,602
URL: http://www.canadacollege.edu
Phone: (650) 306-3100 *Calendar:* Sem. plan
Inst. Accred.: WASC-JR. (1970/2001, Warning)
Prog. Accred.: Radiography

Cerritos College
11110 Alondra Blvd., Norwalk 90650-6296
Type: Public, state/local, two-year
System: Cerritos Community College District
Degrees: A *Enroll:* 11,728
URL: http://www.cerritos.edu
Phone: (562) 860-2451 *Calendar:* Sem. plan
Inst. Accred.: WASC-JR. (1959/2002, Warning)
Prog. Accred.: Dentistry (dental assisting, dental hygiene, general practice residency), Nursing, Physical Therapy Assisting

Cerro Coso Community College
3000 College Heights Blvd., Ridgecrest 93555-9571
Type: Public, state/local, two-year
System: Kern Community College District
Degrees: A *Enroll:* 2,214
URL: http://www.cerrocoso.edu
Phone: (760) 384-6100 *Calendar:* Sem. plan
Inst. Accred.: WASC-JR. (1975/2008)

Chabot College
25555 Hesperian Blvd., Hayward 94545-2447
Type: Public, state/local, two-year
System: Chabot-Las Positas Community College District
Degrees: A *Enroll:* 7,186
URL: http://www.chabotcollege.edu
Phone: (510) 723-6600 *Calendar:* Sem. plan
Inst. Accred.: WASC-JR. (1963/2003)
Prog. Accred.: Allied Health (medical assisting (AMA)), Dentistry (dental hygiene)

Chaffey College
5885 Haven Ave., Rancho Cucamonga 91737-3002
Type: Public, state/local, two-year
System: Chaffey Community College District
Degrees: A *Enroll:* 9,563
URL: http://www.chaffey.edu
Phone: (909) 652-6100 *Calendar:* Sem. plan
Inst. Accred.: WASC-JR. (1952/2004)
Prog. Accred.: Dentistry (dental assisting), Dietetic Technician, Nursing, Radiography

Chapman University
One University Dr., Orange 92866
Type: Private, Disciples of Christ, four-year
Degrees: A, B, M, P, D *Enroll:* 5,210
URL: http://www.chapman.edu
Phone: (714) 997-6815 *Calendar:* 4-1-4 plan
Inst. Accred.: WASC-SR. (1956/2005)
Prog. Accred.: Business (AACSB), Law (ABA only), Music, Physical Therapy

University College
1 University Dr., Orange 92866
Phone: (714) 289-2000

Charles Drew University of Medicine and Science
1731 East 120th St., Los Angeles 90059
Type: Private, independent, four-year
Degrees: A, B, M, D *Enroll:* 126
URL: http://www.cdrewu.edu
Phone: (323) 563-4800 *Calendar:* Sem. plan
Inst. Accred.: WASC-SR. (1995/2003)
Prog. Accred.: Dentistry (general practice residency, oral and maxillofacial surgery), Nuclear Medicine Technology, Physician Assistant, Radiography

Church Divinity School of the Pacific
2451 Ridge Rd., Berkeley 94709-1217
Type: Private, Province of the Pacific of the Episcopal Church, four-year
System: Graduate Theological Union
Degrees: M, D *Enroll:* 100
URL: http://www.cdsp.edu
Phone: (510) 204-0700 *Calendar:* Qtr. plan
Inst. Accred.: ATS (1938/2004)

Citrus College
1000 West Foothill Blvd., Glendora 91741-1899
Type: Public, state/local, two-year
System: Citrus Community College District
Degrees: A *Enroll:* 7,376
URL: http://www.citruscollege.edu
Phone: (626) 963-0323 *Calendar:* Sem. plan
Inst. Accred.: WASC-JR. (1952/2004)
Prog. Accred.: Dentistry (dental assisting)

City College of San Francisco
50 Phelan Ave., San Francisco 94112-1898
Type: Public, state/local, two-year
System: San Francisco Community College District
Degrees: A *Enroll:* 20,151
URL: http://www.ccsf.edu
Phone: (415) 239-3000 *Calendar:* Sem. plan
Inst. Accred.: WASC-JR. (1952/2006)
Prog. Accred.: Allied Health (EMT-paramedic, medical assisting (AMA)), Culinary Education, Dentistry (dental assisting), Radiation Therapy, Radiography

City of Hope National Medical Center
1500 East Duarte Rd., Duarte 91010-3000
Type: Private, independent, four-year
Degrees: D
URL: http://www.cityofhope.org
Phone: (626) 256-8775 *Calendar:* Sem. plan
Inst. Accred.: WASC-SR. (2001/2008)
Prog. Accred.: Radiation Therapy

The Claremont Graduate University
150 East 10th St., Claremont 91711
Type: Private, independent, four-year
System: Claremont University Consortium
Degrees: M, D *Enroll:* 1,793
URL: http://www.cgu.edu
Phone: (909) 621-8000 *Calendar:* Sem. plan
Inst. Accred.: WASC-SR. (1949/2002)
Prog. Accred.: Business (AACSB)

Claremont McKenna College
500 East 9th St., Bauer Center, Claremont 91711-6400
Type: Private, independent, four-year
System: Claremont University Consortium
Degrees: B, M *Enroll:* 1,140
URL: http://www.mckenna.edu
Phone: (909) 621-8111 *Calendar:* Sem. plan
Inst. Accred.: WASC-SR. (1949/2000)

Claremont School of Theology
1325 North College Ave., Claremont 91711
Type: Private, United Methodist Church, four-year
System: Claremont University Consortium
Degrees: M, P, D *Enroll:* 491
URL: http://www.cst.edu
Phone: (909) 447-2500 *Calendar:* Sem. plan
Inst. Accred.: ATS (1944/2004, Probation), WASC-SR. (1949/2006, Probation)

Coastline Community College
11460 Warner Ave., Fountain Valley 92708-2597
Type: Public, state/local, two-year
System: Coast Community College District
Degrees: A *Enroll:* 2,733
URL: http://coastline.cccd.edu
Phone: (714) 546-7600 *Calendar:* Sem. plan
Inst. Accred.: WASC-JR. (1978/2007)

Cogswell Polytechnical College
1175 Bordeaux Dr., Sunnyvale 94089-1299
Type: Private, independent, four-year
Degrees: A, B *Enroll:* 193
URL: http://www.cogswell.edu
Phone: (408) 541-0100 *Calendar:* Sem. plan
Inst. Accred.: WASC-SR. (1977/2008)

The Colburn School of Performing Arts
200 South Grand Ave., Los Angeles 90012
Type: Private, independent, four-year
Degrees: B
URL: http://www.colburnschool.edu
Phone: (213) 621-2200 *Calendar:* Sem. plan
Inst. Accred.: NASM (1980/2005)

Coleman University
8888 Balboa Ave., San Diego 92123-1506
Type: Private, independent, four-year
Degrees: A, B, M *Enroll:* 371
URL: http://www.coleman.edu
Phone: (858) 499-0202 *Calendar:* Qtr. plan
Inst. Accred.: ACICS (1967/2006)

San Marcos Campus
1284 West San Marcos Blvd., San Marcos 92069
Phone: (760) 747-3990

College of Alameda
555 Atlantic Ave., Alameda 94501-2109
Type: Public, state/local, two-year
System: Peralta Community College District
Degrees: A *Enroll:* 2,494
URL: http://alameda.peralta.edu
Phone: (510) 522-7221 *Calendar:* Sem. plan
Inst. Accred.: WASC-JR. (1973/2003)
Prog. Accred.: Dentistry (dental assisting)

College of Marin
835 College Ave., Kentfield 94904-2509
Type: Public, state/local, two-year
System: Marin Community College District
Degrees: A *Enroll:* 3,124
URL: http://www.marin.edu
Phone: (415) 457-8811 *Calendar:* Sem. plan
Inst. Accred.: WASC-JR. (1952/2008)
Prog. Accred.: Dentistry (dental assisting), Nursing

Indian Valley Campus
1800 Ignacio Blvd., Novato 94949
Phone: (415) 457-8811

College of San Mateo
1700 West Hillsdale Blvd., San Mateo 94402-3784
Type: Public, state/local, two-year
System: San Mateo County Community College District
Degrees: A *Enroll:* 5,438
URL: http://collegeofsanmateo.edu
Phone: (650) 574-6161 *Calendar:* Sem. plan
Inst. Accred.: WASC-JR. (1952/2001, Warning)
Prog. Accred.: Dentistry (dental assisting)

College of the Canyons
26455 N. Rockwell Canyon Rd., Santa Clarita 91355-1899
Type: Public, state/local, two-year
System: Santa Clarita Community College District
Degrees: A *Enroll:* 8,334
URL: http://www.canyons.edu
Phone: (661) 259-7800 *Calendar:* Sem. plan
Inst. Accred.: WASC-JR. (1972/2003)
Prog. Accred.: Nursing

College of the Desert
43-500 Monterey Ave., Palm Desert 92260-2499
Type: Public, state/local, two-year
System: Desert Community College District
Degrees: A *Enroll:* 4,645
URL: http://www.collegeofthedesert.edu
Phone: (760) 346-8041 *Calendar:* Sem. plan
Inst. Accred.: WASC-JR. (1963/2005)
Prog. Accred.: Nursing

College of the Redwoods
7351 Tompkins Hill Rd., Eureka 95501-9301
Type: Public, state/local, two-year
System: Redwoods Community College System
Degrees: A *Enroll:* 3,826
URL: http://www.redwoods.edu
Phone: (707) 476-4100 *Calendar:* Sem. plan
Inst. Accred.: WASC-JR. (1967/2000, Warning)
Prog. Accred.: Construction Technology, Dentistry (dental assisting), Design Technology

College of the Sequoias
915 South Mooney Blvd., Visalia 93277-2234
Type: Public, state/local, two-year
System: College of the Sequoias Community College District
Degrees: A *Enroll:* 6,512
URL: http://www.cos.edu
Phone: (559) 730-3700 *Calendar:* Sem. plan
Inst. Accred.: WASC-JR. (1952/2008)

College of the Siskiyous
800 College Ave., Weed 96094-2899
Type: Public, state/local, two-year
System: Siskiyou Joint Community College District
Degrees: A *Enroll:* 1,465
URL: http://www.siskiyous.edu
Phone: (530) 938-4461 *Calendar:* Sem. plan
Inst. Accred.: WASC-JR. (1961/2004)
Prog. Accred.: Allied Health (EMT-paramedic)

Columbia College
11600 Columbia College Dr., Sonora 95370-8518
Type: Public, state/local, two-year
System: Yosemite Community College District
Degrees: A *Enroll:* 1,528
URL: http://www.yosemite.cc.ca.us/columbia
Phone: (209) 588-5100 *Calendar:* Sem. plan
Inst. Accred.: WASC-JR. (1972/2006)
Prog. Accred.: Culinary Education

Columbia College Hollywood
18618 Oxnard St., Tarzana 91356-1411
Type: Private, independent, four-year
Degrees: A, B *Enroll:* 214
URL: http://www.columbiacollege.edu
Phone: (818) 345-8414 *Calendar:* Qtr. plan
Inst. Accred.: ACCSCT (1979/2004)

Community Christian College
251 Tennessee St., Redlands 92373
Type: Private, nondenominational, two-year
Degrees: A
URL: http://www.cccollege.net
Phone: (909) 335-8863 *Calendar:* Qtr. plan
Inst. Accred.: TRACS (2007)

San Bernardino Campus
1777 West Baseline St., San Bernardino 92411
Phone: (909) 327-2554

Sun Valley Campus
9000 Sunland Blvd., Sun Valley 91352
Phone: (818) 252-7940

Concorde Career College
12951 Euclid St., Ste. 101, Garden Grove 92840
Type: Private, proprietary, two-year
System: Concorde Career Colleges, Inc.
Degrees: A *Enroll:* 527
URL: http://www.concordecareercolleges.com
Phone: (714) 703-1900
Inst. Accred.: ACCSCT (1968/2006)
Prog. Accred.: Allied Health (respiratory therapy)

Concorde Career College
12412 Victory Blvd., North Hollywood 91606
Type: Private, proprietary, two-year
System: Concorde Career Colleges, Inc.
Degrees: A *Enroll:* 487
URL: http://www.concordecareercolleges.com
Phone: (818) 766-8151
Inst. Accred.: ACCSCT (1973/2003)
Prog. Accred.: Allied Health (respiratory therapy, surgical technology)

Concorde Career College
4393 Imperial Ave., Ste. 100, San Diego 92113
Type: Private, proprietary, two-year
System: Concorde Career Colleges, Inc.
Degrees: A
URL: http://www.concorde.edu
Phone: (619) 688-0800
Inst. Accred.: ACCSCT (1969/2007)
Prog. Accred.: Allied Health (surgical technology)

Concordia University Irvine
1530 Concordia West, Irvine 92612
Type: Private, Lutheran Church-Missouri Synod, four-year
System: Concordia University System
Degrees: A, B, M *Enroll:* 1,877
URL: http://www.cui.edu
Phone: (949) 854-8002 *Calendar:* Sem. plan
Inst. Accred.: WASC-SR. (1981/2005)

Contra Costa College
2600 Mission Bell Dr., San Pablo 94806-3195
Type: Public, state/local, two-year
System: Contra Costa Community College District
Degrees: A *Enroll:* 3,695
URL: http://www.contracosta.edu
Phone: (510) 235-7800 *Calendar:* Sem. plan
Inst. Accred.: WASC-JR. (1952/2002)
Prog. Accred.: Dentistry (dental assisting), Montessori Teacher Education

Copper Mountain College
6162 Rotary Way, PO Box 1398, Joshua Tree 92252
Type: Public, state/local, two-year
System: Copper Mountain Community College District
Degrees: A *Enroll:* 1,043
URL: http://www.cmccd.edu
Phone: (760) 366-3791 *Calendar:* Sem. plan
Inst. Accred.: WASC-JR. (2001/2007, Warning)

Cosumnes River College
8401 Center Pkwy., Sacramento 95823-5799
Type: Public, state/local, two-year
System: Los Rios Community College District
Degrees: A *Enroll:* 6,408
URL: http://www.crc.losrios.edu
Phone: (916) 691-7344 *Calendar:* Sem. plan
Inst. Accred.: WASC-JR. (1972/2004)
Prog. Accred.: Allied Health (medical assisting (AMA)), Dietetic Technician, Veterinary Technology

Crafton Hills College
11711 Sand Canyon Rd., Yucaipa 92399-1799
Type: Public, state/local, two-year
System: San Bernardino Community College District
Degrees: A *Enroll:* 2,819
URL: http://www.craftonhills.edu
Phone: (909) 794-2161 *Calendar:* Sem. plan
Inst. Accred.: WASC-JR. (1975/2002)
Prog. Accred.: Allied Health (EMT-paramedic, respiratory therapy)

Cuesta College
PO Box 8106, San Luis Obispo 93403-8106
Type: Public, state/local, two-year
System: San Luis Obispo Community College District
Degrees: A *Enroll:* 6,571
URL: http://www.cuesta.edu
Phone: (805) 546-3100 *Calendar:* Sem. plan
Inst. Accred.: WASC-JR. (1968/2003)

Cuyamaca College
900 Rancho San Diego Pkwy., El Cajon 92019-4304
Type: Public, state/local, two-year
System: Grossmont-Cuyamaca Community College District
Degrees: A *Enroll:* 3,747
URL: http://www.cuyamaca.edu
Phone: (619) 660-4000 *Calendar:* Sem. plan
Inst. Accred.: WASC-JR. (1980/2008)

Cypress College
9200 Valley View St., Cypress 90630-5897
Type: Public, state/local, two-year
System: North Orange County Community College District
Degrees: A *Enroll:* 10,651
URL: http://www.cypresscollege.edu
Phone: (714) 484-7000 *Calendar:* Sem. plan
Inst. Accred.: WASC-JR. (1968/2005)
Prog. Accred.: Allied Health (diagnostic medical sonography), Dentistry (dental assisting, dental hygiene), Funeral Service Education (Mortuary Science), Nursing, Radiography

De Anza College
21250 Stevens Creek Blvd., Cupertino 95014-5797
Type: Public, state/local, two-year
System: Foothill-DeAnza Community College District
Degrees: A *Enroll:* 13,582
URL: http://www.deanza.fhda.edu
Phone: (408) 864-5678 *Calendar:* Qtr. plan
Inst. Accred.: WASC-JR. (1969/2006)

Deep Springs College
HC 72 Box 45001, Deep Springs
via Dyer, NV 89010-9803,
Type: Private, independent, two-year
Degrees: A *FTE Enroll:* 26
URL: http://www.deepsprings.edu
Phone: (760) 872-2000 *Calendar:* Sem. plan
Inst. Accred.: WASC-JR. (1952/2005)

Defense Language Institute Foreign Language Center
Presidio of Monterey 93944
Type: Public, federal, two-year
Degrees: A *Enroll:* 4,479
URL: http://pom-www.army.mil
Phone: (831) 242-5000
Inst. Accred.: WASC-JR. (1979/2006)

Dell'Arte Internatinal School of Physical Theater
PO Box 816, Blue Lake 95525
Type: Private, independent, four-year
Degrees: M
URL: http://www.dellarte.com
Phone: (707) 668-5663
Inst. Accred.: NAST (1990/2002)

Design Institute of San Diego
8555 Commerce Ave., San Diego 92121
Type: Private, independent, four-year
Degrees: B *Enroll:* 278
URL: http://www.disd.edu
Phone: (858) 566-1200 *Calendar:* Sem. plan
Inst. Accred.: ACICS (1995/2008)
Prog. Accred.: Interior Design

DeVry University Irvine
3333 Michelson Dr., Ste. 420, Irvine 92612-1682
Type: Private, proprietary, four-year
Degrees: M
URL: http://www.devry.edu
Phone: (949) 752-5631 *Calendar:* Sem. plan
Inst. Accred.: NCA-HLC (2002, *Indirect accreditation through DeVry University, Oakbrook Terrace, IL*)

Fresno Campus
7575 North Fresno St., Fresno 93720
Phone: (559) 439-8595

Sacramento Campus
2216 Kausen Dr., Elk Grove 95758
Phone: (916) 478-2847

San Francisco Campus
455 Market St., Ste. 1650, San Francisco 94105
Phone: (415) 243-8787

DeVry University Pomona
901 Corporate Center Dr., Pomona 91768-2642
Type: Private, proprietary
System: DeVry University
Degrees: A, B, M *Enroll:* 4,406
URL: http://www.devry.edu/pomona
Phone: (909) 622-8866 *Calendar:* Sem. plan
Inst. Accred.: NCA-HLC (2002, *Indirect accreditation through DeVry University, Oakbrook Terrace, IL*)
Prog. Accred.: Engineering Technology (computer, electrical)

Bakersfield Center
3000 Ming Ave., Bakersfield 93304
Phone: (866) 726-9388

Daly City Center
2001 Junipero Serra Blvd., Ste. 161, Daly City 94014-3899
Phone: (650) 991-3520

Fremont Campus
6600 Dumbarton Circle, Fremont 94555
Phone: (510) 574-1100
Prog. Accred: Engineering Technology (computer, electrical)

Fresno Center
7575 North Fresno St., Fresno 93720
Phone: (559) 439-8595

Henderson Campus
2490 Paseo Verde Pkwy., Ste. 150, Henderson, NV 89074
Phone: (702) 933-9700

Inland Empire-Colton Campus
1090 East Washington St., Ste. H, Colton 92324-8180
Phone: (909) 514-1808

Long Beach Campus
3880 Kilroy Airport Way, Long Beach 90806-2449
Phone: (562) 427-0861

Palmdale Center
38256 Sierra Hwy., Ste. D, Palmdale 93550
Phone: (661) 224-2920

Sacramento Center
2216 Kausen Dr., Sacramento 95758
Phone: (916) 478-2847

San Jose Campus
2160 Lundy Ave., Ste. 250, San Jose 95131-1862
Phone: (408) 571-3760

Sherman Oaks Campus
15301 Ventura Blvd., Building D-100, Sherman Oaks 91403
Phone: (818) 932-3001

Diablo Valley College
321 Golf Club Rd., Pleasant Hill 94523-1544
Type: Public, state/local, two-year
System: Contra Costa Community College District
Degrees: A *Enroll:* 11,566
URL: http://www.dvc.edu
Phone: (925) 685-1230 *Calendar:* Sem. plan
Inst. Accred.: WASC-JR. (1952/2008, Warning)
Prog. Accred.: Culinary Education, Dentistry (dental assisting, dental hygiene)

Dominican School of Philosophy and Theology
2401 Ridge Rd., Berkeley 94709
Type: Private, Roman Catholic Church, four-year
System: Graduate Theological Union
Degrees: B, M, P *Enroll:* 73
URL: http://www.dspt.edu
Phone: (510) 849-2030 *Calendar:* Sem. plan
Inst. Accred.: ATS (1978/2002), WASC-SR. (1964/2002)

Dominican University of California
50 Acacia Ave., San Rafael 94901
Type: Private, Roman Catholic Church, four-year
Degrees: B, M *Enroll:* 1,612
URL: http://www.dominican.edu
Phone: (415) 457-4440 *Calendar:* Sem. plan
Inst. Accred.: WASC-SR. (1949/2008)
Prog. Accred.: Allied Health (occupational therapy), Nursing Education

Dongguk Royal University
440 South Shatto Place, Los Angeles 90020
Type: Private, independent, four-year
Degrees: M *Enroll:* 281
URL: http://www.dru.edu
Phone: (213) 487-0110 *Calendar:* Qtr. plan
Inst. Accred.: ACAOM (1994/2007)

East Los Angeles College
1301 Cesar Chavez Ave., Monterey Park 91754-6099
Type: Public, state/local, two-year
System: Los Angeles Community College District
Degrees: A *Enroll:* 11,976
URL: http://www.elac.edu
Phone: (323) 265-8650 *Calendar:* Sem. plan
Inst. Accred.: WASC-JR. (1952/2003)
Prog. Accred.: Allied Health (respiratory therapy)

El Camino College
16007 Crenshaw Blvd., Torrance 90506-0002
Type: Public, state/local, two-year
System: El Camino Community College District
Degrees: A *Enroll:* 12,997
URL: http://www.elcamino.edu
Phone: (310) 532-3670 *Calendar:* Sem. plan
Inst. Accred.: WASC-JR. (1952/2002)
Prog. Accred.: Allied Health (respiratory therapy), Nursing, Radiography

Compton Center Campus
1111 East Artesia Blvd., Compton 90221
Phone: (310) 900-1600

Emperor's College of Traditional Oriental Medicine
1807-B Wilshire Blvd., Santa Monica 90403
Type: Private, proprietary, four-year
Degrees: M *Enroll:* 234
URL: http://www.emperors.edu
Phone: (310) 453-8300 *Calendar:* Qtr. plan
Inst. Accred.: ACAOM (1989/2007)

Los Angeles Campus
3625 West 6th St., Ste. 220, Los Angeles 90020
Phone: (213) 738-8833

Empire College
3035 Cleveland Ave., Santa Rosa 95403
Type: Private, proprietary, two-year
Degrees: A
URL: http://www.empcol.edu
Phone: (707) 546-4000 *Calendar:* Sem. plan
Inst. Accred.: ACICS (1969/2006)

Everest College—City of Industry
12801 Crossroads Pkwy. South, City of Industry 91746
Type: Private, proprietary, two-year
System: Corinthian Colleges, Inc
Degrees: A
URL: http://www.everest.edu
Phone: (562) 908-2500
Inst. Accred.: ACCSCT (1988/2005)

Everest College—Ontario
1460 South Milliken Ave., Ontario 91761
Type: Private, proprietary, two-year
System: Corinthian Colleges, Inc
Degrees: A
URL: http://www.everest.edu
Phone: (909) 984-5027
Inst. Accred.: ACCSCT (1986/2008)

Everest College—San Bernardino
217 East Club Center Dr., Ste. A, San Bernardino 92408
Type: Private, proprietary, two-year
System: Corinthian Colleges, Inc
Degrees: A
URL: http://www.everest.edu
Phone: (909) 783-8810 *Calendar:* Qtr. plan
Inst. Accred.: ACICS (1962/2005)
Prog. Accred.: Allied Health (medical assisting (AMA))

Everest College—West Los Angeles
3000 South Robertson Blvd., Ste. 300, Los Angeles 90034-9158
Type: Private, proprietary, two-year
System: Corinthian Colleges, Inc
Degrees: A *Enroll:* 946
URL: http://www.everest.edu
Phone: (310) 840-5777
Inst. Accred.: ACCSCT (1987/2004)

Evergreen Valley College
3095 Yerba Buena Rd., San Jose 95135-1598
Type: Public, state/local, two-year
System: San Jose-Evergreen Community College District
Degrees: A *Enroll:* 4,903
URL: http://www.evc.edu
Phone: (408) 274-7900 *Calendar:* Sem. plan
Inst. Accred.: WASC-JR. (1977/2006)
Prog. Accred.: Nursing

Expression College for Digital Arts
6601 Shellmound St., Emeryville 94608-1021
Type: Private, proprietary, four-year
Degrees: B
URL: http://www.expression.edu
Phone: (510) 654-2934 *Calendar:* Qtr. plan
Inst. Accred.: ACCSCT (2005/2008)

Fashion Careers College
1923 Morena Blvd., San Diego 92110
Type: Private, proprietary, two-year
Degrees: A *Enroll:* 101
URL: http://www.fashioncollege.com
Phone: (619) 275-4700
Inst. Accred.: ACICS (1983/2006)

The Fashion Institute of Design and Merchandising
919 South Grand Ave., Los Angeles 90015
Type: Private, independent, four-year
Degrees: A, B *Enroll:* 3,070
URL: http://www.fidm.com
Phone: (213) 624-1200 *Calendar:* Qtr. plan
Inst. Accred.: WASC-JR. (1978/2005), WASC-SR. (2007)
Prog. Accred.: Art

Orange County Campus
17590 Gillette Ave., Irvine 92614
Phone: (949) 851-6200

San Diego Campus
1010 Second Ave., Ste. 200, San Diego 92101
Phone: (619) 235-2049

San Francisco Campus
55 Stockton St., San Francisco 94108
Phone: (415) 675-5200

Feather River College
570 Golden Eagle Ave., Quincy 95971-6023
Type: Public, state/local, two-year
System: Feather River Community College District
Degrees: A *Enroll:* 936
URL: http://www.frc.edu
Phone: (530) 283-0202 *Calendar:* Sem. plan
Inst. Accred.: WASC-JR. (1973/2007)

Fielding Graduate University
2112 Santa Barbara St., Santa Barbara 93105
Type: Private, independent, four-year
Degrees: M, P, D *Enroll:* 1,547
URL: http://www.fielding.edu
Phone: (805) 687-1099 *Calendar:* Tri. plan
Inst. Accred.: WASC-SR. (1982/2004)
Prog. Accred.: Clinical Psychology

Five Branches University: Graduate School of Traditional Chinese Medicine
200 7th Ave., Ste. 115, Santa Cruz 95062
Type: Private, proprietary, four-year
Degrees: M *Enroll:* 197
URL: http://www.fivebranches.edu
Phone: (831) 476-9424 *Calendar:* Sem. plan
Inst. Accred.: ACAOM (1996/2007)

San Jose Campus
3031 Tisch Way, Ste. 5PW, San Jose 95128
Phone: (408) 260-0208

Folsom Lake College
100 Scholar Way, Folsom 95630
Type: Public, state/local, two-year
System: Los Rios Community College District
Degrees: A
URL: http://www.flc.losrios.edu
Phone: (916) 608-6500 *Calendar:* Sem. plan
Inst. Accred.: WASC-JR. (2004)

Foothill College
12345 El Monte Rd., Los Altos Hills 94022-4599
Type: Public, state/local, two-year
System: Foothill-DeAnza Community College District
Degrees: A *Enroll:* 8,472
URL: http://www.foothill.fhda.edu
Phone: (650) 949-7777 *Calendar:* Qtr. plan
Inst. Accred.: WASC-JR. (1959/2006)
Prog. Accred.: Allied Health (EMT-paramedic, diagnostic medical sonography, respiratory therapy), Dentistry (dental assisting, dental hygiene), Radiography, Veterinary Technology

Foundation College
404 Camino del Rio South, San Diego 92108-1303
Type: Private, independent, two-year
Degrees: A
Phone: (619) 683-3273
Inst. Accred.: ACCSCT (2001/2006)

Franciscan School of Theology
1712 Euclid Ave., Berkeley 94709
Type: Private, Roman Catholic Church, four-year
System: Graduate Theological Union
Degrees: M *Enroll:* 58
URL: http://www.fst.edu
Phone: (510) 848-5232 *Calendar:* Qtr. plan
Inst. Accred.: ATS (1975/2007), WASC-SR. (1975/2008)

Fremont College
18000 Studebaker Rd., 9th Flr., Cerritos 90703
Type: Private, proprietary, two-year
Degrees: A *Enroll:* 109
URL: http://www.westerncollegesocal.com
Phone: (562) 809-5100
Inst. Accred.: ACCSCT (1986/2004)

Fresno City College
1101 East University Ave., Fresno 93741-0001
Type: Public, state/local, two-year
System: State Center Community College District
Degrees: A *Enroll:* 12,569
URL: http://www.fresnocitycollege.edu
Phone: (559) 442-4600 *Calendar:* Sem. plan
Inst. Accred.: WASC-JR. (1952/2007)
Prog. Accred.: Allied Health (EMT-paramedic, respiratory therapy, surgical technology), Dentistry (dental hygiene), Radiography

Fresno Pacific University
1717 South Chestnut Ave., Fresno 93702
Type: Private, Mennonite Brethren, four-year
Degrees: A, B, M *Enroll:* 1,530
URL: http://www.fresno.edu
Phone: (559) 453-2000 *Calendar:* Sem. plan
Inst. Accred.: WASC-SR. (1961/2003)

Fuller Theological Seminary
135 North Oakland Ave., Pasadena 91182
Type: Private, interdenominational, four-year
Degrees: M, D *Enroll:* 1,893
URL: http://www.fuller.edu
Phone: (626) 584-5200 *Calendar:* Qtr. plan
Inst. Accred.: ATS (1957/2000), WASC-SR. (1969/2008)
Prog. Accred.: Clinical Psychology

Fullerton College
321 East Chapman Ave., Fullerton 92534
Type: Public, state/local, two-year
System: North Orange County Community College District
Degrees: A *Enroll:* 11,965
URL: http://www.fullcoll.edu
Phone: (714) 992-7000 *Calendar:* Sem. plan
Inst. Accred.: WASC-JR. (1952/2005)

Gavilan College
5055 Santa Teresa Blvd., Gilroy 95020-9599
Type: Public, state/local, two-year
System: Gavilan Joint Community College District
Degrees: A *Enroll:* 2,703
URL: http://www.gavilan.edu
Phone: (408) 847-1400 *Calendar:* Sem. plan
Inst. Accred.: WASC-JR. (1952/2007)

Gemological Institute of America School of Business
5345 Armada Dr., Carlsbad 92008
Type: Private, independent, four-year
Degrees: B
URL: http://www.gia.edu/education
Phone: (760) 603-4000
Inst. Accred.: DETC (2002)

Glendale Community College
1500 North Verdugo Rd., Glendale 91208-2894
Type: Public, state/local, two-year
System: Glendale Community College District
Degrees: A *Enroll:* 8,406
URL: http://www.glendale.edu
Phone: (818) 240-1000 *Calendar:* Sem. plan
Inst. Accred.: WASC-JR. (1952/2004)

Golden Gate Baptist Theological Seminary
201 Seminary Dr., Mill Valley 94941-3197
Type: Private, Southern Baptist Convention, four-year
Degrees: M, P, D *Enroll:* 281
URL: http://www.ggbts.edu
Phone: (415) 380-1300 *Calendar:* Sem. plan
Inst. Accred.: ATS (1962/1999), WASC-SR. (1971/2003)
Prog. Accred.: Music

Golden Gate University
536 Mission St., San Francisco 94105-2968
Type: Private, independent, four-year
Degrees: A, B, M, P, D *Enroll:* 2,393
URL: http://www.ggu.edu
Phone: (415) 442-7000 *Calendar:* Tri. plan
Inst. Accred.: WASC-SR. (1959/2002)
Prog. Accred.: Law

Sacramento Campus
3620 Northgate Blvd., Sacramento 95834
Phone: (916) 648-1446

Seattle Campus
1326 5th Ave., Ste. 310, Seattle, WA 98101
Phone: (206) 622-9996

Golden West College
15744 Golden West St., Huntington Beach 92647-0592
Type: Public, state/local, two-year
System: Coast Community College District
Degrees: A *Enroll:* 7,888
URL: http://www.gwc.info
Phone: (714) 892-7711 *Calendar:* Sem. plan
Inst. Accred.: WASC-JR. (1969/2007)
Prog. Accred.: Nursing

Graduate Theological Union
2400 Ridge Rd., Berkeley 94709
Type: Private, interdenominational, four-year
System: Graduate Theological Union
Degrees: M, D *Enroll:* 227
URL: http://www.gtu.edu
Phone: (510) 649-2400 *Calendar:* Sem. plan
Inst. Accred.: ATS (1969/2007), WASC-SR. (1966/2007)

Grossmont College
8800 Grossmont College Dr., El Cajon 92020-1799
Type: Public, state/local, two-year
System: Grossmont-Cuyamaca Community College District
Degrees: A *Enroll:* 9,983
URL: http://www.grossmont.edu
Phone: (619) 644-7000 *Calendar:* Sem. plan
Inst. Accred.: WASC-JR. (1963/2006)
Prog. Accred.: Allied Health (cardiovascular technology, occupational therapy assisting, respiratory therapy), Nursing

Hartnell College
411 Central Ave., Salinas 93901
Type: Public, state/local, two-year
System: Hartnell Community College District
Degrees: A *Enroll:* 4,975
URL: http://www.hartnell.edu
Phone: (831) 755-6700 *Calendar:* Sem. plan
Inst. Accred.: WASC-JR. (1952/2008)
Prog. Accred.: Veterinary Technology

Harvey Mudd College
301 East 12th St., Claremont 91711
Type: Private, independent, four-year
System: Claremont University Consortium
Degrees: B, M *Enroll:* 742
URL: http://www.hmc.edu
Phone: (909) 621-8100 *Calendar:* Sem. plan
Inst. Accred.: WASC-SR. (1959/2000)
Prog. Accred.: Engineering (general)

Heald College—Concord
5130 Commercial Circle, Concord 94520
Type: Private, independent, two-year
System: Heald Colleges
Degrees: A *Enroll:* 570
URL: http://www.heald.edu
Phone: (925) 288-5800 *Calendar:* Qtr. plan
Inst. Accred.: WASC-JR. (1983/2006, *Indirect accreditation through Heald Colleges, San Francisco, CA*)
Prog. Accred.: Allied Health (medical assisting (AMA))

Heald College—Fresno
255 West Bullard Ave., Fresno 93704
Type: Private, independent, two-year
System: Heald Colleges
Degrees: A *Enroll:* 619
URL: http://www.heald.edu
Phone: (559) 438-4222 *Calendar:* Qtr. plan
Inst. Accred.: WASC-JR. (1983/2006, *Indirect accreditation through Heald Colleges, San Francisco, CA*)
Prog. Accred.: Allied Health (medical assisting (AMA))

Heald College—Hayward
25500 Industrial Blvd., Hayward 94545
Type: Private, indepdendent, two-year
System: Heald Colleges
Degrees: A *FTE Enroll:* 359
URL: http://www.heald.edu
Phone: (510) 783-2100 *Calendar:* Qtr. plan
Inst. Accred.: WASC-JR. (1983/2006, *Indirect accreditation through Heald Colleges, San Francisco, CA*)
Prog. Accred.: Allied Health (medical assisting (AMA))

Heald College—Rancho Cordova
2910 Prospect Park Dr., Rancho Cordova 95670
Type: Private, independent, two-year
Degrees: A *Enroll:* 397
URL: http://www.heald.edu
Phone: (916) 638-1616 *Calendar:* Qtr. plan
Inst. Accred.: WASC-JR. (1983/2006, Probation, *Indirect accreditation through Heald Colleges, San Francisco, CA*)
Prog. Accred.: Allied Health (medical assisting (AMA))

Heald College—Roseville
Seven Sierra Gate Plaza, Roseville 95678
Type: Private, independent, two-year
System: Heald Colleges
Degrees: A *Enroll:* 436
URL: http://www.heald.edu
Phone: (916) 789-8600 *Calendar:* Qtr. plan
Inst. Accred.: WASC-JR. (1983/2006, *Indirect accreditation through Heald Colleges, San Francisco, CA*)
Prog. Accred.: Allied Health (medical assisting (AMA))

Heald College—Salinas
1450 North Main St., Salinas 93906
Type: Private, independent, two-year
System: Heald Colleges
Degrees: A *Enroll:* 363
URL: http://www.heald.edu
Phone: (831) 443-1700 *Calendar:* Qtr. plan
Inst. Accred.: WASC-JR. (1983/2006, *Indirect accreditation through Heald Colleges, San Francisco, CA*)
Prog. Accred.: Allied Health (medical assisting (AMA))

Heald College—San Francisco
350 Mission St., San Francisco 94105
Type: Private, independent, two-year
System: Heald Colleges
Degrees: A *Enroll:* 319
URL: http://www.heald.edu
Phone: (415) 808-3000 *Calendar:* Qtr. plan
Inst. Accred.: WASC-JR. (1983/2006, *Indirect accreditation through Heald Colleges, San Francisco, CA*)
Prog. Accred.: Allied Health (medical assisting (AMA))

Heald College—San Jose
341 Great Mall Pkwy., Milpitas 95035
Type: Private, independent, two-year
System: Heald Colleges
Degrees: A *FTE Enroll:* 294
URL: http://www.heald.edu
Phone: (408) 934-4900 *Calendar:* Qtr. plan
Inst. Accred.: WASC-JR. (1983/2006, *Indirect accreditation through Heald Colleges, San Francisco, CA*)
Prog. Accred.: Allied Health (medical assisting (AMA))

Heald College—Stockton
1605 East March Ln., 2nd Flr., Stockton 95210
Type: Private, independent, two-year
System: Heald Colleges
Degrees: A *Enroll:* 450
URL: http://www.heald.edu
Phone: (209) 473-5200 *Calendar:* Qtr. plan
Inst. Accred.: WASC-JR. (1983/2006, *Indirect accreditation through Heald Colleges, San Francisco, CA*)
Prog. Accred.: Allied Health (medical assisting (AMA))

Hebrew Union College-Jewish Institute of Religion
3077 University Ave., Los Angeles 90007-3796
Type: Private, Union for Reform Judaism, four-year
System: Hebrew Union College—Jewish Institute of Religion Central Office
Degrees: B, M, D *Enroll:* 116
URL: http://www.huc.edu
Phone: (213) 749-3424 *Calendar:* Sem. plan
Inst. Accred.: WASC-SR. (1960/2003)

Henley-Putnam University
25 Metro Dr., Ste. 500, San Jose 95110
Type: Private, proprietary, four-year
Degrees: B, M *FTE Enroll:* 6
URL: http://www.henley-putnam.edu
Phone: (408) 453-9900
Inst. Accred.: DETC (2007)

Holmes Institute
2600 West Magnolia Blvd., Burbank 91505
Type: Private, independent, four-year
Degrees: M
URL: http://www.holmesinstitute.org
Phone: (818) 556-7757 *Calendar:* Qtr. plan
Inst. Accred.: DETC (2003)

Holy Names University
3500 Mountain Blvd., Oakland 94619-1699
Type: Private, Roman Catholic Church, four-year
Degrees: B, M *Enroll:* 811
URL: http://www.hnu.edu
Phone: (510) 436-1000 *Calendar:* Sem. plan
Inst. Accred.: WASC-SR. (1949/2003)
Prog. Accred.: Nursing Education

Hope International University
2500 East Nutwood Ave., Fullerton 92831
Type: Private, Christian Churches/Churches of Christ, four-year
Degrees: A, B, M *Enroll:* 925
URL: http://www.hiu.edu
Phone: (714) 879-3901 *Calendar:* 4-1-4 plan
Inst. Accred.: WASC-SR. (1969/2008)
Prog. Accred.: Biblical Studies, Intercultural Studies, Minstry

Humboldt State University
1 Harpst St., Arcata 95521-8999
Type: Public, state, four-year
System: California State University System
Degrees: B, M *Enroll:* 6,833
URL: http://www.humboldt.edu
Phone: (707) 826-3311 *Calendar:* Sem. plan
Inst. Accred.: WASC-SR. (1949/2008)
Prog. Accred.: Art, Engineering (environmental/sanitary), Forestry, Graduate Social Work, Music, Nursing Education, Social Work

Humphreys College
6650 Inglewood St., Stockton 95207
Type: Private, independent, four-year
Degrees: A, B, P *Enroll:* 777
URL: http://www.humphreys.edu
Phone: (209) 478-0800 *Calendar:* Qtr. plan
Inst. Accred.: WASC-SR. (1992/2004)

Imperial Valley College
380 East Aten Rd., PO Box 158, Imperial 92251
Type: Public, state/local, two-year
System: Imperial Community College District
Degrees: A *Enroll:* 4,798
URL: http://www.imperial.edu
Phone: (760) 352-8320 *Calendar:* Sem. plan
Inst. Accred.: WASC-JR. (1952/2001, Warning)

Institute of Transpersonal Psychology
1069 East Meadow Circle, Palo Alto 94303
Type: Private, independent, four-year
Degrees: M, D *Enroll:* 399
URL: http://www.itp.edu
Phone: (650) 493-4430 *Calendar:* Sem. plan
Inst. Accred.: WASC-SR. (1998/2007)

Interior Designers Institute
1061 Camelback Rd., Newport Beach 92660-3228
Type: Private, proprietary, four-year
Degrees: A, B *Enroll:* 285
URL: http://www.idi.edu
Phone: (949) 675-4451 *Calendar:* Qtr. plan
Inst. Accred.: ACCSCT (1987/2003)
Prog. Accred.: Interior Design

International Professional School of Bodywork
9025 Balboa Ave., Ste. 130, San Diego 92123
Type: Private, proprietary, four-year
Degrees: A, B, M
URL: http://www.ipsb.edu
Phone: (858) 505-1100 *Calendar:* Qtr. plan
Inst. Accred.: CMTA (2007)

International Technological University
756 San Aleso Ave., Sunnyvale 94085
Type: Private, proprietary, four-year
Degrees: B, M *Enroll:* 16
URL: http://www.itu.edu
Phone: (408) 331-1014 *Calendar:* Sem. plan
Inst. Accred.: ACICS (2001, Probation)

International Theological Seminary
3215-3225 North Tyler Ave., El Monte 91731
Type: Private, nondenominational, four-year
Degrees: M, D
URL: http://www.itsla.edu
Phone: (626) 448-0023 *Calendar:* Qtr. plan
Inst. Accred.: ATS (2006)

Irvine Valley College
5500 Irvine Center Dr., Irvine 92720-4399
Type: Public, state/local, two-year
System: South Orange County Community College District
Degrees: A *Enroll:* 4,921
URL: http://www.ivc.edu
Phone: (949) 451-5100 *Calendar:* Sem. plan
Inst. Accred.: WASC-JR. (1988/2005)

ITT Technical Institute
650 West Cienega Ave., San Dimas 91773
Type: Private, proprietary, four-year
System: ITT Educational Services, Inc.
Degrees: A, B *Enroll:* 837
URL: http://www.itt-tech.edu
Phone: (626) 960-8681 *Calendar:* Qtr. plan
Inst. Accred.: ACICS (1999/2004)

ITT Technical Institute
9680 Granite Ridge Dr., San Diego 92123-2662
Type: Private, proprietary, four-year
System: ITT Educational Services, Inc.
Degrees: A, B *Enroll:* 948
URL: http://www.itt-tech.edu
Phone: (858) 571-8500 *Calendar:* Qtr. plan
Inst. Accred.: ACICS (1999/2008)

ITT Technical Institute
12669 Encinitas Ave., Sylmar 91342-3664
Type: Private, proprietary, four-year
System: ITT Educational Services, Inc.
Degrees: A, B *Enroll:* 835
URL: http://www.itt-tech.edu
Phone: (818) 364-5151 *Calendar:* Qtr. plan
Inst. Accred.: ACICS (1999/2007)

ITT Technical Institute
10863 Gold Center Dr., Rancho Cordova 95670-6034
Type: Private, proprietary, four-year
System: ITT Educational Services, Inc.
Degrees: A, B *Enroll:* 642
URL: http://www.itt-tech.edu
Phone: (916) 851-3900 *Calendar:* Qtr. plan
Inst. Accred.: ACICS (1999/2004)

ITT Technical Institute
670 East Carnegie Dr., San Bernardino 92408
Type: Private, proprietary, four-year
System: ITT Educational Services, Inc.
Degrees: A, B *Enroll:* 1,018
URL: http://www.itt-tech.edu
Phone: (909) 889-3800 *Calendar:* Qtr. plan
Inst. Accred.: ACICS (1999/2007)

ITT Technical Institute
20050 South Vermont Ave., Torrance 90502
Type: Private, proprietary, four-year
System: ITT Educational Services, Inc.
Degrees: A, B *Enroll:* 558
URL: http://www.itt-tech.edu
Phone: (310) 380-1555 *Calendar:* Qtr. plan
Inst. Accred.: ACICS (1999/2003)

ITT Technical Institute
525 North Muller Ave., Anaheim 92801
Type: Private, proprietary, four-year
System: ITT Educational Services, Inc.
Degrees: A, B *Enroll:* 628
URL: http://www.itt-tech.edu
Phone: (714) 535-3700 *Calendar:* Qtr. plan
Inst. Accred.: ACICS (1999/2007)

Clovis Campus
362 North Clovis Ave., Clovis 93612
Phone: (559) 325-5400

High Point Campus
4050 Piedmont Pkwy., High Point, NC 27265
Phone: (336) 819-5900

Kansas City Campus
9150 East 41st Terrace, Kansas City, MO 64133
Phone: (816) 276-1400

Mobile Campus
3100 Cottage Hill Rd., Office Mall South, Bldg. 3, Mobile, AL 36606
Phone: (251) 472-4760

Modesto-Stockton Campus
16916 South Harlan Rd., Lathrop 95330
Phone: (209) 858-0077

Oxnard Area Campus
2051 Solar Dr., Ste. 150, Oxnard 93030
Phone: (805) 988-0143

Jesuit School of Theology at Berkeley
1735 LeRoy Ave., Berkeley 94709-1193
Type: Private, Roman Catholic Church, four-year
System: Graduate Theological Union
Degrees: M, P, D *Enroll:* 165
URL: http://www.jstb.edu
Phone: (510) 549-5000 *Calendar:* Sem. plan
Inst. Accred.: ATS (1971/1999), WASC-SR. (1971/2000)

John F. Kennedy University
100 Ellinwood Way, Pleasant Hill 94523
Type: Private, independent, four-year
Degrees: B, M, P, D *Enroll:* 1,029
URL: http://www.jfku.edu
Phone: (925) 969-3300 *Calendar:* Qtr. plan
Inst. Accred.: WASC-SR. (1977/2007)
Prog. Accred.: Clinical Psychology

Kaplan College—Fresno
44 Shaw Ave., Clovis 93612
Type: Private, proprietary, two-year
System: Kaplan Higher Education Corporation
Degrees: A
URL: http://getinfo.kaplancollege.com/KaplanCollegePortal
Phone: (559) 325-5100
Inst. Accred.: ACCSCT (2005/2007)

Kaplan College—Modesto
5172 Kiernan Ct., Salida 95368
Type: Private, proprietary, two-year
System: Kaplan Higher Education Corporation
Degrees: A
URL: http://getinfo.kaplancollege.com/KaplanCollegePortal
Phone: (209) 543-7000
Inst. Accred.: ACCSCT (2002/2007)
Prog. Accred.: Medical Assisting (ABHES)

Kaplan College—Palm Springs
2475 East Tahquitz Canyon Way, Palm Springs 92262
Type: Private, proprietary, two-year
System: Kaplan Higher Education Corporation
Degrees: A
URL: http://getinfo.kaplancollege.com/KaplanCollegePortal
Phone: (760) 778-3540
Inst. Accred.: ACCSCT (2006)

Kaplan College—Panorama City
14355 Roscoe Blvd., Panorama City 91402
Type: Private, proprietary, two-year
System: Kaplan Higher Education Corporation
Degrees: A
URL: http://getinfo.kaplancollege.com/KaplanCollegePortal
Phone: (818) 672-8907
Inst. Accred.: ACICS (2005)

Kaplan College—Sacramento
4330 Watt Ave., Ste. 400, Sacramento 95821
Type: Private, proprietary, two-year
System: Kaplan Higher Education Corporation
Degrees: A *Enroll:* 323
URL: http://getinfo.kaplancollege.com/KaplanCollegePortal
Phone: (916) 649-8168 *Calendar:* Qtr. plan
Inst. Accred.: ACICS (1986/2004)

Bakersfield Campus
1914 Wible Rd., Bakersfield 93304
Phone: (661) 836-6300

Kaplan College—San Diego
9055 Balboa Ave., San Diego 92123
Type: Private, proprietary, two-year
System: Kaplan Higher Education Corporation
Degrees: A *Enroll:* 585
URL: http://getinfo.kaplancollege.com/KaplanCollegePortal
Phone: (858) 279-4500
Inst. Accred.: ACCSCT (1982/2008)
Prog. Accred.: Medical Assisting (ABHES)

North County Campus
2022 University Dr., Vista 92083
Phone: (760) 630-1555
Prog. Accred: Medical Assisting (ABHES)

Kaplan College—Stockton
722 West March Ln., Stockton 95207
Type: Private, proprietary, two-year
System: Kaplan Higher Education Corporation
Degrees: A
URL: http://getinfo.kaplancollege.com/KaplanCollegePortal
Phone: (209) 462-8777
Inst. Accred.: ACCSCT (2004)
Prog. Accred.: Medical Assisting (ABHES)

Keck Graduate Institute of Applied Life Science
535 Watson Dr., Claremont 91711
Type: Private, independent, four-year
System: Claremont University Consortium
Degrees: M, D
URL: http://www.kgi.edu
Phone: (909) 607-7855 *Calendar:* Sem. plan
Inst. Accred.: WASC-SR. (2004)

The King's College and Seminary
14800 Sherman Way, Los Angeles 91405-2233
Type: Private, interdenominational, four-year
Degrees: A, B, M, D
URL: http://www.kingscollege.edu
Phone: (818) 779-8040 *Calendar:* Qtr. plan
Inst. Accred.: ABHE (2002/2008), TRACS (2001/2006)

LA College International
3200 Wilshire Blvd., Ste. 400, Los Angeles 90010-1308
Type: Private, proprietary, four-year
Degrees: A, B *Enroll:* 167
URL: http://www.lac.edu
Phone: (213) 381-3333
Inst. Accred.: ACICS (2003/2005)

La Sierra University
4700 Pierce St., Riverside 92515-8247
Type: Private, Seventh-Day Adventist, four-year
Degrees: A, B, M, P, D *Enroll:* 1,739
URL: http://www.lasierra.edu
Phone: (951) 785-2000 *Calendar:* Qtr. plan
Inst. Accred.: WASC-SR. (1960/2002)
Prog. Accred.: Music, Social Work

Laguna College of Art and Design
2222 Laguna Canyon Rd., Laguna Beach 92651-1136
Type: Private, independent, four-year
Degrees: B *Enroll:* 313
URL: http://www.lagunacollege.edu
Phone: (949) 376-6000 *Calendar:* Sem. plan
Inst. Accred.: WASC-SR. (1997/2007)
Prog. Accred.: Art

Lake Tahoe Community College
One College Dr., South Lake Tahoe 96150-4524
Type: Public, state/local, two-year
System: Lake Tahoe Community College District
Degrees: A *Enroll:* 1,466
URL: http://www.ltcc.edu
Phone: (530) 541-4660 *Calendar:* Qtr. plan
Inst. Accred.: WASC-JR. (1979/2006)

Laney College
900 Fallon St., Oakland 94607-4893
Type: Public, state/local, two-year
System: Peralta Community College District
Degrees: A *Enroll:* 5,272
URL: http://laney.peralta.edu
Phone: (510) 834-5740 *Calendar:* Sem. plan
Inst. Accred.: WASC-JR. (1956/2003)

Las Positas College
3033 Collier Canyon Rd., Livermore 94550-7650
Type: Public, state/local, two-year
System: Chabot-Las Positas Community College District
Degrees: A *Enroll:* 4,014
URL: http://www.laspositascollege.edu
Phone: (925) 373-5800 *Calendar:* Sem. plan
Inst. Accred.: WASC-JR. (1991/2003)

Lassen College
PO Box 3000, Susanville 96130-3000
Type: Public, state/local, two-year
System: Lassen Community College District
Degrees: A *Enroll:* 1,225
URL: http://www.lassencollege.edu
Phone: (530) 257-6181 *Calendar:* Sem. plan
Inst. Accred.: WASC-JR. (1952/2002, Probation)

Life Chiropractic College West
25001 Industrial Blvd., Hayward 94545
Type: Private, independent, four-year
Degrees: P *Enroll:* 431
URL: http://www.lifewest.edu
Phone: (510) 780-4500 *Calendar:* Sem. plan
Inst. Accred.: CCE (1987/2003)

LIFE Pacific College
1100 West Covina Blvd., San Dimas 91773-3298
Type: Private, International Church of Foursquare Gospel, four-year
Degrees: A, B *Enroll:* 479
URL: http://www.lifepacific.edu
Phone: (909) 599-5433 *Calendar:* Sem. plan
Inst. Accred.: ABHE (1980/2001), WASC-SR. (2004)

Lincoln University
401 Fifteenth St., Oakland 94612
Type: Private, state, four-year
Degrees: B, M *Enroll:* 117
URL: http://www.lincolnuca.edu
Phone: (510) 628-8016 *Calendar:* Sem. plan
Inst. Accred.: ACICS (1990/2001)

Logos Evangelical Seminary
9358 Telstar Ave., El Monte 91731
Type: Private, Evangelical Formosan Church, four-year
Degrees: M, D
URL: http://www.les.edu
Phone: (626) 571-5110
Inst. Accred.: ATS (1999/2004)

Loma Linda University
Loma Linda 92350-0001
Type: Private, Seventh-Day Adventist Church, four-year
Degrees: A, B, M, P, D *Enroll:* 3,273
URL: http://www.llu.edu
Phone: (909) 558-1000 *Calendar:* Qtr. plan
Inst. Accred.: WASC-SR. (1960/1999)
Prog. Accred.: Allied Health (cytotechnology, diagnostic medical sonography, medicine, occupational therapy, occupational therapy assisting, respiratory therapy, speech-language pathology), Clinical Lab Scientist, Clinical Pastoral Education (ACPEI), Clinical Psychology, Dentistry (combined prosthodontics, dental hygiene, dentistry, endodontics, general practice residency, oral and maxillofacial surgery, orthodontic and dentofacial orthopedics, pediatric dentistry, periodontics), Dietetic Technician, Dietetics (coordinated), Graduate Social Work, Marriage and Family Therapy, Nursing Education, Pharmacy, Phlebotomy, Physical Therapy, Physical Therapy Assisting, Physician Assistant, Public Health, Radiation Therapy, Radiography

Long Beach City College
4901 East Carson St., Long Beach 90808-1706
Type: Public, state/local, two-year
System: Long Beach Community College District
Degrees: A *Enroll:* 12,385
URL: http://www.lbcc.edu
Phone: (562) 938-4353 *Calendar:* Sem. plan
Inst. Accred.: WASC-JR. (1952/2003)
Prog. Accred.: Dietetic Technician, Nursing, Radiography

Los Angeles City College
855 North Vermont Ave., Los Angeles 90029-3590
Type: Public, state/local, two-year
System: Los Angeles Community College District
Degrees: A *Enroll:* 9,183
URL: http://www.lacitycollege.edu
Phone: (323) 953-4000 *Calendar:* Sem. plan
Inst. Accred.: WASC-JR. (1952/2003)
Prog. Accred.: Dentistry (dental laboratory technology), Dietetic Technician, Radiography

Los Angeles County College of Nursing and Allied Health
1200 North State St., Muir Hall, Rm. 114, Los Angeles 90033
Type: Public, local, two-year
Degrees: A *Enroll:* 91
URL: http://www.dhs.co.la.ca.us/lacusc/lacnah
Phone: (323) 226-4911 *Calendar:* Sem. plan
Inst. Accred.: WASC-JR. (1995/2008)

Los Angeles Harbor College
1111 Figueroa Place, Wilmington 90744-2397
Type: Public, state/local, two-year
System: Los Angeles Community College District
Degrees: A *Enroll:* 4,849
URL: http://www.lahc.edu
Phone: (310) 522-8200 *Calendar:* Sem. plan
Inst. Accred.: WASC-JR. (1952/2006)
Prog. Accred.: Nursing

Los Angeles Mission College
13356 Eldridge Ave., Sylmar 91342-3200
Type: Public, state/local, two-year
System: Los Angeles Community College District
Degrees: A *Enroll:* 3,700
URL: http://www.lamission.edu
Phone: (818) 364-7600 *Calendar:* Sem. plan
Inst. Accred.: WASC-JR. (1978/2007)

Los Angeles Pierce College
6201 Winnetka Ave., Woodland Hills 91371-0001
Type: Public, state/local, two-year
System: Los Angeles Community College District
Degrees: A *Enroll:* 9,480
URL: http://www.piercecollege.com
Phone: (818) 347-0551 *Calendar:* Sem. plan
Inst. Accred.: WASC-JR. (1952/2007)
Prog. Accred.: Nursing, Veterinary Technology

Los Angeles Southwest College
1600 West Imperial Hwy., Los Angeles 90047-4899
Type: Public, state/local, two-year
System: Los Angeles Community College District
Degrees: A *Enroll:* 3,098
URL: http://www.lasc.edu
Phone: (323) 241-5225 *Calendar:* Sem. plan
Inst. Accred.: WASC-JR. (1970/2006)

Los Angeles Trade-Technical College
400 West Washington Blvd., Los Angeles 90015-4108
Type: Public, state/local, two-year
System: Los Angeles Community College District
Degrees: A *Enroll:* 7,111
URL: http://www.lattc.edu
Phone: (213) 744-9500 *Calendar:* Sem. plan
Inst. Accred.: WASC-JR. (1952/2003)
Prog. Accred.: Culinary Education

Los Angeles Valley College
5800 Fulton Ave., Van Nuys 91401-4096
Type: Public, state/local, two-year
System: Los Angeles Community College District
Degrees: A *Enroll:* 8,342
URL: http://www.lavc.edu
Phone: (818) 781-1200 *Calendar:* Sem. plan
Inst. Accred.: WASC-JR. (1952/2007)
Prog. Accred.: Allied Health (respiratory therapy), Nursing

Los Medanos College
2700 East Leland Rd., Pittsburg 94565-5197
Type: Public, state/local, two-year
System: Contra Costa Community College District
Degrees: A *Enroll:* 4,313
URL: http://www.losmedanos.edu
Phone: (925) 439-2181 *Calendar:* Sem. plan
Inst. Accred.: WASC-JR. (1977/2002)

Loyola Marymount University
One LMU Dr., Los Angeles 90045-2659
Type: Private, Roman Catholic Church, four-year
Degrees: B, M, P *Enroll:* 8,251
URL: http://www.lmu.edu
Phone: (310) 338-2700 *Calendar:* Sem. plan
Inst. Accred.: ATS (2007), WASC-SR. (1949/2003)
Prog. Accred.: Art, Business (AACSB), Dance, Engineering (civil, electrical, mechanical), Law, Music, Teacher Education (NCATE), Theatre

Marymount College
30800 Palos Verdes Dr. East, Rancho Palos Verdes 90275-6299
Type: Private, Roman Catholic Church, two-year
Degrees: A *Enroll:* 715
URL: http://www.marymountpv.edu
Phone: (310) 377-5501 *Calendar:* Sem. plan
Inst. Accred.: WASC-JR. (1971/2001, Warning)

The Master's College and Seminary
21726 West Placerita Canyon Rd., New Hall 91321-1200
Type: Private, independent, four-year
Degrees: B, M, P, D *Enroll:* 1,308
URL: http://www.masters.edu
Phone: (661) 259-3540 *Calendar:* Sem. plan
Inst. Accred.: WASC-SR. (1975/2003)

Mendocino College
PO Box 3000, Ukiah 95482-0300
Type: Public, state/local, two-year
System: Mendocino-Lake Community College District
Degrees: A *Enroll:* 2,219
URL: http://www.mendocino.edu
Phone: (707) 468-3071 *Calendar:* Sem. plan
Inst. Accred.: WASC-JR. (1980/2008)
Prog. Accred.: Allied Health (EMT-paramedic)

Menlo College
1000 El Camino Real, Atherton 94027-4301
Type: Private, independent, four-year
Degrees: A, B, M *Enroll:* 710
URL: http://www.menlo.edu
Phone: (650) 688-3800 *Calendar:* 4-1-4 plan
Inst. Accred.: WASC-SR. (1952/2000)

Mennonite Brethren Biblical Seminary
4824 East Butler Ave., Fresno 93727-5097
Type: Private, Mennonite Brethren Churches, four-year
Degrees: M *Enroll:* 97
URL: http://www.mbseminary.edu
Phone: (559) 251-8628 *Calendar:* 4-1-4 plan
Inst. Accred.: ATS (1977/2001), WASC-SR. (1972/2002)

Merced College
3600 M St., Merced 95348-2898
Type: Public, state/local, two-year
System: Merced Community College District
Degrees: A *Enroll:* 4,743
URL: http://www.mccd.edu
Phone: (209) 384-6000 *Calendar:* Sem. plan
Inst. Accred.: WASC-JR. (1965/2005)
Prog. Accred.: Allied Health (diagnostic medical sonography), Radiography

Merritt College
12500 Campus Dr., Oakland 94619-3196
Type: Public, state/local, two-year
System: Peralta Community College District
Degrees: A *Enroll:* 3,146
URL: http://www.merritt.edu
Phone: (510) 531-4911 *Calendar:* Sem. plan
Inst. Accred.: WASC-JR. (1956/2003)
Prog. Accred.: Dietetic Technician, Radiography

Mills College
5000 MacArthur Blvd., Oakland 94613
Type: Private, independent, four-year
Degrees: B, M, D *Enroll:* 1,312
URL: http://www.mills.edu
Phone: (510) 430-2096 *Calendar:* Sem. plan
Inst. Accred.: WASC-SR. (1949/1999)

MiraCosta College
One Barnard Dr., Oceanside 92056-3899
Type: Public, state/local, two-year
System: MiraCosta Community College District
Degrees: A *Enroll:* 5,574
URL: http://www.miracosta.edu
Phone: (760) 795-6610 *Calendar:* Sem. plan
Inst. Accred.: WASC-JR. (1952/2004, Warning)

Mission College
3000 Mission College Blvd., Santa Clara 95054-1897
Type: Public, state/local, two-year
System: West Valley-Mission College District
Degrees: A *Enroll:* 4,127
URL: http://www.missioncollege.org
Phone: (408) 988-2200 *Calendar:* Sem. plan
Inst. Accred.: WASC-JR. (1979/2002, Warning)

Modesto Junior College
435 College Ave., Modesto 95350-5800
Type: Public, state/local, two-year
System: Yosemite Community College District
Degrees: A *Enroll:* 10,360
URL: http://mjc.yosemite.cc.ca.us
Phone: (209) 575-6498 *Calendar:* Sem. plan
Inst. Accred.: WASC-JR. (1952/2006, Probation)
Prog. Accred.: Allied Health (medical assisting (AMA), respiratory therapy), Dentistry (dental assisting)

Monterey Institute of International Studies
460 Pierce St., Monterey 93940
Type: Private, independent, four-year
Degrees: B, M *Enroll:* 681
URL: http://www.miis.edu
Phone: (831) 647-4100 *Calendar:* Sem. plan
Inst. Accred.: WASC-SR. (1961/2006)
Prog. Accred.: Business (AACSB)

Monterey Peninsula College
980 Fremont St., Monterey 93940-4799
Type: Public, state/local, two-year
System: Monterey Peninsula Community College District
Degrees: A *Enroll:* 4,219
URL: http://www.mpc.edu
Phone: (831) 646-4000 *Calendar:* Sem. plan
Inst. Accred.: WASC-JR. (1952/2004)
Prog. Accred.: Dentistry (dental assisting), Nursing

Moorpark College
7075 Campus Rd., Moorpark 93021-1695
Type: Public, state/local, two-year
System: Ventura County Community College District
Degrees: A *Enroll:* 8,215
URL: http://www.moorparkcollege.edu
Phone: (805) 378-1400 *Calendar:* Sem. plan
Inst. Accred.: WASC-JR. (1969/2005)
Prog. Accred.: Nursing, Radiography

Mount Saint Mary's College
12001 Chalon Rd., Los Angeles 90049-1599
Type: Private, Roman Catholic Church, four-year
Degrees: A, B, M, D *Enroll:* 2,038
URL: http://www.msmc.la.edu
Phone: (310) 954-4000 *Calendar:* 4-1-4 plan
Inst. Accred.: WASC-SR. (1949/2003)
Prog. Accred.: Music, Nursing Education, Physical Therapy

Doheny Campus
10 Chester Place, Los Angeles 90007
Phone: (310) 746-0450

Mount San Antonio College
1100 North Grand Ave., Walnut 91789-1399
Type: Public, state/local, two-year
System: Mount San Antonio Community College District
Degrees: A *Enroll:* 14,821
URL: http://www.mtsac.edu
Phone: (909) 594-5611 *Calendar:* Sem. plan
Inst. Accred.: WASC-JR. (1952/2005)
Prog. Accred.: Allied Health (EMT-paramedic, respiratory therapy), Radiography, Veterinary Technology

Mount San Jacinto College
1499 North State St., San Jacinto 92583-2399
Type: Public, state/local, two-year
System: Mount San Jacinto Community College District
Degrees: A *Enroll:* 6,505
URL: http://www.msjc.edu
Phone: (951) 487-6752 *Calendar:* Sem. plan
Inst. Accred.: WASC-JR. (1965/2006)

Mount Sierra College
101 East Huntington Dr., Monrovia 91016-3414
Type: Private, proprietary, four-year
Degrees: B
URL: http://www.mtsierra.edu
Phone: (626) 873-2138 *Calendar:* Sem. plan
Inst. Accred.: ACCSCT (1996/2007)

MTI College
5221 Madison Ave., Sacramento 95841
Type: Private, proprietary, two-year
Degrees: A *Enroll:* 765
URL: http://www.mticollege.com
Phone: (916) 339-1500 *Calendar:* Qtr. plan
Inst. Accred.: WASC-JR. (1999/2008)

Musicians Institute
1655 North McCadden Place, Los Angeles 90028-6115
Type: Private, proprietary, four-year
Degrees: A, B
URL: http://www.mi.edu
Phone: (323) 462-1384 *Calendar:* Qtr. plan
Inst. Accred.: NASM (1980/2008)

Napa Valley College
2277 Napa-Vallejo Hwy., Napa 94558-6236
Type: Public, state/local, two-year
System: Napa Valley Community College District
Degrees: A *Enroll:* 3,457
URL: http://www.napavalley.edu
Phone: (707) 253-3000 *Calendar:* Sem. plan
Inst. Accred.: WASC-JR. (1952/2004)
Prog. Accred.: Allied Health (respiratory therapy)

Upper Valley Campus
1088 College Ave., St. Helena 94574
Phone: (707) 967-2900

The National Hispanic University
14271 Story Rd., San Jose 95127-3823
Type: Private, independent, four-year
Degrees: A, B *Enroll:* 387
URL: http://www.nhu.edu
Phone: (408) 254-6900 *Calendar:* Sem. plan
Inst. Accred.: WASC-SR. (2002, Warning)

National Polytechnic College of Science
Los Angeles Harbor, 272 South Fries Ave., Wilmington 90744-6399
Type: Private, independent, two-year
System: National University System
Degrees: A *Enroll:* 246
URL: http://www.natpoly.edu
Phone: (310) 816-5700 *Calendar:* Qtr. plan
Inst. Accred.: WASC-JR. (1982/2004)

Kearny Mesa Campus
3580 Aero Ct., San Diego 92123-1711
Phone: (858) 309-3500

Los Angeles Campus
5245 Pacific Concourse Dr., Ste. 134, Los Angeles 90045
Phone: (310) 816-5700

National University
11255 North Torrey Pines Rd., La Jolla 92037-1011
Type: Private, independent, four-year
System: National University System
Degrees: A, B, M, P *Enroll:* 15,100
URL: http://www.nu.edu
Phone: (858) 642-8000 *Calendar:* 12-mos. pr
Inst. Accred.: WASC-SR. (1977/2008)
Prog. Accred.: Nursing Education

NewSchool of Architecture and Design
1249 F St., San Diego 92101
Type: Private, indepepndent, four-year
System: Laureate Education, Inc.
Degrees: B, M
URL: http://www.newschoolarch.edu
Phone: (619) 235-4100 *Calendar:* Qtr. plan
Inst. Accred.: ACICS (1994/2003)

Northwestern Polytechnic University
47671 Westinghouse Dr., Fremont 94539
Type: Private, independent, four-year
Degrees: B, M *Enroll:* 287
URL: http://www.npu.edu
Phone: (510) 592-9688 *Calendar:* Sem. plan
Inst. Accred.: ACICS (1998/2006)

Notre Dame de Namur University
1500 Ralston Ave., Belmont 94002-1997
Type: Private, Roman Catholic Church, four-year
Degrees: B, M *Enroll:* 1,120
URL: http://www.ndnu.edu
Phone: (650) 508-3500 *Calendar:* Sem. plan
Inst. Accred.: WASC-SR. (1955/2006)
Prog. Accred.: Business (ACBSP), Music

Occidental College
1600 Campus Rd., Los Angeles 90041-3314
Type: Private, independent, four-year
Degrees: B, M *Enroll:* 1,821
URL: http://www.oxy.edu
Phone: (323) 259-2691 *Calendar:* Sem. plan
Inst. Accred.: WASC-SR. (1949/2001)

Ohlone College
PO Box 3909, 43600 Mission Blvd., Fremont 94539-3909
Type: Public, state/local, two-year
System: Ohlone Community College District
Degrees: A *Enroll:* 5,329
URL: http://www.ohlone.edu
Phone: (510) 659-6000 *Calendar:* Sem. plan
Inst. Accred.: WASC-JR. (1970/2002, Warning)
Prog. Accred.: Allied Health (respiratory therapy), Nursing, Physical Therapy Assisting

Orange Coast College
2701 Fairview Rd., PO Box 5005, Costa Mesa 92628-5005
Type: Public, state/local, two-year
System: Coast Community College District
Degrees: A *Enroll:* 13,700
URL: http://www.orangecoastcollege.edu
Phone: (714) 432-0202 *Calendar:* Sem. plan
Inst. Accred.: WASC-JR. (1952/2007, Warning)
Prog. Accred.: Allied Health (cardiovascular technology, diagnostic medical sonography, electroneurodiagnostic technology, medical assisting (AMA), respiratory therapy), Culinary Education, Dentistry (dental assisting), Dietetic Technician, Polysomnographic Technology, Radiography

Otis College of Art and Design
9045 Lincoln Blvd., Westchester 90045
Type: Private, independent, four-year
Degrees: B, M *Enroll:* 1,073
URL: http://www.otis.edu
Phone: (310) 665-6800 *Calendar:* Sem. plan
Inst. Accred.: WASC-SR. (1956/2008)
Prog. Accred.: Art

Oxnard College
4000 South Rose Ave., Oxnard 93033-6699
Type: Public, state/local, two-year
System: Ventura County Community College District
Degrees: A *Enroll:* 3,336
URL: http://www.oxnardcollege.edu
Phone: (805) 986-5800 *Calendar:* Sem. plan
Inst. Accred.: WASC-JR. (1978/2005)
Prog. Accred.: Dentistry (dental hygiene)

Pacific College of Oriental Medicine
7445 Mission Valley Rd., Ste. 105, San Diego 92108-4408
Type: Private, proprietary, four-year
Degrees: M *Enroll:* 397
URL: http://www.pacificcollege.edu
Phone: (619) 574-6909 *Calendar:* Tri. plan
Inst. Accred.: ACAOM (1995/2004)

Chicago Campus
3646 North Broadway, 2nd Flr., Chicago, IL 60613
Phone: (773) 477-4822

Pacific Graduate School of Psychology
940 East Meadow Dr., Palo Alto 94303
Type: Private, independent, four-year
Degrees: D *Enroll:* 334
URL: http://www.pgsp.edu
Phone: (650) 843-3413 *Calendar:* Qtr. plan
Inst. Accred.: WASC-SR. (1986/2008)
Prog. Accred.: Clinical Psychology

Pacific Lutheran Theological Seminary
2770 Marin Ave., Berkeley 94708-1597
Type: Private, Evangelical Lutheran Church in America, four-year
System: Graduate Theological Union
Degrees: M *Enroll:* 104
URL: http://www.plts.edu
Phone: (510) 524-5264 *Calendar:* Sem. plan
Inst. Accred.: ATS (1964/1998)

Pacific Oaks College
5 Westmoreland Place, Pasadena 91103-3592
Type: Private, independent, four-year
Degrees: B, M *Enroll:* 467
URL: http://www.pacificoaks.edu
Phone: (626) 397-1300 *Calendar:* Sem. plan
Inst. Accred.: WASC-SR. (1959/2002)

Pacific School of Religion
1798 Scenic Ave., Berkeley 94709
Type: Private, interdenominational, four-year
System: Graduate Theological Union
Degrees: M, P, D *Enroll:* 201
URL: http://www.psr.edu
Phone: (510) 848-0528 *Calendar:* Sem. plan
Inst. Accred.: ATS (1938/2007), WASC-SR. (1971/2008)

Pacific States University
1516 South Western Ave., Los Angeles 90006
Type: Private, independent, four-year
Degrees: A, B, M *Enroll:* 168
URL: http://www.psuca.edu
Phone: (323) 731-2383 *Calendar:* Qtr. plan
Inst. Accred.: ACICS (1996/2004)

Pacific Union College
One Angwin Ave., Angwin 94508-9707
Type: Private, Seventh-Day Adventist Church, four-year
Degrees: A, B, M *Enroll:* 1,442
URL: http://www.puc.edu
Phone: (707) 965-6234 *Calendar:* Qtr. plan
Inst. Accred.: WASC-SR. (1951/2000)
Prog. Accred.: Music, Nursing, Social Work

Pacifica Graduate Institute
249 Lambert Rd., Carpinteria 93013
Type: Private, proprietary, four-year
Degrees: M, D *Enroll:* 626
URL: http://www.pacifica.edu
Phone: (805) 969-3626 *Calendar:* Qtr. plan
Inst. Accred.: WASC-SR. (1997/2001)

Palmer College of Chiropractic—West
90 East Tasman Dr., San Jose 95134
Type: Private, independent, four-year
System: Palmer Chiropractic University System
Degrees: P *Enroll:* 325
URL: http://www.palmer.edu
Phone: (408) 944-6000 *Calendar:* Qtr. plan
Inst. Accred.: CCE (1985/2001)

Palo Verde College
One College Dr., Blythe 92225
Type: Public, state/local, two-year
System: Palo Verde Community College District
Degrees: A *Enroll:* 2,132
URL: http://www.paloverde.cc.ca.us
Phone: (760) 921-5500 *Calendar:* Sem. plan
Inst. Accred.: WASC-JR. (1951/2002, Warning)

Palomar College
1140 West Mission Rd., San Marcos 92069-1487
Type: Public, state/local, two-year
System: Palomar Community College District
Degrees: A *Enroll:* 13,743
URL: http://www.palomar.edu
Phone: (760) 744-1150 *Calendar:* Sem. plan
Inst. Accred.: WASC-JR. (1951/2002)
Prog. Accred.: Allied Health (EMT-paramedic), Dentistry (dental assisting), Nursing

Pardee Rand Graduate School
1776 Main St., Santa Monica 90401-3208
Type: Private, independent, four-year
Degrees: D *Enroll:* 103
URL: http://www.prgs.edu
Phone: (310) 393-0411 *Calendar:* Qtr. plan
Inst. Accred.: WASC-SR. (1975/2000)

Pasadena City College
1570 East Colorado Blvd., Pasadena 91106-2003
Type: Public, state/local, two-year
System: Pasadena Area Community College District
Degrees: A *Enroll:* 14,460
URL: http://www.pasadena.edu
Phone: (626) 585-7123 *Calendar:* Sem. plan
Inst. Accred.: WASC-JR. (1952/2003)
Prog. Accred.: Allied Health (medical assisting (AMA)), Dentistry (dental assisting, dental hygiene, dental laboratory technology), Radiography

Patten University
2433 Coolidge Ave., Oakland 94601
Type: Private, Christian Evangelical Church of America, four-year
Degrees: A, B, M *Enroll:* 468
URL: http://www.patten.edu
Phone: (510) 261-8500 *Calendar:* Sem. plan
Inst. Accred.: WASC-SR. (1980/2008)

Pepperdine University
24255 Pacific Coast Hwy., Malibu 90263
Type: Private, Churches of Christ, four-year
Degrees: B, M, P, D *Enroll:* 6,101
URL: http://www.pepperdine.edu
Phone: (310) 506-4000 *Calendar:* Tri. plan
Inst. Accred.: WASC-SR. (1949/2001)
Prog. Accred.: Business (AACSB), Clinical Psychology, Dietetics (didactic), Law, Music

Perelandra College
8697-C La Mesa Blvd., PMB 21, La Mesa 91941
Type: Private, independent, four-year
Degrees: M
URL: http://perelandracollege.com
Phone: (619) 677-3308
Inst. Accred.: DETC (2008)

Phillips Graduate Institute
5445 Balboa Blvd., Encino 91316-1509
Type: Private, independent, four-year
Degrees: M, D *Enroll:* 282
URL: http://www.pgi.edu
Phone: (818) 386-5600 *Calendar:* Sem. plan
Inst. Accred.: WASC-SR. (1983/2005)

Pitzer College
1050 North Mills Ave., Claremont 91711-6101
Type: Private, independent, four-year
System: Claremont University Consortium
Degrees: B *Enroll:* 933
URL: http://www.pitzer.edu
Phone: (909) 621-8000 *Calendar:* Sem. plan
Inst. Accred.: WASC-SR. (1965/1999)

Platt College
1000 South Fremont Ave., Ste. A9W, Alhambra 91803
Type: Private, proprietary, four-year
System: ForeFront Education, Inc.
Degrees: A, B *Enroll:* 225
URL: http://www.plattcollege.edu
Phone: (626) 300-5444
Inst. Accred.: ACCSCT (1987/2004)

Ontario Campus
3700 Inland Empire Blvd., Ste. 400, Ontario 91764-4609
Phone: (909) 941-9410

Platt College San Diego
6250 El Cajon Blvd., San Diego 92115-3919
Type: Private, proprietary, four-year
Degrees: A, B *Enroll:* 253
URL: http://www.platt.edu
Phone: (619) 265-0107
Inst. Accred.: ACCSCT (1985/2003)

Point Loma Nazarene University
Mieras Hall, 3900 Lomaland Dr., San Diego 92106-2810
Type: Private, Church of the Nazarene, four-year
Degrees: A, B, M *Enroll:* 3,034
URL: http://www.ptloma.edu
Phone: (619) 849-2200 *Calendar:* Sem. plan
Inst. Accred.: WASC-SR. (1949/2008)
Prog. Accred.: Business (ACBSP), Dietetics (didactic), Music, Nursing Education

Pomona College
550 North College Ave., Claremont 91711
Type: Private, independent, four-year
System: Claremont University Consortium
Degrees: B *Enroll:* 1,533
URL: http://www.pomona.edu
Phone: (909) 621-8131 *Calendar:* Sem. plan
Inst. Accred.: WASC-SR. (1949/2002)

Porterville College
100 East College Ave., Porterville 93257-5901
Type: Public, state/local, two-year
System: Kern Community College District
Degrees: A *Enroll:* 2,472
URL: http://www.portervillecollege.edu
Phone: (559) 791-2200 *Calendar:* Sem. plan
Inst. Accred.: WASC-JR. (1952/2007)

Professional Golfers Career College
26109 Ynez Rd., Temecula 92591
Type: Private, proprietary, two-year
Degrees: A *Enroll:* 200
URL: http://www.progolfed.com
Phone: (951) 719-2994 *Calendar:* Sem. plan
Inst. Accred.: ACICS (1996/2005)

Hilton Head Campus
4454 Bluffton Park Crescent, Building 200, Bluffton, SC 29910
Phone: (866) 797-7422

Orlando Campus
16301 Phil Ritson Way, Winter Garden, FL 34787
Phone: (407) 905-2200

Redstone College—Los Angeles
8911 Aviation Blvd., Inglewood 90301
Type: Private, proprietary, two-year
System: Westwood College
Degrees: A
URL: http://www.redstone.edu
Phone: (310) 337-4444
Inst. Accred.: COE (1988/2006)

Reedley College
995 North Reed Ave., Reedley 93654-2099
Type: Public, state/local, two-year
System: State Center Community College District
Degrees: A *Enroll:* 6,688
URL: http://www.reedleycollege.edu
Phone: (559) 638-3641 *Calendar:* Sem. plan
Inst. Accred.: WASC-JR. (1952/2006)
Prog. Accred.: Dentistry (dental assisting), Forestry

Remington College—San Diego
123 Camino de la Reina, North Bldg., Ste. 100, San Diego 92108
Type: Private, proprietary, four-year
System: Education America, Inc.
Degrees: A, B, M *Enroll:* 242
URL: http://www.remingtoncollege.edu
Phone: (619) 686-8600 *Calendar:* Qtr. plan
Inst. Accred.: ACICS (1998/2008)

Honolulu Campus
1111 Bishop St., Ste. 400, Honolulu, HI 96813-2811
Phone: (808) 942-1000

Rio Hondo College
3600 Workman Mill Rd., Whittier 90601-1699
Type: Public, state/local, two-year
System: Rio Hondo Community College District
Degrees: A *Enroll:* 9,537
URL: http://www.riohondo.edu
Phone: (562) 692-0921 *Calendar:* Sem. plan
Inst. Accred.: WASC-JR. (1967/2002)

Riverside City College
4800 Magnolia Ave., Riverside 92506-1293
Type: Public, state/local, two-year
System: Riverside Community College District
Degrees: A *Enroll:* 15,542
URL: http://www.rcc.edu
Phone: (951) 222-8000 *Calendar:* Sem. plan
Inst. Accred.: WASC-JR. (1952/2008)
Prog. Accred.: Allied Health (EMT-paramedic), Nursing

Sacramento City College
3835 Freeport Blvd., Sacramento 95822-1386
Type: Public, state/local, two-year
System: Los Rios Community College District
Degrees: A *Enroll:* 11,892
URL: http://www.scc.losrios.edu
Phone: (916) 558-2111 *Calendar:* Sem. plan
Inst. Accred.: WASC-JR. (1952/2004)
Prog. Accred.: Allied Health (occupational therapy assisting), Dentistry (dental assisting, dental hygiene), Physical Therapy Assisting

Saddleback College
28000 Marguerite Pkwy., Mission Viejo 92692-3699
Type: Public, state/local, two-year
System: South Orange County Community College District
Degrees: A *Enroll:* 10,371
URL: http://www.saddleback.edu
Phone: (949) 582-4500 *Calendar:* Sem. plan
Inst. Accred.: WASC-JR. (1971/2005)
Prog. Accred.: Allied Health (EMT-paramedic), Nursing

Sage College
12125 Day St., Building L, Moreno Valley 92557-6720
Type: Private, proprietary, two-year
Degrees: A
URL: http://sagecollege.edu
Phone: (951) 781-2727 *Calendar:* Qtr. plan
Inst. Accred.: ACICS (1986/2005)

San Diego Campus
2820 Camino del Rio South, Ste. 100, San Diego 92108-3821
Phone: (619) 683-2727

Saint John's Seminary
5012 Seminary Rd., Camarillo 93012-2598
Type: Private, Roman Catholic Church, four-year
Degrees: B, M, P *Enroll:* 91
URL: http://www.stjohnsem.edu
Phone: (805) 482-2755 *Calendar:* Sem. plan
Inst. Accred.: ATS (1976/2002), WASC-SR. (1951/2002)

Saint Mary's College of California
1928 St. Mary's Rd., Moraga 94556
Type: Private, Roman Catholic Church, four-year
Degrees: A, B, M, D *Enroll:* 3,590
URL: http://www.stmarys-ca.edu
Phone: (925) 631-4000 *Calendar:* 4-1-4 plan
Inst. Accred.: WASC-SR. (1949/2003)
Prog. Accred.: Montessori Teacher Education, Nursing Education

Saint Patrick's Seminary and University
320 Middlefield Rd., Menlo Park 94025-3596
Type: Private, Roman Catholic Church, four-year
Degrees: M, P *Enroll:* 85
URL: http://www.stpatricksseminary.org
Phone: (650) 325-5621 *Calendar:* Sem. plan
Inst. Accred.: ATS (1971/2004), WASC-SR. (1971/2005)

Salvation Army College for Officer Training at Crestmont
30840 Hawthorne Blvd., Rancho Palos Verdes 90274
Type: Private, independent, two-year
Degrees: A
URL: http://www.crestmont.edu
Phone: (310) 377-0481 *Calendar:* Qtr. plan
Inst. Accred.: WASC-JR. (1990/2007, Probation)

Samra University of Oriental Medicine
1730 West Olympic Blvd., 3rd Flr., Los Angeles 90015
Type: Private, proprietary, four-year
Degrees: M *Enroll:* 213
URL: http://www.samra.edu
Phone: (213) 381-2221 *Calendar:* Qtr. plan
Inst. Accred.: ACAOM (1989/2007)

Samuel Merritt College
370 Hawthorne Ave., Oakland 94609
Type: Private, independent, four-year
Degrees: B, M *Enroll:* 936
URL: http://www.samuelmerritt.edu
Phone: (510) 869-6511 *Calendar:* 4-1-4 plan
Inst. Accred.: WASC-SR. (1984/2001)
Prog. Accred.: Allied Health (occupational therapy), Nurse Anesthesia Education, Nursing Education, Physical Therapy, Physician Assistant

California College of Podiatric Medicine at Sameul Merritt College
1210 Scott St., San Francisco 94115
Phone: (415) 563-3444
Prog. Accred: Podiatry

San Bernardino Valley College
701 South Mt. Vernon Ave., San Bernardino 92410-2798
Type: Public, state/local, two-year
System: San Bernardino Community College District
Degrees: A *Enroll:* 6,527
URL: http://www.valleycollege.edu
Phone: (909) 384-4470 *Calendar:* Sem. plan
Inst. Accred.: WASC-JR. (1952/2003)
Prog. Accred.: Nursing

San Diego Christian College
2100 Greenfield Dr., El Cajon 92019
Type: Private, Shadow Mountain Community Church, four-year
Degrees: B *Enroll:* 510
URL: http://www.sdcc.edu
Phone: (619) 441-2200 *Calendar:* Sem. plan
Inst. Accred.: WASC-SR. (1984/2008)

San Diego City College
1313 12th Ave., San Diego 92101-4787
Type: Public, state/local, two-year
System: San Diego Community College District
Degrees: A *Enroll:* 7,088
URL: http://www.sdcity.edu
Phone: (619) 388-3400 *Calendar:* Sem. plan
Inst. Accred.: WASC-JR. (1952/2005)
Prog. Accred.: Nursing

San Diego Mesa College
7250 Mesa College Dr., San Diego 92111-4996
Type: Public, state/local, two-year
System: San Diego Community College District
Degrees: A *Enroll:* 10,896
URL: http://www.sdmesa.edu
Phone: (619) 388-2600 *Calendar:* Sem. plan
Inst. Accred.: WASC-JR. (1966/2005)
Prog. Accred.: Dentistry (dental assisting), Physical Therapy Assisting, Radiography

San Diego Miramar College
10440 Black Mountain Rd., San Diego 92126-2999
Type: Public, state/local, two-year
System: San Diego Community College District
Degrees: A *Enroll:* 4,499
URL: http://www.sdmiramar.edu
Phone: (858) 536-7800 *Calendar:* Sem. plan
Inst. Accred.: WASC-JR. (1982/2005)

San Diego State University
5500 Campanile Dr., San Diego 92182-8143
Type: Public, state, four-year
System: California State University System
Degrees: B, M, D *Enroll:* 27,317
URL: http://www.sdsu.edu
Phone: (619) 594-5200 *Calendar:* Sem. plan
Inst. Accred.: WASC-SR. (1949/2005)
Prog. Accred.: Accounting, Allied Health (audiology, health services administration, kinesiotherapy, speech-language pathology), Applied Science (industrial hygiene), Art, Business (AACSB), Clinical Psychology, Computer Science (ABET-CAC), Dietetics (didactic), Engineering (aerospace, civil, computer, electrical, environmental/sanitary, mechanical), Graduate Social Work, Interior Design, Marriage and Family Therapy, Nurse (Midwifery), Nursing Education, Public Administration, Public Health, Recreation and Leisure Services, Rehabilitation Counseling, Social Work, Teacher Education (NCATE), Theatre

San Francisco Art Institute
800 Chestnut St., San Francisco 94133
Type: Private, independent, four-year
Degrees: B, M *Enroll:* 534
URL: http://www.sfai.edu
Phone: (415) 771-7020 *Calendar:* Sem. plan
Inst. Accred.: WASC-SR. (1954/2005)
Prog. Accred.: Art

San Francisco Conservatory of Music
50 Oak St., San Francisco 94102-6011
Type: Private, independent, four-year
Degrees: B, M *Enroll:* 292
URL: http://www.sfcm.edu
Phone: (415) 564-8086 *Calendar:* Sem. plan
Inst. Accred.: WASC-SR. (1960/2003)
Prog. Accred.: Music

San Francisco State University
1600 Holloway Ave., San Francisco 94132
Type: Public, state, four-year
System: California State University System
Degrees: B, M, D *Enroll:* 24,115
URL: http://www.sfsu.edu
Phone: (415) 338-1111 *Calendar:* Sem. plan
Inst. Accred.: WASC-SR. (1949/2001)
Prog. Accred.: Allied Health (audiology, speech-language pathology), Art, Business (AACSB), Clinical Lab Scientist, Computer Science (ABET-CAC), Counseling, Dietetics (didactic), Dietetics (internship), Engineering (civil, electrical, mechanical), Family & Consumer Science, Graduate Social Work, Journalism, Music, Nursing Education, Physical Therapy, Public Administration, Public Health, Recreation and Leisure Services, Rehabilitation Counseling, Social Work, Teacher Education (NCATE), Theatre

San Francisco Theological Seminary
105 Seminary Rd., San Anselmo 94960
Type: Private, Presbyterian Church (USA), four-year
System: Graduate Theological Union
Degrees: M, P, D *Enroll:* 281
URL: http://www.sfts.edu
Phone: (415) 451-2800 *Calendar:* Sem. plan
Inst. Accred.: ATS (1938/2007), WASC-SR. (1973/2008)

San Joaquin College of Law
901 Fifth St., Clovis 93612-1312
Type: Private, independent, four-year
Degrees: M, P, D *Enroll:* 149
URL: http://www.sjcl.edu
Phone: (559) 323-2100 *Calendar:* Sem. plan
Inst. Accred.: WASC-SR. (1993/1999)

San Joaquin Delta College
5151 Pacific Ave., Stockton 95207-6370
Type: Public, state/local, two-year
System: San Joaquin Delta Community College District
Degrees: A *Enroll:* 10,158
URL: http://www.deltacollege.org
Phone: (209) 954-5151 *Calendar:* Sem. plan
Inst. Accred.: WASC-JR. (1952/2002, Warning)
Prog. Accred.: Culinary Education, Nursing

San Joaquin Valley College—Visalia
8400 West Mineral King Ave., Visalia 93291-9283
Type: Private, proprietary, two-year
System: San Joaquin Valley College System
Degrees: A *Enroll:* 876
URL: http://www.sjvc.com
Phone: (559) 651-2500 *Calendar:* Sem. plan
Inst. Accred.: WASC-JR. (1994/2007)
Prog. Accred.: Allied Health (respiratory therapy, surgical technology), Dentistry (dental hygiene), Physician Assistant

Bakersfield Campus
201 New Stine Rd., Bakersfield 93309-2606
Phone: (661) 834-0126
Prog. Accred: Allied Health (respiratory therapy, surgical technology)

Fresno Aviation Campus
4985 E. Andersen Ave., Fresno 93727-1501
Phone: (559) 453-0380

Fresno Campus
295 East Sierra Ave., Fresno 93710
Phone: (209) 448-8282

Modesto Campus
1700 McHenry Village Way, Ste. 6, Modesto 95350
Phone: (209) 527-7582

Rancho Cordova Campus
11050 Olson Dr., Ste. 100, Rancho Cordova 95670
Phone: (916) 638-7582

Rancho Cucamonga Campus
10641 Church St., Rancho Cucamonga 91703-6862
Phone: (909) 948-7582
Prog. Accred: Allied Health (respiratory therapy)

San Jose City College
2100 Moorpark Ave., San Jose 95128-2799
Type: Public, state/local, two-year
System: San Jose-Evergreen Community College District
Degrees: A *Enroll:* 4,575
URL: http://www.sjcc.edu
Phone: (408) 298-2181 *Calendar:* Sem. plan
Inst. Accred.: WASC-JR. (1953/2006)
Prog. Accred.: Dentistry (dental assisting)

San Jose State University
One Washington Square, San Jose 95192-0031
Type: Public, state, four-year
System: California State University System
Degrees: B, M *Enroll:* 23,897
URL: http://www.sjsu.edu
Phone: (408) 924-1000 *Calendar:* Sem. plan
Inst. Accred.: WASC-SR. (1949/2007)
Prog. Accred.: Allied Health (occupational therapy, speech-language pathology), Art, Business (AACSB), Computer Science (ABET-CAC), Dance, Dietetics (didactic), Dietetics (internship), Engineering (aerospace, chemical, civil, computer, electrical, industrial, materials, mechanical), Graduate Social Work, Industrial Technology, Journalism, Librarianship, Music, Nursing Education, Planning, Public Administration, Public Health, Recreation and Leisure Services, Social Work, Teacher Education (NCATE), Theatre

Santa Ana College
1530 West 17th St., Santa Ana 92706-3398
Type: Public, state/local, two-year
System: Rancho Santiago Community College District
Degrees: A *Enroll:* 13,724
URL: http://www.sac.edu
Phone: (714) 564-6000 *Calendar:* Sem. plan
Inst. Accred.: WASC-JR. (1952/2002)
Prog. Accred.: Allied Health (occupational therapy assisting), Nursing

Santa Barbara Business College
4839 Market St., Ventura 93003
Type: Private, proprietary, two-year
Degrees: A
URL: http://www.sbbcollege.edu
Phone: (805) 339-2999 *Calendar:* Qtr. plan
Inst. Accred.: ACICS (2003/2008)

Santa Barbara Business College
211 South Real Rd., Bakersfield 93309
Type: Private, proprietary, two-year
Degrees: A
URL: http://www.sbbcollege.edu
Phone: (661) 835-1100 *Calendar:* Qtr. plan
Inst. Accred.: ACICS (1985/2008)

Santa Barbara Business College
303 East Plaza Dr., Santa Maria 93454
Type: Private, proprietary, two-year
Degrees: A
URL: http://www.sbbcollege.com
Phone: (805) 922-8256 *Calendar:* Qtr. plan
Inst. Accred.: ACICS (1976/2008)

Palm Desert Campus
75030 Gerald Ford Dr., Palm Desert 92211
Phone: (760) 341-2602

Santa Barbara Campus
506 Chapala St., Santa Barbara 93101
Phone: (805) 967-9677

Santa Barbara City College
721 Cliff Dr., Santa Barbara 93109-2394
Type: Public, state/local, two-year
System: Santa Barbara Community College District
Degrees: A *Enroll:* 9,467
URL: http://www.sbcc.edu
Phone: (805) 965-0581 *Calendar:* Sem. plan
Inst. Accred.: WASC-JR. (1952/2003)
Prog. Accred.: Culinary Education, Dentistry (dental assisting), Nursing, Radiography

Santa Clara University
500 El Camino Real, Santa Clara 95053-0015
Type: Private, Roman Catholic Church, four-year
Degrees: B, M, P, D *Enroll:* 6,814
URL: http://www.scu.edu
Phone: (408) 554-4000 *Calendar:* Qtr. plan
Inst. Accred.: WASC-SR. (1949/2000)
Prog. Accred.: Accounting, Business (AACSB), Engineering (civil, computer, electrical, mechanical), Law

Santa Monica College
1900 Pico Blvd., Santa Monica 90405-1628
Type: Public, state/local, two-year
System: Santa Monica Community College District
Degrees: A *Enroll:* 16,115
URL: http://www.smc.edu
Phone: (310) 434-4000 *Calendar:* Sem. plan
Inst. Accred.: WASC-JR. (1952/2004)
Prog. Accred.: Allied Health (respiratory therapy), Nursing

Santa Rosa Junior College
1501 Mendocino Ave., Santa Rosa 95401-4395
Type: Public, state/local, two-year
System: Sonoma County Junior College District
Degrees: A *Enroll:* 13,329
URL: http://www.santarosa.edu
Phone: (707) 527-4011 *Calendar:* Sem. plan
Inst. Accred.: WASC-JR. (1952/2003)
Prog. Accred.: Allied Health (EMT-paramedic), Dentistry (dental assisting, dental hygiene), Radiography

Petaluma Campus
680 Sonoma Mountain Pkwy., Petaluma 94952
Phone: (707) 778-3801

Santiago Canyon College
8045 East Chapman Ave., Orange 92869-4512
Type: Public, state/local, two-year
System: Rancho Santiago Community College District
Degrees: A
URL: http://www.sccollege.edu
Phone: (714) 628-4900 *Calendar:* Sem. plan
Inst. Accred.: WASC-JR. (2000/2006)

Saybrook Graduate School and Research Center
747 Front St., 3rd Flr., San Francisco 94111-1920
Type: Private, independent, four-year
Degrees: M, D *Enroll:* 486
URL: http://www.saybrook.edu
Phone: (415) 433-9200
Inst. Accred.: WASC-SR. (1984/2007)

Scripps College
1030 North Columbia Ave., Claremont 91711
Type: Private, independent, four-year
System: Claremont University Consortium
Degrees: B *Enroll:* 898
URL: http://www.scrippscollege.edu
Phone: (909) 621-8224 *Calendar:* Sem. plan
Inst. Accred.: WASC-SR. (1949/2002)

The Scripps Research Institute
10550 North Torrey Pines Rd., TCP 19, La Jolla 92037
Type: Private, independent, four-year
Degrees: D
URL: http://www.scripps.edu
Phone: (858) 784-8469 *Calendar:* 9-mos. pro
Inst. Accred.: WASC-SR. (1993/1999)

Shasta Bible College and Graduate School
2951 Goodwater Ave., Redding 96002
Type: Private, Baptist Church, four-year
Degrees: A, B, M *Enroll:* 98
URL: http://www.shasta.edu
Phone: (530) 221-4275 *Calendar:* Sem. plan
Inst. Accred.: TRACS (1997/2002)

Shasta College
1115 Old Oregon Trail, PO Box 496006, Redding 96049-6006
Type: Public, state/local, two-year
System: Shasta-Tehama-Trinity Joint Community College District
Degrees: A *Enroll:* 4,721
URL: http://www.shastacollege.edu
Phone: (530) 225-4600 *Calendar:* Sem. plan
Inst. Accred.: WASC-JR. (1952/2006, Probation)
Prog. Accred.: Dentistry (dental hygiene)

Sierra College
5000 Rocklin Rd., Rocklin 95677-3397
Type: Public, state/local, two-year
System: Sierra Joint Community College District
Degrees: A *Enroll:* 10,649
URL: http://www.sierracollege.edu
Phone: (530) 624-3333 *Calendar:* Sem. plan
Inst. Accred.: WASC-JR. (1952/2001, Warning)

Silicon Valley University
2160 Lundy Ave., Ste. 110, San Jose 95131
Type: Private, independent, four-year
Degrees: B, M *Enroll:* 32
URL: http://www.svuca.edu
Phone: (408) 435-8989 *Calendar:* Tri. plan
Inst. Accred.: ACICS (2003/2006)

Simpson University
2211 College View Dr., Redding 96003-8606
Type: Private, Christian and Missionary Alliance, four-year
Degrees: A, B, M *Enroll:* 1,011
URL: http://www.simpsonuniversity.edu
Phone: (530) 226-4606 *Calendar:* 4-1-4 plan
Inst. Accred.: WASC-SR. (1969/2008)

Skyline College
3300 College Dr., San Bruno 94066-1698
Type: Public, state/local, two-year
System: San Mateo County Community College District
Degrees: A *Enroll:* 4,173
URL: http://skylinecollege.edu
Phone: (650) 738-4100 *Calendar:* Sem. plan
Inst. Accred.: WASC-JR. (1971/2008)
Prog. Accred.: Allied Health (respiratory therapy, surgical technology)

Soka University of America
1 University Dr., Aliso Viejo 92656
Type: Private, independent, four-year
Degrees: B
URL: http://www.soka.edu
Phone: (949) 480-4000
Inst. Accred.: AALE (2005), WASC-SR. (2005)

Solano Community College
4000 Suisun Valley Rd., Fairfield 94534-3197
Type: Public, state/local, two-year
System: Solano County Community College District
Degrees: A *FTE Enroll:* 5,555
URL: http://www.solano.edu
Phone: (707) 864-7000 *Calendar:* Sem. plan
Inst. Accred.: WASC-JR. (1952/2006, Probation)

Sonoma State University
1801 East Cotati Ave., Rohnert Park 94928
Type: Public, state, four-year
System: California State University System
Degrees: B, M *Enroll:* 6,863
URL: http://www.sonoma.edu
Phone: (707) 664-2880 *Calendar:* Sem. plan
Inst. Accred.: WASC-SR. (1963/2008)
Prog. Accred.: Art, Business (AACSB), Counseling, Music, Nursing, Teacher Education (NCATE)

South Baylo University
1126 North Brookhurst St., Anaheim 92801
Type: Private, proprietary, four-year
Degrees: M *Enroll:* 313
URL: http://southbaylo.edu
Phone: (714) 533-1495 *Calendar:* Qtr. plan
Inst. Accred.: ACAOM (1993/2007)

Los Angeles Campus
2727 West 6th St., Los Angeles 90015
Phone: (213) 738-0712
Prog. Accred: Acupuncture

South Coast College
2011 West Chapman Ave., Orange 92868-2616
Type: Private, proprietary, two-year
Degrees: A
URL: http://www.southcoastcollege.com
Phone: (714) 635-6464
Inst. Accred.: ACICS (1984/2008)

Southern California College of Optometry
2575 Yorba Linda Blvd., Fullerton 92631-1699
Type: Private, independent, four-year
Degrees: A, B, P, D *Enroll:* 381
URL: http://www.scco.edu
Phone: (714) 870-7226 *Calendar:* Qtr. plan
Inst. Accred.: WASC-SR. (1961/2001)
Prog. Accred.: Allied Health (optometric residency, optometry)

Southern California Institute of Architecture
960 East Third St., Los Angeles 90013
Type: Private, independent, four-year
Degrees: B, M, P *Enroll:* 474
URL: http://www.sciarc.edu
Phone: (213) 613-2200 *Calendar:* Sem. plan
Inst. Accred.: WASC-SR. (1995/2008)

Southern California Institute of Technology
222 South Harbor Blvd., Ste. 200, Anaheim 92805
Type: Private, proprietary, four-year
Degrees: A, B *Enroll:* 319
URL: http://www.scit-scu.edu
Phone: (714) 300-0300
Inst. Accred.: ACCSCT (1994/2004)

Southern California Seminary
2075 East Madison Ave., El Cajon 92019-1108
Type: Private, independent, four-year
Degrees: A, B, M, D *Enroll:* 176
URL: http://www.socalsem.edu
Phone: (619) 442-9841 *Calendar:* Tri. plan
Inst. Accred.: TRACS (2001/2006)

Fundación ABRE
Santo Domingo St., 34, Santiponce (Seville), Spain 41970
Phone: 011 34 955 997 555

Southern California University of Health Sciences
PO Box 1166, Whittier 90609-1166
Type: Private, independent, four-year
Degrees: M, P *Enroll:* 580
URL: http://www.scuhs.edu
Phone: (562) 947-8755 *Calendar:* Sem. plan
Inst. Accred.: WASC-SR. (1993/2008)
Prog. Accred.: Acupuncture, Chiropractic Education

Southwestern College
900 Otay Lakes Rd., Chula Vista 91910-7299
Type: Public, state/local, two-year
System: Southwestern Community College District
Degrees: A *Enroll:* 10,954
URL: http://www.swc.cc.ca.us
Phone: (619) 421-6700 *Calendar:* Sem. plan
Inst. Accred.: WASC-JR. (1964/2003)
Prog. Accred.: Allied Health (EMT-paramedic, surgical technology), Dentistry (dental hygiene), Nursing

Stanford University
Stanford 94305
Type: Private, independent, four-year
Degrees: B, M, P, D *Enroll:* 15,326
URL: http://www.stanford.edu
Phone: (650) 723-2300 *Calendar:* Qtr. plan
Inst. Accred.: WASC-SR. (1949/2000)
Prog. Accred.: Allied Health (medicine), Business (AACSB), Clinical Pastoral Education (ACPEI), Counseling Psychology, Engineering (chemical, civil, electrical, environmental/sanitary, mechanical), Law, Physician Assistant, Teacher Education (NCATE)

Starr King School for the Ministry
2441 LeConte Ave., Berkeley 94709
Type: Private, Unitarian Universalist Church, four-year
System: Graduate Theological Union
Degrees: M *Enroll:* 78
URL: http://www.sksm.edu
Phone: (510) 845-6232 *Calendar:* Sem. plan
Inst. Accred.: ATS (1978/1998)

Taft Community College
29 Emmons Park Dr., Taft 93268-2317
Type: Public, state/local, two-year
System: West Kern Community College District
Degrees: A *Enroll:* 3,376
URL: http://www.taftcollege.edu
Phone: (661) 763-7700 *Calendar:* Sem. plan
Inst. Accred.: WASC-JR. (1952/2003)
Prog. Accred.: Dentistry (dental hygiene)

Thomas Aquinas College
10000 North Ojai Rd., Santa Paula 93060
Type: Private, Roman Catholic Church, four-year
Degrees: B *Enroll:* 359
URL: http://www.thomasaquinas.edu
Phone: (805) 525-4417 *Calendar:* Sem. plan
Inst. Accred.: WASC-SR. (1980/2002), AALE (1997/2002)

Touro College—Los Angeles
1317 N. Crescent Heights Blvd., West Hollywood 90046
Type: Private, proprietary, four-year
Degrees: B
URL: http://www.touro.edu/losangeles
Phone: (323) 822-9700 *Calendar:* Sem. plan
Inst. Accred.: WASC-JR. (2005)

Touro University—California
1310 Johnson Ln., Mare Island, Vallejo 94592
Type: Private, independent, four-year
Degrees: D
URL: http://www.tumi.edu
Phone: (707) 638-5200 *Calendar:* Sem. plan
Inst. Accred.: WASC-SR. (2005)
Prog. Accred.: Osteopathy, Pharmacy, Physician Assistant

Nevada Campus
874 American Pacific Dr., Henderson, NV 89014
Phone: (702) 777-8687
Prog. Accred: Allied Health (occupational therapy), Nursing Education, Osteopathy, Physician Assistant

Trinity Life Bible College
5225 Hillsdale Blvd., Sacramento 95842
Type: Private, Assemblies of God Church, four-year
Degrees: A, B *Enroll:* 116
URL: http://www.tlbc.edu
Phone: (916) 348-4689 *Calendar:* Qtr. plan
Inst. Accred.: TRACS (2004)

TUI University
5665 Plaza Dr., 3rd Flr., Cypress 90630
Type: Private, independent, four-year
Degrees: B, M, D
URL: http://www.tuiu.edu
Phone: (800) 375-9878 *Calendar:* Sem. plan
Inst. Accred.: WASC-SR. (2005/2007)

The United States Naval Postgraduate School
One University Circle, Monterey 93943-5002
Type: Public, federal, four-year
Degrees: B, M, D *Enroll:* 1,922
URL: http://www.nps.edu
Phone: (831) 656-2023 *Calendar:* Qtr. plan
Inst. Accred.: WASC-SR. (1955/1999)
Prog. Accred.: Business (AACSB), Engineering (aerospace, electrical, mechanical), Public Administration

University of California, Berkeley
Berkeley 94720
Type: Public, state, four-year
System: University of California Office of the President
Degrees: B, M, P, D *Enroll:* 31,893
URL: http://www.berkeley.edu
Phone: (510) 642-6000 *Calendar:* Sem. plan
Inst. Accred.: WASC-SR. (1949/2003)
Prog. Accred.: Allied Health (health services administration, optometric residency, optometry), Business (AACSB), Clinical Psychology, Computer Science (ABET-CAC), Dietetics (didactic), Engineering (chemical, civil, computer, electrical, industrial, mechanical, nuclear), Forestry, Graduate Social Work, Journalism, Landscape Architecture, Law, Planning, Psychology Internship, Public Health, School Psychology

UC Berkeley Extension
1995 University Ave., Berkeley 94720-7007
Phone: (510) 642-4111
Prog. Accred: Interior Architecture

University of California, Davis
One Shields Ave., Davis 95616
Type: Public, state, four-year
System: University of California Office of the President
Degrees: B, M, P, D *Enroll:* 27,261
URL: http://www.ucdavis.edu
Phone: (530) 752-1011 *Calendar:* Qtr. plan
Inst. Accred.: WASC-SR. (1954/2003)
Prog. Accred.: Allied Health (medicine), Business (AACSB), Clinical Lab Scientist, Clinical Pastoral Education (ACPEI), Computer Science (ABET-CAC), Dietetics (didactic), Dietetics (internship), Engineering (aerospace, agricultural, bioengineering, chemical, civil, computer, electrical, materials, mechanical), Landscape Architecture, Law, Physician Assistant, Psychology Internship, Public Health, Veterinary Medicine

University of California, Hastings College of the Law
200 McAllister St., San Francisco 94102
Type: Public, state, four-year
System: University of California Office of the President
Degrees: P *Enroll:* 1,286
URL: http://www.uchastings.edu
Phone: (415) 565-4600 *Calendar:* Sem. plan
Inst. Accred.: ABA (1939/2002)
Prog. Accred.: Law

University of California, Irvine
501 Administration, Irvine 92697-1000
Type: Public, state, four-year
System: University of California Office of the President
Degrees: B, M, P, D *Enroll:* 23,723
URL: http://www.uci.edu
Phone: (949) 824-5011 *Calendar:* Qtr. plan
Inst. Accred.: WASC-SR. (1965/2001)
Prog. Accred.: Allied Health (medicine), Business (AACSB), Clinical Lab Scientist, Engineering (aerospace, chemical, civil, computer, electrical, environmental/sanitary, materials, mechanical), Planning, Psychology Internship

University of California, Los Angeles
405 Hilgard Ave., Los Angeles 90095-1405
Type: Public, state, four-year
System: University of California Office of the President
Degrees: B, M, P, D *Enroll:* 34,909
URL: http://www.ucla.edu
Phone: (310) 825-4321 *Calendar:* Qtr. plan
Inst. Accred.: WASC-SR. (1949/1998)
Prog. Accred.: Allied Health (EMT-paramedic, cytotechnology, health services administration, medicine), Applied Science (industrial hygiene), Business (AACSB), Clinical Pastoral Education (ACPEI), Clinical Psychology, Computer Science (ABET-CAC), Dentistry (advanced education in general dentistry, combined prosthodontics, dental public health, dentistry, endodontics, general dentistry, general practice residency, maxillofacial prosthetics, oral andmaxillofacial surgery, orthodontic and dentofacial orthopedics, pediatric dentistry, periodontics), Engineering (aerospace, chemical, civil, computer, electrical, materials, mechanical), Graduate Social Work, Law, Librarianship, Microbiology, Nursing Education, Planning, Psychology Internship, Public Health, Theatre

UCLA Extension
10995 Le Conte Ave., Los Angeles 90024-2883
Phone: (310) 825-9971
Prog. Accred: Interior Design

University of California, Riverside
900 University Ave., Riverside 92521-4009
Type: Public, state, four-year
System: University of California Office of the President
Degrees: B, M, P, D *Enroll:* 16,089
URL: http://www.ucr.edu
Phone: (951) 827-1012 *Calendar:* Qtr. plan
Inst. Accred.: WASC-SR. (1956/2008)
Prog. Accred.: Business (AACSB), Engineering (chemical, computer, electrical, environmental/sanitary, mechanical), School Psychology

University of California, San Diego
9500 Gilman Dr., La Jolla 92093-0005
Type: Public, state, four-year
System: University of California Office of the President
Degrees: B, M, P, D *Enroll:* 24,552
URL: http://www.ucsd.edu
Phone: (858) 534-2230 *Calendar:* Qtr. plan
Inst. Accred.: WASC-SR. (1964/2008)
Prog. Accred.: Allied Health (diagnostic medical sonography, medicine), Clinical Psychology, Engineering (aerospace, architectural, bioengineering, chemical, electrical, mechanical), Pharmacy, Psychology Internship

University of California, San Francisco
513 Parnassus Ave., San Francisco 94143
Type: Public, state, four-year
System: University of California Office of the President
Degrees: B, M, P, D *Enroll:* 2,863
URL: http://www.ucsf.edu
Phone: (415) 476-9000 *Calendar:* Qtr. plan
Inst. Accred.: WASC-SR. (1976/1999)
Prog. Accred.: Allied Health (medicine), Clinical Pastoral Education (ACPEI), Dentistry (advanced education in general dentistry, combined prosthodontics, dental hygiene, dental public health, dentistry, endodontics, general dentistry, general practice residency, oral and maxillofacial pathology, oral and maxillofacial surgery, orthodontic and dentofacial orthopedics, pediatric dentistry, periodontics), Dietetics (internship), Nurse (Midwifery), Nursing Education, Pharmacy, Physical Therapy, Psychology Internship

University of California, Santa Barbara
Santa Barbara 93106-2030
Type: Public, state, four-year
System: University of California Office of the President
Degrees: B, M, D *Enroll:* 20,570
URL: http://www.ucsb.edu
Phone: (805) 893-8000 *Calendar:* Qtr. plan
Inst. Accred.: WASC-SR. (1949/2001)
Prog. Accred.: Combined Professional-Scientific Psychology, Computer Science (ABET-CAC), Dance, Engineering (chemical, electrical, mechanical), Psychology Internship

University of California, Santa Cruz
1156 High St., Santa Cruz 95064
Type: Public, state, four-year
System: University of California Office of the President
Degrees: B, M, D *Enroll:* 14,669
URL: http://www.ucsc.edu
Phone: (831) 459-2058 *Calendar:* Qtr. plan
Inst. Accred.: WASC-SR. (1965/2005)
Prog. Accred.: Engineering (computer, electrical), Psychology Internship

University of East-West Medicine
970 West EL Camino Real, Sunnyvale 94087
Type: Private, proprietary, four-year
Degrees: M
URL: http://www.uewm.edu
Phone: (408) 733-1878 *Calendar:* Tri. plan
Inst. Accred.: ACAOM (2005)

University of La Verne
1950 Third St., La Verne 91750
Type: Private, independent, four-year
Degrees: A, B, M, P, D *Enroll:* 5,907
URL: http://www.ulv.edu
Phone: (909) 593-3511 *Calendar:* 4-1-4 plan
Inst. Accred.: WASC-SR. (1955/2000)
Prog. Accred.: Clinical Psychology, Law (ABA only), Public Administration

High Desert Campus
15447 Anacapa Rd., Ste. 100, Victorville 92392

Inland Empire Campus
10535 Foothill Blvd., Ste. 400, Ranch Cucamonga 91730
Phone: (909) 484-3858

Kern County Campus
1600 Truxton Ave., Ste. 100, Bakersfield 93301
Phone: (661) 328-1430

Orange County Campus
12951 Euclid St., Ste. 100, Garden Grove 92840-5214
Phone: (714) 534-4860

San Fernando Valley Campus
4001 W. Alameda Ave., Ste. 300, Burbank 91505-4338
Phone: (818) 846-4008

Ventura County Campus
2001 Solar Dr., Ste. 250, Oxnard 93030
Phone: (805) 981-8030

University of Philosophical Research
3910 Los Feliz Blvd., Los Angeles 90027-0299
Type: Private, proprietary, four-year
Degrees: M
URL: http://www.uprs.edu
Phone: (323) 663-2167
Inst. Accred.: DETC (2008)

University of Redlands
PO Box 3080, 1200 East Colton Ave., Redlands 92373-0999
Type: Private, independent, four-year
Degrees: B, M, P, D *Enroll:* 4,215
URL: http://www.redlands.edu
Phone: (909) 793-2121 *Calendar:* Sem. plan
Inst. Accred.: WASC-SR. (1949/2003)
Prog. Accred.: Allied Health (speech-language pathology), Music

University of San Diego
5998 Alcala Park, San Diego 92110-2492
Type: Private, Roman Catholic Church, four-year
Degrees: B, M, P, D *Enroll:* 6,763
URL: http://www.sandiego.edu
Phone: (619) 260-4600 *Calendar:* 4-1-4 plan
Inst. Accred.: WASC-SR. (1956/2001)
Prog. Accred.: Accounting, Business (AACSB), Engineering (electrical, industrial), Law, Marriage and Family Therapy, Nursing Education, Psychology Internship, Teacher Education (NCATE)

University of San Francisco
2130 Fulton St., San Francisco 94117-1080
Type: Private, Roman Catholic Church, four-year
Degrees: B, M, P, D *Enroll:* 7,891
URL: http://www.usfca.edu
Phone: (415) 422-6136 *Calendar:* Sem. plan
Inst. Accred.: WASC-SR. (1949/2008)
Prog. Accred.: Allied Health (surgical technology), Business (AACSB), Law, Nursing Education

University of Southern California
University Park, Los Angeles 90089-0012
Type: Private, independent, four-year
Degrees: B, M, P, D *Enroll:* 30,365
URL: http://www.usc.edu
Phone: (213) 740-2311 *Calendar:* Sem. plan
Inst. Accred.: WASC-SR. (1949/1998)
Prog. Accred.: Accounting, Acupuncture, Allied Health (health services administration, medicine, occupational therapy), Business (AACSB), Clinical Psychology, Computer Science (ABET-CAC), Counseling Psychology, Dentistry (advanced education in general dentistry, combined prosthodontics, dental hygiene, dentistry, endodontics, general dentistry, general practice residency, oral and maxillofacial surgery, orthodontic and dentofacial orthopedics, pediatric dentistry, periodontics), Dietetics (internship), Engineering (aerospace, chemical, civil, computer, electrical, environmental/sanitary, industrial, mechanical), Graduate Social Work, Journalism, Law, Music, Nurse Anesthesia Education, Pharmacy, Physical Therapy, Physician Assistant, Planning, Psychology Internship, Public Administration, Public Health, Radiography

University of the Pacific
3601 Pacific Ave., Stockton 95211
Type: Private, independent, four-year
Degrees: B, M, P, D *Enroll:* 5,772
URL: http://www.uop.edu
Phone: (209) 946-2344 *Calendar:* Sem. plan
Inst. Accred.: WASC-SR. (1949/2000)
Prog. Accred.: Allied Health (speech-language pathology), Art, Business (AACSB), Computer Science (ABET-CAC), Dentistry (dentistry, general dentistry, orthodontic and dentofacial orthopedics), Engineering (civil, computer, electrical, engineering management, engineering physics/science, mechanical), Law, Music, Pharmacy, Physical Therapy, Teacher Education (NCATE)

University of the West
1409 North Walnut Grove Ave., Rosemead 91770
Type: Private, independent, four-year
Degrees: B, M, D *FTE Enroll:* 200
URL: http://www.uwest.edu
Phone: (626) 571-8811 *Calendar:* Sem. plan
Inst. Accred.: WASC-SR. (2006)

Vanguard University of Southern California
55 Fair Dr., Costa Mesa 92626
Type: Private, Southern California District of the Assemblies of God, four-year
Degrees: B, M *Enroll:* 1,863
URL: http://www.vanguard.edu
Phone: (714) 556-3610 *Calendar:* 4-1-4 plan
Inst. Accred.: WASC-SR. (1964/1997)

Ventura College
4667 Telegraph Rd., Ventura 93003-3899
Type: Public, state/local, two-year
System: Ventura County Community College District
Degrees: A *Enroll:* 6,407
URL: http://www.vcccd.net
Phone: (805) 654-6400 *Calendar:* Sem. plan
Inst. Accred.: WASC-JR. (1952/2005)

Victor Valley College
18422 Bear Valley Rd., Victorville 92392-5849
Type: Public, state/local, two-year
System: Victor Valley Community College District
Degrees: A *Enroll:* 6,031
URL: http://www.vvc.edu
Phone: (760) 245-4271 *Calendar:* Sem. plan
Inst. Accred.: WASC-JR. (1963/2005, Warning)
Prog. Accred.: Allied Health (EMT-paramedic, respiratory therapy)

West Coast University
4021 Rosewood Ave., Los Angeles 90004-6818
Type: Private, proprietary, four-year
Degrees: A, B
URL: http://www.westcoastuniversity.edu
Phone: (877) 505-4928
Inst. Accred.: ACICS (2002/2005)

Orange County Campus
1477 South Manchester Ave., Anaheim 92802
Phone: (866) 479-4276

West Hills Community College
300 Cherry Ln., Coalinga 93210
Type: Public, state/local, two-year
System: West Hills Community College District
Degrees: A *Enroll:* 3,059
URL: http://www.westhillscollege.com
Phone: (559) 935-0801 *Calendar:* Sem. plan
Inst. Accred.: WASC-JR. (1952/2005)

West Hills Community College—Lemoore
555 College Ave., Lemoore 93425
Type: Public, state/local, two-year
System: West Hills Community College District
Degrees: A
URL: http://www.westhillscollege.com/lemoore
Phone: (559) 925-3000 *Calendar:* Sem. plan
Inst. Accred.: WASC-JR. (2006)

West Los Angeles College
9000 Overland Ave., Culver City 90230
Type: Public, state/local, two-year
System: Los Angeles Community College District
Degrees: A *Enroll:* 4,354
URL: http://www.wlac.edu
Phone: (310) 287-4200 *Calendar:* Sem. plan
Inst. Accred.: WASC-JR. (1971/2006)
Prog. Accred.: Dentistry (dental hygiene)

West Valley College
14000 Fruitvale Ave., Saratoga 95070-5698
Type: Public, state/local, two-year
System: West Valley-Mission College District
Degrees: A *Enroll:* 5,406
URL: http://www.westvalley.edu
Phone: (408) 867-2200 *Calendar:* Sem. plan
Inst. Accred.: WASC-JR. (1966/2008)
Prog. Accred.: Allied Health (medical assisting (AMA)), Interior Design

Western Career College
8909 Folsom Blvd., Sacramento 95826-9823
Type: Private, proprietary, two-year
System: U.S. Education Corporation
Degrees: A
URL: http://www.westerncollege.edu
Phone: (916) 361-1660 *Calendar:* Sem. plan
Inst. Accred.: WASC-JR. (2001/2008)
Prog. Accred.: Allied Health (medical assisting (AMA)), Veterinary Technology

Citrus Heights Campus
7301 Greenback Ln., Ste. A, Citrus Heights 95621
Phone: (916) 722-8200
Prog. Accred: Allied Health (medical assisting (AMA)), Veterinary Technology

Emeryville Campus
1400 65th St., Ste. 200, Emeryville 94608
Phone: (510) 601-0133
Prog. Accred: Allied Health (medical assisting (AMA))

Pleasant Hill Campus
380 Civic Dr., Ste. 300, Pleasant Hill 94523
Phone: (925) 609-6650
Prog. Accred: Allied Health (medical assisting (AMA)), Veterinary Technology

San Jose Campus
6201 San Ignacio Ave., San Jose 95119
Phone: (408) 360-0840
Prog. Accred: Allied Health (medical assisting (AMA)), Veterinary Technology

San Leandro Campus
15555 East 14th St., Ste. 500, San Leandro 94578
Phone: (510) 276-3888
Prog. Accred: Allied Health (medical assisting (AMA)), Veterinary Technology

Stockton Campus
1313 West Robinhood Dr., Ste. B, Stockton 95207
Phone: (209) 956-1240
Prog. Accred: Allied Health (medical assisting (AMA)), Veterinary Technology

Walnut Creek Campus
2157 Country Hills Rd., Antioch 94509
Phone: (925) 280-0235
Prog. Accred: Allied Health (medical assisting (AMA))

Western State University College of Law
1111 North State College Blvd., Fullerton 92831
Type: Private, proprietary, four-year
System: Argosy University
Degrees: D *Enroll:* 428
URL: http://www.wsulaw.edu
Phone: (714) 738-1000 *Calendar:* Sem. plan
Inst. Accred.: WASC-SR. (1976/2007)
Prog. Accred.: Law (ABA only)

Western University of Health Sciences
309 East Second St., College Plaza, Pomona 91766-1889
Type: Private, independent, four-year
Degrees: M, P *Enroll:* 1,872
URL: http://www.westernu.edu
Phone: (909) 623-6116 *Calendar:* Sem. plan
Inst. Accred.: WASC-SR. (1996/2008)
Prog. Accred.: Nursing Education, Osteopathy, Pharmacy, Physical Therapy, Physician Assistant, Veterinary Medicine

Westminster Theological Seminary in California
1725 Bear Valley Pkwy., Escondido 92027-4128
Type: Private, nondenominational, four-year
Degrees: M, P, D *Enroll:* 105
URL: http://www.wscal.edu
Phone: (760) 480-8474 *Calendar:* 4-1-4 plan
Inst. Accred.: ATS (1997/2002), WASC-SR. (1984/2002)

Westmont College
955 La Paz Rd., Santa Barbara 93108-1089
Type: Private, independent, four-year
Degrees: B *Enroll:* 1,366
URL: http://www.westmont.edu
Phone: (805) 565-6000 *Calendar:* Sem. plan
Inst. Accred.: WASC-SR. (1957/2007)

Westwood College—Los Angeles
3250 Wilshire Blvd., Ste. 400, Los Angeles 90010
Type: Private, proprietary, four-year
System: Westwood College
Degrees: A, B *Enroll:* 944
URL: http://www.westwood.edu
Phone: (213) 739-9999
Inst. Accred.: ACICS (1991/2007), NCA-HLC (2007)

Chicago Loop Campus
17 North State St., 3rd Flr., Chicago, IL 60602
Phone: (312) 739-0850

River Oaks Campus
80 River Oaks Ctr., Ste. D-49, Calumet City, IL 60409
Phone: (708) 832-1988
Prog. Accred: Allied Health (medical assisting (AMA))

Westwood College—South Bay
19700 South Vermont Ave., Ste. 100, Torrance 90502
Type: Private, proprietary, four-year
System: Westwood College
Degrees: A, B
URL: http://www.westwood.edu
Phone: (310) 965-0888
Inst. Accred.: ACCSCT (1973/2008), NCA-HLC (2007, *Indirect accreditation through Westwood College, Denver, CO*)

Whittier College
13406 East Philadelphia St., PO Box 634, Whittier 90608
Type: Private, independent, four-year
Degrees: B, M, P, D *Enroll:* 2,047
URL: http://www.whittier.edu
Phone: (562) 907-4200 *Calendar:* 4-1-4 plan
Inst. Accred.: WASC-SR. (1949/2002, Probation)
Prog. Accred.: Law, Social Work

William Howard Taft University
3700 South Susan St., Office 200, Santa Ana 92704
Type: Private, independent, four-year
System: Taft University System, Inc.
Degrees: B, M, P *FTE Enroll:* 289
URL: http://www.taftu.edu
Phone: (714) 850-4800
Inst. Accred.: DETC (2003/2008)

William Jessup University
333 Sunset Blvd., Rocklin 95765
Type: Private, independent, four-year
Degrees: A, B *Enroll:* 444
URL: http://www.jessup.edu
Phone: (916) 577-2200 *Calendar:* Sem. plan
Inst. Accred.: ABHE (1969/2000), WASC-SR. (2002/2008)

Woodbury University
7500 Glenoaks Blvd., Burbank 91510-7846
Type: Private, independent, four-year
Degrees: B, M *Enroll:* 1,239
URL: http://www.woodbury.edu
Phone: (818) 767-0888 *Calendar:* Sem. plan
Inst. Accred.: WASC-SR. (1961/2008)
Prog. Accred.: Business (ACBSP), Interior Architecture

Woodland Community College
2300 East Gibson Rd., Woodland 95776
Type: Public, state/local, two-year
System: Yuba Community College District
Degrees: A
URL: http://www.yccd.edu/woodland
Phone: (530) 661-5700 *Calendar:* Sem. plan
Inst. Accred.: WASC-JR. (2008)

World Mission University
500 Shatto Place, Ste. 600, Los Angeles 90020
Type: Private, independent, four-year
Degrees: B, M, P
URL: http://www.wmu.edu
Phone: (213) 385-2322 *Calendar:* Sem. plan
Inst. Accred.: ABHE (2006), TRACS (2006)

The Wright Institute
2728 Durant Ave., Berkeley 94702
Type: Private, independent, four-year
Degrees: M, P *Enroll:* 323
URL: http://www.wrightinst.edu
Phone: (510) 841-9230 *Calendar:* Qtr. plan
Inst. Accred.: WASC-SR. (1977/2004)
Prog. Accred.: Clinical Psychology

WyoTech—Fremont
200 Whitney Place, Fremont 94539
Type: Private, proprietary, two-year
System: Corinthian Colleges, Inc
Degrees: A *Enroll:* 1,704
URL: http://www.wyotech.com
Phone: (510) 490-6900
Inst. Accred.: ACCSCT (1977/2005)

Oakland Campus
9636 Earhart Rd., Oakland International Airport, Oakland 94621
Phone: (510) 569-8436

WyoTech—Long Beach
2161 Technology Place, Long Beach 90810
Type: Private, proprietary, two-year
System: Corinthian Colleges, Inc
Degrees: A
URL: http://www.wyotech.edu/campus/long_beach
Phone: (562) 624-9530
Inst. Accred.: ACCSCT (1975/2004)

WyoTech—Sacramento
980 Riverside Pkwy., West Sacramento 95605
Type: Private, proprietary, two-year
System: Corinthian Colleges, Inc
Degrees: A
URL: http://www.wyotech.com
Phone: (916) 376-8888
Inst. Accred.: ACCSCT (2004/2006)

Yeshiva Ohr Elchonon-Chabad/West Coast Talmudic Seminary
7215 Waring Ave., Los Angeles 90046
Type: Private, independent, four-year
Degrees: B *Enroll:* 119
Phone: (323) 937-3763 *Calendar:* Sem. plan
Inst. Accred.: AARTS (1983/2000)

Yo San University of Traditional Chinese Medicine
13315 West Washington Blvd., Los Angeles 90066-5162
Type: Private, independent, four-year
Degrees: M *Enroll:* 98
URL: http://www.yosan.edu
Phone: (310) 577-3000 *Calendar:* Tri. plan
Inst. Accred.: ACAOM (1993/2006)

Yuba College
2088 North Beale Rd., Marysville 95901-7699
Type: Public, state/local, two-year
System: Yuba Community College District
Degrees: A *Enroll:* 5,347
URL: http://www.yccd.edu/yuba
Phone: (530) 741-6700 *Calendar:* Sem. plan
Inst. Accred.: WASC-JR. (1952/2006)
Prog. Accred.: Radiography, Veterinary Technology

COLORADO

Adams State College
208 Edgemont Blvd., Alamosa 81102-0001
Type: Public, state, four-year
System: Colorado Commission on Higher Education
Degrees: A, B, M *Enroll:* 4,686
URL: http://www2.adams.edu
Phone: (719) 589-7011 *Calendar:* Sem. plan
Inst. Accred.: NCA-HLC (1950/2007)
Prog. Accred.: Counseling, Music, Nursing Education, Teacher Education (TEAC)

Aims Community College
5401 West 20th St., PO Box 69, Greeley 80632
Type: Public, state/local, two-year
Degrees: A *Enroll:* 2,678
URL: http://www.aims.edu
Phone: (970) 330-8000 *Calendar:* Qtr. plan
Inst. Accred.: NCA-HLC (1977/1999)
Prog. Accred.: Allied Health (surgical technology), Radiography

Fort Lupton Campus
260 College Ave., Fort Lupton 80621
Phone: (303) 857-4022

Loveland Campus
104 East Fourth St., Loveland 80637
Phone: (970) 667-4611

American Sentinel University
385 Inverness Pkwy., Ste. 310, Englewood 80112
Type: Private, independent, four-year
Degrees: A, B, M
URL: http://www.americansentinel.edu
Phone: (303) 991-1575 *Calendar:* Sem. plan
Inst. Accred.: DETC (2005)

Anthem College
350 Blackhawk St., Aurora 80011
Type: Private, proprietary, two-year
System: High-Tech Institute
Degrees: A
URL: http://www.anthem.edu
Phone: (720) 859-7900
Inst. Accred.: ACCSCT (1997/2004)
Prog. Accred.: Medical Assisting (ABHES), Surgical Technology

Seattle Campus
14432 SE Eastgate Way, Ste. 100, Bellevue, WA 98007
Phone: (425) 747-3433

Arapahoe Community College
5900 South Santa Fe Dr., PO Box 9002, Littleton 80160-9002
Type: Public, state, two-year
System: Colorado Community College System
Degrees: A *Enroll:* 3,855
URL: http://www.arapahoe.edu
Phone: (303) 794-1550 *Calendar:* Sem. plan
Inst. Accred.: NCA-HLC (1970/2007)
Prog. Accred.: Allied Health (medical assisting (AMA)), Clinical Lab Technology, Funeral Service Education (Mortuary Science), Physical Therapy Assisting

Argosy University Denver
1200 Lincoln St., Denver 80203
Type: Private, proprietary, four-year
System: Argosy University
Degrees: A, B, M, D
URL: http://www.argosyu.edu/denver
Phone: (303) 248-2700 *Calendar:* Sem. plan
Inst. Accred.: NCA-HLC (1981/2008, *Indirect accreditation through Argosy University, Chicago, IL*)

The Art Institute of Colorado
1200 Lincoln St., Denver 80203-2983
Type: Private, proprietary, four-year
System: Education Management Corporation
Degrees: A, B *Enroll:* 2,431
URL: http://www.aic.aii.edu
Phone: (303) 837-0825 *Calendar:* Qtr. plan
Inst. Accred.: NCA-HLC (2008)
Prog. Accred.: Culinary Education, Interior Design

Aspen University
501 South Cherry St., Ste. 350, Denver 80246-1326
Type: Private, proprietary, four-year
Degrees: B, M *FTE Enroll:* 600
URL: http://www.aspen.edu
Phone: (303) 333-4224
Inst. Accred.: DETC (1993/2003)
Prog. Accred.: Nursing Education

Bel-Rea Institute of Animal Technology
1681 South Dayton St., Denver 80231-3048
Type: Private, independent, two-year
Degrees: A *Enroll:* 670
URL: http://www.bel-rea.com
Phone: (303) 751-8700 *Calendar:* Qtr. plan
Inst. Accred.: ACCSCT (1975/2003)
Prog. Accred.: Veterinary Technology

Boulder College of Massage Therapy
6255 Longbow Dr., Boulder 80301
Type: Private, proprietary, two-year
Degrees: A
URL: http://www.bcmt.org
Phone: (303) 530-2100
Inst. Accred.: ACCSCT (1990/2006)

College for Financial Planning
8000 E. Maplewood Ave., Ste. 200, Greenwood Village 80111
Type: Private, proprietary, four-year
System: Apollo Group, Inc.
Degrees: M *FTE Enroll:* 5,975
URL: http://www.cffp.edu
Phone: (303) 220-1200
Inst. Accred.: NCA-HLC (1994/2004)

CollegeAmerica—Colorado Springs
3645 Citadel Dr. South, Colorado Springs 80909
Type: Private, proprietary, four-year
Degrees: A, B
URL: http://www.collegeamerica.edu
Phone: (719) 637-0600
Inst. Accred.: ACCSCT (2002/2004)

CollegeAmerica—Denver
1385 S. Colorado Blvd., Ste. A-512, Denver 80222-1912
Type: Private, proprietary, four-year
Degrees: A, B
URL: http://www.collegeamerica.com
Phone: (303) 691-9756
Inst. Accred.: ACCSCT (1984/2004)

CollegeAmerica—Fort Collins
4601 South Mason St., Fort Collins 80525
Type: Private, proprietary, four-year
Degrees: A, B
URL: http://www.collegeamerica.com
Phone: (970) 223-6060
Inst. Accred.: ACCSCT (2001/2003)

Colorado Christian University
8787 West Alameda Ave., Lakewood 80226
Type: Private, independent, four-year
Degrees: A, B, M *Enroll:* 1,625
URL: http://www.ccu.edu
Phone: (303) 963-3000 *Calendar:* Sem. plan
Inst. Accred.: NCA-HLC (1981/2001)

Colorado College
14 East Cache la Pourde St., Colorado Springs 80903
Type: Private, independent, four-year
Degrees: B, M *Enroll:* 1,984
URL: http://www.coloradocollege.edu
Phone: (719) 389-7000 *Calendar:* Sem. plan
Inst. Accred.: NCA-HLC (1915/2008)

Colorado Mountain College
831 Grand Ave., Glenwood Springs 81602
Type: Public, state/local, two-year
Degrees: A *Enroll:* 2,873
URL: http://www.coloradomtn.edu
Phone: (970) 945-7486 *Calendar:* Sem. plan
Inst. Accred.: NCA-HLC (1974/2008)
Prog. Accred.: Veterinary Technology

Alpine Campus
1370 Bob Adams Dr., Steamboat Springs 80477
Phone: (970) 870-4444

Aspen Campus
255 Sage Way, Aspen 81611
Phone: (970) 925-77400

Rifle Campus
703 Railroad Ave., Rifle 81650
Phone: (970) 625-1871

Roaring Fork Campus
3000 County Rd. 114, Glenwood Springs 81601
Phone: (303) 945-7841

Timberline Campus
901 South Hwy. 24, Leadville 80461
Phone: (719) 486-2015

Vail-Eagle Valley Campus
150 Miller Ranch Rd., Edwards 81632
Phone: (970) 569-2900
Prog. Accred: Allied Health (EMT-paramedic)

Colorado Northwestern Community College
500 Kennedy Dr., Rangely 81648
Type: Public, state/local, two-year
System: Colorado Community College System
Degrees: A *Enroll:* 815
URL: http://www.cncc.edu
Phone: (970) 562-1105 *Calendar:* Sem. plan
Inst. Accred.: NCA-HLC (1976/2003)
Prog. Accred.: Dentistry (dental hygiene)

Craig Campus
50 College Dr., Craig 81625
Phone: (970) 824-7071

Colorado School of Healing Arts
7655 West Mississippi, Ste. 100, Lakewood 80226
Type: Private, proprietary, two-year
Degrees: A
URL: http://www.csha.net
Phone: (303) 986-2320
Inst. Accred.: ACCSCT (1998/2003)

Colorado School of Mines
1500 Illinois St., Golden 80401
Type: Public, state, four-year
System: Colorado Commission on Higher Education
Degrees: B, M, P, D *Enroll:* 3,762
URL: http://www.mines.edu
Phone: (303) 273-3280 *Calendar:* Sem. plan
Inst. Accred.: NCA-HLC (1929/2003)
Prog. Accred.: Engineering (chemical, engineering physics/science, general, geological/geophysical, metallurgical, mining, petroleum)

Colorado School of Trades
1575 Hoyt St., Lakewood 80215-2996
Type: Private, proprietary, two-year
Degrees: A *Enroll:* 125
URL: http://www.gunsmithing.com
Phone: (303) 233-4697
Inst. Accred.: ACCSCT (1973/2006)

Colorado School of Traditional Chinese Medicine
1441 York St., Ste. 202, Denver 80206-2127
Type: Private, independent, four-year
Degrees: M
URL: http://www.traditionalhealing.net
Phone: (303) 329-6355 *Calendar:* Sem. plan
Inst. Accred.: ACAOM (2002)

Colorado State University
Fort Collins 80523
Type: Public, state, four-year
System: Colorado Commission on Higher Education
Degrees: B, M, D *Enroll:* 24,031
URL: http://www.colostate.edu
Phone: (970) 491-1101 *Calendar:* Sem. plan
Inst. Accred.: NCA-HLC (1925/2004)
Prog. Accred.: Allied Health (occupational therapy), Applied Science (occupational health & safety), Business (AACSB), Construction Education, Counseling, Counseling Psychology, Dietetics (coordinated), Dietetics (didactic), Engineering (agricultural, chemical, civil, electrical, engineering physics/science, environmental/sanitary, mechanical), Environmental Health, Forestry, Graduate Social Work, Interior Design, Journalism, Landscape Architecture, Marriage and Family Therapy, Music, Psychology Internship, Social Work, Teacher Education (NCATE), Veterinary Medicine

Colorado State University—Pueblo
2200 Bonforte Blvd., Pueblo 81001-4901
Type: Public, state, four-year
System: Colorado Commission on Higher Education
Degrees: B, M *Enroll:* 4,356
URL: http://www.colostate-pueblo.edu
Phone: (719) 549-2100 *Calendar:* Sem. plan
Inst. Accred.: NCA-HLC (1951/2007)
Prog. Accred.: Business (AACSB), Engineering (industrial), Engineering Technology (civil/construction), Music, Nursing, Social Work, Teacher Education (TEAC)

Colorado Technical University
4435 North Chestnut St., Colorado Springs 80907
Type: Private, proprietary, four-year
System: Career Education Corporation
Degrees: A, B, M, D *Enroll:* 1,326
URL: http://www.coloradotech.edu
Phone: (719) 598-0200 *Calendar:* Qtr. plan
Inst. Accred.: NCA-HLC (1980/2002)
Prog. Accred.: Business (ACBSP), Engineering (computer, electrical)

Denver North Campus
1865 West 121st Ave., Building C, Ste. 100, Westminster 80234
Phone: (303) 362-2900

Denver South Campus
5775 Denver Tech Center Blvd., Greenwood Village 80111-3201
Phone: (303) 362-2901

North Kansas City Campus
520 East 19th Ave., North Kansas City, MO 64116
Phone: (816) 472-7400
Prog. Accred: Allied Health (surgical technology), Medical Assisting (ABHES), Radiography

Pueblo Campus
1025 West Sixth St., Pueblo 81003
Phone: (719) 595-0200

Sioux Falls Campus
3901 West 59th St., Sioux Falls, SD 57108
Phone: (605) 361-0200
Prog. Accred: Allied Health (medical assisting (AMA))

Community College of Aurora
16000 East Centretech Pkwy., Aurora 80011
Type: Public, state, two-year
System: Colorado Community College System
Degrees: A *Enroll:* 2,777
URL: http://www.ccaurora.edu
Phone: (303) 360-4700 *Calendar:* Sem. plan
Inst. Accred.: NCA-HLC (1988/2003)
Prog. Accred.: Allied Health (EMT-paramedic)

Community College of Denver
1111 West Colfax Ave., PO Box 173363, Denver 80217-3363
Type: Public, state, two-year
System: Colorado Community College System
Degrees: A *Enroll:* 4,347
URL: http://www.ccd.edu
Phone: (303) 556-2600 *Calendar:* Tri. plan
Inst. Accred.: NCA-HLC (1975/2004)
Prog. Accred.: Allied Health (medical assisting (AMA)), Dentistry (dental hygiene), Radiation Therapy, Veterinary Technology

East Campus
3240 Humboldt St., Denver 80205
Phone: (303) 293-8737

Lowry Campus
1070 Alton Way, Building 849, Denver 80230
Phone: (303) 365-8300
Prog. Accred: Radiography

Concorde Career College
111 North Havana St., Aurora 80010
Type: Private, proprietary, two-year
System: Concorde Career Colleges, Inc.
Degrees: A
URL: http://www.concordecareercolleges.com
Phone: (303) 861-1151
Inst. Accred.: ACCSCT (1969/2006)
Prog. Accred.: Allied Health (surgical technology), Radiography

Denver Academy of Court Reporting
9051 Harlan St., Unit #20, Westminster 80031
Type: Private, proprietary, two-year
System: Stenograph, LLC
Degrees: A *Enroll:* 246
URL: http://www.dacr.org
Phone: (303) 427-5292
Inst. Accred.: ACICS (1982/2003)

Denver Seminary
PO Box 100000, Denver 80250-0100
Type: Private, Conservative Baptist Church of America (CBA), four-year
Degrees: M, D *Enroll:* 641
URL: http://www.denverseminary.edu
Phone: (303) 761-2482 *Calendar:* Qtr. plan
Inst. Accred.: ATS (1970/2002), NCA-HLC (1972/2002)
Prog. Accred.: Counseling

DeVry University Westminster
1870 West 122nd Ave., Westmintser 80234-2010
Type: Private, proprietary, four-year
System: DeVry University
Degrees: A, B, M
URL: http://www.devry.edu/westminster
Phone: (303) 280-7400 *Calendar:* Sem. plan
Inst. Accred.: NCA-HLC (2002, *Indirect accreditation through DeVry University, Oakbrook Terrace, IL*)
Prog. Accred.: Engineering Technology (computer, electrical)

Colorado Springs Campus
225 South Union Blvd., Colorado Springs 80910-3138
Phone: (719) 632-5305

Denver South Campus
6312 South Fiddlers Green Circle, Ste. 105E, Greenwood Village 80111
Phone: (303) 329-3000

Sandy Campus
9350 South 150 East, Ste. 420, Sandy, UT 84070
Phone: (801) 565-5110

Everest College—Colorado Springs
1815 Jet Wing Dr., Colorado Springs 80916
Type: Private, proprietary, two-year
System: Corinthian Colleges, Inc
Degrees: A *Enroll:* 300
URL: http://www.everest.edu
Phone: (719) 638-6580 *Calendar:* Qtr. plan
Inst. Accred.: ACICS (1953/2006)
Prog. Accred.: Allied Health (medical assisting (AMA))

Everest College—Thornton
9065 Grant St., Thornton 80229
Type: Private, proprietary, two-year
System: Corinthian Colleges, Inc
Degrees: A *Enroll:* 709
URL: http://www.everest.edu
Phone: (303) 457-2757 *Calendar:* Qtr. plan
Inst. Accred.: ACICS (1962/2008)
Prog. Accred.: Allied Health (medical assisting (AMA), surgical technology)

Arlington Campus
801 North Quincy St., Ste. 500, Arlington, VA 22203
Phone: (703) 248-8887

Aurora Campus
14280 East Jewell Ave., Aurora 80012
Phone: (303) 745-6244
Prog. Accred: Allied Health (medical assisting (AMA))

Tysons Corner (McLean) Campus
1430 Spring Hill Rd., Ste. 200, McLean, VA 22102
Phone: (703) 288-3131

Fort Lewis College
1000 Rim Dr., Durango 81301-3999
Type: Public, state, four-year
System: Colorado Commission on Higher Education
Degrees: A, B *Enroll:* 3,774
URL: http://www.fortlewis.edu
Phone: (970) 247-7010 *Calendar:* Tri. plan
Inst. Accred.: NCA-HLC (1958/1996)
Prog. Accred.: Business (AACSB), Engineering (engineering physics/science), Music, Teacher Education (TEAC)

Front Range Community College
3645 West 112th Ave., Westminster 80031
Type: Public, state/local, two-year
System: Colorado Community College System
Degrees: A *Enroll:* 8,442
URL: http://www.frontrange.edu
Phone: (303) 466-8811 *Calendar:* Sem. plan
Inst. Accred.: NCA-HLC (1975/2008)
Prog. Accred.: Allied Health (medical assisting (AMA)), Dentistry (dental assisting), Veterinary Technology

Boulder County Campus
2190 Miller Dr., Longmont 80501
Phone: (303) 678-3722

Larimer Campus
4616 South Shields St., Fort Collins 80526
Phone: (970) 226-2500
Prog. Accred: Dentistry (dental assisting)

Westminster Campus
3645 West 112th Ave., Westminster 80031
Phone: (303) 404-5550

Heritage College
12 Lakeside Ln., Denver 80212-7413
Type: Private, proprietary, two-year
Degrees: A
URL: http://www.heritage-education.com
Phone: (303) 477-7240
Inst. Accred.: ACCSCT (1989/2003)

Kansas City Campus
534 East 99th St., Kansas City, MO 64131-4203
Phone: (816) 942-5474

Iliff School of Theology
2201 South University Blvd., Denver 80210
Type: Private, United Methodist Church, four-year
Degrees: M, D *Enroll:* 246
URL: http://www.iliff.edu
Phone: (303) 744-1287 *Calendar:* Qtr. plan
Inst. Accred.: ATS (1938/2008), NCA-HLC (1973/2008)

Institute of Business and Medical Careers
3842 South Mason St., Fort Collins 80525
Type: Private, proprietary, two-year
Degrees: A
URL: http://www.ibmc.edu
Phone: (970) 223-2669
Inst. Accred.: ACICS (1996/2005)

Cheyenne College
3425 Dell Range Blvd., Cheyenne, WY 82009
Phone: (307) 433-8363

Greeley College
5400 West 11th St., Ste. D, Greeley 80634
Phone: (970) 356-4733

Institute of Taoist Education and Acupuncture
608 Main St., Louisville 80027
Type: Public, proprietary, four-year
Degrees: M
URL: http://www.itea-school.com
Phone: (720) 890-8922 *Calendar:* Sem. plan
Inst. Accred.: ACAOM (2006)

Intellitec College—Colorado Springs
2315 E. Pikes Peak Ave., Colorado Springs 80909-6030
Type: Private, proprietary, two-year
Degrees: A *Enroll:* 515
URL: http://www.intelliteccollege.com
Phone: (719) 632-7626
Inst. Accred.: ACCSCT (1983/2005)

Intellitec College—Grand Junction
772 Horizon Dr., Grand Junction 81506
Type: Private, proprietary, two-year
Degrees: A *Enroll:* 486
URL: http://www.intelliteccollege.com
Phone: (970) 245-8101
Inst. Accred.: ACCSCT (1986/2007)

Pueblo Campus
3673 Parker Blvd., Ste. 250, Pueblo 81008
Phone: (719) 542-3181

Intellitec Medical Institute
2345 North Academy Blvd., Colorado Springs 80909
Type: Private, proprietary, two-year
Degrees: A
URL: http://www.intelliteccollege.com
Phone: (719) 596-7400
Inst. Accred.: ABHES (1983/2005)
Prog. Accred.: Medical Assisting (ABHES), Medical Laboratory Technology, Surgical Technology

ITT Technical Institute
500 East 84th Ave., Ste. B-12, Thornton 80229
Type: Private, proprietary, four-year
System: ITT Educational Services, Inc.
Degrees: A, B *Enroll:* 491
URL: http://www.itt-tech.edu
Phone: (303) 288-4488 *Calendar:* Qtr. plan
Inst. Accred.: ACICS (1999/2002)

Clive Campus
1860 NW 118th St., Ste. 110, Clive, IA 50325
Phone: (515) 327-5500

Little Rock Campus
4520 South University Ave., Little Rock, AR 72204
Phone: (501) 565-5550

Liverpool Area Campus
235 Greenfield Pkwy., Liverpool, NY 13088
Phone: (315) 461-8000

Jones International University
9697 East Mineral Ave., Centennial 80112
Type: Private, independent, four-year
Degrees: B, M *FTE Enroll:* 560
URL: http://www.jonesinternational.edu
Phone: (303) 784-8904
Inst. Accred.: NCA-HLC (1999/2001)

Kaplan College—Denver
500 East 84th Ave., Ste. W200, Denver 80229-5316
Type: Private, proprietary, two-year
System: Kaplan Higher Education Corporation
Degrees: A
URL: http://getinfo.kaplancollege.com
Phone: (303) 295-0550 *Calendar:* Qtr. plan
Inst. Accred.: ACCSCT (1979/2004)

Lamar Community College
2401 South Main St., Lamar 81052
Type: Public, state/local, two-year
System: Colorado Community College System
Degrees: A *Enroll:* 625
URL: http://www.lcc.cccoes.edu
Phone: (719) 336-2248 *Calendar:* Sem. plan
Inst. Accred.: NCA-HLC (1976/2000)

Lincoln College of Technology—Denver
460 South Lipan St., Denver 80223-9960
Type: Private, proprietary, two-year
System: Lincoln Educational Services Corporation
Degrees: A *Enroll:* 1,100
URL: http://www.lincolncollegeoftechnology.com
Phone: (303) 722-5724
Inst. Accred.: ACCSCT (1968/2006)

McKinley College
2001 Lowe St., Fort Collins 80525
Type: Private, proprietary, two-year
Degrees: A
URL: http://www.mckinleycollege.edu
Phone: (970) 207-4550 *Calendar:* Sem. plan
Inst. Accred.: DETC (2006)

Mesa State College
1100 North Ave., Ste. 301, Grand Junction 81501
Type: Public, state, four-year
System: Colorado Commission on Higher Education
Degrees: A, B, M *Enroll:* 5,149
URL: http://www.mesastate.edu
Phone: (970) 248-1498 *Calendar:* Sem. plan
Inst. Accred.: NCA-HLC (1957/2004)
Prog. Accred.: Nursing Education, Radiography, Teacher Education (NCATE)

Metropolitan State College of Denver
PO Box 173362, Denver 80217-3362
Type: Public, state, four-year
System: Colorado Commission on Higher Education
Degrees: B *Enroll:* 15,998
URL: http://www.mscd.edu
Phone: (303) 556-2400 *Calendar:* Sem. plan
Inst. Accred.: NCA-HLC (1971/2007)
Prog. Accred.: Applied Science (industrial management), Art, Computer Science (ABET-CAC), Engineering Technology (civil/construction, electrical, mechanical), Music, Nursing, Psychology Internship, Recreation and Leisure Services, Social Work, Teacher Education (NCATE)

Morgan Community College
920 Barlow Rd., Fort Morgan 80701
Type: Public, state, two-year
System: Colorado Community College System
Degrees: A *Enroll:* 858
URL: http://www.morgancc.edu
Phone: (970) 542-3100 *Calendar:* Sem. plan
Inst. Accred.: NCA-HLC (1980/2003)
Prog. Accred.: Physical Therapy Assisting

The Naropa University
2130 Arapahoe Ave., Boulder 80302-6697
Type: Private, independent, four-year
Degrees: B, M *Enroll:* 991
URL: http://www.naropa.edu
Phone: (303) 444-0202 *Calendar:* Sem. plan
Inst. Accred.: NCA-HLC (1986/2001)

National Theatre Conservatory
1050 13th St., Denver 80204
Type: Private, independent, four-year
Degrees: M *FTE Enroll:* 23
URL: http://www.dcpa.org/page.cfm?id=23842027
Phone: (303) 446-4855 *Calendar:* Sem. plan
Inst. Accred.: NCA-HLC (1992/2004)

Nazarene Bible College
1111 Academy Park Loop, Colorado Springs 80910-3704
Type: Private, Church of the Nazarene, four-year
Degrees: A, B *Enroll:* 319
URL: http://www.nbc.edu
Phone: (719) 884-5000 *Calendar:* Tri. plan
Inst. Accred.: ABHE (1976/2007), NCA-HLC (2006)

Emmanuel Bible College
1605 East Elizabeth St., Pasadena, CA 91104
Phone: (626) 791-2575

Northeastern Junior College
100 College Dr., Sterling 80751
Type: Public, state/local, two-year
System: Colorado Community College System
Degrees: A *Enroll:* 1,506
URL: http://www.njc.edu
Phone: (970) 522-6600 *Calendar:* Sem. plan
Inst. Accred.: NCA-HLC (1964/1999)

Otero Junior College
1802 Colorado Ave., La Junta 81050
Type: Public, state, two-year
System: Colorado Community College System
Degrees: A *Enroll:* 1,061
URL: http://www.ojc.edu
Phone: (719) 384-8721 *Calendar:* Sem. plan
Inst. Accred.: NCA-HLC (1967/2007)
Prog. Accred.: Nursing

Pikes Peak Community College
5675 South Academy Blvd., Colorado Springs 80906
Type: Public, state/local, two-year
System: Colorado Community College System
Degrees: A *Enroll:* 6,152
URL: http://www.ppcc.edu
Phone: (719) 502-2000 *Calendar:* Sem. plan
Inst. Accred.: NCA-HLC (1975/2004)
Prog. Accred.: Allied Health (EMT-paramedic), Culinary Education, Dentistry (dental assisting)

Platt College
3100 South Parker Rd., Ste. 200, Aurora 80014-3141
Type: Private, proprietary, four-year
Degrees: A, B *Enroll:* 92
URL: http://www.plattcolorado.edu
Phone: (303) 369-5151
Inst. Accred.: ACCSCT (1986/2007)

Pueblo Community College
900 West Orman Ave., Pueblo 81004
Type: Public, state/local, two-year
System: Colorado Community College System
Degrees: A *Enroll:* 3,173
URL: http://www.pueblocc.edu
Phone: (719) 549-3200 *Calendar:* Sem. plan
Inst. Accred.: NCA-HLC (1979/2001)
Prog. Accred.: Allied Health (EMT-paramedic, occupational therapy assisting, respiratory therapy), Culinary Education, Dentistry (dental assisting, dental hygiene), Nursing, Physical Therapy Assisting, Practical Nursing

Red Rocks Community College
13300 West Sixth Ave., Lakewood 80228
Type: Public, state, two-year
System: Colorado Community College System
Degrees: A *Enroll:* 3,654
URL: http://www.rrcc.edu
Phone: (303) 914-6600 *Calendar:* Sem. plan
Inst. Accred.: NCA-HLC (1975/2005)
Prog. Accred.: Allied Health (medical assisting (AMA)), Physician Assistant, Radiography

Redstone College—Denver
10851 West 120th Ave., Broomfield 80021-3401
Type: Private, proprietary, two-year
System: Westwood College
Degrees: A *Enroll:* 568
URL: http://www.redstone.edu
Phone: (303) 466-1714
Inst. Accred.: ACCSCT (1972/2005)

Regis University
3333 Regis Blvd., Denver 80221-1099
Type: Private, Roman Catholic Church, four-year
Degrees: B, M *Enroll:* 7,904
URL: http://www.regis.edu
Phone: (303) 458-4100
Inst. Accred.: NCA-HLC (1922/2008)
Prog. Accred.: Counseling, Nursing Education, Physical Therapy, Teacher Education (TEAC)

Boulder Campus
6235 Lookout Rd., Ste. H, Boulder 80301
Phone: (303) 458-4100

Remington College—Colorado Springs
6050 Erin Park Dr., Ste. 250, Colorado Springs 80918-3401
Type: Private, proprietary, four-year
Degrees: B
URL: http://www.remingtoncollege.edu
Phone: (719) 532-1234 *Calendar:* Qtr. plan
Inst. Accred.: ACICS (2006)

Rocky Mountain College of Art and Design
1600 Pierce St., Lakewood 80214
Type: Private, proprietary, four-year
Degrees: B *Enroll:* 398
URL: http://www.rmcad.edu
Phone: (800) 888-2787 *Calendar:* Tri. plan
Inst. Accred.: NCA-HLC (2000/2005)
Prog. Accred.: Art, Interior Design

Teikyo Loretto Heights University
3001 South Federal Blvd., Denver 80236
Type: Private, independent, four-year
Degrees: A, B, M *Enroll:* 159
URL: http://www.tlhu.edu
Phone: (303) 937-4200 *Calendar:* Sem. plan
Inst. Accred.: ACICS (1995/2008)

Trinidad State Junior College
600 Prospect St., Trinidad 81082
Type: Public, state, two-year
System: Colorado Community College System
Degrees: A *Enroll:* 1,185
URL: http://www.trinidadstate.edu
Phone: (719) 846-5011 *Calendar:* Sem. plan
Inst. Accred.: NCA-HLC (1962/2008)
Prog. Accred.: Applied Science (occupational health & safety)

United States Air Force Academy
HQ USAFA/CC, 2304 Cadet Dr., Ste. 342, USAF Academy 80840-5001
Type: Public, federal, four-year
Degrees: B *Enroll:* 4,463
URL: http://www.usafa.af.mil
Phone: (719) 333-3970 *Calendar:* Sem. plan
Inst. Accred.: NCA-HLC (1959/1999)
Prog. Accred.: Business (AACSB), Computer Science (ABET-CAC), Engineering (aerospace, civil, computer, electrical, engineering mechanics, environmental/sanitary, mechanical)

University of Colorado at Boulder
17 UCB, Boulder 80309
Type: Public, state, four-year
System: University of Colorado Central Administration
Degrees: B, M, D *Enroll:* 27,919
URL: http://www.colorado.edu
Phone: (303) 492-1411 *Calendar:* Sem. plan
Inst. Accred.: NCA-HLC (1913/2000)
Prog. Accred.: Allied Health (audiology, speech-language pathology), Business (AACSB), Clinical Psychology, Engineering (aerospace, architectural, chemical, civil, computer, electrical, environmental/sanitary, mechanical), English Language Education, Journalism, Law, Music, Psychology Internship, Teacher Education (NCATE)

University of Colorado at Colorado Springs
1420 Austin Bluffs Pkwy., PO Box 7150, Colorado Springs 80933-7150
Type: Public, state, four-year
System: University of Colorado Central Administration
Degrees: B, M, D *Enroll:* 6,821
URL: http://www.uccs.edu
Phone: (719) 262-3000 *Calendar:* Sem. plan
Inst. Accred.: NCA-HLC (1970/2007)
Prog. Accred.: Business (AACSB), Computer Science (ABET-CAC), Counseling, Dietetics (didactic), Engineering (computer, electrical, mechanical), Nursing Education, Public Administration, Teacher Education (NCATE)

University of Colorado Denver
PO Box 173364, Denver 80217-3364
Type: Public, state, four-year
System: University of Colorado Central Administration
Degrees: B, M, P, D *Enroll:* 13,164
URL: http://www.cudenver.edu
Phone: (303) 556-2400 *Calendar:* Sem. plan
Inst. Accred.: NCA-HLC (1970/2001)
Prog. Accred.: Accounting, Allied Health (diagnostic medical sonography, health services administration, medicine), Business (AACSB), Clinical Pastoral Education (ACPEI), Computer Science (ABET-CAC), Counseling, Dentistry (dental hygiene, dentistry, general practice residency, orthodontic and dentofacial orthopedics, periodontics), Engineering (civil, computer, electrical, mechanical), Landscape Architecture, Music, Nurse (Midwifery), Nursing, Nursing Education, Pharmacy, Physical Therapy, Physician Assistant, Planning, Psychology Internship, Public Administration, Public Health, Teacher Education (NCATE)

University of Denver
2199 South University Blvd., Denver 80208
Type: Private, United Methodist Church, four-year
Degrees: B, M, P, D *Enroll:* 8,655
URL: http://www.du.edu
Phone: (303) 871-2000 *Calendar:* Qtr. plan
Inst. Accred.: NCA-HLC (1914/2001)
Prog. Accred.: Accounting, Art, Business (AACSB), Clinical Psychology, Counseling Psychology, Engineering (computer, electrical, general, mechanical), English Language Education, Graduate Social Work, Law, Librarianship, Music, Psychology Internship

University of Northern Colorado
Carter 4000, Campus Box 59, Greeley 80639
Type: Public, state, four-year
System: Colorado Commission on Higher Education
Degrees: B, M, P, D *Enroll:* 11,955
URL: http://www.unco.edu
Phone: (970) 351-1890 *Calendar:* Sem. plan
Inst. Accred.: NCA-HLC (1916/2001)
Prog. Accred.: Accounting, Allied Health (audiology, speech-language pathology), Business (AACSB), Counseling, Counseling Psychology, Dietetics (didactic), Dietetics (internship), Music, Nursing Education, Public Health, Rehabilitation Counseling, School Psychology, Teacher Education (NCATE)

The University of the Rockies
555 East Pikes Peak Ave., Ste. 108, Colorado Springs 80903
Type: Private, proprietary, four-year
System: Bridgepoint Education, Inc.
Degrees: M, D
URL: http://www.rockies.edu
Phone: (877) 442-0505
Inst. Accred.: NCA-HLC (2003/2008)

Western State College of Colorado
210 Taylor Hall, College Heights, Gunnison 81231
Type: Public, state, four-year
System: Colorado Commission on Higher Education
Degrees: B *Enroll:* 2,128
URL: http://www.western.edu
Phone: (970) 943-2114 *Calendar:* Sem. plan
Inst. Accred.: NCA-HLC (1915/2003)
Prog. Accred.: Music, Teacher Education (TEAC)

Westwood College—Denver North
7350 North Broadway, Denver 80221-3653
Type: Private, proprietary, four-year
System: Westwood College
Degrees: A, B, M *Enroll:* 4,167
URL: http://www.westwood.edu
Phone: (303) 426-7000 *Calendar:* Qtr. plan
Inst. Accred.: ACCSCT (2006/2007), NCA-HLC (2007)
Prog. Accred.: Allied Health (medical assisting (AMA))

Anaheim Campus
1551 South Douglass Rd., Anaheim, CA 92806
Phone: (714) 704-2720

Dallas Campus
8390 LBJ Freeway, Executive Center I, Ste. 100, Dallas, TX 75243
Phone: (214) 570-0100
Prog. Accred: Allied Health (medical assisting (AMA))

Denver South Campus
3150 South Sheridan Blvd., Denver 80227-5548
Phone: (303) 934-2790

Houston South Campus
One Arena Place, 7322 Southwest Freeway, Houston, TX 77074
Phone: (713) 777-4433

Inland Empire Campus
20 West Seventh St., Upland, CA 91786-7148
Phone: (909) 931-7550

Yeshiva Toras Chaim Talmudical Seminary
1555 Stuart St., Denver 80204-1246
Type: Private, independent, four-year
Degrees: B, M *Enroll:* 15
Phone: (303) 629-8200 *Calendar:* Sem. plan
Inst. Accred.: AARTS (1979/2004)

Yorktown University
4340 East Kentucky Ave., Ste. 457, Denver 80246
Type: Private, proprietary, four-year
Degrees: M
URL: http://www.yorktownuniversity.com
Phone: (866) 675-0327 *Calendar:* 4-1-4 plan
Inst. Accred.: DETC (2008)

CONNECTICUT

Albertus Magnus College
700 Prospect St., New Haven 06511-1189
Type: Private, Roman Catholic Church, four-year
Degrees: A, B, M *Enroll:* 2,127
URL: http://www.albertus.edu
Phone: (203) 773-8550 *Calendar:* Sem. plan
Inst. Accred.: NEASC-CIHE (1932/2001)

Asnuntuck Community College
170 Elm St., Enfield 06082-3811
Type: Public, state, two-year
System: Board of Trustees of Connecticut Community-Technical Colleges
Degrees: A *Enroll:* 847
URL: http://www.acc.commnet.edu
Phone: (860) 253-3000 *Calendar:* Sem. plan
Inst. Accred.: NEASC-CIHE (1976/2005)

Bais Binyomin Academy
132 Prospect St., Stamford 06901
Type: Private, independent, four-year
Degrees: Talmudic *FTE Enroll:* 54
Phone: (203) 325-4351 *Calendar:* Tri. plan
Inst. Accred.: AARTS (1978/2003)

Berkeley Divinity School
363 St. Ronan St., New Haven 06511
Type: Private, Episcopal Church, four-year
Degrees: M
URL: http://www.yale.edu/berkeleydivinity
Phone: (203) 764-9300 *Calendar:* Sem. plan
Inst. Accred.: ATS (1954/2003)

Briarwood College
2279 Mount Vernon Rd., Southington 06489-1057
Type: Private, proprietary, four-year
System: Lincoln Educational Services Corporation
Degrees: A, B *Enroll:* 490
URL: http://www.briarwood.edu
Phone: (860) 628-4751 *Calendar:* Sem. plan
Inst. Accred.: NEASC-CIHE (2006)
Prog. Accred.: Allied Health (medical assisting (AMA), occupational therapy assisting), Dentistry (dental assisting, dental hygiene), Dietetic Technician, Funeral Service Education (Mortuary Science)

Capital Community College
950 Main St., Hartford 06103
Type: Public, state, two-year
System: Board of Trustees of Connecticut Community-Technical Colleges
Degrees: A *Enroll:* 1,815
URL: http://www.ccc.commnet.edu
Phone: (860) 906-5000 *Calendar:* Sem. plan
Inst. Accred.: NEASC-CIHE (1975/2006)
Prog. Accred.: Allied Health (EMT-paramedic, medical assisting (AMA)), Nursing, Physical Therapy Assisting, Radiography

Flatbush Campus
401 Flatbush Ave., Hartford 06106
Phone: (860) 527-4111

Central Connecticut State University
1615 Stanley St., New Britain 06050-4010
Type: Public, state, four-year
System: Connecticut State University System
Degrees: A, B, M, D *Enroll:* 9,639
URL: http://www.ccsu.edu
Phone: (860) 832-3200 *Calendar:* Sem. plan
Inst. Accred.: NEASC-CIHE (1947/1998)
Prog. Accred.: Computer Science (ABET-CAC), Construction Education, Engineering Technology (civil/construction, manufacturing, mechanical), Industrial Technology, Marriage and Family Therapy, Music, Nursing Education, Rehabilitation Counseling, Social Work, Teacher Education (NCATE)

Charter Oak State College
55 Paul J. Manafort Dr., New Britain 06053-2142
Type: Public, state, four-year
System: State of Connecticut Department of Higher Education
Degrees: A, B *Enroll:* 768
URL: http://www.cosc.edu
Phone: (860) 832-3800 *Calendar:* Sem. plan
Inst. Accred.: NEASC-CIHE (1981/2006)

Clemens College
1760 Mapleton Ave., Suffield 06078
Type: Private, proprietary, two-year
Degrees: A *Enroll:* 46
URL: http://www.clemenscollege.edu
Phone: (860) 668-3515
Inst. Accred.: NEASC-CIHE (2006)

Connecticut College
270 Mohegan Ave., New London 06320-4125
Type: Private, independent, four-year
Degrees: B, M *Enroll:* 1,847
URL: http://www.conncoll.edu
Phone: (860) 447-1911 *Calendar:* Sem. plan
Inst. Accred.: NEASC-CIHE (1932/2007)

Eastern Connecticut State University
83 Windham St., Willimantic 06226
Type: Public, state, four-year
System: Connecticut State University System
Degrees: A, B, M *Enroll:* 4,346
URL: http://www.easternct.edu
Phone: (860) 465-5000 *Calendar:* Sem. plan
Inst. Accred.: NEASC-CIHE (1958/2000)
Prog. Accred.: Social Work, Teacher Education (NCATE)

Fairfield University
1073 North Benson Rd., Fairfield 06824-5195
Type: Private, Society of Jesus, four-year
Degrees: B, M *Enroll:* 4,286
URL: http://www.fairfield.edu
Phone: (203) 254-4000 *Calendar:* Sem. plan
Inst. Accred.: NEASC-CIHE (1953/2007)
Prog. Accred.: Business (AACSB), Counseling, Engineering (computer, electrical, mechanical, software), Marriage and Family Therapy, Nursing Education

Gateway Community College
60 Sargent Dr., New Haven 06511-5970
Type: Public, state/local, two-year
System: Board of Trustees of Connecticut Community-Technical Colleges
Degrees: A *Enroll:* 3,128
URL: http://www.gwctc.commnet.edu
Phone: (203) 285-2000 *Calendar:* Sem. plan
Inst. Accred.: NEASC-CIHE (1981/2006)
Prog. Accred.: Dietetic Technician, Nuclear Medicine Technology, Radiation Therapy, Radiography

North Haven Campus
88 Bassett Rd., North Haven 06473
Phone: (203) 285-2000
Prog. Accred: Engineering Technology (electrical), Nuclear Medicine Technology, Radiography

Gibbs College
10 Norden Place, Norwalk 06855-1436
Type: Private, proprietary, two-year
System: Career Education Corporation
Degrees: A *Enroll:* 693
URL: http://www.gibbsnorwalk.com
Phone: (203) 838-4173 *Calendar:* Sem. plan
Inst. Accred.: ACICS (1975/2005)

Farmington Campus
The Exchange, 270 Farmington Ave., Ste. 183, Farmington 06032-1909
Phone: (860) 882-1690

Goodwin College
745 Burnside Ave., East Hartford 06108
Type: Private, independent, two-year
Degrees: A *Enroll:* 564
URL: http://www.goodwincollege.org
Phone: (860) 528-4111
Inst. Accred.: NEASC-CIHE (2004)
Prog. Accred.: Allied Health (medical assisting (AMA)), Medical Assisting (ABHES), Nursing

Goodwin Institute—Milford Campus
40 Commerce Park, Milford 06460
Phone: 203-877-9889

Hartford Seminary
77 Sherman St., Hartford 06105-2260
Type: Private, interdenominational, four-year
Degrees: M, D *Enroll:* 85
URL: http://www.hartsem.edu
Phone: (860) 509-9500 *Calendar:* Sem. plan
Inst. Accred.: ATS (1938/2003), NEASC-CIHE (1983/2003)

Holy Apostles College and Seminary
33 Prospect Hill Rd., Cromwell 06416
Type: Private, Roman Catholic Church, four-year
Degrees: A, B, M *Enroll:* 136
URL: http://www.holyapostles.edu
Phone: (860) 632-3000 *Calendar:* Sem. plan
Inst. Accred.: NEASC-CIHE (1979/2005)

Housatonic Community College
900 Lafeyette Blvd., Bridgeport 06604-4704
Type: Public, state, two-year
System: Board of Trustees of Connecticut Community-Technical Colleges
Degrees: A *Enroll:* 2,482
URL: http://www.hctc.commnet.edu
Phone: (203) 332-5000 *Calendar:* Sem. plan
Inst. Accred.: NEASC-CIHE (1972/2002)
Prog. Accred.: Allied Health (occupational therapy assisting), Clinical Lab Technology, Physical Therapy Assisting

Lyme Academy College of Fine Arts
84 Lyme St., Old Lyme 06371
Type: Private, independent, four-year
Degrees: B *Enroll:* 109
URL: http://www.lymeacademy.edu
Phone: (860) 434-5232 *Calendar:* Sem. plan
Inst. Accred.: NEASC-CIHE (2001)
Prog. Accred.: Art

Manchester Community College
PO Box 1046, Manchester 06045-1046
Type: Public, state, two-year
System: Board of Trustees of Connecticut Community-Technical Colleges
Degrees: A *Enroll:* 3,862
URL: http://www.mcc.commnet.edu
Phone: (860) 512-3000 *Calendar:* Sem. plan
Inst. Accred.: NEASC-CIHE (1971/2002)
Prog. Accred.: Allied Health (occupational therapy assisting, respiratory therapy, surgical technology), Clinical Lab Technology, Culinary Education, Physical Therapy Assisting

Middlesex Community College
100 Training Hill Rd., Middletown 06457
Type: Public, state, two-year
System: Board of Trustees of Connecticut Community-Technical Colleges
Degrees: A *Enroll:* 1,349
URL: http://www.mxctc.commnet.edu
Phone: (860) 343-5800 *Calendar:* Sem. plan
Inst. Accred.: NEASC-CIHE (1973/2002)
Prog. Accred.: Allied Health (ophthalmic lab technology), Radiography

Mitchell College
437 Pequot Ave., New London 06320
Type: Private, independent, four-year
Degrees: A, B *Enroll:* 677
URL: http://www.mitchell.edu
Phone: (860) 701-5000 *Calendar:* Sem. plan
Inst. Accred.: NEASC-CIHE (1956/2003)

Naugatuck Valley Community College
750 Chase Pkwy., Waterbury 06708-3089
Type: Public, state, two-year
System: Board of Trustees of Connecticut Community-Technical Colleges
Degrees: A *Enroll:* 3,371
URL: http://www.nvcc.commnet.edu
Phone: (203) 575-8040 *Calendar:* Sem. plan
Inst. Accred.: NEASC-CIHE (1973/2002)
Prog. Accred.: Allied Health (respiratory therapy), Engineering Technology (automated systems, electrical, mechanical), Nursing, Physical Therapy Assisting, Radiography

Northwestern Connecticut Community College
Park Place East, Winsted 06098-1798
Type: Public, state, two-year
System: Board of Trustees of Connecticut Community-Technical Colleges
Degrees: A *Enroll:* 877
URL: http://www.nwctc.commnet.edu
Phone: (860) 738-6300 *Calendar:* Sem. plan
Inst. Accred.: NEASC-CIHE (1971/2003)
Prog. Accred.: Allied Health (medical assisting (AMA)), Physical Therapy Assisting, Veterinary Technology

Norwalk Community College
188 Richards Ave., Norwalk 06854-1655
Type: Public, state, two-year
System: Board of Trustees of Connecticut Community-Technical Colleges
Degrees: A *Enroll:* 3,365
URL: http://www.ncc.commnet.edu
Phone: (203) 857-7000 *Calendar:* Sem. plan
Inst. Accred.: NEASC-CIHE (1973/2004)
Prog. Accred.: Allied Health (medical assisting (AMA)), Nursing

Paier College of Art
20 Gorham Ave., Hamden 06517-4025
Type: Private, proprietary, four-year
Degrees: A, B *Enroll:* 225
URL: http://www.paierart.com
Phone: (203) 287-3031 *Calendar:* Sem. plan
Inst. Accred.: ACCSCT (1970/2004)

Post University
800 Country Club Rd., Waterbury 06723-2540
Type: Private, independent, four-year
Degrees: A, B *Enroll:* 836
URL: http://www.post.edu
Phone: (203) 596-4500 *Calendar:* Sem. plan
Inst. Accred.: NEASC-CIHE (1972/2005)

Quinebaug Valley Community College
742 Upper Maple St., Danielson 06239-1440
Type: Public, state, two-year
System: Board of Trustees of Connecticut Community-Technical Colleges
Degrees: A *Enroll:* 1,003
URL: http://www.qvcc.commnet.edu
Phone: (860) 774-1160 *Calendar:* Sem. plan
Inst. Accred.: NEASC-CIHE (1978/2001)
Prog. Accred.: Allied Health (medical assisting (AMA))

Quinnipiac University
Mt. Carmel Ave., Hamden 06518-1908
Type: Private, independent, four-year
Degrees: A, B, M, P, Talmudic *Enroll:* 6,671
URL: http://www.quinnipiac.edu
Phone: (203) 582-8200 *Calendar:* Sem. plan
Inst. Accred.: NEASC-CIHE (1958/1999)
Prog. Accred.: Allied Health (occupational therapy, perfusion, respiratory therapy), Business (AACSB), Clinical Lab Scientist, Law, Nursing, Pathologists' Assistant, Physical Therapy, Physician Assistant, Radiography, Veterinary Technology

Sacred Heart University
5151 Park Ave., Fairfield 06432-1000
Type: Private, Roman Catholic Church, four-year
Degrees: A, B, M, D *Enroll:* 4,443
URL: http://www.sacredheart.edu
Phone: (203) 371-7999 *Calendar:* Sem. plan
Inst. Accred.: NEASC-CIHE (1969/2003)
Prog. Accred.: Allied Health (occupational therapy), Business (AACSB), Nursing Education, Physical Therapy, Social Work

Saint Joseph College
1678 Asylum Ave., West Hartford 06117-2791
Type: Private, independent, four-year
Degrees: B, M *Enroll:* 1,340
URL: http://www.sjc.edu
Phone: (860) 232-4571 *Calendar:* Sem. plan
Inst. Accred.: NEASC-CIHE (1938/2008)
Prog. Accred.: Dietetics (coordinated), Dietetics (didactic), Dietetics (internship), Marriage and Family Therapy, Nursing Education, Social Work

Saint Vincent's College
2800 Main St., Bridgeport 06606-4292
Type: Private, independent, two-year
Degrees: A *Enroll:* 211
URL: http://www.stvincentscollege.edu
Phone: (203) 576-5513 *Calendar:* Sem. plan
Inst. Accred.: NEASC-CIHE (2004)
Prog. Accred.: Allied Health (medical assisting (AMA)), Nursing, Radiography

Southern Connecticut State University
501 Crescent St., New Haven 06515-0901
Type: Public, state, four-year
System: Connecticut State University System
Degrees: A, B, M, D *Enroll:* 9,431
URL: http://www.southernct.edu
Phone: (203) 392-5200 *Calendar:* Sem. plan
Inst. Accred.: NEASC-CIHE (1952/2001)
Prog. Accred.: Allied Health (audiology, speech-language pathology), Computer Science (ABET-CAC), Counseling, Graduate Social Work, Librarianship, Marriage and Family Therapy, Nursing Education, Public Health, Social Work, Teacher Education (NCATE)

Three Rivers Community College
7 Mahan Dr., Norwich 06360-2479
Type: Public, state, two-year
System: Board of Trustees of Connecticut Community-Technical Colleges
Degrees: A *Enroll:* 2,008
URL: http://www.trcc.commnet.edu
Phone: (860) 886-0177 *Calendar:* Sem. plan
Inst. Accred.: NEASC-CIHE (1973/2002)
Prog. Accred.: Business (ACBSP), Engineering Technology (civil/construction, electrical, environmental/sanitary, manufacturing, mechanical, nuclear), Nursing

Thames Valley Campus
574 New London Turnpike, Norwich 06360
Phone: (203) 886-0177

Trinity College
300 Summit St., Hartford 06106-3100
Type: Private, independent, four-year
Degrees: B, M *Enroll:* 2,253
URL: http://www.trincoll.edu
Phone: (860) 297-2000 *Calendar:* Sem. plan
Inst. Accred.: NEASC-CIHE (1929/2006)
Prog. Accred.: Engineering (general)

Tunxis Community College
271 Scott Swamp Rd., Farmington 06032-3187
Type: Public, state, two-year
System: Board of Trustees of Connecticut Community-Technical Colleges
Degrees: A *Enroll:* 2,296
URL: http://www.tunxis.commnet.edu
Phone: (860) 677-7701 *Calendar:* Sem. plan
Inst. Accred.: NEASC-CIHE (1975/2001)
Prog. Accred.: Business (ACBSP), Dentistry (dental assisting, dental hygiene), Physical Therapy Assisting

United States Coast Guard Academy
15 Mohegan Ave., New London 06320-8100
Type: Public, federal, four-year
Degrees: B *Enroll:* 1,005
URL: http://www.cga.edu
Phone: (860) 444-8444 *Calendar:* Sem. plan
Inst. Accred.: NEASC-CIHE (1952/2000)
Prog. Accred.: Business (AACSB), Engineering (civil, electrical, mechanical, naval architecture/marine)

United States Coast Guard Academy
15 Mohegan Ave., New London 06320-8101
Type: Public, federal, four-year
Degrees: B *Enroll:* 1,005
URL: http://www.cga.edu
Phone: (860) 444-8444 *Calendar:* Sem. plan
Inst. Accred.: NEASC-CIHE (1952/2000)
Prog. Accred.: Business (AACSB), Engineering (civil, electrical, mechanical, naval architecture/marine)

University of Bridgeport
380 University Ave., Bridgeport 06601
Type: Private, independent, four-year
Degrees: A, B, M, D *Enroll:* 2,830
URL: http://www.bridgeport.edu
Phone: (203) 576-4000 *Calendar:* Sem. plan
Inst. Accred.: NEASC-CIHE (1951/2004)
Prog. Accred.: Acupuncture, Art, Business (ACBSP), Chiropractic Education, Computer Science (CSAB/CSAC), Dentistry (dental hygiene), Naturopathic Medicine

The University of Connecticut
Storrs 06269-2048
Type: Public, state, four-year
System: State of Connecticut Department of Higher Education
Degrees: B, M, P, D *Enroll:* 20,835
URL: http://www.uconn.edu
Phone: (860) 486-2000 *Calendar:* Sem. plan
Inst. Accred.: NEASC-CIHE (1931/2006)
Prog. Accred.: Accounting, Allied Health (audiology, speech-language pathology), Art, Business (AACSB), Clinical Psychology, Computer Science (ABET-CAC), Cytogenetic Technology, Dentistry (combined prosthodontics, endodontics, general dentistry, oral and maxillofacial surgery, orthodontic and dentofacial orthopedics, pediatric dentistry, periodontics), Dietetics (coordinated), Dietetics (didactic), Dietetics (internship), Engineering (chemical, civil, computer, electrical, mechanical), English Language Education, Graduate Social Work, Journalism, Landscape Architecture, Law, Marriage and Family Therapy, Music, Nursing Education, Pharmacy, Physical Therapy, Public Administration, Public Health, School Psychology, Teacher Education (NCATE), Theatre

Avery Point Regional Campus
1084 Shennecossett Rd., Groton 06340
Phone: (860) 405-9019

Hartford Regional Campus
85 Lawler Rd., West Hartford 06117
Phone: (860) 570-9214

Stamford Regional Campus
One University Place, Stamford 06901-2315
Phone: (203) 251-8400

Torrington Regional Campus
855 University Dr., Torrington 06790
Phone: (860) 626-6800

The University of Connecticut Health Center
263 Farmington Ave., Farmington 06030
Phone: (860) 679-2000
Prog. Accred: Allied Health (medicine), Clinical Pastoral Education (ACPEI), Dentistry (advanced education in general dentistry, combined prosthodontics, dentistry, endodontics, general dentistry, oral and maxillofacial radiology, oral and maxillofacial surgery, orthodontic and dentofacial orthopedics, pediatric dentistry, periodontics)

Waterbury Regional Campus
32 Hillside Ave., Waterbury 06710-2288
Phone: (203) 236-9800

University of Hartford
200 Bloomfield Ave., West Hartford 06117
Type: Private, independent, four-year
Degrees: A, B, M, D *Enroll:* 6,013
URL: http://www.hartford.edu
Phone: (860) 768-4100 *Calendar:* Sem. plan
Inst. Accred.: NEASC-CIHE (1961/2001)
Prog. Accred.: Allied Health (respiratory therapy), Art, Business (AACSB), Clinical Lab Scientist, Clinical Psychology, Dance, Engineering (bioengineering, civil, computer, electrical, mechanical), Engineering Technology (architectural, electrical, mechanical), Music, Nursing Education, Physical Therapy, Radiography, Teacher Education (NCATE)

University of New Haven
300 Boston Post Rd., West Haven 06516
Type: Private, independent, four-year
Degrees: A, B, M, D *Enroll:* 3,682
URL: http://www.newhaven.edu
Phone: (203) 932-7000 *Calendar:* Sem. plan
Inst. Accred.: NEASC-CIHE (1966/2000)
Prog. Accred.: Computer Science (ABET-CAC), Dentistry (dental hygiene), Dietetics (didactic), Engineering (chemical, civil, computer, electrical, industrial, mechanical)

Wesleyan University
237 High St., Middletown 06457
Type: Private, independent, four-year
Degrees: B, M, D *Enroll:* 3,043
URL: http://www.wesleyan.edu
Phone: (860) 685-2000 *Calendar:* Sem. plan
Inst. Accred.: NEASC-CIHE (1929/2002)

Western Connecticut State University
181 White St., Danbury 06810-9972
Type: Public, state, four-year
System: Connecticut State University System
Degrees: A, B, M, D *Enroll:* 4,801
URL: http://www.wcsu.edu
Phone: (203) 837-8200 *Calendar:* Sem. plan
Inst. Accred.: NEASC-CIHE (1954/2003)
Prog. Accred.: Counseling, Music, Nursing Education, Social Work

Yale University
105 Wall St., New Haven 06520-8229
Type: Private, independent, four-year
Degrees: B, M, D *Enroll:* 11,360
URL: http://www.yale.edu
Phone: (203) 432-4771 *Calendar:* Sem. plan
Inst. Accred.: NEASC-CIHE (1929/1999)
Prog. Accred.: Allied Health (health services administration, medicine), Business (AACSB), Clinical Psychology, Engineering (chemical, electrical, mechanical), Forestry, Law, Music, Nurse (Midwifery), Nursing Education, Physician Assistant, Psychology Internship, Public Health

Yale University Divinity School
409 Prospect St., New Haven 06511-2167
Type: Private, interdenominational, four-year
Degrees: M
URL: http://www.yale.edu/divinity/index.html
Phone: (203) 432-5303 *Calendar:* Sem. plan
Inst. Accred.: ATS (1938/2003)

DELAWARE

Delaware College of Art and Design
600 North Market St., Wilmington 19801
Type: Private, independent, two-year
Degrees: A *Enroll:* 165
URL: http://www.dcad.edu
Phone: (302) 622-8000 *Calendar:* Sem. plan
Inst. Accred.: MSA-CHE (2008)

Delaware State University
1200 North Dupont Hwy., Dover 19901
Type: Public, state, four-year
System: Delaware Higher Education Commission
Degrees: B, M, D *Enroll:* 3,329
URL: http://www.desu.edu
Phone: (302) 857-6060 *Calendar:* Sem. plan
Inst. Accred.: MSA-CHE (1945/2007)
Prog. Accred.: Business (AACSB), Dietetics (didactic), Graduate Social Work, Nursing, Nursing Education, Social Work, Teacher Education (NCATE)

Delaware Technical and Community College—Jack F. Owens Campus
PO Box 610, Georgetown 19947
Type: Public, state, two-year
System: Delaware Technical & Community College Office of the President
Degrees: A *Enroll:* 2,384
URL: http://www.dtcc.edu/owens
Phone: (302) 856-5400 *Calendar:* Sem. plan
Inst. Accred.: MSA-CHE (1972/2003)
Prog. Accred.: Allied Health (occupational therapy assisting, respiratory therapy), Business (ACBSP), Clinical Lab Technology, Nursing, Physical Therapy Assisting, Radiography, Veterinary Technology

Delaware Technical and Community College—Stanton/Wilmington Campus
400 Stanton Christiana Rd., Newark 19713
Type: Public, state, two-year
System: Delaware Technical & Community College Office of the President
Degrees: A *Enroll:* 4,347
URL: http://www.dtcc.edu/stanton-wilmington
Phone: (302) 454-3900 *Calendar:* Sem. plan
Inst. Accred.: MSA-CHE (1972/2003)
Prog. Accred.: Allied Health (diagnostic medical sonography, medical assisting (AMA), occupational therapy assisting, respiratory therapy), Business (ACBSP), Dentistry (dental hygiene), Engineering Technology (electrical, mechanical), Histologic Technology, Nursing, Physical Therapy Assisting, Radiography

Wilmington Campus
333 Shipley St., Wilmington 19801
Phone: (302) 571-5300
Prog. Accred: Nuclear Medicine Technology

Delaware Technical and Community College—Terry Campus
100 Campus Dr., Dover 19901
Type: Public, state, two-year
System: Delaware Technical & Community College Office of the President
Degrees: A *Enroll:* 1,444
URL: http://www.dtcc.edu/terry
Phone: (302) 857-1000 *Calendar:* Sem. plan
Inst. Accred.: MSA-CHE (1972/2003)
Prog. Accred.: Allied Health (EMT-paramedic), Business (ACBSP), Culinary Education, Nursing, Practical Nursing, Radiography

Goldey-Beacom College
4701 Limestone Rd., Wilmington 19809
Type: Private, independent, four-year
Degrees: A, B, M *Enroll:* 923
URL: http://www.gbc.edu
Phone: (302) 225-6248 *Calendar:* Sem. plan
Inst. Accred.: MSA-CHE (1976/2006)
Prog. Accred.: Business (ACBSP)

University of Delaware
104 Hullihen Hall, Newark 19716
Type: Public, state-related, four-year
System: Delaware Higher Education Commission
Degrees: A, B, M, D *Enroll:* 19,138
URL: http://www.udel.edu
Phone: (302) 831-2000 *Calendar:* 4-1-4 plan
Inst. Accred.: MSA-CHE (1921/2001)
Prog. Accred.: Accounting, Business (AACSB), Clinical Lab Scientist, Clinical Psychology, Dietetics (didactic), Dietetics (internship), Engineering (chemical, civil, computer, electrical, environmental/sanitary, mechanical), Engineering Technology (general), English Language Education, Music, Nursing, Nursing Education, Physical Therapy, Psychology Internship, Public Administration, Teacher Education (NCATE)

Wesley College
120 North State St., Dover 19901-3875
Type: Private, United Methodist Church, four-year
Degrees: A, B, M *Enroll:* 1,988
URL: http://www.wesley.edu
Phone: (302) 736-2300 *Calendar:* Sem. plan
Inst. Accred.: MSA-CHE (1950/2004)
Prog. Accred.: Nursing, Teacher Education (NCATE)

Wilmington University
320 Dupont Hwy., New Castle 19720
Type: Private, independent, four-year
Degrees: A, B, M, D *Enroll:* 5,158
URL: http://www.wilmu.edu
Phone: (302) 356-4636 *Calendar:* Tri. plan
Inst. Accred.: MSA-CHE (1975/2005)
Prog. Accred.: Counseling, Nursing, Nursing Education, Teacher Education (NCATE)

DISTRICT OF COLUMBIA

American University
4400 Massachusetts Ave. NW, Washington 20016
Type: Private, United Methodist Church, four-year
Degrees: A, B, M, P, D *Enroll:* 9,587
URL: http://www.american.edu
Phone: (202) 885-1000 *Calendar:* Sem. plan
Inst. Accred.: MSA-CHE (1928/2004)
Prog. Accred.: Business (AACSB), Clinical Psychology, Journalism, Law, Music, Psychology Internship, Public Administration, Teacher Education (NCATE)

The Catholic University of America
Cardinal Station, Washington 20064
Type: Private, Roman Catholic Church, four-year
Degrees: A, B, M, P, D *Enroll:* 4,994
URL: http://www.cua.edu
Phone: (202) 319-5000 *Calendar:* Sem. plan
Inst. Accred.: ATS (1980/2007), MSA-CHE (1921/2005)
Prog. Accred.: Clinical Psychology, Engineering (bioengineering, civil, electrical, mechanical), Graduate Social Work, Law, Librarianship, Music, Nursing Education, Social Work, Teacher Education (NCATE)

Corcoran College of Art and Design
500 17th St., NW, Washington 20006-4804
Type: Private, independent, four-year
Degrees: A, B, M *Enroll:* 498
URL: http://www.corcoran.edu
Phone: (202) 639-1800 *Calendar:* Sem. plan
Inst. Accred.: MSA-CHE (1985/2003)
Prog. Accred.: Art

Georgetown Campus
1801 35th St., NW, Washington 20006
Phone: (202) 298-2540

Dominican House of Studies
487 Michigan Ave. NE, Washington 20017
Type: Private, Roman Catholic Church, four-year
Degrees: M, P *Enroll:* 47
URL: http://www.dhs.edu
Phone: (202) 529-5300 *Calendar:* Sem. plan
Inst. Accred.: ATS (1976/2002), MSA-CHE (1976/2007)

Gallaudet University
800 Florida Ave., NE, Washington 20002
Type: Private, independent, four-year
Degrees: B, M, D *Enroll:* 1,542
URL: http://www.gallaudet.edu
Phone: (202) 651-5000 *Calendar:* Sem. plan
Inst. Accred.: MSA-CHE (1957/2008)
Prog. Accred.: Allied Health (audiology, speech-language pathology), Business (ACBSP), Clinical Psychology, Counseling, Graduate Social Work, Recreation and Leisure Services, Social Work, Teacher Education (NCATE)

The George Washington University
2121 I St., Washington 20052
Type: Private, independent, four-year
Degrees: A, B, M, P, D *Enroll:* 18,898
URL: http://www.gwu.edu
Phone: (202) 994-4949 *Calendar:* Sem. plan
Inst. Accred.: MSA-CHE (1922/2008)
Prog. Accred.: Accounting, Allied Health (EMT-paramedic, diagnostic medical sonography, health services administration, medicine, speech-language pathology), Business (AACSB), Clinical Lab Scientist, Clinical Psychology, Computer Science (ABET-CAC), Counseling, Engineering (civil, computer, electrical, mechanical), Law, Music, Nursing Education, Physical Therapy, Physician Assistant, Public Administration, Public Health, Rehabilitation Counseling, Teacher Education (NCATE)

Mount Vernon Campus
2100 Foxhall Rd., N.W., Washington 20007
Phone: (202) 625-0400
Prog. Accred: Interior Design

Georgetown University
37th and O St.s NW, Washington 20057
Type: Private, Roman Catholic Church, four-year
Degrees: B, M, P, D *Enroll:* 12,792
URL: http://www.georgetown.edu
Phone: (202) 687-0100 *Calendar:* Sem. plan
Inst. Accred.: MSA-CHE (1921/2007)
Prog. Accred.: Allied Health (medicine), Business (AACSB), Clinical Pastoral Education (ACPEI), English Language Education, Law, Nurse (Midwifery), Nurse Anesthesia Education, Nursing Education

School of Foreign Service in Qatar
PO Box 23689, Liberal Arts and Science (LAS) Bldg., Education City, Doha, Qatar
Phone: 011 974 492 7652

Howard University
2400 Sixth St. NW, Washington 20059
Type: Private, independent, four-year
Degrees: B, M, P, D *Enroll:* 10,268
URL: http://www.howard.edu
Phone: (202) 806-2500 *Calendar:* Sem. plan
Inst. Accred.: ATS (1940/2002), MSA-CHE (1921/2004)
Prog. Accred.: Accounting, Allied Health (audiology, medicine, occupational therapy, speech-language pathology), Art, Business (AACSB), Clinical Lab Scientist, Clinical Psychology, Computer Science (ABET-CAC), Counseling Psychology, Dentistry (advanced education in general dentistry, dental hygiene, dentistry, general dentistry, general practice residency, oral and maxillofacial surgery, orthodontic and dentofacial orthopedics, pediatric dentistry), Dietetics (coordinated), Engineering (chemical, civil, electrical, mechanical), Graduate Social Work, Journalism, Law, Music, Nursing Education, Pharmacy, Physical Therapy, Physician Assistant, Public Administration, Radiation Therapy, Teacher Education (NCATE), Theatre

Institute of World Politics
1521 16th St. NW, Washington 20036-1423
Type: Private, independent, four-year
Degrees: M *FTE Enroll:* 71
URL: http://www.iwp.edu
Phone: (202) 462 2101 *Calendar:* Sem. plan
Inst. Accred.: MSA-CHE (2006)

National Defense Intelligence College
Defense Intelligence Analysis Center, 200 MacDill Blvd., Washington 20340-5100
Type: Public, federal, four-year
Degrees: B, M, P *FTE Enroll:* 250
URL: http://www.ndic.edu
Phone: (202) 231-3344 *Calendar:* Qtr. plan
Inst. Accred.: MSA-CHE (1983/2008)

National Defense University
Fort Lesley J. McNair, 300 5th Ave. SW, Marshall Hall, Wasington 20319-5066
Type: Public, federal, four-year
Degrees: M *FTE Enroll:* 925
URL: http://www.ndu.edu
Phone: (202) 685-4700 *Calendar:* Sem. plan
Inst. Accred.: MSA-CHE (1997/2007)

Potomac College
4000 Chesapeake St. NW, Washington 20016
Type: Private, proprietary, four-year
Degrees: A, B *Enroll:* 153
URL: http://www.potomac.edu
Phone: (202) 686-0876 *Calendar:* Sem. plan
Inst. Accred.: MSA-CHE (2006)

Northern Virginia Campus
1029 Herndon Pkwy., Herndon, VA 20170
Phone: (703) 709-5875

Southeastern University
501 I St. SW, Washington 20024-2788
Type: Private, independent, four-year
Degrees: A, B, M *Enroll:* 557
URL: http://www.seu.edu
Phone: (202) 488-8162 *Calendar:* Qtr. plan
Inst. Accred.: MSA-CHE (1977/2006, Warning)

Strayer University
1133 15th St. NW, Ste. 200, Washington 20005
Type: Private, proprietary, four-year
Degrees: A, B, M *Enroll:* 14,437
URL: http://www.strayer.edu
Phone: (202) 419-0400 *Calendar:* Qtr. plan
Inst. Accred.: MSA-CHE (1981/2000)

Alexandria Campus
2730 Eisenhower Ave., Alexandria, VA 22314
Phone: (703) 329-9100

Anne Arundel Campus
1520 Jabez Run, Millersville, MD 21108
Phone: (410) 923-4500

Arlington Campus
2121 15th St. North, Arlington, VA 22201-2686
Phone: (703) 892-5100

Baymeadow Campus
8375 Dix Ellis Trail, Ste. 200, Jacksonville, FL 32256

Birmingham Campus
3570 Grandview Pkwy., Birmingham, AL 35243

Center City Campus
1601 Cherry St., Ste. 100, Philadelphia, PA 19102

Chamblee Campus
3355 Northeast Expressway, Ste. 100, Atlanta, GA 30341
Phone: (770) 454-9270

Charleston Campus
5010 Wetland Crossing, North Charleston, SC 29418

Cherry Hill Campus
2201 Route 38, Ste. 100, Cherry Hill, NJ 08002

Chesapeake Campus
700 Independence Pkwy., Ste. 400, Chesapeake, VA 23320
Phone: (757) 382-9900

Chesterfield Campus
2820 Waterford Lake Dr., Ste. 100, Midlothian, VA 23112
Phone: (804) 763-6300

Christiana Campus
240 Continental Dr., Newark, DE 19713

Cobb County Campus
3101 Towercreek Pkwy., Ste. 700, Atlanta, GA 30339
Phone: (770) 612-2170

Columbia, SC Campus
200 Center Circle, Ste. 300, Columbia, SC 29210

Coral Springs Campus
5830 Coral Ridge Dr., Ste. 300, Coral Springs, FL 33076

Cranberry Woods Campus
850 Cranberry Woods Dr., Ste. 2241, Cranberry Township, PA 16066

Delaware County Campus
760 West Sproul Rd., Ste. 200, Springfield, PA 19064
Phone: (610) 543-2500

Douglasville Campus
4655 Timber Ridge Dr., Douglasville, GA 30135
Phone: (678) 715-2200

Fredericksburg Campus
150 Riverside Pkwy., Ste. 100, Frederisckburg, VA 22406
Phone: (504) 785-8800

Ft. Lauderdale Campus
2307 West Broward Blvd., Ste. 100, Fort Lauderdale, FL 33312

Garner Campus
1812 Garner Station Blvd., Raleigh, NC 27603

Greensville Campus
4900 Koger Blvd., Ste. 400, Greensboro, NC 27407

Greenville Campus
555 North Pleasantburg Dr., Ste. 300, Greenville, SC 29607
Phone: (864) 232-4700

Henrico Campus
11501-D Nuckols Rd., Glen Allen, VA 23059
Phone: (804) 527-1000

Huntersville Campus
13620 Reese Blvd., Ste. 130, Huntersville, NC 28078

King of Prussia Campus
234 Mall Blvd., Ste. G50, King of Prussia, PA 19406
Phone: (610) 992-1700

Knoxville Campus
10118 Parkside Dr., Ste. 200, Knoxville, TN 37214

Lexington Campus
220 Lexington Green Circle, Lexington, KY 40503

Lithonia Campus
3120 Stonecrest Blvd., Ste. 200, Lithonia, GA 30038

Loudoun Campus
45150 Russell Branch Pkwy., Ste. 200, Ashburn, VA 20147
Phone: (703) 729-8800

Louisville Campus
2650 Eastpoint Pkwy., Louisville, KY 40223

Lower Bucks County Campus
3600 Horizon Blvd., Ste. 100, Trevose, PA 19053
Phone: (215) 953-5999

Maitland Campus
850 Trafalgar Ct., Maitland, FL 32751

Manassas Campus
9990 Battleview Pkwy., Manassas, VA 20109
Phone: (703) 330-8400

Morrow Campus
3000 Corporate Center Dr., Ste. 100, Morrow, GA 30260

Nashville Campus
30 Rachel Dr., Ste. 200, Nashville, TN 37214
Phone: (615) 871-2260

Newport News Campus
813 Diligence Dr., Ste. 100, Newport News, VA 23606
Phone: (757) 873-3100

North Charlotte Campus
8335 IBM Dr., Ste. 150, Charlotte, NC 28262
Phone: (704) 717-2380

North Raleigh Campus
3200 Spring Forest Rd., Ste. 214, Raleigh, NC 27616
Phone: (919) 878-9900

Online Campus
8382-F Terminal Rd., Lorton, VA 22152
Phone: (703) 339-1850

Orlando East Campus
2200 North Alafaya Trail, Ste. 500, Orlando, FL 32826

Owings Mills Campus
500 Redland Ct., Ste. 100, Owings Mills, MD 21117
Phone: (443) 394-3339

Palm Beach Gardens Campus
11025 RCA Center Dr., Ste. 200, Palm Beach Gardens, FL 33410

Penn Center West Canpus
One Penn Center West, Ste. 320, Pittsburgh, PA 15276

Prince George's Campus
4710 Auth Place, 1st Flr., Suitland, MD 20746
Phone: (301) 423-3600

Rockville Campus
4 Research Place, Ste. 100, Rockville, MD 20850
Phone: (301) 540-8066

Roswell Campus
100 Mansell Ct. East, Ste. 100, Roswell, GA 30076

RTP Campus
4 Copley Pkwy., Morrisville, NC 27560
Phone: (919) 466-1150

Sand Lake Campus
8529 South Park Circle, Ste. 310, Orlando, FL 32819

Savannah Campus
20 Martin Ct., Savannah, GA 31419

Shelby Oaks Campus
6211 Shelby Oaks Dr., Ste. 100, Memphis, TN 38134
Phone: (901) 383-6750

South Charlotte Campus
9101 Kings Parade Blvd., Ste. 200, Charlotte, NC 28273
Phone: (704) 587-5360

Takoma Park Campus
6830 Laurel St., NW, Washington 20012
Phone: (202) 722-8100

Tampa East Campus
6302 East MLK Blvd., Ste. 450, Tampa, FL 33619

Strayer University *(continued)*

Tampa Westshore Campus
4902 Eisenhower Blvd., Ste. 100, Tampa, FL 33634

Thousand Oaks Campus
2620 Thousand Oaks Blvd., Ste. 1100, Memphis, TN 38118
Phone: (901) 369-0835

Virginia Beach Campus
249 Central Park Ave., Ste. 350, Virginia Beach, VA 23462

White Marsh Campus
9409 Philadelphia Rd., Baltimore, MD 21237
Phone: (410) 238-9000

Willingboro Campus
300 Willingboro Pkwy., Ste. 125, Willingboro, NJ 08046

Woodbridge Campus
13385 Minnieville Rd., Woodbridge, VA 22192
Phone: (703) 878-2800

Trinity Washington University
125 Michigan Aveneue NE, Washington 20017
Type: Private, Roman Catholic Church, four-year
Degrees: A, B, M *Enroll:* 1,091
URL: http://www.trinitydc.edu
Phone: (202) 884-9000 *Calendar:* Sem. plan
Inst. Accred.: MSA-CHE (1921/2006)
Prog. Accred.: Teacher Education (NCATE)

University of the District of Columbia
4200 Connecticut Ave., NW, Washington 20008
Type: Public, state, four-year
Degrees: A, B, M, P *Enroll:* 3,382
URL: http://www.udc.edu
Phone: (202) 274-5000 *Calendar:* Sem. plan
Inst. Accred.: MSA-CHE (1971/2005)
Prog. Accred.: Allied Health (respiratory therapy, speech-language pathology), Business (ACBSP), Dietetics (didactic), Engineering (civil, electrical, mechanical), Engineering Technology (architectural, civil/construction, electrical, electromechanical), Funeral Service Education (Mortuary Science), Law (ABA only), Nursing, Radiography, Social Work, Teacher Education (NCATE)

Washington Theological Union
6896 Laurel St. NW, Washington 20012-2016
Type: Private, Roman Catholic Church, four-year
Degrees: M, P, D *Enroll:* 163
URL: http://www.wtu.edu
Phone: (202) 726-8800 *Calendar:* Sem. plan
Inst. Accred.: ATS (1973/1999), MSA-CHE (1973/2004)

Wesley Theological Seminary
4500 Massachusetts Ave. NW, Washington 20016
Type: Private, United Methodist Church, four-year
Degrees: M, P, D *Enroll:* 321
URL: http://www.wesleysem.edu
Phone: (202) 885-8600 *Calendar:* Sem. plan
Inst. Accred.: ATS (1940/2000), MSA-CHE (1975/2001)

FLORIDA

Academy for Five Element Acupuncture
305 SE 2nd Ave., Gainesville 32601
Type: Private, proprietary, four-year
Degrees: M
URL: http://acupuncturist.edu
Phone: (352) 335-2332 *Calendar:* Tri. plan
Inst. Accred.: ACAOM (1998/2001)

Acupuncture and Massage College
10506 North Kendall Dr., Miami 33176
Type: Private, proprietary, four-year
Degrees: M
URL: http://www.amcollege.edu
Phone: (305) 595-9500
Inst. Accred.: ACCSCT (2003)
Prog. Accred.: Acupuncture

Americare School of Nursing
7275 Estapona Circle, Fern Park 32730
Type: Private, proprietary, two-year
Degrees: A
URL: http://www.americareschools.com
Phone: (407) 673-7406
Inst. Accred.: ABHES (1997/2006)
Prog. Accred.: Dentistry (dental assisting)

St. Petersburg Campus
5335 66th St. North, St. Petersburg 33709
Phone: (727) 547-1822
Prog. Accred: Medical Assisting (ABHES), Surgical Technology

Angley College
230 North Woodland Blvd., Ste. 310, Deland 32720
Type: Private, proprietary, two-year
Degrees: A
URL: http://www.angley.edu
Phone: (386) 740-1215 *Calendar:* Sem. plan
Inst. Accred.: ACICS (2003/2008)

Orlando Campus
1819 North Semoran Blvd., Orlando 32807
Phone: (407) 478-5300

Argosy University Sarasota
5250 17th St., Sarasota 34235
Type: Private, proprietary, four-year
System: Argosy University
Degrees: B, M, D *Enroll:* 1,641
URL: http://www.argosyu.edu/sarasota
Phone: (941) 379-0404 *Calendar:* Tri. plan
Inst. Accred.: NCA-HLC (1981/2008, *Indirect accreditation through Argosy University, Chicago, IL*)
Prog. Accred.: Counseling

Argosy University Tampa
Parkside at Tampa Bay Park, 4401 North Himes Ave., Ste. 150, Tampa 33614
Type: Private, proprietary, four-year
System: Argosy University
Degrees: B, M, D
URL: http://www.argosyu.edu/tampa
Phone: (813) 393-5290 *Calendar:* Tri. plan
Inst. Accred.: NCA-HLC (1981/2008, *Indirect accreditation through Argosy University, Chicago, IL*)
Prog. Accred.: Clinical Psychology

The Art Institute of Fort Lauderdale
1799 Southeast 17th St., Fort Lauderdale 33316-3000
Type: Private, proprietary, four-year
System: Education Management Corporation
Degrees: A, B *Enroll:* 2,210
URL: http://www.aifl.edu
Phone: (954) 527-1799 *Calendar:* Qtr. plan
Inst. Accred.: ACICS (2000/2005)
Prog. Accred.: Culinary Education, Interior Design

ATI Career Training Center
3501 NW 9th Ave., Oakland Park 33309-5900
Type: Private, proprietary, two-year
System: ATI Enterprises, Inc.
Degrees: A *Enroll:* 591
URL: http://www.aticareertraining.edu
Phone: (954) 563-5899 *Calendar:* Qtr. plan
Inst. Accred.: ACCSCT (1984/2006)

ATI Career Training Center
2890 NW 62nd St., Fort Lauderdale 33309
Type: Private, proprietary, two-year
System: ATI Enterprises, Inc.
Degrees: A *Enroll:* 623
URL: http://www.aticareertraining.edu
Phone: (954) 973-4760 *Calendar:* Qtr. plan
Inst. Accred.: ACCSCT (1982/2006)

Miami Campus
7625 NW 25th St., Miami 33122
Phone: (305) 573-1600

ATI College of Health
1395 NW 167th St., Ste. 200, Miami 33169-5745
Type: Private, proprietary, two-year
System: ATI Enterprises, Inc.
Degrees: A *Enroll:* 498
URL: http://www.aticareertraining.edu
Phone: (305) 628-1000 *Calendar:* Qtr. plan
Inst. Accred.: ACCSCT (1979/2007)
Prog. Accred.: Allied Health (respiratory therapy)

Atlantic Institute of Oriental Medicine
100 East Broward Blvd., Ste. 100, Fort Lauderdale 33301
Type: Private, proprietary, four-year
Degrees: M
URL: http://www.atom.edu
Phone: (954) 763-9840
Inst. Accred.: ACAOM (1999/2006)

Ave Maria University
1025 Commons Circle, Naples 34119
Type: Private, independent, four-year
Degrees: B
URL: http://www.naples.avemaria.edu
Phone: (239) 280-2500 *Calendar:* Sem. plan
Inst. Accred.: AALE (2008)

Ave Maria College of the Americas
San Marcos, Nicaragua
Phone: 011 505 432 2312

The Baptist College of Florida
5400 College Dr., Graceville 32440-1831
Type: Private, Southern Baptist Church, four-year
Degrees: B *Enroll:* 505
URL: http://www.baptistcollege.edu
Phone: (850) 263-3261 *Calendar:* Sem. plan
Inst. Accred.: SACS (1981/1997)
Prog. Accred.: Music

Barry University
11300 NE Second Ave., Miami Shores 33161-6695
Type: Private, Roman Catholic Church, four-year
Degrees: B, M, P, D *Enroll:* 7,504
URL: http://www.barry.edu
Phone: (305) 899-3000 *Calendar:* Sem. plan
Inst. Accred.: ATS (2004), SACS (1947/2003)
Prog. Accred.: Allied Health (occupational therapy, perfusion), Business (AACSB), Counseling, Graduate Social Work, Histologic Technology, Law (ABA only), Montessori Teacher Education, Nurse Anesthesia Education, Nursing Education, Physician Assistant, Podiatry, Social Work

South Campus
1650 Sandlake Rd., Ste. 111, Orlando 32809-9108
Phone: (407) 438-4150

Bay Medical Center
615 North Bonita Ave., Panama City 32401
Type: Private, independent, four-year
Degrees: M *Enroll:* 40
URL: http://www.baymedical.org/education/index.shtml
Phone: (904) 747-6051
Inst. Accred.: ABHES (2000)
Prog. Accred.: Nurse Anesthesia Education

Beacon College
105 East Main St., Leesburg 34748
Type: Private, independent, four-year
Degrees: A, B *Enroll:* 99
URL: http://www.beaconcollege.edu
Phone: (352) 787-7660 *Calendar:* Sem. plan
Inst. Accred.: SACS (2003)

Bethune-Cookman University
640 Mary McLeod Bethune Blvd., Daytona Beach 32114
Type: Private, United Methodist Church, four-year
Degrees: B, M *Enroll:* 2,911
URL: http://www.cookman.edu
Phone: (386) 481-2000 *Calendar:* Sem. plan
Inst. Accred.: SACS (1947/2000)
Prog. Accred.: Clinical Lab Scientist, Nursing, Teacher Education (NCATE)

Brevard Community College
1519 Clearlake Rd., Cocoa 32922-6597
Type: Public, state/local, two-year
System: Florida State Department of Education, Division of Community Colleges
Degrees: A *Enroll:* 8,120
URL: http://www.brevardcc.edu
Phone: (321) 632-1111 *Calendar:* Sem. plan
Inst. Accred.: SACS (1965/2003)
Prog. Accred.: Allied Health (EMT-paramedic, medical assisting (AMA), surgical technology), Clinical Lab Technology, Dentistry (dental assisting, dental hygiene), Radiography, Veterinary Technology

Broward College
225 East Las Olas Blvd., Fort Lauderdale 33301
Type: Public, local, four-year
System: Florida State Department of Education, Division of Community Colleges
Degrees: A, B *Enroll:* 17,384
URL: http://www.broward.edu
Phone: (954) 201-7400 *Calendar:* Sem. plan
Inst. Accred.: SACS (1965/2003)
Prog. Accred.: Allied Health (EMT-paramedic, diagnostic medical sonography, medical assisting (AMA), respiratory therapy), Dentistry (dental assisting, dental hygiene), Music, Physical Therapy Assisting

A. Hugh Adams Central Campus
3501 SW Davie Rd., Davie 33314
Phone: (954) 201-6500
Prog. Accred: Nursing

Judson A. Samuels South Campus
7200 Pines Blvd., Pembroke Pines 33024
Phone: (954) 201-8835
Prog. Accred: Nursing

North Campus
1000 Coconut Creek Blvd., Coconut Creek 33066
Phone: (954) 973-2240
Prog. Accred: Nursing

Carlos Albizu University—Miami Campus
2173 NW 99th Ave., Miami 33172
Type: Private, independent, four-year
System: Carlos Albizu—Central Administration
Degrees: B, M, D *Enroll:* 831
URL: http://www.albizu.edu
Phone: (305) 593-1223 *Calendar:* Sem. plan
Inst. Accred.: MSA-CHE (1981/2005)
Prog. Accred.: Business (ACBSP), Clinical Psychology

Central Florida Community College
PO Box 1388, Ocala 34474-1388
Type: Public, state/local, two-year
System: Florida State Department of Education, Division of Community Colleges
Degrees: A *Enroll:* 3,652
URL: http://www.cf.edu
Phone: (352) 873-5800 *Calendar:* Sem. plan
Inst. Accred.: SACS (1964/2006)
Prog. Accred.: Allied Health (EMT-paramedic, surgical technology), Nursing, Physical Therapy Assisting, Practical Nursing

Citrus Campus
3800 South Lecanto Hwy., Lecanto 34461
Phone: (352) 746-6721

Central Florida Institute, Inc.
30522 US Hwy. 19 North, Ste. 300, Palm Harbor 34684
Type: Private, proprietary, two-year
Degrees: A
URL: http://www.cfinstitute.com
Phone: (727) 786-4707
Inst. Accred.: ABHES (1999/2003)
Prog. Accred.: Allied Health (cardiovascular technology, surgical technology)

Orlando Campus
6000 Cinderlane Pkwy., Ste. 200, Orlando 32810
Phone: (407) 523-5354
Prog. Accred: Medical Assisting (ABHES)

Centura Institute
6359 Edgewater Dr., Orlando 32810
Type: Private, proprietary, two-year
System: Centura College
Degrees: A
URL: http://www.centurainstitute.edu
Phone: (407) 275-9697
Inst. Accred.: ACCSCT (2004)

Chipola College
3094 Indian Circle, Marianna 32446-2053
Type: Public, state/local, four-year
System: Florida State Department of Education, Division of Community Colleges
Degrees: A, B *Enroll:* 1,516
URL: http://www.chipola.edu
Phone: (850) 526-2761 *Calendar:* Sem. plan
Inst. Accred.: SACS (1957/2008)

City College
2000 W. Commercial Blvd., Ste. 200, Ft. Lauderdale 33309
Type: Private, proprietary, four-year
Degrees: A, B *Enroll:* 388
URL: http://www.citycollege.edu
Phone: (954) 492-5353 *Calendar:* Qtr. plan
Inst. Accred.: ACICS (1986/2008)

Gainesville Campus
2400 SW 13th St., Gainesville 32608
Phone: (352) 335-4000

Miami Campus
9300 South Dadeland Blvd., Miami 33156
Phone: (305) 666-9242

City College Casselberry
853 Semoran Blvd., Ste. 200, Casselberry 32707-5365
Type: Private, proprietary, two-year
Degrees: A
URL: http://www.citycollegeorlando.edu
Phone: (407) 831-8466 *Calendar:* Qtr. plan
Inst. Accred.: ACICS (2000/2003)

Clearwater Christian College
3400 Gulf-to-Bay Blvd., Clearwater 33759-4595
Type: Private, independent, four-year
Degrees: A, B, M *Enroll:* 561
URL: http://www.clearwater.edu
Phone: (727) 726-1153 *Calendar:* Sem. plan
Inst. Accred.: SACS (1984/1999)

College of Business and Technology
8991 SW 107 Ave., Ste. 200, Miami 33176
Type: Private, proprietary, two-year
Degrees: A
URL: http://www.cbt.edu
Phone: (305) 273-4499 *Calendar:* Sem. plan
Inst. Accred.: ACICS (2003)

Flagler Campus
8230 West Flagler St., Miami 33144
Phone: (305) 273-4499 ext 2

Hialeah Campus
935 West 49th St., Hialeah 33012
Phone: (305) 273-4499 ext 3

Daytona College
425 South Nova Rd., Ormond Beach 32174
Type: Private, proprietary, two-year
Degrees: A
URL: http://www.daytonacollege.edu
Phone: (386) 267-0565
Inst. Accred.: ACCSCT (2004)

Daytona State College
PO Box 2811, Daytona Beach 32120-2811
Type: Public, state/local, four-year
System: Florida State Department of Education, Division of Community Colleges
Degrees: A, B *Enroll:* 7,550
URL: http://www.dbc.edu
Phone: (386) 506-3000 *Calendar:* Sem. plan
Inst. Accred.: SACS (1963/2003)
Prog. Accred.: Allied Health (EMT-paramedic, medical assisting (AMA), occupational therapy assisting, respiratory therapy, surgical technology), Dentistry (dental assisting, dental hygiene), Nursing, Physical Therapy Assisting

Delta Connection Academy
2700 Flight Line Ave., Sanford 32773-9683
Type: Private, proprietary, two-year
Degrees: A *Enroll:* 322
URL: http://www.deltaconnectionacademy.com
Phone: (407) 330-7020
Inst. Accred.: ACCSCT (1995/2005)

DeVry University Orlando
4000 Millenia Blvd., Orlando 32839
Type: Private, proprietary
System: DeVry University
Degrees: A, B, M *Enroll:* 1,810
URL: http://www.devry.edu/orlando
Phone: (407) 370-3131 *Calendar:* Sem. plan
Inst. Accred.: NCA-HLC (2002, *Indirect accreditation through DeVry University, Oakbrook Terrace, IL*)
Prog. Accred.: Engineering Technology (computer, electrical)

Ft. Lauderdale Campus
600 Corporate Dr., Ste. 200, Ft. Lauderdale 33334
Phone: (954) 938-3083

Jacksonville Campus
8131 Baymeadows Circle West, Ste. 101, Jacksonville 32256
Phone: (904) 367-4942

Miramar Campus
2300 Southwest 145th Ave., Miramar 33027-4150
Phone: (866) 793-3879

Tampa East Campus
6700 Lakeview Center Dr., Ste. 150, Tampa 33619
Phone: (813) 664-4260

Digital Media Arts College
3785 North Federal Hwy., Boca Raton 33431
Type: Private, proprietary, four-year
Degrees: B, M
URL: http://www.dmac.edu
Phone: (561) 391-1148 *Calendar:* Sem. plan
Inst. Accred.: ACICS (2007)

Dragon Rises College of Oriental Medicine
1000 NE 16th Ave., Building F, Gainesville 32601
Type: Private, proprietary, four-year
Degrees: M
URL: http://www.dragonrises.edu
Phone: (352) 371-2833 *Calendar:* Sem. plan
Inst. Accred.: ACAOM (2002/2007)

East West College of Natural Medicine
3808 North Tamiami Trail, Sarasota 34234
Type: Private, proprietary, four-year
Degrees: M
URL: http://www.ewcollege.org
Phone: (941) 355-9080 *Calendar:* Sem. plan
Inst. Accred.: ACAOM (1999/2007)

Eckerd College
4200 54th Ave. South, St. Petersburg 33711
Type: Private, Presbyterian Church (USA), four-year
Degrees: B *Enroll:* 1,764
URL: http://www.eckerd.edu
Phone: (727) 867-1166 *Calendar:* 4-1-4 plan
Inst. Accred.: SACS (1966/2000)
Prog. Accred.: Liberal Education

Edison State College
PO Box 60210, Fort Myers 33906-6210
Type: Public, state/local, four-year
System: Florida State Department of Education, Division of Community Colleges
Degrees: A, B *Enroll:* 6,323
URL: http://www.edison.edu
Phone: (239) 489-9300 *Calendar:* Sem. plan
Inst. Accred.: SACS (1966/2001)
Prog. Accred.: Allied Health (EMT-paramedic, cardiovascular technology, respiratory therapy), Dentistry (dental assisting, dental hygiene), Nursing, Radiography

Edward Waters College
1658 Kings Rd., Jacksonville 32209
Type: Private, African Methodist Episcopal Church, four-year
Degrees: B *Enroll:* 826
URL: http://www.ewc.edu
Phone: (904) 470-8000 *Calendar:* Sem. plan
Inst. Accred.: SACS (1979/2006)

Embry-Riddle Aeronautical University
600 South Clyde Morris Blvd., Daytona Beach 32114-3900
Type: Private, independent, four-year
Degrees: A, B, M *Enroll:* 4,522
URL: http://www.embryriddle.edu
Phone: (386) 226-6000 *Calendar:* Sem. plan
Inst. Accred.: SACS (1968/2002)
Prog. Accred.: Aviation, Business (ACBSP), Engineering (aerospace, civil, computer, engineering physics/science), Engineering Technology (aerospace)

Arizona Campus
3200 North Willow Creek Rd., Prescott, AZ 86301
Phone: (928) 777-6200
Prog. Accred: Aviation, Engineering (aerospace, computer, electrical)

WorldWide Campus
600 South Clyde Morris Blvd., Daytona Beach 32114-3900
Phone: (386) 226-6910

Everest Institute—Miami
111 NW 183rd St., 2nd Flr., Miami 33169
Type: Private, proprietary, two-year
System: Corinthian Colleges, Inc
Degrees: A *Enroll:* 832
URL: http://www.everest.edu
Phone: (305) 949-9500
Inst. Accred.: ABHES (1978/2008), ACICS (2008)
Prog. Accred.: Allied Health (surgical technology), Criminal Justice (ABHES), Medical Assisting (ABHES)

Hialeah Campus
530 West 49th St., Hialeah 33012
Phone: (305) 558-9500
Prog. Accred: Allied Health (surgical technology), Criminal Justice (ABHES), Medical Assisting (ABHES), Surgical Technology

Everest University—Largo
1199 East Bay Dr., Largo 33770
Type: Private, independent, four-year
System: Corinthian Colleges, Inc
Degrees: A, B, M *FTE Enroll:* 145
URL: http://www.everest.edu
Phone: (727) 725-2688 *Calendar:* Qtr. plan
Inst. Accred.: ACICS (1971/2007)
Prog. Accred.: Allied Health (medical assisting (AMA))

Jacksonville Campus
8226 Phillips Hwy., Jacksonville 32256
Phone: (904) 731-4949

Lakeland Campus
995 East Memorial Blvd., Ste. 110, Lakeland 33801
Phone: (863) 686-1444
Prog. Accred: Allied Health (medical assisting (AMA))

Everest University—North Orlando
5421 Diplomat Circle, Orlando 32810
Type: Private, independent, four-year
System: Corinthian Colleges, Inc
Degrees: A, B, M *Enroll:* 730
URL: http://www.everest.edu
Phone: (407) 628-5870 *Calendar:* Qtr. plan
Inst. Accred.: ACICS (1957/2001)

Melbourne Campus
2401 North Harbor City Blvd., Melbourne 32935
Phone: (321) 253-2929
Prog. Accred: Allied Health (medical assisting (AMA))

Orange Park Campus
805 Wells Rd., Orange Park 32073
Phone: (904) 264-9122

South Orlando Campus
9200 South Park Center Loop, Orlando 32819
Phone: (407) 851-2525
Prog. Accred: Allied Health (medical assisting (AMA))

Everest University—Pompano Beach
225 North Federal Hwy., Pompano Beach 33062
Type: Private, independent, four-year
System: Corinthian Colleges, Inc
Degrees: A, B, M *Enroll:* 1,337
URL: http://www.everest.edu
Phone: (954) 783-7339 *Calendar:* Qtr. plan
Inst. Accred.: ACICS (1968/2003)

Everest University—Tampa
3319 West Hillsborough Ave., Tampa 33614
Type: Private, independent, four-year
System: Corinthian Colleges, Inc
Degrees: A, B, M *Enroll:* 961
URL: http://www.everest.edu
Phone: (813) 879-6000 *Calendar:* Qtr. plan
Inst. Accred.: ACICS (1966/2006)
Prog. Accred.: Allied Health (medical assisting (AMA))

Brandon Campus
3924 Coconut Palm Dr., Tampa 33619
Phone: (813) 621-0041
Prog. Accred: Allied Health (medical assisting (AMA), surgical technology)

Everglades University
5002 T-REX Ave., Ste. 100, Boca Raton 33431
Type: Private, independent, four-year
Degrees: B, M *Enroll:* 458
URL: http://www.evergladesuniversity.edu
Phone: (561) 912-1211 *Calendar:* Tri. plan
Inst. Accred.: ACCSCT (1993/2005), SACS (2008)

Orlando Campus
5600 Lake Underhill Rd., Ste. #200, Orlando 32807
Phone: (407) 277-0311

Sarasota Campus
6151 Lake Osprey Dr., Sarasota 34240
Phone: (941) 907-2262

Flagler College
PO Box 1027, St. Augustine 32085-1027
Type: Private, independent, four-year
Degrees: B *Enroll:* 2,116
URL: http://www.flagler.edu
Phone: (904) 829-6481 *Calendar:* Sem. plan
Inst. Accred.: SACS (1973/1998)

Florida Agricultural and Mechanical University
South Martin Luther King Blvd., Tallahassee 32307-3100
Type: Public, state, four-year
System: State University System of Florida
Degrees: B, M, P, D *Enroll:* 11,249
URL: http://www.famu.edu
Phone: (850) 599-3000 *Calendar:* Sem. plan
Inst. Accred.: SACS (1935/1998)
Prog. Accred.: Allied Health (occupational therapy, respiratory therapy), Computer Science (ABET-CAC), Engineering (agricultural), Engineering Technology (civil/construction, electrical), Graduate Social Work, Journalism, Landscape Architecture, Law (ABA only), Nursing, Pharmacy, Physical Therapy, Public Health, Social Work, Teacher Education (NCATE)

Florida Atlantic University
777 Glades Rd., Boca Raton 33431-0991
Type: Public, state, four-year
System: State University System of Florida
Degrees: B, M, D *Enroll:* 18,220
URL: http://www.fau.edu
Phone: (561) 297-3000 *Calendar:* Sem. plan
Inst. Accred.: SACS (1967/2002)
Prog. Accred.: Allied Health (speech-language pathology), Business (AACSB), Clinical Lab Scientist, Computer Science (ABET-CAC), Counseling, Engineering (civil, computer, electrical, mechanical, ocean), Graduate Social Work, Music, Nursing Education, Planning, Public Administration, Rehabilitation Counseling, Social Work, Teacher Education (NCATE)

Florida Career College
1321 SW 107 Ave., Ste. 201B, Miami 33174-2521
Type: Private, proprietary, four-year
Degrees: A, B
URL: http://www.careercollege.edu
Phone: (305) 553-6065 *Calendar:* Qtr. plan
Inst. Accred.: ACICS (1985/2003)

Florida Career College
410 Park Place Blvd., Clearwater 33759
Type: Private, proprietary, two-year
Degrees: A
URL: http://www.careercollege.edu
Phone: (727) 724-1037
Inst. Accred.: COE (1991/2003)

Florida Career College
7891 Pines Blvd., Pembroke Pines 33024-6916
Type: Private, proprietary, two-year
Degrees: A
URL: http://www.careercollege.edu
Phone: (954) 965-7272 *Calendar:* Qtr. plan
Inst. Accred.: ACICS (2006)

Brandon Campus
2662 South Falkenburg Rd., Riverview 33569
Phone: (813) 621-5775

Hialeah Campus
3750 West 18th Ave., Hialeah 33012
Phone: (305) 825-3231

Lauderdale Lakes Campus
3383 North State Rd. 7, Lauderdale Lakes 33319
Phone: (954) 535-8700

Florida Career College—West Palm Beach Campus
6058 Okeechobee Blvd., West Palm Beach 33417-4326
Type: Private, proprietary, two-year
Degrees: A
URL: http://www.careercollege.edu
Phone: (561) 689-0550 *Calendar:* Qtr. plan
Inst. Accred.: ACICS (2007)

Florida Center for Theological Studies
111 NE First St., 8th Flr., Miami 33132
Type: Private, interdenominational, four-year
Degrees: M, D
URL: http://www.fcts.edu
Phone: (305) 379-3777 *Calendar:* Qtr. plan
Inst. Accred.: ATS (2006)

Florida Christian College
1011 Bill Beck Blvd., Kissimmee 34744-5301
Type: Private, Christian Churches/Churches of Christ, four-year
Degrees: A, B *Enroll:* 235
URL: http://www.fcc.edu
Phone: (407) 847-8966 *Calendar:* Sem. plan
Inst. Accred.: ABHE (1985/2006), SACS (1995/2000)

Florida Coastal School of Law
8787 Baypine Rd., Jacksonville 32256
Type: Private, independent, four-year
Degrees: P
URL: http://www.fcsl.edu
Phone: (904) 680-7700 *Calendar:* Sem. plan
Inst. Accred.: ABA (1999/2002)

Florida College
119 North Glen Arven Ave., Temple Terrace 33617
Type: Private, independent, four-year
Degrees: A, B *Enroll:* 445
URL: http://www.flcoll.edu
Phone: (813) 988-5131 *Calendar:* Sem. plan
Inst. Accred.: SACS (1954/2007)

Florida College of Natural Health
2001 West Sample Rd., Ste. 100, Pompano Beach 33064
Type: Private, proprietary, four-year
Degrees: A, B *Enroll:* 275
URL: http://www.fcnh.com
Phone: (954) 975-6400
Inst. Accred.: ACCSCT (1990/2006)
Prog. Accred.: Allied Health (massage therapy)

Miami Campus
7925 Northwest 12th St., Ste. 201, Miami 33126
Phone: (305) 597-9599
Prog. Accred: Allied Health (massage therapy)

Orlando Campus
2600 Lake Lucien Dr., Ste. 140, Maitland 32751
Phone: (407) 261-0319
Prog. Accred: Allied Health (massage therapy)

Sarasota Campus
616 67th St. Circle East, Bradenton 34208
Phone: (941) 744-1244
Prog. Accred: Allied Health (massage therapy)

Florida Community College at Jacksonville
501 West State St., Jacksonville 32202-4030
Type: Public, state/local, four-year
System: Florida State Department of Education, Division of Community Colleges
Degrees: A, B *Enroll:* 12,685
URL: http://www.fccj.edu
Phone: (904) 646-2300 *Calendar:* Sem. plan
Inst. Accred.: SACS (1969/2004)
Prog. Accred.: Allied Health (EMT-paramedic, respiratory therapy, surgical technology), Business (ACBSP), Clinical Lab Technology, Culinary Education, Dentistry (dental hygiene), Histologic Technology, Nursing, Physical Therapy Assisting

Downtown Campus
101 West State St., Jacksonville 32202
Phone: (904) 633-8100

Kent Campus
3939 Roosevelt Blvd., Jacksonville 32205
Phone: (904) 381-3400

North Campus
4501 Capper Rd., Jacksonville 32218
Phone: (904) 766-6500
Prog. Accred: Dietetic Technician, Funeral Service Education (Mortuary Science)

South Campus
11901 Beach Blvd., Jacksonville 32246
Phone: (904) 646-2111

Florida Gulf Coast University
10501 FGCU Blvd., South, Fort Myers 33965-6565
Type: Public, state, four-year
System: State University System of Florida
Degrees: B, M, D *Enroll:* 5,767
URL: http://www.fgcu.edu
Phone: (239) 590-1000 *Calendar:* Sem. plan
Inst. Accred.: SACS (1999/2005)
Prog. Accred.: Allied Health (occupational therapy), Business (AACSB), Clinical Lab Scientist, Counseling, Graduate Social Work, Nurse Anesthesia Education, Nursing Education, Physical Therapy, Public Administration, Social Work

Florida Hospital College of Health Sciences
800 Lake Estelle Dr., Orlando 32803
Type: Private, Seventh-Day Adventist Church, four-year
Degrees: A, B, M *Enroll:* 1,150
URL: http://www.fhchc.edu
Phone: (407) 303-7742 *Calendar:* Sem. plan
Inst. Accred.: SACS (1996/2001)
Prog. Accred.: Allied Health (diagnostic medical sonography, occupational therapy assisting), Clinical Lab Scientist, Clinical Pastoral Education (ACPEI), Nuclear Medicine Technology, Nurse Anesthesia Education, Nursing, Phlebotomy, Radiography

Florida Institute of Technology
150 West University Blvd., Melbourne 32901-6975
Type: Private, independent, four-year
Degrees: A, B, M, P, D *Enroll:* 3,620
URL: http://www.fit.edu
Phone: (321) 674-8000 *Calendar:* Sem. plan
Inst. Accred.: SACS (1964/2005)
Prog. Accred.: Aviation, Clinical Psychology, Computer Science (ABET-CAC), Engineering (aerospace, chemical, civil, computer, electrical, mechanical, ocean, software)

Florida International University
11200 SW 8th St., University Park, Miami 33199-0001
Type: Public, state, four-year
System: State University System of Florida
Degrees: A, B, M, P, D *Enroll:* 27,799
URL: http://www.fiu.edu
Phone: (305) 348-2000 *Calendar:* Sem. plan
Inst. Accred.: SACS (1974/2000)
Prog. Accred.: Accounting, Allied Health (health services administration, medicine, occupational therapy, speech-language pathology), Art, Business (AACSB), Computer Science (ABET-CAC), Construction Education, Counseling, Dietetics (coordinated), Dietetics (didactic), Engineering (bioengineering, civil, computer, electrical, industrial, mechanical), Graduate Social Work, Interior Architecture, Journalism, Landscape Architecture, Law (ABA only), Music, Nurse Anesthesia Education, Nursing, Nursing Education, Physical Therapy, Public Administration, Public Health, Recreation and Leisure Services, Social Work, Teacher Education (NCATE), Theatre

Florida Keys Community College
5901 West College Rd., Key West 33040-4397
Type: Public, state/local, two-year
System: Florida State Department of Education, Division of Community Colleges
Degrees: A *Enroll:* 553
URL: http://www.fkcc.edu
Phone: (305) 809-3515 *Calendar:* Sem. plan
Inst. Accred.: SACS (1968/2003)

Florida Memorial University
15800 NW 42nd Ave., Miami Gardens 33054-6155
Type: Private, independent, four-year
Degrees: B, M *Enroll:* 1,897
URL: http://www.fmuniv.edu
Phone: (305) 626-3600 *Calendar:* Sem. plan
Inst. Accred.: SACS (1951/2002, Warning)
Prog. Accred.: Business (ACBSP), Music, Social Work, Teacher Education (NCATE)

Florida National College
4425 West 20th Ave., Hialeah 33012-2800
Type: Private, proprietary, four-year
Degrees: A, B *Enroll:* 1,822
URL: http://www.fnc.edu
Phone: (305) 821-3333 *Calendar:* 3-3 plan
Inst. Accred.: SACS (1997/2002)

Bird Road Campus
5761 SW Bird Rd., Miami 33155
Phone: (305) 663-6464

Flagler Campus
11865 SW 26th St., Unit 3, Miami 33175
Phone: (305) 226-9999 x3

Florida Southern College
111 Lake Hollingsworth Dr., Lakeland 33801-5698
Type: Private, United Methodist Church, four-year
Degrees: B, M *Enroll:* 2,045
URL: http://www.flsouthern.edu
Phone: (863) 680-4111 *Calendar:* Sem. plan
Inst. Accred.: SACS (1935/2008)
Prog. Accred.: Nursing Education

Florida State University
Tallahassee 32306
Type: Public, state, four-year
System: State University System of Florida
Degrees: A, B, M, P, D *Enroll:* 35,043
URL: http://www.fsu.edu
Phone: (850) 644-1085 *Calendar:* Sem. plan
Inst. Accred.: SACS (1915/2004)
Prog. Accred.: Accounting, Allied Health (medicine, speech-language pathology), Art, Business (AACSB), Clinical Psychology, Combined Professional-Scientific Psychology, Computer Science (ABET-CAC), Counseling, Dance, Dietetics (didactic), Dietetics (internship), Engineering (chemical, civil, computer, electrical, industrial, mechanical), Family & Consumer Science, Graduate Social Work, Interior Design, Law, Librarianship, Marriage and Family Therapy, Music, Nursing Education, Planning, Psychology Internship, Public Administration, Recreation and Leisure Services, Rehabilitation Counseling, Social Work, Teacher Education (NCATE), Theatre

Florida Technical College
8711 Lone Star Rd., Jacksonville 32211
Type: Private, proprietary, two-year
System: ForeFront Education, Inc.
Degrees: A *Enroll:* 125
URL: http://www.flatech.edu
Phone: (904) 724-2229 *Calendar:* Qtr. plan
Inst. Accred.: ACICS (1988/2006)

Florida Technical College
12689 Challenger Pkwy., Ste. 130, Orlando 32826-2750
Type: Private, proprietary, two-year
System: ForeFront Education, Inc.
Degrees: A *Enroll:* 796
URL: http://www.flatech.edu
Phone: (407) 447-7300 *Calendar:* Qtr. plan
Inst. Accred.: ACICS (1982/2004)

Deland Campus
1199 South Woodland Blvd., Deland 32720-7415
Phone: (386) 734-3303

Lakeland Campus
4715 South Florida Ave., Ste. 4, Lakeland 33813
Phone: (863) 967-8822

Full Sail Real World Education
3300 University Blvd., Winter Park 32792-7429
Type: Private, proprietary, four-year
Degrees: A, B *Enroll:* 4,502
URL: http://www.fullsail.com
Phone: (407) 679-0100
Inst. Accred.: ACCSCT (1986/2003)

Gulf Coast College
3910 U.S. Hwy. 301 North, Ste. 200, Tampa 33619-1290
Type: Private, proprietary, two-year
Degrees: A *Enroll:* 129
Phone: (813) 620-1446 *Calendar:* Qtr. plan
Inst. Accred.: ACICS (1996/2004)

Gulf Coast Community College
5230 West U.S. Hwy. 98, Panama City 32401-1058
Type: Public, state-related, two-year
System: Florida State Department of Education, Division of Community Colleges
Degrees: A *Enroll:* 3,460
URL: http://www.gulfcoast.edu
Phone: (850) 769-1551 *Calendar:* Sem. plan
Inst. Accred.: SACS (1962/2000)
Prog. Accred.: Allied Health (EMT-paramedic, respiratory therapy, surgical technology), Culinary Education, Dentistry (dental assisting, dental hygiene), Nursing, Physical Therapy Assisting, Radiography

Heritage Institute
6811 Palisades Park Ct., Fort Myers 33912
Type: Private, proprietary, two-year
Degrees: A
URL: http://www.heritage-education.com
Phone: (239) 936-5822
Inst. Accred.: ACCSCT (2004)

Heritage Institute
4130 Salisbury Rd., Ste. 1100, Jacksonville 33216
Type: Private, proprietary, two-year
Degrees: A
URL: http://www.heritage-education.com
Phone: (904) 332-0910
Inst. Accred.: ACCSCT (2006)

Hillsborough Community College
PO Box 30030, Tampa 33630-3030
Type: Public, state, two-year
System: Hillsborough Community College District
Degrees: A *Enroll:* 11,717
URL: http://www.hccfl.edu
Phone: (813) 253-7000 *Calendar:* Sem. plan
Inst. Accred.: SACS (1971/2007)
Prog. Accred.: Allied Health (EMT-paramedic, diagnostic medical sonography, opticianry, respiratory therapy), Culinary Education, Dentistry (dental assisting), Nuclear Medicine Technology, Nursing, Radiation Therapy, Radiography

Plant City Campus
1206 North Park Rd., Plant City 33566-2799
Phone: (813) 757-2156
Prog. Accred: Nursing

Hobe Sound Bible College
PO Box 1065, Hobe Sound 33475-1065
Type: Private, independent, four-year
Degrees: A, B *Enroll:* 114
URL: http://www.hsbc.edu
Phone: (772) 546-5534 *Calendar:* Sem. plan
Inst. Accred.: ABHE (1986/2007)

Hodges University
2655 Northbrooke Dr., Naples 34119-7932
Type: Private, independent, four-year
Degrees: A, B, M *Enroll:* 1,315
URL: http://www.hodges.edu
Phone: (239) 513-1122 *Calendar:* Tri. plan
Inst. Accred.: SACS (1998/2003)

Fort Myers Campus
Ste. 120, 8695 College Pkwy., Fort Myers 33919
Phone: (941) 482-0019

IMPAC University
900 West Marion Ave., Punta Gorda 33950
Type: Private, proprietary, four-year
Degrees: M
URL: http://www.impacu.edu
Phone: (941) 639-7512
Inst. Accred.: DETC (2004)

Indian River Community College
3209 Virginia Ave., Fort Pierce 34981-5596
Type: Public, local, four-year
System: Florida State Department of Education, Division of Community Colleges
Degrees: A, B *Enroll:* 7,036
URL: http://www.ircc.edu
Phone: (772) 462-4700 *Calendar:* Sem. plan
Inst. Accred.: SACS (1965/2003)
Prog. Accred.: Allied Health (EMT-paramedic, medical assisting (AMA), respiratory therapy, surgical technology), Clinical Lab Technology, Dentistry (dental assisting, dental hygiene, dental laboratory technology), Nursing, Physical Therapy Assisting, Radiography

Institute of Allied Medical Professions
Delray Medical Center, 5150 Linton Blvd., Ste. 340, Delray Beach 33484
Type: Private, proprietary, two-year
Degrees: A
URL: http://www.iampny.com
Phone: (561) 381-4990
Inst. Accred.: ABHES (2005)

Saint Joseph's Hospital Campus
5673 Peachtree Dunwoody Rd., Ste. 450, Atlanta, GA 30342
Phone: (404) 255-4500

International Academy of Design and Technology
5104 Eisenhower Blvd., Tampa 32809
Type: Private, proprietary, four-year
System: Career Education Corporation
Degrees: A, B, M *Enroll:* 2,166
URL: http://www.academy.edu
Phone: (813) 881-0007
Inst. Accred.: ACICS (1990/2005)
Prog. Accred.: Interior Design

Orlando Campus
5959 Lake Ellenor Dr., Orlando 32809
Phone: (407) 857-2300

Pittsburgh Campus
555 Grant St., Fulton Bldg., Pittsburgh, PA 15219
Phone: (412) 391-4197

ITT Technical Institute
4809 Memorial Hwy., Tampa 33634-7350
Type: Private, proprietary, four-year
System: ITT Educational Services, Inc.
Degrees: A, B *Enroll:* 579
URL: http://www.itt-tech.edu
Phone: (813) 885-2244 *Calendar:* Qtr. plan
Inst. Accred.: ACICS (1999/2008)

ITT Technical Institute
1400 South International Pkwy., Lake Mary 32746
Type: Private, proprietary, four-year
System: ITT Educational Services, Inc.
Degrees: A, B *Enroll:* 453
URL: http://www.itt-tech.edu
Phone: (407) 660-2900 *Calendar:* Qtr. plan
Inst. Accred.: ACICS (1999/2004)

Bensalem Area Campus
3330 Tillman Dr., Bensalem, PA 19020
Phone: (215) 244-8871

Duluth Area Campus
10700 Abbotts Bridge Rd., Ste. 190, Duluth, GA 30097
Phone: (678) 957-8510

Dunmore-Scranton Campus
1000 Meade St., Dunmore, PA 18512
Phone: (570) 330-0600

Jacksonville Campus
6600 Youngerman Circle, Ste. 10, Jacksonville 32244
Phone: (904) 573-9100

Kennesaw Campus
1000 Cobb Place Blvd., NW, Building 300, Kennesaw, GA 30144-3685
Phone: (770) 426-2300

Miami Campus
7955 NW 12th St., Ste. 119, Miami 33126
Phone: (305) 477-3080

Pinellas Park Campus
3491 Gandy Blvd., Ste. 101, Pinellas Park 33781-2658
Phone: (727) 209-4700

Richmond Campus
300 Gateway Centre Pkwy., Richmond, VA 23235-5139
Phone: (804) 330-4992

Springfield Campus
7300 Boston Blvd., Springfield, VA 22153
Phone: (703) 440-9535

Jacksonville University
2800 University Blvd. North, Jacksonville 32211
Type: Private, independent, four-year
Degrees: B, M *Enroll:* 2,362
URL: http://www.ju.edu
Phone: (904) 256-8000 *Calendar:* Sem. plan
Inst. Accred.: SACS (1950/2003)
Prog. Accred.: Dance, Dentistry (orthodontic and dentofacial orthopedics), Music, Nursing Education

Jones College
5353 Arlington Expressway, Jacksonville 32211-5588
Type: Private, independent, four-year
Degrees: A, B *Enroll:* 298
URL: http://www.jones.edu
Phone: (904) 743-1122 *Calendar:* Sem. plan
Inst. Accred.: ACICS (1957/2002)

Miami Campus
11430 North Kendall Dr., Ste. 200, Miami 33176
Phone: (305) 275-9996

West Campus
1195 Edgewood Ave., South, Jacksonville 32205
Phone: (904) 743-1122

Keiser Career College
6812 Forest Hill Blvd., Ste. D-1, Greenacres 33413
Type: Private, proprietary, two-year
Degrees: A
URL: http://www.keisercareer.edu
Phone: (561) 433-2330 *Calendar:* Sem. plan
Inst. Accred.: ACCSCT (2003/2008)
Prog. Accred.: Medical Assisting (ABHES)

Miami Lakes Campus
17395 NW 57th Ave., Miami Lakes 33015
Phone: (305) 820-5003
Prog. Accred: Allied Health (surgical technology), Medical Assisting (ABHES)

St. Petersburg Campus
11208 Blue Heron Blvd., Ste. A, St. Petersburg 33716
Phone: (727) 576-6500
Prog. Accred: Allied Health (surgical technology)

Keiser University
1500 NW 49th St., Fort Lauderdale 33309-3779
Type: Private, proprietary, four-year
Degrees: A, B, M *Enroll:* 6,539
URL: http://www.keiseruniversity.edu
Phone: (954) 776-4456 *Calendar:* Sem. plan
Inst. Accred.: SACS (1991/2007)
Prog. Accred.: Allied Health (diagnostic medical sonography, occupational therapy assisting, surgical technology), Clinical Lab Technology, Medical Assisting (ABHES), Medical Laboratory Technology, Physical Therapy Assisting, Radiography

Daytona Beach Campus
1800 Business Park Blvd., Daytona Beach 32114
Phone: (386) 274-5060
Prog. Accred: Allied Health (diagnostic medical sonography, medical assisting (AMA)), Radiography

Jacksonville Campus
6700 Southpoint Pkwy., Ste. 400, Jacksonville 32216
Phone: (904) 296-3440

Kendall Campus
8505 Mills Dr., Miami 33183
Phone: (305) 596-2226
Prog. Accred: Allied Health (occupational therapy assisting)

Lakeland Campus
2400 Interstate Dr., Lakeland 33805
Phone: (863) 682-6020

Melbourne Campus
900 South Babcock St., Melbourne 32901
Phone: (321) 409-4800
Prog. Accred: Allied Health (occupational therapy assisting), Medical Assisting (ABHES), Nursing

Online Campus
1900 W. Commercial Blvd., Ste. 100, Ft. Lauderdale 33309
Phone: (954) 351-4040

Orlando Campus
5600 Lake Underhill Rd., Orlando 32807
Phone: (407) 273-5800
Prog. Accred: Allied Health (occupational therapy assisting)

Pembroke Pines Campus
12520 Pines Blvd., Pembroke Pines 33027
Phone: (954) 431-4300
Prog. Accred: Allied Health (occupational therapy assisting)

Port St. Lucie Campus
10330 South Federal Hwy., Port St. Lucie 34952
Phone: (772) 398-9990
Prog. Accred: Medical Assisting (ABHES)

Sarasota Campus
6151 Lake Osprey Dr., Sarasota 34240
Phone: (941) 907-3900
Prog. Accred: Medical Assisting (ABHES), Radiography

Tallahassee Campus
1700 Halstead Blvd., Building 2, Tallahassee 32308
Phone: (850) 906-9494
Prog. Accred: Culinary Education, Medical Assisting (ABHES)

Tampa Campus
5225 Memorial Hwy., Tampa 33634
Phone: (813) 885-4900

West Palm Beach Campus
2085 Vista Pkwy., West Palm Beach 33411
Phone: (561) 471-6000

Key College
225 East Dania Beach Blvd., Dania Beach 33004
Type: Private, proprietary, two-year
Degrees: A *Enroll:* 111
URL: http://www.keycollege.edu
Phone: (954) 923-4440
Inst. Accred.: ACICS (1985/2008)

Knox Theological Seminary
5554 North Federal Hwy., Fort Lauderdale 33308
Type: Private, Presbyterian Church in America, four-year
Degrees: M, D
URL: http://www.knoxseminary.org
Phone: (954) 771-0376 *Calendar:* Sem. plan
Inst. Accred.: ATS (2005)

Lake City Community College
149 SE College Place, Lake City 32025-2006
Type: Public, state, two-year
System: Florida State Department of Education, Division of Community Colleges
Degrees: A *Enroll:* 1,649
URL: http://www.lakecitycc.edu
Phone: (386) 752-1822 *Calendar:* Sem. plan
Inst. Accred.: SACS (1966/2000)
Prog. Accred.: Allied Health (EMT-paramedic), Clinical Lab Technology, Nursing, Physical Therapy Assisting

Lake-Sumter Community College
9501 U.S. Hwy. 441, Leesburg 34788-8751
Type: Public, state/local, two-year
System: Florida State Department of Education, Division of Community Colleges
Degrees: A *Enroll:* 1,935
URL: http://www.lscc.edu
Phone: (352) 787-3747 *Calendar:* Sem. plan
Inst. Accred.: SACS (1966/2000)

Le Cordon Bleu College of Culinary Arts—Miami
3221 Enterprise Way, Miramar 33025
Type: Private, proprietary, two-year
System: Career Education Corporation
Degrees: A
URL: http://www.miamiculinary.com
Phone: (954) 438-8882
Inst. Accred.: ACCSCT (2004/2006)

Lincoln College of Technology
2410 Metrocentre Blvd., West Palm Beach 33407
Type: Private, proprietary, four-year
Degrees: A, B *Enroll:* 1,353
URL: http://www.lincolnedu.com/campus/west-palm-beach-fl
Phone: (561) 842-8324 *Calendar:* Qtr. plan
Inst. Accred.: COE (1994/2000), ACICS (2003/2008)
Prog. Accred.: Culinary Education

Green Valley Campus
11041 S. Eastern Ave., Ste. 112, Henderson, NV 89052
Phone: (702) 932-8111

Henderson Campus
2290 Corporate Circle, Ste. 100, Henderson, NV 89014
Phone: (702) 269-7600

Norcross Campus
5675 Jimmy Carter Blvd., Ste. 100, Norcross, GA 30071
Phone: (678) 966-9411

Summerlin Campus
9340 W. Sahara Ave., Ste. 205, Las Vegas, NV 89117
Phone: (702) 341-8111

Lynn University
3601 North Military Trail, Boca Raton 33431
Type: Private, independent, four-year
Degrees: A, B, M, D *Enroll:* 2,554
URL: http://www.lynn.edu
Phone: (561) 237-7000 *Calendar:* Sem. plan
Inst. Accred.: SACS (1967/2001)
Prog. Accred.: Dance, Music

Manatee Community College
PO Box 1849, Bradenton 34206-7046
Type: Public, state/local, two-year
System: Florida State Department of Education, Division of Community Colleges
Degrees: A *Enroll:* 5,840
URL: http://www.mccfl.edu
Phone: (941) 752-5000 *Calendar:* Sem. plan
Inst. Accred.: SACS (1963/2005)
Prog. Accred.: Allied Health (occupational therapy assisting), Dentistry (dental hygiene), Nursing, Physical Therapy Assisting, Radiography

Lakewood Ranch Campus
7131 Professional Pkwy. East, Sarasota 34240
Phone: (941) 363-7000

Venice Campus
8000 South Tamiami Trail, Venice 34293
Phone: (941) 408-1300

The Miami Ad School
955 Alton Rd., Miami Beach 33139
Type: Private, proprietary, two-year
Degrees: A
URL: http://www.adschool.edu
Phone: (305) 538-3193
Inst. Accred.: COE (1995/2007)

Minneapolis Campus
25 North 4th St., #201, Minneapolis, MN 55401
Phone: (612) 339-4089

San Francisco Campus
415 Jackson St., Ste. B, San Francisco, CA 94111
Phone: (415) 837-0966

Miami International University of Art and Design
1501 Biscayne Blvd., Miami 33132
Type: Private, proprietary, four-year
System: Education Management Corporation
Degrees: A, B, M *Enroll:* 1,358
URL: http://www.ifac.edu
Phone: (305) 428-5700 *Calendar:* Sem. plan
Inst. Accred.: SACS (1979/2002, Warning)
Prog. Accred.: Interior Design

The Art Institute of Jacksonville
8775 Baypine Rd., Jacksonville 32256
Phone: (904) 732-9393

Miami-Dade College
300 NE 2nd Ave., Miami 33132
Type: Public, state/local, four-year
System: Florida State Department of Education, Division of Community Colleges
Degrees: A, B *Enroll:* 33,094
URL: http://www.mdc.edu
Phone: (305) 237-3000 *Calendar:* Sem. plan
Inst. Accred.: SACS (1965/2005)
Prog. Accred.: Allied Health (EMT-paramedic, diagnostic medical sonography, respiratory therapy), Clinical Lab Technology, Dentistry (dental hygiene), Funeral Service Education (Mortuary Science), Nursing, Physical Therapy Assisting, Physician Assistant, Radiography

Hialeah Campus
1780 West 49th St., Hialeah 33012
Phone: (305) 237-8700

Homestead Campus
500 College Terrace, Homestead 33030-6009
Phone: (305) 237-5555

InterAmerican Campus
627 Southwest 27th Ave., Miami 33135
Phone: (305) 237-6500

Kendall Campus
11011 SW 104 St., Miami 33176
Phone: (305) 237-2000

Medical Center Campus
950 NW 20th St., Miami 33127
Phone: (305) 237-4400
Prog. Accred: Allied Health (ophthalmic lab technology, opticianry), Dentistry (dental hygiene), Histologic Technology, Radiation Therapy, Radiography, Veterinary Technology

North Campus
11380 NW 27th Ave., Miami 33167-3495
Phone: (305) 237-8500

New College of Florida
5700 North Tamiami Trail, Sarasota 34243-2197
Type: Public, state, four-year
Degrees: B *Enroll:* 761
URL: http://www.ncf.edu
Phone: (941) 359-4700 *Calendar:* 4-1-4 plan
Inst. Accred.: SACS (2004)

New World School of the Arts
300 Northeast Second Ave., Miami 33132
Type: Public, joint partnership of Miami-Dade College & University of Florida, four-year
Degrees: A, B
URL: http://www.mdc.edu/nwsa
Phone: (305) 237-3135 *Calendar:* Sem. plan
Inst. Accred.: SACS (1993/2003, *Indirect accreditation through University of Florida, Gainesville, FL*), SACS (1993/2003, *Indirect accreditation through Miami-Dade College, Miami, FL*)
Prog. Accred.: Art, Dance, Music, Theatre

North Florida Community College
325 NW Turner Davis Dr., Madison 32340-1610
Type: Public, state, two-year
System: Florida State Department of Education, Division of Community Colleges
Degrees: A *Enroll:* 806
URL: http://www.nfcc.edu
Phone: (850) 973-1600 *Calendar:* Sem. plan
Inst. Accred.: SACS (1963/2005)

North Florida Institute
560 Wells Rd., Orange Park 32073
Type: Private, proprietary, two-year
Degrees: A
Phone: (904) 269-7086 *Calendar:* Sem. plan
Inst. Accred.: ACICS (1999/2008)

Jacksonville Campus
5995-3 University Blvd. West, Jacksonville 32216
Phone: (904) 443-6300

Northwest Florida State College
100 College Blvd., Niceville 32578-1295
Type: Public, state/local, four-year
System: Florida State Department of Education, Division of Community Colleges
Degrees: A, B *Enroll:* 4,153
URL: http://www.nwfstatecollege.edu
Phone: (850) 678-5111 *Calendar:* Sem. plan
Inst. Accred.: SACS (1967/2001)
Prog. Accred.: Allied Health (surgical technology)

Nova Southeastern University
1750 N.E. 168th St., North Miami Beach 33162-3097
Type: Private, independent, four-year
Degrees: B, M, P, D *Enroll:* 17,841
URL: http://www.nova.edu
Phone: (954) 262-7300 *Calendar:* Sem. plan
Inst. Accred.: SACS (1971/2007)
Prog. Accred.: Allied Health (anesthesiologist assisting, audiology, diagnostic medical sonography, occupational therapy, optometric residency, optometry, speech-language pathology), Clinical Psychology, Dentistry(advanced education in general dentistry, combined prosthodontics, dentistry, endodontics, general dentistry, oral and maxillofacial surgery, orthodontic and dentofacial orthopedics, pediatric dentistry, periodontics), Law, Marriage and Family Therapy, Nursing, Nursing Education, Osteopathy, Pharmacy, Physical Therapy, Physician Assistant, Psychology Internship, Public Health

Nova Southeastern University
3301 College Ave., Fort Lauderdale 33314
Type: Private, independent, four-year
Degrees: B, M, P, D *Enroll:* 17,841
URL: http://www.nova.edu
Phone: (954) 262-7300 *Calendar:* Sem. plan
Inst. Accred.: SACS (1971/2007)
Prog. Accred.: Allied Health (anesthesiologist assisting, audiology, diagnostic medical sonography, occupational therapy, optometric residency, optometry, speech-language pathology), Clinical Psychology, Dentistry (advanced education in general dentistry, combined prosthodontics, dentistry, endodontics, general dentistry, oral and maxillofacial surgery, orthodontic and dentofacial orthopedics, pediatric dentistry, periodontics), Law, Marriage and Family Therapy, Nursing, Nursing Education, Osteopathy, Pharmacy, Physical Therapy, Physician Assistant, Psychology Internship, Public Health

Palm Beach Atlantic University
PO Box 24708, West Palm Beach 33416-4708
Type: Private, interdenominational, four-year
Degrees: A, B, M, P, D *Enroll:* 2,941
URL: http://www.pba.edu
Phone: (561) 803-2000 *Calendar:* Sem. plan
Inst. Accred.: SACS (1972/2008)
Prog. Accred.: Music, Nursing Education, Pharmacy

Orlando Campus
4700 Millenia Blvd., Ste. 100, Orlando 32839
Phone: (407) 226-5955

Palm Beach Community College
4200 Congress Ave., Lake Worth 33461-4796
Type: Public, local, two-year
System: Florida State Department of Education, Division of Community Colleges
Degrees: A *Enroll:* 11,747
URL: http://www.pbcc.edu
Phone: (561) 868-3350 *Calendar:* Sem. plan
Inst. Accred.: SACS (1942/2001)
Prog. Accred.: Allied Health (EMT-paramedic, diagnostic medical sonography, medical assisting (AMA), respiratory therapy, surgical technology), Dentistry (dental assisting, dental hygiene), Montessori Teacher Education, Nursing, Radiography

Eissey Campus
3160 PGA Blvd., Palm Beach Gardens 33410
Phone: (561) 868-3350
Prog. Accred: Radiography

Glades Campus
1977 College Dr., Belle Glade 33430
Phone: (561) 868-3350

South Campus
3000 Saint Lucie Ave., Boca Raton 33431
Phone: (561) 868-3350

Pasco-Hernando Community College
10230 Ridge Rd., New Port Richey 34654-5199
Type: Public, state/local, two-year
System: Florida State Department of Education, Division of Community Colleges
Degrees: A *Enroll:* 4,240
URL: http://www.phcc.edu
Phone: (727) 847-2727 *Calendar:* Sem. plan
Inst. Accred.: SACS (1974/1999)
Prog. Accred.: Allied Health (EMT-paramedic), Dentistry (dental hygiene), Nursing

East Campus
36727 Blanton Rd., Dade City 33523-7599
Phone: (352) 567-6701

North Campus
11415 Ponce de Leon Blvd., Brooksville 34601-8698
Phone: (352) 796-6726

Pensacola Junior College
1000 College Blvd., Pensacola 32504-8998
Type: Public, state/local, two-year
System: Florida State Department of Education, Division of Community Colleges
Degrees: A *Enroll:* 5,944
URL: http://www.pjc.edu
Phone: (850) 484-1000 *Calendar:* Sem. plan
Inst. Accred.: SACS (1956/1997)
Prog. Accred.: Allied Health (EMT-paramedic, medical assisting (AMA), surgical technology), Culinary Education, Dentistry (dental assisting, dental hygiene), Dietetic Technician, Nursing, Physical Therapy Assisting, Radiography

Milton Campus
5988 Hwy. 90, Milton 32583
Phone: (904) 484-4400

Warrington Campus
5555 Hwy. 98 West, Pensacola 32507
Phone: (904) 484-2230
Prog. Accred: Radiography

Polk Community College
999 Ave. H, NE, Winter Haven 33881-4299
Type: Public, local, two-year
System: Florida State Department of Education, Division of Community Colleges
Degrees: A *Enroll:* 3,720
URL: http://www.polk.edu
Phone: (863) 297-1000 *Calendar:* Sem. plan
Inst. Accred.: SACS (1967/2001)
Prog. Accred.: Allied Health (EMT-paramedic, occupational therapy assisting), Nursing, Physical Therapy Assisting, Radiography

Professional Training Center
13926 SW 47th St., Miami 33175
Type: Private, proprietary, two-year
Degrees: A
URL: http://www.ptcmatt.com
Phone: (305) 220-4120
Inst. Accred.: ABHES (1998/2005), ACICS (2008)
Prog. Accred.: Radiography

Rasmussen College—Fort Myers
9160 Forum Corporate Pkwy., Ste. 100, Fort Myers 33905
Type: Private, proprietary, four-year
System: Rasmussen College System
Degrees: A, B
URL: http://www.rasmussen.edu
Phone: (239) 477-2100 *Calendar:* Qtr. plan
Inst. Accred.: NCA-HLC (2001/2004, *Indirect accreditation through Rasmussen College System, Lake Elmo, MN*)

Rasmussen College—Ocala
2221 Southwest 19th Ave. Rd., Ocala 34474
Type: Private, proprietary, four-year
System: Rasmussen College System
Degrees: A, B
URL: http://www.rasmussen.edu
Phone: (352) 629-1941 *Calendar:* Qtr. plan
Inst. Accred.: NCA-HLC (2001/2004, *Indirect accreditation through Rasmussen College System, Lake Elmo, MN*)

Rasmussen College—Pasco County
2127 Grand Blvd., Holiday 34691
Type: Private, proprietary, four-year
System: Rasmussen College System
Degrees: A, B
URL: http://www.rasmussen.edu
Phone: (727) 942-0069 *Calendar:* Qtr. plan
Inst. Accred.: NCA-HLC (2001/2004, *Indirect accreditation through Rasmussen College System, Lake Elmo, MN*)

Remington College—Tampa
2410 East Busch Blvd., Tampa 33612-8410
Type: Private, proprietary, four-year
System: Education America, Inc.
Degrees: A, B *Enroll:* 866
URL: http://www.remingtoncollege.edu
Phone: (813) 935-5700 *Calendar:* Qtr. plan
Inst. Accred.: ACCSCT (1968/2007)

Fort Worth Campus
300 East Loop 820, Fort Worth, TX 76112-1225
Phone: (817) 451-0017

Largo Campus
8550 Ulmerton Rd., Unit 100, Largo 33771-3842
Phone: (727) 532-1999

RETS College
1573 West Fairbanks Ave., Ste. 100, Winter Park 32789
Type: Private, proprietary, two-year
System: Education Affiliates, Inc.
Degrees: A
URL: http://www.centralfloridacollege.edu
Phone: (407) 843-3984
Inst. Accred.: ACCSCT (1988/2007)

Largo Campus
6565 Ulmerton Rd., Largo 33771
Phone: (727) 531-5900
Prog. Accred: Allied Health (medical assisting (AMA))

Ringling College of Art and Design
2700 North Tamiami Trail, Sarasota 34234-5895
Type: Private, independent, four-year
Degrees: B *Enroll:* 1,065
URL: http://www.ringling.edu
Phone: (941) 351-5100 *Calendar:* Sem. plan
Inst. Accred.: SACS (1979/2006)
Prog. Accred.: Art, Interior Design

Rollins College
1000 Holt Ave., Winter Park 32789-4499
Type: Private, independent, four-year
Degrees: A, B, M *Enroll:* 3,126
URL: http://www.rollins.edu
Phone: (407) 646-2000 *Calendar:* Sem. plan
Inst. Accred.: SACS (1927/2005)
Prog. Accred.: Business (AACSB), Counseling, Music

Saint John Vianney College Seminary
2900 SW 87th Ave., Miami 33165-3244
Type: Private, Roman Catholic Church, four-year
Degrees: B *Enroll:* 43
URL: http://www.sjvcs.edu
Phone: (305) 223-4561 *Calendar:* Sem. plan
Inst. Accred.: SACS (1970/2007)

Saint Johns River Community College
5001 St. Johns Ave., Palatka 32177-3897
Type: Public, state/local, two-year
System: Florida State Department of Education, Division of Community Colleges
Degrees: A *Enroll:* 2,662
URL: http://www.sjrcc.edu
Phone: (386) 312-4200 *Calendar:* Tri. plan
Inst. Accred.: SACS (1963/2003)

Saint Leo University
PO Box 6665, Saint Leo 33574-6665
Type: Private, Roman Catholic Church, four-year
Degrees: A, B, M *Enroll:* 9,764
URL: http://www.saintleo.edu
Phone: (352) 588-8200 *Calendar:* Sem. plan
Inst. Accred.: SACS (1967/2002)
Prog. Accred.: Social Work

Saint Petersburg College
PO Box 13489, St. Petersburg 33733-3489
Type: Public, local, four-year
System: Florida State Department of Education, Division of Community Colleges
Degrees: A, B *Enroll:* 14,564
URL: http://www.spjc.edu
Phone: (727) 341-3600 *Calendar:* Sem. plan
Inst. Accred.: SACS (1931/2000)
Prog. Accred.: Allied Health (EMT-paramedic, respiratory therapy), Clinical Lab Technology, Dentistry (dental hygiene), Funeral Service Education (Mortuary Science), Nursing, Nursing Education, Physical Therapy Assisting, Veterinary Technology

Saint Petersburg Theological Seminary
10830 Navajo Dr., St. Petersburg 33708-3116
Type: Private, interdenominational, four-year
Degrees: B, M, D *Enroll:* 32
URL: http://www.sptseminary.edu
Phone: (727) 399-0276 *Calendar:* Sem. plan
Inst. Accred.: TRACS (2003)

Saint Thomas University
16400 NW 32nd Ave., Miami 33054
Type: Private, Roman Catholic Church, four-year
Degrees: B, M, D *Enroll:* 2,366
URL: http://www.stu.edu
Phone: (305) 625-6000 *Calendar:* Sem. plan
Inst. Accred.: SACS (1968/2003)
Prog. Accred.: Law

Saint Vincent de Paul Regional Seminary
10701 South Military Trail, Boynton Beach 33436-4899
Type: Private, Roman Catholic Church, four-year
Degrees: M *Enroll:* 73
URL: http://www.svdp.edu
Phone: (561) 732-4424 *Calendar:* Sem. plan
Inst. Accred.: ATS (1984/1999), SACS (1968/2000)

Sanford-Brown Institute—Jacksonville
10255 Fortune Pkwy., Ste. 501, Jacksonville 32256
Type: Private, proprietary, two-year
System: Career Education Corporation
Degrees: A *Enroll:* 293
URL: http://www.sbjacksonville.com
Phone: (904) 363-6221
Inst. Accred.: ABHES (1993/2004), ACICS (1999/2008)
Prog. Accred.: Allied Health (surgical technology), Medical Assisting (ABHES), Surgical Technology

Iselin Campus
675 U.S. Route 1, 2nd Flr., Iselin, NJ 08830
Phone: (732) 634-1131
Prog. Accred: Allied Health (diagnostic medical sonography, surgical technology), Medical Assisting (ABHES), Surgical Technology

Tampa Campus
5701 East Hillsborough Ave., Tampa 33610
Phone: (813) 621-0072
Prog. Accred: Allied Health (cardiovascular technology, surgical technology), Medical Assisting (ABHES), Surgical Technology

Santa Fe Community College
3000 NW 83rd St., Gainesville 32606-6200
Type: Public, local, two-year
System: Florida State Department of Education, Division of Community Colleges
Degrees: A *Enroll:* 9,530
URL: http://www.sfcc.edu
Phone: (352) 395-5000 *Calendar:* Sem. plan
Inst. Accred.: SACS (1968/2002)
Prog. Accred.: Allied Health (EMT-paramedic, cardiovascular technology, respiratory therapy, surgical technology), Construction Education, Dentistry (dental assisting, dental hygiene), Nuclear Medicine Technology, Nursing, Practical Nursing, Radiography

Schiller International University
300 East Bay Dr., Largo 33770
Type: Private, proprietary, four-year
System: Knowledge Investment Partners
Degrees: A, B, M *Enroll:* 128
URL: http://www.schiller.edu
Phone: (727) 736-5082 *Calendar:* Sem. plan
Inst. Accred.: ACICS (1983/2003)

American College of Switzerland
The American College of Switzerland, Leysin, Switzerland CH-1854
Phone: 011 41 24 493 03 09

Engelberg, Switzerland Campus
Dortstrasse 40, Engelberg, Switzerland 6390
Phone: 011 41 41 639 74 74

Heidelberg, Germany Campus
Bergstrasse 106, Heidelberg, Germany 69124
Phone: 011 49 62 21 4 58 10

London, England Campus
Royal Waterloo House, 51-55 Waterloo Rd., London, United Kingdom SE1 8TX
Phone: 011 44 207 9288484

Madrid, Spain Campus
Edificio Columina, San Bernardo 97-99, Madrid, Spain 28015
Phone: 011 34 91 448-2488

Paris, France Campus
32 Blvd. de Vaugirard, Paris, France 75015
Phone: 011 33 1 45 38 56 01

Strasbourg, France Campus
Chateau Pourtales, 161 rue Melanie, Strasbourg, France 67000
Phone: 011 33 3 88 45 84 62

Seminole Community College
100 Weldon Blvd., Sanford 32773-6199
Type: Public, local, two-year
System: Florida State Department of Education, Division of Community Colleges
Degrees: A *Enroll:* 6,580
URL: http://www.scc-fl.edu
Phone: (407) 328-4722 *Calendar:* Sem. plan
Inst. Accred.: SACS (1969/2003)
Prog. Accred.: Allied Health (EMT-paramedic, medical assisting (AMA), respiratory therapy), Nursing, Physical Therapy Assisting

South Florida Community College
600 West College Dr., Avon Park 33825-9356
Type: Public, local, two-year
System: Florida State Department of Education, Division of Community Colleges
Degrees: A *Enroll:* 1,325
URL: http://www.southflorida.edu
Phone: (863) 453-6661 *Calendar:* Sem. plan
Inst. Accred.: SACS (1968/2002)
Prog. Accred.: Dentistry (dental assisting, dental hygiene)

Southeastern University
1000 Longfellow Blvd., Lakeland 33801
Type: Private, Assemblies of God, four-year
Degrees: B, M *Enroll:* 2,260
URL: http://www.seuniversity.edu
Phone: (863) 667-5000 *Calendar:* Sem. plan
Inst. Accred.: SACS (1986/2001)
Prog. Accred.: Social Work

Southwest Florida College
1685 Medical Ln., Ste. 200, Fort Myers 33907
Type: Private, independent, four-year
Degrees: A, B *Enroll:* 1,518
URL: http://www.swfc.edu
Phone: (239) 939-4766 *Calendar:* Qtr. plan
Inst. Accred.: ACICS (1984/2003)
Prog. Accred.: Medical Assisting (ABHES), Surgical Technology

Tampa Campus
3910 Riga Blvd., Tampa 33619
Phone: (813) 630-4401
Prog. Accred: Medical Assisting (ABHES), Surgical Technology

Stenotype Institute of Jacksonville
3563 Phillips Hwy., Building E, Ste. 501, Jacksonville 32207
Type: Private, independent, two-year
Degrees: A
URL: http://courtreportingjax.com
Phone: (904) 398-4141
Inst. Accred.: ACICS (1968/2006)

Orlando Campus
1636 West Oakridge Rd., Orlando 32809
Phone: (407) 816-5573

Stetson University
421 North Woodland Blvd., DeLand 32720
Type: Private, Southern Baptist Church, four-year
Degrees: B, M, P, D *Enroll:* 3,369
URL: http://www.stetson.edu
Phone: (386) 822-7000 *Calendar:* Sem. plan
Inst. Accred.: SACS (1932/2001)
Prog. Accred.: Accounting, Business (AACSB), Counseling, Law, Music, Teacher Education (NCATE)

Tallahassee Community College
444 Appleyard Dr., Tallahassee 32304-2895
Type: Public, state/local, two-year
System: Florida State Department of Education, Division of Community Colleges
Degrees: A *Enroll:* 8,816
URL: http://www.tcc.fl.edu
Phone: (850) 201-6200 *Calendar:* Sem. plan
Inst. Accred.: SACS (1969/2005)
Prog. Accred.: Allied Health (EMT-paramedic, respiratory therapy), Dentistry (dental assisting, dental hygiene)

Pat Thomas Law Enforcement Academy
85 Academy Dr., Havana 32333
Phone: (850) 539-4002

Talmudic College of Florida
1910 Alton Rd., Miami Beach 33139
Type: Private, independent, four-year
Degrees: B, M, P, D *Enroll:* 44
Phone: (305) 534-7050 *Calendar:* Sem. plan
Inst. Accred.: AARTS (1977/2005)

Teacher Education University
1079 West Morse Blvd., Ste. B, Winter Park 32789
Type: Private, proprietary, four-year
Degrees: M
URL: http://www.teachereducationuniversity.com
Phone: (800) 523-1578
Inst. Accred.: DETC (2008)

Trinity Baptist College
800 Hammond Blvd., Jacksonville 32221
Type: Private, independent, four-year
Degrees: A, B, M *Enroll:* 399
URL: http://www.tbc.edu
Phone: (904) 596-2400 *Calendar:* Sem. plan
Inst. Accred.: TRACS (1997/2002)

Trinity College of Florida
2430 Welbilt Blvd., Trinity 34655-4401
Type: Private, nondenominational, four-year
Degrees: A, B *Enroll:* 158
URL: http://www.trinitycollege.edu
Phone: (727) 376-6911 *Calendar:* Sem. plan
Inst. Accred.: ABHE (1996/2002)

Universidad FLET
14540 SW 136th St., Ste. 108, Miami 33186
Type: Private, independent, four-year
Degrees: B, M
URL: http://www.flet.edu
Phone: (305) 378-8700
Inst. Accred.: DETC (2003)

University of Central Florida
4000 Central Florida Blvd., Orlando 32816-0002
Type: Public, state, four-year
System: State University System of Florida
Degrees: A, B, M, P, D *Enroll:* 36,757
URL: http://www.ucf.edu
Phone: (407) 823-2000 *Calendar:* Sem. plan
Inst. Accred.: SACS (1970/2006)
Prog. Accred.: Accounting, Allied Health (health information administration, health services administration, medicine, respiratory therapy, speech-language pathology), Business (AACSB), Clinical Lab Scientist, Clinical Psychology, Computer Science (ABET-CAC), Counseling, Engineering (aerospace, civil, computer, electrical, environmental/sanitary, industrial, mechanical), Engineering Technology (computer, electrical, general), English Language Education, Graduate Social Work, Music, Nursing Education, Physical Therapy, Public Administration, Radiography, Social Work, Teacher Education (NCATE)

University of Florida
PO Box 113150, Gainesville 32611-3150
Type: Public, state, four-year
System: State University System of Florida
Degrees: A, B, M, P, D *Enroll:* 45,946
URL: http://www.ufl.edu
Phone: (352) 392-3261 *Calendar:* Sem. plan
Inst. Accred.: SACS (1913/2003)
Prog. Accred.: Accounting, Allied Health (audiology, health services administration, medicine, occupational therapy, speech-language pathology), Applied Science (surveying/geomatics), Art, Business (AACSB), Clinical Psychology, Construction Education, Counseling, Counseling Psychology, Dentistry (combined prosthodontics, dental public health, dentistry, endodontics, oral and maxillofacial pathology, oral and maxillofacial surgery, orthodontic and dentofacial orthopedics, pediatric dentistry, periodontics), Dietetics (didactic), Dietetics (internship), Engineering (aerospace, agricultural, chemical, civil, computer, electrical, engineering physics/science, environmental/sanitary, industrial, materials, mechanical, nuclear, ocean), Forestry, Interior Design, Journalism, Landscape Architecture, Law, Music, Nurse (Midwifery), Nursing Education, Pharmacy, Physical Therapy, Physician Assistant, Planning, Psychology Internship, Recreation and Leisure Services, Rehabilitation Counseling, School Psychology, Teacher Education (NCATE), Theatre, Veterinary Medicine

Shands Jacksonville Medical Center
655 West 8th St., Jacksonville 32209
Phone: (352) 265-0111
Prog. Accred: Clinical Lab Scientist, Dentistry (advanced education in general dentistry, oral and maxillofacial surgery), Radiography

University of Miami
PO Box 248006, Coral Gables 33124-4600
Type: Private, independent, four-year
Degrees: B, M, D *Enroll:* 14,765
URL: http://www.miami.edu
Phone: (305) 284-2211 *Calendar:* Sem. plan
Inst. Accred.: SACS (1940/2008)
Prog. Accred.: Accounting, Allied Health (health services administration, medicine), Business (AACSB), Clinical Psychology, Counseling Psychology, Dentistry (general practice residency, oral and maxillofacial surgery), Engineering (architectural, bioengineering, civil, computer, electrical, environmental/sanitary, industrial, manufacturing, mechanical), English Language Education, Journalism, Law, Music, Nurse (Midwifery), Nurse Anesthesia Education, Nursing Education, Physical Therapy, Psychology Internship, Public Health

University of North Florida
4567 St. John's Bluff Rd. South, Jacksonville 32224-2645
Type: Public, state, four-year
System: State University System of Florida
Degrees: B, M, D *Enroll:* 12,154
URL: http://www.unf.edu
Phone: (904) 620-1000 *Calendar:* Sem. plan
Inst. Accred.: SACS (1974/1999)
Prog. Accred.: Accounting, Allied Health (health services administration), Business (AACSB), Computer Science (ABET-CAC), Construction Education, Counseling, Dietetics (didactic), Dietetics (internship), Engineering (civil, electrical, information systems, mechanical), Music, Nurse Anesthesia Education, Nursing, Nursing Education, Physical Therapy, Public Administration, Rehabilitation Counseling, Teacher Education (NCATE)

University of South Florida
4202 East Fowler Ave., Tampa 33620
Type: Public, state, four-year
System: State University System of Florida
Degrees: A, B, M, P, D *Enroll:* 33,574
URL: http://www.usf.edu
Phone: (813) 974-2011 *Calendar:* Sem. plan
Inst. Accred.: SACS (1965/2005)
Prog. Accred.: Accounting, Allied Health (audiology, medicine, speech-language pathology), Applied Science (industrial hygiene), Art, Business (AACSB), Clinical Psychology, Computer Science (ABET-CAC), Counseling, Engineering (chemical, civil, computer, electrical, industrial, mechanical), English Language Education, Graduate Social Work, Journalism, Librarianship, Music, Nurse Anesthesia Education, Nursing Education, Physical Therapy, Psychology Internship, Public Administration, Public Health, Rehabilitation Counseling, School Psychology, Social Work, Teacher Education (NCATE), Theatre

Lakeland Campus
3433 Winter Lake Rd., Lakeland 33803
Phone: (863) 667-7000

Sarasota Campus
8350 North Tamiami Trail, Sarasota 34243
Phone: (941) 359-4200

University of South Florida St. Petersburg
140 7th Ave. South, St. Petersburg 33701
Type: Public, state, four-year
Degrees: A, B, M, D
URL: http://www.stpt.usf.edu
Phone: (727) 553-4151 *Calendar:* Sem. plan
Inst. Accred.: SACS (2006, Probation)
Prog. Accred.: Accounting, Business (AACSB), Journalism

University of St. Augustine for Health Sciences
One University Blvd., St. Augustine 32086-5783
Type: Private, proprietary, four-year
Degrees: M, D *FTE Enroll:* 380
URL: http://www.usa.edu
Phone: (904) 826-0084 *Calendar:* Sem. plan
Inst. Accred.: DETC (1993/2003)
Prog. Accred.: Allied Health (occupational therapy), Physical Therapy

University of Tampa
401 West Kennedy Blvd., Tampa 33606-1490
Type: Private, independent, four-year
Degrees: A, B, M *Enroll:* 4,648
URL: http://www.ut.edu
Phone: (813) 253-3333 *Calendar:* Sem. plan
Inst. Accred.: SACS (1951/2005)
Prog. Accred.: Business (AACSB), Music, Nursing

University of West Florida
11000 University Pkwy., Pensacola 32514-5750
Type: Public, state, four-year
System: State University System of Florida
Degrees: A, B, M, D *Enroll:* 7,507
URL: http://www.uwf.edu
Phone: (850) 474-2000 *Calendar:* Sem. plan
Inst. Accred.: SACS (1969/2005)
Prog. Accred.: Business (AACSB), Clinical Lab Scientist, Music, Nursing Education, Social Work, Teacher Education (NCATE)

Emerald Coast Campus
1170 Martin Luther King Jr. Blvd., Fort Walton Beach 32547-5068
Phone: (850) 863-6565

Valencia Community College
PO Box 3028, Orlando 32802-3028
Type: Public, state, two-year
System: Florida State Department of Education, Division of Community Colleges
Degrees: A *Enroll:* 17,795
URL: http://valenciacc.edu
Phone: (407) 299-5000 *Calendar:* Sem. plan
Inst. Accred.: SACS (1969/2003)
Prog. Accred.: Allied Health (EMT-paramedic, diagnostic medical sonography, respiratory therapy), Dentistry (dental hygiene), Nursing, Radiography

East Campus
701 North Econlockhatchee Trail, Orlando 32825
Phone: (407) 299-5000

West Campus
1800 South Kirkman Rd., Orlando 32811
Phone: (407) 299-5000

Winter Park Campus
850 West Morse Blvd., Winter Park 32789
Phone: (407) 299-5000

Warner University
13895 Hwy. 27, Lake Wales 33859
Type: Private, Church of God, four-year
Degrees: A, B, M *Enroll:* 883
URL: http://www.warner.edu
Phone: (863) 638-1426 *Calendar:* Sem. plan
Inst. Accred.: SACS (1977/2003)

Webber International University
PO Box 96, Babson Park 33827
Type: Private, independent, four-year
Degrees: A, B, M *Enroll:* 560
URL: http://www.webber.edu
Phone: (800) 741-1844 *Calendar:* Sem. plan
Inst. Accred.: SACS (1969/2007, Probation)

Yeshiva Gedolah Rabbinical College
1140 Alton Rd., Miami Beach 33139
Type: Private, independent, four-year
Degrees: B, M *Enroll:* 51
Phone: (305) 653-8770 *Calendar:* Sem. plan
Inst. Accred.: AARTS (1997/2004)

GEORGIA

Abraham Baldwin Agricultural College
2802 Moore Hwy., Tifton 31794
Type: Public, state, four-year
System: Board of Regents of the University System of Georgia
Degrees: A, B *Enroll:* 2,635
URL: http://www.abac.peachnet.edu
Phone: (229) 391-5000 *Calendar:* Sem. plan
Inst. Accred.: SACS (1953/2007)
Prog. Accred.: Forestry, Nursing

Agnes Scott College
141 East College Ave., Decatur 30030
Type: Private, Presbyterian Church (USA), four-year
Degrees: B, M *Enroll:* 939
URL: http://www.agnesscott.edu
Phone: (404) 471-6000 *Calendar:* Sem. plan
Inst. Accred.: SACS (1907/2004)

Albany State University
504 College Dr., Albany 31705-2794
Type: Public, state, four-year
System: Board of Regents of the University System of Georgia
Degrees: B, M, P *Enroll:* 3,145
URL: http://asuweb.asurams.edu
Phone: (229) 430-4600 *Calendar:* Sem. plan
Inst. Accred.: SACS (1951/200 8)
Prog. Accred.: Business (ACBSP), Nursing, Public Administration, Social Work, Teacher Education (NCATE)

Albany Technical College
1704 South Slappey Blvd., Albany 31701
Type: Public, state, two-year
System: Technical College System of Georgia
Degrees: A *Enroll:* 1,859
URL: http://www.albanytech.edu
Phone: (229) 430-3500 *Calendar:* Qtr. plan
Inst. Accred.: COE (1974/2006), SACS (2005)
Prog. Accred.: Allied Health (medical assisting (AMA), surgical technology), Dentistry (dental assisting), Radiography

Early County Campus
Highway 27 North Bypass, Blakely 31723
Phone: (229) 724-3500

Altamaha Technical College
1777 West Cherry St., Jesup 31545
Type: Public, state/local, two-year
System: Technical College System of Georgia
Degrees: A
URL: http://www.altamahatech.edu
Phone: (912) 427-5800 *Calendar:* Qtr. plan
Inst. Accred.: COE (1992/2003)

Appling Technical Education Center
1334 Golden Isles Pkwy. West, Baxley 31514
Phone: (912) 427-5800

Jeff Davis Community School
677 Douglas Hwy., Hazlehurst 31539
Phone: (912) 379-0041

The American InterContinental University
3300 Peachtree Rd. NE, Atlanta 30326
Type: Private, proprietary, four-year
System: Career Education Corporation
Degrees: A, B, M *Enroll:* 1,369
URL: http://www.aiuniv.edu
Phone: (404) 965-5700 *Calendar:* Qtr. plan
Inst. Accred.: SACS (1987/2002)
Prog. Accred.: Interior Design

American InterContinental University Online
5550 Prairie Stone Pkwy., Hoffman Estates, IL 60192
Phone: (877) 701-3800

Buckhead Campus
3330 Peachtree Rd., NE, Atlanta 30326-1016
Phone: (404) 965-5712

Houston Campus
9999 Richmond Ave., Houston, TX 77042
Phone: (800) 524-3995

London Campus
110 Marylebone High St., London, United Kingdom W1M 3DB
Phone: 011-44-071 486-1772

Los Angeles Campus
12655 West Jefferson Blvd., Los Angeles, CA 90066-7008
Phone: (310) 302-2000
Prog. Accred: Interior Design

Weston/Ft. Lauderdale Campus
2250 North Commerce Parway, Ste. 100, Weston, FL 33326
Phone: (954) 835-0939

Andrew College
413 College St., Cuthbert 31740
Type: Private, United Methodist Church, two-year
Degrees: A *Enroll:* 312
URL: http://www.andrewcollege.edu
Phone: (229) 732-2171 *Calendar:* Sem. plan
Inst. Accred.: SACS (1927/2006)

Appalachian Technical College
100 Campus Dr., Jasper 30143
Type: Public, state, two-year
System: Technical College System of Georgia
Degrees: A *Enroll:* 627
URL: http://www.appalachiantech.edu
Phone: (706) 253-4500
Inst. Accred.: COE (1971/2003), SACS (2007)
Prog. Accred.: Allied Health (medical assisting (AMA))

Argosy University Atlanta
980 Hammond Dr., Ste. 100, Atlanta 30328-6162
Type: Private, proprietary, four-year
System: Argosy University
Degrees: B, M, D
URL: http://www.argosy.edu/locations/atlanta
Phone: (770) 671-1200 *Calendar:* Tri. plan
Inst. Accred.: NCA-HLC (1981/2008, *Indirect accreditation through Argosy University, Chicago, IL*)
Prog. Accred.: Clinical Psychology

Nashville Campus
341 Cool Springs Blvd., Ste. 210, Franklin, TN 37067-7226
Phone: (615) 369-0616

Armstrong Atlantic State University
11935 Abercorn St., Savannah 31419-1997
Type: Public, state, four-year
System: Board of Regents of the University System of Georgia
Degrees: A, B, M *Enroll:* 4,999
URL: http://www.armstrong.edu
Phone: (912) 927-5211 *Calendar:* Sem. plan
Inst. Accred.: SACS (1940/2002)
Prog. Accred.: Allied Health (respiratory therapy), Clinical Lab Scientist, Computer Science (ABET-CAC), Dentistry (dental hygiene), Music, Nuclear Medicine Technology, Nursing Education, Physical Therapy, Public Health, Radiation Therapy, Radiography, Teacher Education (NCATE)

The Art Institute of Atlanta
6600 Peachtree-Dunwoody Rd., 100 Embassy Row, Atlanta 30328
Type: Private, proprietary, four-year
System: Education Management Corporation
Degrees: A, B *Enroll:* 2,421
URL: http://www.aia.artinstitute.edu
Phone: (770) 394-8300 *Calendar:* Qtr. plan
Inst. Accred.: SACS (1985/2000)
Prog. Accred.: Art, Culinary Education, Interior Design

The Art Institute of Charleston
24 North Market St., Charleston, SC 29401
Phone: (843) 727-3500

The Art Institute of Tennessee—Nashville
100 Centerview Dr., Ste. 250, Nashville, TN 37214
Phone: (615) 874-1067

The Art Institute of Washington
1820 North Fort Myer Dr., Arlington, VA 22209-1802
Phone: (703) 358-9550
Prog. Accred: Culinary Education

Decatur Campus
One West Ct. Square, Ste. 110, Decatur 30030-2556
Phone: (866) 856-6203

Ashworth University
430 Technology Pkwy., Norcross 30092-3406
Type: Private, proprietary, four-year
Degrees: A, M
URL: http://www.ashworthuniversity.edu
Phone: (770) 729-8400
Inst. Accred.: DETC (2000/2008)

Athens Technical College
800 U.S. Hwy. 29 North, Athens 30601-1500
Type: Public, state, two-year
System: Technical College System of Georgia
Degrees: A *Enroll:* 2,231
URL: http://www.athenstech.edu
Phone: (706) 355-5000 *Calendar:* Qtr. plan
Inst. Accred.: SACS (1988/2003)
Prog. Accred.: Allied Health (respiratory therapy, surgical technology), Business (ACBSP), Dentistry (dental hygiene), Nursing, Physical Therapy Assisting, Radiography, Veterinary Technology

Atlanta Christian College
2605 Ben Hill Rd., East Point 30344
Type: Private, Christian Churches/Churches of Christ, four-year
Degrees: A, B *Enroll:* 407
URL: http://www.acc.edu
Phone: (404) 761-8861 *Calendar:* Sem. plan
Inst. Accred.: SACS (1990/2006)
Prog. Accred.: Teacher Education (NCATE)

Atlanta Metropolitan College
1630 Metropolitan Pkwy., SW, Atlanta 30310
Type: Public, state, two-year
System: Board of Regents of the University System of Georgia
Degrees: A *Enroll:* 1,163
URL: http://www.atlm.peachnet.edu
Phone: (404) 756-4000 *Calendar:* Sem. plan
Inst. Accred.: SACS (1976/2001)
Prog. Accred.: Business (ACBSP)

Atlanta Technical College
1560 Metropolitan Ave., SW, Atlanta 30310
Type: Public, state, two-year
System: Technical College System of Georgia
Degrees: A *Enroll:* 2,202
URL: http://www.atlantatech.edu
Phone: (404) 225-4400 *Calendar:* Qtr. plan
Inst. Accred.: COE (1971/2003), SACS (2005)
Prog. Accred.: Allied Health (medical assisting (AMA)), Clinical Lab Technology, Dentistry (dental assisting, dental laboratory technology)

Delta Airlines Campus
Hartfield International Airport, Atlanta 30310
Phone: (404) 758-5591

Augusta State University
2500 Walton Way, Augusta 30904-2200
Type: Public, state, four-year
System: Board of Regents of the University System of Georgia
Degrees: A, B, M, P *Enroll:* 4,889
URL: http://www.aug.edu
Phone: (706) 737-1400 *Calendar:* Sem. plan
Inst. Accred.: SACS (1926/2001)
Prog. Accred.: Art, Business (AACSB), Counseling, Music, Nursing, Public Administration, Teacher Education (NCATE)

Augusta Technical College
3200 Augusta Tech Dr., Augusta 30906
Type: Public, state, two-year
System: Technical College System of Georgia
Degrees: A *Enroll:* 2,720
URL: http://www.augustatech.edu
Phone: (706) 771-4000 *Calendar:* Qtr. plan
Inst. Accred.: SACS (1988/2003)
Prog. Accred.: Allied Health (cardiovascular technology, medical assisting (AMA), occupational therapy assisting, respiratory therapy, surgical technology), Dentistry (dental assisting), Engineering Technology (computer, mechanical), Practical Nursing

Thompson McDuffie Campus
388 Tech Dr., NW, Thompson 30824
Phone: (706) 595-0166

Bainbridge College
PO Box 990, Bainbridge 39818-0990
Type: Public, state, two-year
System: Board of Regents of the University System of Georgia
Degrees: A *Enroll:* 1,464
URL: http://www.bainbridge.edu
Phone: (229) 248-2500 *Calendar:* Sem. plan
Inst. Accred.: SACS (1975/2000)

Bauder College
384 Northyards Blvd. NW, Suites 190 and 400, Atlanta 30313
Type: Private, proprietary, four-year
System: Kaplan Higher Education Corporation
Degrees: A, B *Enroll:* 574
URL: http://www.bauder.edu
Phone: (404) 237-7573 *Calendar:* Qtr. plan
Inst. Accred.: SACS (1985/2000)

Beacon University
PO Box 8766, Columbus 31908-8766
Type: Private, interdenominational, four-year
Degrees: A, B, M, D *Enroll:* 176
URL: http://www.beacon.edu
Phone: (706) 323-5364 *Calendar:* Sem. plan
Inst. Accred.: TRACS (2000/2005)

Berry College
PO Box 490039, Mount Berry 30149-0039
Type: Private, independent, four-year
Degrees: B, M, P *Enroll:* 1,894
URL: http://www.berry.edu
Phone: (706) 232-5374 *Calendar:* Sem. plan
Inst. Accred.: SACS (1957/2008)
Prog. Accred.: Business (AACSB), Music, Teacher Education (NCATE)

Beulah Heights University
PO Box 18145, Atlanta 30316-0145
Type: Private, Pentacostal Church of Christ, four-year
Degrees: A, B *Enroll:* 385
URL: http://www.beulah.org
Phone: (404) 627-2681 *Calendar:* Sem. plan
Inst. Accred.: ABHE (1999/2003), TRACS (1997/2002)

Brenau University
500 Washington St. SE, Gainesville 30501
Type: Private, independent, four-year
Degrees: B, M, P *Enroll:* 1,606
URL: http://www.brenau.edu
Phone: (770) 534-6299 *Calendar:* Sem. plan
Inst. Accred.: SACS (1947/2001)
Prog. Accred.: Allied Health (occupational therapy), Dance, Interior Design, Nursing, Nursing Education, Teacher Education (NCATE)

Atlanta Campus
3139 Campus Dr., Ste. 300, Norcross 30071
Phone: (770) 446-2900
Prog. Accred: Allied Health (occupational therapy)

Augusta Campus
115 Davis Rd., Martinez 30907
Phone: (706) 210-2576

Gainesville Campus
500 Washington St. SE, Gainesville 30501
Phone: (770) 531-3135

Kings Bay Campus
918 USS James Madison Rd., Kingsland 31547
Phone: (912) 882-7125

Brewton-Parker College
PO Box 197, Mount Vernon 30445-0197
Type: Private, Georgia Baptist Convention, four-year
Degrees: A, B *Enroll:* 986
URL: http://www.bpc.edu
Phone: (912) 583-2241 *Calendar:* Sem. plan
Inst. Accred.: SACS (1962/2002)
Prog. Accred.: Music, Teacher Education (NCATE)

Brown College of Court Reporting and Medical Transcription
1740 Peachtree St., NW, Atlanta 30309
Type: Private, proprietary, two-year
Degrees: A
URL: http://www.browncollege.com
Phone: (404) 876-1227 *Calendar:* Qtr. plan
Inst. Accred.: COE (1984/2007)

Longview Campus
1125 Judson Plaza, #119, Longview, TX 75601-5120
Phone: (903) 757-4338

Carver Bible College
3870 Cascade Rd. SW, Atlanta 30331-2184
Type: Private, independent, four-year
Degrees: A, B
URL: http://www.carver.edu
Phone: (404) 527-4520 *Calendar:* Sem. plan
Inst. Accred.: ABHE (2006)

Central Georgia Technical College
3300 Macon Tech Dr., Macon 31206
Type: Public, state, two-year
System: Technical College System of Georgia
Degrees: A *Enroll:* 4,061
URL: http://www.cgtcollege.org
Phone: (478) 757-3400 *Calendar:* Qtr. plan
Inst. Accred.: SACS (1999/2005)
Prog. Accred.: Allied Health (surgical technology), Clinical Lab Technology, Dentistry (dental hygiene)

Milledgeville Campus
54 Hwy. 22 West, PO Box 1009, Milledgeville 31206
Phone: (478) 445-2300

Chattahoochee Technical College
980 South Cobb Dr., Marietta 30060
Type: Public, state, two-year
System: Technical College System of Georgia
Degrees: A *Enroll:* 3,597
URL: http://www.chattcollege.com
Phone: (770) 528-4500 *Calendar:* Qtr. plan
Inst. Accred.: SACS (1988/2003)
Prog. Accred.: Allied Health (medical assisting (AMA), surgical technology), Business (ACBSP), Engineering Technology (biomedical, electrical)

Mountain View Campus
2680 Gordy Pkwy., Marietta 30066
Phone: (770) 509-6305
Prog. Accred: Culinary Education

Paulding Campus
400 Nathan Dean Blvd., Dallas 30132
Phone: (770) 443-3600

South Cobb Campus
1578 Veterans Memorial Hwy., Austell 30168
Phone: (770) 732-5900

Clark Atlanta University
223 James P. Brawley Dr., Atlanta 30314
Type: Private, United Methodist Church, four-year
Degrees: B, M, D *Enroll:* 4,115
URL: http://www.cau.edu
Phone: (404) 880-8000 *Calendar:* Sem. plan
Inst. Accred.: SACS (1990/2006)
Prog. Accred.: Business (AACSB), Graduate Social Work, Public Administration, Social Work, Teacher Education (NCATE)

Clayton State University
2000 Clayton State Blvd., Morrow 30260
Type: Public, state, four-year
System: Board of Regents of the University System of Georgia
Degrees: A, B, M *Enroll:* 4,506
URL: http://www.clayton.edu
Phone: (678) 466-4000 *Calendar:* Sem. plan
Inst. Accred.: SACS (1971/2004)
Prog. Accred.: Allied Health (medical assisting (AMA)), Business (AACSB), Dentistry (dental hygiene), Nursing Education, Teacher Education (NCATE)

College of Coastal Georgia
3700 Altama Ave., Brunswick 31520-3644
Type: Public, state, two-year
System: Board of Regents of the University System of Georgia
Degrees: A *Enroll:* 1,694
URL: http://www.ccga.edu
Phone: (912) 264-7235 *Calendar:* Sem. plan
Inst. Accred.: SACS (1967/2001)
Prog. Accred.: Allied Health (surgical technology), Clinical Lab Technology, Culinary Education, Nursing, Radiography

Columbia Theological Seminary
PO Box 520, Decatur 30031-0520
Type: Private, Presbyterian Church (USA), four-year
Degrees: M, D *Enroll:* 281
URL: http://www.ctsnet.edu
Phone: (404) 378-8821 *Calendar:* 4-1-4 plan
Inst. Accred.: ATS (1938/2003), SACS (1983/2003)

Columbus State University
4225 University Ave., Columbus 31907-5645
Type: Public, state, four-year
System: Board of Regents of the University System of Georgia
Degrees: A, B, M, P *Enroll:* 5,798
URL: http://www.colstate.edu
Phone: (706) 568-2001 *Calendar:* Sem. plan
Inst. Accred.: SACS (1963/2006)
Prog. Accred.: Art, Business (AACSB), Counseling, Dentistry (dental hygiene), Music, Nursing, Teacher Education (NCATE), Theatre

Columbus Technical College
928 Manchester Expressway, Columbus 31904-6572
Type: Public, state, two-year
System: Technical College System of Georgia
Degrees: A *Enroll:* 2,205
URL: http://www.columbustech.edu
Phone: (706) 649-1800 *Calendar:* Qtr. plan
Inst. Accred.: SACS (1990/2005)
Prog. Accred.: Allied Health (medical assisting (AMA), surgical technology), Dentistry (dental hygiene), Nursing, Practical Nursing, Radiography

Coosa Valley Technical College
1 Maurice Culberson Dr., Rome 30161-6757
Type: Public, state, two-year
System: Technical College System of Georgia
Degrees: A *Enroll:* 1,781
URL: http://www.coosavalleytech.edu
Phone: (706) 295-6963 *Calendar:* Qtr. plan
Inst. Accred.: COE (1972/2004), SACS (2006)
Prog. Accred.: Allied Health (diagnostic medical sonography, medical assisting (AMA), respiratory therapy, surgical technology), Nuclear Medicine Technology, Radiography

Calhoun/Gordon County Campus
1151 Hwy. 53 Spur, Calhoun 30701
Phone: (706) 295-6927

Polk County Campus
466 Brock Rd., Rockmart 30153
Phone: (770) 684-5696

Covenant College
14049 Scenic Hwy., Lookout Mountain 30750
Type: Private, Reformed Presbyterian Church, four-year
Degrees: A, B, M *Enroll:* 1,224
URL: http://www.covenant.edu
Phone: (706) 820-1560 *Calendar:* Sem. plan
Inst. Accred.: SACS (1971/2007)
Prog. Accred.: Business (ACBSP)

Dalton State College
650 College Dr., Dalton 30720-3778
Type: Public, state, four-year
System: Board of Regents of the University System of Georgia
Degrees: A, B *Enroll:* 2,867
URL: http://www.daltonstate.edu
Phone: (706) 272-4436 *Calendar:* Sem. plan
Inst. Accred.: SACS (1969/2003)
Prog. Accred.: Allied Health (medical assisting (AMA)), Clinical Lab Technology, Nursing, Phlebotomy, Radiography, Social Work

Darton College
2400 Gillionville Rd., Albany 31707-3098
Type: Public, state, two-year
System: Board of Regents of the University System of Georgia
Degrees: A *Enroll:* 2,951
URL: http://www.darton.edu
Phone: (229) 430-6000 *Calendar:* Sem. plan
Inst. Accred.: SACS (1968/2003)
Prog. Accred.: Allied Health (cardiovascular technology, occupational therapy assisting, respiratory therapy), Clinical Lab Technology, Dentistry (dental hygiene), Nursing, Physical Therapy Assisting

DeKalb Technical College
495 North Indian Creek Dr., Clarkston 30021
Type: Public, state, two-year
System: Technical College System of Georgia
Degrees: A *Enroll:* 2,390
URL: http://www.dekalbtech.org
Phone: (404) 297-9522 *Calendar:* Qtr. plan
Inst. Accred.: SACS (1967/2002)
Prog. Accred.: Allied Health (medical assisting (AMA), ophthalmic lab technology, surgical technology), Clinical Lab Technology, Engineering Technology (electrical)

DeVry University Georgia
250 North Arcadia Ave., Decatur 30030-2198
Type: Private, proprietary
System: DeVry University
Degrees: A, B, M *Enroll:* 3,148
URL: http://www.devry.edu/decatur
Phone: (404) 292-7900 *Calendar:* Sem. plan
Inst. Accred.: NCA-HLC (2002, *Indirect accreditation through DeVry University, Oakbrook Terrace, IL*)
Prog. Accred.: Engineering Technology (computer, electrical)

Alpharetta Campus
2555 Northwinds Pkwy., Alpharetta 30004
Phone: (770) 521-4900

Atlanta Buckhead Campus
3575 Piedmont Rd. NE, Plaza Level 100, Atlanta 30305
Phone: (404) 296-7400

Atlanta Cobb-Galleria Campus
100 Galleria Pkwy. SE, Ste. 100, Atlanta 30339
Phone: (678) 424-5630

Gwinnett Campus
3505 Koger Blvd., Ste. 170, Duluth 30096
Phone: (678) 380-9780

Henry County Campus
675 Southcrest Pkwy., Ste. 150, Stockbridge 30281
Phone: (678) 284-4700

East Central Technical College
667 Perry House Rd., Fitzgerald 31750
Type: Public, state/local, two-year
System: Technical College System of Georgia
Degrees: A *Enroll:* 788
URL: http://www.eastcentraltech.edu
Phone: (229) 468-2000 *Calendar:* Qtr. plan
Inst. Accred.: COE (1973/2006)

Coffee Campus
706 West Baker Hwy., Douglas 31533
Phone: (912) 389-4303

East Georgia College
131 College Circle, Swainsboro 30401
Type: Public, state, two-year
System: Board of Regents of the University System of Georgia
Degrees: A *Enroll:* 1,246
URL: http://www.ega.edu
Phone: (478) 289-2000 *Calendar:* Sem. plan
Inst. Accred.: SACS (1975/2000)

Emmanuel College
PO Box 129, Franklin Springs 30639
Type: Private, International Pentecostal Holiness Church, four-year
Degrees: A, B *Enroll:* 638
URL: http://www.emmanuelcollege.edu
Phone: (706) 245-7226 *Calendar:* Sem. plan
Inst. Accred.: SACS (1967/2007)

Emory University
201 Dowman Dr., Atlanta 30322-1061
Type: Private, United Methodist Church, four-year
Degrees: A, B, M, P, D *Enroll:* 11,624
URL: http://www.emory.edu
Phone: (404) 727-6123 *Calendar:* Sem. plan
Inst. Accred.: ATS (1938/2003), SACS (1917/2003)
Prog. Accred.: Allied Health (anesthesiologist assisting, medicine), Business (AACSB), Clinical Pastoral Education (ACPEI), Clinical Psychology, Dentistry (oral and maxillofacial pathology, oral and maxillofacial surgery), Dietetics (internship), Law, Music, Nurse (Midwifery), Nursing Education, Physical Therapy, Physician Assistant, Psychology Internship, Public Health, Radiography, Teacher Education (NCATE)

Everest Institute—Atlanta DeKalb
1706 Northeast Expressway, Atlanta 30329
Type: Private, proprietary, two-year
System: Corinthian Colleges, Inc
Degrees: A
URL: http://www.everest.edu
Phone: (404) 327-8787
Inst. Accred.: ACCSCT (2000/2005)

Flint River Technical College
1533 Hwy. 19, South, Thomaston 30286-4752
Type: Public, state, two-year
System: Technical College System of Georgia
Degrees: A *Enroll:* 553
URL: http://www.flintrivertech.edu
Phone: (706) 646-6148 *Calendar:* Qtr. plan
Inst. Accred.: COE (1973/2003)
Prog. Accred.: Allied Health (surgical technology)

Fort Valley State University
1005 State University Dr., Fort Valley 31030-4313
Type: Public, state, four-year
System: Board of Regents of the University System of Georgia
Degrees: A, B, M, P *Enroll:* 1,947
URL: http://www.fvsu.edu
Phone: (478) 825-6211 *Calendar:* Sem. plan
Inst. Accred.: SACS (1951/2000)
Prog. Accred.: Dietetics (didactic), Engineering Technology (electrical), Family & Consumer Science, Montessori Teacher Education, Rehabilitation Counseling, Veterinary Technology

Gainesville State College
PO Box 1358, Gainesville 30503-1358
Type: Public, state, four-year
System: Board of Regents of the University System of Georgia
Degrees: A, B *Enroll:* 4,367
URL: http://www.gc.peachnet.edu
Phone: (770) 718-3941 *Calendar:* Sem. plan
Inst. Accred.: SACS (1968/2002)
Prog. Accred.: Business (ACBSP), Dentistry (dental assisting)

Georgia College and State University
231 West Hancock St., Milledgeville 31061-3375
Type: Public, state, four-year
System: Board of Regents of the University System of Georgia
Degrees: A, B, M, P *Enroll:* 4,993
URL: http://www.gcsu.edu
Phone: (478) 445-5004 *Calendar:* Sem. plan
Inst. Accred.: SACS (1925/2004)
Prog. Accred.: Business (AACSB), Music, Nursing, Public Administration, Teacher Education (NCATE)

Georgia Highlands College
PO Box 1864, Rome 30162-1864
Type: Public, state, two-year
System: Board of Regents of the University System of Georgia
Degrees: A *Enroll:* 2,649
URL: http://www.highlands.edu
Phone: (706) 802-5000 *Calendar:* Sem. plan
Inst. Accred.: SACS (1972/2008)
Prog. Accred.: Dentistry (dental hygiene), Nursing

Cartersville Campus
5441 Hwy. 20, NE, Cartersville 30121
Phone: (678) 872-8000

Georgia Institute of Technology
225 North Ave., NW, Atlanta 30332-0325
Type: Public, state, four-year
System: Board of Regents of the University System of Georgia
Degrees: B, M, D *Enroll:* 16,050
URL: http://www.gatech.edu
Phone: (404) 894-2000 *Calendar:* Sem. plan
Inst. Accred.: SACS (1923/2005)
Prog. Accred.: Allied Health (orthotist/prothetist), Art, Business (AACSB), Computer Science (ABET-CAC), Construction Education, Engineering (aerospace, bioengineering, chemical, civil, computer, electrical, environmental/sanitary, industrial, materials, mechanical, nuclear, textile), Planning

Institute of Paper Science and Technology at Georgia Tech
500 10th St., N.W., Atlanta 30318
Phone: (404) 894-5700

Georgia Military College
201 East Greene St., Milledgeville 31061-3398
Type: Public, state/local, two-year
Degrees: A *Enroll:* 967
URL: http://www.gmc.cc.ga.us
Phone: (478) 445-2700 *Calendar:* Qtr. plan
Inst. Accred.: SACS (1940/2007)

Georgia Perimeter College
3251 Panthersville Rd., Decatur 30034
Type: Public, state, two-year
System: Board of Regents of the University System of Georgia
Degrees: A *Enroll:* 12,948
URL: http://www.gpc.edu
Phone: (678) 891-2661 *Calendar:* Sem. plan
Inst. Accred.: SACS (1967/2002)

Clarkston Campus
555 North Indian Creek Dr., Clarkston 30021-2396
Phone: (404) 299-4000
Prog. Accred: Nursing

Dunwoody Campus
2101 Womack Rd., Dunwoody 30338-4497
Phone: (770) 551-3000
Prog. Accred: Dentistry (dental hygiene)

Gwinnett University Center
1000 University Center Ln., Lawrenceville 30043
Phone: (678) 407-5000

Georgia Southern University
PO Box 8033, Statesboro 30460-8033
Type: Public, state, four-year
System: Board of Regents of the University System of Georgia
Degrees: A, B, M, P, D *Enroll:* 14,852
URL: http://www.gasou.edu
Phone: (912) 681-5611 *Calendar:* Sem. plan
Inst. Accred.: SACS (1935/2005)
Prog. Accred.: Accounting, Art, Business (AACSB), Computer Science (ABET-CAC), Construction Education, Design Technology, Dietetics (didactic), Engineering Technology (civil/construction, electrical, information systems, mechanical), Industrial Technology, Interior Design, Music, Nursing Education, Public Administration, Recreation and Leisure Services, Teacher Education (NCATE)

Georgia Southwestern State University
800 Wheatley St., Americus 31709-4693
Type: Public, state, four-year
System: Board of Regents of the University System of Georgia
Degrees: A, B, M, P *Enroll:* 2,008
URL: http://www.gsw.edu
Phone: (229) 928-1279 *Calendar:* Sem. plan
Inst. Accred.: SACS (1932/2003)
Prog. Accred.: Business (ACBSP), Nursing, Teacher Education (NCATE)

Georgia State University
PO Box 3965, Atlanta 30302-3965
Type: Public, state, four-year
System: Board of Regents of the University System of Georgia
Degrees: A, B, M, P, D *Enroll:* 20,860
URL: http://www.gsu.edu
Phone: (404) 651-2000 *Calendar:* Sem. plan
Inst. Accred.: SACS (1952/2008)
Prog. Accred.: Accounting, Allied Health (health services administration, respiratory therapy, speech-language pathology), Art, Business (AACSB), Clinical Psychology, Counseling, Counseling Psychology, Dietetics (coordinated), Dietetics (didactic), Dietetics (internship), Exercise Physiology, Exercise Science, Graduate Social Work, Law, Music, Nursing Education, Physical Therapy, Psychology Internship, Public Administration, Public Health, Rehabilitation Counseling, School Psychology, Social Work, Teacher Education (NCATE)

Gordon College
419 College Dr., Barnesville 30204
Type: Public, state, four-year
System: Board of Regents of the University System of Georgia
Degrees: A, B *Enroll:* 2,729
URL: http://www.gdn.edu
Phone: (770) 358-5000 *Calendar:* Sem. plan
Inst. Accred.: SACS (1941/2007)
Prog. Accred.: Nursing

Griffin Technical College
501 Varsity Rd., Griffin 30223
Type: Public, state, two-year
System: Technical College System of Georgia
Degrees: A *Enroll:* 2,136
URL: http://www.griffintech.edu
Phone: (770) 228-7348 *Calendar:* Qtr. plan
Inst. Accred.: SACS (1998/2003)
Prog. Accred.: Allied Health (medical assisting (AMA), respiratory therapy, surgical technology), Radiography

Gupton-Jones College of Funeral Service
5141 Snapfinger Woods Dr., Decatur 30035-4022
Type: Private, independent, two-year
Degrees: A *Enroll:* 190
URL: http://www.gupton-jones.edu
Phone: (770) 593-2257 *Calendar:* Qtr. plan
Inst. Accred.: ABFSE (1965/2007)

Gwinnett College
4230 Hwy. 29, Ste. 11, Liburn 30047
Type: Private, proprietary, two-year
Degrees: A
URL: http://www.gwinnettcollege.com
Phone: (770) 381-7200 *Calendar:* Qtr. plan
Inst. Accred.: ACICS (1988/2008)

Gwinnett Technical College
5150 Sugarloaf Pkwy., Lawrenceville 30043-5702
Type: Public, local, two-year
System: Technical College System of Georgia
Degrees: A *Enroll:* 2,486
URL: http://www.gwinnetttech.edu
Phone: (770) 962-7580 *Calendar:* Qtr. plan
Inst. Accred.: SACS (1991/2007)
Prog. Accred.: Allied Health (EMT-paramedic, medical assisting (AMA), respiratory therapy, surgical technology), Dentistry (dental assisting, dental laboratory technology), Physical Therapy Assisting, Radiography, Veterinary Technology

Heart of Georgia Technical College
560 Pinehill Rd., Dublin 31021-8896
Type: Public, state, two-year
System: Technical College System of Georgia
Degrees: A *Enroll:* 972
URL: http://www.heartofgatech.edu
Phone: (478) 275-6589 *Calendar:* Qtr. plan
Inst. Accred.: COE (1986/2003)
Prog. Accred.: Allied Health (medical assisting (AMA), respiratory therapy), Radiography

Herzing College
3393 Peachtree Rd. NE, Atlanta 30326
Type: Private, proprietary, four-year
System: Herzing College Corporate Offices
Degrees: A, B, M *Enroll:* 203
URL: http://www.herzing.edu
Phone: (404) 816-4533 *Calendar:* Qtr. plan
Inst. Accred.: NCA-HLC (2004, *Indirect accreditation through Herzing College Corporate Offices, Milwaukee, WI*)

New Orleans Campus
2400 Veterans Blvd., Ste. 410, Kenner, LA 70062
Phone: (504) 733-0074

Winter Park Campus
1595 South Semoran Blvd., Winter Park, FL 32792
Phone: (407) 478-0500

Interactive College of Technology
5303 New Peachtree Rd., Chamblee 30341
Type: Private, proprietary, two-year
Degrees: A *Enroll:* 202
URL: http://www.ict-ils.edu
Phone: (770) 216-2960
Inst. Accred.: COE (1989/2006)

Florence Campus
11 Spiral Dr., Ste. 8, Florence, KY 41042
Phone: (859) 282-8989

Gainesville Campus
2323 Browns Bridge Rd., Gainesville 30504
Phone: (678) 450-0550

Morrow Campus
1580 South Lake Pkwy., Ste. C, Morrow 30260
Phone: (770) 960-1298

Interdenominational Theological Center
700 Martin Luther King Jr. Dr., SW, Atlanta 30314-4143
Type: Private, interdenominational, four-year
Degrees: M, D *Enroll:* 363
URL: http://www.itc.edu
Phone: (404) 527-7700 *Calendar:* Sem. plan
Inst. Accred.: ATS (1960/2001), SACS (1984/2001)

Kennesaw State University
1000 Chastain Rd., Kennesaw 30144-5591
Type: Public, state, four-year
System: Board of Regents of the University System of Georgia
Degrees: A, B, M, D *Enroll:* 14,569
URL: http://www.kennesaw.edu
Phone: (770) 423-6000 *Calendar:* Sem. plan
Inst. Accred.: SACS (1968/2007)
Prog. Accred.: Accounting, Art, Business (AACSB), Computer Science (ABET-CAC), Cytogenetic Technology, Engineering (information systems), Graduate Social Work, Music, Nursing Education, Public Administration, Teacher Education (NCATE), Theatre

LaGrange College
601 Broad St., LaGrange 30240-2999
Type: Private, North Georgia Conference of the United Methodist C, four-year
Degrees: A, B, M *Enroll:* 988
URL: http://www.lagrange.edu
Phone: (706) 880-8005 *Calendar:* 4-1-4 plan
Inst. Accred.: SACS (1946/2002)
Prog. Accred.: Business (ACBSP), Nursing

Lanier Technical College
2990 Landrum Education Dr., Oakwood 30566
Type: Public, state, two-year
System: Technical College System of Georgia
Degrees: A *Enroll:* 1,902
URL: http://www.laniertech.edu
Phone: (770) 531-6300 *Calendar:* Qtr. plan
Inst. Accred.: COE (1972/2003)
Prog. Accred.: Allied Health (medical assisting (AMA), surgical technology), Clinical Lab Technology, Dentistry (dental assisting, dental hygiene)

Forsyth Campus
7745 Majors Rd., Cumming 30028-6508
Phone: (770) 781-6800
Prog. Accred: Allied Health (medical assisting (AMA))

Life University
1269 Barclay Circle, Marietta 30060
Type: Private, independent, four-year
Degrees: B, M, D *Enroll:* 1,301
URL: http://www.life.edu
Phone: (770) 426-2600 *Calendar:* Qtr. plan
Inst. Accred.: SACS (1986/2004)
Prog. Accred.: Chiropractic Education, Dietetics (didactic), Dietetics (internship)

Luther Rice University
3038 Evans Mill Rd., Lithonia 30038
Type: Private, Southern Baptist Church, four-year
Degrees: B, M, D
URL: http://www.lru.edu
Phone: (770) 484-1204 *Calendar:* Sem. plan
Inst. Accred.: TRACS (1988/2005)

Macon State College
100 College Station Dr., Macon 31206-5144
Type: Public, state, four-year
System: Board of Regents of the University System of Georgia
Degrees: A, B *Enroll:* 4,144
URL: http://www.maconstate.edu
Phone: (478) 471-2700 *Calendar:* Sem. plan
Inst. Accred.: SACS (1970/2002)
Prog. Accred.: Allied Health (respiratory therapy), Dentistry (dental hygiene), Nursing

Warner Robins Campus
100 University Blvd., Warner Robins 31093-3471
Phone: (478) 929-6700
Prog. Accred: Nursing

Medical College of Georgia
1120 15th St., Augusta 30912
Type: Public, state, four-year
System: Board of Regents of the University System of Georgia
Degrees: A, B, M, D *Enroll:* 2,047
URL: http://www.mcg.edu
Phone: (706) 721-0211 *Calendar:* Sem. plan
Inst. Accred.: SACS (1973/2000)
Prog. Accred.: Allied Health (diagnostic medical sonography, medical illustration, medicine, respiratory therapy), Clinical Lab Scientist, Dentistry (combined prosthodontics, dental assisting, dental hygiene, dentistry, endodontics, general practice residency, oral and maxillofacial surgery, orthodontic and dentofacial orthopedics, pediatric dentistry, periodontics, prosthodontics), Nuclear Medicine Technology, Nurse Anesthesia Education, Nursing Education, Physical Therapy, Physician Assistant, Psychology Internship, Radiation Therapy, Radiography

Mercer University
1400 Coleman Ave., Macon 31207
Type: Private, Cooperative Baptist Fellowship, four-year
Degrees: B, M, P, D *Enroll:* 6,181
URL: http://www.mercer.edu
Phone: (478) 301-2700 *Calendar:* Sem. plan
Inst. Accred.: ATS (2002/2007), SACS (1911/2005)
Prog. Accred.: Allied Health (medicine), Applied Science (industrial management), Business (AACSB), Computer Science (ABET-CAC), Engineering (general), Law, Marriage and Family Therapy, Music, Nurse Anesthesia Education, Public Health

Cecil B. Day Campus
3001 Mercer University Dr., Atlanta 30341
Phone: (678) 547-6000
Prog. Accred: Business (AACSB), Pharmacy

Georgia Baptist College of Nursing
3001 Mercer University Dr., Atlanta 30341
Phone: (678) 547-6799
Prog. Accred: Nursing Education

Middle Georgia College
1100 Second St., SE, Cochran 31014
Type: Public, state, four-year
System: Board of Regents of the University System of Georgia
Degrees: A, B *Enroll:* 2,100
URL: http://www.mgc.edu
Phone: (478) 934-6221 *Calendar:* Sem. plan
Inst. Accred.: SACS (1933/1999)
Prog. Accred.: Allied Health (occupational therapy assisting), Nursing

Georgia Aviation Campus
71 Airport Rd., Eastman 31023
Phone: (478) 374-6980

Middle Georgia Technical College
80 Cohen Walker Dr., Warner Robins 31088
Type: Public, state, two-year
System: Technical College System of Georgia
Degrees: A
URL: http://www.middlegatech.edu
Phone: (478) 988-6800 *Calendar:* Qtr. plan
Inst. Accred.: SACS (2005)
Prog. Accred.: Allied Health (surgical technology), Dentistry (dental assisting, dental hygiene), Nuclear Medicine Technology, Radiography

Morehouse College
830 Westview Dr., SW, Atlanta 30314
Type: Private, independent, four-year
Degrees: B *Enroll:* 2,925
URL: http://www.morehouse.edu
Phone: (404) 681-2800 *Calendar:* Sem. plan
Inst. Accred.: SACS (1932/1998)
Prog. Accred.: Business (AACSB)

Morehouse School of Medicine
720 Westview Dr., SW, Atlanta 30310-1495
Type: Private, independent, four-year
Degrees: M, P, D *Enroll:* 263
URL: http://www.msm.edu
Phone: (404) 752-1500 *Calendar:* Sem. plan
Inst. Accred.: SACS (1986/2001)
Prog. Accred.: Allied Health (medicine), Public Health

Moultrie Technical College
800 Veterans Pkwy. North, Moultrie 31788
Type: Public, state, two-year
System: Technical College System of Georgia
Degrees: A *Enroll:* 1,207
URL: http://www.moultrietech.edu
Phone: (229) 891-7000 *Calendar:* Qtr. plan
Inst. Accred.: COE (1974/2007)
Prog. Accred.: Allied Health (medical assisting (AMA)), Radiography

Industrial Drive Campus
361 Industrial Dr., Moultrie 31768
Phone: (229) 891-7000

Tifton Campus
52 Tech Dr., Tifton 31794
Phone: (229) 391-2600

Turner County Campus
222 Rock House Rd., Ashburn 31714
Phone: (229) 567-2045

Worth County Campus
1210 North Monroe St., Sylvester 31791
Phone: (229) 777-2177

North Georgia College and State University
100 College Circle, Dahlonega 30597-1001
Type: Public, state, four-year
System: Board of Regents of the University System of Georgia
Degrees: A, B, M, P *Enroll:* 3,988
URL: http://www.ngcsu.edu
Phone: (706) 864-1400 *Calendar:* Sem. plan
Inst. Accred.: SACS (1935/2007)
Prog. Accred.: Business (AACSB), Counseling, Nursing, Physical Therapy, Teacher Education (NCATE)

North Georgia Technical College
PO Box 65, Clarkesville 30523
Type: Public, state, two-year
System: Technical College System of Georgia
Degrees: A *Enroll:* 1,255
URL: http://www.northgatech.edu
Phone: (706) 754-7700 *Calendar:* Qtr. plan
Inst. Accred.: COE (1972/2004), SACS (2008)
Prog. Accred.: Allied Health (medical assisting (AMA)), Clinical Lab Technology

Blairsville Campus
434 Meeks Ave., Blairsville 30512
Phone: (706) 781-2300
Prog. Accred: Allied Health (medical assisting (AMA)), Culinary Education

North Metro Technical College
5198 Ross Rd., Acworth 30102
Type: Public, state, two-year
System: Technical College System of Georgia
Degrees: A
URL: http://www.northmetrotech.edu
Phone: (770) 975-4000 *Calendar:* Qtr. plan
Inst. Accred.: COE (1991/2003), SACS (2006)
Prog. Accred.: Radiography

Northwestern Technical College
PO Box 569, Rock Spring 30739-0569
Type: Public, state, two-year
System: Technical College System of Georgia
Degrees: A *Enroll:* 1,365
URL: http://www.northwesterntech.edu
Phone: (706) 764-3510 *Calendar:* Qtr. plan
Inst. Accred.: SACS (1997/2002)
Prog. Accred.: Allied Health (medical assisting (AMA), occupational therapy assisting, surgical technology), Nursing

Ogeechee Technical College
One Joe Kennedy Blvd., Statesboro 30458-8049
Type: Public, state, two-year
System: Technical College System of Georgia
Degrees: A *Enroll:* 1,324
URL: http://www.ogeecheetech.edu
Phone: (912) 681-5500 *Calendar:* Qtr. plan
Inst. Accred.: COE (1992/2004)
Prog. Accred.: Allied Health (diagnostic medical sonography, medical assisting (AMA), opticianry, surgical technology), Dentistry (dental assisting), Funeral Service Education (Mortuary Science), Radiography, Veterinary Technology

Oglethorpe University
4484 Peachtree Rd., NE, Atlanta 30319-2797
Type: Private, independent, four-year
Degrees: B, M *Enroll:* 985
URL: http://www.oglethorpe.edu
Phone: (404) 261-1441 *Calendar:* Sem. plan
Inst. Accred.: SACS (1950/1996, Warning)

Okefenokee Technical College
1701 Carswell Ave., Waycross 31503
Type: Public, state/local, two-year
System: Technical College System of Georgia
Degrees: A *Enroll:* 976
URL: http://www.okefenokeetech.edu
Phone: (912) 287-6584 *Calendar:* Qtr. plan
Inst. Accred.: COE (1972/2003), SACS (2007)
Prog. Accred.: Allied Health (respiratory therapy, surgical technology), Clinical Lab Technology, Radiography

Alma Campus
426 West 12th St., Alma 31510
Phone: (912) 632-0951

Paine College
1235 15th St., Augusta 30901-3182
Type: Private, United Methodist Church, four-year
Degrees: B *Enroll:* 787
URL: http://www.paine.edu
Phone: (706) 821-8200 *Calendar:* Sem. plan
Inst. Accred.: SACS (1944/2001)
Prog. Accred.: Business (ACBSP), Teacher Education (NCATE)

Piedmont College
PO Box 10, Demorest 30535
Type: Private, independent, four-year
Degrees: B, M *Enroll:* 1,461
URL: http://www.piedmont.edu
Phone: (706) 778-3000 *Calendar:* Sem. plan
Inst. Accred.: SACS (1965/2007)
Prog. Accred.: Business (ACBSP), Nursing

Psychological Studies Institute
2055 Mount Paran Rd., NW, McCarty Bldg., Atlanta 30327
Type: Private, independent, four-year
Degrees: M
URL: http://www.psy.edu
Phone: (404) 233-3949 *Calendar:* Sem. plan
Inst. Accred.: SACS (2003)

Chattanooga Campus
1815 McCallie Ave., Chattanooga, TN 37404-3026
Phone: (423) 266-4574

Reinhardt College
7300 Reinhardt College Circle, Waleska 30183-2981
Type: Private, United Methodist Church, four-year
Degrees: A, B, M *Enroll:* 932
URL: http://www.reinhardt.edu
Phone: (770) 720-5600 *Calendar:* Sem. plan
Inst. Accred.: SACS (1953/1999)
Prog. Accred.: Music

Sandersville Technical College
PO Box 6179, Sandersville 31082
Type: Public, state/local, two-year
System: Technical College System of Georgia
Degrees: A
URL: http://www.sandersvilletech.edu
Phone: (478) 553-2060 *Calendar:* Sem. plan
Inst. Accred.: COE (1999/2005)

The Savannah College of Art and Design
PO Box 3146, Savannah 31402-3146
Type: Private, independent, four-year
Degrees: B, M *Enroll:* 6,869
URL: http://www.scad.edu
Phone: (912) 525-5000 *Calendar:* Qtr. plan
Inst. Accred.: SACS (2005)

Atlanta Campus
PO Box 77300, Atlanta 30357-1300
Phone: (404) 253-2700
Prog. Accred: Art

Savannah River College
2528 Center West Pkwy., Building A, Augusta 30909
Type: Private, proprietary, two-year
Degrees: A
URL: http://savannahrivercollege.edu
Phone: (706) 738-5046
Inst. Accred.: ACICS (1976/2004)
Prog. Accred.: Allied Health (medical assisting (AMA))

Savannah State University
PO Box 20449, Savannah 31404-9707
Type: Public, state, four-year
System: Board of Regents of the University System of Georgia
Degrees: B, M *Enroll:* 2,697
URL: http://www.savstate.edu
Phone: (912) 356-2186 *Calendar:* Sem. plan
Inst. Accred.: SACS (1951/2001)
Prog. Accred.: Business (AACSB), Engineering Technology (civil/construction, electrical, mechanical), Graduate Social Work, Journalism, Public Administration, Social Work

Savannah Technical College
5717 White Bluff Rd., Savannah 31405-5521
Type: Public, state, two-year
System: Technical College System of Georgia
Degrees: A *Enroll:* 2,319
URL: http://www.savannahtech.edu
Phone: (912) 443-5700 *Calendar:* Qtr. plan
Inst. Accred.: SACS (1991/2007)
Prog. Accred.: Allied Health (medical assisting (AMA), surgical technology), Culinary Education, Dentistry (dental assisting), Engineering Technology (electrical), Practical Nursing

Liberty Campus
100 Technology Dr., Hinesville 31313
Phone: (912) 408-3024
Prog. Accred: Practical Nursing

Shorter College
315 Shorter Ave., Rome 30165-4298
Type: Private, Georgia Baptist Convention, four-year
Degrees: B, M *Enroll:* 2,635
URL: http://www.shorter.edu
Phone: (706) 291-2121 *Calendar:* Sem. plan
Inst. Accred.: SACS (1923/2002)
Prog. Accred.: Music

South Georgia College
100 West College Park Dr., Douglas 31533-5098
Type: Public, state, two-year
System: Board of Regents of the University System of Georgia
Degrees: A *Enroll:* 1,194
URL: http://www.sga.edu
Phone: (912) 389-4510 *Calendar:* Sem. plan
Inst. Accred.: SACS (1934/1997, Warning)
Prog. Accred.: Nursing

South Georgia Technical College
900 South Georgia Tech Pkwy., Americus 31709
Type: Public, state/local, two-year
System: Technical College System of Georgia
Degrees: A *Enroll:* 1,149
URL: http://www.sgatech.org
Phone: (229) 931-2394 *Calendar:* Qtr. plan
Inst. Accred.: COE (1973/2005)

Crisp County Center
402 North Midway Rd., Cordele 31015
Phone: (229) 271-4040

South University
709 Mall Blvd., Savannah 31406
Type: Private, proprietary, four-year
System: Education Management Corporation
Degrees: A, B, M, P, D *Enroll:* 1,141
URL: http://www.southuniversity.edu
Phone: (912) 201-8000 *Calendar:* Qtr. plan
Inst. Accred.: SACS (1985/2006)
Prog. Accred.: Allied Health (anesthesiologist assisting, medical assisting (AMA)), Pharmacy, Physical Therapy Assisting, Physician Assistant

Columbia Campus
PO Box 1196, 3810 Main St., Columbia, SC 29203
Phone: (803) 799-9082
Prog. Accred: Allied Health (medical assisting (AMA))

Montgomery Campus
5355 Vaughn Rd., Montgomery, AL 36116
Phone: (334) 263-1013
Prog. Accred: Allied Health (medical assisting (AMA)), Physical Therapy Assisting

Online Campus
1400 Penn Ave., Pittsburgh, PA 15222
Phone: (888) 444-3404

Tampa Campus
4401 North Himes Ave., Tampa, FL 33614
Phone: (813) 393-3800
Prog. Accred: Nursing Education

West Palm Beach Campus
1760 North Congress Ave., West Palm Beach, FL 33409-5178
Phone: (561) 697-9200
Prog. Accred: Allied Health (medical assisting (AMA)), Nursing Education, Physical Therapy Assisting

Southeastern Technical College
3001 East First St., Vidalia 30474
Type: Public, state, two-year
System: Technical College System of Georgia
Degrees: A
URL: http://www.southeasterntech.edu
Phone: (912) 538-3100 *Calendar:* Qtr. plan
Inst. Accred.: SACS (2008)
Prog. Accred.: Allied Health (medical assisting (AMA), surgical technology), Dentistry (dental hygiene), Radiography

Glennville Campus
211 S. Tillman St., Glennville 30427
Phone: (912) 654-5276

Southern Polytechnic State University
1100 South Marietta Pkwy., Marietta 30060-2896
Type: Public, state, four-year
System: Board of Regents of the University System of Georgia
Degrees: A, B, M *Enroll:* 2,921
URL: http://www.spsu.edu
Phone: (770) 528-7200 *Calendar:* Sem. plan
Inst. Accred.: SACS (1964/1998)
Prog. Accred.: Applied Science (surveying/geomatics), Business (ACBSP), Computer Science (ABET-CAC), Construction Education, Engineering Technology (apparel, civil/construction, computer, electrical, industrial, mechanical, telecommunications)

Southwest Georgia Technical College
15689 US Hwy. 19 North, Thomasville 31792
Type: Public, state, two-year
System: Technical College System of Georgia
Degrees: A *Enroll:* 891
URL: http://www.southwestgatech.edu
Phone: (229) 225-4096 *Calendar:* Qtr. plan
Inst. Accred.: SACS (1997/2002)
Prog. Accred.: Allied Health (medical assisting (AMA), respiratory therapy, surgical technology), Clinical Lab Technology, Nursing, Radiography

Spelman College
350 Spelman Ln., SW, Atlanta 30314-4399
Type: Private, independent, four-year
Degrees: B *Enroll:* 2,260
URL: http://www.spelman.edu
Phone: (404) 681-3643 *Calendar:* Sem. plan
Inst. Accred.: SACS (1932/2000)
Prog. Accred.: Music, Teacher Education (NCATE)

Thomas University
1501 Millpond Rd., Thomasville 31792
Type: Private, independent, four-year
Degrees: A, B, M *Enroll:* 637
URL: http://www.thomasu.edu
Phone: (229) 226-1621 *Calendar:* Sem. plan
Inst. Accred.: SACS (1984/2006)
Prog. Accred.: Nursing, Rehabilitation Counseling, Social Work

Toccoa Falls College
PO Box 800777, Toccoa Falls 30598-0013
Type: Private, Christian and Missionary Alliance, four-year
Degrees: A, B *Enroll:* 886
URL: http://www.tfc.edu
Phone: (706) 886-6831 *Calendar:* Sem. plan
Inst. Accred.: ABHE (1957/1998), SACS (1983/2001)
Prog. Accred.: Music

Epworth Campus
PO Box 539, Epworth 30541
Phone: (706) 492-5921

Truett McConnell College
100 Alumni Dr., Cleveland 30528
Type: Private, Georgia Baptist Convention, four-year
Degrees: A, B *Enroll:* 354
URL: http://www.truett.edu
Phone: (706) 865-2134 *Calendar:* Sem. plan
Inst. Accred.: SACS (1966/2000)
Prog. Accred.: Music

The University of Georgia
436 East Broad St., Athens 30602
Type: Public, state, four-year
System: Board of Regents of the University System of Georgia
Degrees: A, B, M, P, D *Enroll:* 30,595
URL: http://www.uga.edu
Phone: (706) 542-3000 *Calendar:* Sem. plan
Inst. Accred.: SACS (1909/2001)
Prog. Accred.: Accounting, Allied Health (audiology, speech-language pathology), Art, Business (AACSB), Clinical Psychology, Counseling, Counseling Psychology, Dietetics (didactic), Dietetics (internship),Engineering (agricultural, bioengineering), Environmental Health, Family & Consumer Science, Forestry, Graduate Social Work, Interior Design, Journalism, Landscape Architecture, Law, Marriage and Family Therapy, Music, Pharmacy, Public Administration, Recreation and Leisure Services, School Psychology, Social Work, Teacher Education (NCATE), Theatre, Veterinary Medicine

University of West Georgia
1600 Maple St., Carrollton 30118-0001
Type: Public, state, four-year
System: Board of Regents of the University System of Georgia
Degrees: A, B, M, P, D *Enroll:* 8,419
URL: http://www.westga.edu
Phone: (678) 839-5000 *Calendar:* Sem. plan
Inst. Accred.: SACS (1936/2003)
Prog. Accred.: Accounting, Art, Business (AACSB), Computer Science (ABET-CAC), Counseling, Music, Nursing Education, Public Administration, Teacher Education (NCATE), Theatre

Valdosta State University
1500 North Patterson St., Valdosta 31698
Type: Public, state, four-year
System: Board of Regents of the University System of Georgia
Degrees: A, B, M, P, D *Enroll:* 8,961
URL: http://www.valdosta.edu
Phone: (229) 333-5800 *Calendar:* Sem. plan
Inst. Accred.: SACS (1929/2000)
Prog. Accred.: Allied Health (speech-language pathology), Art, Business (AACSB), Dentistry (dental hygiene), Graduate Social Work, Marriage and Family Therapy, Music, Nursing Education, Public Administration, Teacher Education (NCATE), Theatre

Valdosta Technical College
4089 Val Tech Rd., Valdosta 31602-0929
Type: Public, state, two-year
System: Technical College System of Georgia
Degrees: A *Enroll:* 1,479
URL: http://www.valdostatech.edu
Phone: (229) 333-2100 *Calendar:* Qtr. plan
Inst. Accred.: SACS (2007)
Prog. Accred.: Allied Health (surgical technology), Dentistry (dental assisting, dental hygiene), Radiography

Waycross College
2001 South Georgia Pkwy., Waycross 31503-9248
Type: Public, state, two-year
System: Board of Regents of the University System of Georgia
Degrees: A *Enroll:* 541
URL: http://www.waycross.edu
Phone: (912) 285-6133 *Calendar:* Sem. plan
Inst. Accred.: SACS (1978/2003)

Wesleyan College
4760 Forsyth Rd., Macon 31210-4462
Type: Private, United Methodist Church, four-year
Degrees: B, M *Enroll:* 513
URL: http://www.wesleyancollege.edu
Phone: (478) 477-1110 *Calendar:* Sem. plan
Inst. Accred.: SACS (1919/2005)
Prog. Accred.: Music

West Central Technical College
176 Murphy Campus Blvd., Waco 30182
Type: Public, state, two-year
System: Technical College System of Georgia
Degrees: A *Enroll:* 1,552
URL: http://www.westcentraltech.edu
Phone: (770) 537-6000 *Calendar:* Qtr. plan
Inst. Accred.: SACS (1998/2003)

Carroll Campus
997 South Hwy. 16, Carrollton 30116
Phone: (770) 836-6800

Douglas Campus
4600 Timber Ridge Dr., Douglasville 30135
Phone: (770) 947-7200
Prog. Accred: Allied Health (medical assisting (AMA), surgical technology), Dentistry (dental hygiene), Radiography

Newman Campus
160 Martin Luther King, Jr. Dr., Newman 30263
Phone: (678) 423-2000
Prog. Accred: Dentistry (dental hygiene)

West Georgia Technical College
303 Fort Dr., LaGrange 30240
Type: Public, state, two-year
System: Technical College System of Georgia
Degrees: A *Enroll:* 1,184
URL: http://www.westgatech.edu
Phone: (706) 845-4323 *Calendar:* Qtr. plan
Inst. Accred.: COE (1973/2005), SACS (2007)
Prog. Accred.: Allied Health (medical assisting (AMA)), Radiography

Young Harris College
PO Box 68, Young Harris 30582
Type: Private, United Methodist Church, two-year
Degrees: A *Enroll:* 518
URL: http://www.yhc.edu
Phone: (706) 379-3111 *Calendar:* Sem. plan
Inst. Accred.: SACS (1938/2001)
Prog. Accred.: Music

GUAM

Guam Community College
PO Box 23069, Guam Main Facility, Barrigada 96921
Type: Public, state/local, two-year
Degrees: A *Enroll:* 1,289
URL: http://www.guamcc.edu
Phone: (671) 735-4422 *Calendar:* Sem. plan
Inst. Accred.: WASC-JR. (1979/2006)

Pacific Islands Bible College
PO Box 22619, Guam Main Facility, Barrigada 96921-2619
Type: Private, independent, four-year
Degrees: A, B, M
URL: http://www.pibc-edu.org
Phone: (671) 734-1812 *Calendar:* Sem. plan
Inst. Accred.: TRACS (2004)

University of Guam
UOG Station, Mangilao 96923
Type: Public, state, four-year
Degrees: A, B, M *Enroll:* 2,465
URL: http://www.uog.edu
Phone: (671) 735-2975 *Calendar:* Sem. plan
Inst. Accred.: WASC-SR. (1963/2002)
Prog. Accred.: Nursing, Social Work, Teacher Education (NCATE)

HAWAII

Argosy University Hawai'i
400 Pacific Tower, 1001 Bishop St., Honolulu 96813
Type: Private, proprietary, four-year
System: Argosy University
Degrees: B, M, D
URL: http://www.argosyu.edu/honolulu
Phone: (808) 536-5555 *Calendar:* Tri. plan
Inst. Accred.: NCA-HLC (1981/2008, *Indirect accreditation through Argosy University, Chicago, IL*)
Prog. Accred.: Clinical Psychology

Babel University Professional School of Translation
1720 Ala Moana Blvd., Tradewinds, Ste. A5, Honolulu 96815-1302
Type: Private, proprietary, four-year
Degrees: M
URL: http://www.babel-unv.org
Phone: (808) 946-3773
Inst. Accred.: DETC (2002/2006)

Brigham Young University—Hawaii Campus
55-220 Kulanui St., A152 ASB, Laie 96762-1266
Type: Public, The Church of Jesus Christ of Latter-day Saints, four-year
Degrees: A, B *Enroll:* 2,342
URL: http://www.byuh.edu
Phone: (808) 293-3211 *Calendar:* 4-4-x plan
Inst. Accred.: WASC-SR. (1959/2008)
Prog. Accred.: Social Work

Chaminade University of Honolulu
3140 Waialae Ave., Honolulu 96816-1578
Type: Private, Roman Catholic Church, four-year
Degrees: A, B, M *Enroll:* 2,264
URL: http://www.chaminade.edu
Phone: (808) 735-4711 *Calendar:* Sem. plan
Inst. Accred.: WASC-SR. (1960/2002)

Hawaii Community College
200 West Kawili St., Hilo 96720-4091
Type: Public, state, two-year
System: University of Hawaii System
Degrees: A *Enroll:* 1,519
URL: http://www.hawcc.hawaii.edu
Phone: (808) 974-7611 *Calendar:* Sem. plan
Inst. Accred.: WASC-JR. (1973/2006)
Prog. Accred.: Culinary Education, English Language Education, Nursing

University of Hawaii Center at West Hawaii
81-942 Haleki'i St., Kealakekua 96750
Phone: (808) 322-4850
Prog. Accred: Culinary Education

Hawaii Pacific University
1166 Fort St. Mall, Honolulu 96813
Type: Private, independent, four-year
Degrees: A, B, M *Enroll:* 5,911
URL: http://www.hpu.edu
Phone: (808) 544-0200 *Calendar:* Sem. plan
Inst. Accred.: WASC-SR. (1973/2005)
Prog. Accred.: Graduate Social Work, Social Work

Windward Hawaii Loa Campus
45-045 Kamehameha Hwy., Kaneohe 96744
Phone: (808) 235-3641
Prog. Accred: Nursing

Hawaii Tokai International College
2241 Kapiolani Blvd., Honolulu 96826
Type: Private, independent, two-year
Degrees: A
URL: http://www.tokai.edu
Phone: (808) 983-4100 *Calendar:* Qtr. plan
Inst. Accred.: WASC-JR. (1994/2006, Warning)

Heald College—Honolulu
1500 Kapiolani Blvd., Ste. 201, Honolulu 96814
Type: Private, independent, two-year
System: Heald Colleges
Degrees: A *Enroll:* 677
URL: http://www.heald.edu
Phone: (808) 955-1500 *Calendar:* Qtr. plan
Inst. Accred.: WASC-JR. (1983/2006, *Indirect accreditation through Heald Colleges, San Francisco, CA*)
Prog. Accred.: Allied Health (medical assisting (AMA))

Honolulu Community College
874 Dillingham Blvd., Honolulu 96817
Type: Public, state, two-year
System: University of Hawaii System
Degrees: A *Enroll:* 2,425
URL: http://honolulu.hawaii.edu
Phone: (808) 845-9225 *Calendar:* Sem. plan
Inst. Accred.: WASC-JR. (1970/2007)

Institute of Clinical Acupuncture and Oriental Medicine
100 North Beretania St., Ste. 203B, Honolulu 96817
Type: Private, proprietary, four-year
Degrees: M
URL: http://www.orientalmedicine.edu
Phone: (808) 521-2288 *Calendar:* Sem. plan
Inst. Accred.: ACAOM (2002/2007)

Kapi'olani Community College
4303 Diamond Head Rd., Honolulu 96816
Type: Public, state, two-year
System: University of Hawaii System
Degrees: A *Enroll:* 4,201
URL: http://www.kcc.hawaii.edu
Phone: (808) 734-9000 *Calendar:* Sem. plan
Inst. Accred.: WASC-JR. (1970/2007)
Prog. Accred.: Allied Health (medical assisting (AMA), occupational therapy assisting, respiratory therapy, surgical technology), Clinical Lab Technology, Culinary Education, Nursing, Phlebotomy, Physical Therapy Assisting, Radiography

Kaua'i Community College
University of Hawaii, 3-1901 Kaumaiali, Lihue 96766
Type: Public, state, two-year
System: University of Hawaii System
Degrees: A *Enroll:* 625
URL: http://www.kauaicc.hawaii.edu
Phone: (808) 245-8311 *Calendar:* Sem. plan
Inst. Accred.: WASC-JR. (1971/2007)
Prog. Accred.: Culinary Education, Nursing

Leeward Community College
96-045 Ala Ike, Pearl City 96782
Type: Public, state, two-year
System: University of Hawaii System
Degrees: A *Enroll:* 3,495
URL: http://www.lcc.hawaii.edu
Phone: (808) 455-0011 *Calendar:* Sem. plan
Inst. Accred.: WASC-JR. (1971/2007)
Prog. Accred.: Culinary Education

Maui Community College
310 West Kaahumanu Ave., Kahului 96732
Type: Public, state, four-year
System: University of Hawaii System
Degrees: A, B *Enroll:* 1,865
URL: http://www.maui.hawaii.edu
Phone: (808) 984-3500 *Calendar:* Sem. plan
Inst. Accred.: WASC-JR. (1980/2007), WASC-SR. (2007)
Prog. Accred.: Culinary Education, Nursing

Traditional Chinese Medicine College of Hawaii
65-1206 Mamalohoa Hwy., Building 3, Ste. 9, Kamuela 96743
Type: Private, proprietary, four-year
Degrees: M
URL: http://www.ilhawaii.net/~chinese
Phone: (808) 885-9226
Inst. Accred.: ACAOM (2002/2007)

TransPacific Hawaii College
5257 Kalanianaole Hwy., Honolulu 96821
Type: Private, independent, two-year
Degrees: A
URL: http://www.transpacific.org
Phone: (808) 377-5402 *Calendar:* Sem. plan
Inst. Accred.: WASC-JR. (1985/2002, Warning)

University of Hawaii at Hilo
200 West Kawili St., Hilo 96720
Type: Public, state, four-year
System: University of Hawaii System
Degrees: B, M, P, D *Enroll:* 3,019
URL: http://www.uhh.hawaii.edu
Phone: (808) 974-7414 *Calendar:* Sem. plan
Inst. Accred.: WASC-SR. (1976/2004, Warning)
Prog. Accred.: Business (AACSB), Nursing, Pharmacy

University of Hawaii at Manoa
2500 Campus Rd., Honolulu 96822
Type: Public, state, four-year
System: University of Hawaii System
Degrees: A, B, M, P, D *Enroll:* 17,175
URL: http://manoa.hawaii.edu
Phone: (808) 956-8111 *Calendar:* Sem. plan
Inst. Accred.: WASC-SR. (1952/2005)
Prog. Accred.: Allied Health (audiology, medicine, speech-language pathology), Business (AACSB), Clinical Lab Scientist, Clinical Psychology, Counseling, Dentistry (dental hygiene), Dietetics (didactic), Engineering (bioengineering, civil, electrical, mechanical, ocean), English Language Education, Graduate Social Work, Law, Librarianship, Music, Nursing, Nursing Education, Planning, Psychology Internship, Public Health, Rehabilitation Counseling, Social Work, Teacher Education (NCATE)

University of Hawaii at West Oahu
96-129 Ala Ike, Pearl City 96782
Type: Public, state, four-year
System: University of Hawaii System
Degrees: B *Enroll:* 529
URL: http://www.uhwo.hawaii.edu
Phone: (808) 454-4750 *Calendar:* Sem. plan
Inst. Accred.: WASC-SR. (1981/2005)

Windward Community College
45-720 Keaahala Rd., Kaneohe 96744
Type: Public, state, two-year
System: University of Hawaii System
Degrees: A *Enroll:* 1,059
URL: http://www.wcc.hawaii.edu
Phone: (808) 235-7400 *Calendar:* Sem. plan
Inst. Accred.: WASC-JR. (1977/2007)

World Medicine Institute
1110 University Ave., Ste. 308, Honolulu 96826
Type: Private, proprietary, four-year
Degrees: M *Enroll:* 34
URL: http://www.acupuncture-hi.com
Phone: (808) 949-1050 *Calendar:* Sem. plan
Inst. Accred.: ACAOM (1991/2002)

IDAHO

Apollo College—Boise
1200 North Liberty Rd., Boise 83704
Type: Private, proprietary, two-year
System: U.S. Education Corporation
Degrees: A
URL: http://www.apollocollege.edu/campuses_boise.asp
Phone: (208) 377-8080
Inst. Accred.: ABHES (1982/2005), ACICS (2008)
Prog. Accred.: Dentistry (dental assisting, dental hygiene), Medical Assisting (ABHES)

Boise Bible College
8695 West Marigold St., Boise 83714-1220
Type: Private, Christian Churches/Churches of Christ, four-year
Degrees: A, B *Enroll:* 159
URL: http://www.boisebible.edu
Phone: (208) 376-7731 *Calendar:* Sem. plan
Inst. Accred.: ABHE (1988/1999)

Boise State University
1910 University Dr., Boise 83725
Type: Public, state, four-year
System: State Board of Education and Board of Regents of the University of Idaho
Degrees: A, B, M, D *Enroll:* 14,039
URL: http://www.boisestate.edu
Phone: (208) 426-1011 *Calendar:* Sem. plan
Inst. Accred.: NWCCU (1941/2007)
Prog. Accred.: Accounting, Allied Health (diagnostic medical sonography, respiratory therapy, surgical technology), Art, Business (AACSB), Computer Science (ABET-CAC), Construction Education, Counseling, Culinary Education, Dentistry (dental assisting), Engineering (civil, electrical, mechanical), Environmental Health, Graduate Social Work, Music, Nursing, Public Administration, Radiography, Social Work, Teacher Education (NCATE), Theatre

Brigham Young University—Idaho
525 South Center, Rexburg 83460
Type: Private, The Church of Jesus Christ of Latter-day Saints, four-year
Degrees: A, B *Enroll:* 12,029
URL: http://www.byui.edu
Phone: (208) 496-2011 *Calendar:* Sem. plan
Inst. Accred.: NWCCU (1936/2006)
Prog. Accred.: Engineering Technology (electrical), Interior Design, Music, Nursing, Social Work

The College of Idaho
2112 Cleveland Blvd., Caldwell 83605
Type: Private, independent, four-year
Degrees: B, M *Enroll:* 793
URL: http://www.collegeofidaho.edu
Phone: (208) 459-5011 *Calendar:* 4-1-4 plan
Inst. Accred.: NWCCU (1922/2008)

College of Southern Idaho
315 Falls Ave., PO Box 1238, Twin Falls 83303-1238
Type: Public, local, two-year
System: State Board of Education and Board of Regents of the University of Idaho
Degrees: A *Enroll:* 4,411
URL: http://www.csi.edu
Phone: (208) 733-9554 *Calendar:* Sem. plan
Inst. Accred.: NWCCU (1968/2007)
Prog. Accred.: Allied Health (medical assisting (AMA), surgical technology), Nursing, Radiography, Veterinary Technology

Eastern Idaho Technical College
1600 South 25th East, Idaho Falls 83404-5788
Type: Public, state, two-year
System: State Board of Education and Board of Regents of the University of Idaho
Degrees: A *Enroll:* 420
URL: http://www.eitc.edu
Phone: (208) 524-3000 *Calendar:* Sem. plan
Inst. Accred.: NWCCU (1982/2007)
Prog. Accred.: Allied Health (medical assisting (AMA), surgical technology)

Idaho State University
921 South Eighth Ave., Pocatello 83209
Type: Public, state, four-year
System: State Board of Education and Board of Regents of the University of Idaho
Degrees: A, B, M, P, D *Enroll:* 10,852
URL: http://www.isu.edu
Phone: (208) 282-0211 *Calendar:* Sem. plan
Inst. Accred.: NWCCU (1918/2006)
Prog. Accred.: Accounting, Allied Health (EMT-paramedic, audiology, medical assisting (AMA), occupational therapy, speech-language pathology), Applied Science (health physics), Business (AACSB), Clinical Lab Scientist, Clinical Psychology, Computer Science (ABET-CAC), Counseling, Culinary Education, Dentistry (advanced education in general dentistry, dental hygiene, dental laboratory technology), Design Technology, Dietetics (didactic), Dietetics (internship), Electronic Technology, Engineering (civil, electrical, general, mechanical), Industrial Technology, Mechanical Technology, Music, Nursing, Nursing Education, Pharmacy, Physical Therapy, Physical Therapy Assisting, Physician Assistant, Public Health, Social Work, Teacher Education (NCATE)

ITT Technical Institute
12302 West Explorer Dr., Boise 83713
Type: Private, proprietary, four-year
System: ITT Educational Services, Inc.
Degrees: A, B *Enroll:* 402
URL: http://www.itt-tech.edu
Phone: (208) 322-8844 *Calendar:* Qtr. plan
Inst. Accred.: ACICS (1999/2008)

Albany Campus
13 Airline Dr., Albany, NY 12205
Phone: (518) 452-9300

Owings Mills Campus
11301 Red Run Blvd., Owings Mills, MD 21117
Phone: (443) 394-7115

Lewis-Clark State College
500 8th Ave., Lewiston 83501
Type: Public, state, four-year
System: State Board of Education and Board of Regents of the University of Idaho
Degrees: A, B *Enroll:* 2,753
URL: http://www.lcsc.edu
Phone: (208) 792-5272 *Calendar:* Sem. plan
Inst. Accred.: NWCCU (1964/2003)
Prog. Accred.: Nursing Education, Social Work, Teacher Education (NCATE)

New Saint Andrews College
PO Box 9025, Moscow 83843-1525
Type: Private, Christ Church/Confederation of Reformed Evangelica, four-year
Degrees: A, B, M
URL: http://www.nsa.edu
Phone: (208) 882-1566 *Calendar:* 4-1-4 plan
Inst. Accred.: TRACS (2006)

North Idaho College
1000 West Garden Ave., Coeur d'Alene 83814
Type: Public, local, two-year
System: State Board of Education and Board of Regents of the University of Idaho
Degrees: A *Enroll:* 3,032
URL: http://www.nic.edu
Phone: (208) 769-3300 *Calendar:* Sem. plan
Inst. Accred.: NWCCU (1947/2008)
Prog. Accred.: Nursing

Northwest Nazarene University
623 Holly St., Nampa 83686-5897
Type: Private, Church of the Nazarene, four-year
Degrees: A, B, M *Enroll:* 1,508
URL: http://www.nnu.edu
Phone: (208) 467-8011 *Calendar:* Sem. plan
Inst. Accred.: NWCCU (1930/2007)
Prog. Accred.: Business (ACBSP), Counseling, Graduate Social Work, Music, Nursing Education, Social Work, Teacher Education (NCATE)

University of Idaho
Moscow 83844-3151
Type: Public, state, four-year
System: State Board of Education and Board of Regents of the University of Idaho
Degrees: B, M, D *Enroll:* 10,782
URL: http://www.uidaho.edu
Phone: (208) 885-6111 *Calendar:* Sem. plan
Inst. Accred.: NWCCU (1918/2006)
Prog. Accred.: Accounting, Art, Business (AACSB), Computer Science (ABET-CAC), Counseling, Dietetics (coordinated), Engineering (agricultural, bioengineering, chemical, civil, computer, electrical, mechanical, metallurgical), Forestry, Landscape Architecture, Law, Music, Recreation and Leisure Services, Rehabilitation Counseling, Teacher Education (NCATE)

ILLINOIS

Adler School of Professional Psychology
65 East Wacker Place, Ste. 2100, Chicago 60601
Type: Private, independent, four-year
Degrees: M, D *Enroll:* 276
URL: http://www.adler.edu
Phone: (312) 201-5900 *Calendar:* Sem. plan
Inst. Accred.: NCA-HLC (1978/2002)
Prog. Accred.: Clinical Psychology, Psychology Internship

American Academy of Art
332 South Michigan Ave., #300, Chicago 60604-4302
Type: Private, proprietary, four-year
Degrees: B, M *Enroll:* 372
URL: http://www.aaart.edu
Phone: (312) 461-0600 *Calendar:* Sem. plan
Inst. Accred.: ACCSCT (1974/2004), NCA-HLC (2008)

American College of Education
55 West Monroe St., Ste. 2900, Chicago 60603
Type: Private, proprietary, four-year
Degrees: B, M *Enroll:* 34
URL: http://www.ace.edu
Phone: (312) 332-0854 *Calendar:* Sem. plan
Inst. Accred.: NCA-HLC (2005/2008)

Argosy University Chicago
350 North Orleans St., Chicago 60654
Type: Private, proprietary, four-year
System: Argosy University
Degrees: B, M, D *Enroll:* 794
URL: http://www.argosyu.edu/chicago
Phone: (312) 777-7600 *Calendar:* Tri. plan
Inst. Accred.: NCA-HLC (1981/2008, *Indirect accreditation through Argosy University, Chicago, IL*)
Prog. Accred.: Business (ACBSP), Clinical Psychology

Argosy University Schaumburg
1000 North Plaza Dr., Ste. 100, Schaumburg 60173
Type: Private, proprietary, four-year
System: Argosy University
Degrees: B, M, D
URL: http://www.argosy.edu
Phone: (847) 290-7400 *Calendar:* Tri. plan
Inst. Accred.: NCA-HLC (1981/2008, *Indirect accreditation through Argosy University, Chicago, IL*)
Prog. Accred.: Clinical Psychology, Counseling

Augustana College
639 38th St., Rock Island 61201
Type: Private, Evangelical Lutheran Church in America, four-year
Degrees: B *Enroll:* 2,372
URL: http://www.augustana.edu
Phone: (309) 794-7000 *Calendar:* Qtr. plan
Inst. Accred.: NCA-HLC (1913/2006)
Prog. Accred.: Music, Teacher Education (NCATE)

Aurora University
347 South Gladstone Ave., Aurora 60506-4892
Type: Private, independent, four-year
Degrees: B, M, D *Enroll:* 2,672
URL: http://www.aurora.edu
Phone: (630) 892-6431 *Calendar:* Tri. plan
Inst. Accred.: NCA-HLC (1938/2003)
Prog. Accred.: Graduate Social Work, Nursing Education, Recreation and Leisure Services, Social Work

New College of Aurora University
University Center, 14 North Sheridan Rd., Waukegon 60085
Phone: (708) 662-0100

School of Nursing/Chicago Campus
300 North Michigan, Ste. 300, Chicago 60601
Phone: (312) 357-1080

Wisconsin Campus
PO Box 51687, New Berlin, WI 53151
Phone: (414) 789-6260

Benedictine University
5700 College Rd., Lisle 60532
Type: Private, Roman Catholic Church, four-year
Degrees: A, B, M, D *Enroll:* 2,400
URL: http://www.ben.edu
Phone: (630) 829-6005 *Calendar:* Sem. plan
Inst. Accred.: NCA-HLC (1958/2003)
Prog. Accred.: Dietetics (didactic), Dietetics (internship), Nursing, Nursing Education

Black Hawk College
6600 34th Ave., Moline 61265
Type: Public, local, two-year
System: Illinois Community College Board
Degrees: A *Enroll:* 4,104
URL: http://www.bhc.edu
Phone: (309) 796-1311 *Calendar:* Sem. plan
Inst. Accred.: NCA-HLC (1986/2003)
Prog. Accred.: Allied Health (medical assisting (AMA)), Nursing, Physical Therapy Assisting

Blackburn College
700 College Ave., Carlinville 62626
Type: Private, United Presbyterian Church, four-year
Degrees: B *Enroll:* 595
URL: http://www.blackburn.edu
Phone: (217) 854-3231 *Calendar:* Sem. plan
Inst. Accred.: NCA-HLC (1918/2001)

Blessing-Rieman College of Nursing
Broadway at 11th St., PO Box 7005, Quincy 62305-7005
Type: Private, independent, four-year
Degrees: B *Enroll:* 199
URL: http://www.brcn.edu
Phone: (217) 228-5520 *Calendar:* Sem. plan
Inst. Accred.: NCA-HLC (1994/2003)
Prog. Accred.: Clinical Lab Scientist, Nursing Education

Bradley University
1501 West Bradley Ave., Peoria 61625
Type: Private, independent, four-year
Degrees: B, M, D *Enroll:* 5,607
URL: http://www.bradley.edu
Phone: (309) 676-7611 *Calendar:* Sem. plan
Inst. Accred.: NCA-HLC (1913/2001)
Prog. Accred.: Accounting, Art, Business (AACSB), Construction Education, Counseling, Dietetics (didactic), Engineering (civil, electrical, industrial, manufacturing, mechanical), Engineering Technology (manufacturing), Music, Nurse Anesthesia Education, Nursing, Physical Therapy, Social Work, Teacher Education (NCATE), Theatre

Carl Sandburg College
2400 Tom L. Wilson Blvd., Galesburg 61401
Type: Public, state/local, two-year
System: Illinois Community College Board
Degrees: A *Enroll:* 2,145
URL: http://www.sandburg.edu
Phone: (309) 344-2518 *Calendar:* Sem. plan
Inst. Accred.: NCA-HLC (1974/2001)
Prog. Accred.: Dentistry (dental hygiene), Funeral Service Education (Mortuary Science), Nursing, Practical Nursing, Radiography

Bushnell Extension Campus
380 East Main St., Bushnell 61422
Phone: (309) 772-2177

Carthage Campus
305 Sandburg Dr., Carthage 62321
Phone: (217) 357-3129

Catholic Theological Union
5401 South Cornell Ave., Chicago 60615-5698
Type: Private, Roman Catholic Church, four-year
Degrees: M, D *Enroll:* 327
URL: http://www.ctu.edu
Phone: (773) 324-8000 *Calendar:* Qtr. plan
Inst. Accred.: ATS (1972/2001), NCA-HLC (1972/2002)

The Chicago School of Professional Psychology
325 North Wells St., Chicago 60610
Type: Private, independent, four-year
Degrees: M, D *Enroll:* 862
URL: http://www.thechicagoschool.edu
Phone: (312) 329-6600 *Calendar:* Sem. plan
Inst. Accred.: NCA-HLC (1984/2007)
Prog. Accred.: Clinical Psychology

California Graduate Institute
1145 Gayley Ave., Ste. 322, West Los Angeles, CA 90024
Phone: (310) 208-4240

Chicago State University
9501 South King Dr., Chicago 60628-1598
Type: Public, state, four-year
System: Illinois Board of Higher Education
Degrees: B, M, D *Enroll:* 5,119
URL: http://www.csu.edu
Phone: (773) 995-2000 *Calendar:* Sem. plan
Inst. Accred.: NCA-HLC (1941/2003)
Prog. Accred.: Allied Health (occupational therapy), Business (ACBSP), Counseling, Graduate Social Work, Music, Nursing, Recreation and Leisure Services, Teacher Education (NCATE)

Chicago Theological Seminary
5757 South University Ave., Chicago 60637
Type: Private, United Church of Christ, four-year
Degrees: M, D *Enroll:* 136
URL: http://www.ctschicago.edu
Phone: (773) 752-5757 *Calendar:* Qtr. plan
Inst. Accred.: ATS (1938/2006), NCA-HLC (1982/2007)

Christian Life College
400 East Gregory St., Mount Prospect 60056-2522
Type: Private, Pentecostal/Charismatic Church, four-year
Degrees: A, B *Enroll:* 63
URL: http://www.christianlifecollege.edu
Phone: (847) 259-1840 *Calendar:* Sem. plan
Inst. Accred.: TRACS (2002/2007)

City Colleges of Chicago—Harold Washington College
30 East Lake St., Chicago 60601
Type: Public, state/local, two-year
System: City Colleges of Chicago
Degrees: A *Enroll:* 4,772
URL: http://hwashington.ccc.edu
Phone: (312) 553-5600 *Calendar:* Sem. plan
Inst. Accred.: NCA-HLC (1967/1998)
Prog. Accred.: Business (ACBSP)

City Colleges of Chicago—Harry S Truman College
1145 West Wilson Ave., Chicago 60640
Type: Public, state/local, two-year
System: City Colleges of Chicago
Degrees: A *Enroll:* 5,679
URL: http://www.trumancollege.cc
Phone: (773) 907-4700 *Calendar:* Sem. plan
Inst. Accred.: NCA-HLC (1967/2000)
Prog. Accred.: Nursing

City Colleges of Chicago—Kennedy-King College
6301 South Halsted St., Chicago 60621
Type: Public, state/local, two-year
System: City Colleges of Chicago
Degrees: A *Enroll:* 3,376
URL: http://kennedyking.ccc.edu
Phone: (773) 602-5000 *Calendar:* Sem. plan
Inst. Accred.: NCA-HLC (1967/2006)
Prog. Accred.: Dentistry (dental hygiene)

City Colleges of Chicago—Malcolm X College
1900 West Van Buren St., Chicago 60612
Type: Public, state/local, two-year
System: City Colleges of Chicago
Degrees: A *Enroll:* 4,260
URL: http://malcolmx.ccc.edu
Phone: (312) 850-7000 *Calendar:* Sem. plan
Inst. Accred.: NCA-HLC (1967/2008)
Prog. Accred.: Allied Health (respiratory therapy, surgical technology), Clinical Lab Technology, Funeral Service Education (Mortuary Science), Physician Assistant, Radiography

City Colleges of Chicago—Olive-Harvey College
10001 South Woodlawn Ave., Chicago 60628-1645
Type: Public, state/local, two-year
System: City Colleges of Chicago
Degrees: A *Enroll:* 3,315
URL: http://oliveharvey.ccc.edu
Phone: (773) 291-6100 *Calendar:* Sem. plan
Inst. Accred.: NCA-HLC (1967/2000)
Prog. Accred.: Allied Health (respiratory therapy)

City Colleges of Chicago—Richard J. Daley College
7500 South Pulaski Rd., Chicago 60652
Type: Public, state/local, two-year
System: City Colleges of Chicago
Degrees: A *Enroll:* 5,674
URL: http://daley.ccc.edu
Phone: (773) 838-7500 *Calendar:* Sem. plan
Inst. Accred.: NCA-HLC (1967/2001)
Prog. Accred.: Nursing

City Colleges of Chicago—Wilbur Wright College
4300 North Narragansett Ave., Chicago 60634
Type: Public, state/local, two-year
System: City Colleges of Chicago
Degrees: A *Enroll:* 5,656
URL: http://wright.ccc.edu
Phone: (773) 777-7900 *Calendar:* Sem. plan
Inst. Accred.: NCA-HLC (1967/2002)
Prog. Accred.: Allied Health (occupational therapy assisting), Business (ACBSP), Radiography

College of DuPage
425 Fawell Blvd., Glen Ellyn 60137
Type: Public, state/local, two-year
System: Illinois Community College Board
Degrees: A *Enroll:* 14,939
URL: http://www.cod.edu
Phone: (630) 942-2800 *Calendar:* Qtr. plan
Inst. Accred.: NCA-HLC (1932/2008)
Prog. Accred.: Allied Health (diagnostic medical sonography, respiratory therapy, surgical technology), Culinary Education, Dentistry (dental hygiene), Nuclear Medicine Technology, Nursing, Physical Therapy Assisting, Practical Nursing, Radiography

College of Lake County
19351 West Washington St., Grayslake 60030
Type: Public, state/local, two-year
System: Illinois Community College Board
Degrees: A *Enroll:* 8,285
URL: http://www.clcillinois.edu
Phone: (847) 223-6601 *Calendar:* Sem. plan
Inst. Accred.: NCA-HLC (1974/2002)
Prog. Accred.: Allied Health (surgical technology), Clinical Lab Technology, Dentistry (dental hygiene), Nursing, Phlebotomy, Radiography

Lakeshore Campus
33 North Genesse St., Waukegan 60085
Phone: (847) 623-8686

The College of Office Technology
1520 West Division St., Ste. 20, Chicago 60622
Type: Private, proprietary, two-year
Degrees: A *Enroll:* 388
URL: http://www.cotedu.com
Phone: (773) 278-0042
Inst. Accred.: ACICS (1986/2003)

Columbia College Chicago
600 South Michigan Ave., Chicago 60605
Type: Private, independent, four-year
Degrees: B, M *Enroll:* 9,805
URL: http://www.colum.edu
Phone: (312) 369-7202 *Calendar:* Sem. plan
Inst. Accred.: NCA-HLC (1974/1999)
Prog. Accred.: Interior Architecture

Concordia University Chicago
7400 Augusta St., River Forest 60305
Type: Private, Lutheran Church-Missouri Synod, four-year
System: Concordia University System
Degrees: B, M, D *Enroll:* 1,787
URL: http://www.cuchicago.edu
Phone: (708) 771-8300 *Calendar:* Sem. plan
Inst. Accred.: NCA-HLC (1950/2008)
Prog. Accred.: Counseling, Music, Teacher Education (NCATE)

Cooking and Hospitality Institute of Chicago
361 West Chestnut St., Chicago 60610-3050
Type: Private, proprietary, two-year
System: Career Education Corporation
Degrees: A *Enroll:* 886
URL: http://www.chic.edu
Phone: (312) 944-0884 *Calendar:* Sem. plan
Inst. Accred.: ACCSCT (1986/2002), NCA-HLC (2003/2008)
Prog. Accred.: Culinary Education

Coyne American Institute
330 North Green St., Chicago 60607-1300
Type: Private, proprietary, two-year
Degrees: A
URL: http://www.coyneamerican.edu
Phone: (773) 577-8100 *Calendar:* Sem. plan
Inst. Accred.: ACCSCT (1968/2008)

West Monroe Street Campus
230 West Monroe St., Fourth Flr., Chicago 60606
Phone: (773) 577-8140

Danville Area Community College
2000 East Main St., Danville 61832
Type: Public, state/local, two-year
System: Illinois Community College Board
Degrees: A *Enroll:* 1,718
URL: http://www.dacc.edu
Phone: (217) 443-1811 *Calendar:* Sem. plan
Inst. Accred.: NCA-HLC (1967/1999)
Prog. Accred.: Radiography

DePaul University
1 East Jackson Blvd., Chicago 60604
Type: Private, Roman Catholic Church, four-year
Degrees: B, M, P, D *Enroll:* 18,785
URL: http://www.depaul.edu
Phone: (312) 362-8300 *Calendar:* Qtr. plan
Inst. Accred.: NCA-HLC (1925/2007)
Prog. Accred.: Accounting, Business (AACSB), Clinical Psychology, Law, Music, Nurse Anesthesia Education, Nursing Education, Public Administration, Teacher Education (NCATE)

DeVry University Chicago
3300 North Campbell Ave., Chicago 60618-5994
Type: Private, proprietary
System: DeVry University
Degrees: A, B, M *Enroll:* 8,975
URL: http://www.devry.edu/chicago
Phone: (773) 929-8500 *Calendar:* Sem. plan
Inst. Accred.: NCA-HLC (2002, *Indirect accreditation through DeVry University, Oakbrook Terrace, IL*)
Prog. Accred.: Engineering Technology (computer, electrical)

DeVry University DuPage
1221 North Swift Rd., Addison 60101-6106
Type: Private, proprietary
System: DeVry University
Degrees: A, B, M *FTE Enroll:* 2,980
URL: http://www.devry.edu/addison
Phone: (630) 953-1300 *Calendar:* Sem. plan
Inst. Accred.: NCA-HLC (2002, *Indirect accreditation through DeVry University, Oakbrook Terrace, IL*)
Prog. Accred.: Engineering Technology (computer, electrical)

Tinley Park Campus
18624 West Creek Dr., Ste. 1108, Tinley Park 60477-6243
Phone: (708) 342-3300

DeVry University Oak Brook
One Tower Ln., 9th Flr., Oakbrook Terrace 60181-4624
Type: Private, proprietary
System: DeVry University
Degrees: M *FTE Enroll:* 1,242
URL: http://www.devry.edu
Phone: (630) 571-1818 *Calendar:* Sem. plan
Inst. Accred.: NCA-HLC (2002, *Indirect accreditation through DeVry University, Oakbrook Terrace, IL*)

Atlanta Perimeter Campus
Two Ravinia Dr., Ste. 250, Atlanta, GA 30346-2104
Phone: (770) 671-1744

Chicago Loop Campus
225 West Washington St., Chicago 60606-3418
Phone: (312) 372-4900

Chicago O'Hare Campus
8501 West Higgins Rd., Ste. 410, Chicago 60631
Phone: (773) 695-1000

Crystal City Campus
Arlington Center, 2450 Crystal Dr., Arlington, VA 22202
Phone: (703) 415-0600

Decatur Campus
250 North Arcadia Ave., Decatur, GA 30030-2198
Phone: (404) 298-9444

Edina Campus
7700 France Ave. South, Ste. 575, Edina, MN 55435
Phone: (952) 838-1860

Elgin Campus
2250 Point Blvd., Ste. 250, Elgin 60123
Phone: (847) 622-1135

Gurnee Campus
1075 Tri-State Pkwy., Ste. 800, Gurnee 60031
Phone: (847) 855-2649

Kansas City Downtown Campus
City Center Square, 1100 Main St., Kansas City, MO 64105-2112
Phone: (816) 221-1300

Kansas City South Campus
11224 Holmes Rd., Kansas City, MO 64131
Phone: (816) 941-0367

Lincolnshire Campus
Tri-State International Office Center, Building 25, Ste. 130, Lincolnshire 60069-4460
Phone: (847) 940-7768

Miami Campus
200 South Biscayne Blvd., Ste. 500, Miami, FL 33131-5351
Phone: (786) 425-1113

Milwaukee Center Campus
411 E. Wisconsin Ave., Ste. 300, Milwaukee, WI 53202
Phone: (414) 278-7677

Naperville Campus
2056 Westings Ave., Ste. 40, Naperville 60563-2361
Phone: (630) 428-9086

Northwest Suburban Center Campus
1051 Perimeter Dr., Schaumburg 60173-5009
Phone: (847) 330-0040

Orlando North Campus
1800 Pembrook Dr., Ste. 160, Orlando, FL 32810-6303
Phone: (407) 659-0900

St. Louis Park Campus
400 Hwy. 169 South, Ste. 100, St. Louis Park, MN 55426
Phone: (952) 738-3100

St. Louis West Campus
1801 Park 270 Dr., Ste. 260, St. Louis, MO 63146-4020
Phone: (314) 542-4222

San Diego Campus
2655 Camino Del Rio North, Ste. 201, San Diego, CA 92108-1633
Phone: (619) 683-2446

South Suburban Center Campus
15255 South 94th Ave., Orland Park 60462-3823
Phone: (708) 460-9580

Tampa Bay Campus
3030 North Rocky Point Dr. West, Ste. 100, Tampa, FL 33607-5901
Phone: (813) 288-8994

Tysons Corner Campus
1751 Pinnacle Dr., Ste. 250, McLean, VA 22102-3832
Phone: (703) 556-9669

Waukesha Campus
N14 W23833 Stone Ridge Dr., Ste. 450, Waukesha, WI 53188-1157
Phone: (262) 347-2911

Westminster Campus
1870 West 122nd Ave., Ste. 316, Westminster, CO 80234
Phone: (303) 469-9220

Dominican University
7900 West Division St., River Forest 60305
Type: Private, Roman Catholic Church, four-year
Degrees: B, M *Enroll:* 2,221
URL: http://www.dom.edu
Phone: (708) 366-2490 *Calendar:* Sem. plan
Inst. Accred.: NCA-HLC (1919/2005)
Prog. Accred.: Business (ACBSP), Dietetics (coordinated), Dietetics (didactic), Graduate Social Work, Librarianship

East-West University
816 South Michigan Ave., Chicago 60605
Type: Private, independent, four-year
Degrees: A, B *Enroll:* 1,012
URL: http://www.eastwest.edu
Phone: (312) 939-0111 *Calendar:* Qtr. plan
Inst. Accred.: NCA-HLC (1983/2002)

Eastern Illinois University
600 Lincoln Ave., Charleston 61920
Type: Public, state, four-year
System: Illinois Board of Higher Education
Degrees: B, M, P *Enroll:* 10,754
URL: http://www.eiu.edu
Phone: (217) 581-5000 *Calendar:* Sem. plan
Inst. Accred.: NCA-HLC (1915/2005)
Prog. Accred.: Accounting, Allied Health (speech-language pathology), Art, Business (AACSB), Counseling, Dietetics (didactic), Dietetics (internship), Family & Consumer Science, Industrial Technology, Journalism, Music, Recreation and Leisure Services, Teacher Education (NCATE)

Elgin Community College
1700 Spartan Dr., Elgin 60123
Type: Public, state/local, two-year
System: Illinois Community College Board
Degrees: A *Enroll:* 5,674
URL: http://www.elgin.edu
Phone: (847) 214-7374 *Calendar:* Sem. plan
Inst. Accred.: NCA-HLC (1968/2006)
Prog. Accred.: Allied Health (massage therapy, surgical technology), Clinical Lab Technology, Dentistry (dental assisting), Nursing

Ellis University
111 North Canal St., Ste. 455, Chicago 60606
Type: Private, proprietary, four-year
Degrees: A, B, M *Enroll:* 860
URL: http://www.ellisuonline.com
Phone: (312) 669-5000 *Calendar:* Sem. plan
Inst. Accred.: DETC (2008), NCA-HLC (2008)

Elmhurst College
190 Prospect Ave., Elmhurst 60126-3296
Type: Private, United Church of Christ, four-year
Degrees: B, M *Enroll:* 2,579
URL: http://www.elmhurst.edu
Phone: (630) 617-3500 *Calendar:* 4-1-4 plan
Inst. Accred.: NCA-HLC (1924/1999)
Prog. Accred.: Nursing Education, Teacher Education (NCATE)

Erikson Institute
451 North LaSalle St., Chicago 60654
Type: Private, independent, four-year
Degrees: B, M, P, D *Enroll:* 125
URL: http://www.erikson.edu
Phone: (312) 755-2250 *Calendar:* Tri. plan
Inst. Accred.: NCA-HLC (2000/2005)

Eureka College
300 East College Ave., Eureka 61530-1500
Type: Private, Disciples of Christ, four-year
Degrees: B *Enroll:* 517
URL: http://www.eureka.edu
Phone: (309) 467-3721 *Calendar:* Sem. plan
Inst. Accred.: NCA-HLC (1924/2004)

Fox College
4201 West 93rd St., Oak Lawn 60453
Type: Private, proprietary, two-year
Degrees: A
URL: http://www.foxcollege.edu
Phone: (708) 636-7700 *Calendar:* Sem. plan
Inst. Accred.: NCA-HLC (2007)
Prog. Accred.: Veterinary Technology

Frontier Community College
2 Frontier Dr., Fairfield 62837
Type: Public, state/local, two-year
System: Illinois Eastern Community Colleges System
Degrees: A *Enroll:* 892
URL: http://www.iecc.edu/fcc
Phone: (618) 842-3711 *Calendar:* Sem. plan
Inst. Accred.: NCA-HLC (1984/2005, *Indirect accreditation through Illinois Eastern Community Colleges System, Olney, IL*)
Prog. Accred.: Nursing

Garrett-Evangelical Theological Seminary
2121 Sheridan Rd., Evanston 60201
Type: Private, United Methodist Church, four-year
Degrees: M, D *Enroll:* 259
URL: http://www.garrett.northwestern.edu
Phone: (847) 866-3900 *Calendar:* Qtr. plan
Inst. Accred.: ATS (1938/1998), NCA-HLC (1974/1999)

Governors State University
One University Pkwy., University Park 60466
Type: Public, state, four-year
System: Illinois Board of Higher Education
Degrees: B, M *Enroll:* 2,906
URL: http://www.govst.edu
Phone: (708) 534-5000 *Calendar:* Tri. plan
Inst. Accred.: NCA-HLC (1975/2000)
Prog. Accred.: Allied Health (health services administration, occupational therapy, speech-language pathology), Business (ACBSP), Counseling, Graduate Social Work, Nursing, Physical Therapy, Public Administration, Social Work, Teacher Education (NCATE)

Greenville College
315 East College Ave., PO Box 159, Greenville 62246
Type: Private, Free Methodist Church, four-year
Degrees: B, M *Enroll:* 1,260
URL: http://www.greenville.edu
Phone: (618) 664-2800 *Calendar:* 4-1-4 plan
Inst. Accred.: NCA-HLC (1948/2001)

Harrington College of Design
200 West Madison, Ste. 200, Chicago 60606-3433
Type: Private, proprietary, four-year
System: Career Education Corporation
Degrees: A, B *Enroll:* 1,072
URL: http://www.interiordesign.edu
Phone: (312) 939-4975 *Calendar:* Sem. plan
Inst. Accred.: NASAD (1994/2002), NCA-HLC (2007), ACICS (2004)
Prog. Accred.: Interior Design

Heartland Community College
1500 West Raab Rd., Normal 61761
Type: Public, state/local, two-year
System: Illinois Community College Board
Degrees: A *Enroll:* 2,887
URL: http://www.heartland.edu
Phone: (309) 268-8100 *Calendar:* Sem. plan
Inst. Accred.: NCA-HLC (1994/1999)
Prog. Accred.: Nursing

Hebrew Theological College
7135 North Carpenter Rd., Skokie 60077
Type: Private, independent, four-year
Degrees: B *Enroll:* 413
URL: http://www.htcnet.edu
Phone: (847) 982-2500 *Calendar:* Sem. plan
Inst. Accred.: NCA-HLC (1997/2002)

Highland Community College
2998 West Pearl City Rd., Freeport 61032
Type: Public, state/local, two-year
System: Illinois Community College Board
Degrees: A *Enroll:* 1,557
URL: http://www.highland.edu
Phone: (815) 235-6121 *Calendar:* Sem. plan
Inst. Accred.: NCA-HLC (1973/2003)

Illinois Central College
One College Dr., East Peoria 61635
Type: Public, state/local, two-year
System: Illinois Community College Board
Degrees: A *Enroll:* 7,437
URL: http://www.icc.edu
Phone: (309) 694-5422 *Calendar:* Sem. plan
Inst. Accred.: NCA-HLC (1972/2002)
Prog. Accred.: Allied Health (occupational therapy assisting, respiratory therapy, surgical technology), Clinical Lab Technology, Dentistry (dental hygiene), Music, Nursing, Physical Therapy Assisting, Radiography

Illinois College
1101 West College St., Jacksonville 62650
Type: Private, Presbyterian Church (USA), four-year
Degrees: B *Enroll:* 1,018
URL: http://www.ic.edu
Phone: (217) 245-3000 *Calendar:* Sem. plan
Inst. Accred.: NCA-HLC (1913/2005)

Illinois College of Optometry
3241 South Michigan Ave., Chicago 60616
Type: Private, independent, four-year
Degrees: M, P *Enroll:* 599
URL: http://www.ico.edu
Phone: (312) 225-1700 *Calendar:* Qtr. plan
Inst. Accred.: NCA-HLC (1969/1999)
Prog. Accred.: Allied Health (optometric residency, optometry)

The Illinois Institute of Art
350 North Orleans St., Ste. 136, Chicago 60654
Type: Private, proprietary, four-year
System: Education Management Corporation
Degrees: A, B *Enroll:* 2,190
URL: http://www.artinstitutes.edu/chicago
Phone: (312) 280-3500 *Calendar:* Qtr. plan
Inst. Accred.: ACCSCT (1975/2007), NCA-HLC (2004/2008)
Prog. Accred.: Culinary Education, Interior Design

The Art Institute of Michigan
28125 Cabot Dr., Ste. 120, Novi, MI 48377

The Art Institute of Ohio—Cincinnati
8845 Governor's Hill Dr., Cincinnati, OH 45249-3317
Phone: (513) 833-2400

Illinois Institute of Art—Schaumburg
1000 Plaza Dr., Ste. 100, Schaumburg 60173-4913
Type: Private, proprietary, four-year
System: Education Management Corporation
Degrees: A, B
URL: http://www.ilis.artinstitutes.edu
Phone: (847) 619-3450 *Calendar:* Qtr. plan
Inst. Accred.: ACCSCT (1988/2002), NCA-HLC (2006)
Prog. Accred.: Interior Design

Illinois Institute of Technology
3300 South Federal St., Chicago 60616-3793
Type: Private, independent, four-year
Degrees: B, M, D *Enroll:* 5,344
URL: http://www.iit.edu
Phone: (312) 567-3000 *Calendar:* Sem. plan
Inst. Accred.: NCA-HLC (1941/1997)
Prog. Accred.: Business (AACSB), Clinical Psychology, Computer Science (ABET-CAC), Engineering (aerospace, architectural, chemical, civil, computer, electrical, materials, mechanical), Law, Rehabilitation Counseling

Daniel F. and Ada L. Rice Campus
201 East Loop Rd., Wheaton 60187-8489
Phone: (708) 682-6000

Illinois State University
1000 Illinois State University, Normal 61790-1000
Type: Public, state, four-year
System: Illinois Board of Higher Education
Degrees: B, M, P, D *Enroll:* 18,876
URL: http://www.ilstu.edu
Phone: (309) 438-2111 *Calendar:* Sem. plan
Inst. Accred.: NCA-HLC (1913/2005)
Prog. Accred.: Accounting, Allied Health (audiology, speech-language pathology), Art, Business (AACSB), Clinical Lab Scientist, Computer Science (ABET-CAC), Construction Education, Dietetics (didactic), Dietetics (internship), Engineering (information systems), Environmental Health, Family & Consumer Science, Graduate Social Work, Industrial Technology, Interior Design, Music, Nursing Education, Psychology Internship, Recreation and Leisure Services, School Psychology, Social Work, Teacher Education (NCATE), Theatre

Mennonite College of Nursing
Campus Box 5810, Normal 61790-5810
Phone: (309) 438-7400

Illinois Valley Community College
815 North Orlando Smith Ave., Oglesby 61348
Type: Public, state/local, two-year
System: Illinois Community College Board
Degrees: A *Enroll:* 2,568
URL: http://www.ivcc.edu
Phone: (815) 224-2720 *Calendar:* Sem. plan
Inst. Accred.: NCA-HLC (1929/2002)
Prog. Accred.: Dentistry (dental assisting), Nursing

Illinois Wesleyan University
PO Box 2900, Bloomington 61702
Type: Private, United Methodist Church, four-year
Degrees: B *Enroll:* 2,142
URL: http://www.iwu.edu
Phone: (309) 556-1000 *Calendar:* 4-1-4 plan
Inst. Accred.: NCA-HLC (1916/2003)
Prog. Accred.: Music, Nursing Education

Institute for Clinical Social Work, Inc.
200 North Michigan Ave., Ste. 407, Chicago 60601
Type: Private, independent, four-year
Degrees: D *Enroll:* 65
URL: http://www.icsw.edu
Phone: (312) 726-8480 *Calendar:* Sem. plan
Inst. Accred.: NCA-HLC (1994/1999)

International Academy of Design and Technology
One North State St., Ste. 400, Chicago 60602-3302
Type: Private, proprietary, four-year
System: Career Education Corporation
Degrees: A, B *Enroll:* 2,550
URL: http://www.iadtchicago.edu
Phone: (312) 980-9200 *Calendar:* Qtr. plan
Inst. Accred.: ACICS (1981/2008)
Prog. Accred.: Interior Design

Detroit Campus
1850 Research Dr., Troy, MI 48083
Phone: (248) 526-1700

Sacramento Campus
2450 Del Paso Rd., Sacramento, CA 95834
Phone: (916) 285-9468

Schaumburg Campus
915 National Pkwy., Schaumburg 60173
Phone: (847) 969-2800

Seattle Campus
645 Andover Park West, Seattle, WA 98188
Phone: (206) 575-1865

John A. Logan College
700 Logan College Rd., Carterville 62918
Type: Public, state/local, two-year
System: Illinois Community College Board
Degrees: A *Enroll:* 4,258
URL: http://www.jalc.edu
Phone: (618) 985-3741 *Calendar:* Sem. plan
Inst. Accred.: NCA-HLC (1972/2007)
Prog. Accred.: Allied Health (diagnostic medical sonography), Construction Education, Dentistry (dental assisting, dental hygiene)

The John Marshall Law School
315 South Plymouth Ct., Chicago 60604
Type: Private, independent, four-year
Degrees: M, P *Enroll:* 1,465
URL: http://www.jmls.edu
Phone: (312) 427-2737 *Calendar:* Sem. plan
Inst. Accred.: NCA-HLC (2000/2005)
Prog. Accred.: Law

John Wood Community College
1301 South 48th St., Quincy 62305
Type: Public, state/local, two-year
System: Illinois Community College Board
Degrees: A *Enroll:* 1,645
URL: http://www.jwcc.edu
Phone: (217) 224-6500 *Calendar:* Sem. plan
Inst. Accred.: NCA-HLC (1980/2003)
Prog. Accred.: Allied Health (surgical technology)

Joliet Junior College
1215 Houbolt Rd., Joliet 60431-8938
Type: Public, state/local, two-year
System: Illinois Community College Board
Degrees: A *Enroll:* 7,624
URL: http://www.jjc.edu
Phone: (815) 729-9020 *Calendar:* Sem. plan
Inst. Accred.: NCA-HLC (1917/2008)
Prog. Accred.: Business (ACBSP), Culinary Education, Music, Nursing, Veterinary Technology

Judson University
1151 North State St., Elgin 60123
Type: Private, American Baptist Church, four-year
Degrees: B, M *Enroll:* 1,055
URL: http://www.judsonu.edu
Phone: (847) 695-2500 *Calendar:* 4-1-4 plan
Inst. Accred.: NCA-HLC (1973/2008)

Kankakee Community College
PO Box 888, 817 River Rd., Kankakee 60901
Type: Public, state/local, two-year
System: Illinois Community College Board
Degrees: A *Enroll:* 1,987
URL: http://www.kankakee.edu
Phone: (815) 802-8100 *Calendar:* Sem. plan
Inst. Accred.: NCA-HLC (1974/2004)
Prog. Accred.: Allied Health (respiratory therapy), Clinical Lab Technology

Kaskaskia College
27210 College Rd., Centralia 62801
Type: Public, state/local, two-year
System: Illinois Community College Board
Degrees: A *Enroll:* 2,867
URL: http://www.kaskaskia.edu
Phone: (618) 545-3000 *Calendar:* Sem. plan
Inst. Accred.: NCA-HLC (1964/1999)
Prog. Accred.: Allied Health (respiratory therapy), Dentistry (dental assisting), Nursing, Physical Therapy Assisting, Radiography

Kendall College
900 North Branch St., Chicago 60622
Type: Private, independent, four-year
System: Laureate Education, Inc.
Degrees: A, B *Enroll:* 608
URL: http://www.kendall.edu
Phone: (312) 752-2000 *Calendar:* Qtr. plan
Inst. Accred.: NCA-HLC (1962/2005)
Prog. Accred.: Culinary Education

Kishwaukee College
21193 Malta Rd., Malta 60150
Type: Public, state/local, two-year
System: Illinois Community College Board
Degrees: A *Enroll:* 2,770
URL: http://www.kishwaukeecollege.edu
Phone: (815) 825-2086 *Calendar:* Sem. plan
Inst. Accred.: NCA-HLC (1974/1999)
Prog. Accred.: Allied Health (massage therapy), Radiography

Knowledge Systems Institute
3420 Main St., Skokie 60076
Type: Private, proprietary, four-year
Degrees: M *Enroll:* 60
URL: http://www.ksi.edu
Phone: (847) 679-3135 *Calendar:* Sem. plan
Inst. Accred.: NCA-HLC (1991/2007)

Knox College
2 East South St., Galesburg 61401
Type: Private, independent, four-year
Degrees: B *Enroll:* 1,229
URL: http://www.knox.edu
Phone: (309) 341-7000 *Calendar:* Tri. plan
Inst. Accred.: NCA-HLC (1913/2000)

Lake Forest College
555 North Sheridan Rd., Lake Forest 60045-2399
Type: Private, United Presbyterian Church, four-year
Degrees: B, M *Enroll:* 1,414
URL: http://www.lakeforest.edu
Phone: (847) 234-3100 *Calendar:* Sem. plan
Inst. Accred.: NCA-HLC (1913/2007)

Lake Forest Graduate School of Management
1905 West Field Ct., Lake Forest 60045
Type: Private, independent, four-year
Degrees: M *Enroll:* 313
URL: http://www.lfgsm.edu
Phone: (847) 234-5005 *Calendar:* Qtr. plan
Inst. Accred.: NCA-HLC (1978/2003)

Chicago Campus
176 West Jackson Blvd., Chicago 60604
Phone: (312) 435-5330

Schaumburg Campus
1295 East Algonquin Rd., Schaumburg 60196
Phone: (847) 576-1212

Lake Land College
5001 Lake Land Blvd., Mattoon 61938
Type: Public, state/local, two-year
System: Illinois Community College Board
Degrees: A *Enroll:* 4,394
URL: http://www.lakelandcollege.edu
Phone: (217) 234-5253 *Calendar:* Sem. plan
Inst. Accred.: NCA-HLC (1973/2005)
Prog. Accred.: Dentistry (dental hygiene), Nursing, Physical Therapy Assisting, Practical Nursing

Lakeview College of Nursing
903 North Logan Ave., Danville 61832
Type: Private, independent, four-year
Degrees: B *Enroll:* 191
URL: http://www.lakeviewcol.edu
Phone: (217) 443-5238 *Calendar:* Sem. plan
Inst. Accred.: NCA-HLC (1995/2008)
Prog. Accred.: Nursing, Nursing Education

Lewis and Clark Community College
5800 Godfrey Rd., Godfrey 62035
Type: Public, state/local, two-year
System: Illinois Community College Board
Degrees: A *Enroll:* 4,043
URL: http://www.lc.edu
Phone: (618) 466-3411 *Calendar:* Sem. plan
Inst. Accred.: NCA-HLC (1971/2003)
Prog. Accred.: Allied Health (occupational therapy assisting), Clinical Lab Technology, Dentistry (dental assisting, dental hygiene), Nursing

Lewis University
One University Pkwy., Romeoville 60446-2298
Type: Private, Roman Catholic Church, four-year
Degrees: A, B, M, P *Enroll:* 3,645
URL: http://www.lewisu.edu
Phone: (815) 838-0500 *Calendar:* Sem. plan
Inst. Accred.: NCA-HLC (1963/2004)
Prog. Accred.: Business (ACBSP), Nursing Education, Teacher Education (NCATE)

Lexington College
310 South Peoria St., Ste. 512, Chicago 60607-3534
Type: Private, independent, four-year
Degrees: A, B *Enroll:* 49
URL: http://www.lexingtoncollege.edu
Phone: (312) 226-6294 *Calendar:* Sem. plan
Inst. Accred.: NCA-HLC (1993/2008)

Lincoln Christian College and Seminary
100 Campus View Dr., Lincoln 62656-2167
Type: Private, Christian Churches (Churches of Christ), four-year
Degrees: A, B, M *Enroll:* 868
URL: http://www.lccs.edu
Phone: (217) 732-3168 *Calendar:* Sem. plan
Inst. Accred.: ABHE (1954/2007), ATS (1991/2006), NCA-HLC (1991/2006)

Lincoln College
300 Keokuk St., Lincoln 62656
Type: Private, state/local, two-year
Degrees: A *Enroll:* 1,039
URL: http://www.lincolncollege.edu
Phone: (217) 732-3155 *Calendar:* Sem. plan
Inst. Accred.: NCA-HLC (1929/2004)

Lincoln College at Normal
715 West Raab Rd., Normal 61761
Phone: (309) 452-0500

Lincoln College of Technology—Melrose Park
8317 West North Ave., Melrose Park 60160
Type: Private, proprietary, two-year
System: Lincoln Educational Services Corporation
Degrees: A
URL: http://www.lincolncollegeoftechnology.com
Phone: (708) 344-4700
Inst. Accred.: ACCSCT (1971/2004)

Lincoln Land Community College
5250 Shepard Rd., PO Box 19256, Springfield 62794-9256
Type: Public, local, two-year
System: Illinois Community College Board
Degrees: A *Enroll:* 4,092
URL: http://www.llcc.edu
Phone: (217) 786-2200 *Calendar:* Sem. plan
Inst. Accred.: NCA-HLC (1973/2003)
Prog. Accred.: Allied Health (occupational therapy assisting), Nursing, Radiography

Lincoln Trail College
11220 State Hwy. 1, Robinson 62454
Type: Public, state/local, two-year
System: Illinois Eastern Community Colleges System
Degrees: A *Enroll:* 850
URL: http://www.iecc.edu/ltc
Phone: (618) 544-8657 *Calendar:* Sem. plan
Inst. Accred.: NCA-HLC (1984/2005, *Indirect accreditation through Illinois Eastern Community Colleges System, Olney, IL*)
Prog. Accred.: Nursing

Loyola University of Chicago
820 North Michigan Ave., Chicago 60611
Type: Private, Roman Catholic Church, four-year
Degrees: B, M, D *Enroll:* 13,254
URL: http://www.luc.edu
Phone: (312) 915-6000 *Calendar:* Sem. plan
Inst. Accred.: NCA-HLC (1921/2005)
Prog. Accred.: Accounting, Allied Health (medicine), Business (AACSB), Clinical Pastoral Education (ACPEI), Clinical Pastoral Education (USCC), Clinical Psychology, Counseling Psychology, Dentistry (combined prosthodontics, general practice residency, oral and maxillofacial surgery), Dietetics (internship), Graduate Social Work, Law, Nursing Education, Social Work, Teacher Education (NCATE), Theatre

Lake Shore Campus
6525 N. Sheridan Rd., Chicago 60626
Phone: (773) 274-3000

Loyola University Medical Center
2160 South First Ave., Maywood 60153
Phone: (708) 216-9000
Prog. Accred: Allied Health (EMT-paramedic), Dentistry (general practice residency, oral and maxillofacial surgery)

Mallinckrodt Campus
1041 Ridge Rd., Wilmette 60091
Phone: (847) 853-3000

Lutheran School of Theology at Chicago
1100 East 55th St., Chicago 60615-5199
Type: Private, Evangelical Lutheran Church in America, four-year
Degrees: M, D *Enroll:* 272
URL: http://www.lstc.edu
Phone: (773) 753-0700 *Calendar:* Qtr. plan
Inst. Accred.: ATS (1945/2007), NCA-HLC (1982/2007)

MacCormac College
29 East Madison St., Chicago 60602-4405
Type: Private, independent, two-year
Degrees: A *Enroll:* 206
URL: http://www.maccormac.edu
Phone: (312) 922-1884 *Calendar:* Sem. plan
Inst. Accred.: NCA-HLC (1979/2005)

Elmhurst Campus
615 N. West Ave., Elmhurst 60126
Phone: (708) 941-1200

MacMurray College
447 East College Ave., Jacksonville 62650-2590
Type: Private, United Methodist Church, four-year
Degrees: A, B *Enroll:* 664
URL: http://www.mac.edu
Phone: (217) 479-7000 *Calendar:* 4-1-4 plan
Inst. Accred.: NCA-HLC (1921/2003)
Prog. Accred.: Nursing Education, Social Work

McCormick Theological Seminary
5460 South University Ave., Chicago 60615
Type: Private, Presbyterian Church (USA), four-year
Degrees: M, D *Enroll:* 154
URL: http://www.mccormick.edu
Phone: (773) 947-6300 *Calendar:* Qtr. plan
Inst. Accred.: ATS (1938/2006), NCA-HLC (1982/2007)

McHenry County College
8900 U.S. Hwy. 14, Crystal Lake 60012-2761
Type: Public, state/local, two-year
System: Illinois Community College Board
Degrees: A *Enroll:* 3,209
URL: http://www.mchenry.edu
Phone: (815) 455-3700 *Calendar:* Sem. plan
Inst. Accred.: NCA-HLC (1976/2002)

McKendree University
701 College Rd., Lebanon 62254-1299
Type: Private, United Methodist Church, four-year
Degrees: A, B, M *Enroll:* 2,054
URL: http://www.mckendree.edu
Phone: (618) 537-4481 *Calendar:* Sem. plan
Inst. Accred.: NCA-HLC (1970/1999)
Prog. Accred.: Nursing, Teacher Education (NCATE)

Louisville Campus
11850 Commonwealth Dr., Jeffersontown, KY 40299
Phone: (502) 266-6696
Prog. Accred: Nursing

Radcliff Campus
1635 West Lincoln Trail Blvd., Radcliff, KY 40160
Phone: (270) 351-5003
Prog. Accred: Nursing

Scott AFB Center
375 MSS/DPE, 604 Tyler St., Rm. 73, Scott AFB 62225-5420
Phone: (618) 256-2006

Meadville Lombard Theological School
5701 South Woodlawn Ave., Chicago 60637
Type: Private, Unitarian Universalist Church, four-year
Degrees: M, D *Enroll:* 83
URL: http://www.meadville.edu
Phone: (773) 256-3000 *Calendar:* Qtr. plan
Inst. Accred.: ATS (1940/2003)

Methodist College of Nursing
415 N.E. St. Mark Ct., Peoria 61603
Type: Public, independent, four-year
Degrees: B *Enroll:* 106
URL: http://www.methodistcollegeofnursing.com
Phone: (309) 672-5583 *Calendar:* Sem. plan
Inst. Accred.: NCA-HLC (2008)

Midstate College
411 West Northmoor Rd., Peoria 61614
Type: Private, independent, four-year
Degrees: A, B *Enroll:* 386
URL: http://www.midstate.edu
Phone: (309) 692-4092 *Calendar:* Qtr. plan
Inst. Accred.: NCA-HLC (1982/2003)
Prog. Accred.: Allied Health (medical assisting (AMA))

Carthage Campus
30 South Washington, Carthage 62321
Phone: (217) 357-6626

Midwestern University
555 31st St., Downers Grove 60515
Type: Private, independent, four-year
Degrees: B, M, P, D *Enroll:* 1,857
URL: http://www.midwestern.edu
Phone: (630) 969-4400 *Calendar:* Qtr. plan
Inst. Accred.: NCA-HLC (1993/2008)
Prog. Accred.: Allied Health (occupational therapy), Osteopathy, Pharmacy, Physical Therapy, Physician Assistant

Glendale Campus
19555 North 59th Ave., Glendale, AZ 85308
Phone: (623) 572-3200
Prog. Accred: Allied Health (occupational therapy, perfusion), Dentistry (dentistry), Nurse Anesthesia Education, Osteopathy, Pharmacy, Physician Assistant, Podiatry

Millikin University
1184 West Main St., Decatur 62522
Type: Private, United Presbyterian Church, four-year
Degrees: B, M *Enroll:* 2,533
URL: http://www.millikin.edu
Phone: (217) 424-6211 *Calendar:* Sem. plan
Inst. Accred.: NCA-HLC (1914/2007)
Prog. Accred.: Business (ACBSP), Music, Nursing Education

Monmouth College
700 East Broadway, Monmouth 61462
Type: Private, Presbyterian Church (USA), four-year
Degrees: B *Enroll:* 1,335
URL: http://www.monm.edu
Phone: (309) 457-2311 *Calendar:* Sem. plan
Inst. Accred.: NCA-HLC (1913/2008)

Moody Bible Institute
820 North LaSalle Dr., Chicago 60610-3214
Type: Private, interdenominational, four-year
Degrees: B, M *Enroll:* 1,636
URL: http://www.moody.edu
Phone: (312) 329-4000 *Calendar:* Sem. plan
Inst. Accred.: ABHE (1951/2005), NCA-HLC (1989/2004)
Prog. Accred.: Music

Moraine Valley Community College
10900 South 88th Ave., Palos Hills 60465
Type: Public, state/local, two-year
System: Illinois Community College Board
Degrees: A *Enroll:* 9,768
URL: http://www.morainevalley.edu
Phone: (708) 974-4300 *Calendar:* Sem. plan
Inst. Accred.: NCA-HLC (1975/2004)
Prog. Accred.: Allied Health (medical assisting (AMA), respiratory therapy), Clinical Lab Technology, Nursing, Phlebotomy, Radiography

Morrison Institute of Technology
701 Portland Ave., PO Box 410, Morrison 61270-0410
Type: Private, independent, two-year
Degrees: A *Enroll:* 127
URL: http://www.morrison.tec.il.us
Phone: (815) 772-7218 *Calendar:* Sem. plan
Inst. Accred.: COE (2000/2006)
Prog. Accred.: Engineering Technology (general)

Morton College
3801 South Central Ave., Cicero 60804
Type: Public, state/local, two-year
System: Illinois Community College Board
Degrees: A *Enroll:* 2,468
URL: http://www.morton.edu
Phone: (708) 656-8000 *Calendar:* Sem. plan
Inst. Accred.: NCA-HLC (1927/2004, Warning)
Prog. Accred.: Allied Health (massage therapy), Dentistry (dental assisting), Physical Therapy Assisting

National University of Health Sciences
200 East Roosevelt Rd., Lombard 60148
Type: Private, independent, four-year
Degrees: A, B, M, P *Enroll:* 451
URL: http://www.nuhs.edu
Phone: (630) 629-2000 *Calendar:* Tri. plan
Inst. Accred.: NCA-HLC (1981/2006)
Prog. Accred.: Allied Health (massage therapy), Chiropractic Education

National-Louis University
122 South Michigan Ave., Chicago 60603-6191
Type: Private, independent, four-year
Degrees: B, M, P, D *Enroll:* 4,634
URL: http://www.nl.edu
Phone: (312) 621-9650 *Calendar:* Qtr. plan
Inst. Accred.: NCA-HLC (1946/2001)
Prog. Accred.: Clinical Lab Scientist, Radiation Therapy, Teacher Education (NCATE)

Atlanta Academic Center Campus
Blackstone Center, 1777 N.E. Expressway, Ste. 250, Atlanta, GA 30329
Phone: (404) 633-1223

Chicago Campus
18 South Michigan Ave., Chicago 60603
Phone: (312) 621-9650

Elgin Facility Campus
400 Federation Place, Elgin 60123
Phone: (708) 695-6070

Evanston Campus
2840 Sheridan Rd., Evanston 60201-1796
Phone: (708) 475-1100

Heidelberg Academic Center Campus
Rohrbacher Strasse 47, Heidelberg, Germany 69115
Phone: 011-49-6221-29025

Milwaukee/Beloit Academic Center Campus
325 North Corporate Dr., Ste. 200, Brookfield, WI 53045-5861
Phone: (414) 792-3699

Northern Virginia/Washington, DC Academic Center Campus
8000 Westpark Dr., Ste. 125, McLean, VA 22102
Phone: (703) 749-3000

St. Louis Academic Center Campus
12412 Powerscourt Dr., Ste. LL20, St. Louis, MO 63131
Phone: (314) 822-2110

Tampa Academic Center Campus
4890 West Kennedy Blvd., Ste. 145, Tampa, FL 33609
Phone: (813) 286-8087

Wheaton Campus
200 South Naperville Rd., Wheaton 60187
Phone: (708) 668-3838

Wheeling Campus
1000 Capitol Dr., Wheeling 60090
Phone: (708) 465-0575

North Central College
30 N. Brainard St., PO Box 3063, Naperville 60566-7063
Type: Private, United Methodist Church, four-year
Degrees: B, M *Enroll:* 2,164
URL: http://www.noctrl.edu
Phone: (630) 637-5100 *Calendar:* Tri. plan
Inst. Accred.: NCA-HLC (1914/2000)

North Park Theological Seminary
3225 West Foster Ave., Chicago 60625-4895
Type: Private, Evangelical Covenant Church, four-year
Degrees: M
URL: http://www.northpark.edu/sem
Phone: (773) 244-6229 *Calendar:* Sem. plan
Inst. Accred.: ATS (1963/2007)

North Park University
3225 West Foster Ave., Chicago 60625
Type: Private, Evangelical Covenant Church, four-year
Degrees: B, M, D *Enroll:* 2,178
URL: http://www.northpark.edu
Phone: (773) 244-6200 *Calendar:* Sem. plan
Inst. Accred.: NCA-HLC (1926/2001)
Prog. Accred.: Music, Nursing Education

Northeastern Illinois University
5500 North St. Louis Ave., Chicago 60625
Type: Public, state, four-year
System: Illinois Board of Higher Education
Degrees: B, M *Enroll:* 8,220
URL: http://www.neiu.edu
Phone: (773) 583-4050 *Calendar:* Tri. plan
Inst. Accred.: NCA-HLC (1961/2007)
Prog. Accred.: Counseling, Social Work, Teacher Education (NCATE)

Northern Illinois University
DeKalb 60115
Type: Public, state, four-year
System: Illinois Board of Higher Education
Degrees: B, M, P, D *Enroll:* 21,328
URL: http://www.niu.edu
Phone: (815) 753-1000 *Calendar:* Sem. plan
Inst. Accred.: NCA-HLC (1915/2004)
Prog. Accred.: Accounting, Allied Health (audiology, speech-language pathology), Art, Business (AACSB), Clinical Lab Scientist, Clinical Psychology, Counseling, Dietetics (didactic), Dietetics (internship), Engineering (electrical, industrial, mechanical), Engineering Technology (electrical, mechanical), Industrial Technology, Law, Marriage and Family Therapy, Music, Nursing Education, Physical Therapy, Psychology Internship, Public Administration, Public Health, Rehabilitation Counseling, Teacher Education (NCATE), Theatre

Northern Seminary
660 East Butterfield Rd., Lombard 60148
Type: Private, American Baptish Churches in the USA, four-year
Degrees: M, P, D *FTE Enroll:* 214
URL: http://www.seminary.edu
Phone: (630) 620-2100 *Calendar:* Qtr. plan
Inst. Accred.: ATS (1968/2007), NCA-HLC (1947/2008)

Northwestern Business College
9700 West Higgins Rd., Ste. 750, Rosemont 60018
Type: Private, proprietary, two-year
Degrees: A *Enroll:* 735
URL: http://www.northwesternbc.edu
Phone: (773) 777-4220 *Calendar:* Qtr. plan
Inst. Accred.: NCA-HLC (1997/2002)
Prog. Accred.: Allied Health (medical assisting (AMA)), Business (ACBSP)

Southwestern Campus
8020 West 87th St., Hickory Hills 60457
Phone: (708) 430-0990

Northwestern University
633 Clark St., Evanston 60208
Type: Private, independent, four-year
Degrees: B, M, D *Enroll:* 16,192
URL: http://www.northwestern.edu
Phone: (847) 491-3741 *Calendar:* Qtr. plan
Inst. Accred.: NCA-HLC (1913/2005)
Prog. Accred.: Allied Health (audiology, health services administration, medicine, orthotist/prothetist, speech-language pathology), Business (AACSB), Clinical Psychology, Dentistry (combined prosthodontics, endodontics, general dentistry, oral and maxillofacial surgery, orthodontic and dentofacial orthopedics, pediatric dentistry, periodontics), Engineering (bioengineering, chemical, civil, computer, electrical, environmental/sanitary, industrial, manufacturing, materials, mechanical), Journalism, Law, Marriage and Family Therapy, Music, Physical Therapy, Psychology Internship, Public Health, Theatre

Chicago Campus
303 East Chicago Ave., Chicago 60611-3008
Phone: (312) 503-8649
Prog. Accred: Clinical Psychology

Qatar Campus
2240 Campus Dr., Evanston 60208-3580

Oakton Community College
1600 East Golf Rd., Des Plaines 60016
Type: Public, state/local, two-year
System: Illinois Community College Board
Degrees: A *Enroll:* 5,846
URL: http://www.oakton.edu
Phone: (847) 635-1600 *Calendar:* Sem. plan
Inst. Accred.: NCA-HLC (1976/2008)
Prog. Accred.: Clinical Lab Technology, Nursing, Physical Therapy Assisting

Ray Hartstein Campus
7701 North Lincoln Ave., Skokie 60077
Phone: (847) 635-1400

Olivet Nazarene University
One University Ave., Bourbonnais 60914
Type: Private, Church of the Nazarene, four-year
Degrees: B, M *Enroll:* 3,397
URL: http://www.olivet.edu
Phone: (815) 939-5011 *Calendar:* Sem. plan
Inst. Accred.: NCA-HLC (1956/2005)
Prog. Accred.: Dietetics (didactic), Engineering (general), Music, Nursing Education, Social Work, Teacher Education (NCATE)

Olney Central College
305 North West St., Olney 62450
Type: Public, state/local, two-year
System: Illinois Eastern Community Colleges System
Degrees: A *Enroll:* 1,075
URL: http://www.iecc.edu/occ
Phone: (618) 395-7777 *Calendar:* Sem. plan
Inst. Accred.: NCA-HLC (1984/2005, *Indirect accreditation through Illinois Eastern Community Colleges System, Olney, IL*)
Prog. Accred.: Nursing, Radiography

OSF Saint Francis Medical Center
530 NE Glen Oak Ave., Peoria 61637
Type: Private, Roman Catholic Church, four-year
Degrees: B, M, D *Enroll:* 227
URL: http://www.osfsaintfrancis.org
Phone: (309) 655-2323 *Calendar:* Sem. plan
Inst. Accred.: NCA-HLC (1991/2001)
Prog. Accred.: Clinical Lab Scientist, Dietetics (internship), Histologic Technology, Radiography

Parkland College
2400 West Bradley Ave., Champaign 61821
Type: Public, state/local, two-year
System: Illinois Community College Board
Degrees: A *Enroll:* 6,287
URL: http://www.parkland.edu
Phone: (217) 351-2200 *Calendar:* Sem. plan
Inst. Accred.: NCA-HLC (1972/2003)
Prog. Accred.: Allied Health (occupational therapy assisting, respiratory therapy, surgical technology), Dentistry (dental hygiene), Nursing, Radiography, Veterinary Technology

Prairie State College
202 South Halsted St., Chicago Heights 60411
Type: Public, state/local, two-year
System: Illinois Community College Board
Degrees: A *Enroll:* 2,845
URL: http://www.prairiestate.edu
Phone: (708) 709-3500 *Calendar:* Sem. plan
Inst. Accred.: NCA-HLC (1965/1999)
Prog. Accred.: Allied Health (surgical technology), Dentistry (dental hygiene), Nursing

Principia College
1 Maybeck Place, Elsah 62028
Type: Private, independent, four-year
Degrees: B *Enroll:* 539
URL: http://www.prin.edu/college
Phone: (618) 374-2131 *Calendar:* Qtr. plan
Inst. Accred.: NCA-HLC (1923/2002)

Quincy University
1800 College Ave., Quincy 62301
Type: Private, Roman Catholic Church, four-year
Degrees: B, M *Enroll:* 1,111
URL: http://www.quincy.edu
Phone: (217) 222-8020 *Calendar:* Sem. plan
Inst. Accred.: NCA-HLC (1954/2002)
Prog. Accred.: Music

Rasmussen College—Aurora
2363 Sequoia Dr., Aurora 60506
Type: Private, proprietary, two-year
System: Rasmussen College System
Degrees: A
URL: http://www.rasmussen.edu
Phone: (630) 888-3500 *Calendar:* Qtr. plan
Inst. Accred.: NCA-HLC (2001/2004, *Indirect accreditation through Rasmussen College System, Lake Elmo, MN*)

Rasmussen College—Rockford
6000 East State St., Fourth Flr., Rockford 61108-2513
Type: Private, proprietary, two-year
System: Rasmussen College System
Degrees: A
URL: http://www.rasmussen.edu
Phone: (815) 316-4800 *Calendar:* Qtr. plan
Inst. Accred.: NCA-HLC (2001/2004, *Indirect accreditation through Rasmussen College System, Lake Elmo, MN*)

Rend Lake College
468 N. Ken Gray Pkwy., Ina 62846
Type: Public, state/local, two-year
System: Illinois Community College Board
Degrees: A *Enroll:* 2,724
URL: http://www.rlc.edu
Phone: (618) 437-5321 *Calendar:* Sem. plan
Inst. Accred.: NCA-HLC (1969/1999)

Richland Community College
One College Park, Decatur 62521
Type: Public, state/local, two-year
System: Illinois Community College Board
Degrees: A *Enroll:* 1,715
URL: http://www.richland.edu
Phone: (217) 875-7200 *Calendar:* Sem. plan
Inst. Accred.: NCA-HLC (1978/2008)
Prog. Accred.: Allied Health (surgical technology), Nursing

Robert Morris College
401 South State St., Chicago 60605
Type: Private, independent, four-year
Degrees: A, B *Enroll:* 4,986
URL: http://www.robertmorris.edu
Phone: (312) 935-6600 *Calendar:* Qtr. plan
Inst. Accred.: NCA-HLC (1986/2001)
Prog. Accred.: Allied Health (medical assisting (AMA), surgical technology)

Springfield Campus
1301 Montvale Dr., Springfield 62704-4260
Phone: (800) 762-5960
Prog. Accred: Allied Health (medical assisting (AMA))

Rock Valley College
3301 North Mulford Rd., Rockford 61114-5699
Type: Public, state/local, two-year
System: Illinois Community College Board
Degrees: A *Enroll:* 5,065
URL: http://www.rockvalleycollege.edu
Phone: (815) 921-7821 *Calendar:* Sem. plan
Inst. Accred.: NCA-HLC (1971/2004)
Prog. Accred.: Allied Health (respiratory therapy, surgical technology), Dentistry (dental hygiene)

Rockford Career College
1130 South Alpine Rd., Ste. 100, Rockford 61108
Type: Private, proprietary, two-year
System: American Higher Education Development Corporation
Degrees: A *Enroll:* 332
URL: http://www.rockfordcareercollege.edu
Phone: (815) 965-8616 *Calendar:* Qtr. plan
Inst. Accred.: ACICS (1968/2003)
Prog. Accred.: Allied Health (medical assisting (AMA)), Veterinary Technology

Rockford College
5050 East State St., Rockford 61108-2393
Type: Private, independent, four-year
Degrees: B, M *Enroll:* 1,040
URL: http://www.rockford.edu
Phone: (815) 226-4010 *Calendar:* Sem. plan
Inst. Accred.: NCA-HLC (1913/2001)
Prog. Accred.: Nursing

Roosevelt University
430 South Michigan Ave., Chicago 60605
Type: Private, independent, four-year
Degrees: B, M, D *Enroll:* 4,575
URL: http://www.roosevelt.edu
Phone: (312) 341-3500 *Calendar:* Sem. plan
Inst. Accred.: NCA-HLC (1946/2006)
Prog. Accred.: Business (ACBSP), Clinical Psychology, Counseling, Music, Teacher Education (NCATE)

Albert A. Robin Campus
1400 North Roosevelt Blvd., Schaumburg 60173-4348
Phone: (847) 619-7300

The Rosalind Franklin University of Medicine and Science
3333 Green Bay Rd., North Chicago 60064
Type: Private, independent, four-year
Degrees: B, M, D *Enroll:* 1,591
URL: http://www.rosalindfranklin.edu
Phone: (847) 578-3000 *Calendar:* Qtr. plan
Inst. Accred.: NCA-HLC (1980/2008)
Prog. Accred.: Allied Health (medicine), Clinical Lab Scientist, Clinical Psychology, Immunology, Nurse Anesthesia Education, Pathologists' Assistant, Phlebotomy, Physical Therapy, Physician Assistant

Dr. William M. Scholl College of Podiatric Medicine
3333 Green Bay Rd., North Chicago 60064
Phone: (847) 578-8400
Prog. Accred: Podiatry

Rush University
1653 W. Congress Pkwy., Chicago 60612
Type: Private, independent, four-year
Degrees: B, M, D *Enroll:* 1,201
URL: http://www.rushu.rush.edu
Phone: (312) 942-7120 *Calendar:* Qtr. plan
Inst. Accred.: NCA-HLC (1974/2008)
Prog. Accred.: Allied Health (audiology, blood bank technology, diagnostic medical sonography, health services administration, medicine, occupational therapy, perfusion, speech-language pathology), Clinical Lab Scientist, Dietetics (internship), Nurse Anesthesia Education, Nursing Education

Saint Anthony College of Nursing
5658 East State St., Rockford 61108-2468
Type: Private, Roman Catholic Church, four-year
Degrees: B *Enroll:* 115
URL: http://www.sacn.edu
Phone: (815) 395-5091 *Calendar:* Sem. plan
Inst. Accred.: NCA-HLC (1994/1999)
Prog. Accred.: Nursing Education

Saint Augustine College
1333-45 West Argyle St., Chicago 60640
Type: Private, independent, four-year
Degrees: A, B *Enroll:* 1,314
URL: http://www.staugustinecollege.edu
Phone: (773) 878-8756 *Calendar:* Sem. plan
Inst. Accred.: NCA-HLC (1987/2008)
Prog. Accred.: Allied Health (respiratory therapy technology), Social Work

Saint John's College
421 North Ninth St., Springfield 62702
Type: Private, independent, four-year
Degrees: B *Enroll:* 75
URL: http://www.st-johns.org/education/schools/nursing
Phone: (217) 525-5628 *Calendar:* Sem. plan
Inst. Accred.: NCA-HLC (1995/2000)
Prog. Accred.: Allied Health (electroneurodiagnostic technology, respiratory therapy), Clinical Lab Scientist, Nursing

Saint Xavier University
3700 West 103rd St., Chicago 60655
Type: Private, Roman Catholic Church, four-year
Degrees: B, M *Enroll:* 3,828
URL: http://www.sxu.edu
Phone: (773) 298-3000 *Calendar:* Sem. plan
Inst. Accred.: NCA-HLC (1937/2008)
Prog. Accred.: Allied Health (speech-language pathology), Business (ACBSP), Music, Nursing Education, Teacher Education (NCATE)

Sauk Valley Community College
173 Illinois Route 2, Dixon 61021
Type: Public, state/local, two-year
System: Illinois Community College Board
Degrees: A *Enroll:* 1,688
URL: http://www.svcc.edu
Phone: (815) 288-5511 *Calendar:* Sem. plan
Inst. Accred.: NCA-HLC (1972/2002)
Prog. Accred.: Clinical Lab Technology, Radiography

The School of the Art Institute of Chicago
37 South Wabash Ave., Chicago 60603
Type: Private, independent, four-year
Degrees: B, M *Enroll:* 2,518
URL: http://www.artic.edu/saic/saichome.html
Phone: (312) 899-5219 *Calendar:* Sem. plan
Inst. Accred.: NCA-HLC (1936/2003)
Prog. Accred.: Art

Seabury-Western Theological Seminary
2122 Sheridan Rd., Evanston 60201-2938
Type: Private, Episcopal Church, four-year
Degrees: M, D *Enroll:* 79
URL: http://www.seabury.edu
Phone: (847) 328-9300 *Calendar:* Qtr. plan
Inst. Accred.: ATS (1938/1998), NCA-HLC (1981/1998)

Shawnee Community College
8364 Shawnee College Rd., Ullin 62992-9725
Type: Public, state/local, two-year
System: Illinois Community College Board
Degrees: A *Enroll:* 1,243
URL: http://www.shawneecc.edu
Phone: (618) 634-3200 *Calendar:* Sem. plan
Inst. Accred.: NCA-HLC (1974/2005)
Prog. Accred.: Allied Health (surgical technology)

Shimer College
3424 South State St., Chicago 60616
Type: Private, independent, four-year
Degrees: B *Enroll:* 98
URL: http://www.shimer.edu
Phone: (312) 235-3500 *Calendar:* Sem. plan
Inst. Accred.: NCA-HLC (1991/2006)

South Suburban College of Cook County
15800 South State St., South Holland 60473
Type: Public, state/local, two-year
System: Illinois Community College Board
Degrees: A *Enroll:* 3,935
URL: http://www.southsuburbancollege.edu
Phone: (708) 596-2000 *Calendar:* Sem. plan
Inst. Accred.: NCA-HLC (1933/1999)
Prog. Accred.: Allied Health (diagnostic medical sonography, medical assisting (AMA), occupational therapy assisting), Music, Nursing, Phlebotomy, Practical Nursing, Radiography

Southeastern Illinois College
3575 College Rd., Harrisburg 62946
Type: Public, state/local, two-year
System: Illinois Community College Board
Degrees: A *Enroll:* 1,671
URL: http://www.sic.edu
Phone: (618) 252-6376 *Calendar:* Sem. plan
Inst. Accred.: NCA-HLC (1976/2008)

Southern Illinois University Carbondale
Carbondale 62901-6899
Type: Public, state, four-year
System: Southern Illinois University System
Degrees: A, B, M, D *Enroll:* 18,870
URL: http://www.siuc.edu
Phone: (618) 453-2121 *Calendar:* Sem. plan
Inst. Accred.: NCA-HLC (1913/1999)
Prog. Accred.: Accounting, Allied Health (diagnostic medical sonography, respiratory therapy, speech-language pathology), Art, Business (AACSB), Clinical Psychology, Counseling, Counseling Psychology, Dentistry (dental hygiene, dental laboratory technology), Dietetics (didactic), Dietetics (internship), Engineering (civil, computer, electrical, mechanical, mining), Engineering Technology (electrical, mechanical), Forestry, Funeral Service Education (Mortuary Science), Graduate Social Work, Industrial Technology, Interior Design, Journalism, Law, Music, Physical Therapy Assisting, Physician Assistant, Psychology Internship, Public Administration, Radiography, Recreation and Leisure Services, Rehabilitation Counseling, Social Work, Teacher Education (NCATE), Theatre

Southern Illinois University Carbondale in Niigata
439-1, Oaza Nagahashikami, Nakajo, Kitakanbara, Niigata, Japan 959-26
Phone: 011-81-254-43-6205

School of Medicine
PO Box 19620, Springfield 62794-9620
Phone: (217) 545-8000
Prog. Accred: Allied Health (medicine)

Southern Illinois University Edwardsville
SIUE Campus Box 1151, Edwardsville 62026-1151
Type: Public, state, four-year
System: Southern Illinois University System
Degrees: B, M, P, D *Enroll:* 11,420
URL: http://www.siue.edu
Phone: (618) 650-2000 *Calendar:* Sem. plan
Inst. Accred.: NCA-HLC (1969/2008)
Prog. Accred.: Accounting, Allied Health (speech-language pathology), Business (AACSB), Computer Science (ABET-CAC), Construction Education, Dentistry (dental hygiene, dental laboratory technology, dentistry, general dentistry, general practice residency), Engineering (civil, computer, electrical, industrial, manufacturing, mechanical), Graduate Social Work, Journalism, Music, Nurse Anesthesia Education, Nursing Education, Pharmacy, Public Administration, Social Work, Teacher Education (NCATE)

Southwestern Illinois College
2500 Carlyle Rd., Belleville 62221
Type: Public, state/local, two-year
System: Illinois Community College Board
Degrees: A *Enroll:* 8,379
URL: http://www.swic.edu
Phone: (618) 235-2700 *Calendar:* Sem. plan
Inst. Accred.: NCA-HLC (1961/1999)
Prog. Accred.: Allied Health (medical assisting (AMA), respiratory therapy), Clinical Lab Technology, Culinary Education, Nursing, Physical Therapy Assisting, Radiography

Red Bud Campus
500 West South Fourth St., Red Bud 62278
Phone: (618) 282-6682

Spertus Institute of Jewish Studies
610 South Michigan Ave., Chicago 60605
Type: Private, independent, four-year
Degrees: M, D *Enroll:* 92
URL: http://www.spertus.edu
Phone: (312) 322-1700 *Calendar:* Qtr. plan
Inst. Accred.: NCA-HLC (1971/2008)

Spoon River College
23235 North County 22, Canton 61520
Type: Public, state/local, two-year
System: Illinois Community College Board
Degrees: A *Enroll:* 1,483
URL: http://www.spoonrivercollege.edu
Phone: (309) 647-4645 *Calendar:* Sem. plan
Inst. Accred.: NCA-HLC (1977/2002)

Springfield College in Illinois
1500 North Fifth St., Springfield 62702
Type: Private, Roman Catholic Church, two-year
Degrees: A *Enroll:* 383
URL: http://www.sci.edu
Phone: (217) 525-1420 *Calendar:* Sem. plan
Inst. Accred.: NCA-HLC (1933/2006)

Taylor Business Institute
318 West Adams St., 5th Flr., Chicago 60606-5751
Type: Private, proprietary, two-year
Degrees: A *Enroll:* 95
URL: http://www.tbiil.edu
Phone: (312) 658-5100
Inst. Accred.: ACICS (1973/2006)

Telshe Yeshiva-Chicago
3535 West Foster Ave., Chicago 60625
Type: Private, independent, four-year
Degrees: Rabbinic *Enroll:* 72
Phone: (773) 463-7738 *Calendar:* Sem. plan
Inst. Accred.: AARTS (1976/2002)

Trinity Christian College
6601 West College Dr., Palos Heights 60463
Type: Private, Christian Reformed, four-year
Degrees: B *Enroll:* 1,140
URL: http://www.trnty.edu
Phone: (708) 597-3000 *Calendar:* Sem. plan
Inst. Accred.: NCA-HLC (1976/2001)
Prog. Accred.: Business (ACBSP), Nursing Education, Social Work

Trinity College of Nursing and Health Sciences School
2701 17th St., Rock Island 61201
Type: Private, independent, four-year
Degrees: A, B *Enroll:* 137
URL: http://www.trinitycollegeqc.edu
Phone: (309) 779-7700 *Calendar:* Sem. plan
Inst. Accred.: NCA-HLC (1996/2003)
Prog. Accred.: Allied Health (EMT-paramedic, surgical technology), Nursing, Nursing Education, Radiography

Trinity International University
2065 Half Day Rd., Deerfield 60015
Type: Private, Evangelical Free Church of America, four-year
Degrees: B, M, D *Enroll:* 1,980
URL: http://www.tiu.edu
Phone: (847) 945-8800 *Calendar:* Sem. plan
Inst. Accred.: ATS (1973/1999), NCA-HLC (1996/ 2000)

Florida Regional Center
8190 West State Rd. 84, Davie, FL 33324
Phone: (954) 382-6400

Trinity Law School
2200 North Grand Ave., Santa Ana, CA 92705
Phone: (714) 836-7500

Triton College
2000 Fifth Ave., River Grove 60171
Type: Public, state/local, two-year
System: Illinois Community College Board
Degrees: A *Enroll:* 7,865
URL: http://www.triton.edu
Phone: (708) 456-0300 *Calendar:* Sem. plan
Inst. Accred.: NCA-HLC (1972/2007)
Prog. Accred.: Allied Health (diagnostic medical sonography, respiratory therapy, surgical technology), Construction Education, Dentistry (dental laboratory technology), Nuclear Medicine Technology, Nursing, Practical Nursing, Radiography

University of Chicago
5801 South Ellis Ave., Chicago 60637
Type: Private, independent, four-year
Degrees: B, M, D *Enroll:* 12,474
URL: http://www.uchicago.edu
Phone: (773) 702-1234 *Calendar:* Qtr. plan
Inst. Accred.: ATS (1938/2002), NCA-HLC (1913/2006)
Prog. Accred.: Accounting, Allied Health (medicine), Business (AACSB), Dentistry (general practice residency, maxillofacial prosthetics, oral and maxillofacial surgery), Graduate Social Work, Law, Psychology Internship

Booth School of Business in Singapore
101 Penang Rd., Singapore 238 466
Phone: 011 65 6835 6482

Graduate School of Business
1101 East 58th St., Chicago 60637
Phone: (773) 702-7743

University of Illinois at Chicago
601 South Morgan St., M/C 102, Chicago 60607-7128
Type: Public, state, four-year
System: University of Illinois Central Office
Degrees: B, M, P, D *Enroll:* 21,946
URL: http://www.uic.edu
Phone: (312) 996-7000 *Calendar:* Sem. plan
Inst. Accred.: NCA-HLC (1970/2007)
Prog. Accred.: Accounting, Allied Health (medical illustration, medicine, occupational therapy), Applied Science (industrial hygiene), Art, Business (AACSB), Clinical Lab Scientist, Clinical Pastoral Education (ACPEI), Clinical Psychology, Computer Science (ABET-CAC), Dentistry (combined prosthodontics, dentistry, endodontics, general practice residency, oral and maxillofacial surgery, orthodontic and dentofacial orthopedics, pediatric dentistry, periodontics), Dietetics (coordinated), Dietetics (didactic), Engineering (bioengineering, chemical, civil, computer, electrical, industrial, mechanical), English Language Education, Graduate Social Work, Nurse (Midwifery), Nursing Education, Pharmacy, Physical Therapy, Planning, Psychology Internship, Public Administration, Public Health, Social Work

College of Medicine at Peoria
1 Illini Dr., PO Box 1649, Peoria 62656
Phone: (309) 671-3000

College of Medicine at Rockford
1601 Parkview Ave., Rockford 61107
Phone: (815) 395-0600

University of Illinois at Springfield
One University Plaza, Springfield 62703
Type: Public, state, four-year
System: University of Illinois Central Office
Degrees: B, M, D *Enroll:* 2,983
URL: http://www.uis.edu
Phone: (217) 206-6600 *Calendar:* Sem. plan
Inst. Accred.: NCA-HLC (1975/2008)
Prog. Accred.: Business (AACSB), Clinical Lab Scientist, Counseling, Public Administration, Social Work

University of Illinois at Urbana-Champaign
601 East John St., Champaign 61820
Type: Public, state, four-year
System: University of Illinois Central Office
Degrees: B, M, D *Enroll:* 39,877
URL: http://www.uiuc.edu
Phone: (217) 333-1000 *Calendar:* Sem. plan
Inst. Accred.: NCA-HLC (1913/1999)
Prog. Accred.: Accounting, Allied Health (audiology, speech-language pathology), Art, Business (AACSB), Clinical Psychology, Computer Science (ABET-CAC), Counseling Psychology, Dance, Dietetics (didactic), Dietetics (internship), Engineering (aerospace, agricultural, chemical, civil, computer, electrical, engineering mechanics, general, industrial, materials, mechanical, nuclear), Forestry, Graduate Social Work, Journalism, Landscape Architecture, Law, Librarianship, Music, Planning, Psychology Internship, Recreation and Leisure Services, Rehabilitation Counseling, Theatre, Veterinary Medicine

University of Saint Francis
500 North Wilcox St., Joliet 60435
Type: Private, Roman Catholic Church, four-year
Degrees: B, M *Enroll:* 2,365
URL: http://www.stfrancis.edu
Phone: (815) 740-3360 *Calendar:* Sem. plan
Inst. Accred.: NCA-HLC (1938/1999)
Prog. Accred.: Business (ACBSP), Graduate Social Work, Nursing Education, Recreation and Leisure Services, Social Work

Albuquerque Campus
4401 Silver Ave., SE, Albuquerque, NM 87108
Phone: (505) 266-5565
Prog. Accred: Physician Assistant

University of Saint Mary of the Lake Mundelein Seminary
1000 East Maple Ave., Mundelein 60060
Type: Private, Roman Catholic Church, four-year
Degrees: M, D *Enroll:* 236
URL: http://www.usml.edu
Phone: (847) 566-6401 *Calendar:* Sem. plan
Inst. Accred.: ATS (1972/2002)

VanderCook College of Music
3140 South Federal St., Chicago 60616
Type: Private, independent, four-year
Degrees: B, M *Enroll:* 159
URL: http://www.vandercook.edu
Phone: (312) 225-6288 *Calendar:* Sem. plan
Inst. Accred.: NCA-HLC (1971/2008)
Prog. Accred.: Music

Vatterott College—Quincy
501 North Third St., Quincy 62301-9990
Type: Private, proprietary, two-year
System: Vatterott Educational Centers, Inc.
Degrees: A
URL: http://www.vatterott-college.com
Phone: (217) 224-0600 *Calendar:* Sem. plan
Inst. Accred.: ACCSCT (1977/2006)

Oklahoma City Campus
4621 NW 23rd St., Oklahoma City, OK 73127
Phone: (405) 945-0088

Wabash Valley College
2200 College Dr., Mount Carmel 62863
Type: Public, state/local, two-year
System: Illinois Eastern Community Colleges System
Degrees: A *Enroll:* 1,478
URL: http://www.iecc.edu/wvc
Phone: (618) 262-8641 *Calendar:* Sem. plan
Inst. Accred.: NCA-HLC (1984/2005, *Indirect accreditation through Illinois Eastern Community Colleges System, Olney, IL*)
Prog. Accred.: Nursing

Waubonsee Community College
Illinois Route 47 at Waubonsee Dr., Sugar Grove 60554
Type: Public, state/local, two-year
System: Illinois Community College Board
Degrees: A *Enroll:* 4,709
URL: http://www.waubonsee.edu
Phone: (630) 466-7900 *Calendar:* Sem. plan
Inst. Accred.: NCA-HLC (1972/2003)
Prog. Accred.: Allied Health (medical assisting (AMA), surgical technology)

West Suburban College of Nursing
3 Erie St., Oak Park 60302
Type: Private, independent, four-year
Degrees: B *Enroll:* 116
URL: http://www.wscn.curf.edu
Phone: (708) 763-6530 *Calendar:* Sem. plan
Inst. Accred.: NCA-HLC (1986/2005)
Prog. Accred.: Nursing Education

Western Illinois University
One University Circle, Macomb 61455-1390
Type: Public, state, four-year
System: Illinois Board of Higher Education
Degrees: B, M, P *Enroll:* 11,963
URL: http://www.wiu.edu
Phone: (309) 298-1414 *Calendar:* Sem. plan
Inst. Accred.: NCA-HLC (1913/2001)
Prog. Accred.: Accounting, Allied Health (audiology, speech-language pathology), Business (AACSB), Counseling, Dietetics (didactic), English Language Education, Music, Recreation and Leisure Services, Social Work, Teacher Education (NCATE)

Westwood College—DuPage
7155 Janes Ave., Ste. 100, Woodridge 60517
Type: Private, proprietary, four-year
System: Westwood College
Degrees: A, B
URL: http://www.westwood.edu
Phone: (630) 434-8250
Inst. Accred.: ACICS (1992/2007), NCA-HLC (2007, *Indirect accreditation through Westwood College, Denver, CO*)

Atlanta Midtown Campus
1100 Spring† St., Ste. 102, Atlanta, GA 30309
Phone: (404) 870-8980

Fort Worth Campus
4232 North Freeway, Fort Worth, TX 76137
Phone: (817) 547-9600
Prog. Accred: Allied Health (medical assisting (AMA))

Westwood College—O'Hare Airport
8501 West Higgins Rd., Ste. 100, Chicago 60631
Type: Private, proprietary, four-year
System: Westwood College
Degrees: A, B
URL: http://www.westwoodcollege.com
Phone: (773) 380-6800
Inst. Accred.: ACICS (1985/2004)
Prog. Accred.: Allied Health (medical assisting (AMA))

Atlanta Northlake Campus
2306 Parklake Dr. NE, Atlanta, GA 30345
Phone: (404) 962-2999

Wheaton College
501 College Ave., Wheaton 60187
Type: Private, interdenominational, four-year
Degrees: B, M, D *Enroll:* 2,728
URL: http://www.wheaton.edu
Phone: (630) 752-5000 *Calendar:* Sem. plan
Inst. Accred.: NCA-HLC (1913/2004)
Prog. Accred.: Clinical Psychology, Music, Teacher Education (NCATE)

William Rainey Harper College
1200 West Algonquin Rd., Palatine 60067-7398
Type: Public, state/local, two-year
System: Illinois Community College Board
Degrees: A *Enroll:* 9,146
URL: http://www.harpercollege.edu
Phone: (847) 925-6000 *Calendar:* Sem. plan
Inst. Accred.: NCA-HLC (1971/2008)
Prog. Accred.: Allied Health (medical assisting (AMA)), Business (ACBSP), Dentistry (dental hygiene), Dietetic Technician, English Language Education, Music, Nursing

Worsham College of Mortuary Science
495 Northgate Pkwy., Wheeling 60090-2646
Type: Private, proprietary, two-year
Degrees: A
URL: http://www.worshamcollege.com
Phone: (847) 808-8444 *Calendar:* 12-mos. pr
Inst. Accred.: ABFSE (1952/2001)

INDIANA

Ancilla College
PO Box 1, Union Rd., Donaldson 46513
Type: Private, Roman Catholic Church, two-year
Degrees: A *Enroll:* 490
URL: http://www.ancilla.edu
Phone: (574) 936-8898 *Calendar:* Sem. plan
Inst. Accred.: NCA-HLC (1973/2008)

Anderson University
1100 East Fifth St., Anderson 46012-3495
Type: Private, Church of God, four-year
Degrees: A, B, M, D *Enroll:* 2,454
URL: http://www.anderson.edu
Phone: (765) 649-9071 *Calendar:* Sem. plan
Inst. Accred.: ATS (1965/1999), NCA-HLC (1946/2001)
Prog. Accred.: Business (ACBSP), Music, Nursing Education, Social Work, Teacher Education (NCATE)

Associated Mennonite Biblical Seminary
3003 Benham Ave., Elkhart 46517-1999
Type: Private, Mennonite Church, four-year
Degrees: M *Enroll:* 117
URL: http://www.ambs.edu
Phone: (574) 295-3726 *Calendar:* 4-1-4 plan
Inst. Accred.: ATS (1958/1999), NCA-HLC (1974/1999)

Aviation Institute of Maintenance
7251 West McCarty St., Indianapolis 46241-1445
Type: Private, proprietary, two-year
System: Centura College
Degrees: A *Enroll:* 176
URL: http://www.aviationmaintenance.edu
Phone: (317) 243-4519 *Calendar:* Sem. plan
Inst. Accred.: ACCSCT (1996/2006)

Ball State University
2000 University Ave., Muncie 47306
Type: Public, state, four-year
System: Indiana Commission for Higher Education
Degrees: A, B, M, P, D *Enroll:* 18,334
URL: http://www.bsu.edu
Phone: (765) 289-1241 *Calendar:* Sem. plan
Inst. Accred.: NCA-HLC (1925/2004)
Prog. Accred.: Accounting, Allied Health (audiology, speech-language pathology), Art, Business (AACSB), Counseling, Counseling Psychology, Dance, Dietetics (didactic), Dietetics (internship), Engineering Technology (manufacturing), Interior Design, Journalism, Landscape Architecture, Music, Nursing Education, Planning, Psychology Internship, Radiation Therapy, Radiography, Rehabilitation Counseling, School Psychology, Social Work, Teacher Education (NCATE), Theatre

Bethany Theological Seminary
615 National Rd. West, Richmond 47374-4019
Type: Private, Church of the Brethren, four-year
Degrees: M, D *Enroll:* 57
URL: http://www.bethanyseminary.edu
Phone: (765) 983-1800 *Calendar:* Sem. plan
Inst. Accred.: ATS (1940/2006), NCA-HLC (1971/2007)

Bethel College
1001 West McKinley Ave., Mishawaka 46545
Type: Private, Missionnary Church, four-year
Degrees: A, B, M *Enroll:* 1,604
URL: http://www.bethelcollege.edu
Phone: (219) 259-8511 *Calendar:* Sem. plan
Inst. Accred.: NCA-HLC (1971/2008)
Prog. Accred.: Nursing, Teacher Education (NCATE)

Brown Mackie College—South Bend
1030 East Jefferson Blvd., South Bend 46617
Type: Private, proprietary, four-year
System: Education Management Corporation
Degrees: A, B *Enroll:* 619
URL: http://www.brownmackie.edu/southbend
Phone: (574) 237-0774 *Calendar:* Qtr. plan
Inst. Accred.: ACICS (1960/2003)
Prog. Accred.: Allied Health (medical assisting (AMA), occupational therapy assisting), Physical Therapy Assisting

Boise Campus
9050 West Overland Rd., Ste. 100, Boise, ID 83709
Phone: (208) 321-8800

Tulsa Campus
4608 South Garnett Rd., Ste. 110, Tulsa, OK 74146-5207
Phone: (918) 628-3700

Butler University
4600 Sunset Ave., Indianapolis 46208
Type: Private, independent, four-year
Degrees: A, B, M, P, D *Enroll:* 4,061
URL: http://www.butler.edu
Phone: (317) 940-8000 *Calendar:* Sem. plan
Inst. Accred.: NCA-HLC (1915/2003)
Prog. Accred.: Business (AACSB), Counseling, Dance, Music, Pharmacy, Physician Assistant, Psychology Internship, Teacher Education (NCATE), Theatre

Calumet College of St. Joseph
2400 New York Ave., Whiting 46394
Type: Private, Roman Catholic Church, four-year
Degrees: A, B *Enroll:* 779
URL: http://www.ccsj.edu
Phone: (219) 473-7770 *Calendar:* Sem. plan
Inst. Accred.: NCA-HLC (1968/2001)

Christian Theological Seminary
PO Box 88267, Indianapolis 46208-0267
Type: Private, Christian Churches (Disciples of Christ), four-year
Degrees: M, D *Enroll:* 233
URL: http://www.cts.edu
Phone: (317) 924-1331 *Calendar:* Sem. plan
Inst. Accred.: ATS (1944/2008), NCA-HLC (1973/2008)
Prog. Accred.: Marriage and Family Therapy

College of Court Reporting, Inc.
111 West 10th St., Ste. 111, Hobart 46342
Type: Private, proprietary, two-year
Degrees: A *Enroll:* 165
URL: http://www.ccredu.com
Phone: (219) 942-1459 *Calendar:* Sem. plan
Inst. Accred.: ACICS (1989/2008)

Concordia Theological Seminary
6600 North Clinton St., Fort Wayne 46825-4996
Type: Private, Lutheran Church—Missouri Synod, four-year
System: Concordia University System
Degrees: M, D *Enroll:* 337
URL: http://www.ctsfw.edu
Phone: (260) 452-2100 *Calendar:* Qtr. plan
Inst. Accred.: ATS (1968/2003), NCA-HLC (1981/2003)

Crossroads Bible College
601 North Shortridge Rd., Indianapolis 46219
Type: Private, independent, four-year
Degrees: A, B
URL: http://www.crossroads.edu
Phone: (317) 352-8736 *Calendar:* Sem. plan
Inst. Accred.: ABHE (1999/2005)

DePauw University
313 South Locust St., Greencastle 46135
Type: Private, United Methodist Church, four-year
Degrees: B *Enroll:* 2,369
URL: http://www.depauw.edu
Phone: (765) 658-4800 *Calendar:* 4-1-4 plan
Inst. Accred.: NCA-HLC (1915/2005)
Prog. Accred.: Music, Teacher Education (NCATE)

Earlham College
801 National Rd. West, Richmond 47374-4095
Type: Private, independent, four-year
Degrees: B, M *Enroll:* 1,324
URL: http://www.earlham.edu
Phone: (765) 983-1200 *Calendar:* Sem. plan
Inst. Accred.: ATS (1973/2006), NCA-HLC (1915/2004)

Franklin College
101 Branigin Blvd., Franklin 46131-2623
Type: Private, American Baptist Churches (USA), four-year
Degrees: B *Enroll:* 968
URL: http://www.franklincollege.edu
Phone: (317) 738-8000 *Calendar:* 4-1-4 plan
Inst. Accred.: NCA-HLC (1915/2002)
Prog. Accred.: Teacher Education (NCATE)

Goshen College
1700 South Main St., Goshen 46526
Type: Private, Mennonite Education Agency, four-year
Degrees: B *Enroll:* 863
URL: http://www.goshen.edu
Phone: (574) 535-7000 *Calendar:* 4-1-4 plan
Inst. Accred.: NCA-HLC (1941/2005)
Prog. Accred.: Nursing Education, Social Work, Teacher Education (NCATE)

Grace College and Seminary
200 Seminary Dr., Winona Lake 46590
Type: Private, Fellowship of Grace Brethren Churches, four-year
Degrees: A, B, M, D *Enroll:* 1,127
URL: http://www.grace.edu
Phone: (574) 372-5100 *Calendar:* Sem. plan
Inst. Accred.: ATS (2006), NCA-HLC (1994/1999)
Prog. Accred.: Counseling, Music, Teacher Education (NCATE)

Hanover College
PO Box 108, Hanover 47243-0108
Type: Private, Presbyterian Church (USA), four-year
Degrees: B *Enroll:* 1,006
URL: http://www.hanover.edu
Phone: (812) 866-7000 *Calendar:* 4-1-4 plan
Inst. Accred.: NCA-HLC (1915/2000)
Prog. Accred.: Teacher Education (NCATE)

Holy Cross College
54515 State Rd. 933 North, Notre Dame 46556
Type: Private, Holy-Cross Brothers-Midwest, two-year
Degrees: A *Enroll:* 343
URL: http://www.hcc-nd.edu
Phone: (574) 239-8400 *Calendar:* Sem. plan
Inst. Accred.: NCA-HLC (1987/2007)

Huntington University
2303 College Ave., Huntington 46750
Type: Private, United Brethren in Christ, four-year
Degrees: A, B, M *Enroll:* 902
URL: http://www.huntington.edu
Phone: (260) 356-6000 *Calendar:* 4-1-4 plan
Inst. Accred.: NCA-HLC (1961/2004)
Prog. Accred.: Music, Social Work, Teacher Education (NCATE)

Indiana Business College
411 West Riggin Rd., Muncie 47303
Type: Private, proprietary, two-year
Degrees: A *Enroll:* 341
URL: http://www.ibcschools.edu
Phone: (765) 288-8681
Inst. Accred.: ACICS (1989/2004)
Prog. Accred.: Allied Health (medical assisting (AMA))

Indiana Business College
550 East Washington St., Indianapolis 46204
Type: Private, proprietary, two-year
Degrees: A *Enroll:* 834
URL: http://www.ibcschools.edu
Phone: (317) 264-5656
Inst. Accred.: ACICS (1980/2004)

Anderson Campus
140 East 53rd St., Anderson 46013
Phone: (765) 644-7514
Prog. Accred: Allied Health (medical assisting (AMA))

Indiana Business College *(continued)*

Columbus Campus
2222 Poshard Dr., Columbus 47203
Phone: (812) 379-9000
Prog. Accred: Allied Health (medical assisting (AMA))

Elkhart Campus
56075 Pkwy. Ave., Elkhart 46516
Phone: (574) 522-0397

Evansville Campus
4601 Theater Dr., Evansville 47715
Phone: (812) 476-6000
Prog. Accred: Allied Health (medical assisting (AMA))

Ft. Wayne Campus
6413 North Clinton St., Ft. Wayne 46825
Phone: (260) 471-7667
Prog. Accred: Allied Health (medical assisting (AMA), surgical technology)

Indianapolis Medical Campus
8150 Brookville Rd., Indianapolis 46239
Phone: (317) 375-8000
Prog. Accred: Allied Health (medical assisting (AMA), surgical technology)

Indianapolis Northwest Campus
6300 Technology Center Dr., Indianapolis 46278
Phone: (317) 873-6500

Lafayette Campus
4705 Meijer Ct., Lafayette 47905
Phone: (765) 447-9550

Marion Campus
830 North Miller Ave., Marion 46952
Phone: (765) 662-7497

Terre Haute Campus
1378 South State Rd. 46, Terre Haute 47803
Phone: (812) 877-2100
Prog. Accred: Allied Health (medical assisting (AMA))

Indiana Institute of Technology
1600 East Washington Blvd., Fort Wayne 46803
Type: Private, proprietary, four-year
Degrees: A, B, M *Enroll:* 2,303
URL: http://www.indianatech.edu
Phone: (800) 937-2448 *Calendar:* Sem. plan
Inst. Accred.: NCA-HLC (1962/2004)
Prog. Accred.: Engineering (electrical, mechanical)

Indiana State University
200 North Seventh St., Terre Haute 47809
Type: Public, state, four-year
System: Indiana Commission for Higher Education
Degrees: A, B, M, P, D *Enroll:* 9,285
URL: http://www.indstate.edu
Phone: (812) 237-6311 *Calendar:* Sem. plan
Inst. Accred.: NCA-HLC (1915/2000)
Prog. Accred.: Allied Health (speech-language pathology), Art, Automotive Technology, Business (AACSB), Clinical Psychology, Construction Education, Counseling, Counseling Psychology, Design Technology, Dietetics (coordinated), Electronic Technology, English Language Education, Environmental Health, Family & Consumer Science, Health Technology, Industrial Technology, Interior Design, Mechanical Technology, Music, Nursing, Recreation and Leisure Services, School Psychology, Social Work, Teacher Education (NCATE)

Indiana University Bloomington
107 South Indiana Ave., Bloomington 47405-7000
Type: Public, state, four-year
System: Indiana University System
Degrees: A, B, M, P, D *Enroll:* 35,170
URL: http://www.iub.edu
Phone: (812) 855-4848 *Calendar:* Sem. plan
Inst. Accred.: NCA-HLC (1913/2008)
Prog. Accred.: Accounting, Allied Health (audiology, opticianry, optometric residency, optometric technician, optometry, speech-language pathology), Art, Business (AACSB), Clinical Psychology, Counseling, Counseling Psychology, Interior Design, Journalism, Law, Librarianship, Music, Psychology Internship, Public Administration, Public Health, Recreation and Leisure Services, School Psychology, Teacher Education (NCATE), Theatre

Indiana University East
2325 North Chester Blvd., Richmond 47374
Type: Public, state, four-year
System: Indiana University System
Degrees: A, B *Enroll:* 1,765
URL: http://www.iue.edu
Phone: (317) 973-8200 *Calendar:* Sem. plan
Inst. Accred.: NCA-HLC (1971/2002)
Prog. Accred.: Business (ACBSP), Nursing, Teacher Education (NCATE)

Indiana University Kokomo
PO Box 9003, 2300 South Washington St., Kokomo 46904-9003
Type: Public, state, four-year
System: Indiana University System
Degrees: A, B, M *Enroll:* 2,030
URL: http://www.iuk.edu
Phone: (765) 453-2000 *Calendar:* Sem. plan
Inst. Accred.: NCA-HLC (1969/1999)
Prog. Accred.: Business (AACSB), Nursing, Nursing Education, Radiography, Teacher Education (NCATE)

Indiana University Northwest
3400 Broadway, Gary 46408
Type: Public, state, four-year
System: Indiana University System
Degrees: A, B, M *Enroll:* 3,525
URL: http://www.iun.edu
Phone: (219) 980-6500 *Calendar:* Sem. plan
Inst. Accred.: NCA-HLC (1969/2003)
Prog. Accred.: Allied Health (respiratory therapy), Business (AACSB), Clinical Lab Technology, Dentistry (dental assisting, dental hygiene), Nursing, Nursing Education, Phlebotomy, Public Administration, Radiation Therapy, Radiography, Teacher Education (NCATE)

Indiana University South Bend
1700 Mishawaka Ave., PO Box 7111, South Bend 46634
Type: Public, state, four-year
System: Indiana University System
Degrees: A, B, M *Enroll:* 5,280
URL: http://www.iusb.edu
Phone: (574) 520-4872 *Calendar:* Sem. plan
Inst. Accred.: NCA-HLC (1969/2008)
Prog. Accred.: Business (AACSB), Counseling, Dentistry (dental assisting, dental hygiene), Montessori Teacher Education, Nursing Education, Public Administration, Radiation Therapy, Radiography, Teacher Education (NCATE)

Indiana University Southeast
4201 Grant Line Rd., New Albany 47150
Type: Public, state, four-year
System: Indiana University System
Degrees: A, B, M *Enroll:* 4,400
URL: http://www.ius.edu
Phone: (812) 941-2333 *Calendar:* Sem. plan
Inst. Accred.: NCA-HLC (1969/2000)
Prog. Accred.: Business (AACSB), Nursing Education, Teacher Education (NCATE)

Indiana University-Purdue University Fort Wayne
2101 Coliseum Blvd. East, Fort Wayne 46805-1499
Type: Public, state, four-year
System: Indiana University System
Degrees: A, B, M *Enroll:* 8,857
URL: http://www.ipfw.edu
Phone: (260) 481-6100 *Calendar:* Sem. plan
Inst. Accred.: NCA-HLC (1974/2001)
Prog. Accred.: Business (AACSB), Computer Science (ABET-CAC), Dentistry (dental assisting, dental hygiene, dental laboratory technology), Engineering (computer, electrical, mechanical), Engineering Technology (architectural, civil/construction, electrical, industrial, mechanical), Music, Nursing, Public Administration, Teacher Education (NCATE)

Indiana University-Purdue University Indianapolis
355 North Lansing St., Indianapolis 46202
Type: Public, state, four-year
System: Indiana University System
Degrees: A, B, M, D *Enroll:* 22,369
URL: http://www.iupui.edu
Phone: (317) 274-5555 *Calendar:* Sem. plan
Inst. Accred.: NCA-HLC (1971/2003)
Prog. Accred.: Allied Health (cytotechnology, health services administration, medicine, occupational therapy), Art, Clinical Lab Scientist, Clinical Psychology, Dentistry (combined prosthodontic/maxillofacial prosthetics, combined prosthodontics, dental assisting, dental hygiene, dentistry, endodontics, general practice residency, oral and maxillofacial pathology, oral and maxillofacial surgery, orthodontic and dentofacial orthopedics, pediatric dentistry, periodontics), Dietetics (didactic), Dietetics (internship), Engineering (computer, electrical, mechanical), Engineering Technology (architectural, civil/construction, computer, electrical, mechanical), Graduate Social Work, Histologic Technology, Interior Design, Law, Nuclear Medicine Technology, Nursing, Nursing Education, Physical Therapy, Psychology Internship, Public Administration, Public Health, Radiation Therapy, Radiography, Social Work

Indiana University-Purdue University Columbus
4601 Central Ave., Columbus 47203
Phone: (812) 348-7311
Prog. Accred: Engineering Technology (mechanical)

Indiana Wesleyan University
4201 South Washington St., Marion 46953
Type: Private, The Wesleyan Church, four-year
Degrees: A, B, M *Enroll:* 12,183
URL: http://www.indwes.edu
Phone: (765) 674-6901 *Calendar:* Sem. plan
Inst. Accred.: NCA-HLC (1966/2000)
Prog. Accred.: Counseling, Music, Nursing Education, Social Work, Teacher Education (NCATE)

International Business College
7205 Shadeland Station, Indianapolis 46256
Type: Private, proprietary, two-year
Degrees: A *Enroll:* 289
URL: http://www.ibcindianapolis.edu
Phone: (317) 841-6400
Inst. Accred.: ACICS (1988/2006)
Prog. Accred.: Allied Health (medical assisting (AMA)), Veterinary Technology

International Business College
5699 Coventry Ln., Fort Wayne 46804
Type: Private, proprietary, four-year
Degrees: A, B *Enroll:* 572
URL: http://www.ibcfortwayne.edu
Phone: (260) 459-4500
Inst. Accred.: ACICS (1953/2006)
Prog. Accred.: Allied Health (medical assisting (AMA)), Veterinary Technology

ITT Technical Institute
2810 Dupont Commerce Ct., Fort Wayne 46825
Type: Private, proprietary, four-year
System: ITT Educational Services, Inc.
Degrees: A, B *Enroll:* 600
URL: http://www.itt-tech.edu
Phone: (260) 497-6200 *Calendar:* Qtr. plan
Inst. Accred.: ACICS (1999/2008)

ITT Technical Institute
10999 Stahl Rd., Newburgh 47630
Type: Private, proprietary, four-year
System: ITT Educational Services, Inc.
Degrees: A, B *Enroll:* 291
URL: http://www.itt-tech.edu
Phone: (812) 858-1600 *Calendar:* Qtr. plan
Inst. Accred.: ACICS (1999/2003)

ITT Technical Institute
9511 Angola Ct., Indianapolis 46268-1119
Type: Private, proprietary, four-year
System: ITT Educational Services, Inc.
Degrees: A, B, M *Enroll:* 1,724
URL: http://www.itt-tech.edu
Phone: (317) 875-8640 *Calendar:* Qtr. plan
Inst. Accred.: ACICS (1999/2007)

Arnold Campus
1930 Meyer Drury Dr., Arnold, MO 63010
Phone: (636) 464-6600

Austin Campus
6330 Hwy. 290 East, Ste. 150, Austin, TX 78723
Phone: (512) 467-6800

Burr Ridge Campus
7040 High Grove Blvd., Burr Ridge, IL 60527
Phone: (630) 455-6470

Charlotte Campus
4135 South Stream Blvd., Ste. 200, Charlotte, NC 28217
Phone: (704) 423-3100

Fort Lauderdale Campus
3401 South University Dr., Fort Lauderdale, FL 33328
Phone: (954) 476-9300

Houston North Campus
15621 Blue Ash Dr., Ste. 160, Houston, TX 77090-5821
Phone: (281) 873-0512

Houston West Campus
2950 South Gessner Rd., Houston, TX 77063-3751
Phone: (713) 952-2294

Lexington Campus
2473 Fortune Dr., Ste. 180, Lexington, KY 40509
Phone: (859) 246-3300

Louisville Campus
10509 Timberwood Circle, Louisville, KY 40223
Phone: (502) 327-7424

Mechanicsburg Area Campus
5020 Louise Dr., Mechanicsburg, PA 17055
Phone: (717) 691-9263

Mount Prospect Campus
1401 Freehanville Dr., Mount Prospect, IL 60056
Phone: (847) 375-8800

Norfolk Campus
863 Glenrock Rd., Ste. 100, Norfolk, VA 23502-3701
Phone: (757) 466-1260

Norwood Campus
333 Providence Hwy., Route 1, Norwood, MA 02062
Phone: (781) 278-7200

Troy Campus
1522 East Big Beaver Rd., Troy, MI 48083-1905
Phone: (248) 524-1800

Woburn Campus
10 Forbes Rd., Woburn, MA 01801-2103
Phone: (781) 937-8324

Ivy Tech Community College—Bloomington
200 Daniels Way, Bloomington 47404
Type: Public, state, two-year
System: Ivy Tech Community College—Central Office
Degrees: A *FTE Enroll:* 1,700
URL: http://www.bloomington.ivytech.edu/ivytech
Phone: (812) 332-1559 *Calendar:* Sem. plan
Inst. Accred.: NCA-HLC (1995/1999, *Indirect accreditation through Ivy Tech Community College—Central Indiana, Indianapolis, IN*)
Prog. Accred.: Business (ACBSP), Nursing, Practical Nursing

Ivy Tech Community College—Central Indiana
50 West Fall Creek Pkwy. North Dr., Indianapolis 46208-5752
Type: Public, state, two-year
System: Ivy Tech Community College—Central Office
Degrees: A *Enroll:* 5,836
URL: http://www.ivytech.edu/indianapolis
Phone: (317) 921-4800 *Calendar:* Sem. plan
Inst. Accred.: NCA-HLC (1995/1999)
Prog. Accred.: Allied Health (medical assisting (AMA), respiratory therapy, surgical technology), Business (ACBSP), Culinary Education, Design Technology, Electronic Technology, Manufacturing Technology, Mechanical Technology, Nursing, Practical Nursing, Radiography

Ivy Tech Community College—Columbus
4475 Central Ave., Columbus 47203-1868
Type: Public, state, two-year
System: Ivy Tech Community College—Central Office
Degrees: A *Enroll:* 1,188
URL: http://www.ivytech.edu/columbus
Phone: (812) 372-9925 *Calendar:* Sem. plan
Inst. Accred.: NCA-HLC (1995/1999, *Indirect accreditation through Ivy Tech Community College—Central Indiana, Indianapolis, IN*)
Prog. Accred.: Allied Health (EMT-paramedic, medical assisting (AMA), surgical technology), Business (ACBSP), Dentistry (dental assisting), Nursing, Practical Nursing

Ivy Tech Community College—East Central
4301 South Cowan Rd., Muncie 47302-9448
Type: Public, state, two-year
System: Ivy Tech Community College—Central Office
Degrees: A *Enroll:* 3,485
URL: http://www.ivytech.edu/eastcentral
Phone: (765) 289-2291 *Calendar:* Sem. plan
Inst. Accred.: NCA-HLC (1995/1999, *Indirect accreditation through Ivy Tech Community College—Central Indiana, Indianapolis, IN*)
Prog. Accred.: Allied Health (medical assisting (AMA), surgical technology), Automotive Technology, Business (ACBSP), Construction Technology, Culinary Education, Design Technology, Electronic Technology, Manufacturing Technology, Nursing, Physical Therapy Assisting, Practical Nursing

Anderson Campus
104 West 53rd St., Anderson 46013-1502
Phone: (765) 643-7133
Prog. Accred: Allied Health (medical assisting (AMA)), Practical Nursing

Marion Campus
1015 E. 3rd St., Marion 46952
Phone: (765) 662-9843
Prog. Accred: Allied Health (medical assisting (AMA)), Radiography

Ivy Tech Community College—Kokomo
1815 East Morgan St., Kokomo 46903-1373
Type: Public, state, two-year
System: Ivy Tech Community College—Central Office
Degrees: A *Enroll:* 1,604
URL: http://www.ivytech.edu/kokomo
Phone: (765) 459-0561 *Calendar:* Sem. plan
Inst. Accred.: NCA-HLC (1995/1999, *Indirect accreditation through Ivy Tech Community College—Central Indiana, Indianapolis, IN*)
Prog. Accred.: Allied Health (EMT-paramedic, medical assisting (AMA), surgical technology), Automotive Technology, Business (ACBSP), Construction Technology, Design Technology, Manufacturing Technology, Nursing, Practical Nursing

Logansport Campus
3001 East Market St., Ste. 7, Logansport 46947-2152
Phone: (574) 753-5101

Wabash Campus
277 North Thorne St., Wabash 46992
Phone: (260) 563-8828

Ivy Tech Community College—Lafayette
PO Box 6299, 3101 S. Creasy Ln., Lafayette 47903-6299
Type: Public, state, two-year
System: Ivy Tech Community College—Central Office
Degrees: A *Enroll:* 3,482
URL: http://www.laf.ivytech.edu
Phone: (765) 772-9100 *Calendar:* Sem. plan
Inst. Accred.: NCA-HLC (1995/1999, *Indirect accreditation through Ivy Tech Community College—Central Indiana, Indianapolis, IN*)
Prog. Accred.: Allied Health (medical assisting (AMA), respiratory therapy, surgical technology), Automotive Technology, Business (ACBSP), Dentistry (dental assisting), Design Technology, Manufacturing Technology, Nursing, Practical Nursing

Ivy Tech Community College—Lawrenceburg
50 Walnut Dr., Lawrenceburg 47025
Type: Public, state, two-year
System: Ivy Tech Community College—Central Office
Degrees: A
URL: http://www.ivytech.edu/southeast
Phone: (812) 537-4010 *Calendar:* Sem. plan
Inst. Accred.: NCA-HLC (1995/1999, *Indirect accreditation through Ivy Tech Community College—Central Indiana, Indianapolis, IN*)
Prog. Accred.: Allied Health (medical assisting (AMA))

Ivy Tech Community College—Madison
590 Ivy Tech Dr., Madison 47250-1881
Type: Public, state, two-year
System: Ivy Tech Community College—Central Office
Degrees: A *Enroll:* 958
URL: http://www.ivytech.edu/southeast
Phone: (812) 265-2580 *Calendar:* Sem. plan
Inst. Accred.: NCA-HLC (1995/1999, *Indirect accreditation through Ivy Tech Community College—Central Indiana, Indianapolis, IN*)
Prog. Accred.: Allied Health (medical assisting (AMA)), Business (ACBSP), Nursing, Practical Nursing

Ivy Tech Community College—North Central
220 Dean Johnson Blvd., South Bend 46601-3415
Type: Public, state, two-year
System: Ivy Tech Community College—Central Office
Degrees: A *Enroll:* 2,335
URL: http://www.ivytech.edu/northcentral
Phone: (574) 289-7001 *Calendar:* Sem. plan
Inst. Accred.: NCA-HLC (1995/1999, *Indirect accreditation through Ivy Tech Community College—Central Indiana, Indianapolis, IN*)
Prog. Accred.: Automotive Technology, Business (ACBSP), Clinical Lab Technology, Culinary Education, Dentistry (dental hygiene), Design Technology, Electronic Technology, Manufacturing Technology, Nursing, Phlebotomy, Practical Nursing

Elkhart Campus
2521 Industrial Pkwy., Elkhart 46516-5430
Phone: (219) 293-4657

Warsaw Campus
850 East Smith St., Warsaw 46580-4546
Phone: (219) 267-5428

Ivy Tech Community College—Northeast
3800 North Anthony Blvd., Fort Wayne 46805-1489
Type: Public, state, two-year
System: Ivy Tech Community College—Central Office
Degrees: A *Enroll:* 3,252
URL: http://www.ivytech.edu/fortwayne
Phone: (260) 480-4220 *Calendar:* Sem. plan
Inst. Accred.: NCA-HLC (1995/1999, *Indirect accreditation through Ivy Tech Community College—Central Indiana, Indianapolis, IN*)
Prog. Accred.: Allied Health (medical assisting (AMA), respiratory therapy), Automotive Technology, Business (ACBSP), Construction Technology, Culinary Education, Design Technology, Electronic Technology, Industrial Technology, Manufacturing Technology, Nursing, Practical Nursing

Ivy Tech Community College—Northwest
1440 East 35th Ave., Gary 46409-1499
Type: Public, state, two-year
System: Ivy Tech Community College—Central Office
Degrees: A *Enroll:* 2,334
URL: http://www.gary.ivytech.edu
Phone: (219) 981-1111 *Calendar:* Sem. plan
Inst. Accred.: NCA-HLC (1995/1999, *Indirect accreditation through Ivy Tech Community College—Central Indiana, Indianapolis, IN*)
Prog. Accred.: Business (ACBSP), Culinary Education, Nursing, Physical Therapy Assisting, Practical Nursing

East Chicago Campus
410 Columbus Dr., East Chicago 46312-2714
Phone: (219) 392-3600
Prog. Accred: Funeral Service Education (Mortuary Science)

Michigan City Campus
3714 Franklin, Michigan City 46360
Phone: (219) 879-9137
Prog. Accred: Allied Health (medical assisting (AMA), respiratory therapy, surgical technology)

Valpariso Campus
2401 Valley Dr., Valparaiso 46383-2520
Phone: (219) 464-8514
Prog. Accred: Practical Nursing

Ivy Tech Community College—Richmond
2325 Chester Blvd., Richmond 47374
Type: Public, state, two-year
System: Ivy Tech Community College—Central Office
Degrees: A *Enroll:* 924
URL: http://www.ivytech.edu/richmond
Phone: (317) 966-2656 *Calendar:* Sem. plan
Inst. Accred.: NCA-HLC (1995/1999, *Indirect accreditation through Ivy Tech Community College—Central Indiana, Indianapolis, IN*)
Prog. Accred.: Allied Health (medical assisting (AMA)), Automotive Technology, Business (ACBSP), Construction Technology, Manufacturing Technology, Nursing, Practical Nursing

Ivy Tech Community College—Sellersburg
8204 Hwy. 311, Sellersburg 47172
Type: Public, state, two-year
System: Ivy Tech Community College—Central Office
Degrees: A *Enroll:* 1,587
URL: http://www.ivytech.edu/sellersburg
Phone: (812) 246-3301 *Calendar:* Sem. plan
Inst. Accred.: NCA-HLC (1995/1999, *Indirect accreditation through Ivy Tech Community College—Central Indiana, Indianapolis, IN*)
Prog. Accred.: Allied Health (medical assisting (AMA)), Automotive Technology, Business (ACBSP), Design Technology, Electronic Technology, Manufacturing Technology, Nursing, Practical Nursing

Ivy Tech Community College—Southwest
3501 First Ave., Evansville 47710-3398
Type: Public, state, two-year
System: Ivy Tech Community College—Central Office
Degrees: A *Enroll:* 2,491
URL: http://www.ivytech.edu/evansville
Phone: (812) 426-2865 *Calendar:* Sem. plan
Inst. Accred.: NCA-HLC (1995/1999, *Indirect accreditation through Ivy Tech Community College—Central Indiana, Indianapolis, IN*)
Prog. Accred.: Allied Health (EMT-paramedic, medical assisting (AMA), surgical technology), Business (ACBSP), Design Technology, Electronic Technology, Manufacturing Technology, Nursing, Practical Nursing

Ivy Tech Community College—Wabash Valley
7999 U.S. Hwy. 41, Terre Haute 47802-4898
Type: Public, state, two-year
System: Ivy Tech Community College—Central Office
Degrees: A *Enroll:* 3,053
URL: http://ivytech7.cc.in.us
Phone: (812) 299-1121 *Calendar:* Sem. plan
Inst. Accred.: NCA-HLC (1995/1999, *Indirect accreditation through Ivy Tech Community College—Central Indiana, Indianapolis, IN*)
Prog. Accred.: Allied Health (EMT-paramedic, medical assisting (AMA), respiratory therapy), Business (ACBSP), Clinical Lab Technology, Design Technology, Electronic Technology, Manufacturing Technology, Nursing, Practical Nursing, Radiography

Kaplan College— Northwest Indianapolis
7302 Woodland Dr., Indianapolis 46278-1736
Type: Private, proprietary, two-year
System: Kaplan Higher Education Corporation
Degrees: A *Enroll:* 394
URL: http://getinfo.kaplancollege.com
Phone: (317) 299-6001 *Calendar:* Qtr. plan
Inst. Accred.: ACCSCT (1970/2007)
Prog. Accred.: Dentistry (dental assisting)

Kaplan College—Merrillville
3803 East Lincoln Hwy., Merrillville 46410
Type: Private, proprietary, two-year
Degrees: A
URL: http://getinfo.kaplancollege.com
Phone: (219) 947-8400 *Calendar:* Qtr. plan
Inst. Accred.: ACICS (1985/2006)

Hammond Campus
7833 Indianapolis Blvd., Hammond 46324
Phone: (219) 844-0100

Lincoln College of Technology—Indianapolis
7225 Winton Dr., Building 128, Indianapolis 46268
Type: Private, proprietary, two-year
System: Lincoln Educational Services Corporation
Degrees: A *Enroll:* 1,681
URL: http://www.lincolncollegeoftechnology.com
Phone: (317) 632-5553
Inst. Accred.: ACCSCT (1968/2002)

Manchester College
604 East College Ave., North Manchester 46962
Type: Private, Church of the Brethren, four-year
Degrees: A, B, M *Enroll:* 1,081
URL: http://www.manchester.edu
Phone: (260) 982-5000 *Calendar:* 4-1-4 plan
Inst. Accred.: NCA-HLC (1932/2003)
Prog. Accred.: Social Work, Teacher Education (NCATE)

Marian College
3200 Cold Spring Rd., Indianapolis 46222-1997
Type: Private, Roman Catholic Church, four-year
Degrees: A, B *Enroll:* 1,327
URL: http://www.marian.edu
Phone: (317) 955-6000 *Calendar:* Sem. plan
Inst. Accred.: NCA-HLC (1956/2006)
Prog. Accred.: Nursing, Nursing Education, Teacher Education (NCATE)

Martin University
2171 Avondale Place, Indianapolis 46218
Type: Private, independent, four-year
Degrees: B, M *Enroll:* 384
URL: http://www.martin.edu
Phone: (317) 543-3237 *Calendar:* Sem. plan
Inst. Accred.: NCA-HLC (1987/2008)

MedTech College
6612 East 75th St., Ste. 300, Heritage Park 1, Indianapolis 46250
Type: Private, proprietary, two-year
Degrees: A
URL: http://www.medtechcollege.com
Phone: (317) 845-0100
Inst. Accred.: ACICS (2008)

Greenwood Campus
1500 American Way, South Park, Greenwood 46143
Phone: (317) 534-0322

The Stuart School
2400 Belmar Blvd., Wall, NJ 07719
Phone: (732) 681-7200

Mid-America College of Funeral Service
3111 Hamburg Pike, Jeffersonville 47130
Type: Private, independent, four-year
Degrees: A, B *Enroll:* 76
URL: http://www.mid-america.edu
Phone: (812) 288-8878 *Calendar:* Qtr. plan
Inst. Accred.: ABFSE (1967/2002)

National College—Indianapolis
6060 Castleway West Dr., Indianapolis 46250
Type: Private, proprietary, two-year
Degrees: A
URL: http://www.ncbt.edu
Phone: (317) 578-7352
Inst. Accred.: ACICS (2008)

Oakland City University
138 North Lucretia St., Oakland City 47660-1038
Type: Private, General Association of General Baptists, four-year
Degrees: A, B, M *Enroll:* 1,614
URL: http://www.oak.edu
Phone: (812) 749-4781 *Calendar:* Sem. plan
Inst. Accred.: ATS (2004), NCA-HLC (1977/2004)
Prog. Accred.: Teacher Education (NCATE)

Purdue University
West Lafayette 47907
Type: Public, state, four-year
System: Purdue University System
Degrees: A, B, M, P, D *Enroll:* 37,284
URL: http://www.purdue.edu
Phone: (765) 494-4600 *Calendar:* Sem. plan
Inst. Accred.: NCA-HLC (1913/2000)
Prog. Accred.: Allied Health (audiology, speech-language pathology), Applied Science (industrial hygiene, occupational health & safety), Aviation, Business (AACSB), Clinical Psychology, Construction Education, Counseling, Counseling Psychology, Design Technology, Dietetics (coordinated), Dietetics (didactic), Engineering (aerospace, agricultural, chemical, civil, computer, construction, electrical, food process, industrial, materials, mechanical, nuclear, surveying), Engineering Technology (electrical, manufacturing, mechanical), Forestry, Industrial Technology, Interior Design, Landscape Architecture, Marriage and Family Therapy, Nursing Education, Pharmacy, Psychology Internship, Teacher Education (NCATE), Theatre, Veterinary Medicine, Veterinary Technology

School of Technology at Kokomo
2300 South Washington St., Kokomo 46904-9003
Phone: (765) 455-9339
Prog. Accred: Engineering Technology (electrical)

School of Technology at New Albany
4201 Grant Line Rd., New Albany 47150-6405
Phone: (812) 941-2353
Prog. Accred: Engineering Technology (electrical, mechanical)

School of Technology at South Bend/Elkhart
1733 Northside Blvd., PO Box 711, South Bend 46634-7111
Phone: (219) 237-4180

School of Technology at Versailles
901 West U.S. 50, Versailles 47042-9198
Phone: (812) 689-7040

Purdue University Calumet
2200 169th St., Hammond 46323
Type: Public, state, four-year
System: Purdue University System
Degrees: A, B *Enroll:* 6,802
URL: http://www.calumet.purdue.edu
Phone: (219) 989-2993 *Calendar:* Sem. plan
Inst. Accred.: NCA-HLC (1969/2007)
Prog. Accred.: Engineering (computer, electrical), Engineering Technology (architectural, civil/construction, electrical, industrial, manufacturing, mechanical), Marriage and Family Therapy, Nursing, Teacher Education (NCATE)

Purdue University North Central
1401 South U.S. Hwy. 421, Westville 46391-9528
Type: Public, state, four-year
System: Purdue University System
Degrees: A, B *Enroll:* 2,644
URL: http://www.pnc.edu
Phone: (219) 785-5200 *Calendar:* Sem. plan
Inst. Accred.: NCA-HLC (1971/2001)
Prog. Accred.: Business (ACBSP), Engineering Technology (civil/construction, electrical, industrial, mechanical), Nursing, Teacher Education (NCATE)

Rose-Hulman Institute of Technology
5500 Wabash Ave., Box 20, Terre Haute 47803
Type: Private, independent, four-year
Degrees: B, M *Enroll:* 1,836
URL: http://www.rose-hulman.edu
Phone: (812) 877-8000 *Calendar:* Qtr. plan
Inst. Accred.: NCA-HLC (1916/2008)
Prog. Accred.: Engineering (chemical, civil, computer, electrical, mechanical)

Saint Joseph's College
U.S. Hwy. 231, Rensselaer 47978
Type: Private, Roman Catholic Church, four-year
Degrees: A, B, M *Enroll:* 932
URL: http://www.saintjoe.edu
Phone: (219) 866-6000 *Calendar:* Sem. plan
Inst. Accred.: NCA-HLC (1932/2002)
Prog. Accred.: Teacher Education (NCATE)

Saint Mary's College
Notre Dame 46556
Type: Private, Roman Catholic Church, four-year
Degrees: B *Enroll:* 1,378
URL: http://www.saintmarys.edu
Phone: (574) 284-4000 *Calendar:* Sem. plan
Inst. Accred.: NCA-HLC (1922/2006)
Prog. Accred.: Art, Music, Nursing, Social Work, Teacher Education (NCATE)

Saint Mary-of-the-Woods College
3303 St. Mary's Rd., St. Mary-of-the-Woods 47876
Type: Private, Roman Catholic Church, four-year
Degrees: A, B, M *Enroll:* 998
URL: http://www.smwc.edu
Phone: (812) 535-5151 *Calendar:* Sem. plan
Inst. Accred.: NCA-HLC (1919/2005)
Prog. Accred.: Music, Teacher Education (NCATE)

Saint Meinrad School of Theology
200 Hill Dr., Saint Meinrad 47577-1301
Type: Private, Roman Catholic Church, four-year
Degrees: M *Enroll:* 118
URL: http://www.saintmeinrad.edu
Phone: (812) 357-6611 *Calendar:* 4-1-4 plan
Inst. Accred.: ATS (1968/2003), NCA-HLC (1979/2004)

Taylor University
236 West Reade Ave., Upland 46989
Type: Private, independent, four-year
Degrees: A, B *Enroll:* 1,831
URL: http://www.taylor.edu
Phone: (765) 998-2751 *Calendar:* 4-1-4 plan
Inst. Accred.: NCA-HLC (1947/2004)
Prog. Accred.: Music, Social Work, Teacher Education (NCATE)

Fort Wayne Campus
1025 West Rudisill Blvd., Fort Wayne 46807
Phone: (219) 456-2111

TCM International Institute
6337 Hollister Dr., PO Box 24560, Indianapolis 46224
Type: Private, independent, four-year
Degrees: M
URL: http://www.tcmi.org
Phone: (317) 299-0333
Inst. Accred.: NCA-HLC (2008)

Trine University
One University Ave., Angola 46703
Type: Private, independent, four-year
Degrees: A, B *Enroll:* 1,069
URL: http://www.trine.edu
Phone: (260) 665-4100 *Calendar:* Sem. plan
Inst. Accred.: NCA-HLC (1966/2006)
Prog. Accred.: Business (ACBSP), Engineering (chemical, civil, electrical, mechanical), Teacher Education (NCATE)

University of Evansville
1800 Lincoln Ave., Evansville 47722
Type: Private, United Methodist Church, four-year
Degrees: A, B, M *Enroll:* 2,536
URL: http://www.evansville.edu
Phone: (800) 423-8633 *Calendar:* Sem. plan
Inst. Accred.: NCA-HLC (1931/2006)
Prog. Accred.: Business (AACSB), Computer Science (ABET-CAC), Engineering (civil, computer, electrical, mechanical), Music, Nursing, Physical Therapy, Physical Therapy Assisting, Teacher Education (NCATE)

The University of Indianapolis
1400 East Hanna Ave., Indianapolis 46227-3697
Type: Private, United Methodist Church, four-year
Degrees: A, B, M, D *Enroll:* 3,456
URL: http://www.uindy.edu
Phone: (317) 788-3368
Inst. Accred.: NCA-HLC (1947/2002)
Prog. Accred.: Allied Health (occupational therapy), Business (ACBSP), Clinical Psychology, Music, Nurse (Midwifery), Nursing, Nursing Education, Physical Therapy, Physical Therapy Assisting, Social Work, Teacher Education (NCATE)

Indianapolis International Campus
29, Voulis St., Syntagma Square, Athens, Greece 105 57
Phone: 30 132 39740
Prog. Accred: Business (ACBSP)

Intercollege Campus
17 Heroes Ave., PO Box 4005, Nicosia, Cyprus
Phone: 011 35 723 57735

University of Notre Dame
Notre Dame 46556
Type: Private, Roman Catholic Church, four-year
Degrees: B, M, P, D *Enroll:* 11,307
URL: http://www.nd.edu
Phone: (574) 631-5000 *Calendar:* Sem. plan
Inst. Accred.: ATS (1977/2003), NCA-HLC (1913/2004)
Prog. Accred.: Accounting, Art, Business (AACSB), Computer Science (ABET-CAC), Counseling Psychology, Engineering (aerospace, chemical, civil, computer, electrical, mechanical), Law, Psychology Internship

University of Saint Francis
2701 Spring St., Fort Wayne 46808
Type: Private, Roman Catholic Church, four-year
Degrees: A, B, M *Enroll:* 1,655
URL: http://www.sf.edu
Phone: (219) 434-3100 *Calendar:* Sem. plan
Inst. Accred.: NCA-HLC (1957/2004)
Prog. Accred.: Allied Health (surgical technology), Art, Business (ACBSP), Nursing, Nursing Education, Physical Therapy Assisting, Physician Assistant, Radiography, Social Work, Teacher Education (NCATE)

University of Southern Indiana
8600 University Blvd., Evansville 47712
Type: Public, state, four-year
System: Indiana Commission for Higher Education
Degrees: A, B, M, D *Enroll:* 8,560
URL: http://www.usi.edu
Phone: (812) 464-8600 *Calendar:* Sem. plan
Inst. Accred.: NCA-HLC (1974/2007)
Prog. Accred.: Accounting, Allied Health (occupational therapy, occupational therapy assisting, respiratory therapy), Business (AACSB), Dentistry (dental assisting, dental hygiene), Engineering Technology (mechanical), Graduate Social Work, Journalism, Nursing Education, Radiography, Social Work, Teacher Education (NCATE)

Valparaiso University
U.S. Hwy. 30, Valparaiso 46383
Type: Private, Lutheran University Association, four-year
Degrees: A, B, M, D *Enroll:* 3,655
URL: http://www.valpo.edu
Phone: (219) 464-5000 *Calendar:* Sem. plan
Inst. Accred.: NCA-HLC (1929/2008)
Prog. Accred.: Business (AACSB), Engineering (civil, computer, electrical, mechanical), Law, Music, Nursing Education, Social Work, Teacher Education (NCATE)

Vincennes University
1002 North First St., Vincennes 47591-5201
Type: Public, state, two-year
System: Indiana Commission for Higher Education
Degrees: A *Enroll:* 6,918
URL: http://www.vinu.edu
Phone: (800) 742-9198 *Calendar:* Sem. plan
Inst. Accred.: NCA-HLC (1958/2001)
Prog. Accred.: Allied Health (surgeon assisting, surgical technology), Art, Business (ACBSP), Funeral Service Education (Mortuary Science), Nursing, Physical Therapy Assisting, Practical Nursing, Theatre

Wabash College
301 West Wabash Ave., PO Box 352, Crawfordsville 47933
Type: Private, independent, four-year
Degrees: B *Enroll:* 873
URL: http://www.wabash.edu
Phone: (765) 361-6100 *Calendar:* Sem. plan
Inst. Accred.: NCA-HLC (1913/2003)
Prog. Accred.: Teacher Education (NCATE)

IOWA

AIB College of Business
2500 Fleur Dr., Des Moines 50321-1799
Type: Private, independent, two-year
Degrees: A *Enroll:* 764
URL: http://www.aib.edu
Phone: (515) 244-4221 *Calendar:* Qtr. plan
Inst. Accred.: NCA-HLC (1986/1999)

Allen College
1825 Logan Ave., Waterloo 50703
Type: Private, independent, four-year
Degrees: A, B, M *Enroll:* 358
URL: http://www.allencollege.edu
Phone: (319) 226-3000 *Calendar:* Sem. plan
Inst. Accred.: NCA-HLC (1995/2008)
Prog. Accred.: Nursing, Nursing Education, Radiography

The Ashford University
400 North Bluff Blvd., PO Box 2967, Clinton 52733
Type: Private, proprietary, four-year
System: Bridgepoint Education, Inc.
Degrees: A, B *Enroll:* 789
URL: http://www.ashford.edu
Phone: (866) 974-5700 *Calendar:* Sem. plan
Inst. Accred.: NCA-HLC (2005)

Briar Cliff University
3303 Rebecca St., PO Box 2100, Sioux City 51104
Type: Private, Roman Catholic Church, four-year
Degrees: A, B, M *Enroll:* 1,039
URL: http://www.briarcliff.edu
Phone: (712) 279-5321 *Calendar:* Tri. plan
Inst. Accred.: NCA-HLC (1945/2005)
Prog. Accred.: Nursing, Social Work

Buena Vista University
610 West Fourth St., Storm Lake 50588
Type: Private, Presbyterian Church (USA), four-year
Degrees: B, M *Enroll:* 2,423
URL: http://www.bvu.edu
Phone: (712) 749-2103 *Calendar:* 4-1-4 plan
Inst. Accred.: NCA-HLC (1952/2001)
Prog. Accred.: Social Work

Central College
812 University St., Pella 50219-1902
Type: Private, Reformed Church in America, four-year
Degrees: B *Enroll:* 1,451
URL: http://www.central.edu
Phone: (641) 628-5269 *Calendar:* Sem. plan
Inst. Accred.: NCA-HLC (1942/2004)
Prog. Accred.: Music

Clarke College
1550 Clarke Dr., Dubuque 52001
Type: Private, Roman Catholic Church, four-year
Degrees: A, B, M *Enroll:* 1,049
URL: http://www.clarke.edu
Phone: (319) 588-6300 *Calendar:* Sem. plan
Inst. Accred.: NCA-HLC (1918/2004)
Prog. Accred.: Music, Nursing Education, Physical Therapy, Social Work

Clinton Community College
1000 Lincoln Blvd., Clinton 52732
Type: Public, state/local, two-year
System: Eastern Iowa Community College District
Degrees: A *FTE Enroll:* 612
URL: http://www.eicc.edu/ccc
Phone: (563) 244-7001 *Calendar:* Sem. plan
Inst. Accred.: NCA-HLC (1983/2003, *Indirect accreditation through Eastern Iowa Community College District, Davenport, IA*)

Coe College
1220 First Ave., NE, Cedar Rapids 52402
Type: Private, Iowa Presbyterian Synod, four-year
Degrees: B, M *Enroll:* 1,288
URL: http://www.coe.edu
Phone: (319) 399-8000 *Calendar:* 4-1-4 plan
Inst. Accred.: NCA-HLC (1913/1999)
Prog. Accred.: Music, Nursing Education

Cornell College
600 First St. West, Mount Vernon 52314-1098
Type: Private, United Methodist Church, four-year
Degrees: B *Enroll:* 1,171
URL: http://www.cornellcollege.edu
Phone: (319) 895-4000
Inst. Accred.: NCA-HLC (1913/2003)

Des Moines Area Community College
2006 South Ankeny Blvd., Ankeny 50021
Type: Public, state/local, two-year
System: Iowa Dept. of Educ. Div. of Community Coll. and Workforce Preparation
Degrees: A *Enroll:* 9,625
URL: http://www.dmacc.edu
Phone: (515) 964-6200 *Calendar:* Sem. plan
Inst. Accred.: NCA-HLC (1974/2003)
Prog. Accred.: Allied Health (medical assisting (AMA), respiratory therapy), Clinical Lab Technology, Culinary Education, Dentistry (dental assisting, dental hygiene), Funeral Service Education (Mortuary Science), Nursing, Practical Nursing, Veterinary Technology

Boone Campus
1125 Hancock Dr., Boone 50036
Phone: (515) 432-7203
Prog. Accred: Nursing, Practical Nursing

Des Moines Area Community College *(continued)*

Carroll Campus
906 North Grant Rd., Carroll 51401
Phone: (712) 792-1755
Prog. Accred: Nursing, Practical Nursing

Newton Polytechnic Campus
600 North 2nd Ave., Newton 50208
Phone: (515) 791-3622

Urban Campus
1100 7th St., Des Moines 50314-2597
Phone: (515) 244-4226

Des Moines University—Osteopathic Medical Center
3200 Grand Ave., Des Moines 50312
Type: Private, independent, four-year
Degrees: B, M, D *Enroll:* 1,296
URL: http://www.dmu.edu
Phone: (515) 271-1400
Inst. Accred.: NCA-HLC (1986/2002)
Prog. Accred.: Osteopathy, Physical Therapy, Physician Assistant, Podiatry, Public Health

Divine Word College
102 Jacoby Dr., SW, Epworth 52045
Type: Private, Roman Catholic Church, four-year
Degrees: A, B *Enroll:* 69
URL: http://www.dwci.edu
Phone: (563) 876-3353 *Calendar:* Sem. plan
Inst. Accred.: NCA-HLC (1970/2006)

Dordt College
498 4th Ave., NE, Sioux Center 51250-1697
Type: Private, Christian Reformed Church, four-year
Degrees: A, B, M *Enroll:* 1,221
URL: http://www.dordt.edu
Phone: (712) 722-6000 *Calendar:* Sem. plan
Inst. Accred.: NCA-HLC (1969/2002)
Prog. Accred.: Engineering (general), Nursing Education, Social Work

Drake University
2507 University Ave., Des Moines 50311
Type: Private, independent, four-year
Degrees: B, M, P, D *Enroll:* 4,442
URL: http://www.drake.edu
Phone: (515) 271-2191 *Calendar:* Sem. plan
Inst. Accred.: NCA-HLC (1913/2008)
Prog. Accred.: Accounting, Art, Business (AACSB), Journalism, Law, Music, Pharmacy, Rehabilitation Counseling

Ellsworth Community College
1100 College Ave., Iowa Falls 50126
Type: Public, state/local, two-year
System: Iowa Valley Community College District
Degrees: A *FTE Enroll:* 795
URL: http://iavalley.cc.ia.us/ecc
Phone: (641) 648-4611 *Calendar:* Sem. plan
Inst. Accred.: NCA-HLC (1963/2002, *Indirect accreditation through Iowa Valley Community College District, Marshalltown, IA*)

Emmaus Bible College
2570 Asbury Rd., Dubuque 52001-3096
Type: Private, nondenominational, four-year
Degrees: A, B *Enroll:* 244
URL: http://www.emmaus.edu
Phone: (563) 588-8000 *Calendar:* Sem. plan
Inst. Accred.: ABHE (1986/2007), NCA-HLC (2006)

Faith Baptist Bible College
1900 NW Fourth St., Ankeny 50021-2152
Type: Private, General Association of Regular Baptist Churches, four-year
Degrees: A, B, M *Enroll:* 366
URL: http://www.faith.edu
Phone: (515) 964-0601 *Calendar:* Sem. plan
Inst. Accred.: ABHE (1969/2002), NCA-HLC (1996/2001)

Graceland University
1 University Place, Lamoni 50140-1641
Type: Private, Community of Christ, four-year
Degrees: B, M *Enroll:* 2,153
URL: http://www.graceland.edu
Phone: (641) 784-5000 *Calendar:* 4-1-4 plan
Inst. Accred.: NCA-HLC (1920/2007)
Prog. Accred.: Teacher Education (NCATE)

Independence Campus
1401 West Truman Rd., Independence, MO 64050-3434
Phone: (816) 833-0524
Prog. Accred: Nursing Education

Grand View College
1200 Grandview Ave., Des Moines 50316
Type: Private, Evangelical Lutheran Church in America, four-year
Degrees: A, B, M *Enroll:* 1,521
URL: http://www.gvc.edu
Phone: (515) 263-2800 *Calendar:* Sem. plan
Inst. Accred.: NCA-HLC (1959/2005)
Prog. Accred.: Nursing Education

Grinnell College
1121 Park Ave., Grinnell 50112
Type: Private, independent, four-year
Degrees: B *Enroll:* 1,558
URL: http://www.grinnell.edu
Phone: (641) 269-4000 *Calendar:* Sem. plan
Inst. Accred.: NCA-HLC (1913/1999)

Hamilton Technical College
1011 East 53rd St., Davenport 52807-2616
Type: Private, proprietary, four-year
Degrees: A, B *Enroll:* 293
URL: http://www.hamiltontechcollege.com
Phone: (319) 386-3570 *Calendar:* Sem. plan
Inst. Accred.: ACCSCT (1974/2005)

Hawkeye Community College
1501 East Orange Rd., Waterloo 50701-9014
Type: Public, state/local, two-year
System: Iowa Dept. of Educ. Div. of Community Coll. and Workforce Preparation
Degrees: A *Enroll:* 3,597
URL: http://www.hawkeyecollege.edu
Phone: (319) 296-4201 *Calendar:* Sem. plan
Inst. Accred.: NCA-HLC (1975/1995)
Prog. Accred.: Clinical Lab Technology, Dentistry (dental assisting, dental hygiene)

Indian Hills Community College
525 Grandview Ave., Ottumwa 52501
Type: Public, state/local, two-year
System: Iowa Dept. of Educ. Div. of Community Coll. and Workforce Preparation
Degrees: A *Enroll:* 2,821
URL: http://www.ihcc.cc.ia.us
Phone: (641) 683-5111 *Calendar:* Qtr. plan
Inst. Accred.: NCA-HLC (1980/2001)
Prog. Accred.: Culinary Education, Physical Therapy Assisting, Radiography

Centerville Campus
721 North First St., Centerville 52544
Phone: (641) 856-2143

Institute of Theology by Extension
2302 SW 3rd St., Ankeny 50023
Type: Private, independent, four-year
Degrees: B
URL: http://www.inste.org
Phone: (515) 289-9200 *Calendar:* Sem. plan
Inst. Accred.: DETC (2008)

Iowa Central Community College
330 Ave. M, Fort Dodge 50501
Type: Public, state/local, two-year
System: Iowa Dept. of Educ. Div. of Community Coll. and Workforce Preparation
Degrees: A *Enroll:* 3,439
URL: http://www.iowacentral.edu
Phone: (515) 576-7201 *Calendar:* Sem. plan
Inst. Accred.: NCA-HLC (1974/2001)
Prog. Accred.: Allied Health (medical assisting (AMA)), Clinical Lab Technology, Radiography

Iowa Lakes Community College
300 South 18th St., Estherville 51334
Type: Public, state/local, two-year
System: Iowa Dept. of Educ. Div. of Community Coll. and Workforce Preparation
Degrees: A *Enroll:* 1,950
URL: http://www.iowalakes.edu
Phone: (712) 362-2604 *Calendar:* Sem. plan
Inst. Accred.: NCA-HLC (1976/2004)

Emmetsburg Campus
3200 College Dr., Emmettsburg 50536
Phone: (712) 852-3554

Spencer Campus
Gateway North Shopping Center, 1900 North Grand Ave., Ste. 8, Spencer 51301
Phone: (712) 262-7141
Prog. Accred: Allied Health (medical assisting (AMA), surgical technology)

Iowa State University
117 Beardshear Hall, Ames 50011-2035
Type: Public, state, four-year
System: Board of Regents, State of Iowa
Degrees: B, M, P, D *Enroll:* 23,705
URL: http://www.iastate.edu
Phone: (515) 294-4111 *Calendar:* Sem. plan
Inst. Accred.: NCA-HLC (1916/1996)
Prog. Accred.: Accounting, Business (AACSB), Computer Science (ABET-CAC), Counseling Psychology, Dietetics (didactic), Dietetics (internship), Engineering (aerospace, agricultural, chemical, civil, computer, construction, electrical, industrial, materials, mechanical), Family & Consumer Science, Forestry, Industrial Technology, Interior Design, Journalism, Landscape Architecture, Marriage and Family Therapy, Music, Planning, Psychology Internship, Public Administration, Veterinary Medicine

Iowa Valley Community College District
3702 South Center St., Marshalltown 50158
Type: Public, state/local, two-year
System: Iowa Dept. of Educ. Div. of Community Coll. and Workforce Preparation
Degrees: A
URL: http://www.iavalley.edu
Phone: (515) 752-4643 *Calendar:* Sem. plan
Inst. Accred.: NCA-HLC (1996/2008)

Iowa Wesleyan College
601 North Main St., Mount Pleasant 52641
Type: Private, United Methodist Church, four-year
Degrees: B *Enroll:* 706
URL: http://www.iwc.edu
Phone: (319) 385-8021 *Calendar:* 4-1-4 plan
Inst. Accred.: NCA-HLC (1916/2008)
Prog. Accred.: Nursing

Iowa Western Community College
2700 College Rd., Council Bluffs 51501
Type: Public, state/local, two-year
System: Iowa Dept. of Educ. Div. of Community Coll. and Workforce Preparation
Degrees: A *Enroll:* 3,536
URL: http://www.iwcc.edu
Phone: (712) 325-3200 *Calendar:* Sem. plan
Inst. Accred.: NCA-HLC (1975/2000)
Prog. Accred.: Allied Health (medical assisting (AMA), surgical technology), Culinary Education, Dentistry (dental assisting, dental hygiene), Veterinary Technology

Kaplan University
1801 East Kimberly Rd., Ste. 1, Davenport 52807
Type: Private, proprietary, four-year
System: Kaplan Higher Education Corporation
Degrees: A, B, M *Enroll:* 11,095
URL: http://www.kaplan.edu
Phone: (563) 355-3500 *Calendar:* Qtr. plan
Inst. Accred.: NCA-HLC (1997/2003)
Prog. Accred.: Allied Health (medical assisting (AMA))

Cedar Falls Campus
7009 Nordic Dr., Cedar Falls 50613
Phone: (319) 277-0220
Prog. Accred: Allied Health (medical assisting (AMA))

Cedar Rapids Campus
3165 Edgewood Pkwy., SW, Cedar Rapids 52404
Phone: (319) 363-0481
Prog. Accred: Allied Health (medical assisting (AMA))

Concord Law School
10866 Wilshire Blvd., Ste. 1200, Los Angeles, CA 90024
Phone: (310) 689-3200

Council Bluffs Campus
1751 Madison Ave., Ste. 750, Council Bluffs 51503
Phone: (712) 328-4212
Prog. Accred: Allied Health (medical assisting (AMA))

Des Moines Campus
4655 121st St., Urbandale 50323
Phone: (515) 727-2100
Prog. Accred: Allied Health (medical assisting (AMA))

Lincoln Campus
1821 K St., Lincoln, NE 68508
Phone: (402) 474-5315
Prog. Accred: Allied Health (medical assisting (AMA)), Dentistry (dental assisting)

Mason City Campus
2570 Fourth St. SW, Mason City 50401
Phone: (641) 423-2530

Omaha Campus
5425 North 103 St., Omaha, NE 68134-1002
Phone: (402) 572-8500
Prog. Accred: Allied Health (medical assisting (AMA))

Online Campus
550 West Van Buren, 7th Flr., Chicago, IL 60607
Phone: (866) 527-5268
Prog. Accred: Nursing Education

Kirkwood Community College
6301 Kirkwood Blvd., SW, PO Box 2068, Cedar Rapids 52406-2068
Type: Public, state/local, two-year
System: Iowa Dept. of Educ. Div. of Community Coll. and Workforce Preparation
Degrees: A *Enroll:* 10,714
URL: http://www.kirkwood.edu
Phone: (319) 398-5411 *Calendar:* Sem. plan
Inst. Accred.: NCA-HLC (1970/2000)
Prog. Accred.: Allied Health (EMT-paramedic, electroneurodiagnostic technology, medical assisting (AMA), occupational therapy assisting, respiratory therapy, surgical technology), Business (ACBSP), Culinary Education, Dentistry (dental assisting, dental hygiene, dental laboratory technology), Physical Therapy Assisting, Veterinary Technology

Loras College
1450 Alta Vista, Dubuque 52004-0178
Type: Private, Roman Catholic Church, four-year
Degrees: A, B, M *Enroll:* 1,586
URL: http://www.loras.edu
Phone: (563) 588-7103 *Calendar:* Sem. plan
Inst. Accred.: NCA-HLC (1917/2000)
Prog. Accred.: Social Work

Luther College
700 College Dr., Decorah 52101-1045
Type: Private, Evangelic Lutheran Church in America, four-year
Degrees: B *Enroll:* 2,503
URL: http://www.luther.edu
Phone: (319) 387-2000 *Calendar:* 4-1-4 plan
Inst. Accred.: NCA-HLC (1915/1999)
Prog. Accred.: Music, Nursing Education, Social Work, Teacher Education (NCATE)

Maharishi University of Management
1000 North Fourth St., DB 1113, Fairfield 52557-1113
Type: Private, independent, four-year
Degrees: A, B, M, D *Enroll:* 691
URL: http://www.mum.edu
Phone: (641) 472-1110 *Calendar:* Sem. plan
Inst. Accred.: NCA-HLC (1980/2000)

Marshalltown Community College
3700 South Center St., Marshalltown 50158
Type: Public, state/local, two-year
System: Iowa Valley Community College District
Degrees: A *Enroll:* 1,036
URL: http://www.iavalley.cc.ia.us/mcc
Phone: (641) 752-7106 *Calendar:* Sem. plan
Inst. Accred.: NCA-HLC (1966/2002, *Indirect accreditation through Iowa Valley Community College District, Marshalltown, IA*)
Prog. Accred.: Dentistry (dental assisting)

Mercy College of Health Sciences
928 6th Ave., Des Moines 50309-1239
Type: Private, Religious Sisters of Mercy, four-year
Degrees: A, B *Enroll:* 510
URL: http://www.mchs.edu
Phone: (515) 643-6601 *Calendar:* Sem. plan
Inst. Accred.: NCA-HLC (1999/2004)
Prog. Accred.: Allied Health (cytotechnology, medical assisting (AMA), surgical technology), Clinical Lab Scientist, Nuclear Medicine Technology, Nursing, Nursing Education, Radiography

Morningside College
1501 Morningside Ave., Sioux City 51106
Type: Private, United Methodist Church, four-year
Degrees: B, M *Enroll:* 1,210
URL: http://www.morningside.edu
Phone: (712) 274-5000 *Calendar:* Sem. plan
Inst. Accred.: NCA-HLC (1913/2004)
Prog. Accred.: Music, Nursing

Mount Mercy College
1330 Elmhurst Dr., NE, Cedar Rapids 52402
Type: Private, Roman Catholic Church, four-year
Degrees: A, B, M *Enroll:* 1,207
URL: http://www2.mtmercy.edu
Phone: (319) 363-1323 *Calendar:* 4-1-4 plan
Inst. Accred.: NCA-HLC (1932/2003)
Prog. Accred.: Nursing Education, Social Work

Muscatine Community College
152 Colorado St., Muscatine 52761
Type: Public, state/local, two-year
System: Eastern Iowa Community College District
Degrees: A *FTE Enroll:* 639
URL: http://www.eicc.edu/mcc
Phone: (563) 288-6001 *Calendar:* Sem. plan
Inst. Accred.: NCA-HLC (1983/2003, *Indirect accreditation through Eastern Iowa Community College District, Davenport, IA*)

North Iowa Area Community College
500 College Dr., Mason City 50401
Type: Public, state/local, two-year
System: Iowa Dept. of Educ. Div. of Community Coll. and Workforce Preparation
Degrees: A *Enroll:* 2,180
URL: http://www.niacc.edu
Phone: (515) 422-4000 *Calendar:* Sem. plan
Inst. Accred.: NCA-HLC (1919/2004)
Prog. Accred.: Allied Health (medical assisting (AMA)), Nursing, Physical Therapy Assisting

Northeast Iowa Community College
PO Box 400, Calmar 52132-0400
Type: Public, state/local, two-year
System: Iowa Dept. of Educ. Div. of Community Coll. and Workforce Preparation
Degrees: A *Enroll:* 2,791
URL: http://www.nicc.edu
Phone: (800) 728-2256 *Calendar:* Sem. plan
Inst. Accred.: NCA-HLC (1977/2003)
Prog. Accred.: Allied Health (respiratory therapy), Radiography

Peosta Campus
10250 Sundown Rd., Peosta 52068
Phone: (563) 556-5110
Prog. Accred: Dentistry (dental assisting), Radiography

Northwest Iowa Community College
603 West Park St., Sheldon 51201
Type: Public, state/local, two-year
System: Iowa Dept. of Educ. Div. of Community Coll. and Workforce Preparation
Degrees: A *Enroll:* 708
URL: http://www.nwicc.edu
Phone: (712) 324-5061 *Calendar:* Sem. plan
Inst. Accred.: NCA-HLC (1980/2005)

Northwestern College
101 7th St., SW, Orange City 51041
Type: Private, Reformed Church in America, four-year
Degrees: A, B *Enroll:* 1,244
URL: http://www.nwciowa.edu
Phone: (712) 737-7000 *Calendar:* Sem. plan
Inst. Accred.: NCA-HLC (1953/2006)
Prog. Accred.: Social Work, Teacher Education (NCATE)

Palmer College of Chiropractic
1000 Brady St., Davenport 52803-5287
Type: Private, independent, four-year
System: Palmer Chiropractic University System
Degrees: A, B, M, P *Enroll:* 2,158
URL: http://www.palmer.edu
Phone: (563) 884-5621 *Calendar:* Tri. plan
Inst. Accred.: NCA-HLC (1984/1999)
Prog. Accred.: Chiropractic Education

Florida Campus
4777 City Center Pkwy., Port Orange, FL 32129-4153
Phone: (386) 763-2642
Prog. Accred: Chiropractic Education

Saint Ambrose University
518 West Locust St., Davenport 52803
Type: Private, Roman Catholic Church, four-year
Degrees: B, M, D *Enroll:* 2,920
URL: http://www.sau.edu
Phone: (563) 333-6000 *Calendar:* Sem. plan
Inst. Accred.: NCA-HLC (1927/2008)
Prog. Accred.: Allied Health (occupational therapy), Business (ACBSP), Engineering (industrial), Graduate Social Work, Nursing Education, Physical Therapy, Teacher Education (TEAC)

Saint Luke's College
2720 Stone Park Blvd., PO Box 2000, Sioux City 51104
Type: Private, independent, two-year
Degrees: A *Enroll:* 139
URL: http://www.stlukescollege.com
Phone: (712) 279-3149 *Calendar:* Sem. plan
Inst. Accred.: NCA-HLC (1997/2007)
Prog. Accred.: Allied Health (respiratory therapy), Clinical Lab Scientist, Nursing, Radiography

Scott Community College
500 Belmont Rd., Bettendorf 52722
Type: Public, state/local, two-year
System: Eastern Iowa Community College District
Degrees: A *FTE Enroll:* 3,402
URL: http://www.eicc.edu/scc
Phone: (563) 441-4001 *Calendar:* Sem. plan
Inst. Accred.: NCA-HLC (1983/2003, *Indirect accreditation through Eastern Iowa Community College District, Davenport, IA*)
Prog. Accred.: Allied Health (electroneurodiagnostic technology), Dentistry (dental assisting), Radiography

Simpson College
701 North C St., Indianola 50125
Type: Private, independent, four-year
Degrees: B *Enroll:* 1,702
URL: http://www.simpson.edu
Phone: (515) 961-1560 *Calendar:* Sem. plan
Inst. Accred.: NCA-HLC (1913/2006)
Prog. Accred.: Music

Southeastern Community College
PO Box 180, 1500 West Agency Rd., West Burlington 52655-0180
Type: Public, state/local, two-year
System: Iowa Dept. of Educ. Div. of Community Coll. and Workforce Preparation
Degrees: A *Enroll:* 2,372
URL: http://www.scciowa.edu
Phone: (319) 752-2731 *Calendar:* Sem. plan
Inst. Accred.: NCA-HLC (1974/1999)
Prog. Accred.: Allied Health (medical assisting (AMA), respiratory therapy)

South Campus
335 Messenger Rd., Keokuk 52632-6007
Phone: (319) 524-3221

Southwestern Community College
1501 Townline St., Creston 50801
Type: Public, state/local, two-year
System: Iowa Dept. of Educ. Div. of Community Coll. and Workforce Preparation
Degrees: A *Enroll:* 891
URL: http://www.swcciowa.edu
Phone: (641) 782-7081 *Calendar:* Sem. plan
Inst. Accred.: NCA-HLC (1974/2006)

University of Dubuque
2000 University Ave., Dubuque 52001-5050
Type: Private, Presbyterian Church (USA), four-year
Degrees: A, B, M, D *Enroll:* 1,349
URL: http://www.dbq.edu
Phone: (319) 589-3223 *Calendar:* Sem. plan
Inst. Accred.: ATS (1944/1999), NCA-HLC (1921/2005)
Prog. Accred.: Aviation, Nursing Education

University of Iowa
101 Jessup Hall, Iowa City 52242-1316
Type: Public, state, four-year
System: Board of Regents, State of Iowa
Degrees: B, M, P, D *Enroll:* 25,081
URL: http://www.uiowa.edu
Phone: (319) 335-3500 *Calendar:* Sem. plan
Inst. Accred.: NCA-HLC (1913/2008)
Prog. Accred.: Accounting, Allied Health (EMT-paramedic, audiology, diagnostic medical sonography, health services administration, medicine, perfusion, speech-language pathology), Applied Science (industrial hygiene), Business (AACSB), Clinical Lab Scientist, Clinical Pastoral Education (ACPEI), Clinical Psychology, Counseling, Counseling Psychology, Dentistry (advanced education in general dentistry, combined prosthodontics, dental public health, dentistry, endodontics, general dentistry, general practice residency, oral and maxillofacial pathology, oral and maxillofacial radiology, oral and maxillofacial surgery, orthodontic and dentofacial orthopedics, pediatric dentistry, periodontics), Dietetics (internship), Engineering (bioengineering, chemical, civil, electrical, industrial, mechanical), English Language Education, Graduate Social Work, Journalism, Law, Librarianship, Music, Nuclear Medicine Technology, Nurse Anesthesia Education, Nursing Education, Pharmacy, Physical Therapy, Physician Assistant, Planning, Psychology Internship, Public Health, Radiation Therapy, Radiography, Recreation and Leisure Services, Rehabilitation Counseling, School Psychology, Social Work, Theatre

University of Northern Iowa
1227 West 27th St., Cedar Falls 50614
Type: Public, state, four-year
System: Board of Regents, State of Iowa
Degrees: B, M, P, D *Enroll:* 11,252
URL: http://www.uni.edu
Phone: (319) 273-2311 *Calendar:* Sem. plan
Inst. Accred.: NCA-HLC (1913/2001)
Prog. Accred.: Allied Health (audiology, speech-language pathology), Art, Business (AACSB), Construction Technology, Counseling, Design Technology, Graduate Social Work, Manufacturing Technology, Music, Recreation and Leisure Services, Social Work

Upper Iowa University
PO Box 1857, 605 Washington St., Fayette 52142
Type: Private, independent, four-year
Degrees: A, B, M *Enroll:* 3,433
URL: http://www.uiu.edu
Phone: (563) 425-5200 *Calendar:* Sem. plan
Inst. Accred.: NCA-HLC (1913/1999)
Prog. Accred.: Nursing Education

Vatterott College—Des Moines
6100 Thornton Ave., Ste. 290, Des Moines 50321
Type: Private, proprietary, two-year
System: Vatterott Educational Centers, Inc.
Degrees: A *Enroll:* 153
URL: http://www.vatterott-college.com
Phone: (515) 309-9000 *Calendar:* Sem. plan
Inst. Accred.: ACCSCT (1999/2004)
Prog. Accred.: Medical Assisting (ABHES)

St. Joseph Campus
3131 Frederick Blvd., St. Joseph, MO 64501
Phone: (816) 364-5399

Vennard College
PO Box 29, University Park 52595-0029
Type: Private, independent, four-year
Degrees: A, B *Enroll:* 73
URL: http://www.vennard.edu
Phone: (515) 673-8391 *Calendar:* Sem. plan
Inst. Accred.: ABHE (1997/2002)

Waldorf College
106 South Sixth St., Forest City 50436
Type: Private, Lutheran Church, four-year
Degrees: A, B *Enroll:* 599
URL: http://www.waldorf.edu
Phone: (641) 582-2450 *Calendar:* Sem. plan
Inst. Accred.: NCA-HLC (1948/2001)

Wartburg College
222 9th St., N.W., Waverly 50677-1003
Type: Private, Lutheran Church, four-year
Degrees: B *Enroll:* 1,763
URL: http://www.wartburg.edu
Phone: (319) 352-8200
Inst. Accred.: NCA-HLC (1948/2007)
Prog. Accred.: Music, Social Work, Teacher Education (NCATE)

Wartburg Theological Seminary
333 Wartburg Place, PO Box 5004, Dubuque 52004-5004
Type: Private, Evangelical Lutheran Church in America, four-year
Degrees: M *Enroll:* 168
URL: http://www.wartburgseminary.edu
Phone: (319) 589-0200 *Calendar:* 4-1-4 plan
Inst. Accred.: ATS (1944/2008), NCA-HLC (1976/2008)

Western Iowa Tech Community College
4647 Stone Ave., PO Box 5199, Sioux City 51102-5199
Type: Public, state/local, two-year
System: Iowa Dept. of Educ. Div. of Community Coll. and Workforce Preparation
Degrees: A *Enroll:* 3,176
URL: http://www.witcc.edu
Phone: (712) 274-6400 *Calendar:* Sem. plan
Inst. Accred.: NCA-HLC (1977/2002)
Prog. Accred.: Allied Health (surgical technology), Dentistry (dental assisting), Nursing, Physical Therapy Assisting, Practical Nursing

Cherokee Campus
228-1/2 West Main, Cherokee 51012
Phone: (712) 225-0238
Prog. Accred: Practical Nursing

Denison Campus
11 North 35th St., Denison 51142
Phone: (712) 263-3419
Prog. Accred: Practical Nursing

William Penn University
201 Trueblood Ave., Oskaloosa 52577
Type: Private, Society of Friends, four-year
Degrees: A, B *Enroll:* 1,839
URL: http://www.wmpenn.edu
Phone: (614) 673-1001 *Calendar:* Sem. plan
Inst. Accred.: NCA-HLC (1913/2008)

KANSAS

Allen County Community College
1801 North Cottonwood, Iola 66749
Type: Public, state/local, two-year
System: Kansas Board of Regents
Degrees: A *Enroll:* 1,438
URL: http://www.allencc.edu
Phone: (620) 365-5116 *Calendar:* Sem. plan
Inst. Accred.: NCA-HLC (1974/1999)

Burlingame Campus
PO Box 66, 100 Bloomquist Dr., Burlingame 66413-0066
Phone: (785) 654-2416

Baker University
618 Eighth St., PO Box 65, Baldwin City 66006-0065
Type: Private, United Methodist Church, four-year
Degrees: A, B, M *Enroll:* 882
URL: http://www.bakeru.edu
Phone: (785) 594-6451 *Calendar:* 4-1-4 plan
Inst. Accred.: NCA-HLC (1913/2002)
Prog. Accred.: Business (ACBSP), Music, Teacher Education (NCATE)

School of Nursing Campus
Stormont-Vail Medical Center, 1500 Southwest 10th St., Topeka 66604-1353
Phone: (913) 354-5850
Prog. Accred: Nursing Education

School of Professional and Graduate Studies—Overland
8001 College Blvd., Ste. 100, Overland Park 66210
Phone: (913) 491-4432

School of Professional and Graduate Studies—Wichita
3450 North Rock Rd., #400, Wichita 67206
Phone: (316) 636-2322

Barclay College
PO Box 288, Haviland 67059-0288
Type: Private, Evangelical Friends International, four-year
Degrees: A, B *Enroll:* 106
URL: http://www.barclaycollege.edu
Phone: (620) 862-5252 *Calendar:* Sem. plan
Inst. Accred.: ABHE (1975/2007)

Barton County Community College
243 NE 30th Rd., Great Bend 67530-9283
Type: Public, state/local, two-year
System: Kansas Board of Regents
Degrees: A *Enroll:* 1,909
URL: http://www.bartonccc.edu
Phone: (620) 792-2701 *Calendar:* Sem. plan
Inst. Accred.: NCA-HLC (1974/2003)
Prog. Accred.: Allied Health (EMT-paramedic), Clinical Lab Technology, Nursing

Benedictine College
1020 North Second St., Atchison 66002
Type: Private, Roman Catholic Church, four-year
Degrees: A, B, M *Enroll:* 1,332
URL: http://www.benedictine.edu
Phone: (913) 367-5340 *Calendar:* Sem. plan
Inst. Accred.: NCA-HLC (1971/2000)
Prog. Accred.: Music, Teacher Education (NCATE)

Bethany College
421 North First St., Lindsborg 67456-1897
Type: Private, Evangelical Lutheran Church in America, four-year
Degrees: B *Enroll:* 566
URL: http://www.bethanylb.edu
Phone: (785) 227-3311 *Calendar:* 4-1-4 plan
Inst. Accred.: NCA-HLC (1932/2001)
Prog. Accred.: Music, Social Work, Teacher Education (NCATE)

Bethel College
300 East 27th St., North Newton 67117
Type: Private, Mennonite Education Agency, four-year
Degrees: B *Enroll:* 491
URL: http://www.bethelks.edu
Phone: (316) 283-2500 *Calendar:* 4-1-4 plan
Inst. Accred.: NCA-HLC (1938/1999)
Prog. Accred.: Nursing Education, Social Work, Teacher Education (NCATE)

The Brown Mackie College
2106 South 9th St., Salina 67401
Type: Private, proprietary, two-year
System: Education Management Corporation
Degrees: A *Enroll:* 367
URL: http://www.brownmackie.edu/Salina
Phone: (913) 825-5422 *Calendar:* Sem. plan
Inst. Accred.: NCA-HLC (1980/2008)

Kansas City Campus
9705 Lenexa Dr., Lenexa 66215
Phone: (913) 768-1900

Butler County Community College
901 South Haverhill Rd., El Dorado 67042
Type: Public, state/local, two-year
System: Kansas Board of Regents
Degrees: A *Enroll:* 5,406
URL: http://www.butlercc.edu
Phone: (316) 312-2222 *Calendar:* Sem. plan
Inst. Accred.: NCA-HLC (1970/2000)
Prog. Accred.: Business (ACBSP), Nursing

Central Baptist Theological Seminary
6601 Monticello Rd., Shawnee 66226-3513
Type: Private, American Baptist Churches (USA) Cooperative Baptist Fellowship, four-year
Degrees: M *Enroll:* 80
URL: http://www.cbts.edu
Phone: (913) 667-5700 *Calendar:* Sem. plan
Inst. Accred.: ATS (1962/2007), NCA-HLC (1979/2001)

Central Christian College of Kansas
1200 South Main St., PO Box 1403, McPherson 67460
Type: Private, Free Methodist Church, four-year
Degrees: A, B *Enroll:* 314
URL: http://www.centralcollege.edu
Phone: (620) 241-0723 *Calendar:* 4-1-4 plan
Inst. Accred.: NCA-HLC (1975/2004)

Cleveland Chiropractic College
10850 Lowell Ave., Overland Park 66210-1613
Type: Private, independent, four-year
Degrees: B, P, D *Enroll:* 475
URL: http://www.clevelandchiropractic.edu
Phone: (816) 501-0100 *Calendar:* Tri. plan
Inst. Accred.: NCA-HLC (1984/1997)
Prog. Accred.: Chiropractic Education

Los Angeles Campus
590 North Vermont Ave., Los Angeles, CA 90004
Phone: (323) 660-6166
Prog. Accred: Chiropractic Education

Cloud County Community College
2221 Campus Dr., PO Box 1002, Concordia 66901-1002
Type: Public, state/local, two-year
System: Kansas Board of Regents
Degrees: A *Enroll:* 1,483
URL: http://www.cloud.edu
Phone: (800) 729-5101 *Calendar:* Sem. plan
Inst. Accred.: NCA-HLC (1977/2001)
Prog. Accred.: Nursing

Coffeyville Community College
400 West 11th St., Coffeyville 67337-5064
Type: Public, state/local, two-year
System: Kansas Board of Regents
Degrees: A *Enroll:* 996
URL: http://www.coffeyville.edu
Phone: (620) 251-7700 *Calendar:* Sem. plan
Inst. Accred.: NCA-HLC (1972/2005)
Prog. Accred.: Allied Health (EMT-paramedic)

Technical Campus
600 Roosevelt St., Coffeyville 67337-3421
Phone: (621) 251-3910

Colby Community College
1255 South Range, Colby 67701
Type: Public, state/local, two-year
System: Kansas Board of Regents
Degrees: A *Enroll:* 1,078
URL: http://www.colbycc.edu
Phone: (785) 462-3984 *Calendar:* Sem. plan
Inst. Accred.: NCA-HLC (1972/2005)
Prog. Accred.: Business (ACBSP), Dentistry (dental hygiene), Nursing, Physical Therapy Assisting, Veterinary Technology

Cowley County Community College
125 South Second St., PO Box 1147, Arkansas City 67005-1147
Type: Public, state/local, two-year
System: Kansas Board of Regents
Degrees: A *Enroll:* 3,156
URL: http://www.cowley.edu
Phone: (620) 442-0430 *Calendar:* Sem. plan
Inst. Accred.: NCA-HLC (1975/2000)

Winfield Allied Health Center
1406 East 8th St., Winfield 67156
Phone: (620) 221-3392
Prog. Accred: Allied Health (EMT-paramedic)

Dodge City Community College
2501 North 14th St., Dodge City 67801
Type: Public, state/local, two-year
System: Kansas Board of Regents
Degrees: A *Enroll:* 1,099
URL: http://www.dc3.edu
Phone: (800) 262-4565 *Calendar:* Sem. plan
Inst. Accred.: NCA-HLC (1966/2004)
Prog. Accred.: Nursing, Practical Nursing

Donnelly College
608 North 18th St., Kansas City 66102
Type: Private, Roman Catholic Church, two-year
Degrees: A *Enroll:* 355
URL: http://www.donnelly.edu
Phone: (913) 621-8700 *Calendar:* Sem. plan
Inst. Accred.: NCA-HLC (1958/2006)

Emporia State University
1200 Commercial St., Emporia 66801-5087
Type: Public, state, four-year
System: Kansas Board of Regents
Degrees: B, M, P, D *Enroll:* 4,874
URL: http://www.emporia.edu
Phone: (620) 341-1200 *Calendar:* Sem. plan
Inst. Accred.: NCA-HLC (1915/2005)
Prog. Accred.: Business (AACSB), Counseling, Librarianship, Music, Nursing, Rehabilitation Counseling, Teacher Education (NCATE)

Flint Hills Technical College
3301 West 18th Ave., Emporia 66801
Type: Public, state/local, two-year
System: Kansas Board of Regents
Degrees: A *Enroll:* 261
URL: http://www.fhtc.edu
Phone: (620) 343-4600 *Calendar:* Sem. plan
Inst. Accred.: NCA-HLC (2007)
Prog. Accred.: Allied Health (EMT-paramedic), Dentistry (dental assisting, dental hygiene)

Fort Hays State University
600 Park St., Hays 67601
Type: Public, state, four-year
System: Kansas Board of Regents
Degrees: A, B, M, P *Enroll:* 6,307
URL: http://www.fhsu.edu
Phone: (785) 628-4000 *Calendar:* Sem. plan
Inst. Accred.: NCA-HLC (1915/2008)
Prog. Accred.: Allied Health (speech-language pathology), Music, Nursing Education, Radiography, Social Work, Teacher Education (NCATE)

Fort Scott Community College
2108 South Horton St., Fort Scott 66701
Type: Public, state/local, two-year
System: Kansas Board of Regents
Degrees: A *Enroll:* 1,198
URL: http://www.fortscott.edu
Phone: (620) 223-2700 *Calendar:* Sem. plan
Inst. Accred.: NCA-HLC (1976/2003)
Prog. Accred.: Nursing

Friends University
2100 West University St., Wichita 67213
Type: Private, independent, four-year
Degrees: A, B, M *Enroll:* 2,449
URL: http://www.friends.edu
Phone: (316) 261-5800 *Calendar:* Sem. plan
Inst. Accred.: NCA-HLC (1915/2001)
Prog. Accred.: Marriage and Family Therapy, Music, Teacher Education (NCATE)

Topeka Campus
2820 SW Mission Woods Dr., Topeka 66614
Phone: (800) 794-6945

Garden City Community College
801 Campus Dr., Garden City 67846
Type: Public, state/local, two-year
System: Kansas Board of Regents
Degrees: A *Enroll:* 1,324
URL: http://www.gcccks.edu
Phone: (620) 276-7611 *Calendar:* Sem. plan
Inst. Accred.: NCA-HLC (1975/2005)
Prog. Accred.: Allied Health (EMT-paramedic), Nursing

Haskell Indian Nations University
155 Indian Ave., Lawrence 66046-4800
Type: Public, tribal, four-year
System: American Indian Higher Education Consortium
Degrees: A, B *Enroll:* 869
URL: http://www.haskell.edu
Phone: (785) 749-8404 *Calendar:* Sem. plan
Inst. Accred.: NCA-HLC (1979/2005)

Hesston College
PO Box 3000, Hesston 67062-2093
Type: Private, Mennonite Education Agency, two-year
Degrees: A *Enroll:* 439
URL: http://www.hesston.edu
Phone: (620) 327-4221 *Calendar:* Sem. plan
Inst. Accred.: NCA-HLC (1964/2001)
Prog. Accred.: Nursing

Highland Community College
606 West Main St., Highland 66035-4165
Type: Public, state/local, two-year
System: Kansas Board of Regents
Degrees: A *Enroll:* 1,589
URL: http://www.highlandcc.edu
Phone: (785) 442-6000 *Calendar:* Sem. plan
Inst. Accred.: NCA-HLC (1977/1999)

Northeast Kansas Technical Center
1501 West Riley St., Atchison 66002
Phone: (913) 367-6204

Hutchinson Community College
1300 North Plum St., Hutchinson 67501
Type: Public, state/local, two-year
System: Kansas Board of Regents
Degrees: A *Enroll:* 2,934
URL: http://www.hutchcc.edu
Phone: (620) 665-3500 *Calendar:* Sem. plan
Inst. Accred.: NCA-HLC (1960/2004)
Prog. Accred.: Allied Health (EMT-paramedic, surgical technology), Nursing, Practical Nursing, Radiography

Independence Community College
Independence 67301
Type: Public, state/local, two-year
System: Kansas Board of Regents
Degrees: A *Enroll:* 623
URL: http://www.indycc.edu
Phone: (620) 331-4100 *Calendar:* Sem. plan
Inst. Accred.: NCA-HLC (1957/2003)

Johnson County Community College
12345 College Blvd., Overland Park 66210-1299
Type: Public, state/local, two-year
System: Kansas Board of Regents
Degrees: A *Enroll:* 10,784
URL: http://www.jccc.edu
Phone: (913) 469-8500 *Calendar:* Sem. plan
Inst. Accred.: NCA-HLC (1975/2004)
Prog. Accred.: Allied Health (EMT-paramedic, respiratory therapy), Business (ACBSP), Culinary Education, Dentistry (dental hygiene), Nursing

Kansas City Kansas Community College
7250 State Ave., Kansas City 66112
Type: Public, state/local, two-year
System: Kansas Board of Regents
Degrees: A *Enroll:* 3,098
URL: http://www.kckcc.edu
Phone: (913) 334-1100 *Calendar:* Sem. plan
Inst. Accred.: NCA-HLC (1951/2006)
Prog. Accred.: Allied Health (EMT-paramedic, respiratory therapy), Business (ACBSP), Funeral Service Education (Mortuary Science), Nursing, Physical Therapy Assisting

Kansas State University
Manhattan 66506-0113
Type: Public, state, four-year
System: Kansas Board of Regents
Degrees: A, B, M, D *Enroll:* 20,080
URL: http://www.ksu.edu
Phone: (785) 532-6011 *Calendar:* Sem. plan
Inst. Accred.: NCA-HLC (1916/2002)
Prog. Accred.: Accounting, Allied Health (speech-language pathology), Art, Business (AACSB), Computer Science (ABET-CAC), Construction Education, Counseling, Dietetics (coordinated), Dietetics (didactic), Engineering (agricultural, architectural, chemical, civil, computer, electrical, industrial, manufacturing, mechanical), Interior Architecture, Interior Design, Journalism, Landscape Architecture, Marriage and Family Therapy, Music, Planning, Psychology Internship, Public Administration, Recreation and Leisure Services, Social Work, Teacher Education (NCATE), Theatre, Veterinary Medicine

College of Technology and Aviation
2409 Scanlan Ave., Salina 67401-8196
Phone: (913) 825-0275
Prog. Accred: Aviation, Engineering Technology (civil/construction, computer, mechanical)

Kansas Wesleyan University
100 East Claflin Ave., Salina 67401-6146
Type: Private, United Methodist Church, four-year
Degrees: A, B, M *Enroll:* 764
URL: http://www.kwu.edu
Phone: (785) 827-5541 *Calendar:* Sem. plan
Inst. Accred.: NCA-HLC (1916/2007)
Prog. Accred.: Nursing, Teacher Education (NCATE)

Labette Community College
200 South 14th St., Parsons 67357
Type: Public, state/local, two-year
System: Kansas Board of Regents
Degrees: A *Enroll:* 707
URL: http://www.labette.edu
Phone: (620) 421-6700 *Calendar:* Sem. plan
Inst. Accred.: NCA-HLC (1976/2006)
Prog. Accred.: Allied Health (respiratory therapy), Nursing, Radiography

Manhattan Area Technical College
3136 Dickens Ave., Manhattan 66503-2499
Type: Public, state/local, two-year
Degrees: A *Enroll:* 350
URL: http://www.matc.net
Phone: (785) 587-2800
Inst. Accred.: NCA-HLC (2006)
Prog. Accred.: Nursing

Manhattan Christian College
1415 Anderson Ave., Manhattan 66502-4081
Type: Private, Christian Churches/Churches of Christ, four-year
Degrees: A, B *Enroll:* 298
URL: http://www.mccks.edu
Phone: (785) 539-3571 *Calendar:* Sem. plan
Inst. Accred.: ABHE (1948/2007), NCA-HLC (2000/2005)

McPherson College
1600 East Euclid St., McPherson 67460-3847
Type: Private, Church of the Brethren, four-year
Degrees: A, B *Enroll:* 449
URL: http://www.mcpherson.edu
Phone: (620) 241-0731 *Calendar:* 4-1-4 plan
Inst. Accred.: NCA-HLC (1921/2005)
Prog. Accred.: Teacher Education (NCATE)

MidAmerica Nazarene University
2030 East College Way, Olathe 66062-1899
Type: Private, Church of the Nazarene, four-year
Degrees: A, B, M *Enroll:* 1,540
URL: http://www.mnu.edu
Phone: (913) 791-3750 *Calendar:* Sem. plan
Inst. Accred.: NCA-HLC (1974/1999)
Prog. Accred.: Music, Nursing Education, Teacher Education (NCATE)

European Nazarene College
Junkerstrasse 68-70, Büsingen, Switzerland 8238
Phone: 011 49 7734-80900

Neosho County Community College
800 West 14th St., Chanute 66720
Type: Public, state/local, two-year
System: Kansas Board of Regents
Degrees: A *Enroll:* 1,166
URL: http://www.neosho.edu
Phone: (620) 431-2820 *Calendar:* Sem. plan
Inst. Accred.: NCA-HLC (1976/2004)
Prog. Accred.: Business (ACBSP), Nursing

Newman University
3100 McCormick Ave., Wichita 67213-2097
Type: Private, Roman Catholic Church, four-year
Degrees: A, B, M *Enroll:* 1,574
URL: http://www.newmanu.edu
Phone: (316) 942-4291 *Calendar:* Sem. plan
Inst. Accred.: NCA-HLC (1967/2007)
Prog. Accred.: Allied Health (occupational therapy assisting, respiratory therapy), Graduate Social Work, Nurse Anesthesia Education, Nursing Education, Radiography

North Central Kansas Technical College
PO Box 507, Beloit 67420
Type: Public, state, two-year
Degrees: A *Enroll:* 473
URL: http://www.ncktc.edu
Phone: (785) 738-2276 *Calendar:* Sem. plan
Inst. Accred.: NCA-HLC (1981/2002)

Hays Campus
2205 Wheatland Ave., Hays 67601-4600
Phone: (785) 625-2437
Prog. Accred: Nursing

Northwest Kansas Technical College
1209 Harrison St., Goodland 67211
Type: Public, state, two-year
Degrees: A
URL: http://www.nwktc.edu
Phone: (785) 899-3641
Inst. Accred.: NCA-HLC (2007)
Prog. Accred.: Allied Health (medical assisting (AMA))

Ottawa University
1001 South Cedar St., Ottawa 66067-3399
Type: Private, American Baptist Churches (USA), four-year
Degrees: B, M *Enroll:* 424
URL: http://www.ottawa.edu
Phone: (785) 242-5200 *Calendar:* Sem. plan
Inst. Accred.: NCA-HLC (1914/2004)
Prog. Accred.: Teacher Education (NCATE)

Indiana Campus
287 Quarter Master Ct., Jeffersonville, IN 47130
Phone: (812) 280-7271

Kansas City Campus
4370 West 109th St., Ste. 200, Overland Park 66211
Phone: (913) 451-1431

Milwaukee Campus
300 North Corporate Dr., Ste. 110, Brookfield, WI 53045
Phone: (414) 879-0200

Phoenix Campus
10020 North 25th Ave., Phoenix, AZ 85021
Phone: (602) 371-1188

Pittsburg State University
1701 South Broadway, Pittsburg 66762
Type: Public, state, four-year
System: Kansas Board of Regents
Degrees: A, B, M, P *Enroll:* 5,928
URL: http://www.pittstate.edu
Phone: (620) 231-7000 *Calendar:* Sem. plan
Inst. Accred.: NCA-HLC (1915/2003)
Prog. Accred.: Business (AACSB), Counseling, Engineering Technology (civil/construction, electrical, manufacturing, mechanical, plastics), Music, Nursing Education, Social Work, Teacher Education (NCATE)

Pratt Community College
348 NE SR 61, Pratt 67124
Type: Public, state/local, two-year
System: Kansas Board of Regents
Degrees: A *Enroll:* 934
URL: http://www.prattcc.edu
Phone: (620) 672-9800 *Calendar:* Sem. plan
Inst. Accred.: NCA-HLC (1976/2005)
Prog. Accred.: Business (ACBSP), Nursing

Seward County Community College/Area Technical School
1801 North Kansas St., Box 1137, Liberal 67901
Type: Public, state/local, two-year
System: Kansas Board of Regents
Degrees: A *Enroll:* 990
URL: http://www.sccc.edu
Phone: (620) 624-1951 *Calendar:* Sem. plan
Inst. Accred.: NCA-HLC (1975/2000)
Prog. Accred.: Allied Health (respiratory therapy, surgical technology), Business (ACBSP), Clinical Lab Technology, Nursing

Southwestern College
100 College St., Winfield 67156-2499
Type: Private, United Methodist Church, four-year
Degrees: B, M *Enroll:* 911
URL: http://www.sckans.edu
Phone: (620) 229-6000 *Calendar:* Sem. plan
Inst. Accred.: NCA-HLC (1918/2001)
Prog. Accred.: Music, Nursing Education, Teacher Education (NCATE)

Sterling College
125 West Cooper St., Sterling 67579
Type: Private, Presbyterian Church (USA), four-year
Degrees: B *Enroll:* 466
URL: http://www.sterling.edu
Phone: (316) 278-2173 *Calendar:* 4-1-4 plan
Inst. Accred.: NCA-HLC (1928/1999)
Prog. Accred.: Teacher Education (NCATE)

Tabor College
400 South Jefferson St., Hillsboro 67063
Type: Private, Conference of the Mennonite Brethren Church of North America, four-year
Degrees: A, B, M *Enroll:* 532
URL: http://www.tabor.edu
Phone: (620) 947-3121 *Calendar:* 4-1-4 plan
Inst. Accred.: NCA-HLC (1965/1999)
Prog. Accred.: Music, Nursing Education, Teacher Education (NCATE)

Wichita Campus
7348 West 21st St. North, Ste. 117, Wichita 67205-1765
Phone: (316) 729-6333

United States Army Command and General Staff College
1 Reynolds Ave., Bldg. 111, Fort Leavenworth 66027-1352
Type: Public, federal, four-year
Degrees: M *FTE Enroll:* 1,108
URL: http://cgsc.leavenworth.army.mil
Phone: (913) 684-3097 *Calendar:* Tri. plan
Inst. Accred.: NCA-HLC (1976/2006)

University of Kansas
230 Strong Hall, Lawrence 66045
Type: Public, state, four-year
System: Kansas Board of Regents
Degrees: B, M, P, D *Enroll:* 23,595
URL: http://www.ku.edu
Phone: (785) 864-2700 *Calendar:* Sem. plan
Inst. Accred.: NCA-HLC (1913/2005)
Prog. Accred.: Accounting, Allied Health (audiology, health services administration, speech-language pathology), Art, Business (AACSB), Clinical Psychology, Computer Science (ABET-CAC), Counseling Psychology, Engineering (aerospace, architectural, chemical, civil, computer, electrical, engineering physics/science, mechanical, petroleum), English Language Education, Graduate Social Work, Journalism, Law, Music, Pharmacy, Planning, Psychology Internship, Public Administration, School Psychology, Social Work, Teacher Education (NCATE)

Edwards Campus
12600 Quivira Rd., Overland 66213
Phone: (913) 897-8400

The School of Medicine—Wichita
1010 N. Kansas, Wichita 67214-3199
Phone: (316) 293-2600
Prog. Accred: Public Health

University of Kansas Medical Center
3901 Rainbow Blvd., Kansas City 66160
Phone: (913) 588-1401
Prog. Accred: Allied Health (cytotechnology, diagnostic medical sonography, medicine, occupational therapy, respiratory therapy), Clinical Lab Scientist, Dietetics (internship), Nuclear Medicine Technology, Nurse (Midwifery), Nurse Anesthesia Education, Nursing Education, Physical Therapy

University of Saint Mary
4100 South 4th St., Leavenworth 66048
Type: Private, Roman Catholic Church, four-year
Degrees: A, B, M *Enroll:* 567
URL: http://www.smcks.edu
Phone: (913) 758-6102 *Calendar:* Sem. plan
Inst. Accred.: NCA-HLC (1928/2005)
Prog. Accred.: Nursing Education, Teacher Education (NCATE)

Washburn University
17th and College St.s, Topeka 66621
Type: Public, state/local, four-year
Degrees: A, B, M, D *Enroll:* 5,750
URL: http://www.washburn.edu
Phone: (785) 670-1010 *Calendar:* Sem. plan
Inst. Accred.: NCA-HLC (1913/2008)
Prog. Accred.: Allied Health (diagnostic medical sonography, respiratory therapy), Art, Business (AACSB), Graduate Social Work, Law, Music, Nursing Education, Physical Therapy Assisting, Radiation Therapy, Radiography, Social Work, Teacher Education (NCATE)

Wichita Area Technical College
301 South Grove St., Wichita 67211
Type: Private, proprietary, two-year
Degrees: A *Enroll:* 558
URL: http://www.watc.edu
Phone: (316) 677-9400 *Calendar:* Sem. plan
Inst. Accred.: COE (1995/2007), NCA-HLC (2006)
Prog. Accred.: Allied Health (medical assisting (AMA), surgical technology), Clinical Lab Technology, Practical Nursing

Airport Campus
2021 South Eisenhower St., Wichita 67209-2848
Phone: (316) 973-9550

Central Campus
324 North Emporia St., Wichita 67202-2512
Phone: (316) 973-4340
Prog. Accred: Dentistry (dental assisting)

Dunbar Campus
923 Cleveland St., Wichita 67214-3495
Phone: (316) 973-3150

Schweiter Camous
1400 George Washington Dr., Wichita 67211
Phone: (316) 973-0950

Seneca Campus
4141 North Seneca St., Wichita 67204-3103
Phone: (316) 973-1200

Wichita State University
1845 Fairmont St., Wichita 67260-0001
Type: Public, state, four-year
System: Kansas Board of Regents
Degrees: A, B, M, P, D *Enroll:* 10,451
URL: http://www.wichita.edu
Phone: (800) 362-2594 *Calendar:* Sem. plan
Inst. Accred.: NCA-HLC (1927/2007)
Prog. Accred.: Accounting, Allied Health (audiology, speech-language pathology), Business (AACSB), Clinical Lab Scientist, Clinical Psychology, Dance, Dentistry (dental hygiene), Engineering (aerospace, computer, electrical, industrial, manufacturing, mechanical), Graduate Social Work, Music, Nursing Education, Physical Therapy, Physician Assistant, Psychology Internship, Public Administration, Social Work, Teacher Education (NCATE)

KENTUCKY

Alice Lloyd College
100 Purpose Rd., Pippa Passes 41844-8884
Type: Private, independent, four-year
Degrees: B *Enroll:* 621
URL: http://www.alc.edu
Phone: (606) 368-2101 *Calendar:* Sem. plan
Inst. Accred.: SACS (1952/2008)

Asbury College
One Macklem Dr., Wilmore 40390-1198
Type: Private, independent, four-year
Degrees: B, M *Enroll:* 1,191
URL: http://www.asbury.edu
Phone: (859) 858-3511 *Calendar:* Sem. plan
Inst. Accred.: SACS (1940/1999)
Prog. Accred.: Music, Social Work, Teacher Education (NCATE)

Asbury Theological Seminary
204 North Lexington Ave., Wilmore 40390-1199
Type: Private, interdenominational, four-year
Degrees: M, D *Enroll:* 1,095
URL: http://www.asburyseminary.edu
Phone: (859) 858-3581 *Calendar:* 4-1-4 plan
Inst. Accred.: ATS (1960/2005), SACS (1984/2005)

Florida Campus
8401 Velencia College Ln., Orlando, FL 32825
Phone: (407) 482-7564

Ashland Community and Technical College
1400 College Dr., Ashland 41101-3683
Type: Public, state, two-year
System: Ashland Community and Technical College District
Degrees: A *Enroll:* 2,561
URL: http://www.ashland.kctcs.edu
Phone: (606) 326-2000 *Calendar:* Sem. plan
Inst. Accred.: SACS (2003)
Prog. Accred.: Allied Health (surgical technology), Nursing

Roberts Drive Campus
4818 Roberts Dr., Ashland 41102-9046
Phone: (606) 928-6427

Beckfield College
16 Spiral Dr., Florence 41042
Type: Private, proprietary, four-year
Degrees: A, B *Enroll:* 382
URL: http://www.beckfield.edu
Phone: (859) 371-9393 *Calendar:* Qtr. plan
Inst. Accred.: ACICS (1993/2008)

Bellarmine University
2001 Newburg Rd., Louisville 40205-0671
Type: Private, Roman Catholic Church, four-year
Degrees: A, B, M, D *Enroll:* 2,317
URL: http://www.bellarmine.edu
Phone: (502) 452-8000 *Calendar:* Sem. plan
Inst. Accred.: SACS (1956/2008)
Prog. Accred.: Allied Health (respiratory therapy), Business (AACSB), Clinical Lab Scientist, Nursing Education, Physical Therapy, Teacher Education (NCATE)

Berea College
1001 Chestnut St., Berea 40404
Type: Private, independent, four-year
Degrees: B *Enroll:* 1,555
URL: http://www.berea.edu
Phone: (859) 985-3000 *Calendar:* 4-1-4 plan
Inst. Accred.: SACS (1926/2006)
Prog. Accred.: Nursing Education, Teacher Education (NCATE)

Big Sandy Community and Technical College
One Bert T. Combs Dr., Prestonsburg 41653
Type: Public, state, two-year
System: Big Sandy Community and Technical College District
Degrees: A *Enroll:* 2,897
URL: http://www.bigsandy.kctcs.edu
Phone: (606) 886-3863 *Calendar:* Sem. plan
Inst. Accred.: SACS (2003)
Prog. Accred.: Allied Health (respiratory therapy), Dentistry (dental hygiene)

Mayo Campus
513 Third St., Paintsville 41240
Phone: (606) 789-5321

Pikeville Campus
120 South River Fill Dr., Pikeville 41501
Phone: (606) 218-2060

Bluegrass Community and Technical College
470 Cooper Dr., Lexington 40506-0235
Type: Public, state/local, two-year
System: Bluegrass Community and Technical College District
Degrees: A *Enroll:* 6,089
URL: http://www.bluegrass.kctcs.edu
Phone: (859) 246-6200 *Calendar:* Sem. plan
Inst. Accred.: SACS (2005)
Prog. Accred.: Allied Health (respiratory therapy), Dentistry (dental hygiene, dental laboratory technology), Nursing

Danville Campus
59 Corporate Dr., Danville 40422
Phone: (859) 239-7030

Lawrenceburg Campus
1500 Bypass North, US 127, Lawrenceburg 40342
Phone: (502) 839-8488

Leestown Campus
164 Opportunity Way, Lexington 40511-2623
Phone: (859) 246-6200
Prog. Accred: Allied Health (medical assisting (AMA), surgical technology), Clinical Lab Technology, Dentistry (dental assisting), Radiography

Bowling Green Technical College
1845 Loop Dr., Bowling Green 42101-9202
Type: Public, state, two-year
System: Bowling Green Community and Technical College District
Degrees: A
URL: http://www.bowlinggreen.kctcs.edu
Phone: (270) 901-1000 *Calendar:* Sem. plan
Inst. Accred.: COE (1972/2004), SACS (2008)
Prog. Accred.: Allied Health (diagnostic medical sonography, surgical technology), Culinary Education, Dentistry (dental assisting), Radiography

Glasgow Health Campus
129 State St., Glasgow 42141
Phone: (502) 651-5673

Glasgow Technology Campus
500 Hilltopper Way, Glasgow 42141
Phone: (270) 659-6900

Kentucky Advanced Technology Institute
1127 Morgantown Rd., Bowling Green 42101-9202
Phone: (270) 746-7807

Brescia University
717 Frederica St., Owensboro 42301-3023
Type: Private, Roman Catholic Church, four-year
Degrees: A, B, M *Enroll:* 504
URL: http://www.brescia.edu
Phone: (270) 685-3131 *Calendar:* Sem. plan
Inst. Accred.: SACS (1957/1999)
Prog. Accred.: Social Work

Campbellsville University
1 University Dr., Campbellsville 42718
Type: Private, Southern Baptist Church, four-year
Degrees: A, B, M *Enroll:* 1,673
URL: http://www.campbellsville.edu
Phone: (270) 789-5000 *Calendar:* Sem. plan
Inst. Accred.: SACS (1963/2004)
Prog. Accred.: Music, Social Work, Teacher Education (NCATE)

Louisville Campus
2300 Greene Way, Louisville 40220
Phone: (502) 753-0264

Centre College
600 West Walnut St., Danville 40422-1394
Type: Private, independent, four-year
Degrees: B *Enroll:* 1,128
URL: http://www.centre.edu
Phone: (859) 238-5200 *Calendar:* 4-1-4 plan
Inst. Accred.: SACS (1904/2006)

Clear Creek Baptist Bible College
300 Clear Creek Rd., Pineville 40977-9754
Type: Private, Kentucky Baptist Convention, four-year
Degrees: A, B *Enroll:* 177
URL: http://www.ccbbc.edu
Phone: (606) 337-3196 *Calendar:* Sem. plan
Inst. Accred.: ABHE (1986/2007), SACS (1999/2005)

Daymar College
3361 Buckland Square, Owensboro 42301
Type: Private, proprietary, two-year
Degrees: A *Enroll:* 243
URL: http://www.daymarcollege.edu
Phone: (270) 926-4040 *Calendar:* Qtr. plan
Inst. Accred.: ACICS (1969/2004)

Albany Campus
107 East Water St., Albany 42602
Phone: (606) 387-4600

Lexington Electronics Institute
Clays Mill Shopping Center, 3340 Holwyn Rd., Lexington 40503-9938
Phone: (606) 223-9608

Louisville Campus
4400 Breakenridge Ln., Ste. 415, Louisville 40219
Phone: (502) 495-1040

Newport Campus
76 Carothers Rd., Newport 41071
Phone: (859) 291-0800

Paducah Campus
509 South 30th St., Paducah 42002-4181
Phone: (270) 444-9676

Scottsville Campus
311 North Third St., Scottsville 42164
Phone: (270) 926-1188

Eastern Kentucky University
521 Lancaster Ave., Richmond 40475-3102
Type: Public, state, four-year
System: Kentucky Council on Postsecondary Education
Degrees: A, B, M, P, D *Enroll:* 13,337
URL: http://www.eku.edu
Phone: (859) 622-1000 *Calendar:* Sem. plan
Inst. Accred.: SACS (1928/2007)
Prog. Accred.: Allied Health (EMT-paramedic, medical assisting (AMA), occupational therapy, speech-language pathology), Business (AACSB), Clinical Lab Scientist, Clinical Lab Technology, Computer Science (ABET-CAC), Construction Education, Counseling, Dietetics (didactic), Dietetics (internship), Electronic Technology, Environmental Health, Industrial Technology, Music, Nursing, Nursing Education, Public Administration, Recreation and Leisure Services, Social Work, Teacher Education (NCATE)

Elizabethtown Community and Technical College
600 College St. Rd., Elizabethtown 42701
Type: Public, state, two-year
System: Elizabethtown Community and Technical College District
Degrees: A *Enroll:* 3,219
URL: http://www.elizabethtown.kctcs.edu
Phone: (270) 769-2371 *Calendar:* Sem. plan
Inst. Accred.: SACS (2004)
Prog. Accred.: Dentistry (dental hygiene), Nursing, Radiography

Frontier School of Midwifery and Family Nursing
PO Box 528, Hyden 41749-0528
Type: Private, independent, four-year
Degrees: M, D *Enroll:* 212
URL: http://www.midwives.org
Phone: (606) 672-2312
Inst. Accred.: SACS (2004)
Prog. Accred.: Nurse (Midwifery), Nursing

Galen College of Nursing
1031 Zorn Ave., Louisville 40207
Type: Private, proprietary, four-year
Degrees: A, B
URL: http://www.galencollege.edu
Phone: (502) 582-2305 *Calendar:* Sem. plan
Inst. Accred.: COE (1983/2004)

Cincinnati Campus
100 E-Business Way, Ste. 200, Cincinnati, OH 45241
Phone: (513) 475-3600

San Antonio Campus
4440 Piedras Dr. South, Ste. 200, San Antonio, TX 78228
Phone: (210) 733-3056

Tampa Bay Campus
9549 Koger Blvd., Gadsden Bldg., Ste. 100, St. Petersburg, FL 33702
Phone: (727) 577-1497

Gateway Community and Technical College
1025 Amsterdam Rd., Park Hills 41011-2031
Type: Public, state, two-year
System: Gateway Community and Technical College District
Degrees: A
URL: http://www.gateway.kctcs.edu
Phone: (859) 441-4500 *Calendar:* Sem. plan
Inst. Accred.: COE (1973/2006), SACS (2007)

Boone Campus
10500 Sam Neace Dr., Florence 41042-8969
Phone: (859) 442-1162

Edgewood Campus
790 Thomas More Pkwy., Edgewood 41017
Phone: (606) 341-5200

Highland Heights Campus
90 Campbell Dr., Highland Heights 41076
Phone: (859) 441-2010

Georgetown College
400 East College St., Georgetown 40324
Type: Private, Kentucky Baptist Convention, four-year
Degrees: B, M *Enroll:* 1,583
URL: http://www.georgetowncollege.edu
Phone: (502) 863-8000 *Calendar:* Sem. plan
Inst. Accred.: SACS (1919/2002)

Hazard Community and Technical College
One Community College Dr., Hazard 41701
Type: Public, state, two-year
System: Hazard Community & Technical College District
Degrees: A *Enroll:* 2,523
URL: http://www.hazard.kctcs.edu
Phone: (606) 436-5721 *Calendar:* Sem. plan
Inst. Accred.: SACS (2002/2007)
Prog. Accred.: Clinical Lab Technology, Physical Therapy Assisting, Radiography

Knott County Area Technology Center
PO Box 7498, Hindman 41822
Phone: (606) 785-4114

Lees College Campus
601 Jefferson Ave., Jackson 41339
Phone: (606) 666-7521

Leslie County Area Technology Center
PO Box 1870, Hyden 41749
Phone: (606) 672-6800

Letcher County Area Technology Center
185 Circle Dr., Whitesburg 41858
Phone: (606) 633-5053

Technical Campus
101 Vo-Tech Dr., Hazard 41701
Phone: (606) 435-6101

Henderson Community College
2660 South Green St., Henderson 42420
Type: Public, state, two-year
System: Henderson Community and Technical College District
Degrees: A *Enroll:* 1,071
URL: http://www.hencc.kctcs.edu
Phone: (502) 827-1867 *Calendar:* Sem. plan
Inst. Accred.: SACS (1971/2001)
Prog. Accred.: Allied Health (medical assisting (AMA)), Clinical Lab Technology, Dentistry (dental hygiene), Nursing

Hopkinsville Community College
PO Box 2100, Hopkinsville 42241-2100
Type: Public, state, two-year
System: Hopkinsville Community College District
Degrees: A *Enroll:* 1,965
URL: http://www.hopcc.kctcs.edu
Phone: (270) 886-3921 *Calendar:* Sem. plan
Inst. Accred.: SACS (1971/2001)
Prog. Accred.: Nursing

Jefferson Community and Technical College
109 East Broadway, Louisville 40202-2005
Type: Public, state, two-year
System: Jefferson Community and Technical College District
Degrees: A *Enroll:* 7,939
URL: http://www.jefferson.kctcs.edu
Phone: (502) 213-5333 *Calendar:* Sem. plan
Inst. Accred.: SACS (2005)
Prog. Accred.: Allied Health (occupational therapy assisting, respiratory therapy), Culinary Education, Nuclear Medicine Technology, Nursing, Physical Therapy Assisting, Radiography

Technical Campus
727 West Chestnut St., Louisville 40203-2071
Phone: (502) 213-4200
Prog. Accred: Allied Health (medical assisting (AMA), surgical technology)

Kentucky Christian University
100 Academic Pkwy., Grayson 41143-2205
Type: Private, Chiristian Churches and Churches of Christ, four-year
Degrees: A, B, M *Enroll:* 572
URL: http://www.kcu.edu
Phone: (606) 474-3000 *Calendar:* Sem. plan
Inst. Accred.: SACS (1984/1999)
Prog. Accred.: Nursing Education, Social Work

Kentucky Mountain Bible College
PO Box 10, Vancleve 41385-0010
Type: Private, Kentucky Mountain Holiness Association, four-year
Degrees: A, B *Enroll:* 66
URL: http://www.kmbc.edu
Phone: (606) 666-5000 *Calendar:* Sem. plan
Inst. Accred.: ABHE (1994/1999)

Kentucky State University
400 East Main St., Frankfort 40601
Type: Public, state, four-year
System: Kentucky Council on Postsecondary Education
Degrees: A, B, M *Enroll:* 1,954
URL: http://www.kysu.edu
Phone: (502) 227-6000 *Calendar:* Sem. plan
Inst. Accred.: SACS (1939/1999)
Prog. Accred.: Business (ACBSP), Music, Nursing, Public Administration, Social Work, Teacher Education (NCATE)

Kentucky Wesleyan College
3000 Frederica St., Owensboro 42301
Type: Private, United Methodist Church, four-year
Degrees: A, B *Enroll:* 732
URL: http://www.kwc.edu
Phone: (270) 926-3111 *Calendar:* Sem. plan
Inst. Accred.: SACS (1948/2008)

Lexington Theological Seminary
631 South Limestone St., Lexington 40508
Type: Private, Christian Church (Disciples of Christ), four-year
Degrees: M, D *Enroll:* 72
URL: http://www.lextheo.edu
Phone: (859) 252-0361 *Calendar:* Sem. plan
Inst. Accred.: ATS (1938/2006), SACS (1984/2006)

Lindsey Wilson College
210 Lindsey Wilson St., Columbia 42728
Type: Private, Louisville Conference of the Methodist Church, four-year
Degrees: A, B, M *Enroll:* 1,789
URL: http://www.lindsey.edu
Phone: (270) 384-2126 *Calendar:* Sem. plan
Inst. Accred.: SACS (1951/2003)
Prog. Accred.: Counseling

Louisville Presbyterian Theological Seminary
1044 Alta Vista Rd., Louisville 40205
Type: Private, Presbyterian Church (USA), four-year
Degrees: M, D *Enroll:* 141
URL: http://www.lpts.edu
Phone: (502) 895-3411 *Calendar:* 4-1-4 plan
Inst. Accred.: ATS (1938/1999), SACS (1973/1999)
Prog. Accred.: Marriage and Family Therapy

Louisville Technical Institute
3901 Atkinson Square Dr., Louisville 40218
Type: Private, proprietary, four-year
System: Sullivan Colleges System
Degrees: A, B *Enroll:* 516
URL: http://www.louisvilletech.edu
Phone: (502) 456-6509 *Calendar:* Qtr. plan
Inst. Accred.: ACICS (2000/2008)

Madisonville Community College
2000 College Dr., Madisonville 42431
Type: Public, state, two-year
System: Madisonville Community and Technical College District
Degrees: A *Enroll:* 2,237
URL: http://www.madcc.kctcs.edu
Phone: (270) 821-2250 *Calendar:* Sem. plan
Inst. Accred.: SACS (2001/2007)
Prog. Accred.: Nursing, Physical Therapy Assisting

Health Campus
750 North Laffoon St., Madisonville 42431
Phone: (270) 824-7552
Prog. Accred: Allied Health (occupational therapy assisting, respiratory therapy, surgeon assisting, surgical technology), Radiography

Technical Campus
150 School Ave., Madisonville 42431
Phone: (270) 824-7544

Maysville Community and Technical College
1755 US 68, Maysville 41056
Type: Public, state, two-year
System: Maysville Community and Technical College District
Degrees: A *Enroll:* 1,833
URL: http://www.maycc.kctcs.edu
Phone: (606) 759-7141 *Calendar:* Sem. plan
Inst. Accred.: SACS (2004)

Eastern Kentucky Campus
319 Webster Ave., Cynthiana 41031
Phone: (859) 234-8626

Rowan Campus
609 Viking Dr., Morehead 40351
Phone: (606) 783-1538
Prog. Accred: Allied Health (medical assisting (AMA), respiratory therapy, surgical technology)

Mid-Continent University
99 Powell Rd. East, Mayfield 42066
Type: Private, Baptist Church, four-year
Degrees: B *Enroll:* 860
URL: http://www.midcontinent.edu
Phone: (270) 247-8521 *Calendar:* Sem. plan
Inst. Accred.: SACS (1987/2002)

Midway College
512 East Stephens St., Midway 40347-1120
Type: Private, Disciples of Christ Church, four-year
Degrees: A, B, M *Enroll:* 1,034
URL: http://www.midway.edu
Phone: (859) 846-4421 *Calendar:* Sem. plan
Inst. Accred.: SACS (1949/2005)
Prog. Accred.: Nursing

Morehead State University
150 University Blvd., Morehead 40351-1689
Type: Public, state, four-year
System: Kentucky Council on Postsecondary Education
Degrees: A, B, M, P *Enroll:* 7,308
URL: http://www.morehead-st.edu
Phone: (606) 783-2221 *Calendar:* Sem. plan
Inst. Accred.: SACS (1930/2000)
Prog. Accred.: Allied Health (diagnostic medical sonography), Business (AACSB), Industrial Technology, Music, Nursing, Nursing Education, Phlebotomy, Radiography, Social Work, Teacher Education (NCATE), Veterinary Technology

Murray State University
PO Box 9, Murray 42071
Type: Public, state, four-year
System: Kentucky Council on Postsecondary Education
Degrees: A, B, M, P *Enroll:* 8,683
URL: http://www.murraystate.edu
Phone: (270) 762-3011 *Calendar:* Sem. plan
Inst. Accred.: SACS (1928/2004)
Prog. Accred.: Allied Health (speech-language pathology), Applied Science (occupational health & safety), Art, Business (AACSB), Engineering (engineering physics/science), Engineering Technology (civil/construction), Journalism, Music, Nurse Anesthesia Education, Nursing Education, Social Work, Teacher Education (NCATE), Veterinary Technology

Northern Kentucky University
Nunn Dr., Highland Heights 41099
Type: Public, state, four-year
System: Kentucky Council on Postsecondary Education
Degrees: A, B, M, D *Enroll:* 11,385
URL: http://www.nku.edu
Phone: (859) 578-5100 *Calendar:* Sem. plan
Inst. Accred.: SACS (1973/1998)
Prog. Accred.: Allied Health (respiratory therapy), Business (AACSB), Construction Education, Engineering Technology (electrical, manufacturing), Law, Music, Nursing, Public Administration, Radiography, Social Work, Teacher Education (NCATE)

Owensboro Community and Technical College
4800 New Hartford Rd., Owensboro 42303
Type: Public, state/local, two-year
System: Owensboro Community and Technical College District
Degrees: A *Enroll:* 2,778
URL: http://www.owensboro.kctcs.edu
Phone: (270) 686-4400 *Calendar:* Sem. plan
Inst. Accred.: SACS (2003/2006)
Prog. Accred.: Allied Health (surgical technology), Radiography

Downtown Campus
1501 Frederica St., Owensboro 42301
Phone: (270) 686-4400

Southeastern Campus
1901 Southeastern Pkwy., Owensboro 42303-1677
Phone: (270) 686-4800

Pikeville College
147 Sycamore St., Pikeville 41501
Type: Private, United Presbyterian Church, four-year
Degrees: A, B, D *Enroll:* 1,089
URL: http://www.pc.edu
Phone: (606) 218-5250 *Calendar:* Sem. plan
Inst. Accred.: SACS (1931/2002)
Prog. Accred.: Clinical Lab Scientist, Osteopathy

Saint Catharine College
2735 Bardstown Rd., St. Catharine 40061
Type: Private, Roman Catholic Church, four-year
Degrees: A, B *Enroll:* 584
URL: http://www.sccky.edu
Phone: (859) 336-5082 *Calendar:* Sem. plan
Inst. Accred.: SACS (1957/2008)
Prog. Accred.: Allied Health (diagnostic medical sonography, surgical technology)

Somerset Community College
808 Monticello St., Somerset 42501
Type: Public, state, two-year
System: Somerset Community and Technical College District
Degrees: A *Enroll:* 3,909
URL: http://www.somcc.kctcs.edu
Phone: (606) 679-8501 *Calendar:* Sem. plan
Inst. Accred.: SACS (2003)
Prog. Accred.: Allied Health (surgical technology), Clinical Lab Technology, Nursing, Physical Therapy Assisting, Radiography

Casey County Area Technology Center
3609 North U.S. 127, Liberty 42539
Phone: (606) 787-4732

Clinton County Area Technology Center
1001 West Hwy. 90, Albany 42602
Phone: (606) 387.3236

Green County Area Technology Center
PO Box 167, Carlisle Ave., Greensburg 42743
Phone: (502) 932-4263

Laurel South Campus
235 South Laurel Rd., London 40744
Phone: (606) 864-7311
Prog. Accred: Allied Health (respiratory therapy)

South Campus
230 Airport Rd., Somerset 42501-3043
Phone: (606) 677-4049

Southeast Kentucky Community and Technical College
700 College Rd., Cumberland 40823-1099
Type: Public, state, two-year
System: Southeast Kentucky Community and Technical College District
Degrees: A *Enroll:* 2,719
URL: http://www.secc.kctcs.edu
Phone: (606) 589-2145 *Calendar:* Sem. plan
Inst. Accred.: SACS (2001/2007)
Prog. Accred.: Nursing, Physical Therapy Assisting, Practical Nursing

Harlan Campus
164 Ballpark Rd., Harlan 40831
Phone: (606) 573-1506

Middlesboro Campus
1305 Chichester Ave., Middlesboro 40965-2265
Phone: (606) 242-2145

Pineville Campus
US 25E, PO Box 187, Pineville 40977
Phone: (606) 337-3106
Prog. Accred: Allied Health (respiratory therapy, surgical technology), Clinical Lab Technology, Radiography

The Southern Baptist Theological Seminary
2825 Lexington Rd., Louisville 40280-2899
Type: Private, Southern Baptist Convention, four-year
Degrees: A, B, M, D *Enroll:* 2,681
URL: http://www.sbts.edu
Phone: (502) 897-4011 *Calendar:* Sem. plan
Inst. Accred.: ATS (1938/2002), SACS (1968/2003)
Prog. Accred.: Music

Spalding University
851 South Fourth St., Louisville 40203
Type: Private, Roman Catholic Church, four-year
Degrees: A, B, M, P, D *Enroll:* 1,291
URL: http://www.spalding.edu
Phone: (502) 585-9911 *Calendar:* Sem. plan
Inst. Accred.: SACS (1938/2007)
Prog. Accred.: Allied Health (occupational therapy), Clinical Psychology, Graduate Social Work, Nursing Education, Social Work, Teacher Education (NCATE)

Spencerian College
4627 Dixie Hwy., Louisville 40216
Type: Private, independent, two-year
System: Sullivan Colleges System
Degrees: A *Enroll:* 1,007
URL: http://www.spencerian.edu
Phone: (502) 447-1000 *Calendar:* Qtr. plan
Inst. Accred.: ACICS (1954/2008)
Prog. Accred.: Allied Health (cardiovascular technology, medical assisting (AMA), surgical technology), Medical Assisting (ABHES), Radiography

Lexington Campus
1575 Winchester Rd., Lexington 40505
Phone: (859) 223-9608
Prog. Accred: Allied Health (medical assisting (AMA))

Sullivan University
3101 Bardstown Rd., Louisville 40205
Type: Private, proprietary, four-year
System: Sullivan Colleges System
Degrees: A, B, M, D *Enroll:* 3,722
URL: http://www.sullivan.edu
Phone: (502) 456-6504 *Calendar:* Qtr. plan
Inst. Accred.: SACS (1979/2005)
Prog. Accred.: Culinary Education, Pharmacy

Fort Knox Campus
PO Box 998, Fort Knox 40121-0998
Phone: (502) 942-8500

Lexington Campus
2355 Harrodsburg Rd., Lexington 40504
Phone: (859) 276-4357
Prog. Accred: Allied Health (medical assisting (AMA)), Culinary Education

Thomas More College
333 Thomas More Pkwy., Crestview Hills 41017-3495
Type: Private, Roman Catholic Church, four-year
Degrees: A, B, M *Enroll:* 1,303
URL: http://www.thomasmore.edu
Phone: (859) 341-5800 *Calendar:* Sem. plan
Inst. Accred.: SACS (1959/2002)
Prog. Accred.: Nursing

Transylvania University
300 North Broadway, Lexington 40508-1797
Type: Private, Christian Church/Disciples of Christ, four-year
Degrees: B *Enroll:* 1,141
URL: http://www.transy.edu
Phone: (859) 233-8300 *Calendar:* 4-1-4 plan
Inst. Accred.: SACS (1915/2002)
Prog. Accred.: Teacher Education (NCATE)

Union College
310 College St., Barbourville 40906
Type: Private, United Methodist Church, four-year
Degrees: A, B, M *Enroll:* 936
URL: http://www.unionky.edu
Phone: (606) 546-4151 *Calendar:* Sem. plan
Inst. Accred.: SACS (1932/2005)

University of Kentucky
Lexington 40506
Type: Public, state, four-year
System: University of Kentucky
Degrees: A, B, M, P, D *Enroll:* 23,072
URL: http://www.uky.edu
Phone: (859) 257-9000 *Calendar:* Sem. plan
Inst. Accred.: SACS (1915/2002)
Prog. Accred.: Accounting, Allied Health (health services administration, medicine, speech-language pathology), Business (AACSB), Clinical Lab Scientist, Clinical Pastoral Education (ACPEI), Clinical Psychology, Computer Science (ABET-CAC), Counseling Psychology, Dentistry (dentistry, general practice residency, oral and maxillofacial surgery, orthodontic and dentofacial orthopedics, pediatric dentistry, periodontics), Dietetics (coordinated), Dietetics (didactic), Dietetics (internship), Engineering (agricultural, chemical, civil, electrical, materials, mechanical, mining), Family & Consumer Science, Forestry, Graduate Social Work, Interior Design, Journalism, Landscape Architecture, Law, Librarianship, Marriage and Family Therapy, Music, Nursing Education, Pharmacy, Physical Therapy, Physician Assistant, Public Administration, Public Health, Radiation Therapy, Rehabilitation Counseling, School Psychology, Social Work, Teacher Education (NCATE)

University of Louisville
2301 South Third St., Louisville 40292-0001
Type: Public, state, four-year
System: Kentucky Council on Postsecondary Education
Degrees: A, B, M, P, D *Enroll:* 17,065
URL: http://www.louisville.edu
Phone: (502) 852-5555 *Calendar:* Sem. plan
Inst. Accred.: SACS (1915/2007)
Prog. Accred.: Accounting, Allied Health (audiology, medicine, speech-language pathology), Business (AACSB), Clinical Lab Scientist, Clinical Psychology, Computer Science (ABET-CAC), Counseling Psychology, Dentistry (advanced education in general dentistry, combined prosthodontics, dental hygiene, dentistry, endodontics, general dentistry, general practice residency, oral and maxillofacial surgery, orthodontic and dentofacial orthopedics, periodontics, prosthodontics), Engineering (chemical, civil, computer, electrical, industrial, mechanical), Graduate Social Work, Interior Architecture, Law, Marriage and Family Therapy, Music, Nursing Education, Psychology Internship, Public Administration, Radiation Therapy, Radiography, Teacher Education (NCATE)

University of the Cumberlands
6191 College Station Dr., Williamsburg 40769
Type: Private, Kentucky Baptist (SBC), four-year
Degrees: A, B, M *Enroll:* 1,591
URL: http://www.cumberlandcollege.edu
Phone: (606) 549-2200 *Calendar:* Sem. plan
Inst. Accred.: SACS (1964/2006)

West Kentucky Community and Technical College
PO Box 7380, Paducah 42002-7380
Type: Public, state, two-year
System: West Kentucky Community and Technical College District
Degrees: A *Enroll:* 3,971
URL: http://www.westkentucky.kctcs.edu
Phone: (270) 554-9200 *Calendar:* Sem. plan
Inst. Accred.: SACS (2003)
Prog. Accred.: Allied Health (diagnostic medical sonography, medical assisting (AMA), respiratory therapy), Nursing, Physical Therapy Assisting, Radiography

Paducah Area Technology Center
2400 Adams St., Paducah 42001
Phone: (502) 443-6592

Western Kentucky University
1906 College Heights Blvd., Bowling Green 42101-1000
Type: Public, state, four-year
System: Kentucky Council on Postsecondary Education
Degrees: A, B, M, P, D *Enroll:* 15,714
URL: http://www.wku.edu
Phone: (270) 745-0111 *Calendar:* Sem. plan
Inst. Accred.: SACS (1926/2005)
Prog. Accred.: Allied Health (speech-language pathology), Art, Business (AACSB), Computer Science (ABET-CAC), Construction Education, Counseling, Dentistry (dental hygiene), Dietetics (didactic), Engineering Technology (civil/construction, electrical, mechanical), Graduate Social Work, Industrial Technology, Journalism, Music, Nursing, Nursing Education, Public Health, Recreation and Leisure Services, Social Work, Teacher Education (NCATE)

LOUISIANA

Baton Rouge Community College
5310 Florida Blvd., Baton Rouge 70806
Type: Public, state, two-year
System: Louisiana Community and Technical College System
Degrees: A *Enroll:* 4,926
URL: http://www.brcc.cc.la.us
Phone: (225) 216-8000 *Calendar:* Sem. plan
Inst. Accred.: SACS (2004)
Prog. Accred.: Business (ACBSP)

Baton Rouge School of Computers
10425 Plaza Americana Dr., Baton Rouge 70816
Type: Private, proprietary, two-year
Degrees: A *Enroll:* 62
URL: http://www.brsc.net
Phone: (225) 923-2525
Inst. Accred.: ACCSCT (1982/2007)

Blue Cliff College
803 Barrow St., Houma 70360
Type: Private, proprietary, two-year
Degrees: A
URL: http://www.bluecliffcollege.com
Phone: (985) 601-4000
Inst. Accred.: ACCSCT (2005)

Blue Cliff College
3501 Severn Ave., Ste. 20, Metairie 70002
Type: Private, proprietary, two-year
Degrees: A
URL: http://www.bluecliffcollege.com
Phone: (504) 456-3141 *Calendar:* Qtr. plan
Inst. Accred.: ACCSCT (1998/2003, Probation)

Gulfport Campus
2200 25th Ave., Gulfport, MS 39501-4520
Phone: (228) 896-9727

Lafayette Campus
100 Asma Blvd., Ste. 350, Lafayette 70508
Phone: (337) 269-0620

Shreveport Campus
200 North Thomas Dr., Ste. A, Shreveport 71107
Phone: (318) 425-7941

White River School of Massage
2503 Hiram Davis Place, Fayetteville, AR 72703
Phone: (479) 521-2550

Bossier Parish Community College
6220 East Texas St., Bossier City 71111
Type: Public, state/local, two-year
System: Louisiana Community and Technical College System
Degrees: A *Enroll:* 3,350
URL: http://www.bpcc.edu
Phone: (318) 678-6000 *Calendar:* Sem. plan
Inst. Accred.: SACS (1983/2008)
Prog. Accred.: Allied Health (EMT-paramedic, medical assisting (AMA), respiratory therapy, surgical technology), Culinary Education, Phlebotomy, Physical Therapy Assisting

Camelot College
2618 Wooddale Blvd., Ste. A, Baton Rouge 70805
Type: Private, proprietary, two-year
Degrees: A *Enroll:* 336
URL: http://www.camelotcollege.com
Phone: (225) 928-3005
Inst. Accred.: ACICS (1991/2003)

Cameron College
2740 Canal St., New Orleans 70119
Type: Private, proprietary, two-year
Degrees: A *Enroll:* 217
URL: http://www.cameroncollege.com
Phone: (504) 821-5881
Inst. Accred.: COE (1982/2002)

Career Technical College
2319 Louisville Ave., Monroe 71201
Type: Private, proprietary, two-year
System: Delta Education Corporation
Degrees: A
URL: http://www.careertc.com
Phone: (318) 323-2889
Inst. Accred.: COE (1989/2006)
Prog. Accred.: Allied Health (medical assisting (AMA), surgical technology)

Shreveport Campus
1227 Shreveport-Barksdale Hwy., Shreveport 71005-2405
Phone: (877) 266-7250

Centenary College of Louisiana
PO Box 41188, Shreveport 71134-1188
Type: Private, United Methodist Church, four-year
Degrees: B, M *Enroll:* 952
URL: http://www.centenary.edu
Phone: (318) 869-5011 *Calendar:* Sem. plan
Inst. Accred.: SACS (1925/2008)
Prog. Accred.: Music, Teacher Education (NCATE)

Delgado Community College
615 City Park Ave., New Orleans 70119
Type: Public, state/local, two-year
System: Louisiana Community and Technical College System
Degrees: A *Enroll:* 10,499
URL: http://www.dcc.edu
Phone: (504) 361-6609 *Calendar:* Sem. plan
Inst. Accred.: SACS (1971/2008)
Prog. Accred.: Allied Health (EMT-paramedic, diagnostic medical sonography, occupational therapy assisting, respiratory therapy, surgical technology), Business (ACBSP), Clinical Lab Technology, Construction Technology, Culinary Education, Design Technology, Dietetic Technician, Electronic Technology, Engineering Technology (electromechanical), Funeral Service Education (Mortuary Science), Health Technology, Nuclear Medicine Technology, Nursing, Phlebotomy, Physical Therapy Assisting, Radiation Therapy, Radiography, Veterinary Technology

West Bank Campus
2600 General Meyer Ave., New Orleans 70114-3095
Phone: (504) 361-6402

Delta College of Arts and Technology
7380 Exchange Place, Baton Rouge 70806-3851
Type: Private, proprietary, two-year
Degrees: A *Enroll:* 380
URL: http://www.deltacollege.com
Phone: (225) 928-7770
Inst. Accred.: ACCSCT (1987/2007)

Lafayette Campus
105 Patriot Ave., Lafayette 70508
Phone: (334) 988-5455

Delta School of Business and Technology
517 Broad St., Lake Charles 70601
Type: Private, proprietary, two-year
Degrees: A *Enroll:* 362
URL: http://www.deltatech.edu
Phone: (318) 439-5765 *Calendar:* Qtr. plan
Inst. Accred.: ACICS (1976/2008)

Dillard University
2601 Gentilly Blvd., New Orleans 70122
Type: Private, United Methodist Church, four-year
Degrees: B *Enroll:* 1,881
URL: http://www.dillard.edu
Phone: (504) 283-8822 *Calendar:* Sem. plan
Inst. Accred.: SACS (1938/1999, Probation)
Prog. Accred.: Nursing, Teacher Education (NCATE)

Elaine P. Nunez Community College
3710 Paris Rd., Chalmette 70043
Type: Public, state/local, two-year
System: Louisiana Community and Technical College System
Degrees: A *FTE Enroll:* 1,207
URL: http://www.nunez.edu
Phone: (504) 278-7497 *Calendar:* Sem. plan
Inst. Accred.: SACS (1992/1997)
Prog. Accred.: Design Technology, Electronic Technology

New Orleans Campus
901 Delery St., New Orleans 70117
Phone: (504) 278-7440

Port Sulphur Campus
PO Drawer 944, Port Sulphur 70083
Phone: (504) 564-2701

Grambling State University
PO Drawer 607, Grambling 71245
Type: Public, state, four-year
System: University of Louisiana System
Degrees: A, B, M, P, D *Enroll:* 4,798
URL: http://www.gram.edu
Phone: (318) 247-3811 *Calendar:* Sem. plan
Inst. Accred.: SACS (1949/2003)
Prog. Accred.: Business (AACSB), Computer Science (ABET-CAC), Engineering Technology (electrical, mechanical drafting/design), Graduate Social Work, Journalism, Music, Nursing, Public Administration, Recreation and Leisure Services, Social Work, Teacher Education (NCATE), Theatre

Gretna Career College
1415 Whitney Ave., Gretna 70053-5835
Type: Private, proprietary, two-year
Degrees: A
URL: http://gretnacareercollege.com
Phone: (504) 366-5409
Inst. Accred.: ACCSCT (1993/2003)

ITI Technical College
13944 Airline Hwy., Baton Rouge 70817-5998
Type: Private, proprietary, two-year
Degrees: A *Enroll:* 271
Phone: (225) 752-4233
Inst. Accred.: ACCSCT (1981/2005)

L.E. Fletcher Technical Community College
PO Box 5033, Houma 70361-5033
Type: Public, state, two-year
System: Louisiana Community and Technical College System
Degrees: A *Enroll:* 921
URL: http://www.lefletcher.edu
Phone: (985) 857-3655 *Calendar:* Sem. plan
Inst. Accred.: COE (1975/2001), SACS (2007)

Louisiana College
1140 College Dr., Pineville 71359
Type: Private, Southern Baptist Church, four-year
Degrees: A, B *Enroll:* 908
URL: http://www.lacollege.edu
Phone: (318) 487-7011 *Calendar:* Sem. plan
Inst. Accred.: SACS (1923/2001)
Prog. Accred.: Business (ACBSP), Nursing Education, Social Work, Teacher Education (NCATE)

Louisiana Culinary Institute
5837 Essen Ln., Baton Rouge 70810-1112
Type: Private, proprietary, two-year
Degrees: A
URL: http://www.louisianaculinary.com
Phone: (225) 769-8820 *Calendar:* Sem. plan
Inst. Accred.: COE (2006)

Louisiana State University and Agricultural and Mechanical College
Baton Rouge 70803
Type: Public, state, four-year
System: Louisiana State University System
Degrees: B, M, P, D *Enroll:* 31,711
URL: http://www.lsu.edu
Phone: (225) 578-3202 *Calendar:* Sem. plan
Inst. Accred.: SACS (1913/2004)
Prog. Accred.: Allied Health (audiology, speech-language pathology), Art, Business (AACSB), Clinical Psychology, Construction Education, Counseling, Dietetics (didactic), Engineering (bioengineering, chemical, civil, computer, electrical, environmental/sanitary, industrial, mechanical, petroleum), Family & Consumer Science, Forestry, Graduate Social Work, Interior Design, Journalism, Landscape Architecture, Law, Librarianship, Music, School Psychology, Teacher Education (NCATE), Veterinary Medicine

Louisiana State University at Alexandria
8100 Hwy. 71 South, Alexandria 71302-9121
Type: Public, state, four-year
System: Louisiana State University System
Degrees: A, B *Enroll:* 2,206
URL: http://www.lsua.edu
Phone: (318) 445-3672 *Calendar:* Sem. plan
Inst. Accred.: SACS (1960/2005)
Prog. Accred.: Clinical Lab Technology, Nursing

Louisiana State University at Eunice
PO Box 1129, Eunice 70535
Type: Public, state, two-year
System: Louisiana State University System
Degrees: A *Enroll:* 2,139
URL: http://www.lsue.edu
Phone: (337) 457-7311 *Calendar:* Sem. plan
Inst. Accred.: SACS (1967/2004)
Prog. Accred.: Allied Health (diagnostic medical sonography, respiratory therapy), Nursing, Radiography

Louisiana State University Health Sciences Center in New Orleans
2021 Perdido St., New Orleans 70112-1352
Type: Public, state, four-year
System: Louisiana State University System
Degrees: A, B, M, D *Enroll:* 2,077
URL: http://www.lsuhsc.edu
Phone: (504) 568-4808 *Calendar:* Sem. plan
Inst. Accred.: SACS (1931/2005)
Prog. Accred.: Allied Health (audiology, blood bank technology, cardiovascular technology, medicine, occupational therapy, respiratory therapy, speech-language pathology), Clinical Lab Scientist, Dentistry (advanced education in general dentistry, combined prosthodontics, dental hygiene, dental laboratory technology, dentistry, endodontics, general dentistry, general practice residency, maxillofacial prosthetics, oral and maxillofacial surgery, orthodontic and dentofacial orthopedics, pediatric dentistry, periodontics, prosthodontics), Nurse Anesthesia Education, Nursing Education, Physical Therapy, Psychology Internship, Rehabilitation Counseling

Louisiana State University in Shreveport
One University Place, Shreveport 71115-2399
Type: Public, state, four-year
System: Louisiana State University System
Degrees: B, M, P *Enroll:* 3,409
URL: http://www.lsus.edu
Phone: (318) 797-5000 *Calendar:* Sem. plan
Inst. Accred.: SACS (1975/2005)
Prog. Accred.: Allied Health (medicine), Business (AACSB), Computer Science (ABET-CAC), Physical Therapy, Physician Assistant, Teacher Education (NCATE)

Health Sciences Center—Shreveport
1501 Kings Hwy., Shreveport 71130
Phone: (318) 675-5000
Prog. Accred: Allied Health (occupational therapy, respiratory therapy)

Louisiana Tech University
PO Box 3178, Ruston 71272-3178
Type: Public, state, four-year
System: University of Louisiana System
Degrees: A, B, M, P, D *Enroll:* 9,757
URL: http://www.latech.edu
Phone: (318) 257-2000 *Calendar:* Qtr. plan
Inst. Accred.: SACS (1927/2005)
Prog. Accred.: Accounting, Allied Health (audiology, speech-language pathology), Art, Aviation, Business (AACSB), Computer Science (ABET-CAC), Dietetics (didactic), Dietetics (internship), Engineering (bioengineering, chemical, civil, electrical, industrial, mechanical), Engineering Technology (civil/construction, electrical), Family & Consumer Science, Forestry, Interior Design, Music, Nursing, Teacher Education (NCATE)

Louisiana Technical College—Alexandria Campus
4311 South MacArthur Dr., PO Box 5698, Alexandria 71307-5698
Type: Public, state, two-year
System: Louisiana Community and Technical College System
Degrees: A *Enroll:* 360
URL: http://www.region6.ltc.edu
Phone: (318) 487-5443 *Calendar:* Sem. plan
Inst. Accred.: COE (1976/2003)

Avoyelles Campus
508 Choupique St., PO Box 307, Cottonport 71327
Phone: (318) 876-2401

Hessmer Extension Center
4137 East School St., Hessmer 71341
Phone: (318) 563-8685

Huey P. Long Campus
303 South Jones St., Winnfield 71483
Phone: (318) 628-3815

Lamar Salter Campus
15014 Lake Charles Hwy., Leesville 71446
Phone: (337) 537-3135

Morgan Smith Campus
1230 N. Main St., PO Box 1327, Jennings 70546-1327
Phone: (337) 824-4811

Oakdale Campus
117 Hwy. 1152, PO Drawer EM, Oakdale 71463
Phone: (318) 335-3944

Rod Brady Campus
521 East Bradford Sreet, Jena 71342
Phone: (318) 992-2910

Shelby M. Jackson Campus
2100 E.E. Wallace Blvd., Ferriday 71334
Phone: (318) 757-6501

Louisiana Technical College—Baton Rouge Campus
3250 North Acadian Thruway, Baton Rouge 70805
Type: Public, state, two-year
System: Louisiana Community and Technical College System
Degrees: A *Enroll:* 717
URL: http://www.region2.ltc.edu
Phone: (225) 359-9201 *Calendar:* Sem. plan
Inst. Accred.: COE (1973/2003)
Prog. Accred.: Culinary Education

Angola Correctional Facility
Loiusiana State Penitentiary, Angola 70712
Phone: (504) 655-4411

Folkes Campus
3337 Hwy. 10, Jackson 70748
Phone: (225) 634-2636

Hunt Correctional Center
Hunt Correctional Center, PO Box 40, St. Gabriel 70776
Phone: (504) 642-3306

J.M. Frazier Campus
555 Julia St., Baton Rouge 70802
Phone: (225) 342-5850

Jackson Center
Dixon Correctional Facility, PO Box 788, 5568 Hwy. 68, Jackson 70748
Phone: (504) 342-6661

Jumonville Memorial Campus
605 Hospital Rd., New Roads 70760-2628
Phone: (225) 638-8613

Louisiana Correctional Institute for Women
Louisiana Correctional Inst. for Women, PO Box 40, St. Gabriel 70776
Phone: (504) 642-5529

Westside Campus
59125 Bayou Rd., Plaquemine 70765-0733
Phone: (225) 687-6392

Louisiana Technical College—Delta-Ouachita Campus
609 Vocational Pkwy., West Ouachita Industrial Park, West Monroe 71292-9064
Type: Public, state, two-year
System: Louisiana Community and Technical College System
Degrees: A *Enroll:* 382
URL: http://www.region8.ltc.edu
Phone: (318) 397-6100 *Calendar:* Qtr. plan
Inst. Accred.: COE (1976/2003)

Bastrop Campus
PO Box 1120, Bastrop 71221-1120
Phone: (318) 283-0836

Margaret Surles Center
Highway 883-1, PO Box 368, Lake Providence 71254
Phone: (318) 559-0239

North Central Campus
605 West Boundary, PO Box 548, Farmerville 71241-0548
Phone: (318) 368-3179

Northeast Louisiana Campus
1710 Warren St., Winnsboro 71295
Phone: (318) 435-2163

Ruston Campus
PO Box 1070, Ruston 71273-1070
Phone: (318) 251-4145
Prog. Accred: Counseling Psychology

Tallulah Campus
PO Box 1740, Tallulah 71284-1740
Phone: (318) 574-4820

Louisiana Technical College—Jefferson Campus
5200 Blair Dr., Metairie 70001
Type: Public, state, two-year
System: Louisiana Community and Technical College System
Degrees: A *Enroll:* 318
URL: http://www.dcc.edu/ltc/jeff.htm
Phone: (504) 736-7020 *Calendar:* Qtr. plan
Inst. Accred.: COE (1975/2000)

Louisiana Technical College—Lafayette Campus
1101 Bertrand Dr., Lafayette 70506
Type: Public, state, two-year
System: Louisiana Community and Technical College System
Degrees: A *Enroll:* 770
URL: http://www.ltc.edu/greateracadianaregion
Phone: (337) 262-5962 *Calendar:* Sem. plan
Inst. Accred.: COE (1981/2003)
Prog. Accred.: Allied Health (surgical technology), Clinical Lab Technology, Culinary Education

Acadian Campus
1933 West Hutchinson Ave., Crowley 70526
Phone: (337) 788-7521

Charles B. Coreil Campus
1124 Vocational Dr., Ward 1, Industrial Park, Ville Platte 70586-0296
Phone: (318) 363-2197

Evangeline Campus
PO Box 68, St. Martinville 70582
Phone: (318) 394-6466

Gulf Area Campus
1115 Clover St., Abbeville 70511-0878
Phone: (337) 893-4984

St. Martindale Campus
Main and Martin St., St. Martinsville 70517
Phone: (337) 394-6466

T.H. Harris Campus
322 East South St., Opelousas 70570-6114
Phone: (337) 948-0239

Teche Area Campus
PO Box 11057, New Iberia 70562-1057
Phone: (337) 373-0011

Louisiana Technical College—Shreveport-Bossier Campus
2010 North Market St., PO Box 78527, Shreveport 71137-8527
Type: Public, state, two-year
System: Louisiana Community and Technical College System
Degrees: A *Enroll:* 670
URL: http://www.region7.ltc.edu
Phone: (318) 676-7811 *Calendar:* Sem. plan
Inst. Accred.: COE (1976/2003)
Prog. Accred.: Culinary Education

David Wade Facility
670 Bell Hill Rd., Homer 71040
Phone: (518) 927-9631

Homer Campus
3001 Minden Rd., PO Box 509, Homer 71040-0509
Phone: (318) 927-2034

Mansfield Campus
943 Oxford Rd., PO Box 1236, Mansfield 71052
Phone: (318) 872-2243

Natchitoches Campus
6587 Hwy. 1 Bypass, PO Box 657, Natchitoches 71458-0657
Phone: (318) 357-3162

Northwest Louisiana Campus
814 Constable St., PO Box 835, Minden 71058-0835
Phone: (318) 371-3035

Sabine Valley Campus
1255 Fisher Rd., PO Box 790, Many 71449
Phone: (318) 256-4101

Springhill Campus
102 1st St., NE, Springhill 71075
Phone: (518) 371-3035

Louisiana Technical College—Sullivan Campus
1710 Sullivan Dr., Bogalusa 70427
Type: Public, state, two-year
System: Louisiana Community and Technical College System
Degrees: A *Enroll:* 444
URL: http://www.region9.ltc.edu
Phone: (985) 732-6640 *Calendar:* Sem. plan
Inst. Accred.: COE (1970/2007)

Ascension Campus
9697 Airline Hwy., Sorrento 70778-3007
Phone: (225) 675-5398

Florida Parishes Campus
PO Box 1300, Greensburg 70441
Phone: (225) 222-4251

Hammond Area Campus
PO Box 489, Hammond 70404-0489
Phone: (985) 543-4120

Louisiana Technical College—West Jefferson Campus
475 Manhattan Blvd., Harvey 70058
Type: Public, state, two-year
System: Louisiana Community and Technical College System
Degrees: A *Enroll:* 239
URL: http://www.dcc.edu/ltc/west_jeff.htm
Phone: (504) 361-6464 *Calendar:* Sem. plan
Inst. Accred.: COE (1982/2007)
Prog. Accred.: Allied Health (respiratory therapy technology)

Louisiana Technical College—Young Memorial Campus
PO Box 2148, Morgan City 70381
Type: Public, state, two-year
System: Louisiana Community and Technical College System
Degrees: A
URL: http://www.region3.ltc.edu
Phone: (985) 380-2436 *Calendar:* Qtr. plan
Inst. Accred.: COE (1976/2003)

Franklin Campus
1401 A Cynthia St., Franklin 70538
Phone: (337) 828-1448

LaFourche Campus
PO Box 1831, Thibodaux 70302-1831
Phone: (985) 447-0924
Prog. Accred: Allied Health (surgical technology)

River Parishes Campus
PO Drawer AQ, Reserve 70084
Phone: (985) 536-4418

Loyola University New Orleans
6363 St. Charles Ave., New Orleans 70118
Type: Private, Roman Catholic Church, four-year
Degrees: B, M, D *Enroll:* 333
URL: http://www.loyno.edu
Phone: (504) 865-2011 *Calendar:* Sem. plan
Inst. Accred.: SACS (1929/2006)
Prog. Accred.: Business (AACSB), Counseling, Law, Music, Nursing

McNeese State University
4100 Ryan St., Lake Charles 70609
Type: Public, state, four-year
System: University of Louisiana System
Degrees: A, B, M, P *Enroll:* 7,730
URL: http://www.mcneese.edu
Phone: (337) 475-5000 *Calendar:* Sem. plan
Inst. Accred.: SACS (1954/2007)
Prog. Accred.: Business (AACSB), Clinical Lab Scientist, Computer Science (ABET-CAC), Dietetics (internship), Engineering (general), Engineering Technology (electrical, instrumentation, process/piping design), Family & Consumer Science, Music, Nursing, Nursing Education, Radiography, Teacher Education (NCATE)

New Orleans Baptist Theological Seminary
3939 Gentilly Blvd., New Orleans 70126-4858
Type: Private, Southern Baptist Convention, four-year
Degrees: A, B, M, D *Enroll:* 1,951
URL: http://www.nobts.edu
Phone: (504) 282-4455 *Calendar:* Sem. plan
Inst. Accred.: ATS (1954/2006), SACS (1965/2006)
Prog. Accred.: Music

Nicholls State University
PO Box 2001, Thibodaux 70310-0001
Type: Public, state, four-year
System: University of Louisiana System
Degrees: A, B, M, P *Enroll:* 6,385
URL: http://www.nicholls.edu
Phone: (985) 446-8111 *Calendar:* Sem. plan
Inst. Accred.: SACS (1964/2006)
Prog. Accred.: Accounting, Allied Health (cytotechnology, respiratory therapy), Art, Business (AACSB), Computer Science (ABET-CAC), Family & Consumer Science, Journalism, Music, Nursing, Nursing Education, Teacher Education (NCATE)

Northwestern State University
350 Sam Sibley Rd., Natchitoches 71497-0003
Type: Public, state, four-year
System: University of Louisiana System
Degrees: A, B, M, P, D *Enroll:* 7,939
URL: http://www.nsula.edu
Phone: (318) 357-6011 *Calendar:* Sem. plan
Inst. Accred.: SACS (1941/2007)
Prog. Accred.: Art, Business (AACSB), Counseling, Engineering Technology (electrical, industrial), Family & Consumer Science, Journalism, Music, Nursing, Nursing Education, Radiography, Social Work, Teacher Education (NCATE), Theatre, Veterinary Technology

College of Nursing at Shreveport
1800 Line Ave., Shreveport 71101
Phone: (318) 677-3100
Prog. Accred: Radiography

Notre Dame Seminary
2901 South Carrollton Ave., New Orleans 70118-4391
Type: Private, Roman Catholic Church, four-year
Degrees: M *Enroll:* 97
URL: http://www.nds.edu
Phone: (504) 866-7426 *Calendar:* Sem. plan
Inst. Accred.: ATS (1979/2006), SACS (1951/1996)

Our Lady of Holy Cross College
4123 Woodland Dr., New Orleans 70131-7399
Type: Private, Roman Catholic Church, four-year
Degrees: A, B, M *Enroll:* 1,091
URL: http://www.olhcc.edu
Phone: (504) 394-7744 *Calendar:* Sem. plan
Inst. Accred.: SACS (1972/1996)
Prog. Accred.: Allied Health (respiratory therapy), Counseling, Nursing, Radiography, Teacher Education (NCATE)

Our Lady of the Lake College
7434 Perkins Rd., Baton Rouge 70808-4380
Type: Private, Roman Catholic Church, four-year
Degrees: A, B, M *Enroll:* 1,272
URL: http://www.ololcollege.edu
Phone: (225) 768-1700 *Calendar:* Sem. plan
Inst. Accred.: SACS (1994/1999)
Prog. Accred.: Allied Health (respiratory therapy, surgical technology), Clinical Lab Scientist, Clinical Lab Technology, Nurse Anesthesia Education, Nursing, Physical Therapy Assisting, Radiography

Remington College—Lafayette
303 Rue Louis XIV, Lafayette 70508
Type: Private, proprietary, two-year
System: Education America, Inc.
Degrees: A *Enroll:* 367
URL: http://www.remingtoncollege.edu
Phone: (337) 981-4010 *Calendar:* Qtr. plan
Inst. Accred.: ACICS (1988/2006)

Baton Rouge Campus
10551 Coursey Blvd., Baton Rouge 70816
Phone: (225) 922-3990

River Parishes Community College
PO Box 310, Sorrento 70778-0310
Type: Public, state, two-year
System: Louisiana Community and Technical College System
Degrees: A
URL: http://rpcc.cc.la.us
Phone: (225) 675-8270 *Calendar:* Sem. plan
Inst. Accred.: SACS (2004)

Saint Joseph Seminary College
75376 River Rd., St. Benedict 70457-9990
Type: Private, Roman Catholic Church, four-year
Degrees: B *Enroll:* 96
URL: http://www.stjosephabbey.org
Phone: (985) 892-1800 *Calendar:* Sem. plan
Inst. Accred.: SACS (1956/2003)

School of Urban Missions—New Orleans
PO Box 53344, New Orleans 70153-3344
Type: Private, nondenominational, two-year
Degrees: A
URL: http://www.sumonline.org
Phone: (504) 362-6364 *Calendar:* Tri. plan
Inst. Accred.: ABHE (2006)

Oakland Campus
PO Box 14145, Oakland, CA 94614
Phone: (510) 567-6174

South Louisiana Community College
320 Devalcourt St., Lafayette 70506-4124
Type: Public, state/local, two-year
System: Louisiana Community and Technical College System
Degrees: A
URL: http://www.slcc.cc.la.us
Phone: (337) 521-8896 *Calendar:* Sem. plan
Inst. Accred.: SACS (2007)

Southeastern Louisiana University
SLU 10784, Hammond 70402-0001
Type: Public, state, four-year
System: University of Louisiana System
Degrees: A, B, M, P, D *Enroll:* 13,637
URL: http://www.selu.edu
Phone: (985) 549-2000 *Calendar:* Sem. plan
Inst. Accred.: SACS (1946/2005)
Prog. Accred.: Accounting, Allied Health (speech-language pathology), Business (AACSB), Computer Science (ABET-CAC), Counseling, Industrial Technology, Music, Nursing, Nursing Education, Social Work, Teacher Education (NCATE)

Southern University and Agricultural and Mechanical College
PO Box 9374, Baton Rouge 70813
Type: Public, state, four-year
System: Southern University System
Degrees: A, B, M, P, D *Enroll:* 9,272
URL: http://www.subr.edu
Phone: (225) 771-4500 *Calendar:* Sem. plan
Inst. Accred.: SACS (1938/2000)
Prog. Accred.: Allied Health (speech-language pathology), Business (AACSB), Computer Science (ABET-CAC), Counseling, Dietetics (didactic), Dietetics (internship), Engineering (civil, electrical, mechanical), Engineering Technology (electrical), Family & Consumer Science, Journalism, Law (ABA only), Music, Nursing, Nursing Education, Public Administration, Rehabilitation Counseling, Social Work, Teacher Education (NCATE)

Southern University at New Orleans
6400 Press Dr., New Orleans 70126
Type: Public, state, four-year
System: Southern University System
Degrees: A, B, M *Enroll:* 2,970
URL: http://www.suno.edu
Phone: (504) 286-5000 *Calendar:* Sem. plan
Inst. Accred.: SACS (1970/2000)
Prog. Accred.: Graduate Social Work, Social Work, Teacher Education (NCATE)

Southern University at Shreveport
3050 Martin Luther King, Jr. Dr., Shreveport 71107
Type: Public, state, two-year
System: Southern University System
Degrees: A *Enroll:* 1,921
URL: http://www.susla.edu
Phone: (318) 674-3300 *Calendar:* Sem. plan
Inst. Accred.: SACS (1975/2000)
Prog. Accred.: Allied Health (respiratory therapy, surgical technology), Clinical Lab Technology, Dentistry (dental hygiene), Electronic Technology, Funeral Service Education (Mortuary Science), Nursing, Radiography

Southwest University
2200 Veterans Blvd., Kenner 70062
Type: Private, independent, four-year
Degrees: A, B, M
URL: http://www.southwest.edu
Phone: (504) 468-2900
Inst. Accred.: DETC (2004)

Sowela Technical Community College
3820 Senator J. Bennett Johnston Ave., Lake Charles 70615
Type: Public, state, two-year
System: Louisiana Community and Technical College System
Degrees: A *Enroll:* 1,089
URL: http://www.sowela.edu
Phone: (337) 491-2688 *Calendar:* Sem. plan
Inst. Accred.: COE (1971/2004)

Tulane University
6823 St. Charles Ave., New Orleans 70118
Type: Private, independent, four-year
Degrees: B, M, D *Enroll:* 11,156
URL: http://www.tulane.edu
Phone: (504) 865-5000 *Calendar:* Sem. plan
Inst. Accred.: SACS (1903/2001)
Prog. Accred.: Allied Health (health services administration, medicine), Applied Science (industrial hygiene), Business (AACSB), Computer Science (ABET-CAC), Dietetics (internship), Engineering (bioengineering, chemical, civil, computer, electrical, environmental/sanitary, mechanical), Graduate Social Work, Law, Psychology Internship, Public Health, School Psychology

The University of Louisiana at Lafayette
PO Drawer 41008, Lafayette 70504
Type: Public, state, four-year
System: University of Louisiana System
Degrees: A, B, M, D *Enroll:* 15,082
URL: http://www.louisiana.edu
Phone: (337) 482-1000 *Calendar:* Sem. plan
Inst. Accred.: SACS (1925/2000)
Prog. Accred.: Allied Health (speech-language pathology), Art, Business (AACSB), Computer Science (ABET-CAC), Dietetics (didactic), Dietetics (internship), Engineering (chemical, civil, electrical, mechanical, petroleum), Family & Consumer Science, Industrial Technology, Interior Design, Journalism, Music, Nursing, Nursing Education, Teacher Education (NCATE)

The University of Louisiana at Monroe
700 University Ave., Monroe 71209
Type: Public, state, four-year
System: University of Louisiana System
Degrees: A, B, M, P, D *Enroll:* 8,039
URL: http://www.ulm.edu
Phone: (318) 342-1000 *Calendar:* Sem. plan
Inst. Accred.: SACS (1955/1999)
Prog. Accred.: Accounting, Allied Health (occupational therapy assisting, speech-language pathology), Business (AACSB), Computer Science (ABET-CAC), Construction Education, Counseling, Dentistry (dental hygiene), Exercise Physiology, Exercise Science, Family & Consumer Science, Marriage and Family Therapy, Music, Nursing Education, Pharmacy, Radiography, Social Work, Teacher Education (NCATE)

University of New Orleans
2000 Lakeshore Dr., New Orleans 70122-3520
Type: Public, state, four-year
System: Louisiana State University System
Degrees: A, B, M, D *Enroll:* 4,376
URL: http://www.uno.edu
Phone: (504) 280-6000 *Calendar:* Sem. plan
Inst. Accred.: SACS (1958/2005)
Prog. Accred.: Accounting, Art, Business (AACSB), Computer Science (ABET-CAC), Counseling, Engineering (civil, electrical, mechanical, naval architecture/marine), Music, Planning, Teacher Education (NCATE), Theatre

Xavier University of Louisiana
1 Drexel Dr., New Orleans 70125-1098
Type: Private, Roman Catholic Church, four-year
Degrees: B, M, P, D *Enroll:* 2,963
URL: http://www.xula.edu
Phone: (504) 486-7411 *Calendar:* Sem. plan
Inst. Accred.: SACS (1938/2000)
Prog. Accred.: Business (ACBSP), Music, Pharmacy, Teacher Education (NCATE)

MAINE

Andover College
901 Washington Ave., Portland 04103-2791
Type: Private, proprietary, two-year
System: Kaplan Higher Education Corporation
Degrees: A *Enroll:* 553
URL: http://www.andovercollege.edu
Phone: (207) 774-6126 *Calendar:* Qtr. plan
Inst. Accred.: NEASC-CIHE (2006), NEASC-CTCI (1998)

Lewiston Campus
475 Lisbon St., Lewiston 04240
Phone: (207) 333-3300

Bangor Theological Seminary
PO Box 411, Bangor 04402-0411
Type: Private, United Church of Christ, four-year
Degrees: M, D *Enroll:* 89
URL: http://www.bts.edu
Phone: (207) 942-6781 *Calendar:* Sem. plan
Inst. Accred.: ATS (1974/1998), NEASC-CIHE (1968/1998)

Portland Campus
159 State St., Portland 04102
Phone: (207) 774-5212

Bates College
2 Andrews Rd., Lewiston 04240-6047
Type: Private, independent, four-year
Degrees: B *Enroll:* 1,699
URL: http://www.bates.edu
Phone: (207) 786-6255 *Calendar:* Sem. plan
Inst. Accred.: NEASC-CIHE (1929/2000)

Beal College
99 Farm Rd., Bangor 04401
Type: Private, independent, two-year
Degrees: A *Enroll:* 292
URL: http://www.bealcollege.edu
Phone: (207) 947-4591
Inst. Accred.: ACICS (1966/2006)
Prog. Accred.: Allied Health (medical assisting (AMA))

Bowdoin College
5700 College Station, Brunswick 04011-8448
Type: Private, independent, four-year
Degrees: B *Enroll:* 1,663
URL: http://www.bowdoin.edu
Phone: (207) 725-3000 *Calendar:* Sem. plan
Inst. Accred.: NEASC-CIHE (1929/2006)

Central Maine Community College
1250 Turner St., Auburn 04210-6498
Type: Public, state, two-year
System: Maine Community College System
Degrees: A *Enroll:* 1,318
URL: http://www.cmcc.edu
Phone: (207) 755-5100 *Calendar:* Sem. plan
Inst. Accred.: NEASC-CIHE (2003)
Prog. Accred.: Applied Science (occupational health & safety), Clinical Lab Technology, Engineering Technology (civil/construction), Nursing

Central Maine Medical Center College of Nursing and Health Professions
70 Middle St., Lewiston 04240
Type: Private, independent, two-year
Degrees: A *Enroll:* 61
URL: http://www.cmmcson.edu
Phone: (207) 795-2840 *Calendar:* Sem. plan
Inst. Accred.: NEASC-CIHE (2008), NEASC-CTCI (1978/2000)
Prog. Accred.: Nursing

Colby College
4000 Mayflower Hill, Waterville 04901-8840
Type: Private, independent, four-year
Degrees: B *Enroll:* 1,871
URL: http://www.colby.edu
Phone: (207) 872-3000 *Calendar:* 4-1-4 plan
Inst. Accred.: NEASC-CIHE (1929/2007)

College of the Atlantic
105 Eden St., Bar Harbor 04609-1198
Type: Private, independent, four-year
Degrees: B, M *Enroll:* 309
URL: http://www.coa.edu
Phone: (207) 288-5015 *Calendar:* Tri. plan
Inst. Accred.: NEASC-CIHE (1976/2007)
Prog. Accred.: Business (ACBSP)

Eastern Maine Community College
354 Hogan Rd., Bangor 04401-4280
Type: Public, state, two-year
System: Maine Community College System
Degrees: A *Enroll:* 1,234
URL: http://www.emcc.org
Phone: (207) 941-4600 *Calendar:* Sem. plan
Inst. Accred.: NEASC-CIHE (2004)
Prog. Accred.: Allied Health (medical assisting (AMA)), Nursing, Radiography

Husson University
One College Circle, Bangor 04401-2999
Type: Private, independent, four-year
Degrees: A, B, M, D *Enroll:* 1,663
URL: http://www.husson.edu
Phone: (207) 941-7000 *Calendar:* Sem. plan
Inst. Accred.: NEASC-CIHE (1974/2003)
Prog. Accred.: Allied Health (medical assisting (AMA), occupational therapy), Nursing Education, Physical Therapy

Kennebec Valley Community College
92 Western Ave., Fairfield 04937-1367
Type: Public, state, two-year
System: Maine Community College System
Degrees: A *Enroll:* 946
URL: http://www.kvcc.me.edu
Phone: (207) 453-5000 *Calendar:* Sem. plan
Inst. Accred.: NEASC-CIHE (2003)
Prog. Accred.: Allied Health (medical assisting (AMA), occupational therapy assisting, respiratory therapy), Business (ACBSP), Nursing, Physical Therapy Assisting

Maine College of Art
97 Spring St., Portland 04101-3987
Type: Private, independent, four-year
Degrees: B, M *Enroll:* 478
URL: http://www.meca.edu
Phone: (207) 775-3052 *Calendar:* Sem. plan
Inst. Accred.: NEASC-CIHE (1978/2007)
Prog. Accred.: Art

Maine Maritime Academy
Castine 04420-0001
Type: Public, state, four-year
Degrees: B, M *Enroll:* 826
URL: http://www.mainemaritime.edu
Phone: (207) 326-2217 *Calendar:* Sem. plan
Inst. Accred.: NEASC-CIHE (1971/2006)
Prog. Accred.: Engineering (naval architecture/marine), Engineering Technology (naval architecture/marine)

New England School of Communications
One College Circle, Bangor 04401-2999
Type: Private, independent, four-year
Degrees: A, B *Enroll:* 307
URL: http://www.nescom.edu
Phone: (207) 947-3987 *Calendar:* Sem. plan
Inst. Accred.: ACCSCT (1986/2004)

Northern Maine Community College
33 Edgemont Dr., Presque Isle 04769-2099
Type: Public, state, two-year
System: Maine Community College System
Degrees: A *Enroll:* 711
URL: http://www.nmtc.net
Phone: (207) 768-2700 *Calendar:* Sem. plan
Inst. Accred.: NEASC-CIHE (2003/2008)
Prog. Accred.: Business (ACBSP), Nursing

Saint Joseph's College of Maine
278 Whites Bridge Rd., Standish 04084-5263
Type: Private, Roman Catholic Church, four-year
Degrees: B, M *Enroll:* 2,137
URL: http://www.sjcme.edu
Phone: (207) 892-6766
Inst. Accred.: NEASC-CIHE (1961/2001)
Prog. Accred.: Nursing, Nursing Education

Southern Maine Community College
2 Fort Rd., South Portland 04106
Type: Public, state, two-year
System: Maine Community College System
Degrees: A *Enroll:* 3,032
URL: http://www.smtc.net
Phone: (207) 741-5501 *Calendar:* Sem. plan
Inst. Accred.: NEASC-CIHE (2003/2008)
Prog. Accred.: Allied Health (medical assisting (AMA), respiratory therapy), Dietetic Technician, Nursing, Radiation Therapy, Radiography

Thomas College
180 West River Rd., Waterville 04901-5097
Type: Private, independent, four-year
Degrees: A, B, M *Enroll:* 708
URL: http://www.thomas.edu
Phone: (207) 859-1111 *Calendar:* Sem. plan
Inst. Accred.: NEASC-CIHE (1969/2003)

Unity College
90 Quaker Hill Rd., Unity 04988
Type: Private, independent, four-year
Degrees: A, B *Enroll:* 521
URL: http://www.unity.edu
Phone: (207) 948-3131 *Calendar:* Sem. plan
Inst. Accred.: NEASC-CIHE (1974/2002)

University of Maine
Orono 04469-0001
Type: Public, state, four-year
System: University of Maine System
Degrees: A, B, M, D *Enroll:* 9,810
URL: http://www.umaine.edu
Phone: (207) 581-1110 *Calendar:* Sem. plan
Inst. Accred.: NEASC-CIHE (1929/1999)
Prog. Accred.: Allied Health (speech-language pathology), Business (AACSB), Clinical Psychology, Computer Science (ABET-CAC), Dentistry (dental assisting, dental hygiene), Dietetics (didactic), Dietetics (internship), Engineering (bioengineering, chemical, civil, computer, electrical, engineering physics/science, mechanical, surveying), Engineering Technology (civil/construction, electrical, mechanical), Forestry, Graduate Social Work, Music, Nursing Education, Psychology Internship, Public Administration, Social Work, Teacher Education (NCATE)

University of Maine at Augusta
46 University Dr., Augusta 04330-9410
Type: Public, state, four-year
System: University of Maine System
Degrees: A, B *Enroll:* 3,137
URL: http://www.uma.maine.edu
Phone: (207) 621-3000 *Calendar:* Sem. plan
Inst. Accred.: NEASC-CIHE (1973/2007)
Prog. Accred.: Business (ACBSP), Clinical Lab Technology, Nursing

University College of Bangor
216 Texas Ave., Bangor 04401-4324
Phone: (207) 581-6182
Prog. Accred: Dentistry (dental assisting, dental hygiene), Veterinary Technology

University of Maine at Farmington
111 South St., Farmington 04938-1911
Type: Public, state, four-year
System: University of Maine System
Degrees: B *Enroll:* 2,256
URL: http://www.umf.maine.edu
Phone: (207) 778-7000 *Calendar:* Sem. plan
Inst. Accred.: NEASC-CIHE (1958/2002)
Prog. Accred.: Teacher Education (NCATE)

University of Maine at Fort Kent
23 University Dr., Fort Kent 04743-1292
Type: Public, state, four-year
System: University of Maine System
Degrees: A, B *Enroll:* 936
URL: http://www.umfk.maine.edu
Phone: (207) 834-7500 *Calendar:* Sem. plan
Inst. Accred.: NEASC-CIHE (1970/2006)
Prog. Accred.: Forestry, Nursing Education

University of Maine at Machias
9 O'Brien Ave., Machias 04654-1397
Type: Public, state, four-year
System: University of Maine System
Degrees: A, B *Enroll:* 739
URL: http://www.umm.maine.edu
Phone: (207) 255-1200 *Calendar:* Sem. plan
Inst. Accred.: NEASC-CIHE (1970/2004)
Prog. Accred.: Recreation and Leisure Services

University of Maine at Presque Isle
181 Main St., Presque Isle 04769-2888
Type: Public, state, four-year
System: University of Maine System
Degrees: A, B *Enroll:* 1,288
URL: http://www.umpi.maine.edu
Phone: (207) 768-9400 *Calendar:* Sem. plan
Inst. Accred.: NEASC-CIHE (1968/2003)
Prog. Accred.: Clinical Lab Technology, Social Work

University of New England
11 Hills Beach Rd., Biddeford 04005-9988
Type: Private, independent, four-year
Degrees: A, B, M, D *Enroll:* 2,760
URL: http://www.une.edu
Phone: (207) 283-0171 *Calendar:* Sem. plan
Inst. Accred.: NEASC-CIHE (1966/2007)
Prog. Accred.: Allied Health (occupational therapy), Business (ACBSP), Dentistry (dental hygiene), Graduate Social Work, Nurse Anesthesia Education, Nursing, Osteopathy, Physical Therapy, Physician Assistant

Israel Campus
26 Haim Levanon St., Tel Aviv, Israel
Phone: (207) 221-4476 ext 4
Prog. Accred: Nursing

Westbrook College
716 Stevens Ave., Portland 04103
Phone: (207) 797-7261
Prog. Accred: Dentistry (dental hygiene)

University of Southern Maine
96 Falmouth St., Portland 04104-9300
Type: Public, state, four-year
System: University of Maine System
Degrees: A, B, M, D *Enroll:* 7,953
URL: http://www.usm.maine.edu
Phone: (207) 780-4141 *Calendar:* Sem. plan
Inst. Accred.: NEASC-CIHE (1960/2001)
Prog. Accred.: Allied Health (health services administration), Art, Business (AACSB), Computer Science (ABET-CAC), Counseling, Engineering (electrical), Graduate Social Work, Industrial Technology, Law, Music, Nursing Education, Public Administration, Rehabilitation Counseling, Social Work, Teacher Education (NCATE)

Lewiston-Auburn College
51 Westminster St., Lewiston 04240
Phone: (207) 783-4860
Prog. Accred: Allied Health (occupational therapy)

Washington County Community College
RRI, Box 22C, Calais 04619-9704
Type: Public, state, two-year
System: Maine Community College System
Degrees: A *Enroll:* 329
URL: http://www.wccc.me.edu
Phone: (207) 454-1000 *Calendar:* Sem. plan
Inst. Accred.: NEASC-CIHE (2004)

York County Community College
112 College Dr., Wells 04090-0529
Type: Public, state, two-year
System: Maine Community College System
Degrees: A *Enroll:* 492
URL: http://www.yccc.edu
Phone: (207) 646-9282 *Calendar:* Sem. plan
Inst. Accred.: NEASC-CIHE (2004)

MARYLAND

Allegany College of Maryland
12401 Willowbrook Rd., Southeast, Cumberland 21502
Type: Public, local, two-year
System: Maryland Higher Education Commission
Degrees: A *Enroll:* 2,608
URL: http://www.allegany.edu
Phone: (301) 784-5000 *Calendar:* Sem. plan
Inst. Accred.: MSA-CHE (1965/2005)
Prog. Accred.: Allied Health (massage therapy, medical assisting (AMA), occupational therapy assisting, respiratory therapy), Clinical Lab Technology, Dentistry (dental hygiene), Forestry, Nursing, Physical Therapy Assisting, Radiography

Bedford County Campus
18 North River Ln., Everett, PA 15537
Phone: (814) 652-9528

Somerset County Campus
6022 Glades Pike, Ste. 100, Somerset, PA 15501-4300
Phone: (814) 445-9848

Anne Arundel Community College
101 College Pkwy., Arnold 21012
Type: Public, state/local, two-year
System: Maryland Higher Education Commission
Degrees: A *Enroll:* 8,162
URL: http://www.aacc.edu
Phone: (410) 647-7100 *Calendar:* Sem. plan
Inst. Accred.: MSA-CHE (1968/2004)
Prog. Accred.: Allied Health (EMT-paramedic, medical assisting (AMA)), Culinary Education, Nursing, Physical Therapy Assisting, Physician Assistant, Radiography

Baltimore City Community College
2901 Liberty Heights Ave., Baltimore 21215
Type: Public, state, two-year
System: Maryland Higher Education Commission
Degrees: A *Enroll:* 4,151
URL: http://www.bccc.edu
Phone: (410) 462-8000 *Calendar:* Sem. plan
Inst. Accred.: MSA-CHE (1963/2003)
Prog. Accred.: Allied Health (respiratory therapy, surgical technology), Business (ACBSP), Dentistry (dental hygiene), Dietetic Technician, Nursing, Physical Therapy Assisting

Harbor Campus
600 East Lombard St., Baltimore 21202
Phone: (410) 333-8348

Baltimore Hebrew University
5800 Park Heights Ave., Baltimore 21215
Type: Private, independent, four-year
Degrees: A, B, M, D *Enroll:* 54
URL: http://www.bhu.edu
Phone: (410) 578-6900 *Calendar:* Sem. plan
Inst. Accred.: MSA-CHE (1974/2005)

Baltimore International College
17 Commerce St., Baltimore 21202-3230
Type: Private, independent, four-year
Degrees: A, B, M *Enroll:* 498
URL: http://www.bic.edu
Phone: (410) 752-4710 *Calendar:* Sem. plan
Inst. Accred.: MSA-CHE (1996/2007)
Prog. Accred.: Culinary Education

Bowie State University
14000 Jericho Park Rd., Bowie 20715-9465
Type: Public, state, four-year
System: University System of Maryland
Degrees: B, M, D *Enroll:* 4,233
URL: http://www.bowiestate.edu
Phone: (301) 860-4000 *Calendar:* Sem. plan
Inst. Accred.: MSA-CHE (1961/2001)
Prog. Accred.: Business (ACBSP), Computer Science (ABET-CAC), Nursing, Social Work, Teacher Education (NCATE)

Capital Bible Seminary
6511 Princess Garden Pkwy., Lanham 20706
Type: Private, nondenominational, four-year
Degrees: A, B, M, P *Enroll:* 416
URL: http://www.bible.edu/cbs
Phone: (301) 552-1400 *Calendar:* Sem. plan
Inst. Accred.: ATS (1998/2002), MSA-CHE (2007)

Capitol College
11301 Springfield Rd., Laurel 20708
Type: Private, independent, four-year
Degrees: A, B, M *Enroll:* 469
URL: http://www.capitol-college.edu
Phone: (301) 369-2800 *Calendar:* Sem. plan
Inst. Accred.: MSA-CHE (1976/2001)
Prog. Accred.: Engineering (electrical), Engineering Technology (computer, electrical, telecommunications)

Carroll Community College
1601 Washington Rd., Westminster 21157-6913
Type: Public, local, two-year
System: Maryland Higher Education Commission
Degrees: A *Enroll:* 1,927
URL: http://www.carrollcc.edu
Phone: (410) 386-8000 *Calendar:* Sem. plan
Inst. Accred.: MSA-CHE (1996/2001)
Prog. Accred.: Physical Therapy Assisting

Cecil College
One Seahawk Dr., North East 21901-1999
Type: Public, state/local, two-year
System: Maryland Higher Education Commission
Degrees: A *Enroll:* 1,100
URL: http://www.cecilcc.edu
Phone: (410) 287-1000 *Calendar:* Sem. plan
Inst. Accred.: MSA-CHE (1974/2005)
Prog. Accred.: Allied Health (medical assisting (AMA)), Nursing

Chesapeake College
PO Box 8, Wye Mills 21679-0008
Type: Public, state/local, two-year
System: Maryland Higher Education Commission
Degrees: A *Enroll:* 1,424
URL: http://www.chesapeake.edu
Phone: (410) 822-5400 *Calendar:* Sem. plan
Inst. Accred.: MSA-CHE (1970/2005)
Prog. Accred.: Allied Health (surgical technology), Nursing, Physical Therapy Assisting, Radiography

College of Notre Dame of Maryland
4701 North Charles St., Baltimore 21210
Type: Private, Roman Catholic Church, four-year
Degrees: B, M, P, D *Enroll:* 1,702
URL: http://www.ndm.edu
Phone: (410) 435-0100 *Calendar:* Sem. plan
Inst. Accred.: MSA-CHE (1925/2007)
Prog. Accred.: Nursing, Teacher Education (NCATE)

The College of Southern Maryland
8730 Mitchell Rd., PO Box 910, La Plata 20646-0910
Type: Public, state, two-year
System: Maryland Higher Education Commission
Degrees: A *Enroll:* 4,256
URL: http://www.csmd.edu
Phone: (301) 934-2251 *Calendar:* Sem. plan
Inst. Accred.: MSA-CHE (1969/2004)
Prog. Accred.: Business (ACBSP), Nursing, Physical Therapy Assisting, Practical Nursing

Columbia Union College
7600 Flower Ave., Takoma Park 20912
Type: Private, Seventh-Day Adventist Church, four-year
Degrees: A, B, M *Enroll:* 855
URL: http://www.cuc.edu
Phone: (301) 891-4000 *Calendar:* Sem. plan
Inst. Accred.: MSA-CHE (1942/2007)
Prog. Accred.: Allied Health (respiratory therapy), Nursing

The Community College of Baltimore County
800 South Rolling Rd., Baltimore 21228-5381
Type: Public, state/local, two-year
Degrees: A *FTE Enroll:* 10,331
URL: http://www.ccbcmd.edu
Phone: (410) 455-6050 *Calendar:* Sem. plan
Inst. Accred.: MSA-CHE (1966/2007)
Prog. Accred.: Allied Health (massage therapy, occupational therapy assisting), Business (ACBSP), Dentistry (dental hygiene), Funeral Service Education (Mortuary Science), Music, Nursing, Radiography, Theatre

Dundalk Campus
7200 Sollers Point Rd., Dundalk 21222-4692
Phone: (410) 282-6700
Prog. Accred: Business (ACBSP)

Essex Campus
7201 Rossville Blvd., Baltimore 21237-3899
Phone: (410) 682-6000
Prog. Accred: Allied Health (EMT-paramedic, respiratory therapy, surgical technology), Business (ACBSP), Nursing, Physician Assistant, Radiation Therapy, Radiography, Veterinary Technology

Coppin State University
2500 West North Ave., Baltimore 21216-3698
Type: Public, state, four-year
System: University System of Maryland
Degrees: B, M *Enroll:* 3,477
URL: http://www.coppin.edu
Phone: (410) 951-3000 *Calendar:* Sem. plan
Inst. Accred.: MSA-CHE (1962/2008)
Prog. Accred.: Nursing, Rehabilitation Counseling, Social Work, Teacher Education (NCATE)

Frederick Community College
7932 Opossumtown Pike, Frederick 21702-2097
Type: Public, state/local, two-year
System: Maryland Higher Education Commission
Degrees: A *Enroll:* 2,851
URL: http://www.frederick.edu
Phone: (301) 846-2400 *Calendar:* Sem. plan
Inst. Accred.: MSA-CHE (1971/2006)
Prog. Accred.: Allied Health (respiratory therapy, surgical technology), Nursing

Frostburg State University
101 Braddock Rd., Frostburg 21532-1099
Type: Public, state, four-year
System: University System of Maryland
Degrees: B, M *Enroll:* 4,558
URL: http://www.frostburg.edu
Phone: (301) 687-4000 *Calendar:* Sem. plan
Inst. Accred.: MSA-CHE (1953/2006)
Prog. Accred.: Business (AACSB), Engineering (electrical, mechanical), Recreation and Leisure Services, Social Work, Teacher Education (NCATE)

Garrett College
PO Box 151, 687 Mosser Rd., McHenry 21541
Type: Public, state/local, two-year
System: Maryland Higher Education Commission
Degrees: A *Enroll:* 496
URL: http://www.garrettcollege.edu
Phone: (301) 387-3000 *Calendar:* Sem. plan
Inst. Accred.: MSA-CHE (1975/2003, Warning)

Goucher College
1021 Dulaney Valley Rd., Baltimore 21204-2794
Type: Private, independent, four-year
Degrees: B, M *Enroll:* 1,748
URL: http://www.goucher.edu
Phone: (410) 337-6000 *Calendar:* Sem. plan
Inst. Accred.: MSA-CHE (1921/2004)

Griggs University
12501 Old Columbia Pike, Silver Spring 20904
Type: Private, Seventh-Day Adventist, four-year
Degrees: A, B, M *FTE Enroll:* 289
URL: http://www.griggs.edu
Phone: (301) 680-6586 *Calendar:* Sem. plan
Inst. Accred.: DETC (1991/2003)

Hagerstown Community College
11400 Robinwood Dr., Hagerstown 21740-6590
Type: Public, state/local, two-year
System: Maryland Higher Education Commission
Degrees: A *Enroll:* 1,982
URL: http://www.hagerstowncc.edu
Phone: (301) 790-2800 *Calendar:* Sem. plan
Inst. Accred.: MSA-CHE (1968/2005)
Prog. Accred.: Radiography

Harford Community College
401 Thomas Run Rd., Bel Air 21015-1698
Type: Public, state/local, two-year
System: Maryland Higher Education Commission
Degrees: A *Enroll:* 3,334
URL: http://www.harford.edu
Phone: (410) 836-4000 *Calendar:* Sem. plan
Inst. Accred.: MSA-CHE (1967/2007)
Prog. Accred.: Histologic Technology, Nursing

Hood College
401 Rosemont Ave., Frederick 21701-8575
Type: Private, independent, four-year
Degrees: B, M *Enroll:* 1,469
URL: http://www.hood.edu
Phone: (301) 663-3131 *Calendar:* Sem. plan
Inst. Accred.: MSA-CHE (1922/2007)
Prog. Accred.: Business (ACBSP), Social Work

Howard Community College
10901 Little Patuxent Pkwy., Columbia 21044
Type: Public, state/local, two-year
System: Maryland Higher Education Commission
Degrees: A *Enroll:* 4,047
URL: http://www.howardcc.edu
Phone: (410) 772-4800 *Calendar:* Sem. plan
Inst. Accred.: MSA-CHE (1975/2001)
Prog. Accred.: Allied Health (EMT-paramedic, cardiovascular technology), Nursing, Practical Nursing

Johns Hopkins University
3400 North Charles St., Baltimore 21218
Type: Private, independent, four-year
Degrees: B, M, P, D *Enroll:* 14,021
URL: http://www.jhu.edu
Phone: (410) 516-8000 *Calendar:* Sem. plan
Inst. Accred.: MSA-CHE (1921/2004)
Prog. Accred.: Allied Health (blood bank technology, cytotechnology, diagnostic medical sonography, health services administration, medical illustration, medicine), Applied Science (industrial hygiene), Clinical Pastoral Education (ACPEI), Computer Science (ABET-CAC), Dentistry (general practice residency), Engineering (bioengineering, chemical, civil, computer, electrical, engineering mechanics, environmental/sanitary, materials, mechanical), Music, Nuclear Medicine Technology, Nursing, Nursing Education, Psychology Internship, Public Health, Teacher Education (NCATE)

Columbia Center Campus
6740 Alexander Bell Dr., Columbia 21046
Phone: (410) 290-1777

The Paul H. Nitze School of Advanced International Studies
1740 Massachusetts Ave., NW, Washington, DC 20036
Phone: (202) 663-5600

Peabody Institute of the Johns Hopkins University
One East Mount Vernon Place, Baltimore 21202-2397
Phone: (410) 659-8150
Prog. Accred: Music

Kaplan College—Hagerstown
18618 Crestwood Dr., Hagerstown 21742
Type: Private, proprietary, four-year
System: Kaplan Higher Education Corporation
Degrees: A, B *Enroll:* 983
URL: http://getinfo.kaplancollege.com
Phone: (301) 739-2670 *Calendar:* Qtr. plan
Inst. Accred.: ACICS (1968/2002)
Prog. Accred.: Phlebotomy

Frederick Campus
5301 Buckeystown Pike, Ste. 150, Frederick 21704
Phone: (301) 682-4882

Loyola College in Maryland
4501 North Charles St., Baltimore 21210-2699
Type: Private, Roman Catholic Church, four-year
Degrees: B, M, D *Enroll:* 4,966
URL: http://www.loyola.edu
Phone: (410) 617-2000 *Calendar:* Sem. plan
Inst. Accred.: MSA-CHE (1931/2005)
Prog. Accred.: Accounting, Allied Health (speech-language pathology), Business (AACSB), Clinical Psychology, Computer Science (ABET-CAC), Counseling, Engineering (engineering physics/science), Teacher Education (NCATE)

Maple Springs Baptist Bible College and Seminary
4130 Belt Rd., Capitol Heights 20743
Type: Private, Baptist Church, four-year
Degrees: A, B, M, D
URL: http://www.msbbcs.edu
Phone: (301) 736- 3631 *Calendar:* Sem. plan
Inst. Accred.: TRACS (2000/2004)

The Maryland Institute College of Art
1300 West Mount Royal Ave., Baltimore 21217
Type: Private, independent, four-year
Degrees: B, M *Enroll:* 1,816
URL: http://www.mica.edu
Phone: (410) 669-9200 *Calendar:* Sem. plan
Inst. Accred.: MSA-CHE (1967/2004)
Prog. Accred.: Art

McDaniel College
2 College Hill, Westminster 21157
Type: Private, independent, four-year
Degrees: B, M *Enroll:* 2,463
URL: http://www.mcdaniel.edu
Phone: (410) 848-7000 *Calendar:* Sem. plan
Inst. Accred.: MSA-CHE (1922/2003)
Prog. Accred.: Social Work, Teacher Education (NCATE)

Montgomery College—Germantown Campus
20200 Observation Dr., Germantown 20876
Type: Public, local, two-year
System: Montgomery College
Degrees: A *FTE Enroll:* 1,810
URL: http://www.montgomerycollege.edu
Phone: (240) 353-7700 *Calendar:* Sem. plan
Inst. Accred.: MSA-CHE (1980/2008)

Montgomery College—Rockville Campus
51 Mannakee St., Rockville 20850
Type: Public, local, two-year
System: Montgomery College
Degrees: A *Enroll:* 13,047
URL: http://www.montgomerycollege.edu
Phone: (240) 567-5000 *Calendar:* Sem. plan
Inst. Accred.: MSA-CHE (1968/2008)
Prog. Accred.: Music, Radiography

Montgomery College—Takoma Park Campus
7600 Takoma Ave., Takoma Park 20912
Type: Public, local, two-year
System: Montgomery College
Degrees: A *FTE Enroll:* 2,279
URL: http://www.montgomerycollege.edu
Phone: (240) 567-1300 *Calendar:* Sem. plan
Inst. Accred.: MSA-CHE (1950/2008)
Prog. Accred.: Allied Health (diagnostic medical sonography, surgical technology), Nursing, Physical Therapy Assisting, Radiography

The School of Art and Design at Montgomery College
10500 Georgia Ave., Silver Spring 20902
Phone: (301) 649-4454

Morgan State University
1700 East Cold Spring Ln., Baltimore 21251
Type: Public, state, four-year
System: Maryland Higher Education Commission
Degrees: B, M, D *Enroll:* 5,841
URL: http://www.morgan.edu
Phone: (443) 885-3333 *Calendar:* Sem. plan
Inst. Accred.: MSA-CHE (1925/2008)
Prog. Accred.: Accounting, Business (AACSB), Clinical Lab Scientist, Engineering (civil, electrical, industrial), Graduate Social Work, Landscape Architecture, Music, Planning, Public Health, Social Work, Teacher Education (NCATE)

Mount Saint Mary's University
16300 Old Emmitsburg Rd., Emmitsburg 21727-7797
Type: Private, Roman Catholic Church, four-year
Degrees: B, M, P *Enroll:* 1,887
URL: http://www.msmary.edu
Phone: (301) 447-6122 *Calendar:* Sem. plan
Inst. Accred.: ATS (1987/2005), MSA-CHE (1922/2005)

National Labor College
10000 New Hampshire Ave., Silver Spring 20903
Type: Private, independent, four-year
Degrees: B
URL: http://www.georgemeany.org
Phone: (301) 431-6400 *Calendar:* Sem. plan
Inst. Accred.: MSA-CHE (2004)

Ner Israel Rabbinical College
400 Mount Wilson Ln., Baltimore 21208
Type: Private, independent, four-year
Degrees: B, M, D *Enroll:* 608
Phone: (410) 484-7200 *Calendar:* Sem. plan
Inst. Accred.: AARTS (1974/2004)

Prince George's Community College
301 Largo Rd., Largo 20774
Type: Public, state/local, two-year
System: Maryland Higher Education Commission
Degrees: A *Enroll:* 6,261
URL: http://www.pgcc.edu
Phone: (301) 336-6000 *Calendar:* Sem. plan
Inst. Accred.: MSA-CHE (1969/2005)
Prog. Accred.: Allied Health (respiratory therapy), Engineering Technology (electrical), Nuclear Medicine Technology, Nursing, Radiography

Saint John's College
60 College Ave., PO Box 2800, Annapolis 21404
Type: Private, independent, four-year
Degrees: B, M *Enroll:* 564
URL: http://www.sjca.edu
Phone: (410) 263-2371 *Calendar:* Sem. plan
Inst. Accred.: MSA-CHE (1923/2004), AALE (2004)

Saint Mary's College of Maryland
18952 East Fisher Rd., St. Mary's City 20686-3001
Type: Public, state, four-year
System: Maryland Higher Education Commission
Degrees: B, M *Enroll:* 1,895
URL: http://www.smcm.edu
Phone: (240) 895-2000 *Calendar:* Sem. plan
Inst. Accred.: MSA-CHE (1959/2005)
Prog. Accred.: Music

Saint Mary's Seminary and University
5400 Roland Ave., Baltimore 21210
Type: Private, Roman Catholic Church, four-year
Degrees: B, M, P *Enroll:* 148
URL: http://www.stmarys.edu
Phone: (410) 864-4000 *Calendar:* Sem. plan
Inst. Accred.: ATS (1971/2001), MSA-CHE (1951/2001)

Salisbury University
1101 Camden Ave., Salisbury 21801-6837
Type: Public, state, four-year
System: University System of Maryland
Degrees: B, M *Enroll:* 6,380
URL: http://www.salisbury.edu
Phone: (410) 543-6000 *Calendar:* Sem. plan
Inst. Accred.: MSA-CHE (1956/2006)
Prog. Accred.: Allied Health (respiratory therapy), Business (AACSB), Clinical Lab Scientist, Environmental Health, Exercise Science, Graduate Social Work, Nursing Education, Social Work, Teacher Education (NCATE)

Sojourner-Douglass College
500 North Caroline St., Baltimore 21205
Type: Private, independent, four-year
Degrees: B, M *Enroll:* 795
URL: http://www.sdc.edu
Phone: (410) 276-0306 *Calendar:* Tri. plan
Inst. Accred.: MSA-CHE (1980/2006)

Nassau Campus
Pilot House, 2nd Flr., Nassau, Bahamas
Phone: 011 12423948570

Stevenson University
1525 Green Spring Valley Rd., Stevenson 21153
Type: Private, independent, four-year
Degrees: A, B, M *Enroll:* 2,574
URL: http://www.stevenson.edu
Phone: (410) 486-7000 *Calendar:* Sem. plan
Inst. Accred.: MSA-CHE (1962/2008)
Prog. Accred.: Clinical Lab Technology, Nursing, Nursing Education, Teacher Education (NCATE)

Tai Sophia Institute
7750 Monteplier Rd., Laurel 20723
Type: Private, independent, four-year
Degrees: M *Enroll:* 270
URL: http://www.tai.edu
Phone: (410) 888-9048 *Calendar:* Tri. plan
Inst. Accred.: MSA-CHE (2006), ACAOM (1985/2006)

TESST College of Technology
1520 South Caton Ave., Baltimore 21227-1063
Type: Private, proprietary, two-year
System: Kaplan Higher Education Corporation
Degrees: A
URL: http://www.tesst.com
Phone: (410) 644-6400
Inst. Accred.: ACCSCT (1973/2006)

TESST College of Technology
4600 Powder Mill Rd., Beltsville 20705
Type: Private, proprietary, two-year
System: Kaplan Higher Education Corporation
Degrees: A
URL: http://www.tesst.com
Phone: (301) 937-5327
Inst. Accred.: ACCSCT (1975/2008)

TESST College of Technology
803 Glen Eagles Ct., Towson 21286
Type: Private, proprietary, two-year
System: Kaplan Higher Education Corporation
Degrees: A *Enroll:* 623
URL: http://www.tesst.com
Phone: (410) 296-5350
Inst. Accred.: ACCSCT (2000/2005)

Towson University
8000 York Rd., Towson 21252-0001
Type: Public, state, four-year
System: University System of Maryland
Degrees: B, M, D *Enroll:* 15,286
URL: http://www.towson.edu
Phone: (410) 704-2000 *Calendar:* 4-1-4 plan
Inst. Accred.: MSA-CHE (1949/2005)
Prog. Accred.: Accounting, Allied Health (audiology, occupational therapy, speech-language pathology), Business (AACSB), Computer Science (ABET-CAC), Dance, Music, Nursing Education, Psychology Internship, Teacher Education (NCATE), Theatre

Uniformed Services University of the Health Sciences
4301 Jones Bridge Rd., Bethesda 20814-4799
Type: Public, federal, four-year
Degrees: M, P, D *FTE Enroll:* 835
URL: http://www.usuhs.mil
Phone: (301) 295-3050 *Calendar:* Sem. plan
Inst. Accred.: MSA-CHE (1984/2003)
Prog. Accred.: Allied Health (medicine), Applied Science (industrial hygiene, occupational health & safety), Clinical Psychology, Nurse Anesthesia Education, Nursing, Nursing Education, Public Health

United States Naval Academy
121 Blake Rd., Annapolis 21402-5000
Type: Public, federal, four-year
Degrees: B *Enroll:* 4,422
URL: http://www.usna.edu
Phone: (410) 293-1000 *Calendar:* Sem. plan
Inst. Accred.: MSA-CHE (1947/2006)
Prog. Accred.: Computer Science (ABET-CAC), Engineering (aerospace, electrical, mechanical, naval architecture/marine, ocean, systems)

University of Baltimore
1420 North Charles St., Baltimore 21201
Type: Public, state, four-year
System: University System of Maryland
Degrees: B, M, P, D *Enroll:* 3,393
URL: http://www.ubalt.edu
Phone: (410) 837-4200 *Calendar:* Sem. plan
Inst. Accred.: MSA-CHE (1971/2007)
Prog. Accred.: Business (AACSB), Law, Public Administration

University of Maryland Baltimore
520 West Lombard St., Baltimore 21201-1627
Type: Public, state, four-year
System: University System of Maryland
Degrees: B, M, P, D *Enroll:* 4,864
URL: http://www.umaryland.edu
Phone: (410) 706-3100 *Calendar:* 4-1-4 plan
Inst. Accred.: MSA-CHE (1921/2006)
Prog. Accred.: Allied Health (medicine), Clinical Lab Scientist, Dentistry (advanced education in general dentistry, combined prosthodontics, dental hygiene, dentistry, endodontics, general dentistry, general practice residency, oral and maxillofacial pathology, oral and maxillofacial surgery, orthodontic and dentofacial orthopedics, pediatric dentistry, periodontics, prosthodontics), Graduate Social Work, Law, Nurse (Midwifery), Nursing, Pathologists' Assistant, Pharmacy, Physical Therapy

University of Maryland Baltimore County
1000 Hilltop Circle, Baltimore 21250
Type: Public, state, four-year
System: University System of Maryland
Degrees: B, M, D *Enroll:* 9,929
URL: http://www.umbc.edu
Phone: (410) 455-1000 *Calendar:* 4-1-4 plan
Inst. Accred.: MSA-CHE (1966/2006)
Prog. Accred.: Allied Health (EMT-paramedic, diagnostic medical sonography), Clinical Psychology, Computer Science (ABET-CAC), Engineering (chemical, computer, mechanical), Nurse Anesthesia Education, Public Administration, Social Work, Teacher Education (NCATE)

University of Maryland College Park
College Park 20742
Type: Public, state, four-year
System: University System of Maryland
Degrees: B, M, P, D *Enroll:* 31,973
URL: http://www.umcp.umd.edu
Phone: (301) 405-1000 *Calendar:* Sem. plan
Inst. Accred.: MSA-CHE (1921/2007)
Prog. Accred.: Allied Health (audiology, speech-language pathology), Business (AACSB), Clinical Psychology, Counseling, Counseling Psychology, Dietetics (didactic), Dietetics (internship), Engineering (aerospace, agricultural, chemical, civil, computer, electrical, fire protection, general, materials, mechanical), Forestry, Journalism, Landscape Architecture, Librarianship, Marriage and Family Therapy, Music, Planning, Psychology Internship, Public Administration, Public Health, Rehabilitation Counseling, School Psychology, Teacher Education (NCATE), Theatre

University of Maryland Eastern Shore
11868 Academic Oval, Princess Anne 21853
Type: Public, state, four-year
System: University System of Maryland
Degrees: B, M, D *Enroll:* 3,545
URL: http://www.umes.edu
Phone: (410) 651-2200 *Calendar:* Sem. plan
Inst. Accred.: MSA-CHE (1937/2006)
Prog. Accred.: Construction Education, Dietetics (didactic), Dietetics (internship), Physical Therapy, Physician Assistant, Rehabilitation Counseling, Teacher Education (NCATE)

University of Maryland University College
3501 University Blvd. East, College Park 20783
Type: Public, state, four-year
System: University System of Maryland
Degrees: A, B, M, D *Enroll:* 12,500
URL: http://www.umuc.edu
Phone: (301) 985-7000 *Calendar:* Sem. plan
Inst. Accred.: MSA-CHE (1946/2006)

Washington Bible College
6511 Princess Garden Pkwy., Lanham 20706-3538
Type: Private, independent, four-year
Degrees: A, B, M, P *Enroll:* 416
URL: http://www.bible.edu
Phone: (301) 552-1400 *Calendar:* Sem. plan
Inst. Accred.: ABHE (1962/2002), MSA-CHE (2007)

Washington College
300 Washington Ave., Chestertown 21620-1197
Type: Private, independent, four-year
Degrees: B, M *Enroll:* 1,352
URL: http://www.washcoll.edu
Phone: (410) 778-2800 *Calendar:* Sem. plan
Inst. Accred.: MSA-CHE (1925/2004)

Wor-Wic Community College
32000 Campus Dr., Salisbury 21804
Type: Public, state/local, two-year
System: Maryland Higher Education Commission
Degrees: A *Enroll:* 1,666
URL: http://www.worwic.edu
Phone: (410) 334-2800 *Calendar:* Sem. plan
Inst. Accred.: MSA-CHE (1980/2005)
Prog. Accred.: Radiography

MASSACHUSETTS

American International College
1000 State St., Springfield 01109-3155
Type: Private, independent, four-year
Degrees: B, M, D *Enroll:* 1,530
URL: http://www.aic.edu
Phone: (413) 737-7000 *Calendar:* Sem. plan
Inst. Accred.: NEASC-CIHE (1933/1999)
Prog. Accred.: Allied Health (occupational therapy), Nursing, Nursing Education, Physical Therapy

Amherst College
PO Box 5000, Amherst 01002-5000
Type: Private, independent, four-year
Degrees: B *Enroll:* 1,612
URL: http://www.amherst.edu
Phone: (413) 542-2000 *Calendar:* Sem. plan
Inst. Accred.: NEASC-CIHE (1929/2008)

Andover Newton Theological School
210 Herrick Rd., Newton Centre 02459-2243
Type: Private, American Baptist Churches (USA) and United Church, four-year
Degrees: M, D *Enroll:* 234
URL: http://www.ants.edu
Phone: (617) 964-1100 *Calendar:* Sem. plan
Inst. Accred.: ATS (1938/2008), NEASC-CIHE (1978/2008)

Anna Maria College
Box 32 Sunset Ln., Paxton 01612-1198
Type: Private, Roman Catholic Church, four-year
Degrees: A, B, M *Enroll:* 766
URL: http://www.annamaria.edu
Phone: (508) 849-3300 *Calendar:* 4-1-4 plan
Inst. Accred.: NEASC-CIHE (1955/1998)
Prog. Accred.: Music, Nursing, Social Work

Assumption College
500 Salisbury St., Worchester 01609
Type: Private, Roman Catholic Church, four-year
Degrees: A, B, M *Enroll:* 2,428
URL: http://www.assumption.edu
Phone: (508) 767-7000 *Calendar:* Sem. plan
Inst. Accred.: NEASC-CIHE (1949/2001)
Prog. Accred.: Rehabilitation Counseling

Atlantic Union College
PO Box 1000, South Lancaster 01561-1000
Type: Private, Seventh-Day Adventist Church, four-year
Degrees: A, B, M *Enroll:* 431
URL: http://www.auc.edu
Phone: (978) 368-2000 *Calendar:* Sem. plan
Inst. Accred.: NEASC-CIHE (1945/1998, Probation)
Prog. Accred.: Music, Nursing, Social Work

Babson College
231 Forest St., Babson Park 02457-0310
Type: Private, independent, four-year
Degrees: B, M *Enroll:* 2,570
URL: http://www.babson.edu
Phone: (781) 235-1200 *Calendar:* Sem. plan
Inst. Accred.: NEASC-CIHE (1950/2001)
Prog. Accred.: Business (AACSB)

Bard College at Simon's Rock
84 Alford Rd., Great Barrington 01230-9072
Type: Private, independent, four-year
Degrees: A, B *Enroll:* 380
URL: http://www.simons-rock.edu
Phone: (413) 528-0771 *Calendar:* Sem. plan
Inst. Accred.: NEASC-CIHE (1974/2007)

Bay Path College
588 Longmeadow St., Longmeadow 01106-2292
Type: Private, independent, four-year
Degrees: A, B, M *Enroll:* 1,300
URL: http://www.baypath.edu
Phone: (413) 567-1000 *Calendar:* Sem. plan
Inst. Accred.: NEASC-CIHE (1965/2006)
Prog. Accred.: Allied Health (occupational therapy)

Bay State College
122 Commonwealth Ave., Boston 02116-2975
Type: Private, independent, four-year
Degrees: A, B *Enroll:* 692
URL: http://www.baystate.edu
Phone: (617) 236-8000 *Calendar:* Sem. plan
Inst. Accred.: NEASC-CIHE (2008), NEASC-CTCI (1989/2006)
Prog. Accred.: Medical Assisting (ABHES), Physical Therapy Assisting

Becker College
61 Sever St., PO Box 15071, Worcester 01609
Type: Private, independent, four-year
Degrees: A, B *Enroll:* 1,363
URL: http://www.beckercollege.edu
Phone: (508) 791-9241 *Calendar:* Sem. plan
Inst. Accred.: NEASC-CIHE (1976/2007)
Prog. Accred.: Nursing

Leicester Campus
3 Paxton St., Leicester 01524
Phone: (508) 791-9241
Prog. Accred: Veterinary Technology

Benjamin Franklin Institute of Technology
41 Berkeley St., Boston 02116-6296
Type: Private, independent, four-year
Degrees: A, B *Enroll:* 365
URL: http://www.bfit.edu
Phone: (617) 423-4630 *Calendar:* Sem. plan
Inst. Accred.: NEASC-CIHE (2006)
Prog. Accred.: Engineering Technology (computer, electrical)

Bentley University
175 Forest St., Waltham 02452-4705
Type: Private, independent, four-year
Degrees: A, B, M *Enroll:* 4,841
URL: http://www.bentley.edu
Phone: (781) 891-2000 *Calendar:* Sem. plan
Inst. Accred.: NEASC-CIHE (1966/2002)
Prog. Accred.: Accounting, Business (AACSB)

Berklee College of Music
1140 Boylston St., Boston 02215-3693
Type: Private, independent, four-year
Degrees: B *Enroll:* 3,815
URL: http://www.berklee.edu
Phone: (617) 266-1400 *Calendar:* Sem. plan
Inst. Accred.: NEASC-CIHE (1973/2003)

Berkshire Community College
West St., Pittsfield 01201-5786
Type: Public, state, two-year
System: Massachusetts Department of Higher Education
Degrees: A *Enroll:* 1,395
URL: http://www.berkshirecc.edu
Phone: (413) 499-4660 *Calendar:* Sem. plan
Inst. Accred.: NEASC-CIHE (1964/1999)
Prog. Accred.: Allied Health (respiratory therapy), Nursing, Physical Therapy Assisting

Blessed John XXIII National Seminary
558 South Ave., Weston 02193-2699
Type: Private, Roman Catholic Church, four-year
Degrees: M *Enroll:* 65
URL: http://www.blessedjohnxxiii.edu
Phone: (781) 899-5500 *Calendar:* Sem. plan
Inst. Accred.: ATS (1983/2008)

The Boston Architectural College
320 Newbury St., Boston 02115-2795
Type: Private, independent, four-year
Degrees: B, M *Enroll:* 971
URL: http://www.the-bac.edu
Phone: (617) 262-5000 *Calendar:* Sem. plan
Inst. Accred.: NEASC-CIHE (1991/2006)
Prog. Accred.: Interior Design

Boston Baptist College
950 Metropolitan Ave., Boston 02136
Type: Private, Baptist Church, four-year
Degrees: A, B *Enroll:* 134
URL: http://www.boston.edu
Phone: (617) 364-3510 *Calendar:* Sem. plan
Inst. Accred.: TRACS (1996/2001)

Boston College
140 Commonwealth Ave., Chestnut Hill 02467-3934
Type: Private, Roman Catholic Church, four-year
Degrees: B, M, D *Enroll:* 13,101
URL: http://www.bc.edu
Phone: (617) 552-8000 *Calendar:* Sem. plan
Inst. Accred.: ATS (1968/1998), NEASC-CIHE (1935/2007)
Prog. Accred.: Business (AACSB), Counseling Psychology, Graduate Social Work, Law, Nurse Anesthesia Education, Nursing Education

The Boston Conservatory
8 The Fenway, Boston 02215
Type: Private, independent, four-year
Degrees: B, M *Enroll:* 565
URL: http://www.bostonconservatory.edu
Phone: (617) 536-6340 *Calendar:* Sem. plan
Inst. Accred.: NEASC-CIHE (1968/1999)
Prog. Accred.: Music

Boston Graduate School of Psychoanalysis
1581 Beacon St., Brookline 02446-4602
Type: Private, independent, four-year
Degrees: M, D *Enroll:* 93
URL: http://www.bgsp.edu
Phone: (617) 277-3915 *Calendar:* Sem. plan
Inst. Accred.: NEASC-CIHE (1996/2001)

Boston University
One Sherborne St., Boston 02215
Type: Private, independent, four-year
Degrees: B, M, D *Enroll:* 27,540
URL: http://www.bu.edu
Phone: (617) 353-2000 *Calendar:* Sem. plan
Inst. Accred.: ATS (1938/2001), NEASC-CIHE (1929/1999)
Prog. Accred.: Allied Health (audiology, health services administration, medicine, occupational therapy, speech-language pathology), Business (AACSB), Clinical Psychology, Dentistry (advanced education in general dentistry, combined prosthodontics, dental public health, dentistry, endodontics, general dentistry, oral and maxillofacial pathology, oral and maxillofacial surgery, orthodontic and dentofacial orthopedics, pediatric dentistry, periodontics), Dietetics (coordinated), Dietetics (didactic), Dietetics (internship), Engineering (aerospace, bioengineering, computer, electrical, manufacturing, mechanical), English Language Education, Graduate Social Work, Law, Music, Nurse (Midwifery), Physical Therapy, Psychology Internship, Public Health

Brandeis University
415 South St., Waltham 02454-9110
Type: Private, independent, four-year
Degrees: B, M, D *Enroll:* 4,829
URL: http://www.brandeis.edu
Phone: (781) 736-2000 *Calendar:* Sem. plan
Inst. Accred.: NEASC-CIHE (1953/2006)
Prog. Accred.: Business (AACSB)

Bridgewater State College
131 Summer St., Bridgewater 02325-0002
Type: Public, state, four-year
System: Massachusetts Department of Higher Education
Degrees: B, M *Enroll:* 7,863
URL: http://www.bridgew.edu
Phone: (508) 531-1200 *Calendar:* Sem. plan
Inst. Accred.: NEASC-CIHE (1953/2002)
Prog. Accred.: Graduate Social Work, Social Work, Teacher Education (NCATE)

Bristol Community College
777 Elsbree St., Fall River 02720-7395
Type: Public, state, two-year
System: Massachusetts Department of Higher Education
Degrees: A *Enroll:* 4,365
URL: http://www.bristol.mass.edu
Phone: (508) 678-2811 *Calendar:* Sem. plan
Inst. Accred.: NEASC-CIHE (1970/2004)
Prog. Accred.: Allied Health (medical assisting (AMA), occupational therapy assisting), Clinical Lab Technology, Dentistry (dental hygiene), Nursing

Bunker Hill Community College
250 New Rutherford Ave., Boston 02129-2991
Type: Public, state, two-year
System: Massachusetts Department of Higher Education
Degrees: A *Enroll:* 4,217
URL: http://www.bhcc.mass.edu
Phone: (617) 228-2000 *Calendar:* Sem. plan
Inst. Accred.: NEASC-CIHE (1976/2000)
Prog. Accred.: Allied Health (diagnostic medical sonography), Nursing, Radiography

Chelsea Campus
175 Hawthorne St., Bellingham Square, Chelsea 02150-2917
Phone: (617) 228-2101
Prog. Accred: Allied Health (surgical technology)

Cambridge College
1000 Massachusetts Ave., Cambridge 02138-5304
Type: Private, independent, four-year
Degrees: B, M *Enroll:* 2,888
URL: http://www.cambridgecollege.edu
Phone: (617) 868-1000 *Calendar:* Sem. plan
Inst. Accred.: NEASC-CIHE (1981/2006)

Chesapeake Campus
1403 Greenbrier Pkwy., The Oracle Bldg., Ste. 300, Chesapeake, VA 23320
Phone: (757) 424-0333

Springfield Campus
570 Cottage St., Springfield 01104
Phone: (413) 747-0204

Cape Cod Community College
2240 Iyanough Rd., West Barnstable 02668-1599
Type: Public, state, two-year
System: Massachusetts Department of Higher Education
Degrees: A *Enroll:* 2,280
URL: http://www.capecod.mass.edu
Phone: (508) 362-2131 *Calendar:* Sem. plan
Inst. Accred.: NEASC-CIHE (1967/1998)
Prog. Accred.: Allied Health (medical assisting (AMA)), Dentistry (dental hygiene), Nursing

Caritas Laboure College
2120 Dorchester Ave., Boston 02124-5698
Type: Private, Roman Catholic Church, four-year
Degrees: A, B *Enroll:* 348
URL: http://www.laboure.edu
Phone: (617) 296-8300 *Calendar:* Sem. plan
Inst. Accred.: NEASC-CIHE (2006)
Prog. Accred.: Dietetic Technician, Nursing, Radiation Therapy

Clark University
950 Main St., Worcester 01610-1477
Type: Private, independent, four-year
Degrees: B, M, D *Enroll:* 2,846
URL: http://www.clarku.edu
Phone: (508) 793-7711 *Calendar:* Sem. plan
Inst. Accred.: NEASC-CIHE (1929/2006)
Prog. Accred.: Allied Health (medical assisting (AMA)), Business (AACSB), Clinical Psychology

College of Our Lady of the Elms
291 Springfield St., Chicopee 01013-2839
Type: Private, Roman Catholic Church, four-year
Degrees: B, M *Enroll:* 831
URL: http://www.elms.edu
Phone: (413) 594-2761 *Calendar:* Sem. plan
Inst. Accred.: NEASC-CIHE (1942/2003)
Prog. Accred.: Nursing Education, Social Work

College of the Holy Cross
One College St., Worcester 01610-2395
Type: Private, Society of Jesus, four-year
Degrees: B *Enroll:* 2,799
URL: http://www.holycross.edu
Phone: (508) 793-2011 *Calendar:* Sem. plan
Inst. Accred.: NEASC-CIHE (1930/2000)
Prog. Accred.: Theatre

Conway School of Landscape Design
PO Box 179, Conway 01341-0179
Type: Private, independent, four-year
Degrees: M *Enroll:* 17
URL: http://www.csld.edu
Phone: (413) 369-4044 *Calendar:* Tri. plan
Inst. Accred.: NEASC-CIHE (1989/2005)

Curry College
1071 Blue Hill Ave., Milton 02186-2395
Type: Private, independent, four-year
Degrees: B, M *Enroll:* 2,371
URL: http://www.curry.edu
Phone: (617) 333-0500 *Calendar:* Sem. plan
Inst. Accred.: NEASC-CIHE (1970/2002)
Prog. Accred.: Nursing Education

Dean College
99 Main St., Franklin 02038-1994
Type: Private, independent, four-year
Degrees: A, B *Enroll:* 1,052
URL: http://www.dean.edu
Phone: (508) 528-9100 *Calendar:* Sem. plan
Inst. Accred.: NEASC-CIHE (1957/2006)

Eastern Nazarene College
23 East Elm Ave., Quincy 02170-2999
Type: Private, Church of the Nazarene, four-year
Degrees: A, B, M *Enroll:* 1,206
URL: http://www.enc.edu
Phone: (617) 745-3000 *Calendar:* 4-1-4 plan
Inst. Accred.: NEASC-CIHE (1943/2000)
Prog. Accred.: Social Work

Emerson College
120 Boylston St., Boston 02116-4624
Type: Private, independent, four-year
Degrees: B, M, D *Enroll:* 4,039
URL: http://www.emerson.edu
Phone: (617) 824-8500 *Calendar:* Sem. plan
Inst. Accred.: NEASC-CIHE (1950/2002)
Prog. Accred.: Allied Health (speech-language pathology)

Emmanuel College
400 The Fenway, Boston 02115-5798
Type: Private, Roman Catholic Church, four-year
Degrees: B, M *Enroll:* 1,853
URL: http://www.emmanuel.edu
Phone: (617) 277-9430 *Calendar:* Sem. plan
Inst. Accred.: NEASC-CIHE (1933/2002)
Prog. Accred.: Nursing Education

Endicott College
376 Hale St., Beverly 01915-2098
Type: Private, independent, four-year
Degrees: A, B, M *Enroll:* 2,122
URL: http://www.endicott.edu
Phone: (978) 927-0585 *Calendar:* Sem. plan
Inst. Accred.: NEASC-CIHE (1952/2007)
Prog. Accred.: Interior Design, Nursing

Episcopal Divinity School
99 Brattle St., Cambridge 02138
Type: Private, Episcopal Church, four-year
Degrees: M, D *Enroll:* 73
URL: http://www.episdivschool.edu
Phone: (617) 868-3450 *Calendar:* Sem. plan
Inst. Accred.: ATS (1938/2008)

FINE Mortuary College
150 Kerry Place, Norwood 02062
Type: Private, independent, two-year
Degrees: A
URL: http://www.fine-ne.com
Phone: (781) 762-1211 *Calendar:* Qtr. plan
Inst. Accred.: ABFSE (1969/2004)

Fisher College
118 Beacon St., Boston 02116-1500
Type: Private, independent, four-year
Degrees: A, B *Enroll:* 886
URL: http://www.fisher.edu
Phone: (617) 236-8800 *Calendar:* Sem. plan
Inst. Accred.: NEASC-CIHE (1970/2000)

Fitchburg State College
160 Pearl St., Fitchburg 01420-2697
Type: Public, state, four-year
System: Massachusetts Department of Higher Education
Degrees: B, M *Enroll:* 4,001
URL: http://www.fsc.edu
Phone: (978) 345-2151 *Calendar:* Sem. plan
Inst. Accred.: NEASC-CIHE (1953/2002)
Prog. Accred.: Clinical Lab Scientist, Nursing Education, Teacher Education (NCATE)

Framingham State College
100 State St., Framingham 01701-9101
Type: Public, state, four-year
System: Massachusetts Department of Higher Education
Degrees: B, M *Enroll:* 4,152
URL: http://www.framingham.edu
Phone: (508) 626-1220 *Calendar:* Sem. plan
Inst. Accred.: NEASC-CIHE (1950/2004)
Prog. Accred.: Dietetics (coordinated), Dietetics (didactic), Nursing

Franklin W. Olin College of Engineering
Olin Way, Needham 02492-1245
Type: Private, independent, four-year
Degrees: B
URL: http://www.olin.edu
Phone: (781) 292-2222 *Calendar:* Sem. plan
Inst. Accred.: NEASC-CIHE (2006)

Gibbs College of Boston, Inc.
126 Newbury St., Boston 02116-2904
Type: Private, proprietary, two-year
System: Career Education Corporation
Degrees: A *Enroll:* 476
URL: http://www.gibbsboston.edu
Phone: (617) 578-7100 *Calendar:* Qtr. plan
Inst. Accred.: ACICS (1967/2008)

Gordon College
255 Grapevine Rd., Wenham 01984-1899
Type: Private, independent, four-year
Degrees: B, M *Enroll:* 1,601
URL: http://www.gordon.edu
Phone: (978) 927-2300 *Calendar:* Sem. plan
Inst. Accred.: NEASC-CIHE (1961/2002)
Prog. Accred.: Music, Social Work

Gordon-Conwell Theological Seminary
130 Essex St., South Hamilton 01982-2317
Type: Private, interdenominational, four-year
Degrees: M, D *Enroll:* 1,340
URL: http://www.gordonconwell.edu
Phone: (978) 468-7111 *Calendar:* Sem. plan
Inst. Accred.: ATS (1964/2005), NEASC-CIHE (1985/2006)

Center for Urban Ministerial Education
90 Warren St., Roxbury 02119
Phone: (617) 427- 7293

Southeast Campus
14542 Choate Circle, Charlotte, NC 28273
Phone: (704) 527-9909

Greenfield Community College
One College Dr., Greenfield 01301-9734
Type: Public, state, two-year
System: Massachusetts Department of Higher Education
Degrees: A *Enroll:* 1,405
URL: http://www.gcc.mass.edu
Phone: (413) 775-1000 *Calendar:* Sem. plan
Inst. Accred.: NEASC-CIHE (1966/2000)
Prog. Accred.: Allied Health (massage therapy), Nursing

Hampshire College
893 West St., Amherst 01002
Type: Private, independent, four-year
Degrees: B *Enroll:* 1,376
URL: http://www.hampshire.edu
Phone: (413) 549-4600 *Calendar:* 4-1-4 plan
Inst. Accred.: NEASC-CIHE (1974/2007)

Harvard University
Massachusetts Hall, Cambridge 02138-3800
Type: Private, independent, four-year
Degrees: A, B, M, D *Enroll:* 21,493
URL: http://www.harvard.edu
Phone: (617) 495-1000 *Calendar:* Sem. plan
Inst. Accred.: ATS (1940/2002), NEASC-CIHE (1929/2007)
Prog. Accred.: Allied Health (medicine), Business (AACSB), Dentistry (advanced education in general dentistry, combined prosthodontics, dental public health, dentistry, endodontics, general dentistry, oral and maxillofacial pathology, orthodontic and dentofacial orthopedics, pediatric dentistry, periodontics), Engineering (engineering physics/science), Law, Planning, Public Administration, Public Health

Harvard School of Public Health
677 Huntington Ave., Boston 02115
Phone: (617) 432-1000
Prog. Accred: Applied Science (industrial hygiene)

Radcliffe Institute for Advanced Study
10 Garden St., Cambridge 02138
Phone: (617) 495-8601

Hebrew College
160 Herrick Rd., Newton Centre 02459
Type: Private, independent, four-year
Degrees: B, M *Enroll:* 89
URL: http://www.hebrewcollege.org
Phone: (617) 559-8600 *Calendar:* Sem. plan
Inst. Accred.: NEASC-CIHE (1955/1998)

Hellenic College/Holy Cross Greek Orthodox School of Theology
50 Goddard Ave., Brookline 02445-7496
Type: Private, Greek Orthodox Church, four-year
Degrees: B, M *Enroll:* 180
URL: http://www.hchc.edu
Phone: (617) 731-3500 *Calendar:* Sem. plan
Inst. Accred.: ATS (1974/2001), NEASC-CIHE (1974/2001)

Holyoke Community College
303 Homestead Ave., Holyoke 01040-1099
Type: Public, state/local, two-year
System: Massachusetts Department of Higher Education
Degrees: A *Enroll:* 4,147
URL: http://www.hcc.mass.edu
Phone: (413) 538-7000 *Calendar:* Sem. plan
Inst. Accred.: NEASC-CIHE (1970/2000)
Prog. Accred.: Allied Health (opticianry), Business (ACBSP), Culinary Education, Music, Nursing, Radiography, Veterinary Technology

Hult International Business School
One Education St., Cambridge 02141
Type: Private, proprietary, four-year
Degrees: M *Enroll:* 93
URL: http://www.hult.edu
Phone: (617) 746 1990 *Calendar:* Tri. plan
Inst. Accred.: NEASC-CIHE (1976/2007)

Lasell College
1844 Commonwealth Ave., Newton 02466-2716
Type: Private, independent, four-year
Degrees: A, B, M *Enroll:* 1,217
URL: http://www.lasell.edu
Phone: (617) 243-2000 *Calendar:* Sem. plan
Inst. Accred.: NEASC-CIHE (1932/2002)

Lesley University
29 Everett St., Cambridge 02138-2790
Type: Private, independent, four-year
Degrees: A, B, M, D *Enroll:* 4,190
URL: http://www.lesley.edu
Phone: (617) 868-9600 *Calendar:* Sem. plan
Inst. Accred.: NEASC-CIHE (1952/2005)

The Art Institute of Boston at Lesley University
700 Beacon St., Boston 02215
Phone: (617) 585-6600
Prog. Accred: Art

Longy School of Music
One Follen St., Cambridge 02138-3599
Type: Private, independent, four-year
Degrees: M *Enroll:* 170
URL: http://www.longy.edu
Phone: (617) 876-0956
Inst. Accred.: NEASC-CIHE (1995/2008)
Prog. Accred.: Music

Marian Court College
35 Little's Point Rd., Swampscott 01907
Type: Private, Roman Catholic Church, two-year
Degrees: A *Enroll:* 189
URL: http://www.mariancourt.edu
Phone: (781) 595-6768 *Calendar:* Sem. plan
Inst. Accred.: NEASC-CIHE (2004)

Massachusetts Bay Community College
50 Oakland St., Wellesley Hills 02481-5357
Type: Public, state, two-year
System: Massachusetts Department of Higher Education
Degrees: A *Enroll:* 3,109
URL: http://www.massbay.edu
Phone: (781) 239-3000 *Calendar:* Sem. plan
Inst. Accred.: NEASC-CIHE (1967/2005)
Prog. Accred.: Allied Health (massage therapy, surgical technology), Nursing, Physical Therapy Assisting, Radiography

Massachusetts College of Art and Design
621 Huntington Ave., Boston 02115-5882
Type: Public, state, four-year
System: Massachusetts Department of Higher Education
Degrees: B, M *Enroll:* 1,718
URL: http://www.massart.edu
Phone: (617) 879-7000 *Calendar:* Sem. plan
Inst. Accred.: NEASC-CIHE (1954/2005)
Prog. Accred.: Art

Massachusetts College of Liberal Arts
375 Church St., North Adams 01247-4100
Type: Public, state, four-year
System: Massachusetts Department of Higher Education
Degrees: B, M *Enroll:* 1,472
URL: http://www.mcla.mass.edu
Phone: (413) 662-5000 *Calendar:* Sem. plan
Inst. Accred.: NEASC-CIHE (1953/2003)

Massachusetts College of Pharmacy and Health Sciences
179 Longwood Ave., Boston 02115-5896
Type: Private, independent, four-year
Degrees: A, B, M, P, D *Enroll:* 2,721
URL: http://www.mcp.edu
Phone: (617) 732-2800 *Calendar:* Sem. plan
Inst. Accred.: NEASC-CIHE (1974/2007)
Prog. Accred.: Dentistry (dental hygiene), Nuclear Medicine Technology, Nursing Education, Pharmacy, Physician Assistant, Radiation Therapy, Radiography

Manchester Center for Health Sciences
1528 Elm St., Manchester, NH 03101
Phone: (800) 225-5506
Prog. Accred: Physician Assistant

Worcester Campus
19 Foster St., Worcester 01608
Phone: (508) 890-8855
Prog. Accred: Pharmacy

Massachusetts Institute of Technology
77 Massachusetts Ave., Cambridge 02139-4307
Type: Private, independent, four-year
Degrees: B, M, D *Enroll:* 10,004
URL: http://www.mit.edu
Phone: (617) 253-1000 *Calendar:* 4-1-4 plan
Inst. Accred.: NEASC-CIHE (1929/1999)
Prog. Accred.: Business (AACSB), Computer Science (ABET-CAC), Engineering (aerospace, chemical, civil, computer, electrical, environmental/sanitary, materials, mechanical, nuclear, ocean), Planning

Massachusetts Maritime Academy
101 Academy Dr., Buzzards Bay 02532-3400
Type: Public, state, four-year
System: Massachusetts Department of Higher Education
Degrees: B, M *Enroll:* 969
URL: http://www.mma.mass.edu
Phone: (508) 830-5000 *Calendar:* Sem. plan
Inst. Accred.: NEASC-CIHE (1974/2001)

Massachusetts School of Law
500 Federal St., Andover 01810-1094
Type: Private, independent, four-year
Degrees: D *Enroll:* 494
URL: http://www.mslaw.edu
Phone: (978) 681-0800 *Calendar:* Sem. plan
Inst. Accred.: NEASC-CIHE (1997/2002)

Massachusetts School of Professional Psychology
221 Rivermoor St., Boston 02132-4935
Type: Private, independent, four-year
Degrees: D *Enroll:* 206
URL: http://www.mspp.edu
Phone: (617) 327-6777 *Calendar:* Sem. plan
Inst. Accred.: NEASC-CIHE (1984/2002)
Prog. Accred.: Clinical Psychology

Massasoit Community College
One Massasoit Blvd., Brockton 02402
Type: Public, state, two-year
System: Massachusetts Department of Higher Education
Degrees: A *Enroll:* 4,382
URL: http://www.massasoit.mass.edu
Phone: (508) 588-9100 *Calendar:* Sem. plan
Inst. Accred.: NEASC-CIHE (1971/2006)
Prog. Accred.: Allied Health (medical assisting (AMA), respiratory therapy), Nursing, Radiography

Canton Campus
900 Randolph St., Canton 02021
Phone: (781) 821-2222
Prog. Accred: Dentistry (dental assisting)

Merrimack College
315 Turnpike St., North Andover 01845-5800
Type: Private, Roman Catholic Church, four-year
Degrees: A, B, M *Enroll:* 2,015
URL: http://www.merrimack.edu
Phone: (978) 837-5000 *Calendar:* Sem. plan
Inst. Accred.: NEASC-CIHE (1953/2001)
Prog. Accred.: Engineering (civil, electrical)

MGH Institute of Health Professions
36 First Ave., Charlestown Navy Yard, Boston 02129-4557
Type: Private, independent, four-year
Degrees: M, D *Enroll:* 501
URL: http://www.mghihp.edu
Phone: (617) 726-2947 *Calendar:* Sem. plan
Inst. Accred.: NEASC-CIHE (1985/2000)
Prog. Accred.: Allied Health (speech-language pathology), Nursing, Physical Therapy

Middlesex Community College
590 Springs Rd., Bedford 01730-1197
Type: Public, state, two-year
System: Massachusetts Department of Higher Education
Degrees: A *Enroll:* 4,982
URL: http://www.middlesex.mass.edu
Phone: (781) 280-3200 *Calendar:* Sem. plan
Inst. Accred.: NEASC-CIHE (1973/2004)
Prog. Accred.: Nursing, Radiography

Lowell Campus
33 Kearney Square, Lowell 01852-1987
Phone: (508) 656-3200
Prog. Accred: Allied Health (diagnostic medical sonography, medical assisting (AMA)), Dentistry (dental assisting, dental hygiene, dental laboratory technology)

Montserrat College of Art
23 Essex St., Box 26, Beverly 01915-4508
Type: Private, independent, four-year
Degrees: B *Enroll:* 290
URL: http://www.montserrat.edu
Phone: (978) 922-8222 *Calendar:* Sem. plan
Inst. Accred.: NEASC-CIHE (1995/2001)
Prog. Accred.: Art

Mount Holyoke College
50 College St., South Hadley 01075
Type: Private, independent, four-year
Degrees: B, M *Enroll:* 2,084
URL: http://www.mtholyoke.edu
Phone: (413) 538-2000 *Calendar:* 4-1-4 plan
Inst. Accred.: NEASC-CIHE (1929/2007)

Mount Ida College
777 Dedham St., Newton Centre 02159-3310
Type: Private, independent, four-year
Degrees: A, B *Enroll:* 1,240
URL: http://www.mountida.edu
Phone: (617) 928-4500 *Calendar:* Sem. plan
Inst. Accred.: NEASC-CIHE (1970/2007)
Prog. Accred.: Art, Dentistry (dental hygiene), Funeral Service Education (Mortuary Science), Interior Design, Veterinary Technology

Mount Wachusett Community College
444 Green St., Gardner 01440-1000
Type: Public, state, two-year
System: Massachusetts Department of Higher Education
Degrees: A *Enroll:* 2,701
URL: http://www.mwcc.mass.edu
Phone: (978) 632-6600 *Calendar:* Sem. plan
Inst. Accred.: NEASC-CIHE (1968/2002)
Prog. Accred.: Allied Health (massage therapy, medical assisting (AMA)), Nursing, Physical Therapy Assisting

The National Graduate School
186 Jones Rd., Falmouth 02540
Type: Private, independent, four-year
Degrees: M
URL: http://www.ngs.edu
Phone: (800) 838-2580
Inst. Accred.: NEASC-CIHE (1998/2001)

The New England College of Finance
10 High St., Ste. 204, Boston 02110
Type: Private, independent, four-year
Degrees: A, B, M *Enroll:* 195
URL: http://www.finance.edu
Phone: (617) 951-2350 *Calendar:* Sem. plan
Inst. Accred.: NEASC-CIHE (2007)

New England College of Optometry
424 Beacon St., Boston 02115-1129
Type: Private, independent, four-year
Degrees: B, M, P, D *Enroll:* 423
URL: http://www.ne-optometry.edu
Phone: (617) 266-2030 *Calendar:* Sem. plan
Inst. Accred.: NEASC-CIHE (1976/2003)
Prog. Accred.: Allied Health (optometric residency, optometry)

New England Conservatory of Music
290 Huntington Ave., Boston 02115-5018
Type: Private, independent, four-year
Degrees: B, M, D *Enroll:* 775
URL: http://www.newenglandconservatory.edu
Phone: (617) 585-1100 *Calendar:* Sem. plan
Inst. Accred.: NEASC-CIHE (1951/1998)
Prog. Accred.: Music

The New England Institute of Art
10 Brookline Place West, Brookline 02445
Type: Private, independent, four-year
System: Education Management Corporation
Degrees: A, B *Enroll:* 1,177
URL: http://www.aine.artinstitute.edu
Phone: (617) 739-1700 *Calendar:* Sem. plan
Inst. Accred.: NEASC-CIHE (2004)

New England School of Acupuncture
150 California St., 3rd Flr., Newton 02458
Type: Private, proprietary, four-year
Degrees: M *Enroll:* 173
URL: http://www.nesa.edu
Phone: (617) 558-1788 *Calendar:* Sem. plan
Inst. Accred.: ACAOM (1988/2008)

New England School of Law
154 Stuart St., Boston 02116
Type: Private, independent, four-year
Degrees: P *Enroll:* 926
URL: http://www.nesl.edu
Phone: (617) 451-0010 *Calendar:* Sem. plan
Inst. Accred.: ABA (1969/2002)
Prog. Accred.: Law

Newbury College
129 Fisher Ave., Brookline 02445-5796
Type: Private, independent, four-year
Degrees: A, B *Enroll:* 1,060
URL: http://www.newbury.edu
Phone: (617) 730-7000 *Calendar:* Sem. plan
Inst. Accred.: NEASC-CIHE (2000/2006)
Prog. Accred.: Interior Design

Nichols College
PO Box 5000, Dudley 01571
Type: Private, independent, four-year
Degrees: A, B, M *Enroll:* 1,174
URL: http://www.nichols.edu
Phone: (508) 943-1560 *Calendar:* Sem. plan
Inst. Accred.: NEASC-CIHE (1965/2004)

North Shore Community College
1 Ferncroft Rd., Danvers 01923-0840
Type: Public, state/local, two-year
System: Massachusetts Department of Higher Education
Degrees: A *Enroll:* 4,053
URL: http://www.nscc.mass.edu
Phone: (978) 762-4000 *Calendar:* Sem. plan
Inst. Accred.: NEASC-CIHE (1969/1999)
Prog. Accred.: Allied Health (medical assisting (AMA), occupational therapy assisting, respiratory therapy, surgical technology), Aviation, Nursing, Physical Therapy Assisting, Radiography, Veterinary Technology

Essex Agricultural and Technical Institute
562 Maple St., Hathorne 01937
Phone: (978) 762-4000

Northeastern University
360 Huntington Ave., Boston 02115-0195
Type: Private, independent, four-year
Degrees: A, B, M, P, D *Enroll:* 19,552
URL: http://www.northeastern.edu
Phone: (617) 373-2000 *Calendar:* Qtr. plan
Inst. Accred.: NEASC-CIHE (1940/1998)
Prog. Accred.: Allied Health (audiology, perfusion, respiratory therapy, speech-language pathology), Business (AACSB), Clinical Lab Scientist, Clinical Lab Technology, Combined Professional-Scientific Psychology, Computer Science (ABET-CAC), Engineering (chemical, civil, electrical, industrial, mechanical), Engineering Technology (electrical, mechanical), Law, Nurse Anesthesia Education, Nursing Education, Pharmacy, Physical Therapy, Physician Assistant, Public Administration, Radiography, Rehabilitation Counseling

Northern Essex Community College
100 Elliott Way, Haverhill 01830-2399
Type: Public, state, two-year
System: Massachusetts Department of Higher Education
Degrees: A *Enroll:* 3,664
URL: http://www.necc.mass.edu
Phone: (978) 556-3000 *Calendar:* Sem. plan
Inst. Accred.: NEASC-CIHE (1969/2000)
Prog. Accred.: Allied Health (medical assisting (AMA), respiratory therapy), Nursing, Polysomnographic Technology, Practical Nursing, Radiography

Lawrence Campus
45 Franklin St., Lawrence 01841
Phone: (978) 556-3000
Prog. Accred: Dentistry (dental assisting), Radiography

Pine Manor College
400 Heath St., Chestnut Hill 02467-2332
Type: Private, independent, four-year
Degrees: A, B, M *Enroll:* 450
URL: http://www.pmc.edu
Phone: (617) 731-7000 *Calendar:* Sem. plan
Inst. Accred.: NEASC-CIHE (1939/2003)

Quincy College
34 Coddington St., Quincy 02169-4501
Type: Public, local, two-year
Degrees: A *Enroll:* 2,176
URL: http://www.quincycollege.edu
Phone: (617) 984-1600 *Calendar:* Sem. plan
Inst. Accred.: NEASC-CIHE (1980/2006)
Prog. Accred.: Allied Health (surgical technology), Nursing, Practical Nursing

Quinsigamond Community College
670 West Boylston St., Worcester 01606-2092
Type: Public, state, two-year
System: Massachusetts Department of Higher Education
Degrees: A *Enroll:* 3,838
URL: http://www.qcc.edu
Phone: (508) 853-2300 *Calendar:* Sem. plan
Inst. Accred.: NEASC-CIHE (1967/2003)
Prog. Accred.: Allied Health (medical assisting (AMA), occupational therapy assisting, respiratory therapy, surgical technology), Dentistry (dental assisting, dental hygiene), Nursing, Practical Nursing, Radiography

Regis College
235 Wellesley St., Weston 02493-1571
Type: Private, Roman Catholic Church, four-year
Degrees: B, M *Enroll:* 983
URL: http://www.regiscollege.edu
Phone: (781) 768-7000 *Calendar:* Sem. plan
Inst. Accred.: NEASC-CIHE (1933/2006)
Prog. Accred.: Nursing, Social Work

Roxbury Community College
1234 Columbus Ave., Roxbury Crossing 02120-3400
Type: Public, state, two-year
System: Massachusetts Department of Higher Education
Degrees: A *Enroll:* 1,353
URL: http://www.rcc.mass.edu
Phone: (617) 427-0060 *Calendar:* Sem. plan
Inst. Accred.: NEASC-CIHE (1981/2005)
Prog. Accred.: Nursing

Saint John's Seminary
127 Lake St., Brighton 02135-3898
Type: Private, Roman Catholic Church, four-year
Degrees: B, M, P *Enroll:* 67
URL: http://www.sjs.edu
Phone: (617) 254-2610 *Calendar:* Sem. plan
Inst. Accred.: ATS (1970/2000), NEASC-CIHE (1969/2000)

Salem State College
352 Lafayette St., Salem 01970-5353
Type: Public, state, four-year
System: Massachusetts Department of Higher Education
Degrees: B, M *Enroll:* 7,334
URL: http://www.salemstate.edu
Phone: (978) 542-6000 *Calendar:* Sem. plan
Inst. Accred.: NEASC-CIHE (1953/2001)
Prog. Accred.: Allied Health (occupational therapy), Art, Computer Science (ABET-CAC), Graduate Social Work, Nuclear Medicine Technology, Nursing, Nursing Education, Social Work, Teacher Education (NCATE), Theatre

School of the Museum of Fine Arts, Boston
230 The Fenway, Boston 02115-9975
Type: Private, independent, four-year
Degrees: B, M *Enroll:* 784
URL: http://www.smfa.edu
Phone: (617) 267-6100 *Calendar:* Sem. plan
Inst. Accred.: NASAD (1948/2004)

Simmons College
300 The Fenway, Boston 02115-5898
Type: Private, independent, four-year
Degrees: B, M, D *Enroll:* 3,278
URL: http://www.simmons.edu
Phone: (617) 521-2000 *Calendar:* Sem. plan
Inst. Accred.: NEASC-CIHE (1929/2000)
Prog. Accred.: Allied Health (health services administration), Dietetics (didactic), Dietetics (internship), Graduate Social Work, Librarianship, Nursing Education, Physical Therapy

Smith College
Northampton 01063-0001
Type: Private, independent, four-year
Degrees: B, M, D *Enroll:* 3,056
URL: http://www.smith.edu
Phone: (413) 584-2700 *Calendar:* Sem. plan
Inst. Accred.: NEASC-CIHE (1929/2007)
Prog. Accred.: Engineering (engineering physics/science), Graduate Social Work

Southern New England School of Law
333 Faunce Corner Rd., North Dartmouth 02747-1252
Type: Private, independent, four-year
Degrees: D *Enroll:* 216
URL: http://www.snesl.edu
Phone: (508) 998-9600
Inst. Accred.: NEASC-CIHE (1995/2000)

Springfield College
263 Alder St., Springfield 01109-3788
Type: Private, independent, four-year
Degrees: B, M, D *Enroll:* 4,497
URL: http://www.spfldcol.edu
Phone: (413) 748-3000 *Calendar:* Sem. plan
Inst. Accred.: NEASC-CIHE (1930/2000)
Prog. Accred.: Allied Health (occupational therapy), Graduate Social Work, Physical Therapy, Physician Assistant, Recreation and Leisure Services, Rehabilitation Counseling

Springfield Technical Community College
One Armory Square, Springfield 01105-1296
Type: Public, state, two-year
System: Massachusetts Department of Higher Education
Degrees: A *Enroll:* 3,721
URL: http://www.stcc.edu
Phone: (413) 781-7822 *Calendar:* Sem. plan
Inst. Accred.: NEASC-CIHE (1971/2001)
Prog. Accred.: Allied Health (diagnostic medical sonography, massage therapy, medical assisting (AMA), occupational therapy assisting, respiratory therapy, surgical technology), Clinical Assistant, Clinical Lab Technology, Dentistry (dental assisting, dental hygiene), Nuclear Medicine Technology, Nursing, Physical Therapy Assisting, Radiography

Stonehill College
Washington St., Easton 02357-6110
Type: Private, Roman Catholic Church, four-year
Degrees: B, M *Enroll:* 2,336
URL: http://www.stonehill.edu
Phone: (508) 565-1000 *Calendar:* Sem. plan
Inst. Accred.: NEASC-CIHE (1959/1999)

Suffolk University
8 Ashburton Place, Boston 02108-2701
Type: Private, independent, four-year
Degrees: A, B, M, P, D *Enroll:* 6,799
URL: http://www.suffolk.edu
Phone: (617) 573-8000 *Calendar:* Sem. plan
Inst. Accred.: NEASC-CIHE (1952/2002)
Prog. Accred.: Accounting, Business (AACSB), Clinical Psychology, Engineering (electrical), Law, Psychology Internship, Public Administration, Radiation Therapy

New England School of Art and Design at Suffolk University
81 Arlington St., Boston 02116
Phone: (617) 573-8785
Prog. Accred: Art, Interior Design

Tufts University
Medford 02155
Type: Private, independent, four-year
Degrees: B, M, P, D *Enroll:* 9,210
URL: http://www.tufts.edu
Phone: (617) 628-5000 *Calendar:* Sem. plan
Inst. Accred.: NEASC-CIHE (1929/2003)
Prog. Accred.: Allied Health (medicine, occupational therapy), Computer Science (ABET-CAC), Dentistry (combined prosthodontics, dentistry, endodontics, general practice residency, oral and maxillofacial surgery, orthodontic and dentofacial orthopedics, pediatric dentistry, periodontics), Dietetics (internship), Engineering (chemical, civil, computer, electrical, environmental/sanitary, mechanical), Planning, Psychology Internship, Public Health, Veterinary Medicine

University of Massachusetts Amherst
Whitmore Bldg., 181 President Dr., Amherst 01003-0001
Type: Public, state, four-year
System: University of Massachusetts
Degrees: A, B, M, P, D *Enroll:* 22,024
URL: http://umass.edu
Phone: (413) 545-0111 *Calendar:* Sem. plan
Inst. Accred.: NEASC-CIHE (1932/1998)
Prog. Accred.: Accounting, Allied Health (audiology, speech-language pathology), Business (AACSB), Clinical Psychology, Dietetics (didactic), Dietetics (internship), Engineering (chemical, civil, computer, electrical, environmental/sanitary, industrial, mechanical), Forestry, Landscape Architecture, Music, Nursing Education, Planning, Psychology Internship, Public Health, School Psychology, Teacher Education (NCATE)

University of Massachusetts Boston
100 Morrisey Blvd., Boston 02125-3393
Type: Public, state, four-year
System: University of Massachusetts
Degrees: B, M, D *Enroll:* 8,655
URL: http://www.umb.edu
Phone: (617) 287-5000 *Calendar:* Sem. plan
Inst. Accred.: NEASC-CIHE (1972/2005)
Prog. Accred.: Business (AACSB), Clinical Psychology, Computer Science (ABET-CAC), Marriage and Family Therapy, Nursing Education, Rehabilitation Counseling, Teacher Education (NCATE)

University of Massachusetts Dartmouth
285 Old Westport Rd., North Dartmouth 02747-2300
Type: Public, state, four-year
System: University of Massachusetts
Degrees: B, M, D *Enroll:* 7,481
URL: http://www.umassd.edu
Phone: (508) 999-8000 *Calendar:* Sem. plan
Inst. Accred.: NEASC-CIHE (1964/2000)
Prog. Accred.: Art, Business (AACSB), Clinical Lab Scientist, Computer Science (ABET-CAC), Engineering (civil, computer, electrical, mechanical), Nursing

University of Massachusetts Lowell
One University Ave., Lowell 01854-9985
Type: Public, state, four-year
System: University of Massachusetts
Degrees: A, B, M, D *Enroll:* 8,056
URL: http://www.uml.edu
Phone: (978) 934-4000 *Calendar:* Sem. plan
Inst. Accred.: NEASC-CIHE (1975/2003)
Prog. Accred.: Applied Science (industrial hygiene), Art, Business (AACSB), Clinical Lab Scientist, Computer Science (ABET-CAC), Engineering (chemical, civil, electrical, mechanical, nuclear, plastics), Engineering Technology (civil/construction, electrical, mechanical), Music, Nursing Education, Physical Therapy, Teacher Education (NCATE)

University of Massachusetts Medical School
55 Lake Ave., North, Worcester 01605-0001
Type: Public, state, four-year
System: University of Massachusetts
Degrees: P, D *Enroll:* 975
URL: http://www.umassmed.edu
Phone: (508) 856-8989 *Calendar:* Sem. plan
Inst. Accred.: NEASC-CIHE (1997/2002)
Prog. Accred.: Allied Health (medicine), Nuclear Medicine Technology, Nursing Education, Radiation Therapy

Urban College of Boston
178 Tremont St., Boston 02111-1093
Type: Private, independent, two-year
Degrees: A *Enroll:* 324
URL: http://www.urbancollege.edu
Phone: (617) 292-4723 *Calendar:* Sem. plan
Inst. Accred.: NEASC-CIHE (2001/2006)

Wellesley College
106 Central St., Wellesley 02481-8203
Type: Private, independent, four-year
Degrees: B *Enroll:* 2,261
URL: http://www.wellesley.edu
Phone: (781) 283-1000 *Calendar:* Sem. plan
Inst. Accred.: NEASC-CIHE (1929/1999)

Wentworth Institute of Technology
550 Huntington Ave., Boston 02115-5998
Type: Private, independent, four-year
Degrees: A, B, M *Enroll:* 3,335
URL: http://www.wit.edu
Phone: (617) 989-4590 *Calendar:* Sem. plan
Inst. Accred.: NEASC-CIHE (1967/2001)
Prog. Accred.: Construction Education, Engineering (environmental/sanitary), Engineering Technology (architectural, civil/construction, computer, electrical, mechanical), Interior Design

Western New England College
1215 Wilbraham Rd., Springfield 01119-2684
Type: Private, independent, four-year
Degrees: B, M, P, D *Enroll:* 3,176
URL: http://www.wnec.edu
Phone: (413) 782-3111 *Calendar:* Sem. plan
Inst. Accred.: NEASC-CIHE (1965/2002)
Prog. Accred.: Business (AACSB), Engineering (bioengineering, electrical, industrial, mechanical), Law, Social Work

Westfield State College
PO Box 1630, Westfield 01086-1630
Type: Public, state, four-year
System: Massachusetts Department of Higher Education
Degrees: B, M *Enroll:* 4,632
URL: http://www.wsc.ma.edu
Phone: (413) 572-5300 *Calendar:* Sem. plan
Inst. Accred.: NEASC-CIHE (1957/2002)
Prog. Accred.: Exercise Science, Social Work, Teacher Education (NCATE)

Wheaton College
26 East Main St., Norton 02766-2322
Type: Private, independent, four-year
Degrees: B *Enroll:* 1,563
URL: http://www.wheatonma.edu
Phone: (508) 285-7722 *Calendar:* Sem. plan
Inst. Accred.: NEASC-CIHE (1929/1999)

Wheelock College
200 The Riverway, Boston 02215-4176
Type: Private, independent, four-year
Degrees: A, B, M *Enroll:* 884
URL: http://www.wheelock.edu
Phone: (617) 734-5200 *Calendar:* Sem. plan
Inst. Accred.: NEASC-CIHE (1950/2004)
Prog. Accred.: Graduate Social Work, Social Work, Teacher Education (NCATE)

Williams College
PO Box 687, Williamstown 01267
Type: Private, independent, four-year
Degrees: B, M *Enroll:* 2,074
URL: http://www.williams.edu
Phone: (413) 597-3131 *Calendar:* 4-1-4 plan
Inst. Accred.: NEASC-CIHE (1929/2007)

Woods Hole Oceanographic Institution
Education Off., Clark Laboratory, MS #31, 360 Woods Hole Rd., Woods Hole 02543-1522
Type: Private, independent, four-year
Degrees: D
URL: http://www.whoi.edu
Phone: (508) 289-2000
Inst. Accred.: NEASC-CIHE (2001/2006)

Worcester Polytechnic Institute
100 Institute Rd., Worcester 01609-2280
Type: Private, independent, four-year
Degrees: B, M, D *Enroll:* 3,524
URL: http://www.wpi.edu
Phone: (508) 831-5000 *Calendar:* Sem. plan
Inst. Accred.: NEASC-CIHE (1937/2001)
Prog. Accred.: Business (AACSB), Computer Science (ABET-CAC), Engineering (bioengineering, chemical, civil, computer, electrical, industrial, manufacturing, mechanical)

Worcester State College
486 Chandler St., Worcester 01602-2597
Type: Public, state, four-year
System: Massachusetts Department of Higher Education
Degrees: B, M *Enroll:* 4,164
URL: http://www.worcester.edu
Phone: (508) 793-8000 *Calendar:* Sem. plan
Inst. Accred.: NEASC-CIHE (1957/2002)
Prog. Accred.: Allied Health (occupational therapy, speech-language pathology), Nursing, Nursing Education

Zion Bible College
320 South Main St., Haverhill 01835
Type: Private, Assemblies of God Church, four-year
Degrees: B *Enroll:* 230
URL: http://www.zbc.edu
Phone: (978) 478-3400 *Calendar:* Sem. plan
Inst. Accred.: ABHE (2001/2006)

MICHIGAN

Adrian College
110 South Madison St., Adrian 49221
Type: Private, United Methodist Church, four-year
Degrees: A, B *Enroll:* 950
URL: http://www.adrian.edu
Phone: (517) 264-3867 *Calendar:* Sem. plan
Inst. Accred.: NCA-HLC (1916/1999)
Prog. Accred.: Social Work

Albion College
611 East Porter St., Albion 49224
Type: Private, United Methodist Church, four-year
Degrees: B *Enroll:* 1,956
URL: http://www.albion.edu
Phone: (517) 629-1000 *Calendar:* Sem. plan
Inst. Accred.: NCA-HLC (1915/2001)
Prog. Accred.: Music

Alma College
614 West Superior St., Alma 48801
Type: Private, United Presbyterian Church, four-year
Degrees: B *Enroll:* 1,259
URL: http://www.alma.edu
Phone: (989) 463-7111 *Calendar:* 4-4-x plan
Inst. Accred.: NCA-HLC (1916/2000)
Prog. Accred.: Music

Alpena Community College
666 Johnson St., Alpena 49707-1495
Type: Public, state/local, two-year
System: Michigan Department of Education
Degrees: A *Enroll:* 1,272
URL: http://www.alpenacc.edu
Phone: (989) 356-9021 *Calendar:* Sem. plan
Inst. Accred.: NCA-HLC (1963/2008)
Prog. Accred.: Allied Health (medical assisting (AMA)), Business (ACBSP)

Huron Shores Campus
5800 Skeel Ave., Oscoda 48750-1587
Phone: (517) 739-1449

Andrews University
US 31 North, Berrien Springs 49104-1500
Type: Private, Seventh-Day Adventist Church, four-year
Degrees: A, B, M, P, D *Enroll:* 2,503
URL: http://www.andrews.edu
Phone: (269) 471-7771 *Calendar:* Qtr. plan
Inst. Accred.: ATS (1970/1999), NCA-HLC (1922/1999)
Prog. Accred.: Clinical Lab Scientist, Counseling, Dietetics (didactic), Dietetics (internship), Graduate Social Work, Music, Nursing, Physical Therapy, Social Work, Teacher Education (NCATE)

Aquinas College
1607 Robinson Rd., SE, Grand Rapids 49506-1799
Type: Private, Roman Catholic Church, four-year
Degrees: A, B, M *Enroll:* 1,819
URL: http://www.aquinas.edu
Phone: (616) 632-8900 *Calendar:* Sem. plan
Inst. Accred.: NCA-HLC (1946/2004)

Ave Maria School of Law
3475 Plymouth Rd., Ann Arbor 48105-2550
Type: Private, Roman Catholic Church, four-year
Degrees: P
URL: http://www.avemarialaw.edu
Phone: (734) 827-8040 *Calendar:* Sem. plan
Inst. Accred.: ABA (2002/2005)

Baker College Business and Corporate Services
1195 Centre Rd., Auburn Hills 48326-2603
Type: Private, proprietary, four-year
System: Baker College System
Degrees: A, B, M *Enroll:* 217
URL: https://www.baker.edu
Phone: (248) 276-8260 *Calendar:* Qtr. plan
Inst. Accred.: NCA-HLC (1985/2000, *Indirect accreditation through Baker College System, Flint, MI*)

Baker College Center for Graduate Studies
1116 West Bristol Rd., Flint 48507-9843
Type: Private, proprietary, four-year
System: Baker College System
Degrees: M *Enroll:* 2,888
URL: http://www.baker.edu
Phone: (810) 766-4390 *Calendar:* Qtr. plan
Inst. Accred.: NCA-HLC (1985/2000, *Indirect accreditation through Baker College System, Flint, MI*)

Baker College of Allen Park
4500 Enterprise Dr., Allen Park 48101
Type: Private, proprietary, four-year
Degrees: A, B
URL: https://www.baker.edu
Phone: (313) 425-3700 *Calendar:* Qtr. plan
Inst. Accred.: NCA-HLC (1985/2002, *Indirect accreditation through Baker College System, Flint, MI*)
Prog. Accred.: Allied Health (surgical technology)

Baker College of Auburn Hills
1500 University Dr., Auburn Hills 48326-2642
Type: Private, proprietary, four-year
System: Baker College System
Degrees: A, B, M *Enroll:* 2,399
URL: http://www.baker.edu
Phone: (248) 340-0600 *Calendar:* Qtr. plan
Inst. Accred.: NCA-HLC (1985/2000, *Indirect accreditation through Baker College System, Flint, MI*)
Prog. Accred.: Dentistry (dental assisting, dental hygiene)

Baker College of Cadillac
9600 East 13th St., Cadillac 49601-9600
Type: Private, proprietary, four-year
System: Baker College System
Degrees: A, B *Enroll:* 1,129
URL: http://www.baker.edu
Phone: (231) 775-8458 *Calendar:* Qtr. plan
Inst. Accred.: NCA-HLC (1985/2000, *Indirect accreditation through Baker College System, Flint, MI*)
Prog. Accred.: Allied Health (medical assisting (AMA), surgical technology), Veterinary Technology

Baker College of Clinton Township
34950 Little Mack Ave., Clinton Township 48035-6611
Type: Private, proprietary, four-year
System: Baker College System
Degrees: A, B *Enroll:* 3,683
URL: http://www.baker.edu
Phone: (810) 791-6610 *Calendar:* Qtr. plan
Inst. Accred.: NCA-HLC (1985/2000, *Indirect accreditation through Baker College System, Flint, MI*)
Prog. Accred.: Allied Health (medical assisting (AMA), surgical technology), Veterinary Technology

Baker College of Flint
1050 West Bristol Rd., Flint 48507-5508
Type: Private, proprietary, four-year
System: Baker College System
Degrees: A, B, M *Enroll:* 4,458
URL: http://www.baker.edu
Phone: (810) 766-4000 *Calendar:* Qtr. plan
Inst. Accred.: NCA-HLC (1985/2000, *Indirect accreditation through Baker College System, Flint, MI*)
Prog. Accred.: Allied Health (medical assisting (AMA), occupational therapy, surgical technology), Engineering (mechanical), Physical Therapy Assisting, Polysomnographic Technology, Veterinary Technology

Baker College of Jackson
2800 Springport Rd., Jackson 49202-1299
Type: Private, proprietary, four-year
System: Baker College System
Degrees: A, B *FTE Enroll:* 250
URL: http://www.baker.edu
Phone: (517) 788-7800 *Calendar:* Qtr. plan
Inst. Accred.: NCA-HLC (1985/2000, *Indirect accreditation through Baker College System, Flint, MI*)
Prog. Accred.: Allied Health (medical assisting (AMA), surgical technology), Radiation Therapy, Veterinary Technology

Baker College of Muskegon
1903 Marquette Ave., Muskegon 49442-3404
Type: Private, proprietary, four-year
System: Baker College System
Degrees: A, B, M *Enroll:* 3,615
URL: http://www.baker.edu
Phone: (231) 777-5200 *Calendar:* Qtr. plan
Inst. Accred.: NCA-HLC (1985/2000, *Indirect accreditation through Baker College System, Flint, MI*)
Prog. Accred.: Allied Health (medical assisting (AMA), occupational therapy assisting, surgical technology), Culinary Education, Physical Therapy Assisting, Veterinary Technology

Baker College of Owosso
1020 South Washington St., Owosso 48867-4400
Type: Private, proprietary, four-year
System: Baker College System
Degrees: A, B, M *Enroll:* 2,158
URL: http://www.baker.edu
Phone: (989) 729-3350 *Calendar:* Qtr. plan
Inst. Accred.: NCA-HLC (1985/2000, *Indirect accreditation through Baker College System, Flint, MI*)
Prog. Accred.: Clinical Lab Scientist, Clinical Lab Technology, Phlebotomy, Radiation Therapy, Radiography

Baker College of Port Huron
3403 Lapeer Rd., Port Huron 48060-2597
Type: Private, proprietary, four-year
System: Baker College System
Degrees: A, B *Enroll:* 1,167
URL: http://www.baker.edu
Phone: (810) 985-7000 *Calendar:* Qtr. plan
Inst. Accred.: NCA-HLC (1985/2000, *Indirect accreditation through Baker College System, Flint, MI*)
Prog. Accred.: Allied Health (medical assisting (AMA), surgical technology), Dentistry (dental hygiene), Veterinary Technology

Baker College Online
1116 West Bristol Rd., Flint 48507
Type: Private, proprietary, four-year
Degrees: A, B, M
URL: https://www.baker.edu
Phone: (810) 766-4390
Inst. Accred.: NCA-HLC (1985/2000, *Indirect accreditation through Baker College System, Flint, MI*)

Bay de Noc Community College
2001 North Lincoln Rd., Escanaba 49829-2511
Type: Public, state/local, two-year
System: Michigan Department of Education
Degrees: A *Enroll:* 1,586
URL: http://www.baycollege.edu
Phone: (906) 786-5802 *Calendar:* Sem. plan
Inst. Accred.: NCA-HLC (1976/2001)
Prog. Accred.: Nursing

Bay Mills Community College
12214 West Lakeshore Dr., Brimley 49715
Type: Public, Bay Mills Indian Community, two-year
System: American Indian Higher Education Consortium
Degrees: A *Enroll:* 235
URL: http://www.bmcc.edu
Phone: (906) 248-3354 *Calendar:* Sem. plan
Inst. Accred.: NCA-HLC (1995/2008)

Calvin College
3201 Burton St., SE, Grand Rapids 49546
Type: Private, Christian Reformed Church, four-year
Degrees: B, M *Enroll:* 4,052
URL: http://www.calvin.edu
Phone: (616) 526-6000 *Calendar:* 4-1-4 plan
Inst. Accred.: NCA-HLC (1930/2005)
Prog. Accred.: Computer Science (ABET-CAC), Engineering (general), Music, Nursing Education, Social Work, Teacher Education (NCATE)

Calvin Theological Seminary
3233 Burton St., SE, Grand Rapids 49546
Type: Private, Christian Reformed Church, four-year
Degrees: M, D *Enroll:* 267
URL: http://www.calvinseminary.edu
Phone: (616) 957-6036 *Calendar:* Qtr. plan
Inst. Accred.: ATS (1944/2008)

Central Michigan University
106 Warriner Hall, Mount Pleasant 48859
Type: Public, state, four-year
System: Michigan Department of Education
Degrees: B, M, P, D *Enroll:* 22,431
URL: http://www.cmich.edu
Phone: (989) 774-4000 *Calendar:* Sem. plan
Inst. Accred.: NCA-HLC (1915/2006)
Prog. Accred.: Accounting, Allied Health (audiology, speech-language pathology), Art, Business (AACSB), Clinical Psychology, Dietetics (didactic), Dietetics (internship), Journalism, Music, Physical Therapy, Physician Assistant, Recreation and Leisure Services, School Psychology, Social Work, Teacher Education (NCATE)

Charles Stewart Mott Community College
1401 East Ct. St., Flint 48503
Type: Public, state/local, two-year
System: Michigan Department of Education
Degrees: A *Enroll:* 5,891
URL: http://www.mcc.edu
Phone: (810) 762-0200 *Calendar:* Sem. plan
Inst. Accred.: NCA-HLC (1926/2000)
Prog. Accred.: Allied Health (respiratory therapy), Business (ACBSP), Dentistry (dental assisting, dental hygiene), Nursing, Physical Therapy Assisting

Southern Lakes Campus
2100 West Thompson Rd., Fenton 48430-9798
Phone: (810) 750-8585
Prog. Accred: Allied Health (occupational therapy assisting)

Cleary University
3601 Plymouth Rd., Ann Arbor 48105
Type: Private, independent, four-year
Degrees: A, B, M *Enroll:* 483
URL: http://www.cleary.edu
Phone: (734) 332-4477 *Calendar:* Qtr. plan
Inst. Accred.: NCA-HLC (1988/2003)

Livingston Campus
3750 Cleary Dr., Howell 49943
Phone: (517) 548-3670

The College for Creative Studies
245 East Kirby St., Detroit 48202-4013
Type: Private, independent, four-year
Degrees: B, M *Enroll:* 1,155
URL: http://www.ccscad.edu
Phone: (313) 664-7400 *Calendar:* Sem. plan
Inst. Accred.: NCA-HLC (1977/2006)
Prog. Accred.: Art

Concordia University, Ann Arbor
4090 Geddes Rd., Ann Arbor 48105
Type: Private, Lutheran Church-Missouri Synod, four-year
System: Concordia University System
Degrees: A, B, M *Enroll:* 567
URL: http://www.cuaa.edu
Phone: (734) 995-7300 *Calendar:* Sem. plan
Inst. Accred.: NCA-HLC (1968/2001)
Prog. Accred.: Teacher Education (NCATE)

Cornerstone University
1001 East Beltline Ave., NE, Grand Rapids 49505
Type: Private, Baptist Church, four-year
Degrees: A, B, M, D *Enroll:* 2,204
URL: http://www.cornerstone.edu
Phone: (616) 949-5300 *Calendar:* Sem. plan
Inst. Accred.: NCA-HLC (1977/2002)
Prog. Accred.: Music, Social Work

Cranbrook Academy of Art
39221 Woodward Ave., PO Box 801, Bloomfield Hills 48303-0801
Type: Private, proprietary, four-year
Degrees: M *Enroll:* 155
URL: http://www.cranbrook.edu/art
Phone: (248) 645-3300 *Calendar:* Sem. plan
Inst. Accred.: NCA-HLC (1960/1999)
Prog. Accred.: Art

Davenport University
6191 Kraft Ave. SE, Grand Rapids 49512
Type: Private, independent, four-year
Degrees: A, B, M *Enroll:* 6,984
URL: http://www.davenport.edu
Phone: (616) 698-7111 *Calendar:* Qtr. plan
Inst. Accred.: NCA-HLC (1976/2004)
Prog. Accred.: Allied Health (medical assisting (AMA)), Nursing, Practical Nursing

Caro Campus
1231 Cleaver Rd., Caro 48723
Phone: (989) 673-5857
Prog. Accred: Allied Health (medical assisting (AMA))

Dearborn Campus
4801 Oakman Blvd., Dearborn 48126
Phone: (313) 581-4400

Flint Campus
4318 Miller Rd., Ste. A, Flint 48507
Phone: (810) 732-9977

Holland Campus
643 South Waverly Rd., Holland 49423
Phone: (616) 395-4600

Kalamazoo Campus
4123 West Main St., Kalamazoo 49006
Phone: (269) 382-2835

Lansing Campus
220 East Kalamazoo St., Lansing 48933
Phone: (517) 484-2600
Prog. Accred: Allied Health (medical assisting (AMA))

Merrillville Campus
8200 Georgia St., Merrillville, IN 46410
Phone: (219) 769-5556
Prog. Accred: Allied Health (medical assisting (AMA)), Medical Assisting (ABHES)

Midland Campus
3555 East Patrick Rd., Midland 48642
Phone: (989) 835-5578

Saginaw Campus
5300 Bay Rd., Saginaw 48604
Phone: (989) 799-7800

South Bend/Mishawaka Campus
7121 Grape Rd., Granger, IN 46530
Phone: (574) 277-8447
Prog. Accred: Medical Assisting (ABHES)

Warren Campus
27650 Dequindre Rd., Warren 48092
Phone: (586) 558-8700

Delta College
1961 Delta Dr., University Center 48710
Type: Public, state/local, two-year
System: Michigan Department of Education
Degrees: A *Enroll:* 6,065
URL: http://www.delta.edu
Phone: (517) 686-9000 *Calendar:* Sem. plan
Inst. Accred.: NCA-HLC (1968/2004)
Prog. Accred.: Allied Health (diagnostic medical sonography, respiratory therapy, surgical technology), Dentistry (dental assisting, dental hygiene), Nursing, Physical Therapy Assisting, Radiography

Eastern Michigan University
Ypsilanti 48197-2207
Type: Public, state, four-year
System: Michigan Department of Education
Degrees: B, M, P, D *Enroll:* 17,694
URL: http://www.emich.edu
Phone: (734) 487-1849 *Calendar:* Sem. plan
Inst. Accred.: NCA-HLC (1915/2001)
Prog. Accred.: Allied Health (occupational therapy, orthotist/prothetist, speech-language pathology), Aviation Technology, Business (AACSB), Clinical Lab Scientist, Construction Education, Counseling, Design Technology, Dietetics (coordinated), Electronic Technology, Graduate Social Work, Industrial Technology, Interior Design, Manufacturing Technology, Music, Nursing Education, Planning, Public Administration, Recreation and Leisure Services, Social Work, Teacher Education (NCATE)

Ecumenical Theological Seminary
2930 Woodward Ave., Detroit 48201
Type: Private, interdenominational, four-year
Degrees: M, D
URL: http://www.etseminary.org
Phone: (313) 831-5200 *Calendar:* Qtr. plan
Inst. Accred.: ATS (2005)

Ferris State University
1201 South State St., Big Rapids 49307
Type: Public, state, four-year
System: Michigan Department of Education
Degrees: A, B, M, P, D *Enroll:* 10,775
URL: http://www.ferris.edu
Phone: (231) 591-2000 *Calendar:* Sem. plan
Inst. Accred.: NCA-HLC (1959/2001)
Prog. Accred.: Allied Health (optometric residency, optometry, respiratory therapy), Clinical Lab Scientist, Clinical Lab Technology, Construction Education, Dentistry (dental hygiene), Engineering (surveying), Engineering Technology (electrical, mechanical), Environmental Health, Nuclear Medicine Technology, Nursing, Pharmacy, Radiography, Recreation and Leisure Services, Social Work

Kendall College of Art and Design of Ferris State University
17 Fountain St., Grand Rapids 49503-3102
Phone: (616) 451.2787
Prog. Accred: Art, Interior Design

Northern Michigan Regional Center
1701 Front St., Traverse City 49684-3061
Phone: (616) 922-1734

Southeast Michigan Regional Center
1401 East Ct. St., Flint 48503-2018
Phone: (810) 762-0461

Southwest Michigan Regional Center
Applied Technology Center, 151 Fountain Northeast, Grand Rapids 49503-3263
Phone: (616) 771-3770

Finlandia University
601 Quincy St., Hancock 49930-1882
Type: Private, Evangelic Lutheran Church in America, four-year
Degrees: A, B *Enroll:* 508
URL: http://www.finlandia.edu
Phone: (906) 487-7274 *Calendar:* Tri. plan
Inst. Accred.: NCA-HLC (1969/2007, Warning)
Prog. Accred.: Nursing Education, Physical Therapy Assisting

Glen Oaks Community College
62249 Shimmel Rd., Centreville 49032
Type: Public, state/local, two-year
System: Michigan Department of Education
Degrees: A *Enroll:* 824
URL: http://www.glenoaks.edu
Phone: (269) 467-9945 *Calendar:* Sem. plan
Inst. Accred.: NCA-HLC (1975/2007)
Prog. Accred.: Allied Health (medical assisting (AMA))

Gogebic Community College
E-4946 Jackson Rd., Ironwood 49938
Type: Public, local, two-year
System: Michigan Department of Education
Degrees: A *Enroll:* 649
URL: http://www.gogebic.edu
Phone: (906) 932-4231 *Calendar:* Sem. plan
Inst. Accred.: NCA-HLC (1949/2007)

Grace Bible College
PO Box 910, Wyoming 49509-0910
Type: Private, Grace Gospel Fellowship, four-year
Degrees: A, B *Enroll:* 154
URL: http://www.gbcol.edu
Phone: (616) 538-2330 *Calendar:* Sem. plan
Inst. Accred.: ABHE (1964/2006), NCA-HLC (1990/2000)

Grand Rapids Community College
143 Bostwick St., NE, Grand Rapids 49503-3263
Type: Public, state/local, two-year
System: Michigan Department of Education
Degrees: A *Enroll:* 9,275
URL: http://www.grcc.edu
Phone: (616) 234-4000 *Calendar:* Sem. plan
Inst. Accred.: NCA-HLC (1917/2008)
Prog. Accred.: Allied Health (occupational therapy assisting), Culinary Education, Dentistry (dental assisting, dental hygiene), Music, Nursing, Practical Nursing, Radiography

Grand Rapids Theological Seminary
1001 East Beltline Ave. NE, Grand Rapids 49525
Type: Private, independent, four-year
Degrees: M
URL: http://grts.cornerstone.edu
Phone: (616) 222-1422 *Calendar:* Sem. plan
Inst. Accred.: ATS (2002/2007)

Grand Valley State University
One Campus Dr., Allendale 49401
Type: Public, state, four-year
System: Michigan Department of Education
Degrees: B, M *Enroll:* 19,247
URL: http://www.gvsu.edu
Phone: (616) 331-5000 *Calendar:* Sem. plan
Inst. Accred.: NCA-HLC (1968/1999)
Prog. Accred.: Accounting, Art, Business (AACSB), Engineering (electrical, general, manufacturing, mechanical), Graduate Social Work, Music, Physical Therapy, Physician Assistant, Psychology Internship, Public Administration, Social Work, Teacher Education (NCATE)

Grand Rapids Campus
301 West Fulton St., Grand Rapids 49504
Prog. Accred: Allied Health (occupational therapy), Nursing Education, Radiation Therapy

Great Lakes Christian College
6211 West Willow Hwy., Lansing 48917-1299
Type: Private, Christian Churches/Churches of Christ, four-year
Degrees: A, B *Enroll:* 182
URL: http://www.glcc.edu
Phone: (517) 321-0242 *Calendar:* Sem. plan
Inst. Accred.: ABHE (1977/2008), NCA-HLC (2003/2008)

Henry Ford Community College
5101 Evergreen Rd., Dearborn 48128-1495
Type: Public, state/local, two-year
System: Michigan Department of Education
Degrees: A *Enroll:* 7,390
URL: http://www.hfcc.edu
Phone: (313) 845-9600 *Calendar:* Sem. plan
Inst. Accred.: NCA-HLC (1949/2005)
Prog. Accred.: Allied Health (medical assisting (AMA), respiratory therapy, surgical technology), Culinary Education, Nursing, Physical Therapy Assisting, Radiography

Hillsdale College
33 East College Ave., Hillsdale 49242
Type: Private, independent, four-year
Degrees: B *FTE Enroll:* 1,175
URL: http://www.hillsdale.edu
Phone: (517) 437-7341 *Calendar:* Sem. plan
Inst. Accred.: NCA-HLC (1915/2008)

Hope College
141 East 12th St., PO Box 9000, Holland 49422-9000
Type: Private, Reformed Church in America, four-year
Degrees: B *Enroll:* 3,073
URL: http://www.hope.edu
Phone: (616) 395-7000 *Calendar:* Sem. plan
Inst. Accred.: NCA-HLC (1915/2004)
Prog. Accred.: Art, Dance, Engineering (general), Music, Nursing Education, Social Work, Teacher Education (NCATE), Theatre

ITT Technical Institute
1980 Metro Ct. SW, Wyomong 49519
Type: Private, proprietary, two-year
System: ITT Educational Services, Inc.
Degrees: A *Enroll:* 510
URL: http://www.itt-tech.edu
Phone: (616) 406-1200 *Calendar:* Qtr. plan
Inst. Accred.: ACICS (1999/2008)

Buffalo Campus
2295 Millersport Hwy., Getzville, NY 14068
Phone: (716) 689-2200

Canton Campus
1905 South Haggerty Rd., Canton 48188-2025
Phone: (734) 397-7800

Jackson Community College
2111 Emmons Rd., Jackson 49201
Type: Public, state/local, two-year
System: Michigan Department of Education
Degrees: A *Enroll:* 3,371
URL: http://www.jccmi.edu
Phone: (517) 787-0800 *Calendar:* Sem. plan
Inst. Accred.: NCA-HLC (1933/2000)
Prog. Accred.: Allied Health (diagnostic medical sonography, medical assisting (AMA)), Business (ACBSP), Radiography

Kalamazoo College
1200 Academy St., Kalamazoo 49006-3295
Type: Private, American Baptist Church, four-year
Degrees: B *Enroll:* 1,263
URL: http://www.kzoo.edu
Phone: (616) 337-7000 *Calendar:* Tri. plan
Inst. Accred.: NCA-HLC (1915/2003)

Kalamazoo Valley Community College
6767 West O Ave., PO Box 4070, Kalamazoo 49003-4070
Type: Public, state/local, two-year
System: Michigan Department of Education
Degrees: A *Enroll:* 6,275
URL: http://www.kvcc.edu
Phone: (269) 488-4400 *Calendar:* Sem. plan
Inst. Accred.: NCA-HLC (1972/2006)
Prog. Accred.: Allied Health (medical assisting (AMA), respiratory therapy, surgical technology), Dentistry (dental hygiene)

Arcadia Commons Campus
202 North Rose St., Kalamazoo 49003-4070
Phone: (616) 373-7800

Kellogg Community College
450 North Ave., Battle Creek 49017-3397
Type: Public, state/local, two-year
System: Michigan Department of Education
Degrees: A *Enroll:* 3,380
URL: http://www.kellogg.edu
Phone: (269) 965-3931 *Calendar:* Sem. plan
Inst. Accred.: NCA-HLC (1965/2002)
Prog. Accred.: Clinical Lab Technology, Dentistry (dental hygiene), Physical Therapy Assisting, Radiography

Kettering University
1700 West Third Ave., Flint 48504-4898
Type: Private, independent, four-year
Degrees: B, M *Enroll:* 2,617
URL: http://www.kettering.edu
Phone: (810) 762-9500 *Calendar:* Sem. plan
Inst. Accred.: NCA-HLC (1962/2007)
Prog. Accred.: Business (ACBSP), Engineering (computer, electrical, industrial, mechanical)

Kirtland Community College
10775 North St. Helen Rd., Roscommon 48653
Type: Public, state/local, two-year
System: Michigan Department of Education
Degrees: A *Enroll:* 959
URL: http://www.kirtland.edu
Phone: (989) 275-5000 *Calendar:* Sem. plan
Inst. Accred.: NCA-HLC (1976/1999)

Kuyper College
3333 East Beltline Ave., NE, Grand Rapids 49525-9749
Type: Private, independent, four-year
Degrees: A, B *Enroll:* 242
URL: http://www.kuyper.edu
Phone: (616) 222-3000 *Calendar:* Sem. plan
Inst. Accred.: ABHE (1964/2007), NCA-HLC (1995/2006)
Prog. Accred.: Social Work

Lake Michigan College
2755 East Napier St., Benton Harbor 49022
Type: Public, state/local, two-year
System: Michigan Department of Education
Degrees: A *Enroll:* 2,178
URL: http://www.lakemichigancollege.edu
Phone: (269) 927-8100 *Calendar:* Sem. plan
Inst. Accred.: NCA-HLC (1962/1999)
Prog. Accred.: Dentistry (dental assisting, dental hygiene), Nursing, Radiography

Lake Superior State University
650 West Easterday Ave., Sault Sainte Marie 49783
Type: Public, state, four-year
System: Michigan Department of Education
Degrees: A, B, M *Enroll:* 2,530
URL: http://www.lssu.edu
Phone: (906) 632-6841 *Calendar:* Sem. plan
Inst. Accred.: NCA-HLC (1968/2001)
Prog. Accred.: Engineering (electrical, mechanical), Engineering Technology (manufacturing), Nursing

Lansing Community College
PO Box 40010, Lansing 48901-7210
Type: Public, state/local, two-year
System: Michigan Department of Education
Degrees: A *Enroll:* 10,822
URL: http://www.lansing.cc.mi.us
Phone: (517) 483-1265 *Calendar:* Sem. plan
Inst. Accred.: NCA-HLC (1964/2004)
Prog. Accred.: Allied Health (EMT-paramedic, diagnostic medical sonography, surgical technology), Dentistry (dental assisting, dental hygiene), Histologic Technology, Nursing, Radiography

Lawrence Technological University
21000 West Ten Mile Rd., Ste. M351, Southfield 48075-1058
Type: Private, independent, four-year
Degrees: A, B, M, D *Enroll:* 2,525
URL: http://www.ltu.edu
Phone: (248) 204-2000 *Calendar:* Sem. plan
Inst. Accred.: NCA-HLC (1967/2001)
Prog. Accred.: Art, Business (ACBSP), Engineering (civil, computer, electrical, mechanical), Interior Architecture

Macomb Community College
14500 East Twelve Mile Rd., Warren 48093-3896
Type: Public, state/local, two-year
System: Michigan Department of Education
Degrees: A *Enroll:* 11,910
URL: http://www.macomb.edu
Phone: (586) 445-7999 *Calendar:* Sem. plan
Inst. Accred.: NCA-HLC (1970/2007)
Prog. Accred.: Allied Health (medical assisting (AMA), occupational therapy assisting, respiratory therapy, surgical technology), Culinary Education, Nursing, Physical Therapy Assisting, Veterinary Technology

Center Campus
44575 Garfield Rd., Clinton Township 48038-1139
Phone: (810) 445-7999

Madonna University
36600 Schoolcraft Rd., Livonia 48150
Type: Private, Roman Catholic Church, four-year
Degrees: A, B, M *Enroll:* 2,791
URL: http://www.madonna.edu
Phone: (800) 852-5315 *Calendar:* Sem. plan
Inst. Accred.: NCA-HLC (1959/2008)
Prog. Accred.: Dietetics (didactic), Nursing Education, Social Work, Teacher Education (NCATE)

Orchard Lake Center
3535 Indian Trail, Orchard Lake 48324
Phone: (248) 683-0523

Marygrove College
8425 West McNichols Rd., Detroit 48221
Type: Private, Sisters, Servants of the Immaculate Heart of Mary, four-year
Degrees: A, B, M *Enroll:* 3,302
URL: http://www.marygrove.edu
Phone: (313) 864-8000 *Calendar:* Sem. plan
Inst. Accred.: NCA-HLC (1926/2007)
Prog. Accred.: Radiography, Social Work

Michigan Jewish Institute
25401 Coolidge Hwy., Oak Park 48237-1304
Type: Private, independent, four-year
Degrees: A, B *Enroll:* 43
URL: http://www.mji.edu
Phone: (248) 414-6900 *Calendar:* Sem. plan
Inst. Accred.: ACICS (1998/2007)

Michigan School of Professional Psychology
26811 Orchard Lake Rd., Farmington Hills 48334-4512
Type: Private, independent, four-year
Degrees: M, P, D *Enroll:* 87
URL: http://www.mispp.edu
Phone: (248) 476-1122 *Calendar:* Sem. plan
Inst. Accred.: NCA-HLC (1984/2007)

Michigan State University
450 Administration Bldg., East Lansing 48824
Type: Public, state, four-year
System: Michigan Department of Education
Degrees: B, M, P, D *Enroll:* 41,470
URL: http://www.msu.edu
Phone: (517) 355-1855 *Calendar:* Sem. plan
Inst. Accred.: NCA-HLC (1915/2006)
Prog. Accred.: Accounting, Allied Health (audiology, medicine, speech-language pathology), Business (AACSB), Clinical Lab Scientist, Clinical Psychology, Construction Education, Counseling Psychology, Dietetics (didactic), Dietetics (internship), Engineering (agricultural, chemical, civil, computer, electrical, materials, mechanical), English Language Education, Forestry, Graduate Social Work, Interior Design, Journalism, Landscape Architecture, Marriage and Family Therapy, Music, Nurse Anesthesia Education, Nursing Education, Osteopathy, Planning, Psychology Internship, Recreation and Leisure Services, Rehabilitation Counseling, School Psychology, Social Work, Veterinary Medicine, Veterinary Technology

Detroit College of Law
364 Law College Bldg., East Lansing 48824-1300
Phone: (517) 432-6800
Prog. Accred: Law

James Madison College
368 South Case Hall, East Lansing 48825
Phone: (517) 353-6750
Prog. Accred: Liberal Education

Kalamazoo Center for Medical Studies
1000 Oakland Dr., Kalamazoo 49008-1202
Phone: (269) 337-4415

Michigan Technological University
1400 Townsend Dr., Houghton 49931
Type: Public, state, four-year
System: Michigan Department of Education
Degrees: A, B, M, D *Enroll:* 6,062
URL: http://www.mtu.edu
Phone: (906) 487-1885 *Calendar:* Qtr. plan
Inst. Accred.: NCA-HLC (1928/2005)
Prog. Accred.: Applied Science (surveying/geomatics), Business (AACSB), Engineering (bioengineering, chemical, civil, computer, electrical, environmental/sanitary, general, geological/geophysical, materials, mechanical), Engineering Technology (electrical, mechanical), Forestry

Michigan Theological Seminary
41550 East Ann Arbor Trail, Plymouth 48170
Type: Private, nondenominational, four-year
Degrees: B, M, D *Enroll:* 79
URL: http://www.mts.edu
Phone: (734) 207-9581 *Calendar:* Sem. plan
Inst. Accred.: ATS (2007), TRACS (1998/2003)

Mid Michigan Community College
1375 South Clare Ave., Harrison 48625
Type: Public, state/local, two-year
System: Michigan Department of Education
Degrees: A *Enroll:* 2,104
URL: http://www.midmich.edu
Phone: (989) 386-6622 *Calendar:* Sem. plan
Inst. Accred.: NCA-HLC (1974/2008)
Prog. Accred.: Allied Health (medical assisting (AMA)), Radiography

Monroe County Community College
1555 South Raisinville Rd., Monroe 48161-9746
Type: Public, local, two-year
System: Michigan Department of Education
Degrees: A *Enroll:* 2,566
URL: http://www.monroeccc.edu
Phone: (734) 242-7300 *Calendar:* Sem. plan
Inst. Accred.: NCA-HLC (1972/2000)
Prog. Accred.: Allied Health (respiratory therapy), Culinary Education, Nursing

Montcalm Community College
2800 College Dr., Sidney 48885-9723
Type: Public, state/local, two-year
System: Michigan Department of Education
Degrees: A *Enroll:* 1,221
URL: http://www.montcalm.edu
Phone: (989) 328-2111 *Calendar:* Sem. plan
Inst. Accred.: NCA-HLC (1974/2004)
Prog. Accred.: Allied Health (medical assisting (AMA))

Muskegon Community College
221 South Quarterline Rd., Muskegon 49442
Type: Public, state/local, two-year
System: Michigan Department of Education
Degrees: A *Enroll:* 2,781
URL: http://muskegoncc.edu
Phone: (231) 773-9131 *Calendar:* Sem. plan
Inst. Accred.: NCA-HLC (1929/2001)
Prog. Accred.: Allied Health (respiratory therapy), Nursing

North Central Michigan College
1515 Howard St., Petoskey 49770
Type: Public, state/local, two-year
System: Michigan Department of Education
Degrees: A *Enroll:* 1,473
URL: http://www.ncmich.edu
Phone: (231) 348-6600 *Calendar:* Sem. plan
Inst. Accred.: NCA-HLC (1972/2005)

Northern Michigan University
1401 Presque Isle Ave., Marquette 49855
Type: Public, state, four-year
System: Michigan Department of Education
Degrees: A, B, M, P *Enroll:* 8,558
URL: http://www.nmu.edu
Phone: (906) 227-1000 *Calendar:* Sem. plan
Inst. Accred.: NCA-HLC (1916/2000)
Prog. Accred.: Allied Health (speech-language pathology, surgical technology), Business (AACSB), Clinical Assistant, Clinical Lab Scientist, Clinical Lab Technology, Cytogenetic Technology, Music, Nursing Education, Social Work, Teacher Education (NCATE)

Northwestern Michigan College
1701 East Front St., Traverse City 49686-3061
Type: Public, state/local, two-year
System: Michigan Department of Education
Degrees: A *Enroll:* 2,909
URL: http://www.nmc.edu
Phone: (231) 922-1000 *Calendar:* Sem. plan
Inst. Accred.: NCA-HLC (1961/2000)
Prog. Accred.: Business (ACBSP), Culinary Education, Dentistry (dental assisting)

Northwood University
4000 Whiting Dr., Midland 48640-2398
Type: Private, independent, four-year
Degrees: A, B, M *Enroll:* 3,122
URL: http://www.northwood.edu
Phone: (517) 837-4200 *Calendar:* Tri. plan
Inst. Accred.: NCA-HLC (1974/2003)

Florida Campus
2600 N. Military Trail, W. Palm Beach, FL 33409-2911
Phone: (561) 478-5500

Texas Campus
1114 West FM 1382, Cedar Hill, TX 75104
Phone: (972) 291-1541

University College
4000 Whiting Dr., Midland 48640
Phone: (989) 837-4455

Oakland Community College
2480 Opdyke Rd., Bloomfield Hills 48304-2266
Type: Public, state/local, two-year
System: Michigan Department of Education
Degrees: A *Enroll:* 13,272
URL: http://www.oaklandcc.edu
Phone: (248) 341-2000 *Calendar:* Sem. plan
Inst. Accred.: NCA-HLC (1971/2008)
Prog. Accred.: Allied Health (diagnostic medical sonography, respiratory therapy, surgical technology), Radiography

Auburn Hills Campus
2900 Featherstone Rd., Auburn Hills 48326
Phone: (248) 232-4100

Highland Lakes Campus
7350 Cooley Lake Rd., Waterford 48327-4187
Phone: (248) 942-3100
Prog. Accred: Allied Health (medical assisting (AMA)), Dentistry (dental hygiene), Nursing

Orchard Ridge Campus
27055 Orchard Lake Rd., Farmington Hills 48334
Phone: (248) 522-3400
Prog. Accred: Culinary Education

Royal Oak Campus
739 South Washington, Royal Oak 48067-3898
Phone: (248) 246-2400

Southfield Campus
22322 Rutland Dr., Southfield 48075-4793
Phone: (248) 233-2700
Prog. Accred: Nursing, Radiography

Oakland University
Rochester 48309-4401
Type: Public, state, four-year
System: Michigan Department of Education
Degrees: B, M, P, D *Enroll:* 13,459
URL: http://www3.oakland.edu
Phone: (248) 370-2100 *Calendar:* Sem. plan
Inst. Accred.: NCA-HLC (1966/2001)
Prog. Accred.: Accounting, Applied Science (occupational health & safety), Business (AACSB), Computer Science (ABET-CAC), Counseling, Dance, Engineering (computer, electrical, mechanical, systems), Music, Nurse Anesthesia Education, Nursing Education, Physical Therapy, Public Administration, Theatre

Olivet College
320 South Main St., Olivet 49076
Type: Private, United Church of Christ, four-year
Degrees: B, M *Enroll:* 1,064
URL: http://www.olivetcollege.edu
Phone: (616) 749-7000 *Calendar:* Sem. plan
Inst. Accred.: NCA-HLC (1913/2007)

Robert B. Miller College
450 North Ave., Battle Creek 49017-3397
Type: Private, independent, four-year
Degrees: B
URL: http://www.millercollege.edu
Phone: (269) 660-8021 *Calendar:* Sem. plan
Inst. Accred.: NCA-HLC (2008)

Rochester College
800 West Avon Rd., Rochester Hills 48307
Type: Private, Churches of Christ, four-year
Degrees: A, B *Enroll:* 824
URL: http://www.rc.edu
Phone: (248) 218-2000 *Calendar:* Sem. plan
Inst. Accred.: NCA-HLC (1974/2003)

Sacred Heart Major Seminary
2701 Chicago Blvd., Detroit 48206
Type: Private, Roman Catholic Church, four-year
Degrees: A, B, M *Enroll:* 231
URL: http://www.shmsonline.org
Phone: (313) 883-8501 *Calendar:* Sem. plan
Inst. Accred.: ATS (1991/2004), NCA-HLC (1960/2004)

Saginaw Chippewa Tribal College
2274 Enterprise Dr., Mount Pleasant 48858
Type: Public, tribal, two-year
System: American Indian Higher Education Consortium
Degrees: A
URL: http://www.sagchip.org/tribalcollege
Phone: (989) 775-4123 *Calendar:* Sem. plan
Inst. Accred.: NCA-HLC (2007)

Saginaw Valley State University
7400 Bay Rd., Office of the President, University Center 48710
Type: Public, state, four-year
System: Michigan Department of Education
Degrees: B, M, P *Enroll:* 7,505
URL: http://www.svsu.edu
Phone: (989) 964-4000 *Calendar:* Sem. plan
Inst. Accred.: NCA-HLC (1970/2004)
Prog. Accred.: Allied Health (occupational therapy), Business (AACSB), Engineering (electrical, mechanical), Nursing Education, Social Work, Teacher Education (NCATE)

Saint Clair County Community College
323 Erie St., PO Box 5015, Port Huron 48061-5015
Type: Public, state/local, two-year
System: Michigan Department of Education
Degrees: A *Enroll:* 2,613
URL: http://www.sc4.edu
Phone: (810) 989-5500 *Calendar:* Sem. plan
Inst. Accred.: NCA-HLC (1930/2007)

Schoolcraft College
18600 Haggerty Rd., Livonia 48152-2696
Type: Public, state/local, two-year
System: Michigan Department of Education
Degrees: A *Enroll:* 6,080
URL: http://www.schoolcraft.edu
Phone: (734) 462-4400 *Calendar:* Sem. plan
Inst. Accred.: NCA-HLC (1968/2001)
Prog. Accred.: Allied Health (medical assisting (AMA))

Siena Heights University
1247 East Siena Heights Dr., Adrian 49221
Type: Private, Roman Catholic Church, four-year
Degrees: A, B, M *Enroll:* 1,384
URL: http://www.sienaheights.edu
Phone: (517) 263-0731 *Calendar:* Sem. plan
Inst. Accred.: NCA-HLC (1940/2001)
Prog. Accred.: Art, Social Work

Southwestern Michigan College
58900 Cherry Grove Rd., Dowagiac 49047-9793
Type: Public, state, two-year
System: Michigan Department of Education
Degrees: A *Enroll:* 1,573
URL: http://www.swmich.edu
Phone: (269) 782-1000 *Calendar:* Sem. plan
Inst. Accred.: NCA-HLC (1971/2001)

Spring Arbor University
106 E. Main St., Spring Arbor 49283
Type: Private, Free Methodist Church of North America, four-year
Degrees: A, B, M *Enroll:* 3,046
URL: http://www.arbor.edu
Phone: (517) 750-1200 *Calendar:* Sem. plan
Inst. Accred.: NCA-HLC (1960/2008)
Prog. Accred.: Nursing Education, Social Work, Teacher Education (NCATE)

SS. Cyril and Methodius Seminary
3535 Indian Trail, Orchard Lake 48324
Type: Private, Roman Catholic Church, four-year
Degrees: M *FTE Enroll:* 82
URL: http://www.sscms.edu
Phone: (248) 683-0310 *Calendar:* Sem. plan
Inst. Accred.: ATS (1995/2005)

Thomas M. Cooley Law School
300 South Capitol Ave., Lansing 48933
Type: Private, independent, four-year
Degrees: P *Enroll:* 2,002
URL: http://www.cooley.edu
Phone: (517) 371-5140 *Calendar:* Sem. plan
Inst. Accred.: NCA-HLC (2001/2006)
Prog. Accred.: Law (ABA only)

University of Detroit Mercy
4001 West McNichols Rd., Detroit 48219-0900
Type: Private, Sisters of Mercy and Society of Jesus, four-year
Degrees: A, B, M, P, D *Enroll:* 4,234
URL: http://www.udmercy.edu
Phone: (313) 993-1000 *Calendar:* Sem. plan
Inst. Accred.: NCA-HLC (1931/2007)
Prog. Accred.: Business (AACSB), Clinical Psychology, Counseling, Dentistry (dental hygiene, dentistry, endodontics, orthodontic and dentofacial orthopedics), Engineering (civil, electrical, mechanical), Law, Nurse Anesthesia Education, Nursing Education, Physician Assistant, Social Work

University of Michigan
2074 Fleming Administration Bldg., Ann Arbor 48109-1340
Type: Public, state, four-year
System: Michigan Department of Education
Degrees: B, M, P, D *Enroll:* 38,169
URL: http://www.umich.edu
Phone: (734) 764-1817 *Calendar:* Tri. plan
Inst. Accred.: NCA-HLC (1913/2000)
Prog. Accred.: Allied Health (health services administration, medicine), Applied Science (occupational health & safety), Art, Business (AACSB), Clinical Psychology, Computer Science (ABET-CAC), Dance, Dentistry (advanced education in general dentistry, combined prosthodontics, dental hygiene, dental public health, dentistry, endodontics, general dentistry, general practice residency, oral and maxillofacial surgery, orthodontic and dentofacial orthopedics, pediatric dentistry, periodontics, prosthodontics), Dietetics (didactic), Dietetics (internship), Engineering (aerospace, bioengineering, chemical, civil, computer, electrical, industrial, materials, mechanical, naval architecture/marine, nuclear), Forestry, Graduate Social Work, Landscape Architecture, Law, Librarianship, Music, Nurse (Midwifery), Nursing Education, Pharmacy, Planning, Psychology Internship, Public Health

University of Michigan—Dearborn
4901 Evergreen Rd., Dearborn 48128-1491
Type: Public, state, four-year
System: Michigan Department of Education
Degrees: B, M *Enroll:* 5,806
URL: http://www.umd.umich.edu
Phone: (313) 593-5000 *Calendar:* Sem. plan
Inst. Accred.: NCA-HLC (1970/2003)
Prog. Accred.: Business (AACSB), Computer Science (ABET-CAC), Engineering (computer, electrical, industrial, manufacturing, mechanical, software)

University of Michigan—Flint
303 East Kearsley, Flint 48502-1950
Type: Public, state, four-year
System: Michigan Department of Education
Degrees: B, M *Enroll:* 4,720
URL: http://www.flint.umich.edu
Phone: (810) 762-3000 *Calendar:* Sem. plan
Inst. Accred.: NCA-HLC (1970/2000)
Prog. Accred.: Business (AACSB), Music, Nurse Anesthesia Education, Nursing Education, Physical Therapy, Radiation Therapy, Social Work

Walsh College of Accountancy and Business Administration
3838 Livernois Rd., PO Box 7006, Troy 48007-7006
Type: Private, proprietary, four-year
Degrees: B, M *Enroll:* 1,371
URL: http://www.walshcollege.edu
Phone: (248) 689-8282 *Calendar:* Tri. plan
Inst. Accred.: NCA-HLC (1975/2001)

Novi Campus
41700 Gardenbrook, Novi 48375-1320
Phone: (810) 349-5454

Port Huron Campus
805-B 10th Ave., Port Huron 48060
Phone: (810) 984-4444

University Center Campus
Macomb Community College, 44575 Garfield Rd., Clinton Township 48038-1139
Phone: (810) 263-6630

Washtenaw Community College
4800 E. Huron River Dr., Ann Arbor 48106-1610
Type: Public, local, two-year
System: Michigan Department of Education
Degrees: A *Enroll:* 6,571
URL: http://www.wccnet.edu
Phone: (734) 973-3300 *Calendar:* Sem. plan
Inst. Accred.: NCA-HLC (1973/2000)
Prog. Accred.: Culinary Education, Dentistry (dental assisting), Nursing, Radiography

Wayne County Community College District
801 West Fort St., Detroit 48226-3010
Type: Public, state/local, two-year
System: Michigan Department of Education
Degrees: A *Enroll:* 7,106
URL: http://www.wcccd.edu
Phone: (313) 496-2500 *Calendar:* Sem. plan
Inst. Accred.: NCA-HLC (1976/1999)
Prog. Accred.: Allied Health (occupational therapy assisting, surgical technology), Veterinary Technology

Downriver Campus
21000 Northline Rd., Taylor 48180
Phone: (734) 946-3500

Downtown Campus
1001 West Fort St., Detroit 48226
Phone: (313) 496-2758

Eastern Campus
5901 Connor St., Detroit 48213-3457
Phone: (313) 922-3311

Northwest Campus
8551 Greenfield Rd., Detroit 48228
Phone: (313) 943-4000
Prog. Accred: Dentistry (dental assisting, dental hygiene), Dietetic Technician

Western Campus
9555 Haggerty Rd., Belleville 48111
Phone: (734) 699 7008
Prog. Accred: Allied Health (surgical technology)

Wayne State University
656 West Kirby, Detroit 48202
Type: Public, state, four-year
System: Michigan Department of Education
Degrees: B, M, P, D *Enroll:* 23,437
URL: http://www.wayne.edu
Phone: (313) 577-2424 *Calendar:* Sem. plan
Inst. Accred.: NCA-HLC (1915/2007)
Prog. Accred.: Allied Health (audiology, medicine, occupational therapy, speech-language pathology), Applied Science (occupational health & safety), Business (AACSB), Clinical Lab Scientist, Clinical Psychology, Counseling, Dance, Dietetics (coordinated), Engineering (chemical, civil, electrical, industrial, mechanical), Engineering Technology (electrical, mechanical), Funeral Service Education (Mortuary Science), Graduate Social Work, Law, Librarianship, Music, Nurse (Midwifery), Nurse Anesthesia Education, Nursing Education, Pathologists' Assistant, Pharmacy, Physical Therapy, Physician Assistant, Planning, Psychology Internship, Public Administration, Radiation Therapy, Rehabilitation Counseling, Social Work, Teacher Education (NCATE), Theatre

Detroit Medical Center University Laboratories
4201 St. Antoine Blvd., Detroit 48201-2194
Phone: (313) 993-0482
Prog. Accred: Allied Health (cytotechnology), Clinical Lab Scientist, Histologic Technology

West Shore Community College
3000 North Stiles Rd., Scottville 49454-0277
Type: Public, state/local, two-year
System: Michigan Department of Education
Degrees: A *Enroll:* 810
URL: http://www.westshore.edu
Phone: (231) 845-6211 *Calendar:* Sem. plan
Inst. Accred.: NCA-HLC (1974/2001)

Western Michigan University
1903 West Michigan Ave., Kalamazoo 49008-5130
Type: Public, state, four-year
System: Michigan Department of Education
Degrees: B, M, P, D *Enroll:* 22,193
URL: http://www.wmich.edu
Phone: (616) 387-2351 *Calendar:* Sem. plan
Inst. Accred.: NCA-HLC (1915/2000)
Prog. Accred.: Accounting, Allied Health (audiology, occupational therapy, speech-language pathology), Art, Aviation, Business (AACSB), Clinical Psychology, Computer Science (ABET-CAC), Counseling, Counseling Psychology, Dance, Dietetics (didactic), Dietetics (internship), Engineering (aerospace, chemical, civil, computer, construction, electrical, industrial, mechanical, paper), Engineering Technology (general drafting/design, management, manufacturing), English Language Education, Graduate Social Work, Interior Design, Music, Nursing Education, Physician Assistant, Psychology Internship, Public Administration, Rehabilitation Counseling, Social Work, Teacher Education (NCATE), Theatre

Battle Creek Regional Center/Kendall Center
50 West Jackson St., Battle Creek 49017
Phone: (616) 965-5380

Grand Rapids Regional Center
2333 East Beltline, SE, Grand Rapids 49546
Phone: (616) 771-9470

Lansing Regional Center
300 North Washington Square, Ste. 200, Lansing 48933
Phone: (517) 372-8114

Muskegon Regional Center
221 South Quarterline Rd., Muskegon 49442
Phone: (616) 777-0500

Southwest Regional Center
2510 Lakeview Ave., St. Joseph 49085
Phone: (616) 983-1968

Western Theological Seminary
101 East 13th St., Holland 49423
Type: Private, Reformed Church in America, four-year
Degrees: M, D *Enroll:* 194
URL: http://www.westernsem.edu
Phone: (616) 392-8555 *Calendar:* Sem. plan
Inst. Accred.: ATS (1940/2003)

Yeshiva Beth Yehuda-Yeshiva Gedolah of Greater Detroit
24600 Greenfield Rd., Oak Park 48237-1544
Type: Private, independent, four-year
Degrees: B, M, P, D *Enroll:* 45
Phone: (248) 968-3360 *Calendar:* Sem. plan
Inst. Accred.: AARTS (1986/2002)

MINNESOTA

Academy College
1101 East 78th St., Ste. 100, Minneapolis 55420
Type: Private, proprietary, four-year
Degrees: A, B
URL: http://www.academycollege.edu
Phone: (952) 851-0066 *Calendar:* Qtr. plan
Inst. Accred.: ACICS (1976/2003)

Adler Graduate School
1001 Hwy. 7, Ste. 311, Hopkins 55305
Type: Private, independent, four-year
Degrees: M *Enroll:* 69
URL: http://www.alfredadler.edu
Phone: (952) 988-4170 *Calendar:* Qtr. plan
Inst. Accred.: NCA-HLC (1991/2001)

Alexandria Technical College
1601 Jefferson St., Alexandria 56308
Type: Public, state/local, two-year
System: Minnesota State Colleges and Universities
Degrees: A *Enroll:* 1,771
URL: http://web.alextech.edu
Phone: (320) 762-0221 *Calendar:* Sem. plan
Inst. Accred.: NCA-HLC (1980/2008)
Prog. Accred.: Clinical Lab Technology

American Academy of Acupuncture and Oriental Medicine
1925 West County Rd. B2, Roseville 55113
Type: Private, proprietary, four-year
Degrees: M
URL: http://www.aaaom.org
Phone: (651) 631-0204 *Calendar:* Tri. plan
Inst. Accred.: ACAOM (2003/2007)

Anoka Technical College
1355 West Hwy. 10, Anoka 55303
Type: Private, state, two-year
System: Minnesota State Colleges and Universities
Degrees: A *Enroll:* 1,472
URL: http://www.anokatech.edu
Phone: (763) 576-4700 *Calendar:* Sem. plan
Inst. Accred.: NCA-HLC (1999/2004)
Prog. Accred.: Allied Health (medical assisting (AMA), occupational therapy assisting, surgical technology)

Anoka-Ramsey Community College
11200 Mississippi Blvd. NW, Coon Rapids 55433-3499
Type: Public, state, two-year
System: Minnesota State Colleges and Universities
Degrees: A *Enroll:* 4,478
URL: http://www.anokaramsey.mnscu.edu
Phone: (763) 427-2600 *Calendar:* Sem. plan
Inst. Accred.: NCA-HLC (1975/2007)
Prog. Accred.: Nursing, Physical Therapy Assisting

Cambridge Campus
300 Polk St. South, Cambridge 55008
Phone: (763) 689-7000

Argosy University Twin Cities
1515 Central Pkwy., Eagan 55121
Type: Private, proprietary, four-year
System: Argosy University
Degrees: A, B, M, D *Enroll:* 1,372
URL: http://www.argosyu.edu/twincities
Phone: (651) 846-2882 *Calendar:* Tri. plan
Inst. Accred.: NCA-HLC (1981/2008, *Indirect accreditation through Argosy University, Chicago, IL*)
Prog. Accred.: Allied Health (diagnostic medical sonography, medical assisting (AMA)), Clinical Lab Technology, Clinical Psychology, Dentistry (dental hygiene), Histologic Technology, Radiation Therapy, Radiography, Veterinary Technology

Duluth Learning Center
512 Lonsdale Bldg., 302 West Superior St., Duluth 55802
Phone: (218) 723-8470

Art Institutes International—Minnesota
15 South 9th St., Minneapolis 55402-3137
Type: Private, proprietary, four-year
System: Education Management Corporation
Degrees: A, B *Enroll:* 1,402
URL: http://www.aim.artinstitutes.edu
Phone: (612) 332-3361 *Calendar:* Qtr. plan
Inst. Accred.: ACICS (1971/2003)
Prog. Accred.: Culinary Education

Augsburg College
2211 Riverside Ave., Minneapolis 55454
Type: Private, Evangelic Lutheran Church in America, four-year
Degrees: B, M *Enroll:* 2,984
URL: http://www.augsburg.edu
Phone: (612) 330-1000 *Calendar:* 4-1-4 plan
Inst. Accred.: NCA-HLC (1954/2007)
Prog. Accred.: Graduate Social Work, Music, Nursing Education, Physician Assistant, Social Work, Teacher Education (NCATE)

Bemidji State University
1500 Birchmont Dr., NE, Bemidji 56601-2699
Type: Public, state, four-year
System: Minnesota State Colleges and Universities
Degrees: A, B, M *Enroll:* 3,394
URL: http://www.bemidji.msus.edu
Phone: (218) 755-2000 *Calendar:* Sem. plan
Inst. Accred.: NCA-HLC (1943/2000)
Prog. Accred.: Music, Nursing Education, Social Work

Bethany Lutheran College
700 Luther Dr., Mankato 56001
Type: Private, Evangelic Lutheran Synod, four-year
Degrees: A, B *Enroll:* 549
URL: http://www.blc.edu
Phone: (507) 344-7000 *Calendar:* Sem. plan
Inst. Accred.: NCA-HLC (1974/1999)

Bethel Seminary of Bethel University
3949 Bethel Dr., St. Paul 55112
Type: Private, Baptist General Conference, four-year
Degrees: M, D *Enroll:* 636
URL: http://seminary.bethel.edu
Phone: (651) 638-6180 *Calendar:* Qtr. plan
Inst. Accred.: ATS (1966/2001)

Pennsylvania Campus
1605 North Limekin Pike, Dresher, PA 19025
Phone: (215) 641-4801

San Diego Campus
6116 Arosa St., San Diego, CA 92115-3902
Phone: (619) 582-8188

Bethel University
3900 Bethel Dr., St. Paul 55112
Type: Private, Baptist General Conference, four-year
Degrees: A, B, M, D *Enroll:* 3,485
URL: http://www.bethel.edu
Phone: (651) 638-6400 *Calendar:* Sem. plan
Inst. Accred.: NCA-HLC (1959/2000)
Prog. Accred.: Nursing Education, Social Work, Teacher Education (TEAC)

Brown College
1440 Northland Dr., Mendota Heights 55120
Type: Private, proprietary, four-year
System: Career Education Corporation
Degrees: A, B *Enroll:* 1,955
URL: http://www.browncollege.edu
Phone: (651) 905-3400 *Calendar:* Qtr. plan
Inst. Accred.: ACCSCT (1967/2007)

Brooklyn Center Campus
6860 Shingle Creek Pkwy., Brooklyn Center 55430
Phone: (763) 279-2400

The Capella University
222 South 9th St., Ste. 2000, Minneapolis 55401
Type: Private, proprietary, four-year
System: Capella Education Company
Degrees: B, M, D *Enroll:* 6,370
URL: http://www.capellauniversity.edu
Phone: (888) 227-3552 *Calendar:* Qtr. plan
Inst. Accred.: NCA-HLC (1997/2008)
Prog. Accred.: Counseling

Carleton College
One North College St., Northfield 55057
Type: Private, independent, four-year
Degrees: B *Enroll:* 1,936
URL: http://www.carleton.edu
Phone: (507) 646-4334 *Calendar:* Tri. plan
Inst. Accred.: NCA-HLC (1913/1999)

Central Lakes College
501 West College Dr., Brainerd 56401-3900
Type: Public, state, two-year
System: Minnesota State Colleges and Universities
Degrees: A *Enroll:* 2,191
URL: http://www.clcmn.edu
Phone: (218) 855-8000 *Calendar:* Sem. plan
Inst. Accred.: NCA-HLC (1977/2003)
Prog. Accred.: Dentistry (dental assisting)

Staples Campus
1830 Airport Rd., Staples 56479
Phone: (218) 894-5100

Century College
3300 Century Ave. North, White Bear Lake 55110-5655
Type: Public, state, two-year
System: Minnesota State Colleges and Universities
Degrees: A *FTE Enroll:* 3,000
URL: http://www.century.mnscu.edu
Phone: (651) 779-3200 *Calendar:* Qtr. plan
Inst. Accred.: NCA-HLC (1974/2001)
Prog. Accred.: Allied Health (EMT-paramedic, medical assisting (AMA), orthotist/prothetist), Dentistry (dental assisting, dental hygiene, dental laboratory technology), Nursing, Radiography

College of Saint Benedict
37 South College Ave., St. Joseph 56374
Type: Private, Roman Catholic Church, four-year
Degrees: B *Enroll:* 2,013
URL: http://www.csbsju.edu
Phone: (320) 363-5505
Inst. Accred.: NCA-HLC (1933/1999)
Prog. Accred.: Dietetics (didactic), Music, Nursing Education, Social Work, Teacher Education (NCATE)

College of Saint Catherine
2004 Randolph Ave., St. Paul 55105
Type: Private, Roman Catholic Church, four-year
Degrees: A, B, M *Enroll:* 3,785
URL: http://www.stkate.edu
Phone: (651) 690-6000 *Calendar:* 4-1-4 plan
Inst. Accred.: NCA-HLC (1916/2003)
Prog. Accred.: Allied Health (diagnostic medical sonography, occupational therapy, respiratory therapy), Dietetics (didactic), Graduate Social Work, Montessori Teacher Education, Music, Nursing, Phlebotomy, Radiography, Social Work

Minneapolis Campus
601 25th Ave. South, Minneapolis 55454-1494
Phone: (651) 690-7700
Prog. Accred: Allied Health (occupational therapy assisting), Dietetics (didactic), Nursing, Physical Therapy, Physical Therapy Assisting

The College of Saint Scholastica
1200 Kenwood Ave., Duluth 55811
Type: Private, Roman Catholic Church, four-year
Degrees: B, M *Enroll:* 2,885
URL: http://www.css.edu
Phone: (800) 447-5444 *Calendar:* Sem. plan
Inst. Accred.: NCA-HLC (1931/2001)
Prog. Accred.: Allied Health (occupational therapy), Clinical Lab Scientist, Nursing Education, Physical Therapy, Social Work

College of Visual Arts
344 Summit Ave., St. Paul 55102-2199
Type: Private, independent, four-year
Degrees: B *Enroll:* 178
URL: http://www.cva.edu
Phone: (651) 224-3416 *Calendar:* Sem. plan
Inst. Accred.: NCA-HLC (1998/2003)

Concordia College
901 South 8th St., Moorhead 56562
Type: Private, Evangelical Lutheran Church in America, four-year
Degrees: B *Enroll:* 2,726
URL: http://www.cord.edu
Phone: (218) 299-4000 *Calendar:* Sem. plan
Inst. Accred.: NCA-HLC (1927/2004)
Prog. Accred.: Dietetics (didactic), Dietetics (internship), Music, Nursing Education, Social Work

Concordia University Saint Paul
275 North Syndicate St., St. Paul 55104
Type: Private, Lutheran Church-Missouri Synod, four-year
System: Concordia University System
Degrees: A, B, M *Enroll:* 1,883
URL: http://www.csp.edu
Phone: (651) 641-8278 *Calendar:* Sem. plan
Inst. Accred.: NCA-HLC (1959/2008)
Prog. Accred.: Business (ACBSP), Teacher Education (NCATE)

Crossroads College
920 Mayowood Rd., SW, Rochester 55902
Type: Private, Christian Churches/Churches of Christ, four-year
Degrees: A, B *Enroll:* 159
URL: http://www.crossroadscollege.edu
Phone: (507) 288-4563 *Calendar:* Sem. plan
Inst. Accred.: ABHE (1948/2004)

Crown College
8700 College View Dr., Saint Bonifacius 55375
Type: Private, Christian and Missionary Alliance, four-year
Degrees: A, B, M *Enroll:* 1,077
URL: http://www.crown.edu
Phone: (952) 446-4100 *Calendar:* Sem. plan
Inst. Accred.: ABHE (1950/2002), NCA-HLC (1980/2002)
Prog. Accred.: Nursing Education

Dakota County Technical College
1300 145th St. East, Rosemount 55068
Type: Public, state/local, two-year
System: Minnesota State Colleges and Universities
Degrees: A *Enroll:* 2,044
URL: http://www.dctc.mnscu.edu
Phone: (651) 423-8000 *Calendar:* Sem. plan
Inst. Accred.: NCA-HLC (1996/2001)
Prog. Accred.: Allied Health (medical assisting (AMA)), Dentistry (dental assisting), Interior Design

Duluth Business University
4724 Mike Colalillo Dr., Duluth 55807
Type: Private, proprietary, two-year
Degrees: A *Enroll:* 263
URL: http://www.dbumn.edu
Phone: (218) 722-4000 *Calendar:* Qtr. plan
Inst. Accred.: ACICS (1970/2008)
Prog. Accred.: Allied Health (medical assisting (AMA)), Dentistry (dental assisting), Veterinary Technology

Dunwoody College of Technology
818 Dunwoody Blvd., Minneapolis 55403-1192
Type: Private, independent, two-year
Degrees: A *Enroll:* 1,336
URL: http://www.dunwoody.edu
Phone: (612) 374-5800 *Calendar:* Qtr. plan
Inst. Accred.: NCA-HLC (1998/2007)

Fond du Lac Tribal and Community College
2101 14th St., Cloquet 55720
Type: Public, tribal, two-year
System: Minnesota State Colleges and Universities
Degrees: A *Enroll:* 1,269
URL: http://www.fdltcc.edu
Phone: (218) 879-0800 *Calendar:* Sem. plan
Inst. Accred.: NCA-HLC (1997/1999)

Globe University
8089 Globe Dr., 3rd Flr., Woodbury 55125
Type: Private, proprietary, four-year
Degrees: A, B, M *Enroll:* 666
URL: http://www.globeuniversity.edu
Phone: (651) 730-5100 *Calendar:* Qtr. plan
Inst. Accred.: ACICS (1953/2006)
Prog. Accred.: Allied Health (medical assisting (AMA)), Veterinary Technology

Eau Claire Campus
4955 Bullis Farm Rd., Eau Claire, WI 54702

Sioux Falls Campus
2101 South Broadband Ave., Sioux Falls, SD 57108
Phone: (605) 977-0708

Gustavus Adolphus College
800 West College Ave., St. Peter 56082
Type: Private, Evangelical Lutheran Church in America, four-year
Degrees: B *Enroll:* 2,518
URL: http://www.gustavus.edu
Phone: (507) 933-8000 *Calendar:* 4-1-4 plan
Inst. Accred.: NCA-HLC (1915/2003)
Prog. Accred.: Music, Nursing Education, Teacher Education (NCATE)

Hamline University
1536 Hewitt Ave., St. Paul 55104
Type: Private, United Methodist Church, four-year
Degrees: B, M, D *Enroll:* 3,611
URL: http://www.hamline.edu
Phone: (651) 523-2800 *Calendar:* 4-1-4 plan
Inst. Accred.: NCA-HLC (1914/2008)
Prog. Accred.: Law, Music, Teacher Education (NCATE)

Hazelden Mental Health Center
PO Box 11, Center City 55012-0011
Type: Private, independent, four-year
Degrees: M
URL: http://www.hazelden.org
Phone: (651) 213-4000 *Calendar:* Sem. plan
Inst. Accred.: NCA-HLC (2007)
Prog. Accred.: Psychology Internship

Hennepin Technical College
9000 Brooklyn Blvd., Brooklyn Park 55445-2399
Type: Public, state/local, two-year
System: Minnesota State Colleges and Universities
Degrees: A *Enroll:* 3,292
URL: http://www.hennepintech.edu
Phone: (763) 425-3800 *Calendar:* Sem. plan
Inst. Accred.: NCA-HLC (1999)
Prog. Accred.: Culinary Education, Dentistry (dental assisting)

Eden Prairie Campus
9200 Flying Cloud Dr., Eden Prairie 55347
Phone: (952) 944-2222
Prog. Accred: Culinary Education, Dentistry (dental assisting)

Herzing College—Minneapolis
5700 West Broadway, Minneapolis 55428
Type: Private, proprietary, four-year
System: Herzing College Corporate Offices
Degrees: A, B, M
URL: http://www.herzing.edu
Phone: (763) 535-3000 *Calendar:* Sem. plan
Inst. Accred.: NCA-HLC (2004, *Indirect accreditation through Herzing College Corporate Offices, Milwaukee, WI*)
Prog. Accred.: Allied Health (medical assisting (AMA)), Clinical Lab Technology, Dentistry (dental assisting, dental hygiene)

Hibbing Community College
1515 East 25th St., Hibbing 55746-3354
Type: Public, state, two-year
System: Northeast Higher Education District
Degrees: A *Enroll:* 1,076
URL: http://www.hcc.mnscu.edu
Phone: (218) 262-7200 *Calendar:* Sem. plan
Inst. Accred.: NCA-HLC (1997/2000)
Prog. Accred.: Clinical Lab Technology, Dentistry (dental assisting)

The Institute of Production and Recording
312 Washington Ave. North, Minneapolis 55401
Type: Private, proprietary, two-year
Degrees: A
URL: http://www.ipr.edu
Phone: (612) 375-1900
Inst. Accred.: ACCSCT (2007)

Inver Hills Community College
2500 80th St., East, Inver Grove Heights 55076-3224
Type: Public, state, two-year
System: Minnesota State Colleges and Universities
Degrees: A *Enroll:* 3,143
URL: http://www.inverhills.edu
Phone: (651) 450-8500 *Calendar:* Qtr. plan
Inst. Accred.: NCA-HLC (1976/2002)
Prog. Accred.: Allied Health (EMT-paramedic), Nursing

Itasca Community College
1851 East Hwy. 169, Grand Rapids 55744-3361
Type: Public, state/local, two-year
System: Northeast Higher Education District
Degrees: A *Enroll:* 981
URL: http://www.itascacc.edu
Phone: (218) 327-4460 *Calendar:* Sem. plan
Inst. Accred.: NCA-HLC (1997/1999)
Prog. Accred.: Forestry

Lake Superior College
2101 Trinity Rd., Duluth 55811-3399
Type: Public, state, two-year
System: Minnesota State Colleges and Universities
Degrees: A *Enroll:* 3,177
URL: http://www.lsc.mnscu.edu
Phone: (218) 733-7600 *Calendar:* Sem. plan
Inst. Accred.: NCA-HLC (1998/2008)
Prog. Accred.: Allied Health (medical assisting (AMA), respiratory therapy, surgical technology), Clinical Lab Technology, Dentistry (dental hygiene), Physical Therapy Assisting, Radiography

Leech Lake Tribal College
PO Box 180, Cass Lake 56633-0180
Type: Public, tribal, two-year
System: American Indian Higher Education Consortium
Degrees: A *Enroll:* 153
URL: http://www.leechlaketribalcollege.org
Phone: (218) 335-4200 *Calendar:* Qtr. plan
Inst. Accred.: NCA-HLC (2006)

Luther Seminary
2481 Como Ave., St. Paul 55108
Type: Private, Evangelical Lutheran Church in America, four-year
Degrees: M, D *Enroll:* 713
URL: http://www.luthersem.edu
Phone: (651) 641-3456 *Calendar:* 4-1-4 plan
Inst. Accred.: ATS (1944/2004), NCA-HLC (1979/2005)

Macalester College
1600 Grand Ave., St. Paul 55105-1899
Type: Private, Presbyterian Church (USA), four-year
Degrees: B *Enroll:* 1,843
URL: http://www.macalester.edu
Phone: (651) 696-6000 *Calendar:* Sem. plan
Inst. Accred.: NCA-HLC (1913/2006)

Martin Luther College
1995 Luther Ct., New Ulm 56073
Type: Private, Evangelical Lutheran Synod, four-year
Degrees: B *Enroll:* 831
URL: http://www.mlc-wels.edu
Phone: (507) 354-8221 *Calendar:* Sem. plan
Inst. Accred.: NCA-HLC (1995/1999)

Mayo Graduate School
200 First St., SW, Rochester 55905
Type: Private, independent, four-year
System: Mayo Clinic College of Medicine
Degrees: M, D *Enroll:* 251
URL: http://www.mayo.edu/mgs
Phone: (507) 284-2511 *Calendar:* Sem. plan
Inst. Accred.: NCA-HLC (1984/1999, *Indirect accreditation through Mayo Clinic College of Medicine, Rochester, MN*)
Prog. Accred.: Allied Health (cytotechnology, diagnostic medical sonography, electroneurodiagnostic technology, medicine, respiratory therapy), Dentistry (combined prosthodontic/maxillofacial prosthetics, oral and maxillofacial surgery, orthodontic and dentofacial orthopedics, periodontics), Nuclear Medicine Technology, Nurse Anesthesia Education, Physical Therapy

Mayo Medical School
200 First St., SW, Rochester 55905
Type: Private, independent, four-year
System: Mayo Clinic College of Medicine
Degrees: D *Enroll:* 166
URL: http://www.mayo.edu/mms
Phone: (507) 284-3671
Inst. Accred.: NCA-HLC (1984/1999, *Indirect accreditation through Mayo Clinic College of Medicine, Rochester, MN*)

Mayo School of Health Sciences
200 First St., SW, Rochester 55905
Type: Private, independent, four-year
System: Mayo Clinic College of Medicine
Degrees: A, M *Enroll:* 337
URL: http://www.mayo.edu/mshs
Phone: (507) 284-3678
Inst. Accred.: NCA-HLC (1984/1999, *Indirect accreditation through Mayo Clinic College of Medicine, Rochester, MN*)
Prog. Accred.: Dentistry (combined prosthodontic/maxillofacial prosthetics, oral and maxillofacial surgery, orthodontic and dentofacial orthopedics, periodontics), Dietetics (internship), Radiation Therapy, Radiography

Mayo Clinic—Jacksonville
4500 San Pablo Rd., Jacksonville, FL 32224
Phone: (904) 953-8663
Prog. Accred: Dietetics (internship), Radiography

McNally Smith College of Music
19 Exchange St. East, Saint Paul 55101-2220
Type: Private, proprietary, two-year
Degrees: A
URL: http://www.mcnallysmith.edu
Phone: (651) 291-0177 *Calendar:* Sem. plan
Inst. Accred.: NASM (1989/2007)

Mesabi Range Community and Technical College
1001 West Chestnut St., Virginia 55792
Type: Public, state/local, two-year
System: Northeast Higher Education District
Degrees: A *Enroll:* 1,044
URL: http://www.mesabirange.mnscu.edu
Phone: (218) 749-7700 *Calendar:* Qtr. plan
Inst. Accred.: NCA-HLC (2001)

Eveleth Campus
1100 Industrial Park Dr., PO Box 0648, Eveleth 55734-0648
Phone: (218) 744-3095

Metropolitan State University
700 East 7th St., St. Paul 55106-5000
Type: Public, state, four-year
System: Minnesota State Colleges and Universities
Degrees: B, M *Enroll:* 3,952
URL: http://www.metrostate.edu
Phone: (651) 793-1212 *Calendar:* Sem. plan
Inst. Accred.: NCA-HLC (1975/1995)
Prog. Accred.: Nursing Education, Social Work

Minneapolis Campus
730 Hennepin Ave., Minneapolis 55403
Phone: (651) 772-7777

Minneapolis Business College
1711 West County Rd. B, Roseville 55113
Type: Private, proprietary, two-year
Degrees: A *Enroll:* 445
URL: http://www.minneapolisbusinesscollege.edu
Phone: (651) 636-7406
Inst. Accred.: ACICS (1962/2006)
Prog. Accred.: Allied Health (medical assisting (AMA))

Minneapolis College of Art and Design
2501 Stevens Ave. South, Minneapolis 55404
Type: Private, independent, four-year
Degrees: B, M *Enroll:* 680
URL: http://www.mcad.edu
Phone: (612) 874-3700 *Calendar:* Sem. plan
Inst. Accred.: NCA-HLC (1960/2006)
Prog. Accred.: Art

Minneapolis Community and Technical College
1501 Hennepin Ave., Minneapolis 55403-1779
Type: Public, state/local, two-year
System: Minnesota State Colleges and Universities
Degrees: A *Enroll:* 4,738
URL: http://www.mctc.mnscu.edu
Phone: (612) 341-7000 *Calendar:* Sem. plan
Inst. Accred.: NCA-HLC (1977/2003)
Prog. Accred.: Dentistry (dental assisting), Nursing, Practical Nursing

Minnesota School of Business
1401 West 76th St., Ste. 500, Richfield 55423
Type: Private, proprietary, four-year
Degrees: A, B, M *Enroll:* 601
URL: http://www.msbcollege.edu
Phone: (612) 861-2000 *Calendar:* Qtr. plan
Inst. Accred.: ACICS (1953/2008)
Prog. Accred.: Allied Health (medical assisting (AMA)), Nursing Education

Blaine Campus
3680 Pheasant Ridge Dr. NE, Blaine 55449
Phone: (763) 225-8000
Prog. Accred: Veterinary Technology

Brooklyn Center Campus
5910 Shingle Creek Pkwy., Brooklyn Center 55430
Phone: (763) 566-7777
Prog. Accred: Allied Health (medical assisting (AMA)), Dentistry (dental assisting)

Plymouth Campus
1455 County Rd. 101 North, Plymouth 55447
Phone: (763) 476-2000
Prog. Accred: Veterinary Technology

Rochester Campus
2521 Pennington Dr., NW, Rochester 55901
Phone: (507) 536-9500
Prog. Accred: Veterinary Technology

St. Cloud Campus
1201 2nd St. South, Waite Park 56387
Phone: (320) 257-2000
Prog. Accred: Veterinary Technology

Shakopee Campus
1200 Shakopee Town Square, Shakopee 55379
Phone: (952) 345-1200
Prog. Accred: Veterinary Technology

Minnesota State College-Southeast Technical
1250 Homer Rd., PO Box 409, Winona 55987-0409
Type: Public, state/local, two-year
System: Minnesota State Colleges and Universities
Degrees: A *Enroll:* 1,469
URL: http://www.southeastmn.edu
Phone: (507) 453-2700 *Calendar:* Sem. plan
Inst. Accred.: NCA-HLC (1995/2001)

Red Wing Campus
308 Pioneer Rd. and Hwy. 58, Red Wing 55066
Phone: (651) 385-6300

Minnesota State Community and Technical College
1414 College Way, Fergus Falls 56537-1009
Type: Public, state, two-year
System: Minnesota State Colleges and Universities
Degrees: A *Enroll:* 4,273
URL: http://www.minnesota.edu
Phone: (218) 739-7500 *Calendar:* Sem. plan
Inst. Accred.: NCA-HLC (1972/2003)
Prog. Accred.: Clinical Lab Technology, Histologic Technology

Detroit Lakes Campus
900 Hwy. 34 East, Detroit Lakes 56601-2698
Phone: (218) 846-7444

Moorhead Campus
1900 28th Ave. South, Moorhead 56560-4899
Phone: (218) 236-6277
Prog. Accred: Dentistry (dental assisting, dental hygiene)

Wadena Campus
405 SW Colfax, PO Box 56, Wadena 56482-0566
Phone: (218) 631-3530

Minnesota State University Moorhead
1104 7th Ave. South, Moorhead 56563
Type: Public, state, four-year
System: Minnesota State Colleges and Universities
Degrees: A, B, M, P *Enroll:* 6,840
URL: http://www.mnstate.edu
Phone: (218) 236-2011 *Calendar:* Sem. plan
Inst. Accred.: NCA-HLC (1916/2007)
Prog. Accred.: Allied Health (speech-language pathology), Art, Construction Education, Counseling, Industrial Technology, Music, Nursing Education, Social Work, Teacher Education (NCATE)

Minnesota State University—Mankato
309 Wigley Administration Center, Mankato 56001
Type: Public, state, four-year
System: Minnesota State Colleges and Universities
Degrees: A, B, M, P *Enroll:* 12,861
URL: http://www.mankato.msus.edu
Phone: (507) 389-2463 *Calendar:* Sem. plan
Inst. Accred.: NCA-HLC (1916/2006)
Prog. Accred.: Allied Health (speech-language pathology), Art, Business (AACSB), Counseling, Dentistry (dental hygiene), Engineering (civil, electrical, mechanical), Engineering Technology (automotive, electrical, manufacturing), Music, Nursing, Nursing Education, Recreation and Leisure Services, Rehabilitation Counseling, Social Work, Teacher Education (NCATE)

Minnesota West Community and Technical College—Granite Falls
1593 11th Ave., Granite Falls 56241
Type: Public, state/local, two-year
System: Minnesota State Colleges and Universities
Degrees: A *Enroll:* 1,891
URL: http://www.mnwest.edu
Phone: (320) 564-4511 *Calendar:* Sem. plan
Inst. Accred.: NCA-HLC (1997/2002)
Prog. Accred.: Dentistry (dental assisting)

Canby Campus
1011 1st St. West, Canby 56220
Phone: (507) 223-7252
Prog. Accred: Dentistry (dental assisting)

Jackson Campus
401 West St., Jackson 56143
Phone: (507) 847-3320

Pipestone Campus
1314 North Hiawatha, PO Box 250, Pipestone 56164-0250
Phone: (507) 825-5471
Prog. Accred: Clinical Lab Technology

Worthington Campus
1450 College Way, Worthington 56187-3024
Phone: (507) 372-2107
Prog. Accred: Allied Health (medical assisting (AMA))

Normandale Community College
9700 France Ave. South, Bloomington 55431-4309
Type: Public, state/local, two-year
System: Minnesota State Colleges and Universities
Degrees: A *Enroll:* 5,523
URL: http://www.normandale.mnscu.edu
Phone: (952) 487-8200 *Calendar:* Sem. plan
Inst. Accred.: NCA-HLC (1973/2001)
Prog. Accred.: Business (ACBSP), Dentistry (dental assisting, dental hygiene), Music, Nursing

North Central University
910 Elliot Ave. South, Minneapolis 55404
Type: Private, Assemblies of God, four-year
Degrees: A, B *Enroll:* 1,171
URL: http://www.northcentral.edu
Phone: (612) 343-4400 *Calendar:* Sem. plan
Inst. Accred.: NCA-HLC (1986/2008)

North Hennepin Community College
7411 85th Ave. North, Brooklyn Park 55445-2231
Type: Public, state, two-year
System: Minnesota State Colleges and Universities
Degrees: A *Enroll:* 3,692
URL: http://www.nhcc.mnscu.edu
Phone: (763) 424-0702 *Calendar:* Sem. plan
Inst. Accred.: NCA-HLC (1972/2004)
Prog. Accred.: Business (ACBSP), Clinical Lab Technology, Nursing

Northland Community and Technical College
1101 Hwy. 1 East, Thief River Falls 56701-2598
Type: Public, state, two-year
System: Minnesota State Colleges and Universities
Degrees: A *Enroll:* 2,567
URL: http://www.northlandcollege.edu
Phone: (218) 681-0701 *Calendar:* Sem. plan
Inst. Accred.: NCA-HLC (1976/2000)
Prog. Accred.: Allied Health (EMT-paramedic, cardiovascular technology, medical assisting (AMA), respiratory therapy, surgical technology)

East Grand Forks Campus
2022 Central Ave., NE, East Grand Forks 56721-2702
Phone: (218) 773-3441
Prog. Accred: Allied Health (occupational therapy assisting), Clinical Lab Technology, Radiography

Northwest College
905 Grant Ave., SE, Bemidji 56601
Type: Public, state, two-year
System: Minnesota State Colleges and Universities
Degrees: A *Enroll:* 680
URL: http://www.ntcmn.edu
Phone: (218) 755-4280 *Calendar:* Qtr. plan
Inst. Accred.: NCA-HLC (1995/2008)
Prog. Accred.: Dentistry (dental assisting)

Northwest Technical Institute
950 Blue Gentian Rd., Eagan 55121
Type: Private, proprietary, two-year
Degrees: A *Enroll:* 89
URL: http://www.nti.edu
Phone: (952) 944-0080 *Calendar:* Sem. plan
Inst. Accred.: ACCSCT (1972/2006)

Northwestern College
3003 Snelling Ave. North, Saint Paul 55113-1598
Type: Private, independent, four-year
Degrees: A, B *Enroll:* 2,396
URL: http://www.nwc.edu
Phone: (651) 631-5100 *Calendar:* Sem. plan
Inst. Accred.: NCA-HLC (1978/1999)
Prog. Accred.: Music

Northwestern Health Sciences University
2501 West 84th St., Bloomington 55431-1599
Type: Private, proprietary, four-year
Degrees: B, M, P *Enroll:* 865
URL: http://www.nwhealth.edu
Phone: (952) 888-4777 *Calendar:* Tri. plan
Inst. Accred.: NCA-HLC (1988/2001)
Prog. Accred.: Allied Health (massage therapy), Chiropractic Education

Minnesota Institute of Acupuncture and Oriental Medicine
2501 West 84th St., Bloomington 55431
Phone: (952) 885-5435
Prog. Accred: Acupuncture

Oak Hills Christian College
1600 Oak Hills Rd., SW, Bemidji 56601-8826
Type: Private, interdenominational, four-year
Degrees: A, B *Enroll:* 158
URL: http://www.oakhills.edu
Phone: (218) 751-8670 *Calendar:* Sem. plan
Inst. Accred.: ABHE (1990/2006)

Pillsbury Baptist Bible College
315 South Grove Ave., Owatonna 55060-3068
Type: Private, Minnesota Baptist State Convention, four-year
Degrees: A, B *Enroll:* 178
URL: http://www.pillsbury.edu
Phone: (507) 451-2710 *Calendar:* Sem. plan
Inst. Accred.: ABHE (2005)

Pine Technical College
900 4th St., SE, Pine City 55063
Type: Public, state/local, two-year
System: Minnesota State Colleges and Universities
Degrees: A *Enroll:* 402
URL: http://www.pinetech.edu
Phone: (320) 629-5100 *Calendar:* Sem. plan
Inst. Accred.: NCA-HLC (1994/1999)

Rainy River Community College
1501 Hwy. 71, International Falls 56649-2187
Type: Public, state/local, two-year
System: Northeast Higher Education District
Degrees: A *Enroll:* 344
URL: http://www.rrcc.mnscu.edu
Phone: (218) 254-7976 *Calendar:* Sem. plan
Inst. Accred.: NCA-HLC (1997/2008)

Rasmussen College—Brooklyn Park
8301 93rd Ave. North, Brooklyn Park 55445-1512
Type: Private, proprietary, four-year
System: Rasmussen College System
Degrees: A, B
URL: http://www.rasmussen.edu
Phone: (763) 493-4500 *Calendar:* Qtr. plan
Inst. Accred.: NCA-HLC (2001/2004, *Indirect accreditation through Rasmussen College System, Lake Elmo, MN*)

Rasmussen College—Eagan Campus
3500 Federal Dr., Eagan 55122-1346
Type: Private, proprietary, four-year
System: Rasmussen College System
Degrees: A, B *Enroll:* 305
URL: http://www.rasmussen.edu
Phone: (651) 687-9000 *Calendar:* Qtr. plan
Inst. Accred.: NCA-HLC (1995/2004, *Indirect accreditation through Rasmussen College System, Lake Elmo, MN*)

Rasmussen College—Eden Prairie
7905 Golden Triangle Dr., Eden Prairie 55344
Type: Private, proprietary, four-year
System: Rasmussen College System
Degrees: A, B *Enroll:* 184
URL: http://www.rasmussen.edu
Phone: (952) 545-2000 *Calendar:* Qtr. plan
Inst. Accred.: NCA-HLC (1995/2004, *Indirect accreditation through Rasmussen College System, Lake Elmo, MN*)

Rasmussen College—Lake Elmo/Woodbury
8565 Eagle Point Circle, Lake Elmo 55042
Type: Private, proprietary, four-year
System: Rasmussen College System
Degrees: A, B
URL: http://www.rasmussen.edu
Phone: (651) 259-6600 *Calendar:* Qtr. plan
Inst. Accred.: NCA-HLC (2001/2004, *Indirect accreditation through Rasmussen College System, Lake Elmo, MN*)

Rasmussen College—Mankato Campus
501 Holly Ln., Mankato 56001-6803
Type: Private, proprietary, four-year
System: Rasmussen College System
Degrees: A, B *Enroll:* 360
URL: http://www.rasmussen.edu
Phone: (507) 625-6556 *Calendar:* Qtr. plan
Inst. Accred.: NCA-HLC (1995/2004, *Indirect accreditation through Rasmussen College System, Lake Elmo, MN*)

Rasmussen College—Moorhead
1250 29th Ave. South, Moorhead 56560
Type: Private, proprietary, four-year
System: Rasmussen College System
Degrees: A, B
URL: http://www.rasmussen.edu
Phone: (218) 304-6200 *Calendar:* Qtr. plan
Inst. Accred.: NCA-HLC (2001/2004, *Indirect accreditation through Rasmussen College System, Lake Elmo, MN*)

Rasmussen College—St. Cloud Campus
226 Park Ave. South, St. Cloud 56303-3713
Type: Private, proprietary, four-year
System: Rasmussen College System
Degrees: A, B *Enroll:* 302
URL: http://www.rasmussen.edu
Phone: (320) 251-5600 *Calendar:* Qtr. plan
Inst. Accred.: NCA-HLC (1995/2004, *Indirect accreditation through Rasmussen College System, Lake Elmo, MN*)

Ridgewater College
PO Box 1097, 2101 15th Ave., NW, Wilmar 56201
Type: Public, state, two-year
System: Minnesota State Colleges and Universities
Degrees: A *FTE Enroll:* 970
URL: http://www.ridgewater.mnscu.edu
Phone: (320) 235-5114 *Calendar:* Sem. plan
Inst. Accred.: NCA-HLC (1996/ 2002)
Prog. Accred.: Allied Health (medical assisting (AMA)), Nursing, Practical Nursing, Veterinary Technology

Hutchinson Campus
2 Century Ave., SE, Hutchinson 55350
Phone: (320) 587-3636
Prog. Accred: Nursing, Practical Nursing

Riverland Community College—Austin
1900 8th Ave., NW, Austin 55912-1407
Type: Public, state, two-year
System: Minnesota State Colleges and Universities
Degrees: A *Enroll:* 2,210
URL: http://www.riverland.edu
Phone: (507) 433-0600 *Calendar:* Sem. plan
Inst. Accred.: NCA-HLC (1996/ 2001)
Prog. Accred.: Nursing, Radiography

Albert Lea Campus
2200 Tech Dr., Albert Lea 56007-3499
Phone: (507) 379-3300
Prog. Accred: Dentistry (dental assisting)

Rochester Community and Technical College
851 30th Ave., SE, Rochester 55904-4999
Type: Public, state, two-year
System: Minnesota State Colleges and Universities
Degrees: A *Enroll:* 4,244
URL: http://www.rctc.edu
Phone: (507) 285-7210 *Calendar:* Sem. plan
Inst. Accred.: NCA-HLC (1923/2001)
Prog. Accred.: Allied Health (EMT-paramedic, surgical technology), Dentistry (dental assisting, dental hygiene), Nursing, Practical Nursing, Veterinary Technology

Saint Cloud Technical College
1540 Northway Dr., St. Cloud 56303-1240
Type: Public, state, two-year
System: Minnesota State Colleges and Universities
Degrees: A *Enroll:* 2,633
URL: http://www.sctc.edu
Phone: (320) 654-5017 *Calendar:* Sem. plan
Inst. Accred.: NCA-HLC (1985/1997)
Prog. Accred.: Allied Health (EMT-paramedic, cardiovascular technology, diagnostic medical sonography, surgical technology), Dentistry (dental assisting, dental hygiene)

Saint John's University
PO Box 7155, Collegeville 56321
Type: Private, Roman Catholic Church, four-year
Degrees: B, M *Enroll:* 1,926
URL: http://www.csbsju.edu
Phone: (320) 363-2882 *Calendar:* Sem. plan
Inst. Accred.: ATS (1969/1998), NCA-HLC (1950/1999)
Prog. Accred.: Nursing Education, Social Work

Saint Mary's University of Minnesota
700 Terrace Heights, Winona 55987-1399
Type: Private, Roman Catholic Church, four-year
Degrees: B, M *Enroll:* 3,211
URL: http://www.smumn.edu
Phone: (507) 457-4430 *Calendar:* Sem. plan
Inst. Accred.: NCA-HLC (1934/2007)
Prog. Accred.: Allied Health (surgical technology), Nuclear Medicine Technology, Nurse Anesthesia Education

Twin Cities Campus
2500 Park Ave., Minneapolis 55404-4403
Phone: (800) 328-4827

Saint Olaf College
1520 St. Olaf Ave., Northfield 55057
Type: Private, Evangelical Lutheran Church in America, four-year
Degrees: B *Enroll:* 3,026
URL: http://www.stolaf.edu
Phone: (507) 646-2222 *Calendar:* 4-1-4 plan
Inst. Accred.: NCA-HLC (1915/2004)
Prog. Accred.: Dance, Music, Nursing Education, Social Work, Teacher Education (NCATE), Theatre

Saint Paul College—A Community and Technical College
235 Marshall Ave., St. Paul 55102
Type: Public, state, two-year
System: Minnesota State Colleges and Universities
Degrees: A *Enroll:* 2,636
URL: http://www.saintpaul.edu
Phone: (651) 221-1335 *Calendar:* Sem. plan
Inst. Accred.: NCA-HLC (1983/2003)
Prog. Accred.: Allied Health (respiratory therapy), Clinical Lab Technology, Culinary Education, Practical Nursing

South Central College—Mankato
1920 Lee Blvd., North Mankato 56003
Type: Public, state, two-year
System: Minnesota State Colleges and Universities
Degrees: A *Enroll:* 2,081
URL: http://www.sctc.mnscu.edu
Phone: (507) 389-7200 *Calendar:* Sem. plan
Inst. Accred.: NCA-HLC (1995/2000)
Prog. Accred.: Allied Health (EMT-paramedic), Dentistry (dental assisting)

Faribault Campus
1225 SW Third St., Faribault 55021
Phone: (507) 334-3965
Prog. Accred: Clinical Lab Technology

Southwest Minnesota State University
1501 State St., Marshall 56258
Type: Public, state, four-year
System: Minnesota State Colleges and Universities
Degrees: A, B, M *Enroll:* 4,045
URL: http://www.southwest.msus.edu
Phone: (507) 537-6272 *Calendar:* Sem. plan
Inst. Accred.: NCA-HLC (1972/2004)
Prog. Accred.: Music, Social Work

St. Cloud State University
720 Fourth Ave. South, St. Cloud 56301-4498
Type: Public, state, four-year
System: Minnesota State Colleges and Universities
Degrees: A, B, M, P *Enroll:* 13,558
URL: http://www.stcloudstate.edu
Phone: (320) 255-0121 *Calendar:* Sem. plan
Inst. Accred.: NCA-HLC (1915/2007)
Prog. Accred.: Allied Health (speech-language pathology), Applied Science (surveying/geomatics), Art, Aviation, Business (AACSB), Computer Science (ABET-CAC), Counseling, Engineering (electrical, manufacturing, mechanical), Industrial Technology, Journalism, Marriage and Family Therapy, Music, Nursing Education, Rehabilitation Counseling, Social Work, Teacher Education (NCATE), Theatre

United Theological Seminary of the Twin Cities
3000 Fifth St. NW, New Brighton 55112
Type: Private, United Church of Christ, four-year
Degrees: M, D *Enroll:* 142
URL: http://www.unitedseminary-mn.org
Phone: (651) 633-4311 *Calendar:* 4-1-4 plan
Inst. Accred.: ATS (1966/2002), NCA-HLC (1977/2002)

University of Minnesota—Crookston
2900 University Ave., Crookston 56716
Type: Public, state, four-year
System: University of Minnesota System
Degrees: A, B *Enroll:* 1,437
URL: http://www.crk.umn.edu
Phone: (218) 281-6510 *Calendar:* Sem. plan
Inst. Accred.: NCA-HLC (1971/2006)
Prog. Accred.: Dietetic Technician

University of Minnesota—Duluth
515 Darland Administration Bldg., 10 University Dr., Duluth 55812
Type: Public, state, four-year
System: University of Minnesota System
Degrees: B, M *Enroll:* 9,638
URL: http://www.d.umn.edu
Phone: (218) 726-7106 *Calendar:* Qtr. plan
Inst. Accred.: NCA-HLC (1968/2008)
Prog. Accred.: Allied Health (speech-language pathology), Business (AACSB), Computer Science (ABET-CAC), Engineering (chemical, computer, industrial, mechanical), Graduate Social Work, Music, Teacher Education (NCATE)

University of Minnesota—Morris
600 East Fourth St., Morris 56267
Type: Public, state, four-year
System: University of Minnesota System
Degrees: B *Enroll:* 1,592
URL: http://www.mrs.umn.edu
Phone: (320) 589-6035 *Calendar:* Qtr. plan
Inst. Accred.: NCA-HLC (1970/2000)
Prog. Accred.: Teacher Education (NCATE)

University of Minnesota—Twin Cities
100 Church St., SE, Minneapolis 55455-0213
Type: Public, state, four-year
System: University of Minnesota System
Degrees: B, M, P, D *Enroll:* 41,725
URL: http://www.umn.edu
Phone: (612) 625-5000 *Calendar:* Sem. plan
Inst. Accred.: NCA-HLC (1913/2006)
Prog. Accred.: Accounting, Allied Health (audiology, health services administration, medicine, occupational therapy, speech-language pathology), Applied Science (industrial hygiene), Business (AACSB), Clinical Lab Scientist, Clinical Psychology, Counseling Psychology, Dance, Dentistry (advanced education in general dentistry, combined prosthodontics, dental hygiene, dentistry, endodontics, general dentistry, general practice residency, oral and maxillofacial pathology, oral and maxillofacial surgery, orthodontic and dentofacial orthopedics, pediatric dentistry, periodontics), Dietetics (didactic), Dietetics (internship), Engineering (aerospace, agricultural, bioengineering, chemical, civil, computer, electrical, geological/geophysical, materials, mechanical), Forestry, Funeral Service Education (Mortuary Science), Graduate Social Work, Interior Design, Journalism, Landscape Architecture, Law, Marriage and Family Therapy, Music, Nurse Anesthesia Education, Nursing Education, Nurse (Midwifery), Pharmacy, Pharmacy, Planning, Psychology Internship, Public Administration, Public Health, Radiography, Recreation and Leisure Services, School Psychology, Teacher Education (NCATE), Theatre, Veterinary Medicine

University of Saint Thomas
2115 Summit Ave., St. Paul 55105
Type: Private, Roman Catholic Church, four-year
Degrees: B, M, P, D *Enroll:* 7,890
URL: http://www.stthomas.edu
Phone: (651) 962-5000 *Calendar:* 4-1-4 plan
Inst. Accred.: ATS (1974/2003), NCA-HLC (1916/2004)
Prog. Accred.: Allied Health (health services administration), Engineering (electrical, manufacturing, mechanical), Graduate Social Work, Law (ABA only), Music, Psychology Internship, Social Work, Teacher Education (NCATE)

Bernardi Campus
Lungotevere delle Armi, 16, Rome, RM, Italy 00195
Phone: 011 (39) 06 3260 054

Minneapolis Campus
1000 LaSalle Ave., Ste. 201, Minneapolis 55403
Phone: (612) 962-4000
Prog. Accred: Counseling Psychology

Vermilion Community College
1900 East Camp St., Ely 55731-1918
Type: Public, state/local, two-year
System: Northeast Higher Education District
Degrees: A *Enroll:* 612
URL: http://www.vcc.edu
Phone: (218) 365-7200 *Calendar:* Sem. plan
Inst. Accred.: NCA-HLC (2001)
Prog. Accred.: Forestry

Walden University
155 South Fifth Ave., Minneapolis 55401
Type: Private, proprietary, four-year
System: Laureate Education, Inc.
Degrees: M, D *Enroll:* 18,388
URL: http://www.waldenu.edu
Phone: (866) 925-3364 *Calendar:* Qtr. plan
Inst. Accred.: NCA-HLC (1990/2006)
Prog. Accred.: Nursing Education

NTU School of Engineering and Applied Science
155 Fifth Ave. South, Ste. 600, Minneapolis 55401
Phone: (800) 582-9976

William Mitchell College of Law
875 Summit Ave., St. Paul 55105
Type: Private, independent, four-year
Degrees: P *Enroll:* 940
URL: http://www.wmitchell.edu
Phone: (651) 227-9171 *Calendar:* Sem. plan
Inst. Accred.: ABA (1938/2008)
Prog. Accred.: Law

Winona State University
PO Box 5838, Winona 55987
Type: Public, state, four-year
System: Minnesota State Colleges and Universities
Degrees: A, B, M, P *Enroll:* 7,337
URL: http://www.winona.edu
Phone: (507) 457-5000 *Calendar:* Sem. plan
Inst. Accred.: NCA-HLC (1913/2002)
Prog. Accred.: Counseling, Engineering (materials), Music, Nursing Education, Social Work, Teacher Education (NCATE), Theatre

Rochester Center Campus
Highway 14 East, 859 30th Ave., SE, Rochester 55904
Phone: (507) 285-7100
Prog. Accred: Counseling

MISSISSIPPI

Alcorn State University
1000 ASU Dr. 359, Alcorn State 39096-7510
Type: Public, state, four-year
System: Mississippi Board of Trustees of State Institutions of Higher Learning
Degrees: A, B, M, P *Enroll:* 3,091
URL: http://www.alcorn.edu
Phone: (601) 877-6100 *Calendar:* Sem. plan
Inst. Accred.: SACS (1948/2001)
Prog. Accred.: Dietetics (didactic), Family & Consumer Science, Industrial Technology, Music, Nursing, Teacher Education (NCATE)

Belhaven College
1500 Peachtree St., Jackson 39202
Type: Private, Presbyterian Church, USA, four-year
Degrees: B, M *Enroll:* 2,528
URL: http://www.belhaven.edu
Phone: (601) 968-5940 *Calendar:* Sem. plan
Inst. Accred.: SACS (1946/2007)
Prog. Accred.: Art, Music

Blue Mountain College
PO Box 160, Blue Mountain 38610
Type: Private, Southern Baptist Church, four-year
Degrees: B, M *Enroll:* 315
URL: http://www.bmc.edu
Phone: (662) 685-4771 *Calendar:* Sem. plan
Inst. Accred.: SACS (1927/2005)

Coahoma Community College
3240 Friars Point Rd., Clarksdale 38614
Type: Public, state/local, two-year
System: Mississippi State Board for Community and Junior Colleges
Degrees: A *Enroll:* 1,850
URL: http://www.coahomacc.edu
Phone: (662) 627-2571 *Calendar:* Sem. plan
Inst. Accred.: SACS (1975/2000)
Prog. Accred.: Allied Health (respiratory therapy)

Copiah-Lincoln Community College
PO Box 649, Wesson 39191
Type: Public, state, two-year
System: Mississippi State Board for Community and Junior Colleges
Degrees: A *Enroll:* 1,740
URL: http://www.colin.edu
Phone: (601) 643-5101 *Calendar:* Sem. plan
Inst. Accred.: SACS (1936/2005)
Prog. Accred.: Allied Health (respiratory therapy), Clinical Lab Technology, Nursing, Radiography

Delta State University
Highway 8 West, Cleveland 38733
Type: Public, state, four-year
System: Mississippi Board of Trustees of State Institutions of Higher Learning
Degrees: A, B, M, D *Enroll:* 3,459
URL: http://www.deltastate.edu
Phone: (662) 846-3000 *Calendar:* Sem. plan
Inst. Accred.: SACS (1930/2004)
Prog. Accred.: Art, Business (ACBSP), Counseling, Dietetics (coordinated), Family & Consumer Science, Music, Nursing Education, Social Work, Teacher Education (NCATE)

East Central Community College
PO Box 129, Decatur 39327-0129
Type: Public, state/local, two-year
System: Mississippi State Board for Community and Junior Colleges
Degrees: A *Enroll:* 2,034
URL: http://www.eccc.edu
Phone: (601) 635-2111 *Calendar:* Sem. plan
Inst. Accred.: SACS (1939/2001)
Prog. Accred.: Allied Health (EMT-paramedic, medical assisting (AMA), surgical technology), Nursing

East Mississippi Community College
PO Box 158, Scooba 39358
Type: Public, state/local, two-year
System: Mississippi State Board for Community and Junior Colleges
Degrees: A *Enroll:* 3,166
URL: http://www.eastms.edu
Phone: (662) 476-5000 *Calendar:* Sem. plan
Inst. Accred.: SACS (1949/2007)
Prog. Accred.: Funeral Service Education (Mortuary Science)

Hinds Community College
PO Box 1100, Raymond 39154-1100
Type: Public, state/local, two-year
System: Mississippi State Board for Community and Junior Colleges
Degrees: A *Enroll:* 7,411
URL: http://www.hindscc.edu
Phone: (601) 857-5261 *Calendar:* Sem. plan
Inst. Accred.: SACS (1928/2007, Warning)
Prog. Accred.: Allied Health (diagnostic medical sonography, medical assisting (AMA), respiratory therapy, surgical technology), Clinical Lab Technology, Dentistry (dental assisting), Nursing, Physical Therapy Assisting, Veterinary Technology

Jackson Campus
3925 Sunset Dr., Jackson 39213-5899
Phone: (601) 366-1405

Nursing/Allied Health Center
1750 Chadwick Dr., Jackson 39204-3490
Phone: (601) 372-6507
Prog. Accred: Dentistry (dental assisting)

Rankin Campus
3805 Hwy. 80 East, Pearl 39208-4295
Phone: (601) 932-5237

Raymond Campus
505 East Main St., Raymond 39154-9799
Phone: (601) 352-3011
Prog. Accred: Radiography

Utica Campus
Highway 18 West, Utica 39175-9599
Phone: (601) 885-6062

Vicksburg-Warren County Branch
1624 Hwy. 27, Vicksburg 39180-8699
Phone: (601) 638-0600

Holmes Community College
PO Box 369, Goodman 39079
Type: Public, local, two-year
System: Mississippi State Board for Community and Junior Colleges
Degrees: A *Enroll:* 4,047
URL: http://www.holmescc.edu
Phone: (662) 472-2312 *Calendar:* Sem. plan
Inst. Accred.: SACS (1934/2006)
Prog. Accred.: Allied Health (EMT-paramedic, surgical technology), Funeral Service Education (Mortuary Science), Nursing

Ridgeland Campus
412 W. Ridgeland Ave., Ridgeland 39157
Phone: (801) 856-5400
Prog. Accred: Allied Health (occupational therapy assisting)

Itawamba Community College
602 West Hill St., Fulton 38843
Type: Public, state/local, two-year
System: Mississippi State Board for Community and Junior Colleges
Degrees: A *Enroll:* 4,058
URL: http://www.iccms.edu
Phone: (662) 862-8000 *Calendar:* Sem. plan
Inst. Accred.: SACS (1955/2008)
Prog. Accred.: Allied Health (EMT-paramedic, diagnostic medical sonography, respiratory therapy, surgical technology), Nursing, Physical Therapy Assisting, Radiography

Jackson State University
1400 J.R. Lynch St., Jackson 39217
Type: Public, state, four-year
System: Mississippi Board of Trustees of State Institutions of Higher Learning
Degrees: B, M, P, D *Enroll:* 7,200
URL: http://www.jsums.edu
Phone: (601) 979-2121 *Calendar:* Sem. plan
Inst. Accred.: SACS (1948/2001)
Prog. Accred.: Allied Health (speech-language pathology), Art, Business (AACSB), Clinical Psychology, Computer Science (ABET-CAC), Graduate Social Work, Industrial Technology, Journalism, Music, Public Administration, Rehabilitation Counseling, Social Work, Teacher Education (NCATE)

Jones County Junior College
900 Ct. St., Ellisville 39437
Type: Public, state/local, two-year
System: Mississippi State Board for Community and Junior Colleges
Degrees: A *Enroll:* 4,321
URL: http://www.jcjc.edu
Phone: (601) 477-4000 *Calendar:* Sem. plan
Inst. Accred.: SACS (1940/2008)
Prog. Accred.: Allied Health (EMT-paramedic), Business (ACBSP), Nursing, Radiography

Magnolia Bible College
PO Box 1109, Kosciusko 39090-1109
Type: Private, nondenominational, four-year
Degrees: B *Enroll:* 28
URL: http://www.magnolia.edu
Phone: (622) 289-2896 *Calendar:* Sem. plan
Inst. Accred.: SACS (1990/2005)

Meridian Community College
910 Hwy. 19 North, Meridian 39307
Type: Public, state/local, two-year
System: Mississippi State Board for Community and Junior Colleges
Degrees: A *Enroll:* 2,829
URL: http://www.mcc.cc.ms.us
Phone: (601) 483-8241 *Calendar:* Sem. plan
Inst. Accred.: SACS (1942/2001)
Prog. Accred.: Allied Health (respiratory therapy, surgical technology), Clinical Lab Technology, Dentistry (dental hygiene), Nursing, Physical Therapy Assisting, Practical Nursing, Radiography

Millsaps College
1701 North State St., Jackson 39210
Type: Private, United Methodist Church, four-year
Degrees: B, M *Enroll:* 1,101
URL: http://www.millsaps.edu
Phone: (601) 974-1000 *Calendar:* Sem. plan
Inst. Accred.: SACS (1912/2002)
Prog. Accred.: Business (AACSB), Teacher Education (NCATE)

Mississippi College
PO Box 4001, Clinton 39058
Type: Private, Southern Baptist Church, four-year
Degrees: B, M, P, D *Enroll:* 3,303
URL: http://www.mc.edu
Phone: (601) 925-3000 *Calendar:* Sem. plan
Inst. Accred.: SACS (1922/2002)
Prog. Accred.: Business (ACBSP), Counseling, Law, Music, Social Work, Teacher Education (NCATE)

Mississippi Delta Community College
PO Box 668, Moorhead 38761
Type: Public, state/local, two-year
System: Mississippi State Board for Community and Junior Colleges
Degrees: A *Enroll:* 2,649
URL: http://www.msdelta.edu
Phone: (662) 246-6322 *Calendar:* Sem. plan
Inst. Accred.: SACS (1930/2008)
Prog. Accred.: Clinical Lab Technology, Dentistry (dental hygiene), Nursing, Radiography

Mississippi Gulf Coast Community College
PO Box 609, Perkinston 39573
Type: Public, state/local, two-year
System: Mississippi State Board for Community and Junior Colleges
Degrees: A *Enroll:* 6,081
URL: http://www.mgccc.edu
Phone: (601) 928-5211 *Calendar:* Sem. plan
Inst. Accred.: SACS (1929/1999)
Prog. Accred.: Allied Health (EMT-paramedic, respiratory therapy, surgical technology), Clinical Lab Technology, Funeral Service Education (Mortuary Science), Nursing, Practical Nursing, Radiography

Jackson County Campus
PO Box 100, Gautier 39553
Phone: (228) 497-9602
Prog. Accred: Practical Nursing, Radiography

Jefferson Davis Campus
2226 Switzer Rd., Gulfport 39507
Phone: (228) 896-3355
Prog. Accred: Practical Nursing

Mississippi State University
PO Box 5325, Mississippi State 39762-5325
Type: Public, state, four-year
System: Mississippi Board of Trustees of State Institutions of Higher Learning
Degrees: B, M, P, D *Enroll:* 14,071
URL: http://www.msstate.edu
Phone: (662) 325-2323 *Calendar:* Sem. plan
Inst. Accred.: SACS (1926/2003)
Prog. Accred.: Accounting, Art, Business (AACSB), Computer Science (ABET-CAC), Counseling, Dietetics (didactic), Dietetics (internship), Engineering (aerospace, agricultural, chemical, civil, computer, electrical, industrial, mechanical, software), Family & Consumer Science, Forestry, Interior Design, Landscape Architecture, Music, Public Administration, Rehabilitation Counseling, School Psychology, Social Work, Teacher Education (NCATE), Veterinary Medicine

Meridian Campus
1000 Hwy. 19 North, Meridian 39307
Phone: (601) 484-0144
Prog. Accred: Social Work

Mississippi University for Women
1100 College St., Columbus 39701-5800
Type: Public, state, four-year
System: Mississippi Board of Trustees of State Institutions of Higher Learning
Degrees: A, B, M *Enroll:* 1,967
URL: http://www.muw.edu
Phone: (662) 329-4750 *Calendar:* Sem. plan
Inst. Accred.: SACS (1921/2003)
Prog. Accred.: Allied Health (speech-language pathology), Art, Business (ACBSP), Music, Nursing, Nursing Education, Teacher Education (NCATE)

Mississippi Valley State University
14000 Hwy. 82 West, Itta Bena 38941-1400
Type: Public, state, four-year
System: Mississippi Board of Trustees of State Institutions of Higher Learning
Degrees: B, M *Enroll:* 2,753
URL: http://www.mvsu.edu
Phone: (662) 254-9041 *Calendar:* Sem. plan
Inst. Accred.: SACS (1968/2002)
Prog. Accred.: Art, Business (ACBSP), Computer Science (ABET-CAC), Environmental Health, Graduate Social Work, Music, Social Work, Teacher Education (NCATE)

Northeast Mississippi Community College
101 Cunningham Blvd., Booneville 38829
Type: Public, state/local, two-year
System: Mississippi State Board for Community and Junior Colleges
Degrees: A *Enroll:* 2,817
URL: http://www.nemcc.edu
Phone: (662) 728-7751 *Calendar:* Sem. plan
Inst. Accred.: SACS (1956/2000)
Prog. Accred.: Allied Health (medical assisting (AMA), respiratory therapy), Clinical Lab Technology, Dentistry (dental hygiene), Nursing, Radiography

Northwest Mississippi Community College
4975 Hwy. 51 North, Senatobia 38668
Type: Public, state, two-year
System: Mississippi State Board for Community and Junior Colleges
Degrees: A *Enroll:* 5,203
URL: http://www.northwestms.edu
Phone: (662) 562-3200 *Calendar:* Sem. plan
Inst. Accred.: SACS (1953/2007)
Prog. Accred.: Funeral Service Education (Mortuary Science), Nursing

Southaven Campus
5197 W.E. Ross Pkwy., Southaven 38671
Phone: (662) 342-1570
Prog. Accred: Allied Health (EMT-paramedic, respiratory therapy)

Pearl River Community College
101 Hwy. 11 North, Poplarville 39470-2201
Type: Public, state/local, two-year
System: Mississippi State Board for Community and Junior Colleges
Degrees: A *Enroll:* 3,163
URL: http://www.prcc.edu
Phone: (601) 403-1000 *Calendar:* Sem. plan
Inst. Accred.: SACS (1929/2006)
Prog. Accred.: Clinical Lab Technology, Dentistry (dental assisting, dental hygiene), Nursing

Hattiesburg Campus
5448 US Hwy. 495, Hattiesburg 39401
Phone: (601) 795-6801
Prog. Accred: Allied Health (occupational therapy assisting, respiratory therapy, surgical technology), Dentistry (dental assisting, dental hygiene), Physical Therapy Assisting, Radiography

Reformed Theological Seminary
5422 Clinton Blvd., Jackson 39209-3099
Type: Private, interdenominational, four-year
Degrees: M, D *FTE Enroll:* 160
URL: http://www.rts.edu
Phone: (601) 923-1600 *Calendar:* Sem. plan
Inst. Accred.: ATS (1977/2001), SACS (1977/2003)
Prog. Accred.: Marriage and Family Therapy

Charlotte Campus
2101 Carmel Rd., Charlotte, NC 28226
Phone: (704) 366-5066

Orlando Campus
1231 Reformation Dr., Oviedo, FL 32765
Phone: (407) 366-9493

Rust College
150 East Rust Ave., Holly Springs 38635
Type: Private, United Methodist Church, four-year
Degrees: A, B *Enroll:* 876
URL: http://www.rustcollege.edu
Phone: (662) 252-8000 *Calendar:* Sem. plan
Inst. Accred.: SACS (1970/2004)
Prog. Accred.: Social Work

Southeastern Baptist College
4229 Hwy. 15 North, Laurel 39440-1096
Type: Private, Baptist Missionary Association, four-year
Degrees: A, B *Enroll:* 64
URL: http://www.southeasternbaptist.edu
Phone: (601) 426-6346 *Calendar:* Sem. plan
Inst. Accred.: ABHE (1988/1999)

Southwest Mississippi Community College
1566 College Dr., Summit 39666-9704
Type: Public, state/local, two-year
System: Mississippi State Board for Community and Junior Colleges
Degrees: A *Enroll:* 1,579
URL: http://www.smcc.edu
Phone: (601) 276-2000 *Calendar:* Sem. plan
Inst. Accred.: SACS (1958/2000)
Prog. Accred.: Nursing

Tougaloo College
500 West County Line Rd., Tougaloo 39174
Type: Private, United Church of Christ, four-year
Degrees: A, B *Enroll:* 909
URL: http://www.tougaloo.edu
Phone: (601) 977-7700 *Calendar:* Sem. plan
Inst. Accred.: SACS (1953/2001)

University of Mississippi
PO Box 1848, University 38677-1848
Type: Public, state, four-year
System: Mississippi Board of Trustees of State Institutions of Higher Learning
Degrees: B, M, P, D *Enroll:* 13,728
URL: http://www.olemiss.edu
Phone: (662) 915-7211 *Calendar:* Sem. plan
Inst. Accred.: SACS (1895/1999)
Prog. Accred.: Accounting, Allied Health (audiology, speech-language pathology), Art, Business (AACSB), Clinical Psychology, Computer Science (ABET-CAC), Counseling, Dietetics (didactic), Engineering (chemical, civil, electrical, geological/geophysical, mechanical), Family & Consumer Science, Journalism, Law, Music, Pharmacy, Psychology Internship, Recreation and Leisure Services, Social Work, Teacher Education (NCATE)

University of Mississippi Medical Center
2500 North State St., Jackson 39216-4500
Type: Public, state, four-year
System: Mississippi Board of Trustees of State Institutions of Higher Learning
Degrees: B, M, P, D *Enroll:* 1,876
URL: http://www.umc.edu
Phone: (601) 984-1000 *Calendar:* Qtr. plan
Inst. Accred.: SACS (1991/2001)
Prog. Accred.: Allied Health (EMT-paramedic, cytotechnology, medicine, occupational therapy), Clinical Lab Scientist, Dentistry (advanced education in general dentistry, dental hygiene, dentistry, general dentistry, general practice residency, pediatric dentistry), Nuclear Medicine Technology, Nursing Education, Physical Therapy, Radiography

The University of Southern Mississippi
118 College Dr., Hattiesburg 39406-0001
Type: Public, state, four-year
System: Mississippi Board of Trustees of State Institutions of Higher Learning
Degrees: B, M, P, D *Enroll:* 13,205
URL: http://www.usm.edu
Phone: (601) 266-1000 *Calendar:* Sem. plan
Inst. Accred.: SACS (1929/2006)
Prog. Accred.: Accounting, Allied Health (audiology, kinesiotherapy, speech-language pathology), Art, Business (AACSB), Clinical Lab Scientist, Clinical Psychology, Computer Science (ABET-CAC), Construction Education, Counseling, Counseling Psychology, Dance, Dietetics (didactic), Dietetics (internship), Engineering Technology (architectural, civil/construction, computer, electrical, industrial), Family & Consumer Science, Graduate Social Work, Interior Design, Journalism, Librarianship, Marriage and Family Therapy, Music, Nursing Education, Psychology Internship, Public Health, Recreation and Leisure Services, School Psychology, Social Work, Teacher Education (NCATE), Theatre

Gulf Park Campus
East Beach Blvd., Long Beach 39560
Phone: (601) 865-4500

Wesley Biblical Seminary
PO Box 9938, Jackson 39286-0938
Type: Private, multidenominational, four-year
Degrees: M *Enroll:* 90
URL: http://www.wbs.edu
Phone: (601) 366-8880 *Calendar:* Sem. plan
Inst. Accred.: ATS (1991/2004)

Wesley College
PO Box 1070, Florence 39073-1070
Type: Private, Congregational Methodist Church, four-year
Degrees: B *Enroll:* 80
URL: http://www.wesleycollege.edu
Phone: (601) 845-2265 *Calendar:* Sem. plan
Inst. Accred.: ABHE (1979/2001)

William Carey University
498 Tuscan Ave., Hattiesburg 39401-5499
Type: Private, Southern Baptist Church, four-year
Degrees: B, M, P *Enroll:* 2,007
URL: http://www.wmcarey.edu
Phone: (601) 318-6051 *Calendar:* Tri. plan
Inst. Accred.: SACS (1958/1999)
Prog. Accred.: Music

New Orleans Campus
4103 Chef Mentuer Hwy., New Orleans, LA 70126
Phone: (504) 286-3275
Prog. Accred: Nursing

William Carey University on the Coast
1865 Beach Dr., Gulfport 39507
Phone: (228) 897-7100
Prog. Accred: Nursing

MISSOURI

A.T. Still University of Health Sciences
800 West Jefferson St., Kirksville 63501-1497
Type: Private, independent, four-year
Degrees: M, D *Enroll:* 1,589
URL: http://www.atsu.edu
Phone: (660) 626-2121 *Calendar:* Qtr. plan
Inst. Accred.: NCA-HLC (1994/1999)
Prog. Accred.: Osteopathy

Mesa Campus
5850 East Still Circle, Mesa, AZ 85206-3618
Phone: (480) 219-6000
Prog. Accred: Allied Health (occupational therapy), Dentistry (dentistry, orthodontic and dentofacial orthopedics), Osteopathy, Physical Therapy, Physician Assistant

Allied College
13723 Riverport Dr., Ste. 103, Maryland Heights 63073
Type: Private, proprietary, two-year
System: High-Tech Institute
Degrees: A
URL: http://www.alliedcollege.edu
Phone: (314) 739-4450
Inst. Accred.: ABHES (1985/2005)
Prog. Accred.: Criminal Justice (ABHES), Dentistry (dental assisting), Medical Assisting (ABHES), Surgical Technology

Anthem College Campus
4145 SW Watson Ave., Beaverton, OR 97005
Phone: (503) 646-6000
Prog. Accred: Medical Assisting (ABHES), Surgical Technology

Fenton Campus
645 Gravois Bluffs Blvd., Fenton 63026
Phone: (636) 326-7300
Prog. Accred: Criminal Justice (ABHES), Medical Assisting (ABHES)

High-Tech Institute—Milwaukee
440 S. Executive Dr., Ste. 200, Brookfield, WI 53005
Phone: (262) 641-9944

American College of Technology
2921 North Belt Hwy., Saint Joseph 64506
Type: Private, proprietary, two-year
Degrees: A
URL: http://www.acit.com
Phone: (816) 279-7000
Inst. Accred.: DETC (2006)

Aquinas Institute of Theology
23 South Spring Ave., St. Louis 63108-3323
Type: Private, Roman Catholic Church, four-year
Degrees: M, D *Enroll:* 173
URL: http://www.ai.edu
Phone: (314) 256-8800 *Calendar:* Sem. plan
Inst. Accred.: ATS (1968/2006), NCA-HLC (1964/2006)

Assemblies of God Theological Seminary
1435 North Glenstone Ave., Springfield 65802-2131
Type: Private, Assemblies of God, four-year
Degrees: M, D *Enroll:* 324
URL: http://www.agts.edu
Phone: (417) 268-1000 *Calendar:* Sem. plan
Inst. Accred.: ATS (1992/2001), NCA-HLC (1978/2001)

Avila University
11901 Wornall Rd., Kansas City 64145
Type: Private, Roman Catholic Church, four-year
Degrees: B, M *Enroll:* 1,411
URL: http://www.avila.edu
Phone: (816) 942-8400 *Calendar:* Sem. plan
Inst. Accred.: NCA-HLC (1946/2008)
Prog. Accred.: Nursing Education, Radiography, Social Work

Baptist Bible College
628 East Kearney St., Springfield 65803-3498
Type: Private, Baptist Bible Fellowship International, four-year
Degrees: A, B, M *Enroll:* 632
URL: http://www.bbcnet.edu
Phone: (417) 268-6060 *Calendar:* Sem. plan
Inst. Accred.: ABHE (1978/2007), NCA-HLC (2005)

Bryan College—Springfield
237 South Florence Ave., Springfield 65806-2507
Type: Private, proprietary, two-year
Degrees: A
URL: http://www.bryancolleges.edu
Phone: (417) 862-5700
Inst. Accred.: ACICS (1991/2003)

Rogers Campus
3704 West Walnut St., Rogers, AR 72756-1825
Phone: (479) 899-6644

Calvary Bible College and Theological Seminary
15800 Calvary Rd., Kansas City 64147-1341
Type: Private, interdenominational, four-year
Degrees: A, B, M *Enroll:* 286
URL: http://www.calvary.edu
Phone: (816) 322-0110 *Calendar:* Sem. plan
Inst. Accred.: ABHE (1961/2001), NCA-HLC (2003/2008)

Central Bible College
3000 North Grant Ave., Springfield 65803-1096
Type: Private, Assemblies of God Church, four-year
Degrees: A, B *Enroll:* 715
URL: http://www.cbcag.edu
Phone: (417) 833-2551 *Calendar:* Sem. plan
Inst. Accred.: ABHE (1948/2006), NCA-HLC (2005)

Central Christian College of the Bible
911 East Urbandale Dr., Moberly 65270
Type: Private, Christian Churches/Churches of Christ, four-year
Degrees: A, B *Enroll:* 518
URL: http://cccb.edu
Phone: (660) 263-3900 *Calendar:* Sem. plan
Inst. Accred.: ABHE (1982/2003)

Central Methodist University
411 Central Methodist Square, Fayette 65248
Type: Private, United Methodist Church, four-year
Degrees: A, B, M *Enroll:* 801
URL: http://www.cmc.edu
Phone: (660) 248-3391 *Calendar:* Sem. plan
Inst. Accred.: NCA-HLC (1913/2008)
Prog. Accred.: Music, Nursing Education

Chamberlain College of Nursing
6150 Oakland Ave., St. Louis 63139
Type: Private, proprietary, four-year
System: DeVry University
Degrees: A, B *Enroll:* 461
URL: http://www.chamberlain.edu
Phone: (314) 768-3044 *Calendar:* Sem. plan
Inst. Accred.: NCA-HLC (1985/2006)
Prog. Accred.: Nursing, Nursing Education

Addison (Chicago) Campus
1221 North Swift Rd., Addison, IL 60101
Phone: (630) 953-3680

Columbus (Ohio) Campus
1350 Alum Creek Dr., Columbus, OH 43209
Phone: (614) 252-8890
Prog. Accred: Nursing

Phoenix Campus
2149 West Dunlap Ave., Phoenix, AZ 85021
Phone: (602) 870-0981

City Vision College
PO Box 280046, Kansas City 64128-0046
Type: Private, Association of Gospel Rescue Missions, four-year
Degrees: B
URL: http://www.cityvision.edu
Phone: (816) 960-2008 *Calendar:* Sem. plan
Inst. Accred.: DETC (2005)

College of the Ozarks
PO Box 17, Point Lookout 65726
Type: Private, Presbyterian Church, four-year
Degrees: B *Enroll:* 1,320
URL: http://www.cofo.edu/
Phone: (800) 222-0525 *Calendar:* Sem. plan
Inst. Accred.: NCA-HLC (1961/2001)
Prog. Accred.: Dietetics (didactic)

Columbia College
1001 Rogers St., Columbia 65216
Type: Private, Disciples of Christ, four-year
Degrees: A, B, M *Enroll:* 8,249
URL: http://www.ccis.edu
Phone: (573) 875-8700 *Calendar:* Sem. plan
Inst. Accred.: NCA-HLC (1918/2003)
Prog. Accred.: Social Work

Orlando Campus
2600 Technology Dr., Ste. 100, Orlando, FL 32804
Phone: (407) 293-9911

Conception Seminary College
PO Box 502, Conception 64433
Type: Private, Roman Catholic Church, four-year
Degrees: B *Enroll:* 98
URL: http://www.conception.edu
Phone: (660) 944-2218 *Calendar:* Sem. plan
Inst. Accred.: NCA-HLC (1960/2004)

Concorde Career College
3239 Broadway Blvd., Kansas City 64111-2407
Type: Private, proprietary, two-year
System: Concorde Career Colleges, Inc.
Degrees: A *Enroll:* 524
URL: http://www.concordecareercolleges.com
Phone: (816) 531-5223
Inst. Accred.: ACCSCT (1986/2006)
Prog. Accred.: Allied Health (respiratory therapy), Dentistry (dental assisting)

Concordia Seminary
801 DeMun Ave., St. Louis 63105
Type: Private, Lutheran Church-Missouri Synod, four-year
System: Concordia University System
Degrees: M, D *Enroll:* 700
URL: http://www.csl.edu
Phone: (314) 505-7000 *Calendar:* Qtr. plan
Inst. Accred.: ATS (1963/2003), NCA-HLC (1978/2004)

Concordia University Texas
11400 Concordia University Dr., Lees Summit 78726
Type: Private, Lutheran Church-Missouri Synod, four-year
System: Concordia University System
Degrees: A, B, M *Enroll:* 946
URL: http://www.concordia.edu
Phone: (512) 313-3000 *Calendar:* Sem. plan
Inst. Accred.: SACS (1968/2008)

Cottey College
1000 West Austin St., Nevada 64772
Type: Private, PEO Sisterhood, two-year
Degrees: A *Enroll:* 309
URL: http://www.cottey.edu
Phone: (417) 667-8181 *Calendar:* Sem. plan
Inst. Accred.: NCA-HLC (1918/2003)
Prog. Accred.: Music

Covenant Theological Seminary
12330 Conway Rd., St. Louis 63141
Type: Private, Presbyterian Church in America, four-year
Degrees: M, D *Enroll:* 572
URL: http://www.covenantseminary.edu
Phone: (314) 434-4044 *Calendar:* 4-1-4 plan
Inst. Accred.: ATS (1983/2007), NCA-HLC (1973/2008)

Crowder College
601 Laclede Ave., Neosho 64850
Type: Public, state/local, two-year
System: Missouri Coordinating Board for Higher Education
Degrees: A *Enroll:* 1,754
URL: http://www.crowder.edu
Phone: (417) 451-3226 *Calendar:* Sem. plan
Inst. Accred.: NCA-HLC (1977/2008)
Prog. Accred.: Electronic Technology, Veterinary Technology

Culver-Stockton College
One College Hill, Canton 63435
Type: Private, Christian Church/Disciples of Christ, four-year
Degrees: B *Enroll:* 795
URL: http://www.culver.edu
Phone: (573) 288-6000 *Calendar:* Sem. plan
Inst. Accred.: NCA-HLC (1924/2002)
Prog. Accred.: Music

DeVry University Kansas City
11224 Holmes Rd., Kansas City 64131
Type: Private, proprietary
System: DeVry University
Degrees: A, B, M *Enroll:* 1,003
URL: http://www.devry.edu/kansascity
Phone: (816) 941-0430 *Calendar:* Sem. plan
Inst. Accred.: NCA-HLC (2002, *Indirect accreditation through DeVry University, Oakbrook Terrace, IL*)
Prog. Accred.: Engineering Technology (computer, electrical)

Oklahoma City Campus
4013 NW Expressway St., Ste. 100, Oklahoma City, OK 73116-1695
Phone: (405) 767-9516

DeVry University—Kansas City Downtown
1100 Main St., City Center Square, Ste. 118, Kansas City 64105
Type: Private, proprietary, four-year
System: DeVry University
Degrees: A, B, M
URL: http://www.devry.edu
Phone: (816) 221-1300 *Calendar:* Sem. plan
Inst. Accred.: NCA-HLC (2002, *Indirect accreditation through DeVry University, Oakbrook Terrace, IL*)

DeVry University—St. Louis West
1801 Park 270 Dr., Ste. 260, St. Louis 63146
Type: Private, proprietary, four-year
System: DeVry University
Degrees: A, B, M
URL: http://www.devry.edu
Phone: (314) 542-4222 *Calendar:* Sem. plan
Inst. Accred.: NCA-HLC (2002, *Indirect accreditation through DeVry University, Oakbrook Terrace, IL*)

Drury University
900 North Benton Ave., Springfield 65802
Type: Private, independent, four-year
Degrees: A, B, M *Enroll:* 3,808
URL: http://www.drury.edu
Phone: (417) 873-7879 *Calendar:* Sem. plan
Inst. Accred.: NCA-HLC (1915/2001)
Prog. Accred.: Business (ACBSP), Music, Teacher Education (NCATE)

Cabool Campus
PO Box 526, Cabool 65689
Phone: (417) 962-5314

Fort Leonard Wood Campus
Truman Education Center, 268 Constitution St., Ste. 12, Fort Leonard Wood 65473
Phone: (314) 873-7399

Lebanon Campus
531 West Bland Rd., Lebanon 65536
Phone: (417) 532-9828

Rolla Campus
1280 Forum Dr., Rolla 65401
Phone: (573) 368-4959

East Central College
1964 Prairie Dell Rd., Union 63084
Type: Public, state/local, two-year
System: Missouri Coordinating Board for Higher Education
Degrees: A *Enroll:* 2,132
URL: http://www.eastcentral.edu
Phone: (636) 583-5193 *Calendar:* Sem. plan
Inst. Accred.: NCA-HLC (1976/2000)
Prog. Accred.: Culinary Education, Dentistry (dental assisting)

Eden Theological Seminary
475 East Lockwood Ave., St. Louis 63119-3192
Type: Private, United Church of Christ, four-year
Degrees: M, D *Enroll:* 170
URL: http://www.eden.edu
Phone: (314) 961-6327 *Calendar:* 4-1-4 plan
Inst. Accred.: ATS (1938/1998), NCA-HLC (1973/1999)

Evangel University
1111 North Glenstone Ave., Springfield 65802
Type: Private, General Council of the Assemblies of God, four-year
Degrees: A, B, M *Enroll:* 1,744
URL: http://www.evangel.edu
Phone: (417) 865-2811 *Calendar:* Sem. plan
Inst. Accred.: NCA-HLC (1965/2004)
Prog. Accred.: Music, Social Work, Teacher Education (NCATE)

Everest College—Springfield
1010 West Sunshine St., Springfield 65807
Type: Private, proprietary, four-year
System: Corinthian Colleges, Inc
Degrees: A, B *Enroll:* 399
URL: http://www.everest.edu
Phone: (417) 864-7220 *Calendar:* Qtr. plan
Inst. Accred.: ACICS (1981/2005)
Prog. Accred.: Allied Health (medical assisting (AMA))

Earth City Campus
3420 Rider Trail South, Earth City 63045-1100
Phone: (314) 739-7333

Ontario Metro Campus
1819 South Excise Ave., Ontario, CA 91761-8525
Phone: (909) 484-4311

Fontbonne University
6800 Wydown Blvd., St. Louis 63105
Type: Private, Roman Catholic Church, four-year
Degrees: B, M *Enroll:* 2,267
URL: http://www.fontbonne.edu
Phone: (314) 889-1419 *Calendar:* Sem. plan
Inst. Accred.: NCA-HLC (1926/2000)
Prog. Accred.: Allied Health (speech-language pathology), Business (ACBSP), Dietetics (didactic), Teacher Education (NCATE)

Forest Institute of Professional Psychology
2885 West Battlefield, Springfield 65807
Type: Private, independent, four-year
Degrees: M, D *Enroll:* 188
URL: http://www.forestinstitute.org
Phone: (417) 823-3477
Inst. Accred.: NCA-HLC (1983/2004)
Prog. Accred.: Clinical Psychology, Marriage and Family Therapy, Psychology Internship

Global University
1211 South Glenstone Ave., Springfield 65804
Type: Private, Asemblies of God, four-year
Degrees: A, B, M *FTE Enroll:* 1,200
URL: http://www.globaluniversity.edu
Phone: (417) 862-9533
Inst. Accred.: DETC (2000/2005), NCA-HLC (2006)

Goldfarb School of Nursing at Barnes-Jewish College
306 South Kingshighway Blvd., MS 90 30-625, St. Louis 63110-1091
Type: Private, independent, four-year
Degrees: A, B, M *Enroll:* 481
URL: http://barnesjewishcollege.edu
Phone: (314) 454-7055 *Calendar:* Sem. plan
Inst. Accred.: NCA-HLC (1995/2000)
Prog. Accred.: Allied Health (cytotechnology), Clinical Lab Scientist, Nurse Anesthesia Education, Nursing, Nursing Education, Radiation Therapy

Grantham University
7200 Northwest 86th St., Kansas City 64153
Type: Private, proprietary, four-year
Degrees: A, B, M *FTE Enroll:* 450
URL: http://www.grantham.edu
Phone: (816) 595-5859
Inst. Accred.: DETC (1961/2006)

Hannibal-LaGrange College
2800 Palmyra Rd., Hannibal 63401
Type: Private, Missouri Baptist Convention, four-year
Degrees: A, B *Enroll:* 889
URL: http://www.hlg.edu
Phone: (573) 221-3675 *Calendar:* Sem. plan
Inst. Accred.: NCA-HLC (1958/2005)
Prog. Accred.: Nursing

Harris-Stowe State University
3026 Laclede Ave., St. Louis 63103
Type: Public, state, four-year
System: Missouri Coordinating Board for Higher Education
Degrees: B *Enroll:* 1,249
URL: http://www.hssu.edu
Phone: (314) 340-3366 *Calendar:* Sem. plan
Inst. Accred.: NCA-HLC (1924/2001)
Prog. Accred.: Business (ACBSP), Teacher Education (NCATE)

Hickey College
940 West Port Plaza Dr., St. Louis 63146
Type: Private, proprietary, four-year
Degrees: A, B *Enroll:* 386
URL: http://www.hickeycollege.edu
Phone: (314) 434-2212
Inst. Accred.: ACICS (1971/2007)

ICI University
1211 South Glenstone Ave., Springfield 65804
Type: Private, Assemblies of God, four-year
Degrees: A, B, M *FTE Enroll:* 1,109
URL: http://www.globaluniversity.edu
Phone: (417) 862-9533
Inst. Accred.: DETC (1977/2000)

ITT Technical Institute
3640 Corporate Trail Dr., Earth City 63045
Type: Private, proprietary, four-year
System: ITT Educational Services, Inc.
Degrees: A, B *Enroll:* 672
URL: http://www.itt-tech.edu
Phone: (314) 298-7800 *Calendar:* Qtr. plan
Inst. Accred.: ACICS (1999/2004)

Flint Campus
5405 Gateway Centre Dr., Flint, MI 48507
Phone: (810) 762-2500

Memphis Area Campus
7260 Goodlett Farms Pkwy., Cordova, TN 38016
Phone: (901) 381-0200

Omaha Campus
9814 M St., Omaha, NE 68127-2056
Phone: (402) 331-2900

Warrensville Heights Campus
4700 Richmond Rd., Warrensville Heights, OH 44128
Phone: (216) 896-6500

Jefferson College
1000 Viking Dr., Hillsboro 63050-1000
Type: Public, state/local, two-year
System: Missouri Coordinating Board for Higher Education
Degrees: A *Enroll:* 2,988
URL: http://www.jeffco.edu
Phone: (636) 797-3000 *Calendar:* Sem. plan
Inst. Accred.: NCA-HLC (1969/1999)
Prog. Accred.: Veterinary Technology

Kansas City Art Institute
4415 Warwick Blvd., Kansas City 64111
Type: Private, independent, four-year
Degrees: B *Enroll:* 588
URL: http://www.kcai.edu
Phone: (816) 472-4852 *Calendar:* Sem. plan
Inst. Accred.: NCA-HLC (1964/2007)
Prog. Accred.: Art

The Kansas City University of Medicine and Biosciences
1750 Independence Blvd., Kansas City 64106-1453
Type: Private, independent, four-year
Degrees: D *Enroll:* 958
URL: http://www.uhs.edu
Phone: (816) 283-2000 *Calendar:* Sem. plan
Inst. Accred.: NCA-HLC (1998/2004)
Prog. Accred.: Osteopathy

Kenrick-Glennon Seminary
5200 Glennon Dr., St. Louis 63119-4399
Type: Private, Roman Catholic Church, four-year
Degrees: M *Enroll:* 57
URL: http://www.kenrick.edu
Phone: (314) 792-6100 *Calendar:* Sem. plan
Inst. Accred.: ATS (1973/1999), NCA-HLC (1973/2004)

L'Ecole Culinaire
9811 South Forty Dr., Saint Louis 63124-1103
Type: Private, proprietary, two-year
System: Vatterott Educational Centers, Inc.
Degrees: A
URL: http://www.lecoleculinaire.com
Phone: (314) 587-2433 *Calendar:* Sem. plan
Inst. Accred.: ACCSCT (2004/2006)

Lester L. Cox College of Nursing and Health Sciences
1423 North Jefferson Ave., Springfield 65802
Type: Private, independent, four-year
Degrees: A, B *Enroll:* 402
URL: http://www.coxcollege.edu
Phone: (417) 269-3424 *Calendar:* Sem. plan
Inst. Accred.: NCA-HLC (2000/2005)
Prog. Accred.: Dietetics (internship), Nursing, Nursing Education

Lincoln University
820 Chestnut St., Jefferson City 65101
Type: Public, state, four-year
System: Missouri Coordinating Board for Higher Education
Degrees: A, B, M *Enroll:* 2,527
URL: http://www.lincolnu.edu
Phone: (573) 681-5000 *Calendar:* Sem. plan
Inst. Accred.: NCA-HLC (1926/2003)
Prog. Accred.: Business (ACBSP), Music, Nursing, Teacher Education (NCATE)

Fort Leonard Wood Campus
268 Constitution St., Ste. 5, Fort Leonard Wood 65473-8934
Phone: (573) 329-5160
Prog. Accred: Nursing

Lindenwood University
209 South Kingshighway Blvd., Saint Charles 63301-1695
Type: Private, United Presbyterian Church, four-year
Degrees: B, M, P *Enroll:* 7,474
URL: http://www.lindenwood.edu
Phone: (636) 949-2000
Inst. Accred.: NCA-HLC (1918/2004)
Prog. Accred.: Business (ACBSP), Social Work

Linn State Technical College
One Technology Dr., Linn 65051
Type: Public, state, two-year
Degrees: A *Enroll:* 816
URL: http://www.linnstate.edu
Phone: (573) 897-3603 *Calendar:* Sem. plan
Inst. Accred.: NCA-HLC (2000/2005)
Prog. Accred.: Automotive Technology, Aviation Technology, Design Technology, Electronic Technology, Industrial Technology, Physical Therapy Assisting

Logan University
PO Box 1065, Chesterfield 63006-1065
Type: Private, independent, four-year
Degrees: B, P, D *Enroll:* 1,046
URL: http://www.logan.edu
Phone: (636) 227-2100 *Calendar:* Tri. plan
Inst. Accred.: NCA-HLC (1987/2002)
Prog. Accred.: Chiropractic Education

Longview Community College
500 Longview Rd., Lee's Summit 64081
Type: Public, state/local, two-year
System: Metropolitan Community College—Kansas City
Degrees: A *Enroll:* 3,509
URL: http://www.mcckc.edu
Phone: (816) 672-2000 *Calendar:* Sem. plan
Inst. Accred.: NCA-HLC (1986/2006, *Indirect accreditation through Metropolitan Community College—Kansas City, Kansas City, MO*)

Maple Woods Community College
2601 North East Barry Rd., Kansas City 64156-1299
Type: Public, state/local, two-year
System: Metropolitan Community College—Kansas City
Degrees: A *Enroll:* 2,698
URL: http://www.mcckc.edu
Phone: (816) 437-3000 *Calendar:* Sem. plan
Inst. Accred.: NCA-HLC (1986/2006, *Indirect accreditation through Metropolitan Community College—Kansas City, Kansas City, MO*)
Prog. Accred.: Veterinary Technology

Maryville University of St. Louis
650 Maryville University Dr., St. Louis 63141-7299
Type: Private, independent, four-year
Degrees: B, M *Enroll:* 2,352
URL: http://www.maryville.edu
Phone: (314) 529-9300 *Calendar:* Sem. plan
Inst. Accred.: NCA-HLC (1941/2005)
Prog. Accred.: Art, Business (ACBSP), Interior Design, Music, Nursing Education, Physical Therapy, Rehabilitation Counseling, Teacher Education (NCATE)

Messenger College
PO Box 4050, Joplin 64803
Type: Private, Pentecostal Church of God, four-year
Degrees: A, B *Enroll:* 79
URL: http://www.messengercollege.edu
Phone: (417) 624-7070 *Calendar:* Sem. plan
Inst. Accred.: TRACS (1998/2003)

Metro Business College
1732 North Kingshighway Blvd., Cape Girardeau 63701
Type: Private, proprietary, two-year
Degrees: A *Enroll:* 379
URL: http://www.metrobusinesscollege.edu
Phone: (573) 334-9181 *Calendar:* Qtr. plan
Inst. Accred.: ACICS (1979/2003)

Arnold Campus
2132 Tenbrook Rd., Arnold 63010
Phone: (636) 296-9300

Jefferson City Campus
1407 Southwest Blvd., Jefferson City 65109
Phone: (573) 635-6600

Rolla Campus
1202 East Hwy. 72, Rolla 65401
Phone: (573) 364-8464

Metropolitan Community College Business and Technology College
1775 Universal Ave., Kansas City 64120
Type: Private, local, two-year
System: Metropolitan Community College—Kansas City
Degrees: A
URL: http://www.mcckc.edu
Phone: (816) 482-5200 *Calendar:* Sem. plan
Inst. Accred.: NCA-HLC (1986/2006, *Indirect accreditation through Metropolitan Community College—Kansas City, Kansas City, MO*)

Metropolitan Community College—Blue River
20301 East 78 Hwy., Independence 64057
Type: Public, state/local, two-year
System: Metropolitan Community College—Kansas City
Degrees: A
URL: http://www.mcckc.edu
Phone: (816) 220-6550 *Calendar:* Qtr. plan
Inst. Accred.: NCA-HLC (1986/2006, *Indirect accreditation through Metropolitan Community College—Kansas City, Kansas City, MO*)

Midwest Institute for Medical Assistants
10910 Manchester Rd., Kirkwood 63122
Type: Private, proprietary, two-year
Degrees: A
URL: http://www.midwestinstitute.com
Phone: (314) 965-8363
Inst. Accred.: ABHES (1978/2002)
Prog. Accred.: Medical Assisting (ABHES)

Earth City Campus
4260 Shoreline Dr., Earth City 63045
Phone: (314) 344-4440
Prog. Accred: Medical Assisting (ABHES)

Midwest University
PO Box 365, Wentzville 63385
Type: Private, International Evangelical Association, four-year
Degrees: B, M, D
URL: http://www.midwest.edu
Phone: (636) 327-4645 *Calendar:* Sem. plan
Inst. Accred.: TRACS (2004)

Midwestern Baptist Theological Seminary
5001 North Oak St. Trafficway, Kansas City 64118
Type: Private, Southern Baptist Convention, four-year
Degrees: A, M, D *Enroll:* 467
URL: http://www.mbts.edu
Phone: (816) 414-3700 *Calendar:* Qtr. plan
Inst. Accred.: ATS (1964/2002), NCA-HLC (1971/2003)

Mineral Area College
5270 Flat River Rd., PO Box 1000, Park Hills 63601
Type: Public, state/local, two-year
System: Missouri Coordinating Board for Higher Education
Degrees: A *Enroll:* 2,046
URL: http://www.mineralarea.edu
Phone: (573) 431-4593 *Calendar:* Sem. plan
Inst. Accred.: NCA-HLC (1971/2005)
Prog. Accred.: Dentistry (dental assisting)

Missouri Baptist University
One College Park Dr., St. Louis 63141-8660
Type: Private, Southern Baptist Church, four-year
Degrees: A, B, M *Enroll:* 2,620
URL: http://www.mobap.edu
Phone: (314) 434-1115 *Calendar:* Sem. plan
Inst. Accred.: NCA-HLC (1978/2007)
Prog. Accred.: Music, Teacher Education (NCATE)

Missouri College
10121 Manchester Rd., St. Louis 63122-1583
Type: Private, proprietary, four-year
System: Career Education Corporation
Degrees: A, B *Enroll:* 563
URL: http://www.missouricollege.com
Phone: (314) 821-7700
Inst. Accred.: ACCSCT (1970/2006)
Prog. Accred.: Dentistry (dental assisting, dental hygiene)

Missouri Southern State University
3950 East Newman Rd., Joplin 64801-1595
Type: Public, state, four-year
System: Missouri Coordinating Board for Higher Education
Degrees: A, B, M, D *Enroll:* 4,504
URL: http://www.mssu.edu
Phone: (417) 625-9500 *Calendar:* Sem. plan
Inst. Accred.: NCA-HLC (1949/2008)
Prog. Accred.: Allied Health (respiratory therapy), Business (ACBSP), Dentistry (dental hygiene), Engineering Technology (general drafting/design), Environmental Health, Nursing, Radiography, Teacher Education (NCATE)

Missouri State University
901 South National, Springfield 65897
Type: Public, state, four-year
System: Missouri Coordinating Board for Higher Education
Degrees: A, B, M, P *Enroll:* 15,776
URL: http://www.missouristate.edu
Phone: (417) 836-8500 *Calendar:* Sem. plan
Inst. Accred.: NCA-HLC (1915/2006)
Prog. Accred.: Accounting, Allied Health (audiology, speech-language pathology), Business (AACSB), Computer Science (ABET-CAC), Construction Education, Construction Technology, Family & Consumer Science, Graduate Social Work, Industrial Technology, Music, Nurse Anesthesia Education, Nursing Education, Physical Therapy, Physician Assistant, Planning, Public Administration, Recreation and Leisure Services, Social Work, Teacher Education (NCATE), Theatre

Missouri State University—West Plains
128 Garfield Ave., West Plains 65775
Type: Public, state, two-year
System: Missouri Coordinating Board for Higher Education
Degrees: A *Enroll:* 1,151
URL: http://www.wp.missouristate.edu
Phone: (417) 255-7900 *Calendar:* Sem. plan
Inst. Accred.: NCA-HLC (1994/2004)
Prog. Accred.: Allied Health (respiratory therapy), Nursing

Missouri Tech
1167 Corporate Lake Dr., St. Louis 63132-2907
Type: Private, proprietary, four-year
Degrees: A, B *Enroll:* 94
URL: http://www.motech.edu
Phone: (314) 569-3600 *Calendar:* Sem. plan
Inst. Accred.: ACCSCT (1985/2005)

Missouri University of Science and Technology
206 Parker Hall, Rolla 65409-0470
Type: Public, state, four-year
System: University of Missouri System
Degrees: B, M, D *Enroll:* 5,020
URL: http://www.mst.edu
Phone: (573) 341-4111 *Calendar:* Sem. plan
Inst. Accred.: NCA-HLC (1913/1999)
Prog. Accred.: Computer Science (ABET-CAC), Engineering (aerospace, architectural, ceramic, chemical, civil, computer, electrical, engineering management, geological/geophysical, mechanical, metallurgical, mining, nuclear, petroleum)

Missouri Valley College
500 East College Dr., Marshall 65340
Type: Private, Presbyterian Church (USA), four-year
Degrees: A, B *Enroll:* 1,469
URL: http://www.moval.edu
Phone: (660) 831-4000 *Calendar:* 4-1-4 plan
Inst. Accred.: NCA-HLC (1916/2004)

Missouri Western State University
4525 Downs Dr., St. Joseph 64507-2294
Type: Public, state, four-year
System: Missouri Coordinating Board for Higher Education
Degrees: A, B *Enroll:* 4,384
URL: http://www.missouriwestern.edu
Phone: (816) 271-4200 *Calendar:* Sem. plan
Inst. Accred.: NCA-HLC (1923/2000)
Prog. Accred.: Engineering Technology (civil/construction, electrical), Music, Nursing Education, Physical Therapy Assisting, Social Work, Teacher Education (NCATE)

Moberly Area Community College
101 College Ave., Moberly 65270-1304
Type: Public, state/local, two-year
System: Missouri Coordinating Board for Higher Education
Degrees: A *Enroll:* 2,494
URL: http://www.macc.edu
Phone: (660) 263-4110 *Calendar:* Sem. plan
Inst. Accred.: NCA-HLC (1980/2002)

Nazarene Theological Seminary
1700 East Meyer Blvd., Kansas City 64131-1246
Type: Private, Church of the Nazarene, four-year
Degrees: M, D *Enroll:* 268
URL: http://www.nts.edu
Phone: (816) 333-6254 *Calendar:* Sem. plan
Inst. Accred.: ATS (1970/2000)

North Central Missouri College
1301 Main St., Trenton 64683
Type: Public, state/local, two-year
System: Missouri Coordinating Board for Higher Education
Degrees: A *Enroll:* 917
URL: http://www.ncmc.cc.mo.us
Phone: (660) 359-3948 *Calendar:* Sem. plan
Inst. Accred.: NCA-HLC (1983/2002)

Northwest Missouri State University
800 University Dr., Maryville 64468-6001
Type: Public, state, four-year
System: Missouri Coordinating Board for Higher Education
Degrees: B, M, P *Enroll:* 5,487
URL: http://www.nwmissouri.edu
Phone: (660) 562-1110 *Calendar:* Sem. plan
Inst. Accred.: NCA-HLC (1921/2005)
Prog. Accred.: Business (ACBSP), Dietetics (didactic), Family & Consumer Science, Music, Teacher Education (NCATE)

Ozark Christian College
1111 North Main St., Joplin 64801-4804
Type: Private, Christian Churches/Churches of Christ, four-year
Degrees: A, B *Enroll:* 773
URL: http://www.occ.edu
Phone: (417) 624-2518 *Calendar:* Sem. plan
Inst. Accred.: ABHE (1988/1999)

Ozarks Technical Community College
1001 East Chestnut Expressway, Springfield 65802-3625
Type: Public, local, two-year
System: Missouri Coordinating Board for Higher Education
Degrees: A *Enroll:* 6,253
URL: http://www.otc.edu
Phone: (417) 447-7500 *Calendar:* Sem. plan
Inst. Accred.: NCA-HLC (1996/2001)
Prog. Accred.: Allied Health (occupational therapy assisting, respiratory therapy, surgical technology), Culinary Education, Dentistry (dental assisting, dental hygiene), Physical Therapy Assisting

Park University
8700 NW River Park Dr., Parkville 64152
Type: Private, Church of Latter-Day Saints, four-year
Degrees: A, B, M *Enroll:* 5,822
URL: http://www.park.edu
Phone: (816) 741-2000 *Calendar:* Sem. plan
Inst. Accred.: NCA-HLC (1913/2005)
Prog. Accred.: Nursing, Social Work

Ford Motor Company On-Site Program
Kansas City Assembly Plant, PO Box 11009, Kansas City 64119
Phone: (816) 459-1138

Graduate School of Religion Campus
PO Box 1059, Independence 64051-1059
Phone: (816) 833-1000

Independence Campus
2200 South 291 Hwy., Independence 64057
Phone: (816) 252-9065

MetroPark Campus
934 Wyandotte St., Kansas City 64105-1630
Phone: (816) 842-6182

Patricia Stevens College
300 North 4th St., Ste. 306, St. Louis 63102
Type: Private, proprietary, two-year
Degrees: A *Enroll:* 139
URL: http://www.patriciastevenscollege.edu
Phone: (314) 421-0949 *Calendar:* Qtr. plan
Inst. Accred.: ACICS (1968/2004)

Penn Valley Community College
3201 South West Trafficway, Kansas City 64111
Type: Public, state/local, two-year
System: Metropolitan Community College—Kansas City
Degrees: A *Enroll:* 2,588
URL: http://www.mcckc.edu
Phone: (816) 759-4000 *Calendar:* Sem. plan
Inst. Accred.: NCA-HLC (1986/2006, *Indirect accreditation through Metropolitan Community College—Kansas City, Kansas City, MO*)
Prog. Accred.: Allied Health (occupational therapy assisting, surgical technology), Dentistry (dental assisting), Nursing, Physical Therapy Assisting, Practical Nursing, Radiography

Pinnacle Career Institute
1001 East 101st Terrace, Kansas City 64131-3368
Type: Private, proprietary, two-year
Degrees: A *Enroll:* 146
URL: http://www.pcitraining.edu
Phone: (816) 331-5700 *Calendar:* Qtr. plan
Inst. Accred.: ACCSCT (1971/2006)

Kansas City North
11500 NW Ambassador Dr., Ste. 221, Kansas City 64153

Ranken Technical College
4431 Finney Ave., St. Louis 63113
Type: Private, independent, four-year
Degrees: A, B *Enroll:* 1,273
URL: http://www.ranken.edu
Phone: (314) 371-0233 *Calendar:* Sem. plan
Inst. Accred.: NCA-HLC (1989/1999)

Research College of Nursing
2300 East Meyer Blvd., Kansas City 64132
Type: Private, independent, four-year
Degrees: B, M *Enroll:* 264
URL: http://www.researchcollege.edu
Phone: (816) 276-4721 *Calendar:* Sem. plan
Inst. Accred.: NCA-HLC (1987/2002)
Prog. Accred.: Nursing Education

Rockhurst University
1100 Rockhurst Rd., Kansas City 64110
Type: Private, Roman Catholic Church, four-year
Degrees: B, M *Enroll:* 2,109
URL: http://www.rockhurst.edu
Phone: (816) 501-4250 *Calendar:* Sem. plan
Inst. Accred.: NCA-HLC (1934/2003)
Prog. Accred.: Allied Health (occupational therapy, speech-language pathology), Business (AACSB), Physical Therapy, Teacher Education (TEAC)

Saint Charles Community College
4601 Mid Rivers Mall Dr., St. Peters 63376
Type: Public, state/local, two-year
System: Missouri Coordinating Board for Higher Education
Degrees: A *Enroll:* 4,550
URL: http://www.stchas.edu
Phone: (636) 922-8000 *Calendar:* Sem. plan
Inst. Accred.: NCA-HLC (1991/2002)
Prog. Accred.: Allied Health (occupational therapy assisting), Nursing

Saint Louis Christian College
1360 Grandview Dr., Florissant 63033-6499
Type: Private, independent, four-year
Degrees: A, B *Enroll:* 230
URL: http://www.slcconline.edu
Phone: (314) 837-6777 *Calendar:* Sem. plan
Inst. Accred.: ABHE (1977/1998)

Saint Louis College of Health Careers
909 South Taylor Ave., St. Louis 63110-1511
Type: Private, proprietary, two-year
Degrees: A
URL: http://www.stlouiscollege.com
Phone: (314) 652-0300
Inst. Accred.: ABHES (1986/2006)
Prog. Accred.: Medical Assisting (ABHES)

County Campus
1297 North Hwy. Dr., Fenton 63026
Phone: (636) 529-0000
Prog. Accred: Medical Assisting (ABHES)

Saint Louis College of Pharmacy
4588 Parkview Place, St. Louis 63110
Type: Private, independent, four-year
Degrees: B, M, P, D *Enroll:* 1,087
URL: http://www.stlcop.edu
Phone: (314) 367-8700 *Calendar:* Sem. plan
Inst. Accred.: NCA-HLC (1967/2002)
Prog. Accred.: Pharmacy

Saint Louis Community College at Florissant Valley
3400 Pershall Rd., St. Louis 63135
Type: Public, state/local, two-year
System: Saint Louis Community College District
Degrees: A *Enroll:* 3,844
URL: http://www.stlcc.edu/fv
Phone: (314) 595-4200 *Calendar:* Sem. plan
Inst. Accred.: NCA-HLC (1988/2008, *Indirect accreditation through Saint Louis Community College District, St. Louis, MO*)
Prog. Accred.: Art, Dietetic Technician, Engineering Technology (electrical, mechanical), Nursing

Saint Louis Community College at Forest Park
5600 Oakland Ave., St. Louis 63110
Type: Public, state/local, two-year
System: Saint Louis Community College District
Degrees: A *Enroll:* 4,040
URL: http://www.stlcc.edu/fp
Phone: (314) 644-9100 *Calendar:* Sem. plan
Inst. Accred.: NCA-HLC (1988/2008, *Indirect accreditation through Saint Louis Community College District, St. Louis, MO*)
Prog. Accred.: Allied Health (diagnostic medical sonography, respiratory therapy, surgical technology), Clinical Lab Technology, Culinary Education, Dentistry (dental assisting, dental hygiene), Funeral Service Education (Mortuary Science), Nursing, Radiography

Saint Louis Community College at Meramec
11333 Big Bend Blvd., St. Louis 63122
Type: Public, state/local, two-year
System: Saint Louis Community College District
Degrees: A *Enroll:* 7,444
URL: http://www.stlcc.edu/mc
Phone: (314) 984-7500 *Calendar:* Sem. plan
Inst. Accred.: NCA-HLC (1988/2008, *Indirect accreditation through Saint Louis Community College District, St. Louis, MO*)
Prog. Accred.: Allied Health (occupational therapy assisting), Art, Nursing, Physical Therapy Assisting

Saint Louis Community College at Wildwood
2645 Generations Dr., Wildwood 63040-1168
Type: Public, state/local, two-year
System: Saint Louis Community College District
Degrees: A
URL: http://www.stlcc.edu/ww
Phone: (636) 422-2000 *Calendar:* Sem. plan
Inst. Accred.: NCA-HLC (1988/2008, *Indirect accreditation through Saint Louis Community College District, St. Louis, MO*)

Saint Louis University

221 North Grand Blvd., St. Louis 63103-2097
Type: Private, Society of Jesus, four-year
Degrees: A, B, M, P, D *Enroll:* 11,491
URL: http://www.slu.edu
Phone: (314) 977-2222 *Calendar:* Sem. plan
Inst. Accred.: NCA-HLC (1916/2002)
Prog. Accred.: Allied Health (cytotechnology, health services administration, medicine, occupational therapy, speech-language pathology), Business (AACSB), Clinical Lab Scientist, Clinical Pastoral Education, Clinical Psychology, Dentistry (endodontics, orthodontic and dentofacial orthopedics, periodontics), Dietetics (didactic), Dietetics (internship), Engineering (aerospace, electrical, mechanical), Graduate Social Work, Law, Nuclear Medicine Technology, Nursing Education, Physical Therapy, Physician Assistant, Public Administration, Public Health, Social Work, Teacher Education (NCATE)

Parks College of Engineering, Aviation, and Technology

3450 Lindell Blvd., St. Louis 63103
Phone: (314) 977-8283
Prog. Accred: Aviation

Saint Luke's College

4426 Wornall Rd., Kansas City 64111
Type: Private, independent, four-year
Degrees: B *Enroll:* 104
URL: http://www.saintlukescollege.edu
Phone: (816) 932-2233 *Calendar:* Sem. plan
Inst. Accred.: NCA-HLC (1994/1999)
Prog. Accred.: Nursing Education

Saint Paul School of Theology

5123 Truman Rd., Kansas City 64127
Type: Private, United Methodist Church, four-year
Degrees: M, D *Enroll:* 229
URL: http://www.spst.edu
Phone: (816) 483-9600
Inst. Accred.: ATS (1964/2001), NCA-HLC (1976/2002)

Sanford-Brown College—Fenton

1345 Smizer Mill Rd., Fenton 63026
Type: Private, proprietary, four-year
System: Career Education Corporation
Degrees: A, B *Enroll:* 687
URL: http://www.sbcfenton.com
Phone: (636) 349-4900 *Calendar:* Sem. plan
Inst. Accred.: ACICS (1982/2005)
Prog. Accred.: Allied Health (respiratory therapy), Radiography, Veterinary Technology

Collinsville Campus

1101 Eastport Plaza Dr., Collinsville, IL 62234
Phone: (618) 931-0300
Prog. Accred: Medical Assisting (ABHES)

Hazelwood Campus

75 Village Square, Hazelwood 63042
Phone: (314) 687-2900
Prog. Accred: Allied Health (occupational therapy assisting), Medical Assisting (ABHES)

Houston Campus

10500 Forum Place Dr., Ste. 200, Houston, TX 77036
Phone: (713) 779-1110
Prog. Accred: Allied Health (diagnostic medical sonography, surgical technology), Medical Assisting (ABHES), Medical Laboratory Technology, Surgical Technology

Milwaukee Campus

6737 West Washington St., Ste. 2355, West Allis, WI 53214
Phone: (414) 771-2200

St. Peters Campus

100 Richmond Center Blvd., St. Peters 63376
Phone: (636) 696-2300
Prog. Accred: Veterinary Technology

Southeast Missouri Hospital College of Nursing and Health Sciences

2001 William St., Cape Girardeau 63703-5815
Type: Private, independent, four-year
Degrees: A, P *Enroll:* 100
URL: http://www.southeastmissourihospitalcollege.edu
Phone: (573) 334-6825
Inst. Accred.: NCA-HLC (2005)
Prog. Accred.: Allied Health (surgical technology), Clinical Lab Scientist, Radiography

Southeast Missouri State University

One University Plaza, Cape Girardeau 63701
Type: Public, state, four-year
System: Missouri Coordinating Board for Higher Education
Degrees: A, B, M, P *Enroll:* 8,281
URL: http://www.semo.edu
Phone: (573) 651-2222 *Calendar:* Sem. plan
Inst. Accred.: NCA-HLC (1915/2001)
Prog. Accred.: Allied Health (speech-language pathology), Business (AACSB), Counseling, Dietetics (didactic), Dietetics (internship), Engineering (engineering physics/science), Industrial Technology, Journalism, Music, Nursing, Nursing Education, Recreation and Leisure Services, Social Work, Teacher Education (NCATE)

Southwest Baptist University

1600 University Ave., Bolivar 65613-2496
Type: Private, Southern Baptist Church, four-year
Degrees: A, B, M *Enroll:* 2,521
URL: http://www.sbuniv.edu
Phone: (417) 328-5281 *Calendar:* Sem. plan
Inst. Accred.: NCA-HLC (1957/2006)
Prog. Accred.: Business (ACBSP), Music, Nursing, Physical Therapy

State Fair Community College
3201 West 16th St., Sedalia 65301-2199
Type: Public, state/local, two-year
System: Missouri Coordinating Board for Higher Education
Degrees: A *Enroll:* 2,026
URL: http://sfcc.cc.mo.us
Phone: (660) 530-5800 *Calendar:* Sem. plan
Inst. Accred.: NCA-HLC (1977/1999)
Prog. Accred.: Construction Education, Design Technology, Electronic Technology, Industrial Technology, Manufacturing Technology, Radiography

Stephens College
1200 East Broadway, Columbia 65215
Type: Private, independent, four-year
Degrees: A, B, M *Enroll:* 701
URL: http://www.stephens.edu
Phone: (573) 442-2211 *Calendar:* Sem. plan
Inst. Accred.: NCA-HLC (1918/2008)

Texas County Technical Institute
PO Box 314, Houston 65483-0314
Type: Private, independent, two-year
Degrees: A
URL: http://www.texascountytech.edu
Phone: (417) 967-5466
Inst. Accred.: ACICS (2001/2008)

Bolivar Technical College
PO Box 592, Bolivar 65613
Phone: (417) 777-5062

Branson Technical College
1756 Bee Creek Rd., Branson 65616
Phone: (417) 239-1500

Three Rivers Community College
2080 Three Rivers Blvd., Poplar Bluff 63901
Type: Public, state/local, two-year
System: Missouri Coordinating Board for Higher Education
Degrees: A *Enroll:* 2,063
URL: http://www.trcc.edu
Phone: (573) 840-9600 *Calendar:* Sem. plan
Inst. Accred.: NCA-HLC (1974/2008)
Prog. Accred.: Business (ACBSP), Clinical Lab Technology, Nursing

Truman State University
100 East Normal St., Kirksville 63501-4221
Type: Public, state, four-year
System: Missouri Coordinating Board for Higher Education
Degrees: B, M *Enroll:* 5,735
URL: http://www.truman.edu
Phone: (660) 785-4000 *Calendar:* Sem. plan
Inst. Accred.: NCA-HLC (1914/2005)
Prog. Accred.: Accounting, Allied Health (speech-language pathology), Business (AACSB), Music, Nursing Education, Teacher Education (NCATE)

University of Central Missouri
PO Box 800, Warrensburg 64093
Type: Public, state, four-year
System: Missouri Coordinating Board for Higher Education
Degrees: A, B, M, P *Enroll:* 8,739
URL: http://www.ucmo.edu
Phone: (660) 543-4111 *Calendar:* Sem. plan
Inst. Accred.: NCA-HLC (1915/2004)
Prog. Accred.: Accounting, Allied Health (audiology, speech-language pathology), Applied Science (industrial hygiene, occupational health & safety), Art, Automotive Technology, Aviation, Business (AACSB), Construction Education, Construction Technology, Dietetics (didactic), Electronic Technology, Industrial Technology, Music, Nursing Education, Social Work, Teacher Education (NCATE)

University of Missouri
105 Jesse Hall, Columbia 65211
Type: Public, state, four-year
System: University of Missouri System
Degrees: B, M, P, D *Enroll:* 25,285
URL: http://www.missouri.edu
Phone: (573) 882-2121 *Calendar:* Sem. plan
Inst. Accred.: NCA-HLC (1913/2005)
Prog. Accred.: Accounting, Allied Health (diagnostic medical sonography, health services administration, medicine, occupational therapy, respiratory therapy, speech-language pathology), Business (AACSB), Clinical Psychology, Counseling Psychology, Dietetics (coordinated), Engineering (bioengineering, chemical, civil, computer, electrical, industrial, mechanical), Forestry, Graduate Social Work, Interior Design, Journalism, Law, Librarianship, Music, Nuclear Medicine Technology, Nursing Education, Physical Therapy, Psychology Internship, Public Administration, Radiography, Recreation and Leisure Services, School Psychology, Social Work, Teacher Education (NCATE), Veterinary Medicine

University of Missouri—Kansas City
5100 Rockhill Rd., Kansas City 64110
Type: Public, state, four-year
System: University of Missouri System
Degrees: B, M, P, D *Enroll:* 10,624
URL: http://www.umkc.edu
Phone: (816) 235-1000 *Calendar:* Sem. plan
Inst. Accred.: NCA-HLC (1938/1999)
Prog. Accred.: Allied Health (anesthesiologist assisting, medicine), Business (AACSB), Clinical Psychology, Counseling Psychology, Dentistry (advanced education in general dentistry, combined prosthodontics, dental hygiene, dentistry, endodontics, general dentistry, general practice residency, maxillofacial prosthetics, oral and maxillofacial radiology, oral and maxillofacial surgery, orthodontic and dentofacial orthopedics, pediatric dentistry, periodontics), Engineering (civil, electrical, mechanical), Graduate Social Work, Law, Music, Nursing Education, Pharmacy, Psychology Internship, Public Administration, Teacher Education (NCATE), Theatre

University of Missouri—St. Louis
8001 Natural Bridge Rd., St. Louis 63121
Type: Public, state, four-year
System: University of Missouri System
Degrees: B, M, D *Enroll:* 10,188
URL: http://www.umsl.edu
Phone: (314) 516-5000 *Calendar:* Sem. plan
Inst. Accred.: NCA-HLC (1960/1999)
Prog. Accred.: Accounting, Allied Health (optometric residency, optometry), Business (AACSB), Clinical Psychology, Counseling, Engineering (civil, electrical, mechanical), Graduate Social Work, Music, Nursing Education, Public Administration, Social Work, Teacher Education (NCATE)

Vatterott College—Northpark
8580 Evans Ave., Berkeley 63134
Type: Private, proprietary, four-year
System: Vatterott Educational Centers, Inc.
Degrees: A, B *Enroll:* 911
URL: http://www.vatterott-college.edu
Phone: (314) 264-1000 *Calendar:* Sem. plan
Inst. Accred.: ACCSCT (1982/2008)

Cleveland Campus
5025 East Royalton Rd., Broadview Heights, OH 44147
Phone: (440) 526-1660

Joplin Campus
809 Illinois Ave., Joplin 64801
Phone: (417) 781-5633

Kansas City Campus
8955 East 38th Terrace, Kansas City 64129
Phone: (816) 861-1000

Memphis Campus
2655 Dividend Dr., Memphis, TN 38132
Phone: (901) 761-5730

O'Fallon Campus
927 East Terra Ln., O'Fallon 63366
Phone: (636) 978-7488

Springfield Campus
3850 South Campbell Ave., Springfield 65807-5340
Phone: (417) 831-8116

Sunset Hills (St. Louis) Campus
12970 Maurer Industrial Dr., Sunset Hills 63127-1516
Phone: (314) 843-4200

Tulsa Campus
4343 South 118th East Ave., Ste. A, Tulsa, OK 74146
Phone: (918) 835-8288

Wichita Campus
3639 North Comotara St., Wichita, KS 67226
Phone: (316) 634-0066

Washington University in St. Louis
One Brookings Dr., Box 1192, St. Louis 63130
Type: Private, independent, four-year
Degrees: B, M, D *Enroll:* 11,799
URL: http://www.wustl.edu
Phone: (314) 935-5000 *Calendar:* Sem. plan
Inst. Accred.: NCA-HLC (1913/2004)
Prog. Accred.: Allied Health (audiology, health services administration, medicine, occupational therapy), Art, Business (AACSB), Clinical Psychology, Engineering (chemical, civil, computer, electrical, mechanical, systems), Graduate Social Work, Law, Physical Therapy

Webster University
470 East Lockwood Ave., St. Louis 63119-3194
Type: Private, independent, four-year
Degrees: B, M, P, D *Enroll:* 11,095
URL: http://www.webster.edu
Phone: (314) 968-6900 *Calendar:* Sem. plan
Inst. Accred.: NCA-HLC (1925/2008)
Prog. Accred.: Business (ACBSP), Music, Nurse Anesthesia Education, Nursing, Teacher Education (NCATE)

Wentworth Military Academy and Junior College
1880 Washington Ave., Lexington 64067
Type: Private, independent, two-year
Degrees: A *Enroll:* 387
URL: http://www.wma1880.org
Phone: (660) 259-2221 *Calendar:* Sem. plan
Inst. Accred.: NCA-HLC (1930/2002)

Westminster College
501 Westminster Ave., Fulton 65251-1299
Type: Private, independent, four-year
Degrees: B *Enroll:* 905
URL: http://www.westminster-mo.edu
Phone: (573) 642-3361 *Calendar:* Sem. plan
Inst. Accred.: NCA-HLC (1913/2005)

William Jewell College
500 College Hill, Liberty 64068
Type: Private, Missouri Baptist Convention, four-year
Degrees: B *Enroll:* 1,402
URL: http://www.jewell.edu/
Phone: (816) 781-7700 *Calendar:* Sem. plan
Inst. Accred.: NCA-HLC (1915/2001)
Prog. Accred.: Music, Nursing Education

William Woods University
One University Ave., Fulton 65251
Type: Private, independent, four-year
Degrees: A, B, M *Enroll:* 1,773
URL: http://www.wmwoods.edu
Phone: (573) 642-2251 *Calendar:* Sem. plan
Inst. Accred.: NCA-HLC (1919/2007)
Prog. Accred.: Social Work

MONTANA

Blackfeet Community College
PO Box 819, Browning 59417
Type: Public, tribal, two-year
System: American Indian Higher Education Consortium
Degrees: A *Enroll:* 443
URL: http://www.bfcc.org
Phone: (406) 338-7755 *Calendar:* Qtr. plan
Inst. Accred.: NWCCU (1985/2001)

Carroll College
1601 North Benton Ave., Helena 59625
Type: Private, Roman Catholic Church, four-year
Degrees: B *Enroll:* 1,326
URL: http://www.carroll.edu
Phone: (406) 447-4300 *Calendar:* Sem. plan
Inst. Accred.: NWCCU (1949/2006)
Prog. Accred.: Engineering (civil), Nursing Education

Chief Dull Knife College
PO Box 98, One College Dr., Lame Deer 59043-0098
Type: Public, tribal, two-year
System: American Indian Higher Education Consortium
Degrees: A *Enroll:* 268
URL: http://www.cdkc.edu
Phone: (406) 477-6215 *Calendar:* Sem. plan
Inst. Accred.: NWCCU (1996/2006)

Dawson Community College
300 College Dr., Box 421, Glendive 59330-0421
Type: Public, state/local, two-year
System: Montana University System
Degrees: A *Enroll:* 437
URL: http://www.dawson.edu
Phone: (406) 377-3396 *Calendar:* Sem. plan
Inst. Accred.: NWCCU (1969/2006)

Flathead Valley Community College
777 Grandview Dr., Kalispell 59901-2699
Type: Public, state/local, two-year
System: Montana University System
Degrees: A *Enroll:* 1,305
URL: http://www.fvcc.edu
Phone: (406) 756-3822 *Calendar:* Sem. plan
Inst. Accred.: NWCCU (1970/2007)
Prog. Accred.: Allied Health (medical assisting (AMA), surgical technology)

Fort Belknap College
PO Box 159, Harlem 59526-0159
Type: Public, tribal, two-year
System: American Indian Higher Education Consortium
Degrees: A *Enroll:* 138
URL: http://www.fbcc.edu
Phone: (406) 353-2607 *Calendar:* Qtr. plan
Inst. Accred.: NWCCU (1993/2008)

Fort Peck Community College
605 Indian Ave., Poplar 59255
Type: Public, tribal, two-year
System: American Indian Higher Education Consortium
Degrees: A *Enroll:* 315
URL: http://www.fpcc.edu
Phone: (406) 768-5551 *Calendar:* Sem. plan
Inst. Accred.: NWCCU (1991/2007)

Little Big Horn College
1 Forest Ln., Crow Agency 59022
Type: Public, tribal, two-year
System: American Indian Higher Education Consortium
Degrees: A *Enroll:* 209
URL: http://www.lbhc.cc.mt.us
Phone: (406) 638-3104 *Calendar:* Sem. plan
Inst. Accred.: NWCCU (1989/2007)

Miles Community College
2715 Dickinson, Miles City 59301-4799
Type: Public, state/local, two-year
System: Montana University System
Degrees: A *Enroll:* 403
URL: http://www.milescc.edu
Phone: (406) 234-3031 *Calendar:* Sem. plan
Inst. Accred.: NWCCU (1971/2007)
Prog. Accred.: Nursing

Montana State University
PO Box 17200, Bozeman 59717-2000
Type: Public, state, four-year
System: Montana University System
Degrees: B, M, D *Enroll:* 10,680
URL: http://www.montana.edu
Phone: (406) 994-0211 *Calendar:* Sem. plan
Inst. Accred.: NWCCU (1932/2001)
Prog. Accred.: Art, Business (AACSB), Computer Science (ABET-CAC), Counseling, Engineering (chemical, civil, computer, electrical, industrial, mechanical), Engineering Technology (civil/construction, mechanical), Family & Consumer Science, Music, Nursing Education, Psychology Internship, Teacher Education (NCATE)

Montana State University College of Technology—Great Falls
2100 16th Ave., South, Great Falls 59406-6010
Type: Public, state, two-year
System: Montana University System
Degrees: A *Enroll:* 1,098
URL: http://www.msugf.edu
Phone: (406) 771-4300 *Calendar:* Sem. plan
Inst. Accred.: NWCCU (1979/2007)
Prog. Accred.: Allied Health (respiratory therapy, surgical technology), Dentistry (dental assisting, dental hygiene)

Montana State University—Billings
1500 North 30th St., Billings 59101-0298
Type: Public, state, four-year
System: Montana University System
Degrees: A, B, M *Enroll:* 3,148
URL: http://www.msubillings.edu
Phone: (406) 657-2011 *Calendar:* Sem. plan
Inst. Accred.: NWCCU (1932/2001)
Prog. Accred.: Art, Music, Rehabilitation Counseling, Teacher Education (NCATE)

College of Technology Campus
3803 Central Ave., Billings 59102
Phone: (406) 247-3000
Prog. Accred: Allied Health (EMT-paramedic, medical assisting (AMA))

Montana State University—Northern
PO Box 7751, Havre 59501-7751
Type: Public, state, four-year
System: Montana University System
Degrees: A, B, M *Enroll:* 1,143
URL: http://www.msun.edu
Phone: (406) 265-3700 *Calendar:* Sem. plan
Inst. Accred.: NWCCU (1932/2008)
Prog. Accred.: Engineering Technology (civil/construction, electrical), Nursing, Teacher Education (NCATE)

Great Falls Campus
2100 16th Ave. South, Great Falls 59405
Phone: (406) 771-4302
Prog. Accred: Nursing

Lewistown Campus
215 7th Ave. South, Lewistown 59457
Phone: (406) 535-9022
Prog. Accred: Nursing

Montana Tech of The University of Montana
1300 West Park St., Butte 59701-8997
Type: Public, state, four-year
System: Montana University System
Degrees: A, B, M *Enroll:* 1,582
URL: http://www.mtech.edu
Phone: (406) 496-4101 *Calendar:* Sem. plan
Inst. Accred.: NWCCU (1932/2005)
Prog. Accred.: Applied Science (industrial hygiene), Computer Science (ABET-CAC), Engineering (environmental/sanitary, general, geological/ geophysical, metallurgical, mining, petroleum)

College of Technology
25 Basin Creek Rd., Butte 59701
Phone: (406) 494-2894

Rocky Mountain College
1511 Poly Dr., Billings 59102-1796
Type: Private, interdenominational, four-year
Degrees: A, B, M *Enroll:* 963
URL: http://www.rocky.edu
Phone: (406) 657-1000 *Calendar:* Sem. plan
Inst. Accred.: NWCCU (1949/2007)
Prog. Accred.: Physician Assistant

Salish Kootenai College
PO Box 117, Pablo 59855
Type: Public, tribal, four-year
System: American Indian Higher Education Consortium
Degrees: A, B *Enroll:* 862
URL: http://www.skc.edu
Phone: (406) 675-4800 *Calendar:* Qtr. plan
Inst. Accred.: NWCCU (1984/2005)
Prog. Accred.: Dentistry (dental assisting), Nursing, Social Work

Stone Child College
RRI, Box 1082, Box Elder 59521-9796
Type: Public, tribal, two-year
System: American Indian Higher Education Consortium
Degrees: A *Enroll:* 212
URL: http://www.stonechild.edu
Phone: (406) 395-4875 *Calendar:* Sem. plan
Inst. Accred.: NWCCU (1993/2008)

University of Great Falls
1301 20th St., Great Falls 59405-4996
Type: Private, Roman Catholic Church, four-year
Degrees: A, B, M *Enroll:* 619
URL: http://www.ugf.edu
Phone: (406) 761-8210 *Calendar:* Sem. plan
Inst. Accred.: NWCCU (1935/2006)

The University of Montana
32 Campus Dr., Missoula 59812
Type: Public, state, four-year
System: Montana University System
Degrees: A, B, M, P, D *Enroll:* 12,162
URL: http://www.umt.edu
Phone: (406) 243-0211 *Calendar:* Sem. plan
Inst. Accred.: NWCCU (1932/2005)
Prog. Accred.: Accounting, Art, Business (AACSB), Clinical Psychology, Computer Science (ABET-CAC), Counseling, Forestry, Graduate Social Work, Journalism, Law, Music, Pharmacy, Physical Therapy, Recreation and Leisure Services, Social Work, Teacher Education (NCATE), Theatre

Missoula College of Technology
909 South Ave., West, Missoula 59801
Phone: (406) 243-7811
Prog. Accred: Allied Health (respiratory therapy, surgical technology), Culinary Education

The University of Montana—Helena College of Technology
1115 North Roberts St., Helena 59601
Type: Public, state, two-year
System: Montana University System
Degrees: A *Enroll:* 692
URL: http://www.umh.umontana.edu
Phone: (406) 444-6800 *Calendar:* Sem. plan
Inst. Accred.: NWCCU (1977/2007)

The University of Montana—Western
710 South Atlantic St., Dillon 59725-3598
Type: Public, state, four-year
System: Montana University System
Degrees: A, B *Enroll:* 1,029
URL: http://www.umwestern.edu
Phone: (406) 683-7011 *Calendar:* Sem. plan
Inst. Accred.: NWCCU (1932/2007)
Prog. Accred.: Teacher Education (NCATE)

NEBRASKA

Bellevue University
1000 Galvin Rd. South, Bellevue 68005
Type: Private, independent, four-year
Degrees: B, M *Enroll:* 4,660
URL: http://www.bellevue.edu
Phone: (402) 293-2000 *Calendar:* Sem. plan
Inst. Accred.: NCA-HLC (1977/2008)

Central Community College
PO Box 4903, Grand Island 68802-4903
Type: Public, state, two-year
System: Nebraska State College System
Degrees: A *Enroll:* 3,637
URL: http://www.cccneb.edu
Phone: (308) 398-4222 *Calendar:* Sem. plan
Inst. Accred.: NCA-HLC (1980/2002)
Prog. Accred.: Allied Health (medical assisting (AMA)), Nursing

Columbus Campus
PO Box 1027, 4500 63rd St., Columbus 68602-1027
Phone: (402) 564-7132

Grand Island Campus
PO Box 4903, Grand Island 68802-4903
Phone: (308) 384-5220

Hastings Campus
PO Box 1024, Hastings 68901-1024
Phone: (402) 463-9811
Prog. Accred: Dentistry (dental assisting, dental hygiene, dental laboratory technology)

Chadron State College
1000 Main St., Chadron 69337-2690
Type: Public, state, four-year
System: Nebraska State College System
Degrees: A, B, M, P *Enroll:* 1,988
URL: http://www.csc.edu
Phone: (308) 432-6000 *Calendar:* Sem. plan
Inst. Accred.: NCA-HLC (1915/2007)
Prog. Accred.: Business (ACBSP), Social Work, Teacher Education (NCATE)

Clarkson College
101 South 42nd St., Omaha 68131
Type: Private, Episcopal Church, four-year
Degrees: A, B, M *Enroll:* 515
URL: http://www.clarksoncollege.edu
Phone: (402) 552-3394 *Calendar:* Sem. plan
Inst. Accred.: NCA-HLC (1984/1999)
Prog. Accred.: Nursing, Physical Therapy Assisting, Radiography

College of Saint Mary
7000 Mercy Rd., Omaha 68106-2377
Type: Private, Roman Catholic Church, four-year
Degrees: A, B, M, D *Enroll:* 772
URL: http://www.csm.edu
Phone: (402) 399-2405 *Calendar:* Sem. plan
Inst. Accred.: NCA-HLC (1958/2001)
Prog. Accred.: Dentistry (dental hygiene), Nursing, Radiation Therapy

Concordia University
800 North Columbia Ave., Seward 68434
Type: Private, Lutheran Church-Missouri Synod, four-year
System: Concordia University System
Degrees: B, M *Enroll:* 1,221
URL: http://www.cune.edu
Phone: (402) 643-3651 *Calendar:* Sem. plan
Inst. Accred.: NCA-HLC (1953/2008)
Prog. Accred.: Music, Teacher Education (NCATE)

The Creative Center
10850 Emmet St. South East, Omaha 68164
Type: Private, proprietary, two-year
Degrees: A
URL: http://www.thecreativecenter.com
Phone: (402) 898-1000 *Calendar:* Qtr. plan
Inst. Accred.: ACCSCT (1996/2004)

Creighton University
2500 California Plaza, Omaha 68178
Type: Private, Roman Catholic Church, four-year
Degrees: A, B, M, P, D *Enroll:* 6,387
URL: http://www.creighton.edu
Phone: (402) 280-2700 *Calendar:* Sem. plan
Inst. Accred.: NCA-HLC (1916/2007)
Prog. Accred.: Accounting, Allied Health (EMT-paramedic, medicine, occupational therapy), Business (AACSB), Dentistry (dentistry), Law, Nursing Education, Pharmacy, Physical Therapy, Social Work, Teacher Education (NCATE)

Dana College
2848 College Dr., Blair 68008
Type: Private, Evangelic Lutheran Church in America, four-year
Degrees: B *Enroll:* 660
URL: http://www.dana.edu
Phone: (402) 426-9000 *Calendar:* 4-1-4 plan
Inst. Accred.: NCA-HLC (1958/2002)
Prog. Accred.: Social Work, Teacher Education (NCATE)

Doane College
1014 Boswell Ave., Crete 68333
Type: Private, United Church of Christ, four-year
Degrees: B, M *Enroll:* 1,923
URL: http://www.doane.edu
Phone: (402) 826-2161 *Calendar:* 4-1-4 plan
Inst. Accred.: NCA-HLC (1913/2002)
Prog. Accred.: Business (ACBSP), Teacher Education (NCATE)

Grand Island Campus
180 West US Hwy. 34, Grand Island 68801-7279
Phone: (308) 398-0800

Lincoln Campus
303 North 52nd St., Lincoln 68504
Phone: (402) 466-4774

Grace University
1311 South Ninth St., Omaha 68108
Type: Private, independent, four-year
Degrees: A, B, M *Enroll:* 344
URL: http://www.graceu.edu
Phone: (402) 449-2800 *Calendar:* Sem. plan
Inst. Accred.: ABHE (1948/2006), NCA-HLC (1994/1999)

Hastings College
710 North Turner Ave., Hastings 68901-7621
Type: Private, Presbyterian Church (USA), four-year
Degrees: B, M *Enroll:* 1,167
URL: http://www.hastings.edu
Phone: (402) 463-2402 *Calendar:* 4-1-4 plan
Inst. Accred.: NCA-HLC (1916/2005)
Prog. Accred.: Music, Teacher Education (NCATE)

Little Priest Tribal College
601 East College Dr., Winnebago 68071
Type: Public, tribal, two-year
System: American Indian Higher Education Consortium
Degrees: A *Enroll:* 77
URL: http://www.lptc.bia.edu
Phone: (402) 878-2380 *Calendar:* Sem. plan
Inst. Accred.: NCA-HLC (1998/2003)

McCook Community College
1205 East Third St., McCook 69001
Type: Public, state/local, two-year
System: Mid-Plains Community College Area
Degrees: A *FTE Enroll:* 523
URL: http://www.mpcca.cc.ne.us
Phone: (308) 345-6303 *Calendar:* Sem. plan
Inst. Accred.: NCA-HLC (1986/2004, *Indirect accreditation through Mid-Plains Community College Area, North Platte, NE*)
Prog. Accred.: Dentistry (dental assisting)

Metropolitan Community College
PO Box 3777, Omaha 68103-0777
Type: Public, state/local, two-year
System: Nebraska State College System
Degrees: A *Enroll:* 7,801
URL: http://www.mccneb.edu
Phone: (402) 457-2000 *Calendar:* Qtr. plan
Inst. Accred.: NCA-HLC (1979/2003)
Prog. Accred.: Allied Health (respiratory therapy), Business (ACBSP), Culinary Education, Dentistry (dental assisting), Nursing

Mid-Plains Community College
601 West State Farm Rd., North Platte 69101
Type: Public, state/local, two-year
System: Mid-Plains Community College Area
Degrees: A *FTE Enroll:* 1,113
URL: http://www.mpcca.cc.ne.us
Phone: (308) 535-3600 *Calendar:* Sem. plan
Inst. Accred.: NCA-HLC (1986/2004, *Indirect accreditation through Mid-Plains Community College Area, North Platte, NE*)
Prog. Accred.: Clinical Lab Technology, Dentistry (dental assisting), Nursing

Mid-Plains Community College—North
1101 Halligan Dr., North Platte 69101
Type: Public, state/local, two-year
System: Mid-Plains Community College Area
Degrees: A
URL: http://www.mpcca.cc.ne.us
Phone: (308) 535-3600 *Calendar:* Sem. plan
Inst. Accred.: NCA-HLC (1986/2004, *Indirect accreditation through Mid-Plains Community College Area, North Platte, NE*)

Midland Lutheran College
900 Clarkson St., Fremont 68025
Type: Private, Evangelical Lutheran Church of America, four-year
Degrees: A, B *Enroll:* 909
URL: http://www.mlc.edu
Phone: (402) 941-6001 *Calendar:* 4-1-4 plan
Inst. Accred.: NCA-HLC (1947/1999)
Prog. Accred.: Nursing

Myotherapy Institute
6020 South 58th St., Bldg. D, Lincoln 68516
Type: Private, proprietary, two-year
Degrees: A *Enroll:* 46
URL: http://www.myotherapy.edu
Phone: (402) 421-7410
Inst. Accred.: ACCSCT (1998/2006)

Grand Island Campus
810 North Diers Ave., Ste. J, Grand Island 68803
Phone: (308) 381-4800

Nebraska Christian College
12550 South 114th St., Papillion 68046-4256
Type: Private, Christian Churches/Churches of Christ, four-year
Degrees: A, B *Enroll:* 138
URL: http://www.nechristian.edu
Phone: (402) 935-9400 *Calendar:* Sem. plan
Inst. Accred.: ABHE (1985/2006)

Nebraska College of Technical Agriculture
Rural Route 3, Box 23A, 404 East 7th St., Curtis 69025-9502
Type: Private, independent, two-year
Degrees: A *Enroll:* 250
URL: http://www.ncta.unl.edu
Phone: (308) 367-4124 *Calendar:* Sem. plan
Inst. Accred.: NCA-HLC (2004)
Prog. Accred.: Veterinary Technology

Nebraska Indian Community College
PO Box 428, Macy 68039
Type: Public, tribal, two-year
System: American Indian Higher Education Consortium
Degrees: A *Enroll:* 77
URL: http://www.thenicc.edu
Phone: (402) 837-5078 *Calendar:* Sem. plan
Inst. Accred.: NCA-HLC (1986/2005, Probation)

Nebraska Methodist College
720 North 87th St., Omaha 68114
Type: Private, United Methodist Church, four-year
Degrees: A, B, M *Enroll:* 475
URL: http://nmc.theplacewhereyoubelong.com
Phone: (402) 354-7000 *Calendar:* Sem. plan
Inst. Accred.: NCA-HLC (1989/2003)
Prog. Accred.: Allied Health (diagnostic medical sonography, medical assisting (AMA), respiratory therapy, surgical technology), Nursing Education

Nebraska Wesleyan University
5000 St. Paul Ave., Lincoln 68504-2796
Type: Private, United Methodist Church, four-year
Degrees: B, M *Enroll:* 1,770
URL: http://www.nebrwesleyan.edu
Phone: (402) 466-2371 *Calendar:* Sem. plan
Inst. Accred.: NCA-HLC (1914/2000)
Prog. Accred.: Business (ACBSP), Music, Nursing, Social Work, Teacher Education (NCATE)

Northeast Community College
801 East Benjamin Ave., PO Box 469, Norfolk 68702-0469
Type: Public, state/local, two-year
System: Nebraska State College System
Degrees: A *Enroll:* 3,125
URL: http://www.northeastcollege.com
Phone: (402) 371-2020 *Calendar:* Sem. plan
Inst. Accred.: NCA-HLC (1979/2004)
Prog. Accred.: Nursing, Physical Therapy Assisting, Veterinary Technology

Peru State College
600 Hoyt St., PO Box 10, Peru 68421-0010
Type: Public, state, four-year
System: Nebraska State College System
Degrees: B, M *Enroll:* 1,442
URL: http://www.peru.edu
Phone: (402) 872-3815 *Calendar:* Sem. plan
Inst. Accred.: NCA-HLC (1915/2002)
Prog. Accred.: Teacher Education (NCATE)

Southeast Community College
8800 O St., Lincoln 68520-1299
Type: Public, state/local, two-year
System: Nebraska State College System
Degrees: A *Enroll:* 7,040
URL: http://www.southeast.edu
Phone: (402) 471-3333 *Calendar:* Qtr. plan
Inst. Accred.: NCA-HLC (1983/2003)
Prog. Accred.: Allied Health (medical assisting (AMA), respiratory therapy, surgical technology), Business (ACBSP), Clinical Lab Technology, Culinary Education, Dentistry (dental assisting), Dietetic Technician, Nursing, Practical Nursing, Radiography

Beatrice Campus
4771 West Scott Rd., Beatrice 68310-7042
Phone: (402) 228-3468
Prog. Accred: Practical Nursing

Milford Campus
600 State St., Milford 68405-8498
Phone: (402) 761-2131

Union College
3800 South 48th St., Lincoln 68506
Type: Private, Seventh-Day Adventist Church, four-year
Degrees: A, B *Enroll:* 852
URL: http://www.ucollege.edu
Phone: (402) 486-2500 *Calendar:* Sem. plan
Inst. Accred.: NCA-HLC (1923/2000)
Prog. Accred.: Nursing Education, Physician Assistant, Social Work, Teacher Education (NCATE)

University of Nebraska at Kearney
905 West 25th St., Kearney 68849-0601
Type: Public, state, four-year
System: University of Nebraska Central Administration
Degrees: B, M, P *Enroll:* 5,600
URL: http://www.unk.edu
Phone: (308) 865-8441 *Calendar:* Sem. plan
Inst. Accred.: NCA-HLC (1916/2004)
Prog. Accred.: Allied Health (speech-language pathology), Business (AACSB), Construction Technology, Counseling, Electronic Technology, Industrial Technology, Music, Social Work, Teacher Education (NCATE)

University of Nebraska at Omaha
60th and Dodge, Omaha 68182-0108
Type: Public, state, four-year
System: University of Nebraska Central Administration
Degrees: B, M, P, D *Enroll:* 11,087
URL: http://www.unomaha.edu
Phone: (402) 554-2800 *Calendar:* Sem. plan
Inst. Accred.: NCA-HLC (1939/2004)
Prog. Accred.: Allied Health (speech-language pathology), Art, Aviation, Business (AACSB), Computer Science (ABET-CAC), Counseling, Engineering (information systems), Graduate Social Work, Music, Public Administration, Public Health, Social Work, Teacher Education (NCATE)

University of Nebraska Medical Center
987020 Nebraska Medical Center, Omaha 68198-7020
Type: Public, state, four-year
System: University of Nebraska Central Administration
Degrees: B, M, P, D *Enroll:* 2,746
URL: http://www.unmc.edu
Phone: (402) 559-4000 *Calendar:* Sem. plan
Inst. Accred.: NCA-HLC (1913/2007)
Prog. Accred.: Allied Health (cytotechnology, diagnostic medical sonography, medicine, perfusion), Clinical Lab Scientist, Clinical Pastoral Education, Dietetics (internship), Nuclear Medicine Technology, Nursing Education, Pharmacy, Physical Therapy, Physician Assistant, Public Health, Radiation Therapy, Radiography

University of Nebraska—Lincoln
201 Canfield Admin. Bldg., 14th and R Streets, Lincoln 68588-0419
Type: Public, state, four-year
System: University of Nebraska Central Administration
Degrees: A, B, M, P, D *Enroll:* 19,660
URL: http://www.unl.edu
Phone: (402) 472-7211 *Calendar:* Sem. plan
Inst. Accred.: NCA-HLC (1913/2007)
Prog. Accred.: Accounting, Allied Health (audiology, speech-language pathology), Art, Business (AACSB), Clinical Psychology, Computer Science (ABET-CAC), Construction Education, Counseling Psychology, Dentistry (combined prosthodontics, dental hygiene, dentistry, endodontics, general dentistry, general practice residency, oral and maxillofacial surgery, orthodontic and dentofacial orthopedics, pediatric dentistry, periodontics), Dietetics (didactic), Dietetics (internship), Engineering (agricultural, architectural, bioengineering, chemical, civil, computer, electrical, industrial, mechanical), Family & Consumer Science, Interior Design, Journalism, Law, Marriage and Family Therapy, Music, Planning, School Psychology, Teacher Education (NCATE), Theatre

Vatterott College—Spring Valley
11818 I St., Omaha 68137
Type: Private, proprietary, two-year
System: Vatterott Educational Centers, Inc.
Degrees: A
URL: http://www.vatterott-college.edu/omaha.asp
Phone: (402) 891-9411 *Calendar:* Sem. plan
Inst. Accred.: ACCSCT (1986/2006)
Prog. Accred.: Dentistry (dental assisting), Medical Assisting (ABHES), Veterinary Technology

Wayne State College
1111 Main St., Wayne 68787-1923
Type: Public, state, four-year
System: Nebraska State College System
Degrees: B, M, P *Enroll:* 2,821
URL: http://www.wsc.edu
Phone: (402) 375-7000 *Calendar:* Sem. plan
Inst. Accred.: NCA-HLC (1917/2008)
Prog. Accred.: Teacher Education (NCATE)

Western Nebraska Community College
1601 East 27th St., NE, Scottsbluff 69361
Type: Public, state/local, two-year
System: Nebraska State College System
Degrees: A *Enroll:* 1,342
URL: http://www.wncc.edu
Phone: (308) 635-3606 *Calendar:* Sem. plan
Inst. Accred.: NCA-HLC (1988/2000)
Prog. Accred.: Practical Nursing

Alliance Campus
1750 Sweetwater Ave., Alliance 69301
Phone: (308) 763-2000
Prog. Accred: Practical Nursing

Sidney Campus
371 College Dr., Sidney 69162
Phone: (308) 254-5450
Prog. Accred: Practical Nursing

York College
1125 East 8th St., York 68467-2699
Type: Private, Church of Christ, four-year
Degrees: A, B *Enroll:* 427
URL: http://www.york.edu
Phone: (732) 363-5600 *Calendar:* Sem. plan
Inst. Accred.: NCA-HLC (1970/2004)
Prog. Accred.: Teacher Education (NCATE)

NEVADA

The Art Institute of Las Vegas
2350 Corporate Circle, Henderson 89074
Type: Private, proprietary, four-year
System: Education Management Corporation
Degrees: A, B
URL: http://www.ailv.aii.edu
Phone: (702) 369-9944 *Calendar:* Qtr. plan
Inst. Accred.: ACCSCT (1992/2002)
Prog. Accred.: Culinary Education

The Art Institute of Indianapolis
3500 Depauw Blvd., Indianapolis, IN 46268
Phone: (866) 441-9031

The Art Institute of Salt Lake City
121 West Election Rd., Draper, UT 84020
Phone: (801) 601-4700

Career College of Northern Nevada
1195-A Corporate Blvd., Reno 89502-2331
Type: Private, proprietary, two-year
Degrees: A *Enroll:* 254
URL: http://www.ccnn4u.com
Phone: (775) 856-2266
Inst. Accred.: ACCSCT (1989/2003)

College of Southern Nevada
6375 West Charleston Blvd., Las Vegas 89146
Type: Public, state, four-year
System: Nevada System of Higher Education
Degrees: A, B *Enroll:* 18,920
URL: http://www.csn.edu
Phone: (702) 651-5600 *Calendar:* Sem. plan
Inst. Accred.: NWCCU (1975/2007)
Prog. Accred.: Allied Health (EMT-paramedic, diagnostic medical sonography, medical assisting (AMA), opticianry, respiratory therapy, surgical technology), Business (ACBSP), Clinical Lab Technology, Culinary Education, Engineering Technology (electrical, telecommunications), Nursing, Physical Therapy Assisting, Practical Nursing, Veterinary Technology

Cheyenne Campus
3200 East Cheyenne Ave., North Las Vegas 89030
Phone: (702) 651- 4002
Prog. Accred: Culinary Education, Dentistry (dental assisting, dental hygiene)

Henderson Campus
700 College Dr., Henderson 89015
Phone: (702) 651-3000

West Charleston Campus
6375 West Charleston Blvd., W1A, Las Vegas 89146
Phone: (702) 651-5000
Prog. Accred: Allied Health (occupational therapy assisting), Dentistry (dental assisting)

Great Basin College
1500 College Pkwy., Elko 89801
Type: Public, state, four-year
System: Nevada System of Higher Education
Degrees: A, B *Enroll:* 1,758
URL: http://www.gbcnv.edu
Phone: (775) 738-8493 *Calendar:* Sem. plan
Inst. Accred.: NWCCU (1974/2008)
Prog. Accred.: Nursing

Kaplan College—Las Vegas
3315 Spring Mountain Rd., Ste. 7, Las Vegas 89102
Type: Private, proprietary, two-year
System: Kaplan Higher Education Corporation
Degrees: A
URL: http://getinfo.kaplancollege.com
Phone: (702) 368-2338 *Calendar:* Qtr. plan
Inst. Accred.: ACCSCT (1991/2004)
Prog. Accred.: Medical Assisting (ABHES)

Las Vegas College
170 North Stephanie St., Henderson 89074
Type: Private, proprietary, two-year
System: Corinthian Colleges, Inc
Degrees: A *Enroll:* 199
URL: http://www.lasvegas-college.com
Phone: (702) 567-1920 *Calendar:* Qtr. plan
Inst. Accred.: ACICS (1983/2005)

Le Cordon Bleu College of Culinary Arts—Las Vegas
1451 Center Crossing Rd., Las Vegas 89144
Type: Private, proprietary, two-year
System: Career Education Corporation
Degrees: A
URL: http://www.vegasculinary.com
Phone: (702) 365-7690
Inst. Accred.: ACCSCT (2003/2005)

Sierra Nevada College
999 Tahoe Blvd., Incline Village 89451
Type: Private, independent, four-year
Degrees: B, M *Enroll:* 536
URL: http://www.sierranevada.edu
Phone: (775) 831-1314 *Calendar:* Sem. plan
Inst. Accred.: NWCCU (1977/2006, Probation)

Truckee Meadows Community College
7000 Dandini Blvd., Reno 89512
Type: Public, state, two-year
System: Nevada System of Higher Education
Degrees: A *Enroll:* 5,773
URL: http://www.tmcc.edu
Phone: (775) 673-7000 *Calendar:* Sem. plan
Inst. Accred.: NWCCU (1980/2007)
Prog. Accred.: Culinary Education, Dentistry (dental assisting, dental hygiene), Dietetic Technician, Nursing, Radiography, Veterinary Technology

University of Nevada, Las Vegas
PO Box 451002, 4505 Maryland Pkwy., Las Vegas 89154-1002
Type: Public, state, four-year
System: Nevada System of Higher Education
Degrees: B, M, D *Enroll:* 21,987
URL: http://www.unlv.edu
Phone: (702) 895-3011 *Calendar:* Sem. plan
Inst. Accred.: NWCCU (1964/2005)
Prog. Accred.: Accounting, Applied Science (health physics), Art, Business (AACSB), Clinical Lab Scientist, Clinical Psychology, Computer Science (ABET-CAC), Construction Education, Counseling, Dentistry (dentistry, pediatric dentistry), Dietetics (didactic), Dietetics (internship), Engineering (civil, computer, electrical, mechanical), Graduate Social Work, Interior Architecture, Interior Design, Landscape Architecture, Law, Marriage and Family Therapy, Music, Nuclear Medicine Technology, Nursing, Physical Therapy, Public Administration, Radiography, Social Work, Teacher Education (NCATE), Theatre

University of Nevada, Reno
Reno 89557
Type: Public, state, four-year
System: Nevada System of Higher Education
Degrees: A, B, M, D *Enroll:* 13,408
URL: http://www.unr.edu
Phone: (775) 784-1110 *Calendar:* Sem. plan
Inst. Accred.: NWCCU (1938/2008)
Prog. Accred.: Accounting, Allied Health (medicine, speech-language pathology), Business (AACSB), Clinical Psychology, Computer Science (ABET-CAC), Counseling, Dentistry (general practice residency), Dietetics (didactic), Dietetics (internship), Engineering (chemical, civil, computer, electrical, environmental/sanitary, geological/geophysical, mechanical, mining), Graduate Social Work, Journalism, Music, Nursing Education, Social Work, Teacher Education (NCATE)

University of Southern Nevada
11 Sunset Way, Henderson 89014-2333
Type: Private, independent, four-year
Degrees: B, M, D
URL: http://www.usn.edu
Phone: (702) 990-4433
Inst. Accred.: NWCCU (2008)

Western Nevada College
2201 West College Pkwy., Carson City 89703-7399
Type: Public, state, four-year
System: Nevada System of Higher Education
Degrees: A, B *Enroll:* 2,292
URL: http://www.wnc.edu
Phone: (775) 445-3000 *Calendar:* Sem. plan
Inst. Accred.: NWCCU (1975/2005)
Prog. Accred.: Allied Health (surgical technology), Nursing

NEW HAMPSHIRE

Chester College of New England
40 Chester St., Chester 03036-4331
Type: Private, independent, four-year
Degrees: A, B *Enroll:* 200
URL: http://www.chestercollege.edu
Phone: (603) 887-4401 *Calendar:* Sem. plan
Inst. Accred.: NEASC-CIHE (1975/2003)

Colby-Sawyer College
100 Main St., New London 03257-4648
Type: Private, independent, four-year
Degrees: A, B *Enroll:* 961
URL: http://www.colby-sawyer.edu
Phone: (603) 526-3000 *Calendar:* Sem. plan
Inst. Accred.: NEASC-CIHE (1933/2005)
Prog. Accred.: Nursing Education

Daniel Webster College
20 University Dr., Nashua 03063-1300
Type: Private, independent, four-year
Degrees: A, B, M *Enroll:* 894
URL: http://www.dwc.edu
Phone: (603) 577-6000 *Calendar:* Sem. plan
Inst. Accred.: NEASC-CIHE (1972/2006)
Prog. Accred.: Aviation

Dartmouth College
Hanover 03755-4030
Type: Private, independent, four-year
Degrees: B, M, P, D *Enroll:* 5,693
URL: http://www.dartmouth.edu
Phone: (603) 646-1110 *Calendar:* Qtr. plan
Inst. Accred.: NEASC-CIHE (1929/1999)
Prog. Accred.: Allied Health (medicine), Business (AACSB), Engineering (general), Psychology Internship, Public Health, Theatre

Franklin Pierce Law Center
2 White St., Concord 03301-4197
Type: Private, independent, four-year
Degrees: P, D *Enroll:* 489
URL: http://www.fplc.edu
Phone: (603) 228-1541 *Calendar:* Sem. plan
Inst. Accred.: NEASC-CIHE (2000/2006)
Prog. Accred.: Law (ABA only)

Franklin Pierce University
College Rd., Rindge 03461-0060
Type: Private, independent, four-year
Degrees: B, M *Enroll:* 1,611
URL: http://www.franklinpierce.edu
Phone: (603) 899-4000 *Calendar:* Sem. plan
Inst. Accred.: NEASC-CIHE (1968/2008)
Prog. Accred.: Physical Therapy

Granite State College
8 Old Suncook Rd., Concord 03301
Type: Public, state, four-year
System: University System of New Hampshire
Degrees: A, B *Enroll:* 917
URL: http://www.granite.edu
Phone: (603) 228-3000 *Calendar:* Sem. plan
Inst. Accred.: NEASC-CIHE (1980/2006)

Great Bay Community College
277 Portsmouth Ave., Stratham 03885-2297
Type: Public, state, two-year
Degrees: A *FTE Enroll:* 616
URL: http://www.greatbay.edu
Phone: (603) 772-1194 *Calendar:* Sem. plan
Inst. Accred.: NEASC-CIHE (2002/2007)
Prog. Accred.: Allied Health (surgical technology), Business (ACBSP), Nursing, Veterinary Technology

Hesser College
3 Sundial Ave., Manchester 03103-7245
Type: Private, proprietary, four-year
System: Kaplan Higher Education Corporation
Degrees: A, B *Enroll:* 2,628
URL: http://www.hesser.edu
Phone: (603) 668-6660 *Calendar:* Sem. plan
Inst. Accred.: NEASC-CIHE (2007), NEASC-CTCI (1985/2006)
Prog. Accred.: Allied Health (medical assisting (AMA)), Physical Therapy Assisting

Concord Campus
25 Hall St., Ste. 104, Concord 03301
Phone: (603) 225-9200

Nashua Campus
410 Amherst St., Nashua 03063
Phone: (603) 883-0404

Portsmouth Campus
170 Commerce Way, Portsmouth 03801
Phone: (603) 436-5300

Salem Campus
11 Manor Pkwy., Salem 03079
Phone: (603) 898-3480

Keene State College
229 Main St., Keene 03435-0002
Type: Public, state, four-year
System: University System of New Hampshire
Degrees: A, B, M *Enroll:* 4,456
URL: http://www.keene.edu
Phone: (603) 352-1909 *Calendar:* Sem. plan
Inst. Accred.: NEASC-CIHE (1949/2000)
Prog. Accred.: Dietetics (didactic), Dietetics (internship), Music, Teacher Education (NCATE)

Lakes Region Community College
379 Belmont Rd., Laconia 03246
Type: Public, state, two-year
Degrees: A *FTE Enroll:* 550
URL: http://www.lrcc.edu
Phone: (603) 524-3207 *Calendar:* Sem. plan
Inst. Accred.: NEASC-CIHE (2003)

Lebanon College
15 Hanover St., Lebanon 03766
Type: Private, independent, two-year
Degrees: A
URL: http://www.lebanoncollege.edu
Phone: (603) 448-2445 *Calendar:* Sem. plan
Inst. Accred.: ACICS (2008)
Prog. Accred.: Radiography

Magdalen College
511 Kearsarge Mountain Rd., Warner 03278
Type: Private, independent, four-year
Degrees: A, B *Enroll:* 68
URL: http://www.magdalen.edu
Phone: (603) 456-2656 *Calendar:* Sem. plan
Inst. Accred.: AALE (2004)

Manchester Community College
1066 Front St., Manchester 03102-8518
Type: Public, state, two-year
System: Community College System of New Hampshire
Degrees: A *Enroll:* 2,304
URL: http://www.manchestercommunitycollege.edu
Phone: (603) 668-6706 *Calendar:* Sem. plan
Inst. Accred.: NEASC-CIHE (2002/2007)
Prog. Accred.: Allied Health (medical assisting (AMA)), Nursing

McIntosh College
23 Cataract Ave., Dover 03820-3990
Type: Private, proprietary, two-year
System: Career Education Corporation
Degrees: A *Enroll:* 1,008
URL: http://www.mcintoshcollege.edu
Phone: (603) 742-1234
Inst. Accred.: NEASC-CTCI (1988/1998, *Teach out in process*)
Prog. Accred.: Culinary Education

Nashua Community College
505 Amherst St., Nashua 03063-1092
Type: Public, state, two-year
System: Community College System of New Hampshire
Degrees: A *Enroll:* 1,564
URL: http://www.nashuacc.edu
Phone: (603) 882-6923 *Calendar:* Sem. plan
Inst. Accred.: NEASC-CIHE (2002/2007)
Prog. Accred.: Engineering Technology (computer), Nursing

New England College
7 Main St., Henniker 03242-3244
Type: Private, independent, four-year
Degrees: B, M *Enroll:* 1,176
URL: http://www.nec.edu
Phone: (603) 428-2211 *Calendar:* Sem. plan
Inst. Accred.: NEASC-CIHE (1967/2004)

NHTI, Concord's Community College
31 College Dr., Concord 03301-7412
Type: Public, state, two-year
System: Community College System of New Hampshire
Degrees: A *Enroll:* 2,343
URL: http://www.nhti.edu
Phone: (603) 271-6484 *Calendar:* Sem. plan
Inst. Accred.: NEASC-CIHE (2001/2006)
Prog. Accred.: Allied Health (EMT-paramedic, diagnostic medical sonography), Business (ACBSP), Dentistry (dental assisting, dental hygiene), Engineering Technology (architectural, computer, electrical, manufacturing, mechanical), Nursing, Practical Nursing, Radiation Therapy, Radiography

Plymouth State University
17 High St., Plymouth 03264-1595
Type: Public, state, four-year
System: University System of New Hampshire
Degrees: A, B, M, D *Enroll:* 4,486
URL: http://www.plymouth.edu
Phone: (603) 535-5000 *Calendar:* Sem. plan
Inst. Accred.: NEASC-CIHE (1955/2003)
Prog. Accred.: Business (ACBSP), Computer Science (ABET-CAC), Counseling, Social Work, Teacher Education (NCATE)

River Valley Community College
One College Dr., Claremont 03743-9707
Type: Public, state, two-year
Degrees: A *FTE Enroll:* 400
URL: http://www.rivervalley.edu
Phone: (603) 542-7744 *Calendar:* Sem. plan
Inst. Accred.: NEASC-CIHE (2002/2007)
Prog. Accred.: Allied Health (medical assisting (AMA), occupational therapy assisting, respiratory therapy), Clinical Lab Technology, Nursing, Physical Therapy Assisting

Rivier College
420 Main St., Nashua 03060-5086
Type: Private, Roman Catholic Church, four-year
Degrees: A, B, M *Enroll:* 1,469
URL: http://www.rivier.edu
Phone: (603) 888-1311 *Calendar:* Sem. plan
Inst. Accred.: NEASC-CIHE (1948/2002)
Prog. Accred.: Nursing

Saint Anselm College
100 St. Anselm Dr., Manchester 03102-1310
Type: Private, Roman Catholic Church, four-year
Degrees: A, B *Enroll:* 1,956
URL: http://www.anselm.edu
Phone: (603) 641-7000 *Calendar:* Sem. plan
Inst. Accred.: NEASC-CIHE (1941/1999)
Prog. Accred.: Nursing Education

Southern New Hampshire University
2500 North River Rd., Manchester 03106-1045
Type: Private, independent, four-year
Degrees: A, B, M, D *Enroll:* 4,774
URL: http://www.snhu.edu
Phone: (603) 668-2211 *Calendar:* Sem. plan
Inst. Accred.: NEASC-CIHE (1973/2001)
Prog. Accred.: Business (ACBSP), Culinary Education

The Thomas More College of Liberal Arts
6 Manchester St., Merrimack 03054-4805
Type: Private, Roman Catholic Church, four-year
Degrees: B *Enroll:* 84
URL: http://www.thomasmorecollege.edu
Phone: (603) 880-8308 *Calendar:* Sem. plan
Inst. Accred.: NEASC-CIHE (1996/2001)
Prog. Accred.: Liberal Education

University of New Hampshire
Main St., Durham 03824-3529
Type: Public, state, four-year
System: University System of New Hampshire
Degrees: A, B, M, D *Enroll:* 13,050
URL: http://www.unh.edu
Phone: (603) 862-1234 *Calendar:* Sem. plan
Inst. Accred.: NEASC-CIHE (1929/2003)
Prog. Accred.: Allied Health (occupational therapy, speech-language pathology), Business (AACSB), Clinical Lab Scientist, Computer Science (ABET-CAC), Dietetic Technician, Dietetics (didactic), Dietetics (internship), Engineering (chemical, civil, computer, electrical, environmental/sanitary, mechanical), Engineering Technology (electrical, mechanical), Forestry, Graduate Social Work, Marriage and Family Therapy, Music, Nursing Education, Psychology Internship, Public Health, Recreation and Leisure Services, Social Work

Manchester Campus
400 Commercial St., Manchester 03101-1113
Phone: (603) 641-4321

White Mountains Community College
2020 Riverside Dr., Berlin 03570-3799
Type: Public, state, two-year
System: Community College System of New Hampshire
Degrees: A *Enroll:* 1,137
URL: http://www.wmcc.edu
Phone: (603) 752-1113 *Calendar:* Sem. plan
Inst. Accred.: NEASC-CIHE (2003)

NEW JERSEY

Assumption College for Sisters
350 Bernardsville Rd., Mendham 07945-0800
Type: Private, Roman Catholic Church, two-year
Degrees: A *Enroll:* 34
URL: http://www.acs350.org
Phone: (973) 543-6528 *Calendar:* Sem. plan
Inst. Accred.: MSA-CHE (1965/2005)

Atlantic Cape Community College
5100 Black Horse Pike, Mays Landing 08330-2699
Type: Public, state/local, two-year
System: New Jersey Commission on Higher Education
Degrees: A *Enroll:* 4,340
URL: http://www.atlantic.edu
Phone: (609) 343-4900 *Calendar:* Sem. plan
Inst. Accred.: MSA-CHE (1971/2008)
Prog. Accred.: Allied Health (surgical technology), Dentistry (dental assisting), Nursing

Bergen Community College
400 Paramus Rd., Paramus 07652-1595
Type: Public, state/local, two-year
System: New Jersey Commission on Higher Education
Degrees: A *Enroll:* 9,929
URL: http://www.bergen.edu
Phone: (201) 447-7100 *Calendar:* Sem. plan
Inst. Accred.: MSA-CHE (1972/2006)
Prog. Accred.: Allied Health (diagnostic medical sonography, medical assisting (AMA), respiratory therapy, surgical technology), Clinical Lab Technology, Dentistry (dental hygiene), Nursing, Radiography, Veterinary Technology

Berkeley College—Garret Mountain
44 Rifle Camp Rd., West Paterson 07424
Type: Private, proprietary, four-year
System: Berkeley College of New York and New Jersey
Degrees: A, B *Enroll:* 2,190
URL: http://www.berkeleycollege.edu
Phone: (973) 278-5400 *Calendar:* Qtr. plan
Inst. Accred.: MSA-CHE (1983/2008)

Bergen Campus
64 East Midland Ave., Paramus 07652-2931
Phone: (201) 652-0388

Woodbridge Campus
430 Rahway Ave., Woodbridge 07095
Phone: (732) 750-1800

Beth Medrash Govoha
617 Sixth St., Lakewood 08701
Type: Private, independent, four-year
Degrees: B, M *Enroll:* 4,287
Phone: (732) 367-1060 *Calendar:* Sem. plan
Inst. Accred.: AARTS (1974/2005)

Bloomfield College
467 Franklin St., Bloomfield 07003
Type: Private, Presbyterian Church, USA, four-year
Degrees: B *Enroll:* 1,914
URL: http://www.bloomfield.edu
Phone: (973) 748-9000 *Calendar:* Sem. plan
Inst. Accred.: MSA-CHE (1960/2007)
Prog. Accred.: Nursing Education

Brookdale Community College
765 Newman Springs Rd., Lincroft 07738
Type: Public, local, two-year
System: New Jersey Commission on Higher Education
Degrees: A *Enroll:* 9,181
URL: http://www.brookdalecc.edu
Phone: (732) 224-2345 *Calendar:* 4-4-x plan
Inst. Accred.: MSA-CHE (1972/2008)
Prog. Accred.: Allied Health (respiratory therapy), Clinical Lab Technology, Nursing, Radiography

Burlington County College
County Route 530, Pemberton 08068-1599
Type: Public, state/local, two-year
System: New Jersey Commission on Higher Education
Degrees: A *Enroll:* 5,231
URL: http://www.bcc.edu
Phone: (609) 894-9311 *Calendar:* Sem. plan
Inst. Accred.: MSA-CHE (1972/2004)
Prog. Accred.: Engineering Technology (electrical), Nursing, Radiography

Caldwell College
9 Ryerson Ave., Caldwell 07006-6195
Type: Private, Roman Catholic Church, four-year
Degrees: B, M *Enroll:* 1,596
URL: http://www.caldwell.edu
Phone: (973) 618-3000 *Calendar:* Sem. plan
Inst. Accred.: MSA-CHE (1952/2005)
Prog. Accred.: Business (ACBSP)

Camden County College
PO Box 200, Blackwood 08012
Type: Public, state/local, two-year
System: New Jersey Commission on Higher Education
Degrees: A *Enroll:* 9,763
URL: http://www.camdencc.edu
Phone: (856) 277-7200 *Calendar:* Sem. plan
Inst. Accred.: MSA-CHE (1972/2002, Warning)
Prog. Accred.: Allied Health (opticianry), Clinical Lab Technology, Dentistry (dental assisting, dental hygiene), Dietetic Technician, Veterinary Technology

Camden Campus
Seventh and Cooper St.s, Camden 08102
Phone: (609) 338-1817

Centenary College
400 Jefferson St., Hackettstown 07840
Type: Private, independent, four-year
Degrees: A, B, M *Enroll:* 2,088
URL: http://www.centenarycollege.edu
Phone: (908) 852-1400 *Calendar:* Sem. plan
Inst. Accred.: MSA-CHE (1932/2005)
Prog. Accred.: Social Work, Teacher Education (TEAC)

The College of New Jersey
PO Box 7718, Ewing 08628-0718
Type: Public, state, four-year
System: New Jersey Commission on Higher Education
Degrees: B, M *Enroll:* 6,193
URL: http://www.tcnj.edu
Phone: (609) 771-1855 *Calendar:* Sem. plan
Inst. Accred.: MSA-CHE (1939/2005)
Prog. Accred.: Allied Health (audiology, speech-language pathology), Business (AACSB), Computer Science (ABET-CAC), Counseling, Engineering (computer, electrical, engineering physics/science, mechanical), Music, Nursing Education, Teacher Education (NCATE)

College of Saint Elizabeth
2 Convent Rd., Morristown 07960-6989
Type: Private, Roman Catholic Church, four-year
Degrees: B, M, D *Enroll:* 1,222
URL: http://www.cse.edu
Phone: (973) 290-4000 *Calendar:* Sem. plan
Inst. Accred.: MSA-CHE (1921/2005)
Prog. Accred.: Dietetics (didactic), Dietetics (internship), Nursing

County College of Morris
214 Center Grove Rd., Randolph 07869-2086
Type: Public, state/local, two-year
System: New Jersey Commission on Higher Education
Degrees: A *Enroll:* 5,665
URL: http://www.ccm.edu
Phone: (973) 328-5000 *Calendar:* Sem. plan
Inst. Accred.: MSA-CHE (1972/2008)
Prog. Accred.: Allied Health (respiratory therapy), Business (ACBSP), Clinical Lab Technology, Engineering Technology (electrical, mechanical), Nursing, Phlebotomy, Radiography, Veterinary Technology

Cumberland County College
3322 College Dr., PO Box 1500, Vineland 08362-1500
Type: Public, state/local, two-year
System: New Jersey Commission on Higher Education
Degrees: A *Enroll:* 2,237
URL: http://www.cccnj.edu
Phone: (856) 691-8600 *Calendar:* Sem. plan
Inst. Accred.: MSA-CHE (1970/2001)
Prog. Accred.: Nursing, Radiography

DeVry University North Brunswick
630 U.S. Hwy. One, North Brunswick 08902-3362
Type: Private, proprietary
System: DeVry University
Degrees: A, B *Enroll:* 1,145
URL: http://www.devry.edu/northbrunswick
Phone: (732) 435-4880 *Calendar:* Sem. plan
Inst. Accred.: NCA-HLC (2002, *Indirect accreditation through DeVry University, Oakbrook Terrace, IL*)
Prog. Accred.: Engineering Technology (electrical)

Paramus Center
81 East State Route 4, 35 Plaza, Ste. 102, Paramus 07652
Phone: (877) 613-8669

Drew University
36 Madison Ave., Madison 07940
Type: Private, United Methodist Church, four-year
Degrees: B, M, P, D *Enroll:* 2,287
URL: http://www.drew.edu
Phone: (973) 408-3000 *Calendar:* 4-1-4 plan
Inst. Accred.: ATS (1938/2001), MSA-CHE (1932/2001)

Essex County College
303 University Ave., Newark 07102
Type: Public, state/local, two-year
System: New Jersey Commission on Higher Education
Degrees: A *Enroll:* 7,278
URL: http://www.essex.edu
Phone: (973) 877-3000 *Calendar:* Sem. plan
Inst. Accred.: MSA-CHE (1974/2001)
Prog. Accred.: Allied Health (ophthalmic lab technology), Engineering Technology (civil/construction, electrical, manufacturing), Nursing, Physical Therapy Assisting, Radiography

West Essex Campus
730 Bloomfield Ave., West Caldwell 07006
Phone: (201) 228-3970

Fairleigh Dickinson University
1000 River Rd., Teaneck 07666-1996
Type: Private, independent, four-year
Degrees: A, B, M, D *Enroll:* 5,033
URL: http://www.fdu.edu
Phone: (201) 692-2000 *Calendar:* Sem. plan
Inst. Accred.: MSA-CHE (1948/2006)
Prog. Accred.: Business (AACSB), Computer Science (ABET-CAC), Engineering (electrical), Engineering Technology (civil/construction, electrical, mechanical), Nursing Education

Florham-Madison Campus
285 Madison Ave., Madison 07940
Phone: (201) 593-8500

Felician College
262 South Main St., Lodi 07644
Type: Private, Roman Catholic Church, four-year
Degrees: A, B, M *Enroll:* 1,444
URL: http://www.felician.edu
Phone: (201) 559-6000 *Calendar:* Sem. plan
Inst. Accred.: MSA-CHE (1974/2005)
Prog. Accred.: Clinical Lab Technology, Nursing Education, Teacher Education (TEAC)

Georgian Court University
900 Lakewood Ave., Lakewood 08701-2697
Type: Private, Roman Catholic Church, four-year
Degrees: B, M *Enroll:* 2,181
URL: http://www.georgian.edu
Phone: (732) 987-2200 *Calendar:* Sem. plan
Inst. Accred.: MSA-CHE (1922/2004)
Prog. Accred.: Business (ACBSP), Social Work

Gibbs College
630 West Mount Pleasant Ave., Route 10, Livingston 07039
Type: Private, proprietary, two-year
System: Career Education Corporation
Degrees: A *Enroll:* 1,102
URL: http://www.gibbsnj.edu
Phone: (973) 369-1360 *Calendar:* Sem. plan
Inst. Accred.: ACICS (1967/2004)

Piscataway Campus
180 Centennial Ave., Piscataway 08854
Phone: (732) 885-1580

Gloucester County College
1400 Tanyard Rd., Sewell 08080
Type: Public, state/local, two-year
System: New Jersey Commission on Higher Education
Degrees: A *Enroll:* 4,151
URL: http://www.gccnj.edu
Phone: (856) 468-5000 *Calendar:* 4-1-4 plan
Inst. Accred.: MSA-CHE (1973/2008)
Prog. Accred.: Allied Health (diagnostic medical sonography), Nuclear Medicine Technology, Nursing

Hudson County Community College
25 Journal Square, Jersey City 07307
Type: Public, state/local, two-year
System: New Jersey Commission on Higher Education
Degrees: A *Enroll:* 4,659
URL: http://www.hccc.edu
Phone: (201) 714-7100 *Calendar:* Sem. plan
Inst. Accred.: MSA-CHE (1981/2002, Warning)
Prog. Accred.: Allied Health (medical assisting (AMA)), Culinary Education, Engineering Technology (electrical)

Immaculate Conception Seminary
400 South Orange Ave., South Orange 07079
Type: Private, Roman Catholic Church, four-year
Degrees: M *FTE Enroll:* 141
URL: http://theology.shu.edu
Phone: (973) 761-9575 *Calendar:* Sem. plan
Inst. Accred.: ATS (1977/2004)

Kean University
1000 Morris Ave., Union 07083-7131
Type: Public, state, four-year
System: New Jersey Commission on Higher Education
Degrees: B, M *Enroll:* 10,026
URL: http://www.kean.edu
Phone: (908) 737-5326 *Calendar:* Sem. plan
Inst. Accred.: MSA-CHE (1960/2006)
Prog. Accred.: Allied Health (occupational therapy, speech-language pathology), Art, Counseling, Electronic Technology, Graduate Social Work, Industrial Technology, Interior Design, Music, Nursing, Public Administration, Social Work, Teacher Education (NCATE), Theatre

Mercer County Community College
1200 Old Trenton Rd., West Windsor 08550
Type: Public, state/local, two-year
System: New Jersey Commission on Higher Education
Degrees: A *Enroll:* 5,259
URL: http://www.mccc.edu
Phone: (609) 570-3613 *Calendar:* Sem. plan
Inst. Accred.: MSA-CHE (1967/2005)
Prog. Accred.: Aviation, Clinical Lab Technology, Funeral Service Education (Mortuary Science), Nursing, Physical Therapy Assisting, Radiography

James Kerney Campus
North Broad and Academy Streets, Trenton 08690
Phone: (609) 586-4800

Middlesex County College
PO Box 3050, Edison 08818
Type: Public, state/local, two-year
System: New Jersey Commission on Higher Education
Degrees: A *Enroll:* 7,976
URL: http://www.middlesexcc.edu
Phone: (732) 548-6000 *Calendar:* Sem. plan
Inst. Accred.: MSA-CHE (1970/2000)
Prog. Accred.: Clinical Lab Technology, Dentistry (dental hygiene), Dietetic Technician, Engineering Technology (civil/construction, electrical, mechanical), Nursing, Radiography

Monmouth University
400 Cedar Ave., West Long Branch 07764-1898
Type: Private, independent, four-year
Degrees: A, B, M *Enroll:* 5,282
URL: http://www.monmouth.edu
Phone: (732) 571-3400 *Calendar:* Sem. plan
Inst. Accred.: MSA-CHE (1952/2006)
Prog. Accred.: Business (AACSB), Engineering (software), Graduate Social Work, Nursing Education, Social Work, Teacher Education (NCATE)

Montclair State University
1 University Ave., Upper Montclair 07043-1624
Type: Public, state, four-year
System: New Jersey Commission on Higher Education
Degrees: B, M, D *Enroll:* 12,758
URL: http://www.montclair.edu
Phone: (973) 655-4000 *Calendar:* Sem. plan
Inst. Accred.: MSA-CHE (1937/2007)
Prog. Accred.: Allied Health (speech-language pathology), Art, Business (AACSB), Computer Science (ABET-CAC), Dance, Family & Consumer Science, Music, Teacher Education (NCATE), Theatre

New Brunswick Theological Seminary
17 Seminary Place, New Brunswick 08901-1196
Type: Private, Reformed Church in America, four-year
Degrees: M *Enroll:* 124
URL: http://www.nbts.edu
Phone: (732) 247-5241 *Calendar:* Sem. plan
Inst. Accred.: ATS (1938/2007)

New Jersey City University
2039 Kennedy Blvd., Jersey City 07305-1597
Type: Public, state, four-year
System: New Jersey Commission on Higher Education
Degrees: B, M *Enroll:* 5,867
URL: http://www.njcu.edu
Phone: (201) 200-2000 *Calendar:* Sem. plan
Inst. Accred.: MSA-CHE (1959/2005)
Prog. Accred.: Art, Business (ACBSP), Music, Nursing, Teacher Education (NCATE)

New Jersey Institute of Technology
University Heights, Newark 07102-1982
Type: Public, state, four-year
System: New Jersey Commission on Higher Education
Degrees: B, M, D *Enroll:* 6,416
URL: http://www.njit.edu
Phone: (973) 596-3000 *Calendar:* Sem. plan
Inst. Accred.: MSA-CHE (1934/2007)
Prog. Accred.: Business (AACSB), Computer Science (ABET-CAC), Engineering (chemical, civil, computer, electrical, industrial, information systems, mechanical), Engineering Technology (civil/construction, electrical, mechanical, surveying)

Ocean County College
PO Box 2001, Toms River 08754-2001
Type: Public, state/local, two-year
System: New Jersey Commission on Higher Education
Degrees: A *Enroll:* 5,509
URL: http://www.ocean.edu
Phone: (732) 255-0400 *Calendar:* Sem. plan
Inst. Accred.: MSA-CHE (1969/2004)
Prog. Accred.: Histologic Technology, Nursing

Passaic County Community College
One College Blvd., Paterson 07509-1179
Type: Public, state/local, two-year
System: New Jersey Commission on Higher Education
Degrees: A *Enroll:* 3,817
URL: http://www.pccc.edu
Phone: (973) 684-6888 *Calendar:* Sem. plan
Inst. Accred.: MSA-CHE (1978/2004)
Prog. Accred.: Nursing, Radiography

Princeton Theological Seminary
PO Box 821, Princeton 08542-0803
Type: Private, Presbyterian Church (USA), four-year
Degrees: M, P, D *Enroll:* 659
URL: http://www.ptsem.edu
Phone: (609) 921-8300 *Calendar:* Sem. plan
Inst. Accred.: ATS (1938/1997), MSA-CHE (1968/2003)

Princeton University
Princeton 08544-0015
Type: Private, independent, four-year
Degrees: B, M, D *Enroll:* 6,773
URL: http://www.princeton.edu
Phone: (609) 258-3000 *Calendar:* Sem. plan
Inst. Accred.: MSA-CHE (1921/2004)
Prog. Accred.: Engineering (aerospace, chemical, civil, electrical, engineering physics/science, mechanical), Teacher Education (TEAC)

Rabbi Jacob Joseph School
One Plainfield Ave., Edison 08817
Type: Private, independent, four-year
Degrees: B *Enroll:* 38
Phone: (732) 985-6533 *Calendar:* Sem. plan
Inst. Accred.: AARTS (1991/2002)

Rabbinical College of America
226 Sussex Ave., Morristown 07960
Type: Private, independent, four-year
Degrees: B *Enroll:* 293
URL: http://www.rca.edu/
Phone: (973) 267-9404 *Calendar:* Sem. plan
Inst. Accred.: AARTS (1979/2004)

Ramapo College of New Jersey
505 Ramapo Valley Rd., Mahwah 07430-1680
Type: Public, state, four-year
System: New Jersey Commission on Higher Education
Degrees: B, M *Enroll:* 4,783
URL: http://www.ramapo.edu
Phone: (201) 684-7500 *Calendar:* Sem. plan
Inst. Accred.: MSA-CHE (1975/2005)
Prog. Accred.: Nursing, Social Work

Raritan Valley Community College
PO Box 3300, Somerville 08876
Type: Public, state/local, two-year
System: New Jersey Commission on Higher Education
Degrees: A *Enroll:* 3,809
URL: http://www.raritanval.edu
Phone: (908) 526-1200 *Calendar:* Sem. plan
Inst. Accred.: MSA-CHE (1972/2007)
Prog. Accred.: Allied Health (ophthalmic lab technology), Nursing

The Richard Stockton College of New Jersey
Jimme Leeds Rd., PO Box 195, Pomona 08240-0195
Type: Public, state, four-year
System: New Jersey Commission on Higher Education
Degrees: B, M, P *Enroll:* 6,260
URL: http://www.stockton.edu
Phone: (609) 652-1776 *Calendar:* Sem. plan
Inst. Accred.: MSA-CHE (1975/2007)
Prog. Accred.: Allied Health (occupational therapy), Environmental Health, Nursing Education, Physical Therapy, Social Work

Rider University
2083 Lawrenceville Rd., Lawrenceville 08648-3099
Type: Private, independent, four-year
Degrees: A, B, M *Enroll:* 4,541
URL: http://www.rider.edu
Phone: (609) 896-5000 *Calendar:* Sem. plan
Inst. Accred.: MSA-CHE (1955/2007)
Prog. Accred.: Accounting, Business (AACSB), Counseling, Teacher Education (NCATE)

Westminster Choir College
101 Walnut Ln., Princeton 08540
Phone: (609) 921-7100
Prog. Accred: Music

Rowan University
201 Mullica Hill Rd., Glassboro 08028-1701
Type: Public, state, four-year
System: New Jersey Commission on Higher Education
Degrees: B, M, D *Enroll:* 8,361
URL: http://www.rowan.edu
Phone: (856) 256-4000 *Calendar:* Sem. plan
Inst. Accred.: MSA-CHE (1958/1999)
Prog. Accred.: Art, Business (AACSB), Computer Science (ABET-CAC), Engineering (chemical, civil, electrical, mechanical), Music, Teacher Education (NCATE), Theatre

Camden Campus
One Broadway, Camden 08102
Phone: (856) 756-5400

Rutgers, The State University of New Jersey Camden Campus
Armitage Hall, 311 North 5th St., Camden 08102-1461
Type: Public, state, four-year
System: Rutgers, The State University of New Jersey Central Office
Degrees: B, M, P, D *Enroll:* 4,364
URL: http://www.camden.rutgers.edu
Phone: (856) 225-1766 *Calendar:* Sem. plan
Inst. Accred.: MSA-CHE (1921/2003, *Indirect accreditation through Rutgers, The State University of New Jersey New Brunswick Campus, New Brunswick, NJ*)
Prog. Accred.: Business (AACSB), Law, Nursing Education, Physical Therapy, Public Administration

Rutgers, The State University of New Jersey New Brunswick Campus
83 Somerset St., Old Queens Bldg., New Brunswick 08901-1281
Type: Public, state, four-year
System: Rutgers, The State University of New Jersey Central Office
Degrees: B, M, P, D *Enroll:* 30,577
URL: http://www.rutgers.edu
Phone: (732) 932-4636 *Calendar:* Sem. plan
Inst. Accred.: MSA-CHE (1921/2008)
Prog. Accred.: Clinical Psychology, Dance, Dietetics (didactic), Engineering (agricultural, ceramic, chemical, civil, electrical, industrial, mechanical), Graduate Social Work, Landscape Architecture, Librarianship, Music, Pharmacy, Planning, School Psychology, Social Work

Douglass College
125 George St., New Brunswick 08901
Phone: (732) 932-9721

Rutgers, The State University of New Jersey Newark Campus
15 Washington St., Newark 07102
Type: Public, state, four-year
System: Rutgers, The State University of New Jersey Central Office
Degrees: B, M, P, D *Enroll:* 7,856
URL: http://www.newark.rutgers.edu
Phone: (973) 648-1766 *Calendar:* Sem. plan
Inst. Accred.: MSA-CHE (1921/2003, *Indirect accreditation through Rutgers, The State University of New Jersey New Brunswick Campus, New Brunswick, NJ*)
Prog. Accred.: Business (AACSB), Law, Nursing Education, Public Administration, Social Work

Saint Peter's College
2641 Kennedy Blvd., Jersey City 07306-5997
Type: Private, Roman Catholic Church, four-year
Degrees: A, B, M *Enroll:* 2,369
URL: http://www.spc.edu
Phone: (201) 915-9000 *Calendar:* Sem. plan
Inst. Accred.: MSA-CHE (1935/2003)
Prog. Accred.: Nursing Education

Englewood Cliffs Campus
Hudson Terrace, Englewood Cliffs 07632
Phone: (201) 568-7730

Salem Community College
460 Hollywood Ave., Carneys Point 08069-2799
Type: Public, state/local, two-year
System: New Jersey Commission on Higher Education
Degrees: A *Enroll:* 817
URL: http://www.salemcc.edu
Phone: (856) 299-2100 *Calendar:* Sem. plan
Inst. Accred.: MSA-CHE (1979/2005)

Seton Hall University
400 South Orange Ave., South Orange 07079
Type: Private, Roman Catholic Church, four-year
Degrees: B, M, P, D *Enroll:* 7,903
URL: http://www.shu.edu
Phone: (973) 761-9000 *Calendar:* Sem. plan
Inst. Accred.: MSA-CHE (1932/2004)
Prog. Accred.: Allied Health (audiology, occupational therapy, speech-language pathology), Business (AACSB), Counseling Psychology, Dentistry (oral and maxillofacial surgery), Marriage and Family Therapy, Nursing Education, Physical Therapy, Physician Assistant, Public Administration, Social Work, Teacher Education (NCATE)

School of Law Campus
One Newark Center, Newark 07102-5210
Phone: (201) 642-8500
Prog. Accred: Law

Somerset Christian College
10 Liberty Square, Zarephath 08890
Type: Private, Pillar of Fire, International, two-year
Degrees: A
URL: http://www.somersetchristian.edu
Phone: (732) 356-1595 *Calendar:* Sem. plan
Inst. Accred.: ABHE (2002/2007)

Stevens Institute of Technology
Castle Point on the Hudson, Hoboken 07030
Type: Private, independent, four-year
Degrees: B, M, D *Enroll:* 3,310
URL: http://www.stevens.edu
Phone: (201) 216-5100 *Calendar:* Sem. plan
Inst. Accred.: MSA-CHE (1927/2008)
Prog. Accred.: Computer Science (ABET-CAC), Engineering (chemical, civil, computer, electrical, engineering management, environmental/sanitary, general, mechanical)

Sussex County Community College
One College Hill Rd., Newton 07860-9937
Type: Public, state/local, two-year
System: New Jersey Commission on Higher Education
Degrees: A *Enroll:* 2,295
URL: http://www.sussex.edu
Phone: (973) 300-2100 *Calendar:* Sem. plan
Inst. Accred.: MSA-CHE (1993/2008)
Prog. Accred.: Allied Health (medical assisting (AMA), respiratory therapy, surgical technology), Veterinary Technology

Talmudical Academy of New Jersey
Route 524, Adelphia 07710
Type: Private, independent, four-year
Degrees: B *Enroll:* 52
Phone: (732) 431-1600 *Calendar:* Sem. plan
Inst. Accred.: AARTS (1980/2001)

Thomas Edison State College
101 West State St., Trenton 08608-1176
Type: Public, state, four-year
System: New Jersey Commission on Higher Education
Degrees: A, B, M *Enroll:* 4,516
URL: http://www.tesc.edu
Phone: (609) 984-1100 *Calendar:* Sem. plan
Inst. Accred.: MSA-CHE (1977/2007)
Prog. Accred.: Nursing

Union County College
1033 Springfield Ave., Cranford 07016
Type: Public, state/local, two-year
System: New Jersey Commission on Higher Education
Degrees: A *Enroll:* 7,224
URL: http://www.ucc.edu
Phone: (908) 709-7000 *Calendar:* Sem. plan
Inst. Accred.: MSA-CHE (1957/2007)
Prog. Accred.: Allied Health (respiratory therapy), Physical Therapy Assisting

Elizabeth Campus
12 West Jersey St., Elizabeth 07206
Phone: (908) 965-6000
Prog. Accred: Nursing

Plainfield Campus
232 East Second St., Plainfield 07060
Phone: (908) 412-3550
Prog. Accred: Practical Nursing

Scotch Plains Campus
1700 Raritan Rd., Scotch Plains 07076
Phone: (908) 889-2400

University of Medicine and Dentistry of New Jersey
65 Bergen St., Newark 07101-1709
Type: Public, state, four-year
System: New Jersey Commission on Higher Education
Degrees: A, B, M, P, D *Enroll:* 4,778
URL: http://www.umdnj.edu
Phone: (973) 972-4400 *Calendar:* Sem. plan
Inst. Accred.: MSA-CHE (1979/2008)
Prog. Accred.: Allied Health (cardiovascular technology, cytotechnology, diagnostic medical sonography, massage therapy, respiratory therapy, surgical technology), Clinical Lab Scientist, Clinical Lab Technology, Dentistry (advanced education in general dentistry, combined prosthodontics, endodontics, general practice residency, oral and maxillofacial surgery, pediatric dentistry, periodontics), Dietetics (coordinated), Dietetics (internship), Nurse (Midwifery), Nurse Anesthesia Education, Nursing, Osteopathy, Phlebotomy, Physical Therapy, Radiography

Graduate School of Biomedical Sciences
185 South Orange Ave., Newark 07103
Phone: (973) 972-4511

New Jersey Dental School
110 Bergen St., Newark 07103
Phone: (973) 972-4300
Prog. Accred: Dentistry (combined prosthodontics, dental assisting, dental hygiene, dentistry, endodontics, general dentistry, general practice residency, oral and maxillofacial surgery, orthodontic and dentofacial orthopedics, pediatric dentistry, periodontics)

New Jersey Medical School
185 South Orange Ave., Newark 07103
Phone: (973) 972-4539
Prog. Accred: Allied Health (medicine)

Robert Wood Johnson Medical School
PO Box 2688, University Affiliated Program of New Jersey, New Brunswick 08903-2688
Phone: (732) 235-5600
Prog. Accred: Allied Health (medicine), Clinical Pastoral Education, Dentistry (general practice residency), Physician Assistant, Psychology Internship

School of Health-Related Professions
65 Bergen St., Newark 07107
Phone: (973) 972-5453
Prog. Accred: Dentistry (dental assisting, dental hygiene), Nuclear Medicine Technology, Rehabilitation Counseling

School of Nursing
30 Bergen St., Administrative Complex Bldg. One, Newark 07107
Phone: (973) 972-4322

School of Public Health
170 Frelinghuysen Rd., Rm.236, Piscataway 08854
Phone: (732) 445-0199
Prog. Accred: Public Health

UMDNJ School of Osteopathic Medicine
406 East Laurel Rd., Stratford 08084-1350
Phone: (856) 566-6995
Prog. Accred: Allied Health (respiratory therapy)

Warren County Community College
475 Route 57 West, Washington 07882-4343
Type: Public, state/local, two-year
System: New Jersey Commission on Higher Education
Degrees: A *Enroll:* 963
URL: http://www.warren.edu
Phone: (908) 835-9222 *Calendar:* Sem. plan
Inst. Accred.: MSA-CHE (1993/2008)
Prog. Accred.: Allied Health (medical assisting (AMA)), Nursing

William Paterson University of New Jersey
300 Pompton Rd., Wayne 07470-2152
Type: Public, state, four-year
System: New Jersey Commission on Higher Education
Degrees: B, M *Enroll:* 9,032
URL: http://www.wpunj.edu
Phone: (973) 720-2000 *Calendar:* Sem. plan
Inst. Accred.: MSA-CHE (1958/2001)
Prog. Accred.: Allied Health (speech-language pathology), Business (AACSB), Counseling, Music, Nursing Education, Teacher Education (NCATE)

Yeshiva Toras Chaim
1027 Ridge Ave., Lakewood 08701-2120
Type: Private, independent, four-year
Degrees: Talmudic
Phone: (732) 942-3090 *Calendar:* Sem. plan
Inst. Accred.: AARTS (2007)

Yeshivas Be'er Yitzchok
1391 North Ave., Elizabeth 07208-2480
Type: Private, independent, four-year
Degrees: Talmudic
Phone: (908) 354-6057 *Calendar:* Sem. plan
Inst. Accred.: AARTS (2008)

NEW MEXICO

Central New Mexico Community College
525 Buena Vista Dr., SE, Albuquerque 87106
Type: Public, state/local, two-year
System: New Mexico Commission on Higher Education
Degrees: A *Enroll:* 12,358
URL: http://www.cnm.edu
Phone: (505) 224-3000 *Calendar:* Tri. plan
Inst. Accred.: NCA-HLC (1978/2007)
Prog. Accred.: Allied Health (diagnostic medical sonography, respiratory therapy, surgical technology), Business (ACBSP), Clinical Lab Technology, Construction Education, Culinary Education, Dentistry (dental assisting), Engineering Technology (electrical, general drafting/design), Nursing, Practical Nursing, Veterinary Technology

Clovis Community College
417 Schepps Blvd., Clovis 88101
Type: Public, state, two-year
System: New Mexico Commission on Higher Education
Degrees: A *Enroll:* 1,779
URL: http://www.clovis.edu
Phone: (505) 769-2811 *Calendar:* Sem. plan
Inst. Accred.: NCA-HLC (1987/2002)
Prog. Accred.: Nursing, Radiography

The College of Santa Fe
1600 St. Michael's Dr., Santa Fe 87501
Type: Private, Christian Brothers, four-year
Degrees: A, B, M *Enroll:* 1,113
URL: http://www.csf.edu
Phone: (505) 473-6133 *Calendar:* Sem. plan
Inst. Accred.: NCA-HLC (1965/2001)

Eastern New Mexico University
Campus Station #1, Portales 88130
Type: Public, state, four-year
System: New Mexico Commission on Higher Education
Degrees: A, B, M *Enroll:* 3,216
URL: http://www.enmu.edu
Phone: (505) 562-2121 *Calendar:* Sem. plan
Inst. Accred.: NCA-HLC (1947/2007)
Prog. Accred.: Allied Health (speech-language pathology), Business (ACBSP), Music, Nursing, Social Work, Teacher Education (NCATE)

Eastern New Mexico University—Roswell
PO Box 6000, Roswell 88202
Type: Public, state, two-year
System: New Mexico Commission on Higher Education
Degrees: A *Enroll:* 2,478
URL: http://www.roswell.enmu.edu
Phone: (505) 624-7000 *Calendar:* Sem. plan
Inst. Accred.: NCA-HLC (1971/2007)
Prog. Accred.: Allied Health (EMT-paramedic, medical assisting (AMA), occupational therapy assisting, respiratory therapy), Nursing

Institute of American Indian and Alaskan Native Culture and Arts Development
83 Avon Rd., Santa Fe 87504
Type: Public, federal, four-year
System: American Indian Higher Education Consortium
Degrees: A, B *Enroll:* 95
URL: http://www.iaia.edu/college
Phone: (505) 424-2300 *Calendar:* Sem. plan
Inst. Accred.: NCA-HLC (1984/2004)
Prog. Accred.: Art

Luna Community College
366 Luna Dr., Las Vegas 87701
Type: Public, state/local, two-year
System: New Mexico Commission on Higher Education
Degrees: A *Enroll:* 997
URL: http://www.luna.edu
Phone: (505) 454-2500 *Calendar:* Sem. plan
Inst. Accred.: NCA-HLC (1982/2005)

Mesalands Community College
911 South 10th St., Tucumcari 88401
Type: Public, state, two-year
Degrees: A *Enroll:* 334
URL: http://www.mesalands.edu
Phone: (505) 461-4413 *Calendar:* Sem. plan
Inst. Accred.: NCA-HLC (1999/2004)

National College of Midwifery
#209 State Rd. 240, Taos 87571
Type: Private, independent, four-year
Degrees: A, B, M, D
URL: http://www.midwiferycollege.org
Phone: (505) 758-8914 *Calendar:* Sem. plan
Inst. Accred.: MEAC (2001/2004)

Navajo Technical College
PO Box 849, Crownpoint 87313
Type: Private, tribal, two-year
System: American Indian Higher Education Consortium
Degrees: A
URL: http://navajotech.edu
Phone: (505) 786-4100 *Calendar:* Sem. plan
Inst. Accred.: NCA-HLC (2005)

New Mexico Highlands University
PO Box 9000, Las Vegas 87701
Type: Public, state, four-year
System: New Mexico Commission on Higher Education
Degrees: A, B, M *Enroll:* 2,499
URL: http://www.nmhu.edu
Phone: (877) 850-9064 *Calendar:* Sem. plan
Inst. Accred.: NCA-HLC (1926/2001)
Prog. Accred.: Business (ACBSP), Graduate Social Work, Rehabilitation Counseling, Social Work

New Mexico Institute of Mining and Technology
801 Leroy Place, Socorro 87801
Type: Public, state, four-year
System: New Mexico Commission on Higher Education
Degrees: A, B, M, D *Enroll:* 1,584
URL: http://www.nmt.edu
Phone: (505) 835-5600 *Calendar:* Sem. plan
Inst. Accred.: NCA-HLC (1949/2005)
Prog. Accred.: Engineering (chemical, electrical, environmental/sanitary, materials, mechanical, mineral, petroleum)

New Mexico Junior College
5317 Lovington Hwy., Hobbs 88240
Type: Public, state/local, two-year
System: New Mexico Commission on Higher Education
Degrees: A *Enroll:* 1,592
URL: http://www.nmjc.edu
Phone: (505) 392-4510 *Calendar:* Sem. plan
Inst. Accred.: NCA-HLC (1970/2006)
Prog. Accred.: Nursing

New Mexico Military Institute
101 West College Blvd., Roswell 88201
Type: Public, state, two-year
System: New Mexico Commission on Higher Education
Degrees: A *Enroll:* 470
URL: http://www.nmmi.edu
Phone: (505) 622-6250 *Calendar:* Sem. plan
Inst. Accred.: NCA-HLC (1938/2001)

New Mexico State University
PO Box 30001, Las Cruces 88003-8001
Type: Public, state, four-year
System: New Mexico Commission on Higher Education
Degrees: A, B, M, P, D *Enroll:* 13,526
URL: http://www.nmsu.edu
Phone: (505) 646-2035 *Calendar:* Sem. plan
Inst. Accred.: NCA-HLC (1926/2008)
Prog. Accred.: Accounting, Allied Health (EMT-paramedic, diagnostic medical sonography, respiratory therapy, speech-language pathology), Applied Science (surveying/geomatics), Business (AACSB), Counseling, Counseling Psychology, Engineering (chemical, civil, electrical, industrial, mechanical), Engineering Technology (civil/construction, electrical, mechanical), Graduate Social Work, Journalism, Music, Nursing Education, Public Administration, Public Health, Social Work, Teacher Education (NCATE)

Doña Ana Branch Community College
Box 30001, 3400 South Epina St., Las Cruces 88003
Phone: (505) 527-7500
Prog. Accred: Allied Health (EMT-paramedic, diagnostic medical sonography, respiratory therapy), Business (ACBSP), Nursing, Radiography

Grants Campus
1500 North Third St., Grants 87020
Phone: (505) 287-6678

New Mexico State University at Alamogordo
2400 North Scenic Dr., Alamogordo 88310
Type: Public, state, two-year
Degrees: A *Enroll:* 1,117
URL: http://alamo.nmsu.edu
Phone: (505) 439-3600 *Calendar:* Sem. plan
Inst. Accred.: NCA-HLC (1973/2003)
Prog. Accred.: Clinical Lab Technology, Nursing

New Mexico State University at Carlsbad
1500 University Dr., Carlsbad 88220
Type: Public, state, two-year
Degrees: A *Enroll:* 833
URL: http://cavern.nmsu.edu
Phone: (505) 234-9200 *Calendar:* Sem. plan
Inst. Accred.: NCA-HLC (1980/2008)
Prog. Accred.: Nursing

Northern New Mexico College
921 Paseo de Onate, Espanola 87532
Type: Public, state/local, four-year
System: New Mexico Commission on Higher Education
Degrees: A, B *Enroll:* 1,329
URL: http://nnmcc.edu
Phone: (505) 747-2100 *Calendar:* Sem. plan
Inst. Accred.: NCA-HLC (1982/2004)
Prog. Accred.: Business (ACBSP), Radiography

Saint John's College
1160 Camino Cruz Blanca, Santa Fe 87505-4599
Type: Private, independent, four-year
Degrees: B, M *Enroll:* 527
URL: http://www.sjcsf.edu
Phone: (505) 984-6000 *Calendar:* Sem. plan
Inst. Accred.: NCA-HLC (1969/1999)

San Juan College
4601 College Blvd., Farmington 87402
Type: Public, local, two-year
System: New Mexico Commission on Higher Education
Degrees: A *Enroll:* 3,431
URL: http://www.sanjuancollege.edu
Phone: (505) 326-3311 *Calendar:* Sem. plan
Inst. Accred.: NCA-HLC (1973/2007)
Prog. Accred.: Business (ACBSP), Dentistry (dental assisting, dental hygiene), Engineering Technology (mechanical drafting/design), Nursing, Physical Therapy Assisting, Veterinary Technology

Santa Fe Community College
6401 Richards Ave., Santa Fe 87508
Type: Public, state, two-year
System: New Mexico Commission on Higher Education
Degrees: A *Enroll:* 1,955
URL: http://www.sfccnm.edu
Phone: (505) 428-1000 *Calendar:* Sem. plan
Inst. Accred.: NCA-HLC (1988/2003)
Prog. Accred.: Dentistry (dental assisting), Nursing

Southwest Acupuncture College
2960 Rodeo Park Dr. West, Santa Fe 87505
Type: Private, proprietary, four-year
Degrees: M *Enroll:* 81
URL: http://www.acupuncturecollege.edu
Phone: (505) 438-8884 *Calendar:* Tri. plan
Inst. Accred.: ACAOM (1989/2004)

Albuquerque Campus
7801 Academy Rd., NE, North Towne Bldg., Ste. 1, Albuquerque 87109-3191
Phone: (505) 888-8898
Prog. Accred: Acupuncture

Boulder Campus
6658 Gunpark Dr., Boulder, CO 80301
Phone: (303) 581-9955
Prog. Accred: Acupuncture

Southwestern College
PO Box 4788, Santa Fe 87502
Type: Private, independent, four-year
Degrees: M *Enroll:* 105
URL: http://www.swc.edu
Phone: (505) 471-5756 *Calendar:* Qtr. plan
Inst. Accred.: NCA-HLC (1996/2001)

Southwestern Indian Polytechnic Institute
9169 Coors Rd., NW, Box 10146, Albuquerque 87184
Type: Public, tribal, two-year
System: American Indian Higher Education Consortium
Degrees: A *Enroll:* 516
URL: http://www.sipi.bia.edu
Phone: (505) 346-4766 *Calendar:* Tri. plan
Inst. Accred.: NCA-HLC (1975/2000)
Prog. Accred.: Allied Health (opticianry), Business (ACBSP)

The University of New Mexico
One University of New Mexico, Albuquerque 87131-1001
Type: Public, state, four-year
System: New Mexico Commission on Higher Education
Degrees: A, B, M, P, D *Enroll:* 21,191
URL: http://www.unm.edu
Phone: (505) 277-0111 *Calendar:* Sem. plan
Inst. Accred.: NCA-HLC (1922/1999)
Prog. Accred.: Accounting, Allied Health (EMT-paramedic, audiology, medicine, occupational therapy, speech-language pathology), Business (AACSB), Clinical Lab Scientist, Clinical Psychology, Computer Science (ABET-CAC), Construction Education, Counseling, Dance, Dentistry (dental hygiene, general dentistry), Dietetics (didactic), Dietetics (internship), Engineering (chemical, civil, computer, construction, electrical, mechanical, nuclear), Landscape Architecture, Law, Music, Nurse (Midwifery), Nursing Education, Pharmacy, Physical Therapy, Physician Assistant, Planning, Psychology Internship, Public Administration, Public Health, Radiography, Teacher Education (NCATE), Theatre

Gallup Campus
200 College Rd., Gallup 87301
Phone: (505) 843-7783
Prog. Accred: Clinical Lab Technology, Dentistry (dental assisting), Nursing

Los Alamos Campus
4000 University Dr., Los Alamos 87544
Phone: (505) 867-2379

Taos Education Center Campus
115 Civic Plaza Dr., Taos 87571
Phone: (505) 758-7667

Valencia Campus
280 La Entrada, Los Lunas 87031
Phone: (505) 865-1639

University of the Southwest
6610 Lovington Hwy., Hobbs 88240
Type: Private, independent, four-year
Degrees: B, M *Enroll:* 513
URL: http://www.csw.edu
Phone: (505) 392-6561 *Calendar:* Sem. plan
Inst. Accred.: NCA-HLC (1980/2007)

Western New Mexico University
PO Box 680, 1000 West College Ave., Silver City 88062
Type: Public, state, four-year
System: New Mexico Commission on Higher Education
Degrees: A, B, M *Enroll:* 1,916
URL: http://www.wnmu.edu
Phone: (800) 222-9668 *Calendar:* Sem. plan
Inst. Accred.: NCA-HLC (1926/2007)
Prog. Accred.: Allied Health (occupational therapy assisting), Business (ACBSP), Nursing, Social Work, Teacher Education (NCATE)

NEW YORK

Adelphi University
1 South Ave., Garden City 11530
Type: Private, independent, four-year
Degrees: A, B, M, D *Enroll:* 6,029
URL: http://www.adelphi.edu
Phone: (516) 877-3000 *Calendar:* Sem. plan
Inst. Accred.: MSA-CHE (1921/2004)
Prog. Accred.: Allied Health (audiology, speech-language pathology), Business (AACSB), Clinical Psychology, Graduate Social Work, Nursing Education, Social Work, Teacher Education (NCATE)

Adirondack Community College
640 Bay Rd., Queensbury 12804
Type: Public, state/local, two-year
System: State University of New York Office of Community Colleges
Degrees: A *Enroll:* 2,511
URL: http://www.sunyacc.edu
Phone: (518) 743-2200 *Calendar:* Sem. plan
Inst. Accred.: MSA-CHE (1972/2003, Warning)
Prog. Accred.: Nursing

Albany College of Pharmacy of Union University
106 New Scotland Ave., Albany 12208
Type: Private, independent, four-year
System: Union University
Degrees: B, M, P *Enroll:* 1,145
URL: http://www.acp.edu
Phone: (518) 445-7200 *Calendar:* Sem. plan
Inst. Accred.: MSA-CHE (1921/2004)
Prog. Accred.: Allied Health (cytotechnology), Pharmacy

Albany Law School
80 New Scotland Ave., Albany 12208
Type: Private, independent, four-year
System: Union University
Degrees: M, P, D *Enroll:* 735
URL: http://www.als.edu
Phone: (518) 445-2311 *Calendar:* Sem. plan
Inst. Accred.: ABA (1930/2000)

Albany Medical College
47 New Scotland Ave., Albany 12208
Type: Private, independent, four-year
System: Union University
Degrees: M, P, D *Enroll:* 731
URL: http://www.amc.edu
Phone: (518) 262-6008
Inst. Accred.: MSA-CHE (1921/2005)
Prog. Accred.: Allied Health (medicine), Dentistry (general practice residency), Nurse Anesthesia Education, Physician Assistant, Psychology Internship

Alfred University
One Saxon Dr., Alfred 14802-1205
Type: Private, independent, four-year
System: State University of New York System Office
Degrees: B, M, D *Enroll:* 2,113
URL: http://www.alfred.edu
Phone: (607) 871-2115 *Calendar:* Sem. plan
Inst. Accred.: MSA-CHE (1921/2004)
Prog. Accred.: Business (AACSB), Engineering (ceramic, electrical, materials, mechanical, optical/optics)

New York State College of Ceramics at Alfred University
2 Pine St., Alfred 14802-1296
Phone: (607) 871-2411
Prog. Accred: Art

Alliance Theological Seminary
350 North Highland Ave., Nyack 10960-1416
Type: Private, Christian and Missionary Alliance, four-year
Degrees: M
URL: http://www.nyackcollege.edu/?page=ATSHome
Phone: (845) 353-2020 *Calendar:* Sem. plan
Inst. Accred.: ATS (1990/2000)

American Academy McAllister Institute of Funeral Service, Inc.
619 West 54th St., New York 10019
Type: Private, independent, two-year
Degrees: A *Enroll:* 101
URL: http://www.funeraleducation.org
Phone: (212) 757-1190 *Calendar:* Sem. plan
Inst. Accred.: ABFSE (1964/2006)

American Academy of Dramatic Arts
120 Madison Ave., New York 10016
Type: Private, independent, two-year
Degrees: A *Enroll:* 220
URL: http://www.aada.org
Phone: (212) 686-9244
Inst. Accred.: MSA-CHE (1983/2005), NYBOR (1972/2001)
Prog. Accred.: Theatre

The Art Institute of New York City
75 Varick St., 16th Flr., New York 10013-1917
Type: Private, proprietary, two-year
System: Education Management Corporation
Degrees: A
URL: http://www.ainyc.artinstitutes.edu
Phone: (212) 226-5500 *Calendar:* Sem. plan
Inst. Accred.: ACICS (1999/2008)
Prog. Accred.: Culinary Education

ASA, The College for Excellence
151 Lawrence St., 2nd Flr., Brooklyn 11201
Type: Private, independent, two-year
Degrees: A
URL: http://www.asa.edu
Phone: (718) 522-9073
Inst. Accred.: ACICS (1992/2005), WASC-SR. (2005)
Prog. Accred.: Allied Health (medical assisting (AMA))

Bank Street College of Education
610 West 112th St., New York 10025
Type: Private, independent, four-year
Degrees: M *Enroll:* 675
URL: http://www.bankstreet.edu
Phone: (212) 875-4400 *Calendar:* Sem. plan
Inst. Accred.: MSA-CHE (1960/2005)

Bard College
PO Box 5000, Annandale-on-Hudson 12504-5000
Type: Private, independent, four-year
Degrees: A, B, M, D *Enroll:* 2,049
URL: http://www.bard.edu
Phone: (845) 758-6822 *Calendar:* Sem. plan
Inst. Accred.: MSA-CHE (1922/2007)

Barnard College
3009 Broadway, New York 10027-6598
Type: Private, independent, four-year
Degrees: B *Enroll:* 2,320
URL: http://www.barnard.edu
Phone: (212) 854-5262 *Calendar:* Sem. plan
Inst. Accred.: MSA-CHE (1921/2001)
Prog. Accred.: Dance

Baruch College
One Bernard Baruch Way, New York 10010
Type: Public, state/local, four-year
System: City University of New York System
Degrees: B, M *Enroll:* 12,583
URL: http://www.baruch.cuny.edu
Phone: (646) 312-1000 *Calendar:* Sem. plan
Inst. Accred.: MSA-CHE (1968/2005)
Prog. Accred.: Accounting, Allied Health (health services administration), Business (AACSB), Public Administration

Berkeley College of New York City
3 East 43rd St., New York 10017
Type: Private, proprietary, four-year
System: Berkeley College of New York and New Jersey
Degrees: A, B *Enroll:* 2,792
URL: http://www.berkeleycollege.edu
Phone: (212) 986-4343 *Calendar:* Qtr. plan
Inst. Accred.: MSA-CHE (1993/2008)

Westchester Campus
99 Church St., White Plains 10601
Phone: (914) 694-1122

Beth HaMedrash Shaarei Yosher
4102 16th Ave., Brooklyn 11204
Type: Private, independent, four-year
Degrees: Talmudic *Enroll:* 82
Phone: (718) 854-2290 *Calendar:* Sem. plan
Inst. Accred.: AARTS (1982/2001)

Beth HaTalmud Rabbinical College
2127 82nd St., Brooklyn 11214
Type: Private, independent, four-year
Degrees: Talmudic *Enroll:* 83
Phone: (718) 259-2525 *Calendar:* Sem. plan
Inst. Accred.: AARTS (1978/2002)

Boricua College
3755 Broadway, New York 10032
Type: Private, independent, four-year
Degrees: A, B, M *Enroll:* 1,142
URL: http://www.boricuacollege.edu
Phone: (212) 694-1000 *Calendar:* Sem. plan
Inst. Accred.: MSA-CHE (1980/2004)

Bramson ORT College
69-30 Austin St., Forest Hills 11375-4222
Type: Private, independent, two-year
Degrees: A *Enroll:* 507
URL: http://www.bramsonort.org
Phone: (716) 261-5800 *Calendar:* Sem. plan
Inst. Accred.: NYBOR (1979/2002)

Bensonhurst Campus
5815 20th Ave., Brooklyn 11230
Phone: (718) 259-5800

Briarcliffe College
1055 Stewart Ave., Bethpage 11714-3545
Type: Private, proprietary, four-year
System: Career Education Corporation
Degrees: A, B *Enroll:* 2,230
URL: http://www.bcl.edu
Phone: (516) 918-3600 *Calendar:* Sem. plan
Inst. Accred.: MSA-CHE (1996/2001)

Patchogue Campus
10 Lake St., Patchogue 11772
Phone: (516) 654-5300

Brooklyn Law School
250 Joralemon St., Brooklyn 11201
Type: Private, independent, four-year
Degrees: P *Enroll:* 1,328
URL: http://www.brooklaw.edu
Phone: (718) 625-2200 *Calendar:* Sem. plan
Inst. Accred.: ABA (1937/2003)

Bryant & Stratton College—Albany
1259 Central Ave., Albany 12205-5230
Type: Private, proprietary, four-year
System: Bryant & Stratton College System Office
Degrees: A, B *Enroll:* 400
URL: http://www.bryantstratton.edu
Phone: (518) 437-1802 *Calendar:* Sem. plan
Inst. Accred.: MSA-CHE (2002/2007, *Indirect accreditation through Bryant & Stratton College System Office, Getzville, NY*)
Prog. Accred.: Allied Health (medical assisting (AMA))

Bryant & Stratton College—Buffalo
465 Main St., Ste. 400, Buffalo 14203-1795
Type: Private, proprietary, four-year
System: Bryant & Stratton College System Office
Degrees: A, B *Enroll:* 538
URL: http://www.bryantstratton.edu
Phone: (716) 884-9120 *Calendar:* Sem. plan
Inst. Accred.: MSA-CHE (2002/2007, *Indirect accreditation through Bryant & Stratton College System Office, Getzville, NY*)
Prog. Accred.: Allied Health (medical assisting (AMA))

Amherst Campus
Audubon Bus. Ctr., 40 Hazelwood Dr., Amherst 14228
Phone: (716) 691-0012

Southtowns Campus
Sterling Park, 200 Red Tail, Orchard Park 14127-1562
Phone: (716) 677-9500

Bryant & Stratton College—Greece
150 Bellwood Dr., Rochester 14606
Type: Private, proprietary, two-year
System: Bryant & Stratton College—Buffalo
Degrees: A *Enroll:* 169
URL: http://www.bryantstratton.edu
Phone: (585) 720-0660 *Calendar:* Sem. plan
Inst. Accred.: MSA-CHE (2002/2007, *Indirect accreditation through Bryant & Stratton College System Office, Getzville, NY*)

Henrietta Campus
1225 Jefferson Rd., Rochester 14623-5627
Phone: (585) 292-5627
Prog. Accred: Allied Health (medical assisting (AMA))

Bryant & Stratton College—Syracuse
953 James St., Syracuse 13203-2502
Type: Private, proprietary, four-year
System: Bryant & Stratton College System Office
Degrees: A, B *Enroll:* 550
URL: http://www.bryantstratton.edu
Phone: (315) 472-6603 *Calendar:* Sem. plan
Inst. Accred.: MSA-CHE (2002/2007, *Indirect accreditation through Bryant & Stratton College System Office, Getzville, NY*)
Prog. Accred.: Allied Health (medical assisting (AMA))

Syracuse North Campus
8687 Carling Rd., Liverpool 13090-1315
Phone: (315) 652-6500

Canisius College
2001 Main St., Buffalo 14208-1908
Type: Private, independent, four-year
Degrees: A, B, M *Enroll:* 4,378
URL: http://www.canisius.edu
Phone: (716) 883-7000 *Calendar:* Sem. plan
Inst. Accred.: MSA-CHE (1921/2005)
Prog. Accred.: Business (AACSB), Teacher Education (NCATE)

Cayuga County Community College
197 Franklin St., Auburn 13021-3099
Type: Public, state/local, two-year
System: State University of New York Office of Community Colleges
Degrees: A *Enroll:* 2,694
URL: http://www.cayuga-cc.edu
Phone: (315) 255-1743 *Calendar:* Sem. plan
Inst. Accred.: MSA-CHE (1965/2006)
Prog. Accred.: Nursing

Cazenovia College
22 Sullivan St., Cazenovia 13035-1084
Type: Private, independent, four-year
Degrees: A, B *Enroll:* 896
URL: http://www.cazenovia.edu
Phone: (800) 654-3210 *Calendar:* Sem. plan
Inst. Accred.: MSA-CHE (1961/2003)

Central Yeshiva Tomchei Tmimim-Lubavitch
841-853 Ocean Pkwy., Brooklyn 11230
Type: Private, independent, four-year
Degrees: Rabbinic, Talmudic *Enroll:* 581
Phone: (718) 434-0784 *Calendar:* Sem. plan
Inst. Accred.: AARTS (1976/2005)

Christ the King Seminary
711 Knox Rd., PO Box 607, East Aurora 14052-0607
Type: Private, Roman Catholic Church, four-year
Degrees: M, P *Enroll:* 47
URL: http://www.cks.edu
Phone: (716) 652-8900 *Calendar:* Sem. plan
Inst. Accred.: ATS (1977/2002), MSA-CHE (1974/2003)

Christie's Education
11 West 42nd St., 8th Flr., New York 10036
Type: Public, proprietary, four-year
Degrees: M
URL: http://www.christies.com/education
Phone: (212) 355-1501
Inst. Accred.: NYBOR (2007)

City University of New York
Borough of Manhattan Community College
199 Chambers St., New York 10007
Type: Public, state/local, two-year
System: City University of New York System
Degrees: A *Enroll:* 13,484
URL: http://www.bmcc.cuny.edu
Phone: (212) 220-8000 *Calendar:* Sem. plan
Inst. Accred.: MSA-CHE (1964/2008)
Prog. Accred.: Allied Health (EMT-paramedic, respiratory therapy), Nursing

City University of New York
Bronx Community College
West 181st St. and University Ave., Bronx 10453
Type: Public, state/local, two-year
System: City University of New York System
Degrees: A *Enroll:* 6,223
URL: http://www.bcc.cuny.edu
Phone: (718) 289-5100 *Calendar:* Sem. plan
Inst. Accred.: MSA-CHE (1961/2004)
Prog. Accred.: Business (ACBSP), Engineering Technology (electrical), Nuclear Medicine Technology, Nursing, Radiography

City University of New York Brooklyn College
2900 Bedford Ave., Brooklyn 11210-2889
Type: Public, state/local, four-year
System: City University of New York System
Degrees: B, M *Enroll:* 11,098
URL: http://www.brooklyn.cuny.edu
Phone: (718) 951-5000 *Calendar:* Sem. plan
Inst. Accred.: MSA-CHE (1933/2004)
Prog. Accred.: Allied Health (audiology, speech-language pathology), Dietetics (didactic), Dietetics (internship), Public Health, Teacher Education (NCATE)

City University of New York City College
160 Convent Ave., New York 10031
Type: Public, state/local, four-year
System: City University of New York System
Degrees: B, M *Enroll:* 9,023
URL: http://csauth.ccny.cuny.edu
Phone: (212) 650-7000 *Calendar:* Sem. plan
Inst. Accred.: MSA-CHE (1921/2008)
Prog. Accred.: Clinical Psychology, Computer Science (ABET-CAC), Engineering (chemical, civil, computer, electrical, mechanical), Landscape Architecture, Physician Assistant, Teacher Education (NCATE)

City University of New York
College of Staten Island
2800 Victory Blvd., Staten Island 10314
Type: Public, state/local, four-year
System: City University of New York System
Degrees: A, B, M *Enroll:* 9,240
URL: http://www.csi.cuny.edu
Phone: (718) 982-2000 *Calendar:* Sem. plan
Inst. Accred.: MSA-CHE (1963/2001)
Prog. Accred.: Computer Science (ABET-CAC), Engineering (engineering physics/science), Engineering Technology (electrical), Nursing, Physical Therapy, Teacher Education (NCATE)

City University of New York Graduate Center
365 5th Ave., New York 10016-4309
Type: Public, state/local, four-year
System: City University of New York System
Degrees: M, D *Enroll:* 4,055
URL: http://www.gc.cuny.edu
Phone: (212) 817-7000 *Calendar:* Sem. plan
Inst. Accred.: MSA-CHE (1961/2005)
Prog. Accred.: School Psychology

City University of New York
Hostos Community College
500 Grand Concourse, Bronx 10451-5323
Type: Public, state/local, two-year
System: City University of New York System
Degrees: A *Enroll:* 3,334
URL: http://www.hostos.cuny.edu
Phone: (718) 518-4444 *Calendar:* Sem. plan
Inst. Accred.: MSA-CHE (1974/2007)
Prog. Accred.: Dentistry (dental hygiene), Radiography

City University of New York Hunter College
695 Park Ave., New York 10021-5085
Type: Public, state/local, four-year
System: City University of New York System
Degrees: B, M *Enroll:* 15,045
URL: http://www.hunter.cuny.edu
Phone: (212) 772-4000 *Calendar:* Sem. plan
Inst. Accred.: MSA-CHE (1921/2004)
Prog. Accred.: Allied Health (audiology, speech-language pathology), Applied Science (occupational health & safety), Dietetics (didactic), Dietetics (internship), Graduate Social Work, Nursing Education, Physical Therapy, Planning, Public Health, Rehabilitation Counseling, Teacher Education (NCATE)

City University of New York
John Jay College of Criminal Justice
899 10th Ave., New York 10019
Type: Public, state/local, four-year
System: City University of New York System
Degrees: A, B, M *Enroll:* 11,518
URL: http://www.jjay.cuny.edu
Phone: (212) 237-8800 *Calendar:* Sem. plan
Inst. Accred.: MSA-CHE (1965/2003)
Prog. Accred.: Public Administration

City University of New York Kingsborough Community College
2001 Oriental Blvd., Brooklyn 11235
Type: Public, state/local, two-year
System: City University of New York System
Degrees: A *Enroll:* 10,418
URL: http://www.kbcc.cuny.edu
Phone: (718) 368-5000 *Calendar:* Sem. plan
Inst. Accred.: MSA-CHE (1964/2006)
Prog. Accred.: Nursing, Physical Therapy Assisting

City University of New York LaGuardia Community College
31-10 Thomson Ave., Long Island City 11101-3083
Type: Public, state/local, two-year
System: City University of New York System
Degrees: A *Enroll:* 9,480
URL: http://www.lagcc.cuny.edu
Phone: (718) 482-7200 *Calendar:* Sem. plan
Inst. Accred.: MSA-CHE (1974/2007)
Prog. Accred.: Allied Health (occupational therapy assisting), Dietetic Technician, Nursing, Physical Therapy Assisting, Veterinary Technology

City University of New York Medgar Evers College
1650 Bedford Ave., Brooklyn 11225-2010
Type: Public, state/local, four-year
System: City University of New York System
Degrees: A, B *Enroll:* 3,972
URL: http://www.mec.cuny.edu
Phone: (718) 270-4900 *Calendar:* Sem. plan
Inst. Accred.: MSA-CHE (1976/2007)
Prog. Accred.: Business (ACBSP), Nursing, Teacher Education (NCATE)

City University of New York New York City College of Technology
300 Jay St., Brooklyn 11201-1909
Type: Public, state/local, four-year
System: City University of New York System
Degrees: A, B *Enroll:* 9,258
URL: http://www.citytech.cuny.edu
Phone: (718) 260-5000 *Calendar:* Sem. plan
Inst. Accred.: MSA-CHE (1957/2008)
Prog. Accred.: Allied Health (ophthalmic lab technology, opticianry), Construction Education, Dentistry (dental hygiene, dental laboratory technology), Engineering Technology (civil/construction, computer, electrical, electromechanical, mechanical, telecommunications), Nursing, Radiography, Teacher Education (NCATE)

City University of New York Queens College
65-30 Kissena Blvd., Flushing 11367-1597
Type: Public, state/local, four-year
System: City University of New York System
Degrees: B, M, P *Enroll:* 12,418
URL: http://www.qc.cuny.edu
Phone: (718) 997-5000 *Calendar:* Sem. plan
Inst. Accred.: MSA-CHE (1941/2007)
Prog. Accred.: Allied Health (speech-language pathology), Dietetics (didactic), Dietetics (internship), Family & Consumer Science, Law (ABA only), Librarianship, Teacher Education (NCATE)

City University of New York Queensborough Community College
222-05 56th Ave., Bayside 11364-1497
Type: Public, state/local, two-year
System: City University of New York System
Degrees: A *Enroll:* 8,506
URL: http://www.qcc.cuny.edu
Phone: (718) 631-6262 *Calendar:* Sem. plan
Inst. Accred.: MSA-CHE (1963/2004)
Prog. Accred.: Business (ACBSP), Engineering Technology (computer, electrical, mechanical, optical/optics), Nursing

City University of New York York College
94-20 Guy R. Brewer Blvd., Jamaica 11451-0001
Type: Public, state/local, four-year
System: City University of New York System
Degrees: B, M *Enroll:* 4,694
URL: http://www.york.cuny.edu
Phone: (718) 262-2000 *Calendar:* Sem. plan
Inst. Accred.: MSA-CHE (1967/2008)
Prog. Accred.: Allied Health (occupational therapy), Nursing, Social Work, Teacher Education (NCATE)

Clarkson University
8 Clarkson Ave., Potsdam 13676-1401
Type: Private, independent, four-year
Degrees: B, M, P, D *Enroll:* 3,013
URL: http://www.clarkson.edu
Phone: (315) 268-6400 *Calendar:* Sem. plan
Inst. Accred.: MSA-CHE (1927/2003)
Prog. Accred.: Business (AACSB), Engineering (aerospace, chemical, civil, computer, electrical, mechanical, software), Physical Therapy

Clinton Community College
136 Clinton Point Dr., Plattsburgh 12901-9573
Type: Public, state/local, two-year
System: State University of New York Office of Community Colleges
Degrees: A *Enroll:* 1,621
URL: http://clintoncc.suny.edu
Phone: (518) 562-4200 *Calendar:* Sem. plan
Inst. Accred.: MSA-CHE (1975/2007)
Prog. Accred.: Nursing

Cold Spring Harbor Laboratory
PO Box 100, One Bungtown Rd., Cold Spring Harbor 11724-0100
Type: Private, independent, four-year
Degrees: D
URL: http://www.cshl.edu
Phone: (516) 367-8397
Inst. Accred.: NYBOR (1998/2001)

Colgate Rochester Crozer Divinity School
1100 South Goodman St., Rochester 14620
Type: Private, American Baptist Church (USA), four-year
Degrees: M, D *Enroll:* 70
URL: http://www.crcds.edu
Phone: (585) 271-1320 *Calendar:* Sem. plan
Inst. Accred.: ATS (1938/2007)

Colgate University
13 Oak Dr., Hamilton 13346-1366
Type: Private, independent, four-year
Degrees: B, M *Enroll:* 2,762
URL: http://www.colgate.edu
Phone: (315) 228-1000 *Calendar:* Sem. plan
Inst. Accred.: MSA-CHE (1921/2008)

College of Mount Saint Vincent
6301 Riverdale Ave., Riverdale 10471
Type: Private, independent, four-year
Degrees: A, B, M *Enroll:* 1,498
URL: http://www.mountsaintvincent.edu
Phone: (718) 405-3200 *Calendar:* Sem. plan
Inst. Accred.: MSA-CHE (1921/2007)
Prog. Accred.: Business (ACBSP), Nursing Education, Teacher Education (TEAC)

The College of New Rochelle
29 Castle Place, New Rochelle 10805-2339
Type: Private, independent, four-year
Degrees: B, M *Enroll:* 5,648
URL: http://www.cnr.edu
Phone: (914) 632-5300 *Calendar:* Sem. plan
Inst. Accred.: MSA-CHE (1921/2007)
Prog. Accred.: Nursing Education, Social Work

Brooklyn Campus
1368 Fulton St., Brooklyn 11216
Phone: (718) 638-2500

Co-Op City Campus
755 Co-Op City Blvd., Bronx 10475
Phone: (718) 320-0300

DC 37 Campus
125 Barclay St., New York 10007
Phone: (212) 815-1710

John Cardinal O'Connor Campus
332 East 149th St., Bronx 10451
Phone: (718) 665-1310

Rosa Parks Campus
144 West 125th St., New York 10024
Phone: (212) 662-7500

The College of Saint Rose
432 Western Ave., Albany 12203-1490
Type: Private, independent, four-year
Degrees: B, M *Enroll:* 4,292
URL: http://www.strose.edu
Phone: (518) 454-5111 *Calendar:* Sem. plan
Inst. Accred.: MSA-CHE (1928/2004)
Prog. Accred.: Allied Health (speech-language pathology), Art, Business (ACBSP), Music, Social Work, Teacher Education (NCATE)

The College of Westchester
PO Box 710, 325 Central Park Ave., White Plains 10602
Type: Private, independent, four-year
Degrees: A, B *Enroll:* 912
URL: http://www.cw.edu
Phone: (914) 948-4442 *Calendar:* Qtr. plan
Inst. Accred.: MSA-CHE (2008)

Columbia University in the City of New York
2960 Broadway, New York 10027-6902
Type: Private, independent, four-year
Degrees: B, M, P, D *Enroll:* 20,091
URL: http://www.columbia.edu
Phone: (212) 854-1754 *Calendar:* Sem. plan
Inst. Accred.: MSA-CHE (1921/2006)
Prog. Accred.: Allied Health (medicine, occupational therapy), Business (AACSB), Dentistry (advanced education in general dentistry, combined prosthodontics, dental assisting, dentistry, endodontics, general dentistry, maxillofacial prosthetics, orthodontic and dentofacial orthopedics, pediatric dentistry, periodontics), Engineering (chemical, civil, electrical, environmental/sanitary, industrial, mechanical), Graduate Social Work, Journalism, Law, Nurse (Midwifery), Nurse Anesthesia Education, Nursing Education, Physical Therapy, Planning, Public Health

Columbia-Greene Community College
4400 Route 23, Hudson 12534-9447
Type: Public, state, two-year
System: State University of New York Office of Community Colleges
Degrees: A *Enroll:* 1,218
URL: http://www.sunycgcc.edu
Phone: (518) 828-4181 *Calendar:* Sem. plan
Inst. Accred.: MSA-CHE (1975/2001)
Prog. Accred.: Nursing

Concordia College New York
171 White Plains Rd., Bronxville 10708-1998
Type: Private, Lutheran Church-Missouri Synod, four-year
System: Concordia University System
Degrees: A, B *Enroll:* 614
URL: http://www.concordia-ny.edu
Phone: (914) 337-9300 *Calendar:* Sem. plan
Inst. Accred.: MSA-CHE (1941/2004)
Prog. Accred.: Social Work, Teacher Education (NCATE)

The Cooper Union for the Advancement of Science and Art
30 Cooper Square, New York 10003
Type: Private, independent, four-year
Degrees: B, M *Enroll:* 990
URL: http://www.cooper.edu
Phone: (212) 353-4100 *Calendar:* Sem. plan
Inst. Accred.: MSA-CHE (1946/2008)
Prog. Accred.: Art, Engineering (chemical, civil, electrical, mechanical)

Cornell University
Ithaca 14853
Type: Private, independent, four-year
Degrees: B, M, P, D *Enroll:* 19,616
URL: http://www.cornell.edu
Phone: (607) 255-2000 *Calendar:* Sem. plan
Inst. Accred.: MSA-CHE (1921/2001)
Prog. Accred.: Allied Health (health services administration, medicine), Business (AACSB), Dietetics (didactic), Dietetics (internship), Engineering (bioengineering, chemical, civil, electrical, materials, mechanical), Interior Design, Landscape Architecture, Law, Physician Assistant, Planning, Veterinary Medicine

College of Agriculture and Life Sciences
260 Roberts Hall, Ithaca 14853
Phone: (607) 255-2036

New York State College of Human Ecology
Ithaca 14853-4401
Phone: (607) 255-2138

New York State College of Veterinary Medicine
Ithaca 14853-6401
Phone: (607) 253-3700

New York State School of Industrial and Labor Relations
Ithaca 14853-1296
Phone: (607) 255-2222

Weill Cornell Campus
1300 York Ave., New York 10021-4805
Phone: (914) 682-9100
Prog. Accred: Clinical Pastoral Education, Dentistry (general practice residency, oral and maxillofacial surgery)

Corning Community College
1 Academic Dr., Corning 14830
Type: Public, state/local, two-year
System: State University of New York Office of Community Colleges
Degrees: A *Enroll:* 3,535
URL: http://www.corning-cc.edu
Phone: (607) 962-9222 *Calendar:* Sem. plan
Inst. Accred.: MSA-CHE (1964/2005)
Prog. Accred.: Nursing

Culinary Institute of America
1946 Campus Dr., Hyde Park 12538-1499
Type: Private, independent, four-year
Degrees: A, B *Enroll:* 2,757
URL: http://www.ciachef.edu
Phone: (845) 452-9600
Inst. Accred.: ACCSCT (1983/2004), MSA-CHE (2002/2007)

Center for Foods of the Americas
312 Pearl Pkwy., Building C, San Antonio, TX 78215
Phone: (866) 757-2433

Greystone Campus
2555 Main St., St. Helena, CA 94754-9504
Phone: (914) 452-9600

D'Youville College
320 Porter Ave., Buffalo 14201-1084
Type: Private, independent, four-year
Degrees: B, M, P, D *Enroll:* 2,405
URL: http://www.dyc.edu
Phone: (716) 829-8000 *Calendar:* Sem. plan
Inst. Accred.: MSA-CHE (1928/2005)
Prog. Accred.: Allied Health (occupational therapy), Chiropractic Education, Dietetics (coordinated), Nursing Education, Physical Therapy, Physician Assistant

Daemen College
4380 Main St., Amherst 14226-3592
Type: Private, independent, four-year
Degrees: B, M, P *Enroll:* 1,876
URL: http://www.daemen.edu
Phone: (716) 839-3600 *Calendar:* Sem. plan
Inst. Accred.: MSA-CHE (1956/2006)
Prog. Accred.: Nursing, Physical Therapy, Physician Assistant, Social Work

Darkei No'am Rabbinical College
2822 Ave. J, Brooklyn 11210
Type: Private, independent, four-year
Degrees: Rabbinic *Enroll:* 18
Phone: (718) 338-6464 *Calendar:* Tri. plan
Inst. Accred.: AARTS (1983/2000)

Davis College
PO Box 601, Bible School Park 13737-0601
Type: Private, independent, four-year
Degrees: A, B *Enroll:* 241
URL: http://www.davisny.edu
Phone: (607) 729-1581 *Calendar:* Sem. plan
Inst. Accred.: ABHE (1985/2006), MSA-CHE (2005)

DeVry College of New York
3020 Thomson Ave., Long Island City 11101-3051
Type: Private, proprietary
System: DeVry University
Degrees: A, B *Enroll:* 1,184
URL: http://www.ny.devry.edu
Phone: (718) 269-4200 *Calendar:* Sem. plan
Inst. Accred.: NCA-HLC (2002, *Indirect accreditation through DeVry University, Oakbrook Terrace, IL*)
Prog. Accred.: Engineering Technology (computer, electrical)

Dominican College of Blauvelt
470 Western Hwy., Orangeburg 10956
Type: Private, independent, four-year
Degrees: A, B, M, P, D *Enroll:* 1,297
URL: http://www.dc.edu
Phone: (845) 359-7800 *Calendar:* Sem. plan
Inst. Accred.: MSA-CHE (1972/2007)
Prog. Accred.: Allied Health (occupational therapy), Nursing Education, Physical Therapy, Social Work, Teacher Education (TEAC)

Dowling College
Idle Hour Blvd., Oakdale 11769-1999
Type: Private, independent, four-year
Degrees: B, M, D *Enroll:* 4,378
URL: http://www.dowling.edu
Phone: (631) 244-3000 *Calendar:* 4-1-4 plan
Inst. Accred.: MSA-CHE (1971/2003)
Prog. Accred.: Teacher Education (NCATE)

Dutchess Community College
53 Pendell Rd., Poughkeepsie 12601-1595
Type: Public, state/local, two-year
System: State University of New York Office of Community Colleges
Degrees: A *Enroll:* 5,409
URL: http://www.sunydutchess.edu
Phone: (845) 431-8000 *Calendar:* Sem. plan
Inst. Accred.: MSA-CHE (1964/2005)
Prog. Accred.: Clinical Lab Technology, Nursing

Fishkill Campus
Southern Dutchess Extension Site, Blodgett House, Fishkill 12524
Phone: (914) 896-5775

Poughkeepsie Campus
Martha Lawrence Extension Site, Spackenhill Rd., Poughkeepsie 12603
Phone: (914) 462-0063

Southern Dutchess Extention Site
Hollowbrook Park, Bldg. # 4, Myers Corners Rd., Wappingers Falls 12590
Phone: (914) 298-0755
Prog. Accred: Allied Health (EMT-paramedic)

Elmira Business Institute
Langdon Plaza, 303 North Main St., Elmira 14901
Type: Private, proprietary, two-year
Degrees: A
URL: http://www.ebi-college.com
Phone: (607) 733-7177 *Calendar:* Sem. plan
Inst. Accred.: ACICS (1969/2004)
Prog. Accred.: Allied Health (medical assisting (AMA))

Vestal Campus
Vestal Executive Park, 4100 Old Vestal Rd., Vestal 13850
Phone: (607) 729-8915

Elmira College
One Park Place, Elmira 14901
Type: Private, independent, four-year
Degrees: A, B, M *Enroll:* 1,473
URL: http://www.elmira.edu
Phone: (607) 735-1800
Inst. Accred.: MSA-CHE (1921/2005)
Prog. Accred.: Nursing

Erie Community College
121 Ellicott St., Buffalo 14203
Type: Public, state/local, two-year
System: State University of New York Office of Community Colleges
Degrees: A *Enroll:* 1,751
URL: http://www.ecc.edu
Phone: (716) 842-2770 *Calendar:* Sem. plan
Inst. Accred.: MSA-CHE (1981/2004)
Prog. Accred.: Business (ACBSP), Nursing, Radiation Therapy

North Campus
6205 Main St., Williamsville 14221-7095
Phone: (716) 634-0800
Prog. Accred: Allied Health (medical assisting (AMA), occupational therapy assisting, ophthalmic lab technology, opticianry, respiratory therapy), Clinical Lab Technology, Dentistry (dental hygiene), Dietetic Technician, Engineering Technology (civil/construction, electrical, mechanical)

South Campus
4041 Southwestern Blvd., Orchard Park 14127
Phone: (716) 648-5400
Prog. Accred: Dentistry (dental laboratory technology)

Everest Institute—Rochester
1630 Portland Ave., Rochester 14621
Type: Private, proprietary, two-year
System: Corinthian Colleges, Inc
Degrees: A *Enroll:* 918
URL: http://www.everest.edu
Phone: (585) 266-0430 *Calendar:* Qtr. plan
Inst. Accred.: ACICS (1966/2006)
Prog. Accred.: Allied Health (medical assisting (AMA))

Arlington Campus
2801 East Division St., Ste. 250, Arlington, TX 76011
Phone: (817) 652-7790

Excelsior College
7 Columbia Circle, Albany 12203-5159
Type: Private, independent, four-year
Degrees: A, B, M *Enroll:* 11,174
URL: http://www.excelsior.edu
Phone: (518) 464-8500
Inst. Accred.: MSA-CHE (1977/2007)
Prog. Accred.: Engineering Technology (electrical, nuclear), Nursing

Farmingdale State College
2350 Broadhollow Rd., Farmingdale 11735-1021
Type: Public, state, four-year
System: State University of New York System Office
Degrees: A, B *Enroll:* 5,005
URL: http://www.farmingdale.edu
Phone: (631) 420-2000 *Calendar:* Sem. plan
Inst. Accred.: MSA-CHE (1952/2001)
Prog. Accred.: Clinical Lab Technology, Dentistry (dental hygiene), Engineering Technology (automotive, civil/construction, computer, electrical, manufacturing, mechanical), Nursing

Fashion Institute of Technology
Seventh Ave. at 27th St., New York 10001-5992
Type: Public, state/local, four-year
System: State University of New York Office of Community Colleges
Degrees: A, B, M *Enroll:* 8,224
URL: http://www.fitnyc.edu
Phone: (212) 217-7999 *Calendar:* Sem. plan
Inst. Accred.: MSA-CHE (1957/2007)
Prog. Accred.: Art, Interior Design

Finger Lakes Community College
4355 Lake Shore Dr., Canandaigua 14424
Type: Public, state/local, two-year
System: State University of New York Office of Community Colleges
Degrees: A *Enroll:* 3,375
URL: http://www.flcc.edu
Phone: (585) 394-3500 *Calendar:* Sem. plan
Inst. Accred.: MSA-CHE (1977/2007)
Prog. Accred.: Nursing

Five Towns College
305 North Service Rd., Dix Hills 11746-5871
Type: Private, proprietary, four-year
Degrees: A, B, M, D *Enroll:* 1,105
URL: http://www.fivetowns.edu
Phone: (631) 424-7000 *Calendar:* Sem. plan
Inst. Accred.: MSA-CHE (1988/2001)
Prog. Accred.: Teacher Education (NCATE)

Fordham University
441 East Fordham Rd., Bronx 10458
Type: Private, independent, four-year
Degrees: B, M, P, D *Enroll:* 11,962
URL: http://www.fordham.edu
Phone: (718) 817-1000 *Calendar:* Sem. plan
Inst. Accred.: MSA-CHE (1921/2006)
Prog. Accred.: Business (AACSB), Clinical Psychology, Counseling Psychology, Graduate Social Work, Law, School Psychology, Social Work, Teacher Education (NCATE)

Marymount College of Fordham University
100 Marymount Ave., Tarrytown 10591-3796
Phone: (914) 631-3200
Prog. Accred: Dietetics (didactic)

Fulton-Montgomery Community College
2805 State Hwy. 67, Johnstown 12095-3790
Type: Public, state/local, two-year
System: State University of New York Office of Community Colleges
Degrees: A *Enroll:* 1,670
URL: http://www.fmcc.suny.edu
Phone: (518) 762-4651 *Calendar:* Sem. plan
Inst. Accred.: MSA-CHE (1969/2008)

The General Theological Seminary
175 Ninth Ave., New York 10011-4977
Type: Private, Episcopal Church, four-year
Degrees: M, D *Enroll:* 124
URL: http://www.gts.edu
Phone: (212) 243-5150 *Calendar:* Sem. plan
Inst. Accred.: ATS (1938/2004)

Genesee Community College
One College Rd., Batavia 14020-9704
Type: Public, state/local, two-year
System: State University of New York Office of Community Colleges
Degrees: A *Enroll:* 4,247
URL: http://www.genesee.edu
Phone: (585) 343-0055 *Calendar:* Sem. plan
Inst. Accred.: MSA-CHE (1971/2007)
Prog. Accred.: Allied Health (occupational therapy assisting, respiratory therapy), Nursing, Physical Therapy Assisting

Globe Institute of Technology
291 Broadway, Second Flr., New York 10007-1814
Type: Private, proprietary, four-year
Degrees: A, B *Enroll:* 1,661
URL: http://www.globe.edu
Phone: (212) 349-4330 *Calendar:* Sem. plan
Inst. Accred.: NYBOR (1996/2005)

Graduate School of Figurative Art of the New York Academy of Art
111 Franklin St., New York 10013-2911
Type: Private, independent, four-year
Degrees: M
URL: http://www.nyaa.edu/gschool.html
Phone: (212) 966-0300 *Calendar:* Sem. plan
Inst. Accred.: NYBOR (1989/2006)

Hamilton College
198 College Hill Rd., Clinton 13323
Type: Private, independent, four-year
Degrees: B *Enroll:* 1,802
URL: http://www.hamilton.edu
Phone: (315) 859-4011 *Calendar:* 4-1-4 plan
Inst. Accred.: MSA-CHE (1921/2001)

Hartwick College
One Hartwick Dr., PO Box 4040, Oneonta 13820-4020
Type: Private, independent, four-year
Degrees: B *Enroll:* 1,428
URL: http://www.hartwick.edu
Phone: (607) 431-4000 *Calendar:* 4-1-4 plan
Inst. Accred.: MSA-CHE (1949/2004)
Prog. Accred.: Art, Music, Nursing Education, Teacher Education (TEAC)

Hebrew Union College—Jewish Institute of Religion
One West Fourth St., New York 10012-1186
Type: Private, Union for Reform Judaism, four-year
System: Hebrew Union College—Jewish Institute of Religion Central Office
Degrees: M, P, D *Enroll:* 158
URL: http://www.huc.edu
Phone: (212) 674-5300 *Calendar:* Sem. plan
Inst. Accred.: MSA-CHE (1960/2007)

Helene Fuld College of Nursing
24 East 120th St., New York 10035
Type: Private, independent, two-year
Degrees: A *Enroll:* 209
URL: http://www.helenefuld.edu
Phone: (212) 616-7200 *Calendar:* Qtr. plan
Inst. Accred.: MSA-CHE (1988/2003)
Prog. Accred.: Nursing

Herkimer County Community College
100 Reservoir Rd., Herkimer 13350-9987
Type: Public, state/local, two-year
System: State University of New York Office of Community Colleges
Degrees: A *Enroll:* 2,701
URL: http://www.hccc.suny.edu
Phone: (315) 866-0300 *Calendar:* Sem. plan
Inst. Accred.: MSA-CHE (1972/2003)
Prog. Accred.: Physical Therapy Assisting

Hilbert College
5200 South Park Ave., Hamburg 14075-1597
Type: Private, independent, four-year
Degrees: A, B *Enroll:* 940
URL: http://www.hilbert.edu
Phone: (716) 649-7900 *Calendar:* Sem. plan
Inst. Accred.: MSA-CHE (1976/2006)

Hobart and William Smith Colleges
337 Pulteney St., Geneva 14456
Type: Private, independent, four-year
Degrees: B, M *Enroll:* 1,880
URL: http://www.hws.edu
Phone: (315) 781-3000 *Calendar:* Sem. plan
Inst. Accred.: MSA-CHE (1921/2004)

Hofstra University
100 Hofstra University, Hempstead 11549
Type: Private, independent, four-year
Degrees: B, M, P, D *Enroll:* 11,228
URL: http://www.hofstra.edu
Phone: (516) 463-6600 *Calendar:* Sem. plan
Inst. Accred.: MSA-CHE (1940/2004)
Prog. Accred.: Accounting, Allied Health (audiology, speech-language pathology), Business (AACSB), Combined Professional-Scientific Psychology, Engineering (electrical, engineering physics/science, mechanical), Journalism, Law, Physician Assistant, Rehabilitation Counseling, School Psychology, Teacher Education (NCATE)

Holy Trinity Orthodox Seminary
PO Box 36, Jordanville 13361-1919
Type: Private, independent, four-year
Degrees: B *FTE Enroll:* 37
URL: http://www.hts.edu
Phone: (315) 858-9978 *Calendar:* Sem. plan
Inst. Accred.: NYBOR (1948/2002)

Houghton College
One Willard Ave., PO Box 128, Houghton 14744
Type: Private, Wesleyan Church, four-year
Degrees: A, B, M *Enroll:* 1,369
URL: http://www.houghton.edu
Phone: (585) 567-9200 *Calendar:* Sem. plan
Inst. Accred.: MSA-CHE (1935/2005)
Prog. Accred.: Music, Teacher Education (TEAC)

Hudson Valley Community College
80 Vandenburgh Ave., Troy 12180
Type: Public, state/local, two-year
System: State University of New York Office of Community Colleges
Degrees: A *Enroll:* 8,543
URL: http://www.hvcc.edu
Phone: (518) 629-4822 *Calendar:* Sem. plan
Inst. Accred.: MSA-CHE (1969/2004)
Prog. Accred.: Allied Health (EMT-paramedic, diagnostic medical sonography, respiratory therapy), Clinical Lab Technology, Dentistry (dental hygiene), Engineering Technology (civil/construction, electrical, mechanical), Funeral Service Education (Mortuary Science), Nursing, Radiography

Institute of Design and Construction
141 Willoughby St., Brooklyn 11210-1919
Type: Private, independent, two-year
Degrees: A *Enroll:* 130
URL: http://www.idcbrooklyn.org
Phone: (718) 855-3661
Inst. Accred.: NYBOR (1972/2001)

Iona College
715 North Ave., New Rochelle 10801-1890
Type: Private, independent, four-year
Degrees: B, M *Enroll:* 3,650
URL: http://www.iona.edu
Phone: (914) 633-2000 *Calendar:* Sem. plan
Inst. Accred.: MSA-CHE (1952/2003)
Prog. Accred.: Business (AACSB), Computer Science (ABET-CAC), Journalism, Marriage and Family Therapy, Social Work, Teacher Education (NCATE)

Rockland Graduate Center
PO Box 1522, Pearl River 10965
Phone: (845) 620-1350

Island Drafting & Technical Institute
128 Broadway, Amityville 11701-2789
Type: Private, proprietary, two-year
Degrees: A
Phone: (516) 691-8733
Inst. Accred.: ACCSCT (1967/2004)

Ithaca College
300 Job Hall, Ithaca 14850-7001
Type: Private, independent, four-year
Degrees: B, M, D *Enroll:* 6,315
URL: http://www.ithaca.edu
Phone: (607) 274-3011 *Calendar:* Sem. plan
Inst. Accred.: MSA-CHE (1955/2008)
Prog. Accred.: Allied Health (audiology, occupational therapy, speech-language pathology), Business (AACSB), Music, Physical Therapy, Recreation and Leisure Services, Theatre

Jamestown Business College
PO Box 429, 7 Fairmont Ave., Jamestown 14702-0429
Type: Private, proprietary, four-year
Degrees: A, B *Enroll:* 292
URL: http://www.jbcny.org
Phone: (716) 664-5100 *Calendar:* Qtr. plan
Inst. Accred.: MSA-CHE (2001/2006)

Jamestown Community College
525 Falconer St., PO Box 20, Jamestown 14702-0020
Type: Public, state/local, two-year
System: State University of New York Office of Community Colleges
Degrees: A *Enroll:* 2,864
URL: http://www.sunyjcc.edu
Phone: (716) 665-5220 *Calendar:* Sem. plan
Inst. Accred.: MSA-CHE (1956/2001)
Prog. Accred.: Allied Health (occupational therapy assisting), Nursing

Cattaraugus County Campus
PO Box 5901, Olean 14760-5901
Phone: (716) 376-7500
Prog. Accred: Nursing

Jefferson Community College
1220 Coffeen St., Watertown 13601
Type: Public, state/local, two-year
System: State University of New York Office of Community Colleges
Degrees: A *Enroll:* 2,413
URL: http://www.sunyjefferson.edu
Phone: (315) 786-2200 *Calendar:* Sem. plan
Inst. Accred.: MSA-CHE (1969/2005)
Prog. Accred.: Nursing

The Jewish Theological Seminary
3080 Broadway, New York 10027-4649
Type: Private, independent, four-year
Degrees: B, M, P, D *Enroll:* 580
URL: http://www.jtsa.edu
Phone: (212) 678-8000 *Calendar:* Sem. plan
Inst. Accred.: MSA-CHE (1954/2006)

The Juilliard School
60 Lincoln Center Plaza, New York 10023-6588
Type: Private, independent, four-year
Degrees: B, M, D *Enroll:* 867
URL: http://www.juilliard.edu
Phone: (212) 799-5000 *Calendar:* Sem. plan
Inst. Accred.: MSA-CHE (1956/2003)

Katharine Gibbs School
50 West 40th St., First Flr., New York 10138-1347
Type: Private, proprietary, two-year
System: Career Education Corporation
Degrees: A *Enroll:* 1,999
URL: http://www.gibbsny.com
Phone: (212) 867-9300
Inst. Accred.: ACICS (1967/2004)

Norristown Campus
2501 Monroe Blvd., Norristown, PA 19403
Phone: (610) 676-0500

Kehilath Yakov Rabbinical Seminary
638 Bedford Ave., Brooklyn 11211-8007
Type: Private, independent, four-year
Degrees: Rabbinic *Enroll:* 97
Phone: (718) 963-3940 *Calendar:* Sem. plan
Inst. Accred.: AARTS (1980/2002)

Keuka College
141 Central Ave., Keuka Park 14478
Type: Private, independent, four-year
Degrees: B, M *Enroll:* 1,224
URL: http://www.keuka.edu
Phone: (315) 279-5000 *Calendar:* Sem. plan
Inst. Accred.: MSA-CHE (1927/2003)
Prog. Accred.: Allied Health (occupational therapy), Nursing, Social Work

The King's College
Empire State., 350 Fifth Ave., Ste. 1500, New York 10118
Type: Private, independent, four-year
Degrees: B *FTE Enroll:* 392
URL: http://www.tkc.edu
Phone: (212) 659-7200 *Calendar:* Sem. plan
Inst. Accred.: MSA-CHE (2007), NYBOR (1999/2005)

Kol Yaakov Torah Center
29 West Maple Ave., PO Box 402, Monsey 10952
Type: Private, independent, four-year
Degrees: Rabbinic *Enroll:* 22
Phone: (845) 425-3863 *Calendar:* Sem. plan
Inst. Accred.: AARTS (1984/2003)

Laboratory Institute of Merchandising
12 East 53rd St., New York 10022
Type: Private, proprietary, four-year
Degrees: A, B *Enroll:* 782
URL: http://www.limcollege.edu
Phone: (212) 752-1530 *Calendar:* Sem. plan
Inst. Accred.: MSA-CHE (1977/2007)
Prog. Accred.: Business (ACBSP)

Le Moyne College
1419 Salt Springs Rd., Syracuse 13214
Type: Private, independent, four-year
Degrees: B, M *Enroll:* 2,887
URL: http://www.lemoyne.edu
Phone: (315) 445-4100 *Calendar:* Sem. plan
Inst. Accred.: MSA-CHE (1953/2006)
Prog. Accred.: Nursing Education, Physician Assistant

Lehman College, City University of New York
250 Bedford Park Blvd. West, Bronx 10468
Type: Public, state/local, four-year
System: City University of New York System
Degrees: B, M *Enroll:* 7,323
URL: http://www.lehman.cuny.edu
Phone: (718) 960-8000 *Calendar:* Sem. plan
Inst. Accred.: MSA-CHE (1968/2004)
Prog. Accred.: Allied Health (audiology, speech-language pathology), Dietetics (didactic), Dietetics (internship), Graduate Social Work, Nursing Education, Social Work, Teacher Education (NCATE)

Long Island Business Institute—Queens
136-18 39th Ave., Flushing 11354
Type: Private, proprietary, two-year
Degrees: A
URL: http://www.libi.edu
Phone: (718) 939-5100
Inst. Accred.: ACICS (1978/2006)

Long Island Campus
6500 Jericho Turnpike, Commack 11725
Phone: (631) 499-7100

Long Island University
700 Northern Blvd., Brookville 11548-1326
Type: Private, independent, four-year
Degrees: A, B, M, P, D *FTE Enroll:* 12,975
URL: http://www.liu.edu
Phone: (516) 299-2501 *Calendar:* Sem. plan
Inst. Accred.: MSA-CHE (1955/2003)
Prog. Accred.: Allied Health (speech-language pathology), Dietetics (didactic), Dietetics (internship), Librarianship, Radiography

Brentwood Campus
100 Second Ave., Brentwood 11717
Phone: (631) 273-5112

Brooklyn Campus
One University Plaza, Brooklyn 11201
Phone: (718) 488-1000
Prog. Accred: Allied Health (diagnostic medical sonography, occupational therapy, respiratory therapy, speech-language pathology, surgical technology), Clinical Psychology, Graduate Social Work, Nursing Education, Pharmacy, Physical Therapy, Physician Assistant, Public Administration, Social Work, Teacher Education (TEAC)

C.W. Post Campus
720 Northern Blvd., Brookville 11548-1300
Phone: (516) 299-2000
Prog. Accred: Business (AACSB), Clinical Lab Scientist, Clinical Psychology, Counseling, Graduate Social Work, Nursing Education, Public Administration, Radiography, Social Work

Riverhead Campus
121 Speonk-Riverhead Rd., LIU Bldg., Riverhead 11901
Phone: (631) 287-8010

Rockland Campus
70 Route 340, Orangeburg 10962
Phone: (845) 359-7200

Southampton Graduate Campus
239 Montauk Hwy, Southampton 11968
Phone: (631) 287-8316
Prog. Accred: Teacher Education (TEAC)

Westchester Campus
735 Anderson Hill Rd., Purchase 10577-1400
Phone: (800) 472-3548
Prog. Accred: Teacher Education (TEAC)

Machzikei Hadath Rabbinical College
5407 16th Ave., Brooklyn 11204
Type: Private, independent, four-year
Degrees: Talmudic *Enroll:* 118
Phone: (718) 854-8777 *Calendar:* Sem. plan
Inst. Accred.: AARTS (1980/2003)

Mandl, The College of Allied Health
254 West 54th St., New York 10019-5516
Type: Private, proprietary, two-year
Degrees: A
URL: http://mandlschool.com
Phone: (212) 247-3434
Inst. Accred.: ABHES (1987/2006)

Manhattan College
Manhattan College Pkwy., Bronx 10471
Type: Private, Roman Catholic Church, four-year
Degrees: B, M *Enroll:* 3,135
URL: http://www.manhattan.edu
Phone: (718) 862-8000 *Calendar:* Sem. plan
Inst. Accred.: MSA-CHE (1921/2007)
Prog. Accred.: Business (AACSB), Engineering (chemical, civil, computer, electrical, environmental/sanitary, mechanical), Teacher Education (TEAC)

Manhattan School of Music
120 Claremont Ave., New York 10027-4698
Type: Private, independent, four-year
Degrees: B, M, D *Enroll:* 876
URL: http://www.msmnyc.edu
Phone: (212) 749-2802 *Calendar:* Sem. plan
Inst. Accred.: MSA-CHE (1956/2008)

Manhattanville College
2900 Purchase St., Purchase 10577-2132
Type: Private, independent, four-year
Degrees: B, M *Enroll:* 2,231
URL: http://www.mville.edu
Phone: (914) 694-2200 *Calendar:* Sem. plan
Inst. Accred.: MSA-CHE (1926/2000, Warning)
Prog. Accred.: Teacher Education (NCATE)

Maria College of Albany
700 New Scotland Ave., Albany 12208-1798
Type: Private, independent, two-year
Degrees: A *Enroll:* 434
URL: http://www.mariacollege.edu
Phone: (518) 438-3111 *Calendar:* 4-1-4 plan
Inst. Accred.: MSA-CHE (1973/2008)
Prog. Accred.: Allied Health (occupational therapy assisting), Nursing

Marist College
3399 North Rd., Poughkeepsie 12601-1387
Type: Private, independent, four-year
Degrees: B, M *Enroll:* 5,030
URL: http://www.marist.edu
Phone: (845) 575-3000 *Calendar:* Sem. plan
Inst. Accred.: MSA-CHE (1964/2003)
Prog. Accred.: Business (AACSB), Clinical Lab Scientist, Social Work

Marymount Manhattan College
221 East 71st St., New York 10021-4597
Type: Private, independent, four-year
Degrees: A, B *Enroll:* 1,762
URL: http://www.mmm.edu
Phone: (212) 517-0400 *Calendar:* Sem. plan
Inst. Accred.: MSA-CHE (1961/2007)

Medaille College
18 Agassiz Circle, Buffalo 14214-2695
Type: Private, independent, four-year
Degrees: A, B, M *Enroll:* 2,768
URL: http://www.medaille.edu
Phone: (716) 880-2000 *Calendar:* Sem. plan
Inst. Accred.: MSA-CHE (1951/2003)
Prog. Accred.: Veterinary Technology

Amherst Campus ACCEl Program
400 Essjay Rd., Ste. 100, Center Pointe Corporate park, Williamsville 14221
Phone: (719) 631-1061

Mercy College
555 Broadway, Dobbs Ferry 10522-1189
Type: Private, independent, four-year
Degrees: A, B, M, P *Enroll:* 6,622
URL: http://www.mercy.edu
Phone: (914) 693-4500 *Calendar:* Sem. plan
Inst. Accred.: MSA-CHE (1968/2004)
Prog. Accred.: Acupuncture, Allied Health (occupational therapy, occupational therapy assisting, speech-language pathology), Business (ACBSP), Nursing Education, Physical Therapy, Physician Assistant, Social Work, Veterinary Technology

Bronx Campus
50 Antin Place, Bronx 10462
Phone: (212) 798-8952

White Plains Campus
Martine Ave. and South Broadway, White Plains 10601
Phone: (914) 948-3666

Yorktown Campus
2651 Stang Blvd., Yorktown Heights 10598
Phone: (914) 245-6100

Mesivta of Eastern Parkway Rabbinical Seminary
510 Dahill Rd., Brooklyn 11218
Type: Private, independent, four-year
Degrees: Talmudic *Enroll:* 38
Phone: (718) 438-1002 *Calendar:* Sem. plan
Inst. Accred.: AARTS (1980/2004)

Mesivta Tifereth Jerusalem of America
141 East Broadway, New York 10002
Type: Private, independent, four-year
Degrees: Talmudic *Enroll:* 77
Phone: (212) 964-2830 *Calendar:* Sem. plan
Inst. Accred.: AARTS (1979/2006)

Mesivta Torah Vodaath Seminary
425 East 9th St., Brooklyn 11218
Type: Private, independent, four-year
Degrees: Talmudic *Enroll:* 283
Phone: (718) 941-8000 *Calendar:* Sem. plan
Inst. Accred.: AARTS (1976/2000)

Metropolitan College of New York
431 Canal St., New York 10013
Type: Private, independent, four-year
Degrees: A, B, M *Enroll:* 1,505
URL: http://www.metropolitan.edu
Phone: (212) 343-1234 *Calendar:* Sem. plan
Inst. Accred.: MSA-CHE (1984/2004)

Metropolitan Learning Institute
97-45 Queens Blvd., 4th Flr., Ste. 401, Rego Park 11374
Type: Private, independent, two-year
Degrees: A
URL: http://www.gettraining.org
Phone: (718) 897-0482
Inst. Accred.: COE (2004)

Micropower Computer Institute—Manhattan
243 West 30th St., 9th Flr., New York 10001
Type: Private, proprietary, two-year
Degrees: A
URL: http://www.mpow.com
Phone: (212) 279-2550
Inst. Accred.: COE (2003)

Hauppauge Campus
120 Commerce Dr., Hauppauge 11788
Phone: (631) 656-2940

Linden Campus
1203 St. Georges Ave., Linden, NJ 07036
Phone: (908) 587-9070

Mineola Campus
85 Willis Ave., Mineola 11501
Phone: (516) 742-5913

Queens Campus
75-26 Broadway, Elmhurst 11373
Phone: (718) 507-2663

Mildred Elley
855 Central Ave., Albany 12206-1513
Type: Private, proprietary, two-year
Degrees: A *Enroll:* 376
URL: http://www.mildred-elley.edu
Phone: (518) 786-0855 *Calendar:* Sem. plan
Inst. Accred.: ACICS (1982/2008)

Pittsfield Campus
St. Lukes Square, 505 East St., Ste. 107, Pittsfield, MA 01201
Phone: (413) 499-8618

Mir Yeshiva
1795 Ocean Pkwy., Brooklyn 11223
Type: Private, independent, four-year
Degrees: Talmudic *Enroll:* 313
Phone: (718) 645-0536 *Calendar:* Sem. plan
Inst. Accred.: AARTS (1975/2001)

Mohawk Valley Community College
1101 Sherman Dr., Utica 13501-5394
Type: Public, state/local, two-year
System: State University of New York Office of Community Colleges
Degrees: A *Enroll:* 4,519
URL: http://www.mvcc.edu
Phone: (315) 792-5400 *Calendar:* Sem. plan
Inst. Accred.: MSA-CHE (1960/2008)
Prog. Accred.: Allied Health (respiratory therapy), Engineering Technology (civil/construction, electrical, mechanical, surveying), Nursing

Rome Campus
1101 Floyd Ave., Rome 13440
Phone: (315) 339-3470

Molloy College
1000 Hempstead Ave., Rockville Centre 11571-5002
Type: Private, independent, four-year
Degrees: A, B, M *Enroll:* 2,629
URL: http://www.molloy.edu
Phone: (516) 678-5000 *Calendar:* 4-1-4 plan
Inst. Accred.: MSA-CHE (1967/2004)
Prog. Accred.: Allied Health (cardiovascular technology, respiratory therapy), Nuclear Medicine Technology, Nursing Education, Social Work, Teacher Education (NCATE)

Monroe College
2501 Jerome Ave., Bronx 10468
Type: Private, independent, four-year
Degrees: A, B, M *Enroll:* 3,892
URL: http://www.monroecollege.edu
Phone: (718) 933-6700 *Calendar:* Sem. plan
Inst. Accred.: MSA-CHE (1990/2005)

New Rochelle Campus
434 Main St., New Rochelle 10801
Phone: (914) 632-5400

Monroe Community College
1000 East Henrietta Rd., Rochester 14623
Type: Public, state/local, two-year
System: State University of New York Office of Community Colleges
Degrees: A *Enroll:* 12,590
URL: http://www.monroecc.edu
Phone: (585) 292-2000 *Calendar:* Sem. plan
Inst. Accred.: MSA-CHE (1965/2006)
Prog. Accred.: Allied Health (EMT-paramedic), Dentistry (dental assisting, dental hygiene), Engineering Technology (electrical), Nursing, Radiography

Damon City Center
228 East Main St., Rochester 14604
Phone: (716) 262-1610

Mount Saint Mary College
330 Powell Ave., Newburgh 12550
Type: Private, independent, four-year
Degrees: B, M *Enroll:* 2,068
URL: http://www.msmc.edu
Phone: (845) 561-0800 *Calendar:* Sem. plan
Inst. Accred.: MSA-CHE (1968/2007)
Prog. Accred.: Nursing Education, Teacher Education (NCATE)

Nassau Community College
1 Education Dr., Garden City 11530
Type: Public, state/local, two-year
System: State University of New York Office of Community Colleges
Degrees: A *Enroll:* 16,030
URL: http://www.ncc.edu
Phone: (516) 572-7205 *Calendar:* Sem. plan
Inst. Accred.: MSA-CHE (1967/2004)
Prog. Accred.: Allied Health (respiratory therapy, surgical technology), Engineering Technology (civil/construction, electrical), Funeral Service Education (Mortuary Science), Music, Nursing, Physical Therapy Assisting, Radiation Therapy, Radiography

Nazareth College of Rochester
4245 East Ave., Rochester 14618-3790
Type: Private, independent, four-year
Degrees: B, M, P *Enroll:* 2,586
URL: http://www.naz.edu
Phone: (585) 389-2525 *Calendar:* Sem. plan
Inst. Accred.: MSA-CHE (1930/2006)
Prog. Accred.: Allied Health (speech-language pathology), Graduate Social Work, Music, Nursing Education, Physical Therapy, Social Work, Teacher Education (TEAC)

The New School
66 West 12th St., New York 10011
Type: Private, independent, four-year
Degrees: A, B, M, D *Enroll:* 7,654
URL: http://www.newschool.edu
Phone: (212) 229-5600 *Calendar:* Sem. plan
Inst. Accred.: MSA-CHE (1960/2003)
Prog. Accred.: Clinical Psychology, Public Administration

Parsons School of Design—New York
66 Fifth Ave., New York 10011
Phone: (212) 229-8950
Prog. Accred: Art

Parsons School of Design—Paris, France
14 Rue Letellier, Paris, France 75015
Phone: 011 33 145 77 39 66

New York Career Institute
11 Park Place, New York 10007
Type: Private, proprietary, two-year
Degrees: A *Enroll:* 548
URL: http://www.nyci.edu
Phone: (212) 962-0002
Inst. Accred.: NYBOR (1982/2002)

New York Chiropractic College
PO Box 800, Seneca Falls 13148-0800
Type: Private, independent, four-year
Degrees: B, M, P *Enroll:* 748
URL: http://www.nycc.edu
Phone: (315) 568-3000 *Calendar:* Tri. plan
Inst. Accred.: MSA-CHE (1985/2005)
Prog. Accred.: Chiropractic Education

New York College of Health Professions
6801 Jericho Turnpike, Syosset 11791-4465
Type: Private, proprietary, four-year
Degrees: M
URL: http://www.nycollege.edu
Phone: (516) 364-0808 *Calendar:* Tri. plan
Inst. Accred.: NYBOR (2007)
Prog. Accred.: Acupuncture

New York College of Podiatric Medicine
1800 Park Ave., New York 10035
Type: Private, independent, four-year
Degrees: P *Enroll:* 291
URL: http://www.nycpm.edu
Phone: (212) 410-8000 *Calendar:* Sem. plan
Inst. Accred.: APMA (1923/2003)

New York College of Traditional Chinese Medicine
155 First St., Mineola 11501
Type: Private, proprietary, four-year
Degrees: M
URL: http://www.nyicm.org
Phone: (516) 739-1545 *Calendar:* Sem. plan
Inst. Accred.: ACAOM (2002/2007)

New York Institute of Technology—Old Westbury
PO Box 8000, Old Westbury 11568-8000
Type: Private, independent, four-year
Degrees: A, B, M, P *Enroll:* 5,723
URL: http://www.nyit.edu
Phone: (516) 686-7516 *Calendar:* Sem. plan
Inst. Accred.: MSA-CHE (1969/2003, Warning)
Prog. Accred.: Allied Health (occupational therapy), Dietetics (didactic), Engineering (electrical, mechanical), Engineering Technology (electrical), Interior Design, Osteopathy, Physical Therapy, Physician Assistant, Teacher Education (NCATE)

Central Islip Campus
PO Box 9029, Central Islip 11722-9029
Phone: (516) 348-3000
Prog. Accred: Culinary Education

Manhattan Campus
1855 Broadway, New York 10023-7692
Phone: (212) 399-8300
Prog. Accred: Engineering (electrical), Engineering Technology (electrical)

New York Law School
57 Worth St., New York 10013
Type: Private, independent, four-year
Degrees: P *Enroll:* 1,328
URL: http://www.nyls.edu
Phone: (212) 431-2840 *Calendar:* Sem. plan
Inst. Accred.: ABA (1954/2002)
Prog. Accred.: Law

New York Medical College
Administration Bldg., Valhalla 10595
Type: Private, independent, four-year
Degrees: M, P, D *Enroll:* 1,146
URL: http://www.nymc.edu
Phone: (914) 594-4000
Inst. Accred.: MSA-CHE (1995/2005)
Prog. Accred.: Allied Health (medicine, speech-language pathology), Dentistry (general practice residency, oral and maxillofacial surgery), Physical Therapy, Public Health

New York School of Interior Design
170 70th St., New York 10021-5110
Type: Private, independent, four-year
Degrees: A, B, M *Enroll:* 401
URL: http://www.nysid.edu
Phone: (212) 472-1500 *Calendar:* 4-1-4 plan
Inst. Accred.: NASAD (1996/2007)
Prog. Accred.: Interior Design

New York Theological Seminary
475 Riverside Dr., Ste. 500, New York 10115
Type: Private, interdenominational, four-year
Degrees: M, D *Enroll:* 234
URL: http://www.nyts.edu
Phone: (212) 870-1211 *Calendar:* Sem. plan
Inst. Accred.: ATS (1958/2004)

New York University
70 Washington Square South, New York 10012
Type: Private, independent, four-year
Degrees: A, B, M, P, D *Enroll:* 33,938
URL: http://www.nyu.edu
Phone: (212) 998-1212 *Calendar:* Sem. plan
Inst. Accred.: MSA-CHE (1921/2004)
Prog. Accred.: Allied Health (diagnostic medical sonography, health services administration, medicine, occupational therapy, speech-language pathology, surgical technology), Business (AACSB), Clinical Pastoral Education, Clinical Psychology, Counseling Psychology, Dentistry (advanced education in general dentistry, combined prosthodontics, dental assisting, dental hygiene, dentistry, endodontics, general dentistry, oral and maxillofacial surgery, orthodontic and dentofacial orthopedics, pediatric dentistry, periodontics), Dietetics (didactic), Dietetics (internship), Graduate Social Work, Journalism, Law, Nurse (Midwifery), Nursing Education, Physical Therapy, Planning, Psychology Internship, Public Administration, Public Health, School Psychology, Social Work, Teacher Education (TEAC)

Bellevue Hospital Center
462 First Ave., New York 10016
Phone: (212) 562-4141
Prog. Accred: Clinical Pastoral Education, Psychology Internship, Radiography

Ehrenkranz School of Social Work
125 Route 340, Room 208 The Village, Sparkill 10976
Phone: (845) 359-6084

Medical School Campus
One Gustave L. Levy Place, New York 10029-6574
Phone: (212) 241-6500
Prog. Accred: Allied Health (medicine), Dentistry (general practice residency, oral and maxillofacial surgery), Public Health

Rusk Institute of Rehabilitation Medicine
530 First Ave., New York 10016
Phone: (212) 263-7300
Prog. Accred: Psychology Internship

Stern School of Business
2900 Purchase St., Purchase 10577
Phone: (914) 323-5333

Niagara County Community College
3111 Saunders Settlement Rd., Sanborn 14132-9460
Type: Public, state/local, two-year
System: State University of New York Office of Community Colleges
Degrees: A *Enroll:* 4,215
URL: http://www.niagaracc.suny.edu
Phone: (716) 614-6222 *Calendar:* Sem. plan
Inst. Accred.: MSA-CHE (1970/2006)
Prog. Accred.: Allied Health (medical assisting (AMA), surgical technology), Nursing, Physical Therapy Assisting, Radiography

Niagara University
PO Box 2015, Niagara University 14109
Type: Private, independent, four-year
Degrees: A, B, M *Enroll:* 3,568
URL: http://www.niagara.edu
Phone: (716) 285-1212 *Calendar:* Sem. plan
Inst. Accred.: MSA-CHE (1922/2007)
Prog. Accred.: Business (AACSB), Nursing Education, Social Work, Teacher Education (NCATE)

North Country Community College
PO Box 89, Saranac Lake 12983-0089
Type: Public, state/local, two-year
System: State University of New York Office of Community Colleges
Degrees: A *Enroll:* 1,202
URL: http://www.nccc.edu
Phone: (518) 891-2915 *Calendar:* Sem. plan
Inst. Accred.: MSA-CHE (1975/2005)
Prog. Accred.: Radiography

Malone Campus
College Ave., Malone 12953
Phone: (518) 483-4550

Ticonderoga Campus
Montcalm St., Ticonderoga 12883
Phone: (518) 585-4454

North Shore Long Island Jewish Graduate School of Molecular Medicine
350 Community Dr., Manhasset 11030-3828
Type: Private, independent, four-year
Degrees: D
URL: http://www.northshorelij.com
Phone: (718) 470-7553 *Calendar:* Sem. plan
Inst. Accred.: NYBOR (1994/2006)

Northeastern Seminary
2265 Westside Dr., Rochester 14624
Type: Private, nondenominational, four-year
Degrees: M, P, D
URL: http://www.nes.edu
Phone: (585) 594-6800 *Calendar:* Sem. plan
Inst. Accred.: ATS (2003), MSA-CHE (2005/2008), NYBOR (1998/2002)

Nyack College
One South Blvd., Nyack 10960-3698
Type: Private, Christian Church Missionary Alliance, four-year
Degrees: A, B, M, P *Enroll:* 2,451
URL: http://www.nyackcollege.edu
Phone: (845) 358-1710 *Calendar:* Sem. plan
Inst. Accred.: MSA-CHE (1962/2005)
Prog. Accred.: Music, Social Work, Teacher Education (NCATE)

Alliance Theological Seminary
350 North Highland Ave., Nyack 10960-1416
Phone: (845) 353-2020

Manhattan Center Campus
335 Broadway, New York 10013
Phone: (212) 625-0500

Seminario Teológico de Puerto Rico
Urb. Roosevelt, José Canals #458 Oficina 301, Hato Rey, PR 00918
Phone: (787) 274-1142

Ohr HaMeir Theological Seminary
Furnace Woods Rd., PO Box 2130, Cortland Manor 10567
Type: Private, independent, four-year
Degrees: Talmudic *Enroll:* 90
Phone: (914) 736-1500 *Calendar:* Sem. plan
Inst. Accred.: AARTS (1979/2001)

Ohr Somayach-Tanenbaum Educational Center
PO Box 334, Monsey 10952
Type: Private, independent, four-year
Degrees: Talmudic *Enroll:* 63
URL: http://www.ohrsomayach.edu
Phone: (845) 425-1370 *Calendar:* Tri. plan
Inst. Accred.: AARTS (1984/2003)

Olean Business Institute
301 North Union St., Olean 14760
Type: Private, proprietary, two-year
Degrees: A *Enroll:* 83
URL: http://www.oleanbusinessinstitute.net
Phone: (716) 372-7978 *Calendar:* Sem. plan
Inst. Accred.: ACICS (1969/2003)

Onondaga Community College
4585 West Seneca Turnpike, Syracuse 13215-4585
Type: Public, state/local, two-year
System: State University of New York Office of Community Colleges
Degrees: A *Enroll:* 5,871
URL: http://www.sunyocc.edu
Phone: (315) 498-2622 *Calendar:* Sem. plan
Inst. Accred.: MSA-CHE (1972/2008)
Prog. Accred.: Allied Health (respiratory therapy, surgical technology), Dentistry (dental hygiene), Engineering Technology (computer, electrical), Nursing, Physical Therapy Assisting

Orange County Community College
115 South St., Middletown 10940
Type: Public, state/local, two-year
System: State University of New York Office of Community Colleges
Degrees: A *Enroll:* 4,384
URL: http://www.sunyorange.edu
Phone: (845) 344-6222 *Calendar:* Sem. plan
Inst. Accred.: MSA-CHE (1962/2004)
Prog. Accred.: Allied Health (occupational therapy assisting), Business (ACBSP), Clinical Lab Technology, Dentistry (dental hygiene), Nursing, Phlebotomy, Physical Therapy Assisting, Radiography

Pace University
One Pace Plaza, New York 10038
Type: Private, independent, four-year
Degrees: A, B, M, P, D *Enroll:* 10,497
URL: http://www.pace.edu
Phone: (212) 346-1200 *Calendar:* Sem. plan
Inst. Accred.: MSA-CHE (1957/2003)
Prog. Accred.: Accounting, Business (AACSB), Combined Professional-Scientific Psychology, Computer Science (ABET-CAC), Engineering (information systems), Physician Assistant, Psychology Internship, Teacher Education (NCATE)

Pleasantville/Briarcliff Campus
861 Bedford Rd., Pleasantville 10570
Phone: (914) 773-3200
Prog. Accred: Nursing Education

White Plains Campus
78 North Broadway, White Plains 10603
Phone: (914) 422-4000
Prog. Accred: Law

Pacific College of Oriental Medicine—New York
915 Broadway, 3rd Flr., New York 10010
Type: Private, proprietary, four-year
Degrees: M
URL: http://www.pacificcollege.edu
Phone: (212) 982-3456
Inst. Accred.: ACAOM (1995/2004)

Paul Smith's College of Arts and Sciences
PO Box 265, Paul Smiths 12970-0265
Type: Private, independent, four-year
Degrees: A, B *Enroll:* 831
URL: http://www.paulsmiths.edu
Phone: (518) 327-6227 *Calendar:* Tri. plan
Inst. Accred.: MSA-CHE (1977/2008)
Prog. Accred.: Culinary Education, Engineering Technology (surveying), Forestry

Plaza College
74-09 37th Ave., Jackson Heights 11372-6340
Type: Private, proprietary, four-year
Degrees: A, B *Enroll:* 736
URL: http://www.plazacollege.edu
Phone: (718) 779-1430 *Calendar:* Qtr. plan
Inst. Accred.: MSA-CHE (2002/2007)

Polytechnic Institute of NYU
6 MetroTech Center, Brooklyn 11201
Type: Private, independent, four-year
Degrees: B, M, D *Enroll:* 2,362
URL: http://www.poly.edu
Phone: (718) 260-3600 *Calendar:* Sem. plan
Inst. Accred.: MSA-CHE (1927/2003)
Prog. Accred.: Computer Science (ABET-CAC), Engineering (chemical, civil, computer, electrical, mechanical)

Long Island Center
Route 110, Farmingdale 11735
Phone: (516) 755-4400

Westchester Graduate Center
36 Saw Mill River Rd., Hawthorne 10532
Phone: (914) 347-6940

Pratt Institute
200 Willoughby Ave., Brooklyn 11205
Type: Private, independent, four-year
Degrees: A, B, M, P *Enroll:* 4,459
URL: http://www.pratt.edu
Phone: (718) 636-3600 *Calendar:* Sem. plan
Inst. Accred.: MSA-CHE (1950/2005)
Prog. Accred.: Art, Interior Design, Librarianship, Planning

Manhattan Campus
144 West 14th St., New York 10011
Phone: (718) 636-3600

Pratt MWP
310 Genesee St., Utica 13502
Phone: (315) 797-8260
Prog. Accred.: Art

Professional Business College
125 Canal St., New York 10002
Type: Private, proprietary, two-year
Degrees: A
Phone: (212) 226-7300
Inst. Accred.: ACICS (1985/2008)

Rabbi Isaac Elchanan Theological Seminary
2540 Amsterdam Ave., New York 10033
Type: Private, independent, four-year
Degrees: P *FTE Enroll:* 209
Phone: (212) 960-5344 *Calendar:* Sem. plan
Inst. Accred.: NYBOR (1973/2002)

Rabbinical Academy Mesivta Rabbi Chaim Berlin
1593 Coney Island Ave., Brooklyn 11230
Type: Private, independent, four-year
Degrees: Talmudic *Enroll:* 274
Phone: (718) 377-0777 *Calendar:* Sem. plan
Inst. Accred.: AARTS (1975/2005)

Rabbinical College Beth Shraga
28 Saddle River Rd., Monsey 10952
Type: Private, independent, four-year
Degrees: Talmudic *Enroll:* 43
Phone: (845) 356-1980 *Calendar:* Sem. plan
Inst. Accred.: AARTS (1978/2006)

Rabbinical College Bobover Yeshiva B'nei Zion
1577 48th St., Brooklyn 11219
Type: Private, independent, four-year
Degrees: Rabbinic, Talmudic *Enroll:* 251
Phone: (718) 438-2018 *Calendar:* Sem. plan
Inst. Accred.: AARTS (1979/2001)

Rabbinical College Ch'san Sofer
1876 50th St., Brooklyn 11204
Type: Private, independent, four-year
Degrees: Talmudic *Enroll:* 92
Phone: (718) 236-1171 *Calendar:* Sem. plan
Inst. Accred.: AARTS (1979/2003)

Rabbinical College of Long Island
205 West Beech St., PO Box 630, Long Beach 11561
Type: Private, independent, four-year
Degrees: Talmudic *Enroll:* 123
Phone: (516) 255-4700 *Calendar:* Sem. plan
Inst. Accred.: AARTS (1979/2001)

Rabbinical College of Ohr Shimon Yisroel
215-217 Hewes St., Brooklyn 11211
Type: Private, independent, four-year
Degrees: Talmudic *Enroll:* 159
Phone: (718) 855-4095 *Calendar:* Sem. plan
Inst. Accred.: AARTS (1992/2002)

Rabbinical Seminary Adas Yereim
185 Wilson St., Brooklyn 11211
Type: Private, independent, four-year
Degrees: Talmudic *Enroll:* 77
Phone: (718) 388-1751 *Calendar:* Sem. plan
Inst. Accred.: AARTS (1979/2001)

Rabbinical Seminary M'kor Chaim
1571 55th St., Brooklyn 11219
Type: Private, independent, four-year
Degrees: Talmudic *Enroll:* 49
Phone: (718) 851-0183 *Calendar:* Sem. plan
Inst. Accred.: AARTS (1979/2004)

Rabbinical Seminary of America
76-01 147th St., Flushing 11367
Type: Private, independent, four-year
Degrees: Talmudic *Enroll:* 442
Phone: (718) 268-4700 *Calendar:* Sem. plan
Inst. Accred.: AARTS (1975/2006)

Rensselaer Polytechnic Institute
110 Eighth St., Troy 12180-3590
Type: Private, independent, four-year
Degrees: B, M, D *Enroll:* 6,214
URL: http://www.rpi.edu
Phone: (518) 276-6000 *Calendar:* Sem. plan
Inst. Accred.: MSA-CHE (1927/2006)
Prog. Accred.: Business (AACSB), Engineering (aerospace, bioengineering, chemical, civil, computer, electrical, engineering physics/science, environmental/sanitary, industrial, materials, mechanical, nuclear)

Rensselaer Polytechnic Institute at Hartford
275 Windsor St., Hartford, CT 06120-2991
Phone: (860) 548-2400

Roberts Wesleyan College
2301 Westside Dr., Rochester 14624-1997
Type: Private, independent, four-year
Degrees: A, B, M, D *Enroll:* 1,717
URL: http://www.roberts.edu
Phone: (585) 594-6000 *Calendar:* Sem. plan
Inst. Accred.: MSA-CHE (1963/2006)
Prog. Accred.: Art, Graduate Social Work, Music, Nursing, Nursing Education, Social Work

Rochester Institute of Technology
One Lomb Memorial Dr., Rochester 14623-5603
Type: Private, independent, four-year
Degrees: A, B, M, D *Enroll:* 12,771
URL: http://www.rit.edu
Phone: (585) 475-2411 *Calendar:* Qtr. plan
Inst. Accred.: MSA-CHE (1958/2007)
Prog. Accred.: Allied Health (diagnostic medical sonography), Art, Business (AACSB), Computer Science (ABET-CAC), Dietetics (didactic), Engineering (computer, electrical, industrial, information systems, mechanical, micro/nano-engineering, software), Engineering Technology (civil/construction, computer, electrical, electromechanical, manufacturing, mechanical, telecommunications), Interior Design, Physician Assistant, Teacher Education (TEAC)

American College of Management and Technology
C'ira Caric'a 4, Dubrovnik, Croatia 20000
Phone: 011 38520435555

National Technical Institute for the Deaf
Lyndon Baines Johnson Bldg., 52 Lomd Memorial Dr., Rochester 14623-5604
Phone: (716) 475-6700
Prog. Accred: Art, Teacher Education (TEAC)

U.S. Business School in Prague
Jose Marti 2, Prague, Czech Republic 16200
Phone: (716) 475-7784

Rockefeller University
1230 York Ave., New York 10021
Type: Private, independent, four-year
Degrees: M, D *Enroll:* 200
URL: http://www.rockefeller.edu
Phone: (212) 327-8000 *Calendar:* Sem. plan
Inst. Accred.: NYBOR (1954/2002)

The Sage Colleges
45 Ferry St., Troy 12180
Type: Private, independent, four-year
Degrees: A, B, M, P, D *Enroll:* 790
URL: http://www.sage.edu
Phone: (518) 244-2000 *Calendar:* Sem. plan
Inst. Accred.: MSA-CHE (1928/2005)
Prog. Accred.: Allied Health (occupational therapy), Dietetics (didactic), Dietetics (internship), Nursing Education, Physical Therapy, Teacher Education (NCATE)

Russell Sage College
45 Ferry St., Troy 12180
Phone: (518) 244-2000

Sage College of Albany
140 New Scotland Ave., Albany 12208
Phone: (518) 244-2000
Prog. Accred: Art

Saint Bernard's School of Theology and Ministry
120 French Rd., Rochester 14618
Type: Private, Roman Catholic Church, four-year
Degrees: M *Enroll:* 54
URL: http://www.stbernards.edu
Phone: (585) 271-3657 *Calendar:* Sem. plan
Inst. Accred.: ATS (1970/2003)

Saint Bonaventure University
3261 West State Rd., St. Bonaventure 14778
Type: Private, Roman Catholic Church, four-year
Degrees: B, M *Enroll:* 2,411
URL: http://www.sbu.edu
Phone: (716) 375-2000 *Calendar:* Sem. plan
Inst. Accred.: MSA-CHE (1924/2005)
Prog. Accred.: Business (AACSB), Liberal Education, Teacher Education (NCATE)

Saint Elizabeth College of Nursing
2215 Genesee St., Utica 13501-5998
Type: Private, independent, two-year
Degrees: A *Enroll:* 211
URL: http://www.stemc.org/college/edu.php
Phone: (315) 798-8144 *Calendar:* Sem. plan
Inst. Accred.: MSA-CHE (2005)

Saint Francis College
180 Remsen St., Brooklyn Heights 11201
Type: Private, independent, four-year
Degrees: A, B, M *Enroll:* 2,144
URL: http://www.stfranciscollege.edu
Phone: (718) 522-2300 *Calendar:* Sem. plan
Inst. Accred.: MSA-CHE (1959/2004)
Prog. Accred.: Business (ACBSP), Nursing Education

Saint John Fisher College
3690 East Ave., Rochester 14618
Type: Private, independent, four-year
Degrees: B, M, P, D *Enroll:* 3,006
URL: http://www.sjfc.edu
Phone: (585) 385-8000 *Calendar:* Sem. plan
Inst. Accred.: MSA-CHE (1957/2006)
Prog. Accred.: Business (AACSB), Nursing Education, Pharmacy, Teacher Education (NCATE)

Saint John's University
8000 Utopia Pkwy., Jamaica 11439-0001
Type: Private, Roman Catholic Church, four-year
Degrees: A, B, M, P, D *Enroll:* 16,391
URL: http://new.stjohns.edu
Phone: (718) 990-6161 *Calendar:* Sem. plan
Inst. Accred.: MSA-CHE (1921/2006)
Prog. Accred.: Accounting, Allied Health (audiology, speech-language pathology), Art, Business (AACSB), Clinical Psychology, Counseling, Law, Librarianship, Pharmacy, Rehabilitation Counseling, Teacher Education (TEAC)

Manhattan Campus
101 Murray St., New York 10007
Phone: (212) 962-4111

Staten Island Campus
300 Howard Ave., Staten Island 10301
Phone: (718) 390-4500

Saint Joseph's College
245 Clinton Ave., Brooklyn 11205-3688
Type: Private, independent, four-year
Degrees: B, M *Enroll:* 966
URL: http://www.sjcny.edu
Phone: (718) 636-6800 *Calendar:* Sem. plan
Inst. Accred.: MSA-CHE (1928/2008)
Prog. Accred.: Nursing

Suffolk Campus
155 Roe Blvd., Patchogue 11772
Phone: (631) 447-3200

Saint Joseph's Seminary
Dunwoodie, 201 Seminary Ave., Yonkers 10704
Type: Private, Roman Catholic Church, four-year
Degrees: M, P *Enroll:* 87
URL: http://www.archny.org/seminary/st-josephs-seminary-dunwoodie
Phone: (914) 968-6200 *Calendar:* Qtr. plan
Inst. Accred.: ATS (1973/2004), MSA-CHE (1961/2005)

Saint Lawrence University
23 Romoda Dr., Canton 13617
Type: Private, independent, four-year
Degrees: B, M *Enroll:* 2,191
URL: http://www.stlawu.edu
Phone: (315) 229-5011
Inst. Accred.: MSA-CHE (1921/2008)
Prog. Accred.: Teacher Education (TEAC)

Saint Thomas Aquinas College
125 Route 340, Sparkill 10976-1050
Type: Private, independent, four-year
Degrees: A, B, M *Enroll:* 1,726
URL: http://www.stac.edu
Phone: (845) 398-4000 *Calendar:* 4-1-4 plan
Inst. Accred.: MSA-CHE (1972/2007)
Prog. Accred.: Teacher Education (NCATE)

Saint Vladimir's Orthodox Theological Seminary
575 Scarsdale Rd., Crestwood 10707
Type: Private, Orthodox Church in America, four-year
Degrees: M, D *Enroll:* 94
URL: http://www.svots.edu
Phone: (914) 961-8313 *Calendar:* Sem. plan
Inst. Accred.: ATS (1973/2003)

Salvation Army School for Officer Training
201 Lafayette Ave., Suffern 10901
Type: Private, independent, two-year
Degrees: A
URL: http://www1.salvationarmy.org/use/www_use_sfot.nsf
Phone: (845) 357-3501 *Calendar:* Qtr. plan
Inst. Accred.: NYBOR (2005)

Sanford-Brown Institute—Melville
320 South Service Rd., Melville 11747
Type: Private, proprietary, two-year
System: Career Education Corporation
Degrees: A *Enroll:* 594
URL: http://www.sbmelville.com
Phone: (631) 370-3300 *Calendar:* Qtr. plan
Inst. Accred.: ACICS (1973/2003)

Sarah Lawrence College
One Meadway, Bronxville 10708
Type: Private, independent, four-year
Degrees: B, M *Enroll:* 1,564
URL: http://www.slc.edu
Phone: (914) 337-0700 *Calendar:* Sem. plan
Inst. Accred.: MSA-CHE (1937/2007)

Schenectady County Community College
78 Washington Ave., Schenectady 12305
Type: Public, state/local, two-year
System: State University of New York Office of Community Colleges
Degrees: A *Enroll:* 2,995
URL: http://www.sunysccc.edu
Phone: (518) 381-1200 *Calendar:* Sem. plan
Inst. Accred.: MSA-CHE (1974/2004)
Prog. Accred.: Business (ACBSP), Culinary Education, Music

School of Visual Arts
209 East 23rd St., New York 10010
Type: Private, proprietary, four-year
Degrees: B, M *Enroll:* 3,426
URL: http://www.schoolofvisualarts.edu
Phone: (212) 592-2000 *Calendar:* Sem. plan
Inst. Accred.: MSA-CHE (1978/2007)
Prog. Accred.: Art, Interior Design

Seminary of the Immaculate Conception
440 West Neck Rd., Huntington 11743
Type: Private, Roman Catholic Church, four-year
Degrees: M, P, D *Enroll:* 92
URL: http://www.icseminary.edu
Phone: (631) 423-0483 *Calendar:* Sem. plan
Inst. Accred.: ATS (1976/2001), MSA-CHE (1976/2001)

Sh'or Yoshuv Rabbinical College
1 Cedar Lawn Ave., Lawrence 11559
Type: Private, independent, four-year
Degrees: Talmudic *Enroll:* 128
Phone: (516) 239-9002 *Calendar:* Sem. plan
Inst. Accred.: AARTS (1979/2005)

Siena College
515 Loudon Rd., Loudonville 12211-1462
Type: Private, independent, four-year
Degrees: B, M *Enroll:* 3,166
URL: http://www.siena.edu
Phone: (518) 783-2300 *Calendar:* Sem. plan
Inst. Accred.: MSA-CHE (1943/2004)
Prog. Accred.: Business (AACSB), Social Work, Teacher Education (NCATE)

Simmons Institute of Funeral Service
1828 South Ave., Syracuse 13207
Type: Private, independent, two-year
Degrees: A *Enroll:* 86
URL: http://www.simmonsinstitute.com
Phone: (315) 475-5142 *Calendar:* Sem. plan
Inst. Accred.: ABFSE (2000/2007)

Skidmore College
815 North Broadway, Saratoga Springs 12866-1632
Type: Private, independent, four-year
Degrees: B, M *Enroll:* 2,643
URL: http://www.skidmore.edu
Phone: (518) 580-5000 *Calendar:* Sem. plan
Inst. Accred.: MSA-CHE (1925/2006)
Prog. Accred.: Art, Social Work

State University of New York at Binghamton
PO Box 6000, Binghamton 13902-6000
Type: Public, state, four-year
System: State University of New York System Office
Degrees: B, M, D *Enroll:* 12,974
URL: http://www.binghamton.edu
Phone: (607) 777-2000 *Calendar:* Sem. plan
Inst. Accred.: MSA-CHE (1952/2001)
Prog. Accred.: Business (AACSB), Clinical Psychology, Computer Science (ABET-CAC), Engineering (computer, electrical, industrial, mechanical), Music, Nursing Education, Public Administration, Social Work, Teacher Education (TEAC)

State University of New York at Buffalo
Capen Hall, Buffalo 14260
Type: Public, state, four-year
System: State University of New York System Office
Degrees: A, B, M, P, D *Enroll:* 24,338
URL: http://www.buffalo.edu
Phone: (716) 645-2000 *Calendar:* Sem. plan
Inst. Accred.: MSA-CHE (1921/2004)
Prog. Accred.: Accounting, Allied Health (audiology, medicine, occupational therapy, speech-language pathology), Art, Business (AACSB), Clinical Psychology, Combined Professional-Scientific Psychology, Dentistry (advanced education in general dentistry, combined prosthodontics, dental assisting, dentistry, endodontics, general dentistry, general practice residency, oral and maxillofacial pathology, oral and maxillofacial surgery, orthodontic and dentofacial orthopedics, pediatric dentistry, periodontics), Dietetics (internship), Engineering (aerospace, chemical, civil, computer, electrical, environmental/sanitary, industrial, mechanical), English Language Education, Graduate Social Work, Law, Librarianship, Nuclear Medicine Technology, Nurse Anesthesia Education, Nursing Education, Pharmacy, Physical Therapy, Planning, Psychology Internship, Rehabilitation Counseling, Teacher Education (TEAC)

State University of New York at New Paltz
75 South Manheim Blvd., New Paltz 12561
Type: Public, state, four-year
System: State University of New York System Office
Degrees: B, M *Enroll:* 6,790
URL: http://www.newpaltz.edu
Phone: (845) 257-2121 *Calendar:* Sem. plan
Inst. Accred.: MSA-CHE (1950/2001)
Prog. Accred.: Allied Health (audiology, speech-language pathology), Art, Computer Science (ABET-CAC), Engineering (computer, electrical), Music, Nursing Education, Teacher Education (NCATE), Theatre

State University of New York Broome Community College
Upper Front St., PO Box 1017, Binghamton 13902-1017
Type: Public, state/local, two-year
System: State University of New York Office of Community Colleges
Degrees: A *Enroll:* 4,715
URL: http://www.sunybroome.edu
Phone: (607) 778-5000 *Calendar:* Sem. plan
Inst. Accred.: MSA-CHE (1960/2005)
Prog. Accred.: Allied Health (medical assisting (AMA)), Clinical Lab Technology, Dentistry (dental hygiene), Engineering Technology (civil/construction, electrical, mechanical), Physical Therapy Assisting, Radiography

State University of New York College at Brockport
350 New Campus Dr., Brockport 14420
Type: Public, state, four-year
System: State University of New York System Office
Degrees: B, M *Enroll:* 7,274
URL: http://www.brockport.edu
Phone: (585) 395-2211 *Calendar:* Sem. plan
Inst. Accred.: MSA-CHE (1952/2007)
Prog. Accred.: Business (AACSB), Computer Science (ABET-CAC), Counseling, Dance, Graduate Social Work, Nursing Education, Public Administration, Recreation and Leisure Services, Social Work, Teacher Education (NCATE)

State University of New York College at Buffalo
1300 Elmwood Ave., Buffalo 14222-1095
Type: Public, state, four-year
System: State University of New York System Office
Degrees: B, M *Enroll:* 9,381
URL: http://www.buffalostate.edu
Phone: (716) 878-4000 *Calendar:* Sem. plan
Inst. Accred.: MSA-CHE (1948/2003)
Prog. Accred.: Allied Health (audiology, speech-language pathology), Clinical Lab Scientist, Dietetics (coordinated), Dietetics (didactic), Engineering Technology (electrical, mechanical), Industrial Technology, Interior Design, Social Work, Teacher Education (NCATE)

State University of New York College at Cortland
PO Box 2000, Cortland 13045
Type: Public, state, four-year
System: State University of New York System Office
Degrees: B, M *Enroll:* 6,456
URL: http://www.cortland.edu
Phone: (607) 753-2201 *Calendar:* Sem. plan
Inst. Accred.: MSA-CHE (1949/2007)
Prog. Accred.: Recreation and Leisure Services, Teacher Education (NCATE)

State University of New York College at Fredonia
280 Central Ave., Fredonia 14063
Type: Public, state, four-year
System: State University of New York System Office
Degrees: B, M *Enroll:* 5,165
URL: http://www.fredonia.edu
Phone: (716) 673-3111 *Calendar:* Sem. plan
Inst. Accred.: MSA-CHE (1952/2005)
Prog. Accred.: Allied Health (audiology, speech-language pathology), Music, Social Work, Teacher Education (NCATE), Theatre

State University of New York College at Geneseo
One College Circle, Geneseo 14454
Type: Public, state, four-year
System: State University of New York System Office
Degrees: B, M *Enroll:* 5,335
URL: http://www.geneseo.edu
Phone: (585) 245-5211 *Calendar:* Sem. plan
Inst. Accred.: MSA-CHE (1952/2007)
Prog. Accred.: Allied Health (speech-language pathology), Business (AACSB), Teacher Education (NCATE)

State University of New York College at Old Westbury
PO Box 210, Old Westbury 11568-0210
Type: Public, state, four-year
System: State University of New York System Office
Degrees: B, M *Enroll:* 3,001
URL: http://www.oldwestbury.edu
Phone: (516) 876-3000 *Calendar:* Sem. plan
Inst. Accred.: MSA-CHE (1976/2006)
Prog. Accred.: Teacher Education (NCATE)

State University of New York College at Oneonta
Ravine Pkwy., Oneonta 13820-4015
Type: Public, state, four-year
System: State University of New York System Office
Degrees: B, M *Enroll:* 5,669
URL: http://www.oneonta.edu
Phone: (607) 436-3500 *Calendar:* Sem. plan
Inst. Accred.: MSA-CHE (1949/2003)
Prog. Accred.: Dietetics (didactic), Dietetics (internship), Family & Consumer Science, Music, Teacher Education (NCATE)

State University of New York College at Oswego
7060 State Route 104, Oswego 13126
Type: Public, state, four-year
System: State University of New York System Office
Degrees: B, M *Enroll:* 7,508
URL: http://www.oswego.edu
Phone: (315) 312-2500 *Calendar:* Sem. plan
Inst. Accred.: MSA-CHE (1950/2007)
Prog. Accred.: Business (AACSB), Music, Teacher Education (NCATE)

State University of New York College at Plattsburgh
101 Broad St., Plattsburgh 12901-2681
Type: Public, state, four-year
System: State University of New York System Office
Degrees: B, M *Enroll:* 5,587
URL: http://www.plattsburgh.edu
Phone: (518) 564-2000 *Calendar:* Sem. plan
Inst. Accred.: MSA-CHE (1952/2007)
Prog. Accred.: Allied Health (speech-language pathology), Business (AACSB), Counseling, Dietetics (didactic), Nursing Education, Social Work

State University of New York College at Potsdam
Office of the President, 44 Pierrepont Ave, Potsdam 13676-2200
Type: Public, state, four-year
System: State University of New York System Office
Degrees: B, M *Enroll:* 4,108
URL: http://www.potsdam.edu
Phone: (315) 267-2000 *Calendar:* Sem. plan
Inst. Accred.: MSA-CHE (1952/2007)
Prog. Accred.: Music, Teacher Education (NCATE)

State University of New York College at Purchase
735 Anderson Hill Rd., Purchase 10577-1400
Type: Public, state, four-year
System: State University of New York System Office
Degrees: B, M *Enroll:* 3,536
URL: http://www.purchase.edu
Phone: (914) 251-6000 *Calendar:* Sem. plan
Inst. Accred.: MSA-CHE (1976/2007)
Prog. Accred.: Art, Music

State University of New York College of Agriculture and Technology at Cobleskill
State Route 7, Cobleskill 12043
Type: Public, state, four-year
System: State University of New York System Office
Degrees: A, B *Enroll:* 2,409
URL: http://www.cobleskill.edu
Phone: (518) 255-5700 *Calendar:* Sem. plan
Inst. Accred.: MSA-CHE (1952/2001)
Prog. Accred.: Culinary Education, Histologic Technology

State University of New York College of Agriculture and Technology at Morrisville
PO Box 901, Morrisville 13408
Type: Public, state, four-year
System: State University of New York System Office
Degrees: A, B *Enroll:* 2,933
URL: http://www.morrisville.edu
Phone: (315) 684-6000 *Calendar:* Sem. plan
Inst. Accred.: MSA-CHE (1952/2007)
Prog. Accred.: Business (ACBSP), Dietetic Technician, Engineering Technology (electrical, mechanical), Nursing

State University of New York College of Environmental Science and Forestry
One Forestry Dr., Syracuse 13210-2778
Type: Public, state, four-year
System: State University of New York System Office
Degrees: A, B, M, D *Enroll:* 1,832
URL: http://www.esf.edu
Phone: (315) 470-6500 *Calendar:* Sem. plan
Inst. Accred.: MSA-CHE (1952/2007)
Prog. Accred.: Construction Education, Engineering (forest, paper), Forestry, Landscape Architecture

The Ranger School
PO Box 48, Wanakena 13695
Phone: (315) 848-2566
Prog. Accred: Forestry

State University of New York College of Optometry
33 West 42nd St., New York 10010
Type: Public, state, four-year
System: State University of New York System Office
Degrees: M, P, D *Enroll:* 292
URL: http://www.sunyopt.edu
Phone: (212) 938-4000 *Calendar:* Qtr. plan
Inst. Accred.: MSA-CHE (1976/2003)
Prog. Accred.: Allied Health (optometric residency, optometry)

State University of New York College of Technology at Alfred
Alfred 14802-1196
Type: Public, state, four-year
System: State University of New York System Office
Degrees: A, B *Enroll:* 3,141
URL: http://www.alfredstate.edu
Phone: (607) 587-4111 *Calendar:* Sem. plan
Inst. Accred.: MSA-CHE (1952/2005)
Prog. Accred.: Clinical Lab Technology, Construction Education, Engineering Technology (architectural, civil/construction, computer, electrical, electromechanical, general drafting/design, mechanical, surveying), Nursing, Veterinary Technology

Wellsville Campus
Wellsville 14895
Phone: (607) 587-3105

State University of New York College of Technology at Canton
34 Cornell Dr., Canton 13617
Type: Public, state, four-year
System: State University of New York System Office
Degrees: A, B *Enroll:* 2,242
URL: http://www.canton.edu
Phone: (315) 386-7011 *Calendar:* Sem. plan
Inst. Accred.: MSA-CHE (1952/2003)
Prog. Accred.: Clinical Lab Technology, Engineering Technology (air conditioning, civil/construction, electrical, mechanical), Funeral Service Education (Mortuary Science), Nursing, Physical Therapy Assisting, Veterinary Technology

State University of New York College of Technology at Delhi
2 Main St., Delhi 13753
Type: Public, state, four-year
System: State University of New York System Office
Degrees: A, B *Enroll:* 2,348
URL: http://www.delhi.edu
Phone: (607) 746-4000 *Calendar:* Sem. plan
Inst. Accred.: MSA-CHE (1952/2007)
Prog. Accred.: Construction Education, Culinary Education, Nursing, Veterinary Technology

State University of New York Empire State College
One Union Ave., Saratoga Springs 12866
Type: Public, state, four-year
System: State University of New York System Office
Degrees: A, B, M *Enroll:* 5,936
URL: http://www.esc.edu
Phone: (518) 587-2100
Inst. Accred.: MSA-CHE (1974/2005)

Central New York Regional Center
219 Walton St., Syracuse 13202-1226
Phone: (315) 472-5730

Collegewide Programs Campus
28 Union Ave., Saratoga Springs 12866-4309
Phone: (518) 587-2100

Genessee Valley Regional Center
8 Prince St., Rochester 14607
Phone: (716) 244-3641

Hudson Valley Regional Center
200 North Central Ave., Hartsdale 10530
Phone: (914) 948-6206

Long Island Regional Center
Trainor House, 223 Store Hill Rd., PO Box 130, Old Westbury 11568-0130
Phone: (516) 997-4700

Metropolitan Regional Center
225 Varick St., New York 10014-4382
Phone: (212) 647-7800

Niagara Frontier Center
Market Archade, 3rd Flr., 617 Main St., Buffalo 14203
Phone: (716) 853-7700

Northeast Center
845 Central Ave., Albany 12206
Phone: (518) 485-5964

State University of New York Health Science Center at Brooklyn
450 Clarkson Ave., Box 1, Brooklyn 11203
Type: Public, state, four-year
System: State University of New York System Office
Degrees: B, M, P, D *Enroll:* 1,316
URL: http://www.downstate.edu
Phone: (718) 270-1000 *Calendar:* Sem. plan
Inst. Accred.: MSA-CHE (1952/2006)
Prog. Accred.: Allied Health (diagnostic medical sonography, medicine, occupational therapy, surgical technology), Nurse (Midwifery), Nurse Anesthesia Education, Nursing Education, Physical Therapy, Physician Assistant, Public Health, Radiography

State University of New York Institute of Technology at Utica/Rome
PO Box 3050, Utica 13504-3050
Type: Public, state, four-year
System: State University of New York System Office
Degrees: B, M *Enroll:* 1,846
URL: http://www.sunyit.edu
Phone: (315) 792-7100 *Calendar:* Sem. plan
Inst. Accred.: MSA-CHE (1979/2005)
Prog. Accred.: Engineering Technology (civil/construction, computer, electrical, industrial, mechanical), Nursing Education

State University of New York Maritime College
6 Pennyfield Ave., Bronx 10465
Type: Public, state, four-year
System: State University of New York System Office
Degrees: A, B, M *Enroll:* 1,226
URL: http://www.sunymaritime.edu
Phone: (718) 409-7200 *Calendar:* Sem. plan
Inst. Accred.: MSA-CHE (1952/2002)
Prog. Accred.: Engineering (naval architecture/marine)

State University of New York Rockland Community College
145 College Rd., Suffern 10901
Type: Public, state/local, two-year
System: State University of New York Office of Community Colleges
Degrees: A *Enroll:* 4,567
URL: http://www.sunyrockland.edu
Phone: (845) 574-4000 *Calendar:* Sem. plan
Inst. Accred.: MSA-CHE (1968/2007)
Prog. Accred.: Allied Health (occupational therapy assisting), Nursing

Haverstraw Learning Center
36-39 Main St., Haberstraw 10927
Phone: (914) 942-0624

Nyack Learning Center
92-94 Main St., Nyack 10960
Phone: (914) 358-9392

Spring Valley Learning Center
185 North Main St., Spring Valley 10977
Phone: (914) 352-5535

State University of New York Upstate Medical University
750 East Adams St., Syracuse 13210
Type: Public, state, four-year
System: State University of New York System Office
Degrees: A, B, M, P, D *Enroll:* 1,077
URL: http://www.upstate.edu
Phone: (315) 464-5540 *Calendar:* Sem. plan
Inst. Accred.: MSA-CHE (1952/1999)
Prog. Accred.: Allied Health (EMT-paramedic, cytotechnology, medicine, perfusion, respiratory therapy), Clinical Lab Scientist, Clinical Pastoral Education, Dentistry (general practice residency), Nursing Education, Physical Therapy, Psychology Internship, Radiation Therapy, Radiography

Stony Brook University
Stony Brook 11794-1401
Type: Public, state, four-year
System: State University of New York System Office
Degrees: B, M, P, D *Enroll:* 18,622
URL: http://www.stonybrook.edu
Phone: (631) 689-6000 *Calendar:* Sem. plan
Inst. Accred.: MSA-CHE (1957/2004)
Prog. Accred.: Allied Health (cytotechnology, medicine, occupational therapy, respiratory therapy, surgical technology), Clinical Lab Scientist, Clinical Psychology, Computer Science (ABET-CAC), Dentistry (advanced education in general dentistry, dentistry, endodontics, general dentistry, general practice residency, orthodontic and dentofacial orthopedics, pediatric dentistry, periodontics), Dietetics (internship), Engineering (bioengineering, computer, electrical, engineering physics/science, mechanical), Graduate Social Work, Nurse (Midwifery), Nursing Education, Physical Therapy, Physician Assistant, Psychology Internship, Radiation Therapy, Social Work, Teacher Education (NCATE)

Suffolk County Community College
533 College Rd., Selden 11784
Type: Public, state/local, two-year
System: State University of New York Office of Community Colleges
Degrees: A *Enroll:* 6,963
URL: http://www.sunysuffolk.edu
Phone: (631) 451-4110 *Calendar:* Sem. plan
Inst. Accred.: MSA-CHE (1966/2007)
Prog. Accred.: Nursing, Physical Therapy Assisting

Suffolk County Community College
533 College Rd., NFL37, Selden 11784
Type: Public, state/local, two-year
System: State University of New York Office of Community Colleges
Degrees: A *Enroll:* 6,963
URL: http://www.sunysuffolk.edu
Phone: (631) 451-4110 *Calendar:* Sem. plan
Inst. Accred.: MSA-CHE (1966/2007)
Prog. Accred.: Nursing, Physical Therapy Assisting

Eastern Campus
121 Speonk-Riverhead Rd., Riverhead 11901-3499
Phone: (631) 548-2500
Prog. Accred: Dietetic Technician

Grant Campus
Crooked Hill Rd., Brentwood 11717
Phone: (631) 851-6700
Prog. Accred: Allied Health (occupational therapy assisting), Nursing, Veterinary Technology

Sullivan County Community College
112 College Rd., Loch Sheldrake 12759-5151
Type: Public, state/local, two-year
System: State University of New York Office of Community Colleges
Degrees: A *Enroll:* 1,274
URL: http://www.sullivan.suny.edu
Phone: (845) 434-5750 *Calendar:* Sem. plan
Inst. Accred.: MSA-CHE (1968/2007)
Prog. Accred.: Business (ACBSP), Culinary Education, Nursing

Sunbridge College
285 Hungry Hollow Rd., Spring Valley 10977-6398
Type: Private, independent, four-year
Degrees: M *Enroll:* 44
URL: http://www.sunbridge.edu
Phone: (845) 425-0055 *Calendar:* Sem. plan
Inst. Accred.: NYBOR (1991/2002)

The Swedish Institute: School of Acupuncture and Massage Therapy
226 West 26th St., PO Box 11130, New York 10001
Type: Private, proprietary, two-year
Degrees: A *Enroll:* 212
URL: http://www.swedishinstitute.org
Phone: (212) 924-5900 *Calendar:* Sem. plan
Inst. Accred.: ACCSCT (1981/2004)
Prog. Accred.: Acupuncture

Syracuse University
Syracuse 13244
Type: Private, independent, four-year
Degrees: A, B, M, P, D *Enroll:* 17,081
URL: http://www.syr.edu
Phone: (315) 443-1870 *Calendar:* Sem. plan
Inst. Accred.: MSA-CHE (1921/2008)
Prog. Accred.: Allied Health (audiology, speech-language pathology), Art, Business (AACSB), Clinical Psychology, Computer Science (ABET-CAC), Counseling, Dietetics (coordinated), Dietetics (didactic), Dietetics (internship), Engineering (aerospace, bioengineering, chemical, civil, computer, electrical, environmental/sanitary, mechanical), Graduate Social Work, Interior Design, Journalism, Law, Librarianship, Marriage and Family Therapy, Music, Public Administration, Rehabilitation Counseling, School Psychology, Social Work, Teacher Education (NCATE)

Talmudical Institute of Upstate New York
769 Park Ave., Rochester 14607
Type: Private, independent, four-year
Degrees: Talmudic *Enroll:* 18
Phone: (585) 473-2810 *Calendar:* Sem. plan
Inst. Accred.: AARTS (1984/2006)

Talmudical Seminary of Bobov
4820 16th Ave., Brooklyn 11204
Type: Private, independent, four-year
Degrees: Talmudic
Phone: (718) 436-2122 *Calendar:* Sem. plan
Inst. Accred.: AARTS (2007)

Talmudical Seminary Oholei Torah
667 Eastern Pkwy., Brooklyn 11213
Type: Private, independent, four-year
Degrees: Talmudic *Enroll:* 245
Phone: (718) 774-5050 *Calendar:* Sem. plan
Inst. Accred.: AARTS (1979/2005)

Teachers College of Columbia University
525 West 120th St., New York 10027-6413
Type: Private, independent, four-year
Degrees: M, D *Enroll:* 3,626
URL: http://www.tc.columbia.edu
Phone: (212) 678-3000 *Calendar:* Sem. plan
Inst. Accred.: MSA-CHE (1921/2006)
Prog. Accred.: Allied Health (speech-language pathology), Clinical Psychology, Counseling Psychology, Dietetics (internship), School Psychology, Teacher Education (NCATE)

Technical Career Institutes, Inc.
320 West 31st St., New York 10001-2789
Type: Private, proprietary, two-year
System: EVCI Career Colleges Holding Corp.
Degrees: A *Enroll:* 2,878
URL: http://www.tcicollege.edu
Phone: (212) 594-4000 *Calendar:* Sem. plan
Inst. Accred.: MSA-CHE (2005/2007), NYBOR (1972/2007)
Prog. Accred.: Engineering Technology (electrical)

Tompkins Cortland Community College
PO Box 139, Dryden 13053-0139
Type: Public, state/local, two-year
System: State University of New York Office of Community Colleges
Degrees: A *Enroll:* 2,491
URL: http://www.sunytccc.edu
Phone: (607) 844-8211 *Calendar:* Sem. plan
Inst. Accred.: MSA-CHE (1973/2008)
Prog. Accred.: Nursing

Torah Temimah Talmudical Seminary
507 Ocean Pkwy., Brooklyn 11218
Type: Private, independent, four-year
Degrees: Talmudic *Enroll:* 215
Phone: (718) 853-8500 *Calendar:* Sem. plan
Inst. Accred.: AARTS (1981/1999)

Touro College
27 West 23rd St., 7th Flr., New York 10010
Type: Private, independent, four-year
Degrees: A, B, M, P, D *Enroll:* 16,459
URL: http://www.touro.edu
Phone: (212) 463-0400 *Calendar:* Sem. plan
Inst. Accred.: MSA-CHE (1976/2004)
Prog. Accred.: Acupuncture, Allied Health (occupational therapy, occupational therapy assisting, speech-language pathology), Physical Therapy, Physical Therapy Assisting, Physician Assistant

College of Osteopathic Medicine
2090 Adam Clayton Powell, Jr. Blvd., Ste. 603, New York 10027
Phone: (646) 981-4500
Prog. Accred: Osteopathy

School of Health Sciences
1700 Union Blvd., Bay Shore 11706
Phone: (631) 665-1600
Prog. Accred: Allied Health (occupational therapy), Physician Assistant

Touro Law Center
300 Nassau Rd., Huntington 11743
Phone: (631) 421-2244
Prog. Accred: Law (ABA only)

Tri-State College of Acupuncture
80 8th Ave., 4th Flr., New York 10011
Type: Private, proprietary, four-year
Degrees: M
URL: http://www.tsca.edu
Phone: (212) 242-2255 *Calendar:* Sem. plan
Inst. Accred.: ACAOM (1993/2003)

Trocaire College
360 Choate Ave., Buffalo 14220
Type: Private, independent, two-year
Degrees: A *Enroll:* 837
URL: http://www.trocaire.edu
Phone: (716) 826-1200 *Calendar:* Sem. plan
Inst. Accred.: MSA-CHE (1974/2004)
Prog. Accred.: Allied Health (medical assisting (AMA), surgical technology), Business (ACBSP), Nursing, Phlebotomy, Practical Nursing, Radiography

U.T.A. Mesivta of Kiryas Joel
PO Box 2009, 9 Nicklesburg Rd., Monroe 10950-8509
Type: Private, independent, four-year
Degrees: Rabbinic *FTE Enroll:* 717
Phone: (845) 783-9901 *Calendar:* Sem. plan
Inst. Accred.: AARTS (2003)

Ulster County Community College
Cottekill Rd., Stone Ridge 12484
Type: Public, state/local, two-year
System: State University of New York Office of Community Colleges
Degrees: A *Enroll:* 2,035
URL: http://www.sunyulster.edu
Phone: (845) 687-5000 *Calendar:* Sem. plan
Inst. Accred.: MSA-CHE (1971/2006)
Prog. Accred.: Allied Health (EMT-paramedic), Nursing, Veterinary Technology

Unification Theological Seminary
30 Seminary Dr., Barrytown 12507
Type: Private, Unification Church, four-year
Degrees: M, P *Enroll:* 98
URL: http://www.uts.edu
Phone: (845) 752-3100 *Calendar:* Tri. plan
Inst. Accred.: MSA-CHE (1996/2003, Warning)

Union College
807 Union St., Schenectady 12308
Type: Private, independent, four-year
System: Union University
Degrees: B *Enroll:* 2,226
URL: http://www.union.edu
Phone: (518) 388-6000 *Calendar:* Tri. plan
Inst. Accred.: MSA-CHE (1921/2005)
Prog. Accred.: Allied Health (health services administration), Business (AACSB), Engineering (computer, electrical, mechanical)

The Union Graduate College
807 Union St., Schenectady 12308
Type: Private, independent, four-year
System: Union University
Degrees: M
URL: http://www.uniongraduatecollege.edu
Phone: (518) 388-6148 *Calendar:* Tri. plan
Inst. Accred.: MSA-CHE (2007), NYBOR (2004)
Prog. Accred.: Teacher Education (TEAC)

Union Theological Seminary
3041 Broadway, New York 10027-5710
Type: Private, interdenominational, four-year
Degrees: M, P, D *Enroll:* 197
URL: http://www.utsnyc.edu
Phone: (212) 662-7100 *Calendar:* Sem. plan
Inst. Accred.: ATS (1938/2007), MSA-CHE (1967/2008)

United States Merchant Marine Academy
300 Steamboat Rd., Kings Point 11024-1699
Type: Public, federal, four-year
Degrees: B, M *Enroll:* 927
URL: http://www.usmma.edu
Phone: (516) 773-5000 *Calendar:* Tri. plan
Inst. Accred.: MSA-CHE (1949/2006)
Prog. Accred.: Engineering (naval architecture/marine)

United States Military Academy
West Point 10996-5000
Type: Public, federal, four-year
Degrees: B *Enroll:* 4,448
URL: http://www.usma.edu
Phone: (845) 938-4011 *Calendar:* Sem. plan
Inst. Accred.: MSA-CHE (1949/2005)
Prog. Accred.: Computer Science (ABET-CAC), Engineering (civil, electrical, engineering management, environmental/sanitary, mechanical, systems)

United Talmudical Seminary
45C Williamsburg St., West, Brooklyn 11211-7984
Type: Private, independent, four-year
Degrees: Rabbinic *Enroll:* 1,330
Phone: (718) 963-9770 *Calendar:* Sem. plan
Inst. Accred.: AARTS (1979/2001)

University at Albany
1400 Washington Ave., Albany 12222
Type: Public, state, four-year
System: State University of New York System Office
Degrees: B, M, D *Enroll:* 14,785
URL: http://www.albany.edu
Phone: (518) 442-3300 *Calendar:* Sem. plan
Inst. Accred.: MSA-CHE (1938/2005)
Prog. Accred.: Accounting, Business (AACSB), Clinical Psychology, Counseling Psychology, Dentistry (dental public health), Graduate Social Work, Librarianship, Planning, Public Administration, Public Health, Rehabilitation Counseling, School Psychology, Social Work, Teacher Education (TEAC)

University of Rochester
Rochester 14627
Type: Private, independent, four-year
Degrees: B, M, P, D *Enroll:* 7,711
URL: http://www.rochester.edu
Phone: (585) 275-2121 *Calendar:* Sem. plan
Inst. Accred.: MSA-CHE (1921/2004)
Prog. Accred.: Allied Health (medicine), Business (AACSB), Clinical Pastoral Education, Clinical Psychology, Counseling, Dentistry (advanced education in general dentistry, combined prosthodontics, general dentistry, general practice residency, oral and maxillofacial surgery, orthodontic and dentofacial orthopedics, pediatric dentistry, periodontics), Engineering (bioengineering, chemical, electrical, mechanical), Marriage and Family Therapy, Music, Nursing, Nursing Education, Psychology Internship, Public Health, Teacher Education (NCATE)

Utica College
1600 Burrstone Rd., Utica 13502-4892
Type: Private, independent, four-year
Degrees: B, M, P *Enroll:* 2,438
URL: http://www.utica.edu
Phone: (315) 792-3111 *Calendar:* Sem. plan
Inst. Accred.: MSA-CHE (1946/2008)
Prog. Accred.: Allied Health (occupational therapy), Nursing, Physical Therapy, Teacher Education (TEAC)

Utica School of Commerce
201 Bleecker St., Utica 13501-2280
Type: Private, proprietary, two-year
Degrees: A *Enroll:* 286
URL: http://www.uscny.edu
Phone: (315) 733-2300 *Calendar:* Sem. plan
Inst. Accred.: NYBOR (1972/2001)

Canastota Campus
PO Box 462, Route 5, Canastota 13032-0462
Phone: (315) 697-8200

Oneonta Campus
17 Elm St., Oneonta 138201828
Phone: (607) 432-7003

Vassar College
124 Raymond Ave., Poughkeepsie 12604-0002
Type: Private, independent, four-year
Degrees: B, M *Enroll:* 2,346
URL: http://www.vassar.edu
Phone: (845) 437-7000 *Calendar:* Sem. plan
Inst. Accred.: MSA-CHE (1921/2004)

Vaughn College of Aeronautics and Technology
86-01 23rd Ave., Flushing 11369
Type: Private, independent, four-year
Degrees: A, B, M *Enroll:* 954
URL: http://www.vaughn.edu
Phone: (718) 429-6600 *Calendar:* Sem. plan
Inst. Accred.: MSA-CHE (1969/2007)
Prog. Accred.: Engineering Technology (aerospace, electrical, mechanical)

Villa Maria College of Buffalo
240 Pine Ridge Rd., Buffalo 14225-3999
Type: Private, independent, four-year
Degrees: A, B *Enroll:* 438
URL: http://www.villa.edu
Phone: (716) 896-0700 *Calendar:* Sem. plan
Inst. Accred.: MSA-CHE (1972/2008)
Prog. Accred.: Physical Therapy Assisting

Wagner College
One Campus Rd., Staten Island 10301
Type: Private, independent, four-year
Degrees: B, M *Enroll:* 2,144
URL: http://www.wagner.edu
Phone: (718) 390-3100 *Calendar:* Sem. plan
Inst. Accred.: MSA-CHE (1931/2001)
Prog. Accred.: Business (ACBSP), Nursing, Physician Assistant, Teacher Education (NCATE)

Webb Institute
298 Crescent Beach Rd., Glen Cove 11542-1398
Type: Private, independent, four-year
Degrees: B *Enroll:* 80
URL: http://www.webb-institute.edu
Phone: (516) 671-2213 *Calendar:* Sem. plan
Inst. Accred.: MSA-CHE (1950/2005)
Prog. Accred.: Engineering (naval architecture/marine)

Wells College
PO Box 5000, Aurora 13026-0500
Type: Private, independent, four-year
Degrees: B *Enroll:* 409
URL: http://www.wells.edu
Phone: (315) 364-3265 *Calendar:* Sem. plan
Inst. Accred.: MSA-CHE (1921/2004)

Westchester Community College
75 Grasslands Rd., Valhalla 10595-1698
Type: Public, state/local, two-year
System: State University of New York Office of Community Colleges
Degrees: A *Enroll:* 7,511
URL: http://www.sunywcc.edu
Phone: (914) 606-6600 *Calendar:* Sem. plan
Inst. Accred.: MSA-CHE (1970/2005)
Prog. Accred.: Allied Health (respiratory therapy), Dietetic Technician, Radiography

Wood Tobe-Coburn School
8 East 40th St., New York 10016-0190
Type: Private, proprietary, two-year
Degrees: A *Enroll:* 269
URL: http://www.woodtobecoburn.edu
Phone: (212) 686-9040 *Calendar:* Sem. plan
Inst. Accred.: NYBOR (1972/2005)
Prog. Accred.: Allied Health (medical assisting (AMA))

Yeshiva and Kolel Bais Medrosh Elyon
73 Main St., Monsey 10952
Type: Private, independent, four-year
Degrees: Talmudic *FTE Enroll:* 42
Phone: (845) 356-7064 *Calendar:* Sem. plan
Inst. Accred.: AARTS (1989/2006)

Yeshiva and Kollel Harbotzas Torah
1049 East 15th St., Brooklyn 11230
Type: Private, independent, four-year
Degrees: Talmudic *Enroll:* 28
Phone: (718) 692-0208 *Calendar:* Sem. plan
Inst. Accred.: AARTS (1985/2005)

Yeshiva D'Monsey Rabbinical College
2 Roman Blvd., Monsey 10952
Type: Private, independent, four-year
Degrees: Talmudic *FTE Enroll:* 96
Phone: (845) 426-3276 *Calendar:* Sem. plan
Inst. Accred.: AARTS (2003/2005)

Yeshiva Derech Chaim
1573 39th St., Brooklyn 11218
Type: Private, independent, four-year
Degrees: Talmudic *Enroll:* 171
Phone: (718) 438-5476 *Calendar:* Sem. plan
Inst. Accred.: AARTS (1984/2005)

Yeshiva Gedolah Imrei Yosef D'Spinka
1466 56th St., Brooklyn 11219
Type: Private, independent, four-year
Degrees: Talmudic *Enroll:* 205
Phone: (718) 851-1600 *Calendar:* Sem. plan
Inst. Accred.: AARTS (1989/2005)

Yeshiva Karlin Stolin Beth Aaron V'Israel Rabbinical Institute
1818 54th St., Brooklyn 11204
Type: Private, independent, four-year
Degrees: Rabbinic *Enroll:* 77
Phone: (718) 232-7800 *Calendar:* Sem. plan
Inst. Accred.: AARTS (1975/2006)

Yeshiva Mikdash Melech
1326 Ocean Pkwy., Brooklyn 11230-5655
Type: Private, independent, four-year
Degrees: Rabbinic *Enroll:* 86
Phone: (718) 339-1090 *Calendar:* Sem. plan
Inst. Accred.: AARTS (1984/2005)

Yeshiva Nesivos HaTorah
5 Birchard Ave., Staten Island 10314-4134
Type: Private, independent, four-year
Degrees: Rabbinic
Phone: (718) 982-0239 *Calendar:* Sem. plan
Inst. Accred.: AARTS (2008)

Yeshiva of Machzikai Dadas
1301 47th St., Far Rockaway 11219
Type: Private, independent, four-year
Degrees: Talmudic
Phone: (718) 853-2442 *Calendar:* Sem. plan
Inst. Accred.: AARTS (2007)

Yeshiva of Nitra—Rabbinical College Yeshiva Farm Settlement
Pines Bridge Rd., Mount Kisco 10549
Type: Private, independent, four-year
Degrees: Rabbinic, Talmudic *Enroll:* 211
Phone: (718) 387-0422 *Calendar:* Sem. plan
Inst. Accred.: AARTS (1980/2001)

Yeshiva of the Telshe Alumni
4904 Independence Ave., Riverdale 10471
Type: Private, independent, four-year
Degrees: Talmudic *Enroll:* 112
Phone: (718) 601-3523 *Calendar:* Sem. plan
Inst. Accred.: AARTS (1995/2003)

Yeshiva Shaar HaTorah Talmudic Research Institute
83-96 117th St., Kew Gardens 11415
Type: Private, independent, four-year
Degrees: Rabbinic, Talmudic *Enroll:* 116
Phone: (718) 846-1940 *Calendar:* Sem. plan
Inst. Accred.: AARTS (1984/2002)

Yeshiva Shaarei Torah of Rockland
91 West Carlton Rd., Suffern 10901-4013
Type: Private, independent, four-year
Degrees: Talmudic *FTE Enroll:* 45
Phone: (845) 352-3431 *Calendar:* Sem. plan
Inst. Accred.: AARTS (2000/2004)

Yeshiva University
500 West 185th St., New York 10033-3299
Type: Private, independent, four-year
Degrees: A, B, M, P, D *Enroll:* 5,828
URL: http://www.yu.edu
Phone: (212) 960-5400 *Calendar:* Sem. plan
Inst. Accred.: MSA-CHE (1948/2007)
Prog. Accred.: Allied Health (medicine), Clinical Psychology, Combined Professional-Scientific Psychology, Dentistry (combined prosthodontics, general practice residency, oral and maxillofacial surgery, orthodontic and dentofacial orthopedics, pediatric dentistry), Graduate Social Work, Law, School Psychology

Jack and Pearl Resnick Campus
1300 Morris Park Ave., Bronx 10461
Phone: (718) 430-2000
Prog. Accred: Psychology Internship

Yeshiva Zichron Aryeh
100 Cedarhurst Ave., Cedarhurst 11516-2158
Type: Private, independent, four-year
Degrees: Talmudic *FTE Enroll:* 30
Phone: (516) 295-5700 *Calendar:* Sem. plan
Inst. Accred.: AARTS (2004)

Yeshivas Novominsk
1569 47th St., Brooklyn 11219
Type: Private, independent, four-year
Degrees: Talmudic *Enroll:* 121
Phone: (718) 438-2727 *Calendar:* Sem. plan
Inst. Accred.: AARTS (1992/2005)

Yeshivath Viznitz
15 Elyon Rd., Monsey 10952
Type: Private, independent, four-year
Degrees: Rabbinic *Enroll:* 432
Phone: (845) 356-1010 *Calendar:* Sem. plan
Inst. Accred.: AARTS (1980/2002)

Yeshivath Zichron Moshe
Laurel Park Rd., South Fallsburg 12779
Type: Private, independent, four-year
Degrees: Talmudic *Enroll:* 181
Phone: (845) 434-5240 *Calendar:* Sem. plan
Inst. Accred.: AARTS (1979/2005)

NORTH CAROLINA

Alamance Community College
PO Box 8000, Graham 27253-8000
Type: Public, state/local, two-year
System: North Carolina Community College System
Degrees: A *Enroll:* 2,805
URL: http://www.alamancecc.edu
Phone: (336) 506-4222 *Calendar:* Sem. plan
Inst. Accred.: SACS (1969/2003)
Prog. Accred.: Allied Health (medical assisting (AMA)), Clinical Lab Technology, Culinary Education, Dentistry (dental assisting)

Apex School of Theology
2945 Miami Blvd., Ste. 114, Durham 27703-8024
Type: Private, nondenominational, four-year
Degrees: A, B, M, D
URL: http://www.apexsot.edu
Phone: (919) 572-1625 *Calendar:* Sem. plan
Inst. Accred.: TRACS (2004)

Appalachian State University
Boone 28608
Type: Public, state, four-year
System: University of North Carolina System
Degrees: B, M, P, D *Enroll:* 13,470
URL: http://www.appstate.edu
Phone: (828) 262-2000 *Calendar:* Sem. plan
Inst. Accred.: SACS (1942/2002)
Prog. Accred.: Allied Health (speech-language pathology), Art, Business (AACSB), Computer Science (ABET-CAC), Counseling, Dietetics (didactic), Dietetics (internship), Family & Consumer Science, Graduate Social Work, Marriage and Family Therapy, Music, Nursing Education, Psychology Internship, Public Administration, Recreation and Leisure Services, Social Work, Teacher Education (NCATE), Theatre

The Art Institute of Charlotte
Three LakePointe Plaza, 2110 Water Ridge Pkwy., Charlotte 28217
Type: Private, proprietary, four-year
System: Education Management Corporation
Degrees: A, B
URL: http://www.aich.artinstitutes.edu
Phone: (704) 357-8020 *Calendar:* Qtr. plan
Inst. Accred.: ACICS (1978/2008)

Brown Mackie College—Atlanta
6600 Peachtree Dunwoody NE, 600 Embassy Row, Atlanta, GA 30328
Phone: (770) 510-2310
Prog. Accred: Allied Health (occupational therapy assisting), Surgical Technology

Asheville-Buncombe Technical Community College
340 Victoria Rd., Asheville 28801
Type: Public, state/local, two-year
System: North Carolina Community College System
Degrees: A *Enroll:* 3,766
URL: http://www.abtech.edu
Phone: (828) 254-1921 *Calendar:* Sem. plan
Inst. Accred.: SACS (1969/2004)
Prog. Accred.: Allied Health (diagnostic medical sonography, surgical technology), Clinical Lab Technology, Culinary Education, Dentistry (dental assisting, dental hygiene), Phlebotomy, Radiography, Veterinary Technology

Barton College
PO Box 5000, Wilson 27893-7000
Type: Private, Christian Church/Disciples of Christ, four-year
Degrees: B *Enroll:* 1,024
URL: http://www.barton.edu
Phone: (252) 399-6300 *Calendar:* Sem. plan
Inst. Accred.: SACS (1955/1998)
Prog. Accred.: Nursing, Social Work, Teacher Education (NCATE)

Beaufort County Community College
PO Box 1069, Washington 27889
Type: Public, state/local, two-year
System: North Carolina Community College System
Degrees: A *Enroll:* 971
URL: http://www.beaufortccc.edu
Phone: (252) 946-6194 *Calendar:* Sem. plan
Inst. Accred.: SACS (1973/1998)
Prog. Accred.: Clinical Lab Technology

Belmont Abbey College
100 Belmont-Mount Holly Rd., Belmont 28012-1802
Type: Private, Roman Catholic Church, four-year
Degrees: B *Enroll:* 833
URL: http://www.belmontabbeycollege.edu
Phone: (704) 825-6700 *Calendar:* Sem. plan
Inst. Accred.: SACS (1957/1999)
Prog. Accred.: Teacher Education (NCATE)

Bennett College for Women
900 East Washington St., Greensboro 27401-3239
Type: Private, United Methodist Church, four-year
Degrees: B *Enroll:* 568
URL: http://www.bennett.edu
Phone: (336) 273-4431 *Calendar:* Sem. plan
Inst. Accred.: SACS (1935/1999)
Prog. Accred.: Social Work, Teacher Education (NCATE)

Bladen Community College
PO Box 266, Dublin 28332-0266
Type: Public, state, two-year
System: North Carolina Community College System
Degrees: A *Enroll:* 1,039
URL: http://www.bladencc.edu
Phone: (910) 879-5500 *Calendar:* Sem. plan
Inst. Accred.: SACS (1976/2002)

Blue Ridge Community College
180 West Campus Dr., Flat Rock 28731-4278
Type: Public, state/local, two-year
System: North Carolina Community College System
Degrees: A *Enroll:* 1,093
URL: http://www.blueridge.edu
Phone: (828) 694-1700 *Calendar:* Sem. plan
Inst. Accred.: SACS (1973/1998)
Prog. Accred.: Allied Health (surgical technology)

Brevard College
400 North Broad St., Brevard 28712-3306
Type: Private, United Methodist Church, four-year
Degrees: A, B *Enroll:* 582
URL: http://www.brevard.edu
Phone: (828) 883-8292 *Calendar:* Sem. plan
Inst. Accred.: SACS (1949/2001)
Prog. Accred.: Music

Brunswick Community College
PO Box 30, Supply 28462
Type: Public, state, two-year
System: North Carolina Community College System
Degrees: A *Enroll:* 693
URL: http://www.brunswickcc.edu
Phone: (910) 755-7300 *Calendar:* Sem. plan
Inst. Accred.: SACS (1983/1998)
Prog. Accred.: Phlebotomy

Cabarrus College of Health Sciences
401 Medical Park Dr., Concord 28025-3959
Type: Private, independent, four-year
Degrees: A, B *Enroll:* 249
URL: http://www.cabarruscollege.edu
Phone: (704) 783-1555 *Calendar:* Sem. plan
Inst. Accred.: SACS (1995/2000)
Prog. Accred.: Allied Health (medical assisting (AMA), occupational therapy assisting, surgical technology), Nursing, Nursing Education

Caldwell Community College and Technical Institute
2855 Hickory Blvd., Hudson 28638
Type: Public, state/local, two-year
System: North Carolina Community College System
Degrees: A *Enroll:* 2,108
URL: http://www.cccti.edu
Phone: (828) 726-2200 *Calendar:* Sem. plan
Inst. Accred.: SACS (1969/2007)
Prog. Accred.: Allied Health (diagnostic medical sonography), Nuclear Medicine Technology, Physical Therapy Assisting, Radiography

Campbell University
PO Box 127, Buies Creek 27506-0127
Type: Private, Baptist State Convention of North Carolina, four-year
Degrees: B, M, P, D *Enroll:* 5,104
URL: http://www.campbell.edu
Phone: (910) 893-1200 *Calendar:* Sem. plan
Inst. Accred.: ATS (2002/2007), SACS (1941/2000)
Prog. Accred.: Business (ACBSP), Law (ABA only), Pharmacy, Social Work, Teacher Education (NCATE)

Cape Fear Community College
411 North Front St., Wilmington 28401-3993
Type: Public, state/local, two-year
System: North Carolina Community College System
Degrees: A *Enroll:* 4,617
URL: http://www.cfcc.edu
Phone: (910) 362-7000 *Calendar:* Sem. plan
Inst. Accred.: SACS (1971/2007)
Prog. Accred.: Allied Health (diagnostic medical sonography, occupational therapy assisting), Dentistry (dental assisting, dental hygiene), Nursing, Phlebotomy, Radiography

Carolina Christian College
PO Box 777, Winston-Salem 27102-0777
Type: Private, Christian Churches/Churches of Christ, four-year
Degrees: A, B *Enroll:* 33
URL: http://www.wsbc.edu
Phone: (336) 744-0900 *Calendar:* Sem. plan
Inst. Accred.: ABHE (2006)

Carolina Evangelical Divinity School
1208 Eastchester Dr., Ste. 101, High Point 27265-2384
Type: Private, Friends United Meeting, four-year
Degrees: M, D
URL: http://www.ceds.edu
Phone: (336) 882-3370 *Calendar:* Sem. plan
Inst. Accred.: ATS (2006), TRACS (2006)

Carolinas College of Health Sciences
PO Box 32861, 1200 Blythe Blvd., Charlotte 28232-2861
Type: Public, state-related, two-year
Degrees: A *FTE Enroll:* 7
URL: http://www.carolinascollege.edu
Phone: (704) 355-5043 *Calendar:* Sem. plan
Inst. Accred.: SACS (1995/2000)
Prog. Accred.: Allied Health (surgical technology), Clinical Lab Scientist, Clinical Pastoral Education, Dentistry (general practice residency), Nursing, Phlebotomy, Radiography

Carteret Community College
3505 Arendell St., Morehead City 28557-2989
Type: Public, state/local, two-year
System: North Carolina Community College System
Degrees: A *Enroll:* 822
URL: http://www.carteret.edu
Phone: (252) 222-6000 *Calendar:* Sem. plan
Inst. Accred.: SACS (1974/1999)
Prog. Accred.: Allied Health (medical assisting (AMA), respiratory therapy), Phlebotomy, Radiography

Catawba College
2300 West Innes St., Salisbury 28144
Type: Private, United Church of Christ, four-year
Degrees: B, M *Enroll:* 1,248
URL: http://www.catawba.edu
Phone: (704) 637-4111 *Calendar:* Sem. plan
Inst. Accred.: SACS (1928/2005)
Prog. Accred.: Business (ACBSP), Teacher Education (NCATE)

Catawba Valley Community College
2550 Hwy. 70 SE, Hickory 28602-9699
Type: Public, state/local, two-year
System: North Carolina Community College System
Degrees: A *Enroll:* 3,063
URL: http://www.cvcc.edu
Phone: (828) 327-7000 *Calendar:* Sem. plan
Inst. Accred.: SACS (1969/2006)
Prog. Accred.: Allied Health (EMT-paramedic, respiratory therapy, surgical technology), Dentistry (dental hygiene), Nursing, Polysomnographic Technology

Central Carolina Community College
1105 Kelly Dr., Sanford 27330
Type: Public, state/local, two-year
System: North Carolina Community College System
Degrees: A *Enroll:* 2,565
URL: http://www.cccc.edu
Phone: (919) 775-5401 *Calendar:* Sem. plan
Inst. Accred.: SACS (1972/2008)
Prog. Accred.: Allied Health (medical assisting (AMA)), Dentistry (dental hygiene), Veterinary Technology

Central Piedmont Community College
PO Box 35009, Charlotte 28235-5009
Type: Public, state/local, two-year
System: North Carolina Community College System
Degrees: A *Enroll:* 9,647
URL: http://www.cpcc.edu
Phone: (704) 330-2722 *Calendar:* Sem. plan
Inst. Accred.: SACS (1969/2003)
Prog. Accred.: Allied Health (cytotechnology, medical assisting (AMA), respiratory therapy, surgical technology), Clinical Lab Technology, Culinary Education, Dentistry (dental assisting, dental hygiene), Engineering Technology (computer, electrical, mechanical), Physical Therapy Assisting

Chowan University
200 Jones Dr., Murfreesboro 27855
Type: Private, Baptist State Convention of North Carolina, four-year
Degrees: A, B *Enroll:* 774
URL: http://www.chowan.edu
Phone: (252) 398-6500 *Calendar:* Sem. plan
Inst. Accred.: SACS (1956/1998)
Prog. Accred.: Music, Teacher Education (NCATE)

Cleveland Community College
137 South Post Rd., Shelby 28152
Type: Public, state/local, two-year
System: North Carolina Community College System
Degrees: A *Enroll:* 1,847
URL: http://www.clevelandcommunitycollege.edu
Phone: (704) 484-4000 *Calendar:* Sem. plan
Inst. Accred.: SACS (1975/2001)
Prog. Accred.: Allied Health (surgical technology), Radiography

Coastal Carolina Community College
444 Western Blvd., Jacksonville 28546-6899
Type: Public, state/local, two-year
System: North Carolina Community College System
Degrees: A *Enroll:* 2,757
URL: http://www.coastalcarolina.edu
Phone: (910) 455-1221 *Calendar:* Sem. plan
Inst. Accred.: SACS (1972/2008)
Prog. Accred.: Allied Health (surgical technology), Clinical Lab Technology, Dentistry (dental assisting, dental hygiene)

College of The Albemarle
PO Box 2327, Elizabeth City 27906-2327
Type: Public, state/local, two-year
System: North Carolina Community College System
Degrees: A *Enroll:* 1,166
URL: http://www.albemarle.edu
Phone: (252) 335-0821 *Calendar:* Sem. plan
Inst. Accred.: SACS (1968/2003)
Prog. Accred.: Allied Health (medical assisting (AMA), surgical technology), Nursing

Craven Community College
800 College Ct., New Bern 28562
Type: Public, state/local, two-year
System: North Carolina Community College System
Degrees: A *Enroll:* 1,790
URL: http://www.cravencc.edu
Phone: (252) 638-4131 *Calendar:* Sem. plan
Inst. Accred.: SACS (1971/2007)

Davidson College
PO Box 5000, Davidson 28035-5000
Type: Private, Presbyterian Church (USA), four-year
Degrees: B *Enroll:* 1,683
URL: http://www.davidson.edu
Phone: (704) 894-2000 *Calendar:* Sem. plan
Inst. Accred.: SACS (1917/2007)

Davidson County Community College
PO Box 1287, Lexington 27293-1287
Type: Public, state/local, two-year
System: North Carolina Community College System
Degrees: A *Enroll:* 1,955
URL: http://www.davidsonccc.edu
Phone: (336) 249-8186 *Calendar:* Sem. plan
Inst. Accred.: SACS (1968/2002)
Prog. Accred.: Allied Health (medical assisting (AMA)), Clinical Lab Technology, Nursing

Duke University
207 Allen Bldg., Box 90001, Durham 27708
Type: Private, independent, four-year
Degrees: A, B, M, D *Enroll:* 13,720
URL: http://www.duke.edu
Phone: (919) 684-8111 *Calendar:* Sem. plan
Inst. Accred.: ATS (1938/2005), SACS (1895/1998)
Prog. Accred.: Allied Health (health services administration, medicine), Business (AACSB), Clinical Lab Scientist, Clinical Pastoral Education, Clinical Psychology, Engineering (bioengineering, civil, computer, electrical, mechanical), Forestry, Law, Nurse Anesthesia Education, Nursing Education, Pathologists' Assistant, Physical Therapy, Physician Assistant, Psychology Internship, Teacher Education (NCATE)

Durham Technical Community College
1637 Lawson St., Durham 27703-5023
Type: Public, state/local, two-year
System: North Carolina Community College System
Degrees: A *Enroll:* 2,788
URL: http://www.durhamtech.edu
Phone: (919) 686-3300 *Calendar:* Sem. plan
Inst. Accred.: SACS (1971/2007)
Prog. Accred.: Allied Health (occupational therapy assisting, opticianry, respiratory therapy, surgical technology), Dentistry (dental laboratory technology)

East Carolina University
East Fifth St., Greenville 27858-4353
Type: Public, state, four-year
System: University of North Carolina System
Degrees: B, M, P, D *Enroll:* 19,983
URL: http://www.ecu.edu
Phone: (252) 328-6131 *Calendar:* Sem. plan
Inst. Accred.: SACS (1927/2002)
Prog. Accred.: Allied Health (audiology, medicine, occupational therapy, speech-language pathology), Art, Business (AACSB), Clinical Lab Scientist, Construction Education, Dentistry (general practice residency), Design Technology, Dietetics (didactic), Dietetics (internship), Electronic Technology, Environmental Health, Environmental Health (graduate), Graduate Social Work, Industrial Technology, Interior Design, Manufacturing Technology, Marriage and Family Therapy, Music, Nurse (Midwifery), Nurse Anesthesia Education, Nursing, Physical Therapy, Physician Assistant, Planning, Public Administration, Public Health, Recreation and Leisure Services, Rehabilitation Counseling, Social Work, Teacher Education (NCATE)

Edgecombe Community College
2009 West Wilson St., Tarboro 27886
Type: Public, state/local, two-year
System: North Carolina Community College System
Degrees: A *Enroll:* 1,398
URL: http://www.edgecombe.edu
Phone: (252) 823-5166 *Calendar:* Sem. plan
Inst. Accred.: SACS (1973/1998)
Prog. Accred.: Allied Health (medical assisting (AMA), respiratory therapy, surgical technology), Radiography

Elizabeth City State University
1704 Weeksville Rd., Elizabeth City 27909
Type: Public, state, four-year
System: University of North Carolina System
Degrees: B, M *Enroll:* 2,439
URL: http://www.ecsu.edu
Phone: (252) 335-3400 *Calendar:* Sem. plan
Inst. Accred.: SACS (1947/2001)
Prog. Accred.: Industrial Technology, Social Work, Teacher Education (NCATE)

Elon University
100 Campus Dr., Elon 27244
Type: Private, United Church of Christ, four-year
Degrees: B, M, D *Enroll:* 4,821
URL: http://www.elon.edu
Phone: (336) 278-2000 *Calendar:* Sem. plan
Inst. Accred.: SACS (1947/2002)
Prog. Accred.: Business (AACSB), Journalism, Physical Therapy, Teacher Education (NCATE)

Fayetteville State University
1200 Murchison Rd., Newbold Station, Fayetteville 28301-4298
Type: Public, state, four-year
System: University of North Carolina System
Degrees: A, B, M, D *Enroll:* 5,014
URL: http://www.uncfsu.edu
Phone: (910) 672-1111 *Calendar:* Sem. plan
Inst. Accred.: SACS (1947/2001)
Prog. Accred.: Business (AACSB), Graduate Social Work, Nursing Education, Teacher Education (NCATE)

Fayetteville Technical Community College
PO Box 35236, Fayetteville 28303-0236
Type: Public, state, two-year
System: North Carolina Community College System
Degrees: A *Enroll:* 5,365
URL: http://www.faytechcc.edu
Phone: (910) 678-8400 *Calendar:* Sem. plan
Inst. Accred.: SACS (1967/2001)
Prog. Accred.: Allied Health (respiratory therapy, surgical technology), Dentistry (dental assisting, dental hygiene), Engineering Technology (civil/construction, electrical), Funeral Service Education (Mortuary Science), Nursing, Phlebotomy, Physical Therapy Assisting, Radiography

Forsyth Technical Community College
2100 Silas Creek Pkwy., Winston-Salem 27103
Type: Public, state, two-year
System: North Carolina Community College System
Degrees: A *Enroll:* 4,009
URL: http://www.forsythtech.edu
Phone: (336) 723-0371 *Calendar:* Sem. plan
Inst. Accred.: SACS (1968/2002)
Prog. Accred.: Allied Health (diagnostic medical sonography, medical assisting (AMA), respiratory therapy), Dentistry (dental assisting), Engineering Technology (electrical), Nuclear Medicine Technology, Radiation Therapy, Radiography

Gardner-Webb University
PO Box 897, Boiling Springs 28017
Type: Private, Baptist State Convention of North Carolina, four-year
Degrees: A, B, M, D *Enroll:* 2,866
URL: http://www.gardner-webb.edu
Phone: (704) 406-4000 *Calendar:* Sem. plan
Inst. Accred.: ATS (2000/2004), SACS (1948/2007)
Prog. Accred.: Business (ACBSP), Music, Nursing, Teacher Education (NCATE)

Gaston College
201 Hwy. 321 South, Dallas 28034-1499
Type: Public, state/local, two-year
System: North Carolina Community College System
Degrees: A *Enroll:* 3,204
URL: http://www.gaston.edu
Phone: (704) 922-6200 *Calendar:* Sem. plan
Inst. Accred.: SACS (1967/2001)
Prog. Accred.: Allied Health (medical assisting (AMA)), Business (ACBSP), Dietetic Technician, Engineering Technology (civil/construction, electrical, industrial, mechanical), Veterinary Technology

Greensboro College
815 West Market St., Greensboro 27401-1875
Type: Private, United Methodist Church, four-year
Degrees: B, M *Enroll:* 1,025
URL: http://www.gborocollege.edu
Phone: (336) 272-7102 *Calendar:* Sem. plan
Inst. Accred.: SACS (1926/2005)
Prog. Accred.: Business (ACBSP), Music, Teacher Education (NCATE)

Guilford College
5800 West Friendly Ave., Greensboro 27410
Type: Private, Religious Society of Friends (Quaker), four-year
Degrees: A, B *Enroll:* 2,420
URL: http://www.guilford.edu
Phone: (336) 316-2000 *Calendar:* Sem. plan
Inst. Accred.: SACS (1926/2007)
Prog. Accred.: Teacher Education (NCATE)

Guilford Technical Community College
PO Box 309, Jamestown 27282
Type: Public, state, two-year
System: North Carolina Community College System
Degrees: A *Enroll:* 5,196
URL: http://www.gtcc.edu
Phone: (336) 334-4822 *Calendar:* Sem. plan
Inst. Accred.: SACS (1969/2005)
Prog. Accred.: Allied Health (medical assisting (AMA), surgical technology), Culinary Education, Dentistry (dental assisting, dental hygiene), Physical Therapy Assisting

Halifax Community College
PO Drawer 809, Weldon 27890
Type: Public, state/local, two-year
System: North Carolina Community College System
Degrees: A *Enroll:* 1,048
URL: http://www.halifaxcc.edu
Phone: (252) 536-2551 *Calendar:* Sem. plan
Inst. Accred.: SACS (1975/2000)
Prog. Accred.: Clinical Lab Technology, Phlebotomy

Haywood Community College
185 Freedlander Dr., Clyde 28721
Type: Public, state, two-year
System: North Carolina Community College System
Degrees: A *Enroll:* 1,211
URL: http://www.haywood.edu
Phone: (828) 627-2821 *Calendar:* Sem. plan
Inst. Accred.: SACS (1973/1998)
Prog. Accred.: Allied Health (medical assisting (AMA)), Forestry

Heritage Bible College
PO Box 1628, Dunn 28335-1628
Type: Private, Penticostal Free Will Baptist Church, four-year
Degrees: A, B *Enroll:* 97
URL: http://www.heritagebiblecollege.edu
Phone: (910) 892-3178 *Calendar:* Sem. plan
Inst. Accred.: TRACS (1998/2003)

High Point University
833 Montlieu Ave., High Point 27262
Type: Private, United Methodist Church, four-year
Degrees: B, M *Enroll:* 2,515
URL: http://www.highpoint.edu
Phone: (336) 841-9000 *Calendar:* Sem. plan
Inst. Accred.: SACS (1951/2006)
Prog. Accred.: Business (ACBSP), Interior Design, Teacher Education (NCATE)

Hood Theological Seminary
1810 Lutheran Synod Dr., Salisbury 28144
Type: Private, African Methodist Episcopal Zion Church, four-year
Degrees: M, D
URL: http://www.hoodseminary.edu
Phone: (704) 636-7611 *Calendar:* Sem. plan
Inst. Accred.: ATS (1998/2003)

Isothermal Community College
PO Box 804, Spindale 28160-0804
Type: Public, state/local, two-year
System: North Carolina Community College System
Degrees: A *Enroll:* 1,362
URL: http://www.isothermal.edu
Phone: (828) 286-3636 *Calendar:* Sem. plan
Inst. Accred.: SACS (1970/2006)
Prog. Accred.: Allied Health (surgical technology)

James Sprunt Community College
PO Box 398, Kenansville 28349-0398
Type: Public, state, two-year
System: North Carolina Community College System
Degrees: A *Enroll:* 916
URL: http://www.jamessprunt.edu
Phone: (910) 296-2400 *Calendar:* Sem. plan
Inst. Accred.: SACS (1973/1998)
Prog. Accred.: Allied Health (medical assisting (AMA)), Phlebotomy

John Wesley College
2314 North Centennial St., High Point 27265-3197
Type: Private, independent, four-year
Degrees: A, B *Enroll:* 110
URL: http://www.johnwesley.edu
Phone: (336) 889-2262 *Calendar:* Sem. plan
Inst. Accred.: ABHE (1982/2003)

Johnson C. Smith University
100 Beatties Ford Rd., Charlotte 28216
Type: Private, independent, four-year
Degrees: B *Enroll:* 1,365
URL: http://www.jcsu.edu
Phone: (704) 378-1000 *Calendar:* Sem. plan
Inst. Accred.: SACS (1933/2007)
Prog. Accred.: Business (ACBSP), Social Work, Teacher Education (NCATE)

Johnston Community College
PO Box 2350, Smithfield 27577-2350
Type: Public, state/local, two-year
System: North Carolina Community College System
Degrees: A *Enroll:* 2,456
URL: http://www.johnstoncc.edu
Phone: (919) 934-3051 *Calendar:* Sem. plan
Inst. Accred.: SACS (1977/2002)
Prog. Accred.: Allied Health (diagnostic medical sonography, medical assisting (AMA)), Radiography

King's College
322 Lamar Ave., Charlotte 28204
Type: Private, proprietary, two-year
Degrees: A *FTE Enroll:* 385
URL: http://www.kingscollegecharlotte.edu
Phone: (704) 372-0266 *Calendar:* Qtr. plan
Inst. Accred.: ACICS (1954/2004)
Prog. Accred.: Allied Health (medical assisting (AMA))

Lees-McRae College
PO Box 128, Banner Elk 28604
Type: Private, United Presbyterian Church, USA, four-year
Degrees: A, B *Enroll:* 873
URL: http://www.lmc.edu
Phone: (828) 898-5241 *Calendar:* Sem. plan
Inst. Accred.: SACS (1953/2006)
Prog. Accred.: Nursing Education, Teacher Education (NCATE)

Lenoir Community College
PO Box 188, Kinston 28502-0188
Type: Public, state/local, two-year
System: North Carolina Community College System
Degrees: A *Enroll:* 1,780
URL: http://www.lenoircc.edu
Phone: (252) 527-6223 *Calendar:* Sem. plan
Inst. Accred.: SACS (1968/2003)
Prog. Accred.: Allied Health (medical assisting (AMA), surgical technology)

Lenoir-Rhyne University
PO Box 7163, Hickory 28603-7163
Type: Private, North Carolina Synod of Evangelical Lutheran Churc, four-year
Degrees: B, M *Enroll:* 1,420
URL: http://www.lrc.edu
Phone: (828) 328-1741 *Calendar:* Sem. plan
Inst. Accred.: SACS (1928/2002)
Prog. Accred.: Allied Health (occupational therapy), Business (ACBSP), Nursing Education, Teacher Education (NCATE)

Livingstone College
701 West Monroe St., Salisbury 28144
Type: Private, African Methodist Episcopal Zion Church, four-year
Degrees: B *Enroll:* 876
URL: http://www.livingstone.edu
Phone: (704) 216-6000 *Calendar:* Sem. plan
Inst. Accred.: SACS (1944/2001)
Prog. Accred.: Social Work, Teacher Education (NCATE)

Louisburg College
501 North Main St., Louisburg 27549
Type: Private, North Carolina Conference of the Methodist Church, two-year
Degrees: A *Enroll:* 726
URL: http://www.louisburg.edu
Phone: (919) 496-2521 *Calendar:* Sem. plan
Inst. Accred.: SACS (1952/2006, Probation)

Mars Hill College
PO Box 370, Mars Hill 28754-0370
Type: Private, Baptist State Convention of North Carolina, four-year
Degrees: B *Enroll:* 1,243
URL: http://www.mhc.edu
Phone: (828) 689-1307 *Calendar:* Sem. plan
Inst. Accred.: SACS (1926/2001)
Prog. Accred.: Music, Social Work, Teacher Education (NCATE), Theatre

Martin Community College
1161 Kehukee Park Rd., Williamston 27892-8307
Type: Public, state/local, two-year
System: North Carolina Community College System
Degrees: A *Enroll:* 619
URL: http://www.martincc.edu
Phone: (252) 792-1521 *Calendar:* Sem. plan
Inst. Accred.: SACS (1972/1998)
Prog. Accred.: Allied Health (medical assisting (AMA)), Dentistry (dental assisting), Physical Therapy Assisting

Mayland Community College
PO Box 547, Spruce Pine 28777
Type: Public, state/local, two-year
System: North Carolina Community College System
Degrees: A *Enroll:* 872
URL: http://www.mayland.edu
Phone: (828) 765-7351 *Calendar:* Sem. plan
Inst. Accred.: SACS (1978/2005)
Prog. Accred.: Allied Health (medical assisting (AMA))

McDowell Technical Community College
54 College Dr., Marion 28752-8728
Type: Public, state/local, two-year
System: North Carolina Community College System
Degrees: A *Enroll:* 796
URL: http://www.mcdowelltech.edu
Phone: (828) 652-6021 *Calendar:* Sem. plan
Inst. Accred.: SACS (1975/2000)
Prog. Accred.: Allied Health (surgical technology)

Meredith College
3800 Hillsborough St., Raleigh 27607-5298
Type: Private, independent, four-year
Degrees: B, M *Enroll:* 1,861
URL: http://www.meredith.edu
Phone: (919) 760-8600 *Calendar:* Sem. plan
Inst. Accred.: SACS (1921/2000)
Prog. Accred.: Dietetics (didactic), Dietetics (internship), Interior Design, Music, Social Work, Teacher Education (NCATE)

Methodist University
5400 Ramsey St., Fayetteville 28311-1420
Type: Private, United Methodist Church, four-year
Degrees: A, B, M *Enroll:* 1,906
URL: http://www.methodist.edu
Phone: (910) 630-7000 *Calendar:* Sem. plan
Inst. Accred.: SACS (1966/1999)
Prog. Accred.: Business (ACBSP), Physician Assistant, Social Work, Teacher Education (NCATE)

Mitchell Community College
500 West Broad St., Statesville 28677
Type: Public, state, two-year
System: North Carolina Community College System
Degrees: A *Enroll:* 1,384
URL: http://www.mitchellcc.edu
Phone: (704) 878-3200 *Calendar:* Sem. plan
Inst. Accred.: SACS (1955/2008)
Prog. Accred.: Allied Health (medical assisting (AMA)), Nursing

Montgomery Community College
1011 Page St., Troy 27371-8387
Type: Public, state/local, two-year
System: North Carolina Community College System
Degrees: A *Enroll:* 545
URL: http://www.montgomery.edu
Phone: (910) 576-6222 *Calendar:* Sem. plan
Inst. Accred.: SACS (1978/2003)
Prog. Accred.: Allied Health (medical assisting (AMA))

Montreat College
PO Box 1267, Montreat 28757
Type: Private, Presbyterian Church, USA, four-year
Degrees: A, B, M *Enroll:* 1,008
URL: http://www.montreat.edu
Phone: (828) 669-8011 *Calendar:* Sem. plan
Inst. Accred.: SACS (1960/2000)
Prog. Accred.: Teacher Education (NCATE)

Mount Olive College
634 Henderson St., Mount Olive 28365
Type: Private, Convention of Original Free Will Baptists, four-year
Degrees: A, B *Enroll:* 2,293
URL: http://www.mountolivecollege.edu
Phone: (919) 658-2502 *Calendar:* Sem. plan
Inst. Accred.: SACS (1960/2001)
Prog. Accred.: Business (ACBSP)

Nash Community College
PO Box 7488, Rocky Mount 27804-0488
Type: Public, state/local, two-year
System: North Carolina Community College System
Degrees: A *Enroll:* 1,403
URL: http://www.nashcc.edu
Phone: (252) 443-4011 *Calendar:* Sem. plan
Inst. Accred.: SACS (1976/2001)
Prog. Accred.: Phlebotomy, Physical Therapy Assisting

North Carolina Agricultural and Technical State University
1601 East Market St., Greensboro 27411
Type: Public, state, four-year
System: University of North Carolina System
Degrees: B, M, D *Enroll:* 10,101
URL: http://www.ncat.edu
Phone: (336) 334-7500 *Calendar:* Sem. plan
Inst. Accred.: SACS (1936/2000)
Prog. Accred.: Accounting, Business (AACSB), Computer Science (ABET-CAC), Construction Education, Construction Technology, Counseling, Design Technology, Electronic Technology, Engineering (agricultural, architectural, chemical, civil, electrical, industrial, mechanical), Family & Consumer Science, Graduate Social Work, Health Technology, Journalism, Landscape Architecture, Manufacturing Technology, Music, Nursing, Rehabilitation Counseling, Social Work, Teacher Education (NCATE), Theatre

North Carolina Central University
1801 Fayetteville St., Durham 27707
Type: Public, state, four-year
System: University of North Carolina System
Degrees: B, M, D *Enroll:* 6,827
URL: http://www.nccu.edu
Phone: (919) 560-6100 *Calendar:* Sem. plan
Inst. Accred.: SACS (1938/1999)
Prog. Accred.: Allied Health (speech-language pathology), Business (AACSB), Business (ACBSP), Counseling, Dietetics (didactic), Dietetics (internship), Law (ABA only), Librarianship, Nursing, Recreation and Leisure Services, Social Work, Teacher Education (NCATE), Theatre

North Carolina State University
PO Box 7001, Raleigh 27695-0001
Type: Public, state, four-year
System: University of North Carolina System
Degrees: A, B, M, D *Enroll:* 25,810
URL: http://www.ncsu.edu
Phone: (919) 515-2011 *Calendar:* Sem. plan
Inst. Accred.: SACS (1928/2004)
Prog. Accred.: Art, Business (AACSB), Computer Science (ABET-CAC), Counseling, Engineering (aerospace, agricultural, bioengineering, chemical, civil, computer, construction, electrical, environmental/sanitary, industrial, materials, mechanical, nuclear, paper, textile), Forestry, Graduate Social Work, Landscape Architecture, Public Administration, Recreation and Leisure Services, School Psychology, Social Work, Teacher Education (NCATE), Veterinary Medicine

North Carolina Wesleyan College
3400 North Wesleyan Blvd., Rocky Mount 27804-9906
Type: Private, United Methodist Church, four-year
Degrees: B *Enroll:* 1,483
URL: http://www.ncwc.edu
Phone: (252) 985-5100 *Calendar:* 4-1-4 plan
Inst. Accred.: SACS (1966/2002)
Prog. Accred.: Teacher Education (NCATE)

Pamlico Community College
PO Box 185, Grantsboro 28529
Type: Public, state/local, two-year
System: North Carolina Community College System
Degrees: A *Enroll:* 223
URL: http://www.pamlicocc.edu
Phone: (252) 249-1851 *Calendar:* Sem. plan
Inst. Accred.: SACS (1977/2002)
Prog. Accred.: Allied Health (electroneurodiagnostic technology, medical assisting (AMA))

Peace College
15 East Peace St., Raleigh 27604-1194
Type: Private, Presbyterian Church, USA, four-year
Degrees: B *Enroll:* 655
URL: http://www.peace.edu
Phone: (919) 508-2000 *Calendar:* Sem. plan
Inst. Accred.: SACS (1947/2001)

Pfeiffer University
PO Box 960, Misenheimer 28109-0960
Type: Private, United Methodist Church, four-year
Degrees: B, M *Enroll:* 1,597
URL: http://www.pfeiffer.edu
Phone: (704) 463-1360 *Calendar:* Sem. plan
Inst. Accred.: SACS (1942/2002)
Prog. Accred.: Music, Teacher Education (NCATE)

Charlotte Campus
4701 Park Rd., Charlotte 28209
Phone: (704) 521-9116

Triangle Campus
5001 South Miami Blvd., Ste. 118, Durham 27703
Phone: (919) 941-2920

Piedmont Baptist College and Graduate School
420 South Broad St., Winston-Salem 27101-5025
Type: Private, independent, four-year
Degrees: A, B, M *Enroll:* 280
URL: http://www.pbc.edu
Phone: (336) 725-8344 *Calendar:* Sem. plan
Inst. Accred.: TRACS (1994/2000)

Piedmont Community College
PO Box 1197, Roxboro 27573
Type: Public, state/local, two-year
System: North Carolina Community College System
Degrees: A *Enroll:* 1,572
URL: http://www.piedmontcc.edu
Phone: (336) 599-1181 *Calendar:* Sem. plan
Inst. Accred.: SACS (1977/2002)

Pitt Community College
PO Drawer 7007, Greenville 27835-7007
Type: Public, state, two-year
System: North Carolina Community College System
Degrees: A *Enroll:* 4,321
URL: http://www.pittcc.edu
Phone: (252) 493-7200 *Calendar:* Sem. plan
Inst. Accred.: SACS (1969/2003)
Prog. Accred.: Allied Health (diagnostic medical sonography, medical assisting (AMA), occupational therapy assisting, respiratory therapy), Radiation Therapy, Radiography

Queens University of Charlotte
1900 Selwyn Ave., Charlotte 28274
Type: Private, Presbyterian Church (USA), four-year
Degrees: B, M *Enroll:* 1,544
URL: http://www.queens.edu
Phone: (704) 337-2200 *Calendar:* Sem. plan
Inst. Accred.: SACS (1932/2001)
Prog. Accred.: Business (AACSB), Business (ACBSP), Music, Nursing, Nursing Education, Teacher Education (NCATE)

Randolph Community College
PO Box 1009, Asheboro 27204-1009
Type: Public, state/local, two-year
System: North Carolina Community College System
Degrees: A *Enroll:* 1,270
URL: http://www.randolph.edu
Phone: (336) 633-0200 *Calendar:* Sem. plan
Inst. Accred.: SACS (1974/1999)
Prog. Accred.: Nursing

Richmond Community College
PO Box 1189, Hamlet 28345
Type: Public, state/local, two-year
System: North Carolina Community College System
Degrees: A *Enroll:* 953
URL: http://www.richmondcc.edu
Phone: (910) 582-7000 *Calendar:* Sem. plan
Inst. Accred.: SACS (1969/2003)
Prog. Accred.: Allied Health (medical assisting (AMA))

Roanoke Bible College
715 North Poindexter St., Elizabeth City 27909-4054
Type: Private, Christian Churches/Churches of Christ, four-year
Degrees: A, B *Enroll:* 167
URL: http://www.roanokebible.edu
Phone: (252) 334-2070 *Calendar:* Sem. plan
Inst. Accred.: ABHE (1979/2000), SACS (1999/2005)

Roanoke-Chowan Community College
109 Community College Rd., Ahoskie 27910
Type: Public, state/local, two-year
System: North Carolina Community College System
Degrees: A *Enroll:* 653
URL: http://www.roanokechowan.edu
Phone: (252) 862-1200 *Calendar:* Sem. plan
Inst. Accred.: SACS (1976/2002)

Robeson Community College
PO Box 1420, Lumberton 28359
Type: Public, state/local, two-year
System: North Carolina Community College System
Degrees: A *Enroll:* 1,454
URL: http://www.robeson.cc.nc.us
Phone: (910) 738-7101 *Calendar:* Sem. plan
Inst. Accred.: SACS (1975/2001)
Prog. Accred.: Allied Health (respiratory therapy, surgical technology)

Rockingham Community College
PO Box 38, Wentworth 27375-0038
Type: Public, state/local, two-year
System: North Carolina Community College System
Degrees: A *Enroll:* 1,104
URL: http://www.rockinghamcc.edu
Phone: (336) 342-4261 *Calendar:* Sem. plan
Inst. Accred.: SACS (1968/2003)
Prog. Accred.: Allied Health (respiratory therapy, surgical technology), Phlebotomy

Rowan-Cabarrus Community College
PO Box 1595, Salisbury 28145-1595
Type: Public, state, two-year
System: North Carolina Community College System
Degrees: A *Enroll:* 3,416
URL: http://www.rowancabarrus.edu
Phone: (704) 637-0760 *Calendar:* Sem. plan
Inst. Accred.: SACS (1970/2007)
Prog. Accred.: Dentistry (dental assisting), Nursing, Radiography

Saint Andrews Presbyterian College
1700 Dogwood Mile, Laurinburg 28352
Type: Private, Presbyterian Church, USA, four-year
Degrees: B *Enroll:* 734
URL: http://www.sapc.edu
Phone: (910) 277-5000 *Calendar:* Sem. plan
Inst. Accred.: SACS (1961/2000, Probation)
Prog. Accred.: Teacher Education (NCATE)

Saint Augustine's College
1315 Oakwood Ave., Raleigh 27610-2298
Type: Private, Episcopal Church, four-year
Degrees: B *Enroll:* 1,137
URL: http://www.st-aug.edu
Phone: (919) 516-4000 *Calendar:* Sem. plan
Inst. Accred.: SACS (1942/2002)
Prog. Accred.: Teacher Education (NCATE)

Salem College
PO Box 10548, Winston-Salem 27108-0548
Type: Private, independent, four-year
Degrees: B, M *Enroll:* 872
URL: http://www.salem.edu
Phone: (336) 721-2600 *Calendar:* 4-1-4 plan
Inst. Accred.: SACS (1922/2000)
Prog. Accred.: Music, Teacher Education (NCATE)

Sampson Community College
PO Box 318, Highway 24 West, Clinton 28329-0318
Type: Public, state/local, two-year
System: North Carolina Community College System
Degrees: A *Enroll:* 923
URL: http://www.sampsoncc.edu
Phone: (910) 592-8081 *Calendar:* Sem. plan
Inst. Accred.: SACS (1977/2003)

Sandhills Community College
3395 Airport Rd., Pinehurst 28374
Type: Public, state/local, two-year
System: North Carolina Community College System
Degrees: A *Enroll:* 2,366
URL: http://www.sandhills.edu
Phone: (910) 695-6185 *Calendar:* Sem. plan
Inst. Accred.: SACS (1968/2003)
Prog. Accred.: Allied Health (respiratory therapy, surgical technology), Clinical Lab Technology, Radiography

School of Communication Arts
3000 Wakefield Crossing Dr., Raleigh 27614
Type: Private, proprietary, two-year
Degrees: A
URL: http://www.higherdigital.com
Phone: (919) 488-8500 *Calendar:* Qtr. plan
Inst. Accred.: COE (1994/2006)

Shaw University
118 East South St., Raleigh 27601
Type: Private, American Baptist Churches (USA), four-year
Degrees: A, B, M *Enroll:* 2,569
URL: http://www.shawuniversity.edu
Phone: (919) 546-8200 *Calendar:* Sem. plan
Inst. Accred.: ATS (1997/2004), SACS (1943/2002)
Prog. Accred.: Allied Health (kinesiotherapy), Social Work, Teacher Education (NCATE)

South College
29 Turtle Creek Dr., Asheville 28803
Type: Private, proprietary, four-year
Degrees: A, B *Enroll:* 103
URL: http://www.southcollegenc.com
Phone: (828) 252-2486 *Calendar:* Sem. plan
Inst. Accred.: ACICS (1971/2005)
Prog. Accred.: Allied Health (medical assisting (AMA), surgical technology)

South Piedmont Community College
PO Box 126, Polkton 28135
Type: Public, state/local, two-year
System: North Carolina Community College System
Degrees: A *Enroll:* 1,111
URL: http://www.spcc.edu
Phone: (704) 272-5300 *Calendar:* Sem. plan
Inst. Accred.: SACS (1977/2003)
Prog. Accred.: Allied Health (diagnostic medical sonography, medical assisting (AMA), surgical technology)

Old Charlotte Highway Campus
4209 Old Charlotte Hwy., Monroe 28110
Phone: (704) 290-5100

The Southeastern Baptist Theological Seminary
PO Box 1889, Wake Forest 27588-1889
Type: Private, Southern Baptist Convention, four-year
Degrees: A, B, M, D *Enroll:* 1,653
URL: http://www.sebts.edu
Phone: (919) 761-2100 *Calendar:* Sem. plan
Inst. Accred.: ATS (1958/2001), SACS (1978/2002)
Prog. Accred.: Teacher Education (NCATE)

Southeastern Community College
PO Box 151, Whiteville 28472
Type: Public, state, two-year
System: North Carolina Community College System
Degrees: A *Enroll:* 1,285
URL: http://www.sccnc.edu
Phone: (910) 642-7141 *Calendar:* Sem. plan
Inst. Accred.: SACS (1967/2001)
Prog. Accred.: Clinical Lab Technology

Southern Evangelical Seminary
3000 Tilley Morris Rd., Matthews 28104
Type: Private, nondenominational, four-year
Degrees: B, M, D
URL: http://www.ses.edu
Phone: (704) 847-5600 *Calendar:* Sem. plan
Inst. Accred.: TRACS (2001/2006)

Southwestern Community College
447 College Dr., Sylva 28779
Type: Public, state/local, two-year
System: North Carolina Community College System
Degrees: A *Enroll:* 1,207
URL: http://www.southwesterncc.edu
Phone: (828) 586-4091 *Calendar:* Sem. plan
Inst. Accred.: SACS (1971/2007)
Prog. Accred.: Allied Health (respiratory therapy), Clinical Lab Technology, Phlebotomy, Physical Therapy Assisting, Radiography

Stanly Community College
141 College Dr., Albemarle 28001
Type: Public, state/local, two-year
System: North Carolina Community College System
Degrees: A *Enroll:* 1,275
URL: http://www.stanly.edu
Phone: (704) 982-0121 *Calendar:* Sem. plan
Inst. Accred.: SACS (1979/2005)
Prog. Accred.: Allied Health (medical assisting (AMA), respiratory therapy), Phlebotomy

Surry Community College
PO Box 304, Dobson 27017-0304
Type: Public, state/local, two-year
System: North Carolina Community College System
Degrees: A *Enroll:* 1,884
URL: http://www.surry.edu
Phone: (336) 386-8121 *Calendar:* Sem. plan
Inst. Accred.: SACS (1969/2004)
Prog. Accred.: Allied Health (medical assisting (AMA))

Tri-County Community College
4600 East Hwy. 64, Murphy 28906
Type: Public, state, two-year
System: North Carolina Community College System
Degrees: A *Enroll:* 673
URL: http://www.tricountycc.edu
Phone: (828) 837-6810 *Calendar:* Sem. plan
Inst. Accred.: SACS (1975/2000)
Prog. Accred.: Allied Health (medical assisting (AMA))

The University of North Carolina at Asheville
One University Heights, Asheville 28804-8503
Type: Public, state, four-year
System: University of North Carolina System
Degrees: B, M *Enroll:* 3,096
URL: http://www.unca.edu
Phone: (828) 251-6600 *Calendar:* Sem. plan
Inst. Accred.: SACS (1958/2002)
Prog. Accred.: Business (AACSB), Teacher Education (NCATE)

The University of North Carolina at Chapel Hill
Chapel Hill 27599
Type: Public, state, four-year
System: University of North Carolina System
Degrees: B, M, P, D *Enroll:* 24,251
URL: http://www.unc.edu
Phone: (919) 962-2211 *Calendar:* Sem. plan
Inst. Accred.: SACS (1895/2006)
Prog. Accred.: Allied Health (audiology, cytotechnology, health services administration, medicine, occupational therapy, speech-language pathology), Business (AACSB), Clinical Lab Scientist, Clinical Pastoral Education, Clinical Psychology, Counseling, Dentistry (advanced education in general dentistry, combined prosthodontics, dental assisting, dental hygiene, dentistry, endodontics, general dentistry, general practice residency, oral and maxillofacial pathology, oral and maxillofacial radiology, oral and maxillofacial surgery, orthodontic and dentofacial orthopedics, pediatric dentistry, periodontics), Dietetics (coordinated), Dietetics (didactic), Graduate Social Work, Immunology, Journalism, Law, Librarianship, Nuclear Medicine Technology, Nursing, Nursing Education, Pharmacy, Physical Therapy, Planning, Psychology Internship, Public Administration, Public Health, Radiation Therapy, Radiography, Radiation Therapy, Rehabilitation Counseling, School Psychology, Teacher Education (NCATE)

The University of North Carolina at Charlotte
9201 University City Blvd., Charlotte 28223-0007
Type: Public, state, four-year
System: University of North Carolina System
Degrees: B, M, P, D *Enroll:* 17,079
URL: http://www.uncc.edu
Phone: (704) 687-2000 *Calendar:* Sem. plan
Inst. Accred.: SACS (1957/2002)
Prog. Accred.: Accounting, Business (AACSB), Counseling, Engineering (civil, computer, electrical, mechanical), Engineering Technology (civil/construction, electrical, mechanical), Graduate Social Work, Nurse Anesthesia Education, Nursing Education, Psychology Internship, Public Administration, Social Work, Teacher Education (NCATE)

The University of North Carolina at Greensboro
PO Box 26170, Greensboro 27402
Type: Public, state, four-year
System: University of North Carolina System
Degrees: B, M, P, D *Enroll:* 13,512
URL: http://www.uncg.edu
Phone: (336) 334-5000 *Calendar:* Sem. plan
Inst. Accred.: SACS (1921/2003)
Prog. Accred.: Accounting, Allied Health (audiology, speech-language pathology), Business (AACSB), Clinical Psychology, Computer Science (ABET-CAC), Counseling, Dance, Dietetics (didactic), Dietetics (internship), English Language Education, Graduate Social Work, Interior Architecture, Librarianship, Music, Nursing, Nursing Education, Public Administration, Public Health, Recreation and Leisure Services, Social Work, Teacher Education (NCATE), Theatre

The University of North Carolina at Pembroke
PO Box 1510, Pembroke 28372-1510
Type: Public, state, four-year
System: University of North Carolina System
Degrees: B, M *Enroll:* 4,496
URL: http://www.uncp.edu
Phone: (910) 521-6000 *Calendar:* Sem. plan
Inst. Accred.: SACS (1951/2000)
Prog. Accred.: Music, Nursing Education, Social Work, Teacher Education (NCATE)

The University of North Carolina at Wilmington
601 South College Rd., Wilmington 28403-3297
Type: Public, state, four-year
System: University of North Carolina System
Degrees: B, M, D *Enroll:* 10,768
URL: http://www.uncwil.edu
Phone: (910) 962-3000 *Calendar:* Sem. plan
Inst. Accred.: SACS (1952/2002)
Prog. Accred.: Business (AACSB), Graduate Social Work, Music, Nursing Education, Public Administration, Recreation and Leisure Services, Social Work, Teacher Education (NCATE)

University of North Carolina School of the Arts
1533 South Main St., Winston-Salem 27127-2738
Type: Public, state, four-year
System: University of North Carolina System
Degrees: B, M *Enroll:* 824
URL: http://www.ncarts.edu
Phone: (336) 770-3399 *Calendar:* Tri. plan
Inst. Accred.: SACS (1970/2006)

Vance-Granville Community College
PO Box 917, Henderson 27536
Type: Public, state-related, two-year
System: North Carolina Community College System
Degrees: A *Enroll:* 2,503
URL: http://www.vgcc.edu
Phone: (252) 492-2061 *Calendar:* Sem. plan
Inst. Accred.: SACS (1977/2003)
Prog. Accred.: Allied Health (medical assisting (AMA)), Radiography

Wake Forest University
PO Box 7373, Reynolds Station, Winston-Salem 27109
Type: Private, independent, four-year
Degrees: B, M, D *Enroll:* 6,577
URL: http://www.wfu.edu
Phone: (336) 758-5000 *Calendar:* Sem. plan
Inst. Accred.: ATS (2005), SACS (1921/2006)
Prog. Accred.: Accounting, Allied Health (medicine), Business (AACSB), Clinical Lab Scientist, Clinical Pastoral Education, Counseling, Dentistry (general practice residency), Law, Nurse Anesthesia Education, Physician Assistant, Teacher Education (NCATE)

Wake Technical Community College
9101 Fayetteville Rd., Raleigh 27603-5696
Type: Public, state/local, two-year
System: North Carolina Community College System
Degrees: A *Enroll:* 6,809
URL: http://www.waketech.edu
Phone: (919) 662-3400 *Calendar:* Sem. plan
Inst. Accred.: SACS (1970/2005, Warning)
Prog. Accred.: Allied Health (medical assisting (AMA), surgical technology), Clinical Lab Technology, Culinary Education, Dentistry (dental assisting, dental hygiene), Engineering Technology (automated systems, civil/construction, computer, electrical, mechanical), Phlebotomy, Radiography

Northern Wake Campus
6600 Louisburg Rd., Raleigh 27616
Phone: (919) 532-5502

Western Wake Campus
3434 Kildaire Farm Rd., Cary 27518
Phone: (919) 335-1000

Warren Wilson College
PO Box 9000, Asheville 28815-9000
Type: Private, independent, four-year
Degrees: B, M *Enroll:* 894
URL: http://www.warren-wilson.edu
Phone: (828) 298-3325 *Calendar:* Sem. plan
Inst. Accred.: SACS (1952/2005)
Prog. Accred.: Social Work, Teacher Education (NCATE)

Wayne Community College
Box 8002, Goldsboro 27533-8002
Type: Public, state/local, two-year
System: North Carolina Community College System
Degrees: A *Enroll:* 2,138
URL: http://www.waynecc.edu
Phone: (919) 735-5151 *Calendar:* Sem. plan
Inst. Accred.: SACS (1970/2006)
Prog. Accred.: Allied Health (medical assisting (AMA)), Dentistry (dental assisting, dental hygiene), Nursing, Practical Nursing

Western Carolina University
1 University Dr., Cullowhee 28723
Type: Public, state, four-year
System: University of North Carolina System
Degrees: B, M, P, D *Enroll:* 7,347
URL: http://www.wcu.edu
Phone: (828) 227-7211 *Calendar:* Sem. plan
Inst. Accred.: SACS (1946/2007)
Prog. Accred.: Allied Health (EMT-paramedic, speech-language pathology), Business (AACSB), Clinical Lab Scientist, Construction Education, Counseling, Dietetics (didactic), Dietetics (internship), Engineering Technology (electrical), Environmental Health, Family & Consumer Science, Graduate Social Work, Interior Design, Music, Nurse Anesthesia Education, Nursing Education, Physical Therapy, Social Work, Teacher Education (NCATE)

Western Piedmont Community College
1001 Burkemont Ave., Morganton 28655
Type: Public, state, two-year
System: North Carolina Community College System
Degrees: A *Enroll:* 1,544
URL: http://www.wpcc.edu
Phone: (828) 438-6000 *Calendar:* Sem. plan
Inst. Accred.: SACS (1968/2003)
Prog. Accred.: Allied Health (medical assisting (AMA)), Clinical Lab Technology, Dentistry (dental assisting), Nursing

Wilkes Community College
PO Box 120, Wilkesboro 28697-0120
Type: Public, state, two-year
System: North Carolina Community College System
Degrees: A *Enroll:* 1,772
URL: http://www.wilkescc.edu
Phone: (336) 838-6100 *Calendar:* Sem. plan
Inst. Accred.: SACS (1970/2006)
Prog. Accred.: Allied Health (medical assisting (AMA)), Dentistry (dental assisting)

Wilson Community College
PO Box 4305, Wilson 27893
Type: Public, state, two-year
System: North Carolina Community College System
Degrees: A *Enroll:* 1,233
URL: http://www.wilsoncc.edu
Phone: (252) 291-1195 *Calendar:* Sem. plan
Inst. Accred.: SACS (1969/2005)

Wingate University
PO Box 159, Wingate 28174-0159
Type: Private, Baptist State Convention of North Carolina, four-year
Degrees: A, B, M, D *Enroll:* 1,547
URL: http://www.wingate.edu
Phone: (704) 233-8000 *Calendar:* Sem. plan
Inst. Accred.: SACS (1951/2006)
Prog. Accred.: Business (ACBSP), Music, Pharmacy, Teacher Education (NCATE)

Winston-Salem State University
601 Martin Luther King, Jr. Dr., Winston-Salem 27110-0001
Type: Public, state, four-year
System: University of North Carolina System
Degrees: B, M *Enroll:* 5,092
URL: http://www.wssu.edu
Phone: (336) 750-2000 *Calendar:* Sem. plan
Inst. Accred.: SACS (1947/2001)
Prog. Accred.: Allied Health (occupational therapy), Business (AACSB), Clinical Lab Scientist, Computer Science (ABET-CAC), Music, Nursing Education, Physical Therapy, Recreation and Leisure Services, Rehabilitation Counseling, Teacher Education (NCATE)

NORTH DAKOTA

Bismarck State College
1500 Edwards Ave., PO Box 5587, Bismarck 58506-5587
Type: Public, state, two-year
System: North Dakota University System
Degrees: A *Enroll:* 2,560
URL: http://www.bismarckstate.edu
Phone: (701) 224-5400 *Calendar:* Sem. plan
Inst. Accred.: NCA-HLC (1966/2005)
Prog. Accred.: Allied Health (EMT-paramedic, respiratory therapy, surgical technology), Clinical Lab Technology, Phlebotomy

Cankdeska Cikana Community College
PO Box 269, 214 1st Ave., Fort Totten 58335
Type: Public, tribal, two-year
System: American Indian Higher Education Consortium
Degrees: A *Enroll:* 148
URL: http://www.littlehoop.edu
Phone: (701) 766-4415 *Calendar:* Sem. plan
Inst. Accred.: NCA-HLC (1990/2005)

Dickinson State University
291 Campus Dr., Dickinson 58601-4896
Type: Public, state, four-year
System: North Dakota University System
Degrees: A, B *Enroll:* 2,062
URL: http://www.dickinsonstate.edu
Phone: (701) 483-2507 *Calendar:* Sem. plan
Inst. Accred.: NCA-HLC (1928/2005)
Prog. Accred.: Nursing, Practical Nursing, Teacher Education (NCATE)

Fort Berthold Community College
PO Box 490, 220 8th Ave., New Town 58763
Type: Public, tribal, two-year
System: American Indian Higher Education Consortium
Degrees: A *Enroll:* 183
URL: http://www.fbcc.bia.edu
Phone: (701) 627-4738 *Calendar:* Sem. plan
Inst. Accred.: NCA-HLC (1988/2006)

Jamestown College
6000 College Ln., Jamestown 58405
Type: Private, United Presbyterian Church, four-year
Degrees: B *Enroll:* 986
URL: http://www.jc.edu
Phone: (701) 252-3467 *Calendar:* Sem. plan
Inst. Accred.: NCA-HLC (1920/2001)
Prog. Accred.: Nursing

Lake Region State College
1801 North College Dr., Devils Lake 58301-1598
Type: Public, state, two-year
System: North Dakota University System
Degrees: A *Enroll:* 766
URL: http://www.lrsc.edu
Phone: (701) 662-1600 *Calendar:* Sem. plan
Inst. Accred.: NCA-HLC (1974/2001)

Mayville State University
330 3rd St., NE, Mayville 58257-1299
Type: Public, state, four-year
System: North Dakota University System
Degrees: A, B *Enroll:* 743
URL: http://www.mayvillestate.edu
Phone: (701) 788-4754 *Calendar:* Sem. plan
Inst. Accred.: NCA-HLC (1917/2006)
Prog. Accred.: Teacher Education (NCATE)

Medcenter One Health Systems
300 North 7th St., Bismarck 58501
Type: Private, independent, four-year
Degrees: B *Enroll:* 90
URL: http://www.medcenterone.com
Phone: (701) 323-6000 *Calendar:* Sem. plan
Inst. Accred.: NCA-HLC (1990/2006)
Prog. Accred.: Nursing Education, Radiography

Minot State University
500 University Ave., West, Minot 58707-0001
Type: Public, state, four-year
System: North Dakota University System
Degrees: A, B, M, P, D *Enroll:* 3,069
URL: http://www.minotstateu.edu
Phone: (701) 858-3000 *Calendar:* Sem. plan
Inst. Accred.: NCA-HLC (1917/2008)
Prog. Accred.: Allied Health (audiology, speech-language pathology), Music, Social Work, Teacher Education (NCATE)

Minot State University—Bottineau
105 Simrall Blvd., Bottineau 58318-1198
Type: Public, state, two-year
System: North Dakota University System
Degrees: A *Enroll:* 385
URL: http://www.misu-b.nodak.edu
Phone: (701) 228-2277 *Calendar:* Sem. plan
Inst. Accred.: NCA-HLC (1971/2001)

North Dakota State College of Science
800 North 6th St., Wahpeton 58076-0002
Type: Public, state, two-year
System: North Dakota University System
Degrees: A *Enroll:* 2,055
URL: http://www.ndscs.nodak.edu
Phone: (701) 671-2221 *Calendar:* Sem. plan
Inst. Accred.: NCA-HLC (1971/2001)
Prog. Accred.: Allied Health (occupational therapy assisting), Dentistry (dental assisting, dental hygiene), Practical Nursing

North Dakota State University
1301 12th Ave. North, Fargo 58105
Type: Public, state, four-year
System: North Dakota University System
Degrees: B, M, P, D *Enroll:* 10,738
URL: http://www.ndsu.nodak.edu
Phone: (701) 231-8011 *Calendar:* Sem. plan
Inst. Accred.: NCA-HLC (1915/2006)
Prog. Accred.: Allied Health (respiratory therapy), Art, Business (AACSB), Computer Science (ABET-CAC), Construction Education, Counseling, Dietetics (coordinated), Dietetics (didactic), Engineering (agricultural, civil, construction, electrical, industrial, manufacturing, mechanical), Exercise Science, Interior Design, Landscape Architecture, Marriage and Family Therapy, Music, Nursing Education, Pharmacy, Teacher Education (NCATE), Theatre, Veterinary Technology

Rasmussen College—Bismarck
1701 East Century Ave., Bismarck 58503-0658
Type: Private, proprietary, four-year
System: Rasmussen College System
Degrees: A, B
URL: http://www.rasmussen.edu
Phone: (701) 530-9600 *Calendar:* Qtr. plan
Inst. Accred.: NCA-HLC (2001/2004, *Indirect accreditation through Rasmussen College System, Lake Elmo, MN*)

Rasmussen College—Fargo
4012 19th Ave., SW, Fargo 58103
Type: Private, proprietary, four-year
Degrees: A, B *Enroll:* 435
URL: http://www.rasmussen.edu
Phone: (701) 277-3889 *Calendar:* Qtr. plan
Inst. Accred.: NCA-HLC (2001, *Indirect accreditation through Rasmussen College System, Lake Elmo, MN*)

Sitting Bull College
1341 92nd St., Box 4, Fort Yates 58538
Type: Public, Standing Rock Sioux Tribe, two-year
System: American Indian Higher Education Consortium
Degrees: A *Enroll:* 234
URL: http://www.sittingbull.edu
Phone: (701) 854-3861 *Calendar:* Sem. plan
Inst. Accred.: NCA-HLC (1984/2004)

Trinity Bible College
50 6th Ave. South, Ellendale 58436-7150
Type: Private, Assemblies of God Church, four-year
Degrees: A, B *Enroll:* 280
URL: http://www.trinitybiblecollege.edu
Phone: (701) 349-3621 *Calendar:* Sem. plan
Inst. Accred.: ABHE (1980/2001), NCA-HLC (1991/2007)

Turtle Mountain Community College
PO Box 340, Belcourt 58316
Type: Private, tribal, four-year
System: American Indian Higher Education Consortium
Degrees: A, B *Enroll:* 538
URL: http://www.tm.edu
Phone: (701) 477-5605 *Calendar:* Sem. plan
Inst. Accred.: NCA-HLC (1984/2004)

United Tribes Technical College
3315 University Dr., Bismarck 58504
Type: Private, tribal, two-year
System: American Indian Higher Education Consortium
Degrees: A *Enroll:* 734
URL: http://www.uttc.edu
Phone: (701) 255-3285 *Calendar:* Sem. plan
Inst. Accred.: NCA-HLC (1982/2001)
Prog. Accred.: Practical Nursing

University of Mary
7500 University Dr., Bismarck 58504
Type: Private, Roman Catholic Church, four-year
Degrees: A, B, M *Enroll:* 2,578
URL: http://www.umary.edu
Phone: (701) 255-7500 *Calendar:* Sem. plan
Inst. Accred.: NCA-HLC (1969/2003)
Prog. Accred.: Allied Health (occupational therapy), Nursing Education, Physical Therapy, Social Work

University of North Dakota
Box 8193, University Station, Grand Forks 58202-8193
Type: Public, state, four-year
System: North Dakota University System
Degrees: B, M, P, D *Enroll:* 11,506
URL: http://www.und.nodak.edu
Phone: (701) 777-2011 *Calendar:* Sem. plan
Inst. Accred.: NCA-HLC (1913/2004)
Prog. Accred.: Allied Health (cytotechnology, medicine, occupational therapy, speech-language pathology), Aviation, Business (AACSB), Clinical Lab Scientist, Clinical Psychology, Computer Science (ABET-CAC), Counseling Psychology, Dietetics (coordinated), Engineering (chemical, civil, electrical, geological/geophysical, mechanical), Graduate Social Work, Industrial Technology, Law, Music, Nurse Anesthesia Education, Nursing Education, Physical Therapy, Physician Assistant, Public Administration, Social Work, Teacher Education (NCATE), Theatre

Valley City State University
101 College St. SW, Valley City 58072-4195
Type: Public, state, four-year
System: North Dakota University System
Degrees: B *Enroll:* 885
URL: http://www.vcsu.edu
Phone: (800) 532-8641 *Calendar:* Sem. plan
Inst. Accred.: NCA-HLC (1915/2002)
Prog. Accred.: Music, Teacher Education (NCATE)

Williston State College
PO Box 1326, 1410 University Ave., Williston 58802-1326
Type: Public, state, two-year
System: North Dakota University System
Degrees: A *Enroll:* 688
URL: http://www.wsc.nodak.edu
Phone: (701) 774-4200 *Calendar:* Sem. plan
Inst. Accred.: NCA-HLC (1972/2000)
Prog. Accred.: Physical Therapy Assisting

OHIO

Academy of Court Reporting
2044 Euclid Aveneue, Cleveland 44115
Type: Private, proprietary, two-year
System: Delta Education Corporation
Degrees: A *Enroll:* 327
URL: http://www.acr.edu
Phone: (216) 861-3222
Inst. Accred.: ACICS (1980/2006)

Akron Campus
2930 West Market St., Akron 44313
Phone: (330) 867-4030

Cincinnati Campus
830 Main St., Cincinnati 45202
Phone: (513) 723-0551

Clawson Campus
1330 West 14 Mile Rd., Clawson, MI 48017
Phone: (248) 353-4880

Columbus Campus
630 East Broad St., Columbus 43215
Phone: (614) 221-7770

Pittsburgh Campus
239 Fourth Ave., Pittsburgh, PA 15222
Phone: (412) 535-0560

Air Force Institute of Technology
2950 Hobson Way, Wright-Patterson AFB, Dayton 45433-7765
Type: Public, federal, four-year
System: Air University
Degrees: M, D *FTE Enroll:* 538
URL: http://www.afit.edu
Phone: (937) 255-6565 *Calendar:* Qtr. plan
Inst. Accred.: NCA-HLC (1960/2001)
Prog. Accred.: Engineering (aerospace, computer, electrical, engineering management, nuclear, systems)

Akron Institute of Herzing College
1600 South Arlington St., Ste. 100, Akron 44306
Type: Private, proprietary, two-year
System: Herzing College Corporate Offices
Degrees: A
URL: http://www.akroninstitute.com
Phone: (330) 724-1600 *Calendar:* Qtr. plan
Inst. Accred.: NCA-HLC (2004, *Indirect accreditation through Herzing College Corporate Offices, Milwaukee, WI*)
Prog. Accred.: Allied Health (medical assisting (AMA))

Allegheny Wesleyan College
2161 Woodsdale Rd., Salem 44460
Type: Private, Wesleyan Church, four-year
Degrees: B *Enroll:* 55
URL: http://www.awc.edu
Phone: (330) 337-6403 *Calendar:* Sem. plan
Inst. Accred.: ABHE (2004)

Antioch University
150 East South College St., Yellow Springs 45387
Type: Private, independent, four-year
Degrees: B, M, D *Enroll:* 453
URL: http://www.antioch.edu
Phone: (937) 769-1340
Inst. Accred.: NCA-HLC (1927/2003)

Antioch University McGregor
900 Dayton St., Yellow Springs 45387
Phone: (937) 769-1800
Prog. Accred: Teacher Education (NCATE)

Antioch University New England
40 Avon St., Keene, NH 03431-3516
Phone: (603) 357-3122
Prog. Accred: Clinical Psychology, Marriage and Family Therapy

Antioch University Seattle
2607 Second Ave., Seattle, WA 98121
Phone: (206) 441-5352
Prog. Accred: Marriage and Family Therapy

Antonelli College
124 East Seventh St., Cincinnati 45202-2592
Type: Private, proprietary, two-year
Degrees: A *Enroll:* 338
URL: http://www.antonellic.com
Phone: (513) 241-4338 *Calendar:* Qtr. plan
Inst. Accred.: ACCSCT (1975/2006)

Hattiesburg Campus
1500 North 31st Ave., Hattiesburg, MS 39401
Phone: (601) 583-4100

Jackson Campus
2323 Lakeland Dr., Jackson, MS 39208
Phone: (601) 362-9991

Art Academy of Cincinnati
1212 Jackson St., Cincinnati 45202
Type: Private, independent, four-year
Degrees: A, B, M *Enroll:* 163
URL: http://www.artacademy.edu
Phone: (513) 562 6262 *Calendar:* Sem. plan
Inst. Accred.: NCA-HLC (1990/2002)
Prog. Accred.: Art

The Art Institute of Cincinnati
1171 East Kemper Rd., Cincinnati 45246
Type: Private, independent, two-year
Degrees: A *Enroll:* 76
URL: http://www.theartinstituteofcincinnati.com
Phone: (513) 751-1206 *Calendar:* Qtr. plan
Inst. Accred.: ACCSCT (1979/2003)

Ashland Theological Seminary
910 Center St., Ashland 44805
Type: Private, Brethren Church, four-year
Degrees: M, D
URL: http://www.ashland.edu/seminary
Phone: (419) 289-5161 *Calendar:* Sem. plan
Inst. Accred.: ATS (1969/2008)

Ashland University
401 College Ave., Ashland 44805
Type: Private, Brethren Church, four-year
Degrees: A, B, M, D *Enroll:* 4,854
URL: http://www.ashland.edu
Phone: (419) 289-4142 *Calendar:* Sem. plan
Inst. Accred.: NCA-HLC (1930/2008)
Prog. Accred.: Business (ACBSP), Music, Nursing Education, Social Work, Teacher Education (NCATE)

The Athenaeum of Ohio
6616 Beechmont Ave., Cincinnati 45230-2091
Type: Private, Roman Catholic Archdiocese of Cincinnati, four-year
Degrees: M *Enroll:* 203
URL: http://www.mtsm.org
Phone: (513) 231-2223 *Calendar:* Qtr. plan
Inst. Accred.: ATS (1972/2002), NCA-HLC (1959/2003)

ATS Institute of Technology
230 Alpha Park, Highland Heights 44143
Type: Private, proprietary, two-year
Degrees: A
URL: http://www.atsinstitute.com
Phone: (440) 449-1700 *Calendar:* Qtr. plan
Inst. Accred.: ACICS (2000/2003)

Baldwin-Wallace College
275 Eastland Rd., Berea 44017-2088
Type: Private, United Methodist Church, four-year
Degrees: B, M *Enroll:* 3,807
URL: http://www.bw.edu
Phone: (440) 826-2900 *Calendar:* Sem. plan
Inst. Accred.: NCA-HLC (1913/2008)
Prog. Accred.: Music, Teacher Education (NCATE)

Belmont Technical College
120 Fox-Shannon Place, St. Clairsville 43950-9735
Type: Public, state, two-year
System: University System of Ohio
Degrees: A *Enroll:* 1,269
URL: http://www.btc.edu
Phone: (740) 695-9500 *Calendar:* Qtr. plan
Inst. Accred.: NCA-HLC (1978/1996)
Prog. Accred.: Allied Health (medical assisting (AMA))

Bexley Hall Seminary
583 Sheridan Ave., Columbus 43209-2325
Type: Private, Episcopal Church (USA), four-year
Degrees: M, D
URL: http://www.bexley.edu
Phone: (614) 231-309 *Calendar:* Sem. plan
Inst. Accred.: ATS (1952/2003)

Rochester Campus
26 Broadway, Rochester, NY 14607-1704
Phone: (716) 340-9550

Bluffton University
1 University Dr., Bluffton 45817
Type: Private, Mennonite Education Agency, four-year
Degrees: B, M *Enroll:* 1,152
URL: http://www.bluffton.edu
Phone: (419) 358-3000 *Calendar:* Sem. plan
Inst. Accred.: NCA-HLC (1953/1999)
Prog. Accred.: Dietetics (didactic), Music, Social Work, Teacher Education (NCATE)

Bohecker College
653 Enterprise Pkwy., Ravenna 44266-8058
Type: Private, proprietary, two-year
System: Education Affiliates, Inc.
Degrees: A
URL: http://www.boheckercollege.edu
Phone: (330) 297-7319
Inst. Accred.: ACICS (2006)

Bowling Green State University
Bowling Green 43403-0001
Type: Public, state, four-year
System: University System of Ohio
Degrees: A, B, M, P, D *Enroll:* 17,521
URL: http://www.bgsu.edu
Phone: (419) 372-2531 *Calendar:* Sem. plan
Inst. Accred.: NCA-HLC (1916/2003)
Prog. Accred.: Accounting, Allied Health (respiratory therapy, speech-language pathology), Art, Aviation Technology, Business (AACSB), Clinical Lab Scientist, Clinical Psychology, Construction Education, Construction Technology, Design Technology, Dietetics (didactic), Dietetics (internship), Electronic Technology, Environmental Health, Journalism, Manufacturing Technology, Mechanical Technology, Music, Nursing Education, Public Health, Recreation and Leisure Services, Rehabilitation Counseling, Social Work, Teacher Education (NCATE), Theatre

Firelands College
901 Rye Beach Rd., Huron 44839
Phone: (419) 433-5560

Bradford School
2469 Stelzer Rd., Columbus 43219
Type: Private, proprietary, two-year
Degrees: A *Enroll:* 407
URL: http://www.bradfordschoolcolumbus.edu
Phone: (614) 416-6200 *Calendar:* Qtr. plan
Inst. Accred.: ACICS (1960/2006)
Prog. Accred.: Allied Health (medical assisting (AMA))

Brown Mackie College—Cincinnati
1011 Glendale-Milford Rd., Cincinnati 45215-1107
Type: Private, proprietary, two-year
System: Education Management Corporation
Degrees: A *FTE Enroll:* 1,200
URL: http://www.brownmackie.edu
Phone: (513) 771-2424 *Calendar:* Qtr. plan
Inst. Accred.: ACICS (1964/2005)
Prog. Accred.: Allied Health (medical assisting (AMA))

Akron Campus
2791 Mogadore Rd., Akron 44312
Phone: (330) 733-8766
Prog. Accred: Allied Health (medical assisting (AMA))

Fort Wayne Campus
3000 East Coliseum Blvd., Fort Wayne, IN 46802
Phone: (260) 484-4400
Prog. Accred: Allied Health (medical assisting (AMA), occupational therapy assisting)

Merrillville Campus
1000 East 80th Place, Ste. 101 North, Merrillville, IN 46410-4388
Phone: (219) 769-3321
Prog. Accred: Allied Health (surgical technology), Medical Assisting (ABHES)

Miami Campus
1501 Biscayne Blvd., Miami, FL 33132
Phone: (305) 341-6600

Michigan City Campus
325 East US Hwy. 20, Michigan City, IN 46350
Phone: (219) 877-3100
Prog. Accred: Allied Health (medical assisting (AMA), surgical technology), Medical Assisting (ABHES)

Moline Campus
1527 47th Ave., Moline, IL 61265
Phone: (309) 762-2100

Northern Kentucky Campus
309 Buttermilk Pike, Fort Mitchell, KY 41017
Phone: (859) 341-5627

Brown Mackie College—Findlay
1700 Fostoria Ave., Ste. 100, Findlay 45840
Type: Private, proprietary, two-year
System: Education Management Corporation
Degrees: A *Enroll:* 528
URL: http://www.brownmackie.edu
Phone: (419) 423-2211 *Calendar:* Qtr. plan
Inst. Accred.: ACICS (1989/2003)

Indianapolis Campus
1200 North Meridian St., Ste. 100, Indianapolis, IN 46204
Phone: (866) 255-0279
Prog. Accred: Allied Health (occupational therapy assisting)

Louisville Campus
3605 Fern Valley Rd., Louisville, KY 40219
Phone: (502) 968-7191
Prog. Accred: Surgical Technology

Bryant & Stratton College—Cleveland Downtown Campus
1700 East 13th St., Cleveland 44114-3203
Type: Private, proprietary, four-year
System: Bryant & Stratton College System Office
Degrees: A, B *Enroll:* 339
URL: http://www.bryantstratton.edu
Phone: (216) 771-1700 *Calendar:* Sem. plan
Inst. Accred.: MSA-CHE (2002/2007, *Indirect accreditation through Bryant & Stratton College System Office, Getzville, NY*)

Bryant & Stratton College—Cleveland West Campus
12955 Snow Rd., Parma 44130-1013
Type: Private, proprietary, four-year
System: Bryant & Stratton College System Office
Degrees: A, B *Enroll:* 240
URL: http://www.bryantstratton.edu
Phone: (216) 265-3151 *Calendar:* Sem. plan
Inst. Accred.: MSA-CHE (2002/2007, *Indirect accreditation through Bryant & Stratton College System Office, Getzville, NY*)
Prog. Accred.: Allied Health (medical assisting (AMA))

Willoughby Hills Campus
27557 Chardon Rd., Willoughby Hills 44092
Phone: (440) 944-6800
Prog. Accred: Nursing

Capital University
2199 East Main St., Columbus 43209
Type: Private, Evangelic Lutheran Church in America, four-year
Degrees: B, M, D *Enroll:* 3,289
URL: http://www.capital.edu
Phone: (800) 289-6289 *Calendar:* Sem. plan
Inst. Accred.: NCA-HLC (1921/2004)
Prog. Accred.: Business (ACBSP), Law, Music, Nursing Education, Social Work, Teacher Education (NCATE)

Case Western Reserve University

10900 Euclid Ave., Cleveland 44106-7001
Type: Private, independent, four-year
Degrees: B, M, D *Enroll:* 8,306
URL: http://www.cwru.edu
Phone: (800) 444-6984 *Calendar:* Sem. plan
Inst. Accred.: NCA-HLC (1913/2005)
Prog. Accred.: Accounting, Allied Health (anesthesiologist assisting, medicine, speech-language pathology), Business (AACSB), Clinical Psychology, Computer Science (ABET-CAC), Dentistry (advanced education in general dentistry, dentistry, endodontics, general dentistry, oral and maxillofacial surgery, orthodontic and dentofacial orthopedics, pediatric dentistry, periodontics), Dietetics (didactic), Dietetics (internship), Engineering (aerospace, bioengineering, chemical, civil, computer, electrical, engineering physics/science, materials, mechanical, polymer, systems), Graduate Social Work, Law, Music, Nurse (Midwifery), Nurse Anesthesia Education, Nursing, Public Health

Cedarville University

251 North Main St., Cedarville 45314-0601
Type: Private, Baptist Church, four-year
Degrees: A, B, M, D *Enroll:* 3,002
URL: http://www.cedarville.edu
Phone: (937) 766-7700 *Calendar:* Qtr. plan
Inst. Accred.: NCA-HLC (1975/2007)
Prog. Accred.: Business (ACBSP), Engineering (electrical, mechanical), Nursing Education, Social Work

Central Ohio Technical College

1179 University Dr., Newark 43055-1767
Type: Public, state/local, two-year
System: University System of Ohio
Degrees: A *Enroll:* 1,957
URL: http://www.cotc.edu
Phone: (740) 366-1351 *Calendar:* Qtr. plan
Inst. Accred.: NCA-HLC (1975/2008)
Prog. Accred.: Allied Health (diagnostic medical sonography, surgical technology), Nursing, Radiography

Coshocton Campus

249 Kenwood Dr., Coshocton 43812
Phone: (740) 622-1408

Central State University

PO Box 1004, 1400 Brush Row Rd., Wilberforce 45384-1004
Type: Public, state, four-year
System: University System of Ohio
Degrees: B, M *Enroll:* 1,520
URL: http://www.centralstate.edu
Phone: (937) 376-6011 *Calendar:* Qtr. plan
Inst. Accred.: NCA-HLC (1949/2003)
Prog. Accred.: Engineering (manufacturing), Music, Teacher Education (NCATE)

Chancellor University

3921 Chester Ave., Cleveland 44114
Type: Private, independent, four-year
Degrees: A, B, M *Enroll:* 767
URL: http://www.myers.edu
Phone: (216) 391-6937 *Calendar:* Sem. plan
Inst. Accred.: NCA-HLC (1978/2005, Probation)

Chatfield College

20918 State Route 251, St. Martin 45118
Type: Private, Roman Catholic Church, two-year
Degrees: A *FTE Enroll:* 151
URL: http://www.chatfield.edu
Phone: (513) 875-3344 *Calendar:* Sem. plan
Inst. Accred.: NCA-HLC (1971/2001)

Cincinnati Christian University

PO Box 04320, Cincinnati 45204-3200
Type: Private, Christian Churches (Churches of Christ), four-year
Degrees: A, B, M, P *Enroll:* 917
URL: http://www.ccuniversity.edu
Phone: (513) 244-8100 *Calendar:* Sem. plan
Inst. Accred.: ABHE (1966/2005), ATS (2004), NCA-HLC (1989/2004)

Cincinnati College of Mortuary Science

645 West North Bend Rd., Cincinnati 45224
Type: Private, independent, four-year
Degrees: A, B *Enroll:* 145
URL: http://www.ccms.edu
Phone: (513) 761-2020 *Calendar:* Qtr. plan
Inst. Accred.: NCA-HLC (1982/2001)
Prog. Accred.: Funeral Service Education (Mortuary Science)

Cincinnati State Technical and Community College

3520 Central Pkwy., Cincinnati 45223-2690
Type: Public, state, two-year
System: University System of Ohio
Degrees: A *Enroll:* 5,159
URL: http://www.cincinnatistate.edu
Phone: (513) 569-1500
Inst. Accred.: NCA-HLC (1976/2008)
Prog. Accred.: Allied Health (diagnostic medical sonography, medical assisting (AMA), occupational therapy assisting, respiratory therapy, surgical technology), Clinical Lab Technology, Construction Education, Culinary Education, Dietetic Technician, Engineering Technology (civil/construction, computer, electrical, electromechanical, environmental/sanitary, mechanical), Nursing

Clark State Community College
570 East Leffel Ln., PO Box 570, Springfield 45505-4795
Type: Public, state, two-year
System: University System of Ohio
Degrees: A *Enroll:* 2,228
URL: http://www.clarkstate.edu
Phone: (937) 325-0691 *Calendar:* Qtr. plan
Inst. Accred.: NCA-HLC (1974/1999)
Prog. Accred.: Clinical Lab Technology, Nursing, Physical Therapy Assisting

Cleveland Institute of Art
11141 East Blvd., Cleveland 44106
Type: Private, independent, four-year
Degrees: B, M *Enroll:* 531
URL: http://www.cia.edu
Phone: (216) 421-7000 *Calendar:* Sem. plan
Inst. Accred.: NCA-HLC (1970/2001)
Prog. Accred.: Art

Cleveland Institute of Electronics, Inc.
1776 East 17th St., Cleveland 44114
Type: Private, proprietary, two-year
Degrees: A *FTE Enroll:* 1,826
URL: http://www.cie-wc.edu
Phone: (216) 781-9400
Inst. Accred.: DETC (1956/2008)

Cleveland Institute of Music
11021 East Blvd., Cleveland 44106
Type: Private, independent, four-year
Degrees: B, M, D *Enroll:* 397
URL: http://www.cim.edu
Phone: (216) 791-5000 *Calendar:* Sem. plan
Inst. Accred.: NCA-HLC (1980/2005)
Prog. Accred.: Music

Cleveland State University
2121 Euclid Ave., Cleveland 44115-2214
Type: Public, state, four-year
System: University System of Ohio
Degrees: B, M, P, D *Enroll:* 11,075
URL: http://www.csuohio.edu
Phone: (216) 687-2000 *Calendar:* Sem. plan
Inst. Accred.: NCA-HLC (1940/2001)
Prog. Accred.: Accounting, Allied Health (health services administration, occupational therapy, speech-language pathology), Business (AACSB), Counseling, Engineering (chemical, civil, computer, electrical, industrial, mechanical), Engineering Technology (electrical), Graduate Social Work, Law, Music, Nursing Education, Physical Therapy, Planning, Public Administration, Public Health, Social Work, Teacher Education (NCATE)

College of Mount St. Joseph
5701 Delhi Rd., Cincinnati 45233
Type: Private, Roman Catholic Church, four-year
Degrees: A, B, M *Enroll:* 1,779
URL: http://www.msj.edu
Phone: (513) 244-4200 *Calendar:* Sem. plan
Inst. Accred.: NCA-HLC (1932/2006)
Prog. Accred.: Music, Physical Therapy, Social Work, Teacher Education (TEAC)

The College of Wooster
1189 Beall Ave., Wooster 44691
Type: Private, independent, four-year
Degrees: B *Enroll:* 1,826
URL: http://www.wooster.edu
Phone: (330) 263-2000 *Calendar:* Sem. plan
Inst. Accred.: NCA-HLC (1915/2003)
Prog. Accred.: Music

Columbus College of Art and Design
107 North Ninth St., Columbus 43215
Type: Private, independent, four-year
Degrees: B *Enroll:* 1,334
URL: http://www.ccad.edu
Phone: (614) 224-9101 *Calendar:* Sem. plan
Inst. Accred.: NCA-HLC (1986/2001)
Prog. Accred.: Art, Interior Design

Columbus State Community College
550 East Spring St., PO Box 1609, Columbus 43216
Type: Public, state, two-year
System: University System of Ohio
Degrees: A *Enroll:* 13,434
URL: http://www.cscc.edu
Phone: (614) 287-2400 *Calendar:* Qtr. plan
Inst. Accred.: NCA-HLC (1973/2000)
Prog. Accred.: Allied Health (EMT-paramedic, medical assisting (AMA), respiratory therapy, surgical technology), Business (ACBSP), Clinical Lab Technology, Construction Education, Culinary Education, Dentistry (dental hygiene, dental laboratory technology), Dietetic Technician, Engineering Technology (electrical), Histologic Technology, Nursing, Phlebotomy, Radiography, Veterinary Technology

Cuyahoga Community College
700 Carnegie Ave., Cleveland 44115-2878
Type: Public, state/local, two-year
System: University System of Ohio
Degrees: A *Enroll:* 15,179
URL: http://www.tri-c.edu
Phone: (216) 987-6000 *Calendar:* Sem. plan
Inst. Accred.: NCA-HLC (1979/2000)
Prog. Accred.: Allied Health (diagnostic medical sonography, medical assisting (AMA), respiratory therapy, surgical technology), Dietetic Technician, Phlebotomy, Physician Assistant, Radiography

Corporate Campus
25425 Center Ridge Rd., Westlake 44145-4122
Phone: (866) 806-2677

Eastern Campus
4250 Richmond Rd., Highland Hills 44122
Phone: (216) 987-2000

Metropolitan Campus
2900 Community College Ave., Cleveland 44115
Phone: (216) 987-4000
Prog. Accred: Allied Health (occupational therapy assisting), Culinary Education, Dentistry (dental assisting, dental hygiene), Nursing, Physical Therapy Assisting

Western Campus
11000 West Pleasant Valley Rd., Parma 44130
Phone: (216) 987-5000
Prog. Accred: Nuclear Medicine Technology, Radiography, Veterinary Technology

Davis College
4747 Monroe St., Toledo 43623
Type: Private, proprietary, two-year
Degrees: A *Enroll:* 315
URL: http://www.daviscollege.edu
Phone: (419) 473-2700 *Calendar:* Qtr. plan
Inst. Accred.: NCA-HLC (1991/1999)
Prog. Accred.: Allied Health (medical assisting (AMA))

Daymar College—Chillicothe
1410 Industrial Dr., Chillicothe 45601
Type: Private, proprietary, two-year
Degrees: A *Enroll:* 71
URL: http://www.daymarcollege.edu
Phone: (740) 774-6300 *Calendar:* Qtr. plan
Inst. Accred.: ACICS (1976/2002)

Jackson Campus
504 McCarty Ln., Jackson 45640
Phone: (740) 286-1554

Lancaster Campus
1522 Sheridan Dr., Lancaster 43130
Phone: (740) 687-6126

New Boston Campus
3879 Rhodes Ave., New Boston 45662
Phone: (740) 456-4124

The Defiance College
701 North Clinton St., Defiance 43512
Type: Private, United Church of Christ, four-year
Degrees: A, B, M *Enroll:* 784
URL: http://www.defiance.edu
Phone: (419) 784-4010 *Calendar:* Sem. plan
Inst. Accred.: NCA-HLC (1916/2003)
Prog. Accred.: Social Work

Denison University
1 Main St., Granville 43023
Type: Private, independent, four-year
Degrees: B *Enroll:* 2,304
URL: http://www.denison.edu
Phone: (740) 587-0810 *Calendar:* Sem. plan
Inst. Accred.: NCA-HLC (1913/2000)

DeVry University Cleveland Downtown
200 Public Square, Ste. 150, Cleveland 44114
Type: Private, proprietary, four-year
System: DeVry University
Degrees: M
URL: http://www.devry.edu
Phone: (216) 781-8000 *Calendar:* Sem. plan
Inst. Accred.: NCA-HLC (2002, *Indirect accreditation through DeVry University, Oakbrook Terrace, IL*)

Seven Hills Campus
6000 Lombardo Center, Ste. 200, Seven Hills 44131
Phone: (216) 328-8754

DeVry University Columbus
1350 Alum Creek Dr., Columbus 43209-2705
Type: Private, proprietary
System: DeVry University
Degrees: A, B, M *Enroll:* 2,382
URL: http://www.devry.edu/columbus
Phone: (614) 253-7291 *Calendar:* Sem. plan
Inst. Accred.: NCA-HLC (2002, *Indirect accreditation through DeVry University, Oakbrook Terrace, IL*)
Prog. Accred.: Engineering Technology (computer, electrical)

Cincinnati Campus
8800 Governors Hill Dr., Ste. 100, Cincinnati 45249-1367
Phone: (513) 583-5000

Columbus North Campus
8800 Lyra Dr., Ste. 120, Columbus 43240
Phone: (614) 252-8850

Dayton Campus
3610 New Germany Trebein Rd., Ste. 100, Dayton 45431
Phone: (937) 320-3200

Edison State Community College
1973 Edison Dr., Piqua 45356-9253
Type: Public, state, two-year
System: University System of Ohio
Degrees: A *Enroll:* 1,921
URL: http://www.edisonohio.edu
Phone: (937) 778-8600 *Calendar:* Sem. plan
Inst. Accred.: NCA-HLC (1981/2007)
Prog. Accred.: Nursing

ETI Technical College of Niles
2076-86 Youngstown-Warren Rd., Niles 44446-4398
Type: Private, proprietary, two-year
Degrees: A
URL: http://www.eticollege.edu
Phone: (330) 652-9919
Inst. Accred.: ACCSCT (1992/2006)

Franciscan University of Steubenville
1235 University Blvd., Steubenville 43952
Type: Private, Roman Catholic Church, four-year
Degrees: A, B, M *Enroll:* 2,165
URL: http://www.franciscan.edu
Phone: (740) 283-3771 *Calendar:* Sem. plan
Inst. Accred.: NCA-HLC (1960/2005)
Prog. Accred.: Nursing, Social Work

Franklin University
201 South Grant Ave., Columbus 43215
Type: Private, independent, four-year
Degrees: A, B, M *Enroll:* 4,432
URL: http://www.franklin.edu
Phone: (614) 797-4700 *Calendar:* Tri. plan
Inst. Accred.: NCA-HLC (1976/2008)
Prog. Accred.: Nursing

Gallipolis Career College
1176 Jackson Pike, Ste. 12, Gallipolis 45631
Type: Private, proprietary, two-year
Degrees: A *Enroll:* 149
URL: http://www.gallipoliscareercollege.edu
Phone: (740) 446-4367 *Calendar:* Qtr. plan
Inst. Accred.: ACICS (1989/2008)

God's Bible School and College
1810 Young St., Cincinnati 45210-1599
Type: Private, interdenominational, four-year
Degrees: A, B *Enroll:* 244
URL: http://www.gbs.edu
Phone: (513) 721-7944 *Calendar:* Sem. plan
Inst. Accred.: ABHE (1986/2007), NCA-HLC (2008)

Good Samaritan College of Nursing and Health Science
375 Dixmyth Ave., Cincinnati 45220
Type: Private, independent, two-year
Degrees: A
URL: http://www.goodsamaritancollege.com
Phone: (513) 872-2743 *Calendar:* Sem. plan
Inst. Accred.: NCA-HLC (2006)
Prog. Accred.: Nursing

Hebrew Union College—Jewish Institute of Religion
3101 Clifton Ave., Cincinnati 45220
Type: Private, Union for Reform Judaism, four-year
System: Hebrew Union College—Jewish Institute of Religion Central Office
Degrees: M, P, D *Enroll:* 120
URL: http://www.huc.edu
Phone: (513) 221-1875 *Calendar:* Sem. plan
Inst. Accred.: NCA-HLC (1960/2002)
Prog. Accred.: Clinical Pastoral Education

Heidelberg College
310 East Market St., Tiffin 44883
Type: Private, United Church of Christ, four-year
Degrees: B, M *Enroll:* 1,311
URL: http://www.heidelberg.edu
Phone: (419) 448-2000 *Calendar:* Sem. plan
Inst. Accred.: NCA-HLC (1913/2006)
Prog. Accred.: Music

Hiram College
PO Box 67, Hiram 44234
Type: Private, independent, four-year
Degrees: B, M *Enroll:* 972
URL: http://www.hiram.edu
Phone: (330) 569-3211 *Calendar:* Sem. plan
Inst. Accred.: NCA-HLC (1914/2000)
Prog. Accred.: Music

Hocking College
3301 Hocking Pkwy., Nelsonville 45764-9704
Type: Public, state, two-year
System: University System of Ohio
Degrees: A *Enroll:* 3,591
URL: http://www.hocking.edu
Phone: (740) 753-3591 *Calendar:* Qtr. plan
Inst. Accred.: NCA-HLC (1976/2002)
Prog. Accred.: Allied Health (medical assisting (AMA)), Business (ACBSP), Culinary Education, Dietetic Technician, Engineering Technology (ceramic), Forestry, Nursing, Physical Therapy Assisting, Practical Nursing

Hondros College
4140 Executive Pkwy., Westerville 43081
Type: Private, proprietary, two-year
Degrees: A *FTE Enroll:* 240
URL: http://www.hondros.edu
Phone: (614) 508-7200
Inst. Accred.: ACICS (1990/2004)

Cincinnati Campus
4605 Duke Dr., Ste. 115, Mason 45040
Phone: (513) 573-6093

Dayton Campus
1810 Successful Dr., Fairborn 45324
Phone: (937) 879-1940

International College of Broadcasting
6 South Smithville Rd., Dayton 45431-1833
Type: Private, proprietary, two-year
Degrees: A *Enroll:* 112
URL: http://www.icbcollege.com
Phone: (937) 258-8251
Inst. Accred.: ACCSCT (1976/2003)

ITT Technical Institute
1030 North Meridian Rd., Youngstown 44509-4098
Type: Private, proprietary, two-year
System: ITT Educational Services, Inc.
Degrees: A *Enroll:* 384
URL: http://www.itt-tech.edu
Phone: (330) 270-1600 *Calendar:* Qtr. plan
Inst. Accred.: ACICS (1977/2006)

ITT Technical Institute
3325 Stop Eight Rd., Dayton 45414-9915
Type: Private, proprietary, two-year
System: ITT Educational Services, Inc.
Degrees: A *Enroll:* 434
URL: http://www.itt-tech.edu
Phone: (937) 454-2267 *Calendar:* Qtr. plan
Inst. Accred.: ACICS (1999/2004)

Maumee Campus
1656 Henthorne Dr., Ste. B, Maumee 43537
Phone: (419) 861-6500

Monroeville Area Campus
105 Mall Blvd., Ste. 200 East, Monroeville, PA 15146
Phone: (412) 856-5920

Pittsburgh Area Campus
10 Pkwy. Center, Pittsburgh, PA 15220-3801
Phone: (412) 937-9150

Strongsville Campus
14955 Sprague Rd., Strongsville 44136
Phone: (440) 234-9091

James A. Rhodes State College
4240 Campus Dr., Lima 45804-3597
Type: Public, state, two-year
System: University System of Ohio
Degrees: A *Enroll:* 2,079
URL: http://www.rhodesstate.edu
Phone: (419) 995-8000 *Calendar:* Qtr. plan
Inst. Accred.: NCA-HLC (1979/2002)
Prog. Accred.: Allied Health (medical assisting (AMA), occupational therapy assisting, respiratory therapy), Business (ACBSP), Dentistry (dental hygiene), Engineering Technology (electrical, mechanical), Nursing, Physical Therapy Assisting, Radiography

Jefferson Community College
4000 Sunset Blvd., Steubenville 43952-3594
Type: Public, state, two-year
System: University System of Ohio
Degrees: A *Enroll:* 1,175
URL: http://www.jcc.edu
Phone: (740) 264-5591 *Calendar:* Sem. plan
Inst. Accred.: NCA-HLC (1973/2007)
Prog. Accred.: Allied Health (medical assisting (AMA), respiratory therapy), Clinical Lab Technology, Dentistry (dental assisting), Radiography

John Carroll University
20700 North Park Blvd., University Heights 44118
Type: Private, Roman Catholic Church, four-year
Degrees: B, M *Enroll:* 3,609
URL: http://www.jcu.edu
Phone: (216) 397-1886 *Calendar:* Sem. plan
Inst. Accred.: NCA-HLC (1922/2004)
Prog. Accred.: Accounting, Business (AACSB), Counseling, Teacher Education (NCATE)

Kent State University
PO Box 5190, Kent 44242-0001
Type: Public, state, four-year
System: University System of Ohio
Degrees: A, B, M, P, D *Enroll:* 20,287
URL: http://www.kent.edu
Phone: (330) 672-3000 *Calendar:* Sem. plan
Inst. Accred.: NCA-HLC (1915/2008)
Prog. Accred.: Allied Health (audiology, speech-language pathology), Art, Aviation, Business (AACSB), Business (ACBSP), Clinical Psychology, Counseling, Dance, Dietetics (didactic), Dietetics (internship), Electronic Technology, Industrial Technology, Interior Design, Journalism, Librarianship, Music, Nursing, Nursing Education, Public Administration, Public Health, Radiography, Recreation and Leisure Services, Rehabilitation Counseling, School Psychology, Teacher Education (NCATE), Theatre

Ashtabula Campus
3325 West 13th St., Ashtabula 44004
Phone: (216) 964-3322
Prog. Accred: Allied Health (occupational therapy assisting), Business (ACBSP), Nursing, Physical Therapy Assisting

East Liverpool Campus
400 East Fourth St., East Liverpool 43920
Phone: (216) 385-3805
Prog. Accred: Allied Health (occupational therapy assisting), Business (ACBSP), Nursing, Physical Therapy Assisting

Geauga Campus
14111 Claridon-Troy Rd., Burton Township 44021
Phone: (216) 834-4187
Prog. Accred: Business (ACBSP)

Salem Campus
2491 State Route 45 South, Salem 44460
Phone: (216) 332-0361
Prog. Accred: Business (ACBSP), Nuclear Medicine Technology, Radiography

Stark Campus
6000 Frank Ave., N.W., Canton 44720
Phone: (330) 499-9600

Trumbull Campus
4314 Mahoning Ave., N.W., Warren 44483
Phone: (216) 678-4281
Prog. Accred: Business (ACBSP)

Tuscarawas Campus
University Dr., N.E., New Philadelphia 44663
Phone: (330) 339-3391
Prog. Accred: Business (ACBSP), Engineering Technology (electrical, mechanical), Nursing

Kenyon College
Gambier 43022-9623
Type: Private, Episcopal Church, four-year
Degrees: B *Enroll:* 1,648
URL: http://www.kenyon.edu
Phone: (740) 427-5000 *Calendar:* Sem. plan
Inst. Accred.: NCA-HLC (1913/2001)

Kettering College of Medical Arts
3737 Southern Blvd., Kettering 45429
Type: Private, Seventh-Day Adventist Church, four-year
Degrees: A, B *Enroll:* 604
URL: http://www.kcma.edu
Phone: (937) 296-7201 *Calendar:* Sem. plan
Inst. Accred.: NCA-HLC (1974/2001)
Prog. Accred.: Allied Health (diagnostic medical sonography, respiratory therapy), Clinical Pastoral Education, Nursing, Physician Assistant, Radiography

Lake Erie College
391 West Washington St., Painesville 44077
Type: Private, independent, four-year
Degrees: B, M *Enroll:* 722
URL: http://www.lec.edu
Phone: (440) 296-1856 *Calendar:* Sem. plan
Inst. Accred.: NCA-HLC (1913/1999)

Lakeland Community College
7700 Clocktower Dr., Kirtland 44094-5198
Type: Public, state/local, two-year
System: University System of Ohio
Degrees: A *Enroll:* 4,978
URL: http://www.lakelandcc.edu
Phone: (440) 953-7000 *Calendar:* Sem. plan
Inst. Accred.: NCA-HLC (1973/2000)
Prog. Accred.: Allied Health (respiratory therapy, surgical technology), Clinical Lab Technology, Dentistry (dental hygiene), Engineering Technology (civil/construction, electrical, mechanical), Nursing, Radiography

Laura and Alvin Siegal College of Judaic Studies
26500 Shaker Blvd., Beachwood 44122
Type: Private, independent, four-year
Degrees: B, M *Enroll:* 36
URL: http://www.siegalcollege.edu
Phone: (216) 464-4050 *Calendar:* Sem. plan
Inst. Accred.: NCA-HLC (1988/2003)

Lorain County Community College
1005 North Abbe Rd., Elyria 44035-1691
Type: Public, state/local, two-year
System: University System of Ohio
Degrees: A *Enroll:* 5,990
URL: http://www.lorainccc.edu
Phone: (440) 365-5222 *Calendar:* Sem. plan
Inst. Accred.: NCA-HLC (1971/2004)
Prog. Accred.: Allied Health (diagnostic medical sonography, medical assisting (AMA), surgical technology), Clinical Lab Technology, Dentistry (dental hygiene), Liberal Education, Nursing, Phlebotomy, Physical Therapy Assisting, Practical Nursing, Radiography

Lourdes College
6832 Convent Blvd., Sylvania 43560
Type: Private, Roman Catholic Church, four-year
Degrees: A, B *Enroll:* 1,294
URL: http://www.lourdes.edu
Phone: (419) 885-3211 *Calendar:* Sem. plan
Inst. Accred.: NCA-HLC (1964/2007)
Prog. Accred.: Nursing Education, Social Work

Malone University
5115 25th St., NW, Canton 44709
Type: Private, Evangelical Church Eastern Region, four-year
Degrees: B, M *Enroll:* 1,929
URL: http://www.malone.edu
Phone: (330) 471-8100 *Calendar:* Sem. plan
Inst. Accred.: NCA-HLC (1964/2004)
Prog. Accred.: Nursing Education, Social Work

Marietta College
215 5th St., Marietta 45750
Type: Private, independent, four-year
Degrees: A, B, M *Enroll:* 1,394
URL: http://www.marietta.edu
Phone: (740) 376-4643 *Calendar:* Sem. plan
Inst. Accred.: NCA-HLC (1913/2006)
Prog. Accred.: Engineering (petroleum), Physician Assistant, Teacher Education (NCATE)

Marion Technical College
1467 Mount Vernon Ave., Marion 43302-5694
Type: Public, state, two-year
System: University System of Ohio
Degrees: A *Enroll:* 1,342
URL: http://www.mtc.edu
Phone: (614) 389-4636 *Calendar:* Qtr. plan
Inst. Accred.: NCA-HLC (1977/2007)
Prog. Accred.: Allied Health (medical assisting (AMA)), Clinical Lab Technology, Nursing, Phlebotomy, Physical Therapy Assisting, Radiography

MedCentral College of Nursing
335 Glessner Ave., Mansfield 44903
Type: Private, independent, four-year
Degrees: B
URL: http://www.medcentral.edu
Phone: (419) 520-2600 *Calendar:* Sem. plan
Inst. Accred.: NCA-HLC (2003/2008)
Prog. Accred.: Nursing Education

Mercy College of Northwest Ohio
2221 Madison Ave., Toledo 43624-1132
Type: Private, independent, four-year
Degrees: A, B *Enroll:* 538
URL: http://www.mercycollege.edu
Phone: (419) 251-1313 *Calendar:* Sem. plan
Inst. Accred.: NCA-HLC (1995/2000)
Prog. Accred.: Clinical Lab Technology, Nursing, Nursing Education, Radiography

Methodist Theological School in Ohio
3081 Columbus Pike, Delaware 43015
Type: Private, United Methodist Church, four-year
Degrees: M *Enroll:* 210
URL: http://www.mtso.edu
Phone: (740) 363-1146 *Calendar:* Qtr. plan
Inst. Accred.: ATS (1965/2008), NCA-HLC (1976/1999)

Miami University
501 East High St., Oxford 45056
Type: Public, state, four-year
System: University System of Ohio
Degrees: A, B, M, P, D *Enroll:* 16,083
URL: http://www.muohio.edu
Phone: (513) 529-1809 *Calendar:* Sem. plan
Inst. Accred.: NCA-HLC (1913/2005)
Prog. Accred.: Accounting, Allied Health (audiology, speech-language pathology), Art, Business (AACSB), Clinical Psychology, Computer Science (ABET-CAC), Dietetics (didactic), Engineering (manufacturing, mechanical, paper), Engineering Technology (electrical, electromechanical, mechanical), Interior Design, Music, Psychology Internship, Social Work, Teacher Education (NCATE), Theatre

Hamilton Campus
1601 Peck Blvd., Hamilton 45011
Phone: (513) 863-8833
Prog. Accred: Nursing

Middletown Campus
4200 East University Blvd., Middletown 45042
Phone: (513) 424-4444
Prog. Accred: Nursing

Miami-Jacobs Career College
110 North Patterson Blvd., Dayton 45402-1771
Type: Private, independent, two-year
System: Delta Education Corporation
Degrees: A *Enroll:* 585
URL: http://www.miamijacobs.edu
Phone: (937) 461-5174 *Calendar:* Qtr. plan
Inst. Accred.: ACICS (1957/2005)
Prog. Accred.: Allied Health (medical assisting (AMA), surgical technology)

Springboro Campus
875 West Central Ave., Springboro 45066
Phone: (888) 657-9550

Troy Campus
865 West Market St., Troy 45373
Phone: (888) 657-9551

Mount Carmel College of Nursing
127 South Davis Ave., Columbus 43222
Type: Private, Sisters of the Holy Cross, four-year
Degrees: B *Enroll:* 550
URL: http://www.mccn.edu/
Phone: (614) 225-5800 *Calendar:* Sem. plan
Inst. Accred.: NCA-HLC (1994/1999)
Prog. Accred.: Dietetics (internship)

Mount Union College
1972 Clark Ave., Alliance 44601
Type: Private, United Methodist Church, four-year
Degrees: B *Enroll:* 2,093
URL: http://www.muc.edu
Phone: (330) 821-5320 *Calendar:* Sem. plan
Inst. Accred.: NCA-HLC (1913/2002)
Prog. Accred.: Music, Teacher Education (NCATE)

Mount Vernon Nazarene University
800 Martinsburg Rd., Mount Vernon 43050-5000
Type: Private, Church of the Nazarene, four-year
Degrees: A, B, M *Enroll:* 2,241
URL: http://www.mvnu.edu
Phone: (740) 392-6868 *Calendar:* 4-1-4 plan
Inst. Accred.: NCA-HLC (1972/2001)
Prog. Accred.: Business (ACBSP), Social Work

Muskingum College
163 Stormont St., New Concord 43762
Type: Private, Presbyterian Church (USA), four-year
Degrees: B, M *Enroll:* 1,920
URL: http://www.muskingum.edu
Phone: (740) 826-8211 *Calendar:* Sem. plan
Inst. Accred.: NCA-HLC (1919/2003)
Prog. Accred.: Music, Teacher Education (NCATE)

New Life Technical Institute
114 West Fifth St., East Liverpool 43920
Type: Private, independent, two-year
Degrees: A
URL: http://www.newlife-academy.us
Phone: (330) 386-0445
Inst. Accred.: COE (2007)

North Central State College
2441 Kenwood Circle, PO Box 698, Mansfield 44901-0698
Type: Public, state, two-year
System: University System of Ohio
Degrees: A *Enroll:* 1,756
URL: http://www.ncstatecollege.edu
Phone: (419) 755-4800 *Calendar:* Qtr. plan
Inst. Accred.: NCA-HLC (1976/2005)
Prog. Accred.: Allied Health (respiratory therapy), Business (ACBSP), Nursing, Physical Therapy Assisting, Radiography

Northeastern Ohio Universities Colleges of Medicine and Pharmacy
4209 State Route 44, Rootstown 44272-0095
Type: Public, state, four-year
System: University System of Ohio
Degrees: D *Enroll:* 461
URL: http://www.neoucom.edu
Phone: (330) 325-2511 *Calendar:* Sem. plan
Inst. Accred.: NCA-HLC (1998/2003)
Prog. Accred.: Allied Health (medicine), Pharmacy, Psychology Internship, Public Health

Northwest State Community College
22600 State Route 34, Archbold 43502
Type: Public, state, two-year
System: University System of Ohio
Degrees: A *Enroll:* 1,752
URL: http://www.northweststate.edu
Phone: (419) 267-5511 *Calendar:* Sem. plan
Inst. Accred.: NCA-HLC (1977/2006)
Prog. Accred.: Business (ACBSP), Nursing

Notre Dame College
4545 College Rd., South Euclid 44121
Type: Private, Roman Catholic Church, four-year
Degrees: A, B, M *Enroll:* 837
URL: http://www.notredamecollege.edu
Phone: (216) 381-1680 *Calendar:* Sem. plan
Inst. Accred.: NCA-HLC (1931/2007)
Prog. Accred.: Teacher Education (NCATE)

Oberlin College
101 North Professor St., Oberlin 44074-1075
Type: Private, independent, four-year
Degrees: B, M *Enroll:* 2,809
URL: http://www.oberlin.edu
Phone: (440) 775-8400 *Calendar:* 4-1-4 plan
Inst. Accred.: NCA-HLC (1913/2008)
Prog. Accred.: Music

Ohio Business College
5095 Waterford Dr., Sheffield Village 44035
Type: Private, proprietary, two-year
Degrees: A *Enroll:* 155
URL: http://www.ohiobusinesscollege.edu
Phone: (440) 934-3101
Inst. Accred.: ACICS (1980/2008)

Sandusky Campus
5202 Timber Commons Dr., Sandusky 44870
Phone: (419) 627-8345

Ohio Christian University
PO Box 460, Circleville 43113-0460
Type: Private, Churches of Christ in Christian Union, four-year
Degrees: A, B *Enroll:* 367
URL: http://www.ohiochristian.edu
Phone: (740) 474-8896 *Calendar:* Sem. plan
Inst. Accred.: ABHE (1976/2007), NCA-HLC (2005)

Ohio College of Massotherapy
225 Heritage Woods Dr., Akron 44321
Type: Private, proprietary, two-year
Degrees: A
URL: http://www.ocm.edu
Phone: (330) 665-1084
Inst. Accred.: ACCSCT (1994/2004)

Ohio College of Podiatric Medicine
6000 Rockside Woods Blvd., Independence 44131
Type: Private, independent, four-year
Degrees: D *Enroll:* 271
URL: http://www.ocpm.edu
Phone: (216) 231-3300 *Calendar:* Sem. plan
Inst. Accred.: NCA-HLC (1987/2008)
Prog. Accred.: Podiatry

Ohio Dominican University
1216 Sunbury Rd., Columbus 43219
Type: Private, Roman Catholic Church, four-year
Degrees: A, B *Enroll:* 2,351
URL: http://www.ohiodominican.edu
Phone: (614) 253-2741 *Calendar:* Sem. plan
Inst. Accred.: NCA-HLC (1934/2008)
Prog. Accred.: Business (ACBSP), Social Work

Ohio Institute of Health Careers
1880 East Dublin-Granville Rd., Ste. 100, Columbus 43229
Type: Private, proprietary, two-year
Degrees: A *FTE Enroll:* 654
URL: http://www.ohioinstituteofhealthcareers.edu
Phone: (614) 891-5030
Inst. Accred.: ACCSCT (1985/2005)
Prog. Accred.: Allied Health (medical assisting (AMA))

Elyria Campus
639 Griswold Rd., Elyria 44035
Phone: (440) 324-2293
Prog. Accred: Allied Health (medical assisting (AMA))

Ohio Institute of Photography and Technology

2029 Edgefield Rd., Dayton 45439-1984
Type: Private, proprietary, two-year
System: Kaplan Higher Education Corporation
Degrees: A *Enroll:* 741
URL: http://www.oipt.com
Phone: (937) 294-6155 *Calendar:* Qtr. plan
Inst. Accred.: ACCSCT (1976/2005)
Prog. Accred.: Allied Health (medical assisting (AMA))

Florida Education Center

1299B NW Fortieth Ave. (SR 441), Lauderhill, FL 33313
Phone: (954) 797-6140

Ohio Northern University

525 South Main St., Ada 45810
Type: Private, United Methodist Church, four-year
Degrees: B, P, D *Enroll:* 3,485
URL: http://www.onu.edu
Phone: (419) 772-2000 *Calendar:* Qtr. plan
Inst. Accred.: NCA-HLC (1958/2005)
Prog. Accred.: Business (AACSB), Construction Technology, Design Technology, Engineering (civil, computer, electrical, mechanical), Law, Manufacturing Technology, Music, Nursing Education, Pharmacy, Teacher Education (NCATE)

The Ohio State University

205 Bricker Hall, 190 North Oval Dr., Columbus 43210-1357
Type: Public, state, four-year
System: University System of Ohio
Degrees: A, B, M, P, D *Enroll:* 46,417
URL: http://www.osu.edu
Phone: (614) 292-6446 *Calendar:* Qtr. plan
Inst. Accred.: NCA-HLC (1913/2007)
Prog. Accred.: Accounting, Allied Health (audiology, health services administration, medical assisting (AMA), medicine, occupational therapy, optometric residency, optometry, perfusion, respiratory therapy, speech-language pathology), Applied Science (surveying/geomatics), Art, Business (AACSB), Clinical Lab Scientist, Clinical Pastoral Education, Clinical Psychology, Computer Science (ABET-CAC), Construction Education, Counseling Psychology, Dance, Dentistry (combined prosthodontics, dental hygiene, dentistry, endodontics, general dentistry, general practice residency, oral and maxillofacial pathology, oral and maxillofacial surgery, orthodontic and dentofacial orthopedics, pediatric dentistry, periodontics), Dietetics (coordinated), Dietetics (didactic), Dietetics (internship), Engineering (aerospace, agricultural, chemical, civil, computer, electrical, environmental/sanitary, industrial, materials, mechanical, welding), English Language Education, Forestry, Interior Design, Landscape Architecture, Law, Marriage and Family Therapy, Music, Nuclear Medicine Technology, Nursing Education, Nurse (Midwifery), Pathologists' Assistant, Pharmacy, Physical Therapy, Planning, Psychology Internship, Public Administration, Public Health, Radiography, Radiation Therapy, Social Work, Teacher Education (NCATE), Theatre, Veterinary Medicine

Lima Campus

4240 Campus Dr., Lima 45804
Phone: (419) 221-1641

Mansfield Campus

1680 University Dr., Mansfield 44906
Phone: (419) 755-4011

Marion Campus

1465 Mount Vernon Ave., Marion 43302-5695
Phone: (740) 389-6786

Newark Campus

1179 University Dr., Newark 43055-1797
Phone: (614) 366-3321

The Ohio State University—Agricultural Technical Institute

1328 Dover Rd., Wooster 44691
Type: Public, state, two-year
Degrees: A *Enroll:* 755
URL: http://www.ati.ohio-state.edu
Phone: (330) 264-3911 *Calendar:* Qtr. plan
Inst. Accred.: NCA-HLC (1978/2007)

Ohio University

Athens 45701-2979
Type: Public, state, four-year
System: University System of Ohio
Degrees: A, B, M, D *Enroll:* 19,407
URL: http://www.ohiou.edu
Phone: (740) 593-1000 *Calendar:* Qtr. plan
Inst. Accred.: NCA-HLC (1913/2001)
Prog. Accred.: Accounting, Allied Health (audiology, medical assisting (AMA), speech-language pathology), Applied Science (industrial hygiene), Business (AACSB), Clinical Psychology, Computer Science (ABET-CAC), Counseling, Dance, Dietetics (didactic), Engineering (chemical, civil, electrical, industrial, mechanical), Environmental Health, Family & Consumer Science, Graduate Social Work, Industrial Technology, Interior Architecture, Journalism, Music, Nursing, Nursing Education, Osteopathy, Physical Therapy, Public Health, Recreation and Leisure Services, Rehabilitation Counseling, Social Work, Teacher Education (NCATE), Theatre

Chillicothe Campus

571 West 5th St., Chillicothe 45601
Phone: (614) 774-7200

Eastern Campus

National Rd., West St., St. Clairsville 43950
Phone: (614) 695-1720

Lancaster Campus

1570 Granville Pike, Lancaster 43130
Phone: (614) 654-6711

Southern Campus

1804 Liberty Ave., Ironton 43701
Phone: (614) 533-4600

Zanesville Campus
1425 Neward Rd., Zanesville 43701
Phone: (614) 453-0762

Ohio Valley College of Technology
16808 St. Clair Ave., Liverpool 43920
Type: Private, proprietary, two-year
Degrees: A *Enroll:* 161
URL: http://www.ohiovalleytech.com
Phone: (330) 385-1070
Inst. Accred.: ACICS (1985/2005)
Prog. Accred.: Allied Health (medical assisting (AMA))

Ohio Wesleyan University
61 South Sandusky St., Delaware 43015
Type: Private, United Methodist Church, four-year
Degrees: B *Enroll:* 1,953
URL: http://web.owu.edu
Phone: (740) 368-2000 *Calendar:* Sem. plan
Inst. Accred.: NCA-HLC (1913/1999)
Prog. Accred.: Music, Teacher Education (NCATE)

Otterbein College
One Otterbein College, Westerville 43081
Type: Private, United Methodist Church, four-year
Degrees: B, M *Enroll:* 2,648
URL: http://www.otterbein.edu
Phone: (614) 890-3000 *Calendar:* Qtr. plan
Inst. Accred.: NCA-HLC (1913/2005)
Prog. Accred.: Music, Nursing, Nursing Education, Teacher Education (NCATE), Theatre

Owens Community College
PO Box 10000, Toledo 43699-1947
Type: Public, state, two-year
System: University System of Ohio
Degrees: A *Enroll:* 11,064
URL: http://www.owens.edu
Phone: (419) 661-7000 *Calendar:* Sem. plan
Inst. Accred.: NCA-HLC (1976/2001)
Prog. Accred.: Allied Health (diagnostic medical sonography, occupational therapy assisting, surgical technology), Automotive Technology, Business (ACBSP), Dentistry (dental hygiene), Design Technology, Dietetic Technician, Electronic Technology, Engineering Technology (architectural, electrical, mechanical), Health Technology, Manufacturing Technology, Nursing, Physical Therapy Assisting, Radiography

Findlay Campus
300 Davis St., Findlay 45840-3600
Phone: (567) 429-3604

Payne Theological Seminary
PO Box 474, Wilberforce 45384-0474
Type: Private, African Methodist Episcopal Church, four-year
Degrees: M *Enroll:* 43
URL: http://www.payne.edu
Phone: (937) 376-2946
Inst. Accred.: ATS (1995/2008)

Pontifical College Josephinum
7625 North High St., Columbus 43235
Type: Private, Roman Catholic Church, four-year
Degrees: B, M *Enroll:* 133
URL: http://www.pcj.edu
Phone: (614) 885-5585 *Calendar:* Sem. plan
Inst. Accred.: ATS (1970/2001), NCA-HLC (1977/2001)

Professional Skills Institute
20 Arco Dr., Toledo 43607
Type: Private, proprietary, two-year
Degrees: A *Enroll:* 245
URL: http://www.proskills.com
Phone: (419) 531-9610 *Calendar:* Qtr. plan
Inst. Accred.: ABHES (1986/2003)
Prog. Accred.: Physical Therapy Assisting

Santa Barbara Campus
4213 State St., Ste. 302, Santa Barbara, CA 93110
Phone: (805) 683-1902

Rabbinical College of Telshe
28400 Euclid Ave., Wickliffe 44092-2523
Type: Private, independent, four-year
Degrees: M, D *Enroll:* 58
Phone: (440) 943-5300 *Calendar:* Sem. plan
Inst. Accred.: AARTS (1974/2006)

Remington College—Cleveland
14445 Broadway Ave., Cleveland 44125
Type: Private, proprietary, two-year
System: Education America, Inc.
Degrees: A
URL: http://www.remingtoncollege.edu
Phone: (216) 475-7520 *Calendar:* Qtr. plan
Inst. Accred.: ACCSCT (1990/2005)

Cleveland West Campus
26350 Brookpark Rd., North Olmstead 44070
Phone: (440) 777-2560

Shreveport Campus
2106 Bert Kouns Industrial Loop, Shreveport, LA 71118
Phone: (318) 671-4000

RETS College
555 East Alex-Bell Rd., Centerville 45459
Type: Private, proprietary, two-year
System: Education Affiliates, Inc.
Degrees: A *Enroll:* 533
URL: http://www.rets.edu
Phone: (937) 433-3410 *Calendar:* Sem. plan
Inst. Accred.: ACCSCT (1974/2008)
Prog. Accred.: Allied Health (medical assisting (AMA)), Nursing

Rosedale Bible College
2270 Rosedale Rd., Irwin 43029-9501
Type: Private, Conservative Mennonite Conference, two-year
Degrees: A
URL: http://www.rosedale.edu
Phone: (740) 857-1311
Inst. Accred.: ABHE (2002/2007)

Saint Mary Seminary and Graduate School of Theology
28700 Euclid Ave., Wickliffe 44092-2585
Type: Private, Roman Catholic Church, four-year
Degrees: M, D *Enroll:* 87
URL: http://www.stmarysem.edu
Phone: (440) 943-7600 *Calendar:* Sem. plan
Inst. Accred.: ATS (1970/2005), NCA-HLC (1981/2006)

School of Advertising Art
1725 East David Rd., Dayton 45440-1612
Type: Private, proprietary, two-year
Degrees: A *Enroll:* 141
URL: http://www.saacollege.com
Phone: (937) 294-0592
Inst. Accred.: ACCSCT (1988/2003)

Shawnee State University
940 Second St., Portsmouth 45662-4303
Type: Public, state, four-year
System: University System of Ohio
Degrees: A, B *Enroll:* 3,448
URL: http://www.shawnee.edu
Phone: (740) 354-3205 *Calendar:* Qtr. plan
Inst. Accred.: NCA-HLC (1975/2004)
Prog. Accred.: Allied Health (occupational therapy, occupational therapy assisting, respiratory therapy), Business (ACBSP), Clinical Lab Scientist, Clinical Lab Technology, Dentistry (dental hygiene), Nursing, Physical Therapy Assisting, Radiography, Teacher Education (NCATE)

Sinclair Community College
444 West Third St., Dayton 45402-1460
Type: Public, state/local, two-year
System: University System of Ohio
Degrees: A *Enroll:* 11,273
URL: http://www.sinclair.edu
Phone: (937) 226-2500 *Calendar:* Qtr. plan
Inst. Accred.: NCA-HLC (1970/2003)
Prog. Accred.: Allied Health (medical assisting (AMA), occupational therapy assisting, respiratory therapy, surgical technology), Art, Business (ACBSP), Culinary Education, Dentistry (dental hygiene), Dietetic Technician, Engineering Technology (air conditioning, civil/construction, electrical, environmental/sanitary, fire protection/safety, general drafting/design, industrial, mechanical, quality technology), Music, Nursing, Physical Therapy Assisting, Radiography

Southern State Community College
100 Hobart Dr., Hillsboro 45133-9487
Type: Public, state, two-year
System: University System of Ohio
Degrees: A *Enroll:* 1,633
URL: http://www.sscc.edu
Phone: (937) 393-3431 *Calendar:* Qtr. plan
Inst. Accred.: NCA-HLC (1981/2006)
Prog. Accred.: Allied Health (medical assisting (AMA)), Nursing

Southwestern College
111 West First St., Ste. 1140, Dayton 45402
Type: Private, proprietary, two-year
System: Lincoln Educational Services Corporation
Degrees: A *Enroll:* 304
URL: http://www.swcollege.net
Phone: (937) 224-0061 *Calendar:* Qtr. plan
Inst. Accred.: ACICS (1978/2001)

Florence Campus
8095 Connector Dr., Florence, KY 41042-1466
Phone: (859) 282-9999

Franklin Campus
201 East Second St., Franklin 45005
Phone: (937) 746-6633

Tri-County Campus
149 Northland Blvd., Cincinnati 45246
Phone: (513) 874-0432

Vine Street Campus
632 Vine St., Ste. 200, Cincinnati 45202
Phone: (513) 421-3212

Stark State College of Technology
6200 Frank Ave., NW, Canton 44720-7299
Type: Public, state, two-year
System: University System of Ohio
Degrees: A *Enroll:* 3,828
URL: http://www.starkstate.edu
Phone: (330) 494-6170 *Calendar:* Sem. plan
Inst. Accred.: NCA-HLC (1976/2001)
Prog. Accred.: Allied Health (medical assisting (AMA), occupational therapy assisting, respiratory therapy), Business (ACBSP), Clinical Lab Technology, Dentistry (dental hygiene), Engineering Technology (civil/ construction, electrical, general drafting/design, mechanical), Nursing

Stautzenberger College
1796 Indian Wood Circle, Maumee 43537-4007
Type: Private, proprietary, two-year
System: American Higher Education Development Corporation
Degrees: A *Enroll:* 572
URL: http://www.sctoday.edu
Phone: (419) 866-0261 *Calendar:* Qtr. plan
Inst. Accred.: ACICS (1962/2001)
Prog. Accred.: Allied Health (medical assisting (AMA)), Veterinary Technology

Strongsville Campus
8001 Katherine Blvd., Brecksville 44141
Phone: (440) 846-1999
Prog. Accred: Veterinary Technology

Technology Education College
2745 Winchester Pike, Columbus 43232
Type: Private, proprietary, two-year
System: Kaplan Higher Education Corporation
Degrees: A *Enroll:* 491
URL: http://www.teccollege.com
Phone: (614) 456-4600
Inst. Accred.: ACCSCT (1980/2005)

Temple Baptist College
11965 Kenn Rd., Cincinnati 45240
Type: Private, Baptist Church, four-year
Degrees: B
URL: http://www.templebaptistcollege.net
Phone: (513) 851-3800 *Calendar:* Qtr. plan
Inst. Accred.: TRACS (2005)

Terra State Community College
2830 Napoleon Rd., Fremont 43420-9670
Type: Public, state, two-year
System: University System of Ohio
Degrees: A *Enroll:* 1,517
URL: http://www.terra.edu
Phone: (419) 334-8400 *Calendar:* Qtr. plan
Inst. Accred.: NCA-HLC (1975/2008)

Tiffin University
155 Miami St., Tiffin 44883
Type: Private, independent, four-year
Degrees: A, B, M *Enroll:* 1,415
URL: http://www.tiffin.edu
Phone: (419) 447-6442 *Calendar:* Sem. plan
Inst. Accred.: NCA-HLC (1985/2000)
Prog. Accred.: Business (ACBSP)

Tri-State Bible College
PO Box 445, South Point 45680
Type: Private, independent, four-year
Degrees: A, B *Enroll:* 23
URL: http://www.tsbc.edu
Phone: (740) 377-2520 *Calendar:* Sem. plan
Inst. Accred.: ABHE (2004)

Tri-State College of Massotherapy
9159 Market St., Ste. 26, North Lima 44452
Type: Private, proprietary, two-year
Degrees: A
URL: http://tristatemasso.com
Phone: (330) 629-9998
Inst. Accred.: ACCSCT (2001/2006)

Trinity Lutheran Seminary
2199 East Main St., Columbus 43209-2334
Type: Private, Evangelical Lutheran Church in America, four-year
Degrees: M *Enroll:* 152
URL: http://www.trinitylutheranseminary.edu
Phone: (614) 235-4136 *Calendar:* Sem. plan
Inst. Accred.: ATS (1940/2002), NCA-HLC (1978/2002)

Trumbull Business College
3200 Ridge Rd., Warren 44484
Type: Private, proprietary, two-year
Degrees: A *Enroll:* 356
URL: http://www.tbc-trumbullbusiness.com
Phone: (330) 369-3200
Inst. Accred.: ACICS (1976/2000)

The Union Institute & University
440 East McMillan St., Cincinnati 45206-1947
Type: Private, independent, four-year
Degrees: B, D *Enroll:* 2,107
URL: http://www.tui.edu
Phone: (513) 861-6400 *Calendar:* Sem. plan
Inst. Accred.: NCA-HLC (1985/2000)

United Theological Seminary
4501 Denlinger Rd., Trotwood 45426
Type: Private, The United Methodist Church, four-year
Degrees: M, D *Enroll:* 319
URL: http://www.united.edu
Phone: (937) 529-2201 *Calendar:* Sem. plan
Inst. Accred.: ATS (1938/2006), NCA-HLC (1975/2002)

The University of Akron
302 East Buchtel Common, Akron 44325-4702
Type: Public, state, four-year
System: University System of Ohio
Degrees: A, B, M, D *Enroll:* 17,265
URL: http://www.uakron.edu
Phone: (330) 972-7111 *Calendar:* Sem. plan
Inst. Accred.: NCA-HLC (1914/2003)
Prog. Accred.: Accounting, Allied Health (audiology, medical assisting (AMA), respiratory therapy, speech-language pathology, surgical technology), Art, Business (AACSB), Business (ACBSP), Counseling, Counseling Psychology, Dance, Dietetics (coordinated), Dietetics (didactic), Engineering (bioengineering, chemical, civil, computer, electrical, mechanical, polymer), Engineering Technology (civil/construction, electrical, mechanical, surveying), Family & Consumer Science, Graduate Social Work, Interior Design, Law, Marriage and Family Therapy, Music, Nurse Anesthesia Education, Nursing Education, Psychology Internship, Public Administration, Public Health, Social Work, Teacher Education (NCATE)

University of Akron—Wayne College
1901 Smucker Rd., Orrville 44667
Type: Public, state, two-year
System: University System of Ohio
Degrees: A *Enroll:* 1,124
URL: http://www.wayne.uakron.edu
Phone: (330) 683-2010 *Calendar:* Sem. plan
Inst. Accred.: NCA-HLC (1972/2001)

University of Cincinnati
PO Box 210063, Cincinnati 45221-0063
Type: Public, state, four-year
System: University System of Ohio
Degrees: A, B, M, P, D *Enroll:* 23,748
URL: http://www.uc.edu
Phone: (513) 556-6000 *Calendar:* Qtr. plan
Inst. Accred.: NCA-HLC (1913/1999)
Prog. Accred.: Allied Health (EMT-paramedic, audiology, blood bank technology, medical assisting (AMA), medicine, speech-language pathology), Applied Science (industrial hygiene), Art, Business (AACSB), Clinical Lab Scientist, Clinical Psychology, Computer Science (ABET-CAC), Construction Education, Counseling, Dance, Dentistry (dental hygiene, oral and maxillofacial surgery), Dietetics (coordinated), Dietetics (didactic), Engineering (aerospace, bioengineering, chemical, civil, computer, electrical, environmental/sanitary, industrial, materials, mechanical), Engineering Technology (architectural, civil/construction, electrical, manufacturing, mechanical), Graduate Social Work, Interior Design, Law, Music, Nuclear Medicine Technology, Nurse (Midwifery), Nurse Anesthesia Education, Nursing Education, Pharmacy, Physical Therapy, Physical Therapy Assisting, Planning, Psychology Internship, Radiography, Social Work, Teacher Education (NCATE), Theatre

College-Conservatory of Music
PO Box 210236, Cincinnati 45221-9988
Phone: (513) 556-2595
Prog. Accred: Music

University of Cincinnati—Clermont College
4200 Clermont College Dr., Batavia 45103
Type: Public, state, two-year
System: University System of Ohio
Degrees: A *Enroll:* 2,080
Phone: (513) 732-5200 *Calendar:* Qtr. plan
Inst. Accred.: NCA-HLC (1978/2006)
Prog. Accred.: Allied Health (surgical technology)

University of Cincinnati—Raymond Walters College
9555 Plainfield Rd., Cincinnati 45236-1096
Type: Public, state, four-year
System: University System of Ohio
Degrees: A, B *Enroll:* 3,174
URL: http://www.rwc.uc.edu
Phone: (513) 745-5600 *Calendar:* Qtr. plan
Inst. Accred.: NCA-HLC (1969/1999)
Prog. Accred.: Dentistry (dental hygiene), Nursing, Radiation Therapy, Radiography, Veterinary Technology

University of Dayton
300 College Park Ave., Dayton 45469-1624
Type: Private, Society of Mary, four-year
Degrees: B, M, P, D *Enroll:* 9,403
URL: http://www.udayton.edu
Phone: (937) 229-1000 *Calendar:* Tri. plan
Inst. Accred.: NCA-HLC (1928/2008)
Prog. Accred.: Accounting, Business (AACSB), Dietetics (didactic), Engineering (chemical, civil, computer, electrical, mechanical), Engineering Technology (computer, electrical, industrial, manufacturing, mechanical), Law, Music, Physical Therapy, Public Administration, Teacher Education (NCATE)

University of Findlay
1000 North Main St., Findlay 45840
Type: Private, Churches of God, General Conference, four-year
Degrees: A, B, M *Enroll:* 3,666
URL: http://www.findlay.edu
Phone: (419) 424-8313 *Calendar:* Sem. plan
Inst. Accred.: NCA-HLC (1933/2004)
Prog. Accred.: Allied Health (occupational therapy), Nuclear Medicine Technology, Pharmacy, Physical Therapy, Physician Assistant, Social Work, Teacher Education (NCATE)

University of Northwestern Ohio
1441 North Cable Rd., Lima 45805
Type: Private, independent, four-year
Degrees: A, B *Enroll:* 2,741
URL: http://www.unoh.edu
Phone: (419) 227-3141 *Calendar:* Qtr. plan
Inst. Accred.: NCA-HLC (1987/2006)
Prog. Accred.: Allied Health (medical assisting (AMA)), Business (ACBSP)

University of Rio Grande and Rio Grande Community College
218 North College Ave., Rio Grande 45674
Type: Private, independent, four-year
Degrees: A, B, M *Enroll:* 1,974
URL: http://www.rio.edu
Phone: (740) 245-5353 *Calendar:* Qtr. plan
Inst. Accred.: NCA-HLC (1969/2004)
Prog. Accred.: Allied Health (diagnostic medical sonography), Clinical Lab Technology, Nursing, Social Work, Teacher Education (NCATE)

University of Toledo
2801 West Bancroft St., Toledo 43606-3390
Type: Public, state, four-year
System: University System of Ohio
Degrees: A, B, M, P, D *Enroll:* 16,637
URL: http://www.utoledo.edu
Phone: (419) 530-4636 *Calendar:* Sem. plan
Inst. Accred.: NCA-HLC (1922/2002)
Prog. Accred.: Allied Health (cardiovascular technology, kinesiotherapy, respiratory therapy, speech-language pathology), Art, Business (AACSB), Clinical Psychology, Computer Science (ABET-CAC), Counseling, Engineering (bioengineering, chemical, civil, computer, electrical, industrial, mechanical), Engineering Technology (civil/construction, computer, electrical, mechanical), Graduate Social Work, Law, Music, Nursing, Pharmacy, Public Administration, Recreation and Leisure Services, Social Work, Teacher Education (NCATE)

Health Science Campus
3000 Arlington Ave., Toledo 43614
Phone: (419) 383-4000
Prog. Accred: Allied Health (medicine, occupational therapy), Applied Science (occupational health & safety), Dentistry (general practice residency), Nursing Education, Physical Therapy, Physician Assistant, Psychology Internship, Public Health

Urbana University
579 College Way, Urbana 43078
Type: Private, Swedenborgian, four-year
Degrees: A, B, M *Enroll:* 1,162
URL: http://www.urbana.edu
Phone: (937) 484-1301 *Calendar:* Sem. plan
Inst. Accred.: NCA-HLC (1975/2001)
Prog. Accred.: Nursing Education

Ursuline College
2550 Lander Rd., Pepper Pike 44124
Type: Private, Roman Catholic Church, four-year
Degrees: B, M *Enroll:* 1,094
URL: http://www.ursuline.edu
Phone: (440) 449-4200 *Calendar:* Sem. plan
Inst. Accred.: NCA-HLC (1931/2002)
Prog. Accred.: Nursing Education, Social Work

Virginia Marti College of Art and Design
PO Box 580, 11724 Detroit Ave., Lakewood 44107
Type: Private, independent, two-year
Degrees: A *Enroll:* 285
URL: http://www.virginiamarticollege.com
Phone: (216) 221-8584 *Calendar:* Qtr. plan
Inst. Accred.: ACCSCT (1975/2007)

Walsh University
2020 Easton St., NW, Canton 44720
Type: Private, Roman Catholic Church, four-year
Degrees: A, B, M *Enroll:* 1,753
URL: http://www.walsh.edu
Phone: (330) 499-7090 *Calendar:* Sem. plan
Inst. Accred.: NCA-HLC (1970/2000)
Prog. Accred.: Counseling, Nursing, Physical Therapy

Washington State Community College
710 Colegate Dr., Marietta 45750-9803
Type: Public, state, two-year
System: University System of Ohio
Degrees: A *Enroll:* 1,675
URL: http://www.wscc.edu
Phone: (740) 374-8716 *Calendar:* Qtr. plan
Inst. Accred.: NCA-HLC (1979/2003)
Prog. Accred.: Allied Health (respiratory therapy), Clinical Lab Technology, Physical Therapy Assisting

Wilberforce University
1055 North Bickett Rd., PO Box 1001, Wilberforce 45384-1001
Type: Private, African Methodist Episcopal Church, four-year
Degrees: B, M *Enroll:* 1,162
URL: http://www.wilberforce.edu
Phone: (937) 376-2911 *Calendar:* Tri. plan
Inst. Accred.: NCA-HLC (1939/1999)
Prog. Accred.: Rehabilitation Counseling

Wilmington College
251 Ludovic St., PO Box 1185, Wilmington 45177
Type: Private, Religious Society of Friends (Quaker), four-year
Degrees: B *Enroll:* 1,541
URL: http://www.wilmington.edu
Phone: (937) 382-6661 *Calendar:* Sem. plan
Inst. Accred.: NCA-HLC (1944/2004)

Blue Ash Campus
9987 Carver Rd., Ste. 100, Blue Ash 45242
Phone: (513) 793-1337

Winebrenner Theological Seminary
950 North Main St., Findlay 45840
Type: Private, Churches of God, General Conference, four-year
Degrees: M, D *Enroll:* 56
URL: http://www.winebrenner.edu
Phone: (419) 434-4200 *Calendar:* 4-1-4 plan
Inst. Accred.: ATS (1991/2004), NCA-HLC (1986/2005)

Wittenberg University
PO Box 720, Springfield 45501-0720
Type: Private, Evangelic Church in America, four-year
Degrees: B, M *Enroll:* 1,994
URL: http://www.wittenberg.edu
Phone: (937) 327-6231 *Calendar:* Sem. plan
Inst. Accred.: NCA-HLC (1916/2007)
Prog. Accred.: Music, Teacher Education (NCATE)

Wright State University

3640 Colonel Glenn Hwy., Dayton 45435-0001
Type: Public, state, four-year
System: University System of Ohio
Degrees: A, B, M, P, D *Enroll:* 14,050
URL: http://www.wright.edu
Phone: (937) 775-3333 *Calendar:* Qtr. plan
Inst. Accred.: NCA-HLC (1968/2006)
Prog. Accred.: Accounting, Allied Health (medicine), Business (AACSB), Clinical Lab Scientist, Clinical Psychology, Computer Science (ABET-CAC), Counseling, Engineering (bioengineering, computer, electrical, engineering physics/science, industrial, information systems, materials, mechanical), Environmental Health, Music, Nursing Education, Psychology Internship, Public Administration, Public Health, Rehabilitation Counseling, Social Work, Teacher Education (NCATE)

Lake Campus

7600 State Route 703, Celina 45822
Phone: (419) 586-2365

Xavier University

3800 Victory Pkwy., Cincinnati 45207
Type: Private, Roman Catholic Church, four-year
Degrees: A, B, M, D *Enroll:* 5,091
URL: http://www.xu.edu
Phone: (513) 745-3000 *Calendar:* Sem. plan
Inst. Accred.: NCA-HLC (1925/1999)
Prog. Accred.: Allied Health (health services administration, occupational therapy), Business (AACSB), Clinical Psychology, Counseling, Montessori Teacher Education, Nursing Education, Radiography, Social Work

Youngstown State University

One University Plaza, Youngstown 44555-3101
Type: Public, state, four-year
System: University System of Ohio
Degrees: A, B, M, D *Enroll:* 10,920
URL: http://www.ysu.edu
Phone: (330) 742-3000 *Calendar:* Qtr. plan
Inst. Accred.: NCA-HLC (1945/2008)
Prog. Accred.: Allied Health (EMT-paramedic, medical assisting (AMA), respiratory therapy), Art, Business (AACSB), Clinical Lab Technology, Counseling, Dentistry (dental hygiene), Dietetic Technician, Dietetics (coordinated), Dietetics (didactic), Engineering (chemical, civil, electrical, industrial, mechanical), Engineering Technology (civil/construction, electrical, mechanical), Graduate Social Work, Histologic Technology, Music, Nursing, Physical Therapy, Public Health, Social Work, Teacher Education (NCATE), Theatre

Zane State College

1555 Newark Rd., Zanesville 43701-2694
Type: Public, state, two-year
System: University System of Ohio
Degrees: A *Enroll:* 1,375
URL: http://www.zanestate.edu
Phone: (740) 454-2501 *Calendar:* Qtr. plan
Inst. Accred.: NCA-HLC (1975/2004)
Prog. Accred.: Allied Health (medical assisting (AMA), occupational therapy assisting), Clinical Lab Technology, Culinary Education, Engineering Technology (electrical), Phlebotomy, Physical Therapy Assisting, Radiography

OKLAHOMA

Bacone College
2299 Old Bacone Rd., Muskogee 74403-1597
Type: Private, American Baptist Church, four-year
Degrees: A, B *Enroll:* 687
URL: http://www.bacone.edu
Phone: (918) 683-4581 *Calendar:* 4-1-4 plan
Inst. Accred.: NCA-HLC (1965/2005)
Prog. Accred.: Nursing, Radiography

Cameron University
2800 West Gore Blvd., Lawton 73505-6377
Type: Public, state, four-year
System: Oklahoma State Regents for Higher Education
Degrees: A, B, M *Enroll:* 4,471
URL: http://www.cameron.edu
Phone: (580) 581-2200 *Calendar:* Sem. plan
Inst. Accred.: NCA-HLC (1962/2001)
Prog. Accred.: Business (ACBSP), Music, Teacher Education (NCATE)

Carl Albert State College
1507 South McKenna, Poteau 74953-5208
Type: Public, state, two-year
System: Oklahoma State Regents for Higher Education
Degrees: A *Enroll:* 1,825
URL: http://www.carlalbert.edu
Phone: (918) 647-8660 *Calendar:* Sem. plan
Inst. Accred.: NCA-HLC (1978/2003)
Prog. Accred.: Business (ACBSP), Nursing, Physical Therapy Assisting, Radiography

Sallisaw Campus
PO Box 1437, Sallisaw 77495
Phone: (918) 775-6977

Connors State College
Route 1, Box 1000, Warner 74469
Type: Public, state, two-year
System: Oklahoma State Regents for Higher Education
Degrees: A *Enroll:* 1,619
URL: http://www.connorsstate.edu
Phone: (918) 463-2931 *Calendar:* Sem. plan
Inst. Accred.: NCA-HLC (1963/2000)
Prog. Accred.: Nursing

Muskogee Campus
201 Ct. St., Muskogee 74401
Phone: (918) 687-6747

East Central University
1100 East 14th St., Ada 74820-6999
Type: Public, state, four-year
System: Oklahoma State Regents for Higher Education
Degrees: B, M *Enroll:* 3,819
URL: http://www.ecok.edu
Phone: (928) 428-8322 *Calendar:* Sem. plan
Inst. Accred.: NCA-HLC (1922/2002)
Prog. Accred.: Business (ACBSP), Environmental Health, Music, Nursing, Rehabilitation Counseling, Social Work, Teacher Education (NCATE)

Eastern Oklahoma State College
1301 West Main St., Wilburton 74578-4999
Type: Public, state, two-year
System: Oklahoma State Regents for Higher Education
Degrees: A *Enroll:* 1,352
URL: http://www.eosc.edu
Phone: (918) 465-2361 *Calendar:* Sem. plan
Inst. Accred.: NCA-HLC (1954/2007)
Prog. Accred.: Forestry, Nursing

Family of Faith College
PO Box 1805, Shawnee 74802-1805
Type: Private, independent, four-year
Degrees: B
URL: http://www.familyoffaithcollege.com
Phone: (405) 273-5331 *Calendar:* Sem. plan
Inst. Accred.: ABHE (1998/2008)

Heritage College Hair Design
7100 I-35 Services Rd., Ste. 7118, Oklahoma City 73149
Type: Private, proprietary, two-year
Degrees: A
URL: http://www.heritage-education.com
Phone: (405) 631-3399
Inst. Accred.: ACCSCT (1994/2007)

Hillsdale Free Will Baptist College
PO Box 7208, Moore 73153-1208
Type: Private, Free Will Baptist Church, four-year
Degrees: A, B, M *Enroll:* 221
URL: http://www.hc.edu
Phone: (405) 912-9000 *Calendar:* Sem. plan
Inst. Accred.: TRACS (1999/2004)

Langston University
PO Box 907, Langston 73050-0907
Type: Public, state, four-year
System: Oklahoma State Regents for Higher Education
Degrees: A, B, M *Enroll:* 2,768
URL: http://www.lunet.edu
Phone: (405) 466-3207 *Calendar:* Sem. plan
Inst. Accred.: NCA-HLC (1948/2007)
Prog. Accred.: Business (ACBSP), Dietetics (didactic), Nursing, Physical Therapy, Rehabilitation Counseling

Mid-America Christian University
3500 SW 119th St., Oklahoma City 73170
Type: Private, Church of God, four-year
Degrees: A, B *Enroll:* 619
URL: http://www.macu.edu
Phone: (405) 691-3800 *Calendar:* Sem. plan
Inst. Accred.: NCA-HLC (1985/2007)

Murray State College
1 Murray Campus St., Tishomingo 73460-3137
Type: Public, state, two-year
System: Oklahoma State Regents for Higher Education
Degrees: A *Enroll:* 1,548
URL: http://www.mscok.edu
Phone: (580) 371-2371 *Calendar:* Sem. plan
Inst. Accred.: NCA-HLC (1964/2004)
Prog. Accred.: Nursing, Physical Therapy Assisting, Veterinary Technology

Northeastern Oklahoma A&M College
200 I St. NE, Miami 74354
Type: Public, state, two-year
System: Oklahoma State Regents for Higher Education
Degrees: A *Enroll:* 1,602
URL: http://www.neo.edu
Phone: (918) 542-8441 *Calendar:* Sem. plan
Inst. Accred.: NCA-HLC (1925/2007)
Prog. Accred.: Clinical Lab Technology, Nursing, Physical Therapy Assisting

Northeastern State University
601 North Grand, Tahlequah 74464-2399
Type: Public, state, four-year
System: Oklahoma State Regents for Higher Education
Degrees: B, M, D *Enroll:* 7,854
URL: http://www.nsuok.edu
Phone: (918) 456-5511 *Calendar:* Sem. plan
Inst. Accred.: NCA-HLC (1922/2002)
Prog. Accred.: Allied Health (optometric residency, optometry, speech-language pathology), Business (ACBSP), Music, Nursing, Social Work, Teacher Education (NCATE)

Muskogee Campus
PO Box 549, Muskogee 74402-0549
Phone: (918) 683-0641

Northern Oklahoma College
PO Box 310, 1220 East Grand, Tonkawa 74653-0310
Type: Public, state, two-year
System: Oklahoma State Regents for Higher Education
Degrees: A *Enroll:* 3,429
URL: http://www.north-ok.edu
Phone: (580) 628-6200 *Calendar:* Sem. plan
Inst. Accred.: NCA-HLC (1948/2008)
Prog. Accred.: Business (ACBSP), Nursing

Northwestern Oklahoma State University
709 Oklahoma Blvd., Alva 73717-2799
Type: Public, state, four-year
System: Oklahoma State Regents for Higher Education
Degrees: B, M *Enroll:* 1,767
URL: http://www.nwosu.edu
Phone: (580) 327-1700 *Calendar:* Sem. plan
Inst. Accred.: NCA-HLC (1922/2004)
Prog. Accred.: Nursing, Social Work, Teacher Education (NCATE)

Enid Campus
2929 East Randolph, Enid 73701
Phone: (580) 213-3101

Woodward Campus
High Plains Technical Center, 3921 34th St., Woodward 73801
Phone: (405) 256-0047

Oklahoma Baptist University
500 West University, Shawnee 74801
Type: Private, Southern Baptist Church, four-year
Degrees: A, B, M *Enroll:* 1,501
URL: http://www.okbu.edu
Phone: (405) 275-2850 *Calendar:* Sem. plan
Inst. Accred.: NCA-HLC (1952/2008)
Prog. Accred.: Business (ACBSP), Music, Nursing, Teacher Education (NCATE)

Oklahoma Christian University
PO Box 11000, Oklahoma City 73136-1100
Type: Private, independent, four-year
Degrees: B, M *Enroll:* 1,817
URL: http://www.oc.edu
Phone: (405) 425-5000 *Calendar:* Tri. plan
Inst. Accred.: NCA-HLC (1966/2006)
Prog. Accred.: Business (ACBSP), Engineering (computer, electrical, mechanical), Music, Nursing Education, Teacher Education (NCATE)

Cascade College
9101 East Burnside St., Portland, OR 97216-1515
Phone: (503) 255-7060

Oklahoma City Community College
7777 South May Ave., Oklahoma City 73159-4444
Type: Public, state/local, two-year
System: Oklahoma State Regents for Higher Education
Degrees: A *Enroll:* 7,524
URL: http://www.okccc.edu
Phone: (405) 682-1611 *Calendar:* Sem. plan
Inst. Accred.: NCA-HLC (1977/2002)
Prog. Accred.: Allied Health (EMT-paramedic, occupational therapy assisting), Business (ACBSP), Nursing, Physical Therapy Assisting

Oklahoma City University
2501 North Blackwelder Ave., Oklahoma City 73106
Type: Private, United Methodist Church, four-year
Degrees: B, M, D *Enroll:* 3,300
URL: http://www.okcu.edu
Phone: (405) 521-5000 *Calendar:* Sem. plan
Inst. Accred.: NCA-HLC (1951/2002)
Prog. Accred.: Business (ACBSP), Law, Montessori Teacher Education, Music

Oklahoma Panhandle State University
323 West Eagle Blvd., PO Box 430, Goodwell 73939-9728
Type: Public, state, four-year
System: Oklahoma State Regents for Higher Education
Degrees: A, B *Enroll:* 1,011
URL: http://www.opsu.edu
Phone: (580) 349-2611 *Calendar:* Sem. plan
Inst. Accred.: NCA-HLC (1926/2001)
Prog. Accred.: Nursing, Teacher Education (NCATE)

Oklahoma State University
107 Whitehurst Hall, Stillwater 74078-0004
Type: Public, state, four-year
System: Oklahoma State Regents for Higher Education
Degrees: B, M, P, D *Enroll:* 20,521
URL: http://www.okstate.edu
Phone: (405) 744-5000 *Calendar:* Sem. plan
Inst. Accred.: NCA-HLC (1916/2006)
Prog. Accred.: Accounting, Allied Health (speech-language pathology), Business (AACSB), Clinical Psychology, Counseling, Counseling Psychology, Dietetics (didactic), Dietetics (internship), Engineering (aerospace, agricultural, architectural, chemical, civil, electrical, industrial, mechanical), Engineering Technology (civil/construction, electrical, fire protection/ safety, mechanical), Forestry, Interior Design, Journalism, Landscape Architecture, Marriage and Family Therapy, Music, Recreation and Leisure Services, School Psychology, Teacher Education (NCATE), Theatre, Veterinary Medicine

College of Osteopathic Medicine
1111 West 17th St., Tulsa 74107
Phone: (918) 582-1972
Prog. Accred: Osteopathy

Tulsa Campus
700 N. Greenwood Ave., Tulsa 74106-0203
Phone: (918) 586-0703

Oklahoma State University—Oklahoma City
900 North Portland Ave., Oklahoma City 73107
Type: Public, state, two-year
Degrees: A *Enroll:* 3,168
URL: http://www.osuokc.edu
Phone: (405) 947-4421 *Calendar:* Sem. plan
Inst. Accred.: NCA-HLC (1975/2000)
Prog. Accred.: Nursing, Veterinary Technology

Oklahoma State University—Okmulgee
1801 East Fourth St., Okmulgee 74447-3901
Type: Public, state, four-year
Degrees: A, B *Enroll:* 2,185
URL: http://www.osu-okmulgee.edu
Phone: (918) 293-4636 *Calendar:* Tri. plan
Inst. Accred.: NCA-HLC (1975/2000)
Prog. Accred.: Nursing

Oklahoma Wesleyan University
2201 Silver Lake Rd., Bartlesville 74006
Type: Private, Wesleyan Church, four-year
Degrees: A, B *Enroll:* 766
URL: http://www.okwu.edu
Phone: (918) 335-6200 *Calendar:* Sem. plan
Inst. Accred.: NCA-HLC (1978/2004)
Prog. Accred.: Nursing Education, Teacher Education (NCATE)

Oral Roberts University
7777 South Lewis Ave., Tulsa 74171
Type: Private, interdenominational, four-year
Degrees: B, M, D *Enroll:* 3,152
URL: http://www.oru.edu
Phone: (918) 495-6161 *Calendar:* Sem. plan
Inst. Accred.: ATS (1980/1998), NCA-HLC (1971/2008)
Prog. Accred.: Business (ACBSP), Engineering (general), Music, Nursing Education, Social Work, Teacher Education (NCATE)

Phillips Theological Seminary
901 North Mingo Rd., Tulsa 74116-5612
Type: Private, Christian Church (Disciples of Christ), four-year
Degrees: M, D *Enroll:* 175
URL: http://www.ptstulsa.edu
Phone: (918) 610-8303 *Calendar:* Sem. plan
Inst. Accred.: ATS (1952/1999), NCA-HLC (1992/1999)

Platt College
3801 South Sheridan, Tulsa 74145-1132
Type: Private, proprietary, four-year
Degrees: A, B
URL: http://www.plattcollege.org
Phone: (918) 663-9000
Inst. Accred.: ACCSCT (1985/2006)
Prog. Accred.: Allied Health (surgical technology)

Central Oklahoma City Campus
309 South Ann Arbor, Oklahoma City 73128
Phone: (405) 946-7799
Prog. Accred: Allied Health (surgical technology)

Dallas Campus
2974 LBJ Freeway, Ste. 300, Dallas, TX 75234
Phone: (972) 243-0900

Lawton Campus
112 Southwest Eleventh St., Lawton 73501
Phone: (580) 355-4416

Moore Campus
201 North Eastern Ave., Moore 73160
Phone: (405) 912-3260

Oklahoma City North Campus
2727 West Memorial Rd., Oklahoma City 73134
Phone: (405) 749-2433
Prog. Accred: Culinary Education

Redlands Community College
1300 South Country Club Rd., El Reno 73036-5304
Type: Public, state/local, two-year
System: Oklahoma State Regents for Higher Education
Degrees: A *Enroll:* 1,400
URL: http://www.redlandscc.edu
Phone: (405) 262-2552 *Calendar:* Sem. plan
Inst. Accred.: NCA-HLC (1978/2002)
Prog. Accred.: Nursing

Rogers State University
1701 W. Will Rogers Blvd., Claremore 74017-3252
Type: Public, state, four-year
Degrees: A, B *Enroll:* 2,806
URL: http://www.rsu.edu
Phone: (918) 343-7500 *Calendar:* Sem. plan
Inst. Accred.: NCA-HLC (1950/2000)
Prog. Accred.: Nursing

Rose State College
6420 South East 15th St., Midwest City 73110-2799
Type: Public, state, two-year
System: Oklahoma State Regents for Higher Education
Degrees: A *Enroll:* 4,737
URL: http://www.rose.edu
Phone: (405) 733-7311 *Calendar:* Sem. plan
Inst. Accred.: NCA-HLC (1975/2008)
Prog. Accred.: Allied Health (respiratory therapy), Clinical Lab Technology, Dentistry (dental assisting, dental hygiene), Nursing, Radiography

Saint Gregory's University
1900 West MacArthur, Shawnee 74801
Type: Private, Roman Catholic Church, four-year
Degrees: A, B *Enroll:* 638
URL: http://www.stgregorys.edu
Phone: (405) 878-5100 *Calendar:* Sem. plan
Inst. Accred.: NCA-HLC (1969/2001)

Seminole State College
PO Box 351, Seminole 74818-0351
Type: Public, state, two-year
System: Oklahoma State Regents for Higher Education
Degrees: A *Enroll:* 1,505
URL: http://www.ssc.cc.ok.us
Phone: (405) 382-9950 *Calendar:* Sem. plan
Inst. Accred.: NCA-HLC (1975/2000)
Prog. Accred.: Clinical Lab Technology, Nursing

Southeastern Oklahoma State University
1405 North 4th Ave., Durant 74701-3330
Type: Public, state, four-year
System: Oklahoma State Regents for Higher Education
Degrees: B, M *Enroll:* 3,418
URL: http://www.sosu.edu
Phone: (580) 745-2000 *Calendar:* Sem. plan
Inst. Accred.: NCA-HLC (1922/2004)
Prog. Accred.: Business (ACBSP), Music, Teacher Education (NCATE)

Southern Nazarene University
6729 NW 39th Expressway, Bethany 73008
Type: Private, Church of the Nazarene, four-year
Degrees: A, B, M *Enroll:* 2,130
URL: http://www.snu.edu
Phone: (405) 789-6400 *Calendar:* Sem. plan
Inst. Accred.: NCA-HLC (1956/2000)
Prog. Accred.: Business (ACBSP), Music, Nursing Education, Teacher Education (NCATE)

Southwestern Christian University
PO Box 340, Bethany 73008-0340
Type: Private, International Pentecostal Holiness Church, four-year
Degrees: A, B, M *Enroll:* 278
URL: http://www.swcu.edu
Phone: (405) 789-7661 *Calendar:* Sem. plan
Inst. Accred.: NCA-HLC (1973/2004)

Southwestern Oklahoma State University
100 Campus Dr., Weatherford 73096-3098
Type: Public, state, four-year
System: Oklahoma State Regents for Higher Education
Degrees: A, B, M, P, D *Enroll:* 4,585
URL: http://www.swosu.edu
Phone: (580) 772-6611 *Calendar:* Sem. plan
Inst. Accred.: NCA-HLC (1922/2001)
Prog. Accred.: Engineering Technology (manufacturing), Industrial Technology, Music, Nursing, Pharmacy, Radiography, Social Work, Teacher Education (NCATE)

Sayre Campus
409 East Mississippi, Sayre 73662
Phone: (405) 928-5533
Prog. Accred: Medical Laboratory Technology, Physical Therapy Assisting, Radiography

Spartan College of Aeronautics and Technology
8820 East Pine St., PO Box 582833, Tulsa 74158-2833
Type: Private, proprietary, four-year
Degrees: A, B *Enroll:* 1,010
URL: http://www.spartan.edu
Phone: (918) 836-6886 *Calendar:* Sem. plan
Inst. Accred.: ACCSCT (1969/2006)

Tulsa Community College
6111 East Skelly Dr., Rm. 200, Tulsa 74135-6198
Type: Public, state, two-year
System: Oklahoma State Regents for Higher Education
Degrees: A *Enroll:* 9,668
URL: http://www.tulsacc.edu
Phone: (918) 595-7000 *Calendar:* Sem. plan
Inst. Accred.: NCA-HLC (1974/1999)
Prog. Accred.: Allied Health (medical assisting (AMA), respiratory therapy), Clinical Lab Technology, Dentistry (dental hygiene), Nursing, Phlebotomy, Physical Therapy Assisting, Radiography, Veterinary Technology

Metro Campus
909 South Boston Ave., Tulsa 74119-2095
Phone: (918) 595-7224
Prog. Accred: Allied Health (occupational therapy assisting), Radiography

Northeast Campus
3727 East Apache St., Tulsa 74115-3151
Phone: (918) 595-7524

Southeast Campus
10300 East 81st St., Tulsa 74133-4513
Phone: (918) 595-7724

West Campus
7505 West 41st St., Tulsa 74107-8633
Phone: (918) 595-8100

University of Central Oklahoma
100 North University Dr., Edmond 73034-0170
Type: Public, state, four-year
System: Oklahoma State Regents for Higher Education
Degrees: B, M *Enroll:* 12,685
URL: http://www.ucok.edu
Phone: (405) 341-2980 *Calendar:* Sem. plan
Inst. Accred.: NCA-HLC (1921/2003)
Prog. Accred.: Allied Health (speech-language pathology), Business (ACBSP), Dietetics (didactic), Dietetics (internship), Funeral Service Education (Mortuary Science), Interior Design, Music, Nursing, Teacher Education (NCATE)

University of Oklahoma
660 Parrington Oval, Room 104, Norman 73019-0390
Type: Public, state, four-year
System: Oklahoma State Regents for Higher Education
Degrees: B, M, D *Enroll:* 22,467
URL: http://www.ou.edu
Phone: (405) 325-0311 *Calendar:* Sem. plan
Inst. Accred.: NCA-HLC (1913/2002)
Prog. Accred.: Accounting, Aviation, Business (AACSB), Computer Science (ABET-CAC), Construction Education, Counseling Psychology, Engineering (aerospace, architectural, chemical, civil, computer, electrical, engineering physics/science, environmental/sanitary, general, industrial, mechanical, petroleum), Graduate Social Work, Interior Design, Journalism, Landscape Architecture, Law, Librarianship, Music, Planning, Social Work, Teacher Education (NCATE), Theatre

College of Medicine
City Plaza West, Ste. 200, 5310 31st, Tulsa 74135-5027
Phone: (918) 838-4600
Prog. Accred: Allied Health (occupational therapy)

Health Sciences Center
PO Box 26901, 1000 Stanton L. Young Blvd., Oklahoma City 73126-0901
Phone: (405) 271-4000
Prog. Accred: Allied Health (audiology, diagnostic medical sonography, medicine, occupational therapy, speech-language pathology), Applied Science (industrial hygiene), Dentistry (advanced education in general dentistry, combined prosthodontics, dental hygiene, dentistry, general dentistry, oral and maxillofacial surgery, orthodontic and dentofacial orthopedics, periodontics), Dietetics (coordinated), Dietetics (didactic), Dietetics (internship), Engineering (environmental/sanitary), Nuclear Medicine Technology, Nursing, Pharmacy, Physical Therapy, Physician Assistant, Psychology Internship, Public Health, Radiation Therapy, Radiography

University of Science and Arts of Oklahoma
1727 West Alabama Ave., Chickasha 73018-5322
Type: Public, state, four-year
System: Oklahoma State Regents for Higher Education
Degrees: B *Enroll:* 1,212
URL: http://www.usao.edu
Phone: (405) 224-3140 *Calendar:* Tri. plan
Inst. Accred.: NCA-HLC (1920/1999)
Prog. Accred.: Music, Teacher Education (NCATE)

University of Tulsa
600 South College Ave., Tulsa 74104
Type: Private, United Presbyterian Church, USA, four-year
Degrees: B, M, D *Enroll:* 3,747
URL: http://www.utulsa.edu
Phone: (918) 631-2000 *Calendar:* Sem. plan
Inst. Accred.: NCA-HLC (1929/2008)
Prog. Accred.: Allied Health (speech-language pathology), Business (AACSB), Clinical Psychology, Computer Science (ABET-CAC), Engineering (chemical, electrical, engineering physics/science, mechanical, petroleum), Law, Music, Nursing, Teacher Education (TEAC)

Western Oklahoma State College
2801 North Main St., Altus 73521-1397
Type: Public, state, two-year
System: Oklahoma State Regents for Higher Education
Degrees: A *Enroll:* 1,263
URL: http://www.wosc.edu
Phone: (580) 477-2000 *Calendar:* Sem. plan
Inst. Accred.: NCA-HLC (1976/2008)
Prog. Accred.: Nursing, Radiography

OREGON

Apollo College—Portland
2004 Lloyd Center, 3rd Flr., Portland 97232
Type: Private, proprietary, two-year
System: U.S. Education Corporation
Degrees: A
URL: http://www.apollocollege.com
Phone: (503) 761-6100
Inst. Accred.: ABHES (1985/2002), ACICS (2008)
Prog. Accred.: Dentistry (dental hygiene), Medical Assisting (ABHES)

Las Vegas Campus
5740 South Eastern Ave., Ste. 140, Las Vegas, NV 89119
Phone: (877) 205-1458

Spokane Campus
10102 East Knox Rd., Ste. 200, Spokane, WA 99206
Phone: (509) 532-8888
Prog. Accred: Medical Assisting (ABHES), Radiography

The Art Institute of Portland
1122 NW Davis St., Portland 97209-2911
Type: Private, proprietary, four-year
System: Education Management Corporation
Degrees: A, B *Enroll:* 1,276
URL: http://www.aipd.aii.edu
Phone: (503) 228-6528 *Calendar:* Qtr. plan
Inst. Accred.: NWCCU (1977/2006)

Australasian College of Health Sciences
5940 SW Hood Ave., Portland 97239
Type: Private, independent, four-year
Degrees: M
URL: http://www.achs.edu
Phone: (503) 244-0726 *Calendar:* Sem. plan
Inst. Accred.: DETC (2003/2008)

Blue Mountain Community College
PO Box 100, Pendleton 97801
Type: Public, state/local, two-year
System: Department of Community Colleges and Workforce Development
Degrees: A *Enroll:* 1,278
URL: http://www.bluecc.edu
Phone: (541) 276-1260 *Calendar:* Qtr. plan
Inst. Accred.: NWCCU (1968/2006)
Prog. Accred.: Dentistry (dental assisting), Engineering Technology (electrical)

Central Oregon Community College
2600 NW College Way, Bend 97701-5998
Type: Public, state/local, two-year
System: Department of Community Colleges and Workforce Development
Degrees: A *Enroll:* 2,402
URL: http://www.cocc.edu
Phone: (541) 383-7700 *Calendar:* Qtr. plan
Inst. Accred.: NWCCU (1966/2007)
Prog. Accred.: Allied Health (medical assisting (AMA)), Culinary Education, Dentistry (dental assisting), Forestry

Chemeketa Community College
PO Box 14007, Salem 97309-7070
Type: Public, local, two-year
System: Department of Community Colleges and Workforce Development
Degrees: A *Enroll:* 4,266
URL: http://www.chemeketa.edu
Phone: (503) 399-5000 *Calendar:* Qtr. plan
Inst. Accred.: NWCCU (1972/2006)
Prog. Accred.: Allied Health (EMT-paramedic), Dentistry (dental assisting), Nursing

Clackamas Community College
19600 South Molalla Ave., Oregon City 97045-8980
Type: Public, state/local, two-year
System: Department of Community Colleges and Workforce Development
Degrees: A *Enroll:* 3,947
URL: http://www.clackamas.edu
Phone: (503) 657-6958 *Calendar:* Qtr. plan
Inst. Accred.: NWCCU (1971/2007)
Prog. Accred.: Allied Health (medical assisting (AMA))

Clatsop Community College
1653 Jerome Ave., Astoria 97103
Type: Public, state/local, two-year
System: Department of Community Colleges and Workforce Development
Degrees: A *Enroll:* 788
URL: http://www.clatsopcc.edu
Phone: (503) 325-0910 *Calendar:* Qtr. plan
Inst. Accred.: NWCCU (1965/2006)

Concordia University Portland
2811 NE Holman St., Portland 97211-6099
Type: Private, Lutheran Church-Missouri Synod, four-year
System: Concordia University System
Degrees: A, B, M *Enroll:* 1,294
URL: http://www.cu-portland.edu
Phone: (503) 288-9371 *Calendar:* Sem. plan
Inst. Accred.: NWCCU (1962/2008)

Corban College
5000 Deer Park Dr., SE, Salem 97301-9330
Type: Private, General Association of Regular Baptist Churches, four-year
Degrees: A, B, M *Enroll:* 730
URL: http://www.corban.edu
Phone: (503) 581-8600 *Calendar:* Sem. plan
Inst. Accred.: ABHE (1959/1997), NWCCU (1971/2007)

Eastern Oregon University
One University Blvd., Le Grande 97850-2807
Type: Public, state, four-year
System: Oregon University System
Degrees: A, B, M *Enroll:* 2,575
URL: http://www.eou.edu
Phone: (541) 962-3672 *Calendar:* Qtr. plan
Inst. Accred.: NWCCU (1931/2001)

Eugene Bible College
2155 Bailey Hill Rd., Eugene 97405-1194
Type: Private, Open Bible Standard Churches, four-year
Degrees: B *Enroll:* 173
URL: http://www.ebc.edu
Phone: (541) 485-1780 *Calendar:* Qtr. plan
Inst. Accred.: ABHE (1983/2004), NWCCU (2007, Warning)

Everest College—Portland
425 SW Washington St., Portland 97204
Type: Private, proprietary, two-year
System: Corinthian Colleges, Inc
Degrees: A *Enroll:* 581
URL: http://www.everest.edu
Phone: (503) 222-3225 *Calendar:* Qtr. plan
Inst. Accred.: ACICS (1969/2001)
Prog. Accred.: Allied Health (medical assisting (AMA))

Dallas Campus
6060 North Central Expressway, Ste. 101, Dallas, TX 75206
Phone: (214) 234-4850

Vancouver Campus
120 Northeast 136th Ave., Ste. 130, Vancouver, WA 98684
Phone: (360) 254-3282
Prog. Accred: Allied Health (medical assisting (AMA))

George Fox University
414 North Meridian St., Newberg 97132-2697
Type: Private, The Religious Society of Friends, four-year
Degrees: B, M, D *Enroll:* 2,436
URL: http://www.georgefox.edu
Phone: (503) 554-2142 *Calendar:* Sem. plan
Inst. Accred.: ATS (1974/2006), NWCCU (1959/2006)
Prog. Accred.: Clinical Psychology, Engineering (general), Music, Nursing Education, Social Work

Portland Center
PO Box 23939, Portland 97281-3939
Phone: (503) 639-0559

Heald College—Portland
625 SW Broadway, Ste. 201, Portland 97205
Type: Private, independent, two-year
System: Heald Colleges
Degrees: A
URL: http://www.heald.edu
Phone: (503) 229-0492 *Calendar:* Qtr. plan
Inst. Accred.: WASC-JR. (1996/2006, *Indirect accreditation through Heald Colleges, San Francisco, CA*)
Prog. Accred.: Allied Health (medical assisting (AMA))

ITT Technical Institute
9500 NE Cascades Pkwy., Portland 97220
Type: Private, proprietary, four-year
System: ITT Educational Services, Inc.
Degrees: A, B *Enroll:* 555
URL: http://www.itt-tech.edu
Phone: (503) 255-6500 *Calendar:* Qtr. plan
Inst. Accred.: ACICS (1999/2004)

Orland Park Campus
11551 184th Place, Orland Park, IL 60467
Phone: (708) 326-3200

Klamath Community College
7390 South 6th St., Klamath Falls 97603-7121
Type: Public, state/local, two-year
Degrees: A *Enroll:* 574
URL: http://www.klamathcc.edu
Phone: (541) 882-3521 *Calendar:* Qtr. plan
Inst. Accred.: NWCCU (2004/2007)

Lane Community College
4000 East 30th Ave., Eugene 97405
Type: Public, local, two-year
System: Department of Community Colleges and Workforce Development
Degrees: A *Enroll:* 6,066
URL: http://www.lanecc.edu
Phone: (541) 463-3000 *Calendar:* Qtr. plan
Inst. Accred.: NWCCU (1968/2007)
Prog. Accred.: Allied Health (medical assisting (AMA), respiratory therapy), Culinary Education, Dentistry (dental assisting, dental hygiene)

Lewis and Clark College
0615 South West Palatine Hill Rd., Portland 97219-7899
Type: Private, independent, four-year
Degrees: B, M, D *Enroll:* 3,080
URL: http://www.lclark.edu
Phone: (503) 768-7000 *Calendar:* Sem. plan
Inst. Accred.: NWCCU (1943/2008)
Prog. Accred.: Law, Teacher Education (NCATE)

Linfield College
900 SE Baker St., McMinnville 97128-6894
Type: Private, American Baptist Church, four-year
Degrees: B, M *Enroll:* 1,724
URL: http://www.linfield.edu
Phone: (503) 883-2200 *Calendar:* 4-1-4 plan
Inst. Accred.: NWCCU (1928/1999)
Prog. Accred.: Music

Portland Campus
2215 NW Northrup St., Portland 97210-2932
Phone: (503) 413-8481
Prog. Accred: Nursing Education

Linn-Benton Community College
6500 Pacific Blvd. SW, Albany 97321
Type: Public, local, two-year
System: Department of Community Colleges and Workforce Development
Degrees: A *Enroll:* 3,623
URL: http://www.linnbenton.edu
Phone: (541) 917-4811 *Calendar:* Qtr. plan
Inst. Accred.: NWCCU (1972/2008)
Prog. Accred.: Allied Health (medical assisting (AMA)), Dentistry (dental assisting)

Marylhurst University
PO Box 261, Marylhurst 97036
Type: Private, Roman Catholic Church, four-year
Degrees: B, M *Enroll:* 693
URL: http://www.marylhurst.edu
Phone: (503) 636-8141 *Calendar:* Qtr. plan
Inst. Accred.: NWCCU (1977/2007)
Prog. Accred.: Interior Design, Music

Mount Angel Seminary
One Abbey Dr., St. Benedict 97373
Type: Private, Roman Catholic Church, four-year
Degrees: B, M *Enroll:* 197
URL: http://www.mtangel.edu
Phone: (503) 845-3951 *Calendar:* Sem. plan
Inst. Accred.: ATS (1978/2006), NWCCU (1929/2006)

Mount Hood Community College
26000 South East Stark St., Gresham 97030
Type: Public, state/local, two-year
System: Department of Community Colleges and Workforce Development
Degrees: A *Enroll:* 4,336
URL: http://www.mhcc.edu
Phone: (503) 491-7161 *Calendar:* Qtr. plan
Inst. Accred.: NWCCU (1972/2008)
Prog. Accred.: Allied Health (medical assisting (AMA), respiratory therapy, surgical technology), Dentistry (dental hygiene), Forestry, Funeral Service Education (Mortuary Science), Physical Therapy Assisting

Multnomah University
8435 NE Glisan St., Portland 97220-5814
Type: Private, nondenominational, four-year
Degrees: B, M *Enroll:* 734
URL: http://www.multnomah.edu
Phone: (503) 255-0332 *Calendar:* Sem. plan
Inst. Accred.: ABHE (1953/2004), ATS (1996/2003), NWCCU (2005/2008)

National College of Natural Medicine
049 Southwest Porter St., Portland 97201
Type: Private, proprietary, four-year
Degrees: M, D *Enroll:* 489
URL: http://www.ncnm.edu
Phone: (503) 552-1702 *Calendar:* Qtr. plan
Inst. Accred.: NWCCU (2004/2007)
Prog. Accred.: Acupuncture, Naturopathic Medicine

Northwest Christian University
828 East 11th Ave., Eugene 97401-3745
Type: Private, Disciples of Christ Church, four-year
Degrees: A, B, M *Enroll:* 359
URL: http://www.northwestchristian.edu
Phone: (541) 684-7200 *Calendar:* Sem. plan
Inst. Accred.: NWCCU (1962/2008)

Oregon College of Oriental Medicine
10525 SE Cherry Blossom Dr., Portland 97216
Type: Private, proprietary, four-year
Degrees: M, D *Enroll:* 231
URL: http://www.ocom.edu
Phone: (503) 253-3443 *Calendar:* Qtr. plan
Inst. Accred.: ACAOM (1989/2004), NWCCU (2008)

Oregon Health and Science University
3181 South West Sam Jackson Park Rd., Portland 97201-3098
Type: Public, state, four-year
System: Oregon University System
Degrees: A, B, M, D *Enroll:* 2,089
URL: http://www.ohsu.edu
Phone: (503) 494-8311 *Calendar:* Qtr. plan
Inst. Accred.: NWCCU (1980/2007)
Prog. Accred.: Allied Health (EMT-paramedic, medicine), Clinical Lab Scientist, Dentistry (dental hygiene, dentistry, endodontics, general practice residency, oral and maxillofacial surgery, orthodontic and dentofacial orthopedics, pediatric dentistry, periodontics), Dietetics (internship), Nurse (Midwifery), Nurse Anesthesia Education, Nursing Education, Physician Assistant, Psychology Internship, Public Health, Radiation Therapy

Oregon Graduate Institute School of Science and Engineering at OHSU
PO Box 91000, 20000 N.W. Walker Rd., Beaverton 97006
Phone: (503) 748-1121

Oregon Institute of Technology
3201 Campus Dr., Klamath Falls 97601-8801
Type: Public, state, four-year
System: Oregon University System
Degrees: A, B, M *Enroll:* 2,476
URL: http://www.oit.edu
Phone: (541) 885-1150 *Calendar:* Qtr. plan
Inst. Accred.: NWCCU (1962/2007)
Prog. Accred.: Allied Health (respiratory therapy), Applied Science (surveying/geomatics), Clinical Lab Scientist, Dentistry (dental hygiene), Engineering Technology (computer, electrical, manufacturing, mechanical, surveying), Radiography

Oregon State University
Corvallis 97331-2128
Type: Public, state, four-year
System: Oregon University System
Degrees: B, M, P, D *Enroll:* 17,381
URL: http://oregonstate.edu
Phone: (541) 737-0912 *Calendar:* Qtr. plan
Inst. Accred.: NWCCU (1924/2006)
Prog. Accred.: Accounting, Business (AACSB), Computer Science (ABET-CAC), Construction Education, Counseling, Dietetics (didactic), Engineering (bioengineering, chemical, civil, computer, electrical, environmental/sanitary, forest, industrial, manufacturing, mechanical, nuclear), Environmental Health, Family & Consumer Science, Forestry, Pharmacy, Public Health, Teacher Education (NCATE), Veterinary Medicine

Cascades Campus
2600 NW College Way, Bend 97701
Phone: (541) 322-3100

Pacific Northwest College of Art
1241 NW Johnson Ave., Portland 97209-3023
Type: Private, independent, four-year
Degrees: B, M *Enroll:* 270
URL: http://www.pnca.edu
Phone: (503) 226-4391 *Calendar:* Sem. plan
Inst. Accred.: NWCCU (1961/2008)
Prog. Accred.: Art

Pacific University
2043 College Way, Forest Grove 97116
Type: Private, United Church of Christ, four-year
Degrees: B, M, D *Enroll:* 2,390
URL: http://www.pacificu.edu
Phone: (503) 357-6151 *Calendar:* Sem. plan
Inst. Accred.: NWCCU (1929/2008)
Prog. Accred.: Allied Health (occupational therapy, optometric residency, optometry), Clinical Psychology, Dentistry (dental hygiene), Music, Pharmacy, Physical Therapy, Physician Assistant

Pioneer Pacific College
27501 Southwest Pkwy. Ave., Wilsonville 97070
Type: Private, proprietary, four-year
Degrees: A, B *Enroll:* 1,128
URL: http://www.pioneerpacificcollege.com
Phone: (503) 682-3903
Inst. Accred.: ACICS (1995/2006)

Oregon Culinary Institute
1717 SW Madison St., Portland 97205
Phone: (503) 961-6200

Springfield Campus
3800 Sports Way, Springfield 97477
Phone: (541) 684-4644

Portland Community College
PO Box 19000, Portland 97280-0990
Type: Public, state/local, two-year
System: Department of Community Colleges and Workforce Development
Degrees: A *Enroll:* 13,580
URL: http://www.pcc.edu
Phone: (503) 977-4329 *Calendar:* Qtr. plan
Inst. Accred.: NWCCU (1970/2007)
Prog. Accred.: Allied Health (medical assisting (AMA)), Clinical Lab Technology, Dentistry (dental assisting, dental hygiene, dental laboratory technology), Nursing, Radiography, Veterinary Technology

Rock Creek Campus
17705 NW Springville Rd., Portland 97229
Phone: (503) 244-6111

Sylvania Campus
12000 SW 49th Ave., Portland 97219
Phone: (503) 244-6111

Portland State University
PO Box 751, Portland 97207-0751
Type: Public, state, four-year
System: Oregon University System
Degrees: B, M, D *Enroll:* 17,423
URL: http://www.pdx.edu
Phone: (503) 725-3000 *Calendar:* Qtr. plan
Inst. Accred.: NWCCU (1955/2006)
Prog. Accred.: Accounting, Allied Health (audiology, speech-language pathology), Art, Business (AACSB), Computer Science (ABET-CAC), Counseling, Engineering (civil, electrical, mechanical), Graduate Social Work, Music, Planning, Public Administration, Public Health, Rehabilitation Counseling, Teacher Education (NCATE)

Reed College
3203 SE Woodstock Blvd., Portland 97202-8199
Type: Private, independent, four-year
Degrees: B, M *Enroll:* 1,299
URL: http://www.reed.edu
Phone: (503) 771-1112 *Calendar:* Sem. plan
Inst. Accred.: NWCCU (1920/1999)

Rogue Community College
3345 Redwood Hwy., Grants Pass 97527
Type: Public, state/local, two-year
System: Department of Community Colleges and Workforce Development
Degrees: A *Enroll:* 2,539
URL: http://www.roguecc.edu
Phone: (541) 956-7500 *Calendar:* Qtr. plan
Inst. Accred.: NWCCU (1976/2007)
Prog. Accred.: Allied Health (respiratory therapy)

Southern Oregon University
1250 Siskiyou Blvd., Ashland 97520
Type: Public, state, four-year
System: Oregon University System
Degrees: B, M *Enroll:* 4,130
URL: http://www.sou.edu
Phone: (541) 552-7672 *Calendar:* Qtr. plan
Inst. Accred.: NWCCU (1928/2008)
Prog. Accred.: Counseling, Music

Southwestern Oregon Community College
1988 Newmark Ave., Coos Bay 97420
Type: Public, state/local, two-year
System: Department of Community Colleges and Workforce Development
Degrees: A *Enroll:* 1,313
URL: http://www.socc.edu
Phone: (541) 888-2525 *Calendar:* Qtr. plan
Inst. Accred.: NWCCU (1966/2007)
Prog. Accred.: Culinary Education

Treasure Valley Community College
650 College Blvd., Ontario 97914
Type: Public, state/local, two-year
System: Department of Community Colleges and Workforce Development
Degrees: A *Enroll:* 1,355
URL: http://www.tvcc.cc.or.us
Phone: (541) 881-8822 *Calendar:* Qtr. plan
Inst. Accred.: NWCCU (1966/2006)

Umpqua Community College
1140 College Rd., PO Box 967, Roseburg 97470
Type: Public, state/local, two-year
System: Department of Community Colleges and Workforce Development
Degrees: A *Enroll:* 793
URL: http://www.umpqua.edu
Phone: (541) 440-4600 *Calendar:* Qtr. plan
Inst. Accred.: NWCCU (1970/2007)
Prog. Accred.: Nursing

University of Oregon
Eugene 97403-1226
Type: Public, state, four-year
System: Oregon University System
Degrees: B, M, D *Enroll:* 18,902
URL: http://www.uoregon.edu
Phone: (541) 346-1000 *Calendar:* Qtr. plan
Inst. Accred.: NWCCU (1918/2007)
Prog. Accred.: Accounting, Allied Health (speech-language pathology), Art, Business (AACSB), Clinical Psychology, Counseling Psychology, English Language Education, Interior Architecture, Journalism, Landscape Architecture, Law, Marriage and Family Therapy, Music, Planning, Psychology Internship, Public Administration, School Psychology

University of Portland
5000 North Willamette Blvd., Portland 97203
Type: Private, Roman Catholic Church, four-year
Degrees: B, M *Enroll:* 3,149
URL: http://www.up.edu
Phone: (503) 943-8000 *Calendar:* Sem. plan
Inst. Accred.: NWCCU (1931/2007)
Prog. Accred.: Business (AACSB), Computer Science (ABET-CAC), Engineering (civil, electrical, mechanical), Music, Nursing Education, Social Work, Teacher Education (NCATE), Theatre

Warner Pacific College
2219 S.E. 68th Ave., Portland 97215
Type: Private, Church of God, four-year
Degrees: A, B, M *Enroll:* 562
URL: http://www.warnerpacific.edu
Phone: (503) 517-1000 *Calendar:* Sem. plan
Inst. Accred.: NWCCU (1961/2007)

Western Culinary Institute
600 SW 10th Ave., Ste. 400, Portland 97205
Type: Private, proprietary, two-year
System: Career Education Corporation
Degrees: A
URL: http://www.wci.edu
Phone: (503) 223-2245
Inst. Accred.: ACCSCT (1990/2002)
Prog. Accred.: Culinary Education

Le Cordon Bleu College of Culinary Arts
1927 Lakeside Pkwy., Tucker, GA 30084
Phone: (770) 938-4711
Prog. Accred: Culinary Education

Le Cordon Bleu College of Culinary Arts—Minneapolis/St. Paul
1315 Mendota Heights Rd., Mendota Heights, MN 55120
Phone: (651) 675-4700
Prog. Accred: Culinary Education

Western Oregon University
345 North Monmouth Ave., Monmouth 97361
Type: Public, state, four-year
System: Oregon University System
Degrees: A, B, M *Enroll:* 4,316
URL: http://www.wou.edu
Phone: (503) 838-8000 *Calendar:* Qtr. plan
Inst. Accred.: NWCCU (1924/2007)
Prog. Accred.: Music, Rehabilitation Counseling, Teacher Education (NCATE)

Western Seminary
5511 SE Hawthorne Blvd., Portland 97215
Type: Private, Conservative Baptist Association of America, four-year
Degrees: M, D *Enroll:* 337
URL: http://www.westernseminary.edu
Phone: (503) 517-1800 *Calendar:* Tri. plan
Inst. Accred.: ATS (2000/2002), NWCCU (1969/2008)

Western States Chiropractic College
2900 NE 132nd Ave., Portland 97230
Type: Private, independent, four-year
Degrees: B, P, D *Enroll:* 423
URL: http://www.wschiro.edu
Phone: (503) 251-5712 *Calendar:* Qtr. plan
Inst. Accred.: NWCCU (1986/2007)
Prog. Accred.: Chiropractic Education

Willamette University
900 State St., Salem 97301
Type: Private, independent, four-year
Degrees: B, M *Enroll:* 2,526
URL: http://www.willamette.edu
Phone: (503) 370-6300 *Calendar:* Sem. plan
Inst. Accred.: NWCCU (1924/2006)
Prog. Accred.: Business (AACSB), Law, Music, Public Administration

PENNSYLVANIA

Albright College
13th and Bern St.s, PO Box 15234, Reading 19612-5234
Type: Private, United Methodist Church, four-year
Degrees: B *Enroll:* 2,110
URL: http://www.albright.edu
Phone: (610) 921-2381 *Calendar:* 4-1-4 plan
Inst. Accred.: MSA-CHE (1926/2007)

Allegheny College
520 North Main St., Meadville 16335
Type: Private, independent, four-year
Degrees: B *Enroll:* 2,027
URL: http://www.allegheny.edu
Phone: (814) 332-3100 *Calendar:* Sem. plan
Inst. Accred.: MSA-CHE (1921/2004)

Allied Medical and Technical Institute
166 Slocum St., Forty Fort 18704
Type: Private, proprietary, two-year
System: Education Affiliates, Inc.
Degrees: A
URL: http://www.alliedteched.edu
Phone: (570) 288-8400
Inst. Accred.: ACCSCT (1995/2006)

Alvernia University
400 Saint Bernadine St., Reading 19607
Type: Private, Roman Catholic Church, four-year
Degrees: A, B, M, D *Enroll:* 2,070
URL: http://www.alvernia.edu
Phone: (610) 796-8200 *Calendar:* Sem. plan
Inst. Accred.: MSA-CHE (1967/2005)
Prog. Accred.: Allied Health (occupational therapy), Business (ACBSP), Nursing Education, Social Work

The American College
270 Bryn Mawr Ave., Bryn Mawr 19010
Type: Private, independent, four-year
Degrees: M *Enroll:* 302
URL: http://www.theamericancollege.edu
Phone: (610) 526-1000 *Calendar:* Qtr. plan
Inst. Accred.: MSA-CHE (1978/2003)

Antonelli Institute
300 Montgomery Ave., Erdenheim 19038
Type: Private, proprietary, two-year
Degrees: A *Enroll:* 185
URL: http://www.antonelli.edu
Phone: (215) 836-2222 *Calendar:* Sem. plan
Inst. Accred.: ACCSCT (1975/2003)

Arcadia University
450 South Easton Rd., Glenside 19038-3295
Type: Private, independent, four-year
Degrees: B, M, P, D *Enroll:* 2,653
URL: http://www.arcadia.edu
Phone: (215) 572-2900 *Calendar:* Sem. plan
Inst. Accred.: MSA-CHE (1946/2004)
Prog. Accred.: Art, Business (ACBSP), Physical Therapy, Physician Assistant

The Art Institute of Philadelphia
1622 Chestnut St., Philadelphia 19103-5198
Type: Private, proprietary, four-year
System: Education Management Corporation
Degrees: A, B *Enroll:* 2,799
URL: http://www.aiph.artinstitutes.edu
Phone: (215) 567-7080 *Calendar:* Qtr. plan
Inst. Accred.: MSA-CHE (2007), ACICS (2000/2005)
Prog. Accred.: Culinary Education

The Art Institute of Pittsburgh
420 Blvd. of the Allies, Pittsburgh 15219-1328
Type: Private, proprietary, four-year
System: Education Management Corporation
Degrees: A, B *Enroll:* 4,285
URL: http://www.aip.aii.edu
Phone: (412) 291-6600 *Calendar:* Qtr. plan
Inst. Accred.: ACICS (2000/2003), MSA-CHE (2008)
Prog. Accred.: Culinary Education, Interior Design

The Art Institute of York-Pennsylvania
1409 Williams Rd., York 17402-9012
Type: Private, proprietary, two-year
System: Education Management Corporation
Degrees: A *Enroll:* 619
URL: http://www.artinstitutes.edu/york
Phone: (717) 755-2300 *Calendar:* Sem. plan
Inst. Accred.: ACCSCT (1983/2004)

Baptist Bible College and Seminary
PO Box 800, Clarks Summit 18411-0800
Type: Private, independent, four-year
Degrees: A, B, M, P, D *Enroll:* 841
URL: http://www.bbc.edu
Phone: (570) 586-2400 *Calendar:* Sem. plan
Inst. Accred.: ABHE (1968/2006), MSA-CHE (1984/2005)

Berks Technical Institute
2205 Ridgewood Rd., Wyomissing 19610
Type: Private, proprietary, two-year
System: ForeFront Education, Inc.
Degrees: A *Enroll:* 580
URL: http://www.berks.edu
Phone: (610) 372-1722
Inst. Accred.: ACCSCT (1984/2004)
Prog. Accred.: Allied Health (medical assisting (AMA))

Biblical Theological Seminary
200 North Main St., Hatfield 19440
Type: Private, interdenominational, four-year
Degrees: M, P, D *Enroll:* 223
URL: http://www.biblical.edu
Phone: (215) 368-5000 *Calendar:* Sem. plan
Inst. Accred.: ATS (1996/2006), MSA-CHE (1990/2006)

Bidwell Training Center
1815 Metropolitan St., Pittsburgh 15233-2234
Type: Private, proprietary, two-year
Degrees: A
URL: http://www.bidwell-training.org
Phone: (412) 323-4000
Inst. Accred.: ACCSCT (1993/2006)

Bloomsburg University of Pennsylvania
400 East 2nd St., Bloomsburg 17815
Type: Public, state, four-year
System: Pennsylvania State System of Higher Education
Degrees: A, B, M, D *Enroll:* 7,973
URL: http://www.bloomu.edu
Phone: (570) 389-4000 *Calendar:* Sem. plan
Inst. Accred.: MSA-CHE (1950/2004)
Prog. Accred.: Allied Health (audiology, speech-language pathology), Applied Science (health physics), Business (AACSB), Nursing Education, Social Work, Teacher Education (NCATE)

Bradford School
125 West Station Square Dr., Ste. 129, Pittsburgh 15219
Type: Private, proprietary, two-year
Degrees: A *Enroll:* 441
URL: http://www.bradfordpittsburgh.edu
Phone: (412) 391-6710
Inst. Accred.: ACICS (1970/2005)
Prog. Accred.: Allied Health (medical assisting (AMA))

Bryn Athyn College of the New Church
PO Box 717, 2895 College Dr., Bryn Athyn 19009-0717
Type: Private, The New Church/General Church of the New Jerusalem, four-year
Degrees: A, B, M, P *Enroll:* 151
URL: http://www.brynathyn.edu
Phone: (215) 502-2543 *Calendar:* Tri. plan
Inst. Accred.: MSA-CHE (1952/2003)

Bryn Mawr College
101 North Merion Ave., Bryn Mawr 19010-2899
Type: Private, independent, four-year
Degrees: B, M, D *Enroll:* 1,659
URL: http://www.brynmawr.edu
Phone: (610) 526-5000 *Calendar:* Sem. plan
Inst. Accred.: MSA-CHE (1921/2004)
Prog. Accred.: Graduate Social Work

Bucknell University
701 Moore Ave., Lewisburg 17837
Type: Private, independent, four-year
Degrees: B, M *Enroll:* 3,685
URL: http://www.bucknell.edu
Phone: (570) 577-2000 *Calendar:* Sem. plan
Inst. Accred.: MSA-CHE (1921/2004)
Prog. Accred.: Computer Science (ABET-CAC), Engineering (chemical, civil, computer, electrical, mechanical), Music

Bucks County Community College
275 Swamp Rd., Newtown 18940-4106
Type: Public, state/local, two-year
Degrees: A *Enroll:* 5,872
URL: http://www.bucks.edu
Phone: (215) 968-8000 *Calendar:* Sem. plan
Inst. Accred.: MSA-CHE (1968/2007)
Prog. Accred.: Allied Health (medical assisting (AMA)), Art, Business (ACBSP), Music, Nursing, Radiography

Butler County Community College
College Dr., Oak Hills, PO Box 1203, Butler 16003-1203
Type: Public, state/local, two-year
Degrees: A *Enroll:* 2,599
URL: http://www.bc3.org
Phone: (724) 287-8711 *Calendar:* Sem. plan
Inst. Accred.: MSA-CHE (1971/2006)
Prog. Accred.: Allied Health (medical assisting (AMA)), Business (ACBSP), Nursing, Physical Therapy Assisting

Cabrini College
610 King of Prussia Rd., Radnor 19087-3698
Type: Private, Roman Catholic Church, four-year
Degrees: B, M *Enroll:* 1,896
URL: http://www.cabrini.edu
Phone: (610) 902-8100 *Calendar:* Sem. plan
Inst. Accred.: MSA-CHE (1965/2005)
Prog. Accred.: Social Work

California University of Pennsylvania
250 University Ave., California 15419-1394
Type: Public, state, four-year
System: Pennsylvania State System of Higher Education
Degrees: A, B, M *Enroll:* 6,415
URL: http://www.cup.edu
Phone: (724) 938-4000 *Calendar:* Sem. plan
Inst. Accred.: MSA-CHE (1951/2005)
Prog. Accred.: Allied Health (speech-language pathology), Computer Science (ABET-CAC), Counseling, Engineering Technology (electrical), Graduate Social Work, Industrial Technology, Nursing Education, Physical Therapy Assisting, Social Work, Teacher Education (NCATE)

Cambria-Rowe Business College
221 Central Ave., Johnstown 15902
Type: Private, proprietary, two-year
Degrees: A *Enroll:* 217
URL: http://www.crbc.net
Phone: (814) 536-5168 *Calendar:* Qtr. plan
Inst. Accred.: ACICS (1959/2005)

Indiana Campus
422 South 13th St., Indiana 15701
Phone: (724) 463-0222

Career Training Academy
950 Fifth Ave., New Kensington 15068-6301
Type: Private, proprietary, two-year
Degrees: A *Enroll:* 99
URL: http://www.careerta.com
Phone: (724) 337-1000
Inst. Accred.: ACCSCT (1987/2006)

Monroeville Campus
4314 Old William Penn Hwy., Ste. 103, Monroeville 15146
Phone: (412) 372-3900

Pittsburgh Campus
1500 Northway Mall, Ste. 200, Pittsburgh 15237
Phone: (412) 367-4000

Carlow University
3333 Fifth Ave., Pittsburgh 15213-3165
Type: Private, Roman Catholic Church, four-year
Degrees: B, M, P *Enroll:* 1,607
URL: http://www.carlow.edu
Phone: (412) 578-6000 *Calendar:* Sem. plan
Inst. Accred.: MSA-CHE (1935/2006)
Prog. Accred.: Nursing Education, Social Work

Carnegie Mellon University
5000 Forbes Ave., Pittsburgh 15213
Type: Private, independent, four-year
Degrees: B, M, D *Enroll:* 9,116
URL: http://www.cmu.edu
Phone: (412) 268-2000 *Calendar:* Sem. plan
Inst. Accred.: MSA-CHE (1921/2008)
Prog. Accred.: Art, Business (AACSB), Engineering (chemical, civil, electrical, general, materials, mechanical), Music, Public Administration

Cedar Crest College
100 College Dr., Allentown 18104-6196
Type: Private, United Church of Christ, four-year
Degrees: B, M *Enroll:* 1,328
URL: http://www.cedarcrest.edu
Phone: (610) 437-4471 *Calendar:* Sem. plan
Inst. Accred.: MSA-CHE (1944/2004)
Prog. Accred.: Business (ACBSP), Dietetics (didactic), Nuclear Medicine Technology, Nursing, Social Work

Central Pennsylvania College
College Hill Rd., Summerdale 17093-0309
Type: Private, proprietary, four-year
Degrees: A, B *Enroll:* 811
URL: http://www.centralpenn.edu
Phone: (717) 732-0702 *Calendar:* Qtr. plan
Inst. Accred.: MSA-CHE (1977/2003)
Prog. Accred.: Allied Health (medical assisting (AMA)), Physical Therapy Assisting

Chatham University
Woodland Rd., Pittsburgh 15232
Type: Private, independent, four-year
Degrees: B, M, D *Enroll:* 1,079
URL: http://www.chatham.edu
Phone: (412) 365-1100 *Calendar:* 4-1-4 plan
Inst. Accred.: MSA-CHE (1924/2007)
Prog. Accred.: Allied Health (occupational therapy), Physical Therapy, Physician Assistant, Social Work

Chestnut Hill College
9601 Germantown Ave., Philadelphia 19118-2963
Type: Private, Roman Catholic Church, four-year
Degrees: A, B, M, D *Enroll:* 1,228
URL: http://www.chc.edu
Phone: (215) 248-7000 *Calendar:* Sem. plan
Inst. Accred.: MSA-CHE (1930/2003)
Prog. Accred.: Clinical Psychology, Montessori Teacher Education

Cheyney University of Pennsylvania
1837 University Circle, PO Box 200, Cheyney 19319-0200
Type: Public, state, four-year
System: Pennsylvania State System of Higher Education
Degrees: B, M *Enroll:* 1,434
URL: http://www.cheyney.edu
Phone: (610) 399-2000 *Calendar:* Sem. plan
Inst. Accred.: MSA-CHE (1951/2006)
Prog. Accred.: Teacher Education (NCATE)

CHI Institute
177 Franklin Mills Blvd., Philadelphia 19154
Type: Private, proprietary, two-year
System: Kaplan Higher Education Corporation
Degrees: A *Enroll:* 592
URL: http://www.chitraining.com
Phone: (215) 612-6600
Inst. Accred.: ACCSCT (1985/2004)

Fort Worth Campus
2001 Beach St., Ste. 201, Fort Worth, TX 76103
Phone: (817) 413-2000

Kaplan College—Cincinnati
801 Linn St., Cincinnati, OH 45203
Phone: (888) 517-8050

CHI Institute—Broomall
1991 Sproul Rd., Ste. 42, Lawrence Park Shopping Center, Broomall 19008
Type: Private, proprietary, two-year
System: Kaplan Higher Education Corporation
Degrees: A *Enroll:* 517
URL: http://www.chitraining.com
Phone: (610) 359-7630
Inst. Accred.: ACCSCT (1996/2004)
Prog. Accred.: Allied Health (surgical technology)

Kaplan College—Milwaukee
111 West Pleasant St., Ste. 101, Milwaukee, WI 53212
Phone: (414) 225-4610

Clarion University of Pennsylvania
840 Wood St., Clarion 16214
Type: Public, state, four-year
System: Pennsylvania State System of Higher Education
Degrees: A, B, M *Enroll:* 5,695
URL: http://www.clarion.edu
Phone: (814) 393-2000 *Calendar:* Sem. plan
Inst. Accred.: MSA-CHE (1948/2007)
Prog. Accred.: Allied Health (speech-language pathology), Art, Business (AACSB), Librarianship, Music, Teacher Education (NCATE)

Venango Campus
West First St., Oil City 16301
Phone: (814) 676-6591
Prog. Accred: Nursing

Commonwealth Technical Institute at the Hiram G. Andrews Center
727 Goucher St., Johnstown 15905-3092
Type: Private, proprietary, two-year
Degrees: A
URL: http://www.dli.state.pa.us/landi/cwp/view.asp?a=128&Q=188163
Phone: (814) 255-8200
Inst. Accred.: ACCSCT (1987/2002)
Prog. Accred.: Dentistry (dental assisting)

Community College of Allegheny County
1750 Clairton Rd. (Route 885), West Mifflin 15122-3097
Type: Public, state /local, two-year
System: Community Colleges of Allegheny County
Degrees: A *FTE Enroll:* 4,400
URL: http://www.ccac.edu
Phone: (412) 469-1100 *Calendar:* Sem. plan
Inst. Accred.: MSA-CHE (1970/2006, *Indirect accreditation through Community Colleges of Allegheny County, Pittsburgh, PA*)
Prog. Accred.: Clinical Lab Technology

Community College of Allegheny County
808 Ridge Ave., Pittsburgh 15212
Type: Public, state/local, two-year
System: Community Colleges of Allegheny County
Degrees: A *Enroll:* 11,214
URL: http://www.ccac.edu
Phone: (412) 237-2525 *Calendar:* Sem. plan
Inst. Accred.: MSA-CHE (1970/2006, *Indirect accreditation through Community Colleges of Allegheny County, Pittsburgh, PA*)
Prog. Accred.: Allied Health (medical assisting (AMA), respiratory therapy), Dietetic Technician, Nuclear Medicine Technology, Nursing, Radiation Therapy

Community College of Allegheny County
595 Beatty Rd., Monroeville 15146
Type: Public, state/local, two-year
System: Community Colleges of Allegheny County
Degrees: A *FTE Enroll:* 16,257
URL: http://www.ccac.edu/about/boyce
Phone: (724) 327-1327 *Calendar:* Sem. plan
Inst. Accred.: MSA-CHE (1970/2006, *Indirect accreditation through Community Colleges of Allegheny County, Pittsburgh, PA*)
Prog. Accred.: Allied Health (diagnostic medical sonography, occupational therapy assisting, surgical technology), Physical Therapy Assisting, Radiography

Community College of Allegheny County
8701 Perry Hwy., Pittsburgh 15237
Type: Public, state/local, two-year
System: Community Colleges of Allegheny County
Degrees: A *Enroll:* 11,214
URL: http://www.ccac.edu/about/north
Phone: (412) 366-7000 *Calendar:* Sem. plan
Inst. Accred.: MSA-CHE (1970/2006, *Indirect accreditation through Community Colleges of Allegheny County, Pittsburgh, PA*)

Community College of Beaver County
One Campus Dr., Monaca 15061-2588
Type: Public, state/local, two-year
Degrees: A *Enroll:* 1,691
URL: http://www.ccbc.edu
Phone: (724) 775-8561 *Calendar:* Sem. plan
Inst. Accred.: MSA-CHE (1972/2004)
Prog. Accred.: Clinical Lab Technology, Nursing, Phlebotomy

Community College of Philadelphia
1700 Spring Garden St., Philadelphia 19130-3991
Type: Public, state/local, two-year
Degrees: A *Enroll:* 9,188
URL: http://www.ccp.edu
Phone: (215) 751-8000 *Calendar:* Sem. plan
Inst. Accred.: MSA-CHE (1968/2004)
Prog. Accred.: Allied Health (medical assisting (AMA), respiratory therapy), Clinical Lab Technology, Dentistry (dental assisting, dental hygiene), Nursing, Phlebotomy, Radiography

Consolidated School of Business
1605 Clugston Rd., York 17404
Type: Private, proprietary, two-year
Degrees: A *Enroll:* 137
URL: http://www.csb.edu
Phone: (717) 764-9950
Inst. Accred.: ACICS (1984/2003)

Consolidated School of Business
2124 Ambassador Circle, Lancaster 17603
Type: Private, proprietary, two-year
Degrees: A *Enroll:* 139
URL: http://www.csb.edu
Phone: (717) 394-6211
Inst. Accred.: ACICS (1987/2002)

The Curtis Institute of Music
1726 Locust St., Philadelphia 19103
Type: Private, independent, four-year
Degrees: B, M *Enroll:* 163
URL: http://www.curtis.edu
Phone: (215) 893-5252 *Calendar:* Sem. plan
Inst. Accred.: MSA-CHE (1993/2008)
Prog. Accred.: Music

Dean Institute of Technology
1501 West Liberty Ave., Pittsburgh 15226-1197
Type: Private, proprietary, two-year
Degrees: A *Enroll:* 110
URL: http://www.deantech.edu
Phone: (412) 531-4433 *Calendar:* Qtr. plan
Inst. Accred.: ACCSCT (1969/2005)

Delaware County Community College
901 South Media Line Rd., Media 19063
Type: Public, state/local, two-year
Degrees: A *Enroll:* 6,511
URL: http://www.dccc.edu
Phone: (610) 359-5000 *Calendar:* Sem. plan
Inst. Accred.: MSA-CHE (1970/2001)
Prog. Accred.: Allied Health (medical assisting (AMA), surgical technology), Nursing

Delaware Valley College
700 East Butler Ave., Doylestown 18901-2697
Type: Private, independent, four-year
Degrees: A, B, M *Enroll:* 1,789
URL: http://www.delval.edu
Phone: (215) 345-1500 *Calendar:* Sem. plan
Inst. Accred.: MSA-CHE (1962/2003)

DeSales University
2755 Station Ave., Center Valley 18034-9568
Type: Private, Roman Catholic Church, four-year
Degrees: B, M *Enroll:* 2,178
URL: http://www.desales.edu
Phone: (610) 282-1100 *Calendar:* Sem. plan
Inst. Accred.: MSA-CHE (1970/2008)
Prog. Accred.: Business (ACBSP), Nursing, Physician Assistant

DeVry University Philadelphia
1140 Virginia Dr., Fort Washington 19034
Type: Private, proprietary
System: DeVry University
Degrees: A, B, M
URL: http://www.devry.edu/fortwashington
Phone: (215) 591-5700 *Calendar:* Sem. plan
Inst. Accred.: NCA-HLC (2002, *Indirect accreditation through DeVry University, Oakbrook Terrace, IL*)
Prog. Accred.: Engineering Technology (computer, electrical)

Philadelphia Center City Campus
1800 JFK Blvd., Ste. 104, Philadelphia 19103
Phone: (215) 568-2911

Pittsburgh Campus
210 Sixth Ave., Ste. 200, Pittsburgh 15222
Phone: (412) 642-9072

Valley Forge Campus
701 Lee Rd., Ste. 103, Chesterbrook 19087
Phone: (610) 889-9980

Dickinson College
PO Box 1773, Carlisle 17013-2896
Type: Private, independent, four-year
Degrees: B *Enroll:* 2,327
URL: http://www.dickinson.edu
Phone: (717) 243-5121 *Calendar:* Sem. plan
Inst. Accred.: MSA-CHE (1921/2007)

Douglas Education Center
130 Seventh St., Monessen 15062
Type: Private, proprietary, two-year
Degrees: A *Enroll:* 250
URL: http://www.douglas-school.com
Phone: (724) 684-3684 *Calendar:* Sem. plan
Inst. Accred.: ACICS (1977/2004)

Drexel University
3141 Chestnut St., Philadelphia 19104
Type: Private, independent, four-year
Degrees: A, B, M, P, D *Enroll:* 15,500
URL: http://www.drexel.edu
Phone: (215) 895-2000 *Calendar:* Qtr. plan
Inst. Accred.: MSA-CHE (1927/2007)
Prog. Accred.: Art, Business (AACSB), Clinical Psychology, Computer Science (ABET-CAC), Dietetics (didactic), Engineering (architectural, bioengineering, chemical, civil, computer, electrical, environmental/sanitary, information systems, materials, mechanical), English Language Education, Interior Design, Librarianship, Nursing Education, Public Health

Center City Hahnemann Campus
245 North 15th St., Philadelphia 19102-1192
Phone: (215) 762-8900
Prog. Accred: Allied Health (medicine, perfusion), Dentistry (general practice residency, oral and maxillofacial surgery), Marriage and Family Therapy, Nurse Anesthesia Education, Nursing, Physical Therapy Assisting, Physician Assistant, Radiography

DuBois Business College
One Beaver Dr., DuBois 15801
Type: Private, proprietary, two-year
Degrees: A *Enroll:* 209
URL: http://www.dbcollege.com
Phone: (814) 371-6920 *Calendar:* Qtr. plan
Inst. Accred.: ACICS (1954/2007)

Huntingdon Campus
1001 Moore St., Huntingdon 16652
Phone: (814) 641-0440

Oil City Campus
701 East Third St., Oil City 16301
Phone: (814) 677-1322

Duquesne University
600 Forbes Ave., Pittsburgh 15282
Type: Private, Roman Catholic Church, four-year
Degrees: B, M, P, D *Enroll:* 8,840
URL: http://www.duq.edu
Phone: (412) 396-6000 *Calendar:* Sem. plan
Inst. Accred.: MSA-CHE (1935/2008)
Prog. Accred.: Allied Health (occupational therapy, speech-language pathology), Business (AACSB), Clinical Psychology, Counseling, English Language Education, Law, Music, Nursing Education, Pharmacy, Physical Therapy, Physician Assistant, Teacher Education (NCATE)

East Stroudsburg University of Pennsylvania
200 Prospect St., East Stroudsburg 18301-2999
Type: Public, state, four-year
System: Pennsylvania State System of Higher Education
Degrees: A, B, M *Enroll:* 5,907
URL: http://www.esu.edu
Phone: (570) 422-3545 *Calendar:* Sem. plan
Inst. Accred.: MSA-CHE (1950/2007)
Prog. Accred.: Allied Health (speech-language pathology), Exercise Physiology, Exercise Science, Nursing, Polysomnographic Technology, Public Health, Recreation and Leisure Services, Teacher Education (NCATE)

Eastern University
1300 Eagle Rd., St. Davids 19087-3696
Type: Private, American Baptist Churches in the USA, four-year
Degrees: A, B, M, P, D *Enroll:* 3,147
URL: http://www.eastern.edu
Phone: (610) 341-5800 *Calendar:* Sem. plan
Inst. Accred.: MSA-CHE (1954/2007)
Prog. Accred.: Nursing Education, Social Work

Edinboro University of Pennsylvania
219 Meadville St., Edinboro 16444
Type: Public, state, four-year
System: Pennsylvania State System of Higher Education
Degrees: A, B, M *Enroll:* 6,786
URL: http://www.edinboro.edu
Phone: (814) 732-2000 *Calendar:* Sem. plan
Inst. Accred.: MSA-CHE (1949/2003)
Prog. Accred.: Allied Health (speech-language pathology), Business (ACBSP), Counseling, Dietetics (coordinated), Graduate Social Work, Music, Nursing, Nursing Education, Rehabilitation Counseling, Social Work, Teacher Education (NCATE)

Elizabethtown College
One Alpha Dr., Elizabethtown 17022-2298
Type: Private, Church of the Brethren, four-year
Degrees: A, B, M *Enroll:* 2,017
URL: http://www.etown.edu
Phone: (717) 361-1000 *Calendar:* Sem. plan
Inst. Accred.: MSA-CHE (1948/2004)
Prog. Accred.: Allied Health (occupational therapy), Business (ACBSP), Music, Social Work

Erie Business Center
246 West Ninth St., Erie 16501
Type: Private, proprietary, two-year
Degrees: A *Enroll:* 328
URL: http://www.eriebc.com
Phone: (814) 456-7504
Inst. Accred.: ACICS (1952/2005)

New Castle Campus
170 Cascade Galleria, New Castle 16101
Phone: (724) 658-9066

Erie Institute of Technology
940 Millcreek Mall, Erie 16565
Type: Private, proprietary, two-year
Degrees: A *Enroll:* 139
URL: http://www.erieit.edu
Phone: (814) 868-9900
Inst. Accred.: ACCSCT (1979/2007, Probation)

Evangelical Theological Seminary
121 South College St., Myerstown 17067
Type: Private, Evangelical Congregational Church, four-year
Degrees: M, P *Enroll:* 88
URL: http://www.evangelical.edu
Phone: (717) 866-5775 *Calendar:* Sem. plan
Inst. Accred.: ATS (1987/2000), MSA-CHE (1984/2001)

Everest Institute—Pittsburgh
100 Forbes Ave., Ste. 1200, Pittsburgh 15222
Type: Private, proprietary, two-year
System: Corinthian Colleges, Inc
Degrees: A *Enroll:* 438
URL: http://www.everest.edu
Phone: (412) 261-4520 *Calendar:* Qtr. plan
Inst. Accred.: ACICS (1961/2005)
Prog. Accred.: Allied Health (medical assisting (AMA))

Franklin & Marshall College
PO Box 3003, Lancaster 17604-3003
Type: Private, independent, four-year
Degrees: B *Enroll:* 1,999
URL: http://www.fandm.edu
Phone: (717) 291-3911 *Calendar:* Sem. plan
Inst. Accred.: MSA-CHE (1921/2004)

Gannon University
109 University Square, Erie 16541-0001
Type: Private, Roman Catholic Church, four-year
Degrees: A, B, M, P, D *Enroll:* 2,911
URL: http://www.gannon.edu
Phone: (814) 871-7000 *Calendar:* Sem. plan
Inst. Accred.: MSA-CHE (1951/2003)
Prog. Accred.: Allied Health (occupational therapy, respiratory therapy), Business (ACBSP), Computer Science (ABET-CAC), Dietetics (coordinated), Engineering (electrical, environmental/sanitary, information systems, mechanical), Nurse Anesthesia Education, Nursing Education, Physical Therapy, Physician Assistant, Radiography, Social Work

Geneva College
3200 College Ave., Beaver Falls 15010
Type: Private, Reformed Presbyterian Church of North America, four-year
Degrees: A, B, M *Enroll:* 1,930
URL: http://www.geneva.edu
Phone: (724) 846-5100 *Calendar:* Sem. plan
Inst. Accred.: MSA-CHE (1922/2008)
Prog. Accred.: Allied Health (cardiovascular technology), Business (ACBSP), Engineering (general)

Gettysburg College
300 North Washington St., Gettysburg 17325-1486
Type: Private, Evangelic Lutheran Church, four-year
Degrees: B *Enroll:* 2,488
URL: http://www.gettysburg.edu
Phone: (717) 337-6000 *Calendar:* Sem. plan
Inst. Accred.: MSA-CHE (1921/2004)

Gratz College
7605 Old York Rd., Melrose Park 19027
Type: Private, independent, four-year
Degrees: B, M, D *Enroll:* 145
URL: http://www.gratz.edu
Phone: (215) 635-7300 *Calendar:* Sem. plan
Inst. Accred.: MSA-CHE (1967/2002, Warning)

Grove City College
100 Campus Dr., Grove City 16127-2104
Type: Private, independent, four-year
Degrees: B, M *Enroll:* 2,321
URL: http://www.gcc.edu
Phone: (724) 458-2000 *Calendar:* Sem. plan
Inst. Accred.: MSA-CHE (1922/2003)
Prog. Accred.: Engineering (electrical, mechanical)

Gwynedd-Mercy College
1325 Sumneytown Pike, PO Box 901, Gwynedd Valley 19437-0901
Type: Private, Roman Catholic Church, four-year
Degrees: A, B, M *Enroll:* 1,938
URL: http://www.gmc.edu
Phone: (215) 646-7300 *Calendar:* Sem. plan
Inst. Accred.: MSA-CHE (1958/2006)
Prog. Accred.: Allied Health (cardiovascular technology, respiratory therapy), Nursing, Radiation Therapy

Center for Lifelong Learning
1250 Virginia Dr., Fort Washington 19034-3239
Phone: (877) 499-6333

Harcum College
750 Montgomery Ave., Bryn Mawr 19010
Type: Private, independent, two-year
Degrees: A *Enroll:* 621
URL: http://www.harcum.edu
Phone: (610) 525-4100 *Calendar:* Sem. plan
Inst. Accred.: MSA-CHE (1970/2006)
Prog. Accred.: Clinical Lab Technology, Dentistry (dental assisting, dental hygiene), Nursing, Physical Therapy Assisting, Veterinary Technology

Harrisburg Area Community College
One HACC Dr., Harrisburg 17110-2999
Type: Public, state/local, two-year
Degrees: A *Enroll:* 5,835
URL: http://www.hacc.edu
Phone: (717) 780-2300 *Calendar:* Sem. plan
Inst. Accred.: MSA-CHE (1967/2007)
Prog. Accred.: Allied Health (EMT-paramedic, diagnostic medical sonography, medical assisting (AMA), respiratory therapy, surgical technology), Business (ACBSP), Clinical Lab Technology, Dentistry (dental assisting, dental hygiene), Nursing, Practical Nursing

Lancaster Campus
1008 New Holland Ave., Lancaster 17604
Phone: (717) 293-5000
Prog. Accred: Allied Health (cardiovascular technology, surgical technology)

Lebanon Campus
735 Cumberland St., Lebanon 17042
Phone: (717) 270-6300

Gettysburg Campus
705 Old Harrisburg Rd., Ste. 2, Gettysburg 17325
Phone: (717) 337-3855

Haverford College
370 Lancaster Ave., Haverford 19041-1392
Type: Private, independent, four-year
Degrees: B, M *Enroll:* 1,168
URL: http://www.haverford.edu
Phone: (610) 896-1000 *Calendar:* Sem. plan
Inst. Accred.: MSA-CHE (1921/2004)

Holy Family University
9801 Frankford Ave., Philadelphia 19114-2009
Type: Private, Roman Catholic Church, four-year
Degrees: A, B, M *Enroll:* 2,259
URL: http://www.holyfamily.edu
Phone: (215) 637-7700 *Calendar:* Sem. plan
Inst. Accred.: MSA-CHE (1961/2001)
Prog. Accred.: Nursing, Nursing Education, Radiography, Teacher Education (TEAC)

Hussian School of Art
1118 Market St., Philadelphia 19107-3679
Type: Private, independent, two-year
Degrees: A *Enroll:* 155
URL: http://www.hussianart.edu
Phone: (215) 981-0900 *Calendar:* Sem. plan
Inst. Accred.: ACCSCT (1972/2005)

Immaculata University
1145 King Rd., Immaculata 19345
Type: Private, Roman Catholic Church, four-year
Degrees: A, B, M, D *Enroll:* 2,046
URL: http://www.immaculata.edu
Phone: (610) 647-4400 *Calendar:* Sem. plan
Inst. Accred.: MSA-CHE (1928/2004)
Prog. Accred.: Clinical Psychology, Dietetics (didactic), Dietetics (internship), Music, Nursing Education

Indiana University of Pennsylvania
Sutton Hall, Indiana 15705
Type: Public, state, four-year
System: Pennsylvania State System of Higher Education
Degrees: A, B, M, D *Enroll:* 12,835
URL: http://www.iup.edu
Phone: (724) 357-2100 *Calendar:* Sem. plan
Inst. Accred.: MSA-CHE (1941/2006)
Prog. Accred.: Allied Health (respiratory therapy, speech-language pathology), Applied Science (occupational health & safety), Business (AACSB), Clinical Psychology, Dietetics (didactic), Dietetics (internship), Music, Nursing Education, Teacher Education (NCATE), Theatre

Armstrong County Campus
Kittanning 16201
Phone: (814) 543-1078

Punxsutawney Campus
1012 Winslow St., Punxsutawney 15767
Phone: (814) 938-6711
Prog. Accred: Culinary Education

JNA Institute of Culinary Arts
1212 South Broad St., Philadelphia 19146
Type: Private, proprietary, two-year
Degrees: A
URL: http://www.culinaryarts.com
Phone: (215) 468-8800
Inst. Accred.: ACCSCT (1994/2005)

Johnson College
3427 North Main Ave., Scranton 18508-1495
Type: Private, independent, two-year
Degrees: A *Enroll:* 347
URL: http://www.johnson.edu
Phone: (570) 342-6404 *Calendar:* Sem. plan
Inst. Accred.: ACCSCT (1979/2003)
Prog. Accred.: Radiography, Veterinary Technology

Juniata College
1700 Moore St., Huntingdon 16652-2119
Type: Private, independent, four-year
Degrees: B *Enroll:* 1,413
URL: http://www.juniata.edu
Phone: (814) 641-3000 *Calendar:* Sem. plan
Inst. Accred.: MSA-CHE (1922/2003)
Prog. Accred.: Social Work

Kaplan Career Institute
5650 Derry St., Harrisburg 17111-4112
Type: Private, proprietary, two-year
System: Kaplan Higher Education Corporation
Degrees: A *Enroll:* 510
URL: http://www.getinfokaplancareerinstitute.com
Phone: (717) 564-4112 *Calendar:* Qtr. plan
Inst. Accred.: ACICS (1962/2008)
Prog. Accred.: Allied Health (medical assisting (AMA))

Chambersburg Campus
2593 Philadelphia Ave., Chambersburg 17201
Phone: (717) 709-9400

Philadelphia Campus
University City Science Center, 3010 Market St., Philadelphia 19104
Phone: (215) 594-4000
Prog. Accred: Allied Health (medical assisting (AMA))

Kaplan Career Institute—ICM Campus
10 Wood St., Pittsburgh 15222
Type: Private, proprietary, two-year
System: Kaplan Higher Education Corporation
Degrees: A *Enroll:* 1,154
URL: http://www.kaplancareerinstitute.com
Phone: (412) 261-2647 *Calendar:* Qtr. plan
Inst. Accred.: ACICS (1967/2003)
Prog. Accred.: Allied Health (medical assisting (AMA), occupational therapy assisting)

Keystone College
One College Green, La Plume 18440-0200
Type: Private, independent, four-year
Degrees: A, B *Enroll:* 1,392
URL: http://www.keystone.edu
Phone: (570) 945-8000 *Calendar:* Sem. plan
Inst. Accred.: MSA-CHE (1936/2003)

Keystone Technical Institute
2301 Academy Dr., Harrisburg 17102-2944
Type: Private, proprietary, two-year
Degrees: A
URL: http://www.kti.edu
Phone: (717) 545-4747
Inst. Accred.: ACCSCT (1983/2006)

King's College
133 North River St., Wilkes-Barre 18711
Type: Private, Roman Catholic Church, four-year
Degrees: A, B, M *Enroll:* 2,063
URL: http://www.kings.edu
Phone: (570) 208-5900 *Calendar:* Sem. plan
Inst. Accred.: MSA-CHE (1955/2004)
Prog. Accred.: Allied Health (health services administration), Business (AACSB), Physician Assistant

Kutztown University of Pennsylvania
15200 Kutztown Rd., Kutztown 19530-0730
Type: Public, state, four-year
System: Pennsylvania State System of Higher Education
Degrees: B, M *Enroll:* 8,871
URL: http://www.kutztown.edu
Phone: (610) 683-4000 *Calendar:* Sem. plan
Inst. Accred.: MSA-CHE (1944/2008)
Prog. Accred.: Art, Graduate Social Work, Music, Nursing, Social Work, Teacher Education (NCATE)

La Roche College
9000 Babcock Blvd., Pittsburgh 15237-5828
Type: Private, Roman Catholic Church, four-year
Degrees: A, B, M *Enroll:* 1,459
URL: http://www.laroche.edu
Phone: (412) 367-9300 *Calendar:* Sem. plan
Inst. Accred.: MSA-CHE (1973/2004, Warning)
Prog. Accred.: Art, Business (ACBSP), Interior Design, Nurse Anesthesia Education, Nursing

La Salle University
1900 West Olney Ave., Philadelphia 19141
Type: Private, Roman Catholic Church, four-year
Degrees: A, B, M, D *Enroll:* 4,621
URL: http://www.lasalle.edu
Phone: (215) 951-1000 *Calendar:* Sem. plan
Inst. Accred.: MSA-CHE (1930/2006)
Prog. Accred.: Business (AACSB), Clinical Psychology, Dietetics (coordinated), Dietetics (didactic), Marriage and Family Therapy, Nurse Anesthesia Education, Nursing Education, Social Work

Lackawanna College
501 Vine St., Scranton 18509
Type: Private, independent, two-year
Degrees: A *Enroll:* 987
URL: http://www.lackawanna.edu
Phone: (570) 961-7810 *Calendar:* 4-1-4 plan
Inst. Accred.: MSA-CHE (1973/2005)
Prog. Accred.: Allied Health (diagnostic medical sonography)

Hazleton Center
226 West Broad St., Hazleton 18201
Phone: (717) 459-1573

Honesdale Center
627 Main St., Honesdale 18431
Phone: (717) 253-5408

Towanda Center
201 Main St., Towanda 18848
Phone: (717) 265-3449

Lafayette College
High St., Easton 18042-1768
Type: Private, independent, four-year
Degrees: B *Enroll:* 2,307
URL: http://www.lafayette.edu
Phone: (610) 330-5000 *Calendar:* Sem. plan
Inst. Accred.: MSA-CHE (1921/2003)
Prog. Accred.: Computer Science (ABET-CAC), Engineering (chemical, civil, electrical, mechanical)

Lake Erie College of Osteopathic Medicine
1858 West Grandview Blvd., Erie 16509
Type: Private, independent, four-year
Degrees: M, P *Enroll:* 1,614
URL: http://www.lecom.edu
Phone: (814) 866-6641 *Calendar:* Sem. plan
Inst. Accred.: MSA-CHE (2006)
Prog. Accred.: Osteopathy, Pharmacy

Bradenton Campus
5000 Lakewood Ranch Blvd., Bradenton, FL 34211-4909
Phone: (941) 756-0690

Lancaster Bible College and Graduate School
PO Box 83403, Lancaster 17608-3403
Type: Private, independent, four-year
Degrees: A, B, M *Enroll:* 753
URL: http://www.lbc.edu
Phone: (717) 569-7071 *Calendar:* Sem. plan
Inst. Accred.: ABHE (1964/2008), MSA-CHE (1982/2007)

Lancaster General College of Nursing and Health Sciences
PO Box 3555, 410 North Lime St., Lancaster 17604-3555
Type: Private, independent, two-year
Degrees: A
URL: http://www.lancastergeneral.org
Phone: (717) 544-4912 *Calendar:* 12-mos. pr
Inst. Accred.: MSA-CHE (2006)
Prog. Accred.: Allied Health (cardiovascular technology, diagnostic medical sonography, surgical technology), Nuclear Medicine Technology, Nursing, Radiography

Lancaster Theological Seminary
555 West James St., Lancaster 17603-2897
Type: Private, United Church of Christ, four-year
Degrees: M, P, D *Enroll:* 123
URL: http://www.lts.org
Phone: (717) 393-0654
Inst. Accred.: ATS (1938/2004), MSA-CHE (1978/2004)

Lansdale School of Business
201 Church Rd., North Wales 19454
Type: Private, proprietary, two-year
Degrees: A *Enroll:* 226
URL: http://www.lsbonline.com
Phone: (215) 699-5700
Inst. Accred.: ACICS (1967/2004)

Laurel Business Institute
PO Box 877, Uniontown 15401
Type: Private, proprietary, two-year
Degrees: A *Enroll:* 294
URL: http://www.laurel.edu/lbi
Phone: (724) 439-4900
Inst. Accred.: ACICS (1987/2003)

Laurel Technical Institute
335 Boyd Dr., Sharon 16146
Type: Private, proprietary, two-year
Degrees: A
URL: http://www.laurel.edu/lti
Phone: (724) 983-0700
Inst. Accred.: ACICS (1977/2002)

Meadville Campus
628 Arch St., Ste. B105, Meadville 16335
Phone: (814) 724-0700

Lebanon Valley College
101 North College Ave., Annville 17003-1400
Type: Private, United Methodist Church, four-year
Degrees: A, B, M, P *Enroll:* 1,747
URL: http://www.lvc.edu
Phone: (717) 867-6100 *Calendar:* Sem. plan
Inst. Accred.: MSA-CHE (1922/2007)
Prog. Accred.: Business (ACBSP), Music, Physical Therapy

Lehigh Carbon Community College
4525 Education Park Dr., Schnecksville 18078-2598
Type: Public, state/local, two-year
Degrees: A *Enroll:* 3,923
URL: http://www.lccc.edu
Phone: (610) 799-2121 *Calendar:* Sem. plan
Inst. Accred.: MSA-CHE (1972/2008)
Prog. Accred.: Allied Health (medical assisting (AMA), occupational therapy assisting), Business (ACBSP), Nursing, Physical Therapy Assisting, Practical Nursing, Veterinary Technology

Lehigh University
27 Memorial Dr. West, Bethlehem 18015-3094
Type: Private, independent, four-year
Degrees: B, M, D *Enroll:* 6,034
URL: http://www.lehigh.edu
Phone: (610) 758-3000 *Calendar:* Sem. plan
Inst. Accred.: MSA-CHE (1921/2008)
Prog. Accred.: Accounting, Business (AACSB), Computer Science (ABET-CAC), Counseling Psychology, Engineering (chemical, civil, computer, electrical, industrial, materials, mechanical), School Psychology, Theatre

Lehigh Valley College
2809 East Saucon Valley Rd., Center Valley 18034
Type: Private, proprietary, two-year
System: Career Education Corporation
Degrees: A *Enroll:* 1,049
URL: http://www.lehighvalley.edu
Phone: (610) 791-5100 *Calendar:* Sem. plan
Inst. Accred.: ACICS (1968/2004)

Lincoln Technical Institute
5151 Tilghman St., Allentown 18104-3298
Type: Private, proprietary, two-year
System: Lincoln Educational Services Corporation
Degrees: A *Enroll:* 376
URL: http://www.lincolntech.com
Phone: (610) 398-5300
Inst. Accred.: ACCSCT (1967/2007)

Lincoln Technical Institute
9191 Torresdale Ave., Philadelphia 19136
Type: Private, proprietary, two-year
System: Lincoln Educational Services Corporation
Degrees: A *Enroll:* 600
URL: http://www.lincolntech.com
Phone: (215) 335-0800
Inst. Accred.: ACCSCT (1969/2007)

Lincoln University
PO Box 179, Lincoln University 19352-0999
Type: Public, independent, four-year
Degrees: B, M *Enroll:* 2,138
URL: http://www.lincoln.edu
Phone: (484) 365-8000 *Calendar:* Sem. plan
Inst. Accred.: MSA-CHE (1922/2008)

Lock Haven University of Pennsylvania
401 North Fairview St., Lock Haven 17745-2390
Type: Public, state, four-year
System: Pennsylvania State System of Higher Education
Degrees: A, B, M *Enroll:* 4,923
URL: http://www.lhup.edu
Phone: (570) 893-2011 *Calendar:* Sem. plan
Inst. Accred.: MSA-CHE (1949/2005)
Prog. Accred.: Allied Health (surgical technology), Computer Science (ABET-CAC), Nursing, Physician Assistant, Recreation and Leisure Services, Social Work, Teacher Education (NCATE)

Clearfield Campus
119 Byres St., Clearfield 16830
Phone: (814) 765-0619

Lutheran Theological Seminary at Gettysburg
61 Seminary Ridge, Gettysburg 17325-1795
Type: Private, Evangelical Lutheran Church in America, four-year
Degrees: M, P *Enroll:* 221
URL: http://www.ltsg.edu
Phone: (717) 334-6286 *Calendar:* 4-1-4 plan
Inst. Accred.: ATS (1938/2000), MSA-CHE (1971/2001)

The Lutheran Theological Seminary at Philadelphia
7301 Germantown Ave., Philadelphia 19119
Type: Private, Evangelical Lutheran Church in America, four-year
Degrees: M, P, D *Enroll:* 214
URL: http://www.ltsp.edu
Phone: (215) 248-4616
Inst. Accred.: ATS (1938/2002), MSA-CHE (1971/2007)

Luzerne County Community College
1333 South Prospect St., Nanticoke 18634
Type: Public, local, two-year
Degrees: A *Enroll:* 4,159
URL: http://www.luzerne.edu
Phone: (570) 740-0200 *Calendar:* Sem. plan
Inst. Accred.: MSA-CHE (1975/2001)
Prog. Accred.: Allied Health (respiratory therapy, surgical technology), Business (ACBSP), Dentistry (dental assisting, dental hygiene), Nursing

Lycoming College
700 College Place, Williamsport 17701
Type: Private, United Methodist Church, four-year
Degrees: B *Enroll:* 1,469
URL: http://www.lycoming.edu
Phone: (570) 321-4000 *Calendar:* Sem. plan
Inst. Accred.: MSA-CHE (1934/2001)
Prog. Accred.: Business (ACBSP)

Manor College
700 Fox Chase Rd., Jenkintown 19046
Type: Private, Ukrainian Catholic Church, two-year
Degrees: A *Enroll:* 592
URL: http://www.manor.edu
Phone: (215) 885-2360 *Calendar:* Sem. plan
Inst. Accred.: MSA-CHE (1967/2008)
Prog. Accred.: Clinical Lab Technology, Dentistry (dental assisting, dental hygiene), Veterinary Technology

Mansfield University of Pennsylvania
Academy St., Mansfield 16933
Type: Public, state, four-year
System: Pennsylvania State System of Higher Education
Degrees: A, B, M *Enroll:* 3,030
URL: http://www.mansfield.edu
Phone: (570) 662-4000 *Calendar:* Sem. plan
Inst. Accred.: MSA-CHE (1942/2007)
Prog. Accred.: Allied Health (respiratory therapy), Dietetics (didactic), Music, Nursing, Radiography, Social Work, Teacher Education (NCATE)

Marywood University
2300 Adams Ave., Scranton 18509
Type: Private, Roman Catholic Church, four-year
Degrees: B, M, D *Enroll:* 2,540
URL: http://www.marywood.edu
Phone: (570) 348-6211 *Calendar:* Sem. plan
Inst. Accred.: MSA-CHE (1921/2006)
Prog. Accred.: Allied Health (speech-language pathology), Art, Business (ACBSP), Counseling, Dietetics (coordinated), Dietetics (didactic), Dietetics (internship), Graduate Social Work, Music, Nursing, Physician Assistant, Social Work, Teacher Education (NCATE)

McCann School of Business and Technology—Pottsville
2650 Woodglen Rd., Pottsville 17901
Type: Private, proprietary, two-year
System: Delta Education Corporation
Degrees: A
URL: http://www.mccannschool.com
Phone: (570) 622-7622 *Calendar:* Qtr. plan
Inst. Accred.: ACICS (1962/2006)

Hazelton Campus
14 Maplewood Dr., Humboldt Industrial Park, Hazleton 18202
Phone: (570) 454-6172

Scranton Campus
222 Mulberry St., Third Flr., Scranton 18503
Phone: (570) 969-4330
Prog. Accred: Allied Health (surgical technology)

Sunbury Campus
225 Market St., Third Flr., Sunbury 17801
Phone: (570) 286-3058
Prog. Accred: Allied Health (surgical technology)

Mercyhurst College
501 East 38th St., Erie 16546
Type: Private, Roman Catholic Church, four-year
Degrees: A, B, M *Enroll:* 3,762
URL: http://www.mercyhurst.edu
Phone: (814) 824-2000 *Calendar:* Tri. plan
Inst. Accred.: MSA-CHE (1931/2003)
Prog. Accred.: Dietetics (coordinated), Music, Physical Therapy Assisting, Social Work

North East Campus
16 West Division St., North East 16428
Phone: (814) 725-6100
Prog. Accred: Nursing

Messiah College
One College Ave., Grantham 17027
Type: Private, Brethren in Christ Church, four-year
Degrees: B *Enroll:* 2,884
URL: http://www.messiah.edu
Phone: (717) 766-2511 *Calendar:* Sem. plan
Inst. Accred.: MSA-CHE (1963/2003)
Prog. Accred.: Art, Business (ACBSP), Dietetics (didactic), Engineering (general), Music, Nursing Education, Social Work

City Campus
2026 North Broad St., Philadelphia 19121
Phone: (215) 769-2526

Metropolitan Career Center and Computer Technology Institute
100 South Broad St., #830, Land Title Bldg., Philadelphia 19110
Type: Private, independent, two-year
Degrees: A
URL: http://www.metropolitancareercenter.org
Phone: (215) 568-9215 *Calendar:* Sem. plan
Inst. Accred.: ACCSCT (1999/2002)

Millersville University of Pennsylvania
PO Box 1002, Millersville 17551-0302
Type: Public, state, four-year
System: Pennsylvania State System of Higher Education
Degrees: A, B, M *Enroll:* 7,039
URL: http://muweb.millersville.edu
Phone: (717) 872-3024 *Calendar:* 4-1-4 plan
Inst. Accred.: MSA-CHE (1950/2005)
Prog. Accred.: Allied Health (respiratory therapy), Applied Science (occupational health & safety), Business (ACBSP), Computer Science (ABET-CAC), Graduate Social Work, Industrial Technology, Music, Nursing, Social Work, Teacher Education (NCATE)

Misericordia University
301 Lake St., Dallas 18612-1098
Type: Private, Roman Catholic Church, four-year
Degrees: A, B, M, D *Enroll:* 1,785
URL: http://www.misericordia.edu
Phone: (570) 674-6400 *Calendar:* Sem. plan
Inst. Accred.: MSA-CHE (1935/2004)
Prog. Accred.: Allied Health (diagnostic medical sonography, occupational therapy), Nursing Education, Physical Therapy, Radiography, Social Work

Montgomery County Community College
340 DeKalb Pike, Blue Bell 19422
Type: Public, state/local, two-year
Degrees: A *Enroll:* 5,555
URL: http://www.mc3.edu
Phone: (215) 641-6300 *Calendar:* Sem. plan
Inst. Accred.: MSA-CHE (1970/2005)
Prog. Accred.: Allied Health (medical assisting (AMA), surgical technology), Clinical Lab Technology, Dentistry (dental hygiene), Nursing, Phlebotomy

West Campus
101 College Dr., Pottstown 19464
Phone: (610) 718-1800
Prog. Accred: Radiography

Moore College of Art and Design
The Pkwy. at 20th St., Philadelphia 19103
Type: Private, independent, four-year
Degrees: B, M *Enroll:* 450
URL: http://www.moore.edu
Phone: (215) 568-4515 *Calendar:* Sem. plan
Inst. Accred.: MSA-CHE (1958/2007)
Prog. Accred.: Art, Interior Design

Moravian College
1200 Main St., Bethlehem 18018-6650
Type: Private, Moravian Church, four-year
Degrees: B, M, P *Enroll:* 1,748
URL: http://www.moravian.edu
Phone: (610) 861-1300 *Calendar:* Sem. plan
Inst. Accred.: MSA-CHE (1922/2008)
Prog. Accred.: Music, Nursing Education

Moravian Theological Seminary
1200 Main St., Bethleham 18018
Type: Private, Moravian Church in America, four-year
Degrees: M
URL: http://www.moravianseminary.edu
Phone: (610) 861-1516 *Calendar:* Sem. plan
Inst. Accred.: ATS (1954/2008)

Mount Aloysius College
7373 Admiral Peary Hwy., Cresson 16630-1999
Type: Private, Roman Catholic Church, four-year
Degrees: A, B, M *Enroll:* 1,324
URL: http://www.mtaloy.edu
Phone: (814) 886-4131 *Calendar:* Sem. plan
Inst. Accred.: MSA-CHE (1943/2005)
Prog. Accred.: Allied Health (medical assisting (AMA), surgical technology), Nursing, Physical Therapy Assisting

Muhlenberg College
2400 Chew St., Allentown 18104
Type: Private, Evangelical Lutheran Church in America, four-year
Degrees: A, B *Enroll:* 2,342
URL: http://www.muhlenberg.edu
Phone: (484) 664-3100 *Calendar:* Sem. plan
Inst. Accred.: MSA-CHE (1921/2006)

Neumann College
One Neumann Dr., Aston 19014-1298
Type: Private, Sisters of St. Francis of Philadelphia, four-year
Degrees: A, B, M, P, D *Enroll:* 2,280
URL: http://www.neumann.edu
Phone: (610) 558-5616 *Calendar:* Sem. plan
Inst. Accred.: MSA-CHE (1972/2006)
Prog. Accred.: Business (ACBSP), Clinical Lab Scientist, Nursing, Physical Therapy

New Castle School of Trades
4164 US 422, Pulaski 16143
Type: Private, proprietary, two-year
Degrees: A *Enroll:* 404
URL: http://www.ncstrades.com
Phone: (724) 964-8811
Inst. Accred.: ACCSCT (1973/2005)

Newport Business Institute
941 West Third St., Williamsport 17701
Type: Private, proprietary, two-year
Degrees: A *Enroll:* 103
URL: http://www.nbi.edu
Phone: (570) 326-2869 *Calendar:* Qtr. plan
Inst. Accred.: ACICS (1955/2008)

Newport Business Institute
945 Greensburg Rd., Lower Burrell 15068
Type: Private, proprietary, two-year
Degrees: A *Enroll:* 79
URL: http://www.nbi.edu
Phone: (724) 339-7542 *Calendar:* Qtr. plan
Inst. Accred.: ACICS (1965/2008)

Northampton County Area Community College
3835 Green Pond Rd., Bethlehem 18017
Type: Public, state/local, two-year
Degrees: A *Enroll:* 4,408
URL: http://www.northampton.edu
Phone: (610) 861-5300 *Calendar:* Sem. plan
Inst. Accred.: MSA-CHE (1970/2005)
Prog. Accred.: Allied Health (diagnostic medical sonography, surgical technology), Business (ACBSP), Dentistry (dental hygiene), Funeral Service Education (Mortuary Science), Nursing, Practical Nursing, Radiography

Monroe County Branch Campus
PO Box 639, Tannersville 18372
Phone: (570) 620-9221

Oakbridge Academy of Arts
1250 Greensburg Rd., Lower Burrell 15068
Type: Private, proprietary, two-year
Degrees: A *Enroll:* 66
URL: http://oakbridgeacademy.com
Phone: (724) 335-5336 *Calendar:* Qtr. plan
Inst. Accred.: ACCSCT (1980/2007)

Orleans Technical Institute
1845 Walnut St., Ste. 700, Philadelphia 19103-4707
Type: Private, independent, two-year
Degrees: A
URL: http://www.orleanstech.edu
Phone: (215) 728-4700 *Calendar:* Sem. plan
Inst. Accred.: ACCSCT (1988/2005)

Pace Institute
606 Ct. St., Reading 19601
Type: Private, proprietary, two-year
Degrees: A *Enroll:* 192
URL: http://www.paceinstitute.edu
Phone: (610) 375-1212
Inst. Accred.: ACICS (1984/2008)

The Palmer Theological Seminary
6 East Lancaster Ave., Wynnewood 19096-3494
Type: Private, American Baptist Churches (USA), four-year
Degrees: M, P, D *Enroll:* 306
URL: http://www.palmerseminary.edu
Phone: (610) 896-5000 *Calendar:* 4-1-4 plan
Inst. Accred.: ATS (1954/2005)

Peirce College
1420 Pine St., Philadelphia 19102
Type: Private, independent, four-year
Degrees: A, B *Enroll:* 1,275
URL: http://www.peirce.edu
Phone: (215) 545-6400 *Calendar:* Sem. plan
Inst. Accred.: MSA-CHE (1971/2001)
Prog. Accred.: Business (ACBSP)

Penn Commercial, Inc.
242 Oak Spring Rd., Washington 15301
Type: Private, proprietary, two-year
Degrees: A *Enroll:* 450
URL: http://www.penn-commercial.com
Phone: (724) 222-5330 *Calendar:* Sem. plan
Inst. Accred.: ACICS (1960/2003)
Prog. Accred.: Allied Health (medical assisting (AMA))

Pennco Tech
3815 Otter St., Bristol 19007-3696
Type: Private, proprietary, two-year
Degrees: A *Enroll:* 455
Phone: (215) 824-3200
Inst. Accred.: ACCSCT (1969/2007)

Pennsylvania Academy of the Fine Arts
118 North Broad St., Philadelphia 19102
Type: Private, independent, four-year
Degrees: M *Enroll:* 266
URL: http://www.pafa.edu
Phone: (215) 972-7600 *Calendar:* Sem. plan
Inst. Accred.: NASAD (1979/2007)

Pennsylvania College of Art and Design
204 North Prince St., Lancaster 17603
Type: Private, independent, four-year
Degrees: B
URL: http://www.psad.org
Phone: (717) 396-7833 *Calendar:* Sem. plan
Inst. Accred.: NASAD (1984/2008), MSA-CHE (2008)

Pennsylvania College of Technology
One College Ave., Williamsport 17701
Type: Public, state, four-year
Degrees: A, B *Enroll:* 5,927
URL: http://www.pct.edu
Phone: (570) 326-3761 *Calendar:* Sem. plan
Inst. Accred.: MSA-CHE (1970/2007)
Prog. Accred.: Allied Health (EMT-paramedic, occupational therapy assisting, surgical technology), Automotive Technology, Business (ACBSP), Construction Education, Culinary Education, Dentistry (dental hygiene), Engineering Technology (civil/construction, plastics, surveying), Forestry, Nursing, Physician Assistant, Radiography

North Campus
Mansfield Rd., Wellsboro 16901
Phone: (717) 724-7703

Pennsylvania Culinary Institute
717 Liberty Ave., Pittsburgh 15222-3500
Type: Private, proprietary, two-year
System: Career Education Corporation
Degrees: A *Enroll:* 1,071
URL: http://www.pci.edu
Phone: (412) 566-2433
Inst. Accred.: ACCSCT (1990/2005)
Prog. Accred.: Culinary Education

Pennsylvania Highlands Community College
101 Community College Way, Johnstown 15904
Type: Public, state/local, two-year
Degrees: A *Enroll:* 862
URL: http://www.pennhighlands.edu
Phone: (814) 532-5300 *Calendar:* Sem. plan
Inst. Accred.: MSA-CHE (2002/2007)

Pennsylvania Institute of Technology
800 Manchester Ave., Media 19063
Type: Private, independent, two-year
Degrees: A *Enroll:* 315
URL: http://www.pit.edu
Phone: (610) 892-1500 *Calendar:* Sem. plan
Inst. Accred.: MSA-CHE (1983/2006)

Pennsylvania School of Business
406 West Hamilton St., Allentown 18101
Type: Private, proprietary, two-year
System: EVCI Career Colleges Holding Corp.
Degrees: A
URL: http://www.psb.edu
Phone: (610) 841-3333
Inst. Accred.: ACCSCT (2004, Probation)

The Pennsylvania State University
201 Old Main, University Park 16804-3000
Type: Public, state, four-year
Degrees: A, B, M, P, D *Enroll:* 39,207
URL: http://www.psu.edu
Phone: (814) 865-4700 *Calendar:* Sem. plan
Inst. Accred.: MSA-CHE (1921/2005)
Prog. Accred.: Accounting, Allied Health (audiology, health services administration, speech-language pathology), Applied Science (industrial hygiene), Art, Business (AACSB), Clinical Psychology, Counseling, Counseling Psychology, Dietetic Technician, Dietetics (didactic), Dietetics (internship), Engineering (aerospace, agricultural, architectural, chemical, civil, computer, electrical, engineering physics/science, environmental/ sanitary, industrial, materials, mechanical, mining, nuclear, petroleum), Forestry, Journalism, Landscape Architecture, Music, Nursing, Nursing Education, Psychology Internship, Rehabilitation Counseling, School Psychology, Teacher Education (NCATE), Theatre

Altoona Campus
3000 Ivyside Park, Ste. 1, Altoona 16601-3760
Phone: (724)773-3500
Prog. Accred: Engineering Technology (electrical, electromechanical, mechanical)

Beaver Campus
Brodhead Rd., Monaca 15061
Phone: (412) 773-3500
Prog. Accred: Engineering Technology (electrical)

Berks Campus
Tulpehocken Rd., PO Box 7009, Reading 19610-6009
Phone: (610) 320-4800
Prog. Accred: Allied Health (occupational therapy assisting), Engineering Technology (electrical, electromechanical, mechanical)

Brandywine Campus
25 Yearsley Mill Rd., Media 19063-5596
Phone: (610) 892-1350

Dickinson School of Law
150 South College St., Carlisle 17013
Phone: (717) 243-4611
Prog. Accred: Law

DuBois Campus
College Place, DuBois 15801
Phone: (814) 375-4700
Prog. Accred: Allied Health (occupational therapy assisting), Engineering Technology (electrical, mechanical), Physical Therapy Assisting

Erie Campus
Station Rd., Erie 16563-0101
Phone: (814) 898-6000
Prog. Accred: Business (AACSB), Engineering (computer, electrical, mechanical, software), Engineering Technology (electrical, mechanical, plastics)

Fayette Campus
PO Box 519, Route 119 North, Uniontown 15401
Phone: (724) 430-4100
Prog. Accred: Engineering Technology (architectural, electrical)

Great Valley Graduate Center
30 East Swedesford Rd., Malvern 19355
Phone: (610) 648-3200
Prog. Accred: Business (AACSB)

Greater Allegheny Campus
4000 University Dr., McKeesport 15132
Phone: (412) 675-9000

Harrisburg Campus
777 West Harrisburg Pike, Middletown 17057-4898
Phone: (717) 948-6000
Prog. Accred: Business (AACSB), Engineering (electrical, environmental/sanitary), Engineering Technology (civil/construction, electrical, mechanical), Public Administration

Hazleton Campus
Highacres, Hazleton 18201
Phone: (717) 450-3000
Prog. Accred: Clinical Lab Technology, Engineering Technology (electrical, mechanical), Physical Therapy Assisting

Hershey Medical Center
The Milton S. Hershey Medical Center, 500 University Dr., PO Box 850, Hershey 17033
Phone: (717) 531-8521
Prog. Accred: Allied Health (medicine), Clinical Pastoral Education

Lehigh Valley Campus
8380 Mohr Ln., Fogelsville 18051-9999
Phone: (610) 285-5000

Mont Alto Campus
Campus Dr., Mont Alto 17237-9703
Phone: (717) 749-6000
Prog. Accred: Allied Health (occupational therapy assisting), Forestry, Physical Therapy Assisting

New Kensington Campus
3550 Seventh St. Rd., New Kensington 15068-1798
Phone: (724) 339-5466
Prog. Accred: Clinical Lab Technology, Engineering Technology (bioengineering, electrical, electromechanical, mechanical), Radiography

Ogontz Campus
1600 Woodland Rd., Abington 19001-3990
Phone: (215) 881-7300

Schuylkill Campus
200 University Dr., Schuylkill Haven 17972-2208
Phone: (717) 385-6000
Prog. Accred: Engineering Technology (electrical), Radiography

Shenango Campus
147 Shenango Ave., Sharon 16146
Phone: (724) 983-5800
Prog. Accred: Engineering Technology (mechanical), Physical Therapy Assisting

Wilkes-Barre Campus
PO Box PSU, Lehman 18627
Phone: (717) 675-2171
Prog. Accred: Applied Science (surveying/geomatics), Engineering Technology (electrical, surveying, telecommunications)

Worthington-Scranton Campus
120 Ridge View Dr., Dunmore 18512
Phone: (570) 963-2500
Prog. Accred: Engineering Technology (architectural)

York Campus
1031 Edgecomb Ave., York 17403
Phone: (717) 771-4000
Prog. Accred: Engineering Technology (electrical, mechanical)

Philadelphia Biblical University
200 Manor Ave., Langhorne 19047-2990
Type: Private, interdenominational, four-year
Degrees: A, B, M, P *Enroll:* 1,157
URL: http://www.pbu.edu
Phone: (215) 752-5800 *Calendar:* Sem. plan
Inst. Accred.: ABHE (1950/2006), MSA-CHE (1967/2005)
Prog. Accred.: Music, Social Work

New Jersey Campus
PO Box 19, Liberty Corner, NJ 07938
Phone: (908) 604-2707

Wisconsin Wilderness Campus
HC 60, Box 60, Cable, WI 54821
Phone: (715) 798-3525

Philadelphia College of Osteopathic Medicine
4170 City Ave., Philadelphia 19131
Type: Private, independent, four-year
Degrees: M, P, D *Enroll:* 1,603
URL: http://www.pcom.edu
Phone: (215) 871-6100 *Calendar:* Tri. plan
Inst. Accred.: MSA-CHE (1999/2004)
Prog. Accred.: Clinical Psychology, Osteopathy, Physician Assistant

Georgia Campus
625 Old Peachtree Rd. NW, Suwanee, GA 30024
Phone: (678) 225-7500

Philadelphia University
Schoolhouse Ln. and Henry Ave., Philadelphia 19144
Type: Private, independent, four-year
Degrees: A, B, M, D *Enroll:* 2,864
URL: http://www.philau.edu
Phone: (215) 951-2700 *Calendar:* Sem. plan
Inst. Accred.: MSA-CHE (1955/2006)
Prog. Accred.: Allied Health (occupational therapy), Engineering (textile), Interior Design, Physician Assistant

Midwifery Institute of Philadelphia University
Schoolhouse Ln. and Henry Ave., Philadelphia 19144
Phone: (215) 951-2525
Prog. Accred: Nurse (Midwifery)

Pittsburgh Institute of Aeronautics
PO Box 10897, Pittsburgh 15236-0897
Type: Private, proprietary, two-year
Degrees: A *Enroll:* 318
URL: http://www.pia.edu
Phone: (412) 346-2100 *Calendar:* Qtr. plan
Inst. Accred.: ACCSCT (1970/2004)

Pittsburgh Institute of Mortuary Science
5808 Baum Blvd., Pittsburgh 15206
Type: Private, independent, two-year
Degrees: A *Enroll:* 125
URL: http://www.p-i-m-s.com
Phone: (412) 362-8500 *Calendar:* Tri. plan
Inst. Accred.: ABFSE (1962/2004)

Pittsburgh Technical Institute
1111 McKee Rd., Oakdale 15071-3205
Type: Private, proprietary, two-year
Degrees: A *FTE Enroll:* 1,120
URL: http://www.pittsburghtechnical.com
Phone: (412) 809-5100
Inst. Accred.: MSA-CHE (2002/2007)
Prog. Accred.: Allied Health (medical assisting (AMA))

Pittsburgh Center
635 Smithfield St., Pittsburgh 15222
Phone: (412) 809-5100

Pittsburgh Theological Seminary
616 North Highland Ave., Pittsburgh 15206
Type: Private, Presbyterian Church (USA), four-year
Degrees: M, P, D *Enroll:* 336
URL: http://www.pts.edu
Phone: (412) 362-5610 *Calendar:* Qtr. plan
Inst. Accred.: ATS (1938/2002), MSA-CHE (1970/2003)

The PJA School
7900 West Chester Pike, Upper Darby 19082-1926
Type: Private, proprietary, two-year
Degrees: A
URL: http://www.pjaschool.com
Phone: (610) 789-6700
Inst. Accred.: ACCSCT (1985/2006)

Point Park University
201 Wood St., Pittsburgh 15222
Type: Private, independent, four-year
Degrees: A, B, M *Enroll:* 2,825
URL: http://www.pointpark.edu
Phone: (412) 391-4100 *Calendar:* Sem. plan
Inst. Accred.: MSA-CHE (1968/2001)
Prog. Accred.: Dance, Engineering Technology (civil/construction, electrical, mechanical)

Reading Area Community College
PO Box 1706, Reading 19603-1706
Type: Public, state/local, two-year
Degrees: A *Enroll:* 2,533
URL: http://www.racc.edu
Phone: (610) 372-4721 *Calendar:* Tri. plan
Inst. Accred.: MSA-CHE (1979/2003)
Prog. Accred.: Clinical Lab Technology, Nursing, Practical Nursing

Reconstructionist Rabbinical College
1299 Church Rd., Wyncote 19095
Type: Private, independent, four-year
Degrees: M, P, D *Enroll:* 77
URL: http://www.rrc.edu
Phone: (215) 576-0800 *Calendar:* Sem. plan
Inst. Accred.: MSA-CHE (1990/2005)

Reformed Presbyterian Theological Seminary
7418 Penn Ave., Pittsburgh 15208
Type: Private, Reformed Presbyterian Church of North America, four-year
Degrees: M *Enroll:* 51
URL: http://www.rpts.edu
Phone: (412) 731-8690 *Calendar:* Sem. plan
Inst. Accred.: ATS (1994/2007)

The Restaurant School at Walnut Hill College
4207 Walnut St., Philadelphia 19104-3518
Type: Private, proprietary, four-year
Degrees: A, B *Enroll:* 631
URL: http://www.therestaurantschool.com
Phone: (215) 222-4200
Inst. Accred.: ACCSCT (1982/2008)

Robert Morris University
6001 University Blvd., Moon Township 15108-1189
Type: Private, independent, four-year
Degrees: B, M, D *Enroll:* 3,873
URL: http://www.rmu.edu
Phone: (412) 262-8200 *Calendar:* Sem. plan
Inst. Accred.: MSA-CHE (1968/2007)
Prog. Accred.: Computer Science (ABET-CAC), Engineering (general, information systems, manufacturing), Nursing Education, Radiography

Pittsburgh Campus
600 Fifth Ave., Pittsburgh 15219
Phone: (412) 227-6800
Prog. Accred: Radiography

Rosedale Technical Institute
4634 Browns Hill Rd., Pittsburgh 15217-2919
Type: Private, proprietary, two-year
Degrees: A *Enroll:* 202
URL: http://rosedaletech.org
Phone: (412) 521-6200 *Calendar:* Qtr. plan
Inst. Accred.: ACCSCT (1974/2006)

Rosemont College
1400 Montgomery Ave., Rosemont 19010-1699
Type: Private, Society of the Holy Child Jesus, four-year
Degrees: B, M *Enroll:* 706
URL: http://www.rosemont.edu
Phone: (610) 527-0200
Inst. Accred.: MSA-CHE (1930/2005)

Saint Charles Borromeo Seminary
100 East Wynnewood Rd., Wynnewood 19096-3099
Type: Private, Roman Catholic Church, four-year
Degrees: B, M, P *Enroll:* 225
URL: http://www.scs.edu
Phone: (610) 667-3394 *Calendar:* Sem. plan
Inst. Accred.: ATS (1970/2008), MSA-CHE (1971/2004)

Saint Francis University
PO Box 600, Loretto 15940
Type: Private, Roman Catholic Church, four-year
Degrees: A, B, M, P *Enroll:* 1,681
URL: http://www.sfcpa.edu
Phone: (814) 472-3000 *Calendar:* Sem. plan
Inst. Accred.: MSA-CHE (1939/2006)
Prog. Accred.: Allied Health (occupational therapy), Nursing Education, Physical Therapy, Physician Assistant, Social Work

Saint Joseph's University
5600 City Line Ave., Philadelphia 19131
Type: Private, Roman Catholic Church, four-year
Degrees: A, B, M, D *Enroll:* 5,829
URL: http://www.sju.edu
Phone: (610) 660-1000 *Calendar:* Sem. plan
Inst. Accred.: MSA-CHE (1922/2004)
Prog. Accred.: Accounting, Business (AACSB)

Saint Tikhon's Orthodox Theological Seminary
St. Tikhon's Rd., PO Box 130, South Canaan 18459-0130
Type: Private, Russian Orthodox Greek Catholic Church, four-year
Degrees: M
URL: http://www.stots.edu
Phone: (570) 937-4411 *Calendar:* Sem. plan
Inst. Accred.: ATS (2004)

Saint Vincent College and Seminary
300 Fraser Purchase Rd., Latrobe 15650-2690
Type: Private, Roman Catholic Church, four-year
Degrees: B, M, P *Enroll:* 1,568
URL: http://www.stvincent.edu
Phone: (724) 539-9761 *Calendar:* Sem. plan
Inst. Accred.: ATS (1984/2008), MSA-CHE (1921/2008)
Prog. Accred.: Business (ACBSP), Nurse Anesthesia Education

Salus University
8360 Old York Rd., Elkins Park 19027
Type: Private, independent, four-year
Degrees: B, M, P, D *Enroll:* 887
URL: http://www.pco.edu
Phone: (215) 780-1400 *Calendar:* Qtr. plan
Inst. Accred.: MSA-CHE (1954/2005)
Prog. Accred.: Allied Health (optometric residency, optometry, speech-language pathology)

Sanford-Brown Institute—Pittsburgh
421 Seventh Ave., Pittsburgh 15219
Type: Private, proprietary, two-year
System: Career Education Corporation
Degrees: A
URL: http://www.sanfordbrown.edu
Phone: (412) 281-2600
Inst. Accred.: ACCSCT (1986/2005)
Prog. Accred.: Allied Health (diagnostic medical sonography, respiratory therapy, surgical technology), Medical Assisting (ABHES), Radiography, Veterinary Technology

Monroeville Campus
Penn Center East 777 Penn Center Blvd., Building 7, Pittsburgh 15235
Phone: (412) 373-6400
Prog. Accred: Medical Assisting (ABHES)

Seton Hill University
One Seton Hill Dr., Greensburg 15601
Type: Private, Roman Catholic Church, four-year
Degrees: B, M *Enroll:* 1,538
URL: http://www.setonhill.edu
Phone: (724) 834-2200 *Calendar:* Sem. plan
Inst. Accred.: MSA-CHE (1921/2007)
Prog. Accred.: Dietetics (coordinated), Marriage and Family Therapy, Music, Physician Assistant, Social Work

Shippensburg University of Pennsylvania
1871 Old Main Dr., Shippensburg 17257-2299
Type: Public, state, four-year
System: Pennsylvania State System of Higher Education
Degrees: B, M *Enroll:* 6,821
URL: http://www.ship.edu
Phone: (717) 477-7447 *Calendar:* Sem. plan
Inst. Accred.: MSA-CHE (1939/2004)
Prog. Accred.: Business (AACSB), Computer Science (ABET-CAC), Counseling, Graduate Social Work, Social Work, Teacher Education (NCATE)

Slippery Rock University of Pennsylvania

1 Morrow Way, Slippery Rock 16057-1383
Type: Public, state, four-year
System: Pennsylvania State System of Higher Education
Degrees: B, M, D *Enroll:* 7,539
URL: http://www.sru.edu
Phone: (724) 738-9000 *Calendar:* Sem. plan
Inst. Accred.: MSA-CHE (1943/2001)
Prog. Accred.: Computer Science (ABET-CAC), Counseling, Dance, Engineering (information systems), Exercise Science, Music, Nursing, Physical Therapy, Recreation and Leisure Services, Social Work, Teacher Education (NCATE)

South Hills School of Business and Technology

480 Waupelani Dr., State College 16801-4516
Type: Private, proprietary, two-year
Degrees: A *Enroll:* 632
URL: http://www.southhills.edu
Phone: (814) 234-7755 *Calendar:* Qtr. plan
Inst. Accred.: ACICS (1976/2006)

Altoona Campus

508 58th St., Altoona 16602
Phone: (814) 944-6134

Lewistown Campus

124 East Market St., Lewistown 17044
Phone: (717) 248-8140

Philipsburg Campus

200 Shady Ln., Philipsburg 16866
Phone: (814) 342-7427

Susquehanna University

514 University Ave., Selinsgrove 17870-1025
Type: Private, Evangelical Lutheran Church, four-year
Degrees: A, B *Enroll:* 1,931
URL: http://www.susqu.edu
Phone: (570) 374-0101 *Calendar:* Sem. plan
Inst. Accred.: MSA-CHE (1930/2004)
Prog. Accred.: Business (AACSB), Music

Swarthmore College

500 College Ave., Swarthmore 19081
Type: Private, Religious Society of Friends (Quakers), four-year
Degrees: B *Enroll:* 1,475
URL: http://www.swarthmore.edu
Phone: (610) 328-8000 *Calendar:* Sem. plan
Inst. Accred.: MSA-CHE (1921/2004)
Prog. Accred.: Engineering (general)

Talmudical Yeshiva of Philadelphia

6063 Drexel Rd., Philadelphia 19131
Type: Private, independent, four-year
Degrees: Rabbinic, Talmudic *Enroll:* 111
Phone: (215) 473-1212 *Calendar:* Sem. plan
Inst. Accred.: AARTS (1975/2001)

Temple University

1801 North Broad St., Philadelphia 19122
Type: Private, state-related, four-year
Degrees: A, B, M, P, D *Enroll:* 28,747
URL: http://www.temple.edu
Phone: (215) 204-7000 *Calendar:* Sem. plan
Inst. Accred.: MSA-CHE (1921/2005)
Prog. Accred.: Allied Health (audiology, health services administration, medicine, occupational therapy, speech-language pathology), Art, Business (AACSB), Clinical Psychology, Counseling Psychology, Dance, Dentistry (advanced education in general dentistry, combined prosthodontics, dentistry, endodontics, general dentistry, oral and maxillofacial surgery, orthodontic and dentofacial orthopedics, pediatric dentistry, periodontics), Engineering (civil, electrical, mechanical), Engineering Technology (civil/construction, electrical, environmental/sanitary, general, mechanical), Graduate Social Work, Journalism, Landscape Architecture, Law, Music, Nursing Education, Pharmacy, Physical Therapy, Psychology Internship, Public Health, Recreation and Leisure Services, School Psychology, Social Work, Theatre

Ambler Campus

580 Meeting House Rd., Ambler 19002-3999
Phone: (215) 283-1201

Center City Campus

1616 Walnut St., Philadelphia 19103
Phone: (215) 204-1500

Harrisburg Center

223 Walnut St., Harrisburg 17101
Phone: (717) 232-6400

Japan Campus

2-2 Minami Osewaw, Hachioji-shi, Tokyo, Japan 192-03
Phone: [011] 81-426-77-5116

Rome Campus

Lungotevere Arnaldo da Brescia, 15, Rome, Italy 00196
Phone: [011] 39-6-320-2808

School of Podiatric Medicine

8th and Race Streets, Philadelphia 19107
Phone: (215) 629-0300
Prog. Accred: Podiatry

Thaddeus Stevens College of Technology

750 East King St., Lancaster 17602
Type: Public, state, two-year
Degrees: A *Enroll:* 674
URL: http://www.stevenscollege.edu
Phone: (717) 299-7730 *Calendar:* Sem. plan
Inst. Accred.: MSA-CHE (1991/2007)
Prog. Accred.: Allied Health (respiratory therapy)

Thiel College
75 College Ave., Greenville 16125
Type: Private, Evangelial Lutheran Church in America, four-year
Degrees: A, B *Enroll:* 1,288
URL: http://www.thiel.edu
Phone: (724) 589-2000 *Calendar:* Sem. plan
Inst. Accred.: MSA-CHE (1922/2002, Warning)

Thomas Jefferson University
1020 Walnut St., Philadelphia 19107
Type: Private, independent, four-year
Degrees: A, B, M, P, D *Enroll:* 2,247
URL: http://www.tju.edu
Phone: (215) 955-6000 *Calendar:* Sem. plan
Inst. Accred.: MSA-CHE (1976/2004)
Prog. Accred.: Allied Health (cytotechnology, diagnostic medical sonography, medicine, occupational therapy), Clinical Lab Scientist, Clinical Pastoral Education, Cytogenetic Technology, Dentistry (oral and maxillofacial surgery), Nuclear Medicine Technology, Nurse Anesthesia Education, Nursing Education, Pharmacy, Physical Therapy, Public Health, Radiography

Tri-State Business Institute
5757 West 26th St., Erie 16506
Type: Private, proprietary, two-year
Degrees: A *Enroll:* 337
URL: http://www.tsbi.org
Phone: (814) 838-7673
Inst. Accred.: ACICS (1990/2003)
Prog. Accred.: Allied Health (medical assisting (AMA)), Medical Assisting (ABHES)

Medix School—South
4351 Garden City Dr., Landover, MD 20785
Phone: (301) 459-3650

Triangle Tech
1940 Perrysville Ave., Pittsburgh 15214-3897
Type: Private, proprietary, two-year
Degrees: A *Enroll:* 318
URL: http://www.triangle-tech.com
Phone: (412) 359-1000
Inst. Accred.: ACCSCT (1970/2003)

Triangle Tech
2000 Liberty St., Erie 16502-9987
Type: Private, proprietary, two-year
Degrees: A *Enroll:* 141
URL: http://www.triangle-tech.edu
Phone: (814) 453-6016
Inst. Accred.: ACCSCT (1978/2007)

Triangle Tech
222 Pittsburgh St., Ste. A, Greensburg 15601
Type: Private, proprietary, two-year
Degrees: A *Enroll:* 271
URL: http://www.triangle-tech.edu
Phone: (724) 832-1050
Inst. Accred.: ACCSCT (1979/2008)

Triangle Tech
PO Box 551, DuBois 15801-9990
Type: Private, proprietary, two-year
Degrees: A *Enroll:* 247
URL: http://www.triangle-tech.edu
Phone: (814) 371-2090
Inst. Accred.: ACCSCT (1981/2008)

Business Careers Institute
222 East Pittsburg St., Greensburg 15601-2394
Phone: (412) 834-1258

Business Careers Institute
1940 Perryville Ave., Pittsburgh 15214-3826
Phone: (412) 359-9000

Triangle Tech—Sunbury
RR #1, Box 51, Route 890, Sunbury 17801
Type: Private, proprietary, two-year
Degrees: A
URL: http://www.triangle-tech.edu
Phone: (570) 988-0700
Inst. Accred.: ACCSCT (2002/2004)

Bethlehem Campus
31 South Commerce Way, Lehigh Valley Industrial Park IV, Bethlehem 18017
Phone: (610) 691-1300

Trinity Episcopal School for Ministry
311 Eleventh St., Ambridge 15003
Type: Private, Episcopal Church, four-year
Degrees: M, D *Enroll:* 172
URL: http://www.tesm.edu
Phone: (724) 266-3838 *Calendar:* Sem. plan
Inst. Accred.: ATS (1985/2006)

United States Army War College
122 Forbes Ave., Carlisle 17013
Type: Public, federal, four-year
Degrees: M
URL: http://carlisle-www.army.mil
Phone: (717) 245-3131
Inst. Accred.: MSA-CHE (2004)

University of Pennsylvania
3451 Walnut St., Philadelphia 19104
Type: Private, independent, four-year
Degrees: A, B, M, P, D *Enroll:* 21,293
URL: http://www.upenn.edu
Phone: (215) 898-5000 *Calendar:* Sem. plan
Inst. Accred.: MSA-CHE (1921/2004)
Prog. Accred.: Allied Health (health services administration, medicine), Business (AACSB), Clinical Pastoral Education, Clinical Psychology, Combined Professional-Scientific Psychology, Computer Science (ABET-CAC), Dentistry (advanced education in general dentistry, dentistry, endodontics, general dentistry, general practice residency, oral and maxillofacial surgery, orthodontic and dentofacial orthopedics, pediatric dentistry, periodontics), Engineering (bioengineering, chemical, computer, electrical, materials, mechanical, systems, telecommunications), English Language Education, Graduate Social Work, Landscape Architecture, Law, Nurse (Midwifery), Nurse Anesthesia Education, Nursing Education, Planning, Psychology Internship, Public Health, Radiography, Veterinary Medicine

University of Pittsburgh
4200 Fifth Ave., Pittsburgh 15260
Type: Public, state-related, four-year
Degrees: A, B, M, P, D *Enroll:* 23,587
URL: http://www.pitt.edu
Phone: (412) 624-4200 *Calendar:* Sem. plan
Inst. Accred.: MSA-CHE (1921/2007)
Prog. Accred.: Allied Health (audiology, health services administration, medicine, occupational therapy, speech-language pathology), Business (AACSB), Clinical Psychology, Dentistry (advanced education in general dentistry, combined prosthodontics, dental hygiene, dental public health, dentistry, endodontics, general dentistry, maxillofacial prosthetics, oral and maxillofacial surgery, orthodontic and dentofacial orthopedics, pediatric dentistry, periodontics), Dietetics (coordinated), Dietetics (didactic), Engineering (bioengineering, chemical, civil, computer, electrical, engineering physics/science, industrial, materials, mechanical), English Language Education, Graduate Social Work, Law, Librarianship, Nurse Anesthesia Education, Nursing Education, Pharmacy, Physical Therapy, Psychology Internship, Public Administration, Public Health, Rehabilitation Counseling, Social Work, Theatre

Bradford Campus
300 Campus Dr., Bradford 16701
Phone: (814) 362-7500
Prog. Accred: Nursing

Greensburg Campus
1150 Mount Pleasant Rd., Greensburg 15601
Phone: (724) 837-7040

Johnstown Campus
450 Schoolhouse Rd., Johnstown 15904
Phone: (814) 269-7000
Prog. Accred: Allied Health (respiratory therapy), Engineering Technology (civil/construction, electrical, mechanical)

Titusville Campus
504 East Main St., Titusville 16354
Phone: (814) 827-4400
Prog. Accred: Nursing, Physical Therapy Assisting

University of Scranton
800 Linden St., Scranton 18510-4501
Type: Private, Roman Catholic Church, four-year
Degrees: A, B, M, P *Enroll:* 4,547
URL: http://www.uofs.edu
Phone: (570) 941-7500 *Calendar:* Sem. plan
Inst. Accred.: MSA-CHE (1927/2008)
Prog. Accred.: Allied Health (health services administration, occupational therapy), Business (AACSB), Computer Science (ABET-CAC), Counseling, Engineering (information systems), Nurse Anesthesia Education, Nursing Education, Physical Therapy, Rehabilitation Counseling, Teacher Education (NCATE)

University of the Arts
320 South Broad St., Philadelphia 19102
Type: Private, independent, four-year
Degrees: B, M *Enroll:* 2,213
URL: http://www.uarts.edu
Phone: (215) 717-6000 *Calendar:* Sem. plan
Inst. Accred.: MSA-CHE (1969/2004)
Prog. Accred.: Art, Music

University of the Sciences in Philadelphia
600 South 43rd St., Philadelphia 19104-4495
Type: Private, independent, four-year
Degrees: B, M, P, D *Enroll:* 2,618
URL: http://www.usip.edu
Phone: (215) 596-8800 *Calendar:* Sem. plan
Inst. Accred.: MSA-CHE (1962/2003)
Prog. Accred.: Allied Health (occupational therapy), Pharmacy, Physical Therapy

Ursinus College
Box 1000, Collegeville 19426-1000
Type: Private, independent, four-year
Degrees: A, B *Enroll:* 1,559
URL: http://www.ursinus.edu
Phone: (610) 489-3000 *Calendar:* Sem. plan
Inst. Accred.: MSA-CHE (1921/2004)

Valley Forge Christian College
1401 Charlestown Rd., Phoenixville 19460-2399
Type: Private, Assemblies of God Church, four-year
Degrees: A, B, M *Enroll:* 881
URL: http://www.vfcc.edu
Phone: (610) 935-0450 *Calendar:* Sem. plan
Inst. Accred.: MSA-CHE (2002/2007)

Valley Forge Military College
1001 Eagle Rd., Wayne 19087-3695
Type: Private, independent, two-year
Degrees: A *Enroll:* 165
URL: http://www.vfmac.edu
Phone: (610) 989-1200 *Calendar:* Sem. plan
Inst. Accred.: MSA-CHE (1954/2000)

Vet Tech Institute
125 Seventh St., Pittsburgh 15222-3400
Type: Private, proprietary, two-year
Degrees: A *Enroll:* 296
URL: http://www.vettechinstitute.edu
Phone: (412) 391-7021 *Calendar:* Sem. plan
Inst. Accred.: ACCSCT (1970/2004)

Villanova University
800 Lancaster Ave., Villanova 19085-1699
Type: Private, Roman Catholic Church, four-year
Degrees: A, B, M, P, D *Enroll:* 8,822
URL: http://www.villanova.edu
Phone: (610) 519-4500 *Calendar:* Sem. plan
Inst. Accred.: MSA-CHE (1921/2001)
Prog. Accred.: Accounting, Business (AACSB), Computer Science (ABET-CAC), Engineering (chemical, civil, computer, electrical, mechanical), Law, Nurse Anesthesia Education, Nursing Education

Washington and Jefferson College
60 South Lincoln St., Washington 15301-4801
Type: Private, independent, four-year
Degrees: A, B *Enroll:* 1,407
URL: http://www.washjeff.edu
Phone: (724) 222-4400 *Calendar:* 4-1-4 plan
Inst. Accred.: MSA-CHE (1921/2004)

Waynesburg University
51 West College St., Waynesburg 15370
Type: Private, Presbyterian Church, USA, four-year
Degrees: A, B, M, D *Enroll:* 1,683
URL: http://www.waynesburg.edu
Phone: (724) 627-8191 *Calendar:* Sem. plan
Inst. Accred.: MSA-CHE (1950/2005)
Prog. Accred.: Nursing Education

West Chester University of Pennsylvania
South High St., West Chester 19383
Type: Public, state, four-year
System: Pennsylvania State System of Higher Education
Degrees: B, M *Enroll:* 11,354
URL: http://www.wcupa.edu
Phone: (610) 436-1000 *Calendar:* Sem. plan
Inst. Accred.: MSA-CHE (1946/2001)
Prog. Accred.: Allied Health (respiratory therapy, speech-language pathology), Business (AACSB), Dietetics (didactic), Graduate Social Work, Music, Nursing Education, Public Health, Social Work, Teacher Education (NCATE)

Westminster College
319 South Market St., New Wilmington 16172-0001
Type: Private, Presbyterian Church, four-year
Degrees: B, M *Enroll:* 1,543
URL: http://www.westminster.edu
Phone: (724) 946-8761 *Calendar:* Sem. plan
Inst. Accred.: MSA-CHE (1921/2001)
Prog. Accred.: Music

Westminster Theological Seminary
PO Box 27009, Philadelphia 19118
Type: Private, interdenominational, four-year
Degrees: M, P, D *Enroll:* 525
URL: http://www.wts.edu
Phone: (215) 887-5511 *Calendar:* Sem. plan
Inst. Accred.: ATS (1986/2001), MSA-CHE (1954/2007)

Westmoreland County Community College
400 Armbrust Rd., Youngwood 15697-1895
Type: Public, state/local, two-year
Degrees: A *Enroll:* 3,836
URL: http://www.wccc-pa.edu
Phone: (724) 925-4000 *Calendar:* Sem. plan
Inst. Accred.: MSA-CHE (1978/2003)
Prog. Accred.: Allied Health (medical assisting (AMA), surgical technology), Culinary Education, Dentistry (dental assisting, dental hygiene), Dietetic Technician

Widener University
One University Place, Chester 19013-5792
Type: Private, independent, four-year
Degrees: A, B, M, P, D *Enroll:* 3,515
URL: http://www.widener.edu
Phone: (610) 499-4000 *Calendar:* Sem. plan
Inst. Accred.: MSA-CHE (1954/2007)
Prog. Accred.: Allied Health (health services administration), Business (AACSB), Clinical Psychology, Engineering (chemical, civil, electrical, mechanical), Graduate Social Work, Nursing Education, Physical Therapy, Psychology Internship, Social Work

Harrisburg Campus
3800 Vartan Way, Harrisburg 17110-9450
Phone: (717) 541-3900
Prog. Accred: Law (ABA only)

School of Law Campus
4601 Concord Pike, Wilmington, DE 19803-0474
Phone: (302) 477-2100
Prog. Accred: Law

Wilkes University
84 West South St., Wilkes-Barre 18766
Type: Private, independent, four-year
Degrees: B, M, P, D *Enroll:* 3,195
URL: http://www.wilkes.edu
Phone: (570) 408-5000 *Calendar:* Sem. plan
Inst. Accred.: MSA-CHE (1937/2005)
Prog. Accred.: Business (ACBSP), Engineering (electrical, environmental/sanitary, mechanical), Nursing Education, Pharmacy

The Williamson Free School of Mechanical Trades
106 South New Middletown Rd., Media 19063-5299
Type: Private, independent, two-year
Degrees: A *FTE Enroll:* 250
URL: http://www.williamson.edu
Phone: (610) 566-1776 *Calendar:* Sem. plan
Inst. Accred.: ACCSCT (1970/2008)

Wilson College
1015 Philadelphia Ave., Chambersburg 17201-1285
Type: Private, Presbyterian Church, four-year
Degrees: A, B, M *Enroll:* 499
URL: http://www.wilson.edu
Phone: (717) 264-4141 *Calendar:* 4-1-4 plan
Inst. Accred.: MSA-CHE (1922/2003)
Prog. Accred.: Veterinary Technology

Winner Institute of Arts and Sciences
One Winner Place, Transfer 16154
Type: Private, proprietary, two-year
Degrees: A
URL: http://www.winner-institute.com
Phone: (724) 646-2433
Inst. Accred.: COE (2003)

Won Institute of Graduate Studies
137 South Easton Rd., Glenside 19038
Type: Private, independent, four-year
Degrees: M
URL: http://www.woninstitute.org
Phone: (215) 884-8942
Inst. Accred.: MSA-CHE (2008)

WyoTech—Blairsville
500 Innovation Dr., Blairsville 15717
Type: Private, proprietary, two-year
Degrees: A
URL: http://www.wyotech.com
Phone: (724) 459-9500
Inst. Accred.: ACCSCT (2001/2003)

Yeshiva Beth Moshe
930 Hickory St., PO Box 1141, Scranton 18505
Type: Private, independent, four-year
Degrees: Talmudic *Enroll:* 54
Phone: (570) 346-1747 *Calendar:* Sem. plan
Inst. Accred.: AARTS (1976/2000)

York College of Pennsylvania
Country Club Rd., York 17405-7199
Type: Private, independent, four-year
Degrees: A, B, M *Enroll:* 4,966
URL: http://www.ycp.edu
Phone: (717) 846-7788 *Calendar:* Sem. plan
Inst. Accred.: MSA-CHE (1959/2006)
Prog. Accred.: Allied Health (respiratory therapy), Business (ACBSP), Engineering (mechanical), Nurse Anesthesia Education, Nursing Education, Recreation and Leisure Services

Yorktowne Business Institute
West Seventh Ave., York 17404
Type: Private, proprietary, two-year
Degrees: A *Enroll:* 291
URL: http://www.ybi.edu
Phone: (717) 846-5000
Inst. Accred.: ACICS (1979/2007)

YTI Career Institute
1405 Williams Rd., York 17402-9017
Type: Private, proprietary, two-year
Degrees: A *Enroll:* 1,474
URL: http://www.yti.edu
Phone: (717) 757-1100 *Calendar:* Qtr. plan
Inst. Accred.: ACCSCT (1979/2006)

Lancaster Campus
3050 Hempland Rd., Lancaster 17601
Phone: (717) 295-1100

Inter American University of Puerto Rico Bayamon Campus
500 Rd. Dr., John Will Harris, Bayamon 00957
Type: Private, independent, four-year
System: Inter American University of Puerto Rico Central Office of the System
Degrees: A, B, M *Enroll:* 4,684
URL: http://www.bc.inter.edu
Phone: (787) 279-1912 *Calendar:* Sem. plan
Inst. Accred.: MSA-CHE (1960/2003)

Inter American University of Puerto Rico Fajardo Campus
Call Box 70003, Fajardo 00738-7003
Type: Private, independent, four-year
System: Inter American University of Puerto Rico Central Office of the System
Degrees: A, B, M *Enroll:* 1,992
URL: http://fajardo.inter.edu
Phone: (787) 863-2390 *Calendar:* Sem. plan
Inst. Accred.: MSA-CHE (1961/2003)

Inter American University of Puerto Rico Guayama Campus
PO Box 10004, Guayama 00785
Type: Private, independent, four-year
System: Inter American University of Puerto Rico Central Office of the System
Degrees: A, B, M *Enroll:* 1,982
URL: http://guayama.inter.edu
Phone: (787) 864-2222 *Calendar:* Sem. plan
Inst. Accred.: MSA-CHE (1957/2003)

Inter American University of Puerto Rico Metropolitan Campus
PO Box 191293, San Juan 00919-1293
Type: Private, indepenednt, four-year
System: Inter American University of Puerto Rico Central Office of the System
Degrees: A, B, M, P, D *Enroll:* 7,587
URL: http://www.metro.inter.edu
Phone: (787) 250-1912 *Calendar:* Sem. plan
Inst. Accred.: MSA-CHE (1960/2003)
Prog. Accred.: Allied Health (optometry), Clinical Lab Scientist, Graduate Social Work, Nursing, Social Work

Inter American University of Puerto Rico Ponce Campus
104 Turpo Industrial Park Rd. #1, Mercedita 00715-1602
Type: Private, independent, four-year
System: Inter American University of Puerto Rico Central Office of the System
Degrees: A, B, M *Enroll:* 4,746
URL: http://ponce.inter.edu
Phone: (787) 284-1912 *Calendar:* Sem. plan
Inst. Accred.: MSA-CHE (1962/2003)

Inter American University of Puerto Rico San German Campus
PO Box 5100, San German 00683
Type: Private, independent, four-year
System: Inter American University of Puerto Rico Central Office of the System
Degrees: A, B, M, P, D
URL: http://www.sg.inter.edu
Phone: (787) 264-1912 *Calendar:* Sem. plan
Inst. Accred.: MSA-CHE (1944/2003)
Prog. Accred.: Clinical Lab Scientist

Inter American University of Puerto Rico School of Law
PO Box 70351, San Juan 00936-8351
Type: Private, independent, four-year
System: Inter American University of Puerto Rico Central Office of the System
Degrees: P *Enroll:* 690
URL: http://www.derecho.inter.edu
Phone: (787) 751-1912 *Calendar:* Sem. plan
Inst. Accred.: MSA-CHE (1961/2003)
Prog. Accred.: Law (ABA only)

Inter American University of Puerto Rico School of Optometry
PO Box 191049, San Juan 00919-1049
Type: Private, independent, four-year
System: Inter American University of Puerto Rico Central Office of the System
Degrees: P *Enroll:* 164
URL: http://www.optonet.inter.edu
Phone: (787) 765-1915 *Calendar:* Sem. plan
Inst. Accred.: MSA-CHE (1981/2003)

John Dewey College
PO Box 19538, San Juan 00910-9538
Type: Private, proprietary, four-year
Degrees: A, B
URL: http://www.johndeweycollegepr.com
Phone: (787) 753-0039
Inst. Accred.: ACICS (1994/2004)

Bayamon Campus
Carr. #2, Km 15.9 Bo. Hato Tejas, Bayamon 00959
Phone: (787) 778-1200

Carolina Campus
Carr. #3, Km 11 lote 7, Carolina Industrial Park, Carolina 00986
Phone: (787) 769-1515

National College of Business and Technology
Ramos Bldg., Hwy. No. 2, PO Box 2036, Bayamon 00960
Type: Private, proprietary, four-year
Degrees: A, B *Enroll:* 1,862
URL: http://www.nationalcollegepr.edu
Phone: (787) 780-5134 *Calendar:* Tri. plan
Inst. Accred.: ACICS (1983/2007)

Arecibo Campus
PO Box 4035, Arecibo 00614
Phone: (787) 879-5044

Rio Grande Campus
State Rd. #3 Km.22.1, Barrio Cienaga, Rio Grande 00745
Phone: (787) 780-5134

Ponce Paramedical College
1213 Acacia St., Villa Flores URB, Ponce 00716-2901
Type: Private, independent, two-year
Degrees: A
URL: http://ponce.library.net
Phone: (787) 848-1589
Inst. Accred.: ACCSCT (1987/2003)

Ponce School of Medicine
PO Box 7004, Ponce 00732
Type: Private, independent, four-year
Degrees: M, P, D *Enroll:* 477
URL: http://www.psm.edu
Phone: (787) 840-2575 *Calendar:* Sem. plan
Inst. Accred.: MSA-CHE (2003/2008)
Prog. Accred.: Allied Health (medicine), Clinical Psychology

Pontifical Catholic University of Puerto Rico—Arecibo Campus
PO Box 144045, Arecibo 00614-4045
Type: Private, Roman Catholic Church, four-year
Degrees: A, B, M *Enroll:* 644
URL: http://arecibo.pucpr.edu
Phone: (787) 881-1212 *Calendar:* Sem. plan
Inst. Accred.: MSA-CHE (1981/2005)

Pontifical Catholic University of Puerto Rico—Mayaguez Campus
482 South Post St., PO Box 1326, Mayaguez 00681
Type: Private, Roman Catholic Church, four-year
Degrees: A, B, M *Enroll:* 1,541
URL: http://www.pucpr.edu
Phone: (787) 834-5151 *Calendar:* Sem. plan
Inst. Accred.: MSA-CHE (1962/2004)

Pontifical Catholic University of Puerto Rico—Ponce Campus
2250 Avenida las Americas, Ste. 564, Ponce 00717-0777
Type: Private, Roman Catholic Church, four-year
Degrees: A, B, M, P, D *Enroll:* 6,227
URL: http://www.pucpr.edu
Phone: (787) 841-2000 *Calendar:* Sem. plan
Inst. Accred.: MSA-CHE (1953/2004)
Prog. Accred.: Clinical Lab Scientist, Law (ABA only), Nursing, Rehabilitation Counseling, Social Work

Seminario Major San Juan Bautista
PO Box 11714, San Juan 00922-1714
Phone: (787) 783-0645

Ramirez College of Business and Technology
PO Box 195411, San Juan 00919-5411
Type: Private, proprietary, two-year
Degrees: A *Enroll:* 363
URL: http://ramirezcollege.com
Phone: (787) 763-3120 *Calendar:* Tri. plan
Inst. Accred.: ACICS (1975/2006)

Mayaguez Campus
61 Pilar Defillo Avenida, Mayaguez 00680
Phone: (787) 831-3755

San Juan Bautista School of Medicine
PO Box 4968, Luis Munoz Marin Ave., Caguas 00726-4968
Type: Private, independent, four-year
Degrees: P *Enroll:* 191
URL: http://www.sanjuanbautista.edu
Phone: (787) 743-3038 *Calendar:* Sem. plan
Inst. Accred.: MSA-CHE (2004)

Universidad Adventista de las Antillas
PO Box 118, Mayaguez 00681
Type: Private, Seventh-Day Adventist Church, four-year
Degrees: A, B, M *Enroll:* 778
URL: http://www.uaa.edu
Phone: (787) 834-9595 *Calendar:* Sem. plan
Inst. Accred.: MSA-CHE (1978/2003)
Prog. Accred.: Nursing

Universidad Central del Caribe: School of Medicine
PO Box 60327, Bayamon 00960-6032
Type: Private, independent, four-year
Degrees: A, B, M, P *Enroll:* 355
URL: http://www.uccaribe.edu
Phone: (787) 798-3001 *Calendar:* Sem. plan
Inst. Accred.: MSA-CHE (2003)
Prog. Accred.: Allied Health (medicine), Radiography

Universidad del Este
PO Box 2010, Carolina 00983-2010
Type: Private, independent, four-year
System: Sistema Universitario Ana G. Mendez Central Office
Degrees: A, B, M *Enroll:* 8,629
URL: http://www.suagm.edu/une
Phone: (787) 257-7373 *Calendar:* Sem. plan
Inst. Accred.: MSA-CHE (1959/2005)
Prog. Accred.: Business (ACBSP)

Universidad del Turabo
Box 3030, Gurabo 00778-3030
Type: Private, independent, four-year
System: Sistema Universitario Ana G. Mendez Central Office
Degrees: A, B, M, D *Enroll:* 12,704
URL: http://www.suagm.edu/ut
Phone: (787) 743-7979 *Calendar:* Sem. plan
Inst. Accred.: MSA-CHE (1974/2005)
Prog. Accred.: Dietetics (coordinated), Engineering (mechanical), Nursing Education

Universidad Metropolitana
PO Box 21150, San Juan 00928-1150
Type: Private, independent, four-year
System: Sistema Universitario Ana G. Mendez Central Office
Degrees: A, B, M, D *Enroll:* 8,945
URL: http://www.suagm.edu/umet
Phone: (787) 766-1717 *Calendar:* Sem. plan
Inst. Accred.: MSA-CHE (1980/2007)
Prog. Accred.: Nursing

Universidad Politecnica de Puerto Rico
Box 192017, San Juan 00919-2017
Type: Private, independent, four-year
Degrees: A, B, M *Enroll:* 4,019
URL: http://www.pupr.edu
Phone: (787) 622-8000 *Calendar:* Tri. plan
Inst. Accred.: MSA-CHE (1985/2005)
Prog. Accred.: Engineering (civil, electrical, environmental/sanitary, industrial, mechanical)

Polytechnic University of the Americas
PO Box 526223, Miami, FL 33152-6223
Phone: (305) 418-4220

University College of San Juan
180 Jose Oliver St., Tres Monijitas Industrial Park, San Juan 00918
Type: Public, state/local, four-year
Degrees: A, B *Enroll:* 867
URL: http://www.cunisanjuan.edu
Phone: (787) 250-7111 *Calendar:* Sem. plan
Inst. Accred.: MSA-CHE (1978/2007)
Prog. Accred.: Nursing

University of Puerto Rico at Aguadilla
PO Box 250160, Aguadilla 00604-0160
Type: Public, state, four-year
System: University of Puerto Rico Central Administration
Degrees: A, B *Enroll:* 2,891
URL: http://www.cuna.upr.edu
Phone: (787) 890-2681 *Calendar:* Sem. plan
Inst. Accred.: MSA-CHE (1976/2001)

University of Puerto Rico at Arecibo
PO Box 4010, Arecibo 00614-4010
Type: Public, state, four-year
System: University of Puerto Rico Central Administration
Degrees: A, B *Enroll:* 3,754
URL: http://www.upra.edu
Phone: (787) 815-0000 *Calendar:* Sem. plan
Inst. Accred.: MSA-CHE (1967/2007)
Prog. Accred.: Nursing

University of Puerto Rico at Bayamon
#170 Call.174 Parque Industria Minillas, Bayamon 00959-1919
Type: Public, state, four-year
System: University of Puerto Rico Central Administration
Degrees: A, B *Enroll:* 4,040
URL: http://www.uprb.edu
Phone: (787) 786-2885 *Calendar:* Sem. plan
Inst. Accred.: MSA-CHE (1960/2001)

University of Puerto Rico at Carolina
PO Box 4800, Carolina 00984-4800
Type: Public, state, four-year
System: University of Puerto Rico Central Administration
Degrees: A, B *Enroll:* 3,182
URL: http://www.upr.clu.edu
Phone: (787) 257-0000 *Calendar:* Qtr. plan
Inst. Accred.: MSA-CHE (1978/2001)

University of Puerto Rico at Cayey
205 Antonio R. Barcelo Ave., Cayey 00736
Type: Public, state, four-year
System: University of Puerto Rico Central Administration
Degrees: A, B *Enroll:* 3,371
URL: http://www.cayey.upr.edu
Phone: (787) 738-2161 *Calendar:* Sem. plan
Inst. Accred.: MSA-CHE (1967/2005)

University of Puerto Rico at Humacao
CUH Station, 100 Rd. 908, Humacao 00791-4300
Type: Public, state, four-year
System: University of Puerto Rico Central Administration
Degrees: A, B *Enroll:* 3,827
URL: http://www.uprh.edu
Phone: (787) 850-0000 *Calendar:* Sem. plan
Inst. Accred.: MSA-CHE (1962/2000)
Prog. Accred.: Allied Health (occupational therapy assisting), Nursing, Physical Therapy Assisting, Social Work

University of Puerto Rico at Mayaguez
PO Box 9000, Mayaguez 00681
Type: Public, state, four-year
System: University of Puerto Rico Central Administration
Degrees: A, B, M, D *Enroll:* 11,612
URL: http://www.uprm.edu
Phone: (787) 832-4040 *Calendar:* Sem. plan
Inst. Accred.: MSA-CHE (1946/2005)
Prog. Accred.: Engineering (chemical, civil, computer, electrical, industrial, mechanical), Nursing

University of Puerto Rico at Ponce
PO Box 7186, Ponce 00732
Type: Public, state, four-year
System: University of Puerto Rico Central Administration
Degrees: A, B *Enroll:* 3,161
URL: http://www.upr-ponce.upr.edu
Phone: (787) 844-8181 *Calendar:* Sem. plan
Inst. Accred.: MSA-CHE (1970/2005)
Prog. Accred.: Physical Therapy Assisting

University of Puerto Rico at Rio Piedras
PO Box 23300, San Juan 00931-3300
Type: Public, state, four-year
System: University of Puerto Rico Central Administration
Degrees: B, M, P, D *Enroll:* 17,929
URL: http://www.rrp.upr.edu
Phone: (787) 764-0000 *Calendar:* Sem. plan
Inst. Accred.: MSA-CHE (1946/2005)
Prog. Accred.: Business (ACBSP), Dentistry (oral and maxillofacial surgery), Graduate Social Work, Law, Librarianship, Planning, Rehabilitation Counseling, Social Work, Teacher Education (NCATE)

University of Puerto Rico at Utuado
PO Box 2500, Utuado 00641
Type: Public, state, four-year
System: University of Puerto Rico Central Administration
Degrees: A, B *Enroll:* 1,363
URL: http://upr-utuado.upr.clu.edu
Phone: (787) 894-2828 *Calendar:* Sem. plan
Inst. Accred.: MSA-CHE (1986/2001)

University of Puerto Rico—Medical Sciences Campus
PO Box 365067, San Juan 00936-5067
Type: Public, state, four-year
System: University of Puerto Rico Central Administration
Degrees: A, B, M, P, D *Enroll:* 2,141
URL: http://www.rcm.upr.edu
Phone: (787) 758-2525 *Calendar:* Sem. plan
Inst. Accred.: MSA-CHE (1949/2001)
Prog. Accred.: Allied Health (cytotechnology, health services administration, medicine, occupational therapy), Clinical Lab Scientist, Dentistry (combined prosthodontics, dental assisting, dental hygiene, dentistry, general practice residency, oral and maxillofacial surgery, orthodontic and dentofacial orthopedics, pediatric dentistry), Dietetics (didactic), Dietetics (internship), Nuclear Medicine Technology, Nurse (Midwifery), Nurse Anesthesia Education, Nursing Education, Pharmacy, Physical Therapy, Public Health, Radiography, Veterinary Technology

University of the Sacred Heart
PO Box 12383, San Juan 00914-0383
Type: Private, Roman Catholic Church, four-year
Degrees: A, B, M *Enroll:* 4,239
URL: http://www.sagrado.edu
Phone: (787) 728-1515 *Calendar:* Sem. plan
Inst. Accred.: MSA-CHE (1950/2008)
Prog. Accred.: Clinical Lab Scientist, Nursing, Social Work

RHODE ISLAND

Brown University
Providence 02912
Type: Private, independent, four-year
Degrees: B, M, P, D *Enroll:* 8,041
URL: http://www.brown.edu
Phone: (401) 863-1000 *Calendar:* Sem. plan
Inst. Accred.: NEASC-CIHE (1929/2008)
Prog. Accred.: Allied Health (medicine), Engineering (bioengineering, chemical, civil, computer, electrical, materials, mechanical), Psychology Internship, Public Health

Bryant University
1150 Douglas Pike, Smithfield 02917-1284
Type: Private, independent, four-year
Degrees: A, B, M *Enroll:* 3,279
URL: http://www.bryant.edu
Phone: (401) 232-6000 *Calendar:* Sem. plan
Inst. Accred.: NEASC-CIHE (1964/2000)
Prog. Accred.: Business (AACSB)

Community College of Rhode Island
400 East Ave., Warwick 02886-1807
Type: Public, state, two-year
System: Rhode Island Board of Governors for Higher Education
Degrees: A *Enroll:* 9,215
URL: http://www.ccri.edu
Phone: (401) 825-1000 *Calendar:* Sem. plan
Inst. Accred.: NEASC-CIHE (1969/2004)
Prog. Accred.: Allied Health (massage therapy, respiratory therapy), Business (ACBSP), Clinical Lab Technology, Dentistry (dental assisting, dental hygiene), Nursing, Physical Therapy Assisting

Flanagan Campus
1762 Louisquisset Pike, Lincoln 02865-4585
Phone: (401) 333-7000
Prog. Accred: Nursing, Radiography

Liston Campus
One Hilton St., Providence 02905-2304
Phone: (401) 455-6000
Prog. Accred: Nursing, Practical Nursing

Newport Campus
One John H. Chafee Blvd., Newport 02840
Phone: (401) 851-1600
Prog. Accred: Allied Health (occupational therapy assisting), Nursing

Gibbs College—Cranston
85 Garfield Ave., Cranston 02920
Type: Private, proprietary, two-year
System: Career Education Corporation
Degrees: A *Enroll:* 546
URL: http://www.gibbsri.edu
Phone: (401) 824-5300 *Calendar:* Sem. plan
Inst. Accred.: ACICS (1967/2005)

Johnson and Wales University
8 Abbott Park Place, Providence 02903-3703
Type: Private, independent, four-year
Degrees: A, B, M, P, D *Enroll:* 9,518
URL: http://www.jwu.edu
Phone: (401) 598-1000 *Calendar:* Qtr. plan
Inst. Accred.: NEASC-CIHE (1993/1998)
Prog. Accred.: Dietetics (didactic)

Charlotte Campus
801 West Trade St., Charlotte, NC 28202-1122
Phone: (980) 598-1000

Denver Campus
7150 Montview Blvd., Denver, CO 80220
Phone: (303) 256-9300
Prog. Accred: Dietetics (didactic)

North Miami Campus
1701 NE 127th St., North Miami, FL 33181
Phone: (305) 892-7000

Naval War College
686 Cushing Rd., Newport 02841-1207
Type: Public, federal, four-year
Degrees: M
URL: http://www.nwc.navy.mil
Phone: (401) 841-3089 *Calendar:* Tri. plan
Inst. Accred.: NEASC-CIHE (1989/2004)

New England Institute of Technology
2500 Post Rd., Warwick 02886-2266
Type: Private, independent, four-year
Degrees: A, B *Enroll:* 2,829
URL: http://www.neit.edu
Phone: (401) 467-7744 *Calendar:* Qtr. plan
Inst. Accred.: NEASC-CIHE (2005)
Prog. Accred.: Allied Health (occupational therapy assisting, surgical technology), Engineering Technology (electrical)

Providence College
549 River Ave., Providence 02918-0001
Type: Private, Roman Catholic Church, four-year
Degrees: B, M, D *Enroll:* 4,593
URL: http://www.providence.edu
Phone: (401) 865-1000 *Calendar:* Sem. plan
Inst. Accred.: NEASC-CIHE (1933/2007)
Prog. Accred.: Social Work

Rhode Island College
600 Mount Pleasant Ave., Providence 02908-1991
Type: Public, state, four-year
System: Rhode Island Board of Governors for Higher Education
Degrees: B, M, D *Enroll:* 6,882
URL: http://www.ric.edu
Phone: (401) 456-8000 *Calendar:* Sem. plan
Inst. Accred.: NEASC-CIHE (1958/2000)
Prog. Accred.: Art, Graduate Social Work, Music, Nursing Education, Social Work, Teacher Education (NCATE)

Rhode Island School of Design
2 College St., Providence 02903
Type: Private, independent, four-year
Degrees: B, M *Enroll:* 2,258
URL: http://www.risd.edu
Phone: (401) 454-6100 *Calendar:* Sem. plan
Inst. Accred.: NEASC-CIHE (1949/2006)
Prog. Accred.: Art, Landscape Architecture

Roger Williams University
One Old Ferry Rd., Bristol 02809-2921
Type: Private, independent, four-year
Degrees: A, B, M, P *Enroll:* 4,130
URL: http://www.rwu.edu
Phone: (401) 253-1040 *Calendar:* Sem. plan
Inst. Accred.: NEASC-CIHE (1972/2007)
Prog. Accred.: Business (AACSB), Construction Education, Engineering (general), Law (ABA only)

Salve Regina University
100 Ochre Point Ave., Newport 02840-4192
Type: Private, Roman Catholic Church, four-year
Degrees: A, B, M, D *Enroll:* 2,235
URL: http://www.salve.edu
Phone: (401) 847-6650 *Calendar:* Sem. plan
Inst. Accred.: NEASC-CIHE (1956/2001)
Prog. Accred.: Art, Nursing, Rehabilitation Counseling, Social Work

University of Rhode Island
75 Lower College Rd., Ste. 7, Kingston 02881-1966
Type: Public, state, four-year
System: Rhode Island Board of Governors for Higher Education
Degrees: A, B, M, P, D *Enroll:* 12,771
URL: http://www.uri.edu
Phone: (401) 874-1000 *Calendar:* Sem. plan
Inst. Accred.: NEASC-CIHE (1930/2007)
Prog. Accred.: Accounting, Allied Health (audiology, cytotechnology, speech-language pathology), Business (AACSB), Clinical Psychology, Dentistry (dental hygiene), Dietetics (didactic), Dietetics (internship), Engineering (chemical, civil, computer, electrical, industrial, manufacturing, mechanical, ocean), Landscape Architecture, Librarianship, Marriage and Family Therapy, Music, Nurse (Midwifery), Nursing Education, Pharmacy, Physical Therapy, School Psychology, Teacher Education (NCATE)

SOUTH CAROLINA

Aiken Technical College
PO Box 400, Graniteville 29829
Type: Public, state, two-year
System: South Carolina State Board for Technical and Comprehensive Education
Degrees: A *Enroll:* 1,611
URL: http://www.atc.edu
Phone: (803) 593-9954 *Calendar:* Sem. plan
Inst. Accred.: SACS (1975/2001)
Prog. Accred.: Allied Health (medical assisting (AMA), surgical technology), Business (ACBSP), Dentistry (dental assisting), Engineering Technology (electrical), Nursing, Radiography

Allen University
1530 Harden St., Columbia 29204
Type: Private, African Methodist Episcopal Church, four-year
Degrees: B *Enroll:* 610
URL: http://www.allenuniversity.edu
Phone: (803) 376-5700 *Calendar:* Sem. plan
Inst. Accred.: SACS (1992/2007)

Anderson University
316 Blvd., Anderson 29621
Type: Private, Southern Baptist Convention, four-year
Degrees: A, B, M *Enroll:* 1,422
URL: http://www.anderson-college.edu
Phone: (864) 231-2000 *Calendar:* Sem. plan
Inst. Accred.: SACS (1959/1998)
Prog. Accred.: Business (ACBSP), Music, Teacher Education (NCATE)

Benedict College
1600 Harden St., Columbia 29204
Type: Private, independent, four-year
Degrees: B *Enroll:* 2,514
URL: http://bchome.benedict.edu
Phone: (803) 256-4220 *Calendar:* Sem. plan
Inst. Accred.: SACS (1946/2001)
Prog. Accred.: Business (ACBSP), Recreation and Leisure Services, Social Work, Teacher Education (NCATE)

Bob Jones University
1700 Wade Hampton Blvd., Greenville 29614
Type: Private, independent, four-year
Degrees: A, B, M, D
URL: http://www.bju.edu
Phone: (864) 242-5100 *Calendar:* Sem. plan
Inst. Accred.: TRACS (2006)

Central Carolina Technical College
506 North Guignard Dr., Sumter 29150-2499
Type: Public, state, two-year
System: South Carolina State Board for Technical and Comprehensive Education
Degrees: A *Enroll:* 1,717
URL: http://www.cctech.edu
Phone: (803) 778-1961 *Calendar:* Sem. plan
Inst. Accred.: SACS (1970/2006)
Prog. Accred.: Allied Health (medical assisting (AMA), surgical technology), Business (ACBSP), Engineering Technology (civil/construction), Nursing, Practical Nursing

Charleston Southern University
PO Box 118087, 9200 University Blvd., Charleston 29423-8087
Type: Private, South Carolina Baptist Convention, four-year
Degrees: A, B, M *Enroll:* 2,546
URL: http://www.csuniv.edu
Phone: (843) 863-7000 *Calendar:* 4-1-4 plan
Inst. Accred.: SACS (1970/2006)
Prog. Accred.: Music, Nursing, Teacher Education (NCATE)

The Citadel
171 Moultrie St., Charleston 29409
Type: Public, state, four-year
Degrees: B, M, P *Enroll:* 2,687
URL: http://www.citadel.edu
Phone: (843) 953-5000 *Calendar:* Sem. plan
Inst. Accred.: SACS (1924/2004)
Prog. Accred.: Business (AACSB), Counseling, Engineering (civil, electrical), Teacher Education (NCATE)

Claflin University
400 Magnolia St., Orangeburg 29115
Type: Private, United Methodist Church, four-year
Degrees: B, M *Enroll:* 1,671
URL: http://www.claflin.edu
Phone: (803) 535-5000 *Calendar:* Sem. plan
Inst. Accred.: SACS (1947/2001)
Prog. Accred.: Business (ACBSP), Teacher Education (NCATE)

Clemson University
Clemson 29634
Type: Public, state, four-year
Degrees: B, M, P, D *Enroll:* 16,022
URL: http://www.clemson.edu
Phone: (864) 656-3311 *Calendar:* Sem. plan
Inst. Accred.: SACS (1927/2002)
Prog. Accred.: Accounting, Applied Science (health physics), Art, Business (AACSB), Computer Science (ABET-CAC), Construction Education, Counseling, Dietetics (didactic), Engineering (agricultural, ceramic, chemical, civil, computer, electrical, industrial, mechanical), Forestry, Landscape Architecture, Nursing Education, Planning, Psychology Internship, Recreation and Leisure Services, Teacher Education (NCATE)

Clinton Junior College
1029 Crawford Rd., Rock Hill 29730-5153
Type: Private, African Methodist Episcopal Zion Church, two-year
Degrees: A *Enroll:* 121
URL: http://www.clintonjuniorcollege.edu
Phone: (803) 327-7402 *Calendar:* Sem. plan
Inst. Accred.: TRACS (2000)

Coastal Carolina University
PO Box 261954, Conway 29528-6054
Type: Public, state, four-year
Degrees: A, B, M *Enroll:* 6,520
URL: http://www.coastal.edu
Phone: (843) 347-3161 *Calendar:* Sem. plan
Inst. Accred.: SACS (1976/2001)
Prog. Accred.: Art, Business (AACSB), Computer Science (ABET-CAC), Teacher Education (NCATE)

Coker College
300 East College Ave., Hartsville 29550
Type: Private, independent, four-year
Degrees: B *Enroll:* 990
URL: http://www.coker.edu
Phone: (843) 383-8000 *Calendar:* Sem. plan
Inst. Accred.: SACS (1923/2005)
Prog. Accred.: Music, Social Work

College of Charleston
66 George St., Charleston 29424
Type: Public, state, four-year
Degrees: B, M *Enroll:* 10,104
URL: http://www.cofc.edu
Phone: (843) 953-5507 *Calendar:* Sem. plan
Inst. Accred.: SACS (1916/2007)
Prog. Accred.: Accounting, Business (AACSB), Computer Science (ABET-CAC), Music, Public Administration, Teacher Education (NCATE)

Columbia College
1301 Columbia College Dr., Columbia 29203
Type: Private, United Methodist Church, four-year
Degrees: B, M *Enroll:* 1,321
URL: http://www.colacoll.edu
Phone: (803) 786-3012 *Calendar:* Sem. plan
Inst. Accred.: SACS (1938/2001)
Prog. Accred.: Art, Dance, Music, Teacher Education (NCATE)

Columbia International University
PO Box 3122, Columbia 29230-3122
Type: Private, interdenominational, four-year
Degrees: A, B, M, D *Enroll:* 864
URL: http://www.ciu.edu
Phone: (803) 754-4100 *Calendar:* Sem. plan
Inst. Accred.: ABHE (1948/2004), ATS (1985/2008), SACS (1982/1998 Warning)

Converse College
580 East Main St., Spartanburg 29302-0006
Type: Private, independent, four-year
Degrees: B, M, P *Enroll:* 1,336
URL: http://www.converse.edu
Phone: (864) 596-9000 *Calendar:* Sem. plan
Inst. Accred.: SACS (1912/2007)
Prog. Accred.: Marriage and Family Therapy, Music, Teacher Education (NCATE)

Denmark Technical College
PO Box 327, Denmark 29042-0327
Type: Public, state, two-year
System: South Carolina State Board for Technical and Comprehensive Education
Degrees: A *Enroll:* 1,116
URL: http://www.denmarktech.edu
Phone: (803) 793-5100 *Calendar:* Sem. plan
Inst. Accred.: SACS (1979/2005)
Prog. Accred.: Business (ACBSP), Cosmetology, Engineering Technology (electromechanical)

Erskine College
PO Box 338, Due West 29639-0338
Type: Private, Associate Reformed Presbyterian Church, four-year
Degrees: A, B, M, D *Enroll:* 795
URL: http://www.erskine.edu
Phone: (864) 379-2131 *Calendar:* 4-1-4 plan
Inst. Accred.: ATS (1981/2001), SACS (1925/2002)
Prog. Accred.: Teacher Education (NCATE)

Florence-Darlington Technical College
PO Box 100548, Florence 29501-0548
Type: Public, state, two-year
System: South Carolina State Board for Technical and Comprehensive Education
Degrees: A *Enroll:* 2,948
URL: http://www.fdtc.edu
Phone: (843) 661-8324 *Calendar:* Sem. plan
Inst. Accred.: SACS (1970/2006)
Prog. Accred.: Allied Health (respiratory therapy, surgical technology), Business (ACBSP), Clinical Lab Technology, Cosmetology, Dentistry (dental assisting, dental hygiene), Engineering Technology (civil/construction, electrical, general drafting/design), Nursing, Radiography

Forrest Junior College
601 East River St., Anderson 29624
Type: Private, proprietary, two-year
Degrees: A *Enroll:* 126
URL: http://www.forrestcollege.com
Phone: (864) 225-7653 *Calendar:* Qtr. plan
Inst. Accred.: ACICS (1972/2004)
Prog. Accred.: Allied Health (medical assisting (AMA))

Francis Marion University
PO Box 100547, Florence 29501-0547
Type: Public, state, four-year
Degrees: A, B, M *Enroll:* 3,449
URL: http://www.fmarion.edu
Phone: (843) 661-1362 *Calendar:* Sem. plan
Inst. Accred.: SACS (1972/2008)
Prog. Accred.: Art, Business (AACSB), Nursing, Teacher Education (NCATE), Theatre

Furman University
3300 Poinsett Hwy., Greenville 29613
Type: Private, independent, four-year
Degrees: B, M *Enroll:* 2,931
URL: http://www.furman.edu
Phone: (864) 294-2000 *Calendar:* 3-3 plan
Inst. Accred.: SACS (1924/2008)
Prog. Accred.: Music, Teacher Education (NCATE)

Greenville Technical College
PO Box 5616, Greenville 29606-5616
Type: Public, state, two-year
System: South Carolina State Board for Technical and Comprehensive Education
Degrees: A *Enroll:* 8,033
URL: http://www.greenvilletech.com
Phone: (864) 250-8000 *Calendar:* Sem. plan
Inst. Accred.: SACS (1968/2002)
Prog. Accred.: Allied Health (EMT-paramedic, diagnostic medical sonography, medical assisting (AMA), occupational therapy assisting, respiratory therapy, surgical technology), Business (ACBSP), Clinical Lab Technology, Culinary Education, Dentistry (dental assisting, dental hygiene), Engineering Technology (architectural, civil/construction, electrical, general drafting/design, mechanical, surveying), Nursing, Physical Therapy Assisting, Practical Nursing, Radiography

Horry-Georgetown Technical College
PO Box 261966, Conway 29528
Type: Public, state/local, two-year
System: South Carolina State Board for Technical and Comprehensive Education
Degrees: A *Enroll:* 3,425
URL: http://www.hgtc.edu
Phone: (843) 347-3186 *Calendar:* Sem. plan
Inst. Accred.: SACS (1972/1998)
Prog. Accred.: Allied Health (surgical technology), Business (ACBSP), Culinary Education, Dentistry (dental assisting, dental hygiene), Engineering Technology (civil/construction, electrical), Forestry, Nursing, Practical Nursing, Radiography

Lander University
320 Stanley Ave., Greenwood 29649-2099
Type: Public, state, four-year
Degrees: B, M *Enroll:* 2,441
URL: http://www.lander.edu
Phone: (864) 388-8000 *Calendar:* Sem. plan
Inst. Accred.: SACS (1952/2007)
Prog. Accred.: Art, Business (AACSB), Montessori Teacher Education, Music, Nursing, Teacher Education (NCATE), Theatre

Limestone College
1115 College Dr., Gaffney 29340-3799
Type: Private, independent, four-year
Degrees: B *Enroll:* 2,502
URL: http://www.limestone.edu
Phone: (864) 489-7151 *Calendar:* Sem. plan
Inst. Accred.: SACS (1928/1999)
Prog. Accred.: Music, Social Work

Lutheran Theological Southern Seminary
4201 North Main St., Columbia 29203
Type: Private, Evangelical Lutheran Church in America, four-year
Degrees: M, D *Enroll:* 157
URL: http://www.ltss.edu
Phone: (803) 786-5150 *Calendar:* Sem. plan
Inst. Accred.: ATS (1944/2003), SACS (1983/2003)

Medical University of South Carolina
171 Ashley Ave., Charleston 29425
Type: Public, state, four-year
Degrees: B, M, P, D *Enroll:* 2,315
URL: http://www.musc.edu
Phone: (843) 792-2300 *Calendar:* Sem. plan
Inst. Accred.: SACS (1971/2007)
Prog. Accred.: Allied Health (cytotechnology, health services administration, medicine, occupational therapy, perfusion, speech-language pathology), Dentistry (advanced education in general dentistry, dental public health, dentistry, general dentistry, oral and maxillofacial surgery, orthodontic and dentofacial orthopedics, pediatric dentistry, periodontics), Dietetics (internship), Nurse (Midwifery), Nurse Anesthesia Education, Nursing Education, Pharmacy, Physical Therapy, Physician Assistant, Psychology Internship

Midlands Technical College
PO Box 2408, Columbia 29202
Type: Public, state, two-year
System: South Carolina State Board for Technical and Comprehensive Education
Degrees: A *Enroll:* 6,770
URL: http://www.midlandstech.edu
Phone: (803) 738-1400 *Calendar:* Sem. plan
Inst. Accred.: SACS (1974/1999)
Prog. Accred.: Allied Health (medical assisting (AMA), respiratory therapy, surgical technology), Business (ACBSP), Clinical Lab Technology, Dentistry (dental assisting, dental hygiene), Engineering Technology (architectural, civil/construction, electrical), Nuclear Medicine Technology, Nursing, Physical Therapy Assisting, Practical Nursing, Radiography

Morris College
100 West College St., Sumter 29150-3599
Type: Private, Baptist Educational and Missionary Convention of South Carolina, four-year
Degrees: B *Enroll:* 851
URL: http://www.morris.edu
Phone: (803) 934-3200 *Calendar:* Sem. plan
Inst. Accred.: SACS (1978/2002)
Prog. Accred.: Business (ACBSP), Teacher Education (NCATE)

Newberry College
2100 College St., Newberry 29108
Type: Private, Evangelical Lutheran Church of America, four-year
Degrees: B *Enroll:* 829
URL: http://www.newberry.edu
Phone: (803) 276-5010 *Calendar:* Sem. plan
Inst. Accred.: SACS (1936/2002)
Prog. Accred.: Music, Teacher Education (NCATE), Veterinary Technology

North Greenville University
PO Box 1892, Tigerville 29688-1892
Type: Private, Southern Baptist Church, four-year
Degrees: A, B, M *Enroll:* 1,725
URL: http://www.ngu.edu
Phone: (864) 977-7000 *Calendar:* Sem. plan
Inst. Accred.: SACS (1957/1999)
Prog. Accred.: Teacher Education (NCATE)

Northeastern Technical College
1201 Chesterfield Hwy., Cheraw 29520-1007
Type: Public, state/local, two-year
System: South Carolina State Board for Technical and Comprehensive Education
Degrees: A *Enroll:* 702
URL: http://www.netc.edu
Phone: (843) 921-6900 *Calendar:* Sem. plan
Inst. Accred.: SACS (1973/2008)

Orangeburg-Calhoun Technical College
3250 St. Matthews Rd., NE, Orangeburg 29118
Type: Public, state/local, two-year
System: South Carolina State Board for Technical and Comprehensive Education
Degrees: A *Enroll:* 1,699
URL: http://www.octech.edu
Phone: (803) 536-0311 *Calendar:* Sem. plan
Inst. Accred.: SACS (1970/2006)
Prog. Accred.: Allied Health (medical assisting (AMA), respiratory therapy), Business (ACBSP), Clinical Lab Technology, Engineering Technology (electrical), Nursing, Practical Nursing, Radiography

Piedmont Technical College
PO Box 1467, 620 North Emerald Rd., Greenwood 29648-1467
Type: Public, state, two-year
System: South Carolina State Board for Technical and Comprehensive Education
Degrees: A *Enroll:* 2,750
URL: http://www.ptc.edu
Phone: (864) 941-8324 *Calendar:* Sem. plan
Inst. Accred.: SACS (1972/2008)
Prog. Accred.: Allied Health (medical assisting (AMA), respiratory therapy, surgical technology), Business (ACBSP), Engineering Technology (electrical, general drafting/design), Funeral Service Education (Mortuary Science), Nursing, Radiography

Presbyterian College
503 South Broad St., Clinton 29325
Type: Private, Presbyterian Church (USA), four-year
Degrees: B *Enroll:* 1,161
URL: http://www.presby.edu
Phone: (864) 833-2820 *Calendar:* Sem. plan
Inst. Accred.: SACS (1949/2007)
Prog. Accred.: Teacher Education (NCATE)

Sherman College of Straight Chiropractic
PO Box 1452, Spartanburg 29304
Type: Private, independent, four-year
Degrees: P, D *Enroll:* 346
URL: http://www.sherman.edu
Phone: (864) 578-8770 *Calendar:* Qtr. plan
Inst. Accred.: SACS (2002, Probation)
Prog. Accred.: Chiropractic Education

South Carolina State University
300 College Ave., NE, Orangeburg 29117-0001
Type: Public, state, four-year
Degrees: B, M, P, D *Enroll:* 4,038
URL: http://www.scsu.edu
Phone: (803) 536-7000 *Calendar:* Sem. plan
Inst. Accred.: SACS (1941/2000, Warning)
Prog. Accred.: Allied Health (speech-language pathology), Business (AACSB), Computer Science (ABET-CAC), Counseling, Dietetics (didactic), Engineering Technology (civil/construction, electrical, industrial, mechanical), Family & Consumer Science, Music, Nursing Education, Rehabilitation Counseling, Social Work, Teacher Education (NCATE)

Southern Methodist College
PO Box 1027, Orangeburg 29116-1027
Type: Private, Southern Methodist Church, four-year
Degrees: A, B *Enroll:* 50
URL: http://www.southernmethodistcollege.org
Phone: (803) 534-7826 *Calendar:* Sem. plan
Inst. Accred.: TRACS (2002, Warning)

Southern Wesleyan University
PO Box 1020, Central 29630-1020
Type: Private, Wesleyan Church, four-year
Degrees: A, B, M *Enroll:* 2,580
URL: http://www.swu.edu
Phone: (864) 644-5000 *Calendar:* Sem. plan
Inst. Accred.: SACS (1973/1999)
Prog. Accred.: Music

Spartanburg Community College
PO Box 4386, Spartanburg 29305
Type: Public, state, two-year
System: South Carolina State Board for Technical and Comprehensive Education
Degrees: A *Enroll:* 3,098
URL: http://www.sccsc.edu
Phone: (864) 592-4600 *Calendar:* Sem. plan
Inst. Accred.: SACS (1970/2006)
Prog. Accred.: Allied Health (medical assisting (AMA), respiratory therapy, surgical technology), Business (ACBSP), Clinical Lab Technology, Culinary Education, Dentistry (dental hygiene), Engineering Technology (civil/construction, electrical, mechanical), Radiation Therapy, Radiography

Spartanburg Methodist College
1000 Powell Mill Rd., Spartanburg 29301-5899
Type: Private, United Methodist Church, two-year
Degrees: A *Enroll:* 712
URL: http://www.smcsc.edu
Phone: (864) 587-4000 *Calendar:* Sem. plan
Inst. Accred.: SACS (1957/1998)

Technical College of the Lowcountry
PO Box 1288, Beaufort 29901-1288
Type: Public, state, two-year
System: South Carolina State Board for Technical and Comprehensive Education
Degrees: A *Enroll:* 939
URL: http://www.tcl.edu
Phone: (843) 525-8324 *Calendar:* Sem. plan
Inst. Accred.: SACS (1978/2004)
Prog. Accred.: Allied Health (surgical technology), Business (ACBSP), Cosmetology, Nursing, Practical Nursing, Radiography

New River Campus
100 Community College Dr., Bluffton 29909
Phone: (843) 525-6000

Tri-County Technical College
PO Box 587, Pendleton 29670-0587
Type: Public, state, two-year
System: South Carolina State Board for Technical and Comprehensive Education
Degrees: A *Enroll:* 3,202
URL: http://www.tctc.edu
Phone: (864) 646-8361 *Calendar:* Sem. plan
Inst. Accred.: SACS (1971/2007)
Prog. Accred.: Allied Health (medical assisting (AMA), respiratory therapy, surgical technology), Business (ACBSP), Clinical Lab Technology, Dentistry (dental assisting), Engineering Technology (electrical, general, instrumentation), Nursing, Practical Nursing, Veterinary Technology

Trident Technical College
PO Box 118067, Charleston 29423-8067
Type: Public, state, two-year
System: South Carolina State Board for Technical and Comprehensive Education
Degrees: A *Enroll:* 7,152
URL: http://www.tridenttech.edu
Phone: (843) 574-6111 *Calendar:* Sem. plan
Inst. Accred.: SACS (1974/2000)
Prog. Accred.: Allied Health (EMT-paramedic, medical assisting (AMA), occupational therapy assisting, respiratory therapy), Business (ACBSP), Clinical Lab Technology, Cosmetology, Culinary Education, Dentistry (dental assisting, dental hygiene), Engineering Technology (civil/construction, electrical, mechanical), Nursing, Physical Therapy Assisting, Practical Nursing, Radiography, Veterinary Technology

University of South Carolina—Aiken
471 University Pkwy., Aiken 29801
Type: Public, state, four-year
System: University of South Carolina Central Office
Degrees: A, B, M *Enroll:* 2,697
URL: http://www.usca.edu
Phone: (803) 648-6851 *Calendar:* Sem. plan
Inst. Accred.: SACS (1977/2001)
Prog. Accred.: Business (AACSB), Nursing, Teacher Education (NCATE)

University of South Carolina—Beaufort
801 Carteret St., Beaufort 29902
Type: Public, state, four-year
System: University of South Carolina Central Office
Degrees: A, B *Enroll:* 935
URL: http://www.sc.edu/beaufort
Phone: (843) 521-4100 *Calendar:* Sem. plan
Inst. Accred.: SACS (2004)

University of South Carolina—Columbia
Columbia 29208
Type: Public, state, four-year
System: University of South Carolina Central Office
Degrees: A, B, M, P, D *Enroll:* 23,422
URL: http://www.sc.edu
Phone: (803) 777-7000 *Calendar:* Sem. plan
Inst. Accred.: SACS (1917/2001)
Prog. Accred.: Accounting, Allied Health (health services administration, medicine, speech-language pathology), Applied Science (industrial hygiene), Art, Business (AACSB), Clinical Psychology, Computer Science (ABET-CAC), Counseling, Engineering (chemical, civil, computer, electrical, information systems, mechanical), English Language Education, Graduate Social Work, Journalism, Law, Librarianship, Music, Nurse Anesthesia Education, Nursing Education, Pharmacy, Physical Therapy, Psychology Internship, Public Administration, Public Health, Rehabilitation Counseling, School Psychology, Teacher Education (NCATE), Theatre

Lancaster Campus
PO Box 889, Lancaster 29721-0889
Phone: (803) 313-7000
Prog. Accred: Business (ACBSP)

Salkehatchie Campus
PO Box 617, Allendale 29810-0617
Phone: (803) 584-3446

Sumter Campus
200 Miller Rd., Sumter 29150-2498
Phone: (803) 775-8727

Union Campus
PO Drawer 729, Union 29379-0729
Phone: (864) 429-8728

University of South Carolina—Upstate
800 University Way, Spartanburg 29303
Type: Public, state, four-year
System: University of South Carolina Central Office
Degrees: A, B, M *Enroll:* 3,935
URL: http://www.uscs.edu
Phone: (864) 503-5000 *Calendar:* Sem. plan
Inst. Accred.: SACS (1976/2001)
Prog. Accred.: Business (AACSB), Computer Science (ABET-CAC), Nursing Education, Teacher Education (NCATE)

Voorhees College
PO Box 678, Denmark 29042
Type: Private, Protestant Epispocal Church, four-year
Degrees: A, B *Enroll:* 697
URL: http://www.voorhees.edu
Phone: (803) 793-3351 *Calendar:* Sem. plan
Inst. Accred.: SACS (1946/2003)
Prog. Accred.: Business (ACBSP)

W.L. Bonner College
4430 Argent Ct., Columbia 29203
Type: Private, independent, four-year
Degrees: A, B
URL: http://www.wlbonnercollege.org
Phone: (803) 754-3950 *Calendar:* Sem. plan
Inst. Accred.: ABHE (2008)

Williamsburg Technical College
601 Martin Luther King, Jr. Ave., Kingstree 29556-4192
Type: Public, state, two-year
System: South Carolina State Board for Technical and Comprehensive Education
Degrees: A *Enroll:* 359
URL: http://www.williamsburgtech.com
Phone: (843) 354-2021 *Calendar:* Sem. plan
Inst. Accred.: SACS (1977/2002)
Prog. Accred.: Business (ACBSP)

Winthrop University
701 Oakland Ave., Rock Hill 29733
Type: Public, state, four-year
Degrees: B, M, P *Enroll:* 5,506
URL: http://www.winthrop.edu
Phone: (803) 323-2211 *Calendar:* Sem. plan
Inst. Accred.: SACS (1923/2001)
Prog. Accred.: Art, Business (AACSB), Computer Science (ABET-CAC), Counseling, Dance, Dietetics (didactic), Dietetics (internship), Graduate Social Work, Interior Design, Journalism, Music, Social Work, Teacher Education (NCATE), Theatre

Wofford College
429 North Church St., Spartanburg 29303-3663
Type: Private, United Methodist Church, four-year
Degrees: B *Enroll:* 1,187
URL: http://www.wofford.edu
Phone: (864) 597-4000 *Calendar:* 4-1-4 plan
Inst. Accred.: SACS (1917/2007)

York Technical College
452 South Anderson Rd., Rock Hill 29730
Type: Public, state, two-year
System: South Carolina State Board for Technical and Comprehensive Education
Degrees: A *Enroll:* 2,749
URL: http://www.yorktech.edu
Phone: (803) 327-8000 *Calendar:* Sem. plan
Inst. Accred.: SACS (1970/2006)
Prog. Accred.: Allied Health (surgical technology), Business (ACBSP), Clinical Lab Technology, Dentistry (dental assisting, dental hygiene), Engineering Technology (computer, electrical, general drafting/design, mechanical), Nursing, Radiography

SOUTH DAKOTA

Augustana College
2001 South Summit Ave., Sioux Falls 57197
Type: Private, Evangelical Lutheran Church in America, four-year
Degrees: B, M *Enroll:* 1,669
URL: http://www.augie.edu
Phone: (605) 274-0770 *Calendar:* 4-1-4 plan
Inst. Accred.: NCA-HLC (1931/2002)
Prog. Accred.: Music, Nursing Education, Teacher Education (NCATE)

Black Hills State University
1200 University Ave., Spearfish 57799-9500
Type: Public, state, four-year
System: South Dakota Board of Regents
Degrees: A, B, M *Enroll:* 3,101
URL: http://www.bhsu.edu
Phone: (605) 642-6011 *Calendar:* Sem. plan
Inst. Accred.: NCA-HLC (1928/2003)
Prog. Accred.: Music, Teacher Education (NCATE)

Dakota State University
820 North Washington Ave., Madison 57042-1799
Type: Public, state, four-year
System: South Dakota Board of Regents
Degrees: A, B, M, D *Enroll:* 1,636
URL: http://www.dsu.edu
Phone: (605) 256-5111 *Calendar:* Sem. plan
Inst. Accred.: NCA-HLC (1920/2001)
Prog. Accred.: Allied Health (respiratory therapy), Business (ACBSP), Teacher Education (NCATE)

Dakota Wesleyan University
1200 West University Ave., Mitchell 57301
Type: Private, United Methodist Church, four-year
Degrees: A, B *Enroll:* 803
URL: http://www.dwu.edu
Phone: (605) 995-2600 *Calendar:* Sem. plan
Inst. Accred.: NCA-HLC (1916/2007)
Prog. Accred.: Nursing

Kilian Community College
300 East 6th St., Sioux Falls 57103-7020
Type: Private, independent, two-year
Degrees: A *Enroll:* 279
URL: http://www.kilian.edu
Phone: (605) 221-3100 *Calendar:* Sem. plan
Inst. Accred.: NCA-HLC (1986/2001)

Lake Area Technical Institute
PO Box 730, Watertown 57201-0730
Type: Public, state/local, two-year
Degrees: A *Enroll:* 1,009
URL: http://www.lakeareatech.edu
Phone: (605) 882-5284 *Calendar:* Sem. plan
Inst. Accred.: NCA-HLC (1980/2007)
Prog. Accred.: Allied Health (medical assisting (AMA), occupational therapy assisting), Clinical Lab Technology, Dentistry (dental assisting), Physical Therapy Assisting, Practical Nursing

Mitchell Technical Institute
821 North Capital St., Mitchell 57301
Type: Public, state/local, two-year
Degrees: A *Enroll:* 706
URL: http://mti.tec.sd.us
Phone: (605) 995-3024 *Calendar:* Sem. plan
Inst. Accred.: NCA-HLC (1980/2001)
Prog. Accred.: Allied Health (medical assisting (AMA)), Clinical Lab Technology, Radiography

Mount Marty College
1105 West Eighth St., Yankton 57078
Type: Private, Roman Catholic Church, four-year
Degrees: A, B, M *Enroll:* 933
URL: http://www.mtmc.edu
Phone: (605) 668-1514 *Calendar:* Sem. plan
Inst. Accred.: NCA-HLC (1961/2003)
Prog. Accred.: Nurse Anesthesia Education, Nursing Education

National American University
321 Kansas City St., Rapid City 57701
Type: Private, proprietary, four-year
Degrees: A, B, M *Enroll:* 995
URL: http://www.national.edu
Phone: (605) 394-4800 *Calendar:* Qtr. plan
Inst. Accred.: NCA-HLC (1985/2008)
Prog. Accred.: Nursing, Veterinary Technology

Albuquerque Campus
1202 Pennsylvania Ave., NW, Albuquerque, NM 87110
Phone: (505) 348-3700

Bloomington Campus
7801 Metro Pkwy., Bloomington, MN 55425
Phone: (952) 356-3600

Brooklyn Center Campus
6120 Earle Brown Dr., Ste. 100, Brooklyn Center, MN 55430
Phone: (763) 852-7500

Colorado Springs Campus
5125 North Academy Blvd., Colorado Springs, CO 80918
Phone: (719) 590-8300
Prog. Accred: Allied Health (medical assisting (AMA))

Denver Campus
1325 South Colorado Blvd., #100, Denver, CO 80222
Phone: (303) 876-7100
Prog. Accred: Allied Health (medical assisting (AMA))

Ellsworth AFB Extension Campus
1000 Ellsworth St., Ste. 2400B, Ellsworth AFB 57706
Phone: (605) 718-6550

Independence Campus
3620 Arrowhead Ave., Independence, MO 64057
Phone: (816) 412-7700

National American University *(continued)*

Overland Park Campus
10310 Mastin St., Overland Park, KS 66212-5451
Phone: (913) 981-8700

Roseville Campus
1500 West Hwy. 36, Roseville, MN 55113-4035
Phone: (651) 855-6300

Sioux Falls Campus
2801 South Kiwanis Ave., Ste. 100, Sioux Falls 57105
Phone: (605) 336-4600
Prog. Accred: Allied Health (medical assisting (AMA))

Zona Rosa Campus
7490 NW 87th St., Kansas City, MO 64153
Phone: (816) 412-5500

Northern State University
1200 South Jay St., Aberdeen 57401
Type: Public, state, four-year
System: South Dakota Board of Regents
Degrees: A, B, M *Enroll:* 2,019
URL: http://www.northern.edu
Phone: (605) 626-3000 *Calendar:* Sem. plan
Inst. Accred.: NCA-HLC (1918/2007)
Prog. Accred.: Music, Teacher Education (NCATE)

Oglala Lakota College
PO Box 490, Piya Wiconi Rd., Kyle 57752
Type: Public, tribal, four-year
System: American Indian Higher Education Consortium
Degrees: A, B, M *Enroll:* 950
URL: http://www.olc.edu
Phone: (605) 455-2321 *Calendar:* Sem. plan
Inst. Accred.: NCA-HLC (1983/2003)
Prog. Accred.: Social Work

Presentation College
1500 North Main St., Aberdeen 57401
Type: Private, Roman Catholic Church, four-year
Degrees: A, B *Enroll:* 608
URL: http://www.presentation.edu
Phone: (605) 225-1634 *Calendar:* Sem. plan
Inst. Accred.: NCA-HLC (1971/2006)
Prog. Accred.: Allied Health (medical assisting (AMA), surgical technology), Clinical Lab Technology, Nursing, Radiography, Social Work

Fairmont Campus
714 Victoria St., Fairmont, MN 56031
Phone: (507) 235-4658

Lakota Campus
PO Box 1070, Eagle Butte 57625
Phone: (605) 964-4071
Prog. Accred: Nursing

Sinte Gleska University
PO Box 105, 150 East Second St., Mission 57555-0105
Type: Public, Rosebud Sioux Tribe, four-year
System: American Indian Higher Education Consortium
Degrees: A, B, M *Enroll:* 731
URL: http://sinte.indian.com
Phone: (605) 747-2263 *Calendar:* Sem. plan
Inst. Accred.: NCA-HLC (1983/2003)

Sioux Falls Seminary
1525 South Grange Ave., Sioux Falls 57105-1599
Type: Private, North America Baptist Conference, four-year
Degrees: M, D *Enroll:* 82
URL: http://sfseminary.edu
Phone: (605) 336-6588 *Calendar:* 4-1-4 plan
Inst. Accred.: ATS (1968/2004), NCA-HLC (1979/2004)

Sisseton Wahpeton College
Agency Village Box 689, Sisseton 57262
Type: Public, Sisseton Wahpeton Sioux Tribe, two-year
System: American Indian Higher Education Consortium
Degrees: A *Enroll:* 214
URL: http://www.swc.tc
Phone: (605) 698-3966 *Calendar:* Sem. plan
Inst. Accred.: NCA-HLC (1990/1999)

South Dakota School of Mines and Technology
501 East St. Joseph St., Rapid City 57701-3995
Type: Public, state, four-year
System: South Dakota Board of Regents
Degrees: A, B, M, D *Enroll:* 1,964
URL: http://www.sdsmt.edu
Phone: (605) 394-2400 *Calendar:* Sem. plan
Inst. Accred.: NCA-HLC (1925/2006)
Prog. Accred.: Computer Science (ABET-CAC), Engineering (chemical, civil, computer, electrical, geological/geophysical, industrial, mechanical, metallurgical)

South Dakota State University
Box 2201, Brookings 57007
Type: Public, state, four-year
System: South Dakota Board of Regents
Degrees: A, B, M, P, D *Enroll:* 9,196
URL: http://www.sdstate.edu
Phone: (605) 688-4151 *Calendar:* Sem. plan
Inst. Accred.: NCA-HLC (1916/2001)
Prog. Accred.: Construction Education, Counseling, Dietetics (didactic), Engineering (agricultural, civil, electrical, mechanical), Family & Consumer Science, Interior Design, Journalism, Music, Nursing Education, Pharmacy, Teacher Education (NCATE)

Southeast Technical Institute
2320 North Career Ave., Sioux Falls 57107
Type: Public, state/local, two-year
Degrees: A *Enroll:* 2,046
URL: http://www.southeasttech.com
Phone: (605) 367-7624 *Calendar:* Sem. plan
Inst. Accred.: NCA-HLC (1981/2004)
Prog. Accred.: Allied Health (cardiovascular technology, diagnostic medical sonography, surgical technology), Nuclear Medicine Technology

University of Sioux Falls
1101 West 22nd St., Sioux Falls 57105-1699
Type: Private, American Baptist Churches in the USA, four-year
Degrees: A, B, M *Enroll:* 1,250
URL: http://www.usiouxfalls.edu
Phone: (605) 331-5000 *Calendar:* 4-1-4 plan
Inst. Accred.: NCA-HLC (1931/2002)
Prog. Accred.: Social Work, Teacher Education (NCATE)

The University of South Dakota
414 East Clark St., Vermillion 57069-2390
Type: Public, state, four-year
System: South Dakota Board of Regents
Degrees: A, B, M, P, D *Enroll:* 6,675
URL: http://www.usd.edu
Phone: (605) 677-5276 *Calendar:* Sem. plan
Inst. Accred.: NCA-HLC (1913/2001)
Prog. Accred.: Allied Health (audiology, medicine, occupational therapy, speech-language pathology), Art, Business (AACSB), Clinical Psychology, Counseling, Dentistry (dental hygiene), Dietetics (internship), Journalism, Law, Music, Nursing, Physical Therapy, Physician Assistant, Public Administration, Social Work, Teacher Education (NCATE), Theatre

Western Dakota Technical Institute
800 Mickelson Dr., Rapid City 57701-4178
Type: Public, local, two-year
Degrees: A *Enroll:* 898
URL: http://www.westerndakotatech.org
Phone: (605) 394-4034 *Calendar:* Sem. plan
Inst. Accred.: NCA-HLC (1983/2008)
Prog. Accred.: Allied Health (surgical technology), Phlebotomy

TENNESSEE

American Baptist College
1800 Baptist World Center Dr., Nashville 37207-4994
Type: Private, National Baptist/Southern Baptist Conventions, four-year
Degrees: A, B *Enroll:* 83
URL: http://www.abcnash.edu
Phone: (615) 256-1463 *Calendar:* Sem. plan
Inst. Accred.: ABHE (1971/2003)

Aquinas College
4210 Harding Rd., Nashville 37205
Type: Private, Roman Catholic Church, four-year
Degrees: A, B *Enroll:* 565
URL: http://www.aquinascollege.edu
Phone: (615) 297-7545 *Calendar:* Sem. plan
Inst. Accred.: SACS (1971/2001)
Prog. Accred.: Nursing

Austin Peay State University
PO Box 4505, Clarksville 37044
Type: Public, state, four-year
System: Tennessee Board of Regents
Degrees: A, B, M, P *Enroll:* 7,449
URL: http://www.apsu.edu
Phone: (931) 221-7011 *Calendar:* Sem. plan
Inst. Accred.: SACS (1947/2004)
Prog. Accred.: Art, Clinical Lab Scientist, Music, Nursing, Social Work, Teacher Education (NCATE)

Baptist Memorial College of Health Sciences
1003 Monroe Ave., Memphis 38104
Type: Private, independent, four-year
Degrees: A, B *Enroll:* 672
URL: http://www.bchs.edu
Phone: (901) 572-2468 *Calendar:* Sem. plan
Inst. Accred.: SACS (1999/2005)
Prog. Accred.: Allied Health (diagnostic medical sonography, respiratory therapy), Nuclear Medicine Technology, Nursing Education, Radiation Therapy, Radiography

Belmont University
1900 Belmont Blvd., Nashville 37212-3757
Type: Private, independent, four-year
Degrees: A, B, M, D *Enroll:* 3,864
URL: http://www.belmont.edu
Phone: (615) 460-6000 *Calendar:* Sem. plan
Inst. Accred.: SACS (1959/2000)
Prog. Accred.: Accounting, Allied Health (occupational therapy), Business (AACSB), Music, Nursing Education, Physical Therapy, Social Work, Teacher Education (NCATE)

Bethel College
325 Cherry Ave., McKenzie 38201-1769
Type: Private, West Tennessee Synod, four-year
Degrees: B, M *Enroll:* 1,178
URL: http://www.bethel-college.edu
Phone: (731) 352-4000 *Calendar:* Sem. plan
Inst. Accred.: SACS (1952/2000)
Prog. Accred.: Physician Assistant

Bryan College
PO Box 7000, Dayton 37321
Type: Private, independent, four-year
Degrees: A, B, M *Enroll:* 746
URL: http://www.bryan.edu
Phone: (423) 775-2041 *Calendar:* Sem. plan
Inst. Accred.: SACS (1969/2004)

Carson-Newman College
PO Box 557, Jefferson City 37760
Type: Private, Southern Baptist Church, four-year
Degrees: B, M *Enroll:* 1,903
URL: http://www.cn.edu
Phone: (865) 471-2000 *Calendar:* Sem. plan
Inst. Accred.: SACS (1927/2003)
Prog. Accred.: Art, Dietetics (didactic), Family & Consumer Science, Music, Nursing Education, Teacher Education (NCATE)

Chattanooga College
3805 Brainerd Rd., Chattanooga 37411-3798
Type: Private, proprietary, two-year
Degrees: A *Enroll:* 160
URL: http://www.ecpconline.com
Phone: (423) 624-0077 *Calendar:* Qtr. plan
Inst. Accred.: ACCSCT (1982/2004)

Chattanooga State Technical Community College
4501 Amnicola Hwy., Chattanooga 37406
Type: Public, state, two-year
System: Tennessee Board of Regents
Degrees: A *Enroll:* 4,978
URL: http://www.chattanoogastate.edu
Phone: (423) 697-4400 *Calendar:* Sem. plan
Inst. Accred.: SACS (1967/2001)
Prog. Accred.: Allied Health (EMT-paramedic, diagnostic medical sonography, medical assisting (AMA), respiratory therapy, surgical technology), Business (ACBSP), Dentistry (dental assisting, dental hygiene), Engineering Technology (automated systems, civil/construction, computer, manufacturing, mechanical), Nuclear Medicine Technology, Nursing, Physical Therapy Assisting, Radiation Therapy, Radiography, Veterinary Technology

Christian Brothers University
650 East Pkwy. South, Memphis 38104
Type: Private, Roman Catholic Church, four-year
Degrees: A, B, M *Enroll:* 1,435
URL: http://www.cbu.edu
Phone: (901) 321-3000 *Calendar:* Sem. plan
Inst. Accred.: SACS (1958/2000)
Prog. Accred.: Engineering (chemical, civil, electrical, mechanical)

The Church of God Theological Seminary
PO Box 3330, Cleveland 37320-3330
Type: Private, Church of God, four-year
Degrees: M, D *Enroll:* 196
URL: http://www.cogts.edu
Phone: (423) 478-1131 *Calendar:* 4-1-4 plan
Inst. Accred.: ATS (1989/1999), SACS (1984/1999)

Cleveland State Community College
PO Box 3570, Cleveland 37312-3570
Type: Public, state, two-year
System: Tennessee Board of Regents
Degrees: A *Enroll:* 2,070
URL: http://www.clevelandstatecc.edu
Phone: (423) 472-7141 *Calendar:* Sem. plan
Inst. Accred.: SACS (1969/2004)
Prog. Accred.: Allied Health (medical assisting (AMA)), Industrial Technology, Nursing

Columbia State Community College
PO Box 1315, Columbia 38402-1315
Type: Public, state, two-year
System: Tennessee Board of Regents
Degrees: A *Enroll:* 3,156
URL: http://www.columbiastate.edu
Phone: (931) 540-2722 *Calendar:* Sem. plan
Inst. Accred.: SACS (1968/2003)
Prog. Accred.: Allied Health (EMT-paramedic, respiratory therapy), Business (ACBSP), Nursing, Radiography, Veterinary Technology

Concorde Career College
5100 Poplar Ave., Ste. 132, Memphis 38137
Type: Private, proprietary, two-year
System: Concorde Career Colleges, Inc.
Degrees: A
URL: http://www.concordecareercolleges.com
Phone: (901) 761-9494
Inst. Accred.: COE (1980/2006)
Prog. Accred.: Allied Health (medical assisting (AMA), respiratory therapy, surgical technology), Dentistry (dental assisting, dental hygiene)

Crichton College
255 North Highland St., Memphis 38111-4745
Type: Private, independent, four-year
Degrees: B *Enroll:* 678
URL: http://www.crichton.edu
Phone: (901) 320-9700 *Calendar:* Sem. plan
Inst. Accred.: SACS (1986/2004)

Cumberland University
One Cumberland Square, Lebanon 37087-3554
Type: Private, independent, four-year
Degrees: A, B, M *Enroll:* 1,170
URL: http://www.cumberland.edu
Phone: (615) 444-2562 *Calendar:* Sem. plan
Inst. Accred.: SACS (1962/2000)
Prog. Accred.: Business (ACBSP), Nursing

DeVry University—Nashville
3343 Perimeter Hill Dr., Ste. 200, Nashville 37211
Type: Private, proprietary, four-year
Degrees: B, M
URL: http://www.devry.edu/locations/campuses/loc_nashville.jsp
Phone: (615) 445-3456 *Calendar:* Sem. plan
Inst. Accred.: NCA-HLC (2002, *Indirect accreditation through DeVry University, Oakbrook Terrace, IL*)

Louisville Campus
10172 Linn Station Rd., Ste. 300, Louisville, KY 40223-3887
Phone: (502) 326-2860

Memphis Campus
6401 Poplar Ave., Ste. 600, Memphis 38119
Phone: (901) 537-2560

Draughons Junior College
340 Plus Park at Pavilion Blvd., Nashville 37217
Type: Private, proprietary, two-year
Degrees: A *Enroll:* 388
URL: http://www.draughons.edu
Phone: (615) 361-7555 *Calendar:* Qtr. plan
Inst. Accred.: ACICS (1954/2006)

Bowling Green Campus
2421 Fitzgerald Industrial Dr., Bowling Green, KY 42101
Phone: (270) 843-6750

Clarksville Campus
1860 Wilma Rudolph Blvd., Clarksville 37040
Phone: (931) 552-7600

Murfreesboro Campus
1237 Commerce Park Dr., Murfreesboro 37130
Phone: (615) 217-9347

Dyersburg State Community College
1510 Lake Rd., Dyersburg 38024
Type: Public, state, two-year
System: Tennessee Board of Regents
Degrees: A *Enroll:* 1,773
URL: http://www.dscc.edu
Phone: (731) 286-3200 *Calendar:* Sem. plan
Inst. Accred.: SACS (1971/2008)
Prog. Accred.: Business (ACBSP), Nursing

East Tennessee State University
PO Box 70267, Johnson City 37614-1700
Type: Public, state, four-year
System: Tennessee Board of Regents
Degrees: A, B, M, P, D *Enroll:* 10,394
URL: http://www.etsu.edu
Phone: (423) 439-1000 *Calendar:* Sem. plan
Inst. Accred.: SACS (1927/2002)
Prog. Accred.: Accounting, Allied Health (audiology, medical assisting (AMA), medicine, respiratory therapy, speech-language pathology), Applied Science (surveying/geomatics), Art, Business (AACSB), Clinical Lab Technology, Computer Science (ABET-CAC), Counseling, Dentistry (dental assisting, dental hygiene, dental laboratory technology), Dietetics (didactic), Dietetics (internship), Engineering Technology (civil/construction, electrical, manufacturing), Environmental Health, Environmental Health (graduate), Graduate Social Work, Journalism, Music, Nursing Education, Pharmacy, Physical Therapy, Public Health, Radiography, Social Work, Teacher Education (NCATE)

Emmanuel School of Religion
One Walker Dr., Johnson City 37601
Type: Private, Christian Churches (Churches of Christ), four-year
Degrees: M, D *Enroll:* 118
URL: http://www.esr.edu
Phone: (423) 926-1186 *Calendar:* Sem. plan
Inst. Accred.: ATS (1981/2006), SACS (1986/2006)

Fisk University
1000 17th Ave. North, Nashville 37208-3051
Type: Private, independent, four-year
Degrees: B, M *Enroll:* 873
URL: http://www.fisk.edu
Phone: (615) 329-8500 *Calendar:* Sem. plan
Inst. Accred.: SACS (1930/1999)
Prog. Accred.: Business (ACBSP), Music

Fountainhead College of Technology
3202 Tazewell Pike, Knoxville 37918-2530
Type: Private, proprietary, four-year
Degrees: A, B *Enroll:* 128
URL: http://www.fountainheadcollege.edu
Phone: (865) 688-9422 *Calendar:* Qtr. plan
Inst. Accred.: ACCSCT (1967/2002)

Free Will Baptist Bible College
PO Box 50117, Nashville 37205-0117
Type: Private, National Association of Free Will Baptist Churches, four-year
Degrees: A, B *Enroll:* 327
URL: http://www.fwbbc.edu
Phone: (615) 844-5000 *Calendar:* Sem. plan
Inst. Accred.: ABHE (1958/1999), SACS (1996/2002)

Freed-Hardeman University
158 East Main St., Henderson 38340
Type: Private, Church of Christ, four-year
Degrees: B, M *Enroll:* 1,710
URL: http://www.fhu.edu
Phone: (731) 989-6000 *Calendar:* Sem. plan
Inst. Accred.: SACS (1956/2001)
Prog. Accred.: Business (ACBSP), Social Work, Teacher Education (NCATE)

Harding University Graduate School of Religion
1000 Cherry Rd., Memphis 38117-5499
Type: Private, Churches of Christ, four-year
Degrees: M, D *Enroll:* 113
URL: http://www.hugsr.edu
Phone: (901) 761-1352 *Calendar:* Sem. plan
Inst. Accred.: ATS (1997/2001), NCA-HLC (1954/2005, *Indirect accreditation through Harding University, Searcy, AR*)

Huntington College of Health Sciences
1204 Kenesaw Ave., Knoxville 37919-7736
Type: Private, proprietary, four-year
Degrees: A, M
URL: http://hchs.edu
Phone: (865) 524-8079
Inst. Accred.: DETC (1989/2006)

International Academy of Design and Technology—Nashville
1 Bridgestone Park, Nashville 37214
Type: Private, proprietary, four-year
System: Career Education Corporation
Degrees: A, B
URL: http://www.iadtnashville.com
Phone: (615) 232-7384 *Calendar:* Qtr. plan
Inst. Accred.: ACICS (2005)

Las Vegas Campus
2495 Village View Dr., Henderson, NV 89074
Phone: (702) 990-0150

San Antonio Campus
4511 Horizon Hill Blvd., San Antonio, TX 78229
Phone: (210) 530-9449

ITT Technical Institute
2845 Elm Hill Pike, Nashville 37214-3717
Type: Private, proprietary, four-year
System: ITT Educational Services, Inc.
Degrees: A, B *Enroll:* 744
URL: http://www.itt-tech.edu
Phone: (615) 889-8700 *Calendar:* Qtr. plan
Inst. Accred.: ACICS (1999/2003)

ITT Technical Institute
10208 Technology Dr., Knoxville 37932
Type: Private, proprietary, four-year
System: ITT Educational Services, Inc.
Degrees: A, B *Enroll:* 612
URL: http://www.itt-tech.edu
Phone: (865) 671-2800 *Calendar:* Qtr. plan
Inst. Accred.: ACICS (1999/2004)

Bessemer Campus
6270 Park South Dr., Bessemer, AL 35022
Phone: (205) 991-5410

Chantilly Campus
14420 Albemarle Point Place, Ste. 100, Chantilly, VA 20151
Phone: (703) 263-2541

Cincinnati Campus
4750 Wesley Ave., Norwood, OH 45212
Phone: (513) 531-8300

Columbia Campus
720 Gracern Rd., Ste. 120, Columbia, SC 29210
Phone: (803) 216-6000

Greenville Campus
6 Independence Pointe, Greenville, SC 29615
Phone: (864) 288-0777

Richardson Campus
2101 Waterview Pkwy., Richardson, TX 75080
Phone: (972) 690-9100

Jackson State Community College
2046 North Pkwy., Jackson 38301-3797
Type: Public, state, two-year
System: Tennessee Board of Regents
Degrees: A *Enroll:* 2,655
URL: http://www.jscc.edu
Phone: (731) 424-3520 *Calendar:* Sem. plan
Inst. Accred.: SACS (1969/2006)
Prog. Accred.: Allied Health (EMT-paramedic, respiratory therapy), Business (ACBSP), Clinical Lab Technology, Industrial Technology, Nursing, Physical Therapy Assisting, Radiography

John A. Gupton College
1616 Church St., Nashville 37203
Type: Private, independent, two-year
Degrees: A *Enroll:* 82
URL: http://www.guptoncollege.com
Phone: (615) 327-3927 *Calendar:* Sem. plan
Inst. Accred.: SACS (1971/2006)
Prog. Accred.: Funeral Service Education (Mortuary Science)

Johnson Bible College
7900 Johnson Dr., Knoxville 37998-0001
Type: Private, Christian Churches/Churches of Christ, four-year
Degrees: A, B, M *Enroll:* 849
URL: http://www.jbc.edu
Phone: (865) 573-4517 *Calendar:* Sem. plan
Inst. Accred.: ABHE (1970/2006), SACS (1979/2005)

Kaplan Career Institute—Nashville
750 Envious Ln., Nashville 37217
Type: Private, proprietary, two-year
System: Kaplan Higher Education Corporation
Degrees: A
URL: http://www.kaplancareerinstitute.com
Phone: (615) 279-8300 *Calendar:* Qtr. plan
Inst. Accred.: COE (1985/2002)

King College
1350 King College Rd., Bristol 37620-2699
Type: Private, Presbyterian Church (USA), four-year
Degrees: B, M *Enroll:* 869
URL: http://www.king.edu
Phone: (423) 968-1187 *Calendar:* 4-1-4 plan
Inst. Accred.: SACS (1947/1998)
Prog. Accred.: Nursing Education

Lambuth University
705 Lambuth Blvd., Jackson 38301
Type: Private, United Methodist Church, four-year
Degrees: B *Enroll:* 781
URL: http://www.lambuth.edu
Phone: (731) 425-2500 *Calendar:* Sem. plan
Inst. Accred.: SACS (1954/1999)
Prog. Accred.: Business (ACBSP)

Lane College
545 Ln. Ave., Jackson 38301-4598
Type: Private, Christian Methodist Episcopal Church, four-year
Degrees: B *Enroll:* 1,206
URL: http://www.lanecollege.edu
Phone: (731) 426-7500 *Calendar:* Sem. plan
Inst. Accred.: SACS (1949/2002)

Lee University
PO Box 3450, Cleveland 37320-3450
Type: Private, Church of God, four-year
Degrees: B, M *Enroll:* 3,661
URL: http://www.leeuniversity.edu
Phone: (423) 614-8000 *Calendar:* Sem. plan
Inst. Accred.: SACS (1960/2005)
Prog. Accred.: Business (ACBSP), Music

LeMoyne-Owen College
807 Walker Ave., Memphis 38126
Type: Private, United Church of Christ, four-year
Degrees: B *Enroll:* 733
URL: http://www.loc.edu
Phone: (901) 435-1700 *Calendar:* Sem. plan
Inst. Accred.: SACS (1939/2007)
Prog. Accred.: Teacher Education (NCATE)

Lincoln Memorial University
6965 Cumberland Gap Pkwy., Harrogate 37752
Type: Private, independent, four-year
Degrees: A, B, M, D *Enroll:* 1,846
URL: http://www.lmunet.edu
Phone: (423) 869-3611 *Calendar:* Sem. plan
Inst. Accred.: SACS (1936/2000)
Prog. Accred.: Clinical Lab Scientist, Nursing, Osteopathy, Social Work, Veterinary Technology

Lipscomb University
One University Park Dr., Nashville 37204-3951
Type: Private, Churches of Christ, four-year
Degrees: B, M, D *Enroll:* 2,285
URL: http://www.lipscomb.edu
Phone: (615) 269-1000 *Calendar:* Sem. plan
Inst. Accred.: SACS (1954/2007)
Prog. Accred.: Business (ACBSP), Dietetics (didactic), Dietetics (internship), Engineering (computer, engineering mechanics), Music, Nursing, Social Work, Teacher Education (NCATE)

Martin Methodist College
433 West Madison St., Pulaski 38478
Type: Private, United Methodist Church, four-year
Degrees: A, B *Enroll:* 675
URL: http://www.martinmethodist.edu
Phone: (931) 363-9800 *Calendar:* Sem. plan
Inst. Accred.: SACS (1952/1999)
Prog. Accred.: Nursing Education

Maryville College
502 East Lamar Alexander Pkwy., Maryville 37804-5907
Type: Private, Presbyterian Church (USA), four-year
Degrees: B *Enroll:* 1,130
URL: http://www.maryvillecollege.edu
Phone: (865) 981-8000 *Calendar:* Sem. plan
Inst. Accred.: SACS (1922/2003)
Prog. Accred.: Music

MedVance Institute
1025 Hwy. 111, Cookeville 38501
Type: Private, proprietary, two-year
Degrees: A *Enroll:* 246
URL: http://www.medvance.edu
Phone: (931) 526-3660 *Calendar:* Qtr. plan
Inst. Accred.: COE (1988/2004)
Prog. Accred.: Clinical Lab Technology, Radiography

Miami Campus
9035 Sunset Dr., Ste. 200, Miami, FL 33173
Phone: (305) 596-5553

West Palm Beach Campus
1630 Congress Ave., Palm Springs, FL 33461-2171
Phone: (561) 304-3466
Prog. Accred: Allied Health (surgical technology)

Meharry Medical College
1005 D.B. Todd Blvd., Nashville 37208
Type: Private, United Methodist Church, four-year
Degrees: M, D *Enroll:* 707
URL: http://mmc.edu
Phone: (615) 327-6000 *Calendar:* Sem. plan
Inst. Accred.: SACS (1972/2007)
Prog. Accred.: Allied Health (medicine), Dentistry (dental hygiene, dentistry, general practice residency, oral and maxillofacial surgery)

Memphis College of Art
Overton Park, 1930 Poplar Ave., Memphis 38104-2764
Type: Private, independent, four-year
Degrees: B, M *Enroll:* 298
URL: http://www.mca.edu
Phone: (901) 272-5100 *Calendar:* Sem. plan
Inst. Accred.: SACS (1963/2002)
Prog. Accred.: Art

Memphis Theological Seminary
168 East Pkwy. South, Memphis 38104-4340
Type: Private, Cumberland Presbyterian Church, four-year
Degrees: M, D *Enroll:* 262
URL: http://www.mtscampus.edu
Phone: (901) 458-8232 *Calendar:* Sem. plan
Inst. Accred.: ATS (1973/2008), SACS (1988/2008)

Mid-America Baptist Theological Seminary
2095 Appling Rd., Cordova 38016
Type: Private, independent, four-year
Degrees: A, M, D *FTE Enroll:* 284
URL: http://www.mabts.edu
Phone: (901) 751-8453 *Calendar:* Sem. plan
Inst. Accred.: SACS (1981/2006)

Northeast Campus
2810 Curry Rd., Schenectady, NY 12303
Phone: (518) 355-4000

Middle Tennessee School of Anesthesia
PO Box 6414, Madison 37116
Type: Private, independent, four-year
Degrees: M *Enroll:* 182
URL: http://www.mtsa.edu
Phone: (615) 868-6503 *Calendar:* Qtr. plan
Inst. Accred.: SACS (1994/1999)
Prog. Accred.: Nurse Anesthesia Education

Middle Tennessee State University
1301 East Main St., Murfreesboro 37132
Type: Public, state, four-year
System: Tennessee Board of Regents
Degrees: A, B, M, P, D *Enroll:* 19,765
URL: http://www.mtsu.edu
Phone: (615) 898-2300 *Calendar:* Sem. plan
Inst. Accred.: SACS (1928/2006)
Prog. Accred.: Accounting, Aviation, Business (AACSB), Computer Science (ABET-CAC), Construction Technology, Counseling, Dietetics (didactic), Engineering Technology (computer, electromechanical), Family & Consumer Science, Interior Design, Journalism, Music, Nursing, Nursing Education, Recreation and Leisure Services, Social Work, Teacher Education (NCATE)

Miller-Motte Technical College
1820 Business Park Dr., Clarksville 37040-0415
Type: Private, proprietary, two-year
System: Delta Education Corporation
Degrees: A *Enroll:* 426
URL: http://www.miller-motte.com/clarksvillewelcome.html
Phone: (931) 553-0071 *Calendar:* Qtr. plan
Inst. Accred.: ACICS (1989/2003)
Prog. Accred.: Allied Health (medical assisting (AMA), surgical technology)

Cary Campus
2205 Walnut St., Cary, NC 27511
Phone: (919) 532-7171
Prog. Accred: Allied Health (medical assisting (AMA), surgical technology)

Charleston Campus
8085 Rivers Ave., Ste. E, Charleston, SC 29406
Phone: (843) 574-0101
Prog. Accred: Allied Health (medical assisting (AMA), surgical technology)

Chattanooga Campus
6020 Shallowford Rd., Ste.100, Chattanooga 37421
Phone: (423) 510-9675
Prog. Accred: Allied Health (medical assisting (AMA), surgical technology)

Goodlettsville Campus
801 Spice Park North, Goodlettsville 37072-1870
Phone: (615) 859-8090

Wilmington Campus
5000 Market St., Wilmington, NC 28405
Phone: (910) 392-4660
Prog. Accred: Allied Health (medical assisting (AMA), surgical technology)

Milligan College
PO Box 500, Milligan College 37682-0500
Type: Private, independent, four-year
Degrees: A, B, M *Enroll:* 916
URL: http://www.milligan.edu
Phone: (423) 461-8700 *Calendar:* Sem. plan
Inst. Accred.: SACS (1960/2002)
Prog. Accred.: Allied Health (occupational therapy), Nursing Education, Teacher Education (NCATE)

Motlow State Community College
PO Box 8500, Lynchburg 37352-8500
Type: Public, state, two-year
System: Tennessee Board of Regents
Degrees: A *Enroll:* 2,482
URL: http://www.mscc.edu
Phone: (931) 393-1500 *Calendar:* Sem. plan
Inst. Accred.: SACS (1971/2008)
Prog. Accred.: Business (ACBSP), Nursing

Nashville Auto Diesel College
1524 Gallatin Rd., Nashville 37206-3298
Type: Private, proprietary, two-year
Degrees: A *Enroll:* 2,718
Phone: (615) 226-3990
Inst. Accred.: ACCSCT (1967/2007)

Nashville State Community College
120 White Bridge Rd., Nashville 37209-4515
Type: Public, state, two-year
System: Tennessee Board of Regents
Degrees: A *Enroll:* 4,101
URL: http://www.nscc.edu
Phone: (615) 353-3333 *Calendar:* Sem. plan
Inst. Accred.: SACS (1972/2008)
Prog. Accred.: Allied Health (occupational therapy assisting, surgeon assisting, surgical technology), Business (ACBSP), Culinary Education, Engineering Technology (architectural, electrical)

National College—Nashville
3748 Nolensville Pike, Nashville 37211
Type: Private, proprietary, two-year
Degrees: A
URL: http://www.ncbt.edu
Phone: (615) 333-3344
Inst. Accred.: ACICS (2003/2006)
Prog. Accred.: Allied Health (medical assisting (AMA))

Cincinnati Campus
6871 Steger Dr., Cincinnati, OH 45237
Phone: (513) 761-1291

Danville Campus
115 East Lexington Ave., Danville, KY 40422
Phone: (859) 236-6991
Prog. Accred: Allied Health (medical assisting (AMA))

Dayton Area Campus
1837 Woodman Center Dr., Kettering, OH 45420
Phone: (937) 299-9450
Prog. Accred: Allied Health (surgical technology)

National College—Nashville *(continued)*

Florence Campus
7627 Ewing Blvd., Florence, KY 41042
Phone: (859) 525-6510
Prog. Accred: Allied Health (medical assisting (AMA), surgical technology)

Knoxville Campus
8415 Kingston Pike, Knoxville 37919
Phone: (865) 539-2011
Prog. Accred: Allied Health (medical assisting (AMA))

Lexington Campus
2378 Sir Barton Way, Lexington, KY 40509
Phone: (859) 253-0621
Prog. Accred: Allied Health (medical assisting (AMA))

Louisville Campus
4205 Dixie Hwy., Louisville, KY 40216
Phone: (502) 447-7634
Prog. Accred: Allied Health (medical assisting (AMA), surgical technology)

Madison Campus
900 Madison Square, Madison 37115
Phone: (615) 612-3015

Pikeville Campus
50 National College Blvd., Pikeville, KY 41501
Phone: (606) 478-7200
Prog. Accred: Allied Health (medical assisting (AMA))

Richmond Campus
125 South Killarney Ln., Richmond, KY 40475
Phone: (859) 623-8956
Prog. Accred: Allied Health (medical assisting (AMA))

North Central Institute
168 Jack Miller Blvd., Clarksville 37042-4810
Type: Private, proprietary, two-year
Degrees: A *Enroll:* 107
URL: http://www.nci.edu
Phone: (931) 431-9700
Inst. Accred.: COE (1992/2003)

Northeast State Technical Community College
PO Box 246, Blountville 37617-0246
Type: Public, state, two-year
System: Tennessee Board of Regents
Degrees: A *Enroll:* 3,365
URL: http://www.northeaststate.edu
Phone: (423) 282-0800 *Calendar:* Sem. plan
Inst. Accred.: SACS (1984/2000)
Prog. Accred.: Allied Health (EMT-paramedic, cardiovascular technology, medical assisting (AMA), surgical technology), Business (ACBSP), Design Technology, Electronic Technology, Industrial Technology

Nossi College of Art
907 Rivergate Pkwy., Ste. E6, Goodlettsville 37072-2319
Type: Private, independent, four-year
Degrees: A, B *Enroll:* 330
URL: http://www.nossi.com
Phone: (615) 851-1088 *Calendar:* Sem. plan
Inst. Accred.: ACCSCT (1988/2004)

O'More College of Design
423 South Margin St., Franklin 37064-2816
Type: Private, independent, four-year
Degrees: B *Enroll:* 161
URL: http://www.omorecollege.edu
Phone: (615) 794-4254 *Calendar:* Sem. plan
Inst. Accred.: ACCSCT (1994/2008)
Prog. Accred.: Interior Design

Pellissippi State Technical Community College
PO Box 22990, Knoxville 37933-0990
Type: Public, state, two-year
System: Tennessee Board of Regents
Degrees: A *Enroll:* 5,159
URL: http://www.pstcc.edu
Phone: (865) 694-6752 *Calendar:* Sem. plan
Inst. Accred.: SACS (1977/2002)
Prog. Accred.: Business (ACBSP), Engineering Technology (civil/construction, computer, electrical, mechanical)

Rhodes College
2000 North Pkwy., Memphis 38112-1690
Type: Private, Presbyterian Church (USA), four-year
Degrees: B, M *Enroll:* 1,678
URL: http://www.rhodes.edu
Phone: (901) 843-3000 *Calendar:* Sem. plan
Inst. Accred.: SACS (1911/1999)

Roane State Community College
276 Patton Ln., Harriman 37748-5011
Type: Public, state, two-year
System: Tennessee Board of Regents
Degrees: A *Enroll:* 3,639
URL: http://www.roanestate.edu
Phone: (865) 354-3000 *Calendar:* Sem. plan
Inst. Accred.: SACS (1974/2000)
Prog. Accred.: Allied Health (EMT-paramedic, massage therapy, occupational therapy assisting, opticianry, respiratory therapy), Business (ACBSP), Dentistry (dental hygiene), Nursing, Physical Therapy Assisting, Polysomnographic Technology, Radiography

South College
3904 Lonas Dr., Knoxville 37909
Type: Private, proprietary, four-year
Degrees: A, B, M *Enroll:* 544
URL: http://www.southcollegetn.edu
Phone: (865) 251-1800 *Calendar:* Qtr. plan
Inst. Accred.: SACS (2000/2005)
Prog. Accred.: Allied Health (medical assisting (AMA)), Nuclear Medicine Technology, Physical Therapy Assisting, Radiography

Southern Adventist University
PO Box 370, Collegedale 37315-0370
Type: Private, Seventh-Day Adventist Church, four-year
Degrees: A, B, M *Enroll:* 2,292
URL: http://www.southern.edu
Phone: (423) 236-2000 *Calendar:* Sem. plan
Inst. Accred.: SACS (1950/2002)
Prog. Accred.: Music, Nursing, Social Work, Teacher Education (NCATE)

Southern College of Optometry
1245 Madison Ave., Memphis 38104
Type: Private, independent, four-year
Degrees: D *Enroll:* 481
URL: http://www.sco.edu
Phone: (901) 722-3200 *Calendar:* Qtr. plan
Inst. Accred.: SACS (1967/2002)
Prog. Accred.: Allied Health (optometric residency, optometry)

Southwest Tennessee Community College
5983 Macon Cove, Memphis 38134-7693
Type: Public, state, two-year
System: Tennessee Board of Regents
Degrees: A *Enroll:* 7,637
URL: http://www.southwest.tn.edu
Phone: (901) 333-5000 *Calendar:* Sem. plan
Inst. Accred.: SACS (2000/2005)
Prog. Accred.: Allied Health (EMT-paramedic), Business (ACBSP), Clinical Lab Technology, Dietetic Technician, Nursing, Phlebotomy, Physical Therapy Assisting, Radiography

Macon Cove Campus
5983 Macon Cove, Memphis 38134-7693
Phone: (901) 333-4111
Prog. Accred: Engineering Technology (architectural, civil/construction, computer, electrical, industrial, mechanical, telecommunications)

Temple Baptist Seminary
1815 Union Ave., Chattanooga 37404
Type: Private, Southern Baptist Church, four-year
Degrees: M, D *Enroll:* 25
URL: http://www.templebaptistseminary.edu
Phone: (800) 553-4050 *Calendar:* Sem. plan
Inst. Accred.: TRACS (2000/2005)

Tennessee State University
3500 John Merritt Blvd., Nashville 37209-1561
Type: Public, state, four-year
System: Tennessee Board of Regents
Degrees: A, B, M, P, D *Enroll:* 7,389
URL: http://www.tnstate.edu
Phone: (615) 963-5000 *Calendar:* Sem. plan
Inst. Accred.: SACS (1946/2000)
Prog. Accred.: Allied Health (occupational therapy, respiratory therapy, speech-language pathology), Art, Aviation Technology, Business (AACSB), Clinical Lab Scientist, Counseling Psychology, Dentistry (dental hygiene), Dietetics (didactic), Engineering (architectural, civil, electrical, mechanical), Family & Consumer Science, Industrial Technology, Music, Nursing, Physical Therapy, Public Administration, Social Work, Teacher Education (NCATE)

Tennessee Technological University
1000 North Dixie Ave., Cokkeville 38505-0001
Type: Public, state, four-year
System: Tennessee Board of Regents
Degrees: A, B, M, P, D *Enroll:* 7,899
URL: http://www.tntech.edu
Phone: (931) 372-3101 *Calendar:* Sem. plan
Inst. Accred.: SACS (1939/2006)
Prog. Accred.: Accounting, Allied Health (EMT-paramedic), Art, Business (AACSB), Dietetics (didactic), Engineering (chemical, civil, computer, electrical, industrial, mechanical), Family & Consumer Science, Industrial Technology, Music, Nursing Education, Teacher Education (NCATE)

Tennessee Temple University
1815 Union Ave., Chattanooga 37404-3587
Type: Private, Southern Baptist Church, four-year
Degrees: A, B, M, D *Enroll:* 430
URL: http://www.tntemple.edu
Phone: (423) 493-4100 *Calendar:* Sem. plan
Inst. Accred.: TRACS (2000/2005)

Tennessee Wesleyan College
PO Box 40, Athens 37371-0040
Type: Private, United Methodist Church, four-year
Degrees: B *Enroll:* 785
URL: http://www.twcnet.edu
Phone: (423) 745-7504 *Calendar:* Sem. plan
Inst. Accred.: SACS (1926/2000)
Prog. Accred.: Nursing Education

Trevecca Nazarene University
333 Murfreesboro Rd., Nashville 37210
Type: Private, Church of the Nazarene, four-year
Degrees: A, B, M, D *Enroll:* 1,960
URL: http://www.trevecca.edu
Phone: (615) 248-1200 *Calendar:* Sem. plan
Inst. Accred.: SACS (1969/2003)
Prog. Accred.: Music, Nursing Education, Physician Assistant

Tusculum College
PO Box 5048, Greeneville 37743
Type: Private, Presbyterian Church (USA), four-year
Degrees: B, M *Enroll:* 2,624
URL: http://www.tusculum.edu
Phone: (423) 636-7300 *Calendar:* Sem. plan
Inst. Accred.: SACS (1926/2003)

Union University
1050 Union University Dr., Jackson 38305
Type: Private, Tennessee Baptist Convention, four-year
Degrees: A, B, M, D *Enroll:* 2,471
URL: http://www.uu.edu
Phone: (731) 668-1818 *Calendar:* Sem. plan
Inst. Accred.: SACS (1948/2007)
Prog. Accred.: Art, Engineering (general), Music, Nurse Anesthesia Education, Nursing Education, Social Work, Teacher Education (NCATE)

The University of Memphis
Memphis 38152
Type: Public, state, four-year
System: Tennessee Board of Regents
Degrees: B, M, P, D *Enroll:* 16,318
URL: http://www.memphis.edu
Phone: (901) 678-2000 *Calendar:* Sem. plan
Inst. Accred.: SACS (1927/2005)
Prog. Accred.: Accounting, Allied Health (audiology, health services administration, speech-language pathology), Art, Business (AACSB), Clinical Psychology, Counseling, Counseling Psychology, Dietetics (didactic), Dietetics (internship), Engineering (civil, computer, electrical, mechanical), Engineering Technology (computer, electrical, manufacturing), Family & Consumer Science, Interior Design, Journalism, Law, Music, Nursing, Nursing Education, Planning, Psychology Internship, Public Administration, Rehabilitation Counseling, Social Work, Teacher Education (NCATE), Theatre

The University of Tennessee
527 Andy Holt Tower, Knoxville 37996-0152
Type: Public, state, four-year
System: University of Tennessee System
Degrees: B, M, P, D *Enroll:* 26,132
URL: http://www.tennessee.edu
Phone: (865) 974-1000 *Calendar:* Sem. plan
Inst. Accred.: SACS (2000/2005)
Prog. Accred.: Accounting, Allied Health (audiology, speech-language pathology), Art, Business (AACSB), Clinical Lab Scientist, Clinical Pastoral Education, Clinical Psychology, Counseling, Counseling Psychology, Dentistry (general practice residency, oral and maxillofacial surgery), Dietetics (didactic), Dietetics (internship), Engineering (aerospace, bioengineering, chemical, civil, computer, electrical, industrial, materials, mechanical, nuclear), Family & Consumer Science, Forestry, Graduate Social Work, Interior Design, Journalism, Law, Librarianship, Music, Nuclear Medicine Technology, Nurse Anesthesia Education, Nursing Education, Psychology Internship, Public Administration, Public Health, Radiography, Recreation and Leisure Services, Rehabilitation Counseling, School Psychology, Social Work, Teacher Education (NCATE), Veterinary Medicine

Health Science Center
800 Madison Ave., Memphis 38163
Phone: (901) 448-5500
Prog. Accred: Allied Health (cytotechnology, medicine, occupational therapy), Clinical Lab Scientist, Dentistry (advanced education in general dentistry, combined prosthodontics, dental hygiene, dentistry, general dentistry, oral and maxillofacial surgery, orthodontic and dentofacial orthopedics, pediatric dentistry, periodontics), Nurse Anesthesia Education, Nursing Education, Pharmacy, Physical Therapy, Psychology Internship

The University of Tennessee at Chattanooga
615 McCallie Ave., Chattanooga 37403-2598
Type: Public, state, four-year
System: University of Tennessee System
Degrees: B, M, P, D *Enroll:* 7,473
URL: http://www.utc.edu
Phone: (423) 425-4111 *Calendar:* Sem. plan
Inst. Accred.: SACS (1910/2002)
Prog. Accred.: Accounting, Allied Health (occupational therapy), Art, Business (AACSB), Computer Science (ABET-CAC), Counseling, Dietetics (didactic), Engineering (electrical, general, information systems, mechanical), Interior Design, Journalism, Music, Nurse Anesthesia Education, Nursing Education, Physical Therapy, Public Administration, Social Work, Teacher Education (NCATE)

The University of Tennessee at Martin
University St., Martin 38238
Type: Public, state, four-year
System: University of Tennessee System
Degrees: A, B, M *Enroll:* 5,674
URL: http://www.utm.edu
Phone: (731) 587-7000 *Calendar:* Sem. plan
Inst. Accred.: SACS (1951/2002)
Prog. Accred.: Business (AACSB), Dietetics (didactic), Dietetics (internship), Engineering (general), Family & Consumer Science, Journalism, Music, Nursing, Social Work, Teacher Education (NCATE)

The University of the South
735 University Ave., Sewanee 37383-1000
Type: Private, Prostestant Episcopal Church, four-year
Degrees: B, M, D *Enroll:* 1,509
URL: http://www.sewanee.edu
Phone: (931) 598-1000 *Calendar:* Sem. plan
Inst. Accred.: ATS (1958/2005), SACS (1895/2006)

Vanderbilt University
2201 West End Ave., Nashville 37240
Type: Private, interdenominational, four-year
Degrees: B, M, P, D *Enroll:* 11,122
URL: http://www.vanderbilt.edu
Phone: (615) 322-7311 *Calendar:* Sem. plan
Inst. Accred.: ATS (1938/2005), SACS (1895/2007)
Prog. Accred.: Allied Health (audiology, diagnostic medical sonography, medicine, perfusion, speech-language pathology), Business (AACSB), Clinical Lab Scientist, Clinical Psychology, Counseling, Dentistry (general practice residency, oral and maxillofacial surgery, orthodontic and dentofacial orthopedics), Dietetics (internship), Engineering (bioengineering, chemical, civil, computer, electrical, mechanical), Law, Music, Nuclear Medicine Technology, Nurse (Midwifery), Nursing, Psychology Internship, Radiation Therapy, Teacher Education (NCATE)

Volunteer State Community College
1480 Nashville Pike, Gallatin 37066-3188
Type: Public, state, two-year
System: Tennessee Board of Regents
Degrees: A *Enroll:* 4,707
URL: http://www.volstate.edu
Phone: (615) 452-8600 *Calendar:* Sem. plan
Inst. Accred.: SACS (1973/1999)
Prog. Accred.: Allied Health (EMT-paramedic, diagnostic medical sonography, respiratory therapy), Business (ACBSP), Dentistry (dental assisting), Physical Therapy Assisting, Polysomnographic Technology, Radiography

Walters State Community College
500 South Davy Crockett Pkwy., Morristown 37813-6899
Type: Public, state, two-year
System: Tennessee Board of Regents
Degrees: A *Enroll:* 3,983
URL: http://www.ws.edu
Phone: (423) 585-2600 *Calendar:* Sem. plan
Inst. Accred.: SACS (1972/2008)
Prog. Accred.: Allied Health (EMT-paramedic, respiratory therapy), Business (ACBSP), Culinary Education, Industrial Technology, Nursing, Physical Therapy Assisting

Watkins College of Art and Design
2298 MetroCenter Blvd., Nashville 37228
Type: Private, independent, four-year
Degrees: A, B *Enroll:* 265
URL: http://www.watkins.edu
Phone: (615) 383-4848 *Calendar:* Sem. plan
Inst. Accred.: NASAD (1996/2002)
Prog. Accred.: Interior Design

West Tennessee Business College
1186 Hwy. 45 By-Pass, Jackson 38301-1668
Type: Private, proprietary, two-year
Degrees: A
URL: http://www.wtbc.com
Phone: (731) 668-7240 *Calendar:* Tri. plan
Inst. Accred.: ACICS (1953/2004)

Williamson Christian College
200 Seaboard Ln., Franklin 37067
Type: Private, interdenominational, four-year
Degrees: A, B
URL: http://www.williamsoncc.edu
Phone: (615) 771-7821 *Calendar:* Sem. plan
Inst. Accred.: TRACS (2002/2008), ABHE (2007)

TEXAS

Abilene Christian University
Abilene 79699
Type: Private, Church of Christ, four-year
Degrees: A, B, M, D *Enroll:* 4,409
URL: http://www.acu.edu
Phone: (325) 674-2000 *Calendar:* Sem. plan
Inst. Accred.: ATS (2002/2006), SACS (1971/2001)
Prog. Accred.: Allied Health (speech-language pathology), Business (AACSB), Dietetics (didactic), Interior Design, Journalism, Marriage and Family Therapy, Music, Nursing Education, Social Work

The Academy of Health Care Professions
240 Northwest Mall, Houston 77092-8541
Type: Private, proprietary, two-year
Degrees: A
URL: http://www.academyofhealth.com
Phone: (713) 425-3100
Inst. Accred.: ABHES (1999/2008)
Prog. Accred.: Allied Health (surgical technology)

San Antonio Campus
4738 Northwest Loop 410, San Antonio 78229
Phone: (210) 298-3600

Southwest Freeway Campus
8313 Southwest Freeway, Ste. 300, Houston 77074
Phone: (713) 470-2428
Prog. Accred: Medical Assisting (ABHES), Surgical Technology

Academy of Oriental Medicine at Austin
2700 West Anderson Ln., Ste. 204, Austin 78757
Type: Private, proprietary, four-year
Degrees: M *Enroll:* 181
URL: http://www.aoma.edu
Phone: (512) 454-1188
Inst. Accred.: ACAOM (1996/2004), SACS (2008)

Alvin Community College
3110 Mustang Rd., Alvin 77511-4898
Type: Public, state/local, two-year
Degrees: A *Enroll:* 2,112
URL: http://www.alvincollege.edu
Phone: (281) 756-3500 *Calendar:* Sem. plan
Inst. Accred.: SACS (1959/2000)
Prog. Accred.: Allied Health (diagnostic medical sonography, respiratory therapy), Nursing

Amarillo College
PO Box 447, Amarillo 79178
Type: Public, state/local, two-year
Degrees: A *Enroll:* 5,869
URL: http://www.actx.edu
Phone: (806) 371-5000 *Calendar:* Sem. plan
Inst. Accred.: SACS (1933/2002)
Prog. Accred.: Allied Health (occupational therapy assisting, respiratory therapy, surgical technology), Clinical Lab Technology, Dentistry (dental hygiene), Engineering Technology (electrical), Funeral Service Education (Mortuary Science), Music, Nuclear Medicine Technology, Nursing, Physical Therapy Assisting, Radiation Therapy, Radiography

Amarillo Technical Center
PO Box 11197, Amarillo 79111
Phone: (806) 335-2316

Amberton University
1700 Eastgate Dr., Garland 75041
Type: Private, independent, four-year
Degrees: B, M *Enroll:* 1,008
URL: http://www.amberton.edu
Phone: (972) 279-6511 *Calendar:* Qtr. plan
Inst. Accred.: SACS (1981/2007)

American College of Acupuncture and Oriental Medicine
9100 Park West Dr., Houston 77063
Type: Private, proprietary, four-year
Degrees: M *Enroll:* 118
URL: http://www.acaom.edu
Phone: (713) 780-9777 *Calendar:* Sem. plan
Inst. Accred.: ACAOM (1996/2003), SACS (2008)

Angelina College
PO Box 1768, Lufkin 75902
Type: Public, state/local, two-year
Degrees: A *Enroll:* 2,778
URL: http://www.angelina.edu
Phone: (936) 639-1301 *Calendar:* Sem. plan
Inst. Accred.: SACS (1970/2006)
Prog. Accred.: Allied Health (respiratory therapy), Radiography

Angelo State University
2601 West Ave. North, San Angelo 76909
Type: Public, state, four-year
System: Texas State University System
Degrees: A, B, M *Enroll:* 5,465
URL: http://www.angelo.edu
Phone: (325) 942-2555 *Calendar:* Sem. plan
Inst. Accred.: SACS (1936/2002)
Prog. Accred.: Business (ACBSP), Music, Nursing, Physical Therapy

Argosy University Dallas
8080 Park Ln., Dallas 75231
Type: Private, proprietary, four-year
System: Argosy University
Degrees: M, D
URL: http://www.argosyu.edu/dallas
Phone: (214) 890-9900 *Calendar:* Tri. plan
Inst. Accred.: NCA-HLC (1981/2008, *Indirect accreditation through Argosy University, Chicago, IL*)

Arlington Baptist College
3001 West Division St., Arlington 76012-3497
Type: Private, World Baptist Fellowship, four-year
Degrees: B *Enroll:* 157
URL: http://www.abconline.edu
Phone: (817) 461-8741 *Calendar:* Sem. plan
Inst. Accred.: ABHE (1981/2002)

The Art Institute of Dallas
Two NorthPark East, 8080 Park Ln., Ste. 100, Dallas 75231-5993
Type: Private, proprietary, four-year
System: Education Management Corporation
Degrees: A, B *Enroll:* 1,121
URL: http://www.aid.edu
Phone: (214) 692-8080 *Calendar:* Qtr. plan
Inst. Accred.: SACS (1998/2003)
Prog. Accred.: Culinary Education, Interior Design

The Art Institute of Houston
1900 Yorktown St., Houston 77056
Type: Private, proprietary, four-year
System: Education Management Corporation
Degrees: A, B *Enroll:* 1,298
URL: http://www.artinstitutes.edu/houston
Phone: (713) 623-2040 *Calendar:* Qtr. plan
Inst. Accred.: SACS (2000/2005)
Prog. Accred.: Culinary Education, Interior Design

ATI Career Training Center
10003 Technology Blvd. West, Dallas 75220
Type: Private, proprietary, two-year
System: ATI Enterprises, Inc.
Degrees: A
URL: http://www.aticareertraining.edu
Phone: (972) 902-8191 *Calendar:* Sem. plan
Inst. Accred.: ACCSCT (1986/2004)

Albuquerque Campus
4575 San Mateo Blvd. NE, Ste. G130, Albuquerque, NM 87109-2016
Phone: (505) 903-7035

Garland Campus
3035 South Shiloh Rd., Ste. 150, Garland 75041-2497
Phone: (972) 535-5525

Richardson Campus
1100 East Campbell Rd., Ste. 250, Richardson 75801
Phone: (214) 646-8460

Austin College
900 North Grand Ave., Sherman 75090-4440
Type: Private, Presbyterian Church (USA), four-year
Degrees: B, M *Enroll:* 1,320
URL: http://www.austincollege.edu
Phone: (903) 813-2000 *Calendar:* 4-1-4 plan
Inst. Accred.: SACS (1947/1999)

Austin Community College
5930 Middle Fiskville Rd., Austin 78752-4390
Type: Public, state/local, two-year
Degrees: A *Enroll:* 16,577
URL: http://www.austincc.edu
Phone: (512) 223-7000 *Calendar:* Sem. plan
Inst. Accred.: SACS (1978/2004)
Prog. Accred.: Allied Health (EMT-paramedic, diagnostic medical sonography, occupational therapy assisting, surgical technology), Clinical Lab Technology, Nursing, Phlebotomy, Physical Therapy Assisting, Practical Nursing

Cypress Creek Campus
1555 Cypress Creek Rd., Cedar Park 78613
Phone: (512) 223-2000

Eastview Campus
3401 Webberville Rd., Austin 78702
Phone: (512) 223-5100
Prog. Accred: Culinary Education, Radiography

Northridge Campus
11928 Stonehollow Dr., Austin 78758
Phone: (512) 223-4000

Pinnacle Campus
7748 Hwy. 290 West, Austin 78736
Phone: (512) 223-8001
Prog. Accred: Business (ACBSP)

Rio Grande Campus
1212 Rio Grande St., Austin 78701
Phone: (512) 223-3000

Riverside Campus
1020 Grove Blvd., Austin 78741
Phone: (512) 223-6000

Austin Graduate School of Theology
1909 University Ave., Austin 78705
Type: Private, Church of Christ, four-year
Degrees: B, M *Enroll:* 32
URL: http://www.austingrad.edu
Phone: (512) 476-2772 *Calendar:* Sem. plan
Inst. Accred.: SACS (1987/2003)

Austin Presbyterian Theological Seminary
100 East 27th St., Austin 78705-5797
Type: Private, Presbyterian Church (USA), four-year
Degrees: M, D *Enroll:* 188
URL: http://www.austinseminary.edu
Phone: (512) 472-6736 *Calendar:* 4-1-4 plan
Inst. Accred.: ATS (1940/1999), SACS (1973/1999)

Baptist Health System School of Health Professions
8400 Datapoint Dr., San Antonio 78229-3234
Type: Private, independent, two-year
Degrees: A
URL: http://www.bshp.edu
Phone: (210) 297-9636
Inst. Accred.: ABHES (2005)
Prog. Accred.: Allied Health (surgical technology), Nursing, Surgical Technology

Phoenix Campus
2000 West Bethany Home Rd., Phoenix, AZ 85015-2443
Phone: (877) 493-8238

Baptist Missionary Association Theological Seminary
1530 East Pine St., Jacksonville 75766-5407
Type: Private, Baptist Missionary Association of America, four-year
Degrees: A, B, M *Enroll:* 85
URL: http://www.bmats.edu
Phone: (903) 586-2501 *Calendar:* Sem. plan
Inst. Accred.: ATS (2006), SACS (1986/2001)

Baptist University of the Americas
8019 S. Pan Am Expressway, San Antonio 78224-1397
Type: Private, Southern Baptist Church, four-year
Degrees: B
URL: http://www.bua.edu
Phone: (210) 924-4338 *Calendar:* Sem. plan
Inst. Accred.: ABHE (2003)

Baylor College of Medicine
One Baylor Plaza, Houston 77030-3498
Type: Private, independent, four-year
Degrees: M, D *Enroll:* 1,340
URL: http://www.bcm.tmc.edu
Phone: (713) 798-4029 *Calendar:* Qtr. plan
Inst. Accred.: SACS (1970/2006)
Prog. Accred.: Allied Health (medicine), Clinical Pastoral Education, Nurse Anesthesia Education, Physician Assistant, Psychology Internship

Baylor University
500 Speight Rd., Waco 78798
Type: Private, Baptist General Convention of Texas, four-year
Degrees: B, M, D *Enroll:* 13,550
URL: http://www.baylor.edu
Phone: (254) 710-1011 *Calendar:* Sem. plan
Inst. Accred.: ATS (2002/2007), SACS (1914/2007)
Prog. Accred.: Accounting, Allied Health (health services administration, speech-language pathology), Business (AACSB), Clinical Psychology, Computer Science (ABET-CAC), Dietetics (didactic), Engineering (electrical, general, mechanical), Family & Consumer Science, Graduate Social Work, Interior Design, Journalism, Law, Liberal Education, Montessori Teacher Education, Music, Nursing Education, Physical Therapy, Social Work, Teacher Education (NCATE), Theatre

Blinn College
902 College Ave., Brenham 77833
Type: Public, state/local, two-year
Degrees: A *Enroll:* 9,777
URL: http://www.blinn.edu
Phone: (979) 830-4000 *Calendar:* Sem. plan
Inst. Accred.: SACS (1950/2005)
Prog. Accred.: Nursing, Physical Therapy Assisting, Radiography

Bryan Campus
PO Box 6030, 423 Blinn Blvd., Bryan 77805-6030
Phone: (979) 209-7200
Prog. Accred: Dentistry (dental hygiene)

Bradford School of Business
4669 Southwest Freeway, Ste. 300, Houston 77027
Type: Private, proprietary, two-year
Degrees: A
URL: http://www.bradfordschoolhouston.edu
Phone: (713) 629-8940
Inst. Accred.: ACICS (1980/2004)
Prog. Accred.: Allied Health (medical assisting (AMA))

Brazosport College
500 College Dr., Lake Jackson 77566
Type: Public, state/local, four-year
Degrees: A, B *Enroll:* 1,979
URL: http://www.brazosport.edu
Phone: (979) 230-3000 *Calendar:* Sem. plan
Inst. Accred.: SACS (1970/2006)
Prog. Accred.: Allied Health (EMT-paramedic)

Brite Divinity School
TCU Box 298130, 2800 South University Dr., Fort Worth 76129
Type: Private, Chrstian Church (Disciples of Christ), four-year
Degrees: D
URL: http://www.brite.tcu.edu
Phone: (817) 257-7575 *Calendar:* Sem. plan
Inst. Accred.: ATS (1942/2000), SACS (2007)

Brookhaven College
3939 Valley View Ln., Dallas 75244-4997
Type: Public, state/local, two-year
System: Dallas County Community College District
Degrees: A *Enroll:* 5,318
URL: http://www.brookhavencollege.edu
Phone: (972) 860-4700 *Calendar:* Sem. plan
Inst. Accred.: SACS (1979/2003)
Prog. Accred.: Nursing

Capitol City Trade and Technical School
205 East Riverside Dr., Austin 78704
Type: Private, proprietary, two-year
System: Timberline 1
Degrees: A
URL: http://www.capcitytradetech.com
Phone: (512) 444-3257
Inst. Accred.: COE (1979/2006)

Career Point College
485 Spencer Ln., San Antonio 78201
Type: Private, proprietary, two-year
Degrees: A
URL: http://www.careerpointcollege.edu
Phone: (210) 732-3000
Inst. Accred.: ACICS (1988/2004)

Cedar Valley College
3030 North Dallas Ave., Lancaster 75134
Type: Public, state/local, two-year
System: Dallas County Community College District
Degrees: A *Enroll:* 2,543
URL: http://www.cedarvalleycollege.edu
Phone: (972) 860-8200 *Calendar:* Sem. plan
Inst. Accred.: SACS (1979/2003)
Prog. Accred.: Veterinary Technology

Center for Advanced Legal Studies
3910 Kirby Dr., Ste. 200, Houston 77098
Type: Private, proprietary, two-year
Degrees: A *Enroll:* 74
URL: http://www.paralegalpeople.com
Phone: (713) 529-2778
Inst. Accred.: COE (1989/2007)

Central Texas College
PO Box 1800, Killeen 76540-1800
Type: Public, state, two-year
Degrees: A *Enroll:* 7,899
URL: http://www.ctcd.edu
Phone: (254) 526-7161 *Calendar:* Sem. plan
Inst. Accred.: SACS (1969/2005)
Prog. Accred.: Clinical Lab Technology, Nursing

Cisco Junior College
101 College Heights, Cisco 76437
Type: Public, state, two-year
Degrees: A *Enroll:* 2,196
URL: http://www.cjc.edu
Phone: (254) 442-5000 *Calendar:* Sem. plan
Inst. Accred.: SACS (1958/1999)
Prog. Accred.: Allied Health (medical assisting (AMA), surgical technology), Practical Nursing

Clarendon College
PO Box 968, Clarendon 79226
Type: Public, state/local, two-year
Degrees: A *Enroll:* 652
URL: http://www.clarendoncollege.edu
Phone: (806) 874-3571 *Calendar:* Sem. plan
Inst. Accred.: SACS (1970/2006)

Coastal Bend College
3800 Charco Rd., Beeville 78102
Type: Public, state/local, two-year
Degrees: A *Enroll:* 2,047
URL: http://vct.coastalbend.edu
Phone: (361) 358-2838 *Calendar:* Sem. plan
Inst. Accred.: SACS (1969/2005)
Prog. Accred.: Dentistry (dental hygiene)

College of Biblical Studies—Houston
7000 Regency Square Blvd., Ste. 110, Houston 77036-3211
Type: Private, independent, four-year
Degrees: A, B *Enroll:* 815
URL: http://www.cbshouston.edu
Phone: (713) 785-5995 *Calendar:* Sem. plan
Inst. Accred.: ABHE (1999/2004)

The College of Saint Thomas Moore
3020 Lubbock Ave., Fort Worth 76109-2322
Type: Private, Roman Catholic Church, four-year
Degrees: A, B *Enroll:* 34
URL: http://www.cstm.edu
Phone: (817) 923-8459 *Calendar:* Sem. plan
Inst. Accred.: SACS (1994/1999)

College of the Mainland
1200 Amburn Rd., Texas City 77591
Type: Public, local, two-year
Degrees: A *Enroll:* 2,256
URL: http://www.com.edu
Phone: (409) 938-1211 *Calendar:* Sem. plan
Inst. Accred.: SACS (1969/2003)
Prog. Accred.: Allied Health (EMT-paramedic), Nursing

Collin County Community College District
4800 Preston Park Blvd., Plano 75093
Type: Public, state/local, two-year
Degrees: A *Enroll:* 10,997
URL: http://www.ccccd.edu
Phone: (972) 758-3800 *Calendar:* Sem. plan
Inst. Accred.: SACS (1989/2006)
Prog. Accred.: Nursing, Phlebotomy

Central Park Campus
PO Box 8001, 2200 West University Dr., McKinney 75069-8001
Phone: (972) 548-6790
Prog. Accred: Allied Health (respiratory therapy), Dentistry (dental hygiene)

Commonwealth Institute of Funeral Service
415 Barren Springs Dr., Houston 77090
Type: Private, independent, two-year
Degrees: A *Enroll:* 136
URL: http://www.commonwealthinst.org
Phone: (281) 873-0262 *Calendar:* Qtr. plan
Inst. Accred.: ABFSE (1961/2003)

Computer Career Center
6101 Montana Ave., El Paso 79925
Type: Private, proprietary, two-year
Degrees: A *Enroll:* 269
URL: http://www.computercareercenter.com
Phone: (915) 779-8031 *Calendar:* Sem. plan
Inst. Accred.: COE (1989/2006)
Prog. Accred.: Allied Health (medical assisting (AMA)), Medical Assisting (ABHES)

Court Reporting Institute of Dallas
1341 West Mockingbird Ln., Ste. 200 East, Dallas 75247
Type: Private, proprietary, two-year
System: Vatterott Educational Centers, Inc.
Degrees: A
URL: http://www.crid.com
Phone: (214) 350-9722
Inst. Accred.: ACICS (1986/2004)

Court Reporting Institute of Houston
13101 Northwest Freeway, Ste. 100, Houston 77040
Phone: (713) 996-8300

The Criswell College
4010 Gaston Ave., Dallas 75246-1537
Type: Private, First Baptist Church of Dallas, four-year
Degrees: A, B, M *FTE Enroll:* 283
URL: http://www.criswell.edu
Phone: (214) 821-5433 *Calendar:* Sem. plan
Inst. Accred.: SACS (1985/2002)

Culinary Institute Alain and Marie LeNotre
7070 Allensby St., Houston 77022-4322
Type: Private, proprietary, two-year
Degrees: A
URL: http://www.ciaml.com
Phone: (713) 692-0077 *Calendar:* Qtr. plan
Inst. Accred.: ACCSCT (2002/2007)

Dallas Baptist University
3000 Mountain Creek Pkwy., Dallas 75211-9299
Type: Private, Baptist General Convention of Texas, four-year
Degrees: A, B, M, D *Enroll:* 3,431
URL: http://www.dbu.edu
Phone: (214) 333-7100 *Calendar:* 4-1-4 plan
Inst. Accred.: SACS (1959/2008)
Prog. Accred.: Business (ACBSP), Music

Dallas Christian College
2700 Christian Pkwy., Dallas 75234-7299
Type: Private, Christian Churches/Churches of Christ, four-year
Degrees: B *Enroll:* 322
URL: http://www.dallas.edu
Phone: (972) 241-3371 *Calendar:* Sem. plan
Inst. Accred.: ABHE (1978/1999)

Dallas Institute of Funeral Services
3909 South Buckner Blvd., Dallas 75227
Type: Private, independent, two-year
Degrees: A
URL: http://www.dallasinstitute.edu
Phone: (214) 388-5466 *Calendar:* Qtr. plan
Inst. Accred.: ABFSE (1947/2003)

Dallas Theological Seminary
3909 Swiss Ave., Dallas 75204
Type: Private, interdenominational, four-year
Degrees: M, D *Enroll:* 1,400
URL: http://www.dts.edu
Phone: (214) 824-3094 *Calendar:* Sem. plan
Inst. Accred.: ATS (1994/2003), SACS (1969/2003)

Del Mar College
101 Baldwin Blvd., Corpus Christi 78404-3897
Type: Public, state/local, two-year
Degrees: A *Enroll:* 6,510
URL: http://www.delmar.edu
Phone: (361) 698-1200 *Calendar:* Sem. plan
Inst. Accred.: SACS (1946/2000)
Prog. Accred.: Allied Health (diagnostic medical sonography, occupational therapy assisting, respiratory therapy, surgical technology), Art, Clinical Lab Technology, Culinary Education, Dentistry (dental assisting, dental hygiene), Music, Nuclear Medicine Technology, Nursing, Physical Therapy Assisting, Radiography, Theatre

DeVry University Irving
4800 Regent Blvd., Irving 75063-2440
Type: Private, proprietary
System: DeVry University
Degrees: A, B, M *Enroll:* 1,944
URL: http://www.devry.edu/irving
Phone: (972) 929-6777 *Calendar:* Sem. plan
Inst. Accred.: NCA-HLC (2002, *Indirect accreditation through DeVry University, Oakbrook Terrace, IL*)
Prog. Accred.: Engineering Technology (computer, electrical)

Austin Campus
11044 Research Blvd., Ste. B100, Austin 78759
Phone: (512) 231-2500

Ft. Worth campus
301 Commerce St., DR Horton Tower, Ste. 2000, Ft. Worth 76102
Phone: (817) 810-9114

Houston Campus
11125 Equity Dr., Houston 77041
Phone: (866) 703-3879

Richardson Campus
2201 North Central Expressway, Ste. 149, Richardson 75080
Phone: (972) 792-7450

San Antonio Campus
1919 NW Loop 410, Ste. 150, San Antonio 78213
Phone: (210) 524-5400

East Texas Baptist University
1209 North Grove Ave., Marshall 75670-1498
Type: Private, Baptist General Convention of Texas, four-year
Degrees: B *Enroll:* 1,235
URL: http://www.etbu.edu
Phone: (903) 935-7963 *Calendar:* 4-1-4 plan
Inst. Accred.: SACS (1957/1998)
Prog. Accred.: Music, Nursing Education

Eastfield College
3737 Motley Dr., Mesquite 75150-2099
Type: Public, state/local, two-year
System: Dallas County Community College District
Degrees: A *Enroll:* 6,223
URL: http://www.eastfieldcollege.edu
Phone: (972) 860-7100 *Calendar:* Sem. plan
Inst. Accred.: SACS (1972/2003, Warning)

El Centro College
801 Main St., Dallas 75202-3605
Type: Public, state/local, two-year
System: Dallas County Community College District
Degrees: A *Enroll:* 3,100
URL: http://www.elcentrocollege.edu
Phone: (214) 860-2000 *Calendar:* Sem. plan
Inst. Accred.: SACS (1968/2003)
Prog. Accred.: Allied Health (cardiovascular technology, diagnostic medical sonography, medical assisting (AMA), respiratory therapy, surgical technology), Clinical Lab Technology, Culinary Education, Interior Design, Nursing, Practical Nursing, Radiography

El Paso County Community College District
PO Box 20500, El Paso 79998-0500
Type: Public, state/local, two-year
Degrees: A *Enroll:* 16,099
URL: http://www.epcc.edu
Phone: (915) 831-2000 *Calendar:* Sem. plan
Inst. Accred.: SACS (1978/2003)
Prog. Accred.: Allied Health (diagnostic medical sonography, medical assisting (AMA), ophthalmic lab technology, respiratory therapy, surgical technology), Clinical Lab Technology, Dentistry (dental assisting, dental hygiene), Nursing, Physical Therapy Assisting, Radiography

The Episcopal Theological Seminary of the Southwest
PO Box 2247, Austin 78768-2247
Type: Private, Episcopal Church, four-year
Degrees: M *Enroll:* 91
URL: http://www.etss.edu
Phone: (512) 472-4133 *Calendar:* Sem. plan
Inst. Accred.: ATS (1958/2004), SACS (1983/2005)

Frank Phillips College
PO Box 5118, Borger 79008-5118
Type: Public, local, two-year
Degrees: A *Enroll:* 825
URL: http://www.fpc.cc.tx.us
Phone: (806) 457-4200 *Calendar:* Sem. plan
Inst. Accred.: SACS (1958/1999)

Galveston College
4015 Ave. Q, Galveston 77550
Type: Public, state/local, two-year
Degrees: A *Enroll:* 1,314
URL: http://www.gc.edu
Phone: (409) 944-4242 *Calendar:* Sem. plan
Inst. Accred.: SACS (1969/2005)
Prog. Accred.: Allied Health (EMT-paramedic, surgical technology), Nuclear Medicine Technology, Nursing, Radiation Therapy, Radiography

Graduate Institute of Applied Linguistics
7500 West Camp Wisdom Rd., Dallas 75236
Type: Private, independent, four-year
Degrees: M
URL: http://www.gial.edu
Phone: (972) 708-7340
Inst. Accred.: SACS (2005)

Grayson County College
6101 Grayson Dr., Denison 75020
Type: Public, state/local, two-year
Degrees: A *Enroll:* 2,449
URL: http://www.grayson.edu
Phone: (903) 465-6030 *Calendar:* Sem. plan
Inst. Accred.: SACS (1967/2001)
Prog. Accred.: Clinical Lab Technology, Dentistry (dental assisting), Nursing

Hallmark College
10401 IH 10 West, San Antonio 78216-1737
Type: Private, proprietary, two-year
Degrees: A *Enroll:* 771
URL: http://www.hallmarkcollege.edu
Phone: (210) 690-9000
Inst. Accred.: ACCSCT (1971/2006)
Prog. Accred.: Allied Health (medical assisting (AMA))

Hallmark Institute of Aeronautics
8901 Wetmore Rd., San Antonio 78216
Type: Private, proprietary, two-year
Degrees: A
URL: http://www.hallmarkinstitute.com
Phone: (210) 826-1000
Inst. Accred.: ACCSCT (1973/2006)

Hardin-Simmons University
2200 Hickory St., Abilene 79698
Type: Private, Baptist General Convention of Texas, four-year
Degrees: A, B, M, D *Enroll:* 2,179
URL: http://www.hsutx.edu
Phone: (915) 670-1000 *Calendar:* Sem. plan
Inst. Accred.: ATS (2006), SACS (1927/2007)
Prog. Accred.: Business (ACBSP), Music, Nursing Education, Physical Therapy, Social Work

Hill College
PO Box 619, Hillsboro 76645-0619
Type: Public, local, two-year
Degrees: A *Enroll:* 1,950
URL: http://www.hillcollege.edu
Phone: (254) 582-2555 *Calendar:* Sem. plan
Inst. Accred.: SACS (1966/2000)

Houston Baptist University
7502 Fondren Rd., Houston 77074-3298
Type: Private, Southern Baptist Church, four-year
Degrees: A, B, M *Enroll:* 2,009
URL: http://www.hbu.edu
Phone: (281) 649-3000 *Calendar:* Qtr. plan
Inst. Accred.: SACS (1968/2002)
Prog. Accred.: Business (ACBSP), Nursing

Houston Community College
PO Box 667517, Houston 77266-7517
Type: Public, state, two-year
System: Texas Higher Education Coordinating Board
Degrees: A *Enroll:* 21,370
URL: http://www.hccs.edu
Phone: (713) 718-2000 *Calendar:* Sem. plan
Inst. Accred.: SACS (1977/2002)
Prog. Accred.: Clinical Lab Technology, Dentistry (dental assisting), Histologic Technology, Nuclear Medicine Technology, Physical Therapy Assisting, Radiography

Central Campus
1300 Holman Ave., Houston 77004
Phone: (713) 718-6000

Coleman College for Health Sciences
1900 Pressler St., Houston 77030-3717
Phone: (713) 718-7400
Prog. Accred: Allied Health (EMT-paramedic, diagnostic medical sonography, medical assisting (AMA), occupational therapy assisting, respiratory therapy, surgical technology)

College Without Walls
4310 Dunlavy St., Houston 77270
Phone: (713) 868-0799

Northeast Campus
555 Community College Dr., Houston 77013
Phone: (713) 694-5384
Prog. Accred: Engineering Technology (electrical)

Northwest Campus
1550 Foxlake Dr., Houston 77084
Phone: (713) 718-5757

Southeast Campus
6815 Rustic Ave., Houston 77087
Phone: (713) 718-7000
Prog. Accred: Allied Health (occupational therapy assisting)

Southwest Campus
5407 Gulfton St., Houston 77081
Phone: (713) 718-7760

Houston Graduate School of Theology
2501 Central Pkwy., Ste. A19, Houston 77092
Type: Private, interdenominational, four-year
Degrees: M, D *Enroll:* 185
URL: http://www.hgst.edu
Phone: (713) 942-9505 *Calendar:* Sem. plan
Inst. Accred.: ATS (1997/2004)

Howard College
1001 Birdwell Ln., Big Spring 79720
Type: Public, state/local, two-year
System: Howard County Junior College District
Degrees: A *Enroll:* 1,608
URL: http://www.howardcollege.edu
Phone: (432) 264-5000 *Calendar:* Sem. plan
Inst. Accred.: SACS (1955/2007)
Prog. Accred.: Allied Health (respiratory therapy technology), Dentistry (dental hygiene), Nursing

San Angelo Campus
3501 North US Hwy. 67, San Angelo 76905
Phone: (325) 481-8350
Prog. Accred: Allied Health (surgical technology)

Howard Payne University
1000 Fisk Ave., Brownwood 76801
Type: Private, Southern Baptist Church, four-year
Degrees: B, M *Enroll:* 1,169
URL: http://www.hputx.edu
Phone: (325) 646-2502 *Calendar:* Sem. plan
Inst. Accred.: SACS (1948/2004)
Prog. Accred.: Music, Social Work

Huston-Tillotson University
900 Chicon St., Austin 78702-2795
Type: Private, United Methodist/United Church of Christ, four-year
Degrees: B *Enroll:* 656
URL: http://www.htu.edu
Phone: (512) 505-3000 *Calendar:* Sem. plan
Inst. Accred.: SACS (1943/2002)

ITT Technical Institute
551 Ryan Plaza Dr., Arlington 76011
Type: Private, proprietary, four-year
System: ITT Educational Services, Inc.
Degrees: A, B *Enroll:* 624
URL: http://www.itt-tech.edu
Phone: (817) 794-5100 *Calendar:* Qtr. plan
Inst. Accred.: ACICS (1999/2007)

ITT Technical Institute
5700 Northwest Pkwy., San Antonio 78249-3303
Type: Private, proprietary, four-year
System: ITT Educational Services, Inc.
Degrees: A, B *Enroll:* 706
URL: http://www.itt-tech.edu
Phone: (210) 694-4612 *Calendar:* Qtr. plan
Inst. Accred.: ACICS (1999/2004)

Texas College in Webster
1001 Magnolia Ave., Wesbter 77598
Phone: (281) 316-4700

Jacksonville College
105 B.J. Albritton Dr., Jacksonville 75766-4759
Type: Private, Baptist Missionary Association of Texas, two-year
Degrees: A *Enroll:* 252
URL: http://www.jacksonville-college.edu
Phone: (903) 586-2518 *Calendar:* Sem. plan
Inst. Accred.: SACS (1974/1999)

Jarvis Christian College
PO Box 1470, Hawkins 75765-1470
Type: Private, Disciples of Christ, four-year
Degrees: A, B *Enroll:* 564
URL: http://www.jarvis.edu
Phone: (903) 769-5700 *Calendar:* Sem. plan
Inst. Accred.: SACS (1967/2003)
Prog. Accred.: Business (ACBSP)

KD Studio
2600 Stemmons Freeway, No. 117, Dallas 75207
Type: Private, independent, two-year
Degrees: A *Enroll:* 152
URL: http://www.kdstudio.com
Phone: (214) 638-0484 *Calendar:* Sem. plan
Inst. Accred.: NAST (1988/2003)

Kilgore College
1100 Broadway Blvd., Kilgore 75662
Type: Public, local, two-year
Degrees: A *Enroll:* 3,373
URL: http://www.kilgore.edu
Phone: (903) 984-8531 *Calendar:* Sem. plan
Inst. Accred.: SACS (1939/1999)
Prog. Accred.: Allied Health (medical assisting (AMA), surgical technology), Clinical Lab Technology, Nursing, Physical Therapy Assisting, Radiography

Lamar Institute of Technology
PO Box 10043, Beaumont 77710
Type: Public, state, two-year
System: Texas State University System
Degrees: A
URL: http://www.theinstitute.lamar.edu
Phone: (409) 880-8321 *Calendar:* Sem. plan
Inst. Accred.: SACS (2000/2005)
Prog. Accred.: Radiography

Lamar State College—Orange
410 Front St., Orange 77630
Type: Public, state, two-year
System: Texas State University System
Degrees: A *Enroll:* 1,331
URL: http://www.orange.lamar.edu
Phone: (409) 883-7750 *Calendar:* Sem. plan
Inst. Accred.: SACS (1989/2005)
Prog. Accred.: Clinical Lab Technology, Dentistry (dental assisting)

Lamar State College—Port Arthur
PO Box 310, Port Arthur 77641-0310
Type: Public, state, two-year
System: Texas State University System
Degrees: A *Enroll:* 1,500
URL: http://www.pa.lamar.edu
Phone: (409) 983-4921 *Calendar:* Sem. plan
Inst. Accred.: SACS (1988/2003)
Prog. Accred.: Allied Health (surgical technology), Business (ACBSP)

Lamar University
PO Box 10001, Beaumont 77710-0001
Type: Public, state, four-year
System: Texas State University System
Degrees: A, B, M, D *Enroll:* 8,652
URL: http://www.lamar.edu
Phone: (409) 880-7011 *Calendar:* Sem. plan
Inst. Accred.: SACS (1955/1998)
Prog. Accred.: Allied Health (audiology, respiratory therapy, speech-language pathology, surgical technology), Business (AACSB), Computer Science (ABET-CAC), Culinary Education, Dentistry (dental hygiene), Dietetics (didactic), Dietetics (internship), Engineering (chemical, civil, electrical, industrial, mechanical), Music, Nursing, Radiography, Social Work, Teacher Education (NCATE)

Laredo Community College
West End Washington St., Laredo 78040-4395
Type: Public, state/local, two-year
Degrees: A *Enroll:* 4,912
URL: http://www.laredo.edu
Phone: (956) 722-0521 *Calendar:* Sem. plan
Inst. Accred.: SACS (1957/1999)
Prog. Accred.: Allied Health (occupational therapy assisting), Clinical Lab Technology, Nursing, Physical Therapy Assisting, Radiography

Lee College
PO Box 818, Baytown 77522-0818
Type: Public, state/local, two-year
Degrees: A *Enroll:* 2,823
URL: http://www.lee.edu
Phone: (281) 427-5611 *Calendar:* Sem. plan
Inst. Accred.: SACS (1948/2006)
Prog. Accred.: Allied Health (EMT-paramedic), Nursing

LeTourneau University
PO Box 7001, Longview 75607-7001
Type: Private, independent, four-year
Degrees: A, B, M *Enroll:* 2,539
URL: http://www.letu.edu
Phone: (903) 233-3000 *Calendar:* Sem. plan
Inst. Accred.: SACS (1970/2006)
Prog. Accred.: Engineering (general)

Lon Morris College
800 College Ave., Jacksonville 75766-2900
Type: Private, Texas Annual Conference of The United Methodist Ch, two-year
Degrees: A *Enroll:* 363
URL: http://www.lonmorris.edu
Phone: (903) 589-4000 *Calendar:* Sem. plan
Inst. Accred.: SACS (1927/2006)

Lone Star College System
5000 Research Forest Dr., The Woodlands 77381-4399
Type: Public, state/local, two-year
System: Texas Higher Education Coordinating Board
Degrees: A *Enroll:* 18,198
URL: http://www.lonestar.edu
Phone: (832) 813-6500 *Calendar:* Sem. plan
Inst. Accred.: SACS (1976/2001)
Prog. Accred.: Montessori Teacher Education

Lone Star College—CyFair
9191 Barker Cypress Rd., Cypress 77433
Phone: (281) 290-3200
Prog. Accred: Allied Health (diagnostic medical sonography, medical assisting (AMA)), Nursing

Lone Star College—Kingwood
20000 Kingwood Dr., Kingwood 77339
Phone: (281) 312-1600
Prog. Accred: Allied Health (occupational therapy assisting, respiratory therapy), Nursing

Lone Star College—Montgomery
3200 College Park Dr., Conroe 77384
Phone: (936) 273-7000
Prog. Accred: Nursing, Physical Therapy Assisting, Radiography

Lone Star College—North Harris
2700 W.W. Thorne Dr., Houston 77073
Phone: (281) 618-5400
Prog. Accred: Allied Health (EMT-paramedic), English Language Education, Nursing

Lone Star College—Tomball
30555 Tomball Pkwy., Tomball 77375-4036
Phone: (281) 351-3300
Prog. Accred: Allied Health (occupational therapy assisting), Nursing, Veterinary Technology

Lubbock Christian University
5601 19th St., Lubbock 79407-2099
Type: Private, Church of Christ, four-year
Degrees: A, B, M *Enroll:* 1,674
URL: http://www.lcu.edu
Phone: (806) 796-8800 *Calendar:* Sem. plan
Inst. Accred.: SACS (1963/2008)
Prog. Accred.: Nursing, Social Work

McLennan Community College
1400 College Dr., Waco 76708
Type: Public, state/local, two-year
Degrees: A *Enroll:* 4,945
URL: http://www.mclennan.edu
Phone: (254) 299-8000 *Calendar:* Sem. plan
Inst. Accred.: SACS (1968/2002)
Prog. Accred.: Allied Health (electroneurodiagnostic technology, respiratory therapy, respiratory therapy technology), Clinical Lab Technology, Nursing, Physical Therapy Assisting, Radiography, Veterinary Technology

McMurry University
South 14th St. and Sayles Blvd., Abilene 79697
Type: Private, United Methodist Church, four-year
Degrees: A, B *Enroll:* 1,279
URL: http://www.mcm.edu
Phone: (915) 793-3800 *Calendar:* Sem. plan
Inst. Accred.: SACS (1949/1999)
Prog. Accred.: Nursing Education

Midland College
3600 North Garfield St., Midland 79705
Type: Public, local, four-year
Degrees: A, B *Enroll:* 3,431
URL: http://www.midland.edu
Phone: (432) 685-4500 *Calendar:* Sem. plan
Inst. Accred.: SACS (1975/2001)
Prog. Accred.: Allied Health (diagnostic medical sonography, respiratory therapy), Nursing, Radiography, Veterinary Technology

Midwestern State University
3410 Taft Blvd., Wichita Falls 76308-2099
Type: Public, state, four-year
Degrees: A, B, M *Enroll:* 4,996
URL: http://www.mwsu.edu
Phone: (940) 397-4000 *Calendar:* Sem. plan
Inst. Accred.: SACS (1950/2002)
Prog. Accred.: Allied Health (respiratory therapy), Business (ACBSP), Dentistry (dental hygiene), Engineering Technology (manufacturing), Music, Nursing Education, Radiography, Social Work

Mountain View College
4849 West Illinois Ave., Dallas 75211-6599
Type: Public, state/local, two-year
System: Dallas County Community College District
Degrees: A *Enroll:* 3,388
URL: http://www.mountainviewcollege.edu
Phone: (214) 860-8600 *Calendar:* Sem. plan
Inst. Accred.: SACS (1972/2003)

Navarro College
3200 West Seventh Ave., Corsicana 75110
Type: Public, local, two-year
Degrees: A *Enroll:* 4,386
URL: http://www.navarrocollege.edu
Phone: (903) 874-6501 *Calendar:* Sem. plan
Inst. Accred.: SACS (1954/2006)
Prog. Accred.: Allied Health (occupational therapy assisting), Nursing

North Central Texas College
1525 West California St., Gainesville 76240-4699
Type: Public, state/local, two-year
Degrees: A *Enroll:* 7,346
URL: http://www.nctc.edu
Phone: (940) 668-7731 *Calendar:* Sem. plan
Inst. Accred.: SACS (1961/2001)
Prog. Accred.: Allied Health (surgical technology), Nursing

North Lake College
5001 North MacArthur Blvd., Irving 75038-3899
Type: Public, state/local, two-year
System: Dallas County Community College District
Degrees: A *Enroll:* 5,080
URL: http://www.northlakecollege.edu
Phone: (972) 273-3000 *Calendar:* Sem. plan
Inst. Accred.: SACS (1979/2003)
Prog. Accred.: Construction Education

Northeast Texas Community College
PO Box 1307, Mount Pleasant 75456-1307
Type: Public, state/local, two-year
Degrees: A *Enroll:* 1,350
URL: http://www.ntcc.edu
Phone: (903) 434-8100 *Calendar:* Sem. plan
Inst. Accred.: SACS (1987/2002)

Northwest Vista College
3535 North Ellison Dr., San Antonio 78251
Type: Public, state/local, two-year
System: Alamo Community College District
Degrees: A *Enroll:* 5,243
URL: http://www.accd.edu/nvc
Phone: (210) 348-2000 *Calendar:* Sem. plan
Inst. Accred.: SACS (2001/2006)

Oblate School of Theology
285 Oblate Dr., San Antonio 78216-6693
Type: Private, Roman Catholic Church, four-year
Degrees: M, D *Enroll:* 127
URL: http://www.ost.edu
Phone: (210) 341-1366 *Calendar:* Sem. plan
Inst. Accred.: ATS (1982/1999), SACS (1968/1999)
Prog. Accred.: Clinical Pastoral Education

Odessa College
201 West University Blvd., Odessa 79764-7127
Type: Public, local, two-year
Degrees: A *Enroll:* 2,858
URL: http://www.odessa.edu
Phone: (432) 335-6400 *Calendar:* Sem. plan
Inst. Accred.: SACS (1952/2002)
Prog. Accred.: Clinical Lab Technology, Music, Nursing, Physical Therapy Assisting, Radiography

Our Lady of the Lake University
411 SW 24th St., San Antonio 78207-4689
Type: Private, Roman Catholic Church, four-year
Degrees: B, M, D *Enroll:* 2,021
URL: http://www.ollusa.edu
Phone: (210) 434-6711 *Calendar:* Sem. plan
Inst. Accred.: SACS (1923/2002)
Prog. Accred.: Allied Health (speech-language pathology), Business (ACBSP), Counseling Psychology, Graduate Social Work, Social Work

Palo Alto College
1400 West Villaret Blvd., San Antonio 78224-2499
Type: Public, state/local, two-year
System: Alamo Community College District
Degrees: A *Enroll:* 4,683
URL: http://www.accd.edu/pac
Phone: (210) 921-5000 *Calendar:* Sem. plan
Inst. Accred.: SACS (1987/2002)
Prog. Accred.: Veterinary Technology

Panola College
1109 West Panola St., Carthage 75633
Type: Public, local, two-year
Degrees: A *Enroll:* 1,275
URL: http://www.panola.edu
Phone: (903) 693-2000 *Calendar:* Sem. plan
Inst. Accred.: SACS (1960/2000)
Prog. Accred.: Allied Health (occupational therapy assisting), Nursing

Paris Junior College
2400 Clarksville St., Paris 75460
Type: Public, state/local, two-year
Degrees: A *Enroll:* 2,724
URL: http://www.parisjc.edu
Phone: (903) 785-7661 *Calendar:* Sem. plan
Inst. Accred.: SACS (1934/2002)
Prog. Accred.: Allied Health (surgical technology), Nursing

Parker College of Chiropractic
2500 Walnut Hill Ln., Ste. 100E, Dallas 75229-5668
Type: Private, independent, four-year
Degrees: B, P, D *Enroll:* 983
URL: http://www.parkercc.edu
Phone: (972) 438-6932 *Calendar:* Tri. plan
Inst. Accred.: SACS (1987/2002)
Prog. Accred.: Chiropractic Education

Paul Quinn College
3837 Simpson Stuart Rd., Dallas 75241
Type: Private, African Methodist Episcopal Church, four-year
Degrees: B *Enroll:* 752
URL: http://www.pqc.edu
Phone: (214) 376-1000 *Calendar:* Sem. plan
Inst. Accred.: SACS (1972/1997, Probation)

Prairie View A&M University
PO Box 519, Mail Stop 1001, Prairie View 77446-0519
Type: Public, state, four-year
System: Texas A&M University System
Degrees: B, M, D *Enroll:* 6,637
URL: http://www.pvamu.edu
Phone: (936) 857-3311 *Calendar:* Sem. plan
Inst. Accred.: SACS (1934/2000)
Prog. Accred.: Business (AACSB), Computer Science (ABET-CAC), Dietetics (didactic), Dietetics (internship), Engineering (chemical, civil, electrical, mechanical), Engineering Technology (computer, electrical), Nursing, Nursing Education, Social Work, Teacher Education (NCATE)

Ranger College
College Circle, Ranger 76470-3298
Type: Public, local, two-year
Degrees: A *Enroll:* 622
URL: http://www.ranger.cc.tx.us
Phone: (254) 647-3234 *Calendar:* Sem. plan
Inst. Accred.: SACS (1968/2002)

Remington College—Houston
3110 Hayes Rd., Ste. 380, Houston 77082
Type: Private, proprietary, two-year
System: Education America, Inc.
Degrees: A
URL: http://www.remingtoncollege.edu
Phone: (281) 899-1240 *Calendar:* Qtr. plan
Inst. Accred.: ACCSCT (1990/2004)

Dallas Campus
1800 Eastgate Dr., Garland 75041-5513
Phone: (972) 686-7878

North Houston Campus
11310 Greens Crossing, Ste. 300, Houston 77067
Phone: (281) 885-4450

Richland College
12800 Abrams Rd., Dallas 75243-2199
Type: Public, state/local, two-year
System: Dallas County Community College District
Degrees: A *Enroll:* 7,769
URL: http://www.richlandcollege.edu
Phone: (972) 238-6194 *Calendar:* Sem. plan
Inst. Accred.: SACS (1974/2002)
Prog. Accred.: Allied Health (medical assisting (AMA))

Rio Grande Bible Institute
4300 South Business Hwy. 281, Edinburg 78539
Type: Private, interdenominational, four-year
Degrees: B
URL: http://www.riogrande.edu
Phone: (956) 380-8100 *Calendar:* Sem. plan
Inst. Accred.: ABHE (1999/2004)

Saint Edward's University
3001 South Congress Ave., Austin 78704-6489
Type: Private, Roman Catholic Church, four-year
Degrees: B, M *Enroll:* 3,856
URL: http://www.stedwards.edu
Phone: (512) 448-8400 *Calendar:* Sem. plan
Inst. Accred.: SACS (1958/2007)
Prog. Accred.: Social Work

Saint Mary's University
One Camino Santa Maria, San Antonio 78228-8572
Type: Private, Roman Catholic Church, four-year
Degrees: B, M, D *Enroll:* 3,463
URL: http://www.stmarytx.edu
Phone: (210) 436-3011 *Calendar:* Sem. plan
Inst. Accred.: SACS (1949/2005)
Prog. Accred.: Business (AACSB), Counseling, Engineering (electrical, industrial), Law, Marriage and Family Therapy, Music

Saint Philip's College
1801 Martin Luther King Dr., San Antonio 78203
Type: Public, state/local, two-year
System: Alamo Community College District
Degrees: A *Enroll:* 6,083
URL: http://www.accd.edu/spc
Phone: (210) 531-3500 *Calendar:* Sem. plan
Inst. Accred.: SACS (1951/2006)
Prog. Accred.: Allied Health (occupational therapy assisting, respiratory therapy, surgical technology), Clinical Lab Technology, Culinary Education, Physical Therapy Assisting, Radiography

Sam Houston State University
PO Box 2026, Huntsville 77341-2026
Type: Public, state, four-year
System: Texas State University System
Degrees: B, M, D *Enroll:* 13,245
URL: http://www.shsu.edu
Phone: (936) 294-1111 *Calendar:* Sem. plan
Inst. Accred.: SACS (1925/1999)
Prog. Accred.: Business (AACSB), Counseling, Dietetics (didactic), Dietetics (internship), Music, Teacher Education (NCATE)

San Antonio College
1300 San Pedro Ave., San Antonio 78212-4299
Type: Public, state/local, two-year
System: Alamo Community College District
Degrees: A *Enroll:* 11,768
URL: http://www.accd.edu/sac
Phone: (210) 733-2000 *Calendar:* Sem. plan
Inst. Accred.: SACS (1952/2006)
Prog. Accred.: Allied Health (medical assisting (AMA)), Dentistry (dental assisting), Funeral Service Education (Mortuary Science), Nursing

San Jacinto College Central
8060 Spencer Hwy., PO Box 2007, Pasadena 77501-2007
Type: Public, state/local, two-year
System: San Jacinto College District
Degrees: A
URL: http://www.sjcd.edu
Phone: (281) 476-1501 *Calendar:* Sem. plan
Inst. Accred.: SACS (1966/1999, *Indirect accreditation through San Jacinto College District, Pasadena, TX*)
Prog. Accred.: Dietetic Technician, Radiography

San Jacinto College North
5800 Uvalde Rd., Houston 77049-4599
Type: Public, local, two-year
System: San Jacinto College District
Degrees: A
URL: http://www.sjcd.edu
Phone: (281) 458-4050 *Calendar:* Sem. plan
Inst. Accred.: SACS (1966/1999, *Indirect accreditation through San Jacinto College District, Pasadena, TX*)
Prog. Accred.: Allied Health (EMT-paramedic, medical assisting (AMA))

San Jacinto College South
1373 Beamer Rd., Houston 77089-6099
Type: Public, local, two-year
System: San Jacinto College District
Degrees: A
URL: http://www.sjcd.edu
Phone: (281) 484-1900 *Calendar:* Sem. plan
Inst. Accred.: SACS (1966/1999, *Indirect accreditation through San Jacinto College District, Pasadena, TX*)
Prog. Accred.: Nursing, Physical Therapy Assisting

Schreiner University
2100 Memorial Blvd., Kerrville 78028
Type: Private, Presbyterian Church (USA), four-year
Degrees: A, B, M *Enroll:* 768
URL: http://www.schreiner.edu
Phone: (830) 896-5411 *Calendar:* Sem. plan
Inst. Accred.: SACS (1934/2000)

South Plains College
1401 South College Ave., Levelland 79336
Type: Public, state, two-year
Degrees: A *Enroll:* 6,284
URL: http://www.southplainscollege.edu
Phone: (806) 894-9611 *Calendar:* Sem. plan
Inst. Accred.: SACS (1963/2003)
Prog. Accred.: Allied Health (EMT-paramedic, respiratory therapy, surgeon assisting, surgical technology), Nursing, Radiography

South Texas College
PO Box 9701, McAllen 78502-9701
Type: Public, state, four-year
Degrees: A, B *Enroll:* 10,249
URL: http://www.southtexascollege.edu
Phone: (956) 872-8311 *Calendar:* Sem. plan
Inst. Accred.: SACS (1995/2000)
Prog. Accred.: Allied Health (occupational therapy assisting), Business (ACBSP), Physical Therapy Assisting

South Texas College of Law
1303 San Jacinto St., Houston 77002-7000
Type: Private, independent, four-year
Degrees: P *Enroll:* 1,124
URL: http://www.stcl.edu
Phone: (713) 659-8040 *Calendar:* Sem. plan
Inst. Accred.: ABA (1959/2001)

Southern Methodist University
6425 Boaz St., Dallas 75275
Type: Private, United Methodist Church, four-year
Degrees: B, M, D *Enroll:* 9,314
URL: http://www.smu.edu
Phone: (214) 768-2000 *Calendar:* Sem. plan
Inst. Accred.: ATS (1938/2000), SACS (1921/2000)
Prog. Accred.: Business (AACSB), Computer Science (ABET-CAC), Dance, Engineering (computer, electrical, environmental/sanitary, mechanical), Law, Music, Theatre

Southwest Institute of Technology
5424 Hwy. 290 West, Ste. 200, Austin 78735-8800
Type: Private, proprietary, two-year
System: Timberline 1
Degrees: A *Enroll:* 48
URL: http://www.switaustin.com
Phone: (512) 892-2640
Inst. Accred.: ACCSCT (1978/2006)

Southwest Texas Junior College
2401 Garner Field Rd., Uvalde 78801-6297
Type: Public, local, two-year
Degrees: A *Enroll:* 3,177
URL: http://www.swtjc.edu
Phone: (830) 278-4401 *Calendar:* Sem. plan
Inst. Accred.: SACS (1964/2007)

Southwestern Adventist University
PO Box 567, Keene 76059
Type: Private, Seventh-Day Adventist Church, four-year
Degrees: A, B, M *Enroll:* 813
URL: http://www.swau.edu
Phone: (817) 645-3921 *Calendar:* Sem. plan
Inst. Accred.: SACS (1958/2007)
Prog. Accred.: Nursing

Southwestern Assemblies of God University
1200 Sycamore St., Waxahachie 75165-2397
Type: Private, Assemblies of God Church, four-year
Degrees: A, B, M *Enroll:* 1,425
URL: http://www.sagu.edu
Phone: (972) 937-4010 *Calendar:* Sem. plan
Inst. Accred.: SACS (1968/2002)

Southwestern Baptist Theological Seminary
PO Box 22000, Fort Worth 76122-0001
Type: Private, Southern Baptist Convention, four-year
Degrees: B, M, D *Enroll:* 2,115
URL: http://www.swbts.edu
Phone: (817) 923-1921 *Calendar:* Sem. plan
Inst. Accred.: ATS (1944/2001), SACS (1969/2001)
Prog. Accred.: Music

Southwestern Christian College
PO Box 10, Terrell 75160
Type: Private, Church of Christ, four-year
Degrees: A, B *Enroll:* 239
URL: http://www.swcc.edu
Phone: (972) 524-3341 *Calendar:* Sem. plan
Inst. Accred.: SACS (1973/2001)

Southwestern University
PO Box 770, Georgetown 78627-0770
Type: Private, United Methodist Church, four-year
Degrees: B *Enroll:* 1,295
URL: http://www.southwestern.edu
Phone: (512) 863-6511 *Calendar:* Sem. plan
Inst. Accred.: SACS (1915/2002)
Prog. Accred.: Music

Stephen F. Austin State University
1936 North St., Nacogdoches 75965-3940
Type: Public, state, four-year
Degrees: B, M, D *Enroll:* 10,028
URL: http://www.sfasu.edu
Phone: (936) 468-2011 *Calendar:* Sem. plan
Inst. Accred.: SACS (1927/2000)
Prog. Accred.: Allied Health (speech-language pathology), Art, Business (AACSB), Computer Science (ABET-CAC), Counseling, Dietetics (didactic), Dietetics (internship), Family & Consumer Science, Forestry, Graduate Social Work, Interior Design, Music, Nursing, Rehabilitation Counseling, Social Work, Teacher Education (NCATE), Theatre

Sul Ross State University
400 North Harrison St., Alpine 79830-5105
Type: Public, state, four-year
System: Texas State University System
Degrees: A, B, M *Enroll:* 2,192
URL: http://www.sulross.edu
Phone: (432) 837-8011 *Calendar:* Sem. plan
Inst. Accred.: SACS (1929/2008)
Prog. Accred.: Veterinary Technology

Rio Grande College—Del Rio Campus
205 Wildcat Dr., Del Rio 78840
Phone: (830) 768-4065

Rio Grande College—Eagle Pass Campus
Route 3, PO Box 1200, Eagle Pass 78852
Phone: (830) 758-5005

Rio Grande College—Uvalde Campus
400 Sul Ross Dr., Uvalde 78801
Phone: (830) 279-3001

Tarleton State University
1333 West Washington St., Stephenville 76401-4168
Type: Public, state, four-year
System: Texas A&M University System
Degrees: A, B, M, D *Enroll:* 7,410
URL: http://www.tarleton.edu
Phone: (254) 968-9000 *Calendar:* Sem. plan
Inst. Accred.: SACS (1926/2000)
Prog. Accred.: Business (ACBSP), Clinical Lab Scientist, Engineering (engineering physics/science), Music, Nursing Education, Social Work

Central Texas Campus
1901 South Clear Creek Rd., Kileen 76549-4111
Phone: (254) 519-5435

Tarrant County College District
1500 Houston St., Fort Worth 76102-6599
Type: Public, state/local, two-year
System: Texas Higher Education Coordinating Board
Degrees: A *Enroll:* 19,858
URL: http://www.tccd.edu
Phone: (817) 515-5100 *Calendar:* Sem. plan
Inst. Accred.: SACS (1969/2003)
Prog. Accred.: Allied Health (EMT-paramedic, respiratory therapy, surgical technology), Dentistry (dental hygiene), Nursing, Physical Therapy Assisting, Radiography

Northeast Campus
828 Harwood Rd., Hurst 76054
Phone: (817) 515-6100
Prog. Accred: Dentistry (dental hygiene), Radiography

Northwest Campus
4801 Marine Creek Pkwy., Fort Worth 76179
Phone: (817) 515-7100

South Campus
5301 Campus Dr., Fort Worth 76119
Phone: (817) 515-4100

Southeast Campus
2100 Southeast Pkwy., Arlington 76018
Phone: (817) 515-5100
Prog. Accred: Dietetic Technician

Temple College
2600 South First St., Temple 76504-7435
Type: Public, local, two-year
Degrees: A *Enroll:* 2,210
URL: http://www.templejc.edu
Phone: (254) 298-8282 *Calendar:* Sem. plan
Inst. Accred.: SACS (1959/2000)
Prog. Accred.: Allied Health (respiratory therapy, surgical technology), Clinical Lab Technology, Dentistry (dental hygiene), Nursing

Texarkana College
2500 North Robison Rd., Texarkana 75501
Type: Public, local, two-year
Degrees: A *Enroll:* 2,535
URL: http://www.texarkanacollege.edu
Phone: (903) 838-4541 *Calendar:* Sem. plan
Inst. Accred.: SACS (1931/2006)
Prog. Accred.: Nursing

Texas A&M International University
5201 University Blvd., Laredo 78041-1900
Type: Public, state, four-year
System: Texas A&M University System
Degrees: A, B, M, D *Enroll:* 3,132
URL: http://www.tamiu.edu
Phone: (956) 326-2001 *Calendar:* Sem. plan
Inst. Accred.: SACS (1970/2005)
Prog. Accred.: Business (AACSB), Nursing, Social Work

Texas A&M University
1246 TAMU, College Station 77843-1246
Type: Public, state, four-year
System: Texas A&M University System
Degrees: B, M, D *Enroll:* 41,663
URL: http://www.tamu.edu
Phone: (979) 845-3211 *Calendar:* Sem. plan
Inst. Accred.: SACS (1924/2002)
Prog. Accred.: Accounting, Allied Health (medicine), Business (AACSB), Clinical Psychology, Computer Science (ABET-CAC), Construction Education, Counseling Psychology, Dietetics (didactic), Dietetics (internship), Engineering (aerospace, agricultural, bioengineering, chemical, civil, computer, electrical, industrial, mechanical, nuclear, ocean, petroleum, radiological health), Engineering Technology (electrical, manufacturing, mechanical, telecommunications), English Language Education, Forestry, Landscape Architecture, Planning, Psychology Internship, Public Administration, Recreation and Leisure Services, School Psychology, Teacher Education (NCATE), Veterinary Medicine

Galveston Campus
PO Box 1675, Galveston 77553
Phone: (409) 740-4400
Prog. Accred: Engineering (naval architecture/marine)

Texas A&M University at Qatar
Education City, Doha, Qatar
Phone: (740) 492-7368

Texas A&M University System Health Science Center
301 Tarrow St., John B. Connally Bldg., MS 1361, College Station 77840-7896
Type: Public, state, four-year
System: Texas A&M University System
Degrees: B, M, D *Enroll:* 1,057
URL: http://tamushsc.tamu.edu
Phone: (979) 458-7200 *Calendar:* Sem. plan
Inst. Accred.: SACS (1999/2002)
Prog. Accred.: Dentistry (pediatric dentistry), Public Health

The Baylor College of Dentistry
PO Box 660677, Dallas 75266-0677
Phone: (214) 828-8100
Prog. Accred: Dentistry (advanced education in general dentistry, combined prosthodontics, dental hygiene, dental public health, dentistry, endodontics, general dentistry, general practice residency, oral and maxillofacial pathology, oral and maxillofacial surgery, orthodontic and dentofacial orthopedics, pediatric dentistry, periodontics)

Texas A&M University—Commerce
PO Box 3011, Commerce 75429-3011
Type: Public, state, four-year
System: Texas A&M University System
Degrees: B, M, D *Enroll:* 6,186
URL: http://www.tamu-commerce.edu
Phone: (903) 886-5000 *Calendar:* Sem. plan
Inst. Accred.: SACS (1925/2003)
Prog. Accred.: Business (AACSB), Counseling, Engineering (industrial), Graduate Social Work, Industrial Technology, Music, Social Work

Texas A&M University—Corpus Christi
6300 Ocean Dr., Corpus Christi 78412-5599
Type: Public, state, four-year
System: Texas A&M University System
Degrees: A, B, M, D *Enroll:* 6,807
URL: http://www.tamucc.edu
Phone: (361) 825-5700 *Calendar:* Sem. plan
Inst. Accred.: SACS (1975/2000)
Prog. Accred.: Applied Science (surveying/geomatics), Business (AACSB), Clinical Lab Scientist, Counseling, Engineering Technology (instrumentation, mechanical), Music, Nursing Education

Texas A&M University—Kingsville
700 University Blvd., Kingsville 78363-8202
Type: Public, state, four-year
System: Texas A&M University System
Degrees: B, M, D *Enroll:* 5,195
URL: http://www.tamuk.edu
Phone: (361) 593-2111 *Calendar:* Sem. plan
Inst. Accred.: SACS (1933/2005)
Prog. Accred.: Allied Health (speech-language pathology), Business (ACBSP), Dietetics (didactic), Dietetics (internship), Engineering (chemical, civil, electrical, mechanical), Industrial Technology, Music, Pharmacy, Social Work

Texas A&M University—Texarkana
PO Box 5518, Texarkana 75505-5518
Type: Public, state, four-year
System: Texas A&M University System
Degrees: B, M *Enroll:* 908
URL: http://www.tamut.edu
Phone: (903) 223-3000 *Calendar:* Sem. plan
Inst. Accred.: SACS (1979/2006)
Prog. Accred.: Nursing Education

Texas Chiropractic College
5912 Spencer Hwy., Pasadena 77505-1699
Type: Private, independent, four-year
Degrees: B, P, D *Enroll:* 437
URL: http://www.txchiro.edu
Phone: (281) 487-1170 *Calendar:* Tri. plan
Inst. Accred.: SACS (1984/1999)
Prog. Accred.: Chiropractic Education

Texas Christian University
2800 South University Dr., Fort Worth 76129
Type: Private, Christian Church (Disciples of Christ), four-year
Degrees: B, M, D *Enroll:* 7,889
URL: http://www.tcu.edu
Phone: (817) 257-7000 *Calendar:* Sem. plan
Inst. Accred.: SACS (1922/2003)
Prog. Accred.: Accounting, Allied Health (speech-language pathology), Business (AACSB), Computer Science (ABET-CAC), Dance, Dietetics (coordinated), Dietetics (didactic), Engineering (general), Interior Design, Journalism, Music, Nurse Anesthesia Education, Nursing Education, Social Work

Texas College
PO Box 4500, Tyler 75712-4500
Type: Private, Christian Methodist Episcopal Church, four-year
Degrees: A, B *Enroll:* 772
URL: http://www.texascollege.edu
Phone: (903) 593-8311 *Calendar:* Sem. plan
Inst. Accred.: SACS (2001/2006)

Texas College of Traditional Chinese Medicine
4005 Manchaca Rd., Ste. 200, Austin 78704
Type: Private, proprietary, four-year
Degrees: M *Enroll:* 83
URL: http://www.texastcm.edu
Phone: (512) 444-8082 *Calendar:* Tri. plan
Inst. Accred.: ACAOM (1996/2000)

Texas Culinary Academy
11400 Burnett Rd., Ste. 2100, Austin 78752
Type: Private, proprietary, two-year
System: Career Education Corporation
Degrees: A *Enroll:* 894
URL: http://www.txca.com
Phone: (512) 339-2665
Inst. Accred.: ACICS (2005)
Prog. Accred.: Culinary Education

Le Cordon Bleu Institute of Culinary Arts Dallas
11830 Webb Chapel Rd., Ste. 1200, Dallas 75234
Phone: (214) 647-8500

Orlando Culinary Academy
8511 Commodity Circle, Ste. 100, Orlando, FL 32819
Phone: (407) 888-4000
Prog. Accred: Culinary Education

Texas Lutheran University
1000 West Ct. St., Seguin 78155-5999
Type: Private, Evangelical Lutheran Church in America, four-year
Degrees: A, B *Enroll:* 1,370
URL: http://www.tlu.edu
Phone: (830) 372-8000 *Calendar:* Sem. plan
Inst. Accred.: SACS (1940/2008)
Prog. Accred.: Business (ACBSP), Teacher Education (TEAC)

Texas Southern University
3100 Cleburne St., Houston 77004
Type: Public, state, four-year
Degrees: B, M, P, D *Enroll:* 10,225
URL: http://www.tsu.edu
Phone: (713) 313-7011 *Calendar:* Sem. plan
Inst. Accred.: SACS (1948/2000, Probation)
Prog. Accred.: Allied Health (respiratory therapy), Aviation Technology, Business (AACSB), Clinical Lab Scientist, Dietetics (didactic), Engineering Technology (electrical), Industrial Technology, Law (ABA only), Pharmacy, Planning, Social Work

Texas State Technical College Marshall
PO Box 1269, Marshall 75671-1269
Type: Public, state/local, two-year
System: Texas State Technical College System
Degrees: A
URL: http://www.marshall.tstc.edu
Phone: (903) 935-1010 *Calendar:* Sem. plan
Inst. Accred.: SACS (2002/2007, Warning)

Texas State Technical College—Harlingen
1902 North Loop 499, Harlingen 78550-3697
Type: Public, state, two-year
System: Texas State Technical College System
Degrees: A *Enroll:* 2,466
URL: http://www.harlingen.tstc.edu
Phone: (956) 364-4000 *Calendar:* Sem. plan
Inst. Accred.: SACS (1971/2005)
Prog. Accred.: Allied Health (medical assisting (AMA), surgical technology), Dentistry (dental assisting, dental hygiene)

Texas State Technical College—Waco
3801 Campus Dr., Waco 76705
Type: Public, state, two-year
System: Texas State Technical College System
Degrees: A *Enroll:* 3,480
URL: http://www.waco.tstc.edu
Phone: (254) 799-3611 *Calendar:* Sem. plan
Inst. Accred.: SACS (1968/2003)
Prog. Accred.: Dentistry (dental assisting)

Texas State Technical College—West Texas at Sweetwater
300 Homer K. Tyler Dr., Sweetwater 79556-4108
Type: Public, state, two-year
System: Texas State Technical College System
Degrees: A *Enroll:* 1,125
URL: http://www.westtexas.tstc.edu
Phone: (325) 235-7300 *Calendar:* Sem. plan
Inst. Accred.: SACS (1979/2005)

Texas State University—San Marcos
601 University Dr., San Marcos 78666-4616
Type: Public, state, four-year
System: Texas State University System
Degrees: B, M, D *Enroll:* 22,840
URL: http://www.txstate.edu
Phone: (512) 245-2111 *Calendar:* Sem. plan
Inst. Accred.: SACS (1925/1999)
Prog. Accred.: Allied Health (health services administration, respiratory therapy, speech-language pathology), Business (AACSB), Clinical Lab Scientist, Computer Science (ABET-CAC), Construction Education, Counseling, Dietetics (didactic), Dietetics (internship), Family & Consumer Science, Graduate Social Work, Interior Design, Journalism, Music, Physical Therapy, Public Administration, Radiation Therapy, Recreation and Leisure Services, Social Work

Texas Tech University
PO Box 42005, Lubbock 79409-2005
Type: Public, state, four-year
System: Texas Tech University System
Degrees: B, M, D *Enroll:* 25,743
URL: http://www.texastech.edu
Phone: (806) 742-2011 *Calendar:* Sem. plan
Inst. Accred.: SACS (1928/2005)
Prog. Accred.: Accounting, Allied Health (audiology, health services administration, speech-language pathology), Art, Business (AACSB), Clinical Psychology, Counseling, Counseling Psychology, Dietetics (didactic), Dietetics (internship), Engineering (chemical, civil, computer, electrical, engineering physics/science, environmental/sanitary, industrial, mechanical, petroleum), Engineering Technology (civil/construction, electrical, mechanical), Family & Consumer Science, Interior Design, Journalism, Landscape Architecture, Law, Marriage and Family Therapy, Music, Psychology Internship, Public Administration, Social Work, Teacher Education (NCATE)

Texas Tech University Health Sciences Center
3601 Fourth St., Lubbock 79430
Type: Public, state, four-year
System: Texas Tech University System
Degrees: B, M, P, D *Enroll:* 2,131
URL: http://www.ttuhsc.edu
Phone: (806) 743-1000 *Calendar:* Sem. plan
Inst. Accred.: SACS (2004)
Prog. Accred.: Allied Health (medicine, occupational therapy), Clinical Lab Scientist, Diagnositc Molecular Scientist, Nursing Education, Physical Therapy, Rehabilitation Counseling

Amarillo Campus
1400 Wallace Blvd., Amarillo 79106
Phone: (806) 354-5411
Prog. Accred: Pharmacy

El Paso Campus
4800 Alberta Ave., El Paso 79905
Phone: (915) 545-6500
Prog. Accred: Allied Health (medicine)

Odessa Campus
800 West 4th St., Odessa 79763
Phone: (915) 335-5111
Prog. Accred: Physician Assistant

Texas Wesleyan University
1201 Wesleyan St., Fort Worth 76105-1536
Type: Private, Methodist Episcopal Church, four-year
Degrees: B, M, D *Enroll:* 2,220
URL: http://www.txwesleyan.edu
Phone: (817) 531-4444 *Calendar:* Sem. plan
Inst. Accred.: SACS (1949/2003)
Prog. Accred.: Business (ACBSP), Law (ABA only), Music, Nurse Anesthesia Education

Texas Woman's University
PO Box 425587, Denton 76204-5587
Type: Public, state, four-year
Degrees: B, M, D *Enroll:* 8,070
URL: http://www.twu.edu
Phone: (940) 898-2000 *Calendar:* Sem. plan
Inst. Accred.: SACS (1923/2003)
Prog. Accred.: Allied Health (health services administration, occupational therapy, speech-language pathology), Counseling, Counseling Psychology, Dance, Dentistry (dental hygiene), Dietetics (didactic), Dietetics (internship), Librarianship, Music, Nursing Education, Physical Therapy, Psychology Internship, Social Work

Dallas/Presbyterian Campus
8194 Walnut Hill Ln., Dallas 75231-4365
Phone: (214) 706-2350
Prog. Accred: Allied Health (occupational therapy)

Houston Institute of Health Sciences
1140 M.D. Anderson Blvd., Houston 77030-2897
Phone: (713) 794-2331
Prog. Accred: Allied Health (occupational therapy)

Trinity University
One Trinity Place, San Antonio 78212-7200
Type: Private, Presbyterian Church (USA), four-year
Degrees: B, M *Enroll:* 2,602
URL: http://www.trinity.edu
Phone: (210) 999-7011 *Calendar:* Sem. plan
Inst. Accred.: SACS (1946/1997)
Prog. Accred.: Allied Health (health services administration), Business (AACSB), Engineering (engineering physics/science), Music, Teacher Education (NCATE)

Trinity Valley Community College
100 Cardinal Dr., Athens 75751-3243
Type: Public, state/local, two-year
Degrees: A *Enroll:* 3,611
URL: http://www.tvcc.edu
Phone: (903) 675-6200 *Calendar:* Sem. plan
Inst. Accred.: SACS (1952/2007)
Prog. Accred.: Allied Health (surgical technology), Nursing

Anderson County Campus
Highway 19 North at 287, PO Box 2530, Palestine 75802
Phone: (903) 729-0256

Health Science Center
800 Hwy. 243, Kaufman 75142-1861
Phone: (972) 932-4309

Kaufman County Campus
PO Box 668, Terrell 75160
Phone: (972) 563-9573

Tyler Junior College
PO Box 9020, Tyler 75798-9020
Type: Public, state/local, two-year
Degrees: A *Enroll:* 6,577
URL: http://www.tjc.edu
Phone: (903) 510-2200 *Calendar:* Sem. plan
Inst. Accred.: SACS (1931/2000)
Prog. Accred.: Allied Health (diagnostic medical sonography, ophthalmic lab technology, opticianry, respiratory therapy, surgical technology), Clinical Lab Technology, Dentistry (dental hygiene), Radiography

The University of Dallas
1845 East Northgate Dr., Irving 75062-4799
Type: Private, Roman Catholic Church, four-year
Degrees: B, M, D *Enroll:* 2,092
URL: http://www.udallas.edu
Phone: (972) 721-5000 *Calendar:* Sem. plan
Inst. Accred.: SACS (1963/2004), AALE (1997)
Prog. Accred.: Business (ACBSP)

University of Houston
4800 Calhoun Rd., Houston 77204
Type: Public, state, four-year
System: University of Houston System
Degrees: B, M, P, D *Enroll:* 28,828
URL: http://www.uh.edu
Phone: (713) 743-1000 *Calendar:* Sem. plan
Inst. Accred.: SACS (1954/2008)
Prog. Accred.: Accounting, Allied Health (optometric residency, optometry, speech-language pathology), Business (AACSB), Clinical Psychology, Computer Science (ABET-CAC), Construction Education, Counseling Psychology, Dietetics (didactic), Dietetics (internship), Engineering (chemical, civil, electrical, industrial, mechanical), Engineering Technology (computer, electrical, mechanical), English Language Education, Graduate Social Work, Law, Music, Pharmacy, Psychology Internship, Teacher Education (NCATE)

University of Houston—Clear Lake
2700 Bay Area Blvd., Houston 77058-1098
Type: Public, state, four-year
System: University of Houston System
Degrees: B, M, D *Enroll:* 5,036
URL: http://www.cl.uh.edu
Phone: (281) 283-7600 *Calendar:* Sem. plan
Inst. Accred.: SACS (1976/2002)
Prog. Accred.: Accounting, Allied Health (health services administration), Business (AACSB), Computer Science (ABET-CAC), Engineering (computer, information systems), Marriage and Family Therapy, Social Work, Teacher Education (NCATE)

University of Houston—Downtown
One Main St., Houston 77002
Type: Public, state, four-year
System: University of Houston System
Degrees: B, M *Enroll:* 8,165
URL: http://www.dt.uh.edu
Phone: (713) 221-8000 *Calendar:* Sem. plan
Inst. Accred.: SACS (1976/2006)
Prog. Accred.: Business (AACSB), Engineering Technology (civil/construction, instrumentation, process/piping design)

University of Houston—Victoria
3007 North Ben Wilson, Victoria 77901-4450
Type: Public, state, four-year
System: University of Houston System
Degrees: B, M *Enroll:* 1,386
URL: http://www.vic.uh.edu
Phone: (361) 570-4848 *Calendar:* Sem. plan
Inst. Accred.: SACS (1978/2003)
Prog. Accred.: Business (AACSB)

University of Mary Hardin-Baylor
900 College St., Belton 76513-2599
Type: Private, Southern Baptist Church, four-year
Degrees: B, M, D *Enroll:* 2,473
URL: http://www.umhb.edu
Phone: (254) 295-8642 *Calendar:* Sem. plan
Inst. Accred.: SACS (1926/2003)
Prog. Accred.: Counseling, Nursing Education, Social Work

University of North Texas
PO Box 311277, Denton 76203-1277
Type: Public, state, four-year
System: University of North Texas System
Degrees: B, M, D *Enroll:* 25,924
URL: http://www.unt.edu
Phone: (940) 565-2000 *Calendar:* Sem. plan
Inst. Accred.: SACS (1925/2006)
Prog. Accred.: Accounting, Allied Health (audiology, speech-language pathology), Business (AACSB), Clinical Psychology, Computer Science (ABET-CAC), Counseling, Counseling Psychology, Engineering Technology (electrical, manufacturing, mechanical, nuclear), English Language Education, Interior Design, Journalism, Librarianship, Music, Public Administration, Recreation and Leisure Services, Rehabilitation Counseling, Social Work, Teacher Education (NCATE)

Dallas Campus
7300 Houston School Rd., Dallas 75241
Phone: (972) 780-3600

University of North Texas Health Science Center at Fort Worth
3500 Camp Bowie Blvd., Fort Worth 76107-2699
Type: Public, state, four-year
System: University of North Texas System
Degrees: D *Enroll:* 963
URL: http://www.hsc.unt.edu
Phone: (817) 735-2000 *Calendar:* Sem. plan
Inst. Accred.: SACS (1995/2000)
Prog. Accred.: Clinical Psychology, Osteopathy, Physician Assistant, Public Health

University of Saint Thomas
3800 Montrose Blvd., Houston 77006-4696
Type: Private, Roman Catholic Church, four-year
Degrees: B, M, D *Enroll:* 2,434
URL: http://www.stthom.edu
Phone: (713) 522-7911 *Calendar:* Sem. plan
Inst. Accred.: ATS (1990/2008), SACS (1954/2005)
Prog. Accred.: Business (ACBSP)

The University of Texas at Arlington
1 University of Texas at Arlington, Arlington 76019-0002
Type: Public, state, four-year
System: University of Texas System
Degrees: B, M, D *Enroll:* 20,003
URL: http://www.uta.edu
Phone: (817) 272-2011 *Calendar:* Sem. plan
Inst. Accred.: SACS (1964/2007)
Prog. Accred.: Accounting, Business (AACSB), Computer Science (ABET-CAC), Engineering (aerospace, civil, computer, electrical, industrial, mechanical, software), Graduate Social Work, Interior Design, Landscape Architecture, Music, Nursing Education, Planning, Public Administration, Social Work, Teacher Education (NCATE)

The University of Texas at Austin
Austin 78712-1026
Type: Public, state, four-year
System: University of Texas System
Degrees: B, M, P, D *Enroll:* 46,945
URL: http://www.utexas.edu
Phone: (512) 471-3434 *Calendar:* Sem. plan
Inst. Accred.: SACS (1901/2008)
Prog. Accred.: Accounting, Allied Health (audiology, speech-language pathology), Art, Business (AACSB), Clinical Psychology, Counseling Psychology, Dance, Dietetics (coordinated), Dietetics (didactic), Engineering (aerospace, architectural, chemical, civil, computer, electrical, environmental/sanitary, geological/geophysical, mechanical, petroleum), Graduate Social Work, Interior Design, Journalism, Law, Librarianship, Music, Nursing Education, Pharmacy, Planning, Psychology Internship, Public Administration, Rehabilitation Counseling, School Psychology, Social Work, Theatre

The University of Texas at Brownsville/ Texas Southmost College

80 Fort Brown, Brownsville 78520
Type: Public, state, four-year
System: University of Texas System
Degrees: A, B, M, D *Enroll:* 8,704
URL: http://www.utb.edu
Phone: (956) 544-8200 *Calendar:* Sem. plan
Inst. Accred.: SACS (1995/2008)
Prog. Accred.: Allied Health (EMT-paramedic, diagnostic medical sonography, respiratory therapy), Clinical Lab Technology, Nursing, Radiography

The University of Texas at Dallas

PO Box 830688, Richardson 75083-0688
Type: Public, state, four-year
System: University of Texas System
Degrees: B, M, D *Enroll:* 10,981
URL: http://www.utdallas.edu
Phone: (972) 883-2111 *Calendar:* Sem. plan
Inst. Accred.: SACS (1972/2008)
Prog. Accred.: Accounting, Allied Health (audiology, speech-language pathology), Business (AACSB), Computer Science (ABET-CAC), Engineering (electrical, software, telecommunications), Public Administration

The University of Texas at El Paso

500 West University Ave., El Paso 79968-0500
Type: Public, state, four-year
System: University of Texas System
Degrees: B, M, D *Enroll:* 14,811
URL: http://www.utep.edu
Phone: (915) 747-5000 *Calendar:* Sem. plan
Inst. Accred.: SACS (1936/2006)
Prog. Accred.: Accounting, Allied Health (occupational therapy, speech-language pathology), Business (AACSB), Clinical Lab Scientist, Computer Science (ABET-CAC), Engineering (civil, electrical, industrial, mechanical, metallurgical), Music, Nursing Education, Physical Therapy, Public Administration, Social Work

The University of Texas at San Antonio

One UTSA Circle, San Antonio 78249-1644
Type: Public, state, four-year
System: University of Texas System
Degrees: B, M, D *Enroll:* 22,151
URL: http://www.utsa.edu
Phone: (210) 458-4011 *Calendar:* Sem. plan
Inst. Accred.: SACS (1974/2000)
Prog. Accred.: Accounting, Art, Business (AACSB), Engineering (civil, electrical, mechanical), Graduate Social Work, Histologic Technology, Interior Design, Music, Public Administration

The University of Texas at Tyler

3900 University Blvd., Tyler 75799
Type: Public, state, four-year
System: University of Texas System
Degrees: B, M, D *Enroll:* 4,589
URL: http://www.uttyler.edu
Phone: (903) 566-7000 *Calendar:* Sem. plan
Inst. Accred.: SACS (1974/2000)
Prog. Accred.: Business (AACSB), Clinical Lab Scientist, Engineering (electrical, mechanical), Health Technology, Industrial Technology, Nursing Education

The University of Texas Health Science Center at Houston

PO Box 20036, Houston 77225
Type: Public, state, four-year
System: University of Texas System
Degrees: B, M, D *Enroll:* 3,041
URL: http://www.uth.tmc.edu
Phone: (713) 500-3000 *Calendar:* Sem. plan
Inst. Accred.: SACS (1973/2000)
Prog. Accred.: Allied Health (cytotechnology, medicine), Applied Science (industrial hygiene), Clinical Lab Scientist, Cytogenetic Technology, Dentistry (advanced education in general dentistry, combined prosthodontics, dental hygiene, dental public health, dentistry, endodontics, general dentistry, general practice residency, maxillofacial prosthetics, oral and maxillofacial pathology, oral and maxillofacial surgery, orthodontic and dentofacial orthopedics, pediatric dentistry, periodontics), Dietetics (internship), Histologic Technology, Nurse Anesthesia Education, Nursing Education, Psychology Internship, Public Health, Radiation Therapy

The University of Texas Health Science Center at San Antonio

7703 Floyd Curl Dr., San Antonio 78229-3900
Type: Public, state, four-year
System: University of Texas System
Degrees: B, M, D *Enroll:* 2,464
URL: http://www.uthscsa.edu
Phone: (210) 567-7000 *Calendar:* Sem. plan
Inst. Accred.: SACS (1973/2008)
Prog. Accred.: Allied Health (EMT-paramedic, blood bank technology, medicine, occupational therapy, respiratory therapy), Clinical Lab Scientist, Cytogenetic Technology, Dentistry (advanced education in general dentistry, combined prosthodontics, dental hygiene, dental laboratory technology, dental public health, dentistry, endodontics, general practice residency, oral and maxillofacial pathology, oral and maxillofacial radiology, oral and maxillofacial surgery, orthodontic and dentofacial orthopedics, pediatric dentistry, periodontics, prosthodontics), Nursing Education, Physical Therapy, Physician Assistant, Psychology Internship

The University of Texas M. D. Anderson Cancer Center
1515 Holcombe Blvd., Houston 77030
Type: Public, state, four-year
Degrees: B, M, D
URL: http://www.mdanderson.org
Phone: (713) 792-6161 *Calendar:* Sem. plan
Inst. Accred.: SACS (2005)
Prog. Accred.: Clinical Pastoral Education

The University of Texas Medical Branch at Galveston
301 University Blvd., Galveston 77555-0129
Type: Public, state, four-year
System: University of Texas System
Degrees: B, M, D *Enroll:* 1,894
URL: http://www.utmb.edu
Phone: (409) 772-1011 *Calendar:* Sem. plan
Inst. Accred.: SACS (1973/2008)
Prog. Accred.: Allied Health (blood bank technology, medicine, occupational therapy, respiratory therapy), Clinical Lab Scientist, Dentistry (oral and maxillofacial surgery), Nursing Education, Physical Therapy, Physician Assistant, Public Health

The University of Texas of the Permian Basin
4901 East University Blvd., Odessa 79762-0001
Type: Public, state, four-year
System: University of Texas System
Degrees: B, M *Enroll:* 2,594
URL: http://www.utpb.edu
Phone: (432) 552-2020 *Calendar:* Sem. plan
Inst. Accred.: SACS (1975/2000)
Prog. Accred.: Business (AACSB), Social Work, Teacher Education (NCATE)

The University of Texas Southwestern Medical Center at Dallas
5323 Harry Hines Blvd., Dallas 75390-9002
Type: Public, state, four-year
System: University of Texas System
Degrees: B, M, D *Enroll:* 2,006
URL: http://www.utsouthwestern.edu
Phone: (214) 648-3111 *Calendar:* Sem. plan
Inst. Accred.: SACS (1973/1998)
Prog. Accred.: Allied Health (EMT-paramedic, blood bank technology, medical illustration, medicine, orthotist/prothetist), Clinical Lab Scientist, Clinical Pastoral Education, Clinical Psychology, Dentistry (oral and maxillofacial surgery), Dietetics (coordinated), Nurse (Midwifery), Physical Therapy, Physician Assistant, Psychology Internship, Rehabilitation Counseling

The University of Texas—Pan American
1201 West University Dr., Edinburg 78539-2999
Type: Public, state, four-year
System: University of Texas System
Degrees: A, B, M, D *Enroll:* 13,467
URL: http://www.panam.edu
Phone: (956) 381-2011 *Calendar:* Sem. plan
Inst. Accred.: SACS (1956/2007)
Prog. Accred.: Allied Health (occupational therapy, speech-language pathology), Business (AACSB), Clinical Lab Scientist, Computer Science (ABET-CAC), Dietetics (coordinated), Engineering (electrical, manufacturing, mechanical), Graduate Social Work, Nursing Education, Physician Assistant, Rehabilitation Counseling, Social Work, Theatre

University of the Incarnate Word
4301 Broadway, San Antonio 78209-6397
Type: Private, Roman Catholic Church, four-year
Degrees: B, M, D *Enroll:* 3,478
URL: http://www.uiw.edu
Phone: (210) 829-6000 *Calendar:* Sem. plan
Inst. Accred.: SACS (1925/2005)
Prog. Accred.: Business (ACBSP), Dietetics (didactic), Dietetics (internship), Interior Design, Nuclear Medicine Technology, Nursing Education, Pharmacy, Theatre

Vernon College
4400 College Dr., Vernon 76384-4092
Type: Public, state/local, two-year
Degrees: A *Enroll:* 1,608
URL: http://www.vernoncollege.edu
Phone: (940) 552-6291 *Calendar:* Sem. plan
Inst. Accred.: SACS (1974/1999)

The Victoria College
2200 East Red River St., Victoria 77901-4494
Type: Public, local, two-year
Degrees: A *Enroll:* 2,373
URL: http://www.victoriacollege.edu
Phone: (361) 573-3291 *Calendar:* Sem. plan
Inst. Accred.: SACS (1951/2003)
Prog. Accred.: Allied Health (respiratory therapy), Clinical Lab Technology, Nursing

Wade College
1950 Stemmons Freeway, Ste. 2026, LB #562, Dallas 75207
Type: Private, proprietary, two-year
Degrees: A *Enroll:* 195
URL: http://www.wadecollege.edu
Phone: (214) 637-3530 *Calendar:* Tri. plan
Inst. Accred.: SACS (1985/2000)

Wayland Baptist University
1900 West Seventh St., Plainview 79072
Type: Private, Baptist General Convention of Texas, four-year
Degrees: A, B, M *Enroll:* 3,066
URL: http://www.wbu.edu
Phone: (806) 291-1000 *Calendar:* Sem. plan
Inst. Accred.: SACS (1956/2008)
Prog. Accred.: Music

Weatherford College
225 College Park Dr., Weatherford 76086
Type: Public, local, two-year
Degrees: A *Enroll:* 3,044
URL: http://www.wc.edu
Phone: (817) 594-5471 *Calendar:* Sem. plan
Inst. Accred.: SACS (1956/2001)
Prog. Accred.: Allied Health (respiratory therapy), Nursing

West Texas A&M University
Box 60997, Canyon 79016-0001
Type: Public, state, four-year
System: Texas A&M University System
Degrees: B, M, D *Enroll:* 5,809
URL: http://www.wtamu.edu
Phone: (806) 651-2000 *Calendar:* Sem. plan
Inst. Accred.: SACS (1925/2006)
Prog. Accred.: Allied Health (speech-language pathology), Business (ACBSP), Engineering (mechanical), Music, Nursing Education, Social Work

Western Technical College
9624 Plaza Circle, El Paso 79927
Type: Private, proprietary, two-year
Degrees: A *Enroll:* 493
URL: http://www.wtc-ep.edu
Phone: (915) 532-3737
Inst. Accred.: ACCSCT (1978/2006)
Prog. Accred.: Allied Health (medical assisting (AMA))

Diana Drive Campus
9451 Diana Dr., El Paso 79924
Phone: (915) 566-9621

Western Texas College
6200 South College Ave., Snyder 79549-9599
Type: Public, state/local, two-year
Degrees: A *Enroll:* 891
URL: http://www.wtc.edu
Phone: (325) 573-8511 *Calendar:* Sem. plan
Inst. Accred.: SACS (1973/2008)

Wharton County Junior College
911 Boling Hwy., Wharton 77488
Type: Public, local, two-year
Degrees: A *Enroll:* 3,804
URL: http://www.wcjc.edu
Phone: (979) 532-4560 *Calendar:* Sem. plan
Inst. Accred.: SACS (1951/1998)
Prog. Accred.: Allied Health (EMT-paramedic, surgical technology), Clinical Lab Technology, Dentistry (dental hygiene), Physical Therapy Assisting, Radiography

Wiley College
711 Wiley Ave., Marshall 75670
Type: Private, United Methodist Church, four-year
Degrees: A, B *Enroll:* 794
URL: http://www.wileyc.edu
Phone: (903) 927-3300 *Calendar:* Sem. plan
Inst. Accred.: SACS (1933/2003)

William Marsh Rice University
PO Box 1892, Houston 77251-1892
Type: Private, independent, four-year
Degrees: B, M, D *Enroll:* 5,020
URL: http://www.rice.edu
Phone: (713) 348-0000 *Calendar:* Sem. plan
Inst. Accred.: SACS (1914/2006)
Prog. Accred.: Business (AACSB), Engineering (chemical, civil, electrical, mechanical)

UTAH

Bridgerland Applied Technology College
1301 North 600 West, Logan 84321
Type: Public, state, two-year
System: Utah College of Applied Technology
Degrees: A
URL: http://batc.edu
Phone: (435) 753-6780
Inst. Accred.: COE (2006)
Prog. Accred.: Allied Health (medical assisting (AMA)), Dentistry (dental assisting), Practical Nursing

Brigham Young University
Provo 84602
Type: Private, The Church of Jesus Christ of Latter-day Saints, four-year
Degrees: A, B, M, D *Enroll:* 31,223
URL: http://www.byu.edu
Phone: (801) 378-4636 *Calendar:* Tri. plan
Inst. Accred.: NWCCU (1923/2006)
Prog. Accred.: Accounting, Allied Health (audiology, speech-language pathology), Art, Business (AACSB), Clinical Lab Scientist, Clinical Psychology, Computer Science (ABET-CAC), Construction Education, Counseling, Counseling Psychology, Dance, Dietetics (didactic), Dietetics (internship), Engineering (chemical, civil, computer, electrical, mechanical), Engineering Technology (information systems, manufacturing), Graduate Social Work, Journalism, Law, Marriage and Family Therapy, Music, Nursing Education, Psychology Internship, Public Administration, Public Health, Recreation and Leisure Services, Teacher Education (NCATE), Theatre

Careers Unlimited
575 East University Pkwy., Orem 84097
Type: Private, proprietary, four-year
Degrees: A, B
URL: http://www.ucdh.edu
Phone: (801) 226-1081
Inst. Accred.: ACCSCT (2005)
Prog. Accred.: Dentistry (dental hygiene)

College of Eastern Utah
451 East 400 North, Price 84501-2699
Type: Public, state, two-year
System: Utah System of Higher Education
Degrees: A *Enroll:* 1,605
URL: http://www.ceu.edu
Phone: (435) 637-2120 *Calendar:* Sem. plan
Inst. Accred.: NWCCU (1945/2007)
Prog. Accred.: Nursing, Practical Nursing

San Juan Campus
639 West 100 South, Blanding 84511
Phone: (435) 678-2201

Davis Applied Technology College
550 East 300 South, Kaysville 84037
Type: Public, state, two-year
System: Utah College of Applied Technology
Degrees: A
URL: http://www.datc.net
Phone: (801) 593-2500
Inst. Accred.: COE (2006)
Prog. Accred.: Allied Health (medical assisting (AMA), surgical technology), Dentistry (dental assisting), Practical Nursing

Dixie State College of Utah
225 South 700 East, St. George 84770-3876
Type: Public, state, four-year
System: Utah System of Higher Education
Degrees: A, B *Enroll:* 5,632
URL: http://www.dixie.edu
Phone: (435) 652-7500 *Calendar:* Sem. plan
Inst. Accred.: NWCCU (1945/2008)
Prog. Accred.: Allied Health (EMT-paramedic, surgical technology), Dentistry (dental hygiene), Nursing, Practical Nursing

Eagle Gate College
5588 South Green St., Murray 84123
Type: Private, proprietary, two-year
Degrees: A
URL: http://www.eaglegatecollege.edu
Phone: (801) 281-7700 *Calendar:* Qtr. plan
Inst. Accred.: ACICS (1981/2005)

Layton Campus
915 North 400 West, Layton 84041
Phone: (801) 546-7500

Logan Campus
1350 North 200 West, Logan 84321
Phone: (801) 333-7165

Salt Lake City Downtown Campus
405 South Main St., Ste. 130, Salt Lake City 84111
Phone: (801) 287-9640

Everest College—Salt Lake City
3280 West 3500 South, Salt Lake City 84119
Type: Private, proprietary, four-year
System: Corinthian Colleges, Inc
Degrees: A, B *Enroll:* 412
URL: http://www.everest.edu
Phone: (801) 840-4800
Inst. Accred.: ACICS (1985/2007)
Prog. Accred.: Allied Health (surgical technology)

Ft. Worth Campus
5237 North Riverside Dr., Ste. 100, Ft. Worth, TX 76137
Phone: (817) 838-3000

Independence University
5295 South Commerce Dr., Salt Lake City 84102
Type: Private, proprietary, four-year
Degrees: A, B, M
URL: http://www.independence.edu
Phone: (800) 497-7157 *Calendar:* Sem. plan
Inst. Accred.: DETC (1981/2007)
Prog. Accred.: Allied Health (respiratory therapy)

California College for Health Sciences
5295 South Commerce Dr., Ste. G-50, Salt Lake City 84107
Phone: (801) 290-3280

ITT Technical Institute
920 West LeVoy Dr., Murray 84123-2500
Type: Private, proprietary, four-year
System: ITT Educational Services, Inc.
Degrees: A, B *Enroll:* 622
URL: http://www.itt-tech.edu
Phone: (801) 263-3313 *Calendar:* Qtr. plan
Inst. Accred.: ACICS (1999/2008)

Henderson Campus
168 North Gibson Rd., Henderson, NV 89104
Phone: (702) 558-5404

King of Prussia Campus
760 Moore Rd., King of Prussia, PA 19406-1212
Phone: (610) 491-8004

LDS Business College
95 North 300 West, Salt Lake City 84101-3500
Type: Private, The Church of Jesus Christ of Latter-day Saints, two-year
Degrees: A *Enroll:* 1,067
URL: http://www.ldsbc.edu
Phone: (801) 524-8100 *Calendar:* Sem. plan
Inst. Accred.: NWCCU (1977/2008)
Prog. Accred.: Allied Health (medical assisting (AMA))

Midwives College of Utah
1174 East 2700 South, Ste. 8, Salt Lake City 84106-2671
Type: Private, independent, four-year
Degrees: A, B, M
URL: http://www.midwifery.edu
Phone: (866) 680-2756 *Calendar:* Sem. plan
Inst. Accred.: MEAC (1996/2004)

Mountainland Applied Technology College
987 South Geneva Rd., Orem 84058
Type: Public, state, two-year
System: Utah College of Applied Technology
Degrees: A
URL: http://www.mountainlandatc.org
Phone: (801) 863-7662
Inst. Accred.: COE (2006)

Neumont University
10701 South River Front Pkwy., Ste. 300, South Jordan 84095
Type: Private, proprietary, four-year
Degrees: B, M
URL: http://www.neumont.edu
Phone: (801) 733-2800 *Calendar:* Qtr. plan
Inst. Accred.: ACICS (1990/2008)

Morrison University
10315 Professional Circle, Ste. 201, Reno, NV 89521
Phone: (775) 850-0700

Ogden-Weber Applied Technology College
200 North Washington Blvd., Ogden 84404
Type: Public, state, two-year
System: Utah College of Applied Technology
Degrees: A
URL: http://www.owatc.com
Phone: (801) 627-8300
Inst. Accred.: COE (2005)
Prog. Accred.: Allied Health (medical assisting (AMA)), Dentistry (dental assisting), Practical Nursing

Provo College
1450 West 820 North, Provo 84601
Type: Private, proprietary, two-year
Degrees: A *Enroll:* 445
URL: http://www.provocollege.com
Phone: (801) 375-1861
Inst. Accred.: ACCSCT (1986/2008)
Prog. Accred.: Allied Health (medical assisting (AMA)), Dentistry (dental assisting), Nursing, Physical Therapy Assisting

Salt Lake Community College
4600 South Redwood Rd., Salt Lake City 84123
Type: Public, state, two-year
System: Utah System of Higher Education
Degrees: A *Enroll:* 13,519
URL: http://www.slcc.edu
Phone: (801) 957-4111 *Calendar:* Sem. plan
Inst. Accred.: NWCCU (1969/2006)
Prog. Accred.: Allied Health (medical assisting (AMA), occupational therapy assisting, surgical technology), Business (ACBSP), Clinical Lab Technology, Culinary Education, Dentistry (dental hygiene), Nursing, Physical Therapy Assisting, Radiography

South City Campus
1575 State State St., Salt Lake City 84115
Phone: (801) 957-3413
Prog. Accred: Radiography

Salt Lake-Tooele Applied Technology College
1655 East 3300 South, Salt Lake City 84106
Type: Public, state, two-year
System: Utah College of Applied Technology
Degrees: A
URL: http://www.sltatc.org
Phone: (801) 493-8700
Inst. Accred.: COE (2006)

Snow College
150 East College Ave., Ephraim 84627-1299
Type: Public, state, two-year
System: Utah System of Higher Education
Degrees: A *Enroll:* 2,755
URL: http://www.snow.edu
Phone: (435) 283-7000 *Calendar:* Sem. plan
Inst. Accred.: NWCCU (1953/2008)
Prog. Accred.: Business (ACBSP), Music

Richfield Campus
800 West 200 South, Richfield 84701
Phone: (435) 896-8202
Prog. Accred: Nursing

Southern Utah University
351 West Center, Administration Bldg., Cedar City 84720
Type: Public, state, four-year
System: Utah System of Higher Education
Degrees: A, B, M *Enroll:* 5,567
URL: http://www.suu.edu
Phone: (435) 586-7700 *Calendar:* Sem. plan
Inst. Accred.: NWCCU (1933/2001)
Prog. Accred.: Business (AACSB), Business (ACBSP), Engineering (micro/nano-engineering), Music, Nursing Education, Teacher Education (NCATE)

Stevens-Henager College
1890 South 1350 West, Ogden 84401
Type: Private, proprietary, four-year
Degrees: A, B *Enroll:* 432
URL: http://www.stevenshenager.edu
Phone: (801) 394-7791 *Calendar:* Sem. plan
Inst. Accred.: ACCSCT (2002)
Prog. Accred.: Allied Health (medical assisting (AMA), surgical technology)

Boise Campus
700 Americana Blvd., Boise, ID 83702
Phone: (208) 345-0700

Logan Campus
755 South Main St., Logan 84321
Phone: (435) 713-4777
Prog. Accred: Allied Health (medical assisting (AMA))

Murray Campus
635 West 5300 South, Murray 84123
Phone: (801) 262-7600
Prog. Accred: Allied Health (medical assisting (AMA))

Provo Campus
1476 South Sandhill Rd., Orem 84058
Phone: (801) 375-5455

Uintah Basin Applied Technology College
1100 East Lagoon Sreet, Roosevelt 84066
Type: Public, state, two-year
System: Utah College of Applied Technology
Degrees: A
URL: http://www.ubatc.edu
Phone: (435) 722-4523
Inst. Accred.: COE (2006)
Prog. Accred.: Practical Nursing

University of Utah
201 South Presidents Circle, Ste. 203, Salt Lake City 84112-9008
Type: Public, state, four-year
System: Utah System of Higher Education
Degrees: A, B, M, P, D *Enroll:* 24,396
URL: http://www.utah.edu
Phone: (801) 581-7200 *Calendar:* Sem. plan
Inst. Accred.: NWCCU (1933/2007)
Prog. Accred.: Accounting, Allied Health (audiology, cytotechnology, medicine, occupational therapy, speech-language pathology), Applied Science (industrial hygiene), Business (AACSB), Clinical Lab Scientist, Clinical Psychology, Counseling Psychology, Dentistry (general dentistry, general practice residency), Dietetics (coordinated), Engineering (chemical, civil, computer, electrical, geological/geophysical, materials, mechanical, metallurgical, mining), English Language Education, Graduate Social Work, Journalism, Law, Music, Nuclear Medicine Technology, Nurse (Midwifery), Nursing Education, Pharmacy, Physical Therapy, Physician Assistant, Psychology Internship, Public Administration, Public Health, Recreation and Leisure Services, School Psychology, Social Work

The Utah Career College
1902 West 7800 South, West Jordan 84088
Type: Private, proprietary, four-year
Degrees: A, B *Enroll:* 317
URL: http://www.utahcollege.edu
Phone: (801) 304-4224 *Calendar:* Qtr. plan
Inst. Accred.: ACCSCT (1973/2006)
Prog. Accred.: Allied Health (medical assisting (AMA)), Veterinary Technology

Layton Campus
869 West Hill Field Rd., Layton 84041
Phone: (801) 660-6000

Orem Campus
898 North 1200 West, Orem 84057
Phone: (801) 822-5800

Utah State University
Logan 84322
Type: Public, state, four-year
System: Utah System of Higher Education
Degrees: A, B, M, D *Enroll:* 12,888
URL: http://www.usu.edu
Phone: (435) 797-1157 *Calendar:* Sem. plan
Inst. Accred.: NWCCU (1924/2008)
Prog. Accred.: Accounting, Allied Health (audiology, speech-language pathology), Applied Science (industrial hygiene), Aviation, Business (AACSB), Combined Professional-Scientific Psychology, Computer Science (ABET-CAC), Dietetics (coordinated), Dietetics (didactic), Dietetics (internship), Engineering (agricultural, civil, computer, electrical, environmental/sanitary, mechanical), English Language Education, Forestry, Interior Design, Landscape Architecture, Marriage and Family Therapy, Music, Psychology Internship, Recreation and Leisure Services, Rehabilitation Counseling, Social Work, Teacher Education (NCATE)

Utah Valley University
800 West University Pkwy., Orem 84058-5999
Type: Public, state/local, four-year
System: Utah System of Higher Education
Degrees: A, B *Enroll:* 16,650
URL: http://www.uvu.edu
Phone: (801) 863-8000 *Calendar:* Sem. plan
Inst. Accred.: NWCCU (1969/2007)
Prog. Accred.: Allied Health (EMT-paramedic), Business (AACSB), Computer Science (ABET-CAC), Dentistry (dental hygiene), Engineering Technology (electrical), Nursing

Weber State University
1001 University Circle, Ogden 84408-1001
Type: Public, state, four-year
System: Utah System of Higher Education
Degrees: A, B, M *Enroll:* 13,480
URL: http://www.weber.edu
Phone: (801) 626-6001 *Calendar:* Sem. plan
Inst. Accred.: NWCCU (1932/2007)
Prog. Accred.: Accounting, Allied Health (EMT-paramedic, respiratory therapy), Business (AACSB), Clinical Lab Scientist, Clinical Lab Technology, Construction Education, Dentistry (dental hygiene), Engineering Technology (computer, electrical, general drafting/design, manufacturing, mechanical), Music, Nursing, Practical Nursing, Social Work

Western Governors University
4001 South 700 East, Ste. 700, Salt Lake City 84107-2533
Type: Private, independent, four-year
Degrees: A, B, M *Enroll:* 4,715
URL: http://www.wgu.edu
Phone: (801) 274-3280
Inst. Accred.: DETC (2001/2008), NWCCU (2003/2008), NCA-HLC (2003/2006), WASC-SR. (2003/2006)
Prog. Accred.: Teacher Education (NCATE)

Westminster College
1840 South 1300 East, Salt Lake City 84105
Type: Private, independent, four-year
Degrees: B, M *Enroll:* 2,089
URL: http://www.westminstercollege.edu
Phone: (801) 488-7651 *Calendar:* Sem. plan
Inst. Accred.: NWCCU (1936/2008)
Prog. Accred.: Business (ACBSP), Nurse Anesthesia Education, Nursing Education, Teacher Education (TEAC)

VERMONT

Bennington College
One College Dr., Bennington 05201-6003
Type: Private, independent, four-year
Degrees: B, M *Enroll:* 711
URL: http://www.bennington.edu
Phone: (802) 442-5401 *Calendar:* Sem. plan
Inst. Accred.: NEASC-CIHE (1935/1999)

Burlington College
95 North Ave., Burlington 05401-8477
Type: Private, independent, four-year
Degrees: A, B *Enroll:* 134
URL: http://www.burlcol.edu
Phone: (802) 862-9616 *Calendar:* Sem. plan
Inst. Accred.: NEASC-CIHE (1982/2007)

Castleton State College
86 Seminary St., Castleton 05735
Type: Public, state, four-year
System: Vermont State Colleges
Degrees: A, B, M *Enroll:* 1,975
URL: http://www.csc.vsc.edu
Phone: (802) 468-5611 *Calendar:* Sem. plan
Inst. Accred.: NEASC-CIHE (1960/2001)
Prog. Accred.: Nursing, Social Work

Champlain College
163 South Willard St., Burlington 05402-0670
Type: Private, independent, four-year
Degrees: A, B, M *Enroll:* 2,035
URL: http://www.champlain.edu
Phone: (802) 860-2700 *Calendar:* Sem. plan
Inst. Accred.: NEASC-CIHE (1972/2006)
Prog. Accred.: Radiography

The Woodbury Institute at Champlain College
660 Elm St., Montpelier 05602
Phone: (802) 229-0516

College of Saint Joseph
71 Clement Rd., Rutland 05701-3899
Type: Private, Roman Catholic Church, four-year
Degrees: A, B, M *Enroll:* 328
URL: http://www.csj.edu
Phone: (802) 773-5900 *Calendar:* Sem. plan
Inst. Accred.: NEASC-CIHE (1972/2006)

Community College of Vermont
PO Box 120, Waterbury 05676-0120
Type: Public, state, two-year
System: Vermont State Colleges
Degrees: A *Enroll:* 2,490
URL: http://www.ccv.edu
Phone: (802) 241-3535 *Calendar:* Sem. plan
Inst. Accred.: NEASC-CIHE (1975/2002)

Goddard College
123 Pitkin Rd., Plainfield 05667-9432
Type: Private, independent, four-year
Degrees: B, M *Enroll:* 560
URL: http://www.goddard.edu
Phone: (802) 454-8311 *Calendar:* Sem. plan
Inst. Accred.: NEASC-CIHE (1959/2002)

Green Mountain College
1 College Circle, Poultney 05764-1199
Type: Private, independent, four-year
Degrees: B *Enroll:* 677
URL: http://www.greenmtn.edu
Phone: (802) 287-8000 *Calendar:* Sem. plan
Inst. Accred.: NEASC-CIHE (1934/2006)
Prog. Accred.: Recreation and Leisure Services

Johnson State College
337 College Hill, Johnson 05656-9464
Type: Public, state, four-year
System: Vermont State Colleges
Degrees: A, B, M *Enroll:* 1,394
URL: http://www.jsc.vsc.edu
Phone: (802) 635-2356 *Calendar:* Sem. plan
Inst. Accred.: NEASC-CIHE (1961/2006)

Landmark College
River Rd. South, Putney 05346
Type: Private, independent, two-year
Degrees: A *Enroll:* 334
URL: http://www.landmarkcollege.org
Phone: (802) 387-4767 *Calendar:* Sem. plan
Inst. Accred.: NEASC-CIHE (1991/2006)

Lyndon State College
1001 College Rd., PO Box 919, Lyndonville 05851-0919
Type: Public, state, four-year
System: Vermont State Colleges
Degrees: A, B, M *Enroll:* 1,229
URL: http://www.lsc.vsc.edu
Phone: (802) 626-6200 *Calendar:* Sem. plan
Inst. Accred.: NEASC-CIHE (1965/2000)
Prog. Accred.: Nursing

Marlboro College
PO Box A, Marlboro 05344-9999
Type: Private, independent, four-year
Degrees: B, M *Enroll:* 332
URL: http://www.marlboro.edu
Phone: (802) 257-4333 *Calendar:* Sem. plan
Inst. Accred.: NEASC-CIHE (1965/2004)

Middlebury College
Middlebury 05753-6200
Type: Private, independent, four-year
Degrees: B, M, D *Enroll:* 2,434
URL: http://www.middlebury.edu
Phone: (802) 443-5000 *Calendar:* 4-1-4 plan
Inst. Accred.: NEASC-CIHE (1929/1999)

New England Culinary Institute
56 College St., Montpelier 05602
Type: Private, proprietary, four-year
Degrees: A, B *Enroll:* 262
URL: http://www.neci.edu
Phone: (802) 223-3205 *Calendar:* Sem. plan
Inst. Accred.: ACCSCT (1984/2005)

Essex Campus
5 Franklin St., Essex Junction 05452
Phone: (802) 223-6324

Paraquita Bay Campus
PO Box 3097, Paraquita Bay, Rd. Town, Tortola, Virgin Islands (British)
Phone: 011 284 1494 4994

Norwich University
158 Harmon Dr., Northfield 05663
Type: Private, independent, four-year
Degrees: A, B, M *Enroll:* 2,437
URL: http://www.norwich.edu
Phone: (802) 485-2000 *Calendar:* Sem. plan
Inst. Accred.: NEASC-CIHE (1933/2000)
Prog. Accred.: Business (ACBSP), Engineering (civil, electrical, mechanical), Nursing, Nursing Education

Saint Michael's College
One Winooski Park, Colchester 05439-0001
Type: Private, Roman Catholic Church, four-year
Degrees: B, M *Enroll:* 2,198
URL: http://www.smcvt.edu
Phone: (802) 654-2000 *Calendar:* Sem. plan
Inst. Accred.: NEASC-CIHE (1939/2000)

School for International Training
PO Box 676, Brattleboro 05301-0676
Type: Private, independent, four-year
Degrees: B, M *Enroll:* 370
URL: http://www.sit.edu
Phone: (802) 257-7751 *Calendar:* Sem. plan
Inst. Accred.: NEASC-CIHE (1974/2002)

Southern Vermont College
982 Mansion Dr., Bennington 05201-6002
Type: Private, independent, four-year
Degrees: A, B *Enroll:* 348
URL: http://www.svc.edu
Phone: (802) 442-5427 *Calendar:* Sem. plan
Inst. Accred.: NEASC-CIHE (1979/1999)
Prog. Accred.: Nursing

Sterling College
PO Box 72, Craftsbury Common 05827-0072
Type: Private, independent, four-year
Degrees: A, B *Enroll:* 93
URL: http://www.sterlingcollege.edu
Phone: (802) 586-7711 *Calendar:* Sem. plan
Inst. Accred.: NEASC-CIHE (2006)

University of Vermont
85 South Prospect St., Burlington 05405-0160
Type: Public, state, four-year
Degrees: A, B, M, P, D *Enroll:* 10,420
URL: http://www.uvm.edu
Phone: (802) 656-3131 *Calendar:* Sem. plan
Inst. Accred.: NEASC-CIHE (1929/1999)
Prog. Accred.: Allied Health (medicine, speech-language pathology), Business (AACSB), Clinical Lab Scientist, Clinical Psychology, Counseling, Dentistry (dental hygiene), Dietetics (coordinated), Dietetics (didactic), Engineering (civil, electrical, environmental/sanitary, mechanical), Graduate Social Work, Nuclear Medicine Technology, Nursing Education, Physical Therapy, Radiation Therapy, Social Work, Teacher Education (NCATE)

Vermont Law School
Chelsea St., PO Box 96, South Royalton 05068-0096
Type: Private, independent, four-year
Degrees: M, P, D *Enroll:* 649
URL: http://www.vermontlaw.edu
Phone: (802) 763-8303 *Calendar:* Sem. plan
Inst. Accred.: NEASC-CIHE (1980/2006)
Prog. Accred.: Law

Vermont Technical College
PO Box 500, Randolph Center 05061-0500
Type: Public, state, four-year
System: Vermont State Colleges
Degrees: A, B *Enroll:* 1,137
URL: http://www.vtc.vsc.edu
Phone: (802) 728-1000 *Calendar:* Sem. plan
Inst. Accred.: NEASC-CIHE (2006)
Prog. Accred.: Engineering Technology (architectural, civil/construction, computer, electrical, electromechanical, mechanical), Nursing, Practical Nursing, Veterinary Technology

Fanny Allen Memorial School of Practical Nursing
29 Ethan Allen Ave., Ste. 6, Colchester 05446-3332
Phone: (802) 655-2540
Prog. Accred: Practical Nursing

Thompson School of Practical Nursing
30 Maple St., Brattleboro 05301
Phone: (802) 254-5570
Prog. Accred: Practical Nursing

Williston Campus
201 Lawrence Place, Williston 05495
Phone: (802) 879-2323
Prog. Accred: Practical Nursing

VIRGIN ISLANDS

University of the Virgin Islands
#2 John Brewers Bay, St. Thomas 00802-9990
Type: Public, state, four-year
Degrees: A, B, M *Enroll:* 1,711
URL: http://www.uvi.edu
Phone: (340) 776-9200 *Calendar:* Sem. plan
Inst. Accred.: MSA-CHE (1971/2007)
Prog. Accred.: Business (ACBSP), Nursing

Saint Croix Campus
RR2, Box 10,000, Kingshill, St. Croix 00850-9781
Phone: (340) 778-1620

VIRGINIA

ACT College
1100 Wilson Blvd., Mall Level, Arlington 22209
Type: Private, proprietary, two-year
System: ACT College
Degrees: A
URL: http://www.actcollege.edu
Phone: (703) 527-6660
Inst. Accred.: ABHES (1997/2006)
Prog. Accred.: Medical Assisting (ABHES)

Alexandria Campus
6118 Franconia Rd., Second Flr., Alexandria 22310
Phone: (703) 719-0700
Prog. Accred: Medical Assisting (ABHES)

Manassas Campus
8870 Rixlew Ln., Ste. 201, Manassas 20109
Phone: (703) 365-9286
Prog. Accred: Medical Assisting (ABHES)

Advanced Technology Institute
5700 Southern Blvd., Ste. 100, Virginia Beach 23462
Type: Private, proprietary, two-year
Degrees: A
URL: http://www.auto.edu
Phone: (757) 490-1241
Inst. Accred.: ACCSCT (1996/2006)

Appalachian School of Law
PO Box 1825, Grundy 24614-2825
Type: Private, independent, four-year
Degrees: P *Enroll:* 365
URL: http://www.asl.edu
Phone: (276) 935-4349 *Calendar:* Sem. plan
Inst. Accred.: ABA (2001)

Argosy University Washington, DC
1550 Wilson Blvd., Arlington 22209
Type: Private, proprietary, four-year
System: Argosy University
Degrees: B, M, D
URL: http://www.argosyu.edu/washingtondc
Phone: (703) 526-5800 *Calendar:* Tri. plan
Inst. Accred.: NCA-HLC (1981/2008, *Indirect accreditation through Argosy University, Chicago, IL*)
Prog. Accred.: Clinical Psychology

Atlantic University
215 67th St., Virginia Beach 23451-2061
Type: Private, proprietary, four-year
Degrees: M *Enroll:* 46
URL: http://www.atlanticuniv.edu
Phone: (757) 631-8101 *Calendar:* Sem. plan
Inst. Accred.: DETC (1994/2004)

Averett University
420 West Main St., Danville 24541
Type: Private, independent, four-year
Degrees: B, M *Enroll:* 1,861
URL: http://www.averett.edu
Phone: (434) 791-5600 *Calendar:* Sem. plan
Inst. Accred.: SACS (1928/2007)

Baptist Theological Seminary at Richmond
3400 Brook Rd., Richmond 23227
Type: Private, Cooperative Baptist Fellowship, four-year
Degrees: M, D *Enroll:* 204
URL: http://www.btsr.edu
Phone: (804) 355-8135
Inst. Accred.: ATS (1997/2001)

Blue Ridge Community College
Box 80, Weyers Cave 24486
Type: Public, state, two-year
System: Virginia Community College System
Degrees: A *Enroll:* 2,282
URL: http://www.brcc.edu
Phone: (540) 234-9261 *Calendar:* Sem. plan
Inst. Accred.: SACS (1969/2005)
Prog. Accred.: Nursing, Veterinary Technology

Bluefield College
3000 College Dr., Bluefield 24605
Type: Private, Southern Baptist Church, four-year
Degrees: A, B *Enroll:* 725
URL: http://www.bluefield.edu
Phone: (276) 326-3682 *Calendar:* Sem. plan
Inst. Accred.: SACS (1949/2003)

Bridgewater College
402 East College St., Bridgewater 22812-1599
Type: Private, Church of Brethren, four-year
Degrees: B *Enroll:* 1,499
URL: http://www.bridgewater.edu
Phone: (540) 828-8000 *Calendar:* 4-1-4 plan
Inst. Accred.: SACS (1925/2001)

Bryant & Stratton College—Richmond Campus
8141 Hull St. Rd., Richmond 23235-6411
Type: Private, proprietary, four-year
System: Bryant & Stratton College System Office
Degrees: A, B
URL: http//www.bryantstratton.edu
Phone: (804) 745-2444 *Calendar:* Sem. plan
Inst. Accred.: MSA-CHE (2002/2007, *Indirect accreditation through Bryant & Stratton College System Office, Getzville, NY*)
Prog. Accred.: Allied Health (medical assisting (AMA))

Bryant & Stratton College—Virginia Beach Campus
301 Centre Pointe Dr., Virginia Beach 23462-4417
Type: Private, proprietary, four-year
System: Bryant & Stratton College System Office
Degrees: A, B *Enroll:* 320
URL: http://www.bryantstratton.edu
Phone: (757) 499-7900 *Calendar:* Sem. plan
Inst. Accred.: MSA-CHE (2002/2007, *Indirect accreditation through Bryant & Stratton College System Office, Getzville, NY*)
Prog. Accred.: Allied Health (medical assisting (AMA))

Career Training Solutions
100 Riverside Pkwy., Ste. 123, Fredericksburg 22406
Type: Private, proprietary, two-year
Degrees: A
URL: http://www.careertrainingsolutions.com
Phone: (540) 372-2000
Inst. Accred.: COE (2002/2007)

The Catholic Distance University
120 East Colonial Hwy., Hamilton 20158-9012
Type: Private, independent, four-year
Degrees: B, M
URL: http://www.cdu.edu
Phone: (540) 338-2700
Inst. Accred.: DETC (1986/2006)

Central Baptist Theological Seminary
2221 Centerville Turnpike, Virginia Beach 23464
Type: Private, Baptist Church, four-year
Degrees: M
URL: http://www.baptistseminary.edu
Phone: (757) 479-3706 *Calendar:* Sem. plan
Inst. Accred.: TRACS (2007)

Central Virginia Community College
3506 Wards Rd., Lynchburg 24502-2498
Type: Public, state, two-year
System: Virginia Community College System
Degrees: A *Enroll:* 2,265
URL: http://www.cvcc.vccs.edu
Phone: (434) 832-7600 *Calendar:* Sem. plan
Inst. Accred.: SACS (1969/2004)
Prog. Accred.: Allied Health (respiratory therapy), Radiography

Centura College
2697 Dean Dr., Ste. 100, Virginia Beach 23452-9835
Type: Private, proprietary, two-year
System: Centura College
Degrees: A *Enroll:* 1,192
URL: http://www.centuracollege.edu
Phone: (757) 340-2121
Inst. Accred.: ACCSCT (1986/2007)

Centura College
7914 Midlothian Turnpike, Richmond 23236
Type: Private, proprietary, two-year
System: Centura College
Degrees: A
URL: http://www.centuracollege.edu
Phone: (804) 330-0111
Inst. Accred.: ACCSCT (1994/2004)

Chesapeake Campus
932 B Ventures Way, Ste. 310, Chesapeake 23320
Phone: (757) 549-2121

Newport News Campus
616 Denbigh Blvd., Newport News 23402
Phone: (757) 874-2121
Prog. Accred: Dentistry (dental assisting)

Richmond West Campus
7001 West Broad St., Richmond 23294
Phone: (804) 672-2300

The Christendom College
134 Christendom Dr., Front Royal 22630
Type: Private, Roman Catholic Church, four-year
Degrees: A, B, M *FTE Enroll:* 312
URL: http://www.christendom.edu
Phone: (540) 636-2900 *Calendar:* Sem. plan
Inst. Accred.: SACS (1996/2003)

The Notre Dame Graduate School
4407 Sano St., Alexandria 22312
Phone: (703) 658-4304

Christopher Newport University
One University Place, Newport News 23606-2998
Type: Public, state, four-year
System: State Council of Higher Education for Virginia
Degrees: B, M *Enroll:* 4,440
URL: http://www.cnu.edu
Phone: (757) 594-7000 *Calendar:* Sem. plan
Inst. Accred.: SACS (1971/2007)
Prog. Accred.: Business (AACSB), Engineering (computer), Music, Social Work

The College of William and Mary
PO Box 8795, Williamsburg 23187-8795
Type: Public, state, four-year
System: College of William and Mary Central Office
Degrees: A, B, M, D *Enroll:* 7,215
URL: http://www.wm.edu
Phone: (757) 221-4000 *Calendar:* Sem. plan
Inst. Accred.: SACS (1921/2006)
Prog. Accred.: Accounting, Business (AACSB), Counseling, Law, Teacher Education (NCATE)

Dabney S. Lancaster Community College
PO Box 1000, Clifton Forge 24422-1000
Type: Public, state, two-year
System: Virginia Community College System
Degrees: A *Enroll:* 689
URL: http://www.dl.vccs.edu
Phone: (540) 863-2800 *Calendar:* Sem. plan
Inst. Accred.: SACS (1969/2004)
Prog. Accred.: Forestry, Nursing

Danville Community College
1008 South Main St., Danville 24541
Type: Public, state, two-year
System: Virginia Community College System
Degrees: A *Enroll:* 2,243
URL: http://www.dcc.vccs.edu
Phone: (434) 797-2222 *Calendar:* Sem. plan
Inst. Accred.: SACS (1970/2006)

DeVry University Crystal City
2450 Crystal Dr., Arlington 22202
Type: Private, proprietary
System: DeVry University
Degrees: A, B, M
URL: http://www.devry.edu/arlington
Phone: (866) 338-7932 *Calendar:* Sem. plan
Inst. Accred.: NCA-HLC (2002, *Indirect accreditation through DeVry University, Oakbrook Terrace, IL*)
Prog. Accred.: Engineering Technology (computer, electrical)

South Hampton Roads Campus
1317 Executive Blvd., Ste. 100, Chesapeake 23320
Phone: (757) 382-5680

Eastern Mennonite University
1200 Park Rd., Harrisonburg 22802-2462
Type: Private, Mennonite Education Agency, four-year
Degrees: A, B, M *Enroll:* 1,189
URL: http://www.emu.edu
Phone: (540) 432-4000 *Calendar:* Sem. plan
Inst. Accred.: ATS (1986/1999), SACS (1959/2000)
Prog. Accred.: Clinical Pastoral Education, Counseling, Nursing Education, Social Work, Teacher Education (NCATE)

Eastern Shore Community College
29300 Lankford Hwy., Melfa 23410
Type: Public, state, two-year
System: Virginia Community College System
Degrees: A *Enroll:* 408
URL: http://www.es.vccs.edu
Phone: (757) 789-1789 *Calendar:* Sem. plan
Inst. Accred.: SACS (1973/1998)

Eastern Virginia Medical School
PO Box 1980, Norfolk 23501-1980
Type: Private, independent, four-year
Degrees: M, D *Enroll:* 692
URL: http://www.evms.edu
Phone: (757) 446-5600 *Calendar:* Sem. plan
Inst. Accred.: SACS (1984/1999)
Prog. Accred.: Allied Health (medicine, surgeon assisting), Clinical Psychology, Physician Assistant, Psychology Internship, Public Health

ECPI College of Technology
5555 Greenwich Rd., Virginia Beach 23462
Type: Private, proprietary, four-year
Degrees: A, B *Enroll:* 5,026
URL: http://www.ecpi.edu
Phone: (757) 671-7171 *Calendar:* Sem. plan
Inst. Accred.: SACS (1998/2003)

Charlotte Campus (Concord)
124 Floyd Smith Dr., Charlotte, NC 28262
Phone: (704) 971-5050

Charlotte Campus
4800 Airport Center Pkwy., Charlotte, NC 28208
Phone: (704) 399-1010

Dulles Campus
21020 Dulles Town Center, Dulles 20166
Phone: (703) 421-9191

Greensboro Campus
7802 Airport Center Dr., Greensboro, NC 27409
Phone: (336) 665-1400

Greenville Campus
15 Brendan Way, Ste. 120, Greenville, SC 29615
Phone: (864) 288-2828
Prog. Accred: Medical Assisting (ABHES)

Mansassas Campus
10021 Balls Ford Rd., Manassas 20109
Phone: (703) 330-5300

Newport News Campus
1001 Omni Blvd., Ste. 100, Newport News 23606
Phone: (757) 838-9191

Raleigh Campus
4101 Doie Cope Rd., Raleigh, NC 27613
Phone: (919) 571-0057

ECPI College of Technology—Richmond
800 Moorefield Park Dr., Richmond 23236-3659
Type: Private, proprietary, four-year
Degrees: A, B *Enroll:* 915
URL: http://www.ecpi.edu
Phone: (804) 330-5533 *Calendar:* Sem. plan
Inst. Accred.: ACCSCT (1986/2002)

Glen Allen Campus
4305 Cox Rd., Glen Allen 23060
Phone: (804) 934-0100

Richmond Campus (West End)
2809 Emerywood Pkwy., Ste. 400, Commerce Plaza I, Richmond 23294
Phone: (804) 521-5999

ECPI Technical College
5234 Airport Rd. NW, Roanoke 24012-1603
Type: Private, proprietary, four-year
Degrees: A, B *Enroll:* 350
URL: http://www.ecpi.edu
Phone: (804) 521-5999 *Calendar:* Sem. plan
Inst. Accred.: ACCSCT (1986/2007)

Emory and Henry College
1 Garnand Dr., Emory 24327-0947
Type: Private, United Methodist Church, four-year
Degrees: B, M *Enroll:* 1,040
URL: http://www.ehc.edu
Phone: (276) 944-6107 *Calendar:* Sem. plan
Inst. Accred.: SACS (1925/2007)

Ferrum College
PO Box 1000, Ferrum 24088
Type: Private, United Methodist Church, four-year
Degrees: A, B *Enroll:* 974
URL: http://www.ferrum.edu
Phone: (540) 365-2121 *Calendar:* Sem. plan
Inst. Accred.: SACS (1960/2002)
Prog. Accred.: Business (ACBSP), Social Work

George Mason University
4400 University Dr., Fairfax 22030-4444
Type: Public, state, four-year
System: State Council of Higher Education for Virginia
Degrees: B, M, D *Enroll:* 21,120
URL: http://www.gmu.edu
Phone: (703) 993-1000 *Calendar:* Sem. plan
Inst. Accred.: SACS (1972/2001)
Prog. Accred.: Accounting, Business (AACSB), Clinical Psychology, Computer Science (ABET-CAC), Engineering (civil, computer, electrical, systems), English Language Education, Graduate Social Work, Law, Music, Nursing Education, Public Administration, Recreation and Leisure Services, Social Work, Teacher Education (NCATE)

Ras-Al-Khaimah, United Arab Emirates Campus
Ras-Al-Khaimah, United Arab Emirates

Germanna Community College
2130 Germanna Hwy., Locust Grove 22508-2102
Type: Public, state, two-year
System: Virginia Community College System
Degrees: A *Enroll:* 2,706
URL: http://www.gcc.vccs.edu
Phone: (540) 727-3000 *Calendar:* Sem. plan
Inst. Accred.: SACS (1972/2008)
Prog. Accred.: Nursing

Hampden-Sydney College
PO Box 128, Hampden-Sydney 23943
Type: Private, Presbyterian Church (USA), four-year
Degrees: B *Enroll:* 1,060
URL: http://www.hsc.edu
Phone: (434) 223-6000 *Calendar:* Sem. plan
Inst. Accred.: SACS (1919/2007)

Hampton University
One Hampton University, Hampton 23668-0199
Type: Private, independent, four-year
Degrees: B, M, P, D *Enroll:* 5,752
URL: http://www.hamptonu.edu
Phone: (757) 727-5000 *Calendar:* Sem. plan
Inst. Accred.: SACS (1932/2008)
Prog. Accred.: Allied Health (speech-language pathology), Aviation, Computer Science (ABET-CAC), Engineering (chemical, electrical), Journalism, Music, Nursing, Nursing Education, Pharmacy, Physical Therapy, Teacher Education (NCATE)

Heritage Institute
8255 Shopper's Square, Manassas 22110-5405
Type: Private, proprietary, two-year
Degrees: A
URL: http://www.heritage-education.edu
Phone: (703) 361-7775
Inst. Accred.: ACCSCT (1990/2005)

Hollins University
PO Box 9707, Roanoke 24020-1707
Type: Private, independent, four-year
Degrees: B, M *Enroll:* 965
URL: http://www.hollins.edu
Phone: (540) 362-6000 *Calendar:* 4-1-4 plan
Inst. Accred.: SACS (1932/2007)
Prog. Accred.: Teacher Education (TEAC)

The Institute for the Psychological Sciences
2001 Jefferson Davis Hwy., Ste. 511, Arlington 22202
Type: Private, independent, four-year
Degrees: D
URL: http://www.ipsciences.edu
Phone: (703) 416-1441 *Calendar:* Sem. plan
Inst. Accred.: SACS (2005)

J. Sargeant Reynolds Community College
PO Box 85622, Richmond 23285-5622
Type: Public, state, two-year
System: Virginia Community College System
Degrees: A *Enroll:* 5,831
URL: http://www.jsr.vccs.edu
Phone: (804) 371-3000 *Calendar:* Sem. plan
Inst. Accred.: SACS (1974/1999)
Prog. Accred.: Allied Health (EMT-paramedic, opticianry, respiratory therapy), Clinical Lab Technology, Dentistry (dental assisting, dental laboratory technology), Nursing

James Madison University
800 South Main St., Harrisonburg 22807
Type: Public, state, four-year
System: State Council of Higher Education for Virginia
Degrees: B, M, P, D *Enroll:* 16,098
URL: http://www.jmu.edu
Phone: (540) 568-6211 *Calendar:* Sem. plan
Inst. Accred.: SACS (1927/2002)
Prog. Accred.: Accounting, Allied Health (audiology, occupational therapy, speech-language pathology), Art, Business (AACSB), Combined Professional-Scientific Psychology, Computer Science (ABET-CAC), Counseling, Dance, Dietetics (didactic), Dietetics (internship), Interior Design, Music, Nursing Education, Physician Assistant, Social Work, Teacher Education (NCATE), Theatre

Jefferson College of Health Sciences
PO Box 13186, Roanoke 24031-3186
Type: Private, independent, four-year
Degrees: A, B, M *Enroll:* 708
URL: http://www.jchs.edu
Phone: (540) 985-8483 *Calendar:* Sem. plan
Inst. Accred.: SACS (1986/2000)
Prog. Accred.: Allied Health (EMT-paramedic, occupational therapy, occupational therapy assisting, respiratory therapy), Nursing, Nursing Education, Phlebotomy, Physical Therapy Assisting, Physician Assistant

The John Leland Center for Theological Studies
1301 North Hartford St., Arlington 22201
Type: Private, Baptist World Alliance, four-year
Degrees: M
URL: http://www.johnlelandcenter.edu
Phone: (703) 812-4757 *Calendar:* Sem. plan
Inst. Accred.: ATS (2006)

John Tyler Community College
13101 Jefferson Davis Hwy., Chester 23831-5399
Type: Public, state, two-year
System: Virginia Community College System
Degrees: A *Enroll:* 3,187
URL: http://www.jtcc.edu
Phone: (804) 796-4000 *Calendar:* Sem. plan
Inst. Accred.: SACS (1969/2002)
Prog. Accred.: Funeral Service Education (Mortuary Science), Nursing

The Judge Advocate General's School
600 Massie Rd., Charlottesville 22903-1781
Type: Public, federal, four-year
Degrees: M, P
URL: https://www.jagcnet.army.mil
Phone: (434) 971-3303 *Calendar:* Qtr. plan
Inst. Accred.: ABA (1958/2000)

Liberty University
1971 University Blvd., Lynchburg 24502
Type: Private, independent, four-year
Degrees: A, B, M, D *Enroll:* 10,508
URL: http://www.liberty.edu
Phone: (434) 582-2000 *Calendar:* Sem. plan
Inst. Accred.: SACS (1980/2006)
Prog. Accred.: Law (ABA only), Nursing Education, Teacher Education (NCATE)

Longwood University
201 High St., Farmville 23909-1898
Type: Public, state, four-year
System: State Council of Higher Education for Virginia
Degrees: B, M *Enroll:* 3,923
URL: http://www.longwood.edu
Phone: (434) 395-2000 *Calendar:* Sem. plan
Inst. Accred.: SACS (1927/2003)
Prog. Accred.: Business (AACSB), Music, Recreation and Leisure Services, Social Work, Teacher Education (NCATE), Theatre

Lord Fairfax Community College
173 Skirmisher Ln., Middletown 22645
Type: Public, state, two-year
System: Virginia Community College System
Degrees: A *Enroll:* 2,864
URL: http://www.lfcc.edu
Phone: (540) 868-7000 *Calendar:* Sem. plan
Inst. Accred.: SACS (1972/2008)

Lynchburg College
1501 Lakeside Dr., Lynchburg 24501-3199
Type: Private, Disciples of Christ, four-year
Degrees: B, M *Enroll:* 2,182
URL: http://www.lynchburg.edu
Phone: (434) 544-8100 *Calendar:* Sem. plan
Inst. Accred.: SACS (1927/2003)
Prog. Accred.: Business (ACBSP), Counseling, Nursing Education

Mary Baldwin College
201 East Frederick St., Staunton 24401-3610
Type: Private, Presbyterian Church (USA), four-year
Degrees: B, M *Enroll:* 1,354
URL: http://www.mbc.edu
Phone: (540) 887-7000 *Calendar:* Sem. plan
Inst. Accred.: SACS (1931/2007)

Marymount University
2807 North Glebe Rd., Arlington 22207-4299
Type: Private, Roman Catholic Church, four-year
Degrees: A, B, M, D *Enroll:* 2,845
URL: http://www.marymount.edu
Phone: (703) 522-5600 *Calendar:* Sem. plan
Inst. Accred.: SACS (1958/2008)
Prog. Accred.: Allied Health (health services administration), Business (ACBSP), Counseling, Interior Design, Nursing, Nursing Education, Physical Therapy, Teacher Education (NCATE)

Medical Careers Institute
1001 Omi Blvd., Ste. 200, Newport News 23606
Type: Private, proprietary, two-year
Degrees: A
URL: http://medical.ecpi.edu
Phone: (757) 873-2423
Inst. Accred.: COE (1983/2003)
Prog. Accred.: Allied Health (medical assisting (AMA))

Richmond Campus
800 Moorefield Park Dr., Richmond 23606
Phone: (804) 521-0400

Virginia Beach Campus
5501 Greenwich Rd., Virginia Beach 23462
Phone: (757) 497-8400

Miller-Motte Technical College
1011 Creekside Ln., Lynchburg 24502
Type: Private, proprietary, two-year
System: Delta Education Corporation
Degrees: A
URL: http://www.miller-motte.com/lynchburgwelcome.html
Phone: (434) 239-5222 *Calendar:* Qtr. plan
Inst. Accred.: ACICS (1953/2008)
Prog. Accred.: Allied Health (medical assisting (AMA), surgical technology)

Mountain Empire Community College
3441 Mountain Empire Rd., Big Stone Gap 24219
Type: Public, state, two-year
System: Virginia Community College System
Degrees: A *Enroll:* 1,770
URL: http://www.me.vccs.edu
Phone: (276) 523-2400 *Calendar:* Sem. plan
Inst. Accred.: SACS (1974/1999)
Prog. Accred.: Allied Health (respiratory therapy), Business (ACBSP)

National College—Roanoke Valley
1813 East Main St., Salem 24153
Type: Private, proprietary, four-year
Degrees: A, B, M *Enroll:* 3,011
URL: http://www.ncbt.edu
Phone: (540) 986-1800 *Calendar:* Qtr. plan
Inst. Accred.: ACICS (1954/2006)
Prog. Accred.: Allied Health (medical assisting (AMA))

Bluefield Campus
100 Logan St., PO Box 629, Bluefield 24605
Phone: (276) 326-3621
Prog. Accred: Allied Health (medical assisting (AMA))

Charlottesville Campus
1819 Emmet St., Charlottesville 22901
Phone: (434) 295-0136
Prog. Accred: Allied Health (medical assisting (AMA))

Danville Campus
336 Old Riverside Dr., Danville 24541-3454
Phone: (434) 793-6822
Prog. Accred: Allied Health (medical assisting (AMA))

Harrisonburg Campus
51-B Burgess Rd., Harrisonburg 22801
Phone: (540) 432-0943
Prog. Accred: Allied Health (medical assisting (AMA))

Lynchburg Campus
104 Candlewood Ct., Lynchburg 24502
Phone: (434) 239-3500
Prog. Accred: Allied Health (medical assisting (AMA))

Martinsville Campus
10 Church St., Martinsville 24114
Phone: (276) 632-5621
Prog. Accred: Allied Health (medical assisting (AMA))

Tri-Cities Campus
1328 Hwy. 11 West, Bristol, TN 37620
Phone: (423) 878-4440
Prog. Accred: Allied Health (medical assisting (AMA))

New River Community College
PO Box 1127, Dublin 24084
Type: Public, state, two-year
System: Virginia Community College System
Degrees: A *Enroll:* 2,434
URL: http://www.nr.vccs.edu
Phone: (540) 674-3600 *Calendar:* Sem. plan
Inst. Accred.: SACS (1972/2008)

Norfolk State University
700 Park Ave., Norfolk 23504
Type: Public, state, four-year
System: State Council of Higher Education for Virginia
Degrees: A, B, M, D *Enroll:* 5,296
URL: http://www.nsu.edu
Phone: (757) 823-8600 *Calendar:* Sem. plan
Inst. Accred.: SACS (1969/2008)
Prog. Accred.: Allied Health (kinesiotherapy), Business (AACSB), Clinical Lab Scientist, Computer Science (ABET-CAC), Construction Technology, Electronic Technology, Graduate Social Work, Journalism, Music, Nursing, Social Work, Teacher Education (NCATE)

Northern Virginia Community College
4001 Wakefield Chapel Rd., Annandale 22003
Type: Public, state, two-year
System: Virginia Community College System
Degrees: A *Enroll:* 21,133
URL: http://www.nvcc.edu
Phone: (703) 323-3000 *Calendar:* Sem. plan
Inst. Accred.: SACS (1968/2002)
Prog. Accred.: Allied Health (EMT-paramedic, respiratory therapy), Clinical Lab Technology, Dentistry (dental hygiene), Nursing, Physical Therapy Assisting, Radiography

Alexandria Campus
3001 North Beauregard St., Alexandria 22311
Phone: (703) 845-6200

Annandale Campus
8333 Little River Turnpike, Annandale 22003
Phone: (703) 323-3010

Loudoun Campus
1000 Harry Flood Byrd Hwy., Sterling 22170
Phone: (703) 450-2500
Prog. Accred: Veterinary Technology

Manassas Campus
6901 Sudley Rd., Manassas 22110
Phone: (703) 257-6600

Medical Education Campus
6699 Springfield Center Dr., Springfield 22150-1913
Phone: (703) 822-6500
Prog. Accred: Nursing

Woodbridge Campus
15200 Neabsco Mills Rd., Woodbridge 22191
Phone: (703) 878-5700

Old Dominion University
Norfolk 23529-0001
Type: Public, state, four-year
System: State Council of Higher Education for Virginia
Degrees: B, M, P, D *Enroll:* 15,615
URL: http://www.odu.edu
Phone: (757) 683-3000 *Calendar:* Sem. plan
Inst. Accred.: SACS (1961/2002)
Prog. Accred.: Accounting, Allied Health (cytotechnology, speech-language pathology), Art, Business (AACSB), Clinical Lab Scientist, Counseling, Dentistry (dental assisting, dental hygiene), Engineering (civil, computer, electrical, environmental/sanitary, mechanical), Engineering Technology (civil/construction, electrical, mechanical), Environmental Health, Exercise Science, Music, Nuclear Medicine Technology, Nurse Anesthesia Education, Nursing, Nursing Education, Physical Therapy, Public Administration, Public Health, Recreation and Leisure Services, Teacher Education (NCATE), Theatre

Patrick Henry College
One Patrick Henry Circle, Purcellville 20132-1776
Type: Private, independent, four-year
Degrees: B
URL: http://www.phc.edu
Phone: (540) 338-1776 *Calendar:* Sem. plan
Inst. Accred.: TRACS (2007)

Patrick Henry Community College
PO Box 5311, Martinsville 24115
Type: Public, state/local, two-year
System: Virginia Community College System
Degrees: A *Enroll:* 1,841
URL: http://www.ph.vccs.edu
Phone: (276) 638-8777 *Calendar:* Sem. plan
Inst. Accred.: SACS (1972/2008)
Prog. Accred.: Nursing

Paul D. Camp Community College
PO Box 737, Franklin 23851-0737
Type: Public, state/local, two-year
System: Virginia Community College System
Degrees: A *Enroll:* 756
URL: http://www.pc.vccs.edu
Phone: (757) 569-6700 *Calendar:* Sem. plan
Inst. Accred.: SACS (1973/1998)
Prog. Accred.: Nursing

Piedmont Virginia Community College
501 College Dr., Charlottesville 22902-7589
Type: Public, state, two-year
System: Virginia Community College System
Degrees: A *Enroll:* 2,114
URL: http://www.pvcc.edu
Phone: (434) 977-3900 *Calendar:* Sem. plan
Inst. Accred.: SACS (1974/1999)
Prog. Accred.: Allied Health (EMT-paramedic, surgical technology), Nursing

Protestant Episcopal Theological Seminary in Virginia
3737 Seminary Rd., Alexandria 22304
Type: Private, Episcopal Church, four-year
Degrees: M, D *FTE Enroll:* 111
URL: http://www.vts.edu
Phone: (703) 370-6600 *Calendar:* Sem. plan
Inst. Accred.: ATS (1938/2003)

Radford University
PO Box 6890, Radford 24142-6890
Type: Public, state, four-year
System: State Council of Higher Education for Virginia
Degrees: B, M, P, D *Enroll:* 8,878
URL: http://www.radford.edu
Phone: (540) 831-5000 *Calendar:* Sem. plan
Inst. Accred.: SACS (1928/2002)
Prog. Accred.: Allied Health (audiology, speech-language pathology), Business (AACSB), Computer Science (ABET-CAC), Counseling, Dietetics (didactic), Graduate Social Work, Interior Design, Music, Nursing Education, Recreation and Leisure Services, Social Work, Teacher Education (NCATE), Theatre

Randolph College
2500 Rivermont Ave., Lynchburg 24503-1526
Type: Private, United Methodist Church, four-year
Degrees: B, M *Enroll:* 696
URL: http://www.randolphcollege.edu
Phone: (434) 947-8000 *Calendar:* Sem. plan
Inst. Accred.: SACS (1902/2000)

Randolph-Macon College
PO Box 5005, Ashland 23005-5505
Type: Private, United Methodist Church, four-year
Degrees: B *Enroll:* 1,111
URL: http://www.rmc.edu
Phone: (804) 752-7200 *Calendar:* 4-1-4 plan
Inst. Accred.: SACS (1904/2008)

Rappahannock Community College
12745 College Dr., Glenns 23149-2616
Type: Public, state, two-year
System: Virginia Community College System
Degrees: A *Enroll:* 1,419
URL: http://www.rcc.vccs.edu
Phone: (804) 758-6700 *Calendar:* Sem. plan
Inst. Accred.: SACS (1973/1998)

Regent University
1000 Regent University Dr., Virginia Beach 23464-9801
Type: Private, nondenominational, four-year
Degrees: B, M, D *Enroll:* 2,726
URL: http://www.regent.edu
Phone: (757) 226-4000 *Calendar:* Sem. plan
Inst. Accred.: ATS (1993/2007), SACS (1984/1999)
Prog. Accred.: Clinical Psychology, Counseling, Law (ABA only)

Richard Bland College
11301 Johnson Rd., Petersburg 23805
Type: Public, state, two-year
System: College of William and Mary Central Office
Degrees: A *Enroll:* 1,023
URL: http://www.rbc.edu
Phone: (804) 862-6100 *Calendar:* Sem. plan
Inst. Accred.: SACS (1961/1998)

Roanoke College
221 College Ln., Salem 24153-3794
Type: Private, Evangelical Lutheran Church in America, four-year
Degrees: B *Enroll:* 1,873
URL: http://www.roanoke.edu
Phone: (540) 375-2500 *Calendar:* Sem. plan
Inst. Accred.: SACS (1927/2001)
Prog. Accred.: Business (ACBSP)

RSHT Training Center
1601 Willow Lawn Dr., Ste. 320, Richmond 23230
Type: Private, proprietary, two-year
Degrees: A
URL: http://www.rsht.edu
Phone: (804) 288-1000 *Calendar:* Sem. plan
Inst. Accred.: COE (1999/2005)

Chester Campus
751 West Hundred Rd., Chester 23836-2516
Phone: (804) 751-9191

Saint Paul's College
115 College Dr., Lawrenceville 23868
Type: Private, Episcopal Church, four-year
Degrees: B *Enroll:* 701
URL: http://www.saintpauls.edu
Phone: (434) 848-3111 *Calendar:* Sem. plan
Inst. Accred.: SACS (1950/2000)

Sanford-Brown College—Vienna
1980 Gallows Rd., Vienna 22182
Type: Private, proprietary, four-year
System: Career Education Corporation
Degrees: A, B
URL: http://www.sbcvienna.com
Phone: (703) 556-8888 *Calendar:* Qtr. plan
Inst. Accred.: ACICS (1969/2006)

Shenandoah University
1460 University Dr., Winchester 22601
Type: Private, United Methodist Church, four-year
Degrees: A, B, M, P, D *Enroll:* 2,537
URL: http://www.su.edu
Phone: (540) 665-4500 *Calendar:* Sem. plan
Inst. Accred.: SACS (1973/1999)
Prog. Accred.: Allied Health (occupational therapy, respiratory therapy), Business (AACSB), Music, Nurse (Midwifery), Nursing Education, Pharmacy, Physical Therapy, Physician Assistant

Southeast Culinary and Hospitality College
100 Piedmont Ave., Bristol 24201
Type: Private, proprietary, two-year
Degrees: A
URL: http://www.tricityhospitality.com
Phone: (276) 591-5699
Inst. Accred.: COE (2007)

Southern Virginia University
One College Hill Dr., Buena Vista 24416
Type: Private, independent, two-year
Degrees: A *Enroll:* 661
URL: http://www.southernvirginia.edu
Phone: (540) 261-8400 *Calendar:* Sem. plan
Inst. Accred.: AALE (2003)

Southside Virginia Community College
109 Campus Dr., Alberta 23821
Type: Public, state, two-year
System: Virginia Community College System
Degrees: A *Enroll:* 2,619
URL: http://www.sv.vccs.edu
Phone: (434) 949-1000 *Calendar:* Sem. plan
Inst. Accred.: SACS (1972/2008)

Southwest Virginia Community College
PO Box SVCC, Richlands 24641
Type: Public, state, two-year
System: Virginia Community College System
Degrees: A *Enroll:* 2,237
URL: http://www.sw.edu
Phone: (540) 964-2555 *Calendar:* Sem. plan
Inst. Accred.: SACS (1970/2006)
Prog. Accred.: Allied Health (EMT-paramedic, occupational therapy assisting, respiratory therapy), Nursing, Radiography

Stratford University
7777 Leesburg Pike, Falls Church 22043
Type: Private, proprietary, four-year
Degrees: A, B, M
URL: http://www.stratford.edu
Phone: (703) 821-8570 *Calendar:* Qtr. plan
Inst. Accred.: ACICS (2003/2008)
Prog. Accred.: Culinary Education

Woodbridge Campus
13576 Minneville Rd., Woodbridge 22192
Phone: (703) 897-1982

Sweet Briar College
PO Box C, Sweet Briar 24595
Type: Private, independent, four-year
Degrees: B, M *Enroll:* 728
URL: http://www.sbc.edu
Phone: (434) 381-6100 *Calendar:* Sem. plan
Inst. Accred.: SACS (1920/2001)

TAP—This Valley Works Center for Employment Training
108 North Jefferson St., Roanoke 24001
Type: Private, independent, two-year
Degrees: A
URL: http://www.tapintohope.org/programs/thisvalleyworks.html
Phone: (540) 767-6221
Inst. Accred.: COE (2004)

Thomas Nelson Community College
PO Box 9407, Hampton 23670-0407
Type: Public, state, two-year
System: Virginia Community College System
Degrees: A *Enroll:* 4,651
URL: http://www.tncc.vccs.edu
Phone: (757) 825-2700 *Calendar:* Sem. plan
Inst. Accred.: SACS (1970/2006)
Prog. Accred.: Clinical Lab Technology, Nursing

Tidewater Community College
PO Box 9000, Norfolk 23509-9000
Type: Public, state, two-year
System: Virginia Community College System
Degrees: A *Enroll:* 13,177
URL: http://www.tcc.edu
Phone: (757) 822-1110 *Calendar:* Sem. plan
Inst. Accred.: SACS (1971/2007)
Prog. Accred.: Allied Health (EMT-paramedic, diagnostic medical sonography, medical assisting (AMA), respiratory therapy), Culinary Education, Radiography

Chesapeake Campus
1428 Cedar Rd., Chesapeake 23322-7199
Phone: (757) 822-5100

Portsmouth Campus
7000 College Dr., Portsmouth 23703-6100
Phone: (757) 822-2124
Prog. Accred: Nursing

Virginia Beach Campus
1700 College Crescent, Virginia Beach 23456
Phone: (757) 822-7100
Prog. Accred: Allied Health (occupational therapy assisting), Funeral Service Education (Mortuary Science), Physical Therapy Assisting, Radiography

Union Theological Seminary and Presbyterian School of Christian Education
3401 Brook Rd., Richmond 23227
Type: Private, Presbyterian Church (USA), four-year
Degrees: M, D *Enroll:* 294
URL: http://www.union-psce.edu
Phone: (804) 355-0671 *Calendar:* Sem. plan
Inst. Accred.: ATS (1938/2002), SACS (1997/2002)

United States Marine Corps University
2076 South St., Quantico 22134-5067
Type: Public, federal, four-year
Degrees: M
URL: http://www.mcu.usmc.mil
Phone: (703) 784-2105 *Calendar:* Sem. plan
Inst. Accred.: SACS (1999/2005)

University of Management and Technology
1901 North Fort Meyer Dr., Ste. 700, Arlington 22209-1609
Type: Private, proprietary, four-year
Degrees: A, B, M
URL: http://www.umtweb.edu
Phone: (703) 516-0035
Inst. Accred.: DETC (2002/2007)

University of Mary Washington
1301 College Ave., Fredericksburg 22401-5358
Type: Public, state, four-year
System: State Council of Higher Education for Virginia
Degrees: B, M *Enroll:* 4,040
URL: http://www.umw.edu
Phone: (540) 654-1000 *Calendar:* Sem. plan
Inst. Accred.: SACS (1930/2003)
Prog. Accred.: Music

James Monroe Center for Graduate and Professional Studies
121 University Blvd., Fredericksburg 22406
Phone: (540) 286-8000

University of Richmond
28 Westhampton Way, Richmond 23173
Type: Private, independent, four-year
Degrees: A, B, M, D *Enroll:* 4,045
URL: http://www.richmond.edu
Phone: (804) 289-8000 *Calendar:* Sem. plan
Inst. Accred.: SACS (1910/2008)
Prog. Accred.: Accounting, Business (AACSB), Law, Music

University of Virginia
PO Box 400224, Charlottesville 22904-4224
Type: Public, state, four-year
System: University of Virginia Central Office
Degrees: B, M, P, D *Enroll:* 21,002
URL: http://www.virginia.edu
Phone: (434) 924-0311 *Calendar:* Sem. plan
Inst. Accred.: SACS (1904/2007)
Prog. Accred.: Accounting, Allied Health (audiology, medicine, speech-language pathology), Business (AACSB), Clinical Pastoral Education, Clinical Psychology, Computer Science (ABET-CAC), Counseling, Dentistry (general practice residency), Dietetics (internship), Engineering (aerospace, chemical, civil, computer, electrical, mechanical, systems), Landscape Architecture, Law, Nursing Education, Planning, Psychology Internship, Public Health, Radiography, Teacher Education (TEAC), Theatre

The University of Virginia's College at Wise
One College Ave., Wise 24293
Type: Public, state, four-year
System: State Council of Higher Education for Virginia
Degrees: B *Enroll:* 1,657
URL: http://www.uvawise.edu
Phone: (276) 328-0100 *Calendar:* Sem. plan
Inst. Accred.: SACS (1970/2006)
Prog. Accred.: Nursing Education

Virginia Commonwealth University
PO Box 842512, Richmond 23284-2512
Type: Public, state, four-year
System: State Council of Higher Education for Virginia
Degrees: A, B, M, P, D *Enroll:* 23,594
URL: http://www.vcu.edu
Phone: (804) 828-0100 *Calendar:* Sem. plan
Inst. Accred.: SACS (1953/2004)
Prog. Accred.: Accounting, Allied Health (EMT-paramedic, health services administration, medicine, occupational therapy), Art, Business (AACSB), Clinical Lab Scientist, Clinical Pastoral Education, Clinical Psychology, Computer Science (ABET-CAC), Counseling Psychology, Dance, Dentistry (advanced education in general dentistry, combined prosthodontics, dental hygiene, dentistry, endodontics, general dentistry, general practice residency, oral and maxillofacial surgery, orthodontic and dentofacial orthopedics, pediatric dentistry, periodontics), Dietetics (internship), Engineering (bioengineering, chemical, construction, electrical, information systems, mechanical), Graduate Social Work, Interior Design, Journalism, Music, Nuclear Medicine Technology, Nurse Anesthesia Education, Nursing, Pharmacy, Physical Therapy, Planning, Psychology Internship, Public Administration, Public Health, Radiation Therapy, Radiography, Rehabilitation Counseling, Social Work, Teacher Education (NCATE), Theatre

Virginia Commonwealth University School of the Arts in Qatar
PO Box 8095, Doha, Qatar
Phone: 011 974 492-7200
Prog. Accred: Interior Design

Virginia Highlands Community College
PO Box 828, Abingdon 24212-0828
Type: Public, state, two-year
System: Virginia Community College System
Degrees: A *Enroll:* 1,469
URL: http://www.vhcc.edu
Phone: (276) 739-2400 *Calendar:* Sem. plan
Inst. Accred.: SACS (1972/2008)
Prog. Accred.: Nursing

Virginia Intermont College
1013 Moore St., Bristol 24201
Type: Private, Southern Baptist Church, four-year
Degrees: A, B *Enroll:* 734
URL: http://www.vic.edu
Phone: (276) 669-6101 *Calendar:* Sem. plan
Inst. Accred.: SACS (1925/1997, Probation)
Prog. Accred.: Social Work

Virginia International University
3957 Pender Dr., Fairfax 22030
Type: Private, independent, four-year
System: State Council of Higher Education for Virginia
Degrees: B, M *FTE Enroll:* 331
URL: http://www.viu.edu
Phone: (703) 591-2760 *Calendar:* Sem. plan
Inst. Accred.: ACICS (2008)

Virginia Military Institute
Lexington 24450-0304
Type: Public, state-related, four-year
System: State Council of Higher Education for Virginia
Degrees: B *Enroll:* 1,369
URL: http://www.vmi.edu
Phone: (540) 464-7000 *Calendar:* Sem. plan
Inst. Accred.: SACS (1926/2007)
Prog. Accred.: Computer Science (ABET-CAC), Engineering (civil, electrical, mechanical)

Virginia Polytechnic Institute and State University
Blacksburg 24061-0002
Type: Public, state, four-year
System: State Council of Higher Education for Virginia
Degrees: A, B, M, D *Enroll:* 26,214
URL: http://www.vt.edu
Phone: (540) 231-6000 *Calendar:* Sem. plan
Inst. Accred.: SACS (1923/1998)
Prog. Accred.: Accounting, Art, Business (AACSB), Clinical Psychology, Computer Science (ABET-CAC), Construction Education, Counseling, Dietetics (didactic), Dietetics (internship), Engineering (aerospace, agricultural, chemical, civil, computer, electrical, engineering mechanics, environmental/sanitary, industrial, materials, mechanical, mining, ocean), English Language Education, Family & Consumer Science, Forestry, Interior Design, Landscape Architecture, Marriage and Family Therapy, Planning, Psychology Internship, Public Administration, Teacher Education (NCATE), Theatre, Veterinary Medicine

Northern Virginia Graduate Center
7054 Haycock Rd., Falls Church 22043-2311
Phone: (703) 538-8324
Prog. Accred: Marriage and Family Therapy

Virginia State University
1 Hayden Dr., Petersburg 23806-0001
Type: Public, state, four-year
System: State Council of Higher Education for Virginia
Degrees: B, M, D *Enroll:* 4,501
URL: http://www.vsu.edu
Phone: (804) 524-5000 *Calendar:* Sem. plan
Inst. Accred.: SACS (1933/2008)
Prog. Accred.: Art, Business (AACSB), Dietetics (didactic), Dietetics (internship), Engineering Technology (electrical, mechanical), Music, Nursing, Teacher Education (NCATE)

Virginia Union University
1500 North Lombardy St., Richmond 23220-1711
Type: Private, American Baptist Churches in the USA, four-year
Degrees: B, M, D *Enroll:* 1,669
URL: http://www.vuu.edu
Phone: (804) 257-5600 *Calendar:* Sem. plan
Inst. Accred.: ATS (1971/2007), SACS (1935/2000)
Prog. Accred.: Business (ACBSP), Social Work, Teacher Education (NCATE)

Virginia University of Lynchburg
2058 Garfield Ave., Lynchburg 24501
Type: Private, independent, four-year
Degrees: A, B, M, D *Enroll:* 94
URL: http://vulonline.net
Phone: (434) 528-5276 *Calendar:* Sem. plan
Inst. Accred.: TRACS (2005)

Virginia Wesleyan College
1584 Wesleyan Dr., Norfolk 23502-5599
Type: Private, United Methodist Church, four-year
Degrees: B *Enroll:* 1,227
URL: http://www.vwc.edu
Phone: (757) 455-3200 *Calendar:* Sem. plan
Inst. Accred.: SACS (1970/2006)
Prog. Accred.: Recreation and Leisure Services

Virginia Western Community College
PO Box 14007, Roanoke 24038-4007
Type: Public, state, two-year
System: Virginia Community College System
Degrees: A *Enroll:* 4,099
URL: http://www.vw.vccs.edu
Phone: (540) 857-8922 *Calendar:* Sem. plan
Inst. Accred.: SACS (1969/2003)
Prog. Accred.: Business (ACBSP), Dentistry (dental hygiene), Nursing, Radiography

Washington and Lee University
204 West Washington St., Lexington 24450-2116
Type: Private, independent, four-year
Degrees: B, D *Enroll:* 2,176
URL: http://www.wlu.edu
Phone: (540) 458-8400
Inst. Accred.: SACS (1895/1999)
Prog. Accred.: Business (AACSB), Journalism, Law

Westwood College
4300 Wilson Blvd., Ste. 200, Arlington 22203
Type: Private, proprietary, four-year
System: Westwood College
Degrees: A, B
URL: http://www.westwood.edu
Phone: (703) 243-3900 *Calendar:* Sem. plan
Inst. Accred.: ACCSCT (2005/2007), NCA-HLC (2007, *Indirect accreditation through Westwood College, Denver, CO*)

World College
Lake Shores Plaza, 5193 Shore Dr., Ste. 105, Virginia Beach 23455-2500
Type: Private, proprietary, four-year
Degrees: B *FTE Enroll:* 300
URL: http://www.cie-wc.edu
Phone: (757) 464-4600
Inst. Accred.: DETC (1993/2008)

Wytheville Community College
1000 East Main St., Wytheville 24382
Type: Public, state, two-year
System: Virginia Community College System
Degrees: A *Enroll:* 1,353
URL: http://www.wcc.vccs.edu
Phone: (276) 223-4700 *Calendar:* Sem. plan
Inst. Accred.: SACS (1970/2006)
Prog. Accred.: Clinical Lab Technology, Dentistry (dental hygiene), Nursing, Physical Therapy Assisting

WASHINGTON

Argosy University Seattle
2601-A Elliott Ave., Seattle 98121
Type: Private, proprietary, four-year
System: Argosy University
Degrees: B, M, D
URL: http://www.argosyu.edu/seattle
Phone: (206) 283-4500 *Calendar:* Tri. plan
Inst. Accred.: NCA-HLC (1981/2008, *Indirect accreditation through Argosy University, Chicago, IL*)

The Art Institute of Seattle
2323 Elliott Ave., Seattle 98121-1633
Type: Private, proprietary, four-year
System: Education Management Corporation
Degrees: A, B *Enroll:* 1,989
URL: http://www.ais.edu
Phone: (206) 448-0900 *Calendar:* Qtr. plan
Inst. Accred.: NWCCU (1999/2007)
Prog. Accred.: Culinary Education

Bakke Graduate University
1013 8th Ave., Seattle 98104
Type: Private, nondenominational, four-year
Degrees: M
URL: http://www.bgu.edu
Phone: (206) 264-9100 *Calendar:* Sem. plan
Inst. Accred.: TRACS (1994/2004)

Bastyr University
14500 Juanita Dr. NE, Kenmore 98028-4995
Type: Private, independent, four-year
Degrees: B, M, D *Enroll:* 975
URL: http://www.bastyr.edu
Phone: (425) 823-1300 *Calendar:* Qtr. plan
Inst. Accred.: NWCCU (1989/2007)
Prog. Accred.: Acupuncture, Dietetics (didactic), Dietetics (internship), Midwifery Education, Naturopathic Medicine

Bates Technical College
1101 South Yakima Ave., Tacoma 98405-4895
Type: Public, state, two-year
System: Washington State Board for Community and Technical Colleges
Degrees: A *Enroll:* 3,234
URL: http://www.bates.ctc.edu
Phone: (253) 680-7000 *Calendar:* Qtr. plan
Inst. Accred.: NWCCU (1988/2006)
Prog. Accred.: Dentistry (dental assisting, dental laboratory technology)

Bellevue Community College
3000 Landerholm Circle, SE, Bellevue 98007-6484
Type: Public, state/local, four-year
System: Washington State Board for Community and Technical Colleges
Degrees: A, B *Enroll:* 7,617
URL: http://www.bcc.ctc.edu
Phone: (425) 564-2305 *Calendar:* Qtr. plan
Inst. Accred.: NWCCU (1970/2006)
Prog. Accred.: Allied Health (diagnostic medical sonography), Interior Design, Nuclear Medicine Technology, Nursing, Radiation Therapy, Radiography

Bellingham Technical College
3028 Lindbergh Ave., Bellingham 98225-1599
Type: Public, state/local, two-year
System: Washington State Board for Community and Technical Colleges
Degrees: A *Enroll:* 1,373
URL: http://www.btc.ctc.edu
Phone: (360) 738-3105 *Calendar:* Qtr. plan
Inst. Accred.: NWCCU (1999)
Prog. Accred.: Allied Health (EMT-paramedic, surgical technology), Culinary Education, Dentistry (dental assisting)

Big Bend Community College
7662 Chanute St., Moses Lake 98837-3299
Type: Public, state, two-year
System: Washington State Board for Community and Technical Colleges
Degrees: A *Enroll:* 1,397
URL: http://www.bigbend.edu
Phone: (509) 762-5351 *Calendar:* Qtr. plan
Inst. Accred.: NWCCU (1965/2008)
Prog. Accred.: Nursing

Cascadia Community College
18345 Campus Way, NE, Bothell 98011
Type: Public, state/local, two-year
Degrees: A
URL: http://www.cascadia.ctc.edu
Phone: (425) 352-8000 *Calendar:* Qtr. plan
Inst. Accred.: NWCCU (2006)

Central Washington University
400 East University Way, Ellensburg 98926-7500
Type: Public, state, four-year
System: Washington Higher Education Coordinating Board
Degrees: B, M *Enroll:* 9,373
URL: http://www.cwu.edu
Phone: (509) 963-1111 *Calendar:* Qtr. plan
Inst. Accred.: NWCCU (1918/2001)
Prog. Accred.: Allied Health (EMT-paramedic), Clinical Lab Scientist, Construction Education, Dietetics (didactic), Dietetics (internship), Engineering Technology (electrical, mechanical), Music, Psychology Internship, Teacher Education (NCATE)

Centralia College
600 West Locust, Centralia 98531
Type: Public, state, two-year
System: Washington State Board for Community and Technical Colleges
Degrees: A *Enroll:* 2,263
URL: http://www.centralia.ctc.edu
Phone: (360) 736-9391 *Calendar:* Qtr. plan
Inst. Accred.: NWCCU (1948/2006)

City University of Seattle
11900 NE First St., Bellevue 98005
Type: Private, independent, four-year
Degrees: A, B, M *Enroll:* 3,016
URL: http://www.cityu.edu
Phone: (425) 637-1010 *Calendar:* Qtr. plan
Inst. Accred.: NWCCU (1978/2007)

Clark College
1800 East McLoughlin Blvd., Vancouver 98663
Type: Public, state, two-year
System: Washington State Board for Community and Technical Colleges
Degrees: A *Enroll:* 6,123
URL: http://www.clark.edu
Phone: (360) 992-2000 *Calendar:* Qtr. plan
Inst. Accred.: NWCCU (1948/2000)
Prog. Accred.: Allied Health (EMT-paramedic, medical assisting (AMA)), Dentistry (dental hygiene), Nursing

Clover Park Technical College
4500 Steilacoom Blvd., SW, Lakewood 98499
Type: Public, state, two-year
System: Washington State Board for Community and Technical Colleges
Degrees: A
URL: http://www.cptc.edu
Phone: (253) 589-5800 *Calendar:* Qtr. plan
Inst. Accred.: NWCCU (1999)
Prog. Accred.: Allied Health (medical assisting (AMA), surgical technology), Clinical Lab Technology, Dentistry (dental assisting)

Columbia Basin College
2600 North 20th Ave., Pasco 99301-3397
Type: Public, state, two-year
System: Washington State Board for Community and Technical Colleges
Degrees: A *Enroll:* 3,683
URL: http://www.cbc2.org
Phone: (509) 547-0511 *Calendar:* Qtr. plan
Inst. Accred.: NWCCU (1960/2004)
Prog. Accred.: Allied Health (EMT-paramedic), Dentistry (dental hygiene), Nursing

Cornish College of the Arts
1000 Lenora St., Seattle 98121
Type: Private, independent, four-year
Degrees: B *Enroll:* 750
URL: http://www.cornish.edu
Phone: (206) 726-5151 *Calendar:* Sem. plan
Inst. Accred.: NWCCU (1977/2008)
Prog. Accred.: Art

DeVry University Federal Way
3600 South 344th Way, Federal Way 98001
Type: Private, proprietary, four-year
Degrees: A, B, M
URL: http://www.devry.edu/federalway
Phone: (253) 943-2800 *Calendar:* Sem. plan
Inst. Accred.: NCA-HLC (2002, *Indirect accreditation through DeVry University, Oakbrook Terrace, IL*)
Prog. Accred.: Engineering Technology (computer, electrical)

Bellevue (Seattle) Center
600 108th Ave. NE, Ste. 203, Bellevue 98004
Phone: (425) 455-2242

Portland Campus
9755 SW Barnes Rd., Peterkort Center II, Ste. 150, Portland, OR 97225
Phone: (503) 296-7468

DigiPen Institute of Technology
5001 150th Ave., NE, Redmond 98052
Type: Private, proprietary, four-year
Degrees: A, B
URL: http://www.digipen.edu
Phone: (425) 558-0299 *Calendar:* Sem. plan
Inst. Accred.: ACCSCT (2002/2005)

Eastern Washington University
526 5th St., Cheney 99004-2424
Type: Public, state, four-year
System: Washington Higher Education Coordinating Board
Degrees: B, M, D *Enroll:* 9,690
URL: http://www.ewu.edu
Phone: (509) 359-6200 *Calendar:* Qtr. plan
Inst. Accred.: NWCCU (1919/2006)
Prog. Accred.: Allied Health (occupational therapy, speech-language pathology), Business (AACSB), Computer Science (ABET-CAC), Counseling, Dentistry (dental hygiene), Engineering Technology (computer, mechanical), English Language Education, Graduate Social Work, Music, Nursing Education, Physical Therapy, Planning, Recreation and Leisure Services, Social Work, Teacher Education (NCATE)

Edmonds Community College
20000 68th Ave. West, Lynnwood 98036
Type: Public, state/local, two-year
System: Washington State Board for Community and Technical Colleges
Degrees: A *Enroll:* 4,802
URL: http://www.edcc.edu
Phone: (425) 640-1459 *Calendar:* Qtr. plan
Inst. Accred.: NWCCU (1973/2008)
Prog. Accred.: Construction Education

Everett Community College
2000 Tower St., Everett 98201-1352
Type: Public, state, two-year
System: Washington State Board for Community and Technical Colleges
Degrees: A *Enroll:* 4,271
URL: http://www.evcc.ctc.edu
Phone: (425) 388-9100 *Calendar:* Qtr. plan
Inst. Accred.: NWCCU (1948/2007)
Prog. Accred.: Allied Health (medical assisting (AMA)), Nursing

The Evergreen State College
2700 Evergreen Pkwy., Olympia 98505-0005
Type: Public, state, four-year
System: Washington Higher Education Coordinating Board
Degrees: B, M *Enroll:* 4,063
URL: http://www.evergreen.edu
Phone: (360) 866-6000 *Calendar:* Qtr. plan
Inst. Accred.: NWCCU (1974/2001)

Faith Evangelical Seminary
3504 North Pearl St., Tacoma 98407
Type: Private, Conservative Lutheran Association, four-year
Degrees: B, M, D
URL: http://www.faithseminary.edu
Phone: (253) 752-2020 *Calendar:* Qtr. plan
Inst. Accred.: TRACS (2001/2006)

Gonzaga University
502 East Boone Ave., Spokane 99258-0001
Type: Private, Roman Catholic Church, four-year
Degrees: B, M, D *Enroll:* 5,410
URL: http://www.gonzaga.edu
Phone: (509) 328-4220 *Calendar:* Sem. plan
Inst. Accred.: ATS (1999/2004), NWCCU (1927/2007)
Prog. Accred.: Business (AACSB), Counseling, Engineering (civil, computer, electrical, mechanical), English Language Education, Law, Nurse Anesthesia Education, Nursing Education, Teacher Education (NCATE)

Grays Harbor College
1620 Edward P. Smith Dr., Aberdeen 98520
Type: Public, state/local, two-year
System: Washington State Board for Community and Technical Colleges
Degrees: A *Enroll:* 1,478
URL: http://www.ghc.ctc.edu
Phone: (360) 532-9020 *Calendar:* Qtr. plan
Inst. Accred.: NWCCU (1948/2006)
Prog. Accred.: Nursing

Green River Community College
12401 SE 320th St., Auburn 98002-3699
Type: Public, state, two-year
System: Washington State Board for Community and Technical Colleges
Degrees: A *Enroll:* 4,903
URL: http://www.greenriver.edu
Phone: (253) 833-9111 *Calendar:* Qtr. plan
Inst. Accred.: NWCCU (1967/2007)
Prog. Accred.: Allied Health (occupational therapy assisting), Forestry, Physical Therapy Assisting

Heritage University
3240 Fort Rd., Toppenish 98948
Type: Private, Roman Catholic Church, four-year
Degrees: A, B, M *Enroll:* 908
URL: http://www.heritage.edu
Phone: (509) 865-8500 *Calendar:* Sem. plan
Inst. Accred.: NWCCU (1986/2006)
Prog. Accred.: Social Work

Highline Community College
PO Box 98000, Des Moines 98198-9800
Type: Public, state, two-year
System: Washington State Board for Community and Technical Colleges
Degrees: A *Enroll:* 3,877
URL: http://www.highline.edu
Phone: (206) 878-3710 *Calendar:* Qtr. plan
Inst. Accred.: NWCCU (1965/2003)
Prog. Accred.: Allied Health (medical assisting (AMA), respiratory therapy), Dentistry (dental assisting), Nursing

Interface College
1118 North Washington St., Spokane 99201
Type: Private, proprietary, two-year
Degrees: A
URL: http://www.interface-net.com
Phone: (509) 467-1727
Inst. Accred.: ACCET (1986/2008)

ITT Technical Institute
13518 East Indiana Ave., Spokane Valley 99216
Type: Private, proprietary, four-year
System: ITT Educational Services, Inc.
Degrees: A, B *Enroll:* 514
URL: http://www.itt-tech.edu
Phone: (509) 926-2900 *Calendar:* Qtr. plan
Inst. Accred.: ACICS (1999/2007)

ITT Technical Institute
12720 Gateway Dr., Ste. 100, Seattle 98168-3334
Type: Private, proprietary, four-year
System: ITT Educational Services, Inc.
Degrees: A, B *Enroll:* 373
URL: http://www.itt-tech.edu
Phone: (206) 244-3300 *Calendar:* Qtr. plan
Inst. Accred.: ACICS (1999/2004)

Columbus Area Campus
3781 Park Mill Run Dr., Hilliard, OH 43026
Phone: (614) 771-4888

Everett Campus
1615 75th St. SW, Everett 98203
Phone: (425) 583-0200

Wichita Campus
2024 North Woodlawn St., One Brittany Place, Ste. 100, Wichita, KS 67208-1877
Phone: (316) 681-8400

Kaplan College—Renton
500 SW 39th St., Ste. 115, Renton 98055-4910
Type: Private, proprietary, two-year
System: Kaplan Higher Education Corporation
Degrees: A
URL: http://getinfo.kaplancollege.com
Phone: (425) 291-3620 *Calendar:* Qtr. plan
Inst. Accred.: ACCSCT (2006)

Lake Washington Technical College
11605 132nd Ave., NE, Kirkland 98034-8506
Type: Public, state, two-year
System: Washington State Board for Community and Technical Colleges
Degrees: A *Enroll:* 2,348
URL: http://www.lwtc.ctc.edu
Phone: (425) 739-8100 *Calendar:* Qtr. plan
Inst. Accred.: NWCCU (1981/2007)
Prog. Accred.: Allied Health (medical assisting (AMA)), Culinary Education, Dentistry (dental assisting, dental hygiene)

Lower Columbia College
1600 Maple St., PO Box 3010, Longview 98632-0310
Type: Public, state, two-year
System: Washington State Board for Community and Technical Colleges
Degrees: A *Enroll:* 2,198
URL: http://www.lcc.ctc.edu
Phone: (360) 442-2000 *Calendar:* Qtr. plan
Inst. Accred.: NWCCU (1948/2006)
Prog. Accred.: Allied Health (medical assisting (AMA)), Nursing

Mars Hill Graduate School
2501 Elliot Ave., Seattle 98121
Type: Private, inter-denominational, four-year
Degrees: M
URL: http://www.mhgs.edu
Phone: (206) 876-6100 *Calendar:* Tri. plan
Inst. Accred.: TRACS (2001)

North Seattle Community College
9600 College Way North, Seattle 98103
Type: Public, state/local, two-year
System: Seattle Community Colleges
Degrees: A *Enroll:* 3,216
URL: http://www.northseattle.edu
Phone: (206) 527-3600 *Calendar:* Qtr. plan
Inst. Accred.: NWCCU (1973/2007)
Prog. Accred.: Allied Health (medical assisting (AMA)), Culinary Education

Northwest Aviation College
506 23rd St. NE, Auburn 98002
Type: Private, proprietary, two-year
Degrees: A
URL: http://www.afsnac.com
Phone: (253) 854-4960 *Calendar:* Qtr. plan
Inst. Accred.: ACCSCT (1995/2005)

Northwest Baptist Seminary
4301 North Stevens St., Tacoma 98407
Type: Private, independent, four-year
Degrees: M *Enroll:* 50
URL: http://www.nbs.edu
Phone: (253) 759-6104 *Calendar:* Qtr. plan
Inst. Accred.: TRACS (1999/2003)

Northwest College of Art
16301 Creative Dr. NE, Poulsbo 98370
Type: Private, independent, four-year
Degrees: B *Enroll:* 130
URL: http://www.nca.edu
Phone: (360) 779-9993 *Calendar:* Sem. plan
Inst. Accred.: ACCSCT (1989/2004)

Northwest Indian College
2522 Kwina Rd., Bellingham 98226
Type: Public, tribal, four-year
System: American Indian Higher Education Consortium
Degrees: A, B *Enroll:* 330
URL: http://www.nwic.edu
Phone: (360) 676-2772 *Calendar:* Qtr. plan
Inst. Accred.: NWCCU (1993/2001)

Northwest School of Wooden Boatbuilding
42 North Water St., Port Hadlock 98339
Type: Private, independent, two-year
Degrees: A
URL: http://www.nwboatschool.org
Phone: (360) 385-4948
Inst. Accred.: ACCSCT (1993/2008)

Northwest University
PO Box 579, 5520 108th Ave., NE, Kirkland 98083
Type: Private, Northwest Council of the Assemblies of God, four-year
Degrees: A, B, M *Enroll:* 1,196
URL: http://www.northwestu.edu
Phone: (425) 822-8266 *Calendar:* Sem. plan
Inst. Accred.: NWCCU (1973/2007)
Prog. Accred.: Nursing Education

Olympic College
1600 Chester Ave., Bremerton 98337-1699
Type: Public, state, four-year
System: Washington State Board for Community and Technical Colleges
Degrees: A, B *Enroll:* 4,547
URL: http://www.olympic.edu
Phone: (360) 792-6050 *Calendar:* Qtr. plan
Inst. Accred.: NWCCU (1948/2006)
Prog. Accred.: Allied Health (medical assisting (AMA)), Culinary Education, Nursing

Pacific Lutheran University
Tacoma 98447-0003
Type: Private, Evangelical Lutheran Church in America, four-year
Degrees: B, M *Enroll:* 3,495
URL: http://www.plu.edu
Phone: (253) 535-6900 *Calendar:* Sem. plan
Inst. Accred.: NWCCU (1936/2008)
Prog. Accred.: Accounting, Business (AACSB), Computer Science (ABET-CAC), Marriage and Family Therapy, Music, Nursing Education, Social Work, Teacher Education (NCATE)

Peninsula College
1502 East Lauridsen Blvd., Port Angeles 98362
Type: Public, state/local, four-year
System: Washington State Board for Community and Technical Colleges
Degrees: A, B *Enroll:* 2,367
URL: http://www.pc.ctc.edu
Phone: (360) 452-9277 *Calendar:* Qtr. plan
Inst. Accred.: NWCCU (1965/2007)
Prog. Accred.: Nursing

Pierce College Puyallup
1601 39th Ave., SE, Puyallup 98374-2222
Type: Public, state, two-year
Degrees: A *Enroll:* 4,438
URL: http://www.pierce.ctc.edu
Phone: (253) 840-8400 *Calendar:* Qtr. plan
Inst. Accred.: NWCCU (1972/2008)
Prog. Accred.: Dentistry (dental hygiene), Nursing

Tacoma Campus
9401 Farwest Dr. SW, Lakewood 98498-1919
Phone: (253) 964-6500
Prog. Accred: Dentistry (dental hygiene), Veterinary Technology

Renton Technical College
3000 NE Fourth St., Renton 98056-4195
Type: Public, state, two-year
System: Washington State Board for Community and Technical Colleges
Degrees: A *Enroll:* 3,628
URL: http://www.rtc.edu
Phone: (425) 235-2352 *Calendar:* Qtr. plan
Inst. Accred.: NWCCU (1978/2007)
Prog. Accred.: Allied Health (medical assisting (AMA), surgical technology), Culinary Education, Dentistry (dental assisting)

Saint Martin's University
5300 Pacific Ave. Southeast, Lacey 98513
Type: Private, Roman Catholic Church, four-year
Degrees: A, B, M *Enroll:* 1,204
URL: http://www.stmartin.edu
Phone: (360) 491-4700 *Calendar:* Sem. plan
Inst. Accred.: NWCCU (1933/2008)
Prog. Accred.: Engineering (civil, mechanical)

Seattle Central Community College
1701 Broadway, Seattle 98122
Type: Public, state, two-year
System: Seattle Community Colleges
Degrees: A *Enroll:* 4,292
URL: http://www.seattlecentral.edu
Phone: (206) 587-3800 *Calendar:* Qtr. plan
Inst. Accred.: NWCCU (1970/2007)
Prog. Accred.: Allied Health (ophthalmic lab technology, respiratory therapy, surgical technology), Culinary Education, Nursing

Seattle Vocational Institute
2120 South Jackson St., Seattle 98144
Phone: (206) 587-4950
Prog. Accred: Allied Health (medical assisting (AMA)), Dentistry (dental assisting)

Seattle Institute of Oriental Medicine
916 NE 65th St., Ste. B, Seattle 98115
Type: Private, proprietary, four-year
Degrees: M
URL: http://www.siom.com
Phone: (206) 517-4541
Inst. Accred.: ACAOM (1998/2007)

Seattle Pacific University
3307 Third Ave. West, Seattle 98119-1997
Type: Private, Free Methodist Church, four-year
Degrees: B, M, D *Enroll:* 3,415
URL: http://www.spu.edu
Phone: (206) 281-2800 *Calendar:* Qtr. plan
Inst. Accred.: NWCCU (1933/2007)
Prog. Accred.: Business (AACSB), Dietetics (didactic), Engineering (electrical), Marriage and Family Therapy, Music, Nursing Education, Teacher Education (NCATE)

Seattle University
900 Broadway, Seattle 98122
Type: Private, Roman Catholic Church, four-year
Degrees: B, M, D *Enroll:* 6,442
URL: http://www.seattleu.edu
Phone: (206) 296-6000 *Calendar:* Qtr. plan
Inst. Accred.: ATS (1993/2000), NWCCU (1935/2005)
Prog. Accred.: Allied Health (diagnostic medical sonography), Business (AACSB), Engineering (civil, electrical, mechanical), Law, Montessori Teacher Education, Nursing Education, Public Administration, Social Work, Teacher Education (NCATE)

Shoreline Community College
16101 Greenwood Ave. North, Seattle 98133
Type: Public, state/local, two-year
System: Washington State Board for Community and Technical Colleges
Degrees: A *Enroll:* 4,449
URL: http://www.shoreline.edu
Phone: (206) 546-4552 *Calendar:* Qtr. plan
Inst. Accred.: NWCCU (1966/2008)
Prog. Accred.: Clinical Lab Technology, Dentistry (dental hygiene), Dietetic Technician, Nursing

Skagit Valley College
2405 East College Way, Mount Vernon 98273-5899
Type: Public, state, two-year
System: Washington State Board for Community and Technical Colleges
Degrees: A *Enroll:* 3,446
URL: http://www.skagit.edu
Phone: (360) 416-7600 *Calendar:* Qtr. plan
Inst. Accred.: NWCCU (1948/2004)
Prog. Accred.: Allied Health (medical assisting (AMA)), Culinary Education, Nursing

Whidbey Island Campus
1900 SE Pioneer Way, Oak Harbor 98277-3099
Phone: (360) 675-6656

South Puget Sound Community College
2011 Mottman Rd., SW, Olympia 98512-6292
Type: Public, state, two-year
System: Washington State Board for Community and Technical Colleges
Degrees: A *Enroll:* 2,978
URL: http://www.spscc.ctc.edu
Phone: (360) 754-7711 *Calendar:* Qtr. plan
Inst. Accred.: NWCCU (1975/2007)
Prog. Accred.: Allied Health (medical assisting (AMA)), Culinary Education, Dentistry (dental assisting), Nursing

South Seattle Community College
6000 16th Ave., S.W., Seattle 98106
Type: Public, state, four-year
System: Seattle Community Colleges
Degrees: A, B *Enroll:* 3,457
URL: http://southseattle.edu
Phone: (206) 764-5300 *Calendar:* Qtr. plan
Inst. Accred.: NWCCU (1975/2006)
Prog. Accred.: Culinary Education

Spokane Community College
1810 North Greene St., Spokane 99217-5399
Type: Public, state/local, two-year
System: Community Colleges of Spokane
Degrees: A *Enroll:* 5,256
URL: http://www.scc.spokane.edu
Phone: (509) 533-7000 *Calendar:* Qtr. plan
Inst. Accred.: NWCCU (1967/2005)
Prog. Accred.: Allied Health (EMT-paramedic, cardiovascular technology, medical assisting (AMA), optometric technician, respiratory therapy, surgical technology), Culinary Education, Dentistry (dental assisting, dental hygiene), Forestry, Nursing

Spokane Falls Community College
3410 West Ft. George Wright Dr., Spokane 99224-5288
Type: Public, state/local, two-year
System: Community Colleges of Spokane
Degrees: A *Enroll:* 6,001
URL: http://www.spokanefalls.edu
Phone: (509) 533-3500 *Calendar:* Qtr. plan
Inst. Accred.: NWCCU (1967/2006)
Prog. Accred.: Physical Therapy Assisting

Tacoma Community College
6501 South 19th St., Tacoma 98466
Type: Public, state, two-year
System: Washington State Board for Community and Technical Colleges
Degrees: A *Enroll:* 4,453
URL: http://www.tacoma.ctc.edu
Phone: (253) 566-5000 *Calendar:* Qtr. plan
Inst. Accred.: NWCCU (1967/2006)
Prog. Accred.: Allied Health (EMT-paramedic, respiratory therapy), Nursing, Radiography

Trinity Lutheran College
4221 228th Ave. Southeast, Issaquah 98029-9299
Type: Private, independent, four-year
Degrees: A, B *Enroll:* 94
URL: http://www.tlc.edu
Phone: (425) 392-0400 *Calendar:* Qtr. plan
Inst. Accred.: NWCCU (1982/2008)

University of Puget Sound
1500 North Warner, Tacoma 98416
Type: Private, independent, four-year
Degrees: B, M, D *Enroll:* 2,799
URL: http://www.ups.edu
Phone: (253) 879-3207 *Calendar:* Sem. plan
Inst. Accred.: NWCCU (1923/2004)
Prog. Accred.: Allied Health (occupational therapy), Music, Physical Therapy, Teacher Education (NCATE)

University of Washington
Box 351230, Seattle 98195
Type: Public, state, four-year
System: Washington Higher Education Coordinating Board
Degrees: B, M, P, D *Enroll:* 35,406
URL: http://www.washington.edu
Phone: (206) 543-6616 *Calendar:* Qtr. plan
Inst. Accred.: NWCCU (1918/2008)
Prog. Accred.: Accounting, Allied Health (EMT-paramedic, audiology, health services administration, medicine, occupational therapy, orthotist/prothetist, speech-language pathology), Business (AACSB), Clinical Lab Scientist, Clinical Psychology, Construction Education, Dentistry (combined prosthodontics, dentistry, endodontics, general practice residency, oral and maxillofacial surgery, orthodontic and dentofacial orthopedics, pediatric dentistry, periodontics), Dietetics (coordinated), Engineering (aerospace, chemical, civil, computer, electrical, forest, industrial, materials, mechanical, paper), English Language Education, Environmental Health, Forestry, Graduate Social Work, Journalism, Landscape Architecture, Law, Librarianship, Music, Nurse (Midwifery), Nursing Education, Pharmacy, Physical Therapy, Physician Assistant, Planning, Psychology Internship, Public Administration, Public Health, School Psychology, Social Work

Bothell Campus
PO Box 35800, 18115 Campus Way, NE, Bothell 98011-8246
Phone: (425) 352-5000

University of Washington *(continued)*

Tacoma Campus
1103 A St., Tacoma 98402
Phone: (253) 692-4000

Walla Walla Community College
500 Tausick Way, Walla Walla 99362
Type: Public, state, two-year
System: Washington State Board for Community and Technical Colleges
Degrees: A *Enroll:* 3,087
URL: http://www.wwcc.edu
Phone: (509) 522-2500 *Calendar:* Qtr. plan
Inst. Accred.: NWCCU (1969/2006)
Prog. Accred.: Engineering Technology (civil/construction), Nursing

Walla Walla University
204 South College Ave., College Place 99324-1198
Type: Private, Seventh-Day Adventist Church, four-year
Degrees: A, B, M *Enroll:* 1,830
URL: http://www.wallawalla.edu
Phone: (509) 527-2615 *Calendar:* Qtr. plan
Inst. Accred.: NWCCU (1932/2008)
Prog. Accred.: Business (ACBSP), Engineering (general), Graduate Social Work, Music, Nursing, Social Work

Washington State University
PO Box 641048, Pullman 99164-1048
Type: Public, state, four-year
System: Washington Higher Education Coordinating Board
Degrees: B, M, P, D *Enroll:* 21,061
URL: http://www.wsu.edu
Phone: (509) 335-3564 *Calendar:* Sem. plan
Inst. Accred.: NWCCU (1918/2004)
Prog. Accred.: Accounting, Allied Health (audiology, speech-language pathology), Business (AACSB), Clinical Psychology, Computer Science (ABET-CAC), Construction Education, Counseling Psychology, Dietetics (coordinated), Dietetics (didactic), Engineering (agricultural, chemical, civil, computer, electrical, manufacturing, materials, mechanical), English Language Education, Forestry, Interior Design, Landscape Architecture, Music, Pharmacy, Psychology Internship, Teacher Education (NCATE), Veterinary Medicine

Spokane Campus
310 North Riverpoint Blvd., Spokane 99202
Phone: (509) 358-7500
Prog. Accred: Allied Health (health services administration), Dietetics (coordinated), Nursing Education

Tri-Cities Campus
2710 University Dr., Richland 99352-1643
Phone: (509) 372-7250

Vancouver Campus
14204 NE Salmon Creek Ave., Vancouver 98686-9600
Phone: (360) 546-9788

Wenatchee Valley College
1300 Fifth St., Wenatchee 98801
Type: Public, state, two-year
System: Washington State Board for Community and Technical Colleges
Degrees: A *Enroll:* 2,342
URL: http://www.wvc.edu
Phone: (509) 682-6800 *Calendar:* Qtr. plan
Inst. Accred.: NWCCU (1948/2008)
Prog. Accred.: Allied Health (medical assisting (AMA)), Clinical Lab Technology, Nursing, Radiography

Western Washington University
516 High St., Bellingham 98225-9033
Type: Public, state, four-year
System: Washington Higher Education Coordinating Board
Degrees: B, M *Enroll:* 13,270
URL: http://www.wwu.edu
Phone: (360) 650-3480 *Calendar:* Qtr. plan
Inst. Accred.: NWCCU (1921/2008)
Prog. Accred.: Allied Health (audiology, speech-language pathology), Art, Business (AACSB), Computer Science (ABET-CAC), Counseling, Engineering Technology (electrical, manufacturing, plastics), Music, Recreation and Leisure Services, Rehabilitation Counseling, Teacher Education (NCATE)

Whatcom Community College
237 West Kellogg Rd., Bellingham 98226
Type: Public, state, two-year
System: Washington State Board for Community and Technical Colleges
Degrees: A *Enroll:* 2,637
URL: http://www.whatcom.ctc.edu
Phone: (360) 676-2170 *Calendar:* Qtr. plan
Inst. Accred.: NWCCU (1976/2006)
Prog. Accred.: Allied Health (medical assisting (AMA)), Physical Therapy Assisting

Whitman College
345 Boyer Ave., Walla Walla 99362
Type: Private, independent, four-year
Degrees: B *Enroll:* 1,493
URL: http://www.whitman.edu
Phone: (509) 527-5111 *Calendar:* Sem. plan
Inst. Accred.: NWCCU (1918/2008)

Whitworth University
300 West Hawthorne Rd., Spokane 99251-0001
Type: Private, Presbyterian Church (USA), four-year
Degrees: B, M *Enroll:* 2,245
URL: http://www.whitworth.edu
Phone: (509) 777-1000 *Calendar:* 4-1-4 plan
Inst. Accred.: NWCCU (1933/2001)
Prog. Accred.: Music, Nursing Education, Teacher Education (NCATE)

Yakima Valley Community College
PO Box 22520, Yakima 98907-2520
Type: Public, state, two-year
System: Washington State Board for Community and Technical Colleges
Degrees: A *Enroll:* 3,391
URL: http://www.yvcc.edu
Phone: (509) 574-4600 *Calendar:* Qtr. plan
Inst. Accred.: NWCCU (1948/2007)
Prog. Accred.: Allied Health (medical assisting (AMA), surgical technology), Dentistry (dental hygiene), Nursing, Radiography, Veterinary Technology

WEST VIRGINIA

Alderson-Broaddus College
101 College Hill Dr., Philippi 26416
Type: Private, American Baptist Churches (USA), four-year
Degrees: A, B, M *Enroll:* 735
URL: http://www.ab.edu
Phone: (304) 457-1700 *Calendar:* Sem. plan
Inst. Accred.: NCA-HLC (1959/2003)
Prog. Accred.: Nursing, Physician Assistant, Teacher Education (TEAC)

American Military University
111 West Congress St., Charles Town 25414
Type: Private, proprietary, four-year
System: American Public University System
Degrees: A, B, M *FTE Enroll:* 308
URL: http://www.apus.edu
Phone: (304) 724-3700 *Calendar:* Sem. plan
Inst. Accred.: DETC (1995/2004), NCA-HLC (2006, *Indirect accreditation through American Public University System, Charles Town, WV*)

American Public University
111 West Congress St., Charles Town 25414
Type: Private, proprietary, four-year
System: American Public University System
Degrees: A, B, M
URL: http://www.apus.edu
Phone: (304) 724-3700 *Calendar:* Sem. plan
Inst. Accred.: DETC (2002/2004), NCA-HLC (2006, *Indirect accreditation through American Public University System, Charles Town, WV*)

Appalachian Bible College
PO Box ABC, Bradley 25818-1353
Type: Private, independent, four-year
Degrees: A, B, M *Enroll:* 237
URL: http://www.abc.edu
Phone: (304) 877-6428 *Calendar:* Sem. plan
Inst. Accred.: ABHE (1967/1999), NCA-HLC (2000/2005)

Bethany College
Bethany 26032
Type: Private, Christian Church Disciples of Christ, four-year
Degrees: B *Enroll:* 897
URL: http://www.bethanywv.edu
Phone: (304) 829-7000 *Calendar:* 4-1-4 plan
Inst. Accred.: NCA-HLC (1926/1999)
Prog. Accred.: Social Work, Teacher Education (NCATE)

Blue Ridge Community and Technical College
400 West Stephen St., Martinsburg 25401
Type: Public, state, two-year
System: Community and Technical College System of West Virginia
Degrees: A
URL: http://blueridgectc.edu
Phone: (304) 260-4380 *Calendar:* Sem. plan
Inst. Accred.: NCA-HLC (2005)

Bluefield State College
219 Rock St., Bluefield 24701
Type: Public, state, four-year
System: West Virginia Higher Education Policy Commission
Degrees: A, B *Enroll:* 1,524
URL: http://www.bluefieldstate.edu
Phone: (304) 327-4000 *Calendar:* Sem. plan
Inst. Accred.: NCA-HLC (1951/2002)
Prog. Accred.: Business (ACBSP), Engineering Technology (architectural, civil/construction, electrical, mechanical), Nursing, Nursing Education, Radiography, Teacher Education (NCATE)

Greenbrier Community College Center
Drawer 151, Lewisburg 24901
Phone: (304) 645-3303

Community and Technical College at West Virginia University Institute of Technology
208 Davis Hall, Montgomery 25136
Type: Public, state, two-year
System: Community and Technical College System of West Virginia
Degrees: A
URL: http://ctc.wvutech.edu
Phone: (304) 442-3149 *Calendar:* Sem. plan
Inst. Accred.: NCA-HLC (2004)

Concord University
PO Box 1000, Athens 24712-1000
Type: Public, state, four-year
System: West Virginia Higher Education Policy Commission
Degrees: A, B *Enroll:* 2,431
URL: http://www.concord.edu
Phone: (304) 384-3115 *Calendar:* Sem. plan
Inst. Accred.: NCA-HLC (1931/2008)
Prog. Accred.: Social Work, Teacher Education (NCATE)

Davis and Elkins College
100 Campus Dr., Elkins 26241
Type: Private, Presbyterian Church (USA), four-year
Degrees: A, B *Enroll:* 585
URL: http://www.davisandelkins.edu
Phone: (304) 637-1900 *Calendar:* Sem. plan
Inst. Accred.: NCA-HLC (1946/2000)
Prog. Accred.: Nursing, Teacher Education (TEAC), Theatre

Everest Institute—Cross Lanes
5514 Big Tyler Rd., Cross Lanes 25313-9998
Type: Private, proprietary, two-year
System: Corinthian Colleges, Inc
Degrees: A *Enroll:* 611
URL: http://www.everest.edu
Phone: (304) 776-6290
Inst. Accred.: ACCSCT (1971/2006)

Fairmont State University including Pierpont Community and Technical College
1201 Locust Ave., Fairmont 26554
Type: Public, state, four-year
System: West Virginia Higher Education Policy Commission
Degrees: A, B, M *Enroll:* 4,223
URL: http://www.fairmontstate.edu
Phone: (304) 367-4000 *Calendar:* Sem. plan
Inst. Accred.: NCA-HLC (1928/2003)
Prog. Accred.: Business (ACBSP), Clinical Lab Technology, Engineering Technology (civil/construction, electrical, mechanical, mechanical drafting/design), Nursing, Nursing Education, Teacher Education (NCATE), Veterinary Technology

Glenville State College
200 High St., Glenville 26351
Type: Public, state, four-year
System: West Virginia Higher Education Policy Commission
Degrees: A, B *Enroll:* 1,235
URL: http://www.glenville.edu
Phone: (304) 462-7361 *Calendar:* Sem. plan
Inst. Accred.: NCA-HLC (1949/2003)
Prog. Accred.: Forestry, Teacher Education (NCATE)

Huntington Junior College
900 Fifth Ave., Huntington 25701
Type: Private, proprietary, two-year
Degrees: A *Enroll:* 694
URL: http://www.huntingtonjuniorcollege.com
Phone: (304) 697-7550 *Calendar:* Qtr. plan
Inst. Accred.: NCA-HLC (1997/2002)
Prog. Accred.: Allied Health (medical assisting (AMA))

Marshall Community and Technical College
One John Marshall Dr., Huntington 25755-2700
Type: Public, state, two-year
System: Community and Technical College System of West Virginia
Degrees: A
URL: http://www.marshall.edu/ctc
Phone: (304) 696-6282 *Calendar:* Sem. plan
Inst. Accred.: NCA-HLC (2003/2008)
Prog. Accred.: Business (ACBSP)

Marshall University
One John Marshall Dr., Huntington 25755
Type: Public, state, four-year
System: West Virginia Higher Education Policy Commission
Degrees: A, B, M, P, D *Enroll:* 11,344
URL: http://www.marshall.edu
Phone: (304) 696-2301 *Calendar:* Sem. plan
Inst. Accred.: NCA-HLC (1928/2001)
Prog. Accred.: Allied Health (medicine, speech-language pathology), Applied Science (occupational health & safety), Business (AACSB), Clinical Lab Scientist, Clinical Lab Technology, Clinical Psychology, Dietetics (didactic), Dietetics (internship), Journalism, Music, Nursing, Physical Therapy Assisting, Recreation and Leisure Services, Social Work, Teacher Education (NCATE)

Graduate College Campus
100 Angus E. Peyton Dr., South Charleston 25303-1600
Phone: (304) 746-2500

Mountain State College
Spring at 16th St., Parkersburg 26101
Type: Private, proprietary, two-year
Degrees: A *Enroll:* 118
URL: http://www.mountainstate.org
Phone: (304) 485-5487 *Calendar:* Qtr. plan
Inst. Accred.: ACICS (1950/2005)

The Mountain State University
PO Box 9003, Beckley 25802
Type: Private, independent, four-year
Degrees: A, B, M *Enroll:* 3,775
URL: http://www.mountainstate.edu
Phone: (304) 253-7351 *Calendar:* Sem. plan
Inst. Accred.: NCA-HLC (1981/2001)
Prog. Accred.: Allied Health (diagnostic medical sonography, medical assisting (AMA), occupational therapy assisting, respiratory therapy), Culinary Education, Nurse Anesthesia Education, Nursing, Physical Therapy Assisting, Physician Assistant, Radiography, Social Work

New River Community and Technical College
167 Dye Dr., Beckley 25801
Type: Public, state, two-year
System: Community and Technical College System of West Virginia
Degrees: A
URL: http://www.nrctc.edu
Phone: (304) 255-5812 *Calendar:* Sem. plan
Inst. Accred.: NCA-HLC (2005/2008)

Ohio Valley University
One Campus View Dr., Vienna 26105-8000
Type: Private, Churches of Christ, four-year
Degrees: A, B *Enroll:* 519
URL: http://www.ovu.edu
Phone: (304) 865-6000 *Calendar:* Sem. plan
Inst. Accred.: NCA-HLC (1978/2003)

Potomac State College of West Virginia University
101 Fort Ave., Keyser 26726
Type: Public, state, four-year
System: West Virginia Higher Education Policy Commission
Degrees: A, B *Enroll:* 1,028
URL: http://www.potomacstatecollege.edu
Phone: (304) 788-6800 *Calendar:* Sem. plan
Inst. Accred.: NCA-HLC (1926/2004)

Salem International University
PO Box 500, Salem 26426
Type: Private, independent, four-year
Degrees: A, B, M *Enroll:* 626
URL: http://www.salemu.edu
Phone: (304) 782-5234 *Calendar:* Sem. plan
Inst. Accred.: NCA-HLC (1963/2005)

Shepherd University
PO Box 3210, Shepherdstown 25443-3210
Type: Public, state, four-year
System: West Virginia Higher Education Policy Commission
Degrees: A, B *Enroll:* 3,344
URL: http://www.shepherd.edu
Phone: (304) 876-5000 *Calendar:* Sem. plan
Inst. Accred.: NCA-HLC (1950/2002)
Prog. Accred.: Music, Nursing, Social Work, Teacher Education (NCATE)

Southern West Virginia Community and Technical College
Dempsey Branch Rd., PO Box 2900, Mount Gay 25637
Type: Public, state, two-year
System: Community and Technical College System of West Virginia
Degrees: A *Enroll:* 1,743
URL: http://www.southern.wvnet.edu
Phone: (304) 792-7098 *Calendar:* Sem. plan
Inst. Accred.: NCA-HLC (1971/2004)
Prog. Accred.: Allied Health (surgical technology), Clinical Lab Technology, Nursing, Radiography

The University of Charleston
2300 MacCorkle Ave., Charleston 25304
Type: Private, independent, four-year
Degrees: A, B, M *Enroll:* 915
URL: http://www.ucwv.edu
Phone: (304) 357-4800 *Calendar:* Sem. plan
Inst. Accred.: NCA-HLC (1958/2005)
Prog. Accred.: Nursing, Pharmacy, Radiography, Teacher Education (NCATE)

Valley College of Technology—Beckley
713 South Oakwood Ave., Beckley 25801
Type: Private, proprietary, two-year
Degrees: A
URL: http://www.vct.edu
Phone: (304) 252-9547 *Calendar:* Sem. plan
Inst. Accred.: ACCET (1992/2005)

Valley College of Technology—Martinsburg
287 Aikens Center, Martinsburg 24501
Type: Private, proprietary, two-year
Degrees: A
URL: http://www.vct.edu
Phone: (304) 263-0979 *Calendar:* Sem. plan
Inst. Accred.: ACICS (1996/2004)

Valley College of Technology—Princeton
616 Harrison St., Princeton 24740
Type: Private, proprietary, two-year
Degrees: A
URL: http://www.vct.edu
Phone: (304) 425-2323 *Calendar:* Sem. plan
Inst. Accred.: ACCET (1992/2005)

West Liberty State College
PO Box 295, West Liberty 26074
Type: Public, state, four-year
System: West Virginia Higher Education Policy Commission
Degrees: A, B *Enroll:* 2,080
URL: http://www.wlsc.wvnet.edu
Phone: (866) 937-8542 *Calendar:* Sem. plan
Inst. Accred.: NCA-HLC (1942/2008)
Prog. Accred.: Clinical Lab Scientist, Dentistry (dental hygiene), Music, Nursing Education, Teacher Education (NCATE)

West Virginia Business College
1052 Main St., Wheeling 26003
Type: Private, proprietary, two-year
Degrees: A *FTE Enroll:* 23
URL: http://www.wvbusinesscollege.com
Phone: (304) 232-0631 *Calendar:* Sem. plan
Inst. Accred.: ACICS (1990/2003)

Nutter Fort Campus
116 Pennsylvania Ave., Nutter Fort 26301
Phone: (304) 624-7695

West Virginia Junior College
1000 Virginia St., East, Charleston 25301
Type: Private, proprietary, two-year
Degrees: A *Enroll:* 148
URL: http://www.wvjc.edu
Phone: (304) 345-2820 *Calendar:* Qtr. plan
Inst. Accred.: ACICS (1971/2005)

Bridgeport Campus
176 Thompson Dr., Bridgeport 26330
Phone: (304) 842-4007

West Virginia Junior College at Morgantown
148 Willey St., Morgantown 26505
Type: Private, proprietary, two-year
Degrees: A *Enroll:* 146
URL: http://www.wvjcmorgantown.edu
Phone: (304) 296-8282 *Calendar:* Qtr. plan
Inst. Accred.: ACICS (1953/2005)

West Virginia Career Institute
Mount Braddock Rd., Uniontown, PA 15401
Phone: (724) 437-4600

West Virginia Northern Community College
1704 Market St., College Square, Wheeling 26003
Type: Public, state, two-year
System: Community and Technical College System of West Virginia
Degrees: A *Enroll:* 1,897
URL: http://www.northern.wvnet.edu
Phone: (304) 233-5900 *Calendar:* Sem. plan
Inst. Accred.: NCA-HLC (1972/2003)
Prog. Accred.: Allied Health (respiratory therapy, surgical technology), Clinical Lab Technology, Culinary Education, Nursing

West Virginia School of Osteopathic Medicine
400 North Lee St., Lewisburg 24901
Type: Public, state, four-year
System: West Virginia Higher Education Policy Commission
Degrees: P *Enroll:* 394
URL: http://www.wvsom.edu
Phone: (304) 645-6270 *Calendar:* Sem. plan
Inst. Accred.: AOA-BPE (1976/2006)

West Virginia State Community and Technical College
PO Box 1000, Campus Box 183, Institute 25112-1000
Type: Public, state, two-year
System: Community and Technical College System of West Virginia
Degrees: A
URL: http://www.wvsctc.edu
Phone: (304) 766-3000 *Calendar:* Sem. plan
Inst. Accred.: NCA-HLC (2004)
Prog. Accred.: Nuclear Medicine Technology, Nursing

West Virginia State University
PO Box 1000, Institute 25112
Type: Public, state, four-year
System: West Virginia Higher Education Policy Commission
Degrees: A, B *Enroll:* 2,867
URL: http://www.wvsc.edu
Phone: (304) 766-3000 *Calendar:* Sem. plan
Inst. Accred.: NCA-HLC (1927/2005)
Prog. Accred.: Business (ACBSP), Engineering Technology (electrical), Recreation and Leisure Services, Social Work, Teacher Education (NCATE)

West Virginia University
PO Box 6201, Morgantown 26506-6201
Type: Public, state, four-year
System: West Virginia Higher Education Policy Commission
Degrees: B, M, P, D *Enroll:* 24,003
URL: http://www.wvu.edu
Phone: (304) 293-0111 *Calendar:* Sem. plan
Inst. Accred.: NCA-HLC (1926/2004)
Prog. Accred.: Accounting, Allied Health (audiology, diagnostic medical sonography, medicine, occupational therapy, speech-language pathology), Applied Science (industrial hygiene, occupational health & safety), Art, Business (AACSB), Clinical Lab Scientist, Clinical Pastoral Education, Clinical Psychology, Counseling, Counseling Psychology, Dentistry (advanced education in general dentistry, combined prosthodontics, dental hygiene, dentistry, endodontics, general dentistry, oral and maxillofacial surgery, orthodontic and dentofacial orthopedics), Dietetics (didactic), Dietetics (internship), Engineering (aerospace, chemical, civil, computer, electrical, industrial, mechanical, mining, petroleum), Forestry, Graduate Social Work, Interior Design, Journalism, Landscape Architecture, Law, Music, Nuclear Medicine Technology, Nursing Education, Pharmacy, Physical Therapy, Psychology Internship, Public Administration, Public Health, Radiation Therapy, Radiography, Rehabilitation Counseling, Social Work, Teacher Education (NCATE), Theatre

Charleston Area Medical Center
3110 MacCorkle Ave., SE, Charleston 25304-1299
Phone: (304) 347-1209
Prog. Accred: Dentistry (advanced education in general dentistry, general practice residency), Nurse Anesthesia Education, Psychology Internship

West Virginia University at Parkersburg
300 Campus Dr., Parkersburg 26104
Type: Public, state, four-year
System: Community and Technical College System of West Virginia
Degrees: A, B *Enroll:* 2,834
URL: http://www.wvup.edu
Phone: (304) 424-8200 *Calendar:* Sem. plan
Inst. Accred.: NCA-HLC (1971/2004)
Prog. Accred.: Allied Health (surgical technology), Nursing, Teacher Education (NCATE)

West Virginia University Institute of Technology
405 Fayette Pike, Montgomery 25136
Type: Public, state, four-year
System: West Virginia Higher Education Policy Commission
Degrees: A, B, M *Enroll:* 1,239
URL: http://www.wvutech.edu
Phone: (888) 554-8324 *Calendar:* Sem. plan
Inst. Accred.: NCA-HLC (1956/2000)
Prog. Accred.: Dentistry (dental hygiene), Engineering (chemical, civil, electrical, mechanical), Engineering Technology (civil/construction, electrical, general drafting/design, mechanical)

West Virginia Wesleyan College
59 College Ave., Buckhannon 26201
Type: Private, Methodist Episcopal Church, four-year
Degrees: B, M *Enroll:* 1,347
URL: http://www.wvwc.edu
Phone: (304) 473-8000 *Calendar:* 4-1-4 plan
Inst. Accred.: NCA-HLC (1927/2000)
Prog. Accred.: Music, Nursing, Teacher Education (NCATE)

Wheeling Jesuit University
316 Washington Ave., Wheeling 26003
Type: Private, Roman Catholic Church, four-year
Degrees: B, M *Enroll:* 1,260
URL: http://www.wju.edu
Phone: (304) 243-2000 *Calendar:* Sem. plan
Inst. Accred.: NCA-HLC (1962/2001)
Prog. Accred.: Allied Health (respiratory therapy), Business (ACBSP), Nuclear Medicine Technology, Nursing Education, Physical Therapy

WISCONSIN

Alverno College
3401 South 39th St., PO Box 343922, Milwaukee 53215
Type: Private, Roman Catholic Church, four-year
Degrees: A, B, M *Enroll:* 1,859
URL: http://www.alverno.edu
Phone: (414) 382-6000 *Calendar:* Sem. plan
Inst. Accred.: NCA-HLC (1951/2007)
Prog. Accred.: Music, Nursing Education, Teacher Education (NCATE)

Bellin College of Nursing
725 South Webster Ave., PO Box 23400, Green Bay 54305-3400
Type: Private, independent, four-year
Degrees: B *Enroll:* 241
URL: http://www.bcon.edu
Phone: (920) 433-3560 *Calendar:* 4-1-4 plan
Inst. Accred.: NCA-HLC (1989/2004)
Prog. Accred.: Nursing Education

Beloit College
700 College St., Beloit 53511
Type: Private, independent, four-year
Degrees: B *Enroll:* 1,352
URL: http://www.beloit.edu
Phone: (608) 363-2000 *Calendar:* Sem. plan
Inst. Accred.: NCA-HLC (1913/2007)

Blackhawk Technical College
PO Box 5009, 6004 Praire Rd., Janesville 53547-5009
Type: Public, state/local, two-year
System: Wisconsin Technical College System Board
Degrees: A *Enroll:* 1,476
URL: http://www.blackhawk.edu
Phone: (608) 758-6900 *Calendar:* Sem. plan
Inst. Accred.: NCA-HLC (1978/2000)
Prog. Accred.: Allied Health (medical assisting (AMA)), Culinary Education, Dentistry (dental assisting), Nursing, Physical Therapy Assisting, Radiography

Bryant & Stratton College—Milwaukee Campus
310 West Wisconsin Ave., Ste. 500 E, Milwaukee 53203
Type: Private, proprietary, four-year
System: Bryant & Stratton College System Office
Degrees: A, B *Enroll:* 720
URL: http://www.bryantstratton.edu
Phone: (414) 276-5200 *Calendar:* Qtr. plan
Inst. Accred.: MSA-CHE (2002/2007, *Indirect accreditation through Bryant & Stratton College System Office, Getzville, NY*)
Prog. Accred.: Allied Health (medical assisting (AMA))

Milwaukee West Campus
10950 West Potter Rd., Wauwatosa 53226
Phone: (414) 302-7000

Cardinal Stritch University
6801 North Yates Rd., Milwaukee 53217-3985
Type: Private, Roman Catholic Church, four-year
Degrees: A, B, M, D *Enroll:* 5,337
URL: http://www.stritch.edu
Phone: (414) 410-4000 *Calendar:* Sem. plan
Inst. Accred.: NCA-HLC (1953/2004)
Prog. Accred.: Business (ACBSP), Nursing, Nursing Education, Teacher Education (NCATE)

Edina Campus
3300 Edinborough Way, Ste. 505, Edina, MN 55435
Phone: (612) 835-6418

Madison Campus
8071 Excelsior Dr., Madison 53717
Phone: (608) 831-2722

Carroll University
100 North East Ave., Waukesha 53186
Type: Private, Presbyterian Church (USA), four-year
Degrees: B, M, D *Enroll:* 2,652
URL: http://www.cc.edu
Phone: (262) 547-7247 *Calendar:* Sem. plan
Inst. Accred.: NCA-HLC (1913/2008)
Prog. Accred.: Nursing Education, Physical Therapy

Carthage College
2001 Alford Park Dr., Kenosha 53140-1994
Type: Private, Evangelic Lutheran Church of America, four-year
Degrees: B, M *Enroll:* 2,363
URL: http://www.carthage.edu
Phone: (262) 551-8500 *Calendar:* 4-1-4 plan
Inst. Accred.: NCA-HLC (1916/2005)
Prog. Accred.: Music, Social Work

Chippewa Valley Technical College
620 West Clairemont Ave., Eau Claire 54701
Type: Public, state/local, two-year
System: Wisconsin Technical College System Board
Degrees: A *Enroll:* 3,676
URL: http://www.cvtc.edu
Phone: (715) 833-6200 *Calendar:* Sem. plan
Inst. Accred.: NCA-HLC (1973/2003)
Prog. Accred.: Allied Health (diagnostic medical sonography, medical assisting (AMA), surgical technology), Clinical Lab Technology, Nursing, Practical Nursing, Radiography

College of the Menominee Nation
Highway 47-55, PO Box 1179, Keshena 54135
Type: Public, tribal, four-year
System: American Indian Higher Education Consortium
Degrees: A, B *Enroll:* 353
URL: http://www.menominee.edu
Phone: (715) 799-5600 *Calendar:* Sem. plan
Inst. Accred.: NCA-HLC (1998/2003)

Columbia College of Nursing
2121 East Newport Ave., Milwaukee 53211
Type: Private, independent, four-year
System: Columbia Saint Mary's
Degrees: B *FTE Enroll:* 286
URL: http://www.ccon.edu
Phone: (414) 961-3530 *Calendar:* Sem. plan
Inst. Accred.: NCA-HLC (1988/2008)
Prog. Accred.: Allied Health (diagnostic medical sonography), Nursing

Concordia University Wisconsin
12800 North Lake Shore Dr., Mequon 53097-2402
Type: Private, Lutheran Church—Missouri Synod, four-year
System: Concordia University System
Degrees: A, B, M *Enroll:* 3,893
URL: http://www.cuw.edu
Phone: (262) 243-5700 *Calendar:* 4-1-4 plan
Inst. Accred.: NCA-HLC (1964/2003)
Prog. Accred.: Allied Health (medical assisting (AMA), occupational therapy), Nursing Education, Physical Therapy, Social Work

Edgewood College
1000 Edgewood College Dr., Madison 53711
Type: Private, Roman Catholic Church, four-year
Degrees: A, B, M, D *Enroll:* 2,001
URL: http://www.edgewood.edu
Phone: (800) 444-4861 *Calendar:* 4-1-4 plan
Inst. Accred.: NCA-HLC (1958/2008)
Prog. Accred.: Business (ACBSP), Nursing Education, Teacher Education (NCATE)

Fox Valley Technical College
1825 North Bluemound Dr., PO Box 2277, Appleton 54912-2277
Type: Public, state/local, two-year
System: Wisconsin Technical College System Board
Degrees: A *Enroll:* 3,716
URL: http://www.fvtc.edu
Phone: (920) 735-5600 *Calendar:* Sem. plan
Inst. Accred.: NCA-HLC (1974/2008)
Prog. Accred.: Allied Health (medical assisting (AMA), occupational therapy assisting), Culinary Education, Dentistry (dental assisting), Nursing

Gateway Technical College
3520 30th Ave., Kenosha 53144-1690
Type: Public, state/local, two-year
System: Wisconsin Technical College System Board
Degrees: A *Enroll:* 3,339
URL: http://www.gtc.edu
Phone: (262) 656-6900 *Calendar:* Sem. plan
Inst. Accred.: NCA-HLC (1970/2000)
Prog. Accred.: Allied Health (medical assisting (AMA), surgical technology), Dentistry (dental assisting), Nursing, Physical Therapy Assisting

Elkhorn Campus
400 County Rd. H, Elkhorn 53121-2046
Phone: (262) 741-8200
Prog. Accred: Allied Health (medical assisting (AMA))

Racine Campus
1001 South Main St., Racine 53403-1582
Phone: (262) 619-6200

Herzing College—Madison Campus
5218 East Terrace Dr., Madison 53718
Type: Private, proprietary, four-year
System: Herzing College Corporate Offices
Degrees: A, B, M *Enroll:* 791
URL: http://www.herzing.edu
Phone: (608) 249-6611 *Calendar:* Sem. plan
Inst. Accred.: NCA-HLC (2004, *Indirect accreditation through Herzing College Corporate Offices, Milwaukee, WI*)

ITT Technical Institute
6300 West Layton Ave., Greenfield 53220-4612
Type: Private, proprietary, four-year
System: ITT Educational Services, Inc.
Degrees: A, B *Enroll:* 642
URL: http://www.itt-tech.edu
Phone: (414) 282-9494 *Calendar:* Qtr. plan
Inst. Accred.: ACICS (1999/2004)

Atlanta Campus
1745 Phoenix Blvd., Two Crown Center, Ste. 100, Atlanta, GA 30349
Phone: (770) 909-4606

Eden Prairie Campus
8911 Columbine Rd., Eden Prairie, MN 55347
Phone: (952) 914-5300

Green Bay Campus
470 Security Blvd., Green Bay 54313
Phone: (920) 662-9000

Lac Courte Oreilles Ojibwa Community College
13466 West Trepania Rd., Hayward 54843
Type: Public, tribal, two-year
System: American Indian Higher Education Consortium
Degrees: A *Enroll:* 365
URL: http://www.lco.edu
Phone: (715) 634-4790 *Calendar:* Sem. plan
Inst. Accred.: NCA-HLC (1993/2004)
Prog. Accred.: Allied Health (medical assisting (AMA))

Lakeland College
PO Box 359, Sheboygan 53082-0359
Type: Private, United Church of Christ, four-year
Degrees: A, B, M *Enroll:* 2,462
URL: http://www.lakeland.edu
Phone: (920) 565-2111 *Calendar:* 4-1-4 plan
Inst. Accred.: NCA-HLC (1961/2002)
Prog. Accred.: Teacher Education (TEAC)

Lakeshore Technical College
1290 North Ave., Cleveland 53015
Type: Public, state/local, two-year
System: Wisconsin Technical College System Board
Degrees: A *Enroll:* 1,500
URL: http://www.gotoltc.com
Phone: (920) 693-1000 *Calendar:* Sem. plan
Inst. Accred.: NCA-HLC (1977/2008)
Prog. Accred.: Allied Health (medical assisting (AMA), surgical technology), Dentistry (dental assisting), Medical Assisting (ABHES), Nursing, Radiography

Lawrence University
PO Box 599, Appleton 54912
Type: Private, independent, four-year
Degrees: B *Enroll:* 1,409
URL: http://www.lawrence.edu
Phone: (920) 832-7000 *Calendar:* Qtr. plan
Inst. Accred.: NCA-HLC (1913/1999)
Prog. Accred.: Music

Madison Area Technical College
3550 Anderson St., Madison 53704
Type: Public, state/local, two-year
System: Wisconsin Technical College System Board
Degrees: A *Enroll:* 8,115
URL: http://matcmadison.edu
Phone: (608) 246-6100 *Calendar:* Sem. plan
Inst. Accred.: NCA-HLC (1969/2003)
Prog. Accred.: Allied Health (medical assisting (AMA), occupational therapy assisting, optometric technician, respiratory therapy, surgical technology), Clinical Lab Technology, Culinary Education, Dentistry (dental assisting, dental hygiene), Dietetic Technician, Nursing, Radiography, Veterinary Technology

Madison Media Institute
2702 Agriculture Dr., Madison 53718
Type: Private, proprietary, two-year
Degrees: A
URL: http://www.madisonmedia.com
Phone: (608) 663-2000 *Calendar:* Sem. plan
Inst. Accred.: ACCSCT (1972/2004)

Maranatha Baptist Bible College
745 West Main St., PO Box 438, Watertown 53094
Type: Private, Independent Baptist, four-year
Degrees: A, B, M *Enroll:* 799
URL: http://www.mbbc.edu
Phone: (920) 261-9300 *Calendar:* Sem. plan
Inst. Accred.: NCA-HLC (1993/2008)

Marian University
45 South National Ave., Fond du Lac 54935
Type: Private, Roman Catholic Church, four-year
Degrees: B, M, D *Enroll:* 2,016
URL: http://www.mariancollege.edu
Phone: (920) 923-7600 *Calendar:* Sem. plan
Inst. Accred.: NCA-HLC (1960/2006)
Prog. Accred.: Nursing Education, Social Work, Teacher Education (NCATE)

Marquette University
PO Box 1881, Milwaukee 53201-1881
Type: Private, Roman Catholic Church, four-year
Degrees: A, B, M, P, D *Enroll:* 10,451
URL: http://www.mu.edu
Phone: (414) 288-7223 *Calendar:* Sem. plan
Inst. Accred.: NCA-HLC (1922/2004)
Prog. Accred.: Accounting, Allied Health (speech-language pathology), Business (AACSB), Clinical Lab Scientist, Clinical Psychology, Counseling Psychology, Dentistry (advanced education in general dentistry, combined prosthodontics, dental hygiene, dentistry, endodontics, general dentistry, orthodontic and dentofacial orthopedics), Engineering (bioengineering, civil, computer, electrical, industrial, mechanical), Journalism, Law, Nurse (Midwifery), Nursing Education, Physical Therapy, Physician Assistant, Teacher Education (NCATE)

Medical College of Wisconsin
8701 Watertown Plank Rd., Milwaukee 53226
Type: Private, independent, four-year
Degrees: M, D *Enroll:* 1,134
URL: http://www.mcw.edu
Phone: (414) 456-8296 *Calendar:* Qtr. plan
Inst. Accred.: NCA-HLC (1922/2007)
Prog. Accred.: Allied Health (medicine), Dentistry (oral and maxillofacial surgery), Public Health

Mid-State Technical College
500 32nd St. North, Wisconsin Rapids 54494
Type: Public, state, two-year
System: Wisconsin Technical College System Board
Degrees: A *Enroll:* 1,664
URL: http://www.mstc.edu
Phone: (715) 422-5300 *Calendar:* Sem. plan
Inst. Accred.: NCA-HLC (1979/2002)
Prog. Accred.: Allied Health (medical assisting (AMA), respiratory therapy, surgical technology), Nursing

Marshfield Campus
2600 West 5th St., Marshfield 54449
Phone: (715) 387-2538

Stevens Point Campus
933 Michigan Ave., Stevens Point 54481
Phone: (715) 344-3063
Prog. Accred: Phlebotomy

Midwest College of Oriental Medicine—Wisconsin
6226 Bankers Rd., Racine 53403
Type: Private, proprietary, four-year
Degrees: M *Enroll:* 102
URL: http://www.acupuncture.edu/midwest
Phone: (262) 554-2010 *Calendar:* Qtr. plan
Inst. Accred.: ACAOM (1993/2007)

Chicago Campus
4334 N. Hazel St., Ste. 206, Chicago, IL 60613-1429
Phone: (773) 975-1295

Milwaukee Area Technical College
700 West State St., Milwaukee 53233
Type: Public, state/local, two-year
System: Wisconsin Technical College System Board
Degrees: A *Enroll:* 10,080
URL: http://www.matc.edu
Phone: (414) 297-6600 *Calendar:* Sem. plan
Inst. Accred.: NCA-HLC (1959/1999)
Prog. Accred.: Allied Health (cardiovascular technology, medical assisting (AMA), occupational therapy assisting, opticianry, respiratory therapy, surgical technology), Clinical Lab Technology, Culinary Education, Dentistry (dental hygiene, dental laboratory technology), Dietetic Technician, Nursing, Phlebotomy, Physical Therapy Assisting, Practical Nursing, Radiography

West Allis Campus
1200 South 71st St., West Allis 53214
Phone: (414) 456-5500
Prog. Accred: Funeral Service Education (Mortuary Science)

Milwaukee Institute of Art and Design
273 East Erie St., Milwaukee 53202
Type: Private, independent, four-year
Degrees: B *Enroll:* 621
URL: http://www.miad.edu
Phone: (414) 276-7889 *Calendar:* Sem. plan
Inst. Accred.: NCA-HLC (1987/2000)
Prog. Accred.: Art

Milwaukee School of Engineering
1025 North Broadway, Milwaukee 53202-3109
Type: Private, independent, four-year
Degrees: A, B, M *Enroll:* 2,036
URL: http://www.msoe.edu
Phone: (414) 277-7300 *Calendar:* Qtr. plan
Inst. Accred.: NCA-HLC (1971/2005)
Prog. Accred.: Allied Health (perfusion), Construction Education, Engineering (architectural, bioengineering, computer, electrical, industrial, mechanical, software), Engineering Technology (electrical, mechanical), Nursing Education

Moraine Park Technical College
235 North National Ave., PO Box 1940, Fond Du Lac 54936-1940
Type: Public, state/local, two-year
System: Wisconsin Technical College System Board
Degrees: A *Enroll:* 3,316
URL: http://www.moraine.tec.wi.us
Phone: (920) 929-8611 *Calendar:* Sem. plan
Inst. Accred.: NCA-HLC (1975/2008)
Prog. Accred.: Allied Health (medical assisting (AMA), respiratory therapy, surgical technology), Culinary Education, Nuclear Medicine Technology, Nursing, Veterinary Technology

Mount Mary College
2900 North Menomonee River Pkwy., Milwaukee 53222
Type: Private, School Sisters of Notre Dame, four-year
Degrees: B, M *Enroll:* 1,266
URL: http://www.mtmary.edu
Phone: (414) 258-4810 *Calendar:* Sem. plan
Inst. Accred.: NCA-HLC (1926/2003)
Prog. Accred.: Allied Health (occupational therapy), Dietetics (coordinated), Dietetics (internship), Interior Design, Social Work

Nashotah House
2777 Mission Rd., Nashotah 53058-9793
Type: Private, Episcopal Church, four-year
Degrees: M *Enroll:* 67
URL: http://www.nashotah.edu
Phone: (262) 646-6500 *Calendar:* Sem. plan
Inst. Accred.: ATS (1954/1999)

Nicolet Area Technical College
PO Box 518, County Hwy. G, Rhinelander 54501
Type: Public, state/local, two-year
System: Wisconsin Technical College System Board
Degrees: A *Enroll:* 739
URL: http://www.nicoletcollege.edu
Phone: (715) 365-4410 *Calendar:* Sem. plan
Inst. Accred.: NCA-HLC (1975/2005)
Prog. Accred.: Allied Health (medical assisting (AMA)), Nursing

Northcentral Technical College
1000 West Campus Dr., Wausau 54401
Type: Public, local, two-year
System: Wisconsin Technical College System Board
Degrees: A *Enroll:* 1,994
URL: http://www.ntc.edu
Phone: (715) 675-3331 *Calendar:* Sem. plan
Inst. Accred.: NCA-HLC (1970/2007)
Prog. Accred.: Allied Health (surgical technology), Dentistry (dental hygiene), Nursing, Radiography

Northeast Wisconsin Technical College
PO Box 19042, 2740 W. Mason St., Green Bay 54307-9042
Type: Public, state/local, two-year
System: Wisconsin Technical College System Board
Degrees: A *Enroll:* 5,902
URL: http://www.nwtc.edu
Phone: (920) 498-5400 *Calendar:* Sem. plan
Inst. Accred.: NCA-HLC (1976/2001)
Prog. Accred.: Allied Health (diagnostic medical sonography, medical assisting (AMA), respiratory therapy, surgical technology), Clinical Lab Technology, Dentistry (dental assisting, dental hygiene), Engineering Technology (civil/construction), Nursing, Physical Therapy Assisting

Marinette Campus
1601 University Ave., Marinette 54143
Phone: (715) 735-9361

Sturgeon Bay Campus
229 North 14th Ave., Sturgeon Bay 54235-1317
Phone: (414) 743-2207

Northland Baptist Bible College
W10085 Pike Plains Rd., Dunbar 54119
Type: Private, nondenominational, four-year
Degrees: A, B, M, D
URL: http://www.nbbc.edu
Phone: (715) 324-6900 *Calendar:* Sem. plan
Inst. Accred.: TRACS (2007)

Northland College
1411 Ellis Ave., Ashland 54806
Type: Private, United Church of Christ, four-year
Degrees: B *Enroll:* 693
URL: http://www.northland.edu
Phone: (715) 682-1699
Inst. Accred.: NCA-HLC (1957/2001)

Rasmussen College—Green Bay
904 South Taylor St., Ste. 100, Green Bay 54303
Type: Private, proprietary, four-year
System: Rasmussen College System
Degrees: A, B
URL: http://www.rasmussen.edu
Phone: (920) 593-8400 *Calendar:* Qtr. plan
Inst. Accred.: NCA-HLC (2001/2004, *Indirect accreditation through Rasmussen College System, Lake Elmo, MN*)

Ripon College
300 Seward St., PO Box 248, Ripon 54971
Type: Private, Associated Colleges of the Midwest, four-year
Degrees: B *Enroll:* 963
URL: http://www.ripon.edu
Phone: (920) 748-8115 *Calendar:* Sem. plan
Inst. Accred.: NCA-HLC (1913/2000)

Sacred Heart School of Theology
PO Box 429, Hales Corners 53130-0429
Type: Private, Roman Catholic Church, four-year
Degrees: M *Enroll:* 70
URL: http://www.shst.edu
Phone: (414) 425-8300 *Calendar:* Sem. plan
Inst. Accred.: ATS (1981/1999), NCA-HLC (1995/2000)

Saint Francis Seminary
3257 South Lake Dr., St. Francis 53235
Type: Private, Roman Catholic Church, four-year
Degrees: M *Enroll:* 47
URL: http://www.sfc.edu
Phone: (414) 747-6400 *Calendar:* Sem. plan
Inst. Accred.: ATS (1975/2000), NCA-HLC (1963/2001)

Saint Norbert College
100 Grant St., De Pere 54115-2099
Type: Private, Roman Catholic Church, four-year
Degrees: B, M *Enroll:* 1,972
URL: http://www.snc.edu
Phone: (920) 403-3181 *Calendar:* Sem. plan
Inst. Accred.: NCA-HLC (1934/2002)

Silver Lake College
2406 South Alverno Rd., Manitowoc 54220
Type: Private, Roman Catholic Church, four-year
Degrees: A, B, M *Enroll:* 493
URL: http://www.sl.edu
Phone: (920) 236-4752 *Calendar:* Sem. plan
Inst. Accred.: NCA-HLC (1959/2008)
Prog. Accred.: Music, Teacher Education (NCATE)

Southwest Wisconsin Technical College
1800 Bronson Blvd., Fennimore 53809
Type: Public, state/local, two-year
System: Wisconsin Technical College System Board
Degrees: A *Enroll:* 1,389
URL: http://www.swtc.edu
Phone: (608) 822-3262 *Calendar:* Sem. plan
Inst. Accred.: NCA-HLC (1976/2002)
Prog. Accred.: Allied Health (medical assisting (AMA)), Nursing

University of Wisconsin Colleges
432 North Lake St., Madison 53706-1415
Type: Public, state, two-year
System: University of Wisconsin System
Degrees: A *Enroll:* 9,599
URL: http://www.uwc.edu
Phone: (608) 262-1783 *Calendar:* Sem. plan
Inst. Accred.: NCA-HLC (1977/2003)

Baraboo-Sauk Campus
1006 Connie Rd., Baraboo 53913-1098
Phone: (608) 356-8351

Barron Campus
1800 College Dr., Rice Lake 54868-2497
Phone: (715) 234-8176

Fond du Lac Campus
400 Campus Dr., Fond du Lac 54935-2998
Phone: (920) 929-3600

Fox Valley Campus
1478 Midway Rd., Menasha 54952-8002
Phone: (920) 832-2600

Manitowoc Campus
705 Viebahn St., Manitowoc 54220-6699
Phone: (920) 683-4700

Marathon Campus
518 South Seventh Ave., Wausau 54401-9602
Phone: (715) 261-6100

Marinette Campus
750 West Bay Shore St., Marinette 54143-4300
Phone: (715) 735-4300

Marshfield-Wood County Campus
2000 West 5th St., Marshfield 54449-3310
Phone: (715) 389-6500

University of Wisconsin Colleges *(continued)*

Richland Campus
Highway 14 West, Richland Center 53581-1399
Phone: (608) 647-6186

Rock County Campus
2909 Kellogg Ave., Janesville 53545-5699
Phone: (608) 758-6565

Sheboygan Campus
One University Dr., Sheboygan 53081-4789
Phone: (920) 459-6600

Washington County Campus
400 University Dr., West Bend 53095-3699
Phone: (262) 335-5200

Waukesha Campus
1500 University Dr., Waukesha 53188-2799
Phone: (262) 521-5200

University of Wisconsin-Eau Claire
105 Garfield Ave., PO Box 4004, Eau Claire 54702-4004
Type: Public, state, four-year
System: University of Wisconsin System
Degrees: A, B, M, D *Enroll:* 9,964
URL: http://www.uwec.edu
Phone: (715) 836-2637 *Calendar:* Sem. plan
Inst. Accred.: NCA-HLC (1950/2000)
Prog. Accred.: Allied Health (speech-language pathology), Business (AACSB), Computer Science (ABET-CAC), Environmental Health, Journalism, Music, Nursing Education, Social Work

University of Wisconsin-Green Bay
2420 Nicolet Dr., Green Bay 54311-7001
Type: Public, state, four-year
System: University of Wisconsin System
Degrees: A, B, M *Enroll:* 4,964
URL: http://www.uwgb.edu
Phone: (920) 465-2000 *Calendar:* Sem. plan
Inst. Accred.: NCA-HLC (1972/2008)
Prog. Accred.: Dietetics (didactic), Dietetics (internship), Graduate Social Work, Music, Nursing Education, Social Work

University of Wisconsin-La Crosse
1725 State St., La Crosse 54601
Type: Public, state, four-year
System: University of Wisconsin System
Degrees: A, B, M, D *Enroll:* 8,604
URL: http://www.uwlax.edu
Phone: (608) 785-8000 *Calendar:* Sem. plan
Inst. Accred.: NCA-HLC (1928/2006)
Prog. Accred.: Allied Health (occupational therapy), Business (AACSB), Clinical Lab Scientist, Music, Nurse Anesthesia Education, Physical Therapy, Physician Assistant, Public Health, Radiation Therapy, Recreation and Leisure Services

University of Wisconsin-Madison
500 Lincoln Dr., Madison 53706
Type: Public, state, four-year
System: University of Wisconsin System
Degrees: B, M, P, D *Enroll:* 38,129
URL: http://www.wisc.edu
Phone: (608) 262-1234 *Calendar:* Sem. plan
Inst. Accred.: NCA-HLC (1913/1999)
Prog. Accred.: Accounting, Allied Health (audiology, cytotechnology, medicine, occupational therapy, speech-language pathology), Art, Business (AACSB), Clinical Lab Scientist, Clinical Psychology, Counseling Psychology, Dietetics (coordinated), Dietetics (didactic), Engineering (agricultural, bioengineering, chemical, civil, computer, construction, electrical, engineering mechanics, geological/geophysical, industrial, materials, mechanical, nuclear), Forestry, Graduate Social Work, Interior Design, Landscape Architecture, Law, Librarianship, Music, Nursing Education, Pharmacy, Physical Therapy, Physician Assistant, Planning, Psychology Internship, Rehabilitation Counseling, School Psychology, Social Work, Theatre, Veterinary Medicine

University of Wisconsin-Milwaukee
PO Box 413, Milwaukee 53201
Type: Public, state, four-year
System: University of Wisconsin System
Degrees: B, M, D *Enroll:* 23,464
URL: http://www.uwm.edu
Phone: (414) 229-1122 *Calendar:* Sem. plan
Inst. Accred.: NCA-HLC (1969/2005)
Prog. Accred.: Allied Health (cytotechnology, occupational therapy, speech-language pathology), Business (AACSB), Clinical Lab Scientist, Clinical Psychology, Counseling Psychology, Engineering (civil, electrical, industrial, materials, mechanical), Graduate Social Work, Librarianship, Music, Nursing Education, Planning, School Psychology, Social Work

University of Wisconsin-Oshkosh
800 Algoma Blvd., Oshkosh 54901-8601
Type: Public, state, four-year
System: University of Wisconsin System
Degrees: A, B, M *Enroll:* 9,872
URL: http://www.uwosh.edu
Phone: (920) 424-1234 *Calendar:* Sem. plan
Inst. Accred.: NCA-HLC (1915/2007)
Prog. Accred.: Allied Health (audiology, speech-language pathology), Business (AACSB), Computer Science (ABET-CAC), Counseling, Graduate Social Work, Journalism, Music, Nursing Education, Social Work, Teacher Education (NCATE)

University of Wisconsin-Parkside
900 Wood Rd., PO Box 2000, Kenosha 53141-2000
Type: Public, state, four-year
System: University of Wisconsin System
Degrees: B, M *Enroll:* 4,106
URL: http://www.uwp.edu
Phone: (262) 595-2345 *Calendar:* Sem. plan
Inst. Accred.: NCA-HLC (1972/2003)
Prog. Accred.: Business (AACSB)

University of Wisconsin-Platteville
One University Plaza, Platteville 53818-3099
Type: Public, state, four-year
System: University of Wisconsin System
Degrees: A, B, M *Enroll:* 5,746
URL: http://www.uwplatt.edu
Phone: (608) 342-1491 *Calendar:* Sem. plan
Inst. Accred.: NCA-HLC (1918/2007)
Prog. Accred.: Engineering (civil, electrical, engineering physics/science, environmental/sanitary, industrial, mechanical), Industrial Technology, Music, Teacher Education (NCATE)

University of Wisconsin-River Falls
410 South Third St., River Falls 54022-5001
Type: Public, state, four-year
System: University of Wisconsin System
Degrees: B, M, D *Enroll:* 5,680
URL: http://www.uwrf.edu
Phone: (715) 425-3911 *Calendar:* Sem. plan
Inst. Accred.: NCA-HLC (1935/2008)
Prog. Accred.: Allied Health (speech-language pathology), Business (AACSB), Journalism, Music, Social Work, Teacher Education (NCATE)

University of Wisconsin-Stevens Point
2100 Main St., Stevens Point 54481-3897
Type: Public, state, four-year
System: University of Wisconsin System
Degrees: A, B, M *Enroll:* 8,210
URL: http://www.uwsp.edu
Phone: (715) 346-0123 *Calendar:* Sem. plan
Inst. Accred.: NCA-HLC (1916/2008)
Prog. Accred.: Allied Health (audiology, speech-language pathology), Art, Clinical Lab Scientist, Dance, Dietetics (didactic), Forestry, Interior Design, Music, Theatre

University of Wisconsin-Stout
1 Clock Tower Plaza, Menomonie 54751-0790
Type: Public, state, four-year
System: University of Wisconsin System
Degrees: B, M, P *Enroll:* 7,470
URL: http://www.uwstout.edu
Phone: (715) 232-2441 *Calendar:* Sem. plan
Inst. Accred.: NCA-HLC (1928/2001)
Prog. Accred.: Art, Construction Education, Design Technology, Dietetics (didactic), Dietetics (internship), Engineering (manufacturing), Interior Design, Marriage and Family Therapy, Rehabilitation Counseling

University of Wisconsin-Superior
PO Box 2000, Belknap and Catlin, Superior 54880-4500
Type: Public, state, four-year
System: University of Wisconsin System
Degrees: A, B, M, P *Enroll:* 2,489
URL: http://www.uwsuper.edu
Phone: (715) 394-8101 *Calendar:* Sem. plan
Inst. Accred.: NCA-HLC (1916/2003)
Prog. Accred.: Counseling, Music, Social Work

University of Wisconsin-Whitewater
800 West Main St., Whitewater 53190-1790
Type: Public, state, four-year
System: University of Wisconsin System
Degrees: A, B, M, P *Enroll:* 9,635
URL: http://www.uww.edu
Phone: (262) 472-1234 *Calendar:* Sem. plan
Inst. Accred.: NCA-HLC (1915/2006)
Prog. Accred.: Allied Health (speech-language pathology), Business (AACSB), Counseling, Music, Social Work, Teacher Education (NCATE), Theatre

Viterbo University
815 South Ninth St., La Crosse 54601
Type: Private, Franciscan Sisters, four-year
Degrees: B, M *Enroll:* 1,880
URL: http://www.viterbo.edu
Phone: (608) 796-3000 *Calendar:* Sem. plan
Inst. Accred.: NCA-HLC (1954/1999)
Prog. Accred.: Dietetics (coordinated), Dietetics (internship), Music, Nursing Education, Social Work, Teacher Education (NCATE)

Waukesha County Technical College
800 Main St., Pewaukee 53072
Type: Public, state/local, two-year
System: Wisconsin Technical College System Board
Degrees: A *Enroll:* 3,216
URL: http://www.wctc.edu
Phone: (262) 691-5566 *Calendar:* Sem. plan
Inst. Accred.: NCA-HLC (1975/2000)
Prog. Accred.: Allied Health (medical assisting (AMA), surgical technology), Culinary Education, Dentistry (dental hygiene), Nursing, Practical Nursing

Western Technical College
304 North Sixth St., La Crosse 54602
Type: Public, state/local, two-year
System: Wisconsin Technical College System Board
Degrees: A *Enroll:* 2,869
URL: http://www.westerntc.edu
Phone: (608) 785-9200 *Calendar:* Sem. plan
Inst. Accred.: NCA-HLC (1972/2008)
Prog. Accred.: Allied Health (occupational therapy assisting, respiratory therapy, surgical technology), Clinical Lab Technology, Dentistry (dental assisting), Nursing, Physical Therapy Assisting, Radiography

Wisconsin Indianhead Technical College
505 Pine Ridge Rd., Shell Lake 54871
Type: Public, local, two-year
System: Wisconsin Technical College System Board
Degrees: A *Enroll:* 2,223
URL: http://www.witc.edu
Phone: (715) 468-2815 *Calendar:* Sem. plan
Inst. Accred.: NCA-HLC (1979/2004)
Prog. Accred.: Nursing

Ashland Campus
2100 Beaser Ave., Ashland 54806
Phone: (715) 682-4591
Prog. Accred: Allied Health (medical assisting (AMA), occupational therapy assisting)

New Richmond Campus
1019 South Knowles Ave., New Richmond 54017
Phone: (715) 246-6561
Prog. Accred: Allied Health (medical assisting (AMA))

Superior Campus
600 North 21st St., Superior 54880
Phone: (715) 394-6677
Prog. Accred: Allied Health (medical assisting (AMA))

Wisconsin Lutheran College
8830 West Bluemond Rd., Milwaukee 53226
Type: Private, Wisconsin Evangelical Lutheran Synod, four-year
Degrees: B *Enroll:* 674
URL: http://www.wlc.edu
Phone: (414) 443-8800 *Calendar:* Sem. plan
Inst. Accred.: NCA-HLC (1987/2005)

Wisconsin School of Professional Psychology
9120 West Hampton Ave., Ste. 212, Milwaukee 53225
Type: Private, independent, four-year
Degrees: M, D *Enroll:* 34
URL: http://www.wspp.edu
Phone: (414) 464-9777 *Calendar:* Sem. plan
Inst. Accred.: NCA-HLC (1987/2006)

WYOMING

Casper College
125 College Dr., Casper 82601
Type: Public, local, two-year
System: Wyoming Community College Commission
Degrees: A *Enroll:* 2,636
URL: http://www.caspercollege.edu
Phone: (307) 268-2110 *Calendar:* Sem. plan
Inst. Accred.: NCA-HLC (1960/1999)
Prog. Accred.: Allied Health (occupational therapy, occupational therapy assisting, respiratory therapy), Art, Business (ACBSP), Music, Nursing, Radiography, Theatre

Central Wyoming College
2660 Peck Ave., Riverton 82501
Type: Public, state/local, two-year
System: Wyoming Community College Commission
Degrees: A *Enroll:* 1,009
URL: http://www.cwc.edu
Phone: (307) 855-2000 *Calendar:* Sem. plan
Inst. Accred.: NCA-HLC (1976/2006)
Prog. Accred.: Nursing

CollegeAmerica—Cheyenne
6101 Yellowstone Rd., Cheyenne 82009
Type: Private, proprietary, four-year
Degrees: A, B
URL: http://www.collegeamerica.com
Phone: (307) 432-9200
Inst. Accred.: ACCSCT (2005)

Eastern Wyoming College
3200 West C St., Torrington 82240
Type: Public, state/local, two-year
System: Wyoming Community College Commission
Degrees: A *Enroll:* 799
URL: http://ewc.wy.edu
Phone: (307) 532-8200 *Calendar:* Sem. plan
Inst. Accred.: NCA-HLC (1976/2001)
Prog. Accred.: Veterinary Technology

Laramie County Community College
1400 East College Dr., Cheyenne 82007
Type: Public, state/local, two-year
System: Wyoming Community College Commission
Degrees: A *Enroll:* 2,623
URL: http://www.lccc.wy.edu
Phone: (307) 778-5222 *Calendar:* Sem. plan
Inst. Accred.: NCA-HLC (1975/2000)
Prog. Accred.: Allied Health (surgical technology), Dentistry (dental assisting), Nursing, Radiography

Northern Wyoming Community College District—Sheridan
PO Box 1500, Sheridan 82801
Type: Public, state/local, two-year
System: Wyoming Community College Commission
Degrees: A *Enroll:* 1,652
URL: http://www.sheridan.edu
Phone: (307) 674-6446 *Calendar:* Sem. plan
Inst. Accred.: NCA-HLC (1968/2005)
Prog. Accred.: Dentistry (dental assisting, dental hygiene), Nursing

Gillette Campus
720 West 8th St., Gillette 82716
Phone: (307) 674-6446
Prog. Accred: Nursing

Northwest College
231 West Sixth St., Powell 82435
Type: Public, state/local, two-year
System: Wyoming Community College Commission
Degrees: A *Enroll:* 1,339
URL: http://www.northwestcollege.edu
Phone: (307) 754-6000 *Calendar:* Sem. plan
Inst. Accred.: NCA-HLC (1964/2001)
Prog. Accred.: Music, Nursing

University of Wyoming
1000 East University Ave., Laramie 82071
Type: Public, state, four-year
Degrees: B, M, P, D *Enroll:* 10,546
URL: http://www.uwyo.edu
Phone: (307) 766-4121 *Calendar:* Sem. plan
Inst. Accred.: NCA-HLC (1923/2000)
Prog. Accred.: Allied Health (audiology, speech-language pathology), Business (AACSB), Clinical Psychology, Computer Science (ABET-CAC), Counseling, Dietetics (didactic), Engineering (architectural, chemical, civil, computer, electrical, mechanical), Graduate Social Work, Law, Music, Nursing Education, Pharmacy, Social Work, Teacher Education (NCATE)

Western Wyoming Community College
2500 College Dr., Rock Springs 82901
Type: Public, state/local, two-year
System: Wyoming Community College Commission
Degrees: A *Enroll:* 1,856
URL: http://www.wwcc.wy.edu
Phone: (307) 382-1600 *Calendar:* Sem. plan
Inst. Accred.: NCA-HLC (1976/2004)
Prog. Accred.: Nursing

WyoTech
4373 North Third St., Laramie 82070
Type: Private, proprietary, two-year
System: Corinthian Colleges, Inc
Degrees: A *Enroll:* 2,608
URL: http://www.wyotech.com
Phone: (307) 742-3776
Inst. Accred.: ACCSCT (1969/2004)

AUSTRALIA

Deakin University
Pigdons Rd., Geelong, VI 3217
Type: Private, independent, four-year
Degrees: B, M
URL: http://www.deakin.edu.au
Phone: 011 61 3 9244 5095
Inst. Accred.: DETC (2005)

University of Southern Queensland
Toowoomba, QL 4350
Type: Private, independent, four-year
Degrees: A, B, M, P, D
URL: http://www.usq.edu.au
Phone: 011 61-7-4631-2285 *Calendar:* Tri. plan
Inst. Accred.: DETC (2005)

BULGARIA

The American University in Bulgaria
Blagoevard 2700
Type: Private, independent, four-year
Degrees: B, M
URL: http://www.aubg.bg
Phone: 011 359 73 888218
Inst. Accred.: NEASC-CIHE (2001/2006)

CANADA

Alberta Bible College
635 Northmount Dr., NW, Calgary T2K 3J6
Type: Private, Church of Christ, four-year
Degrees: B
URL: http://www.abc-ca.org
Phone: (403) 282-2994 *Calendar:* Sem. plan
Inst. Accred.: ABHE (2008)

Acadia Divinity College
31 Horton Ave., Wolfville B4P 2R6
Type: Private, Baptist Church, four-year
Degrees: M
URL: http://adc.acadiau.ca
Phone: (902) 585-2210 *Calendar:* Sem. plan
Inst. Accred.: ATS (1984/2000)

Ambrose University College
630-833 4th Ave., SW, Calgary T2P 3TS
Type: Private, Christian and Missionary Alliance, four-year
Degrees: A, B, M, P
URL: http://www.ambrose.edu
Phone: (403) 410-2000 *Calendar:* Sem. plan
Inst. Accred.: ABHE (1961/2004), ATS (1989/2005)

Athabasca University
1 University Dr., Athabasca T9S 3A3
Type: Public, independent, four-year
Degrees: B, M, D
URL: http://www.athabascau.ca
Phone: (780) 675-6100 *Calendar:* Sem. plan
Inst. Accred.: MSA-CHE (2005)

Atlantic School of Theology
660 Francklyn St., Halifax B3H 3B5
Type: Private, interdenominational, four-year
Degrees: M
URL: http://astheology.ns.ca
Phone: (902) 423-6939 *Calendar:* Sem. plan
Inst. Accred.: ATS (1976/1998)

Bethany Bible College
26 Western St., Sussex E4E 1E6
Type: Private, Wesleyan Church, four-year
Degrees: B
URL: http://www.bethany-ca.edu
Phone: (506) 432-4400 *Calendar:* Sem. plan
Inst. Accred.: ABHE (1987/2008)

Bethany College
PO Box 160, Hepburn S0K 1Z0
Type: Private, Mennonite Brethren/Evangelical Mennonite Mission Canada, four-year
Degrees: B
URL: http://www.bethany.sk.ca
Phone: (306) 947-2175 *Calendar:* Sem. plan
Inst. Accred.: ABHE (1996/2005)

Briercrest Biblical Seminary
510 College Dr., Caronport S0H 0S0
Type: Private, nondenominational, four-year
Degrees: M
URL: http://www.briercrest.ca
Phone: (306) 756-3200
Inst. Accred.: ATS (1998/2003)

Briercrest College
510 College Dr., Caronport S0H 0S0
Type: Private, interdenominational, four-year
Degrees: A, B, M
URL: http://www.briercrest.ca
Phone: (306) 756-3200 *Calendar:* Sem. plan
Inst. Accred.: ABHE (1976/2007)

Canadian College of Naturopathic Medicine
1255 Sheppard Ave. East, Toronto M2K 1E2
Type: Private, independent, four-year
Degrees: D
URL: http://www.ccnm.edu
Phone: (416) 498-1255
Inst. Accred.: CNME (2000)

Canadian Southern Baptist Seminary
200 Seminary View, Cochrane T4C 2G1
Type: Private, Canadian Convention of Southern Baptists, four-year
Degrees: M
URL: http://www.csbs.edu
Phone: (403) 932-6622 *Calendar:* Sem. plan
Inst. Accred.: ABHE (208), ATS (2001/2005)

Carey Theological College
5920 Iona Dr., Vancouver V6T 1J6
Type: Private, Baptist Union of Western Canada, four-year
Degrees: M, D
URL: http://www.careycentre.com
Phone: (604) 224-4308
Inst. Accred.: ATS (2002/2007)

Central Pentecostal College
1303 Jackson Ave., Saskatoon S7H 2M9
Type: Private, Pentecostal Assemblies of Canada, four-year
Degrees: B, M
URL: http://www.cpc-paoc.edu
Phone: (306) 374-6655 *Calendar:* Sem. plan
Inst. Accred.: ABHE (1997/2002)

Columbia Bible College
2940 Clearbook Rd., Abbotsford V2T 2Z8
Type: Private, Mennonite Brethren/Conference of Mennonites, four-year
Degrees: B
URL: http://www.columbiabc.edu
Phone: (604) 853-3358 *Calendar:* Sem. plan
Inst. Accred.: ABHE (1991/2008)

Concordia Lutheran Seminary
7040 Ada Blvd., Edmonton T5B 4E3
Type: Private, Lutheran Church-Canada, four-year
Degrees: M
URL: http://www.concordiasem.ab.ca
Phone: (780) 474-1468
Inst. Accred.: ATS (1998/2004)

DeVry Institute of Technology, Calgary
2700 3rd Ave. SE, Calgary T2A 7W4
Type: Private, proprietary
System: DeVry University
Degrees: A, B
URL: http://www.cal.devry.ca
Phone: (403) 235-3450 *Calendar:* Sem. plan
Inst. Accred.: NCA-HLC (2002, *Indirect accreditation through DeVry University, Oakbrook Terrace, IL*)

Emmanuel Bible College
100 Fergus Ave., Kitchener N2A 2H2
Type: Private, Evangelical Missionary Church of Canada East, four-year
Degrees: B, D
URL: http://www.ebcollege.on.ca
Phone: (519) 894-8900 *Calendar:* Sem. plan
Inst. Accred.: ABHE (1982/2003)

Emmanuel College of Victoria University
75 Queen's Park Crescent, East, Toronto M5S 1K7
Type: Private, United Church of Canada, four-year
Degrees: M, D
URL: http://www.vicu.utoronto.ca/emmanuel.htm
Phone: (416) 585-4539 *Calendar:* Sem. plan
Inst. Accred.: ATS (1938/2001)

Eston College
PO Box 579, Eston S0L 1A0
Type: Private, independent, four-year
Degrees: A, B
URL: http://www.estoncollege.ca
Phone: (306) 962-3621 *Calendar:* Sem. plan
Inst. Accred.: ABHE (2008)

Heritage College and Seminary
175 Holiday Inn Dr., Cambridge N3C 3T2
Type: Private, Fellowship of Evangelical Baptist Churches in Canada, four-year
Degrees: B, M
URL: http://www.heritage-theo.edu
Phone: (519) 651-2869 *Calendar:* Sem. plan
Inst. Accred.: ABHE (1996/2001), ATS (2005)

Huron University College Faculty of Theology
1349 Western Rd., London N6G 1H3
Type: Private, Anglican Church of Canada, four-year
Degrees: M
URL: http://www.huronuc.on.ca/theology
Phone: (519) 438-7224 *Calendar:* Sem. plan
Inst. Accred.: ATS (1981/2005)

Knox College
59 St. George St., Toronto M5S 2E6
Type: Private, Presbyterian Church in Canada, four-year
Degrees: M, D
URL: http://www.utoronto.ca/knox
Phone: (416) 978-4500 *Calendar:* Sem. plan
Inst. Accred.: ATS (1948/2001)

Lansbridge University
413 King St., Fredericton E3B 1E5
Type: Private, proprietary, four-year
Degrees: B, M
URL: http://www.lansbridge.com
Phone: (506) 443-0780
Inst. Accred.: DETC (2005)

Lutheran Theological Seminary
114 Seminary Crescent, Saskatoon S7N 0X3
Type: Private, Evangelical Lutheran Church in Canada, four-year
Degrees: M
URL: http://www.usask.ca/stu/luther
Phone: (306) 966-7850 *Calendar:* Sem. plan
Inst. Accred.: ATS (1976/1999)

Master's College and Seminary
3080 Younge St., Ste. 3040, Box 70, Toronto M4N 3N1
Type: Private, Pentacostal Assemblies of Canada, four-year
Degrees: B, M
URL: http://www.mcs.edu
Phone: (416) 482-2224 *Calendar:* Sem. plan
Inst. Accred.: ABHE (1989/2007)

Greater Toronto Campus
2476 Argentia Rd., Missassuaga C5N 6M1
Phone: (905) 819-1936

McGill University
845 Sherbrooke St. West, Montreal H3A 2T5
Type: Private, interdenominational, four-year
Degrees: B, M, D
URL: http://www.mcgill.ca
Phone: (514) 398-4455 *Calendar:* Sem. plan
Inst. Accred.: ATS (1952/2001)
Prog. Accred.: Allied Health (medicine), Clinical Psychology, Counseling Psychology, Dentistry (dentistry, oral and maxillofacial surgery), Librarianship, Psychology Internship, School Psychology

McMaster Divinity College
1280 Main St. West, Hamilton L8S 4K1
Type: Private, Baptist Convention of Ontario and Quebec, four-year
Degrees: M, D
URL: http://www.macdiv.ca
Phone: (905) 525-9140 *Calendar:* Sem. plan
Inst. Accred.: ATS (1954/1998)

Montreal School of Theology
3473 University St., Montreal H3A 2A8
Type: Private, interdenominational, four-year
Degrees: M
URL: http://www.mst-etm.ca
Phone: (514) 849-8511 *Calendar:* Sem. plan
Inst. Accred.: ATS (1989/2001)

Newman Theological College
15611 St. Albert Trail, Edmonton T6V 1H3
Type: Private, Roman Catholic Church, four-year
Degrees: M
URL: http://www.newman.edu
Phone: (403) 447-2993 *Calendar:* Sem. plan
Inst. Accred.: ATS (1992/2006)

Prairie Bible College
PO Box 4000, Three Hills T0M 2N0
Type: Private, interdenominational, four-year
Degrees: A, B
URL: http://www.prairie.edu/biblecollege.htm
Phone: (403) 443-5511 *Calendar:* Sem. plan
Inst. Accred.: ABHE (1997/2002)

Providence College and Theological Seminary
10 College Crescent, Otterburne R0A 1G0
Type: Private, interdenominational, four-year
Degrees: B, M, P, D
URL: http://prov.ca
Phone: (204) 433-7488 *Calendar:* Sem. plan
Inst. Accred.: ABHE (1973/2006), ATS (1992/2002)

Queen's Theological College
Kingston K7L 3N6
Type: Private, United Church of Canada, four-year
Degrees: M
URL: http://www.queensu.ca/theology
Phone: (613) 545-2110 *Calendar:* Sem. plan
Inst. Accred.: ATS (1986/2001)

Regent College
5800 University Blvd., Vancouver V6T 2E4
Type: Private, interdenominational, four-year
Degrees: M
URL: http://www.regent-college.edu
Phone: (604) 224-3245 *Calendar:* Sem. plan
Inst. Accred.: ATS (1985/2000)

Regis College
15 St. Mary St., Toronto M4Y 2R5
Type: Private, Roman Catholic Church, four-year
Degrees: M, D
URL: http://www.regiscollege.ca
Phone: (416) 922-5474 *Calendar:* Sem. plan
Inst. Accred.: ATS (1970/2001)

Rocky Mountain College
4039 Brentwood Rd., NW, Calgary T2L 1L1
Type: Private, Missionary Church of Canada, four-year
Degrees: B
URL: http://www.rockymountaincollege.ca
Phone: (403) 284-5100 *Calendar:* Sem. plan
Inst. Accred.: ABHE (1989/2008)

Saint Andrew's College
1121 College Dr., Saskatoon S7N 0N3
Type: Public, United Church of Canada, four-year
Degrees: B, M
URL: http://www.usask.ca/stu/standrews/index.html
Phone: (306) 966-8970 *Calendar:* Sem. plan
Inst. Accred.: ATS (1996/2007)

Saint Augustine's Seminary of Toronto
2661 Kingston Rd., Toronto M1M 1M3
Type: Private, Roman Catholic Church, four-year
Degrees: M
URL: http://www.staugustines.on.ca
Phone: (416) 261-7207 *Calendar:* Sem. plan
Inst. Accred.: ATS (1980/2001)

Saint Peter's Seminary
1040 Waterloo St. North, London N6A 3Y1
Type: Private, Roman Catholic Church, four-year
Degrees: M
URL: http://www.stpetersseminary.ca
Phone: (519) 432-1824 *Calendar:* Sem. plan
Inst. Accred.: ATS (1986/2001)

Steinbach Bible College
50 PTH 12N, Steinbach R5G 1T4
Type: Private, Evangelical Mennonite Conference, four-year
Degrees: B
URL: http://www.sbcollege.mb.ca
Phone: (204) 326-6451
Inst. Accred.: ABHE (1991/2008)

Summit Pacific College
PO Box 1700, STN MAIN, Abbotsford V2S 7E7
Type: Private, Pentecostal Assemblies of Canada, four-year
Degrees: B
URL: http://www.summitpacific.ca
Phone: (604) 853-7491 *Calendar:* Sem. plan
Inst. Accred.: ABHE (1980/2001)

Taylor University College and Seminary
11525 23rd Ave., Edmonton T6J 4T3
Type: Private, North American Baptist Conference, four-year
Degrees: A, B, M, P, D
URL: http://www.taylor-edu.ca
Phone: (780) 431-5200 *Calendar:* Sem. plan
Inst. Accred.: ATS (1997/2002)

Toronto School of Theology
47 Queen's Park Crescent, East, Toronto M5S 2C3
Type: Private, interdenominational, four-year
Degrees: M, D
URL: http://www.tst.edu
Phone: (416) 978-4039 *Calendar:* Sem. plan
Inst. Accred.: ATS (1980/2001)

Trinity Western University
Fosmark Centre, 7600 Glover Rd., Langley V2Y 1Y1
Type: Private, Evangelical Free Churches of America, four-year
Degrees: B, M
URL: http://www.twu.ca
Phone: (604) 888-7511 *Calendar:* Sem. plan
Inst. Accred.: ATS (1997/2002)
Prog. Accred.: Counseling

Tyndale University College and Seminary
25 Ballyconnor Ct., Toronto M2M 4B3
Type: Private, interdenominational, four-year
Degrees: B, M, P
URL: http://www.tyndale.ca
Phone: (416) 226-6380 *Calendar:* Sem. plan
Inst. Accred.: ABHE (1966/1999), ATS (1989/2008)

University of St. Michael's College
81 St. Mary St., Toronto M5S 1J4
Type: Private, Roman Catholic Church, four-year
Degrees: M, D
URL: http://www.utoronto.ca/stmikes
Phone: (416) 926-7140 *Calendar:* Sem. plan
Inst. Accred.: ATS (1972/2001)

The University of Trinity College in the University of Toronto
6 Hoskin Ave., Toronto M5S 1H8
Type: Private, Anglican Church of Canada, four-year
Degrees: M, D
URL: http://www.trinity.utoronto.ca
Phone: (416) 978-2133 *Calendar:* Sem. plan
Inst. Accred.: ATS (1938/2002)

University of Winnipeg
515 Portage Ave., Winnipeg R3B 2E9
Type: Public, provincial, four-year
Degrees: B, M
URL: http://www.uwinnipeg.ca
Phone: (204) 786-7811
Inst. Accred.: ATS (2006)
Prog. Accred.: Marriage and Family Therapy

Vancouver School of Theology
6000 Iona Dr., Vancouver V6T 1L4
Type: Private, interdenominational, four-year
Degrees: M
URL: http://www.vst.edu
Phone: (604) 822-9031 *Calendar:* Sem. plan
Inst. Accred.: ATS (1976/2003)

Vanguard College
12140 103rd St., Edmonton T5G 2J9
Type: Private, Pentecostal Assembies of Canada, four-year
Degrees: B
URL: http://www.vanguardcollege.com
Phone: (780) 452-0808 *Calendar:* Sem. plan
Inst. Accred.: ABHE (1997/2006)

Waterloo Lutheran Seminary
75 University Ave., West, Waterloo N2L 3C5
Type: Private, Evangelical Lutheran Church, four-year
Degrees: M, D
URL: http://www.wlu.ca/~wwwsem
Phone: (519) 884-1970 *Calendar:* Sem. plan
Inst. Accred.: ATS (1982/2007)

William and Catherine Booth College
447 Webb Place, Winnipeg R3B 2P2
Type: Private, Salvation Army, four-year
Degrees: B
URL: http://www.boothcollege.ca
Phone: (204) 947-6701 *Calendar:* Sem. plan
Inst. Accred.: ABHE (1991/2008)

Wycliffe College
5 Hoskin Ave., Toronto M5S 1H7
Type: Private, Anglican Church of Canada, four-year
Degrees: M, D
URL: http://www.wycliffecollege.ca
Phone: (416) 946-3535 *Calendar:* Sem. plan
Inst. Accred.: ATS (1978/2001)

CAYMAN ISLANDS

International College of the Cayman Islands
PO Box 136 Savannah, Grand Cayman
Type: Private, proprietary, four-year
Degrees: A, B, M
URL: http://www.icci.edu.ky
Phone: (345) 947-1100 *Calendar:* Qtr. plan
Inst. Accred.: ACICS (1979/2008)

COSTA RICA

Instituto Centroamericano de Administracion de Empresas
PO Box 960-4050, Alajuela 4040
Type: Private, independent, four-year
Degrees: M
URL: http://www.incae.ac.cr/ES
Phone: 011 506 437 2200 *Calendar:* Tri. plan
Inst. Accred.: SACS (1994/1999)
Prog. Accred.: Business (AACSB)

EGYPT

The American University in Cairo
PO Box 2511, 113 Sharia Dasr El Aini, Cairo
Type: Private, independent, four-year
Degrees: B, M *FTE Enroll:* 563
URL: http://www.aucegypt.edu
Phone: 011 2 02 794 2964 *Calendar:* Sem. plan
Inst. Accred.: MSA-CHE (1982/2008)
Prog. Accred.: Business (AACSB), Computer Science (ABET-CAC), Engineering (construction, mechanical)

FEDERATED STATES OF MICRONESIA

College of Micronesia-FSM
PO Box 159, Kolonia, Pohnpei, Micronesia, Federated States 96941
Type: Public, state, two-year
Degrees: A *Enroll:* 1,798
URL: http://www.comfsm.fm
Phone: (691) 320-2480 *Calendar:* Sem. plan
Inst. Accred.: WASC-JR. (1978/2004)

FRANCE

American University of Paris
6 Rue du Colonex Combres, Paris 75007
Type: Private, independent, four-year
Degrees: C, B, M
URL: http://www.aup.fr
Phone: 011 331 40 62 07 20 *Calendar:* Sem. plan
Inst. Accred.: MSA-CHE (1973/2003)

GERMANY

European College of Liberal Arts
Platanenstrafle 24, Berlin 13156
Type: Private, independent, four-year
Degrees: B
URL: http://www.ecla.de
Phone: 011 49 (0) 30 43733 *Calendar:* Tri. plan
Inst. Accred.: AALE (2005)

GREECE

American College of Thessaloniki
PO Box 21021, Pylea, Thessaloniki 555 10
Type: Private, independent, four-year
Degrees: B
URL: http://www.act.edu
Phone: 011 2310 398 238
Inst. Accred.: NEASC-CIHE (1997/2002)

Deree College, The American College of Greece
6 Gravitas St., GR-153 42 Aghia Paraskevi, Athens
Type: Private, independent, four-year
Degrees: A, B, M *FTE Enroll:* 4,404
URL: http://www.acg.edu/deree
Phone: 011 301 600-9800 *Calendar:* 4-1-4 plan
Inst. Accred.: NEASC-CIHE (1981/2006)

HUNGARY

Central European University
Nador Utca 9, Budapest H-1051
Type: Private, independent, four-year
Degrees: B, M, D
URL: http://www.ceu.hu
Phone: 011 361327 3000
Inst. Accred.: MSA-CHE (2004)

IRELAND

American College Dublin
2 Merrion Square, Dublin, DU 2
Type: Private, independent, four-year
Degrees: B
URL: http://www.amcd.edu
Phone: 011 353 1 676 8939 *Calendar:* Sem. plan
Inst. Accred.: ACICS (2004)

ITALY

American University of Rome
Via Pietro Roselli 4, Rome 00153
Type: Private, independent, four-year
Degrees: A, B
URL: http://www.aur.edu
Phone: 011 3906 5833 0919 *Calendar:* Sem. plan
Inst. Accred.: ACICS (1992/2008), MSA-CHE (2008)

John Cabot University
Via Della Lungara 233, Rome 00165
Type: Private, independent, four-year
Degrees: A, B
URL: http://www.johncabot.edu
Phone: 011 39 06 681 9121 *Calendar:* Sem. plan
Inst. Accred.: MSA-CHE (2003/2008)

JAPAN

Babel University
1-6-1 Roppongi, Izumi Garden, 7F, Minato-ku, Tokyo 106-6007
Type: Private, proprietary, four-year
Degrees: M
URL: http://www.babel.co.jp
Phone: 011 81 3 6229 2433
Inst. Accred.: DETC (2002/2006)

KENYA

United States International University—Africa
PO Box 14634, Thika Rd., Kasarani, Nairobi
Type: Private, independent, four-year
Degrees: B, M
URL: http://www.usiu.ac.ke
Phone: 011-254-20-360-6000 *Calendar:* Sem. plan
Inst. Accred.: WASC-SR. (2005)

LEBANON

American University of Beirut
PO Box 11-0236, Beirut 1107 2020
Type: Private, independent, four-year
Degrees: B, M, P, D *FTE Enroll:* 1
URL: http://www.aub.edu.lb
Phone: 011 9611-340460 *Calendar:* Sem. plan
Inst. Accred.: MSA-CHE (2004)
Prog. Accred.: Public Health

MARSHALL ISLANDS

College of the Marshall Islands
PO Box 1258, Majuro 96960
Type: Public, state, two-year
Degrees: A *Enroll:* 517
URL: http://64.129.3.54
Phone: (692) 625-3394 *Calendar:* Sem. plan
Inst. Accred.: WASC-JR. (1991/2003, Warning)

MEXICO

Alliant International University—Mexico City
Alvaro Obregon #110, Colonia Roma, Mexico City CP 06700
Type: Private, independent, four-year
System: Alliant International University
Degrees: A, B, M, D
URL: http://www.alliant.edu
Phone: 011 52 5 264 2187 *Calendar:* Sem. plan
Inst. Accred.: WASC-SR. (1977/2006, *Indirect accreditation through Alliant International University, San Francisco, CA*)

Instituto Tecnologico y de Estudios Superiores de Monterrey
Ave. Eugenio Garza Sada, 2501 Sur, Monterrey 64849
Type: Private, independent, four-year
Degrees: B, M, D
URL: http://www.sistema.itesm.mx
Phone: 011 52 8 358 2000
Inst. Accred.: SACS (1950/2008)
Prog. Accred.: Business (AACSB)

Universidad de las Americas, A.C.
Calle de Puebla No. 223, Col. Roma 06700
Type: Private, independent, four-year
Degrees: B, M
URL: http://www.udla.mx
Phone: 011 5255 5209 9800 *Calendar:* Sem. plan
Inst. Accred.: SACS (1991/2007)

Universidad de las Americas—Puebla
Station Catarina Martir, Cholula, PU 72820
Type: Private, independent, four-year
Degrees: B, M, D
URL: http://info.pue.udlap.mx
Phone: 011 52 222 229 2000 *Calendar:* Sem. plan
Inst. Accred.: SACS (1959/2005, Probation)

Universidad de Monterrey
Ave Ignacio Morones Prieto 4500 Pte., San Pedro Garza Garcia 66238
Type: Private, independent, four-year
Degrees: B, M
URL: http://www.udem.edu.mx
Phone: 011 52 8181 24 1000 *Calendar:* Sem. plan
Inst. Accred.: SACS (2001/2006)

Westhill University
Domingo Garcia Ramos 56, Prados de la Montaña I, Santa Fe, Mexico City
Type: Private, independent, two-year
Degrees: A
URL: http://www.westhill.edu.mx
Phone: 011 5292-1729
Inst. Accred.: ACICS (2003/2004)

NORTHERN MARIANA ISLANDS

Northern Marianas College
PO Box 1250, Saipan, CNMI 96950
Type: Public, state, four-year
Degrees: A, B *Enroll:* 833
URL: http://www.nmcnet.edu
Phone: (670) 234-5498 *Calendar:* Sem. plan
Inst. Accred.: WASC-JR. (1985/2007, Warning), WASC-SR. (2001, Probation)

PALAU

Palau Community College
PO Box 9, Koror 96940
Type: Public, federal, two-year
Degrees: A
URL: http://www.palau.edu
Phone: (680) 488-2471 *Calendar:* Sem. plan
Inst. Accred.: WASC-JR. (1977/2004)

SWITZERLAND

Ecole Hoteliere de Lausanne
Le Chalet-a-Gobet, Luasanne CH 1000
Type: Private, proprietary, four-year
Degrees: A, B, M
URL: http://www.ehl.ch
Phone: 011 41 21 785 1111
Inst. Accred.: NEASC-CIHE (2003)

Franklin College Switzerland
Via Ponte Tresa 29, Sorengo CH 6924
Type: Private, independent, four-year
Degrees: A, B
URL: http://www.fc.edu
Phone: 011 4191 985-22-60 *Calendar:* Sem. plan
Inst. Accred.: MSA-CHE (1975/2005)

Glion Institute of Higher Education
Rue de l'Ondine 20, Bulle 1630
Type: Private, proprietary, four-year
System: Laureate Education, Inc.
Degrees: A, B, M
URL: http://www.glion.ch/en
Phone: 011 41 021 966 35 35 *Calendar:* Sem. plan
Inst. Accred.: NEASC-CIHE (2005)

Les Roches School of Hotel Management
Bluche Crans-Montana, Valais CH-3975
Type: Private, proprietary, four-year
System: Laureate Education, Inc.
Degrees: A, B
URL: http://www.les-roches.ch
Phone: 011 41 27 485 96 00 *Calendar:* Sem. plan
Inst. Accred.: NEASC-CIHE (2006)

TAIWAN, PROVINCE OF CHINA

Christ's College
51 Tzu Chiang Rd., Tanshui Taipei 25120
Type: Private, independent, four-year
Degrees: B
URL: http://www.christc.org.tw
Phone: 011 886 2 28097661
Inst. Accred.: TRACS (2006)

UNITED ARAB EMIRATES

American University in Dubai
PO Box 28282, Dubai
Type: Private, proprietary, four-year
Degrees: B, M
URL: http://www.aud.edu
Phone: 011 9714-399-9000 *Calendar:* Sem. plan
Inst. Accred.: SACS (2007)

American University of Sharjah
PO Box 26666, Sharjah
Type: Private, independent, four-year
Degrees: C, B, M
URL: http://www.aus.edu
Phone: 011 971 6 515 5555 *Calendar:* Sem. plan
Inst. Accred.: MSA-CHE (2004)
Prog. Accred.: Computer Science (ABET-CAC), Engineering (chemical, civil, computer, electrical, mechanical)

Zayed University
PO Box 19282, Dubai
Type: Private, state-related, four-year
Degrees: B, M
URL: http://www.zu.ac.ae
Phone: 011 97 714 264-8899
Inst. Accred.: MSA-CHE (2008)

UNITED KINGDOM

London Metropolitan University
166-220 Holloway Rd., London N7 8DB
Type: Private, proprietary, four-year
Degrees: A, B, M, P, D
URL: http://www.londonmet.ac.uk
Phone: 011 44 0 20 7423 000
Inst. Accred.: MSA-CHE (2007)

The Open University, UK
PO Box 75, Walton Hall, Milton Keynes MK7 6AA
Type: Public, independent, four-year
Degrees: B, M, D
URL: http://www.open.ac.uk
Phone: 011 44 190 865-3788
Inst. Accred.: MSA-CHE (2005)
Prog. Accred.: Business (AACSB)

Rhodec International
35 East St., Brighton, E. BN1 1HL
Type: Private, proprietary, four-year
Degrees: A, B
URL: http://www.rhodec.edu
Phone: 011 44 0 1273 327476
Inst. Accred.: DETC (1998/2003)

Massachusetts Campus
59 Coddington St., Ste. 104, Quincy, MA 02169
Phone: (617) 472-4942

Richmond, The American International University in London
Queens Rd., Richmond, SU TW10 6JP
Type: Private, independent, four-year
Degrees: A, B, M
URL: http://www.richmond.ac.uk
Phone: 011 44 20 83329000 *Calendar:* Sem. plan
Inst. Accred.: MSA-CHE (1981/2006)

University of Leicester's Centre for Labour Market Studies
7-9 Salisbury Rd., Leicester LE1 7QR
Type: Private, independent, four-year
Degrees: M
URL: http://www.clms.le.ac.uk
Phone: 011 44 116-252-5950
Inst. Accred.: DETC (1997/2003)

Accredited Non–Degree-Granting Institutions

ALABAMA

Alabama State College of Barber Styling
9480 Pkwy. East, Birmingham 35215-8308
Type: Private, proprietary
Degrees: C
URL: http://www.alabamabarbercollege.com
Phone: (205) 836-2404
Inst. Accred.: ACCSCT (1990/2004)

16th Street Campus
1001 South 16th St., Birmingham 35205
Phone: (205) 933-7600

Blue Cliff Career College
2970 Cottage Hill Rd., Ste. 175, Mobile 36606
Type: Private, proprietary
Degrees: C
URL: http://www.bluecliffmassage.com
Phone: (251) 473-2220
Inst. Accred.: ACCSCT (2003)

Capps College
3590 Pleasant Valley Rd., Mobile 36609
Type: Private, proprietary
Degrees: C
URL: http://www.medcareers.net
Phone: (250) 650-0800
Inst. Accred.: ABHES (1986/2003)

Capps Medical Institute
6420 North 9th Ave., Pensacola, FL 32504
Phone: (850) 476-7607
Prog. Accred: Medical Assisting (ABHES)

Montgomery Campus
3736 Atlanta Hwy., Montgomery 36109
Phone: (334) 272-3857
Prog. Accred: Medical Assisting (ABHES)

Capps College—Foley
914 North McKenzie St., Foley 36535
Type: Private, proprietary
Degrees: C
URL: http://www.medcareers.net
Phone: (334) 970-1460
Inst. Accred.: ABHES (1998/2003)
Prog. Accred.: Medical Assisting (ABHES)

Dothan Campus
200 Vulcan Way, Dothan 36303
Phone: (334) 677-2852
Prog. Accred: Medical Assisting (ABHES)

Cardiac and Vascular Institute of Ultrasound, Inc.
1729 Springhill Ave., Ste. 11, Mobile 36604
Type: Private, proprietary
Degrees: C
URL: http://www.ultrasound.cc
Phone: (251) 433-1600
Inst. Accred.: ABHES (2005)

Gadsden Business College
3225 Rainbow Dr., Ste. 246, Rainbow City 35906-5821
Type: Private, proprietary
Degrees: C
Phone: (256) 442-2805 *Calendar:* Qtr. plan
Inst. Accred.: ACICS (1962/2004)

Anniston Campus
1809 Hillyer Robinson Pkwy., Ste. B, Anniston 36207
Phone: (256) 237-7517

Gaither and Company Beauty College
414 East Willow St., Scottsboro 35768
Type: Private, proprietary
Degrees: C
Phone: (256) 259-1001
Inst. Accred.: NACCAS (1985/2003)

Leadership Development, Inc.
Dale Carnegie Training
300 Cahaba Park Circle, Ste. 118, Birmingham 35242
Type: Private, proprietary
Degrees: C
URL: http://www.birmingham.dale-carnegie.com
Phone: (205) 995-5059
Inst. Accred.: ACCET (1976/2001)

Mimi's Beauty Academy of Cosmetology
2115 Jonathan Dr., Huntsville 35810
Type: Private, proprietary
Degrees: C
URL: http://www.mimisbeautyacademy.com
Phone: (256) 859-1572
Inst. Accred.: NACCAS (2006)

Montgomery Job Corps Center
1145 Air Base Blvd., Montgomery 36108
Type: Private, federal
Degrees: C
URL: http://atlantaregion.jobcorps.gov/jcCenters/montgomeryJCC.html
Phone: (334) 262-8883
Inst. Accred.: COE (2000/2006)

Southeastern School of Cosmetology
849 Dennison Ave. SW, Ste. 101, Birmingham 35211
Type: Private, proprietary
Degrees: C
URL: http://www.southeasternschoolofcosmetology.com
Phone: 323-1011
Inst. Accred.: COE (2002/2006)

Toni Love's Cosmetology Training Center
PO Box 5, Moundville 35474-0005
Type: Private, proprietary
Degrees: C
Phone: (205) 371-8950
Inst. Accred.: NACCAS (2007)

United States Air Force Institute for Advanced Distributed Learning
50 South Turner Blvd., Maxwell AFB-Gunter Annex, Montgomery 36118-5643
Type: Public, federal
System: Air University
Degrees: C
URL: http://www.maxwell.af.mil/au/afiadl
Phone: (334) 416-4252
Inst. Accred.: DETC (1975/2006)

United States Army Ordnance Munitions and Electronic Maintenance School
3300 Patton Rd., Bldg. 3301, Redstone Arsenal 35897-6000
Type: Public, federal
Degrees: C
URL: http://omems.redstone.army.mil
Phone: (256) 876-3349
Inst. Accred.: COE (1976/2003)

ALASKA

Alaska Vocational Technical Center
PO Box 889, Seward 99664-0889
Type: Public, state
Degrees: C
URL: http://www.avtec.alaska.edu
Phone: (907) 224-4159
Inst. Accred.: COE (1983/2003)
Prog. Accred.: Culinary Education

Career Academy
1415 East Tudor Rd., Anchorage 99507-1033
Type: Private, proprietary
Degrees: C
URL: http://www.careeracademy.net
Phone: (907) 563-7575
Inst. Accred.: ACCSCT (1987/2002)

Galena City Schools Post Secondary School
PO Box 359, Antoski Dr., Galena 99741
Type: Private, proprietary
Degrees: C
URL: http://postsec.galenaalaska.org
Phone: (907) 656-2053
Inst. Accred.: NACCAS (1988/2003)

ARIZONA

American Institute of Technology
440 South 54th Ave., Phoenix 85043-4729
Type: Private, proprietary
Degrees: C
URL: http://ait-schools.com
Phone: (602) 233-2222 *Calendar:* Qtr. plan
Inst. Accred.: ACCSCT (1985/2004)

North Las Vegas Campus
4610-A Vandenberg Dr., North Las Vegas, NV 89031
Phone: (702) 644-1234

Arizona Academy of Beauty, Inc.
5631 East Speedway Blvd., Tucson 85712
Type: Private, proprietary
Degrees: C
URL: http://www.arizonaacademy.com
Phone: (520) 885-4120
Inst. Accred.: NACCAS (1971/2006)

Arizona Academy of Beauty—North Inc.
4066 North Oracle Rd., Tucson 85705
Type: Private, proprietary
Degrees: C
URL: http://www.arizonaacademy.com
Phone: (520) 888-0170
Inst. Accred.: NACCAS (1974/2005)

Arizona College of Allied Health
4425 West Olive St., Ste. 300, Glendale 85302
Type: Private, proprietary
Degrees: C
URL: http://www.arizonacollege.edu
Phone: (602) 222-9300
Inst. Accred.: ABHES (1994/2006)

Artistic Beauty Colleges
1790 Route 66, Flagstaff 86004
Type: Private, proprietary
System: Empire Education Group
Degrees: C
URL: http://www.artisticbeautycolleges.com
Phone: (928) 774-7146
Inst. Accred.: NACCAS (1971/2003)

Chandler Campus
2978 North Alma School Rd., Suites 1–3, Chandler 85224
Phone: (480) 855-7901

Prescott Campus
410 West Goodwin St., Prescott 86004
Phone: (520) 778-5064

Artistic Beauty Colleges—Glendale
10820 North 43rd Ave., Glendale 85257
Type: Private, proprietary
System: Empire Education Group
Degrees: C
URL: http://www.artisticbeautycolleges.com
Phone: (623) 937-2749
Inst. Accred.: NACCAS (1974/2005)

Phoenix North Central Campus
402 East Greenway Pkwy., Suites 21 & 28, Phoenix 85022
Phone: (602) 863-2101

Artistic Beauty Colleges—Phoenix
2727 West Glendale Ave., Ste. 200, Phoenix 85051
Type: Private, proprietary
System: Empire Education Group
Degrees: C
URL: http://www.artisticbeautycolleges.com
Phone: (602) 249-1262
Inst. Accred.: NACCAS (1982/2002)

Artistic Beauty Colleges—Scottsdale
7730 East McDowell Rd., Ste. 106, Scottsdale 85257
Type: Private, proprietary
System: Empire Education Group
Degrees: C
URL: http://www.artisticbeautycolleges.com
Phone: (480) 949-7557
Inst. Accred.: NACCAS (1975/2006)

Artistic Beauty Colleges—Tuscon
3030 East Speedway Blvd., Tucson 85716
Type: Private, proprietary
System: Empire Education Group
Degrees: C
URL: http://www.artisticbeautycolleges.com
Phone: (520) 327-6544
Inst. Accred.: NACCAS (1975/2003)

Tucson North Campus
4343 North Oracle Rd., Ste. I, Tucson 85705
Phone: (520) 888-3011

Astrological Institute
7501 East Oak St., Ste. 130, Scottsdale 85257
Type: Private, proprietary
Degrees: C
URL: http://www.primenet.com/astroin
Phone: (480) 423-9494
Inst. Accred.: ACCSCT (2001)

Carsten Institute
3345 South Rural Rd., Tempe 85282
Type: Private, proprietary
Degrees: C
URL: http://www.carsteninstitute.com/institutestempe.html
Phone: (480) 456-4089
Inst. Accred.: NACCAS (1993/2006)

Union Square, NYC Campus
22 East 17th St., Second Flr., New York, NY 10003
Phone: (212) 675-4884

Charles of Italy Beauty College and School of Massage Therapy
1987 McCulloch Blvd., Ste. 205, Lake Havasu City 86403
Type: Private, proprietary
Degrees: C
URL: http://charlesofitaly.com
Phone: (928) 453-6666
Inst. Accred.: NACCAS (1984/2004)

Conservatory of Recording Arts & Sciences
2300 East Broadway Rd., Tempe 85282
Type: Private, independent
Degrees: C
URL: http://www.cras.org
Phone: (480) 858-9400
Inst. Accred.: ACCSCT (1990/2004)

Cortiva Institute—School of Massage Therapy
8010 East McDowell Rd., Ste. 214, Scottsdale 85257
Type: Private, proprietary
Degrees: C
URL: http://www.ptmcaz.com/phoenix
Phone: (480) 945-9461
Inst. Accred.: ACCET (1989/2001)

Flagstaff Campus
1000 North Humphreys St., Ste. 204, Flagstaff 86001-3125
Phone: (520) 213-0010

Phoenix Campus
9201 North 29th Ave., Ste. B-33, Phoenix 85051-3470
Phone: (602) 395-9494

Cortiva Institute-Desert Institute of the Healing Arts
140 East 4th St., Tucson 85705-8330
Type: Private, proprietary
Degrees: C
URL: http://www.cortiva.com/locations/diha
Phone: (520) 882-0899
Inst. Accred.: ACCSCT (1987/2006), CMTA (2001/2004)

DeVoe College of Beauty
750 East Barstow Dr., Sierra Vista 85635
Type: Private, proprietary
Degrees: C
URL: http://personal.riverusers.com/~devoe/index.html
Phone: (520) 458-8660
Inst. Accred.: NACCAS (1981/2006)

Earl's Academy of Beauty
2111 South Alma School Rd., Ste. 21, Mesa 85210
Type: Private, proprietary
Degrees: C
URL: http://www.earlsacademy.com
Phone: (480) 897-1688
Inst. Accred.: NACCAS (1972/2003)

Phoenix Campus
1107 East Bell Rd., Ste. 104, Phoenix 85022
Phone: (602) 443-0076

East Valley Institute of Technology
1601 West Main St., Mesa 85201
Type: Public, state/local
Degrees: C
URL: http://www.evit.com
Phone: (480) 461-4000
Inst. Accred.: NCA-CASI (1986/2004)

The Hair Academy of Safford
1550 West Thatcher Blvd., Safford 85546
Type: Private, proprietary
Degrees: C
Phone: (520) 428-0331
Inst. Accred.: NACCAS (1989/2004)

HDS Truck Driving Institute
6251 South Wilmont Rd., PO Box 17600, Tucson 85706
Type: Private, proprietary
Degrees: C
URL: http://www.hdsdrivers.com
Phone: (520) 721-5825
Inst. Accred.: ACCSCT (2000/2005)

International Academy of Beauty #6
3350 North Arizona Ave., Ste. 4, Chandler 85224
Type: Private, proprietary
Degrees: C
URL: http://www.intlacademy.biz
Phone: (480) 820-9422
Inst. Accred.: NACCAS (1972/2003)

Mesa Campus
42 North Stapley Dr., Mesa 85203
Phone: (480) 964-8675

Laun and Associates, Inc.
4105 North 20th St., Ste. 100, Phoenix 85016
Type: Private, proprietary
Degrees: C
URL: http://www.dalecarnegieaz.com
Phone: (602) 954-8044
Inst. Accred.: ACCET (1977/2004)

Maricopa Beauty College
515 West Western Ave., Avondale 85323
Type: Private, proprietary
Degrees: C
URL: http://www.maricopabeautycollege.com
Phone: (623) 932-4414
Inst. Accred.: NACCAS (1982/2002)

Motorcycle and Marine Mechanics Institute
2844 West Deer Valley Rd., Phoenix 85027-9951
Type: Private, proprietary
Degrees: C
URL: http://www.uticorp.com
Phone: (623) 869-9644
Inst. Accred.: ACCSCT (1979/2004)

Orlando Campus
9751 Delegates Dr., Orlando, FL 32837-9835
Phone: (407) 240-2422

Mundus Institute
2001 West Camelback, Ste. 400, Phoenix 85015
Type: Private, proprietary
Degrees: C
URL: http://www.mundusinstitute.com
Phone: (602) 246-7111
Inst. Accred.: ACCSCT (1989/2004)

Pima Medical Institute—Albuquerque
2301 San Pedro Dr. NE, Ste. D, Albuquerque 87110-4149
Type: Private, proprietary
Degrees: C
URL: http://www.pmi.edu
Phone: (505) 881-1314
Inst. Accred.: ABHES (2001)

Pima Medical Institute—Mesa
941 South Dobson Rd., Mesa 85202
Type: Private, proprietary
Degrees: C
URL: http://www.pmi.edu
Phone: (480) 644-0267
Inst. Accred.: ABHES (2003), ACCSCT (1973/2003)
Prog. Accred.: Allied Health (respiratory therapy), Medical Assisting (ABHES), Radiography

Premier Training, Inc. Dale Carnegie Training
6121 East Broadway Blvd., Ste. 146, Tucson
Type: Private, proprietary
Degrees: C
URL: http://www.tucson.dalecarnegie.com
Phone: (520) 747-4664
Inst. Accred.: ACCET (1977/2004)

Quantum Helicopters
2370 South Airport Blvd., Chandler 85249
Type: Private, proprietary
Degrees: C
URL: http://www.quantumhelicopters.com
Phone: (480) 814-8118
Inst. Accred.: ACCSCT (2002)

Roberto-Venn School of Luthiery
4011 South 16th St., Phoenix 85040-1314
Type: Private, proprietary
Degrees: C
URL: http://www.roberto-venn.com
Phone: (602) 243-1179
Inst. Accred.: ACCSCT (1979/2004)

Sonoran Desert Institute
10245 East Via Linda, Ste. 102, Scottsdale 85258
Type: Private, proprietary
Degrees: C
URL: http://www.sonoranlearning.com
Phone: (480) 314-2102
Inst. Accred.: DETC (2004)

Southwest Institute of Healing Arts
1100 Apache Blvd., Tempe 85281
Type: Private, proprietary
Degrees: C
URL: http://www.swiha.org
Phone: (480) 994-9244
Inst. Accred.: ACCET (2003/2006)

Flagstaff Campus
1000 N. Humphreys St., Ste. 204, Flagstaff 86001-3125
Phone: (928) 213-0010

Toni & Guy Hairdressing Academy
7201 East Camelback Rd., Ste. 100, Scottsdale 85251
Type: Private, proprietary
Degrees: C
URL: http://www.toniguy.com
Phone: (480) 994-4222
Inst. Accred.: NACCAS (1988/2003)

Phoenix Campus
15210 South 50th St., Ste. 150, Phoenix 85044
Phone: (480) 940-5300

Tucson College
7310 East 22nd St., Tucson 85710
Type: Private, proprietary
System: Delta Education Corporation
Degrees: C
URL: http://www.tucsoncollege.edu
Phone: (520) 296-3261
Inst. Accred.: ACICS (1966/2003)

Tucson College of Beauty
3955 North Flowing Wells, Tucson 85705
Type: Private, proprietary
Degrees: C
URL: http://www.tucsoncollegeofbeauty.com
Phone: (520) 887-8262
Inst. Accred.: NACCAS (2005/2006)

Turning Point Beauty College, Inc.
1226 East Florence Blvd., Box #3, Casa Grande 85222
Type: Private, proprietary
Degrees: C
Phone: (520) 836-1476
Inst. Accred.: NACCAS (2003/2006)

ARKANSAS

Arkadelphia Beauty College
2708 Pine St., Arkadelphia 71923
Type: Private, proprietary
Degrees: C
URL: http://www.arkadelphiabeautycollege.com
Phone: (870) 246-6726
Inst. Accred.: NACCAS (1991/2006)

ABC Barber College
103 Brenda St., Hot Springs 71913
Phone: (501) 624-0885

Arkansas Beauty College
109 North Commerce Ave., Russellville 72801-3741
Type: Private, proprietary
Degrees: C
Phone: (479) 968-3075
Inst. Accred.: ACCSCT (2005)

Arkansas Beauty School
5108 Baseline Rd., Little Rock 72209
Type: Private, proprietary
Degrees: C
Phone: (501) 562-5673
Inst. Accred.: NACCAS (1990/2005)

Arkansas Beauty School—Conway
1061 Markham St., Conway 72032
Type: Private, proprietary
Degrees: C
Phone: (501) 329-8303
Inst. Accred.: NACCAS (1990/2003)

Arkansas College of Barbering and Hair Design
200 Washington Ave., North Little Rock 72114-5615
Type: Private, proprietary
Degrees: C
Phone: (501) 376-9696
Inst. Accred.: ACCSCT (1990/2005)

Arthur's Beauty College
2000 North B St., Fort Smith 72901
Type: Private, proprietary
Degrees: C
URL: http://www.arthursbeautycollege.com
Phone: (479) 783-3301
Inst. Accred.: NACCAS (1980/2005)

Arthur's Beauty College
2600 John Harden Dr., Jacksonville 72076
Type: Private, proprietary
Degrees: C
URL: http://www.arthursbeautycollege.com
Phone: (501) 982-8987
Inst. Accred.: NACCAS (1987/2004)

Conway Campus
2320 Washington Ave., Conway 72032
Phone: (50) /329-7770

Pine Bluff Campus
2710 Commerce Dr., Pine Bluff 71601
Phone: (870) 534-0498

Askins Vo-Tech, Inc.
7716 Hwy. 271 South, Fort Smith 72908
Type: Private, proprietary
Degrees: C
Phone: (479) 646-4803
Inst. Accred.: ACCET (1995/2003)

Bee-Jay's Hairstyling Academy
1907 Hinson Loop Rd., Little Rock 72212
Type: Private, proprietary
Degrees: C
URL: http://www.bjacademy.net
Phone: (501) 224-2442
Inst. Accred.: NACCAS (1978/2004)

Batesville Campus
130 West Main St., Batesville 72501
Phone: (501) 793-3898

Blytheville Academy of Cosmetology
100 East Main St., Blytheville 72315
Type: Private, proprietary
Degrees: C
Phone: (870) 763-6326
Inst. Accred.: NACCAS (1995/2006)

Ezp's College of Barbering
3983 Brainerd Rd., Chattanooga, TN 37411
Phone: (423) 316-9936

Career Academy of Hair Design
200 Holcomb St., Springdale 72764
Type: Private, proprietary
Degrees: C
URL: http://www.beautyschool.edu
Phone: (479) 756-6060
Inst. Accred.: NACCAS (1986/2006)

Cass Job Corps Center
21424 North Hwy. 23, Ozark 72949
Type: Public, federal
Degrees: C
Phone: (479) 667-3686
Inst. Accred.: COE (1998/2004)

Crossett School of Cosmetology LLC
121 Pine St., Crossett 71635
Type: Private, proprietary
Degrees: C
Phone: (870) 304-2545
Inst. Accred.: NACCAS (2004)

Crowley's Ridge Technical Institute
1620 Newcastle Rd., Forrest City 72335
Type: Public, local
Degrees: C
URL: http://www.crti.tec.ar.us
Phone: (870) 633-5411 *Calendar:* Sem. plan
Inst. Accred.: COE (2003)

Deluxe Beauty School
1609 West 26th Ave., Pine Bluff 71603-5257
Type: Private, proprietary
Degrees: C
Phone: (870) 534-7609
Inst. Accred.: NACCAS (1994/2002)

Eastern College of Health Vocations
6423 Forbing Rd., Little Rock 72209
Type: Private, proprietary
Degrees: C
URL: http://www.echv.com
Phone: (501) 568-0211
Inst. Accred.: ABHES (1984/2003)

Metairie Campus
201 Evans Rd., Ste. 400, New Orleans, LA 70123
Phone: (504) 885-3353
Prog. Accred: Medical Assisting (ABHES)

Shreveport Campus
9700 St. Vincent Ave., Shreveport, LA 71106
Phone: (318) 861-3246

Eaton Beauty Stylist College, Inc.
814 West Seventh St., Little Rock 72201
Type: Private, proprietary
Degrees: C
Phone: (501) 375-0211
Inst. Accred.: NACCAS (1995/2003)

Fayetteville Beauty College
2167-2177 West 6th St., Fayetteville 72701
Type: Private, proprietary
Degrees: C
Phone: (501) 442-5181
Inst. Accred.: NACCAS (1967/2004)

Hot Springs Beauty College
100 Cones Rd., Hot Springs 71901
Type: Private, proprietary
Degrees: C
Phone: (501) 624-0203
Inst. Accred.: NACCAS (1989/2004)

Jerry Wilson & Associates, Inc.
4 Shackleford Plaza, Ste. 100, Little Rock 72211
Type: Private, proprietary
Degrees: C
URL: http://www.arkansas.dalecarnegie.com
Phone: (501) 224-5000
Inst. Accred.: ACCET (1976/2007)

Lee's School of Cosmetology
2700 West Pershing Blvd., North Little Rock 72114
Type: Private, proprietary
Degrees: C
Phone: (501) 758-2800
Inst. Accred.: NACCAS (1987/2003)

Little Rock Job Corps Center
2020 Vance St., Little Rock 72206
Type: Public, federal
Degrees: C
URL: http://jobcorps.doleta.gov/centers
Phone: (501) 376-4600
Inst. Accred.: NCA-CASI (1995/2005)

Lynndale Fundamentals of Beauty School
1729 Champagnolle Rd., El Dorado 71730
Type: Private, proprietary
Degrees: C
Phone: (870) 863-3919
Inst. Accred.: NACCAS (2003/2006)

Margaret's Hair Academy, Inc.
502 Tyler Rd., Russellville 72812
Type: Private, proprietary
Degrees: C
Phone: (479) 890-0215
Inst. Accred.: NACCAS (1998/2006)

Monticello Campus
305 East Gaines St., Monticello 71655
Phone: (870) 367-5533

Marks-to Beauty Academy
PO Box 7646, Pine Bluff 71611-7646
Type: Private, proprietary
Degrees: C
URL: http://www.markstobeautyacademy.com
Phone: (870) 535-4111
Inst. Accred.: NACCAS (2007)

Marsha Kay Beauty College
408 Hwy. 201 North, Mountain Home 72653-3164
Type: Private, proprietary
Degrees: C
Phone: (870) 425-7575
Inst. Accred.: NACCAS (1984/2004)

Mellie's Beauty College
311 1/2 South Sixteenth St., Fort Smith 72901
Type: Private, proprietary
Degrees: C
Phone: (479) 782-5059
Inst. Accred.: NACCAS (1972/2003)

New Tyler Barber College
1221 East Seventh St., North Little Rock 72114-4973
Type: Private, proprietary
Degrees: C
Phone: (501) 375-0377
Inst. Accred.: ACCSCT (1984/2005)

Northwest Technical Institute
709 South Old Missouri Rd., Springdale 72764
Type: Private, proprietary
Degrees: C
URL: http://www.nti.tec.ar.us
Phone: (479) 751-8824
Inst. Accred.: COE (2003)
Prog. Accred.: Allied Health (surgical technology)

Professional Cosmetology Education Center
2027 North West Ave., El Dorado 71730
Type: Private, proprietary
Degrees: C
Phone: (870) 864-9292
Inst. Accred.: NACCAS (1982/2005)

Searcy Beauty College
1004 South Main St., Searcy 72143
Type: Private, proprietary
Degrees: C
Phone: (501) 268-6300
Inst. Accred.: NACCAS (1988/2003)

Velvatex College of Beauty Culture
1520 Dr. Martin Luther King Jr. Dr., Little Rock 72202
Type: Private, proprietary
Degrees: C
Phone: (501) 372-9678
Inst. Accred.: NACCAS (1997/2005)

CALIFORNIA

A-Technical College
1033 South Broadway St., Los Angeles 90015-4001
Type: Private, proprietary
Degrees: C
URL: http://www.virginiaschoolcenter.com
Phone: (213) 747-8292
Inst. Accred.: ACCET (1995/2006)

Absolute Safety Training Paramedic Program
78 Table Mountain Blvd., Oroville 95965
Type: Private, proprietary
Degrees: C
URL: http://www.absolutesafetytraining.org
Phone: (530) 934-7257
Inst. Accred.: ABHES (2005)
Prog. Accred.: Allied Health (EMT-paramedic)

Academy of Professional Careers
6160 Mission Gorge Rd., La Mesa 92120
Type: Private, proprietary
Degrees: C
URL: http://www.academyofhealthcareers.com/Academy
Phone: (619) 461-5100
Inst. Accred.: ACCET (1993/2005)

Amarillo Campus
2201 S. Western, Suites 102 & 103, Amarillo, TX 79109
Phone: (806) 353-3500

Boise Campus
8590 West Fairview Ave., Boise, ID 83704-8320
Phone: (208) 672-9500

Indio Campus
45-691 Monroe Ave., Indio 92201
Phone: (760) 347-5000

Academy of Radio and Television Broadcasting
16052 Beach Blvd., Ste. 263-N, Huntington Beach 92647
Type: Private, proprietary
Degrees: C
URL: http://www.arbradio.com
Phone: (714) 842-0100
Inst. Accred.: ACCET (1986/2002)

Phoenix Campus
4914 East McDowell Rd., Ste. 107, Phoenix, AZ 85008
Phone: (602) 267-8001

Adelante Career Institute
14547 Titus St., Ste. 100, Van Nuys 91402
Type: Private, proprietary
Degrees: C
URL: http://www.adelantecareerinstitute.com
Phone: (818) 908-9912
Inst. Accred.: ACCET (1990/2005)

Adrian's Beauty College of Turlock
1340 West Main St., Turlock 95380-5116
Type: Private, proprietary
Degrees: C
Phone: (209) 632-2233
Inst. Accred.: NACCAS (1986/2006)

Advance Beauty College
10121 Westminister Ave., Garden Grove 92843
Type: Public, proprietary
Degrees: C
URL: http://www.advancebeautycollege.com
Phone: (714) 530-2131
Inst. Accred.: NACCAS (2003/2006)

Advanced College
13180 Paramount Blvd., South Gate 90280
Type: Private, proprietary
Degrees: C
Phone: (562) 408-6969
Inst. Accred.: COE (2003)

AF International School of Languages, Inc
3625 Thousand Oaks Blvd., Westlake Village 91362
Type: Private, proprietary
Degrees: C
URL: http://www.afint.com
Phone: (805) 496-6694
Inst. Accred.: ACCET (2004)

Alameda Beauty College, Inc.
2318 Central Ave., Alameda 94501
Type: Private, proprietary
Degrees: C
Phone: (510) 523-1050
Inst. Accred.: NACCAS (1977/2004)

Alhambra Beauty College
200 West Main St., PO Box 7494, Alhambra 91802
Type: Private, proprietary
Degrees: C
Phone: (626) 282-7765
Inst. Accred.: NACCAS (1978/2003)

All American Career College
320 North East St., Ste. 513, San Bernardino 92401
Type: Private, proprietary
Degrees: C
Phone: (909) 884-5015
Inst. Accred.: COE (2003)

Allied Business Schools, Inc.
22952 Alcalde Dr., Ste. 150, Laguna Hills 92653
Type: Private, proprietary
Degrees: C
URL: http://www.alliedschools.com
Phone: (949) 598-0875
Inst. Accred.: DETC (2002/2006)

Allied Schools
22952 Alcalde Dr., Laguna Hills 92653
Phone: (949) 598-0875

American Academy of English
530 Golden Gate Ave., San Francisco 94102
Type: Private, proprietary
Degrees: C
URL: http://www.aaesl.com
Phone: (415) 567-0189
Inst. Accred.: ACCET (2001/2007)

American Auto Institute
17522 Studebaker Rd., Cerritos 90703
Type: Private, proprietary
Degrees: C
URL: http://www.americanautoinstitute.com
Phone: (562) 403-2660
Inst. Accred.: ACCSCT (2005)

American Beauty College
16512 Bellflower Blvd., Bellflower 90706
Type: Private, proprietary
Degrees: C
Phone: (562) 866-0728
Inst. Accred.: NACCAS (1977/2002)

American Career College
4021 Rosewood Ave., Los Angeles 90004-2932
Type: Private, proprietary
Degrees: C
URL: http://www.americancareer.com
Phone: (323) 668-7555
Inst. Accred.: ABHES (1983/2005), ACCSCT (2005)
Prog. Accred.: Allied Health (surgical technology)

Orange County Campus
1200 North Magnolia Ave., Anaheim 92801
Phone: (714) 952-9066
Prog. Accred: Allied Health (surgical technology)

American Career College—Norco
3299 Horseless Carriage Rd., Ste. C, Norco 92860
Type: Private, proprietary
Degrees: C
URL: http://www.americancareer.com
Phone: (951) 739-0788
Inst. Accred.: ABHES (2004)

American College of California
760 Market St., Ste. 1009, San Francisco 94102-2305
Type: Private, proprietary
Degrees: C
URL: http://www.acofca.com
Phone: (415) 677-9717
Inst. Accred.: ACCSCT (2004)

American College of Health Professions
3705 La Sierra Ave., Riverside 92505-3038
Type: Private, proprietary
Degrees: C
URL: http://www.achp.edu
Phone: (909) 307-6022 *Calendar:* Qtr. plan
Inst. Accred.: ABHES (1996/2004)
Prog. Accred.: Allied Health (surgical technology)

Riverside Campus
3715 La Sierra Ave., Riverside 92505
Phone: (951) 637-6900
Prog. Accred: Medical Assisting (ABHES), Surgical Technology

American English Academy
111 North Atlantic Blvd., Ste. 112, Monterey Park 91754
Type: Private, proprietary
Degrees: C
URL: http://www.aea-usa.com
Phone: (626) 457-2800
Inst. Accred.: ACCET (2005)

American Institute of Massage Therapy
1570 Brookhollow Dr., Ste. 200, Santa Ana 92705-5428
Type: Private, proprietary
Degrees: C
URL: http://www.aimtinc.com
Phone: (714) 432-7879
Inst. Accred.: ABHES (2004)

American Pacific College
14435 Sherman Way, Ste. 208, Van Nuys 91405
Type: Private, proprietary
Degrees: C
URL: http://www.apc.edu
Phone: (818) 781-0001
Inst. Accred.: ACCSCT (2006)

Los Angeles Campus
1526 West 7th St., Los Angeles 90017
Phone: (213) 251-9777

American Scientific Institute
3540 Wilshire Blvd., Ste. 200, Los Angeles 90010
Type: Private, proprietary
Degrees: C
URL: http://www.asi.edu
Phone: (323) 662-8800
Inst. Accred.: COE (2006)

Antelope Valley Medical College, Inc.
44201 10th St. West, Lancaster 93534
Type: Private, independent
Degrees: C
URL: http://www.antelopevalleymedicalcollege.com
Phone: (661) 726-1911
Inst. Accred.: ABHES (2001/2005)
Prog. Accred.: Allied Health (EMT-paramedic), Medical Assisting (ABHES)

Asian American International Beauty College
7871 Westminster Blvd., Westminster 92683
Type: Private, proprietary
Degrees: C
Phone: (714) 891-0508
Inst. Accred.: NACCAS (1994/2002)

ASPECT International Language Schools
One West Victoria St., Santa Barbara 93101
Type: Private, proprietary
Degrees: C
URL: http://www.aspectworld.com
Phone: (805) 564-8330
Inst. Accred.: ACCET (1992/2001)

Chicago Campus
3424 South State St., Chicago, IL 60616
Phone: (312) 328-0262

Franklin Campus
99 Main St., Franklin, MA 02038
Phone: (508) 541-1776

La Jolla Campus
1111 Torrey Pines Rd., La Jolla 92037
Phone: (858) 551-5750

Orlando Campus
4000 Central Florida Blvd., PC 620, Rm. 102B, Orlando, FL 32837-7662
Phone: (407) 823-3183

Riverdale Campus
4513 Manhattan Coll. Pkwy., de La Salle Hall, 4th Flr., Riverdale, NY 10471
Phone: (718) 549-4838

San Francisco Campus
530 Bush St., Ste. 500, San Francisco 94108
Phone: (415) 362-1588

Santa Barbara Campus
721 Cliff Dr., Building ECC #20, Santa Barbara 93109
Phone: (805) 966-1620

Whittier Campus
13509 Earlham Dr., PO Box 634, Whittier 90608
Phone: (562) 693-9023

Associated Technical College
1670 Wilshire Blvd., Los Angeles 90017-1690
Type: Private, proprietary
Degrees: C
URL: http://www.associatedtechcollege.com
Phone: (213) 353-1845
Inst. Accred.: ACCSCT (1969/2002)

Associated Technical College
1593 East Vista Way, Ste. C, Vista 92084
Type: Private, proprietary
Degrees: C
URL: http://www.associatedtechcollege.com
Phone: (760) 643-0505
Inst. Accred.: ACCSCT (1984/2006)

Associated Technical College
1445 Sixth Ave., San Diego 92101-3245
Type: Private, proprietary
Degrees: C
URL: http://www.associatedtechcollege.com
Phone: (619) 234-2181
Inst. Accred.: ACCSCT (1984/2003)

ATI College
12440 Firestone Blvd., Ste. 2001, Norwalk 90650
Type: Private, proprietary
Degrees: C
URL: http://www.ati.edu
Phone: (562) 864-0506
Inst. Accred.: ACCSCT (2002)

Tustin Campus
17821 East 17th St., Ste. 120, Tustin 92780
Phone: (714) 730-7080

Avalon Beauty College
504 North Milipas St., Santa Barbara 93103
Type: Private, proprietary
Degrees: C
Phone: (805) 966-1931
Inst. Accred.: NACCAS (2001/2004)

Avance Beauty College
750 Beyer Way, Ste. B-D, San Diego 92154
Type: Private, proprietary
Degrees: C
Phone: (619) 575-1511
Inst. Accred.: NACCAS (1987/2002)

Bay Vista College of Beauty
1520 Plaza Blvd., National City 91950
Type: Private, proprietary
Degrees: C
URL: http://www.sandiegobeautyacademy.com
Phone: (619) 474-6607
Inst. Accred.: NACCAS (1974/2006)

Brandon College
25 Kearny St., 2nd Flr., San Francisco 94108
Type: Private, proprietary
Degrees: C
URL: http://www.brandoncollege.com
Phone: (415) 391-5711
Inst. Accred.: ACCET (2000/2006)

Bridges Academy of Beauty
423 East Main St., Barstow 92311
Type: Private, proprietary
Degrees: C
Phone: (760) 256-0515
Inst. Accred.: NACCAS (2005)

Brownson Technical School
1110 Technology Circle, Ste. D, Anaheim 92805
Type: Private, proprietary
Degrees: C
URL: http://www.brownsontechnicalschool.com
Phone: (714) 774-9443
Inst. Accred.: ACCSCT (2002/2005)

California Beauty College
2627 West Florida Ave., Hemet 92545
Type: Private, proprietary
Degrees: C
Phone: (909) 766-5759
Inst. Accred.: NACCAS (1999/2002)

California Beauty College
1115 Fifteenth St., Modesto 95354
Type: Private, proprietary
Degrees: C
Phone: (209) 524-5184
Inst. Accred.: NACCAS (1977/2006)

California Beauty College
35871 Date Palm Dr., Cathedral City 92234
Type: Private, proprietary
Degrees: C
Phone: (760) 251-5373
Inst. Accred.: NACCAS (1999/2002)

California Career College
7108 De Soto Ave., Ste. 207, Canoga Park 91303
Type: Private, proprietary
Degrees: C
Phone: (818) 710-1310
Inst. Accred.: ABHES (2004)

California Career School
1100 Technology Circle, Anaheim 92805-6329
Type: Private, proprietary
Degrees: C
URL: http://www.californiacareerschool.edu
Phone: (714) 635-6585
Inst. Accred.: ACCSCT (1994/2005)

California College of Vocational Careers
2822 F St., Ste. L, Bakersfield 93301
Type: Private, proprietary
Degrees: C
URL: http://www.californiacollegevc.com
Phone: (661) 323-6791
Inst. Accred.: ABHES (2002)

California Cosmetology College, San Jose, Inc.
955 Monroe St., Santa Clara 95050
Type: Private, proprietary
Degrees: C
URL: http://www.cacosmetologycollege.com
Phone: (408) 247-2200
Inst. Accred.: NACCAS (1976/2005)

California Hair Design Academy
8011 University Ave., Auite A-2, La Mesa 91941-5020
Type: Private, proprietary
Degrees: C
Phone: (619) 461-8600
Inst. Accred.: NACCAS (1974/2006)

California Healing Arts College
12217 Santa Monica Blvd., Ste. 206, West Los Angeles 90025
Type: Private, proprietary
Degrees: C
Phone: (310) 826-7622
Inst. Accred.: ACCSCT (2002)

California Institute of the Healing Arts and Sciences
1111 Howe Ave., Ste. 150, Sacramento 95825
Type: Private, proprietary
Degrees: C
URL: http://www.californiainstitute.net
Phone: (916) 484-1700
Inst. Accred.: ACCET (2004)

California Learning Center
222 South Harbor Blvd., Ste. 200, Anaheim 92805
Type: Private, proprietary
Degrees: C
URL: http://ww.aboutclc.com
Phone: (714) 956-5656
Inst. Accred.: ACCSCT (2001/2006)

California Nurses Educational Institute
68-860 Perez Rd., Ste. E, Cathedral City 92234-7248
Type: Private, proprietary
Degrees: C
Phone: (760) 416-5955
Inst. Accred.: COE (2005)

California School of Modern Sciences
291 South La Cienega, Ste. 200, Beverly Hills 90211
Type: Private, proprietary
Degrees: C
Phone: (310) 657-9495
Inst. Accred.: ABHES (1999/2002)

Cambridge Career College
990-A Klamath Ln., Yuba City 95993
Type: Private, proprietary
Degrees: C
URL: http://www.cambridge.edu
Phone: (530) 674-9199
Inst. Accred.: ACICS (2003/2005)

Career Academy of Beauty—West Garden Grove
12471 Valley View Blvd., West Garden Grove 92845
Type: Private, proprietary
Degrees: C
URL: http://www.beautycareers.com
Phone: (704) 897-3010
Inst. Accred.: NACCAS (1977/2003)

Anaheim Campus
663 North Euclid St., Anaheim 92801-4622
Phone: (714) 776-8400

Career Care Institute
43770 15th St. West, Ste. 230, Lancaster 93534
Type: Private, proprietary
Degrees: C
URL: http://www.careercareinstitute.com
Phone: (661) 942-6204
Inst. Accred.: ABHES (2003/2006)

Ventura Campus
1730 South Victoria Ave., Ste. 230, Ventura 93003
Phone: (805) 477-0660
Prog. Accred: Medical Assisting (ABHES)

Career College Consultants, Inc.
5015 Eagle Rock Blvd., Ste. 302, Los Angeles 90041
Type: Private, proprietary
Degrees: C
URL: http://www.sticcc.com
Phone: (323) 254-2203
Inst. Accred.: ACCET (2006)

Career College of California
1720 East Garry Ave., Ste. 101, Santa Ana 92705-5808
Type: Private, proprietary
Degrees: C
URL: http://www.career-college.net
Phone: (949) 222-1033
Inst. Accred.: ACCET (2005)

Career Colleges of America
5612 East Imperial Hwy., South Gate 90280
Type: Private, proprietary
Degrees: C
URL: http://www.careercolleges.org
Phone: (562) 923-4222
Inst. Accred.: ACCET (1999/2006)
Prog. Accred.: Allied Health (surgical technology)

San Bernardino Campus
184 Club Center Dr., San Bernardino 92408
Phone: (909) 876-0919
Prog. Accred: Allied Health (surgical technology)

Casa Loma College
6850 Van Nuys Blvd., Ste. 318, Van Nuys 91405
Type: Private, independent
Degrees: C
URL: http://www.casalomacollege.com
Phone: (818) 785-2726
Inst. Accred.: ABHES (2002/2005)
Prog. Accred.: Medical Assisting (ABHES), Practical Nursing

Hawthorne Campus
12540 South Crenshaw Blvd., Hawthorne 90250-3327
Phone: (310) 290-6440
Prog. Accred: Medical Assisting (ABHES)

CBD College
5724 West Third St., Ste. 314, Los Angeles 90036
Type: Private, proprietary
Degrees: C
URL: http://www.cbdcollege.com
Phone: (323) 937-7772
Inst. Accred.: ACCET (1997/2000)

The Center for Seabees and Facilities Engineering
3502 Godspeed St., Ste. 2, Port Hueneme 93043
Type: Public, federal
Degrees: C
URL: https://www.npdc.navy.mil/csfe
Phone: (805) 982-3300
Inst. Accred.: COE (2005)

Central California School of Continuing Education
271 Ott St., Ste. 23, Corona 91720
Type: Private, proprietary
Degrees: C
URL: http://www.ccsce.org
Phone: (909) 549-0693
Inst. Accred.: ACCSCT (1992/2006)
Prog. Accred.: Radiography

San Luis Obispo Campus
3195 McMillan Ave., Ste. F, San Luis Obispo 93401-6739
Phone: (909) 543-9123

Central Coast College
480 South Main St., Salinas 93901
Type: Private, proprietary
Degrees: C
URL: http://www.centralcoastcollege.edu
Phone: (831) 424-6767
Inst. Accred.: ACCET (1989/2005)
Prog. Accred.: Medical Assisting (ABHES)

Champion Institute of Cosmetology
611 South Palm Canyon Dr., Ste. 22, Palm Springs 92264
Type: Private, proprietary
Degrees: C
Phone: (760) 322-2227
Inst. Accred.: NACCAS (2005)

Clarita Career College
27125 Sierra Hwy., Ste. 329, Canyon Country 91351
Type: Private, proprietary
System: Prospect Colleges, LLC
Degrees: C
URL: http://www.claritacareercollege.com
Phone: (661) 252-1864
Inst. Accred.: ACCSCT (1998/2003)

CNI Vocational College
3420 Bristol St., Ste. 209, Costa Mesa 92626
Type: Private, proprietary
Degrees: C
URL: http://www.cnicollege.edu
Phone: (714) 437-9697
Inst. Accred.: ABHES (1997/2006)

Orange Campus
986 Town and Country Rd., Orange 92868
Phone: (714) 437-9697
Prog. Accred: Allied Health (surgical technology)

Coachella Valley Beauty College
47120 Dune Palms Rd., Ste. D, LaQuinta 92553
Type: Private, proprietary
Degrees: C
Phone: (760) 772-5950
Inst. Accred.: NACCAS (2006)

Coast Career Institute
1354 South Hill St., Los Angeles 90015
Type: Private, proprietary
Degrees: C
URL: http://www.coastcareer.com
Phone: (213) 747-8676
Inst. Accred.: ACCSCT (2007)

Van Nuys Campus
14545 Victory Blvd., 2nd Flr., Van Nuys 91401
Phone: (818) 997-7227

Coastline Beauty College
10840 Warner Ave., Ste. 207, Fountain Valley 92708
Type: Private, proprietary
Degrees: C
URL: http://www.coastlinebeauty.com
Phone: (714) 963-4000
Inst. Accred.: NACCAS (2005/2006)

COBA Academy
102 North Glasselll St., Orange 92866
Type: Private, proprietary
Degrees: C
URL: http://www.coba.edu
Phone: (714) 633-5950
Inst. Accred.: NACCAS (2000/2003)

Colleen O'Hara's Beauty Academy—Santa Ana
109 West 4th St., 2nd Flr., Santa Ana 92701
Type: Private, proprietary
Degrees: C
URL: http://www.californiabeautyschool.com
Phone: (714) 568-5399
Inst. Accred.: NACCAS (1990/2002)

College of Career Training
7220 Fair Oaks Blvd., Ste. A, Carmichael 95608
Type: Private, proprietary
Degrees: C
URL: http://www.collegeofcareertraining.com
Phone: (916) 481-9001
Inst. Accred.: COE (2005)

College of Information Technology
2701 East Chapman Ave., Ste. 101, Fullerton 92831
Type: Private, proprietary
Degrees: C
URL: http://www.collegeofit.com
Phone: (714) 879-5100
Inst. Accred.: ACCSCT (2004, Probation)

Community Business College
3800 McHenry Ave., Ste. M, Modesto 95356
Type: Private, proprietary
Degrees: C
URL: http://www.communitybusinessschool.com
Phone: (209) 529-3648
Inst. Accred.: ACCSCT (2001, Probation)

Community Enhancement Services Adult Education Division
3251 West 6th St., Los Angeles 90020
Type: Private, independent
Degrees: C
URL: http://eduinla.com
Phone: (213) 381-5220
Inst. Accred.: ACCET (2002/2005)

Computer Tutor Business and Technical Institute
4306 Sisk Rd., Modesto 95356
Type: Private, proprietary
Degrees: C
URL: http://www.computertutor.com
Phone: (209) 545-5200
Inst. Accred.: ACCSCT (2003)

Concorde Career College
201 East Airport Dr., Ste. A, San Bernardino 92408
Type: Private, proprietary
System: Concorde Career Colleges, Inc.
Degrees: C *Enroll:* 717
URL: http://www.concordecareercolleges.com
Phone: (909) 884-8891
Inst. Accred.: ACCSCT (1968/2005)
Prog. Accred.: Allied Health (surgical technology), Practical Nursing

Courtesy Career College
8399 Topanga Canyon Blvd., Ste. 200, West Hills 91307
Type: Private, proprietary
Degrees: C
URL: http://courtesycareercollege.com
Phone: (818) 883-9002
Inst. Accred.: ABHES (2006)

CSI Career College
611-K Orange Dr., Vacaville 95687
Type: Private, proprietary
Degrees: C
URL: http://www.traincsi.com
Phone: (707) 455-0557
Inst. Accred.: COE (2004/2005)

Cynthia's Beauty Academy
4130 East Gage Ave., Bell 90201
Type: Private, proprietary
System: B&H Education, Inc.
Degrees: C
Phone: (323) 560-2207
Inst. Accred.: NACCAS (1979/2005)

Dale Carnegie of San Diego
9444 Waples St., Ste. 430, San Diego 92121
Type: Private, proprietary
Degrees: C
URL: http://www.dalecarnegieofsandiego.com
Phone: (858) 452-6444
Inst. Accred.: ACCET (2006)

Dale Carnegie Training of Central California
7208 Darrin Ave., Bakersfield 93305
Type: Private, proprietary
Degrees: C
URL: http://www.centralcalif.dalecarnegie.com
Phone: (661) 393-5050
Inst. Accred.: ACCET (1983/2003)

Dale Carnegie Training of San Joaquin Valley
4629 Pine Valley Circle, Stockton 95202
Type: Private, proprietary
Degrees: C
URL: http://www.modesto.dalecarnegie.com
Phone: (209) 478-3561
Inst. Accred.: ACCET (2006)

Deep Creek Construction School
8280 Deep Creek Rd., Apple Valley 92308
Type: Private, proprietary
Degrees: C
URL: http://www.constructionschool.net
Phone: (760) 240-3045
Inst. Accred.: ACCSCT (2006)

Designs School of Cosmetology
715 24th St., Ste. E, Paso Robles 93446
Type: Private, proprietary
Degrees: C
URL: http://www.designsschool.edu
Phone: (805) 237-8575
Inst. Accred.: NACCAS (2001/2004)

Pleasanton Campus
5572 Springdale Ave., Pleasanton 94588
Phone: (800) 939-9051

Diversified Language Institute—San Diego
1403 Sixth Ave., San Diego 92101
Type: Private, proprietary
Degrees: C
URL: http://www.dliusa.com
Phone: (619) 234-4354
Inst. Accred.: ACCET (2003)

DVS College
3325 Wilshire Blvd., Ste. 200, Los Angeles 90010
Type: Private, proprietary
Degrees: C
URL: http://www.dvusa.com
Phone: (213) 639-1470
Inst. Accred.: ABHES (2000/2005)

Montclair Campus
9740 Central Ave., Montclair 91763
Phone: (909) 447-6750
Prog. Accred: Medical Assisting (ABHES)

Elegance International
1622 North Highland Ave., Hollywood 90028
Type: Private, proprietary
Degrees: C
URL: http://www.eleganceacademy.com
Phone: (323) 871-8318 *Calendar:* Sem. plan
Inst. Accred.: ACCSCT (1978/2004)

Elite Beauty College
8528 Westminster Blvd., Westminster 92683
Type: Private, proprietary
Degrees: C
Phone: (714) 741-0700
Inst. Accred.: NACCAS (1998/2006)

Garden Grove Campus
12141 Brookhurst St., Ste. 101, Garden Grove 92840
Phone: (714) 741-0700

Elite Progressive School of Cosmetology
5522 Garfield Ave., Sacramento 95841
Type: Private, proprietary
Degrees: C
URL: http://www.eliteacademies.com
Phone: (916) 338-1885
Inst. Accred.: ACCSCT (2000/2005, Probation)

Emergency Training Services, Inc.
3050 Paul Sweet Rd., Santa Cruz 95065
Type: Private, proprietary
Degrees: C
URL: http://www.etsclassroom.com
Phone: (831) 476-8813
Inst. Accred.: ABHES (2003/2006)
Prog. Accred.: Allied Health (EMT-paramedic)

English Center for International Women
PO Box 9968, Mills College, 5000 MacArthur Blvd., Oakland 94613
Type: Private, independent
Degrees: C
URL: http://www.eciw.org
Phone: (510) 430-2234
Inst. Accred.: ACCET (1985/2005)

English Language Institute
760 Market St., #401-4, San Francisco 94102
Type: Private, proprietary
Degrees: C
URL: http://www.elisf.com
Phone: (415) 544-0311
Inst. Accred.: ACCET (1999/2005)

Market Street Campus
1177 Polk St., Ste. 200, San Francisco 94109
Phone: (415) 771-4070

Estes Institute of Cosmetology Arts and Sciences
324 East Main St., Visalia 93291
Type: Private, proprietary
Degrees: C
Phone: (209) 733-3617
Inst. Accred.: NACCAS (1980/2004)

Everest College—Alhambra
2215 West Mission Rd., Alhambra 91803
Type: Private, proprietary
System: Corinthian Colleges, Inc
Degrees: C
URL: http://www.everest.edu
Phone: (626) 979-4940
Inst. Accred.: ACCSCT (1968/2004)
Prog. Accred.: Allied Health (medical assisting (AMA))

Everest College—Anaheim
511 North Brookhurst, Ste. 300, Anaheim 92801
Type: Private, proprietary
System: Corinthian Colleges, Inc
Degrees: C
URL: http://www.everest.edu
Phone: (714) 953-6500
Inst. Accred.: ACCSCT (1973/2002)
Prog. Accred.: Allied Health (medical assisting (AMA))

Everest College—Gardena
1045 West Redondo Beach Blvd., Ste. 275, Gardena 90247
Type: Private, proprietary
System: Corinthian Colleges, Inc
Degrees: C
URL: http://www.everest.edu
Phone: (310) 527-7105
Inst. Accred.: ACCSCT (1973/2002)
Prog. Accred.: Allied Health (medical assisting (AMA))

Norcross Campus
1750 Beaver Ruin Rd., Ste. 500, Norcross, GA 30093
Phone: (770) 921-1085

Everest College—Hayward
22336 Main St., First Flr., Hayward 94541
Type: Private, proprietary
System: Corinthian Colleges, Inc
Degrees: C
URL: http://www.everest.edu
Phone: (510) 582-9500
Inst. Accred.: ACCSCT (1973/2006)
Prog. Accred.: Allied Health (surgical technology)

Everest College—Los Angeles
3460 Wilshire Blvd., Ste. 500, Los Angeles 90010
Type: Private, proprietary
System: Corinthian Colleges, Inc
Degrees: C
URL: http://www.everest.edu
Phone: (213) 388-9950
Inst. Accred.: ACCSCT (1962/2005)
Prog. Accred.: Allied Health (medical assisting (AMA))

Everest College—Reseda
18040 Sherman Way, Ste. 400, Reseda 91335-4631
Type: Private, proprietary
System: Corinthian Colleges, Inc
Degrees: C
URL: http://www.everest.edu
Phone: (818) 774-0550
Inst. Accred.: ACCSCT (1974/2006)
Prog. Accred.: Allied Health (surgical technology), Medical Assisting (ABHES)

Everest College—San Francisco
814 Mission St., Ste. 500, San Francisco 94103
Type: Private, proprietary
System: Corinthian Colleges, Inc
Degrees: C
URL: http://www.everest.edu
Phone: (415) 777-2500
Inst. Accred.: ACCSCT (1972/2002, Probation)
Prog. Accred.: Allied Health (medical assisting (AMA))

Chicago Campus
247 South State St., Ste. 400, Chicago, IL 60604
Phone: (312) 913-1616

Everest College—San Jose
1245 South Winchester Blvd., Ste. 102, San Jose 95128
Type: Private, proprietary
System: Corinthian Colleges, Inc
Degrees: C
URL: http://www.everest.edu
Phone: (408) 246-4171
Inst. Accred.: ACCSCT (1973/2003)
Prog. Accred.: Allied Health (medical assisting (AMA))

Everest College—Torrance
1231 Cabrillo Ave., Ste. 201, Torrance 90501
Type: Private, proprietary
System: Corinthian Colleges, Inc
Degrees: C
URL: http://www.everest.edu
Phone: (310) 320-3200
Inst. Accred.: ACCSCT (2004)

Fashion Design Training Center
38268 6th St. East, Palmdale 93550-4635
Type: Private, proprietary
Degrees: C
URL: http://www.fashiondtc.com
Phone: (661) 947-0038
Inst. Accred.: ACCET (2006)

Federico Beauty Institute
1515 Sports Dr., Sacramento 95834
Type: Private, proprietary
Degrees: C
URL: http://www.federicocollege.com
Phone: (916) 929-4242
Inst. Accred.: NACCAS (1967/2005)

FLS International
101 East Green St., Ste. 14, Pasadena 91105
Type: Private, proprietary
Degrees: C
URL: http://www.fls.net
Phone: (626) 795-2912
Inst. Accred.: ACCET (2000/2003)

Franklin Campus
99 Main St., Franklin, MA 02038
Phone: (626) 795-2912

Glendora Campus
1000 West Foothill Blvd., Glendora 91741
Phone: (626) 852-0075

Las Vegas Campus
6375 West Charleston Blvd., Las Vegas, NV 89146
Phone: (702) 651-5653

Lock Haven Campus
151 Susquehanna Ave., Lock Haven, PA 17745
Phone: (570) 893-8474

Oceanside Campus
One Barnard Dr., MiraCosta College, Oceanside 92056
Phone: (760) 795-6663

Oxnard Campus
4000 South Rose Ave., Oxnard 93030
Phone: (805) 986-8200

St. George Campus
225 South 700 East, St. George, UT 84770
Phone: (435) 652-7758

Four-D College
1020 East Washington St., Colton 92324-4117
Type: Private, proprietary
Degrees: C
URL: http://www.4Dcollege.com
Phone: (909) 783-9331
Inst. Accred.: ABHES (1996/2006)

Franklin Career College
1274 Slater Circle, Ontario 91761
Type: Private, proprietary
Degrees: C
URL: http://www.franklincareercollege.com
Phone: (909) 937-9007
Inst. Accred.: ACCET (2005)

Fredrick and Charles Beauty College
831 F St., Eureka 95501
Type: Private, proprietary
Degrees: C
Phone: (707) 443-2733
Inst. Accred.: NACCAS (1976/2003)

Galen College of Medical and Dental Assistants
1325 North Wishon Ave., Fresno 93728-2381
Type: Private, proprietary
Degrees: C
URL: http://www.galencollege.com
Phone: (559) 264-9726
Inst. Accred.: ACCSCT (1974/2003)

Modesto Campus
1604 Ford Ave., Ste. 10, Modesto 95350-4665
Phone: (209) 527-5100

Visalia Campus
3908 West Caldwell, Ste. A, Visalia 93277
Phone: (559) 732-5200

Gates College
4450 West 182nd St., Redondo Beach 90278
Type: Private, proprietary
Degrees: C
URL: http://www.gatescollege.com
Phone: (310) 542-4411 *Calendar:* Qtr. plan
Inst. Accred.: ACCSCT (2003)

GEOS English Academy
949 South Coast Dr., Ste. 450, Costa Mesa 92626
Type: Private, proprietary
Degrees: C
URL: http://www.geos.net
Phone: (714) 662-7413
Inst. Accred.: ACCET (1999/2006)

Boston Campus
40 Ct. St., Ste. 402, Boston, MA 02108
Phone: (617) 277-4600

Honolulu Campus
2222 Kalakaua Ave., Ste. 601, Honolulu, HI 96815
Phone: (808) 924-7733

New York Campus
350 5th Ave., Ste. 612, New York, NY 10118
Phone: (646) 674-0001

San Francisco Campus
1 Sutter St., Ste. 400, San Francisco 94104-4921
Phone: (415) 392-6852

Torrance Campus
21515 Hawthorne Blvd., Ste. G120, Torrance 90503
Phone: (310) 792-7270

Glendale Career College
1015 Grandview Ave., Glendale 91201
Type: Private, proprietary
Degrees: C
URL: http://www.success.edu
Phone: (757) 446-2799
Inst. Accred.: ACCET (1988/2005)
Prog. Accred.: Allied Health (surgical technology)

Nevada Career Institute—East Campus
3025 East Desert Inn Rd., Ste. A, Las Vegas, NV 89121
Phone: (702) 893-3300
Prog. Accred: Allied Health (surgical technology)

Nevada Career Institute—West Campus
3231 North Decatur Blvd., Ste. 250, Las Vegas, NV 89130

Oceanside Campus
2204 El Camino Real, Ste. 315, Oceanside 92054-6306
Phone: (760) 450-0340
Prog. Accred: Allied Health (surgical technology)

Gnomon School of Visual Effects
1015 North Cahuenga Blvd., Ste. 5430i, Hollywood 90038
Type: Private, proprietary
Degrees: C
URL: http://www.gnomonschool.com
Phone: (323) 466-6663
Inst. Accred.: COE (2005)

Golden Gate Language Schools
591 West Hamilton Ave., Ste. 101, Campbell 95008-0521
Type: Private, proprietary
Degrees: C
URL: http://www.goldengatelanguage.com
Phone: (408) 374-9954
Inst. Accred.: ACCET (2003)

Golden State College
3356 South Fairway St., Visalia 93277-8109
Type: Private, proprietary
Degrees: C
URL: http://www.goldenstatecollege.com
Phone: (559) 735-3818
Inst. Accred.: ACCET (1987/2001, Warning)

Fairfield Campus
934 Missouri St., Ste. K,L,Q, Fairfield 94585
Phone: (707) 425-2288

Hair California Beauty Academy
1110 North Tustin St., Orange 92867
Type: Private, proprietary
Degrees: C
URL: http://hairca.com
Phone: (714) 633-7170
Inst. Accred.: NACCAS (2004)

Hair Masters University of Beauty
208-210 West Highland Ave., San Bernadino 92405
Type: Private, proprietary
Degrees: C
Phone: (909) 882-2987
Inst. Accred.: NACCAS (1979/2004)

Healthy Hair Academy, Inc.
2648 West Imperial Hwy., Inglewood 90303
Type: Private, proprietary
Degrees: C
URL: http://www.healthyhairacademy.org
Phone: (310) 671-0614
Inst. Accred.: NACCAS (2005)

Heartwood Institute
220 Harmony Ln., Garberville 95542
Type: Private, proprietary
Degrees: C
URL: http://www.heartwoodinstitute.com
Phone: (707) 923-5000
Inst. Accred.: ACCET (1998/2001)

High-Tech Institute—Sacramento
9738 Lincoln Village Dr., Ste. 100, Sacramento 95827
Type: Private, proprietary
System: High-Tech Institute
Degrees: C
URL: http://www.hightechinstitute.edu
Phone: (916) 929-9700
Inst. Accred.: ACCSCT (1994/2005)
Prog. Accred.: Medical Assisting (ABHES)

Hilltop Beauty School
6317 Mission St., Daly City 94014
Type: Private, proprietary
Degrees: C
URL: http://www.hilltopbeautyschool.com
Phone: (650) 756-2720
Inst. Accred.: NACCAS (1979/2004)

Hypnosis Motivation Institute
18607 Ventura Blvd., Ste. 310, Tarzana 91356
Type: Private, proprietary
Degrees: C
URL: http://www.hypnosismotivation.com
Phone: (800) 600-0464
Inst. Accred.: ACCET (1987/2001, Warning), DETC (1989/2003, Warning)

ICDC College
6363 Wilshire Blvd., Ste. 600, Los Angeles 90048
Type: Private, proprietary
Degrees: C
URL: http://www.learncareer.com
Phone: (323) 655-9100
Inst. Accred.: ACCSCT (1999/2004)

Huntington Park Campus
6330 Pacific Blvd., Ste. 200, Huntington Park 90255
Phone: (323) 277-1900

Lawndale Campus
4415 Redondo Beach Blvd., Lawndale 90260
Phone: (310) 793-4100

San Fernando Valley Campus
14434 Sherman Way, Van Nuys 91405
Phone: (818) 787-0007

Institute for Business and Technology
2400 Walsh Ave., Santa Clara 95050
Type: Private, proprietary
System: Delta Education Corporation
Degrees: C
URL: http://www.ibttech.com
Phone: (408) 727-1060
Inst. Accred.: ACCSCT (1979/2002)

Institute of Network Technology
2727 East Willow St., Signal Hill 90806
Type: Private, proprietary
Degrees: C
Phone: (562) 424-9200
Inst. Accred.: ACCSCT (2001/2004)

Institute of Technology
564 West Herndon Ave., Clovis 93612
Type: Private, proprietary
Degrees: C
URL: http://www.it-colleges.com
Phone: (559) 297-4500
Inst. Accred.: ACCSCT (1991/2006)

Culinary Arts Campus
333 Sunrise Ave., Ste. 400, Roseville 95661
Phone: (916) 797-6337

Mather Campus
3695 Bleckley St., Mather 95655
Phone: (916) 363-4300

Modesto Campus
5737 Stoddard Rd., Modesto 95356
Phone: (209) 545-3100

Integrated Digital Technologies
2555 East Colorado Blvd., Ste. 200, Pasadena 91107
Type: Private, proprietary
Degrees: C
URL: http://www.idtnetwork.com
Phone: (626) 585-6300
Inst. Accred.: ACCSCT (2001/2006)

InterCoast Colleges
3745 West Chapman Ave., Orange 92868
Type: Private, proprietary
Degrees: C
URL: http://www.intercoastcolleges.com
Phone: (714) 712-7900 *Calendar:* Sem. plan
Inst. Accred.: ACCET (1988/2007)

Burbank Campus
401 South Glenoaks Blvd., Ste. 211, Burbank 91502
Phone: (818) 500-8400

Portland, Maine Campus
207 Gannett Dr., South Portland, ME 04106
Phone: (207) 822-9802

Riverside Campus
1115 Spruce St., Ste. C, Riverside 92507
Phone: (909) 779-0700

West Covina Campus
1400 West Covina Pkwy., Second Flr., West Covina 91790-2731
Phone: (626) 337-6800

International Academy of Cosmetology
4085 Tweedy Blvd., South Gate 90280
Type: Private, proprietary
Degrees: C
URL: http://www.internationalacademyofcosmetology.com
Phone: (323) 249-0270
Inst. Accred.: NACCAS (2005)

International Center for American English
1012 Prospect St., #200, La Jolla 92037
Type: Private, proprietary
Degrees: C
URL: http://www.icae-lajolla.com
Phone: (858) 456-1212
Inst. Accred.: ACCET (1993/2001)

International Christian Education College
3807 Wilshire Blvd., Ste. 730, Los Angeles 90010
Type: Private, proprietary
Degrees: C
Phone: (213) 368-0316
Inst. Accred.: ACCSCT (2001/2006)

International School of Beauty, Inc.
72-261 State Hwy. 111, Ste. 121-B, Palm Desert 92260
Type: Private, proprietary
Degrees: C
URL: http://www.internationalschoolofbeauty.com
Phone: (760) 674-1624
Inst. Accred.: NACCAS (2005)

Indio Campus
81695 Hwy. 111, Ste. 1, Indio 92201
Phone: (760) 775-6600

International School of Cosmetology, Inc.
13613 Hawthorne Blvd., Hawthorne 90250
Type: Private, proprietary
Degrees: C
Phone: (310) 973-7774
Inst. Accred.: NACCAS (1979/2002)

INTRAX English Institute
2226 Bush St., San Francisco 94115
Type: Private, proprietary
Degrees: C
URL: http://www.intraxenglish.com
Phone: (415) 434-1221
Inst. Accred.: ACCET (1996/2005)

Chicago Campus
174 North Michigan Ave., 2nd Flr., Chicago, IL 60601
Phone: (312) 236-3208

San Diego Campus
1250 Sixth Ave., Ste. 300A, San Diego 92101
Phone: (619) 702-6300

San Francisco Campus
551 Sutter St., San Francisco 94105
Phone: (415) 835-4766

James Albert School of Cosmetology
281 East 17th St., Costa Mesa 92627
Type: Private, proprietary
Degrees: C
Phone: (949) 642-0606
Inst. Accred.: NACCAS (1999/2002)

Anaheim Campus
2289 West Ball Rd., Anaheim 92804
Phone: (714) 774-8736

Je Boutique College of Beauty
1073 East Main St., El Cajon 92021
Type: Private, proprietary
Degrees: C
URL: http://www.sandiegobeautyacademy.com
Phone: (619) 442-3407
Inst. Accred.: NACCAS (1974/2006)

John Tracy Clinic
806 West Adams Blvd., Los Angeles 90007
Type: Private, proprietary
Degrees: C
URL: http://www.jtc.org
Phone: (213) 748-5481
Inst. Accred.: DETC (1965/2004)

John Wesley International Barber and Beauty College
717 Pine Ave., Long Beach 90813
Type: Private, proprietary
Degrees: C
URL: http://www.johnwesleybarberandbeauty.com
Phone: (562) 435-7060
Inst. Accred.: NACCAS (1994/2002)

Joint Intelligence Training Activity, Pacific
3955 North Harbor Dr., San Diego 92101-1031
Type: Public, federal
Degrees: C
URL: http://www.fas.org/irp/agency/dod/uspacom/jitap/index.html
Phone: (619) 524-5814
Inst. Accred.: COE (2002)

Kensington College
2428 North Grand Ave., Ste. D, Santa Ana 92705-8708
Type: Private, proprietary
Degrees: C
URL: http://www.kensingtoncollege.net
Phone: (714) 542-8086
Inst. Accred.: ACICS (1998/2005)

Kitchen Academy
6370 West Sunset Blvd., Hollywood 90028
Type: Private, proprietary
Degrees: C
URL: http://www.kitchenacademy.com
Phone: (626) 406-0984
Inst. Accred.: ACICS (2006)

Sacramento Campus
2450 Del Paso Rd., Sacramento 95834

Konocti College of Holistic Studies
PO Box 1358, Kelseyville 95451
Type: Private, proprietary
Degrees: C
URL: http://www.konocticollege.com
Phone: (707) 279-2539
Inst. Accred.: ABHES (2007)

Ladera Career Paths Training Center
6820 La Tijera Blvd., Ste. 217, Los Angeles 90045
Type: Private, proprietary
Degrees: C
URL: http://www.laderacareerpathsinc.com
Phone: (310) 568-0244
Inst. Accred.: ACCSCT (2004)

Lake College
2655 Bechelli Ln., Redding 96002
Type: Private, proprietary
Degrees: C
URL: http://www.lakecollege.edu
Phone: (530) 224-7227
Inst. Accred.: ACCSCT (2003/2006)

Lake Forest Beauty College
23600 Rockfield Blvd., Ste. C-3, Lake Forest 92630
Type: Private, proprietary
Degrees: C
Phone: (949) 951-8883
Inst. Accred.: NACCAS (1983/2006)

Lancaster Beauty School
44646 North 10th St. West, Lancaster 93534
Type: Private, proprietary
Degrees: C
URL: http://www.lancasterbeautyschool.com
Phone: (661) 948-1672
Inst. Accred.: NACCAS (1975/2002)

Language Studies International
1706 Fifth Ave., 3rd Flr., San Diego 92101
Type: Private, proprietary
Degrees: C
URL: http://www.lsi.edu/englisch
Phone: (619) 234-2881
Inst. Accred.: ACCET (1997/2005)

Berkeley Campus
2015 Center St., Berkeley 94704
Phone: (510) 841-4695

Boston Campus
105 Beach St., Boston, MA 02111
Phone: (617) 542-3600

New York Campus
75 Varick St., New York, NY
Phone: (212) 965-9940

Leicester School
1940 South Figueroa St., Los Angeles 90007
Type: Private, independent
Degrees: C
Phone: (213) 746-7666
Inst. Accred.: ACCSCT (1992/2004, Probation)

Liberty Training Institute
2706 Wilshire Blvd., 2nd Flr., Los Angeles 90057
Type: Private, proprietary
Degrees: C
URL: http://www.vocrehab.net/liberty
Phone: (213) 383-9545
Inst. Accred.: ACCSCT (2001/2006, Probation)

Lola Beauty College
11883 Valley View St., Garden Grove 92645
Type: Private, proprietary
Degrees: C
Phone: (714) 894-3366
Inst. Accred.: NACCAS (1977/2002)

Los Angeles ORT Technical Institute
6435 Wilshire Blvd., Los Angeles 90048
Type: Private, independent
Degrees: C
URL: http://www.laort.com
Phone: (323) 966-5444
Inst. Accred.: ACCET (1988/2005)

Chicago Campus
3050 West Touhy Ave., Chicago, IL 60645
Phone: (773) 761-5900

Valley Campus
15130 Ventura Blvd., Ste. 250, Sherman Oaks 91403-2122
Phone: (818) 382-6000

Zarem/Golde ORT Technical Institute—Skokie
5440 West Fargo Ave., Skokie, IL 60077
Phone: (847) 324-5588

Los Angeles Recording School
6690 Sunset Blvd., Hollywood 90028
Type: Private, proprietary
Degrees: C
URL: http://www.recordingcareer.com
Phone: (323) 464-5200
Inst. Accred.: ACCET (1989/2006)

Lyle's Bakersfield College of Beauty
2935 F St., Bakersfield 93301
Type: Private, proprietary
Degrees: C
Phone: (661) 327-9784
Inst. Accred.: NACCAS (1975/2005)

Lyle's College of Beauty
6735 North First St., Ste. 112, Fresno 93710
Type: Private, proprietary
Degrees: C
Phone: (559) 431-6060
Inst. Accred.: NACCAS (1994/2002)

Lyle's Fresno College of Beauty
3125 West Shaw Ave., Fresno 93711
Type: Private, proprietary
Degrees: C
Phone: (559) 222-6060
Inst. Accred.: NACCAS (1974/2005)

Lytle's Redwood Empire Beauty College, Inc.
186 Wikiup Dr., Santa Rosa 95403
Type: Private, proprietary
Degrees: C
URL: http://www.lytles-rebc.com
Phone: (707) 545-8490
Inst. Accred.: NACCAS (1976/2002)

Madera Beauty College
325 North Gateway Dr., Madera 93637
Type: Private, proprietary
Degrees: C
Phone: (559) 673-9201
Inst. Accred.: NACCAS (1977/2004)

Make-Up Designory
129 South San Fernando Blvd., Burbank 91502
Type: Private, proprietary
Degrees: C
URL: http://www.mud.edu
Phone: (818) 729-9420
Inst. Accred.: ACCSCT (2003)

Manchester Beauty College
3756 North Blackstone Ave., Fresno 93726
Type: Private, proprietary
Degrees: C
Phone: (559) 224-4242
Inst. Accred.: NACCAS (1974/2005)

Maria Montessori TTC
678 Portola Dr., San Francisco 94127
Type: Private, independent
Degrees: C
Phone: (415) 731-8188
Inst. Accred.: MACTE (2002)

Marian Health Careers Center
3325 Wilshire Blvd., Ste. 1010, Los Angeles 90010
Type: Private, proprietary
Degrees: C
URL: http://www.mariancollege-california.com
Phone: (213) 388-3566
Inst. Accred.: ABHES (1999/2002)

Van Nuys Campus
5900 North Sepulveda Blvd., Ste. 101, Van Nuys 91411
Phone: (818) 782-6163

Maric College—North Hollywood
6180 Laurel Canyon Blvd., Ste. 101, North Hollywood 91606-3231
Type: Private, proprietary
System: Kaplan Higher Education Corporation
Degrees: C
URL: http://www.mariccollege.edu
Phone: (818) 763-2563
Inst. Accred.: ACCSCT (1987/2003)

Maric College—Stockton
722 West March Ln., Stockton 95207
Type: Private, proprietary
System: Kaplan Higher Education Corporation
Degrees: C
URL: http://www.mariccollege.edu
Phone: (209) 462-8777 *Calendar:* Qtr. plan
Inst. Accred.: ACCSCT (2004)
Prog. Accred.: Medical Assisting (ABHES)

Marinello School of Beauty—Burbank
200 North San Fernando Blvd., Burbank 91502
Type: Private, proprietary
System: B&H Education, Inc.
Degrees: C
URL: http://www.marinello.com
Phone: (818) 954-8894
Inst. Accred.: NACCAS (1975/2006)

Marinello School of Beauty—City of Industry
1600 South Azusa Ave., Ste. 244, City of Industry 91748
Type: Private, proprietary
System: B&H Education, Inc.
Degrees: C
URL: http://www.marinello.com
Phone: (626) 965-2532
Inst. Accred.: NACCAS (1975/2006)

Marinello School of Beauty—Eagle Rock
2700 Colorado Blvd., Eagle Rock Plaza, #266, Eagle Rock 90041
Type: Private, proprietary
System: B&H Education, Inc.
Degrees: C
URL: http://www.marinello.com
Phone: (323) 254-6226
Inst. Accred.: NACCAS (1968/2004)

Marinello School of Beauty—East Los Angeles
1241 South Soto St., Ste. 101, Los Angeles 90023
Type: Private, proprietary
System: B&H Education, Inc.
Degrees: C
URL: http://www.marinello.com
Phone: (323) 980-9253
Inst. Accred.: NACCAS (1968/2004)

Marinello School of Beauty—Huntington Beach
19022 Brookhurst St., Huntington Beach 92646
Type: Private, proprietary
System: B&H Education, Inc.
Degrees: C
URL: http://www.marinello.com
Phone: (714) 962-8831
Inst. Accred.: NACCAS (2005)

Marinello School of Beauty—Inglewood
240 South Market St., Inglewood 90301
Type: Private, proprietary
System: B&H Education, Inc.
Degrees: C
URL: http://www.marinello.com
Phone: (310) 674-8100
Inst. Accred.: NACCAS (1968/2004)

Marinello School of Beauty—Lake Forest
23635 El Toro Rd., Ste. K, Lake Forest 92630
Type: Private, proprietary
System: B&H Education, Inc.
Degrees: C
URL: http://www.marinello.com
Phone: (949) 586-4900
Inst. Accred.: NACCAS (1976/2006)

Marinello School of Beauty—Moreno Valley
24741 Alessandro Blvd., Moreno Valley 92553
Type: Private, proprietary
System: B&H Education, Inc.
Degrees: C
URL: http://www.marinello.com
Phone: (951) 247-2047
Inst. Accred.: NACCAS (1976/2005)

Marinello School of Beauty—North Hollywood
6219 Laurel Canyon Blvd., North Hollywood 91606
Type: Private, proprietary
System: B&H Education, Inc.
Degrees: C
URL: http://www.marinello.com
Phone: (818) 980-1300
Inst. Accred.: NACCAS (1968/2005)

Marinello School of Beauty—Ontario
940 North Mountain Ave., Ontario 91762
Type: Private, proprietary
System: B&H Education, Inc.
Degrees: C
URL: http://www.marinello.com
Phone: (909) 984-5884
Inst. Accred.: NACCAS (1972/2003)

Marinello School of Beauty—Paramount
8527 Alondra Blvd., Ste. 129, Paramount 90723
Type: Private, proprietary
System: B&H Education, Inc.
Degrees: C
URL: http://www.marinello.com
Phone: (562) 531-1800
Inst. Accred.: NACCAS (1983/2006)

Marinello School of Beauty—Reseda
18442 Sherman Way, Reseda 91335
Type: Private, proprietary
System: B&H Education, Inc.
Degrees: C
URL: http://www.marinello.com
Phone: (818) 881-2521
Inst. Accred.: NACCAS (1968/2005)

Marinello School of Beauty—San Bernardino
721 West 2nd St., Ste. E, San Bernardino 92410
Type: Private, proprietary
System: B&H Education, Inc.
Degrees: C
URL: http://www.marinello.com
Phone: (909) 884-8747
Inst. Accred.: NACCAS (1968/2003)

Marinello School of Beauty—San Diego
7550 Miramar Rd., Ste. 400, San Diego 92126
Type: Private, proprietary
System: B&H Education, Inc.
Degrees: C
URL: http://www.marinello.com
Phone: (858) 547-9260
Inst. Accred.: NACCAS (1968/2004)

Marinello School of Beauty—West Covina
118 Plaza Dr., West Covina 91790
Type: Private, proprietary
System: B&H Education, Inc.
Degrees: C
URL: http://www.marinello.com
Phone: (626) 962-1021
Inst. Accred.: NACCAS (1968/2005)

Marinello School of Beauty—Whittier
6538 Greenleaf Ave., Whittier 90601
Type: Private, proprietary
System: B&H Education, Inc.
Degrees: C
URL: http://www.marinello.com
Phone: (562) 698-0068
Inst. Accred.: NACCAS (1967/2002)

Lomita Campus
2418 Lomita Blvd., Ste. B, Lomita 90717
Phone: (310) 325-3005

Marinello School of Beauty—Wilshire West
6111 Wilshire Blvd., Los Angeles 90048
Type: Private, proprietary
System: B&H Education, Inc.
Degrees: C
URL: http://www.marinello.com
Phone: (323) 938-2005
Inst. Accred.: NACCAS (1968/2004)

Maritime Institute, Inc.
1310 Rosecrans St., Ste. G, San Diego 92106
Type: Private, proprietary
Degrees: C
URL: http://www.maritimeinstitute.com
Phone: (619) 225-1783
Inst. Accred.: COE (2006)

Mayfield College
35-325 Date Palm Dr., Ste. 101, Cathedral City 92234
Type: Private, proprietary
Degrees: C
URL: http://www.mayfieldcollege.org
Phone: (760) 328-5554
Inst. Accred.: COE (2002)

MCed Career College
2002 North Gateway Blvd., Fresno 93727
Type: Private, proprietary
Degrees: C
URL: http://www.mced.com
Phone: (559) 456-0623
Inst. Accred.: ACCSCT (1994/2004)

Meridian Institute of Massage
4201 Wilshire Blvd., Ste. 515, Los Angeles 90010
Type: Private, proprietary
Degrees: C
URL: http://www.meridianinstitute.com
Phone: (323) 936-1624
Inst. Accred.: ABHES (2006)

Miss Marty's Hair Academy and Esthetics Institute
1087 Mission St., San Francisco 94103
Type: Private, proprietary
Degrees: C
URL: http://www.missmartys.com
Phone: (415) 227-4240
Inst. Accred.: NACCAS (1986/2002)

Modern Beauty Academy
699 South C St., Oxnard 93030
Type: Private, proprietary
Degrees: C
Phone: (805) 483-4994
Inst. Accred.: NACCAS (1972/2003)

Modern Technology School
16560 Harbor Blvd., Fountain Valley 92708
Type: Private, proprietary
Degrees: C
URL: http://www.mtschool.edu
Phone: (714) 418-9100
Inst. Accred.: ACCSCT (1988/2003, Probation)

Mojave Barber College
15505 7th St., Victorville 92392
Type: Private, proprietary
Degrees: C
URL: http://www.mojavebarbercollege.com
Phone: (760) 955-2934
Inst. Accred.: NACCAS (2005)

Moler Barber College
3815 Telegraph Ave., Oakland 94609-2419
Type: Private, proprietary
Degrees: C
Phone: (510) 652-4177
Inst. Accred.: ACCSCT (1980/2006)

Montebello Beauty College
2201 West Whittier Blvd., Montebello 90640
Type: Private, proprietary
Degrees: C
Phone: (323) 727-7851
Inst. Accred.: NACCAS (1986/2004)

Montessori Institute of Advanced Studies
1101 Walpert St., Hayward 94541-6705
Type: Private, independent
Degrees: C
URL: http://www.montessori-training.com/MIAS.htm
Phone: (510) 581-3724
Inst. Accred.: MACTE (2001)

Montessori Teacher Edcuation Center—San Francisco Bay Area
16492 Foothill Blvd., San Leandro 94578
Type: Private, independent
Degrees: C
URL: http://www.montessoritec-sf.com
Phone: (510) 278-1115
Inst. Accred.: MACTE (1999)

Montessori Teachers College of San Diego
4544 Pocahontas Ave., San Diego 92117
Type: Public, independent
Degrees: C
URL: http://www.sandiego-ncme.org
Phone: (858) 270-9350
Inst. Accred.: MACTE (2001)

Montessori Western Teacher Training
6202 Cerulean Ave., Garden Grove 92845-2711
Type: Private, independent
Degrees: C
Phone: (714) 897-3833
Inst. Accred.: MACTE (2001)

MTI Business College of Stockton Inc.
6006 North El Dorado St., Stockton 95207-4349
Type: Private, proprietary
Degrees: C
URL: http://www.mtistockton.com
Phone: (209) 957-3030
Inst. Accred.: ACCSCT (1987/2004)

Mueller College of Holistic Massage Therapies
4607 Park Blvd., San Diego 92116-2630
Type: Private, proprietary
Degrees: C
URL: http://www.muellercollege.com
Phone: (619) 291-9811
Inst. Accred.: CMTA (2001/2004)

My-Le's Beauty College
5972 Stockton Blvd., Sacramento 95824
Type: Private, proprietary
Degrees: C
Phone: (916) 422-0223
Inst. Accred.: ACCSCT (1999/2004)

National Career Education
6060 Sunrise Vista Dr., Ste. 3000, Citrus Heights 95610-7053
Type: Private, proprietary
System: Delta Education Corporation
Degrees: C
URL: http://www.ncecollege.org
Phone: (916) 969-4900
Inst. Accred.: ACCSCT (1986/2005)

National Communications Training Centers
1324 East Mission Rd., San Marcos 92069-3038
Type: Private, proprietary
Degrees: C
URL: http://www.nctc.nu
Phone: (760) 471-9561
Inst. Accred.: ACCSCT (2006)

National Holistic Institute
5900 Hollis St., Ste. J, Emeryville
Type: Private, proprietary
Degrees: C
URL: http://www.nhimassage.com
Phone: (510) 547-6442
Inst. Accred.: ACCET (1987/2006)

Encino Campus
15720 Ventura Blvd., Ste. 101, Encino 91436-2914
Phone: (818) 788-0824

San Jose Campus
3031 Tisch Way, Ste. 1, Plaza South, San Jose 95128
Phone: (408) 423-8004

National Notary Association
PO Box 2402, Chatsworth 91313-2402
Type: Private, independent
Degrees: C
URL: http://www.nationalnotary.org
Phone: (818) 739-4052
Inst. Accred.: ACCET (2006)

National Polytechnic College
2465 West Whittier Blvd., Ste. 201, Montebello 90640
Type: Private, proprietary
Degrees: C
Phone: (323) 728-9636
Inst. Accred.: ACCSCT (2003)

Newberry School of Beauty
16860 Devonshire St., Granada Hills 91344
Type: Private, proprietary
Degrees: C
URL: http://www.newberryschoolofbeauty.net
Phone: (818) 366-3211
Inst. Accred.: NACCAS (1975/2006)

Newbridge College
1840 East 17th St., Santa Ana 92705
Type: Private, proprietary
Degrees: C
URL: http://newbridgecollege.edu
Phone: (714) 550-8000
Inst. Accred.: ACCSCT (1988/2006)
Prog. Accred.: Allied Health (surgical technology)

Long Beach Campus
3799 East Burnett St., Long Beach 90815
Phone: (562) 498-4500

Newbridge College—Burbank
229 East Palm Ave., 2nd Flr., Burbank 91502
Type: Private, proprietary
Degrees: C
URL: http://newbridgecollege.edu
Phone: (818) 557-7677
Inst. Accred.: ACICS (1998/2001)

Newbridge College—Monterey Park
583 South Monterey Pass Rd., Monterey Park 91754
Type: Private, proprietary
Degrees: C
URL: http://newbridgecollege.edu
Phone: (626) 576-2444
Inst. Accred.: ACICS (1994/2005)

Stanton Campus
12362 Beach Blvd., Ste. 100, Stanton 90680-3900
Phone: (714) 901-9447

North Adrian's Beauty College
124 Floyd Ave., Modesto 95350
Type: Private, proprietary
Degrees: C
Phone: (209) 526-2040
Inst. Accred.: NACCAS (1975/2005)

North-West College
530 East Union Ave., Pasadena 91101-1744
Type: Private, proprietary
Degrees: C
URL: http://www.northwestcollege.com
Phone: (626) 796-5815
Inst. Accred.: ACCSCT (1983/2005)

North-West College
2121 West Garvey Ave., West Covina 91790-2097
Type: Private, proprietary
Degrees: C
URL: http://www.northwestcollege.com
Phone: (626) 960-5046
Inst. Accred.: ACCSCT (1973/2003)

Glendale Campus
221 North Brand, Lower Level, Glendale 91205-1109
Phone: (818) 242-0205

Pomona Campus
134 West Holt Ave., Pomona 91768-3199
Phone: (909) 623-1552

Riverside Campus
10020 Indiana Ave., Ste. 202, Second Flr., Riverside 92503
Phone: (951) 351-7750

NTMA Training Centers of Southern California
14926 Bloomfield Ave., Norwalk 90650
Type: Private, independent
Degrees: C
URL: http://www.ntmatrainingcenters.org
Phone: (562) 921-3722
Inst. Accred.: ACCSCT (2001/2006), COE (2004)

Inland Empire Training Center
1717 South Grove Ave., Ontario 91761
Phone: (909) 947-9363

Orange County Training Center
3036 Enterprise St., Costa Mesa 92626
Phone: (714) 545-3202

Occupational Training Services
8799 Balboa Ave., Ste. 100, San Diego 92123
Type: Private, independent
Degrees: C
URL: http://www.ots-sdchc.org
Phone: (858) 560-0411
Inst. Accred.: ACCSCT (1997/2003, Probation)

Oceanside College of Beauty
1575 South Coast Hwy., Oceanside 92054
Type: Private, proprietary
Degrees: C
URL: http://www.ocb.edu
Phone: (760) 757-6161
Inst. Accred.: NACCAS (1976/2006)

OSULA Education Center
3921 Laurel Canyon Blvd., Studio City 91604
Type: Private, independent
Degrees: C
URL: http://www.osula.com
Phone: (818) 509-1484
Inst. Accred.: ACCET (2002)

Oxman College of San Francisco
375 3rd Ave., San Francisco 94118
Type: Private, proprietary
Degrees: C
URL: http://oxmancollege.com
Phone: (415) 751-6461
Inst. Accred.: COE (2005)

Los Angeles Campus
5250 West Century Blvd., Los Angeles 90045
Phone: (415) 751-6461

Pacific Coast Trade School
1690 Universe Circle, Oxnard 93033
Type: Private, proprietary
Degrees: C
Phone: (805) 487-9260
Inst. Accred.: ACCSCT (2004)

Pacific College
3160 Redhill Ave., Costa Mesa 92626
Type: Private, proprietary
Degrees: C
Phone: (714) 662-4402
Inst. Accred.: ACCSCT (1998/2003)

Palace Beauty College
1517 South Western Ave., Los Angeles 90006
Type: Private, proprietary
Degrees: C
Phone: (323) 731-2075
Inst. Accred.: NACCAS (2005)

Palladium Technical Academy
10507 Valley Blvd., Ste. 806, El Monte 91731
Type: Private, proprietary
Degrees: C
URL: http://www.palladiumta.com
Phone: (626) 444-0880
Inst. Accred.: COE (2005)

Palomar Institute of Cosmetology
355 Via Vera Cruz #3, San Marcos 92069
Type: Private, proprietary
Degrees: C
URL: http://pic.edu
Phone: (760) 744-7900
Inst. Accred.: NACCAS (1985/2005)

Paris Beauty College
1655 Willow Pass Rd., Concord 94520-2618
Type: Private, proprietary
Degrees: C
URL: http://www.parisbeautycollege.com
Phone: (925) 685-7600
Inst. Accred.: NACCAS (1976/2003)

PCI College
17215 Studebaker Rd., Ste. 310, Cerritos 90703
Type: Private, proprietary
Degrees: C
URL: http://www.pci-ed.com
Phone: (562) 916-5055
Inst. Accred.: ACCSCT (2000/2005)

Performance Improvement Group, Inc.
Dale Carnegie Training of Los Angeles
1317 West Foothill Blvd., Ste. 235, Upland 91786
Type: Private, proprietary
Degrees: C
URL: http://www.dalecarnegie.com
Phone: (909) 931-3384
Inst. Accred.: ACCET (1979/2005)

POLY Languages Institute
4201 Wilshire Blvd., Ste. 114, Los Angeles 90010
Type: Private, proprietary
Degrees: C
URL: http://www.polylanguages.com
Phone: (323) 933-9399
Inst. Accred.: ACCET (2000/2004, Warning)

Irvine Campus
4255 Campus Dr., Ste. A-200, Irvine 92612
Phone: (949) 737-7628

Pasadena Campus
350 South Lake Ave., Ste. 200, Pasadena 91101
Phone: (626) 499-4441

Poway Academy of Hair Design
13266 Poway Rd., Poway 92064
Type: Private, proprietary
Degrees: C
URL: http://www.sandiegobeautyacademy.com
Phone: (858) 748-1490
Inst. Accred.: NACCAS (1986/2004)

Preferred College of Nursing
4221Wilshire Blvd., Ste. 280 Los Angeles 90010
Type: Private, proprietary
Degrees: C
URL: http://www.pcnla.com
Phone: (323) 857-5000
Inst. Accred.: ABHES (2008)

Bakersfield Campus
1415 18th St., Ste. 205 Bakersfield 93301
Phone: (661) 324-2677

Carson Campus
22010 South Wilmington Ave., Ste. 101 Carson 90745
Phone: (310) 952-1005

Van Nuys Cmpus
6551 Van Nuys Blvd., Ste. 200 Van Nuys 91401
Phone: (818) 902-3708

West Covina Campus
1619 West Garvey Ave, Ste. 103, West Covina 91790
Phone: (626) 856-0111

Premiere Career College
12901 Ramona Blvd., Ste. D, Irwindale 91706
Type: Private, proprietary
Degrees: C
URL: http://www.premcol.com
Phone: (626) 814-2080
Inst. Accred.: ACICS (1995/2004)
Prog. Accred.: Allied Health (surgical technology)

Professional Institute of Beauty
10801 East Valley Mall, El Monte 91731
Type: Private, proprietary
Degrees: C
URL: http://www.pibschool.com
Phone: (626) 443-9401
Inst. Accred.: NACCAS (1975/2006)

Richard's Beauty College
1385 East Foothill Blvd., Upland 91786
Type: Private, proprietary
Degrees: C
Phone: (909) 982-4200
Inst. Accred.: NACCAS (1971/2002)

Robert M. Scherer and Associates, Inc.
1787 Tribute Rd., Ste. K, Sacramento 95815
Type: Private, proprietary
Degrees: C
URL: http://www.sacramento.dalecarnegie.com
Phone: (916) 929-3911
Inst. Accred.: ACCET (1975/2006)

Rosemead Beauty School, Inc.
8531 East Valley Blvd., Rosemead 91770
Type: Private, proprietary
Degrees: C
Phone: (626) 286-2147
Inst. Accred.: NACCAS (1986/2006)

Rosemead College of English
8705 East Valley Blvd., Rosemead 91770
Type: Private, proprietary
Degrees: C
URL: http://www.rosemeadcollege.edu
Phone: (626) 285-9668
Inst. Accred.: ACCET (2007)

Torrance Campus
3848 West Carson St., Ste. 100, Torrance 90503
Phone: (310) 316-3698

Royale College of Beauty
27485 Commerce Center Dr., Temecula 92590
Type: Private, proprietary
Degrees: C
URL: http://www.beautyschool.com/royale
Phone: (909) 676-0833
Inst. Accred.: NACCAS (1991/2006)

Saint Francis Career College
3630 East Imperial Hwy., Lynwood 90262
Type: Private, independent
Degrees: C
Phone: (310) 900-8059
Inst. Accred.: ACCSCT (1998/2006)

San Jose Campus
749 Story Rd., Ste. 50, San Jose 95122
Phone: (408) 286-8903

Saint Giles College
One Hallidie Plaza, Ste. 350, San Francisco 94102
Type: Private, independent
Degrees: C
URL: http://www.stgiles-usa.com
Phone: (415) 788-3552
Inst. Accred.: CEA (2002)

Salon Success Academy
107 North McKinley St., Ste. 109, Corona 92879
Type: Private, proprietary
Degrees: C
Phone: (909) 736-9725
Inst. Accred.: NACCAS (1976/2003)

Santa Monica Montessori Institute
1909 Colorado Ave., Santa Monica 90404
Type: Private, independent
Degrees: C
Phone: (310) 829-3551
Inst. Accred.: MACTE (2000)

Scandinavian Aviation Academy
8665 Gibbs Dr., Ste. 110, San Diego 92123
Type: Private, proprietary
Degrees: C
URL: http://www.scanavia.com
Phone: (858) 278-5770
Inst. Accred.: ACCET (1999/2005)

SEA College of Business and Technology
265 South Randolph Ave., Ste. J230, Brea 92821-5754
Type: Private, proprietary
Degrees: C
Phone: (714) 257-3095
Inst. Accred.: ACCSCT (2000/2005)

Sierra College of Beauty
1340 West 18th St., Merced 95340
Type: Private, proprietary
Degrees: C
Phone: (209) 723-2989
Inst. Accred.: NACCAS (1988/2003)

Sierra Valley College
4747 North First St., Building D, Fresno 93726
Type: Private, proprietary
Degrees: C
URL: http://www.sierravalleycollege.com
Phone: (209) 222-0947
Inst. Accred.: ACICS (1981/2003)

Silvergate Academy
3443 Camino del Rio South, Ste. 119, San Diego 92108
Type: Private, proprietary
Degrees: C
URL: http://www.dliusa.com
Phone: (619) 284-2641
Inst. Accred.: ACCET (1986/2006)

Torrance Campus
3525 Lomita Blvd., Torrance 90505
Phone: (310) 530-4009

Sound Master Recording Engineer School/ Audio-Video Institute
10747 Magnolia Blvd., North Hollywood 91601
Type: Private, proprietary
Degrees: C
Phone: (323) 650-8000
Inst. Accred.: ACCET (1989/2005)

Stanbridge College
2041 Business Center Dr., Ste. 107, Irvine 92612
Type: Private, proprietary
Degrees: C
URL: http://www1.stanbridge.edu
Phone: (949) 794-9090
Inst. Accred.: ACCSCT (2004)

Summit Career College, Inc.
1250 East Cooley Dr., Colton 92324
Type: Private, proprietary
Degrees: C
URL: http://www.summitcollege.com
Phone: (909) 422-8950
Inst. Accred.: ACCET (1994/2005)

Anaheim Campus
1830 West Romneya Dr., Anaheim 92801-1833
Phone: (714) 635-6232

TechSkills—Sacramento
1510 Arden Way, Ste. 102, Sacramento 95815
Type: Private, proprietary
Degrees: C
URL: http://www.techskills.com
Phone: (916) 649-9600
Inst. Accred.: ACCET (2006)

Thanh Le College, School of Cosmetology
12875 Chapman Ave., Garden Grove 92640
Type: Private, proprietary
Degrees: C
Phone: (714) 748-7019
Inst. Accred.: NACCAS (1983/2003)

Thomas J. Kiblen and Associates
3530 Atlantic Ave., Ste. 200, Long Beach 90807-4569
Type: Private, proprietary
Degrees: C
URL: http://www.longbeach.dalecarnegie.com
Phone: (562) 427-1040
Inst. Accred.: ACCET (1979/2005)

Thuy Princess Beauty College
252 East Second St., Pomona 91766
Type: Private, proprietary
Degrees: C
Phone: (909) 620-6893
Inst. Accred.: NACCAS (2005)

Transworld Schools
701 Sutter St., 2nd Flr., San Francisco 94109
Type: Private, proprietary
Degrees: C
URL: http://www.transworldschools.com
Phone: (415) 928-2835
Inst. Accred.: ACCET (2003/2006)

Truck Marketing Institute
1090 Eugenia Place, Ste. 101, Carpinteria 93014-5000
Type: Private, proprietary
Degrees: C
URL: http://www.truckmarketinginstitute.com
Phone: (805) 684-4558
Inst. Accred.: DETC (1968/2006)

Tulare Beauty College
325 North Gateway Dr., Madera 93637
Type: Private, proprietary
Degrees: C
Phone: (209) 688-2901
Inst. Accred.: NACCAS (1974/2005)

United Beauty College, Inc.
10229 Lower Azusa Rd., Temple City 91780
Type: Private, proprietary
Degrees: C
URL: http://www.unitedbeautycollege.com
Phone: (626) 443-0900
Inst. Accred.: NACCAS (2001/2004)

United Education Institute
3020 Wilshire Blvd., Ste. 250, Los Angeles 90010
Type: Private, proprietary
Degrees: C
URL: http://www.uei-edu.com
Phone: (213) 427-3700
Inst. Accred.: ACCET (1988/2005, Warning)

Chula Vista Campus
310 Third Ave., Chula Vista 91910
Phone: (619) 409-4111

El Monte Campus
9330 Flair Dr., Ste. 100, El Monte 91731
Phone: (949) 794-9999

Huntington Park Capmus
6812 Pacific Blvd., Huntington Park 90255
Phone: (323) 277-8000

Ontario Campus
3380 Shelby St., Ste. 150, Ontario 91764
Phone: (909) 476-2424

San Bernardino Campus
295 East Caroline St., Ste. E, San Bernardino 92408
Phone: (909) 554-1999

San Diego Campus
1323 6th Ave., San Diego 92101
Phone: (619) 544-9800

Van Nuys Campus
7335 Van Nuys Blvd., Van Nuys 91405
Phone: (818) 756-1200

United Truck and Car Driving School
2425 Camino del Rio South, San Diego 92108
Type: Private, proprietary
Degrees: C
URL: http://www.drivetrucks.com
Phone: (619) 296-2020
Inst. Accred.: ACCSCT (2003/2006)

Universal College of Beauty, Inc.—South Vermont Avenue
8619 South Vermont Ave., Los Angeles 90044
Type: Private, proprietary
Degrees: C
Phone: (323) 750-5750
Inst. Accred.: NACCAS (1975/2004)

Compton Campus
718 West Compton Blvd., Compton 90220
Phone: (310) 635-6969

Universal College of Beauty, Inc.—West 43rd Place
3419 West 43rd Place, Los Angeles 90008
Type: Private, proprietary
Degrees: C
Phone: (323) 298-0045
Inst. Accred.: NACCAS (1985/2004)

Valley Career College
878 Jackman St., El Cajon 92020
Type: Private, proprietary
Degrees: C
URL: http://www.valleycareercollege.com
Phone: (619) 593-5111 *Calendar:* Qtr. plan
Inst. Accred.: ACCET (1999/2002)

Victor Valley Beauty College
16515 Mojave Dr., Victorville 92392
Type: Private, proprietary
Degrees: C
URL: http://www.victorvalleybeautycollege.com
Phone: (760) 245-2522
Inst. Accred.: NACCAS (1976/2003)

Video Symphony EnterTraining, Inc.
731 North Hollywood Way, Burbank 91505-3183
Type: Private, proprietary
Degrees: C
URL: http://www.videosymphony.com
Phone: (818) 557-7200
Inst. Accred.: ACCET (2003/2006)

Walter Jay M.D. Institute An Educational Center
1930 Wilshire Blvd., Ste. 700, Los Angeles 90057
Type: Private, proprietary
Degrees: C
Phone: (213) 353-0722
Inst. Accred.: ACCET (2003)

West Coast Ultrasound Institute
291 South La Cienega Blvd., Ste. 500, Beverly Hills 90211
Type: Private, proprietary
Degrees: C
URL: http://www.ultrasoundinstitute.com
Phone: (310) 289-5123
Inst. Accred.: ACCSCT (2001/2006)

Westech College
3491 East Concours, Ontario 91764-5916
Type: Private, proprietary
Degrees: C
URL: http://www.westech.edu
Phone: (909) 980-4474
Inst. Accred.: ACCSCT (1991/2003, Probation)

Western Beauty Institute—San Fernando Valley
8700 Van Nuys Blvd., Panorama City 91402
Type: Private, proprietary
Degrees: C
URL: http://www.sanfernandobeautyacademy.com
Phone: (818) 894-9550
Inst. Accred.: NACCAS (1974/2003)

Antelope Valley Campus
2733 West Ave. L, Lancaster 93536
Phone: (661) 718-8410

WestMed College
5300 Stevens Creek Blvd., Ste. 200, San Jose 95129
Type: Private, proprietary
System: National University System
Degrees: C
URL: http://www.westmedtraining.com
Phone: (408) 977-0723
Inst. Accred.: ACCSCT (2005)
Prog. Accred.: Allied Health (EMT-paramedic)

COLORADO

Academy of Beauty Culture
2938 North Ave., Units B & C, Grand Junction 81504
Type: Private, proprietary
Degrees: C
Phone: (970) 245-1110
Inst. Accred.: NACCAS (1981/2006)

Academy of Natural Therapy
123 Elm Ave., Eaton 80615
Type: Private, proprietary
Degrees: C
URL: http://www.natural-therapy.com
Phone: (970) 454-2628
Inst. Accred.: CMTA (2006)

Americana Beauty College II
3650 Austin Bluff Pkwy., Ste. 174, Colorado Springs 80918
Type: Private, proprietary
Degrees: C
URL: http://www.americanabeautycollege.com
Phone: (719) 598-4188
Inst. Accred.: NACCAS (1976/2003)

Artistic Beauty Colleges
3049-A West 74th Ave., Westminister 80030
Type: Private, proprietary
System: Empire Education Group
Degrees: C
URL: http://www.artisticbeautycolleges.com
Phone: (303) 428-5100
Inst. Accred.: NACCAS (1980/2005)

Aurora Campus
16800 East Mississippi Ave., Aurora 80017
Phone: (303) 745-6300

Littleton Campus
8996 West Bowles Ave., Suites E-F, Littleton 80123
Phone: (303) 904-4400

Artistic Beauty Colleges—Denver
6520 Wadsworth Blvd., Ste. 209, Arvada 80003
Type: Private, proprietary
System: Empire Education Group
Degrees: C
URL: http://www.artisticbeautycolleges.com
Phone: (303) 455-0100
Inst. Accred.: NACCAS (1977/2002)

Artistic Beauty Colleges—Lakewood
441 Wadsworth Blvd., Lakewood 80226
Type: Private, proprietary
System: Empire Education Group
Degrees: C
URL: http://www.artisticbeautycolleges.com
Phone: (303) 238-7501
Inst. Accred.: NACCAS (1972/2003)

Artistic Beauty Colleges—Thornton
3811 East 120th Ave., Thornton 80241
Type: Private, proprietary
System: Empire Education Group
Degrees: C
URL: http://www.artisticbeautycolleges.com
Phone: (303) 451-5808
Inst. Accred.: NACCAS (1981/2006)

At-Home Professions
2001 Lowe St., Fort Collins 80525
Type: Private, proprietary
Degrees: C
URL: http://www.ahpseminars.com
Phone: (970) 225-6300
Inst. Accred.: DETC (2004)

Bridge Linguatec
915 South Colorado Blvd., Denver 80246
Type: Private, proprietary
Degrees: C
URL: http://www.bridgelinguatec.com
Phone: (303) 777-7783
Inst. Accred.: ACCET (1998/2007)

Center of Advanced Therapeutics
1212 South Broadway, Ste. 200, Denver 80210
Type: Private, proprietary
Degrees: C
URL: http://www.catinc.net
Phone: (303) 765-2201
Inst. Accred.: ACCSCT (2000/2005)

Colorado School of English
331 14th St., Ste. 300, Denver 80202
Type: Private, proprietary
Degrees: C
URL: http://www.englishamerica.com
Phone: (720) 932-8900
Inst. Accred.: ACCET (1998/2004)

Corporate Change Catalysts Dale Carnegie Training
5619 DTC Pkwy., Ste. 620, Greenwood Village 80111
Type: Private, proprietary
Degrees: C
URL: http://www.denver.dalecarnegie.com
Phone: (303) 964-8688
Inst. Accred.: ACCET (2004)

Cortiva Institute—Colorado
390 Interlocken Crescent, Broomfield 80021
Type: Private, proprietary
Degrees: C
URL: http://www.cortiva.com
Phone: (303) 996-5050
Inst. Accred.: ACCSCT (2003)

Culinary School of the Rockies
637 South Broadway, Ste. H, Boulder 80305
Type: Private, independent
Degrees: C
URL: http://www.cookingschoolrockies.com
Phone: (303) 494-7988
Inst. Accred.: ACCET (2002/2006)

Cuttin Up Beauty Academy
8101 East Colfax Ave., Denver 80220
Type: Private, proprietary
Degrees: C
Phone: (303) 388-5700
Inst. Accred.: NACCAS (2005)

Delta-Montrose Technical College
1765 Hwy. 50, Delta 81416
Type: Public, state/local
Degrees: C
URL: http://www.dmavtc.edu
Phone: (970) 874-7671
Inst. Accred.: NCA-CASI (1977/2005)

Emily Griffith Opportunity School
1250 Welton St., Denver 80204
Type: Private, independent
Degrees: C
URL: http://www.egos-school.com
Phone: (303) 575-4700 *Calendar:* Sem. plan
Inst. Accred.: NCA-CASI (1926/2003)
Prog. Accred.: Dentistry (dental assisting)

Glenwood Beauty Academy
51241 Hwy. 6 & 24, West Glenwood Plaza, Ste. 1, Glenwood Springs 81601
Type: Private, proprietary
Degrees: C
Phone: (970) 945-0485
Inst. Accred.: NACCAS (1984/2004)

Hair Dynamics Education Center
6464 South College Ave., Fort Collins 80525
Type: Private, proprietary
Degrees: C
Phone: (970) 223-9943
Inst. Accred.: NACCAS (1987/2002)

Language Consultants International, LLC
2055 South Oneida, Ste. 300, Denver 80224
Type: Private, proprietary
Degrees: C
URL: http://www.languageconsultants.org
Phone: (303) 756-0760
Inst. Accred.: ACCET (2000)

Massage Therapy Institute of Colorado
1441 York St., Ste. 301, Denver 80206-2127
Type: Private, proprietary
Degrees: C
URL: http://www.mtic-co.com
Phone: (303) 329-6345
Inst. Accred.: CMTA (2005)

Ohio Center for Broadcasting—Colorado
1310 Wadsworth Blvd., Ste. 100, Lakewood 80214
Type: Private, proprietary
Degrees: C
URL: http://www.beonair.com
Phone: (303) 937-7070
Inst. Accred.: ACCSCT (2001/2003)

San Juan Basin Technical College
33057 Hwy. 160, Mancos 81328
Type: Public, state/local
Degrees: C
URL: http://www.sjbtc.edu
Phone: (970) 565-8457 *Calendar:* Sem. plan
Inst. Accred.: NCA-CASI (1975/2005)

Spring Institute for Intercultural Learning
1610 Emerson St., Denver 80218
Type: Private, independent
Degrees: C
URL: http://www.spring-institute.org
Phone: (303) 863-0188
Inst. Accred.: ACCET (2001/2004)

Spring International Language Center, Inc.
5900 South Santa Fe Dr., Littleton 80120
Type: Private, proprietary
Degrees: C
URL: http://www.spring-usa.com
Phone: (303) 797-0100
Inst. Accred.: ACCET (2000/2005)

Denver Campus
900 Auraria Pkwy., Tivoli Bldg., #454, Auraria Higher Education Center, Denver 80204
Phone: (303) 534-1616

Fayetteville Campus
300 Hotz Hall, University of Arkansas, Fayetteville, AR 72701
Phone: (479) 575-7600

T.H. Pickens Technical Center
500 Airport Blvd., Aurora 80011-9307
Type: Public, state/local
Degrees: C
URL: http://www.aps.k12.co.us/pickens
Phone: (303) 344-4910
Inst. Accred.: NCA-CASI (1975/2002)
Prog. Accred.: Allied Health (respiratory therapy), Dentistry (dental assisting)

Technical Education College
2458 Waynoka Rd., Colorado Springs 80915
Type: Private, independent
Degrees: C
URL: http://www.technicaleducationcollege.com
Phone: (719) 597-8446
Inst. Accred.: NCA-CASI (2003)

Toni & Guy Hairdressing Academy
332 Main St., Colorado Springs 80911
Type: Private, proprietary
Degrees: C
URL: http://www.toniguy.com/academy
Phone: (719) 390-9898
Inst. Accred.: ACCSCT (2001/2006)

U.S. Career Institute
2001 Lowe St., Fort Collins 80525
Type: Private, proprietary
Degrees: C
URL: http://www.uscareerinstitute.com
Phone: (970) 207-4500
Inst. Accred.: DETC (2004)

Xenon International School of Hair Design III
2231 South Peoria St., Aurora 80014
Type: Private, proprietary
Degrees: C
URL: http://www.xenonintl.com
Phone: (303) 752-1560
Inst. Accred.: NACCAS (1990/2005)

CONNECTICUT

Academy Di Capelli School of Cosmetology
950 Yale Ave., Yale Plaza, Unit 20, Wallingford 06492
Type: Private, proprietary
Degrees: C
URL: http://www.academydicapelli.com
Phone: (203) 294-9496
Inst. Accred.: NACCAS (2006)

Albert I. Prince Regional Vocational-Technical School
401 Flatbush Ave., Hartford 06106
Type: Public, state
Degrees: C
URL: http://www.cttech.org/prince/adult-ed/adult-ed.htm
Phone: (860) 951-7112
Inst. Accred.: NEASC-CTCI (1968/2005)
Prog. Accred.: Allied Health (surgical technology), Dentistry (dental assisting)

Baran Institute of Technology
97 Newberry Rd., East Windsor 06088
Type: Private, proprietary
Degrees: C
URL: http://www.baraninstitute.com
Phone: (800) 243-4242
Inst. Accred.: ACCSCT (1983/2003)

Branford Hall Career Institute
1 Summit Place, Branford 06405
Type: Private, proprietary
System: Premier Education Group
Degrees: C
URL: http://www.branfordhall.com
Phone: (203) 488-2525
Inst. Accred.: ACICS (1977/2006)
Prog. Accred.: Allied Health (medical assisting (AMA))

Albany Campus
500 New Karner Rd., Albany, NY 12205
Phone: (518) 456-4464

Bohemia Campus
565 Johnson Ave., Bohemia, NY 11716
Phone: (631) 471-9100

Chicopee Campus
54 Center St., Chicopee, MA 01013
Phone: (413) 598-8300

Southington Campus
35 North Main St., Southington 06489
Phone: (860) 276-0600

Springfield Campus
112 Industry Ave., Springfield, MA 01104
Phone: (413) 781-2276
Prog. Accred: Medical Assisting (ABHES)

Windsor Campus
995 Day Hill Rd., Windsor 06095
Phone: (860) 683-4900
Prog. Accred: Medical Assisting (ABHES)

Brio Academy of Cosmetology
1000 Main St., East Hartford 06108-2220
Type: Private, proprietary
Degrees: C
URL: http://www.brioacademy.com
Phone: (860) 528-7178
Inst. Accred.: NACCAS (1971/2002)

Brio Academy of Cosmetology
1231 East Main St., Meriden 06450
Type: Private, proprietary
Degrees: C
URL: http://www.brioacademy.com
Phone: (203) 237-6683
Inst. Accred.: NACCAS (1975/2005)

Fairfield Campus
675 Kings Hwy. East, Fairfield 06824
Phone: (203) 331-0852

New Haven Campus
514 Orchard St., New Haven 06511
Phone: (203) 787-1264

Williamantic Campus
1320 Main St., Ste. 23, Willimantic 06226
Phone: (860) 423-6339

The Brio Academy of Cosmetology—Niantic
63 Pennsylvania Ave., Niantic 06357
Type: Private, proprietary
Degrees: C
URL: http://www.brioacademy.com
Phone: (860) 739-2466
Inst. Accred.: NACCAS (2004)

Bullard-Havens Technical High School
500 Pallisade Ave., Bridgeport 06610
Type: Public, state
Degrees: C
URL: http://www.cttech.org/bullard%2Dhavens
Phone: (203) 579-6333
Inst. Accred.: NEASC-CTCI (1968/2004)

Butler Business School
2710 North Ave., Bridgeport 06604
Type: Private, proprietary
Degrees: C
Phone: (203) 333-3601
Inst. Accred.: ACICS (1979/2001)

Connecticut Center for Massage Therapy
75 Kitts Ln., Newington 06111-3954
Type: Private, proprietary
Degrees: C
URL: http://www.ccmt.com
Phone: (860) 667-1886
Inst. Accred.: CMTA (1995/2005)

Groton Campus
1154 Poquonnock Rd., Groton 06340
Phone: (860) 446-2299
Prog. Accred: Allied Health (massage therapy)

Westport Campus
25 Sylvan Rd. South, Westport 06880
Phone: (877) 292-2268
Prog. Accred: Allied Health (massage therapy)

Connecticut Culinary Institute
230 Farmington Ave., Farmington 06032
Type: Private, proprietary
Degrees: C
URL: http://www.ctculinary.com
Phone: (860) 677-7869
Inst. Accred.: ACCSCT (1994/2004)
Prog. Accred.: Culinary Education

Suffield Campus
1760 Mapleton Ave., Suffield 06078
Phone: (860) 668-3500
Prog. Accred: Culinary Education

Connecticut Institute of Hair Design
1681 Meriden Rd., Wolcott 06716-3322
Type: Private, proprietary
Degrees: C
Phone: (203) 879-4247
Inst. Accred.: ACCSCT (1980/2004)

Connecticut School of Electronics
221 West Main St., Branford 06405-4049
Type: Private, proprietary
Degrees: C
URL: http://www.ctschoolofelectronics.com
Phone: (203) 624-2121 *Calendar:* Sem. plan
Inst. Accred.: ACCSCT (1968/2002)
Prog. Accred.: Medical Assisting (ABHES)

Connecticut Training Center
1137 Main St., East Hartford 06108-2236
Type: Private, independent
Degrees: C
URL: http://www.cttraining.org
Phone: (860) 291-9898
Inst. Accred.: ACICS (1998/2005)

Dale Carnegie Training of Western Connecticut
21 Maple St., Naugatuck 06770
Type: Private, proprietary
Degrees: C
URL: http://www.westernct.dalecarnegie.com
Phone: (203) 723-9888
Inst. Accred.: ACCET (1975/2006)

Eli Whitney Regional Vocational-Technical School
71 Jones Rd., Hamden 06514
Type: Public, state/local
Degrees: C
URL: http://www.cttech.org/whitney
Phone: (203) 397-4031 ext 3
Inst. Accred.: NEASC-CTCI (1968/2007)
Prog. Accred.: Allied Health (surgical technology), Dentistry (dental assisting)

Fifth Avenue Academy of Hairdressing and Cosmetology
466 Washington Ave., North Haven 06473
Type: Private, proprietary
Degrees: C
Phone: (203) 234-7540
Inst. Accred.: NACCAS (2006)

Fox Institute of Business
99 South St., West Hartford 06110
Type: Private, proprietary
Degrees: C
URL: http://www.foxinstitute.com
Phone: (860) 947-2299 *Calendar:* Qtr. plan
Inst. Accred.: ACICS (1979/2001)
Prog. Accred.: Allied Health (medical assisting (AMA))

Clifton, NJ Campus
346 Lexington Ave., Clifton, NJ 07011
Phone: (973) 340-9500

Grasso Southeastern Technical High School Adult Education Program
189 Fort Hill Rd., Groton 06340
Type: Public, state/local
Degrees: C
URL: http://www.cttech.org/grasso
Phone: (860) 448-0220 *Calendar:* Sem. plan
Inst. Accred.: NEASC-CTCI (1982/2002)

Hartford Conservatory
834 Asylum Ave., Hartford 06105
Type: Private, independent
Degrees: C
URL: http://www.hartfordconservatory.org
Phone: (860) 246-2588 *Calendar:* Sem. plan
Inst. Accred.: NEASC-CTCI (1979/2007)

Industrial Management and Training Institute
233 Mill St., Waterbury 06706
Type: Private, proprietary
Degrees: C
URL: http://www.imtiusa.com
Phone: (203) 753-7910
Inst. Accred.: ACCSCT (1993/2004)

New York Campus
43-82 Vernon Blvd., Con Edison Learning Center, Long Island City, NY 11101
Phone: (718) 786-9298

J.M. Wright Technical High School
PO Box 1416, Stamford 06904
Type: Public, state
Degrees: C
URL: http://www.cttech.org/wright
Phone: (203) 324-4363
Inst. Accred.: NEASC-CTCI (1968/2007)

Leon Institute of Hair Design
111 Wall St., Bridgeport 06604
Type: Private, proprietary
Degrees: C
Phone: (203) 335-0364
Inst. Accred.: NACCAS (1975/2005)

Lincoln Technical Institute—New Britain
200 John Downey Dr., New Britain 06051-2904
Type: Private, proprietary
Degrees: C
URL: http://www.lincolntech.com
Phone: (860) 225-8641
Inst. Accred.: ACCSCT (1983/2003)
Prog. Accred.: Allied Health (medical assisting (AMA))

Cromwell Campus
106 Sebethe Dr., Cromwell 06416
Phone: (860) 613-3350
Prog. Accred: Culinary Education

Hamden Campus
109 Sanford St., Hamden 06514
Phone: (203) 287-7300

Shelton Campus
8 Progress Dr., Shelton 06484
Phone: (203) 929-0592
Prog. Accred: Culinary Education

New England Tractor Trailer Training School
32 Field Rd., Somers 06071-0326
Type: Private, proprietary
Degrees: C
URL: http://www.nettts.com
Phone: (860) 749-0711
Inst. Accred.: ACCSCT (1982/2003)

North Haven Academy
97 Washington Ave., North Haven 06473
Type: Private, proprietary
Degrees: C
URL: http://www.northhavenacademy.com
Phone: (203) 985-0222
Inst. Accred.: NACCAS (1979/2002)

Norwich Technical High School Adult Education Program
590 New London Turnpike, Norwich 06360
Type: Public, state/local
Degrees: C
URL: http://www.cttech.org/norwich
Phone: (860) 889-8453 *Calendar:* Sem. plan
Inst. Accred.: NEASC-CTCI (1971/2007)

Nutmeg Conservatory for the Arts
58 Main St., Torrington 06790
Type: Private, independent
Degrees: C
URL: http://www.nutmegballet.org
Phone: (860) 482-4413
Inst. Accred.: NASD (1995/2002)

Paul Mitchell the School—Danbury
109 South St., Danbury 06810
Type: Private, proprietary
Degrees: C
URL: http://www.paulmitchelltheschool.com
Phone: (203) 740-0443
Inst. Accred.: NACCAS (1971/2004)

Porter and Chester Institute
670 Lordship Blvd., PO Box 364, Stratford 06615-7123
Type: Private, proprietary
Degrees: C
URL: http://www.porterchester.com
Phone: (203) 375-4463 *Calendar:* Qtr. plan
Inst. Accred.: ACCSCT (1972/2003)
Prog. Accred.: Medical Assisting (ABHES)

Chicopee Campus
134 Dulong Circle, Chicopee, MA 01022
Phone: (413) 593-3339
Prog. Accred: Allied Health (medical assisting (AMA))

Enfield Campus
138 Weymouth Rd., Enfield 06082
Phone: (860) 741-2561
Prog. Accred: Dentistry (dental assisting)

Watertown Campus
320 Sylvan Lake Rd., Watertown 06779-1400
Phone: (860) 274-9294
Prog. Accred: Medical Assisting (ABHES)

Westborough Campus
129 Flanders Rd., Westborough, MA 01581
Phone: (508) 366-0296

Wethersfield Campus
125 Silas Deane Hwy., Wethersfield 06109-1238
Phone: (860) 529-2519
Prog. Accred: Medical Assisting (ABHES)

Renasci Academy of Hair, Inc.
486 Bridgeport Ave., Milford 06460
Type: Private, proprietary
Degrees: C
URL: http://www.renasciacademy.com
Phone: (203) 878-4228
Inst. Accred.: NACCAS (1975/2004)

Results, Inc.
Dale Carnegie Training
8 Ellsworth Rd., West Hartford 06107
Type: Private, proprietary
Degrees: C
URL: http://www.hartford.dalecarnegie.com
Phone: (860) 232-6000
Inst. Accred.: ACCET (1978/2006)

Stone Academy
1315 Dixwell Ave., Hamden 06514
Type: Private, proprietary
Degrees: C
URL: http://www.stoneacademy.com
Phone: (203) 288-7474
Inst. Accred.: ACICS (1974/2001)
Prog. Accred.: Allied Health (medical assisting (AMA))

East Hartford Campus
403 Main St., East Hartford 06118
Phone: (860) 569-0618

Waterbury Campus
101 Pierpont Rd., Waterbury 06705
Phone: (203) 756-5500

Submarine Learning Center
PO Box 5029, Groton 06349-5029
Type: Public, federal
Degrees: C
URL: https://www.npdc.navy.mil/slc
Phone: (860) 694-1710
Inst. Accred.: COE (2004)

Vinal Technical High School Adult Education Program
60 Daniels St., Middletown 06457
Type: Public, state/local
Degrees: C
URL: http://www.cttech.org/vinal
Phone: (860) 344-7100 *Calendar:* Sem. plan
Inst. Accred.: NEASC-CTCI (1968/2007)

Westlawn Institute of Marine Technology
PO Box 6000, Mystic 06355-0990
Type: Private, proprietary
Degrees: C
URL: http://www.westlawn.org
Phone: (860) 572-7900
Inst. Accred.: DETC (1971/2007)

DELAWARE

ComputerTraining.com
100 Commerce Dr., Ste. 2, Newark 19713
Type: Private, proprietary
Degrees: C
URL: http://www.computertraining-delaware.com
Phone: (800) 733-5641
Inst. Accred.: ACCET (2006)

Dawn Training Centre
3700 Lancaster Ave., Ste. 105, Wilmington 19805
Type: Private, proprietary
Degrees: C
URL: http://www.dawntrainingcentre.edu
Phone: (302) 575-1322
Inst. Accred.: ACCSCT (1990/2006)

The Delaware Learning Institute of Cosmetology
Country Garden Business Center, Route 113, Ste. F2, Dagsboro 19939
Type: Private, proprietary
Degrees: C
URL: http://www.delawarecosmetology.com
Phone: (888) 663-1121
Inst. Accred.: NACCAS (2003/2006)
Prog. Accred.: Allied Health (massage therapy)

Delaware School of Hotel Management
3005 Philadelphia Pike, Claymont 19703
Type: Private, proprietary
Degrees: C
URL: http://www.delawareschoolofhotel.com
Phone: (302) 793-1101 *Calendar:* Sem. plan
Inst. Accred.: ACICS (2004)

Harris School—Wilmington
1413 Foulk Rd., Foulkstone Plaza, Wilmington 19803
Type: Private, proprietary
System: Premier Education Group
Degrees: C
URL: http://www.harrisschool.com
Phone: (302) 478-8890
Inst. Accred.: ACCET (2000/2006)

Montessori Institute for Teacher Education
PO Box 408, Yorklyn 19736
Type: Private, independent
Degrees: C
Phone: (610) 444-4643
Inst. Accred.: MACTE (1999/2006)

National Massage Therapy Institute
1601 Concord Pike, Suites 82-84, Wilmington 19803
Type: Private, proprietary
Degrees: C
URL: http://www.studymassage.com
Phone: (888) 663-1121
Inst. Accred.: CMTA (2001/2005)

Schilling-Douglas School of Hair Design
70 Amstel Ave., Newark 19711
Type: Private, proprietary
Degrees: C
URL: http://www.schillingdouglas.com
Phone: (302) 737-5100
Inst. Accred.: NACCAS (1981/2006)

DISTRICT OF COLUMBIA

Bennett Career Institute, Inc.
700 Monroe St. NE, Washington 20017
Type: Private, proprietary
Degrees: C
Phone: (202) 526-1400
Inst. Accred.: NACCAS (1999/2002)

Career Skills Institute—Washington, D.C.
2131 K St. NW, Washington 20037
Type: Private, proprietary
Degrees: C
URL: http://www.careerskills.com
Phone: (202) 467-4223
Inst. Accred.: COE (2004)

Dudley Beauty College—Washington
2031 Rhode Island Ave. NE, Washington 20018
Type: Private, proprietary
Degrees: C
URL: http://www.dudleyq.com/Education/educationindex.html
Phone: (202) 269-3666
Inst. Accred.: NACCAS (1984/2004)

Inter-American Institute for Social Development
1350 New York Ave. NW, Stop B200, Washington 20577
Type: Private, independent
Degrees: C
URL: http://indes.iadb.org
Inst. Accred.: ACCET (2007)

Joint Military Intelligence Training Center, Defense Intelligence Agency
Defense Intelligence Agency, Building 6000, Washington 20340-5100
Type: Public, federal
Degrees: C
URL: http://www.dia.mil
Phone: (202) 231-2800
Inst. Accred.: COE (2003)

Lado International College
2233 Wisconsin Ave. NW, Washington 20007
Type: Private, proprietary
Degrees: C
URL: http://www.lado.com
Phone: (202) 223-0023
Inst. Accred.: ACCET (1996/2002)

Arlington Campus
1550 Wilson Blvd., Garden Level, Arlington, VA 22209
Phone: (703) 524-1100

Silver Spring Campus
1400 Spring St., #250, Silver Spring, MD 20910
Phone: (301) 565-5236

Levine School of Music
Sallie Mae Hall, 2801 Upton St. NW, Washington 20008
Type: Public, independent
Degrees: C
URL: http://www.levineschool.org
Phone: (202) 686-8000 *Calendar:* Sem. plan
Inst. Accred.: NASM (1989/2003)

The Middle East Institute
1761 N St. NW, Washington 20036-2882
Type: Private, independent
Degrees: C
URL: http://www.mideasti.org
Phone: (202) 785-1141
Inst. Accred.: ACCET (2005)

The National Conservatory of Dramatic Arts
1556 Wisconsin Ave. NW, Washington 20007-2758
Type: Private, independent
Degrees: C
URL: http://www.theconservatory.org
Phone: (202) 333-2202
Inst. Accred.: ACCSCT (1980/2003)

Potomac Massage Training Institute
5028 Wisconsin Ave. NW, Ste. LL, Washington 20016-4118
Type: Private, proprietary
Degrees: C
URL: http://www.pmti.org
Phone: (202) 686-7046
Inst. Accred.: CMTA (1999/2004)

Sanz College
1720 I St. NW, Washington 20006
Type: Private, proprietary
Degrees: C
URL: http://www.sanzschool.com
Phone: (202) 872-4700
Inst. Accred.: ACCET (1988/2004, Warning)

Falls Church Campus
2930 Patrick Henry Dr., Falls Church, VA 22044
Phone: (703) 237-6200

Silver Spring Campus
8455 Colesville Rd., Silver Spring, MD 20910
Phone: (301) 608-2300

School of Tomorrow
810 5th St. NW, Washington 20001
Type: Private, proprietary
Degrees: C
URL: http://www.grm.org
Phone: (202) 789-1810
Inst. Accred.: ACCET (2000/2006)

Technical Learning Centers, Inc.
1012 14th St. NW, Ste. 309, Washington 20005
Type: Private, proprietary
Degrees: C
URL: http://www.tlc-corp.com
Phone: (202) 393-7100
Inst. Accred.: ACCET (2003/2006)

United States Marine Corps Institute
Washington Navy Yard, 912 Charles Poor St. SE, Washington 20391-5680
Type: Public, federal
Degrees: C
URL: http://www.mci.usmc.mil
Phone: (202) 685-7463
Inst. Accred.: DETC (1977/2003)

FLORIDA

Academy for Practical Nursing and Health Occupations
5154 Okeechobee Blvd., Ste. 201, West Palm Beach 33417
Type: Public, state-related
Degrees: C
URL: http://www.apnho.edu
Phone: (561) 683-1400
Inst. Accred.: COE (1999/2005)

Academy of Career Training
3501 West Vine St., #111, Kissimmee 34741
Type: Public, proprietary
Degrees: C
URL: http://academyofcareertraining.com
Phone: (417) 943-8777
Inst. Accred.: NACCAS (2007)

Academy of Cosmetology
2088 North Ct.enay Pkwy., Merritt Island 32953
Type: Private, proprietary
Degrees: C
URL: http://floridacosmetologyschools.com
Phone: (321) 452-8490
Inst. Accred.: NACCAS (1987/2002)

Academy of Cosmetology
1975 Palm Bay Rd. NE, Palm Bay 32905
Type: Private, proprietary
Degrees: C
URL: floridacosmetologyschools.com
Phone: (321) 951-0595
Inst. Accred.: NACCAS (1989/2004)

Academy of Healing Arts, Massage and Facial Skin Care
3141 South Military Trail, Lake Worth 33463-2113
Type: Private, proprietary
Degrees: C
URL: http://www.ahamassage.com
Phone: (561) 965-5550
Inst. Accred.: ACCSCT (1992/2003)

Academy of Professional Careers
114 South Semoran Blvd., Winter Park 32792
Type: Private, proprietary
Degrees: C
Phone: (407) 673-8477
Inst. Accred.: NACCAS (2006)

Advance Science Institute
3750 West 12th Ave., Hialeah 33012
Type: Private, proprietary
Degrees: C
Phone: (305) 827-5452
Inst. Accred.: ACCSCT (2003)

Advanced Technical Centers
5600 NW 36th St., Ste. 104, Miami 33166-2787
Type: Private, independent
Degrees: C
URL: http://www.advancedtechnicalcenters.com
Phone: (305) 871-2808
Inst. Accred.: COE (1985/2005)

American Advanced Technicians Institute Corporation
6801 West 20th Ave., Hialeah 33014
Type: Private, proprietary
Degrees: C
URL: http://www.aationline.com
Phone: (305) 362-5519
Inst. Accred.: ACCET (2002/2006)

American Institute of Beauty, Inc
13244 66th St. North, Largo 33773
Type: Private, proprietary
Degrees: C
URL: http://aibschool.com
Phone: (727) 532-2125
Inst. Accred.: NACCAS (2005)

Americare School of Nursing
7275 Estapona Circle, Fern Park 32730
Type: Private, proprietary
Degrees: C
Phone: (407) 673-7406
Inst. Accred.: ABHES (1997/2006)
Prog. Accred.: Dentistry (dental assisting)

St. Petersburg Campus
5335 66th St. North, St. Petersburg 33709
Phone: (727) 547-1822
Prog. Accred: Medical Assisting (ABHES), Surgical Technology

Ari-Ben Aviator
3800 St. Lucie Blvd., Ft. Pierce 34946
Type: Private, proprietary
Degrees: C
URL: http://www.aribenaviator.com
Phone: (561) 466-4822
Inst. Accred.: ACCSCT (1997/2006)

Artistic Nails and Beauty Academy
4951-A Adamo Dr., Tampa 33605
Type: Private, proprietary
Degrees: C
URL: http://www.artisticbeautyschool.com
Phone: (813) 654-4529
Inst. Accred.: NACCAS (2003/2006)

ASM Beauty World Academy
6423 Stirling Rd., Davie 33314
Type: Private, proprietary
Degrees: C
Phone: (954) 966-5998
Inst. Accred.: NACCAS (1990/2005)

Atlantic Technical Center
4700 Coconut Creek Pkwy., Coconut Creek 33063
Type: Public, state/local
Degrees: C
URL: http://www.atlantictechcenter.com
Phone: (754) 321-5100
Inst. Accred.: COE (1978/2007)
Prog. Accred.: Culinary Education, Practical Nursing

Pompano Beach Campus
1400 NE 6th St., Pompano Beach 33060
Phone: (305) 786-7600

Audio Recording Technology Institute
4525 Vineland Rd., Ste. 201B, Orlando 32811
Type: Private, proprietary
Degrees: C
URL: http://www.audiocareer.com
Phone: (407) 423-2784
Inst. Accred.: ACCSCT (1999/2004)

Aveda Institute
235 3rd St. South, Ste. 100, St. Petersburg 33709
Type: Private, proprietary
Degrees: C
URL: http://avedaflorida.com
Phone: (727) 820-3162
Inst. Accred.: NACCAS (2007)

B Naturale Beauty School, Inc.
3772 West Oakland Park Blvd., Lauderdale Lakes 33311-1109
Type: Private, proprietary
Degrees: C
Phone: (954) 733-4800
Inst. Accred.: NACCAS (2007)

The Beauty Institute, Inc.
2215 North Military Trail, #1, West Palm Beach 33409
Type: Private, proprietary
Degrees: C
Phone: (561) 688-0225
Inst. Accred.: NACCAS (2003/2006)

Beauty Schools of America
1060 West 49 St., Hialeah 33012
Type: Private, proprietary
Degrees: C
URL: http://www.bsa.edu
Phone: (305) 362-9003
Inst. Accred.: COE (1989/2007)

Miami Campus
1176 SW 67th Ave., Miami 33144
Phone: (305) 267-6604

North Miami Beach Campus
1813 NE 163 St., North Miami Beach 33162
Phone: (888) 456-4272

Bene's International School of Beauty, Inc.
7127 U.S. Hwy. 19, New Port Richey 34652
Type: Private, proprietary
Degrees: C
URL: http://www.isbschool.com
Phone: (727) 848-8415
Inst. Accred.: NACCAS (1979/2005)

Bradenton Beauty and Barber Academy, Inc.
5505 Manatee Ave. West, Bradenton 34209
Type: Private, proprietary
Degrees: C
URL: http://www.beauty-academy.us
Phone: (941) 761-4400
Inst. Accred.: NACCAS (1982/2007)

Bradford-Union Area Vocational-Technical Center
609 North Orange St., Starke 32091
Type: Public, local
Degrees: C
URL: http://www.bradfordvotech.com
Phone: (966) 966-6760
Inst. Accred.: COE (1998/2003)

Cambridge Institute of Allied Health
1912 Boothe Circle, Ste. 200, Longwood 32750
Type: Private, proprietary
Degrees: C
Phone: (407) 265-8383
Inst. Accred.: ABHES (2004/2007)
Prog. Accred.: Medical Assisting (ABHES)

Career Institute of Florida
701 94th Ave. North, Ste. 100, St. Petersburg 33702
Type: Private, proprietary
Degrees: C
URL: http://www.cifontheweb.com
Phone: (727) 576-9597
Inst. Accred.: ACCSCT (2004)

Career Training Institute
3318 Edgewater Dr., Orlando 32804
Type: Private, proprietary
Degrees: C
Phone: (407) 884-1816
Inst. Accred.: ACCSCT (1988/2002)

Center for Explosive Ordnance Disposal and Diving
350 South Crag Rd., Panama City 32407-7016
Type: Public, federal
Degrees: C
URL: https://www.npdc.navy.mil/ceneoddive
Phone: (850) 235-5241
Inst. Accred.: COE (1983/2005)

Center for Information Dominance Corry Station
640 Roberts Ave., Code CIS, Pensacola 32511-5138
Type: Public, federal
Degrees: C
URL: https://www.npdc.navy.mil/ceninfodom
Phone: (850) 452-6516
Inst. Accred.: COE (1975/2007)

Center for Naval Aviation Technical Training
230 Chevalier Field Ave., Building 3460, Ste. C, Pensacola 32508-5168
Type: Public, federal
Degrees: C
URL: https://www.npdc.navy.mil/cnatt
Phone: (850) 452-7163
Inst. Accred.: COE (1976/2004)

Trident Training Facility
1040 USS Georgia Ave., Kings Bay 31547-6300
URL: https://www.cnet.navy.mil/ttfkb/index1.html
Phone: (912)-673-2926

Charlotte Technical Center
18150 Murdock Circle, Port Charlotte 33948
Type: Public, state
Degrees: C
URL: http://charlottetechcenter.ccps.k12.fl.us
Phone: (941) 255-7500
Inst. Accred.: COE (1983/2005)
Prog. Accred.: Dentistry (dental assisting)

Commercial Diving Academy
8137 North Main St., Jacksonville 32208
Type: Private, proprietary
Degrees: C
URL: http://www.commercialdivingacademy.com
Phone: (904) 766-7736
Inst. Accred.: ACCET (2005)

Compu-Med Vocational Careers
2900 West 12th Ave., 3rd Flr., Hialeah 33012
Type: Private, proprietary
Degrees: C
Phone: (305) 888-9200
Inst. Accred.: ACCSCT (1994/2004)

Compu-Med Vocational Careers
9738 SW 24th St., Miami 33165
Type: Private, proprietary
Degrees: C
Phone: (305) 553-2898
Inst. Accred.: ACCSCT (1999/2004)

Concorde Career Institute
7960 Arlington Expressway, Jacksonville 32211-7429
Type: Private, proprietary
System: Concorde Career Colleges, Inc.
Degrees: C
URL: http://www.concordecareercolleges.com
Phone: (904) 725-0525
Inst. Accred.: ACCSCT (1977/2004)
Prog. Accred.: Allied Health (surgical technology)

Concorde Career Institute
4000 N. State Rd. 7, Ste. 100, Lauderdale Lakes 33319
Type: Private, proprietary
System: Concorde Career Colleges, Inc.
Degrees: C
URL: http://www.concordecareercolleges.com
Phone: (954) 731-8880
Inst. Accred.: ACCSCT (1983/2005)
Prog. Accred.: Allied Health (surgical technology)

Concorde Career Institute
4202 West Spruce St., Tampa 33607-4127
Type: Private, proprietary
System: Concorde Career Colleges, Inc.
Degrees: C
URL: http://www.concordecareercolleges.com
Phone: (813) 874-0094
Inst. Accred.: ACCSCT (1981/2004)
Prog. Accred.: Allied Health (surgical technology)

Coral Ridge Training School
2740 E. Oakland Park Blvd., Ste. 301, Fort Lauderdale 33306
Type: Private, proprietary
Degrees: C
URL: http://www.geocities.com/CRTrainingSchool
Phone: (954) 561-2022
Inst. Accred.: COE (1996/2007)

CORE Institute
223 West Carolina St., Tallahassee 32301
Type: Private, proprietary
Degrees: C
URL: http://www.coreinstitute.com
Phone: (850) 222-8673
Inst. Accred.: CMTA (1999/2004, Warning)

Cortiva Institute-Humanities Center Institute of Allied Health/School of Massage
4045 Park Blvd., Pinellas Park 33718
Type: Private, proprietary
Degrees: C
URL: http://www.cortiva.com/locations/tampa
Phone: (727) 541-5200
Inst. Accred.: ACCSCT (1984/2005)

Dade Medical Institute
3401 NW 7th St., Miami 33125
Type: Private, proprietary
Degrees: C
URL: http://www.dademedicalinstitute.com
Phone: (305) 644-1171
Inst. Accred.: ABHES (2003/2005)

David G. Erwin Technical Center
2010 East Hillsborough Ave., Tampa 33612
Type: Public, state
Degrees: C
URL: http://erwin.edu
Phone: (813) 231-1800
Inst. Accred.: COE (1981/2003)
Prog. Accred.: Allied Health (electroneurodiagnostic technology, medical assisting (AMA), respiratory therapy technology, surgical technology), Clinical Lab Technology, Dentistry (dental assisting)

Defense Equal Opportunity Management Institute
366 Tuskegee Airmen Dr., Patrick AFB 32925-3399
Type: Public, federal
Degrees: C
URL: https://www.deomi.org
Phone: (321) 494-6976
Inst. Accred.: COE (1983/2007)

Duwayne E. Keller and Associates, Inc.
12415 SW Sheri Ave., Ste. A, Lake Suzy 34269
Type: Private, proprietary
Degrees: C
URL: http://www.swflorida.dale-carnegie.com
Phone: (941) 766-7227
Inst. Accred.: ACCET (1976/2007)

Educating Hands School of Massage
120 SW 8th St., Miami 33130-3513
Type: Private, proprietary
Degrees: C
URL: http://www.educatinghands.com
Phone: (305) 285-6991
Inst. Accred.: CMTA (1999/2007)

Embassy CES
301 East Las Olas Blvd., 6th Flr., Ft. Lauderdale 33301
Type: Private, proprietary
Degrees: C
URL: http://www.studygroup.com/embassyces
Phone: (954) 522-0081
Inst. Accred.: ACCET (1984/2002)

Boston Campus
Eager House, 49 Seminary Ave., Lasell College, Newton, MA 02466
Phone: (617) 796-4303

Federal Way Campus
3600 South 344th Way, Federal Way, WA 98001

New York Campus
330 7th Ave., 5th & 6th Flr.s, New York, NY 10001
Phone: (212) 629-7300

San Diego Campus
600 B St., Ste. 1700, San Diego, CA 92101
Phone: (619) 235-9222

San Francisco Campus
1462 Pine St., San Francisco, CA 94109
Phone: (415) 447-9014

West Hills Campus
22801 Roscoe Blvd., West Hills, CA 91304
Phone: (813) 731-8111

Westminster Campus
1870 West 122nd Ave., Westminster, CO 80234

The English Center
3501 SW 28 St., Miami 33133
Type: Public, local
Degrees: C
URL: http://www.tecmiami.com
Phone: (305) 448-7731
Inst. Accred.: COE (2004)

Fashion Focus Hair Academy
2184 Gulf Gate Dr., Sarasota 34231
Type: Private, proprietary
Degrees: C
URL: http://www.dudleyq.com/cosmetology.html
Phone: (941) 921-4877
Inst. Accred.: NACCAS (1980/2003)

Federal Correctional Institution—Tallahassee
501 Capital Circle, NE, Tallahassee 32301-3572
Type: Public, federal
Degrees: C
URL: http://www.bop.gov/locations/institutions/tal/index
Phone: (850) 878-2173
Inst. Accred.: COE (1985/2002)
Prog. Accred.: Psychology Internship

First Coast Technical Institute
2980 Collins Ave., St. Augustine 32095-1919
Type: Public, state-chartered
Degrees: C
URL: http://www.fcti.org
Phone: (904) 826-3284
Inst. Accred.: COE (1980/2002)
Prog. Accred.: Allied Health (medical assisting (AMA)), Culinary Education

Clay County Campus
4035 Reynolds Blvd., Bldg. 91, Green Cove Springs 32043-8360
Phone: (904) 824-4401

Putnam County Campus
820 Reid St., Ste. D, Palatka 32177
Phone: (904) 329-3550

FlightSafety Academy
Vero Beach Airport, PO Box 2708, Vero Beach 32961-2708
Type: Private, proprietary
Degrees: C
URL: http://www.flightsafetyacademy.com
Phone: (561) 564-7600
Inst. Accred.: ACCSCT (1975/2003)

Florida Academy of Health and Beauty
2300 NW 9th Ave., Wilton Manors 33311
Type: Private, proprietary
Degrees: C
Phone: (954) 563-9098
Inst. Accred.: NACCAS (2003/2006)

Florida Barber Academy
3269 North Federal Hwy., Pompano Beach 33064
Type: Private, proprietary
Degrees: C
Phone: (954) 781-6066
Inst. Accred.: COE (2001/2007)

Florida Career Institute
5925 Imperial Pkwy., Ste. 200, Mulberry 33860
Type: Private, proprietary
Degrees: C
URL: http://www.floridacareerinstitute.com
Phone: (863) 646-1400
Inst. Accred.: ACCET (1989/2004)
Prog. Accred.: Allied Health (medical assisting (AMA))

Florida Education Institute
5818 SW 8th St., Miami 33144
Type: Private, proprietary
Degrees: C
URL: http://www.fei.edu
Phone: (305) 263-9990
Inst. Accred.: COE (2001/2007)

The Florida Institute of Animal Arts
3776 Howell Branch Rd., Winter Park 32792
Type: Private, proprietary
Degrees: C
URL: http://www.fifi-inc.com
Phone: (407) 657-8088
Inst. Accred.: ACCSCT (2001/2006)

Florida Institute of Montessori Studies
1240 Banana River Dr., Indian Harbour Beach 32937-4105
Type: Private, independent
Degrees: C
URL: http://www.montessorischools.org
Phone: (321) 779-0031
Inst. Accred.: MACTE (1999/2002)

Florida Institute of Ultrasound, Inc.
8800 University Pkwy., Building A4, Pensacola 32514
Type: Private, proprietary
Degrees: C
URL: http://www.fiuonline.net
Phone: (850) 478-7611
Inst. Accred.: ABHES (1985/2002)

Florida Language Center
5975 North Federal Hwy., Ste. 243, Ft. Lauderdale 33308
Type: Private, proprietary
Degrees: C
URL: http://www.lalgroup.com/florida
Phone: (954) 771-0222
Inst. Accred.: CEA (2006)

Florida Medical Training Institute
4400 West Sample Rd., Ste. 134, Coconut Creek 33073
Type: Private, proprietary
Degrees: C
URL: http://www.fmti.edu
Phone: (954) 979-6500
Inst. Accred.: ABHES (2003)

Florida Medical Training Institute
478 Ballard Dr., Melbourne 32935
Type: Private, proprietary
Degrees: C
URL: http://www.ems-training.com
Phone: (321) 751-9696
Inst. Accred.: ABHES (2003)

Miami Campus
7902 NW 36th St., Ste. 214-215, Miami 33166
Phone: (305) 715-0377

Orlando Campus
5575 South Semoran Blvd., Ste. 34-35, Orlando 32822
Phone: (407) 275-9660

Florida School of Massage
6421 SW 13th St., Gainesville 32608
Type: Private, proprietary
Degrees: C
URL: http://www.floridaschoolofmassage.com
Phone: (352) 378-7891
Inst. Accred.: CMTA (1999/2004)

Florida School of Traditional Midwifery
810 East University Ave., Gainesville 32601
Type: Private, independent
Degrees: C
URL: http://www.fstmgainesville.com
Phone: (352) 338-0766 *Calendar:* Sem. plan
Inst. Accred.: MEAC (2000/2005)

Folkner Training Associates, Inc.
8641 Baypine Rd., Ste. 2, Jacksonville 32256
Type: Private, proprietary
Degrees: C
URL: http://www.jacksonvill.dale-carnegie.com
Phone: (904) 443-2929
Inst. Accred.: ACCET (1978/2004)

Fort Pierce Beauty Academy
3028 South U.S. 1, Fort Pierce 34982
Type: Private, proprietary
Degrees: C
Phone: (772) 464-4885
Inst. Accred.: NACCAS (1985/2005)

Beauty and Massage Institute
719 17th St., Vero Beach 32960
Phone: (772) 978-7178

Port St. Lucie Beauty Academy
7644 South U.S. 1, Port St. Lucie 34983
Phone: (772) 340-3540

Galiano Career Academy
1140 East Altamonte Dr., Ste. 1020, Altamonte Springs 32701
Type: Private, proprietary
Degrees: C
URL: http://www.galianocareeracademy.com
Phone: (407) 331-7443
Inst. Accred.: ABHES (2004/2006)

George Stone Vocational-Technical Center
2400 Longleaf Dr., Pensacola 32526-8922
Type: Public, state/local
Degrees: C
URL: http://www.georgestonecenter.com
Phone: (850) 941-6200
Inst. Accred.: COE (1981/2003)

George T. Baker Aviation School
3275 NW 42nd Ave., Miami 33142
Type: Public, state
Degrees: C
URL: http://bakeraviation.dadeschools.net
Phone: (305) 871-3143
Inst. Accred.: COE (1978/2005)

The Harid Conservatory
2285 Potomac Rd., Boca Raton 33431-5518
Type: Private, independent
Degrees: C
URL: http://www.harid.edu
Phone: (561) 997-2677
Inst. Accred.: NASD (1993/2004)

Health Opportunity Technical Center, Inc.
18441 NW 2nd Ave., Ste. 300, Miami 33169
Type: Private, proprietary
Degrees: C
Phone: (305) 249-2275
Inst. Accred.: ABHES (2005)

Helicopter Adventures
365 Golden Knights Blvd., Titusville 32780
Type: Private, proprietary
Degrees: C
URL: http://www.heli.com
Phone: (321) 385-2919
Inst. Accred.: ACCSCT (1994/2004)

Henry W. Brewster Technical Center
2222 North Tampa St., Tampa 33602
Type: Public, state
Degrees: C
URL: http://www.brewstertech.org
Phone: (813) 276-5448
Inst. Accred.: COE (1989/2002)

Hi-Tech The School of Cosmetology
1303 SW 107th Ave., Miami 33174
Type: Private, proprietary
Degrees: C
URL: http://www.hitechtheschool.com
Phone: (305) 487-9997
Inst. Accred.: NACCAS (2006/2007)

Hollywood Institute of Beauty Careers
2642 Hollywood Blvd., Hollywood 33020
Type: Private, proprietary
Degrees: C
Phone: (954) 922-5505
Inst. Accred.: NACCAS (2002/2005)

I.C.E. Beauty School and Spa Training Center
280 South State Rd. 434, Ste. 2045, Altamonte Springs 32714
Type: Private, proprietary
Degrees: C
Phone: (407) 862-4001
Inst. Accred.: NACCAS (2004)

International Academy
2550 South Ridgewood Ave., South Daytona 32119
Type: Private, proprietary
Degrees: C
URL: http://www.iahd.net
Phone: (386) 767-4600
Inst. Accred.: NACCAS (1984/2004)

International School of Health and Beauty
2045 North University Dr., Sunrise 33322
Type: Private, proprietary
Degrees: C
URL: http://www.ishb.edu
Phone: (954) 741-0088
Inst. Accred.: COE (1999/2005)

International School of Health and Beauty
3714 West Oakland Park Blvd., Lauderdale Lakes 33311
Type: Private, proprietary
Degrees: C
URL: http://www.ishb.edu
Phone: (954) 741-0088
Inst. Accred.: COE (1999/2005)

International Training Careers
7360 SW 24th St., Blue Gables Plaza, Ste. 31, Miami 33155
Type: Private, independent
Degrees: C
URL: http://www.internationaltrainingcareers.com
Phone: (305) 263-9696
Inst. Accred.: COE (2001/2007)

Jacksonville Beauty Institute, Inc.
5045 Sontel Dr., Ste. 80, Jacksonville 32208
Type: Private, proprietary
Degrees: C
Phone: (904) 768-9001
Inst. Accred.: NACCAS (2001/2004)

Tampa Bay Beauty Institute
6211 East Hillsborough Ave., Tampa 33610
Phone: (813) 514-9100

Ken Roberts Corporation
4295 South Atlantic Ave., Wilbur by the Sea 32119
Type: Private, proprietary
Degrees: C
URL: http://www.centralflorida.dalecarnegie.com
Phone: (904) 767-6346
Inst. Accred.: ACCET (1976/2004)

La Belle Beauty Academy—Miami
2960 SW 8th St., Miami 33135
Type: Private, proprietary
Degrees: C
URL: http://www.beautyacademy.com
Phone: (305) 649-2800
Inst. Accred.: NACCAS (1988/2003)

La Belle Beauty School—Hialeah
775 West 49th St., Ste. 5, Hialeah 33012
Type: Private, proprietary
Degrees: C
URL: http://www.beautyacademy.com
Phone: (305) 558-0562
Inst. Accred.: NACCAS (1979/2003)

Lake Technical Center
2001 Kurt St., Eustis 32726
Type: Public, state
Degrees: C
URL: http://www.laketech.org
Phone: (352) 589-2250
Inst. Accred.: COE (1974/2007)
Prog. Accred.: Allied Health (EMT-paramedic), Culinary Education

Kenneth Bragg Public Safety Complex
12900 Ln. Park Cutoff, Tavares 32778-9653
Phone: (352) 742-6463

The Langauge Academy
300 NE 3rd Ave., Ste. 100, Fort Lauderdale 33301
Type: Private, proprietary
Degrees: C
URL: http://www.languageacademy.com
Phone: (954) 462-8373
Inst. Accred.: ACCET (2002)

Lee County High Tech Center North
360 Santa Barbara Blvd. North, Cape Coral 33993
Type: Public, state
Degrees: C
URL: http://www.hightechnorth.com
Phone: (239) 574-4440
Inst. Accred.: COE (1996/2002)
Prog. Accred.: Allied Health (medical assisting (AMA), surgical technology)

Lee County High Tech Center—Central
3800 Michigan Ave., Fort Myers 33916
Type: Public, state/local
Degrees: C
URL: http://www.leeschools.net/schools/voc
Phone: (941) 334-4544
Inst. Accred.: COE (1978/2005)

Levin School of Health Care
2206 West Atlantic Ave., Delray Beach 33445
Type: Private, proprietary
Degrees: C
URL: http://levinschoolofhealthcare.com
Phone: (561) 274-9663
Inst. Accred.: ACICS (2004)

Lindsey Hopkins Technical Education Center
750 NW 20th St., Miami 33127
Type: Public, state/local
Degrees: C
URL: http://lindsey.dadeschools.net
Phone: (305) 324-6070
Inst. Accred.: COE (1972/2005)
Prog. Accred.: Allied Health (surgical technology), Dentistry (dental assisting, dental laboratory technology)

Lively Technical Center
500 North Appleyard Dr., Tallahassee 32304-2895
Type: Public, state
Degrees: C
URL: http://www.livelytech.com
Phone: (850) 487-7555
Inst. Accred.: COE (1977/2004)
Prog. Accred.: Allied Health (medical assisting (AMA))

Florida State Hospital
HRS, District 2, Chattahoochee 32324
Phone: (850) 663-7202

Lively Aviation Center
3290 Capital Circle, SW, Tallahassee 32310
Phone: (850) 488-2460

Loraine's Academy, Inc.
1012 58th St. North, Tyrone Garden Center, St. Petersburg 33710
Type: Private, proprietary
Degrees: C
URL: http://www.lorainesacademy.net
Phone: (727) 347-4247
Inst. Accred.: NACCAS (1968/2004)

Lorenzo Walker Institute of Technology
3702 Estey Ave., Naples 34104-4498
Type: Public, state
Degrees: C
URL: http://www.collier.k12.fl.us/workforce/lwit
Phone: (239) 430-6900
Inst. Accred.: COE (1980/2002)
Prog. Accred.: Allied Health (medical assisting (AMA), surgical technology), Dentistry (dental assisting)

Management Resources Institute
4343 West Flagler St., Ste. 203, Miami 33134-1586
Type: Private, proprietary
Degrees: C
URL: http://www.managementresourcesinstitute.com
Phone: (305) 442-9223
Inst. Accred.: COE (2007)

Manatee Technical Institute
5603 34th St., West, Bradenton 34210-5297
Type: Public, state
Degrees: C
URL: http://www.manateetechnicalinstitute.org
Phone: (941) 751-7900
Inst. Accred.: COE (1980/2002)
Prog. Accred.: Allied Health (EMT (paramedic), medical assisting (AMA)), Cosmetology, Dentistry (dental assisting)

Manhattan Hairstyling Academy
1906 West Platt St., Tampa 33606
Type: Private, proprietary
Degrees: C
URL: http://www.manhattanhairstylingacademy.com
Phone: (813) 837-2525
Inst. Accred.: NACCAS (1980/2006)

Manhattan Beauty School, Inc.
1720 16th St. North, St. Petersburg 33705
Phone: (727) 821-7575

Tampa Campus
2317 East Fletcher Ave., Tampa 33612
Phone: (813) 264-3535

Valrico Campus
Royal Oak Plaza, 3244 Lithia Pinecrest, #103-104, Valrico 33594
Phone: (813) /258-0505

Marion County Community Technical and Adult Education
1014 SW 7th Rd., Ocala 34474
Type: Public, state/local
Degrees: C
URL: http://www.marion.k12.fl.us/schools/chs
Phone: (352) 671-7200
Inst. Accred.: COE (2003)
Prog. Accred.: Allied Health (medical assisting (AMA)), Radiography

Melbourne Beauty School
686 North Wickham Rd., Melbourne 32935
Type: Private, proprietary
Degrees: C
Phone: (321) 259-0001
Inst. Accred.: NACCAS (1981/2005)

Miami Job Corps Center
3050 NW 183rd St., Miami 33056-3536
Type: Public, federal
Degrees: C
URL: http://miami.jobcorps.gov
Phone: (305) 626-7800
Inst. Accred.: COE (1986/2003)

Miami Lakes Educational Center
5780 NW 158th St., Miami 33014
Type: Public, state/local
Degrees: C
URL: http://mlec.dadeschools.net
Phone: (305) 557-1100
Inst. Accred.: COE (1983/2004, Probation)

Mid Florida Tech
2900 West Oak Ridge Rd., Orlando 32809
Type: Public, state
Degrees: C
URL: http://www.mft.ocps.net
Phone: (407) 251-6047
Inst. Accred.: COE (1974/2005)

Montessori Academy Training Institute
19620 Pines Blvd., Ste. 115, Pembroke Pines 33029
Type: Private, independent
Degrees: C
URL: http://www.montessori-academy.org/mati.htm
Phone: (954) 437-2329 *Calendar:* Sem. plan
Inst. Accred.: MACTE (2006)

Montessori Teacher Training Institute
6050 SW 57th Ave., Miami 33143
Type: Private, independent
Degrees: C
URL: http://www.alexandermontessori.com
Phone: (305) 665-6033
Inst. Accred.: MACTE (2001)

National Aviation Academy
6225 Ulmerton Rd., Clearwater 33760
Type: Private, proprietary
Degrees: C
URL: http://www.naa.edu
Phone: (727) 531-2080
Inst. Accred.: COE (1991/2003)

National Training, Inc.
PO Box 65789, Orange Park 32065-0014
Type: Private, proprietary
Degrees: C
URL: http://www.truckschool.com
Phone: (904) 272-4000
Inst. Accred.: DETC (1982/2003)

Truck Driving and Heavy Equipment Operating Training Site
SR 202, Green Cove Springs 32043
Phone: (904) 272-4000

New Concept Massage & Beauty School, Inc.
2022 SW 1st St., Miami 33135
Type: Private, proprietary
Degrees: C
Phone: (305) 642-3020
Inst. Accred.: NACCAS (2000/2006)

New Dimension Academy of Beauty
4551 Gunn Hwy., Tampa 33624
Type: Private, proprietary
Degrees: C
URL: http://www.newdimensionacademy.com
Phone: (813) 264-9677
Inst. Accred.: COE (2006)

New Gate Center for Montessori Studies
5237 Ashton Rd., Sarasota 34233
Type: Private, independent
Degrees: C
URL: http://www.thenewgateschool.org
Phone: (941) 504-2640
Inst. Accred.: MACTE (2001)

New Professions Technical Institute
4100 West Flagler St., Miami 33134
Type: Private, proprietary
Degrees: C
URL: http://www.npti.com
Phone: (305) 461-2223
Inst. Accred.: ACCET (1997/2006)

New World Symphony
541 Lincoln Rd., Miami Beach 33139
Type: Private, independent
Degrees: C
URL: http://www.nws.org
Phone: (305) 673-3330
Inst. Accred.: NASM (1999/2004)

Normandy Beauty School of Jacksonville
5373 Lenox Ave., Jacksonville 32205
Type: Private, proprietary
Degrees: C
Phone: (904) 786-6250
Inst. Accred.: NACCAS (1979/2004)

North Florida Cosmetology Institute, Inc.
2424 Allen Rd., Tallahassee 32312
Type: Private, proprietary
Degrees: C
URL: http://www.cosmetologyinst.com
Phone: (850) 878-5269
Inst. Accred.: NACCAS (2001/2004)

Nouvelle Institute
3271 Northwest 7th St., Ste. 106, Miami 33125
Type: Private, proprietary
Degrees: C
Phone: (305) 643-3360
Inst. Accred.: NACCAS (1992/2005)

Hialeah Campus
500 West 49th St., Second Flr., Hialeah 33012
Phone: (305) 557-3017

Okaloosa Applied Technology Center
1976 Lewis Turner Blvd., Fort Walton Beach 32547
Type: Public, state
Degrees: C
URL: http://www.okaloosa.k12.fl.us/oatc
Phone: (850) 833-3500
Inst. Accred.: COE (1979/2007)

Orlando Montessori Teacher Education Institute
901 Begonia Rd., Celebration 34747
Type: Private, independent
Degrees: C
Phone: (407) 566-1561
Inst. Accred.: MACTE (1996/2003)

Orlando Tech
301 West Amelia St., Orlando 32801
Type: Public, state/local
Degrees: C
URL: http://www.orlandotech.ocps.net
Phone: (407) 246-7060
Inst. Accred.: COE (1983/2006)
Prog. Accred.: Allied Health (surgical technology), Dentistry (dental assisting)

Palm Beach Academy of Health and Beauty
1220A 10th St., Lake Park 33403
Type: Private, proprietary
Degrees: C
URL: http://www.pbacademy.net
Phone: (561) 845-1400
Inst. Accred.: ACCSCT (2004)

PC Professor of Boca Raton
7056 Beracasa Way, Boca Raton 33433
Type: Private, proprietary
Degrees: C
URL: http://www.pcprofessor.com
Phone: (561) 750-7879
Inst. Accred.: ACCSCT (2001/2006)

PC Professor of Pembroke Pines
600 North Hiatus Rd., Ste. 105, Pembroke Pines 33026
Type: Private, proprietary
Degrees: C
URL: http://www.pcprofessor.edu
Phone: (954) 704-4444
Inst. Accred.: ACCSCT (2003/2006, Probation)

PC Professor of West Palm Beach
6080 Okeechobee Blvd., Ste. 200, West Palm Beach 33417
Type: Private, proprietary
Degrees: C
URL: http://www.pcprofessor.com
Phone: (561) 684-3333
Inst. Accred.: ACCSCT (2001/2006)

Pelican Flight Training Center
1601 SW 75th Ave., Pembroke Pines 33023
Type: Private, proprietary
Degrees: C
URL: http://www.pelican-airways.com
Phone: (954) 966-9750
Inst. Accred.: ACCSCT (2000/2003)

Pensacola School of Massage Therapy and Health Careers
2409 Creighton Rd., Pensacola 32504
Type: Private, proprietary
Degrees: C
URL: http://www.pensacolamassageschool.com
Phone: (850) 474-1330
Inst. Accred.: COE (2006)

Phoenix East Aviation, Inc.
561 Pearl Harbor Dr., Daytona Beach 32114
Type: Private, proprietary
Degrees: C
URL: http://www.pea.com
Phone: (386) 258-0703
Inst. Accred.: ACCET (1995/2004)

Pinellas Technical Education Center
6100 154th Ave., North, Clearwater 34620
Type: Public, state
Degrees: C
URL: http://www.myptec.org
Phone: (727) 538-7167
Inst. Accred.: COE (1970/2002)
Prog. Accred.: Allied Health (surgical technology), Culinary Education

Pinellas Technical Education Center
901 34th St., St. Petersburg 33711-2298
Type: Public, state
Degrees: C
URL: http://www.myptec.org
Phone: (727) 893-2500
Inst. Accred.: COE (1975/1995)
Prog. Accred.: Allied Health (medical assisting (AMA)), Dentistry (dental assisting)

Clearwater Extension Campus
2735 Whitney Rd., Clearwater 33760-1610
Phone: (727) 538-7167

Pinellas County Jail
14400 49th St., North, Clearwater 34620
Phone: (813) 531-3531

The Poynter Institute for Media Studies
801 Third St., South, St. Petersburg 33701
Type: Private, proprietary
Degrees: C
URL: http://www.poynter.org
Phone: (727) 821-9494
Inst. Accred.: COE (1983/2005)

Praxis Institute
1850 SW 8th St., 4th Flr., Miami 33135
Type: Private, proprietary
Degrees: C
URL: http://www.thepraxisinstitute.com
Phone: (305) 642-4104
Inst. Accred.: COE (1994/2006)

Professional Health Training Academy
1240 SE Hwy. 484, Ocala 34480
Type: Private, proprietary
Degrees: C
URL: http://www.phtacademy.com
Phone: (352) 245-4119
Inst. Accred.: COE (2006)

Radford M. Locklin Technical Center
5330 Berryhill Rd., Milton 32571
Type: Public, state
Degrees: C
URL: http://www.santarosa.k12.fl.us/ltc
Phone: (850) 983-5700
Inst. Accred.: COE (1988/2005)

Rick J. Gallegos and Associates, Inc.
1408 North Westshore Blvd., Ste. 912, Tampa 33607
Type: Private, proprietary
Degrees: C
URL: http://www.tampabay.dale-carnegie.com
Phone: (813) 288-8778
Inst. Accred.: ACCET (1976/2001)

Ridge Career Center
7700 State Rd. 544, Winter Haven 33881
Type: Public, state/local
Degrees: C
URL: http://www.polk-fl.net/ridge
Phone: (863) 419-3060
Inst. Accred.: COE (1982/2005)

Riverside Hairstyling Academy
3530 Beach Blvd., Jacksonville 32207
Type: Private, proprietary
Degrees: C
URL: http://www.riversidehair.com
Phone: (904) 398-0502
Inst. Accred.: NACCAS (1974/2004)

Robert Morgan Educational Center
18180 SW 122nd Ave., Miami 33177
Type: Public, state/local
Degrees: C
URL: http://rmec.dadeschools.net
Phone: (305) 253-9920
Inst. Accred.: COE (1983/2006)
Prog. Accred.: Allied Health (medical assisting (AMA)), Dentistry (dental assisting)

Community Habilitation Center
11450 Southwest 79th St., Miami 33173
Phone: (305) 279-7999

Haven Center
11300 SW 80 Terrace, Miami 33173
Phone: (305) 271-3232

Princeton Agribusiness Training Center
24315 South Dixie Hwy., Princeton 33030
Phone: (305) 279-7999

SABER
3990 West Flagler St., Ste. 100, Miami 33134
Type: Private, independent
Degrees: C
Phone: (305) 443-7601
Inst. Accred.: COE (2005)

Sarasota County Technical Institute
4748 Beneva Rd., Sarasota 34233
Type: Public, state
Degrees: C *Enroll:* 657
URL: http://www.sarasotatech.org
Phone: (941) 924-1365
Inst. Accred.: COE (1971/2003)
Prog. Accred.: Allied Health (EMT (paramedic), surgical technology), Practical Nursing

Sarasota School of Massage Therapy
1932 Ringling Blvd., Sarasota 34326
Type: Private, proprietary
Degrees: C
URL: http://www.sarasotamassageschool.com
Phone: (941) 957-0577
Inst. Accred.: COE (1994/2006)
Prog. Accred.: Allied Health (massage therapy)

The School of Health Careers
3190 North State Rd. 7, Lauderdale Lakes 33319
Type: Private, proprietary
Degrees: C
URL: http://www.schoolofhealth.edu
Phone: (954) 777-0083
Inst. Accred.: ACCSCT (2002)

American Institute of Massage Therapy
416 East Atlantic Blvd., Pompano Beach 33060
Phone: (954) 781-2468

Sheridan Technical Center
5400 Sheridan St., Hollywood 33021
Type: Public, state
Degrees: C
URL: http://www.sheridantechnical.com
Phone: (754) 321-5400
Inst. Accred.: COE (1974/2006)
Prog. Accred.: Allied Health (surgical technology), Clinical Lab Technology, Culinary Education, Practical Nursing

South Florida Institute of Technology
720 NW 27th Ave., 2nd Flr., Miami 33125
Type: Private, proprietary
Degrees: C
URL: http://www.sf-institute.com
Phone: (305) 649-2050
Inst. Accred.: ACCSCT (2002/2007)

South Florida Montessori Education Center
606 S. Palmway, Lake Worth 33460
Type: Private, independent
Degrees: C
Phone: (561) 493-3093
Inst. Accred.: MACTE (2002)

Southeast Florida Institute, Inc.
2401 PGA Blvd., Ste. 196, Palm Beach Gardens 33410
Type: Private, proprietary
Degrees: C
URL: http://www.southflorida.dalecarnegie.com
Phone: (561) 624-3660
Inst. Accred.: ACCET (1976/2005)

Southeastern School of Neuromuscular and Massage Therapy, Inc.
9424 Baymeadows Rd., Ste. 200, Jacksonville 32256
Type: Private, proprietary
Degrees: C
URL: http://se-massage.com
Phone: (904) 448-9499 *Calendar:* Tri. plan
Inst. Accred.: ACCSCT (2001/2006)

Southern Technical Institute
1819 North Semoran Blvd., Orlando 32807
Type: Private, proprietary
Degrees: C
URL: http://www.stiorlando.com
Phone: (407) 478-5300
Inst. Accred.: ACICS (2004/2006)

Space Coast Health Institute
1070 South Wickham Rd., West Melbourne 32904
Type: Private, proprietary
Degrees: C
URL: http://www.jodystork.com/school
Phone: (321) 729-9000
Inst. Accred.: ACCSCT (2003)

SunCoast II—The Tampa Bay School of Health/ Suncoast School
2005 Pan Am Circle, Ste. 100, Tampa 33607
Type: Private, proprietary
Degrees: C
URL: http://www.suncoastii.com
Phone: (813) 879-1500
Inst. Accred.: ACCSCT (1986/2006)

Sunstate Academy of Hair Design
4424 Bee Ridge Rd., Sarasota 34233-2502
Type: Private, proprietary
Degrees: C
Phone: (941) 377-4880
Inst. Accred.: ACCSCT (1983/2006)

Sunstate Academy of Hair Design
18453 U.S. Hwy. 19, Clearwater 33764
Type: Private, proprietary
Degrees: C
Phone: (727) 538-3827
Inst. Accred.: ACCSCT (1984/2004)

Sunstate Academy of Hair Design
2418 Colonial Blvd., Fort Myers 33907-1415
Type: Private, proprietary
Degrees: C
Phone: (941) 278-1311
Inst. Accred.: ACCSCT (1988/2004)

Suwanee-Hamilton Technical Center
415 Pinewood Dr., SW, Live Oak 32060
Type: Public, state/local
Degrees: C
URL: http://www.suwannee.k12.fl.us/shtc
Phone: (386) 364-2750
Inst. Accred.: COE (1973/2001)

TALK International
2455 East Sunrise Blvd., Ste. 200, Fort Lauderdale 33304
Type: Private, proprietary
Degrees: C
URL: http://www.talkinusa.com
Phone: (954) 565-8505
Inst. Accred.: ACCET (1999/2004)

Taylor Technical Institute
3233 Hwy. 19, South, Perry 32347
Type: Public, state
Degrees: C
URL: http://www.taylortech.org
Phone: (850) 838-2545
Inst. Accred.: COE (1993/2005)

Technical Career Institute
7757 North Flagler St., Miami 33144
Type: Private, proprietary
Degrees: C
URL: http://www.technicalcareerinstitute.com
Phone: (305) 261-5511
Inst. Accred.: COE (1991/2001)

Technical Education Center—Osceola
501 Simpson Rd., Kissimmee 34744
Type: Public, state/local
Degrees: C
URL: http://www.teco.osceola.k12.fl.us
Phone: (407) 344-5080
Inst. Accred.: COE (1996/2002)

Tom P. Haney Technical Center
3016 Hwy. 77, Panama City 32444
Type: Public, state
Degrees: C
URL: http://www.bay.k12.fl.us/schools/htc
Phone: (850) 747-5500
Inst. Accred.: COE (1977/2004)

Total International Career Institute
3060 West 12th Ave., Hialeah 33012
Type: Private, proprietary
Degrees: C
Phone: (305) 681-6622
Inst. Accred.: ACCSCT (2004)

Traviss Technical Center
3225 Winter Lake Rd., Lakeland 33803
Type: Public, state/local
Degrees: C
URL: http://www.travisstech.org
Phone: (863) 499-2700
Inst. Accred.: COE (1978/2006)
Prog. Accred.: Allied Health (surgical technology), Dentistry (dental assisting)

Trendsetters Florida School of Beauty and Barbering
5337 Lenox Ave., Jacksonville 32205
Type: Private, proprietary
Degrees: C
Phone: (904) 764-9932
Inst. Accred.: NACCAS (2005)

Ultimate Medical Academy
1218 Ct. St., Ste. B, Clearwater 33756
Type: Private, proprietary
Degrees: C
URL: http://www.studymedical.com
Phone: (727) 446-8655
Inst. Accred.: ABHES (2000/2005)

Universal Massage and Beauty Institute
10720 West Flagler St., Suites 21-22, Miami 33174
Type: Private, proprietary
Degrees: C
URL: http://www.universalbeautyschool.com
Phone: (305) 485-7700
Inst. Accred.: COE (2004)

Lauder Hill Campus
4944 University Dr., Lauderdale 33351
Phone: (954) 747-8055

Washington-Holmes Technical Center
757 Hoyt St., Chipley 32428
Type: Public, state
Degrees: C
URL: http://www.whtc.org
Phone: (850) 638-1180
Inst. Accred.: COE (1976/2003)

Westside Tech
955 East Story Rd., Winter Garden 34787
Type: Public, state/local
Degrees: C
URL: http://www.westside.ocps.net
Phone: (407) 905-2000
Inst. Accred.: COE (1981/2003)

William T. McFatter Technical Center
6500 Nova Dr., Davie 33314
Type: Public, state
Degrees: C
URL: http://www.mcfattertech.com
Phone: (954) 321-5700
Inst. Accred.: COE (1989/2006)
Prog. Accred.: Allied Health (medical assisting (AMA)), Dentistry (dental laboratory technology), Practical Nursing

Davie Campus
Broward Fire Academy, 2600 S.W. 71 Terrace, Davie 33314
Phone: (954) 370-8324

Winter Park Tech
901 Webster Ave., Winter Park 32789
Type: Public, state
Degrees: C
URL: http://www.wpt.ocps.net
Phone: (407) 622-2900
Inst. Accred.: COE (1986/2005)
Prog. Accred.: Allied Health (medical assisting (AMA))

Withlacoochee Technical Institute
1201 West Main St., Inverness 34450-4696
Type: Public, state/local
Degrees: C
URL: http://www.wtionline.cc
Phone: (352) 726-2430
Inst. Accred.: COE (1984/2000)

WyoTech—Daytona
3042 West International Speedway Blvd., Daytona Beach 32124
Type: Private, proprietary
System: Corinthian Colleges, Inc
Degrees: C
URL: http://wyotech.com
Phone: (386) 255-0295
Inst. Accred.: ACCET (1986/2002)

WyoTech—Daytona
470 Destination Daytona Ln., Ormond Beach 32174
Type: Private, proprietary
System: Corinthian Colleges, Inc
Degrees: C
URL: http://wyotech.com
Phone: (386) 255-0295
Inst. Accred.: ACCET (1986/2002)

Zoni Regent Language Training U.S.A.
765 41st St. (Arthur Godfrey Rd.), Miami Beach 33140
Type: Private, proprietary
Degrees: C
URL: http://www.regentusa.com
Phone: (305) 673-8760
Inst. Accred.: ACCET (1999/2002)

GEORGIA

Academy of Somatic Healing Arts
7094 Peachtree Industrial Blvd., Building 4, Norcross 30071
Type: Private, proprietary
Degrees: C
URL: http://www.ashamassage.com
Phone: (770) 368-2661
Inst. Accred.: CMTA (2007)

Advanced Career Training
2 Executive Park West, Ste. 100, Atlanta 30329
Type: Private, proprietary
Degrees: C
URL: http://www.act-edu.com
Phone: (404) 321-2929
Inst. Accred.: ACCET (1987/2006, Warning)

Jacksonville Campus
7660 Phillips Hwy., Ste. 14, Jacksonville, FL 32256
Phone: (904) 737-6911

Riverdale Campus
7165 Georgia Hwy. 85, Riverdale 30274
Phone: (770) 991-9356

American Professional Institute
1990 Riverside Dr., Macon 31211
Type: Private, proprietary
Degrees: C
Phone: (478) 314-4444
Inst. Accred.: COE (1983/2002)

Arnold/Padrick's University of Cosmetology
4971 Ct.ney Dr., Forest Park 30297
Type: Private, proprietary
Degrees: C
Phone: (404) 361-5641
Inst. Accred.: NACCAS (1988/2003)

Ashworth University Career Diploma
430 Technology Pkwy., Norcross 30092-3406
Type: Private, proprietary
Degrees: C
URL: http://www.pcdi.com
Phone: (770) 729-8400
Inst. Accred.: DETC (1993/2003)

National College of Appraisal and Property Management
430 Technology Pkwy., Norcross 30092
Phone: (770) 729-8400

The Atlanta Ballet Centre for Dance Education
1400 West Peachtree St., NW, Atlanta 30309
Type: Private, independent
Degrees: C
URL: http://www.atlantaballet.com/new/fs_centre.htm
Phone: (404) 873-5811 ext 1
Inst. Accred.: NASD (2003)

Atlanta Institute of Music
5985 Financial Dr., Ste. 200, Norcross 30071
Type: Private, proprietary
Degrees: C
URL: http://www.aim-music.com
Phone: (770) 242-7717 *Calendar:* Qtr. plan
Inst. Accred.: COE (1994/2004)

Atlanta Job Corps Center
239 West Lake Ave., NW, Atlanta 30314
Type: Public, federal
Degrees: C
URL: http://www.atljcc.org
Phone: (404) 794-9512
Inst. Accred.: COE (1985/2001)

Atlanta School of Massage
2 Dunwoody Park South, Atlanta 30338
Type: Private, proprietary
Degrees: C
URL: http://www.atlantaschoolofmassage.com
Phone: (770) 454-7167
Inst. Accred.: ACCSCT (1988/2003)

Augusta School of Massage
608 Ponder Place Dr., Evans 30809
Type: Private, proprietary
Degrees: C
URL: http://www.augustamassage.com
Phone: (706) 863-4799
Inst. Accred.: ACCSCT (2005)

Aviation Institute of Maintenance
500 Briscoe Blvd., Lawrenceville 30045
Type: Private, proprietary
Degrees: C
URL: http://www.aim-atlanta.com
Phone: (678) 377-5600
Inst. Accred.: ACCSCT (2000/2005)

Manassas Campus
9821 Godwin Dr., Manassas, VA 20110
Phone: (703) 257-5515

Virginia Beach Campus
1429 Miller Store Rd., Virginia Beach, VA 23455-3324
Phone: (757) 363-2121

Beauty College of America
1171 Main St., Forest Park 30050
Type: Private, proprietary
Degrees: C
Phone: (404) 361-4098
Inst. Accred.: NACCAS (1988/2003)

Brown College of Court Reporting and Medical Transcription
1740 Peachtree St., NW, Atlanta 30309
Type: Private, proprietary
Degrees: C
URL: http://www.browncollege.com
Phone: (404) 876-1227 *Calendar:* Qtr. plan
Inst. Accred.: COE (1984/2001)

Longview Campus
1125 Judson Plaza, #119, Longview, TX 75601-5120
Phone: (903) 757-4338

Cobb Beauty College
3096 Cherokee St., Kennesaw 30144
Type: Private, proprietary
Degrees: C
URL: http://www.cobbbeautycollege.com
Phone: (770) 424-6915
Inst. Accred.: COE (1993/2005)

The Creative Circus
812 Lambert St., Atlanta 30324
Type: Private, proprietary
System: Delta Education Corporation
Degrees: C
URL: http://www.creativecircus.com
Phone: (404) 607-8880
Inst. Accred.: COE (1983/2005)

Dale Carnegie of Georgia
Three Ravinia Dr., Ste. 1950, Atlanta 30346
Type: Private, proprietary
Degrees: C
URL: http://www.atlanta.dalecarnegie.com
Phone: (404) 634-8100
Inst. Accred.: ACCET (2006)

Empire Beauty School
425 Ernest-Barrett Pkwy., Ste. H-2, Kennesaw 30144
Type: Private, proprietary
Degrees: C
URL: http://www.empirebeauty.com
Phone: (770) 419-2303
Inst. Accred.: NACCAS (1971/2003)

Empire Beauty School—Dunwoody
4719 Ashford-Dunwwody Rd., Ste. 205, Dunwoody 30338
Type: Private, proprietary
System: Empire Education Group
Degrees: C
URL: http://www.empirebeauty.com
Phone: (770) 671-1448
Inst. Accred.: NACCAS (1989/2004)

Empire Beauty School—Lawrenceville, GA
1455 Pleasant Rd., Ste. 105, Lawrenceville 30044
Type: Private, proprietary
Degrees: C
URL: http://www.empirebeauty.com
Phone: (704) 564-0725
Inst. Accred.: NACCAS (1975/2004)

English for Internationals
575 Colonial Park Dr., Roswell 30075
Type: Private, proprietary
Degrees: C
URL: http://www.eng4intl.com
Phone: (770) 587-9640
Inst. Accred.: ACCET (2002)

ETI Career Institute
1150 Lake Hearn Dr., Ste. 260, Atlanta 30342
Type: Private, proprietary
Degrees: C
URL: http://www.etimedicalschool.com
Phone: (404) 303-2929
Inst. Accred.: ACCSCT (1991/2006)

Jonesboro Campus
9500 South Main St., Jonesboro 30236
Phone: (770) 477-2799

Everest Institute—Atlanta Downtown
101 Marietta St., NW, Ste. 600, Atlanta 30303
Type: Private, proprietary
System: Corinthian Colleges, Inc
Degrees: C
URL: http://www.everest.edu
Phone: (404) 525-1111
Inst. Accred.: ABHES (1985/2004)
Prog. Accred.: Medical Assisting (ABHES)

Jonesboro Campus
6431 Tara Blvd., Jonesboro 30236
Phone: (770) 603-0000
Prog. Accred: Medical Assisting (ABHES)

Marietta Campus
1600 Terrell Mill Rd., Ste. G, Marietta 30067
Phone: (770) 303-7997
Prog. Accred: Allied Health (surgical technology), Medical Assisting (ABHES), Surgical Technology

Fayette Beauty Academy
386 North Glynn St., Fayetteville 30214
Type: Private, proprietary
Degrees: C
Phone: (770) 461-4669
Inst. Accred.: NACCAS (1999/2002)

Georgia Career Institute
1820 Hwy. 20, Ste. 200, Conyers 30013
Type: Private, proprietary
Degrees: C
URL: http://www.georgiacareerinstitute.com
Phone: (770) 922-7653
Inst. Accred.: COE (1990/2004)

McMinnville Campus
755 North Chancery St., McMinnville, TN 37110
Phone: (931) 506-5343

Murfreesboro Campus
1233 Commerce Park Dr., Murfreesboro, TN 37130
Phone: (931) 506-5343

Nave Cosmetology Academy
112 East James Campbell Blvd., Columbia, TN 38401
Phone: (931) 388-7717

Georgia Driving Academy
1449 V.F.W. Dr., SW, Conyers 30012
Type: Private, proprietary
Degrees: C
URL: http://www.gadrivingacademy.com
Phone: (770) 918-8501
Inst. Accred.: COE (1998/2004)

Georgia Institute of Cosmetology
3529 Atlanta Hwy., Athens 30606-3152
Type: Private, proprietary
Degrees: C
URL: http://www.gicschool.com
Phone: (706) 549-6400
Inst. Accred.: COE (1993/2003)

Augusta Campus
2803 Wrightsboro Rd., Augusta 30909
Phone: (706) 736-1819

Buford Campus
1605 Buford Hwy., Suites M, N, & O, Buford 30518-3635
Phone: (770) 945-4008

International City Beauty College
1859 Watson Blvd., Warner Robins 31093
Type: Private, proprietary
Degrees: C
URL: http://www.icbeauty.edu
Phone: (478) 923-0915
Inst. Accred.: NACCAS (1988/2003)

International School of Skin & Nailcare
5600 Roswell Rd., NE, Atlanta 30342
Type: Private, proprietary
Degrees: C
URL: http://www.skin-nails.com
Phone: (404) 843-1005
Inst. Accred.: COE (1987/2004)

Lake Lanier School of Massage
675 E.E. Butler Pkwy., Ste. K, Gainesville 30501
Type: Private, proprietary
Degrees: C
URL: http://www.school-of-massage.com
Phone: (770) 287-0377
Inst. Accred.: ABHES (2007)

Medix School
2108 Cobb Pkwy., Smyrna 30080
Type: Private, proprietary
Degrees: C
URL: http://www.medixschool.com
Phone: (770) 980-0002
Inst. Accred.: ABHES (1999/2005)
Prog. Accred.: Allied Health (medical assisting (AMA)), Dentistry (dental assisting), Medical Assisting (ABHES)

Michael's School of Beauty
630 North Ave., Ste. J, Macon 31211
Type: Private, proprietary
Degrees: C
URL: http://www.michaelsschoolofbeauty.com
Phone: (478) 741-0030
Inst. Accred.: NACCAS (2003/2006)

Augusta Campus
1325 Augusta West Pkwy., Ste. C, Augusta 30909
Phone: (706) 854-0010

Nightingale Medical Institute
2260 Northlake Pkwy., Ste. 1-100, Tucker 30084
Type: Private, proprietary
Degrees: C
URL: http://www.nmiatlanta.com
Phone: (770) 270-5708
Inst. Accred.: COE (2005)

OmniTech Institute
4319 Covington Hwy., Ste. 202, Decatur 30035
Type: Private, proprietary
Degrees: C
URL: http://www.omnitechinc.com
Phone: (404) 284-8121
Inst. Accred.: COE (2003)

Portfolio Center
125 Bennett St., NW, Atlanta 30308
Type: Private, proprietary
Degrees: C
URL: http://www.portfoliocenter.com
Phone: (404) 351-5055
Inst. Accred.: COE (1982/2004)

Powder Springs Beauty College
4114 Austell Powder Springs Rd., Powder Springs 30073
Type: Private, proprietary
Degrees: C
Phone: (770) 439-9432
Inst. Accred.: NACCAS (2000/2006)

Pro Way Hair School
5684 Memorial Dr., Stone Mountain 30083
Type: Private, proprietary
Degrees: C
URL: http://www.prowayhairschool.com
Phone: (404) 299-5156
Inst. Accred.: COE (1993/2005)

Rising Spirit Institute of Natural Health
4536 Chamblee Dunwoody Rd., Ste. 250, Atlanta 30338
Type: Private, proprietary
Degrees: C
URL: http://www.risingspiritinstitute.com
Phone: (770) 457-2021
Inst. Accred.: ACCSCT (1999/2004)

Rivertown School of Beauty
4747-B Hamilton Rd., Columbus 31904
Type: Private, proprietary
Degrees: C
URL: http://rivertownschoolofbeauty.com
Phone: (706) 653-8032
Inst. Accred.: COE (1994/2003)

Roffler-Moler Hairstyling College
1311 Roswell Rd, Marietta 30062
Type: Private, proprietary
Degrees: C
Phone: (770) 366-2838
Inst. Accred.: ACCSCT (1988/2005)

Roswell Road Campus
1311 Roswell Rd., Marietta 30062
Phone: (770) 565-3285

Ross Medical Education Center
2645 North Decatur Rd., Decatur 30033
Type: Private, proprietary
Degrees: C
URL: http://www.rossmedicaleducation.com
Phone: (404) 377-5744
Inst. Accred.: ABHES (1999/2005)
Prog. Accred.: Medical Assisting (ABHES)

Smyrna Campus
2534 Cobb Pkwy., Smyrna 30080
Phone: (770) 951-9255
Prog. Accred: Medical Assisting (ABHES)

Sanford-Brown Institute—Atlanta
1140 Hammond Dr., Ste. C-3200, Atlanta 30328
Type: Private, proprietary
System: Career Education Corporation
Degrees: C *Enroll:* 689
URL: http://www.sb-atlanta.com
Phone: (770) 350-0009
Inst. Accred.: ABHES (1990/2002), ACICS (2004)
Prog. Accred.: Allied Health (diagnostic medical sonography)

Cleveland Campus
17535 Rosbough Dr., Ste. 100, Middleburg Heights, OH 44130
Phone: (440) 239-9640
Prog. Accred: Allied Health (diagnostic medical sonography), Medical Assisting (ABHES)

Fort Lauderdale Campus
1201 West Cypress Creek Rd., Ft. Lauderdale, FL 33309
Phone: 954) 308-7400
Prog. Accred: Allied Health (surgical technology), Medical Assisting (ABHES), Surgical Technology

Houston Campus
10500 Forum Place Dr., Ste. 200, Houston, TX 77036
Phone: (713) 779-1110
Prog. Accred: Allied Health (diagnostic medical sonography, surgical technology), Medical Assisting (ABHES), Medical Laboratory Technology, Surgical Technology

Houston North Loop Campus
2627 Northloop West, Ste. 100, Houston, TX 77008
Phone: (713) 863-0429
Prog. Accred: Medical Assisting (ABHES), Surgical Technology

Landover Campus
8401 Corporate Dr., Ste. 500, Landover, MD 20785
Phone: (301) 918-8221
Prog. Accred: Medical Assisting (ABHES)

New York Campus
120 East 16th St., 2nd Flr., New York, NY 10003
Phone: (212) 460-8567
Prog. Accred: Medical Assisting (ABHES)

Philadelphia Campus
3600 Horizon Blvd., Ste. GL-1, Trevose, PA 19053
Phone: (215) 244-4906
Prog. Accred: Medical Assisting (ABHES)

Savannah School of Massage Therapy Training, Inc.
6413 Waters Ave., Savannah 31406
Type: Private, proprietary
Degrees: C
URL: http://www.ssomt.com
Phone: (912) 355-3011
Inst. Accred.: ACCET (2006)

Southeastern Beauty School—Midtown
PO Box 12483, Columbus 31907
Type: Private, proprietary
Degrees: C
Phone: (706) 687-1054
Inst. Accred.: NACCAS (1986/2004)

Southeastern Beauty School—North Lumpkin
3448 North Lumpkin Rd., Columbus 31903
Type: Private, proprietary
Degrees: C
Phone: (706) 687-1054
Inst. Accred.: NACCAS (1987/2005)

Turner Job Corps Center
2000 Schilling Ave., Albany 31705-1524
Type: Public, federal
Degrees: C
URL: http://atlantaregion.jobcorps.gov
Phone: (229) 883-8500
Inst. Accred.: COE (1984/2007)

United States Army Infantry School
6751 Constitution Loop, Ste. 650, Ft. Benning 31905
Type: Public, federal
Degrees: C
URL: https://www.benning.army.mil/infantry/toc/school.htm
Phone: (706) 545-6105
Inst. Accred.: COE (1999/2006)

United States Navy Supply Corps School
1425 Prince Ave., Athens 30606-2205
Type: Public, federal
Degrees: C
URL: http://www.nscs.com
Phone: (706) 355-7501
Inst. Accred.: COE (1981/2004)

Vogue Beauty School
3655 Macland Rd., Ste. H, Hiram 30141
Type: Private, proprietary
Degrees: C
URL: http://www.voguebeautyschool.com
Phone: (770) 943-6811
Inst. Accred.: COE (1995/2001)

Cartersville Campus
238 Nelson St., Bldg. 10, Cartersville 30120
Phone: (770) 943-6811

HAWAII

Center for Asia Pacific Exchange
1616 Makiki St., Honolulu 96822
Type: Public, independent
Degrees: C
URL: http://www.cape.edu
Phone: (808) 942-8553
Inst. Accred.: ACCET (1998/2003)

Hawaii Institute of Hair Design
71 South Hotel St., Honolulu 96813-3112
Type: Private, proprietary
Degrees: C
Phone: (808) 533-6596
Inst. Accred.: ACCSCT (1978/2005)

Hawaii Technology Institute
629 Pohukaina St., Honolulu 96813
Type: Private, proprietary
Degrees: C
URL: http://www.hti.edu
Phone: (808) 522-2700
Inst. Accred.: ACCSCT (2000/2005, Probation)

Hollywood Beauty College
99-084 Kauhale St., Building A, Aiea 96701
Type: Private, proprietary
Degrees: C
URL: http://www.hollywoodbeautycollege.com
Phone: (808) 486-7255
Inst. Accred.: NACCAS (1973/2006)

Institute of Intensive English
2155 Kalakaua Ave., Ste. 700, Honolulu 96815
Type: Private, proprietary
Degrees: C
URL: http://www.studyenglishhawaii.com
Phone: (808) 924-2117
Inst. Accred.: ACCET (2005)

Intercultural Communications College
1601 Kapiolani Blvd., Ste. 1000, Honolulu 96814
Type: Private, proprietary
Degrees: C
URL: http://www.gvenglish.com
Phone: (808) 946-2445
Inst. Accred.: ACCET (1996/2004)

International Mid Pac College
1311 Kapiolani Blvd., Ste. 400, Honolulu 96814
Type: Private, proprietary
Degrees: C
URL: http://www.impachawaii.com
Phone: (808) 593-9388
Inst. Accred.: ACCET (2007)

James E. Varner & Associates, Inc.
Gentry Pacific Center, 560 North Nimitz Hwy., #112, Honolulu 96817
Type: Private, proprietary
Degrees: C
URL: http://www.hawaii.dalecarnegie.com
Phone: (808) 536-1400
Inst. Accred.: ACCET (1975/2001)

Med-Assist School of Hawaii
33 South King St., Ste. 223, Honolulu 96813
Type: Private, proprietary
Degrees: C
Phone: (808) 524-3363
Inst. Accred.: ABHES (1984/2002)

New York Technical Institute of Hawaii
1375 Dillingham Blvd., Honolulu 96817-4415
Type: Private, proprietary
Degrees: C
Phone: (808) 841-5827
Inst. Accred.: ACCSCT (1990/2005, Probation)

Travel Institute of the Pacific
1314 South King St., Ste. 1164, Honolulu 96814-2004
Type: Private, proprietary
Degrees: C
Phone: (808) 591-2708
Inst. Accred.: ACCSCT (1990/2005)

IDAHO

Ballet Idaho Academy
501 South 8th St., Boise 83702
Type: Private, independent
Degrees: C
URL: http://www.balletidaho.org/academy.html
Phone: (208) 343-0556
Inst. Accred.: NASD (2003)

Career Beauty College
57 College Ave., Rexburg 83440
Type: Private, proprietary
Degrees: C
Phone: (208) 356-0222
Inst. Accred.: NACCAS (1982/2002)

Cosmetology School of Arts and Sciences
529 Overland Ave., Burley 83318
Type: Private, proprietary
Degrees: C
Phone: (208) 678-0741
Inst. Accred.: NACCAS (2003/2006)

The Headmasters School of Hair Design
317 East Coeur D'Alene Ave., Coeur D'Alene 83814
Type: Private, proprietary
Degrees: C
URL: http://www.headmastersschool.com
Phone: (208) 664-0541
Inst. Accred.: NACCAS (1985/2005)

Boise Campus
5823 West Franklin Rd., Boise 83709
Phone: (208) 429-8070

Headmasters School of Hair Design—Lewiston
602 Main St., Lewiston 83501
Type: Private, proprietary
Degrees: C
URL: http://www.headmastersschoolhairdesign.com
Phone: (208) 743-1512
Inst. Accred.: NACCAS (1986/2006)

Mr. Juan's College of Hair Design
586 Blue Lakes Blvd. North, Twin Falls 83301
Type: Private, proprietary
Degrees: C
Phone: (208) 733-7777
Inst. Accred.: NACCAS (1969/2005)

Mr. Leon's School of Hair Design
618 South Main St., Moscow 83843
Type: Private, proprietary
Degrees: C
Phone: (208) 882-2923
Inst. Accred.: NACCAS (1984/2004)

Lewiston Campus
205 10th St., Lewiston 83501
Phone: (208) 743-6822

Northwest Lineman College
7600 South Meridian Rd., Meridian 83642
Type: Private, proprietary
Degrees: C
URL: http://www.lineman.com
Phone: (208) 888-4817
Inst. Accred.: ACCSCT (2000/2005)

Razzle Dazzle College of Hair Design
214 Holly St., Nampa 83686-5163
Type: Private, proprietary
Degrees: C
URL: http://www.razzledazzlecollege.com
Phone: (208) 465-7660
Inst. Accred.: NACCAS (1988/2003)

Sage Technical Services
2845 West Seltice Way, Coeur d'Alene 83814
Type: Private, proprietary
Degrees: C
URL: http://www.sageschools.com
Phone: (208) 765-6346
Inst. Accred.: ACCSCT (1998/2003)

The School of Hairstyling
141 East Chubbuck Rd., Chubbuck 83202
Type: Private, proprietary
Degrees: C
Phone: (208) 232-9170
Inst. Accred.: NACCAS (1985/2005)

Scot Lewis Schools-Paul Mitchell Partner School—Boise
1270 South Vinnell Way, Boise 83709
Type: Private, proprietary
Degrees: C
URL: http://www.scotlewisschools.com
Phone: (208) 375-0190
Inst. Accred.: NACCAS (1989/2004)

ILLINOIS

Alvareita's College of Cosmetology
333 South Kansas St., Edwardsville 62025
Type: Private, proprietary
Degrees: C
Phone: (618) 656-2593
Inst. Accred.: NACCAS (1984/2004)

Belleville Campus
5400 West Main St., Belleville 62226
Phone: (618) 257-9193

Alvareita's College of Cosmetology—Godfrey Campus
3048 Godfrey Rd., Godfrey 62035
Type: Private, proprietary
Degrees: C
Phone: (618) 466-8952
Inst. Accred.: NACCAS (1986/2005)

American Career College of Hair Design. Inc.
7000 West Cermak Rd., Berwyn 60402
Type: Private, proprietary
Degrees: C
Phone: (708) 795-1500
Inst. Accred.: NACCAS (2002/2005)

American Health Information Management Association
233 North Michigan Ave., Ste. 2150, Chicago 60601
Type: Private, proprietary
Degrees: C
URL: http://www.ahima.org
Phone: (312) 233-1184
Inst. Accred.: DETC (2003)

American Institute for Paralegal Studies
17W705 Butterfield Rd., Ste. A, Oakbrook 60181
Type: Private, proprietary
Degrees: C
URL: http://www.americanparalegal.edu
Phone: (630) 916-6680
Inst. Accred.: ACCET (1981/2005)

Beck Area Career Center
6137 Beck Rd., Red Bud 62278
Type: Public, state/local
Degrees: C
URL: http://www.schools.lth5.k12.il.us/beck
Phone: (618) 473-2222
Inst. Accred.: NCA-CASI (1977/2005)

Bell Mar Beauty College
5717 West Cermak Rd., Cicero 60650
Type: Private, proprietary
Degrees: C
Phone: (708) 863-6644
Inst. Accred.: NACCAS (1987/2002)

BIR Training Center—North
3601 West Devon Ave., Ste. 210, Chicago 60659
Type: Private, independent
Degrees: C
URL: http://birtraining.com
Phone: (773) 866-0111
Inst. Accred.: NCA-CASI (1997/2004)

Loop Campus
828 South Wabash Ave., Ste. 290, Chicago 60605-2182
Phone: (312) 229-7600

Cain's Barber College
365 East 51st St., Chicago 60615-3510
Type: Private, proprietary
Degrees: C
URL: http://www.cainsbarbers.com
Phone: (773) 536-4441
Inst. Accred.: ACCSCT (1993/2006)

Cameo Beauty Academy
9714 South Cicero Ave., Oak Lawn 60453
Type: Private, proprietary
Degrees: C
URL: http://www.caemeobeautyacademy.com
Phone: (708) 636-4660
Inst. Accred.: NACCAS (1992/2002)

Cannella School of Hair Design—Blue Island
12840 South Western Ave., Blue Island 60406
Type: Private, proprietary
Degrees: C
URL: http://www.cannellabeautyschools.com
Phone: (708) 388-4949
Inst. Accred.: NACCAS (1975/2005)

Cannella School of Hair Design—Elgin
117 West Chicago St., Elgin 60120
Type: Private, proprietary
Degrees: C
URL: http://www.cannellabeautyschools.com
Phone: (847) 742-6611
Inst. Accred.: NACCAS (1984/2003)

Cannella School of Hair Design—South Archer
4269 South Archer Ave., Chicago 60632
Type: Private, proprietary
Degrees: C
URL: http://www.cannellabeautyschools.com
Phone: (773) 890-0412
Inst. Accred.: NACCAS (1986/2004)

West Belmont Campus
6000 West Belmont, Chicago 60653
Phone: (773) 283-8340

Cannella School of Hair Design—South Commercial
9012 South Commercial Ave., Chicago 60617-4303
Type: Private, proprietary
Degrees: C
URL: http://www.cannellabeautyschools.com
Phone: (773) 221-4700
Inst. Accred.: NACCAS (1969/2004)

Cannella School of Hair Design—Villa Park
617 West North Ave., Villa Park 60181
Type: Private, proprietary
Degrees: C
URL: http://www.cannellabeautyschools.com
Phone: (630) 833-6118
Inst. Accred.: NACCAS (1982/2002)

Cannella School of Hair Design—West North Avenue
4217 West North Ave., Chicago 60639
Type: Private, proprietary
Degrees: C
URL: http://www.cannellabeautyschools.com
Phone: (773) 278-4477
Inst. Accred.: NACCAS (1984/2003)

Capital Area Career Center
12201 Toronto Rd., Springfield 62707
Type: Public, state/local
Degrees: C
URL: http://www.capital.tec.il.us
Phone: (217) 529-5431 *Calendar:* Qtr. plan
Inst. Accred.: NCA-CASI (1998/2005)
Prog. Accred.: Allied Health (surgical technology), Practical Nursing

Capri Garfield Ridge School of Beauty Culture
2659 West 63rd St., Chicago 60629
Type: Private, proprietary
Degrees: C
URL: http://www.capribeautyschool.com
Phone: (773) 778-8161
Inst. Accred.: NACCAS (1976/2002)

Capri Oak Forest College of Beauty Culture
15815 Rob Roy Dr., Oak Forest 60452
Type: Private, proprietary
Degrees: C
URL: http://www.capribeautyschool.com
Phone: (708) 687-3020
Inst. Accred.: NACCAS (1976/2002)

Chicago Urban League Computer Training Center
220 South State St., 11th Flr., Chicago 60604
Type: Private, independent
Degrees: C
URL: http://www.cul-chicago.org
Phone: (312) 692-0766
Inst. Accred.: ACCET (2000/2006)

Computer Systems Institute
8930 Gross Point Rd., Skokie 60077
Type: Private, proprietary
Degrees: C
URL: http://www.csinow.com
Phone: (847) 967-5030
Inst. Accred.: NCA-CASI (1998/2006)

Computer Systems Institute
318 West Adams St., Floor 10, Chicago 60606
Type: Private, proprietary
Degrees: C
URL: http://www.csinow.com
Phone: (312) 346-6774
Inst. Accred.: NCA-CASI (2004/2006)

Concept College of Cosmetology
2500 Georgetown Rd., Danville 61832
Type: Private, proprietary
Degrees: C
URL: http://conceptcollege.com
Phone: (217) 442-9329
Inst. Accred.: NACCAS (1985/2003)

Urbana Campus
129 North Race St., Urbana 61801
Phone: (217) 344-7550

Cortiva Institute-Chicago School of Massage Therapy
17 North State St., 5th Flr., Chicago 60602
Type: Private, proprietary
Degrees: C
URL: http://www.cortiva.com/locations/csmt
Phone: (312) 753-7900
Inst. Accred.: CMTA (1999/2006)

McHenry County Campus
100 South Main St., Crystal Lake 60012
Phone: (312) 753-7900

The Cosmetology and Spa Institute
700 East Terra Cotta Ave., Crystal Lake 60014
Type: Private, proprietary
Degrees: C
Phone: (815) 455-5900
Inst. Accred.: NACCAS (1980/2006)

The Don Adams Corporation
1333 Butterfield Rd., Ste. 140, Downers Grove 60515
Type: Private, proprietary
Degrees: C
URL: http://www.chicago.dalecarnegie.com
Phone: (630) 971-1900
Inst. Accred.: ACCET (1975/2006)

Educators of Beauty—La Salle
122 Wright St., La Salle 61301
Type: Private, proprietary
Degrees: C
URL: http://www.educatorsofbeauty.com
Phone: (815) 223-7326
Inst. Accred.: NACCAS (1970/2003)

Educators of Beauty—Sterling
211 East Third St., Sterling 61081
Type: Private, proprietary
Degrees: C
URL: http://www.educatorsofbeauty.com
Phone: (815) 625-0247
Inst. Accred.: NACCAS (1967/2005)

Rockford Campus
128 South Fifth St., Rockford 61104
Phone: (815) 969-7030

Empire Beauty School—Hanover Park
1166 West Lake St., Hanover Park 60103
Type: Private, proprietary
Degrees: C
URL: http://www.empirebeauty.com
Phone: (630) 830-6560
Inst. Accred.: NACCAS (1984/2002)

Environmental Technical Institute
1101 West Thorndale Ave., Itasca 60143-1334
Type: Private, proprietary
Degrees: C
URL: http://www.eticampus.com
Phone: (630) 285-9100
Inst. Accred.: ACCSCT (1988/2004)

Blue Island Campus
13010 South Division St., Blue Island 60406-2606
Phone: (708) 385-0707

European Massage Therapy School
8707 Skokie Blvd., Ste. 106, Skokie 60077
Type: Private, proprietary
Degrees: C
URL: http://www.school-for-massage.com
Phone: (847) 673-7585
Inst. Accred.: ABHES (2003)

Las Vegas Campus
8751 W. Charleston Blvd., Ste. 295, Las Vegas, NV 89117
Phone: (702) 202-2455

Everest College—Skokie
9811 Woods Dr., 2nd Flr., Skokie 60077
Type: Private, proprietary
System: Corinthian Colleges, Inc
Degrees: C
URL: http://www.everest.edu
Phone: (847) 470-0277 *Calendar:* Qtr. plan
Inst. Accred.: ACCSCT (1973/2005)
Prog. Accred.: Allied Health (medical assisting (AMA))

Burr Ridge Campus
6880 North Frontage Rd., Ste. 400, Burr Ridge 60527
Phone: (630) 920-1102

First Institute, Inc.
790 McHenry Ave., Crystal Lake 60014
Type: Private, proprietary
Degrees: C
URL: http://www.firstinstitute.com
Phone: (815) 459-3500
Inst. Accred.: ACCET (1988/2005)

Gem City College
700 State St., Quincy 62301
Type: Private, proprietary
Degrees: C *Enroll:* 75
URL: http://www.gemcitycollege.com
Phone: (217) 222-0391
Inst. Accred.: ACICS (1954/2004)

Greater West Town Training Partnership
2021 West Fulton St., Ste. 204, Chicago 60612
Type: Private, proprietary
Degrees: C
URL: http://www.gwtp.org
Phone: (312) 563-9028
Inst. Accred.: ACCSCT (1999/2004)

The Hadley School for the Blind
700 Elm St., Winnetka 60093
Type: Private, independent
Degrees: C
URL: http://www.hadley-school.org
Phone: (847) 446-8111
Inst. Accred.: DETC (1958/2004)

Hair Professionals Academy of Cosmetology—West Dundee
825 B Village Quarter Rd., West Dundee 60118
Type: Private, proprietary
Degrees: C
URL: http://www.hairprofessionalschool.com/schools.html
Phone: (847) 836-5900
Inst. Accred.: NACCAS (1984/2004)

G Skin and Beauty Institute
2585 East Flamingo Rd., Suites 5-8, Las Vegas, NV 89121
Phone: (702) 953-9695

Hair Professionals Academy of Cosmetology—Wheaton
1145 East Butterfield, Wheaton 60187
Type: Private, proprietary
Degrees: C
URL: http://www.hairprofessionalschool.com/schools.html
Phone: (630) 653-6630
Inst. Accred.: NACCAS (1987/2007)

Naperville Skin Institute
1100 North Sherman Ave., Naperville 60563
Phone: (630) 369-7546

Hair Professionals Career College
10321 South Roberts Rd., Palos Hills 60465
Type: Private, proprietary
Degrees: C
URL: http://www.hairpros.edu/schools.html
Phone: (708) 430-1755
Inst. Accred.: NACCAS (1988/2003)

Hair Professionals Career College, Inc.—Sycamore
2245 Gateway Dr., Sycamore 60542
Type: Private, proprietary
Degrees: C
URL: http://www.hairpros.edu/schools.html
Phone: (815) 756-3596
Inst. Accred.: NACCAS (1986/2006)

Hair Professionals School of Cosmetology, Inc.—Oswego
PO Box 40, Oswego 60543-0040
Type: Private, proprietary
Degrees: C
URL: http://www.hairpros.edu/schools.html
Phone: (630) 554-2266
Inst. Accred.: NACCAS (1984/2004)

Hairmasters Institute of Cosmetology, Inc.
506 South McClun St., Bloomington 61701
Type: Private, proprietary
Degrees: C
Phone: (309) 828-1884
Inst. Accred.: NACCAS (1990/2005)

Illinois Center for Broadcasting
55 West 22nd St., Lombard 60148-4854
Type: Private, proprietary
Degrees: C
URL: http://www.beonair.com
Phone: (630) 916-1700
Inst. Accred.: ACCSCT (1993/2003)

Illinois School of Health Careers
11 East Adams St., Ste. 200, Chicago 60603
Type: Private, proprietary
System: ForeFront Education, Inc.
Degrees: C
URL: http://www.ishc.edu
Phone: (312) 913-1230
Inst. Accred.: ABHES (1993/2002)
Prog. Accred.: Medical Assisting (ABHES)

Chicago O'Hare Airport Campus
8750 West Bryn Mawr Ave., Chicago 60631
Phone: (773) 444-0300

Illinois Welding School
5901 Washington St., Bartonville 61607
Type: Private, proprietary
Degrees: C
URL: http://www.illinoisweldingschool.com
Phone: (309) 633-0379
Inst. Accred.: ACCSCT (2001/2006)

John Amico's School of Hair Design
15301 South Cicero Ave., Oak Forest 60452
Type: Private, proprietary
Degrees: C
Phone: (708) 687-7800
Inst. Accred.: NACCAS (1981/2004)

La' James International College—East Moline
485 42nd Ave., East Moline 61244
Type: Private, proprietary
Degrees: C
URL: http://www.lajames.net
Phone: (309) 755-1313
Inst. Accred.: NACCAS (1967/2004)

Mac Daniel's Beauty School
5228 North Clark St., Second Flr., Chicago 60640
Type: Private, proprietary
Degrees: C
Phone: (773) 561-2376
Inst. Accred.: NACCAS (1977/2003)

Midwest Institute of Massage Therapy
4715 West Main St., Belleville 62223
Type: Private, proprietary
Degrees: C
URL: http://www.midwest-institute.com
Phone: (618) 239-6468
Inst. Accred.: ABHES (2004)

Midwest Montessori TTC
926 Noyes St., Evanston 60201
Type: Private, independent
Degrees: C
Phone: (847) 276-0405
Inst. Accred.: MACTE (1998/2005)

Midwest Technical Institute
405 North Limit St., Lincoln 62656
Type: Private, proprietary
Degrees: C
URL: http://www.midwesttechnicalinstitute.com
Phone: (217) 735-3105
Inst. Accred.: ACCSCT (1999/2004)
Prog. Accred.: Allied Health (medical assisting (AMA))

Delta Technical College
1090 Main St., Southaven, MS 38671
Phone: (662) 280-1442

Montessori Education Centers Associated-Seton
5728 Virginia St., Clarendon Hills 60514
Type: Public, independent
Degrees: C
URL: http://www.meca-seton.com
Phone: (630) 654-0151
Inst. Accred.: MACTE (1999/2006)

Mr. John's School of Cosmetology, Esthetics and Nails
1745 East Eldorado, Decatur 62521
Type: Private, proprietary
Degrees: C
URL: http://www.mrjohns.com
Phone: (217) 423-8173
Inst. Accred.: NACCAS (1982/2002)

Mr. John's School of Cosmetology, Esthetics and Nails
300 Broadway Lincoln Square, Ste. 111, Urbana 61801
Type: Private, proprietary
Degrees: C
URL: http://www.mrjohns.com
Phone: (217) 328-2590
Inst. Accred.: NACCAS (1987/2002)

Mr. John's School of Cosmetology, Esthetics and Nails
1429 South Main St., Jacksonville 62650
Type: Private, proprietary
Degrees: C
URL: http://www.mrjohns.com
Phone: (217) 243-1744
Inst. Accred.: NACCAS (2001/2004)

Ms. Robert's Academy of Beauty Culture
17-19 East Park Blvd., Villa Park 60181
Type: Private, proprietary
Degrees: C
Phone: (630) 941-3880
Inst. Accred.: NACCAS (1974/2003)

Hillsdale Campus
552 Mannheim Rd., Hillsdale 60162
Phone: (708) 649-9088

Music Institute of Chicago
300 Green Bay Rd., Winnetka 60093
Type: Private, independent
Degrees: C
URL: http://www.musicinst.com
Phone: (847) 446-3822 *Calendar:* Sem. plan
Inst. Accred.: NASM (1978/2003)

Niles School of Beauty Culture
8057 North Milwaukee Ave., Niles 60648
Type: Private, proprietary
Degrees: C
Phone: (847) 965-8061
Inst. Accred.: NACCAS (1987/2002)

Oehrlein School of Cosmetology, Inc.
100 Meadow Ave., East Peoria 61611
Type: Private, proprietary
Degrees: C
Phone: (309) 699-1561
Inst. Accred.: NACCAS (1985/2005)

Pivot Point International Academy
1560 Sherman Ave., Annex, Evanston 60201
Type: Private, proprietary
Degrees: C
URL: http://www.pivot-point.com
Phone: (847) 866-4247
Inst. Accred.: NACCAS (1967/2004)

Bloomingdale Campus
144 C East Lake St., Bloomingdale 60108
Phone: (847) 985-5900

Cosmetology Research Center
3901 West Irving Park Rd., Chicago 60618
Phone: (773) 463-3121

Pivot Point the Masters
8215 Stephanie Dr., Huntsville, AL 35802
Phone: (256) 881-8587

Professional's Choice Hair Design Academy
2719 West Jefferson St., Joliet 60435
Type: Private, proprietary
Degrees: C
URL: http://www.pchairdesign.com
Phone: (815) 741-8224
Inst. Accred.: NACCAS (1985/2005)

Pyramid Career Institute
3051 North Lincoln Ave., Chicago 60657
Type: Private, proprietary
Degrees: C
URL: http://www.pyramid-pci.com
Phone: (773) 975-9898
Inst. Accred.: ACCSCT (1996/2006)

Rosel School of Cosmetology
2444 West Devon, Chicago 60659
Type: Private, proprietary
Degrees: C
Phone: (773) 508-5600
Inst. Accred.: NACCAS (1992/2005)

S.J. Grant and Associates, Inc.
806 West Tailcreek Dr., Peoria 61615
Type: Private, proprietary
Degrees: C
URL: http://www.centralil.dale-carnegie.com
Phone: (309) 691-6808
Inst. Accred.: ACCET (1976/2007)

Sanford-Brown College—Collinsville
1101 Eastport Plaza Dr., Collinsville 62234
Type: Private, proprietary
System: Career Education Corporation
Degrees: C *Enroll:* 493
URL: http://www.sbcollinsville.com
Phone: (618) 931-0300
Inst. Accred.: ACICS (1991/2005)
Prog. Accred.: Medical Assisting (ABHES)

Solex Academy
350 East Dundee Rd., Ste. 200, Wheeling 60090
Type: Private, proprietary
Degrees: C
URL: http://www.academicvisa.com
Phone: (847) 229-9595
Inst. Accred.: CMTA (2006)

The Soma Institute
14 East Jackson Blvd., Ste. 1300, Chicago 60604
Type: Private, proprietary
Degrees: C
URL: http://www.soma.edu
Phone: (312) 939-2723
Inst. Accred.: ACCET (2003/2006)

Spanish Coalition for Jobs, Inc.
2011 West Pershing Rd., Chicago 60609
Type: Private, independent
Degrees: C
URL: http://www.scj-usa.org
Phone: (773) 247-0707
Inst. Accred.: ACICS (1994/2006)
Prog. Accred.: Allied Health (medical assisting (AMA))

Sparks College
131 South Morgan St., Shelbyville 62565
Type: Private, independent
Degrees: C
URL: http://www.sparkscollege.org
Phone: (217) 774-5112
Inst. Accred.: ACICS (1954/2006)

Trend Setters College of Cosmetology
605 East North St., Bradley 60915
Type: Private, proprietary
Degrees: C
URL: http://www.trendsetterscollege.com
Phone: (815) 932-5049
Inst. Accred.: NACCAS (1991/2005)

Mokena Campus
19031 Old La Grange Rd., Ste. 209, Mokena 60448
Phone: (708) 478-6907

Tri-County Beauty Academy
219 North State St., Litchfield 62056
Type: Private, proprietary
Degrees: C
Phone: (217) 324-9062
Inst. Accred.: NACCAS (1973/2004)

University of Spa and Cosmetology Art
2913 West White Oaks Dr., Springfield 62704
Type: Private, proprietary
Degrees: C
URL: http://www.uscart.com
Phone: (217) 753-8990
Inst. Accred.: NACCAS (1979/2005)

Vee's School of Beauty Culture
2701 State St., East St. Louis 62205
Type: Private, proprietary
Degrees: C
Phone: (618) 247-1751
Inst. Accred.: NACCAS (2001/2004)

Your School of Beauty Culture
116 East Pershing Rd., Chicago 60653
Type: Private, proprietary
Degrees: C
URL: http://www.yourschofbeauty.com
Phone: (773) 538-4886
Inst. Accred.: NACCAS (2003/2006)

INDIANA

A Cut Above Beauty College
3810 East Southport Rd., Indianapolis 46237
Type: Private, proprietary
System: Empire Education Group
Degrees: C
URL: http://www.acutabovebeautyschool.com
Phone: (317) 781-0959
Inst. Accred.: NACCAS (1986/2006)

Alexandria School of Scientific Therapeutics, Inc.
809 South Harrison St., PO Box 287, Alexandria 46001
Type: Private, proprietary
Degrees: C
URL: http://www.assti.com
Phone: (765) 724-9152
Inst. Accred.: CMTA (1999/2005)

Apex Academy of Hair Design
333 Jackson St., Anderson 46016
Type: Private, proprietary
Degrees: C
Phone: (765) 642-7560
Inst. Accred.: NACCAS (1966/2003)

Charles D. Eubank & Associates, Inc.
747 Oak Hill Rd., Evansville
Type: Private, proprietary
Degrees: C
URL: http://www.southillinois.dale-carnegie.com
Phone: (812) 424-3253
Inst. Accred.: ACCET (1976/2002)

Creative Hair Styling Academy
2549 Hwy. Ave., Highland 46322
Type: Private, proprietary
Degrees: C
URL: http://www.creativehair.com
Phone: (219) 838-2004
Inst. Accred.: NACCAS (1973/2004)

David Demuth Institute of Cosmetology
1301 South 8th St., Richmond 47374
Type: Private, proprietary
Degrees: C
Phone: (765) 935-7964
Inst. Accred.: NACCAS (1997/2005)

Don Roberts Beauty School
1354 Lincoln Way, Valparaiso 46383
Type: Private, proprietary
Degrees: C
Phone: (219) 462-5189
Inst. Accred.: NACCAS (1978/2003)

Don Roberts School of Hair Design
152 East Route 30, Schererville 46375
Type: Private, proprietary
Degrees: C
Phone: (219) 864-1600
Inst. Accred.: NACCAS (1977/2003)

Evansville Tri-State Beauty College
4920 Tippecanoe Ave., Evansville 47715
Type: Private, proprietary
Degrees: C
Phone: (812) 479-6989
Inst. Accred.: NACCAS (1978/2004)

Hair Arts Academy
933 North Walnut St., Bloomington 47404
Type: Private, proprietary
Degrees: C
Phone: (812) 339-1117
Inst. Accred.: NACCAS (1989/2002)

Hair Fashions by Kaye Beauty College—Indianapolis
6346 East 82nd St., Indianapolis 46250
Type: Private, proprietary
Degrees: C
Phone: (317) 576-8000
Inst. Accred.: NACCAS (1986/2006)

Hair Fashions by Kaye Beauty College—Noblesville
1111 South 10th St., Noblesville 46060
Type: Private, proprietary
Degrees: C
Phone: (317) 773-6189
Inst. Accred.: NACCAS (1986/2006)

Hanes and Associates, Inc.
9296 Waldemar Rd., Indianapolis 46268
Type: Private, proprietary
Degrees: C
URL: http://www.centralindiana.dalecarnegie.com
Phone: (317) 875-4229
Inst. Accred.: ACCET (1976/2004)

Ideal Beauty Academy, Inc.
1401 Youngstown Rd., Jeffersonville 47130
Type: Private, proprietary
Degrees: C
URL: http://www.idealbeautyacademy.net
Phone: (812) 282-1371
Inst. Accred.: NACCAS (2005)

J. Everett Light Career Center
1901 East 86 St., Indianapolis 46240
Type: Public, state/local
Degrees: C
URL: http://www.jelcc.com
Phone: (317) 259-5265
Inst. Accred.: NCA-CASI (1984/2005)

J. Michael Harrold Beauty Academy, Inc.
2232 Wabash Ave., Terre Haute 47807
Type: Private, proprietary
Degrees: C
URL: http://www.harroldbeautyacademy.com
Phone: (812) 232-8334
Inst. Accred.: NACCAS (1966/2004)

Knox Beauty College
320 East Culver Rd., Knox 46534
Type: Private, proprietary
Degrees: C
Phone: (574) 772-5500
Inst. Accred.: NACCAS (1986/2006)

Lafayette Beauty Academy, Inc.
833 Ferry St., Lafayette 47901
Type: Private, proprietary
Degrees: C
Phone: (765) 742-0068
Inst. Accred.: NACCAS (2000/2006)

The Masters of Cosmetology College, Inc.
1732 Bluffton Rd., Fort Wayne 46809
Type: Private, proprietary
Degrees: C
URL: http://www.mastersofcosmetology.com
Phone: (260) 747-6667
Inst. Accred.: NACCAS (1985/2005)

Merrillville Beauty College
48 West 67th Place, Merrillville 46410
Type: Private, proprietary
Degrees: C
URL: http://www.merrillvillebeautycollege.com
Phone: (219) 769-2232
Inst. Accred.: NACCAS (1968/2004)

Moler Hairstyling College, Inc.
4391 West 5th Ave., Gary 46406-1745
Type: Private, proprietary
Degrees: C
Phone: (219) 944-0960
Inst. Accred.: NACCAS (2006)

PJ's College of Cosmetology—Clarksville
1414 Blackiston Mill Rd., Clarksville 47129
Type: Private, proprietary
System: PJ's College of Cosmetology
Degrees: C
URL: http://www.gotopjs.com
Phone: (812) 282-0459
Inst. Accred.: NACCAS (1983/2003)

PJ's College of Cosmetology—Richmond
115 North 9th St., Richmond 47374
Type: Private, proprietary
System: PJ's College of Cosmetology
Degrees: C
URL: http://www.gotopjs.com
Phone: (765) 962-3005
Inst. Accred.: NACCAS (1984/2004)

Ravenscroft Beauty College
6110 Stellhorn Rd., Fort Wayne 46815
Type: Private, proprietary
Degrees: C
Phone: (260) 486-8868
Inst. Accred.: NACCAS (1978/2004)

Roger's Academy of Hair Design, Inc.
2903 Mount Vernon Ave., Evansville 47712
Type: Private, proprietary
Degrees: C
URL: http://rogershairacademy.com
Phone: (812) 429-0110
Inst. Accred.: NACCAS (1986/2006)

Rudae's School of Beauty Culture
208 West Jefferson St., Kokomo 46901
Type: Private, proprietary
Degrees: C
URL: http://www.rudaes.com
Phone: (765) 459-4197
Inst. Accred.: NACCAS (1965/2003)

Fort Wayne Campus
5317 Coldwater Rd., Coldwater Crossings, Fort Wayne 46825
Phone: (260) 483-2466

Success Schools, LLC
8101 Polo Club Dr., Merrillville 46410
Type: Private, proprietary
Degrees: C
Phone: (219) 736-9999
Inst. Accred.: COE (2003)

Vincennes Beauty College
12 South Second St., Vincennes 47591
Type: Private, proprietary
Degrees: C
Phone: (812) 882-1086
Inst. Accred.: NACCAS (1971/2003)

IOWA

American College of Hairstyling—Cedar Rapids
1531 First Ave., SE, Cedar Rapids 52402-5123
Type: Private, proprietary
Degrees: C
URL: http://www.americancollegeofhair.com
Phone: (319) 362-1488
Inst. Accred.: ACCSCT (1977/2006)

American College of Hairstyling—Des Moines
603 East Sixth St., Des Moines 50309-5478
Type: Private, proprietary
Degrees: C
URL: http://www.americancollegeofhair.com
Phone: (515) 244-0971
Inst. Accred.: ACCSCT (1975/2005, Probation)

Bill Hill's College of Cosmetology
910 Ave. G, Fort Madison 52627
Type: Private, proprietary
Degrees: C
Phone: (319) 372-6248
Inst. Accred.: NACCAS (1984/2003)

Bio-Chi Institute of Massage Therapy
1925 Geneva St., Sioux City 51103-2138
Type: Private, proprietary
Degrees: C
URL: http://www.bcimassage.com
Phone: (712) 252-1157
Inst. Accred.: ACCSCT (2006)

Capri College
395 Main St., PO Box 873, Dubuque 52004-0873
Type: Private, proprietary
Degrees: C
URL: http://www.capricollege.com
Phone: (563) 588-2379
Inst. Accred.: ACCSCT (1990/2005)

Capri College
425 East 59th St., Davenport 52807-2622
Type: Private, proprietary
Degrees: C
URL: http://www.capricollege.com
Phone: (319) 388-6642
Inst. Accred.: ACCSCT (1994/2004)

Capri College
2945 Williams Pkwy., SW, Cedar Rapids 52404
Type: Private, proprietary
Degrees: C
URL: http://www.capricollege.com
Phone: (319) 364-1541
Inst. Accred.: ACCSCT (1994/2004)

Carlson College of Massage Therapy
11809 County Rd. X28, Stone City 52205
Type: Private, proprietary
Degrees: C
URL: http://www.carlsoncollege.com
Phone: (319) 462-3402
Inst. Accred.: CMTA (1999/2004)

College of Hair Design
722 Water St, Ste 201, Waterloo 50702-1834
Type: Private, proprietary
Degrees: C
Phone: (319) 232-9995
Inst. Accred.: ACCSCT (1989/2005)

Davenport Barber-Styling College
730 East Kimberly Rd., Davenport 52807
Type: Private, proprietary
Degrees: C
Phone: (319) 391-9950
Inst. Accred.: ACCSCT (1996/2006)

Dayton's School of Hair Design—Burlington
315 North Main St., Burlington 52601
Type: Private, proprietary
Degrees: C
Phone: (319) 752-3193
Inst. Accred.: NACCAS (1975/2005)

Dayton's School of Hair Design—Keokuk
23 South Second St., Keokuk 52632
Type: Private, proprietary
Degrees: C
Phone: (319) 524-6445
Inst. Accred.: NACCAS (1985/2005)

EQ School of Hair Design
536 West Broadway, Council Bluffs 51503
Type: Private, proprietary
Degrees: C
Phone: (712) 328-2613
Inst. Accred.: NACCAS (1972/2003)

The Faust Institute of Cosmetology
1290 North Lake Ave., Storm Lake 50588
Type: Private, proprietary
Degrees: C
Phone: (712) 732-6571
Inst. Accred.: NACCAS (1984/2004)

Spirit Lake Campus
1543 18th St., Spirit Lake 51360
Phone: (712) 336-0512

Institute of Therapeutic Massage and Wellness
1730 Wilkes Ave., Davenport 52804
Type: Private, proprietary
Degrees: C
URL: http://www.learntomassage.com/school.htm
Phone: (563) 445-1055
Inst. Accred.: CMTA (2006)

Iowa School of Beauty—Des Moines
3305 70th St., Des Moines 50322
Type: Private, proprietary
Degrees: C
URL: http://www.iowaschoolofbeauty.com
Phone: (515) 278-9939
Inst. Accred.: NACCAS (1980/2005)

Iowa School of Beauty—Marshalltown
112 Nicholas Dr., Marshalltown 50158
Type: Private, proprietary
Degrees: C
URL: http://www.iowaschoolofbeauty.com
Phone: (515) 752-4223
Inst. Accred.: NACCAS (1985/2005)

Iowa School of Beauty—Ottumwa
609 West Second St., Ottumwa 52501
Type: Private, proprietary
Degrees: C
URL: http://www.iowaschoolofbeauty.com
Phone: (641) 684-6504
Inst. Accred.: NACCAS (1977/2003)

Iowa School of Beauty—Sioux City
2524 Glenn Ave., Sioux City 51106
Type: Private, proprietary
Degrees: C
URL: http://www.iowaschoolofbeauty.com
Phone: (712) 274-9733
Inst. Accred.: NACCAS (1972/2003)

La' James College of Hairstyling—Mason City
24 Second St., NE, Mason City 50401
Type: Private, proprietary
Degrees: C
URL: http://www.lajames.net
Phone: (641) 424-2161
Inst. Accred.: NACCAS (1974/2005)

La' James International College—Cedar Falls
6322 University Ave., Cedar Falls 50613
Type: Private, proprietary
Degrees: C
URL: http://www.lajames.net
Phone: (319) 277-2150
Inst. Accred.: NACCAS (1976/2003)

La' James International College—Davenport
3802 East 53rd St., Davenport 52807
Type: Private, proprietary
Degrees: C
URL: http://www.lajames.net
Phone: (563) 441-7900
Inst. Accred.: NACCAS (1980/2005)

La' James International College—Des Moines
8805 Chambery Boulvard, Johnston 50131
Type: Private, proprietary
Degrees: C
URL: http://www.lajames.net
Phone: (515) 278-2208
Inst. Accred.: NACCAS (1984/2004)

La' James International College—Fort Dodge
2419 5th Ave. South, Fort Dodge 50501
Type: Private, proprietary
Degrees: C
URL: http://www.lajames.net
Phone: (515) 576-3119
Inst. Accred.: NACCAS (1974/2005)

La' James International College—Iowa City
227 East Market St., Brewery Square, Iowa City 52240
Type: Private, proprietary
Degrees: C
URL: http://www.lajames.net
Phone: (319) 338-3926
Inst. Accred.: NACCAS (1965/2003)

The Professional Cosmetology Institute
309 Kitty Hawk Dr., Ames 50010-8592
Type: Private, proprietary
Degrees: C
URL: http://www.professionalcosmetologyinstitute.com
Phone: (515) 232-7250
Inst. Accred.: NACCAS (1981/2006)

Salon Professional Academy
4411 Winnetka Ave. North, New Hope, MN 55446
Phone: (763) 536-0772

Total Look School of Cosmetology and Massage Therapy
806 West Third St., Cresco 52136
Type: Private, proprietary
Degrees: C
Phone: (563) 547-3624
Inst. Accred.: NACCAS (2001/2004)

KANSAS

Academy of Hair Design
115 South Fifth St., Salina 67401
Type: Private, proprietary
Degrees: C
Phone: (785) 825-8155
Inst. Accred.: NACCAS (1970/2003)

American Academy of Hair Design
901 SW 37th St., Topeka 66611
Type: Private, proprietary
Degrees: C
URL: http://www.aaahairdesign.com
Phone: (785) 267-5800
Inst. Accred.: NACCAS (1982/2002)

American Institute of Baking
1213 Bakers Way, Manhattan 66502
Type: Private, independent
Degrees: C
URL: http://www.aibonline.org
Phone: (785) 537-4750
Inst. Accred.: NCA-CASI (1985/2001)

B-Street Design School of International Hair Styling
3602 Topeka Blvd., SW, Topeka 66611
Type: Private, proprietary
Degrees: C
URL: http://www.bstreetdesign.com
Phone: (785) 267-7701
Inst. Accred.: NACCAS (2000/2006)

B-Street Design School of International Hair Styling
1215 East Santa Fe, Olathe 66061
Type: Private, proprietary
Degrees: C
URL: http://www.bstreetdesign.com
Phone: (913) 782-4004
Inst. Accred.: NACCAS (1990/2005)

Overland Park Campus
10324 Mastin St., Overland Park 66212
Phone: (913) 492-4114

Wichita Campus
1675 South Rock Rd., Ste. 101, Wichita 67207
Phone: (316) 681-2288

BMSI Institute, LLC
8665 West 96th St., Ste. 300, Overland Park 66212
Type: Private, proprietary
Degrees: C
URL: http://www.bmsi-institute.com
Phone: (913) 649-3322 *Calendar:* Sem. plan
Inst. Accred.: CMTA (2004)

Bryan College—Topeka
1527 SW Fairlawn Rd., Topeka 66604
Type: Private, proprietary
Degrees: C
URL: http://www.bryancareercolleges.com
Phone: (785) 272-0889
Inst. Accred.: ACICS (1991/2005)

CB&T, Inc
5700 Broadmoor, #202, Mission 66202
Type: Private, proprietary
Degrees: C
URL: http://www.kansascity.dalecarnegie.com
Phone: (913) 831-9330
Inst. Accred.: ACCET (1976/2007)

Crum's Beauty College
512 Poyntz Ave., Manhattan 66502
Type: Private, proprietary
Degrees: C
URL: http://www.crumsbeautycollege.com
Phone: (785) 776-4794
Inst. Accred.: NACCAS (1967/2003)

Cutting Edge Hairstyling Academy
4323 State Ave., Kansas City 66101
Type: Private, proprietary
Degrees: C
URL: http://cuttingedge-kc.com
Phone: (913) 321-0214
Inst. Accred.: ACCSCT (1987/2004)

Cutting Edge Hairstyling Academy
4327 State Ave., Kansas City 66102
Type: Private, proprietary
Degrees: C
URL: http://cuttingedge-kc.com
Phone: (913) 321-0214
Inst. Accred.: ACCSCT (1987/2004)

Shawnee Campus
12148 Shawnee Mission Pkwy., Shawnee 66216
Phone: (913) 962-0076

Tampa Campus
3942 South Dale Mabry Hwy., Tampa, FL 33611
Phone: (813) 902-9400

Hays Academy of Hair Design
1214 East 27th St., Hays 67601
Type: Private, proprietary
Degrees: C
Phone: (785) 628-6624
Inst. Accred.: NACCAS (1984/2005)

Kansas City Kansas Area Technical School
2220 North 59th St., Kansas City 66104
Type: Public, state/local
Degrees: C
URL: http://www.kckats.com
Phone: (913) 627-4100
Inst. Accred.: NCA-CASI (1996/2002)

Kaw Area Technical School
5724 SW Huntoon St., Topeka 66604-2199
Type: Public, local
Degrees: C
URL: http://www.kats.tec.ks.us
Phone: (785) 273-7140 *Calendar:* Qtr. plan
Inst. Accred.: COE (2004)
Prog. Accred.: Allied Health (surgical technology)

LaBaron Hairdressing Academy—Overland Park
8119 Robinson St., Overland Park 66204
Type: Private, proprietary
Degrees: C
URL: http://www.labaronacademy.com
Phone: (913) 642-0077
Inst. Accred.: NACCAS (1986/2006)

Old Town Barber and Beauty College
1207 East Douglas Ave., Wichita 67211-1693
Type: Private, proprietary
Degrees: C
URL: http://otbbcollege.com
Phone: (316) 264-4891
Inst. Accred.: ACCSCT (1980/2006)

Pinnacle Career Institute—Lawrence
1601 West 23rd St., Ste. 200, Lawrence 66046
Type: Private, proprietary
Degrees: C
URL: http://www.pcitraining.edu
Phone: (785) 841-9640
Inst. Accred.: ACICS (1989/2005)

Salina Area Technical College
2562 Centennial Rd., Salina 67401
Type: Public, state/local
Degrees: C
URL: http://www.salinatech.com
Phone: (785) 309-3100 *Calendar:* Sem. plan
Inst. Accred.: NCA-CASI (1997/2004)
Prog. Accred.: Dentistry (dental assisting)

Sidney's Hairdressing College, Inc.
916 East 4th Ave., Hutchinson 67501
Type: Private, proprietary
Degrees: C
URL: http://www.sidneyshair.com
Phone: (620) 662-5481
Inst. Accred.: NACCAS (2001/2004)

Southwest Kansas Technical School
2215 North Kansas Ave., Liberal 67901-2013
Type: Public, state/local
Degrees: C
URL: http://www.usd480.net/swkts
Phone: (620) 626-3819
Inst. Accred.: NCA-CASI (1983/2002)

Vernon's Kansas School of Cosmetology
2531 South Seneca St., Wichita 67217
Type: Private, proprietary
Degrees: C
URL: http://www.vksc.edu
Phone: (316) 265-2629
Inst. Accred.: NACCAS (1965/2005)

Wichita Technical Institute
2051 South Meridian Ave., Wichita 67213-1927
Type: Private, proprietary
Degrees: C
URL: http://www.wtielectronics.com
Phone: (316) 943-2241
Inst. Accred.: ACCSCT (1971/2004)
Prog. Accred.: Dentistry (dental assisting)

Joplin Campus
1531 East 32nd St., Joplin, MO 64804
Phone: (417) 206-9115

Tulsa Campus
708 South Sheridan Rd., Tulsa, OK 74112-3140
Phone: (918) 292-8166

Wichita Campus
3712 SW Burlingame Rd., Topeka 66609
Phone: (785) 354-4568

Wright Business School
8951 Metcalf Ave., Overland Park 66212
Type: Private, proprietary
Degrees: C
URL: http://www.wrightbusinessschool.edu
Phone: (913) 385-7700
Inst. Accred.: ACICS (1988/2004)

Oklahoma City Campus
2219 SW 74th St., Ste. 124, Oklahoma City, OK 73159
Phone: (405) 681-2300

Tulsa Campus
4908 South Sheridan Rd., Tulsa, OK 74145
Phone: (918) 628-7700

Xenon International School of Hair Design
3804 West Douglas Ave., Wichita 67203
Type: Private, proprietary
Degrees: C
URL: http://www.xenonintl.com
Phone: (316) 943-5516
Inst. Accred.: NACCAS (1989/2004)

KENTUCKY

Appalachian Beauty School
609 Central Ave., US Hwy. 119 South, South Williamson 41503
Type: Private, proprietary
Degrees: C
Phone: (606) 237-6650
Inst. Accred.: NACCAS (1980/2005)

ATA Career Education
10180 Linn Station Rd., Ste. A-200, Louisville 40223
Type: Private, proprietary
Degrees: C
URL: http://www.ata.edu
Phone: (502) 371-8330
Inst. Accred.: ABHES (2005)

Barrett and Company School of Hair Design
973 Kimberly Square, Nicholasville 40356
Type: Private, proprietary
Degrees: C
URL: http://www.barrett.edu
Phone: (859) 885-9135
Inst. Accred.: COE (1987/2004)

Bellefonte Academy of Beauty
420 Belfont St., PO Box 40, Russell 41169
Type: Private, proprietary
Degrees: C
URL: http://www.bellefonteacademyofbeauty.com
Phone: (606) 833-5446
Inst. Accred.: NACCAS (2003/2006)

Maysville Campus
111 West Second St., Maysville 41056
Phone: (606) 833-5446

Carl D. Perkins Job Corps Center
478 Meadows Branch Rd., Prestonsburg 41653-1501
Type: Public, federal
Degrees: C
URL: http://jobcorps.dol.gov/centers/ky.htm
Phone: (606) 886-1037
Inst. Accred.: COE (1985/2001)

Center for Employment Training
601 Washington St., Ste. 106, Newport 41071
Type: Private, independent
Degrees: C
URL: http://www.brightoncenter.com/cet
Phone: (859) 491-8303 ext 2
Inst. Accred.: COE (2001/2007)

Collins School of Cosmetology
PO Box 1370, Middlesboro 40965-3170
Type: Private, proprietary
Degrees: C
Phone: (606) 248-3602
Inst. Accred.: NACCAS (1973/2003)

Donta School of Beauty Culture
515 West Oak St., Louisville 40203
Type: Private, proprietary
Degrees: C
Phone: (502) 583-1018
Inst. Accred.: NACCAS (1980/2005)

Earle C. Clements Job Corps Center
2302 US Hwy. 60 East, Morganfield 42437
Type: Public, federal
Degrees: C
URL: http://earlecclements.jobcorps.gov
Phone: (270) 389-2419
Inst. Accred.: COE (1983/2005)

Elizabethtown Beauty School
308 North Miles St., Elizabethtown 42701
Type: Private, proprietary
Degrees: C
Phone: (270) 765-2118
Inst. Accred.: NACCAS (1984/2004)

Employment Solutions—College for Technical Education
1165 Centre Pkwy., Ste. 120, Lexington 40517
Type: Private, independent
Degrees: C
URL: http://www.employmentsolutionsinc.org
Phone: (859) 272-5225
Inst. Accred.: COE (2006)

Ezell's Cosmetology School
PO Box 1431, Murray 42071-0026
Type: Private, proprietary
Degrees: C
Phone: (270) 753-4723
Inst. Accred.: NACCAS (2000/2003)

Federal Medical Center Lexington
3301 Leestown Rd., Lexington 40511-8799
Type: Public, federal
Degrees: C
URL: http://www.bop.gov/locations/institutions/lex
Phone: (859) 255-6812
Inst. Accred.: COE (2000)
Prog. Accred.: Psychology Internship

The Hair Design School
1049 Bardstown Rd., Louisville 40204
Type: Private, proprietary
System: Empire Education Group
Degrees: C
URL: http://www.hairdesignschool.com
Phone: (502) 459-8150
Inst. Accred.: NACCAS (1980/2005)

The Hair Design School
5120 Dixie Hwy., Louisville 40216
Type: Private, proprietary
System: Empire Education Group
Degrees: C
URL: http://www.hairdesignschool.com
Phone: (502) 447-0111
Inst. Accred.: NACCAS (1975/2006)

The Hair Design School
151 Chenoweth Ln., Louisville 40207
Type: Private, proprietary
System: Empire Education Group
Degrees: C
URL: http://www.hairdesignschool.com
Phone: (502) 897-9401
Inst. Accred.: COE (1989/2002)

The Hair Design School
554 Westport Rd., Elizabethtown 42701
Type: Private, proprietary
System: Empire Education Group
Degrees: C
URL: http://www.hairdesignschool.com
Phone: (270) 765-3374
Inst. Accred.: NACCAS (1976/2006)

The Hair Design School
7285 Turfway Rd., Florence 41042
Type: Private, proprietary
System: Empire Education Group
Degrees: C
URL: http://www.hairdesignschool.com
Phone: (859) 283-2690
Inst. Accred.: NACCAS (1975/2006)

The Hair Design School—Louisville
5314 Bardstown Rd., Louisville 40291
Type: Private, proprietary
System: Empire Education Group
Degrees: C
URL: http://www.hairdesignschool.com
Phone: (502) 499-0070
Inst. Accred.: NACCAS (1975/2006)

Head's West Kentucky Beauty College
Briarwood Shopping Center, Madisonville 42431
Type: Private, proprietary
Degrees: C
Phone: (270) 825-3019
Inst. Accred.: NACCAS (1990/2005)

J & M Academy of Cosmetology, Inc.
110 A Brighton Park Blvd., Frankfort 40601
Type: Private, proprietary
Degrees: C
Phone: (502) 695-8001
Inst. Accred.: NACCAS (1986/2004)

Jenny Lea Academy of Cosmetology—Harlan
114 North Cumberland Ave., Harlan 40831
Type: Private, proprietary
Degrees: C
Phone: (606) 573-4276
Inst. Accred.: NACCAS (1984/2004)

Johnson City Campus
222 East Unaka Ave., Johnson City, TN 37601
Phone: (423) 926-9095

Jenny Lea Academy of Cosmetology—Whitesburg
74 Pkwy. Plaza Loop, Whitesburg 41858
Type: Private, proprietary
Degrees: C
Phone: (606) 633-8784
Inst. Accred.: NACCAS (1987/2005)

Kaufman Beauty School
701 East High St., Lexington 40502
Type: Private, proprietary
Degrees: C
URL: http://www.kaufmaneducation.com
Phone: (859) 266-5531
Inst. Accred.: NACCAS (1971/2003)

Lexington Beauty College, Inc.
90 Southport Dr., Lexington 40503-1819
Type: Private, proprietary
Degrees: C
URL: http://lexingtonbeautycollege.com
Phone: (859) 278-7483
Inst. Accred.: COE (2004)

Lexington Healing Arts Academy
272 Southland Dr., Lexington 40503
Type: Private, proprietary
Degrees: C
URL: http://www.lexingtonhealingarts.com
Phone: (859) 252-5656
Inst. Accred.: ABHES (2006)

Motif Beauty Academy
23 West Lexington Ave., Winchester 40391
Type: Private, proprietary
Degrees: C
URL: http://motifbeautyacademy.com
Phone: (859) 745-5886
Inst. Accred.: NACCAS (1993/2006)

Mr. Jim's Beauty College
1240 Carter Rd., Owensboro 42301
Type: Private, proprietary
Degrees: C
URL: http://www.mrjimscollegeofcosmetology.com
Phone: (270) 684-3505
Inst. Accred.: NACCAS (1994/2002)

Northern Kentucky School of Medical Massage
1793 Patrick Rd., Burlington 41005
Type: Private, proprietary
Degrees: C
URL: http://www.massageschools.com
Phone: (859) 578-8868
Inst. Accred.: CMTA (2006)

Nu-Tek Academy of Beauty
153 Evans Dr., Mount Sterling 40353
Type: Private, proprietary
Degrees: C
Phone: (859) 498-4460
Inst. Accred.: COE (1990/2005)

Pat Wilson Beauty College, Inc.
326 North Main St., Henderson 42420
Type: Private, proprietary
Degrees: C
Phone: (270) 826-5195
Inst. Accred.: NACCAS (1985/2003)

PJ's College of Cosmetology
1901 Russellville Rd., Ste. 10, Bowling Green 42101
Type: Private, proprietary
System: PJ's College of Cosmetology
Degrees: C
URL: http://www.gotopjs.com
Phone: (270) 842-8149
Inst. Accred.: COE (1986/2003)

PJ's College of Cosmetology
124 South Public Square, Glasgow 42141
Type: Private, proprietary
System: PJ's College of Cosmetology
Degrees: C
URL: http://www.gotopjs.com
Phone: (270) 651-6553
Inst. Accred.: COE (1987/2004)

Greenfield Campus
1400 West Main St., Greenfield, IN 46140
Phone: (317) 462-9239

Indianapolis Campus
5539 South Madison St., Indianapolis, IN 46227
Phone: (317) 781-9600

Louisville Campus
10434 Shelbyville Rd., Louisville 40223-3120
Phone: (502) 489-3757

Muncie Campus
2006 North Walnut St., Muncie, IN 47303
Phone: (765) 289-6144

Plainfield Campus
2026 Stafford Rd., Plainfield, IN 46168
Phone: (317) 839-2761

Regency School of Hair Design
567 North Lake Dr., Prestonsburg 41653
Type: Private, proprietary
Degrees: C
Phone: (606) 886-6457
Inst. Accred.: NACCAS (2003/2006)

Southeast School of Cosmetology
356 Manchester Square Center, PO Box 493, Manchester 40962
Type: Private, proprietary
Degrees: C
Phone: (606) 598-7901
Inst. Accred.: NACCAS (1988/2003)

Trend Setter's Academy of Beauty Culture
7283 Dixie Hwy., Louisville 40258
Type: Private, proprietary
Degrees: C
Phone: (502) 937-6704
Inst. Accred.: NACCAS (1981/2006)

Crestwood Campus
PO Box 1124, Crestwood 40014-1124
Phone: (502) 241-0565

Elizabethtown Campus
622 Westport Rd., Ste. B, Elizabethtown 42701
Phone: (270) 765-5243

Louisville Dale Carnegie Group
2100 Gardiner Ln., Ste. 316, Louisville 40205
Type: Private, proprietary
Degrees: C
URL: http://www.kentuckiana.dalecarnegie.com
Phone: (502) 413-8870
Inst. Accred.: ACCET (1998/2003)

LOUISIANA

Alden's School of Cosmetology
4321 Airline Hwy., Baton Rouge 70805-1502
Type: Private, proprietary
Degrees: C
URL: http://www.aldensschoolofcosmetology.com
Phone: (225) 355-5776
Inst. Accred.: NACCAS (2006)

Alexandria Academy of Beauty
2305 Rapides Ave., Alexandria 71301
Type: Private, proprietary
Degrees: C
Phone: (318) 442-7715
Inst. Accred.: NACCAS (1987/2002)

American School of Business
702 Professional Dr. North, Shreveport 71105
Type: Private, proprietary
Degrees: C
URL: http://www.americanschoolofbusiness.com
Phone: (318) 798-3333
Inst. Accred.: ACICS (1988/2004)

Ascension College
320 East Ascension St., Gonzales 70737
Type: Private, proprietary
Degrees: C
URL: http://www.ascensioncollege.org
Phone: (225) 647-6609
Inst. Accred.: ACICS (2006)

Aveda Institute
1355 Polders Ln., Covington 70434
Type: Private, proprietary
Degrees: C
URL: http://www.avedainstitutes.com
Phone: (985) 892-9953
Inst. Accred.: NACCAS (1988/2006)

Atlanta Campus
3402 Piedmont Rd., Atlanta, GA 30305
Phone: (404) 649-7119

Charlotte Campus
1520 South Blvd., Ste. 150, Charlotte, NC 28203
Phone: (704) 333-9940

New Orleans Campus
3330 Veterans Blvd., Ste. A, Metairie 70002
Phone: (504) 454-1400

Shenandoah Campus
19245 David Memorial Dr., Ste. 100, Shenandoah, TX 77385
Phone: (936) 539-6770

Aveda Institute Baton Rouge
2834 South Sherwood Forest Blvd., Ste. A, Baton Rouge 70816
Type: Private, proprietary
Degrees: C
URL: http://www.avedainstitutes.com
Phone: (225) 295-1435
Inst. Accred.: NACCAS (1981/2006)

Aveda Institute Lafayette
2922 Johnston St., Lafayette 70503
Type: Private, proprietary
Degrees: C
URL: http://www.avedainstitutes.com
Phone: (337) 233-0511
Inst. Accred.: NACCAS (1979/2006)

Ayers Career College
8820 Jewella Ave., Shreveport 71108
Type: Private, proprietary
Degrees: C
URL: http://www.ayersinstitute.com
Phone: (318) 868-3000
Inst. Accred.: COE (1995/2001)

Bastrop Beauty School #1
117 South Vine St., Bastrop 71220
Type: Private, proprietary
Degrees: C
Phone: (318) 281-8652
Inst. Accred.: NACCAS (1984/2004)

Baton Rouge College
2834 South Sherwood Forest Blvd., B-12, Baton Rouge
Type: Private, proprietary
Degrees: C
URL: http://www.brcollege.edu
Phone: (225) 292-5464
Inst. Accred.: ACCET (1989/2002)

Blue Cliff College—Baton Rouge
6160 Perkins Rd., Ste. 200, Baton Rouge 70808-4191
Type: Private, proprietary
Degrees: C
URL: http://www.bluecliffcollege.com
Phone: (225) 757-3770
Inst. Accred.: CMTA (1999/2006, Warning)

Cloyd's Beauty School #1
603 Natchitoches St., West Monroe 71291
Type: Private, proprietary
Degrees: C
Phone: (318) 322-5314
Inst. Accred.: NACCAS (1986/2006)

Cloyd's Beauty School #2
1311 Winnsboro Rd., Monroe 71201
Type: Private, proprietary
Degrees: C
Phone: (318) 322-5314
Inst. Accred.: COE (1991/2001)

Cloyd's Beauty School #3
2514 Ferrand St., West Monroe 71294
Type: Private, proprietary
Degrees: C
Phone: (318) 322-5314
Inst. Accred.: COE (1991/2001)

Compass Career College
42353 Deluxe Plaza, Suites 16-20, Hammond 70403
Type: Private, proprietary
Degrees: C
URL: http://www.compasscareercollege.com
Phone: (985) 419-2050
Inst. Accred.: COE (2005)

Cosmetology Business and Management Institute
59 West Bank Expressway, Gretna 70053
Type: Private, proprietary
Degrees: C
Phone: (504) 362-1999
Inst. Accred.: NACCAS (1982/2006)

Cosmetology Training Center
2516 Johnston St., Lafayette 70503
Type: Private, proprietary
Degrees: C
Phone: (337) 237-6868
Inst. Accred.: NACCAS (1987/2002)

Court Reporting Institute of Louisiana, Inc.
12090 South Harrells Ferry Rd., Ste. A, Baton Rouge 70816
Type: Private, proprietary
Degrees: C
URL: http://www.courtreportinginstituteoflouisiana.com
Phone: (225) 292-1950
Inst. Accred.: COE (2003)

Crescent Schools
209 North Broad St., New Orleans 70119
Type: Private, proprietary
Degrees: C
URL: http://www.crescentschools.com
Phone: (504) 822-3362
Inst. Accred.: ACCET (1990/2003)

Gulfport Campus
1306 259th Ave., Gulfport, MS 39501
Phone: (228) 822-2444

Las Vegas Campus
4180 South Sandhill Rd., Ste. B8/9, Las Vegas, NV 89121
Phone: (702) 458-9910

D-Jay's School of Beauty Arts and Sciences
5131 Government St., Baton Rouge 70806
Type: Private, proprietary
Degrees: C
Phone: (225) 926-2530
Inst. Accred.: NACCAS (1974/2003)

Delta College
19231 North 6th St., Covington 70433
Type: Private, proprietary
Degrees: C
URL: http://www.deltacollege.com
Phone: (225) 892-6651
Inst. Accred.: COE (1998/2004)

Baton Rouge Campus
7380 Exchange Place, Baton Rouge 70806
Phone: (225)928-7770

Lafayette Campus
105 Patriot Ave., Lafayette 70508
Phone: (337) 988-5455

Slidell Campus
105 Gause Blvd., West Slidell 70406
Phone: (985) 643-7730

Demmon School of Beauty
1222 Ryan St., Lake Charles 70601
Type: Private, proprietary
Degrees: C
Phone: (337) 439-9265
Inst. Accred.: NACCAS (1967/2005)

Denham Springs Beauty College
923 Florida Ave., SE, Denham Springs 70726
Type: Private, proprietary
Degrees: C
Phone: (225) 665-6188
Inst. Accred.: COE (1989/2006)

Diesel Driving Academy
8136 Airline Hwy., Baton Rouge 70815
Type: Private, proprietary
Degrees: C
URL: http://www.dieseldrivingacademy.com
Phone: (225) 929-9990
Inst. Accred.: COE (1990/2004)

Diesel Driving Academy
4709 Greenwood Rd., Shreveport 71133-6949
Type: Private, proprietary
Degrees: C
URL: http://www.dieseldrivingacademy.com
Phone: (318) 636-6300
Inst. Accred.: COE (1982/2002)

Lafayette Campus
3225-A Hwy. 90 East, Broussard 70518
Phone: (800) 551-8900

Little Rock Campus
1 Harold Ives Dr., North Little Rock, AR 72117
Phone: (800) 551-8900

Domestic Health Care Institute
4826 Jamestown Ave., Baton Rouge 70808
Type: Private, proprietary
Degrees: C
Phone: (225) 925-5312
Inst. Accred.: ABHES (1990/2005)

Guy's Academy Hair, Skin, and Nails
1141 Shreveport-Barksdale Hwy., Shreveport 71105
Type: Private, proprietary
Degrees: C
URL: http://www.guysacademy.com
Phone: (318) 865-5591
Inst. Accred.: NACCAS (1988/2003)

John Jay Beauty College
540 Robert E. Lee Blvd., New Orleans 70124
Type: Private, proprietary
Degrees: C
Phone: (504) 467-2774
Inst. Accred.: NACCAS (1966/2006)

Slidell Campus
3144 Pontchartrain Dr., Slidell 70458
Phone: (985) 643-0677

John Jay Kenner Academy
2844 Tennessee Ave., Kenner 70062
Type: Private, proprietary
Degrees: C
Phone: (504) 647-2774
Inst. Accred.: NACCAS (1983/2003)

Jonesville Beauty School
208 Westside Dr., Vidalia 71373
Type: Private, proprietary
Degrees: C
Phone: (318) 336-2377
Inst. Accred.: NACCAS (1997/2005)

Vidalia Beauty School
208 Westside Dr., Vidalia 71373
Phone: (318) 336-2377

King's Career College—Florida Boulevard Campus
3875 Florida Blvd., Baton Rouge 70806
Type: Private, proprietary
Degrees: C
Phone: (225) 387-5535
Inst. Accred.: ABHES (1999/2001)

King's Career College—Ocean Drive Campus
1771 North Lobdell Blvd., Baton Rouge 70806
Type: Private, proprietary
Degrees: C
Phone: (225) 644-4432
Inst. Accred.: ABHES (1999/2001)

Louisiana Academy of Beauty
550 East Laurel St., Eunice 70535
Type: Private, proprietary
Degrees: C
Phone: (337) 457-7627
Inst. Accred.: NACCAS (1987/2002)

Louisiana Culinary Institute
5837 Essen Ln., Baton Rouge 70810-1112
Type: Private, proprietary
Degrees: C
URL: http://www.louisianaculinary.com
Phone: (225) 769-8820 *Calendar:* Qtr. plan
Inst. Accred.: COE (2006)

Medical Training College
10525 Plaza Americana Dr., Baton Rouge 70816
Type: Private, proprietary
Degrees: C
URL: http://mtcbr.com
Phone: (225) 926-5820
Inst. Accred.: COE (1998/2004)

MedVance Institute of Baton Rouge
9255 Interline Ave., Baton Rouge 70809
Type: Private, proprietary
Degrees: C
URL: http://www.medvance.edu
Phone: (225) 248-1015 *Calendar:* Qtr. plan
Inst. Accred.: ABHES (1995/2006)
Prog. Accred.: Allied Health (surgical technology), Radiography

Fort Lauderdale Campus
4850 West Oakland Park Blvd., Ste. 200, Ft. Lauderdale, FL 33313
Phone: (954) 332-3086
Prog. Accred: Allied Health (surgical technology), Medical Assisting (ABHES), Radiography, Surgical Technology

Nashville Campus
2400 Parman Place, Building B, Ste. 3, Nashville, TN 37203
Phone: (561) 832-3535
Prog. Accred: Medical Assisting (ABHES)

Stuart Campus
851 Johnson Ave., Stuart, FL 34994
Phone: (772) 221-9799
Prog. Accred: Medical Assisting (ABHES), Surgical Technology

Omega Institute of Cosmetology
229 South Hollywood Rd., Houma 70360
Type: Private, proprietary
Degrees: C
URL: http://www.omegainstitutes.com
Phone: (985) 876-9334
Inst. Accred.: NACCAS (2000/2003)

Opelousas School of Cosmetology, Inc
529 East Vine St., Opelousas 70570
Type: Private, proprietary
Degrees: C
Phone: (337) 942-6147
Inst. Accred.: NACCAS (1989/2004)

Pat Goins Beauty School
3138 Louisville Ave., Monroe 71201
Type: Private, proprietary
Degrees: C
Phone: (318) 322-2500
Inst. Accred.: NACCAS (1975/2005)

Pat Goins Benton Road Beauty School
1701 Old Minden Rd., Ste. 36, Bossier City 71111
Type: Private, proprietary
Degrees: C
Phone: (318) 746-7674
Inst. Accred.: NACCAS (1975/2005)

Pat Goins Ruston Beauty School
213 West Alabama St., Ruston 71270
Type: Private, proprietary
Degrees: C
Phone: (318) 255-2717
Inst. Accred.: NACCAS (1971/2005)

Pat Goins Shreveport Beauty School
6363 Hearne Ave., Ste. 106, Shreveport 71108
Type: Private, proprietary
Degrees: C
Phone: (318) 631-1833
Inst. Accred.: NACCAS (1979/2005)

Paul Phillips and Associates, Inc.
2540 Severn Ave., Ste. 211, Metairie 70002
Type: Private, proprietary
Degrees: C
URL: http://www.neworleans.dalecarnegie.com
Phone: (985) 727-4636
Inst. Accred.: ACCET (1978/2004)

Pineville Beauty School
1008 Main St., Pineville 71360
Type: Private, proprietary
Degrees: C
Phone: (318) 445-1040
Inst. Accred.: NACCAS (1985/2005)

Ray's Faith Academy of Beauty Education
1064 East Worthey Rd., Gonzales 70737
Type: Private, proprietary
Degrees: C
Phone: (225) 644-2872
Inst. Accred.: NACCAS (2004)

Ronnie and Dorman's School of Hair Design
2002 Johnston St., Lafayette 70503
Type: Private, proprietary
Degrees: C
Phone: (337) 232-1806
Inst. Accred.: NACCAS (1975/2006)

Shreveport Job Corps Center
2815 Lillian St., Shreveport 71109
Type: Public, federal
Degrees: C
URL: http://jobcorps.dol.gov/centers/la.htm
Phone: (318) 227-9331
Inst. Accred.: COE (1997/2003)

South Louisiana Beauty College
300 Howard Ave., Houma 70363
Type: Private, proprietary
Degrees: C
URL: http://slbc-houma.com
Phone: (985) 873-8978
Inst. Accred.: COE (1987/2004)

Stage One- The Hair School, Inc.
209 West College St., Lake Charles 70605
Type: Private, proprietary
Degrees: C
URL: http://www.stage-one.org
Phone: (337) 474-0533
Inst. Accred.: NACCAS (1986/2004)

Stevenson's Academy of Hair Design
401 Opelousas Ave., New Orleans 70114
Type: Private, proprietary
Degrees: C
URL: http://www.stevensonsacademy.com
Phone: (504) 368-6377
Inst. Accred.: NACCAS (1978/2004)

West Bank Campus
401 Opelousas St., New Orleans 70114
Phone: (504) 945-2312

Unitech Training Academy
3605 Ambassador Caffery Pkwy., Lafayette 70503
Type: Private, proprietary
Degrees: C
URL: http://www.unitechtrainingacademy.com
Phone: (337) 988-6764
Inst. Accred.: COE (2002/2003)

Houma Campus
1227 Grand Caillou Rd., Houma 70863
Phone: (985) 223-1755

West Monroe Campus
111 Crosley St., West Monroe 71291
Phone: (318) 651-8001

Vanguard College of Cosmetology
740 Oak Harbor Blvd., Slidell 70458
Type: Private, proprietary
Degrees: C
Phone: (985) 643-2614
Inst. Accred.: NACCAS (1988/2003)

Vortex Helicopters, Inc.
PO Box 9789, New Iberia 70560
Type: Private, proprietary
Degrees: C
URL: http://vortex-helicopters.com
Phone: (337) 364-8909
Inst. Accred.: ACCSCT (2002)

Winner Institute, Inc.
519 Kimmeridge Dr., PO Box 40188, Baton Rouge
Type: Private, proprietary
Degrees: C
URL: http://www.batonrouge.dalecarnegie.com
Phone: (225) 273-8447
Inst. Accred.: ACCET (1977/2004)

MAINE

Birthwise Midwifery School
24 South High St., Bridgton 04009
Type: Private, independent
Degrees: C
URL: http://wwwbirthwisemidwifery.org
Phone: (207) 647-5968 *Calendar:* Sem. plan
Inst. Accred.: MEAC (1998/2006)

Dale Carnegie Training of Maine
75 John Roberts Rd., Ste. B11, South Portland 04106
Type: Private, proprietary
Degrees: C
URL: http://www.maine.dalecarnegie.com
Phone: (207) 775-3253
Inst. Accred.: ACCET (1997/2002)

Downeast School of Massage
PO Box 24, 99 Moose Meadow Ln., Waldoboro 04572-0024
Type: Private, proprietary
Degrees: C
URL: http://www.downeastschoolofmassage.net
Phone: (207) 832-5531
Inst. Accred.: CMTA (2004/2007, Probation)

Fuller Circles School for Therapeutic Massage
169 Rice Rips Rd., Oakland 04963
Type: Private, proprietary
Degrees: C
URL: http://www.fullercircles.com
Phone: (207) 877-5650
Inst. Accred.: ABHES (2002/2005)

The Landing School of Boat Building and Design
PO Box 1490, Kennebunkport 04046-1490
Type: Private, proprietary
Degrees: C
URL: http://www.landingschool.org
Phone: (207) 985-7976
Inst. Accred.: ACCSCT (1987/2004)

Mid-Maine Technical Center
Three Brooklyn Ave., Waterville 04901-1151
Type: Public, state
Degrees: C
URL: http://www.midmainetech.org
Phone: (207) 873-0102
Inst. Accred.: NEASC-CTCI (1981/2006)

Mr. Bernard's School of Hair Fashion, Inc.
711 Lisbon St., PO Box 1163, Lewiston 04243
Type: Private, proprietary
Degrees: C
URL: http://www.bernardschoolofhair.com
Phone: (207) 783-7250
Inst. Accred.: NACCAS (1966/2003)

New Hampshire Institute for Therapeutic Arts
27 Sandy Creek Rd., Bridgton 04009
Type: Private, proprietary
Degrees: C
URL: http://www.nhita.com
Phone: (207) 647-3794
Inst. Accred.: CMTA (1999/2007)

Hudson Campus
153 Lowell Rd., Hudson, NH 03051
Phone: (603) 882-3022

Northeast Montessori Institute
PO Box 68, Rockport 04856
Type: Private, independent
Degrees: C
URL: http://www.nemontessori.org
Phone: (207) 236-6316
Inst. Accred.: MACTE (2001/2006)

Beijing Campus
7 Sanlitun Beiziaojie, Beijing, China 100027
Phone: 011 86 10 6532 6713

Pierre's School of Cosmetology
319 Marginal Way, Ste. 2, Portland 04101
Type: Private, proprietary
System: Empire Education Group
Degrees: C
URL: http://www.pierresschool.com
Phone: (207) 774-9413
Inst. Accred.: NACCAS (1967/2002)

Caribou Campus
30 Skyway Dr., Syway Plaza, Caribou 04736
Phone: (207) 498-6067

Sanford Campus
913 Main St., Sanford 04073
Phone: (207) 490-1274

Pierre's School of Cosmetology—Bangor
635 Broadway, Bangor 04401
Type: Private, proprietary
System: Empire Education Group
Degrees: C
URL: http://www.pierresschool.com
Phone: (207) 942-0039
Inst. Accred.: NACCAS (1996/2004)

Waterville Campus
215 Kennedy Memorial Dr., Waterville 04901
Phone: (207) 873-0682

Seacoast Career Schools
One Eagle Dr., Ste. 1, Sanford 04073
Type: Private, proprietary
System: Premier Education Group
Degrees: C
URL: http://www.seacoastcareerschools.com
Phone: (207) 490-0509
Inst. Accred.: ACCET (1999/2006)

Manchester Campus
670 North Commercial St., Manchester, NH 03101
Phone: (603) 624-7222

Spa Tech Institute
1041 Brighton Ave., Portland 04102
Type: Private, proprietary
Degrees: C
URL: http://www.spatech.edu
Phone: (207) 772-2591
Inst. Accred.: NACCAS (1979/2006)

Ipswich Campus
126 High St., Ipswich, MA 01938
Phone: (978) 356-0980

Plymouth Campus
59 Industrial Park Rd., Plymouth, MA 02360
Phone: (508) 747-3130

Westboro Campus
227 Turnpike Rd., Ste. 1, Westboro, MA 01581
Phone: (508) 836-8864

Westbrook Campus
100 Larrabee Rd., Westbrook 04093
Phone: (207) 591-4141

Worldwide Language Resources, Inc.
449 Upton Rd., Andover 04216
Type: Private, proprietary
Degrees: C
URL: http://www.wwlr.com
Phone: (207) 392-1403
Inst. Accred.: ACCET (2000/2003, Warning)

MARYLAND

Aaron's Academy of Beauty
11690 Doolittle Dr., Waldorf 20602
Type: Private, proprietary
Degrees: C
Phone: (301) 645-3681
Inst. Accred.: NACCAS (1991/2006)

Academy of Computer Education
7833 Walker Dr., Ste. 520C, Greenbelt 20770
Type: Private, proprietary
Degrees: C
URL: http://www.trainace.com
Phone: (301)220-2802
Inst. Accred.: ACCSCT (2005)

AccuTech Career Institute
5310 Spectrum Dr., Frederick 21703
Type: Private, proprietary
Degrees: C
URL: http://www.accutech.edu
Phone: (301) 694-0211
Inst. Accred.: ACICS (1987/2001)

Aesthetics Institute of Cosmetology
15958-C Shady Grove Rd., Gaithersburg
Type: Private, proprietary
Degrees: C
Phone: (301) 330-9252
Inst. Accred.: NACCAS (1992/2005)

American Beauty Academy
11006 Viers Mill Rd., Wheaton 20902
Type: Private, proprietary
Degrees: C
URL: http://www.americanbeautyacademy.org
Phone: (301) 949-3000
Inst. Accred.: NACCAS (1996/2004)

Baltimore Campus
4719 Harford Rd., Baltimore 21214
Phone: (410) 444-3100

Americare School of Allied Health
11141 Georgia Ave., Ste. 418, Wheaton 20902
Type: Private, proprietary
Degrees: C
URL: http://www.americareschool.com
Phone: (301) 933-4660
Inst. Accred.: ABHES (1997), ACCET (2003/2006)

Award Beauty School, Inc.
26 East Antietam St., Hagerstown 21740
Type: Private, proprietary
Degrees: C
URL: http://www.awardbeautyschool.net
Phone: (301) 733-4520
Inst. Accred.: NACCAS (1966/2002)

Chambersburg Beauty School
171 Cedar St., Chambersburg, PA 17201-2435
Phone: (717) 267-0041

The Baltimore School of Massage
517 Progress Dr., Suites A-L, Linthicum 21090
Type: Private, proprietary
Degrees: C
URL: http://www.bsom.com
Phone: (410) 636-7929
Inst. Accred.: ACCSCT (1998/2003)
Prog. Accred.: Allied Health (massage therapy)

York Campus
170 Redrock Rd., York, PA 17402
Phone: (717) 268-1881
Prog. Accred: Allied Health (massage therapy)

Baltimore Studio of Hair Design, Inc.
318 North Howard St., Baltimore 21201
Type: Private, proprietary
Degrees: C
URL: http://www.baltimorestudio.net
Phone: (410) 539-1935
Inst. Accred.: NACCAS (1987/2007)

Blades School of Hair Design
22576 McArthur Blvd., PO Box 226, California 20619
Type: Private, proprietary
Degrees: C
Phone: (301) 862-9797
Inst. Accred.: NACCAS (1990/2003)

Brescook, LLC
2331 York Rd., Ste. 202, Timonium 21093
Type: Private, proprietary
Degrees: C
URL: http://www.baltimore.dale-carnegie.com
Phone: (410) 560-2188
Inst. Accred.: ACCET (1976/2002)

Harrisburg Campus
4813 Jonestown Rd., Ste. 206, Harrisburg, PA 17109
Phone: (717) 540-0801

Broadcasting Institute of Maryland
7200 Harford Rd., Baltimore 21234-7765
Type: Private, proprietary
Degrees: C
URL: http://www.bim.org
Phone: (410) 254-2770 *Calendar:* Sem. plan
Inst. Accred.: ACCSCT (1980/2005)

ComputerTraining.com
1447 York Rd., Sutie 610, Lutherville 21093
Type: Private, proprietary
Degrees: C
URL: http://www.computertraining-towson.com
Phone: (800) 733-5641
Inst. Accred.: ACCET (2006)

Annapolis Junction Campus
8975 Henkels Ln., Ste. 704, Annapolis Junction 20701
Phone: (800) 733-5641

Defense Information School
6500 Mapes Rd., Fort Meade 20755-5620
Type: Public, federal
Degrees: C
URL: http://www.dinfos.osd.mil
Phone: (301) 677-2173
Inst. Accred.: COE (1995/2004)

Defense Security Service Academy
938 Elkridge Landing Rd., Linthicum 21090
Type: Public, federal
Degrees: C
URL: http://dssa.dss.mil/seta/seta.html
Phone: (888) 282-7682
Inst. Accred.: COE (2003)

Del-Mar-Va Beauty Academy
111 Milford St., Salisbury 21801
Type: Private, proprietary
Degrees: C
Phone: (410) 742-7929
Inst. Accred.: NACCAS (1966/2004)

English House
26 North Summit Ave., Gaithersburg 20877
Type: Private, proprietary
Degrees: C
URL: http://www.englishhouseusa.com
Phone: (301) 527-0600
Inst. Accred.: ACCET (2004)

Everest Institute—Silver Spring
8757 Georgia Ave., Silver Spring 20910
Type: Private, proprietary
System: Corinthian Colleges, Inc
Degrees: C
URL: http://www.everest.edu
Phone: (301) 495-4400
Inst. Accred.: ACICS (2004)

The Fila Academy-A Paul Mitchell Partner School
6320 Ritchie Hwy., Glen Burnie 21061
Type: Private, propietary
Degrees: C
URL: http://www.filaacademy.com
Phone: (410) 789-9516
Inst. Accred.: NACCAS (2006/2007)

Hair Academy, Inc.
8435 Annapolis Rd., New Carrolton 20784
Type: Private, proprietary
Degrees: C
Phone: (301) 459-2509
Inst. Accred.: NACCAS (1986/2006)

Hair Expressions Academy, Inc.
12450 Parklawn Dr., Rockville 20852
Type: Private, proprietary
Degrees: C
URL: http://www.hairex.com
Phone: (301) 984-8182
Inst. Accred.: NACCAS (2005)

Institute for Advanced Montessori Studies
13500 Layhill Rd., Silver Spring 20906-3299
Type: Private, independent
Degrees: C
URL: http://www.barrie.org/iams
Phone: (301) 576-2866
Inst. Accred.: MACTE (2000/2007)

International Beauty School—Bel Air
227 Archer St., Bel Air 21014
Type: Private, proprietary
Degrees: C
Phone: (410) 838-0845
Inst. Accred.: NACCAS (1984/2004)

International Beauty School—Cumberland
119 North Centre St., Cumberland 21502
Type: Private, proprietary
Degrees: C
Phone: (301) 777-3020
Inst. Accred.: NACCAS (1969/2004)

L'Academie de Cuisine
16006 Industrial Dr., Gaithersburg 20877-1414
Type: Private, proprietary
Degrees: C
URL: http://www.lacademie.com
Phone: (301) 670-8670
Inst. Accred.: ACCET (1988/2002)

Bethesda Campus
5021 Wilson Ln., Bethesda 20814
Phone: (301) 986-9490

Lincoln Technical Institute
9325 Snowden River Pkwy., Columbia 21046
Type: Private, proprietary
System: Lincoln Educational Services Corporation
Degrees: C
URL: http://www.lincolntech.com
Phone: (410) 290-7100
Inst. Accred.: ACCSCT (1968/2007)

Maryland Beauty Academy
152 Chartley Dr., Chartley Park Shopping Center, Reisterstown 21136
Type: Private, proprietary
Degrees: C
URL: http://www.baltimorestudio.net
Phone: (410) 517-0442
Inst. Accred.: NACCAS (1987/2007)

Maryland Beauty Academy of Essex, Inc.
505 Eastern Blvd., Baltimore 21221
Type: Private, proprietary
Degrees: C
URL: http://www.baltimorestudio.net
Phone: (410) 686-4477
Inst. Accred.: NACCAS (1986/2006)

Maryland Center for Montessori Studies
10807 Tony Dr., Lutherville 21093
Type: Private, independent
Degrees: C
Phone: (410) 321-8555
Inst. Accred.: MACTE (2000/2007)

The Massage Institute of Maryland
816 Frederick Rd., Catonsville 21228
Type: Private, proprietary
Degrees: C
URL: http://www.massageinstitutemd.org
Phone: (410) 744-9130
Inst. Accred.: ABHES (2006)

Medix School
700 York Rd., Towson 21204-2511
Type: Private, proprietary
Degrees: C
URL: http://www.medixschool.com
Phone: (410) 337-5155
Inst. Accred.: ABHES (1999/2006)
Prog. Accred.: Allied Health (medical assisting (AMA)), Dentistry (dental assisting), Medical Assisting (ABHES)

Bohecker College—Columbus
4151 Executive Pkwy., Ste. 240, Westerville, OH 43081-3860
Phone: (330) 297-7319

Cincinnati Campus
11499 Chester Rd., Cincinnati, OH 45246-4012
Phone: (877) 873-1818

Montgomery Beauty School
8736 Arliss St., Silver Spring 20901
Type: Private, proprietary
Degrees: C
Phone: (301) 588-3570
Inst. Accred.: NACCAS (1986/2006)

Montgomery Montessori Institute
10500 Darnestown Rd., Rockville 20850
Type: Private, independent
Degrees: C
URL: http://www.montessori-mmi.com
Phone: (301) 279-2799
Inst. Accred.: MACTE (2001)

National Cryptologic School
9800 Savage Rd., Ste. 6801, S309, Fort Meade 20755
Type: Public, federal
Degrees: C
URL: http://www.nsa.gov/about/about00004.cfm
Phone: (410) 859-6321
Inst. Accred.: COE (1990/2002)

New Creations Academy of Hair Design
3930 Bexley Place, Suitland 20746
Type: Private, proprietary
Degrees: C
Phone: (301) 899-9100
Inst. Accred.: NACCAS (1998/2004)

North American Trade Schools
6901 Security Blvd., Ste. 16, Baltimore 21244
Type: Private, proprietary
Degrees: C
URL: http://www.natradeschools.com
Phone: (410) 298-4844
Inst. Accred.: ACCSCT (1988/2003)

Omega Studio's School of Applied Recording Arts and Sciences
5609 Fishers Ln., Rockville 20852
Type: Private, proprietary
Degrees: C
URL: http://www.omegastudios.com
Phone: (301) 230-9100
Inst. Accred.: ACCSCT (2002)

Robert Paul Academy of Cosmetology Arts and Sciences
1811 York Rd., Timonium 21093
Type: Private, proprietary
Degrees: C
URL: http://www.robertpaulacademy.com
Phone: (410) 252-4481
Inst. Accred.: NACCAS (1986/2006)

United States Army Ordnance Center and School
3701 Aberdeen Blvd., Building 3071, Rm. 217, Aberdeen 21005
Type: Public, federal
Degrees: C
URL: http://www.goordnance.apg.army.mil
Phone: (410) 278-3642
Inst. Accred.: COE (1978/2005)

United States Navy Medicine Manpower, Personnel, Training and Education Command
8901 Wisconsin Ave., Bethesda 20889-5611
Type: Public, federal
Degrees: C
URL: http://navmedmpte.med.navy.mil/index.htm
Phone: (202) 762-3830
Inst. Accred.: COE (1984/2002)
Prog. Accred.: Radiography

Bethesda Campus
8901 Wisconsin Ave., Bethesda 20889-5602
Phone: (301) 295-0064
Prog. Accred: Dentistry (combined prosthodontics, endodontics, general dentistry, maxillofacial prosthetics, oral and maxillofacial pathology, periodontics)

Field Medical Service School Camp LeJeune
PSC Box 20042, Marine Corps Base, Camp LeJeune, NC 28542-0042
Phone: (910) 450-0915

Field Medical Training School Camp Pendleton
PO Box 555041, Camp Pendleton, CA 92055-5031
Phone: (760) 725-2559

Groton Campus
Naval Submarine Base New London, PO Box 159, Groton, CT 06349-5159
Phone: (860) 449-2874

Naval Hospital Corps School Great Lakes
601 D St., Bldg. 130-H, Great Lakes, IL 60088-5257
Phone: (847) 688-3412

Naval Medical Education and Training Command
8901 Wisconsin Ave., Bethesda 20889-5611
Phone: (301) 295-1204
Prog. Accred: Nuclear Medicine Technology, Nurse Anesthesia Education

Naval Operational Medicine Institute
220 Hovey Rd., Ste. A, Pensacola, FL 32508-1047
Phone: (850) 452-4554

Naval Ophthalmic Support and Training Activity
160 Main Rd., Ste. 350, Naval Weapons Station, Bldg. 1794, Yorktown, VA 23691-9984
Phone: (757) 887-7600
Prog. Accred: Allied Health (ophthalmic lab technology)

Naval Postgraduate Dental School
8901 Wisconsin Ave., Bethesda 20889-5602
Phone: (301) 295-0064
Prog. Accred: Dentistry (combined prosthodontics, endodontics, general dentistry, oral and maxillofacial pathology, periodontics)

Opthalmis Support and Training Campus
Yorktown, VA 23691-5071
Phone: (804) 887-7611

Portsmouth Campus
10001 Holcomb Rd., Portsmouth, VA 23708-5200
Phone: (757) 953-5040

San Diego Farenholt Avenue Campus
34101 Farenholt Ave., San Diego, CA 92134-5291
Phone: (619) 532-7700

San Diego Norman Scott Road Campus
4170 Norman Scott Rd., P.O. Box 368147, San Diego, CA 92136-5597
Phone: (619) 556-7640
Prog. Accred: Dentistry (dental laboratory technology)

Washington Conservatory of Music, Inc.
5144 Massachusetts Ave., Bethesda 20816
Type: Private, independent
Degrees: C
URL: http://www.washingtonconservatory.com
Phone: (301) 320-2770 *Calendar:* Sem. plan
Inst. Accred.: NASM (1991/2003)

MASSACHUSETTS

Ailano School of Cosmetology
541 West St., Brockton 02301
Type: Private, proprietary
Degrees: C
URL: http://ailanoschool.com
Phone: (508) 583-5433
Inst. Accred.: NACCAS (1991/2006)

Assabet Valley Regional Technical High School
215 Fitchburg St., Marlborough 01752
Type: Public, state/local
Degrees: C
URL: http://www.assabettech.com
Phone: (508) 460-3472 *Calendar:* Sem. plan
Inst. Accred.: NEASC-CTCI (1976/2007)

Bancroft School of Massage Therapy
333 Shrewsbury St., Worcester 01604
Type: Private, proprietary
Degrees: C
URL: http://www.bancroftsmt.com
Phone: (508) 757-7923
Inst. Accred.: ACCSCT (1986/2002)

Bay State School of Technology
225 Turnpike St., Route 138, Canton 02021
Type: Private, proprietary
Degrees: C
URL: http://www.ultranet.com/bssanet
Phone: (781) 828-3434
Inst. Accred.: ACCSCT (1986/2002)

Blaine, The Beauty Career Schools—Boston
30 West St., Downtown Crossing, Boston 02111
Type: Private, proprietary
System: Empire Education Group
Degrees: C
URL: http://www.blainebeautyschools.com
Phone: (617) 266-2661
Inst. Accred.: NACCAS (1975/2006)

Hyannis Campus
259 North St., Hyannis 02601
Phone: (508) 771-1680

Blaine, The Beauty Career Schools—Lowell
231 Central St., Lowell 01852
Type: Private, proprietary
System: Empire Education Group
Degrees: C
URL: http://www.blainebeautyschools.com
Phone: (978) 459-9959
Inst. Accred.: NACCAS (1978/2004)

Blaine, The Beauty Career Schools—Malden
347 Pleasant St., Malden 02148
Type: Private, proprietary
System: Empire Education Group
Degrees: C
URL: http://www.blainebeautyschools.com
Phone: (781) 397-7400
Inst. Accred.: NACCAS (1977/2004)

Blaine, The Beauty Career Schools—Waltham
314 Moody St., Waltham 02154
Type: Private, proprietary
System: Empire Education Group
Degrees: C
URL: http://www.blainebeautyschools.com
Phone: (781) 899-1500
Inst. Accred.: NACCAS (1977/2004)

Framingham Campus
624 Worcester Rd., Route 9, Framingham 01702
Phone: (508) 370-3700

Blue Hills Regional Technical School
800 Randolph St., Canton 02021
Type: Public, state/local
Degrees: C
URL: http://www.bluehills.org
Phone: (781) 828-5800 *Calendar:* Sem. plan
Inst. Accred.: NEASC-CTCI (1968/2007)

Boston Academy of English
59 Temple Place, 2nd Flr., Boston 02111
Type: Private, proprietary
Degrees: C
URL: http://www.bostonacademyofenglish.com
Phone: (617) 338-6243
Inst. Accred.: ACCET (2003/2006)

Boston School of Modern Languages, Inc.
814 South St., Boston 02131
Type: Private, proprietary
Degrees: C
URL: http://www.studyenglish.com
Phone: (617) 325-2760
Inst. Accred.: ACCET (2004)

Butera School of Art
111 Beacon St., Boston 02116-1597
Type: Private, proprietary
Degrees: C
URL: http://www.buteraschool.com
Phone: (617) 536-4623 *Calendar:* Sem. plan
Inst. Accred.: ACCSCT (1977/2005)

The Cambridge School of Culinary Arts
2020 Massachusetts Ave., Cambridge 02140-2124
Type: Private, proprietary
Degrees: C
URL: http://www.cambridgeculinary.com
Phone: (617) 354-2020
Inst. Accred.: ACCSCT (1989/2005)

Catherine E. Hinds Institute of Esthetics
300 Wildwood Ave., Woburn 01801
Type: Private, proprietary
Degrees: C
URL: http://catherinehinds.com
Phone: (781) 935-3344
Inst. Accred.: ACCSCT (1983/2003)

Olympia Avenue Campus
82 Olympia Ave., Woburn 01801
Phone: (617) 933-2501

Central Mass School of Massage and Therapy
200 Main St., Spencer 01562
Type: Private, proprietary
Degrees: C
URL: http://www.centralmassschool.com
Phone: (508) 885-0306
Inst. Accred.: ACCSCT (2007)

Charles H. McCann Technical School
70 Hodges Cross Rd., North Adams 01247
Type: Public, local
Degrees: C
URL: http://www.mccanntech.org
Phone: (413) 663-5383
Inst. Accred.: NEASC-CTCI (1968/2006)
Prog. Accred.: Allied Health (medical assisting (AMA), surgical technology), Dentistry (dental assisting)

Cortiva Institute-Muscular Therapy Institute
103 Morse St., Watertown 02472
Type: Private, proprietary
Degrees: C
URL: http://www.cortiva.com/locations/mti
Phone: (617) 688-1000
Inst. Accred.: CMTA (2004)

DiGrigoli School of Cosmetology, Inc.
1578 Riverdale St., West Springfield 01089
Type: Private, proprietary
Degrees: C
URL: http://www.digrigoli.com/school
Phone: (413) 827-0037
Inst. Accred.: NACCAS (2006)

EF International Language Schools, Inc.
200 Lake St., Brighton 02135-3104
Type: Private, proprietary
Degrees: C
URL: http://www.ef.com
Phone: (617) 619-1700
Inst. Accred.: ACCET (1986/2007)

California State University Campus
9757 Zelzah, Building 12, Saguaro Hall, Ste. 112, Northridge, CA 91330-8363
Phone: (818) 772-0903

Corporate Center Campus
EF Corporate Center, One Education St., Cambridge 02141
Phone: (617) 619-1800

Evergreen State College Campus
Seminar Bldg., Rm. 4154, 2700 Evergreen Pkwy., NW, Olympia, WA 98505
Phone: (360) 867-6423

Marymount College Campus
100 Marymount Ave., Ursula Hall, Tarrytown, NY 10591-3796
Phone: (914) 332-1072

Miami Beach Campus
2469 Collins Ave., Miami Beach, FL 33140
Phone: (305) 674-6535

Mills College Campus
White Hall, 5000 MacArthur Blvd., Oakland, CA 94613
Phone: (510) 430-3209

San Diego Campus
10455 Pomerado Rd., M-4, San Diego, CA 92131
Phone: (619) 693-0771

Santa Barbara Campus
1421 Chapala St., Santa Barbara, CA 93101
Phone: (805) 962-8680

Electrology Institute of New England
1501 Main St., Ste. 50, Tewksbury 01876
Type: Private, proprietary
Degrees: C
URL: http://www.electrologyinstitute.com
Phone: (978) 851-4444
Inst. Accred.: NACCAS (2004)

The Elizabeth Grady School of Esthetics
222 Boston Ave., Medford 02155
Type: Private, proprietary
Degrees: C
URL: http://www.elizabethgrady.com
Phone: (781) 391-9380
Inst. Accred.: NACCAS (1987/2002)

Empire Beauty School—Boston
867 Boylston St., Boston 02116
Type: Private, proprietary
Degrees: C
URL: http://www.empire.edu
Phone: (617) 424-6565
Inst. Accred.: NACCAS (1976/2002)

Empire Beauty School—Malden
384 Main St., Malden 02148
Type: Private, proprietary
Degrees: C
URL: http://www.empire.edu
Phone: (781) 324-3400
Inst. Accred.: NACCAS (1976/2002)

Everest Institute—Brighton
1505 Commonwealth Ave., Brighton 02135
Type: Private, proprietary
System: Corinthian Colleges, Inc
Degrees: C
URL: http://www.everest.edu
Phone: (617) 783-9955
Inst. Accred.: ACCSCT (1973/2006)

Everest Institute—Chelsea
70 Everett Ave., Chelsea 02150
Type: Private, proprietary
System: Corinthian Colleges, Inc
Degrees: C
URL: http://www.everest.edu
Phone: (617) 889-5999
Inst. Accred.: ACCSCT (2004/2006)

Hair In Motion Beauty Academy
73 Hamilton St., Worcester 01604
Type: Private, proprietary
Degrees: C
URL: http://hairmotion.net
Phone: (508) 756-6060
Inst. Accred.: NACCAS (1997/2005)

Hallmark Institute of Photography
PO Box 308, Turners Falls 01376-0308
Type: Private, proprietary
Degrees: C
URL: http://www.hallmark-institute.com
Phone: (413) 863-2478
Inst. Accred.: ACCSCT (1982/2005)

Henri's School of Hair Design
276 Water St., PO Box 2244, Fitchburg 01420
Type: Private, proprietary
Degrees: C
Phone: (978) 342-6061
Inst. Accred.: NACCAS (1969/2005)

International Language Institute of Massachusetts
25 New South St., Northampton 01060
Type: Private, independent
Degrees: C
URL: http://www.languageschoolusa.org
Phone: (413) 586-8927
Inst. Accred.: ACCET (1982/2001)

Jolie Hair and Beauty Academy, Inc.
44 Sewall St., Ludlow 01056
Type: Private, proprietary
Degrees: C
Phone: (413) 589-0747
Inst. Accred.: NACCAS (1997/2005)

Joseph P. Keefe Technical School
750 Winter St., Framingham 01702
Type: Public, state/local
Degrees: C
URL: http://www.jpkeefehs.org
Phone: (508) 416-2100 *Calendar:* Sem. plan
Inst. Accred.: NEASC-CTCI (1977/2007)

Kay Harvey Hairdressing Academy
11 Central St., West Springfield 01089
Type: Private, proprietary
Degrees: C
URL: http://www.labaronacademy.com
Phone: (413) 732-7117
Inst. Accred.: NACCAS (1995/2003)

LaBaron Hairdressing Academy—Brockton
240 Liberty St., Brockton 02401
Type: Private, proprietary
Degrees: C
URL: http://www.labaronacademy.com
Phone: (508) 583-1700
Inst. Accred.: NACCAS (1978/2005)

LaBaron Hairdressing Academy—New Bedford
281 Union St., New Bedford 02074
Type: Private, proprietary
Degrees: C
URL: http://www.labaronacademy.com
Phone: (508) 996-6611
Inst. Accred.: NACCAS (1977/2003)

Lincoln Technical Institute—Somerville
5 Middlesex Ave., Somerville 02145
Type: Private, proprietary
System: Lincoln Educational Services Corporation
Degrees: C
URL: http://www.lincolntech.com
Phone: (617) 776-3500
Inst. Accred.: ACICS (1997/2004)

Lowell Campus
211 Plain St., Lowell 01852
Phone: (978) 458-4800

Lowell Academy Hairstyling Institute
136 Central St., Lowell 01852
Type: Private, proprietary
Degrees: C
URL: http://www.lahair.net
Phone: (978) 453-3235
Inst. Accred.: NACCAS (1966/2002)

Mansfield Beauty School—Quincy
200 Parkingway St., Quincy 02169
Type: Private, proprietary
Degrees: C
Phone: (617) 479-1090
Inst. Accred.: NACCAS (1974/2006)

Mansfield Beauty School—Springfield
266 Bridge St., Springfield 01103
Type: Private, proprietary
Degrees: C
Phone: (413) 788-7575
Inst. Accred.: NACCAS (1974/2006)

Massachusetts School of Barbering and Men's Hairstyling
1585 Hancock St, Quincy 02169-5058
Type: Private, proprietary
Degrees: C
Phone: (617) 770-4444 *Calendar:* Sem. plan
Inst. Accred.: ACCSCT (1978/2005)

Medical Professional Institute
388 Pleasant St., Ste. 302, Malden 02148
Type: Private, proprietary
Degrees: C
URL: http://www.mpi.edu
Phone: (781) 397-6822
Inst. Accred.: ABHES (2002/2005)
Prog. Accred.: Medical Assisting (ABHES)

Millennium Training Institute
600 West Cummings Park, Ste. 2450, Woburn 01801
Type: Private, proprietary
Degrees: C
URL: http://www.mtiedu.com/career
Phone: (781) 933-8877
Inst. Accred.: ACCSCT (2007)

Montachusett Regional Vocational Technical School
1050 Westminster St., Fitchburg 01420
Type: Public, state
Degrees: C
URL: http://www.montytech.net
Phone: (978) 345-9200
Inst. Accred.: NEASC-CTCI (1975/2006)

NCME—New England
243 Essex St., Beverly 01915
Type: Private, independent
Degrees: C
URL: http://www.harborlightmontessori.org
Phone: (978) 927-9600
Inst. Accred.: MACTE (1999/2006)

New England Hair Academy
110 Florence St., Ste. 203, Malden 02148
Type: Private, proprietary
Degrees: C
Phone: (781) 324-6799
Inst. Accred.: ACCSCT (1979/2005)

Haverhill Campus
80 Merrimack St., Haverhill 01830
Phone: (978) 521-6500

The New England School of English
36 John F. Kennedy St., Cambridge 02138
Type: Private, proprietary
Degrees: C
URL: http://www.nese.com
Phone: (617) 864-7170
Inst. Accred.: ACCET (1998/2003)

New England School of Photography
537 Commonwealth Ave., Boston 02215-2005
Type: Private, proprietary
Degrees: C
Phone: (617) 437-1868
Inst. Accred.: ACCSCT (1995/2005)

North Bennet Street School
39 North Bennet St., Boston 02113-1998
Type: Private, indepepdent
Degrees: C
URL: http://www.nbss.org
Phone: (617) 227-0155
Inst. Accred.: ACCSCT (1982/2004)

OISE Boston
31 St. James Ave., Ste. 940, Boston 02116
Type: Private, proprietary
Degrees: C
URL: http://www.boston.oise.net
Phone: (617) 357-6473
Inst. Accred.: CEA (2005)

The Olin Center
729 Boylston St., Boston 02116
Type: Private, independent
Degrees: C
URL: http://www.olincenter.com
Phone: (617) 247-3033
Inst. Accred.: ACCET (2003)

Performance Training Associates, Inc.
135 Beaver St., Waltham 02452
Type: Private, proprietary
Degrees: C
URL: http://www.boston.dalecarnegie.com
Phone: (781) 894-2700
Inst. Accred.: ACCET (1977/2002)

RETS Technical Center
570 Rutherford Ave., Charlestown 02129
Type: Private, proprietary
System: Kaplan Higher Education Corporation
Degrees: C
URL: http://www.retstech.com
Phone: (617) 580-4010
Inst. Accred.: ACCSCT (1974/2005)

Rob Roy Academy, Inc.—New Bedford
1872 Acushnet Ave., New Bedford 02746
Type: Private, proprietary
Degrees: C
URL: http://www.rob-roy.com
Phone: (508) 995-8711
Inst. Accred.: NACCAS (1985/2005)

Rob Roy Academy, Inc.—Taunton Campus
One School St., Taunton 02780
Type: Private, proprietary
Degrees: C
URL: http://www.rob-roy.com
Phone: (508) 822-1405
Inst. Accred.: NACCAS (1969/2002)

Rob Roy Academy, Inc.—Worcester
150 Pleasant St., Worcester 01609
Type: Private, proprietary
Degrees: C
URL: http://www.rob-roy.com
Phone: (508) 799-2111
Inst. Accred.: NACCAS (1981/2006)

Woonsocket Campus
800 Clinton St., Woonsocket, RI 02895
Phone: (401) 769-1777

Rob Roy Academy—Fall River Campus
260 South Main St., Fall River 02721
Type: Private, proprietary
Degrees: C
URL: http://www.rob-roy.com
Phone: (508) 672-4751
Inst. Accred.: NACCAS (1970/2007)

Salter College
184 West Boylston St., West Boylston 01583
Type: Private, proprietary
System: Premier Education Group
Degrees: C
URL: http://www.salterschool.com
Phone: (508) 853-1074 *Calendar:* Sem. plan
Inst. Accred.: ACICS (1953/2003)
Prog. Accred.: Allied Health (medical assisting (AMA))

Fall River Campus
82 Hartwell St., Fall River 02720
Phone: (508) 730-2740

Malden Campus
2 Florence St., Malden 02148
Phone: (781) 324-5454

Tewksbury Campus
515 Woburn St., Tewksbury 01876
Phone: (978) 934-9300

Southeastern Technical Institute
250 Foundry St., South Easton 02375
Type: Public, state/local
Degrees: C
URL: http://ti.sersd.org
Phone: (508) 238-4371 *Calendar:* Sem. plan
Inst. Accred.: NEASC-CTCI (1968/2007)
Prog. Accred.: Allied Health (medical assisting (AMA)), Dentistry (dental assisting)

Sullivan and Cogliano Training Centers
365 Westgate Dr., Brockton 02301
Type: Private, proprietary
Degrees: C
URL: http://www.sctrain.com
Phone: (508) 584-9909
Inst. Accred.: COE (2005)

Miami Campus
7740 North Kendall Dr., Miami, FL 33156
Phone: (305) 279-5877

North Miami Campus
4724 North West 167th St., Miami, FL 33014
Phone: (305) 624-3030

Upper Cape Cod Regional Technical School
220 Sandwich Rd., Bourne 02532
Type: Public, state/local
Degrees: C
URL: http://www.uppercapetech.com
Phone: (508) 759-7711 *Calendar:* Sem. plan
Inst. Accred.: NEASC-CTCI (1975/2007)

WyoTech—Boston
150 Hanscom Dr., Bedford 01730
Type: Private, proprietary
System: Corinthian Colleges, Inc
Degrees: C
URL: http://www.wyotech.com
Phone: (781) 274-8448
Inst. Accred.: ACCSCT (1970/2002)

MICHIGAN

Access International Business Institute
PO Box 7710, Ann Arbor 48107
Type: Private, independent
Degrees: C
URL: http://www.accessesl.org
Phone: (734) 994-1456
Inst. Accred.: ACCET (2007)

Adrian Beauty Academy, Inc.
329 1/2 East Maumee St., Adrian 49221
Type: Private, proprietary
Degrees: C
Phone: (517) 263-0000
Inst. Accred.: NACCAS (1977/2003)

Adrian Dominican Montessori Teacher Institute
1257 East Siena Heights Dr., Adrian 49221
Type: Private, independent
Degrees: C
URL: http://www.admtei.com
Phone: (517) 266-3415
Inst. Accred.: MACTE (2000/2007)

Ann Arbor Institute of Massage Therapy
180 Jackson Plaza, Ste. 100, Ann Arbor 48103
Type: Private, proprietary
Degrees: C
URL: http://www.aaimt.com
Phone: (734) 677-4430
Inst. Accred.: CMTA (2001/2006)

Bayshire Beauty Academy
917 Saginaw St., Bay City 48708
Type: Private, proprietary
Degrees: C
Phone: (989) 894-2431
Inst. Accred.: NACCAS (1984/2004)

Blue Water College of Cosmetology
1871 Gratiot Blvd., Marysville 48080
Type: Private, proprietary
Degrees: C
Phone: (810) 364-9595
Inst. Accred.: NACCAS (2002/2005)

Booker Institute of Cosmetology
1989 Lakeshore Dr., Muskegon 49441
Type: Private, proprietary
Degrees: C
URL: http://www.bookerinstitute.com
Phone: (231) 759-9800
Inst. Accred.: NACCAS (2005)

Carnegie Institute
550 Stephenson Hwy., Ste. 100, Troy 48083-1159
Type: Private, independent
Degrees: C
URL: http://www.carnegie-institute.com
Phone: (248) 589-1078 *Calendar:* Qtr. plan
Inst. Accred.: ACCSCT (1968/2003)
Prog. Accred.: Allied Health (cardiovascular technology, electroneurodiagnostic technology, medical assisting (AMA))

Career Quest Learning Center
5000 Northwind Dr., Ste. 120, East Lansing 48823
Type: Private, proprietary
Degrees: C
URL: http://www.careerquest1.com
Phone: (517) 318-3330
Inst. Accred.: COE (2004)

Chic University of Cosmetology—Grand Rapids
1735 Four Mile Rd., NE, Grand Rapids 49525
Type: Private, proprietary
System: Empire Education Group
Degrees: C
URL: http://www.chicuniversity.com
Phone: (616) 363-9853
Inst. Accred.: NACCAS (1965/2003)

Portage Campus
6091 Constitution Blvd., Portage 49024
Phone: (269) 329-3333

Standale Plaza Campus
455 Standale Plaza, NW, Grand Rapids 49544
Phone: (616) 735-9680

Creative Hair School of Cosmetology
G-4439 Clio Rd., Flint 48504
Type: Private, proprietary
Degrees: C
Phone: (810) 787-4247
Inst. Accred.: NACCAS (2005)

David Pressley Professional School of Cosmetology
1127 South Washington St., Royal Oak 48067
Type: Private, proprietary
Degrees: C
URL: http://www.davidpressleyschool.com
Phone: (248) 548-5090
Inst. Accred.: NACCAS (1965/2003)

Taylor Campus
21255 Wick Rd., Taylor 48180
Phone: (313) 291-7381

Detroit Business Institute—Downriver
19100 Fort St., Riverview 48192
Type: Private, proprietary
Degrees: C
URL: http://www.dbidownriver.com
Phone: (734) 479-0660 *Calendar:* Qtr. plan
Inst. Accred.: ACICS (1983/2005)

Southfield Campus
23077 Greenfield Rd., Ste. LL28, Southfield 48075
Phone: (248) 552-6300

Dorsey Business School
15755 Northline Rd., Southgate 48195
Type: Private, proprietary
Degrees: C
URL: http://www.dorseyschools.com
Phone: (734) 285-5400 *Calendar:* Qtr. plan
Inst. Accred.: ACICS (1972/2002)

Madison Heights Campus
30821 Barrington Ave., Madison Heights 48071
Phone: (248) 588-9660

Roseville Campus
31542 Gratiot Ave., Roseville 48066
Phone: (586) 296-3225

Wayne-Westland Campus
34841 Veteran's Plaza, Wayne 48184
Phone: (734) 595-1540

Douglas J Aveda Institute
331 East Grand River Ave., East Lansing 48823
Type: Private, proprietary
Degrees: C
URL: http://douglasj.seal-server.com/institute_about_el.html
Phone: (517) 333-9656
Inst. Accred.: NACCAS (1988/2003)

Ann Arbor Campus
333 Maynard St., Ann Arbor 48104
Phone: (734) 929-0453

Everest Institute—Grand Rapids
1750 Woodworth St., NE, Grand Rapids 49505
Type: Private, proprietary
System: Corinthian Colleges, Inc
Degrees: C
URL: http://www.everest.edu
Phone: (616) 364-8464
Inst. Accred.: ABHES (1985/2005)
Prog. Accred.: Medical Assisting (ABHES), Surgical Technology

Kalamazoo Campus
5177 West Main St., Kalamazoo 49009
Phone: (269) 381-9616
Prog. Accred: Medical Assisting (ABHES)

Merrillville Campus
707 East 80th Place, Ste. 200, Merrillville, IN 46410
Phone: (219) 756-6811
Prog. Accred: Allied Health (surgical technology)

Merrionette Park Campus
11560 South Kedzie Ave., Merrionette Park, IL 60803
Phone: (708) 239-0055

North Aurora Campus
150 S. Lincolnway, Ste. 100, North Aurora, IL 60542
Phone: (630) 896-2140
Prog. Accred: Allied Health (medical assisting (AMA))

Everest Institute—Southfield
26111 Evergreen Rd., Ste. 201, Southfield 48076-4491
Type: Private, proprietary
System: Corinthian Colleges, Inc
Degrees: C
URL: http://www.everest.edu
Phone: (248) 799-9933 *Calendar:* Qtr. plan
Inst. Accred.: ACCSCT (1970/2003)
Prog. Accred.: Allied Health (medical assisting (AMA))

Austin Campus
9100 US Hwy 290 East, Building 1, Ste. 100, Austin, TX 78754
Phone: (512) 928-1933

Dearborn Campus
23400 Michigan Ave., Ste. 200, Dearborn 48124
Phone: (313) 562-4228

Detroit Campus
300 River Place Dr., Ste. 1000, Detroit 48207
Phone: (313) 567-5350

Flint Institute of Barbering
3214 Flushing Rd., Flint 48504-4395
Type: Private, proprietary
Degrees: C
Phone: (810) 232-4711
Inst. Accred.: ACCSCT (1972/2005)

Focus: Hope Information Technologies Center
1400 Oakman Blvd., Detroit 48238
Type: Private, proprietary
Degrees: C
URL: http://www.focushope.edu
Phone: (313) 494-4888
Inst. Accred.: ACCET (2004/2007)

Focus: Hope Machinist Training Institute
1200 Oakman Blvd., Detroit 48238
Type: Private, independent
Degrees: C
URL: http://www.focushope.edu
Phone: (313) 494-4200
Inst. Accred.: ACCET (1986/2006)

The Gallery College of Beauty
38132 South Gratiot Ave., Clinton Township 48036-3591
Type: Private, proprietary
Degrees: C
URL: http://www.gallerycollegeofbeauty.com
Phone: (586) 783-7358
Inst. Accred.: NACCAS (2005)

Great Lakes Academy of Hair Design
2950 Lapeer Rd., Port Huron 48060
Type: Private, proprietary
Degrees: C
URL: http://www.glahd.com
Phone: (810) 987-8118
Inst. Accred.: NACCAS (2004)

Handley and Associates, Inc.
5800 Gratiot Rd., Ste. 102, Saginaw 48603-6090
Type: Private, proprietary
Degrees: C
URL: http://www.mid-northernmichigan.dalecarnegie.com
Phone: (989) 799-7760
Inst. Accred.: ACCET (2006)

Health Enrichment Center
204 East Nepessing Rd., Lapeer 48446
Type: Private, proprietary
Degrees: C
URL: http://www.healthenrichment.com
Phone: (810) 667-9453
Inst. Accred.: ACCSCT (1995/2005)

Hillsdale Beauty College
64 Waldron St., Hillsdale 49242
Type: Private, proprietary
Degrees: C
Phone: (517) 437-4670
Inst. Accred.: NACCAS (1989/2004)

Houghton Lake Institute of Cosmetology
5921 West Houghton Lake Dr., PO Box 669, Houghton Lake 48629
Type: Private, proprietary
Degrees: C
Phone: (989) 422-4573
Inst. Accred.: NACCAS (1994/2007)

In Session, Arts of Cosmetology Beauty School
7212 Gratiot Rd., Ste. D, Saginaw 48609
Type: Private, proprietary
Degrees: C
Phone: (989) 781-6282
Inst. Accred.: NACCAS (2003/2006)

Irene's Myomassology Institute
26061 Franklin Rd., Southfield 48034
Type: Private, proprietary
Degrees: C
URL: http://www.myomassology.com
Phone: (248) 350-1400
Inst. Accred.: ACCET (2001/2007)

Kaplan Institute—Detroit
3031 West Grand Blvd., Ste. 236, Detroit 48202
Type: Private, proprietary
Degrees: C
URL: http://www.getinfokaplancareerinstitute.com
Phone: (313) 456-8100
Inst. Accred.: ACCSCT (2006)

Lakewood School of Therapeutic Massage
1102 6th St., Port Huron 48060
Type: Private, proprietary
Degrees: C
URL: http://www.lakewoodschool.com
Phone: (810) 987-3959
Inst. Accred.: CMTA (2004)

Lawton School
20755 Greenfield, Ste. 300, Southfield 48075
Type: Private, proprietary
Degrees: C
Phone: (248) 569-7787
Inst. Accred.: ACCSCT (1988/2005)

M.J. Murphy Beauty College
201 West Broadway, Mt. Pleasant 48858
Type: Private, proprietary
Degrees: C
Phone: (989) 772-2339
Inst. Accred.: NACCAS (1976/2003)

Clare Campus
210 Wilcox Pkwy., Clare 48617
Phone: (989) 386-6151

Michigan Barber School, Inc.
8988-90 Grand River Ave., Detroit 48204-2244
Type: Private, proprietary
Degrees: C
Phone: (313) 894-2300
Inst. Accred.: ACCSCT (1986/2002)

Michigan Career and Technical Institute
11611 West Pine Lake Rd., Plainwell 49080
Type: Public, state
Degrees: C
URL: http://www.michigan.gov/mdcd
Phone: (269) 664-4461
Inst. Accred.: NCA-CASI (1999/2005)

Michigan College of Beauty—Monroe
15233 South Dixie Hwy., Monroe 48161
Type: Private, proprietary
Degrees: C
URL: http://www.michigancollegebeauty.com
Phone: (734) 241-8877
Inst. Accred.: NACCAS (1985/2005)

Michigan College of Beauty—Troy
3498 Rochester Rd., Troy 48083
Type: Private, proprietary
Degrees: C
URL: http://www.michigancollege.nv.switchboard.com
Phone: (248) 528-0303
Inst. Accred.: NACCAS (1977/2003)

Michigan College of Beauty—Waterford
5620 Dixie Hwy., Waterford 48329
Type: Private, proprietary
Degrees: C
Phone: (248) 623-9494
Inst. Accred.: NACCAS (1968/2004)

Michigan Institute of Aviation and Technology
Willow Run Airport, 47884 D St., Belleville 48111-1278
Type: Private, proprietary
Degrees: C
URL: http://www.miat.edu
Phone: (734) 483-3758
Inst. Accred.: ACCSCT (1976/2006)

Michigan Montessori Teacher Education Center
1263 South Adams Rd., Rochester Hills 48309
Type: Private, independent
Degrees: C
URL: http://www.mmtec.org
Phone: (248) 375-2800
Inst. Accred.: MACTE (2000/2007)

Mr. Bela's School of Cosmetology
5580 East 12 Mile Rd., Warren 48092
Type: Private, proprietary
Degrees: C
URL: http://www.mrbelas.com
Phone: (586) 751-4000
Inst. Accred.: NACCAS (1980/2005)

Mr. David's School of Cosmetology, Ltd.
4000 South Saginaw St., Flint 48507
Type: Private, proprietary
Degrees: C
URL: http://www.mrdavids.com
Phone: (810) 762-7474
Inst. Accred.: NACCAS (1990/2006)

Northwestern Technological Institute
24567 Northwestern Hwy., Ste. 200, Southfield 48075
Type: Private, proprietary
Degrees: C
URL: http://www.northwesterntech.org
Phone: (248) 358-4006
Inst. Accred.: ACCSCT (1995/2005)

Nuvo College of Cosmetology
4236 Grand Have Rd., Norton Shores 49441
Type: Private, proprietary
Degrees: C
URL: http://www.nuvocollege.com
Phone: (231) 799-1500
Inst. Accred.: NACCAS (2005)

P & A Scholars Beauty School, Inc.
12001 Grand River Ave., Ste. A, Detroit 48204
Type: Private, proprietary
Degrees: C
Phone: (313) 933-9393
Inst. Accred.: NACCAS (2005)

Ralph Nichols Group, Inc.
19500 Victor Pkwy., Ste. 275, Livonia
Type: Private, proprietary
Degrees: C
URL: http://www.michigan.dalecarnegie.com
Phone: (734) 953-1200
Inst. Accred.: ACCET (1975/2001)

Ross Medical Education Center
5757 Whitmore Lake Rd., Ste. 800, Brighton 48116-1091
Type: Private, proprietary
Degrees: C
URL: http://www.rossmedicaleducation.com
Phone: (810) 227-0160
Inst. Accred.: ACCSCT (1986/2003)
Prog. Accred.: Medical Assisting (ABHES)

Ross Medical Education Center
1036 Gilbert Rd., Flint 48532-3527
Type: Private, proprietary
Degrees: C
URL: http://www.rossmedicaleducation.com
Phone: (810) 230-1100
Inst. Accred.: ACCSCT (1978/2006)
Prog. Accred.: Medical Assisting (ABHES)

Ross Medical Education Center
913 West Holmes Rd., Ste. 260, Lansing 48910-4490
Type: Private, proprietary
Degrees: C
URL: http://www.rossmedicaleducation.com
Phone: (517) 887-0180
Inst. Accred.: ACCSCT (1982/2006)
Prog. Accred.: Medical Assisting (ABHES)

Ross Medical Education Center
27120 Dequindre Rd., Warren 48092
Type: Private, proprietary
Degrees: C
URL: http://www.rossmedicaleducation.com
Phone: (586) 574-0830
Inst. Accred.: ACCSCT (1981/2003)
Prog. Accred.: Medical Assisting (ABHES)

Ann Arbor Campus
4741 Washtenaw Ave., Ann Arbor 48108-1411
Phone: (734) 434-7320
Prog. Accred: Medical Assisting (ABHES)

Grand Rapids Campus
2035 28th St., SE, Ste. O, Grand Rapids 49508-1539
Phone: (616) 243-3070
Prog. Accred: Medical Assisting (ABHES)

Hollywood Campus
6847 Taft St., Hollywood, FL 33024
Phone: (954) 963-0043
Prog. Accred: Medical Assisting (ABHES)

Port Huron Campus
3568 Pine Grove Ave., Port Huron 48060
Phone: (810) 982-0454
Prog. Accred: Medical Assisting (ABHES)

Redford Campus
9327 Telegraph Rd., Redford 48239
Phone: (313) 794-6448
Prog. Accred: Medical Assisting (ABHES)

Roosevelt Park Campus
950 West Norton Ave., Roosevelt Park 49441-4156
Phone: (231) 739-1531
Prog. Accred: Medical Assisting (ABHES)

Saginaw Campus
4054 Bay Rd., Saginaw 48603-1201
Phone: (989) 793-9800
Prog. Accred: Medical Assisting (ABHES)

West Palm Beach Campus
2601 S. Military Trail, Ste. 29, W. Palm Beach, FL 33415
Phone: (561) 433-1288
Prog. Accred: Medical Assisting (ABHES)

Sally Esser Beauty School
27201 West Warren St., Dearborn Heights 48127-1804
Type: Private, proprietary
Degrees: C
Phone: (313) 724-0404
Inst. Accred.: NACCAS (2005)

The School of Creative Hair Designs, Inc.
470 Marshall St., Fairfield Plaza, Coldwater 49036
Type: Private, proprietary
Degrees: C
URL: http://www.schoolofhair.com
Phone: (517) 279-2355
Inst. Accred.: NACCAS (1994/2002)

Sharp's Academy of Hairstyling
8166 Holly Rd., Grand Blanc 48439
Type: Private, proprietary
Degrees: C
Phone: (810) 695-6742
Inst. Accred.: ACCSCT (1993/2003)

Grand Blanc Campus
8166 Holly Rd., Grand Blanc 48499
Phone: (810) 695-6742

Specs Howard School of Broadcast Arts, Inc.
19900 West Nine Mile Rd., Southfield 48075-5273
Type: Private, proprietary
Degrees: C
URL: http://www.specshoward.edu
Phone: (248) 358-9000
Inst. Accred.: ACCSCT (1978/2005)

Taylortown School of Beauty
23015 Ecorse Rd., Taylor 48180
Type: Private, proprietary
Degrees: C
Phone: (313) 291-2177
Inst. Accred.: NACCAS (1982/2002)

Twin City Beauty College
2600 Lincoln Ave., St. Joseph 49085
Type: Private, proprietary
Degrees: C
URL: http://tcbeautycollege.com
Phone: (269) 428-2900
Inst. Accred.: NACCAS (1992/2006)

Michiana Beauty College
6323 University Commons, South Bend, IN 46635
Phone: (574) 271-1542

Traverse City Beauty College
1144 Boon St., Ste. D, Traverse City 49686
Phone: (231) 929-0710

U.P. Academy of Hair Design, Inc.
1625 Sheridan Rd., Escanaba 49829
Type: Private, proprietary
Degrees: C
Phone: (906) 786-5750
Inst. Accred.: NACCAS (2000/2003)

Virginia Farrell Beauty School—Ferndale
22925 Woodward Ave., Ferndale 48220
Type: Private, proprietary
Degrees: C
URL: http://www.virginiafarrell.com
Phone: (248) 398-4647
Inst. Accred.: NACCAS (1969/2006)

Virginia Farrell Beauty School—Livonia
33425 Five Mile Rd., Livonia 48154
Type: Private, proprietary
Degrees: C
URL: http://www.virginiafarrell.com
Phone: (734) 427-3970
Inst. Accred.: NACCAS (1987/2007)

Virginia Farrell Beauty School—St. Clair Shores
23620 Harper Ave., St. Clair Shores 48080
Type: Private, proprietary
Degrees: C
URL: http://www.virginiafarrell.com
Phone: (586) 775-6640
Inst. Accred.: NACCAS (1969/2006)

Virginia Farrell Beauty School—Westland
34580 Ford Rd., Westland 48185
Type: Private, proprietary
Degrees: C
URL: http://www.virginiafarrell.com
Phone: (734) 729-9220
Inst. Accred.: NACCAS (1973/2002)

Warren Woods Vocational Adult Education
13400 East 12 Mile Rd., Warren 48088-4036
Type: Public, state/local
Degrees: C
URL: http://www.warrenwoods.misd.net
Phone: (810) 439-4408
Inst. Accred.: NCA-CASI (2001/2005)

West Michigan College of Barbering and Beauty
3026 Lovers Ln., Kalamazoo 49001
Type: Private, proprietary
Degrees: C
Phone: (269) 381-4424
Inst. Accred.: NACCAS (1986/2002)

Wright Beauty Academy—Battle Creek
492 Capital Ave., SW, Battle Creek 49015
Type: Private, proprietary
Degrees: C
URL: http://www.wrightbeautyacademy.com
Phone: (269) 964-4016
Inst. Accred.: NACCAS (1973/2005)

Wright Beauty Academy—Portage
6666 Lovers Ln., Portage 49002
Type: Private, proprietary
Degrees: C
URL: http://www.wrightbeautyacademy.com
Phone: (269) 321-8708
Inst. Accred.: NACCAS (1971/2004)

MINNESOTA

American Indian Opportunities Industrial Center
1845 East Franklin Ave., Minneapolis 55404
Type: Public, independent
Degrees: C
URL: http://www.aioic.org
Phone: (612) 341-3358 *Calendar:* Qtr. plan
Inst. Accred.: NCA-CASI (1985/2004)

Art Instruction Schools
3400 Technology Dr., Minneapolis 55418
Type: Private, proprietary
Degrees: C
URL: http://www.artists-ais.com
Phone: (612) 362-5000
Inst. Accred.: DETC (1956/2006)

Aveda Institute, Inc.
400 Central Ave., Minneapolis 55414
Type: Private, proprietary
Degrees: C
Phone: (612) 378-7403
Inst. Accred.: NACCAS (1979/2006)

Cosmetology Careers Unlimited—Duluth
121 West Superior St., Duluth 55802
Type: Private, proprietary
Degrees: C
URL: http://www.coscareers.com
Phone: (218) 722-7484
Inst. Accred.: NACCAS (1970/2002)

Cosmetology Careers Unlimited—Hibbing
110 East Howard St., Hibbing 55746
Type: Private, proprietary
Degrees: C
URL: http://www.coscareers.com
Phone: (218) 263-8354
Inst. Accred.: NACCAS (1975/2005)

East Metro Opportunities Industrialization Center
1919 University Ave., St. Paul 55104
Type: Public, state/local
Degrees: C
URL: http://www.eastmetrooic.org
Phone: (651) 291-5088
Inst. Accred.: NCA-CASI (1987/2004)

Everest Institute—Eagan
1000 Blue Gentian Rd., Ste. 250, Eagan 55122
Type: Private, proprietary
System: Corinthian Colleges, Inc
Degrees: C
URL: http://www.everest.edu
Phone: (651) 688-2145
Inst. Accred.: ACCSCT (2004/2006)

Global Language Institute, Inc.
1536 Hewitt Ave., St. Paul 55104
Type: Private, proprietary
Degrees: C
URL: http://www.gli.org
Phone: (651) 523-2934
Inst. Accred.: ACCET (1995/2006)

Herzing College—Minneapolis Drafting School Campus
5700 West Broadway, Minneapolis 55428-3548
Type: Private, proprietary
Degrees: C
URL: http://www.herzing.edu
Phone: (763) 535-8843 *Calendar:* Sem. plan
Inst. Accred.: NCA-HLC (2004, *Indirect accreditation through Herzing College Corporate Offices, Milwaukee, WI*)

Ing'enue Beauty School
1024 Center Ave., Moorhead 56560
Type: Private, proprietary
Degrees: C
Phone: (218) 236-7201
Inst. Accred.: NACCAS (1987/2002)

Minneapolis School of Massage and Bodywork
81 Lowry Ave. NE, Minneapolis 55418
Type: Private, proprietary
Degrees: C
Phone: (612) 788-8907
Inst. Accred.: ACCSCT (1994/2004)

Minnesota School of Cosmetology
1750 Weir Dr., Woodbury 55125
Type: Private, proprietary
Degrees: C
URL: http://www.msccollege.edu
Phone: (651) 287-2180
Inst. Accred.: NACCAS (1983/2003)

Model College of Hair Design
201 Eighth Ave. South, St. Cloud 56301
Type: Private, proprietary
Degrees: C
URL: http://www.mcohd.com
Phone: (320) 253-4222
Inst. Accred.: NACCAS (1966/2003)

Montessori Training Center of Minnesota
683 Dodd Rd., St. Paul 55107
Type: Private, independent
Degrees: C
URL: http://www.mtcm.org
Phone: (651) 298-1120
Inst. Accred.: MACTE (1995/2004)

Norman and Associates
4938 Lincoln Dr., Edina 55436
Type: Private, proprietary
Degrees: C
URL: http://www.minnesota.dalecarnegie.com
Phone: (952) 935-0515
Inst. Accred.: ACCET (1976/2007)

Regency Beauty Institute
40 County Rd. 10 NE, Blaine 55434
Type: Private, proprietary
Degrees: C
URL: http://www.regencybeauty.com
Phone: (763) 784-9102
Inst. Accred.: NACCAS (1971/2003)

Regency Beauty Institute
14350 Buck Hill Rd., Burnsville 55306
Type: Private, proprietary
Degrees: C
URL: http://www.regencybeauty.com
Phone: (952) 435-3882
Inst. Accred.: NACCAS (1977/2003)

Aurora-Naperville Campus
4374 East New York St., Aurora, IL 60504
Phone: (630) 723-5051

Champaign Campus
Champaign Town Center, Town Center Blvd., Ste. 6, Champaign, IL 61822
Phone: (800) 787-6456

Darien-Downers Grove Campus
7411 South Cass Ave., Darien, IL 60651
Phone: (630) 824-4022

Duluth Campus
5115 Burning Tree Rd., Ste. 307, Duluth 55811
Phone: (800) 787-6456

Fairview Heights Campus
10850 Lincoln Trail, Ste. 15, Fairview Heights, IL 62208
Phone: (800) 787-6456

Greenwood Campus
Shoppes at County Line, 8811 Hardegan St., Ste. 305, Indianapolis, IN 46227
Phone: (800) 787-6456

Kansas City Campus
14133 East US Hwy. 40, Ste. 7A, Kansas City, MO 64136
Phone: (800) 787-6456

Madison Campus
2358 East Springs Dr., Ste. 300, Madison, WI 53704
Phone: (608) 819-0469

Maplewood Campus
3000 White Bear Ave. North, Maplewood 55109
Phone: (651) 773-3951

Mehlville Campus
4468 Lemay Ferry Rd., Ste. 16, Mehlville, MO 63129
Phone: (800) 787-6456

Olathe Campus
12517 South Rogers Rd., Cornerstone Point, Olathe, KS 66062
Phone: (800) 787-6456

Peoria Campus
Westlake Shopping Center, 2601 West Lake Ave., Ste. B-1A, Peoria, IL 61614
Phone: (800) 787-6456

St. Cloud Campus
Market Place of Waite, 110 2nd St. South, Waite Park 56387
Phone: (320) 251-0500

St. Cloud Regency Beauty Academy
912 West St. Germain St., St. Cloud 56301
Phone: (320) 251-0500

St. Peters Campus
Dierbergs 79 Crossing, 259 Salt Lick Rd., Ste. E2-E5, St. Peters, MO 63376
Phone: (800) 787-6456

Scot Lewis School-Paul Mitchell Partner School—Bloomington
9749 Lyndale Ave South, Bloomington 55420
Type: Private, proprietary
System: Empire Education Group
Degrees: C
URL: http://www.scotlewis.com
Phone: (952) 881-9327
Inst. Accred.: NACCAS (1968/2006)

Eden Prairie Campus
964 Prairie Center Dr., Eden Prairie 55344
Phone: (952) 906-2117

Scot Lewis School-Paul Mitchell Partner School—Plymouth
4124 Lancaster Ln., Plymouth 55441
Type: Private, proprietary
System: Empire Education Group
Degrees: C
URL: http://www.scotlewis.com
Phone: (763) 551-0562
Inst. Accred.: NACCAS (1966/2006)

St. Paul Campus
1905 Suburban Ave., St. Paul 55119
Phone: (651) 209-6930

Sister Rosalind Gefre Schools and Clinics of Massage
149 East Thompson Ave., Ste. 160, West St. Paul 55118
Type: Private, independent
Degrees: C
URL: http://www.sisterrosalind.org
Phone: (651) 554-3010
Inst. Accred.: ACCSCT (2002/2005)

Fargo Campus
3101 39th St. South, Ste. E, Fargo, ND 58104
Phone: (701) 297-5993

Summit Academy OIC
935 Olson Memorial Hwy., Minneapolis 55405
Type: Public, state/local
Degrees: C
URL: http://www.saoic.org
Phone: (612) 377-0150
Inst. Accred.: NCA-CASI (1983/2005)

MISSISSIPPI

The Academy of Hair Design #1
2003-B South Commerce St., Grenada 38901
Type: Private, proprietary
Degrees: C
Phone: (662) 226-2462
Inst. Accred.: NACCAS (1978/2004)

The Academy of Hair Design #3
1815 Terry Rd., Jackson 39204
Phone: (601) 372-9800

The Academy of Hair Design #8
4031 Popps Ferry Rd., D'Iberville 39532
Phone: (228) 354-8282

The Academy of Hair Design #4
3167 Hwy 80 East, McLaurin Mart, Pearl 39280
Type: Private, proprietary
Degrees: C
Phone: (601) 939-4441
Inst. Accred.: NACCAS (1983/2003)

The Academy of Hair Design #6
Cloverleaf Mall D-4, 5912 U.S. Hwy. 49, Hattiesburg 39401
Type: Private, proprietary
Degrees: C
Phone: (601) 583-1290
Inst. Accred.: NACCAS (1983/2006)

Batesville Job Corps Center
821 Hwy. 51 South, Batesville 38606
Type: Public, federal
Degrees: C
Phone: (662) 563-4656
Inst. Accred.: COE (1989/2000)

Chris' Beauty College
1265 Pass Rd., Gulfport 39501
Type: Private, proprietary
Degrees: C
URL: http://www.chrisbeautycollege.com
Phone: (228) 864-2920
Inst. Accred.: NACCAS (1977/2003)

Creations College of Cosmetology
2419 West Main St., PO Box 2635, Tupelo 38803
Type: Private, proprietary
Degrees: C
Phone: (662) 844-9264
Inst. Accred.: NACCAS (1987/2007)

Day Spa Career College
3900 Bienville Blvd., Ocean Springs 39564-5802
Type: Private, proprietary
Degrees: C
URL: http://www.dayspacareercollege.com
Phone: (228) 875-4809
Inst. Accred.: COE (2004)

Delta Beauty College
697 Delta Plaza, Greenville 38701
Type: Private, proprietary
Degrees: C
Phone: (662) 332-0587
Inst. Accred.: NACCAS (1978/2003)

The Final Touch Beauty School
5700 North Hills St., Meridian 39307
Type: Private, proprietary
Degrees: C
Phone: (601) 485-7733
Inst. Accred.: NACCAS (1990/2005)

Foster's Cosmetology College
1813 Hwy. 15 North, PO Box 66, Ripley 38663
Type: Private, proprietary
Degrees: C
Phone: (662) 837-9334
Inst. Accred.: NACCAS (1983/2006)

Gibson's Barber and Beauty College
120 East Main St., PO Box 990, West Point 39773
Type: Private, proprietary
Degrees: C
Phone: (662) 494-5444
Inst. Accred.: NACCAS (1988/2003)

Healing Touch School of Massage Therapy
4700 Hardy St., Ste. J-1, Hattiesburg 39402
Type: Private, proprietary
Degrees: C
URL: http://www.healingtouchms.com
Phone: (601) 261-0111
Inst. Accred.: ABHES (2004)

Healthcare Institute of Jackson
405 Briarwood Dr., Ste. 110, Jackson 39206
Type: Private, proprietary
Degrees: C
URL: http://www.hcijackson.com
Phone: (601) 956-3940
Inst. Accred.: ACICS (2007)

ICS The Wright Beauty College
2077 Hwy. 72 East—Annex, Corinth 38834
Type: Private, proprietary
Degrees: C
Phone: (662) 287-0944
Inst. Accred.: NACCAS (1986/2006)

J & J Hair Design College
116 East Franklin St., Carthage 39050
Type: Private, proprietary
Degrees: C
Phone: (601) 267-3678
Inst. Accred.: ACCSCT (1985/2002)

J & J Hair Design College
333 Pass Rd., Gulfport 39507
Type: Private, proprietary
Degrees: C
Phone: (228) 864-4663
Inst. Accred.: COE (2000/2006)

Greenwood Campus
502 Howard St., Greenwood 38930

Senatobia Campus
562B West Main St., Senatobia 38668
Phone: (662) 562-8010

Magnolia College of Cosmetology
4725 I-55 North, Jackson 39206
Type: Private, proprietary
Degrees: C
URL: http://www.magnoliacollegeofcosmetology.com
Phone: (601) 362-6940
Inst. Accred.: NACCAS (1985/2005)

Mississippi College of Beauty Culture
732 Sawmill Rd., Laurel 39440
Type: Private, proprietary
Degrees: C
Phone: (601) 428-7127
Inst. Accred.: NACCAS (1976/2004)

Mississippi Job Corps Center
400 Harmony Rd., Crystal Springs 39059
Type: Public, federal
Degrees: C
URL: http://atlantaregion.jobcorps.gov
Phone: (601) 892-3348
Inst. Accred.: COE (1984/2006)

Mississippi School of Therapeutic Massage
5120 Galaxie Dr., Jackson 39206
Type: Private, proprietary
Degrees: C
URL: http://www.mstm.info
Phone: (601) 362-3624
Inst. Accred.: CMTA (1999/2006)

Traxler School of Hair
2845 Suncrest Dr., Jackson 39212
Type: Private, proprietary
Degrees: C
Phone: (601) 371-0226
Inst. Accred.: ACCSCT (1997/2006, Probation)

MISSOURI

Abbott Academy of Cosmetology Arts and Sciences
2101 Pkwy. Dr., St. Peters 63376
Type: Private, proprietary
Degrees: C
URL: http://www.missouribeauty.com
Phone: (636) 447-0100
Inst. Accred.: NACCAS (1985/2005)

Academy of Hair Design, Inc.
1832 South Glenstone Ave., #4, Springfield 65804
Type: Private, proprietary
Degrees: C
Phone: (417) 881-3900
Inst. Accred.: NACCAS (2003/2006)

Advance Beauty College, Inc.
202 East Main St., Warrenton 63383-2006
Type: Private, proprietary
Degrees: C
URL: http://www.esbc.edu/~abc123/index.html
Phone: (636) 456-1180
Inst. Accred.: NACCAS (2004)

American College of Hair Design, Inc.
125 Duke Rd., Sedalia 65301
Type: Private, proprietary
Degrees: C
URL: http://www.americancollegeofhairdesign.com
Phone: (660) 827-1270
Inst. Accred.: NACCAS (1999/2007)

Andrews Academy of Cosmetology
100 West Main, Sullivan 63080
Type: Private, proprietary
Degrees: C
Phone: (573) 468-3864
Inst. Accred.: NACCAS (2002/2005)

University of Cosmetology
201 East 5th St., Washington 63090
Phone: (636) 390-4554

Aviation Institute of Maintenance
3130 Terrace St., Kansas City 64141
Type: Private, proprietary
Degrees: C
URL: http://www.tidetech.com
Phone: (816) 753-9920
Inst. Accred.: ACCSCT (2001/2006)

Broadcast Center
2360 Hampton Ave., St. Louis 63139
Type: Private, proprietary
Degrees: C
URL: http://www.broadcastcenterinfo.com
Phone: (314) 647-8181
Inst. Accred.: ACCET (1990/2005)

C.J. Sealey and Associates, LLC
1869 Craig Park Ct., Ste. A, St. Louis 63146
Type: Private, proprietary
Degrees: C
URL: http://www.carnegiestl.com
Phone: (314) 439-8090
Inst. Accred.: ACCET (1999/2005)

Career Alternatives Learning Center
12158 Natural Bridge Rd., Ste. 101, St. Louis 63044
Type: Private, proprietary
Degrees: C
URL: http://www.calearningcenter.com
Phone: (314) 209-1777
Inst. Accred.: COE (2006)

Central College of Cosmetology
1012 Missouri Ave., St. Robert 65584
Type: Private, proprietary
Degrees: C
Phone: (573) 336-3888
Inst. Accred.: NACCAS (1991/2006)

Camdenton Campus
1159 North Hwy. 5, Camdenton 65020
Phone: (573) 346-7800

Chillicothe Beauty Academy
505 Elm St., Chillicothe 64601
Type: Private, proprietary
Degrees: C
URL: http://www.chillicothecosmetology.com
Phone: (660) 646-4198
Inst. Accred.: NACCAS (1975/2006)

Cosmetology Concepts Institute
1611 Burlington St., Ste. A, Columbia 65202
Type: Private, proprietary
Degrees: C
Phone: (573) 449-7527
Inst. Accred.: NACCAS (1992/2007)

Diva's Unlimited Academy
3306 Brown Rd., St. Louis 63114
Type: Private, proprietary
Degrees: C
Phone: (314) 428-3482
Inst. Accred.: NACCAS (2005)

Elaine Steven Beauty College, Inc.
10420 West Florissant, St. Louis 63136
Type: Private, proprietary
Degrees: C
URL: http://www.esbc.edu
Phone: (314) 868-8196
Inst. Accred.: NACCAS (1988/2003)

Grabber School of Hair Design
14557 Manchester Rd., Ballwin 63011
Type: Private, proprietary
Degrees: C
Phone: (636) 227-4440
Inst. Accred.: NACCAS (1988/2003)

The Hair Academy—110
110 North Franklin St., Kirksville 63501
Type: Private, proprietary
Degrees: C
Phone: (660) 665-1028
Inst. Accred.: NACCAS (2005)

Hannibal Career and Technical Center
4500 McMasters Ave., Hannibal 63401
Type: Public, state/local
Degrees: C
URL: http://www.hannibal.tec.mo.us
Phone: (573) 221-4430
Inst. Accred.: NCA-CASI (1991/2005)
Prog. Accred.: Allied Health (respiratory therapy)

House of Heavilin Beauty College—Blue Springs
2000 South 7 Hwy., Blue Springs 64014
Type: Private, proprietary
Degrees: C
URL: http://www.kc-hair.com
Phone: (816) 229-9000
Inst. Accred.: NACCAS (1979/2005)

House of Heavilin Beauty College—Grandview
12020 Blue Ridge Blvd., Grandview 64030
Type: Private, proprietary
Degrees: C
URL: http://www.kc-hair.com
Phone: (816) 767-8000
Inst. Accred.: NACCAS (1992/2003)

House of Heavilin Beauty College—Kansas City
5720 Troost Ave., Kansas City 64110
Type: Private, proprietary
Degrees: C
URL: http://www.kc-hair.com
Phone: (816) 523-2471
Inst. Accred.: NACCAS (1968/2004)

Independence College of Cosmetology
815 West 23rd St., Independence 64055
Type: Private, proprietary
Degrees: C
URL: http://www.hair-skin-nails.com
Phone: (816) 252-4247
Inst. Accred.: NACCAS (1966/2004)

Martinez School of Cosmetology
248 1/2 East Broadway, Excelsior Springs 64024
Type: Private, proprietary
Degrees: C
Phone: (816) 630-3900
Inst. Accred.: NACCAS (1989/2004)

Massage Therapy Training Institute
9140 Ward Pkwy., Ste. 100, Kansas City 64114
Type: Private, proprietary
Degrees: C
URL: http://www.mtti.net
Phone: (816) 523-9140
Inst. Accred.: ABHES (2005)

Topeka Campus
4123 Gage Center Dr., Ste. 240, Topeka, KS 66604
Phone: (785) 273-6884

Merrell University of Beauty Arts and Science
1101-R Southwest Blvd., Jefferson City 65109
Type: Private, proprietary
Degrees: C
URL: http://www.merrelluniversity.edu
Phone: (573) 635-4433
Inst. Accred.: NACCAS (1987/2005)

Missouri College of Cosmetology and Esthetics
401 West Reed St., Moberly 65270
Phone: (660) 263-9600

Missouri Beauty Academy
224 East Columbia St., Farmington 63640
Type: Private, proprietary
Degrees: C
URL: http://www.missouribeauty.com
Phone: (573) 756-2730
Inst. Accred.: NACCAS (1984/2004)

Festus Campus
109 A Main St., Festus 63028
Phone: (636) 933-3627

Missouri College of Cosmetology North
2555 West Kearney St., Springfield 65803
Type: Private, proprietary
Degrees: C
URL: http://missouricosmo.com
Phone: (417) 866-2786
Inst. Accred.: NACCAS (2000/2003)

Missouri College of Cosmetology—Bolivar
1820 Springfield Rd., Bolivar 65613
Type: Private, proprietary
Degrees: C
URL: http://missouricosmo.com
Phone: (417) 326-3002
Inst. Accred.: NACCAS (2002/2005)

Missouri College of Cosmetology—South
3636 South Campbell Ave., Springfield 65807-5202
Type: Private, proprietary
Degrees: C
URL: http://missouricosmo.com
Phone: (417) 887-6511
Inst. Accred.: NACCAS (2002/2005)

Missouri Montessori Teacher Education Program
1100 White Rd., Chesterfield 63017
Type: Private, independent
Degrees: C
URL: http://www.chesterfielddayschool.org/MOMTEP
Phone: (314) 469-6622
Inst. Accred.: MACTE (1999/2006)

National Academy of Beauty Arts
157 Concord Plaza, St. Louis 63128
Type: Private, proprietary
Degrees: C
URL: http://www.nationalacademyofbeautyarts.com
Phone: (314) 842-3616
Inst. Accred.: NACCAS (1967/2005)

Crystal City Campus
26 Twin City Plaza, Crystal City 63019
Phone: (636) 931-7100

Neosho Beauty College
116 North Wood St., Neosho 64850
Type: Private, proprietary
Degrees: C
URL: http://www.neoshobeautycollege.com
Phone: (417) 451-7216
Inst. Accred.: NACCAS (1989/2004)

Class Act I School of Cosmetology
512 Main St., Joplin 64801
Phone: (417) 781-7070

New Dimensions School of Hair Design
621 Kentucky Ave., Ste. 12, Joplin 64801
Type: Private, proprietary
Degrees: C
Phone: (417) 782-2875
Inst. Accred.: NACCAS (1993/2006)

Paris II Educational Center
6840 North Oak Trafficway, Gladstone 64118
Type: Private, proprietary
Degrees: C
URL: http://parisii.net
Phone: (816) 468-6666
Inst. Accred.: NACCAS (1987/2002)

Patsy and Rob's Academy of Beauty
18 Northwest Plaza, St. Ann 63074
Type: Private, proprietary
Degrees: C
URL: http://www.praob.edu
Phone: (314) 298-8808
Inst. Accred.: NACCAS (1988/2003)

Professional Massage Training Center
229 East Commercial St., Springfield 65803
Type: Private, proprietary
Degrees: C
URL: http://www.pmtc.edu
Phone: (417) 863-7682
Inst. Accred.: ACCSCT (2000/2005)

Saint Charles School of Massage Therapy
2440 Executive Dr., Ste. 100, St. Charles 63303
Type: Private, proprietary
Degrees: C
URL: http://www.spastcharles.com/school/index.html
Phone: (636) 498-0777
Inst. Accred.: CMTA (2003/2006)

Saint Louis Hair Academy, Inc.
3701 Kossuth Ave., St. Louis 63107
Type: Private, proprietary
Degrees: C
Phone: (314) 533-3125
Inst. Accred.: NACCAS (1992/2003)

Salem College of Hairstyling
1051 Kings Hwy., Ste. 1, Rolla 65401
Type: Private, proprietary
Degrees: C
Phone: (573) 368-3136
Inst. Accred.: NACCAS (1982/2002)

SEMO Hairstyling Academy
904 Broadway St., Cape Girardeau 63701
Type: Private, proprietary
Degrees: C
Phone: (573) 651-0333
Inst. Accred.: NACCAS (2004)

MONTANA

Academy of Cosmetology
133 West Mendenhall, Bozeman 59715
Type: Private, proprietary
Degrees: C
URL: http://academycosmetology.com
Phone: (406) 587-1265
Inst. Accred.: NACCAS (1989/2004)

Academy of Nail and Skin and Hair, LLP
928 Broadwater Ave., Ste. C, Billings 59101
Type: Private, proprietary
Degrees: C
URL: http://www.academyofnailandskin.com
Phone: (406) 252-3232
Inst. Accred.: NACCAS (2003/2006)

Butte Academy of Beauty Culture, Inc.
303 West Park St., Butte 59701
Type: Private, proprietary
Degrees: C
Phone: (406) 723-8565
Inst. Accred.: NACCAS (1965/2003)

The College of Coiffure Art
1423 Wyoming Ave., Billings 59102
Type: Private, proprietary
Degrees: C
Phone: (406) 656-9114
Inst. Accred.: NACCAS (1974/2005)

Dahl's College of Beauty, Inc.
716 Central Ave., Great Falls 59401
Type: Private, proprietary
Degrees: C
Phone: (406) 454-3453
Inst. Accred.: NACCAS (1972/2006)

David L. Pals and Associates, Inc.
632 Luther Circle, PO Box 21502, Billings 59104
Type: Private, proprietary
Degrees: C
URL: http://www.montana.dalecarnegie.com
Phone: (406) 652-4442
Inst. Accred.: ACCET (1978/2004)

Health Works Institute
111 South Grand, Annex 3, Bozeman 59715
Type: Private, proprietary
Degrees: C
URL: http://www.healthworksinstitute.com
Phone: (406) 582-1555
Inst. Accred.: CMTA (1999/2004)

Modern Beauty School, Inc.
2700 Paxson Plaza, Ste. G, Missoula 59801
Type: Private, proprietary
Degrees: C
Phone: (406) 549-9608
Inst. Accred.: NACCAS (1997/2005)

Sage Technical Services
3044 Hesper Rd., Billings 59102
Type: Private, proprietary
Degrees: C
URL: http://www.sageschools.com
Phone: (406) 652-3030
Inst. Accred.: ACCSCT (1994/2007)

NEBRASKA

Alegent Health Immanuel Medical Center
6901 North 72nd St., Omaha 68122
Type: Private, independent
Degrees: C
URL: http://www.alegent.com
Phone: (402) 572-2676
Inst. Accred.: ABHES (2005)
Prog. Accred.: Allied Health (medical assisting (AMA), respiratory therapy), Clinical Pastoral Education, Medical Assisting (ABHES)

Capitol School of Hairstyling and Esthetics
2819 South 125th Ave., Ste. 268, Omaha 68144
Type: Private, proprietary
Degrees: C
URL: http://www.capitollook.com
Phone: (402) 333-3329
Inst. Accred.: NACCAS (1988/2003)

College of Hair Design
304 South 11th St., Lincoln 68508-2199
Type: Private, proprietary
Degrees: C
Phone: (402) 477-4040 *Calendar:* Qtr. plan
Inst. Accred.: ACCSCT (1977/2004)

Joseph's College of Beauty—Beatrice
618 Count St., Beatrice 68310
Type: Private, proprietary
Degrees: C
URL: http://josephscollege.com
Phone: (402) 223-3588
Inst. Accred.: NACCAS (1973/2004)

Joseph's College of Beauty—Hastings
828 West 2nd St., Hastings 68901
Type: Private, proprietary
Degrees: C
URL: http://josephscollege.com
Phone: (402) 463-1357
Inst. Accred.: NACCAS (1973/2004)

Grand Island Campus
305 West 3rd St., Grand Island 68801
Phone: (308) 381-8848

Joseph's College of Beauty—Lincoln
2241 O St., Ste. 2, Lincoln 68510
Type: Private, proprietary
Degrees: C
URL: http://josephscollege.com
Phone: (402) 435-2333
Inst. Accred.: NACCAS (1973/2004)

Omaha Campus
3724 Farnam St., Omaha 68131
Phone: (402) 345-4152

Joseph's College of Beauty—Norfolk
202 Madison Ave., Norfolk 68701
Type: Private, proprietary
Degrees: C
URL: http://josephscollege.com
Phone: (402) 371-3358
Inst. Accred.: NACCAS (1968/2005)

Joseph's of Kearney, School of Hair Design
2213 Central Ave., Kearney 68847
Type: Private, proprietary
Degrees: C
URL: http://josephscollege.com
Phone: (308) 234-6594
Inst. Accred.: NACCAS (1983/2003)

La' James International College
1660 North Grant St., Fremont 68025
Type: Private, proprietary
Degrees: C
URL: http://www.bahnercollege.com
Phone: (402) 721-6500
Inst. Accred.: NACCAS (1966/2003)

Mid-America Montessori Teacher Training Center
10730 Pacific St., Ste. 234, Omaha 68114
Type: Private, independent
Degrees: C
Phone: (402) 393-1311
Inst. Accred.: MACTE (2001)

North Platte Beauty Academy
107 West Sixth St., North Platte 69101
Type: Private, proprietary
Degrees: C
Phone: (308) 532-4664
Inst. Accred.: NACCAS (1987/2002)

Omaha School of Massage Therapy
9748 Park Dr., Omaha 68128
Type: Private, proprietary
Degrees: C
URL: http://www.osmt.com
Phone: (402) 331-3694
Inst. Accred.: ACCSCT (1995/2005)

Universal College of Healing Arts
8702 North 30th St., Omaha 68112
Type: Private, proprietary
Degrees: C
URL: http://www.ucha.com
Phone: (402) 556-4456
Inst. Accred.: ABHES (2002/2006)

Xenon International School of Hair Design II
8516 Park Dr., Omaha 68127
Type: Private, proprietary
Degrees: C
URL: http://www.xenonintl.com
Phone: (402) 393-2933
Inst. Accred.: NACCAS (1989/2004)

Grand Island Campus
804 North Webb Rd., Grand Island 68803
Phone: (308) 395-8600

NEVADA

Academy of Hair Design
5191 West Charleston Blvd., Las Vegas 89146
Type: Private, proprietary
Degrees: C
URL: http://www.ahdvegas.com
Phone: (702) 878-1185
Inst. Accred.: NACCAS (1976/2005)

Academy of Healing Arts
710 South Tonopah Dr., Las Vegas 89106
Type: Private, proprietary
Degrees: C
URL: http://www.academylasvegas.com
Phone: (702) 671-4242
Inst. Accred.: COE (2005)

American Career Institute
2340 Paseo Del Prado, Ste. D-208, Las Vegas 89102
Type: Private, proprietary
Degrees: C
URL: http://www.acinst.com
Phone: (702) 222-3522
Inst. Accred.: DETC (2002)

Carson City Beauty Academy
2531 North Carson St., Carson City 89706
Type: Private, proprietary
Degrees: C
Phone: (775) 885-9977
Inst. Accred.: NACCAS (1992/2005)

Expertise Cosmetology Institute
1911 Stella Lake St., Las Vegas 89106
Type: Private, proprietary
Degrees: C
URL: http://www.expertisebeauty.com
Phone: (702) 636-8686
Inst. Accred.: NACCAS (2003/2006)

Institute of Professional Careers
4472 South Eastern Ave., Las Vegas 89119
Type: Private, proprietary
Degrees: C
Phone: (702) 734-9900
Inst. Accred.: ACCSCT (2005)

J. R. Rodgers and Associates, Inc.
1100 East Sahara, Ste. 105, Las Vegas 89104
Type: Private, proprietary
Degrees: C
URL: http://www.nevada.dalecarnegie.com
Phone: (702) 735-2115
Inst. Accred.: ACCET (1979/2005)

Marinello School of Beauty—Las Vegas
5001 East Bonanza Rd., Ste. 110, Las Vegas 89110
Type: Private, proprietary
System: B&H Education, Inc.
Degrees: C
URL: http://www.marinello.com
Phone: (702) 431-6200
Inst. Accred.: NACCAS (1965/2003)

Henderson Campus
4451 East Sunset Rd., Ste. 16, Henderson 89014
Phone: (702) 450-9988

Montessori Training of Southern Nevada
1401 Amador Ln., Henderson 89012
Type: Private, independent
Degrees: C
Phone: (702) 407-0790
Inst. Accred.: MACTE (2006)

Northwest Health Careers
7398 Smoke Ranch Rd., Ste. 100, Las Vegas 89128
Type: Private, proprietary
Degrees: C
URL: http://www.northwesthealthcareers.com
Phone: (702) 254-7577
Inst. Accred.: ABHES (2003)
Prog. Accred.: Medical Assisting (ABHES)

Prater Way College of Beauty, Inc.
1627 Prater Way, Sparks 89431
Type: Private, proprietary
Degrees: C
URL: http://www.praterway.net
Phone: (775) 355-6677
Inst. Accred.: NACCAS (2006)

NEW HAMPSHIRE

Continental Academie of Hair Design—Hudson
102 Derry Rd., Hudson 03051
Type: Private, proprietary
Degrees: C
URL: http://continentalacademie.net
Phone: (603) 889-1614
Inst. Accred.: NACCAS (1976/2002)

Continental Academie of Hair Design—Manchester
228 Maple St., Manchester 03103
Type: Private, proprietary
Degrees: C
URL: http://continentalacademie.net
Phone: (603) 622-5851
Inst. Accred.: NACCAS (1972/2003)

Empire Beauty School—Laconia
556 Main St., Laconia 03246
Type: Private, proprietary
Degrees: C
URL: http://www.empirebeautyschools.com
Phone: (603) 524-8777
Inst. Accred.: NACCAS (1977/2004)

Hooksett Campus
1328 Hooksett Rd., Hooksett 03106
Phone: (603) 792-1400

Empire Beauty School—Somersworth
362 Route 108, Somersworth 03878
Type: Private, proprietary
Degrees: C
URL: http://www.empirebeautyschools.com
Phone: (603) 692-1515
Inst. Accred.: NACCAS (1981/2006)

Portsmouth Campus
2454 Lafayette Rd., Southgate Plaza, Portsmouth 03801
Phone: (603) 433-6664

Esthetics Institute at Concord Academy
20 South Main St., Concord 03301
Type: Private, proprietary
Degrees: C
URL: http://www.estheticsinstitute.net
Phone: (603) 224-2211
Inst. Accred.: NACCAS (1985/2005)

Keene Beauty Academy, Inc.
800 Park Ave., Keene 03431
Type: Private, proprietary
Degrees: C
URL: http://www.keenebeautyacademy.com
Phone: (603) 357-3736
Inst. Accred.: NACCAS (1983/2003)

Michael's School of Hair Design and Esthetics
73 South River Rd., Bedford Mall, Bedford 03110
Type: Private, proprietary
Degrees: C
URL: http://www.michaelsschool.com
Phone: (603) 668-4300
Inst. Accred.: NACCAS (1981/2006)

New England Montessori Teacher Education Center
30 Moose Club Rd., Goffstown 03045
Type: Private, independent
Degrees: C
URL: http://www.nemtecmontessoritraining.com
Phone: (603) 641-5256
Inst. Accred.: MACTE (1999)

New England School of Hair Design, Inc.
12 Interchange Dr., West Lebanon 03784
Type: Private, proprietary
Degrees: C
URL: http://www.neschoolofhairdesign.com
Phone: (603) 298-5199
Inst. Accred.: NACCAS (1983/2003)

The New Hampshire Career Institute
17 Knight St., Concord 03301
Type: Private, independent
Degrees: C
URL: http://www.second-start.org
Phone: (603) 228-1341
Inst. Accred.: ACCET (1998/2004)

Portsmouth Beauty School of Hair Design
140 Congress St., Portsmouth 03801
Type: Private, proprietary
Degrees: C
Phone: (603) 436-5456
Inst. Accred.: NACCAS (1976/2002)

Seacoast Center
PO Box 323, Greenland 03840
Type: Private, independent
Degrees: C
URL: http://www.seacoastcenter.com
Phone: (603) 772-0181
Inst. Accred.: MACTE (1999/2006)

Upper Valley Teacher Institute
One Ct. St., Ste. 210, Lebanon 03766
Type: Private, independent
Degrees: C
URL: http://www.uvti.org
Phone: (603) 448-6507 *Calendar:* Sem. plan
Inst. Accred.: NEASC-CTCI (1999/2007)

NEW JERSEY

Academy of Massage Therapy
321 Main St., 2nd Flr., Hackensack 07601
Type: Private, proprietary
Degrees: C
URL: http://www.academyofmassage.com
Phone: (201) 568-3220 *Calendar:* Sem. plan
Inst. Accred.: CMTA (1999/2004)

Allied Medical and Technical Institute
201 Willowbrook Blvd., 2nd Flr., Wayne 07470
Type: Private, proprietary
Degrees: C
URL: http://www.alliedteched.com
Phone: (973) 837-1818
Inst. Accred.: ACICS (1985/2005)

The Artistic Academy of Hair Design
301 Gibraltar Dr., Ste. 1-A, Morris Plains 07950
Type: Private, proprietary
Degrees: C
URL: http://www.artisticacademy.com
Phone: (973) 656-1401
Inst. Accred.: NACCAS (1987/2002)

Avtech Institute of Technology
4500 New Brunswick Ave., Piscataway 08854
Type: Private, proprietary
Degrees: C
Phone: (732) 424-8008
Inst. Accred.: ACCSCT (2005)

Berdan Institute
201 Willowbrook Blvd., 2nd Flr., Wayne 07470
Type: Private, proprietary
Degrees: C
URL: http://www.berdaninstitute.com
Phone: (973) 837-1818
Inst. Accred.: ABHES (2002/2006)
Prog. Accred.: Allied Health (medical assisting (AMA)), Dentistry (dental assisting), Medical Assisting (ABHES)

Bergen County Technical Schools
200 Hackensack Ave., Hackensack 07601
Type: Public, local
Degrees: C
URL: http://www.bergen.org/academy
Phone: (201) 343-6000
Inst. Accred.: COE (2005)

Berlitz International, Inc.
400 Alexander Park, Princeton 08540
Type: Private, proprietary
Degrees: C
URL: http://www.berlitz.com
Phone: (609) 514-3127
Inst. Accred.: ACCET (1984/2000)

Akron Campus
156 South Main St., Akron, OH 44308
Phone: (330) 762-0991

Atlanta Campus
Tower Place 200, Ste. 130, 3348 Peachtree Rd., NE, Atlanta, GA 30326
Phone: (404) 261-5062

Austin Campus
8400 North MoPac, Ste. 302, Austin, TX 78759
Phone: (512) 343-0087

Baltimore Campus
1467 York Rd., Ste. 312, Baltimore, MD 21093
Phone: (410) 296-8365

Bellevue Campus
520 112th Ave., NE, Ste. 210, Bellevue, WA 98004
Phone: (425) 451-0162

Beverly Hills Campus
9454 Wilshire Blvd., Ste. 100, Beverly Hills, CA 91212
Phone: (310) 276-1101

Bingham Farms Campus
30700 Telegraph Rd., Ste. 1660, Bingham Center, Bingham Farms, MI 48025
Phone: (248) 642-9335

Boston Campus
437 Boylston St., Boston, MA 02116
Phone: (617) 266-6858

Campbell Campus
Creekside Business Mall, 1475 South Bascom Ave., Campbell, CA 95008
Phone: (408) 377-9513

Charlotte Campus
5821 Fairview Rd., Ste. 202, Charlotte, NC 28209
Phone: (704) 554-8169

Chicago Campus
2 North Lasalle St., Ste. 1810, Chicago, IL 60602
Phone: (312) 782-6820

Cincinnati Campus
580 Walnut St., Plaza Level, Ste. 172-E, Cincinnati, OH 45202
Phone: (513) 381-4650

Cleveland Campus
1300 East Ninth St., Ste. 112, Bond Ct. Bldg., Cleveland, OH 44114
Phone: (216) 861-0950

Coral Gables Campus
2199 Ponce de Leon Blvd., Ste. 101, Coral Gables, FL 33134
Phone: (305) 444-7665

Costa Mesa Campus
3070 Bristol St., Ste. 150, Costa Mesa, CA 92626
Phone: (714) 557-3535

Dallas Campus
17194 Preston Rd., Ste. 207, Dallas, TX 75248
Phone: (972) 380-0404

Denver Campus
55 Madison St., #175, Denver, CO 80206
Phone: (303) 399-8686

Ft. Lauderdale Campus
2400 East Commercial Blvd., Ste. 100, Ft. Lauderdale, FL 33308
Phone: (954) 491-9393

Houston Campus
520 Post Oak Blvd., Ste. 500, Houston, TX 77027
Phone: (713) 626-7844

Indianapolis Campus
8888 Keystone Crossing, Ste. 848, Indianapolis, IN 46240
Phone: (317) 844-4303

Miami Campus
777 Brickell Ave., Ste. 970, Sun Bank Bldg., Miami, FL 33131
Phone: (305) 371-3686

Mineola Campus
47 Mineola Blvd., Mineola, NY 11501
Phone: (516) 741-9220

Minneapolis Campus
6800 South France Ave., Ste. 190, Minneapolis, MN 55435
Phone: (952) 920-4100

New York Rector Street Campus
2 Rector St., New York, NY 10006
Phone: (212) 766-2388

New York West 51st Campus
40 West 51st St., New York, NY 10020
Phone: (212) 765-1000

Northbrook Campus
One Northbrook Place, 5 Revere Dr., Ste. 505, Northbrook, IL 60062
Phone: (847) 509-0338

Oakbrook Campus
1200 Harger Rd., Ste. 722, Oakbrook, IL 60521
Phone: (630) 954-3822

Orange Campus
1835 Orangewood Ave., Ste. 102, Orange, CA 92668
Phone: (714) 935-0828

Pasadena Campus
600 South Lake Ave., Ste. 101, Pasadena, CA 91106
Phone: (626) 795-5888

Philadelphia Campus
1608 Walnut St., Philadelphia, PA 19103
Phone: (215) 735-8500

Phoenix Campus
3333 E. Camelback Rd., #160, Phoenix, AZ 85018
Phone: (602) 468-9494

Pittsburgh Campus
Penn Center West, Building 3, Ste. 400, Pittsburgh, PA 15222
Phone: (412) 494-9122

Princeton Campus
400 Alexander Park, Princeton 08540-6306
Phone: (609) 514-3400

Raleigh Campus
5974-A Six Forks Rd., Raleigh, NC 27609
Phone: (919) 848-1888

Ridgewood Campus
40 West Ridgewood Ave., Ste. 201, Ridgewood 07450
Phone: (201) 444-6400

Rochester Campus
36 Main St. West, Rochester, NY 14614
Phone: (716) 232-6424

Rockville Campus
11300 Rockville Pike, Ste. 911, Rockville, MD 20852
Phone: (301) 770-7551

St. Louis Campus
200 South Hanley Rd., Ste. 208, St. Louis, MO 63105
Phone: (314) 721-1070

San Antonio Campus
5825 Callaghan Rd., Ste. 200, San Antonio, TX 78228
Phone: (210) 681-7050

San Diego Campus
Home Savings Bldg., 225 Broadway, Ste. 200, San Diego, CA 92101
Phone: (619) 235-8344

San Francisco Campus
180 Montgomery St., Ste. 1580, San Francisco, CA 94104
Phone: (415) 986-6464

Santa Monica Campus
616 Santa Monica Blvd., Santa Monica, CA 90401
Phone: (310) 458-0330

Schaumburg Campus
1821 Walden Office Square, Ste. 230, Schaumburg, IL 60173
Phone: (847) 397-9422

Stamford Campus
350 Bedford St., Ste. 407, Stamford, CT 06901
Phone: (203) 324-9551

Summit Campus
47 Maple St., Summit 07901
Phone: (908) 277-0300

Berlitz International, Inc. *(continued)*

Torrance Campus
Park Del Amo, 2355 Crenshaw Blvd., Building A, Ste. 185, Torrance, CA 90501
Phone: (310) 328-7722

Vienna Campus
Tyson Ct.house Bldg., 2070 Chain Bridge Rd., Ste. 140, Vienna, VA 22182
Phone: (703) 883-0627

Walnut Creek Campus
1646 North California Blvd., Ste. P-112, Walnut Creek, CA 94596
Phone: (925) 935-1386

Washington, DC Campus
1050 Connecticut Ave., NW, Washington, DC 20036
Phone: (202) 331-1160

Wauwatosa Campus
2675 North Mayfair Rd., Ste. 204, Wauwatosa, WI 53226
Phone: (414) 454-2744

Wayne Campus
Sugartown Square, 230 Sugartown Rd., Ste. 103, Wayne, PA 19087
Phone: (610) 964-8404

Wellesley Hills Campus
40 Washington St., Wellesley Hills, MA 02181
Phone: (781) 237-2220

West Hartford Campus
61 South Main St., West Hartford, CT 06107
Phone: (860) 231-7310

Westport Campus
The Market Place, 125 Main St., Ste. 340, Westport, CT 06880
Phone: (203) 226-4223

White Plains Campus
One North Broadway, Rm. 15, White Plains, NY 10601
Phone: (914) 946-8389

Woodland Hills Campus
6300 Canoga Ave., Ste. 1002, Woodland Hills, CA 91367
Phone: (818) 999-1870

Brookside Business and Training Institute
25 Brookside Ave., Sussex 07461-2223
Type: Private, proprietary
Degrees: C
URL: http://www.bbti.edu
Phone: (973) 875-4445
Inst. Accred.: ACICS (2003)

Capri Institute of Hair Design—Bricktown
268 Brick Blvd., Bricktown 08723
Type: Private, proprietary
Degrees: C
URL: http://www.capriinstitute.com
Phone: (732) 920-3600
Inst. Accred.: NACCAS (1984/2004)

Capri Institute of Hair Design—Clifton
1595 Main Ave., Clifton 07011
Type: Private, proprietary
Degrees: C
URL: http://www.capriinstitute.com
Phone: (973) 772-4610
Inst. Accred.: NACCAS (1972/2003)

Capri Institute of Hair Design—Kenilworth
660 North Michigan Ave., Kenilworth 07033
Type: Private, proprietary
Degrees: C
URL: http://www.capriinstitute.com
Phone: (908) 964-1330
Inst. Accred.: NACCAS (1981/2005)

Roxbury Campus
Roxbury Mall, 45 Sunset Strip & Route 10 East, Succasunna 07876
Phone: (973) 584-9030

Capri Institute of Hair Design—Paramus
615 Winters Ave., Paramus 07652
Type: Private, proprietary
Degrees: C
URL: http://www.capriinstitute.com
Phone: (201) 599-0880
Inst. Accred.: NACCAS (1978/2005)

Central Career Schools
126 Corporate Blvd., South Plainfield 07080
Type: Private, proprietary
Degrees: C
URL: http://www.centralcareer.com
Phone: (908) 412-8600
Inst. Accred.: ACCSCT (1998/2003)

The Chubb Institute—Parsippany
8 Sylvan Way, First Flr., Parsippany 07054-0342
Type: Private, proprietary
System: High-Tech Institute
Degrees: C
URL: http://www.chubbinstitute.edu
Phone: (973) 682-4900
Inst. Accred.: ACCSCT (1972/2005, Probation)

Jersey City Campus
40 Journal Square, Jersey City 07306-4009
Phone: (201) 876-3800

Concorde School of Hair Design, Inc.
1458 State Route 35, Highway 35 and Dean Rd., Ocean 07712
Type: Private, proprietary
System: Empire Education Group
Degrees: C
URL: http://www.natural-motion.com
Phone: (732) 493-1355
Inst. Accred.: NACCAS (1983/2003)

Bloomfield Campus
15 Ward St., Bloomfield 07003
Phone: (973) 680-0099

Cortiva Institute-Somerset School of Massage Therapy
180 Centennial Ave., Piscataway 08854
Type: Private, proprietary
Degrees: C
URL: http://www.cortiva.com/locations/ssmt
Phone: (732) 885-3400
Inst. Accred.: CMTA (2001/2004)

Wall Township Campus
1985 Hwy. 34, Wall Township 07719
Phone: (732) 282-0100

Dale Carnegie Training of Central New Jersey
243 Route 130, Bordentown 08505-2111
Type: Private, proprietary
Degrees: C
URL: http://www.centralnj.dalecarnegie.com
Phone: (609) 324-9200
Inst. Accred.: ACCET (1976/2007)

Divers Academy International
1500 Liberty Place, lakeside Business Park, Erial 08081
Type: Private, proprietary
Degrees: C
URL: http://www.diversacademy.com
Phone: (856) 404-6100
Inst. Accred.: ACCSCT (1981/2002)

Dover Business College
600 Getty Ave., Clifton 07011
Type: Private, proprietary
Degrees: C
URL: http://www.doverbusinesscollege.org
Phone: (973) 546-0123 *Calendar:* Qtr. plan
Inst. Accred.: ACICS (1974/2006)
Prog. Accred.: Allied Health (medical assisting (AMA))

Dover Campus
15 East Blackwell St., Dover 07801
Phone: (973) 366-6700

duCret School of the Arts
1030 Central Ave., Plainfield 07060-2898
Type: Private, independent
Degrees: C
URL: http://www.ducret.edu
Phone: (908) 757-7171 *Calendar:* Sem. plan
Inst. Accred.: ACCSCT (1979/2005)

Eastern School of Acupuncture and Traditional Medicine
215 Glenridge Ave., Montclair 07042
Type: Private, proprietary
Degrees: C
URL: http://www.easternschool.com
Phone: (973) 746-8717
Inst. Accred.: ACAOM (2003/2007)

ELS Language Centers
400 Alexander Park, Princeton 08540-6306
Type: Private, proprietary
Degrees: C
URL: http://www.els.edu
Phone: (609) 750-3510
Inst. Accred.: ACCET (1978/2004)

Boston Campus
400 The Fenway, Boston, MA 02115-5798
Phone: (617) 731-3600

Bristol Campus
One Old Ferry Rd., Roger Williams University, Bristol, RI 02809
Phone: (401) 254-5300

Charlotte Campus
2324 Wellesley Ave., Barnhardt Hall, Charlotte, NC 28207-2448
Phone: (704) 337-2364

Cleveland Campus
Case Western Reserve University, 10900 Euclid Ave., Stone Commons, Cleveland, OH 44106
Phone: (216) 368-2716

Culver City Campus
9000 Overland Ave., Culver City, CA 90230-3519
Phone: (310) 451-4544

DeLand Campus
145 East Michigan Ave., Campus Box 8416, DeLand, FL 32720-6306
Phone: (386) 736-6330

Denver Campus
7150 Montview Blvd., Foote Hall, Denver, CO 80220
Phone: (303) 256-9480

Garden City Campus
Adelphi University, South Ave., Linen Hall, Garden City, NY 11530
Phone: (516) 877-3910

Goleta Campus
Francisco Torres Student Center, 6850 El Colegio Rd., Goleta, CA 93117
Phone: (805) 685-7878

ELS Language Centers *(continued)*

Grand Rapids Campus
301 Michigan St. NE, 5th Flr., Rm. 546, Grand Rapids, MI 49503
Phone: (616) 331-5720

Hayward Campus
25555 Hesperian Blvd., Building 1800, Rm. 1814A, Hayward, CA 94545
Phone: (510) 723-6885

Houston Campus
4200 Montrose Blvd., Ste. 120, Houston, TX 77006
Phone: (713) 521-2030

Indianapolis Campus
Indiana University°Purdue University Indianapolis, 620 Union Dr., Rm. 242, Indianapolis, IN 46202
Phone: (317) 274-2371

Laramie Campus
406 South 21st St., Room 215, Laramie, WY 82071
Phone: (307) 766-3900

Louisville Campus
2001 Newburg Rd., Bonaventure Hall, Louisville, KY 40205
Phone: (502) 473-3357

Marietta Campus
1100 South Marietta Pkwy., Building D, Marietta, GA 30060-2896
Phone: (770) 528-4960

Melbourne Campus
Florida Institute of Technology, 150 West University Blvd., Melbourne, FL 32901
Phone: (321) 727-3990

Miami Shores Campus
11300 Northeast Second Ave., Miami Shores, FL 33161-6695
Phone: (305) 899-3390

Nashville Campus
1900 Belmont Blvd., Nashville, TN 37212
Phone: (615) 460-6011

New York Campus
75 Varick St., 2nd Flr., New York, NY 10013-1919
Phone: (212) 431-9330

Oklahoma City Campus
Oklahoma City University, 1915 NW 24th St., Harris Hall, Oklahoma City, OK 73106
Phone: (405) 525-3738

Orange Campus
Chapman University, 410 North Glassell St., Orange, CA 92866
Phone: (714) 538-6800

Philadelphia Campus
St. Joseph's University, 5414 Overbrook Ave., Philadelphia, PA 19131
Phone: (215) 473-4430

Portland Campus
1881 Southwest Naito Pkwy., Ste. 150, Portland, OR 97201
Phone: (971) 544-1655

River Forest Campus
7900 West Division St., River Forest, IL 60305-1499
Phone: (704) 488-5010

Riverdale Campus
College of Mount Saint Vincent-Seton Hall, 6301 Riverdale Ave., Riverdale, NY 10471
Phone: (718) 796-6325

Ruston Campus
PO Box 3006, Ruston, LA 71272
Phone: (318) 257-2012

St. Paul Campus
2115 Summit Ave., Mail CHC 203, St. Paul, MN 55105-1096
Phone: (651) 962-5990

St. Petersburg Campus
Eckerd College, 4200 54th Ave., South, St. Petersburg, FL 33711
Phone: (727) 864-7820

San Antonio Campus
4301 Broadway, CPO #498, San Antonio, TX 78209
Phone: (210) 283-5077

San Diego Campus
225 Broadway, Ste. 200, San Diego, CA 92101
Phone: (619) 233-5433

San Francisco Campus
1825 Sacramento St., 3rd Flr., San Francisco, CA 94109
Phone: (415) 561-0438

San Rafael Campus
50 Acacia Ave., San Rafael, CA 94901-8008
Phone: (415) 485-3224

Santa Clarita Campus
26455 Rockwell Canyon Rd., Santa Clarita, CA 91355
Phone: (661) 362-5554

Seattle Campus
718 12th Ave., Seattle, WA 98122
Phone: (206) 623-1481

Teaneck Campus
1000 River Rd., Robinson Hall, 4th Flr., Teaneck 07666
Phone: (201) 907-0004

West Haven Campus
300 Orange Ave., Bethel Hall, West Haven, CT 06516-1916
Phone: (203) 931-3000

White Plains Campus
99 Church St., White Plains, NY 10601
Phone: (914) 948-0635

Empire Beauty School—Bordentown
610 Route 206, Bordentown 08505
Type: Private, proprietary
Degrees: C
URL: http://www.empirebeauty.com
Phone: (609) 392-4545
Inst. Accred.: NACCAS (1990/2004)

Empire Beauty School—Cherry Hill
2100 State Hwy. 38, Cherry Hill Plaza, Cherry Hill 08002
Type: Private, proprietary
Degrees: C
URL: http://www.empirebeauty.com
Phone: (856) 667-8326
Inst. Accred.: NACCAS (1983/2001)

Empire Beauty School—Laurel Springs
1305 Blackwood-Clemton Rd., Laurel Springs 08021
Type: Private, proprietary
Degrees: C
URL: http://www.empirebeauty.com
Phone: (856) 425-8100
Inst. Accred.: NACCAS (1979/2004)

Engine City Technical Institute
901 Hadley Rd., South Plainfield 07080
Type: Private, proprietary
Degrees: C
URL: http://www.enginecitytech.com
Phone: (800) 305-3487
Inst. Accred.: ACCSCT (1984/2004)

European Academy of Cosmetology, Inc.
1126 Morris Ave., Union 07083
Type: Private, proprietary
System: Empire Education Group
Degrees: C
URL: http://www.natural-motion.com
Phone: (908) 686-4422
Inst. Accred.: NACCAS (1983/2003)

Everest Institute—South Plainfield
5000 Hadley Rd., Ste. 100, South Plainfield 07080
Type: Private, proprietary
System: Corinthian Colleges, Inc
Degrees: C
URL: http://www.everest.edu
Phone: (908) 222-9300 *Calendar:* Qtr. plan
Inst. Accred.: ACCSCT (2005)

G. Mitchell Hartman and Associates, Inc.
155 Route 46 West, Wayne Plaza II, Wayne 07470
Type: Private, proprietary
Degrees: C
URL: http://www.northernnj.dale-carnegie.com
Phone: (973) 890-0909
Inst. Accred.: ACCET (1977/2004)

Gentle Healing School of Massage
1274 South River Rd., Cranbury 08512
Type: Private, proprietary
Degrees: C
URL: http://www.gentlehealingschool.com
Phone: (609) 409-2700
Inst. Accred.: ACCSCT (2007)

Harris School of Business
1 Cherry Hill, 1 Mall Dr., Ste. 700, Cherry Hill 08002
Type: Private, proprietary
System: Premier Education Group
Degrees: C
URL: http://www.harrisschool.edu
Phone: (856) 662-5300
Inst. Accred.: ACICS (1978/2004)

Linwood Campus
1201 New Rd., Ste. 226, Linwood 08221
Phone: (609) 927-4310

Healing Hands Institute
41 Bergenline Ave., Westwood 07675
Type: Private, proprietary
Degrees: C
URL: http://www.healinghandsinstitute.com
Phone: (201) 722-0099
Inst. Accred.: CMTA (1999/2007, Probation)

Healthcare Training Institute
1969 Morris Ave., Union 07083
Type: Private, proprietary
Degrees: C
URL: http://www.healthcareti.com
Phone: (908) 851-7711
Inst. Accred.: ACCSCT (2003/2006)

Helma Institute of Massage Therapy
190 Midland Ave., Saddle Brook 07663
Type: Private, proprietary
Degrees: C
URL: http://www.helma.com
Phone: (201) 226-0056
Inst. Accred.: ACCSCT (2001/2006, Probation)
Prog. Accred.: Allied Health (massage therapy)

HoHoKus RETS—Nutley
103 Park Ave., Nutley 07110-3505
Type: Private, proprietary
System: Eastwick Colleges
Degrees: C
URL: http://www.hohokusrets.com
Phone: (973) 661-0600
Inst. Accred.: ACCSCT (1977/2002)

HoHoKus School of Business and Medical Sciences
10 South Franklin Turnpike, Ramsey 07446
Type: Private, proprietary
System: Eastwick Colleges
Degrees: C
URL: http://www.hohokus.com
Phone: (201) 327-8877
Inst. Accred.: ACICS (1976/2005)

HoHoKus School of Trade and Technical Sciences
634 Market St., Paterson 07513
Type: Private, proprietary
System: Eastwick Colleges
Degrees: C
URL: http://www.hohokustrades.com
Phone: (908) 486-9353
Inst. Accred.: ACCSCT (2005)

HoHoKus-Hackensack School of Business and Medical Science
66 Moore St., Hackensack 07601
Type: Private, proprietary
System: Eastwick Colleges
Degrees: C
URL: http://www.hohokushackensack.com
Phone: (201) 488-9400 *Calendar:* Qtr. plan
Inst. Accred.: ACICS (1976/2006)

The Institute for Health Education
7 Spielman Rd., Fairfield 07004
Type: Private, proprietary
Degrees: C
URL: http://www.instituteforhealtheducation.com
Phone: (973) 808-1110 *Calendar:* Qtr. plan
Inst. Accred.: ACCSCT (1997/2007)
Prog. Accred.: Dentistry (dental assisting)

Institute for Therapeutic Massage, Inc.
125 Wanaque Ave., Pompton Lakes 07442
Type: Private, proprietary
Degrees: C
URL: http://www.massageprogram.com
Phone: (973) 839-6131
Inst. Accred.: CMTA (1999/2006)

Atlantic Mind Body Center
Morristown Memorial Hospital, 95 Mt. Kemble Ave., Morristown 07962
Phone: (973) 839-613

Brown Mills Campus
Deborah Heart & Lung Center, 200 Trenton Rd., Brown Mills 08015
Phone: (732) 936-9111

Red Bank Campus
213 State Route 35, Red Bank 07701
Phone: (732) 936-9111

Institute of Logistical Management
PO Box 427, Burlington 08016-0427
Type: Private, proprietary
Degrees: C
URL: http://www.logisticseducation.edu
Phone: (609) 747-1515
Inst. Accred.: DETC (2001/2006)

Joe Kubert School of Cartoon and Graphic Art
37 Myrtle Ave., Dover 07801-4054
Type: Private, proprietary
Degrees: C
Phone: (973) 361-1327 *Calendar:* Sem. plan
Inst. Accred.: ACCSCT (1980/2005)

KeySkills Learning, Inc.
50 Mount Prospect Ave., Clifton 07013
Type: Private, proprietary
Degrees: C
URL: http://www.keyskillslearning.com
Phone: (973) 778-8136
Inst. Accred.: ACCSCT (2000/2005)

Maywood Campus
99 Essex St., Maywood 07607
Phone: (201) 587-0221

Lincoln Technical Institute
2299 Vauxhall Rd., Union 07083-5032
Type: Private, proprietary
System: Lincoln Educational Services Corporation
Degrees: C
URL: http://www.lincolntech.com
Phone: (908) 964-7800
Inst. Accred.: ACCSCT (1967/2004)

Mahwah Campus
70 McKee Dr., Mahwah 07430
Phone: (201) 529-1414

Lincoln Technical Institute—Edison
1697 Oak Tree Rd., Edison 08820-2896
Type: Private, proprietary
System: Lincoln Educational Services Corporation
Degrees: C
URL: http://www.lincolntech.com
Phone: (732) 548-8798
Inst. Accred.: ACICS (1975/2007)

Mount Laurel Campus
1000 Howard Blvd., Mount Laurel 08054-3414
Phone: (856) 722-9333

Northeast Philadelphia Campus
2180 Horing Rd., Building A, Philadelphia, PA 19116
Phone: (215) 969-0869

Paramus Campus
160 East Route 4, Paramus 07652
Phone: (201) 845-6868

Plymouth Meeting Campus
1 Plymouth Mtg., Ste. 300, Plymouth Meeting, PA 19462
Phone: (610) 941-0319

Mercer County Technical Schools Health Careers Center
1070 Klockner Rd., Trenton 08619
Type: Public, local
Degrees: C
URL: http://www.mcts.edu/health/index.htm
Phone: (609) 587-7640
Inst. Accred.: COE (2005)
Prog. Accred.: Allied Health (medical assisting (AMA)), Dentistry (dental assisting, dental hygiene)

Metro Auto Electronics Training Institute, Inc.
111 Market St., Kenilworth 07033
Type: Private, proprietary
Degrees: C
URL: http://www.metro-auto.com
Phone: (908) 245-5335
Inst. Accred.: ACCET (2002/2006)

Micro Tech Training Center
3000 Kennedy Blvd., 3rd Flr., Jersey City 07306
Type: Private, proprietary
Degrees: C
URL: http://www.microtechtrainingcenter.com
Phone: (201) 216-9901
Inst. Accred.: ACCSCT (1995/2005)

Belleville Campus
251 Washington Ave., Belleville 07109
Phone: (973) 751-9051

Monmouth County Vocational School
105 Neptune Blvd., Ste. 307, Neptune 07753
Type: Public, local
Degrees: C
URL: http://www.mcvsd.org
Phone: (732) 869-1181 *Calendar:* Sem. plan
Inst. Accred.: COE (2003)

Practical Nursing Campus
60 Neptune Blvd., 4th Flr., Neptune 07753
Phone: (732) 869-1181

Morris County School of Technology
400 East Main St., Denville 07834
Type: Public, local
Degrees: C
URL: http://www.mcvts.org
Phone: (973) 627-4600
Inst. Accred.: COE (2004)

National Massage Therapy Institute
108-L Greentree Rd. & Black Horse Pike, Turnersville 08012
Type: Private, proprietary
Degrees: C
Phone: (856) 227-8363
Inst. Accred.: CMTA (1999/2005)

National Massage Therapy Institute
Washington Square West, 6712 Washington Ave., Ste. 302, Egg Harbor 08234
Type: Private, proprietary
Degrees: C
Phone: (609) 227-8363
Inst. Accred.: CMTA (1999/2005)

National Tax Training School
PO Box 767, Mahwah 07430-0767
Type: Private, proprietary
Degrees: C
URL: http://nattax.com
Phone: (201) 684-0828
Inst. Accred.: DETC (1965/2003)

Natural Motion Institute of Hair Design
2800 Kennedy Blvd., Jersey City 07306
Type: Private, proprietary
System: Empire Education Group
Degrees: C
URL: http://www.natural-motion.com
Phone: (201) 659-0303
Inst. Accred.: NACCAS (1973/2006)

New Community Workforce Development Center
201 Bergen St., Newark 07103
Type: Private, independent
Degrees: C
URL: http://www.newcommunity.org
Phone: (973) 639-5604
Inst. Accred.: COE (2002/2007, Probation)

New Horizons Beauty School
5518 Bergenline Ave., West New York 07093
Type: Private, proprietary
Degrees: C
Phone: (201) 866-4000
Inst. Accred.: NACCAS (1983/2006)

North Jersey Community Coordinated Child Care Agency, Inc.
101 Oliver St., Paterson 07501
Type: Private, independent
Degrees: C
URL: http://www.nj4c.com
Phone: (973) 684-1904
Inst. Accred.: ACCET (2005)

Ocean County Vocational Technical School
1299 Old Freehold Rd., Toms River 08753-4201
Type: Public, state/local
Degrees: C
URL: http://www.ocvts.org
Phone: (732) 473-3159
Inst. Accred.: COE (2004)

Brick Campus
350 Chambers Ridge Rd., Brick 08723
Phone: (732) 920-0050

Jackson Campus
850 Toms River Rd., Jackson 08527
Phone: (732) 928-3830

Lakehurst Campus
Hanger One NAVAIR, Lakehurst 08733
Phone: (732) 657-4000

Southern Ocean Campus
423 Wells Mill Rd., Route 532, Waretown 08758
Phone: (609) 693-3434

Omega Institute
7050 Route 38 East, Pennsauken 08109
Type: Private, proprietary
Degrees: C
URL: http://www.omegacareers.com
Phone: (856) 663-4299
Inst. Accred.: ACICS (1982/2004)
Prog. Accred.: Allied Health (massage therapy)

P. B. Cosmetology Education Centre
110 Monmouth St., Gloucester 08030
Type: Private, proprietary
Degrees: C
URL: http://www.cosedcenter.com
Phone: (856) 456-4927
Inst. Accred.: NACCAS (1972/2003)

Parisian Beauty Academy
362 State St., Hackensack 07601
Type: Private, proprietary
Degrees: C
URL: http://www.parisianbeautyacademy.com
Phone: (201) 487-2203
Inst. Accred.: NACCAS (1965/2003)

PC AGE Career Institute—Newark
89 Market St., 3rd Flr., Newark 07102
Type: Private, proprietary
Degrees: C
URL: http://www.pcage.com
Phone: (973) 565-9800
Inst. Accred.: ACCET (2001/2005)

Edison Campus
3 Ethel Rd., Durham Center, Ste. 301, Edison 08817
Phone: (732) 287-3622

PC Tech Learning Center
895 Bergen Ave., Jersey City 07306
Type: Private, proprietary
Degrees: C
URL: http://www.pctech2000.com
Phone: (201) 761-0038
Inst. Accred.: ACCET (2003, Warning)

Pennco Tech
PO Box 1427, Blackwood 08012-9961
Type: Private, proprietary
Degrees: C
Phone: (856) 232-0310
Inst. Accred.: ACCSCT (1980/2003)

Performance Training Institute
1012 Cox Cro Rd., Toms River 08753
Type: Private, proprietary
Degrees: C
URL: http://www.ptitraining.com
Phone: (732) 505-9119
Inst. Accred.: ACCSCT (2001/2006)

Princeton Center for Teacher Education
487 Cherry Valley Rd., Princeton 08540
Type: Private, independent
Degrees: C
URL: http://www.pctemontessori.org
Phone: (609) 924-4594
Inst. Accred.: MACTE (1999/2006)

Prism Career Institute
Bayport One Bldg., 8025 Black Horse Pike, West Atlantic City 08232
Type: Private, proprietary
Degrees: C
URL: http://www.prismcareerinstitute.com
Phone: (215) 331-4600
Inst. Accred.: ACCET (1988/2006)

Philadelphia Campus
8040 Roosevelt Blvd., Philadelphia, PA 19152
Phone: (215) 331-4600

Reignbow Beauty Academy, Inc.
312 State St., Perth Amboy 08861
Type: Private, proprietary
Degrees: C
URL: http://www.reignbowbeautyacademy.com
Phone: (732) 442-6007
Inst. Accred.: NACCAS (1974/2005)

Reignbow Hair Fashion Institute
121 Watchung Ave., North Plainfield 07060
Type: Private, proprietary
Degrees: C
URL: http://www.reignbowbeautyacademy.com
Phone: (908) 754-4247
Inst. Accred.: NACCAS (1987/2005)

Rizzieri Aveda School for Beauty and Wellness
6001 West Lincoln Dr., Marlton 08053
Type: Private, proprietary
Degrees: C
URL: http://www.rizzieri.com
Phone: (856) 985-8600
Inst. Accred.: NACCAS (1972/2004)

Roman Academy of Beauty Culture
431 Lafayette Ave., Hawthorne 07506
Type: Private, proprietary
Degrees: C
URL: http://www.romanacademy.com
Phone: (973) 423-2223
Inst. Accred.: NACCAS (1976/2002)

Shore Beauty School
103 West Washington Ave., Pleasantville 08232
Type: Private, proprietary
Degrees: C
URL: http://www.shorebeautyschool.com
Phone: (609) 645-3635
Inst. Accred.: NACCAS (1983/2003)

Somerset County Technology Institute
PO Box 6350, Bridgewater 08807
Type: Public, state/local
Degrees: C
URL: http://www.scti.org
Phone: (908) 526-8900 *Calendar:* Sem. plan
Inst. Accred.: COE (2003)

Southern New Jersey Technical School
1833 Glassboro Rd. (Rt. 322), Williamstown 08094
Type: Private, proprietary
Degrees: C
URL: http://www.snjts.com
Phone: (856) 442-0006
Inst. Accred.: ABHES (2004)

Willingboro Campus
429 John F Kennedy Way, Willingboro 08046
Phone: (609) 877-8600

Star Technical Institute—Stratford
43 South White Horse Pike, Stratford 08084
Type: Private, proprietary
Degrees: C
URL: http://www.startechinstitute.com
Phone: (856) 435-7827
Inst. Accred.: ACCSCT (1985/2005)

Dover Campus
655 South Bay Rd., Ste. 562, Dover, DE 19901
Phone: (302) 736-6111

Lakewood Campus
1255 Hwy. 70, Ste. 12N, Lakewood 08701-5900
Phone: (732) 901-9710

StenoTech Career Institute
20 Just Rd., Fairfield 07004-3490
Type: Private, proprietary
Degrees: C
URL: http://www.stenotechcareerinst.com
Phone: (973) 882-4875
Inst. Accred.: ACICS (1996/2005)

Piscataway Campus
262-A Old New Brunswick Rd., Piscataway 08854-3756
Phone: (732) 562-1200

The Stuart School
2400 Belmar Blvd., Wall 07719
Type: Private, proprietary
Degrees: C
URL: http://www.stuartschool.com
Phone: (732) 681-7200 *Calendar:* Sem. plan
Inst. Accred.: ACICS (1967/2003)

MedTech College
6602 East 75th St., Heritage Park 1, Indianapolis, IN 46250
Phone: (317) 845-0100

Success Unlimited, Inc.
1301 East Route 70, Cherry Hill 08034-2101
Type: Private, proprietary
Degrees: C
URL: http://www.southjersey.dalecarenegie.com
Phone: (856) 428-4243
Inst. Accred.: ACCET (1977/2003)

Teterboro School of Aeronautics
80 Moonachie Ave., Teterboro Airport, Teterboro 07608-1083
Type: Private, proprietary
Degrees: C
URL: http://www.teterboroschool.com
Phone: (201) 288-6300
Inst. Accred.: ACCSCT (1973/2002)

Union County Vocational-Technical School
1776 Raritan Rd., Scotch Plains 07076
Type: Public, state/local
Degrees: C
URL: http://www.ucvts.tec.nj.us
Phone: (908) 889-8288
Inst. Accred.: COE (2003)

NEW MEXICO

Albuquerque Barber College
601 San Pedro Dr. NE, Ste. 100, Albuquerque 87108-1860
Type: Private, proprietary
Degrees: C
Phone: (505) 266-4900
Inst. Accred.: ACCSCT (1987/2005)

Business Skills Institute
1400 El Paseo Dr., Las Cruces 88001
Type: Private, proprietary
Degrees: C
URL: http://www.ibclubbock.com
Phone: (505) 526-5579
Inst. Accred.: ACICS (1987/2006)

El Paso Campus
8037 Lockheed Dr., El Paso, TX 79925-2400
Phone: (915) 845-7772

Crystal Mountain School of Massage Therapy
4775 Indian School Rd., NE, Ste. 102, Albuquerque 87110
Type: Private, proprietary
Degrees: C
URL: http://crystalmtnmassage.com
Phone: (505) 872-2030
Inst. Accred.: CMTA (2005)

DeWolff College of Hairstyling and Cosmetology
1500 Eubank Blvd. NE, Albuquerque 87112
Type: Private, proprietary
Degrees: C
URL: http://www/dewolffcollege.com
Phone: (505) 296-4100
Inst. Accred.: NACCAS (1972/2003)

International Schools
PO Box 1919, Sunland Park 88063
Type: Private, proprietary
Degrees: C
URL: http://www.internationalschools.com
Phone: (505) 589-1414
Inst. Accred.: ACCSCT (1990/2006)

Kaplan Career Institute—Albuquerque
5981 Jefferson NE, Ste. A, Albuquerque 87109
Type: Private, proprietary
Degrees: C
URL: http://www.getinfokaplancareerinstitute.com
Phone: (505) 345-6800
Inst. Accred.: ABHES (1996/2002)

Massage Therapy Training Institute
2701 West Picacho Ave., Ste. 4, Las Cruces 88007
Type: Private, proprietary
Degrees: C
URL: http://www.mtti.org
Phone: (505) 523-6811
Inst. Accred.: ABHES (2002/2005)

National Training Center
PO Box 18041, Kirtland AFB, Albuquerque 87185
Type: Public, federal
Degrees: C
URL: http://www.ntc.doe.gov
Phone: (505) 845-5170
Inst. Accred.: COE (2001)

New Mexico Aveda Institute de Bellas Artes
2614 Pennsylvania St., NE, Albuquerque 87110
Type: Private, proprietary
Degrees: C
URL: http://www.nmaveda.com
Phone: (505) 298-3357
Inst. Accred.: NACCAS (1998/2006)

Olympian University of Cosmetology
1810 East Tenth St., Alamogordo 88310
Type: Private, proprietary
Degrees: C
Phone: (505) 437-2221
Inst. Accred.: NACCAS (1976/2005)

Aladdin Beauty College #5
793 East Park Row Dr., Arlington, TX 76010-4408
Phone: (817) 460-7061

Aladdin Beauty College #7
1113 West Pipeline Rd., Ste. 133, Hurst, TX 76053-4759
Phone: (817) 282-1371

Aladdin Beauty College #11
1026 NW 38th St., Lawton, OK 73505-3704
Phone: (580) 355-6573

Aladdin Beauty College #15
8151 Camp Bowie West, Fort Worth, TX 76116-6314
Phone: (817) 244-5406

Aladdin Beauty College #20
1406 Gary Blvd., Clinton, OK 73601-3238
Phone: (580) 323-6279

Aladdin Beauty College #22
108 South Union Ave., Roswell 88203
Phone: (505) 623-6331

Aladdin Beauty College #26
3330 North Galloway Ave., Ste. 160, Mesquite, TX 75150
Phone: (972) 682-5333

Albuquerque Campus
800 Juan Tabo, NE, Suites I-J, Albuquerque 87123
Phone: (505) 765-1044

ITS Academy of Beauty #4
1541 J.B.S. Pkwy., Ste. 9, Odessa, TX 79761-1952
Phone: (432) 367-7500

ITS Academy of Beauty #17
1717 East Spring Creek Pkwy., Ste. 191, Plano, TX 75074-3081
Phone: (972) 881-0577

ITS Academy of Beauty #18
6600 Montana Ave., Ste. G, El Paso, TX 79925-2149
Phone: (915) 779-8000

ITS Academy of Beauty #21
1010 West University Dr., Denton, TX 76201-1848
Phone: (940) 382-6734

Las Cruces Campus
1460 Missouri Ave., Ste. 5, Las Cruces 88005
Phone: (505) 523-7181

Ron L. Straughan and Associates, Inc.
4108 Alcazar, NE, Ste. B, Albuquerque 87109
Type: Private, proprietary
Degrees: C
URL: http://www.newmexico.dalecarnegie.com
Phone: (505) 296-0408
Inst. Accred.: ACCET (2000/2005)

Universal Therapeutic Massage Institute
3410 Aztec Rd., NE, Albuquerque 87107
Type: Private, proprietary
Degrees: C
URL: http://www.utmi.com
Phone: (505) 888-0020
Inst. Accred.: ACCSCT (1999/2004)

NEW YORK

A.B.I. School of Barbering and Cosmetology
252 West 29th St., New York 10001-5271
Type: Private, proprietary
Degrees: C
URL: http://www.americanbarberinstitute.com
Phone: (212) 290-2289
Inst. Accred.: COE (1998/2005)

ACE Computer Training Center
109-19 72nd Rd., Ste. 4F, Forest Hills 11375
Type: Private, proprietary
Degrees: C
URL: http://www.aceedu.com
Phone: (718) 575-3223
Inst. Accred.: COE (2005)

Adirondack Beauty School
108 Dix Ave., Glens Falls 12801
Type: Private, proprietary
Degrees: C
Phone: (518) 745-1646
Inst. Accred.: NACCAS (1993/2004)

Allen School
163-18 Jamaica Ave., Jamaica 11432
Type: Private, independent
System: Allen School, Inc.
Degrees: C
URL: http://online.allenschool.edu
Phone: (718) 243-1700
Inst. Accred.: COE (2000/2005)

Brooklyn Campus
188 Montague St., Brooklyn 11201-3609
Phone: (718) 243-1700

The Alvin Ailey American Dance Center
405 West 55th St., New York 10019
Type: Private, independent
Degrees: C
URL: http://www.alvinailey.org/aileyschool.asp
Phone: (212) 405-9000
Inst. Accred.: NASD (1982/2005)

American Ballet Center/Joffrey Ballet School
434 Ave. of the Americas, New York 10011
Type: Private, independent
Degrees: C
URL: http://www.joffreyballetschool.com
Phone: (212) 254-8520
Inst. Accred.: NASD (1982/2002)

American Beauty School
1380 Metropolitan Ave., Bronx 10462
Type: Private, proprietary
Degrees: C
URL: http://www.americanbeautyschool.com
Phone: (718) 931-7400
Inst. Accred.: NACCAS (2004)

The American Musical and Dramatic Academy
2109 Broadway, New York 10023
Type: Private, independent
Degrees: C
URL: http://www.amda.edu
Phone: (212) 787-5300 *Calendar:* Sem. plan
Inst. Accred.: NAST (1984/2004)

Los Angeles Campus
6305 Yucca St., Los Angeles, CA 90028
Phone: (323) 469-3300

Andrew Terranova and Associates, Inc.
2350 North Forest Rd., Getzville 14068
Type: Private, proprietary
Degrees: C
URL: http://www.dalecarnegiewny.com
Phone: (716) 688-8100
Inst. Accred.: ACCET (2000/2005)

Apex Technical School
635 Ave. of the Americas, New York 10011-2030
Type: Private, proprietary
Degrees: C
URL: http://www.apextechnical.com
Phone: (212) 645-3300
Inst. Accred.: ACCSCT (1968/2005)

Associated Beth Rivkah Schools
310 Crown St., Brooklyn 11225
Type: Private, independent
Degrees: C
URL: http://www.bethrivkahschools.org
Phone: (718) 735-0400
Inst. Accred.: ACCET (1990/2006)

Austin's School of Spa Technology
527 Central Ave., Albany 12206
Type: Private, proprietary
Degrees: C
URL: http://www.austin.edu
Phone: (518) 438-7879
Inst. Accred.: NACCAS (1967/2003)

Beauty Salon School
426 Kings High Way, Brooklyn 11223
Type: Private, proprietary
Degrees: C
URL: http://www.beautysalonschool.com
Phone: (718) 998-9388
Inst. Accred.: NACCAS (2005)

Beauty School of Middletown, Inc.
225 Dolson Ave., Ste. 100, Middletown 10940
Type: Private, proprietary
Degrees: C
Phone: (914) 343-2171
Inst. Accred.: NACCAS (1974/2006)

Hyde Park Campus
Route 9, Hyde Park Mall, Hyde Park 12538
Phone: (914) 229-6541

Berk Trade and Business School
383 Pearl St., Brooklyn 11201
Type: Private, proprietary
Degrees: C
URL: http://www.berktradeschool.com
Phone: (718) 625-6037
Inst. Accred.: ACCSCT (1973/2004)

Brittany Beauty School—Levittown
2981 Hempstead Turnpike, Levittown 11756
Type: Private, proprietary
Degrees: C
URL: http://www.libsbeautyschool.com
Phone: (516) 731-8300
Inst. Accred.: NACCAS (1973/2006)

Bronx Campus
210 East 188th St., 2nd Flr., Bronx 10458
Phone: (718) 220-0400

Brooklyn Institute of Business Technology
9 Bond St., Third Flr., Brooklyn 11201
Type: Private, proprietary
Degrees: C
Phone: (718) 859-3900
Inst. Accred.: ACICS (1999/2006)

Buffalo Montessori Teacher Education Program
630 Youngs Rd., Unit D, Williamsville 14221
Type: Private, independent
Degrees: C
Phone: (716) 630-5955
Inst. Accred.: MACTE (1998/2004)

Business Informatics Center
134 South Central Ave., Valley Stream 11580-5431
Type: Private, proprietary
Degrees: C
Phone: (516) 561-0050
Inst. Accred.: ACCSCT (1988/2004)

Caliber Training Institute
500 Seventh Ave., 2nd & 3rd Flr.s, New York 10018
Type: Private, proprietary
Degrees: C
URL: http://www.caliberny.com
Phone: (212) 564-0500
Inst. Accred.: ACCSCT (1985/2005)

Capri Cosmetology Learning Center
251 West Route 59, Nanuet 10954
Type: Private, proprietary
Degrees: C
URL: http://www.caprinow.com
Phone: (845) 623-6339
Inst. Accred.: NACCAS (1976/2002)

Career and Educational Consultants
270 Flatbush Ave. Extension, Brooklyn 11201
Type: Private, proprietary
Degrees: C
Phone: (718) 858-8500
Inst. Accred.: ACCSCT (2000/2005)

Career Institute of Health and Technology
200 Garden City Plaza, Ste. 519, Garden City 11530
Type: Private, proprietary
Degrees: C
URL: http://www.careerinstitute.edu
Phone: (516) 877-1225
Inst. Accred.: ACICS (1992/2002)

Brooklyn Campus
340 Flatbush Ave. Extension, Brooklyn 11201
Phone: (718) 422-1212

Rego Park Campus
95-25 Queens Blvd., Ste. 600, Rego Park 11374
Phone: (718) 897-4868

Career Skills Institute
290 Madison Ave., Third Flr., New York 10017
Type: Private, proprietary
Degrees: C
URL: http://www.careerskills.com
Phone: (212) 725-7900
Inst. Accred.: ACCET (1985/2004)

The Center for Natural Wellness School of Massage Therapy
3 Cerone Commercial Dr., Albany 12205
Type: Private, proprietary
Degrees: C
URL: http://www.cnwsmt.com
Phone: (518) 489-4026
Inst. Accred.: ACCSCT (2004)

Charles Stuart School of Locksmithing
1420 Kings Hwy., Brooklyn 11229
Type: Private, proprietary
Degrees: C
URL: http://www.charlesstuartschool.com
Phone: (718) 339-2640
Inst. Accred.: ACCSCT (1993/2004)

New Jersey School of Locksmithing
392 Summit Ave., Jersey City, NJ 07306
Phone: (201) 963-9688

Cheryl Fell's School of Business
2541 Military Rd., Niagara Falls 14304
Type: Private, proprietary
Degrees: C
Phone: (716) 297-2750
Inst. Accred.: ACICS (1981/2002)

The Chubb Institute—New York City
498 Seventh Ave., 17th Flr., New York 10019
Type: Private, proprietary
System: High-Tech Institute
Degrees: C
URL: http://www.chubbinstitute.edu
Phone: (212) 659-2116 *Calendar:* Sem. plan
Inst. Accred.: ACCET (1999/2004)

The Chubb Institute—Westbury
1400 Old Country Rd., Westbury 11590
Type: Private, proprietary
System: High-Tech Institute
Degrees: C
URL: http://www.chubbinstitute.edu
Phone: (516) 997-1400 *Calendar:* Sem. plan
Inst. Accred.: ACCET (2001/2004)

Circle in the Square Theatre School
1633 Broadway, New York 10019
Type: Private, independent
Degrees: C
URL: http://www.circlesquare.org
Phone: (212) 307-0388
Inst. Accred.: NAST (1979/2004)

Commercial Driver Training
600 Patton Ave., West Babylon 11704-1421
Type: Private, proprietary
Degrees: C
URL: http://www.cdtschool.com
Phone: (845) 336-2300
Inst. Accred.: ACCSCT (1984/2002)

Continental School of Beauty Culture, Ltd.
633 Jefferson Rd., Rochester 14623
Type: Private, proprietary
Degrees: C
URL: http://www.continentalschbeauty.com
Phone: (716) 272-8060
Inst. Accred.: NACCAS (1973/2004)

Continental School of Beauty Culture—Batavia
215 Main St., Batavia 14020
Type: Private, proprietary
Degrees: C
URL: http://www.continentalschbeauty.com
Phone: (716) 344-0886
Inst. Accred.: NACCAS (1985/2005)

Olean Campus
515 North Union St., Olean 14760
Phone: (716) 372-5095

Continental School of Beauty Culture—Kenmore
326 Kenmore Ave., Buffalo 04223
Type: Private, proprietary
Degrees: C
URL: http://www.continentalschbeauty.com
Phone: (716) 833-5016
Inst. Accred.: NACCAS (1973/2004)

West Seneca Campus
1050 Union Rd., Southgate Plaza, West Seneca 14224
Phone: (716) 675-8205

Cope Institute
225 Broadway, 2nd Flr., New York 10007
Type: Private, independent
Degrees: C
Phone: (212) 809-5935 *Calendar:* Qtr. plan
Inst. Accred.: ACICS (1981/2004)

Culinary Academy of Long Island
125 Michael Dr., Syosset 11791
Type: Private, proprietary
Degrees: C
URL: http://www.culinaryacademyli.com
Phone: (516) 364-4344
Inst. Accred.: ACCSCT (1999/2004)

Culinary Academy of New York Management School
154 West 14th St., New York 10011-7307
Type: Private, proprietary
Degrees: C
URL: http://www.culinaryacademy.edu/ny
Phone: (212) 675-6655 *Calendar:* Sem. plan
Inst. Accred.: ACCSCT (1973/2006)

Dale Carnegie and Associates, Inc.
290 Motor Pkwy., Hauppauge 11788-5105
Type: Private, proprietary
Degrees: C
URL: http://www.longisland.dalecarnegie.com
Phone: (631) 415-9336
Inst. Accred.: ACCET (1975/2006)

New York City Campus
780 Third Ave., 22nd Flr., New York 10017
Phone: (212) 750-4455

San Francisco Campus
465 California St., Ste. 830, San Francisco, CA 94104
Phone: (415) 394-3253

Dance Theatre of Harlem, Inc.
466 West 152nd St., New York 10031
Type: Private, independent
Degrees: C
URL: http://www.dancetheatreofharlem.com
Phone: (212) 690-2800
Inst. Accred.: NASD (1982/2005)

David Hochstein Memorial Music School
50 North Plymouth Ave., Rochester 14614
Type: Private, independent
Degrees: C
URL: http://www.hochstein.org
Phone: (585) 454-4596 *Calendar:* Qtr. plan
Inst. Accred.: NASM (1976/2003)

EDP School of Computer Programming, Inc.
1601 Voorhies Ave., Brooklyn 11235
Type: Private, proprietary
Degrees: C
URL: http://www.edpschool.com
Phone: (718) 332-6469
Inst. Accred.: ACICS (2005)

FEGS Trades and Business School
80 Vandam St., New York 10013
Type: Private, Federation of Jewish Philanthropies of New York
Degrees: C
URL: http://www.fegs.org
Phone: (212) 366-8400
Inst. Accred.: ACCSCT (1986/2005)

Brooklyn Campus
199 Jay St., Brooklyn 11201
Phone: (718) 448-0120

Franklin Career Institute
91 North Franklin St., Ste. 300, Hempstead 11550-3003
Type: Private, proprietary
Degrees: C
URL: http://www.franklincareer.edu
Phone: (516) 481-4444
Inst. Accred.: COE (2000/2005)

Brooklyn Campus
5323 Fifth Ave., Brooklyn 11220
Phone: (718) 535-3333

French Culinary Institute
462 Broadway, New York 10013
Type: Private, proprietary
Degrees: C
URL: http://www.frenchculinary.com
Phone: (212) 219-8890
Inst. Accred.: ACCSCT (1985/2006)

Global Business Institute
1931 Mott Ave., Far Rockaway 11691
Type: Private, proprietary
Degrees: C
URL: http://www.gbi.org
Phone: (718) 327-2220
Inst. Accred.: ACICS (1984/2006)

New York City Campus
209 West 125th St., New York 10027
Phone: (212) 663-1500

Hair Design Institute at Fifth Avenue
6711 Fifth Ave., Brooklyn 11220
Type: Private, proprietary
Degrees: C
URL: http://www.hairdesigninstitute.com
Phone: (718) 745-1000
Inst. Accred.: NACCAS (1979/2004)

Harlem School of Technology
215 West 25th St., New York 10027
Type: Private, proprietary
Degrees: C
Phone: (212) 932-2849
Inst. Accred.: ACCSCT (1998/2003)

Holy Trinity Orthodox Seminary
PO Box 36, Jordanville 13361-1919
Type: Private, independent
Degrees: C *FTE Enroll:* 37
URL: http://www.hts.edu
Phone: (315) 858-0945 *Calendar:* Sem. plan
Inst. Accred.: NYBOR (1948/2002)

Hudson Valley School of Advanced Aesthetic Skin Care, Inc.
256 Main St., New Paltz 12561
Type: Private, proprietary
Degrees: C
URL: http://www.hvsaesthetics.com
Phone: (845) 255-0013
Inst. Accred.: NACCAS (2004)

Hudson Valley School of Massage Therapy, Inc.
72 Vineyard Ave., Highland 12528
Type: Public, proprietary
Degrees: C
URL: http://www.hvsmassagetherapy.com
Phone: (845) 691-2547
Inst. Accred.: NACCAS (2006)

Hunter Business School
3601 Hempstead Turnpike, Levittown 11756
Type: Private, proprietary
Degrees: C
URL: http://www.hunterbusinessschool.com
Phone: (516) 796-1000
Inst. Accred.: ACICS (1982/2002)

Medford Campus
3247 Route 112, Building #3, Medford 11763
Phone: (631) 736-7360

Institute of Allied Medical Professions
405 Park Ave., Ste. 501, New York 10022
Type: Private, proprietary
Degrees: C
URL: http://www.iamp.edu
Phone: (212) 758-1410
Inst. Accred.: ABHES (2006)
Prog. Accred.: Nuclear Medicine Technology

Westchester Medical Center Campus
95 Grasslands Rd., Elmwood Hall, 2nd Flr., Valhalla 10595
Phone: (914) 345-0900

Institute of Audio Research
64 University Place, New York 10003-4595
Type: Private, proprietary
Degrees: C
URL: http://www.audioschool.com
Phone: (212) 677-7590
Inst. Accred.: ACCSCT (1985/2006)

The Institute of Culinary Education
50 West 23rd St., New York 10010
Type: Private, proprietary
Degrees: C
URL: http://www.newyorkculinary.com
Phone: (212) 847-0711
Inst. Accred.: ACCSCT (2000/2005, Probation)

John Paul's Hair, Nails and Skin Care Institute
2144 Saratoga Ave., Saratoga Springs 12020
Type: Private, proprietary
Degrees: C
URL: http://johnpaulinstitute.saratoga.com
Phone: (518) 583-3700
Inst. Accred.: NACCAS (2006)

Kaplan Test Prep
888 Seventh Ave., 22nd Flr., New York 10106-0001
Type: Private, proprietary
Degrees: C
URL: http://www.kaplan.com
Phone: (212) 492-5800
Inst. Accred.: ACCET (1979/2007)

Akron Campus
59 E. Market St., 2nd Flr., Akron, OH 44308
Phone: (330) 384-9499

Albany Campus
Executive Park Dr., Stuyvesant Plaza, Albany 12203
Phone: http://www.kaptest.c

Albuquerque Campus
2501 San Pedro Dr. NE, Ste. 203, Albuquerque, NM 87110-4131
Phone: (505) 884-8880

Allentown Campus
1926 Catasauqua Rd., Allentown, PA 18103
Phone: (610) 231-2065

Amherst, MA Campus
150 Fearing St., Ste. 1, Amherst, MA 01002
Phone: (413) 549-5780

Amherst, NY Campus
520 Lee Entrance, UB Commons, Ste. 201, Amherst 14228
Phone: (716) 636-1882

Ann Arbor Campus
337 East Liberty St., Ann Arbor, MI 48104
Phone: (734) 662-3149

Arlington Campus
1100 North Glebe Rd., Ballston Plaza, 1st Flr., Arlington, VA 22201
Phone: (703) 552-5882

Athens Campus
225 North Lumpkin St., Athens, GA 30601-2801
Phone: (706) 353-3202

Atlanta Campus
3867 Roswell Rd., Ste. 200, Atlanta, GA 30342
Phone: (404) 365-9004

Austin Campus
811 West 24th St., University Towers, Austin, TX 78705-9965
Phone: (512) 472-8085

Baltimore Campus
733 West 40th St., Ste. 200, Baltimore, MD 21211
Phone: (410) 243-1456

Beachwood Campus
24700 Chagrin Blvd., Ste. 309, Beachwood, OH 44122-5360
Phone: (216) 831-2233

Berkeley Campus
150 Beckley Square, Berkeley, CA 94724
Phone: (510) 204-8980

Birmingham Campus
1900 28th Ave. South, Ste. 100, Birmingham, AL 35209-2604
Phone: (205) 879-1307

Blacksburg Campus
460 Turner St., Ste. 214, Blacksburg, VA 24060
Phone: (540) 552-8186

Bloomington Campus
421 East 3rd, Suites 6-7, Bloomington, IN 47401-3601
Phone: (812) 339-0084

Boca Raton Campus
2900 North Military Trail, Ste. 150, Boca Raton, FL 33431-6308
Phone: (561) 997-6388

Boston Campus
One Congress St., Boston, MA 02116-5198
Phone: (617) 722-4180

Boulder Campus
1310 College Ave., Hilltop Bldg., Upper Level, Ste. 400, Boulder, CO 80302-7324
Phone: (303) 444-1683

Brooklyn Campus
1602 Kings Hwy., 3rd Flr., Brooklyn 11229-1208
Phone: (718) 336-5300

Bryn Mawr Campus
950 Haverford Rd., Lower Level, Bryn Mawr, PA 19010-3820
Phone: (610) 526-9744

Cambridge Campus
727 Massachusetts Ave., Cambridge, MA 02139-3303
Phone: (617) 964-8378

Central Park Campus
131 West 56th St., New York 10019-3894
Phone: (212) 977-8200

Champaign Campus
405 East Green St., Champaign, IL 61820-5702
Phone: (217) 367-0011

Chapel Hill Campus
308 West Rosemary St., Ste. 103, Chapel Hill, NC 27514
Phone: (919) 960-4600

Charleston Campus
1650 Sam Rittenberg Blvd., Charleston, SC 29407-5768
Phone: (843) 571-6080

Charlotte Campus
1515 Mockingbird Ln., Ste. 203, Charlotte, NC 28209
Phone: (704) 522-7600

Charlottesville Campus
1928 Arlington Blvd., Ste. 200, Charlottesville, VA 22903-1561
Phone: (804) 979-3001

Chicago/North Clark Campus
2828 North Clark St., 4th Flr., Chicago, IL 60657
Phone: (773) 764-5151

Chicago/West Randolph Campus
205 West Randolph St., Ste. 200, Chicago, IL 60606-1814
Phone: (312) 606-8905

Cincinnati Campus
4600 Montgomery Rd., Ste. 100, Cincinnati, OH 45212
Phone: (513) 731-8378

College Park Campus
College Park Shopping Center, 7338 Baltimore Ave., College Park, MD 20740
Phone: (301) 779-8136

College Station Campus
707 Texas Ave., Ste. 106-E, College Station, TX 77840-1917
Phone: (409) 696-7737

Columbia, MO Campus
1103 East Broadway, Ste. 200, Columbia, MO 65201-4909
Phone: (573) 443-8378

Columbia, SC Campus
1717 Gervais St., Columbia, SC 29201
Phone: (803) 256-0673

Columbus Campus
1778 North High St., 2nd Flr., Columbus, OH 43201
Phone: (614) 294-7035

Coral Gables Campus
1320 South Dixie Hwy., Ste. 100, Coral Gables, FL 33146-2911
Phone: (305) 284-0090

Dallas Campus
10500 Steppington St., Ste. 150, Dallas, TX 75230
Phone: (214) 265-9805

Davie Campus
3501 South University Dr., Ste. 1, Davie, FL 33328-2023
Phone: (954) 370-2500

Davis Campus
132 E St., Davis, CA 95616-4515
Phone: (916) 753-4800

Dayton Campus
3077 Kettering Blvd., Ste. 319, Dayton, OH 45435-1922
Phone: (937) 293-1725

Decatur Campus
1248 Clairmont Rd., Ste. 4-B, Decatur, GA 30030
Phone: (404) 321-0801

Denver Campus
720 South Colorado Blvd., Ste. 140-A, Denver, CO 80246
Phone: (303) 757-5400

Des Moines Campus
Highline Community College, 2400 South 240th St., MS25-516, Des Moines, IA 98198
Phone: (206) 870-3740

Downers Grove Campus
3130 Finley Rd., Ste. 500, Downers Grove, IL 60515
Phone: (630) 271-4410

Kaplan Test Prep *(continued)*

Durham Campus
501 Washington St., South Park Office Center, Durham, NC 27701
Phone: (919) 956-7374

East Hanover Campus
188 Route 10 West, East Hanover, NJ 07936
Phone: (973) 884-3500

East Lansing Campus
333 Albert St., Ste. 214, East Lansing, MI 48823
Phone: (517) 332-2539

Encino Campus
17167 Ventura Blvd., Plaza De Oro, 2nd Level, Encino, CA 91316
Phone: (818) 382-2421

Eugene Campus
720 East 13th Ave., Ste. 303, Eugene, OR 97401
Phone: (541) 345-4420

Fayetteville Campus
7 Colt Square Dr., Ste. 4, Fayetteville, AR 72703-2842
Phone: (479) 521-8599

Flushing Campus
65-30 Kissena Blvd., Queens College Student Union, Flushing 11367-1575
Phone: (718) 575-2400

Ft. Worth Campus
1701 River Run Rd., Ste. 102, Ft. Worth, TX 76107
Phone: (817) 877-0024

Fresno Campus
1630 East Shaw Ave., Ste. 140, Fresno, CA 93710
Phone: (559) 225-4203

Gainesville Campus
409 SW 2nd Ave., Gainesville, FL 32601-6225
Phone: (352) 377-0014

Garden City Campus
400 Garden City Plaza, Ste. 110, Garden City 11530-3336
Phone: (516) 248-1134

Goleta Campus
6464 Hollister Ave., Ste. 7, Goleta, CA 93117-3113
Phone: (805) 685-5767

Greenville Campus
216 South Pleasantburg Dr., University Center of Greenville, Greenville, SC 29607
Phone: (864) 250-8832

Greenwich Village Campus
16 Cooper Square, New York, NY 10003-7110
Phone: (212) 590-2800

Highland Park Campus
1893 Sheridan Rd., Ste. 200, Highland Park, IL 60035-9906
Phone: (847) 433-7410

Honolulu Campus
1580 Makaloa St., Ste. 500, Honolulu, HI 96814
Phone: (808) 946-5600

Houston Campus
2500 Dunstan Rd., 5th Flr., Houston, TX 77005-2523
Phone: (713) 988-4700

Indianapolis Campus
9102 N. Meridian St., Ste. 440, Indianapolis, IN 46260
Phone: (317) 571-1009

Iowa City Campus
325 East Washington St., Ste. 208, Iowa City, IA 52240-3923
Phone: (319) 338-2588

Irvine Campus
2646 Dupont Dr., Ste. 50, Irvine, CA 92612-1688
Phone: (949) 756-2950

Irvine Valley College Campus
5500 Irvine Center Dr., Irvine, CA 92620
Phone: (949) 651-1163

Ithaca Campus
409 College Ave., 3rd Flr., Ithaca 14850
Phone: (607) 277-3307

Kalamazoo Campus
151 South Rose St., Ste. 106, Kalamazoo, MI 49007
Phone: (616) 342-8333

Kensington Campus
11301 Rockville Pike, 3rd Flr., Kensington, MD 20895-1021
Phone: (301) 770-2843

Knoxville Campus
100 Concord St., Cherokee Place, Knoxville, TN 37919-2329
Phone: (423) 971-5455

Las Vegas Campus
4632 S. Maryland Pkwy., Ste. 23, Las Vegas, NV 89119
Phone: (702) 798-5005

Lawrence Campus
1000 Massachusetts St., Lawrence, KS 66044
Phone: (785) 842-5442

Lexington Campus
1050 Chinoe Rd., Ste. 200, Lexington, KY 40502
Phone: (859) 269-1172

Lincoln Campus
1821 K St., Lincoln, NE 68508-1401
Phone: (314) 997-7791

Little Rock Campus
10220 West Markham, Ste. 220, Centre Mark Bldg., Little Rock, AR 72205-2185
Phone: (501) 224-1060

Los Angeles Campus
750 W 7th St., Garden Level, Ste. RG024, Los Angeles, CA 90017
Phone: (213) 896-1844

Louisville Campus
420 South Hurstbourne Pkwy., Ste. 204, Louisville, KY 40222
Phone: (502) 339-8021

Lubbock Campus
4620 50th St., Ste. 1, Lubbock, TX 79414-3508
Phone: (806) 795-0344

Madison Campus
315-B West Gorham St., Madison, WI 53703
Phone: (608) 255-0575

Marlton Campus
169 Route 73 S., Marlton Crossing, Marlton, NJ 08053
Phone: (856) 988-6306

Memphis Campus
4515 Popular Ave., Ste. 330, Memphis, TN 38117-7503
Phone: (901) 767-1861

Miami Campus
11900 Biscayne Blvd., First Flr., Miami, FL 33181
Phone: (305) 892-9019

Milwaukee Campus
316 North Milwaukee St., Ste. 210, Milwaukee, WI 53202-5803
Phone: (414) 277-9990

Montreal Campus
550 Sherbrooke Quest, Ste. 550, Montreal, QC, Canada H3A 1B9
Phone: (514) 287-1896

Nashville Campus
2404 West End Ave., Ste. 201, Nashville, TN 37203
Phone: (615) 321-5199

New Brunswick Campus
390 George St., 3rd Flr., New Brunswick, NJ 08901
Phone: (732) 628-0111

New Haven Campus
970 Chapel St., New Haven, CT 06510-1011
Phone: (203) 789-1169

Newton Centre Campus
792 Beacon St., Newton Centre, MA 02459-1963
Phone: (617) 332-8241

Norfolk Campus
861 Glenrock Rd., Circle East Bldg., Ste. 155, Norfolk, VA 23502-3701
Phone: (757) 466-1100

Norman Campus
408 West Main St., Norman, OK 73069-1327
Phone: (405) 321-7362

Oklahoma City Campus
777 NW Grand Blvd., Ste. 100, Oklahoma City, OK 73118-6103
Phone: (405) 848-3922

Omaha Campus
1020 South 74th Plaza, Omaha, NE 68114
Phone: (402) 393-8570

Orlando Campus
3403 Technological Ave., Ste. 13, Orlando, FL 32817-1478
Phone: (407) 273-7111

Oxford Campus
13-B East High St., Second Flr., Oxford, OH 45056
Phone: (513) 523-4429

Palo Alto Campus
299 California Ave., Ste. 210, Palo Alto, CA 94306
Phone: (650) 327-4040

Paramus Campus
10 Forest Ave., Paramus, NJ 07652
Phone: (201) 845-6652

Pasadena Campus
251 South Lake Ave., Ste. 130, Pasadena, CA 91101
Phone: (626) 584-9613

Philadelphia Campus
1528 Walnut St., First Flr., Philadelphia, PA 19102-3615
Phone: (215) 546-3317

Pittsburgh Campus
130 North Bellefield Ave., 3rd Flr., Pittsburgh, PA 15213
Phone: (412) 621-4620

Portland Campus
The Galleria, Rm. 402, 600 SW 10th St., Portland, OR 97205-2733
Phone: (503) 222-5556

Providence Campus
144 Wayland Ave., Providence, RI 02906
Phone: (401) 521-3926

Provo Campus
Brigham's Landing, 1774 North University Pkwy., Ste. 22, Provo, UT 84604
Phone: (801) 375-9955

Kaplan Test Prep *(continued)*

Reno Campus
1048 North Sierra, Unit A, Reno, NV 89503
Phone: (775) 329-1755

Richmond Campus
1601 Willow Lawn Dr., Ste. 109-C, The Shops at Willow Lawn, Richmond, VA 23230-3023
Phone: (804) 285-3414

Ridgeland Campus
731 South Pear Orchard Rd., Ste. 32, Ridgeland, MS 39157-4802
Phone: (601) 957-0084

Riverside Campus
3637 Canyon Crest Dr., Ste. J-115, Riverside, CA 92507
Phone: (909) 683-2221

Rochester Campus
1544 Mount Hope Ave., Rochester 14620-4240
Phone: (716) 461-9320

Rutherford Campus
223 Montrose Ave., Rutherford, NJ 07070
Phone: (201) 964-0997

Sacramento Campus
955 University Ave., Sacramento, CA 95825
Phone: (916) 929-4402

St. Paul Campus
2610 University Ave. West, St. Paul, MN 55114-1066
Phone: (651) 641-1200

St. Petersburg Campus
1700 66th St. North, Ste. 103, St. Petersburg, FL 33710
Phone: (727) 381-8378

Salt Lake City Campus
515 South 700 East, Ste. 3-J, Salt Lake City, UT 84102-2801
Phone: (801) 363-4446

San Antonio Campus
8401 Datapoint Dr., Ste. B-100, San Antonio, TX 78229-2974
Phone: (210) 614-2924

San Diego Campus
4350 Executive Dr., Ste. 305, San Diego, CA 92121
Phone: (858) 457-7595

San Francisco Campus
50 First St., Ste. 601, San Francisco, CA 94105-2405
Phone: (415) 905-9000

San Jose Campus
100 Park Center Plaza, Ste. 112, San Jose, CA 95113
Phone: (408) 275-0100

Santa Cruz Campus
740 Front St., Ste. 130, Santa Cruz, CA 95060
Phone: (831) 457-3900

Schaumburg Campus
1014 East Algonquin Rd., Ste. 114, Schaumburg, IL 60173
Phone: (847) 397-5630

Seattle Campus
4216 University Way, NE, Seattle, WA 98105
Phone: (206) 632-0634

Shawnee Mission Campus
5800 Foxridge Dr., Ste. 103, Shawnee Mission, KS 66202
Phone: (913) 262-8378

Shreveport Campus
106 East King's Hwy., Ste. 211, Shreveport, LA 71104
Phone: (318) 868-6400

South Bend Campus
1717 East South Bend Ave., South Bend, IN 46637-5639
Phone: (219) 272-4135

Stamford Campus
189 Bedford St., Stamford, CT 06901-1902
Phone: (203) 353-1466

State College, PA Campus
522 East College Ave., Ste. 201, State College, PA 16801-5585
Phone: (814) 238-1423

Staten Island Campus
2795 Richmond Ave., Pergament Shopping Center, Staten Island 10314-5857
Phone: (718) 477-6343

Syracuse Campus
720 University Ave., Ste. 206, Marshall Square Mall, Syracuse 13210-1791
Phone: (315) 472-3702

Tallahassee Campus
675 West Jefferson St., Tallahassee, FL 32304
Phone: (850) 224-3555

Tempe Campus
310 S. Mill Ave., Ste. A-103, Tempe, AZ 85281
Phone: (602) 967-2967

Temple Terrace Campus
5405 East Fowler Ave., Temple Terrace, FL 33617
Phone: (813) 899-2355

Toledo Campus
3450 West Central Ave., The Westgate Bldg., Ste. 102, Toledo, OH 43606-1403
Phone: (419) 536-3701

Toronto Campus
180 Bloor St. West, 4th Flr., Toronto, ON, Canada M5S 2V6
Phone: (416) 967-4733

Tulsa Campus
2865 East Skelly Dr., Ste. 228, Tulsa, OK 74105-6221
Phone: (918) 748-8065

Tucson Campus
845 East University, Ste. 175, Tucson, AZ 85719-5048
Phone: (502) 622-4256

Vancouver, BC Campus
1490 West Broadway Ave., 3rd Flr., Vancouver, BC, Canada V6H 1H5
Phone: (604) 734-8378

Vestal Campus
3951 Vestal Pkwy. East, Vestal 13850-2336
Phone: (607) 797-2302

Washington, DC Campus
2025 M St., NW, Kaplan Computer Lab Location, Washington, DC 20036
Phone: (202) 835-9745

West Hartford Campus
967-D Farmington Ave., West Hartford, CT 06107-2123
Phone: (860) 236-6851

Westwood Village Square Campus
1133 Westwood Blvd., Ste. 201, Westwood Village Square, Los Angeles, CA 90024
Phone: (310) 209-0554

White Plains Campus
220 East Post Rd., White Plains 10601-4903
Phone: (914) 948-7801

Wilmington Campus
4758-D Limestone Rd., Wilmington, DE 19808
Phone: (302) 992-0980

Winooski Campus
20 West Canal St., The Woolen Mill, Winooski, VT 05404-2131
Phone: (802) 655-3300

Winston-Salem Campus
100 Northgate Park Dr., Ste. 102, Winston-Salem, NC 27106-3226
Phone: (336) 759-9987

Worcester Campus
352 Belmont St., Route 9, Worcester, MA 01604
Phone: (508) 757-8378

Laban/Bartenieff Institute of Movement Studies, Inc.
520 8th Ave., Ste. 304, 3rd Flr., New York 10018-6507
Type: Private, independent
Degrees: C
URL: http://www.limsonline.org
Phone: (212) 477-4299
Inst. Accred.: NASD (1983/2004)

Learning Institute for Beauty Sciences—Astoria
38-15 Broadway, Astoria 11103
Type: Private, proprietary
Degrees: C
URL: http://www.libsbeautyschool.com
Phone: (718) 726-8383
Inst. Accred.: NACCAS (1986/2006)

Learning Institute for Beauty Sciences—New York
22 West 34th St., New York 10001
Type: Private, proprietary
Degrees: C
URL: http://www.libsbeautyschool.com
Phone: (212) 967-1717
Inst. Accred.: NACCAS (1981/2006)

Bensonhurst Campus
2384 86th St., Bensonhurst 11214
Phone: (718) 373-2400

Leon Studio One School of Hair Design
5221 Main St., Williamsville 14221
Type: Private, proprietary
Degrees: C
URL: http://www.leonstudioone.com
Phone: (716) 631-3878
Inst. Accred.: NACCAS (2001/2004)

Lia Schorr Institute of Cosmetic Skin Care
686 Lexington Ave., New York 10022
Type: Private, proprietary
Degrees: C
URL: http://www.liaschorrinstitute.com
Phone: (212) 486-9541
Inst. Accred.: NACCAS (2000/2003)

Limón Dance Institute
611 Broadway, Ste. 905, New York 10012
Type: Private, independent
Degrees: C
URL: http://www.limon.org
Phone: (212) 777-3353
Inst. Accred.: NASD (2003)

Lincoln Technical Institute—Queens
15-30 Petracca Place, Whitestone 11357
Type: Private, proprietary
Degrees: C
URL: http://www.lincolntech.com/queens_ny.htm
Phone: (718) 640-9800
Inst. Accred.: ACCSCT (2006)

Long Island Beauty School—Hauppauge
544 Route 111, Hauppauge 11788
Type: Private, proprietary
Degrees: C
URL: http://www.libsbeautyschool.com
Phone: (516) 724-0440
Inst. Accred.: NACCAS (1974/2005)

Long Island Beauty School—Hempstead
173 A Fulton Ave., Hempstead 11550
Type: Private, proprietary
Degrees: C
URL: http://www.libsbeautyschool.com
Phone: (516) 483-6259
Inst. Accred.: NACCAS (1975/2007)

Manhattan School of Computer Technology
42 Broadway, 22nd Flr., New York 10004-1638
Type: Private, proprietary
Degrees: C
URL: http://www.manhattanschool.com
Phone: (212) 349-9768
Inst. Accred.: ACICS (1996/2004)

MarJon School of Beauty Culture
1154 Niagara Falls Blvd., Tonawanda 14150
Type: Private, proprietary
Degrees: C
URL: http://www.marjonbeautyschool.com
Phone: (716) 836-6240
Inst. Accred.: NACCAS (1982/2007)

Martha Graham School of Contemporary Dance
316 East 63rd St., New York 10021
Type: Private, independent
Degrees: C
URL: http://www.marthagrahamdance.org/school.htm
Phone: (212) 838-5886
Inst. Accred.: NASD (1982/2002)

Merce Cunningham Studio
55 Bethune St., New York 10014
Type: Private, independent
Degrees: C *Enroll:* 34
URL: http://www.merce.org
Phone: (212) 691-9751
Inst. Accred.: NASD (1982/2006)

Merkaz Bnos Business School
2115 Benson Ave., Brooklyn 11214
Type: Private, proprietary
Degrees: C
URL: http://www.mbs-career.org
Phone: (718) 234-4000
Inst. Accred.: COE (2006)

Midway Paris Beauty School—Queens
54-40 Myrtle Ave., Ridgewood 11385
Type: Private, proprietary
Degrees: C
URL: http://www.naccas.org/midway-paris/index.htm
Phone: (718) 418-2790
Inst. Accred.: NACCAS (1975/2006)

Modern Welding School
1842 State St., Schenectady 12304
Type: Private, proprietary
Degrees: C
URL: http://www.modernwelding.com
Phone: (518) 374-1216
Inst. Accred.: ACCSCT (1984/2004)

Music Conservatory of Westchester
216 Central Ave., White Plains 10606
Type: Private, independent
Degrees: C
URL: http://www.musicconservatory.org
Phone: (914) 761-3900
Inst. Accred.: NASM (1977/2004)

The Nail Academy
162-04 Jamaica Ave., 5th Flr., Jamaica 11432
Type: Private, proprietary
Degrees: C
URL: http://beautytech.com/nailacademy
Phone: (718) 297-6330
Inst. Accred.: ACCSCT (2002, Probation)

National Tractor Trailer School
PO Box 208, Liverpool 13088-0208
Type: Private, proprietary
Degrees: C
URL: http://www.ntts.edu
Phone: (315) 451-2430
Inst. Accred.: ACCSCT (1984/2004)

Buffalo Campus
175 Katherine St., Buffalo 14210-2007
Phone: (716) 849-6887

Natural Gourmet Cookery School
48 West 21st St., 2nd Flr., New York 10010
Type: Private, proprietary
Degrees: C
URL: http://www.naturalgourmetschool.com
Phone: (212) 645-5170
Inst. Accred.: ACCET (2000/2003)

Neighborhood Playhouse School of Theatre
340 East 54th St., New York 10022-5017
Type: Private, independent
Degrees: C
URL: http://www.the-neiplay.org
Phone: (212) 688-3770
Inst. Accred.: NAST (1994/2000)

New Age Training
500 8th Ave., 5th Flr., New York 10018
Type: Private, proprietary
Degrees: C
URL: http://www.newagetraining.com
Phone: (212) 947-7940
Inst. Accred.: ACCET (2005)

New York Automotive and Diesel Institute
178-18 Liberty Ave., Jamaica 11433
Type: Private, proprietary
Degrees: C
URL: http://www.nyadi.com
Phone: (718) 361-1300
Inst. Accred.: ACCSCT (1999/2004)

New York Institute of English and Business
248 West 35th St., 2nd Flr., New York 10016
Type: Private, proprietary
Degrees: C
URL: http://www.nyieb.com
Phone: (212) 725-9400
Inst. Accred.: ACICS (1985/2005)

New York Institute of Massage
PO Box 645, 4701 Transit Rd., Buffalo 14231
Type: Private, proprietary
Degrees: C
URL: http://www.nyinstituteofmassage.com
Phone: (716) 633-0355
Inst. Accred.: ACCSCT (1999/2004)

New York Institute of Photography
211 East 43rd St., Ste. 2402, New York 10017
Type: Private, proprietary
Degrees: C
URL: http://www.nyip.com
Phone: (212) 867-8260
Inst. Accred.: DETC (2006)

New York International Beauty School, LTD
800 8th Ave., New York 10019-7410
Type: Private, proprietary
Degrees: C
URL: http://www.nyibs.baweb.com
Phone: (212) 868-7171
Inst. Accred.: NACCAS (1992/2003)

New York Paralegal School
299 Broadway, Ste. 200, New York 10007
Type: Private, proprietary
Degrees: C
URL: http://www.nyparalegal.com
Phone: (212) 349-8800
Inst. Accred.: ACICS (1994/2001)

New York School for Medical and Dental Assistants
33-10 Queens Blvd., Long Island City 11101-2327
Type: Private, proprietary
Degrees: C
URL: http://www.nysmda.com
Phone: (718) 793-2330
Inst. Accred.: ACCSCT (1973/2004)

Northern Westchester School of Hairdressing and Cosmetology
19 Bank St., Peekskill 10566
Type: Private, proprietary
Degrees: C
Phone: (914) 739-8400
Inst. Accred.: NACCAS (1985/2005)

Onondaga-Cortland-Madison BOCES
4500 Crown Rd., Liverpool 13090
Type: Public, local
Degrees: C
URL: http://www.ocmboces.org
Phone: (315) 433-2600 *Calendar:* Sem. plan
Inst. Accred.: COE (2005)

Center for New Careers
242 Port Watson St., Cortland 13045-2823

The Orlo School of Hair Design and Cosmetology
232 North Allen St., Albany 12206
Type: Private, proprietary
Degrees: C
URL: http://www.theorloschool.com
Phone: (518) 459-7832
Inst. Accred.: NACCAS (1988/2003)

Phillips Hairstyling Institute
709 East Genesee St., Syracuse 13210
Type: Private, proprietary
Degrees: C
URL: http://www.phillipshairinstitute.com
Phone: (315) 422-9656
Inst. Accred.: NACCAS (1974/2004)

R.L. Heron and Associates, Inc.
290 Elwood Davis Rd., Ste. 340, Liverpool 13088
Type: Private, proprietary
Degrees: C
URL: http://www.centralny.dalecarnegie.com
Phone: (315) 457-1300
Inst. Accred.: ACCET (1977/2002)

Ridley-Lowell Business and Technical Institute
116 Front St., Binghamton 13905
Type: Private, proprietary
Degrees: C
URL: http://www.ridley.edu
Phone: (607) 724-2941
Inst. Accred.: ACICS (1977/2004)
Prog. Accred.: Allied Health (medical assisting (AMA))

New London Campus
470 Bank St., New London, CT 06320
Phone: (860) 443-7441
Prog. Accred: Allied Health (medical assisting (AMA))

Poughkeepsie Campus
26 South Hamilton St., Poughkeepsie 12601
Phone: (914) 471-0330
Prog. Accred: Allied Health (medical assisting (AMA))

Russian and East European Partnerships, Inc.
PO Box 227, Fineview 13640
Type: Private, proprietary
Degrees: C
URL: http://www.usereep.com
Phone: (613) 545-3034
Inst. Accred.: ACCET (2002/2005)

SAE Institute of Technology
1293 Broadway, 9th Flr., Herald Square, New York 10001
Type: Private, proprietary
Degrees: C
URL: http://www.sae.edu
Phone: (212) 944-9121
Inst. Accred.: ACCSCT (2005)

Sanford-Brown Institute—White Plains
333 Westchester Ave., First Flr., White Plains 10604
Type: Private, proprietary
System: Career Education Corporation
Degrees: C
URL: http://www.sbiwhiteplains.com
Phone: (914) 874-2500
Inst. Accred.: ABHES (1985/2002)

Springfield Campus
365 Cadwell Dr., First Flr., Springfield, MA 01104-1739
Phone: (413) 739-4700
Prog. Accred: Medical Assisting (ABHES)

School for Film and Television at Three of Us Studio
39 West 19th St., 12th Flr., New York 10011
Type: Private, independent
Degrees: C *Enroll:* 214
URL: http://www.filmandtelevision.com
Phone: (212) 645-0030
Inst. Accred.: NAST (1995/2001)

School of Professional Horticulture at the New York Botanical Garden
Bronx River Pkwy. and Fordham Rd., Bronx 10458-5126
Type: Private, independent
Degrees: C
URL: http://www.nybg.org/edu/soph/overview.php
Phone: (718) 817-8797
Inst. Accred.: ACCET (2005)

Seminar L'Moros Bais Yaakov
4409 15th Ave., Brooklyn 11219
Type: Private, proprietary
Degrees: C
Phone: (718) 851-2900
Inst. Accred.: ACCET (1988/2003)

Sessions Online School of Design
350 Seventh Ave., Ste. 1203, New York 10001
Type: Private, proprietary
Degrees: C
URL: http://www.sessions.edu
Phone: (212) 239-3080
Inst. Accred.: DETC (2001/2006)

Shear Ego International School of Hair Design
525 Titus Ave., Rochester 14617
Type: Private, proprietary
Degrees: C
URL: http://shearego.com
Phone: (585) 342-0070
Inst. Accred.: NACCAS (1989/2004)

Sheffield School of Interior Design
211 East 43rd St., New York 10017
Type: Private, proprietary
Degrees: C
URL: http://www.sheffield.edu
Phone: (212) 661-7270
Inst. Accred.: DETC (2006)

Sotheby's Institute of Art
1334 York Ave., New York 10021
Type: Private, independent
Degrees: C
URL: http://search.sothebys.com/about/institute
Phone: (212) 894-1111
Inst. Accred.: NASAD (1989/2006)

Spanish-American Institute
215 West 43rd St., New York 10036-3913
Type: Private, proprietary
Degrees: C
URL: http://www.sai2000.org
Phone: (212) 840-7111
Inst. Accred.: ACICS (1986/2004)

Stella Adler Studio of Acting
31 West 27th St., Third Flr., New York 10001
Type: Private, independent
Degrees: C
URL: http://www.stellaadler.com
Phone: (212) 260-0525 *Calendar:* Sem. plan
Inst. Accred.: NAST (1994/2003)

Studio Art Centers International
809 United Nations Plaza, c/o Institute of International Education, New York 10017-3580
Type: Private, proprietary
Degrees: C
URL: http://www.saci-florence.org
Phone: (212) 984-5548
Inst. Accred.: NASAD (1996/2002)

Studio Jewelers, Ltd.
32 East 31st St., New York 10016
Type: Private, proprietary
Degrees: C
URL: http://www.studiojewelersltd.com
Phone: (212) 686-1944
Inst. Accred.: ACCSCT (1999/2004)

Suburban Technical School
175 Fulton Ave., Sixth Flr., Hempstead 11550-3771
Type: Private, proprietary
System: Premier Education Group
Degrees: C
URL: http://www.suburbantech.com
Phone: (516) 481-6660
Inst. Accred.: ACCSCT (1972/2004)

Training Solutions, Inc.
450 West 41st St., 6th Flr., New York 10036
Type: Private, proprietary
Degrees: C
URL: http://www.trainsol.com
Phone: (212) 947-3039
Inst. Accred.: ACICS (2000/2006)

U.S.A. Beauty School International, Inc.
87 Walker St., New York 10013
Type: Private, proprietary
Degrees: C
Phone: (212) 431-0505
Inst. Accred.: NACCAS (2002/2005)

West Side Montessori School Teacher Education Program
309 West 92nd St., New York 10025-7213
Type: Public, independent
Degrees: C
URL: http://www.wsmsnyc.org
Phone: (212) 662-8000
Inst. Accred.: MACTE (1996/2003)

Westchester School of Beauty Culture
6 Gramatan Ave., Mt. Vernon 10550
Type: Private, proprietary
Degrees: C
URL: http://www.westchesterschoolofbeauty.com
Phone: (914) 699-2344
Inst. Accred.: NACCAS (1974/2005)

Western Suffolk BOCES
152 Laurel Hill Rd., Northport 11764
Type: Public, local
Degrees: C
URL: http://www.wsboces.org
Phone: (631) 549-4900
Inst. Accred.: NACCAS (2002/2005)
Prog. Accred.: Allied Health (diagnostic medical sonography, surgical technology), Cosmetology, Practical Nursing

Willsey Institute
120 Stuyvesant Place, Staten Island 10301
Type: Private, proprietary
Degrees: C
URL: http://www.willsey.org
Phone: (718) 442-5706
Inst. Accred.: ACCET (1997/2004)

Word of Life Bible Institute
PO Box 129, Pottersville 12860-0129
Type: Private, nondenominational
Degrees: C
URL: http://www.wol.org
Phone: (518) 494-4723 *Calendar:* Qtr. plan
Inst. Accred.: TRACS (1997/2002)

NORTH CAROLINA

American Institute of Applied Science
100 Hunter Place, Youngsville 27596-9909
Type: Private, proprietary
Degrees: C
URL: http://www.aiasinc.com
Phone: (919) 554-2500
Inst. Accred.: DETC (1999/2004)

Anson College of Cosmetology
1217 East Carswell St., Wadesboro 28170
Type: Private, proprietary
Degrees: C
Phone: (704) 694-6677
Inst. Accred.: COE (1997/2003)

Asheboro Beauty School
736 South Fayetteville St., Asheboro 27203
Type: Private, proprietary
Degrees: C
URL: http://www.asheborobeautyschool.com
Phone: (336) 629-9639
Inst. Accred.: NACCAS (2006/2007)

Body Therapy Institute
300 Southwind Rd., Siler City 27344
Type: Private, proprietary
Degrees: C
URL: http://www.bti.edu
Phone: (919) 663-3111
Inst. Accred.: CMTA (1999/2005)

Brookstone College of Business
10125 Berkeley Place Dr., Charlotte 28262
Type: Private, proprietary
Degrees: C *FTE Enroll:* 118
URL: http://www.brookstone.edu
Phone: (704) 547-8600 *Calendar:* Qtr. plan
Inst. Accred.: ACICS (1987/2006)
Prog. Accred.: Allied Health (medical assisting (AMA))

Greensboro Campus
7815 National Service Rd., Greensboro 27409
Phone: (336) 668-2627

Carolina Academy of Cosmetic Art and Science
284 East Garrison Blvd., Gastonia 28054
Type: Private, proprietary
Degrees: C
URL: http://www.carolinaacademy.com
Phone: (704) 864-8723
Inst. Accred.: NACCAS (2003/2006)

Carolina Beauty College
2001 East Wendover Ave., Greensboro 27405
Type: Private, proprietary
Degrees: C
Phone: (336) 379-9404
Inst. Accred.: COE (1984/2004)

Charlotte Campus
1904-B North Tryon St., Charlotte 28213
Phone: (704) 597-5641

Durham Campus
5106 North Roxboro Rd., Durham 22704
Phone: (919) 477-4014

Winston-Salem Campus
7736-C Northpoint Blvd., Winston-Salem 27106
Phone: (910) 759-7969

Carolina School of Broadcasting
3435 Performance Rd., Charlotte 28214
Type: Private, proprietary
Degrees: C
URL: http://www.csbradiotv.com
Phone: (704) 395-9272
Inst. Accred.: ACCSCT (2006)

Center for Massage and Natural Health
530 Upper Flat Creek Rd., Weaverville 28787
Type: Private, proprietary
Degrees: C
URL: http://www.centerformassage.com
Phone: (828) 658-0814
Inst. Accred.: CMTA (2007)

Cheveux School Hair Design and Hairport, Inc.
4781 Gum Branch Rd., Ste. #1, Jacksonville 28540
Type: Private, proprietary
Degrees: C
Phone: (910) 455-5767
Inst. Accred.: NACCAS (1988/2003)

Cosmetic Arts Center
2703 High Point Rd., Ste. E, Greensboro 27403
Type: Private, proprietary
Degrees: C
Phone: (336) 855-8882
Inst. Accred.: NACCAS (2006/2007)

The Cosmetology Institute of Beauty Arts and Science
807 Silas Creek Pkwy., Winston Salem 27127
Type: Private, proprietary
Degrees: C
Phone: (336) 773-1472
Inst. Accred.: NACCAS (1991/2006)

Dudley Beauty College—Charlotte
1950 Bishop Madison Ln., Charlotte 28216
Type: Private, proprietary
Degrees: C
URL: http://dudleybeautycollege-charlotte.com
Phone: (704) 392-2565
Inst. Accred.: NACCAS (1998/2006)

Dudley Cosmetology University
900 East Mountain St., Kernersville 27284
Type: Private, proprietary
Degrees: C
URL: http://www.dudleyq.com/cosmetology.html
Phone: (336) 996-2030
Inst. Accred.: NACCAS (1992/2003)

Durham Beauty Academy
4600 Durham Chapel Hill Blvd., Durham 27707
Type: Private, proprietary
Degrees: C
Phone: (919) 493-9557
Inst. Accred.: NACCAS (2003/2006)

E. J. Taylor Corporation
4814 Fox Chase Rd., Greensboro 27410
Type: Private, proprietary
Degrees: C
URL: http://www.nc.dale-carnegie.com
Phone: (336) 292-6102
Inst. Accred.: ACCET (1978/2004)

Empire Beauty School—Matthew
11032 East Independence Blvd., Matthew 28105
Type: Private, proprietary
Degrees: C
URL: http://www.empirebeauty.com
Phone: (704) 845-8064
Inst. Accred.: NACCAS (1965/2002)

Concord Campus
10075 Weddington Rd. Extension, Concord 28027
Phone: (704) 979-3500

Fayetteville Beauty College
3442 Bragg Blvd., Fayetteville 28303
Type: Private, proprietary
Degrees: C
Phone: (910) 484-0227
Inst. Accred.: COE (1989/2006)

Hairstyling Institute of Charlotte
209-B South Kings Dr., Charlotte 28204-2621
Type: Private, proprietary
Degrees: C
URL: http://www.yp.bellsouth.com/sites/hairstyling
Phone: (704) 334-5511
Inst. Accred.: ACCSCT (1983/2004)

InovaTech School of Applied Technology
6408 Brookstone Ln., Ste. C, Fayetteville 28314
Type: Private, proprietary
Degrees: C
URL: http://www.inovatech.edu
Phone: (910) 764-1111
Inst. Accred.: ACCET (2005)

Jung Tao School of Classical Chinese Medicine
207 Dale Adams Rd., Sugar Grove 28679
Type: Private, proprietary
Degrees: C
URL: http://www.jungtao.edu
Phone: (828) 297-4181 *Calendar:* 12-mos. pr
Inst. Accred.: ACAOM (2006)

Leon's Beauty School
1410 West Lee St., Greensboro 27403
Type: Private, proprietary
Degrees: C
Phone: (336) 274-4601
Inst. Accred.: NACCAS (1966/2005)

The Medical Arts School
6541 Meridien Dr., Ste. 113, Raleigh 27612
Type: Private, proprietary
Degrees: C
URL: http://www.medicalartsschool.com
Phone: (919) 783-9290
Inst. Accred.: ACCET (1998/2001, Warning)

Mitchell's Hairstyling Academy—Goldsboro
1021 North Spence Ave., Goldsboro 27534
Type: Private, proprietary
Degrees: C
Phone: (919) 778-8200
Inst. Accred.: NACCAS (1976/2002)

Mitchell's Hairstyling Academy—Greenville
426 Arlington Blvd., Greenville 27858
Type: Private, proprietary
Degrees: C
Phone: (252) 756-3050
Inst. Accred.: NACCAS (1978/2004)

Mitchell's Hairstyling Academy—Wilson
2620 Forest Hills Rd., Ste. A, Wilson 27893
Type: Private, proprietary
Degrees: C
Phone: (252) 243-3158
Inst. Accred.: NACCAS (1973/2003)

Raleigh Campus
1301 Buck Jones Rd., Raleigh 27606
Phone: (919) 469-5807

Montgomery's Hair Styling Academy
222 Tallywood Shopping Center, Fayetteville 28303
Type: Private, proprietary
Degrees: C
Phone: (910) 485-6310
Inst. Accred.: NACCAS (1973/2004)

Mr. David's School of Hair Design
4348 Market St., N-17, Wilmington 28403-1411
Type: Private, proprietary
Degrees: C
Phone: (910) 763-4418
Inst. Accred.: COE (1989/2002)

North Carolina Center for Montessori Teacher Education
4817 Johnson Pond Rd., Apex 27502
Type: Private, independent
Degrees: C
Phone: (919) 779-6671
Inst. Accred.: MACTE (2000)

Franklin Montessori School
10500 Darnestown Rd., Rockville, MD 20850
Phone: (301) 279-2799

Oconaluftee Job Corps Center
502 Oconaluftee Job Corps Rd., Cherokee 28719
Type: Public, federal
Degrees: C
URL: http://oconaluftee.jobcorps.gov
Phone: (828) 497-5411
Inst. Accred.: COE (1984/2006)

Pinnacle Institute of Cosmetology, Inc
461 Plaza Dr., Ste. C, Moorseville 28115
Type: Private, proprietary
Degrees: C
URL: http://www.pinnacleinst.com
Phone: (704) 235-0185
Inst. Accred.: NACCAS (1988/2003)

Regina's College of Beauty
1201 Stafford St., Ste. B, Monroe 28110
Type: Private, proprietary
Degrees: C
URL: http://reginascollegeofbeauty.com
Phone: (704) 226-8830
Inst. Accred.: NACCAS (2006)

Schenck Civilian Conservation Center
98 Schenck Dr., Pisgah Forest 28768
Type: Public, federal
Degrees: C
URL: http://atlantaregion.jobcorps.gov/jcCenters/schenckJCC.html
Phone: (828) 862-6100
Inst. Accred.: COE (1985/2004)

Southeastern School of Neuromuscular and Massage Therapy, Inc.
4 Woodlawn Green, Ste. 200, Charlotte 28217
Type: Private, proprietary
Degrees: C
URL: http://www.se-massage.com
Phone: (704) 527-4979 *Calendar:* Tri. plan
Inst. Accred.: ACCSCT (2001/2006)

TechSkills, LLC
4944 Pkwy. Plaza Blvd., Ste. 310, Charlotte 28217
Type: Private, proprietary
Degrees: C
URL: http://www.techskills.com
Phone: (704) 357-0606
Inst. Accred.: ACCET (2006)

TechSkills, LLC.
4015 Meeting Way, Ste. 150, High Point 27409
Type: Private, proprietary
Degrees: C
URL: http://www.techskills.com
Phone: (336) 668-3000
Inst. Accred.: ACCET (2007)

TechSkills, LLC.
5400 Trinity Rd., Ste. 102, Raleigh 27607
Type: Private, proprietary
Degrees: C
URL: http://www.techskills.com
Phone: (919) 851-1700
Inst. Accred.: ACCET (2007)

Winston-Salem Barber School
1531 Silas Creek Pkwy., Winston-Salem 27127-3757
Type: Private, proprietary
Degrees: C
Phone: (336) 724-1459
Inst. Accred.: ACCSCT (1990/2005)

NORTH DAKOTA

The Headquarters Academy of Hair Design, Inc.
108 South Main St., Minot 58701
Type: Private, proprietary
Degrees: C
Phone: (701) 852-8329
Inst. Accred.: NACCAS (1985/2005)

Josef's School of Hair Design Inc—Fargo
627 NP Ave., Fargo
Type: Private, proprietary
Degrees: C
URL: http://www.josefsschoolofhairdesign.com
Phone: (701) 235-0011
Inst. Accred.: NACCAS (1967/2003)

Josef's School of Hair Design, Inc—Grand Forks
2011 South Washington St., Grand Forks 58201
Type: Private, proprietary
Degrees: C
URL: http://www.josefsschoolofhairdesign.com
Phone: (701) 772-2728
Inst. Accred.: NACCAS (1972/2003)

Moler Barber College of Hairstyling
16 South Eighth St., Fargo 58103-1805
Type: Private, proprietary
Degrees: C
Phone: (701) 232-6773
Inst. Accred.: ACCSCT (1992/2002)

R.D. Hairstyling College, Inc.
124 North Fourth St., Bismarck 58501
Type: Private, proprietary
Degrees: C
URL: http://www.rdhairstylingcollege.com
Phone: (701) 223-8804
Inst. Accred.: NACCAS (1975/2006)

The Salon Professionals Academy Fargo, Inc.
1435 University Dr. South, Fargo 58103
Type: Private, proprietary
Degrees: C
URL: http://www.spafargo.com
Phone: (701) 478-1772
Inst. Accred.: NACCAS (2005)

OHIO

Adult and Continuing Education—Cleveland Extension
4600 Detroit Ave., Room 169, Cleveland 44102
Type: Public, state/local
Degrees: C
URL: http://www.cmsdnet.net/schools/schoolbuildings/extensionhigh.htm
Phone: (216) 631-2885
Inst. Accred.: NCA-CASI (1994/2004)

Adult Center for Education
400 Richards Rd., Zanesville 43701
Type: Public, state/local
Degrees: C
URL: http://adultcentereducation.org
Phone: (740) 455-3111
Inst. Accred.: NCA-CASI (1974/2005)

Adult Community Education Full Service Center
1510 Clarendon Ave. NW, Room 4, Canton 44708
Type: Public, state/local
Degrees: C
URL: http://www.ccsdistrict.org/adult
Phone: (330) 438-2603 *Calendar:* Sem. plan
Inst. Accred.: NCA-CASI (1950/2004)
Prog. Accred.: Allied Health (medical assisting (AMA))

Adult Vocational Services
147 Park St., Akron 44308
Type: Public, state/local
Degrees: C
URL: http://www.akron.k12.oh.us/dept/776
Phone: (330) 761-1385
Inst. Accred.: NCA-CASI (1985/2004)

Akron Machining Institute Inc.
2959 Barber Rd., Barberton 44203-1005
Type: Private, proprietary
Degrees: C
URL: http://www.akronmach.com
Phone: (330) 745-1111
Inst. Accred.: ACCSCT (1986/2006)

Alliance City Schools Career Centre
200 Glamorgan St., Alliance 44601
Type: Public, state/local
Degrees: C
URL: http://www.aviators.stark.k12.oh.us
Phone: (330) 821-2102 *Calendar:* Sem. plan
Inst. Accred.: NCA-CASI (1912/2005)

American Institute of Alternative Medicine
6685 Doubletree Ave., Columbus 43229
Type: Private, proprietary
Degrees: C
URL: http://www.aiam.net
Phone: (614) 825-6278
Inst. Accred.: ACAOM (2007), ACCSCT (2000/2005)

American School of Technology
2100 Morse Rd., Building 4599, Columbus 43229-6665
Type: Private, proprietary
Degrees: C
URL: http://www.americanschooloftech.com
Phone: (614) 436-4820
Inst. Accred.: ACCSCT (1985/2003)
Prog. Accred.: Allied Health (medical assisting (AMA))

American Winds Flight Academy
1600 Triplett Blvd., Akron Fulton Airport, Akron 44306
Type: Private, proprietary
Degrees: C
URL: http://www.teachmetofly.com
Phone: (330) 733-2500
Inst. Accred.: ACCET (2007)

Apollo Career Center
3325 Shawnee Rd., Lima 45806-1497
Type: Public, state/local
Degrees: C
URL: http://www.apollocareercenter.com
Phone: (419) 998-2999
Inst. Accred.: NCA-CASI (1988/2004)
Prog. Accred.: Allied Health (medical assisting (AMA), surgical technology)

Ashland County-West Holmes Career Center
1783 State Route 60, Ashland 44805
Type: Public, state/local
Degrees: C
URL: http://www.acwhcc-jvs.k12.oh.us
Phone: (419) 289-3313
Inst. Accred.: NCA-CASI (1995/2005)
Prog. Accred.: Allied Health (medical assisting (AMA))

Ashtabula County Joint Vocational School
1565 State Route 167, Jefferson 44047
Type: Public, state/local
Degrees: C
URL: http://www.acjvs.org
Phone: (440) 576-6015 *Calendar:* Sem. plan
Inst. Accred.: NCA-CASI (1986/2005)

Auburn Career Center
8140 Auburn Rd., Concord Township 44077
Type: Public, state/local
Degrees: C
URL: http://www.auburncc.org/adult.asp
Phone: (440) 357-7542
Inst. Accred.: NCA-CASI (1990/2005)

Aveda Fredric's Institute
3654 Edwards Rd., Cincinnati 45208
Type: Private, proprietary
Degrees: C
URL: http://www.avedafredricsinstitute.com
Phone: (513) 533-0700
Inst. Accred.: NACCAS (2003/2007)

Beatrice Academy of Beauty
10500 Cedar Ave., Cleveland 44106
Type: Private, proprietary
Degrees: C
Phone: (216) 421-2313
Inst. Accred.: NACCAS (1980/2003)

Brighton College
85 South Main St., Ste. G, Hudson 44326
Type: Private, proprietary
Degrees: C
URL: http://www.brightoncollege.edu
Phone: (330) 342-5579
Inst. Accred.: DETC (1986/2006)

Brown Aveda Institute
8816 Mentor Ave., Mentor 44606
Type: Private, proprietary
Degrees: C
URL: http://brownaveda.com
Phone: (440) 255-9494
Inst. Accred.: NACCAS (2001/2004)

Rocky River Campus
19336 Detroit Rd., Ste. B102, Rocky River 44116
Phone: (440) 255-9494

Buckeye Career Center
545 University Dr. NE, New Philadelphia 44663-9439
Type: Public, state/local
Degrees: C
URL: http://web.bjvs.k12.oh.us
Phone: (330) 308-5720
Inst. Accred.: NCA-CASI (1988/2004)

Buckeye Hills Career Center
351 Buckeye Hills Rd., Rio Grande 45674
Type: Public, state/local
Degrees: C
URL: http://www.bhcc.k12.oh.us
Phone: (740) 245-5334
Inst. Accred.: NCA-CASI (1990/2005)
Prog. Accred.: Allied Health (surgical technology)

Butler Technology and Career Development Schools
3603 Hamilton-Middletown Rd., Fairfield Township 45011
Type: Public, state/local
Degrees: C
URL: http://www.butlertech.org/adult
Phone: (513) 868-6300
Inst. Accred.: NCA-CASI (1982/2005)

Career and Technology Centers of Licking County
222 Price Rd., Newark 43055
Type: Public, state/local
Degrees: C
URL: http://www.c-tec.edu/adults
Phone: (740) 366-3358
Inst. Accred.: NCA-CASI (1981/2004)

The Career Center Adult Technical Training
21740 State Route 676, Marietta 45750
Type: Public, state/local
Degrees: C
URL: http://www.mycareerschool.com
Phone: (740) 373-6283
Inst. Accred.: NCA-CASI (1988/2004)
Prog. Accred.: Allied Health (medical assisting (AMA))

Carnegie Institute of Integrative Medicine and Massotherapy
1292 Waterloo Rd., Suffield 44260
Type: Private, proprietary
Degrees: C
URL: http://www.cimassotherapy.org
Phone: (330) 630-1132
Inst. Accred.: ABHES (2002/2006)
Prog. Accred.: Medical Assisting (ABHES)

Carousel Beauty College—Dayton
125 East Second St., Dayton 45402
Type: Private, proprietary
Degrees: C
URL: http://carouselbeauty.com
Phone: (937) 224-1454
Inst. Accred.: NACCAS (1974/2005)

Kettering Campus
3120 Woodman Dr., Kettering 45420
Phone: (937) 298-5752

Springfield Campus
1475 Upper Valley Pike, Room 956, Springfield 45504
Phone: (937) 323-0277

Carousel Beauty College—Middletown
633 South Breiel Blvd., Middletown 45044
Type: Private, proprietary
Degrees: C
URL: http://carouselbeauty.com
Phone: (513) 422-2962
Inst. Accred.: NACCAS (1975/2005)

Carousel of Miami Valley Beauty College
7809 Waynetown Blvd., Huber Heights 45424
Type: Private, proprietary
Degrees: C
URL: http://carouselbeauty.com
Phone: (937) 233-8818
Inst. Accred.: NACCAS (1975/2005)

Casal Aveda Institute
6000 Mahoning Ave., Austintown 44512
Type: Private, proprietary
Degrees: C
URL: http://www.casalsspa.com
Phone: (330) 792-6504
Inst. Accred.: NACCAS (1988/2003)

Central School of Practical Nursing
4600 Carnegie Ave., Cleveland 44103-4371
Type: Private, independent
Degrees: C
URL: http://www.cspnohio.org
Phone: (216) 391-8434
Inst. Accred.: ABHES (2004)
Prog. Accred.: Practical Nursing

Choffin Career and Technical Center
200 East Wood St., Youngstown 44503
Type: Public, state/local
Degrees: C
URL: http://www.youngstown.k12.oh.us/choffin
Phone: (330) 744-8710 *Calendar:* Sem. plan
Inst. Accred.: NCA-CASI (1990/2005)
Prog. Accred.: Allied Health (surgical technology), Dentistry (dental assisting), Practical Nursing

Cincinnati School of Medical Massage
11250 Cornell Park Dr., Ste. 203, Cincinnati 45242
Type: Private, proprietary
Degrees: C
URL: http://www.massageschools.com
Phone: (513) 469-6300
Inst. Accred.: CMTA (2006)

Cleveland Institute of Dental-Medical Assistants, Inc.
2450 Prospect Ave., 2nd Flr., Cleveland 44115-2285
Type: Private, proprietary
Degrees: C
URL: http://www.cidma.com
Phone: (216) 241-2930
Inst. Accred.: ACCSCT (1979/2006)

Lyndhurst Campus
5564 Mayfield Rd., Lyndhurst 44124-2928
Phone: (440) 473-6273

Mentor Campus
5733 Hopkins Rd., Mentor 44060-2035
Phone: (440) 946-9530

Cleveland Institute of Medical Massage
7285 Old Oak Blvd., Middleburg Heights 44130-3375
Type: Private, proprietary
Degrees: C
URL: http://www.massageschools.com
Phone: (440) 243-8650
Inst. Accred.: CMTA (2006)

The Cleveland Music School Settlement
11125 Magnolia Dr., Cleveland 44106
Type: Private, independent
Degrees: C
URL: http://www.thecmss.org
Phone: (216) 421-5806 *Calendar:* Sem. plan
Inst. Accred.: NASM (2000)

Collins Career Center
11627 State Route 243, Chesapeake 45619
Type: Public, state/local
Degrees: C
URL: http://www.collins-cc.k12.oh.us
Phone: (740) 867-6641
Inst. Accred.: NCA-CASI (1982/2002)
Prog. Accred.: Allied Health (respiratory therapy, surgical technology), Phlebotomy

Columbiana County Career and Technical Center
9364 State Route 45, Lisbon 44432
Type: Public, state/local
Degrees: C
URL: http://www.columbianajvs.k12.oh.us
Phone: (330) 424-9561
Inst. Accred.: NCA-CASI (1982/2005)

Columbus Montessori Center/COMET
933 Hamlet St., Columbus 43201
Type: Private, independent
Degrees: C
Phone: (614) 291-8601
Inst. Accred.: MACTE (2000)

Columbus Montessori Teacher Education Program
979 South James Rd., Columbus 43227
Type: Private, independent
Degrees: C
URL: http://www.columbusmontessori.org
Phone: (614) 231-3790
Inst. Accred.: MACTE (1995/2001)

Creative Images—A Certified Matrix Design Academy
1076 Kauffman Ave., Fairborn 45324
Type: Private, proprietary
Degrees: C
Phone: (937) 878-9555
Inst. Accred.: NACCAS (1998/2006)

Dayton Campus
568 Miamisburg-Centerville Rd., Dayton 45459
Phone: (937) 433-1944

The Cut Beauty School, Inc.
1007 Ivanhoe Rd., Cleveland 44110
Type: Private, proprietary
Degrees: C
Phone: (216) 458-0448
Inst. Accred.: NACCAS (2007)

Cuyahoga Valley Career Center
8001 Brecksville Rd., Brecksville 44141
Type: Public, state/local
Degrees: C
URL: http://www.cvcc.k12.oh.us/cvccworks
Phone: (440) 526-5200
Inst. Accred.: NCA-CASI (1930/2005)

Dale Carnegie Training of Central Ohio Tyson Eppley, LLC
6029 Cleveland Ave., Columbus 43231
Type: Private, proprietary
Degrees: C
URL: http://www.columbus.dalecarnegie.com
Phone: (614) 523-1080
Inst. Accred.: ACCET (1977/2006)

Dale Carnegie Training of Greater Cincinnati
4243 Hunt Rd., Ste. 100, Cincinnati 45242-6657
Type: Private, proprietary
Degrees: C
URL: http://www.cincinnati.dalecarnegie.com
Phone: (513) 984-4448
Inst. Accred.: ACCET (1977/2003)

Dale Carnegie Training of Northwest Ohio and Northern Indiana
580 Carol Ln., Perrysburg 43551
Type: Private, proprietary
Degrees: C
URL: http://www.nwohio.dalecarnegie.com
Phone: (419) 872-9040
Inst. Accred.: ACCET (1996/2006)

Dayton Barber College
28 West Fifth St., Dayton 45402
Type: Private, proprietary
Degrees: C
URL: http://www.daytonbarbercollege.com
Phone: (937) 222-9101
Inst. Accred.: NACCAS (1994/2002)

Dayton School of Medical Massage
4457 Far Hills Ave., Dayton 45429
Type: Private, proprietary
Degrees: C
URL: http://www.massageschools.com
Phone: (937) 294-6994
Inst. Accred.: CMTA (2006)

Defense Institute of Security Assistance Management
2335 7th St., Wright-Patterson 45433-7803
Type: Public, federal
Degrees: C
URL: http://www.disam.dsca.mil
Phone: (937) 255-5850 *Calendar:* Qtr. plan
Inst. Accred.: COE (2001)

Delaware Area Career Center
4565 Columbus Pike, Delawar 43015
Type: Public, state/local
Degrees: C
URL: http://www.delawarejvs.org
Phone: (740) 548-0708
Inst. Accred.: NCA-CASI (1988/2005)

Eastern Hills Academy of Hair Design
7681 Beechmont Ave., Cincinnati 45255
Type: Private, proprietary
Degrees: C
Phone: (513) 231-8621
Inst. Accred.: NACCAS (1977/2003)

Eastland Career Center—Adult Workforce Development Center
4300 Amalgamated Place, Groveport 43125
Type: Public, state/local
Degrees: C
URL: http://www.eastland.k12.oh.us
Phone: (614) 836-454 *Calendar:* Qtr. plan
Inst. Accred.: NCA-CASI (1987/2004)

EHOVE Career Center
316 West Mason Rd., Milan 44846
Type: Public, state/local
Degrees: C
URL: http://www.ehove-jvs.k12.oh.us
Phone: (419) 499-4663 *Calendar:* Qtr. plan
Inst. Accred.: NCA-CASI (1990/2004)
Prog. Accred.: Allied Health (medical assisting (AMA), surgical technology)

Euclid Beauty College
22741 Shore Center Dr., Euclid 44123
Type: Private, proprietary
Degrees: C
Phone: (216) 261-2600
Inst. Accred.: NACCAS (2002/2005)

Everest Institute—Gahanna
825 Tech Center Dr., Gahanna 43230-6653
Type: Private, proprietary
System: Corinthian Colleges, Inc
Degrees: C
URL: http://www.everest.edu
Phone: (614) 322-3414
Inst. Accred.: ACCSCT (2004/2006)

Fairfield Career Center
4000 Columbus-Lancaster Rd., Carroll 43112
Type: Public, state/local
Degrees: C
URL: http://www.eastland.k12.oh.us
Phone: (614) 837-9443 *Calendar:* Qtr. plan
Inst. Accred.: NCA-CASI (1989/2004)
Prog. Accred.: Allied Health (medical assisting (AMA))

Fairview Academy
22610 Lorain Rd., Fairview Park 44126
Type: Private, proprietary
Degrees: C
Phone: (440) 734-5555
Inst. Accred.: NACCAS (1990/2003)

Four County Career Center
22900 State Route 34, Archbold 43502-9586
Type: Public, state/local
Degrees: C
URL: http://www.fourcounty.net
Phone: (419) 267-3331
Inst. Accred.: NCA-CASI (1975/2005)

Gerber Akron Beauty School
33 Shiawassee Ave., Fairlawn 44333
Type: Private, proprietary
Degrees: C
Phone: (330) 867-6200
Inst. Accred.: NACCAS (1965/2003)

Great Oaks Institute of Technology and Career Development—Diamond Oaks Campus
6375 Harrison Ave., Cincinnati 45247-7898
Type: Public, state/local
Degrees: C
URL: http://www.greatoaks.com
Phone: (513) 574-1300
Inst. Accred.: NCA-CASI (1981/2004)

Great Oaks Institute of Technology and Career Development—Laurel Oaks Campus
300 Oak Dr., Wilmington 45177
Type: Public, state/local
Degrees: C
URL: http://www.greatoaks.com
Phone: (937) 382-1411
Inst. Accred.: NCA-CASI (1981/2004)

Great Oaks Institute of Technology and Career Development—Live Oaks Campus
5956 Buckwheat Rd., Milford 45150
Type: Public, state/local
Degrees: C
URL: http://www.greatoaks.com
Phone: (513) 575-1900
Inst. Accred.: NCA-CASI (1981/2004)

Great Oaks Institute of Technology and Career Development—Scarlet Oaks Campus
3254 East Kemper Rd., Cincinnati 45241
Type: Public, state/local
Degrees: C
URL: http://www.greatoaks.com
Phone: (513) 771-8810
Inst. Accred.: NCA-CASI (1981/2004)
Prog. Accred.: Practical Nursing

Greene County Career Center
2960 West Enon Rd., Xenia 45385
Type: Public, state/local
Degrees: C
URL: http://www.greeneccc.com
Phone: (937) 372-6941
Inst. Accred.: NCA-CASI (1987/2005)

Hamrick School
1156 Medina Rd., Medina 44256-9615
Type: Private, proprietary
Degrees: C
URL: http://www.hamricktruck.com
Phone: (330) 239-2229
Inst. Accred.: ACCSCT (1987/2006)

HARDI Home Study Institute
1389 Dublin Rd., PO Box 16790, Columbus 43216
Type: Private, independent
Degrees: C
URL: http://www.hardinet.org
Phone: (614) 488-1835
Inst. Accred.: DETC (1969/2006)

Healing Arts Institute
340 Three Meadows Dr., Perrysburg 43551
Type: Private, proprietary
Degrees: C
URL: http://www.haiohio.com
Phone: (419) 874-4496
Inst. Accred.: ACCSCT (2003)

Hobart Institute of Welding Technology
400 Trade Square East, Troy 45373-9989
Type: Private, proprietary
Degrees: C
URL: http://www.welding.org
Phone: (937) 332-5610
Inst. Accred.: ACCSCT (1972/2004)

Inner State Beauty School
5150 Mayfield Rd., Lyndhurst 44124
Type: Private, proprietary
Degrees: C
URL: http://www.innerstatebeautyschool.com
Phone: (440) 442-4500
Inst. Accred.: NACCAS (1987/2004)

Institute of Medical and Dental Technology
375 Glensprings Dr., Cincinnati 45246
Type: Private, proprietary
Degrees: C
URL: http://www.imdtcareers.com
Phone: (513) 851-8500
Inst. Accred.: ABHES (1983/2006)

Eastgate Boulevard Campus
4452 Eastgate Blvd., Ste. 209, Cincinnati 45245
Phone: (513) 753-5030

International Academy of Hair Design
8419 Colerain Ave., Cincinnati 45239
Type: Private, proprietary
Degrees: C
URL: http://www.mybeautycareer.com
Phone: (513) 741-4777
Inst. Accred.: NACCAS (1986/2006)

Kaplan Career Institute—Cleveland
8720 Brookpark Rd., Brooklyn 44129
Type: Private, proprietary
System: Kaplan Higher Education Corporation
Degrees: C
URL: http://www.getinfokaplancareerinstitute.com
Phone: (216) 485-0900
Inst. Accred.: ACCSCT (1984/2004)

Knox County Career Center
306 Martinsburg Rd., Mount Vernon 43050
Type: Private, state/local
Degrees: C
URL: http://www.knoxcc.org
Phone: (740) 397-5820 *Calendar:* Sem. plan
Inst. Accred.: NCA-CASI (1986/2005)
Prog. Accred.: Allied Health (medical assisting (AMA))

Lance Tyson and Associates Dale Carnegie Training of Northeast Ohio
5350 Transportation Blvd., Ste. 14, Cleveland 44125
Type: Private, proprietary
Degrees: C
URL: http://www.cleveland.dalecarnegie.com
Phone: (216) 663-2500
Inst. Accred.: ACCET (1975/2004)

Lima School of Medical Massage
3325 Shawnee Rd., Lima 45806
Type: Private, proprietary
Degrees: C
URL: http://www.massageschools.com
Phone: (888) 860-4544
Inst. Accred.: CMTA (2006)

Lorain County Joint Vocational School Adult Career Center
15181 State Route 58, Oberlin 44074
Type: Public, state/local
Degrees: C
URL: http://adult.lcjvs.com/adult
Phone: (440) 774-1051
Inst. Accred.: NCA-CASI (1988/2005)
Prog. Accred.: Allied Health (medical assisting (AMA))

Madison Adult Education
600 Esley Ln., Mansfield 44905
Type: Public, state/local
Degrees: C
URL: http://www.madison-richland.k12.oh.us/adulted
Phone: (419) 589-6363
Inst. Accred.: NCA-CASI (1961/2005)

Mahoning County Career and Technical Center
7300 North Palmyra Rd., Canfield 44406
Type: Public, state/local
Degrees: C
URL: http://www.mahoningctc.com
Phone: (330) 729-4100
Inst. Accred.: NCA-CASI (1988/2004)
Prog. Accred.: Allied Health (medical assisting (AMA))

Medina County Career Center
1101 West Liberty St., Medina 44256-9969
Type: Public, state/local
Degrees: C
URL: http://www.mccc-jvsd.org
Phone: (330) 725-8461
Inst. Accred.: NCA-CASI (1978/2004)
Prog. Accred.: Allied Health (medical assisting (AMA))

Miami Valley Career Technology Center
6800 Hoke Rd., Clayton 45315
Type: Public, state/local
Degrees: C
URL: http://www.mvctc.com/home.htm
Phone: (937) 837-7781
Inst. Accred.: NCA-CASI (1976/2004)
Prog. Accred.: Allied Health (medical assisting (AMA))

Moler-Hollywood Beauty College
130 East 6th St., Cincinnati 45202
Type: Private, proprietary
Degrees: C
Phone: (513) 621-5262
Inst. Accred.: NACCAS (1975/2005)

Moler-Pickens Beauty College
5951-S Boymel Dr., Fairfield 45014
Type: Private, proprietary
Degrees: C
Phone: (513) 874-5116
Inst. Accred.: NACCAS (1985/2005)

Montessori Opportunities, Inc.
2381 Plymouth Ln., Cuyahoga Falls 44221-3642
Type: Private, independent
Degrees: C
Phone: (330) 929-5581
Inst. Accred.: MACTE (2002)

Montessori Teacher Education Institute of Bowling Green
630 South Maple St., Bowling Green 43402
Type: Private, independent
Degrees: C
URL: http://www.wcnet.org/~montesso/tibg
Phone: (419) 352-4203
Inst. Accred.: MACTE (2000)

Moore Université of Hair Design, Inc.
7030 Reading Rd., Ste. 640, Cincinnati 45237
Type: Private, proprietary
Degrees: C
URL: http://www.mooreuniversiteofhairdesign.com
Phone: (513) 531-3100
Inst. Accred.: NACCAS (1971/2002)

National Beauty College—Canton
4642 Cleveland Ave., NW, Canton 44709
Type: Private, proprietary
Degrees: C
Phone: (330) 499-9444
Inst. Accred.: NACCAS (1965/2002)

National Institute of Massotherapy, Inc.
2110 Copley Rd., Akron 44320
Type: Private, proprietary
Degrees: C
URL: http://www.naturalhealers.com
Phone: (330) 867-1996
Inst. Accred.: ACCET (1999/2006)

National Institute of Technology—Cuyahoga Falls
2545 Bailey Rd., First Flr., Cuyahoga Falls 44221-2949
Type: Private, proprietary
Degrees: C
URL: http://www.nationalinstituteoftechnology.org
Phone: (330) 923-9959 *Calendar:* Qtr. plan
Inst. Accred.: ACCSCT (1969/2003)

Nationwide Beauty Academy
5300 WestPointe Plaza Dr., Columbus 43228
Type: Private, proprietary
System: Salon Schools Group
Degrees: C
URL: http://www.salonschools.com
Phone: (614) 921-9101
Inst. Accred.: NACCAS (1968/2004)

North Education Center
100 Arcadia Ave., Columbus 43202
Type: Public, state/local
Degrees: C
URL: http://www.cpsadulted.org
Phone: (614) 365-6000
Inst. Accred.: NCA-CASI (1983/2004)

Northcoast Medical Training Academy
1832 State Route 59, Kent 44240
Type: Private, proprietary
Degrees: C
URL: http://www.northcoastmedicalacademy.com
Phone: (330) 678-6600 *Calendar:* Qtr. plan
Inst. Accred.: ACCSCT (2006)

Northern Institute of Cosmetology
667-669 Broadway, Lorain 44052
Type: Private, proprietary
Degrees: C
Phone: (440) 244-4282
Inst. Accred.: NACCAS (1967/2003)

Ohio Academy of Holistic Health, Inc.
2380 Bellbrook Ave., Xenia 45385
Type: Private, proprietary
Degrees: C
URL: http://www.oahh.com
Phone: (937) 708-3232
Inst. Accred.: ACCET (2001/2005, Warning)

The Ohio Academy—Paul Mitchell Partner School
434 Market St., Steubenville 43952
Type: Private, proprietary
Degrees: C
URL: http://www.theohioacademy.com
Phone: (740) 282-3312
Inst. Accred.: NACCAS (1978/2004)

Ohio Center for Broadcasting
6703 Madison Rd., Cincinnati 45227
Type: Private, proprietary
Degrees: C
URL: http://www.beonair.com
Phone: (513) 271-6060
Inst. Accred.: ACCSCT (1992/2003)

Ohio Center for Broadcasting
9000 Sweet Valley Dr., Valley View 44125
Type: Private, proprietary
Degrees: C
URL: http://www.beonair.com
Phone: (216) 447-9117
Inst. Accred.: ACCSCT (1991/2006)

Ohio Hi Point Career Center
2280 State Route 540, Bellefontaine 43311
Type: Public, state/local
Degrees: C
URL: www.ohp.k12.oh.us
Phone: (937) 599-6275
Inst. Accred.: NCA-CASI (1984/2004)

Ohio State Beauty Academy
57 Town Square, Lima 45801
Type: Private, proprietary
Degrees: C
URL: http://www.ohiostatebeauty.com
Phone: (419) 229-7896
Inst. Accred.: NACCAS (1969/2005)

Ohio State College of Barber Styling
4614 East Broad St., Columbus 43213
Type: Private, proprietary
Degrees: C
Phone: (614) 868-1015
Inst. Accred.: ACCSCT (1977/2004)

Ohio State School of Cosmetology—Columbus
3717 South High St., Columbus 43207
Type: Private, proprietary
System: Salon Schools Group
Degrees: C
URL: http://www.salonschools.com
Phone: (614) 491-0492
Inst. Accred.: NACCAS (1982/2002)

Ohio State School of Cosmetology—East
6320 East Livingston Ave., Reynoldsburg 43068
Type: Private, proprietary
System: Salon Schools Group
Degrees: C
URL: http://www.salonschools.com
Phone: (614) 868-1601
Inst. Accred.: NACCAS (1976/2002)

Ohio State School of Cosmetology—Northland
4390 Karl Rd., Columbus 43224
Type: Private, proprietary
System: Salon Schools Group
Degrees: C
URL: http://www.salonschools.com
Phone: (614) 263-1861
Inst. Accred.: NACCAS (1973/2004)

Ohio State School of Cosmetology—Westerville
5970 Westerville Rd., Westerville 43081
Type: Private, proprietary
System: Salon Schools Group
Degrees: C
URL: http://www.salonschools.com
Phone: (614) 890-3535
Inst. Accred.: NACCAS (1983/2003)

Ohio Technical College
1374 East 51st St., Cleveland 44103-1269
Type: Private, proprietary
Degrees: C
Phone: (216) 881-1700
Inst. Accred.: ACCSCT (1973/2004)

Oregon Career and Technology Center
5721 Seaman Rd., Oregon 43616
Type: Public, state/local
Degrees: C
URL: http://www.oregon.k12.oh.us/pages/adulted.html
Phone: (419) 697-3450
Inst. Accred.: NCA-CASI (1931/2006)

Paramount Beauty Academy
1745 11th St., Portsmouth 45662
Type: Private, proprietary
Degrees: C
URL: http://www.paramountbeautyacademy.com
Phone: (740) 353-2436
Inst. Accred.: NACCAS (1993/2006)

Penta Career Center
30095 Oregon Rd., Perrysburg 43551
Type: Public, state/local
Degrees: C
URL: http://www.pentacareercenter.org
Phone: (419) 661-6555
Inst. Accred.: NCA-CASI (1973/2005)

Pickaway-Ross Career and Technology Center
895 Crouse Chapel Rd., Chillicothe 45601
Type: Public, state/local
Degrees: C
URL: http://www.pickawayross.com
Phone: (740) 642-1200
Inst. Accred.: NCA-CASI (1988/2003)
Prog. Accred.: Allied Health (medical assisting (AMA))

Pioneer Career and Technical Center
27 Ryan Rd., Shelby 44875
Type: Public, state/local
Degrees: C
URL: http://www.pctc.k12.oh.us
Phone: (419) 347-7744
Inst. Accred.: NCA-CASI (1981/2004)

Polaris Career Center
7285 Old Oak Blvd., Middleburg Heights 44130
Type: Public, state/local
Degrees: C
URL: http://www.polaris.edu
Phone: (440) 891-7750
Inst. Accred.: NCA-CASI (1985/2005)
Prog. Accred.: Allied Health (medical assisting (AMA)), Dentistry (dental assisting)

Portage Lakes Career Center
4401 Shriver Rd., Green 44232
Type: Public, state/local
Degrees: C
URL: http://www.plcc.k12.oh.us
Phone: (330) 896-8200
Inst. Accred.: NCA-CASI (1988/2004)
Prog. Accred.: Allied Health (medical assisting (AMA))

Quest Career College
6248 Pearl Rd., Parma Heights 44130
Type: Private, proprietary
Degrees: C
URL: http://www.computerquest.com
Phone: (440) 886-5544
Inst. Accred.: ACCET (2001/2004)

Raphael's Salem Beauty Academy
2445 West State St., Alliance 44601
Type: Private, proprietary
Degrees: C
Phone: (330) 823-3884
Inst. Accred.: NACCAS (1988/2003)

Raphael's School of Beauty Culture
1324 Youngstown Warren Rd., Niles 44446
Type: Private, proprietary
Degrees: C
Phone: (330) 652-1559
Inst. Accred.: NACCAS (1978/2004)

Raphael's School of Beauty Culture
5311 Market St., Boardman 44512
Type: Private, proprietary
Degrees: C
Phone: (330) 782-3395
Inst. Accred.: NACCAS (1991/2006)

Raphael's School of Beauty Culture, Inc.
3307 Center Rd., Brunswick 44212
Type: Private, proprietary
Degrees: C
Phone: (330) 225-0195
Inst. Accred.: NACCAS (1985/2005)

Sandusky High School Adult Education
2130 Hayes Ave., sandusky 44870
Type: Public, state/local
Degrees: C
URL: http://webserver.sandusky.k12.mi.us
Phone: (419) 621-2743
Inst. Accred.: NCA-CASI (1994/2005)

Scioto County Joint Vocational School
951 Vern Riffe Dr., Lucasville 45648
Type: Public, state/local
Degrees: C
URL: http://www.scjvs.com
Phone: (740) 259-5526
Inst. Accred.: NCA-CASI (1986/2004)
Prog. Accred.: Allied Health (surgical technology)

The Spa School
5050 North High St., Columbus 43214
Type: Private, proprietary
System: Salon Schools Group
Degrees: C
URL: http://www.salonschools.com
Phone: (614) 888-0725
Inst. Accred.: NACCAS (1965/2003)

Springfield-Clark County Joint Vocational School
1901 Selma Rd., Springfield 45505
Type: Public, state/local
Degrees: C
URL: http://sccjvs.org
Phone: (937) 325-7368 *Calendar:* Sem. plan
Inst. Accred.: NCA-CASI (1973/2005)

TDDS Technical Institute
1688 North Princetown Rd., Lake Milton 44429
Type: Private, proprietary
Degrees: C
URL: http://www.tdds.edu
Phone: (330) 538-2216
Inst. Accred.: ACCSCT (1987/2003)

TechSkills—Columbus
2400 Corporate Exchange Dr., Ste. 2400, Columbus 43231
Type: Private, proprietary
Degrees: C
URL: http://www.techskills.com
Phone: (614) 891-3200
Inst. Accred.: ACCET (2006)

TechSkills—Cincinnati
4460 Carver Woods Dr., Ste. 100, Cincinnati 45242
Type: Private, proprietary
Degrees: C
URL: http://www.techskills.com
Phone: (513) 489-2600
Inst. Accred.: ACCET (2006)

TechSkills—Independence
6500 Rockside Rd., Ste. 130, Independence 44131
Type: Private, proprietary
Degrees: C
URL: http://www.techskills.com
Phone: (216) 446-1010
Inst. Accred.: ACCET (2006)

Tiffin Academy of Hair Design
104 East Market St., Tiffin 44883
Type: Private, proprietary
Degrees: C
URL: http://tiffinacademy.com
Phone: (419) 447-3117
Inst. Accred.: NACCAS (1966/2003)

Toledo Academy of Beauty Culture—North
5020 Lewis Ave., Toledo 43612
Type: Private, proprietary
Degrees: C
Phone: (419) 478-5325
Inst. Accred.: NACCAS (1985/2005)

Northwood Campus
2592 Woodville Rd., Northwood 43619
Phone: (419) 693-7257

Toledo Academy of Beauty Culture—South
1554 South Byrne Rd., Glenbyrne Center, Toledo 43614
Type: Private, proprietary
Degrees: C
Phone: (419) 381-7218
Inst. Accred.: NACCAS (1987/2002)

Toledo Public Schools Adult Education Center
3301 Upton Ave., Ellis Center, Toledo 43613
Type: Public, state/local
Degrees: C
URL: http://www.tps.org
Phone: (419) 671-8700
Inst. Accred.: NCA-CASI (1994/2004)

Tri County Beauty College
155 Northland Blvd., Cincinnati 45246
Type: Private, proprietary
Degrees: C
Phone: (513) 671-8340
Inst. Accred.: NACCAS (1975/2003)

Tri-County Career Center
15676 State Route 691, Nelsonville 45764
Type: Public, state/local
Degrees: C
URL: http://www.tricountyhightech.com
Phone: (740) 753-3511
Inst. Accred.: NCA-CASI (1981/2004)

Tri-Rivers Career Center
2222 Marion-Mount Gilead Rd., Marion 43302
Type: Public, state/local
Degrees: C
URL: http://www.tririvers.com
Phone: (740) 389-4681
Inst. Accred.: NCA-CASI (1985/2004)

Trumbull Career and Technical Center
1776 Salt Springs Rd., Lordstown 44481
Type: Public, state/local
Degrees: C
URL: http://www.tctcadulttraining.org
Phone: (330) 824-2588
Inst. Accred.: NCA-CASI (1988/2005)

U.S. Grant Joint Vocational School
718 West Plane St., Bethel 45106
Type: Public, state/local
Degrees: C
URL: http://www.grantcareer.com
Phone: (513) 734-6222
Inst. Accred.: NCA-CASI (1992/2004)

Upper Valley Joint Vocational School
5 East State Route 36, Piqua 45356
Type: Public, state/local
Degrees: C
URL: http://www.uvjvs.org/adulted/atc/index.htm
Phone: (937) 778-1980 ext 2
Inst. Accred.: NCA-CASI (1977/2005)

Valley Beauty School
706 Wheeling Ave., Cambridge 43725
Type: Private, proprietary
Degrees: C
Phone: (740) 439-5559
Inst. Accred.: NACCAS (1990/2002)

Parkersburg Campus
707 Market St., Parkersburg, WV 26101
Phone: (304) 422-2226

Valley Beauty School—Zanesville
627 Main St., Zanesville 43701
Type: Private, proprietary
Degrees: C
Phone: (740) 452-6821
Inst. Accred.: NACCAS (1999/2002)

Vanguard-Sentinel Joint Vocational School District
1220 Cedar St., Ste. B, Fremont 43420
Type: Public, state/local
Degrees: C
URL: http://www.vscc.k12.oh.us/adulted.html
Phone: (419) 332-2626
Inst. Accred.: NCA-CASI (1995/2004)

Vantage Career Center
818 North Franklin St., Van Wert 45891-1304
Type: Public, state/local
Degrees: C
URL: http://www.vantagecareercenter.com
Phone: (419) 238-5411
Inst. Accred.: NCA-CASI (1993/2004)

Vocational Guidance Services
2239 East 55th St., Cleveland 44103
Type: Private, independent
Degrees: C
URL: http://www.vgsjob.org
Phone: (216) 881-6007
Inst. Accred.: NCA-CASI (2003)

Warren County Career Center
3525 North State Route 48, Lebanon 45036
Type: Public, state/local
Degrees: C
URL: http://www.wccareercenter.com
Phone: (513) 932-8145
Inst. Accred.: NCA-CASI (1983/2004)

Wayne County Career Center
518 West Prospect St., Smithville 44677
Type: Public, state/local
Degrees: C
URL: http://www.wayne-jvs.k12.oh.us
Phone: (330) 669-9611
Inst. Accred.: NCA-CASI (1977/2004)

Western Hills School of Beauty and Hair Design
6490 Glenway Ave., Cincinnati 45211
Type: Private, proprietary
Degrees: C
Phone: (513) 574-3818
Inst. Accred.: NACCAS (1977/2003)

The Youngstown College of Massotherapy
14 Highland Ave., Struthers 44471
Type: Private, proprietary
Degrees: C
URL: http://www.yocm.com
Phone: (330) 755-1406
Inst. Accred.: ACCSCT (1999/2004, Probation)

OKLAHOMA

4-States Okmulgee Academy of Cosmetology, Inc.
308 East 6th St., Okmulgee 74447
Type: Private, proprietary
Degrees: C
Phone: (918) 756-5566
Inst. Accred.: NACCAS (2006/2007)

American Beauty Institute
2009 North Main St., McAlester 74501
Type: Private, proprietary
Degrees: C
URL: http://www.americanbeautyinstitutes.com
Phone: (918) 420-4247
Inst. Accred.: NACCAS (1988/2003)

Ardmore International College of Beauty
Broadlawn Shopping Center, Ste. 16, Ardmore 73401
Phone: (580) 223-0711

American Broadcasting School
4511 SE 29th St., Oklahoma City 73115
Type: Private, proprietary
Degrees: C
URL: http://www.radioschool.com
Phone: (405) 672-6511
Inst. Accred.: ACCET (1990/2004)

Arlington Campus
712 North Watson Rd., Ste. 200, Arlington, TX 76011
Phone: (817) 695-2474

Garland Campus
1914 Pendleton Dr., Garland, TX 75041-4840
Phone: (972) 682-5500

Tulsa Campus
2843 East 51st St., Tulsa 74105-1701
Phone: (918) 293-9100

American Institute of Medical Technology
7040 Ste. Yale Ave., Ste. 100, Tulsa 74136
Type: Private, proprietary
Degrees: C
URL: http://www.aimt-edu.com
Phone: (918) 496-0800
Inst. Accred.: ABHES (2005)

ATI Career Training Center
2401 NW 23rd St., Ste. 14, Oklahoma City 73107
Type: Private, proprietary
System: ATI Enterprises, Inc.
Degrees: C
URL: http://www.aticareertraining.edu
Phone: (405) 445-5760
Inst. Accred.: ACICS (2006)

Autry Technology Center
1201 West Willow St., Enid 73703
Type: Public, state/local
Degrees: C
URL: http://www.autrytech.com
Phone: (580) 242-2750
Inst. Accred.: NCA-CASI (1992/2003)
Prog. Accred.: Allied Health (respiratory therapy, surgical technology), Practical Nursing, Radiography

Beauty Technical College
1600 East Downing St., Tahlequah 74465
Type: Private, proprietary
Degrees: C
Phone: (918) 456-9431
Inst. Accred.: NACCAS (1988/2003)

Broken Arrow Beauty College, Inc.
400 South Elm Place, Broken Arrow 74012
Type: Private, proprietary
Degrees: C
Phone: (918) 251-9660
Inst. Accred.: NACCAS (1983/2003)

Cosmetology Education Center
11122 East 71st St. South, Tulsa 74133
Phone: (918) 294-8627

Caddo-Kiowa Technology Center
PO Box 90, Ft. Cobb 73015
Type: Public, state/local
Degrees: C
URL: http://www.caddokiowa.com
Phone: (405) 643-5511
Inst. Accred.: NCA-CASI (1973/2004)
Prog. Accred.: Allied Health (occupational therapy assisting), Practical Nursing

CC's Cosmetology College
11630 East 21st St. South, Tulsa 74129
Type: Private, proprietary
Degrees: C
URL: http://www.ccscosmetology.edu
Phone: (918) 234-9444
Inst. Accred.: NACCAS (1988/2003)

Oklahoma City Campus
4439 NW 50th St., Oklahoma City 73112
Phone: (918) 943-2300

Tulsa Campus
11630 East 21st St. South, Tulsa 74129
Phone: (918) 234-9444

Central State Beauty Academy
8494 NW Expressway, Oklahoma City 73162
Type: Private, proprietary
Degrees: C
Phone: (405) 722-4499
Inst. Accred.: NACCAS (1983/2003)

Central State Massage Academy
8494 NW Expressway, OKC Market Square, Oklahoma City 73162
Type: Private, proprietary
Degrees: C
URL: http://www.centralstatemassageacademy.net
Phone: (405) 722-4560
Inst. Accred.: NACCAS (2004)

Central Technology Center—Drumright
3 CT Circle, Drumright 74030
Type: Public, state/local
Degrees: C
URL: http://www.ctechok.org
Phone: (918) 352-2551
Inst. Accred.: NCA-CASI (1973/2005)
Prog. Accred.: Allied Health (surgical technology), Practical Nursing

Central Technology Center—Sapulpa
1720 South Main St., Sapulpa 74066
Type: Public, state/local
Degrees: C
URL: http://www.ctechok.org
Phone: (918) 224-9300
Inst. Accred.: NCA-CASI (1987/2000)

Claremore Beauty College
200 North Cherokee Ave., Claremore 74017
Type: Private, proprietary
Degrees: C
URL: http://claremorebeautycollege.com
Phone: (918) 341-4370
Inst. Accred.: NACCAS (1988/2003)

Community Care College
4242 South Sheridan Rd., Tulsa 74145-1119
Type: Private, proprietary
Degrees: C
URL: http://www.communitycarecollege.com
Phone: (918) 610-0027
Inst. Accred.: ABHES (1998/2001)
Prog. Accred.: Allied Health (surgical technology)

Enid Beauty College, Inc.
1601 East Broadway, Enid 73701
Type: Private, proprietary
Degrees: C
Phone: (580) 237-6677
Inst. Accred.: NACCAS (1977/2004)

Eve's College of Hairstyling
912 C Ave., Lawton 73501
Type: Private, proprietary
Degrees: C
Phone: (580) 355-6620
Inst. Accred.: NACCAS (1968/2004)

Gordon Cooper Technology Center
One John C Bruton Blvd., Shawnee 74804
Type: Public, state/local
Degrees: C
URL: http://www.gctech.org
Phone: (405) 273-7493
Inst. Accred.: NCA-CASI (1972/2003)

Great Plains Technology Center
4500 West Lee Blvd., Lawton 73505
Type: Public, local
Degrees: C
URL: http://www.gptech.org
Phone: (580) 355-6371
Inst. Accred.: NCA-CASI (1973/2004)
Prog. Accred.: Allied Health (respiratory therapy, surgical technology), Practical Nursing, Radiography

Frederick Campus
2001 East Gladstone Ave., Frederick 73542-4645
Phone: (580) 335-5525

Guthrie Job Corps Center
3106 West University Ave., Guthrie 73044-8712
Type: Public, federal
Degrees: C
URL: http://guthrie.jobcorps.gov/html/home
Phone: (405) 282-9518
Inst. Accred.: COE (2006)

Hollywood Cosmetology Center
PO Box 89048, Oklahoma City 73189-0488
Type: Private, proprietary
Degrees: C
Phone: (405) 364-3375
Inst. Accred.: ACCSCT (1991/2002)

Indian Capital Technology Center
HC 61 Box 12, 401 Houser Rd., Sallisaw 74955
Type: Public, state/local
Degrees: C
URL: http://www.icavts.tec.ok.us
Phone: (918) 775-9119
Inst. Accred.: NCA-CASI (1994/2005)

Indian Capital Technology Center
Rural Route 4, Box 3320, Stilwell 74960
Type: Public, state/local
Degrees: C
URL: http://www.icavts.tec.ok.us
Phone: (918) 696-3111
Inst. Accred.: NCA-CASI (1994/2005)

Indian Capital Technology Center
240 Vo-Tech Rd., Tahlequah 74464-3466
Type: Public, state/local
Degrees: C
URL: http://www.icavts.tec.ok.us
Phone: (918) 456-2594
Inst. Accred.: NCA-CASI (1994/2005)

Indian Capital Technology Center
2403 North 41st St. East, Muskogee 74403
Type: Public, state/local
Degrees: C
URL: http://www.icavts.tec.ok.us
Phone: (918) 687-6383
Inst. Accred.: NCA-CASI (1974/2005)
Prog. Accred.: Radiography

Institute of Hair Design Barber College
1601 1/2 North Harrison St., Shawnee 74804
Type: Private, proprietary
Degrees: C
URL: http://www.ihdbarberschool.com
Phone: (405) 275-8000
Inst. Accred.: NACCAS (2003/2007)

Kiamichi Technology Center—Atoka
1301 West Liberty Rd., Atoka 74525
Type: Public, state/local
Degrees: C
URL: http://www.kiamichi-atoka.tec.ok.us
Phone: (580) 889-7321
Inst. Accred.: NCA-CASI (1982/2002)

Kiamichi Technology Center—Durant
810 Waldron Rd., Durant 74701
Type: Public, state/local
Degrees: C
URL: http://www.kiamichi-durant.tec.ok.us
Phone: (580) 924-7081
Inst. Accred.: NCA-CASI (1992/2002)

Kiamichi Technology Center—Hugo
107 South 15th St., Hugo 74743-4254
Type: Public, state/local
Degrees: C
URL: http://www.kiamichi-hugo.tec.ok.us
Phone: (580) 326-6491
Inst. Accred.: NCA-CASI (1973/2002)

Kiamichi Technology Center—Idabel
Rural Route 3 Box 177, Idabel 74745-9534
Type: Public, state/local
Degrees: C
URL: http://www.kiamichi-idabel.tec.ok.us
Phone: (580) 286-7555
Inst. Accred.: NCA-CASI (1984/2002)

Kiamichi Technology Center—McAlester
301 Kiamichi Dr., McAlester 74501
Type: Public, state/local
Degrees: C
URL: http://www.kiamichi-mcalester.tec.ok.us
Phone: (918) 426-0940
Inst. Accred.: NCA-CASI (1973/2002)

Kiamichi Technology Center—Poteau
1509 South McKenna St., Poteau 74953-5207
Type: Public, state/local
Degrees: C
URL: www.kiamichi-poteau.tec.ok.us
Phone: (918) 647-4525
Inst. Accred.: NCA-CASI (1973/2002)

Kiamichi Technology Center—Spiro
610 SW Third St., Spiro 74959
Type: Public, state/local
Degrees: C
URL: http://www.kiamichi-spiro.tec.ok.us
Phone: (918) 962-3722
Inst. Accred.: NCA-CASI (1996/2002)

Kiamichi Technology Center—Stigler
1410 Old Military Rd., Stigler 74462
Type: Public, state/local
Degrees: C
URL: http://www.kiamichi-stigler.tec.ok.us
Phone: (918) 967-2801
Inst. Accred.: NCA-CASI (1996/2002)

Kiamichi Technology Center—Talihina
Route 2, Box 1800, Talihina 74571
Type: Public, state/local
Degrees: C
URL: http://www.kiamichi-talihina.tec.ok.us
Phone: (918) 567-2264
Inst. Accred.: NCA-CASI (1987/2002)
Prog. Accred.: Practical Nursing

The Language Company
189 West 15th St., Edmond 73013
Type: Private, proprietary
Degrees: C
URL: http://www.thelanguagecompany.com
Phone: (405) 636-1333
Inst. Accred.: ACCET (2000/2006)

Edmond Language Institute
University of Central Oklahoma, 100 North University Dr., PO Box 341881, Edmond 73034
Phone: (405) 341-2125

Hays Language Institute
Fort Hays State University, 600 Picken Hall, Rm. 200, Hays, KS 67601
Phone: (785) 628-2121

Orlando English Institute
Florida Mall Business Center, 1650 Sand Lake Rd., Ste. 100, Orlando, FL 32809
Phone: (407) 859-5444

Pennsylvania Language Institute
Widener University, One Unversity Place, Chester, PA 19013
Phone: (610) 499-4550

The Shawnee Language Institute
1900 West MacArthur Dr., Shawnee 74804
Phone: (405) 273-8229

South Bend English Institute
1720 Ruskin St., Ste. 100, South Bend, IN 46615
Phone: (219) 287-3622

Tahlequah Campus
622 North Lewis Ave., Tahlequah 74464-2303
Phone: (918) 456-5511 x4730

The Tulsa English Institute
3115 South Winston, Tulsa 74135
Phone: (918) 742-8855

Metro Technology Center—South Bryant
4901 South Bryant Ave., Oklahoma City 73129
Type: Private, proprietary
Degrees: C
URL: http://www.metrotech.org
Phone: (405) 605-4488
Inst. Accred.: NCA-CASI (2001/2006)

Metro Technology Centers—Springlake
1900 Springlake Dr., Oklahoma City 73111-5240
Type: Private, proprietary
Degrees: C
URL: http://www.metrotech.org
Phone: (405) 605-4488
Inst. Accred.: NCA-CASI (1996/2006)
Prog. Accred.: Allied Health (medical assisting (AMA), surgical technology), Dentistry (dental assisting), Practical Nursing, Radiography

Mid-America Technology Center
PO Box H, Wayne 73095-0210
Type: Public, state/local
Degrees: C
URL: http://www.matech.org
Phone: (405) 449-3391
Inst. Accred.: NCA-CASI (1972/2002)

Mid-Del Technology Center
1612 Maple Dr., Midwest City 73110
Type: Public, state/local
Degrees: C
URL: http://www.mid-del.tec.ok.us
Phone: (405) 739-1707
Inst. Accred.: NCA-CASI (2001/2003)

Moore Norman Technology Center
4701 12th Ave., NW, Norman 73069
Type: Public, state/local
Degrees: C
URL: http://mntechnology.com
Phone: (405) 364-5763
Inst. Accred.: NCA-CASI (2001/2006)
Prog. Accred.: Allied Health (diagnostic medical sonography, medical assisting (AMA), surgical technology), Practical Nursing

Northeast Technology Center
PO Box 825, Pryor 74362
Type: Public, state/local
Degrees: C
URL: http://www.netechcenters.com
Phone: (918) 825-55550
Inst. Accred.: NCA-CASI (1989/2004)
Prog. Accred.: Practical Nursing

Northeast Technology Center
PO Box 30, Kansas 74347
Type: Public, state/local
Degrees: C
URL: http://www.netechcenters.com
Phone: (918) 868-3535
Inst. Accred.: NCA-CASI (1998/2004)

Northeast Technology Center
19901 South Hwy. 69, Afton 74331
Type: Public, state/local
Degrees: C
URL: http://www.netechcenters.com
Phone: (918) 257-8324
Inst. Accred.: NCA-CASI (1989/2004)

Oklahoma Health Academy—Moore
1939 North Moore Ave., Moore 73160
Type: Private, proprietary
Degrees: C
URL: http://www.oklahomahealthacademy.org
Phone: (405) 912-2777
Inst. Accred.: ACCSCT (1999/2004)
Prog. Accred.: Allied Health (surgical technology)

Oklahoma Health Academy—Tulsa
2865 East Skelly Dr., Ste. 224, Tulsa 74105
Type: Private, proprietary
Degrees: C
URL: http://www.oklahomahealthacademy.org
Phone: (918) 748-9900
Inst. Accred.: ACCSCT (1999/2004)

Oklahoma School of Photography, Inc.
2306 North Moore Ave., Oklahoma City 73160
Type: Private, proprietary
Degrees: C
URL: http://www.photocareers.com
Phone: (405) 799-1411
Inst. Accred.: ACCET (1990/2004)

Oklahoma Technology Institute
9801 Broadway Extension, Oklahoma City 73114
Type: Private, proprietary
Degrees: C
URL: http://www.oti-okc.edu
Phone: (405) 842-9400
Inst. Accred.: COE (2005)

Ponca City Beauty College
122 North 1st St., Ponca City 74601
Type: Private, proprietary
Degrees: C
Phone: (580) 762-1470
Inst. Accred.: NACCAS (1994/2002)

Pontotoc Technology Center
601 West 33rd St., Ada 74820
Type: Public, state/local
Degrees: C
URL: http://www.pontotoc.com
Phone: (580) 310-2200
Inst. Accred.: NCA-CASI (2001/2004)

Poteau Beauty College
301 Turman St., Poteau 74953
Type: Private, proprietary
Degrees: C
Phone: (918) 647-4119
Inst. Accred.: NACCAS (1989/2004)

Mena Cosmetology College
1310 Hwy. 71 North, Mena, AR 71953
Phone: (479) 394-7272

Pryor Beauty College
330 West Graham Ave., Pryor 74361
Type: Private, proprietary
Degrees: C
Phone: (918) 825-2795
Inst. Accred.: NACCAS (1998/2006)

Grove Beauty College
63155 East 290 Rd., Grove 74345
Phone: (918) 787-5810

North East Oklahoma Academy of Hair Design
3918 West Hwy. 412, West Siloam Springs 74338
Phone: (918) 422-4314

Ron Moore and Associates
300 North Meridian, Ste. 110N, Oklahoma City 73107
Type: Private, proprietary
Degrees: C
URL: http://www.oklahoma.dalecarnegie.com
Phone: (405) 947-2111
Inst. Accred.: ACCET (1977/2005)

Sand Springs Beauty College
28 East Second St., Sand Springs 74063
Type: Private, proprietary
Degrees: C
URL: http://www.jenksbeautycollege.com
Phone: (918) 245-6627
Inst. Accred.: NACCAS (1981/2004)

Jenks Beauty College
535 West Main St., Jenks 74037
Phone: (918) 299-0901

Shawnee Beauty College
410 East Main St., Shawnee 74801
Type: Private, proprietary
Degrees: C
Phone: (405) 275-8698
Inst. Accred.: NACCAS (2000/2003)

Southern School of Beauty
140 West Main, Durant 74701-5008
Type: Private, proprietary
Degrees: C
URL: http://www.durantmainstreet.org/southern_school_beauty.htm
Phone: (580) 924-1049
Inst. Accred.: NACCAS (1993/2006)

Stanton Beauty College
127 West Main St., Ada 74820
Phone: (580) 924-1049

State Barber & Hair Design College Inc.
2514 South Agnew Ave., Oklahoma City 73108-6220
Type: Private, proprietary
Degrees: C
Phone: (405) 631-8621
Inst. Accred.: ACCSCT (1987/2004)

Stillwater Beauty Academy
1684 Cimarron Plaza, Stillwater 74075
Type: Private, proprietary
Degrees: C
Phone: (405) 377-4100
Inst. Accred.: NACCAS (1990/2005)

Academy of Cosmetology
607 West Grand Ave., Chickasha 73018
Phone: (405) 377-4100

Technical Institute of Cosmetology Arts and Sciences
822 East 6th St., Tulsa 74120
Type: Private, proprietary
Degrees: C
Phone: (918) 660-8828
Inst. Accred.: NACCAS (1992/2002)

Tri County Technology Center
6101 Nowata Rd., Bartlesville 74006
Type: Public, state/local
Degrees: C
URL: http://www.tctc.org
Phone: (918) 331-3333
Inst. Accred.: NCA-CASI (1975/2005)
Prog. Accred.: Culinary Education, Practical Nursing

Tulsa Job Corps Center
1133 North Lewis Ave., Tulsa 74110
Type: Public, federal
Degrees: C
URL: http://tulsa.jobcorps.gov/html/home
Phone: (918) 591-5644
Inst. Accred.: COE (2006)

Tulsa Technology Center—Broken Arrow
4600 South Olive Ave., Tulsa 74011-1706
Type: Public, state/local
System: Tulsa Technology Center
Degrees: C
URL: http://www.tulsatech.com
Phone: (918) 828-3000 *Calendar:* Qtr. plan
Inst. Accred.: NCA-CASI (1985/2003)

Tulsa Technology Center—Lemley
3420 South Memorial Dr., Tulsa 74145-1390
Type: Public, state/local
System: Tulsa Technology Center
Degrees: C
URL: http://www.tulsatech.com
Phone: (918) 828-1000 *Calendar:* Qtr. plan
Inst. Accred.: NCA-CASI (1972/2003)
Prog. Accred.: Allied Health (surgical technology), Practical Nursing, Radiography

Tulsa Technology Center—Peoria
3850 North Peoria Ave., Tulsa 74106-1619
Type: Public, state/local
System: Tulsa Technology Center
Degrees: C
URL: http://www.tulsatech.com
Phone: (918) 828-2000 *Calendar:* Qtr. plan
Inst. Accred.: NCA-CASI (1977/2003)

Tulsa Technology Center—Riverside
801 East 91st St., Tulsa 74132-4008
Type: Public, state/local
System: Tulsa Technology Center
Degrees: C
URL: http://www.tulsatech.com
Phone: (918) 828-4000 *Calendar:* Qtr. plan
Inst. Accred.: NCA-CASI (1992/2003)
Prog. Accred.: Radiography

Tulsa Welding School
2545 East 11th St., Tulsa 74107-3818
Type: Private, proprietary
Degrees: C
URL: http://www.tulsaweldingschool.com
Phone: (918) 587-6789
Inst. Accred.: ACCSCT (1970/2002)

Jacksonville Campus
3500 Southside Blvd., Jacksonville, FL 32216
Phone: (904) 646-9353

University Language Institute
2448 East 81st St., Ste. 1400, Tulsa 74137
Type: Private, independent
Degrees: C
URL: http://uli.net
Phone: (918) 493-8088
Inst. Accred.: CEA (2002)

Virgil's Beauty College
111 South Ninth St., Muskogee 74401
Type: Private, proprietary
Degrees: C
URL: http://www.virgilsbeautycollege.com
Phone: (918) 682-9429
Inst. Accred.: NACCAS (1970/2006)

Wes Watkins Technology Center
7892 Hwy. 9, Wetumka 74883-9522
Type: Public, state/local
Degrees: C
URL: http://www.wwtech.org
Phone: (405) 452-5500 *Calendar:* Sem. plan
Inst. Accred.: NCA-CASI (2001/2005)
Prog. Accred.: Allied Health (surgical technology)

Woodward Beauty College
502 Texas St., Woodward 73801
Type: Private, proprietary
Degrees: C
Phone: (580) 256-7520
Inst. Accred.: NACCAS (1987/2002)

Yukon Beauty College
221 West Main St., Yukon 73099-1414
Type: Private, proprietary
Degrees: C
Phone: (405) 354-3172
Inst. Accred.: NACCAS (1988/2003)

OREGON

Abdill Career College
843 East Main St., Ste. 203, Medford 97504
Type: Private, proprietary
Degrees: C
URL: http://www.abdill.com
Phone: (541) 779-8384
Inst. Accred.: ACCSCT (2003)

Academy of Hair Design, Inc.
305 Ct. St., NE, Salem 97301
Type: Private, proprietary
Degrees: C
Phone: (503) 585-8122
Inst. Accred.: NACCAS (1972/2003)

Airman's Proficiency Center
3565 NE Cornell Rd., Hillsboro 97124
Type: Private, proprietary
Degrees: C
URL: http://www.hillsboro-aviation.com
Phone: (503) 648-2831
Inst. Accred.: ACCSCT (1992/2005)

Australasian College of Health Sciences
5940 SW Hood Ave., Portland 97239
Type: Private, independent
Degrees: C
URL: http://www.achs.edu
Phone: (503) 244-0726
Inst. Accred.: DETC (2003)

Beau Monde College of Hair Design
1221 SW 12th Ave., Portland 97205
Type: Private, proprietary
Degrees: C
URL: http://www.beaumondecollege.com
Phone: (503) 226-1427
Inst. Accred.: NACCAS (1980/2005)

Beaverton School of Beauty
18295 SW Tualatin Valley Hwy., Ste. A, Aloha 97007
Type: Private, proprietary
Degrees: C
URL: http://www.beavertonschoolofbeauty.com
Phone: (503) 649-0357
Inst. Accred.: NACCAS (1988/2006)

Birthingway College of Midwifery
12113 SE Foster Rd., Portland 97266
Type: Private, independent
Degrees: C
URL: http://www.birthingway.org
Phone: (503) 760-3131
Inst. Accred.: MEAC (2001/2006)

College of Cosmetology, Inc.
357 East Main St., Klamath Falls 97601
Type: Private, proprietary
Degrees: C
URL: http://www.collegeofcos.com
Phone: (541) 882-6644
Inst. Accred.: NACCAS (1977/2003)

College of Hair Design Careers
1684 Clay St., NE, Salem 97301
Type: Private, proprietary
Degrees: C
Phone: (503) 588-5888
Inst. Accred.: NACCAS (1986/2006)

College of Legal Arts
8909 SW Barbur Blvd., Ste. 100, Portland 97219
Type: Private, proprietary
Degrees: C
URL: http://www.collegeoflegalarts.com
Phone: (503) 223-5100
Inst. Accred.: ACICS (1978/2004)

Concorde Career Institute
1425 NE Irving St., Ste. 300, Portland 97232
Type: Private, proprietary
System: Concorde Career Colleges, Inc.
Degrees: C
URL: http://www.concordecareercolleges.com
Phone: (503) 281-4181
Inst. Accred.: ACCSCT (1969/2002)
Prog. Accred.: Allied Health (medical assisting (AMA), surgical technology), Dentistry (dental assisting)

East-West College of the Healing Arts
525 NE Oregon St., Portland 97232
Type: Private, proprietary
Degrees: C
URL: http://www.eastwestcollege.com
Phone: (503) 231-1500
Inst. Accred.: CMTA (2001/2004)

Beaverton Campus
The Cedar Hills Shopping Center, 10226 SW Park Way, Beaverton 97225
Phone: (503) 297-3800
Prog. Accred: Allied Health (massage therapy)

IITR Truck Driving School
15828 SE 114th St., Clackamas 97015
Type: Private, proprietary
Degrees: C
URL: http://www.iitr.net
Phone: (503) 657-8225
Inst. Accred.: ACCET (1986/2006)

Montessori Institute Northwest
4506 Southeast Belmont St., Ste. 100, Portland 97215-1658
Type: Private, independent
Degrees: C
URL: http://www.montessori-nw.org/
Phone: (503) 963-8992
Inst. Accred.: MACTE (1996/2003)

Northwest College
8307 SE Monterey Ave., Clackamas 97266
Type: Private, proprietary
Degrees: C
URL: http://www.nwcollege.edu
Phone: (503) 659-2834
Inst. Accred.: NACCAS (1977/2003)

Hillsboro Campus
210 SE Fourth Ave., Hillsboro 97123
Phone: (503) 844-7320

Northwest Nannies Institute
11830 SW Kerr Pkwy., Ste. 100, Lake Oswego 97035
Type: Private, proprietary
Degrees: C
URL: http://www.nwnanny.com
Phone: (503) 245-5288
Inst. Accred.: ACCET (1988/2005)

Pacific International Academy
17600 Pacific Hwy. 43, Marylhurst 97036-0267
Type: Private, proprietary
Degrees: C
URL: http://www.piaschools.edu
Phone: (503) 699-6310
Inst. Accred.: ACCET (2003/2006)

Paul Mitchell The School
1180 Commercial St., Astoria 97103
Type: Private, proprietary
System: Paul Mitchell The School—Corporate Office
Degrees: C
URL: http://pmts.paulmitchelltheschool.com
Phone: (503) 325-3163
Inst. Accred.: NACCAS (1985/2003)

Phagans' Beauty College
142 SW Second St., Corvallis 97333
Type: Private, proprietary
Degrees: C
URL: http://www.phagans-schools.com
Phone: (541) 753-6466
Inst. Accred.: NACCAS (1975/2007)

Phagans' Central Oregon Beauty College
355 NE Second St., Bend 97701
Type: Private, proprietary
Degrees: C
URL: http://www.phagans-schools.com
Phone: (541) 382-6171
Inst. Accred.: NACCAS (1975/2007)

Phagans' Grants Pass College of Beauty
304 Agness Ave., Ste. F, Grants Pass 97526
Type: Private, proprietary
Degrees: C
URL: http://www.phagans-schools.com
Phone: (541) 479-6678
Inst. Accred.: NACCAS (1995/2003)

Phagans' Medford Beauty School
2320 Poplar Dr., Medord 97504
Type: Private, proprietary
Degrees: C
URL: http://www.phagans-schools.com
Phone: (541) 772-6155
Inst. Accred.: NACCAS (1967/2004)

Phagans' Newport Academy of Cosmetology Careers
158 East Olive St., Newport 97365
Type: Private, proprietary
Degrees: C
URL: http://www.phagans-schools.com
Phone: (541) 265-3083
Inst. Accred.: NACCAS (1991/2006)

Phagans' School of Beauty
622 Lancaster Dr. NE, Salem 97303
Type: Private, proprietary
Degrees: C
URL: http://www.phagans-schools.com
Phone: (503) 363-6800
Inst. Accred.: NACCAS (1975/2007)

Phagans' School of Hair Design
16550 SE McLoughlin Blvd., Milwaukie 97267
Type: Private, proprietary
Degrees: C
URL: http://www.phagans.com
Phone: (503) 652-2668
Inst. Accred.: NACCAS (1981/2006)

Phagans' School of Hair Design
1542 NE Weidler Ave., Portland 97232
Type: Private, proprietary
Degrees: C
URL: http://www.phagans.com
Phone: (503) 239-0838
Inst. Accred.: NACCAS (1977/2003)

Phagans' Tigard Beauty School
8820 SW Center St., Tigard 97223
Type: Private, proprietary
Degrees: C
URL: http://www.phagansnw.com
Phone: (503) 639-6107
Inst. Accred.: NACCAS (1976/2006)

Roseburg Beauty College, Inc.
700 SE Stephens St., Roseburg 97470
Type: Private, proprietary
Degrees: C
Phone: (541) 673-5533
Inst. Accred.: NACCAS (1986/2006)

Springfield College of Beauty
307 Q St., Springfield 97477
Type: Private, proprietary
Degrees: C
Phone: (541) 746-4473
Inst. Accred.: NACCAS (1966/2004)

Valley Medical College, Inc.
3886 Beverly St., Building I-16, Salem 97305
Type: Private, proprietary
Degrees: C
URL: http://www.valleymedicalcollege.com
Phone: (503) 363-9001
Inst. Accred.: ACCET (2001/2004)

PENNSYLVANIA

The Academy of Creative Hair Design
125 North Wilkes Barre Blvd., Kingston 18702
Type: Private, proprietary
Degrees: C
Phone: (570) 825-8363
Inst. Accred.: NACCAS (1984/2004)

Academy of Hair Design
1057 A North Church St., Hazleton 18202
Type: Private, proprietary
Degrees: C
Phone: (570) 459-5501
Inst. Accred.: NACCAS (1981/2006)

Academy of Vocal Arts
1920 Spruce St., Philadelphia 19103
Type: Private, independent
Degrees: C
URL: http://www.avaopera.com
Phone: (215) 735-1685
Inst. Accred.: NASM (2000)

All-State Career School
97 Second St., North Versailles 15137-1000
Type: Private, proprietary
Degrees: C
URL: http://www.allstatecareer.edu
Phone: (412) 823-1818
Inst. Accred.: ACCSCT (1991/2005)

All-State Career School
501 Seminole St., Lester 19029-1827
Type: Private, proprietary
Degrees: C
URL: http://www.allstatecareer.edu
Phone: (610) 521-1818
Inst. Accred.: ACCSCT (1987/2003)

Baltimore Campus
2200 Broening Hwy., Ste. 160, Baltimore, MD 21224-6658
Phone: (410) 631-1818

Allied Medical and Technical Institute
517 Ash St., Scranton 18510-2903
Type: Private, proprietary
Degrees: C
URL: http://www.alliedteched.com
Phone: (570) 558-1818
Inst. Accred.: ACCSCT (1995/2006)

The Alternative Conjunction Clinic and School of Massage Therapy
716 State St., Lemoyne 17043
Type: Private, proprietary
Degrees: C
Phone: (717) 737-6001
Inst. Accred.: NACCAS (1999/2002)

Altoona Beauty School, Inc.
1528 Valley View Blvd., Altoona 16602
Type: Private, proprietary
Degrees: C
URL: http://www.altoonabeautyschool.com
Phone: (814) 942-3141
Inst. Accred.: NACCAS (1984/2004)

Antonelli Medical and Professional Institute
1700 Industrial Hwy., Pottstown 19464-9250
Type: Private, proprietary
Degrees: C
Phone: (610) 323-7270
Inst. Accred.: ACCSCT (1989/2004)

Automotive Training Center
114 Pickering Way, Exton 19341-1310
Type: Private, proprietary
Degrees: C
URL: http://www.autotraining.edu
Phone: (610) 363-6716
Inst. Accred.: ACCSCT (1973/2003)

Warminster Campus
900 Johnsville Blvd., Warminster 18974
Phone: (215) 259-1900

Aviation Institute of Maintenance
3001 Grant Ave., Philadelphia 19114
Type: Private, proprietary
Degrees: C
URL: http://www.tidetech.com
Phone: (215) 676-7700
Inst. Accred.: ACCSCT (1994/2003)

Beaver Falls Beauty Academy
720 13th St., Beaver Falls 15010
Type: Private, proprietary
Degrees: C
URL: http://www.bfbeauty.com
Phone: (724) 843-7700
Inst. Accred.: NACCAS (1980/2006)

Blackstone Career Institute
218 Main St., PO Box 899, Emmaus 18049
Type: Private, proprietary
Degrees: C
URL: http://www.blackstone.edu
Phone: (610) 967-3323
Inst. Accred.: DETC (2005)

Bucks County School of Beauty Culture, Inc.
1761 Bustleton Pike, Feasterville
Type: Private, proprietary
Degrees: C
URL: http://www.bcsbc.com
Phone: (215) 322-0666
Inst. Accred.: NACCAS (1984/2004)

Butler Beauty School
233 South Main St., Butler 16001
Type: Private, proprietary
Degrees: C
Phone: (412) 287-0708
Inst. Accred.: NACCAS (1987/2002)

Career Development and Employment
100 North Wilkes-Barre Blvd., Ste. 203, Wilkes-Barre 18702
Type: Private, proprietary
Degrees: C
URL: http://www.cdetraining.com
Phone: (570) 823-3891
Inst. Accred.: COE (2007)

Center for Innovative Training and Education
714 Market St., Ste. 433, Philadelphia 19106
Type: Private, independent
Degrees: C
Phone: (215) 922-6555
Inst. Accred.: ACCSCT (1996/2005)

The Chubb Institute—Keystone
400 South State Rd., Marple Crossroads, Springfield 19064
Type: Private, proprietary
System: High-Tech Institute
Degrees: C
FTE Enroll: 195
URL: http://www.chubbinstitute.edu
Phone: (610) 338-2300
Calendar: Sem. plan
Inst. Accred.: ACICS (1968/2006)

Cherry Hill Campus
The Plaza at Cherry Hill, 2100 Route 38 and Mall Dr., Cherry Hill, NJ 08002
Phone: (856) 755-4800

North Brunswick Campus
651 US Route 1, North Brunswick, NJ 08902
Phone: (732) 448-2600

Computer Learning Network
401 East Winding Hill Rd., Mechanicsburg 17055-4989
Type: Private, proprietary
Degrees: C
URL: http://www.clncamphill.com
Phone: (717) 761-1481
Inst. Accred.: ACCSCT (1985/2004)

Altoona Campus
2900 Fairway Dr., Altoona 16602-4457
Phone: (814) 944-5643

Cortiva Institute-Pennsylvania School of Muscle Therapy
1173 Egypt Rd., Oaks 19456-0400
Type: Private, proprietary
Degrees: C
URL: http://www.cortiva.com/locations/psmt
Phone: (610) 666-9060
Inst. Accred.: CMTA (1999/2004)

DCI Career Institute
One Data Plaza, 561 Wallace Run Rd., Beaver Falls 15010
Type: Private, proprietary
Degrees: C
URL: http://www.dcitraining.com
Phone: (724) 847-0152
Inst. Accred.: ACCET (1991/2004)

Delaware Valley Academy of Medical and Dental Assistants
3330 Grant Ave., Grant Academy Shopping Center, Philadelphia 19114
Type: Private, proprietary
Degrees: C
URL: http://www.delawarevalleyacademy.com
Phone: (215) 676-1200
Inst. Accred.: ABHES (1986/2005)

DPT Business School
11000 Roosevelt Blvd., Ste. 200, Philadelphia 19116
Type: Private, proprietary
Degrees: C
URL: http://www.dptschools.com
Phone: (215) 637-8140
Inst. Accred.: ACCET (1990/2005)

Denver Campus
405 South Platte River Dr., Ste. 3A, Denver, CO 80223
Phone: (303) 744-3075

Philadelphia Center City Campus
125-27 North 4th St., Philadelphia 19106
Phone: (215) 627-8140

Education and Technology Institute
Rural Route 12, PO Box 213, Greensburg 15601
Type: Public, independent
Degrees: C
URL: http://www.eti.edu
Phone: (724) 836-2395
Inst. Accred.: ACICS (2004)

Empire Beauty School
The Plaza on Mall Blvd., Monroeville 15146
Type: Private, proprietary
Degrees: C
URL: http://www.empirebeauty.com
Phone: (412) 373-7727
Inst. Accred.: NACCAS (1992/2005)

West Mifflin Campus
2393 Mountain View Dr., West Mifflin 15122
Phone: (412) 653-2870

Empire Beauty School—Center City Philadelphia
1522 Chestnut St., Philadelphia 19102
Type: Private, proprietary
Degrees: C
URL: http://www.empirebeauty.com
Phone: (215) 568-3980
Inst. Accred.: NACCAS (1967/2003)

Empire Beauty School—Exton
454 West Lincoln Hwy., Exton 19341
Type: Private, proprietary
Degrees: C
URL: http://www.empirebeauty.com
Phone: (610) 594-6181
Inst. Accred.: NACCAS (1979/2005)

Empire Beauty School, Inc—Hanover
Clearview Shopping Center, Carlise St., Hanover 17331
Type: Private, proprietary
Degrees: C
URL: http://www.empirebeauty.com
Phone: (570) 633-6201
Inst. Accred.: NACCAS (1990/2005)

Empire Beauty School—Harrisburg
3941 Jonestown Rd., Harrisburg 17901
Type: Private, proprietary
System: Empire Beauty School—Harrisburg
Degrees: C
URL: http://www.empirebeauty.com
Phone: (570) 652-8500
Inst. Accred.: NACCAS (1967/2004)

Empire Beauty School—Lancaster
801 Columbia Ave., Wheatland Shopping Center, Lancaster 17604
Type: Private, proprietary
System: Empire Education Group
Degrees: C
URL: http://www.empirebeauty.com
Phone: (570) 394-8561
Inst. Accred.: NACCAS (1972/2004)

Empire Beauty School—Lebanon
1776 Quentin Rd., Cedar Crest Square, Lebanon 17042
Type: Private, proprietary
System: Empire Education Group
Degrees: C
URL: http://www.empirebeauty.com
Phone: (570) 272-3323
Inst. Accred.: NACCAS (1973/2004)

Empire Beauty School—Moosic
3409 Birney Ave., Birney Mall, Moosic 18507
Type: Private, proprietary
Degrees: C
URL: http://www.empirebeauty.com
Phone: (570) 343-4730
Inst. Accred.: NACCAS (1971/2004)

Lisle Campus
2709 Maple Ave., Unit 3, Green Trails Shopping Center, Lisle, IL 60532
Phone: (630) 717-1777

Empire Beauty School—Northeast Philadelphia
Knights Rd. Shopping Center, 4026 Woodhaven Rd., Philadelphia 19154
Type: Private, proprietary
Degrees: C
URL: http://www.empirebeautyschools.com
Phone: (215) 637-3700
Inst. Accred.: NACCAS (1965/2003)

Arlington Heights Campus
264 West Rand Rd., Arlington Heights, IL 60004
Phone: (847) 394-8365

Empire Beauty School—Pottsville
324 North Centre St., Pottsville 17901
Type: Private, proprietary
Degrees: C
URL: http://www.empirebeauty.com
Phone: (570) 622-6060
Inst. Accred.: NACCAS (1975/2005)

Empire Beauty School—Reading
2302 North Fifth St., Reading 19605
Type: Private, proprietary
System: Empire Education Group
Degrees: C
URL: http://www.empirebeauty.com
Phone: (610) 372-2777
Inst. Accred.: NACCAS (1967/2004)

Midlothian Campus
10807 Hull St. Rd., Midlothian, VA 23112
Phone: (804) 745-9062

Empire Beauty School—Shamokin Dam
Orchard Hills Plaza, PO Box397, Shamokin Dam 17876
Type: Private, proprietary
System: Empire Education Group
Degrees: C
URL: http://www.empirebeauty.com
Phone: (570) 743-1410
Inst. Accred.: NACCAS (1972/2004)

Empire Beauty School—State College
208 West Hamilton St., State College 16801
Type: Private, proprietary
Degrees: C
URL: http://www.empirebeauty.com
Phone: (814) 238-1961
Inst. Accred.: NACCAS (1975/2005)

Empire Beauty School—Warminster
435 York Rd., Warminster 18974
Type: Private, proprietary
Degrees: C
URL: http://www.empirebeauty.com
Phone: (215) 443-8446
Inst. Accred.: NACCAS (1981/2006)

Empire Beauty School—Whitehall
1634 MacArthur Rd., Whitehall 18052
Type: Private, proprietary
Degrees: C
URL: http://www.empirebeauty.com
Phone: (610) 776-8908
Inst. Accred.: NACCAS (1967/2004)

Owings Mills Campus
9616 Reisterstown Rd., Ste. 105, Owings Mills, MD 21117
Phone: (410) 581-2373

Empire Beauty School—Williamsport
1808 East Third St., Williamsport 17701
Type: Private, proprietary
Degrees: C
URL: http://www.empirebeauty.com
Phone: (570) 322-8243
Inst. Accred.: NACCAS (1971/2003)

Pittsburgh Campus
4768 McKnight Rd., Pittsburgh 15237
Phone: (412) 367-9704

Empire Beauty School—York
2592 Eastern Blvd., Kingston Square, York 17402
Type: Private, proprietary
System: Empire Education Group
Degrees: C
URL: http://www.empirebeauty.com
Phone: (717) 600-8111
Inst. Accred.: NACCAS (1972/2004)

Richmond Campus
9049 West Broad St., #3, West Broad Commons, Richmond, VA 23294
Phone: (804) 270-2095

GECAC Training Institute
1006 West Tenth St., Erie 16502
Type: Private, state-related
Degrees: C
URL: http://www.gecac.org/gti.htm
Phone: (814) 451-5610
Inst. Accred.: ACICS (1996/2005)

Great Lakes Institute of Technology
5100 Peach St., Erie 16509
Type: Private, proprietary
Degrees: C
URL: http://www.glit.edu
Phone: (814) 846-6666
Inst. Accred.: ACCSCT (1979/2002, Probation)
Prog. Accred.: Allied Health (diagnostic medical sonography, surgical technology)

Greater Altoona Career and Technology Center
1500 Fourth Ave., Altoona 16602
Type: Public, state/local
Degrees: C
URL: http://www.gactc.com
Phone: (814) 946-8450
Inst. Accred.: COE (2003)
Prog. Accred.: Allied Health (medical assisting (AMA))

Greater Johnstown Career and Technology Center
445 Schoolhouse Rd., Johnstown 15904-2998
Type: Public, state/local
Degrees: C
URL: http://www.gjctc.tec.pa.us
Phone: (814) 269-3874
Inst. Accred.: COE (2004, Probation)
Prog. Accred.: Practical Nursing

Indiana Cosmetology Academy
441 Hamill Rd., Indiana 15701
Type: Public, state/local
Degrees: C
URL: http://www.ictc.ws/ica/index.htm
Phone: (724) 349-6700
Inst. Accred.: NACCAS (2005)

Jean Madeline Aveda Institute
315A Bainbridge St., Philadelphia 19147
Type: Private, proprietary
Degrees: C
URL: http://www.jeanmadeline.com
Phone: (215) 238-9998
Inst. Accred.: NACCAS (1989/2002)

Frankford Avenue Campus
7248 Frankford Ave., Philadelphia 19135
Phone: (215) 332-2000

JR Rodgers and Associates, Inc.
824 Struble Rd., State College 16801
Type: Private, proprietary
Degrees: C
URL: http://www.centralpa.dalecarnegie.com
Phone: (814) 238-2677
Inst. Accred.: ACCET (1997/2001)

Kittanning Beauty School of Cosmetology Arts
120 Market St., Kittanning 16201
Type: Private, proprietary
Degrees: C
Phone: (724) 548-2031
Inst. Accred.: NACCAS (1990/2005)

L.T. International Beauty School
830 North Broad St., Philadelphia 19130
Type: Private, proprietary
Degrees: C
Phone: (215) 922-4478
Inst. Accred.: NACCAS (1997/2004)

Lancaster County Career and Technology Center
1730 Hans-Herr Dr., Willow Street 17584-0527
Type: Public, local
Degrees: C
URL: http://www.lcctc.org
Phone: (717) 464-7050
Inst. Accred.: COE (2001)
Prog. Accred.: Practical Nursing

Lancaster School of Cosmetology, Inc.
50 Ranck Ave., Lancaster 17602
Type: Private, proprietary
Degrees: C
URL: http://www.lancasterschoolofcosmetology.com
Phone: (717) 299-0200
Inst. Accred.: NACCAS (1982/2002)

Lansdale School of Cosmetology, Inc.
215 West Main St., Lansdale 19446
Type: Private, proprietary
Degrees: C
URL: http://www.lansdalebeauty.com
Phone: (215) 362-2322
Inst. Accred.: NACCAS (1984/2004)

Leadership Institute, Inc.
5050 Tilghman St., Ste. 430, Allentown 18104
Type: Private, proprietary
Degrees: C
URL: http://www.dalecarnegie.com
Phone: (610) 783-6500
Inst. Accred.: ACCET (1977/2001)

LearnQuest
225 City Ave., Ste. 106, Bala Cynwyd 19004
Type: Private, proprietary
Degrees: C
URL: http://www.learnquest.com
Phone: (610) 206-0101
Inst. Accred.: ACCET (2000/2005)

Lebanon County Career and Technology Center
833 Metro Dr., Lebanon 17042
Type: Public, local
Degrees: C
URL: http://www.lcctc.k12.pa.us
Phone: (717) 273-8551
Inst. Accred.: COE (2001)
Prog. Accred.: Practical Nursing

Lebanon County Career School
18 East Weidman St., Lebanon 17046
Type: Private, proprietary
Degrees: C
URL: http://www.sageschools.com
Phone: (717) 274-8804
Inst. Accred.: ACCSCT (1998/2003)

Levittown Beauty Academy
8919 New Falls Rd., Levittown 19054
Type: Private, proprietary
Degrees: C
URL: http://www.levittownbeautyacademy.com
Phone: (215) 943-0298
Inst. Accred.: NACCAS (1978/2004)

Magnolia School
50 East Butler Pike, Ambler 19002
Type: Private, proprietary
Degrees: C
URL: http://www.ababeauty.com
Phone: (215) 643-5994
Inst. Accred.: NACCAS (1982/2006)

American Beauty Academy, Inc.
6912 Frankford Ave., Philadelphia 19135
Phone: (215) 331-1515

Mercer County Career Center
776 Greenville Rd., Mercer 16137
Type: Public, state/local
Degrees: C
URL: http://www.mccc.onlinecommunity.com
Phone: (724) 662-3000
Inst. Accred.: COE (2003)

National Massage Therapy Institute
10050 Roosevelt Blvd., Philadelphia 19116
Type: Private, proprietary
Degrees: C
Phone: (215) 698-0702
Inst. Accred.: CMTA (1999/2005)

NAWCC School of Horology
514 Poplar St., Columbia 17512-2130
Type: Private, independent
Degrees: C
URL: http://www.nawcc.org
Phone: (717) 684-8261
Inst. Accred.: ACCSCT (1999/2005)

New Castle School of Beauty Culture
314 East Washington St., New Castle 16101
Type: Private, proprietary
Degrees: C
Phone: (724) 654-6611
Inst. Accred.: NACCAS (1975/2005)

Northwest Regional Technology Institute
3104 State St., Erie 16508
Type: Private, proprietary
Degrees: C
URL: http://www.nwrti.com
Phone: (814) 455-4446
Inst. Accred.: ACCSCT (2004)

Orleans Technical Institute
1330 Rhawn St., Philadelphia 19111-2899
Type: Private, independent
Degrees: C
URL: http://www.orleanstech.org
Phone: (215) 728-4700
Inst. Accred.: ACCSCT (1981/2005)

Penn Foster Career School
925 Oak St., Scranton 18515
Type: Private, proprietary
Degrees: C
URL: http://www.pennfoster.edu
Phone: (570) 342-7701
Inst. Accred.: DETC (1956/2004)

Pennsylvania Academy of Cosmetology Arts and Sciences—DuBois
19 North Brady St., DuBois 15801
Type: Private, proprietary
Degrees: C
URL: http://www.pacas.com
Phone: (814) 371-4151
Inst. Accred.: NACCAS (1979/2005)

Pennsylvania Academy of Cosmetology Arts and Sciences—Johnstown
2445 Bedford St., Johnstown 15904
Type: Private, proprietary
Degrees: C
URL: http://www.pacas.com
Phone: (814) 269-3444
Inst. Accred.: NACCAS (1979/2005)

The Pennsylvania Academy of Music
42 North Prince St., Lancaster 17603-3840
Type: Private, independent
URL: http://paacademymusic.com
Phone: (717) 399-9733 *Calendar:* Sem. plan
Inst. Accred.: NASM (2003)

Pennsylvania Gunsmith School
812 Ohio River Blvd., Pittsburgh 15202-2699
Type: Private, proprietary
Degrees: C
URL: http://www.pagunsmith.com
Phone: (412) 766-1812
Inst. Accred.: ACCSCT (1985/2002)

Pennsylvania Institute of Taxidermy
118 Industrial Park Rd., Ebensburg 15931-8947
Type: Private, proprietary
Degrees: C
URL: http://www.studytaxidermy.com
Phone: (814) 472-4510
Inst. Accred.: ACCSCT (1988/2004)

Pennsylvania Myotherapy Institute
2904 Carlisle Pike, New Oxford 17350
Type: Private, proprietary
Degrees: C
URL: http://www.pamyotherapyinstitute.com
Phone: (717) 624-3333
Inst. Accred.: NACCAS (2006/2007)

Pittsburgh Fillmmakers' School of Film, Video and Photography
477 Melwood Ave., Pittsburgh 15213
Type: Private, independent
Degrees: C
URL: http://www.pghfilmmakers.org/school.html
Phone: (412) 681-5449
Inst. Accred.: NASAD (1999/ 2007)

Pittsburgh School of Pain Management
1312 East Carson St., Pittsburgh 15203
Type: Private, proprietary
Degrees: C
URL: http://www.painschool.com
Phone: (412) 481-2553 *Calendar:* Qtr. plan
Inst. Accred.: ABHES (2006)

Precision Manufacturing Institute
18282 Technology Dr., Meadville 16335
Type: Private, proprietary
Degrees: C
URL: http://www.pmionline.edu
Phone: (814) 333-2415
Inst. Accred.: ACCSCT (2004)

Princeton Information Technology Center
140 South Easton Rd., Glenside 19038
Type: Private, proprietary
Degrees: C
URL: http://www.princetonweb.com
Phone: (215) 576-5650
Inst. Accred.: ACCSCT (2003/2006)

Professional Academy of Cosmetology, LLC
516 East Marshall St., Norristown 19401
Type: Private, proprietary
Degrees: C
URL: http://www.penncosmetology.com
Phone: (610) 277-7390
Inst. Accred.: NACCAS (2007)

Pruonto's Hair Design Institute
705 12th St., Altoona 16602
Type: Private, proprietary
Degrees: C
URL: http://www.pruontos.com
Phone: (814) 944-4494
Inst. Accred.: NACCAS (1983/2003)

PSC Academy
2200 East State St., Hermitage 16148
Type: Private, proprietary
Degrees: C
URL: http://www.pscacademy.com
Phone: (724) 347-4503
Inst. Accred.: NACCAS (1982/2002)

Punxy Beauty School of Cosmetology Arts and Science
222 North Findley St., Punxsutawney 15767
Type: Private, proprietary
Degrees: C
Phone: (814) 938-8811
Inst. Accred.: NACCAS (1990/2005)

Schuylkill Training and Technology Center
101 Technology Dr., Frackville 17931
Type: Public, state/local
Degrees: C
URL: http://www.iu29.org/STCenters
Phone: (570) 874-1034
Inst. Accred.: COE (2002)
Prog. Accred.: Practical Nursing

Settlement Music School
PO Box 63966, Philadelphia 19147-3966
Type: Private, independent
Degrees: C
URL: http://www.smsmusic.org
Phone: (215) 320-2600
Inst. Accred.: NASM (1989/2004)

Camden School of Musical Arts
531-35 Market St., Camden, NJ 08105
Phone: (856) 541-6375

Germantown Campus
6128 Germantown Ave., Philadelphia 19144
Phone: (215) 320-2610

Jenkintown Music School
515 Meetinghouse Rd., Jenkintown 19046
Phone: (215) 320-2630

Kardon-Northeast Campus
3745 Clarendon Ave., Philadelphia 19114
Phone: (215) 320-2620

Mary Louise Curtis Campus
416 Queen St., Philadelphia 19147
Phone: (215) 320-2600

West Philadelphia Campus
4910 Wynnefield Ave., Philadelphia 19131
Phone: (215) 320-2640

South Hills Beauty Academy
3269 West Liberty Ave., Pittsburgh 15216
Type: Private, proprietary
Degrees: C
URL: http://www.shnhbeauty.com
Phone: (412) 561-3381
Inst. Accred.: NACCAS (1975/2007)

North Hills Beauty Academy
434 Perry Hwy., Pittsburgh 15229
Phone: (412) 931-8563

Springhouse Education and Consulting Services
770 Pennsylvania Dr., Ste. 120, Exton 19341-1129
Type: Private, proprietary
Degrees: C
URL: http://www.springhouse.com
Phone: (610) 321-2090
Inst. Accred.: ACCET (2001/2004)

Star Technical Institute—Philadelphia
9121-49 Roosevelt Blvd., Philadelphia 19114
Type: Private, proprietary
Degrees: C
URL: http://www.startechinstitute.com
Phone: (215) 969-5877
Inst. Accred.: ACCSCT (1994/2005)

Newark Campus
550 Broad St., Third Flr., Newark, NJ 07102
Phone: (973) 639-0789

Star Technical Institute—Upper Darby
1570 Garrett Rd., Upper Darby 19082
Type: Private, proprietary
Degrees: C
URL: http://www.startechinstitute.com
Phone: (610) 626-2700
Inst. Accred.: ACCSCT (1994/2004)

Egg Harbor Campus
3003 English Creek Ave., Unit 212, Egg Harbor, NJ 08234
Phone: (609) 407-2999

Stroudsburg School of Cosmetology
100 North Eighth St., Stroudsburg 18360
Type: Private, proprietary
Degrees: C
Phone: (570) 421-3387
Inst. Accred.: NACCAS (1982/2002)

Susquehanna Career and Technology Center
PO Box 100, Schoolhouse Rd., Dimmock 18816-0100
Type: Public, state/local
Degrees: C
URL: http://scctc.elklakeschool.org
Phone: (570) 278-9229
Inst. Accred.: COE (2004)

Synergy Healing Arts Center and Massage School
13593 Monterey Ln., Blue Ridge Summit 17214
Type: Private, proprietary
Degrees: C
URL: http://www.synergymassage.com
Phone: (717) 794-5778
Inst. Accred.: CMTA (2005)

Tony and Guy Hairdressing Academy at Great Lakes Institute of Technology
930 Peach St., Erie 16501
Type: Private, proprietary
Degrees: C
URL: http://www.toniguy-erie.edu
Phone: (814) 452-1900
Inst. Accred.: NACCAS (2003/2006)

Upper Bucks Institute of Aeronautics
2375 Milford Square Pike, Quakertown 18951
Type: Public, state/local
Degrees: C
Phone: (215) 536-6786
Inst. Accred.: COE (2003)

Venus Beauty Academy
1033 Chester Pike, Sharon Hill 19079
Type: Private, proprietary
Degrees: C
URL: http://www.venusbeautyacademy.com
Phone: (610) 586-2500
Inst. Accred.: NACCAS (1976/2002)

Aston Campus
600 Turner Industrial Way, Aston 19014
Phone: (610) 494-1000

The Vision Academy—A Paul Mitchell Partner School
1921 Union Blvd., Allentown 18103
Type: Private, proprietary
Degrees: C
URL: http://www.thevisionacademy.com
Phone: (610) 437-4626
Inst. Accred.: NACCAS (1980/2005)

Welder Training and Testing Institute
729 East Highland St., Allentown 18103-1263
Type: Private, proprietary
Degrees: C *Enroll:* 34
URL: http://www.welderinstitute.com
Phone: (215) 437-9720
Inst. Accred.: ACCSCT (1973/2006)

Wrightco Technologies Technical Training Institute
728 Ben Franklin Hwy., Edensburg 15931
Type: Private, proprietary
Degrees: C
URL: http://www.wrightco.com
Phone: (814) 472-5211
Inst. Accred.: ACCSCT (2000/2005)

Alexandria Campus
PO Box 22, Alexandria 16611
Phone: (814) 669-4241

Chambersburg Campus
225 Sollenberger Rd., Chambersburg 17201
Phone: (717) 263-8142

Shelocta Campus
Route 422 West, Shelocta 15774
Phone: (724) 354-5162

Uniontown Campus
National City Bank Bldg. 2, 2 West Main St., Ste. 200, Uniontown 15401
Phone: (724) 439-2080

PUERTO RICO

A1 Business and Technical College
Dr. Rufo St. #14, Ponce 00726
Type: Private, proprietary
Degrees: C
URL: http://www.a1college.com
Phone: (787) 746-1074
Inst. Accred.: ACCSCT (1994/2004)

Academia Maison D'Esthetique
904 Ave. Ponce De Leon, Santurce 00907-3330
Type: Private, proprietary
Degrees: C
URL: http://www.maisondesthetique.com
Phone: (787) 723-4672
Inst. Accred.: NACCAS (1987/2003)

Mayaguez Campus
Calle Pilar Defillo # 61, Mayaguez 00680
Phone: (787) 806-6666

Academia Morales
Bo. Guaniquilla Carretera 441 Km 0.4, Aguada 00602
Type: Private, proprietary
Degrees: C
Phone: (787) 868-4041
Inst. Accred.: COE (2004)

San Sebastian Campus
Calle Andres Veelazquez #49, San Sebastian 00602
Phone: (787) 868-4041

Academia Serrant
8180 Concordia St., Ponce 00717-1568
Type: Private, proprietary
Degrees: C
URL: http://www.serrant.com
Phone: (787) 259-4900
Inst. Accred.: ACCSCT (1995/2002)

Academia Vocational Del Turabo
Campio Alonso #41, Caquas 00725
Type: Private, proprietary
Degrees: C
Phone: (787) 746-6634
Inst. Accred.: ACCSCT (1996/2005)

Advance Tech College
#24 Barboas St., Bayamon 00961
Type: Private, proprietary
Degrees: C
Phone: (787) 785-6841
Inst. Accred.: ACCSCT (2003/2006)

Aguadilla Technical College
PO Box 988, Manati 00674
Type: Private, independent
Degrees: C
Phone: (787) 891-6966
Inst. Accred.: ACCSCT (2003)

Allegro Music College
1851 Ponce de Leon, Santurce 00909-1907
Type: Private, proprietary
Degrees: C
Phone: (787) 727-6996
Inst. Accred.: ACCSCT (2005)

American Educational College
45 Santa Cruz St., Bayamon 00961
Type: Private, proprietary
Degrees: C
Phone: (787) 798-2970
Inst. Accred.: ACICS (1985/2001)

Toa Alta Campus
25 Munoz Rivera St., Toa Alta 00961
Phone: (787) 870-2552

Antilles School of Technical Careers
1851 & 1905 Ave Fernandez Juncos #1851, Santurce 00907
Type: Private, proprietary
Degrees: C
Phone: (787) 268-2244
Inst. Accred.: ABHES (1985/2006)
Prog. Accred.: Practical Nursing

ASPIRA, Inc. de Puerto Rico
8887 St., Km.11.19, San Anton, San Juan 00929-0132
Type: Private, proprietary
Degrees: C
URL: http://www.aspirapr.org
Phone: (787) 641-1985
Inst. Accred.: ACCET (2005)

Atenas College
PO Box 365, Manati 00674
Type: Private, proprietary
Degrees: C
URL: http://www.atenascollege.com
Phone: (787) 884-3838
Inst. Accred.: ACCSCT (2005)

Automeca Technical College
Carr #2, Km. 14, Bayamon 00960
Type: Private, proprietary
Degrees: C
URL: http://www.automeca.com
Phone: (787) 792-5915
Inst. Accred.: ACCET (1985/2004)

Aguadilla Campus
Parque Industrial La Montana Lot #14, Carretera #459, Km 0.9, Edificio #932, Aguadilla 00605
Phone: (787) 882-2828

Caguas Campus
Calle Munoz Rivera #69, Caguas 00725
Phone: (787) 746-3468

Automeca Technical College—Ponce
452 Calle Villa, Ponce 00731
Type: Private, proprietary
Degrees: C
URL: http://www.automeca.com
Phone: (787) 840-7880
Inst. Accred.: ACCET (1990/2005)

Bayamon Community College
Maceo 17, Bayamon 00960
Type: Private, proprietary
Degrees: C
URL: http://www.bccpr.org
Phone: (787) 780-4370
Inst. Accred.: ACCSCT (2003)

Caguas Central College
Calle Betances 39, Caguas 00726-7199
Type: Private, proprietary
Degrees: C
Phone: (787) 703-2704
Inst. Accred.: ACCSCT (1995/2005)

Caguas Institute of Mechanical Technology
Calle B, No. 39-40, Caguas West Industrial Park, Caguas 00726
Type: Private, proprietary
Degrees: C
Phone: (787) 743-0484
Inst. Accred.: ACCET (1990/2004)

Bayamon Campus
Carr #174 KM 3.0 Sector, Industrial Minillas, Solar 51 Lomas Verd, Bayamon 00856

Mayaguez Campus
Calle Balboa No. 69-71, Caguas West Industrial Park, Mayaguez 00680
Phone: (787) 834-5225

Carib Technological Institute
Calle #39 UU-1 Santa Huanita, Bayamon 00956
Type: Private, proprietary
Degrees: C
Phone: (787) 644-0512
Inst. Accred.: ACCSCT (2006)

Caribbean Forensic and Technical College
Paseo de Diego #5, 3er Piso, Rio Piedras 00919
Type: Private, proprietary
Degrees: C
URL: http://www.cafotech.com
Phone: (787) 751-6961
Inst. Accred.: ACCSCT (2001/2006)

Century College
125 Progress St., Aguadilla 00603
Type: Private, independent
Degrees: C
URL: http://www.centurycollegepr.com
Phone: (787) 882-5086 *Calendar:* Sem. plan
Inst. Accred.: COE (2000/2003)

Charlie's Guard, Detective Bureau, and Academy
PO Box 3087 Carr. 107, Km 3.1 Bo. Borinquen, Aguadilla 00605
Type: Private, proprietary
Degrees: C
Phone: (787) 882-7222
Inst. Accred.: ACCSCT (2005)

Colegio Educativo Tecnologico Industrial
Calle Eugenio Maria de Hsotos, Esq. Puro Girau, Arecibo 00613
Type: Private, independent
Degrees: C
Phone: (787) 879-3300
Inst. Accred.: COE (2003)

Colegio Mayor de Tecnologia
151 Morse St., Arroyo 00714
Type: Private, proprietary
Degrees: C
Phone: (787) 839-5266
Inst. Accred.: ACCSCT (1988/2004)

Colegio Tecnico de Electricidad Galloza
HC 03 Box 32562, Aguada 00602
Type: Private, proprietary
Degrees: C
Phone: (787) 252-0922
Inst. Accred.: ACCSCT (2004)

Colegio Tecnico Metropolitano
1251 Franklin D. Roosevelt Ave., Puerto Nuevo 00920
Type: Private, proprietary
Degrees: C
Phone: (787) 781-5140
Inst. Accred.: ACCSCT (1992/2002)

Colegio Tecnologico y Comercial de Puerto Rico
Calle Paz 165 Altos, Aguada 00602
Type: Private, proprietary
Degrees: C
Phone: (787) 868-2688
Inst. Accred.: ACICS (1990/2003)

D'Mart Institute
Centro Commercial San Cristobal, Ste. 202, Barranquitas 00974
Type: Private, proprietary
Degrees: C
URL: http://www.dmartpr.com
Phone: (787) 857-6929
Inst. Accred.: ACCSCT (1991/2006)

Corozal Campus
Carr. 159 (Desvlo de Corozal) Km 1.5, Corozal 00783
Phone: (787) 859-5391

Ponce Campus
Calle Mayor #46 Esquina Sol, Ponce 00731
Phone: (787) 290-2089

Educational Technical College
Calle Degetau No. 5, Esq. Betances, Bayamon 00961-6208
Type: Private, proprietary
Degrees: C
Phone: (787) 785-2388
Inst. Accred.: ACCSCT (1988/2004)

Coamo Campus
Calle Ramon Power #5, Coamo 00769
Phone: (787) 825-0370

San Sebastian Campus
Calle Hostos #20, Annex at Calle Pavia, San Sebastian 00669
Phone: (787) 896-7655

Emma's Beauty Academy—Juana Diaz
Carr. 149 Barrio Amuelas, Sector Guanabanos, Juana Diaz 00795
Type: Private, proprietary
Degrees: C
Phone: (787) 837-0303
Inst. Accred.: NACCAS (1986/2005)

Emma's Beauty Academy—Mayaguez
Munoz Rivera #9 Oeste, Mayaguez 00680
Type: Private, proprietary
Degrees: C
URL: http://www.emmasbeautyacademy.com
Phone: (787) 833-0980
Inst. Accred.: NACCAS (1979/2007)

Aguada Campus
Bo. Guan·banos Carr 417, Aguada 00602
Phone: (787) 868-4711

Escuela de Peritos Electricistas de Isabel
PO Box 457, Avenida Aguadilla No. 242, Isabel 00662
Type: Private, proprietary
Degrees: C
Phone: (787) 872-1747
Inst. Accred.: ACCSCT (1993/2003)

Escuela Hotelera de San Juan
229 Guayama St., Hato Rey 00917
Type: Private, proprietary
Degrees: C
URL: http://www.escuelahotelera.com
Phone: (787) 759-7599
Inst. Accred.: ACCSCT (2005)

Escuela Tecnica de Electricidad, Inc.
Calle Villa #190, Ponce 00730-4875
Type: Private, proprietary
Degrees: C
URL: http://www.etepr.edu
Phone: (787) 843-3588
Inst. Accred.: ACCET (1988/2002)

Fajardo Campus
Calle Antonio R Barcelo #6, Fajardo
Phone: (787) 801-5555

Rio Piedras Campus
Ave Campo Rico 767, Country Club, PO Box 29743, 65th Infantry Station, Rio Piedras 00924
Phone: (787) 750-1020

Globelle Technical Institute
Call Marginal #114, Urbanizacion Monte Carlo, Veja Baja 00693
Type: Private, proprietary
Degrees: C
Phone: (787) 858-0236
Inst. Accred.: ACCSCT (1995/2005)

Hispanic American College
Calle Ruiz Belvis #52-54, Caguas 00725
Type: Private, proprietary
Degrees: C
Phone: (787) 258-4851
Inst. Accred.: ACCSCT (1997/2002)

Industrial Technical College
16 Carreras St., Humacao 00792-8480
Type: Private, proprietary
Degrees: C
Phone: (787) 852-8806
Inst. Accred.: ACCSCT (2003)

Institucion Chaviano de Mayaguez
Calle Ramos Antonini, No. 116 Este, Mayaguez 00608-5045
Type: Private, independent
Degrees: C
Phone: (787) 833-2474
Inst. Accred.: ACCSCT (1987/2003)

Institute of Beauty Careers
Ave. Llorens Torres #199 Esq. Coll y Toste, Arecibo 00613
Type: Private, proprietary
Degrees: C
Phone: (787) 878-2880
Inst. Accred.: NACCAS (1982/2002)

Manati Campus
Mc Kinley #21, Manati 00674
Phone: (787) 884-0099

Institute of Beauty Occupation and Technology
Calle Concepcion Vera #500, Moca 00676
Type: Private, proprietary
Degrees: C
Phone: (787) 818-0355
Inst. Accred.: ACCSCT (2003)

Instituto de Banca y Comercio
61 Ponce de Leon Ave., Hato Rey 00919
Type: Private, proprietary
Degrees: C
URL: http://www.ibanca.net
Phone: (787) 754-7120
Inst. Accred.: ACICS (1978/2005)

Caguas Campus
52 Ruiz Belvis St., Caguas 00725
Phone: (787) 745-9525

Cayey Campus
Calle José de Diego 164, Cayey 00736
Phone: (787) 738-5555

Fajardo Campus
Calle Muñoz Rivera 205, Fajardo 00738
Phone: (787) 860-6262

Guayama Campus
Calle Derkes 4, Guayama 00784
Phone: (787) 864-3220

Manati Campus
56 Carrera No 2, Manati 00674
Phone: (787) 854-6634

Mayaguez Campus
Calle Méndez Vigo (Este) 155, Mayaguez 00680
Phone: (787) 833-4748

Ponce Campus
Calle Ferrocarril 609, Ponce 00731
Phone: (787) 840-6119

Instituto de Educacion Tecnica Ocupacional "LaReine"
Avenida Colon No. 8A, Manati 00674
Type: Private, proprietary
Degrees: C
Phone: (787) 854-1119
Inst. Accred.: ACCSCT (1991/2007)

Aguadilla Campus
Mercedes Moreno St., #3, Aguadilla 00603
Phone: (787) 819-0222

Instituto de Educacion Vocacional
Carr. 159 km 13.4—HC-03 Box 17272, Corozal 00783
Type: Private, independent
Degrees: C
Phone: (787) 859-9259
Inst. Accred.: ACCSCT (1995/2005)

Morovis Campus
Calle Comercio, Esquina Betances, Morovis 00687
Phone: (787) 862-6758

Instituto Merlix
Betances #20, #5 Degetau, Bayamon 00960
Type: Private, proprietary
Degrees: C
URL: http://www.institutomerlix.com
Phone: (787) 786-7035
Inst. Accred.: ACCSCT (1989/2006)

Instituto Postsecundario de Educación a Distancia
PO Box 8517, Carretera 183, Km.1.7, Caguas 00726-8517
Type: Private, independent
Degrees: C
URL: http://www.columbiaco.edu
Phone: (787) 743-4041
Inst. Accred.: DETC (2003)

Instituto Tecnologico Empresarial
22 Munoz Rivera Ave., Trujillo Alto 00976
Type: Private, proprietary
Degrees: C
Phone: (787) 748-5577
Inst. Accred.: ACICS (2002/2004)

Lares Campus
8 Calle Munoz Rivera, Lares 00669-2422
Phone: (787) 748-5577

Instituto Vocacional Aurea E. Mendez
14 Intendente Ramirez St., Caguas 00726
Type: Private, proprietary
Degrees: C
URL: http://www.ivaempr.com
Phone: (787) 743-5327
Inst. Accred.: ACCSCT (2005)

International Technical College
104 Loaiza Cordero St., San Juan 00918
Type: Private, proprietary
Degrees: C
Phone: (787) 767-8389
Inst. Accred.: ACCSCT (1988/2004)

J G Guaynabo Technical College
67 Carazo St., Guaynabo 00969
Type: Private, proprietary
Degrees: C
Phone: (787) 648-3628
Inst. Accred.: ACCSCT (2003/2006)

Leston College
Calle Dr. Veve #52, Bayamon 00961
Type: Private, proprietary
Degrees: C
Phone: (787) 787-9661
Inst. Accred.: ACCSCT (2001/2006)

Liberty Technical College
Carretera #735, KM 0.4, Cayey 00736
Type: Private, independent
Degrees: C
URL: http://www.radiansschool.org/liberty-tech.htm
Phone: (787) 738-4822
Inst. Accred.: ABHES (2007)

Liceo de Arte y Tecnologia
PO Box 192346, San Juan 00919-2346
Type: Private, proprietary
Degrees: C
URL: http://www.liceopr.com
Phone: (787) 759-9800
Inst. Accred.: ACCSCT (1978/2006)

Liceo de Arte, Disenos y Comercio
Calle Acosta No. 47-49, PO Box 1889, Caguas 00626-1889
Type: Private, proprietary
Degrees: C
Phone: (787) 743-7447
Inst. Accred.: ACCSCT (1990/2003)

MBTI Business Training Institute
1256 Ponce de Leon Ave., Santurce 00907
Type: Private, proprietary
Degrees: C
Phone: (787) 723-9403
Inst. Accred.: ACICS (1969/2002)

Aguadilla Campus
99 Progreso St., Aguadilla 00831
Phone: (787) 891-9403

Modern Hairstyling Institute—Arecibo
Vista Azul Shopping Center, Carr. 2, Km. 30.0 Marginal, Arecibo 00612
Type: Private, proprietary
Degrees: C
Phone: (787) 816-2991
Inst. Accred.: NACCAS (1980/2003)

Modern Hairstyling Institute—Carolina
Avenue Fernandez Juncos #60, 2nd Flr., Carolina 00980
Type: Private, proprietary
Degrees: C
Phone: (787) 752-8383
Inst. Accred.: NACCAS (1980/2003)

Fajardo Campus
Celis Aguilera 51, Fajardo 00648
Phone: (787) 863-9922

Modern Hairstyling Institute—Fajardo
Oeste Num 10, Calle Dr., Lopez Lopez, Fajardo 00738
Type: Private, proprietary
Degrees: C
Phone: (787) 778-0300
Inst. Accred.: ACCSCT (2004)

Monteclaro: Escuela de Hoteleria y Artes Servicios de Hospitalidad
PO Box 447, Palmer 00721
Type: Private, proprietary
Degrees: C
URL: http://monteclaro.edu
Phone: (787) 888-1135
Inst. Accred.: ACCSCT (1999/2004)

MyrAngel Beauty Institute
Calle Munoz Rivera #57 Sur, San Lorenzo 00754
Type: Private, proprietary
Degrees: C
Phone: (787) 736-0435
Inst. Accred.: NACCAS (2005)

Nova College of Puerto Rico
PO Box 55016, Station #1, Bayamon 00960
Type: Private, proprietary
Degrees: C
Phone: (787) 740-5030
Inst. Accred.: ACCSCT (2005)

Politec Institute
Guadalupe St. #78, PO Box 335577, Ponce 00733-5577
Type: Private, proprietary
Degrees: C
Phone: (787) 843-4725
Inst. Accred.: ACCSCT (1999/2002)

Professional Electrical School
Ramos Velez No. 3, PO Box 1797, Manati 00674-1797
Type: Private, proprietary
Degrees: C
Phone: (787) 854-4776
Inst. Accred.: ACCSCT (1993/2003)

Professional Technical Institution
PO Box 607061-BMS 491, Bayamon 00960
Type: Private, proprietary
Degrees: C
Phone: (787) 740-6810
Inst. Accred.: ACCSCT (1992/2002)

Puerto Rico Barber College
Ave General Valero #300, Fajardo 00738
Type: Private, proprietary
Degrees: C
Phone: (787) 863-2970
Inst. Accred.: ACCSCT (1987/2005)

Quality Technical and Beauty College
Calle Betances Esquina de Parque #12, Bayamon 00960
Type: Private, proprietary
Degrees: C
Phone: (787) 787-1809
Inst. Accred.: NACCAS (1991/2006)

Rogie's School of Beauty Culture
1315 Ponce de Leon Ave., PO Box 19828, San Juan 00910
Type: Private, proprietary
Degrees: C
Phone: (787) 722-2293
Inst. Accred.: NACCAS (1987/2004)

Caguas Campus
Paseo Gautier Benitez #26 Altos, Caguas 00725
Phone: (787) 746-3797

Rosslyn Training Academy of Cosmetology, Inc.
Calle Paz #213, Aguada 00602
Type: Private, proprietary
Degrees: C
Phone: (787) 868-2902
Inst. Accred.: NACCAS (2002/2005)

RTP Hispanic American College
Ruiz Belvis #52-54, Second Flr., Caquas 00725
Type: Private, proprietary
Degrees: C
Phone: (787) 258-4851
Inst. Accred.: COE (2006)

Serbia's Technical College
Calle Hostos Esquina Vicente Pales #27, Guayama 00785
Type: Private, proprietary
Degrees: C
Phone: (787) 864-7254
Inst. Accred.: ACCSCT (2000/2005)

Trinity College of Puerto Rico
PO Box 34360, Ponce 00734-4360
Type: Private, proprietary
Degrees: C
Phone: (787) 842-0000 *Calendar:* Qtr. plan
Inst. Accred.: ACICS (1994/2006)

Universal Career Counseling Center
1902 Fernandez Juncos Ave., Stop 26/1/2, San Juan 00909
Type: Private, proprietary
Degrees: C
URL: http://www.universalcareer.org
Phone: (787) 728-7233
Inst. Accred.: ACCSCT (1999/2004)

Universal Career Counseling Center
McKinley #113 St., Manati 00674
Type: Private, proprietary
Degrees: C
URL: http://www.universalcareer.org
Phone: (787) 854-1636
Inst. Accred.: ACCSCT (1999/2004)

Humacao Center
#6 Antonio Lopez St., Humacao 00791
Phone: (787) 728-7211

Universal Technology College of Puerto Rico
Apartado 1955, Victoria Station, Aguadilla 00605
Type: Private, proprietary
Degrees: C
URL: http://www.unitecpr.net
Phone: (787) 882-2065 *Calendar:* Qtr. plan
Inst. Accred.: ACCSCT (2000/2005, Probation)

Camuy Campus
Calle Munoz Rivera Oeste 167, Ste. 2, Camuy 00627
Phone: (787) 262-5786

World Training Academy, Inc.
M-4 F St., Urb. HermanasDavila, Bayamon 00959
Type: Private, proprietary
Degrees: C
Phone: (787) 740-7372
Inst. Accred.: NACCAS (2007)

RHODE ISLAND

Arthur Angelo School of Cosmetology and Hair Design
151 Broadway, Providence 02903
Type: Private, proprietary
System: Empire Education Group
Degrees: C
URL: http://www.arthurangelo.com
Phone: (401) 272-4300
Inst. Accred.: NACCAS (1977/2003)

Arthur Angelo School of Cosmetology and Hair Design—Warwick
1276 Bald Hill Rd., Ste. 100, Warwick 02886
Type: Private, proprietary
System: Empire Education Group
Degrees: C
URL: http://www.arthurangelo.com
Phone: (401) 826-2022
Inst. Accred.: NACCAS (1981/2006)

International Yacht Restoration School
449 Thames St., Newport 02840
Type: Private, proprietary
Degrees: C
URL: http://www.iyrs.org
Phone: (401) 848-5777
Inst. Accred.: ACCSCT (2002)

Lincoln Technical Institute—Lincoln
622 George Washington Hwy., Lincoln Mall, Lincoln 02865
Type: Private, proprietary
System: Lincoln Educational Services Corporation
Degrees: C
URL: http://www.lincolntech.com
Phone: (401) 344-2430
Inst. Accred.: ACICS (1997/2005)

Brockton Campus
375 Westgate Dr., Brockton, MA 02401
Phone: (508) 941-0730

Marietta Campus
2359 Windy Hill Rd., Marietta, GA 30067
Phone: (770) 226-0056

MotoRing Technical Training Institute
54 Water St., East Providence 02914
Type: Private, proprietary
Degrees: C
URL: http://www.mtti.tec.ri.us
Phone: (401) 434-4840
Inst. Accred.: ACCSCT (1995/2005)

New England Tractor Trailer Training School
600 Moshassuck Valley Industrial Hwy., Pawtucket 02860
Type: Private, proprietary
Degrees: C
URL: http://www.nettts.com
Phone: (401) 725-1220
Inst. Accred.: ACCSCT (1985/2004)

Newport School of Hairdressing, Inc.—Pawtucket
226 Main St., Pawtucket 02860
Type: Private, proprietary
Degrees: C
Phone: (401) 725-6882
Inst. Accred.: NACCAS (1983/2004)

Sawyer School
101 Main St., Pawtucket 02860
Type: Private, proprietary
Degrees: C
URL: http://www.sawyerschool.org
Phone: (401) 272-8400
Inst. Accred.: ACICS (1975/2006)

Hamden Campus
1125 Dixwell Ave., Hamden, CT 06514
Phone: (203) 865-2900

Hartford Campus
141 Washington St., Hartford, CT 06106
Phone: (860) 247-4440

Narragansett Campus
Mariner Square, 140 Point Judith Rd., Unit 3a, Narragansett 02882
Phone: (401) 348-8383

New London Campus
PO Box 510, New London, CT 06320
Phone: (860) 439-0065

Providence Campus
550 Hartford Ave., Providence 02909
Phone: (401) 272-3280

SOUTH CAROLINA

Academy of Cosmetology, Inc.
5117 Dorchester Rd., Charleston 29418
Type: Private, proprietary
Degrees: C
URL: http://www.aoccharleston.com
Phone: (843) 225-4151
Inst. Accred.: NACCAS (1993/2003)

Academy of Hair Technology
3715 East North St., Ste. F, Greenville 29615
Type: Private, proprietary
Degrees: C
URL: http://www.hairchamps.com
Phone: (864) 322-0300
Inst. Accred.: NACCAS (1987/2006)

Bamberg Job Corps Center
19 Job Corps Ave., Bamberg 29003
Type: Public, federal
Degrees: C
URL: http://atlantaregion.jobcorps.gov
Phone: (803) 245-6300
Inst. Accred.: COE (1994/2006)

Beta Tech
8088 Rivers Ave., North Charleston 29406
Type: Private, proprietary
Degrees: C
URL: http://www.betatech.edu
Phone: (843) 569-0889
Inst. Accred.: ACCSCT (1998/2003)

Columbia Campus
6699 Two Notch Rd., Columbia 29223
Phone: (803) 754-7544

Charleston Cosmetology Institute
8484 Dorchester Rd., Charleston 29420
Type: Private, proprietary
Degrees: C
URL: http://www.charlestoncosmetology.com
Phone: (843) 552-3670
Inst. Accred.: COE (1986/2003)

Charleston School of Massage
778 Folly Rd., Charleston 29412
Type: Private, proprietary
Degrees: C
URL: http://www.charlestonmassage.com
Phone: (843) 762-7727
Inst. Accred.: ACCET (2001/2004)

Charzanne Beauty College
1549 Hwy. 72, East, Greenwood 29649
Type: Private, proprietary
Degrees: C
Phone: (864) 223-7321
Inst. Accred.: COE (1986/2001)

Columbia Beauty School
1824 Airport Blvd., Cayce 29033
Type: Private, proprietary
Degrees: C
Phone: (803) 796-5252
Inst. Accred.: NACCAS (1979/2004)

Dale Carnegie Training of South Carolina, LLC
4120 Colonel Vanderhorst Circle, Mt. Pleasant 29466-8044
Type: Private, proprietary
Degrees: C
URL: http://www.sc.dalecarnegie.com
Phone: (843) 884-4848
Inst. Accred.: ACCET (1977/2004)

Department of Defense Polygraph Institute
7540 Pickens Ave., Fort Jackson 29207
Type: Public, federal
Degrees: C
URL: http://www.dodpoly.army.mil
Phone: (803) 751-9100 *Calendar:* 3-3 plan
Inst. Accred.: ACICS (2003)

Harley's Beauty and Barber Career Institute
1527 Lyon St., Columbia 29204
Type: Private, proprietary
Degrees: C
Phone: (803) 254-0050
Inst. Accred.: NACCAS (2004/2007)

Kenneth Shuler's School of Cosmetology
736 Martintown Rd., North Augusta 29841
Type: Private, proprietary
Degrees: C
URL: http://www.kennethshuler.com
Phone: (803) 278-1200
Inst. Accred.: NACCAS (1991/2006)

Kenneth Shulers School of Cosmetology, Nail Design
449 Saint Andrews Rd., Columbia 29210
Type: Private, proprietary
Degrees: C
URL: http://www.kennethshuler.com
Phone: (803) 772-6042
Inst. Accred.: NACCAS (1985/2005)

Columbia South East Campus
7474 Garners Ferry Rd., Columbia 29209
Phone: (803) 776-9100

Spartanburg Campus
1515 John B White Sr. Blvd., Spartanburg 29301
Phone: (864) 587-2006

Lacy Cosmetology School
3084 Whiskey Rd., Aiken 29803
Type: Private, proprietary
Degrees: C
URL: http://www.lacyschools.com
Phone: (803) 648-6181
Inst. Accred.: COE (2000/2006)

LeGrand Institute of Cosmetology
PO Box 2102, Camden 29020
Type: Private, proprietary
Degrees: C
URL: http://www.legrandinstitute.com
Phone: (803) 425-8449
Inst. Accred.: NACCAS (2003/2006)

Platinum Shear School of Cosmetology
1520 Russell St., Orangeburg 29115
Type: Private, proprietary
Degrees: C
Phone: (803) 534-3384
Inst. Accred.: NACCAS (2004/2007)

Plaza School of Beauty Culture
946 Oakland Ave., Rock Hill 29730
Type: Private, proprietary
Degrees: C
URL: http://plazaschoolofbeauty.com
Phone: (803) 328-5166
Inst. Accred.: NACCAS (1996/2002)

Southeastern School of Neuromuscular and Massage Therapy, Inc.
1420 Colonial Life Blvd. West, Ste. 80, Columbia 29210
Type: Private, proprietary
Degrees: C
URL: http://se-massage.com
Phone: (803) 798-8800 *Calendar:* Tri. plan
Inst. Accred.: ACCSCT (2002/2006)

Southeastern School of Neuromuscular and Massage Therapy, Inc.
4600 Goer Dr., Ste. 105, North Charleston 29406
Type: Private, proprietary
Degrees: C
URL: http://charlotte.se-massage.com
Phone: (843) 747-1279 *Calendar:* Tri. plan
Inst. Accred.: ACCSCT (2001/2006)

Strand College of Hair Design
423 79th Ave. West, Myrtle Beach 29572
Type: Private, proprietary
Degrees: C
URL: http://www.strandcollege.com
Phone: (843) 449-1017
Inst. Accred.: NACCAS (1996/2004)

Styletrends Barber and Hairstyling Academy, Inc.
239 Hampton St., Rock Hill 29730
Type: Private, proprietary
Degrees: C
Phone: (803) 328-0807
Inst. Accred.: NACCAS (2003/2006)

Sumter Beauty College
921 Carolina Ave., Sumter 29150-2871
Type: Private, proprietary
Degrees: C
URL: http://www.sumterbeautycollege.com
Phone: (803) 773-7311
Inst. Accred.: COE (1988/2005)

Wackenhut Services, Inc.—Savannah River Site
Building 703-1B, Aiken 29802
Type: Private, proprietary
Degrees: C
URL: http://www.srs.gov/general/people/wackenhut/over.htm
Phone: (803) 952-7778
Inst. Accred.: COE (2000/2006)

SOUTH DAKOTA

Black Hills Beauty College
623 Saint Joseph St., Rapid City 57701
Type: Private, proprietary
Degrees: C
Phone: (605) 342-0697
Inst. Accred.: NACCAS (1980/2005)

Sioux Falls Campus
3501 South Kelley Ave., Sioux Falls 57106
Phone: (605) 361-2787

Headlines Academy, Inc.
508 Sixth St., Rapid City 57701
Type: Private, proprietary
Degrees: C
Phone: (605) 348-4247
Inst. Accred.: NACCAS (1985/2005)

Leadership Training Institute
3109 West 41st St., Ste. 101B, Sioux Falls 57105
Type: Private, proprietary
Degrees: C
URL: http://www.dalecarnegiesd.com
Phone: (605) 332-0699
Inst. Accred.: ACCET (1977/2004)

Stewart School
604 North West Ave., Sioux Falls 57104
Type: Private, proprietary
Degrees: C
URL: http://www.stewartschool.com
Phone: (605) 336-2775
Inst. Accred.: ACCSCT (2004)

TENNESSEE

Arnold's Beauty School
1179 South Second St., Milan 38358
Type: Private, proprietary
Degrees: C
Phone: (901) 686-7351
Inst. Accred.: COE (1983/2005)

The Barber School
1309 Jackson Ave., Memphis 38107
Type: Private, proprietary
Degrees: C
Phone: (901) 726-4247
Inst. Accred.: NACCAS (2003/2006)

Buchanan Beauty College
925 Sevier St., Shelbyville 37160
Type: Private, proprietary
Degrees: C
URL: http://www.buchananbeautycollege.com
Phone: (931) 684-4080
Inst. Accred.: NACCAS (2004)

Career Beauty College
110 Waterloo St., Lawrenceburg 38464
Type: Private, proprietary
Degrees: C
Phone: (931) 766-9900
Inst. Accred.: NACCAS (2003/2006)

Defense Contract Audit Institute
4075 Park Ave., Memphis 38111
Type: Public, federal
Degrees: C
URL: http://www.dcaa.mil
Phone: (901) 925-6100
Inst. Accred.: COE (2004)

Diamond Council of America
3212 West End Ave., Ste. 202, Nashville 37203
Type: Private, proprietary
Degrees: C
URL: http://www.diamondcouncil.org
Phone: (615) 385-5301
Inst. Accred.: DETC (1984/2003)

Dudley Nwani, The School
3532 West Hamilton Rd., Nashville 37218
Type: Private, proprietary
Degrees: C
URL: http://1wcu.org/main.htm
Phone: (615) 868-4003
Inst. Accred.: NACCAS (2002/2005)

Madison Campus
966 Madison Square, Madison 37115
Phone: (615) 860-4247

Elite College of Cosmetology
459 North Main St., Lexington 38351
Type: Private, proprietary
Degrees: C
Phone: (731) 968-5400
Inst. Accred.: NACCAS (2007)

Fayetteville Beauty School
201 South Main Ave., Fayetteville 37334
Type: Private, proprietary
Degrees: C
URL: http://www.fayettevillebeautyschool.com
Phone: (931) 433-1305
Inst. Accred.: NACCAS (1989/2004)

Franklin Academy
633 Mimosa Dr., NW, Cleveland 37320
Type: Private, proprietary
Degrees: C
Phone: (423) 476-3742
Inst. Accred.: COE (1994/2001, Probation)

Glyn Ed Newton and Associates, Inc.
1321 Murfreesboro Rd., Ste. 311, Nashville 37217
Type: Private, proprietary
Degrees: C
URL: http://www.nashville.dalecarnegie.com
Phone: (615) 399-5101
Inst. Accred.: ACCET (1976/2005)

Institute of Hair Design, Inc.
205 Enterprise Dr., Adamsville 38310
Type: Private, proprietary
Degrees: C
URL: http://www.ihd4me.com
Phone: (731) 632-9533
Inst. Accred.: NACCAS (2005)

International English Institute
1228 16th Ave. South, Nashville 37212
Type: Private, independent
Degrees: C
URL: http://www.eslnashville.org
Phone: (615) 327-1715
Inst. Accred.: CEA (2000)

Jacobs Creek Job Corps
984 Denton Valley Rd., Bristol 37620
Type: Private, federal
Degrees: C
URL: http://atlantaregion.jobcorps.gov/jcCenters/jacobscreekJCC.html
Phone: (423) 878-4021
Inst. Accred.: COE (1997/2003)

Knox International 2000 Beauty College
3641 Brainerd Rd., Ste. F & G, Chattanooga 37411
Type: Private, proprietary
Degrees: C
Phone: (423) 622-1515
Inst. Accred.: NACCAS (2003/2006)

Last Minute Cut School of Barbering and Cosmetology
2195 South Third St., Memphis 38116
Type: Private, proprietary
Degrees: C
URL: http://www.lastminutecuts.com
Phone: (901) 774-9699
Inst. Accred.: NACCAS (2005)

Mason Academy of Cosmetology
12198 Main St., PO Box 581, Mason 38049
Type: Private, proprietary
Degrees: C
Phone: (901) 294-2590
Inst. Accred.: NACCAS (2005)

McCollum and Ross, The Hair School
1433 Hollywood Dr., Jackson 38301
Type: Private, proprietary
Degrees: C
URL: http://www.leadersinbeautyed.com
Phone: (901) 427-6642
Inst. Accred.: NACCAS (1989/2004)

Memphis Montessori Institute
8563 Fay Rd., Cordova 38018
Type: Private, independent
Degrees: C
URL: http://www.lamplighterschool.org
Phone: (901) 751-2000
Inst. Accred.: MACTE (1995/2002)

Middle Tennessee School of Cosmetology
868 A East 10th St., Cookeville 38501
Type: Private, proprietary
Degrees: C
URL: http://www.midtncosmo.com
Phone: (931) 526-8735
Inst. Accred.: COE (1994/2006)

Mister Wayne's School of Unisex Hair Design
170 South Willow Ave., Cookeville 38501
Type: Private, proprietary
Degrees: C
Phone: (931) 526-1478
Inst. Accred.: ACCSCT (1984/2004)

Nashville College of Medical Careers
1556 Crestview Dr., Madison 37115
Type: Private, proprietary
Degrees: C
Phone: (615) 868-2963
Inst. Accred.: ACCSCT (1990/2005)

New Directions Hair Academy-The Beauty Institute
3744 Old Hickory Blvd., Ste. A-2, Nashville 37209
Type: Private, proprietary
Degrees: C
Phone: (615) 353-8333
Inst. Accred.: NACCAS (1996/2004)

The Beauty Institute
568 Colonial Rd., Memphis 38117
Phone: (901) 761-1888

New Wave Hair Academy—Coleman Road
3250 Coleman Rd., Memphis 38128
Type: Private, proprietary
Degrees: C
URL: http://www.leadersinbeautyed.com
Phone: (901) 323-6100
Inst. Accred.: NACCAS (1987/2000)

New Wave Hair Academy—South Highland Street
804 South Highland St., Memphis 38111
Type: Private, proprietary
Degrees: C
URL: http://www.leadersinbeautyed.com
Phone: (901) 320-9283
Inst. Accred.: NACCAS (1989/2004)

Paul Mitchell the School—Nashville
5510 Crossings Circle, Antioch 37013
Type: Private, proprietary
Degrees: C
URL: http://www.paulmitchelltheschool.com
Phone: (615) 283-1000
Inst. Accred.: NACCAS (1980/2005)

Plaza Beauty School
4682 Spottswood Ave., Memphis 38117
Type: Private, proprietary
Degrees: C
URL: http://www.plazabeautyschool.com
Phone: (901) 761-4445
Inst. Accred.: NACCAS (1966/2003)

Pyramid Beauty School
1292 Madison Ave., Memphis 38104
Type: Private, proprietary
Degrees: C
URL: http://www.pyramidbeautyschool.org
Phone: (901) 276-5325
Inst. Accred.: NACCAS (2003/2006)

Queen City College
1594 Fort Campbell Blvd., Clarksville 37042
Type: Private, proprietary
Degrees: C
URL: http://www.queencitycollege.com
Phone: (931) 645-3736
Inst. Accred.: COE (1987/2004)

Reuben Allen College
120 Center Park Dr., Knoxville 37922
Type: Private, proprietary
Degrees: C
Phone: (865) 966-0400
Inst. Accred.: NACCAS (1976/2003)

SAE Institute of Technology
7 Music Circle North, Nashville 37203
Type: Private, proprietary
Degrees: C
URL: http://www.sae-nashville.com
Phone: (615) 244-5848
Inst. Accred.: ACCSCT (2003)

Seminary Extension Independent Study Institute
901 Commerce St., Ste. 500, Nashville 37203-3631
Type: Private, independent
Degrees: C
URL: http://www.seminaryextension.org
Phone: (615) 242-2453
Inst. Accred.: DETC (1972/2003)

Shear Academy
780 West Academy, Crossville 38555
Type: Private, proprietary
Degrees: C
Phone: (931) 456-5391
Inst. Accred.: NACCAS (2004)

Shear Majik School of Beauty
121-A Oak Valley Dr., Nashville 37207
Type: Private, proprietary
Degrees: C
URL: http://www.shearmajik.com
Phone: (615) 228-2112
Inst. Accred.: NACCAS (2006/2007)

Southern Institute of Cosmetology
3099 South Perkins Rd., Memphis 38118-3239
Type: Private, proprietary
Degrees: C
Phone: (901) 363-3553
Inst. Accred.: NACCAS (1986/2006)

Memphis Campus
3099 South Perkins, Memphis 38118
Phone: (901) 363-3553

Stylemasters Beauty Academy
223 North Cumberland St., Lebanon 37087
Type: Private, proprietary
Degrees: C
URL: http://www.stylemasters.net
Phone: (615) 453-7066
Inst. Accred.: NACCAS (1991/2001)

Dalton Beauty College
505 Underwood St., Dalton, GA 30721
Phone: (706) 278-1300

Styles and Profiles Beauty College
119 South Second St., PO Box 402, Selmer 38375
Type: Private, proprietary
Degrees: C
Phone: (731) 645-9728
Inst. Accred.: ACCSCT (1996/2006)

Tennessee Academy of Cosmetology—East Shelby Drive
7020 East Shelby Dr., Ste. 104, Memphis 38125
Type: Private, proprietary
Degrees: C
URL: http://www.tennesseeacademy.com
Phone: (901) 757-4166
Inst. Accred.: NACCAS (1990/2005)

Tennessee Academy of Cosmetology—Highway 64
7041 Hwy. 64, Ste. 101, Memphis 38133
Type: Private, proprietary
Degrees: C
URL: http://www.tennesseeacademy.com
Phone: (901) 388-1687
Inst. Accred.: NACCAS (1987/2005)

Tennessee Career College
443 Donelson Pike, Nashville 37214
Type: Private, proprietary
Degrees: C
URL: http://www.tennesseecareercollege.com
Phone: (615) 874-0774
Inst. Accred.: ACCET (1999/2002)

Tennessee Career Institute
1412 Trotwood Ave., Ste. #1, Columbia 38401
Type: Private, proprietary
Degrees: C
URL: http://www.tennesseecareerinstitute.com
Phone: (931) 388-7717
Inst. Accred.: NACCAS (2005)

Tennessee School of Beauty, Inc.
4704 Western Ave., Knoxville 37921
Type: Private, proprietary
Degrees: C
URL: http://www.tennesseeschoolofbeauty.com
Phone: (865) 588-7878
Inst. Accred.: NACCAS (1965/2006)

Tennessee Technology Center at Athens
PO Box 848, Athens 37371-0848
Type: Public, state
System: Tennessee Board of Regents
Degrees: C
URL: http://www.athens.tec.tn.us
Phone: (423) 744-2814 *Calendar:* Tri. plan
Inst. Accred.: COE (1971/2004)

Tennessee Technology Center at Covington
PO Box 249, Covington 38019-0249
Type: Public, state
System: Tennessee Board of Regents
Degrees: C
URL: http://www.covington.tec.tn.us
Phone: (901) 475-2526 *Calendar:* Tri. plan
Inst. Accred.: COE (1972/2004)

Tennessee Technology Center at Crossville
PO Box 2959, Crossville 38557-2959
Type: Public, state
System: Tennessee Board of Regents
Degrees: C
URL: http://www.crossville.tec.tn.us
Phone: (931) 484-7502 *Calendar:* Tri. plan
Inst. Accred.: COE (1971/2004)
Prog. Accred.: Allied Health (surgical technology)

Tennessee Technology Center at Crump
PO Box 89, Crump 38327-0089
Type: Public, state
System: Tennessee Board of Regents
Degrees: C
URL: http://www.crumpttc.edu
Phone: (731) 632-3393 *Calendar:* Tri. plan
Inst. Accred.: COE (1974/2005)

Tennessee Technology Center at Dickson
740 Hwy. 46, Dickson 37055
Type: Public, state
System: Tennessee Board of Regents
Degrees: C
URL: http://www.dickson.tec.tn.us
Phone: (615) 441-6220 *Calendar:* Tri. plan
Inst. Accred.: COE (1974/2006)
Prog. Accred.: Allied Health (surgical technology), Dentistry (dental assisting)

Tennessee Technology Center at Elizabethton
426 Hwy. 91, Elizabethton 37644
Type: Public, state
System: Tennessee Board of Regents
Degrees: C
URL: http://www.elizabethton.tec.tn.us
Phone: (423) 543-0070 *Calendar:* Tri. plan
Inst. Accred.: COE (1973/2005)

Tennessee Technology Center at Harriman
PO Box 1109, Harriman 37748-1109
Type: Public, state
System: Tennessee Board of Regents
Degrees: C
URL: http://www.harriman.tec.tn.us
Phone: (865) 882-6703 *Calendar:* Tri. plan
Inst. Accred.: COE (1973/2005)

Tennessee Technology Center at Hartsville
716 McMurry Blvd., Hartsville 37074
Type: Public, state
System: Tennessee Board of Regents
Degrees: C
URL: http://www.hartsville.tec.tn.us
Phone: (615) 374-2147 *Calendar:* Tri. plan
Inst. Accred.: COE (1971/2004)

Tennessee Technology Center at Hohenwald
813 West Main St., Hohenwald 38462-2201
Type: Public, state
System: Tennessee Board of Regents
Degrees: C
URL: http://www.hohenwald.tec.tn.us
Phone: (931) 796-5351 *Calendar:* Tri. plan
Inst. Accred.: COE (1972/2004)
Prog. Accred.: Allied Health (surgical technology)

Tennessee Technology Center at Jacksboro
PO Box 419, Jacksboro 37757
Type: Public, state
System: Tennessee Board of Regents
Degrees: C
URL: http://www.jacksboro.tec.tn.us
Phone: (423) 566-9629 *Calendar:* Tri. plan
Inst. Accred.: COE (1972/2004)

Tennessee Technology Center at Jackson
2468 Technology Center Dr., Jackson 38301
Type: Public, state
System: Tennessee Board of Regents
Degrees: C
URL: http://www.jackson.tec.tn.us
Phone: (731) 424-0691 *Calendar:* Tri. plan
Inst. Accred.: COE (1972/2004)
Prog. Accred.: Allied Health (surgical technology)

Tennessee Technology Center at Knoxville
1100 Liberty St., Knoxville 37919
Type: Public, state
System: Tennessee Board of Regents
Degrees: C
URL: http://www.knoxville.tec.tn.us
Phone: (865) 546-5567 *Calendar:* Tri. plan
Inst. Accred.: COE (1971/2004)
Prog. Accred.: Allied Health (medical assisting (AMA), surgical technology), Dentistry (dental assisting)

Tennessee Technology Center at Livingston
PO Box 219, Livingston 38570-0219
Type: Public, state
System: Tennessee Board of Regents
Degrees: C
URL: http://www.livingston.tec.tn.us
Phone: (931) 823-5525 *Calendar:* Tri. plan
Inst. Accred.: COE (1971/2004)

Tennessee Technology Center at McKenzie
PO Box 427, McKenzie 38201-0427
Type: Public, state
System: Tennessee Board of Regents
Degrees: C
URL: http://www.mckenzie.tec.tn.us
Phone: (731) 352-5364 *Calendar:* Tri. plan
Inst. Accred.: COE (1971/2005)

Tennessee Technology Center at McMinnville
241 Vo-Tech Dr., McMinnville 37110
Type: Public, state
System: Tennessee Board of Regents
Degrees: C
URL: http://www.ttcmcminnville.edu
Phone: (931) 473-5587 *Calendar:* Tri. plan
Inst. Accred.: COE (1971/2005)
Prog. Accred.: Allied Health (medical assisting (AMA), surgical technology)

Tennessee Technology Center at Memphis
550 Alabama Ave., Memphis 38105-3604
Type: Public, state
System: Tennessee Board of Regents
Degrees: C
URL: http://www.memphis.tec.tn.us
Phone: (901) 543-6100 *Calendar:* Tri. plan
Inst. Accred.: COE (1970/2002)
Prog. Accred.: Allied Health (medical assisting (AMA), surgical technology), Dentistry (dental assisting)

Aviation Campus
3435 Tchulahoma Rd., Memphis 38116
Phone: (901) 543-6180

Tennessee Technology Center at Morristown
821 West Louise Ave., Morristown 37813-2094
Type: Public, state
System: Tennessee Board of Regents
Degrees: C
URL: http://www.morristown.tec.tn.us
Phone: (423) 586-5771 *Calendar:* Tri. plan
Inst. Accred.: COE (1971/2004)

Hawkins County Campus
323 Phipps Bend Rd., Surgoinsville 37873
Phone: (423) 586-5771

Tennessee Technology Center at Murfreesboro
1303 Old Fort Pkwy., Murfreesboro 37129-3312
Type: Public, state
System: Tennessee Board of Regents
Degrees: C
URL: http://www.murfreesboro.tec.tn.us
Phone: (615) 898-8010 *Calendar:* Tri. plan
Inst. Accred.: COE (1980/2007)
Prog. Accred.: Allied Health (surgical technology), Dentistry (dental assisting)

Tennessee Technology Center at Nashville
100 White Bridge Rd., Nashville 37209
Type: Public, state
System: Tennessee Board of Regents
Degrees: C
URL: http://www.nashville.tec.tn.us
Phone: (615) 425-5500 *Calendar:* Tri. plan
Inst. Accred.: COE (1972/2004)

Cockrill Bend Campus
7204 Cockrill Bend Rd., Cockrill Bend Industrial Park, Nashville 37209
Phone: (615) 350-6224

Tennessee Technology Center at Newbern
340 Washington St., Newbern 38059
Type: Public, state
System: Tennessee Board of Regents
Degrees: C
URL: http://www.newbern.tec.tn.us
Phone: (731) 627-2511 *Calendar:* Tri. plan
Inst. Accred.: COE (1972/2004)

Tennessee Technology Center at Oneida/ Huntsville
355 Scott High Dr., Huntsville 37756-4120
Type: Public, state
System: Tennessee Board of Regents
Degrees: C
URL: http://www.huntsville.tec.tn.us
Phone: (423) 663-4900 *Calendar:* Tri. plan
Inst. Accred.: COE (1973/2005)

Tennessee Technology Center at Paris
312 South Wilson St., Paris 38242
Type: Public, state
System: Tennessee Board of Regents
Degrees: C
URL: http://www.paris.tec.tn.us
Phone: (731) 644-7365 *Calendar:* Tri. plan
Inst. Accred.: COE (1974/2004)
Prog. Accred.: Allied Health (surgical technology)

Tennessee Technology Center at Pulaski
PO Box 614, Pulaski 38478-0614
Type: Public, state
System: Tennessee Board of Regents
Degrees: C
URL: http://www.pulaski.tec.tn.us
Phone: (931) 424-4014 *Calendar:* Tri. plan
Inst. Accred.: COE (1973/2004)

Tennessee Technology Center at Ripley
North Industrial Park, 127 Industrial Dr., Ripley 38063
Type: Public, state
System: Tennessee Board of Regents
Degrees: C
URL: http://www.ttcripley.edu
Phone: (731) 635-3368 *Calendar:* Tri. plan
Inst. Accred.: COE (1973/2005)

Tennessee Technology Center at Shelbyville
1405 Madison St., Shelbyville 37160
Type: Public, state
System: Tennessee Board of Regents
Degrees: C
URL: http://www.shelbyville.tec.tn.us
Phone: (931) 685-5013 *Calendar:* Tri. plan
Inst. Accred.: COE (1972/2005)

Tennessee Technology Center at Whiteville
PO Box 489, Whiteville 38075-0489
Type: Public, state
System: Tennessee Board of Regents
Degrees: C
URL: http://www.whiteville.tec.tn.us
Phone: (731) 254-8521 *Calendar:* Tri. plan
Inst. Accred.: COE (1980/2002)

Volunteer Beauty Academy of Lawrenceburg
5666 Nolensville Rd., Nashville 37211
Type: Private, proprietary
Degrees: C
URL: http://www.volunteerbeauty.com
Phone: (615) 781-1500
Inst. Accred.: NACCAS (1986/2006)

Volunteer Beauty Academy—Dyersburg
2440 Lake Rd., Dyersburg 38024
Type: Private, proprietary
Degrees: C
URL: http://www.volunteerbeauty.com
Phone: (901) 285-1453
Inst. Accred.: NACCAS (1984/2004)

Volunteer Beauty Academy—Madison
1791 North Gallatin Rd., Madison 37115
Type: Private, proprietary
Degrees: C
URL: http://www.volunteerbeauty.com
Phone: (615) 860-4200
Inst. Accred.: NACCAS (1984/2004)

William R. Moore College of Technology
1200 Poplar Ave., Memphis 38104
Type: Private, independent
Degrees: C
URL: http://www.williammoore.org
Phone: (901) 726-1977
Inst. Accred.: COE (1971/20003)

TEXAS

A New Beginning School of Massage
2525 Wallingwood Dr., Ste. 1501, Austin 78746
Type: Private, proprietary
Degrees: C
URL: http://www.nbegin.com
Phone: (512) 306-0975
Inst. Accred.: ACCSCT (2002)

The Academy at Austin
15635 Vision Dr., Ste. 107, Pflugerville 78660
Type: Private, proprietary
Degrees: C
URL: http://www.theacademyaustin.com
Phone: (512) 251-1644
Inst. Accred.: NACCAS (2007)

Academy of Cosmetology
1901 West William Cannon Dr., Ste. 143, Austin 78745
Type: Private, proprietary
Degrees: C
Phone: (512) 444-2249
Inst. Accred.: NACCAS (2002/2005)

Academy of Hair Design, Inc.
3141 College St., Ste. A-10, Beaumont 77701
Type: Private, proprietary
Degrees: C
Phone: (409) 813-3100
Inst. Accred.: NACCAS (1997/2005)

Academy of Hair Design, Inc.
512 South Chestnut, Lufkin 75901
Type: Private, proprietary
Degrees: C
Phone: (409) 634-8440
Inst. Accred.: NACCAS (1997/2005)

Jasper Campus
348 Springhill St., Jasper 75951
Phone: (409) 384-8200

Academy of Health Care Professions
6505 Airport Blvd., Ste. 102, Austin 78752
Type: Private, proprietary
Degrees: C
URL: http://www.academyofhealth.com
Phone: (512) 892-2835
Inst. Accred.: ABHES (1999/2006)

Advanced Barber College and Hair Design
2818 South International, FM 1015, Weslaco 78596
Type: Private, proprietary
Degrees: C
Phone: (956) 969-0341
Inst. Accred.: COE (1999/2003)

AIMS Academy
1106 North Hwy. 360, Ste. 305, Grand Prairie 75050
Type: Private, proprietary
Degrees: C
URL: http://www.aimsacademy.com
Phone: (972) 988-3202
Inst. Accred.: COE (1990/1999)

Dallas Campus
3300 Oak Lawn Ave. Ste. 100, Dallas 75219
Phone: (214) 520-6848

Allied Career Center
1933 East Frankford Rd., Ste. 110, Carrollton 75007
Type: Private, proprietary
Degrees: C
URL: http://www.alliedcareercenter.com
Phone: (972) 939-5482
Inst. Accred.: ACCET (2005)

Dallas Campus
9330 Amberton Pkwy., Ste. 1395, Dallas 75243
Phone: (972) 939-5482

Allied Health Careers
5424 Hwy. 290, West, Ste. 105, Austin 78735
Type: Private, proprietary
Degrees: C
Phone: (512) 892-5210
Inst. Accred.: COE (1991/2000)

American Commercial College
2007 34th St., Lubbock 79411
Type: Private, proprietary
Degrees: C
URL: http://www.acc-careers.com
Phone: (806) 747-4339
Inst. Accred.: ACICS (1982/2003)

American Commercial College
5119 Twin Towers Blvd., Odessa 79762
Type: Private, proprietary
Degrees: C
URL: http://www.acc-careers.com
Phone: (432) 362-6768
Inst. Accred.: ACICS (1970/2006)

American Commercial College
3177 Executive Dr., San Angelo 76904
Type: Private, proprietary
Degrees: C
URL: http://www.acc-careers.com
Phone: (915) 942-6797
Inst. Accred.: ACICS (1976/2006)

American Commercial College
402 Butternut St., Abilene 79602
Type: Private, proprietary
Degrees: C
URL: http://www.acc-careers.com
Phone: (915) 672-8495
Inst. Accred.: ACICS (1970/2004)

Shreveport Campus
3014 Knight St., Shreveport, LA 71105
Phone: (318) 861-2112

Wichita Falls Campus
4317 Barnett Rd., Wichita Falls 76310
Phone: (940) 691-0454

American Institute of Allied Health
1310 South Stemmons Freeway, Lewisville 75067
Type: Private, proprietary
Degrees: C
URL: http://www.aioah.com
Phone: (972) 221-7717
Inst. Accred.: ABHES (2006)

AmesEd
3863 Southwest Loop 820, Fort Worth 76133
Type: Private, proprietary
Degrees: C
Phone: (972) 968-0600
Inst. Accred.: COE (2003)

Anamarc Educational Institute
3210 Dyer St., El Paso 79930-6230
Type: Private, proprietary
Degrees: C
URL: http://www.anamarc.com
Phone: (915) 351-8100
Inst. Accred.: ACICS (2003/2006)

Santa Teresa Campus
2660 Airport Rd., Ste. 500, Santa Teresa, NM 88008
Phone: (505) 589-3158

Arlington Career Institute
901 Ave. K., Grand Prairie 75050
Type: Private, proprietary
Degrees: C
URL: http://www.themetro.com/aci
Phone: (972) 647-1607
Inst. Accred.: ACCSCT (1987/2003)

Arlington Medical Institute
2301 North Collins, Ste. 100, Arlington 76011
Type: Private, proprietary
Degrees: C
Phone: (817) 265-0706
Inst. Accred.: ABHES (1996/2004)

Astrodome Dental Career Center
2646 South Loop West, Ste. 415, Houston 77054
Type: Private, proprietary
Degrees: C
URL: http://www.astrodomeresource.com
Phone: (713) 664-5300
Inst. Accred.: COE (2001/2006)

ATI Career Training Center
10003 Technology Blvd. West, Dallas 75220
Type: Private, proprietary
System: ATI Enterprises, Inc.
Degrees: C
URL: http://www.aticareertraining.com
Phone: (214) 902-8191
Inst. Accred.: ACCSCT (1986/2005)

ATI Career Training Center
6351 Blvd. 26, North Richland Hills 76180
Type: Private, proprietary
System: ATI Enterprises, Inc.
Degrees: C
URL: http://www.aticareertraining.edu
Phone: (817) 284-1141
Inst. Accred.: ACCSCT (1986/2005)

Albuquerque Campus
4575 San Mateo Blvd. NE, Ste. G130, Albuquerque, NM 87109-2016
Phone: (888) 209-8264

Garland Campus
3035 South Shiloh Rd., Ste. 150, Garland 75041-2497
Phone: (888) 209-8264

Richardson Campus
1100 East Campbell Rd., Ste. 250, Richardson 75801
Phone: (888) 209-8264

ATI Technical Training Center
6627 Maple Ave., Dallas 75235-9990
Type: Private, proprietary
System: ATI Enterprises, Inc.
Degrees: C
URL: http://www.aticareertraining.edu
Phone: (214) 352-2222
Inst. Accred.: ACCSCT (1975/2005)

Aviation Institute of Maintenance—Dallas
7555 Lemmon Ave., Dallas 75209
Type: Private, proprietary
Degrees: C
URL: http://www.aviationmaintenance.edu
Phone: (214) 333-9711
Inst. Accred.: ACCSCT (2001/2004)

Baldwin Beauty School
3005 South Lamar, Ste. 103, Austin 78704
Type: Private, proprietary
Degrees: C
Phone: (512) 441-6898
Inst. Accred.: NACCAS (1978/2004)

Burnet Road Campus
8440 Burnet Rd., Austin 78758
Phone: (512) 458-4127

Behold! Beauty Academy
9937 Homestead Rd., Houston 77016
Type: Private, proprietary
Degrees: C
Phone: (713) 635-5252
Inst. Accred.: NACCAS (2001/2004)

Bilingual Education Institute
8989 Westheimer Rd., Ste. 110, PO Box 570596, Houston 77063
Type: Private, proprietary
Degrees: C
URL: http://www.aetas.com
Phone: (713) 789-4555
Inst. Accred.: ACCET (1997/2005)

Capitol City Careers
5424 Hwy. 290 West, Ste. 200, Austin 78745
Type: Private, proprietary
Degrees: C
URL: http://www.capcitycareers.com
Phone: (512) 892-4270
Inst. Accred.: COE (1989/2004)

Capitol City Trade and Technical School
205 East Riverside Dr., Austin 78704
Type: Private, proprietary
Degrees: C
URL: http://www.capcitytradetech.com
Phone: (512) 444-3257
Inst. Accred.: COE (1979/2006, Probation)

Career Academy
32 Oaklawn Village, Texarkana 75501
Type: Private, proprietary
Degrees: C
Phone: (903) 832-1021
Inst. Accred.: COE (1988/2001)

Career Advancement and Applied Technical Training Division
9350 South Presa, San Antonio 78223-4799
Type: Public, state/local
Degrees: C
URL: http://teexweb.tamu.edu
Phone: (210) 633-1000
Inst. Accred.: COE (1984/2000)

Hemisfair Park Campus
600 Hemisfair Park, Building 22, San Antonio 78291-0040
Phone: (210) 633-1000

Career Centers of Texas—El Paso
8360 Burnham Rd., Ste. 100, El Paso 79907
Type: Private, proprietary
System: Kaplan Higher Education Corporation
Degrees: C
URL: http://www.careercenters.edu
Phone: (915) 595-1935
Inst. Accred.: ACCSCT (1995/2003)
Prog. Accred.: Allied Health (medical assisting (AMA), surgical technology)

Brownsville Campus
1900 North Expressway, Brownsville 78521
Phone: (956) 547-8200

Career Point Institute
485 Spencer Ln., San Antonio 78201
Type: Private, proprietary
Degrees: C
URL: http://www.career-point.org
Phone: (210) 732-3000
Inst. Accred.: ACICS (1988/2004)

Tulsa Campus
3138 South Garnett Rd., Tulsa, OK 74146-1933
Phone: (918) 622-4100

Career Quest
5430 Fredericksburg, Ste. 310, San Antonio 78229
Type: Private, proprietary
Degrees: C
URL: http://www.careerquestusa.com
Phone: (210) 366-2701
Inst. Accred.: COE (1999/2005)

Career Tech Institute
2715 Cornerstone Blvd., Edinburg 78539
Type: Private, proprietary
Degrees: C
Phone: (956) 687-8138
Inst. Accred.: ABHES (1998/2001)

Careers Unlimited
335 South Bonner St., Tyler 75702
Type: Private, proprietary
Degrees: C
Phone: (903) 593-4424
Inst. Accred.: ACCSCT (1993/2003)

CCI Training Center
768 Lincoln Square, Arlington 76011
Type: Private, proprietary
Degrees: C
URL: http://www.cci-training.com
Phone: (817) 226-1900
Inst. Accred.: ACCET (2005)

Center of English Language
3434 Forest Ln., Dallas 75234
Type: Private, proprietary
Degrees: C
URL: http://www.english-classes.com
Phone: (214) 696-0027
Inst. Accred.: ACCET (2001/2005)

Central Texas Beauty College
2010 South 57th St., Temple 76501
Type: Private, proprietary
Degrees: C
URL: http://www.centraltexasbeautycollege.com
Phone: (254) 773-9911
Inst. Accred.: NACCAS (1985/2005)

Central Texas Beauty College #2
1400 North Mays St., Ste. A, Round Rock 78664-4209
Type: Private, proprietary
Degrees: C
Phone: (512) 244-2235
Inst. Accred.: NACCAS (1977/2003)

Central Texas Commercial College
9400 N. Central Expressway, Ste. 200, Dallas 75231-4347
Type: Private, proprietary
Degrees: C
URL: http://ctcc-dallas.com
Phone: (214) 368-3680
Inst. Accred.: ACICS (1971/2004)

Champion Beauty College, Inc.
4714 FM 1960 Rd. West, Ste. 104, Houston 77069-4634
Type: Private, proprietary
Degrees: C
URL: http://www.championbeautycollege.com
Phone: (281) 583-9117
Inst. Accred.: COE (2006)

Charles and Sue's School of Hair Design
1711 Briarcrest Dr., Bryan 77802
Type: Private, proprietary
Degrees: C
URL: http://www.charlesandsues.com
Phone: (979) 776-4375
Inst. Accred.: NACCAS (1976/2006)

Computer Labs, Inc.
#3 Butterfield Trail, El Paso 79906
Type: Private, proprietary
Degrees: C
URL: http://geocities.com/computerlabsinc
Phone: (915) 591-8899
Inst. Accred.: ACICS (2003/2006)

Concorde Career Institute—Arlington
601 Ryan Plaza Dr., Ste. 200, Arlington 76011
Type: Private, proprietary
System: Concorde Career Colleges, Inc.
Degrees: C
URL: http://www.concordecareercolleges.com
Phone: (817) 261-1594
Inst. Accred.: ABHES (1998/2006)
Prog. Accred.: Allied Health (surgical technology)

Conlee's College of Cosmetology
402 Quinlan St., Kerrville 78028
Type: Private, proprietary
Degrees: C
Phone: (830) 896-2380
Inst. Accred.: NACCAS (1976/2005)

Coryell Cosmetology College
608 East Leon St., Galesville 76528-2036
Type: Private, proprietary
Degrees: C
Phone: (254) 248-1716
Inst. Accred.: COE (2000/2006)

Cosmetology Career Center
2389A Midway Rd., Carrollton 75006
Type: Private, proprietary
Degrees: C
URL: http://www.cccdallastexas.com
Phone: (972) 669-0494
Inst. Accred.: NACCAS (1976/2006)

Culinary Academy of Austin
6020-B Dillard Circle, Austin 78752-4438
Type: Private, proprietary
Degrees: C
URL: http://www.culinaryacademyofaustin.com
Phone: (512) 451-5743
Inst. Accred.: COE (2002/2006)

Dallas Barber and Stylist College
9357 Forest Ln., Dallas 75243
Type: Private, proprietary
Degrees: C
URL: http://www.dallasbarberandstylistcollege.com
Phone: (214) 575-2168
Inst. Accred.: COE (2002/2005)

Dallas Montessori Teacher Education Programs
5757 Samuell Blvd., Ste. 200, Dallas 75227
Type: Private, independent
Degrees: C
URL: http://www.dallasmontessori.com
Phone: (214) 388-0091
Inst. Accred.: MACTE (1998/2005)

Dallas Nursing Institute
12170 North Abrams Rd., Ste. 200, Dallas 75243
Type: Private, proprietary
Degrees: C
URL: http://www.ntpci.com
Phone: (214) 351-0223
Inst. Accred.: ABHES (1999/2006)

David L. Carrasco Job Corps Center
11155 Gateway West, El Paso 79935
Type: Public, federal
Degrees: C
URL: http://www.jobcorpsworks.org
Phone: (915) 594-0022
Inst. Accred.: COE (1986/2006)

Defense Language Institute English Language Center
2235 Andrews Ave., Lackland AFB 78236-5514
Type: Public, federal
Degrees: C
URL: http://www.dlielc.org
Phone: (210) 671-3540
Inst. Accred.: CEA (2000)

Dolphin Technical Institute
4835 Concord Rd., Beaumont 77703
Type: Private, proprietary
Degrees: C
Phone: (409) 892-0677
Inst. Accred.: NACCAS (2005)

Everest Institute—San Antonio
6550 First Park Ten Blvd., San Antonio 78213
Type: Private, proprietary
System: Corinthian Colleges, Inc
Degrees: C *Enroll:* 1,033
URL: http://www.everest.edu
Phone: (210) 732-7800 *Calendar:* Qtr. plan
Inst. Accred.: ACCSCT (1969/2006)

Bissonnet Campus
9700 Bissonnet St., Ste. 1400, Houston 77036-8014
Phone: (713) 772-4200

Houston Greenspoint Campus
255 Northpoint Dr., Ste. 100, Houston 77060
Phone: (281) 447-7037

Houston (Hobby) Campus
7151 Office City Dr., Ste. 100, Houston 77087
Phone: (713) 645-7404

Galleria Campus
4150 Westheimer, Ste. 200, Houston 77027
Phone: (713) 629-1637

Exposito School of Hair Design
3710 Mockingbird Ln., Amarillo 79109
Type: Private, proprietary
Degrees: C
URL: http://www.expositoschoolofhair.com
Phone: (806) 355-9111
Inst. Accred.: NACCAS (1984/2004)

Faris Computer School
1119 Kent Ave., Nederland 77627
Type: Private, proprietary
Degrees: C
URL: http://www.fariscomputerschool.com
Phone: (409) 722-4072
Inst. Accred.: COE (1997/2003)

Fort Worth Beauty School
6785 Camp Bowie Blvd., Ste. 100, Fort Worth 76116-7158
Type: Private, proprietary
Degrees: C
Phone: (817) 732-2232
Inst. Accred.: NACCAS (1978/2002)

Franklin Beauty School #2
4965 Martin Luther King Blvd., Houston 77021
Type: Private, proprietary
Degrees: C
URL: http://thefranklinbeautyschool.com
Phone: (713) 645-9060
Inst. Accred.: NACCAS (1976/2003)

Gulf Coast Trades Center
143 Forest Service Rd., Ste. 233, New Waverly 77358
Type: Private, independent
Degrees: C
URL: http://www.gctc.us
Phone: (936) 344-6677
Inst. Accred.: COE (1984/2006)

HandsOn Therapy School of Massage
1804 North Galloway Ave., Mesquite 75149-2294
Type: Private, proprietary
Degrees: C
URL: http://www.handsontherapyschools.com
Phone: (972) 285-6133
Inst. Accred.: ACCSCT (2005)

House of Tutors Learning Centers USA, Inc
2400 Pearl St., Austin 78705
Type: Private, proprietary
Degrees: C
URL: http://www.houseoftutors.com
Phone: (512) 472-6996
Inst. Accred.: ACCET (2003)

Houston Ballet's Ben Stevenson Academy
1921 West Bell St., PO Box 130487, Houston 77219-0487
Type: Private, independent
Degrees: C
URL: http://www.houstonballet.org
Phone: (713) 523-6300 ext 201 *Calendar:* Sem. plan
Inst. Accred.: NASD (1985/2005)

Houston Montessori Center
9601 Katy Freeway, Ste. 350, Houston 77024-1330
Type: Private, independent
Degrees: C
URL: http://www.houstonmontessoricenter.org
Phone: (713) 465-7670
Inst. Accred.: MACTE (2001)

Houston Training Schools
709 Shotwell St., Houston 77020-4813
Type: Private, proprietary
Degrees: C
Phone: (713) 675-4300
Inst. Accred.: COE (1979/2005)

Gulf Freeway Campus
6969 Gulf Freeway, Ste. 200, Houston 77087
Phone: (713) 649-5050

Houston's Training and Education Center
7457 Harwin Dr., Ste. 190, Houston 77036
Type: Private, proprietary
Degrees: C
URL: http://www.houston-tec.com
Phone: (713) 783-2221
Inst. Accred.: COE (2004)

ICC Technical Institute
3333 Fannin St., Ste. 203, Houston 77004
Type: Private, independent
Degrees: C
Phone: (713) 522-7799
Inst. Accred.: COE (1995/2002)

Institute of Cosmetology and Esthetics
7011 Harwin Dr., Ste. 100, Houston
Type: Private, proprietary
Degrees: C
Phone: (713) 783-9988
Inst. Accred.: NACCAS (1988/2003)

Inter-American Air Forces Academy
2431 Carswell Ave., Lackland AFB 78236-2247
Type: Public, federal
Degrees: C
URL: http://www.lackland.af.mil/iaafa
Phone: (210) 671-0215
Inst. Accred.: COE (2003)

Interactive College of Technology
8585 North Stemmons Freeway, Ste. M-30, Dallas 75247
Type: Private, proprietary
Degrees: C
URL: http://www.ict-ils.edu
Phone: (214) 637-3377
Inst. Accred.: COE (1989/2004)

Hillcroft Campus
6200 Hillcroft Ave., Houston 77081
Phone: (713) 771-5336

Pasadena Campus
213 West Southmore Ave., Ste. 101, Pasadena 77502-1026
Phone: (713) 920-1120

International Beauty College
2716 West Irving Blvd., Irving 75061
Type: Private, proprietary
Degrees: C
URL: http://www.jonesbeautycollege.com
Phone: (972) 255-1176
Inst. Accred.: NACCAS (1976/2005)

International Beauty College #3
1225 Beltline Rd., Ste. 7, Garland 75040
Type: Private, proprietary
Degrees: C
Phone: (972) 530-1103
Inst. Accred.: NACCAS (1987/2002)

International Business College
5700 Cromo Dr., El Paso 79912
Type: Private, proprietary
Degrees: C
URL: http://www.ibcelpaso.com
Phone: (915) 842-0422
Inst. Accred.: ACICS (1969/2006)

International Business College
4630 50th St., Ste. 100, Lubbock 79414
Type: Private, proprietary
Degrees: C
URL: http://www.ibclubbock.com
Phone: (806) 797-1933
Inst. Accred.: ACICS (1987/2004)

Denton Campus
2006 West University Dr., Denton 76201
Phone: (940) 380-0024

McKinney Campus
901 North McDonald St., Building 7, Ste. 702, McKinney 75069-2169
Phone: (972) 548-0774

Midland Campus
3305 Andrews Hwy., Midland 79703
Phone: (915) 694-7584

Sherman Campus
4107 North Texoma Pkwy., Sherman 75090
Phone: (903) 893-6604

Zaragosa Campus
1155 North Zaragosa Rd., El Paso 79907
Phone: (915) 859-0422

ITS Academy of Beauty #1
4701 Southwest Pkwy., Ste. 2, Wichita Falls 76310-3268
Type: Private, proprietary
Degrees: C
URL: http://www.itsacademyofbeauty.com
Phone: (940) 691-3875
Inst. Accred.: NACCAS (2003/2006)

Iverson Business School and Court Reporting Institute
1600 East Pioneer Pkwy., Ste. 200, Arlington 76010
Type: Private, proprietary
Degrees: C
URL: http://www.iversonschool.edu
Phone: (817) 274-6465
Inst. Accred.: COE (1988/2005)

Norcross Campus
6685 Peachtree Industrial Blvd., Atlanta, GA 30360
Phone: (770) 446-1333

Jay's Technical Institute
9000 West Bellfort St., Houston 77031
Type: Private, proprietary
Degrees: C
Phone: (713) 772-2410
Inst. Accred.: COE (2002/2006)

John M. Jennings and Associates, Inc.
16990 North Dallas Pkwy., Ste. 108, Dallas 75248-1926
Type: Private, proprietary
Degrees: C
URL: http://www.dallas.dalecarnegie.com
Phone: (972) 702-9600
Inst. Accred.: ACCET (1996/2006)

Jones Beauty College
10909 Webb Chapel Rd., Ste. 129, Dallas 75229
Type: Private, proprietary
Degrees: C
URL: http://www.jonesbeautycollege.com
Phone: (214) 956-0088
Inst. Accred.: NACCAS (1991/2006)

Jones Beauty College #2
311-A East Hwy. 303, Grand Prairie 75051
Phone: (214) 956-0088

Jones Beauty College #4
1305 South Hwy. 121, Ste. A150, Lewisville 75067
Phone: (972) 221-3500

Kussad Institute of Court Reporting
2800 South IH-35, Ste. 110, Austin 78704
Type: Private, proprietary
Degrees: C
URL: http://www.kicr1.com
Phone: (512) 443-7286
Inst. Accred.: COE (2001/2006)

Language Plus, Inc.
4110 Rio Bravo, Ste. 202, El Paso 79902
Type: Private, proprietary
Degrees: C
URL: http://www.languageplus.com
Phone: (915) 544-8600
Inst. Accred.: ACCET (1998/2004)

Laredo Beauty College
3002 North Malinche Ave., Laredo 78043
Type: Private, proprietary
Degrees: C
Phone: (956) 723-2059
Inst. Accred.: NACCAS (1974/2005)

Leadership Excellence, Inc.
9100 Southwest Freeway, Ste. 200, Houston 77074
Type: Private, proprietary
Degrees: C
URL: http://www.houston.dalecarnegie.com
Phone: (713) 779-8080
Inst. Accred.: ACCET (1975/2005)

Leadership Training
1616 South Kentucky, Building A, Ste. 110, Amarillo 79102
Type: Private, proprietary
Degrees: C
URL: http://www.dalecarnegie.com
Phone: (806) 355-5033
Inst. Accred.: ACCET (1977/2003)

Lincoln Technical Institute
2915 Alouette Dr., Grand Prairie 75052
Type: Private, proprietary
System: Lincoln Educational Services Corporation
Degrees: C
URL: http://www.lincolntech.com
Phone: (972) 660-5701
Inst. Accred.: ACCSCT (1968/2006)

Lubbock Hair Academy
2844 34th St., Lubbock 79410-3524
Type: Private, proprietary
Degrees: C
URL: http://www.lubbockhairacademy.com
Phone: (806) 795-0806
Inst. Accred.: COE (2000/2006)

Lumberton Adult Educational Center
103 South LHS Dr., Lumberton 77657
Type: Public, local
Degrees: C
URL: http://www.lisdcontinuinged.org
Phone: (409) 923-7835
Inst. Accred.: COE (2004)

Mai-trix Beauty College
5999 West 34th St., Ste. 100, Houston 77092
Type: Private, proprietary
Degrees: C
Phone: (713) 957-0050
Inst. Accred.: NACCAS (2005/2006)

Manuel and Theresa's School of Hair Design
220 North Main St., Bryan 77803-3236
Type: Private, proprietary
Degrees: C
Phone: (979) 821-0076
Inst. Accred.: NACCAS (2007)

Maternidad La Luz
1308 Magoffin St., El Paso 79901
Type: Private, independent
Degrees: C
URL: http://www.maternidadlaluz.com
Phone: (915) 532-4540
Inst. Accred.: MEAC (1999/2005)

Mediatech Institute
350 East Royal Ln., Building 4, Ste. 119, Irving 75039
Type: Private, proprietary
Degrees: C
URL: http://www.mediatechinstitute.com
Phone: (972) 869-1122
Inst. Accred.: ACCSCT (2007)

Austin Sound Lab Campus
200 Academy Dr., Ste. A, Austin 78704
Phone: (512) 447-2002

Houston Sound Lab Campus
3330 Walnut Bend Ln., Houston 77042-4712
Phone: (832) 242-3426

MedVance Institute of Houston
6220 Westpark Dr., Ste. 180, Houston 77057-7378
Type: Private, proprietary
Degrees: C
URL: http://www.medvance.edu
Phone: (713) 266-6594
Inst. Accred.: COE (1996/2006)
Prog. Accred.: Allied Health (surgical technology), Radiography

Metroplex Beauty School
519 North Galloway Ave., Mesquite 75149
Type: Private, proprietary
Degrees: C
URL: http://www.metroplexbeautyschool.com
Phone: (972) 288-5485
Inst. Accred.: NACCAS (1975/2007)

Mid Cities Barber College
2345 SW 3rd St., Ste. 101, Grand Prairie 75051-4892
Type: Private, proprietary
Degrees: C
Phone: (214) 642-1892
Inst. Accred.: ACCSCT (1994/2002)

Milan Institute of Cosmetology
2400 SE 27th Ave., Amarillo 79103-4306
Type: Private, proprietary
Degrees: C
URL: http://www.milaninstitute.edu
Phone: (559) 735-3818
Inst. Accred.: NACCAS (1976/2006)

Wind Crest Campus
5403 Walzem Rd., San Antonio 78218
Phone: (210) 656-1991

South San Antonio Campus
605 SW Military Dr., San Antonio 78221
Phone: (210) 647-5100

Milan Institute San Antonio
6151 NW Loop 410, Ingram Park, Ste. 201, San Antonio 78238
Type: Private, proprietary
Degrees: C
URL: http://www.milaninstitute.edu
Phone: (210) 647-5100
Inst. Accred.: COE (1999/2005, Probation)

Clovis Campus
731 West Shaw Ave., Clovis, CA 93621

Mims Classic Beauty College
5121 Blanco Rd., San Antonio 78216
Type: Private, proprietary
Degrees: C
URL: http://www.mimsclassic.com
Phone: (210) 344-2041
Inst. Accred.: NACCAS (1989/2004)

MJ's Beauty Academy, Inc.
3939 South Polk St., Ste. 505, Dallas 75224
Type: Private, proprietary
Degrees: C
Phone: (214) 374-7500
Inst. Accred.: NACCAS (2001/2004)

National Beauty College—Garland
149 West Kingsley, Ste. 230, Garland 75040
Type: Private, proprietary
Degrees: C
URL: http://www.nationalbeautycollege.com
Phone: (972) 278-2020
Inst. Accred.: NACCAS (1996/2004)

Neilson Beauty College, Inc.
416 West Jefferson Blvd., Dallas 75208
Type: Private, proprietary
Degrees: C
Phone: (214) 941-8756
Inst. Accred.: NACCAS (1975/2002)

North West Beauty School
6770 Antoine Dr., Houston 77091-1208
Type: Private, proprietary
Degrees: C
Phone: (713) 263-8333
Inst. Accred.: NACCAS (2005/2006)

Northwest Educational Center
2910 Antoine Dr., Ste. B-100, Houston 77092
Type: Private, proprietary
Degrees: C
Phone: (713) 680-2929
Inst. Accred.: COE (1998/2003)

The Ocean Corporation
10840 Rockley Rd., Houston 77099-3416
Type: Private, proprietary
Degrees: C
Phone: (281) 530-0202
Inst. Accred.: ACCSCT (1989/2005)

Ogle School of Hair Design—Ft. Worth
5063 Old Granbury Rd., Ft. Worth 76133
Type: Private, proprietary
Degrees: C
URL: http://www.ogleschool.com
Phone: (817) 294-2950
Inst. Accred.: NACCAS (1982/2007)

Dallas Campus
6333 East Mockingbird Ln., Ste. 201, Dallas 75214
Phone: (214) 821-0819

Ogle School of Hair Design—Hurst
720 Arcadia St., Apartment B, Hurst 76053
Type: Private, proprietary
Degrees: C
URL: http://www.ogleschool.com
Phone: (817) 284-9231
Inst. Accred.: NACCAS (1982/2007)

Ogle School of Hair, Skin and Nails
2200 West Park Row Dr., Ste. 106, Arlington 76013
Type: Private, proprietary
Degrees: C
URL: http://www.ogleschool.com
Phone: (817) 460-8181
Inst. Accred.: NACCAS (1975/2007)

Paul Mitchell the School—Houston
744 F. M. 1960 West, Ste. G, Houston 77090
Type: Private, proprietary
Degrees: C
URL: http://www.paulmitchelltheschool.com
Phone: (281) 893-1960
Inst. Accred.: NACCAS (1986/2006)

PCI Health Training Center
8101 John Carpenter Freeway, Dallas 75247-4720
Type: Private, proprietary
Degrees: C
URL: http://www.pcihealth.edu
Phone: (214) 630-0568
Inst. Accred.: ACCSCT (1986/2002)

Richardson Campus
1300 International Pkwy., Richardson 75081
Phone: (214) 576-2600

Pipo Academy of Hair Design
3000 Pershing Dr., El Paso 79903
Type: Private, proprietary
Degrees: C
Phone: (915) 565-3491
Inst. Accred.: NACCAS (1981/2004)

Polytechnic Institute
5206 Airline, Houston 77022-2929
Type: Private, proprietary
Degrees: C
Phone: (713) 694-6027
Inst. Accred.: ACCSCT (1990/2006)

Professional Careers Institute, Inc.
6666 Harwin Dr., Ste. 160, Houston 77036
Type: Private, proprietary
Degrees: C
URL: http://www.pcitraining.org
Phone: (713) 783-3999
Inst. Accred.: ACCET (2004)

Ronny J's Barber and Styling College
443 Bruton Terrace Center, Dallas 75227
Type: Private, proprietary
Degrees: C
Phone: (214) 275-7151
Inst. Accred.: NACCAS (2002/2005)

Royal Beauty Careers
5020 F.M. 1960 West, Ste. A-12, Houston 77069-4611
Type: Private, proprietary
Degrees: C
URL: http://www.rb.edu
Phone: (281) 580-2554
Inst. Accred.: COE (1994/2005)

Royal Beauty Careers
1611 Spencer Hwy., Ste. E, South San Antonio 77587
Type: Private, proprietary
Degrees: C
URL: http://www.rb.edu
Phone: (713) 946-5055
Inst. Accred.: NACCAS (1990/2005)

Jackson Beauty School
223 West Main, Ste. C, League City 77573
Phone: (281) 332-6604

San Antonio Beauty College #3
4021 Naco Perrin Blvd., San Antonio 78217
Type: Private, proprietary
Degrees: C
Phone: (210) 654-9734
Inst. Accred.: NACCAS (1986/2006)

San Antonio Beauty College #4
2423 Jamar St., San Antonio 78226-1194
Type: Private, proprietary
Degrees: C
Phone: (210) 433-7222
Inst. Accred.: NACCAS (1990/2005)

San Antonio College of Medical and Dental Assistants
4205 San Pedro Ave., San Antonio 78212-1899
Type: Private, proprietary
System: Kaplan Higher Education Corporation
Degrees: C
URL: http://www.sacmda.com
Phone: (210) 733-0777
Inst. Accred.: ACCSCT (1970/2003)
Prog. Accred.: Allied Health (medical assisting (AMA))

Corpus Christi Campus
1620 South Padre Island, Ste. 600, Corpus Christi 78416
Phone: (361) 852-2900

McAllen Campus
1500 South Jackson Rd., McAllen 78503
Phone: (956) 360-1499

Sanford-Brown Institute—Dallas
1250 West Mockingbird Ln., Dallas 75247
Type: Private, proprietary
System: Career Education Corporation
Degrees: C
URL: http://www.sbdallas.com
Phone: (214) 459-8490
Inst. Accred.: ABHES (1993/2003)
Prog. Accred.: Allied Health (diagnostic medical sonography, surgical technology)

Garden City Campus
711 Stewart Ave., 2nd Flr., Garden City, NY 11530
Phone: (516) 247-2900
Prog. Accred: Medical Assisting (ABHES)

School of Automotive Machinists
1911 Antoine Dr., Houston 77055-1803
Type: Private, proprietary
Degrees: C
URL: http://www.samracing.com
Phone: (713) 683-3817
Inst. Accred.: ACCSCT (1991/2006)

School of Hair Design
4115 North Kings Hwy., Ste. 110, Texarkana 75503
Type: Private, proprietary
Degrees: C
Phone: (903) 831-3737
Inst. Accred.: NACCAS (1993/2006)

Sherman Cosmetology College
4800 North Texoma Pkwy., Ste. 404, Sherman 75090
Phone: (903) 893-9400

Sebring Career Schools
7060 Bissonnet St., Houston 77074
Type: Private, proprietary
Degrees: C
URL: http://www.sebringbeautyschool.com
Phone: (713) 772-6209
Inst. Accred.: COE (1985/2002)

Barker Campus
6672 Hwy. 6, South, Houston 77413-0277
Phone: (713) 561-0592

Huntsville Campus
2505 Lake Rd., Ste. 1, Huntsville 77340
Phone: (409) 291-6299

Seguin Beauty School
102 East Ct. St., Seguin 78155
Type: Private, proprietary
Degrees: C
URL: http://www.seguinbeautyschool.net
Phone: (830) 372-0935
Inst. Accred.: COE (1987/2004)

New Braunfels Campus
214 West San Antonio St., New Braunfels 78130
Phone: (830) 620-1301

South Texas Barber College
3917 Ayers St., Corpus Christi 78415
Type: Private, proprietary
Degrees: C
Phone: (361) 855-2297
Inst. Accred.: COE (2004)

South Texas Training Center
213 East Ferguson St., Pharr 78577-1826
Type: Private, proprietary
Degrees: C
URL: http://southtexastraining.com
Phone: (956) 782-7100
Inst. Accred.: COE (2006)

Laredo Campus
5460 Springfield Ave., Ste. 1111, Laredo 78041-3884
Phone: (956) 727-4909

San Benito Campus
1901 West Hwy. 77 Sunshine Strip, San Benito 78586
Phone: (956) 399-9698

South Texas Vo-Tech Institute—McAllen
2400 West Daffodil Ave., Mcallen 78501
Type: Private, proprietary
Degrees: C
URL: http://www.stvt.edu
Phone: (956) 631-1107
Inst. Accred.: COE (1982/2004)

South Texas Vo-Tech Institute—Weslaco
2419 East Haggar Ave., Weslaco 78596
Type: Private, proprietary
Degrees: C
URL: http://www.stvt.edu
Phone: (956) 969-1564
Inst. Accred.: COE (1982/2004)

Brownsville Campus
2144 Central Blvd., Brownsville 78520
Phone: (888) 509-3584

Southeastern Career Institute
12005 Ford Rd., Ste. 100, Dallas 75234
Type: Private, proprietary
System: Kaplan Higher Education Corporation
Degrees: C
URL: http://www.southeasterncareerinstitute.com
Phone: (972) 385-1446
Inst. Accred.: COE (1989/2002)

Midland Campus
4320 West Illinois Ave., Ste. A, Westwood Village Shopping Center, Midland 79703-5591
Phone: (432) 681-3390

Southern Careers Institute
2301 South Congress Ave., Ste. #27, Austin 78704
Type: Private, proprietary
Degrees: C
URL: http://www.scitexas.com
Phone: (512) 326-1415
Inst. Accred.: COE (1991/2003)

Corpus Christi Campus
2422 Airline Rd., Corpus Christi 78414
Phone: (361) 857-5700

Laredo campus
4805 Maher Ave., Laredo 78041-3846
Phone: (956) 723-2345

Pharr Campus
1414 North Jackson Rd., Pharr 78577
Phone: (956) 687-1415

San Antonio Campus
1405 North Main # 100, San Antonio 78212
Phone: (210) 271-0096

Southern Educational Alliance
6420 Richmond Ave., Ste. 610, Houston 77057
Type: Private, proprietary
Degrees: C
URL: http://www.seainstantlearning.com
Phone: (713) 975-9642
Inst. Accred.: ABHES (2001)

Southwest Career Institute
1414 Geronimo Dr., El Paso 79925-1814
Type: Private, proprietary
Degrees: C
Phone: (915) 778-4001
Inst. Accred.: ABHES (2007)

Southwest School of Business and Technical Careers
272 Commercial St., Eagle Pass 78852
Type: Private, proprietary
Degrees: C
Phone: (210) 773-1373
Inst. Accred.: COE (1989/2001)

Southwest School of Business and Technical Careers
2402 San Pedro Ave., San Antonio 78212-2840
Type: Private, proprietary
Degrees: C
Phone: (210) 225-7287
Inst. Accred.: COE (1992/2004)

Del Rio Campus
1909 Ave. F, Del Rio 78840

Southwest School of Business and Technical Careers
602 West Southcross Blvd., San Antonio 78221
Type: Private, proprietary
Degrees: C
Phone: (210) 921-0951
Inst. Accred.: COE (1982/2003)

Southwestern Montessori Training Center
PO Box 310947 NT Station, Denton 76207
Type: Private, independent
Degrees: C
Phone: (940)566-1640
Inst. Accred.: MACTE (2003)

Star College of Cosmetology—Nacogdoches
705 North University Dr., Nacogdoches 75961-4645
Type: Private, proprietary
Degrees: C
Phone: (936) 462-7232
Inst. Accred.: NACCAS (1988/2003)

Longview Campus
700 East Whaley St., Longview 75601-6527
Phone: (903) 758-8611

Star College of Cosmetology—Tyler
520 East Front St., Tyler 75702
Type: Private, proprietary
Degrees: C
URL: http://www.starcollegeofcosmetology.com
Phone: (903) 596-7860
Inst. Accred.: NACCAS (1991/2004)

State Beauty Academy, Inc.
663 Oriole Blvd., Duncanville 75116
Type: Private, proprietary
Degrees: C
Phone: (972) 298-0100
Inst. Accred.: NACCAS (2001/2004)

Stephenville Beauty College
951 South Lillian St., Stephenville 76401
Type: Private, proprietary
Degrees: C
Phone: (254) 968-2111
Inst. Accred.: NACCAS (1977/2002)

Sterling Health Center
15070 Beltwood Pkwy., Addison 75001-3715
Type: Private, proprietary
Degrees: C
URL: http://sterlinghealthcenter.com
Phone: (972) 991-9293
Inst. Accred.: ACCSCT (2003)

Sylvia's International School of Beauty
434 West Parker Rd., Houston 77091
Type: Private, proprietary
Degrees: C
Phone: (713) 697-1200
Inst. Accred.: COE (2000/2006)

Texas Barber College and Hairstyling Schools
9275 Richmond Ave., Ste. 180, Houston 77063
Type: Private, proprietary
Degrees: C
URL: http://www.texasbarbercolleges.com
Phone: (713) 953-0262
Inst. Accred.: COE (1988/2006)

Conroe Campus
1212 South Frazier St., Conroe 77301

Dallas Campus
2406 Gus Thomason Rd., Dallas 75228
Phone: (214) 324-2851

South Lancaster Campus
5148 South Lancaster Rd., Dallas 75241

West Cavalcade Campus
610 West Cavalcade St., Houston 77009
Phone: (972) 644-4106

Texas Careers
1015 Jackson-Keller Rd., Ste. 102A, San Antonio 78213
Type: Private, proprietary
System: Kaplan Higher Education Corporation
Degrees: C
URL: http://www.texascareers.com
Phone: (210) 308-8584
Inst. Accred.: COE (1995/2001, Probation)

Laredo Campus
6410 McPherson Ave., Laredo 78041-6191
Phone: (956) 717-5909

Texas College of Cosmetology
918 North Chadbourne St., San Angelo 76903
Type: Private, proprietary
Degrees: C
Phone: (325) 659-2622
Inst. Accred.: COE (1994/2001)

Texas College of Cosmetology
117 Sayles Blvd., Abilene 79605
Type: Private, proprietary
Degrees: C
Phone: (915) 677-0532
Inst. Accred.: NACCAS (1990/2005)

Texas Health School
11211 Katy Freeway, Ste. 170, Houston 77079
Type: Private, proprietary
Degrees: C
URL: http://www.texashealthschool.org
Phone: (713) 932-9333
Inst. Accred.: COE (2005)

Texas School of Business
711 East Airtex Dr., Houston 77073
Type: Private, proprietary
System: Kaplan Higher Education Corporation
Degrees: C
URL: http://www.tsb.edu
Phone: (281) 443-8900
Inst. Accred.: ACICS (1985/2006)

East Houston Campus
12030 East Freeway, Houston 77029
Phone: (713) 455-8555
Prog. Accred: Allied Health (medical assisting (AMA))

Friendswood Campus
3208 Farm Rd. 528, Friendswood 77546-8938
Phone: (281) 648-0880

Southwest Campus
6363 Richmond Ave., Ste. 300, Houston 77057
Phone: (713) 975-7527
Prog. Accred: Allied Health (medical assisting (AMA))

Texas Vocational Schools
1921 East Red River, Victoria 77901
Type: Private, proprietary
Degrees: C
URL: http://www.texasvocationalschools.com
Phone: (361) 575-4768
Inst. Accred.: COE (1983/2005)

Victoria Campus
201 East Rio Grande, Victoria 77901
Phone: (512) 575-4768

Touch of Class School of Cosmetology
5015 Weslet St., Ste. A, Greenville 75402
Type: Private, proprietary
Degrees: C
URL: http://www.tocsoc.com
Phone: (903) 455-1144
Inst. Accred.: NACCAS (1998/2006)

McKinney Campus
405 North McDonald St., Ste. A, McKinney 75069-3911
Phone: (972) 369-1020

Trend Barber College
7725 West Bellfort St., Houston 77071-2104
Type: Private, proprietary
Degrees: C
URL: http://www.trendbarbercollege.com
Phone: (713) 721-0000
Inst. Accred.: COE (2002/2006)

Tri-State Cosmetology Institute—Doniphan Drive
3910 Doniphan Dr., Ste. C-F, El Paso 79922
Type: Private, proprietary
Degrees: C
URL: http://www.tristatecosmetology.com
Phone: (915) 585-8777
Inst. Accred.: NACCAS (1982/2002)

Tri-State Cosmetology Institute—Gateway East
6800 Gateway East, #4-A, El Paso 79915
Type: Private, proprietary
Degrees: C
URL: http://www.tristatecosmetology.com
Phone: (915) 778-1741
Inst. Accred.: NACCAS (1982/2002)

United States Army Medical Department Center and School
2250 Stanley Rd., Building 2840, Rm. 301, MCCS-Z, San Antonio 78234-6100
Type: Public, federal
Degrees: C
URL: http://www.cs.amedd.army.mil
Phone: (210) 221-8715
Inst. Accred.: COE (1983/2005)
Prog. Accred.: Allied Health (cardiovascular technology, occupational therapy assisting, respiratory therapy), Dentistry (dental laboratory technology), Nurse Anesthesia Education, Physician Assistant, Radiography

Army Medical Equipment and Optician School
Aurora, CO 80045-7040
Phone: (303) 943-4107

School of Aviation Medicine
Fort Rucker, AL 36362-5377
Phone: (205) 558-7409

Universal Technical Institute
721 Lockhaven Dr., Houston 77073-5598
Type: Private, proprietary
Degrees: C *Enroll:* 3,338
URL: http://www.uticorp.com
Phone: (281) 443-6262
Inst. Accred.: ACCSCT (1983/2004)

Exton Campus
750 Pennsylvania Ave., Exton, PA 19341
Phone: (610) 646-8301

University of Cosmetology Arts and Sciences
8401 North 10th St., PO Box 720391, McAllen 78504
Type: Private, proprietary
Degrees: C
URL: http://www.ucasinc.com
Phone: (956) 687-9444
Inst. Accred.: NACCAS (1978/2005)

Harlingen Campus
913 North Thirteenth St., Harlingen 78550
Phone: (956) 412-1212

Valley Grande Institute for Academic Studies
414 South Missouri Ave., Weslaco 78596-6018
Type: Private, proprietary
Degrees: C
URL: http://www.valleygrandeinstitute.com
Phone: (956) 973-1945
Inst. Accred.: ABHES (2001/2006)

Vanguard Institute of Technology
3107 North Sugar Rd., Pharr 78577
Type: Private, proprietary
Degrees: C
Phone: (956) 787-4388
Inst. Accred.: COE (1990/2001)

Ed Carey Drive Campus
603 Ed Carey Dr., Harlingen 78550
Phone: (210) 428-4999

West Price Road Campus
1424 West Price Rd, #K, Harlingen 78550
Phone: (210) 472-6668

Velma B's Beauty Academy
1511 South Ewing Ave., Dallas 75216
Type: Private, proprietary
Degrees: C
URL: http://www.velmabs.com
Phone: (214) 942-1541
Inst. Accred.: NACCAS (1975/2003)

Victoria Beauty College
1508 North Laurent St., Victoria 77901
Type: Private, proprietary
Degrees: C
Phone: (361) 575-4526
Inst. Accred.: NACCAS (1989/2004)

UTAH

Ameritech College
1675 North Freedom Blvd., Building 3, Provo 84604
Type: Private, proprietary
Degrees: C
URL: http://www.ameritech.edu
Phone: (801) 377-2900
Inst. Accred.: ABHES (1984/2003)
Prog. Accred.: Allied Health (medical assisting (AMA), surgical technology), Dentistry (dental assisting), Medical Assisting (ABHES), Surgical Technology

Draper Campus
12257 Business Park Dr., Ste. 108, Draper 84020
Phone: (801) 816-1444
Prog. Accred: Dentistry (dental assisting)

Bio Kosmetique Institute of Aesthetics
11075 South State St., Crescent Office Park, Ste. 21, Sandy 84070
Type: Private, proprietary
Degrees: C
URL: http://www.biokosmetique.com
Phone: (801) 523-0395
Inst. Accred.: NACCAS (2007)

Bon Losee Academy of Hair Artistry
2230 North University Pkwy., Building #5, Provo 84604
Type: Private, proprietary
Degrees: C
URL: http://www.bonlosse.com
Phone: (801) 375-8000
Inst. Accred.: NACCAS (1989/2004)

Cameo College of Essential Beauty
124 East 5770 South, Murray 84107-6106
Type: Private, proprietary
Degrees: C
URL: http://www.cameocollege.com
Phone: (801) 747-5700
Inst. Accred.: NACCAS (1994/2002)

Color My Nails School of Nail Technology
85 East 7200 South, Midvale 84047
Type: Private, proprietary
Degrees: C
URL: http://www.colormynails.com
Phone: (801) 561-9112
Inst. Accred.: NACCAS (2005)

Dale Carnegie Training Utah
180 South 300 West, Ste. 315, Salt Lake City 84101
Type: Private, proprietary
Degrees: C
URL: http://www.utah.dalecarnegie.com
Phone: (801) 363-5294
Inst. Accred.: ACCET (1988/2006)

Dallas Roberts Academy of Hair Design
1700 North State St., Ste. 18, Provo 84604
Type: Private, proprietary
Degrees: C
URL: http://www.dallasroberts.com
Phone: (801) 375-1501
Inst. Accred.: NACCAS (2000/2003)

Evan's Hairstyling College—Cedar City
169 North 100 West, Cedar City 84720
Type: Private, proprietary
Degrees: C
URL: http://www.evanscollege.com
Phone: (435) 586-4486
Inst. Accred.: NACCAS (1988/2003)

Evan's Hairstyling College—Orem
798 West 400 North, Orem 84057
Type: Private, proprietary
Degrees: C
URL: http://www.evanscollege.com
Phone: (801) 224-6034
Inst. Accred.: NACCAS (2001/2004)

Evan's Hairstyling College—St. George
955 East Tabernacle St., St. George 84770
Type: Private, proprietary
Degrees: C
URL: http://www.evanscollege.com
Phone: (435) 673-6128
Inst. Accred.: NACCAS (1988/2003)

Fran Brown College of Beauty
521 West 600 North, Layton 84041
Type: Private, proprietary
Degrees: C
URL: http://www.franschool.com
Phone: (801) 546-1377
Inst. Accred.: NACCAS (1988/2003)

Francois D. Hair Design Academy
111 West 9000 South, Sandy 84070
Type: Private, proprietary
Degrees: C
URL: http://www.francoisd.com
Phone: (801) 561-2244
Inst. Accred.: NACCAS (1994/2002)

Hairitage Hair Academy
900 South Bluff St., Ste. 9, St. George 84770
Type: Private, proprietary
Degrees: C
Phone: (435) 673-5233
Inst. Accred.: NACCAS (1994/2007)

Healing Mountain Massage School
455 South 300 East, Ste. 103, Salt Lake City 84111
Type: Private, proprietary
Degrees: C
URL: http://www.healingmountain.org
Phone: (801) 355-6300
Inst. Accred.: ABHES (2001/2006)

Image Works Academy of Hair Design, Inc.
77 East 800 North, Spanish Fork 84660
Type: Private, proprietary
Degrees: C
Phone: (801) 798-0448
Inst. Accred.: NACCAS (2006)

Jean's Nails, Etc.
356 North 100 West, Provo 84601
Type: Private, proprietary
Degrees: C
Phone: (801) 377-8267
Inst. Accred.: COE (2006)

Maximum Style Tec School of Cosmetology
130 South Main St., Ste. 230, Logan 84321
Type: Private, proprietary
Degrees: C
Phone: (435) 752-3599
Inst. Accred.: NACCAS (2004/2007)

Myotherapy College of Utah
1174 East 2700 South, Ste. 19, Graystone Plaza, Salt Lake City 84106
Type: Private, proprietary
Degrees: C
URL: http://www.myomassage.net
Phone: (801) 484-7624
Inst. Accred.: ACCSCT (1992/2006)

New Horizons Beauty College
550 North Main St., Ste. 115, Logan 84321
Type: Private, proprietary
Degrees: C
URL: http://newhorizonsbeautycollege.com
Phone: (435) 753-9779
Inst. Accred.: NACCAS (1993/2006)

Ogden Institute of Massage Therapy
3500 Harrison Blvd., Ogden 84403
Type: Private, proprietary
Degrees: C
URL: http://www.oimt.net
Phone: (801) 627-8227
Inst. Accred.: ABHES (2002/2005)

Paul Mitchell The School
480 North 900 East, Provo 84606
Type: Private, proprietary
System: Paul Mitchell The School—Corporate Office
Degrees: C
URL: http://pmts.paulmitchelltheschool.com
Phone: (801) 374-5111
Inst. Accred.: NACCAS (1987/2006)

Paul Mitchell The School
1969 East Murray Holiday Rd., Salt Lake City 84117
Type: Private, proprietary
System: Paul Mitchell The School—Corporate Office
Degrees: C
URL: http://pmts.paulmitchelltheschool.com
Phone: (801) 266-4693
Inst. Accred.: NACCAS (1988/2003)

Casselberry Campus
1271 Semoran Boulvard, Ste. 131, Casselberry, FL 32707
Phone: (407) 677-7695

Cranston Campus
379 Atwood Ave., Cranston, RI 02920
Phone: (401) 946-9920

Paul Mitchell—The School
1534 Adams Ave., Costa Mesa, CA 92626
Phone: (714) 546-8786

San Diego Campus
410 A St., Unit C, San Diego, CA 92101
Phone: (619) 595-1633

Tampa Campus
14210 North Nebraska Ave., Unit C, Ste. 200, Tampa, FL 33613
Phone: (813) 972-9838

Premier Hair Academy
4616 South 4000 West, West Valley 84120
Type: Private, proprietary
Degrees: C
Phone: (801) 966-8414
Inst. Accred.: NACCAS (1988/2003)

Prime Cut Academy of Hair and Nail Artistry
341 East Main St., Vernal 84078-2607
Type: Private, proprietary
Degrees: C
URL: http://www.primecutacademy.com
Phone: (435) 789-3098
Inst. Accred.: NACCAS (2005)

Renaissance School of Therapeutic Massage
566 West 1350 South, Ste. 100, Bountiful 84010
Type: Private, proprietary
Degrees: C
URL: http://www.renaissancemassageschool.com
Phone: (801) 292-8515
Inst. Accred.: ABHES (2004)

Sherman Kendall's Academy of Beauty Arts and Science—Midvale
7353 South 900 East, Midvale 84047
Type: Private, proprietary
Degrees: C
URL: http://www.shermankendallsacademy.com
Phone: (801) 561-5610
Inst. Accred.: NACCAS (1976/2003)

Sherman Kendall's Academy of Beauty Arts and Science—Salt Lake City
2230 South 700 East, Salt Lake City 84106
Type: Private, proprietary
Degrees: C
URL: http://www.shermankendallsacademy.com
Phone: (801) 486-0101
Inst. Accred.: NACCAS (1973/2003)

The Skin Institute, LLC
992 North Westridge Dr., Building A, St. George 84770
Type: Private, proprietary
Degrees: C
Phone: (435) 673-7696
Inst. Accred.: NACCAS (2005/2006)

Skin Works School of Advanced Skin Care
2121 South 230 East, Salt Lake City 84115
Type: Private, proprietary
Degrees: C
URL: http://www.skin-works.com
Phone: (801) 530-0001
Inst. Accred.: COE (2003)

Stacey's Hands of Champions Beauty College, Inc.
3721 South 250 West, Ogden 84405
Type: Private, proprietary
Degrees: C
URL: http://www.staceyscollege.com
Phone: (801) 394-5718
Inst. Accred.: NACCAS (1987/2007)

Taylor Andrews Academy of Hair Design
9052 South 1510 West, West Jordan 84088-6577
Type: Private, proprietary
Degrees: C
URL: http://www.taylorandrew.com
Phone: (801) 748-2288
Inst. Accred.: NACCAS (2005/2006)

TechSkills, LLC.
756 East Winchester St., Ste. 190, Murray 84107
Type: Private, proprietary
Degrees: C
URL: http://www.techskills.com
Phone: (801) 313-9200
Inst. Accred.: ACCET (2007)

Utah College of Massage Therapy
25 South 300 East, Salt Lake City
Type: Private, proprietary
Degrees: C
URL: http://www.ucmt.com
Phone: (801) 521-3330
Inst. Accred.: ACCET (1990/2001)

Denver School of Massage Therapy—Aurora Campus
14104 East Exposition Ave., Aurora, CO 80019
Phone: (800) 617-3302

Denver School of Massage Therapy—Westminster Campus
8991 Harlan St., Ste. B, Westminster, CO 80031
Phone: (303) 426-5621

Las Vegas Campus
2381 East Windmill Ln., Ste. 14, Las Vegas, NV 89123
Phone: (702) 456-4325

Lindon Campus
135 South State St., Ste. 12, Lindon 84042
Phone: (801) 796-0300

Nevada School of Massage Therapy
2381 East Windmill Ln., Ste. 14, Las Vegas, NV 89123
Phone: (702) 456-4325

Phoenix Campus
9201 North 29th Ave., Ste. 35, Phoenix, AZ 85051-3436
Phone: (602) 331-4325

Tempe Campus
1409 West Southern Ave., Ste. 6, Tempe, AZ 85282
Phone: (480) 983-2222

Vista College
1385 West 2200 South, Salt Lake City 84119
Type: Private, proprietary
Degrees: C *Enroll:* 27
URL: http://www.vistacollege.edu
Phone: (801) 973-7008
Inst. Accred.: ACCSCT (1988/2005)

Clearfield Campus
775 South 2000 East, Clearfield 84015
Phone: (801) 774-9900

VERMONT

National Midwifery Institute
PO Box 128, Bristol 05443-0128
Type: Private, proprietary
Degrees: C
URL: http://www.nationalmidwiferyinstitute.com
Phone: (802) 453-3332
Inst. Accred.: MEAC (2002/2005)

O'Brien's Training Center
1475 Shelburne Rd., Ste. 200, South Burlington 05403
Type: Private, proprietary
Degrees: C
Phone: (802) 658-9591
Inst. Accred.: NACCAS (1966/2003)

Vermont College of Cosmetology
400 Cornerstone Dr., Ste. 220, Williston 05495
Type: Private, proprietary
Degrees: C
URL: http://www.vtcollegeofcosmo.com
Phone: (802) 879-4811
Inst. Accred.: NACCAS (1972/2005)

Vermont Training Solutions, Inc.
23 Athens Dr., Essex 05452
Type: Private, proprietary
Degrees: C
URL: http://www.vts-dalecarnegie.com
Phone: (802) 879-7219
Inst. Accred.: ACCET (1998/2003)

VIRGINIA

AKS Massage School
462 Herndon Pkwy., Ste. 208, Herndon 20170
Type: Private, proprietary
Degrees: C
URL: http://www.aksmassageschool.com
Phone: (703) 464-0333
Inst. Accred.: ACCSCT (2004)

Ana Visage Academy
10130-B Colvin Run Rd., Great Falls 22066
Type: Private, proprietary
Degrees: C
URL: http://www.anavisage.com
Phone: (703) 759-2200
Inst. Accred.: COE (2005)

The Banner College
2300 Wilson Blvd., Ste. 600, Arlington 22201
Type: Private, proprietary
System: High-Tech Institute
Degrees: C
URL: http://www.bannercollege.edu
Phone: (703) 908-8300
Inst. Accred.: ACCET (2001/2004, Warning)

BarPalma Beauty Careers Academy
3535 Franklin Rd., SW, Unit D, Roanoke 24014
Type: Private, proprietary
Degrees: C
URL: http://www.barpalma.com
Phone: (540) 343-0153
Inst. Accred.: COE (1989/2004)

Blue Ridge Job Corps Center
245 West Main St., Marion 24354
Type: Public, federal
Degrees: C
URL: http://blueridge.jobcorps.gov
Phone: (276) 783-7221
Inst. Accred.: COE (2004)

Career Training Solutions
100 Riverside Pkwy., Ste. 123, Fredericksburg 22406
Type: Private, proprietary
Degrees: C
URL: http://www.careertrainingsolutions.com
Phone: (540) 372-2000
Inst. Accred.: COE (2002/2007)

Cayce/Reilly School of Massotherqapy
215 67th St., Virginia Beach 23451
Type: Private, proprietary
Degrees: C
URL: http://edgarcayce.org/health/crsm_index.html
Phone: (757) 457-7270
Inst. Accred.: CMTA (1999/2004)

Center for Naval Engineering
1534 Piersey St., Ste. 321, Norfolk 23511-2613
Type: Public, federal
Degrees: C
URL: https://www.npdc.navy.mil/cne
Phone: (757) 444-5332
Inst. Accred.: COE (2004/2006)

Center for Naval Intelligence
2088 Regulus Ave., Virginia Beach 23461-2099
Type: Public, federal
Degrees: C
URL: https://www.npdc.navy.mil/cennavintel
Phone: (757) 492-0001
Inst. Accred.: COE (2000/2006)

Center for Personal and Professional Development
2025 Tartar Ave., Ste. 218, Virginia Beach 23461-1933
Type: Public, federal
Degrees: C
URL: https://www.npdc.navy.mil
Phone: (757) 492-0771
Inst. Accred.: COE (2004)

Center for Surface Combat Systems
5395 First St., Building 1520, Dahlgren 22448
Type: Public, federal
Degrees: C
URL: https://www.npdc.navy.mil/cscs
Phone: (540)-653-1023
Inst. Accred.: COE (2004)

Colonial Heights Beauty Academy
3233-B Blvd., Colonial Heights 23834
Type: Private, proprietary
Degrees: C
Phone: (804) 526-6363
Inst. Accred.: NACCAS (1986/2004)

ComputerTraining.com
4465 Brookfield Corporate Dr., Ste. 300, Chantilly 20151
Type: Private, proprietary
Degrees: C
URL: http://www.computertraining.com
Phone: (800) 733-5641
Inst. Accred.: ACCET (2007)

Culpeper Cosmetology Training Center
311 South East St., Ste. 120, Culpeper 22701
Type: Private, proprietary
Degrees: C
Phone: (540) 727-8003
Inst. Accred.: NACCAS (2004/2007)

Danville Regional Medical Center
142 South Main St., Danville 24541
Type: Private, independent
Degrees: C
URL: http://www.danvilleregional.org
Phone: (434) 799-4510
Inst. Accred.: ABHES (2002/2006)
Prog. Accred.: Radiography

Defense Acquisition University
9820 Belvior Rd., Building 202, Fort Belvior 22060-5565
Type: Public, federal
Degrees: C
URL: http://www.dau.mil
Phone: (703) 805-3360
Inst. Accred.: COE (2003)

Defense Commissary Agency
1300 East Ave., Building 11200, Fort Lee 23801-1800
Type: Public, federal
Degrees: C
URL: http://www.commissaries.com
Phone: (804) 734-8860
Inst. Accred.: COE (1995/2001)

Dominion School of Hair Design
7118 Hayes Shopping Center, Hayes 23072
Type: Private, proprietary
Degrees: C
URL: http://www.dominionschoolofhairdesign.com
Phone: (804) 684-9150
Inst. Accred.: NACCAS (2007)

Everest Institute—Newport News
803 Dilligence Dr., Newport News 23606
Type: Private, proprietary
System: Corinthian Colleges, Inc
Degrees: C
URL: http://www.everest.edu
Phone: (757) 873-1111 *Calendar:* Qtr. plan
Inst. Accred.: ACICS (1955/2004)

Chesapeake Campus
Greenbriar Circle Corporate Center, 825 Greenbriar Circle, Ste. 100, Chesapeake 23320-2637
Phone: (757) 361-3900

Flatwoods Civilian Conservation Center
2803 Dungannon Rd., Coeburn 24230
Type: Public, federal
Degrees: C
Phone: (540) 395-3384
Inst. Accred.: COE (1989/2005, Warning)

Graham Webb International Academy of Hair
1621 North Kent St., Ste. 1617 LL, Rosslyn Plaza, Arlington 22209
Type: Private, proprietary
Degrees: C
URL: http://www.grahamwebbacademyonline.com
Phone: (703) 243-9322
Inst. Accred.: NACCAS (1989/2004)

Hicks Academy of Beauty Culture
904 Loudoun Ave., Portsmouth 23707
Type: Private, proprietary
Degrees: C
Phone: (757) 399-2400
Inst. Accred.: NACCAS (1965/2007)

Inlingua English Center
1901 North Moore St., Ste. LL-01, Arlington 22209
Type: Private, proprietary
Degrees: C
URL: http://www.inlinguadc.com
Phone: (703) 527-7888
Inst. Accred.: CEA (2003)

J.J. White and Associates, Inc. Dale Carnegie Training
1320 Grandin Rd., Ste. B, Roanoke 24015
Type: Private, proprietary
Degrees: C
URL: http://www.swvirginia.dalecarnegie.com
Phone: (540) 400-8415
Inst. Accred.: ACCET (2000/2005)

Legends Institute
2323 Memorial Ave., Ste. 27, Lynchburg 24501-2652
Type: Private, proprietary
Degrees: C
Phone: (434) 385-7722
Inst. Accred.: NACCAS (1973/2007)

National Court Reporters Association
8224 Old Ct.house Rd., Vienna 22182-3808
Type: Private, independent
Degrees: C
URL: http://www.ncraonline.org
Phone: (703) 556-6272
Inst. Accred.: ACCET (1982/2004)

National Geospatial-Intelligence College
5855 21st St., Ste. 101, Fort Belvior 22060-5921
Type: Public, federal
Degrees: C
URL: http://www.nima.mil
Phone: (703) 805-3268
Inst. Accred.: COE (2001)

Bethesda Campus
4600 Sangamore Rd., Bethesda, MD 20816-5003

National Imagery and Analysis School
1200 First St., SE, Washington Navy Yard, Bldg. 213, Washington, DC 20303-0001

National Institute for Learning Development
107 Seekel St., Norfolk 23505
Type: Private, independent
Degrees: C
URL: http://www.nild.net
Phone: (757) 423-8646
Inst. Accred.: ACCET (2006)

National Massage Therapy Institute
803 West Broad St., Ste. 110, Falls Church 22046
Type: Private, proprietary
Degrees: C
Phone: (703) 237-3905
Inst. Accred.: CMTA (1999/2005)

Norfolk Skills Center
922 West 21st St., Norfolk 23517-1516
Type: Public, local
Degrees: C
URL: http://www.nps.k12.va.us/schools/skillscenter
Phone: (757) 628-3300
Inst. Accred.: COE (1988/2004)

Northrop Grumman Newport News Apprentice School
4101 Washington Ave., Newport News 23607
Type: Private, proprietary
Degrees: C
URL: http://www.apprenticeschool.com
Phone: (757) 380-2000
Inst. Accred.: COE (1982/2004)

Rudy & Kelly Academy of Hair and Nails
5606-8 Princess Anne Rd., Virginia Beach 23462
Type: Private, proprietary
Degrees: C
Phone: (757) 473-0994
Inst. Accred.: NACCAS (2001/2004)

Sentara School of Health Professions
1441 Crossways Blvd., Crossways I, Ste. 105, Chesapeake 23320
Type: Private, independent
Degrees: C
URL: http://www.sentara.com
Phone: (757) 388-2900
Inst. Accred.: ABHES (1999/2004)
Prog. Accred.: Allied Health (cardiovascular technology)

SM Consulting, Inc.
1835 Alexander Bell Dr., Ste. 240, Reston 20191
Type: Private, proprietary
Degrees: C
URL: http://www.smcteam.com
Phone: (703) 319-9030
Inst. Accred.: ACCET (2006)

Springfield Beauty Academy, Inc.
4223 Annandale Rd., Annandale 22003
Type: Private, proprietary
Degrees: C
Phone: (703) 256-5662
Inst. Accred.: NACCAS (1993/2006)

Staunton School of Cosmetology, Inc.
PO Box 2385, Staunton 24402-2385
Type: Private, proprietary
Degrees: C
URL: http://hairstylingschool.com
Phone: (540) 885-0808
Inst. Accred.: NACCAS (1969/2002)

Suffolk Beauty Academy
860 Portsmouth Blvd., Suffolk 23434
Type: Private, proprietary
Degrees: C
Phone: (757) 934-0656
Inst. Accred.: NACCAS (1987/2002)

The United States Army Institute for Professional Development
U.S. Army Training Support Center, Attn: ATIC-ITS, Fort Eustis 23604-5166
Type: Public, federal
Degrees: C
URL: http://www.atsc.army.mil/accp/dlsd.htm
Phone: (757) 878-3866
Inst. Accred.: DETC (1978/2003)

United States Army Logistics Management College
2401 Quarters Rd., Fort Lee 23801-1705
Type: Public, federal
Degrees: C
URL: http://www.almc.army.mil
Phone: (804) 765-4605
Inst. Accred.: COE (2002)

United States Army Management Staff College
5500 21st St., Fort Belvior 22060-5934
Type: Public, federal
Degrees: C
URL: http://www.amsc.belvoir.army.mil
Phone: (703) 805-4714
Inst. Accred.: COE (2002)

United States Army Quartermaster Center and School
1201 22nd St., Fort Lee 23801-1601
Type: Public, federal
Degrees: C
URL: http://www.quartermaster.army.mil
Phone: (804) 734-3458
Inst. Accred.: COE (1975/2004)

United States Army Transportation and Aviation Logistics School
705 Read St., Ft Eustis 23604
Type: Public, federal
Degrees: C
URL: http://www.transchool.eustis.army.mil
Phone: (757) 878-0400
Inst. Accred.: COE (1975/2004)

Virginia Career Institute
100 Constitution Dr., Ste. 101, Virginia Beach 23462
Type: Private, proprietary
Degrees: C
URL: http://www.vstsuccess.com
Phone: (757) 499-5447 *Calendar:* Qtr. plan
Inst. Accred.: ACICS (1986/2003)

Richmond Campus
9210 Arboretum Pkwy., Richmond 23236-3472
Phone: (804) 323-1020

Virginia School of Hair Design
101 West Queens Way, Hampton 23669
Type: Private, proprietary
Degrees: C
Phone: (757) 722-0211
Inst. Accred.: NACCAS (1967/2003)

Virginia School of Massage
2008 Morton Dr., Charlottesville 22903
Type: Private, proprietary
Degrees: C
URL: http://www.vasom.com
Phone: (804) 293-4031
Inst. Accred.: ACCSCT (1998/2003)
Prog. Accred.: Allied Health (massage therapy)

Wade Powell & Associates, Inc.
291 Independence Blvd., Ste. 515, Pembroke Four, Virginia Beach 23462-5473
Type: Private, proprietary
Degrees: C
URL: http://www.easternvirginia.dalecarnegie.com
Phone: (757) 490-1611
Inst. Accred.: ACCET (1975/2006)

Wards Corner Beauty Academy
7525 Tidewater Dr., Ste. 45, Norfolk 23505
Type: Private, proprietary
Degrees: C
Phone: (757) 583-3300
Inst. Accred.: NACCAS (1977/2003)

Virginia Beach Campus
103 South Witchduck Rd., Virginia Beach 23462
Phone: (757) 473-5555

Washington County Adult Skill Center
848 Thompson Dr., Abingdon 24210
Type: Public, local
Degrees: C
URL: http://wcsc.wcs.k12.va.us
Phone: (276) 676-1948
Inst. Accred.: COE (1990/2002)

Woodrow Wilson Rehabilitation Center
Materials Management Division, Box W-146, PO Box 1500, Fishersville 22939-1500
Type: Public, state
Degrees: C
URL: http://www.wwrc.net
Phone: (540) 332-7000
Inst. Accred.: COE (1983/2005)

Wray K. Powell and Associates, Inc.
2800 North Parham Rd., Ste. 102, Richmond 23294
Type: Private, proprietary
Degrees: C
URL: http://www.centralvirginia.dalecarnegie.com
Phone: (804) 270-0020
Inst. Accred.: ACCET (2000/2005)

WASHINGTON

The Academy of Hair Design
208 South Wenatchee Ave., Wenatchee 98801
Type: Private, proprietary
Degrees: C
Phone: (509) 662-9082
Inst. Accred.: NACCAS (1987/2007)

Alpine College
International Gateway Corporate Park, 10020 East Knox Ave., Ste. 500, Spokane Valley 99206-5097
Type: Private, proprietary
Degrees: C
URL: http://www.alpinecollege.com
Phone: (509) 892-0155
Inst. Accred.: COE (2005)

ALPS Language School
216 Broadway East, Ste. 202, Seattle 98102
Type: Private, proprietary
Degrees: C
URL: http://www.enlishintheusa.com
Phone: (206) 720-6363
Inst. Accred.: ACCET (1995/2000)

Ashmead College
2111 North Northgate Way, Ste. 218, Seattle 98133
Type: Private, proprietary
System: Corinthian Colleges, Inc
Degrees: C
URL: http://cci.edu/ashmead
Phone: (206) 527-0807
Inst. Accred.: ACCET (1989/2004)

Everett Campus
3019 Colby Ave., Everett 98201
Phone: (425) 339-2678

Fife Campus
5005 Pacific Hwy. East, Ste. 20, Fife 98424
Phone: (253) 922-2967

Tigard Campus
9600 SW Oak, 4th Flr., Tigard, OR 97223
Phone: (503) 892-8100

Vancouver Campus
120 136th Ave., NE, Ste. 220, Vancouver 98684
Phone: (360) 885-3152

B.J.'s Beauty and Barber College
5239 South Tacoma Way, Tacoma 98409
Type: Private, proprietary
Degrees: C
Phone: (253) 473-4320
Inst. Accred.: NACCAS (1987/2005)

Puyallup Campus
12020 Meridian East, Ste. K, Puyallup 98373
Phone: (253) 848-1595

Bellevue Beauty School
14045 NE 20th St., Bellevue 98007
Type: Private, proprietary
Degrees: C
Phone: (425) 643-0270
Inst. Accred.: NACCAS (1979/2004)

Bellingham Beauty School, Inc.
4192 Meridian St., Bellingham 98226
Type: Private, proprietary
Degrees: C
URL: http://bellinghambeautyschool.edu
Phone: (360) 734-1090
Inst. Accred.: NACCAS (1976/2003)

Chetta's Academy of Hair and Nails, Inc.
1222 East Front St., Port Angeles 98362
Type: Private, proprietary
Degrees: C
Phone: (360) 417-0388
Inst. Accred.: NACCAS (2002/2005)

Clare's Beauty College
104 North Fourth Ave., Pasco 99301
Type: Private, proprietary
Degrees: C
Phone: (509) 547-8871
Inst. Accred.: NACCAS (1991/2006)

Cortiva Institute-Brian Utting School of Massage
900 Thomas St., Ste. 200, Seattle 98109
Type: Private, proprietary
Degrees: C
URL: http://www.cortiva.com/locations/busm
Phone: (206) 292-8055
Inst. Accred.: CMTA (2001)

Crace and Associates
325 118th Ave., SE, Ste. 104, Bellevue 98005
Type: Private, proprietary
Degrees: C
URL: http://www.washington,dalecarnegie.com
Phone: (425) 453-8822
Inst. Accred.: ACCET (1978/2004)

Divers Institute of Technology
PO Box 70667, 4315 11th Ave., NW, Seattle 98107-0667
Type: Private, proprietary
Degrees: C
URL: http://www.diveweb.com/dit
Phone: (206) 783-5542
Inst. Accred.: ACCSCT (1973/2005)

Emil Fries School of Piano Tuning and Technology
2510 East Evergreen Blvd., Vancouver 98661
Type: Private, proprietary
Degrees: C
URL: http://www.pianotuningschool.org
Phone: (360) 693-1511
Inst. Accred.: ACCSCT (1993/2004)

Everest College—Bremerton
155 Washington Ave., Ste. 200, Bremerton 98337
Type: Private, proprietary
System: Corinthian Colleges, Inc
Degrees: C
URL: http://www.everest.edu
Phone: (360) 473-1120
Inst. Accred.: ACICS (1979/2006)
Prog. Accred.: Allied Health (medical assisting (AMA))

Everett Campus
906 Everett Mall Way, Ste. 600, Everett 98208
Phone: (425) 789-7960
Prog. Accred: Allied Health (medical assisting (AMA))

Tacoma Campus
2156 Pacific Ave., Tacoma 98402
Phone: (253) 207-4000

Everest College—Renton
981 Powell Ave. SW, Ste. 200, Renton 98057-2990
Type: Private, proprietary
System: Corinthian Colleges, Inc
Degrees: C
URL: http://www.everest.edu
Phone: (425) 255-3281
Inst. Accred.: ACCSCT (1989/2002)
Prog. Accred.: Allied Health (medical assisting (AMA))

Evergreen Beauty and Barber College
802 SE Everett Mall Way, Ste. A, Everett 98208
Type: Private, propietary
Degrees: C
URL: http://www.evergreenbeautybarber.com
Phone: (425) 423-9186
Inst. Accred.: NACCAS (2004)

Gene Juarez Academy of Beauty
10715 8th Ave., NE, Seattle 98125
Type: Private, proprietary
Degrees: C
URL: http://www.genejuarezacademy.com
Phone: (206) 368-0210
Inst. Accred.: NACCAS (1977/2003)

Federal Way Campus
2222 South 314th St., Federal Way 98003
Phone: (253) 839-4338

Glen Dow Academy of Hair Design, Inc.
309 West Riverside Ave., Spokane 99201
Type: Private, proprietary
Degrees: C
URL: http://www.glendow.com
Phone: (509) 624-3244
Inst. Accred.: NACCAS (1970/2006)

Greenwood Academy of Hair Design
8501 Greenwood North, Seattle 98103
Type: Private, proprietary
Degrees: C
Phone: (206) 782-0220
Inst. Accred.: NACCAS (1975/2007)

Interface Computer School
9921 North Nevada St., Nevada 99218
Type: Private, proprietary
Degrees: C
URL: http://www.interface-net.com
Phone: (509) 467-1727
Inst. Accred.: ACCET (1986/2003)

Central Spokane Campus
1118 North Washington St., Spokane 99201
Phone: (509) 323-0070

International Air and Hospitality Academy
2901 East Mill Plain Blvd., Vancouver 98661-4899
Type: Private, proprietary
Degrees: C
URL: http://www.airacademy.com
Phone: (360) 695-2500
Inst. Accred.: ACCSCT (1983/2003)

Ontario Campus
2980 Inland Empire Blvd., Ontario, CA 91764-4804
Phone: (909) 989-5222

Kaplan College—Renton
500 SW 39th St., Ste. 115, Renton 98055-4910
Type: Private, proprietary
Degrees: C
URL: http://getinfo.kaplancollege.com
Phone: (425) 291-3620
Inst. Accred.: ACCSCT (2006)

Kirkland Beauty School
17311 140th Ave., NE, Woodinville 98072
Type: Private, proprietary
Degrees: C
Phone: (425) 487-0437
Inst. Accred.: NACCAS (1980/2005)

Milan Institute of Cosmetology
607 SE Everett Mall Way, Ste. 5, Everett 98208
Type: Private, proprietary
Degrees: C
URL: http://www.milaninstitute.edu
Phone: (425) 353-8193
Inst. Accred.: NACCAS (1978/2005)

Montessori Teacher Preparation of Washington
23807 98th Ave. South, Kent 98031
Type: Private, independent
Degrees: C
URL: http://www.montessoriplus.org
Phone: (253) 859-2262
Inst. Accred.: MACTE (1996/2003)

Northwest Hair Academy
615 South First St., Mount Vernon 98273
Type: Private, proprietary
Degrees: C
URL: http://www.northwesthairacademy.com
Phone: (360) 336-6553
Inst. Accred.: NACCAS (1986/2006)

Everett Campus
520 128th St., SW, Everett 98204
Phone: (425) 710-0888

Northwest HVAC/R Association and Training Center
811 East Sprague, Ste. 6, Spokane 99202
Type: Private, independent
Degrees: C
URL: http://www.inwhvac.org/nate.htm
Phone: (509) 747-8810
Inst. Accred.: COE (2000/2006)

Northwest Regional Training Center
11606 NE 66th Circle, Ste. 103, Vancouver 98662
Type: Public, local
Degrees: C
URL: http://www.nwrtc.org
Phone: (360) 759-4404
Inst. Accred.: ACCET (2006)

Perry Technical Institute
2011 West Washington Ave., Yakima 98903-1296
Type: Private, proprietary
Degrees: C
URL: http://www.perrytech.edu
Phone: (509) 453-0374
Inst. Accred.: ACCSCT (1969/2006)

Phagans' Orchards Beauty School
10411 NE Fourth Plain Blvd., Ste. 109, Vancouver 98662
Type: Private, proprietary
Degrees: C
URL: http://www.phagansnw.com
Phone: (360) 254-9517
Inst. Accred.: NACCAS (1986/2006)

The Photographic Center Northwest
900 Twelfth Ave., Seattle 98122
Type: Private, independent
Degrees: C
URL: http://www.pcnw.org
Phone: (206) 720-7222 *Calendar:* 10-mos. pr
Inst. Accred.: NASAD (1996/2002)

Professional Beauty School
PO Box 9243, Yakima 98909-0243
Type: Private, proprietary
Degrees: C
Phone: (509) 576-0966
Inst. Accred.: NACCAS (1994/2003)

Sunnyside Campus
214 South 6th St., Sunnyside 98944
Phone: (509) 837-4040

Sage College
929 North 130th St., Ste. 2, Seattle 98133
Type: Private, proprietary
Degrees: C
URL: http://www.cri.org
Phone: (206) 363-8300
Inst. Accred.: ACICS (1991/2004)

Boise Campus
1951 South Saturn Way, Ste. 120, Boise, ID 83709
Phone: (208) 322-8517

CRI Career Training—Tacoma
15 Oregon Ave., Ste. 40, Tacoma 98409
Phone: (253) 474-4744

San Diego Campus
1333 Camino del Rio South, San Diego, CA 92108
Phone: (619) 294-5700

Sakie International College of Cosmetology
2106 West Nob Hill Blvd., Ste. 104, Yakima 98902
Type: Private, proprietary
Degrees: C
URL: http://sakieintl.com
Phone: (509) 457-2773
Inst. Accred.: NACCAS (2005)

Seattle Midwifery School
4000 NE 41st St., Building D, Ste. 3, Seattle 98105
Type: Private, independent
Degrees: C
URL: http://www.seattlemidwifery.org
Phone: (206) 322-8834 *Calendar:* Qtr. plan
Inst. Accred.: MEAC (1999/2005)

Stylemasters College of Hair Design
1224 Commerce Ave., Longview 98632
Type: Private, proprietary
Degrees: C
URL: http://stylemasters.edu
Phone: (360) 636-2720
Inst. Accred.: NACCAS (1982/2002)

Sunnyside Beauty Academy
440 Barnard Blvd., Ste. 2, Sunnyside 98944
Type: Private, proprietary
Degrees: C
Phone: (509) 839-3700
Inst. Accred.: NACCAS (2006/2007)

Total Cosmetology Training Center
5303 North Market St., Spokane 99207
Type: Private, proprietary
Degrees: C
URL: http://www.totalcosmetology.com
Phone: (509) 487-5500
Inst. Accred.: NACCAS (2004)

Victoria's Academy of Cosmetology
314 West Kennewick Ave., Kennewick 99336-3826
Type: Private, proprietary
Degrees: C
URL: http://www.victoriasacademy.com
Phone: (509) 586-9979
Inst. Accred.: NACCAS (2007)

Yakima Beauty School Beauty Works
401 North First St., Yakima 98901
Type: Private, proprietary
Degrees: C
URL: http://www.yakimabeautyschool.com
Phone: (509) 248-2288
Inst. Accred.: NACCAS (2005)

WEST VIRGINIA

Academy of Careers and Technology
390 Stanaford Rd., Beckley 25801
Type: Public, state/local
Degrees: C
URL: http://www.wvact.net
Phone: (304) 256-4615 *Calendar:* Sem. plan
Inst. Accred.: NCA-CASI (1980/2004)

APUS Center for Professional and Workforce Development
111 West Congress St., Charles Town 25414
Type: Private, proprietary
Degrees: C
URL: http://www.apustraining.com
Phone: (877) 468-6269
Inst. Accred.: DETC (2005)

Art and Science Institute of Cosmetology and Massage Therapy
33 Corey Rd., Fairmont 26554
Type: Private, proprietary
Degrees: C
Phone: (304) 363-2015
Inst. Accred.: NACCAS (2004)

Beckley Beauty Academy
109 South Fayette St., Beckley 25801
Type: Private, proprietary
Degrees: C
Phone: (304) 253-8326
Inst. Accred.: NACCAS (1977/2004)

Ben Franklin Career Center
500 28th St., Dunbar 25064
Type: Public, state/local
Degrees: C
URL: http://bfcc.kana.tec.wv.us
Phone: (304) 766-0369
Inst. Accred.: NCA-CASI (1974/2003)
Prog. Accred.: Allied Health (medical assisting (AMA))

Cabell County Career Technology Center
1035 Norway Ave., Huntington 25705
Type: Public, state/local
Degrees: C
URL: http://boe.cabe.k12.wv.us/ctc
Phone: (304) 528-5106
Inst. Accred.: NCA-CASI (1977/2004)

Carver Career and Technical Education Center
4799 Midland Dr., Charleston 25306
Type: Public, state/local
Degrees: C
URL: http://kcs.kana.k12.wv.us/carver
Phone: (304) 348-1965
Inst. Accred.: NCA-CASI (1973/2004)
Prog. Accred.: Allied Health (respiratory therapy, surgical technology)

Charleston School of Beauty Culture
210 Capitol St., Charleston 25301
Type: Private, proprietary
Degrees: C
URL: http://www.csbcwv.com
Phone: (304) 346-9603
Inst. Accred.: NACCAS (1981/2003)

Clarksburg Beauty Academy
120 South Third St., Clarksburg 26301
Type: Private, proprietary
Degrees: C
URL: http://www.clarksburgbeautyacademy.com
Phone: (304) 624-6475
Inst. Accred.: NACCAS (1970/2006)

Fayette Plateau Vocational Technology Center
300 West Oyler Ave., Oak Hill 25901
Type: Public, state/local
Degrees: C
URL: http://boe.faye.k12.wv.us
Phone: (304) 469-2911
Inst. Accred.: NCA-CASI (1992/2004)

Fred W. Eberle Technical Center
Rural Route 5 Box 2, Buckhannon 26201-9102
Type: Public, state/local
Degrees: C
URL: http://fetc.upsh.tec.wv.us
Phone: (304) 472-1259
Inst. Accred.: NCA-CASI (1980/2003)

Garnet Career Center
422 Dickinson St., Charleston 25301
Type: Public, state/local
Degrees: C
URL: http://kcs.kana.k12.wv.us/garnet
Phone: (304) 348-6195
Inst. Accred.: NCA-CASI (1982/2004)
Prog. Accred.: Practical Nursing

Harpers Ferry Job Corps Center
146 Buffalo Dr., Harpers Ferry 25425
Type: Public, federal
Degrees: C
URL: http://philadelphiaregion.jobcorps.gov
Phone: (304) 724-3403
Inst. Accred.: COE (2001)

Huntington School of Beauty Culture, Inc.
East Hills Mall, 5185 U.S. Route 60 East, Rm. 115, Huntington 25705
Type: Private, proprietary
Degrees: C
Phone: (304) 736-6289
Inst. Accred.: NACCAS (1971/2007)

Ashland School of Beauty Culture
1653 Greenup Ave., Ashland, KY 41101
Phone: (606) 329-8720

International Beauty School—Martinsburg
201 West King St., Martinsburg 25401
Type: Private, proprietary
Degrees: C
Phone: (304) 263-4929
Inst. Accred.: NACCAS (1969/2005)

James Rumsey Technical Institute
3274 Hedgesville Rd., Martinsburg 25401-0259
Type: Public, state/local
Degrees: C
URL: http://www.jamesrumsey.com
Phone: (304) 754-7925
Inst. Accred.: NCA-CASI (1975/2002)

John D Rockefeller IV Career Center
Rural Route 4 Box 500, New Cumberland 26047
Type: Public, state/local
Degrees: C
URL: http://jdrcc.hanc.tec.wv.us
Phone: (304) 564-3337
Inst. Accred.: NCA-CASI (2004)

McDowell County Vocational Technical Center
PO Drawer V, Welch 24801
Type: Public, state/local
Degrees: C
URL: http://boe.mcdo.k12.wv.us/votech
Phone: (304) 436-3488
Inst. Accred.: NCA-CASI (1984/2003)

Mercer County Technical Education Center
1397 Stafford Dr., Princeton 24740
Type: Public, state/local
Degrees: C
URL: http://mctec.merc.tec.wv.us
Phone: (304) 425-9551
Inst. Accred.: NCA-CASI (1982/2004)

Meredith Manor International Equestrian Centre
Route 1, Box 66, Waverly 26184
Type: Private, proprietary
Degrees: C
URL: http://www.meredithmanor.com
Phone: (304) 679-3128
Inst. Accred.: ACCET (1987/2000)

Mineral County Technical Center
600 Harley O Staggers Dr., Keyser 26726
Type: Public, state/local
Degrees: C
URL: http://mctc.mine.tec.wv.us
Phone: (304) 788-4240
Inst. Accred.: NCA-CASI (1977/2002)

Monongalia County Technical Education Center
1000 Mississippi St., Morgantown 26505
Type: Public, state/local
Degrees: C
URL: http://boe.mono.k12.wv.us/mtec
Phone: (304) 291-9240
Inst. Accred.: NCA-CASI (1973/2005)
Prog. Accred.: Allied Health (surgical technology)

Morgantown Beauty College, Inc.
276 Walnut St., Morgantown 26505
Type: Private, proprietary
Degrees: C
URL: http://morgantownbeautycollege.homestead.com
Phone: (304) 292-8475
Inst. Accred.: NACCAS (1993/2006)

Mountain State School of Massage
601 50th St., Charleston 25304
Type: Private, proprietary
Degrees: C
URL: http://www.mtnstmassage.com
Phone: (304) 926-8822
Inst. Accred.: CMTA (2004)

Mountaineer Beauty College, Inc.
700 6th Ave., PO Box 547, St. Albans 25177
Type: Private, proprietary
Degrees: C
URL: http://www.webmbc.com
Phone: (304) 727-9999
Inst. Accred.: NACCAS (1993/2004)

North Central West Virginia Opportunities Industrialization Center
120 Jackson St., Fairmont 26554
Type: Public, state/local
Degrees: C
URL: http://www.oicwv.org
Phone: (304) 366-8142
Inst. Accred.: NCA-CASI (1988/2004)

Putnam Career and Technical Center
101 Roosevelt Blvd., Eleanor 25070
Type: Public, state/local
Degrees: C
URL: http://boe.putn.k12.wv.us/pctc
Phone: (304) 586-3494
Inst. Accred.: NCA-CASI (1974/2005)

Ralph R. Willis Vocational Technical Center
PO Box 1747, Logan 25601
Type: Public, state/local
Degrees: C
URL: http://www.williscareercenter.com
Phone: (304) 752-4687
Inst. Accred.: NCA-CASI (1986/2005)

Roane Jackson Technical Center
4800 Spencer Rd., Leroy 25252
Type: Public, state/local
Degrees: C
URL: http://boe.jack.k12.wv.us/RJTCpage/Index.html
Phone: (304) 372-7335
Inst. Accred.: NCA-CASI (1975/2002)

Scott College of Cosmetology
1502 Market St., Wheeling 26003
Type: Private, proprietary
Degrees: C
Phone: (304) 232-7798
Inst. Accred.: NACCAS (1978/2004)

South Branch Career and Technical Center
401 Pierpont St., Petersburg 26847
Type: Public, state/local
Degrees: C
URL: http://sbvc.gran.tec.wv.us
Phone: (304) 257-1331
Inst. Accred.: NCA-CASI (1978/2004)

Stanley Technical Institute
1644 Mileground, Morgantown 26505
Type: Private, proprietary
Degrees: C
URL: http://www.hrdfwv.org
Phone: (304) 296-8223
Inst. Accred.: NCA-CASI (1997/2005)

Clarksburg Campus
120 Linden Ave., Clarksburg 26301
Phone: (304) 296-8223

Hinton Campus
McCreery Center, 320 Ω Second Ave., Hinton 25951
Phone: (304) 466-4805

Parkersburg Campus
800 Camden Ave., Parkersburg 26101
Phone: (304) 296-8223

United Technical Center
Route 3 Box 43-C, Clarksburg 26301
Type: Public, state/local
Degrees: C
URL: http://www.wvonline.com/utc
Phone: (304) 624-3280
Inst. Accred.: NCA-CASI (1975/2003)

West Virginia Career and Technical Center
PO Box 1004, Institute 25112
Type: Public, state/local
Degrees: C
Phone: (304) 766-4700
Inst. Accred.: NCA-CASI (1984/2002)

WISCONSIN

Academy of Cosmetology
2310 West Ct. St., Janesville 53545
Type: Private, proprietary
Degrees: C
URL: http://www.cosmetologycareer.net
Phone: (608) 758-4810
Inst. Accred.: NACCAS (2006)

Blue Sky School of Professional Massage and Therapeutic Bodywork
220 Oak St., Manchester Mall, Grafton 53024
Type: Private, proprietary
Degrees: C
URL: http://www.blueskyedu.org
Phone: (262) 376-1011
Inst. Accred.: CMTA (2004/2007)

DePere/Green Bay Campus
2200 American Blvd., DePere 54115
Phone: (920) 406-9770

Madison Campus
2122 Luann Ln., Madison 53713
Phone: (608) 270-5245

Gill-Tech Academy of Hair Design
423 West College Ave., Appleton 54911
Type: Private, proprietary
Degrees: C
URL: http://www.gill-tech.com
Phone: (920) 739-8684
Inst. Accred.: NACCAS (1987/2007)

The Institute of Beauty and Wellness
342 North Water St., Milwaukee 53202
Type: Private, proprietary
Degrees: C
URL: http://www.institutebw.com
Phone: (414) 227-2889
Inst. Accred.: NACCAS (2003/2006)

J. R. Rodgers and Associates, Inc.
2300 North Mayfair Rd., Ste. 945, Wauwatosa 53226
Type: Private, proprietary
Degrees: C
URL: http://www.sewis.dalecarnegie.com
Phone: (414) 771-3200
Inst. Accred.: ACCET (2000/2005)

Lakeside School of Massage Therapy
1726 North First St., Ste. 100, Milwaukee 53212
Type: Private, proprietary
Degrees: C
URL: http://www.lakesideschoolmassage.org
Phone: (414) 372-4345
Inst. Accred.: CMTA (2001)

Madison Campus
6121 Odana Rd., Madison 53719
Phone: (608) 274-2484

Madison Cosmetology College
310 Westgate Mall, Madison 53711
Type: Private, proprietary
Degrees: C
URL: http://www.cosmetologycollege.com
Phone: (608) 271-4204
Inst. Accred.: NACCAS (1975/2006)

Martin's College of Cosmetology—Green Bay
2575 West Mason St., Green Bay 54304
Type: Private, proprietary
System: Empire Education Group
Degrees: C
URL: http://www.mcofc.com
Phone: (920) 494-1430
Inst. Accred.: NACCAS (1989/2004)

Milwaukee Campus
5655 South 27th St., Milwaukee 53221
Phone: (414) 282-4110

Martin's College of Cosmetology—Madison
6414 Odana Rd., Madison 53717
Type: Private, proprietary
System: Empire Education Group
Degrees: C
URL: http://www.mcofc.com
Phone: (608) 270-0270
Inst. Accred.: NACCAS (1985/2005)

Martin's College of Cosmetology—Manitowoc
1034 South 18th St., Manitowoc 54220
Type: Private, proprietary
System: Empire Education Group
Degrees: C
URL: http://www.mcofc.com
Phone: (920) 684-0177
Inst. Accred.: NACCAS (1986/2006)

Appleton Campus
525 North Westhill Blvd., Appleton 54914
Phone: (920) 832-8686

Meyer Uebelher Associates, LLC
1463 County Rd. X, Mosinee 54455
Type: Private, proprietary
Degrees: C
URL: http://www.cwdalecarnegie.com
Phone: (715) 693-5007
Inst. Accred.: ACCET (2004)

Milwaukee Career College
3077 North Mayfair Rd., Ste. 300, Milwaukee 53222
Type: Private, proprietary
Degrees: C
URL: http://www.mkecc.edu
Phone: (414) 257-2939
Inst. Accred.: ABHES (2006)

Montessori Institute of Milwaukee, Inc.
3195 South Superior St., Ste. L428, Milwaukee 53207
Type: Public, independent
Degrees: C
URL: http://www.montessori6-12ami.org
Phone: (414) 481-5050
Inst. Accred.: MACTE (1998/2005)

Professional Hair Design Academy
3408 Mall Dr., Eau Claire 54701
Type: Private, proprietary
Degrees: C
URL: http://www.phdacademy.com
Phone: (715) 835-2345
Inst. Accred.: NACCAS (1997/2005)

Scientific College of Beauty and Barbering
326 Pearl St., LaCrosse 54601
Type: Private, proprietary
Degrees: C
URL: http://www.lacrossebeautyschool.com
Phone: (608) 784-4702
Inst. Accred.: NACCAS (1976/2007)

Siebert Associates, Inc.
802 West Broadway, Ste. L-9, Madison 53713
Type: Private, proprietary
Degrees: C
URL: http://www.swwis.dalecarnegie.com
Phone: (608) 222-5363
Inst. Accred.: ACCET (1999/2004)

State College of Beauty Culture
1930 Grand Ave., Wausau 54401
Type: Private, proprietary
Degrees: C
URL: http://www.statecollegeofbeauty.com
Phone: (715) 845-2888
Inst. Accred.: NACCAS (1971/2002)

Vici Beauty School
4111 South 108th St., Greenfield 53228
Type: Private, proprietary
Degrees: C
URL: http://www.vicibeautyschool.com
Phone: (414) 425-1700
Inst. Accred.: NACCAS (1985/2003)

Vici Beauty School
11010 West Hampton Ave., Milwaukee 53225
Type: Private, proprietary
Degrees: C
URL: http://www.vicibeautyschool.com
Phone: (414) 464-5002
Inst. Accred.: NACCAS (1972/2003)

Wisconsin College of Cosmetology, Inc.
2960 Allied St., Green Bay 54304
Type: Private, proprietary
Degrees: C
URL: http://www.wccgb.com
Phone: (920) 336-8888
Inst. Accred.: NACCAS (1970/2005)

Wisconsin English Second Language Institute
19 North Pinckney St., Madison 53703
Type: Private, independent
Degrees: C
URL: http://www.ies-ed.com/descriptions/wiscesl_inst
Phone: (608) 257-4300
Inst. Accred.: CEA (2000)

WYOMING

Business Skills Institute
336 Summit St., Evanston 82930
Type: Private, proprietary
Degrees: C
URL: http://www.llc-evanston.org/llc/bsi.htm
Phone: (307) 789-5742
Inst. Accred.: ACCET (1998/2004)

Cheeks International Academy of Beauty Culture
207 West 18th St., Cheyenne 82001
Type: Private, proprietary
Degrees: C
URL: http://www.cheeksusa.com
Phone: (307) 637-8700
Inst. Accred.: NACCAS (1982/2002)

Fort Collins Campus
4025 South Mason St., Unit 5, Fort Collins, CO 80525
Phone: (970) 226-1416

Greeley Campus
2547-B 11th Ave., Greeley, CO 80631
Phone: (970) 352-4500

CANADA

Angela Martin Montessori Training Center
4052 Wilkerson Rd., Victoria V8Z 5A5
Type: Private, independent
Degrees: C
URL: http://www.montessori.bc.ca/ammtc/ammtc.htm
Phone: (250) 479-4746
Inst. Accred.: MACTE (2000)

ICT Northumberland College
1888 Brunswick St., Halifax B3J 3J8
Type: Private, proprietary
Degrees: C
URL: http://www.ictschools.com
Phone: (902) 425-2869
Inst. Accred.: CMTA (2001)

ICT Kikkawa College
2340 Dundas St., West, Unit G-04, Toronto M6P 4A9
Type: Private, proprietary
Degrees: C
URL: http://www.ictschools.com
Phone: (416) 762-4857
Inst. Accred.: CMTA (2001/2004)

The Massage Therapy College of Manitoba, Inc.
692 Wolseley Ave., 2nd Flr., Winnipeg R3G 1C3
Type: Private, proprietary
Degrees: C
URL: http://www.massagetherapycollege.com
Phone: (204) 772-8999
Inst. Accred.: CMTA (1999/2006)

Montessori House of Children
711 Waterloo St., London N6A 3WI
Phone: (519) 433-9121

Toronto Montessori Schools
8569 Bayview Ave., Richmond Hill L4B 3M7
Phone: (905) 857-0953

Nightingale Medical Institute
11111 Jasper Ave., Main Flr., Rm. 3C04, Edmonton T5K 0L4
Type: Private, proprietary
Degrees: C
URL: http://www.nightingaleacademy.com
Phone: (780) 482-8928
Inst. Accred.: COE (2005)

Toronto Montessori Teacher Training Institute
13650 Caledon King Townline S., RR #1, Bolton L7E 5R7
Type: Private, independent
Degrees: C
URL: http://www.torontomontessoriinstitute.on.ca
Phone: (905) 857-0953
Inst. Accred.: MACTE (2000)

DOMINICAN REPUBLIC

Montessori Training Center of Santo Domingo
Prol. Hatuey Esquina Olegario Tenares, Santo Domingo
Type: Private, independent
Degrees: C
Phone: (809) 530-1838
Inst. Accred.: MACTE (2000)

JAPAN

Babel University
1-6-1 Roppongi, Izumi Garden, 7F, Minato-ku, Tokyo 106-6007
Type: Private, proprietary
Degrees: C
URL: http://www.babel.co.jp
Phone: 011 81 3 6229 2433
Inst. Accred.: DETC (2002/2006)

MEXICO

Centro de Entrenamiento Montessori
PO Box 145, Garza Garcia 66230
Type: Private, independent
Degrees: C
URL: http://www.giga.com/~montsm/cem.htm
Phone: 011 52 8 336 5150
Inst. Accred.: MACTE (2000)

REPUBLIC OF KOREA

Dr. Jun Institute of Montessori Education
1072 Tae Jong Dong, Buk, Dae Gu City 702-866
Type: Private, independent
Degrees: C
Phone: 011 822-979-8293
Inst. Accred.: MACTE (2006)

Korean Institute for Montessori
#188, Taegen-Bldg. 3FL, Sang-do-5 dong, Dong-Zak-Ku, Seoul 156-833
Type: Private, independent
Degrees: C
Phone: 011 82 2 825 6231
Inst. Accred.: MACTE (1996/2006)

SAUDI ARABIA

Saudi Arabian Oil Company Training and Career Development

Dhahran 31311
Type: Private, proprietary
Degrees: C
URL: http://www.saudiaramco.com
Phone: 011 966 3874 6043
Inst. Accred.: ACCET (1993/2001)

Abqaiq Campus

Abqaiq
Phone: 011 966 3874 6043

Al Hasa/Mubarraz Campus

Al Hasa/Mubarraz
Phone: 011 966 3874 6043

Jeddah Campus

Jeddah
Phone: 011 966 3874 6043

Ras Tanura Campus

Ras Tanura
Phone: 011 966 3874 6043

Udhailiyah Campus

Udhailiyah
Phone: 011 966 3874 6043

Yenbu Campus

Yenbu
Phone: 011 966 3874 6043

Jeddah Campus

Jeddah
Phone: 011 966 3874 6043

Saudi Electricity Company—Eastern Region Branch

SECTI, PO Box 5190, Damman
Type: Private, proprietary
Degrees: C
URL: http://www.sceco-east.com.sa/English/index.htm
Phone: 011 3 842-5222
Inst. Accred.: ACCET (2004)

SOUTH AFRICA

The College of Modern Montessori

PO Box 119, Linbro Park, South Africa 2065
Type: Private, independent
Degrees: C
URL: http://www.montessoriint.com
Phone: 011 27 11 608 1584
Inst. Accred.: MACTE (1995/2002)

Durban Campus

PO Box 110, Linbro Park, South Africa 2065
Phone: 011 27 11 608 1584

Stepping Stones Montessori School

Sigmouth Ave., Oranjezicht, Cape Town 2065
Phone: 011 27 11 608 1584

SPAIN

Les Roches Marbella School of Hotel Management

Urbanización Las Lomas de Rio Verde, Carretera de Ist·n, Km. 1, Marbella, Spain E-29602
Type: Private, proprietary
System: Laureate Education, Inc.
Degrees: C
URL: http://www.lesroches.es
Phone: 011 34 95 276 41 45
Inst. Accred.: NEASC-CTCI (2004)

SWEDEN

IHM Business School

Warfvinges Vag 21, Box 30163, Stockholm 104 25
Type: Private, proprietary
Degrees: C
URL: http://www.ihm.se
Phone: 011 46 8 657 0000
Inst. Accred.: NEASC-CTCI (2000)

Gotenberg Campus

Fabriksgatan 21-25, Box 5273, Gotenborg 402 25
Phone: 011 46 31 335 2000

Malmo Campus

Carlsgatatn 12C, Malmo 211 20
Phone: 011 46 40 601 2300

SWITZERLAND

DCT International Hotel and Business Management School
Seestrasse, Vitznau CH 6354
Type: Private, independent
Degrees: C
URL: http://www.dct.ch
Phone: 011 41 41 418-0707
Inst. Accred.: NEASC-CTCI (2006)
Prog. Accred.: Business (ACBSP), Culinary Education

Hotel Institute Montreux
Avenue des Alpes, Montreux CH-1820
Type: Private, proprietary
Degrees: C
URL: http://www.him.ch
Phone: 011 41 21 966 4646 *Calendar:* Sem. plan
Inst. Accred.: NEASC-CTCI (1996/2006)

Institut Hotelier "Cesar Ritz"
Le Bouveret CH-1897
Type: Private, proprietary
Degrees: C
URL: http://www.ihcritz.ch
Phone: 011 41 24 481 8282 *Calendar:* Sem. plan
Inst. Accred.: NEASC-CTCI (1999)

TAIWAN, PROVINCE OF CHINA

Trillium Montessori Teacher Education Institute of Taiwan
67, Ln. 270, Chuing Yang Rd., Chang Hua
Type: Private, independent
Degrees: C
URL: http://www.tschool.org
Phone: 011 8-864-763-7377
Inst. Accred.: MACTE (2006)

TRINIDAD AND TOBAGO

Trinidad and Tobago College of Therapeutic Massage
68 Market St., Gopaul Lands, Marabella
Type: Private, proprietary
Degrees: C
Phone: (868) 658-3907
Inst. Accred.: CMTA (2005)

UNITED ARAB EMIRATES

The Petroleum Institute
PO Box 2533, Abu Dhabi
Type: Private, independent
Degrees: C
URL: http://www.pi.ac.ae/fp/index.html
Phone: 011 971 2 5085 157
Inst. Accred.: CEA (2002)

UNITED KINGDOM

The Kent and Sussex Montessori Centre
Hoath Hall, Walnut Tree Cross, Chiddingstone Hoath, Edenbridge, KE TN8 7DB
Type: Private, independent
Degrees: C
URL: http://www.montessoricentre.com
Phone: 011 44 1892 870740
Inst. Accred.: MACTE (1997/2005)

VENEZUELA

Centro Electronico de Idiomas y Computacion
Av. 11 con 78 Edif. Centro Electronico de Idiomas, Planta Baja, Maracaibo 4001
Type: Private, proprietary
Degrees: C
URL: http://www.centroelectronic.com
Phone: (261) 797-6089
Inst. Accred.: ACCET (2001/2005)

Accredited Programs at Other Facilities

This section lists accredited programs offered at facilities that are independent of any affiliation or connection with an accredited institution of postsecondary education.

ALABAMA

Alabama Reference Laboratories/LabSouth, Inc.
543 South Hull St., PO Box 4600, Montgomery 36103-4600
Type: Private, proprietary
Degrees: C
Phone: (205) 263-5745
Prog. Accred.: Clinical Lab Scientist

Baptist Health System of Alabama
701 Princeton Ave. SW, Birmingham 35211-1399
Type: Private, Birmingham Baptist Association
Degrees: C
URL: http://www.bhsala.com
Phone: (205) 783-3395
Prog. Accred.: Clinical Pastoral Education

Baptist Medical Center South School of Medical Technology
PO Box 11010, 2105 East South Blvd., Montgomery 36116
Type: Private, independent
Degrees: C
URL: http://www.baptistfirst.org
Phone: (334) 288-2100
Prog. Accred.: Allied Health (diagnostic medical sonography), Clinical Lab Scientist, Radiography

Carraway Methodist Medical Center
1600 Carraway Blvd., Birmingham 35234-1913
Type: Private, independent
Degrees: C
URL: Carraway Methodist Medical Center
Phone: (205) 502-6000
Prog. Accred.: Radiography

DCH Regional Medical Center
809 University Blvd. East, Tuscaloosa 35401
Type: Private, independent
Degrees: C
URL: http://www.dchsystem.com
Phone: (205) 759-7111
Prog. Accred.: Radiography

Flowers Hospital
4370 West Main St., Dothan 36305
Type: Private, independent
Degrees: C
URL: http://www.flowershospital.com
Phone: (334) 793-5000
Prog. Accred.: Allied Health (surgical technology)

Huntsville Hospital
101 Sivley Rd., Huntsville 35801
Type: Private, independent
Degrees: C
URL: http://www.hhsys.org
Phone: (256) 265-1000
Prog. Accred.: Radiography

Institute of Ultrasound Diagnostics
1230 Montimar Dr., Ste. A, Mobile 36609
Type: Private, proprietary
Degrees: C
URL: http://www.iudmed.com
Phone: (800) 473-2485
Prog. Accred.: Allied Health (diagnostic medical sonography)

Morning Pilgrim Baptist Church
1309 Goode St., Montgomery 36104-5458
Type: Private, Southern Baptist Convention
Degrees: C
Phone: (334) 265-0766
Prog. Accred.: Clinical Pastoral Education

Tuscaloosa Veterans Affairs Medical Center
3701 Loop Rd. East, Tuscaloosa 35404
Type: Public, federal
Degrees: C
URL: http://www.tuscaloosa.va.gov
Phone: (205) 554-2000
Prog. Accred.: Allied Health (optometric residency)

Veterans Affairs Medical Center—Birmingham
700 South 19th St., Birmingham 35233
Type: Public, federal
Degrees: C
Phone: (205) 933-8101
Prog. Accred.: Allied Health (optometric residency), Dentistry (general practice residency)

ALASKA

3rd Medical Group
5955 Zeamer Ave., Elmendorf AFB 99506
Type: Public, federal
Degrees: C
URL: http://www.elmendorf.af.mil
Phone: (907) 552-1110
Prog. Accred.: Dentistry (dental assisting)

Southcentral Foundation-Alaska Native Medical Center
4315 Diplomacy Dr., Anchorage 99508
Type: Private, independent
Degrees: C
URL: http://www.southcentralfoundation.com
Phone: (907) 563-2662
Prog. Accred.: Dentistry (general practice residency)

ARIZONA

Arizona State Hospital
2500 East Van Buren St., Phoenix 85008-6037
Type: Public, state
Degrees: C
URL: http://www.azdhs.gov/azsh
Phone: (602) 244-1331
Prog. Accred.: Psychology Internship

Banner Desert Medical Center
1400 South Dobson Rd., Mesa 85202
Type: Private, independent
Degrees: C
URL: http://www.bannerhealth.com
Phone: (480) 512-3000
Prog. Accred.: Clinical Pastoral Education

Banner Good Samaritan Medical Center
PO Box 2989, Phoenix 85006-2612
Type: Private, independent
Degrees: C
URL: http://www.bannerhealth.com
Phone: (602) 239-2000
Prog. Accred.: Clinical Pastoral Education

Carl T. Hayden Veterans Affairs Medical Center
650 East Indian School Rd., Phoenix 85012-1892
Type: Public, federal
Degrees: C
URL: http://www.phoenix.med.va.gov
Phone: (602) 277-5551
Prog. Accred.: Psychology Internship

Hu Hu Kam Memorial Hospital
PO Box 38, Sacaton 85247
Type: Private, tribal
Degrees: C
URL: http://members.cox.net/huhukam
Phone: (602) 528-1230
Prog. Accred.: Allied Health (optometric residency)

Kayenta Health Center of the Indian Health Service
PO Box 368, Kayenta 86033
Type: Public, federal
Degrees: C
URL: http://www.ihs.gov
Phone: (928) 697-4232
Prog. Accred.: Allied Health (optometric residency)

Kino Community Hospital
2800 East Ajo Way, Tucson 85713-6204
Type: Private, independent
Degrees: C
Phone: (520) 294-4471
Prog. Accred.: Dentistry (general practice residency)

Maricopa County Department of Public Health
4041 North Central Ave., Ste. 1400, Phoenix 85012
Type: Public, local
Degrees: C
URL: http://www.maricopa.gov/public_health
Phone: (602) 506-6900
Prog. Accred.: Dietetics (internship)

Paradise Valley Unified School District
20621 North 32nd St., Phoenix 85050
Type: Public, local
Degrees: C
URL: http://cmweb.pvschools.net/nutritionandwellnessweb
Phone: (602) 449-2000
Prog. Accred.: Dietetics (internship)

Phoenix Indian Medical Center
4212 North 16th St., Phoenix 85016
Type: Private, tribal
Degrees: C
URL: http://www.ihs.gov
Phone: (602) 263-1532
Prog. Accred.: Dietetics (internship)

RainStar University
4130 North Goldwater Blvd., Rm. 110, Scottsdale 85251
Type: Private, proprietary, four-year
Degrees: C, A, M
URL: http://www.rainstaruniversity.com
Phone: (480) 423-0375 *Calendar:* Qtr. plan
Prog. Accred.: Acupuncture

Saint Mary's Hospital
1601 West St. Mary's Rd., Tucson 85745
Type: Private, independent
Degrees: C
URL: http://www.carondelet.org/information/csm.htm
Phone: (520) 872-6109
Prog. Accred.: Dietetics (internship)

Southern Arizona Psychology Internship Consortium
502 West 29th St., Tucson 85713-3394
Type: Private, independent
Degrees: C
URL: http://www.u.arizona.edu/~penn/sapic
Phone: (520) 838-3923
Prog. Accred.: Psychology Internship

Southern Arizona Veterans Affairs Health Care System
3601 South 6th Ave., Tucson 85723
Type: Public, federal
Degrees: C
URL: http://www.va.gov/678savahcs
Phone: (520) 792-1450
Prog. Accred.: Allied Health (optometric residency), Psychology Internship

University Medical Center
1501 North Campbell Ave., Tucson 85724
Type: Private, independent
Degrees: C
URL: http://www.azumc.com
Phone: (520) 694-0111
Prog. Accred.: Dietetics (internship)

Yavapai County Community Health Services
1090 Commerce Dr., Prescott 86305-3700
Type: Public, local
Degrees: C
URL: http://www.co.yavapai.az.us
Phone: (928) 442-5488
Prog. Accred.: Dietetics (internship)

Yuma Regional Medical Center
2400 South Ave. A, Yuma 85364
Type: Private, independent
Degrees: C
URL: http://www.yumaregional.org
Phone: (520) 344-7002
Prog. Accred.: Clinical Pastoral Education

ARKANSAS

Baptist Health System, Nursing and Allied Health Schools
11900 Colonel Glenn Rd., Ste. 1000, Little Rock 72210-2820
Type: Private, independent
Degrees: C
URL: http://www.baptist-health.org
Phone: (501) 202-2000
Prog. Accred.: Allied Health (surgical technology), Clinical Lab Scientist, Histologic Technology, Nuclear Medicine Technology, Nursing, Practical Nursing, Radiography

Central Arkansas Radiation Therapy Institute
PO Box 55050, Little Rock 72215
Type: Private, independent
Degrees: C
URL: http://www.carti.com
Phone: (501) 664-8573
Prog. Accred.: Radiation Therapy

Central Arkansas Veterans Healthcare System
4300 West 7th St., Little Rock 72205-5484
Type: Private, federal
Degrees: C
URL: http://www1.va.gov/directory/guide/facility.asp
Phone: (501) 257-1000
Prog. Accred.: Psychology Internship

Jefferson Regional Medical Center
1515 West 42nd Ave., Pine Bluff 71306-7004
Type: Private, independent
Degrees: C
URL: http://www.jrmc.org
Phone: (870) 541-7167
Prog. Accred.: Clinical Pastoral Education, Nursing

Saint Vincent Infirmary Medical Center
Two St. Vincent Circle, Little Rock 72205
Type: Private, independent
Degrees: C
URL: https://www.stvincenthealth.com
Phone: (501) 552-3000
Prog. Accred.: Radiography

CALIFORNIA

1st Dental Battalion/NDC
13128 14th St., Camp Pendleton 92055-5221
Type: Public, federal
Degrees: C
URL: http://www.ndc.cpen.med.navy.mil
Phone: (760) 725-5578
Prog. Accred.: Dentistry (advanced education in general dentistry)

60th Medical Group
101 Bodin Circle, Travis AFB 94535-1800
Type: Public, federal
Degrees: C
URL: https://www.travis.af.mil/dgmc
Phone: (707) 423-7000
Prog. Accred.: Dentistry (advanced education in general dentistry, oral and maxillofacial surgery)

Alta Bates Summit Medical Center
2450 Ashby Ave, Berkeley
Type: Private, independent
Degrees: C
URL: http://www.altabates.com
Phone: (510) 204-6730
Prog. Accred.: Clinical Pastoral Education

American Academy of Dramatic Arts Los Angeles
1336 North LaBrea Ave., Hollywood 90028
Type: Private, independent, two-year
Degrees: A *Enroll:* 278
URL: http://www.aada.org
Phone: (323) 464-2777 *Calendar:* Sem. plan
Prog. Accred.: Theatre

American Red Cross Blood Services—Pomona
100 Red Cross Circle, Pomona 91768
Type: Private, independent
Degrees: C
URL: http://www.redcross.org
Phone: (909) 859-7405
Prog. Accred.: Allied Health (blood bank technology)

Arrowhead Regional Medical Center
400 North Pepper Ave., Colton 92324-1819
Type: Private, independent
Degrees: C
URL: http://www.co.san-bernardino.ca.us/armc
Phone: (909) 580-1000 *Calendar:* 24-mos. pr
Prog. Accred.: Radiography

Atascadero State Hospital
PO Box 7001, Atascadero 93423-7001
Type: Public, state
Degrees: C
URL: http://www.dmh.ca.gov/Statehospitals/Atascadero
Phone: (805) 468-2000
Prog. Accred.: Psychology Internship

California Department of Mental Health Vacaville Psychiatric Program
1600 California Dr., Vacaville 95696-2297
Type: Public, state
Degrees: C
URL: http://www.dmh.ca.gov/Statehospitals/Vacaville
Phone: (707) 449-6571
Prog. Accred.: Psychology Internship

California EMS Academy
1098 Foster City Blvd., Ste. 106, Foster City 94404
Type: Private, proprietary
Degrees: C
URL: http://www.caems-academy.com
Phone: (650) 701-0739
Prog. Accred.: Allied Health (EMT (paramedic))

California Pacific Medical Center
Institute for Health and Healing, PO Box 7999, San Francisco 94120-7999
Type: Private, independent
Degrees: C
Phone: (415) 600-3660
Prog. Accred.: Clinical Pastoral Education

California Paramedic Institute
23141 Lake Center Dr., Lake Forest 92630
Type: Private, proprietary
Degrees: C
URL: http://www.cpimedic.com
Phone: (949) 452-0606
Prog. Accred.: Allied Health (EMT (paramedic))

Cedars Sinai Medical Center
8700 Beverly Blvd., Los Angeles 90048
Type: Private, independent
Degrees: C
URL: http://www.cedars-sinai.edu
Phone: (310) 423-3277
Prog. Accred.: Dentistry (general practice residency)

The Center for Aging Resources
447 North El Molino Ave., Pasadena 91101-1403
Type: Private, independent
Degrees: C
URL: http://www.centerforagingresources.org
Phone: (626) 577-8480
Prog. Accred.: Psychology Internship

The Center for Urban Ministry
2859 El Cajon Blvd., Ste. 2A, San Diego
Type: Private, independent
Degrees: C
Phone: (619) 260-7118 x5122
Prog. Accred.: Clinical Pastoral Education

Central Valley WIC Dietetic Internship
1560 East Manning Ave., Reedley 93654-2346
Type: Private, independent
Degrees: C
URL: http://www.cvwdi.org
Phone: (559) 646-6611
Prog. Accred.: Dietetics (internship)

Children's Hospital of Los Angeles
4650 West Sunset Blvd., Los Angeles 90027
Type: Private, independent
Degrees: C
URL: http://www.chla.usc.edu
Phone: (323) 669-2482
Prog. Accred.: Clinical Pastoral Education, Dietetics (internship), Psychology Internship

Children's Hospital of Orange County
455 South Main St., Orange 92868-3874
Type: Private, independent
Degrees: C
URL: http://www.choc.com
Phone: (714) 997-3000
Prog. Accred.: Psychology Internship

Clinica Sierra Vista
1430 Truxtun Ave., Ste. 120, Bakersfield 93301-3834
Type: Private, independent
Degrees: C
URL: http://www.clinicasierravista.org
Phone: (661) 635-3050
Prog. Accred.: Dietetics (internship)

Community Reach Center
8931 Huron St., Thornton 80260
Type: Private, independent
Degrees: C
URL: http://www.communityreachcenter.org
Phone: (303) 853-3500
Prog. Accred.: Psychology Internship

Converse International School of Languages
636 Broadway St., Ste. 210, San Diego 92101
Type: Private, proprietary
Degrees: C
URL: http://www.cisl.org
Phone: (619) 239-3363
Prog. Accred.: English Language Education

The Crystal Cathedral
12141 Lewis St, Garden Grove
Type: Private, independent
Degrees: C
URL: http://www.crystalcathedral.org
Phone: (714) 971-4038
Prog. Accred.: Clinical Pastoral Education

Didi Hirsch Community Mental Health Center
4760 South Sepulveda Blvd., Culver City 90230-4888
Type: Private, independent
Degrees: C
URL: http://www.didihirsch.org
Phone: (310) 390-6612
Prog. Accred.: Psychology Internship

East Los Angeles Education and Career Center
2100 Marengo St., Los Angeles 90033
Type: Public, local
Degrees: C
URL: http://www.lausd.k12.ca.us/East_LA_OC
Phone: (213) 223-1283
Prog. Accred.: Dentistry (dental assisting)

East San Gabriel Valley Occupational Program
1501 Del Norte St., West Covina 91790-2105
Type: Public, local
Degrees: C
URL: http://www.esgvop.org
Phone: (626) 472-5100
Prog. Accred.: Allied Health (medical assisting (AMA))

Eisenhower Medical Center School of Medical Technology
39000 Bob Hope Dr., Rancho Mirage 92270-3202
Type: Private, proprietary
Degrees: C
URL: http://www.emc.org
Phone: (760) 773-4525
Prog. Accred.: Clinical Lab Scientist

Emergency Medical Sciences Training Institute
1801 East March Ln., Ste. 260, Stockton 95210
Type: Private, proprietary
Degrees: C
URL: http://www.emsti.com
Phone: (209) 461-5550
Prog. Accred.: Allied Health (EMT (paramedic))

Glendale Memorial Hospital and Health Center
1420 South Central Ave., Glendale 91204
Type: Private, independent
Degrees: C
URL: http://www.glendalememorialhospital.org
Phone: (818) 502-1900
Prog. Accred.: Dietetics (internship)

The Guidance Center
3711 Long Beach Blvd., Ste. 600, Long Beach 90807
Type: Private, independent
Degrees: C
URL: http://www.glbcgc.org
Phone: (562) 424-4227
Prog. Accred.: Psychology Internship

Hacienda La Puente Adult Education
15540 East Fairgrove Ave., La Puente 91744
Type: Public, local
Degrees: C
URL: http://www.hlpusd.k12.ca.us/hlpae/
Phone: (818) 855-3138
Prog. Accred.: Dentistry (dental assisting)

Highland General Hospital
1411 East 31st St., Oakland 94602
Type: Private, independent
Degrees: C
URL: http://community.hghed.com
Phone: (510) 437-8497
Prog. Accred.: Dentistry (oral and maxillofacial surgery)

John Muir Medical Center, Concord Campus
2540 East St., Concord 94520-1906
Type: Private, independent
Degrees: C
URL: http://www.johnmuirhealth.com
Phone: (925) 682-8200
Prog. Accred.: Clinical Pastoral Education

Kaiser Permanente Los Angeles Medical Center
4700 Sunset Blvd., 5th and 6th Flr.s, Los Angeles 90027-6082
Type: Private, independent
Degrees: C
URL: http://members.kaiserpermanente.org
Phone: (323) 783-2600
Prog. Accred.: Psychology Internship

Kaiser Permanente School of Allied Health Sciences
938 Marina Way South, Richmond 94804
Type: Private, independent
Degrees: C
URL: http://kpsahs.kp.org
Phone: (510) 231-5000
Prog. Accred.: Allied Health (diagnostic medical sonography), Nuclear Medicine Technology, Radiation Therapy, Radiography

Kaiser Permanente Vista Medical Offices
780 Shadowridge Dr., Vista 92083
Type: Private, independent
Degrees: C
URL: http://members.kaiserpermanente.org
Phone: (760) 599-2350
Prog. Accred.: Psychology Internship

Loma Linda Veterans Affairs Healthcare System
11201 Benton St., Loma Linda 92357
Type: Public, federal
Degrees: C
URL: http://www.lom.med.va.gov
Phone: (909) 825-7084
Prog. Accred.: Dentistry (general practice residency), Psychology Internship

Los Angeles County Emergency Medical Services Agency
5555 Ferguson Dr., Room 220, Commerce 90022
Type: Public, local
Degrees: C
URL: http://www.ladhs.org/ems
Phone: (323) 890-7500
Prog. Accred.: Allied Health (EMT (paramedic))

Los Angeles County Harbor-UCLA Medical Center
1000 West Carson St., Torrance 90502
Type: Private, independent
Degrees: C
URL: http://www.humc.edu
Phone: (310) 222-2345
Prog. Accred.: Nuclear Medicine Technology, Psychology Internship, Radiography

Los Angeles County-USC Medical Center
1200 North State St., Los Angeles 90033
Type: Public, independent
Degrees: C
URL: http://www.ladhs.org
Phone: (323) 226-2800
Prog. Accred.: Dentistry (general practice residency)

Lucile Packard Children's Hospital
725 Welch Rd., Palo Alto 94304
Type: Private, independent
Degrees: C
URL: http://www.lpch.org
Phone: (650) 497-8000
Prog. Accred.: Psychology Internship

Methodist Hospital of Southern California
PO Box 60016, Arcadia 91066-6016
Type: Private, independent
Degrees: C
URL: http://www.methodisthospital.org
Phone: (626) 574-3433
Prog. Accred.: Clinical Pastoral Education

The Metropolitan Detention Center
535 North Alameda St., Los Angeles 90012
Type: Public, federal
Degrees: C
URL: http://www.bop.gov/locations/institutions/los/index.jsp
Phone: (213) 485-0439
Prog. Accred.: Psychology Internship

Metropolitan State Hospital
11401 Bloomfield Ave., Norwalk 90650
Type: Public, state
Degrees: C
URL: http://www.dmh.ca.gov/Statehospitals/Metro
Phone: (562) 863-7011
Prog. Accred.: Psychology Internship

Mills-Peninsula Health Services
1783 El Camino Real, Burlingame 94010
Type: Private, independent
Degrees: C
URL: http://www.mills-peninsula.org
Phone: (650) 696 5400
Prog. Accred.: Radiography

Mount Diablo Adult Education
1266 San Carlos Ave., Concord 94518
Type: Public, local
Degrees: C
URL: http://www.mdusd.k12.ca.us/adulted
Phone: (925) 685-7340
Prog. Accred.: Allied Health (surgical technology)

National College of Technical Instruction—Buellton
240 East Hwy. 246, Ste. 200, Buellton 93427
Type: Private, proprietary
Degrees: C
URL: http://www.ncti-online.com
Prog. Accred.: Allied Health (EMT (paramedic))

National College of Technical Instruction—Livermore
7543 Southfront Rd., Livermore 94551
Type: Private, proprietary
Degrees: C
URL: http://www.ncti-online.com
Prog. Accred.: Allied Health (EMT (paramedic))

National College of Technical Instruction—Roseville
333 Sunrise Ave., Ste. 500, Roseville 95661
Type: Private, proprietary
Degrees: C
URL: http://www.ncti-online.com
Prog. Accred.: Allied Health (EMT (paramedic))

Naval Dental Center—San Diego
2310 Craven St., San Diego 92136-5596
Type: Public, federal
Degrees: C
URL: http://www-nmcsd.med.navy.mil
Phone: (619) 556-8239
Prog. Accred.: Dentistry (general dentistry)

Naval Hospital—Camp Pendelton
PO Box 555191, Camp Pendleton 92055-5191
Type: Public, federal
Degrees: C
URL: http://www.cpen.med.navy.mil
Phone: (760) 725-1288
Prog. Accred.: Dentistry (general practice residency)

Naval Medical Center—San Diego
34800 Bob Willson Dr., San Diego 92134-5001
Type: Public, federal
Degrees: C
URL: http://www-nmcsd.med.navy.mil
Phone: (619) 532-6400
Prog. Accred.: Dentistry (general practice residency, oral and maxillofacial surgery), Psychology Internship

Naval School of Health Sciences
34101 Farenholt Ave., Bldg. 14, San Diego 92021-5291
Type: Public, federal
Degrees: C
URL: http://nshssd.med.navy.mil
Phone: (619) 532-9712
Prog. Accred.: Allied Health (cardiovascular technology, surgical technology), Clinical Lab Technology (C), Dentistry (dental laboratory technology), Radiation Therapy, Radiography

Olive View-UCLA Medical Center
14445 Olive View Dr., Sylmar 91342
Type: Public, local
Degrees: C
URL: http://www.ladhs.org
Phone: (818) 364-1555
Prog. Accred.: Dietetics (internship)

Patton State Hospital
3102 East Highland Ave., Patton 92369
Type: Public, state
Degrees: C
URL: http://www.dmh.ca.gov/Statehospitals/Patton
Phone: (909) 425-7000
Prog. Accred.: Dietetics (internship)

Porterville Developmental Center
PO Box 2000, Porterville 93258-2000
Type: Public, state
Degrees: C
URL: http://www.portervilledc.info
Phone: (559) 782-2751
Prog. Accred.: Dietetics (internship)

Public Health Foundation Enterprises-WIC Dietetic Internship Program
12781 Schabarum Ave., Irwindale 91706-6802
Type: Private, independent
Degrees: C
URL: http://www.phfewic.org
Phone: (626) 856-6650
Prog. Accred.: Dietetics (internship)

Richmond Area Multi-Services, Inc.
3626 Balboa St., San Francisco 94121
Type: Private, independent
Degrees: C
URL: http://www.ramsinc.org/ramshome.html
Phone: (415) 668-5955
Prog. Accred.: Psychology Internship

River Oak Center for Children
4330 Auburn Blvd., Ste. 2000, Sacramento 95841
Type: Private, independent
Degrees: C
URL: http://www.riveroak.org
Phone: (916) 609-5100
Prog. Accred.: Psychology Internship

Saint John's Child and Family Development Center
1339 20th St., Santa Monica 90404
Type: Private, independent
Degrees: C
Phone: (310) 829-8921
Prog. Accred.: Psychology Internship

Saint Joseph Hospital
1100 West Stewart Dr., Orange 92868-5600
Type: Private, independent
Degrees: C
URL: http://www.sjo.org
Phone: (714) 633-9111
Prog. Accred.: Clinical Pastoral Education

Saint Mary's Medical Center
450 Stanyan St., San Francisco 94117-1079
Type: Private, independent
Degrees: C
URL: http://www.stmarysmedicalcenter.org
Phone: (415) 750-5718
Prog. Accred.: Clinical Pastoral Education

San Bernardino County Department of Behavioral Health
700 East Gilbert St., San Bernardino 92415
Type: Public, state
Degrees: C
URL: http://www.co.san-bernardino.ca.us/dbh
Phone: (909) 873-4478
Prog. Accred.: Psychology Internship

San Diego WIC Dietetic Internship
8057 Vickers St., San Diego 92111
Type: Private, independent
Degrees: C
URL: http://www.wic-sdsu.org
Phone: (858) 505-3070
Prog. Accred.: Dietetics (internship)

San Joaquin General Hospital
500 West Hospital Rd., French Camp 95231
Type: Private, independent
Degrees: C
URL: http://www.sjgeneralhospital.com
Phone: (209) 468-6000
Prog. Accred.: Radiography

Santa Barbara Cottage Hospital
PO Box 689, Santa Barbara 93102-0689
Type: Private, independent
Degrees: C
URL: http://www.cottagehealthsystem.org
Phone: (805) 682-7111
Prog. Accred.: Clinical Lab Scientist

Sharp Memorial Hospital
7901 Frost St., San Diego 92123-2701
Type: Private, proprietary
Degrees: C
URL: http://www.sharp.com/hospital/index.cfm?id=919
Phone: (858) 939-3400
Prog. Accred.: Clinical Pastoral Education, Psychology Internship

Sharp Mesa Vista Hospital
7850 Vista Hill Ave., San Diego 92123
Type: Private, proprietary
Degrees: C
URL: http://www.sharp.com/hospital/index.cfm?id=921
Phone: (858) 278-4110
Prog. Accred.: Psychology Internship

Simi Valley Adult School and Career Institute
1880 Blackstock St., Simi Valley 93065
Type: Public, local
Degrees: C
URL: http://www.simi.tec.ca.us
Phone: (805) 527-6200 *Calendar:* Sem. plan
Prog. Accred.: Allied Health (respiratory therapy technology, surgical technology)

Southern California Regional Occupational Center
2300 Crenshaw Blvd., Torrance 90501
Type: Public, state/local
Degrees: C
URL: http://www.scroc.com
Phone: (310) 224-4200 *Calendar:* Sem. plan
Prog. Accred.: Allied Health (medical assisting (AMA))

Southwestern University School of Law
3050 Wilshire Blvd., Los Angeles 90010
Type: Private, independent, four-year
Degrees: M, P *Enroll:* 807
URL: http://www.swlaw.edu
Phone: (213) 738-6700 *Calendar:* Sem. plan
Prog. Accred.: Law

Sutter Medical Center
2801 L St., Sacramento 95816
Type: Private, independent
Degrees: C
URL: http://suttermedicalcenter.org
Phone: (916) 454-2222
Prog. Accred.: Clinical Pastoral Education

Thomas Jefferson School of Law
2121 San Diego Ave., San Diego 92110-2905
Type: Private, independent, four-year
Degrees: P, D *Enroll:* 683
URL: http://www.tjsl.edu
Phone: (619) 297-9700 *Calendar:* Sem. plan
Prog. Accred.: Law (ABA only)

Tri-City Mental Health Center
790 East Bonita Ave., Pomona 91767-1906
Type: Public, state/local
Degrees: C
URL: http://www.tricitymhs.org
Phone: (909) 623-6131
Prog. Accred.: Psychology Internship

Veterans Affairs Central California Health Care System
2615 East Clinton Ave., Fresno 93703
Type: Public, federal
Degrees: C
URL: http://www.fresno.va.gov
Phone: (559) 225-6100
Prog. Accred.: Allied Health (optometric residency)

Veterans Affairs Greater Los Angeles Healthcare System
11301 Wilshire Blvd., West Los Angeles 90073
Type: Public, federal
Degrees: C
URL: http://www.gla.med.va.gov
Phone: (310) 478-3711
Prog. Accred.: Allied Health (optometric residency), Dentistry (combined prosthodontics, general practice residency, periodontics), Dietetics (internship), Psychology Internship

Los Angeles Ambulatory Care Center
351 East Temple St., Los Angeles 90012
Phone: (213) 253-2677
Prog. Accred: Psychology Internship

Sepulveda Ambulatory Care Center
16111 Plummer St., Sepulveda 91343
Phone: (818) 891-7711
Prog. Accred: Allied Health (optometric residency), Dentistry (general practice residency), Psychology Internship

Veterans Affairs Long Beach Healthcare System
5901 East 7th St., Long Beach 90822-5201
Type: Public, federal
Degrees: C
URL: http://www.long-beach.med.va.gov
Phone: (562) 826-8000
Prog. Accred.: Dentistry (endodontics, general practice residency), Psychology Internship

Veterans Affairs Medical Center—San Francisco
4150 Clement St., San Francisco 94121
Type: Public, federal
Degrees: C
URL: http://www.sf.med.va.gov
Phone: 415) 221-4810
Prog. Accred.: Allied Health (optometric residency), Dentistry (general practice residency), Psychology Internship

Veterans Affairs Northern California Health Care System—Mare Island
201 Walnut Ave., Vallejo 94592
Type: Public, federal
Degrees: C
URL: http://www.va.gov/sta/guide
Phone: (707) 562-8200
Prog. Accred.: Dentistry (general practice residency)

Veterans Affairs Northern California Health Care System—Martinez
150 Muir Rd., Martinez 94553
Type: Private, federal
Degrees: C
URL: http://www1.va.gov/directory
Phone: (925) 372-2000
Prog. Accred.: Psychology Internship

Veterans Affairs Palo Alto Health Care System
3801 Miranda Ave., Palo Alto 94304
Type: Public, federal
Degrees: C
URL: http://www.palo-alto.med.va.gov
Phone: (650) 493-5000
Prog. Accred.: Allied Health (optometric residency), Clinical Pastoral Education, Dentistry (general practice residency), Nuclear Medicine Technology, Psychology Internship

Veterans Affairs San Diego Healthcare System
3350 La Jolla Village Dr., San Diego 92161
Type: Public, federal
Degrees: C
URL: http://www.sandiego.va.gov
Phone: (858) 552-8585
Prog. Accred.: Allied Health (optometric residency), Dentistry (general practice residency), Dietetics (internship)

VITAS Innovative Hospice Care—San Diego
9655 Granite Ridge Dr., Ste. 300, San Diego 92123
Type: Private, independent
System: VITAS Innovative Hospice Care
Degrees: C
URL: http://www.vitas.com
Phone: (858) 499-8901
Prog. Accred.: Clinical Pastoral Education

COLORADO

10th Medical Group/SGFL
4102 Pinion Dr., Ste. 3, USAF Academy 80840
Type: Public, federal
Degrees: C
URL: http://www.usafa.af.mil/10abw/10mdg/?catname=10mdg
Phone: (719) 333-5111
Prog. Accred.: Dentistry (advanced education in general dentistry)

Aurora Mental Health Center
14301 East Hampden Ave., Aurora 80014
Type: Private, independent
Degrees: C
URL: http://www.aumhc.org
Phone: (303) 617-2300
Prog. Accred.: Psychology Internship

The Children's Hospital
1056 East 19th Ave., Denver 80218
Type: Private, independent
Degrees: C
URL: http://www.tchden.org
Phone: (303) 861-8888
Prog. Accred.: Dentistry (pediatric dentistry), Psychology Internship

Colorado Mental Health Institute at Fort Logan
3520 West Oxford Ave., Denver 80236-3108
Type: Public, proprietary
Degrees: C
URL: http://www.cdhs.state.co.us/cmhifl
Phone: (303) 866-7066
Prog. Accred.: Psychology Internship

The Colorado School for Family Therapy
12101 East Second Ave., Aurora 80011-8328
Type: Private, independent
Degrees: C
URL: http://www.familyplaytherapy.net
Phone: (720) 859-0464
Prog. Accred.: Marriage and Family Therapy

Denver Family Institute
7200 East Hampden Ave., Ste. 301, Denver 80224-3021
Type: Private, independent
Degrees: C
URL: http://www.denverfamilyinstitute.org
Phone: (303) 756-3340 *Calendar:* Qtr. plan
Prog. Accred.: Marriage and Family Therapy

Denver Health Medical Center
777 Bannock St., Denver 80204
Type: Private, independent
Degrees: C
URL: http://www.denverhealth.org
Phone: (303) 436-6000
Prog. Accred.: Allied Health (EMT (paramedic)), Dentistry (general practice residency, oral and maxillofacial surgery), Psychology Internship

HealthONE Center for Health Science Education
1719 East 19th Ave., Denver 80218
Type: Private, independent
Degrees: C
URL: http://www.pslmc.com
Phone: (303) 839-6000
Prog. Accred.: Clinical Lab Scientist, Radiography

HealthONE Emergency Medical Services
333 West Hampton Ave., Ste. 200, Englewood 80110
Type: Private, independent
Degrees: C
URL: http://www.healthoneems.com
Phone: (303) 788-6317
Prog. Accred.: Allied Health (EMT (paramedic))

Memorial Hospital
1400 East Boulder, Colorado Springs 80909
Type: Private, independent
Degrees: C
URL: http://www.memorialhospital.com
Phone: (719) 365-5000
Prog. Accred.: Radiography

Parkview Medical Center
400 West 16th St., Pueblo 81003-2781
Type: Private, independent
Degrees: C
URL: http://www.parkviewmc.com
Phone: (719) 584-4000
Prog. Accred.: Clinical Lab Scientist

Penrose-St. Francis Health Services
825 East Pikes Peak Ave., Colorado Springs 80933-7021
Type: Private, independent
System: Centura Health System
Degrees: C
URL: http://www.penrosestfrancis.org
Phone: (719) 776-5000
Prog. Accred.: Clinical Pastoral Education, Dietetics (internship)

Penrose Hospital School of Clinical Laboratory Science
PO Box 7021, Colorado Springs 80933
Phone: (719) 776-5221
Prog. Accred: Clinical Lab Scientist

Porter Adventist Hospital
2525 South Downing St., Denver 80210-5817
Type: Private, independent
System: Centura Health System
Degrees: C
URL: http://www.porterhospital.org
Phone: (303) 778-1955
Prog. Accred.: Clinical Pastoral Education

Saint Anthony Central Hospital
4231 West 16th Ave., Denver 80204
Type: Private, independent
System: Centura Health System
Degrees: C
URL: http://www.stanthonyhosp.org
Phone: (303) 629-3511
Prog. Accred.: Clinical Pastoral Education, Radiography

Saint Mary-Corwin Medical Center
1008 Minnequa Ave., Pueblo 81004
Type: Private, independent
System: Centura Health System
Degrees: C
URL: http://www.stmarycorwin.org
Phone: (719) 560-4000
Prog. Accred.: Clinical Pastoral Education

Samaritan Counseling and Education Center
420 North Nevada Ave., Colorado Springs 80903
Type: Private, independent
Degrees: C
URL: http://www.samaritancs.com
Phone: (719) 471-2500
Prog. Accred.: Clinical Pastoral Education

Swedish Medical Center
501 East Hampden Ave., Englewood 80110-2702
Type: Private, independent
Degrees: C
URL: http://www.swedishhospital.com
Phone: (303) 788-6233
Prog. Accred.: Clinical Pastoral Education

Tri-County Health Department
7000 E. Belleview Ave., Ste. 301, Greenwood Village 80111
Type: Public, state/local
Degrees: C
URL: http://www.tchd.org
Phone: (303) 220-9200
Prog. Accred.: Dietetics (internship)

United States Army Dental Activity—Ft. Carson
Ft. Carson 80913-5207
Type: Public, federal
Degrees: C
URL: http://evans.amedd.army.mil/dentac
Phone: (719) 526-2006
Prog. Accred.: Dentistry (general dentistry)

Veterans Affairs Eastern Colorado Healthcare System
1055 Clermont St., Denver 80220
Type: Public, federal
Degrees: C
URL: http://www1.va.gov/directory
Phone: (303) 399-8020
Prog. Accred.: Dentistry (general practice residency), Psychology Internship

CONNECTICUT

Bridgeport Hospital
267 Grant St., Bridgeport 06610-2805
Type: Private, independent
Degrees: C
URL: http://www.bridgeporthospital.org
Phone: (203) 384-3881
Prog. Accred.: Allied Health (surgical technology), Clinical Pastoral Education, Nurse Anesthesia Education, Nursing

Capitol Region Mental Health Center
500 Vine St., Hartford 06112
Type: Public, state
Degrees: C
URL: http://www.dmhas.state.ct.us
Phone: (860) 297-0800
Prog. Accred.: Psychology Internship

Connecticut Valley Psychology Internship
PO Box 351, Silver St., Middletown 06457
Type: Private, independent
Degrees: C
URL: http://www.dmhas.state.ct.us/RVS/PsychIntern.htm
Phone: (860) 262-5200
Prog. Accred.: Psychology Internship

Danbury Hospital
24 Hospital Ave., Danbury 06810-5988
Type: Private, independent
Degrees: C
URL: http://www.danhosp.org
Phone: (203) 797-7804
Prog. Accred.: Allied Health (surgical technology), Clinical Lab Scientist, Dentistry (general practice residency), Dietetics (internship), Radiography

Griffin Hospital
130 Division St., Derby 06418
Type: Private, independent
Degrees: C
URL: http://www.griffinhealth.org
Phone: (203) 735-7421
Prog. Accred.: Clinical Pastoral Education

Hanger Orthopedic Group, Inc.
181 Patricia M. Genova Dr., Newington 06111
Type: Private, proprietary
Degrees: C
URL: http://www.hanger.com
Phone: (860) 667-5361
Prog. Accred.: Allied Health (orthotist/prothetist)

Hartford Hospital School of Allied Health
560 Hudson St., Hartford 06102
Type: Private, independent
Degrees: C
URL: http://www.harthosp.org/alliedhealth
Phone: (860) 545-2611
Prog. Accred.: Clinical Lab Scientist, Clinical Pastoral Education, Dentistry (general practice residency), Histologic Technology, Radiation Therapy, Radiography

Hospital of Saint Raphael
1450 Chapel St., New Haven 06511
Type: Private, independent
Degrees: C
URL: http://www.srhs.org
Phone: (203) 789-3245
Prog. Accred.: Clinical Pastoral Education, Clinical Pastoral Education (USCC), Dentistry (oral and maxillofacial surgery), Nurse Anesthesia Education

The Institute of Living
400 Washington St., Hartford 06106
Type: Private, independent
Degrees: C
URL: http://www.instituteofliving.org
Phone: (800) 673-2411
Prog. Accred.: Psychology Internship

Masonic Geriatric Healthcare Center
22 Masonic Ave., Wallingford 06492-0070
Type: Private, proprietary
Degrees: C
URL: http://www.masonicare.org
Phone: (203) 679-5900
Prog. Accred.: Clinical Pastoral Education

New Britain School of Nurse Anesthesia
100 Grand St., New Britain 06050
Type: Private, independent
Degrees: C
URL: http://www.nbsna.org
Phone: (860) 224-5612
Prog. Accred.: Nurse Anesthesia Education

Norwalk Hospital
34 Maple St., Norwalk 06856
Type: Private, independent
Degrees: C
URL: http://www.norwalkhosp.org
Phone: (203) 852-2000
Prog. Accred.: Allied Health (respiratory therapy), Clinical Pastoral Education

Saint Francis Hospital
114 Woodland St., Hartford 06105-1208
Type: Private, independent
Degrees: C
URL: http://www.stfranciscare.org
Phone: (860) 714-4000
Prog. Accred.: Allied Health (diagnostic medical sonography), Dentistry (general practice residency)

Saint Mary's Hospital
56 Franklin St., Waterbury 06706
Type: Private, independent
Degrees: C
URL: http://www.stmh.org
Phone: (203) 574-6000
Prog. Accred.: Clinical Lab Scientist, Dentistry (general practice residency)

Stamford Health System
30 Shelburne Rd., Stamford 06904-9317
Type: Private, independent
Degrees: C
URL: http://www.stamhealth.org
Phone: (203) 276-1000
Prog. Accred.: Clinical Pastoral Education, Radiography

Veterans Affairs Connecticut Healthcare System
555 Willard Ave., Newington 06111
Type: Private, federal
Degrees: C
URL: http://www.avapl.org/training/Hartford
Phone: (860) 666-6951
Prog. Accred.: Allied Health (optometric residency), Psychology Internship

Veterans Affairs Connecticut Healthcare System West Haven
950 Campbell Ave., West Haven 06516
Type: Public, federal
Degrees: C
URL: http://www.visn1.med.va.gov/vact
Phone: (203) 932-5711
Prog. Accred.: Allied Health (optometric residency), Psychology Internship

The Village for Families and Children, Inc.
1680 Albany Ave., Hartford 06105
Type: Private, independent
Degrees: C
URL: http://www.villageforchildren.org
Phone: (860) 236-4511
Prog. Accred.: Psychology Internship

Waterbury Hospital Health Center
64 Robbins St., Waterbury 06721
Type: Private, independent
Degrees: C
URL: http://www.waterburyhospital.com
Phone: (203) 573-6000
Prog. Accred.: Dentistry (general practice residency)

Windham Community Memorial Hospital
112 Mansfield Ave., Willimantic 06226
Type: Private, independent
Degrees: C
URL: http://www.wcmh.org
Phone: (860) 456-9116
Prog. Accred.: Radiography

Windham Regional Vocational-Technical School
210 Birch St., Willimantic 06226
Type: Public, state/local
Degrees: C
URL: http://www.cttech.org/windham/adult-ed
Phone: (860) 456-3879
Prog. Accred.: Dentistry (dental assisting)

Yale-New Haven Hospital
20 York St., New Haven 06504
Type: Private, independent
Degrees: C
Phone: (203) 688-2151
Prog. Accred.: Allied Health (diagnostic medical sonography), Clinical Pastoral Education, Dentistry (general practice residency), Dietetics (internship)

DELAWARE

Alfred I. duPont Hospital for Children
PO Box 269, Wilmington 19899
Type: Private, independent
Degrees: C
URL: http://www.nemours.org
Phone: (302) 651-4000
Prog. Accred.: Psychology Internship

Beebe School of Nursing
424 Savannah Rd., Lewes 19958
Type: Private, independent
Degrees: C
URL: http://www.beebeschoolofnursing.org
Phone: (302) 645-3251
Prog. Accred.: Nursing

Christiana Care Health System
501 West 14th St., Wilmington 19801
Type: Private, independent
Degrees: C
URL: http://www.christianacare.org
Phone: (302) 428-2780
Prog. Accred.: Clinical Pastoral Education, Dentistry (general practice residency, oral and maxillofacial surgery)

Christiana Care Health System
Broadlawn Shopping Center, Ste. 16, Ardmore, OK 73401
Type: Private, independent
Degrees: C
URL: http://www.christianacare.org
Phone: (302) 428-2780
Prog. Accred.: Clinical Pastoral Education, Dentistry (general practice residency, oral and maxillofacial surgery)

Medical Center of Delaware
501 W. 14th St., Box 1668, Wilmington 19899
Type: Private, independent
Degrees: C
Prog. Accred.: Dentistry (general practice residency, oral and maxillofacial surgery)

Terry Children's Psychiatric Center
10 Central Ave., New Castle 19720
Type: Private, independent
Degrees: C
Phone: (302) 577-4270
Prog. Accred.: Psychology Internship

Wilmington Veterans Affairs Medical Center
1601 Kirkwood Hwy., Wilmington` 19805
Type: Public, federal
Degrees: C
URL: http://www.va.gov/Wilmington
Phone: (302) 994-2511
Prog. Accred.: Allied Health (optometric residency)

DISTRICT OF COLUMBIA

579th Medical Group
260 Brookley Ave., Ste. 2-48, Bolling AFB 20032
Type: Public, federal
Degrees: C
URL: http://www.bolling.af.mil
Phone: (202) 767-5536
Prog. Accred.: Dentistry (advanced education in general dentistry)

The Armed Forces Institute of Pathology
6825 16th St., NW, Washington 20306-6000
Type: Public, federal
Degrees: C
URL: http://www.afip.org
Phone: (202) 782-2100
Prog. Accred.: Histologic Technology

Children's National Medical Center
111 Michigan Ave., NW, Washington 20010
Type: Private, independent
Degrees: C
URL: http://www.cnmc.org
Phone: (202) 884-5000
Prog. Accred.: Clinical Pastoral Education, Dentistry (orthodontic and dentofacial orthopedics, pediatric dentistry), Psychology Internship

District of Columbia School of Law
4250 Connecticut Ave., NW, Washington 20008
Type: Public, state, four-year
Degrees: P *Enroll:* 232
URL: http://www.law.udc.edu
Phone: (202) 727-5225 *Calendar:* Sem. plan
Prog. Accred.: Law (ABA only)

Margaret Murray Washington Vocational School
27 O St., NW, Washington 20001
Type: Public, state
Degrees: C
URL: http://www.k12.dc.us/schools/mmwashington/index2.htm
Phone: (202) 673-7224
Prog. Accred.: Dentistry (dental assisting)

Saint Elizabeths Hospital
2700 Martin Luther King Jr. Dr., SE, Washington 20032
Type: Public, city
Degrees: C
URL: http://dmh.dc.gov/dmh/cwp/view,a,3,q,516064.asp
Phone: (202) 373-7035
Prog. Accred.: Clinical Pastoral Education, Clinical Pastoral Education (USCC)

Sibley Memorial Hospital
5255 Loughboro Rd., NW, Washington 20016-2633
Type: Private, independent
Degrees: C
URL: http://www.sibley.org
Phone: (202) 537-4000
Prog. Accred.: Clinical Pastoral Education

Walter Reed Army Medical Center
6900 Georgia Ave., Washington 20307
Type: Public, federal
Degrees: C
URL: http://www.wramc.amedd.army.mil
Phone: (202) 782-1104
Prog. Accred.: Allied Health (blood bank technology, perfusion), Clinical Lab Scientist, Clinical Pastoral Education, Psychology Internship

Washington DC Veterans Affairs Medical Center
50 Irving St., NW, Washington 20422
Type: Public, federal
Degrees: C
URL: http://www1.va.gov/washington
Phone: (202) 745-8000
Prog. Accred.: Dentistry (prosthodontics), Psychology Internship

Washington Hospital Center
110 Irving St., NW, Washington 20010-2975
Type: Private, independent
Degrees: C
URL: http://www.whcenter.org
Phone: (202) 877-7000
Prog. Accred.: Clinical Lab Scientist, Clinical Pastoral Education, Dentistry (oral and maxillofacial surgery), Radiography

FLORIDA

96th Medical Group
Eglin AFB 32542-5000
Type: Public, federal
Degrees: C
URL: http://www.eglin.af.mil
Phone: (850) 883-8242
Prog. Accred.: Dentistry (advanced education in general dentistry)

Baptist Hospital
1000 West Moreno St., Pensacola 32522-7500
Type: Private, independent
Degrees: C
URL: http://www.ebaptisthealthcare.org
Phone: (850) 434-4011
Prog. Accred.: Clinical Pastoral Education

Baptist Medical Center Downtown
800 Prudential Dr., Jacksonville 32207-8202
Type: Private, independent
Degrees: C
URL: http://www.bmcjax.com
Phone: (904) 202-2000
Prog. Accred.: Clinical Pastoral Education

Bay Pines Veterans Affairs Medical Center
10,000 Bay Pines Blvd., Bay Pines 33744
Type: Public, federal
Degrees: C
URL: http://www.visn8.med.va.gov/baypines
Phone: (727) 398-6661
Prog. Accred.: Allied Health (optometric residency), Dietetics (internship), Psychology Internship

Bayfront Medical Center
701 6th St., South, St. Petersburg 33701-4814
Type: Private, proprietary
Degrees: C
URL: http://www.bayfront.org
Phone: (727) 823-1234
Prog. Accred.: Clinical Lab Scientist

Bethesda Memorial Hospital
2815 South Seacrest Blvd., Boynton Beach 33435
Type: Private, independent
Degrees: C
URL: http://www.bethesdaweb.com
Phone: (561) 737-7733
Prog. Accred.: Radiography

Broward County Practical Nursing Program
600 S. East 3rd Ave., 11th Flr., Ft. Lauderdale 33301-3125
Type: Public, state
Degrees: C
URL: http://www.browardschools.com/schoolboard
Phone: (954) 760-7409
Prog. Accred.: Practical Nursing

The Children's Psychiatric Center, Inc.
15490 NW 7th Ave., Ste. 200, Miami 33169-6231
Type: Private, independent
Degrees: C
URL: http://www.fostercaremiami.org
Phone: (305) 235-8105
Prog. Accred.: Psychology Internship

Citrus Health Network, Inc.
175 West 20th Ave., Hialeah 33012-5875
Type: Private, proprietary
Degrees: C
URL: http://www.citrushealth.org
Phone: (305) 825-0300
Prog. Accred.: Psychology Internship

Coastal Behavioral Healthcare, Inc.
PO Box 1599, Sarasota 34230
Type: Private, proprietary
Degrees: C
URL: http://www.coastalbh.org
Phone: (941) 927-8900
Prog. Accred.: Psychology Internship

Florida College of Integrative Medicine
7100 Lake Ellenor Dr., Orlando 32809
Type: Private, proprietary, four-year
Degrees: C, M
URL: http://www.fcim.edu
Phone: (407) 888-8689 *Calendar:* Sem. plan
Prog. Accred.: Acupuncture

Florida Department of Education Dietetic Internship Program
325 West Gaines St., Rm. 1024, Tallahassee 32399-0400
Type: Public, state
Degrees: C
URL: http://www.fldoe.org/FNM/internship/default.asp
Phone: (850) 245-9267
Prog. Accred.: Dietetics (internship)

Florida State Hospital
100 North Main St., Chattahoochee 32324
Type: Public, state
Degrees: C
URL: http://www.dcf.state.fl.us/institutions/fsh
Phone: (850) 663-7001
Prog. Accred.: Psychology Internship

Halifax Medical Center
303 North Clyde Morris Blvd., Daytona Beach 32114
Type: Private, independent
Degrees: C
URL: http://www.hfch.org
Phone: (386) 254-4000
Prog. Accred.: Radiation Therapy, Radiography

Jackson Memorial Hospital
1611 NW 12th Ave., Miami 33136-1094
Type: Private, independent
Degrees: C
URL: http://um-jmh.org
Phone: (305) 585-1111
Prog. Accred.: Clinical Pastoral Education, Psychology Internship, Radiography

James A. Haley Veterans Affairs Medical Center
13000 Bruce B. Downs Blvd., Tampa 33612
Type: Public, federal
Degrees: C
URL: http://www.visn8.med.va.gov/Tampa
Phone: (813) 972-2000
Prog. Accred.: Clinical Pastoral Education, Dietetics (internship), Psychology Internship

Lake City Veterans Affairs Medical Center
619 South Marion Ave., Lake City 32025-5808
Type: Public, federal
Degrees: C
URL: http://www.northflorida.va.gov
Phone: (386) 755-3016
Prog. Accred.: Allied Health (optometric residency)

Lakeland Regional Medical Center
1324 Lakeland Hills Blvd., Lakeland 33805
Type: Private, independent
Degrees: C
URL: http://www.lakelandcc.edu
Phone: (863) 687-1100
Prog. Accred.: Radiography

Malcom Randall Veterans Affairs Medical Center
1601 SW Archer Rd., Gainesville 32608-1197
Type: Public, federal
Degrees: C
URL: http://www.northflorida.va.gov
Phone: (352) 376-1611
Prog. Accred.: Allied Health (optometric residency), Dentistry (general practice residency), Psychology Internship

Mercy Hospital
3663 South Miami Ave., Miami 33133
Type: Private, independent
Degrees: C
URL: http://www.mercymiami.org
Phone: (305) 854-4400 *Calendar:* Sem. plan
Prog. Accred.: Practical Nursing

Miami Children's Hospital
3100 SW 62nd Ave., Miami 33155
Type: Private, independent
Degrees: C
URL: http://www.mch.com
Phone: (305) 666-6511
Prog. Accred.: Dentistry (pediatric dentistry)

Miami Veterans Affairs Medical Center
1201 NW 16th St., Miami 33125
Type: Public, federal
Degrees: C
URL: http://www.visn8.med.va.gov/miami
Phone: (305) 575-7000
Prog. Accred.: Dentistry (general practice residency), Psychology Internship

Miami-Dade County Department of Human Services
11025 SW 84 St., Miami 33173
Type: Public, state/local
Degrees: C
URL: http://www.miamidade.gov/dhs
Phone: (305) 270-2930
Prog. Accred.: Psychology Internship

Miami-Dade County Public Schools Health Science Education
1450 Northeast Second Ave., Room 817, Miami 33132
Type: Public, local
Degrees: C
URL: http://healthscience.dadeschools.net
Phone: (305) 995-1832
Prog. Accred.: Practical Nursing

Miami-Dade County Public Schools Health Science Education
6161 Northwest Fifth Ct., Miami 33127
Type: Public, local
Degrees: C
URL: healthscience.dadeschools.net
Phone: (305) 995-1832
Prog. Accred.: Practical Nursing

Naval Dental Center Southeast
PO Box 74, Jacksonville 32212-0074
Type: Public, federal
Degrees: C
URL: http://ndcse.med.navy.mil
Phone: (904) 542-3441
Prog. Accred.: Dentistry (general dentistry)

Naval Dental Center—Gulf Coast
161 Turner St., Ste. B, Pensacola 32508-5526
Type: Public, federal
Degrees: C
Phone: (850) 452-5600
Prog. Accred.: Dentistry (general dentistry)

NCH Downtown Naples Hospital
350 7th St., Naples 34102-5754
Type: Private, independent
Degrees: C
URL: http://www.nchhcs.org
Phone: (239) 436-5000
Prog. Accred.: Clinical Pastoral Education

Northeast Florida State Hospital
7487 South State Rd. 121, Macclenny 32063-5451
Type: Public, state
Degrees: C
URL: http://www.dcf.state.fl.us/institutions/nefsh
Phone: (904) 259-6211
Prog. Accred.: Psychology Internship

Orlando Veterans Affairs Medical Center
5201 Raymond St., Orlando 32803
Type: Public, federal
Degrees: C
URL: http://www1.va.gov/orlando
Phone: (407) 629-1599
Prog. Accred.: Allied Health (optometric residency)

Pasco County Health Department
10841 Little Rd., New Port Richey 34654
Type: Public, local
Degrees: C
URL: http://www.doh.state.fl.us/chdpasco
Phone: (727) 861-5250
Prog. Accred.: Dietetics (internship)

Radiation Therapy School for Radiation Therapy
1419 SE 8th Terrace, Cape Coral 33990
Type: Private, proprietary
Degrees: C
URL: http://www.rtsx.com/school/index.htm
Phone: (239) 573-5972
Prog. Accred.: Radiation Therapy

Saint Vincent's Medical Center
1800 Barrs St., Jacksonville 32203-2982
Type: Private, independent
Degrees: C
URL: http://www.jaxhealth.com
Phone: (904) 308-7300
Prog. Accred.: Allied Health (diagnostic medical sonography), Clinical Lab Scientist, Nuclear Medicine Technology, Radiography

Sarasota District Schools' Dietetic Internship Program
101 Old Venice Rd., Osprey 34229
Type: Public, local
Degrees: C
URL: http://www.sarasota.k12.fl.us/fns/dietetic_internship.htm
Phone: (941) 486-2199
Prog. Accred.: Dietetics (internship)

Sarasota Memorial Hospital
1700 South Tamiami Trail, Sarasota 34239-3555
Type: Private, independent
Degrees: C
URL: http://www.smh.com
Phone: (941) 917-9000
Prog. Accred.: Dietetics (internship)

South Florida State Hospital
800 East Cypress Dr., Pembroke Pines 33025
Type: Private, independent
Degrees: C
URL: http://www.sfsh.org
Phone: (954) 392-3000
Prog. Accred.: Psychology Internship

Tampa General Hospital
PO Box 1289, Tampa 33601-1289
Type: Private, independent
Degrees: C
URL: http://www.tgh.org
Phone: (813) 844-7000
Prog. Accred.: Clinical Lab Scientist, Clinical Pastoral Education

Veterans Affairs Medical Center—West Palm Beach
7305 North Military Trail, West Palm Beach 33410-6400
Type: Public, federal
Degrees: C
URL: http://www.va.gov/sta
Phone: (561) 882-8262
Prog. Accred.: Dentistry (general practice residency)

VITAS Innovative Hospice Care—Broward
5420 NW 33rd Ave., Ste. 100, Ft Lauderdale 33309
Type: Private, independent
System: VITAS Innovative Hospice Care
Degrees: C
URL: http://www.vitas.com
Phone: (954) 777-5388
Prog. Accred.: Clinical Pastoral Education

VITAS Innovative Hospice Care—Miami
100 Biscayne Blvd., Ste. 1700, Miami 31331-2011
Type: Private, independent
System: VITAS Innovative Hospice Care
Degrees: C
URL: http://www.vitas.com
Phone: (305) 350-5946
Prog. Accred.: Clinical Pastoral Education

West Boca Medical Center
21644 State Rd. 7, Boca Raton 33428
Type: Private, independent
Degrees: C
URL: http://www.westbocamedctr.com
Phone: (561) 488-8000
Prog. Accred.: Radiography

William V. Chappell, Jr., Veterans Affairs Outpatient Clinic
551 National Health Care Dr., Daytona Beach 32114
Type: Public, federal
Degrees: C
URL: http://www.orlando.va.gov
Phone: (386) 323-7500
Prog. Accred.: Allied Health (optometric residency)

Wolford College
4933 Tamiami Trail North, Ste. 200, Naples 34103
Type: Private, independent, four-year
Degrees: M
URL: http://www.wolford.edu
Phone: (239) 649-0238
Prog. Accred.: Nurse Anesthesia Education

GEORGIA

Atlanta Medical Center
303 Pkwy. Dr. NE, Atlanta 30312
Type: Private, independent
Degrees: C
URL: http://www.atlantamedcenter.com
Phone: (404) 265-4000
Prog. Accred.: Radiography

Atlanta Veterans Affairs Medical Center
1670 Clairmont Rd., Decatur 30033-4004
Type: Public, federal
Degrees: C
URL: http://www1.va.gov/atlanta
Phone: (404) 329-2220
Prog. Accred.: Psychology Internship

Care and Counseling Center of Georgia
1814 Clairmont Rd., Decatur 30033-3405
Type: Private, independent
Degrees: C
URL: http://www.cccgeorgia.org
Phone: (404) 636-1457
Prog. Accred.: Clinical Pastoral Education

Centers for Disease Control and Prevention
1600 Clifton Rd., Atlanta 30333
Type: Public, federal
Degrees: C
URL: http://www.cdc.gov
Phone: 404) 639-3311
Prog. Accred.: Dentistry (dental public health)

Charlie Norwood Veterans Affairs Medical Center
1 Freedom Way, Augusta 30904-6285
Type: Public, federal
Degrees: C
URL: http://www1.va.gov/augustaga
Phone: (706) 733-0188
Prog. Accred.: Dentistry (dental assisting)

Covenant Counseling and Family Resource Center
2219 Scenic Dr., Snelville 30078-3131
Type: Private, independent
Degrees: C
URL: http://www.covenantcounseling.org/cpe.htm
Phone: (770) 985-0837
Prog. Accred.: Clinical Pastoral Education

DeKalb Medical Center Decatur
2701 North Decatur Rd., Decatur 30033
Type: Public, local
Degrees: C
URL: http://www.dekalbmedicalcenter.org
Phone: (404) 501-1000
Prog. Accred.: Radiography

Dwight David Eisenhower Army Medical Center
300 Hospital Rd., Fort Gordon 30905-5650
Type: Public, federal
Degrees: C
URL: http://www.ddeamc.amedd.army.mil
Phone: (706) 787-5811
Prog. Accred.: Clinical Pastoral Education, Psychology Internship

Grady Memorial Hospital
80 Jesse Hill Jr. Dr., SE, PO Box 26095, Atlanta 30303
Type: Private, independent
Degrees: C
URL: http://www.gradyhealthsystem.org
Phone: (404) 616-4307
Prog. Accred.: Allied Health (diagnostic medical sonography), Radiation Therapy, Radiography

The Marcus Institute
1920 Briarcliff Rd., Atlanta 30329
Type: Private, independent
Degrees: C
URL: http://www.marcus.org
Phone: (404) 419-4000
Prog. Accred.: Psychology Internship

Northwest Georgia Regional Hospital
1305 Redmond Circle, Rome 30165
Type: Public, state
Degrees: C
URL: http://www.nwgahealth.com/irsweb/n50pwkd8.htm
Phone: (706) 295-6011
Prog. Accred.: Psychology Internship

Phoebe Putney Memorial Hospital
417 Third Ave., Albany 31701
Type: Private, independent
Degrees: C
URL: http://www.phoebeputney.com
Phone: (229) 312-1000
Prog. Accred.: Clinical Pastoral Education

Saint Francis Hospital
2122 Machester Expressway, Columbus 31908-7000
Type: Private, independent
Degrees: C
URL: http://www.sfhga.com
Phone: (706) 596-4000
Prog. Accred.: Clinical Pastoral Education

Saint Joseph's Hospital
5665 Peachtree Dunwoody Rd. NE, Atlanta 30342
Type: Private, independent
Degrees: C
URL: http://www.sjha.org
Phone: (404) 851-7001
Prog. Accred.: Clinical Pastoral Education

Southern Regional Medical Center
11 Upper Riverdale Rd., Riverdale 30274-2615
Type: Private, independent
Degrees: C
URL: http://www.southernregional.org
Phone: (770) 991-8000
Prog. Accred.: Dietetics (internship)

Training and Counseling Center at Saint Luke's
435 Peachtree St., NE, Atlanta 30308-3228
Type: Private, independent
Degrees: C
URL: http://www.trainingandcounselingcenter.org
Phone: (404) 876-6266
Prog. Accred.: Clinical Pastoral Education

United States Army Dental Activity, Southeast Regional
38th St., Building 38717, Fort Gordon 30905-5660
Type: Public, federal
Degrees: C
URL: http://serdc.amedd.army.mil
Phone: (706) 787-5738
Prog. Accred.: Dentistry (combined prosthodontics, endodontics, oral and maxillofacial surgery, periodontics)

University Hospital
1350 Walton Way, Augusta 30901-3599
Type: Private, independent
Degrees: C
URL: http://www.universityhealth.org
Phone: (706) 722-9011
Prog. Accred.: Dietetics (internship), Radiography

HAWAII

Pacific Health Ministry
1245 Young St., Ste. 204, Honolulu 96814
Type: Private, independent
Degrees: C
URL: http://www.pacifichealthministry.org
Phone: (808) 591-6556
Prog. Accred.: Clinical Pastoral Education

The Queen's Medical Center
1301 Punchbowl St., Honolulu 96813
Type: Private, independent
Degrees: C
URL: http://www.queens.org
Phone: (808) 538-9011
Prog. Accred.: Dentistry (general practice residency)

Tripler Army Medical Center
1 Jarrett White Rd., Honolulu 96859-5000
Type: Public, federal
Degrees: C
URL: http://www.tamc.amedd.army.mil
Phone: (808) 433-6661
Prog. Accred.: Dentistry (general dentistry, oral and maxillofacial surgery), Psychology Internship

Veterans Affairs Pacific Islands Healthcare System
459 Patterson Rd., Honolulu 96819-1522
Type: Public, federal
Degrees: C
URL: http://www.va.gov/hawaii
Phone: (808) 433-0600
Prog. Accred.: Psychology Internship

IDAHO

Saint Luke's Boise Medical Center
190 East Bannock St., Boise 83712-6261
Type: Private, independent
Degrees: C
URL: http://www.stlukesonline.org/boise
Phone: (208) 381-2100
Prog. Accred.: Clinical Pastoral Education

ILLINOIS

375th Medical Group
310 West Losey St., Scott AFB 62225-5252
Type: Public, federal
Degrees: C
URL: http://www.scott.af.mil/units/375thmedicalgroup.asp
Phone: (618) 256-7500
Prog. Accred.: Dentistry (advanced education in general dentistry)

Advocate Bethany Hospital
3435 West Van Buren St., Chicago 60624
Type: Private, independent
System: Advocate Health Care System
Degrees: C
URL: http://www.advocatehealth.com/beth
Phone: (773) 265-7000
Prog. Accred.: Clinical Pastoral Education

Advocate Christ Medical Center
4440 West 95th St., Oak Lawn 60453
Type: Private, independent
System: Advocate Health Care System
Degrees: C
URL: http://www.advocatehealth.com
Phone: (708) 425-8000
Prog. Accred.: Clinical Pastoral Education, Dentistry (general practice residency), Psychology Internship

Advocate Illinois Masonic Medical Center
836 West Wellington Ave., Chicago 60657
Phone: (773) 975-1600
Prog. Accred: Clinical Pastoral Education, Psychology Internship

Advocate Good Samaritan Hospital
3815 Highland Ave., Downers Grove 60515
Type: Private, independent
System: Advocate Health Care System
Degrees: C
URL: http://www.advocatehealth.com/gsam
Phone: (630) 275-5900
Prog. Accred.: Clinical Pastoral Education

Advocate Good Shepherd Hospital
450 West Hwy. 22, Barrington 60010
Type: Private, independent
System: Advocate Health Care System
Degrees: C
URL: http://www.advocatehealth.com/gshp
Phone: (847) 381-0123
Prog. Accred.: Clinical Pastoral Education

Advocate Lutheran General Hospital
1775 Dempster St., Park Ridge 60068
Type: Private, independent
System: Advocate Health Care System
Degrees: C
URL: http://www.advocatehealth.com/luth
Phone: (847) 723-2210
Prog. Accred.: Clinical Pastoral Education

Advocate South Suburban Hospital
17800 South Kedzie Ave., Hazel Crest 60429
Type: Private, independent
System: Advocate Health Care System
Degrees: C
URL: http://www.advocatehealth.com/ssub
Phone: (708) 799-8000
Prog. Accred.: Clinical Pastoral Education

Advocate Trinity Hospital
2320 East 93rd St., Chicago 60617
Type: Private, independent
System: Advocate Health Care System
Degrees: C
URL: http://www.advocatehealth.com/trin
Phone: (773) 967-2000
Prog. Accred.: Clinical Pastoral Education, Radiography

Alexian Brothers Health System
600 Alexian Way, Elk Grove Village 60007-3370
Type: Private, independent
System: Alexian Brothers (System Center)
Degrees: C
URL: http://www.alexianhealthsystem.org
Phone: (847) 981-3621
Prog. Accred.: Clinical Pastoral Education

Alexian Brothers Medical Center
800 Biesterfield Rd., Elk Grove Village 60007-3311
Type: Private, independent
System: Alexian Brothers (System Center)
Degrees: C
URL: http://www.alexianhealthsystem.org
Phone: (847) 437-5500 x4744
Prog. Accred.: Clinical Pastoral Education

Allendale Association
PO Box 1088, Lake Villa 60046
Type: Private, independent
Degrees: C
URL: http://www.allendale4kids.org
Phone: (888) 255-3631
Prog. Accred.: Psychology Internship

Blessing Hospital
1005 Broadway, PO Box 7005, Quincy 62305-7005
Type: Private, independent
Degrees: C
URL: http://www.blessinghospital.org
Phone: (217) 223-1200
Prog. Accred.: Radiography

Bloomington-Normal School of Radiography
900 Franklin Ave., Normal 61761
Type: Private, independent
Degrees: C
URL: http://www.bnradiography.com
Phone: (309) 452-2834 *Calendar:* 24-mos. pr
Prog. Accred.: Radiography

BroMenn Regional Medical Center
1304 Franklin Ave., Normal 61761
Type: Private, independent
Degrees: C
URL: http://www.BroMenn.com
Phone: (309) 454-1400
Prog. Accred.: Clinical Pastoral Education

Carle Foundation Hospital
611 West Park St., Urbana 61801
Type: Private, independent
Degrees: C
URL: http://www.carle.com
Phone: (217) 383-3311
Prog. Accred.: Clinical Pastoral Education, Dentistry (oral and maxillofacial surgery)

Cermak Health Services of Cook County
2800 South California Ave., Chicago 60608
Type: Public, state-affiliated
Degrees: C
URL: http://www.cookcountyresearch.net/cer.html
Phone: (773) 890-5641
Prog. Accred.: Psychology Internship

Chicago Area Christian Training Consortium
336 Gunderson Dr., Ste. B, Carol Stream 60188
Type: Private, independent
Degrees: C
URL: http://www.cactc.org
Phone: (630) 871-2100
Prog. Accred.: Psychology Internship

Chicago Public Schools
2245 West Jackson Blvd., Chicago 60612
Type: Public, state/local
Degrees: C
Phone: (773) 534-7890
Prog. Accred.: Practical Nursing

Children's Memorial Hospital
2300 Children's Plaza, Chicago 60614-3394
Type: Private, independent
Degrees: C
URL: http://www.childrensmemorial.org
Phone: (773) 880-4000
Prog. Accred.: Dentistry (pediatric dentistry), Psychology Internship

Christian Homes, Inc.
200 North Postville Dr., Lincoln 62656
Type: Private, independent
Degrees: C
URL: http://www.christianhomes.org
Phone: (217) 732-5168
Prog. Accred.: Clinical Pastoral Education

Fair Havens Christian Home
1790 South Fairview Ave., Decatur 62521
Phone: (217) 429-2551
Prog. Accred: Clinical Pastoral Education

Lewis Memorial Christian Village
3400 West Washington St., Springfield 62711
Phone: (217) 787-9600
Prog. Accred: Clinical Pastoral Education

Spring River Christian Village
201 South Northpark Ln., Joplin, MO 64801
Phone: (417) 623-4313
Prog. Accred: Clinical Pastoral Education

The Church Home at Montgomery Place
5550 South Shore Dr., Chicago 60637-1550
Type: Private, Episcopal Charities and Community Services
Degrees: C
URL: http://montgomeryplace.org/church.html
Phone: (773) 753-4102
Prog. Accred.: Clinical Pastoral Education

Cook County Hospital
1900 West Polk St., Chicago 60612
Type: Private, independent
Degrees: C
URL: http://www.cchil.org
Phone: (312) 864-6000
Prog. Accred.: Dentistry (oral and maxillofacial surgery)

Deaconess Hospital
600 Mary St., Evanston 47747-0001
Type: Private, independent
Degrees: C
URL: http://www.deaconess.com
Phone: (812) 450-5000
Prog. Accred.: Clinical Pastoral Education

Edward Hines, Jr. Veterans Affairs Hospital
5th Ave. & Roosevelt Rd., PO Box 5000, Hines 60141
Type: Public, federal
Degrees: C
URL: http://www.visn12.med.va.gov/hines
Phone: (708) 202-8387
Prog. Accred.: Clinical Lab Scientist, Dietetics (internship), Nuclear Medicine Technology, Psychology Internship

Edward Hospital
801 South Washington St., Naperville 60540-7430
Type: Private, independent
Degrees: C
URL: http://www.edward.org
Phone: (630) 527-3000
Prog. Accred.: Clinical Pastoral Education

Elmhurst Memorial Hospital
200 Berteau Ave., Elmhurst 60126-2966
Type: Private, independent
Degrees: C
URL: http://www.emhc.org
Phone: (630) 833-1400
Prog. Accred.: Clinical Pastoral Education

Evanston Hospital
2650 Ridge Ave., Evanston 60201
Type: Private, independent
Degrees: C
URL: http://www.enh.org/locations/evanston
Phone: (847) 570-2000
Prog. Accred.: Clinical Pastoral Education, Dentistry (general practice residency)

Graham Hospital School of Nursing
210 West Walnut St., Canton 61520
Type: Private, independent
Degrees: C
URL: http://grahamschoolofnursing.org
Phone: (309) 647-4086 *Calendar:* Sem. plan
Prog. Accred.: Nursing

Ingalls Memorial Hospital
One Ingalls Dr., Harvey 60426
Type: Private, independet
Degrees: C
URL: http://www.ingallshealthsystem.org
Phone: (708) 333-2300
Prog. Accred.: Dietetics (internship)

Jesse Brown Veterans Affairs Medical Center
820 South Damen Ave., Chicago 60612
Type: Public, federal
Degrees: C
URL: http://www.chicago.med.va.gov
Phone: (312) 569-8387
Prog. Accred.: Allied Health (optometric residency), Psychology Internship

Jewish Child and Family Services
255 Revere Dr., Ste. 200, Northbrook 60062
Type: Private, independent
Degrees: C
URL: http://www.jcbchicago.org
Phone: (847) 412-4350
Prog. Accred.: Psychology Internship

La Rabida Children's Hospital
East 65th St. at Lake Michigan, Chicago 60649
Type: Private, independent
Degrees: C
URL: http://www.larabida.org
Phone: (773) 363-6700
Prog. Accred.: Psychology Internship

MacNeal Hospital
3249 Oak Park Ave., Berwyn 60402-3429
Type: Private, independent
Degrees: C
URL: http://www.macneal.com
Phone: (708) 795-3107
Prog. Accred.: Clinical Pastoral Education

McDonough District Hospital
525 East Grant St., Macomb 61455
Type: Public, local
Degrees: C
URL: http://www.mdh.org
Phone: (309) 833-4101
Prog. Accred.: Radiography

The Menta Group
900 Jorie Blvd., Ste. 59, Oak Brook 60521
Type: Private, independent
Degrees: C
URL: http://www.thementagroup.org
Phone: (630) 907-2400
Prog. Accred.: Psychology Internship

Naval Dental Center—Great Lakes
2730 Sampson Rd., Great Lakes 60088
Type: Public, federal
Degrees: C
URL: http://www.nsgreatlakes.navy.mil
Phone: (847) 688-5650
Prog. Accred.: Dentistry (general dentistry)

Naval Health Clinic, Great Lakes
3001A Sixth St., Great Lakes 60088-2833
Type: Public, federal
Degrees: C
URL: http://greatlakes.med.navy.mil
Phone: (847) 688-4560
Prog. Accred.: Dentistry (general practice residency)

Nazareth Family Center-Family Practice Center
1127 North Oakley Blvd., Chicago 60622
Type: Private, Catholic-sponsored
Degrees: C
URL: http://www.reshealthcare.org
Phone: (312) 770-2040
Prog. Accred.: Clinical Pastoral Education

North Chicago Veterans Affairs Medical Center
3001 Green Bay Rd., North Chicago 60064
Type: Public, federal
Degrees: C
URL: http://www.visn12.med.va.gov/northchicago
Phone: (847) 688-1900
Prog. Accred.: Dentistry (general practice residency), Psychology Internship

Northwest Community Hospital
800 West Central Rd., Arlington Heights 60005-2349
Type: Private, independent
Degrees: C
URL: http://www.nch.org
Phone: (847) 618-1000
Prog. Accred.: Clinical Pastoral Education

Northwestern Memorial Hospital
251 East Huron St., Galter Pavillion L-178, Chicago 60611-2908
Type: Private, independent, four-year
Degrees: C, B
URL: http://www.nmh.org
Phone: (31) 926-2000
Prog. Accred.: Allied Health (diagnostic medical sonography), Clinical Pastoral Education, Dentistry (general practice residency), Nuclear Medicine Technology, Radiation Therapy

Oak Forest Hospital
15900 South Cicero Ave., Oak Forest 60452
Type: Private, independent
Degrees: C
Phone: (708) 633-2000
Prog. Accred.: Psychology Internship

Rockford Memorial Hospital
2400 North Rockton Ave., Rockford 61103-3655
Type: Private, independent
Degrees: C
URL: http://www.rhsnet.org
Phone: (815) 971-5000
Prog. Accred.: Clinical Pastoral Education, Radiography

Rush-Presbyterian-Saint Luke's Medical Center
1725 West Harrison, Rm. 717-PB, Chicago 60612
Type: Private, independent
Degrees: C
URL: http://www.rush.edu
Phone: (312) 942-5000
Prog. Accred.: Clinical Pastoral Education, Dentistry (general practice residency), Psychology Internship

Lake Forest Hospital
660 North Westmoreland Rd., Lake Forest 60045-1659
Phone: (847) 535-6070
Prog. Accred: Clinical Pastoral Education

Saint Elizabeth's Hospital
211 South 3rd St., Belleville 62222
Type: Private, independent
Degrees: C
URL: http://www.steliz.org
Phone: (618) 234-2120
Prog. Accred.: Clinical Lab Scientist

Saint Francis Hospital
355 Ridge Ave., Evanston 60202-3328
Type: Private, independent
Degrees: C
URL: http://www.reshealth.org/sub_sfh/default.cfm
Phone: (847) 316-4000
Prog. Accred.: Radiography

Saint Joseph Hospital
2900 North Lake Shore Dr., Chicago 60657
Type: Private, independent
Degrees: C
URL: http://www.reshealth.org/sub_sjh/default.cfm
Phone: (773) 665-3000
Prog. Accred.: Clinical Pastoral Education

Saints Mary and Elizabeth Medical Center
Saint Mary Campus, 2233 West Division St., Chicago 60622
Type: Private, independent
Degrees: C
URL: http://www.reshealth.org/sub_smemc/default.cfm
Phone: (312) 770-2000
Prog. Accred.: Clinical Pastoral Education

Southern Illinois Collegiate Common Market
3213 South Park Ave., Herrin 62948
Type: Private, independent
Degrees: C
URL: http://www.siccm.com
Phone: (618) 942-6902
Prog. Accred.: Allied Health (occupational therapy assisting, surgical technology)

Swedish American Hospital
1401 East State St., Rockford 61104
Type: Private, independent
Degrees: C
URL: http://www.swedishamerican.org
Phone: (815) 968-4400
Prog. Accred.: Radiation Therapy, Radiography

Urban CPE Consortium, Inc.
332 South Michigan Ave., Ste. 500, Chicago 60604-4306
Type: Private, independent
Degrees: C
Phone: (312) 673-3833
Prog. Accred.: Clinical Pastoral Education

Veterans Affairs Illiana Health Care System
1900 East Main St., Danville 61832-5198
Type: Public, federal
Degrees: C
URL: http://www.danville.va.gov
Phone: (217) 554-3000
Prog. Accred.: Allied Health (optometric residency), Psychology Internship

VITAS Innovative Hospice Care—Chicagoland Central
1340 South Damen Ave., Ste. 200A, Chicago 60608
Type: Private, independent
System: VITAS Innovative Hospice Care
Degrees: C
URL: http://www.vitas.com
Phone: (312) 997-7200
Prog. Accred.: Clinical Pastoral Education

Wheaton Franciscan Healthcare
PO Box 667, Wheaton 60189-0667
Type: Private, independent
Degrees: C
URL: http://www.wfhealthcare.org
Phone: (630) 462-9271
Prog. Accred.: Clinical Pastoral Education

INDIANA

Ball Memorial Hospital
2401 University Ave., Muncie 47303
Type: Private, independent, two-year
Degrees: C, A
URL: http://www.cardinalhealthsystem.org
Phone: (765) 747-3111
Prog. Accred.: Clinical Lab Scientist, Radiography

Bloomington Hospital
601 West Second St., Bloomington 47402
Type: Private, independent
Degrees: C
URL: http://www.bloomingtonhospital.org
Phone: (812) 353-6821
Prog. Accred.: Allied Health (surgical technology)

The Center for Behavioral Health
645 South Rogers St., Bloomington 47403-2367
Type: Private, independent
Degrees: C
URL: http://www.the-center.org
Phone: (812) 339-1691
Prog. Accred.: Psychology Internship

Columbus Regional Hospital
2400 East 17th St., Columbus 47201
Type: Private, independent
Degrees: C
URL: http://www.crh.org
Phone: (812) 379-4441
Prog. Accred.: Radiography

Community Hospital East
1500 North Ritter Ave., Indianapolis 46219
Type: Private, independent
Degrees: C
URL: http://ecommunity.com
Phone: (317) 355-1411
Prog. Accred.: Radiography

Elkhart General Hospital
600 East Blvd., Elkhart 46514
Type: Private, independent
Degrees: C
URL: http://www.egh.org
Phone: (574) 294-2621
Prog. Accred.: Allied Health (EMT (paramedic))

Fort Wayne School of Radiography
700 Broadway, Fort Wayne 46802-1402
Type: Private, independent
Degrees: C
Phone: (219) 425-3990 *Calendar:* 24-mos. pr
Prog. Accred.: Radiography

Good Samaritan Hospital
520 South 7th St., Vincennes 47591
Type: Private, independent
Degrees: C
URL: http://www.gshvin.org
Phone: (812) 882-5220
Prog. Accred.: Clinical Lab Scientist, Radiography

Hamilton Center Inc.
620 Eighth Ave., Terre Haute 47804
Type: Private, independent
Degrees: C
URL: http://www.hamiltoncenter.org
Phone: (812) 231-8320
Prog. Accred.: Psychology Internship

Hancock Regional Hospital
801 North State St., Greenfield 46140
Type: Private, independent
Degrees: C
URL: http://www.hmhhs.org
Phone: (317) 462-5544
Prog. Accred.: Radiography

Howard Community Hospital
3500 South Lafountain St., Kokomo 46904-9001
Type: Private, independent
Degrees: C
URL: http://www.howardcommunity.org
Phone: (765) 453-0702
Prog. Accred.: Clinical Pastoral Education

Indiana Blood Center
3450 North Meridian St., Indianapolis 46208
Type: Private, independent
Degrees: C
URL: http://www.indianablood.org
Phone: (317) 916-5265
Prog. Accred.: Allied Health (blood bank technology)

King's Daughters' Hospital and Health Service
One King's Daughters' Dr., PO Box 447, Madison 47250
Type: Private, independent
Degrees: C
URL: http://www.kingsdaughtershospital.org
Phone: (812) 265-5211
Prog. Accred.: Radiography

Lutheran Hospital of Indiana
7950 West Jefferson Blvd., Fort Wayne 46804-4160
Type: Private, independent
Degrees: C
URL: http://www.lutheranhospital.com
Phone: (219) 435-7117
Prog. Accred.: Clinical Pastoral Education

Methodist Hospital
PO Box 1367, Indianapolis 46206-1367
Type: Private, independent
Degrees: C
URL: http://www.clarian.org
Phone: (317) 962-2000
Prog. Accred.: Clinical Pastoral Education

Methodist Hospital
PO Box 1367, Indianapolis 46206-1367
Type: Private, independent
Degrees: C
URL: http://www.clarian.org
Phone: (317) 962-2000
Prog. Accred.: Allied Health (EMT (paramedic), electroneurodiagnostic technology, respiratory therapy, surgical technology), Clinical Lab Scientist, Clinical Pastoral Education, Medical Assisting (ABHES), Physician Assistant, Radiation Therapy

Methodist Hospitals Northlake
600 Grant St., Gary 46402
Type: Private, independent
Degrees: C
URL: http://www.methodisthospitals.org
Phone: (219) 886-4000
Prog. Accred.: Allied Health (EMT (paramedic))

Park Center, Inc.
909 East State Blvd., Fort Wayne 46805
Type: Private, independent
Degrees: C
URL: http://www.parkcenter.org
Phone: (260) 481-2700
Prog. Accred.: Psychology Internship

Parkview Hospital
2200 Randallia Dr., Fort Wayne 46805
Type: Private, independent
Degrees: C
URL: http://www.parkview.com
Phone: (260) 373-4000
Prog. Accred.: Clinical Lab Scientist

Porter Valparaiso Hospital
814 LaPorte Ave., Valparaiso 46383
Type: Private, independent
Degrees: C
URL: http://www.porterhealth.org
Phone: (219) 263-4600
Prog. Accred.: Radiography

Quinco Behavioral Health Systems
720 North Marr Rd., Columbus 47201
Type: Private, independent
Degrees: C
URL: http://www.quincobhs.org
Phone: (812) 348-7449
Prog. Accred.: Psychology Internship

Reid Hospital and Health Care Services
1401 Chester Blvd., Richmond 47374
Type: Private, independent
Degrees: C
URL: http://www.reidhosp.com
Phone: (765) 983-3000
Prog. Accred.: Radiography

Richard L. Roudebush Veterans Affairs Medical Center
1481 West Tenth St., Indianapolis 46202
Type: Public, federal
Degrees: C
URL: http://www1.va.gov/directory/guide/home.asp
Phone: (317) 554-0000
Prog. Accred.: Dentistry (endodontics, general practice residency, periodontics)

Saint Elizabeth School of Nursing
1508 Tippecanoe St., Lafayette 47904
Type: Private, independent
Degrees: C
URL: http://www.steson.org
Phone: (765) 423-6400 *Calendar:* Sem. plan
Prog. Accred.: Nursing

Saint Francis Hospital and Health Centers
1600 Albany St., Beech Grove 46107-1593
Type: Private, independent
Degrees: C
URL: http://stfrancishospitals.org
Phone: (317) 787-3311
Prog. Accred.: Allied Health (EMT (paramedic)), Clinical Lab Scientist

Saint Joseph Regional Medical Center
801 East La Salle Ave., South Bend 46617-2814
Type: Private, independent
Degrees: C
URL: http://www.sjmed.com
Phone: (219) 237-7249
Prog. Accred.: Clinical Pastoral Education

Saint Margaret Mercy Healthcare Center
5454 Hohman Ave., Hammond 46320
Type: Private, independent
Degrees: C
URL: http://www.smmhc.com
Phone: (219) 932-2300
Prog. Accred.: Clinical Lab Scientist

Saint Vincent Indianapolis Hospital
2001 East 86th St., Indianapolis 46240-0970
Type: Private, independent
Degrees: C
URL: http://www.indianapolis.stvincent.org
Phone: (317) 338-2345
Prog. Accred.: Clinical Pastoral Education, Radiography

Southlake Center for Mental Health
8555 Taft St., Merrillville 46410-6199
Type: Private, independent
Degrees: C
URL: http://www.southlakecenter.com
Phone: (219) 769-4005
Prog. Accred.: Psychology Internship

Tri-City Community Mental Health Center
3903 Indianapolis Blvd., East Chicago 46312-2555
Type: Private, independent
Degrees: C
URL: http://www.tricitycenter.org
Phone: (219) 392-6001
Prog. Accred.: Psychology Internship

Veterans Affairs Northern Indiana Health Care System
2121 Lake Ave., Fort Wayne 46805
Type: Public, federal, four-year
Degrees: B
URL: http://www.northernindiana.va.gov
Phone: (260) 426-5431
Prog. Accred.: Allied Health (optometric residency)

IOWA

Blank Children's Hospital
1200 Pleasant St., Des Moines 50309-1406
Type: Private, independent
Degrees: C
URL: http://www.blankchildrens.org
Phone: (515) 241-5437
Prog. Accred.: Clinical Pastoral Education

Covenant Medical Center
3421 West Ninth St., Waterloo 50702
Type: Private, independent
Degrees: C
URL: http://www.covhealth.com
Phone: (319) 272-8000
Prog. Accred.: Radiography

The Ecumenical Institute
1275 Dodge Ave., Holstein 51025-8025
Type: Private, nondenominational
Degrees: C
Phone: (712) 368-2500
Prog. Accred.: Clinical Pastoral Education

Genesis Medical Center
1227 East Rusholme St., Davenport 52803-2459
Type: Private, independent
Degrees: C
URL: http://www.genesishealth.com
Phone: (563) 421-1000
Prog. Accred.: Clinical Pastoral Education

Jennie Edmundson Hospital
933 East Pierce St., Council Bluffs 51503
Type: Private, independent
Degrees: C
URL: http://www.bestcare.org
Phone: (712) 396-6000
Prog. Accred.: Radiography

Mercy Medical Center Des Moines
1111 6th Ave., Des Moines 50314
Type: Private, independent
Degrees: C
URL: http://www.mercydesmoines.org
Phone: (515) 247-3121
Prog. Accred.: Allied Health (EMT (paramedic), cytotechnology)

Mercy Medical Center North Iowa
1000 4th St. SW, Mason City 50401
Type: Private, independent
Degrees: C
URL: http://www.mercynorthiowa.com
Phone: (641) 422-7000
Prog. Accred.: Radiography

Mercy Medical Center Sioux City
801 Fifth St., Sioux City 51102
Type: Private, independent
Degrees: C
URL: http://www.mercysiouxcity.com
Phone: (712) 279-2010
Prog. Accred.: Clinical Lab Scientist

Mercy/St. Luke's School of Radiologic Technology
810 First Ave. NE, Cedar Rapids 52402
Type: Private, independent
Degrees: C
URL: http://www.mercycare.org/services/radiology/school/index.aspx
Phone: (319) 369-7097
Prog. Accred.: Radiography

Saint Luke's Hospital
PO Box 3026, Cedar Rapids 52406-3026
Type: Private, independent
Degrees: C
URL: http://www.crstlukes.com/lab/school.htm
Phone: (319) 369-7211
Prog. Accred.: Clinical Lab Scientist, Clinical Pastoral Education

Saint Luke's Regional Medical Center
2720 Stone Park Blvd., Sioux City 51104
Type: Private, independent
Degrees: C
URL: http://www.stlukes.org
Phone: (712) 279-3500
Prog. Accred.: Clinical Pastoral Education

Veterans Affairs Central Iowa Healthcare System—Knoxville Division
1515 West Pleasant St., Knoxville 50138
Type: Public, federal
Degrees: C
URL: http://www1.va.gov/directory/guide
Phone: (515) 699-5999
Prog. Accred.: Psychology Internship

KANSAS

Counseling and Mediation Center, Inc.
200 West Douglas Ave., Ste. 560, Wichita 67202-3020
Type: Private, proprietary
Degrees: C
URL: http://www.counselingandmediation.org
Phone: (316) 269-2322
Prog. Accred.: Clinical Pastoral Education

Dwight D. Eisenhower Veterans Affairs Medical Center
4101 South 4th St., Leavenworth 66048-5055
Type: Public, federal
Degrees: C
URL: http://www1.va.gov/directory/guide/home.asp
Phone: (913) 682-2000
Prog. Accred.: Psychology Internship

Family Service and Guidance Center of Topeka, Inc.
325 SW Frazier Ave., Topeka 66606-1963
Type: Private, independent
Degrees: C
URL: http://www.fsgctopeka.com
Phone: (785) 232-5005
Prog. Accred.: Psychology Internship

Menorah Medical Center
5721 West 119th St., Overland Park 66209-3722
Type: Private, independent
System: HCA Midwest Health System
Degrees: C
URL: http://www.menorahmedicalcenter.com
Phone: (913) 498-6000
Prog. Accred.: Clinical Pastoral Education

North Coast Emergency Medical Services
3340 Glenwood Ave., Eureka 95501
Type: Private, proprietary
Degrees: C
URL: http://www.northcoastems.com
Phone: (707) 445-2081
Prog. Accred.: Allied Health (EMT (paramedic))

Overland Park Regional Medical Center
10500 Quivira Rd., Overland Park 66215
Type: Private, independent
System: HCA Midwest Health System
Degrees: C
URL: http://www.oprmc.com
Phone: (913) 541-5000
Prog. Accred.: Clinical Pastoral Education

Wesley Medical Center
550 North Hillside St., Wichita 67214-4910
Type: Private, independent
Degrees: C
URL: http://www.wesleymc.com
Phone: (316) 962-2000
Prog. Accred.: Clinical Pastoral Education

KENTUCKY

Baptist Hospital East
4000 Kresge Way, Louisville 40207-4605
Type: Private, independent
Degrees: C
URL: http://www.baptisteast.com
Phone: (502) 897-8100
Prog. Accred.: Clinical Pastoral Education

Fort Campbell Dental Activity
650 Joel Dr., Fort Campbell 42223
Type: Public, federal
Degrees: C
URL: http://www.campbell.amedd.army.mil/clinicalresources/dentac.html
Phone: (270) 798-8400
Prog. Accred.: Dentistry (general dentistry)

Hospice of the Bluegrass
2312 Alexandria Dr., Lexington 40504-3229
Type: Private, independent
Degrees: C
URL: http://www.hospicebg.com
Phone: (859) 276-5344
Prog. Accred.: Clinical Pastoral Education

Jefferson County Internship Consortium
914 East Broadway, Ste. 200, Louisville 40204
Type: Private, independent
Degrees: C
URL: http://www.sevencounties.org
Phone: (502) 587-8833
Prog. Accred.: Psychology Internship

King's Daughters Medical Center
2201 Lexington Ave., Ashland 41101
Type: Private, independent
Degrees: C
URL: http://www.kdmc.com
Phone: (606) 327-4000
Prog. Accred.: Radiography

Lexington Veterans Affairs Medical Center
1101 Veterans Dr., Lexington 40502-2236
Type: Public, federal
Degrees: C
URL: http://www1.va.gov/Lexington
Phone: (859) 233-4511
Prog. Accred.: Psychology Internship

Louisville Medical Center
530 South Jackson St., Louisville 40202-1675
Type: Private, independent
Degrees: C
URL: http://www.uoflhealthcare.org
Phone: (502) 562-3000
Prog. Accred.: Clinical Pastoral Education

Norton Hospital
315 East Broadway, Norton Healthcare Pavilion, Ste. 525, Louisville 40202
Type: Private, independent
Degrees: C
URL: http://www.nortonhealthcare.com
Phone: (502) 629-8000
Prog. Accred.: Clinical Pastoral Education

Norton Hospital
PO Box 35070, Louisville 40232-5070
Type: Private, independent
Degrees: C
URL: http://www.nortonhealthcare.com
Phone: (502) 629-8000
Prog. Accred.: Clinical Pastoral Education

Owensboro Mercy Health System
811 East Parrish Ave., Ownsboro 42303
Type: Private, independent
Degrees: C
URL: http://www.omhs.org
Phone: (270) 688-2000
Prog. Accred.: Clinical Lab Scientist

Pathology and Cytology Laboratories, Inc.
290 Big Run Rd., Lexington 40503
Type: Private, proprietary
Degrees: C
URL: http://www.pandclab.com
Phone: (859) 278-9513
Prog. Accred.: Allied Health (cytotechnology)

Saint Elizabeth Medical Center
One Medical Village Dr., Edgewood 41017
Type: Private, independent
Degrees: C
URL: http://www.stelizabeth.com
Phone: (859) 301-2000
Prog. Accred.: Clinical Lab Scientist

Saint Joseph Healthcare
One Saint Joseph Dr., Lexington 40504
Type: Private, independent
Degrees: C
URL: http://www.sjhlex.org
Phone: (859) 313-1000
Prog. Accred.: Radiography

LOUISIANA

2nd Medical Group/SGDDT
1067 Twining Dr., Barksdale AFB 71110-2486
Type: Public, federal
Degrees: C
Phone: (318) 456-6000
Prog. Accred.: Dentistry (advanced education in general dentistry)

Alexandria Veterans Affairs Medical Center
PO Box 69004, Alexandria 71306-9004
Type: Public, federal
Degrees: C
URL: http://www.alexandria.med.va.gov
Phone: (318) 473-0010
Prog. Accred.: Clinical Pastoral Education

Baton Rouge General
3600 Florida Blvd., Baton Rouge 70806
Type: Private, independent
Degrees: C
URL: http://www.brgeneral.org
Phone: (225) 387-7000
Prog. Accred.: Nursing, Radiography

East Jefferson General Hospital
4200 Houma Blvd., Metairie 70006-2970
Type: Private, independent
Degrees: C
URL: http://www.ejgh.org
Phone: (504) 454-4000
Prog. Accred.: Clinical Pastoral Education

Lafayette General Medical Center
1214 Coolidge St., PO Box 52009, Lafayette 70503
Type: Private, independent
Degrees: C
URL: http://www.lafayettegeneral.com
Phone: (337) 289-7991
Prog. Accred.: Radiography

Lake Charles Memorial Hospital School of Medical Technology
1701 Oak Park Blvd., Lake Charles 70601
Type: Private, independent
Degrees: C
URL: http://www.lcmh.com
Phone: (337) 494-3196
Prog. Accred.: Clinical Lab Scientist

The McFarland Institute
400 Poydras St., Ste. 2525, New Orleans 70130
Type: Private, independent
Degrees: C
URL: http://www.tmcfi.org
Phone: (504) 593-2320
Prog. Accred.: Clinical Pastoral Education

North Oaks Medical Center
15790 Paul Vega M.D. Dr., Hammond 70403
Type: Private, independent
Degrees: C
URL: http://www.northoaks.org
Phone: (985) 345-2700
Prog. Accred.: Radiography

Ochsner School of Allied Health Sciences
1516 Jefferson Hwy., New Orleans 70123-3335
Type: Private, independent
Degrees: C
URL: http://academics.ochsner.org/allied.aspx
Phone: (504) 842-3267
Prog. Accred.: Allied Health (respiratory therapy), Radiography

The Overton Brooks Veterans Affairs Medical Center
510 East Stoner Ave., Shreveport 71101-4295
Type: Public, federal
Degrees: C
URL: http://www.shreveport.va.gov
Phone: (318) 221-8411
Prog. Accred.: Clinical Lab Scientist

Pinecrest Developmental Center
100 Pinecrest Dr., Pineville 71360
Type: Public, state
Degrees: C
Phone: (318) 641-2000
Prog. Accred.: Psychology Internship

Rapides Regional Medical Center
211 4th St., Box 30101, Alexandria 71301
Type: Private, independent
Degrees: C
URL: http://www.rapidesregional.com
Phone: (318) 473-3000
Prog. Accred.: Clinical Lab Scientist, Phlebotomy

Saint Francis Medical Center
309 Jackson St., PO Box 1901, Monroe 71201-7407
Type: Private, independent
Degrees: C
URL: http://www.stfran.com
Phone: (318) 327-4000
Prog. Accred.: Clinical Lab Scientist

Southeast Louisiana Veterans Health Care System
1601 Perdido St., New Orleans 70146
Type: Public, federal
Degrees: C
URL: http://www1.va.gov/new-orleans
Phone: (800) 935-8387
Prog. Accred.: Dentistry (general practice residency), Psychology Internship

Touro Infirmary
1401 Foucher St., New Orleans 70115-3515
Type: Private, independent
Degrees: C
URL: http://www.touro.com
Phone: (504) 897-7011
Prog. Accred.: Dietetics (internship)

MAINE

Central Maine Medical Center
300 Main St., Lewiston 04240
Type: Private, independent
Degrees: C
URL: http://www.cmmc.org
Phone: (207) 795-0111
Prog. Accred.: Clinical Pastoral Education, Nuclear Medicine Technology, Radiography

Eastern Maine Medical Center
489 State St., PO Box 404, Bangor 04401
Type: Private, independent
Degrees: C
URL: http://www.emh.org/emmc
Phone: (207) 973-7000
Prog. Accred.: Clinical Lab Scientist

Maine Medical Center
27 Bramhall St., Portland 04102-3134
Type: Private, independent
Degrees: C
URL: http://www.mmc.org
Phone: (207) 871-2951
Prog. Accred.: Allied Health (surgical technology), Clinical Pastoral Education

Mercy Hospital
144 State St., Portland 04101-3776
Type: Private, independent
Degrees: C
URL: http://www.mercyhospital.com
Phone: (207) 879-3000
Prog. Accred.: Radiography

Togus Veterans Affairs Medical Center
1 VA Center, Augusta 04330
Type: Public, federal
Degrees: C
URL: http://www.visn1.med.va.gov/togus
Phone: (207) 623-8411
Prog. Accred.: Psychology Internship

MARYLAND

Asbury Methodist Village
201 Russell Ave., Gaithersburg 20877-2813
Type: Private, proprietary
Degrees: C
URL: http://www.asburymethodistvillage.org
Phone: (301) 216-4001
Prog. Accred.: Clinical Pastoral Education

Associates in Emergency Care, LLC
PO Box 490, Damascus 20872
Type: Private, proprietary
Degrees: C
URL: http://aecare911.org
Prog. Accred.: Allied Health (EMT (paramedic))

Baltimore Veterans Affairs Medical Center
10 North Greene St., Baltimore 21201
Type: Public, federal
Degrees: C
URL: http://www.vamhcs.med.va.gov
Phone: (410) 605-7000
Prog. Accred.: Allied Health (optometric residency), Dentistry (general practice residency), Psychology Internship

Greater Baltimore Medical Center
6701 North Charles St., Baltimore 21204
Type: Private, independent
Degrees: C
URL: http://www.gbmc.org
Phone: (443) 849-2000
Prog. Accred.: Radiography

Holy Cross Hospital
1500 Forest Glen Rd., Silver Spring 20910
Type: Private, independent
Degrees: C
URL: http://www.holycrosshealth.org
Phone: (301) 754-7000
Prog. Accred.: Radiography

John L. Gildner Regional Institute for Children and Adolescents
15000 Broschart Rd., Rockville 20850
Type: Public, state
Degrees: C
Prog. Accred.: Psychology Internship

Johns Hopkins Bayview Medical Center
4940 Eastern Ave., Baltimore 21224-2735
Type: Private, independent
Degrees: C
URL: http://www.hopkinsbayview.org
Phone: (410) 550-0100
Prog. Accred.: Dietetics (coordinated), Dietetics (internship)

The Johns Hopkins Hospital
600 North Wolfe St., Baltimore 21287
Type: Private, independent
Degrees: C
URL: http://www.hopkinshospital.org
Phone: (410) 955-5000
Prog. Accred.: Radiography

Kennedy Krieger Institute
707 North Broadway, Baltimore 21205
Type: Private, independent
Degrees: C
URL: http://www.kennedykrieger.org
Phone: (443) 923-9200
Prog. Accred.: Psychology Internship

Maryland General Hospital
827 Linden Ave., Baltimore 21201
Type: Private, independent
Degrees: C
URL: http://www.marylandgeneral.org
Phone: (410) 225-8000
Prog. Accred.: Radiography

Memorial Hospital and Medical Center of Cumberland Maryland
600 Memorial Ave., Cumberland 21502
Type: Private, independent
Degrees: C
URL: http://www.wmhs.com
Phone: (301) 723-4000
Prog. Accred.: Clinical Pastoral Education

Mercy Medical Center
301 Saint Paul Place, Baltimore 21202
Type: Private, independent
Degrees: C
URL: http://www.mercymed.com
Phone: (410) 332-9000
Prog. Accred.: Dentistry (general practice residency)

National Capital Consortium
4301 Jones Bridge Rd., Bethesda 20814-4799
Type: Private, independent
Degrees: C
URL: http://www.usuhs.mil/gme
Phone: (301) 295-3436
Prog. Accred.: Dentistry (oral and maxillofacial surgery)

National Institute of Dental and Craniofacial Research
National Institutes of Health, Bethesda 20892-2190
Type: Public, federal
Degrees: C
URL: http://www.nidcr.nih.gov
Phone: (301) 496-4261
Prog. Accred.: Dentistry (dental public health)

National Institutes of Health Clinical Center
6100 Executive Blvd., Bethesda 20892
Type: Public, federal
Degrees: C
URL: http://www.cc.nih.gov
Phone: (301) 496-2563
Prog. Accred.: Allied Health (blood bank technology), Clinical Pastoral Education, Microbiology

National Naval Medical Center
8901 Wisconsin Ave., Bethesda 20889
Type: Public, federal
Degrees: C
URL: http://www.bethesda.med.navy.mil
Phone: (301) 295-4611
Prog. Accred.: Dentistry (general practice residency), Psychology Internship

Perry Point Veterans Affairs Medical Center
Dental Service, Perry Point 21902
Type: Public, federal
Degrees: C
URL: http://www.maryland.va.gov/facilities/perrypoint.htm
Phone: (410) 642-2411
Prog. Accred.: Allied Health (optometric residency), Dentistry (dental public health)

Prince George's Hospital Center
3001 Hospital Dr., Cheverly 20785
Type: Private, independent
Degrees: C
URL: http://www.dimensionshealth.org/website/c/pghc
Phone: (301) 618-2000
Prog. Accred.: Dentistry (general practice residency)

Sodexo Health Care Services Mid-Atlantic
10500 Little Patuxent Pkwy., Ste. 620, Columbia 21044
Type: Private, proprietary
Degrees: C
URL: http://www.dieteticintern.com/Mid-Atlantic
Phone: (410) 744-2798
Prog. Accred.: Dietetics (internship)

Spring Grove Hospital Center
55 Wade Ave., Catonsville 21228
Type: Public, state
Degrees: C
URL: http://www.springgrove.com
Phone: (410) 402-6000
Prog. Accred.: Psychology Internship

Springfield Hospital Center
6655 Sykesville Rd., Sykesville 21784
Type: Public, state
Degrees: C
URL: http://www.dhmh.state.md.us/springfield
Phone: (410) 970-7000
Prog. Accred.: Psychology Internship

University of Maryland Medical Center
22 South Greene St., Baltimore 21201
Type: Private, independent
Degrees: C
URL: http://www.umm.edu
Phone: (410) 328-8667
Prog. Accred.: Dietetics (internship)

Washington Adventist Hospital
7600 Carroll Ave., Takoma Park 20912
Type: Private, independent
Degrees: C
URL: http://www.adventisthealthcare.com/WAH
Phone: (301) 891-7600
Prog. Accred.: Radiography

MASSACHUSETTS

Baystate Medical Center
689 Chestnut St., Springfield 01199
Type: Private, independent
Degrees: C
URL: http://www.baystatehealth.com/baystatemidwifery
Phone: (413) 794-4448
Prog. Accred.: Clinical Pastoral Education, Nurse (Midwifery)

Berkshire Medical Center
725 North St., Pittsfield 01201
Type: Private, independent
Degrees: C
URL: http://www.bhs1.org
Phone: (413) 447-2000
Prog. Accred.: Allied Health (cytotechnology), Clinical Lab Scientist, Dentistry (general practice residency)

Beth Israel Deaconess Medical Center
330 Brookline Ave., Boston 02215
Type: Private, independent
Degrees: C
URL: http://www.bidmc.harvard.edu
Phone: (617) 667-7000
Prog. Accred.: Clinical Pastoral Education, Dietetics (internship), Nuclear Medicine Technology

Beverly Hospital
85 Herrick St., Beverly 01915-1776
Type: Private, independent
Degrees: C
URL: http://www.beverlyhospital.org
Phone: (978) 922-3000
Prog. Accred.: Clinical Pastoral Education

Boston Medical Center
One Boston Medical Center Place, Boston 02118-2908
Type: Private, independent
Degrees: C
URL: http://www.bmc.org
Phone: (617) 638-8000
Prog. Accred.: Dentistry (general practice residency), Psychology Internship

Brigham and Women's Hospital
75 Francis St., Boston 02115
Type: Private, independent
Degrees: C
URL: http://www.brighamandwomens.org
Phone: (617) 732-5500
Prog. Accred.: Clinical Pastoral Education, Dentistry (general practice residency), Dietetics (internship)

The Cambridge Hospital
1493 Cambridge St., Cambridge 02139
Type: Private, independent
Degrees: C
URL: http://www.challiance.org/cambridge_hospital/cambridge_hospital.shtml
Phone: (617) 665-1000
Prog. Accred.: Psychology Internship

Caritas Christi Health Care System
736 Cambridge St., Brighton 02135-2997
Type: Private, independent
Degrees: C
URL: http://www.cchcs.org
Phone: (617) 789-3228
Prog. Accred.: Clinical Pastoral Education

Caritas Holy Family Hospital and Medical Center
70 East St., Methuen 01844-4597
Phone: (978) 687-0156

Caritas Saint Elizabeth's Medical Center
736 Cambridge St., Brighton 02135-2907
Phone: (617) 789-3000

Saint Anne's Hospital
795 Middle St., Fall River 02721-1733
Phone: (508) 674-5600

Children's Hospital Boston
300 Longwood Ave., Boston 02115
Type: Private, independent
Degrees: C
URL: http://www.childrenshospital.org
Phone: (617) 355-6000
Prog. Accred.: Psychology Internship

Community Healthlink Youth and Family Services
275 Belmont St., Worcester 01604-1693
Type: Private, independent
Degrees: C
Phone: (508) 791-3261
Prog. Accred.: Psychology Internship

Edith Nourse Rogers Memorial Veterans Hospital
200 Springs Rd., Bedford 01730
Type: Public, federal
Degrees: C
URL: http://www.visn1.med.va.gov/bedford
Phone: (781) 275-7500
Prog. Accred.: Allied Health (optometric residency), Psychology Internship

Federal Medical Center Devens
PO Box 879, Devens 01434
Type: Public, federal
Degrees: C
URL: http://www.bop.gov/locations/institutions/dev/index.jsp
Phone: (978) 796-1000
Prog. Accred.: Psychology Internship

Franciscan Hospital for Children
30 Warren St., Boston 02135
Type: Private, Franciscan Missionaries of Mary
Degrees: C
URL: http://www.franciscanhospital.org
Phone: (617) 254-3800
Prog. Accred.: Psychology Internship

Lawrence Memorial Hospital
170 Governors Ave., Medford 02155-1643
Type: Private, independent, two-year
Degrees: A
URL: http://www.lmregisnurse.org
Phone: (781) 306-6600 *Calendar:* Sem. plan
Prog. Accred.: Nursing

Massachusetts General Hospital
55 Fruit St., Boston 02114
Type: Private, independent
Degrees: C
URL: http://www.mgh.harvard.edu
Phone: (617) 726-2000
Prog. Accred.: Clinical Pastoral Education, Dentistry (oral and maxillofacial surgery), Dietetics (internship), Psychology Internship

Massachusetts Mental Health Center
180 Morton St., Jamaica Plain 02130
Type: Private, independent
Degrees: C
URL: http://www.massmentalhealthcenter.org
Phone: (617) 626-9300
Prog. Accred.: Psychology Internship

New England Baptist Hospital
125 Parker Hill Ave., Boston 02120-2847
Type: Private, independent
Degrees: C
URL: http://nebh.org
Phone: (617) 754-5800
Prog. Accred.: Clinical Pastoral Education

Saint Lukes Hospital
101 Page St., New Bedford 02740-3464
Type: Private, independent
Degrees: C
URL: http://www.southcoast.org/services/stlukes.html
Phone: (508) 997-1515
Prog. Accred.: Dietetics (internship)

Saint Vincent Hospital at Worcester Medical Center
123 Summer St., Worcester 01608
Type: Private, independent
Degrees: C
URL: http://www.stvincenthospital.com
Phone: (508) 363-5000
Prog. Accred.: Clinical Pastoral Education

Showa Boston Institute for Language and Culture
420 Pond St., Boston 02130
Type: Private, independent
Degrees: C
URL: http://www.showaboston.org
Phone: (617) 522-0080
Prog. Accred.: English Language Education

Signature Healthcare Brockton Hospital
680 Centre St., Brockton 02302-3395
Type: Private, independent
Degrees: C
URL: http://signature-healthcare.org
Phone: (508) 941-7000
Prog. Accred.: Nursing

Sodexo Health Care Services Distance Education Dietetic Internship
200 Fifth Ave., 4th Flr., Waltham 02451
Type: Private, proprietary
Degrees: C
URL: http://www.dieteticintern.com/distance
Phone: (603) 487-5293
Prog. Accred.: Dietetics (internship)

Veterans Affairs Boston Healthcare System
940 Belmont St., Brockton 02301
Type: Public, federal
Degrees: C
URL: http://www.boston.va.gov
Phone: (508) 583-4500
Prog. Accred.: Allied Health (optometric residency)

Westborough State Hospital
PO Box 288, Westborough 01581
Type: Public, state
Degrees: C
Phone: (508) 616-3500
Prog. Accred.: Clinical Pastoral Education

MICHIGAN

Battle Creek Veterans Affairs Medical Center
5500 Armstrong Rd., Battle Creek 49015
Type: Public, federal
Degrees: C
URL: http://www.battlecreek.va.gov
Phone: (269) 966-5600
Prog. Accred.: Allied Health (optometric residency)

Bronson Methodist Hospital
601 John St., Kalamazoo 49007
Type: Private, proprietary
Degrees: C
URL: http://www.bronsonhealth.com
Phone: (269) 341-7654
Prog. Accred.: Clinical Pastoral Education

Butterworth Hospital
100 Michigan St. NE, Grand Rapids 49503
Type: Private, independent
Degrees: C
URL: http://www.spectrum-health.org
Phone: (616) 391-1774
Prog. Accred.: Clinical Lab Scientist

Children's Hospital of Michigan
3901 Beaubien St., Detroit 48201-2119
Type: Private, independent
Degrees: C
URL: http://www.childrensdmc.org
Phone: (313) 745-5437
Prog. Accred.: Dietetics (internship), Psychology Internship

Covenant Medical Center Harrison
1447 North Harrison St., Saginaw 48602-4727
Type: Private, independent
Degrees: C
URL: http://www.covenanthealthcare.com
Phone: (989) 583-7000
Prog. Accred.: Clinical Pastoral Education

Detroit Department of Health and Wellness Promotion
1151 Taylor St., Detroit 48202-1732
Type: Public, local
Degrees: C
URL: http://www.dethealth.org
Phone: (313) 876-4000
Prog. Accred.: Dietetics (internship)

Detroit Receiving Hospital
4201 St. Antoine St., Detroit 48201
Type: Private, independent
Degrees: C
URL: http://www.drhuhc.org
Phone: (313) 745-3000
Prog. Accred.: Dentistry (oral and maxillofacial surgery)

DMC Sinai-Grace Hospital
6701 West Outer Dr., Detroit 48235-2624
Type: Private, independent
Degrees: C
URL: http://www.sinaigrace.org
Phone: (313) 966-3300
Prog. Accred.: Clinical Pastoral Education

Hawthorn Center
18471 Haggerty Rd., Northville 48167
Type: Public, state
Degrees: C
URL: http://www.michigan.gov/mdch
Phone: (248) 349-3000
Prog. Accred.: Psychology Internship

Henry Ford Hospital
1 Ford Place, Detroit 48202
Type: Private, independent
Degrees: C
URL: http://www.henryfordhealth.org
Phone: (313) 916-2600
Prog. Accred.: Allied Health (diagnostic medical sonography), Dentistry (oral and maxillofacial surgery), Dietetics (internship), Psychology Internship, Radiation Therapy, Radiography

Hurley Medical Center
One Hurley Plaza, Flint 48503-5993
Type: Private, independent
Degrees: C
URL: http://www.hurleymc.com
Phone: (810) 257-9000
Prog. Accred.: Clinical Lab Scientist, Dietetics (internship), Radiography

Huron Valley Ambulance
1200 State Circle, Ann Arbor 48108
Type: Private, independent
Degrees: C
URL: http://www.hva.org
Phone: (734) 971-4420
Prog. Accred.: Allied Health (EMT (paramedic))

Interlochen Center for the Arts
PO Box 199, Interlochen 49643-0199
Type: Private, independent
Degrees: C
URL: http://www.interlochen.org
Phone: (231) 276-7200
Prog. Accred.: Music

John D. Dingell Veterans Affairs Medical Center
4646 John R. St., Detroit 48201
Type: Public, federal
Degrees: C
URL: http://www1.va.gov/directory
Phone: (313) 576-1000
Prog. Accred.: Allied Health (optometric residency), Dentistry (general practice residency)

Marquette General Health System
580 West College Ave., Marquette 49855
Type: Private, independent
Degrees: C
URL: http://www.mgh.org
Phone: (906) 228-9440
Prog. Accred.: Radiography

MEDRIGHT-Professional Medical Education
427 Allen St., Ferndale 48220-2442
Type: Private, proprietary
Degrees: C
Phone: (248) 547-0834
Prog. Accred.: Phlebotomy

Pine Rest Christian Mental Health Services
PO Box 165, Grand Rapids 49501-0165
Type: Private, independent
Degrees: C
URL: http://www.pinerest.org
Phone: (616) 455-5000
Prog. Accred.: Clinical Pastoral Education

Port Huron Hospital
1221 Pine Grove Ave., Port Huron 48060
Type: Private, independent
Degrees: C
URL: http://www.porthuronhosp.org
Phone: (810) 987-5000
Prog. Accred.: Radiography

Providence Hospital and Medical Centers
16001 West Nine Mile Rd., Southfield 48075
Type: Private, independent
Degrees: C
URL: http://www.realmedicine.org/Providence
Phone: (248) 849-3000
Prog. Accred.: Allied Health (diagnostic medical sonography), Radiography

Saint John Hospital and Medical Center
22101 Moross Rd., Grosse Pointe 48236-2148
Type: Private, independent
Degrees: C
URL: http://www.realmedicine.org/StJohnHospital
Phone: (313) 343-4000
Prog. Accred.: Radiography

Saint John Hospital School of Medical Technology
19251 Mack Ave., Ste. 460, Grosse Pointe Woods 48236
Type: Private, independent
Degrees: C
URL: http://www.stjohn.org/LabCareers
Phone: (313) 343-3508
Prog. Accred.: Clinical Lab Scientist

Saint John Macomb-Oakland Hospital Detroit Riverview Center
7733 East Jefferson Ave., Detroit 48214
Type: Private, independent
Degrees: C
URL: http://www.stjohn.org/DetroitRiverview
Phone: (313) 499-4000
Prog. Accred.: Dentistry (oral and maxillofacial surgery)

Saint Joseph Mercy Oakland
900 Woodward Ave., Pontiac 48341-2985
Type: Private, independent
Degrees: C
URL: http://www.mercyoakland.com
Phone: (248) 858-3000
Prog. Accred.: Dentistry (oral and maxillofacial surgery)

Sinai-Grace Hospital
6071 West Outer Dr., Detroit 48235-2624
Type: Private, independent
Degrees: C
URL: http://www.sinaigrace.org
Phone: (313) 966-3300
Prog. Accred.: Clinical Pastoral Education, Dentistry (general practice residency), Radiography

Veterans Affairs Medical Center—Ann Arbor
2215 Fuller Rd., Ann Arbor 48105
Type: Public, federal
Degrees: C
Prog. Accred.: Dentistry (general practice residency)

William Beaumont Hospital Schools of Allied Health
3601 West Thirteen Mile Rd., Royal Oak 48073-6769
Type: Private, independent
Degrees: C
URL: http://www.beaumonthospitals.com
Phone: (248) 551-5135
Prog. Accred.: Allied Health (surgeon assisting), Clinical Lab Scientist, Clinical Pastoral Education, Histologic Technology, Nuclear Medicine Technology, Radiation Therapy, Radiography

MINNESOTA

Allina Hospitals and Clinics
800 East 28th St., Minneapolis 55417
Type: Private, independent
Degrees: C
URL: http://www.allina.com
Phone: (612) 863-4370
Prog. Accred.: Clinical Pastoral Education

Abbott Northwestern Hospital/Children's Hospitals and Clinics
800 East 28th St., Minneapolis 55407
Phone: (612) 863-4000
Prog. Accred: Clinical Pastoral Education

Mercy-Unity Hospitals and Convalescent Center
550 Osborne Rd., Fridley 55432
Phone: (763) 236-5000
Prog. Accred: Clinical Pastoral Education

United Hospital/Children's Hospital and Clinic
333 North Smith Ave., St. Paul 55102
Phone: (651) 241-8000
Prog. Accred: Clinical Pastoral Education

Bethesda Hospital
559 Capitol Blvd., St. Paul 55103-2101
Type: Private, independent
Degrees: C
URL: http://www.bethesdahospital.org
Phone: (651) 232-2000
Prog. Accred.: Clinical Pastoral Education

Children's Hospitals and Clinics of Minnesota
2525 Chicago Ave., Minneapolis 55404
Type: Private, independent
Degrees: C
URL: http://www.childrensmn.org
Phone: (612) 813-6100
Prog. Accred.: Psychology Internship

Emergency Training Associates, Inc.
PO Box 1014, Fergus Falls 56538
Type: Private, proprietary
Degrees: C
URL: http://www.emergencytrainingassociates.com
Phone: (218) 998-2739
Prog. Accred.: Allied Health (EMT (paramedic))

Fairview-University Medical Center
2450 Riverside Ave., Minneapolis 55454
Type: Private, independent
Degrees: C
URL: http://fairview-university.fairview.org
Phone: (612) 273-3000
Prog. Accred.: Clinical Pastoral Education, Dietetics (internship), Radiation Therapy, Radiography

Federal Medical Center Rochester
PO Box 4000, Rochester 55903
Type: Public, federal
Degrees: C
URL: http://www.bop.gov/locations/institutions/rch/index.jsp
Phone: (507) 287-0674
Prog. Accred.: Psychology Internship

Hamm Clinic
408 St. Peter St., Ste. 429, St. Paul 55102
Type: Private, independent
Degrees: C
URL: http://www.hammclinic.org
Phone: (651) 224-0614
Prog. Accred.: Psychology Internship

Hennepin County Medical Center
701 Park Ave., Minneapolis 55415
Type: Public, local
Degrees: C
URL: http://www.hcmc.org
Phone: (612) 873-3000
Prog. Accred.: Clinical Lab Scientist, Dentistry (general practice residency), Psychology Internship

Methodist Hospital
6500 Excelsior Blvd., St. Louis Park 55426
Type: Private, independent
Degrees: C
URL: http://www.parknicollet.com/methodist
Phone: (952) 993-5000
Prog. Accred.: Clinical Pastoral Education, Radiography

Minneapolis School of Anesthesia
6715 Minnetonka Blvd., St. Louis Park 55426
Type: Private, independent, four-year
Degrees: M
URL: http://www.nurseanesthesia.org
Phone: (952) 925-5222
Prog. Accred.: Nurse Anesthesia Education

North Memorial Medical Center
3300 Oakdale Ave. North, Robbinsdale 55422-2900
Type: Private, independent
Degrees: C
URL: http://www.northmemorial.com
Phone: (763) 520-5200
Prog. Accred.: Radiography

Rice Memorial Hospital
301 SW Becker Ave., Willmar 56201
Type: Private, independent
Degrees: C
URL: http://www.ricehospital.com
Phone: (320) 235-4543
Prog. Accred.: Radiography

Rochester Methodist Hospital
201 West Center St., Rochester 55902
Type: Private, independent
Degrees: C
URL: http://www.mayoclinic.org/methodisthospital
Phone: (507) 266-7890
Prog. Accred.: Clinical Pastoral Education

Saint Cloud Hospital
1406 Sixth Ave. North, St. Cloud 56303
Type: Private, independent
Degrees: C
URL: http://www.centracare.com/sch
Phone: (320) 251-2700
Prog. Accred.: Radiography

Saint Cloud Veterans Affairs Medical Center
4801 Veterans Dr., St. Cloud 56303-2015
Type: Public, federal
Degrees: C
URL: http://www1.va.gov
Phone: (320) 252-1670
Prog. Accred.: Clinical Pastoral Education

University Good Samaritan Center
22 27th Ave., SE, Minneapolis 55414-3198
Type: Private, independent
Degrees: C
URL: http://www.good-sam.com/cpe
Phone: (612) 673-6298
Prog. Accred.: Clinical Pastoral Education

Veterans Affairs Medical Center—Minneapolis
One Veterans Dr., Minneapolis 55417
Type: Public, federal
Degrees: C
URL: http://www.visn23.med.va.gov/Service-Areas/Minneapolis-VAMC.asp
Phone: (612) 725-2000
Prog. Accred.: Dentistry (general practice residency), Radiography

MISSISSIPPI

81 Dental Squadron/SGDDT
606 Fisher St., Keesler AFB 39534-2513
Type: Public, federal
Degrees: C
URL: http://www.keesler.af.mil/units/81stmedicalgroup.asp
Phone: (210) 565-0645
Prog. Accred.: Dentistry (advanced education in general dentistry, general practice residency)

G.V. (Sonny) Montgomery Veterans Affairs Medical Center
1500 East Woodrow Wilson Dr., Jackson 39216-5119
Type: Private, federal
Degrees: C
URL: http://www1.va.gov/directory/guide/facility.asp?ID=64
Phone: (601) 364-1397
Prog. Accred.: Clinical Pastoral Education

Mississippi Baptist Medical Center
1225 North State St., PO Box 23668, Jackson 39202
Type: Private, independent
Degrees: C
URL: http://www.mbhs.org
Phone: (601) 968-3070
Prog. Accred.: Clinical Lab Scientist, Clinical Pastoral Education

North Mississippi Medical Center
830 South Gloster St., Tupelo 38801-4934
Type: Private, independent
Degrees: C
URL: http://www.nmhs.net/nmmc
Phone: (662) 377-3000
Prog. Accred.: Clinical Lab Scientist

Oral and Facial Surgical Center
300 Hospital Dr., Columbus 39701
Type: Private, independent
Degrees: C
URL: http://www.ofsc.info
Phone: (662) 327-2100
Prog. Accred.: Dentistry (oral and maxillofacial surgery)

MISSOURI

Barnes-Jewish Hospital
One Barnes-Jewish Hospital Plaza, St. Louis 63110
Type: Private, independent, four-year
Degrees: C, B, M
URL: http://www.barnesjewish.org
Phone: (314) 747-3000
Prog. Accred.: Clinical Pastoral Education, Dentistry (general practice residency), Microbiology, Radiography

Children's Mercy Hospital
2401 Gillham Rd., Kansas City 64108
Type: Private, independent
Degrees: C
URL: http://www.childrensmercy.org
Phone: (816) 234-3000
Prog. Accred.: Psychology Internship

Christian Hospital
11133 Dunn Rd., St. Louis 63136-6119
Type: Private, independent
System: Saint Louis Cluster
Degrees: C
URL: http://www.christianhospital.org
Phone: (314) 653-5000
Prog. Accred.: Clinical Pastoral Education

Cox Medical Center South
3801 South National Ave., Springfield 65807
Type: Private, independent
Degrees: C
URL: http://www.coxhealth.com
Phone: (417) 269-6000
Prog. Accred.: Allied Health (diagnostic medical sonography), Clinical Lab Scientist, Radiation Therapy, Radiography

Forest Park Hospital
6150 Oakland Ave., St. Louis 63139-3215
Type: Private, independent
Degrees: C
URL: http://www.forestparkhospital.com
Phone: (314) 768-3000
Prog. Accred.: Clinical Pastoral Education

Fulton State Hospital
600 East 5th St., Fulton 65251
Type: Public, state
Degrees: C
URL: http://www.dmh.missouri.gov/fulton
Phone: (573) 592-4100
Prog. Accred.: Psychology Internship

Harry S. Truman Memorial Veterans' Hospital
800 Hospital Dr., Columbia 65201-5297
Type: Public, federal
Degrees: C
URL: http://www.va.gov/cmo
Phone: (573)814-6000
Prog. Accred.: Allied Health (optometric residency), Psychology Internship

Heartland Health
5325 Faraon St., Saint Joseph 64506-3373
Type: Private, proprietary
Degrees: C
URL: http://www.heartland-health.com
Phone: (816) 271-6040
Prog. Accred.: Clinical Pastoral Education

IHM Health Studies Center
2500 Abbott Place, St. Louis 63143-2636
Type: Private, independent, two-year
Degrees: C, A
URL: http://www.ihmhealthstudies.com
Phone: (314) 768-1234
Prog. Accred.: Allied Health (EMT (paramedic))

Kansas City Veterans Affairs Medical Center
4801 East Linwood Blvd., Kansas City 64128-2226
Type: Public, federal
Degrees: C
URL: http://www1.va.gov/directory/guide/facility.asp?id=65
Phone: (816) 861-4700
Prog. Accred.: Allied Health (optometric residency), Clinical Pastoral Education

Lutheran School of Nursing
3547 South Jefferson Ave., St. Louis 63118-3909
Type: Private, independent
Degrees: C
URL: http://www.nursingschoollmc.com
Phone: (314) 577-5850
Prog. Accred.: Nursing

Lutheran Senior Services CPE
709 South Laclede Station Rd., St. Louis 63119
Type: Private, independent
Degrees: C
URL: http://www.lssmo.org
Phone: (314) 446-2580
Prog. Accred.: Clinical Pastoral Education

Mineral Area Regional Medical Center
1212 Weber Rd., Farmington 63640
Type: Private, independent
Degrees: C
URL: http://marmc.org
Phone: (573) 756-4581
Prog. Accred.: Radiography

Nichols Career Center
605 Union St., Jefferson City 65101
Type: Public, local
Degrees: C
URL: http://www.jcps.k12.mo.us/education/school
Phone: (573) 659-3100
Prog. Accred.: Dentistry (dental assisting), Radiography

North Kansas City Hospital
2800 Clay Edwards Dr., North Kansas City 64116
Type: Private, independent
Degrees: C
URL: https://www.nkch.org
Phone: (816) 691-2000
Prog. Accred.: Clinical Lab Scientist

Research Medical Center
2316 East Meyer Blvd., Kansas City 64132-1136
Type: Private, independent
System: HCA Midwest Health System
Degrees: C
URL: http://researchmedicalcenter.com
Phone: (816) 276-4000
Prog. Accred.: Clinical Pastoral Education, Nuclear Medicine Technology, Radiography

Research Medical Center
2316 East Meyer Blvd., Kansas City 64132-1199
Type: Private, independent
System: HCA Midwest Health System
Degrees: C
URL: http://researchmedicalcenter.com
Phone: (816) 276-4000
Prog. Accred.: Clinical Pastoral Education, Nuclear Medicine Technology, Radiography

Saint John's Mercy Medical Center
615 South New Ballas Rd., St. Louis 63141
Type: Private, independent
Degrees: C
URL: http://www.stjohnsmercy.org/sjmmc
Phone: (314) 251-6000
Prog. Accred.: Dentistry (general practice residency), Radiography

Saint John's Regional Health System
1235 East Cherokee St., Springfield 65804-2263
Type: Private, independent
Degrees: C
URL: http://www.stjohns.com
Phone: (417) 820-2000
Prog. Accred.: Radiography

Saint John's Regional Medical Center
2727 McClelland Blvd., Joplin 64804
Type: Private, independent
Degrees: C
URL: http://www.stj.com
Phone: (417) 625-2727
Prog. Accred.: Clinical Lab Scientist, Clinical Pastoral Education (USCC)

Saint Joseph Medical Center
1000 Carondelet Dr., Kansas City 64114-4673
Type: Private, independent
Degrees: C
URL: http://www.carondelethealth.org/sj
Phone: (816) 942-4400
Prog. Accred.: Clinical Pastoral Education, Dietetics (internship)

Saint Luke's Hospital
4401 Wornall Rd., Kansas City 64111
Type: Private, independent
Degrees: C
URL: http://www.saint-lukes.org
Phone: (816) 932-2000
Prog. Accred.: Clinical Lab Scientist, Clinical Pastoral Education, Radiography

South Central Career Center
610 East Olden St., West Plains 65775
Type: Public, local
Degrees: C
URL: http://wphs.k12.mo.us/education/school/
Phone: (417) 256-6152
Prog. Accred.: Allied Health (surgical technology)

St. Louis Children's Hospital
One Children's Place, St. Louis 63110
Type: Private, independent
Degrees: C
URL: http://www.stlouischildrens.org
Phone: (314) 454-6000
Prog. Accred.: Microbiology

St. Louis Veterans Affairs Medical Center—Jefferson Barracks
1 Jefferson Barracks Dr., St. Louis 63125-4101
Type: Public, federal
Degrees: C
URL: http://www.visn15.med.va.gov/st-louis
Phone: (314) 652-4100
Prog. Accred.: Clinical Pastoral Education, Dietetics (internship)

St. Louis Veterans Affairs Medical Center—John Cochran Division
915 North Grand Blvd., St. Louis 63106
Type: Public, federal
Degrees: C
URL: http://www.stlouis.va.gov
Phone: (314) 652-4100
Prog. Accred.: Allied Health (optometric residency)

Truman Medical Center Hospital Hill
2301 Holmes St., Kansas City 64108
Type: Private, independent, four-year
Degrees: M
URL: http://www.trumed.org/tmc
Phone: (816) 404-1000
Prog. Accred.: Nurse Anesthesia Education

NEBRASKA

55th Dental Squadron
2501 Capehart Rd., Ste. 1K47, Offutt AFB 68113-2160
Type: Public, federal
Degrees: C
URL: http://www.offutt.af.mil
Phone: (402) 294-9760
Prog. Accred.: Dentistry (advanced education in general dentistry)

Alegent Health Bergan Mercy Medical Center
7500 Mercy Rd., Omaha 68124
Type: Private, independent
Degrees: C
URL: http://www.alegent.com
Phone: (402) 398-6060
Prog. Accred.: Radiography

Mary Lanning Memorial Hospital
715 North St. Joseph Ave., Hastings 68901
Type: Private, independent
Degrees: C
URL: http://www.mlmh.org
Phone: (402) 463-4521
Prog. Accred.: Radiography

Regional West Medical Center
4021 Ave. B, Scottsbluff 69361
Type: Private, independent
Degrees: C
URL: http://www.rwmc.net
Phone: (308) 635-3711
Prog. Accred.: Radiography

NEVADA

Las Vegas Veterans Affairs Medical Center
901 Rancho Ln., Las Vegas 89106
Type: Public, federal
Degrees: C
URL: http://www.lasvegas.va.gov
Phone: (702) 636-3000
Prog. Accred.: Allied Health (optometric residency)

Veterans Affairs Sierra Nevada Health Care System
1000 Locust St., Reno 89502
Type: Public, federal
Degrees: C
URL: http://www.reno.va.gov
Phone: (775) 786-7200
Prog. Accred.: Allied Health (optometric residency)

NEW HAMPSHIRE

Dartmouth-Hitchcock Medical Center
1 Medical Center Dr., Lebanon 03756-0001
Type: Private, independent
Degrees: C
URL: http://www.hitchcock.org
Phone: (603) 650-5000
Prog. Accred.: Allied Health (surgical technology), Clinical Pastoral Education

Havenwood-Heritage Heights
33 Christian Ave., Concord 03301
Type: Private, United Church of Christ
Degrees: C
URL: http://www.hhhinfo.com
Phone: (603) 229-1103
Prog. Accred.: Clinical Pastoral Education

Manchester Veterans Affairs Medical Center
718 Smyth Rd., Manchester 03104
Type: Public, federal
Degrees: C
URL: http://www.manchester.va.gov
Phone: (603) 624-4366
Prog. Accred.: Allied Health (optometric residency), Dentistry (general practice residency)

New England EMS Institute
One Elliot Way, Manchester 03103
Type: Private, proprietary
Degrees: C
URL: http://www.neemsi.com
Phone: (603) 663-4402
Prog. Accred.: Allied Health (EMT (paramedic))

New England School of Practical Nursing
60 Rogers St., Manchester 03103
Type: Private, proprietary
Degrees: C
URL: http://www.hcta.net
Phone: (603) 622-8400
Prog. Accred.: Practical Nursing

Saint Joseph School of Nursing
5 Woodward Ave., Nashua 03060
Type: Private, independent
Degrees: C
URL: http://www.sjhacademiccenter.org
Phone: (603) 594-2567
Prog. Accred.: Practical Nursing

NEW JERSEY

Ancora Psychiatric Hospital
202 Spring Garden Rd., Ancora 08037
Type: Public, state
Degrees: C
URL: http://www.state.nj.us/humanservices/pfnurse/ancora.htm
Phone: (609)567-7321
Prog. Accred.: Psychology Internship

Bayonne Medical Center
69-71 New Hook Rd., Bayonne 07002
Type: Private, independent
Degrees: C
URL: http://www.bayonnemedicalcenter.com
Phone: (201) 858-5000
Prog. Accred.: Nursing

Cape May County Technical Institute
188 Crest Haven Rd., Cape May Courthouse 08210
Type: Public, local
Degrees: C
URL: http://www.capemaytech.com
Phone: (609) 465-3064 *Calendar:* Sem. plan
Prog. Accred.: Dentistry (dental assisting)

Capital Health System—Mercer Campus
446 Bellevue Ave., Trenton 08618
Type: Private, independent
Degrees: C
URL: http://www.capitalhealth.org
Phone: (609) 394-4000
Prog. Accred.: Nursing

Christ Hospital
176 Palisade Ave., Jersey City 07306-1121
Type: Private, independent
Degrees: C
URL: http://www.christhospital.org
Phone: (201) 795-8200
Prog. Accred.: Clinical Pastoral Education, Nursing

Cooper University Hospital
One Cooper Plaza, Camden 08103
Type: Private, independent
Degrees: C
URL: http://www.cooperhealth.org
Phone: (856) 342-2000
Prog. Accred.: Allied Health (perfusion), Clinical Pastoral Education, Radiation Therapy, Radiography

Cumberland County Technical Education Center
601 Bridgeton Ave., Bridgeton 08302
Type: Public, local
Degrees: C
URL: http://www.cumberland.tec.nj.us
Phone: (856) 451-9000
Prog. Accred.: Dentistry (dental assisting)

Englewood Hospital and Medical Center
350 Engle St., Englewood 07631
Type: Private, independent
Degrees: C
URL: http://www.englewoodhospital.com
Phone: (201) 894-3000
Prog. Accred.: Radiography

Hackensack University Medical Center
30 Prospect Ave., Hackensack 07601
Type: Private, independent
Degrees: C
URL: http://www.humed.com
Phone: (201) 996-2000
Prog. Accred.: Dentistry (general practice residency)

Helene Fuld School of Nursing in Camden County
PO Box 1669, College Dr., Blackwood 08012
Type: Private, independent
Degrees: C
URL: http://www.helenefuld.virtua.org
Phone: (856) 481-9100 *Calendar:* Sem. plan
Prog. Accred.: Nursing

Holy Name Hospital
718 Teaneck Rd., Teaneck 07666
Type: Private, independent
Degrees: C
URL: http://www.holyname.org
Phone: (201) 833-3000 *Calendar:* Sem. plan
Prog. Accred.: Nursing

Hudson Area School of Radiologic Technology
176 Palisade Ave., Jersey City 07006
Type: Private, independent
Degrees: C
URL: http://www.bayonnemedicalcenter.org/schoolofradiology.html
Phone: (201) 795-8246
Prog. Accred.: Radiography

Jersey City Medical Center
50 Baldwin Ave., Jersey City 07304
Type: Private, independent
Degrees: C
URL: http://www.libertyhealth.org/jcmc.html
Phone: (201) 915-2000
Prog. Accred.: Dentistry (general practice residency)

Jersey Shore University Medical Center
1945 Rte 33, Neptune 07753
Type: Private, independent
Degrees: C
URL: http://www.meridianhealth.com/jsmc.cfm
Phone: (732) 775-5500
Prog. Accred.: Dentistry (general practice residency)

John F. Kennedy Medical Center
65 James St., Edison 08818-3059
Type: Private, independent
Degrees: C
URL: http://jfkmc.org
Phone: (732) 321-7000
Prog. Accred.: Allied Health (diagnostic medical sonography), Dentistry (general practice residency), Nuclear Medicine Technology, Nursing, Radiation Therapy, Radiography

Monmouth Medical Center
300 Second Ave., Long Branch 07740
Type: Private, independent
System: Saint Barnabas Health Care System
Degrees: C
URL: http://www.sbhcs.com/hospitals/monmouth_medical
Phone: (732) 222-5200
Prog. Accred.: Dentistry (general practice residency)

Morristown Memorial Hospital
100 Madison Ave., Morristown 07962
Type: Private, independent
Degrees: C
URL: http://www.atlantichealth.org/cons/hospitals/at_MMH
Phone: (973) 971-5000
Prog. Accred.: Allied Health (cardiovascular technology), Dentistry (general practice residency)

Mountainside Hospital
1 Bay Ave., Montclair 07042
Type: Private, independent
Degrees: C
URL: http://www.mountainsidenow.com
Phone: (973) 429-6000
Prog. Accred.: Dentistry (general practice residency), Nursing

Newark Beth Israel Medical Center
201 Lyons Ave. at Osborne Ave., Newark 07112
Type: Private, independent
System: Saint Barnabas Health Care System
Degrees: C
URL: http://www.sbhcs.com/hospitals/newark_beth_israel
Phone: (973) 926-7000
Prog. Accred.: Dentistry (general practice residency)

Our Lady of Lourdes Medical Center
1600 Haddon Ave., Camden 08103
Type: Private, Franciscan Sisters of Allegany, four-year
Degrees: C, M
URL: http://www.lourdesnet.org/lourdes
Phone: (856) 757-3500
Prog. Accred.: Nurse Anesthesia Education, Nursing

Overlook Hospital
99 Beauvoir Ave., Summit 07902
Type: Private, independent
Degrees: C
URL: http://www.overlookhospital.org/en/overlook
Phone: (908) 522-2000
Prog. Accred.: Clinical Pastoral Education, Dentistry (general practice residency)

Pascack Valley Hospital
250 Old Hook Rd., Westwood 07675
Type: Public, local
Degrees: C
URL: http://www.pvhospital.org
Phone: (201) 358-3000
Prog. Accred.: Radiography

Saint Barnabas Medical Center
94 Old Short Hills Rd., Livingston 07039
Type: Private, independent
Degrees: C
URL: http://www.sbhcs.com
Phone: (973) 322-5000
Prog. Accred.: Radiation Therapy

Saint Francis Medical Center
601 Hamilton Ave., Trenton 08629
Type: Private, independent
Degrees: C
URL: http://www.stfrancismedical.com
Phone: (609) 599-5000
Prog. Accred.: Nursing, Radiography

Saint Joseph's Regional Medical Center
703 Main St., Paterson 07503
Type: Private, independent
Degrees: C
URL: http://www.stjosephshealth.org
Phone: (973) 754-2000
Prog. Accred.: Dentistry (general practice residency)

Shore Memorial Hospital
1 East New York Ave., Somers Point 08244-2387
Type: Private, independent
Degrees: C
URL: http://www.shorememorial.org
Phone: (609) 653-3500
Prog. Accred.: Radiography

South Jersey Healthcare Regional Medical Center
1505 West Sherman Ave., Vineland 08360
Type: Private, independent
Degrees: C
URL: http://www.sjhealthcare.net/content/SJHRegionalMedicalCenter.htm
Phone: (856) 641-8000
Prog. Accred.: Dietetics (internship)

Technical Institute of Camden County
343 Berlin-Cross Keys Rd., Sicklerville 08081-9709
Type: Private, local
Degrees: C
URL: http://www.ccts.tec.nj.us/ti
Phone: (856) 767-7000
Prog. Accred.: Allied Health (medical assisting (AMA)), Dentistry (dental assisting)

Trinitas Hospital School of Nursing Williamson Street Campus
225 Williamson St., Elizabeth 07207
Type: Private, independent
Degrees: C
URL: http://www.trinitashospital.org
Phone: (908) 994-5000 *Calendar:* Qtr. plan
Prog. Accred.: Nursing

New Point Campus
655 East Jersey St., Elizabeth 07201
Prog. Accred: Nursing

The Valley Hospital
223 North Van Dien Ave., Ridgewood 07450
Type: Private, independent
Degrees: C
URL: http://www.valleyhealth.com
Phone: (201) 447-8000
Prog. Accred.: Clinical Pastoral Education, Radiography

Veterans Affairs Medical Center—East Orange
385 Tremont Ave., East Orange 07018-1095
Type: Public, federal
Degrees: C
Prog. Accred.: Dentistry (general practice residency)

Veterans Affairs New Jersey Health Care System—Lyons
151 Knollcroft Rd., Lyons 07019
Type: Public, federal
Degrees: C
URL: http://www.lyons.va.gov
Phone: (908) 647-0180
Prog. Accred.: Allied Health (optometric residency)

Virtua Health Camden
1000 Atlantic Ave., Camden 08104
Type: Private, independent
Degrees: C
URL: http://www.virtua.org
Phone: (856) 246-3000
Prog. Accred.: Dentistry (general practice residency)

NEW MEXICO

Albuquerque Area Indian Health Service
5300 Homestead Rd. NE, Albuquerque 87110
Type: Public, federal
Degrees: C
URL: http://www.ihs.gov/FacilitiesServices/AreaOffices/Albuquerque
Phone: (505) 248-4500
Prog. Accred.: Dentistry (dental public health)

Albuquerque Public Schools Career Enrichment Center
807 Mountain Rd. NE, Albuquerque 87102
Type: Public, local
Degrees: C
URL: http://www.cec.aps.edu
Phone: (505) 247-3658
Prog. Accred.: Nursing

Crownpoint Health Care Facility
PO Box 358, Highway Junction 57, Route 9, Crownpoint 87313-0358
Type: Public, federal
Degrees: C
URL: http://www.ihs.gov
Phone: (505) 786-5291
Prog. Accred.: Allied Health (optometric residency)

Gallup Indian Medical Center
PO Box 1337, Gallup 87301
Type: Private, federal
Degrees: C
URL: http://www.ihs.gov
Phone: (505) 722-1000
Prog. Accred.: Allied Health (optometric residency), Dentistry (general practice residency)

Northern Navajo Medical Center
PO Box 160, Shiprock 87420
Type: Private, federal
Degrees: C
URL: http://www.ihs.gov
Phone: (505) 368-6001
Prog. Accred.: Allied Health (optometric residency)

Presbyterian Hospital
1100 Central Ave. SE, Albuquerque 87106
Type: Private, independent
Degrees: C
URL: http://www.phs.org/PHS/hospitals/hospitals/abqpres/index.htm
Phone: (505) 841-1234
Prog. Accred.: Clinical Pastoral Education

Raymond G. Murphy Veterans Affairs Medical Center
1501 San Pedro SE, Albuquerque 87108
Type: Public, federal
Degrees: C
URL: http://www.albuquerque.va.gov
Phone: (505) 265-1711
Prog. Accred.: Allied Health (optometric residency)

NEW YORK

Albany Medical Center
43 New Scotland Ave., Albany 12208
Type: Private, independent
Degrees: C
URL: http://www.amc.edu
Phone: (518) 262-3125
Prog. Accred.: Clinical Pastoral Education

Albany Veterans Affairs Medical Center
113 Holland Ave., Albany 12208
Type: Public, federal
Degrees: C
Prog. Accred.: Dentistry (general practice residency)

ARAMARK Healthcare Metropolitan New York Dietetic Internship Program
90-15 158th Ave., Jamaica 11414-3125
Type: Private, proprietary
Degrees: C
URL: http://www.aramark.com
Phone: (718) 835-7087
Prog. Accred.: Dietetics (internship)

Arnot-Ogden Medical Center
600 Roe Ave., Elmira 14905
Type: Private, independent
Degrees: C
URL: http://www.aomc.org
Phone: (607) 737-4100 *Calendar:* 24-mos. pr
Prog. Accred.: Nursing, Radiography

Association for the Help of Retarded Children
200 Park Ave. South, New York 10003
Type: Private, independent
Degrees: C
URL: http://www.ahrcnyc.org
Phone: (212) 780-2500
Prog. Accred.: Psychology Internship

The Astor Home for Children
PO Box 5005, Rhinebeck 12572-5005
Type: Private, independent
Degrees: C
URL: http://www.astorservices.org
Phone: (845) 871-1000
Prog. Accred.: Psychology Internship

Bassett Healthcare
One Atwell Rd., Cooperstown 13326
Type: Private, independent
Degrees: C
URL: http://www.bassett.org
Phone: (607) 547-3456
Prog. Accred.: Allied Health (EMT (paramedic))

Bath Veterans Affairs Medical Center
76 Veterans Ave., Bath 14810
Type: Public, federal
Degrees: C
URL: http://www.va.gov/visns/visn02/bath.cfm
Phone: (607) 664-4000
Prog. Accred.: Dentistry (general dentistry)

Beth Israel Medical Center
First Ave. at 16th St., New York 10003
Type: Private, independent
Degrees: C
URL: http://www.wehealnewyork.org/patients/bimc_description.html
Phone: (212) 420-2000
Prog. Accred.: Clinical Pastoral Education, Psychology Internship

Blanton-Peale Institute
3 West 29th St., New York 10001-4597
Type: Private, nondenominational, four-year
Degrees: C, P
URL: http://www.blantonpeale.org
Phone: (212) 725-7850 *Calendar:* Sem. plan
Prog. Accred.: Marriage and Family Therapy

Bronx Lebanon Hospital Center
1650 Grand Concourse, Bronx 10457-7606
Type: Private, independent
Degrees: C
URL: http://www.bronx-leb.org
Phone: (718) 590-1800
Prog. Accred.: Dentistry (general practice residency, pediatric dentistry)

The Brookdale University Hospital and Medical Center
One Brookdale Plaza, Brooklyn 11212
Type: Private, independent
Degrees: C
URL: http://www.brookdale.edu
Phone: (718) 240-6785
Prog. Accred.: Dentistry (general practice residency, pediatric dentistry), Psychology Internship

Brooklyn Hospital Center
121 DeKalb Ave., Brooklyn 11201
Type: Private, independent
Degrees: C
URL: http://www.tbh.org
Phone: (718) 250-8000
Prog. Accred.: Dentistry (general practice residency, oral and maxillofacial surgery)

Center for Montessori Teacher Education/NY
785 Mamaroneck Ave., White Plains 10605
Type: Private, independent
Degrees: C
URL: http://www.cmteny.com
Phone: (914) 948-2501
Prog. Accred.: Montessori Teacher Education

Villa Montessori School
4535 North 28th St., Phoenix, AZ 85016
Phone: (914) 948-2210

The Village School for Children
865 East Glen Ave., Ridgewood, NJ 07450
Phone: (914) 948-2501

Center for Preventive Psychiatry
19 Greenridge Ave., White Plains 10605
Type: Private, independent
Degrees: C
URL: http://www.andruschildren.org
Phone: (914) 949-7680
Prog. Accred.: Psychology Internship

Central Suffolk Hospital
1300 Roanoke Ave., Riverhead 11944
Type: Private, independent
Degrees: C
URL: http://www.centralsuffolkhospital.org
Phone: (631) 548-6000
Prog. Accred.: Radiography

Champlain Valley Physicians Hospital Medical Center
75 Beekman St., Plattsburgh 12901
Type: Private, independent
Degrees: C
URL: http://www.cvph.org
Phone: (518) 561-2000
Prog. Accred.: Radiography

Coler-Goldwater Specialty Hospital and Nursing Facility
One Main St., Roosevelt Island 10044
Type: Private, independent
Degrees: C
URL: http://www.nyc.gov/html/hhc/coler-goldwater/home.html
Phone: (212) 848-6000
Prog. Accred.: Dentistry (general practice residency)

Creedmoor Psychiatric Center
80-45 Winchester Blvd., Queens Village 11427
Type: Public, state-related
Degrees: C
URL: http://www.omh.state.ny.us/omhweb/facilities/crpc/facility.htm
Phone: (718) 264-4000
Prog. Accred.: Psychology Internship

Crouse Hospital
736 Irving Ave., Syracuse 13210
Type: Private, independent, two-year
Degrees: A
URL: http://www.crouse.org
Phone: (315) 470-7511
Prog. Accred.: Nursing

Dutchess County Department of Mental Hygiene
230 North Rd., Poughkeepsie 12601
Type: Public, state
Degrees: C
URL: http://www.dutchessny.gov/CountyGov/Departments/MentalHygiene/MHIndex.htm
Phone: (845) 485-9700
Prog. Accred.: Psychology Internship

Eger Health Care Center of Staten Island
140 Meisner Ave., Staten Island 10306-1200
Type: Private, independent
Degrees: C
URL: http://www.eger.org
Phone: (718) 979-1800
Prog. Accred.: Clinical Pastoral Education

Ellis Hospital School of Nursing
1101 Nott St., Schenectady 12308
Type: Private, independent, two-year
Degrees: A
URL: http://www.ehson.org
Phone: (518) 243-4471 *Calendar:* Sem. plan
Prog. Accred.: Nursing

Erie County Medical Center
462 Grider St., Buffalo 14215
Type: Private, independent
Degrees: C
URL: http://www.ecmc.edu
Phone: (716) 898-3000
Prog. Accred.: Dentistry (general practice residency)

Faxton-St. Luke's Healthcare
PO Box 479, Utica 13503
Type: Private, independent
Degrees: C
URL: http://www.faxtonstlukes.com
Phone: (315) 624-6000
Prog. Accred.: Dentistry (general practice residency), Radiography

Flushing Hospital Medical Center
4500 Parsons Blvd., Flushing 11355
Type: Private, independent
Degrees: C
URL: http://www.flushinghospital.org
Phone: (718) 670-5000
Prog. Accred.: Dentistry (general practice residency)

Glens Falls Hospital
100 Park St., Glens Falls 12801
Type: Private, independent
Degrees: C
URL: https://www.glensfallshospital.org
Phone: (518) 926-1000
Prog. Accred.: Radiography

Harlem Hospital Center
506 Lenox Ave., New York 10037
Type: Private, independent
Degrees: C
URL: http://www.ci.nyc.ny.us/html/hhc/html/harlem.html
Phone: (212) 939-1000 *Calendar:* 24-mos. pr
Prog. Accred.: Dentistry (general practice residency, oral and maxillofacial surgery, pediatric dentistry), Radiography

The HealthCare Chaplaincy
315 East 62nd St., New York 10021-7767
Type: Private, independent
Degrees: C
URL: http://www.healthcarechaplaincy.org
Phone: (212) 644-1111
Prog. Accred.: Clinical Pastoral Education

Interfaith Medical Center
1545 Atlantic Ave., Brooklyn 11213
Type: Private, independent
Degrees: C
URL: http://www.interfaithmedical.com
Phone: (718) 613-4000
Prog. Accred.: Dentistry (general practice residency, pediatric dentistry)

Isabella G. Hart School of Practical Nursing
333 Humboldt St., Rochester 14610-1044
Type: Private, independent
Degrees: C
URL: http://www.viahealth.org/body_education.cfm?id=120
Phone: (716) 338-4784
Prog. Accred.: Practical Nursing

Jamaica Hospital Medical Center
8900 Van Wyck Expressway, Jamaica 11418
Type: Private, independent
Degrees: C
URL: http://www.jamaicahospital.org
Phone: (718) 206-6000
Prog. Accred.: Dentistry (general practice residency)

James J. Peters Veterans Affairs Medical Center
130 West Kingsbridge Rd., Bronx 10468
Type: Public, federal
Degrees: C
URL: http://www.bronx.va.gov
Phone: (718) 584-9000
Prog. Accred.: Dietetics (internship)

Keller Army Community Hospital
900 Washington Rd., West Point 10996-1197
Type: Public, federal
Degrees: C
URL: http://kach.amedd.army.mil
Phone: (845) 938-5169
Prog. Accred.: Allied Health (optometric residency)

Kings County Hospital Center
451 Clarkson Ave., Brooklyn 11203
Type: Private, city-owned
Degrees: C
URL: http://www.ci.nyc.ny.us/html/hhc/html/facilities/kings.shtml
Phone: (718) 245-3131
Prog. Accred.: Dentistry (general practice residency, oral and maxillofacial surgery)

Kingsbrook Jewish Medical Center
585 Schnectady Ave., Brooklyn 11203
Type: Private, independent
Degrees: C
URL: http://www.kingsbrook.org
Phone: (718) 604-5000
Prog. Accred.: Dentistry (general practice residency)

Lenox Hill Hospital
100 East 77th St., New York 10021
Type: Private, independent
Degrees: C
URL: http://www.lenoxhillhospital.org
Phone: (212) 434-2000
Prog. Accred.: Clinical Pastoral Education

Lincoln Medical and Mental Health Center
234 East 149th St., Bronx 10451
Type: Public, city-owned
Degrees: C
URL: http://www.ci.nyc.ny.us/html/hhc/html/lincoln.html
Phone: (718) 579-5000
Prog. Accred.: Dentistry (general practice residency)

Long Island College Hospital
340 Henry St., Brooklyn 11201
Type: Private, independent, two-year
Degrees: C, A
URL: http://www.wehealny.org/patients/lich_description
Phone: (718) 780-1000
Prog. Accred.: Dentistry (general practice residency), Nursing, Radiography

Long Island Jewish Medical Center
270-05 76th Ave., New Hyde Park 11040
Type: Private, independent
Degrees: C
URL: http://www.northshorelij.com
Phone: (718) 470-7000
Prog. Accred.: Dentistry (general practice residency, oral and maxillofacial pathology, oral and maxillofacial surgery, pediatric dentistry)

Lutheran Medical Center
150 55th St., Brooklyn 11220
Type: Private, independent
Degrees: C
URL: http://www.lutheranmedicalcenter.com
Phone: (718) 630-7000
Prog. Accred.: Dentistry (general dentistry, general practice residency, pediatric dentistry)

Maimonides Medical Center
4802 Tenth Ave., Brooklyn 11219
Type: Private, independent
Degrees: C
URL: http://www.maimonidesmed.org
Phone: (718) 283-6000
Prog. Accred.: Dentistry (general practice residency, pediatric dentistry)

Marion S. Whelan School of Practical Nursing
196-198 North St., Geneva 14456
Type: Private, independent
Degrees: C
URL: http://www.flhealth.org/body.cfm?id=37#Marion
Phone: (315) 787-4005
Prog. Accred.: Practical Nursing

Memorial Sloan-Kettering Cancer Center
1275 York Ave., New York 10021
Type: Private, independent
Degrees: C
URL: http://www.mskcc.org
Phone: (212) 639-2000
Prog. Accred.: Allied Health (cytotechnology), Radiation Therapy

Mercy Medical Center
1000 North Village Ave., PO Box 9024, Rockville Centre 11571-9024
Type: Private, Diocese of Rockville Centre
Degrees: C
URL: http://mercymedicalcenter.chsli.org
Phone: (516) 705-2525
Prog. Accred.: Radiography

Montefiore Medical Center East Campus
1825 Eastchester Rd., Bronx 10461
Type: Private, independent
Degrees: C
URL: http://www.montefiore.org
Phone: (718) 904-2000
Prog. Accred.: Dentistry (general practice residency)

Montefiore Medical Center West Campus
111 East 210th St., Bronx 10467
Type: Private, independent
Degrees: C
URL: http://www.montefiore.org
Phone: (718) 920-4321
Prog. Accred.: Dentistry (combined prosthodontics, general practice residency, oral and maxillofacial surgery, orthodontic and dentofacial orthopedics, pediatric dentistry), Radiation Therapy

Mount Sinai Hospital
One Gustave L. Levy Place, New York 10029
Type: Private, independent
Degrees: C
URL: http://www.mountsinai.org
Phone: (212) 241-6500
Prog. Accred.: Dentistry (general dentistry, oral and maxillofacial surgery)

Nassau County Vocational Educational and Extension (VEEB)
899-A Jerusalem Ave., Uniondale 11553
Type: Public, state/local
Degrees: C
URL: http://www.veeb.org
Phone: (516) 572-1704 *Calendar:* Tri. plan
Prog. Accred.: Practical Nursing

Nassau University Medical Center
2201 Hempstead Turnpike, East Meadow 11554
Type: Private, independent
Degrees: C
URL: http://www.ncmc.edu
Phone: (516) 572-0123
Prog. Accred.: Dentistry (general practice residency, oral and maxillofacial surgery)

The New York Hospital Queens
56-45 Main St., Flushing 11355
Type: Private, independent
Degrees: C
URL: http://www.nyhq.org
Phone: (718) 670-1231
Prog. Accred.: Dentistry (general practice residency, oral and maxillofacial pathology)

New York Methodist Hospital
506 Sixth St., Brooklyn 11215
Type: Private, independent
Degrees: C
URL: http://www.nym.org
Phone: (718) 780-3000
Prog. Accred.: Allied Health (EMT (paramedic)), Clinical Pastoral Education, Dentistry (general practice residency), Radiation Therapy, Radiography

New York Presbyterian Hospital—Columbia University
622 West 168th St., New York 10032
Type: Private, independent
Degrees: C
URL: http://www.nyp.org
Phone: (212) 305-2500
Prog. Accred.: Clinical Pastoral Education, Dentistry (general dentistry, general practice residency, oral and maxillofacial surgery, pediatric dentistry), Psychology Internship

New York State Department of Health
NYSDOH Bureau of Dental Health, ESP Corning Tower, Albany 12237-0619
Type: Public, state
Degrees: C
URL: http://www.health.state.ny.us/prevention/dental/public.htm
Phone: (518) 474-1961
Prog. Accred.: Dentistry (dental public health)

Nicholas H. Noyes Memorial Hospital
111 Clara Barton St., Dansville 14437
Type: Private, independent
Degrees: C
URL: http://www.noyes-health.org
Phone: (585) 335-6001
Prog. Accred.: Phlebotomy

North Shore University Hospital at Manhasset
300 Community Dr., Manhasset 11030
Type: Private, independent
Degrees: C
URL: http://www.northshorelij.com
Phone: (516) 562-0100
Prog. Accred.: Allied Health (perfusion), Clinical Pastoral Education, Dentistry (general practice residency), Psychology Internship

Northport Veterans Affairs Medical Center
79 Middleville Rd., Northport 11768
Type: Public, federal
Degrees: C
URL: http://www.va.gov/visns/visn03/nrptinfo.asp
Phone: (631) 261-4400
Prog. Accred.: Allied Health (optometry), Dentistry (general practice residency)

Peninsula Hospital Center
51-15 Beach Channel Dr., Far Rockaway 11691-1074
Type: Private, independent
Degrees: C
URL: http://www.peninsulahospital.org
Phone: (718) 734-2000
Prog. Accred.: Dentistry (general practice residency)

Phillips Beth Israel School of Nursing
776 Ave. of the Americas, 4th Flr., New York 10001-6354
Type: Private, independent, two-year
Degrees: A *Enroll:* 100
URL: http://www.futurenursebi.org
Phone: (212) 614-6110 *Calendar:* Sem. plan
Prog. Accred.: Nursing

Queens Hospital Center
82-70 164th Streey, Jamaica 11432
Type: Private, city-owned
Degrees: C
URL: http://www.ci.nyc.ny.us/html/hhc/html/queens.html
Phone: (718) 883-3000
Prog. Accred.: Dentistry (general practice residency)

Rochester General Hospital
1425 Portland Ave., Rochester 14621
Type: Private, independent
Degrees: C
URL: http://www.viahealth.org/rgh
Phone: (585) 922-4000
Prog. Accred.: Phlebotomy

Saint Barnabas Hospital
4422 Third Ave., Bronx 10457
Type: Private, independent
Degrees: C
URL: http://www.stbarnabashospital.org
Phone: (718) 960-9000
Prog. Accred.: Dentistry (general practice residency, oral and maxillofacial surgery, pediatric dentistry)

Saint Charles Hospital
200 Belle Terre Rd., Port Jefferson 11777
Type: Private, independent
Degrees: C
URL: http://stcharleshospital.chsli.org
Phone: (631) 474-6000
Prog. Accred.: Clinical Pastoral Education, Dentistry (general practice residency)

Saint Elizabeth Medical Center
2209 Genesee St., Utica 13501
Type: Private, independent, two-year
Degrees: C, A
URL: http://www.stemc.org
Phone: (315) 798-8100
Prog. Accred.: Nursing, Radiography

Saint James Mercy Health System
411 Canisteo St., Hornell 14843
Type: Private, independent
Degrees: C
URL: http://www.stjamesmercy.org
Phone: (607) 324-8000
Prog. Accred.: Radiography

Saint Joseph's Medical Center
127 South Broadway, Yonkers 10701
Type: Private, independent
Degrees: C
URL: http://www.saintjosephs.org
Phone: (914) 378-7000
Prog. Accred.: Radiography

Saint Luke's-Roosevelt Hospital Center
1111 Amsterdam Ave., New York 10025
Type: Private, independent
Degrees: C
URL: http://www.wehealny.org
Phone: (212) 523-4000
Prog. Accred.: Clinical Pastoral Education, Dentistry (general practice residency, oral and maxillofacial surgery)

Saint Peter's Hospital
315 South Manning Blvd., Albany 12208
Type: Private, independent
Degrees: C
URL: http://www.stpetershealthcare.org
Phone: (518) 525-1293
Prog. Accred.: Dentistry (general practice residency)

Saint Vincent Catholic Medical Centers of New York
175-05 Horace Harding Expressway, Fresh Meadows 11365
Type: Private, independent, four-year
Degrees: C, B
URL: http://www.svcmc.org
Phone: (718) 357-0500 *Calendar:* Sem. plan
Prog. Accred.: Allied Health (EMT (paramedic)), Clinical Lab Scientist, Physician Assistant, Radiography

Mary Immaculate Hospital
88-25 153rd St., Jamaica 11432
Phone: (718) 558-7280
Prog. Accred: Dentistry (general practice residency, oral and maxillofacial surgery)

Staten Island Campus
75 Vanderbilt Ave., Staten Island 10304-3850
Phone: (718) 818-6470

Saint Vincent's Hospital Manhattan
170 West 12th St., New York 10011
Type: Private, independent
Degrees: C
URL: http://www.svcmc.org
Phone: (212) 604-7000 *Calendar:* 12-mos. pr
Prog. Accred.: Clinical Lab Scientist, Nuclear Medicine Technology

Sisters of Charity Hospital
2157 Main St., Buffalo 14214
Type: Private, independent
Degrees: C
URL: http://www.chsbuffalo.org
Phone: (716) 862-1000
Prog. Accred.: Clinical Pastoral Education

Sodexo Health Care Services New York Metropolitan
90 Merrick Ave., Ste. 210, East Meadow 11554-1573
Type: Private, proprietary
Degrees: C
URL: http://www.dieteticintern.com/NYmetro
Phone: (215) 612-4615
Prog. Accred.: Dietetics (internship)

South Nassau Communities Hospital
One Healthy Way, Oceanside 11572
Type: Private, independent
Degrees: C
URL: http://www.southnassau.org
Phone: (516) 632-4678
Prog. Accred.: Radiography

Staten Island University Hospital
475 Seaview Ave., Staten Island 10305
Type: Private, independent
Degrees: C
URL: http://www.siuh.edu
Phone: (718) 226-9000
Prog. Accred.: Dentistry (general practice residency)

Strong Memorial Hospital
601 Elmwood Ave., Rochester 14642
Type: Private, independent
Degrees: C
URL: http://www.stronghealth.com
Phone: (585) 275-2100
Prog. Accred.: Dentistry (general practice residency, oral and maxillofacial surgery)

Ulster County Board of Cooperative Educational Services
175 Route 32 North, New Paltz 12561
Type: Public, state
Degrees: C
URL: http://www.ulsterboces.org
Phone: (845) 255-1400
Prog. Accred.: Allied Health (surgical technology)

University at Buffalo Educational Opportunity Center
465 Washington St., Buffalo 14203-1707
Type: Public, state
Degrees: C
URL: http://www.eoc.buffalo.edu
Phone: (716) 849-6727 ext 5
Prog. Accred.: Dentistry (dental assisting)

Veterans Affairs Hudson Valley Health Care System—Castle Point
Route 9D, Castle Point 12511
Type: Public, federal
Degrees: C
URL: http://www.hudsonvalley.va.gov
Phone: (845) 831-2000
Prog. Accred.: Dentistry (general dentistry)

Veterans Affairs Hudson Valley Health Care System—Montrose
2094 Albany Post Rd., Montrose 12508
Type: Public, federal
Degrees: C
URL: http://www.hudsonvalley.va.gov
Phone: (914) 737-4400
Prog. Accred.: Allied Health (optometric residency)

Veterans Affairs New York Harbor Healthcare System—Brooklyn
800 Poly Place, Brooklyn 11209
Type: Public, federal
Degrees: C
URL: http://www.va.gov/visns/visn03/brooklyninfo.asp
Phone: (718) 836-6600
Prog. Accred.: Allied Health (optometric residency), Dentistry (general practice residency)

Veterans Affairs NewYork Harbor Healthcare System—New York City
423 East 23rd St., New York 10010
Type: Public, federal
Degrees: C
URL: http://www.va.gov/visns/visn03/nyinfo.asp
Phone: (212) 686-7500
Prog. Accred.: Clinical Pastoral Education, Dentistry (combined prosthodontics, endodontics, general practice residency, periodontics)

Veterans Affairs Western New York Healthcare System at Buffalo
3495 Bailey Ave., Buffalo 14215
Type: Public, federal
Degrees: C
URL: http://www1.va.gov/visns/visn02/buffalo.cfm
Phone: (716) 834-9200
Prog. Accred.: Dentistry (combined prosthodontics, general practice residency)

Westchester Medical Center
95 Grasslands Rd., Valhalla 10595
Type: Private, independent
Degrees: C
URL: http://www.wcmc.com
Phone: (914) 493-7000
Prog. Accred.: Clinical Pastoral Education, Dentistry (general practice residency, oral and maxillofacial surgery)

Winthrop University Hospital
259 1st St., Mineola
Type: Private, independent
Degrees: C
URL: http://www.winthrop.org
Phone: (516) 663-4749
Prog. Accred.: Radiography

Women's Christian Association Hospital
PO Box 840, Jamestown 14702-0840
Type: Private, independent
Degrees: C
URL: http://www.wcahospital.org
Phone: (716) 487-0141
Prog. Accred.: Clinical Lab Scientist, Radiography

Woodhull Medical and Mental Health Center
760 Broadway Ave., Brooklyn 11206
Type: Public, city-owned
Degrees: C
URL: http://www.ci.nyc.ny.us/html/hhc/html/woodhull.html
Phone: (718) 963-8000
Prog. Accred.: Dentistry (general practice residency, oral and maxillofacial surgery)

Wyckoff Heights Medical Center
374 Stockholm St., Brooklyn 11237
Type: Private, independent
Degrees: C
URL: http://www.wyckoffhospital.org
Phone: (718) 963-7272
Prog. Accred.: Dentistry (general practice residency)

NORTH CAROLINA

2nd Dental Battalion—Naval Dental Center
315 Main Service Rd., Camp LeJeune 28542-2508
Type: Public, federal
Degrees: C
URL: http://ndc-cl-www.med.navy.mil
Phone: (910) 451-2775
Prog. Accred.: Dentistry (advanced education in general dentistry)

Alamance Regional Medical Center
1240 Huffman Mill Rd., Burlington 27216
Type: Private, independent
Degrees: C
URL: http://www.armc.com
Phone: (336) 538-7000
Prog. Accred.: Clinical Pastoral Education

Asheville Veterans Affairs Medical Center
1100 Tunnel Rd., Asheville 28805-2043
Type: Public, federal
Degrees: C
URL: http://www.asheville.va.gov
Phone: (828) 298-7911
Prog. Accred.: Clinical Pastoral Education

Behavioral Health Center CMC—Randolph
501 Billingsley Rd., Charlotte 28211
Type: Private, independent
Degrees: C
URL: http://www.carolinashealthcare.org/services/behavioral/Centers/Randolph.cfm
Phone: (704) 444-2400
Prog. Accred.: Psychology Internship

Broughton Hospital
1000 South Sterling St., Morganton 28655
Type: Public, state
Degrees: C
URL: http://www.broughtonhospital.org
Phone: (828) 433-2111
Prog. Accred.: Psychology Internship

Dorothea Dix Hospital
820 South Boylan Ave., Raleigh 27603-2176
Type: Public, state-related
Degrees: C
URL: http://www.dhhs.state.nc.us/mhddsas/DIX/
Phone: (919) 733-5540
Prog. Accred.: Psychology Internship

Durham Veterans Affairs Medical Center
508 Fulton St., Durham 27705-3875
Type: Public, federal
Degrees: C
URL: http://www.durham.va.gov
Phone: (919) 286-0411
Prog. Accred.: Clinical Pastoral Education

Fayetteville Veterans Affairs Medical Center
2300 Ramsey St., Fayetteville 28301
Type: Public, federal
Degrees: C
URL: http://www.fayettevillenc.va.gov
Phone: (910) 488-2120
Prog. Accred.: Allied Health (optometric residency)

Federal Medical Center Butner
PO Box 1600, Butner 27509
Type: Public, federal
Degrees: C
URL: http://www.bop.gov/locations/institutions/buh/index.jsp
Phone: (919) 575-3900
Prog. Accred.: Psychology Internship

John Umstead Hospital
1003 12th St., Butner 27509
Type: Private, independent
Degrees: C
URL: http://www.dhhs.state.nc.us/mhddsas/Umstead.htm
Phone: (919) 575-7211
Prog. Accred.: Clinical Pastoral Education

The Moses H. Cone Memorial Hospital
1200 North Elm St., Greensboro 27401
Type: Private, independent
Degrees: C
URL: http://www.mosescone.com
Phone: (336) 832-7000
Prog. Accred.: Clinical Pastoral Education, Radiography

Mountain Area Health Education Center
501 Biltmore Ave., Asheville 28801
Type: Public, state
Degrees: C
URL: http://www.mahec.net
Phone: (828) 257-4400
Prog. Accred.: Dentistry (general practice residency)

New Hanover Regional Medical Center
2131 South 17th St., Wilmington 28401
Type: Private, independent
Degrees: C
URL: http://www.nhrmc.org
Phone: (910) 343-7000
Prog. Accred.: Clinical Pastoral Education

North Carolina Division of Dental Health
1931 Mail Service Center, Raleigh 27699-1931
Type: Public, state
Degrees: C
URL: http://www.ncpublichealth.com
Phone: (919) 707-5000
Prog. Accred.: Dentistry (dental public health)

Pitt County Memorial Hospital
PO Box 6028, Greenville 27835-6028
Type: Private, independent
Degrees: C
URL: http://www.uhseast.com
Phone: (252) 847-4100
Prog. Accred.: Clinical Pastoral Education

Presbyterian Hospital
PO Box 33549, Charlotte 28233-3549
Type: Private, independent
Degrees: C
URL: http://www.presbyterian.org
Phone: (704) 384-4000
Prog. Accred.: Radiography

Raleigh School of Nurse Anesthesia
23 Sunnybrook Rd., Ste. 163, Raleigh 27610
Type: Private, independent, four-year
Degrees: C, M
URL: http://www.rsna-edu.org
Phone: (919) 250-9740
Prog. Accred.: Nurse Anesthesia Education

Rex Healthcare
4420 Lake Boone Trail, Raleigh 27607
Type: Private, independent
Degrees: C
URL: http://www.rexhealth.com
Phone: (919) 784-3100
Prog. Accred.: Clinical Pastoral Education

Rutherford Hospital, Inc.
288 South Ridgecrest Ave., Rutherfordton 28139
Type: Private, independent
URL: http://www.rutherfordhosp.org
Phone: (828) 286-5000
Prog. Accred.: Clinical Pastoral Education

United States Army DENTAC—Ft. Bragg
Fort Bragg 28310-5000
Type: Public, federal
Degrees: C
Prog. Accred.: Dentistry (general dentistry)

United States Army John F. Kennedy Special Warfare Center and School
Joint Special Operations Medical Training Facility, Building 5-3845, Fort Bragg 28307-5000
Type: Public, federal
Degrees: C
URL: https://arsofu.army.mil
Phone: (910) 432-6393
Prog. Accred.: Allied Health (EMT (paramedic))

W.G. (Bill) Hefner Veterans Affairs Medical Center
1601 Brenner Ave., Salisbury 28144
Type: Public, federal
Degrees: C
URL: http://www.salisbury.va.gov
Phone: (704) 638-9000
Prog. Accred.: Allied Health (optometric residency)

Wake Forest University Baptist Medical Center
Medical Center Blvd., Winston-Salem 27157
Type: Private, independent
Degrees: C
URL: http://www.wfubmc.edu
Phone: (800) 446-2255
Prog. Accred.: Clinical Pastoral Education

WakeMed Raleigh
3000 New Bern Ave., Raleigh 27610-1231
Type: Private, independent
Degrees: C
URL: http://www.wakemed.org
Phone: (919) 350-8000
Prog. Accred.: Clinical Pastoral Education

Watts School of Nursing
2828 Croasdaile Dr., Ste. 200, Durham 27705
Type: Private, independent
Degrees: C
URL: http://www.wattsschoolofnursing.org
Phone: (919) 470-7348 *Calendar:* Sem. plan
Prog. Accred.: Nursing

Wilkes Regional Medical Center
1370 West D St., North Wilkesboro 28659
Type: Private, independent
Degrees: C
URL: http://www.wilkesregional.org
Phone: (336) 651-8100
Prog. Accred.: Radiography

NORTH DAKOTA

Altru Hospital
1200 South Columbia Rd., PO Box 6002, Grand Forks 58201
Type: Private, independent
Degrees: C
URL: http://www.altru.org
Phone: (701) 780-5300
Prog. Accred.: Clinical Pastoral Education

Meritcare Hospital
720 4th St. North, Fargo 58122
Type: Private, proprietary
Degrees: C
URL: http://www.meritcare.com
Phone: (701) 234-6000
Prog. Accred.: Radiography

Trinity Medical Center
407 3rd St. SE, Minot 58701
Type: Private, independent
Degrees: C
URL: http://trinity.minot.org
Phone: (701) 857-5000
Prog. Accred.: Radiography

OHIO

88th Medical Group
4881 Sugar Maple Dr., Wright-Patterson AFB 45433-5529
Type: Public, federal
Degrees: C
URL: http://www.wpafb.af.mil/units/wpmc
Phone: (937) 257-9575
Prog. Accred.: Dentistry (advanced education in general dentistry)

Akron General Medical Center
400 Wabash Ave., Akron 44307
Type: Private, independent
Degrees: C
URL: http://www.agmc.org
Phone: (330) 384-6411
Prog. Accred.: Allied Health (EMT (paramedic), cytotechnology), Clinical Pastoral Education

American Red Cross Blood Services—Columbus
995 East Broad St., Columbus 43205
Type: Private, independent
Degrees: C
URL: http://www.bloodsaveslives.org
Phone: (614) 253-7981
Prog. Accred.: Allied Health (blood bank technology)

Applewood Centers, Inc.
2525 East 22nd St., Cleveland 44115-3266
Type: Private, independent
Degrees: C
URL: http://www.applewoodcenters.org
Phone: (216) 696-5800
Prog. Accred.: Psychology Internship

Child and Adolescent Service Center
4801 Dressler Rd., Ste. 130, Belden Village 44718
Type: Private, independent
Degrees: C
URL: http://www.casrv.org
Phone: (330) 649-7373
Prog. Accred.: Psychology Internship

Children's Hospital Medical Center of Akron
One Perkins Square, Akron 44308
Type: Private, independent
Degrees: C
URL: http://www.akronchildrens.org
Phone: (330) 543-1000
Prog. Accred.: Radiography

Chillicothe Veterans Affairs Medical Center
17273 State Route 104, Chillicothe 45601
Type: Public, federal
Degrees: C
URL: http://www.chillicothe.va.gov
Phone: (740) 773-1141
Prog. Accred.: Allied Health (optometric residency)

The Christ Hospital
2139 Auburn Ave., Cincinnati 45219-2906
Type: Private, independent
Degrees: C
Phone: (513) 585-2265
Prog. Accred.: Allied Health (perfusion), Clinical Pastoral Education, Dietetics (internship)

Cincinnati Children's Hospital Medical Center
3333 Burnet Ave., Cincinnati
Type: Private, independent
Degrees: C
URL: http://www.cincinnatichildrens.org
Phone: (513) 636-4200
Prog. Accred.: Clinical Pastoral Education, Dentistry (pediatric dentistry), Psychology Internship

The Cleveland Clinic
9500 Euclid Ave., Cleveland 44195
Type: Private, independent
System: Cleveland Clinic Health System
Degrees: C
URL: http://www.clevelandclinic.org
Phone: (216) 444-2200
Prog. Accred.: Allied Health (perfusion), Clinical Pastoral Education, Dentistry (general practice residency), Dietetics (internship), Nurse Anesthesia Education, Radiation Therapy

Columbus Children's Hospital
700 Children's Dr., Columbus 43205
Type: Private, independent
Degrees: C
URL: http://www.childrenscolumbus.org
Phone: (614) 722-2000
Prog. Accred.: Clinical Pastoral Education

Dayton Veterans Affairs Medical Center
4100 West 3rd St., Dayton 45428
Type: Public, federal
Degrees: C
URL: http://www.dayton.va.gov
Phone: (937) 268-6511
Prog. Accred.: Allied Health (optometric residency), Clinical Pastoral Education, Dentistry (general practice residency)

Euclid Hospital
18901 Lake Shore Blvd., Euclid 44119
Type: Private, independent
System: Cleveland Clinic Health System
Degrees: C
URL: http://www.euclidhospital.org
Phone: (216) 531-9000
Prog. Accred.: Radiography

Firelands Regional Medical Center
1101 Decatur St., Sandusky 44870
Type: Private, independent
Degrees: C
URL: http://www.firelands.com
Phone: (419) 557-7400
Prog. Accred.: Nursing

Hannah E. Mullins School of Practical Nursing
230 North Lincoln Ave., Ste. 3, Salem 44460
Type: Public, local
Degrees: C
URL: http://www.salem.k12.oh.us/Mullins/Mullins.html
Phone: (330) 332-8940
Prog. Accred.: Practical Nursing

Huron Hospital
13951 Terrace Rd., East Cleveland 44112-4399
Type: Private, independent
Degrees: C
URL: http://www.huronhospital.org
Phone: (216) 761-3300
Prog. Accred.: Nursing

Louis Stokes Cleveland Veterans Affairs Medical Center
10701 East Blvd., Cleveland 44106
Type: Public, federal
Degrees: C
URL: http://www.cleveland.va.gov
Phone: (216) 791-3800
Prog. Accred.: Allied Health (optometric residency), Dentistry (general practice residency), Dietetics (internship)

Marietta Memorial Hospital
401 Matthew St., Marietta 45750
Type: Private, independent
Degrees: C
URL: http://www.mmhospital.org
Phone: (740) 374-1400
Prog. Accred.: Radiography

Maxillofacial and Facial Aesthetic Surgery
280 East Town St., Ste. C, Columbus 43215
Type: Private, independent
Degrees: C
Phone: (614) 224-0905
Prog. Accred.: Dentistry (oral and maxillofacial surgery)

Mercy Medical Center
1320 Mercy Dr. NW, Canton 44708
Type: Private, independent
Degrees: C
URL: http://www.cantonmercy.com
Phone: (330) 489-1105
Prog. Accred.: Allied Health (diagnostic medical sonography), Dentistry (general practice residency), Radiography

The MetroHealth Medical Center
2500 MetroHealth Dr., Cleveland 44109-1998
Type: Private, independent
Degrees: C
URL: http://www.metrohealth.org
Phone: (216) 778-7800
Prog. Accred.: Dentistry (general dentistry, general practice residency, oral and maxillofacial surgery, pediatric dentistry), Dietetics (internship)

Miami Valley Hospital
1 Wyoming St., Dayton 45409
Type: Private, independent
Degrees: C
URL: http://www.miamivalleyhospital.com
Phone: (937) 208-8000
Prog. Accred.: Dentistry (general practice residency), Dietetics (internship)

Mount Carmel West
793 West State St., Columbus 43222
Type: Private, independent
Degrees: C
URL: http://www.mountcarmelhealth.com
Phone: (614) 234-5000
Prog. Accred.: Clinical Pastoral Education

Parma Community General Hospital
7007 Powers Blvd., Parma 44129
Type: Private, independent
Degrees: C
URL: http://www.parmahospital.org
Phone: (440) 743-4900
Prog. Accred.: Allied Health (EMT (paramedic))

Riverside Methodist Hospital
3535 Olentangy River Rd., Columbus 43214
Type: Private, independent
Degrees: C
URL: http://www.ohiohealth.com
Phone: (614) 566-5000
Prog. Accred.: Clinical Pastoral Education

Saint Elizabeth Health Center
1044 Belmont Ave., PO Box 1790, Youngstown 44501
Type: Private, independent
Degrees: C
URL: http://www.ehealthconnection.com/regions/youngstown
Phone: (330) 746-7211 *Calendar:* 24-mos. pr
Prog. Accred.: Dentistry (general practice residency), Nurse Anesthesia Education

Saint Elizabeth Health Center
1044 Belmont Ave., Youngstown 44501-1790
Type: Private, independent
Degrees: C
URL: http://www.ehealthconnection.com/regions/youngstown
Phone: (330) 746-7211 *Calendar:* 24-mos. pr
Prog. Accred.: Dentistry (general practice residency), Nurse Anesthesia Education

Saint Vincent Charity Hospital
2351 East 22nd St., Cleveland 44115
Type: Private, independent
Degrees: C
URL: http://www.svch.net
Phone: (216) 861-6200
Prog. Accred.: Clinical Pastoral Education

HealthCare Center at Saint Luke's Pointe
11201 Shaker Blvd., Cleveland 44104
Phone: (216) 721-6900
Prog. Accred: Dentistry (general practice residency)

Saint Vincent Mercy Medical Center
2213 Cherry St., Toledo 43608-2801
Type: Private, independent
Degrees: C
URL: http://www.mercyweb.org
Phone: (419) 251-3232
Prog. Accred.: Clinical Lab Scientist, Clinical Pastoral Education

Sleep Care, Inc.
7634 Rivers Edge Dr., Columbus 43235
Type: Private, proprietary
Degrees: C
URL: http://www.sleepcareinc.com
Phone: (866) 320-8989
Prog. Accred.: Polysomnographic Technology

Spiritual Care and Education Center
915 North Reynolds Rd., Toledo 43615
Type: Private, independent
Degrees: C
URL: http://www.scec-cpe.org
Phone: (419) 536-9351
Prog. Accred.: Clinical Pastoral Education

Spiritual Care and Education Center
915 North Reynolds Rd., Toledo 43615
Type: Private, independent
Degrees: C
URL: http://www.scec-cpe.org
Phone: (419) 536-9351
Prog. Accred.: Clinical Pastoral Education

Springfield Regional Medical Center
2615 East High St., Springfield 45505
Type: Private, independent
Degrees: C
URL: http://www.ehealthconnection.com/regions/springfield
Phone: (937) 328-8900 *Calendar:* Sem. plan
Prog. Accred.: Nursing

TriHealth Good Samaritan Hospital
375 Dixmyth Ave., Cincinnati 45220-2489
Type: Private, independent
Degrees: C
URL: http://www.trihealth.com
Phone: (513) 872-1400
Prog. Accred.: Clinical Pastoral Education, Dietetics (internship)

Trinity Health System School of Nursing
380 Summit Ave., Steubenville 43952
Type: Private, independent
Degrees: C
URL: http://www.trinityson.com
Phone: (740) 283-7467 *Calendar:* Sem. plan
Prog. Accred.: Nursing

Trumbull Memorial Hospital
1350 East Market St., Warren 44482
Type: Private, independent
Degrees: C
URL: http://www.forumhealth.com
Phone: (330) 841-9011
Prog. Accred.: Phlebotomy

Twin Towers Senior Living Community
5343 Hamilton Ave., Cincinnati 45224-3130
Type: Private, independent
Degrees: C
URL: http://www.twintowers.org/twintowers.htm
Phone: (513) 719-3556
Prog. Accred.: Clinical Pastoral Education

Upper Valley Medical Center
3130 North Dixie Hwy., Troy 45373-1337
Type: Private, independent
Degrees: C
URL: http://www.uvmc.com
Phone: (937) 440-4000
Prog. Accred.: Clinical Pastoral Education

Veterans Affairs Medical Center Cincinnati
3200 Vine St., Cincinnati 45828
Type: Public, federal
Degrees: C
URL: http://www.cincinnati.va.gov
Phone: (513) 861-3100
Prog. Accred.: Allied Health (optometric residency)

Western Reserve Care System
345 Oak Hill Ave., Youngstown 44501
Type: Private, independent
Degrees: C
URL: http://www.forumhealth.org/forumhealth/med_ed/intro.php
Phone: (330) 884-3572
Prog. Accred.: Dentistry (general practice residency)

OKLAHOMA

Canadian Valley Technology Center
1401 Michigan Ave., Chickasha 73018
Type: Public, local
Degrees: C
URL: http://www.cvtech.org/Chickasha
Phone: (405) 224-7220
Prog. Accred.: Practical Nursing

El Reno Campus
6505 East Hwy. 66, El Reno 73036
Phone: (405) 262-2629
Prog. Accred: Allied Health (surgical technology), Practical Nursing

The Children's Hospital at OU Medical Center
940 NE 13th St., Oklahoma City 73104
Type: Private, independent
Degrees: C
URL: http://www.oumedical.com
Phone: (405) 271-4700
Prog. Accred.: Dentistry (general practice residency)

Francis Tuttle Technology Center
12777 North Rockwell Ave., Oklahoma City 73142-2789
Type: Public, local
Degrees: C
URL: http://www.francistuttle.com
Phone: (405) 717-7799
Prog. Accred.: Allied Health (medical assisting (AMA), respiratory therapy), Practical Nursing

Heritage College
7100 South I-35 Service Rd., Ste. 7118, Oklahoma City 73149
Type: Private, proprietary, two-year
Degrees: A
URL: http://www.heritage-education.com
Phone: (888) 334-7339
Prog. Accred.: Allied Health (surgical technology)

Hillcrest Medical Center
1120 South Utica Ave., Tulsa 74104-4012
Type: Private, independent
Degrees: C
URL: http://www.hillcrest.com
Phone: (918) 579-1000
Prog. Accred.: Clinical Pastoral Education

Integris Baptist Medical Center
3030 Northwest Expressway, Oklahoma City 73112
Type: Private, independent
Degrees: C
URL: http://www.integris-health.com
Phone: (405) 949-3011
Prog. Accred.: Clinical Pastoral Education

Jack C. Montgomery Veterans Affairs Medical Center
1011 Honor Heights Dr., Muskogee 74401
Type: Public, federal
Degrees: C
URL: http://www.muskogee.va.gov
Phone: (918) 577-3000
Prog. Accred.: Allied Health (optometric residency)

Meridian Technology Center
1312 South Sangre St., Stillwater 74074
Type: Public, local
Degrees: C
URL: http://www.meridian-technology.com
Phone: (405) 377-3333 *Calendar:* Qtr. plan
Prog. Accred.: Practical Nursing, Radiography

Oklahoma City Veterans Affairs Medical Center
921 NE 13th St., Oklahoma City 73104
Type: Public, federal
Degrees: C
URL: http://www.oklahoma.va.gov
Phone: (405) 270-0501
Prog. Accred.: Clinical Pastoral Education, Dentistry (general practice residency)

OU Medical Center
1200 Everett Dr., Oklahoma City 73104
Type: Private, independent
Degrees: C
URL: http://www.oumedical.com
Phone: (405) 271-4700
Prog. Accred.: Clinical Pastoral Education

Red River Technology Center
PO Box 1087, Duncan 73533
Type: Public, local
Degrees: C
URL: http://www.redriver.tec.ok.us
Phone: (580) 255-2903
Prog. Accred.: Practical Nursing

Saint Anthony Hospital
1000 North Lee St., Oklahoma City 73102
Type: Private, independent
Degrees: C
URL: http://www.saintsok.com
Phone: (405) 272-7000
Prog. Accred.: Dentistry (general practice residency)

Saint Francis Hospital
6161 South Yale Ave., Tulsa 74136
Type: Private, independent
Degrees: C
URL: http://www.sfh-tulsa.com
Phone: (918) 494-2200
Prog. Accred.: Clinical Lab Scientist

Southern Oklahoma Technology Center
2610 Sam Noble Pkwy., Ardmore 73401
Type: Private, independent
Degrees: C
URL: http://www.sotc.org
Phone: (580) 223-2070
Prog. Accred.: Allied Health (surgical technology), Practical Nursing

W. W. Hastings Indian Hospital
100 South Bliss, Tahlequah 74464
Type: Private, tribal
Degrees: C
Phone: (918) 458-3100
Prog. Accred.: Dentistry (general practice residency)

Western Technology Center
621 Sooner Dr., Burns Flat 73624
Type: Public, local
Degrees: C
URL: http://www.wtc.tec.ok.us
Phone: (580) 562-3181
Prog. Accred.: Practical Nursing

OREGON

Capital Manor Retirement Community
1955 Salem Dallas Hwy. NW, Ste. 1200, Salem 97304
Type: Private, proprietary
Degrees: C
URL: http://www.capitalmanor.com
Phone: (503) 362-4101
Prog. Accred.: Dietetics (internship)

College of Emergency Services
2016 SE Sherrett St., Clackamas 97202
Type: Private, proprietary
Degrees: C
URL: http://www.ces-ems.org
Phone: (503) 502-5229
Prog. Accred.: Allied Health (EMT (paramedic))

Legacy Emanuel Children's Hospital
2801 North Gantenbein Ave., Portland 97227
Type: Private, independent
Degrees: C
URL: http://www.legacyhealth.org
Phone: (503) 413-2200
Prog. Accred.: Clinical Pastoral Education

Oregon State Hospital
2600 Center St., NE, Salem 97310
Type: Public, state
Degrees: C
URL: http://www.oregon.gov/DHS/mentalhealth/osh/main.shtml
Phone: (503) 945-2800
Prog. Accred.: Clinical Pastoral Education

Portland Veterans Affairs Medical Center
3710 SW U.S. Veterans Hospital Rd., Portland 97207-1034
Type: Public, federal
Degrees: C
URL: http://www.visn20.med.va.gov/portland
Phone: (503) 220-8262
Prog. Accred.: Allied Health (optometric residency), Clinical Pastoral Education, Dentistry (combined prosthodontics, general practice residency)

Providence Portland Medical Center
4805 NE Glisan St., Portland 97213
Type: Private, independent
Degrees: C
URL: http://www.providence.org/oregon/facilities/hospitals
Phone: (503) 215-1111
Prog. Accred.: Clinical Pastoral Education

Roseburg Veterans Affairs Medical Center
913 NW Garden Valley Blvd., Roseburg 97470-6513
Type: Public, federal
Degrees: C
URL: http://www.visn20.med.va.gov/roseburg
Phone: (541) 440-1000
Prog. Accred.: Allied Health (optometric residency)

Sacred Heart Medical Center
1255 Hilyard St., Eugene 97401
Type: Private, independent
Degrees: C
URL: http://www.peacehealth.org/Oregon/WhoWeAreSHMC.htm
Phone: (541) 686-7300
Prog. Accred.: Clinical Pastoral Education

Salem Veterans Affairs Medical Center
617 Chemeketa St., NE, Salem 97301
Type: Public, federal, four-year
Degrees: P
URL: http://www1.va.gov
Phone: (503) 362-9911
Prog. Accred.: Allied Health (optometric residency)

Veterans Affairs Southern Oregon Rehabilitation Center and Clinics
8495 Crater Lake Hwy., White City 97503
Type: Public, federal
Degrees: C
URL: http://www1.va.gov
Phone: (541) 826-2111
Prog. Accred.: Clinical Pastoral Education

PENNSYLVANIA

Abington Memorial Health Center—Schilling Campus
2500 Maryland Rd., Willow Grove 19090-1284
Type: Private, independent
Degrees: C
URL: http://www.amh.org
Phone: (215) 481-5526
Prog. Accred.: Nuclear Medicine Technology, Nursing, Radiography

Abington Memorial Hospital
1200 Old York Rd., Abington 19001
Type: Private, independent
Degrees: C
URL: http://www.amh.org
Phone: (215) 481-2000
Prog. Accred.: Clinical Pastoral Education, Dentistry (general practice residency)

Adagio Healthcare
960 Penn Ave., Ste. 600, Pittsburgh 15222-1417
Type: Private, independent
Degrees: C
URL: http://www.adagiohealth.org
Phone: (412) 288-2130 ext 1
Prog. Accred.: Dietetics (internship)

Albert Einstein Medical Center
5501 Old York Rd., Philadelphia 19141
Type: Private, independent
Degrees: C
URL: http://www.einstein.edu
Phone: (215) 456-7890
Prog. Accred.: Clinical Pastoral Education, Dentistry (endodontics, general practice residency, orthodontic and dentofacial orthopedics), Radiography

Allegheny General Hospital
320 East North Ave., Pittsburgh 15212
Type: Private, independent
Degrees: C
URL: http://www.allhealth.edu/agh
Phone: (412) 359-3131
Prog. Accred.: Dentistry (general practice residency, oral and maxillofacial surgery), Psychology Internship

ARAMARK Healthcare Mid-Atlantic Dietetic Internship Program
1717 Arch St.,, Bell Atlantic Tower, 42nd Flr., Philadelphia 19103
Type: Private, proprietary
Degrees: C
URL: http://www.aramark.com
Phone: (215) 409-7653
Prog. Accred.: Dietetics (internship)

Armstrong County Memorial Hospital
One Nolte Dr., Kittanning 16201
Type: Private, independent
Degrees: C
URL: http://www.acmh.org
Phone: (724) 543-8500 *Calendar:* 24-mos. pr
Prog. Accred.: Radiography

Bradford Regional Medical Center
116 Interstate Pkwy., Bradford 16701
Type: Private, independent
Degrees: C
URL: http://www.brmc.com
Phone: (814) 368-4143
Prog. Accred.: Radiography

Brandywine Hospital
201 Reeceville Rd., Coatesville 19320
Type: Private, independent
Degrees: C
URL: http://www.brandywinehospital.com
Phone: (610) 383-8000
Prog. Accred.: Nursing

Career Technology Center of Lackawanna County
3201 Rockwell Ave., Scranton 18508
Type: Public, local
Degrees: C
URL: http://www.ctc.tec.pa.us
Phone: (717) 346-8728
Prog. Accred.: Practical Nursing

Center for Arts and Technology
1635 E. Lincoln Hwy., Coatesville 19320
Type: Public, local
Degrees: C
URL: http://www.cciu.org/pnp
Phone: (610) 384-1585
Prog. Accred.: Practical Nursing

Center for Emergency Medicine of Western Pennsylvania
230 McKee Place, Ste. 500, Pittsburgh 15213
Type: Private, independent
Degrees: C
URL: http://www.centerem.org
Phone: (412) 647-5300
Prog. Accred.: Allied Health (EMT (paramedic))

Central Pennsylvania Institute of Science and Technology
540 North Harrison Rd., Pleasant Gap 16823
Type: Public, state/local
Degrees: C
URL: http://www.cpi.tec.pa.us
Phone: (814) 359-2582
Prog. Accred.: Practical Nursing

Central Susquehanna LPN Career Center
1145 North 4th St., Sunbury 17801
Type: Public, state/local
Degrees: C
URL: http://www.csiu.org/lpn
Phone: (570) 988-6760
Prog. Accred.: Practical Nursing

Children's Hospital of Philadelphia
34th St. and Civic Center Blvd., Philadelphia 19104-4399
Type: Private, independent
Degrees: C
URL: http://www.chop.edu
Phone: (215) 590-1000
Prog. Accred.: Psychology Internship

Children's Hospital of Pittsburgh
3705 Fifth Ave., Pittsburgh 15213
Type: Private, independent
Degrees: C
URL: http://www.chp.edu
Phone: (412) 692-5325
Prog. Accred.: Dentistry (pediatric dentistry)

Citizens School of Nursing
651Fourth Ave., New Kensington 15068
Type: Private, independent
Degrees: C
URL: http://www.wpahs.org/akmc
Phone: (724) 337-5090
Prog. Accred.: Nursing

Clarion County Career Center
447 Career Rd., Shippenville 16254-8975
Type: Public, local
Degrees: C
URL: http://www.ccccntr.org
Phone: (814) 226-4391
Prog. Accred.: Practical Nursing

Clearfield County Career and Technology Center
1620 River Rd., Clearfield 16830
Type: Public, local
Degrees: C
URL: http://www.ccctc.org
Phone: (814) 765-5308
Prog. Accred.: Practical Nursing

Clearfield Hospital
809 Turnpike Ave., PO Box 992, Clearfield 16830
Type: Private, independent
Degrees: C
URL: http://www.clearfieldhosp.org
Phone: (814) 765-5341
Prog. Accred.: Radiography

Conemaugh Memorial Medical Center
1086 Franklin St., Johnstown 15905
Type: Private, independent
Degrees: C
URL: http://www.conemaugh.org
Phone: (814) 534-9000
Prog. Accred.: Allied Health (surgical technology), Histologic Technology, Nursing, Radiography

Council for Relationahips
4025 Chestnut St., Philadelphia 19104
Type: Private, proprietary
Degrees: C
URL: http://www.councilforrelationships.org
Phone: (215) 382-6680
Prog. Accred.: Marriage and Family Therapy

Crawford County Area Vocational Technical School
860 Thurston Rd., Meadville 16335
Type: Public, local
Degrees: C
URL: http://www.ccvts.org
Phone: (814) 724-6024
Prog. Accred.: Practical Nursing

Crozer-Chester Medical Center
One Medical Center Blvd., Upland 19013
Type: Private, independent
Degrees: C
URL: http://www.crozer.org
Phone: (610) 447-2000
Prog. Accred.: Allied Health (diagnostic medical sonography, electroneurodiagnostic technology, respiratory therapy), Radiography

Delaware County Technical School
Delmar Dr. & Henderson Blvd., Folcroft 19032
Type: Public, state/local
Degrees: C
URL: http://www.dciu.org/dccte
Phone: (610) 583-7620
Prog. Accred.: Practical Nursing

The Devereux Institute of Clinical Training and Research
444 Devereux Dr., Villanova 19085
Type: Private, independent
Degrees: C
URL: http://www.devereux.org
Phone: (610) 542-3059
Prog. Accred.: Psychology Internship

Eastern Center for Arts and Technology
3075 Terwood Rd., Willow Grove 19090
Type: Public, local
Degrees: C
URL: http://www.eastech.org
Phone: (215) 784-4805
Prog. Accred.: Practical Nursing

Erie Psychological Consortium
120 East 2nd St., Third Flr., Erie 16550
Type: Private, independent
Degrees: C
URL: http://www.safeharborbh.org/eriepsychcons.htm
Phone: (814) 878-1200
Prog. Accred.: Psychology Internship

Fayette County Area Vocational Technical School
175 Georges Fairchance Rd., Uniontown 15401
Type: Public, local
Degrees: C
URL: http://www.fayettevo-tech.org
Phone: (724) 437-2721
Prog. Accred.: Practical Nursing

Frankford Hospital
4918 Penn St., Philadelphia 19124-2696
Type: Private, independent
Degrees: C
URL: http://www.frankfordhospitals.org
Phone: (215) 831-6740 *Calendar:* Sem. plan
Prog. Accred.: Nursing

Franklin County Career and Technology Center
2463 Loop Rd., Chambersberg 17201
Type: Public, local
Degrees: C
URL: http://www.franklinctc.com
Phone: (717) 263-9033
Prog. Accred.: Practical Nursing

Friends Hospital
4641 Roosevelt Blvd., Philadelphia 19124
Type: Private, Religious Society of Friends
Degrees: C
URL: http://www.friendshospitalonline.org
Phone: (800) 889-0548
Prog. Accred.: Psychology Internship

Geisinger Medical Center
100 North Academy Ave., Danville 17822
Type: Private, independent
Degrees: C
URL: http://www.geisinger.org
Phone: (570) 271-3700
Prog. Accred.: Allied Health (cardiovascular technology), Clinical Pastoral Education, Dietetics (internship), Psychology Internship, Radiography

Gettysburg Hospital
PO Box 3786, Gettysburg 17325-0786
Type: Private, independent
Degrees: C
URL: http://www.wellspan.org
Phone: (717) 334-2121
Prog. Accred.: Clinical Pastoral Education

Greene County Career and Technology Center
60 Zimmerman Dr., Waynesburg 15370-8281
Type: Public, local
Degrees: C
URL: http://www.grvt.org
Phone: (412) 627-3106
Prog. Accred.: Practical Nursing

Hanover Public School District
403 Moul Ave., Hanover 17331-1541
Type: Public, local
Degrees: C
URL: http://www.hpsd.k12.pa.us
Phone: (717) 637-2111
Prog. Accred.: Practical Nursing

Hazelton Area Career Center
1451 West 23rd St., Hazleton 18201
Type: Public, local
Degrees: C
URL: http://www.hasd.k12.pa.us
Phone: (570) 459-3178
Prog. Accred.: Practical Nursing

Heritage Valley Sewickley School of Nursing
420 Rouser Rd., Airport Office Park, Bldg. 3, Moon Township 15108
Type: Private, independent
Degrees: C
URL: http://www.heritagevalley.org
Phone: (412) 741-6600
Prog. Accred.: Nursing, Radiography

Holy Spirit Hospital
503 North 21st St., Camp Hill 17011-2288
Type: Private, Roman Catholic Church
Degrees: C
URL: http://www.hsh.org
Phone: (717) 763-2100
Prog. Accred.: Radiography

Huntingdon County Career and Technology Center
PO Box E, Mill Creek 17060
Type: Public, state/local
Degrees: C
URL: http://www.tiu.k12.pa.us/~hcctcwp
Phone: (814) 643-0951
Prog. Accred.: Practical Nursing

Jameson Hospital—North
1211 Wilmington Ave., New Castle 16105
Type: Private, independent
Degrees: C
URL: http://www.jamesonhealthsystem.com
Phone: (724) 658-9001
Prog. Accred.: Nursing, Radiography

Jameson Hospital—South
1000 South Mercer St., New Castle 16101
Type: Private, independent
Degrees: C
URL: http://www.jamesonhealthsystem.com
Phone: (724) 656-4134
Prog. Accred.: Nuclear Medicine Technology

Jeanes Hospital
7600 Central Ave., Philadelphia 19111-2442
Type: Private, independent
Degrees: C
URL: http://www.jeanes.com
Phone: (215) 728-2036
Prog. Accred.: Clinical Pastoral Education

Jefferson County-DuBois Area Vocational Technical School
100 Jeff Tech Dr., Reynoldsville 15851
Type: Public, local
Degrees: C
URL: http://www.jefftech.tec.pa.us
Phone: (814) 653-8265
Prog. Accred.: Practical Nursing

Lancaster General Hospital
555 North Duke St., Lancaster 17604-3555
Type: Private, independent
Degrees: C
URL: http://www.lancastergeneral.org
Phone: (717) 544-5511
Prog. Accred.: Clinical Pastoral Education

Lancaster Cleft Palate Clinic
223 North Lime St., Lancaster 17602
Phone: (717) 394-3793
Prog. Accred: Dentistry (general dentistry)

Lawrence County Career and Technical Center
750 Phelps Way, New Castle 16101
Type: Public, local
Degrees: C
URL: http://www.lcvt.tec.pa.us
Phone: (724) 658-3583
Prog. Accred.: Practical Nursing

Lebanon County Career and Technology Center
833 Metro Dr., Lebanon 17042
Type: Public, local
Degrees: C
URL: http://www.lcctc.k12.pa.us
Phone: (717) 273-8551
Prog. Accred.: Practical Nursing

Lehigh Valley Hospital—17th and Chew Streets
PO Box 7017, Allentown 18105-7017
Type: Private, independent
Degrees: C
URL: http://www.lvh.org/lvh/Locations/17th__Chew
Phone: (610) 402-8000
Prog. Accred.: Dentistry (general practice residency)

Lehigh Valley Hospital—Cedar Crest & I-78
PO Box 689, Allentown 18105
Type: Private, independent
Degrees: C
URL: http://www.lvh.org/lvh/Locations/Cedar_Crest
Phone: (610) 402-2273
Prog. Accred.: Allied Health (EMT (paramedic)), Clinical Pastoral Education

Lehigh Valley Hospital—Muhlenberg
2545 Schoenersville Rd., Bethlehem 18017
Type: Private, independent
Degrees: C
URL: http://www.lvh.org/lvh/Locations/Muhlenberg
Phone: (610) 402-2273
Prog. Accred.: Dentistry (general practice residency)

Lenape Area Vocational Technical School
2215 Chaplin Ave., Ford City 16226
Type: Public, local
Degrees: C
URL: http://www.lenape.k12.pa.us
Phone: (724) 763-7116
Prog. Accred.: Practical Nursing

Magee-Womens Hospital
300 Halket St., Pittsburgh 15213-3180
Type: Private, independent
Degrees: C
URL: http://magee.upmc.com
Phone: (412) 641-1000
Prog. Accred.: Allied Health (cytotechnology)

Mifflin Juniata Career and Technology Center
700 Pitt St., Lewistown 17044
Type: Public, local
Degrees: C
URL: http://www.mjctc.org
Phone: (717) 248-3933
Prog. Accred.: Practical Nursing

Nazareth Hospital
2601 Holme Ave., Philadelphia 19152
Type: Private, independent, four-year
Degrees: C, M
URL: http://www.nazarethhospital.org
Phone: (215) 335-6000
Prog. Accred.: Nurse Anesthesia Education

Northeastern Hospital School of Nursing
Helene Fuld Bldg., 2301 East Allegheny Ave., Philadelphia 19134
Type: Private, independent
Degrees: C
URL: http://www.nehson.templehealth.org
Phone: (215) 291-3172 *Calendar:* Sem. plan
Prog. Accred.: Nursing

Northern Tier Career Center
Rural Route 1, PO Box 157A, Towanda 18848-9731
Type: Public, local
Degrees: C
URL: http://www.ntccschool.org
Phone: (570) 265-8111
Prog. Accred.: Practical Nursing

Ohio Valley General Hospital
25 Heckel Rd., McKees Rocks 15136
Type: Private, independent, two-year
Degrees: C, A
URL: http://www.ohiovalleyhospital.org
Phone: (412) 777-6200
Prog. Accred.: Nursing, Radiography

Penn Foundation, Inc.
807 Lawn Ave., Sellersville 18960
Type: Private, independent
Degrees: C
URL: http://www.pennfoundation.org
Phone: (215) 257-6551
Prog. Accred.: Clinical Pastoral Education

Philadelphia Child and Family Therapy Training Center
PO Box 4092, Philadelphia 19118-8092
Type: Private, proprietary
Degrees: C
URL: http://www.philafamily.com
Phone: (215) 242-0949
Prog. Accred.: Marriage and Family Therapy

Philadelphia Veterans Affairs Medical Center
University & Woodland Avenues, Philadelphia 19104
Type: Public, federal
Degrees: C
URL: http://www.philadelphia.va.gov
Phone: (215) 823-5800
Prog. Accred.: Allied Health (optometric residency), Dentistry (general practice residency)

Philhaven
283 South Butler Rd., Mt. Gretna 17064
Type: Private, Lancaster Conference of Mennonite Churches
Degrees: C
URL: http://www.philhaven.com
Phone: (717) 273-8871
Prog. Accred.: Clinical Pastoral Education

Phoebe Ministries
1925 Turner St., Allentown 18104
Type: Private, independent
Degrees: C
URL: http://www.phoebe.org
Phone: (610) 794-5119
Prog. Accred.: Clinical Pastoral Education

The Pottsville Hospital and Warne Clinic
420 South Jackson St., Pottsville 17901
Type: Private, independent
Degrees: C
URL: http://www.pottsvillehospital.com
Phone: (570) 621-5000 *Calendar:* Sem. plan
Prog. Accred.: Nursing

The Reading Hospital and Medical Center
Sixth Ave. and Spruce St., PO Box 16052, West Reading 19612-6052
Type: Private, independent
Degrees: C
URL: http://www.readinghospital.org
Phone: (610) 988-4357
Prog. Accred.: Allied Health (surgical technology), Clinical Pastoral Education, Nursing, Radiography

Roxborough Memorial Hospital
5800 Ridge Ave., Philadelphia 19128
Type: Private, independent
Degrees: C
URL: http://www.roxboroughmemorial.com
Phone: (215) 483-9900 *Calendar:* Qtr. plan
Prog. Accred.: Nursing

Sacred Heart Hospital
421 Chew St., Allentown 18102
Type: Private, independent
Degrees: C
URL: http://www.shh.org
Phone: (610) 776-4500
Prog. Accred.: Dentistry (general practice residency)

Saint Christopher's Hospital for Children
Erie Ave. at Front St., Philadelphia 19134
Type: Private, independent
Degrees: C
URL: http://www.stchristophershospital.com
Phone: (215) 427-5000
Prog. Accred.: Dentistry (pediatric dentistry), Radiography

Saint Joseph Medical Center
145 North Sixth St., Reading 19604
Type: Private, independent
Degrees: C
URL: http://www.sjmcberks.org
Phone: (610) 378-2000
Prog. Accred.: Dentistry (general practice residency), Radiography

Saint Luke's Hospital
801 Ostrum St., Bethlehem 18015-1014
Type: Private, independent
Degrees: C
URL: http://www.slhn-lehighvalley.org
Phone: (610) 954-4000
Prog. Accred.: Allied Health (surgical technology), Clinical Pastoral Education, Nursing

Saint Mary Medical Center
Langhorne-Newtown Rd., Langhorne 19047-1295
Type: Private, independent
Degrees: C
URL: http://www.stmaryhealthcare.org
Phone: (215) 938-3820
Prog. Accred.: Clinical Pastoral Education

Sharon Regional Health System
740 East State State, Sharon 16146
Type: Private, independent
Degrees: C
URL: http://www.sharonregional.com
Phone: (724) 983-5518
Prog. Accred.: Nursing, Radiography

Sodexo Health Care Services Allentown
PO Box 3501, Allentown 18106-0501
Type: Private, proprietary
Degrees: C
URL: http://www.dieteticintern.com
Phone: (484) 201-2533
Prog. Accred.: Dietetics (internship)

Sodexo Health Care Services NJ/Philadelphia Metro Dietetic Internship
PO Box 602-0601, Washington Cross 18977
Type: Private, proprietary
Degrees: C
URL: http://www.dieteticintern.com/NJ-Phila
Phone: (215) 612-4615
Prog. Accred.: Dietetics (internship)

Somerset County Technology Center
281 Technology Dr., Somerset 15501
Type: Public, local
Degrees: C
URL: http://www.sctc.net
Phone: (814) 443-3651
Prog. Accred.: Allied Health (medical assisting (AMA))

Temple University Hospital—Episcopal Campus
100 East Lehigh Ave., Philadelphia 19125-1098
Type: Private, independent
Degrees: C
URL: www.health.temple.edu
Phone: (215) 707-1200
Prog. Accred.: Nursing

University of Pittsburgh Medical Center Northwest
100 Fairfield Dr., Seneca 16346
Type: Public, independent
Degrees: C
URL: http://northwest.upmc.com
Phone: (814) 676-7600 *Calendar:* Sem. plan
Prog. Accred.: Radiography

University of Pittsburgh Medical Center Shadyside
5230 Centre Ave., Pittsburgh 15232-1381
Type: Private, independent
Degrees: C
URL: http://shadyside.upmc.com
Phone: (412) 623-2121
Prog. Accred.: Dietetics (internship), Nursing

University of Pittsburgh Medical Center Presbyterian
200 Lothrop St., Pittsburgh 15213-2582
Phone: (412) 647-2345
Prog. Accred: Allied Health (perfusion), Dentistry (oral and maxillofacial pathology), Radiography

UPMC Mercy
1401 Blvd. of the Allies, Pittsburgh 15219
Type: Private, independent
Degrees: C
URL: http://www.pmhs.org/schoolofnursing
Phone: (412) 232-8111 *Calendar:* Qtr. plan
Prog. Accred.: Nursing

UPMC Saint Margaret Hospital
221 Seventh St., Commons Bldg., Pittsburgh 15238
Type: Private, independent
Degrees: C
URL: http://stmargaret.upmc.com
Phone: (412) 784-4980
Prog. Accred.: Nursing, Practical Nursing

Venango Technology Center
1 Vo-Tech Dr., Oil City 16301
Type: Public, local
Degrees: C
URL: http://www.vtc1.org
Phone: (814) 677-3097
Prog. Accred.: Practical Nursing

Vet Tech Institute
125 Seventh St., Pittsburgh 15222
Type: Private, proprietary
Degrees: C
URL: http://www.vettechinstitute.edu
Phone: (412) 391-7021
Prog. Accred.: Veterinary Technology

Veterans Affairs Pittsburgh Healthcare System, Highland Drive Division
7180 Highland Dr., Pittsburgh 15206
Type: Private, federal
Degrees: C
URL: http://www.va.gov/pittsburgh/highland.htm
Phone: (412) 365-4900
Prog. Accred.: Clinical Pastoral Education, Dentistry (general practice residency)

The Washington Hospital
155 Wilson Ave., Washington 15301
Type: Private, independent
Degrees: C
URL: http://www.washingtonhospital.org
Phone: (724) 225-7000
Prog. Accred.: Radiography

Wilkes-Barre General Hospital
575 North River St., Wilkes-Barre 18764-0001
Type: Private, independent
Degrees: C
URL: http://www.wvhc.org
Phone: (570) 829-8111 *Calendar:* 12-mos. pr
Prog. Accred.: Allied Health (diagnostic medical sonography), Nuclear Medicine Technology, Radiography

Wilkes-Barre Veterans Affairs Medical Center
1111 East End Blvd., Wilkes-Barre 18711
Type: Public, federal
Degrees: C
URL: http://www.va.gov/vamcwb
Phone: (570) 824-3521
Prog. Accred.: Allied Health (optometric residency), Dentistry (general practice residency)

York County School of Technology
2179 South Queen St., York 17402
Type: Public, local
Degrees: C
URL: http://www.ycstech.org
Phone: (717) 741-0820
Prog. Accred.: Practical Nursing

York Hospital Community Health Center
605 South George St., York 17401
Type: Private, independent
Degrees: C
URL: http://www.wellspan.org
Phone: (717) 851-2334
Prog. Accred.: Clinical Pastoral Education, Dentistry (general practice residency)

PUERTO RICO

Puerto Rico Department of Health
PO Box 70184, San Juan 00936
Type: Public, state
Degrees: C
Phone: (787) 977-2128
Prog. Accred.: Dietetics (internship)

Ryder Memorial Hospital, Inc.
355 Font Martelo, Humacao 00791
Type: Private, proprietary
Degrees: C
Phone: (787) 656-0711
Prog. Accred.: Practical Nursing

Veterans Affairs Caribbean Healthcare System
10 Casia St., San Juan 00921-3201
Type: Public, federal
Degrees: C
URL: http://www1.va.gov/directory
Phone: (787) 641-7582
Prog. Accred.: Allied Health (optometric residency), Dentistry (general practice residency), Dietetics (internship)

RHODE ISLAND

The Chaplaincy Center
Gerry House #36, 593 Eddy St., Providence 02903-4970
Type: Private, independent
Degrees: C
URL: http://www.thechaplaincycenter.com
Phone: (401) 444-8356
Prog. Accred.: Clinical Pastoral Education

Memorial Hospital of Rhode Island
111 Brewster St., Pawtucket 02860
Type: Private, independent, four-year
Degrees: M
URL: http://www.howtocms.com/6
Phone: (401) 729-2000
Prog. Accred.: Nurse Anesthesia Education

Rhode Island Hospital
593 Eddy St., Providence 02903
Type: Private, independent
Degrees: C
URL: http://ww.nwcr.ws/rih
Phone: (401) 444-4000
Prog. Accred.: Allied Health (diagnostic medical sonography), Dentistry (general practice residency), Nuclear Medicine Technology, Radiography

Saint Joseph Hospital School of Anesthesia for Nurses
200 High Service Ave., North Providence 02904
Type: Private, independent, four-year
Degrees: M
URL: http://www.fatimahospital.com/services/anesthesia.asp
Phone: (401) 456-3639
Prog. Accred.: Nurse Anesthesia Education

Saint Joseph School of Nursing
200 High Service Ave., Our Lady of Fatima Hospital, Marian Hall, North Providence 02904
Type: Private, independent
Degrees: C
URL: http://www.nursingri.com
Phone: (401) 456-3050
Prog. Accred.: Nursing

SOUTH CAROLINA

Anderson Area Medical Center
800 North Fant St., Anderson 29621
Type: Private, independent
Degrees: C
URL: http://www.anmed.com
Phone: (864) 261-1000
Prog. Accred.: Clinical Pastoral Education, Radiography

Bon Secours Saint Francis Hospital
2095 Henry Tecklenburg Dr., Charleston 29414-5733
Type: Private, independent
Degrees: C
URL: http://www.carealliance.com
Phone: (843) 402-1000
Prog. Accred.: Clinical Pastoral Education, Clinical Pastoral Education (USCC)

C.M. Tucker, Jr. Nursing Care Center
2200 Harden St., Columbia 29203
Type: Private, independent
Degrees: C
URL: http://www.state.sc.us/dmh/cmtucker_dowdy/
Phone: (803) 737-5301
Prog. Accred.: Clinical Pastoral Education

Marion County Technical Education Center
PO Box 890, Marion 29571
Type: Public, local
Degrees: C
URL: http://www.mctec.org
Phone: (843) 423-1941
Prog. Accred.: Practical Nursing

Palmetto Health Baptist Hospital
Taylor at Marion St.s, Columbia 29220
Type: Private, independent
Degrees: C
URL: http://www.palmettohealth.org
Phone: (803) 296-5010
Prog. Accred.: Clinical Pastoral Education

Palmetto Richland Memorial Hospital
Five Richland Medical Park, Columbia 29203
Type: Private, independent
Degrees: C
URL: http://www.palmettohealth.org
Phone: (803) 434-7000
Prog. Accred.: Clinical Pastoral Education, Dentistry (general practice residency)

Providence Hospital
2435 Forest Dr., Columbia 29204
Type: Private, independent
Degrees: C
URL: http://www.provhosp.com
Phone: (803) 256-5300
Prog. Accred.: Allied Health (cardiovascular technology)

Self Regional Healthcare
1325 Spring St., Greenwood 29646
Type: Private, independent
Degrees: C
URL: http://www.selfmemorial.org
Phone: (864) 227-4150
Prog. Accred.: Clinical Pastoral Education

South Carolina College of Pharmacy
PO Box 250141, Charleston 29425
Type: Public, state, four-year
Degrees: D
URL: http://www.sccp.sc.edu
Phone: (843) 792-2300 *Calendar:* Sem. plan
Prog. Accred.: Pharmacy

South Carolina Department of Health and Environmental Control
Mills Complex, Box 101106, Columbia 29211-0106
Type: Public, state
Degrees: C
URL: http://www.scdhec.gov
Phone: (803) 898-3432
Prog. Accred.: Dietetics (internship)

Spartanburg Regional Medical Center
101 East Wood St., Spartanburg 29303
Type: Private, independent
Degrees: C
URL: http://www.spartanburgregional.com
Phone: (864) 560-6000
Prog. Accred.: Clinical Pastoral Education

United States Army Dental Activity—Ft. Jackson
4590 Strom Thurmond Blvd., Ft. Jackson 29207-5720
Type: Public, federal
Degrees: C
Prog. Accred.: Dentistry (advanced education in general dentistry)

WestGate Training & Consultation Network
167 Alabama St., Spartansburg 29302
Type: Private, independent
Degrees: C
Phone: (864) 583-1010 *Calendar:* Sem. plan
Prog. Accred.: Marriage and Family Therapy

SOUTH DAKOTA

Avera Health
3900 West Avera Dr., Sioux Falls 57108
Type: Private, independent
Degrees: C
URL: http://www.avera.org
Phone: (605) 322-4700
Prog. Accred.: Clinical Pastoral Education

Avera McKennan Hospital and University Health Center
800 East 21st St., Sioux Falls 57117-5045
Type: Private, independent
Degrees: C
URL: http://www.averamckennan.com
Phone: (605) 322-8000 *Calendar:* 24-mos. pr
Prog. Accred.: Allied Health (EMT (paramedic)), Radiography

Avera Sacred Heart Hospital
501 Summit St., Yankton 57078
Type: Private, independent
Degrees: C
URL: http://www.averasacredheart.com
Phone: (605) 668-8000 *Calendar:* 24-mos. pr
Prog. Accred.: Radiography

Bethesda Christian Counseling Midwest, Inc.
400 South Sycamore Ave., Ste. 105-3, Sioux Falls 57110
Type: Private, independent
Degrees: C
URL: http://www.bethesdachristiancounseling.org
Phone: (605) 334-3739
Prog. Accred.: Clinical Pastoral Education

Rapid City Regional Hospital
353 Fairmont Blvd., Rapid City 57701
Type: Private, independent
Degrees: C
URL: http://www.rcrh.org
Phone: (605) 719-1000
Prog. Accred.: Radiography

Sioux Valley Hospital
1305 West 18th St., Sioux Falls 57117-5039
Type: Private, independent
Degrees: C
URL: http://www.siouxvalley.org
Phone: (605) 333-1000
Prog. Accred.: Radiography

TENNESSEE

Chattanooga Association for Clinical Pastoral Care
975 East Third St., Chattanooga 37403
Type: Private, independent
Degrees: C
URL: http://www.cacpc.org
Phone: (423) 778-7177
Prog. Accred.: Clinical Pastoral Education

Cherokee Health Systems
140 Dameron Ave., Knoxville 37917-6413
Type: Private, independent
Degrees: C
URL: http://www.cherokeehealth.com
Phone: (865) 544-0406
Prog. Accred.: Psychology Internship

The Guidance Center
118 North Church St., Murfreesboro 37113-1559
Type: Private, independent
Degrees: C
Phone: (615) 893-0770
Prog. Accred.: Psychology Internship

James H. Quillen Veterans Affairs Medical Center
PO Box 1058, Mountain Home 37684-1058
Type: Public, federal
Degrees: C
URL: http://www1.va.gov/directory
Phone: (423) 926-1171 x2432
Prog. Accred.: Allied Health (optometric residency), Clinical Pastoral Education

Johnson City Medical Center
400 North State of Franklin Rd., Johnson City 37604-6094
Type: Private, independent
Degrees: C
URL: http://www.msha.com/facility.cfm?id=47
Phone: (423) 431-6111
Prog. Accred.: Clinical Pastoral Education

Memphis Veterans Affairs Medical Center
1030 Jefferson Ave., Memphis 38104-2127
Type: Public, federal
Degrees: C
URL: http://www.memphis.va.gov
Phone: (901) 577-7326
Prog. Accred.: Allied Health (optometric residency), Clinical Pastoral Education

Meridian Institute of Surgical Assisting
PO Box 758, Joelton 37080
Type: Private, proprietary
Degrees: C
URL: http://www.meridian-institute.com
Phone: (877) 954-1500
Prog. Accred.: Allied Health (surgeon assisting)

Methodist University Hospital
1265 Union Ave., Memphis 38104
Type: Private, independent
Degrees: C
URL: http://www.methodisthealth.org
Phone: (901) 516-7000
Prog. Accred.: Allied Health (diagnostic medical sonography), Clinical Pastoral Education, Nuclear Medicine Technology, Radiography

Nashville General Hospital at Meharry
1818 Albion St., Nashville 37208
Type: Public, city-owned
Degrees: C
URL: http://www.nashville.gov/general_hospital/index.htm
Phone: (615) 341-4000
Prog. Accred.: Radiography

Nashville Veterans Affairs Medical Center
1310 24th Ave. South, Nashville 37212-2637
Type: Public, federal
Degrees: C
URL: http://www.tennesseevalley.va.gov
Phone: (615) 327-5362
Prog. Accred.: Clinical Pastoral Education

Tennessee Board of Regents Online Degree Programs
1415 Murfreesboro Rd., Nashville 37217-2833
Type: Public, state, four-year
System: Tennessee Board of Regents
Degrees: M
URL: http://www.tn.regentsdegrees.org/msn
Phone: (615) 366-3972 *Calendar:* Sem. plan
Prog. Accred.: Nursing

TEXAS

82nd Medical Group
149 Hart St., Ste. 4, Sheppard AFB 76311-3477
Type: Public, federal
Degrees: C
URL: http://www.sheppard.af.mil/units
Phone: (940) 676-2511
Prog. Accred.: Dentistry (advanced education in general dentistry)

Baptist Medical Center
111 Dallas St., San Antonio 78205-1230
Type: Private, independent
Degrees: C
URL: http://www.baptisthealthsystem.org
Phone: (210) 297-7000
Prog. Accred.: Clinical Pastoral Education, Dietetics (internship), Radiography

Baylor University Medical Center
3500 Gaston Ave., Dallas 75246
Type: Private, independent
Degrees: C
URL: http://www.baylorhealth.com
Phone: (214) 820-0111
Prog. Accred.: Dietetics (internship), Nuclear Medicine Technology, Radiography

Ben Taub General Hospital
1504 Taub Loop, Houston 77030
Type: Public, local
Degrees: C
URL: http://www.hchdonline.com
Phone: (713) 873-2000
Prog. Accred.: Clinical Pastoral Education, Radiography

Brooke Army Medical Center
3851 Roger Brooke Dr., Fort Sam Houston 78234
Type: Public, federal
Degrees: C
URL: http://www.bamc.amedd.army.mil
Phone: (210) 226-2225
Prog. Accred.: Allied Health (cytotechnology, optometric residency), Clinical Pastoral Education, Dentistry (oral and maxillofacial surgery), Psychology Internship, Radiography

Central Texas Veterans Health Care System
1901 Veterans Memorial Dr., Temple 76504-7451
Type: Public, federal
Degrees: C
URL: http://www.central-texas.med.va.gov/main
Phone: (254) 778-4811
Prog. Accred.: Dentistry (general practice residency)

Children's Medical Center of Dallas
1935 Motor St., Dallas 75235-7701
Type: Private, independent
Degrees: C
URL: http://www.childrens.com
Phone: (214) 456-7000
Prog. Accred.: Clinical Pastoral Education

CHRISTUS Hospital-Saint Elizabeth
2830 Calder St., Beaumont 77702-1809
Type: Private, independent
Degrees: C
URL: http://www.christusste.org
Phone: (409) 892-7171
Prog. Accred.: Phlebotomy

CHRISTUS Spohn Hospital Corpus Christi—Memorial
2606 Hospital Blvd., Corpus Christi 78405
Type: Private, independent
Degrees: C
URL: http://www.christusspohn.org/facilities_memorial.html
Phone: (361) 902-4000
Prog. Accred.: Clinical Pastoral Education

Citizens Medical Center
2701 Hospital Dr., Victoria 77901
Type: Private, independent
Degrees: C
URL: http://www.citizensmedicalcenter.org
Phone: (361) 573-9181
Prog. Accred.: Radiography

Covenant Medical Center
3615 19th St., Lubbock 79410
Type: Private, independent
Degrees: C
URL: http://www.covenanthealth.org
Phone: (806) 725-1011
Prog. Accred.: Clinical Pastoral Education, Nursing, Radiography

Cypress-Fairbanks Independent School District
14103 Reo St., Department of Psychological Services, Houston 77040
Type: Public, state-local
Degrees: C
URL: http://www.cfisd.net
Phone: (713) 460-7825
Prog. Accred.: Psychology Internship

Dallas Independent School District
Nolan Estes Plaza, 3434 South R.L. Thornton Freeway, Dallas 75224
Type: Public, state/local
Degrees: C
URL: http://www.dallasisd.org
Phone: (972) 925-3700
Prog. Accred.: Psychology Internship

Dallas Veterans Affairs Medical Center
4500 South Lancaster Rd., Dallas 75216
Type: Public, federal
Degrees: C
URL: http://www.north-texas.med.va.gov
Phone: (214) 742-8387
Prog. Accred.: Clinical Pastoral Education, Dentistry (dental public health, general practice residency)

Deer Oaks Mental Health Associates
7272 Wurzbach Rd., Ste. 601, San Antonio 78240-4803
Type: Private, independent
Degrees: C
URL: http://www.deeroaks.com/deer-oaks-mental-health-associates
Phone: (210) 615-8880
Prog. Accred.: Psychology Internship

Federal Medical Center Carswell
PO Box 27137, Fort Worth 76127
Type: Public, federal
Degrees: C
URL: http://www.bop.gov/locations/institutions/crw/index.jsp
Phone: (817) 782-4000
Prog. Accred.: Psychology Internship

Fort Worth Independent School District
100 North University Dr., Ste. NE 229, Fort Worth 76107
Type: Public, state/local
Degrees: C
URL: http://www.fortworthisd.org
Phone: (817) 871-2486
Prog. Accred.: Psychology Internship

Gulf Coast School of Blood Bank Technology
1400 La Concha Ln., Houston 77054
Type: Private, independent
Degrees: C
URL: http://www.giveblood.org/education/distance.htm
Phone: (713) 790-1200
Prog. Accred.: Allied Health (blood bank technology)

Harris Methodist Fort Worth Hospital
1301 Pennsylvania Ave., Fort Worth 76104
Type: Private, independent
Degrees: C
URL: http://www.texashealth.org
Phone: (817) 882-2000
Prog. Accred.: Clinical Pastoral Education

Hendrick Medical Center
1900 Pine St., Abilene 79601
Type: Private, Baptist General Convention of Texas
Degrees: C
URL: http://www.ehendrick.org
Phone: (325) 670-2000
Prog. Accred.: Allied Health (respiratory therapy), Radiography

Hillcrest Health System
3000 Herring Ave., Waco 76708-0100
Type: Private, Baptist General Convention of Texas
Degrees: C
URL: http://www.hillcrest.net
Phone: (254) 202-2000
Prog. Accred.: Clinical Pastoral Education

Huguley Memorial Medical Center
PO Box 6337, Fort Worth 76115-0337
Type: Private, Seventh-day Adventist Church
Degrees: C
URL: http://www.huguley.org
Phone: (817) 293-9110
Prog. Accred.: Clinical Pastoral Education

JPS Institute for Health Career Development
2500 Circle Dr., Fort Worth 76119
Type: Private, independent
Degrees: C
URL: http://www.jpshealthnet.org
Phone: (817) 920-7340
Prog. Accred.: Radiography

Memorial Hermann Baptist Beaumont Hospital
3080 College St., Beaumont 77701
Type: Private, independent
Degrees: C
URL: http://www.memorialhermann.org
Phone: (409) 212-5000
Prog. Accred.: Radiography

Memorial Hermann Memorial City Hospital
921 Gessner Rd., Houston 77024
Type: Private, independent
Degrees: C
URL: http://www.memorialhermann.org
Phone: (713) 242-3000
Prog. Accred.: Radiography

Memorial Hermann Southwest Hospital
7600 Beechnut St., Houston 77074-4302
Type: Private, independent
Degrees: C
URL: http://www.memorialhermann.org
Phone: (713) 456-5000
Prog. Accred.: Clinical Pastoral Education

Methodist Dallas Medical Center
1441 North Beckley Ave., Dallas 75203-1201
Type: Private, independent
Degrees: C
URL: http://www.methodisthealthsystem.org
Phone: (214) 947-8181
Prog. Accred.: Clinical Pastoral Education

The Methodist Hospital
6565 Fannin St., Houston 77030
Type: Private, independent
Degrees: C
URL: http://www.methodisthealth.com
Phone: (713) 790-3311
Prog. Accred.: Clinical Pastoral Education

Methodist Hospital
7700 Floyd Curl Dr., San Antonio 78229
Type: Private, independent
Degrees: C
URL: http://mh.sahealth.com
Phone: (210) 575-4000
Prog. Accred.: Clinical Pastoral Education

Michael E. DeBakey Veterans Affairs Medical Center
2002 Holcombe Blvd., Houston 77030
Type: Public, federal
Degrees: C
URL: http://www.houston.med.va.gov
Phone: (713) 791-1414
Prog. Accred.: Dentistry (advanced education in general dentistry, combined prosthodontics, general practice residency), Dietetics (internship)

Parkland Memorial Hospital
5201 Harry Hines Blvd., Dallas 75235
Type: Private, independent
Degrees: C
URL: http://www.parklandhospital.com
Phone: (214) 590-8000
Prog. Accred.: Clinical Pastoral Education

Presbyterian Hospital of Dallas
8200 Walnut Hill Ln., Dallas 75231-4402
Type: Private, independent
Degrees: C
URL: http://www.texashealth.org
Phone: (214) 345-6789
Prog. Accred.: Dietetics (internship)

Saint Joseph Regional Health Center
2801 Franciscan Dr., Bryan 77802
Type: Private, independent
Degrees: C
URL: http://www.st-joseph.org/sjrhc
Phone: (979) 776-3777
Prog. Accred.: Allied Health (surgical technology), Clinical Pastoral Education

Saint Luke's Episcopal Hospital
6720 Bertner Ave., Houston 77030-2604
Type: Private, independent
Degrees: C
URL: http://www.sleh.com
Phone: (832) 355-1000
Prog. Accred.: Allied Health (perfusion), Clinical Pastoral Education

Scenic Mountain Medical Center
1601 West 11th Place, Big Spring 79720-9990
Type: Private, independent
Degrees: C
URL: http://www.smmccares.com
Phone: (432) 268-4885
Prog. Accred.: Radiography

Scott and White Clinic in Temple
2401 South 31st St., Temple 76508
Type: Private, independent
Degrees: C
URL: http://www.sw.org
Phone: (254) 724-2111
Prog. Accred.: Clinical Pastoral Education

Seton Shoal Creek Hospital
3501 Mills Ave., Austin 78731
Type: Private, independent
Degrees: C
URL: http://www.seton.net/locations/shoal_creek
Phone: (512) 324-2000
Prog. Accred.: Clinical Pastoral Education

South Texas Veterans Health Care System
7400 Merton Minter Blvd., San Antonio 78284
Type: Public, federal
Degrees: C
URL: http://www.vasthcs.med.va.gov
Phone: (210) 617-5300
Prog. Accred.: Clinical Pastoral Education, Dentistry (advanced education in general dentistry), Psychology Internship

South Texas Veterans Health Care System
7400 Merton Minter St., San Antonio 78284-5700
Type: Public, federal
Degrees: C
URL: http://www.vasthcs.med.va.gov
Phone: (210) 617-5300
Prog. Accred.: Clinical Pastoral Education, Dentistry (advanced education in general dentistry), Psychology Internship

Terrell State Hospital
1200 East Brin, Terrell 75160-9000
Type: Public, state
Degrees: C
URL: http://www.dshs.state.tx.us/mhhospitals/TerrellSH/default.shtm
Phone: (972) 563-6452
Prog. Accred.: Clinical Pastoral Education

Texas Department of State Health Services
1100 West 49th St., Mail Code 1933, Austin 78756
Type: Public, state
Degrees: C
URL: http://www.dshs.state.tx.us/wichd/nut/intern-intro.shtm
Phone: (512) 458-7111 ext 2
Prog. Accred.: Dietetics (internship)

Texas International Education Consortium
1103 West 24th St., Austin 78705
Type: Private, independent
Degrees: C
URL: http://www.tiec.org
Phone: (512) 477-9283
Prog. Accred.: English Language Education

Thomas E. Creek Veterans Affairs Medical Center
6010 Amarillo Blvd., West Amarillo 79106
Type: Public, federal
Degrees: C
URL: http://www.amarillo.va.gov
Phone: (806) 355-9703
Prog. Accred.: Allied Health (optometric residency)

United States Air Force School of Health Care Sciences
917 Missile Rd., Sheppard AFB 76311-2246
Type: Public, federal
Degrees: C
URL: http://www.sheppard.af.mil/units
Phone: (940) 676-2511
Prog. Accred.: Allied Health (optometric technician, respiratory therapy), Dentistry (dental assisting, dental laboratory technology), Radiography

United States AMEDD Center and School Department of Pastoral Ministry Training
3151 Scott Rd., Ste. 400, Fort Sam Houston 78234-6106
Type: Public, federal
Degrees: C
URL: http://www.samhouston.army.mil/chaplain/DPMT/default.aspx
Phone: (210) 221-8609
Prog. Accred.: Clinical Pastoral Education

United States Army Dental Activity—Fort Hood
3600 Darnall Loop, Fort Hood 76544-5063
Type: Public, federal
Degrees: C
Phone: (254) 286-7412
Prog. Accred.: Dentistry (advanced education in general dentistry)

Valley Baptist Medical Center—Harlingen
2101 Pease St., Harlingen 78550
Type: Private, independent
Degrees: C
URL: http://www.valleybaptist.net/harlingen
Phone: (956) 389-1100
Prog. Accred.: Clinical Pastoral Education

VITAS Innovative Hospice Care—Fort Worth
2501 Parkview Dr., Ste. 600, Fort Worth 76102
Type: Private, independent
System: VITAS Innovative Hospice Care
Degrees: C
URL: http://www.vitas.com
Phone: (817) 870-7000
Prog. Accred.: Clinical Pastoral Education

Wilford Hall Medical Center
2200 Berquist Dr., Lackland AFB 78236-9908
Type: Public, federal
Degrees: C
URL: http://www.whmc.af.mil
Phone: (210) 292-7100
Prog. Accred.: Allied Health (optometric residency), Clinical Pastoral Education, Dentistry (combined prosthodontics, endodontics, oral and maxillofacial surgery, orthodontic and dentofacial orthopedics, pediatric dentistry, periodontics), Dietetics (internship)

UTAH

George E. Wahlen Department of Veterans Affairs Medical Center
500 Foothill Dr., Salt Lake City 84148
Type: Public, federal
Degrees: C
URL: http://www.saltlakecity.va.gov
Phone: (801) 582-1565
Prog. Accred.: Allied Health (optometric residency), Dentistry (general practice residency)

LDS Hospital
8th Ave. and C St., Salt Lake City 84143-0001
Type: Private, independent
Degrees: C
URL: http://intermountainhealthcare.org
Phone: (801) 408-1100
Prog. Accred.: Allied Health (surgical technology)

Saint Mark's Hospital
1250 East 3900 South, Salt Lake City 84123
Type: Private, independent
Degrees: C
URL: http://www.stmarkshospital.com
Phone: (801) 268-7111
Prog. Accred.: Clinical Pastoral Education

Utah State Hospital
1300 East Center St., Provo 84606
Type: Public, state
Degrees: C
URL: http://www.hsush.state.ut.us
Phone: (801) 344-4400
Prog. Accred.: Psychology Internship

VERMONT

The Center for Technology, Essex
3 Educational Dr., Essex Junction 05452
Type: Public, local
Degrees: C
URL: http://www.go-cte.org
Phone: (802) 879-5558 *Calendar:* Qtr. plan
Prog. Accred.: Dentistry (dental assisting)

Fletcher Allen Health Care
111 Colchester Ave., Burlington 05401
Type: Private, independent
Degrees: C
URL: http://www.fahc.org
Phone: (802) 847-2770
Prog. Accred.: Allied Health (cytotechnology), Clinical Pastoral Education, Dentistry (general practice residency)

New England School of Radiologic Technology
Rutland Regional Med. Ctr., 160 Allen St., Rotland 05701
Type: Private, independent
Degrees: C
URL: http://www.rrmc.org/progandserv/radiology.html
Phone: (802) 775-7111
Prog. Accred.: Radiography

White River Junction Veterans Affairs Medical Center
215 North Main St., White River Junction 05009-0001
Type: Public, federal
Degrees: C
URL: http://www.whiteriver.va.gov
Phone: (802) 295-9363
Prog. Accred.: Allied Health (optometric residency)

VIRGINIA

1st Dental Squadron
73 Cherry St., Building 272, Langley AFB 23665
Type: Public, federal
Degrees: C
URL: http://www.langley.af.mil/units
Phone: (757) 764-1403
Prog. Accred.: Dentistry (advanced education in general dentistry)

Bon Secours Maryview Medical Center
3636 High St., Portsmouth 23707
Type: Private, independent
Degrees: C
URL: http://www.bonsecourshamptonroads.com/facilities/maryview.html
Phone: (757) 398-2200
Prog. Accred.: Clinical Pastoral Education

Centra Lynchburg General Hospital
1901 Tate Springs Rd., Lynchburg 24501
Type: Private, independent
Degrees: C
URL: http://www.centrahealth.com
Phone: (434) 200-3000
Prog. Accred.: Nursing, Practical Nursing

Global Health Nurse Training Services
25 South Quaker Ln., Alexandria 22314
Type: Private, proprietary
Degrees: C
URL: http://www.ghnts.com
Phone: (703) 212-7410
Prog. Accred.: Practical Nursing

Goodwin House Alexandria
4800 Fillmore Ave., Alexandria 22311
Type: Private, Episcopal Church in the Diocese of Virginia
Degrees: C
URL: http://www.goodwinhouse.org
Phone: (703) 578-1000
Prog. Accred.: Clinical Pastoral Education

Hampton Veterans Affairs Medical Center
100 Emancipation Dr., Hampton 23667
Type: Public, federal
Degrees: C
URL: http://www.hampton.va.gov
Phone: (757) 722-9961
Prog. Accred.: Allied Health (optometric residency), Clinical Pastoral Education, Dentistry (general practice residency)

Mary Washington Hospital
1001 Sam Perry Blvd., Fredericksburg 22401
Type: Private, independent
Degrees: C
URL: http://www.medicorp.org/mwh
Phone: (540) 741-1100
Prog. Accred.: Radiography

Memorial Regional Medical Center
8260 Atlee Rd., Mechanicsville 23116
Type: Private, independent
Degrees: C
URL: http://www.bonsecours.com/hospitals/memorial
Phone: (804) 764-6000
Prog. Accred.: Nursing

Naval Dental Clinic Mid-Atlantic
1647 Taussig Blvd., Norfolk 23511-2896
Type: Public, federal
Degrees: C
Phone: (757) 314-6561
Prog. Accred.: Dentistry (advanced education in general dentistry)

Naval Medical Center Portsmouth
620 John Paul Jones Circle, Portsmouth 23708-2197
Type: Public, federal
Degrees: C
URL: http://www-nmcp.med.navy.mil
Phone: (757) 953-5000
Prog. Accred.: Dentistry (general dentistry, oral and maxillofacial surgery)

Naval School of Health Sciences
1001 Holcomb Rd., Portsmouth 23708-5200
Type: Public, federal
Degrees: C
URL: https://www-nshspts.med.navy.mil
Phone: (757) 953-5040 *Calendar:* 12-mos. pr
Prog. Accred.: Allied Health (electroneurodiagnostic technology, surgical technology), Nuclear Medicine Technology, Radiography

Norfolk Technical Vocational Center
1330 North Military Hwy., Norfolk 23502
Type: Private, proprietary
Degrees: C
URL: http://www.nps.k12.va.us/schools/ntvc
Phone: (757) 892-3300
Prog. Accred.: Practical Nursing

Riverside School of Health Careers
316 Main St., Newport News 23601
Type: Private, independent
Degrees: C
URL: http://www.riverside-online.com/rshc
Phone: (757) 240-2200
Prog. Accred.: Allied Health (surgical technology), Clinical Pastoral Education, Practical Nursing, Radiography

Rockingham Memorial Hospital
235 Cantrell Ave., Harrisonburg 22801-3293
Type: Private, independent
Degrees: C
URL: http://www.rmhonline.com
Phone: (540) 433-4100
Prog. Accred.: Radiography

Saint Mary's Hospital
5801 Bremo Rd., Richmond 23226
Type: Private, independent
Degrees: C
URL: http://www.bonsecours.com/hospitals/stmarys
Phone: (804) 285-2011
Prog. Accred.: Practical Nursing, Radiography

Sentara Norfolk General Hospital
600 Gresham Dr., Norfolk 23507
Type: Private, independent
Degrees: C
URL: http://www.sentara.com
Phone: (757) 388-3000
Prog. Accred.: Clinical Pastoral Education

Southside Regional Medical Center
801 South Adams St., Petersburg 23803
Type: Private, independent
Degrees: C
URL: http://www.srmconline.com
Phone: (804) 862-5000
Prog. Accred.: Nursing, Radiography

Suffolk Public Schools Sentara Obici Hospital School of Practical Nursing
PO Box 1100, Suffolk 23439-1100
Type: Public, public
Degrees: C
URL: http://www.sentara.com/obicilpnschool
Phone: (757) 934-4826
Prog. Accred.: Practical Nursing

University of Appalachia College of Pharmacy
Route 3, Box 182, Grundy 24614
Type: Private, independent, four-year
Degrees: D
URL: http://www.uacp.org
Phone: (276) 935-4277 *Calendar:* Sem. plan
Prog. Accred.: Pharmacy

Virginia Beach School of Practical Nursing
2925 North Landing Rd., Virginia Beach 23456-2499
Type: Public, local
Degrees: C
URL: http://www.adultlearning.vbschools.com
Phone: (757) 648-6050
Prog. Accred.: Practical Nursing

Virginia Department of Health
109 Governor St., 9th Flr., Richmond 23219
Type: Public, state
Degrees: C
URL: http://www.vahealth.org/WIC
Phone: (804) 864-7832
Prog. Accred.: Dietetics (internship)

Winchester Medical Center, Inc.
1840 Amherst St., PO Box 3340, Winchester 22601
Type: Private, independent
Degrees: C
URL: http://www.valleyhealthlink.com
Phone: (540) 536-8000
Prog. Accred.: Radiography

WASHINGTON

The Chaplaincy
2108 West Entiat Ave., Kennewick 99336
Type: Private, independent
Degrees: C
URL: http://www.tricitieschaplaincy.org
Phone: (509) 783-7416
Prog. Accred.: Clinical Pastoral Education

Evergreen Health Care
12040 NE 128th St., Kirkland 98034
Type: Private, independent
Degrees: C
URL: http://www.evergreenhealthcare.org
Phone: (425) 899-1000
Prog. Accred.: Clinical Pastoral Education

Good Samaritan Hospital
407 14th Ave. SE, Puyallup 98372
Type: Private, independent
Degrees: C
URL: http://www.goodsamhealth.org
Phone: (253) 697-4000
Prog. Accred.: Clinical Pastoral Education

Harborview Medical Center
325 Ninth Ave., Seattle 98104
Type: Private, independent
Degrees: C
URL: http://www.uwmedicine.org/Facilities/Harborview
Phone: (206) 731-3000
Prog. Accred.: Clinical Pastoral Education

Jonathan M. Wainwright Memorial Veterans Affairs Medical Center
77 Wainwright Dr., Walla Walla 99362
Type: Public, federal
Degrees: C
URL: http://www.visn20.med.va.gov/walla-walla
Phone: (509) 525-5200
Prog. Accred.: Allied Health (optometric residency)

Madigan Army Medical Center
Building 9040 Fitzsimmons Dr., Tacoma 98431
Type: Public, federal
Degrees: C
URL: http://www.mamc.amedd.army.mil/wrmc
Phone: (253) 968-1110
Prog. Accred.: Clinical Pastoral Education, Dentistry (general dentistry, oral and maxillofacial surgery)

Providence Saint Peter Hospital
413 Lilly Rd. NE, Olympia 98506
Type: Private, independent
Degrees: C
URL: http://www.providence.org/swsa/facilities/St_Peter_Hospital
Phone: (360) 491-9480
Prog. Accred.: Clinical Pastoral Education

Sacred Heart Medical Center
101 West Eighth Ave., PO Box 2555, Spokane 99220
Type: Private, independent
Degrees: C
URL: http://www.shmc.org
Phone: (509) 474-3131
Prog. Accred.: Radiography

Saint Joseph Hospital
2901 Squalicum Pkwy., Bellingham 98225-1898
Type: Private, independent
Degrees: C
URL: http://www.peacehealth.org
Phone: (360) 734-5400
Prog. Accred.: Clinical Pastoral Education

Saint Joseph Medical Center
1717 South J St., Tacoma 98405
Type: Private, independent
Degrees: C
URL: https://www.fhshealth.org/location/sjmc.asp
Phone: (253) 426-4101
Prog. Accred.: Clinical Pastoral Education, Clinical Pastoral Education (USCC)

Sea Mar Community Health Center
1040 South Henderson St., Seattle 98108-4720
Type: Private, independent
Degrees: C
URL: http://www.seamar.org
Phone: (206) 763-5277
Prog. Accred.: Dietetics (internship)

Spokane Veterans Affairs Medical Center
4815 North Assembly St., Spokane 99205
Type: Public, federal
Degrees: C
URL: http://www.visn20.med.va.gov/spokane
Phone: (509) 434-7000
Prog. Accred.: Allied Health (optometric residency)

Spring Valley Montessori Teacher Education Program
36605 Pacific Hwy. South, Federal Way 98003
Type: Private, independent
Degrees: C
URL: http://www.springvalley.org
Phone: (253) 927-2557
Prog. Accred.: Montessori Teacher Education

Swedish Medical Center
747 Broadway, Seattle 98122-4307
Type: Private, independent
Degrees: C
URL: http://www.swedish.org
Phone: (206) 386-6000
Prog. Accred.: Clinical Pastoral Education

Veterans Affairs Puget Sound Health Care System
1660 South Columbian Way, Seattle 98108-1532
Type: Public, federal
Degrees: C
URL: http://www.puget-sound.med.va.gov
Phone: (206) 762-1010
Prog. Accred.: Clinical Pastoral Education

Veterans Affairs Puget Sound Health Care System—American Lake Division
9900 Veterans Dr., Tacoma 98493
Type: Public, federal
Degrees: C
URL: http://www1.va.gov/pugetsound
Phone: (253) 582-8440
Prog. Accred.: Allied Health (optometric residency), Dentistry (general practice residency)

Yakima Valley Farm Workers Clinic
518 West First Ave., Toppenish 98948
Type: Private, independent
Degrees: C
URL: http://www.yvfwc.com/toppenish.html
Phone: (509) 865-3886
Prog. Accred.: Dentistry (advanced education in general dentistry)

WEST VIRGINIA

B.M. Spurr School of Practical Nursing
800 Wheeling Ave., Glen Dale 26038
Type: Private, independent
Degrees: C
URL: http://www.reynoldsmemorial.com/programs.php?id=12
Phone: (304) 845-3211
Prog. Accred.: Practical Nursing

Cabell Huntington Hospital
1340 Hal Greer Blvd., Huntington 25701
Type: Private, independent
Degrees: C
URL: http://www.cabellhuntington.org
Phone: (304) 526-2000
Prog. Accred.: Allied Health (cytotechnology), Clinical Pastoral Education

Huntington Veterans Affairs Medical Center
1540 Spring Valley Dr., Huntington 25704
Type: Public, federal
Degrees: C
URL: http://www.huntington.va.gov
Phone: (304) 429-6741
Prog. Accred.: Allied Health (optometric residency)

Ohio Valley Medical Center
2000 Eoff St., Wheeling 26003
Type: Private, independent
Degrees: C
URL: http://www.ohiovalleymedicalcenter.com
Phone: (304) 234-0123
Prog. Accred.: Radiography

Saint Mary's Medical Center
2900 First Ave., Huntington 25702
Type: Private, independent, two-year
Degrees: C, A
URL: http://www.st-marys.org
Phone: (304) 526-1234
Prog. Accred.: Nursing, Radiography

United Hospital Center
3 Hospital Plaza, PO Box 1680, Clarksburg 26301
Type: Private, independent
Degrees: C
URL: http://www.uhcwv.org
Phone: (304) 624-2121
Prog. Accred.: Radiography

Veterans Affairs Medical Center—Martinsburg
510 Butler Ave., Martinsburg 25405
Type: Public, federal
Degrees: C
URL: http://www.martinsburg.va.gov
Phone: (304) 263-0811
Prog. Accred.: Dentistry (general dentistry)

Wheeling Hospital
1 Medical Park, Wheeling 26003
Type: Private, independent
Degrees: C
URL: http://www.wheelinghospital.com
Phone: (304) 243-3000
Prog. Accred.: Radiography

Wood County Vocational School
300 Campus Dr., Parkersburg 26104
Type: Public, local
Degrees: C
URL: http://wcvt.wood.tec.wv.us/wcsopn
Phone: (304) 420-9501
Prog. Accred.: Practical Nursing

WISCONSIN

Alexian Village of Milwaukee
7979 West Glenbrook Rd., Milwaukee 53223-1062
Type: Private, independent
System: Alexian Brothers (System Center)
Degrees: C
URL: http://www.alexianhealthsystem.org
Phone: (414) 355-9300
Prog. Accred.: Clinical Pastoral Education

All Saints Healthcare—St. Mary's Campus
3801 Spring St., Racine 53405
Type: Private, independent
Degrees: C
URL: http://www.allsaintshealth.com
Phone: (262) 687-4011
Prog. Accred.: Radiography

Aspirus Wausau Hospital
425 Pine Ridge Blvd., Wausau 54401
Type: Private, independent
Degrees: C
URL: http://www.aspirus.org
Phone: (715) 847-2118
Prog. Accred.: Clinical Pastoral Education

Aurora Lakeland Medical Center
W3985 County Rd. NN, Elkhorn 53121
Type: Private, independent
Degrees: C
URL: http://www.aurorahealthcare.org
Phone: (262) 741-2000
Prog. Accred.: Clinical Pastoral Education

Aurora Saint Luke's Medical Center
2900 West Oklahoma Ave., Milwaukee 53201-2901
Type: Private, independent
Degrees: C
URL: http://www.aurorahealthcare.org
Phone: (414) 649-6000
Prog. Accred.: Allied Health (diagnostic medical sonography), Clinical Pastoral Education, Nuclear Medicine Technology, Radiography

Aurora Sinai Medical Center
945 North 12th St., Milwaukee 53233
Type: Private, independent
Degrees: C
URL: http://www.aurorahealthcare.org
Phone: (414) 219-2000
Prog. Accred.: Clinical Pastoral Education

Bellin School of Radiology
PO Box 23400, Green Bay 54301
Type: Private, independent
Degrees: C
URL: http://www.bellin.org/careers/radiology.shtml
Phone: (920) 433-3497
Prog. Accred.: Radiography

BloodCenter of Wisconsin
638 North 18th St., Milwaukee 53233
Type: Private, independent
Degrees: C
URL: http://www.bcw.edu
Phone: (414) 933-5000
Prog. Accred.: Allied Health (blood bank technology)

Catholic Diocese of Green Bay Clinical Pastoral Education Program
212 Iroquois Ave., Green Bay 54301-1995
Type: Private, Roman Catholic Church
Degrees: C
Phone: (920) 431-0367
Prog. Accred.: Clinical Pastoral Education

Children's Hospital of Wisconsin—Appleton
1825 Bluemound Dr., Appleton 54913
Type: Private, independent
Degrees: C
URL: http://www.foxvalley.tec.wi.us
Phone: (920) 735-5600
Prog. Accred.: Dentistry (dental assisting)

Children's Hospital of Wisconsin—Milwaukee
9000 West Wisconsin Ave., PO Box 1997, Milwaukee 53201-1997
Type: Private, independent
Degrees: C
URL: http://www.chw.org/default.htm
Phone: (414) 266-2000
Prog. Accred.: Dentistry (pediatric dentistry)

Clement J. Zablocki Veterans Affairs Medical Center
5000 West National Ave., Milwaukee 53295
Type: Public, federal
Degrees: C
URL: http://www.visn12.med.va.gov/milwaukee
Phone: (414) 384-2000
Prog. Accred.: Dentistry (general practice residency), Psychology Internship

Columbia Hospital
2025 East Newport Ave., Milwaukee 53211
Type: Private, independent
System: Columbia Saint Mary's
Degrees: C
URL: http://columbia-stmarys.com
Phone: (414) 961-3300
Prog. Accred.: Radiography

Ethan Allen School
PO Box 900, Wales 53183-0900
Type: Public, state
Degrees: C
Phone: (262) 646-3341
Prog. Accred.: Psychology Internship

Family Therapy Training Institute
3200 West Highland Blvd., Milwaukee 53208-0440
Type: Private, proprietary
Degrees: C
URL: http://www.aurorahealthcare.org
Phone: (414) 345-4970
Prog. Accred.: Marriage and Family Therapy

Froedtert and Medical College Health Services
9200 West Wisconsin Ave., Milwaukee 53226
Type: Private, independent, four-year
Degrees: C, B
URL: http://www.froedtert.com
Phone: (414) 805-3666
Prog. Accred.: Nuclear Medicine Technology, Radiography

Gundersen Lutheran Medical Center
1900 South Ave., La Crosse 54601
Type: Private, independent, four-year
Degrees: C, B
URL: http://www.gundluth.org
Phone: (608) 782-7300
Prog. Accred.: Clinical Pastoral Education, Dentistry (oral and maxillofacial surgery), Nuclear Medicine Technology

Luther Midelfort
1221 Whipple St., Eau Claire 54702-4105
Type: Private, independent
Degrees: C
URL: http://www.mayohealthsystem.org
Phone: (715) 838-3311
Prog. Accred.: Clinical Pastoral Education

Lutheran Homes of Oshkosh
225 North Eagle St., Oshkosh 54902-4125
Type: Private, Evangelical Lutheran Church in America
Degrees: C
URL: http://www.lutheranhomes.com
Phone: (920) 235-4653
Prog. Accred.: Clinical Pastoral Education

Marshfield Clinic
1000 North Oak Ave., Marshfield 54449
Type: Private, independent
Degrees: C
URL: http://www.marshfieldclinic.org
Phone: (715) 387-5511
Prog. Accred.: Allied Health (cytotechnology)

Mercy Medical Center
500 South Oakwood Rd., Oshkosh 54904
Type: Private, independent
Degrees: C
URL: http://www.affinityhealth.org/object/mmchospital.html
Phone: (920) 223-2000
Prog. Accred.: Radiography

Meriter Hospital
202 South Park St., Madison 53715
Type: Private, independent
Degrees: C
URL: http://www.meriter.com
Phone: (608) 267-6000
Prog. Accred.: Clinical Pastoral Education, Dentistry (general practice residency)

Saint Camillus Campus
10200 West Bluemound Rd., Wauwatosa 53226
Type: Private, Order of Saint Camillius
Degrees: C
URL: http://www.stcam.com
Phone: (414) 259-6333
Prog. Accred.: Clinical Pastoral Education

Saint Joseph's Hospital of Marshfield
611 Saint Joseph Ave., Marshfield 54449
Type: Private, independent
Degrees: C
URL: http://www.stjosephs-marshfield.org
Phone: (715) 387-1713
Prog. Accred.: Histologic Technology, Nuclear Medicine Technology, Radiography

Saint Michael Hospital
2400 West Villard Ave., Milwaukee 53209
Type: Private, independent
Degrees: C
URL: http://www.covhealth.org
Phone: (414) 527-8000
Prog. Accred.: Radiography

Theda Clark Medical Center
130 Second St., PO Box 2021, Neenah 54956-2021
Type: Private, independent
Degrees: C
URL: http://www.thedacare.org
Phone: (920) 729-3100
Prog. Accred.: Radiography

University of Wisconsin Hospital and Clinics
600 Highland Ave., Madison 53792
Type: Private, independent
Degrees: C
URL: http://www.uwhealth.org
Phone: (608) 263-6400
Prog. Accred.: Allied Health (diagnostic medical sonography), Dietetics (internship), Radiography

The Village at Manor Park
3023 South 84th St., Milwaukee 53227-3703
Type: Private, independent
Degrees: C
URL: http://www.vmpcares.com
Phone: (414) 607-4100
Prog. Accred.: Clinical Pastoral Education

Wheaton Franciscan Healthcare—St. Francis Hospital
3237 South 16th St., Milwaukee 53215
Type: Private, independent
Degrees: C
URL: http://www.wfhealthcare.org
Phone: (414) 647-5000
Prog. Accred.: Allied Health (diagnostic medical sonography)

WYOMING

Cornerstone Behavioral Health
PO Box 6005, Evanston 82931-6005
Type: Private, independent
Degrees: C
URL: http://www.cornerstonebh.com
Phone: (307) 789-0715
Prog. Accred.: Psychology Internship

ARGENTINA

Universidad Argentina de la Empresa
Lima 717 . C1073AAO, Buenos Aires
Type: Private, independent, four-year
Degrees: B, M
URL: http://www.uade.edu.ar
Phone: 011 0800-122-8233
Prog. Accred.: Business (ACBSP)

IAE Universidad Austral
Casilla de Correo n 49, Mariano Acosta s/n y Ruta Nac. 8 (1629) Pilar, Buenos Aires
Type: Private, independent, four-year
Degrees: M
URL: http://www.iae.edu.ar
Phone: 011 54 2322 48 1000
Prog. Accred.: Business (AACSB)

AUSTRALIA

Australian Graduate School of Management
University of New South Wales, Gate 11, Botany St., Randwick, NSW 2031
Type: Public, federal, four-year
Degrees: M, D
URL: http://www2.agsm.edu.au
Phone: 011 61 2 9931 9200
Prog. Accred.: Business (AACSB)

Murdoch University
South St., Murdoch 6150
Type: Public, federal, four-year
Degrees: D
URL: http://www.murdoch.edu.au
Phone: 011 61 08 9360 6000 *Calendar:* Qtr. plan
Prog. Accred.: Veterinary Medicine

Queensland University of Technology
GPO Box 2434, Brisbane, Queensland 4001
Type: Public, federal, four-year
Degrees: B, M
URL: http://www.qut.edu.au
Phone: 011 61 7 3138 2111 *Calendar:* Qtr. plan
Prog. Accred.: Business (AACSB)

The University of Melbourne
500 Yarra Blvd., Richmond, VIC 3121
Type: Public, provincial, four-year
Degrees: B
URL: http://www.unimelb.edu.au
Phone: 011 61 3 8344 4000 *Calendar:* Sem. plan
Prog. Accred.: Veterinary Medicine

The University of Queensland
Brisbane, QL 4072
Type: Public, federal, four-year
Degrees: B, M, D
URL: http://www.uq.edu.au
Phone: 011 61 7 3365 1111
Prog. Accred.: Business (AACSB)

University of South Australia
GPO Box 2471, Adelaide 5001
Type: Public, provincial, four-year
Degrees: B
URL: http://www.unisa.edu.au
Phone: 011 61 8 8302 6611 *Calendar:* Sem. plan
Prog. Accred.: Construction Education

The University of Sydney
Sydney, NSW 2006
Type: Public, federal, four-year
Degrees: C, B, M
URL: http://www.usyd.edu.au
Phone: 011 61 2 9351 2222 *Calendar:* Sem. plan
Prog. Accred.: Accounting, Business (AACSB), Veterinary Medicine

University of Technology Sydney
PO Box 123, Broadway, NSW 2007
Type: Public, state-controlled, four-year
Degrees: B, M
URL: http://www.uts.edu.au
Phone: 011 61 2 9514 2000
Prog. Accred.: Business (AACSB)

BANGLADESH

Stamford University Bangladesh
744, Satmosjid Rd., Dhanmondi, DHAKA-1209
Type: Private, independent, four-year
Degrees: B, M
URL: http://www.stamforduniversity.info
Phone: 011 8153168-69
Prog. Accred.: Business (ACBSP)

BELGIUM

Vlerick Leuven Gent Management School
Reep 1, Ghent 9000
Type: Private, independent, four-year
Degrees: M
URL: http://www.vlerick.be
Phone: 011 32 9 210 97 11 *Calendar:* Qtr. plan
Prog. Accred.: Business (AACSB)

CANADA

Alberta Children's Hospital
1820 Richmond Rd. SW, Calgary T2T 5C7
Type: Private, provincial government
Degrees: C
URL: http://www.calgaryhealthregion.ca/ACH
Phone: (403) 943-7211
Prog. Accred.: Psychology Internship

Algonquin College
1385 Woodroffe Ave., Ottawa K2G 1V8
Type: Public, provincial
Degrees: C
URL: http://www.algonquincollege.com
Phone: (613) 727-4723
Prog. Accred.: Dentistry (dental assisting, dental hygiene), Interior Design

APLUS Institute of Technology, Healthcare and Business
4950 Yonge St., Concourse Level Unit 15, Toronto M2N 6K1
Type: Private, proprietary
Degrees: C
URL: http://www.aplusinstitute.com
Phone: (416) 222-0500 *Calendar:* Sem. plan
Prog. Accred.: Dentistry (dental hygiene)

Argyle Institute of Human Relations
4114 Sherbrook St. West, 5th Flr., Montreal H3Z 1K9
Type: Private, independent
Degrees: C
URL: http://home.total.net/~argyle
Phone: (514) 931-5629 *Calendar:* Sem. plan
Prog. Accred.: Marriage and Family Therapy

Aurora College
PO Box 600, Fort Smith X0E 0P0
Type: Public, provincial
Degrees: C
URL: http://www.auroracollege.nt.ca
Phone: (867) 872-7500
Prog. Accred.: Forestry

British Columbia Cancer Agency—Vancouver Centre
600 West 10th Ave., Vancouver V5Z 4E6
Type: Public, provincial
Degrees: C
URL: http://www.bccancer.bc.ca/RS/VancouverCentre
Phone: (604) 877-6000
Prog. Accred.: Dentistry (general practice residency)

British Columbia Children's Hospital
4500 Oak St., Vancouver V6H 3N1
Type: Private, independent
Degrees: C
URL: http://www.bcchildrens.ca
Phone: (604) 875-2000
Prog. Accred.: Dentistry (general practice residency), Psychology Internship

Brock University
500 Glenridge Ave., St. Catharines L2S 3A1
Type: Public, provincial, four-year
Degrees: B
URL: http://www.brocku.ca
Phone: (905) 688-5550 *Calendar:* Sem. plan
Prog. Accred.: Business (AACSB)

Calgary Regional Health Authority
1213 4th St., SW, First Flr., Colonel Belcher Hospital, Calgary T2R 0X7
Type: Public, provincial
Degrees: C
URL: http://www.crha-health.ab.ca
Phone: (403) 541-2104 *Calendar:* Sem. plan
Prog. Accred.: Marriage and Family Therapy

Cambrian College
1400 Barrydowne Rd., Sudbury P3A 3V8
Type: Public, provincial, two-year
Degrees: A
URL: http://www.cambriancollege.ca
Phone: (705) 566-8101 *Calendar:* Sem. plan
Prog. Accred.: Dentistry (dental hygiene)

Camosun College
3100 Foul Bay Rd., Victoria V8P 5J2
Type: Public, provincial, four-year
Degrees: A, B
URL: http://www.camosun.bc.ca
Phone: (250) 370-3000 *Calendar:* Qtr. plan
Prog. Accred.: Dentistry (dental assisting, dental hygiene)

Canadian Academy of Dental Hygiene
165 Dundas St. West, Mississauga L5B 2N6
Type: Private, proprietary
Degrees: C
URL: http://www.canadianacademyofdentalhygiene.ca
Phone: (905) 896-2234
Prog. Accred.: Dentistry (dental hygiene)

Canadian College of Dental Health
760 Brant St., Burlington L7R 4B7
Type: Private, independent
Degrees: C
URL: http://www.ccdh.ca
Phone: (905) 632-3200
Prog. Accred.: Dentistry (dental hygiene)

Canadian Institute of Dental Hygiene
145 King St. East, Hamilton L8N 1B1
Type: Private, independent
Degrees: C
URL: http://www.cidh.on.ca
Phone: (905) 524-2434
Prog. Accred.: Dentistry (dental hygiene)

Canadian Montessori Academy Teacher Education Program
70 Fieldrow St., Ottawa K2G 2Y7
Type: Private, independent
Degrees: C
URL: http://www.montessori-academy.com/tt/tt_ec.htm
Phone: (613) 727-9427
Prog. Accred.: Montessori Teacher Education

Canadore College
PO Box 5001, North Bay P1B 8K9
Type: Public, provincial
Degrees: C
URL: http://www.canadorec.on.ca
Phone: (705) 474-7600 *Calendar:* Sem. plan
Prog. Accred.: Dentistry (dental hygiene)

Cape Breton Business College
PO Box 33 Whitney Pier, Sydney B1N 3B1
Type: Private, proprietary
Degrees: C
URL: http://www.cbbc.ns.ca
Phone: (902) 564-2222
Prog. Accred.: Dentistry (dental assisting)

CDI College—Burnaby
603 Kingsway, Suite 101, Burnaby V5H 4M4
Type: Private, proprietary
Degrees: C
URL: http://www.cdischool.com
Phone: (604) 437-8585
Prog. Accred.: Dentistry (dental assisting)

CDI College—Winnipeg
280 Main St., Winnipeg R3C 1A9
Type: Private, proprietary
Degrees: C
URL: http://www.cdischool.com
Phone: (204) 942-1773
Prog. Accred.: Dentistry (dental assisting)

Centre for Addiction and Mental Health
250 College St., Toronto M5T 1R8
Type: Public, provincial
Degrees: C
URL: http://www.camh.net
Phone: (416) 535-8501
Prog. Accred.: Psychology Internship

Chicoutimi College
534 Jacques-Cartier, Est, Chicoutimi G7H 1Z6
Type: Public, provincial
Degrees: C
URL: http://www.cegep-chicoutimi.qc.ca
Phone: (418) 549-9520
Prog. Accred.: Dentistry (dental hygiene)

Children's Hospital of Eastern Ontario
401 Smyth Rd., Ottawa K1H 8L1
Type: Private, independent
Degrees: C
URL: http://www.cheo.on.ca
Phone: (613) 737-7600
Prog. Accred.: Psychology Internship

Collége Boréal
21, Lasalle Blvd., Sudbury P3A 6B1
Type: Public, provincial
Degrees: C
URL: http://www.borealc.on.ca
Phone: (705) 560-6673
Prog. Accred.: Dentistry (dental assisting, dental hygiene)

Collége Édouard-Montpetit
945, chemin de Chambly, Longueuil J4H 3M6
Type: Public, provincial
Degrees: C
URL: http://www.college-em.qc.ca
Phone: (450) 679-2631
Prog. Accred.: Dentistry (dental hygiene)

College of New Caledonia
3330 22nd Ave., Prince George V2N 1P8
Type: Public, provincial, two-year
Degrees: C, A
URL: http://www.cnc.bc.ca
Phone: (250) 562-2131
Prog. Accred.: Dentistry (dental assisting, dental hygiene)

College of the North Atlantic
432 Massachussetts Dr., Stephenville A2N 2Z6
Type: Public, provincial, four-year
Degrees: B
URL: http://www.cna.nl.ca
Phone: (709) 643-7730
Prog. Accred.: Business (ACBSP)

Clarenville Campus
69 Pleasant St., Clarenville A5A 1V9
Phone: (709) 466-6900
Prog. Accred: Business (ACBSP)

Corner Brook Campus
PO Box 822, Corner Brook A2H 6H6
Phone: (709) 637-8530
Prog. Accred: Business (ACBSP), Forestry

Prince Phillip Drive Campus
PO Box 1693, St. John's A1C 5P7
Phone: (709) 758-7284
Prog. Accred: Business (ACBSP)

Qatar Campus
PO Box 24449, 68 Al Tarafa, Duhail North, Doha, Qatar
Phone: 011 974 495-2222
Prog. Accred: Business (ACBSP)

College of Outaouais
333 boul. de la Cité-des-Jeunes Gatineau, Hull J8Y 6M
Type: Public, provincial
Degrees: C
URL: http://www.cegepoutaouais.qc.ca
Phone: (819) 770-4012
Prog. Accred.: Dentistry (dental hygiene)

College of the Rockies
2700 College Way, PO Box 8500, Cranbrook V1C 5L7
Type: Public, local, four-year
Degrees: C, A, B
URL: http://www.cotr.bc.ca
Phone: (250) 489-2751
Prog. Accred.: Dentistry (dental assisting)

Columbia College
802 Manning Rd. NE, Calgary T2E 7N8
Type: Public, provincial
Degrees: C
URL: http://www.columbia.ab.ca
Phone: (403) 235-9300
Prog. Accred.: Dentistry (dental assisting)

Concordia University
1455 de Maisonneuve Blvd. West, Montreal H3G 1M8
Type: Private, independent, four-year
Degrees: A, B, M, D
URL: http://www.concordia.ca
Phone: (514) 848-2424 *Calendar:* Sem. plan
Prog. Accred.: Business (AACSB), Clinical Psychology

Confederation College
PO Box 398, Thunder Bay P7C 4W1
Type: Public, provincial
Degrees: C
URL: http://www.confederationc.on.ca
Phone: (807) 475-6110 *Calendar:* Sem. plan
Prog. Accred.: Dentistry (dental hygiene)

Dalhousie University
Halifax B3H 3J5
Type: Private, independent, four-year
Degrees: B, M, P, D
URL: http://www.dal.ca
Phone: (902) 424-2211 *Calendar:* Sem. plan
Prog. Accred.: Allied Health (health services administration, medicine), Business (AACSB), Dentistry (dental hygiene, dentistry, oral and maxillofacial surgery, prosthodontics), Librarianship

Dawson College
2120 Sherbrooke St. East, Montreal H2K 1C1
Type: Private, independent
Degrees: C
URL: http://www.dawsoncollege.qc.ca
Phone: (514) 931-8371 *Calendar:* Sem. plan
Prog. Accred.: Interior Design

Douglas College
PO Box 2503, 700 Royal Ave., New Westminster V3L 5B2
Type: Public, provincial, two-year
Degrees: C, A
URL: http://www.douglas.bc.ca
Phone: (604) 527-5400 *Calendar:* Sem. plan
Prog. Accred.: Dentistry (dental assisting)

Durham College
2000 Simcoe St. North, Oshawa L1H 7K4
Type: Public, provincial
Degrees: C
URL: http://www.durhamcollege.ca
Phone: (905) 721-2000 *Calendar:* Sem. plan
Prog. Accred.: Dentistry (dental hygiene)

Fanshawe College
PO Box 7005, London N5Y 5R6
Type: Public, provincial
Degrees: C
URL: http://www.fanshawec.ca/EN
Phone: (519) 452-4430
Prog. Accred.: Dentistry (dental assisting, dental hygiene)

Franáois-Xavier Garneau College
1660, Blvd. de l'Entente, Québec G1S 4S3
Type: Public, provincial
Degrees: C
URL: http://www.cegep-fxg.qc.ca
Phone: (418) 688-8310 *Calendar:* Sem. plan
Prog. Accred.: Dentistry (dental hygiene)

George Brown College
PO Box 1015, Station B, Toronto M5T 2T9
Type: Public, provincial
Degrees: C
URL: http://www.georgebrown.ca
Phone: (416) 415-2000 *Calendar:* Sem. plan
Prog. Accred.: Dentistry (dental assisting, dental hygiene)

Georgian College
One Georgian Dr., Barrie L4M 3X9
Type: Public, provincial
Degrees: C
URL: http://www.georgianc.on.ca
Phone: (705) 728-1968 *Calendar:* Sem. plan
Prog. Accred.: Dentistry (dental assisting, dental hygiene)

HEC Montréal
3000 Chemin de la Cùte-Sainte-Catherine, Montréal H3T 2A7
Type: Private, independent, four-year
Degrees: C, B, M, D
URL: http://www.hec.ca
Phone: (514) 340-6000 *Calendar:* Sem. plan
Prog. Accred.: Business (AACSB)

Holland College
140 Weymouth St., Charlottetown C1A 4Z1
Type: Public, provincial
Degrees: C
URL: http://www.hollandc.pe.ca
Phone: (902) 629-4217
Prog. Accred.: Dentistry (dental assisting)

Humber College of Applied Arts and Technology
205 Humber College Blvd., Toronto M9W 5L7
Type: Public, provincial, four-year
Degrees: C, B
URL: http://www.humberc.on.ca
Phone: (416) 675-3111 *Calendar:* Sem. plan
Prog. Accred.: Interior Design

Interfaith Institute for Couples and Families
480 Charles St. East, Kitchener N2G 4K5
Type: Private, independent, four-year
Degrees: M
URL: http://www.interfaithmft.on.ca
Phone: (519) 884-0000
Prog. Accred.: Marriage and Family Therapy

International Academy of Merchandising and Design—Toronto
31 Wellesley St., East, Toronto M4V 1G7
Type: Private, proprietary
Degrees: C
URL: http://www.iadt.ca
Phone: (416) 927-7811
Prog. Accred.: Interior Design

Izaak Walton Killam Health Centre
5850 University Ave., Halifax B3J 3G9
Type: Private, independent
Degrees: C
URL: http://www.iwk.nshealth.ca
Phone: (902) 470-8888
Prog. Accred.: Dentistry (general practice residency)

Jewish General Hospital
3755 Cùte-Sainte-Catherine Rd., Montréal H3T 1E2
Type: Private, independent
Degrees: C
URL: http://www.jgh.ca
Phone: (514) 340-8210
Prog. Accred.: Marriage and Family Therapy

John Abbott College
PO Box 2000, Ste. Anne de Bellevue H9X 3L9
Type: Public, provincial
Degrees: C
URL: http://www.johnabbott.qc.ca
Phone: (514) 457-6610 *Calendar:* Sem. plan
Prog. Accred.: Dentistry (dental hygiene)

Keyin College
PO Box 13609, Station A, St. John's A1B 4G1
Type: Private, proprietry
Degrees: C
URL: http://www.keyin.com
Phone: (709) 579-1061
Prog. Accred.: Dentistry (dental assisting)

Kwantlen Polytechnic University
12666 - 72nd Ave., Surrey V3W 2M8
Type: Public, provincial
Degrees: C
URL: http://www.kwantlen.bc.ca
Phone: (604) 599-2100 *Calendar:* Sem. plan
Prog. Accred.: Business (ACBSP), Interior Design

La Cité Collégiale
801, promenade de l'Aviation, Ottawa K1K 4R3
Type: Public, provincial
Degrees: C
URL: http://www3.lacitec.on.ca
Phone: (613) 742-2483
Prog. Accred.: Dentistry (dental hygiene)

Maisonneuve College
3800, rue Sherbrooke Est, Montréal H1X 2A2
Type: Public, provincial
Degrees: C
URL: http://www.cmaisonneuve.qc.ca
Phone: (514) 254-7131
Prog. Accred.: Dentistry (dental hygiene)

Malaspina University-College
900 Fifth St., Nanaimo V9R 5S5
Type: Public, provincial, four-year
Degrees: C, A, B, M
URL: http://www.mala.ca
Phone: (250) 753-3245 *Calendar:* Sem. plan
Prog. Accred.: Dentistry (dental assisting)

Maritime College of Forest Technology
1350 Regent St., Fredericton E3C 2G6
Type: Public, provincial
Degrees: C
URL: http://www.mcft.ca/English.htm
Phone: (506) 458-0653 *Calendar:* Sem. plan
Prog. Accred.: Forestry

McMaster University
1280 Main St., West, Hamilton L8S 4L8
Type: Private, Baptist Convention of Ontario and Quebec, four-year
Degrees: B, M, P, D
URL: http://www.mcmaster.ca
Phone: (905) 525-9140 *Calendar:* Sem. plan
Prog. Accred.: Allied Health (medicine), Business (AACSB)

Memorial University of Newfoundland
St. John's A1C 5S7
Type: Public, provincial, four-year
Degrees: B, M, P, D
URL: http://www.mun.ca
Phone: (709) 737-8000 *Calendar:* Sem. plan
Prog. Accred.: Allied Health (medicine), Business (AACSB)

Michener Institute for Applied Health Sciences
222 St. Patrick St., Toronto M5T 1V4
Type: Private, independent
Degrees: C
URL: http://www.michener.on.ca
Phone: (416) 596-3101 *Calendar:* Sem. plan
Prog. Accred.: Acupuncture

Mount Royal College
4825 Mount Royal Gate SW, Calgary T3E 6K6
Type: Private, independent, four-year
Degrees: B
URL: http://www.mtroyal.ab.ca
Phone: (403) 440-6111 *Calendar:* Sem. plan
Prog. Accred.: Interior Design

New Brunswick Community College
505, rue du Collège, Dieppe E1A 7H9
Type: Public, provincial
Degrees: C
URL: http://collegecommunautaire.ccnb.nb.ca
Phone: (506) 856-2200 *Calendar:* Sem. plan
Prog. Accred.: Interior Design

Niagara College
300 Woodlawn Rd., Welland L3C 7L3
Type: Public, provincial
Degrees: C
URL: http://www.niagaracollege.ca
Phone: (905) 735-2211 *Calendar:* Qtr. plan
Prog. Accred.: Dentistry (dental assisting, dental hygiene)

Northern Alberta Institute of Technology
11762 106 St., Edmonton T5G 2R1
Type: Public, provincial
Degrees: C
URL: http://www.nait.ca
Phone: (780) 471-7400 *Calendar:* Sem. plan
Prog. Accred.: Dentistry (dental assisting)

Northern Ontario School of Medicine
935 Ramsey Lake Rd., Sudbury P3E 2C6
Type: Public, independent, four-year
Degrees: B, P
URL: http://www.normed.ca
Phone: (705) 675-4883 *Calendar:* Sem. plan
Prog. Accred.: Allied Health (medicine)

Thunder Bay Campus
955 Oliver Rd., Thunder Bay P7B 5E1
Phone: (807) 766-7300

Nova Scotia Community College
PO Box 220, Halifax B3J 2M4
Type: Public, provincial
Degrees: C
URL: http://www.nscc.ca
Phone: (902) 491-4911 *Calendar:* Sem. plan
Prog. Accred.: Dentistry (dental assisting)

Okanagan College
1000 KLO Rd., Kelowna V1Y 4X8
Type: Public, provincial, four-year
Degrees: C, B
URL: http://www.okanagan.bc.ca
Phone: (250) 762-5445
Prog. Accred.: Dentistry (dental assisting)

Ontario Dental Education Institute
201 Wilson St. East, Level 1, Ancaster L9G 2B8
Type: Private, independent
Degrees: C
URL: http://www.on-dei.com
Phone: (905) 304 4706
Prog. Accred.: Dentistry (dental hygiene)

Oulton College
55 Lutz St., Moncton E1C 0L2
Type: Private, proprietary
Degrees: C
URL: http://www.oultoncollege.com
Phone: (506) 858-9696
Prog. Accred.: Dentistry (dental assisting)

Oxford College of Arts, Business and Technology
670 Progress Ave., Scarborough M1H 3A4
Type: Private, proprietary
Degrees: C
URL: http://oxfordedu.ca
Phone: (416) 439-8668 *Calendar:* Sem. plan
Prog. Accred.: Dentistry (dental hygiene)

Queen's University at Kingston
99 University Ave., Kingston K7L 3N6
Type: Public, provincial, four-year
Degrees: M, D
URL: http://www.queensu.ca
Phone: (613) 533-2000 *Calendar:* Sem. plan
Prog. Accred.: Allied Health (medicine), Business (AACSB), Clinical Psychology

Red River College
2055 Notre Dame Ave., Winnipeg R3H 0J9
Type: Public, provincial
Degrees: C
URL: http://www.rrc.mb.ca
Phone: (204) 632-3960
Prog. Accred.: Dentistry (dental assisting)

Regency Dental Hygiene Academy
481 University Ave., Suite 400, Toronto M5G 2E9
Type: Private, proprietary, four-year
Degrees: D
URL: http://www.regencydha.com
Phone: (416) 341-0100 ext 1
Prog. Accred.: Dentistry (dental hygiene)

Ryerson University
350 Victoria St., Toronto M5B 2K3
Type: Private, independent, four-year
Degrees: B
URL: http://www.ryerson.ca
Phone: (416) 979-5000 *Calendar:* Sem. plan
Prog. Accred.: Interior Design

Saint Clair College of Applied Arts and Technology
2000 Talbot Rd. West, Windsor N9A 6S4
Type: Private, independent
Degrees: C
URL: http://www.stclairc.on.ca
Phone: (519) 966-1656
Prog. Accred.: Dentistry (dental assisting, dental hygiene), Interior Design

Saint-Hyacinthe College
3000, Ave. Boullé, Saint-Hyacinthe J2S 1H9
Type: Public, provincial
Degrees: C
URL: http://www.cegepsth.qc.ca
Phone: (450) 773-6800 *Calendar:* Qtr. plan
Prog. Accred.: Dentistry (dental hygiene)

Saint Mary's University
923 Robie St., Halifax B3H 3C3
Type: Private, independent, four-year
Degrees: B, M, D
URL: http://www.smu.ca
Phone: (902) 420-5400 *Calendar:* Sem. plan
Prog. Accred.: Business (AACSB)

Saskatchewan Institute of Applied Science and Technology—Palliser
Box 1420, Moose Jaw S6H 4R4
Type: Public, provincial
Degrees: C
URL: http://www.siast.sk.ca
Phone: (306) 694-3200
Prog. Accred.: Construction Education

Wascana Campus
PO Box 556, Regina S4P 3A3
Phone: (306) 798-4356
Prog. Accred: Dentistry (dental assisting, dental hygiene)

Sheridan College
1430 Trafalger Rd., Oakville L6H 2L1
Type: Public, provincial, four-year
Degrees: C, B
URL: http://www.sheridanc.on.ca
Phone: (905) 845-9430
Prog. Accred.: Interior Design, Montessori Teacher Education

Simon Fraser University
8888 University Dr., Burnaby V5A 1S6
Type: Public, provincial, four-year
Degrees: C, A, B
URL: http://www.sfu.ca
Phone: (604) 291-3111 *Calendar:* Sem. plan
Prog. Accred.: Business (AACSB), Clinical Psychology

Southern Alberta Institute of Technology
1301-16 Ave. NW, Calgary T2M 0L4
Type: Public, provincial
Degrees: C
URL: http://www.sait.ab.ca
Phone: (403) 284-7248
Prog. Accred.: Dentistry (dental assisting)

Three Rivers College
3500 De courval, Trois-Rivieres G9A 5E6
Type: Public, provincial
Degrees: C
URL: https://cegeptr.qc.ca
Phone: (819) 376-1721
Prog. Accred.: Dentistry (dental hygiene)

Toronto College for Dental Hygiene and Auxiliaries
300 Steeprock Dr., Toronto M3J 2W9
Type: Private, proprietary
Degrees: C
URL: http://www.toronto-college-dental.org/en
Phone: (416) 423-3099
Prog. Accred.: Dentistry (dental hygiene)

Université de Montréal
Case Postal 6128, Succursale A, Montréal H3C 3J7
Type: Private, independent, four-year
Degrees: B, M, P, D
URL: http://www.umontreal.ca
Phone: (514) 343-6111 *Calendar:* Sem. plan
Prog. Accred.: Allied Health (health services administration, medicine, optometric residency, optometry), Dentistry (combined prosthodontics, dentistry, general practice residency, orthodontic and dentofacial orthopedics, pediatric dentistry), Landscape Architecture, Librarianship, Planning, Public Health, Veterinary Medicine

Université de Sherbrooke
2500 Blvd. de l'Université, Sherbrooke J1K 2R1
Type: Private, independent, four-year
Degrees: B, M, P, D
URL: http://www.usherbrooke.ca
Phone: (819) 821-7000 *Calendar:* Sem. plan
Prog. Accred.: Allied Health (medicine)

Université Laval
Cité Universitairé, Québec City G1K 7P4
Type: Private, independent, four-year
Degrees: B, M, P, D
URL: http://www.ulaval.ca
Phone: (418) 656-2131 *Calendar:* Sem. plan
Prog. Accred.: Allied Health (medicine), Business (AACSB), Dentistry (dentistry, oral and maxillofacial surgery, periodontics)

University College of the North
PO Box 3000, The Pas R9A 1M7
Type: Public, provincial, two-year
Degrees: C, A
URL: https://www.ucn.ca/ics
Phone: (204) 627-8500
Prog. Accred.: Dentistry (dental assisting)

University of Alberta
3-1 University Hall, Edmonton, Alberta T6G-2E1
Type: Public, provincial, four-year
Degrees: B, P, M, D
URL: http://www.ualberta.ca
Phone: (780) 492-3111 *Calendar:* Sem. plan
Prog. Accred.: Allied Health (medicine), Business (AACSB), Dentistry (dental hygiene, dentistry, orthodontic and dentofacial orthopedics), Librarianship

University of British Columbia
6328 Memorial Rd., Vancouver, BC V6T 1Z2
Type: Public, provincial, four-year
Degrees: B, P, M, D
URL: http://www.ubc.ca
Phone: (604) 822-5017 *Calendar:* Sem. plan
Prog. Accred.: Allied Health (medicine), Business (AACSB), Clinical Psychology, Counseling Psychology, Dentistry (dentistry, general practice residency, oral and maxillofacial radiology, periodontics), Landscape Architecture, Librarianship, Planning

University of Calgary
2500 University Dr. NW, Calgary T2N 1N4
Type: Public, provincial, four-year
Degrees: B, M, P, D
URL: http://www.ucalgary.ca
Phone: (403) 220-5110 *Calendar:* Sem. plan
Prog. Accred.: Allied Health (medicine), Business (AACSB), Veterinary Medicine

University of Guelph
50 Stone Rd. East, Guelph N1G 2W1
Type: Public, provincial, four-year
Degrees: B, M
URL: http://www.uoguelph.ca
Phone: (519) 824-4120 *Calendar:* Sem. plan
Prog. Accred.: Landscape Architecture, Marriage and Family Therapy, Veterinary Medicine

Ridgetown Campus
120 Main St. East, Ridgetown N0P 2C0
Prog. Accred: Veterinary Technology

University of Manitoba
Winnipeg R3T 2N2
Type: Public, provincial, four-year
Degrees: B, M, P, D
URL: http://www.umanitoba.ca
Phone: (204) 474-8880 *Calendar:* Sem. plan
Prog. Accred.: Allied Health (medicine), Business (AACSB), Clinical Psychology, Dentistry (dental hygiene, dentistry, oral and maxillofacial surgery, orthodontic and dentofacial orthopedics, periodontics), Interior Design, Landscape Architecture, Psychology Internship

University of Ottawa
550 Cumberland, Ottawa K1N 6N5
Type: Public, provincial, four-year
Degrees: B, M, P, D
URL: http://www.uottawa.ca
Phone: (613) 562-5700 *Calendar:* Sem. plan
Prog. Accred.: Allied Health (medicine), Business (AACSB), Clinical Psychology, Psychology Internship

University of Prince Edward Island
550 University Ave., Charlottetown C1A 4P3
Type: Public, provincial, four-year
Degrees: C, A, B
URL: http://www.upei.ca
Phone: (902) 566-0439 *Calendar:* Sem. plan
Prog. Accred.: Veterinary Medicine

University of Saskatchewan
Saskatoon S7N 0W0
Type: Public, provincial, four-year
Degrees: B, M, P, D
URL: http://www.usask.ca
Phone: (306) 966-4343 *Calendar:* Sem. plan
Prog. Accred.: Allied Health (medicine), Clinical Psychology, Dentistry (dentistry), Veterinary Medicine

University of the Fraser Valley—Chilliwack Campus
45635 Yale Rd., Chilliwack V2P 6T4
Type: Public, provincial
Degrees: C
URL: http://www.ucfv.ca
Phone: (604) 792-0025
Prog. Accred.: Dentistry (dental assisting)

University of Toronto
27 King's College Circle, Toronto M5S 1A1
Type: Public, provincial, four-year
Degrees: B, M, P, D
URL: http://www.utoronto.ca
Phone: (416) 978-2011 *Calendar:* Sem. plan
Prog. Accred.: Allied Health (health services administration, medical illustration, medicine), Business (AACSB), Combined Professional-Scientific Psychology, Dentistry (combined prosthodontics, dental public health, dentistry, endodontics, oral and maxillofacial pathology, oral and maxillofacial radiology, oral and maxillofacial surgery, orthodontic and dentofacial orthopedics, pediatric dentistry, periodontics), Landscape Architecture, Librarianship, Physical Therapy

University of Victoria
Victoria V8W 3P5
Type: Public, provincial, four-year
Degrees: B, M, D
URL: http://www.uvic.ca
Phone: (250) 721-7211 *Calendar:* Qtr. plan
Prog. Accred.: Clinical Psychology

University of Waterloo
University Ave., Waterloo N2L 3G1
Type: Public, provincial, four-year
Degrees: B, M, P
URL: http://www.uwaterloo.ca
Phone: (519) 888-4567 *Calendar:* Sem. plan
Prog. Accred.: Allied Health (optometry), Clinical Psychology

University of Western Ontario
1151 Richmond St., Suite 2, London N6A 5B8
Type: Private, independent, four-year
Degrees: B, M, P, D
URL: http://www.uwo.ca
Phone: (519) 679-2111 *Calendar:* Sem. plan
Prog. Accred.: Allied Health (medicine), Clinical Psychology, Dentistry (dentistry, oral and maxillofacial surgery, orthodontic and dentofacial orthopedics), Librarianship, Physical Therapy

University of Windsor
401 Sunset Ave., Windsor N9B 3P4
Type: Public, provincial, four-year
Degrees: B, M, P, D
URL: http://www.uwindsor.ca
Phone: (519) 253-3000 *Calendar:* Sem. plan
Prog. Accred.: Clinical Psychology

Vancouver College of Dental Hygiene
3030 East Broadway, Vancouver V5M 1Z4
Type: Private, proprietary
Degrees: C
URL: http://www.vancouver-college-dental.org
Phone: (604) 215-7611
Prog. Accred.: Dentistry (dental hygiene)

Vancouver Community College
250 West Pender St., Vancouver V6B 1S9
Type: Public, local, two-year
Degrees: C, A
URL: http://www.vcc.ca
Phone: (604) 443-8300 *Calendar:* Sem. plan
Prog. Accred.: Dentistry (dental assisting, dental hygiene)

Vancouver Island University
900 Fifth St., Nanaimo V9R 5S5
Type: Public, provincial, four-year
Degrees: B, M
URL: http://www.mala.ca
Phone: (250) 753-3245 *Calendar:* Sem. plan
Prog. Accred.: Business (ACBSP)

West Coast College of Health Care
#204-9648 128 St., Surrey V3T 2X9
Type: Private, proprietary
Degrees: C
URL: http://www.westcoastcollege.com
Phone: (604) 951-6644
Prog. Accred.: Dentistry (dental assisting)

Wilfrid Laurier University
75 University Ave. West, Waterloo N2L 3C5
Type: Public, provincial, four-year
Degrees: B, M, D
URL: http://www.wlu.ca
Phone: (519) 884-1970 *Calendar:* Tri. plan
Prog. Accred.: Business (AACSB)

York University
4700 Keele St., Toronto M3J 1P3
Type: Public, independent, four-year
Degrees: B, M, D
URL: http://www.yorku.ca
Phone: (416) 736-2100 *Calendar:* Sem. plan
Prog. Accred.: Clinical Psychology

CHILE

Adolfo Ibanez University
Balmaceda 1625, Recreo, Viòa del Mar
Type: Private, independent, four-year
Degrees: B, M
URL: http://www.uai.cl
Phone: 011 (56-32) 503-727
Prog. Accred.: Business (AACSB)

Pontificia Universidad Catolica de Chile
Casilla 114-D, Avienda Bernardo O'Higgins 340, Santiago
Type: Private, independent, four-year
Degrees: M
URL: http://www.per.puc.cl
Phone: 011 56 2 222-4516
Prog. Accred.: Business (AACSB), Journalism

CHINA

Tsinghua University
Beijing 100084
Type: Public, state-controlled, four-year
Degrees: B, M, D
URL: http://www.tsinghua.edu.cn/eng
Phone: 011 86-10-6278-2015 *Calendar:* Sem. plan
Prog. Accred.: Accounting, Business (AACSB)

COLOMBIA

EAN University
Calle 72 No. 9-71, Bogota
Type: Private, independent, four-year
Degrees: B, M
URL: http://www.ean.edu.co
Phone: 011 571 540-0330
Prog. Accred.: Business (ACBSP)

FINLAND

Helsinki School of Economics
PO Box 1210, Helsinki 00101
Type: Public, independent, four-year
Degrees: B, M, D
URL: http://www.hse.fi/EN/
Phone: 011 358 9 43131
Prog. Accred.: Business (AACSB)

FRANCE

Audencia Nantes Ecole de Management
8 route de la Joneliëre, BP 31222, 44312, Nantes CEDEX 3
Type: Private, independent, four-year
Degrees: B, M
URL: http://www.audencia.com
Phone: 011 33 (0) 2 40 37 3
Prog. Accred.: Business (AACSB)

Centre Européan de Management Hôtelier International
52 Rue Saint Lazare, Paris 75009
Type: Private, proprietary, four-year
Degrees: C, B, M
URL: http://www.cmh-school.com
Phone: 011 33 01 45 26 59 2
Prog. Accred.: Business (ACBSP)

Ecole de hautes Etudes commerciales du Nord
58, rue du Port, Lille 59046
Type: Private, independent, four-year
Degrees: M
URL: http://www.edhec.com
Phone: 011 33 3 20 15 45 00
Prog. Accred.: Business (AACSB)

Nice Campus
393, Promenade des Anglais, BP3116, Nice, 59 06202
Phone: 011 33 04 93 18 99 6

Ecole de Management de Lyon
23 Ave. Guy de Collongue, BP 174, Ecully 69134
Type: Private, independent, four-year
Degrees: M
URL: http://www.em-lyon.com
Phone: 011 33 4 78 33 78 00 *Calendar:* Tri. plan
Prog. Accred.: Business (AACSB)

Ecole des Hautes Etudes Commerciales
1, rue de la Libération, Jouy en Josas 78351
Type: Private, independent, four-year
Degrees: M
URL: http://www.hec.edu
Phone: 011 33 1 4409 3400
Prog. Accred.: Business (AACSB)

Ecole supérieure de Commerce de Grenoble
BP 127, 12, rue Pierre Sémard, Grenoble 38003
Type: Private, independent, four-year
Degrees: C, B, M, D
URL: http://www.grenoble-em.com
Phone: 011 33 4 76 70 60 60 *Calendar:* Sem. plan
Prog. Accred.: Business (AACSB)

Ecole supérieure de Commerce de Paris
79, Ave. de la Répoblique, Paris CEDEX 75543
Type: Private, independent, four-year
Degrees: M
URL: http://www.escp-eap.net
Phone: 011 33 3 49 23 20 00
Prog. Accred.: Business (AACSB)

Ecole Superieure des Sciences Economiques et Commerciales
Avenue Bernard Hirsch, BP 50105, Cergy-Pontoise Cedex 95021
Type: Private, independent, four-year
Degrees: M
URL: http://www.essec.edu
Phone: 011 33 1 34 43 30 00
Prog. Accred.: Business (AACSB)

Groupe Ecole supérieure de Commerce et de Management
1 rue Léo Delibes, BP 0535, Tours 37205
Type: Private, federal, four-year
Degrees: M
URL: http://www.escem.fr
Phone: 011 33 247 71 71 71
Prog. Accred.: Business (AACSB)

Groupe ESC Clermont
4 Blvd. Trudaine, Clermont-Ferrand 63037
Type: Private, independent, four-year
Degrees: M
URL: http://www.esc-clermont.fr
Phone: 011 33 04 73 98 24 2
Prog. Accred.: Business (AACSB)

Groupe ESC Toulouse
BP 7010, 20, Blvd. Lascrosses, Toulouse 31068
Type: Private, independent, four-year
Degrees: B, M
URL: http://www.esc-toulouse.fr
Phone: 011 33 5 61 29 49 49
Prog. Accred.: Business (AACSB)

INSEAD
Boulevard de Constance, Fontainebleau 77305
Type: Private, independent, four-year
Degrees: M, D
URL: http://www.insead.edu
Phone: 011 33 1 60 72 40 00 *Calendar:* Tri. plan
Prog. Accred.: Business (AACSB)

Singapore Campus
1 Ayer Rajah Ave., Singapore 138676

Institut Européen de Management International
52 Rue Saint Lazare, Paris 75009
Type: Private, independent, four-year
Degrees: M
URL: http://www.iemi.com
Phone: 011 33 01 45 26 59
Prog. Accred.: Business (ACBSP)

Institut Supérieur de Gestion
8, rue de Lota, Paris 75116
Type: Private, independent, four-year
Degrees: B
URL: http://www.isg.fr
Phone: 011 330 1-56-26-11-1
Prog. Accred.: Business (ACBSP)

International School of Management
148, rue de Grenelle, Paris 75007
Type: Private, independent, four-year
Degrees: M, D
URL: http://www.ism.edu
Phone: 011 33 (0)1 45 51 09
Prog. Accred.: Business (ACBSP)

GEORGIA

American University for Humanities
Agmashenebeli Ave., Tbilisi
Type: Private, independent, four-year
Degrees: C, B
URL: http://www.auhtc.net
Phone: 011 995-32 956993 *Calendar:* Sem. plan
Prog. Accred.: Liberal Education

GERMANY

HHL-Leipzig Graduate School of Management
Jahnallee 59, Leipzig 04109
Type: Private, independent, four-year
Degrees: M
URL: http://www.hhl.de
Phone: 011 49 341 985-1600
Prog. Accred.: Business (AACSB)

Johann Wolfgang Goethe-Universitüt Frankfurt am Main
Senckenberganlage 31, Frankfurt am Main 60325
Type: Public, state, four-year
Degrees: B, M, D
URL: http://www.uni-frankfurt.de
Phone: 011 49 69 7980
Prog. Accred.: Business (AACSB)

University of Mannheim
Schloss, Mannheim 68131
Type: Public, state, four-year
Degrees: M
URL: http://www.uni-mannheim.de
Phone: 011 49 621 181 1013
Prog. Accred.: Business (AACSB)

HONG KONG

The Chinese University of Hong Kong
Shatin SAR
Type: Private, independent, four-year
Degrees: B, M
URL: http://www.cuhk.edu.hk/v6/en
Phone: 011 852 2609 6000 *Calendar:* Qtr. plan
Prog. Accred.: Accounting, Business (AACSB)

City University of Hong Kong
Tat Chee Ave., Kowloon SAR
Type: Private, independent, four-year
Degrees: A, B, M, D
URL: http://www.cityu.edu.hk
Phone: 011 (852) 2788 7654 *Calendar:* Sem. plan
Prog. Accred.: Business (AACSB)

Hong Kong University of Science and Technology
Clear Water Bay, Kowloon, SAR
Type: Public, Hong Kong Government, four-year
Degrees: B, M
URL: http://www.ust.hk
Phone: 011 852 2258 6000 *Calendar:* Sem. plan
Prog. Accred.: Accounting, Business (AACSB)

IRELAND

Liberties College
Bull Alley St., Dublin 8
Type: Public, government-supported
Degrees: C
URL: http://www.libertiescollege.ie
Phone: 011 353 1 454 0044
Prog. Accred.: Montessori Teacher Education

University College Dublin
Belfield, DU 4
Type: Public, federal, four-year
Degrees: B
URL: http://www.ucd.ie
Phone: 011 353 1 716 7777 *Calendar:* Sem. plan
Prog. Accred.: Business (AACSB), Veterinary Medicine

ISRAEL

Tel Aviv University
PO Box 39040, Ramat-Aviv 69978
Type: Public, autonomous, four-year
Degrees: B, M
URL: http://www.tau.ac.il
Phone: 011 972 3 6408-111 *Calendar:* Sem. plan
Prog. Accred.: Business (AACSB)

JAPAN

3rd Dental Battalion/NDC Okinawa
Unit 38450, FPO AP 96604-8450, Okinawa
Type: Public, federal
Degrees: C
URL: http://www.3fssg.usmc.mil/legacy/dentalbn
Phone: 011 81 61 745 7157
Prog. Accred.: Dentistry (advanced education in general dentistry)

International Christian University
10-2, Osawa 3-chome, Mitaka-shi
Type: Private, nondenominational, four-year
Degrees: B
URL: http://www.icu.ac.jp
Phone: 011 81-422-33-3043
Prog. Accred.: Liberal Education

Keio University
2-15-45 Mita, Minato-ku 108-8345
Type: Private, independent, four-year
Degrees: M
URL: http://www.keio.ac.jp
Phone: 011 81 3 3453 4511
Prog. Accred.: Business (AACSB)

Nagoya University of Commerce and Business
4-4 Sagamine, Komenoki-cho, Nisshin City 470-0193
Type: Private, independent, four-year
Degrees: B, M
URL: http://www.nucba.ac.jp
Phone: 011 81 561-73-2111
Prog. Accred.: Business (AACSB)

KUWAIT

American University of Kuwait
PO Box 3323, Safat 13034
Type: Private, independent, four-year
Degrees: B
URL: http://www.auk.edu.kw
Phone: 011 965-224-8399 *Calendar:* Sem. plan
Prog. Accred.: Business (ACBSP)

Kuwait University
PO Box 5969, Khaldiya, Sarat 13060
Type: Public, state, four-year
Degrees: B, M
URL: http://www.kuniv.edu.kw
Phone: 011 965 481-1188
Prog. Accred.: Business (AACSB)

MEXICO

Autonomous Technical Institute of Mexico
Rio Honda 1, Tizapan, San Angel, Alvaro Obregon 01000
Type: Public, state, four-year
Degrees: M
URL: http://www.itam.mx/en
Phone: 011 52 55 56 28 4000
Prog. Accred.: Business (AACSB)

National Institute of Public Health
Avienda Universidad 655, Col. Santa Maria Ahuacatitlan, Cuernavacas, MO 62508
Type: Public, federal, four-year
Degrees: B, M
URL: http://www.insp.mx
Phone: 011 52 73 11-03-45
Prog. Accred.: Public Health

Universidad Panamericana
Floresta 20, Col. Claveria, Del. Azcapotzalco
Type: Private, independent, four-year
Degrees: M
URL: http://www.ipade.mx
Phone: 011 52 5 527-02-62
Prog. Accred.: Business (AACSB)

NETHERLANDS

Erasmus University Rotterdam
Postbus 1738, Burgermeester Oudlaan 50, Rotterdam 3000 DR
Type: Private, independent, four-year
Degrees: M, D
URL: http://www.eur.nl
Phone: 011 31 10 408 1649 *Calendar:* Sem. plan
Prog. Accred.: Business (AACSB)

Maastricht School of Management
PO Box 1203, Maastricht, 00 6201
Type: Private, independent
URL: http://www.msm.nl
Phone: 011 31 43 387 08 08
Prog. Accred.: Business (ACBSP)

Maastricht University
Postbus 616, Maastricht 6200 MD
Type: Private, independent, four-year
Degrees: M, D
URL: http://www.unimaas.nl
Phone: 011 31 43 388 2222
Prog. Accred.: Business (AACSB)

Tilburg University
Warandelaan 2, PO Box 90153, Tilburg 5000 LE
Type: Public, provincial, four-year
Degrees: C, M
URL: http://www.tilburguniversity.nl
Phone: 011 31 13 466 9111
Prog. Accred.: Business (AACSB)

University of Utrecht
PO Box 80.163, 3508 TD, Utrecht
Type: Public, provincial, four-year
Degrees: P
URL: http://www.ruu.nl
Phone: 011 31 30 2531815
Prog. Accred.: Veterinary Medicine

NEW ZEALAND

Massey University—Palmerston North
Private Bag 11 222, Palmerston North
Type: Public, national, four-year
Degrees: B, M, D
URL: http://palmerstonnorth.massey.ac.nz
Phone: 011 64 6 356 9099
Prog. Accred.: Veterinary Medicine

The University of Auckland
Private Bag 92019, Auckland Mail Centre, Auckland 1142
Type: Public, national, four-year
Degrees: B, M, D
URL: http://www.auckland.ac.nz
Phone: 011 64 9 373 7999 *Calendar:* Sem. plan
Prog. Accred.: Business (AACSB)

University of Otago
PO Box 56, Dunedin 9054
Type: Public, national, four-year
Degrees: B, M
URL: http://www.otago.ac.nz
Phone: 011 64 3 479 1100
Prog. Accred.: Business (AACSB)

The University of Waikato
Private Bag 3105, Gate 1 Knighton Rd., Hamilton 3240
Type: Public, national, four-year
Degrees: B, M, D
URL: http://www.waikato.ac.nz
Phone: 011 64 7 856-2889 *Calendar:* Sem. plan
Prog. Accred.: Business (AACSB)

PANAMA

ADEN Business School Panama
Edificio Nueva PH Torre Global Piso 30 Calle 50
Type: Private, independent, four-year
Degrees: B
URL: http://www.aden.org
Phone: 011 2630-299
Prog. Accred.: Business (ACBSP)

PERU

Universidad de San Martin de Porres
Ciudad Universitaria Avenida, Las Calandrias, Santa Anita, Lima
Type: Private, independent, four-year
Degrees: B, M
URL: http://www.usmp.edu.pe
Phone: 011 511 362-0064
Prog. Accred.: Business (ACBSP)

PHILIPPINES

Asian Institute of Management
123 Paseo de Roxas, MCPO Box 2095, Makati City 1260
Type: Private, independent, four-year
Degrees: B, M
URL: http://www.aim.edu
Phone: 011 (632) 8924011
Prog. Accred.: Business (AACSB)

Center for Culinary Arts, Manila
287 Katipunan Ave., Loyola Heights, Quezon City 1108
Type: Private, proprietary
Degrees: C
URL: http://www.cca-manila.com
Phone: 011 63 2 426-4840
Prog. Accred.: Culinary Education

PORTUGAL

Universidade Católica Portuguesa
Palma de Cima, Lisbon 1649-023
Type: Private, independent, four-year
Degrees: B, M
URL: http://www.fcee.ucp.pt
Phone: 011 351 21 721-4000
Prog. Accred.: Business (AACSB)

REPUBLIC OF KOREA

Korea Advanced Institute of Science and Technology
373-1 Guseoung-dong, Yuseong-gu, Daejeon 305-701
Type: Private, independent, four-year
Degrees: B, M
URL: http://www.kaist.edu
Phone: 011 042 869-2114 *Calendar:* Sem. plan
Prog. Accred.: Business (AACSB)

Korea University
1 Aman-dong 5-ga, Sungbuk-gu, Seoul 136-701
Type: Private, independent, four-year
Degrees: B, M, D
URL: http://www.korea.edu
Phone: 011 82 2 926-3522 *Calendar:* Sem. plan
Prog. Accred.: Business (AACSB)

Sejong University
98 Gunja-Dong, Gwangjin-Gu, Seoul 143-747
Type: Private, independent, four-year
Degrees: B, M
URL: http://www.sejong.ac.kr/eng
Phone: 011 82-2 3408-3114
Prog. Accred.: Business (AACSB)

Seoul National University
San 56-1, Shillim-dong, Kwanak-gu, Seoul 151-742
Type: Public, national, four-year
Degrees: B, M
URL: http://www.snu.ac.kr
Phone: 011 82 2 880 5114 *Calendar:* Sem. plan
Prog. Accred.: Business (AACSB)

SAUDI ARABIA

Jubail Industrial College
PO Box 10099, Jubail Industrial City
Type: Private, royal charter, two-year
Degrees: A
URL: http://www.jic.edu.sa
Phone: 011 966 33402000 *Calendar:* Sem. plan
Prog. Accred.: Business (ACBSP)

King Fahd University of Petroleum and Minerals
Dhahran 31261
Type: Public, national, four-year
Degrees: B, M, D
URL: http://www.kfupm.edu.sa
Phone: 011 966 (3) 860 0000 *Calendar:* Sem. plan
Prog. Accred.: Business (AACSB)

Yanbu Industrial College
PO Box 30426, Madinat Yanbu Al Sinaiyah
Type: Public, royal-charter, two-year
Degrees: A
URL: http://www.yic.edu.sa
Phone: 011 966-04-3946111
Prog. Accred.: Business (ACBSP)

SINGAPORE

Nanyang Technological University
Nanyang Ave. 639798
Type: Private, independent, four-year
Degrees: B, M
URL: http://www.ntu.edu.sg
Phone: 011 (65) 6791-1744 *Calendar:* Sem. plan
Prog. Accred.: Accounting, Business (AACSB)

National University of Singapore
21 Lower Kent Ridge Rd. 119077
Type: Private, independent, four-year
Degrees: B, M, D
URL: http://www.nus.edu.sg
Phone: 011 65 6516 1811 *Calendar:* Sem. plan
Prog. Accred.: Business (AACSB)

SPAIN

ESADE Business School
Avenida de Pedralbes 60-62, Barcelona 08034
Type: Private, independent, four-year
Degrees: B, M, D
URL: http://www.esade.es
Prog. Accred.: Business (AACSB)

European University—Barcelona
Ganduxer 70, Barcelona E-08021
Type: Private, proprietary, four-year
Degrees: B, M
URL: http://www.euruni.es
Phone: 011 34 93 201 81 71 *Calendar:* Sem. plan
Prog. Accred.: Business (ACBSP)

Instituto de Empresa Business School
Maria de Molina, 11, Madrid 28006
Type: Private, independent, four-year
Degrees: M
URL: http://www.ie.edu
Phone: 011 34 91 568 9600
Prog. Accred.: Business (AACSB)

Institut Quimic de Sarria de Universitat Ramôn Llull
Via Augusta 390, Barcelona 08017
Type: Private, independent, four-year
Degrees: B, M
URL: http://www.iqs.url.es
Phone: 011 34 932 672 000
Prog. Accred.: Business (AACSB)

SWITZERLAND

BHMS-Business and Hotel Management School
Baselstrasse 57 CH-6003
Type: Private, proprietary
Degrees: C
URL: http://www.bhms.ch
Phone: 011 41 41 248 70 70
Prog. Accred.: Culinary Education

Business School Lausanne
Av. Dapples 38, PO Box 160, Lausanne CH-1001
Type: Private, independent, four-year
Degrees: B, M
URL: http://www.bsl-lausanne.ch
Phone: 011 41 21 619 06 06
Prog. Accred.: Business (ACBSP)

IMD International Institute
Ch. de Bellerive 23, PO Box 915, Lausanne CH-1001
Type: Private, independent, four-year
Degrees: M
URL: http://www.imd.ch
Phone: 011 41 21 618 0111
Prog. Accred.: Business (AACSB)

Swiss Management Center
Baarerstrasse 112, Zug CH-6302
Type: Private, independent, four-year
Degrees: B, M, D
URL: http://www.swissmc.ch
Phone: 011 410 41 500 16 22
Prog. Accred.: Business (ACBSP)

University of Saint Gallen
Dufourstrasse 50, St. Gallen CH-9000
Type: Private, independent, four-year
Degrees: B, M
URL: http://www.unisg.ch
Phone: 011 41 71 224 2111 *Calendar:* Sem. plan
Prog. Accred.: Business (AACSB)

TAIWAN, PROVINCE OF CHINA

Fu Jen Catholic University
510 Chung Cheng Rd., Taipei County, Hsinchuang 24205
Type: Private, Roman Catholic Church, four-year
Degrees: M, D
URL: http://www.fju.edu.tw
Phone: 011 886-2-29052000 *Calendar:* Sem. plan
Prog. Accred.: Business (AACSB)

National Chengchi University
No. 64, Sec. 2, ZhiNan Rd., Wenshan District, Taipei City 11605
Type: Public, state-controlled, four-year
Degrees: B, M
URL: http://2007.nccu.edu.tw/english
Phone: 011 886-2-29393091 *Calendar:* Sem. plan
Prog. Accred.: Business (AACSB)

National Chiao Tung University, College of Management
1001 Ta Hsueh Rd., Hsinchu 30050
Type: Private, independent, four-year
Degrees: B, M, D
URL: http://www.icom.nctu.edu.tw
Phone: 011 886 3 5731683 *Calendar:* Sem. plan
Prog. Accred.: Business (AACSB)

National Sun Yat-Sen University
70 Lien-hai Rd., Kaohsiung 804
Type: Public, state, four-year
Degrees: B, M, D
URL: http://www.oia.nsysu.edu.tw/english
Phone: 011 886-7-525-2633
Prog. Accred.: Business (AACSB)

TURKEY

Bilkent University
Bilkent, Ankara 06800
Type: Private, independent, four-year
Degrees: A, B, M
URL: http://www.bilkent.edu.tr
Phone: 011 90 312 290 4000 *Calendar:* Sem. plan
Prog. Accred.: Business (AACSB)

UNITED ARAB EMIRATES

Higher Colleges of Technology Abu Dhabi Men's College
PO Box 25035, Abu Dhabi
Type: Private, independent, four-year
Degrees: A, B
URL: http://www.admc.hct.ac.ae
Phone: 011 02 445 1514
Prog. Accred.: Business (ACBSP)

Higher Colleges of Technology Abu Dhabi Women's College
PO Box 41012, Abu Dhabi
Type: Private, independent, four-year
Degrees: A, B
URL: http://adw.hct.ac.ae
Phone: 011 02 6413839
Prog. Accred.: Business (ACBSP)

Higher Colleges of Technology Al Ain Men's College
PO Box 17155, Al Ain
Type: Private, independent, four-year
Degrees: A, B
URL: http://aam.hct.ac.ae
Phone: 011 971-3-782088
Prog. Accred.: Business (ACBSP)

Higher Colleges of Technology Al Ain Women's College
PO Box 17258, Al Ain
Type: Private, independent, four-year
Degrees: A, B
URL: http://aaw.hct.ac.ae
Phone: 011 03 782 0777
Prog. Accred.: Business (ACBSP)

Higher Colleges of Technology Dubai Men's College
PO Box 15825, Dubai
Type: Private, independent, four-year
Degrees: A, B
URL: http://dbm.hct.ac.ae
Phone: 011 971-4-3260333
Prog. Accred.: Business (ACBSP)

Higher Colleges of Technology Dubai Women's College
PO Box 16062, Dubai
Type: Private, independent, four-year
Degrees: A, B
URL: http://dwc.hct.ac.ae
Phone: 011 971 4 267 2929
Prog. Accred.: Business (ACBSP)

Higher Colleges of Technology Fujairah Men's College
PO Box 1626, Fujairah
Type: Private, independent, four-year
Degrees: C, B
URL: http://fjw.hct.ac.ae
Phone: 011 971-9-2011-100
Prog. Accred.: Business (ACBSP)

Higher Colleges of Technology Fujairah Women's College
PO Box 1626, Fujairah
Type: Private, independent, four-year
Degrees: C, B
URL: http://fjw.hct.ac.ae
Phone: 011 971-9-2011-100
Prog. Accred.: Business (ACBSP)

Higher Colleges of Technology Ras Al Khaimah Men's College
PO Box 4793, Ras Al Khaimah
Type: Private, independent, four-year
Degrees: A, B
URL: http://rkm.hct.ac.ae
Phone: 011 07-2462999
Prog. Accred.: Business (ACBSP)

Higher Colleges of Technology Ras Al Khaimah Women's College
PO Box 4792, Ras Al Khaimah
Type: Private, independent, four-year
Degrees: A, B
URL: http://rkw.hct.ac.ae
Phone: 011 07-2210550
Prog. Accred.: Business (ACBSP)

Higher Colleges of Technology Sharjah Men's College
PO Box 7947, Sharjah
Type: Private, independent, four-year
Degrees: A, B
URL: http://sjm.hct.ac.ae
Phone: 011 9716 5585333
Prog. Accred.: Business (ACBSP)

Higher Colleges of Technology Sharjah Women's College
PO Box 7947, Sharjah
Type: Private, independent, four-year
Degrees: A, B
URL: http://swcweb.sjwc.hct.ac.ae
Phone: 011 9716 5585333
Prog. Accred.: Business (ACBSP)

United Arab Emirates University
PO Box 15551, Al-Ain
Type: Public, national, four-year
Degrees: B
URL: http://www.uaeu.ac.ae
Phone: 011 971 3 642 500
Prog. Accred.: Business (AACSB)

UNITED KINGDOM

Ashridge Business School
Berkhamsted, HE HP4 1NS
Type: Public, independent, four-year
Degrees: B, M
URL: http://www.ashridge.org.uk
Phone: 011 44 0 1442 843491
Prog. Accred.: Business (AACSB)

Aston University
Aston Triangle, Birmingham B4 7ET
Type: Public, independent with public funding, four-year
Degrees: B
URL: http://www.aston.ac.uk
Phone: 011 44 0 121 359 361
Prog. Accred.: Business (AACSB)

Cranfield University
Cranfield, BE MK43 0AL
Type: Public, independent with public funding, four-year
Degrees: M
URL: http://www.cranfield.ac.uk
Phone: 011 44 1234 750 111
Prog. Accred.: Business (AACSB)

Henley Management College
Greenlands, Henley-on-Thames RG9 3AU
Type: Private, independent, four-year
Degrees: M
URL: http://www.henleymc.ac.uk
Phone: 011 44 01491 418802
Prog. Accred.: Business (AACSB)

The Robert Gordon University
Schoolhill, Aberdeen, Scotland AB10 1FR
Type: Public, independent with public funding, four-year
Degrees: M
URL: http://www.rgu.ac.uk
Phone: 011 44 1224 262-000
Prog. Accred.: Physical Therapy

University of Dundee
Nethergate, Dundee DD1 4HN
Type: Private, independent, four-year
Degrees: B, M
URL: http://www.dundee.ac.uk
Phone: 011 44 1382 383 000
Prog. Accred.: Nursing

The University of Edinburgh
Old College, South Bridge, Edinburgh EH8 9YL
Type: Public, independent with public funding, four-year
Degrees: B, M, D
URL: http://www.ed.ac.uk
Phone: 011 44 0131 650 1000
Prog. Accred.: Veterinary Medicine

University of Glasgow
Glasgow G12 8QQ
Type: Public, independent with public funding, four-year
Degrees: B, M, D
URL: http://www.gla.ac.uk
Phone: 011 0141 339 8855
Prog. Accred.: Business (AACSB), Veterinary Medicine

The University of Lancaster
Lancaster, LA LA1 4YW
Type: Public, Royal Charter, four-year
Degrees: B
URL: http://www.lancs.ac.uk
Phone: 011 44 0 1524 65201
Prog. Accred.: Business (AACSB)

University of London—External Programme
Senate House, University of London, Malet St., London WC1E 7HU
Type: Private, independent with public funding, four-year
Degrees: C, B
URL: http://www.londonexternal.ac.uk
Phone: 011 44 0 20 7862 836
Prog. Accred.: Liberal Education

University of London—London Business School
Sussex Place, Regent's Park, London NW1 4SA
Type: Public, independent with public funding, four-year
Degrees: M, D
URL: http://www.lbs.ac.uk
Phone: 011 44 20 7262 5050
Prog. Accred.: Business (AACSB)

University of London—Royal Veterinary College
Royal College St., London NW1 0TU
Type: Public, independent with public funding, four-year
Degrees: P, D
URL: http://www.rvc.ac.uk
Phone: 011 44 20 7468 5000
Prog. Accred.: Veterinary Medicine

University of Manchester
Oxford Rd., Manchester M13 9PL
Type: Public, independent with public funding, four-year
Degrees: B, M
URL: http://www.man.ac.uk
Phone: 011 44 161 275 2000
Prog. Accred.: Business (AACSB)

University of Strathclyde
16 Richmond St., Glasgow, Scotland G1 1XQ
Type: Public, independent with public funding, four-year
Degrees: B, M, D
URL: http://www.strath.ac.uk
Phone: 011 44 141 552 4400 *Calendar:* Sem. plan
Prog. Accred.: Business (AACSB)

University of Surrey
Guilford, Surrey GU2 5XH
Type: Private, independent, four-year
Degrees: B, M
URL: http://www.surrey.ac.uk
Phone: 011 44 (0) 1483 300800
Prog. Accred.: Business (AACSB)

University of Warwick
Heath Park, Cardiff, Wales CF4 4XN
Type: Public, independent with public funding, four-year
Degrees: B, M, D
URL: http://www.uwcm.ac.uk
Phone: 011 44 29 2074 7747
Prog. Accred.: Business (AACSB)

VENEZUELA

Instituto de Estudios Superiores de Administración
Avenida IESA, Edificio IESA, San Bernardino CARACAS 10
Type: Private, independent, four-year
Degrees: B, M
URL: http://www.iesa.edu.ve
Phone: 011 58 212- 5521533
Prog. Accred.: Business (AACSB)

Major Institutional Changes

ALABAMA

American College of Computer & Information Sciences merged with American Graduate School of Management and changed its name to American Sentinel University (Winter 2006)

American Graduate School of Management merged with American College of Computer & Information Sciences and changed its name to American Sentinel University (Winter 2006)

Bessemer State Technical College merged with Lawson State Community College and changed its name to T.A. Lawson State Community College—Bessemer (Summer 2005)

Blue Cliff School of Therapeutic Massage changed its name to Blue Cliff Career College (Summer 2006)

Chauncey Sparks State Technical College changed its name to Sparks State Technical College (Spring 1996)

Lawson State Community College merged with Bessemer State Technical College (Summer 2005)

Medical Institute changed its name to Capps College—Foley (Summer 1996)

Oakwood College changed its name to Oakwood University (Winter 2008)

Regions University changed its name to Amridge University (Winter 2008)

Southern Christian University changed its name to Regions University (Summer 2006)

Troy State University changed its name to Troy University (Spring 2004)

Troy State University Dothan changed its name to Troy University Dothan (Spring 2004)

Troy State University Dothan merged with Troy State University in Montgomery (Summer 2005)

Troy State University in Montgomery merged with Troy State University Dothan (Summer 2005)

Virginia College School of Construction—Birmingham closed (Winter 2007)

Virginia College—Technical closed (Winter 2007)

ALASKA

Sheldon Jackson College closed. *Accreditation remains valid unitl March 31, 2009* (Summer 2007)

ARIZONA

Arizona State University East changed its name to Arizona State University Polytechnic Campus (Summer 2005)

Arizona State University West merged with Arizona State University (Spring 2006)

Chaparral College changed its name to Brown Mackie College—Tucson (Winter 2008)

College of the Humanities and Sciences changed its name to College of the Humanities and Sciences Harrison Middleton University (Summer 2005)

Cortiva Institute-Desert Institute of the Healing Arts changed its name to Cortiva Institute-Tucson (Fall 2007)

Desert Institute of the Healing Arts changed its name to Cortiva Institute-Desert Institute of the Healing Arts (Summer 2005)

High-Tech Institute—Phoenix Campus changed its name to Anthem College—Phoenix (Summer 2007)

International Import-Export Institute merged with, and became a division of, Dunlap-Stone University (Spring 2008)

International Institute of the Americas changed its name to IIA College (Winter 2008)

Long Technical College changed its name to Kaplan College, Phoenix (Summer 2007)

Long Technical College—East Valley closed (Spring 2007)

Metropolitan College—Phoenix Campus closed (Spring 2006)

Phoenix Therapeutic Massage College changed its name to Cortiva Institute—School of Massage Therapy (Summer 2005)

Premier Training, Inc. changed its name to Success Development Group, Inc. (Winter 2002)

Remington College—Tempe closed (Summer 2008)

Safford College of Beauty changed its name to The Hair Academy of Safford (Summer 2005)

Thunderbird, The Garvin Graduate School of International Management changed its name to Thunderbird School of Global Management (Winter 2007)

Tucson Design College changed its name to Art Institute of Tucson (Fall 2007)

ARKANSAS

Arkansas Northeastern College merged with Cotton Boll Technical Institute (Summer 2003)

Arkansas Tech University merged with Arkansas Valley Technical College (Summer 2003)

Forest Echoes Technical Institute merged with University of Arkansas at Monticello and changed its name to University of Arkansas at Monticello College of Technology-Crossett (Summer 2003)

University of Arkansas at Monticello merged with Forest Echoes Technical Institute (Summer 2003)

CALIFORNIA

Academy Pacific Travel College closed (Summer 2006)

Advanced Career Technologies Institute closed (Summer 2005)

Alliant University—San Diego changed its name to Alliant International University—Cornerstone Court Campus (Summer 2001)

American Academy of Dramatic Arts West changed its name to American Academy of Dramatic Arts Los Angeles (Winter 2006)

American Institute of Health Sciences changed its name to American University of Health Sciences (Summer 2006)

American Medical Sciences Center—North Hollwood closed (Winter 2006)

Bethany College changed its name to Bethany University (Summer 2005)

Brooks College closed (Fall 2008)

Brown Mackie College—Los Angeles merged with Argosy University Orange County and changed its name to Argosy University Santa Monica (Spring 2006)

Brown Mackie College—San Diego merged with Argosy University Orange County and changed its name to Argosy University San Diego (Spring 2006)

Bryman College—Alhambra changed its name to Everest College—Alhambra (Spring 2007)

Bryman College—Anaheim changed its name to Everest College—Anaheim (Spring 2007)

Bryman College—City of Industry changed its name to Everest College—City of Industry (Spring 2007)

Bryman College—Gardena changed its name to Everest College—Gardena (Spring 2007)

Bryman College—Hayward changed its name to Everest College—Hayward (Spring 2007)

Bryman College—Los Angeles changed its name to Everest College—Los Angeles (Spring 2007)

Bryman College—Ontario changed its name to Everest College—Ontario (Spring 2007)

Bryman College—Reseda changed its name to Everest College—Reseda (Spring 2007)

Bryman College—San Bernardino changed its name to Everest College—San Bernardino (Spring 2007)

Bryman College—San Francisco changed its name to Everest College—San Francisco (Spring 2007)

Bryman College—San Jose changed its name to Everest College—San Jose (Spring 2007)

Bryman College—Torrance changed its name to Everest College—Torrance (Spring 2007)

Bryman College—West Los Angeles changed its name to Everest College—West Los Angeles (Spring 2007)

California State University—Hayward changed its name to California State University, East Bay (Winter 2005)

Career Management Institute closed (Summer 2006)

Career Networks Institute changed its name to CNI Vocational College (Summer 2006)

Christian Heritage College changed its name to San Diego Christian College (Summer 2005)

Coachella Valley Technical Skills Center changed its name to Mayfield College (Summer 2006)

Colleen O'Hara's Beauty Academy changed its name to COBA Academy (Winter 2007)

College for Recording Arts closed (Summer 1994)

Community Business School changed its name to Community Business College (Summer 2006)

Compton Community College merged with El Camino College and changed its name to El Camino College—Compton Center (Summer 2006)

Computer Education Institute changed its name to Maric College (Spring 2004)

Computer Education Institute—San Marcos closed (Spring 2004)

Computer Services and Instruction, Inc. changed its name to CSI Career College (Summer 2005)

Computer Training Institute changed its name to Medacom College (Summer 2005)

Concord School of Law merged with Kaplan University and changed its name to Concord Law School of Kaplan University (Fall 2007)

Concord University School of Law changed its name to Concord Law School (Summer 2003)

Concorde Career Institute—Garden Grove changed its name to Concorde Career College—Garden Grove (Winter 2003)

Concorde Career Institute—North Hollywood changed its name to Concorde Career College—North Hollywood (Winter 2003)

Concorde Career Institute—San Bernardino changed its name to Concorde Career College—San Bernardino (Winter 2003)

Concorde Career Institute—San Diego changed its name to Concorde Career College—San Diego (Winter 2003)

Dale Carnegie Training of Los Angeles changed its name to Performance Improvement Group, Inc. Dale Carnegie Training of Los Angeles (Summer 2006)

Diversified Language Institute changed its name to Silvergate Academy (Summer 2005)

Domincan College of San Rafael changed its name to Dominican University of California (Spring 2000)

Don Bosco Technical Institute closed (Summer 2006)

Donald Vocational School changed its name to DVS College (Summer 2003)

East Los Angeles Occupational Center changed its name to East Los Angeles Education and Career Center (Summer 2007)

El Camino College merged with Compton Community College (Summer 2006)

Elegante Beauty College—City of Industry merged with Marinello School of Beauty and changed its name to Marinello School of Beauty—City of Industry (Summer 2004)

Elegante Beauty College—Lake Forest merged with Marinello School of Beauty and changed its name to Marinello School of Beauty—Lake Forest (Summer 2004)

Elegante Beauty College—Moreno merged with and Marinello School of Beauty changed its name to Marinello School of Beauty—Moreno Valley (Summer 2004)

Elegante Beauty College—Moreno merged with and Marinello School of Beauty changed its name to Marinello School of Beauty—Burbank (Summer 2004)

Fashion Careers of California College changed its name to Fashion Careers College (Summer 2003)

Federico College of Hairstyling changed its name to Federico Beauty Institute (Winter 2005)

Fielding Graduate Institute changed its name to Fielding Graduate University (Winter 2005)

Foundation College closed (Fall 1999)

Four-D Success Academy changed its name to Four-D College (Summer 2004)

Greater Long Beach Child Guidance Center changed its name to The Guidance Center (Summer 2005)

Heald College—Santa Rosa closed (Spring 2003)

Holy Names College changed its name to Holy Names University (Spring 2004)

Image Schools of Cosmetology—Cathedral City changed its name to California Beauty College—Cathedral City (Summer 2006)

Image Schools of Cosmetology—Hemet changed its name to California Beauty College—Hemet (Summer 2006)

Institute of Computer Technology changed its name to LA College International (Spring 2006)

Intelisource closed (Winter 2002)

International School of Theology closed (Summer 2002)

ITT Technical Institute—Hayward closed (Winter 2004)

Keller Graduate School of Management—Irvine Center changed its name to DeVry University Irvine (Summer 2004)

Kim Anh Academy of Beauty changed its name to Elite Beauty College (Summer 2006)

Learning Tree University closed (Summer 2004)

Los Angeles Recording Workshop changed its name to Los Angeles Recording School (Summer 2006)

Management College of San Francisco closed (Spring 2000)

Maric College—Anaheim closed (Fall 2006)

Maric College—East County closed (Fall 2006)

Maric College—Irwindale closed (Summer 2006)

Maric College—Los Angeles closed (Summer 2007)

Maric College—Modesto changed its name to Kaplan College—Modesto (Fall 2008)

Maric College—North Hollywood changed its name to Kaplan College—North Hollywood (Fall 2008)

Maric College—Sacramento changed its name to Kaplan College—Sacramento (Fall 2008)

Maric College—Stockton changed its name to Kaplan College—Stockton (Fall 2008)

Masters Institute closed (Spring 2001)

Medacom College closed (Spring 2007)

Miss Marty's School of Beauty & Hairstyling changed its name to Miss Marty's Hair Academy and Esthetics Institute (Summer 2005)

Monterey Park College changed its name to Newbridge College—Monterey Park (Summer 2005)

Monterey Park College—Walnut closed (Spring 2004)
Mount Diablo Medical Center changed its name to John Muir Medical Center, Concord Campus (Summer 2006)
National Institute of Technology—Long Beach changed its name to WyoTech—Long Beach (Summer 2007)
National Institute of Technology—San Jose closed (Fall 2003)
National Polytechnic College of Engineering and Oceaneering changed its name to National Polytechnic College of Science (Summer 2007)
New College of California closed (Summer 2008)
Newbridge College—Burbank closed (Spring 2006)
Newbridge College—Monterey Park closed (Summer 2008)
Northwestern College changed its name to Bryan College—Sacramento (Summer 2006)
Northwestern Technical College changed its name to Northwestern College (Fall 2003)
Pacific Travel Trade School—Los Angeles closed (Winter 2000)
Paramount School of Beauty merged with Marinello School of Beauty and changed its name to Marinello School of Beauty—Paramount (Summer 2004)
Platt College changed its name to Western College of Southern California (Summer 2005)
Professional Career Institute changed its name to PCI College (Summer 2005)
Quality College of Culinary Careers closed (Fall 2007)
Rand Graduate School changed its name to Pardee Rand Graduate School (Fall 2003)
Richard's Beauty College merged with Marinello School of Beauty and changed its name to Marinello School of Beauty—Huntington Beach (Summer 2004)
Ross Business Institute changed its name to Newbridge College—Burbank (Summer 2005)
Salvation Army Crestmont College changed its name to Salvation Army College for Officer Training at Crestmont (Summer 2005)
Samuel Merritt College merged with California College of Podiatric Medicine (Summer 2002)
San Fernando Beauty Academy, Inc. changed its name to Western Beauty Institute—San Fernando Valley (Summer 2006)
SEA College of Business and Technology closed (Winter 2005)
Sequoia Institute changed its name to WyoTech—Fremont (Summer 2004)
Sierra Valley Business College changed its name to Sierra Valley College (Summer 2005)
Silicon Valley College merged with Western Career College—Sacramento and changed its name to Western Career College—Fremont (Summer 2005)
Software Education of America changed its name to SEA College of Business and Technology (Summer 2006)
Sonoma College—Petaluma closed (Summer 2007)
Touro University College of Osteopathic Medicine changed its name to Touro University—California (Summer 2005)
Touro University International changed its name to TUI University (Fall 2007)
Travel and Trade Career Institute closed (Fall 2005)
University of Judaism changed its name to American Jewish University (Summer 2007)
University of West Los Angeles merged with San Fernando College of Law (Summer 2002)
Virginia Sewing Machines & School Center changed its name to A-Technical College (Summer 2006)
Vista Community College changed its name to Berkeley City College (Summer 2006)
Western Career College—Fremont closed (Summer 2006)
Western Career College—Sacramento merged with Silicon Valley College (Summer 2005)
Western College of Southern California changed its name to Fremont College (Summer 2006)
Westwood College of Aviation Technology—Los Angeles changed its name to Redstone College—Los Angeles (Spring 2006)
Westwood College of Technology—Anaheim changed its name to Westwood College—Anaheim (Winter 2005)
Westwood College of Technology—Inland Empire changed its name to Westwood College—Inland Empire (Winter 2005)
Westwood College of Technology—Long Beach changed its name to Westwood College—Long Beach (Winter 2005)
Westwood College of Technology—Los Angeles changed its name to Westwood College—Los Angeles (Winter 2005)
Westwood College—Long Beach changed its name to Westwood College—South Bay (Fall 2006)

COLORADO

Blair College changed its name to Everest College—Colordao Springs (Spring 2006)

Brown Mackie College—Denver merged with Argosy University and changed its name to Argosy University—Denver (Spring 2006)

Cardean University and New York Institute of Technology formed a partnership known as Ellis College (Winter 2007)

Colorado School of Professional Psychology changed its name to University of the Rockies (Fall 2007)

Concorde Career Institute—Aurora changed its name to Concorde Career College—Aurora (Winter 2003)

Denver Automotive and Diesel College changed its name to Lincoln College of Technology—Denver (Winter 2007)

Denver Career College—Colorado Springs closed (Spring 2003)

Denver Career College—Denver changed its name to Kaplan College—Denver (Spring 2007)

Family Therapy/Play Therapy Institute changed its name to Colorado School for Family Therapy (Winter 2006)

International Beauty Academy closed (Spring 2007)

National Technological University merged with Walden University and changed its name to NTU School of Engineering and Applied Science at Walden University (Summer 2005)

Parks College changed its name to Everest College (Summer 2006)

Remington College—Denver closed (Winter 2006)

T.H. Pickens Technical Center changed its name to Pickens Technical College (Spring 2006)

University of Colorado at Denver and Health Sciences Center changed its name to University of Colorado Denver (Fall 2007)

Westwood College of Aviation Technology—Denver changed its name to Redstone College—Denver (Spring 2006)

Westwood College of Technology—Denver North changed its name to Westwood College—Denver North (Winter 2005)

Westwood College of Technology—Denver South changed its name to Westwood College—Denver South (Winter 2005)

CONNECTICUT

Albert School changed its name to Brio Academy—Niantic (Fall 2006)

American Academy of Cosmetology changed its name to Paul Mitchell the School—Danbury (Summer 2006)

B. Dickson and Associates, LLC changed its name to Dale Carnegie Training of Western Connecticut (Summer 2006)

Baran Institute of Technology closed (Fall 2001)

Beth Benjamin Academy of Connecticut changed its name to Bais Binyomin Academy (Summer 2005)

Bradley College changed its name to Clemens College (Summer 2007)

Connecticut Business Institute—New Haven closed (Winter 1999)

Connecticut Institute of Hair Design changed its name to Brio Academy of Cosmetology (Summer 2005)

Gal Mar Academy of Hairdressing changed its name to North Haven Academy (Summer 2005)

Huntington Institute closed (Fall 2001)

International College of Hospitality Management "César Ritz" changed its name to Bradley College (Summer 2007)

M.J. Francoeur & Associates changed its name to Results, Inc. Dale Carnegie Training (Summer 2006)

Naugatuck Valley Community-Technical College changed its name to Naugatuck Valley Community College (Summer 2000)

New England Technical Institute—Cromwell changed its name to Lincoln Technical Institute—Cromwell (Summer 2006)

New England Technical Institute—Hamden changed its name to Lincoln Technical Institute—Hamden (Summer 2006)

New England Technical Institute—New Britain changed its name to Lincoln Technical Institute—New Britain (Summer 2006)

New England Technical Institute—Shelton changed its name to Lincoln Technical Institute—Shelton (Summer 2006)

Teikyo Post University changed its name to Post University (Fall 2004)

Walker & Associates, Inc. changed its name to B. Dickson and Associates, LLC (Winter 2004)

DELAWARE

Deep Muscle Therapy School changed its name to Harris School (Summer 2006)

Harrison Career Institute—Wilmington closed (Winter 2007)

Wilmington College changed its name to Wilmington University (Fall 2007)

DISTRICT OF COLUMBIA

11th Medical Group/SGD changed its name to 579th Medical Group (Spring 2006)
Bennett Beauty Institute, Inc. changed its name to Bennett Career Institute, Inc. (Summer 2005)
Career Blazers Learning Center of Washington, DC changed its name to Career Skills Institute (Summer 2007)
Instructional Telecommunications Council changed its name to Instructional Technology Council (Summer 2004)
Joint Military Intelligence College changed its name to National Defense Intelligence College (Summer 2006)
Trinity University changed its name to Trinity Washington University (Winter 2006)

FLORIDA

A.M.I., Inc. changed its name to WyoTech—Daytona (Fall 2006)
Academy of Health & Beauty Care changed its name to International School of Health and Beauty (Summer 2005)
Advanced/Basic Hair Design Training Center changed its name to Academy of Cosmetology (Winter 2005)
ATI Health Education Center changed its name to ATI College of Health (Summer 2005)
Bethune-Cookman College changed its name to Bethune-Cookman University (Winter 2007)
Business Etcetera Institute closed (Summer 2002)
Career Training Institute changed its name to Central Florida College (Summer 2006)
Central Florida College changed its name to RETS College (Summer 2008)
Comair Aviation Academy changed its name to Delta Connection Academy (Summer 2003)
Cooper Career Institute closed (Winter 2005)
Darlyne McGee's Academy of Cosmetology, Inc. changed its name to Academy of Cosmetology (Winter 2005)
Daytona Beach College changed its name to Daytona State College (Summer 2008)
Daytona Beach Community College changed its name to Daytona Beach College (Fall 2007)
Edison College changed its name to Edison State College (Summer 2008)
Edison Community College changed its name to Edison College (Winter 2005)
EduTech Centers changed its name to Florida Career College (Winter 2006)
Euro Hair Design Institute—Jacksonville closed (Fall 2002)
Euro Hair Design Institute—Tallahassee closed (Fall 2002)
Florida Computer & Business School changed its name to Florida Career College (Spring 2003)
Florida Institute of Traditional Chinese Medicine closed (Winter 2002)
Florida Memorial College changed its name to Florida Memorial University (Summer 2004)
Florida Metropolitan University—Orlando North changed its name to Everest University—Orlando North (Fall 2007)
Florida Metropolitan University—Pinellas changed its name to Everest University—Pinellas (Fall 2007)
Florida Metropolitan University—Pompano Beach changed its name to Everest University—Pompano Beach (Fall 2007)
Florida Metropolitan University—Tampa changed its name to Everest University—Tampa (Fall 2007)
Hi-Tech School of Miami closed (Winter 2005)
International B Naturale Beauty School changed its name to B Naturale Beauty School (Summer 2006)
International College changed its name to Hodges University (Summer 2007)
International School of Beauty changed its name to Bene's International School of Beauty (Winter 2005)
Keiser College changed its name to Keiser University (Spring 2007)
Lane Institute of Health Sciences closed (Spring 2007)
Meridian Technical Institute merged with Venord Institute and changed its name to Lane Institute of Health Sciences (Summer 2004)
Miami Technical Istitute—North Miami closed (Winter 2001)
National Aviation Academy merged with WyoTech—Boston (Spring 2008)
Naval Air Technical Training Center changed its name to Center for Naval Aviation Technical Training (Winter 2005)
Naval Diving and Salvage Training Center changed its name to Center for Explosive Ordnance Disposal and Diving (Winter 2005)
Naval Technical Training Center changed its name to Center for Information Dominance (CID) (Winter 2005)
New England Institute of Technology at Palm Beach changed its name to Lincoln College of Technology—West Palm Beach (Summer 2006)
Okaloosa-Walton College changed its name to Northwest Florida State College (Summer 2008)

Okaloosa-Walton Community College changed its name to Okaloosa-Walton College (Summer 2004)
Omni Technical School closed (Fall 2002)
Polytechnic Institute of America changed its name to Centura Institute (Fall 2007)
Regent Language Training U.S.A. changed its name to Zoni Regent Language Training U.S.A. (Winter 2007)
Remington College—Jacksonville closed (Summer 2008)
Ridge Vocational-Technical Center changed its name to Ridge Career Center (Fall 2006)
Ringling School of Art and Design changed its name to Ringling College of Art and Design (Spring 2007)
Robert Morgan Vocational-Technical Institute changed its name to Robert Morgan Educational Center (Fall 2001)
SER-IBM Business Institute changed its name to Advanced Technical Centers (Spring 2006)
Somerset School of Massage Therapy changed its name to Cortiva Institute-Humanities Center Institute of Allied Health/School of Massage (Summer 2005)
Southeastern College of the Assemblies of God changed its name to Southeastern University (Spring 2005)
Southern Technical Center closed (Winter 2000)
Southern Technical Institute changed its name to Southern Technical College (Summer 2007)
Suncoast Center for Natural Health/Suncoast School changed its name to SunCoast II—The Tampa Bay School of Health/Suncoast School (Summer 2003)
The College for Professional Studies closed (Summer 2007)
Webster College—Ocala changed its name to Rasmussen College—Ocala (Fall 2007)
Webster College—Tampa changed its name to Gulf Coast College (Winter 2005)

GEORGIA

Ashworth College changed its name to Ashworth University (Spring 2007)
Atlanta College of Art merged with Savannah College of Art and Design and changed its name to Savannah College of Art and Design—Atlanta (Summer 2006)
Beulah Heights Bible College changed its name to Beulah Heights University (Summer 2006)
Career Education Institute—Marietta changed its name to Lincoln College of Technology—Marietta (Summer 2006)
Career Education Institute—Norcross changed its name to Lincoln College of Technology—Norcross (Summer 2006)
Dalton Beauty Inc. changed its name to Dalton Beauty College (Spring 2005)
Executive Travel Institute changed its name to ETI Career Institute (Summer 2005)
Floyd College changed its name to Georgia Highlands College (Summer 2005)
Gainesville College changed its name to Gainesville State College (Winter 2006)
Georgia Association for Pastoral Care merged with Georgia Baptist Health Care System and changed its name to Care and Counseling Center of Georgia (Winter 2007)
Georgia Aviation and Technical College merged with Middle Georgia College and changed its name to Middle Gerogia College—Georgia Aviation Campus (Summer 2007)
Georgia Baptist Health Care System merged with Georgia Association for Pastoral Care and closed (Winter 2007)
Georgia Career Institute merged with Nave Cosmetology Academy, Inc. (Spring 2007)
Georgia Medical Institute—Atlanta changed its name to Everest Institute—Atlanta Downtown (Spring 2007)
Georgia Medical Institute—DeKalb changed its name to Everest Institute—Atlanta DeKalb (Spring 2007)
Georgia School of Professional Psychology changed its name to Argosy University Atlanta (Fall 2001)
Gwinnett Technical Institute changed its name to Gwinnett Technical College (Summer 2000)
Institute for Medical Services, Inc. closed (Spring 2006)
Kerr Business College changed its name to Savannah River College (Winter 2005)
Luther Rice Bible College and Seminary changed its name to Luther Rice University (Summer 2004)
Middle Georgia College merged with Georgia Aviation and Technical College (Summer 2007)
North Georgia Technical Institute changed its name to North Georgia Technical College (Summer 2008)
Professional Career Development Institute changed its name to Ashworth University Career Diploma (Spring 2007)
Quest Education Corporation changed its name to Kaplan Higher Education Corporation (Winter 2002)
Savannah College of Art and Design merged with Atlanta College of Art (Summer 2006)
State University of West Georgia changed its name to University of West Georgia (Winter 2005)
West Georgia Technical Institute changed its name to West Georgia Technical College (Summer 2000)

HAWAII

American Schools of Professional Psychology merged Argosy University with and changed its name to Argosy University Honolulu (Fall 2001)

Argosy University Honolulu changed its name to Argosy University Hawai'i (Summer 2004)

Hawaii Business College closed (Summer 2007)

Tai Hsuan Foundation College of Acupuncture and Herbal Medicine changed its name to World Medicine Institute (Spring 2005)

IDAHO

Albertson College of Idaho changed its name to The College of Idaho (Fall 2007)

American Institute of Health Technology, Inc. changed its name to Apollo College—Boise (Winter 2005)

New Images Academy of Beauty changed its name to Scot Lewis School (Summer 2005)

Rasmussen College closed (Winter 1996)

ILLINOIS

American Schools of Professional Psychology merged with Illinois School of Professional Psychology—Chicago and changed its name to Argosy University (Fall 2001)

Argosy University Chicago Northwest changed its name to Argosy University Schaumburg (Summer 2004)

Barat College of DePaul University changed its name to American College of Education (Winter 2004)

Cannella School of Hair Design—South Halstead closed (Fall 2002)

Cannella School of Hair Design—West Roosevelt closed (Winter 2006)

Career Colleges of Chicago closed (Summer 2006)

Chicago School of Massage Therapy changed its name to Cortiva Institute-Chicago School of Massage Therapy (Summer 2005)

Chubb Institute—Chicago changed its name to Banner Institute (Summer 2005)

Chubb Institute—Villa Park closed (Winter 2004)

Cortiva Institute-Chicago School of Massage Therapy changed its name to Cortiva Institute—Chicago (Winter 2008)

DuQuoin Beauty College closed (Spring 2006)

Ellis College changed its name to Ellis University (Summer 2008)

Hanover Park College of Beauty Culture, Inc. changed its name to Empire Beauty School—Hanover Park (Fall 2004)

Herman M. Finch University of Health Sciences/The Chicago Medical School changed its name to Rosalind Franklin University of Medicine & Science (Spring 2004)

Jewish Children's Bureau of Chicago changed its name to Jewish Child and Family Services (Summer 2006)

Judson College changed its name to Judson University (Summer 2007)

Kankakee Academy of Hair Design closed (Winter 2004)

La' James College of Hairstyling—East Moline changed its name to La' James International College—East Moline (Summer 2005)

Lincoln Technical Institute—Melrose Park changed its name to Lincoln College of Technology—Melrose Park (Summer 2006)

Northern Baptist Theological Seminary changed its name to Northern Seminary (Spring 2005)

Olympia College—Skokie changed its name to Everest College—Skokie (Spring 2007)

Trend Beauty College closed (Spring 2006)

Westwood College of Technology—Chicago Loop changed its name to Westwood College—Chicago Loop (Winter 2005)

Westwood College of Technology—DuPage changed its name to Westwood College—DuPage (Winter 2005)

Westwood College of Technology—O'Hare changed its name to Westwood College—O'Hare Airport (Winter 2005)

Westwood College of Technology—River Oaks changed its name to Westwood College—River Oaks (Winter 2005)

INDIANA

Apex School of Beauty Culture changed its name to Apex Academy of Hair Design (Summer 2005)

Huntington College changed its name to Huntington University (Summer 2005)

Ivy Tech State College—Bloomington changed its name to Ivy Tech Community College of Indiana—Bloomington (Summer 2005)

Ivy Tech State College—Columbus changed its name to Ivy Tech Community College of Indiana—Columbus (Summer 2005)

Ivy Tech State College—East Central changed its name to Ivy Tech Community College of Indiana—East Central (Summer 2005)

Ivy Tech State College—Indianapolis changed its name to Ivy Tech Community College (Fall 2000)

Ivy Tech State College—Kokomo changed its name to Ivy Tech Community College of Indiana—Kokomo (Summer 2005)

Ivy Tech State College—Lafayette changed its name to Ivy Tech Community College of Indiana—Lafayette (Summer 2005)

Ivy Tech State College—North Central changed its name to Ivy Tech Community College of Indiana—North Central (Summer 2005)

Ivy Tech State College—Northeast changed its name to Ivy Tech Community College of Indiana—Northeast (Summer 2005)

Ivy Tech State College—Sellersburg changed its name to Ivy Tech Community College of Indiana—Sellersburg (Summer 2005)

Ivy Tech State College—Southeast changed its name to Ivy Tech Community College of Indiana—Madison (Summer 2005)

Ivy Tech State College—Southwest changed its name to Ivy Tech Community College of Indiana—Southwest (Summer 2005)

Ivy Tech State College—Wabash Valley changed its name to Ivy Tech Community College of Indiana—Wabash Valley (Summer 2005)

Ivy Tech State College—Whitewater changed its name to Ivy Tech Community College of Indiana—Richmond (Summer 2005)

Lincoln Technical Institute—Indianapolis changed its name to Lincoln College of Technology—Indianapolis (Summer 2006)

Professional Careers Institute—Indianapolis changed its name to Kaplan College—Indianapolis (Spring 2007)

Sawyer College, Inc. changed its name to Kaplan College (Summer 2006)

Tri-State University changed its name to Trine University (Summer 2008)

IOWA

The Franciscan University of the Prairies changed its name to Ashford University (Spring 2005)

Kaplan University merged with Concord School of Law (Fall 2007)

La' James College of Hairstyling—Cedar Falls changed its name to La' James International College—Cedar Falls (Summer 2005)

La' James College of Hairstyling—Davenport changed its name to La' James International College—Davenport (Summer 2005)

La' James College of Hairstyling—Des Moines changed its name to La' James International College—Des Moines (Summer 2005)

La' James College of Hairstyling—Fort Dodge changed its name to La' James International College—Fort Dodge (Summer 2005)

La' James College of Hairstyling—Iowa City changed its name to La' James International College—Iowa City (Summer 2005)

Professional Cosmetology Institute, Ltd. changed its name to Salon Professional Academy (Spring 2005)

Salon Professional Academy changed its name to Professional Cosmetology Institute (Summer 2006)

KANSAS

Classic College of Hair Design changed its name to B-Street Design School of International Hair Styling—Wichita (Fall 2006)

College of Hair Design changed its name to B-Street Design School of International Hair Styling—Overland Park (Fall 2006)

Community College of Cosmetology changed its name to B-Street Design School of International Hair Styling (Fall 2006)

Superior School of Hairstyling changed its name to B-Street Design School of International Hair Styling (Fall 2006)

Wright Business School changed its name to Wright Career College (Summer 2007)

KENTUCKY

Central Kentucky Technical College merged with Lexington Community College and changed its name to Bluegrass Community and Technical College—Central (Winter 2005)

Cumberland College changed its name to University of the Cumberlands (Summer 2005)

Decker College of Business Technology closed (Fall 2005)

Health Institute of Louisville changed its name to Galen College of Nursing (Winter 2005)

Jefferson Community College merged with Jefferson Technical College and changed its name to Jefferson Community and Technical College (Summer 2005)

Jefferson Technical College merged with Jefferson Community College and changed its name to Jefferson Community and Technical College (Summer 2005)

Lexington Community College merged with Central Kentucky Technical College and changed its name to Bluegrass Community and Technical College—Cooper (Winter 2005)

Mid-Continent College changed its name to Mid-Continent University (Spring 2004)

Paducah Technical College changed its name to Daymar College—Paducah (Summer 2008)

William F. Lea & Associates, Inc. changed its name to Louisville Dale Carnegie Group (Summer 2007)

LOUISIANA

Academy of Creative Hair Design changed its name to Vanguard College of Cosmetology (Summer 2005)

Ayers Institute changed its name to Ayers Career College (Summer 2006)

Blue Cliff College—Baton Rouge changed its name to Moore Career College (Winter 2008)

Bryman College—New Orleans closed (Winter 2006)

Cosmetology Business and Management Institute closed (Fall 2004)

Culinary Arts Institute of Louisiana closed (Fall 2002)

Culinary Institute of New Orleans closed (Summer 2006)

Gulfport Job Corps Center closed (Fall 2005)

Guy's Shreveport Academy of Cosmetology changed its name to Guy's Academy Hair, Skin, and Nails (Summer 2005)

Lockworks Academy of Hairdressing—Baton Rouge changed its name to Aveda Institute Baton Rouge (Summer 2005)

Lockworks Academy of Hairdressing—Lafayette changed its name to Aveda Institute Lafayette (Summer 2005)

Louisiana Hair Design College closed (Summer 1997)

Louisiana State University Medical Center changed its name to Louisiana State University Health Sciences Center (Summer 2000)

Louisiana Technical College—L.E. Fletcher Campus changed its name to L.E. Fletcher Technical Community College (Winter 2002)

Louisiana Technical College—Sidney N. Collier Campus closed (Summer 2005)

Louisiana Technical College—Slidell Campus closed (Summer 2005)

Louisiana Technical College—Sowela Campus changed its name to Sowela Technical Community College (Winter 2002)

Massage Therapy College of Baton Rouge changed its name to Blue Cliff College—Baton Rouge (Winter 2006)

Moler Beauty College—Canal Street closed (Winter 2004)

Moler Beauty College—Gretna changed its name to Cosmetology Business and Management Instiute (Summer 2005)

New Orleans Veterans Affairs Medical Center changed its name to Southeast Louisiana Veterans Health Care System (Summer 2005)

Professional Chefs Institute of the South closed (Spring 2006)

Remington College—New Orleans closed (Summer 2005)

MAINE

Headhunter Institute changed its name to Spa Tech Institute (Spring 2005)

MARYLAND

Cecil Community College changed its name to Cecil College (Summer 2007)

Diesel Institute of America changed its name to North American Trade Schools (Spring 2004)

George Meany Center for Labor Studies-National Labor College changed its name to National Labor College (Summer 2004)

Gordon Phillips School of Beauty Culture—Baltimore closed (Summer 1997)
Hagerstown Business College changed its name to Kaplan College—Hagerstown (Spring 2007)
Hagerstown Business College—Frederick changed its name to Kaplan College—Frederick (Spring 2007)
Harrison Career Institute—Baltimore closed (Summer 2006)
Home Study International changed its name to Griggs International Academy (Winter 2006)
Villa Julie College changed its name to Stevenson University (Summer 2008)

MASSACHUSETTS

Bentley College changed its name to Bentley University (Fall 2008)
Boston Architectural Center changed its name to Boston Architectural College (Summer 2006)
Boston College merged with Weston Jesuit School of Theology (Summer 2008)
Bryman Institute—Brighton changed its name to Everest Institute—Brighton (Spring 2007)
Bryman Institute—Chelsea changed its name to Everest Institute—Chelsea (Spring 2007)
Career Education Institute—Brockton changed its name to Lincoln Technical Institute—Brockton (Summer 2006)
Career Education Institute—Lowell changed its name to Lincoln Technical Institute—Lowell (Summer 2006)
Career Education Institute—Somerville changed its name to Lincoln Technical Institute—Somerville (Summer 2006)
Computer Processing Institute closed (Winter 1999)
Cortiva Institute-Muscular Therapy Institute changed its name to Cortiva Institute—Boston (Winter 2008)
East Coast Aero Tech changed its name to WyoTech—Boston (Summer 2004)
Laboure College changed its name to Caritas Laboure College (Spring 2005)
Learning Institute for Beauty Sciences—Boston changed its name to Empire Beauty School—Boston (Winter 2007)
Learning Institute for Beauty Sciences—Malden changed its name to Empire Beauty School—Malden (Winter 2007)
Muscular Therapy Institute changed its name to Cortiva Institute-Muscular Therapy Institute (Summer 2005)
Northeast Institute of Industrial Technology closed (Winter 1998)
RETS Electronic School—Charlestown changed its name to RETS Technical Center—Charlestown (Summer 2005)
Simon's Rock College of Bard changed its name to Bard College at Simon's Rock (Summer 2007)
Western Massachusetts Precision Institute closed (Fall 2002)
Weston Jesuit School of Theology merged with Boston College and closed (Summer 2008)
WyoTech—Boston merged with National Aviation Academy and changed its name to National Aviation Academy—New England (Spring 2008)

MICHIGAN

Ave Maria College closed (Spring 2007)
Center for Humanistic Studies changed its name to Michigan School of Professional Psychology (Fall 2006)
Davenport University—Bad Axe Campus closed (Summer 2008)
Davenport University—Bay City Campus closed (Summer 2008)
Detroit Barber College, Inc. closed (Summer 2002)
Detroit Practical Nursing Center closed (Summer 1996)
Howell College of Cosmetology closed (Winter 2007)
JTPA School of Practical Nursing closed (Winter 2003)
Michigan Institute of Aeronautics changed its name to Michigan Institute of Aviation and Technology (Summer 2005)
National Institute of Technology—Southfield changed its name to Everest Institute—Southfield (Fall 2006)
Olympia Career Training Institute changed its name to Everest Institute—Grand Rapids (Spring 2007)
Reformed Bible College changed its name to Kuyper College (Spring 2006)
SER Business and Technical Institute closed (Winter 2004)
Travel Education Institute closed (Winter 2003)

MINNESOTA

Bethel College merged with Bethel Seminary and changed its name to Bethel University (Summer 2004)
Bryman Institute—Eagan changed its name to Everest Institute—Eagan (Fall 2006)
Globe College changed its name to Globe University (Summer 2007)

Herzing College—Lakeland Medical-Dental College changed its name to Herzing College—Minneapolis (Summer 2007)

Herzing College—Minneapolis Drafting School Campus merged with Herzing College—Lakeland Medical-Dental College and closed (Summer 2007)

McConnell School closed (Spring 2002)

Medical Institute of Minnesota merged with Minnesota School of Professional Psychology and changed its name to Argosy University Twin Cities (Fall 2001)

Medical Institute of Minnesota merged with Argosy University and changed its name to Argosy University Twin Cities (Fall 2001)

Minnesota Cosmetology Education Center, Inc. changed its name to Minnesota School of Cosmetology (Fall 2003)

Minnesota Institute of Technologies closed (Spring 2004)

Minnesota School of Professional Psychology merged with Medical Institute of Minnesota and closed (Fall 2001

Musictech College changed its name to McNally Smith College of Music (Winter 2005)

Northwest Technical Institute changed its name to NTI School of CAD Technology (Summer 2001)

NTI School of CAD Technology changed its name to Northwest Technical Institute (Spring 2005)

Oliver Thein Beauty School changed its name to Regency Beauty Institute (Winter 2004)

Regency Beauty Academy changed its name to Regency Beauty Institute (Winter 2005)

Rita's Moorhead Beauty College changed its name to Ing'enue Beauty School (Spring 2005)

South Central Technical College—Mankato changed its name to South Central College—Mankato (Spring 2005)

Walden University merged with National Technological University (Summer 2005)

MISSISSIPPI

Traxler School of Hair closed (Summer 1995)

William Carey College changed its name to William Carey University (Summer 2006)

MISSOURI

ATA Career Education—Arnold closed (Winter 2007)

Barnes College of Nursing merged with University of Missouri—St. Louis and changed its name to Barnes College of Nursing and Health Studies at the University of MIssouri—St. Louis (Summer 2004)

Blue River Community College—Blue Springs merged with Blue River Community College—Independence Campus and closed (Summer 2004)

Blue River Community College—Independence Campus changed its name to Metropolitan Community College—Blue River (Summer 2006)

Bryman College—Earth City changed its name to Everest College—Earth City (Summer 2006)

Career Alternatives Learning Center closed (Fall 2007)

Central Missouri State University changed its name to University of Central Missouri (Fall 2006)

Columbia Beauty Academy closed (Summer 2006)

Concorde Career Institute—Kansas City changed its name to Concorde Career College—Kansas City (Summer 2005)

Deaconess College of Nursing changed its name to Chamberlain College of Nursing (Summer 2006)

Harris-Stowe State College changed its name to Harris-Stowe State University (Winter 2006)

Jerry's School of Hairstyling, Inc. changed its name to Cosmetology Concepts Institute (Spring 2005)

Kansas City College closed (Summer 2006)

Metropolitan Community College District changed its name to Metropolitan Community College—Kansas City (Spring 2006)

Midwest Theological Seminary changed its name to Midwest University (Winter 2006)

Missouri Southern State University-Joplin changed its name to Missouri Southern State University (Summer 2005)

Missouri Western State College changed its name to Missouri Western State University (Summer 2005)

Rescue College changed its name to City Vision College (Winter 2008)

St. Louis Tech closed (Winter 1997)

Sanford-Brown College—North Kansas City changed its name to Colorado Technical University—North Kansas City (Winter 2005)

Southwest Missouri State University changed its name to Missouri State University (Summer 2005)

Southwest Missouri State University—West Plains changed its name to Missouri State University—West Plains (Summer 2005)
Springfield College changed its name to Everest College—Springfield (Summer 2006)
University of Missouri—Rolla changed its name to Missouri University of Science and Technology (Winter 2008)
University of Missouri—St. Louis merged with Barnes College of Nursing (Summer 2004)

NEBRASKA

Bahner College of Hairstyling changed its name to La' James International College (Spring 2006)
Vatterott College—Deerfield merged with Vatterott College—Spring Valley and closed (Winter 2004)
Vatterott College—Spring Valley merged with Vatterott College—Deerfield (Winter 2004)

NEVADA

Career Education Institute—Henderson changed its name to Lincoln College of Technology—Henderson (Summer 2006)
Community College of Southern Nevada changed its name to College of Southern Nevada (Summer 2007)
Dahan Institute of Massage Studies closed (Summer 2003)
Expertise School of Beauty changed its name to Expertise Cosmetology Institute (Summer 2006)
Heritage College changed its name to Kaplan College—Las Vegas (Summer 2008)
Las Vegas College—Henderson merged with Las Vegas College—Las Vegas and closed (Summer 2005)
Las Vegas College—Las Vegas merged with Las Vegas College—Henderson (Summer 2005)
Nevada College of Pharmacy changed its name to University of Southern Nevada (Fall 2004)
Southern Nevada University of Cosmetology closed (Winter 2007)
Western Nevada Community College changed its name to Western Nevada College (Summer 2007)

NEW HAMPSHIRE

Antioch New England Graduate School changed its name to Antioch University New England (Summer 2006)
College for Lifelong Learning changed its name to Granite State College (Spring 2005)
Concord Academy of Hair Design changed its name to Esthetics Institute at Concord Academy (Winter 2005)
Franklin Pierce College changed its name to Franklin Pierce University (Summer 2007)
New Hampshire Community Technical College—Berlin changed its name to White Mountains Community College (Winter 2008)
New Hampshire Community Technical College—Berlin/Laconia split to become New Hampshire Community Technical College—Berlin and New Hampshire Community Technical College—Laconia (Summer 2005)
New Hampshire Community Technical College—Claremont changed its name to River Valley Community College (Winter 2008)
New Hampshire Community Technical College—Laconia changed its name to Lakes Region Community College (Winter 2008)
New Hampshire Community Technical College—Manchester changed its name to Manchester Community College (Winter 2008)
New Hampshire Community Technical College—Manchester/Stratham split to become New Hampshire Community Technical College—Manchester and New Hampshire Community Technical College—Stratham (Summer 2005)
New Hampshire Community Technical College—Nashua changed its name to Nashua Community College (Winter 2008)
New Hampshire Community Technical College—Nashua/Claermont split to become New Hampshire Community Technical College—Nashua and New Hampshire Community Technical College—Claremont (Summer 2005)
New Hampshire Community Technical College—Stratham changed its name to Great Bay Community College (Winter 2008)
New Hampshire Technical Institute changed its name to NHTI, Concord's Community College (Winter 2008)

NEW JERSEY

Allied Medical and Technical Careers changed its name to Allied Medical and Technical Institute (Summer 2004)
Allied Medical and Technical Institute closed (Spring 2006)
Boardwalk and Marina Casino Dealers School closed (Summer 2001)
Brick Computer Science Institute closed (Summer 2004)

Bryman Institute—South Plainfield changed its name to Everest Institute—South Plainfield (Fall 2006)
Cittone Institute—Edison changed its name to Lincoln Technical Institute—Edison (Summer 2006)
Cittone Institute—Mount Laurel changed its name to Lincoln Technical Institute—Mount Laurel (Summer 2006)
Cittone Institute—Paramus changed its name to Lincoln Technical Institute—Paramus (Summer 2006)
DeVry College of Technology—North Brunswick changed its name to DeVry University—North Brunswick (Summer 2006)
Harrison Career Institute—Clifton closed (Winter 2006)
Harrison Career Institute—Delran closed (Winter 2007)
Harrison Career Institute—Depford closed (Winter 2007)
Harrison Career Institute—Ewing closed (Winter 2007)
Harrison Career Institute—Jersey City closed (Winter 2007)
Harrison Career Institute—Oakhurst closed (Winter 2007)
Harrison Career Institute—South Orange closed (Winter 2006)
HoHoKus School of Business and Medical Sciences changed its name to Eastwick College (Summer 2008)
Metropolitan Technical Institute closed (Fall 2002)
PC AGE Career Institute closed (Summer 2004)
Plaza School of Technology closed (Fall 1990)
Prism Career Institute—Sewell Campus closed (Fall 2005)
RETS Institute-Nutley changed its name to HoHoKus RETS—Nutley (Summer 2005)
Rizzieri Institute changed its name to Rizzieri Aveda School for Beauty and Wellness (Summer 2005)
Software Sense Computer Learning Center, Inc. closed (Summer 2004)
Somerset School of Massage Therapy changed its name to Cortiva Institute-Somerset School of Massage Therapy (Summer 2005)
Worldwide Educational Services—Clifton closed (Summer 2003)
Worldwide Educational Services—Jersey City closed (Fall 2003)
Worldwide Educational Services—Newark closed (Summer 2003)

NEW MEXICO

Albuquerque Technical Vocational Institute changed its name to Central New Mexico Community College (Winter 2006)
College of the Southwest changed its name to University of the Southwest (Spring 2008)
Crownpoint Institute of Technology changed its name to Navajo Technical College (Fall 2006)
Metropolitan College—Albuquerque Campus closed (Summer 2006)
Nonproliferation and National Security Institute changed its name to National Training Center (Summer 2004)
Northern New Mexico Community College changed its name to Northern New Mexico College (Spring 2005)
Southwest Health Career Institute, Inc. changed its name to Kaplan Career Institute (Summer 2006)

NEW YORK

American Barber Institute changed its name to A.B.I. School of Barbering and Cosmetology (Summer 2007)
ASA Institute, The College of Advanced Technology changed its name to ASA, The College for Excellence (Spring 2006)
Austin Beauty School changed its name to Austin's School of Spa Technology (Spring 2005)
Brooklyn Institute of Business Technology closed (Summer 2007)
Career Blazers, Inc. changed its name to Career Skills Institute (Summer 2007)
Centurion Professional Training closed (Spring 2006)
City University of New York Bernard M. Baruch College changed its name to Baruch College (Summer 2006)
Columbia-Greene Beauty School, Inc. closed (Winter 2006)
Computer Career Center changed its name to Career Institute of Health and Technology (Summer 2006)
Culinary Academy of New York Management School changed its name to Career Academy of New York (Winter 2006)
Farmingdale State University of New York changed its name to Farmingdale State College (Fall 2006)
Grace Institute of Business Technology changed its name to Brooklyn Institute of Business Technology (Summer 2006)
Graduate College of Union University changed its name to Union Graduate College (Spring 2006)
Interboro Institute closed (Winter 2007)

Learning Institute for Beauty Sciences—Hauppauge changed its name to Long Island Beauty School—Hauppauge (Fall 2007)

Learning Institute for Beauty Sciences—Hempstead changed its name to Long Island Beauty School—Hempstead (Fall 2007)

Learning Institute for Beauty Sciences—Levittown changed its name to Brittany Beauty School—Levittown (Fall 2007)

Mandl School changed its name to Mandl, The College of Allied Health (Summer 2006)

New School University changed its name to The New School (Summer 2005)

New York Food & Hotel Management School changed its name to Culinary Academy of New York Management School (Summer 2005)

New York Institute of Technology and Cardean University formed a partnership known as Ellis College (Winter 2007)

New York Restaurant School changed its name to The Art Institute of New York City (Winter 2002)

ParalegalTech Institute changed its name to National Paralegal College (Summer 2007)

Polytechnic University changed its name to Polytechnic Institute of NYU (Summer 2008)

Professional Business Institute changed its name to Professional Business College (Winter 2005)

Rochester Business Institute changed its name to Everest Institute—Rochester (Fall 2006)

Saint Francis School of Practical Nursing closed (Summer 2002)

Sessions Online School of Design changed its name to Sessions Online Schools of Art and Design (Summer 2008)

State University of New York at Stony Brook changed its name to Stony Brook University (Summer 2002)

State University of New York College of Technology at Farmingdale changed its name to Farmingdale State University of New York (Summer 2002)

Taylor Business Institute closed (Summer 2007)

NORTH CAROLINA

Chowan College changed its name to Chowan University (Fall 2006)

ECPI Technical College—Raleigh closed (Spring 2005)

Institute of Textile Technology merged with North Carolina State University and closed (Winter 2003)

LaShe' Beauty Academy changed its name to Durham Beauty Academy (Summer 2006)

Medical Arts Massage School changed its name to Medical Arts School (Fall 2006)

Methodist College changed its name to Methodist University (Fall 2006)

Mitchell's Hairstyling Academy—Fayetteville changed its name to Montgomery's Hair Styling Academy (Summer 2005)

North Carolina State University merged with Institute of Textile Technology (Winter 2003)

Winston-Salem Bible College changed its name to Carolina Christian College (Summer 2007)

NORTH DAKOTA

Aaker's Business College changed its name to Aaker's College (Spring 2005)

Aaker's College changed its name to Rasmussen College—Fargo (Fall 2007)

OHIO

Academy of Hair Design closed (Winter 2001)

Brown Aveda Institute changed its name to Ladies and Gentlemen Hair Stylists (Winter 2005)

Bryman Institute—Gahanna changed its name to Everest Institute—Gahanna (Fall 2006)

Casal's De Spa and Salon changed its name to Casal Aveda Institute (Summer 2006)

Century School of Cosmetology, Inc. changed its name to The Ohio Academy—Paul Mitchell Partner School (Fall 2006)

Charmayne Beauty Academy closed (Fall 2003)

Choffin Career Center changed its name to Choffin Career and Technical Center (Summer 2004)

CIMS College closed (Winter 2004)

Circleville Bible College changed its name to Ohio Christian University (Spring 2006)

College of Art Advertising closed (Winter 2006)

Columbus Para-Professional Institute changed its name to Ohio Institute of Health Careers—Columbus (Summer 2002)

Conservatory of Cosmetology closed (Fall 2005)

Ed W. Grooms & Associates, Inc. changed its name to Dale Carnegie Training of Greater Cincinnati (Winter 2004)

Hair Academy changed its name to Casal's De Spa and Salon (Winter 2005)
Hamrick Truck Driving School changed its name to Hamrick School (Summer 2006)
Kaplan Career Institute—Cleveland changed its name to Kaplan College—Cleveland (Summer 2007)
Ladies and Gentlemen Hair Stylists changed its name to Brown Aveda Institute (Winter 2006)
Medical College of Ohio changed its name to Medical University of Ohio (Spring 2005)
Medical University of Ohio merged with University of Toledo and changed its name to University of Toledo Health Science Campus (Summer 2006)
Michael W. Jones & Associates, Inc. changed its name to Dale Carnegie Training of Central Ohio Tyson Eppley, LLC (Winter 2006)
Myers University changed its name to Chancellor University (Fall 2008)
New Life Academy of Information Technology changed its name to New Life Technical Institute (Summer 2007)
Northwestern College changed its name to University of Northwestern Ohio (Winter 1999)
Ohio Board of Regents changed its name to University System of Ohio (Spring 2008)
Omni Technical School closed (Fall 2002)
Riggs Le Mar Beauty College closed (Summer 2006)
Samuel Stephen College changed its name to Daymar College—Chillicothe (Summer 2008)
Southeastern Business College changed its name to Samuel Stephen College (Summer 2006)
TDDS—Professional Training Center changed its name to TDDS Technical Institute (Summer 2004)
Total Technical Institute changed its name to Kaplan Career Institute—Cleveland (Spring 2007)
University of Toledo merged with Medical University of Ohio (Summer 2006)
Vogue Beauty Academy—Cleveland closed (Fall 2003)
Vogue Beauty Academy—Cleveland Heights closed (Fall 2003)
Wilmington College—Eastgate merged with Wilmington College—Tri-County, changed its name to Wilmington College—Blue Ash and closed (Summer 2007)

OKLAHOMA

Canadian Valley Area Vocational Technical School changed its name to Canadian Valley Technology Center (Summer 2001)
Central Oklahoma Area Vocational-Technical Center changed its name to Central Technology Center—Drumright (Summer 2004)
Chisholm Trail Area Vocational Technical School changed its name to Chisholm Trail Technology Center (Summer 2001)
City College, Inc. closed (Spring 2007)
DeMarge College closed (Fall 2004)
Francis Tuttle Vocational-Technical Center changed its name to Francis Tuttle Technology Center (Summer 2001)
Magee Brothers Beaverton School of Beauty changed its name to Beaverton School of Beauty (Summer 2006)
Metropolitan College—Oklahoma City closed (Summer 2006)
Metropolitan College—Tulsa closed (Summer 2006)
Moore-Norman Area Vocational Technical School changed its name to Moore Norman Technology Center (Summer 2005)
Northeast Area Vocational Technical School changed its name to Northeast Technology Center (Summer 2003)
Spartan School of Aeronautics changed its name to Spartan College of Aeronautics and Technology (Summer 2004)
Western Oklahoma Area Vocational Technical School changed its name to Western Technology Center (Summer 2001)

OREGON

Astoria Beauty College changed its name to Paul Mitchell The School (Summer 2005)
Northwest Christian College changed its name to Northwest Christian University (Summer 2008)
Northwest College of Hair Design changed its name to Northwest College (Fall 2006)
Western Baptist College changed its name to Corban College (Summer 2005)
Western Business College changed its name to Everest College—Portland (Fall 2005)

PENNSYLVANIA

Academy of Hair Design changed its name to Academy of Creative Hair Design (Summer 2005)
Academy of Medical Arts and Business changed its name to Keystone Technical Institute (Winter 2007)

Allentown Business School changed its name to Lehigh Valley College (Winter 2005)

Allentown School of Cosmetology, Inc. changed its name to The Vision Academy—A Paul Mitchell Partner School (Spring 2006)

Allied Medical and Technical Careers merged with Business Training Institute (Summer 2004)

Ambler Beauty Academy, Inc. changed its name to Magnolia School (Spring 2005)

The Boyd School—Oakdale changed its name to Pittsburgh Technical Institute (Summer 2000)

Business Institute of Pennsylvania—Pulaski closed (Summer 2002)

Business Institute of Pennsylvania changed its name to Laurel Technical Institute (Spring 2008)

Cambria County Area Community College changed its name to Pennsylvania Highlands Community College (Summer 2004)

Center for Advanced Manufacturing and Technology closed (Fall 2004)

Centre County Area Vocational Technical School changed its name to Central Pennsylvania Institute of Science and Technology (Summer 2004)

Chatham College changed its name to Chatham University (Spring 2007)

Churchman Business School closed (Winter 2004)

Cittone Institute—Center City changed its name to Lincoln Technical Institute—Center City (Summer 2006)

Cittone Institute—Northeast changed its name to Lincoln Technical Institute—Northeast Philadelphia (Summer 2006)

Cittone Institute—Plymouth Meeting changed its name to Lincoln Technical Institute—Plymouth Meeting (Summer 2006)

Clarion County Area Vocational Technical School changed its name to Clarion County Career Center (Summer 2006)

Clearfield Beauty Academy closed (Fall 2005)

Clearfield County Area Vocational Technical School changed its name to Clearfield County Career and Technology Center (Summer 2006)

College Misericordia changed its name to Misericordia University (Summer 2007)

Connelley Technical Institute and Adult Education Center closed (Summer 2004)

CSC Institute closed (Winter 2005)

Dale Carnegie Systems changed its name to JR Rodgers and Associates, Inc. (Winter 2004)

Duff's Business Institute changed its name to Everest Institute—Pittsburgh (Fall 2006)

East Montgomery County Area Vocational Technical School changed its name to Eastern Center for Arts and Technology (Summer 2006)

Eastern Baptist Theological Seminary changed its name to Palmer Theological Seminary (Summer 2005)

Education Direct changed its name to Penn Foster Career School (Winter 2005)

Education Direct Center for Degree Studies changed its name to Penn Foster College (Winter 2005)

Electronic Institutes changed its name to Harrisburg Institute of Trade and Technology (Spring 2005)

Empire Beauty School—Pottstown closed (Winter 2005)

Evangelical School of Theology changed its name to Evangelical Theological Seminary (Summer 2007)

Franklin County Area Vocational Technical School changed its name to Franklin County Career and Technology Center (Summer 2006)

Gordon Phillips School of Beauty Culture—Norristown closed (Spring 2003)

Gordon Phillips School of Beauty Culture—Philadelphia closed (Fall 1994)

Gordon Phillips School of Beauty Culture—Upper Darby closed (Spring 2003)

Greene County Area Vocational Technical School changed its name to Greene County Career and Technology Center (Summer 2006)

Harrisburg Institute of Trade and Technology closed (Winter 2006)

Harrison Career Institute—Allentown closed (Winter 2007)

Harrison Career Institute—Philadelphia closed (Winter 2007)

Harrison Career Institute—Reading closed (Summer 2006)

Hazleton Area Vocational Technical School changed its name to Hazelton Area Career Center (Summer 2006)

ICM School of Business and Medical Careers changed its name to Kaplan Career Institute—ICM Campus (Summer 2006)

Information Computer Systems Institute changed its name to Pennsylvania School of Business (Spring 2005)

Institute of Midwifery, Women and Health merged with Philadelphia University and changed its name to Midwifery Institute of Philadelphia University (Summer 2005)

International Academy of Design and Technology closed (Winter 2008)

Lackawanna County Area Vocational Technical School changed its name to Career Technology Center of Lackawanna County (Winter 2004)

Lawrence County Area Vocational Technical School changed its name to Lawrence County Career and Technical Center (Summer 2006)

Median School of Allied Health Careers changed its name to Vet Tech Institute (Spring 2006)

Medical College of Pennsylvania merged with Hahnamann University and changed its name to MCP Hahnamann University (Fall 1999)

Monroe County Area Vocational Technical School changed its name to Monroe Career and Technical Institute (Summer 2006)

North Central Industrial Technical Education Center closed (Winter 2007)

North Hills School of Health Occupations closed (Spring 2000)

Parkway West Vocational Technical School changed its name to Parkway West Career and Technical Institute (Summer 2006)

Penn Council for Relationships changed its name to Council for Relationships (Summer 2004)

Penn State Cosmetology Academy changed its name to PSC Academy (Spring 2003)

Pennsylvania College of Optometry changed its name to Salus University (Summer 2008)

Pennsylvania Institute of Culinary Arts changed its name to Pennsylvania Culinary Institute (Summer 2004)

Pennsylvania School of Muscle Therapy, Ltd. changed its name to Cortiva Institute-Pennsylvania School of Muscle Therapy (Summer 2005)

Pennsylvania State University Fayette Campus changed its name to Pennsylvania State University Fayette, The Eberly Campus (Spring 2004)

Philadelphia University merged with Institute of Midwifery, Women and Health (Summer 2005)

Pittsburgh Beauty Academy of Charleroi closed (Summer 2003)

Pittsburgh Beauty Academy of Greensburg closed (Summer 2003)

Pittsburgh Beauty Academy of Pittsburgh closed (Summer 2003)

PSC Academy closed (Summer 2008)

The Sawyer School closed (Winter 1999)

Somerset County Area Vocational Technical School changed its name to Somerset County Technology Center (Summer 2006)

South Philadelphia Beauty Academy closed (Spring 2004)

Springhouse Computer School changed its name to Springhouse Education and Consulting Services (Winter 2003)

Talent Academy closed (Winter 2005)

Thompson Institute changed its name to Kaplan Career Institute (Summer 2006)

Venango County Area Vocational Technical School changed its name to Venango Technology Center (Summer 2006)

Venus Beauty School changed its name to Venus Beauty Academy (Summer 2006)

Waynesburg College changed its name to Waynesburg University (Summer 2007)

Western Area Vocational Technical School changed its name to Western Area Career and Technology Center (Summer 2006)

York County Area Vocational Technical School changed its name to York County School of Technology (Summer 2006)

York Technical Institute changed its name to YTI Career Institute (Summer 2006)

PUERTO RICO

American Business College closed (Fall 2002)

Electronic Data Processing College changed its name to EDP College (Winter 2006)

Instituto del Arte Moderno closed (Spring 1996)

Instituto Irma Valentin—Aricebo closed (Fall 2006)

Instituto Irma Valentin—Manati closed (Fall 2006)

Instituto Irma Valentin—Mayaguez closed (Fall 2006)

Instituto Vocacional Aurea E. Mendez changed its name to IVAEM College (Summer 2006)

J G Guaynabo Technical College changed its name to Cambridge Technical Institute (Summer 2006)

Marugie Beauty and Technical College closed (Spring 2002)

Pontifical Catholic University of Puerto Rico—Guayama Campus closed (Spring 2006)

Star Career College changed its name to Quality Technical and Beauty College (Summer 2006)

Technological College of the Municipality of San Juan changed its name to Technological College of San Juan (Winter 2000)

Teddy Ulmo Institute closed (Spring 2003)

Universal Career Counseling Center changed its name to Universal Career Community College (Summer 2006)

Veterans Affairs Medical Center—San Juan changed its name to Veterans Affairs Caribbean Healthcare System (Spring 2006)

RHODE ISLAND

Career Education Institute—Lincoln changed its name to Lincoln Technical Institute—Lincoln (Summer 2006)

Rhode Island Beauty Academy closed (Winter 2003)

Warwick Academy of Beauty Culture changed its name to Arthur Angelo School of Cosmetology & Hair Design—Warwick (Winter 2007)

Zion Bible Institute changed its name to Zion Bible College (Summer 2005)

SOUTH CAROLINA

Anderson College changed its name to Anderson University (Winter 2006)

Beta Tech changed its name to Centura College (Fall 2007)

Johnson & Wales University—Charleston closed (Spring 2006)

North Greenville College changed its name to North Greenville University (Fall 2005)

Spartanburg Technical College changed its name to Spartanburg Community College (Fall 2006)

SOUTH DAKOTA

North American Baptist Seminary changed its name to Sioux Falls Seminary (Spring 2007)

Si Tanka University closed (Winter 2005)

Si Tanka University—Huron closed (Spring 2005)

TENNESSEE

Academy of Beauty Arts changed its name to Franklin Academy (Summer 2005)

Ambassador Institute of Travel closed (Spring 2001)

American Academy of Nutrition changed its name to Huntington College of Health Sciences (Summer 2005)

Electronic Computer Programming College changed its name to Chattanooga College (Summer 2007)

Fort Sanders School of Nursing merged with Tennessee Wesleyan College to become the Fort Sanders Nursing Department of Tennessee Wesleyan College (Summer 2005)

Methodist Healthcare—University Hospital changed its name to Methodist University Hospital (Summer 2002)

Middle Tennessee School of Cosmetology changed its name to Genesis Career College (Winter 2008)

Nave Cosmetology Academy, Inc. merged with Georgia Career Institute and changed its name to Georgia Career Institute—Nave Cosmetology Academy (Spring 2007)

Southeastern Career College changed its name to Kaplan Career Institute—Nashville (Spring 2007)

Stylemasters Beauty Academy changed its name to Genesis Career College (Winter 2008)

Tennessee Career College closed (Spring 2008)

Tennessee Wesleyan College merged with Fort Sanders School of Nursing (Summer 2005)

World Class University changed its name to Dudley Nwani, The School (Spring 2007)

TEXAS

Academy of Hair Design changed its name to Paul Mitchell the School—Houston (Summer 2006)

Aeronautical Institute of Technologies merged with Aviation Institute of Maintenance and changed its name to Aviation Institute of Maintenance—Dallas (Summer 2006)

Amarillo College of Hairdressing, Inc. changed its name to Milan Institute of Cosmetology (Spring 2005)

Border Institute of Technology closed (Summer 2007)

Career Point Institute changed its name to Career Point College (Summer 2008)

Careers Unlimited closed (Winter 2007)

Circle J Beauty School changed its name to Royal Beauty Careers (Summer 2006)

Concordia University at Austin changed its name to Concordia University Texas (Summer 2008)
Dallas College of Oriental Medicine closed (Winter 2005)
DSU Training Institute closed (Spring 2004)
English Language Specialists closed (Summer 2003)
Euro Hair School closed (Winter 2002)
Genesis Vocational Training closed (Summer 2004)
Houston Allied Health Careers, Inc. closed (Summer 2005)
Huston-Tillotson College changed its name to Huston-Tillotson University (Winter 2005)
IMTI College of Business and Technology—Regency Square closed (Summer 2007)
MTI College of Business and Technology—Space Park closed (Summer 2006)
National Institute of Technology—San Antonio changed its name to Everest Institute—San Antonio (Fall 2006)
North Harris Montgomery Community College District changed its name to Lone Star College System (Winter 2008)
North Texas Professional Career Institute changed its name to Dallas Nursing Institute (Summer 2007)
R. C. Leffke & Associates, Inc. changed its name to John M. Jennings and Associates, Inc. (Spring 2005)
Southwest School of Business & Technical Careers closed (Winter 2006)
Southwestern Adventist College changed its name to Southwestern Adventist University (Summer 1996)
Southwestern Professional Institute closed (Fall 2006)
Texas Beauty College changed its name to Milan Institute of Cosmetology (Spring 2005)
Texas Career Institute closed (Winter 2005)
U.S. Army Academy of Health Sciences changed its name to Army Medical Department Center and School (AMEDD) (Winter 2000)
Valley Grande College of Health and Technology changed its name to Valley Grande Institute for Academic Studies (Fall 2001)
Western Technical Institute changed its name to Western Technical College (Fall 2005)
Westwood College of Aviation Technology—Houston changed its name to Westwood Aviation Institute—Houston (Winter 2005)
Westwood College of Technology—Dallas changed its name to Westwood College—Dallas (Winter 2005)
Westwood College of Technology—Fort Worth changed its name to Westwood College—Fort Worth (Winter 2005)
Westwood Institute of Technology—Houston South changed its name to Westwood College—Houston South (Winter 2005)

UTAH

American Institute of Medical-Dental Technology changed its name to Ameritech College (Summer 2006)
California College for Health Sciences changed its name to Independence University (Summer 2005)
Chatterton, Inc. changed its name to Dale Carnegie Training Utah (Summer 2005)
College of Eastern Utah merged with Southeast Applied Technology College (Summer 2007)
Hairitage College of Beauty changed its name to Paul Mitchell The School (Summer 2005)
International Institute of Hair Design closed (Summer 2004)
Mountain West College changed its name to Everest College—Salt Lake City (Summer 2006)
Northface University changed its name to Neumont University (Winter 2005)
Southeast Applied Technology College merged with College of Eastern Utah and closed (Summer 2007)
Utah College of Midwifery changed its name to Midwives College of Utah (Fall 2004)
Utah Valley State College changed its name to Utah Valley University (Summer 2008)
Von Curtis Academy of Hair Design changed its name to Paul Mitchell The School (Summer 2005)

VERMONT

Woodbury College merged with Champlain College and changed its name to The Woodbury Institute at Champlain College (Fall 2008)

VIRGINIA

American School of Professional Psychology—Virginia Campus merged with Argosy University and changed its name to Argosy University Washington, DC (Fall 2001)
Applied Career Training, Inc. changed its name to ACT College (Summer 2003)
ATI—Hollywood changed its name to BarPalma Beauty Careers Academy (Summer 2005)
Banner College closed (Summer 2008)
Beta Tech changed its name to Centura College (Fall 2007)
Braxton School of Business closed (Fall 2007)
Center for Naval Leadership merged with Center for Personal and Professional Development (Spring 2008)
Center for Personal and Professional Development merged with Center for Naval Leadership and closed (Spring 2008)
Chubb Institute—Arlington changed its name to Banner College (Summer 2005)
Cosmopolitan Beauty and Barber School changed its name to Cosmopolitan Beauty and Tech School (Summer 2005)
Dickerson Beauty Academy closed (Fall 2003)
EasTech closed (Fall 2000)
ECPI Technical College—Roanoke changed its name to ECPI College of Technology—Richmond (West End) (Summer 2008)
Ghent Beauty Academy closed (Summer 2004)
Gibbs College—Vienna changed its name to Sanford-Brown College—Vienna (Summer 2008)
Heritage Institute—Falls Church merged with Heritage Institute—Manassas and closed (Fall 2007)
Indian River Beauty Academy closed (Winter 2004)
International Beauty School—Charlottesville closed (Fall 2005)
Johnson & Wales University—Norfolk closed (Spring 2006)
Kee Business College—Newport News changed its name to Everest Institute—Newport News (Spring 2007)
Lawrence-White Associates, Inc. changed its name to J.J. White & Associates, Inc. Dale Carnegie Training (Summer 2006)
LIFE Bible College East closed (Spring 2004)
National Imagery and Mapping College changed its name to National Geospatial-Intelligence College (Fall 2005)
Potomac Academy of Hair Design changed its name to Heritage Institute (Summer 2004)
Potomac Academy of Hair Design—Falls Church changed its name to Heritage Institute (Summer 2004)
Ralph's Virginia School of Cosmetology, Inc. changed its name to Legends Institute (Summer 2005)
Randolph-Macon Woman's College changed its name to Randolph College (Summer 2007)
Richmond School of Health and Technology changed its name to RSHT Training Center (Summer 2005)
TESST College of Technology closed (Summer 2007)
United States Navy and Marine Corps Intelligence Training Center changed its name to Center for Naval Intelligence (Summer 2003)
Virginia Careers Academy closed (Spring 2001)
Virginia Center for Montessori Training changed its name to Virginia Montessori Teacher Education Center (Summer 2007)
Virginia School of Technology changed its name to Virginia Career Institute (Summer 2006)

WASHINGTON

American College of Professional Education closed (Summer 2000)
Brenneke School of Massage changed its name to Cortiva Institute-Brenneke School of Massage (Summer 2005)
Brian Utting School of Massage changed its name to Cortiva Institute-Brian Utting School of Massage (Summer 2005)
Bryman College—Federal Way closed (Winter 2005)
Bryman College—Lynnwood closed (Fall 2007)
Bryman College—Port Orchard changed its name to Everest College—Bremerton (Spring 2007)
Bryman College—Renton changed its name to Everest College—Renton (Spring 2007)
Business Career Training Institute closed (Spring 2005)
Cortiva Institute-Brenneke School of Massage changed its name to Cortiva Institute-Seattle (Fall 2007)
Cortiva Institute-Brian Utting School of Massage closed (Spring 2007)
Court Reporting Institute changed its name to Sage College (Fall 2003)
Crown College closed (Summer 2007)

Everett Beauty Academy changed its name to Milan Institute of Cosmetology (Spring 2005)
Faith Evangelical Lutheran Seminary changed its name to Faith Evangelical Seminary (Summer 2006)
Henry Cogswell College closed (Fall 2006)
Heritage College changed its name to Heritage University (Summer 2004)
Inland Northwest Heating, Ventilation, and Air Conditioning Training Center changed its name to Northwest HVAC/R Association and Training Center (Summer 2004)
International Air Academy changed its name to International Air and Hospitality Academy (Summer 2006)
Northwest College of the Assemblies of God changed its name to Northwest University (Winter 2005)
Puget Sound Christian College closed (Spring 2007)
Sage College closed (Summer 2006)
Saint Martin's College changed its name to Saint Martin's University (Summer 2005)
Tri-Cities Chaplaincy changed its name to The Chaplaincy (Fall 2007)
Walla Walla College changed its name to Walla Walla University (Fall 2007)
Whitworth College changed its name to Whitworth University (Summer 2007)

WEST VIRGINIA

American Community College closed (Winter 2004)
Community and Technical College of Shepherd changed its name to Blue Ridge Community and Technical College (Summer 2006)
Fairmont State Community and Technical College changed its name to Pierpont Community and Technical College (Summer 2006)
Fairmont State University merged with Pierpont Community and Technical College and changed its name to Fairmont State University including Pierpont Community and Technical College (Summer 2007)
International Academy of Design and Technology—Fairmont closed (Spring 2006)
National Institute of Technology—Cross Lanes changed its name to Everest Institute—Cross Lanes (Fall 2006)
Ohio Valley College changed its name to Ohio Valley University (Summer 2005)
Pierpont Community and Technical College merged with Fairmont State University (Summer 2006)
Webster College—Fairmont closed (Winter 2001)

WISCONSIN

Carroll College changed its name to Carroll University (Summer 2008)
Community Health Care Wausau Hospital changed its name to Aspirus Wausau Hospital (Summer 2007)
Marian College of Fond du Lac changed its name to Marian University (Spring 2008)
Western Wisconsin Technical College changed its name to Western Technical College (Spring 2006)

CANADA

Alliance University College changed its name to Ambrose University College (Spring 2007)
Full Gospel Bible College changed its name to Eston College (Winter 2008)
Full Gospel Bible Institute changed its name to Full Gospel Bible College (Winter 2005)
Keewatin Community College changed its name to University College of the North (Summer 2004)
Kwantlen University College changed its name to Kwantlen Polytechnic University (Summer 2008)
Okanagan University College changed its name to Okanagan College (Summer 2005)
Ryerson Polytechnic University changed its name to Ryerson University (Summer 2002)

Candidates for Accreditation

Candidate for Accreditation is a status of affiliation with a recognized accrediting organization that indicates that an institution has achieved initial recognition and is progressing toward, but has not been assured, accreditation.

The Candidate for Accreditation classification is designed for postsecondary institutions that may or may not be fully operative. In either case, the institution must provide evidence of sound planning, the resources to implement these plans, and appear to have the potential for attaining its goals within a reasonable time.

To be considered for Candidate for Accreditation status, the applicant must be a postsecondary education institution with the following characteristics:

(1) Have a charter and/or formal authority from an appropriate governmental agency to award a certificate, diploma, or degree.

(2) Have a governing board that includes representation reflecting the public interest.

(3) Have employed a chief administrative officer.

(4) Offer, or plan to offer, one or more educational programs of at least one academic year in length, or the equivalent at the postsecondary level, with clearly defined and published educational objectives, as well as a clear statement of the means for achieving them.

(5) Include general education at the postsecondary level as a prerequisite to or as an essential element in its principal educational programs.

(6) Have admission policies compatible with its stated objectives.

(7) Have developed a preliminary survey or evidence of basic planning for the development of the institution.

(8) Have established an adequate financial base of funding commitments and have available a summary of its latest audited financial statement.

ALABAMA

Selma University
1501 Lapsley St., Selma 36701
Type: Private, Baptist Church, four-year
System: Alabama Association of Independent Colleges and Universities
Degrees: A, B, M *FTE Enroll:* 183
Phone: (334) 872-2533 *Calendar:* Sem. plan
Inst. Accred.: ABHE (2005)

ARIZONA

Phoenix Seminary
4222 East Thomas Rd., Ste. 400, Phoenix 85018
Type: Private, nondenominational, four-year
Degrees: M, D
URL: http://www.phoenixseminary.edu
Phone: (602) 850-8000 *Calendar:* Sem. plan
Inst. Accred.: ATS (2000/2007), NCA-HLC (2007)

CALIFORNIA

Horizon College San Diego
10625 Scripps Ranch Blvd., San Diego 92131
Type: Private, nondenominational, four-year
Degrees: B
URL: http://www.horizoncollege.org
Phone: (858) 695-8587 *Calendar:* Sem. plan
Inst. Accred.: ABHE (2008)

InterAmerican College
140 West 16th St., National City 91950-4413
Type: Private, independent, four-year
Degrees: B
URL: http://www.iacnc.edu
Phone: (619) 477-6310 *Calendar:* Sem. plan
Inst. Accred.: WASC-SR. (2005)

International Reformed University and Seminary
2853 West Seventh St., Los Angeles 90005
Type: Private, nondenominational, four-year
Degrees: B
URL: http://www.iruniv.org
Phone: (213) 381-0081 *Calendar:* Sem. plan
Inst. Accred.: ABHE (2007)

KPCA College and Theological Seminary
13353 Alondra Blvd., Ste. 200K, Santa Fe Springs 90670
Type: Private, Korean Presbyterian Church in America, four-year
Degrees: B, M
URL: http://www.kpcas.com
Phone: (562) 926-1023 *Calendar:* Sem. plan
Inst. Accred.: ABHE (2006)

KPCA Presbyterian Theological Seminary
14300 Leffingwell Rd., Whittier 90604
Type: Private, Presbyterian Church, four-year
Degrees: B, M
Phone: (562) 906-4747
Inst. Accred.: ABHE (2006)

Olivet University and Seminary
250 Fourth St., San Francisco 94103
Type: Private, Evangelical Assembly of Presbyterian Churches, four-year
Degrees: B, M
URL: http://www.olivetuniversity.org
Phone: (415) 371-0002 *Calendar:* Sem. plan
Inst. Accred.: ABHE (2007)

Riverside City College—Moreno Valley Campus
16130 Lasselle St., Moreno Valley 92551-2045
Type: Public, state/local, two-year
System: Riverside Community College District
Degrees: A
URL: http://www.rcc.edu/morenovalley
Phone: (951) 571-6100 *Calendar:* Sem. plan
Inst. Accred.: WASC-JR. (2008)

Riverside Community College—Norco
2001 Third St., Norco 92860-2600
Type: Public, state/local, two-year
System: Riverside Community College District
Degrees: A
URL: http://www.rcc.edu/norco
Phone: (951) 372-7000 *Calendar:* Sem. plan
Inst. Accred.: WASC-JR. (2008)

University of California, Merced
PO Box 2039, Merced 95344
Type: Public, state, four-year
System: University of California Office of the President
Degrees: B, M, D
URL: http://www.ucmerced.edu
Phone: (209) 724-4417 *Calendar:* Sem. plan
Inst. Accred.: WASC-SR. (2007)

Westwood College—Los Angeles
3250 Wilshire Blvd., Ste. 400, Los Angeles 90010
Type: Private, proprietary, four-year
System: Westwood College
Degrees: A, B *Enroll:* 944
URL: http://www.westwood.edu
Phone: (213) 739-9999
Inst. Accred.: NCA-HLC (2007)

Westwood College—South Bay
19700 South Vermont Ave., Ste. 100, Torrance 90502
Type: Private, proprietary, four-year
System: Westwood College
Degrees: A, B
URL: http://www.westwood.edu
Phone: (310) 965-0888
Inst. Accred.: NCA-HLC (2007, *Indirect accreditation through Westwood College, Denver, CO*)

World Mission University
500 Shatto Place, Ste. 600, Los Angeles 90020
Type: Private, independent, four-year
Degrees: B, M, P
URL: http://www.wmu.edu
Phone: (213) 385-2322 *Calendar:* Sem. plan
Inst. Accred.: TRACS (2006)

COLORADO

American Pathways University
2227 Franklin St., Denver 80205
Type: Private, proprietary, four-year
Degrees: A, B
URL: http://www.apudenver.org
Phone: (303) 839-9491 *Calendar:* Sem. plan
Inst. Accred.: AALE (2007)

Rocky Vista University College of Osteopathic Medicine
8401 South Chambers Rd., Parker 80134
Type: Private, independent, four-year
Degrees: P
URL: http://www.rockyvistauniversity.org
Phone: (303) 373-2008 *Calendar:* Sem. plan
Inst. Accred.: AOA-BPE (2007)

Saint John Vianney Theological Seminary
1300 South Steele St., Denver 80210-2599
Type: Private, Roman Catholic Church, four-year
Degrees: M
URL: http://www.sjvdenver.org
Phone: (303) 282-3427 *Calendar:* Sem. plan
Inst. Accred.: ATS (2006)

Westwood College—Denver North
7350 North Broadway, Denver 80221-3653
Type: Private, proprietary, four-year
System: Westwood College
Degrees: A, B, M *Enroll:* 4,167
URL: http://www.westwood.edu
Phone: (303) 426-7000 *Calendar:* Qtr. plan
Inst. Accred.: NCA-HLC (2007)

CONNECTICUT

Saint Basil College Seminary
195 Glenbrook Rd., Stamford, CO 06902
Type: Private, Roman Catholic Church, four-year
Degrees: B *FTE Enroll:* 6
URL: http://www.stbasilcollegesem.net
Phone: (203) 324-4578 *Calendar:* Sem. plan
Inst. Accred.: AALE (2005), NEASC-CIHE (2007)

Saint Basil College Seminary
195 Glenbrook Rd., Stamford 06902
Type: Private, Roman Catholic Church, four-year
Degrees: B *FTE Enroll:* 6
URL: http://www.stbasilcollegesem.net
Phone: (203) 324-4578 *Calendar:* Sem. plan
Inst. Accred.: NEASC-CIHE (2007)

DISTRICT OF COLUMBIA

Pontifical John Paul II Institute for Studies on Marriage and Family
620 Michigan Ave. NE, Washington 20017
Type: Private, Roman Catholic Church, four-year
Degrees: M, D
URL: http://www.johnpaulii.edu
Phone: (202) 526-3799 *Calendar:* Sem. plan
Inst. Accred.: MSA-CHE (2008)

FLORIDA

Everglades University
5002 T-REX Ave., Ste. 100, Boca Raton 33431
Type: Private, independent, four-year
Degrees: B, M *Enroll:* 458
URL: http://www.evergladesuniversity.edu
Phone: (561) 912-1211 *Calendar:* Tri. plan
Inst. Accred.: SACS (2008)

The Robert E. Webber Institute for Worship Studies
151 Kingsley Ave., Orange Park 32073
Type: Private, nondenominational, four-year
Degrees: M, D
URL: http://www.iwsfla.org
Phone: (904) 264-2172
Inst. Accred.: ABHE (2008)

South Florida Bible College and Theological Seminary
747 South Federal Hwy., Deerfield Beach 33441
Type: Private, independent, four-year
Degrees: A, B, M, D
URL: http://www.sfbc.edu
Phone: (954) 426-8652 *Calendar:* Sem. plan
Inst. Accred.: ABHE (2008)

GEORGIA

Appalachian Technical College
100 Campus Dr., Jasper 30143
Type: Public, state, two-year
System: Technical College System of Georgia
Degrees: A *Enroll:* 627
URL: http://www.appalachiantech.edu
Phone: (706) 253-4500
Inst. Accred.: SACS (2007)

Georgia Gwinnett College
1000 University Ln., Lawrenceville 30043
Type: Public, state, four-year
System: Board of Regents of the University System of Georgia
Degrees: A, B
URL: http://www.ggc.usg.edu
Phone: (678) 407-5016 *Calendar:* Sem. plan
Inst. Accred.: SACS (2008)

Holy Spirit Preparatory School
4449 Northside Dr., Atlanta 30327
Type: Private, Roman Catholic Church, two-year
Degrees: A
URL: http://www.holyspiritprep.org
Phone: (678) 904-2811
Inst. Accred.: AALE (2006)

John Marshall Law School—Atlanta
1422 West Peachtree St. NW, Atlanta 30309
Type: Private, independent, four-year
Degrees: P
URL: http://www.johnmarshall.edu
Phone: (404) 872-3593 *Calendar:* Sem. plan
Inst. Accred.: ABA (2005)

Okefenokee Technical College
1701 Carswell Ave., Waycross 31503
Type: Public, state/local, two-year
System: Technical College System of Georgia
Degrees: A *Enroll:* 976
URL: http://www.okefenokeetech.edu
Phone: (912) 287-6584 *Calendar:* Qtr. plan
Inst. Accred.: SACS (2007)

Southern Catholic College
330 Southern Catholic Dr., Dawsonville 30534
Type: Private, independent, four-year
Degrees: B
URL: http://www.southerncatholic.org
Phone: (706) 344-4000 *Calendar:* Sem. plan
Inst. Accred.: AALE (2007)

Swainsboro Technical College
346 Kite Rd., Swainsboro 30401
Type: Public, state, two-year
System: Technical College System of Georgia
Degrees: A *Enroll:* 420
URL: http://www.swainsborotech.edu
Phone: (478) 289-2200 *Calendar:* Qtr. plan
Inst. Accred.: SACS (2007)

ILLINOIS

Harrington College of Design
200 West Madison, Ste. 200, Chicago 60606-3433
Type: Private, proprietary, four-year
System: Career Education Corporation
Degrees: A, B *Enroll:* 1,072
URL: http://www.interiordesign.edu
Phone: (312) 939-4975 *Calendar:* Sem. plan
Inst. Accred.: NCA-HLC (2007)

Toyota Technological Institute at Chicago
1427 East 60th St., Second Flr., Chicago 60637
Type: Private, proprietary, four-year
Degrees: M, D
URL: http://www.tti-c.org
Phone: (773) 834-2500 *Calendar:* Qtr. plan
Inst. Accred.: NCA-HLC (2005)

Westwood College—DuPage
7155 Janes Ave., Ste. 100, Woodridge 60517
Type: Private, proprietary, four-year
System: Westwood College
Degrees: A, B
URL: http://www.westwood.edu
Phone: (630) 434-8250
Inst. Accred.: NCA-HLC (2007, *Indirect accreditation through Westwood College, Denver, CO*)

INDIANA

Grace College and Seminary
200 Seminary Dr., Winona Lake 46590
Type: Private, Fellowship of Grace Brethren Churches, four-year
Degrees: A, B, M, D *Enroll:* 1,127
URL: http://www.grace.edu
Phone: (574) 372-5100 *Calendar:* Sem. plan
Inst. Accred.: ATS (2006)

Mid-America Reformed Seminary
229 Seminary Dr., Dyer 46311
Type: Private, Reformed and Presbyterian Churches, four-year
Degrees: M
URL: http://www.midamerica.edu
Phone: (219) 864-2400 *Calendar:* Sem. plan
Inst. Accred.: ATS (2007), TRACS (2005)

KANSAS

Wichita Area Technical College
301 South Grove St., Wichita 67211
Type: Private, proprietary, two-year
Degrees: A *Enroll:* 558
URL: http://www.watc.edu
Phone: (316) 677-9400 *Calendar:* Sem. plan
Inst. Accred.: NCA-HLC (2006)

KENTUCKY

Bowling Green Technical College
1845 Loop Dr., Bowling Green 42101-9202
Type: Public, state, two-year
System: Bowling Green Community and Technical College District
Degrees: A
URL: http://www.bowlinggreen.kctcs.edu
Phone: (270) 901-1000 *Calendar:* Sem. plan
Inst. Accred.: SACS (2008)

Gateway Community and Technical College
1025 Amsterdam Rd., Park Hills 41011-2031
Type: Public, state, two-year
System: Gateway Community and Technical College District
Degrees: A
URL: http://www.gateway.kctcs.edu
Phone: (859) 441-4500 *Calendar:* Sem. plan
Inst. Accred.: SACS (2007)

Louisville Bible College
PO Box 91046, Louisville 40291-0046
Type: Private, nondenominational, four-year
Degrees: A, B, M
URL: http://www.louisvillebiblecollege.org
Phone: (502) 231-5221 *Calendar:* Sem. plan
Inst. Accred.: ABHE (2008)

LOUISIANA

L.E. Fletcher Technical Community College
PO Box 5033, Houma 70361-5033
Type: Public, state, two-year
System: Louisiana Community and Technical College System
Degrees: A *Enroll:* 921
URL: http://www.lefletcher.edu
Phone: (985) 857-3655 *Calendar:* Sem. plan
Inst. Accred.: SACS (2007)

Louisiana Delta Community College
1201 Bayou Dr., Monroe 71203
Type: Public, state, two-year
System: Louisiana Community and Technical College System
Degrees: A
URL: http://www.ladelta.cc.la.us
Phone: (318) 342-3700 *Calendar:* Sem. plan
Inst. Accred.: SACS (2007)

MARYLAND

Yeshiva College of the Nation's Capital
1216 Arcola Ave., Silver Spring 20902
Type: Private, independent, four-year
Degrees: B *FTE Enroll:* 56
Phone: (301) 593-2534 *Calendar:* Sem. plan
Inst. Accred.: AARTS (2003)

MINNESOTA

Central Baptist Theological Seminary of Minneapolis
900 Forestview Ln. North, Plymouth 55441
Type: Private, Fourth Baptist Church, four-year
Degrees: M, D
URL: http://www.centralseminary.edu
Phone: (763) 417-8250 *Calendar:* Sem. plan
Inst. Accred.: TRACS (2007)

White Earth Tribal and Community College
PO Box 478, 202-210 South Main St., Mahnomen 56557
Type: Public, tribal, two-year
System: American Indian Higher Education Consortium
Degrees: A
URL: http://www.wetcc.org
Phone: (218) 935-0417 *Calendar:* Sem. plan
Inst. Accred.: NCA-HLC (2004)

MISSOURI

Central Bible College
3000 North Grant Ave., Springfield 65803-1096
Type: Private, Assemblies of God Church, four-year
Degrees: A, B *Enroll:* 715
URL: http://www.cbcag.edu
Phone: (417) 833-2551 *Calendar:* Sem. plan
Inst. Accred.: NCA-HLC (2005)

Franklin Technology Center
2020 Iowa Ave., Joplin 64804-2131
Type: Public, local, two-year
Degrees: A
URL: http://www.ftcjoplin.com
Phone: (417) 625-5269
Inst. Accred.: NCA-CASI (2006)

Global University
1211 South Glenstone Ave., Springfield 65804
Type: Private, Asemblies of God, four-year
Degrees: A, B, M *FTE Enroll:* 1,200
URL: http://www.globaluniversity.edu
Phone: (417) 862-9533
Inst. Accred.: NCA-HLC (2006)

Urshan Graduate School of Theology
704 Howdershell Rd., Florissant 63031
Type: Private, United Pentecostal Church, four-year
Degrees: M
URL: http://www.ugst.org
Phone: (314) 921-9290 *Calendar:* Sem. plan
Inst. Accred.: ATS (2008)

MONTANA

Montana Bible College
3625 South 19th Ave., Bozeman 59718
Type: Private, nondenominational, four-year
Degrees: B
URL: http://www.montanabiblecollege.edu
Phone: (406) 586-3585 *Calendar:* Sem. plan
Inst. Accred.: ABHE (2008)

NEBRASKA

BryanLGH College of Health Sciences
5035 Everett St., Lincoln 68506-1315
Type: Private, independent, four-year
Degrees: A, B, M
URL: http://www.bryanlghcollege.org
Phone: (402) 481- 3801 *Calendar:* Sem. plan
Inst. Accred.: NCA-HLC (2006)

BryanLGH College of Health Sciences
5035 Everett St., Lincoln 68506-1398
Type: Private, independent, four-year
Degrees: A, B, M
URL: http://www.bryanlghcollege.org
Phone: (402) 481- 3801 *Calendar:* Sem. plan
Inst. Accred.: NCA-HLC (2006)

NEVADA

Nevada State College at Henderson
1125 Nevada State Dr., Henderson 89015
Type: Public, state, four-year
Degrees: B, M
URL: http://www.nsc.nevada.edu
Phone: (702) 992-2000 *Calendar:* Sem. plan
Inst. Accred.: NWCCU (2006)

NEW HAMPSHIRE

New Hampshire Institute of Art
148 Concord St., Manchester 03104-4158
Type: Private, independent, four-year
Degrees: B
URL: http://www.nhia.edu
Phone: (603) 623-0313 *Calendar:* Sem. plan
Inst. Accred.: NEASC-CIHE (2006)

NEW JERSEY

Bais Medrash Toras Chesed
910 Monmouth Ave., Lakewood 08701
Type: Private, independent, four-year
Degrees: B
Phone: (732) 901-6786
Inst. Accred.: AARTS (2006)

NEW YORK

ASA, The College for Excellence
151 Lawrence St., 2nd Flr., Brooklyn 11201
Type: Private, independent, two-year
Degrees: A
URL: http://www.asa.edu
Phone: (718) 522-9073
Inst. Accred.: WASC-SR. (2005)

Beis Medrash Heichal Dovid
257 Beach 17th St., Far Rockaway 11691
Type: Private, independent, four-year
Degrees: Talmudic *FTE Enroll:* 70
Phone: (718) 868-2300 *Calendar:* Sem. plan
Inst. Accred.: AARTS (2002)

Career School of New York
350 St. Marks Place, Room 105, Staten Island 10301
Type: Private, proprietary, two-year
Degrees: A
URL: http://www.careerschoolny.com
Phone: (718) 420-6440
Inst. Accred.: COE (2007)

Derech Ayson Rabbinical Seminary
802 Hicksville Rd., Far Rockaway 11691
Type: Private, independent, four-year
Degrees: Talmudic
Phone: (718) 327-7600
Inst. Accred.: AARTS (2006)

The King's College
Empire State Bldg., 350 Fifth Ave., Ste. 1500, New York 10118
Type: Private, independent, four-year
Degrees: B *FTE Enroll:* 392
URL: http://www.tkc.edu
Phone: (212) 659-7200 *Calendar:* Sem. plan
Inst. Accred.: MSA-CHE (2007)

Saint Joseph's College of Nursing
301 Prospect Ave., Syracuse 13203-1898
Type: Private, independent, two-year
Degrees: A
URL: http://www.sjhsyr.org/nursing
Phone: (315) 448-5040
Inst. Accred.: MSA-CHE (2008)

NORTH CAROLINA

Carolina Evangelical Divinity School
1208 Eastchester Dr., Ste. 101, High Point 27265-2384
Type: Private, Friends United Meeting, four-year
Degrees: M, D
URL: http://www.ceds.edu
Phone: (336) 882-3370 *Calendar:* Sem. plan
Inst. Accred.: ATS (2006)

New Life Theological Seminary
PO Box 790106, Charlotte 28206-7901
Type: Private, independent, four-year
Degrees: B, M
URL: http://www.nlts.org
Phone: (704) 334-6882 *Calendar:* Sem. plan
Inst. Accred.: TRACS (2006)

Shepherds Theological Seminary
6051 Tyron Rd., Cary 27511
Type: Private, nondenominational, four-year
Degrees: A, B, M
URL: http://www.shepherdsseminary.org
Phone: (919) 573-5350 *Calendar:* Sem. plan
Inst. Accred.: TRACS (2008)

OREGON

Columbia Gorge Community College
400 East Scenic Dr., The Dalles 97058
Type: Public, local, two-year
Degrees: A
URL: http://www.cgcc.cc.or.us
Phone: (541) 506-6000 *Calendar:* Qtr. plan
Inst. Accred.: NWCCU (2008)

Gutenberg College
1883 University St., Eugene 97403
Type: Private, independent, four-year
Degrees: B
URL: http://www.gutenberg.edu
Phone: (541) 683-5141 *Calendar:* Qtr. plan
Inst. Accred.: TRACS (2007)

Oregon College of Art and Craft
8245 SW Barnes Rd., Portland 97225
Type: Private, independent, four-year
Degrees: B
URL: http://www.ocac.edu
Phone: (503) 297-5544 *Calendar:* Sem. plan
Inst. Accred.: NWCCU (2006)

Oregon College of Oriental Medicine
10525 SE Cherry Blossom Dr., Portland 97216
Type: Private, proprietary, four-year
Degrees: M, D *Enroll:* 231
URL: http://www.ocom.edu
Phone: (503) 253-3443 *Calendar:* Qtr. plan
Inst. Accred.: NWCCU (2008)

Tillamook Bay Community College
2510 First St., Tillamook 97141
Type: Public, local, two-year
Degrees: A
URL: http://www.tbcc.cc.or.us
Phone: (503) 842-8222 *Calendar:* Qtr. plan
Inst. Accred.: NWCCU (2009)

PENNSYLVANIA

The Art Institute of Philadelphia
1622 Chestnut St., Philadelphia 19103-5198
Type: Private, proprietary, four-year
System: Education Management Corporation
Degrees: A, B *Enroll:* 2,799
URL: http://www.aiph.artinstitutes.edu
Phone: (215) 567-7080 *Calendar:* Qtr. plan
Inst. Accred.: MSA-CHE (2007)

Byzantine Catholic Seminary of SS. Cyril and Methodius Seminary
3605 Perrysville Ave., Pittsburgh 15214
Type: Private, Byzantine Catholic Church, four-year
Degrees: M
URL: http://www.byzcathsem.org
Phone: (412) 321-8383 *Calendar:* Sem. plan
Inst. Accred.: ATS (2006)

Calvary Baptist Theological Seminary
1380 South Valley Forge Rd., Lansdale 19446
Type: Private, Calvary Baptist Church, four-year
Degrees: M, P, D
URL: http://seminary.cbs.edu
Phone: (215) 368-7538 ext 1 *Calendar:* Sem. plan
Inst. Accred.: MSA-CHE (2004)

Harrisburg University of Science and Technology
304 Market St., Harrisburg 17101
Type: Private, proprietary, four-year
Degrees: B, M *FTE Enroll:* 67
URL: http://www.harrisburgu.net
Phone: (717) 901-5100 *Calendar:* Sem. plan
Inst. Accred.: MSA-CHE (2006)

RHODE ISLAND

Mater Ecclesiae College
60 Austin Ave., Greenville 02828
Type: Private, Roman Catholic Church, four-year
Degrees: B
URL: http://www.materecclesiae.net
Phone: (401) 949-2820 *Calendar:* Sem. plan
Inst. Accred.: NEASC-CIHE (2005)

TENNESSEE

Oxford Graduate School
500 Oxford Dr., Dayton 37321-6736
Type: Private, independent, four-year
Degrees: M, D
URL: http://www.oxnetedu.org
Phone: (423) 775-6596 *Calendar:* Qtr. plan
Inst. Accred.: TRACS (2006)

Visible School, Music and Worship Arts College
9817 Huff N Puff Rd., Lakeland 38002
Type: Private, independent, four-year
Degrees: B
URL: http://www.visibleschool.com
Phone: (901) 381-3939 *Calendar:* Sem. plan
Inst. Accred.: TRACS (2007)

TEXAS

Academy of Oriental Medicine at Austin
2700 West Anderson Ln., Ste. 204, Austin 78757
Type: Private, proprietary, four-year
Degrees: M *Enroll:* 181
URL: http://www.aoma.edu
Phone: (512) 454-1188
Inst. Accred.: SACS (2008)

American College of Acupuncture and Oriental Medicine
9100 Park West Dr., Houston 77063
Type: Private, proprietary, four-year
Degrees: M *Enroll:* 118
URL: http://www.acaom.edu
Phone: (713) 780-9777 *Calendar:* Sem. plan
Inst. Accred.: SACS (2008)

Baptist Missionary Association Theological Seminary
1530 East Pine St., Jacksonville 75766-5407
Type: Private, Baptist Missionary Association of America, four-year
Degrees: A, B, M *Enroll:* 85
URL: http://www.bmats.edu
Phone: (903) 586-2501 *Calendar:* Sem. plan
Inst. Accred.: ATS (2006)

UTAH

Rocky Mountain University of Health Professions
1662 West 820 North, Provo 84601
Type: Private, independent, four-year
Degrees: M, D
URL: http://www.rmuohp.edu
Phone: (801) 375-5125
Inst. Accred.: NWCCU (2005)

VERMONT

Vermont College of Fine Arts
36 College St., Montpelier 05602-3128
Type: Private, independent, four-year
Degrees: M
URL: http://www.tui.edu/vcfa
Phone: (800) 336-6794 *Calendar:* Sem. plan
Inst. Accred.: NEASC-CIHE (2008)

VIRGINIA

Virginia Baptist College
4105 Plank Rd., Fredericksburg 22407
Type: Private, Baptist Church, four-year
Degrees: A, B, M
URL: http://www.vbc.edu
Phone: (540) 785-5440 *Calendar:* Sem. plan
Inst. Accred.: TRACS (2008)

Washington Baptist University
4300 Evergreen Ln., Annandale 22003
Type: Private, Baptist Church, four-year
Degrees: B, M
URL: http://www.wbcs.edu
Phone: (703) 333-5904 *Calendar:* Sem. plan
Inst. Accred.: ATS (2006)

Westwood College
4300 Wilson Blvd., Ste. 200, Arlington 22203
Type: Private, proprietary, four-year
System: Westwood College
Degrees: A, B
URL: http://www.westwood.edu
Phone: (703) 243-3900 *Calendar:* Sem. plan
Inst. Accred.: NCA-HLC (2007, *Indirect accreditation through Westwood College, Denver, CO*)

WASHINGTON

Pacific Northwest University of Health Sciences College of Osteopathic Medicine
111 South 33rd St., Ste. 104, Yakima 98901
Type: Private, independent, four-year
Degrees: P
URL: http://www.pnwu.org
Phone: (509) 452-3627 *Calendar:* Sem. plan
Inst. Accred.: AOA-BPE (2007)

WEST VIRGINIA

Eastern West Virginia Community and Technical College
1929 State Rd. 55, Moorefield 26836
Type: Public, state, two-year
System: Community and Technical College System of West Virginia
Degrees: A
URL: http://www.eastern.wvnet.edu
Phone: (304) 434-8000 *Calendar:* Sem. plan
Inst. Accred.: NCA-HLC (2006)

Future Generations Graduate School
HC 73 Box 100 North Mountain, Franklin 26807
Type: Private, independent, four-year
Degrees: M
URL: http://www.future.org
Phone: (304) 358-2000
Inst. Accred.: NCA-HLC (2008)

BERMUDA

Bermuda College
PO Box PG 297, Paget PG BX
Type: Private, independent, two-year
Degrees: A
URL: http://www.bercol.bm
Phone: (441) 236-9000 *Calendar:* Sem. plan
Inst. Accred.: NEASC-CIHE (2005)

CANADA

Boucher Institute of Naturopathic Medicine
200-668 Carnarvon St., New Westminster V3M 5Y6
Type: Private, independent, four-year
Degrees: D
URL: http://www.binm.org
Phone: (604) 777-9981
Inst. Accred.: CNME (2003)

Capilano College
2055 Purcell Way, North Vancouver V7J 3H5
Type: Private, independent, four-year
Degrees: A, B
URL: http://www.capcollege.bc.ca
Phone: (604) 986-1911 *Calendar:* Sem. plan
Inst. Accred.: NWCCU (2008)

Concordia Lutheran Theological Seminary
470 Glenridge Ave., St. Catharines L2T 4C3
Type: Private, Lutheran Church-Canada, four-year
Degrees: B, M
URL: http://www.concordia-seminary.ca
Phone: (905) 688-2362 *Calendar:* Sem. plan
Inst. Accred.: ATS (2008)

CHILE

Universidad Mayor
Av. Américo Vespucio Sur 357, Las Condes, Santiago
Type: Private, independent, four-year
Degrees: B, M, P
URL: http://www.umayor.cl
Phone: 011 56 2 240-3800
Inst. Accred.: MSA-CHE (2006)

ITALY

American University of Rome
Via Pietro Roselli 4, Rome 00153
Type: Private, independent, four-year
Degrees: A, B
URL: http://www.aur.edu
Phone: 011 3906 5833 0919 *Calendar:* Sem. plan
Inst. Accred.: MSA-CHE (2008)

LEBANON

Lebanese American University
PO Box 13-5053, Beirut
Type: Private, independent, four-year
Degrees: P
URL: http://www.lau.edu.lb
Phone: 011 961 1 867 620
Inst. Accred.: NEASC-CIHE (2007)

MEXICO

CETYS University
Calzada CETYS s/n Colonia Rivera, Apartado Postal 3-797, Mexicali, BC 21259
Type: Private, independent, four-year
System: Sistema CETYS Universidad
Degrees: B, M, D
URL: http://www.mxl.cetys.mx
Phone: 011 5256 73230
Inst. Accred.: WASC-SR. (2008)

NORTHERN MARIANA ISLANDS

EUCON International College
PO Box 500087 CK, Saipan 96950-0087
Type: Private, independent, four-year
Degrees: B
URL: http://www.eucon.edu
Phone: (670) 234-3207 *Calendar:* Sem. plan
Inst. Accred.: TRACS (2007)

ALABAMA

Xcell Academy-A Paul Mitchell Partner School
1694 Montgomery Hwy., Hoover 35126
Type: Private, proprietary
Degrees: C
URL: https://www.xcellacademy.com
Phone: (205) 824-4442
Inst. Accred.: NACCAS (2008)

ALASKA

Alaska Christian College
35109 Royal Place, Soldotna 99669
Type: Private, independent
Degrees: C
URL: http://akcc.org/home/akcc.org
Phone: (907) 260-7422 *Calendar:* Sem. plan
Inst. Accred.: ABHE (2008)

ARIZONA

The Studio Academy of Beauty
610 North Alma School Rd., Ste. 38, Chandler 85224
Type: Private, proprietary
Degrees: C
URL: http://www.tsaob.com
Phone: (480) 857-1138
Inst. Accred.: NACCAS (2008)

ARKANSAS

Blackwood Beauty School
2105 Hwy. 67 South, Pocahontas 72444
Type: Private, proprietary
Degrees: C
Phone: (870) 892-3879
Inst. Accred.: NACCAS (2005)

CALIFORNIA

Beyond 21st Century Beauty Academy
13640 Imperial Hwy., Ste. 7, Santa Fe Springs 90670-6315
Type: Private, proprietary
Degrees: C
Phone: (562) 404-6193
Inst. Accred.: NACCAS (2008)

The California Academy-A Paul Mitchell Partner School
2100 Arden Way, Ste. 265, Sacramento 95825
Type: Private, proprietary
Degrees: C
URL: http://www.thecaliforniaacademy.com
Phone: (916) 646-3523
Inst. Accred.: NACCAS (2008)

Career College of San Diego
3350 Market St., Ste. C, San Diego 92102
Type: Private, proprietary
Degrees: C
URL: http://www.careercollegesandiego.com
Phone: (619) 338-0813
Inst. Accred.: COE (2007)

Cosmetology School of Fresno-A Paul Mitchell Partner School
5091 North Fresno St., Ste. 104, Fresno 93710
Type: Private, proprietary
Degrees: C
URL: http://www.fresnopaulmitchellschool.com
Phone: (559) 224-2700
Inst. Accred.: NACCAS (2008)

Diamond Beauty College
10301 Garvey Ave., Ste. 200, El Monte 91733
Type: Private, proprietary
Degrees: C
Phone: (626) 350-1195
Inst. Accred.: NACCAS (2008)

Dior School of Cosmetology
3121 Yosemite Blvd., Ste. D1, Modesto 95354
Type: Private, proprietary
Degrees: C
URL: http://www.go2dior.com
Phone: (209) 521-1000
Inst. Accred.: NACCAS (2008)

Federico Career College of Bakersfield, Inc
4105 Ming Ave., Bakersfield 93309-4994
Type: Private, proprietary
Degrees: C
URL: http://www.federicocareercolleges.com
Phone: (661) 397-9293
Inst. Accred.: NACCAS (2008)

Federico Career College of Fresno, Inc
5660 North Blackstone Ave., Fresno 93710-5004
Type: Private, proprietary
Degrees: C
URL: http://www.federicocareercolleges.com
Phone: (559) 432-4343
Inst. Accred.: NACCAS (2008)

Flair Beauty College
18914 Soledad Canyon Rd., Canyon Country 91351
Type: Private, proprietary
Degrees: C
URL: http://flairbeautycollege.com
Phone: (661) 251-3261
Inst. Accred.: NACCAS (2008)

Foreign Trade Institute—LA
3333 Wilshire Blvd., Ste. 209, Los Angeles 90005
Type: Private, proprietary
Degrees: C
URL: http://www.fti-la.org
Phone: (213) 368-1231
Inst. Accred.: COE (2007)

Hollywood Beauty College
1024 East March Ln., Stockton 95210
Type: Private, proprietary
Degrees: C
URL: http://hollywoodbeautycollege.org
Phone: (209) 951-7572
Inst. Accred.: NACCAS (2008)

Institute of Beauty Culture
533 Five Cities Dr., Pismo Beach 93449
Type: Private, proprietary
Degrees: C
URL: http://institutebeautyculture.org
Phone: (805) 556-0912
Inst. Accred.: NACCAS (2008)

International Dermal Institute Los Angeles
1535 Beachey Place, Carson 90746
Type: Private, proprietary
Degrees: C
URL: http://www.dermalinstitute.com
Phone: (310) 352-4784
Inst. Accred.: NACCAS (2008)

Los Angeles Music Academy
370 South Fair Oaks Ave., Pasadena 91105
Type: Private, independent
Degrees: C
URL: http://www.lamusicacademy.com
Phone: (626) 568-8850 *Calendar:* Qtr. plan
Inst. Accred.: NASM (2003)

Lu Ross Academy
470 East Thompson Blvd., Ventura 93001
Type: Private, proprietary
Degrees: C
URL: http://www.lurossacademy.com
Phone: (805) 643-5690
Inst. Accred.: NACCAS (2008)

Northern California Institute of Cosmetology
644 East 14th St., San Leandro 94577
Type: Private, proprietary
Degrees: C
URL: http://ncinstitutecosmetology.com
Phone: (510) 635-4371
Inst. Accred.: NACCAS (2008)

NTMA Training Centers of Southern California
14926 Bloomfield Ave., Norwalk 90650
Type: Private, independent
Degrees: C
URL: http://www.ntmatrainingcenters.org
Phone: (562) 921-3722
Inst. Accred.: COE (2004)

The Real Barbers College
528 West Lincoln Ave., Anaheim 92805
Type: Private, proprietary
Degrees: C
URL: http://www.therealbarberscollege.com
Phone: (714) 772-4423
Inst. Accred.: NACCAS (2008)

San Francisco College of Cosmetology
2075 Mission St., San Francisco 94110
Type: Private, proprietary
Degrees: C
URL: http://www.sfcosmetology.com
Phone: (415) 621-1333
Inst. Accred.: NACCAS (2008)

San Rafael Beauty Academy
827 Fourth St., San Rafael 94901
Type: Private, proprietary
Degrees: C
URL: http://www.sanrafaelbeautyacademy.org
Phone: (415) 454-5432
Inst. Accred.: NACCAS (2008)

Santa Ana Beauty Academy
2231 North Tustin Avenu, Santa Ana 92705
Type: Private, proprietary
Degrees: C
Phone: (714) 547-5177
Inst. Accred.: NACCAS (2008)

Tony and Guy Hairdressing Academy
1358 5th St., Santa Monica 90401
Type: Private, proprietary
Degrees: C
URL: http://toniguy.com
Phone: (310) 451-0101
Inst. Accred.: NACCAS (2008)

COLORADO

Aveda Institute Denver
700 16th St., Denver 80202
Type: Private, proprietary
Degrees: C
URL: http://www.avedadenver.com
Phone: (303) 567-7500
Inst. Accred.: NACCAS (2008)

Summit Salon and Beauty School
PO Box 4569, Woodland Park 80863
Type: Private, proprietary
Degrees: C
Phone: (719) 686-0205
Inst. Accred.: NACCAS (2008)

CONNECTICUT

B Beautiful Hair Institute
60 Access Rd., Stratford 06615
Type: Private, proprietary
Degrees: C
Phone: (203) 375-2849
Inst. Accred.: NACCAS (2008)

The European Academy of Cosmetology and Hairdressing
1575 Boston Post Rd., Building C, Guilford 06437
Type: Private, proprietary
Degrees: C
URL: http://www.teachbeauty.com
Phone: (203) 458-3334
Inst. Accred.: NACCAS (2008)

International Institute of Cosmetology
632 Silas Deane Hwy., Wethersfield 06109
Type: Private, proprietary
Degrees: C
URL: http://www.studyhair.com
Phone: (860) 571-0330
Inst. Accred.: NACCAS (2008)

New Haven Job Corps Center
455 Wintergreen Ave., New Haven 06515
Type: Public, federal
Degrees: C
URL: http://www.ctdol.state.ct.us/JobCorps/newhaven_desc.html
Phone: (203) 397-3775
Inst. Accred.: NEASC-CTCI (2007)

Oxford Academy of Hair Design
225 West St., Seymour 06483
Type: Private, proprietary
Degrees: C
URL: http://www.oxfordhairacademy.com
Phone: (203) 888-9075
Inst. Accred.: NACCAS (2008)

Shear Style School of Cosmetology and Hair Design
488 North Main St., Norwich 06360-3941
Type: Private, proprietary
Degrees: C
URL: http://www.shearstyleschool.com
Phone: (860) 887-1364
Inst. Accred.: NACCAS (2008)

Tonsorial Academy of Cosmetology and Barber Styling
217-219 Boston Post Rd., West Haven 06516
Type: Private, proprietary
Degrees: C
URL: http://tonsorialacademy.org
Phone: (203) 937-8263
Inst. Accred.: NACCAS (2008)

DISTRICT OF COLUMBIA

Aveda Institute Washington DC
713 7th St. NW, Washington 20001
Type: Private, proprietary
Degrees: C
URL: http://www.avedainstitutedc.com
Phone: (202) 824-1624
Inst. Accred.: NACCAS (2008)

Joint Military Attache School
MacDill Air Force Base, 200 MacDill Blvd., Bldg. 6000, Washington 20340-5100
Type: Public, federal
Degrees: C
URL: http://www.dia.mil
Phone: (202) 231-5691
Inst. Accred.: COE (2006)

FLORIDA

Academy of Health and Beauty
2115 West Colonial Dr., Orlando 32804
Type: Private, proprietary
Degrees: C
URL: http://www.aohab.com
Phone: (407) 447-5565
Inst. Accred.: NACCAS (2008)

American Academy of Cosmetology
1330 Blanding Blvd., Ste. 125, Orange Park 32065
Type: Private, proprietary
Degrees: C
URL: http://americanacademyfl.com
Phone: (904) 213-1444
Inst. Accred.: NACCAS (2008)

Beauty Academy of South Florida
1305 West 49th St., Hialeah 33012
Type: Private, proprietary
Degrees: C
URL: http://beautyacademyofsouthflorida.net
Phone: (305) 817-3577
Inst. Accred.: COE (2007)

Celebrity School of Beauty
8478 SW 8 St., Miami 33144
Type: Private, proprietary
Degrees: C
URL: http://www.celebrity-beauty.com
Phone: (305) 267-7277
Inst. Accred.: NACCAS (2008)

D.A. Dorsey Educational Center
7100 NW 17th Ave., Miami 33147
Type: Public, local
Degrees: C
URL: http://dadorsey.dadeschools.net
Phone: (305) 693-2490 *Calendar:* Tri. plan
Inst. Accred.: COE (2007)

Eternity Cosmetology School
4698 Forest Hill Blvd., West Palm Beach 33415
Type: Private, proprietary
Degrees: C
Phone: (561) 963-5551
Inst. Accred.: NACCAS (2008)

Eureka Institute of Health and Beauty
11373 W Flagler St., Ste. 209, Miami 33174
Type: Private, proprietary
Degrees: C
URL: http://www.eurekainstituteofhealthandbeauty.com
Phone: (305) 480-1005
Inst. Accred.: COE (2008)

Flagler Technical Center
One Corporate Dr., Ste. 2J, Palm Coast 32137
Type: Public, local
Degrees: C
URL: http://www.flagleradulted.com
Phone: (386) 446-7612
Inst. Accred.: COE (2007)

Florida Academy of Cosmetology, Inc.
5802 North Armenia Ave., Ste. 1, Tampa 33603
Type: Private, proprietary
Degrees: C
URL: http://floridaacademyofcosmetology.info
Phone: (813) 872-7888
Inst. Accred.: NACCAS (2008)

Margate School of Beauty
5281 Coconut Creek Pkwy., Coco Centre 33063
Type: Private, proprietary
Degrees: C
URL: http://www.margateschoolofbeauty.net
Phone: (954) 972-9630
Inst. Accred.: NACCAS (2008)

Margate School of Beauty
5281 Coconut Creek Pkwy., Coco Center, Margate 33063
Type: Private, proprietary
Degrees: C
URL: http://www.margateschoolofbeauty.net
Phone: (954) 972-9630
Inst. Accred.: NACCAS (2008)

Medical Career Institute of South Florida
1750 45th St., West Palm Beach 33407
Type: Private, proprietary
Degrees: C
URL: http://www.mcisf.com
Phone: (561) 296-0824
Inst. Accred.: COE (2004)

Medical Institute of Palm Beach
802 South Dixie Hwy., Lake Worth 33460
Type: Private, proprietary
Degrees: C
Phone: (561) 493-5022
Inst. Accred.: COE (2007)

Professional Hands Institute
2128 West Flagler St., Ste. 100, Miami 33135
Type: Private, proprietary
Degrees: C
Phone: (305) 541-8845
Inst. Accred.: COE (2007)

Progressive Training Centers
98 East McNab Rd., Ste. 98, Pompano Beach 33060
Type: Private, proprietary
Degrees: C
URL: http://www.progressivetc.com
Phone: (954) 946-2022
Inst. Accred.: COE (2007)

Walton Career Development Center
761 North 20th St., DeFuniak Springs 32433
Type: Public, local
Degrees: C
URL: http://www.walton.k12.fl.us
Phone: (850) 892-1240
Inst. Accred.: COE (2007)

GEORGIA

Atlanta Beauty Academy
6088 Buford Hwy., Doraville 30340
Type: Private, proprietary
Degrees: C
URL: http://www.atlantabeautyacademy.com
Phone: (770) 449-1740
Inst. Accred.: NACCAS (2008)

EnSynergy Southeastern School of Esthetics
105 Glendalough Ct., Ste.s H & I, Tyrone 30290
Type: Private, proprietary
Degrees: C
URL: http://www.ensynergyskin.com
Phone: (770) 486-8801
Inst. Accred.: NACCAS (2008)

Georgia Beauty Academy
303 Fernwood Ave., Dalton 30721-3952
Type: Private, proprietary
Degrees: C
URL: http://www.georgiabeautyacademy.com
Phone: (706) 278-9606
Inst. Accred.: COE (2007)

Ke Vos Nik School of Hair Design, Inc.
400 West Moore St., Dublin 31021
Type: Private, proprietary
Degrees: C
Phone: (478) 275-7251
Inst. Accred.: NACCAS (2008)

Malix College of Medical and Computer Technology
5115 New Peachtree Rd., Ste. 100, Chamblee 30341
Type: Private, proprietary
Degrees: C
URL: http://www.malix.edu
Phone: (770) 451-9115
Inst. Accred.: COE (2007)

Paul Mitchell the School—Atlanta
887 Marietta St., King Plow Arts Center Northwest, Atlanta 30318
Type: Private, proprietary
Degrees: C
URL: http://www.pmtheschoolatl.com
Phone: (404) 888-0070
Inst. Accred.: NACCAS (2008)

The Process Institute of Cosmetology
860 Duluth Hwy., Lawrenceville 30043
Type: Private, proprietary
Degrees: C
URL: http://www.theprocessinstitute.com
Phone: (678) 990-0762
Inst. Accred.: NACCAS (2008)

Profile Institute of Barber-Styling
24 Cleveland Ave. SE, Ste. A, Atlanta 30315
Type: Private, proprietary
Degrees: C
URL: http://profileinstitute.com
Phone: (404) 559-0704
Inst. Accred.: NACCAS (2008)

GUAM

Mariacy Beauty Academy
601 South Biang St., Route 8, Maite 96910
Type: Private, proprietary
Degrees: C
URL: http://mariacy.com
Phone: (671) 472-1981
Inst. Accred.: NACCAS (2008)

HAWAII

Paul Brown Institute of Beauty and Wellness Technologies
1132 Bishop St., Ste. 550, Honolulu 96813
Type: Private, proprietary
Degrees: C
URL: http://www.paulbrownhawaii.com
Phone: (808) 587-8448
Inst. Accred.: NACCAS (2008)

Spa Luna Holistic School for Estheticians and Massage Therapists
810 Haiku Rd., Ste. 209, Haiku 96708
Type: Private, proprietary
Degrees: C
URL: http://www.spaluna.com
Phone: (808) 575-9267
Inst. Accred.: NACCAS (2008)

IDAHO

Burton Academy of Beauty Culture and Hair Design
780 North Cecil Rd., Ste. 105, Post Falls 83854-8966
Type: Private, proprietary
Degrees: C
URL: http://www.burtonbeautyschool.com
Phone: (208) 618-0120
Inst. Accred.: NACCAS (2008)

D & L Academy of Hair Design
113 Main Ave. East, Twin Falls 83301
Type: Private, proprietary
Degrees: C
Phone: (208) 736-4972
Inst. Accred.: NACCAS (2008)

Master Educators of Beauty
1205 Filer Ave. E, Twin Falls 83301
Type: Private, proprietary
Degrees: C
URL: http://www.themastereducators.com
Phone: (208) 736-0044
Inst. Accred.: NACCAS (2008)

Oliver Finley Academy of Cosmetology
10222 West Fairview Ave., Boise 83704
Type: Private, proprietary
Degrees: C
URL: http://www.oliverfinley.com
Phone: (208) 658-1115
Inst. Accred.: NACCAS (2008)

ILLINOIS

CALC, Institute of Technology
235A East Center Dr., Alton 62002
Type: Private, proprietary
Degrees: C
URL: http://www.calc4it.com
Phone: (618) 474-0616
Inst. Accred.: COE (2004)

Chazap Inc. Barber College School for Haircutting
325 West 103rd St., Chicago 60628
Type: Private, proprietary
Degrees: C
URL: http://www.chazap.com
Phone: (773) 209-6283
Inst. Accred.: NACCAS (2008)

Dudley Beauty College—Chicago
8501 South Green St., Chicago 60620
Type: Private, proprietary
Degrees: C
URL: http://www.dudleyq.com/Education/DBSS/chicagofees.html
Phone: (773) 488-5900
Inst. Accred.: NACCAS (2008)

International Institute for the Advancement of Aesthetics
1315 Butterfield Rd., Ste. 200, Downers Grove 60515
Type: Private, proprietary
Degrees: C
Phone: (630) 434-9053
Inst. Accred.: NACCAS (2008)

Larry's Barber College 1
10350 South Halsted, Chicago 60628
Type: Private, proprietary
Degrees: C
URL: http://larrysbarbercollege.com
Phone: (773) 779-2100
Inst. Accred.: NACCAS (2008)

Northwestern Institute of Health and Technology
4641 North Ashland Ave., Chicago 60640
Type: Private, proprietary
Degrees: C
URL: http://www.nwiht.org
Phone: (773) 506-2136
Inst. Accred.: NCA-CASI (2006)

Shear Learning Academy of Cosmetology
241 North Main St., Decatur 62523-1208
Type: Private, proprietary
Degrees: C
URL: http://shearlearning.com
Phone: (217) 425-9117
Inst. Accred.: NACCAS (2008)

Tricoci University of Beauty Culture
5485 East State St., Rockford 61108
Type: Private, proprietary
Degrees: C
URL: http://www.tricociuniversity.com
Phone: (815) 226-9848
Inst. Accred.: NACCAS (2008)

Tricoci University of Beauty Culture
602 West Glen Ave., Peoria 61602
Type: Private, proprietary
Degrees: C
URL: http://www.tricociuniversity.com
Phone: (309) 679-4500
Inst. Accred.: NACCAS (2008)

Tricoci University of Beauty Culture
7350 West 87th St., Bridgeview 60455
Type: Private, proprietary
Degrees: C
URL: http://www.tricociuniversity.com
Phone: (708) 233-9933
Inst. Accred.: NACCAS (2008)

Tricoci University of Beauty Culture
751 East Park Ave., Libertyville 60048
Type: Private, proprietary
Degrees: C
URL: http://www.tricociuniversity.com
Phone: (847) 247-8100
Inst. Accred.: NACCAS (2008)

KANSAS

Kansas College of Chinese Medicine
9235 East Harry St., Wichita 67207
Type: Private, proprietary
Degrees: C
URL: http://www.kccm.edu
Phone: (316) 691-8822 *Calendar:* Sem. plan
Inst. Accred.: ACAOM (2007)

KENTUCKY

Lindsey Institute of Cosmetology
1059 Shive Ln., Bowling Green 42103
Type: Private, proprietary
Degrees: C
URL: http://www.lindseyinstituteofcosmetology.wisebuyingmall.com
Phone: (270) 796-3661
Inst. Accred.: NACCAS (2008)

Michael's College of Hair Design
7535 Burlington Pike, Florence 41042
Type: Private, proprietary
Degrees: C
URL: http://www.michaelscollege.com
Phone: (859) 282-7333
Inst. Accred.: NACCAS (2008)

LOUISIANA

My Le Beauty College
601 Terry Pkwy., Ste. A, Gretna 70056
Type: Private, proprietary
Degrees: C
URL: http://www.mylebeautycollege.com
Phone: (504) 362-3150
Inst. Accred.: NACCAS (2008)

MARYLAND

The Temple: A Paul Mitchell Partner School
22 West Church St., Frederick 21701
Type: Private, proprietary
Degrees: C
URL: http://www.pmthetemple.com
Phone: (301) 682-7550
Inst. Accred.: NACCAS (2008)

MASSACHUSETTS

Alexander Academy
112-114 River St., Fitchburg 01420
Type: Private, proprietary
Degrees: C
URL: http://www.alexanderacademy.com
Phone: (978) 345-0011
Inst. Accred.: NACCAS (2008)

MICHIGAN

Abcott Institute
Crossroads Bldg., 16250 Northland Dr., Ste. 205, Southfield 48075
Type: Private, proprietary
Degrees: C
URL: http://www.abcottinstitute.com
Phone: (248) 440-6020
Inst. Accred.: COE (2006)

L'esprit Academy
31501 Schoolcraft Rd., Livonia 48150
Type: Private, proprietary
Degrees: C
URL: http://www.lespritacademy.com
Phone: (734) 762-0200
Inst. Accred.: NACCAS (2008)

Marketti Academy of Cosmetology
4390 Dixie Hwy., Waterford 48329
Type: Private, proprietary
Degrees: C
URL: http://www.marketticosmetology.com
Phone: (248) 618-6832
Inst. Accred.: NACCAS (2008)

MINNESOTA

Allure School of Cosmetology
1610 West Third St., Red Wing 55066
Type: Private, proprietary
Degrees: C
URL: http://www.allureschool.com
Phone: (651) 388-8224
Inst. Accred.: NACCAS (2008)

Hastings Beauty School
221 East 2nd St., Hastings 55033-1205
Type: Private, proprietary
Degrees: C
URL: http://www.hastingsbeautyschool.com
Phone: (651) 437-1225
Inst. Accred.: NACCAS (2008)

Schwan's University
800 East Southview Dr., Marshall 56258
Type: Private, proprietary
Degrees: C
URL: http://www.schwansuniversity.com
Phone: (507) 537-8102
Inst. Accred.: COE (2007)

MISSOURI

Cape Girardeau Career and Technology Center
1080 South Silver Springs Rd., Cape Girardeau 63703
Type: Public, local
Degrees: C
URL: http://www.cape.k12.mo.us/cc
Phone: (573) 334-0826
Inst. Accred.: NCA-CASI (2006)

Cass Career Center
1600 East Elm St., Harrisonville 64701
Type: Public, local
Degrees: C
URL: http://www.casscareercenter.com
Phone: (816) 380-3253 ext 2
Inst. Accred.: NCA-CASI (2006)

Columbia Area Career Center
4203 South Providence Rd., Columbia 65203
Type: Public, local
Degrees: C
URL: http://www.career-center.org
Phone: (573) 214-3800 *Calendar:* Qtr. plan
Inst. Accred.: NCA-CASI (2006)

Cosmetology College of Franklin County
550 East Springfield South, Main Plaza, Saint Clair 63077
Type: Private, proprietary
Degrees: C
Phone: (636) 629-3433
Inst. Accred.: NACCAS (2008)

Northland Career Center
1801 Branch St., Platte City 64079
Type: Public, local
Degrees: C
URL: http://www.northlandcareercenter.com
Phone: (816) 858-5505
Inst. Accred.: NCA-CASI (2006)

Rolla Technical Institute/Center
1304 East Tenth St., Rolla 65401-3699
Type: Public, local
Degrees: C
URL: http://www.rolla.k12.mo.us/rti/index.htm
Phone: (573) 458-0150 *Calendar:* Sem. plan
Inst. Accred.: NCA-CASI (2006)

The System, A Paul Mitchell Partner School
3017 South Kansas Expressway, Springfield 65807
Type: Private, proprietary
Degrees: C
URL: http://www.thesystemonline.com
Phone: (417) 881-2110 ext 1
Inst. Accred.: NACCAS (2008)

Transformed Barber and Cosmetology Academy
5720 East Bannister Rd., Kansas City 64137
Type: Private, proprietary
Degrees: C
URL: http://www.transformedbca.com
Phone: (816) 765-8222
Inst. Accred.: NACCAS (2008)

Waynesville Technical Academy
810 Roosevelt St., Waynesville 65583-2131
Type: Public, local
Degrees: C
URL: http://waynesville.k12.mo.us/Schools/WTA/home.htm
Phone: (573) 774-6106
Inst. Accred.: NCA-CASI (2006)

NEVADA

Casal Institute of Las Vegas
4856 South Eastern Ave., Las Vegas 89119
Type: Private, proprietary
Degrees: C
Phone: (702) 459-2900
Inst. Accred.: NACCAS (2008)

DeLoux Schools of Cosmetology
7685 South Virginia St., Reno 89511
Type: Private, proprietary
Degrees: C
URL: http://www.deloux.com
Phone: (775) 329-9494
Inst. Accred.: NACCAS (2008)

NEW HAMPSHIRE

Laird Institute of Spa Therapy
38-40 South River Rd., Bedford 03110
Type: Private, proprietary
Degrees: C
URL: http://www.lairdinstitute.com
Phone: (603) 625-6100
Inst. Accred.: NACCAS (2008)

NEW JERSEY

National Career Institute
134 Evergreen Place, East Orange 07018
Type: Private, proprietary
Degrees: C
URL: http://www.nciedu.com
Phone: (973) 678-3901
Inst. Accred.: COE (2008)

NEW MEXICO

Urban Academy
2122 Central Ave. SE, Albuquerque 87106
Type: Private, proprietary
Degrees: C
URL: http://www.urbanacademy.com
Phone: (505) 842-1900
Inst. Accred.: NACCAS (2008)

NEW YORK

Access Careers
25 Elm Place, Ste. 201, Brooklyn 11201
Type: Private, proprietary
Degrees: C
URL: http://www.accesscareers.net
Phone: (718) 643-9060
Inst. Accred.: COE (2007)

Ann Marie's World of Beauty School
389 State St., Binghamton 13901
Type: Private, proprietary
Degrees: C
Phone: (607) 724-1113
Inst. Accred.: NACCAS (2008)

Aveda Institute New York
233 Spring St., New York 10013
Type: Private, proprietary
Degrees: C
Phone: (212) 367-0321
Inst. Accred.: NACCAS (2004)

Erie 1 Board of Cooperative Educational Services
355 Harlem Rd., West Seneca 14224
Type: Public, state
Degrees: C
URL: http://eboces.wnyric.org
Phone: (716) 821-7000
Inst. Accred.: COE (2008)

Manhattan Institute
255 Fifth Ave., New York 10016
Type: Private, proprietary
Degrees: C
URL: http://www.manhattaninstitute.com
Phone: (212) 564-1234
Inst. Accred.: COE (2008)

Monroe 2—Orleans BOCES, Center for Workforce Development
3545 Buffalo Rd., Rochester 14624
Type: Public, state/local
Degrees: C
URL: http://www.monroe2boces.org
Phone: (585) 349-9100
Inst. Accred.: COE (2006)

New York Medical Career Training Center
36-09 Main St., 5th Flr., Flushing 11354
Type: Private, proprietary
Degrees: C
URL: http://www.nymedtraining.com
Phone: (718) 460-1717
Inst. Accred.: COE (2006)

The Salon Professional Academy Buffalo
2309 Eggert Rd., Tonawanda 14150
Type: Private, proprietary
Degrees: C
URL: http://www.thesalonprofessionalacademy.com
Phone: (716) 833-8772
Inst. Accred.: NACCAS (2008)

Wayne-Finger Lakes Board of Cooperative Educational Services
121 Drumlin Ct., Newark 14513
Type: Public, state/local
Degrees: C
URL: http://www.wflboces.org
Phone: (315) 332-7284
Inst. Accred.: COE (2006)

Western Suffolk Board of Cooperative Educational Services
17 Westminster Ave., Dix Hills 11746
Type: Public, local
Degrees: C
URL: http://www.wilsontech.org
Phone: (631) 667-6000
Inst. Accred.: COE (2007)

NORTH CAROLINA

Daoist Traditions College of Chinese Medical Arts
382 Montford Ave., Asheville 28801
Type: Private, proprietary
Degrees: C
URL: http://www.daoisttraditions.com
Phone: (828) 225-3993 *Calendar:* Sem. plan
Inst. Accred.: ACAOM (2006)

Park West Barber School
931 East Main St., Durham 27701
Type: Private, proprietary
Degrees: C
URL: http://www.parkwest1.com
Phone: (919) 688-2914
Inst. Accred.: NACCAS (2008)

OHIO

Aultman College of Nursing and Health Sciences
2600 Sixth St., SW, Canton 44710
Type: Private, independent
Degrees: C
URL: http://www.aultmancollege.org
Phone: (330) 363-6347 *Calendar:* Sem. plan
Inst. Accred.: NCA-HLC (2007)

Cincinnati Academy-A Paul Mitchell Partner School
11956 Lebanon Rd., Cincinnati 45241
Type: Private, proprietary
Degrees: C
URL: http://www.cincinnatiacademy.com
Phone: (513) 769-7699
Inst. Accred.: NACCAS (2008)

Cincinnati Job Corps Center
1409 Western Ave., Cincinnati 45214
Type: Public, federal
Degrees: C
URL: http://jobcorps.doleta.gov/centers/oh.cfm
Phone: (513) 651-2000
Inst. Accred.: NCA-CASI (2005)

Cisoria Academy of Cosmetology
20880 Southgate Park Blvd., Maple Heights 44137
Type: Private, proprietary
Degrees: C
URL: http://cisoria.web.officelive.com
Phone: (216) 475-3535
Inst. Accred.: NACCAS (2008)

Darnell Institute of Cosmetology
2930 Market St., Youngstown 44507
Type: Private, proprietary
Degrees: C
Phone: (330) 783-9759
Inst. Accred.: NACCAS (2005)

The Ohio Academy-A Paul Mitchell Partner School
3000 Morse Rd., Columbus 43231
Type: Private, proprietary
Degrees: C
URL: https://www.theohioacademy.com
Phone: (614) 478-0922
Inst. Accred.: NACCAS (2008)

OKLAHOMA

Arleen's Clinton Beauty Academy
502 South 13th St., Clinton 73601
Type: Private, proprietary
Degrees: C
Phone: (580) 323-6700
Inst. Accred.: NACCAS (2008)

Elite Academy of Cosmetology
1206 North Hwy. 81, Ste. 59A, Duncan 73533
Type: Private, proprietary
Degrees: C
Phone: (580) 252-6620
Inst. Accred.: NACCAS (2008)

United States Army Defense Ammunition Center, Training Directorate
1 C Tree Rd., McAlester 74501
Type: Public, federal
Degrees: C
URL: https://www3.dac.army.mil/AS
Phone: (918) 420-8938
Inst. Accred.: COE (2008)

OREGON

European Institute of Cosmetology
2540 NE MLK Jr Blvd., Portland 97212
Type: Private, proprietary
Degrees: C
URL: http://www.eicschool.com
Phone: (503) 525-0200
Inst. Accred.: NACCAS (2008)

PENNSYLVANIA

District Council 21 Joint Apprenticeship and Training Fund
2190 Hornig Rd., Philadelphia 19116
Type: Private, independent
Degrees: C
URL: http://www.dc21.org
Phone: (215) 501-0130
Inst. Accred.: COE (2008)

Metro Beauty Academy
4977 Medical Center Dr., Allentown 18106
Type: Private, proprietary
Degrees: C
URL: http://www.metrobeautyacademy.com
Phone: (610) 398-6227
Inst. Accred.: NACCAS (2008)

World A Cuts Barber Institute
121 North George St., York 17401
Type: Private, proprietary
Degrees: C
URL: http://www.worldacuts.com
Phone: (717) 846-8711
Inst. Accred.: NACCAS (2008)

SOUTH CAROLINA

Betty's Career College of Cosmetology
311 South Hampton Ave., Johnsonville 29555
Type: Private, proprietary
Degrees: C
Phone: (843) 386-3346
Inst. Accred.: NACCAS (2008)

Contemporary Hair Care Institution Inc.
1701 Leesburg Rd., Columbia 29209
Type: Private, proprietary
Degrees: C
Phone: (803) 776-4101
Inst. Accred.: NACCAS (2008)

Cosmetic Arts Institute
248 Robertson Blvd., Walterboro 29488
Type: Private, proprietary
Degrees: C
Phone: (843) 549-8590
Inst. Accred.: COE (2007)

Jolies Hair Institute
203 East Main St., Olanta 29114
Type: Private, proprietary
Degrees: C
Phone: (843) 396-9010
Inst. Accred.: NACCAS (2008)

Salon 496 Barber Academy
496 South Pleasantburg Dr., Ste. H, Greenville 29607
Type: Private, proprietary
Degrees: C
Phone: (864) 242-0800
Inst. Accred.: NACCAS (2008)

TENNESSEE

Bodyworks School of Massage
2752-B North Highland Ave., Jackson 38305
Type: Private, proprietary
Degrees: C
Phone: (731) 664-8704
Inst. Accred.: COE (2007)

New Concepts School of Cosmetology
1701-M South Lee Hwy., Cleveland 37311
Type: Private, proprietary
Degrees: C
Phone: (423) 478-3231
Inst. Accred.: NACCAS (2004)

TEXAS

ABC Beauty Academy
1841 North Jupiter Rd., Ste. 120, Garland 75042
Type: Private, proprietary
Degrees: C
Phone: (972) 485-1222
Inst. Accred.: NACCAS (2007)

Advanced Beauty College
1735 North Story Rd., Irving 75061
Type: Private, proprietary
Degrees: C
Phone: (214) 492-2076
Inst. Accred.: NACCAS (2008)

Austin Beauty Academy
623 West Ben White Blvd., Austin 78704-7031
Type: Private, proprietary
Degrees: C
Phone: (512) 444-5599
Inst. Accred.: NACCAS (2008)

Austin Cosmetology and Permanent Cosmetics Institute
2521 Rutland Dr., Ste. 500, Austin 78758
Type: Private, proprietary
Degrees: C
Phone: (512) 821-2259
Inst. Accred.: NACCAS (2008)

Austin Schools of Massage
2600 West Stassney Ln., Austin 78745
Type: Private, proprietary
Degrees: C
URL: http://www.asmt.com
Phone: (512) 462-3005
Inst. Accred.: NACCAS (2008)

Aveda Institute San Antonio
250 Grayson St., Ste. 101, San Antonio 78215
Type: Private, proprietary
Degrees: C
URL: http://www.avedaisa.com
Phone: (210) 222-0023
Inst. Accred.: NACCAS (2008)

Career Academy of Texas
925 Minters Chapel Rd., Grapevine 76051
Type: Private, proprietary
Degrees: C
Phone: (817) 310-0440
Inst. Accred.: COE (2005)

Diamond's Barber College
2832 Miller Ave., Fort Worth 76105
Type: Private, proprietary
Degrees: C
Phone: (817) 534-6203
Inst. Accred.: NACCAS (2008)

DuVall's School of Cosmetology
201 Harwood Rd., Ste. 218, Bedford 76021
Type: Private, proprietary
Degrees: C
URL: http://www.duvallsschool.com
Phone: (817) 281-8819
Inst. Accred.: NACCAS (2008)

G.G.O. Beauty School
2033 Military Pkwy., Ste. 203B, Mesquite 75149
Type: Private, proprietary
Degrees: C
URL: http://ggobeautyschool.com
Phone: (972) 285-5043
Inst. Accred.: NACCAS (2008)

International Renowned Beauty Academy
3536 East Lancaster Ave., Fort Worth 76103
Type: Private, proprietary
Degrees: C
URL: http://www.irba.net
Phone: (817) 531-3716
Inst. Accred.: NACCAS (2008)

Job Ready Training
314 East Highland Mall Blvd., Ste. 507, Austin 78752
Type: Private, proprietary
Degrees: C
URL: http://www.jobreadytraining.com
Phone: (512) 300-2245
Inst. Accred.: COE (2006)

Salon and Spa Institute
1425 Ruben M. Torres Blvd., Ste. P, Brownsville 78521
Type: Private, proprietary
Degrees: C
URL: http://www.salonspainstitute.com
Phone: (956) 541-3330
Inst. Accred.: NACCAS (2008)

Texas Beauty College
3534 Denton Hwy., Haltom City 76117
Type: Private, proprietary
Degrees: C
Phone: (682) 647-1505
Inst. Accred.: NACCAS (2008)

Vogue Beauty Academy
1712-34th St., Lubbock 79411
Type: Private, proprietary
Degrees: C
Phone: (806) 763-0711
Inst. Accred.: NACCAS (2008)

UTAH

Acaydia School of Aesthetics
86 North University Ave., Ste. 130, Provo 84601
Type: Private, proprietary
Degrees: C
URL: http://www.acaydia.com
Phone: (801) 377-0025
Inst. Accred.: NACCAS (2008)

American Beauty Academy, LLC
61 South 100 West, Payson 81651
Type: Private, proprietary
Degrees: C
URL: http://www.americanbeautyacademy.info
Phone: (801) 465-1650
Inst. Accred.: NACCAS (2008)

Capelli Institute of Hair
200 East State Rd., Pleasant Grove 84062
Type: Private, proprietary
Degrees: C
URL: http://capellihair.com
Phone: (801) 785-3113
Inst. Accred.: NACCAS (2008)

Envision Academy of Hair Design
212 South State St., Orem 84058-5422
Type: Private, proprietary
Degrees: C
Phone: (801) 226-2300
Inst. Accred.: NACCAS (2008)

hair-A Paul Mitchell Partner School
568 West Telegraph Rd., Washington 84780
Type: Private, proprietary
Degrees: C
URL: https://www.hairpm.com
Phone: (435) 656-2178
Inst. Accred.: NACCAS (2008)

Mandalyn Academy, Inc.
648 East State Rd., Ste. B, American Fork 84003
Type: Private, proprietary
Degrees: C
URL: http://www.mandalynacademy.com
Phone: (801) 772-3131
Inst. Accred.: NACCAS (2004)

Nail Techniques School of Nail Technology
1930 West Sunset Blvd., Ste. 108, Saint George 84770
Type: Private, proprietary
Degrees: C
Phone: (435) 632-6200
Inst. Accred.: NACCAS (2008)

Renaissance Academie de Hair Design
227 West 1230 North, Provo 84604
Type: Private, proprietary
Degrees: C
URL: http://www.hairschoolonline.com
Phone: (801) 592-0156
Inst. Accred.: NACCAS (2008)

SkinScience Institute of Laser and Esthetics
28 East 2100 South, Ste. 101, Salt Lake City 84115
Type: Private, proprietary
Degrees: C
URL: http://www.skinscienceinstitute.com
Phone: (801) 983-0619
Inst. Accred.: NACCAS (2008)

Top Nails and Hair Beauty School
1735 West 5400 South, Taylorsville 84118
Type: Private, proprietary
Degrees: C
Phone: (801) 964-5400
Inst. Accred.: NACCAS (2008)

VIRGINIA

American Beauty College
1057 West Broad St., Ste. 217, Falls Church 22046
Type: Private, proprietary
Degrees: C
URL: http://www.americanbeautycollege.org
Phone: (703) 536-8700
Inst. Accred.: NACCAS (2008)

Center for Naval Leadership
1905 Regulus Ave., Virginia Beach 23461-2019
Type: Public, federal
Degrees: C
URL: https://www.netc.navy.mil/centers/cnl/default.cfm
Phone: (757) 492-5600
Inst. Accred.: COE (2007)

Cosmopolitan Beauty and Tech School
4201 John Marr Dr., Ste. 206, Annandale 22003
Type: Private, proprietary
Degrees: C
URL: http://cosmopolitanbeautyschool.com/eng
Phone: (703) 354-5475
Inst. Accred.: NACCAS (2008)

Genesis Beauty and Barber School
3535 Tidewater Dr., Ste. F, Norfolk 23509-1333
Type: Private, proprietary
Degrees: C
Phone: (757) 622-9400
Inst. Accred.: NACCAS (2008)

The Institute of Advanced Medical Esthetics
8547 Mayland Dr., Richmond 23294
Type: Private, proprietary
Degrees: C
URL: http://www.theinstituteofadvancedmedicalesthetics.com
Phone: (804) 346-1979
Inst. Accred.: NACCAS (2008)

Northern Virginia School of Therapeutic Massage
200 Little Falls St., Ste. 303, Falls Church 22046
Type: Private, proprietary
Degrees: C
URL: http://www.nvschoolofmassage.com
Phone: (703) 533-3113
Inst. Accred.: NACCAS (2008)

Otis Cosmetology School
3946 Maple Ln., Alexandria 22302
Type: Private, proprietary
Degrees: C
Phone: (301) 420-7590
Inst. Accred.: NACCAS (2008)

WASHINGTON

Gary Manuel Aveda Institute
1514 10th Ave., Seattle 98122-3807
Type: Private, proprietary
Degrees: C
URL: http://www.gmaveda.com
Phone: (206) 329-9933
Inst. Accred.: NACCAS (2008)

GP Institute of Cosmetology
3401 Rainier Ave., Seattle 98144
Type: Private, proprietary
Degrees: C
URL: http://www.gpiofcosmetology.com
Phone: (206) 760-3333
Inst. Accred.: NACCAS (2008)

Lee-Lee's Creative Images Salon and Academy, Inc.
7308 Creek Wood Place NE, Bremerton 98311
Type: Private, proprietary
Degrees: C
Phone: (360) 478-2732
Inst. Accred.: NACCAS (2008)

Wu Hsing Tao School
Talaris World Campus, Building D, Ste. One 4000 NE 41st St., Seattle 98105
Type: Private, proprietary
Degrees: C
URL: http://www.wuhsing.org
Phone: (206) 324-7188
Inst. Accred.: ACAOM (2006)

WISCONSIN

The Academy Waukesha-A Paul Mitchell Partner School
2000 Silvernail Rd., Waukesha 53072
Type: Private, proprietary
Degrees: C
URL: http://www.theacademywaukesha.com
Phone: (262) 549-3100
Inst. Accred.: NACCAS (2008)

There are no non–degree-granting candidates for accreditation outside the United States at this time.

Appendices

AN OVERVIEW OF U.S. ACCREDITATION

Accreditation is a process of external quality review used by higher education to scrutinize colleges, universities, and higher education programs for quality assurance and quality improvement. Accreditation in the United States is more than 100 years old, emerging from concerns to protect public health and safety and to serve the public interest.

In the United States, accreditation is carried out by private, nonprofit organizations designed for this specific purpose. External quality review of higher education is a non governmental enterprise. The U.S. accreditation structure is decentralized and complex, mirroring the decentralization and complexity of American higher education. The higher education enterprise is made up of degree-granting and non–degree-granting institutions. These may be public or private, two- or four-year, nonprofit or for-profit. They spend more than $250 billion per year, enroll more than 16 million credit students and employ approximately 3.1 million full- and part-time people.[1]

U.S. accreditors review colleges and universities in 50 states and 95 other countries. They review many thousands of programs in a range of professions and specialties including law, medicine, business, nursing, social work, pharmacy, arts and journalism.

Both federal and state government consider accreditation to be a reliable authority on academic quality. The federal government relies on accreditation to assure the quality of institutions and programs for which the government provides federal funds and for which the government provides federal aid to students. Most state governments will initially license institutions and programs without accreditation. However, states will subsequently require accreditation to make state funds available to institutions and students. States often require that individuals who sit for state licensure in various professions have graduated from accredited institutions and programs.

Types of U.S. Accrediting Organizations

There are four types of accrediting organizations:

Regional accreditors: Accredit public and private, mainly nonprofit and degree-granting, two- and four-year institutions.

Faith-based accreditors: Accredit religiously affiliated and doctrinally based institutions, mainly nonprofit and degree-granting.

Private career accreditors: Accredit mainly for-profit, career-based, singlepurpose institutions, both degree and non-degree.

Programmatic accreditors: Accredit specific programs, professions and free-standing schools, e.g., law, medicine, engineering, and health professions.

HOW U.S. ACCREDITATION IS ORGANIZED

Approximately 80 recognized institutional and programmatic accrediting organizations operate in the United States.[2] Accrediting organizations derive their legitimacy from the colleges, universities and programs that created accreditation, not government. In 2004–2005, accrediting organizations employed approximately 650 paid full- and part-time staff and worked with more than 16,000 volunteers.[3]

1 *The Chronicle of Higher Education Almanac Issue 2005-2006*, Volume LII, Number 1, August 26, 2005.

2 *2005 CHEA Almanac of External Quality Review.* The number of recognized accreditors varies depending on whether an existing accreditor maintains recognition or a new accreditor earns recognition. These variations have been modest, perhaps one or two per year.

3 *2005 CHEA Almanac of External Quality Review.*

The Roles of Accreditation

Accreditation carries out the following roles:

Assuring quality. Accreditation is the primary means by which colleges, universities and programs assure quality to students and the public. Accredited status is a signal to students and the public that an institution or program meets at least threshold standards for, e.g., its faculty, curriculum, student services, and libraries. Accredited status is conveyed only if institutions and programs provide evidence of fiscal stability.

Access to federal and state funds. Accreditation is required for access to federal funds such as student aid and other federal programs. Federal student aid funds are available to students only if the institution or program they are attending is accredited by a recognized accrediting organization. The federal government awarded $69 billion in student grants and loans in 2002 alone. State funds to institutions and students are contingent on accredited status.

Engendering private sector confidence. Accreditation status of an institution or program is important to employers when evaluating credentials of job applicants and when deciding whether to provide tuition support for current employees seeking additional education. Private individuals and foundations look for evidence of accreditation when making decisions about private giving.

Easing transfer. Accreditation is important to students for smooth transfer of courses and programs among colleges and universities. Receiving institutions take note of whether or not the credits a student wishes to transfer have been earned at an accredited institution. Although accreditation is but one among several factors taken into account by receiving institutions, it is viewed carefully and is considered an important indicator of quality.

Values and Benefits of Accreditation

U.S. accreditation is built upon a core set of traditional academic values and beliefs. These are described by the following statements:

- Higher education institutions have primary responsibility for academic quality; colleges and universities are the leaders and the key sources of authority in academic matters.
- Institutional mission is central to judgments of academic quality.
- Institutional autonomy is essential to sustaining and enhancing academic quality.
- Academic freedom flourishes in an environment of academic leadership of institutions.
- The higher education enterprise and our society thrive on decentralization and diversity of institutional purpose and mission.

How U.S. Accreditation Is Funded

Accrediting organizations are funded primarily by annual dues from institutions and programs that are accredited and fees that institutions and programs pay for accreditation reviews. In some instances, an accrediting organization may receive financial assistance from sponsoring organizations. Accrediting organizations sometimes obtain funds for special initiatives from government or from private foundations. Accrediting organizations report that they spent approximately $70 million in 2004–2005.[4]

4 *2005 CHEA Almanac of External Quality Review.*

The Operation of U.S. Accreditation

Accreditation of institutions and programs takes place on a cycle that may range from every few years to as many as ten years. Accreditation is ongoing; the initial earning of accreditation is not entry to indefinite accredited status. Periodic review is a fact of life for accredited institutions and programs. Self-accreditation is not an option.

An institution or program seeking accreditation must go through a number of steps stipulated by an accrediting organization. These steps involve a combination of several tasks: preparation of evidence of accomplishment by the institution or program, scrutiny of this evidence and a site visit by faculty and administrative peers, and action to determine accreditation status by the accrediting organization.

Self-study: Institutions and programs prepare a written summary of performance, based on accrediting organizations' standards.

Peer review: Accreditation review is conducted primarily by faculty and administrative peers in the profession. These colleagues review the self-study and serve on visiting teams that review institutions and programs after the selfstudy is completed. Peers constitute the majority of members of the accrediting commissions or boards that make judgments about accrediting status.

Site visit: Accrediting organizations normally send a visiting team to review an institution or program. The self-study provides the foundation for the team visit. Teams, in addition to the peers described above, may also include public members (non-academics who have an interest in higher education). All team members are volunteers and are generally not compensated.

Judgment by accrediting organization: Accrediting organizations have decision-making bodies (commissions) made up of administrators and faculty from institutions and programs as well as public members. These commissions may affirm accreditation for new institutions and programs, reaffirm accreditation for ongoing institutions and programs, and deny accreditation to institutions and programs.

Periodic external review: Institutions and programs continue to be reviewed over time. They normally prepare a self-study and undergo a site visit each time.

Accreditation is a trust-based, standards-based, evidence-based, judgment-based, peer-based process.

Holding Accreditors Accountable: "Recognition" of Accrediting Organizations

In the United States, accreditors are accountable to the institutions and programs they accredit. They are accountable to the public and government that have invested heavily in higher education and expect quality. Accreditors undertake an organizational self-assessment on a routine basis and are required to have internal complaint procedures.

Accreditors also undergo a periodic external review of their organizations known as "recognition." Recognition is carried out either by another private organization, the Council for Higher Education Accreditation (CHEA, a national coordinating body for national, regional, and specialized accreditation) or the United States Department of Education (USDE). Although accreditation is strictly a nongovernmental activity, recognition is not.

How Recognition Operates

The process of recognition is similar to accreditation in a number of ways:

- CHEA and USDE each develop standards that must be met by an accrediting organization in order to be recognized.
- An accrediting organization undertakes self-evaluation based on recognition standards.
- CHEA or USDE may require a staff site visit to the accreditor and staff report on the visit.
- CHEA and USDE award (or do not award) recognition status.
- An accrediting organization undergoes periodic review to maintain recognition.

As of 2005, 19 institutional accrediting organizations were or had been recognized by either CHEA or USDE or both. These organizations accredit approximately 7,000 institutions that make up U.S. higher education. Sixty-one (61) programmatic accrediting organizations were or had been recognized and accredit more than 18,000 programs, as indicated above.[5]

Council For Higher Education Accreditation (CHEA)

CHEA has six recognition standards by which it reviews accrediting organizations for recognition. The standards place primary emphasis on academic quality assurance and improvement for an institution or program. They require accreditors to advance academic quality, demonstrate accountability, encourage purposeful change and needed improvement, employ appropriate and fair procedures in decision making, continually reassess accreditation practices, and sustain fiscal stability.

CHEA accreditors are normally reviewed on a 10-year cycle with two interim reports. The review is carried out by the CHEA Committee on Recognition, a group of institutional representatives, accreditors, and public members who scrutinize accreditors for their eligibility for CHEA recognition and review accreditors based on an accreditor self-evaluation. The review may also include a site visit. The Committee on Recognition makes recommendations to the CHEA governing board to affirm or deny recognition to an accreditor.

CHEA (Nongovernmental) Recognition Standards[6]

- ***Advance academic quality.*** Accreditors have a clear description of academic quality and clear expectations that the institutions or programs they accredit have processes to determine whether quality standards are being met.
- ***Demonstrate accountability.*** Accreditors have standards that call for institutions and programs to provide consistent, reliable information about academic quality and student achievement to foster continuing public confidence and investment.
- ***Encourage, where appropriate, self scrutiny and planning for change and needed improvement.*** Accreditors encourage self scrutiny for change and needed improvement through ongoing self-examination in institutions and programs.
- ***Employ appropriate and fair procedures in decision making.*** Accreditors maintain appropriate and fair organizational policies and procedures that include effective checks and balances.
- ***Demonstrate ongoing review of accreditation practice***. Accreditors undertake self scrutiny of their accrediting activities.
- ***Possess sufficient resources.*** Accreditors have and maintain predictable and stable resources.

5 *2005 CHEA Almanac of External Quality Review.*

6 As of January 2006. This language illustrates the recognition standards and is not the full or official CHEA policy statement.

United States Department of Education (USDE)

USDE recognition standards place primary emphasis on whether an institution or program is of sufficient quality to qualify for federal funds for student financial aid and other federal programs. These standards require accreditors to maintain criteria or standards in specific areas: student achievement, curricula, faculty, facilities (includes equipment and supplies), fiscal and administrative capacity, student support services, recruiting and admissions practices, measures of the degree and objectives of degrees or credentials offered, record of student complaints, and record of compliance with program responsibilities for student aid as required by the 1965 federal Higher Education Act (Title IV) as amended.

USDE recognition review normally takes place every five years. USDE staff conduct the review based on communication with the accreditor, a written report from the accreditor and, from time to time, a visit to the accreditor. USDE staff make recommendations to the National Advisory Committee on Institutional Quality and Integrity (NACIQI), an appointed group of educators and public members, to recognize or not recognize an accrediting organization. The committee, in turn, recommends action to the U.S. Secretary of Education.

Federal (Governmental) Recognition Standards[7]

- Success with respect to student achievement in relation to the institution's mission, including as appropriate, consideration of course completion, state licensing examination and job placement rates
- Curricula
- Faculty
- Facilities, equipment, and supplies
- Fiscal and administrative capacity as appropriate to the specified scale of operations
- Student support services
- Recruiting and admissions practices, academic calendars, catalogs, publications, grading, and advertising
- Measures of program length and the objectives of the degrees or credentials offered
- Record of student complaints received by, or available to, the agency
- Record of compliance with the institution's program responsibilities under Title IV of the Act, based on the most recent student loan default rate data provided by the Secretary, the results of financial or compliance audits, program reviews and any other information that the Secretary may provide to the agency.

CHEA and USDE recognize many of the same accrediting organizations, but not all. Accreditors seek CHEA or USDE recognition for different reasons. CHEA recognition confers an academic legitimacy on accrediting organizations, helping to solidify the place of these organizations and their institutions and programs in the national higher education community. USDE recognition is required for accreditors whose institutions or programs seek eligibility for federal student aid funds.

How Recognition Is Funded

CHEA funds its recognition activity through annual fees charged to its institutional members. The federal government funds its recognition activity through a budget allocation from Congress to USDE.

Adapted from *An Overview of U.S. Accreditation (revised)*, 2006, Judith S. Eaton. Available through the courtesy of the Council for Higher Education Accreditation (CHEA), http://www.chea.org/pdf/OverviewAccred_rev0706.pdf

7 As of July 2000.

RECOGNIZED ACCREDITING ORGANIZATIONS

The accrediting activities of institutional and professional associations are periodically evaluated through a formal recognition process by either CHEA, USDE, or both. Specific standards of quality in the accreditation process are ensured through this recognition process.

Key to Accrediting Organizations

Regional Institutional Accrediting Organizations

MSA .... Middle States Association of Colleges and Schools, Commission on Higher Education
NWCCU .... Northwest Commission on Colleges and Universities
NCA-HLC .... North Central Association of Colleges and Schools, Higher Learning Commission
NCA-CASI .... North Central Association of Colleges and Schools, Commission on Accreditation and School Improvement, Board of Trustees
NEASC-CIHE .... New England Association of Schools and Colleges, Inc., Commission on Institutions of Higher Education
NEASC-CTCI .... New England Association of Schools and Colleges, Inc., Commission on Technical and Career Institutions
SACS .... Southern Association of Colleges and Schools, Commission on Colleges
WASC-ACCJC .... Western Association of Schools and Colleges, Accrediting Commission for Community and Junior Colleges
WASC-ACSCU .... Western Association of Schools and Colleges, Accrediting Commission for Senior Colleges and Universities

National Career-related Accrediting Organizations

ABHES .... Accrediting Bureau of Health Education Schools
ACCET .... Accrediting Council for Continuing Education and Training
ACCSCT .... Accrediting Commission for Career Schools and Colleges of Technology
ACICS .... Accrediting Council for Independent Colleges and Schools
COE .... Council on Occupational Education
DETC .... Distance Education and Training Council Accrediting Commission
NACCAS .... National Accrediting Commission for Cosmetology Arts and Sciences

National Faith-related Accrediting Organizations

ABHE .... Association for Biblical Higher Education
AARTS .... Association of Advanced Rabbinical and Talmudic Schools
ATS .... Commission on Accrediting of the Association of Theological Schools
TRACS .... Transnational Association of Christian Colleges and Schools

Appendix B

Professional and Specialized Accrediting Organizations

Some professional and specialized accrediting organizations are recognized to accredit whole institutions as well as programs at other accredited and/or non-accredited facilities.

AACSB........................ AACSB International-The Association to Advance Collegiate Schools of Business
AABI........................ Aviation Accreditation Board International
AAFCS........................ American Association of Family and Consumer Sciences, Council for Accreditation
AALE........................ American Academy for Liberal Education
AAMFT........................ American Association for Marriage and Family Therapy, Commission on Accreditation for Marriage and Family Therapy Education
AANA........................ American Association of Nurse Anesthetists, Council on Accreditation of Nurse Anesthesia Educational Programs
ABA........................ American Bar Association, Council of the Section of Legal Education and Admissions to the Bar
ABET........................ Accreditation Board for Engineering and Technology, Inc.
ABFSE-CA........................ American Board of Funeral Service Education, Committee on Accreditation
ACAOM........................ Accreditation Commission for Acupuncture and Oriental Medicine
ACBSP........................ Association of Collegiate Business Schools and Programs
ACCE........................ American Council for Construction Education
ACEJMC........................ Accrediting Council on Education in Journalism and Mass Communication
ACF........................ American Culinary Federation Foundation, Accrediting Commission
ACNM........................ American College of Nurse-Midwives, Accreditation Commission for Midwifery Education
ACPE........................ Accreditation Council for Pharmacy Education
ACPEI........................ Association for Clinical Pastoral Education, Inc., Accreditation Commission
ADA-CADE........................ American Dietetic Association, Commission on Accreditation for Dietetics Education
ADA-CDA........................ American Dental Association, Commission on Dental Accreditation
ALA........................ American Library Association, Committee on Accreditation
AOA-COCA........................ American Osteopathic Association, Commission on Osteopathic College Accreditation
AOA-COE........................ American Optometric Association, Accreditation Council on Optometric Education
AOTA-ACOTE........................ American Occupational Therapy Association, Accreditation Council for Occupational Therapy Education
APA........................ American Psychological Association, Committee on Accreditation
APMA........................ American Podiatric Medical Association, Council on Podiatric Medical Education
APTA........................ American Physical Therapy Association, Commission on Accreditation in Physical Therapy Education
ARC-PA........................ Accreditation Review Commission on Education for the Physician Assistant, Inc.
ASHA........................ American Speech-Language-Hearing Association, Council on Academic Accreditation in Audiology and Speech-Language Pathology
ASLA........................ American Society of Landscape Architects, Landscape Architectural Accreditation Board
AVMA........................ American Veterinary Medical Association, Council on Education
CAAHEP........................ Commission on Accreditation of Allied Health Education Programs
CACREP........................ Council for Accreditation of Counseling and Related Educational Programs
CAHME........................ Commission on Accreditation of Healthcare Management Education
CCE........................ Council on Chiropractic Education, Commission on Accreditation
CCNE........................ Commission on Collegiate Nursing Education

CEA........................... Commission on English Language Program Accreditation
CEPH......................... Council on Education for Public Health
CIDA.......................... Council for Interior Design Accreditation (formerly FIDER)
CMTA .... Commission on Massage Therapy Accreditation
CNME........................ Council on Naturopathic Medical Education
COA........................... Commission on Opticianry Accreditation
CORE......................... Council on Rehabilitation Education, Commission on Standards and Accreditation
CSWE .... Council on Social Work Education, Office of Social Work Accreditation and Educational Excellence
JRCERT .... Joint Review Committee on Education in Radiologic Technology
JRCNMT.................... Joint Review Committee on Educational Programs in Nuclear Medicine Technology
LCME .... Liaison Committee on Medical Education
MACTE .... Montessori Accreditation Council for Teacher Education, Commission on Accreditation
MEAC .... Midwifery Education Accreditation Council
NAACLS.................... National Accrediting Agency for Clinical Laboratory Science
NAIT .... National Association of Industrial Technology
NASAD .... National Association of Schools of Art and Design
NASD .... National Association of Schools of Dance
NASM........................ National Association of Schools of Music
NASPAA.................... National Association of Schools of Public Affairs and Administration, Commission on Peer Review and Accreditation
NAST......................... National Association of Schools of Theatre
NCATE....................... National Council for Accreditation of Teacher Education
NLNAC .... National League for Nursing Accrediting Commission, Inc.
NRPA......................... National Recreation and Park Association, Council on Accreditation
PAB .... Planning Accreditation Board (formerly American Institute of Certified Planners/ Association of Collegiate Schools of Planning, Planning Accreditation Board)
SAF .... Society of American Foresters, Commission on Accreditation
TEAC .... Teacher Education Accreditation Council, Accreditation Committee

State-based Accrediting Organizations

NYBOR .... New York Board of Regents

Programs Accredited by Specialized and Professional Programmatic Accrediting Organizations

Program	Accrediting Organization
Accounting	AACSB International-The Association to Advance Collegiate Schools of Business (AACSB)
Acupuncture	Accreditation Commission for Acupuncture and Oriental Medicine (ACAOM)
Allied Health	Commission on Accreditation of Allied Health Education Programs (CAAHEP)
Applied Science	Accreditation Board for Engineering and Technology, Inc. (ABET)
Art	National Association of Schools of Art and Design (NASAD)
Audiology	American Speech-Language-Hearing Association (ASHA)
Aviation	Aviation Accreditation Board International (AABI)
Aviation Technology	National Association of Industrial Technology (NAIT)
Business	AACSB International-The Association to Advance Collegiate Schools of Business (AACSB)
also	Association of Collegiate Business Schools and Programs (ACBSP)
Chiropractic Education	Council on Chiropractic Education (CCE)
Clinical Assistant	National Accrediting Agency for Clinical Laboratory Science (NAACLS)
Clinical Lab Scientist	National Accrediting Agency for Clinical Laboratory Science (NAACLS)
Clinical Lab Technology	National Accrediting Agency for Clinical Laboratory Science (NAACLS)
Clinical Pastoral Education	Association for Clinical Pastoral Education, Inc. (ACPEI)
Clinical Psychology	American Psychological Association (APA)
Combined Professional-Scientific Psychology	American Psychological Association (APA)
Community Health	Council on Education for Public Health (CEPH)
Community Health/Preventative Medicine	Council on Education for Public Health (CEPH)
Computer Science	Accreditation Board for Engineering and Technology, Inc. (ABET)
Construction Education	American Council for Construction Education (ACCE)
Construction Technology	National Association of Industrial Technology (NAIT)
Counseling	Council for Accreditation of Counseling and Related Educational Programs (CACREP)
Counseling Psychology	American Psychological Association (APA)
Culinary Education	American Culinary Federation Foundation (ACF)
Cytogenetic Technology	National Accrediting Agency for Clinical Laboratory Science (NAACLS)
Dance	National Association of Schools of Dance (NASD)
Dentistry	American Dental Association (ADA-CDA)
Design Technology	National Association of Industrial Technology (NAIT)
Diagnostic Molecular Scientist	National Accrediting Agency for Clinical Laboratory Science (NAACLS)
Dietetics	American Dietetic Association (ADA-CADE)
Electronic Technology	National Association of Industrial Technology (NAIT)
Engineering	Accreditation Board for Engineering and Technology, Inc. (ABET)
Engineering Technology	Accreditation Board for Engineering and Technology, Inc. (ABET)
English Language Education	Commission on English Language Program Accreditation (CEA)
Family and Consumer Science	American Association of Family and Consumer Sciences (AAFCS)
Forestry	Society of American Foresters (SAF)

Program	Accrediting Agency
Funeral Service Education	American Board of Funeral Service Education (ABFSE-CA)
Graduate Social Work	Council on Social Work Education (CSWE)
Health Services Administration	Commission on Accreditation of Healthcare Management Education (CAHME)
Histologic Technology	National Accrediting Agency for Clinical Laboratory Science (NAACLS)
Industrial Technology	National Association of Industrial Technology (NAIT)
Interior Architecture	Council for Interior Design Accreditation (CIDA)
Interior Design	Council for Interior Design Accreditation (CIDA)
Journalism	Accrediting Council on Education in Journalism and Mass Communication (ACEJMC)
Landscape Architecture	American Society of Landscape Architects (ASLA)
Law	American Bar Association (ABA)
Liberal Education	American Academy for Liberal Education (AALE)
Librarianship	American Library Association (ALA)
Manufacturing Technology	National Association of Industrial Technology (NAIT)
Marriage and Family Therapy	American Association for Marriage and Family Therapy (AAMFT)
Massage Therapy	Commission on Massage Therapy Accreditation (CMTA)
Medical Assisiting	Accrediting Bureau of Health Education Schools (ABHES)
also	Commission on Accreditation of Allied Health Education Programs (CAAHEP)
Medical Laboratory Technology	Accrediting Bureau of Health Education Schools (ABHES)
Medicine	Liaison Committee on Medical Education (LCME)
Midwifery Education	Midwifery Education Accreditation Council (MEAC)
Montessori Teacher Education	Montessori Accreditation Council for Teacher Education (MACTE)
Mortuary Science	American Board of Funeral Service Education (ABFSE-CA)
Music	National Association of Schools of Music (NASM)
Naturopathic Medicine	Council on Naturopathic Medical Education (CNME)
Nuclear Medicine Technology	Joint Review Committee on Educational Programs in Nuclear Medicine Technology (JRCNMT)
Nurse Anesthesia Education	American Association of Nurse Anesthetists (AANA)
Nurse-Midwifery	American College of Nurse-Midwives, Accreditation Commission for Midwifery Education (ACNM-ACME)
Nursing	National League for Nursing Accrediting Commission, Inc. (NLNAC)
Nursing Education	Commission on Collegiate Nursing Education (CCNE)
Occupational Therapy	American Occupational Therapy Association (AOTA)
Occupational Therapy Assisting	American Occupational Therapy Association (AOTA)
Ophthalmic Lab Technology	Commission on Opticianry Accreditation (COA)
Optometric Residency	American Optometric Association (AOA-COE)
Optometric Technician	American Optometric Association (AOA-COE)
Opticianry	Commission on Opticianry Accreditation (COA)
Optometry	American Optometric Association (AOA-COE)
Osteopathy	American Osteopathic Association (AOA-COCA)
Pharmacy	Accreditation Council for Pharmacy Education (ACPE)
Physical Therapy	American Physical Therapy Association (APTA)
Physical Therapy Assisting	American Physical Therapy Association (APTA)
Physician Assisting	Accreditation Review Commission on Education for the Physician Assistant, Inc. (ARC-PA)
Planning	Planning Accreditation Board (PAB)
Podiatry	American Podiatric Medical Association (APMA)

Program	Accrediting Agency
Practical Nursing	National League for Nursing Accrediting Commission, Inc. (NLNAC)
Psychology Internship	American Psychological Association (APA)
Public Administration	National Association of Schools of Public Affairs and Administration (NASPAA)
Public Health	Council on Education for Public Health (CEPH)
Radiation Therapy	Joint Review Committee on Education in Radiologic Technology (JRCERT)
Radiography	Joint Review Committee on Education in Radiologic Technology (JRCERT)
Recreation and Leisure Services	National Recreation and Park Association (NRPA)
Rehabilitation Counseling	Council on Rehabilitation Education (CORE)
School Psychology	American Psychological Association (APA)
Social Work	Council on Social Work Education (CSWE)
Speech-Language Pathology	American Speech-Language-Hearing Association (ASHA)
Surgeon Assisting	Accreditation Review Commission on Education for the Physician Assistant, Inc. (ARC-PA)
also	Commission on Accreditation of Allied Health Education Programs (CAAHEP)
Teacher Education	National Council for Accreditation of Teacher Education (NCATE)
also	Teacher Education Accreditation Council (TEAC)
Theater	National Association of Schools of Theatre (NAST)
Veterinary Medicine	American Veterinary Medical Association (AVMA)
Veterinary Technology	American Veterinary Medical Association (AVMA)

Detailed Description of Broad Program Categories

Some of the categories in the previous list contain subcategories within the same general field of study. The following list details the subcategories appearing in this directory.

Allied Health .... Anesthesiologist Assisting, Athletic Training, Blood Bank Technology, Cardiovascular Technology, Cytotechnology, Diagnostic Medical Sonography, Electroneurodiagnostic Technology, EMT-Paramedic, Kinesiotherapy, Medical Assisting, Medical Illustration, Health Information Administration, Health Information Technician, Ophthalmic Medical Technology, Orthotist/Prothetist, Perfusion, Phlebotomy, Physician Assisting, Radiation Therapy Technology, Radiography, Respiratory Therapy, Respiratory Therapy Technology, Surgeon Assisting, Surgical Technology

Applied Science .... Health Physics, Industrial Hygiene, Industrial Management, Occupational Health and Safety, Surveying/Geomatics

Dentistry .... Advanced Education in General Dentistry, Combined Prosthodontics, Combined Prosthodontic/Maxillofacial Prosthetics, Dental Assisting, Dental Hygiene, Dental Laboratory Technology, Dental Public Health, Endodontics, General Dentistry, General Practice Residency, Maxillofacial Prosthetics, Oral and Maxillofacial Pathology, Oral and Maxillofacial Radiology, Oral and Maxillofacial Surgery, Orthodontic and Dentofacial Orthopedics, Pediatric Dentistry, Periodontics, Prosthodontics

Engineering .... Aerospace, Agricultural, Architectural, Bioengineering, Ceramic, Chemical, Civil, Computer, Construction, Electrical, Engineering Management, Engineering Mechanics, Engineering Physics/Science, Environmental/Sanitary, Fire Protection, Food Process, Forest, General, Geological/Geophysical, Industrial, Information Systems, Manufacturing, Materials, Mechanical, Metallurgical, Micro/Nano-Engineering, Mineral, Mining, Naval Architecture/Marine, Nuclear, Ocean, Optical/Optics, Paper, Petroleum, Plastics, Polymer, Radiological Health, Software, Surveying, Systems, Telecommunications, Textile, Transportation, Welding

Engineering Technology .... Aerospace, Agricultural, Air Conditioning, Apparel, Architectural, Automated Systems, Automation-Robotic Technology, Automotive, Bioengineering, Biomedical, Ceramic, Chemical, Civil/Construction, Computer, Electrical, Electromechanical, Energy, Environmental/Sanitary, Facilities, Fire Protection/Safety, General, General Drafting/Design, Industrial, Information Systems, Instrumentation, Management, Manufacturing, Marine Group, Mechanical, Mechanical Drafting/Design, Mining, Naval Architecture/Marine, Nuclear, Operations Technology, Optical/Optics, Packaging, Petroleum, Plastics, Process/Piping Design, Quality Technology, Software, Surveying, Systems, Telecommunications, Textile, Welding

National Career-related Accrediting Organizations

Accrediting Bureau of Health Education Schools (ABHES)

Board of Commissioners

Carol A. Moneymaker, Executive Director
7777 Leesburg Pike, Ste. 314N
Falls Church, VA 22043
(703) 917-9503, Fax: (703) 917-4109
http://www.abhes.org

Accrediting Commission of Career Schools and Colleges of Technology (ACCSCT)

Michale S. McComis, Executive Director
2101 Wilson Blvd., Ste. 302
Arlington, VA 22201
(703) 247-4212, Fax: (703) 247-4533
http://www.accsct.org

Accrediting Council for Continuing Education and Training (ACCET)

Roger J. Williams, Executive Director
1722 N St. NW
Washington, DC 20036
(202) 955-1113, Fax: (202) 955-1118
http://www.accet.org

Accrediting Council for Independent Colleges and Schools (ACICS)

Albert C. Gray, Executive Director and
Chief Executive Officer
750 First St. NE, Ste. 980
Washington, DC 20002-4241
(202) 336-6780, Fax: (202) 842-2593
http://www.acics.org

Council on Occupational Education (COE)

Gary Puckett, Executive Director/President
41 Perimeter Center East NE, Ste. 640
Atlanta, GA 30346
(770) 396-3898, Fax: (770) 396-3790
http://www.council.org

Distance Education and Training Council Accrediting Commission (DETC)

Michael P. Lambert, Executive Director
1601 18th St. NW, Ste. 2
Washington, DC 20009-2529
(202) 234-5100, Fax: (202) 332-1386
http://www.detc.org

National Accrediting Commission on Cosmetology Arts and Sciences, Inc. (NACCAS)

Tony Mirando, Executive Director
4401 Ford Ave., Ste. 1300
Alexandria, VA 22302
(703) 600-7600, Fax: (703) 379-2200
http://www.naccas.org

National Faith-related Accrediting Organizations

Association for Biblical Higher Education (ABHE)

Commission on Accreditation

Ralph E. Enlow Jr., Executive Director
5575 South Semoran Blvd., Ste. 26
Orlando, FL 32822-1781
(407) 207-0808, Fax: (407) 207-0840
http://www.abhe.org

Association of Advanced Rabbinical and Talmudic Schools (AARTS)

Bernard Fryshman, Executive Vice President
11 Broadway, Ste. 405
New York, NY 10004-1392
(212) 363-1991, Fax: (212) 533-5335

Commission on Accrediting of the Association of Theological Schools (ATS)

Daniel O. Aleshire, Executive Director
10 Summit Park Dr.
Pittsburgh, PA 15275-1110
(412) 788-6505, Fax: (412) 788-6510
http://www.ats.edu

Transnational Association of Christian Colleges and Schools (TRACS)

Accreditation Commission

Russell G. Fitzgerald, Executive Director
PO Box 328
Forest, VA 24551
(434) 525-9539, Fax: (434) 525-9538
http://www.tracs.org

Regional Institutional Accrediting Organizations

Middle States Association of Colleges and Schools (MSA-CHE)
Commission on Higher Education
Jean Avnet Morse, President
3624 Market St.
Philadelphia, PA 19104-2680
(267) 284-5000, Fax: (215) 662-5501
http://www.msche.org

New England Association of Schools and Colleges (NEASC-CIHE)
Commission on Institutions of Higher Education
Barbara E. Brittingham, President/Director of the Commission
209 Burlington Rd., Ste. 201
Bedford, MA 01730-1433
(781) 271-0022, Fax: (781) 271-0950
http://cihe.neasc.org

New England Association of Schools and Colleges (NEASC-CTCI)
Commission on Technical and Career Institutions
Paul Bento, Director
209 Burlington Rd., Ste. 201
Bedford, MA 01730-1433
(781) 271-0022, Fax: (781) 271-0950
http://ctci.neasc.org

North Central Association (NCA-CASI)
Commission on Accreditation and School Improvement, Board of Trustees
Kenneth F. Gose, Executive Director
PO Box 871008
Tempe, AZ 85287-1008
(800) 525-9517, Fax: (480) 965-8658
http://www.ncacasi.org

North Central Association of Colleges and Schools (NCA-HLC)
The Higher Learning Commission
Sylvia Manning, President
30 North LaSalle St., Ste. 2400
Chicago, IL 60602-2504
(312) 263-0456, Fax: (312) 263-7462
http://www.ncahigherlearningcommission.org

Northwest Commission on Colleges and Universities (NWCCU)
Sandra E. Elman, President
8060 165th Ave. NE, Ste. 100
Redmond, WA 98052
(425) 558-4224, Fax: (425) 376-0596
http://www.nwccu.org

Southern Association of Colleges and Schools (SACS)
Commission on Colleges
Belle S. Wheelan, President
1866 Southern Ln.
Decatur, GA 30033-4097
(404) 679-4500, Fax: (404) 679-4528
http://www.sacscoc.org

Western Association of Schools and Colleges (WASC-ACSCU)
Accrediting Commission for Senior Colleges and Universities
Ralph A. Wolff, President and Executive Director
985 Atlantic Ave., Ste. 100
Alameda, CA 94501
(510) 748-9001, Fax: (510) 748-9797
http://www.wascsenior.org

Western Association of Schools and Colleges (WASC-ACCJC)
Accrediting Commission for Community and Junior Colleges
Barbara A. Beno, President
10 Commercial Blvd., Ste. 204
Novato, CA 94949-6175
(415) 506-0234, Fax: (415) 506-0238
http://www.accjc.org

State-based Accrediting Organization

New York State Board of Regents (NYBOR)
The Commissioner of Education
Richard P. Mills, Commissioner of Education
89 Washington Ave., Rm. 110 EB
Albany, NY 12234
(518) 474-5844, Fax: (518) 474-4909
http://www.highered.nysed.gov

Specialized and Professional Programmatic Accrediting Organizations

AACSB International-The Association to Advance Collegiate Schools of Business (AACSB)

Jerry E. Trapnell, Executive Vice President and Chief Accreditation Officer
777 South Harbour Island Blvd., Ste. 750
Tampa, FL 33602-5730
(813) 769-6500, Fax: (813) 769-6559
http://www.aacsb.edu

Accreditation Board for Engineering and Technology, Inc. (ABET)

Applied Science Accreditation Commission (ASAC)
Computing Accreditation Commission (CAC)
Engineering Accreditation Commission (EAC)
Technology Accreditation Commission (TAC)
Lance K. Hoboy, Interim Executive Director
111 Market Place, Ste. 1050
Baltimore, MD 21202
(410) 347-7700, Fax: (410) 625-2238
http://www.abet.org

Accreditation Commission for Acupuncture and Oriental Medicine (ACAOM)

Dort S. Bigg, Executive Director
Maryland Trade Ctr. 3, 7501 Greenway Center Dr., Ste. 760
Greenbelt, MD 20770
(301) 313-0855, Fax: (301) 313-0912
http://www.acaom.org

Accreditation Council for Pharmacy Education (ACPE)

Peter H. Vlasses, Executive Director
20 North Clark St., Ste. 2500
Chicago, IL 60602-5109
(312) 664-3575, Fax: (312) 664-4652
http://www.acpe-accredit.org

Accreditation Review Commission on Education for the Physician Assistant, Inc. (ARC-PA)

John E. McCarty, Executive Director
12000 Findley Rd., Ste. 240
Johns Creek, GA 30097
(770) 476-1224, Fax: (770) 476-1738
http://www.arc-pa.org

Accrediting Council on Education in Journalism and Mass Communication (ACEJMC)

Susanne Shaw, Executive Director
Stauffer-Flint Hall, 1435 Jayhawk Blvd., University of Kansas
Lawrence, KS 66045-7575
(785) 864-3973, Fax: (785) 864-5225
http://www2.ku.edu/~acejmc

American Academy for Liberal Education (AALE)

Jeffrey D. Wallin, President
1050 17th St. NW, Ste. 400
Washington, DC 20036
(202) 452-8611, Fax: (202) 452-8620
http://www.aale.org

American Association for Marriage and Family Therapy (AAMFT)

Commission on Accreditation for Marriage and Family Therapy Education
Jeffrey S. Harmon, Director of Educational Services
112 South Alfred St.
Alexandria, VA 22314-3061
(703) 838-9808, Fax: (703) 838-9805
http://www.aamft.org

American Association of Family and Consumer Sciences (AAFCS)

Council for Accreditation
Gay Nell McGinnis, Director of Credentialing and Professional Development
400 North Columbus St., Ste. 202
Alexandria, VA 22314
(703) 706-4600, Fax: (703) 706-4663
http://www.aafcs.org

American Association of Nurse Anesthetists (AANA)

Council on Accreditation of Nurse Anesthesia Educational Programs
Francis R. Gerbasi, Executive Director, Council on Accreditation of Nurse Anesthesia Educational Programs
222 South Prospect Ave.
Park Ridge, IL 60068-4001
(847) 692-7050, Fax: (847) 692-6968
http://www.aana.com

American Bar Association (ABA)

Council of the Section of Legal Education and Admissions to the Bar
Hulett H. Askew, Consultant on Legal Education, ABA
321 North Clark St., 21st Flr.
Chicago, IL 60610-4714
(312) 988-6746, Fax: (312) 988-5681
http://www.abanet.org/legaled

American Board of Funeral Service Education (ABFSE)

Committee on Accreditation
Michael Smith, Executive Director
3432 Ashland Ave., Ste. U
St. Joseph, MO 64506
(816) 233-3747, Fax: (816) 233-3793
http://www.abfse.org

American College of Nurse-Midwives (ACNM)
Accreditation Commission for Midwifery Education
Lorrie Kaplan, Executive Director
8403 Colesville Rd., Ste. 1550
Silver Spring, MD 20910-6374
(240) 485-1800, Fax: (240) 485-1818
http://www.midwife.org

American Council for Construction Education (ACCE)
Michael M. Holland, Executive Vice President
1717 North Loop 1604 East, Ste. 320
San Antonio, TX 78232-1570
(210) 495-6161, Fax: (210) 495-6168
http://www.acce-hq.org

American Culinary Federation Foundation (ACF)
Accrediting Commission
Kristy Begley, Director of Education and Professional Development
180 Center Place Way
St. Augustine, FL 32095
(904) 824-4468, Fax: (904) 825-4758
http://www.acfchefs.org

American Dental Association (ADA-CDA)
Commission on Dental Accreditation
Anthony Ziebert, Director
211 East Chicago Ave., 18th Floor
Chicago, IL 60611-2678
(312) 440-2712, Fax: (312) 440-2915
http://www.ada.org

American Dietetic Association (ADA-CADE)
Commission on Accreditation for Dietetics Education
Ulric K. Chung, Senior Director, Accreditation and Education Programs
120 South Riverside Plaza, Ste. 2000
Chicago, IL 60606-6995
(312) 899-4872, Fax: (312) 899-4817
http://www.eatright.org/cade

American Library Association (ALA)
Committee on Accreditation
Karen O'Brien, Director, Office for Accreditation
50 East Huron St.
Chicago, IL 60611-2795
(312) 280-2434, Fax: (312) 280-2433
http://www.ala.org/accreditation.html

American Occupational Therapy Association (AOTA)
Accreditation Council for Occupational Therapy Education
Neil Harvison, Director of Accreditation and Academic Affairs
PO Box 31220
Bethesda, MD 20824-1220
(301) 652-6611 ext 2914, Fax: (301) 652-7711
http://www.aota.org/educate/accredit.aspx

American Optometric Association (AOA-COE)
Accreditation Council on Optometric Education
Joyce L. Urbeck, Administrative Director
243 North Lindbergh Blvd.
St. Louis, MO 63141-7881
(314) 991-4100, Fax: (314) 991-4101
http://www.aoa.org

American Osteopathic Association (AOA-COCA)
Commission on Osteopathic College Accreditation
Konrad C. Miskowicz-Retz, Director, Department of Accreditation
142 East Ontario St.
Chicago, IL 60611-2864
(312) 202-8097, Fax: (312) 202-8397
http://www.osteopathic.org

American Physical Therapy Association (APTA)
Commission on Accreditation in Physical Therapy Education
Mary Jane Harris, Director
1111 North Fairfax St.
Alexandria, VA 22314-3229
(703) 684-2782, Fax: (703) 684-7343
http://www.apta.org

American Podiatric Medical Association (APMA)
Council on Podiatric Medical Education
Alan R. Tinkleman, Executive Director
9312 Old Georgetown Rd.
Bethesda, MD 20814-1612
(301) 581-9200, Fax: (301) 571-4903
http://www.cpme.org

American Psychological Association (APA)
Commission on Accreditation
Susan F. Zlotlow, Executive Director, Office of Program Consultation and Accreditation
750 First St. NE
Washington, DC 20002-4242
(202) 336-5979, Fax: (202) 336-5978
http://www.apa.org/ed/accreditation

American Society of Landscape Architects (ASLA)
Landscape Architectural Accreditation Board
Ronald C. Leighton, Executive Director
636 I St. NW
Washington, DC 20001-3736
(202) 898-2444, Fax: (202) 898-1185
http://www.asla.org

American Speech-Language-Hearing Association (ASHA)
Council on Academic Accreditation in Audiology and Speech-Language Pathology
Patrima L. Tice, Director of Credentialing
2200 Research Boulevard
Rockville, MD 20850-3289
(301) 296-5700, Fax: (301) 296-8580
http://www.asha.org

American Veterinary Medical Association (AVMA)

Council on Education

David Granstrom, Director, AVMA Education and Research Division
1931 North Meacham Rd., Ste. 100
Schaumburg, IL 60173-4360
(847) 925-8070, Fax: (847) 925-1329
http://www.avma.org/education/cvea

Association for Clinical Pastoral Education, Inc. (ACPEI)

Accreditation Commmission

Rev. Teresa E. Snorton, Executive Director
1549 Clairmont Rd., Ste. 103
Decatur, GA 30033-4611
(404) 320-1472, Fax: (404) 320-0849
http://www.acpe.edu

Association of Collegiate Business Schools and Programs (ACBSP)

Douglas G. Viehland, Executive Director
7007 College Blvd., Ste. 420
Overland Park, KS 66211
(913) 339-9356, Fax: (913) 339-6226
http://www.acbsp.org

Aviation Accreditation Board International (AABI)

Gary W. Kiteley, Executive Director
3410 Skyway Dr.
Auburn, AL 36830
(334) 844-2431, Fax: (334) 844-2432
http://www.aabi.aero

Commission on Accreditation of Allied Health Education Programs (CAAHEP)

CHEA recognizes the Commission on Accreditation of Allied Health Education Programs (CAAHEP) as an umbrella agency for 16 review committees representing professional organizations collaborating in the accreditation of programs in the following areas of allied health. All questions concerning accreditation of these programs should be directed to CAAHEP at the address given. The review committees are:

- AABB (*American Association of Blood Banks*)
- Accreditation Committee-Perfusion Education
- Accreditation Review Committee for the Anesthesiologists Assistant
- Accreditation Review Committee for the Medical Illustrator
- Accreditation Review Committee on Education in Surgical Technology
- American Association of Medical Assistants
- Committee on Accreditation for Education in Electroneurodiagnostic Technology
- Committee on Accreditation for Respiratory Care
- Committee on Accreditation for the Exercise Sciences
- Committee on Accreditation of Education for Polysomnographic Technologists
- Committee on Accreditation of Education Programs for Kinesiotherapy
- Committee on Accreditation of Educational Programs for the Emergency Medical Services Professions
- Cytotechnology Programs Review Committee
- Joint Review Committee on Education in Cardiovascular Technology
- Joint Review Committee on Education in Diagnostic Medical Sonography
- National Commission on Orthotic and Prosthetic Education

Kathleen Megivern, Executive Director
1361 Park St.
Clearwater, FL 33756
(727) 210-2350, Fax: (727) 210-2354
http://www.caahep.org

Commission on Accreditation of Healthcare Management Education (CAHME)

John S. Lloyd, President and CEO
2000 14th St. North, Ste. 780
Arlington, VA 22201
(703) 894-0960, Fax: (703) 894-0941
http://www.cahme.org

Commission on Collegiate Nursing Education (CCNE)

Jennifer L. Butlin, Director
One Dupont Circle NW, Ste. 530
Washington, DC 20036-1120
(202) 887-6791, Fax: (202) 887-8476
http://www.aacn.nche.edu/accreditation

Commission on English Language Program Accreditation (CEA)

Teresa D. O'Donnell, Executive Director
801 North Fairfax Street
Alexandria, VA 22314
(703) 519-2070, Fax: (703) 683-8099
http://www.cea-accredit.org

Commission on Massage Therapy Accreditation (CMTA)

John R. Goss III, Interim Executive Director
5335 Wisconsin Avenue NW, Suite 440
Washington DC 20015
(202) 895-1518, Fax: (202) 895-1519
http://www.comta.org

Commission on Opticianry Accreditation (COA)

Ellen Stoner, Director of Accreditation
PO Box 142
Florence, IN 47020
(703) 468-0566, Fax: (703) 306-9036
http://www.coaccreditation.com

Council for Accreditation of Counseling and Related Educational Programs (CACREP)
Carol L. Bobby, Executive Director
1001 North Fairfax St., Ste. 510
Alexandria, VA 22314
(703) 535-5990, Fax: (703) 739-6209
http://www.cacrep.org

Council for Interior Design Accreditation (CIDA)
Holly Mattson, Executive Director
146 Monroe Center NW, Ste. 1318
Grand Rapids, MI 49503-2822
(616) 458-0400, Fax: (616) 458-0460
http://www.accredit-id.org

Council on Chiropractic Education (CCE)
Commission on Accreditation
G. Lansing Blackshaw, Interim Executive Director
8049 North 85th Way
Scottsdale, AZ 85258-4321
(480) 443-8877, Fax: (480) 483-7333
http://www.cce-usa.org

Council on Education for Public Health (CEPH)
Laura Rasar King, Executive Director
800 Eye St. NW, Ste. 202
Washington, DC 20001-3710
(202) 789-1050, Fax: (202) 789-1895
http://www.ceph.org

Council on Naturopathic Medical Education (CNME)
Daniel Seitz, Executive Director
PO Box 178
Great Barrington, MA 01230
(413) 528-8877, Fax: (413) 528-8880
http://www.cnme.org

Council on Rehabilitation Education (CORE)
Commission on Standards and Accreditation
Marvin D. Kuehn, Executive Director
1699 Woodfield Rd., Ste. 300
Schaumburg 60173
(847) 944-1345, Fax: (847) 944-1324
http://www.core-rehab.org

Council on Social Work Education (CSWE)
Office of Social Work Accreditation and Educational Excellence
Dean Pierce, Director, Office of Social Work Accreditation and Educational Excellence
1725 Duke St., Ste. 500
Alexandria, VA 22314-3457
(703) 683-8080, Fax: (703) 683-8099
http://www.cswe.org

Joint Review Committee on Education in Radiologic Technology (JRCERT)
Leslie F. Winter, Chief Executive Officer
20 North Wacker Dr., Ste. 2850
Chicago, IL 60606-3182
(312) 704-5300, Fax: (312) 704-5304
http://www.jrcert.org

Joint Review Committee on Educational Programs in Nuclear Medicine Technology (JRCNMT)
Jan M. Winn, Executive Director
2000 West Danforth Rd., Ste. 130 #203
Edmond, OK 73003
(405) 285-0546, Fax: (405) 285-0579
http://www.jrcnmt.org

Liaison Committee on Medical Education [EVEN YEARS] (LCME)
Dan Hunt, LCME Secretary and Senior Director of Accreditation Services
Association of American Medical Colleges
2450 N St. NW
Washington, DC 20037
(202) 828-0596, Fax: (202) 828-1125
http://www.lcme.org

Liaison Committee on Medical Education [ODD YEARS] (LCME)
Barbara Barzansky, LCME Secretary and Director of Undergraduate Medical Education
American Medical Association
515 North State St.
Chicago, IL 60654
(312) 464-4933, Fax: (312) 464-5830
http://www.lcme.org

Midwifery Education Accreditation Council (MEAC)
Jo Anne Myers-Ciecko, Executive Director
PO Box 984
La Conner WA 98257
(360) 466-2080, Fax: (480) 907-2936
http://www.meacschools.org

Montessori Accreditation Council for Teacher Education (MACTE)
Commission on Accreditation
Gretchen L. Warner, Executive Director
524 Main St., Ste. 202
Racine, WI 53403
(262) 898-1846, Fax: (262) 898-1849
http://www.macte.org

National Accrediting Agency for Clinical Laboratory Science (NAACLS)
Dianne M. Cearlock, Chief Executive Officer
5600 N. River Rd., Ste. 720
Rosemont, IL 60018-5119
(773) 714-8880, Fax: (773) 714-8886
http://www.naacls.org

National Association of Industrial Technology (NAIT)
Rick Coscarelli, Executive Director
3300 Washtenaw Ave., Ste. 220
Ann Arbor, MI 48104-4200
(734) 677-0720, Fax: (734) 677-0046
http://www.nait.org

National Association of Schools of Art and Design (NASAD)
Commission on Accreditation
Samuel Hope, Executive Director
Karen P. Moynahan, Associate Director
11250 Roger Bacon Dr., Ste. 21
Reston, VA 20190
(703) 437-0700, Fax: (703) 437-6312
http://www.arts-accredit.org

National Association of Schools of Dance (NASD)
Commission on Accreditation
Samuel Hope, Executive Director
Karen P. Moynahan, Associate Director
11250 Roger Bacon Dr., Ste. 21
Reston, VA 20190
(703) 437-0700, Fax: (703) 437-6312
http://www.arts-accredit.org

National Association of Schools of Music (NASM)
Commission on Accreditation
Samuel Hope, Executive Director
Karen P. Moynahan, Associate Director
11250 Roger Bacon Dr., Ste. 21
Reston, VA 20190
(703) 437-0700, Fax: (703) 437-6312
http://www.arts-accredit.org

National Association of Schools of Public Affairs and Administration (NASPAA)
Commission on Peer Review and Accreditation
Laurel L. McFarland, Executive Director
1029 Vermont Ave. NW, Ste. 1100
Washington, DC 20005
(202) 628-8965, Fax: (202) 626-4978
http://www.naspaa.org

National Association of Schools of Theatre (NAST)
Commission on Accreditation
Samuel Hope, Executive Director
Karen P. Moynahan, Associate Director
11250 Roger Bacon Dr., Ste. 21
Reston, VA 20190
(703) 437-0700, Fax: (703) 437-6312
http://www.arts-accredit.org

National Council for Accreditation of Teacher Education (NCATE)
James G. Cibulka, President
2010 Massachusetts Ave. NW, Ste. 500
Washington, DC 20036-1023
(202) 466-7496, Fax: (202) 296-6620
http://www.ncate.org

National League for Nursing Accrediting Commission, Inc. (NLNAC)
Sharon J. Tanner, Executive Director
61 Broadway, 33rd Floor
New York, NY 10006
(212) 363-5555 ext. 153, Fax: (212) 812-0390
http://www.nlnac.org

National Recreation and Park Association (NRPA/AALR)
Council on Accreditation
James O'Connor, Accreditation Manager
22377 Belmont Ridge Rd.
Ashburn, VA 20148-4150
(703) 858-0784, Fax: (703) 858-0794
http://www.nrpa.org

Planning Accreditation Board (PAB)
Shonagh Merits, Executive Director
122 South Michigan Ave., Ste. 1600
Chicago, IL 60603-6147
(312) 334-1271, Fax: (312) 334-1273
http://www.planningaccreditationboard.org

Society of American Foresters (SAF)
Commission on Accreditation
Terrance Clark, Director of Science and Education
5400 Grosvenor Ln.
Bethesda, MD 20814-2198
(301) 897-8720, Fax: (301) 897-3690
http://www.safnet.org

Teacher Education Accreditation Council (TEAC)
Accreditation Committee
Frank B. Murray, President
One Dupont Circle NW, Ste. 320
Washington, DC 20036-0110
(202) 466-7236, Fax: (302) 831-3013
http://www.teac.org

Recognized and Participating Organizations 2007

This chart lists regional, faith-related, career-related, and specialized accreditors that are or have been recognized by the Council for Higher Education Accreditation (CHEA) or the U.S. Department of Education (USDE) or both. Organizations identified by (●) are recognized; (—) indicates those not currently recognized. This symbol (O) identifies accrediting organizations that were formerly recognized.

CHEA-recognized organizations must meet CHEA eligibility standards (*www.chea.org/recognition/recognition.asp*). Accreditors exercise independent judgment about whether to seek CHEA recognition. For USDE recognition, accreditation from the organization is used by an institution or program to establish eligibility to participate in federal student aid or other federal programs (*www.ed.gov/about/offices/list/ope/index.html*). Some accreditors cannot be considered for USDE recognition because they do not provide access to federal funds. Other accreditors have chosen not to pursue USDE recognition.

Because CHEA affiliation and USDE recognition depend on a range of factors, readers are strongly cautioned against making judgments about the quality of an accrediting organization and its institutions and programs based solely on CHEA or USDE status. Additional inquiry is essential. If you have any questions about CHEA affiliation or USDE recognition status of an accreditor, please contact the accrediting organization.

ACCREDITOR	CHEA-Recognized Organization	USDE-Recognized Organization
REGIONAL ACCREDITING ORGANIZATIONS		
Middle States Association of Colleges and Schools, Commission on Higher Education	●	●
New England Association of Schools and Colleges, Commission on Institutions of Higher Education	●	●
New England Association of Schools and Colleges, Commission on Technical and Career Institutions	●	●
North Central Association of Colleges and Schools, The Higher Learning Commission	●	●
Northwest Commission on Colleges and Universities	●	●
Southern Association of Colleges and Schools, Commission on Colleges	●	●
Western Association of Schools and Colleges, Accrediting Commission for Community and Junior Colleges	●	●
Western Association of Schools and Colleges, Accrediting Commission for Senior Colleges and Universities	●	●
PRIVATE CAREER ACCREDITING ORGANIZATIONS		
Accrediting Bureau of Health Education Schools	—	●
Accrediting Commission of Career Schools and Colleges of Technology	—	●
Accrediting Council for Continuing Education and Training	—	●
Accrediting Council for Independent Colleges and Schools	●	●
Council on Occupational Education	—	●
Distance Education and Training Council Accrediting Commission	●	●
National Accrediting Commission on Cosmetology Arts and Sciences, Inc.	—	●

Source: *2007 CHEA Almanac of External Quality Review.* Washington, DC: Council for Higher Education Accreditation, 2008.

Note: This chart is updated when the CHEA Board of Directors recognizes or withdraws recognition of an accrediting organization or when the U.S. Secretary of Education recognizes or withdraws recognition of an accrediting organization.

ACCREDITOR	CHEA-Recognized Organization	USDE-Recognized Organization
FAITH-BASED ACCREDITING ORGANIZATIONS		
Association for Biblical Higher Education, Commission on Accreditation	●	●
Association of Advanced Rabbinical and Talmudic Schools, Accreditation Commission	●	●
Commission on Accrediting of the Association of Theological Schools in the U.S. and Canada	●	●
Transnational Association of Christian Colleges and Schools, Accreditation Commission	●	●
SPECIALIZED AND PROFESSIONAL ACCREDITING ORGANIZATIONS		
AACSB International—The Association to Advance Collegiate Schools of Business	●	○
Accreditation Board for Engineering and Technology, Inc.	●	○
Accreditation Commission for Acupuncture and Oriental Medicine	—	●
Accreditation Council for Pharmacy Education	●	●
Accredition Review Commission on Education for the Physician Assistant, Inc.	●	—
Accrediting Council on Education in Journalism and Mass Communication	●	○
American Academy for Liberal Education	—	●
American Association for Marriage and Family Therapy, Commission on Accreditation for Marriage and Family Therapy Education	●	●
American Association of Family and Consumer Sciences, Council for Accreditation	●	—
American Association of Nurse Anesthetists, Council on Accreditation of Nurse Anesthesia Educational Programs	●	●
American Bar Association, Council of the Section of Legal Education and Admissions to the Bar	—	●
American Board of Funeral Service Education, Committee on Accreditation	●	●
American College of Nurse-Midwives, Accreditation Commission for Midwifery Education	—	●
American Council for Construction Education	●	○
American Counseling Association, Council for Accreditation of Counseling and Related Educational Programs	●	—
American Culinary Federation Foundation, Accrediting Commission	●	○
American Dental Association, Commission on Dental Accreditation	—	●
American Dietetic Association, Commission on Accreditation for Dietetics Education	●	●
American Library Association, Committee on Accreditation	●	○
American Occupational Therapy Association, Accreditation Council for Occupational Therapy Education	●	●
American Optometric Association, Accreditation Council on Optometric Education	●	●
American Osteopathic Association, Commission on Osteopathic College Accreditation	○	●
American Physical Therapy Association, Commission on Accreditation in Physical Therapy Education	●	●
American Podiatric Medical Association, Council on Podiatric Medical Education	●	●
American Psychological Association, Committee on Accreditation	●	●
American Society for Microbiology/American College of Microbiology	—	○

○ *Accreditors that were not recognized by CHEA or USDE but have been recognized in prior years.*

ACCREDITOR	CHEA-Recognized Organization	USDE-Recognized Organization
SPECIALIZED AND PROFESSIONAL ACCREDITING ORGANIZATIONS *(Continued)*		
American Society of Landscape Architects, Landscape Architectural Accreditation Board	●	○
American Speech-Language-Hearing Association, Council on Academic Accreditation in Audiology and Speech-Language Pathology	●	●
American Veterinary Medical Association, Council on Education	●	●
Association for Clinical Pastoral Education, Inc., Accreditation Commission	—	●
Association of Collegiate Business Schools and Programs	●	○
Aviation Accreditation Board International	●	—
Commission on Accreditation of Allied Health Education Programs	●	○
Commission on Accreditation of Healthcare Management Education	●	●
Commission on Collegiate Nursing Education	●	●
Commission on English Language Program Accreditation	—	●
Commission on Massage Therapy Accreditation	—	●
Commission on Opticianry Accreditation	—	○
Council for Interior Design Accreditation	●	○
Council on Chiropractic Education, Commission on Accreditation	●	●
Council on Education for Public Health	—	●
Council on Naturopathic Medical Education	—	●
Council on Rehabilitation Education, Commission on Standards and Accreditation	●	○
Council on Social Work Education, Office of Social Work Accreditation and Educational Excellence	●	○
Joint Review Committee on Education in Radiologic Technology	●	●
Joint Review Committee on Educational Programs in Nuclear Medicine Technology	●	●
Liaison Committee on Medical Education	—	●
Midwifery Education Accreditation Council	—	●
Montessori Accreditation Council for Teacher Education, Commission on Accreditation	—	●
National Accrediting Agency for Clinical Laboratory Sciences	●	—
National Architectural Accrediting Board, Inc.	—	○
National Association of Industrial Technology	●	○
National Association of Schools of Art and Design, Commission on Accreditation	●	●
National Association of Schools of Dance, Commission on Accreditation	●	●
National Association of Schools of Music, Commission on Accreditation and Commission on Community/Junior College Accreditation	●	●
National Association of Schools of Public Affairs and Administration, Commission on Peer Review and Accreditation	●	—
National Association of Nurse Practioners in Women's Health	—	○

○ *Accreditors that were not recognized by CHEA or USDE but have been recognized in prior years.*

ACCREDITOR	CHEA-Recognized Organization	USDE-Recognized Organization
SPECIALIZED AND PROFESSIONAL ACCREDITING ORGANIZATIONS *(Continued)*		
National Association of Schools of Theatre, Commission on Accreditation	●	●
National Council for Accreditation of Teacher Education	●	●
National Environmental Health Science and Protection Accreditation Council	—	○
National League for Nursing, Accrediting Commission, Inc.	●	●
National Recreation and Park Association	●	—
Planning Accreditation Board	●	—
Society of American Foresters, Committee on Accreditation	●	○
Teacher Education Accreditation Council	●	●
United States Catholic Conference, Commission on Certification and Accreditation	—	○

○ *Accreditors that were not recognized by CHEA or USDE but have been recognized in prior years.*

Other Recognized Accrediting Organizations

Two accrediting organizations recognized by the U.S. Department of Education are not included in the preceding chart developed by the Council for Higher Education Accreditation.

The *North Central Association of Colleges and Schools, Commission on Accreditation and School Improvement* accredits schools ranging from pre-kindergarten through postsecondary. Only the adult education, vocational, and non–degree-granting postsecondary schools they evaulate are included in this directory.

The *New York Board of Regents* accredits postsecondary institutions only within the confines of the State of New York.

JOINT STATEMENT ON TRANSFER AND AWARD OF ACADEMIC CREDIT

The following set of guidelines has been developed by the three national associations whose member institutions are directly involved in the transfer and award of academic credit: the American Association of Collegiate Registrars and Admissions Officers, the American Council on Education, and the Council for Higher Education Accreditation. The need for such a statement came from an awareness of the growing complexity of transfer policies and practices, which have been brought about, in part, by the changing nature of postsecondary education. With increasing frequency, students are pursuing their education in a variety of institutional and extrainstitutional settings. Social equity and the intelligent use of resources require that validated learning be recognized wherever it takes place.

The statement is thus intended to serve as a guide for institutions developing or reviewing policies dealing with transfer, acceptance, and award of credit. "Transfer" as used here refers to the movement of students from one college, university, or other education provider to another and to the process by which credits representing educational experiences, courses, degrees, or credentials that are awarded by an education provider are accepted or not accepted by a receiving institution.

Basic Assumptions

This statement is directed to institutions of postsecondary education and others concerned with the transfer of academic credit among institutions and the award of academic credit for learning that takes place at another institution or education provider. Basic to this statement is the principle that each institution is responsible for determining its own policies and practices with regard to the transfer, acceptance, and award of credit. Institutions are encouraged to review their policies and practices periodically to assure that they accomplish the institutions' objectives and that they function in a manner that is fair and equitable to students. General statements of policy such as this one or others referred to, should be used as guides, not as substitutes, for institutional policies and practices.

Transfer and award of credit is a concept that increasingly involves transfer between dissimilar institutions and curricula and recognition of extrainstitutional learning, as well as transfer between institutions and curricula with similar characteristics. As their personal circumstances and educational objectives change, students seek to have their learning, wherever and however attained, recognized by institutions where they enroll for further study. It is important for reasons of social equity and educational effectiveness for all institutions to develop reasonable and definitive policies and procedures for acceptance of such learning experiences, as well as for the transfer of credits earned at another institution. Such policies and procedures should provide maximum consideration for the individual student who has changed institutions or objectives. It is the receiving institution's responsibility to provide reasonable and definitive policies and procedures for determining a student's knowledge in required subject areas. All sending institutions have a responsibility to furnish transcripts and other documents necessary for a receiving institution to judge the quality and quantity of the student's work. Institutions also have a responsibility to advise the student that the work reflected on the transcript may or may not be accepted by a receiving institution as bearing the same (or any) credits as those awarded by the provider institution, or that the credits awarded will be applicable to the academic credential the student is pursuing.

Interinstitutional Transfer of Credit

Transfer of credit from one institution to another involves at least three considerations:

(1) the educational quality of the learning experience which the student transfers;

(2) the comparability of the nature, content, and level of the learning experience to that offered by the receiving institution; and

(3) the appropriateness and applicability of the learning experience to the programs offered by the receiving institution, in light of the student's educational goals.

Accredited Institutions

Accreditation speaks primarily to the first of these considerations, serving as the basic indicator that an institution meets certain minimum standards. Users of accreditation are urged to give careful attention to the accreditation conferred by accrediting bodies recognized by the Council for Higher Education Accreditation (CHEA). CHEA has a formal process of recognition which requires that all accrediting bodies so recognized must meet the same standards. Under these standards, CHEA has recognized a number of accrediting bodies, including:

(1) regional accrediting commissions (which historically accredited the more traditional colleges and universities but which now accredit proprietary, vocational-technical, distance learning providers, and single-purpose institutions as well);

(2) national accrediting bodies that accredit various kinds of specialized institutions, including distance learning providers and freestanding professional schools; and

(3) professional organizations that accredit programs within multipurpose institutions.

Although accrediting agencies vary in the ways they are organized and in their statements of scope and mission, all accrediting bodies that meet CHEA's standards for recognition function to ensure that the institutions or programs they accredit have met generally accepted minimum standards for accreditation.

Accreditation thus affords reason for confidence in an institution's or a program's purposes, in the appropriateness of its resources and plans for carrying out these purposes, and in its effectiveness in accomplishing its goals, insofar as these things can be judged. Accreditation speaks to the probability, but does not guarantee, that students have met acceptable standards of educational accomplishment.

Comparability and Applicability

Comparability of the nature, content, and level of transfer credit and the appropriateness and applicability of the credit earned to programs offered by the receiving institution are as important in the evaluation process as the accreditation status of the institution at which the transfer credit was awarded. Since accreditation does not address these questions, this information must be obtained from catalogues and other materials and from direct contact between knowledgeable and experienced faculty and staff at both the receiving and sending institutions. When such considerations as comparability and appropriateness of credit are satisfied, however, the receiving institution should have reasonable confidence that students from accredited institutions are qualified to undertake the receiving institution's educational program. In its articulation and transfer policies, the institution should judge courses, programs, and other learning experiences on their learning outcomes and the existence of valid evaluation measures, including third-party expert review, and not on modes of delivery.

Admissions and Degree Purposes

At some institutions there may be differences between the acceptance of credit for admission purposes and the applicability of credit for degree purposes. A receiving institution may accept previous work, place a credit value on it, and enter it on the transcript. However, that previous work, because of its nature and not its inherent quality, may be determined to have no applicability to a specific degree to be pursued by the student. Institutions have a responsibility to make this distinction, and its implications, clear to students before they decide to enroll. This should be a matter of full disclosure, with the best interests of the student in mind. Institutions also should make every reasonable effort to reduce the gap between credits accepted and credits applied toward an educational credential.

Additional Criteria for Transfer Decisions

The following additional criteria are offered to assist institutions, accreditors, and higher education associations in future transfer decisions. These criteria are intended to sustain academic quality in an environment of more varied transfer, assure consistency of transfer practice, and encourage appropriate accountability about transfer policy and practice.

Balance in the Use of Accreditation Status in Transfer Decisions. Institutions and accreditors need to assure that transfer decisions are not made solely on the source of accreditation of a sending program or institution. While acknowledging that accreditation is an important factor, receiving institutions ought to make clear their institutional reasons for accepting or not accepting credits that students seek to transfer. Students should have reasonable explanations about how work offered for credit is or is not of sufficient quality when compared with the receiving institution and how work is or is not comparable with curricula and standards to meet degree requirements of the receiving institution.

Consistency. Institutions and accreditors need to reaffirm that the considerations that inform transfer decisions are applied consistently in the context of changing student attendance patterns (students likely to engage in more transfer) and emerging new providers of higher education (new sources of credits and experience to be evaluated). New providers and new attendance patterns increase the number and type of transfer issues that institutions will address—making consistency even more important in the future.

Accountability for Effective Public Communication. Institutions and accreditors need to assure that students and the public are fully and accurately informed about their respective transfer policies and practices. The public has a significant interest in higher education's effective management of transfer, especially in an environment of expanding access and mobility. Public funding is routinely provided to colleges and universities. This funding is accompanied by public expectations that the transfer process is built on a strong commitment to fairness and efficiency.

Commitment to Address Innovation. Institutions and accreditors need to be flexible and open in considering alternative approaches to managing transfer when these approaches will benefit students. Distance learning and other applications of technology generate alternative approaches to many functions of colleges and universities. Transfer is inevitably among these.

Foreign Institutions

In most cases, foreign institutions are chartered and authorized to grant degrees by their national governments, usually through a Ministry of Education or similar appropriate ministerial body. No other nation has a system comparable with voluntary accreditation as it exists in the United States. At an operational level, AACRAO's Office of International Education Services can assist institutions by providing general or specific guidelines on admission and placement of foreign students, or by providing evaluations of foreign educational credentials.

Evaluation of Extrainstitutional and Experiential Learning for Purposes of Transfer and Award of Credit

Transfer and award of credit policies should encompass educational accomplishment attained in extrainstitutional settings. In deciding on the award of credit for extrainstitutional learning, institutions will find the services of the American Council on Education's Center for Adult Learning and Educational Credentials helpful. One of the Center's functions is to operate and foster programs to determine credit equivalencies for various modes of extrainstitutional learning. The Center maintains evaluation programs for formal courses offered by the military and civilian organizations such as business, corporations, government agencies, training providers, institutes, and labor unions. Evaluation services are also available for examination programs, for occupations with validated job proficiency evaluation systems, and for correspondence courses offered by schools accredited by the Distance Education and Training Council. The results are published in a Guide series. Another resource is the General Educational Development (GED) Testing Program, which provides a means for assessing high school equivalency.

For learning that has not been evaluated through the ACE evaluation processes, institutions are encouraged to explore the Council for Adult and Experiential Learning (CAEL) procedures and processes.

Uses of This Statement

Institutions are encouraged to use this statement as a basis for discussions in developing or reviewing institutional policies with regard to the transfer and award of credit. If the statement reflects an institution's policies, that institution may wish to use these guidelines to inform faculty, staff, and students.

It is also recommended that accrediting bodies reflect the essential precepts of this statement in their criteria.

Ratified on September 28, 2001, by:

- The American Association of Collegiate Registrars and Admissions Officers
- The American Council on Education
- The Council for Higher Education Accreditation

Institutional Index

Abbreviations Used in This Index

Acad	Academy
Assoc	Association
Bus	Business
Ctr	Center
Coll	College
Comm	Community
Dept	Department
Dist	District
Edu	Education
Grad	Graduate
Hosp	Hospital
Inst	Institute
Int'l	International
Jr	Junior
Mgmnt	Management
Maint.	Maintenance
Med	Medical
Mem	Memorial
Prof	Professional
Reg	Regional
Sch	School
Sem	Seminary
Sr	Senior
Sys.	System
Tech	Technical
Techno	Technology
Univ	University

1st Dental Battalion *(see 1st Dental Battalion/NDC)*
1st Dental Battalion/NDC 685
1st Dental Squadron 750
1st Dental Squadron/SGD *(see 1st Dental Squadron)*
1st MDG *(see 1st Dental Squadron)*
1st Med. Group *(see 1st Dental Squadron)*
2nd Dental Battalio—Naval Dental Ctr. 729
2nd Med. Group/SGDDT 709
3rd Dental Battalion/NDC Okinawa 766
3rd Dental Squadron *(see 3rd Med. Group)*
3rd Med. Group 683
4Cs The Ctr. for Child Care Careers *(see North Jersey Comm. Coordinated Child Care Agency, Inc.)*
4-States Acad. of Cosmetology *(see 4-States Okmulgee Acad. of Cosmetology, Inc.)*
4-States Okmulgee Acad. of Cosmetology, Inc. 614
5th Avenue Acad. of Hairdressing & Cosmetology *(see Fifth Avenue Acad. of Hairdressing & Cosmetology)*
10th Med. Group/SGFL 691
11th Infantry Regiment *(see United States Army Infantry Sch.)*
11th Med. Group/SGD *(see 579th Med. Group)*
11th Med. Group/SGD 780
21st Century Beauty Acad. *(see Beyond 21st Century Beauty Acad.)*
55th Dental Squadron 719
55th Dental Squadron/SGD *(see 55th Dental Squadron)*
55th MDG *(see 55th Dental Squadron)*
55th Med. Group *(see 55th Dental Squadron)*
60th Med. Group 685
74th Dental Squadron/SGD *(see 88th Med. Group)*
79th Med. Wing *(see 579th Med. Group)*
81 Dental Squadron/SGDDT 717
81 DS/SGDDT *(see 81 Dental Squadron/SGDDT)*
81st MDG *(see 81 Dental Squadron/SGDDT)*
81st Med. Group 745 *(see also 81 Dental Squadron/SGDDT; United States Air Force Sch. of Health Care Sciences)*
82nd Dental Squadron *(see 82nd Med. Group)*
82nd MDG *(see United States Air Force Sch. of Health Care Sciences)*
82nd Med. Group/Squadron *(see 82nd Med. Group)*
82nd Training Group *(see United States Air Force Sch. of Health Care Sciences)*
88th MDG *(see 88th Med. Group)*
88th Med. Group 731
96th Air Base Wing *(see 96th Med. Group)*
96th Dental Squadron *(see 96th Med. Group)*
96th Med. Group 695
96th Med. Group/SGD *(see 96th Med. Group)*
199th Infantry Brigade *(see United States Army Infantry Sch.)*
375th Dental Squadron *(see 375th Med. Group)*
375th Med. Group 700
375th Med. Group/SGDDT *(see 375th Med. Group)*
579th MDG *(see 579th Med. Group)*
579th Med. Group 695, 780

A

A Cut Above Beauty Coll. 530
A Gathering Place Massage Sch. & Clinic *(see A Gathering Place Wellness Edu. Ctr.)*
A New Beginning Sch. of Massage 647
A&M Commerce *(see Texas A&M Univ—Commerce)*
A&M Corpus Christi *(see Texas A&M Univ—Corpus Christi)*
A&M Kingsville *(see Texas A&M Univ—Kingsville)*
A&M Texarkana *(see Texas A&M Univ—Texarkana)*
A.B.I. Sch. of Barbering & Cosmetology 586, 788
A.I. Prince Reg. Vocational-Tech. Sch. *(see Albert I. Prince Reg. Vocational-Tech. Sch.)*
A.I. Prince Tech. High Sch. *(see Albert I. Prince Reg. Vocational-Tech. Sch.)*
A.M.I., Inc. 780 *(see also WyoTec—Daytona)*
A.R.T. Tech. Coll. *(see Hamilton Tech. Coll.)*
A.T. Still Univ. of Health Sciences 235
A.T.E.S. Tech. Sch. *(see Erie Inst. of Techno.)*
A1 Bus. & Tech. Coll. 631
Aaker's Bus. Coll. 789 *(see also Rasmussen Coll—Bismarck, Rasmussen Coll—Fargo)*
Aaker's Coll. 789 *(see also Rasmussen Coll—Bismarck, Rasmussen Coll—Fargo)*
Aaron's Acad. of Beauty 546
AB Tech *(see Asheville-Buncombe Tech. Comm. Coll.)*
Abbey, The *(see Belmont Abbey Coll.)*
Abbott Acad. of Cosmetology Arts & Sciences 565 *(see also Missouri Beauty Acad.)*
Abbott Coll. *(see John Abbott Coll.)*
Abbott Hosp. for Women *(see Abbott Northwestern Hosp/Children's Hospitals & Clinics)*
Abbott Northwestern Hosp/Children's Hospitals & Clinics 715
ABC Beauty Acad. 819
ABC Training Ctr. of Maryland, Inc. *(see Americare Sch. of Allied Health)*
ABC Training Ctr., Inc. *(see Americare Sch. of Nursing)*
Abcott Inst. 815
Abdill Career Coll. 620
Abilene Baptist Coll. *(see Hardin-Simmons Univ.)*
Abilene Christian Coll. *(see Abilene Christian Univ.)*
Abilene Christian Univ. 392
Abilene Christian Univ. Grad. Sch. of Theology *(see Abilene Christian Univ.)*
Abington Mem. Health Ctr—Schilling Campus 736
Abington Mem. Hosp. 736 *(see also Abington Mem. Health Ctr—Schilling Campus)*
Abraham Baldwin Agricultural Coll. 108
Abraham Baldwin Coll. *(see Abraham Baldwin Agricultural Coll.)*
Absolute Safety Training Paramedic Program 472
Abu Dhabi Men's Coll. *(see Higher Colleges of Techno. Abu Dhabi Men's Coll.)*
Abu Dhabi Women's Coll. *(see Higher Colleges of Techno. Abu Dhabi Women's Coll.)*
ACA Coll. of Design *(see Art Inst. of Cincinnati)*
Academia Maison D'Esthetique 631
Academia Morales 631
Academia Serrant 631
Academia Vocational Del Turabo 631
Academic Sixth Form Centre *(see Bermuda Coll.)*
Acad. at Austin, The 647
Acad. Coll. 219
Acad. Di Capelli Sch. of Cosmetology 497
Acad. Edu. Ctr., Inc. *(see Acad. Coll.)*
Acad. for Construction & Engineering *(see Washington-Holmes Tech. Ctr.)*
Acad. for Five Element Acupuncture 89
Acad. for Med. & Dental Assistants *(see PCI Health Training Ctr.)*

AIBT Inst. *(see IIA Coll.)*
AIBT Int'l. Inst. of the Americas *(see IIA Coll.)*
Aiken Coll. *(see Aiken Tech. Coll.)*
Aiken Tech. Coll. 373
Aiken Tech. Edu. Ctr. *(see Aiken Tech. Coll.)*
Ailano Sch. of Cosmetology 550
Ailey American Dance Ctr. *(see Alvin Ailey American Dance Ctr.)*
Ailey Sch., The *(see Alvin Ailey American Dance Ctr.)*
AI—Indianapolis *(see Aviation Inst. of Maint.)*
AI—Kansas City *(see Aviation Inst. of Maint.)*
AI—Lawrenceville *(see Aviation Inst. of Maint.)*
AI—Manassas *(see Aviation Inst. of Maint—Manassas)*
AI—Philadelphia *(see Aviation Inst. of Maint.)*
AIMS Acad. 647 *(see also AimsEd Inc.)*
Aims Coll. *(see Aims Comm. Coll.)*
Aims Comm. Coll. 69
AI—Virginia Beach *(see Aviation Inst. of Maint—Virgina Beach)*
AI—Washington, DC *(see Aviation Inst. of Maint—Manassas)*
Air Command & Staff Coll. *(see Air Univ.)*
Air Corps Engineering Sch. *(see Air Force Inst. of Techno.)*
Air Force Acad. *(see United States Air Force Acad.)*
Air Force Acad. Hosp. *(see 10th Med. Group/SGFL)*
Air Force Inst. for Advanced Distributed Learning *(see Air Univ. Extension Course Program)*
Air Force Inst. of Techno. 313 *(see also Air Univ.)*
Air Force Sch. of Health Care Sciences *(see United States Air Force Sch. of Health Care Sciences)*
Air Sch. of Application *(see Air Force Inst. of Techno.)*
Air Univ. 3
Air Univ. Sch. of Air & Space Studies *(see Sch. of Advanced Air & Space Studies)*
Airman's Proficiency Ctr. 620
Air-Vu Sch. of Drawing *(see DeVry Univ. Westminster)*
AIU Online *(see American InterContinental Univ. Online)*
Akers Computerized Learning Ctr.s *(see Interactive Coll. of Techno.)*
Akron Beauty Sch. *(see Gerber Akron Beauty Sch.)*
Akron Children's Hosp. *(see Children's Hosp. Med. Ctr. of Akron)*
Akron City Schools *(see Akron Sch. of Practical Nursing)*
Akron General Med. Ctr. 731
Akron Hosp. *(see Akron General Med. Ctr.)*
Akron Inst. of Herzing Coll. 313
Akron Machining Inst. Inc. 604
Akron Med.-Dental Inst. *(see Akron Inst. of Herzing Coll.)*
Akron Public Schools *(see Adult Vocational Services, Akron Sch. of Practical Nursing)*
Akron Univ. *(see Univ. of Akron)*
AKS Massage Sch. 664
Al Ain Women's Coll. *(see Higher Colleges of Techno. Al Ain Women's Coll.)*
Al Collins Graphic Design Sch. *(see Collins Coll.)*
Alabama A&M Univ. *(see Alabama Agricultural & Mechanical Univ.)*
Alabama Agricultural & Mechanical Univ. 3
Alabama Aviation & Tech. Coll. *(see Enterprise-Ozark Comm. Coll.; George C. Wallace State Comm. Coll—Dothan)*
Alabama Baptist Normal & Theological Sch. *(see Selma Univ.)*
Alabama Career Coll. *(see Virginia Coll.)*
Alabama Christian Coll. *(see Amridge Univ., Faulkner Univ.)*
Alabama Christian Sch. of Religion *(see Amridge Univ.)*
Alabama Coll. of Barber Styling *(see Alabama State Coll. of Barber Styling)*
Alabama Colored People's Univ. *(see Alabama State Univ.)*
Alabama Conference Female Coll. *(see Huntingdon Coll.)*
Alabama Lutheran Acad. & Jr. Coll. *(see Concordia Coll. Selma)*
Alabama Polytechnic Inst. *(see Auburn Univ.)*
Alabama Reference Laboratories/LabSouth, Inc. 683
Alabama Southern Coll. *(see Alabama Southern Comm. Coll.)*
Alabama Southern Comm. Coll. 3
Alabama State Barber Coll. *(see Alabama State Coll. of Barber Styling)*
Alabama State Coll. for Negroes *(see Alabama State Univ.)*
Alabama State Coll. of Barber Styling 463
Alabama State Univ. 3
Alabama Tech. Coll. *(see Gadsden State Comm. Coll.)*
Aladdin Beauty Coll. #11 584
Aladdin Beauty Coll. #15 584
Aladdin Beauty Coll. #20 584
Aladdin Beauty Coll. #22 584
Aladdin Beauty Coll. #26 584
Aladdin Beauty Coll. #5 584
Aladdin Beauty Coll. #7 584
Aladdin Beauty Coll—Mesquite *(see Aladdin Beauty Coll. #26)*
Alamance Comm. Coll. 299
Alamance Reg. Med. Ctr. 729
Alameda Beauty Coll., Inc. 472
Alameda Coll. *(see Coll. of Alameda)*
Alameda County Hosp. Authority *(see Highland General Hosp.)*
Alameda County Med. Ctr. *(see Highland General Hosp.)*
Alamogordo Branch Comm. Coll. *(see New Mexico State Univ. at Alamogordo)*
Alaska Bible Coll. 12
Alaska Christian Coll. 809
Alaska Coll. *(see Alaska Bible Coll., Alaska Christian Coll.)*
Alaska Eye Care Ctr. *(see Pacific Univ.)*
Alaska Methodist Univ. *(see Alaska Pacific Univ.)*
Alaska Native Med. Ctr. *(see Southcentral Foundation-Alaska Native Med. Ctr.)*
Alaska Pacific Univ. 12
Alaska Vocational Tech. Ctr. 465
Alaska Vo-Tech Ctr. *(see Alaska Vocational Tech. Ctr.)*
Albany Area Vocational-Tech. Sch. *(see Albany Tech. Coll.)*
Albany Bible & Manual Training Inst. *(see Albany State Univ.)*
Albany Coll. of Pharmacy of Union Univ. 269
Albany Collegiate Inst. *(see Lewis & Clark Coll.)*
Albany Jr. Coll. *(see Darton Coll.)*
Albany Law Coll. *(see Albany Law Sch.)*
Albany Law Sch. 269
Albany Med. Ctr. 723
Albany Med. Coll. 269
Albany Med. Coll. of Union Univ. *(see Albany Med. Coll.)*
Albany Pharmacy Coll. *(see Albany Coll. of Pharmacy of Union Univ.)*
Albany State Coll. *(see Albany State Univ.)*
Albany State Univ. 108 *(see also Univ. at Albany)*
Albany Tech. Coll. 108
Albany Tech. Inst. *(see Albany Tech. Coll.)*
Albany Univ. *(see Univ. at Albany)*
Albany VA Med. Ctr. *(see Albany Veterans Affairs Med. Ctr.)*
Albany VAMC *(see Albany Veterans Affairs Med. Ctr.)*
Albany Veterans Affairs Med. Ctr. 723

Albemarle Coll. *(see Coll. of The Albemarle)*
Albert Einstein Coll. of Medicine *(see Yeshiva Univ.)*
Albert Einstein Healthcare Network *(see Albert Einstein Med. Ctr.)*
Albert Einstein Med. Ctr. 736
Albert I. Prince Reg. Vocational-Tech. Sch. 497
Albert I. Prince Tech. High Sch. *(see Albert I. Prince Reg. Vocational-Tech. Sch.)*
Albert Sch. 779 *(see also Brio Acad. of Cosmetolog—Niantic)*
Albert Sch. of Cosmetology *(see James Albert Sch. of Cosmetology)*
Albert State Coll. *(see Carl Albert State Coll.)*
Alberta Bible Coll. 454
Alberta Children's Hosp. 756
Alberta Coll. *(see Alberta Bible Coll.)*
Alberta Crippled Children's Hosp. *(see Alberta Children's Hosp.)*
Alberta Univ. *(see Univ. of Alberta)*
Albertson Coll. of Idaho 782 *(see also Coll. of Idaho)*
Albertus Magnus Coll. 78
Albion Coll. 207
Albion Female Collegiate Inst. *(see Albion Coll.)*
Albizu Univ—Miami Campus *(see Carlos Albizu Univ—Miami Campus)*
Albizu Univ—San Juan Campus *(see Carlos Albizu Univ—San Juan Campus)*
Albright Art Sch. *(see State Univ. of New York at Buffalo)*
Albright Coll. 343
Albuquerque Area Indian Health Service 722
Albuquerque Barber Coll. 584
Albuquerque Public Schools Career Enrichment Ctr. 722
Albuquerque Tech. Inst. *(see Central New Mexico Comm. Coll.)*
Albuquerque Tech. Vocational Inst. 788 *(see also Central New Mexico Comm. Coll.)*
Albuquerque TVI Coll. *(see Central New Mexico Comm. Coll.)*
Albuquerque TVI Comm. Coll. *(see Central New Mexico Comm. Coll.)*
Albuquerque VA Med. Ctr. *(see Raymond G. Murphy Veterans Affairs Med. Ctr.)*
Albuquerque VAMC *(see Raymond G. Murphy Veterans Affairs Med. Ctr.)*
Albuquerque Veterans Affairs Med. Ctr. *(see Raymond G. Murphy Veterans Affairs Med. Ctr.)*
Alcorn A&M Coll. *(see Alcorn State Univ.)*
Alcorn Agricultural & Mechanical Coll. *(see Alcorn State Univ.)*
Alcorn State Univ. 230
Alcorn Univ. *(see Alcorn State Univ.)*
Alden's Cosmetology Sch. *(see Alden's Sch. of Cosmetology)*
Alden's Sch. of Cosmetology 539
Alderson Acad. & Jr. Coll. *(see Alderson-Broaddus Coll.)*
Alderson-Broaddus Coll. 440
Alegent Health Bergan Mercy Med. Ctr. 719
Alegent Health Immanuel Med. Ctr. 570
Alegent Health Sch. of Med. Assisiting *(see Alegent Health Immanuel Med. Ctr.)*
Alexander Acad. 815
Alexander City State Jr. Coll. *(see Central Alabama Comm. Coll.)*
Alexander Inst. *(see Lon Morris Coll.)*
Alexandria Acad. of Beauty 539
Alexandria Coll. *(see Alexandria Tech. Coll.)*
Alexandria Sch. of Scientific Therapeutics, Inc. 530
Alexandria Tech. Coll. 219
Alexandria VA Med. Ctr. *(see Alexandria Veterans Affairs Med. Ctr.)*
Alexandria VAMC *(see Alexandria Veterans Affairs Med. Ctr.)*
Alexandria Veterans Affairs Med. Ctr. 709
Alexian Brothers Health Sys. 701
Alexian Brothers Med. Ctr. 701
Alexian Village of Milwaukee 753
Alfred Adler Grad. Sch. *(see Adler Grad. Sch.)*
Alfred Adler Inst. of Chicago *(see Adler Sch. of Prof. Psychology)*
Alfred Adler Inst. of Minnesota *(see Adler Grad. Sch.)*
Alfred Coll. of Techno. *(see State Univ. of New York Coll. of Techno. at Alfred)*
Alfred I. duPont Hosp. for Children 694
Alfred I. duPont Inst. of the Nemeurs Foundation *(see Alfred I. duPont Hosp. for Children)*
Alfred Select Sch. *(see Alfred Univ.)*
Alfred State Coll. *(see State Univ. of New York Coll. of Techno. at Alfred)*
Alfred Univ. 269
Alfred Univ—New York State Coll. of Ceramics *(see New York State Coll. of Ceramics at Alfred Univ.)*
Algonquin Coll. 757
Algonquin Coll. of Applied Arts & Techno. *(see Algonquin Coll.)*
Alhambra Beauty Coll. 472
Alice Lloyd Coll. 170
All American Career Coll. 472
All Saints Healthcare Sys. *(see All Saints Healthcar—St. Mary's Campus)*
All Saints Healthcar—St. Mary's Campus 753
Allan Hancock Coll. 31
Allegany Coll. of Maryland 189
Allegany Comm. Coll. *(see Allegany Coll. of Maryland)*
Allegheny Coll. 343
Allegheny County Comm. Coll. Allegheny Campus *(see Comm. Coll. of Allegheny County)*
Allegheny County Comm. Coll. Boyce Campus *(see Comm. Coll. of Allegheny County)*
Allegheny County Comm. Coll. North Campus *(see Comm. Coll. of Allegheny County)*
Allegheny County Comm. Coll. South Campus *(see Comm. Coll. of Allegheny County)*
Allegheny General Hosp. 737
Allegheny Valley Hosp. *(see La Roche Coll.)*
Allegheny Wesleyan Coll. 313
Allegro Music Coll. 631
Alle-Kiski Med. Ctr. *(see Citizens Sch. of Nursing)*
Allen Coll. 157
Allen Coll. of Nursing *(see Allen Coll.)*
Allen County Comm. Coll. 164
Allen Health Systems, Inc. *(see Allen Coll.)*
Allen Mem. Hosp. Sch. of Nursing *(see Allen Coll.)*
Allen Mem. Sch. of Practical Nursing *(see Vermont Tech. Coll.)*
Allen Sch. 586
Allen Univ. 373
Allendale Assoc. 701
Allentown Bus. Sch. 791 *(see also Lehigh Valley Coll.)*
Allentown Coll. of St. Francis De Sales *(see DeSales Univ.)*
Allentown Sch. of Cosmetology, Inc. 791 *(see also Vision Acad—A Paul Mitchell Partner Sch.)*
Alliance Career Centre *(see Alliance City Schools Career Centre)*
Alliance City Schools Career Centre 604
Alliance Coll. *(see Ambrose Univ. Coll.)*
Alliance Sch. of Theology & Missions *(see Alliance Theological Sem.)*
Alliance Sem. *(see Alliance Theological Sem.)*
Alliance Theological Sem. 269 *(see also Nyack Coll.)*
Alliance Univ. Coll. 797 *(see also Ambrose Univ. Coll.)*

Alliant Int'l. Univ—Cornerstone Court Campus 776
Alliant Int'l. Univ—Cornerstone Court Campus 776
Alliant Int'l. Univ—Fresno 31
Alliant Int'l. Univ—Irvine 31
Alliant Int'l. Univ—Los Angeles 31
Alliant Int'l. Univ—Mexico City 459
Alliant Int'l. Univ—Nairobi *(see United States Int'l. Univ—Africa)*
Alliant Int'l. Univ—San Diego Cornerstone Court 31
Alliant Int'l. Univ—San Diego Scripps Ranch 32
Alliant Int'l. Univ—San Francisco Bay 32
Alliant Univ—Fresno *(see Alliant Int'l. Univ—Fresno)*
Alliant Univ—Los Angeles *(see Alliant Int'l. Univ—Los Angeles)*
Alliant Univ—San Diego 776 *(see also Alliant Int'l. Univ—San Diego Cornerstone Court)*
Alliant Univ—San Francisco Bay *(see Alliant Int'l. Univ—San Francisco Bay)*
Allied American Univ. 32
Allied Bus. Schools, Inc. 473 *(see also Allied American Univ.)*
Allied Career Ctr. 647
Allied Coll. 235
Allied Health & Nursing Edu. Ctr. *(see Ctr. for Allied Health & Nursing Edu.)*
Allied Health Careers 647
Allied Health Coll. of Arizona *(see Arizona Coll. of Allied Health)*
Allied Med. & Tech. Careers *(see Allied Med. & Tech. Inst.)*
Allied Med. & Tech. Careers 787, 791
Allied Med. & Tech. Inst. 343, 574, 623, 787
Allied Med. Careers *(see Allied Med. & Tech. Inst.)*
Allied Med. Coll. *(see Allied Coll.)*
Allied Schools 473
Allied Univ. *(see Allied American Univ.)*
Allina Clinical Pastoral Edu. Ctr. *(see Allina Hospitals & Clinics)*
Allina Health Sys. *(see Abbott Northwestern Hosp/Children's Hospitals & Clinics; Allina Hospitals & Clinics; United Hosp/ Children's Hosp. & Clinic; Unity Hosp.)*
Allina Hospitals & Clinics 715
All-State Career Sch. 623
Allstate Vocational Training *(see Northwestern Technological Inst.)*
Allure Sch. of Cosmetology 815
Alma Coll. 207
Al-Med Acad. *(see Allied Coll.)*
Alpena Coll. *(see Alpena Comm. Coll.)*
Alpena Comm. Coll. 207
Alpine Coll. 668
ALPS Educational Services, Inc. *(see ALPS Language Sch.)*
ALPS Language Sch. 668
Alta Bates Med. Ctr. *(see Alta Bates Summit Med. Ctr.)*
Alta Bates Summit Med. Ctr. 685
Altamaha Coll. *(see Altamaha Tech. Coll.)*
Altamaha Tech. Coll. 108
Altamaha Tech. Inst. *(see Altamaha Tech. Coll.)*
Alternative Conjunction Clinic & Sch. of Massage Therapy, The 623
Alton Ochsner Med. Foundation *(see Ochsner Sch. of Allied Health Sciences; Our Lady of Holy Cross Coll.)*
Altoona Beauty Sch., Inc. 623
Altoona Career & Techno. Ctr. *(see Greater Altoona Career & Techno. Ctr.)*
Altoona Sch. of Commerce *(see South Hills Sch. of Bus. & Techno.)*
Altru Hosp. 731
Altus Jr. Coll. *(see Western Oklahoma State Coll.)*
Alvareita's Coll. of Cosmetology 524
Alvareita's Coll. of Cosmetolog—Godfrey Campus 524
Alvernia Coll. *(see Alvernia Univ.)*
Alvernia Univ. 343
Alverno Coll. 445
Alverno Teachers Coll. *(see Alverno Coll.)*
Alvin Ailey American Dance Ctr., The 586
Alvin Coll. *(see Alvin Comm. Coll.)*
Alvin Comm. Coll. 392
Alvin Jr. Coll. *(see Alvin Comm. Coll.)*
Amarillo Coll. 392
Amarillo Coll. of Hairdressing, Inc. 793 *(see also Milan Inst. of Cosmetology)*
Amarillo Jr. Coll. *(see Amarillo Coll.)*
Amarillo Tech. Ctr. 392 *(see also Amarillo Coll.)*
Amarillo VA Health Care Sys. *(see Thomas E. Creek Veterans Affairs Med. Ctr.)*
Amarillo Veterans Affairs Health Care Sys. *(see Thomas E. Creek Veterans Affairs Med. Ctr.)*
Ambassador Inst. of Travel 793
Amber Univ. *(see Amberton Univ.)*
Amberton Univ. 392
Ambler Beauty Acad., Inc. 791 *(see also Magnolia Sch.)*
Ambrose Univ. *(see Ambrose Univ. Coll.)*
Ambrose Univ. Coll. 454, 797
AMEDD Acad. of Health Sciences *(see United States Army Med. Dept. Ctr. & Sch.)*
AMEDD Ctr. & Sch. *(see United States Army Med. Dept. Ctr. & Sch.)*
AMEDD Ctr. & Sch. DPMT *(see United States AMEDD Ctr. & Sch. Dept. of Pastoral Ministry Training)*
American Acad. McAllister Inst. of Funeral Service, Inc. 269
American Acad. of Acupuncture & Oriental Medicine 219
American Acad. of Acupuncture & Traditional Chinese Medicine *(see American Coll. of Acupuncture & Oriental Medicine)*
American Acad. of Art 127
American Acad. of Cosmetology 779, 811 *(see also Paul Mitchell the Sch—Danbury)*
American Acad. of Dramatic Arts 269
American Acad. of Dramatic Arts Los Angeles 685, 776
American Acad. of Dramatic Arts West 776
American Acad. of English 473
American Acad. of Hair Design 534
American Acad. of Music & Drama *(see American Musical & Dramatic Acad.)*
American Acad. of Nutrition 793 *(see also Huntington Coll. of Health Sciences)*
American Acupuncture & Oriental Medicine Acad. *(see American Acad. of Acupuncture & Oriental Medicine)*
American Advanced Technicians Inst. Corporation 504
American Art Acad. *(see American Acad. of Art)*
American Auto Inst. 473
American Ballet Ctr/Joffrey Ballet Sch. 586
American Baptist Coll. 382
American Baptist Coll. of the Bible *(see American Baptist Coll.)*
American Baptist Sem. of the West 32
American Barber Inst. 788 *(see also A.B.I. Sch. of Barbering & Cosmetology)*
American Beauty Acad. 546 *(see also Magnolia Sch.)*
American Beauty Acad., Inc. 627
American Beauty Acad., LLC 820
American Beauty Coll. 473, 820
American Beauty Inst. 614 *(see also American Inst. of Beauty, Inc)*
American Beauty Sch. 586
American Broadcasting Sch. 614

Antonelli Inst. of Art & Photography *(see Antonelli Coll.)*
Antonelli Med. & Prof. Inst. 623
Apex Acad. of Hair Design 530, 782
Apex Sch. of Beauty Culture 782 *(see also Apex Acad. of Hair Design)*
Apex Sch. of Theology 299
Apex Tech. Sch. 586
Apex Theology Sch. *(see Apex Sch. of Theology)*
APLUS Inst. of Techno., Healthcare & Bus. 757
Apollo Career Ctr. 604 *(see also Lima Sch. of Med. Massage)*
Apollo Coll. of Med. & Dental Assistants *(see Apollo Coll—Tri-City)*
Apollo Coll. of Med.-Dental Careers *(see Apollo Coll—Portland)*
Apollo Coll—Boise 125, 782
Apollo Coll—Boise 782
Apollo Coll—Mesa *(see Apollo Coll—Tri-City)*
Apollo Coll—Phoenix Campus 15
Apollo Coll.-Portland 337
App State *(see Appalachian State Univ.)*
Appalachia Univ. Coll. of Pharmacy *(see Univ. of Appalachia Coll. of Pharmacy)*
Appalachian Beauty Sch. 536
Appalachian Bible Coll. 440
Appalachian Coll. *(see Appalachian Bible Coll.; Appalachian Tech. Coll.)*
Appalachian Sch. of Law 420
Appalachian State Teachers' Coll. *(see Appalachian State Univ.)*
Appalachian State Univ. 299
Appalachian Tech. Coll. 109, 802
Appalachian Tech. Inst. *(see Appalachian Tech. Coll.)*
Appalachian Training Sch. for Teachers *(see Appalachian State Univ.)*
Applewood Ctr.s, Inc. 732
Applied Career Training, Inc. 795 *(see also ACT Coll.)*
Applied Career Training, Inc—Alexandria Campus *(see ACT Coll—Alexandria)*
Applied Prof. Training, Inc. 33
Appling Tech. Edu. Ctr. 108
Appraisal & Property Mgmnt. Coll. *(see National Coll. of Appraisal & Property Mgmnt.)*
Apprentice Sch—Newport News Shipbuilding *(see Northrop Grumman Newport News Apprentice Sch.)*
APUS Ctr. for Prof. & Workforce Development 672
Aquinas Coll. 207, 382 *(see also Saint Thomas Aquinas Coll.; Thomas Aquinas Coll.)*
Aquinas Inst. of Philosophy & Theology *(see Aquinas Inst. of Theology)*
Aquinas Inst. of Theology 235
Aquinas Jr. Coll. *(see Aquinas Coll.)*
Aquinas Theology Inst. *(see Aquinas Inst. of Theology)*
ARAMARK Healthcare Kansas City Dietetic Internship Program *(see Saint Joseph Med. Ctr.)*
ARAMARK Healthcare Metropolitan New York Dietetic Internship Program 723
ARAMARK Healthcare Mid-Atlantic Dietetic Internship Program 737
Aran Eye Associates *(see Nova Southeastern Univ.)*
Arapahoe Coll. *(see Arapahoe Comm. Coll.)*
Arapahoe Comm. Coll. 69 *(see also HealthONE Emergency Med. Services)*
Arapahoe Jr. Coll. *(see Arapahoe Comm. Coll.)*
Arcadia Univ. 343
Architectural Ctr. of Boston *(see Boston Architectural Coll.)*
Architecture Inst. of Southern California *(see Southern California Inst. of Architecture)*
Arctic Sivunmun Ilisagvik Coll. *(see Ilisagvik Coll.)*
Ardmore Int'l. Coll. of Beauty 614 *(see also American Beauty Inst.)*
Area One Vocational-Tech. Sch. *(see Northeast Iowa Comm. Coll.)*
Area Vocational Sch. for Alachua County *(see Santa Fe Comm. Coll.)*
Argentina Bus. Univ. *(see Universidad Argentina de la Empresa)*
Argosy Atlanta *(see Argosy Univ. Atlanta)*
Argosy Univ. 779, 782, 795
Argosy Univ. Atlanta 109, 781
Argosy Univ. Chicago 127
Argosy Univ. Chicago Northwest 782 *(see also Argosy Univ. Schaumburg)*
Argosy Univ. Coll. of Health Sciences *(see Argosy Univ. Twin Cities)*
Argosy Univ. Dallas 393
Argosy Univ. Denver 69
Argosy Univ. Hawai'i 123, 782
Argosy Univ. Honolulu 782 *(see also Argosy Univ. Hawai'i)*
Argosy Univ. Los Angeles *(see Argosy Univ. Orange County)*
Argosy Univ. Orange County 33, 776
Argosy Univ. Phoenix 15
Argosy Univ. San Diego 776
Argosy Univ. San Francisco Bay Area 33
Argosy Univ. Santa Monica 776 *(see also Argosy Univ. Los Angeles)*
Argosy Univ. Sarasota 89
Argosy Univ. Schaumburg 127 782
Argosy Univ. Seattle 432
Argosy Univ. Tampa 89
Argosy Univ. Twin Cities 219, 786
Argosy Univ. Washington, DC 420, 795
Argosy Univ—Denver 779 *(see also Argosy Univ. Denver)*
Argyle Inst. of Human Relations 757
Ari-Ben Aviator 504
Arizona Acad. of Beauty, Inc. 466
Arizona Acad. of Beaut—North Inc. 466
Arizona Acupunture & Oriental Medicine Sch. *(see Arizona Sch. of Acupunture & Oriental Medicine)*
Arizona Automotive Inst. 15
Arizona Coll. *(see Arizona Coll. of Allied Health)*
Arizona Coll. of Allied Health 466
Arizona Coll. of Osteopathic Medicine *(see Midwestern Univ.)*
Arizona Dept. of Health Services *(see Arizona State Hosp.)*
Arizona Dietetic Practicum Advisory Committee *(see Maricopa County Dept. of Public Health; Phoenix Indian Med. Ctr.)*
Arizona Golf Acad. *(see Golf Acad. of America; Virginia Coll.)*
Arizona Health & Techno. Park *(see A.T. Still Univ—Mesa Campus)*
Arizona Inst. of Bus. & Techno. *(see IIA Coll.)*
Arizona Int'l. Campus of The Univ. of Arizona *(see Arizona Int'l. Coll.)*
Arizona Int'l. Coll. 23
Arizona Int'l. Univ. *(see Arizona Int'l. Coll.)*
Arizona Sch. of Acupunture & Oriental Medicine 15
Arizona Sch. of Dentistry & Oral Health *(see A.T. Still Univ—Mesa Campus)*
Arizona Sch. of Health Sciences *(see A.T. Still Univ. of Health Sciences; A.T. Still Univ—Mesa Campus)*
Arizona Sch. of Osteopathic Medicine *(see A.T. Still Univ—Mesa Campus)*
Arizona Sch. of Pharmacy Techno. *(see Arizona Coll. of Allied Health)*
Arizona Sch. of Prof. Psychology *(see Argosy Univ. Phoenix)*
Arizona State Coll. at Flagstaff *(see Northern Arizona Univ.)*
Arizona State Coll. at Tempe *(see Arizona State Univ.)*
Arizona State Hosp. 683
Arizona State Teachers Coll. at Tempe *(see Arizona State Univ.)*

Austin Schools of Massage 819
Austin Sem. *(see Austin Presbyterian Theological Sem.)*
Austin State Univ. *(see Stephen F. Austin State Univ.)*
Austin Theology Sch. *(see Austin Grad. Sch. of Theology)*
Austin's Sch. of Spa Techno. 586, 788
Austral Univ. *(see IAE Universidad Austral)*
Australasian Coll. of Health Sciences 337, 620
Australasian Coll. of Herbal Sciences *(see Australasian Coll. of Health Sciences)*
Australasian Coll. of Herbal Studies *(see Australasian Coll. of Health Sciences)*
Australasian Herbal Studies Coll. *(see Australasian Coll. of Health Sciences)*
Australian Grad. Sch. of Mgmnt. 756 *(see also Univ. of New South Wales)*
Auto Diesel Coll. of Nashville *(see Nashville Auto Diesel Coll.)*
Automeca Tech. Coll. 631
Automeca Tech. Coll—Ponce 632
Automotive Inst. of Arizona *(see Arizona Automotive Inst.)*
Automotive Machinists Sch. *(see Sch. of Automotive Machinists)*
Automotive Mgmnt. Coll. *(see Coll. of Automotive Mgmnt.)*
Automotive Training Ctr. 623
Autonomous Tech. Inst. of Mexico 767
Autry Area Vocational-Tech. Ctr. *(see Autry Techno. Ctr.)*
Autry Tech *(see Autry Techno. Ctr.)*
Autry Techno. Ctr. 614
Avalon Beauty Coll. 474
Avance Beauty Coll. 474
Ave Maria Coll. 785
Ave Maria Coll. of the Americas 90
Ave Maria Sch. of Law 207
Ave Maria Univ. 90
Aveda DC Inst. *(see Aveda Inst. Washington DC)*
Aveda Fredric's Inst. 604
Aveda Inst. 505, 539 *(see also Carsten Inst.; Douglas J Aveda Inst.)*
Aveda Inst. Baton Rouge 539, 784
Aveda Inst. de Bellas Artes *(see New Mexico Aveda Inst. de Bellas Artes)*
Aveda Inst. Denver 810
Aveda Inst. Lafayette 539, 784
Aveda Inst. Las Vegas *(see Casal Inst. of Las Vegas)*
Aveda Inst. Nevada *(see Casal Inst. of Las Vegas)*
Aveda Inst. New York 816
Aveda Inst. San Antonio 819
Aveda Inst. Vegas *(see Casal Inst. of Las Vegas)*
Aveda Inst. Washington DC 811
Aveda Inst., Inc. 561
Aveda Sch. *(see Carsten Inst. New York)*
Avera Health 744
Avera Health ACPE Ctr. *(see Avera Health)*
Avera McKennan Hosp. & Univ. Health Ctr. 744
Avera Sacred Heart Hosp. 744
Averett Coll. *(see Averett Univ.)*
Averett Univ. 420
Aviation & Electronic Sch. of America 34
Aviation Inst. of Maint. 146, 517, 566, 623, 793
Aviation Inst. of Maint. Training Acad. *(see Aviation Inst. of Maint.)*
Aviation Inst. of Maint—Dallas 648, 793
Aviation Inst. of Maint—Indianapolis *(see Aviation Inst. of Maint.)*
Aviation Maint. Campus *(see Tennessee Techno. Ctr. at Memphis)*
Aviation Maint. Training, Inc. *(see Aviation Inst. of Maint—Dallas)*
Aviation Techno. Division *(see Hallmark Inst. of Aeronautics)*
Avila Coll. *(see Avila Univ.)*
Avila Univ. 235
Avtech Inst. of Techno. 574
Avtech Techno. Inc. *(see Avtech Inst. of Techno.)*
Award Beauty Sch., Inc. 546
Awesome Kneading Sch. *(see AKS Massage Sch.)*
Axia Coll. *(see Univ. of Phoenix)*
Axia Coll. of Univ. of Phoenix 23
Axia Univ. *(see Axia Coll. of Univ. of Phoenix)*
Ayers Career Coll. 539, 784
Ayers Inst. 784 *(see also Ayers Career Coll.)*
Ayers Sch. of Bus., Inc. *(see Ayers Career Coll.)*
Azusa Coll. *(see Azusa Pacific Univ.)*
Azusa Pacific Univ. 34

B

B Beautiful Hair Inst. 810
B Naturale Beauty Sch. 780
B Naturale Beauty Sch., Inc. 505
B. Dickson & Associates, LLC 779 *(see also Dale Carnegie Training of Western Connecticut)*
B.J.'s Beauty & Barber Coll. 668
B.M. Spurr Sch. of Practical Nursing 753
Babcock Grad. Sch. of Mgmnt. *(see Wake Forest Univ.)*
Babel Univ. 458, 678
Babel Univ. Hawaii *(see Babel Univ. Prof. Sch. of Translation)*
Babel Univ. Prof. Sch. of Translation 123 *(see also Babel Univ.)*
Babel Univ. PST *(see Babel Univ. Prof. Sch. of Translation)*
Babson Coll. 196
Babson Inst. *(see Babson Coll.)*
Bacone Coll. 331
Bahner Coll. of Hairstyling 787 *(see also La' James Int'l. Coll.)*
Bailey Tech. Sch., Inc. *(see ITT Tech. Inst.)*
Bainbridge Coll. 110
Bais Binyomin Acad. 78, 779
Bais Medrash Toras Chesed 805
Baker Aviation Sch. *(see George T. Baker Aviation Sch.)*
Baker Coll. Bus. & Corporate Services 207
Baker Coll. Ctr. for Grad. Studies 207
Baker Coll. Corporate Services *(see Baker Coll. Bus. & Corporate Services)*
Baker Coll. of Allen Park 207
Baker Coll. of Auburn Hills 207
Baker Coll. of Cadillac 208
Baker Coll. of Clinton Township 208
Baker Coll. of Flint 208
Baker Coll. of Jackson 208
Baker Coll. of Mount Clemens *(see Baker Coll. of Clinton Township)*
Baker Coll. of Muskegon 208
Baker Coll. of Owosso 208
Baker Coll. of Port Huron 208
Baker Coll. Online 208
Baker Sch. of Aviation *(see George T. Baker Aviation Sch.; Baker Univ—Sch. of Nursing)*
Baker Sch. of Prof. & Grad. Studies *(see Baker Univ.)*
Baker Univ. 164
Bakersfield Coll. 34
Baking Inst. of America *(see American Inst. of Baking)*
Bakke Grad. Univ. 432
Bakke Grad. Univ. of Ministry *(see Bakke Grad. Univ.)*
Bakke Univ. *(see Bakke Grad. Univ.)*
Baldwin Agricultural Coll. *(see Abraham Baldwin Agricultural Coll.)*
Baldwin Beauty Sch. 649
Baldwin Coll. *(see Mary Baldwin Coll.)*
Baldwin Inst. *(see Baldwin-Wallace Coll.)*
Baldwin Sch. *(see Macalester Coll.)*
Baldwin Univ. *(see Baldwin-Wallace Coll.; Macalester Coll.)*
Baldwin-Wallace Coll. 314

Ball Mem. Hosp. 704
Ball State Univ. 146
Ballet Acad. of Idaho *(see Ballet Idaho Acad.)*
Ballet Idaho Acad. 523
Ballet Sch. of the Pacific Northwest *(see Pacific Northwest Ballet Sch.)*
Baltimore City Coll. *(see Baltimore City Comm. Coll.)*
Baltimore City Comm. Coll. 189
Baltimore City Hosp. *(see Mercy Med. Ctr.)*
Baltimore Coll. *(see Baltimore Int'l. Coll.)*
Baltimore County Comm. Coll. *(see Comm. Coll. of Baltimore County)*
Baltimore Hebrew Univ. 189
Baltimore Infirmary *(see Univ. of Maryland Med. Ctr.)*
Baltimore Int'l. Coll. 189
Baltimore Int'l. Culinary Coll. *(see Baltimore Int'l. Coll.)*
Baltimore Jr. Coll. *(see Baltimore City Comm. Coll.)*
Baltimore Massage Sch. *(see Baltimore Sch. of Massage)*
Baltimore Med. Coll. *(see Maryland General Hosp.)*
Baltimore Normal Sch. *(see Bowie State Univ.)*
Baltimore Sch. of Hair Design *(see Baltimore Studio of Hair Design, Inc.)*
Baltimore Sch. of Massage, The 546
Baltimore Studio of Hair Design, Inc. 546
Baltimore Univ. *(see Univ. of Baltimore)*
Baltimore VAMC *(see Baltimore Veterans Affairs Med. Ctr.)*
Baltimore Veterans Affairs Med. Ctr. 710
Bamberg Job Corps Ctr. 638
Bancroft Health Ctr. *(see Bancroft Sch. of Massage Therapy)*
Bancroft Massage Therapy Sch. *(see Bancroft Sch. of Massage Therapy)*
Bancroft Sch. of Massage Therapy 550
Bangor Comm. Coll. *(see Univ. of Maine at Augusta)*
Bangor Sem. *(see Bangor Theological Sem.)*
Bangor Theological Sem. 186
Bank Street Coll. of Edu. 270
Banking & Commerce Inst. *(see Instituto de Banca y Comercio)*
Banner Coll. 795
Banner Coll., The 664
Banner Desert Med. Ctr. 684
Banner Good Samaritan Med. Ctr. 684
Banner Health *(see Banner Desert Med. Ctr.; Banner Good Samaritan Med. Ctr.)*
Banner Inst. 782
Baptist Bible Coll. 235
Baptist Bible Coll. & Grad. Sch. of Theology *(see Baptist Bible Coll.)*
Baptist Bible Coll. & Sem. 343
Baptist Bible Coll. East *(see Boston Baptist Coll.)*
Baptist Bible Coll. of Indianapolis *(see Crossroads Bible Coll.)*
Baptist Bible Coll. of Pennsylvania *(see Baptist Bible Coll. & Sem.)*
Baptist Bible Grad. Sch. of Theology *(see Baptist Bible Coll.)*
Baptist Bible Inst. *(see Baptist Coll. of Florida; New Orleans Baptist Theological Sem.)*
Baptist Bible Inst. of Grand Rapids *(see Cornerstone Univ.)*
Baptist Bible Sem. *(see Baptist Bible Coll. & Sem.)*
Baptist Coll. & Sem. of Washington *(see Washington Baptist Univ.)*
Baptist Coll. at McMinnville *(see Linfield Coll.)*
Baptist Coll. of Arkansas *(see Arkansas Baptist Coll.)*
Baptist Coll. of Florida, The 90
Baptist Coll. of Health Sciences *(see Baptist Mem. Coll. of Health Sciences)*
Baptist Coll. of Hillsdale *(see Hillsdale Free Will Baptist Coll.)*
Baptist Coll. of Houston *(see Houston Baptist Univ.)*
Baptist Coll. of Missouri *(see Missouri Baptist Univ.)*
Baptist Downtown *(see Baptist Med. Ctr. Downtown)*
Baptist Health *(see Baptist Med. Ctr. Downtown; Baptist Med. Ctr. South Sch. of Med. Techno.)*
Baptist Health Care *(see Baptist Hosp.)*
Baptist Health Med. Ctr—Little Rock *(see Baptist Health Sys., Nursing & Allied Health Schools)*
Baptist Health Schools Little Rock *(see Baptist Health Sys., Nursing & Allied Health Schools)*
Baptist Health Sys. *(see Baptist Med. Ctr.)*
Baptist Health Sys. Dietetic Internship *(see Baptist Med. Ctr.)*
Baptist Health Sys. of Alabama 683
Baptist Health Sys. Sch. of Health Professions 394
Baptist Health Sys. Sch. of Nursing *(see Baptist Health Sys. Sch. of Health Professions)*
Baptist Health Sys., Nursing & Allied Health Schools 685
Baptist Health Systems *(see Mississippi Baptist Med. Ctr.)*
Baptist Healthcare Sys. of South Carolina *(see Palmetto Richland Mem. Hosp.)*
Baptist Hosp. 695
Baptist Hosp. East 708
Baptist Hosp. of New England *(see New England Baptist Hosp.)*
Baptist Inst., The *(see Arkansas Baptist Coll.)*
Baptist Med. Ctr. 745 *(see also Mississippi Baptist Med. Ctr.)*
Baptist Med. Ctr. Downtown 695
Baptist Med. Ctr. South Sch. of Med. Techno. 683
Baptist Mem. Coll. of Health Sciences 382
Baptist Mem. Hosp. *(see Baptist Mem. Coll. of Health Sciences)*
Baptist Missionary Assoc. Theological Sem. 394, 807
Baptist Missionary Training Sch. *(see Colgate Rochester Crozer Divinity Sch.)*
Baptist Sem. of North America *(see Sioux Falls Sem.)*
Baptist Sem. of the Northwest *(see Northwest Baptist Sem.)*
Baptist Theological Sem. at Richmond 420
Baptist Theological Sem. of New Orleans *(see New Orleans Baptist Theological Sem.)*
Baptist Univ. of California *(see California Baptist Univ.)*
Baptist Univ. of Dallas *(see Dallas Baptist Univ.)*
Baptist Univ. of Houston *(see Houston Baptist Univ.)*
Baptist Univ. of Missouri *(see Missouri Baptist Univ.)*
Baptist Univ. of the Americas 394
Baran Inst. of Techno. 497, 779
Baran Techno. Inst. *(see Baran Inst. of Techno.)*
Barat Coll. of DePaul Univ. 782 *(see also American Coll. of Edu.)*
Barber Acad. of Bradenton *(see Bradenton Beauty & Barber Acad., Inc.)*
Barber Acad. of Florida *(see Florida Barber Acad.)*
Barber Coll. of Albuquerque *(see Albuquerque Barber Coll.)*
Barber Coll. of Puerto Rico *(see Puerto Rico Barber Coll.)*
Barber Coll. of South Texas *(see South Texas Barber Coll.)*
Barber Coll. of West Michigan *(see West Michigan Coll. of Barbering & Beauty)*

Bellingham Vocational Tech. Inst. *(see Bellingham Tech. Coll.)*
Bellport Academic Ctr. *(see Eastern Suffolk Sch. for Practical Nursing)*
Belmont Abbey Coll. 299
Belmont Coll. *(see Belmont Tech. Coll.; Belmont Univ.)*
Belmont Tech. Coll. 314
Belmont Tech. Inst. *(see Belmont Tech. Coll.)*
Belmont Univ. 382
Beloit Coll. 445
Bel-Rea Inst. of Animal Techno. 69
Bemidji Area Vocational Tech. Inst. *(see Northwest Coll.)*
Bemidji State Univ. 219
Bemidji Univ. *(see Bemidji State Univ.)*
Ben Franklin Career & Techno. Ctr. *(see Ben Franklin Career Ctr.)*
Ben Franklin Career Ctr. 672
Ben Hill-Irwin Area Vocational Inst. *(see East Central Tech. Coll.)*
Ben Hill-Irwin Tech *(see East Central Tech. Coll.)*
Ben Hill-Irwin Vocational-Tech. Ctr. *(see East Central Tech. Coll.)*
Ben Hill-Irwin Vo-Tech Ctr. *(see East Central Tech. Coll.)*
Ben Stevenson Acad. of Ballet *(see Houston Ballet's Ben Stevenson Acad.)*
Ben Taub General Hosp. 746
Benedict Coll. 373 *(see also Tech. Coll. of the Lowcountry)*
Benedict Inst. *(see Benedict Coll.)*
Benedictine Coll. 164 *(see also Benedictine Univ.)*
Benedictine Health Sys. *(see City of Lakes Transitional Care Ctr.)*
Benedictine Univ. 127
Benedictine Univ. Springfield Coll. of Illinois *(see Springfield Coll. in Illinois)*
Benefis Healthcare Sch. of Radiologic Techno. *(see Benefis Healthcar—West Campus)*
Bene's Int'l. Sch. of Beauty 780
Bene's Int'l. Sch. of Beauty, Inc. 505
Benjamin Franklin Career & Techno. Ctr. *(see Ben Franklin Career Ctr.)*
Benjamin Franklin Career Ctr. *(see Ben Franklin Career Ctr.)*
Benjamin Franklin Inst. of Techno. 196
Benjamin Franklin Techno. Inst. *(see Benjamin Franklin Inst. of Techno.)*
Benjamin P. Cheney Acad. *(see Eastern Washington Univ.)*
Bennett Beauty Inst., Inc. 780 *(see also Bennett Career Inst., Inc.)*
Bennett Career Inst., Inc. 502, 780
Bennett Coll. for Women 299
Bennett-Clarkson Hosp. *(see Rapid City Reg. Hosp.)*
Bennington Coll. 417
Bentley Coll. 785 *(see also Bentley Univ.)*
Bentley Univ. 197, 785
Benton Harbor Comm. Coll. & Tech. Inst. *(see Lake Michigan Coll.)*
Benton Harbor Jr. Coll. *(see Lake Michigan Coll.)*
Berdan Inst. 574
Berdan Sch. for Med. Secretaries *(see Berdan Inst.)*
Berea Coll. 170
Berean Baptist Inst. *(see Virginia Baptist Coll.)*
Berean Sch. of the Bible *(see Global Univ.)*
Berean Univ. *(see Global Univ.)*
Bergan Mercy Med. Ctr. *(see Alegent Health Bergan Mercy Med. Ctr.)*
Bergen Coll. *(see Bergen Comm. Coll.)*
Bergen Comm. Coll. 259
Bergen County Academies *(see Bergen County Tech. Schools)*
Bergen County One-Stop Career Ctr. *(see Bergen County Tech. Schools)*
Bergen County Tech. Schools 574
Berk Trade & Bus. Sch. 587
Berkeley Baptist Divinity Sch. *(see American Baptist Sem. of the West)*
Berkeley City Coll. 34, 778
Berkeley Coll. of Acupuncture & Integrative Medicine *(see Acupuncture & Integrative Medicine Coll., Berkeley)*
Berkeley Coll. of Bus. *(see Berkeley Coll—Garret Mountain)*
Berkeley Coll. of New York City 270
Berkeley Coll.-Garret Mountain 259
Berkeley Coll—Middlesex Campus *(see Berkeley Coll—Woodbridge Campus)*
Berkeley Divinity Sch. 78
Berkeley Divinity Sch. at Yale *(see Berkeley Divinity Sch.)*
Berkeley Learning Pavilion *(see Berkeley City Coll.)*
Berkeley Sch. of New York, The *(see Berkeley Coll. of New York City)*
Berkeley Univ. *(see Univ. of California, Berkeley)*
Berkeley-Charleston-Dorchester Tech. Edu. Ctr. *(see Trident Tech. Coll.)*
Berklee Coll. of Music 197
Berklee Music Coll. *(see Berklee Coll. of Music)*
Berklee Sch. of Music *(see Berklee Coll. of Music)*
Berks Tech. Inst. 343
Berkshire Coll. *(see Berkshire Comm. Coll.)*
Berkshire Comm. Coll. 197
Berkshire Health Systems *(see Berkshire Med. Ctr.)*
Berkshire Med. Ctr. 712
Berlitz Int'l., Inc. 574–576
Berlitz Language Ctr.s *(see Berlitz Int'l., Inc.)*
Bermuda Coll. 808
Bermuda Hotel & Catering Coll. *(see Bermuda Coll.)*
Bermuda Tech. Inst. *(see Bermuda Coll.)*
Bernard M. Baruch Coll. *(see Baruch Coll.)*
Bernard's Sch. of Hair Fashion *(see Mr. Bernard's Sch. of Hair Fashion, Inc.)*
Berry Coll. 110
Berry Jr. Coll. *(see Berry Coll.)*
Bessemer State Tech. Coll. 775 *(see also T.A. Lawson State Comm. Coll.)*
Bessemer State Tech. Inst. *(see T.A. Lawson State Comm. Coll.)*
Beta Tech 638, 793, 795 *(see also Centura Coll.)*
Beth Benjamin Acad. of Connecticut 779 *(see also Bais Binyomin Acad.)*
Beth HaMedrash Shaarei Yosher 270
Beth HaTalmud Rabbinical Coll. 270
Beth Israel Deaconess Med. Ctr. 712
Beth Israel Med. Ctr. 723 *(see also Phillips Beth Israel Sch. of Nursing)*
Beth Medrash Govoha 259
Beth Moses Hosp. *(see Maimonides Med. Ctr.)*
Beth Rivkah Schools *(see Associated Beth Rivkah Schools)*
Beth Shraga Rabbinical Coll. *(see Rabbinical Coll. Beth Shraga)*
Bethany Acad. *(see Bethany Coll.)*
Bethany Bible Coll. 454
Bethany Bible Inst. *(see Bethany Coll.)*
Bethany Coll. 164, 440, 454, 776 *(see also Bethany Bible Coll.; Bethany Lutheran Coll.)*
Bethany Coll. of the Assemblies of God *(see Bethany Univ.)*
Bethany Hosp. *(see Advocate Bethany Hosp.)*
Bethany Ladies Coll. *(see Bethany Lutheran Coll.)*
Bethany Lutheran Coll. 219
Bethany Med. Ctr. *(see Kansas City Kansas Comm. Coll.)*
Bethany Sem. *(see Bethany Theological Sem.)*
Bethany Theological Sem. 146
Bethany Univ. 34, 776

Braverman Eye Ctr. *(see Nova Southeastern Univ.)*
Brawley Jr. Coll. *(see Imperial Valley Coll.)*
Braxton Sch. of Bus. 795
Brazosport Coll. 394
Brazosport Jr. Coll. *(see Brazosport Coll.)*
BRC Paralegal Studies *(see Baton Rouge Coll.)*
Breckinridge Job Corps Ctr. *(see Earle C. Clements Job Corps Ctr.)*
Breeden Sch. of Welding *(see Welder Training & Testing Inst.)*
Bremerton Bus. Coll. *(see Everest Coll—Bremerton)*
Brenau Coll. *(see Brenau Univ.)*
Brenau Univ. 110
Brenneke Massage Sch. *(see Cortiva Inst—Seattle)*
Brenneke Sch. of Massage 795 *(see also Cortiva Inst—Seattle)*
Brescia Coll. *(see Brescia Univ.)*
Brescia Univ. 171
Brescook, LLC 546
Brevard Coll. 300 *(see also Brevard Comm. Coll.)*
Brevard Comm. Coll. 90
Brevard Inst. *(see Brevard Coll.)*
Brewer State Jr. Coll. *(see Bevill State Comm. Coll.)*
Brewster Tech. Ctr. *(see Henry W. Brewster Tech. Ctr.)*
Brewton-Parker Coll. 111
Brian Utting Sch. of Massage 795
Briar Cliff Coll. *(see Briar Cliff Univ.)*
Briar Cliff Univ. 157
Briarcliffe Coll. 270
Briarcliffe Sch., Inc. *(see Briarcliffe Coll.)*
Briarwood Coll. 78
Brick Computer Science Inst. 787
Bridge Int'l. Sch. *(see Bridge Linguatec)*
Bridge Linguatec 494
Bridgeport Hosp. 692
Bridgeport Hosp. Nurse Anesthesia Program *(see Bridgeport Hosp.)*
Bridgeport Hosp. Sch. of Nursing *(see Bridgeport Hosp.)*
Bridgeport Univ. *(see Univ. of Bridgeport)*
Bridgerland Applied Techno. Coll. 413
Bridgerland Coll. *(see Bridgerland Applied Techno. Coll.)*
Bridges Acad. of Beauty 475
Bridgewater Coll. 420 *(see also Bridgewater State Coll.)*
Bridgewater State Coll. 197
Bridgewater State Teacher's Coll. *(see Bridgewater State Coll.)*
Briercrest Bible Coll. *(see Briercrest Coll.)*
Briercrest Bible Inst. *(see Briercrest Coll.)*
Briercrest Biblical Sem. 454
Briercrest Coll. 454
Briercrest Family of Schools *(see Briercrest Biblical Sem.; Briercrest Coll.)*
Briercrest Sem. *(see Briercrest Biblical Sem.)*
Brigham & Women's Hosp. 712
Brigham Young Acad. *(see Brigham Young Univ.)*
Brigham Young Univ. 413
Brigham Young Univ—Hawaii Campus 123
Brigham Young Univ—Idaho 125
Brighton Ctr., Inc. *(see Ctr. for Employment Training)*
Brighton Coll. 605
Brio Acad. of Cosmetology 497, 779
Brio Acad. of Cosmetolog—Niantic, The 497
Brio Acad—Niantic 779 *(see also Brio Acad. of Cosmetolog—Niantic)*
Bristol Comm. Coll. 198
Brite Coll. of the Bible *(see Brite Divinity Sch.)*
Brite Divinity Sch. 394 *(see also Texas Christian Univ.)*
British Columbia Cancer Agency—Vancouver Centre 757
British Columbia Children's Hosp. 757
British Columbia's Children's Hosp. *(see British Columbia Children's Hosp.)*
British Columbia Cancer Agency—Vancouver Centre *(see British Columbia Cancer Agency—Vancouver Centre)*
British Columbia Univ. *(see Univ. of British Columbia)*
Brittany Beauty Sch—Levittown 587, 789
Britton Training Inst. *(see Cisco Jr. Coll.)*
Britton Vision Associates Advanced Surgical Eyecare *(see Northeastern State Univ.)*
Broadcast Ctr. 566
Broadcast Services, Inc. *(see Broadcast Ctr.)*
Broadcasting Ctr. of Illinois *(see Illinois Ctr. for Broadcasting)*
Broadcasting Inst. of Maryland 546
Broadcasting Sch. of Carolina *(see Carolina Sch. of Broadcasting)*
Broaddus Coll. *(see Alderson-Broaddus Coll.)*
Brock Univ. 757
Brockport Coll. *(see State Univ. of New York Coll. at Brockport)*
Brockport Collegiate Inst. *(see State Univ. of New York Coll. at Brockport)*
Brockport State Normal Sch. *(see State Univ. of New York Coll. at Brockport)*
Brock's Hair Design Coll. *(see J & J Hair Design Coll.)*
Brockton Hosp. Sch. of Nursing *(see Signature Healthcare Brockton Hosp.)*
Broken Arrow Beauty Coll., Inc. 614
BroMenn Healthcare *(see BroMenn Reg. Med. Ctr.)*
BroMenn Reg. Med. Ctr. 701 *(see also Bloomington-Normal Sch. of Radiography)*
Bronson Healthcare Group Inc. *(see Bronson Methodist Hosp.)*
Bronson Hosp. *(see Bronson Methodist Hosp.)*
Bronson Methodist Hosp. 714
Bronx Comm. Coll. *(see City Univ. of New York Bronx Comm. Coll.)*
Bronx Hosp. *(see Bronx Lebanon Hosp. Ctr.)*
Bronx Lebanon Hosp. Ctr. 723
Bronx Psychiatric Ctr. *(see Yeshiva Univ.)*
Bronx VA Med. Ctr. *(see James J. Peters Veterans Affairs Med. Ctr.)*
Bronx VAMC *(see James J. Peters Veterans Affairs Med. Ctr.)*
Bronx Veterans Affairs Med. Ctr. *(see James J. Peters Veterans Affairs Med. Ctr.)*
Brookdale Coll. *(see Brookdale Comm. Coll.)*
Brookdale Comm. Coll. 259
Brookdale Hosp. *(see Brookdale Univ. Hosp. & Med. Ctr.)*
Brookdale Med. Ctr. *(see Brookdale Univ. Hosp. & Med. Ctr.)*
Brookdale Univ. Hosp. & Med. Ctr., The 724
Brooke Army Med. Ctr. 746
Brooke General Hosp. *(see Brooke Army Med. Ctr.)*
Brookhaven Coll. 394
Brooklyn City Hosp. *(see Brooklyn Hosp. Ctr.)*
Brooklyn Coll. *(see City Univ. of New York Brooklyn Coll.)*
Brooklyn Coll. of the Coll. of the City of New York *(see City Univ. of New York Brooklyn Coll.)*
Brooklyn Collegiate & Polytechnic Inst. *(see Polytechnic Inst. of NYU)*
Brooklyn Hosp. Ctr. 724
Brooklyn Inst. of Bus. Techno. 587, 788
Brooklyn Law Sch. 270
Brooklyn VA Med. Ctr. *(see Veterans Affairs New York Harbor Healthcare Sys—Brooklyn)*

C

CENEODDIVE *(see Ctr. for Explosive Ordnance Disposal & Diving)*
CENINFOCOM *(see Ctr. for Information Dominance Corry Station)*
CENNAVINTEL *(see Ctr. for Naval Intelligence)*
Centenary Biblical Inst. *(see Morgan State Univ.)*
Centenary Coll. 260
Centenary Coll. for Women *(see Centenary Coll.)*
Centenary Coll. of Louisiana 178
Centenary Collegiate Inst. *(see Centenary Coll.)*
Centenary Jr. Coll. *(see Centenary Coll.)*
Ctr. for Advanced Legal Studies 395
Ctr. for Advanced Manufacturing & Techno. 791
Ctr. for Advanced Studies of Puerto Rico & the Caribbean *(see Centro de Estudios Avanzados de Puerto Rico y El Caribe)*
Ctr. for Aging Resources, The 686
Ctr. for Arts & Techno. 737
Ctr. for Asia Pacific Exchange 522
Ctr. for Automotive Edu. & Training *(see Lincoln Tech. Inst.)*
Ctr. for Behavioral Health, The 704
Ctr. for Child Development & Developmental Disabilities *(see Children's Hosp. of Los Angeles)*
Ctr. for Creative Studie—Coll. of Art & Design *(see Coll. for Creative Studies)*
Ctr. for Cryptology Training *(see Ctr. for Information Dominance Corry Station)*
Ctr. for Culinary Arts *(see Lincoln Tech. Inst—New Britain)*
Ctr. for Culinary Arts, Manila 768
Ctr. for Degree Studies *(see Penn Foster Coll.)*
Ctr. for EM *(see Ctr. for Emergency Medicine of Western Pennsylvania)*
Ctr. for Emergency Medicine of Western Pennsylvania 737
Ctr. for Employment Training 536
Ctr. for English Studies *(see Embassy CES)*
Ctr. for Explosive Ordnance Disposal & Diving 506, 780
Ctr. for Foods of the Americas 275
Ctr. for Humanistic Studies 785 *(see also Michigan Sch. of Prof. Psychology)*
Ctr. for Information Dominance (CID) 780
Ctr. for Information Dominance Corry Station 506
Ctr. for Innovative Training & Edu. 624
Ctr. for Labor Studies *(see National Labor Coll.)*
Ctr. for Languages & Electronic Computation *(see Centro Electronico de Idiomas y Computacion)*
Ctr. for Mgmnt. Studies *(see European Univ—Barcelona)*
Ctr. for Massage & Natural Health 600
Ctr. for Montessori Teacher Edu/NY 724
Ctr. for Natural Wellness Sch. of Massage Therapy, The 587
Ctr. for Naval Aviation Tech. Training 506, 780
Ctr. for Naval Engineering 664
Ctr. for Naval Intelligence 664, 795
Ctr. for Naval Leadership 795, 820
Ctr. for Personal & Prof. Development 664, 795 *(see also Ctr. for Naval Leadership)*
Ctr. for Preventive Psychiatry 724
Ctr. for Seabees & Facilities Engineering, The 476
Ctr. for Service Support *(see United States Navy Supply Corps Sch.)*
Ctr. for Studies in Jewish Pastoral Care, The *(see HealthCare Chaplaincy)*
Ctr. for Surface Combat Systems 664
Ctr. for Techno., Essex, The 749
Ctr. for the Partially-Sighted *(see Southern California Coll. of Optometry)*
Ctr. for Theological Studies of Florida *(see Florida Ctr. for Theological Studies)*
Ctr. for Training in Bus. & Industry *(see Pinnacle Career Inst—Lawrence)*
Ctr. for Urban Ministerial Edu. 199
Ctr. for Urban Ministry, The 686
Ctr. for Workforce Development *(see Monroe —Orleans BOCES, Ctr. for Workforce Development)*
Ctr. of Advanced Therapeutics 494
Ctr. of English Language 650
Ctr. of Excellence Long Island Ctr. *(see Dale Carnegie & Associates, Inc.)*
Ctr.s for Disease Control & Prevention 699
Centra Health *(see Centra Lynchburg General Hosp.)*
Centra Lynchburg General Hosp. 750
CentraCare Health Sys. *(see Saint Cloud Hosp.)*
Central Acad. & Coll. *(see Central Christian Coll. of Kansas)*
Central Alabama Coll. *(see Central Alabama Comm. Coll.)*
Central Alabama Comm. Coll. 4
Central Arizona Coll. 17
Central Arkansas Radiation Therapy Inst. 685
Central Arkansas Univ. *(see Univ. of Central Arkansas)*
Central Arkansas VA Med. Ctr. *(see Central Arkansas Veterans Healthcare Sys.)*
Central Arkansas Veterans Affairs Med. Ctr. *(see Central Arkansas Veterans Healthcare Sys.)*
Central Arkansas Veterans Healthcare Sys. 685
Central Baptist Coll. 26
Central Baptist Sem. *(see Central Baptist Theological Sem.; Central Baptist Theological Sem. of Minneapolis; Heritage Coll. & Sem.)*
Central Baptist Theological Sem. 165, 421
Central Baptist Theological Sem. of Minneapolis 804
Central Bible Coll. 235, 804
Central Cadre Sch. *(see National Chengchi Univ.)*
Central California Dale Carnegie Training *(see Dale Carnegie Training of Central California)*
Central California Psychology Internship Consortium *(see Alliant Int'l. Univ—Fresno)*
Central California Sch. of Continuing Edu. 476
Central Career Schools 576
Central Caribbean Univ. *(see Universidad Central del Caribe: Sch. of Medicine)*
Central Carolina Coll. *(see Central Carolina Comm. Coll.; Central Carolina Tech. Coll.)*
Central Carolina Comm. Coll. 301
Central Carolina Tech. Coll. 373
Central Chiropractic Coll. *(see Cleveland Chiropractic Coll.)*
Central Christian Coll. *(see Central Christian Coll. of the Bible)*
Central Christian Coll. of Kansas 165
Central Christian Coll. of the Bible 236
Central Clinic at Delta Point *(see Las Vegas Veterans Affairs Med. Ctr.)*
Central Coast Coll. 476
Central Coll. 157 *(see also Central Christian Coll. of Kansas; Central Comm. Coll.)*
Central Coll. of Cosmetology 566
Central Coll. of The Free Methodist Church *(see Central Christian Coll. of Kansas)*
Central Collegiate Inst. *(see Hendrix Coll.)*
Central Comm. Coll. 250
Central Connecticut State Coll. *(see Central Connecticut State Univ.)*
Central Connecticut State Univ. 78
Central European Univ. 458
Central Florida Bible Coll. *(see Florida Christian Coll.)*

Central Washington Coll. of Edu. *(see Central Washington Univ.)*
Central Washington State Coll. *(see Central Washington Univ.)*
Central Washington Univ. 432
Central Wesleyan Coll. *(see Southern Wesleyan Univ.)*
Central Wisconsin Dale Carnegie *(see Meyer Uebelher Associates, LLC)*
Central Wyoming Coll. 453
Central Yeshiva Tomchei Tmimim-Lubavitch 271
Centralia Coll. 433
Centre Coll. 171
Centre County Area Vocational Tech. Sch. 791 *(see also Central Pennsylvania Inst. of Science & Techno.)*
Centre Européan de Mgmnt. Hôtelier Int'l. 765
Centre for Addiction & Mental Health, Clarke Division 758
Centre for Dance Edu., The *(see Atlanta Ballet Centre for Dance Edu.)*
Centre for Labour Market Studies *(see Univ. of Leicester's Centre for Labour Market Studies)*
Centre Hosptalier pour Enfants de l'est de l'Ontario *(see Children's Hosp. of Eastern Ontario)*
Centre of Tech. & Higher Studies *(see CETYS Univ.)*
Centro de Capacitacion y Asesoramient—Aquadilla *(see Centro de Capacitacion y Asesoramiento Vetelb—Aquadilla)*
Centro de Capacitacion y Asesoramient—Caguas *(see Centro de Capacitacion y Asesoramiento Vetelb—Caguas)*
Centro de Enseñanza Téchnica y Superior *(see CETYS Univ.)*
Centro de Entrenamiento Montessori 678
Centro de Estudios Avanzados de Puerto Rico y El Caribe 365
Centro de Estudios de los Dominicos del Caribe *(see Dominican Study Ctr. of the Caribbean)*
Centro de Estudios Multidisciplinarios 365
Centro Electronico de Idiomas y Computacion 680
Centro Entrenamiento Montessori de Santo Domingo *(see Montessori Training Ctr. of Santo Domingo)*
Centro Politec de Puerto Rico *(see Politec Inst.)*
Centura Coll. 421, 793, 795
Centura Health *(see Penrose-St. Francis Health Services; Porter Adventist Hosp.; Saint Anthony Central Hosp.; Saint Mary-Corwin Med. Ctr.)*
Centura Inst. 91, 781
Centurion Prof. Training 788
Century Coll. 220, 632
Century Comm. & Tech. Coll. *(see Century Coll.)*
Century Sch. of Cosmetology, Inc. 789 *(see also Ohio Acad.-Paul Mitchell Partner Sch.)*
Cermak Health Services of Cook County 701
Cerritos Coll. 39
Cerro Coso Coll. *(see Cerro Coso Comm. Coll.)*
Cerro Coso Comm. Coll. 39
CES Coll. *(see Comm. Enhancement Services Adult Edu. Division)*
"Cesar Ritz" *(see Clemens Coll.)*
"Cesar Ritz" Hotel Mgmnt. Inst. *(see Institut Hotelier "Cesar Ritz")*
CETYS Univ. 808
Chabot Coll. 39
Chabot Coll. Valley Campus *(see Las Positas Coll.)*
Chadron Coll. *(see Chadron State Coll.)*
Chadron State Coll. 250
Chaffey Coll. 39
Chaffey Jr. Coll. of Agriculture *(see Chaffey Coll.)*
Chamberlain Coll. of Nursing 236, 786
Chamberlayne Jr. Coll. *(see Mount Ida Coll.)*
Chaminade Coll. of Honolulu *(see Chaminade Univ. of Honolulu)*
Chaminade Univ. of Honolulu 123
Champaign Sch. of Beauty Culture *(see Mr. John's Sch. of Cosmetology, Esthetics & Nails)*
Champion Beauty Coll., Inc. 650
Champion Inst. of Cosmetology 476
Champlain Coll. 417, 794
Champlain Valley Hosp. *(see Champlain Valley Physicians Hosp. Med. Ctr.)*
Champlain Valley Physicians Hosp. Med. Ctr. 724
Chancellor Univ. 316, 790
Chandler Med. Ctr. *(see Univ. of Kentucky)*
Chandler-Gilbert Coll. *(see Chandler-Gilbert Comm. Coll.)*
Chandler-Gilbert Comm. Coll. 17
Chandler-Gilbert Edu. Ctr. *(see Chandler-Gilbert Comm. Coll.)*
Changsha Temporary Univ. *(see Tsinghua Univ.)*
Chaparral Career Coll. *(see Brown Mackie Coll—Tucson)*
Chaparral Coll. 775 *(see also Brown Mackie Coll—Tucson)*
Chaplaincy Ctr., The 743
Chaplaincy, The 751, 796
Chapman Sch. of Religious Studies *(see Oakland City Univ.)*
Chapman Sem. of Oakland City Univ. *(see Oakland City Univ.)*
Chapman Univ. 39
Chapman Univ., Univ. Coll. *(see Chapman Univ. Coll.)*
Chappell, Jr., VA OPC *(see William V. Chappell, Jr., Veterans Affairs Outpatient Clinic)*
Chappell, Jr., VA Outpatient Clinic *(see William V. Chappell, Jr., Veterans Affairs Outpatient Clinic)*
Chappell, Jr., Veterans Affairs Outpatient Clinic *(see William V. Chappell, Jr., Veterans Affairs Outpatient Clinic)*
Charity Hosp. *(see Saint Vincent Infirmary Med. Ctr.)*
Charles & Sue's Sch. of Hair Design 650
Charles County Coll. *(see Coll. of Southern Maryland)*
Charles County Comm. Coll. *(see Coll. of Southern Maryland)*
Charles D. Eubank & Associates, Inc. 530
Charles Drew Univ. of Medicine & Science 39
Charles F. Kettering Mem. Hosp. *(see Kettering Coll. of Med. Arts)*
Charles H. Mason Theological Sem. *(see Interdenominational Theological Ctr.)*
Charles H. McCann Tech. Sch. 551
Charles of Italy Beauty Coll. & Sch. of Massage Therapy 467
Charles R. Drew Univ. of Medicine & Science *(see Charles Drew Univ. of Medicine & Science)*
Charles Stewart Mott Comm. Coll. 209
Charles Stuart Sch. of Diamond Setting *(see Charles Stuart Sch. of Locksmithing)*
Charles Stuart Sch. of Locksmithing 587
Charles T. Miller Hosp. *(see United Hosp/ Children's Hosp. & Clinic)*
Charleston Area Med. Ctr. 443 *(see also West Virginia Univ.)*
Charleston Art Inst. *(see Art Inst. of Charleston)*
Charleston Coll. *(see Coll. of Charleston)*
Charleston Cosmetology Inst. 638
Charleston Culinary Inst. *(see Trident Tech. Coll.)*
Charleston Inst. of Cosmetology *(see Charleston Cosmetology Inst.)*
Charleston Med. Ctr. *(see West Virginia Univ.)*
Charleston Sch. of Beauty Culture 672
Charleston Sch. of Massage 638
Charleston Southern Univ. 373
Charleston Univ. *(see Univ. of Charleston)*

City Coll. of Santa Barbara *(see Santa Barbara City Coll.)*
City Coll. of the City Univ. of New York, The *(see City Univ. of New York City Coll.)*
City Coll. Orlando *(see City Coll. Casselberry)*
City Coll., Inc. 790
City Colleges of Chicag—Harold Washington Coll. 128
City Colleges of Chicag—Harry S Truman Coll. 128
City Colleges of Chicag—Kennedy-King Coll. 128
City Colleges of Chicag—Malcolm X Coll. 129
City Colleges of Chicag—Olive-Harvey Coll. 129
City Colleges of Chicag—Richard J. Daley Coll. 129
City Colleges of Chicag—Wilbur Wright Coll. 129
City Hosp. *(see Hennepin County Med. Ctr.; Univ. Hosp.)*
City of Hope Grad. Sch. of Biological Sciences *(see City of Hope National Med. Ctr.)*
City of Hope National Med. Ctr. 39
City Polytechnic of Hong Kong *(see City Univ. of Hong Kong)*
City Tech *(see City Univ. of New York New York City Coll. of Techno.)*
City Univ. *(see City Univ. of Seattle)*
City Univ. of Hong Kong 766
City Univ. of New Jersey *(see New Jersey City Univ.)*
City Univ. of New York Baruch Coll. *(see Baruch Coll.)*
City Univ. of New York Bernard M. Baruch Coll. 788 *(see also Baruch Coll.)*
City Univ. of New York Borough of Manhattan Comm. Coll. 272
City Univ. of New York Bronx Comm. Coll. 272
City Univ. of New York Brooklyn Coll. 272
City Univ. of New York City Coll. 272
City Univ. of New York Coll. of Staten Island 272
City Univ. of New York Grad. Ctr. 272
City Univ. of New York Grad. Sch. & Univ. Ctr. *(see City Univ. of New York Grad. Ctr.)*
City Univ. of New York Herbert H. Lehman Coll. *(see Lehman Coll., City Univ. of New York)*
City Univ. of New York Hostos Comm. Coll. 272
City Univ. of New York Hunter Coll. 272
City Univ. of New York John Jay Coll. of Criminal Justice 272
City Univ. of New York Kingsborough Comm. Coll. 273
City Univ. of New York LaGuardia Comm. Coll. 273
City Univ. of New York Medgar Evers Coll. 273
City Univ. of New York Mount Sinai Sch. of Medicine *(see Mount Sinai Sch. of Medicine)*
City Univ. of New York New York City Coll. of Techno. 273
City Univ. of New York New York City Tech. Coll. *(see City Univ. of New York New York City Coll. of Techno.)*
City Univ. of New York Queens Coll. 273
City Univ. of New York Queensborough Comm. Coll. 273
City Univ. of New York York Coll. 273
City Univ. of Seattle 433
City Univ. Sch. of Law at Queens Coll. *(see City Univ. of New York Queens Coll.)*
City Vision Coll. 236, 786
Clackamas Coll. *(see Clackamas Comm. Coll.)*
Clackamas Comm. Coll. 337
Clackamas County Coll. *(see Clackamas Comm. Coll.)*
Claflin Coll. *(see Claflin Univ.)*
Claflin Univ. 373
Claremont Colleges *(see Pitzer Coll.)*
Claremont Grad. Sch. *(see Claremont Grad. Univ.)*
Claremont Grad. Univ., The 39
Claremont McKenna Coll. 40
Claremont Sch. of Theology 40
Claremont Tech *(see River Valley Comm. Coll.)*
Claremont Tech. Coll. *(see River Valley Comm. Coll.)*
Claremont Theology Sch. *(see Claremont Sch. of Theology)*
Claremont Univ. *(see Claremont Grad. Univ.)*
Claremore Beauty Coll. 615
Claremore Jr. Coll. *(see Rogers State Univ.)*
Clarendon Coll. 395
Clarendon Jr. Coll. *(see Clarendon Coll.)*
Clare's Beauty Coll. 668
Clarian Health Partners, Inc. *(see Methodist Hosp.)*
Clarion County Area Vocational Tech. Sch. 791 *(see also Clarion County Career Ctr.)*
Clarion County Career Ctr. 737, 791
Clarion County Vo-Tech Sch. *(see Clarion County Career Ctr.)*
Clarion Health Partners *(see Methodist Hosp.)*
Clarion State Coll. *(see Clarion Univ. of Pennsylvania)*
Clarion State Teachers Coll. *(see Clarion Univ. of Pennsylvania)*
Clarion Univ. of Pennsylvania 346
Clarita Career Coll. 477
Clarita Coll. *(see Clarita Career Coll.)*
Clark Art Inst., The *(see Williams Coll.)*
Clark Atlanta Univ. 111
Clark Coll. 433 *(see also Clark Atlanta Univ.; Clark State Comm. Coll.)*
Clark Comm. Coll. *(see Clark State Comm. Coll.)*
Clark County Fire Dist. 5 Northwest Reg. Training Ctr. *(see Northwest Reg. Training Ctr.)*
Clark County Tech. Inst. *(see Clark State Comm. Coll.)*
Clark F. Miller Sch. of Radiologic Techno. *(see Central Maine Med. Ctr.)*
Clark State Coll. *(see Clark State Comm. Coll.)*
Clark State Comm. Coll. 317
Clark Tech. Coll. *(see Clark State Comm. Coll.)*
Clark Univ. 198
Clarke Coll. 157
Clarke Inst. of Psychiatry *(see Centre for Addiction & Mental Health, Clarke Division)*
Clark's Bus. Coll. *(see Erie Bus. Ctr.)*
Clarksburg Beauty Acad. 672
Clarksburg Skills Training Ctr. *(see Stanley Tech. Inst.)*
Clarkson Coll. 250
Clarkson Univ. 273
Clary Sage Coll. *(see Comm. Care Coll.)*
Classic Coll. of Hair Design 783 *(see also B-Street Design Sch. of Int'l. Hair Styling)*
Classical Chinese Medicine Clinic *(see National Coll. of Natural Medicine)*
Clatsop Coll. *(see Clatsop Comm. Coll.)*
Clatsop Comm. Coll. 337
Clayton Coll. *(see Clayton State Univ.)*
Clayton Coll. & State Univ. *(see Clayton State Univ.)*
Clayton Eye Ctr. *(see Nova Southeastern Univ.)*
Clayton Jr. Coll. *(see Clayton State Univ.)*
Clayton State Coll. *(see Clayton State Univ.)*
Clayton State Univ. 111
Clayton Univ. *(see Clayton State Univ.)*
Clear Creek Baptist Bible Coll. 171
Clear Creek Baptist Sch. *(see Clear Creek Baptist Bible Coll.)*
Clear Creek Coll. *(see Clear Creek Baptist Bible Coll.)*

Clear Creek Mountain Preacher's Bible Sch. *(see Clear Creek Baptist Bible Coll.)*
Clearfield Beauty Acad. 791
Clearfield County Area Vocational Tech. Sch. 791 *(see also Clearfield County Career & Techno. Ctr.)*
Clearfield County Career & Techno. Ctr. 738, 791
Clearfield County Career Ctr. *(see Clearfield County Career & Techno. Ctr.)*
Clearfield County Vo-Tech Sch. *(see Clearfield County Career & Techno. Ctr.)*
Clearfield Hosp. 738
Clearwater Christian Coll. 91
Clearwater Coll. *(see Clearwater Christian Coll.)*
Cleary Bus. Coll. *(see Cleary Univ.)*
Cleary Coll. *(see Cleary Univ.)*
Cleary Jr. Coll. *(see Cleary Univ.)*
Cleary Sch. of Penmanship, The *(see Cleary Univ.)*
Cleary Univ. 209
Cleft Palate Clinic of Lancaster *(see Lancaster Cleft Palate Clinic)*
Clemens Coll. 78, 779
Clement J. Zablocki Veterans Affairs Med. Ctr. 754
Clements Job Corps Acad. *(see Earle C. Clements Job Corps Ctr.)*
Clements Job Corps Ctr. *(see Earle C. Clements Job Corps Ctr.)*
Clemson Agricultural Coll. *(see Clemson Univ.)*
Clemson Coll. *(see Clemson Univ.)*
Clemson Univ. 374
Clermont Coll. *(see Univ. of Cincinnat—Clermont Coll.)*
Cleveland Art Inst. *(see Cleveland Inst. of Art)*
Cleveland Bible Coll. *(see Malone Univ.)*
Cleveland Chiropractic Coll. 165
Cleveland Clinic Foundation *(see Cleveland Clinic)*
Cleveland Clinic Health Sys—East Region *(see Huron Hosp.)*
Cleveland Clinic, The 732
Cleveland Coll. *(see Cleveland Comm. Coll.)*
Cleveland Coll. of Chiropractic *(see Cleveland Chiropractic Coll.)*
Cleveland Coll. of Jewish Studies *(see Laura & Alvin Siegal Coll. of Judaic Studies)*
Cleveland Comm. Coll. 301 *(see also Cleveland State Comm. Coll.)*
Cleveland County Tech. Inst. *(see Cleveland Comm. Coll.)*
Cleveland Dental-Med. Assistants Inst. *(see Cleveland Inst. of Dental-Med. Assistants, Inc.)*
Cleveland Extension High Sch. *(see Adult & Continuing Edu—Cleveland Extension)*
Cleveland General Hosp. *(see Saint Vincent Charity Hosp.)*
Cleveland Inst. of Art 317
Cleveland Inst. of Dental-Med. Assistants, Inc. 606
Cleveland Inst. of Electronics, Inc. 317
Cleveland Inst. of Med. Massage 606
Cleveland Inst. of Music 317
Cleveland Music Inst. *(see Cleveland Inst. of Music)*
Cleveland Music Sch. Settlement, The 606
Cleveland State Coll. *(see Cleveland State Comm. Coll.)*
Cleveland State Comm. Coll. 383
Cleveland State Univ. 317
Cleveland Tech. Coll. *(see Cleveland Comm. Coll.)*
Cleveland Univ. *(see Cleveland State Univ.)*
Cleveland VA Med. Ctr. *(see Louis Stokes Cleveland Veterans Affairs Med. Ctr.)*
Cleveland VAMC *(see Louis Stokes Cleveland Veterans Affairs Med. Ctr.)*
Cleveland Veterans Affairs Med. Ctr. *(see Louis Stokes Cleveland Veterans Affairs Med. Ctr.)*
Clinch Valley Coll. of the Univ. of Virginia *(see Univ. of Virginia's Coll. at Wise)*
Clinica Sierra Vista 686
Clinical Acupuncture & Oriental Medicine Inst. *(see Inst. of Clinical Acupuncture & Oriental Medicine)*
Clinical Social Work Inst. *(see Inst. for Clinical Social Work, Inc.)*
Clinton Beauty Acad. *(see Arleen's Clinton Beauty Acad.)*
Clinton Coll. *(see Clinton Comm. Coll.; Clinton Jr. Coll.; Presbyterian Coll.)*
Clinton Comm. Coll. 157, 273
Clinton County Area Techno. Ctr. 175 *(see also Somerset Comm. Coll.)*
Clinton Jr. Coll. 374 *(see also Clinton Comm. Coll.)*
Clinton Tech. Inst. *(see Motorcycle & Marine Mechanics Inst.)*
Cloud Coll. *(see Cloud County Comm. Coll.)*
Cloud County Coll. *(see Cloud County Comm. Coll.)*
Cloud County Comm. Coll. 165
Cloud County Jr. Coll. *(see Cloud County Comm. Coll.)*
Clover Park Coll. *(see Clover Park Tech. Coll.; Pierce Coll. Fort Steilacoom; Pierce Coll. Puyallup)*
Clover Park Comm. Coll. *(see Pierce Coll. Fort Steilacoom; Pierce Coll. Puyallup)*
Clover Park Tech. Coll. 433
Clovis Coll. *(see Clovis Comm. Coll.)*
Clovis Comm. Coll. 266
Cloyd's Beauty Sch. #1 539
Cloyd's Beauty Sch. #2 540
Cloyd's Beauty Sch. #3 540
CMHA Sch. of Nursing *(see Carolinas Coll. of Health Sciences)*
CNATT *(see Ctr. for Naval Aviation Tech. Training)*
Cncinnati Eye Inst. *(see Ohio State Univ.)*
CNI Vocational Coll. 477, 776
Coachella Valley Beauty Coll. 477
Coachella Valley Tech Ctr. *(see Mayfield Coll.)*
Coachella Valley Tech. Skills Ctr. 776 *(see also Mayfield Coll.)*
Coahoma Coll. *(see Coahoma Comm. Coll.)*
Coahoma Comm. Coll. 230
Coalinga Jr. Coll. *(see West Hills Comm. Coll.)*
Coast Career Inst. 477
Coast Guard Acad. *(see United States Coast Guard Acad.)*
Coastal Behavioral Healthcare, Inc. 696
Coastal Bend Coll. 395
Coastal Bend Health Edu. Ctr. *(see Texas A&M Univ. Sys. Health Science Ctr.)*
Coastal Carolina Coll. *(see Coastal Carolina Comm. Coll.)*
Coastal Carolina Comm. Coll. 301
Coastal Carolina Jr. Coll. *(see Coastal Carolina Univ.)*
Coastal Carolina Univ. 374
Coastal Georgia Coll. *(see Coll. of Coastal Georgia)*
Coastal Georgia Comm. Coll. *(see Coll. of Coastal Georgia)*
Coastal Law Sch. *(see Florida Coastal Sch. of Law)*
Coastal Valley Coll. *(see Expression Coll. for Digital Arts)*
Coastline Beauty Coll. 477
Coastline Coll. *(see Coastline Comm. Coll.)*
Coastline Comm. Coll. 40
COBA Acad. 477, 776
Cobb Beauty Coll. 518
Cobleskill Coll. of Agriculture & Techno. *(see State Univ. of New York Coll. of Agriculture & Techno. at Cobleskill)*
Cochise Coll. 17

Coll. of Bennington *(see Bennington Coll.)*
Coll. of Berea *(see Berea Coll.)*
Coll. of Bermuda *(see Bermuda Coll.)*
Coll. of Biblical Studie—Houston 395
Coll. of Boston *(see Boston Coll.)*
Coll. of Brooklyn *(see City Univ. of New York Brooklyn Coll.)*
Coll. of Bryn Athyn *(see Bryn Athyn Coll. of the New Church)*
Coll. of Bryn Mawr *(see Bryn Mawr Coll.)*
Coll. of Burlington County *(see Burlington County Coll.)*
Coll. of Bus. & Techno. 91
Coll. of Butte County *(see Butte Coll.)*
Coll. of Bytown *(see Univ. of Ottawa)*
Coll. of Caldwell *(see Caldwell Coll.)*
Coll. of California *(see Univ. of California, Berkeley)*
Coll. of Camden County *(see Camden County Coll.)*
Coll. of Career Training 477
Coll. of Casper *(see Casper Coll.)*
Coll. of Castleton *(see Castleton State Coll.)*
Coll. of Cazenovia *(see Cazenovia Coll.)*
Coll. of Central Arizona *(see Central Arizona Coll.)*
Coll. of Central Georgia *(see Central Georgia Tech. Coll.)*
Coll. of Central Illinois *(see Illinois Central Coll.)*
Coll. of Central Iowa *(see Iowa Central Comm. Coll.)*
Coll. of Central Pennsylvania *(see Central Pennsylvania Coll.)*
Coll. of Central Texas *(see Central Texas Coll.)*
Coll. of Central Virginia *(see Central Virginia Comm. Coll.)*
Coll. of Central Wyoming *(see Central Wyoming Coll.)*
Coll. of Centralia *(see Centralia Coll.)*
Coll. of Charleston 374
Coll. of Chicoutimi *(see Chicoutimi Coll.)*
Coll. of Chinese Acupuncture, U.S. *(see Tai Sophia Inst.)*
Coll. of Chiropractic Physicians & Surgeons *(see Southern California Univ. of Health Sciences)*
Coll. of Christ the King *(see Regis Coll.)*
Coll. of Cinema Arts & Television *(see Colegio de las Ciencias Artes y Television)*
Coll. of Cisco *(see Cisco Jr. Coll.)*
Coll. of Clinton *(see Presbyterian Coll.)*
Coll. of Coastal Georgia 111
Coll. of Coiffure Art, The 569
Coll. of Connecticut *(see Connecticut Coll.)*
Coll. of Cosmetology, Inc. 620
Coll. of Court Reporting, Inc. 147
Coll. of Crowley's Ridge *(see Crowley's Ridge Coll.)*
Coll. of Culinary Arts of Atlanta *(see Western Culinary Inst.)*
Coll. of Culinary Arts of Las Vegas *(see Le Cordon Bleu Coll. of Culinary Art—Las Vegas)*
Coll. of Culinary Arts of Miami *(see Le Cordon Bleu Coll. of Culinary Art—Miami)*
Coll. of Culinary Arts of Minneapolis/St. Paul *(see Western Culinary Inst.)*
Coll. of Cumberland County *(see Cumberland County Coll.)*
Coll. of Cypress *(see Cypress Coll.)*
Coll. of DuPage 129
Coll. of East Georgia *(see East Georgia Coll.)*
Coll. of East Los Angeles *(see East Los Angeles Coll.)*
Coll. of Eastern Arizona *(see Eastern Arizona Coll.)*
Coll. of Eastern Oklahoma *(see Eastern Oklahoma State Coll.)*
Coll. of Eastern Utah 413, 794
Coll. of Eastern Wyoming *(see Eastern Wyoming Coll.)*
Coll. of Edu. & Industrial Arts at Wilberforce *(see Central State Univ.)*
Coll. of Electronic Computer Programming *(see Chattanooga Coll.)*
Coll. of Electronic Data Processing *(see EDP Coll.)*
Coll. of Elizabethtown *(see Elizabethtown Coll.)*
Coll. of Elmhurst *(see Elmhurst Coll.)*
Coll. of Elmira *(see Elmira Coll.)*
Coll. of Emergency Services 736
Coll. of Environmental Science & Forestry at Syracuse *(see State Univ. of New York Coll. of Environmental Science & Forestry)*
Coll. of Essex & Franklin, The *(see North Country Comm. Coll.)*
Coll. of Essex County *(see Essex County Coll.)*
Coll. of Framingham *(see Framingham State Coll.)*
Coll. of François-Xavier Garneau *(see François-Xavier Garneau Coll.)*
Coll. of Galveston *(see Galveston Coll.)*
Coll. of Georgetown *(see Georgetown Coll.)*
Coll. of Gettysburg *(see Gettysburg Coll.)*
Coll. of Gloucester County *(see Gloucester County Coll.)*
Coll. of Great Falls *(see Univ. of Great Falls)*
Coll. of Greensboro *(see Greensboro Coll.)*
Coll. of Greenville *(see Greenville Coll.)*
Coll. of Grove City *(see Grove City Coll.)*
Coll. of Guilford County *(see Guilford Coll.)*
Coll. of Hair Design 532, 570, 783
Coll. of Hair Design Careers 620
Coll. of Hampton Roads *(see Everest Inst—Newport News)*
Coll. of Hanover *(see Hanover Coll.)*
Coll. of Hastings *(see Hastings Coll.)*
Coll. of Health Professions of New York *(see New York Coll. of Health Professions)*
Coll. of Health Sciences *(see Jefferson Coll. of Health Sciences)*
Coll. of Hesston *(see Hesston Coll.)*
Coll. of Hillsdale *(see Hillsdale Coll.)*
Coll. of Hiram *(see Hiram Coll.)*
Coll. of Hobe Sound *(see Hobe Sound Bible Coll.)*
Coll. of Hosp.ity Mgmnt. *(see Clemens Coll.)*
Coll. of Houghton *(see Houghton Coll.)*
Coll. of Houston *(see Univ. of Houston)*
Coll. of Humanities & Sciences *(see Coll. of the Humanities & Sciences Harrison Middleton Univ.)*
Coll. of Huntington *(see Huntington Jr. Coll.)*
Coll. of Idaho, The 125, 782
Coll. of Industrial Arts *(see Texas Woman's Univ.)*
Coll. of Information Techno. 477
Coll. of Insurance *(see Saint John's Univ.)*
Coll. of Integrative Medicine of Florida *(see Florida Coll. of Integrative Medicine)*
Coll. of Irvine Valley *(see Irvine Valley Coll.)*
Coll. of Ithaca *(see Ithaca Coll.)*
Coll. of Jacksonville *(see Jacksonville Coll.)*
Coll. of Jamestown *(see Jamestown Coll.)*
Coll. of Jewish Studies *(see Spertus Inst. of Jewish Studies)*
Coll. of Jones County *(see Jones County Jr. Coll.)*
Coll. of Knox County *(see Knox Coll.)*
Coll. of LaGrange *(see LaGrange Coll.)*
Coll. of Lake County 129
Coll. of Lake Erie *(see Lake Erie Coll.)*
Coll. of Lake Forest *(see Lake Forest Coll.)*
Coll. of Lake Michigan *(see Lake Michigan Coll.)*
Coll. of Las Vegas *(see Las Vegas Coll.)*
Coll. of Lebanon *(see Lebanon Coll.)*

Colorado Agricultural Coll. *(see Colorado State Univ.)*
Colorado Art Inst. *(see Art Inst. of Colorado)*
Colorado Baptist Univ. *(see Colorado Christian Univ.)*
Colorado Christian Coll. *(see Colorado Christian Univ.)*
Colorado Christian Univ. 70
Colorado Coll. 70
Colorado Dept. of Human Services *(see Colorado Mental Health Inst. at Fort Logan)*
Colorado Healing Arts Sch. *(see Colorado Sch. of Healing Arts)*
Colorado Inst. Massage Therapy *(see Massage Therapy Inst. of Colorado)*
Colorado Inst. of Art *(see Art Inst. of Colorado)*
Colorado Massage Therapy Inst. *(see Massage Therapy Inst. of Colorado)*
Colorado Mental Health Inst. at Fort Logan 691
Colorado Mines Sch. *(see Colorado Sch. of Mines)*
Colorado Mountain Coll. 70
Colorado Northwestern Coll. *(see Colorado Northwestern Comm. Coll.)*
Colorado Northwestern Comm. Coll. 70
Colorado Sch. for Family Therapy 691, 779
Colorado Sch. of English 494
Colorado Sch. of Healing Arts 70
Colorado Sch. of Mines 70
Colorado Sch. of Prof. Psychology 779 *(see also Univ. of the Rockies)*
Colorado Sch. of Trades 70
Colorado Sch. of Traditional Chinese Medicine 71
Colorado Springs Academic Ctr. *(see Univ. of the Rockies)*
Colorado Springs Bible Coll. *(see Oklahoma Wesleyan Univ.)*
Colorado Springs Mem. Hosp. *(see Mem. Hosp.)*
Colorado State Coll. of Agriculture & Mechanic Arts *(see Fort Lewis Coll.)*
Colorado State Coll. of Edu. *(see Univ. of Northern Colorado)*
Colorado State Teachers Coll. *(see Univ. of Northern Colorado)*
Colorado State Univ. 71
Colorado State Univ—Pueblo 71
Colorado Tech. Univ. 71
Colorado Tech. Univ. Online *(see Colorado Tech. Univ.)*
Colorado Tech. Univ—North Kansas City 786
Colorado Univ. at Boulder *(see Univ. of Colorado at Boulder)*
Colorado Univ. at Colorado Springs *(see Univ. of Colorado at Colorado Springs)*
Colorado Women's Coll. *(see Univ. of Denver)*
Colored Industrial & Agricultural Sch., The *(see Grambling State Univ.)*
Columbia Area Career Ctr. 815
Columbia Basin Coll. 433
Columbia Beauty Acad. 786
Columbia Beauty Sch. 638
Columbia Bible Coll. *(see Columbia Int'l. Univ.)*
Columbia Bible Coll. 455
Columbia Bible Sch. *(see Columbia Int'l. Univ.)*
Columbia Career Ctr. *(see Columbia Area Career Ctr.)*
Columbia Ctr. Univ. 365
Columbia Centro Universitario *(see Columbia Ctr. Univ.)*
Columbia Coll. 41, 236, 374, 759 *(see also Columbia Bible Coll.; Columbia Ctr. Univ.; Columbia Coll. Chicago; Columbia Univ. in the City of New York; Loras Coll.; Pacific Lutheran Univ.)*
Columbia Coll. Chicago 129
Columbia Coll. Hollywood 41
Columbia Coll. of Missouri *(see Columbia Coll.)*
Columbia Coll. of Nursing 446
Columbia Commercial Coll. *(see South Univ.)*
Columbia Female Acad. *(see Stephens Coll.)*
Columbia Female Baptist Acad. *(see Stephens Coll.)*
Columbia Female Coll. *(see Columbia Coll.)*
Columbia Forest Ranger Sch. *(see Lake City Comm. Coll.)*
Columbia Gorge Comm. Coll. 806 *(see also Columbia Gorge Comm. Coll.)*
Columbia Hosp. 754 *(see also Palmetto Richland Mem. Hosp.)*
Columbia Inst. of Chiropractic *(see New York Chiropractic Coll.)*
Columbia Institution for the Instruction of the Deaf & Dumb & the Blind *(see Gallaudet Univ.)*
Columbia Int'l. Univ. 374
Columbia Jr. Coll. *(see Columbia Coll.; Columbia Union Coll.; South Univ.)*
Columbia Nursing Coll. *(see Columbia Coll. of Nursing)*
Columbia Public Schools *(see Columbia Area Career Ctr.)*
Columbia Saint Mary's *(see Columbia Coll. of Nursing)*
Columbia Sch. Dist. 93 *(see Columbia Area Career Ctr.)*
Columbia Sem. *(see Columbia Theological Sem.)*
Columbia Southern Univ. 4
Columbia St. Mary's *(see Columbia Coll. of Nursing; Columbia Hosp.)*
Columbia State Comm. Coll. 383
Columbia Tech. Edu. Ctr. *(see Midlands Tech. Coll.)*
Columbia Theological Sem. 112
Columbia Union Coll. 190
Columbia Univ. *(see Columbia Univ. in the City of New York; Univ. of Portland)*
Columbia Univ. in the City of New York 274
Columbia Univ. Med. Ctr. *(see New York Presbyterian Hosp—Columbia Univ.)*
Columbia Univ. Teachers Coll. *(see Teachers Coll. of Columbia Univ.)*
Columbia-CSA HS Cleveland Partnership *(see Saint Vincent Charity Hosp.)*
Columbia-CSA/HS Greater Cleveland Area Healthcare Sys., L.P. *(see Saint Vincent Charity Hosp.)*
Columbia-Greene Beauty Sch., Inc. 788
Columbia-Greene Coll. *(see Columbia-Greene Comm. Coll.)*
Columbia-Greene Comm. Coll. 274
Columbian Coll., The *(see George Washington Univ.)*
Columbian Univ. *(see George Washington Univ.)*
Columbiana County Career & Tech. Ctr. 606
Columbiana County Joint Vocational Sch. *(see Columbiana County Career & Tech. Ctr.)*
Columbiana County Vocational Sch. Dist. *(see Columbiana County Career & Tech. Ctr.)*
Columbia-Presbyterian Med. Ctr. *(see New York Presbyterian Hosp—Columbia Univ.)*
Columbus Area Vocational-Tech. Sch. *(see Columbus Tech. Coll.)*
Columbus Children's Hosp. 732
Columbus Coll. *(see Columbus State Univ.)*
Columbus Coll. of Art & Design 317
Columbus Coll. of Design *(see Columbus Coll. of Art & Design)*
Columbus Montessori Ctr/COMET 606
Columbus Montessori Teacher Edu. Program 606

Comm. Coll. of Coffeyville *(see Coffeyville Comm. Coll.)*
Comm. Coll. of Colby *(see Colby Comm. Coll.)*
Comm. Coll. of Collin County *(see Collin County Comm. Coll. Dist.)*
Comm. Coll. of Compton *(see El Camino Coll.)*
Comm. Coll. of Cosmetology 783 *(see also B-Street Design Sch. of Int'l. Hair Styling)*
Comm. Coll. of Cowley County *(see Cowley County Comm. Coll.)*
Comm. Coll. of Danville *(see Danville Comm. Coll.)*
Comm. Coll. of Davidson County *(see Davidson County Comm. Coll.)*
Comm. Coll. of Daytona Beach *(see Daytona State Coll.)*
Comm. Coll. of Delaware County *(see Delaware County Comm. Coll.)*
Comm. Coll. of Denver 71 *(see also Red Rocks Comm. Coll.)*
Comm. Coll. of Denver Health Sciences Ctr. *(see Comm. Coll. of Denver)*
Comm. Coll. of Denver North Campus *(see Front Range Comm. Coll.)*
Comm. Coll. of Dodge City *(see Dodge City Comm. Coll.)*
Comm. Coll. of Doña Ana County *(see New Mexico State Univ.)*
Comm. Coll. of Dutchess County *(see Dutchess Comm. Coll.)*
Comm. Coll. of Dyersburg *(see Dyersburg State Comm. Coll.)*
Comm. Coll. of East Arkansas *(see East Arkansas Comm. Coll.)*
Comm. Coll. of East Mississippi *(see East Mississippi Comm. Coll.)*
Comm. Coll. of Eastern Los Angeles County *(see Mount San Antonio Coll.)*
Comm. Coll. of Eastern Maine *(see Eastern Maine Comm. Coll.)*
Comm. Coll. of Eastern West Virginia *(see Eastern West Virginia Comm. & Tech. Coll.)*
Comm. Coll. of El Paso *(see El Paso County Comm. Coll. Dist.)*
Comm. Coll. of Elgin *(see Elgin Comm. Coll.)*
Comm. Coll. of Elizabethtown *(see Elizabethtown Comm. & Tech. Coll.)*
Comm. Coll. of Erie County *(see Erie Comm. Coll.)*
Comm. Coll. of Everett *(see Everett Comm. Coll.)*
Comm. Coll. of Fayetteville *(see Fayetteville Tech. Comm. Coll.)*
Comm. Coll. of Fort Scott *(see Fort Scott Comm. Coll.)*
Comm. Coll. of Frederick *(see Frederick Comm. Coll.)*
Comm. Coll. of Garden City *(see Garden City Comm. Coll.)*
Comm. Coll. of Gila County *(see Eastern Arizona Coll.)*
Comm. Coll. of Glen Oaks *(see Glen Oaks Comm. Coll.)*
Comm. Coll. of Glendale *(see Glendale Comm. Coll.)*
Comm. Coll. of Grand Rapids *(see Grand Rapids Comm. Coll.)*
Comm. Coll. of Greenfield *(see Greenfield Comm. Coll.)*
Comm. Coll. of Guam *(see Guam Comm. Coll.)*
Comm. Coll. of Hagerstown *(see Hagerstown Comm. Coll.)*
Comm. Coll. of Halifax County *(see Halifax Comm. Coll.)*
Comm. Coll. of Harrisburg *(see Harrisburg Area Comm. Coll.)*
Comm. Coll. of Hawaii *(see Hawaii Comm. Coll.)*
Comm. Coll. of Henderson *(see Henderson Comm. Coll.)*
Comm. Coll. of Herkimer County *(see Herkimer County Comm. Coll.)*
Comm. Coll. of Highland *(see Highland Comm. Coll.)*
Comm. Coll. of Holmes County *(see Holmes Comm. Coll.)*
Comm. Coll. of Holyoke *(see Holyoke Comm. Coll.)*
Comm. Coll. of Honolulu *(see Honolulu Comm. Coll.)*
Comm. Coll. of Houston *(see Houston Comm. Coll.)*
Comm. Coll. of Howard County *(see Howard Comm. Coll.)*
Comm. Coll. of Hudson County *(see Hudson County Comm. Coll.)*
Comm. Coll. of Hudson Valley *(see Hudson Valley Comm. Coll.)*
Comm. Coll. of Humacao *(see Humacao Comm. Coll.)*
Comm. Coll. of Hutchinson *(see Hutchinson Comm. Coll.)*
Comm. Coll. of Illinois Valley *(see Illinois Valley Comm. Coll.)*
Comm. Coll. of Independence *(see Independence Comm. Coll.)*
Comm. Coll. of Jackson *(see Jackson Comm. Coll.)*
Comm. Coll. of Jefferson County *(see Jefferson Comm. Coll.)*
Comm. Coll. of Johnson County *(see Johnson County Comm. Coll.)*
Comm. Coll. of Kalamazoo Valley *(see Kalamazoo Valley Comm. Coll.)*
Comm. Coll. of Kankakee County *(see Kankakee Comm. Coll.)*
Comm. Coll. of Kansas City *(see Kansas City Kansas Comm. Coll.)*
Comm. Coll. of Kingsborough *(see City Univ. of New York Kingsborough Comm. Coll.)*
Comm. Coll. of Klamath County *(see Klamath Comm. Coll.)*
Comm. Coll. of Lake Tahoe *(see Lake Tahoe Comm. Coll.)*
Comm. Coll. of Lamar *(see Lamar Comm. Coll.)*
Comm. Coll. of Lansing *(see Lansing Comm. Coll.)*
Comm. Coll. of Laramie County *(see Laramie County Comm. Coll.)*
Comm. Coll. of Laredo *(see Laredo Comm. Coll.)*
Comm. Coll. of Lexington *(see Bluegrass Comm. & Tech. Coll.)*
Comm. Coll. of Lorain County *(see Lorain County Comm. Coll.)*
Comm. Coll. of Luzerne County *(see Luzerne County Comm. Coll.)*
Comm. Coll. of Macomb County *(see Macomb Comm. Coll.)*
Comm. Coll. of Madisonville *(see Madisonville Comm. Coll.)*
Comm. Coll. of Manatee County *(see Manatee Comm. Coll.)*
Comm. Coll. of Marshall County *(see Marshalltown Comm. Coll.)*
Comm. Coll. of Marshalltown *(see Marshalltown Comm. Coll.)*
Comm. Coll. of Massachusetts Bay *(see Massachusetts Bay Comm. Coll.)*
Comm. Coll. of Mercer County *(see Mercer County Comm. Coll.)*
Comm. Coll. of Meridian *(see Meridian Comm. Coll.)*
Comm. Coll. of Micronesia *(see Coll. of Micronesia-FSM)*
Comm. Coll. of Mid Michigan *(see Mid Michigan Comm. Coll.)*
Comm. Coll. of Middlesex *(see Middlesex Comm. Coll.)*
Comm. Coll. of Monroe County *(see Monroe Comm. Coll.; Monroe County Comm. Coll.)*
Comm. Coll. of Montgomery County *(see Montgomery County Comm. Coll.)*
Comm. Coll. of Moraine Valley *(see Moraine Valley Comm. Coll.)*
Comm. Coll. of Muskegon *(see Muskegon Comm. Coll.)*
Comm. Coll. of Nashville *(see Nashville State Comm. Coll.)*

Creek VA Med. Ctr. *(see Thomas E. Creek Veterans Affairs Med. Ctr.)*
Creek VAMC *(see Thomas E. Creek Veterans Affairs Med. Ctr.)*
Creek Veterans Affairs Med. Ctr. *(see Thomas E. Creek Veterans Affairs Med. Ctr.)*
Creighton Univ. 250
Crescent City Sch. of Gaming & Bartending, Inc. *(see Crescent Schools)*
Crescent Schools 540
Crestmont Coll. *(see Salvation Army Coll. for Officer Training at Crestmont)*
CRI Career Trainin—Tacoma 670
Crichton Coll. 383
Crippled Children's Hosp. *(see British Columbia Children's Hosp.)*
Criswell Ctr. for Biblical Studies *(see Criswell Coll.)*
Criswell Coll., The 396
Critical Health Systems of North Carolina *(see Raleigh Sch. of Nurse Anesthesia)*
Croatan Normal Sch. *(see Univ. of North Carolina at Pembroke)*
Cross Lanes National Inst. of Techno. *(see Everest Inst—Cross Lanes)*
Crossett Sch. of Cosmetology LLC 470
Crossroads Bible Coll. 147
Crossroads Coll. 221 *(see also Crossroads Bible Coll.)*
Crossville Area Vocational-Tech. Sch. *(see Tennessee Techno. Ctr. at Crossville)*
Crossville Vocational-Tech. Sch. *(see Tennessee Techno. Ctr. at Crossville)*
Crossville Vo-Tech Sch. *(see Tennessee Techno. Ctr. at Crossville)*
Crouse Hosp. 724
Crouse Irving Hosp. *(see Crouse Hosp.)*
Crouse Irving Mem. Hosp. *(see Crouse Hosp.)*
Crowder Coll. 237
Crowley's Ridge Coll. 27
Crowley's Ridge Tech. Inst. 470
Crown Coll. 221, 795
Crownpoint Health Care Facility 722
Crownpoint Inst. of Techno. 788 *(see also Navajo Tech. Coll.)*
Crozer Hosp. *(see Crozer-Chester Med. Ctr.)*
Crozer Theological Sem. *(see Colgate Rochester Crozer Divinity Sch.)*
Crozer-Chester Med. Ctr. 738
Crozer-Keystone Health Sys. *(see Crozer-Chester Med. Ctr.)*
Cruise Career Training Inst. *(see Keiser Career Coll.)*
Crump Area Vocational-Tech. Sch. *(see Tennessee Techno. Ctr. at Crump)*
Crump Area Vo-Tech Sch. *(see Tennessee Techno. Ctr. at Crump)*
Crump Vocational-Tech. Sch. *(see Tennessee Techno. Ctr. at Crump)*
Crump Vo-Tech Sch. *(see Tennessee Techno. Ctr. at Crump)*
Crum's Beauty Coll. 534
Crystal Cathedral, The 686
Crystal Mountain Sch. of Massage Therapy 584
CSC Inst. 791
CSI Career Coll. 478, 776
CSI, Inc. *(see CSI Career Coll.)*
CSU Bakersfield *(see California State Univ., Bakersfield)*
CSU Channel Islands *(see California State Univ., Channel Islands)*
CSU Dominguez Hills *(see California State Univ., Dominguez Hills)*
CSU East Bay *(see California State Univ., East Bay)*
CSU Fresno *(see California State Univ., Fresno)*
CSU Fullerton *(see California State Univ., Fullerton)*
CSU Hayward *(see California State Univ., East Bay)*
CSU Humboldt *(see Humboldt State Univ.)*
CSU LA *(see California State Univ., Los Angeles)*
CSU Long Beach *(see California State Univ., Long Beach)*
CSU Los Angeles *(see California State Univ., Los Angeles)*
CSU Monterey Bay *(see California State Univ., Monterey Bay)*
CSU Northridge *(see California State Univ., Northridge)*
CSU Sacramento *(see California State Univ., Sacramento)*
CSU San Bernardino *(see California State Univ., San Bernardino)*
CSU San Jose *(see San Jose State Univ.)*
CSU San Marcos *(see California State Univ., San Marcos)*
CSU Stanislaus *(see California State Univ., Stanislaus)*
CTC at WVU Inst. of Techno. *(see Comm. & Tech. Coll. at West Virginia Univ. Inst. of Techno.)*
CTC Shepherd *(see Blue Ridge Comm. & Tech. Coll.)*
C-TEC Adult Edu. Ctr. *(see Career & Techno. Ctr.s of Licking County)*
CU Denver *(see Univ. of Colorado Denver)*
CUA Sch. of Theology & Religious Studies *(see Catholic Univ. of America)*
C—Colorado Springs *(see Univ. of Colorado at Colorado Springs)*
Cuesta Coll. 42
Culinard *(see Virginia Coll.)*
Culinard at Virginia Coll. 10
Culinary Acad. of Austin 650
Culinary Acad. of California *(see California Culinary Acad.)*
Culinary Acad. of Long Island 588
Culinary Acad. of New York Mgmnt. Sch. 588, 788–789 *(see also Career Acad. of New York)*
Culinary Acad. of Orlando *(see Orlando Culinary Acad.; Texas Culinary Acad.)*
Culinary Acad. of Texas *(see Texas Culinary Acad.)*
Culinary Arts Inst. of Louisiana 784
Culinary Arts Inst. of San Antonio *(see Culinary Inst. of America)*
Culinary Arts Sch. of California *(see California Sch. of Culinary Arts)*
Culinary Edu. Inst. *(see Inst. of Culinary Edu.)*
Culinary Inst. Alain & Marie LeNotre 396
Culinary Inst. of America 275
Culinary Inst. of Americ—Graystone *(see Culinary Inst. of Americ—Greystone)*
Culinary Inst. of Charleston *(see Trident Tech. Coll.)*
Culinary Inst. of Connecticut *(see Connecticut Culinary Inst.)*
Culinary Inst. of Dallas *(see Texas Culinary Acad.)*
Culinary Inst. of Florida *(see Lincoln Coll. of Techno.)*
Culinary Inst. of Houston *(see Culinary Inst. Alain & Marie LeNotre)*
Culinary Inst. of Las Vegas *(see Art Inst. of Las Vegas)*
Culinary Inst. of Louisiana *(see Louisiana Culinary Inst.)*
Culinary Inst. of New England *(see New England Culinary Inst.)*
Culinary Inst. of New Orleans 784
Culinary Inst. of Oregon *(see Oregon Culinary Inst.)*
Culinary Inst. of Pennsylvania *(see Pennsylvania Culinary Inst.)*
Culinary Inst. of Portland *(see Western Culinary Inst.)*
Culinary Inst. of Scottsdale *(see Scottsdale Culinary Inst.)*
Culinary Sch. of the Rockies 495
Culpeper Cosmetology Training Ctr. 664
Culver-Stockton Coll. 237

D

Detroit Riverview Ctr. *(see Saint John Macomb-Oakland Hosp. Detroit Riverview Ctr.)*
Detroit Sinai Hosp. *(see Sinai-Grace Hosp.)*
Detroit-Macomb Hosp. Corporation *(see Saint John Macomb-Oakland Hosp. Detroit Riverview Ctr.)*
Dettmer Hosp. *(see Upper Valley Med. Ctr.)*
Devereux Foundation *(see Devereux Inst. of Clinical Training & Research)*
Devereux ICTR *(see Devereux Inst. of Clinical Training & Research)*
Devereux Inst. of Clinical Training & Research, The 738
Devils Lake Jr. Coll. & Bus. Sch. *(see Lake Region State Coll.)*
DeVoe Coll. of Beauty 467
DeVry Calgary *(see DeVry Inst. of Techno., Calgary)*
DeVry Coll. of New York 276
DeVry Coll. of Techno—North Brunswick 788 *(see also DeVry Univ. North Brunswick)*
DeVry Inst. of Techno. *(see DeVry Coll. of New York; DeVry Univ. Georgia; DeVry Univ. Pomona)*
DeVry Inst. of Techno. City of Industry *(see DeVry Univ. Pomona)*
DeVry Inst. of Techno. Denver *(see DeVry Univ. Westminster)*
DeVry Inst. of Techno., Calgary 455
DeVry Inst. of Techno—Addison *(see DeVry Univ. DuPage)*
DeVry Inst. of Techno—Alpharetta *(see DeVry Univ. Georgia)*
DeVry Inst. of Techno—Chicago *(see DeVry Univ. Chicago)*
DeVry Inst. of Techno—Columbus *(see DeVry Univ. Columbus)*
DeVry Inst. of Techno—DuPage *(see DeVry Univ. DuPage)*
DeVry Inst. of Techno—Irving *(see DeVry Univ. Irving)*
DeVry Inst. of Techno—Kansas City *(see DeVry Univ. Kansas City)*
DeVry Inst. of Techno—Lombard *(see DeVry Univ. DuPage)*
DeVry Inst. of Techno—Long Beach *(see DeVry Univ. Pomona)*
DeVry Inst. of Techno—North Brunswick *(see DeVry Univ. North Brunswick)*
DeVry Inst. of Techno—Orlando *(see DeVry Univ. Orlando)*
DeVry Inst. of Techno—Phoenix *(see DeVry Univ. Northeast Phoenix)*
DeVry Inst. of Techno—Pomona *(see DeVry Univ. Pomona)*
DeVry Inst. of Techno—Tinley Park *(see DeVry Univ. DuPage)*
DeVry Long Island *(see DeVry Coll. of New York)*
DeVry New York *(see DeVry Coll. of New York)*
DeVry Tech. Inst. *(see DeVry Univ. Chicago; DeVry Univ. Pomona; DeVry Univ. Westminster)*
DeVry Tech. Inst—Woodbridge *(see DeVry Univ. North Brunswick)*
DeVry Univ. Arlington *(see DeVry Univ. Crystal City)*
DeVry Univ. Calgary *(see DeVry Inst. of Techno., Calgary)*
DeVry Univ. Chicago 130
DeVry Univ. Cleveland Downtown 318
DeVry Univ. Columbus 318
DeVry Univ. Crystal City 422
DeVry Univ. Dallas *(see DeVry Univ. Irving)*
DeVry Univ. Denver *(see DeVry Univ. Westminster)*
DeVry Univ. DuPage 130
DeVry Univ. Federal Way 433
DeVry Univ. Fort Washington *(see DeVry Univ. Philadelphia)*
DeVry Univ. Georgia 112
DeVry Univ. Georgi—Alpharetta *(see DeVry Univ. Georgia)*
DeVry Univ. Grad. Sch. of Mgmnt. *(see DeVry Univ. Oak Brook)*
DeVry Univ. Irvine 42, 777
DeVry Univ. Irving 396
DeVry Univ. Kansas City 237
DeVry Univ. North Brunswick 260
DeVry Univ. Northeast Phoenix 17
DeVry Univ. Oak Brook 130
DeVry Univ. Orlando 92
DeVry Univ. Philadelphia 347
DeVry Univ. Phoenix 18
DeVry Univ. Pomona 43
DeVry Univ. Seattle *(see DeVry Univ. Federal Way)*
DeVry Univ. Southern California *(see DeVry Univ. Pomona)*
DeVry Univ. West Hills *(see DeVry Univ. Pomona)*
DeVry Univ. Westminster 72
DeVry Univ.-Kansas City Downtown 237
DeVry Univ—Mesa Ctr. 18
DeVry Univ—Nashville 383
DeVry Univ—North Brunswick 788
DeVry Univ—Scottsdale Ctr. *(see DeVry Univ. Northeast Phoenix)*
DeVry Univ—St. Louis West 237
Dewey Coll. *(see John Dewey Coll.)*
DeWolff Coll. of Hairstyling & Cosmetology 584
Diablo Valley Coll. 43
Diamond Beauty Coll. 809
Diamond Council of America 641
Diamond Oaks Career Development Campus *(see Great Oaks Inst. of Techno. & Career Developmen—Diamond Oaks Campus)*
Diamond's Barber Coll. 819
Dickerson Beauty Acad. 795
Dickinson Bus. Sch. *(see Career Point Coll.; Wright Career Coll.)*
Dickinson Coll. 347 *(see also Fairleigh Dickinson Univ.)*
Dickinson Normal Sch. *(see Dickinson State Univ.)*
Dickinson Sch. of Law 356 *(see also Pennsylvania State Univ.)*
Dickinson State Coll. *(see Dickinson State Univ.)*
Dickinson State Teachers Coll. *(see Dickinson State Univ.)*
Dickinson State Univ. 311
Dickinson Univ. *(see Fairleigh Dickinson Univ.)*
Dickson & Associates, LLC *(see Dale Carnegie Training of Western Connecticut)*
Dickson Area Vocational-Tech. Sch. *(see Tennessee Techno. Ctr. at Dickson)*
Dickson Area Vo-Tech Sch. *(see Tennessee Techno. Ctr. at Dickson)*
Dickson Vocational-Tech. Sch. *(see Tennessee Techno. Ctr. at Dickson)*
Dickson Vo-Tech Sch. *(see Tennessee Techno. Ctr. at Dickson)*
Didi Hirsch Comm. Mental Health Ctr. 686
Diesel Driving Acad. 540
Diesel Inst. of America 784 *(see also North American Trade Schools)*
DigiPen Applied Computer Graphics Sch. *(see DigiPen Inst. of Techno.)*
DigiPen Inst. of Techno. 433
Digital Circus *(see Sch. of Communication Arts)*
Digital Media Arts Coll. 92
DiGrigoli Sch. of Cosmetology, Inc. 551
Dillard Univ. 179
Dimensions Healthcare Sys. *(see Prince George's Hosp. Ctr.)*
Dimrock Comm. Health CCtr. *(see New England Coll. of Optometry)*
Diné Coll. 18
Dingell VA Med. Ctr. *(see John D. Dingell Veterans Affairs Med. Ctr.)*
Dingell VAMC *(see John D. Dingell Veterans Affairs Med. Ctr.)*
Dingell Veterans Affairs Med. Ctr. *(see John D. Dingell Veterans Affairs Med. Ctr.)*

Drew Univ. 260
Drew Univ. of Medicine & Science *(see Charles Drew Univ. of Medicine & Science)*
Drew Univ. Theological Sch. *(see Drew Univ.)*
Drexel Inst. *(see Drexel Univ.)*
Drexel Univ. 347
Driving Acad. of Georgia *(see Georgia Driving Acad.)*
Druid City Hosp. *(see DCH Reg. Med. Ctr.)*
Drury Coll. *(see Drury Univ.)*
Drury Univ. 237
DSU Training Inst. 794
du Cret Sch. of the Arts *(see duCret Sch. of the Arts)*
Dubai Men's Coll. *(see Higher Colleges of Techno. Dubai Men's Coll.)*
Dubai Women's Coll. *(see Higher Colleges of Techno. Dubai Women's Coll.)*
DuBois Bus. Coll. 347
DuBois Coll. of Bus. *(see DuBois Bus. Coll.)*
Dubuque Coll. *(see Loras Coll.)*
Dubuque Univ. *(see Univ. of Dubuque)*
duCret Sch. of the Arts 577
Dudley Beauty Coll—Charlotte 601
Dudley Beauty Coll—Chicago 813
Dudley Beauty Coll—Kernersville *(see Dudley Cosmetology Univ.)*
Dudley Beauty Coll—Washington 502
Dudley Beauty Sch. *(see Dudley Beauty Coll—Washington)*
Dudley Beauty Sch. Sys. of Illinois *(see Dudley Beauty Coll—Chicago)*
Dudley Beauty Sch—Chicago *(see Dudley Beauty Coll—Chicago)*
Dudley Beauty Sch—Kernersville *(see Dudley Cosmetology Univ.)*
Dudley Cosmetology Univ. 601
Dudley Nwani Int'l. Barber & Styling Coll. *(see Dudley Nwani, The Sch.)*
Dudley Nwani, The Sch. 641, 793
Due West Female Coll. *(see Erskine Coll.)*
Duff's Bus. Inst. 791 *(see also Everest Inst—Pittsburgh)*
Duff's Iron City Coll. *(see Everest Inst—Pittsburgh)*
Duff's Mercantile Coll. *(see Everest Inst—Pittsburgh)*
Duke Divinity Sch. *(see Duke Univ.)*
Duke Univ. 302
Duke Univ. Divinity Sch. *(see Duke Univ.)*
Duke Univ. Health Sys. *(see Watts Sch. of Nursing)*
Dull Knife Mem. Coll. *(see Chief Dull Knife Coll.)*
Duluth Area Inst. of Techno. *(see Lake Superior Coll.)*
Duluth Area Vocational Tech. Inst. *(see Lake Superior Coll.)*
Duluth Bus. Univ. 221
Duluth Comm. Coll. Ctr. *(see Lake Superior Coll.)*
Duluth Tech. Coll. *(see Lake Superior Coll.)*
Duncan Area Vocational-Tech. Ctr. *(see Red River Techno. Ctr.)*
Dundalk Comm. Coll. *(see Comm. Coll. of Baltimore County)*
Dunlap-Stone Univ. 18, 775
Dunwoody Coll. of Techno. 221
Dunwoody Inst. *(see Dunwoody Coll. of Techno.)*
duPont Children's Hosp. *(see Alfred I. duPont Hosp. for Children)*
duPont Hosp. for Children *(see Alfred I. duPont Hosp. for Children)*
duPont Inst. *(see Alfred I. duPont Hosp. for Children)*
Duquesne Univ. 348
DuQuoin Beauty Coll. 782
Durham Beauty Acad. 601, 789
Durham Coll. 759 *(see also Durham Tech. Comm. Coll.)*
Durham Comm. Coll. *(see Durham Tech. Comm. Coll.)*
Durham Reg. Hosp. *(see Watts Sch. of Nursing)*
Durham State Normal Sch. *(see North Carolina Central Univ.)*
Durham Tech. Coll. *(see Durham Tech. Comm. Coll.)*
Durham Tech. Comm. Coll. 302
Durham VA Med. Ctr. *(see Durham Veterans Affairs Med. Ctr.)*
Durham VAMC *(see Durham Veterans Affairs Med. Ctr.)*
Durham Veterans Affairs Med. Ctr. 730
Dutchess Coll. *(see Dutchess Comm. Coll.)*
Dutchess Comm. Coll. 276
Dutchess County Dept. of Mental Hygiene 724
DuVall's Sch. of Cosmetology 819
Duwayne E. Keller & Associates, Inc. 507
Duwayne Keller & Associates *(see Duwayne E. Keller & Associates, Inc.)*
DVS Coll. 478, 777
Dwight D. Eisenhower Veterans Affairs Med. Ctr. 707
Dwight David Eisenhower Army Med. Ctr. 699
Dyersburg Coll. *(see Dyersburg State Comm. Coll.)*
Dyersburg Comm. Coll. *(see Dyersburg State Comm. Coll.)*
Dyersburg State Comm. Coll. 383
Dyke Coll. *(see Chancellor Univ.)*
Dynamic Educational Systems, Inc. *(see Carl D. Perkins Job Corps Ctr.)*
D'Youville Coll. 275

E

E. J. Taylor Corporation 601
E.I.N.E., Inc. *(see Electrology Inst. of New England)*
Eagle Gate Coll. 413
EAN Univ. 764
Earle C. Clements Job Corps Acad. *(see Earle C. Clements Job Corps Ctr.)*
Earle C. Clements Job Corps Ctr. 536
Earlham Coll. 147
Earlham Sch. of Religion *(see Earlham Coll.)*
Earl's Acad. of Beauty 467
Early Coll., The *(see Bard Coll. at Simon's Rock)*
East Alabama Male Coll. *(see Auburn Univ.)*
East Arkansas Coll. *(see East Arkansas Comm. Coll.)*
East Arkansas Comm. Coll. 27
East Carolina Coll. *(see East Carolina Univ.)*
East Carolina Univ. 302
East Central Coll. 237 *(see also East Central Comm. Coll.; East Central Tech. Coll.)*
East Central Comm. Coll. 230
East Central Tech. Coll. 113
East Central Tech. Inst. *(see East Central Tech. Coll.; Ivy Tech Comm. Coll—East Central)*
East Central Univ. 331
East Coast Aero Tech 785 *(see also National Aviation Acad—New England)*
East Coast Aero Tech. Sch. *(see National Aviation Acad—New England)*
East Florida Sem. *(see Univ. of Florida)*
East Georgia Coll. 113
East Grand Forks Tech. Coll. *(see Northland Comm. & Tech. Coll.)*
East Grand Forks Tech. Inst. *(see Northland Comm. & Tech. Coll.)*
East Jefferson General Hosp. 709
East Jefferson Hosp. *(see East Jefferson General Hosp.)*
East LA Coll. *(see East Los Angeles Coll.)*
East Los Angeles Coll. 43
East Los Angeles Edu. & Career Ctr. 687, 777

Eastern Washington State Coll. *(see Eastern Washington Univ.)*
Eastern Washington Univ. 433
Eastern West Virginia Coll. *(see Eastern West Virginia Comm. & Tech. Coll.)*
Eastern West Virginia Comm. & Tech. Coll. 807
Eastern Wyoming Coll. 453
Eastfield Coll. 397
Eastland Career Ctr—Adult Workforce Development Ctr. 607
Eastland-Fairfield Career & Tech. Schools *(see Eastland Career Ctr—Adult Workforce Development Ctr.; Fairfield Career Ctr.)*
Eastman Sch. of Music *(see Univ. of Rochester)*
East-West Coll. of the Healing Arts 620
East-West Medicne Univ. *(see Univ. of East-West Medicine)*
East-West Univ. 131
Eastwick Coll. 788
Eaton Beauty Stylist Coll., Inc. 470
Eaton Therapeutic Ctr. *(see Acad. of Natural Therapy)*
Eau Claire State Normal Sch. *(see Univ. of Wisconsin-Eau Claire)*
Eau Claire State Teachers Coll. *(see Univ. of Wisconsin-Eau Claire)*
Eberle Tech. Ctr. *(see Fred W. Eberle Tech. Ctr.)*
Ecclesia Coll. 27
Ecclesiastical Faculty at Boston Coll. *(see Boston Coll.)*
Echelon Edge Acad. of Hair, Skin & Nails *(see Francois D. Hair Design Acad.)*
Eckerd Coll. 92
Eclectic Coll. of Chiropractic *(see Southern California Univ. of Health Sciences)*
Ecole de hautes Etudes commerciales du Nord 764
Ecole de Mgmnt. de Lyon 764
Ecole des Hautes Etudes Commerciales 765
Ecole des Hautes Etudes Commerciales de Montréal *(see HEC Montréal)*
Ecole Hoteliere de Lausanne 459
Ecole "Les Roches" *(see "Les Roches" Sch. of Hotel Mgmnt.)*
Ecole Supérieure de Commerce de Clermont-Ferrand *(see Groupe ESC Clermont)*
Ecole supérieure de Commerce de Grenoble 765
Ecole supérieure de Commerce de Paris 765
Ecole Superieure de Commerce et de Mgmnt. *(see Groupe Ecole supérieure de Commerce et de Mgmnt.)*
Ecole Superieure des Sciences Economiques et Commerciales 765
Ecole supériuer de Commerce de Toulouse *(see Groupe ESC Toulouse)*
École Théologique de Montréal *(see Montreal Sch. of Theology)*
ECPI Coll. of Techno. *(see Med. Careers Inst.)*
ECPI Coll. of Techno. 422
ECPI Coll. of Techno—Richmond 423, 795
ECPI Computer Inst. *(see ECPI Coll. of Techno.; ECPI Coll. of Techno—Richmond)*
ECPI Computer Inst—Roanoke *(see ECPI Tech. Coll.)*
ECPI Tech. Coll. *(see ECPI Coll. of Techno—Richmond)*
ECPI Tech. Coll. 423
ECPI Tech. Coll—Raleigh 789
ECPI Tech. Coll—Roanoke 795
Ecumenical Inst., The 706
Ecumenical Theological Sem. 210
Ed W. Grooms & Associates, Inc. 789 *(see also Dale Carnegie Training of Greater Cincinnati)*
Ed Waters Coll. *(see Edward Waters Coll.)*
Eden Sem. *(see Eden Theological Sem.)*
Eden Theological Sem. 237
Edgecombe Coll. *(see Edgecombe Comm. Coll.)*
Edgecombe Comm. Coll. 302
Edgewood Coll. 446
EDHEC Bus. Sch. *(see Ecole de hautes Etudes commerciales du Nord)*
EDHEC Grande Ecole *(see Ecole de hautes Etudes commerciales du Nord)*
EDHEC Sch. of Bus. *(see Ecole de hautes Etudes commerciales du Nord)*
EDIC Coll. 366
Edinboro Acad. *(see Edinboro Univ. of Pennsylvania)*
Edinboro State Coll. *(see Edinboro Univ. of Pennsylvania)*
Edinboro State Teachers Coll. *(see Edinboro Univ. of Pennsylvania)*
Edinboro Univ. of Pennsylvania 348
Edinburg Jr. Coll. *(see Univ. of Texa—Pan American)*
Edison Coll. 780 *(see also Edison State Coll.; Edison State Comm. Coll.; Thomas Edison State Coll.)*
Edison Comm. Coll. 780 *(see also Edison State Coll.; Edison State Comm. Coll.)*
Edison State Coll. 92, 780 *(see also Edison State Comm. Coll.; Thomas Edison State Coll.)*
Edison State Comm. Coll. 319
Edison State General & Tech. Coll. *(see Edison State Comm. Coll.)*
Edison Tech. Sch. *(see Seattle Central Comm. Coll.)*
Edith Nourse Rogers Mem. Veterans Hosp. 712
Edith Nourse Rogers VA Med. Ctr. *(see Edith Nourse Rogers Mem. Veterans Hosp.)*
Edith Nourse Rogers VAMC *(see Edith Nourse Rogers Mem. Veterans Hosp.)*
Edith Nourse Rogers Veterans Affairs Med. Ctr. *(see Edith Nourse Rogers Mem. Veterans Hosp.)*
Edmond Language Inst. 616
Edmonds Coll. *(see Edmonds Comm. Coll.)*
Edmonds Comm. Coll. 434
Edmonton Baptist Sem. *(see Taylor Univ. Coll. & Sem.)*
Edmonton General Continuing Care Centre *(see Nightingale Med. Inst.)*
Edmonton Sem. *(see Taylor Univ. Coll. & Sem.)*
Edmundson Hosp. *(see Jennie Edmundson Hosp.)*
Edmundson Mem. Hosp. *(see Jennie Edmundson Hosp.)*
Édouard-Montpetit Coll. *(see Collége Édouard-Montpetit)*
EDP Coll. 366, 792
EDP Coll. of PR *(see EDP Coll.)*
EDP Coll. of Puerto Rico *(see EDP Coll.)*
EDP Sch. of Computer Programming, Inc. 589
Educatinal Tech. Coll. *(see Educational Tech. Coll.)*
Educatinal Tech. Coll—Coamo *(see Educational Tech. Coll—Coamo)*
Educating Hands Sch. of Massage 507
Edu. America Univ. *(see Remington Coll—San Diego)*
Edu. Americ—Colorado Springs *(see Remington Coll—Colorado Springs)*
Edu. Americ—Dallas *(see Remington Coll—Houston)*
Edu. Americ—Honolulu *(see Remington Coll—San Diego)*
Edu. Americ—Houston *(see Remington Coll—Houston)*

Elizabethton Vo-Tech Sch. *(see Tennessee Techno. Ctr. at Elizabethton)*
Elizabethtown Beauty Sch. 536
Elizabethtown Coll. 348 *(see also Elizabethtown Comm. & Tech. Coll.)*
Elizabethtown Comm. & Tech. Coll. 172
Elizabethtown Comm. Coll. *(see Elizabethtown Comm. & Tech. Coll.)*
Elk Lake Sch. Dist. *(see Susquehanna Career & Techno. Ctr.)*
Elkhart General Healthcare Sys. *(see Elkhart General Hosp.)*
Elkhart General Hosp. 705
Elkhart Hosp. *(see Elkhart General Hosp.)*
Elkhart Inst. *(see Goshen Coll.)*
Elkins Coll. *(see Davis & Elkins Coll.)*
Elko Comm. Coll. *(see Great Basin Coll.)*
Elley Bus. Sch. *(see Mildred Elley)*
Ellis Coll. 779, 782, 789
Ellis Coll. of New York Inst. of Techno. *(see Ellis Univ.; New York Inst. of Techno—Old Westbury)*
Ellis Coll. of NYIT *(see Ellis Univ.)*
Ellis Hosp. Sch. of Nursing 724
Ellis Univ. 131, 782
Ellsworth Coll. *(see Ellsworth Comm. Coll.)*
Ellsworth Comm. Coll. 158
Elmhurst Acad. & Jr. Coll. *(see Elmhurst Coll.)*
Elmhurst Coll. 131
Elmhurst Hosp. *(see Elmhurst Mem. Hosp.)*
Elmhurst Mem. Healthcare *(see Elmhurst Mem. Hosp.)*
Elmhurst Mem. Hosp. 702
Elmira Bus. & Shorthand Coll. *(see Elmira Bus. Inst.)*
Elmira Bus. Inst. 276
Elmira Coll. 276
Elms Coll. *(see Coll. of Our Lady of the Elms)*
Elon Coll. *(see Elon Univ.)*
Elon Univ. 302
ELS Language Ctr.s 577–578
Ely State Jr. Coll. *(see Vermilion Comm. Coll.)*
EM Lyon *(see Ecole de Mgmnt. de Lyon)*
Emanuel Children's Hosp. *(see Legacy Emanuel Children's Hosp.)*
Embassy CES 507
Embry-Riddle Aeronautical Univ. 92
Emergency Med. Sciences Training Inst. 687
Emergency Training Associates, Inc. 716
Emergency Training Services, Inc. 479
Emerson Coll. 199
Emes Investment Corporation *(see Career Colleges of America)*
Emil Fries Piano & Training Ctr. *(see Emil Fries Sch. of Piano Tuning & Techno.)*
Emil Fries Sch. of Piano Tuning & Techno. 669
Emily Griffith Opportunity Sch. 495
Emmanuel Bible Coll. 74, 455 *(see also Nazarene Bible Coll.)*
Emmanuel Coll. 113, 199 *(see also Emmanuel Bible Coll.; Nazarene Bible Coll.)*
Emmanuel Coll. of Victoria Univ. 455
Emmanuel Missionary Coll. *(see Andrews Univ.)*
Emmanuel Sch. of Religion 384
Emma's Beauty Acad—Juana Diaz 633
Emma's Beauty Acad—Mayaguez 633
Emmaus Bible Coll. 158
Emmaus Coll. *(see Emmaus Bible Coll.)*
Emmett Comm. Coll. *(see North Central Michigan Coll.)*
Emory & Henry Coll. 423
Emory Coll. *(see Emory Univ.)*
Emory Healthcare *(see Emory Univ.)*
Emory Hospitals *(see Emory Univ.)*
Emory Univ. 113
Emperor's Coll. of Traditional Oriental Medicine 44
Empire Beauty Sch. #3 *(see Empire Beauty Sch—Somersworth)*
Empire Beauty Sch. 518, 624
Empire Beauty Sch., Inc—Woodhaven Road Campus *(see Empire Beauty Sch—Northeast Philadelphia)*
Empire Beauty Sch., In—Hanover 625
Empire Beauty Sch—Bordentown 579
Empire Beauty Sch—Boston 551, 785
Empire Beauty Sch—Ctr. City Philadelphia 624
Empire Beauty Sch—Chambersburg *(see Chambersburg Beauty Sch.)*
Empire Beauty Sch—Cherry Hill 579
Empire Beauty Sch—Dunwoody 518
Empire Beauty Sch—Exton 625
Empire Beauty Sch—Frankford Avenue *(see Empire Beauty Sch—Ctr. City Philadelphia)*
Empire Beauty Sch—Hanover Park 526, 782
Empire Beauty Sch—Harrisburg 625
Empire Beauty Sch—Laconia 573
Empire Beauty Sch—Lancaster 625
Empire Beauty Sch—Laurel Springs 579
Empire Beauty Sch—Lawrenceville, GA 518
Empire Beauty Sch—Lawrenceville, NJ *(see Empire Beauty Sch—Bordentown)*
Empire Beauty Sch—Lebanon 625
Empire Beauty Sch—Malden 551, 785
Empire Beauty Sch—Matthew 601
Empire Beauty Sch—Moosic 625
Empire Beauty Sch—Northeast Philadelphia 625
Empire Beauty Sch—Pottstown 791
Empire Beauty Sch—Pottsville 625
Empire Beauty Sch—Reading 625
Empire Beauty Sch—Shamokin Dam 625
Empire Beauty Sch—Somersworth 573
Empire Beauty Sch—State Coll. 625
Empire Beauty Sch—Warminster 625
Empire Beauty Sch—West Chester *(see Empire Beauty Sch—Exton)*
Empire Beauty Sch—Whitehall 626
Empire Beauty Sch—Williamsport 626
Empire Beauty Sch—York 626
Empire Coll. 44
Empire State Coll. *(see State Univ. of New York Empire State Coll.)*
Employment Solutions, Inc. *(see Employment Solution—Coll. for Tech. Edu.)*
Employment Solution—Coll. for Tech. Edu. 536
Emporia Kansas State Coll. *(see Emporia State Univ.)*
Emporia State Univ. 165
Emporia Univ. *(see Emporia State Univ.)*
Endicott Coll. 199
Engine City Tech. Inst. 579
Engineering Sch. of Milwaukee *(see Milwaukee Sch. of Engineering)*
Englewood Hosp. & Med. Ctr. 720
English Ctr. for Int'l. Women 479
English Ctr., The 507
English for Int'l.s 518
English House 547
English Language Ctr. *(see Ctr. of English Language; Defense Language Inst. English Language Ctr.)*
English Language Inst. 479
English Language Specialists 794
Enid Beauty Coll., Inc. 615
EnSynergy Southeastern Sch. of Esthetics 812
Enterprise Comm. Coll. *(see Enterprise-Ozark Comm. Coll.)*
Enterprise State Jr. Coll. *(see Enterprise-Ozark Comm. Coll.)*
Enterprise-Ozark Coll. *(see Enterprise-Ozark Comm. Coll.)*
Enterprise-Ozark Comm. Coll. 5
Entourage Beauty Coll. *(see Larry's Barber Coll. 1)*
Environmental Science & Forestry Coll. *(see State Univ. of New York Coll. of Environmental Science & Forestry)*

Evangelical Sem. of Puerto Rico 366
Evangelical Theological Coll. *(see Dallas Theological Sem.)*
Evangelical Theological Sem. 348, 791 *(see also Garrett-Evangelical Theological Sem.)*
Evan's Hairstyling Coll—Cedar City 660
Evan's Hairstyling Coll—Orem 660
Evan's Hairstyling Coll—St. George 660
Evanston Collegiate Inst. *(see Kendall Coll.)*
Evanston Hosp. 702
Evanston Northwestern Healthcare *(see DePaul Univ.; Evanston Hosp.)*
Evanston-Glenbrook Hosp. *(see Evanston Hosp.)*
Evansville Coll. *(see Univ. of Evansville)*
Evansville Tri-State Beauty Coll. 530
Evansville Univ. *(see Univ. of Evansville)*
Eveleth Jr. Coll. *(see Mesabi Range Comm. & Tech. Coll.)*
Everest Coll. 779 *(see also Everest Coll—Phoenix)*
Everest Coll—Alhambra 479, 776
Everest Coll—Anaheim 479, 776
Everest Coll—Atlanta DeKalb *(see Everest Inst—Atlanta DeKalb)*
Everest Coll—Atlanta Downtown *(see Everest Inst—Atlanta Downtown)*
Everest Coll—Bremerton 669, 795
Everest Coll—City of Industry 44, 776
Everest Coll—Colorado Springs 72, 779
Everest Coll—Denver *(see Everest Coll—Thornton)*
Everest Coll—Earth City 786
Everest Coll—Gardena 479, 776
Everest Coll—Hayward 479, 776
Everest Coll—Los Angeles 479, 776
Everest Coll—Ontario 44, 776
Everest Coll—Phoenix 18
Everest Coll—Pittsburgh *(see Everest Inst—Pittsburgh)*
Everest Coll—Portland 338, 790
Everest Coll—Rancho Cucamonga *(see Everest Coll—Springfield)*
Everest Coll—Renton 669, 795
Everest Coll—Reseda 479, 776
Everest Coll—Salt Lake City 413, 794
Everest Coll—San Bernardino 44, 776
Everest Coll—San Francisco 479, 776
Everest Coll—San Jose 480, 776
Everest Coll—Skokie 526, 782
Everest Coll—Springfield 238, 787
Everest Coll—Thornton 72
Everest Coll—Torrance 480, 776
Everest Coll—West Los Angeles 44, 776
Everest Coll—West Valley City *(see Everest Coll—Salt Lake City)*
Everest Inst—Atlanta DeKalb 113, 781
Everest Inst—Atlanta Downtown 518, 781
Everest Inst—Brighton 552, 785
Everest Inst—Chelsea 552, 785
Everest Inst—Cross Lanes 440, 796
Everest Inst—Eagan 561, 785
Everest Inst—Gahanna 607, 789
Everest Inst—Grand Rapids 556, 785
Everest Inst—Miami 93
Everest Inst—Newport News 665, 795
Everest Inst—Pittsburgh 348, 791
Everest Inst—Rochester 276, 789
Everest Inst—San Antonio 651, 794
Everest Inst—Silver Spring 547
Everest Inst—South Plainfield 579, 788
Everest Inst—Southfield 556, 785
Everest Univ—Clearwater *(see Everest Univ—Largo)*
Everest Univ—Largo 93
Everest Univ—North Orlando 93
Everest Univ—Orlando North 780 *(see also Everest Univ—North Orlando)*
Everest Univ—Pinellas 780 *(see also Everest Univ—Largo)*
Everest Univ—Pompano Beach 93, 780
Everest Univ—Tampa 93, 780
Everett Beauty Acad. 796 *(see also Milan Inst. of Cosmetology)*
Everett Coll. *(see Everett Comm. Coll.)*
Everett Comm. Coll. 434
Everglades Coll. *(see Everglades Univ.)*
Everglades Univ. 802
Everglades Univ. 93
Evergreen Barber Coll. *(see Evergreen Beauty & Barber Coll.)*
Evergreen Beauty & Barber Coll. 669
Evergreen Coll. *(see Evergreen State Coll.; Evergreen Valley Coll.)*
Evergreen Comm. Coll. *(see Evergreen Valley Coll.)*
Evergreen General Hosp. *(see Evergreen Health Care)*
Evergreen Health Care 751
Evergreen Hosp. Med. Ctr. *(see Evergreen Health Care)*
Evergreen State Coll., The 434
Evergreen Valley Coll. 44
Evergreen Valley Comm. Coll. *(see Evergreen Valley Coll.)*
Evergreen Wellness Ctr. *(see Kansas Coll. of Chinese Medicine)*
Evers Coll. *(see City Univ. of New York Medgar Evers Coll.)*
Eve's Coll. of Hairstyling 615
EWTGPAC *(see Naval Expeditionary Warfare Training Grou—Pacific)*
Excela Health Sch. of Anesthesia *(see Saint Vincent Coll. & Sem.)*
Excelsior Coll. 277
Executive 2000, Inc. *(see Stanbridge Coll.)*
Executive Travel Inst. 781 *(see also ETI Career Inst.)*
Expeditionary Warfare Training Group Pacific *(see Naval Expeditionary Warfare Training Grou—Pacific)*
Expertise Cosmetology Inst. 572, 787
Expertise Sch. of Beauty 787 *(see also Expertise Cosmetology Inst.)*
Exposito Sch. of Hair Design 651
Ex'pression Coll. for Digital Arts *(see Expression Coll. for Digital Arts)*
Expression Coll. for Digital Arts 44
Extended Home Health Edu. *(see Concorde Career Inst—Arlington)*
Eye Ctr. of Toledo *(see Ohio State Univ.)*
Eye Ctr.s of Florida *(see Southern Coll. of Optometry)*
Eye Health Partners of Middle Tennessee *(see Southern Coll. of Optometry)*
Ezell's Cosmetology Sch. 536
Ezp's Coll. of Barbering 469

F

F.D. Learey Tech. Ctr. *(see Learey Tech. Ctr.)*
F.K. Marchman Edu. Ctr. *(see Marchman Tech. Edu. Ctr.)*
F.W. Olin Coll. of Engineering *(see Franklin W. Olin Coll. of Engineering)*
Faculdade de Ciencias Economicas e Empresariais (FCEE) *(see Universidade Católica Portuguesa)*
Facultad Latinoamericano de Estudios Teológicos *(see Universidad FLET)*
Fair Havens Christian Home 702 *(see also Christian Homes, Inc.)*
Fairfax Comm. Coll. *(see Lord Fairfax Comm. Coll.)*
Fairfield Career Ctr. 607
Fairfield Coll. *(see Fairfield Univ.)*
Fairfield Univ. 79
Fairhavens Christian Home *(see Christian Homes, Inc.; Fair Havens Christian Home)*
Fairleigh Dickinson Coll. *(see Fairleigh Dickinson Univ.)*
Fairleigh Dickinson Univ. 260
Fairmont Coll. *(see Fairmont State Univ. including Pierpont Comm. & Tech. Coll.; Pierpont Comm. & Tech. Coll.)*
Fairmont State Coll. *(see Fairmont State Univ. including Pierpont Comm. & Tech. Coll.)*
Fairmont State Comm. & Tech. Coll. 796 *(see also Pierpont Comm. & Tech. Coll.)*
Fairmont State Comm. Coll. *(see Pierpont Comm. & Tech. Coll.)*

Folsom Lake Coll. 45
Folsom's Mercantile Coll. *(see Chancellor Univ.)*
Fond du Lac Coll. *(see Fond du Lac Tribal & Comm. Coll.)*
Fond du Lac Tribal & Comm. Coll. 221
Fontbonne Coll. *(see Fontbonne Univ.)*
Fontbonne Univ. 238
Foothill Coll. 45
Foothills Montessori Sch. *(see Montessori Training of Southern Nevada)*
Foothills Surgical Techno. Consortium *(see Cleveland Comm. Coll.; Isothermal Comm. Coll.; McDowell Tech. Comm. Coll.)*
Ford Comm. Coll. *(see Henry Ford Comm. Coll.)*
Ford Hosp. *(see Henry Ford Hosp.)*
Fordham Univ. 277
Foreign Language Ctr. *(see Defense Language Inst. Foreign Language Ctr.)*
Foreign Trade Inst—LA 809
Forest Echoes Tech. Inst. 776 *(see also Univ. of Arkansas at Monticello Coll. of Techno.-Crossett)*
Forest Inst. of Prof. Psychology 238
Forest Inst. of Psychology *(see Forest Inst. of Prof. Psychology)*
Forest Park Coll. *(see Saint Louis Comm. Coll. at Forest Park)*
Forest Park Hosp. 717
Forrest Coll. *(see Forrest Jr. Coll.)*
Forrest Jr. Coll. 375
Forsyth Sch. for Dental Hygienists *(see Massachusetts Coll. of Pharmacy & Health Sciences)*
Forsyth Tech *(see Forsyth Tech. Comm. Coll.)*
Forsyth Tech. Coll. *(see Forsyth Tech. Comm. Coll.)*
Forsyth Tech. Comm. Coll. 303
Forsyth Tech. Inst. *(see Forsyth Tech. Comm. Coll.)*
Fort Belknap Coll. 247
Fort Berthold Coll. *(see Fort Berthold Comm. Coll.)*
Fort Berthold Comm. Coll. 311
Fort Campbell Dental Activity 708
Fort Collins Coll. *(see Inst. of Bus. & Med. Careers)*
Fort Hays Kansas State Coll. *(see Fort Hays State Univ.)*
Fort Hays Kansas State Normal Sch. *(see Fort Hays State Univ.)*
Fort Hays State Univ. 166
Fort Kent State Coll. *(see Univ. of Maine at Fort Kent)*
Fort Kent State Teacher's Coll. *(see Univ. of Maine at Fort Kent)*
Fort Lauderdale Art Inst. *(see Art Inst. of Fort Lauderdale)*
Fort Lauderdale City Coll. *(see City Coll.)*
Fort Lauderdale Coll. *(see Everest Univ—Pompano Beach)*
Fort Lauderdale Inst. of Art *(see Art Inst. of Fort Lauderdale)*
Fort Lewis A&M Coll. *(see Fort Lewis Coll.)*
Fort Lewis Agricultural & Mechanical Coll. *(see Fort Lewis Coll.)*
Fort Lewis Coll. 72
Fort Peck Coll. *(see Fort Peck Comm. Coll.)*
Fort Peck Comm. Coll. 247
Fort Pierce Beauty Acad. 508
Fort Sanders Nursing Dept. of Tennessee Wesleyan Coll. 793
Fort Sanders Sch. of Nursing 793 *(see also Tennessee Wesleyan Coll.)*
Fort Scott Coll. *(see Fort Scott Comm. Coll.)*
Fort Scott Comm. Coll. 166
Fort Smith Jr. Coll. *(see Univ. of Arkansas at Fort Smith)*
Fort Steilacoom Comm. Coll. *(see Pierce Coll. Puyallup)*
Fort Valley High & Industrial Sch. *(see Fort Valley State Univ.)*
Fort Valley State Coll. *(see Fort Valley State Univ.)*
Fort Valley State Univ. 113
Fort Wayne Bible Coll. *(see Taylor Univ.)*
Fort Wayne Child Guidance Clinic *(see Park Ctr., Inc.)*
Fort Wayne Coll. *(see Taylor Univ.)*
Fort Wayne Coll. of Medicine *(see Taylor Univ.)*
Fort Wayne Commercial Coll. *(see Brown Mackie Coll—South Bend)*
Fort Wayne Female Coll. *(see Taylor Univ.)*
Fort Wayne Sch. of Radiography 705
Fort Worth Beauty Sch. 651
Fort Worth Hosp. *(see Harris Methodist Fort Worth Hosp.)*
Fort Worth Independent Sch. Dist. 747
Fort Wright Coll. *(see Heritage Univ.)*
Forum Health *(see Western Reserve Care Sys.)*
Foster Estes Vocational Ctr. *(see Metro Techno. Ctr—South Bryant)*
Foster G. McGaw Hosp. *(see Loyola Univ. of Chicago)*
Foster's Cosmetology Coll. 564
Foundation Coll. 45, 777
Foundation Coll. San Diego *(see Foundation Coll.)*
Foundation Opens *(see Fundación ABRE)*
Foundation Program of the Petroleum Inst. *(see Petroleum Inst.)*
Fountainhead Coll. of Techno. 384
Four County Career Ctr. 608
Four Seasons Cosmetology Sch. *(see Four Seasons Salon & Day Spa)*
Four-D Coll. 480, 777
Four-D Success Acad. 777 *(see also Four-D Coll.)*
Fox Coll. 132
Fox Inst. of Bus. 498
Fox Secretarial Coll. *(see Fox Coll.)*
Fox Univ. *(see George Fox Univ.)*
Fox Valley Coll. *(see Fox Valley Tech. Coll.)*
Fox Valley Tech. Coll. 446
Fox Valley Tech. Inst. *(see Fox Valley Tech. Coll.)*
Framingham Coll. *(see Framingham State Coll.)*
Framingham State Coll. 199
Fran Brown Coll. of Beauty 660
Franáois-Xavier Garneau Coll. 759
Frances Payne Bolton Sch. of Nursing *(see Cleveland Clinic)*
Francis Marion Univ. 375
Francis T. Nicholls Jr. Coll. of Louisiana State Univ. *(see Nicholls State Univ.)*
Francis T. Nicholls State Coll. *(see Nicholls State Univ.)*
Francis Tuttle Techno. Ctr. 734, 790
Francis Tuttle Vocational-Tech. Ctr. 790 *(see also Francis Tuttle Techno. Ctr.)*
Francis Tuttle Vo-Tech Ctr. *(see Francis Tuttle Techno. Ctr.)*
Franciscan Children's Hosp. & Rehabilitation Ctr. *(see Franciscan Hosp. for Children)*
Franciscan Health Sys. *(see Saint Joseph Med. Ctr.)*
Franciscan Hosp. for Children 713
Franciscan Missionaries of Our Lady Health Sys. *(see Saint Francis Med. Ctr.)*
Franciscan Sch. of Theology 45
Franciscan Services Corporation *(see Trinity Health Sys. Sch. of Nursing)*
Franciscan Skemp Healthcare *(see Univ. of Wisconsin-La Crosse)*
Franciscan Univ. of Steubenville 319
Franciscan Univ. of the Prairies, The 783 *(see also Ashford Univ.)*
Franciscan Univ., The *(see Ashford Univ.)*
Francoeur & Associates *(see Results, Inc. Dale Carnegie Training)*
Francois D. Hair Design Acad. 660
Frank Lloyd Wright Sch. of Architecture 18
Frank Phillips Coll. 397

Frank Wiggins Trade Sch. *(see Los Angeles Trade-Tech. Coll.)*
Frankford Hosp. 738
Frankford Hosp. Sch. of Nursing *(see Frankford Hosp.)*
Frankfurt Univ. *(see Johann Wolfgang Goethe-Universität Frankfurt am Main)*
Franklin & Marshall Coll. 348
Franklin Acad. 641, 793 *(see also Louisburg Coll.)*
Franklin Beauty Sch. #2 651
Franklin Career Ctr. *(see Ben Franklin Career Ctr.)*
Franklin Career Coll. 480
Franklin Career Inst. 589
Franklin Coll. 147 *(see Franklin & Marshall Coll.; Franklin Career Coll.; Franklin Coll. Switzerland; Franklin Univ.)*
Franklin Coll. of Indiana *(see Franklin Coll.)*
Franklin Coll. Switzerland 460
Franklin County Area Vocational Tech. Sch. 791 *(see also Franklin County Career & Techno. Ctr.)*
Franklin County Career & Techno. Ctr. 738, 791
Franklin County Cosmetology Coll. *(see Cosmetology Coll. of Franklin County)*
Franklin County Vo-Tech Sch. *(see Franklin County Career & Techno. Ctr.)*
Franklin Delano Roosevelt Hosp. *(see Veterans Affairs Hudson Valley Health Care Sys—Montrose)*
Franklin Inst. of Boston *(see Benjamin Franklin Inst. of Techno.)*
Franklin Inst. of Techno. *(see Benjamin Franklin Inst. of Techno.)*
Franklin Montessori Sch. 602
Franklin Pierce Coll. 787 *(see also Franklin Pierce Univ.)*
Franklin Pierce Law Ctr. 256
Franklin Pierce Univ. 256, 787
Franklin Techno. Ctr. 804
Franklin Union *(see Benjamin Franklin Inst. of Techno.)*
Franklin Univ. 319
Franklin Univ. of Medicine & Science *(see Rosalind Franklin Univ. of Medicine & Science)*
Franklin W. Olin Coll. of Engineering 199
Fraser Univ. *(see Simon Fraser Univ.)*
Frazier Vocational-Tech. Sch. *(see Louisiana Tech. Coll—Baton Rouge Campus)*
Fred D. Learey Tech. Ctr. *(see Learey Tech. Ctr.)*
Fred K. Marchman Edu. Ctr. *(see Marchman Tech. Edu. Ctr.)*
Fred W. Eberle Tech. Ctr. 672
Frederick Coll. *(see Frederick Comm. Coll.)*
Frederick Comm. Coll. 190
Frederick S. Pardee RAND Grad. Sch. *(see Pardee Rand Grad. Sch.)*
Fredonia Acad. *(see State Univ. of New York Coll. at Fredonia)*
Fredonia Coll. *(see State Univ. of New York Coll. at Fredonia)*
Fredonia Normal & Training Sch. *(see State Univ. of New York Coll. at Fredonia)*
Fredonia State Coll. *(see State Univ. of New York Coll. at Fredonia)*
Fredrick & Charles Beauty Coll. 480
Fredric's Inst. *(see Aveda Fredric's Inst.)*
Free Acad., The *(see City Univ. of New York City Coll.)*
Free Will Baptist Bible Coll. 384
Free Will Bible Coll. *(see Free Will Baptist Bible Coll.)*
Freed-Hardeman Coll. *(see Freed-Hardeman Univ.)*
Freed-Hardeman Univ. 384
Freedom Ministries, Inc. *(see Oblate Sch. of Theology)*
Fremont Coll. 45, 778
French Broad Baptist Acad. *(see Mars Hill Coll.)*
French Culinary Inst. 589
Fresno City Coll. 45
Fresno Coll. *(see Fresno City Coll.)*
Fresno Cosmetology Sch. *(see Cosmetology Sch. of Fresno-A Paul Mitchell Partner Sch.)*
Fresno County Paramedic Program *(see Fresno City Coll.)*
Fresno Inst. of Techno. *(see Inst. of Techno.)*
Fresno Jr. Coll. *(see Fresno City Coll.)*
Fresno Pacific Coll. *(see Fresno Pacific Univ.)*
Fresno Pacific Univ. 45
Fresno State *(see California State Univ., Fresno)*
Fresno State Normal Sch. *(see California State Univ., Fresno)*
Fresno VA Med. Ctr. *(see Veterans Affairs Central California Health Care Sys.)*
Fresno VAMC *(see Veterans Affairs Central California Health Care Sys.)*
Fresno Veterans Affairs Med. Ctr. *(see Veterans Affairs Central California Health Care Sys.)*
Friends Asylum *(see Friends Hosp.)*
Friends Bible Coll. *(see Barclay Coll.)*
Friends Coll. *(see George Fox Univ.)*
Friends Hosp. 738
Friends Pacific Acad. *(see George Fox Univ.)*
Friends Univ. 166
Fries Sch. of Piano Tuning & Techno. *(see Emil Fries Sch. of Piano Tuning & Techno.)*
Froedtert & Med. Coll. Health Services 754
Front Range Coll. *(see Front Range Comm. Coll.)*
Front Range Comm. Coll. 72
Frontier Coll. *(see Frontier Comm. Coll.)*
Frontier Comm. Coll. 132
Frontier Grad. Sch. of Midwifery *(see Frontier Sch. of Midwifery & Family Nursing)*
Frontier Midwifery Sch. *(see Frontier Sch. of Midwifery & Family Nursing)*
Frontier Sch. of Midwifery & Family Nursing 172
Frostburg State Coll. *(see Frostburg State Univ.)*
Frostburg State Teachers Coll. *(see Frostburg State Univ.)*
Frostburg State Univ. 190
Frostburg Univ. *(see Frostburg State Univ.)*
Ft. Belknap Coll. *(see Fort Belknap Coll.)*
Ft. Berthold Coll. *(see Fort Berthold Comm. Coll.)*
Ft. Berthold Comm. Coll. *(see Fort Berthold Comm. Coll.)*
Ft. Collins Coll. *(see Inst. of Bus. & Med. Careers)*
Ft. Hays Kansas State Coll. *(see Fort Hays State Univ.)*
Ft. Hays Kansas State Normal Sch. *(see Fort Hays State Univ.)*
Ft. Hays State Univ. *(see Fort Hays State Univ.)*
Ft. Lewis A&M Coll. *(see Fort Lewis Coll.)*
Ft. Lewis Agricultural & Mechanical Coll. *(see Fort Lewis Coll.)*
Ft. Lewis Coll. *(see Fort Lewis Coll.)*
Ft. Peck Coll. *(see Fort Peck Comm. Coll.)*
Ft. Peck Comm. Coll. *(see Fort Peck Comm. Coll.)*
Ft. Pierce Beauty Acad. *(see Fort Pierce Beauty Acad.)*
Ft. Sanders Sch. of Nursing *(see Tennessee Wesleyan Coll.)*
Ft. Scott Coll. *(see Fort Scott Comm. Coll.)*
Ft. Scott Comm. Coll. *(see Fort Scott Comm. Coll.)*
Ft. Smith Jr. Coll. *(see Univ. of Arkansas at Fort Smith)*

Ft. Wayne Child Guidance Clinic *(see Park Ctr., Inc.)*
Ft. Wayne Commercial Coll. *(see Brown Mackie Coll—South Bend)*
Ft. Worth Hosp. *(see Harris Methodist Fort Worth Hosp.)*
Ft. Worth Independent Sch. Dist. *(see Fort Worth Independent Sch. Dist.)*
Ft. Wright Coll. *(see Heritage Univ.)*
Fu Jen Acad. *(see Fu Jen Catholic Univ.)*
Fu Jen Catholic Univ. 770
Fu Jen Univ. *(see Fu Jen Catholic Univ.)*
Fugazzi Coll. *(see National Coll—Nashville)*
Fujairah Men's Coll. *(see Higher Colleges of Techno. Fujairah Men's Coll.)*
Fujairah Women's Coll. *(see Higher Colleges of Techno. Fujairah Women's Coll.)*
Fuld Coll. of Nursing *(see Helene Fuld Coll. of Nursing)*
Fuld Sch. of Nursing *(see Helene Fuld Coll. of Nursing)*
Fuld Sch. of Nursing in Camden County *(see Helene Fuld Sch. of Nursing in Camden County)*
Full Gospel Bible Coll. 797 *(see also Eston Coll.)*
Full Gospel Bible Inst. 797 *(see also Eston Coll.)*
Full Sail Real World Edu. 96
Fuller Circles Sch. for Therapeutic Massage 544
Fuller Circles Therapeutic Massage Sch. *(see Fuller Circles Sch. for Therapeutic Massage)*
Fuller Sem. *(see Fuller Theological Sem.)*
Fuller Theological Sem. 45
Fullerton Coll. 45
Fullerton Jr. Coll. *(see Fullerton Coll.)*
Fulton Comm. Coll. *(see Fulton-Montgomery Comm. Coll.)*
Fulton Hosp. *(see Fulton State Hosp.)*
Fulton State Hosp. 717
Fulton-Montgomery Coll. *(see Fulton-Montgomery Comm. Coll.)*
Fulton-Montgomery Comm. Coll. 277
Fundacion Universidad de las Americas - Puebla *(see Universidad de las America—Puebla)*
Fundamental Bible Inst. *(see Arlington Baptist Coll.)*
Funeral Inst. of the North East *(see FINE Mortuary Coll.)*
Funeral Inst. of the Northeast *(see FINE Mortuary Coll.)*
Funeral Services Inst. of Dallas *(see Dallas Inst. of Funeral Services)*
Furman Univ. 375
Future Generations Grad. Sch. 807
FWISD Psychological Services Dept. *(see Fort Worth Independent Sch. Dist.)*

G

G Skin & Beauty Inst. 526
G. Mitchell Hartman & Associates, Inc. 579
G.G.O. Beauty Sch. 819
G.V. (Sonny) Montgomery Veterans Affairs Med. Ctr. 717
Gadsden Bus. Coll. 463
Gadsden Coll. *(see Gadsden State Comm. Coll.)*
Gadsden Comm. Coll. *(see Gadsden State Comm. Coll.)*
Gadsden State Comm. Coll. 5
Gadsden State Jr. Coll. *(see Gadsden State Comm. Coll.)*
Gadsden State Tech. Inst. *(see Gadsden State Comm. Coll.)*
Gainesville Coll. 781 *(see also Gainesville State Coll.)*
Gainesville Jr. Coll. *(see North Central Texas Coll.)*
Gainesville State Coll. 113, 781
Gainesville VA Med. Ctr. *(see Malcom Randall Veterans Affairs Med. Ctr.)*
Gainesville VAMC *(see Malcom Randall Veterans Affairs Med. Ctr.)*
Gainesville Veterans Affairs Med. Ctr. *(see Malcom Randall Veterans Affairs Med. Ctr.)*
Gaither & Company Beauty Coll. 463
Gaither Beauty Coll. *(see Gaither & Company Beauty Coll.)*
Gaither, Inc. *(see Gaither & Company Beauty Coll.)*
Gal Mar Acad. of Hairdressing 779 *(see also North Haven Acad.)*
Galen Coll. of Med. & Dental Assistants 480
Galen Coll. of Nursing 172, 784
Galen Health Inst.s, Inc. *(see Galen Coll. of Nursing)*
Galen Nursing Coll. *(see Galen Coll. of Nursing)*
Galen Sch. of Nursing *(see Galen Coll. of Nursing)*
Galena City Schools Post Secondary Sch. 465
Galena Interior Learning Acad. Adult Programs *(see Galena City Schools Post Secondary Sch.)*
Galena Tech. Ctr. *(see Galena City Schools Post Secondary Sch.)*
Galiano Career Acad. 509
Gallaudet Coll. *(see Gallaudet Univ.)*
Gallaudet Univ. 85
Gallegos & Associates, Inc. *(see Rick J. Gallegos & Associates, Inc.)*
Gallery Coll. of Beauty, The 557
Gallia-Jackson-Vinton Joint Career-Tech. Sch. Dist. *(see Buckeye Hills Career Ctr.)*
Gallipolis Bus. Coll. *(see Gallipolis Career Coll.)*
Gallipolis Career Coll. 319
Galloza Tech. Sch. of Electricity *(see Colegio Tecnico de Electricidad Galloza)*
Gallup Indian Med. Ctr. 722
Galveston Coll. 397
Gammon Sch. of Theology *(see Interdenominational Theological Ctr.)*
Gammon Theological Sem. *(see Interdenominational Theological Ctr.)*
Gannon Coll. *(see Gannon Univ.)*
Gannon Univ. 348
Garden City Coll. *(see Garden City Comm. Coll.)*
Garden City Comm. Coll. 166
Garden City Comm. Jr. Coll. *(see Garden City Comm. Coll.)*
Garden City Jr. Coll. *(see Garden City Comm. Coll.)*
Gardner-Webb Coll. *(see Gardner-Webb Univ.)*
Gardner-Webb Univ. 303
Garland County Comm. Coll. *(see National Park Comm. Coll. at Hot Springs)*
Garnet Career Ctr. 672
Garnet Career Ctr. Sch. of Practical Nursing *(see Garnet Career Ctr.)*
Garrett Biblical Inst. *(see Garrett-Evangelical Theological Sem.)*
Garrett Coll. 191
Garrett Comm. Coll. *(see Garrett Coll.)*
Garrett-Evangelical Theological Sem. 132
Garvin Grad. Sch. of Int'l. Mgmnt., The *(see Thunderbird Sch. of Global Mgmnt.)*
Gary General Hosp. *(see Methodist Hospitals Northlake)*
Gary Manuel Aveda Inst. 821
Gary Manuel Salon *(see Gary Manuel Aveda Inst.)*
Gaston Coll. 303
Gates Coll. 480
Gateway Coll. *(see Gateway Comm. & Tech. Coll.; Gateway Comm. Coll.; Gateway Tech. Coll.)*
Gateway Comm. & Tech. Coll. 172, 804
Gateway Comm. Coll. 18, 79
Gateway Comm.-Tech. Coll. *(see Gateway Comm. Coll.)*

Georgia State Coll. *(see Savannah State Univ.)*
Georgia State Coll. for Women *(see Georgia Coll. & State Univ.)*
Georgia State Industrial Coll. *(see Savannah State Univ.)*
Georgia State Univ. 114 *(see also Georgia Coll. & State Univ.)*
Georgia State Women's Coll. *(see Valdosta State Univ.)*
Georgia Tech *(see Georgia Inst. of Techno.)*
Georgia Univ. *(see Univ. of Georgia)*
Georgian Coll. 759
Georgian Court Coll. *(see Georgian Court Univ.)*
Georgian Court Univ. 261
Georgie Robertson Christian Coll. *(see Freed-Hardeman Univ.)*
GEOS English Acad. 481
GEOS New York Corporation *(see GEOS English Acad.)*
Gerber Akron Beauty Sch. 608
Gerber Beauty Sch. *(see Gerber Akron Beauty Sch.)*
German Evangelical ProSem. *(see Elmhurst Coll.)*
German Hosp. Training Sch. for Nurses *(see Research Coll. of Nursing)*
German Theological Sem. *(see Bloomfield Coll.)*
German Wallace Coll. *(see Baldwin-Wallace Coll.)*
Germanna Coll. *(see Germanna Comm. Coll.)*
Germanna Comm. Coll. 423
Gettysburg Coll. 349
Gettysburg Hosp. 739
Gettysburg Lutheran Theological Sem. *(see Lutheran Theological Sem. at Gettysburg)*
Ghent Beauty Acad. 795
GIA Sch. of Bus. *(see Gemological Inst. of America; Gemological Inst. of America Sch. of Bus.)*
GIA's Sch. of Bus. *(see Gemological Inst. of America Sch. of Bus.)*
Gibbs Boston *(see Gibbs Coll. of Boston, Inc.)*
Gibbs Coll. 79, 261
Gibbs Coll. Connecticut *(see Gibbs Coll.)*
Gibbs Coll. Livingston *(see Gibbs Coll.)*
Gibbs Coll. of Boston, Inc. 199
Gibbs Coll—Cranston 371
Gibbs Coll—Vienna 795 *(see also Sanford-Brown Coll—Vienna)*
Gibbs Jr. Coll. *(see Saint Petersburg Coll.)*
Gibbs Melville *(see Sanford-Brown Inst—Melville)*
Gibbs New York *(see Katharine Gibbs Sch.)*
Gibbs Sch. *(see Gibbs Coll. of Boston, Inc.; Gibbs Coll—Cranston; Katharine Gibbs Sch.; Sanford-Brown Coll—Vienna; Sanford-Brown Inst—Melville)*
Gibson's Barber & Beauty Coll. 564
Gibson's Beauty Coll. *(see Gibson's Barber & Beauty Coll.)*
Gila Acad. *(see Eastern Arizona Coll.)*
Gila Coll. *(see Eastern Arizona Coll.)*
Gila Comm. Coll. *(see Eastern Arizona Coll.)*
Gila County Comm. Coll. *(see Eastern Arizona Coll.)*
Gila Jr. Coll. *(see Eastern Arizona Coll.)*
Gila Normal Coll. *(see Eastern Arizona Coll.)*
Gildner Reg. Inst. for Children & Adolescents *(see John L. Gildner Reg. Inst. for Children & Adolescents)*
Gill-Tech Acad. of Hair Design 675
Girls Industrial Coll. *(see Texas Woman's Univ.)*
Glad Tidings Bible Inst. *(see Bethany Univ.)*
Glasgow Univ. *(see Univ. of Glasgow)*
Glassboro Normal Sch. *(see Rowan Univ.)*
Glassboro State Coll. *(see Rowan Univ.)*
Glen Dow Acad. of Hair Design, Inc. 669
Glen Oaks Coll. *(see Glen Oaks Comm. Coll.)*
Glen Oaks Comm. Coll. 211
Glendale Career Coll. 481
Glendale Career Schools, Inc. *(see Glendale Career Coll.)*
Glendale Coll. *(see Glendale Comm. Coll.)*
Glendale Comm. Coll. 18, 46
Glendale Hosp. *(see Glendale Mem. Hosp. & Health Ctr.)*
Glendale Jr. Coll. *(see Glendale Comm. Coll.)*
Glendale Mem. Hosp. & Health Ctr. 687
Glens Falls Hosp. 725
Glenville Coll. *(see Glenville State Coll.)*
Glenville Hosp. *(see Euclid Hosp.)*
Glenville State Coll. 441
Glenville State Normal Sch. *(see Glenville State Coll.)*
Glenwood Beauty Acad. 495
Glion Hotel Sch. *(see Glion Inst. of Higher Edu.)*
Glion Inst. of Higher Edu. 460
Global Bus. Inst. 589
Global Health Nurse Training Services 750
Global Language Inst., Inc. 561
Global Univ. 238, 804 *(see also ICI Univ.)*
Globe Coll. 785 *(see also Globe Univ.; Minnesota Sch. of Bus.)*
Globe Coll. of Bus. *(see Globe Univ.)*
Globe Inst. of Techno. 277
Globe Techno. Inst. *(see Globe Inst. of Techno.)*
Globe Univ. 221, 785 *(see also Minnesota Sch. of Bus.)*
Globelle Tech. Inst. 633
Glockner Sanatorium & Hosp. *(see Penrose-St. Francis Health Services)*
Glockner-Penrose Hosp. *(see Penrose-St. Francis Health Services)*
Gloucester Coll. *(see Gloucester County Coll.)*
Gloucester County Coll. 261
Glouco Coll. *(see Gloucester County Coll.)*
Glyn Ed Newton & Associates, Inc. 641
GMI Engineering & Mgmnt. Inst. *(see Kettering Univ.)*
Gnomon Sch. of Visual Effects 481
Goddard Coll. 417
Goddard Jr. Coll. *(see Goddard Coll.)*
Goddard Sch. for Girls *(see Goddard Coll.)*
Goddard Sem. *(see Goddard Coll.)*
God's Bible Coll. *(see God's Bible Sch. & Coll.)*
God's Bible Sch. & Coll. 319
Gogebic Coll. *(see Gogebic Comm. Coll.)*
Gogebic Comm. Coll. 211
Going Places Travel Sch. *(see Newbridge Coll.)*
Golden Gate Baptist Theological Sem. 46
Golden Gate Coll. *(see Golden Gate Univ.)*
Golden Gate Language Schools 481
Golden Gate Sem. *(see Golden Gate Baptist Theological Sem.)*
Golden Gate Univ. 46
Golden State Bus. Coll. *(see Golden State Coll.)*
Golden State Coll. 481
Golden State Coll. of Chiropractic *(see Southern California Univ. of Health Sciences)*
Golden State Sch. *(see Golden State Coll.)*
Golden Valley Inst. *(see Toccoa Falls Coll.)*
Golden West Coll. 46
Goldey-Beacom Coll. 84
Goldfarb Sch. of Nursing at Barnes-Jewish Coll. 238
Goldsboro Industrial Edu. Ctr. *(see Wayne Comm. Coll.)*

Goldwater Mem. Hosp. *(see Coler-Goldwater Specialty Hosp. & Nursing Facility)*
Golf Acad. of America Orlando 10 *(see also Virginia Coll.)*
Golf Acad. of America Phoenix 10 *(see also Virginia Coll.)*
Golf Acad. of America San Diego 10 *(see also Virginia Coll.)*
Golf Acad. of America The Carolinas *(see Virginia Coll.)*
Golf Acad. of Arizona *(see Golf Acad. of America)*
Golf Acad. of San Diego *(see Golf Acad. of America; Virginia Coll.)*
Golf Acad. of the Carolinas 10 *(see also Golf Acad. of America; Virginia Coll.)*
Golf Acad. of the South *(see Golf Acad. of America; Virginia Coll.)*
Gonzaga Coll. *(see Gonzaga Univ.)*
Gonzaga Univ. 434
Gonzaga Univ. Dept. of Religious Studies *(see Gonzaga Univ.)*
Good Samaritan Coll. of Nursing & Health Science 319
Good Samaritan Hosp. 705, 751 *(see also Advocate Good Samaritan Hosp.; Banner Desert Med. Ctr.; Banner Good Samaritan Med. Ctr.; TriHealth Good Samaritan Hosp.)*
Good Samaritan Hosp. of Cincinnati *(see Good Samaritan Coll. of Nursing & Health Science)*
Good Samaritan Med. Ctr. *(see Banner Good Samaritan Med. Ctr.)*
Good Samaritan Nursing Coll. *(see Good Samaritan Coll. of Nursing & Health Science)*
Good Shepherd Hosp. *(see Advocate Good Shepherd Hosp.)*
Goodman Child & Adolescent Inst. *(see Jewish Child & Family Services)*
Goodwin Coll. 79 *(see also Goodwin Inst—Milford)*
Goodwin House Alexandria 750
Goodwin House Foundation *(see Goodwin House Alexandria)*
Goodwin Inst—Milford 79
Goodwin Inst—Waterbury *(see Stone Acad—Waterbury)*
Gordon Coll. 115, 199
Gordon Cooper Techno. Ctr. 615
Gordon Divinity Sch. *(see Gordon-Conwell Theological Sem.)*
Gordon Inst. *(see Gordon Coll.)*
Gordon Inst. of Techno. *(see Robert Gordon Univ.)*
Gordon Jr. Coll. *(see Gordon Coll.)*
Gordon Phillips Sch. of Beauty Cultur—Baltimore 785
Gordon Phillips Sch. of Beauty Cultur—Norristown 791
Gordon Phillips Sch. of Beauty Cultur—Philadelphia 791
Gordon Phillips Sch. of Beauty Cultur—Upper Darby 791
Gordon Univ. *(see Robert Gordon Univ.)*
Gordon-Barrington Coll. *(see Gordon Coll.)*
Gordon-Conwell Theological Sem. 199
Gordon's Coll. *(see Robert Gordon Univ.)*
Gordon's Inst. of Techno. *(see Robert Gordon Univ.)*
Goshen Coll. 147
Gospel Rescue Ministries *(see Sch. of Tomorrow)*
Goss Military Acad. *(see New Mexico Military Inst.)*
Goucher Coll. 191
Gourmet Cookery Sch. *(see Natural Gourmet Cookery Sch.)*
Government Hosp. for the Insane *(see Saint Elizabeths Hosp.)*
Governors State Univ. 132
Governors Univ. *(see Governors State Univ.)*
GP Inst. of Cosmetology 821
Grabber Sch. of Hair Design 567
Grace Bible Coll. 211 *(see also Grace Univ.)*
Grace Coll. *(see Grace Bible Coll.)*
Grace Coll. & Sem. 147, 803
Grace Coll. of the Bible *(see Grace Univ.)*
Grace Conaway Inst. *(see Evangelical Sem. of Puerto Rico)*
Grace Grad. Sch. of Theology *(see Grace Coll. & Sem.)*
Grace Hosp. *(see DMC Sinai-Grace Hosp.)*
Grace Inst. of Bus. Techno. 788
Grace Maternity Hosp. *(see Izaak Walton Killam Health Centre)*
Grace Sch. of Theology *(see Grace Coll. & Sem.)*
Grace Theological Sem. *(see Grace Coll. & Sem.)*
Grace Univ. 251
Graceland Coll. *(see Graceland Univ.)*
Graceland Univ. 158
Grad. Ctr. of New York *(see City Univ. of New York Grad. Ctr.)*
Grad. Coll. of Union Univ. 788 *(see also Union Grad. Coll.)*
Grad. Inst. of Applied Linguistics 397
Grad. Inst. of California *(see California Grad. Inst.)*
Grad. Research Ctr. of the Southwest *(see Univ. of Texas at Dallas)*
Grad. Sch. & Univ. Ctr. *(see City Univ. of New York Grad. Ctr.)*
Grad. Sch. of America *(see Capella Univ.)*
Grad. Sch. of BioMed. Sciences *(see Texas A&M Univ. Sys. Health Science Ctr.; Univ. of Medicine & Dentistry of NJ Grad. Sch. of BioMed. Sciences)*
Grad. Sch. of Figurative Art of the New York Acad. of Art 278
Grad. Sch. of Molecular Medicine *(see North Shore Long Island Jewish Grad. Sch. of Molecular Medicine)*
Grad. Sem. of Phillips Univ., The *(see Phillips Theological Sem.)*
Grad. Theological Sem. *(see Grad. Theological Union)*
Grad. Theological Union 46
Grad. Theology Sch. of Austin *(see Austin Grad. Sch. of Theology)*
Grad. Theology Sch. of Houston *(see Houston Grad. Sch. of Theology)*
Grady Health Sys. *(see Grady Mem. Hosp.)*
Grady Mem. Hosp. 699
Grady Sch. of Esthetics *(see Elizabeth Grady Sch. of Esthetics)*
Graham Hosp. Sch. of Nursing 702
Graham Sch. of Contemporary Dance *(see Martha Graham Sch. of Contemporary Dance, Inc.)*
Graham Webb Acad. *(see Graham Webb Int'l. Acad. of Hair)*
Graham Webb Int'l. Acad. of Hair 665
Grambling Coll. of Louisiana *(see Grambling State Univ.)*
Grambling State Univ. 179
Grand Canyon Coll. *(see Grand Canyon Univ.)*
Grand Canyon Univ. 18
Grand Island Coll. *(see Univ. of Sioux Falls)*
Grand Rapids Baptist Bible Coll. *(see Cornerstone Univ.)*
Grand Rapids Baptist Sem. *(see Cornerstone Univ.)*
Grand Rapids Bible Inst. & Theological Sem. *(see Grand Rapids Theological Sem.)*
Grand Rapids Coll. *(see Grand Rapids Comm. Coll.)*
Grand Rapids Comm. Coll. 211
Grand Rapids Educational Ctr. *(see Everest Inst—Grand Rapids)*
Grand Rapids Jr. Coll. *(see Grand Rapids Comm. Coll.)*
Grand Rapids Theological Sem. 211
Grand Rapids Theological Sem. of Cornerstone Univ. *(see Cornerstone Univ.)*
Grand Valley State Univ. 211
Grand Valley Univ. *(see Grand Valley State Univ.)*
Grand View Coll. 158

Green Bay Catholic Diocese *(see Catholic Diocese of Green Bay Clinical Pastoral Edu. Program)*
Green County Area Techno. Ctr. 175 *(see also Somerset Comm. Coll.)*
Green Mountain Coll. 417
Green River Coll. *(see Green River Comm. Coll.)*
Green River Comm. Coll. 434
Greenbrier Coll. of Osteopathic Medicine *(see West Virginia Sch. of Osteopathic Medicine)*
Greenbrier Comm. Coll. Ctr. 440 *(see also Bluefield State Coll.)*
Greene County Area Vocational Tech. Sch. 791 *(see also Greene County Career & Techno. Ctr.)*
Greene County Career & Techno. Ctr. 739, 791
Greene County Career Ctr. 608 *(see also Greene County Career & Techno. Ctr.)*
Greene County Vo-Tech Sch. *(see Greene County Career & Techno. Ctr.)*
Greenfield Coll. *(see Greenfield Comm. Coll.)*
Greenfield Comm. Coll. 200
Greensboro Coll. 303
Greenville Coll. 132
Greenville Mem. Hosp. *(see Greenville Hosp. Sys.)*
Greenville Tech *(see Greenville Tech. Coll.)*
Greenville Tech. Coll. 375
Greenville Woman's Coll. *(see Furman Univ.)*
Greenwood Acad. of Hair Design 669
Grenoble Ecole de Mgmnt. *(see Ecole supérieure de Commerce de Grenoble)*
Grenoble Sch. of Mgmnt. *(see Ecole supérieure de Commerce de Grenoble)*
Gretna Career Coll. 179
Gretna Career Coll. Training Inst. *(see Gretna Career Coll.)*
Greys Harbor Coll. *(see Grays Harbor Coll.)*
Griffin Coll. *(see Griffin Tech. Coll.)*
Griffin Health Services Corporation *(see Griffin Hosp.)*
Griffin Hosp. 693
Griffin Tech *(see Griffin Tech. Coll.)*
Griffin Tech. Coll. 115
Griffin Tech. Inst. *(see Griffin Tech. Coll.)*
Griffin-Spalding County Area Vocational Tech. Sch. *(see Griffin Tech. Coll.)*
Griffith Opportunity Sch. *(see Emily Griffith Opportunity Sch.)*
Griggs Int'l. Acad. 785
Griggs Univ. 191
Grinnell Coll. 158
Grooms & Associates, Inc. *(see Dale Carnegie Training of Greater Cincinnati)*
Grossmont Coll. 46
Group Theatre, The *(see Stella Adler Studio of Acting)*
Groupe Ecole supérieure de Commerce et de Mgmnt. 765
Groupe ESC Clermont 765
Groupe ESC Toulouse 765
Groupe HEC *(see Ecole des Hautes Etudes Commerciales)*
Grove Beauty Coll. 618
Grove City Coll. 349
Grubbs Vocational Coll. *(see Univ. of Texas at Arlington)*
Guam Coll. *(see Guam Comm. Coll.)*
Guam Comm. Coll. 122
Guam Univ. *(see Univ. of Guam)*
Guelph Univ. *(see Univ. of Guelph)*
Guidance Ctr. of Rutherford County *(see Guidance Ctr.)*
Guidance Ctr., The 687, 745, 777
Guidance Ctr.s, The *(see Applewood Ctr.s, Inc.)*
Guilford Coll. 303
Guilford County Coll. *(see Guilford Coll.)*
Guilford Industrial Edu. Ctr. *(see Guilford Tech. Comm. Coll.)*
Guilford Tech. Comm. Coll. 303
Guilford Tech. Inst. *(see Guilford Tech. Comm. Coll.)*
Guitar Inst. of Techno., The *(see Musicians Inst.)*
Gulf Coast Bible Coll. *(see Mid-America Christian Univ.)*
Gulf Coast Coll. 96, 781 *(see also Gulf Coast Comm. Coll.)*
Gulf Coast Comm. Coll. 96
Gulf Coast Reg. Blood Ctr. *(see Gulf Coast Sch. of Blood Bank Techno.)*
Gulf Coast Sch. of Blood Bank Techno. 747
Gulf Coast Trades Ctr. 651
Gulfport Job Corps Ctr. 784
Gundersen Clinic *(see Gundersen Lutheran Med. Ctr.)*
Gundersen Lutheran Med. Ctr. 754
Gunsmith Sch. of Pennsylvania *(see Pennsylvania Gunsmith Sch.)*
Gupton Coll. *(see John A. Gupton Coll.)*
Gupton-Jones Coll. of Funeral Service 115
Gupton-Jones Coll. of Mortuary Science *(see Gupton-Jones Coll. of Funeral Service)*
Gupton-Jones Sch. of Embalming *(see Gupton-Jones Coll. of Funeral Service)*
Gustavus Adolphus Coll. 222
Gustavus Coll. *(see Gustavus Adolphus Coll.)*
Gutenberg Coll. 806
Guthrie Job Corps Ctr. 615
Guy's Acad. Hair, Skin, & Nails 541, 784
Guy's Beauty Sch. *(see Guy's Acad. Hair, Skin, & Nails)*
Guy's Shreveport Acad. of Cosmetology 784 *(see also Guy's Acad. Hair, Skin, & Nails)*
GW Univ. *(see George Washington Univ.)*
Gwin & Associates *(see J. R. Rodgers & Associates, Inc.)*
Gwinnett Coll. 115 *(see also Georgia Gwinnett Coll.; Gwinnett Tech. Coll.)*
Gwinnett Tech. Coll. 115, 781
Gwinnett Tech. Inst. 781 *(see also Gwinnett Tech. Coll.)*
Gwinnett Univ. Ctr. *(see Georgia Perimeter Coll.)*
Gwynedd-Mercy Coll. 349
Gwynedd-Mercy Jr. Coll. *(see Gwynedd-Mercy Coll.)*

H

H. Councill Trenholm State Tech. Coll. 5
H. Sophie Newcomb Mem. Coll. *(see Tulane Univ.)*
Hablespana *(see Boston Acad. of English)*
Hacienda La Puente Adult Edu. 687
Hackensack Hosp. *(see Hackensack Univ. Med. Ctr.)*
Hackensack Med. Ctr. *(see Hackensack Univ. Med. Ctr.)*
Hackensack Univ. Med. Ctr. 720
Hadley Sch. for the Blind, The 526
Hagerstown Bus. Coll. 785 *(see also Kaplan Coll—Hagerstown)*
Hagerstown Bus. Coll—Frederick 785 *(see also Kaplan Coll—Hagerstown)*
Hagerstown Coll. *(see Hagerstown Comm. Coll.)*
Hagerstown Comm. Coll. 191
Hagerstown Jr. Coll. *(see Hagerstown Comm. Coll.)*
Haggard Sch. of Theology of Azusa Pacific Univ. *(see Azusa Pacific Univ.)*
Hahnamann Univ. 792
Hair Acad. *(see Casal Aveda Inst.)*
Hair Acad. 790
Hair Acad. of Safford, The 467, 775
Hair Acad., Inc. 547
Hair Acad—110, The 567
Hair Arts Acad. 530
Hair California Beauty Acad. 481
Hair Design Acad. of Tiffin *(see Tiffin Acad. of Hair Design)*

Hair Design Coll. *(see Coll. of Hair Design)*
Hair Design Inst. *(see Inst. of Hair Design, Inc.)*
Hair Design Inst. at Fifth Avenue 589
Hair Design Inst. of Connecticut *(see Brio Acad. of Cosmetology; Connecticut Inst. of Hair Design)*
Hair Design Sch. of New England *(see New England Sch. of Hair Design, Inc.)*
Hair Design Sch., The 53—537
Hair Design Sch—Louisville, The 537
Hair Dynamics Edu. Ctr. 495
Hair Expressions Acad., Inc. 547
Hair Fashions by Kaye Beauty Coll—Indianapolis 530
Hair Fashions by Kaye Beauty Coll—Noblesville 530
Hair In Motion Beauty Acad. 552
Hair Masters Univ. of Beauty 481
Hair Prof.s Acad. of Cosmetolog—Elgin *(see Hair Prof.s Acad. of Cosmetolog—West Dundee)*
Hair Prof.s Acad. of Cosmetolog—West Dundee 526
Hair Prof.s Acad. of Cosmetolog—Wheaton 526
Hair Prof.s Career Coll. 527 *(see also Hair Prof.s Sch. of Cosmetology, Inc—Oswego)*
Hair Prof.s Career Coll., Inc—Sycamore 527
Hair Prof.s Sch. of Cosmetology, Inc—Oswego 527
Hair Sch., Inc. *(see Stage One- The Hair Sch., Inc.)*
Hair Sch., The *(see McCollum & Ross, The Hair Sch.)*
hair-A Paul Mitchell Partner Sch. 820
Hairitage Beauty Coll. *(see Paul Mitchell The Sch.)*
Hairitage Coll. of Beauty 794 *(see also Paul Mitchell The Sch.)*
Hairitage Hair Acad. 660
Hairmasters Inst. of Cosmetology, Inc. 527
Hairstyling Inst. of Charlotte 601
Haley VA Med. Ctr. *(see James A. Haley Veterans Affairs Med. Ctr.)*
Haley VAMC *(see James A. Haley Veterans Affairs Med. Ctr.)*
Haley Veterans Affairs Med. Ctr. *(see James A. Haley Veterans Affairs Med. Ctr.)*
Halifax Coll. *(see Halifax Comm. Coll.)*
Halifax Comm. Coll. 303
Halifax County Comm. Coll. *(see Halifax Comm. Coll.)*
Halifax County Tech. Inst. *(see Halifax Comm. Coll.)*
Halifax Med. Ctr. 696
Halifax Tech. Inst. *(see Halifax Comm. Coll.)*
Hallmark Aero-Tech *(see Hallmark Coll.)*
Hallmark Coll. 397
Hallmark Coll. of Aeronautics *(see Hallmark Coll.)*
Hallmark Inst. of Aeronautics 397
Hallmark Inst. of Photography 552
Hallmark Inst. of Techno. *(see Hallmark Coll.)*
Hall-Moody Inst. *(see Univ. of Tennessee at Martin)*
Hall-Moody Jr. Coll. of Martin *(see Union Univ.)*
Hamilton Bus. Coll. *(see Kaplan Univ.)*
Hamilton Ctr. Inc. 705
Hamilton Coll. 278 *(see also Hamilton Tech. Coll.)*
Hamilton Coll—Cedar Falls *(see Kaplan Univ.)*
Hamilton Coll—Cedar Rapids *(see Kaplan Univ.)*
Hamilton Coll—Council Bluffs *(see Kaplan Univ.)*
Hamilton Coll—Des Moines *(see Kaplan Univ.)*
Hamilton Coll—Lincoln *(see Kaplan Univ.)*
Hamilton Coll—Mason City *(see Kaplan Univ.)*
Hamilton Coll—Omaha *(see Kaplan Univ.)*
Hamilton Inst. *(see Colgate Univ.)*
Hamilton Jr. Coll. *(see Kaplan Univ.)*
Hamilton Tech. Coll. 159
Hamilton-Oneida Acad. *(see Hamilton Coll.)*
Hamline Univ. 222
Hamm Clinic 716
Hamm Mem. Psychiatric Clinic *(see Hamm Clinic)*
Hamma Divinity Sch. *(see Wittenberg Univ.)*
Hamma Sch. of Theology *(see Trinity Lutheran Sem.)*
Hampden-Sydney Coll. 423
Hampshire Coll. 200
Hampstead Acad. *(see Mississippi Coll.)*
Hampton Jr. Coll. *(see Central Florida Comm. Coll.)*
Hampton Roads CPE Ctr. *(see Hampton Veterans Affairs Med. Ctr.)*
Hampton Univ. 423
Hampton VA Med. Ctr. *(see Hampton Veterans Affairs Med. Ctr.)*
Hampton VAMC *(see Hampton Veterans Affairs Med. Ctr.)*
Hampton Veterans Affairs Med. Ctr. 750
Hamrick Sch. 608, 790
Hamrick Truck Driving Sch. 790 *(see also Hamrick Sch.)*
Hancock Coll. *(see Allan Hancock Coll.)*
Hancock Mem. Hosp. *(see Hancock Reg. Hosp.)*
Hancock Reg. Hosp. 705
Handley & Associates, Inc. 557
Hands of Champions Beauty Coll. *(see Stacey's Hands of Champions Beauty Coll., Inc.)*
HandsOn Therapy Sch. of Massage 651
Hanes & Associates, Inc. 530
Haney Tech. Ctr. *(see Tom P. Haney Tech. Ctr.)*
Hanger Orthopedic Group, Inc. 693
Hanger Prosthetics & Orthotics, Inc. *(see Hanger Orthopedic Group, Inc.)*
Hannah E. Mullins Sch. of Practical Nursing 732
Hannibal Area Vocational-Tech. Sch. *(see Hannibal Career & Tech. Ctr.)*
Hannibal Career & Tech. Ctr. 567
Hannibal Coll. *(see Hannibal-LaGrange Coll.)*
Hannibal Vo-Tech Sch. *(see Hannibal Career & Tech. Ctr.)*
Hannibal-LaGrange Coll. 238
Hanover Acad. *(see Hanover Coll.)*
Hanover Coll. 147
Hanover Park Coll. of Beauty Culture, Inc. 782 *(see also Empire Beauty Sch—Hanover Park)*
Hanover Practical Nursing Program *(see Hanover Public Sch. Dist.)*
Hanover Public Sch. Dist. 739
Harbor Coll. *(see Los Angeles Harbor Coll.)*
Harbor Healthcare Sys. *(see Veterans Affairs NewYork Harbor Healthcare Sys—New York City)*
Harbor Med. Coll. *(see Everest Coll—Torrance)*
Harborlight Montessori Sch. *(see NCM—New England)*
Harborview Med. Ctr. 751
Harcourt Learning Direct *(see Penn Foster Career Sch.Penn Foster Coll.)*
Harcourt Learning Direct Ctr. for Degree Studies *(see Penn Foster Coll.)*
Harcum Coll. 349
Harcum Post Grad. Sch. *(see Harcum Coll.)*
HARDI Home Study Inst. 608
Hardin Coll. *(see Midwestern State Univ.)*
Hardin Jr. Coll. *(see Midwestern State Univ.)*
Harding Coll. *(see Harding Univ.)*
Harding Univ. 27
Harding Univ. Grad. Sch. of Religion 384
Hardin-Simmons Univ. 397
Harford Coll. *(see Harford Comm. Coll.)*

Hohenwald Vo-Tech Sch. *(see Tennessee Techno. Ctr. at Hohenwald)*
HoHoKus RET—Nutley 579, 788
HoHoKus Sch. *(see Eastwick Coll.)*
HoHoKus Sch. of Bus. & Med. Sciences 580, 788 *(see also Eastwick Coll.)*
HoHoKus Sch. of Trade & Tech. Sciences 580
HoHoKus-Hackensack Sch. of Bus. & Med. Science 580
Hoke Smith Tech. Inst. *(see Atlanta Tech. Coll.)*
Holiness Evangelistic Inst. *(see Oklahoma Wesleyan Univ.)*
Holistic Health Acad. of Ohio *(see Ohio Acad. of Holistic Health, Inc.)*
Holistic Home Nursing, Inc. *(see Midwest Inst. of Massage Therapy)*
Holland Acad., The *(see Hope Coll.)*
Holland Coll. 759
Holland Comm. Coll. *(see Holland Coll.)*
Hollins Coll. *(see Hollins Univ.)*
Hollins Inst. *(see Hollins Univ.)*
Hollins Univ. 423
Hollywood Beauty Coll. 522, 810 *(see also Moler-Hollywood Beauty Coll.)*
Hollywood Coll. of Chiropractic *(see Southern California Univ. of Health Sciences)*
Hollywood Cosmetology Ctr. 615
Hollywood Inst. of Beauty Careers 509
Holmes Coll. *(see Holmes Comm. Coll.)*
Holmes Comm. Coll. 231
Holmes Inst. 47
Holmes Jr. Coll. *(see Holmes Comm. Coll.)*
Holy Apostles Coll. & Sem. 79
Holy Apostles Sem. *(see Holy Apostles Coll. & Sem.)*
Holy Cross Coll. 147 *(see also Coll. of the Holy Cross; Our Lady of Holy Cross Coll.)*
Holy Cross Greek Orthodox Sch. of Theology *(see Hellenic Coll/Holy Cross Greek Orthodox Sch. of Theology)*
Holy Cross Hosp. 710
Holy Cross Jr. Coll. *(see Holy Cross Coll.)*
Holy Cross Normal Sch. *(see Our Lady of Holy Cross Coll.)*
Holy Cross Theological Sch. *(see Hellenic Coll/Holy Cross Greek Orthodox Sch. of Theology)*
Holy Family Coll. *(see Holy Family Univ.)*
Holy Family Hosp. & Med. Ctr. *(see Caritas Christi Health Care Sys.)*
Holy Family Med. Ctr. *(see Holy Family Hosp. & Med. Ctr.)*
Holy Family Univ. 349
Holy Heart Sem. *(see Atlantic Sch. of Theology)*
Holy Name Hosp. 721
Holy Name Tech. Sch. *(see Lewis Univ.)*
Holy Names Coll. 777 *(see also Heritage Univ.; Holy Names Univ.)*
Holy Names Univ. 47, 777
Holy Spirit Coll. *(see Holy Spirit Preparatory Sch.)*
Holy Spirit Health Sys. *(see Holy Spirit Hosp.)*
Holy Spirit Hosp. 739
Holy Spirit Preparatory Sch. 803
Holy Spirit Preparatory Sch. Upper Level Sch. *(see Holy Spirit Preparatory Sch.)*
Holy Trinity Orthodox Sem. 278, 589
Holy Trinity Sem. *(see Holy Trinity Orthodox Sem.)*
Holyoke Coll. *(see Holyoke Comm. Coll.)*
Holyoke Comm. Coll. 200
Holyoke Jr. Coll. *(see Holyoke Comm. Coll.)*
Home of the Sick *(see Danville Reg. Med. Ctr.)*
Home Study Int'l. 785
Homestead Sr. High Sch. *(see Miami-Dade County Public Schools Health Science Edu.)*
Hondros Career Ctr.s *(see Hondros Coll.)*
Hondros Coll. 319
Hondros Coll—Beaver Creek *(see Hondros Coll.)*
Hong Kong City Univ. *(see City Univ. of Hong Kong)*
Hong Kong Univ. of Science & Techno. 766
Honolulu Bus. Coll. *(see Heald Coll—Honolulu)*
Honolulu Christian Coll. *(see Hawaii Pacific Univ.)*
Honolulu Coll. *(see Honolulu Comm. Coll.)*
Honolulu Comm. Coll. 123
Honolulu Tech. Sch. *(see Honolulu Comm. Coll.)*
Honolulu VA Med. Ctr. *(see Veterans Affairs Pacific Islands Healthcare Sys.)*
Honolulu VAMC *(see Veterans Affairs Pacific Islands Healthcare Sys.)*
Honolulu Veterans Affairs Med. Ctr. *(see Veterans Affairs Pacific Islands Healthcare Sys.)*
Honolulu Vocational Sch. *(see Honolulu Comm. Coll.)*
Honors Coll. of Florida *(see New Coll. of Florida)*
Hood Coll. 191
Hood Sem. *(see Hood Theological Sem.)*
Hood Theological Sem. 303
Hope Career Inst. *(see Int'l. Sch. of Health & Beauty)*
Hope Coll. 212
Hope Comm. Coll. *(see Univ. of Arkansas Comm. Coll. at Hope)*
Hope Hospice *(see Hope Hospice & Comm. Services)*
Hope Int'l. Univ. 48
Hope Univ. *(see Hope Int'l. Univ.)*
Hôpital général juif *(see Jewish General Hosp.)*
Hopkins Edu. Ctr. *(see Lindsey Hopkins Tech. Edu. Ctr.)*
Hopkins Hosp. *(see Johns Hopkins Hosp.)*
Hopkins Sch. of Medicine *(see Johns Hopkins Hosp.)*
Hopkins Tech. Edu. Ctr. *(see Lindsey Hopkins Tech. Edu. Ctr.)*
Hopkins Univ. *(see Johns Hopkins Univ.)*
Hopkinsville Comm. Coll. 173
Horizon Bible Inst. *(see Horizon Coll. San Diego)*
Horizon Career Coll. *(see Everest Inst—Grand Rapids)*
Horizon Coll. of San Diego *(see Horizon Coll. San Diego)*
Horizon Coll. San Diego 801
Horry-Georgetown Coll. *(see Horry-Georgetown Tech. Coll.)*
Horry-Georgetown Tech. Coll. 375
Horton Acad. *(see Acadia Divinity Coll.)*
Hospice of the Bluegrass 708
Hosp. Ctr. of Brooklyn *(see Brooklyn Hosp. Ctr.)*
Hosp. Ctr. of Harlem *(see Harlem Hosp. Ctr.)*
Hosp. Ctr. of Washington *(see Washington Hosp. Ctr.)*
Hosp. of Oak Forest *(see Oak Forest Hosp.)*
Hosp. of Port Huron *(see Port Huron Hosp.)*
Hosp. of Rockford *(see Rockford Mem. Hosp.)*
Hosp. of Saint Raphael 693
Hosp. of the Protestant Episcopal Church *(see Cincinnati Children's Hosp. Med. Ctr.)*
Hosp. of the Univ. of Pennsylvania *(see Univ. of Pennsylvania)*
Hosp. Sisters Health Sys. *(see Saint Elizabeth's Hosp.)*
Hosp.ity Training Ctr. *(see Brighton Coll.)*
Hostos Comm. Coll. *(see City Univ. of New York Hostos Comm. Coll.)*
Hot Springs Beauty Coll. 470
Hotel Inst. "Cesar Ritz" *(see Institut Hotelier "Cesar Ritz")*
Hotel Inst. Montreux 680

Humboldt State Univ. 48
Humphreys Coll. 48
Hunt Correctional Ctr. *(see Jumonville Mem. Tech. Inst.)*
Hunter Bus. & Tech. Programs *(see Hunter Bus. Sch.)*
Hunter Bus. Sch. 589
Hunter Coll. *(see City Univ. of New York Brooklyn Coll.; City Univ. of New York Hunter Coll.)*
Hunter Coll. of The City of New York *(see City Univ. of New York Hunter Coll.)*
Huntingdon Coll. 5
Huntingdon County Career & Techno. Ctr. 739
Huntington Coll. 782 *(see also Huntington Jr. Coll.; Huntington Univ.)*
Huntington Coll. of Health Sciences 384, 793
Huntington Dental Techno. Coll. *(see Huntington Coll. of Dental Techno.)*
Huntington Hosp. *(see Cabell Huntington Hosp.)*
Huntington Inst. 779
Huntington Jr. Coll. 441
Huntington Jr. Coll. of Bus. *(see Huntington Jr. Coll.)*
Huntington Sch. of Beauty Culture, Inc. 672
Huntington Univ. 147, 782
Huntington VA Med. Ctr. *(see Huntington Veterans Affairs Med. Ctr.)*
Huntington VAMC *(see Huntington Veterans Affairs Med. Ctr.)*
Huntington Veterans Affairs Med. Ctr. 753
Huntsville Baptist Inst. *(see Huntsville Bible Coll.)*
Huntsville Bible Coll. 6
Huntsville Coll. *(see Huntsville Bible Coll.)*
Huntsville Hosp. 683
Huntsville Hosp. Sys. *(see Huntsville Hosp.)*
Hurley Health Group *(see Hurley Med. Ctr.)*
Hurley Hosp. *(see Hurley Med. Ctr.)*
Hurley Med. Ctr. 714
Huron Coll. *(see Huron Univ. Coll. Faculty of Theology)*
Huron Hosp. 732
Huron Sch. of Nursing *(see Huron Hosp.)*
Huron Univ. Coll. Faculty of Theology 455
Huron Valley Ambulance 714
Hussian Sch. of Art 349
Husson Coll. *(see Husson Univ.)*
Husson Univ. 187
Huston-Tillotson Coll. 794 *(see also Huston-Tillotson Univ.)*
Huston-Tillotson Univ. 398, 794
Hutchinson Coll. *(see Hutchinson Comm. Coll.)*
Hutchinson Comm. Coll. 166
Hutchinson Comm. Jr. Coll. *(see Hutchinson Comm. Coll.)*
Hutchinson Jr. Coll. *(see Hutchinson Comm. Coll.)*
Hutchinson-Willmar Reg. Tech. Coll. *(see Ridgewater Coll.)*
Hypnosis Motivation Inst. 482
Hypnosis Motivation Inst., Extension Sch. *(see Hypnosis Motivation Inst.)*

I

I.C.E. Beauty Sch. & Spa Training Ctr. 509
I.C.E. Spa Training Ctr. *(see I.C.E. Beauty Sch. & Spa Training Ctr.)*
IADT Detroit *(see Int'l. Acad. of Design & Techno.)*
IADT Nashville *(see Int'l. Acad. of Design & Techno—Nashville)*
IADT Pittsburgh *(see Int'l. Acad. of Design & Techno.)*
IADT Tampa *(see Int'l. Acad. of Design & Techno.)*
IAE Bus. & Mgmnt. Sch. *(see IAE Universidad Austral)*
IAE Universidad Austral 756
IAUPR Sch. of Law *(see Inter American Univ. of Puerto Rico Sch. of Law)*
IAUPR Sch. of Optometry *(see Inter American Univ. of Puerto Rico Sch. of Optometry)*
IBM—Fort Collins Coll. *(see Inst. of Bus. & Med. Careers)*
ICC Tech. Inst. 652
ICDC Coll. 482
ICE Beauty Sch. & Spa Training Ctr. *(see I.C.E. Beauty Sch. & Spa Training Ctr.)*
ICI Univ. 238 *(see also Global Univ.)*
ICI Univ. Int'l. *(see Global Univ.)*
ICM Sch. of Bus. & Med. Careers 791 *(see also Kaplan Career Inst—ICM Campus)*
ICPR Jr. Coll. *(see Instituto Comercial de Puerto Rico Jr. Coll.)*
ICS Ctr. for Degree Studies *(see Penn Foster Coll.)*
ICS Learning Systems *(see Penn Foster Career Sch.; Penn Foster Coll.)*
ICS The Wright Beauty Coll. 564
ICT Coll. *(see LA Coll. Int'l.)*
ICT Kikkawa Coll. 678
ICT Northumberland Coll. 678
Idaho Ballet Acad. *(see Ballet Idaho Acad.)*
Idaho State Coll. *(see Idaho State Univ.)*
Idaho State Univ. 125
Idaho Tech. Inst. *(see Idaho State Univ.)*
Idaho Univ. *(see Idaho State Univ.)*
Ideal Beauty Acad., Inc. 530
IE Bus. Sch. *(see Instituto de Empresa Bus. Sch.)*
IHM Bus. Sch. 679
IHM Health Studies Ctr. 718
IIA Coll. 19, 775
IITR Truck Driving Sch. 620
Iliff Sch. of Theology 73
Iliff Theology Sch. *(see Iliff Sch. of Theology)*
Ilisagvik Coll. 12
Illiana Health Care Sys. *(see Veterans Affairs Illiana Health Care Sys.)*
Illiana VA Health Care Sys. *(see Veterans Affairs Illiana Health Care Sys.)*
Illiana Veterans Affairs Health Care Sys. *(see Veterans Affairs Illiana Health Care Sys.)*
Illinois Art Inst. *(see Illinois Inst. of Art)*
Illinois Benedictine Coll. *(see Benedictine Univ.)*
Illinois Ctr. for Broadcasting 527
Illinois Central Coll. 132
Illinois Coll. 132
Illinois Coll. of Optometry 133
Illinois Conference Female Acad. *(see MacMurray Coll.)*
Illinois Dale Carnegie Training *(see S.J. Grant & Associates, Inc.)*
Illinois Female Coll. *(see MacMurray Coll.)*
Illinois Holiness Univ. *(see Olivet Nazarene Univ.)*
Illinois Industrial Univ. *(see Univ. of Illinois at Urbana-Champaign)*
Illinois Inst. *(see Wheaton Coll.)*
Illinois Inst. of Art, The 133
Illinois Inst. of Ar—Chicago *(see Illinois Inst. of Art)*
Illinois Inst. of Ar—Schaumburg 133
Illinois Inst. of Techno. 133
Illinois Liberal Inst. *(see Meadville Lombard Theological Sch.)*
Illinois Masonic Med. Ctr. *(see Advocate Illinois Masonic Med. Ctr.)*
Illinois Sch. of Health Careers 527
Illinois Sch. of Prof. Psychology Chicago 782 *(see also Argosy Univ. Chicago)*
Illinois Sch. of Prof. Psychology—Rolling Meadows *(see Argosy Univ. Schaumburg)*
Illinois State Univ. 133 *(see also Carthage Coll.)*
Illinois Teachers Coll. Chicago South *(see Chicago State Univ.)*
Illinois Valley Coll. *(see Illinois Valley Comm. Coll.)*
Illinois Valley Comm. Coll. 133

Inland Empire Training Ctr. 489
Inland North West Culinary Acad. *(see Spokane Comm. Coll.)*
Inland Northwest Heating, Ventilation, & Air Conditioning Training Ctr. 796 *(see also Northwest HVAC/R Assoc. & Training Ctr.)*
Inland Northwest HVAC Training Ctr. *(see Northwest HVAC/R Assoc. & Training Ctr.)*
Inlingua English Ctr. 665
Inlingua Int'l. Language Ctr.s *(see Inlingua English Ctr.)*
Inlingua Int'l., Inc. *(see Inlingua English Ctr.)*
Inner State Beauty Sch. 608
Innovative Corporate Solutions *(see Dale Carnegie of San Diego)*
InovaTech Coll. of Bus. & Techno. *(see InovaTech Sch. of Applied Techno.)*
InovaTech Sch. of Applied Techno. 601
InovaTech, Inc. *(see InovaTech Sch. of Applied Techno.)*
INSEAD 765
Inservicer's Coll. of Health Edu. *(see Everest Inst—Grand Rapids)*
Institucion Chaviano de Mayaguez 633
Institut Européen d'Administration des Affaires *(see INSEAD)*
Institut Européen de Mgmnt. Int'l. 765
Institut Hotelier "Cesar Ritz" 680
Institut Quimic de Sarria de Universitat Ramôn Llull 769
Institut Supérieur de Gestion 765
Inst. for Advanced Distributed Learning *(see Air Univ. Extension Course Program)*
Inst. for Advanced Montessori Studies 547
Inst. for Bus. & Techno. 482
Inst. for Chaplaincy & Clinical Pastoral Edu., The *(see Care & Counseling Ctr. of Georgia)*
Inst. for Christian Studies *(see Austin Grad. Sch. of Theology)*
Inst. for Clinical Social Work, Inc. 133
Inst. for Colored Youth *(see Cheyney Univ. of Pennsylvania)*
Inst. for Health Edu., The 580
Inst. for Med. Services, Inc. 781
Inst. for Prof. Development *(see United States Army Inst. for Prof. Development; Univ. of Phoenix)*
Inst. for the Culinary Arts *(see Metropolitan Comm. Coll.)*
Inst. for the Psychological Sciences, The 423
Inst. for Therapeutic Massage *(see Univ. of Medicine & Dentistry of New Jersey)*
Inst. for Therapeutic Massage, Inc. 580
Inst. for Worship Studies *(see Robert E. Webber Inst. for Worship Studies)*
Inst. of Advanced Med. Esthetics, The 821
Inst. of Aeronautical Technologies *(see Aviation Inst. of Maint—Dallas)*
Inst. of Agriculture & Natural Resources *(see Nebraska Coll. of Tech. Agriculture)*
Inst. of Allied Med. Professions 97, 590
Inst. of American Indian & Alaskan Native Culture & Arts Development 266
Inst. of American Indian Arts *(see Inst. of American Indian & Alaskan Native Culture & Arts Development)*
Inst. of Animal Arts of Florida *(see Florida Inst. of Animal Arts)*
Inst. of Applied Linguistics *(see Grad. Inst. of Applied Linguistics)*
Inst. of Audio Recording Techno. *(see Audio Recording Techno. Inst.)*
Inst. of Audio Research 590
Inst. of Banking & Commerce *(see Instituto de Banca y Comercio)*
Inst. of Beauty & Wellness, The 675
Inst. of Beauty Careers 633
Inst. of Beauty Culture 810
Inst. of Beauty Occupation & Techno. 634
Inst. of Biosciences & Techno. *(see Texas A&M Univ. Sys. Health Science Ctr.)*
Inst. of Bus. & Med. Careers 73
Inst. of Central Florida *(see Central Florida Inst., Inc.)*
Inst. of Chinese Medicine of New York *(see New York Coll. of Traditional Chinese Medicine)*
Inst. of Clinical Acupuncture & Oriental Medicine 123
Inst. of Computer Mgmnt. *(see Kaplan Career Inst—ICM Campus)*
Inst. of Computer Techno. 777 *(see also LA Coll. Int'l.)*
Inst. of Cosmetology *(see Inst. of Cosmetology & Esthetics)*
Inst. of Cosmetology & Esthetics 652
Inst. of Culinary Edu., The 590
Inst. of Dental-Med. Assistants of Cleveland *(see Cleveland Inst. of Dental-Med. Assistants, Inc.)*
Inst. of Design *(see Illinois Inst. of Techno.)*
Inst. of Design & Construction 279
Inst. of Electronic Techno. *(see Daymar Coll.)*
Inst. of Entertainment Media Production *(see Video Symphony EnterTraining, Inc.)*
Inst. of Fashion Design & Merchandising *(see Fashion Inst. of Design & Merchandising)*
Inst. of Fashion Techno. *(see Fashion Inst. of Techno.)*
Inst. of Grad. Health Sciences *(see Univ. of St. Augustine for Health Sciences)*
Inst. of Hair Design Barber Coll. 616
Inst. of Hair Design, Inc. 641
Inst. of Health Professions *(see MGH Inst. of Health Professions)*
Inst. of Healthcare Training *(see Healthcare Training Inst.)*
Inst. of Hypnosis Motivation *(see Hypnosis Motivation Inst.)*
Inst. of Industrial Mgmnt. & Training *(see Industrial Mgmnt. & Training Inst.)*
Inst. of Intensive English 522
Inst. of Living, The 693
Inst. of Logistical Mgmnt. 580
Inst. of Med. & Dental Techno. 608 *(see also Kaplan Coll., Phoenix)*
Inst. of Midwifery, Women & Health 791–792 *(see also Midwifery Inst. of Philadelphia Univ.)*
Inst. of Modern Hairstylin—Bayamon *(see Modern Hairstyling Inst—Fajardo)*
Inst. of Movement Studies *(see Laban/Bartenieff Inst. of Movement Studies, Inc.)*
Inst. of Muscular Therapy *(see Cortiva Inst—Boston)*
Inst. of Musical Art *(see Juilliard Sch.)*
Inst. of Network Techno. 482
Inst. of North Florida *(see North Florida Inst.)*
Inst. of Open Edu. at Newton Coll. of the Sacred Heart *(see Cambridge Coll.)*
Inst. of Oriental Medicine of Seattle *(see Seattle Inst. of Oriental Medicine)*
Inst. of Paper Chemistry *(see Georgia Inst. of Techno.; Inst. of Paper Science & Techno. at Georgia Tech)*
Inst. of Paper Science & Techno. *(see Inst. of Paper Science & Techno. at Georgia Tech)*
Inst. of Paper Science & Techno. at Georgia Tech 114 *(see also Georgia Inst. of Techno.)*
Inst. of Physical Therapy *(see Univ. of St. Augustine for Health Sciences)*
Inst. of Production & Recording, The 222
Inst. of Prof. Careers 572
Inst. of Prof. Skills *(see Prof. Skills Inst.)*
Inst. of Psychological Studies *(see Psychological Studies Inst.)*
Inst. of Psycho-Structural Balancing *(see Int'l. Prof. Sch. of Bodywork)*
Inst. of Specialized Training & Mgmnt. *(see City Coll. Casselberry)*

J

Jackson Area Vocational-Tech. Sch. *(see Tennessee Techno. Ctr. at Jackson)*
Jackson Area Vo-Tech Sch. *(see Tennessee Techno. Ctr. at Jackson)*
Jackson Coll. *(see Jackson Comm. Coll.; Jackson State Comm. Coll.; Tufts Univ.)*
Jackson Comm. Coll. 212 *(see also Jackson State Comm. Coll.)*
Jackson County Industrial Edu. Ctr. *(see Southwestern Comm. Coll.)*
Jackson County Tech. Ctr. *(see Roane Jackson Tech. Ctr.)*
Jackson Health Sys. *(see Jackson Mem. Hosp.)*
Jackson Healthcare Inst. *(see Healthcare Inst. of Jackson)*
Jackson Jr. Coll. *(see Jackson Comm. Coll.)*
Jackson Male Acad. *(see Union Univ.)*
Jackson Mem. Hosp. 696
Jackson Mem. Med. Ctr. *(see Jackson Mem. Hosp.)*
Jackson Sch. of Bus. *(see West Tennessee Bus. Coll.)*
Jackson State Coll. *(see Jackson State Comm. Coll.)*
Jackson State Comm. Coll. 385
Jackson State Univ. 231
Jackson Univ. *(see Andrew Jackson Univ.; Jackson State Univ.)*
Jackson Vocational-Tech. Sch. *(see Tennessee Techno. Ctr. at Jackson)*
Jackson Vo-Tech Sch. *(see Tennessee Techno. Ctr. at Jackson)*
Jacksonville Baptist Coll. *(see Jacksonville Coll.)*
Jacksonville Beauty Inst., Inc. 509
Jacksonville Coll. 399 *(see also Florida Comm. Coll. at Jacksonville)*
Jacksonville Coll. Sem. *(see Baptist Missionary Assoc. Theological Sem.)*
Jacksonville Comm. Coll. *(see Florida Comm. Coll. at Jacksonville)*
Jacksonville Dale Carnegie Training *(see Folkner Training Associates, Inc.)*
Jacksonville Female Acad. *(see Illinois Coll.)*
Jacksonville Jr. Coll. *(see Jacksonville Univ.)*
Jacksonville Med. Ctr. *(see Shands Jacksonville Med. Ctr.)*
Jacksonville State Normal Sch. *(see Jacksonville State Univ.)*
Jacksonville State Teachers Coll. *(see Jacksonville State Univ.)*
Jacksonville State Univ. 6
Jacksonville Stenotype Inst. *(see Stenotype Inst. of Jacksonville)*
Jacksonville Univ. 98 *(see also Jacksonville State Univ.)*
Jacobi/Montefiore Hosp/East *(see Montefiore Med. Ctr. East Campus)*
Jacobs Creek Job Corps 641
Jaffray Sch. of Missions *(see Alliance Theological Sem.)*
JAG Sch. *(see Judge Advocate General's Sch.)*
Jamaica Hosp. *(see Jamaica Hosp. Med. Ctr.)*
Jamaica Hosp. Med. Ctr. 725
Jameat Alemarat Al Arabia Al Mutaheda *(see United Arab Emirates Univ.)*
James A. Haley VA Med. Ctr. *(see James A. Haley Veterans Affairs Med. Ctr.)*
James A. Haley Veterans Affairs Med. Ctr. 696
James A. Rhodes State Coll. 320
James Albert Sch. of Cosmetology 483
James & Carolyn McAfee Sch. of Theology *(see Mercer Univ.)*
James Cancer Hosp. *(see Ohio State Univ.)*
James Connally Tech. Inst. *(see Texas State Tech. Coll. Marshall; Texas State Tech. Coll—Harlingen; Texas State Tech. Coll—Waco; Texas State Tech. Coll—West Texas at Sweetwater)*
James E. Varner & Associates, Inc. 522
James Graham Brown Cancer Ctr. *(see Univ. of Louisville)*
James H. Faulkner State Comm. Coll. 6
James H. Quillen VA Med. Ctr. *(see James H. Quillen Veterans Affairs Med. Ctr.)*
James H. Quillen Veterans Affairs Med. Ctr. 745
James J. Peters VA Med. Ctr. *(see James J. Peters Veterans Affairs Med. Ctr.)*
James J. Peters VAMC *(see James J. Peters Veterans Affairs Med. Ctr.)*
James J. Peters Veterans Affairs Med. Ctr. 725
James King Coll. *(see King Coll.)*
James L. Walker Vocational-Tech. Ctr. *(see Lorenzo Walker Inst. of Techno.)*
James Madison Coll. 213 *(see also Michigan State Univ.)*
James Madison Univ. 424
James Millikin Univ., The *(see Millikin Univ.)*
James Monroe Ctr. for Grad. & Prof. Studies 429 *(see also Univ. of Mary Washington)*
James Rumsey Tech. Inst. 673
James Sprunt Coll. *(see James Sprunt Comm. Coll.)*
James Sprunt Comm. Coll. 304
Jameson Health Sys. *(see Jameson Hosp—North; Jameson Hosp—South)*
Jameson Hosp. *(see Jameson Hosp—North; Jameson Hosp—South)*
Jameson Hosp—North 739
Jameson Hosp—South 739
Jameson Mem. Hosp. *(see Jameson Hosp—North; Jameson Hosp—South)*
Jameson Mem. Hosp. Sch. of Nursing *(see Jameson Hosp—North)*
Jamestown Bus. Coll. 279
Jamestown Coll. 311 *(see also Jamestown Comm. Coll.)*
Jamestown Coll. of Bus. *(see Jamestown Bus. Coll.)*
Jamestown Comm. Coll. 279
Janesville Acad. of Cosmetology *(see Acad. of Cosmetology)*
Jarvis Christian Coll. 399
Jarvis Coll. *(see Jarvis Christian Coll.)*
Jasper County Jr. Coll. *(see Missouri Southern State Univ.)*
Javelin Tech *(see Javelin Tech. Training Ctr.)*
Jay Coll. of Criminal Justice *(see City Univ. of New York John Jay Coll. of Criminal Justice)*
Jay Inst. *(see Walter Jay M.D. Inst. An Educational Ctr.)*
Jay's Tech. Inst. 653
Je Boutique Coll. of Beauty 483
Jean Madeline Aveda Inst. 626
Jean Madeline Edu. Ctr. for Cosmetology *(see Jean Madeline Aveda Inst.)*
Jeanes Hosp. 739
Jean's Nails, Etc. 661
Jeff Davis Comm. Sch. 108
Jeff Tech *(see Jefferson County-Dubois Area Vocational Tech. Sch.)*
Jefferson Coll. 239 *(see also Jefferson Comm. & Tech. Coll.; Jefferson Comm. Coll.; Jefferson State Comm. Coll.; Washington & Jefferson Coll.)*
Jefferson Coll. of Health Sciences 424
Jefferson Comm. & Tech. Coll. 173, 784
Jefferson Comm. Coll. 279, 320, 784 *(see also Jefferson Comm. & Tech. Coll.; Jefferson State Comm. Coll.)*
Jefferson Comm. Tech. Colleges *(see Jefferson Comm. & Tech. Coll.)*

Jefferson County Internship Consortium 708
Jefferson County Manpower Skills Ctr. *(see Jefferson Comm. & Tech. Coll.)*
Jefferson County State Vocational-Tech. Sch. & Manpower Skills Ctr. *(see Jefferson Comm. & Tech. Coll.)*
Jefferson County Tech. Inst. *(see Jefferson Comm. Coll.)*
Jefferson County-Dubois Area Vocational Tech. Sch. 739
Jefferson County-Dubois Vo-Tech Sch. *(see Jefferson County-Dubois Area Vocational Tech. Sch.)*
Jefferson Davis Comm. Coll. 6
Jefferson Health Sys. *(see Frankford Hosp.)*
Jefferson Law Sch. *(see Thomas Jefferson Sch. of Law)*
Jefferson Med. Coll. *(see Thomas Jefferson Univ.)*
Jefferson Reg. Med. Ctr. 685
Jefferson Sch. of Law *(see Thomas Jefferson Sch. of Law)*
Jefferson State Coll. *(see Jefferson State Comm. Coll.)*
Jefferson State Comm. Coll. 6
Jefferson Tech. *(see Louisiana Tech. Coll—Jefferson Campus)*
Jefferson Tech. Coll. 784 *(see also Jefferson Comm. & Tech. Coll.; Jefferson Comm. Coll.)*
Jefferson Univ. *(see Thomas Jefferson Univ.)*
Jenkintown Music Sch. *(see Settlement Music Sch.)*
Jenks Beauty Coll. *(see Sand Springs Beauty Coll.)*
Jenks Beauty Coll. 618
Jennie Edmundson Hosp. 707
Jennie Edmundson Mem. Hosp. *(see Jennie Edmundson Hosp.)*
Jennings & Associates, Inc. *(see John M. Jennings & Associates, Inc.)*
Jenny Lea Acad. of Cosmetolog—Harlan 537
Jenny Lea Acad. of Cosmetolog—Whitesburg 537
Jerry L. Pettis Mem. Veterans Affairs Hosp. *(see Loma Linda Veterans Affairs Healthcare Sys.)*
Jerry Wilson & Associates, Inc. 470
Jerry's Sch. of Hairstyling, Inc. 786 *(see also Cosmetology Concepts Inst.)*
Jersey City Med. Ctr. 721
Jersey City State Coll. *(see New Jersey City Univ.)*
Jersey Sch. of Locksmithing *(see New Jersey Sch. of Locksmithing)*
Jersey Shore Med. Ctr. *(see Jersey Shore Univ. Med. Ctr.)*
Jersey Shore Univ. Med. Ctr. 721
Jesse Brown VA Med. Ctr. *(see Jesse Brown Veterans Affairs Med. Ctr.)*
Jesse Brown Veterans Affairs Med. Ctr. 702
Jessup Univ. *(see William Jessup Univ.)*
Jesuit Comm. Santa Clara Univ. *(see Santa Clara Univ.)*
Jesuit Sch. of Theology at Berkeley 49
Jesuit Sem/Coll. of Christ the King *(see Regis Coll.)*
Jesus Coll. *(see Macalester Coll.)*
Jewell Coll. *(see William Jewell Coll.)*
Jewish Child & Family Services 702, 782
Jewish Children's Bureau of Chicago 782 *(see also Jewish Child & Family Services)*
Jewish Employment & Vocational Service *(see Orleans Tech. Inst.)*
Jewish Family & Comm. Service *(see Jewish Child & Family Services)*
Jewish General Hosp. 760
Jewish Hosp. Coll. of Nursing & Allied Health *(see Goldfarb Sch. of Nursing at Barnes-Jewish Coll.)*
Jewish Inst. for Pastoral Care *(see HealthCare Chaplaincy)*
Jewish Inst. of Michigan *(see Michigan Jewish Inst.)*
Jewish Inst. of Religion *(see Hebrew Union Coll—Jewish Inst. of Religion)*
Jewish Sem. of America *(see Jewish Theological Sem.)*
Jewish Theological Sem. of America *(see Jewish Theological Sem.)*
Jewish Theological Sem., The 279
JFK Med. Ctr. *(see John F. Kennedy Med. Ctr.)*
JFK Snyder Schools of Nursing & Med. Imaging *(see John F. Kennedy Med. Ctr.)*
JFK Special Warfare Ctr. & Sch. *(see United States Army John F. Kennedy Special Warfare Ctr. & Sch.)*
JFK Univ. *(see John F. Kennedy Univ.)*
Jim's Coll. of Cosmetology *(see Mr. Jim's Beauty Coll.)*
JNA Culinary Inst. *(see JNA Inst. of Culinary Arts)*
JNA Inst. of Culinary Arts 350
Job Corps Ctr. at Montgomery *(see Montgomery Job Corps Ctr.)*
Job Corps Ctr. of Atlanta *(see Atlanta Job Corps Ctr.)*
Job Corps Ctr. of Bamberg *(see Bamberg Job Corps Ctr.)*
Job Corps Ctr. of Brunswick *(see Brunswick Job Corps Ctr.)*
Job Corps Ctr. of Cincinnati *(see Cincinnati Job Corps Ctr.)*
Job Corps Ctr. of Denison *(see Denison Job Corps Ctr.)*
Job Corps Ctr. of Guthrie *(see Guthrie Job Corps Ctr.)*
Job Corps Ctr. of Little Rock *(see Little Rock Job Corps Ctr.)*
Job Corps Ctr. of Miami *(see Miami Job Corps Ctr.)*
Job Corps Ctr. of Shreveport *(see Shreveport Job Corps Ctr.)*
Job Corps Ctr. of Tulsa *(see Tulsa Job Corps Ctr.)*
Job Corps Region One *(see New Haven Job Corps Ctr.)*
Job Ready Training 819
Joe Kubert Sch. of Cartoon & Graphic Art 580
Joffrey Ballet Sch. *(see American Ballet Ctr/Joffrey Ballet Sch.)*
Johann Wolfgang Goethe-Universitüt Frankfurt am Main 766
John A. Gupton Coll. 385
John A. Logan Coll. 134
John Abbott Coll. 760
John Amico's Sch. of Hair Design 527
John B. Stetson Univ. *(see Stetson Univ.)*
John Bastyr Coll. of Naturopathic Medicine *(see Bastyr Univ.)*
John Brown Coll. & Acad. *(see John Brown Univ.)*
John Brown Univ. 27
John C. Calhoun State Comm. Coll. *(see Calhoun Comm. Coll.)*
John Cabot Univ. 458
John Calvin Jr. Coll. *(see Calvin Coll.)*
John Carroll Univ. 320
John D Rockefeller IV Career Ctr. 673
John D. Dingell VA Med. Ctr. *(see John D. Dingell Veterans Affairs Med. Ctr.)*
John D. Dingell Veterans Affairs Med. Ctr. 714
John D. Langdon & Associates, Inc. *(see Lance Tyson & Associates Dale Carnegie Training of Northeast Ohio)*
John Dempsey Hosp. *(see Univ. of Connecticut)*
John Dewey Coll. 367
John E. Brown Acad. *(see John Brown Univ.)*
John E. Brown Coll. & Acad. *(see John Brown Univ.)*
John F. Kennedy Med. Ctr. 721
John F. Kennedy Special Warfare Ctr. & Sch. *(see United States Army John F. Kennedy Special Warfare Ctr. & Sch.)*

K

Keller Grad. Sch. of Mgmnt. Seattle/ Bellevue *(see DeVry Univ. Federal Way)*
Keller Grad. Sch. of Mgmnt. Waukesha Ctr. *(see DeVry Univ. Oak Brook)*
Keller Grad. Sch. of Mgmnt—Irvine Ctr. 777 *(see also DeVry Univ. Irvine)*
Keller Grad. Sch. of Mgmnt—Nashville *(see DeVry Univ—Nashville)*
Keller Grad. Sch. of Mgmnt—Scottsdale Ctr. *(see DeVry Univ. Northeast Phoenix)*
Keller Hosp. *(see Keller Army Comm. Hosp.)*
Kellogg Coll. *(see Kellogg Comm. Coll.)*
Kellogg Comm. Coll. 212
Ken Roberts Corporation 510
Kenai Coll. *(see Kenai Peninsula Coll.)*
Kenai Peninsula Coll. 12
Kendall Coll. 134
Kendall Coll. of Art & Design *(see Ferris State Univ.)*
Kendall Coll. of Art & Design of Ferris State Univ. 210 *(see also Ferris State Univ.)*
Kendall Coll. of Design *(see Ferris State Univ.)*
Kendall Sch. of Art *(see Ferris State Univ.)*
Kendall Sch. of Design *(see Ferris State Univ.)*
Kendall's Acad. of Beauty Arts & Science *(see Sherman Kendall's Acad. of Beauty Arts & Scienc—Midvale; Sherman Kendall's Acad. of Beauty Arts & Scienc—Salt Lake City)*
Kennebec Valley Coll. *(see Kennebec Valley Comm. Coll.)*
Kennebec Valley Comm. Coll. 187
Kennebec Valley Tech. Coll. *(see Kennebec Valley Comm. Coll.)*
Kennedy Inst. *(see Kennedy Krieger Inst.)*
Kennedy Krieger Inst. 711
Kennedy Med. Ctr. *(see John F. Kennedy Med. Ctr.)*
Kennedy Univ. *(see John F. Kennedy Univ.)*
Kennedy-King Coll. *(see City Colleges of Chicag—Kennedy-King Coll.)*
Kennesaw Coll. *(see Kennesaw State Univ.)*
Kennesaw Jr. Coll. *(see Kennesaw State Univ.)*
Kennesaw State Coll. *(see Kennesaw State Univ.)*
Kennesaw State Univ. 115
Kenneth Bragg Public Safety Complex 510 *(see also Lake Tech. Ctr.)*
Kenneth Shuler's Sch. of Cosmetology 638
Kenneth Shulers Sch. of Cosmetology, Nail Design 638
Kenrick Sch. of Theology *(see Kenrick-Glennon Sem.)*
Kenrick-Glennon Sem. 239
Kensington Coll. 483
Kent & Sussex Montessori Centre, The 680
Kent State Coll. *(see Kent State Univ.)*
Kent State Normal Coll. *(see Kent State Univ.)*
Kent State Normal Sch. *(see Kent State Univ.)*
Kent State Univ. 320
Kentucky Advanced Techno. Ctr. *(see Kentucky Advanced Techno. Inst.)*
Kentucky Advanced Techno. Inst. 171
Kentucky Career Inst. *(see Beckfield Coll.)*
Kentucky Career Inst—Louisville *(see Daymar Coll.)*
Kentucky Christian Coll. *(see Kentucky Christian Univ.)*
Kentucky Christian Univ. 173
Kentucky Coll. of Bus. *(see National Coll—Nashville)*
Kentucky Inst. of Advanced Techno. *(see Kentucky Advanced Techno. Inst.)*
Kentucky Mountain Bible Coll. 173
Kentucky Mountain Coll. *(see Kentucky Mountain Bible Coll.)*
Kentucky Sch. of Mortuary Science, The *(see Mid-America Coll. of Funeral Service)*
Kentucky State Univ. 173
Kentucky Tech *(see Jefferson Comm. & Tech. Coll.)*
Kentucky Tec—Ashland State Vocational Tech. Sch. *(see Ashland Comm. & Tech. Coll.)*
Kentucky Tec—Jefferson State Vocational-Tech. Ctr. *(see Jefferson Comm. & Tech. Coll.)*
Kentucky Tec—Owensboro Campus *(see Owensboro Comm. & Tech. Coll.)*
Kentucky Tec—Rowan State Vocational-Tech. Sch. *(see Maysville Comm. & Tech. Coll.)*
Kentucky Tec—Somerset Reg. Techno. Ctr. *(see Somerset Comm. Coll.)*
Kentucky Univ. Coll. of Agriculture & Mechanical Arts *(see Univ. of Kentucky)*
Kentucky Univ. Sch. of Biblical Literature & Moral Sciences *(see Lexington Theological Sem.)*
Kentucky Wesleyan Coll. 173
Kenyon Coll. 321
Kerr Bus. Coll. 781 *(see also Savannah River Coll.)*
Kerrville VA Med. Ctr. *(see South Texas Veterans Health Care Sys.)*
Kerrville VAMC *(see South Texas Veterans Health Care Sys.)*
Kerrville Veterans Affairs Med. Ctr. *(see South Texas Veterans Health Care Sys.)*
Kettering Coll. of Med. Arts 321
Kettering Med. Ctr. *(see Kettering Coll. of Med. Arts)*
Kettering Univ. 212
Keuka Coll. 280
KeVosnik Sch. of Hair Design *(see Ke Vos Nik Sch. of Hair Design, Inc.)*
Key Coll. 99
Keyin Coll. 760
KeySkills Learning, Inc. 580
Keystone Coll. 350
Keystone Normal Sch. *(see Kutztown Univ. of Pennsylvania)*
Keystone Sch. *(see Anthem Inst—Springfield)*
Keystone Tech. Inst. 350, 790
Kiamichi Area Vocational-Tech. Sch. *(see Kiamichi Techno. Ctr—Atoka; Kiamichi Techno. Ctr—Durant; Kiamichi Techno. Ctr—Hugo; Kiamichi Techno. Ctr—Idabel; Kiamichi Techno. Ctr—McAlester; Kiamichi Techno. Ctr—Poteau; Kiamichi Techno. Ctr—Spiro; Kiamichi Techno. Ctr—Stigler; Kiamichi Techno. Ctr—Talihina)*
Kiamichi Area Vo-Tec *(see Kiamichi Techno. Ctr—Atoka; Kiamichi Techno. Ctr—Durant; Kiamichi Techno. Ctr—Hugo; Kiamichi Techno. Ctr—Idabel; Kiamichi Techno. Ctr—McAlester; Kiamichi Techno. Ctr—Poteau; Kiamichi Techno. Ctr—Spiro; Kiamichi Techno. Ctr—Stigler; Kiamichi Techno. Ctr—Talihina)*
Kiamichi Techno. Ctr—Atoka 616
Kiamichi Techno. Ctr—Durant 616
Kiamichi Techno. Ctr—Hugo 616
Kiamichi Techno. Ctr—Idabel 616
Kiamichi Techno. Ctr—McAlester 616
Kiamichi Techno. Ctr—Poteau 616
Kiamichi Techno. Ctr—Spiro 616
Kiamichi Techno. Ctr—Stigler 616
Kiamichi Techno. Ctr—Talihina 616
Kiblen & Associates *(see Thomas J. Kiblen & Associates)*
Kilgore Coll. 399
Kilian Coll. *(see Kilian Comm. Coll.)*
Kilian Comm. Coll. 379
Kim Anh Acad. of Beauty 777 *(see also Elite Beauty Coll.)*

KIMC Investments, L.P. *(see MedVance Inst.)*
King Beauty Careers *(see Royal Beauty Careers)*
King Coll. 385
King Fahd Univ. of Petroleum & Minerals 769
King's Career Coll—Florida Boulevard Campus 541
King's Career Coll—Ocean Drive Campus 541
King's Coll. 304, 350 *(see also Columbia Univ. in the City of New York; Univ. of Toronto)*
King's Coll. & Sem., The 50
King's Coll., Charlotte *(see King's Coll.)*
King's Coll., New York *(see King's Coll.)*
King's Coll., The 280, 805
Kings County Hosp. *(see Kings County Hosp. Ctr.)*
Kings County Hosp. Ctr. 725
Kings County Hosp. Downstate Med. Ctr. *(see Kings County Hosp. Ctr.)*
King's Daughters' Hosp. & Health Service 705
King's Daughters Med. Ctr. 708
Kings River Comm. Coll. *(see Reedley Coll.)*
King's Sem., The *(see King's Coll. & Sem.)*
Kingsborough Comm. Coll. *(see City Univ. of New York Kingsborough Comm. Coll.)*
Kingsbrook Jewish Hosp. *(see Kingsbrook Jewish Med. Ctr.)*
Kingsbrook Jewish Med. Ctr. 725
Kingsbury Acad. in Ocala *(see Univ. of Florida)*
Kingwood Coll. *(see Lone Star Coll. Sys.)*
Kino Comm. Hosp. 684
Kirkland Beauty Sch. 669
Kirksville Coll. of Osteopathic Medicine *(see A.T. Still Univ. of Health Sciences)*
Kirkwood Coll. *(see Kirkwood Comm. Coll.)*
Kirkwood Comm. Coll. 160
Kirtland Coll. *(see Kirtland Comm. Coll.)*
Kirtland Comm. Coll. 212
Kishwaukee Coll. 134
Kitchen Acad. 483
Kittanning Beauty Sch. of Cosmetology Arts 626
Klamath Coll. *(see Klamath Comm. Coll.)*
Klamath Comm. Coll. 338
Klein Sch. of Optics *(see New England Coll. of Optometry)*
Knott County Area Techno. Ctr. *(see Hazard Comm. & Tech. Coll.)*
Knott County Area Techno. Ctr. 172
Knowledge Systems Inst. 135
Knox Beauty Coll. 531
Knox Coll. 135, 455
Knox County Career Ctr. 609
Knox Int'l. 2000 Beauty Coll. 642
Knox Sem. *(see Knox Theological Sem.)*
Knox Theological Sem. 99
Knoxville Area Vocational-Tech. Sch. *(see Tennessee Techno. Ctr. at Knoxville)*
Knoxville Area Vo-Tech Sch. *(see Tennessee Techno. Ctr. at Knoxville)*
Knoxville Bus. Coll. *(see South Coll.)*
Knoxville Tech *(see Tennessee Techno. Ctr. at Knoxville)*
Knoxville VA Med. Ctr. *(see Veterans Affairs Central Iowa Healthcare Sys—Knoxville Division)*
Knoxville Veterans Affairs Med. Ctr. *(see Veterans Affairs Central Iowa Healthcare Sys—Knoxville Division)*
Knoxville Vocational-Tech. Sch. *(see Tennessee Techno. Ctr. at Knoxville)*
Knoxville Vo-Tech Sch. *(see Tennessee Techno. Ctr. at Knoxville)*
Kodiak Coll. 12
Kokomo Tech. Inst. *(see Ivy Tech Comm. Coll—Kokomo)*
Kol Yaakov Torah Ctr. 280
Konocti Coll. of Holistic Studies 483
Kootenai Coll. *(see Salish Kootenai Coll.)*
Korea Advanced Inst. of Science & Techno. 768
Korea Inst. of Techno. *(see Korea Advanced Inst. of Science & Techno.)*
Korea Univ. 768
Korean Inst. for Montessori 678
Korean Presbyterian Church in America *(see KPCA Coll. & Theological Sem.)*
KPCA Coll. & Theological Sem. 801 *(see also KPCA Presbyterian Theological Sem.)*
KPCA Presbyterian Theological Sem. 801
Krolak Bus. Inst. *(see Las Vegas Coll.)*
K-State *(see Kansas State Univ.)*
K-State at Salina *(see Kansas State Univ.)*
Kubert Sch. of Cartoon & Graphic Art *(see Joe Kubert Sch. of Cartoon & Graphic Art)*
Kuring-gai Coll. of Advanced Edu. *(see Univ. of Techno. Sydney)*
Kussad Court Reporting Inst. *(see Kussad Inst. of Court Reporting)*
Kussad Inst. of Court Reporting 653
Kutztown State Coll. *(see Kutztown Univ. of Pennsylvania)*
Kutztown State Teachers Coll. *(see Kutztown Univ. of Pennsylvania)*
Kutztown Univ. of Pennsylvania 351
Kuwait Univ. 767
Kuyper Coll. 212, 785
K-W Counselling Services *(see Interfaith Inst. for Couples & Families)*
Kwangtung Provincial Agricultural Tech. Sch. *(see National Sun Yat-Sen Univ.)*
Kwangtung Provincial Law Coll. *(see National Sun Yat-Sen Univ.)*
Kwantlen Coll. *(see Kwantlen Polytechnic Univ.)*
Kwantlen Polytechnic Univ. 760, 797
Kwantlen Univ. Coll. 797 *(see also Kwantlen Polytechnic Univ.)*
K-Wes, LLC *(see Cortiva Inst—Sch. of Massage Therapy)*
Kyung Sung Humanities Inst. *(see Sejong Univ.)*

L

L.E. Fletcher Tech. Comm. Coll. 179, 784, 804
L.T. Int'l. Beauty Sch. 626
La Belle Beauty Acad—Miami 510
La Belle Beauty Sch—Hialeah 510
La Carrera Universal que Aconseja los Centros *(see Universal Career Comm. Coll.)*
La Cité Collégiale 760
LA Coll. Int'l. 50, 777
LA County Coll. of Nursing *(see Los Angeles County Coll. of Nursing & Allied Health)*
LA County Dept. of Health Services *(see Los Angeles County Emergency Med. Services Agency)*
LA County EMS Agency *(see Los Angeles County Emergency Med. Services Agency)*
LA County Health Services *(see Los Angeles County Emergency Med. Services Agency)*
LA County Hosp. Coll. of Nursing *(see Los Angeles County Coll. of Nursing & Allied Health)*
LA County Med. Ctr. Sch. of Nursing *(see Los Angeles County Coll. of Nursing & Allied Health)*
LA County-USC Med. Ctr. *(see Los Angeles County-USC Med. Ctr.)*
La Crosse Normal Sch. *(see Univ. of Wisconsin-La Crosse)*

La Crosse State Teachers Coll. *(see Univ. of Wisconsin-La Crosse)*
La Frontera Ctr., Inc *(see Southern Arizona Psychology Internship Consortium)*
La Grange Coll. *(see Hannibal-LaGrange Coll.)*
La Guardia Coll. *(see City Univ. of New York LaGuardia Comm. Coll.)*
La Guardia Comm. Coll. *(see City Univ. of New York LaGuardia Comm. Coll.)*
LA Harbor Coll. *(see Los Angeles Harbor Coll.)*
La' James Coll. of Hairstylin—Cedar Falls 783
La' James Coll. of Hairstylin—Davenport 783
La' James Coll. of Hairstylin—Des Moines 783
La' James Coll. of Hairstylin—East Moline 782
La' James Coll. of Hairstylin—Fort Dodge 783
La' James Coll. of Hairstylin—Iowa City 783
La' James Coll. of Hairstylin—Mason City 533
La' James Int'l. Coll. 570, 787
La' James Int'l. Coll—Cedar Falls 533, 783
La' James Int'l. Coll—Davenport 533, 783
La' James Int'l. Coll—Des Moines 533, 783
La' James Int'l. Coll—East Moline 527, 782
La' James Int'l. Coll—Fort Dodge 533, 783
La' James Int'l. Coll—Iowa City 533, 783
La Jolla Acad. of Advertising Arts *(see Art Inst. of Californi—San Diego)*
La Jolla Med. Ctr. *(see Veterans Affairs San Diego Healthcare Sys.)*
La Junta Jr. Coll. *(see Otero Jr. Coll.)*
LA Mission Coll. *(see Los Angeles Mission Coll.)*
LA Music Acad. *(see Los Angeles Music Acad.)*
LA ORT Tech. Inst. *(see Los Angeles ORT Tech. Inst.)*
LA Pierce Coll. *(see Los Angeles Pierce Coll.)*
La Rabida Children's Hosp. 702
LA Recording Sch. *(see Los Angeles Recording Sch.)*
LA Recording Workshop *(see Los Angeles Recording Sch.)*
La Roche Coll. 351
La Roche Coll. Sch. of Radiography *(see Ohio Valley General Hosp.)*
La Salle Univ. 351
La Sierra Acad. & Normal Sch. *(see La Sierra Univ.)*
La Sierra Univ. 50
LA Southwest Coll. *(see Los Angeles Southwest Coll.)*
LA Trade-Tech. Coll. *(see Los Angeles Trade-Tech. Coll.)*
La Universidad San Agustín *(see Saint Augustine Coll.)*
LA Valley Coll. *(see Los Angeles Valley Coll.)*
La Verne Coll. *(see Univ. of La Verne)*
La Verne Univ. *(see Univ. of La Verne)*
Laban/Bartenieff Inst. of Movement Studies, Inc. 595
LaBaron Hairdressing Acad—Brockton 552
LaBaron Hairdressing Acad—New Bedford 552
LaBaron Hairdressing Acad—Overland Park 535
Labette Coll. *(see Labette Comm. Coll.)*
Labette Comm. Coll. 167
Labette Comm. Jr. Coll. *(see Labette Comm. Coll.)*
Laboratorio Químico del Ebro *(see Institut Quimic de Sarria de Universitat Ramón Llull)*
Laboratory Inst. of Merchandising 280
Laboure Coll. 785 *(see also Caritas Laboure Coll.)*
LabSouth, Inc. *(see Alabama Reference Laboratories/LabSouth, Inc.)*
Lac Courte Oreilles Ojibwa Comm. Coll. 446
LAC+USC Healthcare Network *(see Los Angeles County-USC Med. Ctr.)*
L'Academie de Cuisine 547
LaCarm Sch. of Cosmetology *(see Pro Way Hair Sch.)*
Lackawanna Coll. 351
Lackawanna County Area Vocational Tech. Sch. 792 *(see also Career Techno. Ctr. of Lackawanna County)*
Lackawanna County Career Techno. Ctr. *(see Career Techno. Ctr. of Lackawanna County)*
Lackawanna County Vo-Tech Sch. *(see Career Techno. Ctr. of Lackawanna County)*
Lackawanna Jr. Coll. *(see Lackawanna Coll.)*
Laclede Groves Retirement Comm. *(see Lutheran Sr. Services CPE)*
LaCrosse Beauty Sch. *(see Scientific Coll. of Beauty & Barbering)*
Lacy Cosmetology Sch. 639
Ladera Career Paths Training Ctr. 484
Ladera Career Paths, Inc. *(see Ladera Career Paths Training Ctr.)*
Ladies & Gentlemen Hair Stylists 789–790 *(see also Brown Aveda Inst.)*
Lado Enterprises, Inc. *(see Lado Int'l. Coll.)*
Lado Int'l. Coll. 502
Lady of the Elms Coll. *(see Coll. of Our Lady of the Elms)*
Lady of the Lake Coll. *(see Our Lady of the Lake Coll.; Our Lady of the Lake Univ.)*
Lady of the Lake Univ. *(see Our Lady of the Lake Univ.)*
Lafayette Beauty Acad., Inc. 531
Lafayette Coll. 351
Lafayette General Med. Ctr. 709
Lafayette Tech. Inst. *(see Ivy Tech Comm. Coll—Lafayette)*
LaGrange Acad. *(see LaGrange Coll.)*
LaGrange Coll. 116 *(see also Hannibal-LaGrange Coll.; Univ. of North Alabama)*
LaGrange Cosmetology Sch. *(see Rivertown Sch. of Beauty, Barber, Skin Care & Nails)*
LaGrange Female Coll. *(see LaGrange Coll.)*
LaGuardia Coll. *(see City Univ. of New York LaGuardia Comm. Coll.)*
LaGuardia Comm. Coll. *(see City Univ. of New York LaGuardia Comm. Coll.)*
Laguna Beach Sch. of Art *(see Laguna Coll. of Art & Design)*
Laguna Coll. of Art & Design 50
Laird Inst. of Spa Therapy 816
Lake Area Tech *(see Lake Area Tech. Inst.)*
Lake Area Tech. Inst. 379
Lake Charles Hosp. *(see Lake Charles Mem. Hosp. Sch. of Med. Techno.)*
Lake Charles Jr. Coll. *(see McNeese State Univ.)*
Lake Charles Mem. Hosp. Sch. of Med. Techno. 709
Lake City Comm. Coll. 99
Lake City Jr. Coll. *(see Lake City Comm. Coll.)*
Lake City VA Med. Ctr. *(see Lake City Veterans Affairs Med. Ctr.)*
Lake City VAMC *(see Lake City Veterans Affairs Med. Ctr.)*
Lake City Veterans Affairs Med. Ctr. 696
Lake Coll. 484
Lake County Area Vocationa—Tech. Ctr. *(see Lake Tech. Ctr.)*
Lake County Coll. *(see Coll. of Lake County)*
Lake County Consortium of Public & Private Universities *(see Northeastern Illinois Univ.)*
Lake County Joint Vocational Sch. *(see Auburn Career Ctr.)*

Loop Coll. *(see City Colleges of Chicag—Harold Washington Coll.)*
Lorain County Adult Career Ctr. *(see Lorain County Joint Vocational Sch. Adult Career Ctr.)*
Lorain County Coll. *(see Lorain County Comm. Coll.)*
Lorain County Comm. Coll. 321
Lorain County Joint Vocational Sch. Adult Career Ctr. 609
Lorain County JVS Adult Career Ctr. *(see Lorain County Joint Vocational Sch. Adult Career Ctr.)*
Lorain Sch. of Techno. *(see Lorain County Comm. Coll.)*
Loraine's Acad., Inc. 510
Loras Coll. 160
Lord Fairfax Coll. *(see Lord Fairfax Comm. Coll.)*
Lord Fairfax Comm. Coll. 424
Lordsburg Coll. *(see Univ. of La Verne)*
Lorenzo Walker Inst. of Techno. 510
Loretto Coll. *(see Webster Univ.)*
Loretto Heights Coll. *(see Teikyo Loretto Heights Univ.)*
Los Angeles Ambulatory Care Ctr. 690 *(see also Veterans Affairs Greater Los Angeles Healthcare Sys—Los Angeles)*
Los Angeles Art Inst. *(see Art Inst. of Californi—Los Angeles)*
Los Angeles Aviation Inst. *(see Redstone Coll—Los Angeles)*
Los Angeles Baptist Coll. & Theological Sem. *(see Northwest Baptist Sem.)*
Los Angeles Baptist Theological Sem. *(see Northwest Baptist Sem.)*
Los Angeles Children's Hosp. *(see Children's Hosp. of Los Angeles)*
Los Angeles City Coll. 51
Los Angeles Coll. *(see Loyola Marymount Univ.)*
Los Angeles Coll. of Chiropractic *(see Southern California Univ. of Health Sciences)*
Los Angeles Coll. of Culinary Arts *(see California Sch. of Culinary Arts)*
Los Angeles Coll. of Nursing *(see Los Angeles County Coll. of Nursing & Allied Health)*
Los Angeles Colleges of Med. & Dental Assistants *(see Everest Inst—Brighton)*
Los Angeles Conservatory of Music *(see California Inst. of the Arts)*
Los Angeles County + USC Med. Ctr. *(see Los Angeles County-USC Med. Ctr.)*
Los Angeles County Coll. of Nursing & Allied Health 51
Los Angeles County Dept. of Health Services *(see Los Angeles County Emergency Med. Services Agency)*
Los Angeles County Emergency Med. Services Agency 687
Los Angeles County EMS Agency *(see Los Angeles County Emergency Med. Services Agency)*
Los Angeles County Harbor-UCLA Med. Ctr. 688
Los Angeles County Health Services *(see Los Angeles County Emergency Med. Services Agency)*
Los Angeles County Hosp. Coll. of Nursing *(see Los Angeles County Coll. of Nursing & Allied Health)*
Los Angeles County Med. Ctr. Sch. of Nursing *(see Los Angeles County Coll. of Nursing & Allied Health)*
Los Angeles County-USC Med. Ctr. 688
Los Angeles Harbor Coll. 51
Los Angeles Jr. Coll. *(see Los Angeles City Coll.)*
Los Angeles Metropolitan Detention Ctr. *(see Metropolitan Detention Ctr.)*
Los Angeles Mission Coll. 51
Los Angeles Music Acad. 810
Los Angeles ORT Tech. Inst. 484
Los Angeles Pacific Coll. *(see Azusa Pacific Univ.)*
Los Angeles Pierce Coll. 51
Los Angeles Recording Sch. 484, 777
Los Angeles Recording Workshop 777 *(see also Los Angeles Recording Sch.)*
Los Angeles Southwest Coll. 52
Los Angeles State Coll. *(see California State Univ., Los Angeles)*
Los Angeles State Coll. of Applied Arts & Sciences *(see California State Univ., Los Angeles)*
Los Angeles State Coll. of Applied Arts & Science—San Fernando Valley *(see California State Univ., Northridge)*
Los Angeles Trade-Tech. Coll. 52
Los Angeles Unified Sch. Dist. *(see East Los Angeles Edu. & Career Ctr.)*
Los Angeles Valley Coll. 52
Los Medanos Coll. 52
Louis D. Brandeis Sch. of Law *(see Univ. of Louisville)*
Louis Stokes Cleveland VA Med. Ctr. *(see Louis Stokes Cleveland Veterans Affairs Med. Ctr.)*
Louis Stokes Cleveland VAMC *(see Louis Stokes Cleveland Veterans Affairs Med. Ctr.)*
Louis Stokes Cleveland Veterans Affairs Med. Ctr. 732
Louisburg Coll. 304
Louisburg Female Acad. *(see Louisburg Coll.)*
Louisburg Female Coll. *(see Louisburg Coll.)*
Louise Harkey Sch. of Nursing *(see Cabarrus Coll. of Health Sciences)*
Louise Salinger Acad. of Fashion *(see Art Inst. of Californi—San Francisco)*
Louisiana A & M Coll. *(see Louisiana State Univ. & Agricultural & Mechanical Coll.)*
Louisiana Acad. of Beauty 541
Louisiana Agricultural & Mechanical Coll. *(see Louisiana State Univ. & Agricultural & Mechanical Coll.)*
Louisiana Art Inst. *(see Delta Coll. of Arts & Techno.)*
Louisiana Coll. 180
Louisiana Correctional Inst. for Women *(see Jumonville Mem. Tech. Inst.)*
Louisiana Court Reporting Inst. *(see Court Reporting Inst. of Louisiana, Inc.)*
Louisiana Culinary Inst. 180, 541
Louisiana Delta Coll. *(see Louisiana Delta Comm. Coll.)*
Louisiana Delta Comm. Coll. 804
Louisiana Hair Design Coll. 784
Louisiana Inst. of Court Reporting *(see Court Reporting Inst. of Louisiana, Inc.)*
Louisiana Negro Normal & Industrial Inst. *(see Grambling State Univ.)*
Louisiana State Normal Sch. *(see Northwestern State Univ.)*
Louisiana State Univ. & Agricultural & Mechanical Coll. 180
Louisiana State Univ. at Alexandria 180
Louisiana State Univ. at Eunice 180
Louisiana State Univ. Health Sciences Ctr. 784
Louisiana State Univ. Health Sciences Ctr. in New Orleans 180
Louisiana State Univ. in New Orleans *(see Univ. of New Orleans)*
Louisiana State Univ. in Shreveport 180
Louisiana State Univ. Med. Ctr. 784 *(see also Louisiana State Univ. Health Sciences Ctr. in New Orleans)*
Louisiana Tech Univ. 180
Louisiana Tech. Coll. Region 1 *(see Louisiana Tech. Coll—Jefferson Campus; Louisiana Tech. Coll—West Jefferson Campus)*
Louisiana Tech. Coll. Region 2 *(see Jumonville Mem. Tech. Inst.; Louisiana Tech. Coll—Baton Rouge Campus)*
Louisiana Tech. Coll. Region 3 *(see Louisiana Tech. Coll—Young Mem. Campus)*

Louisville Presbyterian Theological Sem. 173
Louisville Sem. *(see Louisville Presbyterian Theological Sem.)*
Louisville Tech *(see Louisville Tech. Inst.)*
Louisville Tech. Inst. 173
Louisville Univ. *(see Univ. of Louisville)*
Lourdes Coll. 321
Lourdes Jr. Coll. *(see Lourdes Coll.)*
Lowcountry Tech. Coll. *(see Tech. Coll. of the Lowcountry)*
Lowell Acad. Hairstyling Inst. 552
Lowell Normal Sch. *(see Univ. of Massachusetts Lowell)*
Lowell Sch. of Bus. *(see Ridley-Lowell Bus. & Tech. Inst.)*
Lowell State Coll. *(see Univ. of Massachusetts Lowell)*
Lowell Technological Inst. *(see Univ. of Massachusetts Lowell)*
Lowell Textile Inst. *(see Univ. of Massachusetts Lowell)*
Lowell's Commercial Coll. *(see Ridley-Lowell Bus. & Tech. Inst.)*
Lower Columbia Coll. 435
Lowthian Coll. *(see Art Inst.s Int'l—Minnesota)*
Loyola Coll. *(see Concordia Univ.)*
Loyola Coll. in Maryland 192
Loyola Coll. of Los Angeles *(see Loyola Marymount Univ.)*
Loyola Marymount Univ. 52
Loyola Univ. *(see Loyola Marymount Univ.)*
Loyola Univ. Chicago *(see Loyola Univ. of Chicago)*
Loyola Univ. Health Sys. *(see Loyola Univ. of Chicago)*
Loyola Univ. Hosp. *(see Loyola Univ. of Chicago)*
Loyola Univ. Med. Ctr. 136 *(see also Loyola Univ. of Chicago)*
Loyola Univ. New Orleans 183
Loyola Univ. of Chicago 136
Loyola Univ. of Chicag—Med. Ctr. *(see Loyola Univ. of Chicago)*
LPN Career Ctr. *(see Central Susquehanna LPN Career Ctr.)*
LSU Alexandria *(see Louisiana State Univ. at Alexandria)*
LSU Eunice *(see Louisiana State Univ. at Eunice)*
LSU Health Sciences Ctr., New Orleans *(see Louisiana State Univ. Health Sciences Ctr. in New Orleans)*
LSU Shreveport *(see Louisiana State Univ. in Shreveport)*
LTC Jefferson Tech. *(see Louisiana Tech. Coll—Jefferson Campus)*
LTC Region 1 *(see Louisiana Tech. Coll—Jefferson Campus; Louisiana Tech. Coll—West Jefferson Campus)*
LTC Region 2 *(see Jumonville Mem. Tech. Inst.; Louisiana Tech. Coll—Baton Rouge Campus)*
LTC Region 3 *(see Louisiana Tech. Coll—Young Mem. Campus)*
LTC Region 4 *(see Louisiana Tech. Coll—Gulf Area Campus; Louisiana Tech. Coll—Lafayette Campus)*
LTC Region 6 *(see Louisiana Tech. Coll—Alexandria Campus; Louisiana Tech. Coll—Avoyelles Campus)*
LTC Region 7 *(see Louisiana Tech. Coll—Shreveport-Bossier Campus)*
LTC Region 8 *(see Louisiana Tech. Coll—Delta-Ouachita Campus; Louisiana Tech. Coll—Northeast Louisiana Campus)*
LTC Region 9 *(see Louisiana Tech. Coll—Sullivan Campus)*
LTC West Jefferson Tech. *(see Louisiana Tech. Coll—West Jefferson Campus)*
LTC-Margaret Surles Ctr. *(see Louisiana Tech. Coll—Delta-Ouachita Campus)*
LTT Enterprises, Inc. *(see Gwinnett Coll.)*
Lu Ross Acad. 810
Lubbock Barber Coll. *(see Lubbock Hair Acad.)*
Lubbock Christian Univ. 400
Lubbock Hair Acad. 653
Lucile Packard Children's Hosp. 688
Lumberton Adult Educational Ctr. 653
Lumberton Independent Sch. Dist. *(see Lumberton Adult Educational Ctr.)*
Lummi Comm. Coll. *(see Northwest Indian Coll.)*
Lummi Indian Sch. of Aquaculture *(see Northwest Indian Coll.)*
Luna Area Vocational Tech. Sch. *(see Luna Comm. Coll.)*
Luna Comm. Coll. 266
Luna Vocational Tech. Inst. *(see Luna Comm. Coll.)*
Lurleen B. Wallace Comm. Coll. 6
Lurleen B. Wallace State Jr. Coll. *(see Lurleen B. Wallace Comm. Coll.)*
Luther Coll. 160
Luther Hosp. *(see Luther Midelfort)*
Luther Midelfort 754
Luther Northwestern Theological Sem. *(see Luther Sem.)*
Luther Rice Bible Coll. & Sem. 781 *(see also Luther Rice Univ.)*
Luther Rice Sem. *(see Luther Rice Univ.)*
Luther Rice Univ. 116, 781
Luther Sem. 223
Luther Theological Sem. *(see Luther Sem.)*
Lutheran Altenheim Society *(see Lutheran Sr. Services CPE)*
Lutheran Bible Inst. of Seattle *(see Trinity Lutheran Coll.)*
Lutheran Charities Assoc. *(see Lutheran Sr. Services CPE)*
Lutheran Coll. & Sem. *(see Lutheran Theological Sem.)*
Lutheran Coll. of Wisconsin *(see Wisconsin Lutheran Coll.)*
Lutheran General Hosp. *(see Advocate Lutheran General Hosp.)*
Lutheran HealthCare *(see Lutheran Med. Ctr.)*
Lutheran Homes of Oshkosh 754
Lutheran Hosp. of Indiana 705
Lutheran Hosp.-La Crosse *(see Gundersen Lutheran Med. Ctr.)*
Lutheran Jr. Coll. *(see Midland Lutheran Coll.)*
Lutheran Med. Ctr. 726
Lutheran Normal Sch. *(see Augustana Coll.)*
Lutheran Sch. of Nursing 718
Lutheran Sch. of Theology at Chicago 136
Lutheran Sem. at Philadelphia *(see Lutheran Theological Sem. at Philadelphia)*
Lutheran Sr. Services CPE 718
Lutheran Services New York Alliance *(see Eger Health Care Ctr. of Staten Island)*
Lutheran Services NY Alliance *(see Eger Health Care Ctr. of Staten Island)*
Lutheran Southern Sem. *(see Lutheran Theological Southern Sem.)*
Lutheran Theological Sem. 455
Lutheran Theological Sem. at Gettysburg 352
Lutheran Theological Sem. at Philadelphia, The 352
Lutheran Theological Southern Sem. 375
Lutheran Univ. of Texas *(see Texas Lutheran Univ.)*
Luzerne Coll. *(see Luzerne County Comm. Coll.)*
Luzerne Comm. Coll. *(see Luzerne County Comm. Coll.)*
Luzerne County Comm. Coll. 353
Lyceum of Art & Techno. *(see Liceo de Arte y Tecnologia)*
Lyceum of Art, Design & Commerce *(see Liceo de Arte, Disenos y Comercio)*
Lyceum Theatre Sch. of Acting, The *(see American Acad. of Dramatic Arts)*

Lycoming Coll. 353
Lyle's Bakersfield Coll. of Beauty 484
Lyle's Coll. of Beauty 484
Lyle's Coll. of Beauty of Bakersfield *(see Lyle's Bakersfield Coll. of Beauty)*
Lyle's Coll. of Beauty of Fresno *(see Lyle's Fresno Coll. of Beauty)*
Lyle's Fresno Coll. of Beauty 485
Lyme Acad. Coll. of Fine Arts 79
Lyme Coll. of Fine Arts *(see Lyme Acad. Coll. of Fine Arts)*
Lynchburg Baptist Sem. *(see Virginia Univ. of Lynchburg)*
Lynchburg Coll. 424
Lynchburg General Hosp. Sch. of Nursing *(see Centra Lynchburg General Hosp.)*
Lyndon B. Johnson Comm. Health Ctr. *(see Ben Taub General Hosp.)*
Lyndon Coll. *(see Lyndon State Coll.)*
Lyndon State Coll. 417
Lynn Univ. 100
Lynndale Fundamentals of Beauty Sch. 470
Lyon Coll. 27
Lyon Grad. Sch. of Bus. *(see Ecole de Mgmnt. de Lyon)*
Lyon Mgmnt. Sch. *(see Ecole de Mgmnt. de Lyon)*
Lytle's Beauty Coll. *(see Lytle's Redwood Empire Beauty Coll., Inc.)*
Lytle's Redwood Empire Beauty Coll., Inc. 485

M

M & M Word Processing Inst. *(see Remington Coll—Houston)*
M. Christopher White Sch. of Divinity of Gardner-Webb Univ. *(see Gardner-Webb Univ.)*
M. D. Anderson Cancer Ctr. *(see Univ. of Texas M. D. Anderson Cancer Ctr.)*
M. M. Washington Vocational Sch. *(see Margaret Murray Washington Vocational Sch.)*
M.J. Francoeur & Associates 779 *(see also Results, Inc. Dale Carnegie Training)*
M.J. Lewi Coll. of Podiatry *(see New York Coll. of Podiatric Medicine)*
M.J. Murphy Beauty Coll. 557
Maastricht Sch. of Mgmnt. 767
Maastricht Univ. 767
Mac Daniel's Beauty Sch. 527
Macalester Coll. 223
MacArthur Coll. *(see Lurleen B. Wallace Comm. Coll.)*
MacArthur State Tech. Coll. *(see Lurleen B. Wallace Comm. Coll.)*
MacCormac Bus. Coll. *(see MacCormac Coll.)*
MacCormac Coll. 136
MacCormac Jr. Coll. *(see MacCormac Coll.)*
MacCormac Sch. *(see MacCormac Coll.)*
MacDiv *(see McMaster Divinity Coll.)*
Machining Inst. of Akron *(see Akron Machining Inst. Inc.)*
Machzikei Hadath Rabbinical Coll. 281
Maclay Coll. of Theology *(see Claremont Sch. of Theology)*
MacMurray Coll. 136
MacNeal Health Network *(see MacNeal Hosp.)*
MacNeal Hosp. 703
Macomb Coll. *(see Macomb Comm. Coll.)*
Macomb Comm. Coll. 213
Macomb Culinary Inst. *(see Macomb Comm. Coll.)*
Macon Beauty Sch. *(see American Prof. Inst.)*
Macon Coll. *(see Macon State Coll.)*
Macon Jr. Coll. *(see Macon State Coll.)*
Macon State Coll. 116
Macon Tech. Inst. *(see Central Georgia Tech. Coll.)*
Madame Walkers' Beauty Coll. *(see Velma B's Beauty Acad.)*
Madawaska Training Sch. *(see Univ. of Maine at Fort Kent)*
Madeline Aveda Inst. *(see Jean Madeline Aveda Inst.)*
Madera Beauty Coll. 485
Madigan Army Med. Ctr. 752
Madison Adult Edu. 609
Madison Area Tech. Coll. 447
Madison Coll. *(see James Madison Univ.)*
Madison Cosmetology Coll. 675
Madison General Hosp. *(see Meriter Hosp.)*
Madison Hosp. Sch. of Anesthesia *(see Middle Tennessee Sch. of Anesthesia)*
Madison Media Inst. 447
Madison Normal Coll. *(see Dakota State Univ.)*
Madison Tech *(see Madison Area Tech. Coll.)*
Madison Tech. Coll. *(see Madison Area Tech. Coll.)*
Madison Univ. *(see Colgate Univ.; James Madison Univ.)*
Madisonville Coll. *(see Madisonville Comm. Coll.)*
Madisonville Comm. Coll. 174
Madisonville Health Occupations Sch. *(see Madisonville Comm. Coll.)*
Madisonville State Vocational-Tech. Sch. *(see Madisonville Comm. Coll.)*
Madisonville Tech. Coll. *(see Madisonville Comm. Coll.)*
Madonna Coll. *(see Madonna Univ.)*
Madonna Univ. 213
Magdalen Coll. 257
Magee Brothers Beaverton Sch. of Beauty 790 *(see also Beaverton Sch. of Beauty)*
Magee-Womens Hosp. 740
Magnolia Bible Coll. 231
Magnolia Coll. *(see Magnolia Bible Coll.)*
Magnolia Coll. of Cosmetology 565
Magnolia Sch. 627, 791
Magnus Coll. *(see Albertus Magnus Coll.)*
Maharishi Int'l. Univ. *(see Maharishi Univ. of Mgmnt.)*
Maharishi Univ. of Mgmnt. 160
Mahoning County Career & Tech. Ctr. 609
Mahoning County Joint Vocational Sch. *(see Mahoning County Career & Tech. Ctr.)*
Mahoning County JVS *(see Mahoning County Career & Tech. Ctr.)*
Mailman Ctr. for Child Development *(see Univ. of Miami)*
Maimonides Med. Ctr. 726
Maine Coll. of Agriculture & the Mechanic Arts *(see Univ. of Maine)*
Maine Coll. of Art 187
Maine Dale Carnegie Training *(see Dale Carnegie Training of Maine)*
Maine Eye & Ear Infirmary *(see Maine Med. Ctr.)*
Maine General Hosp. *(see Maine Med. Ctr.)*
Maine Hosp. *(see Maine Med. Ctr.)*
Maine Law Sch. *(see Univ. of Southern Maine)*
Maine Literary & Theological Institution *(see Colby Coll.)*
Maine Maritime Acad. 187
Maine Med. Ctr. 710
Maine Sch. of Commerce *(see Husson Univ.)*
Maine State Sem. *(see Bates Coll.)*
Maine Vocational Tech. Inst. *(see Southern Maine Comm. Coll.)*
Mainland Coll. *(see Coll. of the Mainland)*
Maison D'Esthetique Acad. *(see Academia Maison D'Esthetique)*
Maisonneuve Coll. 760
Mai-trix Beauty Coll. 653
Make-Up Designory 485
Malaspina Univ.-Coll. 760 *(see also Vancouver Island Univ.)*
Malcolm X Coll. *(see City Colleges of Chicag—Malcolm X Coll.)*

Malcom Randall VA Med. Ctr. *(see Malcom Randall Veterans Affairs Med. Ctr.)*
Malcom Randall Veterans Affairs Med. Ctr. 697
Malix Coll. of Med. & Computer Techno. 812
Malone Coll. *(see Malone Univ.)*
Malone Univ. 321
Mgmnt. Sch. of Lake Forest Sch. *(see Lake Forest Grad. Sch. of Mgmnt.)*
Mgmnt. & Techno. Univ. *(see Univ. of Mgmnt. & Techno.)*
Mgmnt. Coll. of San Francisco 777
Mgmnt. Resources Inst. 510
Mgmnt. Sch. of Lyon *(see Ecole de Mgmnt. de Lyon)*
Mgmnt. Sch. of Vlerick Leuven, Gent *(see Vlerick Leuven Gent Mgmnt. Sch.)*
Manatee Coll. *(see Manatee Comm. Coll.)*
Manatee Comm. Coll. 100
Manatee County Tech. Ctr. *(see Manatee Tech. Inst.)*
Manatee County Tech. Inst. *(see Manatee Tech. Inst.)*
Manatee Tech. Inst. 511
Manchester Beauty Coll. 485
Manchester Ctr. for Health Sciences 201
Manchester Coll. 153 *(see also Manchester Comm. Coll.)*
Manchester Comm. Coll. 80, 257, 787
Manchester Comm. Coll—Middlesex *(see Middlesex Comm. Coll.)*
Manchester Comm.-Tech. Coll. *(see Manchester Comm. Coll.)*
Manchester Inst. of Arts & Sciences *(see New Hampshire Inst. of Art)*
Manchester Univ. *(see Univ. of Manchester)*
Manchester VA Med. Ctr. *(see Manchester Veterans Affairs Med. Ctr.)*
Manchester VAMC *(see Manchester Veterans Affairs Med. Ctr.)*
Manchester Veterans Affairs Med. Ctr. 720
Mandalyn Acad., Inc. 820
Mandl Sch. 789 *(see also Mandl, The Coll. of Allied Health)*
Mandl Sch. for Med. & Dental Assistants *(see Mandl, The Coll. of Allied Health)*
Mandl Sch. for Med. Office Assistants *(see Mandl, The Coll. of Allied Health)*
Mandl, The Coll. of Allied Health 281, 789
Manhattan Area Coll. *(see Manhattan Area Tech. Coll.)*
Manhattan Area Tech. Ctr. *(see Manhattan Area Tech. Coll.)*
Manhattan Area Tech. Coll. 167
Manhattan Area Vocational -Tech. Sch. *(see Manhattan Area Tech. Coll.)*
Manhattan Beauty Sch., Inc. *(see Manhattan Hairstyling Acad.)*
Manhattan Beauty Sch., Inc. 511
Manhattan Bible Coll. *(see Manhattan Christian Coll.)*
Manhattan Christian Coll. 167
Manhattan Coll. 281
Manhattan Comm. Coll. *(see City Univ. of New York Borough of Manhattan Comm. Coll.)*
Manhattan Hairstyling Acad. 511
Manhattan Inst. 817
Manhattan Marymount Coll. *(see Marymount Manhattan Coll.)*
Manhattan Sch. of Computer Techno. 596
Manhattan Sch. of Music 281
Manhattanville Coll. 281
Manitoba Coll. *(see Univ. of Winnipeg)*
Manitoba Coll. of Massage Therapy, The *(see Massage Therapy Coll. of Manitoba, Inc.)*
Manitoba Univ. *(see Univ. of Manitoba)*
Mankato Normal Sch. *(see Minnesota State Univ—Mankato)*
Mankato State Coll. *(see Minnesota State Univ—Mankato)*
Mankato State Teachers Coll. *(see Minnesota State Univ—Mankato)*
Mankato State Univ. *(see Minnesota State Univ—Mankato)*
Mannes Coll. of Music *(see New Sch.)*
Mannes Coll. The New Sch. for Music *(see New Sch.)*
Mannheim Univ. *(see Univ. of Mannheim)*
Manor Coll. 353
Manor Int'l. Equestrian Centre *(see Meredith Manor Int'l. Equestrian Centre)*
Manor Jr. Coll. *(see Manor Coll.)*
Manpower Development Training Ctr. *(see Pinellas Tech. Edu. Ctr.)*
Mansfield Beauty Sch—Quincy 552
Mansfield Beauty Sch—Springfield 552
Mansfield Bus. Coll. *(see Centura Coll.)*
Mansfield Sch. of Techno. *(see North Central State Coll.)*
Mansfield Univ. of Pennsylvania 353
Manual Training Sch. *(see Univ. of Toledo)*
Manuel & Theresa's Sch. of Hair Design 653
Maple Springs Baptist Bible Coll. & Sem. 192
Maple Springs Coll. *(see Maple Springs Baptist Bible Coll. & Sem.)*
Maple Springs Sem. *(see Maple Springs Baptist Bible Coll. & Sem.)*
Maple Woods Coll. *(see Maple Woods Comm. Coll.)*
Maple Woods Comm. Coll. 240
Maranatha Baptist Bible Coll. 447
Maranatha Coll. *(see Maranatha Baptist Bible Coll.)*
Marchman Edu. Ctr. *(see Marchman Tech. Edu. Ctr.)*
Marcus Inst., The 699
Mare Island Outpatient Clinic *(see Veterans Affairs Northern California Health Care Sys—Mare Island)*
Mare Island VA Med. Ctr. *(see Veterans Affairs Northern California Health Care Sys—Mare Island)*
Mare Island VAMC *(see Veterans Affairs Northern California Health Care Sys—Mare Island)*
Mare Island Veterans Affairs Med. Ctr. *(see Veterans Affairs Northern California Health Care Sys—Mare Island)*
Margaret Murray Washington Vocational Sch. 695
Margaret Surles Ctr. *(see Louisiana Tech. Coll—Delta-Ouachita Campus)*
Margaret's Hair Acad., Inc. 470
Margate Sch. of Beauty 812
Maria Coll. of Albany 281
Maria Montessori TTC 485
Mariacy Beauty Acad. 813
Marian Coll. 153 *(see also Marian Health Careers Ctr.; Marist Coll.)*
Marian Coll. of Fond du Lac 796 *(see also Marian Univ.)*
Marian Court Coll. 200
Marian Health Careers Ctr. 485
Marian Health Ctr. *(see Mercy Med. Ctr. Sioux City)*
Marian Univ. 447, 796
Maric Coll. 776
Maric Coll. of Med. Careers *(see Kaplan Coll—San Diego)*
Maric Coll. Sch. of X-ray *(see Kaplan Coll—North Hollywood)*
Maric Coll—Anaheim 777
Maric Coll—Bakersfield *(see Kaplan Coll—Sacramento)*
Maric Coll—East County 777
Maric Coll—Fresno *(see Kaplan Coll—Fresno)*
Maric Coll—Irwindale 777
Maric Coll—Lake Forest *(see Kaplan Coll—Palm Springs)*
Maric Coll—Los Angeles 777
Maric Coll—Modesto *(see Kaplan Coll—Modesto)*
Maric Coll—Modesto 777

Marshall Univ. 441
Marshalls Theological Coll. *(see Pacific Islands Bible Coll.)*
Marshalltown Coll. *(see Marshalltown Comm. Coll.)*
Marshalltown Comm. Coll. 160
Marshalltown Jr. Coll. *(see Marshalltown Comm. Coll.)*
Marshfield Clinic 755
Martha Graham Dance Sch. *(see Martha Graham Sch. of Contemporary Dance, Inc.)*
Martha Graham Sch. of Contemporary Dance, 596
Marti Coll. of Fashion & Art *(see Virginia Marti Coll. of Art & Design)*
Martin Ctr. Coll. *(see Martin Univ.)*
Martin Coll. *(see Martin Comm. Coll.)*
Martin Comm. Coll. 305
Martin Luther Coll. 223
Martin Methodist Coll. 386
Martin Tech. Inst. *(see Martin Comm. Coll.)*
Martin Univ. 153
Martinez Sch. of Cosmetology 567
Martinez VA Outpatient Clinic *(see Veterans Affairs Northern California Health Care Sys—Martinez)*
Martinez Veterans Affairs Outpatient Clinic *(see Veterans Affairs Northern California Health Care Sys—Martinez)*
Martin's Coll. of Cosmetolog—Green Bay 675
Martin's Coll. of Cosmetolog—Madison 675
Martin's Coll. of Cosmetolog—Manitowoc 675
Martinsburg VA Med. Ctr. *(see Veterans Affairs Med. Ctr—Martinsburg)*
Martinsburg VAMC *(see Veterans Affairs Med. Ctr—Martinsburg)*
Martinsburg Veterans Affairs Med. Ctr. *(see Veterans Affairs Med. Ctr—Martinsburg)*
Marugie Beauty & Tech. Coll. 792
Mary Baldwin Coll. 424
Mary Baldwin Sem. *(see Mary Baldwin Coll.)*
Mary C. Gwin & Associates *(see J. R. Rodgers & Associates, Inc.)*
Mary Coll. *(see Univ. of Mary)*
Mary Fletcher Hosp. *(see Fletcher Allen Health Care)*
Mary Hardin-Baylor Univ. *(see Univ. of Mary Hardin-Baylor)*
Mary Hitchcock Mem. Hosp. *(see Dartmouth-Hitchcock Med. Ctr.)*
Mary Immaculate Hosp. 728
Mary Imogene Bassett Hosp. *(see Bassett Healthcare)*
Mary Karl Vocational Sch. *(see Daytona State Coll.)*
Mary Lanning Mem. Hosp. 719
Mary Univ. *(see Univ. of Mary)*
Mary Washington Coll. *(see Univ. of Mary Washington)*
Mary Washington Hosp. 750
Marygrove Coll. 213
Maryland Agricultural Coll. *(see Univ. of Maryland Coll. Park)*
Maryland Art & Design Coll. *(see Sch. of Art & Design at Montgomery Coll.)*
Maryland Beauty Acad. 547
Maryland Beauty Acad. of Essex, Inc. 547
Maryland Broadcasting Inst. *(see Broadcasting Inst. of Maryland)*
Maryland Ctr. for Montessori Studies 548
Maryland Coll. of Art *(see Maryland Inst. Coll. of Art)*
Maryland Coll. of Art & Design *(see Sch. of Art & Design at Montgomery Coll.)*
Maryland General Hosp. 711
Maryland Inst. Coll. of Art, The 192
Maryland Inst. for the Promotion of the Mechanic Arts *(see Maryland Inst. Coll. of Art)*
Maryland Inst. of Art *(see Maryland Inst. Coll. of Art)*
Maryland Inst. of Contemporary Art *(see Maryland Inst. Coll. of Art)*
Maryland Inst. of Massage *(see Massage Inst. of Maryland)*
Maryland Massage Inst. *(see Massage Inst. of Maryland)*
Maryland Med. Secretarial Sch. *(see Kaplan Coll—Hagerstown)*
Maryland Normal & Industrial Sch. at Bowie *(see Bowie State Univ.)*
Maryland Normal Sch. #3 *(see Bowie State Univ.)*
Maryland State Coll. *(see Univ. of Maryland Coll. Park)*
Maryland State Normal Sch. *(see Towson Univ.)*
Maryland State Normal Sch. No. 2 at Frostburg *(see Frostburg State Univ.)*
Maryland State Teachers Coll. at Bowie *(see Bowie State Univ.)*
Maryland State Teachers Coll. at Towson *(see Towson Univ.)*
Marylhurst Coll. *(see Marylhurst Univ.)*
Marylhurst Univ. 339
Marymount Coll. 52 *(see also Loyola Marymount Univ.)*
Marymount Coll. of Fordham Univ. 277 *(see also Fordham Univ.)*
Marymount Coll. of Manhattan *(see Marymount Manhattan Coll.)*
Marymount Health Care Systems *(see Marymount Sch. of Practical Nursing)*
Marymount Hosp. *(see Marymount Sch. of Practical Nursing)*
Marymount Jr. Coll. *(see Marymount Coll.)*
Marymount Manhattan Coll. 281
Marymount Univ. 425
Mary-of-the-Woods Coll. *(see Saint Mary-of-the-Woods Coll.)*
Maryview Med. Ctr. *(see Bon Secours Maryview Med. Ctr.)*
Maryville Coll. 386
Maryville Univ. of St. Louis 240
Marywood Coll. *(see Marywood Univ.)*
Marywood Univ. 353
Mason Acad. of Cosmetology 642
Mason City Jr. Coll. *(see North Iowa Area Comm. Coll.)*
Mason Coll. *(see George Mason Univ.)*
Mason County Techno. Ctr. *(see Maysville Comm. & Tech. Coll.)*
Mason Univ. *(see George Mason Univ.)*
Masonic Geriatric Healthcare Ctr. 693
Masonic Healthcare Ctr. *(see Masonic Geriatric Healthcare Ctr.)*
Masonicare *(see Masonic Geriatric Healthcare Ctr.)*
Massachusetts Agricultural Coll. *(see Univ. of Massachusetts Boston)*
Massachusetts Barber Sch. *(see Massachusetts Sch. of Barbering & Men's Hairstyling)*
Massachusetts Bay Coll. *(see Massachusetts Bay Comm. Coll.)*
Massachusetts Bay Comm. Coll. 201
Massachusetts Coll. of Art *(see Massachusetts Coll. of Art & Design)*
Massachusetts Coll. of Art & Design 201
Massachusetts Coll. of Embalming *(see Mount Ida Coll.)*
Massachusetts Coll. of Liberal Arts 201
Massachusetts Coll. of Optometry *(see New England Coll. of Optometry)*
Massachusetts Coll. of Pharmacy & Allied Health Sciences *(see Massachusetts Coll. of Pharmacy & Health Sciences)*
Massachusetts Coll. of Pharmacy & Health Sciences 201
Massachusetts Communications Coll. *(see New England Inst. of Art)*
Massachusetts General Hosp. 713
Massachusetts General Hosp. Inst. of Health Professions *(see MGH Inst. of Health Professions)*
Massachusetts Inst. of Techno. 201

Mayville Normal Sch. *(see Mayville State Univ.)*
Mayville State Coll. *(see Mayville State Univ.)*
Mayville State Univ. 311
Mayville Univ. *(see Mayville State Univ.)*
MBTI Bus. Training Inst. 635
MBTI Training *(see MBTI Bus. Training Inst.)*
McAfee Sch. of Theology *(see Mercer Univ.)*
McAllister Inst. of Funeral Service, Inc. *(see American Acad. McAllister Inst. of Funeral Service, Inc.)*
McCann Sch. of Bus. & Techno.-Pottsville 353
McCann Tech *(see Charles H. McCann Tech. Sch.)*
McCann Tech. Sch. *(see Charles H. McCann Tech. Sch.)*
MC—Blue River *(see Metropolitan Comm. Coll—Blue River)*
MC—Bus. & Techno. Coll. *(see Metropolitan Comm. Coll. Bus. & Techno. Coll.)*
MC—Kansas City *(see Penn Valley Comm. Coll.)*
McClellan Mem. Veterans Hosp. *(see Central Arkansas Veterans Healthcare Sys.)*
MC—Longview *(see Longview Comm. Coll.)*
MC—Maple Woods *(see Maple Woods Comm. Coll.)*
McCollum & Ross, The Hair Sch. 642
McComb Female Inst. *(see Belhaven Coll.)*
McConnell Coll. *(see Truett McConnell Coll.)*
McConnell Sch. 786
McCook Comm. Coll. 251 *(see also Mid-Plains Comm. Coll.)*
McCook Jr. Coll. *(see McCook Comm. Coll.; Mid-Plains Comm. Coll.)*
McCormick Theological Sem. 136
MC—Penn Valley *(see Penn Valley Comm. Coll.)*
McDaniel Coll. 192
McDonough County Hosp. Dist. *(see McDonough Dist. Hosp.)*
McDonough Dist. Hosp. 703
McDonough Hosp. *(see McDonough Dist. Hosp.)*
McDowell Coll. *(see McDowell Tech. Comm. Coll.)*
McDowell Comm. Coll. *(see McDowell Tech. Comm. Coll.)*
McDowell County Vocational Tech. Ctr. 673
McDowell County Voc-Tech Ctr. *(see McDowell County Vocational Tech. Ctr.)*
McDowell Tech. Coll. *(see McDowell Tech. Comm. Coll.)*
McDowell Tech. Comm. Coll. 305
McDowell Tech. Inst. *(see McDowell Tech. Comm. Coll.)*
MCed *(see MCed Career Coll.)*
MCed Career Coll. 487
McFarland Inst., The 709
McFatter Tech. Ctr. *(see William T. McFatter Tech. Ctr.)*
McFatter Vocational-Tech. Ctr. *(see William T. McFatter Tech. Ctr.)*
McGarvey Bible Coll. *(see Cincinnati Christian Univ.)*
McGaw Hosp. *(see Loyola Univ. of Chicago)*
McGee's Acad. of Cosmetology, Inc. *(see Acad. of Cosmetology)*
McGeorge Sch. of Law *(see Univ. of the Pacific)*
McGill Faculty of Religious Studies *(see Montreal Sch. of Theology)*
McGill Univ. 456
McGill Univ. Faculty of Religious Studies *(see McGill Univ.)*
McGill Univ. Teaching Hosp. *(see Jewish General Hosp.)*
McGregor Sch. of Antioch Univ. *(see Antioch Univ. McGregor)*
McHenry Coll. *(see McHenry County Coll.)*
McHenry County Coll. 136
McIntire Sch. of Commerce *(see Univ. of Virginia)*
McIntosh Coll. 257
McKees Rocks General Hosp. *(see Ohio Valley General Hosp.)*
McKendree Coll. *(see McKendree Univ.)*
McKendree Univ. 136
McKenna Coll. *(see Claremont McKenna Coll.)*
McKennan Hosp. *(see Avera McKennan Hosp. & Univ. Health Ctr.)*
McKenzie Area Vocational-Tech. Sch. *(see Tennessee Techno. Ctr. at McKenzie)*
McKenzie Area Vo-Tech Sch. *(see Tennessee Techno. Ctr. at McKenzie)*
McKenzie Coll. *(see Southwestern Univ.)*
McKenzie Study Ctr. *(see Gutenberg Coll.)*
McKenzie Vocational-Tech. Sch. *(see Tennessee Techno. Ctr. at McKenzie)*
McKenzie Vo-Tech Sch. *(see Tennessee Techno. Ctr. at McKenzie)*
McKinley Coll. 74
McLennan Coll. *(see McLennan Comm. Coll.)*
McLennan Comm. Coll. 400
McMaster Divinity Coll. 456 *(see also McMaster Univ.)*
McMaster Univ. 760 *(see also McMaster Divinity Coll.)*
McMinnville Area Vocational-Tech. Sch. *(see Tennessee Techno. Ctr. at McMinnville)*
McMinnville Area Vo-Tech Sch. *(see Tennessee Techno. Ctr. at McMinnville)*
McMinnville Coll. *(see Linfield Coll.)*
McMinnville Vocational-Tech. Sch. *(see Tennessee Techno. Ctr. at McMinnville)*
McMinnville Vo-Tech Sch. *(see Tennessee Techno. Ctr. at McMinnville)*
McMurry Univ. 400
McNally Smith Coll. of Music 223, 786
McNeese State Coll. *(see McNeese State Univ.)*
McNeese State Univ. 183
MCP Hahnamann Univ. 792 *(see also Drexel Univ.)*
McPherson Coll. 167
MD Anderson Cancer Ctr. *(see Univ. of Texas M. D. Anderson Cancer Ctr.)*
Meadville Lombard Theological Sch. 137
Meadville Theological Sch. *(see Meadville Lombard Theological Sch.)*
Meany Ctr. for Labor Studies *(see National Labor Coll.)*
MECA-Seton *(see Montessori Edu. Ctr.s Associated-Seton)*
Mechanical Techno. Inst. of Caguas *(see Caguas Inst. of Mechanical Techno.)*
Mecklenburg Coll. *(see Central Piedmont Comm. Coll.)*
Med Tech Coll. *(see MedTech Coll.; Stuart Sch.)*
Medaille Coll. 281
Med-Assist Sch. of Hawaii 522
MedCtr. One Coll. of Nursing *(see MedCtr. One Health Systems)*
MedCtr. One Health Systems 311
MedCtr. One Hosp. *(see MedCtr. One Health Systems)*
MedCentral Coll. of Nursing 322
Medgar Evers Coll. *(see City Univ. of New York Medgar Evers Coll.)*
Median Sch. of Allied Health Careers 792 *(see also Vet Tech Inst.)*
Mediatech Inst. 654
Med. & Dental Assistants Coll. of San Antonio *(see San Antonio Coll. of Med. & Dental Assistants)*
Med. & Dental Assistants Sch. of New York *(see New York Sch. for Med. & Dental Assistants)*

Michael D. Norman & Associates, Inc. *(see Norman & Associates)*
Michael E. DeBakey Veterans Affairs Med. Ctr. 747
Michael W. Jones & Associates, Inc. 790 *(see also Dale Carnegie Training of Central Ohio Tyson Eppley, LLC)*
Michael's Coll. of Hair Design 814
Michael's Sch. of Beauty 519
Michael's Sch. of Hair Design & Esthetics-A Paul Mitchell Partner Sch. *(see Michael's Sch. of Hair Design & Esthetics)*
Michael's Sch. of Hair Design & Esthetics 573
Michener Inst. for Applied Health Sciences 760
Michiana Beauty Coll. 559 *(see also Twin City Beauty Coll.)*
Michiana Coll. *(see Brown Mackie Coll—Cincinnati; Brown Mackie Coll—South Bend)*
Michigan Aeronautics Inst. *(see Michigan Inst. of Aviation & Techno.)*
Michigan Agricultural Coll. *(see Michigan State Univ.)*
Michigan & Huron Inst., the *(see Kalamazoo Coll.)*
Michigan Barber Sch., Inc. 557
Michigan Career & Tech. Inst. 557
Michigan Central Coll. *(see Hillsdale Coll.)*
Michigan Christian Coll. *(see Rochester Coll.)*
Michigan Coll. of Beaut—Monroe 557
Michigan Coll. of Beaut—Troy 558
Michigan Coll. of Beaut—Waterford 558
Michigan Coll. of Edu. *(see Northern Michigan Univ.)*
Michigan Coll. of Mines *(see Michigan Technological Univ.)*
Michigan Coll. of Mining & Techno. *(see Michigan Technological Univ.)*
Michigan Coll. of Optometry *(see Ferris State Univ.)*
Michigan Dale Carnegie Training *(see Ralph Nichols Group, Inc.)*
Michigan Dept. of Comm. Health *(see Hawthorn Ctr.)*
Michigan Inst. of Aeronautics 785 *(see also Michigan Inst. of Aviation & Techno.)*
Michigan Inst. of Aviation & Techno. 558, 785
Michigan Jewish Inst. 213
Michigan Mining Sch. *(see Michigan Technological Univ.)*
Michigan Montessori Teacher Edu. Ctr. 558
Michigan Sch. of Prof. Psychology 213, 785
Michigan Sem. *(see Michigan Theological Sem.)*
Michigan State Coll. of Agriculture & Applied Science *(see Michigan State Univ.)*
Michigan State Univ. 213
Michigan State Univ. Oakland *(see Oakland Univ.)*
Michigan State Univ. of Agriculture & Applied Science *(see Michigan State Univ.)*
Michigan Tech *(see Michigan Technological Univ.)*
Michigan Technological Univ. 214
Michigan Technological Univ—Sault Ste. Marie Campus *(see Lake Superior State Univ.)*
Michigan Theological Coll. *(see Michigan Theological Sem.)*
Michigan Theological Sem. 214
Michigan Theological Sem. & Coll. *(see Michigan Theological Sem.)*
Michigan Univ. *(see Univ. of Michigan)*
Michigan Veterans Vocational Sch. *(see Michigan Career & Tech. Inst.)*
Micro Tech Training Ctr. 581
Microcomputer Edu. Ctr. *(see MCed Career Coll.)*
Micronesia Coll. *(see Coll. of Micronesia-FSM)*
Micronesia Comm. Coll. *(see Coll. of Micronesia-FSM)*
Micronesian Inst. of Biblical Studies *(see Pacific Islands Bible Coll.)*
Micropower Computer Inst.-Manhattan 282
Mid Cities Barber Coll. 654
Mid Florida Tech 511
Mid Michigan Coll. *(see Mid Michigan Comm. Coll.)*
Mid Michigan Comm. Coll. 214
Mid Pac Coll. *(see Int'l. Mid Pac Coll.)*
Mid-America Baptist Theological Sem. 386
Mid-America Bible Coll. *(see Mid-America Christian Univ.)*
Mid-America Christian Univ. 331
Mid-America Coll. of Funeral Service 153
Mid-America Montessori Teacher Training Ctr. 570
MidAmerica Nazarene Coll. *(see MidAmerica Nazarene Univ.)*
MidAmerica Nazarene Univ. 167
Mid-America Reformed Sem. 803
Mid-America Sem. *(see Mid-America Baptist Theological Sem.)*
Mid-America Techno. Ctr. 617
MidAmerica Univ. *(see MidAmerica Nazarene Univ.)*
Mid-America Univ. *(see Mid-America Christian Univ.)*
Mid-Atlantic Healthcare Network *(see Asheville Veterans Affairs Med. Ctr.; Durham Veterans Affairs Med. Ctr.)*
Mid-Atlantic Naval Dental Clinic *(see Naval Dental Clinic Mid-Atlantic)*
Mid-Continent Baptist Bible Coll. *(see Mid-Continent Univ.)*
Mid-Continent Coll. 784 *(see also Mid-Continent Univ.)*
Mid-Continent Univ. 174, 784
Mid-Del Area Vocational-Tech. Sch. *(see Mid-Del Techno. Ctr.)*
Mid-Del Area Vo-Tech *(see Mid-Del Techno. Ctr.)*
Mid-Del Lewis Eubanks Area Vocational-Tech. Sch. *(see Mid-Del Techno. Ctr.)*
Mid-Del Lewis Eubanks Area Vo-Tech *(see Mid-Del Techno. Ctr.)*
Mid-Del Lewis Eubanks Techno. Ctr. *(see Mid-Del Techno. Ctr.)*
Mid-Del Techno. Ctr. 617
Mid-Del Vocational-Tech. Ctr. *(see Mid-Del Techno. Ctr.)*
Middle East Inst., The 502
Middle Georgia Agricultural & Mechanical Jr. Coll. *(see Middle Georgia Coll.)*
Middle Georgia Coll. 116, 781 *(see also Middle Georgia Tech. Coll.)*
Middle Georgia Military & Agricultural Coll. *(see Georgia Military Coll.)*
Middle Georgia Tech. Coll. 117
Middle Georgia Tech. Inst. *(see Middle Georgia Tech. Coll.)*
Middle Gerogia Coll—Georgia Aviation Campus 781
Middle Tennessee Cosmetology Sch. *(see also Genesis Career Coll.)*
Middle Tennessee Sch. of Anesthesia 386
Middle Tennessee Sch. of Cosmetology 642, 793 *(see also Genesis Career Coll.)*
Middle Tennessee State Coll. *(see Middle Tennessee State Univ.)*
Middle Tennessee State Normal Sch. *(see Middle Tennessee State Univ.)*
Middle Tennessee State Teachers Coll. *(see Middle Tennessee State Univ.)*
Middle Tennessee State Univ. 387
Middle Tennessee Univ. *(see Middle Tennessee State Univ.)*
Middlebury Coll. 417 *(see Monterey Inst. of Int'l. Studies)*
Middlesex Coll. *(see also Middlesex Comm. Coll.; Middlesex County Coll.)*
Middlesex Comm. Coll. 80, 202
Middlesex Comm.-Tech. Coll. *(see Middlesex Comm. Coll.)*

Minneapolis Central Baptist Theological Sem. *(see Central Baptist Theological Sem. of Minneapolis)*
Minneapolis Children's Med. Ctr. *(see Children's Hospitals & Clinics of Minnesota)*
Minneapolis City Hosp. *(see Hennepin County Med. Ctr.)*
Minneapolis Coll. of Art & Design 224
Minneapolis Coll. of Culinary Arts *(see Western Culinary Inst.)*
Minneapolis Coll. of Design *(see Minneapolis Coll. of Art & Design)*
Minneapolis Comm. & Tech. Coll. 224
Minneapolis Comm. Coll. *(see Minneapolis Comm. & Tech. Coll.)*
Minneapolis Drafting Sch. Division *(see Herzing Coll—Minneapolis)*
Minneapolis General Sch. of Anesthesia *(see Minneapolis Sch. of Anesthesia)*
Minneapolis Massage Sch. *(see Minneapolis Sch. of Massage & Bodywork)*
Minneapolis Sch. of Anesthesia 716
Minneapolis Sch. of Art *(see Minneapolis Coll. of Art & Design)*
Minneapolis Sch. of Massage & Bodywork 561
Minneapolis VA Med. Ctr. *(see Veterans Affairs Med. Ctr—Minneapolis)*
Minneapolis VAMC *(see Veterans Affairs Med. Ctr—Minneapolis)*
Minneapolis Veterans Affairs Med. Ctr. *(see Veterans Affairs Med. Ctr—Minneapolis)*
Minnequa Hosp. *(see Saint Mary-Corwin Med. Ctr.)*
Minnesota Acad. *(see Pillsbury Baptist Bible Coll.)*
Minnesota Adlerian Society *(see Adler Grad. Sch.)*
Minnesota Art Inst. *(see Art Inst.s Int'l—Minnesota)*
Minnesota Bible Coll. *(see Crossroads Coll.)*
Minnesota Central Univ. *(see Pillsbury Baptist Bible Coll.)*
Minnesota Cosmetology Edu. Ctr., Inc. 786 *(see also Minnesota Sch. of Cosmetology)*
Minnesota Dale Carnegie Training *(see Norman & Associates)*
Minnesota Eye Consultants *(see Illinois Coll. of Optometry)*
Minnesota Inst. of Acupuncture & Herbal Studies *(see Minnesota Inst. of Acupuncture & Oriental Medicine)*
Minnesota Inst. of Acupuncture & Oriental Medicine 226 *(see also Northwestern Health Sciences Univ.)*
Minnesota Inst. of Art *(see Art Inst.s Int'l—Minnesota)*
Minnesota Inst. of Technologies 786
Minnesota Intercollegiate Nursing Consortium *(see Gustavus Adolphus Coll.; Saint Olaf Coll.)*
Minnesota Med. Inst. *(see Argosy Univ. Twin Cities)*
Minnesota Methodist Hosp. *(see Methodist Hosp.)*
Minnesota Montessori Training Ctr. *(see Montessori Training Ctr. of Minnesota)*
Minnesota Riverland Tech. Coll. *(see South Central Coll—Faribault; South Central Coll—Mankato)*
Minnesota Riverland Tech. Coll—Austin *(see Riverland Comm. Coll—Austin)*
Minnesota Sch. of Bus. 224 *(see also Duluth Bus. Univ.; Globe Univ.; Inst. of Production & Recording; Minnesota Sch. of Cosmetology; Utah Career Coll.)*
Minnesota Sch. of Cosmetology 561, 786
Minnesota Sch. of Prof. Psychology 786 *(see also Argosy Univ. Twin Cities)*
Minnesota State Coll.-Southeast Tech. 224
Minnesota State Comm. & Tech. Coll. 224
Minnesota State Teachers Coll. *(see Univ. of Minnesot—Duluth)*
Minnesota State Univ. Moorhead 224
Minnesota State Univ.-Mankato 225
Minnesota Tech. Coll. *(see Minnesota State Coll.-Southeast Tech.)*
Minnesota Tech. Inst. *(see Minnesota State Coll.-Southeast Tech.)*
Minnesota West Comm. & Tech. Coll.-Granite Falls 225
Minot State Univ. 311
Minot State Univ.-Bottineau 311
Mir Yeshiva 282
Mira Costa Coll. *(see MiraCosta Coll.)*
MiraCosta Coll. 53
Miramar Coll. *(see San Diego Miramar Coll.)*
Mirrer Yeshiva *(see Mir Yeshiva)*
Misericordia Coll. *(see Misericordia Univ.)*
Misericordia Univ. 354, 791
Miss Marty's Beauty Sch. *(see Miss Marty's Hair Acad. & Esthetics Inst.)*
Miss Marty's Hair Acad. & Esthetics Inst. 487, 777
Miss Marty's Sch. of Beauty & Hairstyling 777 *(see also Miss Marty's Hair Acad. & Esthetics Inst.)*
Miss Wade's Fashion Merchandising Coll. *(see Wade Coll.)*
Mission Coll. 53 *(see also Los Angeles Mission Coll.)*
Mission Comm. Coll. *(see Mission Coll.)*
Mission House *(see Lakeland Coll.)*
Mission House Sem. *(see United Theological Sem. of the Twin Cities)*
Mission Institution *(see Blinn Coll.)*
Missionary Training Inst. *(see Nyack Coll.)*
Missionshaus *(see Lakeland Coll.)*
Mississippi Acad. *(see Mississippi Coll.)*
Mississippi Baptist Health Systems, Inc. *(see Mississippi Baptist Med. Ctr.)*
Mississippi Baptist Hosp. *(see Mississippi Baptist Med. Ctr.)*
Mississippi Baptist Med. Ctr. 717
Mississippi Coll. 232
Mississippi Coll. of Beauty Culture 565
Mississippi Consortium of Religion & Pastoral Care *(see G.V. (Sonny) Montgomery Veterans Affairs Med. Ctr.)*
Mississippi County Coll. *(see Arkansas Northeastern Coll.)*
Mississippi County Comm. Coll. *(see Arkansas Northeastern Coll.)*
Mississippi Delta Coll. *(see Mississippi Delta Comm. Coll.)*
Mississippi Delta Comm. Coll. 232
Mississippi Gulf Coast Coll. *(see Mississippi Gulf Coast Comm. Coll.)*
Mississippi Gulf Coast Comm. Coll. 232
Mississippi Job Corps Ctr. 565
Mississippi Normal Coll. *(see Univ. of Southern Mississippi)*
Mississippi Sch. of Therapeutic Massage 565
Mississippi Southern Coll. *(see Univ. of Southern Mississippi)*
Mississippi State Coll. *(see Mississippi State Univ.)*
Mississippi State Coll. for Women *(see Mississippi Univ. for Women)*
Mississippi State Univ. 232
Mississippi Synodical Coll. *(see Belhaven Coll.)*
Mississippi Univ. for Women 232
Mississippi Valley State Coll. *(see Mississippi Valley State Univ.)*
Mississippi Valley State Univ. 232
Mississippi Valley Univ. *(see Mississippi Valley State Univ.)*
Mississippi Vocational Coll. *(see Mississippi Valley State Univ.)*

Mississippi Woman's Coll. *(see William Carey Univ.)*
Mississippi Women's Univ. *(see Mississippi Univ. for Women)*
Missoula Coll. of Techno. *(see Univ. of Montana)*
Missoula Coll. of Techno. 248
Missoula Vocational-Tech. Ctr. *(see Univ. of Montana; Univ. of Montan—Missoula Coll. of Techno.)*
Missouri Baptist Coll. *(see Missouri Baptist Univ.)*
Missouri Baptist Univ. 241
Missouri Beauty Acad. 567
Missouri Coll. 241
Missouri Coll. of Cosmetology And Esthetics *(see Merrell Univ. of Beauty Arts & Science)*
Missouri Coll. of Cosmetology & Esthetics 567
Missouri Coll. of Cosmetology North 567
Missouri Coll. of Cosmetolog—Bolivar 567
Missouri Coll. of Cosmetolog—South 567
Missouri Inst. of Techno. *(see DeVry Univ. Kansas City)*
Missouri Montessori Teacher Edu. Program 568
Missouri S&T *(see Missouri Univ. of Science & Techno.)*
Missouri Sch. for Doctors' Assistants *(see Missouri Coll.)*
Missouri Sch. of Mines & Metallurgy *(see Missouri Univ. of Science & Techno.)*
Missouri Southern State Coll. *(see Missouri Southern State Univ.)*
Missouri Southern State Univ. 241, 786 *(see also Franklin Techno. Ctr.)*
Missouri Southern State Univ—Joplin 786
Missouri Southern Univ. *(see Missouri Southern State Univ.)*
Missouri State Univ. 241, 786
Missouri State Univ—West Plains 241, 787
Missouri Tech 241
Missouri Tech. Sch. *(see Missouri Tech)*
Missouri Univ. of Science & Techno. 241, 787
Missouri Valley Coll. 241
Missouri Western State Coll. 786 *(see also Missouri Western State Univ.)*
Missouri Western State Univ. 241, 786
Mister Wayne's Sch. of Unisex Hair Design 642
MIT *(see Massachusetts Inst. of Techno.)*
Mitchell Coll. 80 *(see also Mitchell Comm. Coll.)*
Mitchell Coll. of Law *(see William Mitchell Coll. of Law)*
Mitchell Comm. Coll. 305
Mitchell Jr. Coll. *(see Pfeiffer Univ.)*
Mitchell Tech *(see Mitchell Tech. Inst.)*
Mitchell Tech. Inst. 379
Mitchell's Hairstyling Acad—Fayetteville 789
Mitchell's Hairstyling Acad—Fayetteville 789 *(see also Montgomery's Hair Styling Acad.)*
Mitchell's Hairstyling Acad—Goldsboro 601
Mitchell's Hairstyling Acad—Greenville 601
Mitchell's Hairstyling Acad—Wilson 601
Mizpa Pentacostal Coll. *(see Colegio Pentecostal Mizpa)*
Mizzou *(see Univ. of Missouri)*
MJ's Beauty Acad., Inc. 654
M'kor Chaim Rabbinical Sem. *(see Rabbinical Sem. M'kor Chaim)*
MM—Arizona *(see Motorcycle & Marine Mechanics Inst.)*
Moats & Associates, Inc. *(see CB&T, Inc)*
Moberly Area Comm. Coll. 241
Moberly Coll. *(see Moberly Area Comm. Coll.)*
Mobile Campus of Techno. *(see Remington Coll—Mobile)*
Mobile State Jr. Coll. *(see Bishop State Comm. Coll.)*
Mobile Univ. *(see Univ. of Mobile)*
Model Coll. of Hair Design 561
Modern Beauty Acad. 487
Modern Beauty Sch., Inc. 569
Modern Bus. Sch. *(see Everest Coll—Thornton)*
Modern Hairstyling Inst—Arecibo 635
Modern Hairstyling Inst—Bayamon *(see Modern Hairstyling Inst—Fajardo)*
Modern Hairstyling Inst—Carolina 635
Modern Hairstyling Inst—Fajardo 635
Modern Techno. Coll. *(see Kaplan Coll—North Hollywood)*
Modern Techno. Sch. 487
Modern Welding Sch. 596
Moderncare, Inc. *(see Texas Careers)*
Modesto Coll. *(see Modesto Jr. Coll.)*
Modesto Jr. Coll. 53
Modi Apollo Int'l. Inst. 25 *(see also Western Int'l. Univ.)*
Mohave Coll. *(see Mohave Comm. Coll.)*
Mohave Comm. Coll. 20
Mohawk Valley Coll. *(see Mohawk Valley Comm. Coll.)*
Mohawk Valley Comm. Coll. 282
Mohawk Valley Network *(see Faxton-St. Luke's Healthcare)*
Mohegan Comm. Coll. *(see Three Rivers Comm. Coll.)*
Mojave Barber Coll. 487
Moler Barber Coll. 487 *(see also American Coll. of Hairstylin—Cedar Rapids, American Coll. of Hairstylin—Des Moines)*
Moler Barber Coll. of Hairstyling 603
Moler Beauty Coll—Canal Street 784
Moler Beauty Coll—Gretna 784 *(see also Cosmetology Bus. & Mgmnt. Inst.)*
Moler Coll. of Hairstyling *(see Moler Hairstyling Coll., Inc.)*
Moler Hairstyling Coll., Inc. 531
Moler-Hollywood Beauty Coll. 609
Moler-Pickens Beauty Coll. 609
Molloy Catholic Coll. for Women *(see Molloy Coll.)*
Molloy Coll. 282
Monmouth Coll. 137 *(see also Monmouth Univ.)*
Monmouth County Vocational Sch. 581
Monmouth Jr. Coll. *(see Monmouth Univ.)*
Monmouth Med. Ctr. 721
Monmouth Univ. 261
Monongalia County Tech. Ctr. *(see Monongalia County Tech. Edu. Ctr.)*
Monongalia County Tech. Edu. Ctr. 673
Monroe —Orleans BOCES, Ctr. for Workforce Development 817
Monroe Area Vocational-Tech. Sch. *(see Albany Tech. Coll.)*
Monroe Career & Tech. Inst. 792
Monroe Ctr. for Grad. & Prof. Studies *(see Univ. of Mary Washington)*
Monroe Coll. 282 *(see also Monroe Comm. Coll.; Monroe County Comm. Coll.)*
Monroe Comm. Coll. 282
Monroe County Area Vocational Tech. Sch. 792
Monroe County Coll. *(see Monroe County Comm. Coll.)*
Monroe County Comm. Coll. 214
Monroe Sch. of Bus. *(see Monroe Coll.)*
Monroe Univ. *(see Univ. of Louisiana at Monroe)*
Monroeville Sch. of Bus. *(see Bus. Careers Inst.)*
Montachusett Reg. Vocational Tech. Sch. 553
Montana Agricultural Coll. *(see Montana State Univ.)*
Montana Bible Coll. 804
Montana Coll. *(see also Montana Bible Coll.)*
Montana Coll. of Agriculture & Mechanic Arts, The *(see Montana State Univ.)*
Montana Coll. of Mineral Science & Techno. *(see Montana Tech of The Univ. of Montana)*

Moraine Valley Coll. *(see Moraine Valley Comm. Coll.)*
Moraine Valley Comm. Coll. 137
Morales Acad. *(see Academia Morales)*
Moravian Coll. 354 *(see also Moravian Theological Sem.)*
Moravian Sem. *(see Moravian Coll.; Moravian Theological Sem.)*
Moravian Theological Sem. 354 *(see also Moravian Coll.)*
More Coll. *(see Thomas More Coll.)*
More Coll. of Liberal Arts *(see Thomas More Coll. of Liberal Arts)*
Morehead Normal Sch. *(see Morehead State Univ.)*
Morehead State Coll. *(see Morehead State Univ.)*
Morehead State Univ. 174
Morehouse Coll. 117
Morehouse Coll. & Sch. of Religion *(see Interdenominational Theological Ctr.)*
Morehouse Med. Sch. *(see Morehouse Sch. of Medicine)*
Morehouse Sch. of Medicine 117
Morgan Bus. Coll. *(see Thomas Coll.)*
Morgan Coll. *(see Morgan State Univ.)*
Morgan Comm. Coll. 74
Morgan County Comm. Coll. *(see Morgan Comm. Coll.)*
Morgan County Jr. Coll. *(see Morgan Comm. Coll.)*
Morgan Educational Ctr. *(see Robert Morgan Educational Ctr.)*
Morgan State Univ. 192
Morgan Vocational-Tech. Inst. *(see Robert Morgan Educational Ctr.)*
Morgan-Thomas Bus. Coll. *(see Thomas Coll.)*
Morgantown Beauty Coll., Inc. 673
Morgantown Skills Training Ctr. *(see Stanley Tech. Inst.)*
Morning Pilgrim Baptist Church 683
Morningside Coll. 161
Morrilton Comm. Coll. *(see Univ. of Arkansas Comm. Coll. at Morrilton)*
Morris Coll. 376 *(see also Lon Morris Coll.; Robert Morris Coll.; Robert Morris Univ.)*
Morris County Coll. *(see County Coll. of Morris)*
Morris County Sch. of Techno. 581
Morris County Vocational Sch. Dist. *(see Morris County Sch. of Techno.)*
Morris County Vocational Tech. Sch. *(see Morris County Sch. of Techno.)*
Morris Harvey Coll. *(see Univ. of Charleston)*
Morris Univ. *(see Robert Morris Univ.)*
Morrison Inst. of Techno. 137
Morrison Univ. *(see Neumont Univ.)*
Morristown Area Vocational-Tech. Sch. *(see Tennessee Techno. Ctr. at Morristown)*
Morristown Area Vo-Tech Sch. *(see Tennessee Techno. Ctr. at Morristown)*
Morristown Hosp. *(see Morristown Mem. Hosp.)*
Morristown Mem. Hosp. 721 *(see also Inst. for Therapeutic Massage, Inc.)*
Morristown Vocational-Tech. Sch. *(see Tennessee Techno. Ctr. at Morristown)*
Morristown Vo-Tech Sch. *(see Tennessee Techno. Ctr. at Morristown)*
Morrisville Coll. of Agriculture & Techno. *(see State Univ. of New York Coll. of Agriculture & Techno. at Morrisville)*
Morrisville State Coll. *(see State Univ. of New York Coll. of Agriculture & Techno. at Morrisville)*
Morton Coll. 137
Mortuary Science Coll. of Cincinnati *(see Cincinnati Coll. of Mortuary Science)*
Mortuary Science Inst. of Pittsburgh *(see Pittsburgh Inst. of Mortuary Science)*
Moses Cone Health Sys. *(see Moses H. Cone Mem. Hosp.)*
Moses Cone Hosp. *(see Moses H. Cone Mem. Hosp.)*
Moses Division of Montefiore Med. Ctr. *(see Montefiore Med. Ctr. West Campus)*
Moses H. Cone Mem. Hosp., The 730
Mossy Creek Coll. *(see Carson-Newman Coll.)*
Motif Beauty Acad. 537
Motlow Coll. *(see Motlow State Comm. Coll.)*
Motlow State Comm. Coll. 387
Motorcycle & Marine Mechanics Inst. 468
Motorcycle Mechanics Inst. *(see Motorcycle & Marine Mechanics Inst.)*
MotoRing Inst. *(see MotoRing Tech. Training Inst.)*
MotoRing Tech. Training Inst. 637
Mott Comm. Coll. *(see Charles Stewart Mott Comm. Coll.)*
Mott Middle Coll. *(see Charles Stewart Mott Comm. Coll.)*
Moultrie Area Tech. Inst. *(see Moultrie Tech. Coll.)*
Moultrie Coll. *(see Moultrie Tech. Coll.)*
Moultrie Tech. Coll. 117
Moultrie Tech. Coll—East 14th St. Campus *(see Moultrie Tech. Coll.)*
Moultrie Tech. Coll—Tech Drive Campus *(see Moultrie Tech. Coll.)*
Moultrie Tech. Coll—Tiftarea Campus *(see Moultrie Tech. Coll.)*
Moultrie Vocational-Tech. Sch. *(see Moultrie Tech. Coll.)*
Mount Allen Jr. Coll. *(see Mount Olive Coll.)*
Mount Aloysius Coll. 354
Mount Aloysius Jr. Coll. *(see Mount Aloysius Coll.)*
Mount Angel Sem. 339
Mount Carmel Coll. of Nursing 322
Mount Carmel Health Sys. *(see Mount Carmel West)*
Mount Carmel Med. Ctr. *(see Mount Carmel West)*
Mount Carmel West 733
Mount Diablo Adult Edu. 688
Mount Diablo Med. Ctr. 778 *(see also John Muir Med. Ctr., Concord Campus)*
Mount Diablo Unified Sch. Dist. *(see Mount Diablo Adult Edu.)*
Mount Holyoke Coll. 202
Mount Holyoke Female Sem. *(see Mount Holyoke Coll.)*
Mount Hood Coll. *(see Mount Hood Comm. Coll.)*
Mount Hood Comm. Coll. 339
Mount Ida Coll. 202
Mount Lebanon Univ. *(see Louisiana Coll.)*
Mount Marty Coll. 379
Mount Mary Coll. 448
Mount Mercy Coll. 161 *(see also Carlow Univ.)*
Mount Morris Coll. *(see Manchester Coll.)*
Mount of Praise Bible Coll. *(see Ohio Christian Univ.)*
Mount Olive Coll. 305
Mount Olive Jr. Coll. *(see Mount Olive Coll.)*
Mount Royal Coll. 760
Mount SAC *(see Mount San Antonio Coll.)*
Mount Saint Agnes Coll. *(see Loyola Coll. in Maryland)*
Mount Saint Bernard Coll. *(see Loras Coll.)*
Mount Saint Charles Coll. *(see Carroll Coll.)*
Mount Saint Clare Coll. *(see Ashford Univ.)*
Mount Saint Joseph Acad. & Coll. *(see Clarke Coll.)*
Mount Saint Joseph Coll. *(see Chestnut Hill Coll.)*

MTI Coll. of Bus. & Techno. *(see MTI Coll.)*
MTI Coll. of Bus. & Techno—Space Park 794
MTI Western Bus. Coll. *(see MTI Coll.)*
Mudd Coll. *(see Harvey Mudd Coll.)*
Mueller Coll. of Holistic Massage Therapies 487
Muhlenberg Coll. 354
Muhlenberg Hosp. Ctr. *(see Lehigh Valley Hosp—Muhlenberg)*
Muhlenberg Reg. Med. Ctr. *(see Lehigh Valley Hosp—Muhlenberg)*
Muhlenberg Schools of Nursing, Med. Imaging & Therapeutic Sciences *(see John F. Kennedy Med. Ctr.)*
Muhlenberg Snyder Schools of Nursing & Med. Imaging *(see John F. Kennedy Med. Ctr.)*
Mullins Sch. of Practical Nursing *(see Hannah E. Mullins Sch. of Practical Nursing)*
MultiCare Health Sys. *(see Good Samaritan Hosp.)*
Multnomah Bible Coll. & Biblical Sem. *(see Multnomah Univ.)*
Multnomah Biblical Sem. *(see Multnomah Univ.)*
Multnomah Coll. *(see Multnomah Univ.)*
Multnomah Grad. Sch. of Ministry *(see Multnomah Univ.)*
Multnomah Sch. of the Bible *(see Multnomah Univ.)*
Multnomah Univ. 339
Muncy Valley Hosp. *(see Susquehanna Health Sys.)*
Mundelein Coll. *(see Loyola Univ. of Chicago)*
Mundelein Sem. *(see Univ. of Saint Mary of the Lake Mundelein Sem.)*
Mundus Inst. 468
Municipal Univ. of Omaha *(see Univ. of Nebraska at Omaha)*
Municipal Univ. of Wichita, The *(see Wichita State Univ.)*
Munson-Williams-Proctor Inst. *(see Pratt Inst.)*
Murdoch Univ. 756
Murfreesboro Area Vocational-Tech. Sch. *(see Tennessee Techno. Ctr. at Murfreesboro)*
Murfreesboro Area Vo-Tech Sch. *(see Tennessee Techno. Ctr. at Murfreesboro)*
Murfreesboro Vocational-Tech. Sch. *(see Tennessee Techno. Ctr. at Murfreesboro)*
Murfreesboro Vo-Tech Sch. *(see Tennessee Techno. Ctr. at Murfreesboro)*
Murphy Mem. Veterans Hosp. *(see South Texas Veterans Health Care Sys.)*
Murphy VA Med. Ctr. *(see Raymond G. Murphy Veterans Affairs Med. Ctr.)*
Murphy VAMC *(see Raymond G. Murphy Veterans Affairs Med. Ctr.)*
Murphy Veterans Affairs Med. Ctr. *(see Raymond G. Murphy Veterans Affairs Med. Ctr.)*
Murray Coll. *(see Murray State Coll.)*
Murray State Coll. 332
Murray State Univ. 174
Murray Univ. *(see Murray State Univ.)*
Muscatine Comm. Coll. 161
Muscatine Jr. Coll. *(see Muscatine Comm. Coll.)*
Muscogee Area Vocational-Tech. Sch. *(see Columbus Tech. Coll.)*
Muscular Therapy Inst. 785 *(see also Cortiva Inst—Boston)*
Museum Art Sch. of the Portland Art Assoc. *(see Pacific Northwest Coll. of Art)*
Museum of American Folk Art Folk Art Inst. *(see Folk Art Inst. of the Museum of American Folk Art)*
Music Acad. of Los Angeles *(see Los Angeles Music Acad.)*
Music Acad. of Pennsylvania, The *(see Pennsylvania Acad. of Music)*
Music & Worship Arts Coll. *(see Visible Sch., Music & Worship Arts Coll.)*
Music Ctr. of the North Shore *(see Music Inst. of Chicago)*
Music Conservatory of San Francisco *(see San Francisco Conservatory of Music)*
Music Conservatory of Washington *(see Washington Conservatory of Music, Inc.)*
Music Conservatory of Westchester 596
Music Conservatory of Wisconsin *(see Wisconsin Conservatory of Music, Inc.)*
Music Inst. of Atlanta *(see Atlanta Inst. of Music)*
Music Inst. of Chicago 528
Music Inst. of Cleveland *(see Cleveland Inst. of Music)*
Music Sch. of Cleveland *(see Cleveland Music Sch. Settlement)*
Music Sch. of Manhattan *(see Manhattan Sch. of Music)*
Music Tech *(see McNally Smith Coll. of Music)*
Musical & Dramatic Acad. of America *(see American Musical & Dramatic Acad.)*
Musicians Inst. 53
Musictech Coll. 786 *(see also McNally Smith Coll. of Music)*
Muskegon Coll. *(see Muskegon Comm. Coll.)*
Muskegon Comm. Coll. 214
Muskegon Jr. Coll. *(see Muskegon Comm. Coll.)*
Muskingum Acad. *(see Marietta Coll.)*
Muskingum Area Tech. Coll. *(see Zane State Coll.)*
Muskingum Area Tech. Inst. *(see Zane State Coll.)*
Muskingum Coll. 322
Muskogee VA Med. Ctr. *(see Jack C. Montgomery Veterans Affairs Med. Ctr.)*
Muskogee VAMC *(see Jack C. Montgomery Veterans Affairs Med. Ctr.)*
Muskogee Veterans Affairs Med. Ctr. *(see Jack C. Montgomery Veterans Affairs Med. Ctr.)*
My Le Beauty Coll. 814
Myers Univ. 790 *(see also Chancellor Univ.)*
My-Le's Beauty Coll. 488 *(see also My Le Beauty Coll.)*
Myndall Cain Beauty Sch. *(see Regency Beauty Inst.)*
Myotherapy Coll. of Utah 661
Myotherapy Inst. 251
Myotherapy Inst. of Utah *(see Myotherapy Coll. of Utah)*
MyrAngel Beauty Inst. 635

N

Nacogdoches Univ. *(see Stephen F. Austin State Univ.)*
Nagoya Univ. of Commerce & Bus. 767
Nail Acad., The 596
Nail Techniques Sch. of Nail Techno. 820
Nancy Taylor Secretarial Sch. *(see Taylor Bus. Inst.)*
Nankai Univ. *(see Tsinghua Univ.)*
Nanyang Technological Univ. 769
Nanyang Univ. *(see Nanyang Technological Univ.; National Univ. of Singapore)*
Napa Coll. *(see Napa Valley Coll.)*
Napa Valley Coll. 54
Naperville Skin Inst. 526 *(see also Hair Prof.s Acad. of Cosmetolog—Wheaton)*
Naples Mem. Hosp., Inc. *(see NCH Downtown Naples Hosp.)*
Naropa Inst. *(see Naropa Univ.)*
Naropa Univ., The 74
NASCAR Tech. Inst. *(see Universal Tech. Inst.)*
Nash Coll. *(see Nash Comm. Coll.)*
Nash Comm. Coll. 305

National Univ. of Health Sciences 138
National Univ. of Ireland, Dublin *(see Univ. Coll. Dublin)*
National Univ. of Singapore 769
National-Louis Univ. 138
Nationwide Beauty Acad. 610
Natural Gourmet Cookery Corporation *(see Natural Gourmet Cookery Sch.)*
Natural Gourmet Cookery Sch. 596
Natural Health Ctr. Clinic *(see National Coll. of Natural Medicine)*
Natural Motion Inst. *(see Concorde Sch. of Hair Design, Inc.; European Acad. of Cosmetology, Inc.)*
Natural Motion Inst. of Hair Design 581
Naugatuck Valley Coll. *(see Naugatuck Valley Comm. Coll.)*
Naugatuck Valley Comm. Coll. 80, 779
Naugatuck Valley Comm. Coll. in Consortium *(see Capital Comm. Coll.; Housatonic Comm. Coll.; Manchester Comm. Coll. Northwestern Connecticut Comm. Coll.; Tunxis Comm. Coll.)*
Naugatuck Valley Comm.-Tech. Coll. 779
Navajo Area Indian Health Service *(see Crownpoint Health Care Facility; Kayenta Health Ctr. of the Indian Health Service; Northern Navajo Med. Ctr.)*
Navajo Coll. *(see Diné Coll.)*
Navajo Comm. Coll. *(see Diné Coll.)*
Navajo County Comm. Coll. Dist. *(see Northland Pioneer Coll.)*
Navajo Skills Ctr. *(see Navajo Tech. Coll.)*
Navajo Tech. Coll. 266, 788
Naval Acad. *(see United States Naval Acad.)*
Naval Air Tech. Training Ctr. 780 *(see also Ctr. for Naval Aviation Tech. Training)*
Naval Ctr. for Security Forces *(see Ctr. for Security Forces)*
Naval Construction Training Ctr. *(see Ctr. for Seabees & Facilities Engineering)*
Naval Dental Ctr. Southeast 697
Naval Dental Ctr—Great Lakes 703
Naval Dental Ctr—Gulf Coast 697
Naval Dental Ctr—Jacksonville *(see Naval Dental Ctr. Southeast)*
Naval Dental Ctr—San Diego 688
Naval Dental Clinic *(see Naval Dental Clinic Mid-Atlantic)*
Naval Dental Clinic Mid-Atlantic 750
Naval Dental Clinic Norfolk *(see Naval Dental Clinic Mid-Atlantic)*
Naval Dental Sch. *(see Naval PostGrad. Dental Sch.)*
Naval Diving & Salvage Training Ctr. 780 *(see also Ctr. for Explosive Ordnance Disposal & Diving)*
Naval Expeditionary Warfare Training Grou—Pacific *(see Naval Expeditionary Warfare Training Grou—Pacific)*
Naval Health Clinic, Great Lakes 703
Naval Hosp. Corps Sch. Great Lakes 549
Naval Hosp—Camp Pendelton 688
Naval Hosp—Great Lakes *(see Naval Health Clinic, Great Lakes)*
Naval Leadership Ctr. *(see Ctr. for Naval Leadership)*
Naval Med. Ctr. *(see National Naval Med. Ctr.)*
Naval Med. Ctr. Bethesda *(see Naval Med. Edu. & Training Command)*
Naval Med. Ctr. Portsmouth 750
Naval Med. Ctr—San Diego 688 *(see also Naval Dental Ctr—San Diego)*
Naval Med. Edu. & Training Command 549 *(see also United States Navy Medicine Manpower, Personnel, Training & Edu. Command)*
Naval Operational Medicine Inst. 549
Naval Ophthalmic Support & Training Activity 549
Naval PostGrad. Dental Sch. 549
Naval PostGrad. Sch. *(see United States Naval PostGrad. Sch.)*
Naval Sch. *(see United States Naval Acad.)*
Naval Sch. of Health Sciences 689, 750
Naval Surface Warfare Training Ctr. *(see Ctr. for Surface Combat Systems)*
Naval Tech. Training Ctr. 780 *(see also Ctr. for Information Dominance Corry Station)*
Naval Tech. Training Ctr., Corry Station *(see Ctr. for Information Dominance Corry Station)*
Naval War Coll. 371
Navarro Coll. 400
Navarro Jr. Coll. *(see Navarro Coll.)*
NAVCONSTRACEN *(see Ctr. for Seabees & Facilities Engineering)*
Nave Cosmetology Acad. 519
Nave Cosmetology Acad., Inc. 781, 793 *(see also Georgia Career Inst.)*
NAVMED MPT&E *(see United States Navy Medicine Manpower, Personnel, Training & Edu. Command)*
Navy & Marine Corps Intelligence Training Ctr. *(see Ctr. for Naval Intelligence)*
Navy Ctr. for Naval Intelligence *(see Ctr. for Naval Intelligence)*
Navy Ctr. for Personal Development *(see Ctr. for Naval Leadership)*
Navy Field Med. Service Sch. *(see Navy Manpower Command)*
Navy Nurse Corps Anesthesia Program *(see Naval Med. Edu. & Training Command)*
Navy Supply Corps Sch. *(see United States Navy Supply Corps Sch.)*
NAWCC Sch. of Horology 627
Nazarene Bible Coll. 74
Nazarene Coll. *(see Nazarene Bible Coll.)*
Nazarene Sem. *(see Nazarene Theological Sem.)*
Nazarene Theological Sem. 242
Nazarene Univ. *(see Point Loma Nazarene Univ.)*
Nazarene Univ. Coll. *(see Ambrose Univ. Coll.)*
Nazareth Coll. of Rochester 283
Nazareth Family Ctr.-Family Practice Ctr. 703
Nazareth Hosp. 740
NC State Univ. *(see North Carolina State Univ.)*
NCH Downtown Naples Hosp. 697
NCH Healthcare Sys. *(see NCH Downtown Naples Hosp.)*
NCH Naples Hosp. *(see NCH Downtown Naples Hosp.)*
NCM—New England 553
NCT—Bay Area Counties *(see National Coll. of Tech. Instructio—Livermore)*
NCT—Buellton *(see National Coll. of Tech. Instructio—Buellton)*
NCT—Livermore *(see National Coll. of Tech. Instructio—Livermore)*
NCT—Roseville *(see National Coll. of Tech. Instructio—Roseville)*
NCT—Siskiyous County *(see Coll. of the Siskiyous)*
Nebraska Christian Coll. 252
Nebraska Coll. *(see Nebraska Methodist Coll.)*
Nebraska Coll. of Bus. *(see Kaplan Univ.)*
Nebraska Coll. of Tech. Agriculture 252
Nebraska Indian Comm. Coll. 252
Nebraska Med. Ctr., The *(see Univ. of Nebraska Med. Ctr.)*
Nebraska Methodist Coll. 252
Nebraska Methodist Coll. of Nursing & Allied Health *(see Nebraska Methodist Coll.)*
Nebraska Normal Coll. of Wayne *(see Wayne State Coll.)*
Nebraska State Normal Sch. at Kearney *(see Univ. of Nebraska at Kearney)*
Nebraska State Teachers Coll. at Kearney *(see Univ. of Nebraska at Kearney)*
Nebraska State Teachers Coll. of Chadron *(see Chadron State Coll.)*

New York Interior Design Sch. *(see New York Sch. of Interior Design)*
New York Int'l. Beauty Sch., LTD 597
New York Law Sch. 284
New York Massage Inst. *(see New York Inst. of Massage)*
New York Med. Assistants Sch. *(see New York Sch. for Med. & Dental Assistants)*
New York Med. Career Training Ctr. 817
New York Med. Ctr. of Queens *(see New York Hosp. Queens)*
New York Med. Coll. 284
New York Methodist Hosp. 727
New York Optometry Coll. *(see State Univ. of New York Coll. of Optometry)*
New York Paralegal Sch. 597
New York Presbyterian Hosp—Columbia Univ. 727
New York Restaurant Sch. 789 *(see also Art Inst. of New York City)*
New York Sch. for Med. & Dental Assistants 597
New York Sch. for the Training of Teachers *(see Teachers Coll. of Columbia Univ.)*
New York Sch. of Chiropody *(see New York Coll. of Podiatric Medicine)*
New York Sch. of Interior Design 284
New York State Agricultural & Tech. Coll. at Alfred *(see Alfred Univ.)*
New York State Agricultural & Tech. Inst. *(see State Univ. of New York Coll. of Techno. at Canton)*
New York State Assoc. for Retarded Children *(see Assoc. for the Help of Retarded Children)*
New York State Coll. for Teachers *(see Univ. at Albany)*
New York State Coll. of Agriculture & Life Sciences *(see Cornell Univ.)*
New York State Coll. of Ceramics at Alfred Univ. 269 *(see also Alfred Univ.; New York State Coll. of Ceramics at Alfred Univ.)*
New York State Coll. of Human Ecology 275 *(see also Cornell Univ.)*
New York State Coll. of Veterinary Medicine 275 *(see also Cornell Univ.)*
New York State Dept. of Health 727 *(see also Univ. at Albany)*
New York State Inst. of Applied Arts & Sciences *(see Westchester Comm. Coll.)*
New York State Inst. of Applied Arts & Sciences at Binghamton *(see State Univ. of New York Broome Comm. Coll.)*
New York State Psychiatric Inst. *(see New York Presbyterian Hosp—Columbia Univ.)*
New York State Sch. of Industrial & Labor Relations 275 *(see also Cornell Univ.)*
New York Tech. Inst. of Hawaii 522
New York Techno. Inst. *(see New York Inst. of Techno—Old Westbury)*
New York Theological Sem. 284
New York Univ. 284
New York Univ. Med. Ctr. *(see New York Univ.)*
New York Univ. Sch. of Medicine *(see Bellevue Hosp. Ctr.; New York Univ.; Rusk Inst. of Rehabilitation Medicine)*
Newark Beth Israel Med. Ctr. 721
Newark Coll. *(see Univ. of Delaware)*
Newark Coll. of Engineering *(see New Jersey Inst. of Techno.)*
Newark Tech. Sch. *(see New Jersey Inst. of Techno.)*
Newbern Area Vocational-Tech. Sch. *(see Tennessee Techno. Ctr. at Newbern)*
Newbern Area Vo-Tech Sch. *(see Tennessee Techno. Ctr. at Newbern)*
Newbern Vocational-Tech. Sch. *(see Tennessee Techno. Ctr. at Newbern)*
Newbern Vo-Tech Sch. *(see Tennessee Techno. Ctr. at Newbern)*
Newberry Coll. 376
Newberry Sch. of Beauty 488
Newbridge Coll. 488
Newbridge Coll—Burbank 488, 778
Newbridge Coll—Monterey Park 488, 777–778
Newbury Coll. 203
NewCoast Coll., Inc. *(see Newbridge Coll.)*
Newcomb Coll. *(see Tulane Univ.)*
Newcomb Mem. Coll. *(see Tulane Univ.)*
Newman Coll. *(see Carson-Newman Coll.; Newman Theological Coll.; Newman Univ.)*
Newman Theological Coll. 456
Newman Univ. 167
Newport Acad. of Cosmetology Careers *(see Phagans' Newport Acad. of Cosmetology Careers)*
Newport Bus. Inst. 355
Newport News Shipbuilding Apprentice Sch. *(see Northrop Grumman Newport News Apprentice Sch.)*
Newport Sch. of Hairdressing, Inc—Cranston *(see Paul Mitchell The Sch.)*
Newport Sch. of Hairdressing, Inc—Pawtucket 637
Newport Univ. *(see Christopher Newport Univ.)*
NewSch. of Architecture & Design 54
Newton & Associates, Inc. *(see Glyn Ed Newton & Associates, Inc.)*
Newton Coll. of the Sacred Heart *(see Boston Coll.)*
Newton Theological Institution *(see Andover Newton Theological Sch.)*
NHC Great Lakes *(see Naval Health Clinic, Great Lakes)*
NHCS Great Lakes *(see Naval Hosp. Corps Sch. Great Lakes)*
NHCT—Berlin *(see White Mountains Comm. Coll.)*
NHCT—Claremont *(see River Valley Comm. Coll.)*
NHCT—Laconia *(see Lakes Region Comm. Coll.)*
NHCT—Nashua *(see Nashua Comm. Coll.)*
NHCT—Stratham *(see Great Bay Comm. Coll.)*
NHRAW Home Study Inst. *(see HARDI Home Study Inst.)*
NHTI, Concord's Comm. Coll. 257, 787
Niagara Coll. 761
Niagara Comm. Coll. *(see Niagara County Comm. Coll.)*
Niagara County Coll. *(see Niagara County Comm. Coll.)*
Niagara County Comm. Coll. 284
Niagara Frontier Ctr. *(see State Univ. of New York Empire State Coll.)*
Niagara Sem. *(see Niagara Univ.)*
Niagara Univ. 285
Nicholas H. Noyes Mem. Hosp. 727
Nicholls Jr. Coll. *(see Nicholls State Univ.)*
Nicholls State Coll. *(see Nicholls State Univ.)*
Nicholls State Univ. 183
Nichols Acad. *(see Nichols Coll.)*
Nichols Career Ctr. 718
Nichols Coll. 203
Nichols Jr. Coll. *(see Nichols Coll.)*
Nick Randazzo Vocational Training Inst. *(see Gretna Career Coll.)*
Nicolet Area Tech. Coll. 448
Nicolet Coll. *(see Nicolet Area Tech. Coll.)*
Nicolet Tech. Coll. *(see Nicolet Area Tech. Coll.)*
Nightingale Acad. *(see Nightingale Med. Inst.)*
Nightingale Med. Inst. 519, 678
Niles Coll. of Loyola Univ. *(see Univ. of Saint Mary of the Lake Mundelein Sem.)*

NTU Sch. of Engineering & Applied Science 229
NTU Sch. of Engineering & Applied Science at Walden Univ. 779 *(see also Walden Univ.)*
Nunez Coll. *(see Elaine P. Nunez Comm. Coll.)*
Nunez Comm. Coll. *(see Elaine P. Nunez Comm. Coll.)*
Nunnelley State Tech. Coll. *(see Central Alabama Comm. Coll.)*
Nurse Anesthesia Sch. of New Britain Sch. *(see New Britain Sch. of Nurse Anesthesia)*
Nurse Assistant Training Sch. *(see Acad. for Practical Nursing & Health Occupations)*
Nursing Coll. of Lancaster General Hosp. *(see Lancaster General Coll. of Nursing & Health Sciences)*
Nursing Sch. of Central Maine *(see Central Maine Med. Ctr. Coll. of Nursing & Health Professions)*
Nu-Tek Acad. of Beauty 538
Nu-Tek Beauty Acad. *(see Nu-Tek Acad. of Beauty)*
Nutmeg Ballet *(see Nutmeg Conservatory for the Arts)*
Nutmeg Conservatory for the Arts 499
Nuvo Coll. of Cosmetology 558
NW Georgia Reg. Hosp. *(see Northwest Georgia Reg. Hosp.)*
Nwani Int'l. Barber & Styling Coll. *(see Dudley Nwani, The Sch.)*
Nwani Sch. *(see Dudley Nwani, The Sch.)*
NY DOH Dental Public Health Residency Program *(see New York State Dept. of Health)*
NY Harbor Healthcare Sys. *(see Veterans Affairs New York Harbor Healthcare Sys—Brooklyn)*
Nyack Coll. *(see Alliance Theological Sem.)*
Nyack Coll. 285
Nyack Missionary Coll. *(see Nyack Coll.)*
NYC Health & Hospitals Corporation *(see Kings County Hosp. Ctr.; Lincoln Med. & Mental Health Ctr.; Woodhull Med. & Mental Health Ctr.)*
NYS Coll. of Agriculture & Life Sciences *(see Cornell Univ.)*
NYS Coll. of Human Ecology *(see Cornell Univ.)*
NYS Coll. of Veterinary Medicine *(see Cornell Univ.)*
NYS Sch. of Industrial & Labor Relations *(see Cornell Univ.)*
NYU Med. Ctr. *(see New York Univ.)*
NYU Sch. of Medicine *(see Bellevue Hosp. Ctr.; New York Univ.)*
NYU-Poly *(see Polytechnic Inst. of NYU)*

O

O Street Vocational Sch. *(see Margaret Murray Washington Vocational Sch.)*
O.T. Autry Area Vocational-Tech. Ctr. *(see Autry Techno. Ctr.)*
Oak Forest Hosp. 703
Oak Hills Bible Coll. *(see Oak Hills Christian Coll.)*
Oak Hills Bible Inst. *(see Oak Hills Christian Coll.)*
Oak Hills Christian Coll. 226
Oak Hills Christian Training Sch. *(see Oak Hills Christian Coll.)*
Oak Hills Coll. *(see Oak Hills Christian Coll.)*
Oakbridge Acad. of Arts 355
Oakland Bible Inst. *(see Patten Univ.)*
Oakland City Coll. *(see Oakland City Univ.)*
Oakland City Univ. 154
Oakland Comm. Coll. 215
Oakland Univ. 215
Oaklawn Psychiatric/Comm. Mental Health Ctr. *(see Univ. of Notre Dame)*
Oakton Coll. *(see Oakton Comm. Coll.)*
Oakton Comm. Coll. 139
Oakwood Coll. 775 *(see also Oakwood Univ.)*
Oakwood Inst. *(see Eden Theological Sem.)*
Oakwood Univ. 7, 775
Oberlin Coll. 323
Oberlin Collegiate Inst. *(see Oberlin Coll.)*
Oberlin Conservatory of Music *(see Oberlin Coll.)*
Oblate Sch. of Theology 401
O'Brien's Training Ctr. 663
OC Tech *(see Orangeburg-Calhoun Tech. Coll.)*
Occidental Coll. 54
Occupational Training Services 489
Ocean Coll. *(see Ocean County Coll.)*
Ocean Corporation, The 654
Ocean County Coll. 262
Ocean County Vocational Tech. Sch. 582
Oceaneering Coll. *(see National Polytechnic Coll. of Science)*
Oceanside Coll. of Beauty 489
Oceanside-Carlsbad Jr. Coll. *(see MiraCosta Coll.)*
Ochsner Allied Health Sciences Sch. *(see Ochsner Sch. of Allied Health Sciences; Our Lady of Holy Cross Coll.)*
Ochsner Clinic Foundation *(see Our Lady of Holy Cross Coll.)*
Ochsner Clinic Foundation Sch. of Allied Health Sciences *(see Ochsner Sch. of Allied Health Sciences)*
Ochsner Health Sys. *(see Ochsner Sch. of Allied Health Sciences)*
Ochsner Sch. of Allied Health Sciences 709 *(see also Our Lady of Holy Cross Coll.)*
OCM BOCES *(see Onondaga-Cortland-Madison BOCES)*
Oconaluftee Civilian Conservation Ctr. *(see Oconaluftee Job Corps Ctr.)*
Oconaluftee Job Corps Ctr. 602
Oconaluftee Job Corps Civilian Conservation Ctr. *(see Oconaluftee Job Corps Ctr.)*
Odessa Coll. 401
Oehrlein Sch. of Cosmetology, Inc. 528
Office Techno. Coll. *(see Coll. of Office Techno.)*
Ogden Inst. of Massage Therapy 661
Ogden-Weber Applied Techno. Ctr. *(see Ogden-Weber Applied Techno. Coll.)*
Ogden-Weber Applied Techno. Coll. 414
Ogden-Weber Coll. *(see Ogden-Weber Applied Techno. Coll.)*
Ogeechee Coll. *(see Ogeechee Tech. Coll.)*
Ogeechee Tech. Coll. 118
Ogeechee Tech. Inst. *(see Ogeechee Tech. Coll.)*
Oglala Coll. *(see Oglala Lakota Coll.)*
Oglala Lakota Coll. 380
Oglala Sioux Comm. Coll. *(see Oglala Lakota Coll.)*
Ogle Sch. of Hair Desig—Ft. Worth 655
Ogle Sch. of Hair Desig—Hurst 655
Ogle Sch. of Hair, Skin & Nails 655
Oglethorpe Univ. 118
O'Hara's Beauty Acad. *(see COBA Acad.; Colleen O'Hara's Beauty Acad—Santa Ana)*
Ohio Acad. of Holistic Health, Inc. 610
Ohio Acad.-A Paul Mitchell Partner Sch., The 817
Ohio Acad—Columbus *(see Ohio Acad.-A Paul Mitchell Partner Sch.)*
Ohio Acad—Paul Mitchell Partner Sch., The 610, 789
Ohio Acad.-Paul Mitchell Partner Sch., The 789
Ohio Agricultural & Mechanical Coll. *(see Ohio State Univ.)*

Overland Park Hosp. *(see Overland Park Reg. Med. Ctr.)*
Overland Park Reg. Med. Ctr. 708
Overlook Hosp. 721
Overton Brooks VA Med. Ctr. *(see Overton Brooks Veterans Affairs Med. Ctr.)*
Overton Brooks VAMC *(see Overton Brooks Veterans Affairs Med. Ctr.)*
Overton Brooks Veterans Affairs Med. Ctr., The 709
Owens Campus of the Delaware Tech. & Comm. Coll. *(see Delaware Tech. & Comm. Coll—Jack F. Owens Campus)*
Owens Coll. *(see Owens Comm. Coll.)*
Owens Comm. Coll. 325
Owens Tech. Coll. *(see Owens Comm. Coll.)*
Owensboro Coll. *(see Owensboro Comm. & Tech. Coll.)*
Owensboro Comm. & Tech. Coll. 174
Owensboro Comm. Coll. *(see Owensboro Comm. & Tech. Coll.)*
Owensboro Hosp. *(see Owensboro Mercy Health Sys.)*
Owensboro Jr. Coll. of Bus. *(see Daymar Coll.)*
Owensboro Mercy Health Sys. 708
Owensboro Tech. Coll. *(see Owensboro Comm. & Tech. Coll.)*
Oxford Acad. of Hair Design 811
Oxford Coll. of Arts, Bus. & Techno. 761
Oxford Grad. Sch. 806
Oxman Coll. of San Francisco 489
Oxnard Coll. 55
Ozark Bible Coll. *(see Ozark Christian Coll.)*
Ozark Christian Coll. 242
Ozark Coll. *(see Ozark Christian Coll.)*
Ozark Comm. Coll. *(see Enterprise-Ozark Comm. Coll.)*
Ozarka Coll. 28
Ozarka Tech. Coll. *(see Ozarka Coll.)*
Ozarka Vocational-Tech. Sch. *(see Ozarka Coll.)*
Ozarks Coll. *(see Coll. of the Ozarks; Ozarks Tech. Comm. Coll.)*
Ozarks Comm. Coll. *(see Ozarks Tech. Comm. Coll.)*
Ozarks Tech. Comm. Coll. 242

P

P & A Scholars Beauty Sch., Inc. 558
P & C Lab *(see Pathology & Cytology Laboratories, Inc.)*
P. B. Cosmetology Edu. Centre 582
Pace Coll. *(see Pace Univ.)*
Pace Inst. 355 *(see also Pace Univ.)*
Pace Sch. of Accountancy *(see Pace Univ.)*
Pace Univ. 286
Pace Univ. Sch. of Law *(see Pace Univ. White Plains Campus)*
Pacific Univ. *(see Univ. of the Pacific)*
Pacific Bible Coll. *(see Azusa Pacific Univ.; Point Loma Nazarene Univ.; Warner Pacific Coll.)*
Pacific Bible Inst. *(see Fresno Pacific Univ.)*
Pacific Christian Coll. *(see Hope Int'l. Univ.)*
Pacific Church Divinity Sch. *(see Church Divinity Sch. of the Pacific)*
Pacific Coast Baptist Theological Sem. *(see American Baptist Sem. of the West)*
Pacific Coast Trade Sch. 489
Pacific Coll. 489
Pacific Coll. of Chiropractic *(see Western States Chiropractic Coll.)*
Pacific Coll. of Oriental Medicine 55
Pacific Coll. of Oriental Medicin—New York 286
Pacific Grad. Sch. of Psychology 55
Pacific Health Ministry 700
Pacific Int'l. Acad. 621
Pacific Islands Bible Coll. 122
Pacific Islands VA Healthcare Sys. *(see Veterans Affairs Pacific Islands Healthcare Sys.)*
Pacific Islands Veterans Affairs Healthcare Sys. *(see Veterans Affairs Pacific Islands Healthcare Sys.)*
Pacific Lutheran Coll. *(see Pacific Lutheran Univ.)*
Pacific Lutheran Sem. *(see Pacific Lutheran Theological Sem.)*
Pacific Lutheran Theological Sem. 55
Pacific Lutheran Univ. 436
Pacific Northwest Coll. of Art 340
Pacific Northwest Univ. of Health Sciences Coll. of Osteopathic Medicine 807
Pacific Oaks Coll. 55
Pacific Oriental Coll. of Medicine *(see Pacific Coll. of Oriental Medicine)*
Pacific Sch. of Religion 55
Pacific States Chiropractic Coll. *(see Life Chiropractic Coll. West)*
Pacific States Univ. 55
Pacific Tech. Inst. *(see Lake Coll.)*
Pacific Theological Sem. *(see Pacific Sch. of Religion)*
Pacific Travel Inst. *(see Travel Inst. of the Pacific)*
Pacific Travel Trade Sch—Los Angeles 778
Pacific Union Coll. 55
Pacific Unitarian Sch. for the Ministry *(see Starr King Sch. for the Ministry)*
Pacific Unitarian Sch. of Religion *(see Starr King Sch. for the Ministry)*
Pacific Univ. 340
Pacifica Grad. Inst. 55
Pacifica Inst. *(see Pacifica Grad. Inst.)*
Packard Children's Hosp. *(see Lucile Packard Children's Hosp.)*
Padrick's Univ. of Cosmetology *(see Arnold/Padrick's Univ. of Cosmetology)*
Paducah Area Techno. Ctr. 177
Paducah Coll. *(see Daymar Coll.)*
Paducah Comm. Coll. *(see West Kentucky Comm. & Tech. Coll.)*
Paducah Jr. Coll. *(see West Kentucky Comm. & Tech. Coll.)*
Paducah Tech. Coll. 784 *(see also Daymar Coll.)*
Paier Coll. of Art 80
Pain Mgmnt. Sch. of Pittsburgh *(see Pittsburgh Sch. of Pain Mgmnt.)*
Paine Coll. 118
Paine Inst., The *(see Paine Coll.)*
Palace Beauty Coll. 489
Palladium Tech. Acad. 489
Palau Coll. 459
Palau Comm. Coll. 459
Palm Beach Acad. of Health & Beauty 512
Palm Beach Atlantic Coll. *(see Palm Beach Atlantic Univ.)*
Palm Beach Atlantic Univ. 101
Palm Beach Coll. *(see Palm Beach Comm. Coll.)*
Palm Beach Comm. Coll. 101
Palm Beach Med. Inst. *(see Med. Inst. of Palm Beach)*
Palmer Coll. *(see Midlands Tech. Coll.; Trident Tech. Coll.)*
Palmer Coll. of Chiropractic 161
Palmer Coll. of Chiropracti—West 55
Palmer Sch. & Cure *(see Palmer Coll. of Chiropractic)*
Palmer Theological Sem. 355, 791
Palmetto Health *(see Palmetto Richland Mem. Hosp.)*
Palmetto Health Alliance *(see Palmetto Health Baptist Hosp.)*
Palmetto Health Baptist Hosp. 743
Palmetto Richland Mem. Hosp. 743
Palo Alto Coll. 401
Palo Alto VA Med. Ctr. *(see Veterans Affairs Palo Alto Health Care Sys.)*
Palo Alto VAMC *(see Veterans Affairs Palo Alto Health Care Sys.)*
Palo Alto Veterans Affairs Med. Ctr. *(see Veterans Affairs Palo Alto Health Care Sys.)*
Palo Verde Coll. 55
Palo Verde Comm. Coll. *(see Palo Verde Coll.)*
Palo Verde Jr. Coll. *(see Palo Verde Coll.)*

Pivot Point Int'l. Cosmetology Research Ctr. *(see Pivot Point Int'l. Acad.)*
Pivot Point the Masters 528
PJA Sch., The 358
PJ's Coll. of Cosmetology 538
PJ's Coll. of Cosmetolog—Clarksville 531
PJ's Coll. of Cosmetolog—Richmond 531
Placer Coll. *(see Sierra Coll.)*
Placer Jr. Coll. *(see Sierra Coll.)*
Plainfield Coll. *(see North Central Coll.)*
Planned Parenthood of Colorado *(see Planned Parenthood of the Rocky Mountains)*
Platinum Shear Sch. of Cosmetology 639
Platt Coll. 56, 74, 334, 778 *(see also Fremont Coll.)*
Platt Coll. San Diego 56
Platt Culinary Inst. *(see Platt Coll.)*
Platteville Normal Sch. *(see Univ. of Wisconsin-Platteville)*
Platteville State Teachers Coll. *(see Univ. of Wisconsin-Platteville)*
Plattsburgh Coll. *(see State Univ. of New York Coll. at Plattsburgh)*
Plattsburgh State Univ. *(see State Univ. of New York Coll. at Plattsburgh)*
Play Therapy Inst. *(see Colorado Sch. for Family Therapy)*
Plaza Beauty Sch. 642
Plaza Bus. Inst. *(see Plaza Coll.)*
Plaza Coll. 286
Plaza Sch. of Beauty Culture 639
Plaza Sch. of Techno. 788
Plymouth State Coll. *(see Plymouth State Univ.)*
Plymouth State Univ. 257
PMC Colleges *(see Widener Univ.)*
PMG HealthCom, Inc. *(see Ctr. for Massage & Natural Health)*
Point Loma Coll. *(see Point Loma Nazarene Univ.)*
Point Loma Nazarene Coll. *(see Point Loma Nazarene Univ.)*
Point Loma Nazarene Univ. 56
Point Park Coll. *(see Point Park Univ.)*
Point Park Univ. 358
Polaris Adult Edu. Ctr. *(see Polaris Career Ctr.)*
Polaris Career Ctr. 611
Polaris Vocational Ctr—Adult Edu. *(see Polaris Career Ctr.)*
Politec Inst. 635
Politechnic Inst. of Puerto Rico *(see Inter American Univ. of Puerto Rico San German Campus)*
Polk Coll. *(see Polk Comm. Coll.)*
Polk Comm. Coll. 102
Polk County Public Schools *(see Ridge Career Ctr.)*
Polk County Sch. Sys. *(see Traviss Tech. Ctr.)*
Polk State Coll. *(see Polk Comm. Coll.)*
POLY Languages Inst. 490
Polygraph Inst. *(see Defense Acad. for Credibility Assessment)*
Polytechnic Coll. *(see Texas Wesleyan Univ.)*
Polytechnic Inst. 655
Polytechnic Inst. of America 781 *(see also Centura Inst.)*
Polytechnic Inst. of Brooklyn *(see Polytechnic Inst. of NYU)*
Polytechnic Inst. of New York *(see Polytechnic Inst. of NYU)*
Polytechnic Inst. of NYU 286, 789
Polytechnic of Dubrovnik *(see American Coll. of Mgmnt. & Techno.)*
Polytechnic Univ. 789 *(see also Polytechnic Inst. of NYU)*
Polytechnic Univ. of New York Univ. *(see Polytechnic Inst. of NYU)*
Polytechnic Univ. of NYU *(see Polytechnic Inst. of NYU)*
Polytechnic Univ. of Puerto Rico *(see Universidad Politecnica de Puerto Rico)*
Polytechnic Univ. of the Americas 369 *(see also Universidad Politecnica de Puerto Rico)*
Pomona Coll. 56
Ponca City Beauty Coll. 618
Ponce el Colegio Paramédico *(see Ponce ParaMed. Coll.)*
Ponce ParaMed. Coll. 368
Ponce Sch. of Medicine 368
Pontifica Universidad Catolica de Puerto Ric—Arecibo *(see Pontifical Catholic Univ. of Puerto Ric—Arecibo Campus)*
Pontifica Universidad Catolica de Puerto Ric—Mayaguez *(see Pontifical Catholic Univ. of Puerto Ric—Mayaguez Campus)*
Pontifica Universidad Catolica de Puerto Ric—Ponce *(see Pontifical Catholic Univ. of Puerto Ric—Ponce Campus)*
Pontifical Catholic Univ. of Puerto Ric—Arecibo Campus 368
Pontifical Catholic Univ. of Puerto Ric—Guayama Campus 792
Pontifical Catholic Univ. of Puerto Ric—Mayaguez Campus 368
Pontifical Catholic Univ. of Puerto Ric—Ponce Campus 368
Pontifical Coll. Josephinum 325
Pontifical John Paul II Inst. for Studies on Marriage & Family 802
Pontifical Theological Faculty of the Immaculate Conception *(see Dominican House of Studies)*
Pontificia Universidad Catolica de Chile 764
Pontotoc County Techno. Ctr. *(see Pontotoc Techno. Ctr.)*
Pontotoc Techno. Ctr. 618
Pope John XXIII National Sem. *(see Blessed John XXIII National Sem.)*
Port Huron Hosp. 715
Port Huron Jr. Coll. *(see Saint Clair County Comm. Coll.)*
Port St. Lucie Beauty Acad. 508 *(see also Fort Pierce Beauty Acad.)*
Portage Lakes Career Ctr. 611
Porter Adventist Hosp. 692
Porter & Chester Inst. 499 *(see also Connecticut Sch. of Electronics)*
Porter Mem. Health Sys. *(see Porter Valparaiso Hosp.)*
Porter Sch. of Engineering Design *(see Porter & Chester Inst.)*
Porter Valparaiso Hosp. 705
Porter's Valparaiso Hosp. *(see Porter Valparaiso Hosp.)*
Porterville Coll. 56
Porterville Developmental Ctr. 689
Porterville State Hosp. *(see Porterville Developmental Ctr.)*
Portfolio Ctr. 519
Portia Law Sch. *(see New England Sch. of Law)*
Portland Art Inst. *(see Art Inst. of Portland)*
Portland Coll. *(see Portland Comm. Coll.)*
Portland Coll. of Art *(see Pacific Northwest Coll. of Art)*
Portland Comm. Coll. 340
Portland Comm. Coll. Dist. *(see Portland Comm. Coll.)*
Portland Culinary Inst. *(see Western Culinary Inst.)*
Portland Inst. of Art *(see Art Inst. of Portland)*
Portland Med. Ctr. *(see Providence Portland Med. Ctr.)*
Portland Sch. of Art *(see Maine Coll. of Art)*
Portland Society of Art *(see Maine Coll. of Art)*
Portland State Univ. 340
Portland Univ. *(see Portland State Univ.; Univ. of Portland)*
Portland VA Med. Ctr. *(see Portland Veterans Affairs Med. Ctr.)*
Portland VAMC *(see Portland Veterans Affairs Med. Ctr.)*
Portland Veterans Affairs Med. Ctr. 736
Portsmouth Beauty Sch. of Hair Design 573
Portsmouth Naval Med. Ctr. *(see Naval Med. Ctr. Portsmouth)*

Prof. Health Training Acad. 513 *(see also Taylor Coll.)*
Prof. Inst. of Beauty 490
Prof. Massage Training Ctr. 568
Prof. Practice Mgmnt. Assoc. Inst. *(see Pace Inst.)*
Prof. Psychology Sch. of Chicago *(see Chicago Sch. of Prof. Psychology)*
Prof. Psychology Sch. of Colorado *(see Univ. of the Rockies)*
Prof. Psychology Sch. of Wisconsin *(see Wisconsin Sch. of Prof. Psychology)*
Prof. Sch. of Translation *(see Babel Univ. Prof. Sch. of Translation)*
Prof. Skills Inst. 325
Prof. Tech. Institution 635
Prof. Training Ctr. 102
Prof. Truck Driving Sch. *(see Lebanon County Career Sch.)*
Prof.'s Choice Hair Design Acad. 528
Profile Inst. of Barber-Styling 813
Profile Inst. of Hair Care *(see Profile Inst. of Barber-Styling)*
Progressive Training Ctr.s 812
Promentor Techno. Training *(see Milwaukee Career Coll.)*
Protestant Episcopal Theological Sem. in Virginia 427
Providence Coll. 371
Providence Coll. & Theological Sem. 456
Providence Health & Services *(see Providence Portland Med. Ctr.)*
Providence Health Care *(see Sacred Heart Med. Ctr.)*
Providence Hosp. 744
Providence Hosp. & Med. Ctr.s 715
Providence Hosp. & Med. Ctr—Grad. Med. Edu. *(see Providence Hosp. & Med. Ctr.s)*
Providence Med. Ctr. *(see Kansas City Kansas Comm. Coll.)*
Providence Portland Med. Ctr. 736
Providence Saint Peter Hosp. 752
Providence Services *(see Benefis Healthcar—West Campus)*
Providence St. Peter Hosp. *(see Providence Saint Peter Hosp.)*
Providence Theological Sem. *(see Providence Coll. & Theological Sem.)*
Provincial Health Services Authority *(see British Columbia Cancer Agency—Vancouver Centre)*
Provo Coll. 414
Pruonto's Hair Design Inst. 628
Pryor Beauty Coll. 618
PSC Acad. 629, 792
PSU Worthington-Scranton *(see Pennsylvania State Univ.)*
Psychoanalysis Grad. Sch. of Boston *(see Boston Grad. Sch. of Psychoanalysis)*
Psychological Sciences Inst. *(see Inst. for the Psychological Sciences)*
Psychological Studies Inst. 118
Psychosocial Services *(see Dallas Independent Sch. Dist.)*
Psycho-Structural Balancing *(see Int'l. Prof. Sch. of Bodywork)*
Public Health Foundation Enterprises-WIC Dietetic Internship Program 689
Public Health Service Dept. of Human Health Services *(see Crownpoint Health Care Facility; Kayenta Health Ctr. of the Indian Health Service; Northern Navajo Med. Ctr.)*
Pueblo Coll. *(see Pueblo Comm. Coll.)*
Pueblo Comm. Coll. 75
Pueblo Jr. Coll. *(see Colorado Tech. Univ.; Pueblo Comm. Coll.)*
Pueblo Vocational Comm. Coll. *(see Pueblo Comm. Coll.)*
Puerto Rican Adventist Coll. *(see Universidad Adventista de las Antillas)*
Puerto Rico Barber Coll. 635
Puerto Rico Conservatory of Music *(see Conservatory of Music of Puerto Rico)*
Puerto Rico Dept. of Health 742
Puerto Rico Evangelical Sem. *(see Evangelical Sem. of Puerto Rico)*
Puerto Rico Jr. Coll. *(see Universidad del Este; Universidad del Turabo; Universidad Metropolitana)*
Puerto Rico Sch. of Plastic Arts *(see Escuela de Artes Plasticas de Puerto Rico)*
Puerto Rico Techno. & Commercial Coll. *(see Colegio Tecnologico y Comercial de Puerto Rico)*
Puerto Rico Theological Sem. *(see Nyack Coll.)*
Puerto Rico Univ. at Utuado *(see Univ. of Puerto Rico at Utuado)*
Puerto Rico Univ—Aguadilla *(see Univ. of Puerto Rico at Aguadilla)*
Puerto Rico Univ—Arecibo *(see Univ. of Puerto Rico at Arecibo)*
Puerto Rico Univ—Bayamon *(see Univ. of Puerto Rico at Bayamon)*
Puerto Rico Univ—Carolina *(see Univ. of Puerto Rico at Carolina)*
Puerto Rico Univ—Cayey *(see Univ. of Puerto Rico at Cayey)*
Puerto Rico Univ—Humacao *(see Univ. of Puerto Rico at Humacao)*
Puerto Rico Univ—Mayaguez *(see Univ. of Puerto Rico at Mayaguez)*
Puerto Rico Univ—Med. Sciences Campus *(see Univ. of Puerto Ric—Med. Sciences Campus)*
Puerto Rico Univ—Ponce *(see Univ. of Puerto Rico at Ponce)*
Puerto Rico Univ—Rio Piedras *(see Univ. of Puerto Rico at Rio Piedras)*
Puget Sound Christian Coll. 796
Puget Sound Inst. of Techno. *(see Everest Coll—Bremerton)*
Puget Sound Univ. *(see Univ. of Puget Sound)*
Pulaski Area Vocational-Tech. Sch. *(see Tennessee Techno. Ctr. at Pulaski)*
Pulaski Area Vo-Tech Sch. *(see Tennessee Techno. Ctr. at Pulaski)*
Pulaski Coll. *(see Pulaski Tech. Coll.)*
Pulaski Tech *(see Pulaski Tech. Coll.)*
Pulaski Tech. Coll. 28
Pulaski Vocational-Tech. Sch. *(see Tennessee Techno. Ctr. at Pulaski)*
Pulaski Vo-Tech Sch. *(see Tennessee Techno. Ctr. at Pulaski)*
Punxy Beauty Sch. of Cosmetology Arts & Science 629
Purchase Coll. *(see State Univ. of New York Coll. at Purchase)*
Purdue North Central *(see Purdue Univ. North Central)*
Purdue Univ. 154
Purdue Univ. Calumet 154
Purdue Univ. Fort Wayne *(see Indiana Univ.-Purdue Univ. Fort Wayne)*
Purdue Univ. Indianapolis *(see Indiana Univ.-Purdue Univ. Indianapolis)*
Purdue Univ. North Central 154
Purdue Univ. Sch. of Techno. at New Albany *(see Purdue Univ. Coll. of Techno. at New Albany)*
Putnam Career & Tech. Ctr. 673
Putnam County Career & Tech. Ctr. *(see Putnam Career & Tech. Ctr.)*
Puyallup General Hosp. *(see Good Samaritan Hosp.)*
PVUSD Nutrition & Wellness Dept. *(see Paradise Valley Unified Sch. Dist.)*
Pyramid Beauty Sch. 642
Pyramid Career Inst. 528

Q

Qe2 Systems, Inc. *(see Laurus Coll.)*
Quaker City Inst. of Aviation *(see Aviation Inst. of Maint.)*
Quality Coll. of Culinary Careers 778
Quality Systems Mgmnt. Grad. Sch. *(see National Grad. Sch.)*
Quality Tech. & Beauty Coll. 636, 792
Quantum Helicopters 468

R

Roseburg VA Med. Ctr. *(see Roseburg Veterans Affairs Med. Ctr.)*
Roseburg VAMC *(see Roseburg Veterans Affairs Med. Ctr.)*
Roseburg Veterans Affairs Med. Ctr. 736
Rosedale Bible Coll. 326
Rosedale Bible Inst. *(see Rosedale Bible Coll.)*
Rosedale Coll. *(see Rosedale Bible Coll.)*
Rosedale Tech *(see Rosedale Tech. Inst.)*
Rosedale Tech. Inst. 359
Rose-Hulman Inst. of Techno. 154
Rosel Sch. of Cosmetology 528
Rosemead Beauty Sch., Inc. 490
Rosemead Coll. of English 490
Rosemont Coll. 359
Ross Bus. Inst. 778
Ross Med. Edu. Ctr. 520, 558
Ross Med. Inst. *(see Ross Med. Edu. Ctr.)*
Ross Tech. Inst. *(see Ross Med. Edu. Ctr.)*
Rosslyn Acad. of Cosmetology *(see Rosslyn Training Acad. of Cosmetology, Inc.)*
Rosslyn Training Acad. of Cosmetology, Inc. 636
Rosston Sch. *(see WyoTec—Long Beach)*
Roswell Comm. Coll. *(see Eastern New Mexico Univ—Roswell)*
Rotterdam Sch. of Mgmnt. *(see Erasmus Univ. Rotterdam)*
Roudebush VA Med. Ctr. *(see Richard L. Roudebush Veterans Affairs Med. Ctr.)*
Roudebush Veterans Affairs Med. Ctr. *(see Richard L. Roudebush Veterans Affairs Med. Ctr.)*
Rowan Coll. of New Jersey *(see Rowan Univ.)*
Rowan Tech. Coll. *(see Maysville Comm. & Tech. Coll.; Rowan-Cabarrus Comm. Coll.)*
Rowan Tech. Coll—Eastern Kentucky Campus *(see Maysville Comm. & Tech. Coll.)*
Rowan Tech. Inst. *(see Rowan-Cabarrus Comm. Coll.)*
Rowan Univ. 263
Rowan-Cabarrus Coll. *(see Rowan-Cabarrus Comm. Coll.)*
Rowan-Cabarrus Comm. Coll. 307
Roxborough Hosp. *(see Roxborough Mem. Hosp.)*
Roxborough Mem. Hosp. 741
Roxbury Coll. *(see Roxbury Comm. Coll.)*
Roxbury Comm. Coll. 204
Royal Beauty Careers 655, 793
Royal Coll. of Beauty *(see Royale Coll. of Beauty)*
Royal Commission for Jubail & Yanbu *(see Yanbu Industrial Coll.)*
Royal Commission Jubail Human Resources Development Inst. *(see Jubail Industrial Coll.)*
Royal Tech. Coll. *(see Univ. of Strathclyde)*
Royal Univ. of America *(see Dongguk Royal Univ.)*
Royal Veterinary Coll. *(see Univ. of London—Royal Veterinary Coll.)*
Royale Beauty Coll. *(see Royale Coll. of Beauty)*
Royale Coll. of Beauty 490
Roy's Beauty Acad. *(see Hair Design Sch.)*
Roy's of Louisville Beauty Acad. *(see Hair Design Sch.)*
RSHT Training Ctr. 427, 795
RTP Hispanic American Coll. 636
Rudae's Sch. of Beauty Culture 531
Rudy & Kelly Acad. of Hair & Nails 666
Rumsey Tech. Inst. *(see James Rumsey Tech. Inst.)*
Rush Med. Ctr. *(see Rush Univ.)*
Rush Univ. 141
Rush-Presbyterian-Saint Luke's Med. Ctr. 703
Rusk Inst. of Rehabilitation Medicine 284
Russell Sage Coll. 288 *(see also Sage Colleges)*
Russelville Area Techno. Ctr. *(see Bowling Green Tech. Coll.)*
Russian & East European Partnerships, Inc. 598
Rust Coll. 233
Rust Univ. *(see Rust Coll.)*
Rutersville Coll. *(see Southwestern Univ.)*
Rutgers Coll. *(see Rutgers, The State Univ. of New Jersey New Brunswick Campus)*
Rutgers Univ. *(see Rutgers, The State Univ. of New Jersey Camden Campus; Rutgers, The State Univ. of New Jersey New Brunswick Campus; Rutgers, The State Univ. of New Jersey Newark Campus)*
Rutgers, The State Univ. of New Jersey Camden Campus 263
Rutgers, The State Univ. of New Jersey New Brunswick Campus 263
Rutgers, The State Univ. of New Jersey Newark Campus 263
Rutger—Camden *(see Rutgers, The State Univ. of New Jersey Camden Campus)*
Rutger—New Brunswick *(see Rutgers, The State Univ. of New Jersey New Brunswick Campus)*
Rutger—Newark *(see Rutgers, The State Univ. of New Jersey Newark Campus)*
Rutherford County Guidance Ctr. *(see Guidance Ctr.)*
Rutherford County Hosp. *(see Rutherford Hosp., Inc.)*
Rutherford Hosp., Inc. 731
Rutland Reg. Med. Ctr. *(see New England Sch. of Radiologic Techno.)*
Ryder Hosp. *(see Ryder Mem. Hosp., Inc.)*
Ryder Mem. Hosp., Inc. 743
Ryerson Inst. of Techno. *(see Ryerson Univ.)*
Ryerson Polytechnic Univ. 797 *(see also Ryerson Univ.)*
Ryerson PolyTech. Inst. *(see Ryerson Univ.)*
Ryerson Univ. 761, 797

S

S.A. Owen Jr. Coll. *(see LeMoyne-Owen Coll.)*
S.C. Johnson Grad. Sch. of Mgmnt. *(see Cornell Univ.)*
S.D. Bishop State Jr. Coll. *(see Bishop State Comm. Coll.)*
S.J. Grant & Associates, Inc. 528
SAA Coll. *(see Sch. of Advertising Art)*
SABER 514
Sac City Coll. *(see Sacramento City Coll.)*
Sac State *(see California State Univ., Sacramento)*
Sacramento City Coll. 57
Sacramento State Coll. *(see California State Univ., Sacramento)*
Sacred Heart Coll. *(see Belmont Abbey Coll.; Newman Univ.; Regis Univ.)*
Sacred Heart Hosp. 741 *(see also Avera Sacred Heart Hosp.)*
Sacred Heart Major Sem. 215
Sacred Heart Med. Ctr. 736, 752 *(see also Gonzaga Univ.)*
Sacred Heart Monastery *(see Sacred Heart Sch. of Theology)*
Sacred Heart Sch. of Theology 449
Sacred Heart Sem. *(see Sacred Heart Major Sem.)*
Sacred Heart Univ. 80 *(see also Univ. of the Sacred Heart)*
Saddleback Coll. 57
Saddleback Coll—North Campus *(see Irvine Valley Coll.)*
SAE Inst. of Techno. 598, 643

Southern Nevada Univ. *(see Univ. of Southern Nevada)*
Southern Nevada Univ. of Cosmetology 787
Southern New England Sch. of Law 204
Southern New Hampshire Univ. 258
Southern New Jersey Dale Carnegie Training *(see Success Unlimited, Inc.)*
Southern New Jersey Tech. Sch. 583
Southern Normal Sch. of Bowling Green *(see Western Kentucky Univ.)*
Southern Ohio Coll. *(see Brown Mackie Coll—Cincinnati)*
Southern Ohio Coll—Findlay *(see Brown Mackie Coll—Findlay)*
Southern Ohio Coll—Northern Kentucky *(see Brown Mackie Coll—Cincinnati)*
Southern Oklahoma Techno. Ctr. 735
Southern Optometry Coll. *(see Southern Coll. of Optometry)*
Southern Oregon State Coll. *(see Southern Oregon Univ.)*
Southern Oregon Univ. 341
Southern Polytech *(see Southern Polytechnic State Univ.)*
Southern Polytechnic State Univ. 120
Southern Queensland Univ. *(see Univ. of Southern Queensland)*
Southern Reg. Health Sys. *(see Southern Reg. Med. Ctr.)*
Southern Reg. Med. Ctr. 699
Southern Sch. of Beauty 618
Southern Sem. Coll. *(see Southern Virginia Univ.)*
Southern Sem. Jr. Coll. *(see Southern Virginia Univ.)*
Southern State Coll. *(see Southern State Comm. Coll.)*
Southern State Comm. Coll. 326
Southern State General & Tech. Coll. *(see Southern State Comm. Coll.)*
Southern Tech. Ctr. 781
Southern Tech. Coll. 781 *(see also Remington Coll—Lafayette)*
Southern Tech. Inst. 514, 781 *(see also Southern Polytechnic State Univ.; Southern Tech. Coll.)*
Southern Texas Univ. *(see Texas Southern Univ.)*
Southern Training Sch. *(see Southern Adventist Univ.)*
Southern Union Coll. *(see Southern Union State Comm. Coll.)*
Southern Union Comm. Coll. *(see Southern Union State Comm. Coll.)*
Southern Union State Comm. Coll. 8
Southern Union State Jr. Coll. *(see Southern Union State Comm. Coll.)*
Southern Univ. *(see Birmingham-Southern Coll.)*
Southern Univ. & A&M Coll. *(see Southern Univ. & Agricultural & Mechanical Coll.)*
Southern Univ. & Agricultural & Mechanical Coll. 184
Southern Univ. & Agricultural & Mechanical Coll. at Baton Rouge *(see Southern Univ. & Agricultural & Mechanical Coll.)*
Southern Univ. at New Orleans 184
Southern Univ. at Shreveport 185
Southern Univ. at Shreveport-Bossier City *(see Southern Univ. at Shreveport)*
Southern Univ. Law Ctr. *(see Southern Univ. & Agricultural & Mechanical Coll.)*
Southern Utah State Coll. *(see Southern Utah Univ.)*
Southern Utah Univ. 415
Southern Vermont Coll. 418
Southern Virginia Coll. for Women *(see Southern Virginia Univ.)*
Southern Virginia Univ. 428
Southern Wesleyan Univ. 377
Southern West Virginia Comm. & Tech. Coll. 442
Southern West Virginia Comm. Coll. *(see Southern West Virginia Comm. & Tech. Coll.)*
Southlake Ctr. for Mental Health 706
Southside Dist. Hosp. *(see Banner Desert Med. Ctr.)*
Southside Reg. Med. Ctr. 751
Southside Virginia Coll. *(see Southside Virginia Comm. Coll.)*
Southside Virginia Comm. Coll. 428
Southwest Acupuncture Coll. 268
Southwest Associated Univ. *(see Tsinghua Univ.)*
Southwest Baptist Coll. *(see Southwest Baptist Univ.)*
Southwest Baptist Univ. 244
Southwest Career Inst. 657
Southwest Ctr. for Advanced Studies *(see Univ. of Texas at Dallas)*
Southwest Coll. *(see City Colleges of Chicag—Richard J. Daley Coll.; Los Angeles Southwest Coll.; Southwest Applied Techno. Coll.; Univ. of the Southwest)*
Southwest Coll. of Naturopathic Medicine & Health Sciences 22
SouthWest Collegiate Inst. for the Deaf *(see Howard Coll.)*
Southwest Colorado Area Vocational-Tech. Sch. *(see San Juan Basin Tech. Coll.)*
Southwest Episcopal Theological Sem. *(see Episcopal Theological Sem. of the Southwest)*
Southwest Florida Coll. 105
Southwest Florida Coll. of Bus. *(see Southwest Florida Coll.)*
Southwest Georgia Tech. Coll. 120
Southwest Georgia Tech. Inst. *(see Southwest Georgia Tech. Coll.)*
Southwest Health Career Inst., Inc. 788
Southwest Hosp. of Houston *(see Mem. Hermann Southwest Hosp.)*
Southwest Inst. of Healing Arts 468
Southwest Inst. of Myotherapy *(see Southwest Inst. of Healing Arts)*
Southwest Inst. of Techno. 403
Southwest Kansas Conference Coll. *(see Southwestern Coll.)*
Southwest Kansas Tech. Sch. 535
Southwest Los Angeles Coll. *(see Los Angeles Southwest Coll.)*
Southwest Minnesota State Univ. 228
Southwest Mississippi Coll. *(see Southwest Mississippi Comm. Coll.)*
Southwest Mississippi Comm. Coll. 233
Southwest Missouri State Coll. *(see Missouri State Univ.)*
Southwest Missouri State Teachers Coll. *(see Missouri State Univ.)*
Southwest Missouri State Univ. 786 *(see also Missouri State Univ.)*
Southwest Missouri State Univ—West Plains 787
Southwest Naturpathic Coll. *(see Southwest Coll. of Naturopathic Medicine & Health Sciences)*
Southwest Sch. of Bus. & Tech. Careers 794
Southwest Sch. of Bus. & Tech. Careers 657
Southwest Sch. of Electronics *(see Southwest Inst. of Techno.)*
Southwest State Tech. Coll. *(see Bishop State Comm. Coll.)*
Southwest State Univ. *(see Southwest Minnesota State Univ.)*
Southwest Tech *(see Southwest Wisconsin Tech. Coll.)*
Southwest Tech. Inst. *(see Ivy Tech Comm. Coll—Southwest; Southern Arkansas Univ—Tech)*
Southwest Tennessee Coll. *(see Southwest Tennessee Comm. Coll.)*
Southwest Tennessee Comm. Coll. 389
Southwest Texas Coll. *(see Southwest Texas Jr. Coll.)*

St. Luke's Med. Ctr. *(see Aurora Saint Luke's Med. Ctr.; HealthCare Ctr. at Saint Luke's Pointe; Rush-Presbyterian-Saint Luke's Med. Ctr.)*
St. Luke's Mem. Hosp. Ctr. *(see Faxton-St. Luke's Healthcare)*
St. Luke's Reg. Med. Ctr. *(see Saint Luke's Reg. Med. Ctr.)*
St. Margaret Mercy Healthcare Ctr. *(see Saint Margaret Mercy Healthcare Ctr.)*
St. Margaret Sch. of Nursing *(see UPMC Saint Margaret Hosp.)*
St. Mark's Home & Hosp. *(see Butterworth Hosp.)*
St. Mark's Hosp. *(see Saint Mark's Hosp.)*
St. Martin's Coll. *(see Saint Martin's Univ.)*
St. Martin's Univ. *(see Saint Martin's Univ.)*
St. Mary Acad. *(see Marygrove Coll.)*
St. Mary Coll. *(see Coll. of Saint Mary; Marygrove Coll.; Univ. of Saint Mary)*
St. Mary Grad. Sch. of Theology *(see Saint Mary Sem. & Grad. Sch. of Theology)*
St. Mary Hosp. *(see Reg. West Med. Ctr.; Saints Mary & Elizabeth Med. Ctr.)*
St. Mary of Nazareth Hosp. Ctr. *(see Saints Mary & Elizabeth Med. Ctr.)*
St. Mary of the Lake Univ. *(see Univ. of Saint Mary of the Lake Mundelein Sem.)*
St. Mary Sem. & Grad. Sch. of Theology *(see Saint Mary Sem. & Grad. Sch. of Theology)*
St. Mary-Corwin Med. Ctr. *(see Saint Mary-Corwin Med. Ctr.)*
St. Mary-of-the-Woods Coll. *(see Saint Mary-of-the-Woods Coll.)*
St. Mary's Acad. *(see Clarke Coll.)*
St. Mary's Acad. & Coll. *(see Marylhurst Univ.)*
St. Mary's Bay Area CPE Ctr. *(see Saint Mary's Med. Ctr.)*
St. Mary's Coll. *(see Belmont Abbey Coll.)*
St. Mary's Coll. *(see Madonna Univ. Orchard Lake Ctr.; Saint Mary's Coll.; Univ. of Saint Mary of the Lake Mundelein Sem.)*
St. Mary's Coll. of Ave Maria Univ. *(see Madonna Univ. Orchard Lake Ctr.)*
St. Mary's Coll. of California *(see Saint Mary's Coll. of California)*
St. Mary's Coll. of Madonna Univ. *(see Madonna Univ. Orchard Lake Ctr.)*
St. Mary's Coll. of Maryland *(see Saint Mary's Coll. of Maryland)*
St. Mary's Coll. of Minnesota *(see Saint Mary's Univ. of Minnesota)*
St. Mary's Female Sem. *(see Saint Mary's Coll. of Maryland)*
St. Mary's Hosp. *(see Inst. of Allied Med. Professions; Marquette General Health Sys.; Mayo Sch. of Health Sciences; Saint Mary-Corwin Med. Ctr.; Saint Mary's Hosp.; Saint Mary's Hosp.; Saint Mary's Med. Ctr.; United Hosp. Ctr.)*
St. Mary's Hosp. of Franciscan Sisters *(see All Saints Healthcar—St. Mary's Campus)*
St. Mary's Hosp. Sch. of Nursing *(see Saint Mary's Med. Ctr.)*
St. Mary's Jr. Coll. *(see Coll. of Saint Catherine)*
St. Mary's Med. Ctr. *(see All Saints Healthcar—St. Mary's Campus; Saint Mary's Med. Ctr.)*
St. Mary's Sch. of Nursing *(see Coll. of Saint Catherine)*
St. Mary's Sem. & Univ. *(see Saint Mary's Sem. & Univ.)*
St. Mary's Univ. *(see Saint Mary's Sem. & Univ.; Saint Mary's Univ.)*
St. Mary's Univ. of Minnesota *(see Saint Mary's Univ. of Minnesota)*
St. Meinrad Sch. of Theology *(see Saint Meinrad Sch. of Theology)*
St. Michael Hosp. *(see Saint Michael Hosp.)*
St. Michael's Coll. *(see Coll. of Santa Fe; Saint Michael's Coll.; Univ. of St. Michael's Coll.)*
St. Michael's Inst. *(see Saint Michael's Coll.)*
St. Norbert Coll. *(see Saint Norbert Coll.)*
St. Olaf Coll. *(see Saint Olaf Coll.)*
St. Patrick's Sem. & Univ. *(see Saint Patrick's Sem. & Univ.)*
St. Patrick's Univ. *(see Saint Patrick's Sem. & Univ.)*
St. Paul Bible Coll. *(see Crown Coll.)*
St. Paul Bible Inst. *(see Crown Coll.)*
St. Paul Coll. *(see Saint Paul Coll—A Comm. & Tech. Coll.)*
St. Paul Coll. of Law *(see William Mitchell Coll. of Law)*
St. Paul Luther Sem. *(see Wartburg Theological Sem.)*
St. Paul Sch. of Theology *(see Saint Paul Sch. of Theology)*
St. Paul Sem. Sch. of Divinity *(see Univ. of Saint Thomas)*
St. Paul Tech. Coll. *(see Saint Paul Coll—A Comm. & Tech. Coll.)*
St. Paul's Coll. *(see Saint Paul's Coll.)*
St. Peter Hosp. *(see Providence Saint Peter Hosp.)*
St. Peter's Coll. *(see Saint Peter's Coll.)*
St. Peter's Health Care Services *(see Saint Peter's Hosp.)*
St. Peter's Hosp. *(see Saint Peter's Hosp.)*
St. Peter's Sem. *(see Saint Peter's Sem.)*
St. Petersburg Coll. *(see Saint Petersburg Coll.)*
St. Petersburg Jr. Coll. *(see Saint Petersburg Coll.)*
St. Petersburg Sem. *(see Saint Petersburg Theological Sem.)*
St. Petersburg State Coll. *(see Saint Petersburg Coll.)*
St. Petersburg Theological Sem. *(see Saint Petersburg Theological Sem.)*
St. Petersburg Vocational Tech. Inst. *(see Pinellas Tech. Edu. Ctr.)*
St. Philip's Coll. *(see Saint Philip's Coll.)*
St. Procopius Coll. *(see Benedictine Univ.)*
St. Raphael Hosp. *(see Hosp. of Saint Raphael)*
St. Raphael Sem. *(see Loras Coll.)*
St. Rose Coll. *(see Coll. of Saint Rose)*
St. Rose Jr. Coll. *(see Viterbo Univ.)*
St. Rose Normal Sch. *(see Viterbo Univ.)*
St. Scholastica Coll. *(see Coll. of Saint Scholastica)*
St. Stephen's Coll. *(see Bard Coll.)*
St. Teresa Coll. *(see Avila Univ.)*
St. Thomas Aquinas Coll. *(see Saint Thomas Aquinas Coll.)*
St. Thomas More Coll. *(see Coll. of Saint Thomas Moore; Thomas More Coll.)*
St. Thomas More Inst. *(see Coll. of Saint Thomas Moore)*
St. Thomas Univ. *(see Saint Thomas Univ.; Univ. of Saint Thomas)*
St. Tikhon of Zadonsk *(see Saint Tikhon's Orthodox Theological Sem.)*
St. Tikhon's Orthodox Theological Sem. *(see Saint Tikhon's Orthodox Theological Sem.)*
St. Vincent Archabbey & Coll. *(see Saint Vincent Coll. & Sem.)*
St. Vincent Catholic Med. Ctr.s of New York *(see Saint Vincent Catholic Med. Ctr.s of New York)*
St. Vincent Catholic Med. Ctr.s Staten Island *(see Saint Vincent Catholic Med. Ctr.s of New Yor—Staten Island)*
St. Vincent Charity Hosp. *(see Saint Vincent Charity Hosp.)*

SUNY Dehli Coll. *(see State Univ. of New York Coll. of Techno. at Delhi)*
SUNY Downstate Med. Ctr. *(see State Univ. of New York Health Science Ctr. at Brooklyn)*
SUNY Dutchess Comm. Coll. *(see Dutchess Comm. Coll.)*
SUNY Empire State Coll. *(see State Univ. of New York Empire State Coll.)*
SUNY Environmental Science & Forestry Coll. *(see State Univ. of New York Coll. of Environmental Science & Forestry)*
SUNY Erie Comm. Coll. *(see Erie Comm. Coll.)*
SUNY ESF *(see State Univ. of New York Coll. of Environmental Science & Forestry)*
SUNY Farmingdale *(see Farmingdale State Coll.)*
SUNY Fashion Inst. of Techno. *(see Fashion Inst. of Techno.)*
SUNY Fulton-Montgomery Comm. Coll. *(see Fulton-Montgomery Comm. Coll.)*
SUNY Genesee *(see Genesee Comm. Coll.)*
SUNY Genesee Comm. Coll. *(see Genesee Comm. Coll.)*
SUNY Genesseo *(see State Univ. of New York Coll. at Geneseo)*
SUNY Health Science Ctr. at Brooklyn *(see State Univ. of New York Health Science Ctr. at Brooklyn)*
SUNY Herkimer County Comm. Coll. *(see Herkimer County Comm. Coll.)*
SUNY Hudson Valley Comm. Coll. *(see Hudson Valley Comm. Coll.)*
SUNY Instittue of Techno. at Utica/Rome *(see State Univ. of New York Inst. of Techno. at Utica/Rome)*
SUNY IT *(see State Univ. of New York Inst. of Techno. at Utica/Rome)*
SUNY Jamestown Comm. Coll. *(see Jamestown Comm. Coll.)*
SUNY Jefferson Comm. Coll. *(see Jefferson Comm. Coll.)*
SUNY Maritime Coll. *(see State Univ. of New York Maritime Coll.)*
SUNY Mohawk Valley Comm. Coll. *(see Mohawk Valley Comm. Coll.)*
SUNY Nassau Comm. Coll. *(see Nassau Comm. Coll.)*
SUNY New Paltz *(see State Univ. of New York at New Paltz)*
SUNY New York State Coll. of Ceramics at Alfred Univ. *(see New York State Coll. of Ceramics at Alfred Univ.)*
SUNY Niagara County Comm. Coll. *(see Niagara County Comm. Coll.)*
SUNY North Country Comm. Coll. *(see North Country Comm. Coll.)*
SUNY Oneonta *(see State Univ. of New York Coll. at Oneonta)*
SUNY Onondaga Comm. Coll. *(see Onondaga Comm. Coll.)*
SUNY Optometry Coll. *(see State Univ. of New York Coll. of Optometry)*
SUNY Orange County Comm. Coll. *(see Orange County Comm. Coll.)*
SUNY Oswego *(see State Univ. of New York Coll. at Oswego)*
SUNY Plattsburgh *(see State Univ. of New York Coll. at Plattsburgh)*
SUNY Purchase *(see State Univ. of New York Coll. at Purchase)*
SUNY Rockland Comm. Coll. *(see State Univ. of New York Rockland Comm. Coll.)*
SUNY Schenectady County Comm. Coll. *(see Schenectady County Comm. Coll.)*
SUNY State Coll. of Optometry *(see State Univ. of New York Coll. of Optometry)*
SUNY Suffolk *(see Suffolk County Comm. Coll.)*
SUNY Tompkins Cortland Comm. Coll. *(see Tompkins Cortland Comm. Coll.)*
SUNY Ulster *(see Ulster County Comm. Coll.)*
SUNY Upstate Med. Univ. *(see State Univ. of New York Upstate Med. Univ.)*
SUNY Westchester Comm. Coll. *(see Westchester Comm. Coll.)*
Suomi Coll. *(see Finlandia Univ.)*
Suomi Theological Sem. *(see Lutheran Sch. of Theology at Chicago)*
Superior Career Inst. *(see Int'l. Sch. of Health & Beauty)*
Superior Normal Sch. *(see Univ. of Wisconsin-Superior)*
Superior Sch. of Hairstyling 783 *(see also B-Street Design Sch. of Int'l. Hair Styling)*
Superior State Teachers Coll. *(see Univ. of Wisconsin-Superior)*
Surrey Univ. *(see Univ. of Surrey)*
Surry Coll. *(see Surry Comm. Coll.)*
Surry Comm. Coll. 308
Susquehanna Career & Techno. Ctr. 629
Susquehanna Career Ctr. *(see Susquehanna Career & Techno. Ctr.)*
Susquehanna Techno. Ctr. *(see Susquehanna Career & Techno. Ctr.)*
Susquehanna Univ. 360
Sussex Coll. *(see Sussex County Comm. Coll.)*
Sussex Comm. Coll. *(see Sussex County Comm. Coll.)*
Sussex County Coll. *(see Sussex County Comm. Coll.)*
Sussex County Comm. Coll. 264
Sutter General Hosp. *(see Sutter Med. Ctr.)*
Sutter Health Network *(see Alta Bates Summit Med. Ctr.)*
Sutter Med. Ctr. 690
Suwanee-Hamilton Tech. Ctr. 515
Swainsboro Coll. *(see Swainsboro Tech. Coll.)*
Swainsboro Tech. Coll. 803
Swainsboro Tech. Inst. *(see Swainsboro Tech. Coll.)*
Swanson's Driving Schools, Inc. *(see All-State Career Sch.)*
Swarthmore Coll. 360
Swayne Sch. *(see Talladega Coll.)*
Swedish American Hosp. 704
Swedish Bible Inst. of Chicago *(see Trinity Int'l. Univ.)*
Swedish Health Services *(see Swedish Med. Ctr.)*
Swedish Inst.: Sch. of Acupuncture & Massage Therapy, The 294
Swedish Med. Ctr. 692, 752 *(see also HealthONE Emergency Med. Services)*
Swedish Sch. of Acupuncture & Massage Therapy *(see Swedish Inst.: Sch. of Acupuncture & Massage Therapy)*
SwedishAmerican Health Sys. *(see Swedish American Hosp.)*
Sweet Briar Coll. 428
Swiss Hosp.ity Inst. "Cesar Ritz" *(see Clemens Coll.)*
Swiss Hotel Assoc. Hotel Mgmnt. Sch. "Les Roches" *(see "Les Roches" Sch. of Hotel Mgmnt.)*
Swiss Mgmnt. Ctr. 769
SWOSU at Sayre *(see Southwestern Oklahoma State Univ.)*
Sydney Univ. *(see Univ. of Sydney)*
Sylacauga Sch. of Nursing *(see Central Alabama Comm. Coll.)*
Sylvia's Beauty Sch. *(see Sylvia's Int'l. Sch. of Beauty)*
Sylvia's Int'l. Sch. of Beauty 658
Sylvia's Sch. of Beauty *(see Sylvia's Int'l. Sch. of Beauty)*
Synergy Healing Arts Ctr. & Massage Sch. 630
Synergy Therapeutic Massage Ctr. & Training Sch. *(see Synergy Healing Arts Ctr. & Massage Sch.)*
Syracuse Hosp. for Women & Children *(see Crouse Hosp.)*

T

Tech. Coll. of Milwaukee *(see Milwaukee Area Tech. Coll.)*
Tech. Coll. of Moultrie *(see Moultrie Tech. Coll.)*
Tech. Coll. of North Central Kansas *(see North Central Kansas Tech. Coll.)*
Tech. Coll. of Northeast Kansas *(see Highland Comm. Coll.; Northeast Kansas Tech. Ctr. of Highland Comm. Coll.)*
Tech. Coll. of Northeast Wisconsin *(see Northeast Wisconsin Tech. Coll.)*
Tech. Coll. of Northwest Kansas *(see Northwest Kansas Tech. Coll.)*
Tech. Coll. of Ohio *(see Ohio Tech. Coll.)*
Tech. Coll. of Paducah *(see Daymar Coll.)*
Tech. Coll. of Savannah *(see Savannah Tech. Coll.)*
Tech. Coll. of South Georgia *(see South Georgia Tech. Coll.)*
Tech. Coll. of Southwest Georgia *(see Southwest Georgia Tech. Coll.)*
Tech. Coll. of Southwest Wisconsin *(see Southwest Wisconsin Tech. Coll.)*
Tech. Coll. of Spartanburg *(see Spartanburg Comm. Coll.)*
Tech. Coll. of the Greater Madison Area *(see Madison Area Tech. Coll.)*
Tech. Coll. of the Lowcountry 377
Tech. Coll. of the San Juan Basin *(see San Juan Basin Tech. Coll.)*
Tech. Coll. of Vermont *(see Vermont Tech. Coll.)*
Tech. Coll. of Waukesha County *(see Waukesha County Tech. Coll.)*
Tech. Coll. of West Georgia *(see West Georgia Tech. Coll.)*
Tech. Coll. of Western Wisconsin *(see Western Tech. Coll.)*
Tech. Coll. of York *(see York Tech. Coll.)*
Tech. Edu. Ctr. of Mercer County *(see Mercer County Tech. Edu. Ctr.)*
Tech. Edu. Ctr—Osceola 515
Tech. Edu. Coll. 495
Tech. Inst. in Chamblee *(see Southern Polytechnic State Univ.)*
Tech. Inst. of Alamance *(see Alamance Comm. Coll.)*
Tech. Inst. of Camden County 722
Tech. Inst. of Cape May County *(see Cape May County Tech. Inst.)*
Tech. Inst. of Cosmetology Arts & Sciences 618
Tech. Inst. of Mitchell *(see Mitchell Tech. Inst.)*
Tech. Inst. of New England *(see Lincoln Tech. Inst—New Britain)*
Tech. Inst. of New Hampshire *(see NHTI, Concord's Comm. Coll.)*
Tech. Inst. of Pittsburgh *(see Pittsburgh Tech. Inst.)*
Tech. Inst. of Texas County *(see Texas County Tech. Inst.)*
Tech. Inst. of Wichita *(see Wichita Tech. Inst.)*
Tech. Inst. of York *(see YTI Career Inst.)*
Tech. Learning Ctr.s, Inc. 503
Tech. Metropolitan Sch. *(see Colegio Tecnico Metropolitano)*
Tech. Sch. of Southern New Jersey *(see Southern New Jersey Tech. Sch.)*
Tech. Sch. of Southwest Kansas *(see Southwest Kansas Tech. Sch.)*
Tech. Schools of Bergen County *(see Bergen County Tech. Schools)*
Tech. Skills Ctr. of Coachella Valley *(see Mayfield Coll.)*
Tech. Trades Inst. *(see Intellitec Coll—Colorado Springs; Intellitec Coll—Grand Junction)*
Tech. Univ. of Colorado *(see Colorado Tech. Univ.)*
Tech. Vocational Inst. of Albuquerque *(see Central New Mexico Comm. Coll.)*
Technological Coll. of San Juan 793 *(see also Univ. Coll. of San Juan)*
Technological Coll. of the Municipality of San Juan 793 *(see Univ. Coll. of San Juan)*
Technológico de Monterrey *(see Instituto Tecnologico y de Estudios Superiores de Monterrey)*
Techno. & Commercial Coll. of Puerto Rico *(see Colegio Tecnologico y Comercial de Puerto Rico)*
Techno. Ctr. of Essex *(see Ctr. for Techno., Essex)*
Techno. Ctr. of Indiana County *(see Indiana Cosmetology Acad.)*
Techno. Ctr. of Pontotoc County *(see Pontotoc Techno. Ctr.)*
Techno. Coll. of Pennsylvania *(see Pennsylvania Coll. of Techno.)*
Techno. Coll. of the Delaware Valley *(see Pennsylvania Inst. of Techno.)*
Techno. Edu. Ctr. *(see Techno. Edu. Coll.)*
Techno. Edu. Coll. 327
Techno. Inst. of California *(see California Inst. of Techno.)*
Techno. Inst. of Erie *(see Erie Inst. of Techno.)*
Techno. Inst. of Hawaii *(see Hawaii Techno. Inst.)*
Techno. Inst. of New England *(see New England Inst. of Techno.)*
Techno. Inst. of New Jersey *(see New Jersey Inst. of Techno.)*
Techno. Inst. of New York *(see New York Inst. of Techno—Old Westbury)*
Techno. Inst. of Northern Alberta *(see Northern Alberta Inst. of Techno.)*
Techno. Inst. of Oregon *(see Oregon Inst. of Techno.)*
Techno. Inst. of Pennsylvania *(see Pennsylvania Inst. of Techno.)*
Techno. Inst. of South Florida *(see South Florida Inst. of Techno.)*
Techno. Inst. of Southern California *(see Southern California Inst. of Techno.)*
Techno. Sch. of Morris County *(see Morris County Sch. of Techno.)*
Techno. Sch. of Virginia *(see Virginia Career Inst.)*
TechSkills *(see TechSkills, LLC)*
TechSkills, LLC 602, 662
TechSkill—Cilumbus *(see TechSkill—Columbus)*
TechSkill—Cincinnati 612
TechSkill—Columbus 612
TechSkill—Independence 612
TechSkill—Sacramento 491
TECO/PATHS *(see Tech. Edu. Ctr—Osceola)*
Teddy Ulmo Inst. 793
Teikyo Loretto Heights Univ. 75
Teikyo Post Univ. 779 *(see also Post Univ.)*
Teikyo Univ. *(see Teikyo Loretto Heights Univ.)*
Tel Aviv Univ. 766
Teletronic Tech. Inst. *(see ITT Tech. Inst.)*
Television Broadcasting Acad. *(see Acad. of Radio & Television Broadcasting)*
Telluride Inst. *(see Deep Springs Coll.)*
Telshe Rabbinical Coll. *(see Rabbinical Coll. of Telshe)*
Telshe Yeshiva-Chicago 143
Tempe Normal Sch. of Arizona *(see Arizona State Univ.)*
Tempe State Teachers Coll. *(see Arizona State Univ.)*
Temple Acad. *(see Temple: A Paul Mitchell Partner Sch.)*
Temple Baptist Coll. 327
Temple Baptist Sem. 389 *(see also Tennessee Temple Univ.)*
Temple Baptist Theological Sem. *(see Temple Baptist Sem.)*
Temple Coll. 404 *(see also Temple Baptist Coll.; Temple Univ.)*
Temple Jr. Coll. *(see Temple Coll.)*
Temple Sem. *(see Temple Baptist Sem.)*
Temple Univ. 360
Temple Univ. Health Sys. *(see Northeastern Hosp. Sch. of Nursing; Temple Univ. Hosp—Episcopal Campus)*
Temple Univ. Hosp—Episcopal Campus 742

U

UCSD/VA Psychlogy Internship Program *(see Univ. of California, San Diego)*
Uebehler Associates, LLC *(see Meyer Uebelher Associates, LLC)*
U—Clear Lake *(see Univ. of Housto—Clear Lake)*
U—Downtown *(see Univ. of Housto—Downtown)*
UHHS/CSAHS-Cuyahoga, Inc. *(see Saint Vincent Charity Hosp.)*
U—Victoria *(see Univ. of Housto—Victoria)*
UIC Coll. of Medicine at Peoria *(see Univ. of Illinois at Chicago)*
UIC Coll. of Medicine at Rockford *(see Univ. of Illinois at Chicago)*
Uintah Basin Applied Techno. Coll. 415 *(see also Uintah Basin Applied Techno. Coll.)*
Uintah Basin Area Vocational Ctr. *(see Uintah Basin Applied Techno. Coll.)*
Uintah Basin Coll. *(see Uintah Basin Applied Techno. Coll.)*
Ukrainian Catholic Sem. *(see Saint Basil Coll. Sem.)*
Ulster Coll. *(see Ulster County Comm. Coll.)*
Ulster Comm. Coll. *(see Ulster County Comm. Coll.)*
Ulster County Board of Cooperative Educational Services 728
Ulster County BOCES *(see Ulster County Board of Cooperative Educational Services)*
Ulster County Coll. *(see Ulster County Comm. Coll.)*
Ulster County Comm. Coll. 295
Ultima Coll. of Cosmetology *(see Artistic Beauty Colleges)*
Ultimate Med. Acad. 515
Ultrasound Diagnostic Sch. *(see Sanford-Brown Coll—Houston; Sanford-Brown Inst—Atlanta; Sanford-Brown Inst—Ft. Lauderdale; Sanford-Brown Inst—Garden City; Sanford-Brown Inst—Iselin; Sanford-Brown Inst—Jacksonville; Sanford-Brown Inst—Landover; Sanford-Brown Inst—New York, NY; Sanford-Brown Inst—Philadelphia; Sanford-Brown Inst—Springfield; Sanford-Brown Inst—Tampa; Sanford-Brown Inst—White Plains)*
Ultrasound Diagnostic Sch—Irving Campus *(see Sanford-Brown Inst—Dallas)*
Ultrasound Inst. of Florida *(see Florida Inst. of Ultrasound, Inc.)*
UM Dearborn *(see Univ. of Michiga—Dearborn)*
UMaine *(see Univ. of Maine)*
UMass Amherst *(see Univ. of Massachusetts Amherst)*
UMass Boston *(see Univ. of Massachusetts Boston)*
UMass Dartmouth *(see Univ. of Massachusetts Dartmouth)*
UMass Lowell *(see Univ. of Massachusetts Lowell)*
UMass Mem. Med. Ctr. *(see Univ. of Massachusetts Med. Sch.)*
UMass Worcester *(see Univ. of Massachusetts Med. Sch.)*
UMDNJ Sch. of Osteopathic Medicine 265 *(see also Univ. of Medicine & Dentistry of New Jersey)*
U—Helena Coll. of Techno. *(see Univ. of Montan—Helena Coll. of Techno.)*
UMMDNJ Sch. of Nursing *(see Univ. of Medicine & Dentistry of New Jersey)*
Umpqua Coll. *(see Umpqua Comm. Coll.)*
Umpqua Comm. Coll. 341
U—St. Louis *(see Univ. of Missour—St. Louis)*
Umstead Hosp. *(see John Umstead Hosp.)*
U—Western *(see Univ. of Montan—Western)*
UNC Health Care Sys. *(see Rex Healthcare)*
UnderGrad. Sch. of Cosmetology *(see Univ. of Spa & Cosmetology Art)*
Unification Theological Sem. 295
Uniformed Services Univ. of the Health Sciences 194 *(see also National Capital Consortium)*
Union Biblical Sem. *(see United Theological Sem.)*
Union Bus. Coll. *(see Peirce Coll.)*
Union Coll. 176, 252, 295
Union County Coll. 264
Union County Vocational-Tech. Sch. 583
Union for Experimenting Colleges & Universities (UECU) *(see Union Inst. & Univ.)*
Union for Research & Experimentation in Higher Edu. (UREHE) *(see Union Inst. & Univ.)*
Union Grad. Coll. 295, 788
Union Inst. & Univ., The 327 *(see also Vermont Coll. of Fine Arts)*
Union Inst., The *(see Union Inst. & Univ.)*
Union Prof. Training Sch. *(see Hondros Coll.)*
Union Protestant Hosp. *(see United Hosp. Ctr.)*
Union PSCE *(see Union Theological Sem. & Presbyterian Sch. of Christian Edu.)*
Union Sem. *(see Union Theological Sem. & Presbyterian Sch. of Christian Edu.)*
Union Tech. Edu. Ctr. *(see South Piedmont Comm. Coll.)*
Union Teological Sem. in Virginia *(see Union Theological Sem. & Presbyterian Sch. of Christian Edu.)*
Union Theological Sem. 296
Union Theological Sem. & Presbyterian Sch. of Christian Edu. 428
Union Univ. 390 *(see also Union Inst. & Univ.)*
Union Univ—Albany Law Sch. *(see Albany Law Sch.)*
Unitech Acad. *(see Unitech Training Acad.)*
Unitech Training Acad. 542
United Arab Emirates Univ. 771
United Beauty Coll., Inc. 492
United Church Sem. *(see Luther Sem.)*
United Coll. *(see Univ. of Winnipeg)*
United Driving Sch. *(see United Truck & Car Driving Sch.)*
United Edu. Inst. 492
United Electronics Inst. *(see Everest Inst—Cross Lanes; ITT Tech. Inst.)*
United Hosp. Ctr. 753
United Hosp/Children's Hosp. & Clinic 715
United Israel Zion Hosp. *(see Maimonides Med. Ctr.)*
United States Air Force Acad. 75
United States Air Force Acad. Hosp. *(see 10th Med. Group/SGFL)*
United States Air Force Inst. for Advanced Distributed Learning 464 *(see also Air Univ. Extension Course Program)*
United States Air Force Inst. of Techno. *(see Air Force Inst. of Techno.)*
United States Air Force Sch. of Health Care Sciences 749
United States AMEDD Ctr. & Sch. Dept. of Pastoral Ministry Training 749
United States AMEDD Ctr. & Sch. DPMT *(see United States AMEDD Ctr. & Sch. Dept. of Pastoral Ministry Training)*
United States Army Acad. of Health Sciences *(see United States Army Med. Dept. Ctr. & Sch.)*
United States Army Command & General Staff Coll. 169

Universidad Interamericana de Puerto Rico Recinto de Bayamon *(see Inter American Univ. of Puerto Rico Bayamon Campus)*
Universidad Interamericana de Puerto Rico Recinto de Fajardo *(see Inter American Univ. of Puerto Rico Fajardo Campus)*
Universidad Interamericana de Puerto Rico Recinto de Guayama *(see Inter American Univ. of Puerto Rico Guayama Campus)*
Universidad Interamericana de Puerto Rico Recinto de Ponce *(see Inter American Univ. of Puerto Rico Ponce Campus)*
Universidad Interamericana de Puerto Rico Recinto Metropolitano *(see Inter American Univ. of Puerto Rico Metropolitan Campus)*
Universidad Internacional de Mexico, A.C. *(see Alliant Int'l. Univ—Mexico City)*
Universidad Mayor 808
Universidad Metropolitana 369 *(see also Universidad Metropolitana)*
Universidad Panamericana 767
Universidad Politecnica de Puerto Rico 369
Universidade Católica Portuguesa 768
Universität Frankfurt *(see Johann Wolfgang Goethe-Universität Frankfurt am Main)*
Universitat Mannheim *(see Univ. of Mannheim)*
Universitat Ramon Llull *(see ESADE Bus. Sch.; Institut Quimic de Sarria de Universitat Ramón Llull)*
Université de Montréal 762
Université de Sherbrooke 762
Université d'Ottawa *(see Univ. of Ottawa)*
Université du Maine *(see Univ. of Maine at Fort Kent)*
Université Laval 762
Universiteit Maastricht *(see Maastricht Univ.)*
Universiteit Tilburg *(see Tilburg Univ.)*
Universiteit Utrecht *(see Univ. of Utrecht)*
Univ. of Lowell *(see Univ. of Massachusetts Lowell)*
Univ. at Albany 296
Univ. at Albany, State Univ. of New York *(see Univ. at Albany)*
Univ. at Buffalo *(see State Univ. of New York at Buffalo)*
Univ. at Buffalo Educational Opportunity Ctr. 728
Univ. at Buffalo EOC *(see Univ. at Buffalo Educational Opportunity Ctr.)*
Univ. at Lewisburg *(see Bucknell Univ.)*
Univ. Ctr. for Excellence in Developmental Disabilities *(see Children's Hosp. of Los Angeles)*
Univ. Coll. Dublin 766
Univ. Coll. of Bangor 188 *(see also Univ. of Maine at Augusta)*
Univ. Coll. of Maryland *(see Univ. of Maryland Univ. Coll.)*
Univ. Coll. of San Juan 369
Univ. Coll. of Southern Queensland *(see Univ. of Southern Queensland)*
Univ. Coll. of the North 762, 797
Univ. Good Samaritan Ctr. 716
Univ. Health Care Sys. *(see Univ. Hosp.)*
Univ. Health Ctr. *(see Detroit Receiving Hosp.)*
Univ. Health Ctr. of Pittsburgh *(see Magee-Womens Hosp.)*
Univ. Health Sciences Ctr. (Consortium) *(see Univ. of North Texas)*
Univ. Health Systems of Eastern Carolina *(see Pitt County Mem. Hosp.)*
Univ. Hosp. 700 *(see Louisville Med. Ctr.; State Univ. of New York Upstate Med. Univ.)*
Univ. Hosp. in Birmingham 9
Univ. Hosp. of Columbia & Cornell *(see New York Presbyterian Hosp—Columbia Univ.)*
Univ. Hospitals *(see Saint Vincent Charity Hosp.)*
Univ. Hospitals Case Med. Ctr. *(see Case Western Reserve Univ.)*
Univ. Hospitals Health Sys. *(see Mercy Med. Ctr.)*
Univ. Language Inst. 619
Univ. Mayor *(see Universidad Mayor)*
Univ. Med. Ctr. 684 *(see also Louisville Med. Ctr.; Univ. of Mississippi Med. Ctr.)*
Univ. of Advancing Computer Techno. *(see Univ. of Advancing Techno.)*
Univ. of Advancing Techno. 23
Univ. of Akron, The 327
Univ. of Akro—Comm. & Tech. Coll., The *(see Univ. of Akron)*
Univ. of Akron-Wayne Coll. 328
Univ. of Alabama at Birmingham, The 9
Univ. of Alabama at Tuscaloosa *(see Univ. of Alabama)*
Univ. of Alabama Birmingha—Walker Coll. *(see Bevill State Comm. Coll.)*
Univ. of Alabama Health Sys. *(see Univ. Hosp. in Birmingham)*
Univ. of Alabama in Huntsville, The 9
Univ. of Alabama, The 9
Univ. of Alaska Anchorage 12
Univ. of Alaska Fairbanks 12
Univ. of Alaska Fairbanks Chukchi Campus *(see Univ. of Alaska Fairbanks)*
Univ. of Alaska Fairbanks Kuskokwim Campus *(see Univ. of Alaska Fairbanks)*
Univ. of Alaska Fairbanks Northwest Campus *(see Univ. of Alaska Fairbanks)*
Univ. of Alaska Southeast 13
Univ. of Alaska Southeast Ketchikan Campus *(see Univ. of Alaska Fairbanks)*
Univ. of Alberta 762
Univ. of Alfred *(see Alfred Univ.)*
Univ. of Anderson *(see Anderson Univ.)*
Univ. of Appalachia Coll. of Pharmacy 751
Univ. of Arizona 23
Univ. of Arizon—Arizona Int'l. Coll. *(see Arizona Int'l. Coll.)*
Univ. of Arkansas at Fayetteville 29
Univ. of Arkansas at Fort Smith 29
Univ. of Arkansas at Little Rock 29
Univ. of Arkansas at Monticello 29, 776
Univ. of Arkansas at Monticello Coll. of Techno—Crossett 29, 776
Univ. of Arkansas at Pine Bluff 29
Univ. of Arkansas Comm. Coll. at Batesville 29
Univ. of Arkansas Comm. Coll. at Hope 30
Univ. of Arkansas Comm. Coll. at Morrilton 30
Univ. of Arkansas Cossatot Comm. Coll. *(see Cossatot Comm. Coll. of the Univ. of Arkansas)*
Univ. of Arkansas for Med. Sciences 30
Univ. of Atlanta 9
Univ. of Auckland, The 767
Univ. of Aurora *(see Aurora Univ.)*
Univ. of Baltimore 194
Univ. of Bayamon *(see Bayamon Central Univ.)*
Univ. of Bellevue *(see Bellevue Univ.)*
Univ. of Boston *(see Boston Univ.)*
Univ. of Boulder *(see Univ. of Colorado at Boulder)*
Univ. of Bowie *(see Bowie State Univ.)*
Univ. of Bridgeport 81
Univ. of British Columbia 763
Univ. of Buffalo *(see State Univ. of New York at Buffalo)*
Univ. of Calgary 763
Univ. of California at Los Angeles *(see Univ. of California, Los Angeles)*
Univ. of California Ctr. for Health Sciences *(see Univ. of California, Los Angeles)*
Univ. of California Southern Branch *(see Univ. of California, Los Angeles)*
Univ. of California, Berkeley 63
Univ. of California, Davis 63
Univ. of California, Davis Med. Ctr. *(see Univ. of California, Davis)*

Univ. of Valley City *(see Valley City State Univ.)*
Univ. of Valparaiso *(see Valparaiso Univ.)*
Univ. of Vancouver Island *(see Vancouver Island Univ.)*
Univ. of Vermont 418
Univ. of Victoria 763
Univ. of Villanova *(see Villanova Univ.)*
Univ. of Virginia Health Sys. *(see Univ. of Virginia)*
Univ. of Virginia Med. Ctr. *(see Univ. of Virginia)*
Univ. of Virginia, The 429
Univ. of Virginia's Coll. at Wise, The 429
Univ. of Waikato, The 768
Univ. of Warwick 772
Univ. of Washington 437–438
Univ. of Washington Medicine *(see Harborview Med. Ctr.)*
Univ. of Washington State *(see Washington State Univ.)*
Univ. of Waterloo 763
Univ. of West Alabama, The 10
Univ. of West Florida 107
Univ. of West Georgia 120, 781
Univ. of West Los Angeles 778
Univ. of Western Carolina *(see Western Carolina Univ.)*
Univ. of Western Connecticut *(see Western Connecticut State Univ.)*
Univ. of Western Illinois *(see Western Illinois Univ.)*
Univ. of Western Kentucky *(see Western Kentucky Univ.)*
Univ. of Western Michigan *(see Western Michigan Univ.)*
Univ. of Western New Mexico *(see Western New Mexico Univ.)*
Univ. of Western Ontario 763 *(see also Huron Univ. Coll. Faculty of Theology)*
Univ. of Western Oregon *(see Western Oregon Univ.)*
Univ. of Western Washington *(see Western Washington Univ.)*
Univ. of Wichita *(see Wichita State Univ.)*
Univ. of Windsor 764
Univ. of Wingate *(see Wingate Univ.)*
Univ. of Winnipeg 457
Univ. of Winnipeg Faculty of Theology *(see Univ. of Winnipeg)*
Univ. of Winona *(see Winona State Univ.)*
Univ. of Wisconsin at Eau Claire *(see Univ. of Wisconsin-Eau Claire)*
Univ. of Wisconsin at Green Bay *(see Univ. of Wisconsin-Green Bay)*
Univ. of Wisconsin at La Crosse *(see Univ. of Wisconsin-La Crosse)*
Univ. of Wisconsin at Madison *(see Univ. of Wisconsin-Madison)*
Univ. of Wisconsin at Milwaukee *(see Univ. of Wisconsin-Milwaukee)*
Univ. of Wisconsin at Oshkosh *(see Univ. of Wisconsin-Oshkosh)*
Univ. of Wisconsin at Parkside *(see Univ. of Wisconsin-Parkside)*
Univ. of Wisconsin at Platteville *(see Univ. of Wisconsin-Platteville)*
Univ. of Wisconsin at River Falls *(see Univ. of Wisconsin-River Falls)*
Univ. of Wisconsin at Stevens Point *(see Univ. of Wisconsin-Stevens Point)*
Univ. of Wisconsin at Stout *(see Univ. of Wisconsin-Stout)*
Univ. of Wisconsin at Superior *(see Univ. of Wisconsin-Superior)*
Univ. of Wisconsin at Whitewater *(see Univ. of Wisconsin-Whitewater)*
Univ. of Wisconsin Ctr—Baraboo-Sauk County *(see Univ. of Wisconsin Colleges)*
Univ. of Wisconsin Ctr—Barron County *(see Univ. of Wisconsin Colleges)*
Univ. of Wisconsin Ctr—Fond du Lac *(see Univ. of Wisconsin Colleges)*
Univ. of Wisconsin Ctr—Fox Valley *(see Univ. of Wisconsin Colleges)*
Univ. of Wisconsin Ctr—Manitowoc County *(see Univ. of Wisconsin Colleges)*
Univ. of Wisconsin Ctr—Marathon County *(see Univ. of Wisconsin Colleges)*
Univ. of Wisconsin Ctr—Marinette County *(see Univ. of Wisconsin Colleges)*
Univ. of Wisconsin Ctr—Marshfield-Wood County *(see Univ. of Wisconsin Colleges)*
Univ. of Wisconsin Ctr—Richland *(see Univ. of Wisconsin-Richland)*
Univ. of Wisconsin Ctr—Rock County *(see Univ. of Wisconsin Colleges)*
Univ. of Wisconsin Ctr—Sheboygan County *(see Univ. of Wisconsin Colleges)*
Univ. of Wisconsin Ctr—Washington County *(see Univ. of Wisconsin Colleges)*
Univ. of Wisconsin Ctr—Waukesha County *(see Univ. of Wisconsin Colleges)*
Univ. of Wisconsin Colleges 449–450
Univ. of Wisconsin Eau Claire *(see Univ. of Wisconsin-Eau Claire)*
Univ. of Wisconsin Green Bay *(see Univ. of Wisconsin-Green Bay)*
Univ. of Wisconsin Hosp. & Clinics 755
Univ. of Wisconsin Hospitals & Clinics Authority *(see Univ. of Wisconsin Hosp. & Clinics)*
Univ. of Wisconsin La Crosse *(see Univ. of Wisconsin-La Crosse)*
Univ. of Wisconsin Milwaukee *(see Univ. of Wisconsin-Milwaukee)*
Univ. of Wisconsin Oshkosh *(see Univ. of Wisconsin-Oshkosh)*
Univ. of Wisconsin Parkside *(see Univ. of Wisconsin-Parkside)*
Univ. of Wisconsin Platteville *(see Univ. of Wisconsin-Platteville)*
Univ. of Wisconsin River Falls *(see Univ. of Wisconsin-River Falls)*
Univ. of Wisconsin Stevens Point *(see Univ. of Wisconsin-Stevens Point)*
Univ. of Wisconsin Stout *(see Univ. of Wisconsin-Stout)*
Univ. of Wisconsin Superior *(see Univ. of Wisconsin-Superior)*
Univ. of Wisconsin Whitewater *(see Univ. of Wisconsin-Whitewater)*
Univ. of Wisconsin-Eau Claire 450
Univ. of Wisconsin-Green Bay 450
Univ. of Wisconsin-La Crosse 450
Univ. of Wisconsin-Madison 450
Univ. of Wisconsin-Milwaukee 450
Univ. of Wisconsin-Oshkosh 450
Univ. of Wisconsin-Parkside 450
Univ. of Wisconsin-Platteville 451
Univ. of Wisconsin-River Falls 451
Univ. of Wisconsin-Stevens Point 451
Univ. of Wisconsin-Stout 451
Univ. of Wisconsin-Superior 451
Univ. of Wisconsi—Waukesha County *(see Univ. of Wisconsin Colleges)*
Univ. of Wisconsin-Whitewater 451
Univ. of Wyoming 453
Univ. of Wyoming Northwest Ctr. *(see Northwest Coll.)*
Univ. Otago *(see Univ. of Otago)*
Univ. Ramon Llull *(see ESADE Bus. Sch.)*
Univ. 'San Martin de Porres' *(see Universidad de San Martin de Porres)*
Univ. Sch. of Turabo *(see Universidad del Turabo)*
Univ. Sys. of New Hampshire Coll. for Lifelong Learning *(see Granite State Coll.)*
Univ. Sys. of New Hampshire Sch. of Continuing Studies *(see Granite State Coll.)*
Univ. Sys. of Ohio 790
UNLV *(see Univ. of Nevada, Las Vegas)*
UPMC Mercy 742
UPMC Montefiore Hosp. *(see Univ. of Pittsburgh Med. Ctr. Shadyside)*
UPMC Northwest *(see Univ. of Pittsburgh Med. Ctr. Northwest)*
UPMC Presbyterian *(see Univ. of Pittsburgh Med. Ctr. Shadyside)*
UPMC Presbyterian Shadyside *(see Univ. of Pittsburgh Med. Ctr. Shadyside)*
UPMC Saint Margaret Hosp. 742

Utica Coll. of Syracuse Univ. *(see Utica Coll.)*
Utica Homeopathic Hosp. *(see Faxton-St. Luke's Healthcare)*
Utica Mem. Hosp. *(see Faxton-St. Luke's Healthcare)*
Utica Sch. of Commerce 296
UT—Houston *(see Universal Tech. Inst.)*
UT—Illinois *(see Universal Tech. Inst.)*
UT—Massachusetts *(see Universal Tech. Inst.)*
UT—Orlando *(see Motorcycle & Marine Mechanics Inst.)*
UT—Pennsylvania *(see Universal Tech. Inst.)*
UT—Phoenix *(see Motorcycle & Marine Mechanics Inst.; Universal Tech. Inst.)*
UT—Sacramento *(see Universal Tech. Inst.)*
UT—Southern California *(see Universal Tech. Inst.)*
UT—Texas *(see Universal Tech. Inst.)*
Utrecht Univ. *(see Univ. of Utrecht)*
UVA Coll. at Wise *(see Univ. of Virginia's Coll. at Wise)*
UVA Wise *(see Univ. of Virginia's Coll. at Wise)*
UVMC Health Sys. *(see Upper Valley Med. Ctr.)*
UW at La Crosse *(see Univ. of Wisconsin-La Crosse)*
UW at Madison *(see Univ. of Wisconsin-Madison)*
UW Health *(see Univ. of Wisconsin Hosp. & Clinics)*
UW Medicine *(see Harborview Med. Ctr.)*
UW-Baraboo-Sauk County *(see Univ. of Wisconsin Colleges)*
UW-Barron County *(see Univ. of Wisconsin Colleges)*
UW-Eau Claire *(see Univ. of Wisconsin-Eau Claire)*
UW-Fond du Lac *(see Univ. of Wisconsin Colleges)*
UW-Fox Valley *(see Univ. of Wisconsin Colleges)*
UW-Green Bay *(see Univ. of Wisconsin-Green Bay)*
UW-La Crosse *(see Univ. of Wisconsin-La Crosse)*
UW-Madison *(see Univ. of Wisconsin-Madison)*
UW-Manitowoc County *(see Univ. of Wisconsin Colleges)*
UW-Marathon County *(see Univ. of Wisconsin Colleges)*
UW-Marinette County *(see Univ. of Wisconsin Colleges)*
UW-Marshfield-Wood County *(see Univ. of Wisconsin Colleges)*
UW-Milwaukee *(see Univ. of Wisconsin-Milwaukee)*
UW-Oshkosh *(see Univ. of Wisconsin-Oshkosh)*
UW-Parkside *(see Univ. of Wisconsin-Parkside)*
UW-Platteville *(see Univ. of Wisconsin-Platteville)*
UW-Richland *(see Univ. of Wisconsin-Richland)*
UW-River Falls *(see Univ. of Wisconsin-River Falls)*
UW-Rock County *(see Univ. of Wisconsin Colleges)*
UW-Sheboygan County *(see Univ. of Wisconsin Colleges)*
UW-Stevens Point *(see Univ. of Wisconsin-Stevens Point)*
UW-Stout *(see Univ. of Wisconsin-Stout)*
UW-Superior *(see Univ. of Wisconsin-Superior)*
UW-Washington County *(see Univ. of Wisconsin Colleges)*
UW-Whitewater *(see Univ. of Wisconsin-Whitewater)*

V

V.M. Delgado & Associates *(see Dale Carnegie Training of San Joaquin Valley)*
VA Boston Healthcare Sys. *(see Veterans Affairs Boston Healthcare Sys.)*
VA Central California Health Care Sys. *(see Veterans Affairs Central California Health Care Sys.)*
VA Central Iowa Healthcare Sys. *(see Veterans Affairs Central Iowa Healthcare Sys—Knoxville Division)*
VA Connecticut Healthcare Sys. Newington *(see Veterans Affairs Connecticut Healthcare Sys.)*
VA Connecticut Healthcare Sys. West Haven *(see Veterans Affairs Connecticut Healthcare Sys. West Haven)*
VA Eastern Kansas Healthcare Sys. *(see Colmery-O'Neil Veterans Affairs Med. Ctr.; Dwight D. Eisenhower Veterans Affairs Med. Ctr.)*
VA Greater Los Angeles Healthcare Sys. *(see Veterans Affairs Greater Los Angeles Healthcare Sys.; Veterans Affairs Greater Los Angeles Healthcare Sys—Los Angeles; Veterans Affairs Greater Los Angeles Healthcare Sys—Sepulveda)*
VA Healthcare Sys. of Ohio *(see Chillicothe Veterans Affairs Med. Ctr.; Dayton Veterans Affairs Med. Ctr.; Veterans Affairs Med. Ctr. Cincinnati)*
VA Heartland Network *(see Kansas City Veterans Affairs Med. Ctr.; St. Louis Veterans Affairs Med. Ctr—Jefferson Barracks; St. Louis Veterans Affairs Med. Ctr—John Cochran Division)*
VA Hudson Valley Health Care Sys—Castle Point *(see Veterans Affairs Hudson Valley Health Care Sys—Castle Point)*
VA Hudson Valley Health Care Sys—Montrose *(see Veterans Affairs Hudson Valley Health Care Sys—Montrose)*
VA Hudson Valle—Montrose *(see Veterans Affairs Hudson Valley Health Care Sys—Montrose)*
VA Illiana Health Care Sys. *(see Veterans Affairs Illiana Health Care Sys.)*
VA Long Beach Healthcare Sys. *(see Veterans Affairs Long Beach Healthcare Sys.)*
VA Long Beach Med. Ctr. *(see Veterans Affairs Long Beach Healthcare Sys.)*
VA Maryland Health Care Sys. *(see Baltimore Veterans Affairs Med. Ctr.; Perry Point Veterans Affairs Med. Ctr.)*
VA Med. Ctr. at Asheville *(see Asheville Veterans Affairs Med. Ctr.)*
VA Med. Ctr. at Decatur *(see Atlanta Veterans Affairs Med. Ctr.)*
VA Med. Ctr. at Durham *(see Durham Veterans Affairs Med. Ctr.)*
VA Med. Ctr. at East Orange *(see Veterans Affairs Med. Ctr—East Orange)*
VA Med. Ctr. at Manchester *(see Manchester Veterans Affairs Med. Ctr.)*
VA Med. Ctr. at Philadelphia *(see Philadelphia Veterans Affairs Med. Ctr.)*
VA Med. Ctr. at San Juan *(see Veterans Affairs Caribbean Healthcare Sys.)*
VA Med. Ctr. at Wilkes-Barre *(see Wilkes-Barre Veterans Affairs Med. Ctr.)*

VA Med. Ctr. Atlanta *(see Atlanta Veterans Affairs Med. Ctr.)*
VA Med. Ctr. Augusta *(see Charlie Norwood Veterans Affairs Med. Ctr.)*
VA Med. Ctr. Cincinnati *(see Veterans Affairs Med. Ctr. Cincinnati)*
VA Med. Ctr. Fayetteville *(see Fayetteville Veterans Affairs Med. Ctr.)*
VA Med. Ctr. Honolulu *(see Veterans Affairs Pacific Islands Healthcare Sys.)*
VA Med. Ctr. Lyons *(see Veterans Affairs New Jersey Health Care Sys—Lyons)*
VA Med. Ctr. Northport *(see Northport Veterans Affairs Med. Ctr.)*
VA Med. Ctr. of Alexandria *(see Alexandria Veterans Affairs Med. Ctr.)*
VA Med. Ctr. of Allen Park *(see John D. Dingell Veterans Affairs Med. Ctr.)*
VA Med. Ctr. of Ann Arbor *(see Veterans Affairs Med. Ctr—Ann Arbor)*
VA Med. Ctr. of Baltimore *(see Baltimore Veterans Affairs Med. Ctr.)*
VA Med. Ctr. of Bay Pines *(see Bay Pines Veterans Affairs Med. Ctr.)*
VA Med. Ctr. of Bedford *(see Edith Nourse Rogers Mem. Veterans Hosp.)*
VA Med. Ctr. of Birmingham *(see Veterans Affairs Med. Ctr—Birmingham)*
VA Med. Ctr. of Brooklyn *(see Veterans Affairs New York Harbor Healthcare Sys—Brooklyn)*
VA Med. Ctr. of Castle Point *(see Veterans Affairs Hudson Valley Health Care Sys—Castle Point)*
VA Med. Ctr. of Chicago *(see Jesse Brown Veterans Affairs Med. Ctr.)*
VA Med. Ctr. of Cleveland *(see Louis Stokes Cleveland Veterans Affairs Med. Ctr.)*
VA Med. Ctr. of Dallas *(see Michael E. DeBakey Veterans Affairs Med. Ctr.)*
VA Med. Ctr. of Dayton *(see Dayton Veterans Affairs Med. Ctr.)*
VA Med. Ctr. of DC *(see Washington DC Veterans Affairs Med. Ctr.)*
VA Med. Ctr. of Des Moines *(see Veterans Affairs Central Iowa Healthcare Sys—Knoxville Division)*
VA Med. Ctr. of Gainesville *(see Malcom Randall Veterans Affairs Med. Ctr.)*
VA Med. Ctr. of Hampton *(see Hampton Veterans Affairs Med. Ctr.)*
VA Med. Ctr. of Indianapolis *(see Richard L. Roudebush Veterans Affairs Med. Ctr.)*
VA Med. Ctr. of Kansas City *(see Kansas City Veterans Affairs Med. Ctr.)*
VA Med. Ctr. of Knoxville *(see Veterans Affairs Central Iowa Healthcare Sys—Knoxville Division)*
VA Med. Ctr. of Leavenworth *(see Dwight D. Eisenhower Veterans Affairs Med. Ctr.)*
VA Med. Ctr. of Lexington *(see Lexington Veterans Affairs Med. Ctr.)*
VA Med. Ctr. of Loma Linda *(see Loma Linda Veterans Affairs Healthcare Sys.)*
VA Med. Ctr. of Long Beach *(see Veterans Affairs Long Beach Healthcare Sys.)*
VA Med. Ctr. of Mare Island *(see Veterans Affairs Northern California Health Care Sys—Mare Island)*
VA Med. Ctr. of Martinsburg *(see Veterans Affairs Med. Ctr—Martinsburg)*
VA Med. Ctr. of Memphis *(see Memphis Veterans Affairs Med. Ctr.)*
VA Med. Ctr. of Miami *(see Miami Veterans Affairs Med. Ctr.)*
VA Med. Ctr. of Milwaukee *(see Clement J. Zablocki Veterans Affairs Med. Ctr.)*
VA Med. Ctr. of Minneapolis *(see Veterans Affairs Med. Ctr—Minneapolis)*
VA Med. Ctr. of Montrose *(see Veterans Affairs Hudson Valley Health Care Sys—Montrose)*
VA Med. Ctr. of Mountain Home *(see James H. Quillen Veterans Affairs Med. Ctr.)*
VA Med. Ctr. of Nashville *(see Nashville Veterans Affairs Med. Ctr.)*
VA Med. Ctr. of New Orleans *(see Southeast Louisiana Veterans Health Care Sys.)*
VA Med. Ctr. of New York City *(see Veterans Affairs NewYork Harbor Healthcare Sys—New York City)*
VA Med. Ctr. of North Chicago *(see North Chicago Veterans Affairs Med. Ctr.)*
VA Med. Ctr. of Palo Alto *(see Veterans Affairs Palo Alto Health Care Sys.)*
VA Med. Ctr. of Perry Point *(see Perry Point Veterans Affairs Med. Ctr.)*
VA Med. Ctr. of Pittsburgh *(see Veterans Affairs Pittsburgh Healthcare Sys., Highland Drive Division)*
VA Med. Ctr. of Portland *(see Portland Veterans Affairs Med. Ctr.)*
VA Med. Ctr. of Reno *(see Veterans Affairs Sierra Nevada Health Care Sys.)*
VA Med. Ctr. of Salem *(see Salem Veterans Affairs Med. Ctr.)*
VA Med. Ctr. of Salt Lake City *(see George E. Wahlen Dept. of Veterans Affairs Med. Ctr.)*
VA Med. Ctr. of San Antonio *(see South Texas Veterans Health Care Sys.)*
VA Med. Ctr. of San Diego *(see Veterans Affairs San Diego Healthcare Sys.)*
VA Med. Ctr. of San Francisco *(see Veterans Affairs Med. Ctr—San Francisco)*
VA Med. Ctr. of Seattle *(see Veterans Affairs Puget Sound Health Care Sys.)*
VA Med. Ctr. of Sepulveda *(see Veterans Affairs Greater Los Angeles Healthcare Sys—Sepulveda)*
VA Med. Ctr. of Spokane *(see Spokane Veterans Affairs Med. Ctr.)*
VA Med. Ctr. of Tampa *(see James A. Haley Veterans Affairs Med. Ctr.)*
VA Med. Ctr. of Temple *(see Central Texas Veterans Health Care Sys.)*
VA Med. Ctr. of the Puget Sound *(see Veterans Affairs Puget Sound Health Care Sys.)*
VA Med. Ctr. of Togus *(see Togus Veterans Affairs Med. Ctr.)*
VA Med. Ctr. of Topeka *(see Colmery-O'Neil Veterans Affairs Med. Ctr.)*
VA Med. Ctr. of Tucson *(see Southern Arizona Veterans Affairs Health Care Sys.)*
VA Med. Ctr. of West Haven *(see Veterans Affairs Connecticut Healthcare Sys. West Haven)*
VA Med. Ctr. of West Los Angeles *(see Veterans Affairs Greater Los Angeles Healthcare Sys.)*
VA Med. Ctr. of West Palm Beach *(see Veterans Affairs Med. Ctr—West Palm Beach)*
VA Med. Ctr. Salisbury *(see W.G. (Bill) Hefner Veterans Affairs Med. Ctr.)*
VA Med. Ctr. St. Louis *(see St. Louis Veterans Affairs Med. Ctr—Jefferson Barracks)*
VA Med. Ctr., Washington, DC *(see Washington DC Veterans Affairs Med. Ctr.)*
VA Med. Ctr—Little Rock *(see Central Arkansas Veterans Healthcare Sys.)*
VA Med. Ctr—Phoenix *(see Carl T. Hayden Veterans Affairs Med. Ctr.)*

W

Warner Coll. *(see Warner Pacific Coll.; Warner Univ.)*
Warner Pacific Coll. 341
Warner Pacific Univ. *(see Warner Pacific Coll.)*
Warner Southern Coll. *(see Warner Univ.)*
Warner Univ. 107
Warren Coll. *(see Warren County Comm. Coll.)*
Warren Comm. Coll. *(see Warren County Comm. Coll.)*
Warren County Area Vo-Tech Sch. *(see Warren County Area Vocational Tech. Sch.)*
Warren County Career Ctr. 613
Warren County Career Ctr. Adult & Comm. Edu. Workforce Training *(see Warren County Career Ctr.)*
Warren County Coll. *(see Warren County Comm. Coll.)*
Warren County Comm. Coll. 265
Warren H. Wilson Vocational Jr. Coll. & Associated Schools *(see Warren Wilson Coll.)*
Warren Wilson Coll. 310
Warren Woods Vocational Adult Edu. 560
Warren Woods Vocational Ctr. *(see Warren Woods Vocational Adult Edu.)*
Wartburg Coll. 163
Wartburg Sem. *(see Wartburg Theological Sem.)*
Wartburg Theological Sem. 163
Warwick Acad. of Beauty Culture 793 *(see also Arthur Angelo Sch. of Cosmetology & Hair Desig—Warwick)*
Warwick Beauty Acad. *(see Arthur Angelo Sch. of Cosmetology & Hair Desig—Warwick)*
Warwick Univ. *(see Univ. of Warwick)*
Wasatch Front South *(see Salt Lake-Tooele Applied Techno. Coll.)*
Wasco Area Edu. Service Dist. *(see Columbia Gorge Comm. Coll.)*
Washburn Coll. *(see Washburn Univ.)*
Washburn Municipal Univ. *(see Washburn Univ.)*
Washburn Univ. 169
Washburn Univ. of Topeka *(see Washburn Univ.)*
Washburne Culinary Inst. *(see City Colleges of Chicag—Kennedy-King Coll.)*
Washington Acad. *(see Washington & Lee Univ.)*
Washington Adventist Hosp. 712
Washington & Jefferson Coll. 363
Washington & Lee Univ. 430
Washington Art Inst. *(see Art Inst. of Atlanta)*
Washington Baptist Coll. & Sem. *(see Washington Baptist Univ.)*
Washington Baptist Sem. *(see Washington Baptist Univ.)*
Washington Baptist Theological Sem. *(see Washington Baptist Univ.)*
Washington Baptist Univ. 807
Washington Baptist Univ. & Sem. *(see Washington Baptist Univ.)*
Washington Bible Coll. 195 *(see also Capital Bible Sem.)*
Washington Bible Inst. *(see Washington Bible Coll.)*
Washington Bus. Sch. of Northern Virginia *(see Sanford-Brown Coll—Vienna)*
Washington Coll. 195 *(see also City Colleges of Chicag—Harold Washington Coll.; Trinity Coll.; Univ. of Mary Washington; Washington & Jefferson Coll.; Washington & Lee Univ.; Washington State Comm. Coll.)*
Washington Comm. Coll. *(see Washington County Comm. Coll.; Washington State Comm. Coll.)*
Washington Conservatory of Music, Inc. 549
Washington County Adult Skill Ctr. 667
Washington County Career Ctr. *(see Career Ctr. Adult Tech. Training)*
Washington County Coll. *(see Washington County Comm. Coll.; Washington State Comm. Coll.)*
Washington County Comm. Coll. 188 *(see also Washington State Comm. Coll.)*
Washington County Hosp. *(see Washington Hosp.)*
Washington County Tech. Coll. *(see Washington County Comm. Coll.)*
Washington DC VA Med. Ctr. *(see Washington DC Veterans Affairs Med. Ctr.)*
Washington DC Veterans Affairs Med. Ctr. 695
Washington Foreign Mission Sem. *(see Columbia Union Coll.)*
Washington Hosp. 742 *(see also Washington Adventist Hosp.)*
Washington Hosp. Ctr. 695
Washington Inst. in St. Louis *(see Washington Univ. in St. Louis)*
Washington Jr. Coll. *(see Pensacola Jr. Coll.)*
Washington Missionary Coll. *(see Columbia Union Coll.)*
Washington Sch. of Prof. Psychology *(see Argosy Univ. Seattle)*
Washington Sch. of the Bible *(see Washington Bible Coll.)*
Washington State Comm. Coll. 329
Washington State Dale Carnegie Training *(see Crace & Associates)*
Washington State Normal Sch. *(see Central Washington Univ.)*
Washington State Univ. 438
Washington State Univ. Intercollegiate Coll. of Nursing *(see Eastern Washington Univ.; Whitworth Univ.)*
Washington Tech. Coll. *(see Washington State Comm. Coll.)*
Washington Tech. Inst. *(see Univ. of the Dist. of Columbia; Washington State Comm. Coll.)*
Washington Theological Union 88
Washington Township Metropolitan Sch. Dist. *(see J. Everett Light Career Ctr.)*
Washington Training Inst. *(see Columbia Union Coll.)*
Washington Univ. *(see George Washington Univ.; Washington Univ. in St. Louis)*
Washington Univ. in St. Louis 246
Washington Vocational Sch. *(see Margaret Murray Washington Vocational Sch.)*
Washington-Holmes Area Tech. Ctr. *(see Washington-Holmes Tech. Ctr.)*
Washington-Holmes Area Vocational-Tech. Ctr. *(see Washington-Holmes Tech. Ctr.)*
Washington-Holmes Tech. Ctr. 516
Washington-Holmes Vo-Tech Ctr. *(see Washington-Holmes Tech. Ctr.)*
Washtenaw Coll. *(see Washtenaw Comm. Coll.)*
Washtenaw Comm. Coll. 217
Wash'-uh-taw Baptist Univ. *(see Ouachita Baptist Univ.)*
Watauga Acad. *(see Appalachian State Univ.)*
Waterbury Hosp. Health Ctr. 694
Waterbury State Tech. Coll. *(see Naugatuck Valley Comm. Coll.)*
Waterloo Area Vocational Sch. *(see Hawkeye Comm. Coll.)*
Waterloo Coll. *(see Univ. of Waterloo)*
Waterloo Lutheran Sem. 457
Waterloo Sem. *(see Waterloo Lutheran Sem.)*
Waterloo Univ. *(see Univ. of Waterloo)*
Waterman Inst. *(see Waterman Training Inst.)*
Waters Coll. *(see Edward Waters Coll.)*
Waterville Coll. *(see Colby Coll.)*
Watkins Coll. of Art & Design 391
Watkins Film Sch., The *(see Watkins Coll. of Art & Design)*

West Virginia Wesleyan Coll. 444
Westark Comm. Coll. *(see Univ. of Arkansas at Fort Smith)*
Westark Jr. Coll. *(see Univ. of Arkansas at Fort Smith)*
Westborough State Hosp. 713
Westbrook Coll. *(see Univ. of New England)*
Westchester Bus. Inst. *(see Coll. of Westchester)*
Westchester Coll. *(see Coll. of Westchester; Westchester Comm. Coll.)*
Westchester Comm. Coll. 297
Westchester Conservatory of Music *(see Music Conservatory of Westchester)*
Westchester County Med. Ctr. *(see Inst. of Allied Med. Professions; Westchester Med. Ctr.)*
Westchester Med. Ctr. 729
Westchester Sch. of Beauty Culture 599
WestConn *(see Western Connecticut State Univ.)*
Westech Coll. 493
Western Area Career & Techno. Ctr. 792
Western Area Vocational Tech. Sch. 792
Western Baptist Coll. 790 *(see also Corban Coll.)*
Western Baptist Theological Sem. *(see Western Sem.)*
Western Beauty Inst—San Fernando Valley 493, 778
Western Bible Inst. *(see Colorado Christian Univ.)*
Western Branch of the Kansas Normal Sch. *(see Fort Hays State Univ.)*
Western Bus. Coll. 790 *(see also Everest Coll—Portland)*
Western Bus. Coll—Vancouver *(see Everest Coll—Portland)*
Western Career Coll. 66
Western Career Coll—Fremont 778
Western Career Coll—Sacramento 778
Western Carolina Univ. 310
Western Coll. *(see Western Career Coll.; Western Christian Coll.)*
Western Coll. of Southern California 778 *(see also Fremont Coll.)*
Western Colorado Coll. *(see Western State Coll. of Colorado)*
Western Connecticut State Univ. 82
Western Culinary Inst. 341 *(see also Brown Coll.)*
Western Dakota Tech. Inst. 381
Western Evangelical Sem. *(see George Fox Univ.)*
Western Governors Univ. 416
Western Hills Sch. of Beauty & Hair Design 613
Western Illinois Edu. Consortium *(see Sauk Valley Comm. Coll.)*
Western Illinois Univ. 145
Western Int'l. Univ. 25
Western Iowa Coll. *(see Western Iowa Tech Comm. Coll.)*
Western Iowa Comm. Coll. *(see Western Iowa Tech Comm. Coll.)*
Western Iowa Tech *(see Western Iowa Tech Comm. Coll.)*
Western Iowa Tech Comm. Coll. 163
Western Kentucky State Coll. *(see Western Kentucky Univ.)*
Western Kentucky Univ. 177
Western Maryland Coll. *(see McDaniel Coll.)*
Western Massachusetts Precision Inst. 785
Western Michigan Coll. *(see Western Michigan Univ.)*
Western Michigan Coll. of Edu. *(see Western Michigan Univ.)*
Western Michigan Univ. 218
Western Montana Coll. of the Univ. of Montana *(see Univ. of Montan—Western)*
Western Nebraska Coll. *(see Western Nebraska Comm. Coll.)*
Western Nebraska Comm. Coll. 253
Western Nebraska Tech. Coll. *(see Western Nebraska Comm. Coll.)*
Western Nebraska Vocational Tech. Sch. *(see Western Nebraska Comm. Coll.)*
Western Nevada Coll. 255, 787
Western Nevada Comm. Coll. 787 *(see also Western Nevada Coll.)*
Western New England Coll. 206
Western New Mexico Univ. 268
Western New York Healthcare Sys. at Buffalo *(see Veterans Affairs Western New York Healthcare Sys. at Buffalo)*
Western North Carolina Insane Asylum *(see Broughton Hosp.)*
Western Oklahoma Area Vocational Tech. Sch. 790 *(see also Western Techno. Ctr.)*
Western Oklahoma Coll. *(see Western Oklahoma State Coll.)*
Western Oklahoma State Coll. 336
Western Oklahoma Techno. Ctr. *(see Western Techno. Ctr.)*
Western Oklahoma Vo-Tech Sch. *(see Western Techno. Ctr.)*
Western Ontario Inst. of Techno. *(see Saint Clair Coll. of Applied Arts & Techno.)*
Western Oregon Univ. 342 *(see also Univ. of Western Ontario)*
Western Pennsylvania Ctr. for Emergency Medicine *(see Ctr. for Emergency Medicine of Western Pennsylvania)*
Western Pentecostal Bible Coll. *(see Summit Pacific Coll.)*
Western Pentecostal Coll. *(see Summit Pacific Coll.)*
Western Piedmont Coll. *(see Western Piedmont Comm. Coll.)*
Western Piedmont Comm. Coll. 310
Western Pilgrim Coll. *(see Oklahoma Wesleyan Univ.)*
Western Reg. Med. Command *(see Madigan Army Med. Ctr.)*
Western Reserve Care Sys. 734
Western Reserve Coll. *(see Case Western Reserve Univ.)*
Western Reserve Eclectic Inst. *(see Hiram Coll.)*
Western Reserve Univ. *(see Case Western Reserve Univ.)*
Western Sch. of Commerce *(see Humphreys Coll.)*
Western Sch. of Health & Bus. Careers *(see Sanford-Brown Inst—Monroeville; Sanford-Brown Inst—Pittsburgh)*
Western Sem. 342
Western Sem. Phoenix *(see Phoenix Sem.)*
Western State Coll. of Colorado 76
Western State Normal Sch. *(see Univ. of Maine at Farmington; Western Michigan Univ.)*
Western State Teachers Coll. *(see Western Michigan Univ.)*
Western State Univ. Coll. of Law 67
Western State Univ. Coll. of Law of San Diego *(see Thomas Jefferson Sch. of Law)*
Western States Chiropractic Coll. 342
Western States Coll. *(see Western States Chiropractic Coll.)*
Western Suffolk Board of Cooperative Educational Services 817
Western Suffolk BOCES 599 *(see also Western Suffolk Board of Cooperative Educational Services)*
Western Tech *(see Western Tech. Coll.)*
Western Tech. Coll. 412, 451, 794, 796
Western Tech. Inst. 794 *(see also Western Tech. Coll.)*
Western Techno. Ctr. 735, 790
Western Texas Coll. 412
Western Theological Sem. 218 *(see also Seabury-Western Theological Sem.)*
Western Truck Sch. *(see Western Pacific Truck Sch.)*
Western Univ. of Health Sciences 67

Western Washington Coll. *(see Western Washington Univ.)*
Western Washington Coll. of Edu. *(see Western Washington Univ.)*
Western Washington Univ. 438
Western Wisconsin Coll. *(see Western Tech. Coll.)*
Western Wisconsin Tech. Coll. 796 *(see also Western Tech. Coll.)*
Western Wisconsin Tech. Inst. *(see Western Tech. Coll.)*
Western Wyoming Coll. *(see Western Wyoming Comm. Coll.)*
Western Wyoming Comm. Coll. 453
Westfield Normal Sch. *(see Westfield State Coll.)*
Westfield State Coll. 206
Westfield State Teachers Coll. *(see Westfield State Coll.)*
WestGate Training & Consultation Network 744
Westhampton Coll. *(see Univ. of Richmond)*
Westhill Inst. *(see Westhill Univ.)*
Westhill Univ. 459
Westlawn Inst. of Marine Techno. 500
Westlawn Marine Techno. Inst. *(see Westlawn Inst. of Marine Techno.)*
Westlawn Sch. of Yacht Design *(see Westlawn Inst. of Marine Techno.)*
WestMed Coll. 493
Westminster Choir Coll. 263 *(see also Rider Univ.)*
Westminster Coll. 246, 363, 416
Westminster Coll. & Bible Inst. *(see Wesley Coll.)*
Westminster Coll. of Salt Lake City *(see Westminster Coll.)*
Westminster Sem. *(see Westminster Theological Sem.)*
Westminster Sem. in California *(see Westminster Theological Sem. in California)*
Westminster Theological Sem. 363 *(see also Wesley Theological Sem.)*
Westminster Theological Sem. in California 67
Westmont Coll. 67
Westmoreland Coll. *(see Westmoreland County Comm. Coll.)*
Westmoreland Comm. Coll. *(see Westmoreland County Comm. Coll.)*
Westmoreland County Coll. *(see Westmoreland County Comm. Coll.)*
Westmoreland County Comm. Coll. 363
Weston Enterprises, Inc. *(see McKinley Coll.)*
Weston Jesuit Sch. of Theology 785 *(see also Boston Coll.)*
Westside Tech 516
Westside VA Med. Ctr. *(see Jesse Brown Veterans Affairs Med. Ctr.)*
Westside Veterans Affairs Med. Ctr. *(see Jesse Brown Veterans Affairs Med. Ctr.)*
Westside Vocational Tech. Ctr. *(see Westside Tech)*
Westwood Aviation Inst. *(see Redstone Coll—Denver)*
Westwood Aviation Inst—Houston 794 *(see also Aviation Inst. of Maint—Houston)*
Westwood Coll. 431, 807
Westwood Coll. of Aviation Techno. *(see Redstone Coll—Denver; Redstone Coll—Los Angeles)*
Westwood Coll. of Aviation Techno—Denver 779
Westwood Coll. of Aviation Techno—Houston 794 *(see also Aviation Inst. of Maint—Houston)*
Westwood Coll. of Aviation Techno—Los Angeles 778
Westwood Coll. of Techno. *(see Westwood Coll—DuPage; Westwood Coll—Los Angeles; Westwood Coll—O'Hare Airport; Westwood Coll—South Bay)*
Westwood Coll. of Techno—Anaheim 778
Westwood Coll. of Techno—Chicago Loop 782 *(see also Westwood Coll—Chicago Loop)*
Westwood Coll. of Techno—Dallas 794
Westwood Coll. of Techno—Denver North 779 *(see also Westwood Coll—Denver North)*
Westwood Coll. of Techno—Denver South 779 *(see also Westwood Coll—Denver South)*
Westwood Coll. of Techno—DuPage 782 *(see also Westwood Coll—DuPage)*
Westwood Coll. of Techno—Fort Worth 794
Westwood Coll. of Techno—Inland Empire 778
Westwood Coll. of Techno—Long Beach 778
Westwood Coll. of Techno—Los Angeles 778 *(see also Westwood Coll—Los Angeles)*
Westwood Coll. of Techno—O'Hare 782 *(see also Westwood Coll—O'Hare Airport)*
Westwood Coll. of Techno—River Oaks 782 *(see also Westwood Coll—Los Angeles)*
Westwood Coll. of Techno—Schiller Park *(see Westwood Coll—O'Hare Airport)*
Westwood Coll. of Techno—Upland *(see Westwood Coll—Denver North)*
Westwood Coll—Anaheim 778
Westwood Coll—Calumet City *(see also Westwood Coll—Los Angeles)*
Westwood Coll—Chicago Loop 782
Westwood Coll—Dallas 794
Westwood Coll—Denver North 76, 779, 802
Westwood Coll—Denver South 779
Westwood Coll—DuPage 145, 782, 803
Westwood Coll—Fort Worth 794
Westwood Coll—Houston South 794
Westwood Coll—Inland Empire 778
Westwood Coll—Long Beach 778 *(see also Westwood Coll—South Bay)*
Westwood Coll—Los Angeles 67, 778, 801
Westwood Coll—O'Hare Airport 145, 782
Westwood Coll—River Oaks 782
Westwood Coll—South Bay 67, 778, 801
Westwood Inst. of Techno. *(see Westwood Coll—Denver North)*
Westwood Inst. of Techno—Houston South 794
Wharton Coll. *(see Wharton County Jr. Coll.)*
Wharton County Coll. *(see Wharton County Jr. Coll.)*
Wharton County Jr. Coll. 412
Whatcom Coll. *(see Whatcom Comm. Coll.)*
Whatcom Comm. Coll. 438
Wheaton Coll. 145, 206
Wheaton Female Sem. *(see Wheaton Coll.)*
Wheaton Franciscan Healthcare 704
Wheaton Franciscan Healthcar—St. Francis Hosp. 755
Wheaton Franciscan Services, Inc. *(see Wheaton Franciscan Healthcare)*
Wheeling Hosp. 753
Wheeling Jesuit Coll. *(see Wheeling Jesuit Univ.)*
Wheeling Jesuit Univ. 444
Wheelock Coll. 206
Whelan Sch. of Practical Nursing *(see Marion S. Whelan Sch. of Practical Nursing)*
White & Associates *(see J.J. White & Associates, Inc. Dale Carnegie Training)*
White Earth Coll. *(see White Earth Tribal & Comm. Coll.)*
White Earth Comm. Coll. *(see White Earth Tribal & Comm. Coll.)*
White Earth Tribal & Comm. Coll. 804
White Mountains Coll. *(see White Mountains Comm. Coll.)*
White Mountains Comm. Coll. 258, 787

Williamsport Acad. *(see Lycoming Coll.)*
Williamsport Area Comm. Coll. *(see Pennsylvania Coll. of Techno.)*
Williamsport Dickinson Jr. Coll. *(see Lycoming Coll.)*
Williamsport Dickinson Sem. *(see Lycoming Coll.)*
Williamsport Hosp. & Med. Ctr., The *(see Susquehanna Health Sys.)*
Williamsport Sch. of Commerce *(see Newport Bus. Inst.)*
Williamsport Tech. Inst. *(see Pennsylvania Coll. of Techno.)*
Williamston Female Coll. *(see Lander Univ.)*
Willimantic Inst. of Hair *(see Brio Acad. of Cosmetolog—Williamantic)*
Willis Career Ctr. *(see Ralph R. Willis Vocational Tech. Ctr.)*
Willis Vocational Tech. Ctr. *(see Ralph R. Willis Vocational Tech. Ctr.)*
Willis Vo-Tech Ctr. *(see Ralph R. Willis Vocational Tech. Ctr.)*
Williston Coll. *(see Williston State Coll.)*
Williston State Coll. 312
Willmar Comm. Coll. *(see Ridgewater Coll.)*
Willsey Inst. 599
Willsey Limited Rockland, Inc. *(see Willsey Inst.)*
Wilmington Campus of the Delaware Tech. & Comm. Coll. *(see Delaware Tech. & Comm. Coll—Stanton/ Wilmington Campus)*
Wilmington Coll. 329, 779 *(see also Univ. of North Carolina at Wilmington; Wilmington Univ.)*
Wilmington Coll—Blue Ash 790
Wilmington Coll—Eastgate 790
Wilmington Coll—Tri-County 790
Wilmington Commercial Coll. *(see Goldey-Beacom Coll.)*
Wilmington Hosp. *(see Christiana Care Health Sys.)*
Wilmington Univ. 84, 779
Wilmington VA Med. Ctr. *(see Wilmington Veterans Affairs Med. Ctr.)*
Wilmington VAMC *(see Wilmington Veterans Affairs Med. Ctr.)*
Wilmington Veterans Affairs Med. Ctr. 694
Wilson & Associates, Inc. *(see Jerry Wilson & Associates, Inc.)*
Wilson Beauty Coll., Inc. *(see Pat Wilson Beauty Coll., Inc.)*
Wilson Coll. 364 *(see Lindsey Wilson Coll.; Warren Wilson Coll.; Wilson Comm. Coll.)*
Wilson Comm. Coll. 310
Wilson County Tech. Inst. *(see Wilson Comm. Coll.)*
Wilson Industrial Edu. Ctr. *(see Wilson Comm. Coll.)*
Wilson Rehabilitation Ctr. *(see Woodrow Wilson Rehabilitation Ctr.)*
Wilson Tech *(see Wilson Comm. Coll.)*
Wilson Tech. Coll. *(see Wilson Comm. Coll.)*
Wilson Tech. Comm. Coll. *(see Wilson Comm. Coll.)*
Wilson Technological Ctr. *(see Western Suffolk Board of Cooperative Educational Services)*
Winchester Med. Ctr., Inc. 751
Windham Comm. Mem. Hosp. 694
Windham Reg. Vocational-Tech. Sch. 694
Windham Tech. High Sch. *(see Windham Reg. Vocational-Tech. Sch.)*
Windsor Univ. *(see Univ. of Windsor)*
Windward Coll. *(see Windward Comm. Coll.)*
Windward Comm. Coll. 124
Winebrenner Sem. *(see Winebrenner Theological Sem.)*
Winebrenner Theological Sem. 329
Winfield Allied Health Ctr. *(see Cowley County Comm. Coll.)*
Wingate Coll. *(see Wingate Univ.)*
Wingate Univ. 310
Winner Inst. of Arts & Sciences 364
Winner Inst., Inc. 543
Winnipeg Bible Coll. *(see Providence Coll. & Theological Sem.)*
Winnipeg Univ. *(see Univ. of Winnipeg)*
Winona State Coll. *(see Winona State Univ.)*
Winona State Normal Sch. *(see Winona State Univ.)*
Winona State Teachers Coll. *(see Winona State Univ.)*
Winona State Univ. 229
Winona Tech. Coll. *(see Minnesota State Coll.-Southeast Tech.)*
Winston-Salem Barber Sch. 602
Winston-Salem Bible Coll. 789 *(see also Carolina Christian Coll.)*
Winston-Salem Coll. *(see Carolina Christian Coll.; Winston-Salem State Univ.)*
Winston-Salem State Coll. *(see Winston-Salem State Univ.)*
Winston-Salem State Univ. 310
Winston-Salem Teachers Coll. *(see Winston-Salem State Univ.)*
Winston-Salem Univ. *(see Winston-Salem State Univ.)*
Winston-Salem/Forsyth County Industrial Edu. Ctr. *(see Forsyth Tech. Comm. Coll.)*
Winter Park Tech 516
Winthrop Coll. *(see Winthrop Univ.)*
Winthrop South Nassau Univ. Health Sys. *(see Winthrop Univ. Hosp.)*
Winthrop Training Sch. *(see Winthrop Univ.)*
Winthrop Univ. 378
Winthrop Univ. Hosp. 729
Wisconsin Coll. of Cosmetology, Inc. 676
Wisconsin Coll. of Physicians & Surgeons *(see Med. Coll. of Wisconsin)*
Wisconsin Deaconess Training Sch. *(see Bellin Coll. of Nursing)*
Wisconsin Dept. of Health & Social Services *(see Ethan Allen Sch.)*
Wisconsin English Second Language Inst. 676
Wisconsin General Hosp. *(see Univ. of Wisconsin Hosp. & Clinics)*
Wisconsin Indianhead Tech. Coll. 452
Wisconsin Inst. of Techno. *(see Univ. of Wisconsin-Platteville)*
Wisconsin Lutheran Coll. 452
Wisconsin Med. Coll. *(see Med. Coll. of Wisconsin)*
Wisconsin Mining Sch. *(see Univ. of Wisconsin-Platteville)*
Wisconsin Mining Trade Sch. *(see Univ. of Wisconsin-Platteville)*
Wisconsin Music Conservatory *(see Wisconsin Conservatory of Music, Inc.)*
Wisconsin Sch. of Electronics *(see Herzing Coll—Madison Campus)*
Wisconsin Sch. of Prof. Psychology 452
Wisconsin State Coll. & Inst. of Techno. *(see Univ. of Wisconsin-Platteville)*
Wisconsin State Coll. at Eau Claire *(see Univ. of Wisconsin-Eau Claire)*
Wisconsin State Coll. at River Falls *(see Univ. of Wisconsin-River Falls)*
Wisconsin State Coll. Oshkosh *(see Univ. of Wisconsin-Oshkosh)*
Wisconsin State Coll., La Crosse *(see Univ. of Wisconsin-La Crosse)*
Wisconsin State Coll., Milwaukee *(see Univ. of Wisconsin-Milwaukee)*
Wisconsin State Coll—Stevens Point *(see Univ. of Wisconsin-Stevens Point)*
Wisconsin State Coll—Superior *(see Univ. of Wisconsin-Superior)*
Wisconsin State Coll—Whitewater *(see Univ. of Wisconsin-Whitewater)*
Wisconsin State Laboratory of Hygiene *(see Univ. of Wisconsin-Madison)*
Wisconsin State Univ. at Eau Claire *(see Univ. of Wisconsin-Eau Claire)*
Wisconsin State Univ. at River Falls *(see Univ. of Wisconsin-River Falls)*
Wisconsin State Univ. Oshkosh *(see Univ. of Wisconsin-Oshkosh)*
Withlacoochee Tech. Inst. 516

X

Y

Z